2010 FULLY UPDATED Edition
WRITER'S MARKET
UK & Ireland

Newton Abbot: David   0715332856

2010 FULLY UPDATED Edition

WRITER'S MARKET

UK & Ireland

Your guide to making money from your writing

Foreword by Katie Fforde

Edited by Caroline Taggart

David and Charles

EDITOR'S ACKNOWLEDGEMENTS
Many thanks to all those who have contributed articles to this year's edition,
particularly Katie for the foreword and Mary for putting me in touch with her;
and to the many people I have met at festivals and workshops for their ideas and
enthusiasm – this book is all the stronger for their input. Thanks also to Em, Ali,
James, Susie, Steve, Gemma and everyone else at David and Charles who beavers
away in the background to make the *Writer's Market UK* book and website happen,
leaving me to do the fun bits.

A DAVID & CHARLES BOOK
Copyright © David & Charles Limited 2009

David & Charles is an F+W Media, Inc. company
4700 East Galbraith Road
Cincinnati, OH 45236

First published in the UK in 2009

A catalogue record for this book is available from the British Library.

ISBN-13: 978-0-7153-3285-6
ISBN-10: 0-7153-3285-6

Printed in Finland by WS Bookwell
for David & Charles Ltd.
Brunel House, Newton Abbot, Devon

Editor: Caroline Taggart
Director of Editorial and Design: Ali Myer
Editorial Manager: Emily Pitcher
Editorial Assistant: James Brooks
Designer: Joanna Ley
Proofreader: Susan Pitcher
Production Director: Roger Lane

Visit our website at www.davidandcharles.co.uk

David & Charles books are available from all good bookshops; alternatively you can
contact our Orderline on 0870 9908222 or write to us at FREEPOST EX2 110, D&C
Direct, Newton Abbot, TQ12 4ZZ (no stamp required UK only);
US customers call 800-289-0963 and
Canadian customers call 800-840-5220.

www.writersmarket.co.uk

D&C
David and Charles

CONTENTS

FOREWORD
KATIE FFORDE

If you decide to start training for a marathon someone you know will see you puffing up the hill looking less like Paula Radcliffe than a walrus in shorts. The joy of deciding to write a novel – or indeed to write anything – is that while it's just as hard as running a marathon and probably takes far longer to achieve, it is at least private. You don't need to tell anyone what you're getting up to unless and until you choose to.

Even knowing this, that first attempt at any sort of writing beyond an 'off-games' note for your child is hard. While computers have mostly got rid of the blank sheet of paper that is so utterly terrifying, there is still that blank computer screen. The way I got over this was simple but blush-making: I typed out the first paragraph of someone else's book, a book I had thought bad for various reasons. My cunning plan was to re-write it, thus saving myself hours of agony.

The first paragraph was enough. I was so frustrated with the other book, and so full of the story I wanted to tell, that I forgot about not knowing how to start and just jumped straight in.

So why would any apparently sane person want to write? Why would anyone want to shut themselves up in a room on their own, for the most part, making things up? I suspect there are as many answers as there are writers, but it's something to do with getting the story out of your head, onto the page and then into the head of another person. They won't get it exactly as you've thought it, however well you've written it, but if they are convinced, that's enough.

Lots of writers have always written, always had scenarios running through their heads. For them getting all this on paper or onto a computer is logical, and may feel slightly less dotty than chatting away in their heads to people who don't exist.

Others, like me, come to it later. For me it was a desire to do for others what Mills and Boon novels had done for me. The fact that I never managed to get my camel through the eye of that particular needle hasn't changed my motive.

WHAT DO YOU WANT TO WRITE?

Some people think they'd like to write a novel if only they had time (I meet lots of them!) but if you're taking it seriously, the only way to find out if you can write one is by starting.

But supposing you think you'd like to write a novel but are not sure you have the stamina? Consider short stories. Many novelists declare they can't write them and they are difficult. Shorter, yes, but they have to have to be the perfect shape. You can't waste space explaining too much, or having too many characters, or indulging yourself in too much description. Short stories are an excellent discipline, satisfying to read and write, and a great way of developing your writing technique. There is no room for extraneous material in them and if, having written short stories, you move on to novels and apply the same strict rules, your novels will be better.

Articles too are very satisfying, if you can get them right. To the practised article writer, ideas are everywhere – you just need to train yourself to spot them. I have a non-fiction writing friend who rarely goes to any social occasion without collecting at least three ideas for articles. She then does some of the research, pitches the idea to relevant editors and, having established interest, writes the piece. The work often has to be done very quickly, thus instilling discipline and a professional attitude to her work.

> " I WAS SO FRUSTRATED WITH THE OTHER BOOK, AND SO FULL OF THE STORY I WANTED TO TELL, THAT I FORGOT ABOUT NOT KNOWING HOW TO START AND JUST JUMPED STRAIGHT IN "

UNTIL YOU TREAT WRITING AS A JOB, EVEN IF A PART-TIME ONE, YOU WON'T EVER BE ABLE TO THINK OF YOURSELF AS A WRITER

It is not only journalists writing non-fiction who need to find out if what they are considering writing is likely to find a home. Research your markets; if you want to write stories for magazines, read the magazines you are aiming for first. Send away for their tip sheets and follow what they say.

If the first submission comes back to you, try to work out why it didn't work, think where else you might offer it and, after a few adjustments, send it out again.

Novel writing does take longer, but the same rules apply. Find out which agents might be interested in your work and pitch it to them. See which publishers are producing what and make sure you don't offer your *Sex and the City For Men* to a publisher of car maintenance manuals.

BE PROFESSIONAL

You may not have a deadline other than a self-imposed one, but you need some sense of discipline or you'll never get anything finished. It might be very pleasant to drift along enjoying the beauties of nature, writing the odd line as it occurs, but it won't get you anywhere. Until you treat writing as a job, even if a part-time one, you won't ever be able to think of yourself as a writer.

A very disciplined writer friend of mine makes her deadline a couple of months sooner than the one her publisher has set. This gives her extra time to polish, to put the book away for a while so she can read it afresh. This is the perfect way, but for me it's rather like being a size ten – infinitely desirable but not ever going to happen. Achieving the original deadline has to be good enough for most of us.

FINDING THE TIME

Having established that you want to write and have the proper professional attitude, but assuming that you already have a job, or a family, or both, how do you find the time? The only answer is to steal it. I gave up ironing, cut down on housework drastically (such a hardship!) and became adept at throwing an onion into a pan as my husband came through the door, to give an impression of cooking, and producing a meal rapidly after that. I started with an hour a day and loved the process so much it soon became stretched to as much time as I could get away with, given that I had small children and the same day-to-day demands on my time that everybody has. Most of us can find an hour a day if we really want to, although if you have children and/or a full-time job you may have to get up very early or stay up very late.

So assemble your tools, your desire to express yourself on paper, your writing equipment (a pencil and paper, typewriter or diamond-studded laptop, whichever works for you) and the perseverance of a marathon runner times ten and write. Then buy your copy of *Writer's Market UK* and sell what you've written!

Katie Fforde

9

INTRODUCTION
CAROLINE TAGGART

Hello, and welcome to the new and completely updated edition of *Writer's Market UK*, with revised listings and many new articles, covering – I hope – a lot of areas in which you as aspiring writers are looking for help. Since I last sat down to write an introduction to this book – a year ago – I've been travelling the country talking to some of you and usually (and happily) spending more time answering your questions than I do in giving my own prepared speech.

Which is one of the reasons why I've commissioned some different articles for this edition. One of the questions I have been asked most frequently concerns how to approach a publisher – what to include, what not to include in a submission, and how to write a covering letter. Answering these questions is part of literary consultant Hilary Johnson's day job, and she gives you something like a blueprint on page 49.

I say 'something like' a blueprint, because a book like this can't hope to cover every individual case and because in a lot of areas there simply aren't any hard and fast rules. At the very first talk I gave somebody asked me how much sex she should include in a particular type of novel and there really is no answer to that. It's the sort of decision that has to be taken by you, the writer, following your own creative instincts but having had a good rummage round your local bookshop to see what other people writing in your genre are doing. That said, it inspired me to ask my friend Lyn Wood, queen of erotic fiction, to advise on some of the dos and don'ts of writing about sex! Find out what she has to say on page 40.

Another frequently occurring subject is how to find an agent, and Jonathan Pegg, newly set up on his own since leaving agency giant Curtis Brown, has some useful tips on page 73.

TALENT WILL OUT
Aspiring writers – and when I use that term I mean writers who aspire to be *published* – often seem to feel that they won't succeed if they don't have connections, if they don't know 'the right people'. All I can say is that, while knowing people can obviously do you no harm, it won't make you talented, it won't improve your technique, it won't make you a real writer. I'm assuming, just for the moment, that you are not a television chef, a footballer's wife or a former member of the SAS. If you are the sort of person whose name alone will sell a book, no matter what the pages contain, then I am flattered that you have read so far, but really (at the risk of appearing rude) I am not talking to you. For everyone else, the way the reader responds to the words you have put on paper is paramount, and anything you can do to improve your writing will help. Read as widely as possible – the idea that you shouldn't read too much in case it influences your work is nonsense. If you don't read good writers, how can you know what good writing is? As Simon Brett puts it on page 21, 'Decide why you like some authors and dislike others, why some books are crystal clear and others deeply muddled. Identify the qualities you would like to see in your own writing, and then try to reproduce them.'

PRACTISE, PRACTISE, PRACTISE
Which brings me to another thing you must do: write. I realise that sounds obvious, but like so many clichés, this is a wise one: writing is like a muscle

> THE WAY THE READER RESPONDS TO WORDS YOU HAVE PUT ON PAPER IS PARAMOUNT, AND ANYTHING YOU CAN DO TO IMPROVE YOUR WRITING WILL HELP

> **ONLY ABOUT 20 PER CENT OF PEOPLE WHO DESCRIBE THEMSELVES AS WRITERS EARN ALL OF THEIR INCOME FROM WRITING**

– use it or lose it. Only by constantly practising your writing, honing your skills, trying to do it better, will you make progress. One of the ways you can improve your chances of selling your work is by becoming as good a writer as you can possibly be.

For many of us, being as good a writer as we can possibly be may have to remain satisfaction enough; even if we are published, it is unlikely to bring us fame and fortune. Only about 20 per cent of people who describe themselves as writers earn all of their income from writing, and 10 per cent of the writers earn 50 per cent of the money, leaving not an enormous amount for the rest of us. So be realistic – enjoy your writing as an end in itself and treat publication and payment as a bonus.

HOW TO HELP YOURSELF

On the other hand, this is, of course, a book about where and how to *sell* what you write, so you can help yourself in other ways too:

• **Get the work finished**. Two chapters of a novel are no good to anyone. Keep at it, keep polishing it and once it is in as good a state as you can get it, send it out.

• **Do your homework**. Don't send a literary novel to someone who is interested in science fiction or vice versa. Don't send a completed novel to an agent who wants to see three chapters (but do make it clear that the rest of the book exists). And find out the name of the person to send it to – nobody likes 'Dear Sir or Madam' letters.

• **Don't boast** and don't tell publishers how to do their job, or how excited they are going to be to read your work. They know how to do their job, and they can judge for themselves whether they are excited or not.

• **Network**. Get online and look for people who are doing the same sort of thing as you are. Check out sites such as www.authonomy. com and www.youwriteon.com: agents and publishers look at these sites and you may just get spotted. Enter competitions. Join a local writing group, attend literary festivals and writers' conferences (there are sections giving details about these events towards the back of the book). Who knows, you may meet your future agent or publisher over coffee (nobody is denying that having contacts is useful).

• **Think laterally**. Does your work have to be a novel? Could it become a radio play or a screenplay? (See page 46 for Helen Cross's advice on these areas.) Can you get your stories published on a website (see Sarah Salway's article on page 43 for suggestions) or in a parish magazine, or read on hospital radio?

• **Read the *Writer's Market* website**, www.writersmarket.co.uk. We do our very best to keep you informed about what is going on in the world of publishing, and we're always eager to hear from you and find out what *you* would like to see on the site.

Above all, **keep writing**. Whether or not the world succumbs to the e-book revolution, it's still going to need material. It needs writers. And that means you.

YOUR QUESTIONS ANSWERED

Is it possible to learn to be a writer?
Yes, up to a point. As Jem Poster says, literary talent may be partly innate, but it can also be nurtured. See his article on page 17 or, for journalism, Peter Cole on page 24.

I haven't the time or money to go on a full-time course. Are there other options?
Yes. There are plenty of short courses – see Simon Brett on page 21. In addition, there is a surprising number of grants available, as Victoria Patch details on page 30.

Do I need an agent?
Probably. See the agent's point of view expressed by Jonathan Pegg on page 73.

I know oodles of people are trying to be published. How can I make my efforts stand out?
Present your work professionally and write an eye-catching synopsis. Look at Hilary Johnson's advice on page 49.

There are so many brilliant novelists out there – what can I do to improve my writing?
Lots of things. On page 36 Sophie Hannah helps you with the psychology of your characters; on page 33 Caro Fraser talks about drawing on your own experience; and, if you are trying to write sex scenes, have a look at what Lyn Wood has to say on page 40.

I want to write articles, not a full-length book. How do I go about it?
Editors are always on the lookout for good ideas. See what Susan Grossman has to say on page 66.

Everyone says there's no market for short stories or poetry. Is this true?
Getting collections published is difficult, but there are plenty of outlets for single pieces. Read Sarah Salway's article on page 43 and Neil Astley's on page 55 for advice.

What about children's books?
Lindsey Heaven describes what a commissioning editor is looking for on page 52.

What other outlets might I consider?
You could try writing for the screen: read Helen Cross's article on page 46. Or the web: Anthony Pearson has some suggestions on page 70. If you want to try your hand at non-fiction, read Heather Angel (page 62) on becoming a writer/photographer and David Reynolds (page 59) on memoirs.

I've written the book. The publisher has accepted it. I thought that was the end of the story.
Oh no. You've still got work to do. For more about what happens to your manuscript after you've delivered it – and who does what in the publishing house – see my articles on pages 93 and 98.

My contract is 14 pages long – what's *that* all about?
See page 86 for my explanation of the small print and your legal responsibilities.

My book's been published – can I help it to sell?
You certainly can. There's no hiding your light under a bushel here: read Mary Cavanagh's article on page 82. And for an insight into what is important to a bookseller, see Sarah Rees on page 78.

I'm earning money from my writing. What do I tell the tax office?
The truth, the whole truth and... see my thoughts on page 100.

You hear so much doom and gloom about bookshops closing, supermarkets taking over and only bestsellers selling – is it worth all the effort?
Of course it is. The market is just changing, not dying. Read what Philip Jones has to say about it on page 13.

CARRY ON PUBLISHING

AN INSIDER'S LOOK AT THE CURRENT STATE OF THE UK BOOK TRADE

PHILIP JONES

Philip Jones is managing editor of theBookseller.com, the website of the weekly book-trade bible *The Bookseller*. Except for a short stint travelling across Eastern Europe, he has worked at the magazine for over ten years, first as financial news reporter, and most recently as its web editor. He lives in North London.

If 2007 was a year of possibilities for publishers, authors and booksellers, then 2008 could be classified as a year of certainties – not all of them welcome.

On the plus side, the digital book definitely arrived with the successful launch of the Sony Reader into the UK; publishers continued to invest in and break new authors (think Stephenie Meyer internationally or Sadie Jones in the UK); and Waterstone's, still the largest dedicated retailer of books in the UK, got back on the front foot with some innovative marketing initiatives such as its Writer's Table, and began to look as if it might again be able to grow its business profitably.

On the down side, no retailer weathered the credit crunch particularly well and – to the surprise of some – booksellers were not immune: after a positive start to the year, book sales declined year-on-year for the first time since 'records began' in the late 1990s. The market was not helped by the collapse of Woolworth's just before Christmas 2008. The group was a small-time bookseller but, through its subsidiary Entertainment UK, a big-time supplier of books to other retailers, including the supermarkets:

there are estimates that the collapse could cost UK publishers as much as £10m in bad debts and irretrievable stock, as big a hit as they have suffered since the collapse of Dillons in the mid-1990s. Last, the single biggest influence on book sales in the UK, television duo Richard and Judy, moved to a digital channel. With their *New Position* on Watch TV attracting a fraction of the viewers who tuned in on Channel 4, the switch raised genuine doubts over whether this key driver of book sales could be lost to the trade for good.

THE CREDIT CRUNCH TAKES HOLD

It all began so much better. In fact, if 2008 could be summarised in a phrase, then it was a year of two halves. A good start saw sales up 3.7 per cent by July, thanks to some of the most reliable names in the industry – Delia Smith, Katie Price and Jamie Oliver. But as the credit crunch worsened so did book sales: the market found itself down on last year for 20 of the last 26 weeks, with total revenue down 5 per cent.

By the end of 2008, 236.9 million books had been purchased at a total value of £1.773bn – figures down 0.4 per cent and 1.6 per cent respectively on 2007. It is perhaps not the first time in publishing history that sales have shrunk, but it is certainly the first dip since Nielsen BookScan began recording retail book sales in the late 1990s.

> **IF 2008 COULD BE SUMMARISED IN A PHRASE, THEN IT WAS A YEAR OF TWO HALVES**

CARRY ON PUBLISHING

PHILIP JONES

FEATURE

13

Of course some of the blame for this can be laid at the enchanted doors of Hogwarts, the final edition of J K Rowling's Harry Potter series, *Harry Potter and the Deathly Hallows*, having been a phenomenal – and more importantly unrepeatable – hit the previous summer. Taking this book out of the equation puts the figures back into the black, but only marginally, with volume sales up 1.1 per cent and market value up a much flatter 0.4 per cent.

The publishers' own measure, the Publishers Association's Sales Monitor (PASM), has witnessed a similar pattern, with both home and export markets down strongly in the third quarter after a good first half. Between July and September UK publishers saw their sales decline by 9.4 per cent, with unit sales down by 8.2 per cent. The fourth quarter figures (yet to be released at the time of writing) will almost certainly show that sales have been nudged into the red.

THE BIG FOUR PUBLISHERS...

Perhaps one indicator of the slowing market in 2008 was the inability of the top publishers to build on their already hefty dominance. There were few, if any, notable company acquisitions over the year, as finance became harder to come by and the big groups looked to shore up rather than expand their borders. Even Bloomsbury, still carrying a pot of Harry Potter gold on its balance sheet, only managed a few small purchases, two in the academic field and, towards the end of the year, cricket stats compiler Wisden and the Arden Shakespeare series.

The lack of movement was evidenced in the market share statistics. Hachette UK remained narrowly ahead of Random House UK, with Penguin and HarperCollins well behind in third and fourth spots. Even in a bad year, as highlighted in the previous edition of this book, the UK publishing market is dominated by these big four. Last year just 17 out of the top 100 bestselling books came from a publisher that was not part of this grouping; this year that number remarkably remained unchanged. Remove the smaller conglomerates (such as Bloomsbury, Guinness and Macmillan) and the number of different imprints reduces even further, to seven – also the same as last year.

...AND THE REST

In such times it is often the smaller, more agile publishers who take the lead. Witness the Scottish independent Canongate: its business has arguably stewed since it published the 2002 Booker winner *Life of Pi*, yet in 2008 it scored remarkable successes having taken on two books by a then little-known American senator called Barack Obama, whose *Dreams of my Father* and *The Audacity of Hope* were both among the top 50 bestselling books of the year.

Not all small publishers will be so fortunate. During 2008 Faber chief executive Stephen Page admitted that the market for literary publishing had 'been becoming tougher for some time'. Faber has diversified into own-branded mugs and literary courses. New independent Quercus also reported tough conditions but, lacking the brand name to move into other areas, was forced to raise additional investment and planned a review both of its forward publishing programme and of its staffing requirements. It is unlikely to be the only publisher, whether big or small, undergoing the same process.

However, authors viewing the structure of the UK publishing landscape in the first half of 2009 will likely see little change, in spite of the poor 2008 numbers. As this book went to press – though there have been pay and recruitment freezes – UK publishers (and indeed booksellers) have yet to begin the wholesale restructurings and slashing of lists that have been witnessed during previous recessions. The US has not been so lucky, with 11 December 2008 now known as 'Black Wednesday' after five publishing houses announced either job cuts or salary freezes in the space of just 24 hours.

Those writers who read this article later in the year may be seeing something different – both structurally and in the types of books being commissioned.

SO WHAT ARE PUBLISHERS BUYING?

There is already evidence that publishers are avoiding risk. The annual rights fair at Frankfurt certainly lacked some 'buzz' in 2008: the concept of the 'big' Frankfurt book disappeared some years ago, but now even the 'biggish' books are off the table. Towards the end of the year a few agents noted a decline in adventurous buying, with some struggling to sell début and literary fiction, and more failing to find a buyer at all. According to one agent, tough times were 'undoubtedly affecting confidence about acquisitions'.

Despite the chastening conditions no-one expects UK publishers to stop acquiring books, as the US publisher Harcourt was oddly forced to in December. But what is very likely is that the risk-averse will chase the guaranteed hits. Simon Trewin of United Agents reckons that brand names with the feel-good factor or within the 'comfort zone' will flourish in coming months as credit-crunched book buyers turn to tried and trusted names.

If that is the case then it probably means more, not fewer, celebrity titles. Contrary to some newspaper reports, sales of celebrity memoirs in 2008 were bigger than ever. Paul O'Grady's *At My Mother's Knee* sold 664,474 copies, for example, almost 150,000 more than Richard Hammond's *On the Edge* managed last year. Twenty months ago Random House's £2m deal for Dawn French's memoir looked bad business, but *Dear Fatty* was the number one non-fiction title during Christmas week, and came in second only to O'Grady as the top-selling non-fiction title of the year.

The most likely impact of this will be felt on the already hard-pressed booksellers, particularly those with the expensive overheads of a high-street presence. 'Popular' titles such as those just mentioned do not sell well through the UK's 4,000 independent bookshops and are also increasingly difficult territory for the chains. Just before Christmas HMV admitted that its subsidiary Waterstone's was not selling as many celebrity titles as it had done in previous years, while in their annual accounts both Blackwell's and British Bookshops – a small chain of mainly Sussex-based shops – warned that heavy discounting of bestselling books was having a damaging effect on their businesses. For independents, 2008 was reported to be lacking that big unexpected hit in the manner of the *Schott's* miscellanies and *Does Anything Eat Wasps?* of previous years. As Nigel Jones of Devon independent Totnes Bookshop said, 'I can't see many good books – did nobody bother commissioning last year?' The situation in 2009 might not be much better.

> **UK PUBLISHERS HAVE YET TO BEGIN THE WHOLESALE RESTRUCTURINGS AND SLASHING OF LISTS THAT HAVE BEEN WITNESSED DURING PREVIOUS RECESSIONS**

GOING DIGITAL

Looking deeper into 2009 and aside from the recession, publishing is likely to witness two big debates. The first will be how to make money from the burgeoning digital channels, and the second how to make money after discounting.

There were two significant digital developments over the year that will inform how the former issue is discussed in 2009. First, Waterstone's successful launch of the Sony Reader meant that for the first time UK publishers had a viable digital platform. This led to many of them rushing to digitise their backlists and make changes to author contracts, allowing them the right to digitise the authors' work in the first place. The market remains small: according to one medium-sized publisher, sales of its entire digital catalogue in one month accounted for roughly one week's sales of a single printed bestseller. But it is growing: figures from the more developed US market showed that publishers' digital sales had quadrupled over the year, with Amazon.com's Kindle having a similar kind of 'breakthrough' impact as the Sony Reader has had in the UK. For authors looking at the fresh wording in their contracts, the advice from agents is to negotiate only a short-term deal, so that royalty rates can grow as sales increase and the initial conversion costs recede.

The second big digital development over the year (and one wonders whether this will, over time, kick the first one into touch) was the deal negotiated between the digital giant Google on the one hand, and US publishers and authors' representatives on the other. Google won the right to index books in its search engine (legally) for a one-off fee of $125m, meaning that users will be able to search and preview millions of additional titles, including out-of-print books. Money will be made from advertising, subscriptions and sales, and will be split 63:37 between the rights holders and Google. In addition, Google will build a Books Rights Registry so that rights holders can be correctly identified and the revenue passed on. Though the deal was done in the US, where Google was being sued by US publishers and author groups, it is inconceivable that a similar arrangement won't be made in the UK and Europe.

For authors the advantages are obvious: suddenly their works can be put before an almost unmeasurable audience, and money can be made. As the *Guardian* newspaper commented at the time, if only the music industry had negotiated such an arrangement.

But booksellers were less happy: once again they look like missing out, as yet another competitor to their selling of the printed word arrives. In an unusually strongly worded statement, the UK's Booksellers Association said the deal 'would have a hugely damaging effect on the publishing and bookselling industry and, consequently, on authors and the public as well'. This reaction was swiftly echoed across Europe and beyond, with only the American booksellers noticeably quiet.

THE DISCOUNTING WARS

If booksellers find themselves marginalised by the first debate, they will be central to the second. In 2008 a report commissioned by the UK Booksellers Association found that UK bookshops were making less money, seeing less market growth and giving away more in discounts than their counterparts overseas. As BA president Graham Rand said, 'We have to ask ourselves whether the industry has gone too far in creating this "lowest price" environment for consumers.'

It is almost as if, ten years after the loss of the Net Book Agreement, which prevented retailers offering discounts off the price printed on the

> **WATERSTONE'S SUCCESSFUL LAUNCH OF THE SONY READER MEANT THAT FOR THE FIRST TIME UK PUBLISHERS HAD A VIABLE DIGITAL PLATFORM**

book, the trade is now asking, 'What went wrong?' Authors who feel they will be untouched by this 'industry issue' are mistaken – witness the announced closure of Murder One, the specialist crime bookshop on London's Charing Cross Road. Discounting has allowed a smaller number of mega-books to sell more than anyone could have dreamed of selling ten years ago, across an increasing number of outlets from supermarkets to websites. But those booksellers who wish to champion good writing by selling fewer copies of a more diverse range at higher prices are without doubt being squeezed out.

Authors may well find that the new channels offered by the likes of Google, Amazon and Sony more than make up for any loss of exposure on the high street: but it won't happen overnight. Macmillan US has estimated that Google has helped sell about 16,400 copies of the 11,000 titles in its book search programme, but that is not much more than one copy of each book.

LOOKING FORWARD

As 2009 moves forward, the shape the industry will take as its readies itself for a new decade of publishing will – of course – become clearer. There will certainly be casualties. But we should be cautious about writing off any part of the book business. Though it might not always seem so for readers of this book, the publishing world in its entirety exists to help authors and readers find each other. It has been and remains remarkably adroit at performing this task.

STUDYING CREATIVE WRITING

THE OPTIONS AVAILABLE TO THOSE WHO WANT TO EMBARK ON A CREATIVE WRITING COURSE

JEM POSTER

Jem Poster is the author of a collection of poetry, *Brought to Light* (Bloodaxe, 2001) and two novels, *Courting Shadows* (Sceptre, 2002) and *Rifling Paradise* (Sceptre, 2006). He is Professor and Director of Creative Writing at Aberystwyth University.

First of all, let's dispose of the myth that creative writing can't – or shouldn't – be taught or learned. Like all artistic talent, literary talent may be partly innate but this doesn't mean that it can't also be nurtured, or that courses similar to those available for would-be composers or painters shouldn't be made available to emergent writers. If you find the course that's right for you, your work is likely to improve significantly and the improvement may well mark a crucial stage in your discovery of yourself as a writer.

Most of those who think of discovering themselves as writers also imagine being discovered as writers by others: dreams of literary achievement are usually partly – and sometimes primarily – dreams of commercial success and/or critical acclaim. The ambition to be published is natural and entirely understandable, but it's worth remembering that there are many forms of creative fulfilment. No reputable creative writing course will offer you a guarantee of success in the crowded field of literary publishing but all good courses will help you to advance in your understanding of the craft of writing. For some, this will give readily measurable results – an agent, a publisher, good sales figures – while for others the benefits may be more modest, but no less important: for a student who begins with limited confidence and ability, the eventual production of a handful of well-written poems can represent a very real achievement.

I'm emphasising this point because even the most basic statistical analysis will make it clear that many of those who complete programmes of creative writing study don't in fact go on to achieve literary success in the public sphere. But if you bear in mind that publication isn't the only measure of a course's value, you'll be open to the full range of possible benefits. As a result of signing up for a creative writing course, you may conceivably become a well-known writer; but even if you don't, you're likely to find that your life has been enriched in other ways.

> **AS A RESULT OF SIGNING UP FOR A CREATIVE WRITING COURSE, YOU MAY CONCEIVABLY BECOME A WELL-KNOWN WRITER; BUT EVEN IF YOU DON'T, YOU'RE LIKELY TO FIND THAT YOUR LIFE HAS BEEN ENRICHED IN OTHER WAYS**

WHAT KIND OF COURSE?

I'm going to look at several different kinds of course: the short course (by which I mean a course of a week's duration or less); the longer course of the kind provided mainly by university departments of continuing education and often leading to a qualification such as a certificate or diploma; and the range of full-scale degree courses now offered by many universities in the UK.

This is a large and complex field, and my necessarily broad survey is simply an indicative guide. The organisations mentioned in this article are prominent providers of creative writing courses, but there are many others, and you may wish to research options beyond the framework offered here.

Short courses
Many aspiring writers will already have attended at least one short creative writing course but if you haven't yet done so, this might be a good starting point. Short courses offer an opportunity to get the flavour of working with a small group under tutorial guidance. The best known are those run by the Arvon Foundation at their four UK centres; and you might also look at the courses at Ty Newydd, the National Writers' Centre for Wales, which works in close collaboration with Arvon. Keep an eye open, too, for courses organised as part of literary festivals: the Cheltenham Festival of Literature sometimes offers two-day courses, while the Oxford Literary Festival offers a six-day residential programme.

It would perhaps be unwise to base any significant decision solely on your experience of a single short course, but it's fair to say that if you've enjoyed one or more of them (and particularly if enjoyment has been accompanied by a noticeable improvement in your writing ability), then there's a good chance that you're ready for a more sustained programme of study.

Longer courses
If you feel that you want to commit to a more sustained programme of creative writing study, a good option would be one of the part-time certificate or diploma courses organised for mature students by the continuing education departments of a number of universities. In London, for example, there's Birkbeck's two-year certificate course, while those living in or near Oxford might take advantage of the two-year diploma course offered by Oxford University's Department for Continuing Education. Other continuing education departments offer similar opportunities. Because these courses are designed to accommodate those with domestic or professional commitments, classes tend to take place in the evenings and at weekends.

Technically, certificate courses operate at first-year undergraduate level and diploma courses at second-year level: the former might therefore seem most suitable for beginners and the latter for more advanced writers. However, there is often some flexibility on entrance requirements, and the standard is in any case defined partly by the quality of your fellow students – so don't automatically assume that you're restricted to one or the other.

University degree courses
Undergraduate (BA) programmes mix creative writing with literary study. There are historical reasons for this – creative writing programmes have usually grown out of existing English departments – but there are also sound practical reasons. It's simple: good creative writers need to be good analytical readers and the intermingling of the two strands is both natural and necessary.

The programme of study is likely to last for three years, and to be dominated by participants of standard undergraduate age (18–21), though mature students are usually welcome. The courses differ significantly from one university to another, so it's difficult to generalise; all offer guidance on the elements of good writing, while helping students to understand the relationship of their own work to a wider literary tradition.

MA programmes offer more specialised training in the craft of writing and they are more likely than undergraduate courses to emphasise the goal of publication. Since they assume a certain level of critical and creative expertise, it follows that the majority of successful applicants will be graduates in English or closely related disciplines – classics or modern languages, for example. But you shouldn't be deterred if your previous degree is in a subject only loosely related to English studies: if you have a good degree in any subject and can show a convincing portfolio of creative work, it's well worth discussing your situation with the institution concerned in the hope that it will consider an application.

It's often possible to study for an MA on a part-time basis, but those with other commitments will usually need to juggle them carefully since – unlike the certificate and diploma courses discussed above – MA courses normally require daytime attendance. Courses last for a year (two years in part-time mode).

PhD programmes in creative writing are not as widely available as MA programmes, but are offered by a substantial number of universities, including Aberystwyth, Bath Spa, Lancaster, Manchester and St Andrews. Typically, a PhD

> IF YOU HAVE A GOOD DEGREE IN ANY SUBJECT AND CAN SHOW A CONVINCING PORTFOLIO OF CREATIVE WORK, IT'S WELL WORTH DISCUSSING YOUR SITUATION WITH THE INSTITUTION CONCERNED IN THE HOPE THAT IT WILL CONSIDER AN APPLICATION

USEFUL WEBSITES FOR DEGREE COURSES

Aberystwyth University www.aber.ac.uk/english
Bath Spa University www.bathspa.ac.uk
University of East Anglia www.uea.ac.uk
Glamorgan University www.glam.ac.uk
Lancaster University www.lancs.ac.uk/fass/english
Manchester University www.arts.manchester.ac.uk/newwriting
St Andrews University www.st-andrews.ac.uk
Warwick University www.warwick.ac.uk

student will spend three years on a major creative project (a novel, a collection of short stories or a substantial collection of poems) together with a critical account which both analyses and contextualises that work. PhD study tends to be less communally focused than the programmes of study discussed above, but a good department will ensure that there are ample opportunities for meeting up with other students.

An MA in creative writing may not be a prerequisite for PhD study, but it arguably provides the best grounding. You'll certainly need to provide evidence of a high level of prior attainment both as a creative writer and as a critical thinker. If you're interested in the possibility but have doubts about your eligibility, don't hesitate to discuss the matter with a representative of the department concerned.

WHAT FORM WILL THE TEACHING TAKE?

Except in the case of PhD programmes, you can normally expect the workshop to figure centrally in your course of study: a workshop is essentially a small-group discussion focusing on writing produced by course members. A good creative writing tutor will ensure that group work of this kind is simultaneously stringent and supportive – that is, it offers suggestions for the improvement of the work under review while at the same time acknowledging its strengths. A successful, well-run group will operate collaboratively rather than competitively, working towards insights which will be useful to all of its members.

Try to find out the probable size of workshop groups when you check on other course details: somewhere between 8 and 15 students is an appropriate size. You might also want to find out whether the course provides any one-to-one tutorials: a programme that offers individual tuition as part of its provision has obvious advantages over one that doesn't.

> " AS YOUR CRITICAL AWARENESS DEVELOPS, YOU'LL ALMOST CERTAINLY FIND YOURSELF APPRECIATING THE SUBTLETIES OF THE WRITING PROCESS IN NEW AND INCREASINGLY SOPHISTICATED WAYS "

WHO ARE THE TEACHERS?

These will be writers, often well-known ones. The short courses tend to draw on a wide range of writers, ringing the changes each year. University departments are likely to have a stable core of full-time creative writing staff, often augmented by part-time tutors; again, all are likely to be practising writers.

It's worth looking closely at the published work of these tutors before making your decision: if you like the work of a particular writer, it's probable that you will enjoy the classes s/he teaches. A word of warning, however: the presence of a particular writer's name on the list of a university department's teaching staff is no guarantee that s/he will be teaching extensively (or even at all) on the course you sign up for. If this matter is important to you, be sure to make the necessary enquiries in advance.

A tutor's publishing profile is a significant indicator but not the only one. In the case of university courses, it's important to be taught by appropriately qualified tutors: academic qualifications don't outweigh creative achievements, but if good writers are also academically well qualified they are likely to be in a stronger position to offer academic guidance.

HOW WILL I BENEFIT?

As I suggested in my introduction, it's conceivable that the benefits of creative writing study will be tangible and obvious; but even if you don't end up with a contract for your next novel or poetry collection, you're likely to have benefited in other ways. Think, for example, about the advantages of working within a structured learning environment: as a student on a creative writing course, you'll usually be expected to produce work by a particular time or date. This may sound intimidating, even restrictive, but it can actually be surprisingly empowering to know that other people are waiting to see your work. And then there's the feedback you get on that work – not to mention the feedback you'll be invited to give to other members of your group: again, this may seem intimidating at first, but as your critical awareness develops, you'll find yourself appreciating the subtleties of the writing process in new and increasingly sophisticated ways.

The ability to write and speak well is an immensely important social and professional skill. Many employers are, for obvious reasons, interested in job applicants with well-developed powers of expression, while social relationships almost invariably benefit from the participants' ability to say what they mean in suitably nuanced language. A well-taught course in creative writing will, at the very least, offer you fresh insights into language and the ways in which we use it; it will almost certainly heighten your awareness of the world around you and help you to express that awareness; and it's always possible that – as with any serious programme of study – it will radically change your life.

LEARNING TO WRITE
A GUIDE TO WHAT YOU CAN AND CAN'T BE TAUGHT

SIMON BRETT

Simon Brett started his professional career as a comedy producer, first for BBC radio and then for London Weekend Television, before becoming a full-time writer. He has published over 70 books, many of them crime novels or psychological thrillers, as well as the Charles Paris, Mrs Pargeter and Fethering series. His humorous writings include the bestselling *How To Be A Little Sod*. For radio and television he has written many plays and series, like *After Henry* and *No Commitments*.

Is it possible to teach anyone to write? The answer to that question would have to be no. You can't teach *anyone* to write. If the person you're trying to teach has no interest in or aptitude for writing, then the task is impossible. And even when you're dealing with people who are motivated, there is still a question mark over whether they can actually be *taught*.

I speak as someone who has spent a lot of time conducting Creative Writing Classes. I have been a tutor on numerous occasions for the Arvon Foundation (about which more below), I have led workshops in libraries and at literary festivals. I have taught courses in rural France and on the Greek island of Skyros. I have even run a week of workshops on short-story writing for the British Council in Enugu, Nigeria. And yet I'm still ambivalent about whether writing can be taught.

One thing I'm certain of, though, is that an experienced writer can facilitate the work of an aspiring writer. You can save people time; you can stop them from pursuing their craft in directions that will prove unrewarding. For example, you can point out that, however good a 72-minute radio play someone has written may be, there are no slots on BBC radio for 72-minute plays. Or you can gently suggest that writing a novel about a writer with writer's block is possibly not the most rewarding route to travel. Often all you're doing is giving aspiring writers a bit of confidence in their own abilities. Above all, you can encourage them in the belief that the ambition to write is not an unnatural one.

In the various courses I've conducted, I have observed that the participants get at least as much stimulus from each other as they do from the tutors. A few people grow up in literary families or even dynasties, but for the great majority wanting to write is a slightly unusual aspiration and feeling that urge can sometimes lead to a sense of isolation. Just being with other people who share the ambition has a very liberating effect.

The prerequisite then for any writer must be the desire to write. At school most students will at one stage or another have been set a Creative Writing task. For the majority the demand was sheer purgatory, for the few it was a moment of great excitement and liberation. The same majority would regard continuing to do such homework for the rest of one's life as a bizarre and masochistic concept. But for someone who wants to do it, writing offers an unrivalled sense of power when it's going well (and an unrivalled sense of despair when it's going badly).

IMPROVING YOUR SKILLS
There is no lack of titles in the Creative Writing section of bookshops, but it's a striking fact that few of them seem to have been written by people you've ever heard of. The cruel question inevitably arises: if you know so much about the subject, why aren't you writing your own bestsellers rather

than 'How To' manuals? So I'm afraid I don't have that much faith in books on creative writing.

The exception I would make to this general rule concerns works by William Goldman, screenwriter of *The Sting, Butch Cassidy and the Sundance Kid* and many other great movies. His two books, *Adventures in the Screen Trade* and *Which Lie Did I Tell?*, are full not only of good jokes but also of great wisdom about the business of writing for the movies – wisdom which applies to a lot of other literary forms too.

What I would recommend an aspiring writer to read, however, is as much fiction as they can lay their hands on. Read good writing, read bad writing – work out for yourself what the difference is. Read classics, read potboilers, read so-called literary fiction, read genre fiction – you will learn something from every word of it. Decide why you like some authors and dislike others, why some books are crystal clear and others deeply muddled. Identify the qualities you would like to see in your own writing and then try to reproduce them.

> FOR SOMEONE WHO WANTS TO DO IT, WRITING OFFERS AN UNRIVALLED SENSE OF POWER WHEN IT'S GOING WELL (AND AN UNRIVALLED SENSE OF DESPAIR WHEN IT'S GOING BADLY)

SEEKING HELP

But that invaluable basis of broad reading may still need to be built on by some form of teaching. So where should the aspiring writer turn for help in developing his or her skills? The answer, of course, depends on how much time the individual wants to invest. Twenty years ago East Anglia was about the only university in the British Isles which offered a degree course in Creative Writing. Now there is an enormous number to choose from in other universities (see Jem Poster's article on page 17 for more about these), and you should assess them from reading prospectuses and talking to people who have experienced them, just as you would choose any other course.

It should be pointed out, however, that gaining a degree in Creative Writing offers no guarantee of success in the commercial world of literature. Such training may help focus the energies of a talented writer but it won't help a no-hoper to get published.

Anyway, many aspirant writers don't have the time to devote to a full-time degree course. Most have to hold down a day job while they dream of the bestseller that will one day free them from the thrall of going out to work. For them the solution must be something part-time.

There are local Writers' Circles all over the country (information about those in your area can be found through your library or from www.writers-circles.com). They are of variable quality but they do offer the aspirant an opportunity to mix with like-minded people. Many also organise programmes of talks by professional writers, from whom useful tips may be gleaned. And the practice of completing set exercises and critiquing each other's work can be of benefit (though there is always the danger of the same people constantly repeating the same criticisms).

> READ GOOD WRITING, READ BAD WRITING – WORK OUT FOR YOURSELF WHAT THE DIFFERENCE IS

SHORT COURSES

Another worthwhile experience for would-be writers who can spare the time is The Writers' Summer School at Swanwick in Derbyshire. This week-long event has been taking place every August since 1949. It exists, to quote from its website (www.wss.org.uk), 'to give writers at all levels of experience an opportunity to learn from expert tutors and excellent speakers in a comfortable and friendly atmosphere'. I have tutored and spoken there on many occasions and can vouch for the fact that it is a unique and nurturing environment.

Many local authorities also run Creative Writing courses, of which details can be found in libraries or on council websites. The quality of these tends to depend on the quality of the individual tutors involved, and it would be best to do a bit of homework before enrolling.

Then again, newspapers are full of advertisements for correspondence courses in Creative Writing, and there are also plenty to be found on the internet. I have never actually taken one of these myself, but the anecdotal evidence I have gleaned from those who have has not been encouraging. The general view is that the people running them are more concerned with taking your money than with turning you into a better writer.

THE CRÈME DE LA CRÈME

The best courses I have encountered – and indeed been involved in – are those run by the Arvon Foundation (www.arvonfoundation.org). These take place in four large houses in the country, one in Devon, one in Yorkshire, one in Shropshire and one in Inverness-shire. They usually run from Monday evening till Saturday morning and different weeks concentrate on different aspects of writing – poetry, the novel, short stories, radio, television and so on. There is a maximum of 16 participants on each course, with two professional writers as tutors. The structure of individual courses differs, but generally speaking participants take part in group sessions and workshops, where they are set short writing exercises to be read out at the next session. Among the other valuable components in the programme are one-to-one tutorials with the professional writers. And in the middle of the week there is a visit for one evening from a Guest Reader, another writer whose work is relevant to the course but whose insights can open up a wider perspective on the subject.

Arvon's admission policy is very broad. Basically, places are awarded to the first 16 people who try to book. As a result, there is a wide range of skills and backgrounds amongst the participants who may vary, in my experience, from published novelists to the man who joined a course of mine 'because the Spanish course was full'.

The concentration during these Arvon weeks is intensified by the lack of outside distractions, and the experience of communal living never fails to create something greater than the sum of its parts. Unexpected talents are discovered and developed, and the participants frequently keep in touch with each other once the course has finished. (The participants in my most recent one have set up a Yahoo Group and supportive emails are constantly flying back and forth between them.) As a tutor, I always return from a week at Arvon totally exhausted but with the feeling that something worthwhile has been achieved.

The courses are not cheap but there are bursaries and grants available for qualifying applicants.

A final important thing that's worth saying about writing courses is that they can be just another form of procrastination. The members of no other profession are as skilled as writers in finding things to do other than what they should be doing. Going on a course is a very effective way of postponing the actual putting down of words on the page. As a tutor I have encountered many 'courseoholics'. More than once, when I have met truly talented people in such circumstances, I have given them one stern piece of advice: 'Never go on another course. You've already got as much as you're ever going to get from courses. From now on, just bite the bullet and write!'

> **THE CONCENTRATION DURING THESE ARVON WEEKS IS INTENSIFIED BY THE LACK OF OUTSIDE DISTRACTIONS, AND THE EXPERIENCE OF COMMUNAL LIVING NEVER FAILS TO CREATE SOMETHING GREATER THAN THE SUM OF ITS PARTS**

SO YOU WANT TO BECOME A JOURNALIST...

SOME POINTS FOR THOSE STILL AT SCHOOL, OR COLLEGE, OR UNIVERSITY, OR IN ANOTHER JOB AND THINKING ABOUT THE POSSIBILITIES

PETER COLE

Peter Cole is Professor of Journalism at the University of Sheffield and Director of Journalism in the University's Department of Journalism Studies. His journalism career took him from the *London Evening News*, to the *Guardian*, to the *London Evening Standard*, back to the *Guardian* as news editor and deputy editor, to the *Sunday Correspondent*, which he edited, and to the *Sunday Times*, where he was News Review editor.

FOR STARTERS

Many people think they want to go 'into the media'. It is one of the most popular careers. I've seen it from two vantage points: the hundreds of job applications I received as news editor of the *Guardian*; the hundreds I now receive for places on journalism courses at Sheffield University. It's understandable – glamorous job, do exciting things, meet famous people, get on television, travel the world. And although it isn't like that for many much of the time, it can be all those things. I never pretend it's not exciting or that it cannot be glamorous, but I do stress that some of it can be humdrum and particularly that much of it is lowly paid at the beginning of your career. But many will still want to do it, so fine. I loved it.

It helps to be a bit realistic. It's hard to get into journalism, but if you are determined you will. Talent usually outs. There is also a greater variety of jobs in journalism than you may realise. For every 'face' on the screen, 'byline' in a newspaper, presenter on a radio current affairs programme, magazine fashion writer, blogger, *Newsnight* presenter, chief football writer or foreign correspondent, there are those who plan, edit, produce, direct, design and organise. The latter group is just as important and their jobs can be just as satisfying. If there is one commodity that is essential to all jobs in journalism it is 'ideas'. If there is another, it is getting off on pressure, unpredictable hours and some madness.

It does not really help to have written poems when you were six or novels when you were 12. But it does help to have read widely, to be interested in a lot of things, to enjoy talking to people, and more importantly listening to them, to be inquisitive, sceptical, gossipy, numerate, to know about popular culture, even when you don't like it, about soaps, even when you cannot bear watching them, to have heard of celebrities, even those for whom you feel contempt, and to consume all forms of media avidly.

> IF THERE IS ONE COMMODITY THAT IS ESSENTIAL TO ALL JOBS IN JOURNALISM IT IS 'IDEAS'. IF THERE IS ANOTHER, IT IS GETTING OFF ON PRESSURE, UNPREDICTABLE HOURS AND SOME MADNESS

TRADITIONAL MEDIA ARE CONVERGING, SO DON'T THINK TRADITIONALLY

Increasingly there is convergence in the media, with employers asking young recruits to carry cameras or video or audio recorders as well as notebooks. This will continue to develop. More importantly, digital technology is bringing about convergence between print, broadcast and online platforms. Magazines and newspapers have their websites; so do radio and television companies. They require words and pictures, audio and video. While journalism remains what it has always been – the gathering of accurate information and presenting it in a clear and accessible way to the audience at which it is aimed – publication has changed and will continue to change.

The jargon words are multi-platform, re-purposing and content. Journalists provide content for a variety of platforms, and the same content must be repurposed to suit various platforms: print, broadcast and digital. These days digital is not only the website; it may be the mobile telephone. A recent recruit to a news agency may be writing copy for the news service, for teletext and for the website, or indeed for web clients. A young broadcast journalist at the BBC may be preparing text for Ceefax or BBC Online, as well as making radio or TV programmes.

This is the trend. The old distinctions are disappearing. Increasingly journalism educators are reflecting this media convergence in the courses they offer and it should be borne in mind when deciding where to go. Employers are greedy these days: they want you to be aware of the way the media are developing; they want you to have a variety of skills before they will give you a job; and they want you to be flexible enough to work across the various platforms on which they publish. So it is important when choosing a course to investigate whether the curriculum takes account of converged media needs.

But there are still the traditional, core requirements for becoming a journalist and they must not be forgotten in all the hysteria about new media. News sense, good writing, good research skills, interviewing and note-taking technique are needed, wherever your journalism is published. So is knowledge of media law and ethics. And an understanding of how society is organised – local and national politics, who runs education and health, transport and planning – is also required.

JOURNALISM IS A GRADUATE CAREER, MOSTLY

While journalism is not a profession (although it is often referred to as such) in that access to the media is rightly open rather than restricted, it requires great professionalism. As more and more young people have moved into further and higher education, and government continues to encourage this, entrants into journalism are increasingly graduates. And, more than ever before, entrants need what is called pre-entry training. The days of a school leaver getting an apprenticeship on a local paper which provides the training are virtually gone. With so many young people having studied journalism before applying for a job, those with no knowledge have little chance of being interviewed. There are some graduate traineeships offered by some of the bigger media organisations which require aptitude for journalism rather than prior training, but they are few and far between, and numbers of applicants are vast. In the main you need the basic skills to be eligible for employment. There are a variety of ways of acquiring them.

PRE-ENTRY COURSES

The school leaver with A-levels faces the following options:
- do any degree
- do a media-related degree
- do a short (up to a year) school-leaver course
- try to gain direct entry to a media organisation

ANY DEGREE

Most entrants to the media these days are graduates. And anyway, any school leaver who wants to go to university, and is able to, should. There are dinosaur editors around, particularly on a few local newspapers, who are still suspicious of graduates, but they are dying out rapidly.

So question one is: should the aspiring journalist do a media-related degree or a more traditional degree? Most graduates who have gone into the media up until now tend to have non-media degrees, because Media Studies degrees are relatively recent. History, English and Politics have perhaps been the most common, but really anything goes, because (we'll come to this) these graduates will tend to do further training. Enlightened editors, on the bigger papers, are interested in people who have done other things – science, languages, economics – because this knowledge will be useful. More important is the kind of person you are: a self-starter with social and team skills, initiative, inquisitiveness, scepticism, the ability to order and organise information, to distil, to write fluently, comprehensibly and briefly; and, probably most important, buzzing with ideas.

It is important for non-media-related degree students hoping to enter the media or take a postgraduate journalism course to do relevant things – work on the student paper or radio station, do some work experience on a local paper or radio station (or hospital radio) in vacations. It will help later.

Advantages
Taking a non-media-related degree delays your career decision, keeps more options open, may produce a broader-minded graduate. Some employers are sceptical of all media degrees, particularly because they have built up a prejudice against Media Studies.

Disadvantages
It may delay entry into the media by one year. There are the costs of further study, becoming more relevant as undergraduate debts mount

MEDIA-RELATED UNDERGRADUATE DEGREE

These are very popular at present – at Sheffield, for example, BA Journalism Studies is one of the most applied-for courses, with 800 applicants for 60 places – and are proliferating all the time. Numbers doing them bear no relation to jobs available. A difficulty for school leavers and their advisers is the badging and content of such degrees: Media Studies, Communication Studies, Journalism Studies, Journalism, Multi-Media Journalism, Experience of Writing, Film and Media Studies, Audio Visual and Media Studies – all these and many more exist, to the confusion

> **MOST GRADUATES WHO HAVE GONE INTO THE MEDIA UP UNTIL NOW TEND TO HAVE NON-MEDIA-RELATED DEGREES, BECAUSE MEDIA-RELATED DEGREES ARE RELATIVELY RECENT**

of all. Essentially there are theory courses and applied/practical courses, but there are practical courses with varying amounts of theory, and theoretical courses with a dollop of practice. How do you choose the right one?

Media theory
Think of Media Studies as a branch of Cultural Studies, another thing it is often called. The curriculum may include linguistics and sociology, history and philosophy, media ownership and organisation. Students will look at bias and gender and representation. Put simply, they will study media products, print, film, television etc. But they will tend not to study how to make those products, how to 'do' journalism. They are likely to graduate ill-equipped to be practitioners.

A lot of students feel let down by these courses, particularly when they approach the jobs market and encounter hostility from editors, who seek people who can already 'do' journalism. That is a fact. Fine to study media in a theoretical way; it is an interesting and rewarding area. But you should be aware that such courses are often not vocational, so the decision can have a major effect on your future.

And do not be deceived by equipment. A lot of Media Studies courses are richly resourced with cameras and computers. That does not make them vocational. It is the curriculum and teaching that does that.

There are such Media Studies courses at a large number of universities and colleges, some good, many not so good.

Media practice
There are far fewer vocational/applied undergraduate courses – courses which concentrate on preparing students for journalism jobs, teaching them writing, reporting and

broadcasting skills, media law, ethics and codes of practice, central and local government and shorthand. There will be some more academic work, perhaps a little media theory, but more media history and organisation and issues. The students will spend a high proportion of their time 'doing' journalism. Employers are undoubtedly much more receptive to these graduates.

Below is a basic list of questions applicants or their advisers should ask in order to clarify which sort of course is on offer.

- Is the course recognised by the National Council for the Training of Journalists, the Broadcast Journalism Training Council and/ or the Periodicals Training Council?
- Is some of the course taught by former practitioners, people who have worked in mainstream media?
- Do the students spend a fair amount of time reporting, going out, making newspapers, radio and TV programmes, websites?
- Is the university equipped with electronic newsrooms, studios, cameras, tape-recorders, edit facilities?
- Do the students learn relevant media law and public administration? And shorthand?
- Do the students undertake media work placements and does the university organise or help to organise these?
- What is the university's record on the employment of graduating students?
- What are the links – in terms of visitors, teaching, provision of professional expertise – with the relevant industries?
- Does the course place emphasis on new (converged) media? Does it integrate writing, audio and video skills and teach you to bring them together on the website? Does it teach you to think about different interpretations of the same material for different publishing platforms?

The answer yes to all or most of these questions will tell potential students that this is a vocational course. There are such courses with a good reputation, but not all that many of them, and usually at institutions with a good reputation. My own, biased, view is that it is only worth doing an undergraduate course at one of the better places. Look at Quality Assurance Agency reports. Look at league tables. Look at research ratings. Look at employment records. Talk to employers. Talk to practising journalists who have done courses, particularly the younger ones! Application rates for these courses are high. Ten to one, even 15 to one, is not unusual at the best places. A-level requirements will be three Bs and better. Admissions tutors will also look for 'evidence of commitment' to journalism – some work experience on a local paper or hospital radio, involvement in the school magazine, etc. – and for the sort of personal qualities mentioned on page 24.

There are also some 'combined' or 'joint' honours courses where journalism is studied alongside, say, a social science, modern history or a modern language. These will provide less teaching in journalism, obviously, but remain vocational. Basic journalism skills are acquired, as well as education in another subject. A good compromise for some, particularly those who want to continue more explicitly 'academic' work through university.

Advantages
Vocational journalism courses are increasingly recognised by the relevant industries as equipping students for work in the media. They provide transferable skills – writing, teamwork, handling information, communication, presentation – that can be applied to a wide range of employment. It doesn't have to be journalism just because you've done a journalism course.

> ESSENTIALLY THERE ARE THEORY COURSES AND APPLIED/ PRACTICAL COURSES, BUT THERE ARE PRACTICAL COURSES WITH VARYING AMOUNTS OF THEORY, AND THEORETICAL COURSES WITH A DOLLOP OF PRACTICE. HOW DO YOU CHOOSE THE RIGHT ONE?

PETER COLE

FEATURE

Disadvantages

Media-related degrees demand an early concentration on journalism for those not certain that this is what they want to do and provide a lower level 'academic' experience for those who want to go to university to study hard in a more traditional way. On the other hand, some Journalism degrees are very good. If you are sure about what you want to do, why not get on and do it?

As mentioned above, some so-called Journalism degrees are really academic Media Studies degrees – if you are doing an academic as opposed to a vocational degree you might want to pursue something you loved and in which you gained a good A-level. Some employers remain sceptical about media-related degrees in general.

SCHOOL-LEAVER COURSES

There are some one-year or shorter courses for school leavers, some of them run under the auspices of the NCTJ, which awards its Preliminary Certificate to successful students. These courses are often undertaken by students with A-levels who for some reason, perhaps financial, do not want to do a degree course, and by mature students. It is easier to get a place on one of these courses than on an undergraduate or postgraduate course, but when making a choice the same list of questions as above should be applied. Those who have completed these courses tend to join local papers in the area they come from – editors like local knowledge.

SOME USEFUL BOOKS FOR THOSE CONSIDERING A COURSE IN JOURNALISM

Randall, David (2007) *The Universal Journalist*, London: Pluto Press

Harcup, Tony (2004) *Journalism Principles and Practice*, London: Sage

Fletcher, Kim (2005) *The Journalist's Handbook*, London: Macmillan

DIRECT ENTRY

Some papers, but hardly any broadcasters, will recruit direct from school, usually only on to the paper in the town where the school leaver lives. They will provide some form of training towards NCTJ exams. Some trainees will be sent to college, on day or block release, some even on courses such as those mentioned in the previous section.

POSTGRADUATES AND JOURNALISM

Postgraduate vocational journalism courses have been around longer than undergraduate ones and, perhaps for that reason, tend to be better liked by publishers, who remark on the benefits of a broader educational base and the knowledge of a subject other than journalism itself. They also say that those from postgraduate courses are more serious about journalism, more focused and, due to the intensive nature of postgraduate courses, more attuned to everyday journalistic work.

There are relatively few postgraduate vocational courses – Diploma or MA – in Journalism, and they tend to be badged specifically as Print, Newspaper, Magazine, Broadcast or Web Journalism. But whatever the badge, it is now vital that the course addresses itself to converged journalism on the website, makes you aware of the different requirements of the different platforms and the different skills needed to deliver them. The best postgraduate courses tend to be offered by the same institutions that run the best undergraduate courses.

These courses are intensive and practical, providing all the basic journalism skills, the law, public administration, shorthand, etc., as well as work placements and masses of hands-on experience. They are training courses with more reflective components on law, ethics, politics and current media issues. They have a near 100 per cent success rate in providing jobs for students at the completion of the course. The good ones are hard to get on to: applicants need to demonstrate commitment to a journalistic career, through involvement in student journalism or perhaps work experience in the media; aptitude for journalism; knowledge of current affairs and current media debates; and the personal qualities which have already been outlined.

The further education short courses, mentioned as an alternative to undergraduate courses above, are also open to graduates. There are also commercial courses, outside the higher and further education system. Choice of course should be influenced by the checklist set out in the section on undergraduate courses.

Fees for postgraduate courses tend to be between £4,000 and £6,000, with living costs on top of that. Some of the short courses run by further education colleges are much cheaper, and shorter, and are an alternative to the postgraduate courses run by universities.

There is some financial help available for postgraduate courses. The Guardian (Scott Trust) bursaries are aimed at ethnic and other minorities but do not recruit only in this area. The Journalism Diversity Fund bursaries, administered by the NCTJ, again seek to increase access to journalism and are available to students on undergraduate and short courses as well. The Arts and Humanities Research Council offers 'professional masters' bursaries, the main criteria being the quality of the applicant's first degree and the standing of the course offering the place.

OTHER THINGS

Some employers take on graduates straight after their degrees. Again these tend to be the bigger employers who run their own company training schemes. The *Financial Times, Telegraph*, Reuters, *Guardian* and *Times* are examples. And some send their trainees on university postgraduate courses. It is of course very competitive, because these graduates will be up against those who have already done the postgraduate courses. Crudely, in the case of the latter, the employers have had a lot of the basic training done for them, at no cost.

PAY

Journalism may be glamorous and attractive, but it tends to be badly paid, particularly at the very beginning. Those who have done postgraduate

USEFUL SITES FOR CAREER INFORMATION

Broadcast Journalism Training Council
www.bjtc.org.uk

National Council for the Training of Journalism
www.nctj.com

Periodicals Training Council
www.ppa.co.uk

National Union of Journalists
www.nujtraining.org.uk

courses often take a first newspaper job on little more than £12,000–£14,000 a year, with debts to be paid off. Broadcast jobs often pay a bit more, maybe £14,000–£16,000, although some researcher jobs are as badly paid as the local paper. The big money (and it's not as big as it was) tends to be on the national papers, and some major broadcast organisations. The media are suffering greatly from falling advertising revenues and the migration of some advertising to the internet. Consequently they are cutting staff.

This is the reality but young aspiring journalists should not be put off. Changing media provide new opportunities. Just make sure you are abreast of change, aware of what is happening and do not present yourself at interview as an old-fashioned romantic from the old world of delineated print and broadcast media.

OTHER JOBS

It doesn't have to be journalism. Many of the big companies are looking for graduates with the communication skills a journalism course teaches. There is public relations, which is more than gin, tonic and parties but an important corporate activity these days. There is political communication, working for politicians, parties, NGOs, charities. As I said at the beginning, keep trying and talent will out!

SO YOU WANT TO BECOME A JOURNALIST...

PETER COLE

FEATURE

GRANTS AND AWARDS FOR NEW WRITERS

TIPS ABOUT WHO'S OFFERING WHAT TO WHOM AND HOW TO LAY YOUR HANDS ON IT

VICTORIA PATCH

Victoria Patch lives in the West Country and has worked in the arts for the last seven years. She is completing her first novel after receiving a Grants for the Arts award from the Arts Council and has been shortlisted for the 2008 Asham Award, the foremost short story prize for unpublished women writers.

For the first time in four years, thanks to the Arts Council and a Grants for the Arts award, I am completely and utterly free to write. I have never really wanted to do anything else. When all my friends at university were planning their future careers, I was dreaming about the wild and romantic life I would lead before becoming a writer. I wanted to travel the world, live and work in different communities, maybe rent a flat in Paris, then return at some point in the distant future and translate it all into fiction. Which was lucky, really, as I graduated in the last recession and most of the graduates I knew ended up working in bars or shops or temping.

I worked briefly in investment banking before I started to take my writing seriously. I think it was panic about the idea of really becoming a banker – not so wild or romantic – that gave me that extra push and I joined a writing group, organised a day off from work and started to write my first novel. Of course it wasn't very good, it was about my family (un-publishable anyway until they are all dead), but it did get me an interview on the MA course in Creative Writing at UEA. Two gin and tonics to steady the nerves, and a meeting with the Poet Laureate later I had a place. This was it – I was going to give writing my best shot.

Which is all very well, but I needed a job as soon as I graduated. I applied for a position as a trainee in an arts development agency, and unexpectedly was offered the job. Given my literary interests, I was handed any project to do with literature to manage. As a result I met a local author, Jill Dawson (*Fred and Edie*, *Wild Boy*), who became a friend and sort of unofficial mentor. I was working a 40-hour week plus evenings and weekends, so my novel was temporarily put on hold. This was frustrating but in the end hugely beneficial – I was learning all about the opportunities, both regional and national, there are for writers and, most usefully, the grants writers can apply for to help them on their way.

So this is basically a mini-guide to the awards and grants that are available to new writers, most

> ❝ I WAS LEARNING ALL ABOUT THE OPPORTUNITIES, BOTH REGIONAL AND NATIONAL, THERE ARE FOR WRITERS AND, MOST USEFULLY, THE GRANTS WRITERS CAN APPLY FOR TO HELP THEM ON THEIR WAY ❞

of which I have successfully obtained for myself (back to financial advising – maybe I missed my true vocation?).

SO YOU WANT TO BE A WRITER...

You have decided you want to take your writing more seriously, maybe even make it your career. Perhaps you are a member of a writers' group and have been working on some short stories or started a novel. A short course or a BA could be the next step.

Arvon (www.arvonfoundation.org, see page 23) runs residential courses in subjects ranging from screenwriting to various genres of novels in different locations around the country. If you are hard up they have a grant scheme to enable writers to attend for a reduced rate. Alternatively you could try applying to the Arts Council, under their Grants for the Arts strand (of which more in a minute) – one of the aims being professional development for writers. It is worth contacting your regional office to find out more, or downloading funding guidelines from www. artscouncil.org.uk/funding.

BAs and MAs are expensive but normally you have the option of going part-time. Alternatively, with a postgraduate degree, if you can argue the case that the course will have some sort of beneficial effect on your current career, the Arts and Humanities Research Council (www.ahrb.ac.uk) may go some way to meeting the cost.

YOU'VE WRITTEN YOUR FIRST DRAFT BUT IT IS NOT QUITE RIGHT...

You could send your manuscript off to one of the literary consultancies that are springing up around the country. For a fee, a professional reader will give you feedback in the form of a written report. These are of varying quality, so check them out if possible (find out which readers they use, compare costs) before committing. Some, such as the Literary Consultancy (www.literaryconsultancy.co.uk) and the Hilary Johnson Authors' Advisory Service (see page 49) have links with agents and will pass on manuscripts they think are good. Don't waste this opportunity by sending in a first draft – write and rewrite your manuscript until it is as good as

> ❝ WRITE AND REWRITE YOUR MANUSCRIPT UNTIL IT IS AS GOOD AS YOU CAN MAKE IT. THE READER WILL THEN HAVE A BETTER IDEA WHERE YOUR STRENGTHS AND WEAKNESSES LIE, AND BE ABLE TO OFFER YOU CONSTRUCTIVE CRITICISM ❞

you can make it. The reader will then have a better idea where your strengths and weaknesses lie and be able to offer you constructive criticism.

This can be an expensive service but there are occasional grants available; I received one from Cambridgeshire County Council. Keep an eye out for offers like this – sign up for email newsletters from your local Arts or Literature Development Officer and have a look at websites such as www. literaturetraining.com, which has an up-to-date and extensive list of jobs, awards and funding opportunities for writers.

A much more personal and I believe rewarding experience is mentoring – again this is becoming very popular. I was a guinea pig for a mentoring scheme set up by Jill Dawson with funding from the Royal Literary Fund and the Arts Council. I was partnered with Kathryn Heyman, an Aussie novelist who went through my work with me by email and in person. The best thing about this scheme is the way it sharpens your writing (it's amazing what the anxiety induced by face-to-face criticism can do for quality) and a dialogue can develop. With readers from a literary consultancy you can't argue your point, and who is to say the reader is always right? Jill Dawson has gone on to set up her own mentoring scheme (www. golddust.org.uk) and uses only well-established authors like Michèle Roberts and Louise Doughty, who also have a track record in teaching creative writing. Again, this is quite expensive but some of Jill's mentees have received grants from the Arts Council.

New Writing North (www.newwritingnorth. com) also has a mentoring scheme. This organisation is particularly useful for writing opportunities in the north east (it is based at Newcastle University) but also keep an eye on what's happening nationally. In 2009 Arvon is running its excellent mentoring scheme in partnership with Jerwood – writers who completed one of Arvon's courses in 2008 are eligible if they asked in their booking forms for their names to be put forward. Worth finding out more from their website for 2010.

YOU HAVE COMPLETED AN MA/BEEN WORKING ON A MANUSCRIPT FOR SOME TIME – AGENTS HAVE SHOWN AN INTEREST BUT NOT COMMITTED

Perhaps now is the time to take six or seven months out and finish that novel. If you can take a sabbatical from work, great. If not – I took the plunge anyway and handed in my notice. Maybe a bit fool-hardy in the current climate but if I'd wanted a stable career I'd have stuck with banking. I had a wonderful job working for a literary festival (www.wayswithwords.org.uk) and being surrounded by successful writers, hearing their stories about their first breaks, inspired me. The director of Ways With Words has promised me a spot in the programme in 2010, so no pressure…

If you're looking for financial support, the Arts Council is the obvious place to start – www. artscouncil.org.uk. Under their Grants for the Arts funding stream, writers can apply to take time out – i.e. get their living costs paid – to work on a project, whether it's a novel or a book of poetry. The Arts Council is inundated with applicants, so your application needs to stand out. You need a reference, two or three if possible. An agent or publisher is ideal; failing that, ask a creative writing tutor, a fellow writer or someone in the business whose opinion the AC will take seriously. I have an agent who likes my work but is not prepared to sign me at this stage. (I'm a new writer with a half-finished manuscript – how does she know that I can write a beginning, a middle and an end?)

So she has written me a reference supporting my application for a grant, with the request to be the first to see the manuscript in its polished state. My mentor gave me a second reference and Jill Dawson a third.

If you live in the east of England you are eligible to apply to Escalator (www.artscouncil.org.uk/escalator), a regional talent scheme that aims to help artists get funding to complete a particular project. If successful you are guided through a Grants for the Arts application by an Arts Officer and your chances of receiving the grant are much higher.

Also in the east is the New Writing Partnership. This is another great organisation that partners UEA, the city and county council and the Arts Council – check out their website, www.newwritingpartnership.org.uk, for details of their new writers' award; this is closed for evaluation in 2008 but hopefully it will be reintroduced by 2010.

Perhaps we should be careful what we wish for. I have just come back from Paris where I was staying in a friend's flat and working on my manuscript. I am waiting to hear about an application for a grant to go to Can Serrat (www.canserrat.org), an artists' community in the foot of the mountains just outside Barcelona. They offer occasional grants to artists in all fields to live and work there for free. Maybe by the time you read this I shall be fluent in Spanish and have a completed manuscript under my belt. If not there's always banking – or maybe writing is the more reliable career in the current economic climate.

> ❝ THE ARTS COUNCIL IS INUNDATED WITH APPLICANTS, SO YOUR APPLICATION NEEDS TO STAND OUT ❞

WRITING FROM EXPERIENCE

SHOULD YOU ONLY WRITE ABOUT WHAT YOU KNOW?

CARO FRASER

Caro Fraser is the author of the bestselling Caper Court series of legal novels, numbering seven to date, and of six stand-alone novels, including *A Little Learning* and *A World Apart*. She is currently working on the eighth in the Caper Court series.

'Write about what you know' is one of those tired old adages guaranteed to polarise professional writers. In some it arouses spittle-flecked invective about the stifling of creativity and encouragement of dreary, introverted navel-gazing. There are even those who say it's particularly bad advice to give writers because, as a breed, we tend not to get out a lot. There are, on the other hand, those who believe it to be a sound precept, on the basis that if you're not writing from within the scope of your own experience, you can't possibly write with authenticity or with a truthful voice.

So, for the aspiring writer, is the advice good or bad – or what?

The answer probably lies somewhere in between. Let's first of all try to establish what is meant by 'writing about what you know'. If it means using only the material of your own life, working solely with events and characters from within your personal experience, then that, at first glance, seems extremely restricting. However, if you possess the talents of Jane Austen, if you can handle social and domestic microcosms with dexterity and humour, and have a brilliant ear for dialogue and eye for detail, then what you 'know', in a strict sense, may be all you need. Yet even writers who are using only the material of their own life, like Austen, have to expand beyond the confines of their knowledge – that is, they need to manipulate and explore their experiences in creative ways that make them interesting to readers. It isn't so much what you know, as how you use it.

> IF YOU POSSESS THE TALENTS OF JANE AUSTEN, IF YOU CAN HANDLE SOCIAL AND DOMESTIC MICROCOSMS WITH DEXTERITY AND HUMOUR, AND HAVE A BRILLIANT EAR FOR DIALOGUE AND EYE FOR DETAIL, THEN WHAT YOU 'KNOW', IN A STRICT SENSE, MAY BE ALL YOU NEED

USE WHAT YOU KNOW

When I wrote *The Pupil*, the first of my Caper Court novels, I used the legal world as its setting. This wasn't because I especially wanted to write about lawyers or the law – my main interest is in people, exploring human emotions and motivation – but because setting the novel in a world with which I was familiar gave the story authenticity. I'm a barrister by training, so the legal world is one I understand. I'm familiar with lawyers' concerns, with law courts and with legal jargon. Leo Davies, perhaps my best-known character, is a successful, bisexual commercial barrister. I don't need to be bisexual to write him, because sexual impulses, passion, love, are universal emotions. All that's needed there is a little imagination and emotional empathy. But knowing what makes a commercial barrister tick enables me to write about Leo's world with a fluidity and confidence that I couldn't possibly bring to bear if I'd made him a brain surgeon. As a writer, I believe it's important to get to the essential truth of a character and it seems self-evident that this can only be achieved by properly understanding the motivation and preoccupations of that character.

Inside knowledge is invaluable if you decide to set your stories within a very particular world – take Patricia Cornwell and her experience of forensic science, or Dick Francis and his knowledge of horses and the world of racing. In such instances, 'what you know' allows you to manipulate your knowledge and use it deftly – even to subvert it for the purposes of plot. If you're not sure of your territory, your lack of confidence will transmit itself to the reader and hamper your ability to develop plot and character. The point is, use what you know to its best advantage: your own life or experience may not strike you as a promising basis for fiction but, if you handle it with imagination and inventiveness, and create believable and empathetic characters about whom the reader can care, you may be surprised how much potential it possesses.

Invention and manipulation lie at the heart of all good fiction. Writers constantly range beyond themselves, but within their own experience, to find the material upon which they build their stories. Even enthralling fantasy worlds populated by fantastical characters, such as those created by JRR Tolkein and Terry Pratchett, while obviously the products of extraordinarily fertile imaginations, must have as their essence the writer's own experience and understanding. It is the magical, combined power of both the writer's and the reader's imaginations that enables these worlds to come so vividly to life.

When it comes to characterisation, most writers create a range of characters widely diverse and different from themselves. The characters I write about in my books aren't based on real individuals – though certain people claim, mistakenly, to have identified themselves – but are amalgamations of different aspects of personalities I have encountered, with other traits and idiosyncrasies thrown in. Look around you, and you'll find a wealth of promising character material among your own family and friends. Just be aware of the dangers of putting people directly on to the page – be inventive!

PUT YOUR OWN SLANT ON YOUR EXPERIENCE

Writing from your own experience needn't be a limiting concept. We are all capable of extending our breadth of knowledge and depth of insight. Dickens did it by walking the streets of London, by watching, observing and noting with meticulous detail the everyday business of a city which, in another writer's hands, might be humdrum and pedestrian. So it's important to build up what you 'know', to keep your perceptions alert, observe, investigate and take notes. Note-taking can be particularly helpful later when you want to recapture certain sensations, sounds or visual effects which are difficult to recollect, and notes can act as an excellent means of reviving certain trains of thought. Because it involves exercising one's powers of observation, recall and self-examination, working from personal experience can be useful for a beginner who is just learning the skills of plot, characterisation, dialogue and pacing. But only the magical power of imagination can transform that experience into good fiction.

You also 'know' more than you think. Through the process of writing, new truths often emerge. Your interpretation of a commonly shared

> **AS A WRITER I BELIEVE IT'S IMPORTANT TO GET TO THE ESSENTIAL TRUTH OF A CHARACTER, AND IT SEEMS SELF-EVIDENT THAT THIS CAN ONLY BE ACHIEVED BY PROPERLY UNDERSTANDING THE MOTIVATIONS AND PREOCCUPATION OF THAT CHARACTER**

experience, or an everyday event – done humorously, darkly or in whatever way you wish to explore it – can bring readers alive to a new understanding of their own experience. We all have a shared humanity, an understanding of the common links and trivia which inform everyone's life. Much of the success of writing lies in making readers identify their own experiences or responses to familiar situations. Truth is more than just bare facts. As a writer you may aim to write something with which others will identify but, as often as not, they will identify with things you never intended or find truths you didn't know you'd uttered.

DO YOUR RESEARCH – BUT DON'T FLAUNT IT

Maybe you want to write beyond the scope of your personal experience, in an area where you don't feel you know enough? Make yourself an expert! Thorough research can prove an excellent substitute for working knowledge and experience. Stef Penney demonstrated this in the writing of her hugely successful novel, *Tenderness of Wolves*. Penney has reportedly never been near the desolate interior of northern Canada where her novel is set and whose landscape and atmosphere she so powerfully describes and evokes. She did, however, spend over two years researching the political, cultural and social history of the area in order to write the book. This provoked controversy among certain reviewers, who seemed to suggest that lack of direct experience might make for a less credible novel. But why should it? If it works for the reader, if the ambience which the author is striving for has been successfully created, does the book somehow lack authenticity because the author hasn't tramped the snowy wastes of Canada? Grafted on to a fertile imagination and a strong storyline, good research can be just as resonant as first-hand experience, as is demonstrated by the best historical novelists.

Don't forget, however, that one of the dangers of working largely from research is that you can get carried away by your own discoveries. There is a temptation, when researching some incidental aspect of a novel, to use a wealth of interesting information and fact in the novel itself. Most of it isn't needed. It may have helped you to write with confidence but the reader can usually do without it. More than a few writers fall into the trap of imagining that their sudden, profound depth of knowledge about some esoteric subject will be just as fascinating to the reader as it is to them. In my most recent novel I had to create a character who develops dementia and I spent a lot of time researching dementia and its effects on the individual. At the end of the day, however, I took what I had learned and used my imagination to create what I hoped was a believable characterisation. The research stayed in my notes.

So don't assume you don't know enough or don't have anything interesting to write about. The most apparently mundane material can become inspiring in the right hands. Use what you know, research the things you don't know and you may find that your own everyday experiences can be turned into absorbing fiction. Follow the excellent advice of Henry James – 'Try to be one of those people on whom nothing is lost.'

> **WORKING FROM PERSONAL EXPERIENCE CAN BE USEFUL FOR A BEGINNER WHO IS JUST LEARNING THE SKILLS OF PLOT, CHARACTERISATION, DIALOGUE AND PACING. BUT ONLY THE MAGICAL POWER OF IMAGINATION CAN TRANSFORM THAT EXPERIENCE INTO GOOD FICTION**

WRITING FROM EXPERIENCE

CARO FRASER

FEATURE

CREATING BELIEVABLE CHARACTERS

IT DOESN'T MATTER WHAT THEY EAT FOR BREAKFAST

SOPHIE HANNAH

Sophie Hannah is a bestselling crime writer. Her latest novel is *The Other Half Lives* (Hodder, February 2009). She lives in West Yorkshire. Her website is www.sophiehannah.com

When I read 'How To…' articles and books about writing, the sections on characterisation are the parts I agree with least. Invariably, the advice will go something like this: 'You need to know your characters inside out and be able to answer the following questions about them: what do they like to eat for breakfast? What is their favourite colour? Are they night owls or early risers?' Usually, the list of questions is endless and enough, in my opinion, to crush anyone's creative enthusiasm.

> IN REAL LIFE, WE DON'T KNOW ANYONE INSIDE OUT, NOT EVEN THOSE CLOSEST TO US

GETTING TO KNOW YOUR CHARACTERS

When you begin a work of fiction, you need to feel energised and excited about every aspect of it, including the characters with whom you'll be spending so much time. You must be eager to get to know them – ideally, you should feel magnetically drawn to them – and so to force yourself to answer a list of (often irrelevant) questions about them seems to me to be a silly task to set yourself, as silly as saying to someone who has just fallen in love, 'If you've met a gorgeous stranger who you hope might be "the one", the first thing to do is sit down and fill in a complicated tax return with him.'

Why should we strive to know the characters in our novels inside out? In real life, we don't know anyone inside out, not even those closest to us. People are unpredictable and full of secrets; many lack self-awareness and have an image of their own character that is entirely out of kilter with the reality. Sometimes the people who seem most stable are presenting a façade to the world which might eventually crack to reveal an entirely different personality underneath. Often (as with the falling in love example above) we are keenest to spend time with – to try to get a grip on – those who are in some way elusive to us.

This is as true in fiction as in life. Therefore, writing fiction is going to be far more compelling for any writer struggling with the fascinating ambiguities presented by a character he/she has invented. In writing the novel, or story, you are striving to know your characters. To a certain extent you'll succeed and to a certain extent you'll fail – ideally, by the end of the writing process, your characters will still feel slightly intangible and out of your reach. That, in my view, is how you know you've created a genuinely plausible and rounded character.

WHAT DO YOU *NEED* TO KNOW?

You can answer questions about how early someone likes to get up or what their favourite colour is till the cows come home – and yes, some of these details might be useful to include – but what do they really tell you about the core of a person? Their taste in music, the messy versus the tidy – these are peripheral details, not real

> ## THEIR TASTE IN MUSIC, THE MESSY VERSUS THE TIDY – THESE ARE PERIPHERAL DETAILS, NOT REAL CHARACTER

character. They're the sorts of things you can easily tick off on a checklist, and, in doing so, give yourself the illusion that you know someone. I know the preferred getting-up times of all my close relatives, for example, but I'm not sure how a single one of them would react if I killed someone in a hit-and-run accident and begged them not to tell the police.

Tomorrow, I'm going to start writing my fifth psychological thriller. One of my main characters is a woman called Rachel. I have no idea whether she likes to rise early or sleep late – if it matters to the story, then I suppose that information will come to me when I need it but I suspect it won't matter a jot. I also don't know what her favourite subject was at school. All that seems too boring even to consider. I started off knowing only three things about her: the situation in which she finds herself at the beginning of the story, what she is hiding and why she is hiding it. All three were things I was not conscious of 'making up' – they were simply there in my mind, as if they already existed, in accordance with the needs of the story I wanted to tell. From these needs my main characters grew. The concept of the overall story comes first every time for me; my approach to characterisation is a plot-based one.

PLOT AND CHARACTER: YOU CAN'T SEPARATE THEM

I've often heard writers asked, 'Which is more important to you: character or plot?' Most writers choose character. I've only ever heard one answer, 'Plot, plot, plot' – that was the American thriller writer Jeffery Deaver. But it's a crazy question, because plot and character are inextricably linked. The best way to start a novel is with a character in a compelling or intriguing situation. There's no character in the world unique and amazing enough to sustain readers' interest if they're not

doing anything fascinating or if not much is at stake for them. Equally, the most gripping plot will fall flat if the characters acting it out are one-dimensional.

The element of 'puzzle' here is crucial, in relation to plot and character and how they can and ought to develop together. As a crime writer, I frequently take part in panel discussions on various aspects of crime writing and recently was on an Agatha Christie panel. The topic was, basically: are her novels now obsolete or is there still a place for them? I was amazed to hear a respected crime writer explain vehemently why Christie's work was worthless because her novels are merely 'puzzles'. I have often heard crime

> ## THERE'S NO CHARACTER IN THE WORLD UNIQUE AND AMAZING ENOUGH TO SUSTAIN READERS' INTEREST IF THEY'RE NOT DOING ANYTHING FASCINATING, OR IF NOT MUCH IS AT STAKE FOR THEM

writers deride the puzzle element of crime fiction. The contemporary orthodoxy seems to be that too much emphasis on puzzle and plot is somehow shallow, reducing both the writer and the reader to the status of crossword-obsessed, anorak-wearing geeks who care little for the deep concerns of humanity and want nothing more than to fill in their grid of boxes with the right symbols.

I couldn't disagree more. It is the unknown and the mysterious that drive us forward in life and sharpen our motivation: not knowing what's going to happen next, not knowing what others are really thinking. The known has a feeling of 'been there, done that'; this applies to people as well as to happenings. There is no deeper concern for humanity than puzzle-solving, and no such thing as 'just a puzzle', if the writer truly understands the crucial importance of mystery and solution in our narratives about our lives. This is as true of general fiction as it is of crime fiction. As one of my favourite poets, C H Sisson, wrote:

Human uncertainty is all
That makes the human reason strong.

I ended up using that quote in my second crime novel, *Hurting Distance*, in a scene where a witness (who knows exactly what's going on and could solve the mystery in a heartbeat if she chose to) is refusing to share any information with the detectives who are interviewing her, and taunting them with her knowledge and their lack of it. I was pleased with the scene because it sharpens the desire to know, in relation to both the plot and the withholding character. The reader wonders not only, 'What's going on here?' but also, 'Why would someone who knows be determined not to share that knowledge?'

Character and plot should, ideally, develop in tandem, organically. (I'm having visions of braided hair as I write this – that's as close a visual image as I can come up with of the process I'm trying to describe.) Each new piece of plot should bring with it further insights about the characters; each new foray into the mind of a character should point the way for the plot. The way we know people in real life is not with any sort of inside-out comprehensiveness – it's not like buying a new car and reading its manual from cover to cover. We get to know people in glimpses – that remark, that behaviour on that occasion. When we have enough experience of the person, we can start to try to put the pieces together. Sometimes those pieces seem to add up and sometimes they seem contradictory. I suppose the first question I might ask myself about a character for one of my books is: what's my first glimpse of him or her? Whatever it is, it should contain the seeds of some kind of compulsion; it should breed a need to see more of that character, spend more time with her and discover more about her.

> **EACH NEW PIECE OF PLOT SHOULD BRING WITH IT FURTHER INSIGHTS ABOUT THE CHARACTERS; EACH NEW FORAY INTO THE MIND OF A CHARACTER SHOULD POINT THE WAY FOR THE PLOT**

FIRST IMPRESSIONS

To go back to Rachel, one of the heroines of the novel I'm currently writing, my first glimpse of her was through the eyes of another character in the book, Fliss. Fliss has arranged to meet Rachel at her (Fliss's) flat, and is watching through the window as Rachel drives up the road. Suddenly, Rachel swerves her car round and drives away. Why? Because she doesn't like the look of Fliss's flat from the outside and suspects she'll like it even less on the inside. Rachel (I realised as this scene unfolded in my head) is someone who is obsessed with everything being perfect. Fliss's flat is merely ordinary, perhaps a little shabby, so Rachel doesn't want to be in it, not even for half an hour. In suspense fiction it's important to answer some questions straight away while leaving others – the over-arching ones – unanswered until the end of the book. So, almost

> **IT IS THE UNKNOWN AND THE MYSTERIOUS THAT DRIVE US FORWARD IN LIFE AND SHARPEN OUR MOTIVATION**

immediately, Rachel tells Fliss about her obsession with high standards and aesthetic beauty, with some things being objectively better than others, and it making sense, therefore, to deal exclusively with the better things in life and avoid the worse.

In answering one question, Rachel is creating another: *why* would it disturb her so much to spend a short time in a flat that is ordinary rather than stunning? It's not as if she has to live there. Rachel is a puzzle to Fliss – after a brief glimpse and a question-raising answer, she's become more puzzling as we have seen more of her. Sometimes, the only way in which we get to know characters better during the course of a book is as they confuse us more and more with their behaviour (as in Ford Madox Ford's *The Good Soldier*, for example).

As soon as I'd seen, in my imaginings, Rachel driving away from Fliss's flat and understood why she'd done it, I found I was able to catch a few more glimpses of her. At some point in the book, someone is going to offer her a brew and she's going to turn it down on the grounds that there are no one-off-work-of-art pottery mugs for her to drink it from, and she doesn't like to drink from mass-produced mugs.

Do I know why Rachel is like this? Absolutely, and it's tied up with her psychological relationship to the main mystery in the novel; it's not an irrelevant detail. I am now able to see and feel her as a fully present actor in the book. She's wholly 'there' and I know that I can write about her accurately: present her behaviour and speech and some of her thoughts. But if you said to me, 'What sort of a person is Rachel?' I'd find that very difficult to answer, because that would involve labelling and summarising rather than my preferred impressionistic method of getting to know characters.

A DIFFERENT SORT OF CHECKLIST

If I were going to attempt a list of questions for fiction writers to answer about their characters, I would try to formulate questions that could be answered impressionistically, such as:

- what opinions/beliefs does this person seem to have about himself?
- how, if at all, does this differ from other people's opinions of him?
- how well does this character seem to know himself?

- Is he dishonest with himself but honest with others, or honest with himself and dishonest with others?
- what doesn't make sense, or add up, about this person? What contradictions are there?
- what memorable scenes do you associate with this character?
- in what way might your other characters, or you as a writer, misjudge this person because of your own behaviours or attitudes?
- what do you fear you might never find out about this person?

These questions are more useful because they relate to insights about character that have some depth, rather than simply to details that anyone who knew that person might know.

> DO I KNOW WHY RACHEL IS LIKE THIS? ABSOLUTELY, AND IT'S TIED UP WITH HER PSYCHOLOGICAL RELATIONSHIP TO THE MAIN MYSTERY IN THE NOVEL; IT'S NOT AN IRRELEVANT DETAIL. I AM NOW ABLE TO SEE AND FEEL HER AS A FULLY PRESENT ACTOR IN THE BOOK

THE OTHER SIDE OF THE BEDROOM DOOR

HOW TO WRITE SEX SCENES

LYN WOOD

Lyn Wood has written many short stories, both literary and commercial, that feature sex scenes; she is also the author of two novels for Black Lace. All of the quotations in this article are taken from her work.

> When that bedroom door looms before you, does your blood run cold at the prospect of opening it? Do you feel that you're damned if you do and damned if you don't? If you skip to coffee and croissants the following morning your readers are going to feel cheated – but if you write the scene without sufficient care, we're either going to howl with laughter or stop reading altogether.

BAD SEX

Some really big names have won the Bad Sex in Fiction Award, which has been run since 1993 by the *Literary Review* to 'draw attention to the crude, tasteless, often perfunctory use of redundant passages of sexual description in the modern novel, and to discourage it'. Genuine pornographers need not apply; this is for writers who want to be taken seriously (and maybe a little roughly, preferably in a haystack).

Four *slithers* in a row, followed by *otorhinolaryngological caverns* ensured Tom Wolfe's win in 2004, and a reference to an *old battering ram* made Norman Mailer the first posthumous recipient in 2007. Paul Theroux's *demon eel thrashing in his loins* was only bad enough for a shortlisting in 2005.

It's easy to poke fun at passages that don't succeed, and much harder to write ones that do. The reason it's particularly easy to have a good giggle at extracts is that they are precisely that – extracts. Taken out of context, sex frequently becomes simply funny.

WHO ARE YOU WRITING *FOR*?

True eroticism in literature nearly always depends upon characterisation, and characters take time – and quite a few pages – to develop. It's people's motivation we really care about – why they behave the way they do. One of the most erotic stories ever written is John Fowles' *The Ebony Tower* where, in the end, nothing actually happens. Fowles uses the characters to represent artistic movements, and there's a sense of justification in reading about sex when it's a literary device for something highbrow. Cardboard characters have cardboard sex; complex characters have interesting sex.

In an out-and-out romance, the bedroom scene is often the culmination of the whole plot, sometimes after many near-misses. You are aiming to get an emotional response from your reader, which means that your reader has to care what happens.

Imagine you're writing an updated *Jane Eyre*. After 400 pages of frustration 'Reader, I married him' will fall a bit flat. Charlotte Bronte did, however, give us a few hints.

No woman was ever nearer to her mate than I am: ever more absolutely bone of his bone and flesh of his flesh.

> *IMAGINE YOU'RE WRITING AN UPDATED JANE EYRE. AFTER 400 PAGES OF FRUSTRATION 'READER, I MARRIED HIM' WILL FALL A BIT FLAT.*

But remember, she was writing in a time when a large percentage of her female readers wouldn't have had a clue what she meant. It's a bit different today.

The build-up is crucial, sexual tension is a must and we need to feel a real sense of relief when your characters finally get it together. An ellipsis as they climb into bed just isn't acceptable any more...

If you're setting out to write soft porn for an imprint such as Black Lace or Nexus, you need to read a few of them to get an idea of what's wanted. Black Lace accepts only female authors and gives comprehensive guidelines online, for writing women's erotica isn't the same as writing for men. Women want a connection between characters, men want the act and the anatomy, and there's a surprisingly high demand for sado-masochism. These books are not for the faint-hearted, nor are they simply one bonk after another. There has to be a story. The secret is to create a world in which erotic events can happen, without seeming to be too unlikely or gratuitous. A suspension of disbelief is vital, so interruptions in the way of factual errors are bad news. The purpose of these books is to arouse. If it didn't arouse you, the writer, it is in all likelihood going to be a bit of a damp squib. You need to invent characters you find devastatingly attractive and situations in which just about anything seems possible, with perhaps a hint of the forbidden. And, at the same time, you need to try to be original…

'It is a bit of a problem,' said Tad.
'What is?'
'Having a shower. You have to stick the bandaged arm out of the curtain, and do everything one-handed. Takes forever. On your own.'

She looked at him. He was smiling.
'What are you suggesting?' she said.
'We could combine it with an anatomy lesson.'

Because the reader becomes a voyeur it may help to imagine the action as a scene from a film, and write it accordingly. But the characters themselves can be voyeurs too, and watching them watching someone else can work equally well:

What she'd thought was a patch of sunlight was, in fact, Gerald's right buttock. And the dead branch wasn't a piece of wood at all, it was Lettie's left leg. And the way the ferns were moving had nothing to do with the breeze. There wasn't a breeze.
'I think we ought to... well, go,' whispered Nan. 'Why?' said Tad softly in her ear. 'When elephants do it, the whole herd gathers to watch.'

If you're writing a book where the central theme is something else entirely, your purpose may be rather different. The reader's arousal isn't necessarily the object of the exercise. The sex may be intentionally unfulfilling, and the style of writing needs to reflect that:

So what happened last night? I had a bath, he cut his toenails, I plumped up the pillows, he drew the curtains. I switched out the light, he put his left arm round me, I rolled slightly in his direction, he said, 'Fingers crossed' and we coupled like two halves of a goods train. There was a job to be done.

And just occasionally, your plot may require the truly horrific, such as a rape scene, when you need to choose your words very carefully indeed. Absolutely no humour, no trivialisation, no glamour. The tiny details that have nothing to do with the act itself can have the most impact.

'You cannot refuse me, Airam,' said Iktar. With one movement of his hand he ripped the shift from her body. Her emerald pendant, the most precious thing she possessed, caught in the material and went with it.

THE TOOLS OF THE TRADE...

Body parts. There's no getting away from them, you're going to have to describe those naughty bits – and, in all probability, more than once. *Roget's Thesaurus* is invaluable for alternatives, as is *Roger's Profanisaurus* for the terms to avoid. Sound too technical or medical and it's a turn-off. Sound too colloquial and it's sliding down the lubricated slope of pornography. Similes and metaphors work rather better, but transport is generally best avoided. Trains going into tunnels, submarines surfacing and planes taking off have all become clichés, because sex is the subject that's been written about more than anything else. Those verbs can be a problem, too. Clench, thrust, slam, writhe, slide... taken in isolation, they raise a smile rather than anything else.

Sex is sensual. Using as many senses as possible is, on the whole, a good idea. The visual presents the fewest problems. You're describing either a character or a setting and the rules here are no different from anywhere else. But what about the sounds? Squelches and slurps and sucking noises are a quagmire of sibilance, and finding new words to describe the oldest performance of all is a tough one. The most important sense is, of course, touch. Silky, satiny, muscular, moist... Once again, there are certain sounds that predominate. Use them; alliteration is a very effective device for making a piece of prose memorable. And, last but not least, don't forget the smells. Because not everyone remembers to put them in they don't have the cliché rating of the other senses, and they can be used to great effect in creating atmosphere.

Everything seemed very focused and sharp, the predictable squeak of the door-handle, the staccato click of the latch moving back. Their shadows on the stairs, the creak on the top step, the smell of beeswax and lavender, the softer click as the bedroom door closed behind them.

IMPEDIMENTS

One hundred and fifty years ago it was mad wives in the attic. These days, it's buttons, zips, hooks and eyes, ribbons, laces... even Velcro. Ignore them, and suddenly we go from fully dressed to naked. Gaps in the narrative draw attention to the artifice of fiction just as much as the superfluous, so you do need to undress your characters unless it's a quickie in a car park. You can be concise about it, but you still have to do it:

Maxim lit the fat yellow candle, placed it on the table and turned to her. Then he started to undress her, and there was no bumping of elbows or zips that got stuck or buttons that wouldn't undo.

And then there's safe sex to be considered. This is where historical, fantasy and science-fiction novels have a definite advantage, as it's irrelevant. Sometimes, the best way to deal with an issue is to confront it head-on – as long as you can find a device that fits the bill.

He started to unbutton her shirt. 'At this juncture,' he smiled, 'as you'll be a little out of date, we say things like I have no known diseases, and as luck would have it I've got a condom in my pocket.'

This moves the story along and develops the characters, at the same time as being responsible authorship. Dialogue can often achieve things better than a straight description and it breaks up the page in an interesting way. And don't forget, post-coital cigarettes are out these days unless your characters have a *real* penchant for danger.

Georges Mikes, in his book *How to Be an Alien*, remarked that 'Continental people have sex lives; the English have hot-water bottles'. Not any longer, they don't.

A COUPLE OF USEFUL WEBSITES

- www.blacklace-books.co.uk/guidelines.html
- www.millsandboon.co.uk/aspiringauthors.asp

WRITING SHORTER
THE CRAFT OF THE SHORT STORY

SARAH SALWAY

Sarah Salway's short story collection, *Leading the Dance*, is published by Bluechrome. She is also the author of the novels *Something Beginning With* and *Tell Me Everything* (both Bloomsbury). Sarah keeps an online writing journal at www.sarahsalway. blogspot.com.

> *Not that the story need be long, but it will take a long while to make it short.*
> Henry David Thoreau

I love both reading and writing short stories. But I also know how much hard work and skill it takes to get them right, so I ignore the warnings that normally accompany such a statement – that they are 'easy' to write and therefore a cheat, that no one wants to read them, that they don't sell, that somehow they are less satisfying than either poetry or novels because they fall somewhere in between.

'The art of the glimpse,' William Trevor called them. The phrase describes perfectly the chance the short story offers to peek in at someone's life. Writing one is like being asked to fill in a page of someone else's diary. Indeed, one of the best pieces of writing advice I received was to cut the first and the last paragraph of every short story. I don't always follow it but it was useful when I started out because it made me realise how painstakingly keen I'd been to explain everything

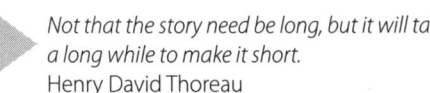

> **ONE OF THE BEST PIECES OF WRITING ADVICE I RECEIVED WAS TO CUT THE FIRST AND THE LAST PARAGRAPH OF EVERY SHORT STORY**

FIVE SHORT STORY WEBSITES

www.pulp.net
A useful site for new writing, updated regularly
www.shortstory.org.uk
Dedicated to the short story
www.theshortreview.com
Reviews of short story anthologies
www.eastoftheweb.com
An online library of classic and contemporary stories
www.mcsweeneys.net
Good resource for US short story news

that was going to happen and then to wrap everything up at the end just in case the reader hadn't understood the story. But to write good short stories, we have to learn to trust the reader. Ernest Hemingway's six-word classic, 'For sale: baby shoes, never worn', is perhaps the best example of this.

Writing a short story is like meeting a stranger you want to confide in. You need the other person to really feel what you have to say. Given the limited length of time you will be together, images become important, senses vital. Perhaps this heightened visual sense is one of the reasons why so many short stories – *Crash*, *The Swimmer*, *Brokeback Mountain*, *In the Gloaming**– have been made into successful films.

And then there's the chance for the writer to experiment. I've now written over 30 short stories and my subjects have included a bored housewife who commissions a portrait of her fridge (*Painting the Family Pet*), the art of survival a schoolboy has to learn when his gang turns against him (*Toad in the Hole*) and how a dance between a husband and a wife at a school ceilidh becomes a battle (*Leading the Dance*).

I've written from every available point of view, including (in *Quiet Hour*) a child who happily narrates events without realising how his life has just changed in front of him. More than one of my stories has taken the lexicon format. *Dictionary of Death Dreams* consists of an alphabetically organised list of nightmare images, all designed to explore the violence present in my narrator's relationship, and I even used bullet points in *Instructions for Reading this Story*. Given what's possible, it's not surprising that there's often an exuberance detectable in the short story that hints at just how liberated the author feels. However hard she might wrestle with the form, it doesn't demand the same commitment that a novel needs in terms of time and energy.

HOW LONG SHOULD THEY BE?

The shortest story I've written is just 30 words, and my longest is a bit over 5,000. Although common wisdom says that the average length is about 2,000 words, as the Hemingway example above shows, short stories can be very short indeed. Edge over 8,000 words and you need to think whether you wouldn't be better off writing a novel. The rise in internet publishing has led to an increase in 'flash fiction'; very compact intense stories that are read in one sitting and that deal often in one moment – or flash – of someone's life. Generally these will be between 500 and

> ## WRITING A SHORT STORY IS LIKE MEETING A STRANGER YOU WANT TO CONFIDE IN. YOU NEED THE OTHER PERSON TO REALLY FEEL WHAT YOU HAVE TO SAY. GIVEN THE LIMITED LENGTH OF TIME YOU WILL BE TOGETHER, IMAGES BECOME IMPORTANT, SENSES VITAL

1,000 words and so, not surprisingly, experienced writers of flash fiction often talk about how what they leave out of the story is as important as what remains.

MAKING EVERYTHING COUNT

Take apart any successful short story and you will find skilful use of nearly every tool in the writer's kit. Everything counts. This might be in an attention-grabbing title – Karen Russell's *St Lucy's Home for Girls Raised by Wolves* is one of my current favourites. The structure also has to be there to add to either the theme or the character. Lorrie Moore's collection *Self-Help* is excellent to see how it can be done. In her *How to Talk To Your Mother (notes)*, the story is broken into a list of dates starting with the daughter's birth. By the end, it is the mother who has become the child and so the silent cycle relentlessly continues.

Rhythm is important too. David Foster Wallace's *Incarnations of Burnt Children* is a story about a child being scalded in a domestic accident. It consists of just nine very long sentences used to build up an almost unbearable tension. Every time I read it, it's only when I reach the end that I realise I stopped breathing after the first line.

In contrast, there can be a playfulness that makes me smile. Carol Shields's story *Absence* is about a writer who has one key broken on her typewriter. It's the letter 'I' and yes, you've guessed it, the story is written completely without that particular letter. This conceit fits in with the theme of how the narrator is wrestling with her identity.

But this isn't to suggest that short stories are the trick ponies of literature. Most are character-led, and contain what James Joyce called

FIVE SHORT STORY COMPETITIONS

The Bridport Prize
(www.bridportprize.org.uk) – one of the big ones
New Writer Magazine
(www.thenewwriter.com/prizes.htm) – annual prose and poetry competition
Fish Short Story Prize
(www.fishpublishing.com) – a number of different themed competitions
The Willesden Herald Competition
(www.willesdenherald.com/competition/rules.php)
Momaya Press
(www.momayapress.com)

the epiphany or, as I often tell my students, 'something needs to happen'. In Joyce's *Dubliners*, this takes the form of an insight each of the characters has which changes the way he or she sees their world. Like Joyce's, the best epiphanies are subtle; indeed in the very best it's the reader who has the insight, viewing the character in a completely different light by the end of the story. On the surface nothing really has happened, but underneath everything has changed. It's this integrity of the relationship between reader and writer that's important. You're only together a little while so you need to build up trust quickly. Which is why stories which have the character waking up from a dream, or turning out to be a cat are so difficult to write effectively. Although someone like Roald Dahl is a master at the 'twist in the tale', too often as a reader I can end up feeling cheated.

WHERE CAN YOU PUBLISH THEM?

Because of their length and immediacy, short stories work well on the internet. When Lynne Rees and I wanted to celebrate the reprint of our collaborative collection, *Messages*, we started a website, Your Messages, for responses to our daily prompts (www.yourmessages.org). The challenge was that the stories had to be 300 words exactly. It's now in its second year, and we have writers participating from all over the world. This is just one example of the thriving online market for writers and readers. Nearly every month, a new web-based magazine for short stories is launched, and even established print magazines like the *New Yorker* now offer their stories as podcasts.

And if you wonder whether all this writing is ever read online let me tell you my own story. In 2003, I put one of my short stories, *A Girls Alphabet* up on the site East of the Web (see box on page 43). Within a couple of weeks, I received a letter from an editor at a large publishing house asking if I was interested in talking further.

Of course I was; so interested, in fact, that I didn't reply at first, presuming it was a joke by one of my friends. However a couple of days later, I had also had separate emails from two agents. Six months later, I had a two-novel deal with both an English and an American publisher. A modern day fairytale to be sure, with the short story as a perfect prince!

TEN SHORT STORY COLLECTIONS FOR YOUR LIBRARY

- **Anton Chekhov**, *Tales of Anton Chekhov*
- **Katherine Mansfield**, *Collected Stories of Katherine Mansfield*
- **James Joyce**, *Dubliners*
- **Guy de Maupassant**, *Selected Short Stories*
- **Donald Barthelme**, *Sixty Stories*
- **Raymond Carver**, *Cathedral*
- **Lydia Davis**, *Samuel Johnson is Indignant*
- **Z Z Packer**, *Drinking Coffee Elsewhere*
- **Alice Munro**, *The Love of A Good Woman*
- **William Trevor**, *The Collected Stories*

FIVE SHORT STORY WRITING GUIDES

Ailsa Cox, *Writing Short Stories*
Damon Knight, *Creating Short Fiction*
Rust Hills, *Writing in General and the Short Story in Particular*
Tom Bailey (ed.), *On Writing Short Stories*
Paul Mandelbaum, *12 Short Stories and their Making*

ON THE SURFACE NOTHING REALLY HAS HAPPENED, BUT UNDERNEATH EVERYTHING HAS CHANGED. IT'S THIS INTEGRITY OF THE RELATIONSHIP BETWEEN READER AND WRITER THAT'S IMPORTANT

SARAH SALWAY

FEATURE

MOVING INTO MOVIES

WRITING ACROSS A VARIETY OF FORMS

HELEN CROSS

Helen Cross is the author of three novels, including, *My Summer of Love*, which became a BAFTA-award-winning feature film, and most recently, *Spilt Milk, Black Coffee* (Bloomsbury, 2009). Her plays have been broadcast on radio, and her stories have appeared in various anthologies. Her original screenplay, *Stratford Road*, is currently in development with Red Room Films.

Screenwriting is to novel-writing what marching is to wandering. It's quite a step from wrestling with novel characters, who hang around in a vague unstructured way, to tussling with screen characters who never just hang around but do everything – even their loitering – in a concise and purposeful way.

For years I tiptoed across the divide between prose and drama. I'd always known I wanted to be a writer, but what kind of writing did I want to do? I began with novels; not because of any timeless tender literary sensibilities, but because novel-writing seemed solitary and personal and you needed no permission to begin. You did not have to convince anyone of your abilities, or ask them to come on the journey with you. You did not need a team, a cast or a crew. Just a pen, paper and peace, and if it turned out that you were an embarrassing disaster, only you would know you'd ever considered yourself otherwise.

But I still had drama in my sights. While studying for my undergraduate degree in English and Drama at Goldsmiths, I'd been impressed by the energy and self-confidence of the emerging playwrights who would trumpet the arrival of

their new plays, then wait open-armed as actors, stage managers and an entire creative team galloped forth.

I couldn't imagine anything worse. Opening up? No, thanks, I'm shutting down and hiding away to write. After university I worked for the Royal Shakespeare Company, and at night I wrote in an icy-cold cottage in the Cotswolds. Where it took me three years to write my first novel, which was everything I feared it might be: deeply, darkly, dreadful. At least I realised it was too crazy and uneven even to consider sending it out to publishers.

BRANCHING OUT

Writing alone and obsessively had taught me one important lesson, though: there is more to successful writing than just having the iron will to do it. There is the tricky question of talent. Then the headache of skill; of structure and plot and style. So, I quit the day job, applied to study for an MA in Creative Writing at the University of East Anglia and hoped to explore what some say absolutely can't be taught: the craft of writing.

Under the expert tuition of Andrew Motion, I did learn: about character and theme and voice.

USEFUL BOOKS ON SCREENWRITING

- Syd Field, *The Screenwriter's Workbook*
- Linda Seger, *Advanced Screenwriting*
- Linda Seger, *Making a Good Script Great*
- Robert McKee, *Story*
- Christopher Vogler, *The Writer's Journey*
- William Goldman, *Which Lie Did I Tell?*

> ## "
> ## FOR THE FIRST TIME IT WASN'T ALL ABOUT ME – NOW THE DIRECTOR, THE ACTORS, THE TECHNICIANS ALL SHARED IN THE FINAL SUCCESS, OR FAILURE
> "

I wrote stories and plays as well as my second 'first' novel, *My Summer of Love*. After *My Summer of Love* was published I began a play for radio. Again, I wrote the whole play without any permission, or commission, and without telling anyone I was dipping into drama. *The Typist Who Flew to Australia* was an ambitious historical drama about the 1930s aviator Amy Johnson. It ranged backwards and forwards in time and space, crossing continents. There were cannibals and sharks and crashes in the desert. Compared to a novel it was quick work, and when finished that slim sheaf of 42 pages seemed delightfully lean.

Then, what a relief, what a liberation, to suddenly have a team, a crew, a cast; all these talented people making my writing better. For the first time it wasn't all about me – now the director, the actors, the technicians all shared in the final success, or failure.

When I had written a few radio plays, monologues and stories for broadcast, and another novel, I began noting ideas for screenplays. *My Summer of Love* had just been made into a successful film, directed by Pawel Pawlikowski, and won a BAFTA in 2005 for Best British Film.

AN ASIDE ABOUT MONEY

Let's stop here and talk about cash. If you are a writer, particularly a female one with children, you need to buy the time to write. In order to get the money to buy the time, you have to sell something. I'd suggest that you sell your writing. Screenwriting is useful here as it pays well. Much more than writing for radio or newspapers or magazines, and often more than writing a big fat novel. Even scripts that never hit the screen might be optioned and developed at good rates of pay. So, if you are serious about making a career out

of story-writing, you can't afford not to think of giving your stories some valuable screen time. You can check rates of pay through The Writers' Guild of Great Britain (www.writersguild.org.uk).

GETTING TO GRIPS WITH CHARACTERISATION

It was a revelation to me when I realised that a good film script should be as gripping to read as a novel. The characterisation on the page should be just as deep and the reader should care just as fully for the characters and their situation as they would when reading any successful story. The script is everything the film should be, and more.

Great characterisation, the bedrock of fine novel-writing, is the foundation of fine film-writing too, though screenwriters present their characters differently: unlike their book-bound buddies, film characters need to actually do something as well as talking about doing something. They need not just desire, but desire that will lead to actions. Check this out by reading as many screenplays as you can. Many are easily available online at www.simplyscripts.com.

GETTING HELP

If you've spent years creating novelistic slackers with deep interiorities but little get up and go, you might need a bit of help here. Grab whatever training you can. There are often schemes to help writers move into film and TV. Regional screen agencies (such as Screen WM in Birmingham, where I live) are wonderfully supportive of emerging screenwriters. Skillset and the Film Council also offer valuable funding and guidance.

I was part of a very helpful scheme, The Writers' Circle, funded by Skillset and arranged by a training organisation called The Script Factory. It took nine writers with a track record in other literary forms and, over a year, introduced them to the film industry. It was as much about networking as it was about training. It proved an illuminating insight into an industry I'd had many preconceptions about; mainly that it was a closed club run by rich public-school boys. It's not – entirely.

I'd never read a book on how to write a novel, but for scriptwriting I felt there were more nuts and bolts. There were a few books that I found interesting, particularly those by gurus Linda Seger and Syd Field (see box on page 46), whose truths are so elemental it's as if they're reminding you of what you already know about writing, rather than teaching you something new.

KEEPING YOUR IDEAS IN ORDER

If you are going to write for lots of different forms, you need to keep careful track of your ideas. Some days ideas come like bubbles from a bubble machine, rolling out one after another, only to drift up to the ceiling and pop. So, make a note of everything that comes to you. And then push it. Try to develop each idea into a scenario and on into a little story. Push yourself forward to make a narrative that is memorable – at least to yourself. It's better than stumbling upon 'goat in front of a train' two years later and having no idea where that goat came from, or where the goat was going. Keep all your ideas together, because ideas in close proximity cross-fertilise.

An astronaut who didn't fit into a story can take flight in a radio play; a ballerina can leap from a stage play into a short film.

Some ideas come with their exact form in their DNA. My monologue for radio, *The Restless Home*, about an OAP living in a rest home and

KEEP ALL YOUR IDEAS TOGETHER, BECAUSE IDEAS IN CLOSE PROXIMITY CROSS-FERTILISE

who might be a ghost, was possible only on the radio, because the mystery needed the invisibility of the narrator. My screenplay, *Stratford Road*, was inspired in part by the stunning visual disparity between Stratford-upon-Avon and South Birmingham. Initially, I wanted simply to show these widely divergent modern places as they appear right now in contemporary England.

IS IT FOR YOU?

Writing drama is not for all novelists. If your novels are primarily concerned with language and style, or if they are wonderfully rambling and expansive and led purely by the boundless flights of the imagination, then the compression and emphasis on story and structure and action that drama demands could seem crass and constraining.

But since I began writing screenplays I've appreciated much more the wonderful mess of a novel, the unstructured nature of it, the collisions and the cul-de-sacs, the flops and the repetitions and the detours. Reading a novel you come very close to the raw creative mind, and muddle, of the writer writing. You are on her shoulder as she thinks. It's wonderfully one on one. And in turn I've come to admire the strict structure and muscularity of a good screenplay – as one admires, with envy and awe, the super-fit.

It's one of the great consolations offered to writers that, no matter what happens to you in your life, whatever amount of poverty or failure, it's all material. I think this is particularly comforting if you write across a variety of forms. If you can make all your creative ideas fluid and malleable, as well as brilliant and true, you can hop happily from one form to another. And you might not be so impoverished either.

REFERENCE AND INFORMATION FOR SCREENWRITERS

- **British Film Institute**
  www.bfi.org.uk
- **The Script Factory**
  www.scriptfactory.co.uk
- **Skillset**
  www.skillset.org
- **Film Council**
  www.ukfilmcouncil.org.uk
- **BBC**
  www.bbc.co.uk/writersroom
- **The Writers' Guild of Great Britain**
  www.writersguild.org.uk

FIRST IMPRESSIONS

HOW TO ENSURE *YOUR* SUBMISSION ATTRACTS INSTANT ATTENTION

HILARY JOHNSON

Dr Hilary Johnson has edited a writers' magazine, taught creative writing and judged writing competitions. She has been organiser of The Romantic Novelists' Association's New Writers' Scheme and worked as a publisher's reader. For many years she has run her own authors' advisory service (www.hilaryjohnson.com) and is a scout for a leading literary agent.

> 'My novel came back exactly as I sent it. I don't think they even read it!'

How often have I heard these words from aspiring authors, the tone at once angry and disappointed? My immediate answer, I'm afraid, is harsh: 'They probably didn't need to.'

Aspiring novelists these days are generally pretty well-informed. Thanks to writers' groups, specialist magazines and, of course, the internet, the intensity of the competition to be published and the towering height of most agents' and editors' slush piles are common knowledge. Most writers know how to present a typescript properly. With a wealth of advice available on every possible aspect of novel-writing, many believe they have done a pretty decent job – especially, as some claim, when they compare their own work with 'the rubbish which does get published.'

This, incidentally, is not a productive line of thinking. Should you feel your thoughts travelling in this direction, you should curb them at once, instead taking the trouble to analyse the very book for which you have such scorn, particularly if it is a first novel by an unknown author. Why, you should ask yourself, would an editor have seen fit to pluck this particular novel from among thousands of submissions and commit his/her employer to making a substantial financial investment in it so that it might be put before the public? It must have some merit, so try to discern what that is. (Although I do appreciate that sometimes this is difficult!)

But the basic mystery remains: when you believe that you have done everything right, how can it be that your typescript is returned, accompanied by a standard rejection letter and with the pages as apparently untouched as when you put it in the post ? How, you may wonder, can an agent or editor know that a submission will be of no interest to them if they have read barely a word of it?

> " WITH A WEALTH OF ADVICE AVAILABLE ON EVERY POSSIBLE ASPECT OF NOVEL-WRITING, MANY BELIEVE THEY HAVE DONE A PRETTY DECENT JOB – ESPECIALLY, AS SOME CLAIM, WHEN THEY COMPARE THEIR OWN WORK WITH 'THE RUBBISH WHICH DOES GET PUBLISHED' "

The answers are several. In theory, they could begin with the way the typescript has been packaged, although in practice the average agent or editor wouldn't be involved with the struggles sometimes required to release novels from their bonds. All the same, it's worth mentioning that an ordinary padded envelope is the simplest and safest way of sending a bulky wad of paper. No staples, no yards of sticky tape – and, within, no ring-binders, plastic folders to infuriate as they slide from desk to floor, or other hindrances to easy access to the actual typescript.

New authors who have done their homework don't make these mistakes, so let's assume that packaging and presentation are professional, not the instant off-putters I have described.

THE COVERING LETTER

Where so many hopefuls appear to shoot themselves disastrously in the foot is with the covering letter. As a part of my service, I regularly assess these for clients, a job which is often time-consuming out of all proportion to the letter's length.

It is astonishing how often these sample letters contain careless errors of the most basic kind: mistakes in the spelling of the author's own name, address or title of his novel; typos, accidental omission of words; sloppy constructions and general evidence of a failure to proof-read the letter before printing the final version. Errors of grammar, spelling and punctuation in a covering letter, especially when all three are present, do not inspire confidence in the author's ability to write a novel of publishable standard. Neither does extensive use of cliché or the repetition of words, phrases or ideas.

I have been addressed in all manner of ways, my favourite being 'Dear Person', but for these letters it's important to use the name of an individual rather than 'Dear Sir or Madam'. Extreme as it may sound, there are those who would be minded to reject on that alone. The phrase 'for your perusal' virtually guarantees rejection.

Indulgence in irrelevancies, extended explanations of the plot – pointless when a synopsis is included – and talking up your own book are all bad signs. Agents and editors don't want to be told how the novel should be marketed; it's amazing how often authors fail to credit these people with knowing their own business! Detailed cvs showing your personal history from primary school on are not a good idea, especially if they are so lengthy as to suggest a commensurate length of tooth. (Age is not necessarily a disadvantage, but, then again, no need to bring it to the fore at the outset.) 'I was for a period PA to a Premier League football manager until he was sacked last year' gives less away – and will attract swifter attention – than 'I worked with the same company from leaving school until retirement five years ago'.

Unless anything different is specifically requested, stick to businesslike – but without business-speak, be it dated or modern jargon – courteous and correct. The aim is that the recipient will be keen to read the synopsis, and after that the actual novel, rather than becoming bogged down in a verbose and messy covering letter. A letter which indicates that you have a professional attitude and also shows true originality of thought and voice is, of course, one which instantly excites interest in a submission.

So does a really good title. To the extent that these can be changed before publication, titles may not be that important but there is no question that a really eye-catching title does attract immediate attention.

SUMMING IT UP

Once the hurdles of the letter and the title have been successfully surmounted, there then presents that most formidable of obstacles, the synopsis. The ability to write a strong synopsis is a vital part of the aspiring author's armoury. It is no good lamenting the difficulty of the task – and anyway, if the novel has already been written, boiling it down to its essence shouldn't be *that* hard!

Different agents and editors vary in their expectations of a synopsis, so it is always sensible to check these individually. But in the absence of specific guidelines, following these should result in a professional-looking approach:

For most adult fiction two A4 pages single spaced is the norm, but some editors ask for one page only. For the majority of relatively

> I HAVE BEEN ADDRESSED IN ALL MANNER OF WAYS, MY FAVOURITE BEING 'DEAR PERSON', BUT FOR THESE LETTERS IT'S IMPORTANT TO USE THE NAME OF AN INDIVIDUAL RATHER THAN 'DEAR SIR OR MADAM'

short children's novels, one page is likely to be sufficient.

Begin with two or three sentences stating what kind of novel it is. Say what it is about, who it features and when and where it is set:

Girly Gang is a novel aimed at girls in their mid-teens. A contemporary story with a Tyneside setting, it shows how 15-year old Jess Curtis, seeking an exciting alternative to her drab and difficult home life, finds herself embroiled with a notorious girl gang. When her new friends' activities lead her into a world far scarier than she could have imagined, she discovers that leaving the gang is a lot harder than joining it.

> **THE ABILITY TO WRITE A STRONG SYNOPSIS IS A VITAL PART OF THE ASPIRING AUTHOR'S ARMOURY. IT IS NO GOOD LAMENTING THE DIFFICULTY OF THE TASK – AND ANYWAY, IF THE NOVEL HAS ALREADY BEEN WRITTEN, BOILING IT DOWN TO ITS ESSENCE SHOULDN'T BE *THAT* HARD!**

The remainder of the synopsis should encapsulate the whole story within the proverbial nutshell. There is nothing to be gained by including teasers or leaving the reader guessing as to the ending. The purpose of this piece of writing is to enable someone who is permanently inundated with stuff to be read to absorb the gist of the story within a few minutes; it is not in any way the same as a jacket blurb, designed to whet the appetites of bookshop browsers.

Omit unimportant detail and minor sub-plots or characters. Make sure that the overall tone is lively, giving a sense of the narrative drive and resonating with your own individual voice. A flat retelling of the story will not help your cause. And crucially, avoid the temptation to include anything which may smack of personal opinion concerning the novel's qualities. Allow the agent/editor to make up his/her own mind as to these.

Quite a few submissions may, frustratingly, come crashing down at this point for purely commercial reasons. You may have written a faultless outline of your novel, but if the first couple of sentences show themes or subject matter known to be unpopular with readers, or a background or a historical period proven to have little appeal, the chances are that any early enthusiasm rapidly wanes. (Unless the agent/editor decides to have a quick look at the opening chapter anyway and is so hooked that perhaps the novel is on its way to becoming one of those rare exceptions to the usual rule.)

A synopsis may be perfectly well-written, but reveal a story which, though attractive, is too closely similar to others recently published or in the pipeline. Too many, despite being competent in all respects, lack the essential spark.

A good synopsis should create in the reader a strong desire to read the novel itself or, at any rate, the first three chapters which nowadays usually comprise the initial submission. A reasonable one might prompt a decision just to have a look. Either way, if you have begun your novel with a brilliant opening sentence, a marvellous first paragraph and two or three pages which draw the professional reader into the story almost without noticing and compelling him/her to read on, even if ultimately the novel is for some reason turned down, you will at least have the satisfaction of knowing that your typescript was indeed read. And, who knows, maybe it won't come back at all and you will be en route to publication, all because you took care to ensure a sequence of irresistible first impressions!

> **THE PURPOSE OF THIS PIECE OF WRITING IS TO ENABLE SOMEONE WHO IS PERMANENTLY INUNDATED WITH STUFF TO BE READ TO ABSORB THE GIST OF THE STORY WITHIN A FEW MINUTES**

JUST SO STORIES
LOOKING OUT FOR THAT SPECIAL 'SOMETHING' IN CHILDREN'S BOOKS

LINDSEY HEAVEN

Lindsey Heaven has worked in children's publishing for eight years. She is a Senior Commissioning Editor for Fiction at Puffin Books, where she is lucky enough to be working not only with some of the most exciting new writers in the children's book world but also with some of her childhood heroes.

Being a children's editor can be like being a child in a sweetshop. Nearly all of us would have grown up with our nose continually in a book; courtesy of the genius of the author, immersed in the magic of a different world and maybe a different time, emerging only when we were told to 'put the book down and concentrate on what you're doing' (this being anything from eating dinner, doing homework or even walking along the pavement in a straight line). Books were the most indulgent and very best of any treats you gratefully received. But now as adult editors we are *asked* to read these very books, and the excitement of having a children's story land on our desk or, mostly these days, ping its arrival in our in-box hasn't lessened from when we were little. It's a privilege to have so much to read and so much to choose from.

> "WE'RE LOOKING FOR THAT LITTLE 'GEM' IN EVERY MANUSCRIPT, DESPERATELY HOPING THAT THE NEXT STORY WE READ WILL BE THE ONE TO KNOCK US OFF OUR FEET. WE WANT TO FIND AND PUBLISH IT SO THAT EVERYONE ELSE CAN DISCOVER THE MAGIC IN IT THAT WE LOVED"

At Puffin HQ, in the fiction department alone, we probably receive around ten submissions a week (sometimes many more if it's just before or after a book fair) and that's just from agents and publishers from other countries – if you included the picture books department and the unsolicited pile it would run to hundreds. So everything that comes in to us is, already, generally very good; it's good enough for an agent to send out expecting a UK publisher to buy it or even good enough for a publisher abroad to have bought it and be about to put it out there as a fully formed book themselves.

So given that we are in this wonderful position, reading so many good children's stories every day, ranging from chapter books for five-year-olds to teen and even crossover fiction, something obviously has to call out to us in a very special way, appealing to our publishing minds and pulling on our editorial heartstrings so that we can't do anything but declare that we *have* to publish it.

STANDING OUT FROM THE CROWD

There is a common misconception that editors enjoy writing rejection letters and that they're always looking for that one thing that will allow them to say no (understandably, it is a difficult and thankless journey for many aspiring and unpublished writers). But in fact it's quite the opposite – a disappointing and not very nice task. We're looking for that little 'gem' in every manuscript, desperately hoping that the next story we read will be the one to knock us off our feet. We want to find and publish it so that everyone else can discover the magic in it that we loved.

There are various different gems that we may be looking for at any one time; those special things to make a book stand out from the crowd. These can differ depending on the type of readership it's for, our list at the time or even the editor reading it.

Whilst the act of reading is as subjective as that of writing a book, there are the same things at every book's heart that all editors will see. Even if a book isn't to one editor's taste, we at Puffin all recognise great writing and will pass the manuscript on to another person in the team – we know each other's tastes well.

But there are two key things that really do impress upon us when reading a brilliant book – the 'voice' and the concept. Both, together or by themselves, must be utterly engaging, striking and original. There are many books out there that are easily readable and a pleasantly unchallenging experience, but then there are those that take you aback in their originality and stay with you well after you've finished reading them – sometimes even forever.

These are the books that can have the power to make you a different 'you' from the one who began the very first chapter; the books that make you stand up and take notice as an editor and that you know will make a child reader do the same. Who can forget Meg Rosoff's Daisy from *How I Live Now*, with her damaged, grammatically anarchic and incredibly powerful narrative voice that haunts you long after the final page of this award-winning novel? Or the complete genius of Road Dahl's *The BFG* and the wonderfully magical premise of a dream-catching, vegetarian giant with whom everyone falls a little bit in love?

MORE, PLEASE

There are, of course, trends in children's books as there are in adult ones and it's up to editors not only to predict and publish for a future trend, but also to respond to the success of current ones. At the turn of the millennium children and adults alike were gripped by Harry Potter fever, the magical escapist fantasy that turned much-deserved attention back on to the world of children's books and also spawned the acquisition of many other fantasy series and trilogies for several years after that. At the time of writing this article, there has been real resurgence in teen fiction and most noticeably in 'goth lit' – other-worldly, gothic romances, in which the objects of one's affection are characters such as vampires,

werewolves or fallen angels. The current leading light is Stephenie Meyer with her incredibly successful *Twilight* series.

Obviously there have been amazing and even seminal fantasy novels and dark teen romances before either of these series, as there will continue to be afterwards, but when children really latch on to a series they can be voracious readers and, if there are no more books in that particular series, will want to continue a similar experience through another author. At these moments, editors will be particularly looking out for books in this genre. However the stories can't just be the same book with another cover and copy-cat plots – they must have their own hook that sets them apart from everything else whilst remaining very much of the current trend. The quality of writing must be no less brilliant than in any other book we would buy for the list. As with all our other books, it must stand up in its own right.

WHERE HAVE ALL THE OTHERS GONE?

Conversely, as with any other industry, trends also leave gaps in the market. Filling a niche, at a time when no one else is doing what you are as an author (obviously doing it well and bearing in mind all the above points about good writing), can lead to great success. Publishers are very aware of this and once gaps have been recognised it's up to the editor to acquire the book that will fill it. Publishing can be quite a cyclical market – a trend may leave a gap for a certain neglected type of book; that book, as the only one or one of few filling the gap, becomes

> " THESE ARE THE BOOKS THAT CAN EVEN HAVE THE POWER TO MAKE YOU A DIFFERENT 'YOU' FROM THE ONE WHO BEGAN THE VERY FIRST CHAPTER; THE BOOKS THAT MAKE YOU STAND UP AND TAKE NOTICE AS AN EDITOR AND THAT YOU KNOW WILL MAKE A CHILD READER DO THE SAME "

LINDSEY HEAVEN

FEATURE

successful and its success starts a trend in itself. It's about the perfect book at the perfect moment.

NOT THE FINAL CHAPTER

It's important to remember, however, that not all books come to editors fully formed and word-for-word as the reader will eventually find them. We may receive a submission that on the surface is a little poorly; but should we see a glimmer of any of the aforementioned promise, then it's our job to dust it off and let everyone else discover it for the real treasure it is, also not forgetting that behind every amazing book is an even more impressive author. We're looking for someone whom we can grow and promote and for whom we can build a reputation in the trade so that the launch of any of their books is a much anticipated event.

The journey from the first read of the manuscript to this point is a long one, so in that first draft we're looking to be struck down by the beginnings of something brilliant. We want it to make us laugh, cry, feel shocked, surprised, even hurt. And if you are that perfect book, show yourself to me! I can't wait to read you.

> ❝ THE STORIES CAN'T JUST BE THE SAME BOOK WITH ANOTHER COVER AND COPY-CAT PLOTS – THEY MUST HAVE THEIR OWN HOOK THAT SETS THEM APART FROM EVERYTHING ELSE WHILST REMAINING VERY MUCH OF THE CURRENT TREND ❞

> ❝ AS WITH ANY OTHER INDUSTRY, TRENDS ALSO LEAVE GAPS IN THE MARKET. FILLING A NICHE, AT A TIME WHEN NO ONE ELSE IS DOING WHAT YOU ARE AS AN AUTHOR, CAN LEAD TO GREAT SUCCESS ❞

USEFUL WEBSITES

To keep up to date with what is being published for children and to get in touch with other authors, the *Writer's Market* team recommend that you look at these websites:

- www.writeaway.org.uk
- www.wordpool.co.uk
- www.carouselguide.co.uk
- www.armadillomagazine.com
- www.booktrusted.co.uk
- www.btinternet.com/~martin.kromer/

For more information about the children's book market, specialist listings and articles, read the companion volume to this one, *Children's Writer's and Illustrator's Market UK*, or go to the website www.writersmarket.co.uk/childrens

POETRY PUBLICATION
AN EDITOR'S VIEW

NEIL ASTLEY

Neil Astley is editor of Bloodaxe Books, which he founded in 1978. He has edited nearly a thousand poetry books and published several bestselling anthologies, including *Staying Alive* and *Being Alive*; two collaborations with Pamela Robertson-Pearce, *Soul Food* and *In Person;* two poetry collections; and two novels, *The End of My Tether* (Scribners), which was shortlisted for the Whitbread First Novel Award, and *The Sheep Who Changed the World* (Flambard).

> **TECHNIQUE IS BEST LEARNED BY READING OTHER POETS. READING IS THE MOST ESSENTIAL PART OF ANY WRITER'S DEVELOPMENT. RHYTHM AND TONE ARE FIRST ABSORBED FROM READING AND THEN BECOME INTUITIVE, PART OF THE UNIQUE REGISTER OF YOUR OWN INDIVIDUAL VOICE**

While a poet may not write *for* other readers, it's the *readership* which justifies publication. All editors are flooded with submissions from people whose desire to be *published* is greater than their desire to write well or to communicate.

At Bloodaxe I receive around a hundred manuscripts, samples or letters offering collections every week. That's 5,000 poets a year wanting to be taken on by just one publisher. Bloodaxe publishes 30 or so new books of poetry a year, but only one or two of these will be first collections: we have a stable of over 300 already published poets with new books coming out every month, as well as poets from America, Europe and other parts of the world whose work we want to introduce to our readers. So this is the first thing to remember: given the competition, your work has to be *really strong* if a publisher is going to want to take up your work. The numbers are against you.

The books I publish are those I respond to as a *reader* of poetry, and the things that interest me most as a reader are subject matter, breadth of vision and engagement with language. When considering manuscripts by new writers, I'm looking for an original voice, assured technique and poetry showing a lively interplay of intellect and emotion.

IMPROVING TECHNIQUE

Technique has to be a *given* if a writer is expecting to publish a book. Before I even begin to read and absorb a manuscript, I register immediately whether or not the work is well crafted. If it's prose chopped into lines, or rhyming verse with no metre or rhythmical sense (the two most common crimes against poetry committed by unpublished writers), it goes straight back into the envelope.

Technique is best learned by reading other poets. Reading is the most essential part of any writer's development. Rhythm and tone are first absorbed from reading and then become intuitive, part of the unique register of your own individual voice. Only bad writers 'avoid' influences (or so they claim when sending me their dreadful work). If you do not read much contemporary poetry or if you write poetry 'as a hobby', I'm unlikely to be interested in what you produce.

I think you need to read poetry from all periods as well as contemporary poetry, and to have both an awareness and a *love* of English poetry from Shakespeare to the present day. If your knowledge and sense of poetry stops at the beginning of the last century, there's no point in sending your work to any publisher or magazine. In poetry terms, you are an anachronism. If you don't talk like a person from the 18th or 19th century, why should you write like one? And yet a large proportion of the submissions I receive from would-be writers are appalling pastiches of Romantic or Victorian verse, complete with invocations, poeticisms, inversions of word order (usually to contrive a rhyme), clangy rhymes and jingly or jumbled metre. Doggerel.

You must also be passionate about *wanting to write*: wanting to be a *writer* must be secondary to that. Too often new writers want to get that first collection finished and published because they want to be writers. They want a career and opportunities.

Many people seem to believe that you need connections to get published. 'It's not what you write but who you know that matters,' is what they say. But connections won't make you a writer. Before anything else, you need to have *talent* and to be *passionate* about poetry: reading it, writing it, thinking it, feeling it, living it. And you have to put in time nurturing your own talent before you start thinking of how to take your work out into the world.

Many promising new writers lose their way and squander their talent because they get caught up too early in the processes of promoting their work. They get drawn into the quagmire of networking and opportunities instead of devoting their creative energies to reading and writing. They start giving public readings, or performances of quick-fire poems in slams, and soon they find themselves writing more of the kinds of poems which go down well with audiences. They let down their guard and allow their writing to be influenced by ways of writing and perceiving which aren't their own.

At a critical time in the development of their own work, they've gone out into the marketplace and allowed their own still-developing voice to be drowned by the clamour of all the others. And that crucial fostering of a new voice in poetry is something which can only be achieved in private, in isolation, through much reading, much writing and much thought. Yes, you have to read all the other poets, but then you have to assimilate those influences and eventually find yourself writing poetry which is distinctively yours, unlike anyone else's.

And that's what I look for as an editor interested in publishing new poets: a writer who is doing something new, something different. I want a book which is more than just a collection of good, well-written poems: there are plenty of those about as it is. I'm looking for poetry which is recognisably the work of this particular new writer. The poems in the collection must read unlike anyone else's and the writer's stamp has to be felt right through the book. Then it's not just in reading the individual poems that I feel this writer is doing something different but in how the whole book feels as a coherent, consistently strong collection, imbued with the writer's particular imagination and way of writing.

The manuscript also has to convince me that the writer isn't a one-trick pony who's done everything they're likely to do in that one book, especially if it is a strong focus on a particular theme or set of experiences which is what makes the book unusual. In some cases the writing may be especially powerful because the subject is so compelling but, having written those poems which had to be written, where does the poet go next? I'm looking for new writers whose work makes me sit up, not just because it is distinctively different but because it suggests that this writer will stay the course and go on to produce even stronger second and third collections. A publisher taking on your first collection is making an upfront investment in your talent and sees your first book as a first step. This is a partnership:

> **THAT CRUCIAL FOSTERING OF A NEW VOICE IN POETRY IS SOMETHING WHICH CAN ONLY BE ACHIEVED IN PRIVATE, IN ISOLATION, THROUGH MUCH READING, MUCH WRITING AND MUCH THOUGHT**

the publisher wants to work with you to help establish your professional career and then to share in your success as your subsequent books take off.

DEVELOPING YOUR WORK

As well as intensive reading, other ways of stimulating the development of your work include poetry workshops, courses and writing groups – once you've reached the right stage for these. But again: these gatherings are about your work and the work of the other writers and how you can help each other creatively, *not* about making connections or networking. There are many national and local organisations offering critical services, writers' courses, workshops and mentoring, some of them via the Poetry Society. The magazine *Poetry London* has the most comprehensive listings. Week-long courses tutored by poets are offered by the Arvon Foundation at three centres in England and one in Scotland and at Ty Newydd in Wales (see Jem Poster's article on page 17 and Simon Brett's on page 21 for more about these courses). The Poetry School in London offers workshops, courses and online tuition, and there is a growing number of creative writing programmes at universities. Many people who have gone on to become published poets have been helped at a crucial stage in their development by working with established poets in one or other of these ways.

ESTABLISHING A TRACK RECORD

However, before you even think about putting a book together, you should be submitting poems to magazines and then to pamphlet or chapbook

> ❝ I'M LOOKING FOR NEW WRITERS WHOSE WORK MAKES ME SIT UP NOT JUST BECAUSE IT IS DISTINCTIVELY DIFFERENT BUT BECAUSE IT SUGGESTS THAT THIS WRITER WILL STAY THE COURSE AND GO ON TO PRODUCE EVEN STRONGER SECOND AND THIRD COLLECTIONS ❞

SOME USEFUL WEBSITES

- **The Poetry Society**
www.poetrysoc.com whose aim is to advance the study, use and enjoyment of poetry. Organizes events and promotions and has an educational programme that includes opportunities for emerging writers.

- **Poetry London magazine**
www.poetrylondon.co.uk for listings of courses, workshops and more.

- **The Poetry School**
www.poetryschool.com for workshops, courses and online tuition.

- **The Poetry Library**
www.poetrylibrary.org.uk for a list of poetry magazines and presses.

presses, which produce small collections sold mainly at readings, from websites or by their authors. Book publishers use such a 'track record' not as a guarantee of quality but as an indication that you have spent time building up a publishable collection. Trying to publish a book before you have had work taken by magazines is perceived as much the same as thinking you can run before you can walk.

Don't submit to publishers unless you've read their books, or to magazines unless you're familiar with the kind of work they publish. I have very wide taste – from traditional to post-modern – but there are publishers whose editors are interested only in certain kinds or schools of poetry. Every imprint is different, and you won't be able to publish much unless you research the field and send to publishers or magazines whose output you like and respect. The Poetry Library has a comprehensive listing of poetry presses and magazines on its website (see box above) and you can read back-issues of leading journals at www.poetrymagazines.org.

APPROACHING A PUBLISHER

Building up a coherent body of work can take years. As your work matures, so your confidence grows and you start getting more and more poems taken by magazines and perhaps win prizes in poetry competitions. Then you may find a small press willing to publish a pamphlet or chapbook (15 to 20 poems). Finally, you have a book-length manuscript (= typescript) of around 50 poems which you and other writers (not your friends or family!) think worthy of publication. At this stage, if there is a particular writer who has helped you with your work, ask if they will write a supporting paragraph for you to include in a covering letter to publishers.

Make your covering letter strong, straightforward and factual, setting out your publication credentials, and include a stamped addressed envelope (you won't get a response without this). Because editors are swamped, they can't read and respond to new work promptly and it may be months before you hear back. Do not use e-mail for submitting work unless asked to do so but do include your e-mail address in the covering letter.

While you should only submit your book to one publisher at a time, it's acceptable to send a small sample (half a dozen of your best poems) to several publishers with a letter asking if they'd like to see the full manuscript. Sending an s.a.e. with this should get you a response within a fortnight. Then you can send your book to an editor who wants to read it. But even then, don't hold out too much hope: most of the poetry books published are by already known writers and there are very few openings for new poets.

If you are lucky enough to have your book accepted, don't expect to make much money from it. Most poetry books are published in editions of fewer than a thousand copies and don't earn their writers much more than £500 in royalties. Because poetry sales are tiny in book-trade terms and the field is so small – with just ten imprints publishing most of the significant poets – literary agents don't usually handle poetry. You have to do it all yourself.

Lastly, it's fine to pay fees to enter competitions which support the work of poetry organisations or other worthy causes, but you should never pay to have your work published. Think twice before approaching the kinds of publishers who advertise for new writers in the small ads columns of newspapers and magazines or on the internet.

Reputable publishers or magazines of any size will pay authors for their work, usually with royalties in the case of books. The normal arrangements for publishing also involve the author receiving complimentary copies of a book or a free contributor's copy of a magazine or anthology (with additional copies at author's discount). If you're asked to pay for the production of your book by a 'publisher' who sends you a flattering 'reader's report' on your work, try asking a local printer to give you an estimate for printing a few hundred copies. The likelihood is that the cost to you will be considerably lower and, if you want your work to be read by friends, colleagues and people in your local community, the circulation you will achieve by this DIY method will be more effective.

And lest all of this sound discouraging, remember that although you may not get your first collection published by one of the big poetry houses, there are numerous small presses, magazines and websites which are always on the lookout for new writers. If you research all the different outlets and try those you think are most likely to be interested in your work, you should be lucky somewhere. If you have real talent, that should not go unrecognised for long.

> TRYING TO PUBLISH A BOOK BEFORE YOU HAVE HAD WORK TAKEN BY MAGAZINES IS PERCEIVED AS MUCH THE SAME AS THINKING YOU CAN RUN BEFORE YOU CAN WALK

WHAT MAKES A GOOD MEMOIR?

NOT JUST THE STORY OF YOUR LIFE

DAVID REYNOLDS

David Reynolds is a director of Old Street Publishing. His book *Swan River: A Family Memoir* is published by Picador. He was one of the four founders of Bloomsbury Publishing and worked there from 1986 until 1999 as Publishing Director for Non-fiction.

> **THESE WRITERS AND THEIR MEMOIRS PROVED SOMETHING THAT SHOULD HAVE BEEN OBVIOUS BUT HAD PERHAPS BEEN OBSCURED IN THE CLIQUEY, RAREFIED WORLD OF BOOK PUBLISHING: NO PERSON IS 'ORDINARY'; EVERYONE HAS A UNIQUE STORY**

In France *mémoire* means memory. In the English-speaking world, and anglicised to memoir, it becomes a fancy word for something less than autobiography: a book that contains recollections of events in which the author was involved, but that does not tell the story of his or her entire life to date. Until about 15 years ago memoirs tended to be written by posh or powerful people, statesmen and generals who had come to the ends of their careers and felt a need to tell the world about the important things they thought they had done or, perhaps, witnessed. With a few exceptions – Lord Curzon, T E Lawrence, Winston Churchill – their books are likely to contain huge amounts of dry information, often of interest only to historians and to the author's family and friends.

In the 1990s gusts of fresh air blew into this stuffy arena as books by people who were not posh or important – people who, superficially at least, were just 'ordinary' – reached the bookshops and proved popular. The first of these, the pioneer as I see it, was Blake Morrison's *And When Did You Last See Your Father?* The author was a poet and journalist who had not previously published narrative prose. The book, which came out in 1993, intersperses vignettes from the author's life as a child, teenager and adult with moving description of the last illness and death of his father. Its appeal lies in the vivid portrait of Morrison senior, a supposedly 'ordinary' man who worked as a GP but who, in the eyes of his son, had other personae. Morrison senior, with his fallibilities, is, in a sense, everyman; everyone's father – and Morrison's description of his death is raw but consoling reading for anyone thinking about or experiencing the death of someone close.

Other examples of this type of memoir followed – notably Tim Lott's *The Scent of Dried Roses* and Frank McCourt's *Angela's Ashes* – and soon the genre not only had a new and more approachable identity but had given birth to a sub-genre, the 'misery memoir', of which McCourt's tale of childhood poverty in Ireland was perhaps the first, soon to be followed by Angela Ashworth's *Once in a House on Fire* and Lorna Sage's *Bad Blood*. From America came Mary Karr's *The Liar's Club*, Dave Eggers' part-fictionalised *A Heartbreaking Work of Staggering Genius* and Dave Pelzer's *A Child Called It*.

All these and many more, some of them by established authors – Diana Athill's memoir of a privileged childhood *Yesterday Morning*; William Styron's examination of his own depression *Darkness Visible*; Joan Didion's account of her husband's death *The Year of Magical Thinking* – describe slices of the lives of 'ordinary' people and families; they have nothing to do with fame and are of no apparent historical significance. These writers and their memoirs proved something that should have been obvious but had perhaps been obscured in the cliquey, rarefied world of book publishing: no person is 'ordinary'; everyone has a unique story, including siblings who grew up in the same home with the same parents.

IT'S THE WAY YOU TELL IT

Although everyone has their story, many do not know how to tell it. Yet at the same time a surprising number *want* to tell it. As a publisher, I frequently come across people who think that hordes of strangers will march into bookshops and pay money for a book that they will write when they get round to it – which might be when the bar we are in closes or perhaps when I agree to pay them some money. It will be a book about something remarkable that happened to them, perhaps about something terrible that took place when they were children; or about their experiences in World War II – or in the Falklands, or in Iraq or Afghanistan; or about their addiction to drugs or alcohol or sex or gambling; or about how they coped with a killer illness, or their experiences as a criminal; or their years in prison; or their relationship with someone famous – they might have been a rock star's lover or a princess's butler. Or perhaps they have had a series of experiences which they think in total will make an interesting book: a career in the RAF followed, say, by years of flying celebrities around the world,

> WHAT MANY SUCH WOULD-BE AUTHORS DON'T APPRECIATE IS THAT THE WAY YOU TELL A STORY IS MORE IMPORTANT THAN THE STORY ITSELF

rounded off with wrongful imprisonment in Abu Dhabi on suspicion of smuggling alcohol. The common supposition is: 'Something extraordinary happened to me. Other people will want to read about this.'

What many such would-be authors don't appreciate is that the way you tell a story is more important than the story itself. Or, to put it another way, the likelihood of your reminiscences being of interest to others depends less on your experiences themselves than on the way you relate them. In that sense writing a memoir is like telling a joke. It's all – well, almost all – in the way you tell it.

This means that a successful memoir does not have to describe some apparently extraordinary experience. It can describe anything – the daily life of a shelf stacker in Asda or the fun someone had designing and planting a garden – as long as the story is exceptionally well told, as long as it has something original and universally enlightening about it, something fresh to say to others about life on earth, about the experiences that all of us, or groups of us, have in common. It can be sad, funny or moving – or all those things, preferably all those things, but not necessarily at the same time – as long as it lives and it captivates the reader.

In the life of a shelf stacker, just as much as in the life of a vet or of a Spitfire pilot, things will happen that stand out. However, a frequent mistake is to concentrate exclusively on the dramatic, exciting, unusual events and emotions while ignoring the apparently ordinary, but in fact unique, stretches of life that led up to them, continued around them and ultimately followed them. The best memoir-writing features the mundane and the routine and brings it to life. It provides a background, establishes characters and provides a relief against which the dramatic events can stand out – and ordinary life is not dull; written with care and attention to detail, one person's mundane routine can be another person's (a reader's) revelation.

Crucially, it is no good writing a true story, however thrilling or revealing or poignant, in a dull, flat way, with characters who do not come to life or who are larger than life and therefore unbelievable; with settings too thinly sketched or described at too great a length; at a plodding pace or too hastily; without suspense or overstocked with melodrama; without human feeling or with how you felt laid on too thickly, like artificial cream.

GETTING STARTED – WITH OR WITHOUT A PLAN

Those who want to learn to write a memoir will gain by reading good memoirs, such as those mentioned above, and by studying how the authors get their effects. But writing is a skill, and writing a memoir is a subset of the same skill, and the best way to learn a skill is to do it, to practise, to write something and keep writing regularly. Write short pieces about things that happen or that you observe around you. Or start writing a memoir – and be prepared to change it, revise it, scrap bits later.

Different writers have different ways of approaching a story or a book. There are those who plan meticulously before starting, those who start with no planning whatever and those who plan a little, but not too much. I find that the middle way is best for most writers. Too much planning can create a straitjacket and stifle spontaneity; too little can cause a writer to go off in the wrong direction and in time become discouraged.

I would suggest thinking about – and, if necessary, researching – the subject, making notes and perhaps looking at different ways into the book. It might be that a less obvious, oblique, route in is best. When I was thinking about writing a book that was eventually published under the title *Swan River*, I wanted at first to write about my paternal grandfather, a man I had never met, who died years before I was born, of whom there were no photographs and whom no one in my family liked to talk about. As a child I had become intrigued by this mysterious man, and by pestering relations I discovered just a little about him. Then, as an adult, I came across five letters written by him and sent from Swan River, a remote town in northern Canada, in the early years of the 20th century. They described a strange, hard lifestyle, a cold, bleak, winter landscape, and they revealed why he was there,

exiled from his family – including his son, my father, who was growing up in the East End of London.

I wanted to write about him but decided that the best way to start was to write about my own childhood and my memories of asking my father to tell me about his father. The book developed from there in two timescales, that of my childhood in the 1950s and '60s, and that of my grandfather's exile in the 1900s. I put much effort into knitting those two periods together. The contrast between them became interesting in itself. The book expanded into areas I hadn't considered during my brief planning stage and I found that the whole thing worked. I mention this because I believe it is worth looking at your subject from as many angles as possible before you start, but at the same time I believe you should start writing without too much ado because, as you write, ideas will flow.

To end where I started, it is significant that memoir is less than autobiography for, after all, as a wise man once wrote, 'less is more'. And it's perhaps instructive that that wise man was an architect, the German-born American Ludwig Mies van der Rohe, and that he popularised another piece of wisdom, 'God is in the details'. Writing memoirs – writing many things, but *not* autobiography – has much in common with architecture. The aim of both is to devise an appropriate and pleasing shape, and within it place some – but not too many – well-wrought, unfussy details. It is hardly surprising that Mies van der Rohe took both aphorisms from writers: respectively, Robert Browning and Gustave Flaubert.

> ❝ TOO MUCH PLANNING CAN CREATE A STRAITJACKET AND STIFLE SPONTANEITY; TOO LITTLE CAN CAUSE A WRITER TO GO OFF IN THE WRONG DIRECTION AND IN TIME BECOME DISCOURAGED ❞

HAVE CAMERA, WILL TRAVEL
TIPS ON TRAVEL WRITING

HEATHER ANGEL

Heather Angel worked as a marine biologist before she became a peripatetic wildlife photographer and took up writing. She is the author of over 50 books on photographic techniques and natural history topics. In 2007 and early 2008 she made seven one-month-long trips to China in 15 months to research and photograph for her latest book *Green China*, a celebration of China's natural heritage. See www.naturalvisions.co.uk and www.heatherangel.co.uk

> ❝ AS A PENNILESS RESEARCH STUDENT I WAS THRILLED TO GET (WHAT I THOUGHT THEN) THE PRINCELY SUM OF 25 GUINEAS FOR AN ARTICLE ON SEA ANEMONES – THE ONLY SUBJECT FOR WHICH I HAD PLENTY OF PHOTOGRAPHS ❞

▶ Years ago, I took a small photographic group to India during a petrol shortage. When our coach driver told me he would have to queue up all night to get petrol, I asked our guide to arrange alternative transport to the Taj Mahal so we could arrive for the 6 a.m. opening. We set off in half a dozen tuk tuks and were rewarded with a magical dawn light painting the iconic building.

This was the icing on the cake of the whole trip. While we had no control over the weather, I am a firm believer in attempting to make your own luck by being in the right place at the right time. By rising early to capture the dawn light, we had been rewarded with striking photos and a fresh-angled account of one of the world's most visited buildings – and there is always a market for that.

GETTING STARTED

As a child, I was taught the names of wild flowers on my grandparents' Suffolk farm, which inspired me with a zest to learn more. So it was a natural progression to study zoology and then take up marine biology, which I assumed would see me through my working life: neither photography nor writing was on my list of ambitions. But when my father gave me my first camera as a twenty-first birthday present, a new interest was triggered.

Initially I used my camera to document the marine life I was studying, then realised I could use some of these pictures to illustrate the articles I was beginning to write. During this time, I sold my very first article to *Animal Life* (no longer published). Before submitting, I spent time in W H Smith's thumbing through magazines to check out the ratio of text to pictures and the length of articles each magazine preferred. As a penniless research student I was thrilled to get (what I thought then) the princely sum of 25 guineas for an article on sea anemones – the only subject for which I had plenty of photographs. It was some years later, when I began to travel to remote islands to study their marine life, that I began writing on a regular basis.

If you are serious about pursuing this genre of writing, the first thing you need to do is what I did – research your market. Find out which magazines take travel stories and buy a few to study in more depth. Many have regular writers and columnists but there is always scope for fresh faces. The features editor of any travel magazine will welcome original text and eye-catching pictures on a popular or novel location: it makes their work much easier than if they are presented with just the text and have to find suitable images to marry with it.

Find out who to submit to: get a name from the switchboard or check the website for contact details. Then send off a proposal with a snappy title, outlining how it will appeal to that particular magazine's readers and including a few low-res (100dpi) images. (Some magazines now produce Contributor's Guidelines, which are a big help.) Never send a complete article, or even an outline, to an unnamed person or generic email address.

When I started writing, I travelled first and then approached a magazine when I knew I had the photos. Nowadays, my articles tend to be spin-offs from my book assignments and I prefer to wait until I have the images in the can, as it were, before making an approach. Once I have the pictures, but before writing a word of the article, I either call or email the editor or features editor to confirm an interest in my idea. At this stage he or she may ask to see a few images, which I send as low-res files.

However, I know of other people who like to get a nod before they set off. Many professional travel writers expect to have all their expenses paid if they are writing about a resort such as an upmarket tented camp in Africa but as a beginner you will have to fund your own trips until you can produce some published articles. An economic way to start is to glean a story from a holiday – without being so obsessive that you antagonise your travelling companions!

> **THE FEATURES EDITOR OF ANY TRAVEL MAGAZINE WILL WELCOME ORIGINAL TEXT AND EYE-CATCHING PICTURES ON A POPULAR OR NOVEL LOCATION: IT MAKES THEIR WORK MUCH EASIER THAN IF THEY ARE PRESENTED WITH JUST THE TEXT AND HAVE TO FIND SUITABLE IMAGES TO MARRY WITH IT**

When you get a commission, don't whatever you do blow it by not meeting a deadline. Many articles I have written late at night for a desperate editor who has called saying he has been let down – could I bail him out? I am always happy to do this providing I can squeeze the fee up a little for burning the midnight oil.

PREPARATION

When you are about to go on a trip, don't leave where you go and what you see to chance. Researching the best time is easy via the internet, but be sure to check more than one source, for by no means everything on the web is 100 per cent accurate.

Then research what you want to photograph. If it is an annual festival, make sure you know what date it is *this year*: the Pushkar Camel Fair in Rajasthan, for example, is usually held in November but the precise date depends on the lunar calendar. If you use anything other than right up-to-the-minute information, you may turn up to find that it happened last week. Also remember that your article may not be published until the festival comes around next year, so check the dates for that too.

Bear in mind, also, that other writers and photographers may well have the same idea as you. Make your approach more original by combining a special interest with your travels. In my case, this could range from garden designs to local vegetables on sale in markets to following in the steps of plant hunters.

Whenever I travel to Africa, India or China, I always request a naturalist guide from my local ground agent. They tend to be enthusiastic and generous in passing on their invaluable knowledge. I take photocopies or make sketches to show my guide of any unusual plants and animals I particularly want to find. I did this once with a bizarre insect native to Madagascar. Quite unfazed, my guide produced the small red and black beetle with the distinctive giraffe-like neck the following day, because he knew which shrub it fed on. Whatever your main interest, it is always fruitful to talk to local people and, if possible, get and use a quotable quote. Don't be shy about asking questions because you never know what spin-off leads may develop as a result.

WHAT IMAGES TO TAKE

The quality of the images is, of course, crucial and for reproduction you must provide high-quality jpegs saved at 300dpi, preferably at A4 size (30 x 21cm or 3543 x 2480 pixels) with Adobe RGB colour space, which is the industry standard.

When faced with a plethora of possible subjects in a new location, I adopt a two-pronged approach. On the one hand I make lists of prime locations and species I want to find; on the other I am always on the lookout for the unexpected. Like the time I spotted a huge pile of rose blossoms beside a street in Hotan on China's Silk Road. Quite fortuitously I was given a glass of *mei gei* (rose wine) that evening. It took two more days to track down the rose bushes and early one morning I entered the back garden of a family home to take pictures of women and girls plucking rose heads at first light, specifically for the wine production. It was pure luck that my visit to Hotan coincided with the peak time for the rose blooms and only by asking lots of questions did I get the chance to produce a colourful photo story.

The chances are that anything which catches my eye will also appeal to other people, whether I use the pictures to illustrate an article or accompany a lecture. It makes sense to make your research pay dividends and get as much out of a journey as possible. Indeed, as a result of that single trip, a large feature on Silk Road traditions appeared in *World Magazine*, with annotated photo essays on wine production, hand-made silk (my main objective), hand-made paper (stumbled upon) and hand-made noodles (ditto).

No matter what your subject is, be careful to change the pace by taking different types of shot – wide-angles to set the scene, with or without people; detailed cameos to add colour or texture. Shoot both landscape (horizontal) and portrait (vertical) formats. It is always worth remembering that a striking vertical shot with empty space at the top for the banner and room at the bottom sides for the dreaded barcode and teaser text could be a contender for a cover. The fee for a cover shot is much higher than for a picture that appears inside a magazine.

Automatic digital compact cameras keep getting better; even images taken with camera phones are used on television news if no photojournalist was on the spot, though these images won't normally be 'reproduction quality' for a magazine. Before buying a camera check the maximum jpeg file size it can produce, since this will be the main limitation to getting a cover shot published. Compact digital cameras with a single zoom lens are lightweight and easy to use and can produce some great shots. Digital single lens reflex (DSLR) cameras come with a higher price tag but enable you to see precisely which part of the image is in focus, so are best for critical close-ups and wildlife. They also allow you to interchange lenses.

SO WHAT ABOUT THE WORDS?

Writing came later for me and at the outset it was laborious. Then a chance encounter fired my imagination to write more and in a different way. On a whale-watching trip off the coast of Mexico's Baja California, I met an author who told me she never left home without paper and pen so she could jot down thoughts that came to her in cafés or on trains or planes.

That was when it dawned on me how much downtime I had spent at airports, on long-haul flights or steaming south to Antarctica in an ice breaker; so the first thing I now pack in my hand luggage is a thick A4 pad and several pens. Because I think so much faster than I can type,

I prefer to jot down ideas for articles or a synopsis for a book or even to write a complete article which can be tidied up later. If you are a better typist than I am and are able to travel with a laptop, then you can compose directly on to that. Either way, the more you write the easier it will become.

TAKING NOTES

My bible is my field notebook – one for each trip – with the country and date written on the spine. As I write this I can see hundreds stacked up on a shelf above my desk. My favourite is a plain paper Moleskine (www.moleskine.com) which can be closed with a strip of elastic – as used by artists and authors including Van Gogh, Picasso and Hemingway.

In addition to writing down local names of places, plants and animals, I record smells and sounds, which cannot be captured in a photograph but are invaluable for painting a verbal picture. It can also be useful to refer to the weather at a particular time, so I write a brief daily weather resumé. And I keep notes on bizarre food such as jellyfish, giant salamander or sea cucumber – all of which I have eaten in China – which can be woven into a story.

After years of working this way, I was able to write almost all the text for my *Green China* book while I was travelling in China getting the photographs. My hand-written copy was faxed back to my office peppered with 'check date' or 'more info here', so that Lucy, my researcher, could fill in the facts and figures before I returned.

I cannot think of a more congenial way of earning a living than travelling to photograph and write about my experiences off the beaten track. As a frequent visitor to Japan, I have become fascinated by haiku and have begun writing my own – but that's another story!

TEN TIPS ON WRITING ILLUSTRATED TRAVEL FEATURES

- **Research, research, research**…before you fix a date to travel.
- **Find out about annual events** by googling or contacting the relevant tourist board and make sure your information is up to date.
- **Check out the average weather** for the time you plan to be there on www.bbc.co.uk/weather/world/country_guides, and try to avoid the hurricane season.
- **Take a multi-adaptor** for recharging a mobile phone as well as rechargeable camera batteries.
- **Number all memory cards for your camera** before you leave home. Use them in chronological order – it helps to remind you what you have been shooting when you come to write captions.
- **Jot down article ideas before you leave.** Expand them with headings on location.
- **Buy local postcards on arrival** to check out the best viewpoints. Mark these on a local map.
- **Take lots of different shots** in both landscape (horizontal) and portrait (vertical) formats.
- **Record what you shoot** in a notebook, or photograph a sign to remind you where you were. This is another way to avoid mistakes with captioning: by the time you get home you may not remember the names of a series of formal gardens in Italy or waterfalls in Iceland.
- **Be organised with your filing of images.** Place them in folders clearly marked with the destination, so that you can retrieve them quickly and easily at a later date.
- **Back up your images** on a downloader or external hard drive.

WRITING FOR NEWSPAPERS AND MAGAZINES
GETTING OUT THERE AND GETTING PUBLISHED

SUSAN GROSSMAN

Susan Grossman is a visiting lecturer in journalism at two London universities and a professional writing coach. Her travel features appear regularly in the national press and she has contributed to BBC Radio 4 and BBC TV. A former magazine editor at Redwood Publishing, she is also author of half a dozen travel guides. Susan runs journalism workshops for freelancers looking to approach editors with confidence; and 'Get your Message Across' workshops for marketing and media professionals. Her 'Selling Freelance Features' workshops are held regularly in central London. For more information see www.susangrossman. co.uk. Part of this article may appear in Susan's forthcoming book on getting published.

Without contributions from freelancers, newspapers and magazines would struggle to survive. The travel section would be as empty |as an undiscovered beach, the health pages ailing and the money pages even more depressing than they are already. Readers would lose interest and advertisers stop buying space. As a freelance writer you are a vital cog in the wheel. So why are so many aspiring writers fearful of approaching editors? What are your chances of getting a commission, and how do you avoid rejection?

Editors are often perceived as having a reliable band of trusted freelancers who provide them with everything they need at the click of a mouse.

This is certainly true of editors who have been in the job for some time (probably too long) and who want an easy life. But as every freelancer who has just established a rapport with an editor knows, editors (eventually) retire, get fired or move on. Sad? Not necessarily. Their replacements are often on the hunt for a new entourage, especially in the early days when they are finding their feet and there is a continuous stream of new magazines being launched. A lot of doors are constantly opening.

> **FOLLOW UP ANY FACE-TO-FACE MEETINGS WITH EMAILS AND KEEP IN TOUCH WITH YOUR IDEAS AND NEEDS. ONE JOURNALIST I KNOW SENDS ALL HIS CONTACTS POSTCARDS FROM WHEREVER HE IS IN THE WORLD**

A FOOT IN THE DOOR

Gone are the days when editors knew their contributors by face as well as by name. The publication may be based in Brighton but its pages may be filled by writers as far afield as Bali or Bangkok. There is rarely a need to set eyes on an editor, but if you did you would probably feel a lot less fearful of approaching him or her. So it may help your cause to get out there and meet as many editors and other journalists as you can.

One of the best ways of networking is to go

to shows and exhibitions that cover your area of interest, such as the Ideal Home exhibition or the World Travel Market. You should register in advance online to get a press pass (and therefore get in free) and hang around in the press room when you arrive. Press rooms are usually very informal places, where you can chat to other journalists over coffee and pick up press releases and a (free to press) Exhibitors' Directory which will be full of useful contacts. To get on the mailing lists of PR companies that promote products or services you are interested in, you can subscribe (free) to websites like www.TravMedia. com, www.Food4Media.com, www.Health4Media. com and their sister sites on other topics and customise the press releases you want to receive according to your interests. You will receive a steady stream of invitations to product launches, lunches, press parties and occasional journalist alerts asking for feature contributions, as well as material that might support your stories. Do not be afraid to go along to events as a freelance.

Get yourself a business card with 'journalist' and your email address on it and start handing them out. www.vistaprint.com are cheap and quick and you can design your own card online. Follow up any face-to-face meetings with emails and keep in touch with your ideas and needs. One journalist I know sends all his contacts postcards from wherever he is in the world!

But rest assured, all of you outside the main metropolises, editors buy ideas, not people. If your idea is both interesting and topical and it matches the interests of the readership, you stand as good a chance as any of getting a commission. So first you need to do some homework.

'Contributors' guidelines' on a publisher's website are useful but bear in mind that these are designed to prevent editors receiving a mailbox full of unsolicited and unsuitable material from readers who fancy they can write. It's a bit like a double-glazing salesman knocking on your door without an appointment and asking if you need metal windows when you live in a 16th-century farmhouse in a conservation area. What immediately sorts the professional from the punter is the approach. A professional journalist in the UK rarely sends in a fully written feature 'on spec'. Editors respond to a synopsis (pitch, query letter, proposal) and only if that appeals will they commission a feature. And, although it should go without saying – whatever your subject and whomever you are approaching, get your facts right and make sure your synopsis and letter have no spelling errors.

> ## WHAT IMMEDIATELY SORTS THE PROFESSIONAL FROM THE PUNTER IS THE APPROACH

RESEARCH

The first thing you need to do before you even start is to identify who might be interested in your story, i.e. your target audience (bearing in mind, that there may be more than one). Don't assume you know a magazine's readership because you have flicked through a copy. To find out more about the demographics of the readership, get in touch with the advertising department and ask for a 'media pack'. (This might involve a bit of ingenuity on your part – you could always say you were a student.) This gives a breakdown of the age, gender, interests and income of the reader and will help you decide whether your feature idea is suitable or not. You also need to find out if it's weekly, monthly or biannual, so that you can establish their 'lead times'. A magazine published in January may make editorial decisions about content as far back as July or August.

The more back issues of a magazine you read, the more familiar you will become with what the editor or section editor might find interesting. Targeting your idea to the right person is essential. Look at the 'masthead' of the publication for the commissioning editor of the section you are interested in, whether it is health, food, beauty, finance or travel. Sometimes one editor oversees everything, while other publications have individual editors who look after specific sections. Look at published by-lines. If the writers' names seem to change regularly and you cannot find those names on the masthead, you know they use freelancers so you are in with a chance. This book and the Writer's Market UK website will help you find the contact details of publishers or you might also want to look online at websites like www.ppa.co.uk, www.apa.co.uk, www.mediauk.com or www.world-newspapers.com, which also includes magazines.

> ## DON'T ASSUME YOU KNOW A MAGAZINE'S READERSHIP BECAUSE YOU HAVE FLICKED THROUGH A COPY

THE PERFECT PITCH

The best pitches are succinct, detailed and include a topical peg or what I call a 'why now'. You might find this 'hook' or 'sell' in a new book or film, a trend, news story or survey. Many feature ideas are rejected because there is no good reason to publish them *now*!

Imagine your pitch is like a recipe for a cake. If you hand the editor bags of flour and sugar, half a dozen eggs and a pack of butter, he or she won't have a clue what to do with them. Don't hold anything back, tell the editor exactly what you intend to write about with precise ingredients, and make sure that it is suitable for their target audience – by adding 80 candles and some icing!

If you are unknown to the editor, remember it is your idea that they are buying, not you. But they *will* be looking for reassurance that you are capable, reliable, have good research skills, are passionate about your subject and can meet a deadline, which might mean putting in something about yourself. Your pitch should demonstrate as much of the above as possible and in so doing will also give the editor a good idea of your writing capabilities.

> *'I am a freelance journalist, would you be interested in a feature on a hotel in an old prison in Helsinki?'*

says very little, apart from that you want to write about your holiday and that you are probably not a journalist. However:

> *'As a probation officer used to visiting prison inmates as part of my job, I wonder if you would be interested in a write-up of a new hotel in Helsinki built on the site of a prison?'*

offers the editor an interesting angle. Despite this being the writer's first attempt at a feature, the angle and idea appealed, and it was published in a daily newspaper.

Several travel editors rejected an offer of a travel feature on Bruges when the writer wrote:

> *'I am planning to visit Bruges with its intricate network of canals, lace and chocolates.'*

She tried again:

> *'Bruges is the setting for the new blackly comic gangster movie,* In Bruges. *The director, taking the Hieronymus Bosch painting* The Last Judgement *as his inspiration, weaves a fast-paced story of three restless characters who find their minds and souls being expanded by the storybook Gothic architecture, canals and cobbled streets of this Flemish city. At the same time he offers a hilarious parody on tourism and the tensions between young and middle-aged visitors. The Bruges tourist office have produced a 'movie map' to tie in with the film, showing all the key locations. I intend to offer an insight into the culture, history and city behind the film, weaving colour from the film and interviews with the actors on their experiences while filming.'*

It worked. Similarly:

> *'I am planning to go to Odessa in the Ukraine as I am very interested in old films'*

says very little. However the writer went on to say:

> *'This year is the centenary of the historical events dramatised in* Battleship Potemkin. *In the light of this and the deep suspicion Odessans feel about Ukraine's 'orange revolution', I wondered if the very mention of the film might provoke some interesting conversation.'*

It did, and the feature was published in the *New Statesman*.

Although some newspapers, especially the supplements and weekly magazines, seem to thrive on first-hand accounts of doom and disaster from readers, a professional writer will develop the subject and use case histories to illustrate the bigger picture:

'My dog Ringo sleeps with me as he suffers from terrible depression'

would become:

'A drug company has developed an anti-depressant for dogs. My feature will look at how to spot the telltale signs and suggest alternatives to medication.'

In this instance your pitch would need to include statistics, the names of experts who will give authoritative views and advice on where readers, or their dogs, can get help.

REJECTION

This might have absolutely nothing to do with you or your idea. There may be all sorts of things going on behind the scenes, from budgeting restraints to the whims of editorial directors. But you could have slipped up without realising it, by not following the style of the publication. For example, you may have written in the first person, when all the other features are reported objectively. You may have missed deadlines for magazine issues or sent it to the wrong person. To avoid this happening, you could telephone the editorial assistant before you decide whom to pitch to and when. Don't always assume the worst. If the editor you have written to fails to reply, don't assume that they are being rude

– they may be away or no longer in the job. Pick up the phone. If you do get a *'No thank you, not this time'*, try again with another idea. Lastly, never tell an editor what they *ought* to be covering: it will only put their backs up.

THE WRITING

Here's the tricky part – or is it? Now that you have a commission you are probably panicking. There is no need. The editor has seen your synopsis, liked the way you write and accepted the ingredients of your story. If you are in any doubt, open up a dialogue, confirm your understanding and ask questions. Also remember that sub-editors are employed to straighten out your words, add headings and tighten up any phrases if English is not your first language. One way to start is to do as my students do: get a copy of the magazine or newspaper you are contributing to, find a feature or two on a similar topic and follow the formula! Most publications have websites on which you can read previous published features, to help identify the style of writing and the format. Imagine the feature is made up of layers, like one of those glass jars of coloured sand. The first layer may be a 'quote', the second a statistic, the third a fact or description, and so on.

Who said journalism was difficult? It's a doddle. Whether you can make a living out of doing it depends on your needs. But when the cheques start to arrive and you can't remember who they're from, you'll know you've made it! Good luck.

> **MANY FEATURE IDEAS ARE REJECTED BECAUSE THERE IS NO GOOD REASON TO PUBLISH THEM *NOW!***

WRITING FOR THE WEB
GETTING THE WORDS RIGHT ON A WEBSITE

ANTHONY PEARSON

Anthony Pearson is a consultant editor specialising in online and interactive media. He has devised, written and produced content and services for the BBC, Dorling Kindersley, HM Revenue & Customs, Directgov and many others.

▶ It wasn't so long ago that to find a writer in a web team was a rare thing – content (as words are called on the web) was something programmers wrote on buttons and web designers got from, ah, somewhere. That has changed – hurrah – and now editors and authors are central to many web projects. I've worked on a number of large, public service projects recently that have been led by editors – which is as it should be.

So the work is there. How to get it is, as ever, the tricky bit. As with all things publishing, it's often down to making contacts. If you already make money out of writing for print you'll have contacts – use them. And if your old-media clients aren't thinking about the web as a platform, take the initiative and educate them.

> ❝ IF YOU AREN'T ALREADY A PROFESSIONAL WRITER, THEN WORK OUT WHAT IT IS YOU HAVE TO OFFER AND SELL IT ❞

Then there are agencies. Don't just try the editorial ones. I've found a lot of web work through IT agencies – a hangover from the days when editors and authors didn't get involved in web stuff. To find them search for 'IT agency UK', or similar, on the internet. And when using job search sites don't restrict your searches to 'writer' or 'author' – try something more new-media such as 'information architect' or 'content manager'.

The other, very nice, hangover from those days is that wordy types working on the web often get paid at IT rates, and that can mean two or three times what you would expect in the world of print. (You'll get paid even more if you call yourself an Information Architect or a Content Manager.)

If you aren't already a professional writer, then work out what it is you have to offer and sell it. Getting a head start by writing for free (think forums, blogging, reviewing) can only help. One great thing about the web is that it is easy to get your words out there (if you don't mind doing it for free).

GENERAL RULES
Whether you are being paid or not, you'll need to adapt your style to the medium.

- Stick to your point and keep it short (stop reading here if you like).
- Make your writing work. Be clear about what you want to achieve and re-read what you've written to make sure it delivers.
- Know your audience and use words and style they'll understand.
- Be positive (don't be negative).

- Be direct and confident. (It is, perhaps, best not to be indirect.)
- Use plain language. Buzzwords and jargon make your strategic innovations mission statements look unoriginal and insincere.
- Studiously avoid the loquacious, endeavour to shun baroque locutions and spurn labyrinthine grammatical structures else you may earn the disapprobation of your esteemed readership. (Don't show off. Keep it simple.)
- DUA (don't use acronyms) unless they really do save space and your audience will understand them. Even then, always explain what they mean the first time you use them. Acronymfinder.com is a good place to find out how ambiguous you are being – DUA also stands for Distal Uterine Artery and Dead or Unable to Attend.
- Contractions (you'll, we'll, they're) are good things – they save space and make your writing more direct.
- Avoid colons and semi-colons. Much as I love them in print, they usually mean your sentence is too complicated: split your sentence into several, shorter ones; or write your points as a bulleted list.
- And don't worry about starting sentences with 'and' and 'but' – it makes your writing snappier. Good grammar is important, but on the web accessible writing is more important. Having said that, do brush up on your grammar. Quality counts on the web as much as it does in print. Knowing the difference between 'which' and 'that' and putting apostrophes and commas in the right places make all the difference. If your writing is clear and accurate (check your spelling), people will take notice of, and trust, your message.

SOME SPECIFICS

You'll need to adapt your writing to its destination. Here are a few varieties of web publishing, and some points to bear in mind.

Websites
It's the words – not the interactive media plug-ins and curvy corners – that matter on the web.

- Be clear about your site's purpose, and tell people what that purpose is – if not in the site's name then in a strapline.
- Split your site into bite-sized chunks under meaningful headings. You can now call yourself an Information Architect and take a pay rise.
- If you're repetitively repeating the same information under different headings, re-jig your site structure. (This makes you a Senior Information Architect – more money.)
- It's hard to read long chunks of writing from a screen, so keep it short, break it up and put the important bits first so your readers don't have to scroll down to find them.
- Search engines look for keywords (words that describe what your site is about) at the top of pages. Which means that meaningful headlines and first paragraphs will help your readers find your site. You are now an expert in search engine optimisation (SEO) – take another pay rise.
- Make links descriptive. Tell people why they should click on a link and what they'll find there.
- Test your site on as many people as you can. Take note of what they say – you may not agree, but the site is for your audience, not for you. Then change your site until it works for your audience. You are now a usability expert – you had better put your day rate up again.

Blogs
Sometimes books and films get made out of them…there's proper money for you (well, one in 20 million of you).

- Keep it simple, keep it focused. (There is a theme emerging here… have you spotted it yet?)
- Write about something you know for an audience you understand.
- Stick with it – dedication is all when it comes to diaries.
- Think twice before sharing too much. Anything you write can be saved (don't rely on being able to delete it), copied and passed around.

Forums

Great places to get your words out into the world (and have 50 people pull you up on your mistakes instantly).

- What you write will be published. Keep it simple, focused and accurate.
- Keep to the forum's topic, and the specific point being discussed.
- Don't post contentious messages in haste.
- Don't get drawn into arguments ('flame wars'). Make your point clearly and concisely without getting personal.
- Don't post personal, especially financial, information.
- Be suspicious. Would you believe me if I told you I was an 18-year-old Adonis?

Ads

Beyond the banners and promotions that are clearly adverts, much of what you write is probably selling something to someone.

- Be snappy, direct and keep it simple – don't try to be clever.
- Be honest about what you are selling.
- But be positive – there's no need to sell something's faults.
- Know your audience, and sell them the benefits of the thing from their point of view. A lot of people sell technologies on the web when they should be selling what the technology does.
- Check your spelling and grammar. If your writing is dodgy, people will think you are too.

Emails

You may not think of it as publishing, but whether you are delivering an ad campaign or writing to your mum think of email as a publishing platform and take it seriously.

- Write in haste, repent at your leisure. Imagine everyone you know and thousands of complete strangers reading that email. It can happen.
- Keep it simple, focused and accurate.
- Make the subject line meaningful – people get a lot of email and you need to tell them up-front why they should read yours.
- Don't send personal, especially financial, information by email. Email isn't secure and it isn't private. Assume lots of people have access to every message you send.
- Make sure you are sending it to the right person – check the address before you hit the send button.

Just remember (you know what I'm going to say) stick to your point and keep it short.

> " USE PLAIN LANGUAGE. BUZZWORDS AND JARGON MAKE YOUR STRATEGIC INNOVATIONS MISSION STATEMENTS LOOK UNORIGINAL AND INSINCERE "

THE AGENT'S VIEW
A GUIDE TO FINDING AND WORKING WITH AN AGENT

JONATHAN PEGG

Jonathan Pegg recently founded his own agency after 12 years at Curtis Brown where he was a senior agent. Prior to becoming an agent he was an agent's assistant, foreign rights executive, and publicist for books. He has worked with a range of prestigious authors, and his interests include both fiction (literary fiction, thrillers, historical and quality commercial) and a broad range of non-fiction. Visit www.jonathanpegg.com.

If I meet a first-time author with a view to representing them, they often seem hesitant about asking what they can expect from me. Yet there are many elements to agency work and equally as many considerations that I try to anticipate for the author at such meetings.

Since the whole purpose of a literary agent is to take care of publishing processes for their client, to the extent that many details can go without saying if an author's career is in good hands, the important question to begin with is how one agent differs from another. At the same time, the considerations involved in choosing an agent are meaningless without basic prior knowledge of publishing processes. So I have provided a ten-step guide to the least an agent does for a client, hoping to address not just the kinds of questions that first-time authors often have but also the issue of which are reasonable or realistic questions to ask at an initial meeting.

FINDING AND APPROACHING A LITERARY AGENT

It can be difficult to secure an agent's attention in the first place, so I'll begin with a very basic guide to going about that.

- First, look up the websites of the agents listed in this book's directory.
- Check that the agency's commission rates are acceptable to you (see box on The Agency Agreement on page 76).
- Study the agency's guidelines for submitting material. Most will request you to enclose a stamped addressed envelope if you would like your material returned. A typical requirement for fiction might be to enclose a covering letter, biographical information, one-page synopsis and two chapters; for non-fiction it might be to enclose the same but also a longer 'proposal' for the book. Some agencies' sites go into more detail than I have done here.
- Prepare and send off your submission (see box overleaf). It is reasonable to expect a swift acknowledgement. After that, be prepared to wait patiently for a further response – agencies receive a lot of manuscripts and it sometimes takes them up to two months to clear their backlog, although most try to respond within four to six weeks. If they are potentially interested in taking you on, they should invite you for the introductory meeting I mentioned earlier.
- An agent's main resource in a time-devouring occupation is their time, so it is advisable to direct your work accurately by doing your research. You should, of course, also present your work carefully and conduct yourself professionally.

So what does an agent actually do for you? Here is my ten-stage description of an agent's role.

1. Preliminaries – content preparation
Agents vary in the amount of editorial guidance they will offer. Sometimes they will suggest further work as a pre-requisite to formalising your

PREPARING YOUR SUBMISSION

The covering letter should be brief but not so brief as to be meaningless. State what kind of book it is – e.g. literary, thriller, romantic etc. for fiction; memoir, travelogue, history etc. for non-fiction. You could mention why you feel the book deserves a place in the bookshops, and include information that will be relevant or interesting to someone considering your work.

The biographical information should largely, though not necessarily exclusively, focus on what is of relevance to the book. There is no need to send a full CV.

The synopsis should capture the heart of the book, summarising the plot: not a blow-by-blow account so much as a characterisation of what the reader can expect, as with the blurbs on the back of books.

A non-fiction proposal should be 5–15 pages long and should introduce the basic idea of the book and your relationship to the idea (that is, why you feel you are qualified to write it), followed by a few pages expanding on the idea, a 'chapter breakdown' summarising each chapter in a paragraph or two, your thoughts about what the market for the book might be, and information about how long you plan the book to be and how long it might take to write.

For more detail about preparing a submission, see Hilary Johnson's article on page 49.

relationship with a written agreement (see box on page 76). If a formal agreement is produced before editorial suggestions have been made, it is reasonable to check whether the agent feels more work will be needed before submitting the material to publishers. It may be that they correctly feel the material is ready – after all, you should have got it into the best possible state before you sent it to them. But if they do think more work will be necessary, it is reasonable to ask roughly how much editorial guidance they will be prepared to give you. I say 'roughly' because it's difficult for an agent to say how much detail they'll go into without going into the detail itself!

2. Submission strategy
The agent will decide in due course which publishers, and specifically which commissioning editors, are likely to be interested in – and most suitable for – any particular project. Sometimes an agent will submit a project to one editor at a time; sometimes they will make a 'multiple submission'. They are unlikely to have decided this until after your initial meeting and it is probably unrealistic to request too much information about strategy at this stage for two reasons: first, the agent might understandably be reticent to give away all their ideas before you have committed to them; second, the process does require flexibility.

Once a project has been submitted by an agent, it may be difficult to find another agent to take it on if it is rejected and the author loses steam, so it is worth trying to ascertain the extent to which an agent will persevere with your project. The response will be necessarily vague because the question of how many publishers they'll approach may depend on the kind of feedback they get, or indeed a number of circumstances. Yet I personally believe it is only fair for an agent to be as clear as possible about their intentions so that you have a rough idea of where you stand with them – are they undertaking to stick with the project to the bitter end if necessary or will it be a staged process in which, after a number of unsuccessful submissions, they will review their commitment and the valid question of whether it is in your best interests to continue?

3. Pitching

The agent's next step is to represent your book to commissioning editors in a way that is appealing without being misleading. It is important that an agent enthusiastically 'gets' your work. Whether they do or not will probably be apparent from the way they talk about it to you. If not, I think it is reasonable to ask an agent how, in broad terms, they see themselves characterising your work. How would they summarise the book, and what strengths would they emphasise?

4. Exploitation of subsidiary rights

Should a publishing deal be secured, there are early decisions for an agent to make about which rights are included in the deal (see the glossary on page 104 for an explanation of the various types of subsidiary rights). From a publisher's point of view, the sale of these rights will often be an important means of recouping their initial investment in producing the book. So the question of which rights are being granted and which are being withheld will have some impact on the level of advance they are prepared to pay. The relative value of different rights will vary according to the project in question, and the agent will need to try to judge whether the advance is a fair return for the rights that are being requested.

If a publisher which has been granted the opportunity to sub-license these rights makes a successful sale, they will share with you a portion as set out in the original publishing contract (see the article on contracts, page 86, for more about this). However, as with the royalties from sales of the book, that share will initially go towards 'earning out' the up-front 'advance' sum the publisher has paid for the book, with the result that you may receive payments from sub-licensed subsidiary rights only some time later, if at all.

If, on the other hand, an agent handles the subsidiary rights, further up-front advances are guaranteed as soon as the sale is made. You are also one step closer to the publishing activities that will ensue and will therefore have that much more control over what happens with your work.

So there is a variety of considerations involved in the granting of subsidiary rights. Apart from the question of what a publisher is prepared to pay

for them, another factor is how energetically they will pursue the sale of these rights. At the same time, this latter factor is equally true of your agent. So it is important to ascertain how an agent is set up for exploitation of the more important subsidiary rights such as US, translation and serialisation.

A few will sell US and translation rights directly to publishers, some will work with a network of co-agents in the territories concerned and some will have in-house foreign rights staff selling directly or via co-agents. Having dedicated staff selling your foreign rights is obviously attractive, but the impact on sales of the primary agent's enthusiastic familiarity with a book should never be underestimated. So there are pros and cons whichever way you look at it. In these days of easy telecommunications, what is important is for the agent to have sufficient knowledge of the market in question if they are working directly and a good network of co-agents (together with sufficient knowledge to oversee them) if they are working indirectly.

Serialisation rights are more relevant to non-fiction, and usually non-fiction of topical interest at that. Most non-fiction agents will sell these rights directly.

I am sometimes asked whether money can be saved by coming to independent arrangements with agents in several territories. In my view the savings are small and such an arrangement may prevent you benefiting from the strategic overview your primary agent can provide.

> ## IT IS IMPORTANT THAT AN AGENT ENTHUSIASTICALLY 'GETS' YOUR WORK

5. TV/Film representation

Some literary agencies offer TV and film representation; others partner with independent specialist agents. There are advantages and disadvantages to each: in a larger agency with a TV department, there is the convenience of having all the activities under one roof but, even so, the TV agent is unlikely to commit to all their book department's offerings. An independent literary agent may or may not be prepared to network with independent TV and film agents on your behalf, but if they are there is the advantage of a more bespoke service. If you've aspirations in this direction, ask whether the agent feels that they are realistic, and how they would help you if so.

6. Deal negotiation
Rather than bombard the agent with too many questions about the deal initially, since they are somewhat hypothetical until the moment has arrived, it is worth remembering that at this point an agent's time is best spent focusing on making the deal happen in the first place. They will probably have a rough idea of what they might expect by way of an advance but be understandably reluctant to make predictions. However, it may be helpful to touch on the question of their attitude to advances.

Since agents work on commission, they share your financial interest but a good agent will also take other things into consideration on their clients' behalf. Too high an advance might put you under unconstructive commercial pressure and, if a publisher ends up making a large loss on a book, this can affect your future opportunities. At the same time, it's worth bearing in mind that a publisher's marketing budget for a book is sometimes influenced by the advance they have paid, with a higher advance meaning more to recoup and therefore more reason to put resources into making a success of the book. The agent is there to advise you in these matters and then secure your aim to the best of their ability according to the circumstances.

7. Contracts
There are many negotiable points in a publisher's contract. Some have financial implications, such as royalty rates and the way royalties are accounted. An agent's commission is based on all future income, so it is in their interest to take care over these matters. Many points are to do with your control over the book in the longer term, your obligations to the publisher in the overall life of the book and sometimes even your next book.

Negotiating contracts is a very important part of an agent's duties, requiring willingness to fight a corner, attention to detail and not least patience to interpret the legalese for you insofar as you wish to be concerned.

8. Quality control and diplomacy
There are some areas that can't be definitively covered in a contract but do need to be considered as your relationship with a publisher develops. It is in a publisher's interest to succeed with a book once they have committed to it, but every book will be published amongst a number of other books and a publisher's time and overall resources are finite. There's rarely a certain science in the realms of publicity or advertising and promotions, and most authors find it difficult to press their own case even if they're confident there's a case to be pressed.

It might be that your expectations are a little high or that the publishing team as a whole is insufficiently behind a book; in these circumstances an agent may be able to step in and mediate or contribute support and ideas.

THE AGENCY AGREEMENT

Reputable agencies offer a formal contract, either immediately or once you have done the suggested work to make your material ready for submission to publishers. The agreement is usually subject to a reasonable notice period invoked by either party, since a successful relationship is dependent on mutual enthusiasm. Most agencies charge a commission of between 10 and 15 per cent of earnings on deals done in the UK, and 20 per cent on international deals. Most also charge expenses such as photocopying, couriers or ordering finished copies of your book for the purpose of selling subsidiary rights, but not phone calls, standard postage or entertaining. It is not advisable to sign with an agent who charges a reading fee or any other sort of fee (including fees if they are unsuccessful in placing your work).

Most publishers will take your views into account in matters like the book's format, the cover design and the publication date, but these are ultimately the publisher's decision. This is as it should be, given the degree of specialist expertise arrayed within a publishing house, but even then it is sometimes necessary for an agent to help you get your point of view across and liaise for both parties.

Sometimes an agent has to stamp a foot on behalf of their client, but most of the time their relationship with publishers is not adversarial. As a first-time author you don't necessarily know what it is realistic to try to change, or how best to go about things if you have a complaint, so the agent's role is to take all that off your shoulders. An agent can hopefully pre-empt any communication breakdowns between author and publisher, thus keeping the creative channels clear in everyone's best interest.

9. Invoicing, statement processing and general paperwork relief
The agent will also invoice and check payments and statements for you. Aside from the advance payments, there are usually biannual royalty statements (and payments if the advance has been earned out). These statements can be complex and impenetrable to the layman.

There are also other bits of paperwork as you go forward, such as when the publisher seeks consent to a sub-licence or to sell copies at a discount not allowed for in the original contract. The agent is there to advise you each time this happens, manage the paperwork and check that the receipts from these deals have been properly accounted for.

10. Career building
In the last 20 years or so the role of agents has grown in importance and become better known. This is not just for all the reasons given above. Another major reason, at least if you have more than one book in mind, is that editors tend to move jobs a lot these days. They aren't looking out for your overall trajectory in the same way as an agent who is often your most reliable industry contact and ally. In theory your career is the agent's career, so the agent is always thinking about your profile and taking care of it in the small world of publishing and the media.

IN SUMMARY
In all these ways and more, agents earns their commission. If you are successful in securing an agent's attention, remember that the effort they commit is based on belief in you and your work. I would certainly advise against signing up with an agent without first meeting them in person. A good meeting provides opportunity for comfortable, informal discussion around a lot of the points above and of course it enables both you and the agent to establish whether you are likely to enjoy a happy working rapport together.

> **NEGOTIATING CONTRACTS IS A VERY IMPORTANT PART OF AN AGENT'S DUTIES, REQUIRING WILLINGNESS TO FIGHT A CORNER, ATTENTION TO DETAIL AND NOT LEAST PATIENCE TO INTERPRET THE LEGALESE FOR YOU INSOFAR AS YOU WISH TO BE CONCERNED**

THE AGENT'S VIEW

JONATHAN PEGG

FEATURE

SO HOW *DO* BOOKS GET INTO SHOPS?

AN INDEPENDENT BOOKSELLER'S VIEW

SARAH REES

Sarah Rees graduated from Oxford Polytechnic in 1983, then worked in various publishing companies, including W H Allen in export sales, Time Life as Production Controller and finally Reed Illustrated Books as Production Manager on Hamlyn and Mitchell Beazley titles.

After 11 years in London, she moved back to South Wales, working for a small family print company. She also explored the opportunity of having her own business and finally opened Cover to Cover in the Mumbles area of Swansea in 1999 (www.cover-to-cover.co.uk). Predominately a bookshop, Cover to Cover also sells interesting gifts for all ages, cards and stationery.

The business of bookselling in the UK is as competitive, price-conscious and vulnerable as any other sector of the retail industry. Since the abolition of the Net Book Agreement in 1998, which meant that books no longer had to be sold for the price printed on the cover, bookselling has become a growth area in supermarkets, a huge worldwide internet business and a significantly more challenging one for the chain shops and surviving independent booksellers.

Today's independent booksellers have had to become innovative entrepreneurs, always coming up with new marketing ideas and improvements to customer service. We must also be relative experts in technology. Many have diversified and opened in-store coffee shops, developed excellent websites and offered more non-book products.

Cover to Cover has always sold a lot of non-book products. My range is large, from soft toys to moneyboxes, from toiletries to jewellery. However, nearly two-thirds of my shop space is dedicated to books. Not least because of space constraints, I have to be careful about what books I choose to stock, so I'm going to start by highlighting some of the criteria I use in making my decision to take a particular title. In so doing, I hope that I shall provide some useful pointers to authors wanting to publish their own work and give those who are lucky enough to have their books taken on by a publisher an insight into the reasons publishing decisions are made.

HOW DO I CHOOSE WHICH BOOKS TO SELL?

Probably my main consideration when choosing whether or not to stock a book is the cover. A good cover will sell a mediocre book; a poor cover will hinder the sales of even the best book. In the small space available on a cover or even the spine, the design and typography have to convey sufficient interest to make the browser pick it off the shelf. The spine is often overlooked but it is very important: think how many books spend their entire shelf life with just the spine on display. I find the history of cover design fascinating. It was a bold decision by Penguin to produce their early books in such a distinctive style, but see how that decision has filtered through into today's publishing and influenced such modern covers

> TODAY'S INDEPENDENT BOOKSELLERS HAVE HAD TO BECOME INNOVATIVE ENTREPRENEURS, ALWAYS COMING UP WITH NEW MARKETING IDEAS AND IMPROVEMENTS TO CUSTOMER SERVICE

as those of Alexander McCall Smith's *No. 1 Ladies' Detective Agency* series.

Price

The second major factor is the recommended price of the book. As a result of price-cutting by internet sites, supermarkets and chain shops, the independent bookseller is faced with an unbelievable price war: to sell a hardcover book at the full price is almost retail suicide. Price has become such a major factor in a customer's purchasing decision that I believe the book's intrinsic worth has been devalued, which is a very sad state of affairs. As a potential author, and particularly if you are self-publishing, be careful in pricing your title. A young photographer came into the shop recently to show me his first book, which he had self-financed. The photos were excellent and of local interest but he had produced a paperback priced at £20. Unfortunately there are two successful books of local photos currently available. Both sell equally well, both hardcover, both at £14.99. To date I have sold only one copy of the £20 title.

Format: getting the 'package' right

This example leads me onto the format of the book. That is, its size, whether it is hardback or paperback, and how highly illustrated it is. I find this particularly sensitive in the children's market where I choose few hardcover picture books. The average price now for a picture paperback is £5.99, for a hardcover £10.99. Jumping over the £10 threshold really does affect sales. Some children's fiction titles, such as the Lemony Snicket books and the Spiderwick Chronicles, have been very successful as small hardcovers, but that is

at least in part because they were attractively packaged and priced. In the case of the local photography book mentioned above, sales might have been better had the book been a hardcover, so that it looked better value for its £20 price tag.

Format also is a strong factor in the sales of adult non-fiction. Like many people, I like cookery and gardening books to include colour photos. However, once in a while, a title will become a bestseller because the quality of the writing needs no embellishments. A few years ago, Simon Hopkinson's cookery title *Roast Chicken and Other Stories*, which has only a few colour illustrations and no photographs of finished dishes, was a great bestseller, particularly for the independent bookshops. But again, it was an attractive 'gifty-looking' book, sensibly priced.

Knowing my customers

During my process of selection, I also take into account seasonality and topicality. I am near the coast and any children's books relating to the seaside sell well during the summer, whatever the weather. As for topicality, the most obvious example is a current TV or film tie-in, though I realise that if you are writing one of those you probably don't need my help! An author with a strong track record will always appeal, as will a book whose cover features any promising endorsements by reviewers or fellow authors. Obtaining this sort of quote is one of the best ways you can help promote sales of your book, if you know anyone who is willing to support you, or know anyone who knows anyone… it is personal and direct. Publicity in the local press is another thing that usually has an excellent effect on sales.

HOW *DO* BOOKS GET INTO SHOPS?

SARAH REES

FEATURE

Finally, I need to be sure that the new title will fit in with my existing stock holding. Because I know a lot of my customers well, I am able to hone my stock to appeal to them; I am also able to 'hand sell', so I can probably entice a good customer to try something new. This is something that the bigger chain shops and supermarkets cannot do, so it is a vital area in which the independent bookseller has to shine.

Although I use the above criteria, I think it important to stress that good independent booksellers also strive for quality – both in presentation and of course in writing. This is obviously difficult to assess on an initial presentation; however, as booksellers become more experienced, so their ability to judge a book by more than just the cover becomes more acute.

HOW DO I BUY MY BOOKS?

There are a number of avenues open to me from which to source my books. A knowledge of these might enable you as a prospective author to target the appropriate suppliers.

Today there are few sales representatives 'on the road' visiting bookshops: I see only four, all of them from children's publishers, despite the fact that I sell adult books too. They come once a month to subscribe (that is, sell) titles that are being published in a given month, usually about six months ahead. For each title a presentation consists of an information sheet, possibly a cover proof or a mock-up of the book, even a final copy, and the rep will give me a very brief description of the appeal of each title. That is another way in which you as an author can help sales – give your publishers just a sentence or two which sums up your book in an irresistible way!

Wholesalers and telesales

As I see so few representatives I source the majority of my books from one UK wholesaler, based over 500km away. Book wholesalers are vital tools to the independent bookselling trade. Mine stocks over half a million titles from which I can order daily if necessary. I receive a monthly catalogue of the new titles they intend to stock. Titles are organised by genre and given star highlights to indicate their predicted sales, from five stars for the bestsellers down to one for the less notable. The catalogue does not allow for a picture of every front cover but all titles include a very brief synopsis/sales pitch. I believe it is vital, as a new author, that you endeavour to have the major UK wholesalers (there are only two) stock your book. This may reduce your profit margin on a self-financed title, but it makes it easier for independent bookshops to order and hopefully sell your work.

Publishers also use 'telesales' to supplement reps' visits and the work of the wholesalers. This involves sending out a monthly catalogue of titles, often including extra discount offers as an incentive to buy, and following up the mail shot with a telephone call to take the order. This sort of selling relies heavily on the visual impact of the cover and the 'blurb' written about the book.

Special interest

As I am based in Wales, I stock Welsh interest/ Welsh language books and I source these via the Welsh Books Council. Again, if there is a specialist wholesaler or distributor who might stock your title, I strongly recommend that you

> **WHILE YOU ARE WRITING YOUR BOOK, TALK TO YOUR LOCAL BOOKSELLER, FIND OUT WHAT IS CURRENTLY AVAILABLE AND WHETHER OR NOT YOUR BOOK WILL SIT COMFORTABLY ALONGSIDE ANOTHER SIMILAR TITLE**

investigate the possibility. For example, Marston Book Services distribute Lion Hudson and other Christian publishers and John Wiley stock many art publishers' titles. These companies will warehouse, invoice and distribute for you. They might even help market the book, although this is not always their priority.

Not only am I made aware of new titles via these avenues, I also pick up information through the same channels as any other consumer. The media plays a huge part in promoting books. All serious newspapers carry book review pages. TV and particularly radio have book-related programmes. Other booksellers publish book guides on their websites, and there are various 'good book' guides available. I also listen constantly to my customers. They are a huge resource, telling me what books they have read or want to read. As a new author, I recommend that new authors scout out their nearest bookshop and library, and make friends with the staff. Also look out for the book guides in Waterstone's and other booksellers.

IN CONCLUSION

Finally I encourage any future authors to do as much market research as possible *prior* to publication. This might seem obvious, but I have often been confronted by an excited author who wants me to stock a book that I would have been happy to buy had it been produced in a slightly different way. This puts me in a difficult position. So while you are writing your book, talk to your local bookseller, find out what is currently available and whether or not your book will sit comfortably alongside another similar title. Any knowledge of bookselling you can pick up will help you to realise your dream. Bookselling, like writing, is a task not easily undertaken but if done well gives the ultimate in satisfaction.

SARAH REES

FEATURE

BECOMING YOUR OWN SALES REP
MARKETING ADVICE FOR AUTHORS

MARY CAVANAGH

Mary Cavanagh is the author of two novels, *A Man Like Any Other*, published by Matador in 2008, and *The Crowded Bed*, published by Transita in 2007. She has a third nearly completed and another in progress. As a member of The Oxford Writers Group, she has co-written and self-published two anthologies, *The Sixpenny Debt and Other Oxford Stories* and *The Lost College and Other Oxford Stories,* under the imprint OxPens. This article is based on extracts from Mary's book *The Seriously Useful Authors' Guide to Marketing: Publicity, Marketing and the Books Trade,* published by Troubador Publishing Ltd.

▶ Your newly published book is in your hands. Congratulations. Isn't it a great feeling to see your name emblazoned on the front cover as the author? If you are a household name and with a long backlist of successes, then don't bother to read any more – cheerio – you will have the luxury of not having to lift a finger to publicise and market your book. The majority of us are not so lucky, especially in the current economic climate, so if you are *not* a household name, particularly if you have been published by a small publisher or have self-published, then *do* read on!

> ❝ ONE THING TO REMEMBER AT ALL TIMES: YOUR BOOK IS NOT LIKE A POP RECORD THAT HAS TO SELL MULTIPLE COPIES IN THE FIRST FIVE MINUTES OR BE DEEMED A FLOP ❞

At this stage I am envisaging that 98 per cent of you will still be on board.

It's a sad fact that, with very, very few exceptions, only books with a large publicity budget behind them stand a chance of stardom. Did you know that only 5 per cent of all published books sell over 3,000 copies? Or that large publishing houses spend 95 per cent of their marketing budgets on 5 per cent of their authors? Thus the marketplace is saturated with first-time and lesser known authors fighting to stick their heads above the parapet. It may well be up to you to create a reputation for your book and make yours the one to go that extra mile.

HARE VERSUS TORTOISE

One thing to remember at all times: your book is not like a pop record that has to sell multiple copies in the first five minutes or be deemed a flop. Yes, flash-in-the-pan books come and go in the publishing world like shooting stars. They make a huge killing over about six weeks and then the star falls, never to be heard of again. But it's much better to have gradual and steady sales over a period of time and it matters not a whit that a month after your book comes out sales are sluggish. I favour a tortoise (rather than a hare) philosophy, taking each stage slowly and thoroughly. If you're going to do a job properly you can concentrate on only one thing at a time, and information often takes a while to permeate through to your targets. It's also a fact that not everything works first time, and some things never work, no matter how many times you try.

I have been involved in three different types of publication: I've been published by a mainstream publisher, and I have self-published via both print-on-demand (POD) and a commissioned print run. In each case I have had to roll up my sleeves and get on with the task of being my own marketing manager. I'm not wealthy, young and beautiful, or well-connected socially, nor do I have a far-reaching network of career and leisure pursuits to boost my sales. I call myself a kitchen-table author: hard working, ambitious, dedicated to my craft and eager to use any opportunity to the best effect. Because I don't write science fiction, romance, crime or any other dedicated genre, I fall into the 'mid-list' category – the hardest type to market these days – and had I not put my shoulder to the wheel it's doubtful I'd have made many sales at all. The advice I give to everyone, whether writing fiction or non-fiction, is that if you are prepared to work hard and with vision, you can make excellent sales.

Three years ago I knew nothing – and I really do mean absolutely nothing – about dealing with the book industry. Like most authors, I'd been so neurotically obsessed with getting into print that it hadn't occurred to me how much I would have to be involved in the sales side. When I found out, nothing daunted, I jumped on the learning curve. At times I must have seemed maniacally driven but I was determined to act upon every suggestion I could glean from the grapevine.

There are many, many areas to investigate and pursue for sales possibilities and I explore them in more depth in my book *The Seriously Useful Authors' Guide to Marketing*. For the purpose of this article I will concentrate on the skills you need if you are to be your own sales rep and communicator. *You* are about to become the all-important person who approaches bookshops (both chain and independent), libraries, reading groups and the editorial offices of the press and the media. Although I am focusing on bookshops here, the same general rules apply to anyone else you might decide to contact.

With regard to bookshops, my experience

> ## THE ADVICE I GIVE TO EVERYONE, WHETHER WRITING FICTION OR NON-FICTION, IS THAT IF YOU ARE PREPARED TO WORK HARD AND WITH VISION, YOU CAN MAKE EXCELLENT SALES

is that less well-known writers are more likely to have success with the independents, as the chains are very much driven by the commercial market. However, *The Sixpenny Debt* and *The Lost College*, two self-published anthologies produced by the Oxford Writers Group, of which I am a member, have sold amazingly well at our local Waterstone's. This is the exception rather than the norm, but I will quote Colin Shone, the manager:

The policy of Waterstone's is very much on the side of the author, but the company is in the business of selling books to … sell books! Thus, they will stock any book, self-published or mainstream, as long as they think they can shift it. The reason they have sold so many hundreds of copies of The Sixpenny Debt *is that it is a slim volume, has an attractive cover, is well produced and has Oxford in the title. Generally, in order for a self-published book to be of interest to them, it should have a very strong local theme as a 'peg'. Even if it has been talked up at a Literary Festival, or in the broadsheets, that doesn't really sell it. The local connection is paramount.*

YOU AS A SALES REPRESENTATIVE

The first thing to remember when you go out into the world of hand-selling is that neither you nor your book will initially dazzle anyone. We all, especially first-time authors, are so thrilled at being published that – even if only subconsciously – we desire interest and ideally some admiration. But the book trade and the media deal with authors, agents and publishing houses on a daily basis, and one more hopeful author among thousands won't get them very excited. What *can* make a difference is the way you appeal to them, and it's really a question of life skills, confidence and planning.

So here you are, cold calling, trying to make an impact. How do you start? First, think of how many times you've been pounced upon by overpowering shop assistants or confronted by doorstep or street traders. If you're anything like me, being cornered is off-putting to say the least.

The rule is to keep your enthusiasm contained and accept that every time you make an approach you are dealing with a unique situation and an unknown person. We all have our own very different personalities, from bombastic to painfully shy, and there's no way anyone can give you a blueprint for toning yourself down or boosting yourself up: only experience will help you get the balance right. It's very tempting to become intimidated, gushing or flustered, and obviously some people are easier to deal with than others, but I try not to be too influenced by general demeanour. Try to be exactly the same, whoever you're dealing with.

When I'm planning a trip to a bookshop (in fact whenever I do anything to promote my books), I pay a lot of attention to my personal appearance, having no intention of being remembered as a bag lady. If, when I enter a shop, the assistant is busy, I don't join a queue at the till. I hover, looking at the shelves, behaving like a customer, and approach them only when they are clearly free. I make positive eye contact, smile, introduce myself as an author with a newly published book, and ensure that I say my name *very* clearly. To avoid gabbling or getting tongue-tied, I have rehearsed a modest but confident opening speech that doesn't come across as either mouse-like or overbearing. I then say I would like to 'leave them some information' on my latest publication, and 'would it be at all possible' to speak to the bookshop owner or the manager. Whoever I end up dealing with, I never give the impression that I'm assuming they will take it, but once I have their attention I make the most of my opportunities, even if the person *is* clearly trying to get rid of me. If they do show some interest and engage me in conversation, I stay strictly focused on the merits of the book and my background as an author. The conversation might then drift into which books are selling well, and I find it useful to be *au fait* with the current bestsellers or prizewinners. Don't be tempted to outstay your welcome, but as a

parting shot, do tell them that they have a lovely shop. It isn't patronising – it's a thing they will remember and be pleased about.

I conclude by producing an A4 envelope containing some well-produced publicity material. This will include an advance information sheet, a press release, any reviews, a talk-up sheet Matador produced for libraries and reading groups, and any other promotional material, such as postcards and bookmarks. (For more information on this, see my article 'Calling All Authors', which appeared in the 2009 edition of *Writer's Market UK* and is now available on the website, www.writersmarket.co.uk.)

THE PAPERWORK

Another essential part of my pack is information on how the book can be ordered. The bookselling chain is complex, and far too intricate to detail here (the flow chart of book sales, including wholesalers' and retailers' terms, is covered extensively in *The Seriously Useful Authors' Guide to Marketing*), but a bookshop will generally purchase from a wholesaler at agreed discounts. If you are self-published, the shop can order either from their usual wholesaler (to regularise their paperwork) or directly from you. This must be the bookshop's decision, but if they want to order from you – usually on a 'sale or return' basis, which means you have to take back any copies that haven't been sold after a specified time – then agree a deal that makes you both a fair profit.

I always make sure I have some copies in the car to save a repeat journey or postage if a shop does order immediately. I follow up with a dated and numbered invoice and, should it not be paid within three months, I present it again. This might seem a long time but the book trade works several weeks in arrears and they may wish to make 'returns' to you before they pay up.

If they don't agree to purchase on the spot but say 'they will look into it', don't push the issue. Make a final gesture of eye contact, offer them your hand to shake, smile, thank them very much for 'the chat' and bid them farewell. I personally don't 'follow up' a contact as I'm of the opinion that being pushy might be irritating. If they look at my presentation pack and decide not to bother, that must be the end of the matter.

If you do hit an obvious brick wall (and it will be obvious), you have to accept it graciously – as in all aspects of life, disappointments abound – but don't show any sign of intimidation. Remember that you are an author, you are proud of your work and if they are snotty just let it roll off you. Cross them off the list as no-hopes and move on.

INSIDE THE BOOKSELLER'S HEAD

It's a happy coincidence that I have become involved with one of the most dynamic 'indies' in the book trade. My local shop, Mostly Books of Abingdon, opened in the summer of 2006 and is run by husband-and-wife team Mark and Nicki Thornton. Thanks to their drive and enthusiasm they quickly soared in recognition, winning the inaugural New Bookshop of the Year award at the British Book Industry Awards (the Nibbies) in 2008, as well as being shortlisted for Children's Bookshop of the Year at the Bookseller Retail Awards.

Mark has also had the insight to start a day course, Shelf Secrets, advising writers on how to approach bookshops. From a bookseller's point of view, he says, there are right and wrong ways:

The overriding message of the course is very simple: when you approach a bookshop, stop thinking like an author, and instead think like a bookseller. As soon as you see things from the bookseller's perspective, the whole experience becomes less stressful and more rewarding

A bookseller has to carry in his or her head hundreds of books in summary form to recommend to a customer. Often there are only a few moments to place a book in the hands of a customer and make a recommendation (usually with several other books). As the author, you need to give the bookseller something

powerful – a sentence or two, memorable, unique – that they can then use when making their recommendations. This makes it easy for a bookseller – and means your book is likely to be recommended more often.

A good and bad example might be useful here. The description 'a gripping page turner' isn't very strong; 'this story of an adulterous priest looking back over his life is compelling and thought-provoking' is much better.

The less stress that occurs between author/ sales rep and bookseller, the better the chance of sales. Instead of a battle of wills to get your book on their shelves, you have the chance to become a partner with the bookshop in achieving the same goal: to sell more of your book.

IN CONCLUSION

Having read all this, you may feel something like alarm at the tasks ahead. As authors we tend to be creative and sensitive and we so enjoy the solitary life, immersed in our precious characters and plot lines. But the hard fact is that, as a published author with no claim to fame, you *have* to become a Jekyll and Hyde. However difficult you may find it, publicising and marketing your work are things you need to do in order to create a career and enjoy the satisfaction of sales.

To conclude on an upbeat note. Working in isolation can actually limit your enjoyment of the literary world; 'getting out there' into the marketplace may provide a life-enhancing boost. I have found a real invigoration to my life, a huge number of new friends and, most importantly, potentially several thousands reading and enjoying my work. This is, after all, what authors want, isn't it? Readers!

> ## REMEMBER THAT YOU ARE AN AUTHOR, YOU ARE PROUD OF YOUR WORK AND IF THEY ARE SNOTTY JUST LET IT ROLL OFF YOU. CROSS THEM OFF THE LIST AND MOVE ON

More information on Shelf Secrets, and course dates for 2009/2010 can be found at www.mostly-books.co.uk/courses.html. A useful internet site for searching for local independent bookshops is www.localbookshops.co.uk.

CONTRACTS AND LEGAL ISSUES
A GUIDE TO WHAT THE SMALL PRINT MEANS

CAROLINE TAGGART

Caroline Taggart has been editing non-fiction for longer than she cares to remember and, in addition to commissioning the articles for this book and travelling the country talking about it, has recently become the best-selling author of *I Used to Know That* and co-author of *My Grammar and I (or should that be 'Me'?)*. Another book in the same series, *A Classical Education,* will be published in 2009.

▶ Once your work is accepted by a publisher or by a newspaper or magazine you're likely to be paid in one of two ways: a flat fee or an advance against royalties.

FLAT FEE

This means exactly what it says: you are paid a one-off fee for your work and that is an end of it. This is the norm if you write a piece for a newspaper or magazine. In the case of an article or short story, the fee might be paid on delivery or on publication; for a longer piece of work it might be paid in stages, perhaps a third on signature of a letter of agreement, a third on delivery and a third on publication. If you have been commissioned to write something on the basis of an outline, rather than having a finished piece

> **EVEN IF YOU ASSIGN COPYRIGHT TO THE PUBLISHER OF YOUR WORK, YOU ARE STILL RESPONSIBLE FOR ITS CONTENT**

of work accepted, read the paragraph on 'delivery and acceptance' below.

For work contracted on this basis, you may receive something as simple as a purchase order, outlining what you have agreed to do, the date by which you have agreed to do it, the fee and when it will be paid. Or you may be asked to sign a letter of agreement which covers similar ground but may also mention who will own copyright in your work and, most importantly, some form of warranty (see below).

Even if you assign copyright to the publisher of your work, you are still responsible for its content, so in addition to the warranty, see *Libel, plagiarism and breach of copyright* below.

ADVANCE AGAINST ROYALTIES

Strictly speaking, this should be called 'an advance against all earnings', but 'royalties' is the more common term.

What it means is that you are paid a lump sum in advance of anything you may earn on sales of your book and you then have to 'earn it out' before you receive any more money.

So, for the sake of keeping the sums easy, say you are paid an advance of £5000 on a book that is going to sell for £10 and you are paid a royalty of 10 per cent of the cover price. That means that for every copy sold at a full royalty rate, you earn £1 (10 per cent of £10). In order to earn out, therefore, you have to sell 5000 copies (5000 x £1 = £5000, the amount of the advance).

It's more complicated than that in real life, because books may be sold at other than the full royalty rate (overseas, for example, or to a book club) and there may be other sources of income such as the sale of an extract to a newspaper, but that is the principle.

The good news is that this advance is non-refundable. If the book in our example fails to sell 5000 copies, you have what is called an 'unearned balance' in the publisher's accounts but that is the publisher's problem. They took a punt on you and for whatever reason failed to do what they hoped to do with your book. It may make them less likely to buy another book from you but at least you don't have to pay that money back.

THE PUBLISHER'S OFFER

The normal procedure when a publisher makes an offer to publish your book is that you agree (verbally or by letter or email) the outline terms: probably the advance and main royalty rates, the territory for which the publisher is offering and the length, nature and delivery date of the book. The publisher will then send you two copies of a draft contract, for you to pore over the small print. If you agree with everything, sign both copies and return them. If not, ring up and discuss the points that you are unhappy about and agree amendments. Ask if your publisher needs to receive an invoice at this point (they certainly will if you are liable for VAT and may well want one anyway).

You will then receive a counter-signed copy of the contract for your files. If you have an agent, there will probably be three copies, so that the agent has one too and they will do the negotiating, administration and invoicing for you; but you should always keep a copy of the final signed agreement in your own files just in case.

THE CONTRACT

Publishers' contracts vary in detail but are pretty similar in outline. If you have an agent who has dealt with your publisher before, they may well have agreed a boilerplate so that they don't waste time haggling over the small print every time. Even if you have an agent it is as well to understand what is going on. It is your name on the contract, not the agent's, and you are the one who will be liable if things go badly wrong.

An important word of advice here: however well you know your editor and however much you like and trust her, *a contract is not a friendly agreement between two mates*. When negotiating a contract, you should always imagine a worst-case scenario: what if your editor leaves? What if the company is taken over and nobody cares what happens to your book? What if you go under a bus and someone else has to deal with the mess you have left behind? Implicit understandings between the two of you are no good here – get it down on paper and make sure it is clear.

At first glance a publisher's contract can look pretty daunting. Some run to 15 pages and include things that seem irrelevant (how likely is it that a literary first novel is going to be made into a strip cartoon?), so let's look at some key points.

Delivery, acceptance and grant of rights
The first clauses are likely to detail the parties to the contract (you and the publisher) and the nature of the work – provisional title, whether it is fiction or non-fiction, approximately how many words it is and when it is to be delivered. If you are providing illustrations in any form, this will be specified too.

Of course, you can't just deliver any old rubbish and expect the publisher to publish it. The contract will probably contain a clause specifying that the work must be of a professional and publishable standard and that it must be along the lines of the agreed outline. If what you deliver doesn't meet these standards, the publisher may decline to publish and cancel the contract. That doesn't mean that your outline is a complete straightjacket, however. If you said in the outline that the chapter on diet was to be chapter 7 and the one on exercise chapter 8 but, as you write, you realise that it makes more sense for diet to come earlier, no one is going to mind. If you are planning a more major departure from the script, keep your editor informed.

These clauses will also specify the territory and languages in which the publisher is permitted to sell the book. For an expensively illustrated book, where the publisher needs to recoup its investment by printing a lot of copies for worldwide distribution, this might be throughout the world in all languages. With a novel or non-illustrated non-fiction, an agent is likely to advise you to sell US and translation rights separately (see Jonathan Pegg's article on page 73 for more about this).

Publication
Assuming you deliver what you are supposed to deliver, the publisher has an obligation to publish it within a specified timeframe, usually 12 or 18 months from delivery, at their own expense.

Warranty
As author, you have to assure the publisher that your book has not previously been published in the territories covered by the agreement, that it is not an infringement of any existing copyright or licence, that it is not libellous, blasphemous or obscene, that anything purporting to be a fact is true and, if it contains recipes or formulae, that they are not likely to poison anyone or blow anyone up. See *Libel, Plagiarism and Breach of copyright* below for more about this.

Advance and royalties
The amount of the advance and the stages in which it will be paid are spelled out. Payment in thirds on signature of the agreement, on delivery and acceptance of the manuscript and on publication is normal. If the writing is going to take place over a considerable period of time, or if the publisher wants you to deliver part of the material early for sales purposes, a fourth stage (sometimes called evidence of progress) may be introduced. If you are going to incur a lot of expense in the course of your research – because you have to travel – perhaps you may be able to negotiate to get half of the advance on signature.

> YOU CAN'T BLATANTLY RECYCLE YOUR OWN MATERIAL. YOU CERTAINLY CAN'T USE IT VERBATIM

> NO PUBLISHER IN THEIR RIGHT MIND IS GOING TO HAND OVER MORE THAN HALF THE ADVANCE TO AN UNPROVEN AUTHOR UNTIL THEY HAVE AN ACCEPTABLE MANUSCRIPT IN THEIR HAND

But no publisher in their right mind is going to hand over more than half the advance to an unproven author until they have an acceptable manuscript in their hand.

Next come the details about the royalty you will be paid for each type of sale. The highest royalties are on home sales (i.e. books sold in the UK) through conventional outlets such as high-street booksellers. This will be specified as either a percentage of the published price or a percentage of the publisher's receipts, and will vary according to the nature of the book and whether it is a hardback or a paperback. A starting royalty of 7½ per cent of the published price of an unillustrated hardback would be pretty good for an unproven writer. Expect to earn less for a paperback (they are cheaper, so margins are tighter but, on the other hand, you should sell more copies) or for an illustrated book, unless you have also provided the illustrations. It is perfectly reasonable to ask for what is called an escalating royalty: if you start at 7½ per cent, you might ask to go up to 10 per cent after 5,000 copies have been sold, because by the time the publisher has sold 5,000 copies they have recouped a lot of their original investment and can afford to be more generous to you.

On other types of sales where margins may be lower – for example export sales or sales to a high-discount outlet such as a mail order company – you are likely to be paid a proportion of the above percentages.

Then there are what are called subsidiary rights, which may include:

- sales to a book club or to a foreign publisher
- sales of an extract to a newspaper or magazine (often known as first serial rights

if the extract appears before the book is published and second serial if it appears afterwards)

- sales to a large-print or condensed book publisher, or a publisher of talking books
- anthology and quotation rights; that is if someone wants to quote a substantial part of your work in their own book
- dramatic and film, television and sound broadcasting rights
- digital media rights, which may say something like 'the licensing of the work for use through any digital or online system now in existence or yet to be invented'! It sounds daft, but 20 years ago no-one would have thought of including a clause about online publishing, so who knows what we will be talking about in 20 years' time?

In all these instances you will receive a specified portion of the publishers' receipts. This is an area where you or your agent may want to negotiate or even to retain rights. For example, if you have no contacts outside the UK, it makes sense for the publisher to handle translation rights; but if you already write for radio and think you can use your own contacts to sell a radio play based on the book, you could ask for a higher royalty or simply hang on to the rights yourself. After all, they are your rights – you are under no obligation to sell them to anyone. On the other hand, if the main reason the publisher is taking you on is that they think they can exploit the radio rights, you may jeopardise the deal if you dig your heels in too deeply. It's all about negotiation, with a dash of swings and roundabouts thrown in.

Accounting
Once you have 'earned out' your advance, royalties are normally paid every six months, three or four months after the end of the half-year in question. So any royalties you earn from 1 January to 30 June will be paid to you on 1 October or 1 November. Many publishers don't send a royalty statement for books that are not due any royalties but they still have to do the accounting, so if you don't receive a statement and you want one, ask.

The contract is likely to specify that the publisher is entitled to set aside a reserve against returns for the first one, two or three royalty periods. The key to having a successful book is not selling it into the bookshops, but selling it out the other end, to a member of the public. Many books sell in quite successfully and then fail to sell out; when this happens bookshops return books to the publisher – sometimes in terrifying quantities – as much as a year after first publication. So a publisher who has paid out royalties on sales with no provision for returns could be badly out of pocket. This sort of crisis normally occurs in the early stages of a book's life and you may later receive a gratifying backlog of royalty payments.

Non-competing titles
It is a standard clause in most contracts that you are not allowed to write another book for another publisher on a subject similar enough that it is likely to 'affect prejudicially' the sales of your book. So if your book is a biography of Mary Queen of Scots for adults, you could write a children's book on the same subject for another publisher, or a novel based on Mary's life, or a history of sixteenth-century Scotland, but not another 'grown-up' biography of the woman herself. This also means – and this is something that has been known to take authors by surprise – that you can't blatantly recycle your own material. You certainly can't use it verbatim. So, for example, if you have written a book about antiques and you are now writing a book about porcelain (whether for the same publisher or for another) you can't just copy chunks of your porcelain chapter from the previous book – you have to rewrite it.

Revision, remaindering and reversion
So what happens later in the book's life? Well, you may be asked to update it and the clause about

> **IT IS A STANDARD CLAUSE IN MOST CONTRACTS THAT YOU ARE NOT ALLOWED TO WRITE ANOTHER BOOK FOR ANOTHER PUBLISHER ON A SUBJECT SIMILAR ENOUGH THAT IT IS LIKELY TO 'AFFECT PREJUDICIALLY' THE SALES OF YOUR BOOK**

> **IF YOUR BOOK IS REMAINDERED, OR IF THE PUBLISHER ALLOWS IT TO GO OUT OF PRINT AND DOES NOT INTEND TO REPRINT IT, YOU ARE ENTITLED TO RECLAIM THE RIGHTS**

USING THE INTERNET

This is a particular hobbyhorse of mine, so forgive me if I rant a little. It is *extraordinary* how many otherwise perfectly sensible people think that it is OK to copy and paste material from the internet willynilly into their work. It isn't. I don't know who owns the information on Wikipedia or any other of the myriad websites that I have searched over the last few months – but I do know that it isn't me. And it probably isn't you either.

Please don't copy text verbatim from a website, any more than you would copy it from a printed book or article. For one thing, it is a breach of *somebody's* copyright, even if you don't know who that somebody is; for another, it may or may not be accurate; and – perhaps most importantly for anyone who takes a pride in their work – it will stick out like a sore thumb. It won't be your 'voice', it won't fit in with the paragraphs before and after it, and it will devalue your work in the eyes of anyone who notices what you have done.

revision covers whether or not you will be paid for this, what the time frame might be and what happens if you are unable or unwilling to do it.

Then comes the time when the book has ceased to sell and the publisher wants to dispose of it ('remainder') at the best price it can get. This is almost certain to be below cost price (so you receive no royalties). The contract should specify the minimum time after first publication when this is allowed to happen: some publishers like as little as 12 months, others 18.

If your book is remaindered, or if the publisher allows it to go out of print and does not intend to reprint it, you are entitled to reclaim (revert) the rights. In that case your contract with that publisher is terminated and you can enter into a contract with another publisher for the same work. Reversion can be complicated by the existence of sub-licences; your book may not be selling in this country, but it may be successful elsewhere, so it may be possible to revert the UK rights while leaving the sub-licences in place.

Free copies, moral right, option and arbitration
We're getting into the small print now. Other clauses specify:

- the number of complimentary copies you will receive on first publication (it varies, but fewer than six hardbacks or ten paperbacks would be pretty mean).
- your moral right to be identified as the author. This means that your name goes on the front of the book and, assuming that the copyright remains yours, the copyright © notice and year of first publication will be followed by your name on the relevant page.
- that you grant the publisher an option to publish your next book or, if you cover a

number of subject areas, your next book of a similar nature. If this is something that you are unhappy about, perhaps because of other contractual commitments, you should be able to negotiate to have it omitted.
- what happens if there is a dispute over the terms of the contract: with a UK publisher, this normally simply says that the contract is subject to English (or Scottish) law.

LIBEL, PLAGIARISM AND BREACH OF COPYRIGHT

In signing the warranty mentioned above, you have taken on certain responsibilities *throughout the life of your book* (even if the contract with this particular publisher is terminated). Ignorance of the law is no excuse so, if you are in any doubt at all, warn your editor of your concerns and if need be, ask professional advice.

Libel
It is your responsibility to ensure that you have not defamed any living person who is identifiable from what you have written. (Libel laws do not

protect the dead.) It is possible to libel someone – or something, such as a company or an institution – even if you change their name and even if you are writing about them in a novel –
if their real identity is recognisable. Avoid expensive legal fees by being aware of the risks, doing your research thoroughly and keeping detailed and accurate records of your sources of information.

Plagiarism

There is no copyright in ideas but if you steal (or appear to steal) someone else's ideas, you can be sued for plagiarism. The recent well-publicised case revolving round *The Da Vinci Code* cost the losing parties huge sums of money and you don't want to go there.

Plagiarism is a difficult area because we all consciously or unconsciously absorb ideas and even turns of phrase from everything we read and hear, but you can help your own cause by remembering the cynical maxim that taking ideas from one source is plagiarism, taking them from a number of sources is research. Don't base too much of your book on a single source; if you want to quote someone else's work acknowledge the fact (but see copyright, below); and even if your work is a synthesis of other people's, make sure you draw your own, original conclusion.

Copyright

Copyright protects not only the written word but many other forms of creativity, such as photography, art and dramatic performance. It is a complicated business but what it boils down to is that the work is the property of the person who created it and cannot be used by anyone else without their permission. For written work, under British and EC law, copyright lasts for 70 years after the end of the year in which the author

> **IF YOU ARE SUPPLYING ILLUSTRATIONS – WHETHER PHOTOGRAPHS, PAINTINGS, CARTOONS OR MAPS – AND THEY ARE NOT YOUR OWN WORK, YOU NEED TO CLEAR COPYRIGHT**

dies, so anyone who died in 1939 will come out of copyright on 1 January 2010.

The law of copyright protects 'a substantial part' of a written work. If you want to quote a couple of lines from a 500-page history book, you would probably not be in breach of copyright (though you should always acknowledge your source); two lines of a haiku, a limerick or even a sonnet might actually involve fewer words but could still be considered 'a substantial part', simply because the 'whole' is so much smaller.

If quoting a substantial passage from a copyright work is essential to your own work, you must seek permission. Your first approach should be to the publisher of the work in question who may then refer you to the author's agent or estate, or to the author himself. The right to grant permission to quote from a song probably lies with the music publisher: unless you are an industry insider, Google is as good a place as any to start tracking them down. You will probably have to pay a fee, which will vary according to the length of the passage you want to quote and the fame of the author.

Letters are often a pitfall in terms of copyright clearance: a letter that was written to you and is in your possession is still the copyright of the author and needs to be cleared in the same way.

Dealing with copyright issues can be frustrating, so leave yourself plenty of time. You may find that the UK publisher can grant UK and Commonwealth rights only, and if the contract for your book covers the entire English-speaking world you need to go to the New York publisher too. Your urgent request may be the recipient's boring piece of admin and they may not reply for weeks. Or at all.

> **IT IS YOUR RESPONSIBILITY TO ENSURE THAT YOU HAVE NOT DEFAMED ANY LIVING PERSON WHO IS IDENTIFIABLE FROM WHAT YOU HAVE WRITTEN**

All of the above applies to illustrative material too. If you are supplying illustrations – whether photographs, paintings, cartoons or maps – and they are not your own work, you need to clear copyright. And remember that copyright rests with the *creator* of the work, so a photograph that has been in your family for years (even if it is your parents' wedding photo) may not belong to you in the copyright sense.

DISCLAIMERS

You often see on the imprint page of a book (or at the end of the acknowledgements) a statement to the effect that 'the author and publishers have made every effort to trace copyright holders; they apologise in advance for any omissions and will be pleased to make due acknowledgement in any future editions of this book'. Would this stand up in court? It might. If there is any doubt, you and your editor should jointly make a decision as to whether or not to include the material. Your parents' wedding photo is probably OK; the lyric of a recent pop song whose copyright holder you can't trace (or who hasn't bothered to reply to your request) is more dodgy ground.

If a book contains recipes or instructions, publishers often include a disclaimer along the lines of 'the publisher can accept no responsibility for any accident or injury as a result of anyone

> **REMEMBER THAT COPYRIGHT RESTS WITH THE CREATOR OF THE WORK**

> **IT IS UP TO YOU AS THE AUTHOR TO ADHERE CLOSELY TO THE WARRANTY IN YOUR CONTRACT AND TO MAKE SURE THAT 'EVERYTHING PURPORTING TO BE A FACT IS TRUE'**

using this book' or 'this book is not intended as a substitute for professional medical attention'. This may or may not stand up in court either, so it is up to you as the author to adhere closely to the warranty in your contract and to make sure that 'everything purporting to be a fact is true'.

IN CONCLUSION

A lot of this article may sound like scaremongering and indeed the vast majority of the things I have told you to be careful about will never happen. But publishing contracts are founded in common sense and protect the interests of everyone concerned. Read yours carefully, make sure you understand it and are prepared to commit to it, sign it and get on with the exciting business of publishing your book.

A longer version of this article is available on the website, www.writersmarket.co.uk

THE PUBLISHING PROCESS
A LOOK AT HOW YOUR MANUSCRIPT IS TURNED INTO A BOOK

CAROLINE TAGGART

▶ **Congratulations. You've written your book and you've got a publisher. An enormous amount of the hard work that goes into being a published author is behind you.**

An enormous amount. Not all of it.

Not understanding the publishing process is a cause of woe for a lot of first-time authors, so here is a rough guide to what happens after you have delivered your manuscript.

EDITING

You and your book will be assigned to an editor who will steer your book through the production process and be your main point of contact with the company. At least one person is now going to read your book very closely and ask you questions and make comments about it. There are likely to be two levels of queries and they may come from two different people. Broadly speaking:

- a commissioning editor or senior editor or project editor cares about the structure and content of the book. She will tell you that the action takes too long to get going and you should drop Chapter 2 altogether, that Chapter 4 would be better if it came after Chapter 7, or that your hero simply isn't romantic enough. If you're writing non-fiction, she will point out that you haven't mentioned James II in your list of Stuart monarchs, that you've written a whole chapter about John Wayne but only two pages about Clint Eastwood in your guide to classic westerns and that your analysis of the muscles of the knee is too technical for the target audience. So you may be asked to add, subtract, rewrite or shuffle

- a copy editor or line editor or desk editor (who in many companies will be a freelancer employed on a project-by-project basis) cares about consistency, spelling, grammar, punctuation and repetition. Her job is to notice that you spell 'organisation' with an s but 'realize' with a z, or that you have told that anecdote about your first day at work three times. A lot of this will seem like nit-picking, but that is what a copy editor is paid for. Good publishers believe in 'getting it right' and that includes putting the apostrophes in the right place and not saying 'imply' when you mean 'infer'

- either or both of these will care about factual accuracy, copyright issues and potential libel problems. Copyright and libel are dealt with in more detail elsewhere in this book (see page 90). Accuracy, of course, means 'getting it right' again, and it's just as important in historical novels as it is in non-fiction. If you are old enough to remember the 1960s film *El Cid*, you probably know that at one point the eleventh-century heroine, played by Sophia Loren, is seen wearing a dress with

> **AT LEAST ONE PERSON IS NOW GOING TO READ YOUR BOOK VERY CLOSELY AND ASK YOU QUESTIONS AND MAKE COMMENTS ABOUT IT**

a zip, a device that was patented in 1851. It may well be the only thing you do know about the film – a sad reflection on what was probably several years' work for hundreds of people. Don't let that sort of carelessness spoil your own opus.

How you deal with editorial queries is a matter of give and take. Obviously, the more personal your book, the more sensitive you are going to feel but no good editor (and I draw your attention to the adjective there) is going to change your text just to satisfy her own ego. Try to listen objectively to what she is saying and remember that it is in her interests to make you look good by making the book as good as it can possibly be. If she says a section is boring (she may phrase it differently but you will get the gist), look at it again. Is there anything you can take out? Or can you add to it to make it more appealing? If you really want to dig your heels in, consider giving way on some other point that is less important to you.

With non-fiction, you are likely to know more about the subject than your editor. That's why you are writing the book. But unless you are writing for a specialist audience – MBA students, for example, or medical practitioners – who can be expected to understand the jargon, your editor's knowledge may be typical of your target readership. In other words, if she doesn't understand it, chances are your readers won't either.

DESIGN AND PRODUCTION

When you have a text that everyone is happy with, you start making it into a book.

If a book isn't illustrated, this is a fairly straightforward process. First the size of the book will be decided and, unless you are a

THE AQUISITION PROCESS

Most publishing companies hold a regular meeting to discuss whether or not to offer to publish a book or proposed book. This is usually called an acquisitions meeting, and typically involves editors pitching projects to other members of the company – their editorial bosses, the sales, publicity and rights departments, the accountants. In a small firm where one person makes most of the decisions, this can happen very quickly; in others it can be frustratingly slow. The sales director may want to sound out W H Smith before making a large commitment or, if you are a new author, the publicist may want to meet you to see how promotable you are. Be patient: remember that publishing is a business like any other, and every book has to pay its way. If you hassle for a decision, you may provoke a rejection.

photographer or artist working on something that is going to display your work in a glamorous way, you are unlikely to have much say in this. Paper comes in standard sizes and most paperbacks are published in something called A, B or C format, according to their perceived market. (Give or take the odd millimetre, A format is 178 x 110mm, the size all paperbacks used to be; B is 20mm bigger each way, C is bigger again and as a general rule the larger the page size the more upmarket the book is deemed to be.) Someone will mark up the type, which means that they will decide on the typeface (font) to be used, the type size, the number and length of lines on a page, what the chapter openers will look like and myriad other things. Then the book will be typeset and you will be sent page proofs to read. If you don't have illustrations to worry about, skip the next few sections and go straight to the bit about proof-reading, below.

ILLUSTRATIONS

If your book is illustrated, whether by black and white 'inserts', colour photography throughout or just a few diagrams, you have one crucial job as an author: to make sure that they are right. 'Right' may mean accurate, correctly captioned, in the right order, alongside the right bit of text or simply the right way up. Other people will be checking them too but you may be the only person with the knowledge to spot a silly mistake before it is too late.

Images may come from a variety of sources. Most commonly:

*   you, the author, provide them. This is particularly likely in the case of memoirs, when pictures may come from your private collection; or if you are the photographer or artist as well as the author
*   you, the author, provide roughs or reference (diagrams, graphs, flow charts, garden designs, anatomical sketches) and the publisher gets them drawn up professionally. Roughs can be pencil scribbles as long as they are clear; reference can be photocopied from other books or downloaded from the internet and annotated to tell the artist what you are trying to show. If your book needs a map of India, for example, copy a page from an atlas and highlight the places that need to be mentioned or draw in the route of your character's journey
*   the publisher employs a picture researcher to find images. This may be the best approach to, say, history or travel, allowing

pictures to be gleaned from a number of sources to provide comprehensive coverage of the subject

*   the publisher commissions a photographer to take pictures especially for the book. This happens, for example, with cookery, where photographs are taken of specific recipes that have been created for that book or gardening, when a photographer may trace the progress of a garden through the course of a year. Alternatively, the publisher may commission cartoons for a humorous work or line drawings to produce a 'retro' look.

If you are providing pictures, make sure everyone knows who is responsible for clearing permission to use them and paying any necessary fees (see page 91).

With illustrated books, each page is designed individually and a lot of people have a say in how the book looks. You may be forced to take into consideration what the rights department says the American (or Dutch or Korean) market wants: I once worked on a 'lifestyle' book about kitchens where a picture had to be taken out at a late stage because they don't have Agas in Norway. If we changed it we could sell 3000 copies to a Norwegian publisher, so the Aga bit the dust.

You should see layouts for approval at a stage when everything is still on a screen and it is easy to make changes. If you would prefer the picture the designer has used big to be small and vice versa, say so. But remember that the designer is an expert in his field just as you are in yours. He will be considering such things as the balance of the pages, the pace of the book and the quality of the individual images. Be prepared for a bit of give and take.

THE PUBLISHING PROCESS

CAROLINE TAGGART

FEATURE

PROOF-READING

Whatever the nature of your book, your editor should warn you when you are expected to read your text for the final time. This is not an invitation to rewrite it, just to get it right. The publisher will also employ a professional proof-reader to do a final check, so in addition to any spelling or grammar mistakes that may have slipped through you should be looking out for things that only you will notice, such as errors of fact or statistics that need to be updated.

Mark any corrections on the pages you have been given in something bold like black felt tip or red pen. Timid pencil marks are easy to overlook. And try not to raise questions at this stage – find answers. Write your corrections clearly, accurately and completely. Don't leave the person who is typing in your amendments to guess at what you mean or to finish your sentences for you.

PRELIMS AND ENDMATTER

Easy to forget but very important are the bits that come at the beginning and the end of the book. The prelims (short for preliminary pages but no one ever calls them that) are the bits before the main text starts: the 'half-title' and 'title' pages, the imprint (which gives the publisher's name and address and copyright information), the contents page, dedication and acknowledgements. Most of this the publisher will supply, but you should be asked if you want to dedicate the book to anyone and if you have any acknowledgements that should be included.

A dedication is a completely personal thing. Have one or not, just as you like. Dedicate your book to your lover, your dog or the waiters in your local curry house if the fancy takes you. It's entirely up to you.

Acknowledgements are a combination of the personal and the dutiful. Who you thank for support while writing your book is a matter of choice and courtesy. Staff at your local library, your friend with a degree in maths who put you right on Pythagoras, your husband who made you copious cups of hot chocolate when the going was tough, your agent, your editor, your editor's assistant who was always there even when the editor wasn't – these are all people who may appreciate a mention. If you have used copyright material such as photographs or a verse from a song, you should acknowledge your sources. If in doubt, consult your editor to make sure that you don't miss out anyone who will be offended and that you fulfil any copyright obligations.

The endmatter varies according to the book but may include notes, sources, further reading,

> PUT A COLOUR PRINT-OUT OF THE COVER ON A SHELF OR MANTELPIECE, WITH A COUPLE OF OTHER BOOKS ALONGSIDE IT, AND LOOK AT IT FROM THE OTHER SIDE OF THE ROOM. DOES IT LEAP OUT AT YOU? CAN YOU READ THE WORDS? DOES IT MAKE YOU WANT TO PICK IT UP? IF SO, IT IS DOING ITS JOB

THE JACKET OR COVER

What goes on the front of the book is the single most important selling tool a publisher has. Your contract may well say that you will be consulted about jacket /cover design. But consulting means just that: the publisher has the final say and publishers do vary enormously in their attitude to author input. If they produce something you don't like or weren't expecting, again try to be objective about it. You should certainly point out if they have got the concept of the book wrong e.g. if it is aimed at teenagers and the cover is more likely to appeal to seven-year-olds, or if you have written a work of literary fiction and they have made it look like a thriller. But otherwise, imagine that you are a book buyer for a large chain store, seeing a million covers a day and spending perhaps ten seconds considering each one. Would this cover attract you and make you want to stock the book in your shops? Put a colour print-out of the cover on a shelf or mantelpiece, with a couple of other books alongside it and look at it from the other side of the room. Does it leap out at you? Can you read the words? Does it make you want to pick it up? If so, it is doing its job.

glossary, useful addresses and an index. If your work is academic, you will probably be used to compiling this sort of thing anyway; if not, discuss with your editor what you both think is necessary. Many contracts contain a clause saying that the author will supply the index or that it can be commissioned at the author's expense. Please don't offer to compile an index unless you are genuinely competent to do so. Professional indexers are not expensive, the publisher will have a stable of them, and there is nothing in the world more annoying than a bad index.

AND THEN...

Once the index has been compiled, the job is just about done. The editor will get a plotter proof – that's the modern-day term for what used to be called an ozalid or a printer's blue – for a final check before the printing press starts to roll and then you have to wait for as much as two months for the book to be printed and bound.

But one day, a finished copy appears. It is an extraordinarily exciting moment. In 30 years I have

JACKET COPY

The blurb – the couple of paragraphs about the book designed to whet the buyer's appetite which appear on the front flap of a hardback jacket or on the back cover of a paperback – is also an important selling tool. Your editor may ask you if would like to write your own blurb. Some authors are brilliant at this, but many feel uncomfortable writing selling copy about their own book and are happier leaving it to their editor. That's fine. She should then send it to you for approval and you can alter it as you see fit. But remember that this is a selling tool, not a summary of the plot or a table of contents. It has to grab the reader in the first sentence, and keep him grabbed. If you haven't already done so, you may also be asked to provide a brief autobiography at this stage. This is in my experience harder (and more embarrassing) than it sounds, so be prepared.

never got used to it, and I am only the midwife. This is your baby. The anxiety and hard work have been worth it. Now all you have to do is get out there and sell it.

If you feel strong enough, turn to page 82.

A longer version of this article is available on the website, www.writersmarket.co.uk.

THE PUBLISHING PROCESS

CAROLINE TAGGART

FEATURE

THE PUBLISHING HOUSE

WHO DOES WHAT

CAROLINE TAGGART

▶ Every business has its own structure, its own jargon and its own assumptions, which can make the simplest thing mystifying to the outsider, so here is a guide to some of what you may meet on your journey through publishing.

EDITORIAL

Editors acquire or commission books and then edit them – or pass them on to a more junior editor to edit, as explained in The Publishing Process, page 93. Acquiring, by the way, means buying a book that has already been written, which is what happens with most novels; commissioning means agreeing to publish a book before it has been written, usually on the strength of an outline and some sample material (see the articles beginning on pages 49 and 73).

THE PRODUCTION DEPARTMENT

Production's job is to turn your raw material into a book. They deal primarily with typesetters (not as common a breed as they used to be), repro houses (the people who take your pictures and turn them into something that the printer can use – normally a digital file) and printers, but also have to worry about costs, schedules, paper, binding, jackets, shipping, quality control and why in the world editors can't do anything on time.

DESIGN

Many publishing houses have large in-house design departments; others make extensive use of freelances. Whatever the set-up, these are the people who create the look for both the outside and the inside of the book. This may involve:

- commissioning illustration(s) or photograph(s) for the cover
- designing the type to go on it – choosing the typeface ('font'), the size, the colour and the balance of the words
- designing the type for the inside of the book
- commissioning illustrations, photographs, diagrams or maps
- if necessary, designing the individual pages and 'marrying' words and pictures.

SALES, MARKETING AND PUBLICITY

Different companies divide these functions in different ways, but basically the sales department sells copies of your book, marketing spends money on promoting it (through booksellers' catalogues, advertising, 3 for 2 offers, etc) and publicity promotes it without spending money – by arranging for it to be reviewed or for you to be interviewed about it. Publicity also sometimes handles serial rights, which means that a newspaper or magazine buys the rights to print an exclusive extract or extracts from your book (confusingly, it is still called serial even if it is only one extract). In some companies, serial rights are handled by the Rights Department (see opposite).

> **BASICALLY, THE SALES DEPARTMENT SELLS COPIES OF YOUR BOOK, MARKETING SPENDS MONEY ON PROMOTING IT, AND PUBLICITY PROMOTES IT WITHOUT SPENDING MONEY**

JARGON BUSTING

- Many publishing companies are still referred to by the old-fashioned term 'publishing houses', which is why we often talk about work being done 'in house'. It means nothing more nor less than 'in the office'. You don't have to be a member of staff to be in house – it is not uncommon for a freelance to work in house for a couple of days a week on a given project.

- From the same source comes the expression 'house style', which means 'the way we do things'. House style means do you write realise or realize, do you write 11 or eleven, and do you spell the President of the United States with a capital or not. Most publishing companies have a house style sheet which details their preferences. As a first-time author you may be given one of these and asked to follow its guidelines, or you may find that the copy editor makes changes to ensure that your book conforms.

- Another common word with a meaning of its own is 'list', which means the books that a publishing company or an imprint is publishing in a given year or season. 'Front list' titles are generally those that are being published this year; 'back list' refers to anything older.

THE RIGHTS DEPARTMENT

If the sales department sells copies of your book, the rights department sells pretty much everything else. This can include serial rights (see above), book club rights, translation and other foreign rights, large print rights and much more besides.

Deals to produce other editions of your book take one of two forms: a co-edition deal or a rights deal.

A co-edition deal is most likely to happen with an illustrated book where the costs of production are high. Your publisher will print copies for the other editions, be they American, Australian, Danish or UK book club, and sell finished books. The idea is to produce a lot of books at the same time and substantially reduce the unit cost of each one. Assuming you are being paid a royalty, it will be a percentage of the price your publisher receives.

A rights deal means that your publisher (or your agent, if you have retained these rights) sells another publisher the right to publish your book in a given form and/or language and/or part of the world. The local publisher produces the book and pays your publisher or agent an advance against royalties, and again you receive a percentage.

A longer version of this article is available on the website, www.writersmarket.co.uk.

THE PUBLISHING HOUSE · CAROLINE TAGGART · FEATURE

THE FINANCIAL SIDE

A FEW TIPS ON LOOKING AFTER YOUR MONEY – AND FULFILLING YOUR LEGAL OBLIGATIONS

CAROLINE TAGGART

> If you are just starting out on a writing career, you may have another job and pay tax and national insurance through the Pay As You Earn (PAYE) system. If you have no other source of income, you may never have had to fill in a tax return because all the tax you owe is deducted at source. Once you start earning money from your writing, it becomes a little (but not necessarily a lot) more complicated. If you are not employed but you are earning money from your writing, you are responsible for your own tax and national insurance payments and you must register yourself as self-employed with Her Majesty's Revenue and Customs (HMRC). In either case you will have to fill in a tax return.

You can get all the forms you need online from the HMRC website (www.hmrc.gov.uk) or from your local tax office. The self-assessment tax return is surprisingly easy to follow, and the website is very helpful. If you don't want to calculate your tax liability yourself, you must return the form to your local tax office by the end of October each year (under most circumstances you have till the end of January if you do it online).

And if all this is too much for you, you can employ an accountant to do it for you, but expect to pay several hundred pounds a year if your affairs are straightforward, and rather more if they are not.

KEEPING RECORDS

Whichever category you fall into, you must keep a record of any writing income you receive and any

> **YOUR RECORDS SHOULD BE METICULOUS. COPIES OF EVERY INVOICE YOU SUBMIT AND EVERY PAYMENT YOU RECEIVE SHOULD BE FILED – EITHER ON PAPER OR ON YOUR COMPUTER**

business expenditure you may incur (see *Expenses*, below).

Your records should be meticulous. Copies of every invoice you submit and every payment you receive should be filed – either on paper or on your computer. Many writers use Excel or other spreadsheet software to build a document that they can use again and again. There are also a number of simple business software packages, such as Quicken or Microsoft Money, that help you to keep the records and manage your invoicing and other personal finances. Your system need not be complex, but it does need to be complete.

Keep these records separate from any others you may have and do not muddle the payments with any other income. If you are earning more than a pittance from your writing, it is worth opening a separate bank account for that income.

EXPENSES

As a self-employed person, or an employed person who has an additional freelance income, you are legally entitled to set certain items of expenditure against your earnings to reduce the amount of tax you have to pay. If you are working from home, using electricity to keep you warm and to power your laptop, then some of your electricity bill is a genuine business expense. So are stationery, computer supplies, work-related travel and various other relevant items: I once went to the cinema with an author who kept her ticket to file away as a business receipt because her accountant considered that looking for ideas by watching a film was legitimate research in her line of work.

Reasonableness should be the watch word when claiming a proportion of 'use of home as office' expenses. You can't claim your entire phone bill, for example, unless you can show that you never use the phone for other than business calls.

You can also claim capital allowances for the cost of equipment that you use in your writing business: typically your computer and hardware attached to it, such as the printer. Again, if you use these for personal matters as well as business, you should claim only a proportion of the allowance.

> **IF YOU ARE WORKING FROM HOME, USING ELECTRICITY TO KEEP YOU WARM AND TO POWER YOUR LAPTOP, THEN SOME OF YOUR ELECTRICITY BILL IS A GENUINE BUSINESS EXPENSE**

Sometimes, publishers will allow you to add 'reasonable expenses' to your invoice: for postage, say, or travel to a meeting. It is always worth asking but don't charge expenses without asking – you'll get the reputation of being money-grubbing. Keep any relevant receipts and attach a photocopy of them to your invoice to show that you've actually spent the money. Keeping and filing receipts is good practice anyway – unsubstantiated expenses are harder to justify to the tax man.

If your expenses are considerable– as they might be if you are a travel writer, say, or needed to buy a lot of expensive books for research – it is a good idea to have a separate credit card so that you don't confuse business with personal expenditure.

> **CONSIDERING THAT INCOME TAX IS A PERCENTAGE OF MONEY YOU HAVE ALREADY RECEIVED, IT IS EXTRAORDINARY HOW MANY PEOPLE DON'T MAKE PROVISION TO PAY IT**

PAYING THE TAX

If you pay tax under PAYE but have declared additional freelance earnings on a tax return, your tax code may be adjusted accordingly. This means that you pay a bit more tax every month, rather than building up a substantial tax bill.

If you are self-employed, it is usual to pay your national insurance monthly by direct debit. But if you earn more than a few thousand pounds a year from your writing – that is, more than your personal tax-free allowance – there will come a time when you have to pay the income tax. Payments are due twice a year, at the end of January and the end of July. HMRC will write to you in plenty of time telling you what you owe but it is your responsibility to pay it on time, otherwise you may be charged interest. Considering that income tax is a percentage of money you have already received, it is extraordinary how many people don't make provision to pay it. It is a sound strategy to put some money aside from each job, or perhaps to save every fourth fee for tax.

It is worth noting that if you can defer invoicing or being paid for a job until after 5 April (the end of the tax year) you can also defer having to pay the tax on it for a further year. Royalties – including the advance against royalties – are taxed as income, but there is a system called averaging which allows you to average out your profits over two or more consecutive years if the profit for one of these years is less than 75 per cent of the profits of your highest earning year. This can be an advantage if your earnings are irregular, or it may enable you to avoid paying higher rate tax in a year when you do a one-off highly paid piece of work.

VAT

If your earnings as a self-employed person are above a certain threshold (£67,000 in the financial year 2008/9), it is compulsory to register for VAT and to add VAT to all your invoices. If you earn less than the threshold, you may choose to register anyway because you can then claim back VAT on business purchases. This matters less for writers than for many other professions, though, as a lot of business purchases, such as books, newspapers and magazines, are zero-rated for VAT anyway.

An alternative is to go for the 'flat-rate' VAT available to certain small businesses. At the time of writing, VAT is charged at 15 per cent on most goods and services in the UK, but if you register for this scheme as a writer or journalist you pay only 11 per cent. The downside is that you can't then claim back the VAT on your purchases.

Some people worry that charging VAT will make their services less competitive, but if you are working for a company that is itself registered for VAT (and unless you are dealing with a very small business such as, say, a parish magazine, it almost certainly will be), the company can claim the VAT back at the end of each quarter and there is no long-term disadvantage. The real disadvantage from your point of view is that you have to do more complicated paperwork – and do it regularly. It is a lot more work than a tax return. Unless you are really clued up about this, you will be well advised to employ an accountant to do it for you. Again, you can find out more on the Revenue and Customs website.

GETTING PAID

When you get work – whether from a publisher or a magazine or whatever – ask what the form is about payment. Do you send in an invoice, or do you have to wait for a purchase order or contract? If there is no formal contract, send an

> THE COMPANY CAN CLAIM THE VAT BACK AT THE END OF EACH QUARTER AND THERE IS NO LONG-TERM DISADVANTAGE

> IF THERE IS NO FORMAL CONTRACT, SEND AN EMAIL CONFIRMING A VERBAL AGREEMENT WHILE THE CONVERSATION IS FRESH IN YOUR MIND, JUST SO THAT YOU BOTH HAVE IT ON RECORD

email confirming a verbal agreement while the conversation is fresh in your mind, just so that you both have it on record.

Ask also when you might expect to be paid and put this on your invoice. In theory, as the supplier of the service, it is for you to dictate the terms – lots of freelancers optimistically ask for payment within 14 days please. In practice, you are likely to be paid 30 days from the end of the month in which you invoice. So if you send in your invoice in early May, you should realistically expect to be paid at the end of June. (A tip: if you are invoicing in the first week of a month, date your invoice the last day of the month before. It sometimes works.)

It is a sad fact of life that some publishers are prompt payers but others are not. At the beginning of your career you probably have to put up with this; as you begin to build up a list of clients you may be in the happy position of refusing to work for people who mess you about.

If your payment is overdue, call the person who commissioned you and ask her to chase it; only if she fails should you call the accounts department yourself. Be polite but, if necessary, persistent. Don't be fobbed off with talk of the next cheque run. Most publishers of any size make payments on regular cycles once a week or once or twice a month but they can always write a cheque manually, so if your payment is overdue you should not have to wait.

HOW MUCH WILL THEY PAY YOU?

A tricky one, this. Newspapers and some magazines pay the going NUJ rate (see www.nuj.org.uk for whether you are eligible to join and whether it feels right for you). Smaller magazines pay what they can. Some don't pay at all. If you are at the bottom of the writing ladder you may agree to do your first jobs for nothing just to build up a portfolio of published work.

Book publishers' rates vary a lot. More and more non-fiction publishers pay a flat, one-off fee (see Contracts and legal issues, page 86), particularly if you are one of a number of contributors to a book. Like this one, for instance. The downside of this is that you are surrendering control of your work; the upside is that you are paid a guaranteed fee with no waiting around to see if the book is a success before you earn more.

Whether or not you accept the fee that is offered to you (with or without negotiation) is a matter of judgement. How much do you want the job? How easy will it be for the publisher to find someone else if you refuse? Will you be out of pocket if you do it? Is it worth it to get it on your CV? Only you can answer these questions.

For novels and some other books of which you are the sole author you can expect an advance and royalties, about which there is more on page 86. But a word of caution here. The vast majority of first novels earn modest advances. If you read in the papers about someone's first novel being snapped up for a massive six-figure sum, remember that this is highly unusual – that's why it is in the papers. Some publishers are currently experimenting with the idea of royalty but no advance, which reduces their risk and means you still earn money if the book is a success. Check out www.panmacmillan.com/imprints/macmillan new writing/ for one such scheme.

> **WHETHER OR NOT YOU ACCEPT THE FEE THAT IS OFFERED TO YOU (WITH OR WITHOUT NEGOTIATION) IS A MATTER OF JUDGEMENT. HOW MUCH DO YOU WANT THE JOB? HOW EASY WILL IT BE FOR THE PUBLISHER TO FIND SOMEONE ELSE IF YOU REFUSE?**

PUBLIC LENDING RIGHT

- PLR, as it is commonly known, can be a useful addition to a writer's earnings. It is the system whereby you as sole author or substantial contributor earn money because your book is borrowed from a library.

- Not every library is surveyed for PLR; different boroughs are selected every year, with a view to giving a representative sample across the country. The borrowings from the sample are then used to estimate the number of borrowings nation-wide and a fixed rate per loan is paid to each registered contributor. In 2008 this rate was 5.98 pence, as a result of which close to 24,000 people received a payment of at least £1 and around 1,500 people received £1,000 or more, up to a maximum of £6,600 a head.

- You don't have to be the sole author or the copyright holder to qualify for PLR; you just have to be mentioned on the title page or entitled to a royalty from the publisher. Photographers, illustrators, ghost writers and translators may all be eligible. But you have to register. It doesnt happen automatically and your publisher can't do it for you. Furthermore, before you can do it, everyone involved has to agree what percentage of the whole they will claim.

For more information and application forms, go to the PLR website: www.plr.uk.com

THE FINANCIAL SIDE

CAROLINE TAGGART

FEATURE

GLOSSARY

of Book Trade Terminology

acquiring/acquisitions editor: a person within a publishing house whose primary function is to identify and negotiate to acquire new titles for publication. Also known as a commissioning editor.

advance: the non-returnable payment to authors by publishers against which the royalty earnings are offset.

A format: format of mass market paperbacks, most commonly with a trimmed page size of 178 x 111 mm.

agent: see literary agent.

AI: (sometimes AIS) abbreviation for Advance Information (Sheet), a document produced by publishers to provide information about new titles for the purpose of subscription to book buyers and initiating promotional opportunities. Typical contents would include a blurb, author biography, review of the author's previous works, provisional specification, working cover, publication date and price.

appendix: material which is not part of the main text, appearing at the end of a book.

auction: a process whereby a title is submitted, particularly by a literary agent, to a number of selected publishers in order to secure the best offer or highest price.

BA: abbreviation for The Booksellers Association of Great Britain and Ireland, the trade association for booksellers.

bar code: the machine-readable image of lines of varying thickness which encodes a book's ISBN and which is printed on the back cover. When 'read' by electronic till equipment it plays a vital part in booksellers' EPOS systems for sales monitoring and stock control. Also used in distribution centres for various functions, such as processing returns.

B format: a format for paperbacks particularly favoured for non-fiction and literary fiction, normally of a trimmed size 198 x 126 mm.

BIC: see Book Industry Communication.

BL: see British Library.

blad: Basic (or Book) Layout And Design – a term used to describe advance sales material, most commonly consisting of a jacket, sales blurb and a selection of pages of text and illustration, printed professionally.

bleed: term used for an illustration or image which extends beyond the trimmed page.

blocking: the use of metallic foils, often on covers and jackets, for visual impact or as a routine operation on the spine of a hardback book.

blurb: brief description of a book which appears on the back of a paperback or on the inside front flap of a book jacket.

Bologna Book Fair: the pre-eminent book fair for children's publishers, particularly those buying and selling rights, held in Bologna in Italy each spring.

Bookbank: a bibliographic product on CD-ROM, listing titles currently in print in the UK.

book block: the sewn or bound pages of a hardback book before they are cased in.

book club: a mail order operation through which selected books are sold direct to the public at a price significantly below the RRP in return for a commitment to buy a particular number of books over a period.

BookData: company established in the UK to market bibliographical information supplied by publishers

Book fairs: exhibitions and conventions used by publishers as locations for meetings and business dealings. Many such fairs take place internationally, of widely differing purpose and focus, of which much the most important is Frankfurt.

Book House Training Centre: the book trade's training organisation, based in south London.

Book Industry Communication: a company set up by the Booksellers Association, the British Library, the Library Association and the Publishers Association to encourage the establishment of standards in the book trade. Among other activities, BIC has responsibility for bar codes.

Book Marketing Ltd: formed from the Book Marketing Council of the Publishers Association, this company provides statistical and market research information to the industry, notably in the form of the annual publication Books and the Consumer.

Book proof: a specially produced advance copy of the uncorrected text of a title, used by publishers' sales teams and as early review copies.

Bookseller (The): a weekly journal of the UK book trade, with up-to-date bestseller lists.

BookTrack: an operation set up by Whitaker to monitor sales out of bookshops and produce accurate bestseller lists.

British Library: the national book collection based in London.

bulk: the thickness of a book.

byline: the name of the author of a given piece, indicating credit for having written a book or article (most commonly used in newspaper and magazine publishing).

cased: hardback; derived from the case into which the book block is inserted (cased in) at the conclusion of hardback binding.

CD-ROM: compact disc with read-only memory; a non-interactive CD which is the platform for almost all offline electronic publishing.

C format: an imprecise term for any paperback format other than A and B.

CMYK: Cyan, Magenta, Yellow and blacK – the four colours of ink used in four-colour printing.

colophon: originally the bibliographic information printed at the end of a book, the term is now used almost exclusively for the device or logo of the publisher commonly printed on the title page and the spine of the cover or jacket.

commissioning editor: a person employed in a publishing house to seek out authors to write particular books for publication.

contract: the agreement drawn up between the publisher and the author to confirm payment terms, royalty, respective responsibilities etc. at the point of acquisition.

copy editor: the person employed in a publishing house (or as a freelance) who works on the detail of a book, ensuring accuracy and completeness and preparing it for typesetting.

copyright: the right of an author, artist, publisher etc. to retain ownership of works and to produce or contract others to produce copies. In 1996, the full term of copyright was extended throughout the European Union to 70 years (previously 50 years in the UK) from the end of the year in which the author died.

cover copy: blurb that is written by the publishing house, generally on the back of paperbacks, or on the front flap of hardbacks, to give the reader information on the book's content; extended to include any other copy that appears on the cover, such as author biography, price, acknowledgements etc.

crown quarto: book format, trimmed page size 246 x 189 mm, frequently an economical choice for illustrated books.

demy octavo: very popular book format, trimmed page size 216 x 138 mm sewn (135 mm unsewn).

DPI: Dots Per Inch – a measure of printing resolution, in particular the number of individual dots of ink a printer or toner can produce within a linear one-inch (2.54 cm) space.

DPS: Double Page Spread.

dust jacket: See jacket

EAN: European Article Numbering – a convention of product numbering on all sorts of retail products, not just books, in the form of a bar code and incorporating the recommended retail price.

edition: the whole (usually first) printing of a title. See new edition, first edition.

editorial: the department within a publishing house responsible for the content of its titles, both by commissioning and acquiring but also subsequently ensuring accuracy and completeness of the finished publication.

em: a typographical measurement, so called because it represents the width of the widest character in the alphabet.

en: half an em; used as a measurement of the number of characters (text and spaces) in a given text.

end matter: the last pages of the book, after the main text, usually containing glossary, index, picture credits etc.

end-paper: the pages of heavy cartridge paper at the front and back of a hardback book which join the book block to the hardback binding; sometimes used for maps or carrying a decorative colour or design.

erratum: the correction of errors in a book, normally inserted as a slip of paper (an erratum slip) into the finished book.

extent: the number of pages in a book.

finish: special treatment applied to a book's cover. Can include gloss, matt etc. See lamination.

first edition: first printing of a book; occasionally gains substantial second-hand value if the book or its author becomes especially collectable.

folio: the page number which is printed at the top or bottom of each printed page.

foot-note: explanatory note inserted at the foot of the page referring to a point within the text

fore-edge: the right-hand edge of a book when closed, opposite the spine.

format: the shape of a book defined by its height and depth.

Frankfurt Book Fair: the most important international book fair of the year, especially for the buying and selling of rights, held in Frankfurt, Germany, at the beginning of October.

frontispiece: an illustration inserted to face the title-page.

FTP: File Transfer Protocol is used to connect two computers or a server and a client (computer) over the internet so that large files can be transferred. The client connects to the server by running FTP client software (such as Fetch or Cyberduck), and can then transfer the file to their computer. It is a common way for publishers to send large files to printers or repro houses, and sometimes for large files to be passed quickly between author and publisher.

furnish: the pulp and chemical components of a quality or grade of paper.

gutter: the white space in the centre of a double page spread, some of which disappears into the binding of the book.

half-title: the first page of a book, on which the title is displayed, sometimes with a blurb, biography of the author or quotations from reviews.

half-tone: result of the process whereby continuous tone illustrations are broken down into dots for printing.

headline: the line which commonly appears at the top of each printed page, typically showing the book title on the left-hand side and chapter title on the right; sometimes also incorporates the folio. Sometimes also known as a running head.

high-res: Picture resolution over 300dpi. Publishers will always want high-res images for printing as they give the best quality reproduction. The images can either be supplied to the publisher as digital files or as artwork or transparencies for them to scan at an appropriate size.

house: an old-fashioned term for a publishing company.

house style: details of spelling, punctuation and presentation to which a publishing company's books conform.

imprint:
• the name of the publisher under which a title is issued. Increasingly in conglomerate publishing the term represents a publishing brand rather than a publishing company in its own right.
• also used to refer to the printer's name and address which by law must appear in all printed books.

InDesign: Adobe's equivalent of Quark Xpress. It is now widely used in the book, magazine and newspaper industries for graphic page design and layout.

in-house: used of people who work, permanently or temporarily, in the publisher's office and the work that they do, as opposed to freelance or 'out of house'.

ISBN: universal abbreviation for International Standard Book Number, a ten or thirteen-digit unique identifier for each title published, which is used in a wide range of applications in all stages of the supply chain throughout the world. The number – made up of a language prefix (0 or 1 for the English language), followed by a publisher prefix, then a number relating to the individual title, and finally a check digit (used to validate the remainder of the code) – is customarily encoded in a bar code printed on the back of the book and normally appears also in the bibliographical details on the reverse of the title-page.

ISSN: abbreviation for International Standard Serials Number, the equivalent of the ISBN in the journal and magazine publishing business.

jacket: the paper cover wrapped round a hardback book, and normally the publisher's main marketing tool.

JPEG/JPG: A colour image compression format which allows the storage of high-quality images in relatively small files by balancing compression against loss of detail.

kill fee: A fee paid by a magazine when it cancels a commissioned article. The fee is only a certain percentage of the agreed payment for the whole assignment (rarely more than 50 per cent). Not all publishers pay kill fees, so any arrangements should be formally agreed in advance.

lamination: the coating of film applied to book jackets to give added durability. Gloss and matt versions are available and go in and out of fashion for certain types of book.

landscape: a format which is wider than it is deep.

large crown octavo: a hardback format with identical measurements to those of B format paperbacks, 198 x 129 mm sewn (126 mm unsewn).

lead time: the time it takes from a publishing house accepting your work to its actual publication.

leaf: a page of the book comprising both recto and verso.

legal deposit: the legal requirement for publishers to deposit with the British Library and five regional libraries (University Library in Cambridge, the Bodleian Library in Oxford and the national libraries of Scotland, Wales and Ireland) a single copy of each publication.

Library of Congress: the USA's national book collection, based in Washington, DC.

licence: a subsidiary right granted for a fixed term or a particular usage by the holder of the head contract in a work.

limited edition: a book published on the basis that a stated number of copies will be printed regardless of demand. Such titles are often individually numbered by hand and may achieve rarity value for collectors.

literary agent/agency: a person or company

looking after the interests of author clients and managing the exploitation of rights in an author's work. Includes submission of a book to publishers, negotiating a contract, collecting money, and dealing with other rights not held by the publisher, such as (in many cases) broadcasting and film rights.

London International Book Fair: held annually in the spring, this fair has grown rapidly as a meeting place for all those involved in the book trade in the UK, Europe and beyond.

low-res: image file that is less than 300dpi in resolution size. Often used by designers for layout purposes, because the smaller files use up less of the computer's memory than high-res images.

Mac: common name for the Apple Macintosh computer, much favoured by publishers' art and design departments for its flexibility and suitability for graphics programs.

margin: the white space surrounding a page of type.

market:
- the potential readership for a title.
- the territories of the world in which a title may contractually be sold.

marketing: the department in a publishing house with responsibility for promoting titles published; this may include the creation of point of sale display material, press and other advertising, and securing free coverage through PR and publicity.

Minimum Terms Agreement: a contractual agreement negotiated between the Society of Authors and a number of publishers laying down the minimum acceptable terms for individual book contracts. The most contentious ingredient is the requirement that the work should be contracted on a limited licence rather than for the full term of copyright.

monochrome: printing in one colour, usually black.

MTA: see Minimum Terms Agreement.

new edition: a reprint of an existing title, usually incorporating substantial textual alterations, or republication of a title which has been out of print.

Nielsen BookScan: the industry-standard database providing weekly point-of-sale data with the highest possible degree of accuracy. The sales figures come from all the major booksellers. Nielsen BookScan functions as a central clearing house for book industry data, and enables its subscribers to access comprehensive and up-to-the-minute reports on a wide variety of perspectives within the industry. Widely used by publishers as a central resource to track sales figures for similar titles when at the acquisitions process and also to monitor sales of specific titles.

NIP: New In Paperback.

NYP: common abbreviation for Not Yet Published.

offset, offset fee: so named after the process of offset lithography which, in the days when letterpress was still the predominant printing method, was used for the reprinting of books when the metal type was no longer available. The term describes the practice of photographically reproducing the text of one edition of a book in order to create another (for instance, from the US edition to the UK edition, or from an original hardback to a reduced size paperback) and paying an agreed fee per page for the right to do so.

OP: universal abbreviation for Out Of Print.

ozalid: a form of proof made from a film assembly used to check the position of text and illustrations as a final stage of approval before printing. Called in the US 'blues' after the colour of the image on the proof. Rarely used now thanks to digital printing.

packager: company which creates and originates, sometimes manufactures, books for publishers.

page proof: proof of the made-up pages in a book, often used not only to check accuracy of typesetting but also as an advance promotional tool.

part-title: a page in a book which divides it into separate parts, usually printed with the name of the forthcoming section on the recto page but having a blank verso.

partwork: a publication which appears in weekly or fortnightly instalments and which may be bound together to make a complete book.

PDF: Portable Document Format – a file format that maintains the original look of the document, regardless of the software it was created in, and allows it to be read on any machine that has Adobe Acrobat installed.

permissions: the granting of rights by one publisher to another to quote extracts from a previously published title; a permission fee is often charged.

picture research: the process of finding suitable illustrations for a book, normally involving contact with photo libraries, art galleries, museums and so on.

plates: illustrations printed separately from the text of a book and inserted in the appropriate place by the binder. These may appear as a single section, or be wrapped round text sections, or occasionally individually pasted in.

PLC: Paper Laminated Case. See PPC.

point: a size measurement for type. Most books are set in 10 or 11 point type. Twelve points equal one pica em.

point of sale: merchandising display material provided by publishers to bookshops to promote particular titles.

portrait: description of a format which is deeper than it is wide.

POS: see Point of Sale.

PPC: Paper Printed Case – printed paper cover adhered to book boards to create a casebound book, without the need for a protective jacket.

prelims: universal abbreviation for the preliminary pages of a book before the start of the main text, often numbered in roman numerals. May include half-title, title, imprint page, table of contents, acknowledgements and introduction.

print run: the number of copies printed in a single impression.

process colours: the four colours used in printing to represent the full spectrum. See CMYK. Black is represented with a K because B is used for Blue in the RGB profile.

production: the department within a publishing house responsible for print and paper buying and cost and quality control; in some cases has responsibility for typographic design also.

proof: general description of any kind of check of accuracy and quality control of a book's content; might be used of typesetting, of the reproduction of illustrations, or as a final check before printing (see ozalid).

proof-reader: person employed in a publishing house (or freelance) to read proofs and ensure accuracy of typesetting.

publicity: the department within a publishing house which organises 'free' promotion of titles published, often through the sending out of review copies or soliciting coverage in the broadcast media; often nowadays in larger firms a part of the marketing department.

pulping: a system of destroying unsold books, which are then usually recycled into paper or cardboard products.

Quark Xpress: a graphic design software package used on the Apple Mac, which enables a designer to manipulate words and images to produce an integrated design concept.

recommended retail price: since the abolition of the Net Book Agreement, the price at which the publisher recommends that a book should be sold; to which the bookseller's discount is applied and on which the royalty payment to the author is customarily calculated.

recto: the right-hand page of an opening in a book.

register: the accurate printing of each of the four process colours on top of the others to produce a near-perfect representation of a colour original.

remainder: a publisher's overstock sold off cheaply for resale through bargain bookshops etc.

reprint: a second or subsequent printing of a title with minimal alteration to the text.

repro: a common abbreviation for the reproduction of illustrations; a company carrying out such work is called a 'repro house'.

returns: books returned unsold from bookshops to publishers for full credit.

review copy: advance copy of a book sent out without charge to the press or other media for the purposes of review.

RGB: Red, Green, Blue – the colours used by a computer monitor which are converted to CMYK for printing.

royal octavo: book format, 234 x 156 mm (153 mm unsewn), very common in all sectors of the market.

royalty: the payment made by publishers on sales made; typically a percentage of the recommended retail price in the home market and of the monies received from export sales. These payments are frequently set off against an advance and accounted for at six-monthly intervals.

RRP: Recommended Retail Price.

running head: see headline.

sale or return: the arrangement whereby books supplied by publishers to booksellers may be returned for credit if subsequently unsold.

scanning:
• the electronic process of breaking down an image into dots for printing.
• the electronic process of reading a document into a digital memory, from which it can be retrieved and manipulated.

serial rights: a subsidiary right involving the sale of extracts from a title to a newspaper or magazine.

slam: a high-energy performance poetry event, with the audience voting on who they think is the best poet.

slip-case: a cardboard box open at one end into which single copies of a book (or two or three related volumes) are inserted; nowadays used for decorative effect.

spot varnish: the varnishing of a particular part only of a cover or jacket for visual impact.

Society of Authors: organisation representing the interests of writers of books in the UK.

spine: the round edge of a book where the title, author's and publisher's name or logo normally appear.

spread: common name for a double page spread – i.e. two facing pages.

strip and re-bind: process where a book which is already printed and bound has the cover stripped off and replaced with a new one. No changes are made to internal pages. This is done by publishers wanting to invigorate sales, or to correct an error on a cover after printing.

subsidiary rights: rights acquired by publishers for resale, such as serial rights, translation rights, etc.

terms: the percentage discount from the recommended retail price given to the bookseller.

TIFF/TIF: Tagged Image File – a format for bitmapped colour images produced by a scanner. The most common image file format for the industry.

title page: the page, normally the second leaf in a book, which displays the title, author and publisher's name.

title verso: the reverse of the title page, on which the publisher's name and address, the book's printing history, the copyright notice, ISBN and other bibliographical details and the printer's name are customarily printed.

translation rights: the right acquired to translate and publish a work into another language.

typeface: a style or design of type encompassing shape, weight and proportions that make it distinct from the many hundreds of other typefaces. There are around 20 that are commonly used in books.

UV varnish: a varnish cured by ultraviolet light normally applied to covers and jackets as part of the printing process.

verso: the reverse of a page in a book, thus the left-hand page of an opening.

WIPO: abbreviation for World Intellectual Property Organisation, a body concerned with international copyright.

Writers Guild: an organisation representing the interests of writers in the UK.

BOOKS

UK & IRISH BOOK PUBLISHERS

A&A Farmar
Beech House, 78 Ranelagh Village, Dublin 6, Republic of Ireland
- 00353 1 496 3625
- afarmar@iol.ie
- www.aafarmar.ie

Contact Editorial Director, Anna Farmar; Production Director, Tony Farmar
Insider Info Catalogue available online.
Non-Fiction Publishes Biography and Non-Fiction titles on the following subjects:
Biography, Business, Food & Drink, History, Irish Literature, Travel, mostly of Irish interest.
Recent Title(s) *Two in a Million*, Ben Murnane (Biography); *101 Great Wines Under €12*, Mary Dowey (Food & Drink)
Tips Deals mainly with Irish interest titles.

A&C Black Publishers Ltd
38 Soho Square, London, W1D 3HB
- 020 7758 0200
- 020 7758 0222
- See 'Tips'.
- www.acblack.com

Parent Company Bloomsbury Publishing Plc
Contact Chairman/Chief Executive, Nigel Newton; Managing Director, Jill Coleman
Established 1807
Imprint(s) Adlard Coles Nautical
Andrew Brodie Publications
Christopher Helm
Pica Press
T&D Poyser
Herbert Press
Methuen Drama
Fitness Trainers
Insider Info Publishes roughly 170 titles per year. Receives approximately 3,000 queries and 650 manuscripts per year. Five per cent of books published are from first-time authors and 70 per cent are from unagented authors. Offers an advance. Average lead time is nine months, with simultaneous submissions accepted. Aims to respond within two months to proposals and manuscripts. Catalogue is free on request.
Non-Fiction Publishes Children's/Teenage, General Non-Fiction, Gift Books, How-To, Humour, Illustrated, Scholarly, Dictionary, Who's Who (Biography/Reference) and Reference titles on the following subjects:
Language/Literature, Marine Subjects, Sports, Travel, Fitness Training, Arts & Crafts, Glass, Ceramics, Printmaking, Ornithology, Performing Arts and Stagecraft, Drama and Writing, Children's Educational
Fiction Publishes Children's titles.
Recent Title(s) *The Letters of Noël Coward*, Noël Coward and Barry Day (ed.) (Essays & Letters)
Tips A&C Black was acquired by Bloomsbury Publishing Plc in 2000. The editorial contact email addresses are displayed by department on the website.

AA Publishing
Fanum House, Basing View, Basingstoke, RG21 4EA
- 01256 491524
- 01256 322575
- www.theaa.com

Contact Publishing Director, David Watchus
Insider Info AA Publishing is one of the world's leading publishers of travel guides and books on Britain, as well as illustrated reference titles, atlases and maps. Catalogue available online.
Non-Fiction Publishes Travel Guides (including *Citypack*, *Essential*, *Spiral* and *KeyGuide* series, as well as *National Geographic Travellers*), Maps and Atlases, Driving Test Books, Lifestyle Guides (including *Pub Guide*, *Hotel Guide*, *Bed & Breakfast Guide*, *Golf Course Guide*), Leisure Guides, Walking Guides and Illustrated Reference titles.

Aard Press
c/o Aardverx, 31 Mountearl Gardens, London, SW16 2NL
Contact Managing Director, Dawn Redwood
Established 1971

UK & IRISH BOOKS

PUBLISHERS

LISTINGS

Non-Fiction Publishes Booklets, General Non-Fiction, Multimedia and Illustrated titles on the following subjects:
Art/Architecture, Crafts, Creative Non-Fiction, Literary Criticism
Fiction Publishes Experimental and Picture Book titles.
Poetry Publishes Poetry titles.
Recent Title(s) *Actuary*, Dawn Redwood
Tips Aard Press only does small print runs and does not accept any form of unsolicited submission proposals, or even enquiries.

Abacus

100 Victoria Embankment, London, EC4Y 0DY
- 020 7911 8000
- 020 7911 8100
- info@littlebrown.co.uk
- www.littlebrown.co.uk

Parent Company Little, Brown Book Group
Contact Publishing Director, Richard Beswick
Established 1973
Insider Info Submissions accompanied by SAE will be returned. Aims to respond to proposals within eight weeks. Catalogue available online.
Non-Fiction Publishes General Non-Fiction on the following subjects:
Biography/Autobiography, Memoirs, Nature/Environment, Science
* Began as a strictly non-fiction imprint with an ecological focus. Now publishes over a wider range of subjects.
Submission Guidelines Accepts query with SAE. Submit proposal package (including outline, three sample chapters and a covering letter).
Fiction Publishes Literary and Mainstream/Contemporary Fiction.
* Publishes both original fiction and paperback editions of Little, Brown's hardback fiction.
Submission Guidelines Accepts query with SAE. Submit proposal package (including outline, three sample chapters and a covering letter).

Abbey Home Media

435–437 Edgware Road, London, W2 1TH
- 020 7563 3910
- 020 7563 3911
- anne.miles@abbeyhomemedia.com
- www.abbeyhomemedia.com

Contact Managing Director, Acquisitions & Programme Development, Anne Miles
Insider Info Catalogue available online.
Non-Fiction Publishes Children's Non-Fiction, Educational and Reference titles based on licensed characters.

Fiction Publishes Children's Fiction and Picture Books based on licensed brands.
* Brands include *Superted* and *Teddy Trucks*.
Recent Title(s) *Wide Eye* (Animated TV Series)
Tips Abbey Home Media produce CDs, DVDs and other resources for children, as well as their book publishing programme. Note that most ranges are linked in some way to characters or brands either created and licensed themselves, or bought from other licence holders.

Abbey Press

Courtenay Hill, Newry, Co. Down, BT34 2ED
- 028 3026 3142
- 028 3026 2514
- adrianrice@earthlink.net
- www.abbeypressbooks.com

Contact Co-Founder/Editor, Adrian Rice (Poetry/Essays); Co-Founder/Administrator, Mel McMahon (Poetry)
Established 1997
Insider Info Publishes three titles per year. Receives approximately 200 queries and 100 manuscripts per year. 20 per cent of books published are from first-time authors, and 75 per cent are from unagented authors. Does not publish author subsidy books. Authors paid by small fee, plus free books. Average lead time is seven months. Does not accept simultaneous submissions. Submissions accompanied by SAE will be returned. Aims to respond to queries, proposals and manuscript submissions within four months. Catalogue available online, or via email. Author guidelines available by sending SAE, online, or via email.
Non-Fiction Publishes Autobiography/Biography and Scholarly titles on the following subjects:
Academic Subjects, Art, Government/Politics, History, Memoirs
Submission Guidelines Accepts query with SAE. Submit proposal package (including outline, one sample chapter, your publishing history, author biography and SAE). Does not review artwork/photographs.
Fiction Publishes Historical and Literary fiction, and Short Story Collections.
Poetry Publishes Poetry and Translated Poetry.
Submission Guidelines Submit seven sample poems.
Recent Title(s) *43 Poems*, Attilla Jozsef (Translated Poetry); *Whereabouts*, Mark Roper (Paperback)
Tips Abbey's target audience is literary or academic readers with an interest in either poetry or history.

ABC-Clio

PO Box 1437, Oxford, OX4 9AZ
- 01844 238448

salesinternational@abc-clio.com
www.abc-clio.com
Contact President and CEO (US), Ron Boehm
Established 1955
Insider Info Catalogue available online.
Non-Fiction Publishes Reference and Scholarly on the followin subjects:
Education and General Reference, History, Social Sciences, World Affairs.
Submission Guidelines Contact the Oxford office for information on submission methods.
Recent Title(s) *The Encyclopedia of the Arab-Israeli Conflict*, Spencer C. Tucker (Reference)
Tips The company is US based with an office in the UK. The website is US authored, but does contain information for UK authors and readers. Also has an online subscription reference database.

Absolute Press
Scarborough House, 29 James Street West, Bath, BA1 2BT
01225 316013
01225 445836
office@absolutepress.co.uk
www.absolutepress.co.uk
Contact Publisher, Jon Croft; Commissioning Editor, Meg Avent
Established 1979
Insider Info Authors paid by royalties. Catalogue available online.
Non-Fiction Publishes Cookbooks, General Non-Fiction, Gift, How-To, Humour and Reference titles on the following subjects:
Cooking/Foods/Nutrition, Health/Medicine, House & Home, Travel
Submission Guidelines No unsolicited manuscripts.
Recent Title(s) *Aga Year*, Louise Walker (Cookery); *Curry: Classic and Contemporary Recipes*, Vivek Singh (Cookery)
Tips Target audience is chefs, cooks, homeowners, etc. As well as not accepting unsolicited manuscripts, Absolute Press is also unable to offer any proofreading or copyediting commissions for freelancers.

Abson Books London
5 Sidney Square, London, E1 2EY
020 7790 4737
020 7790 7346
books@absonbooks.co.uk
www.absonbooks.co.uk
Contact Publisher, M.J. Ellison
Established 1971
Insider Info Catalogue is available online.

Non-Fiction Publishes Language Glossaries, Literary Quiz, Puzzle Books and Curiosity titles.
Recent Title(s) *West of England English*, Abson Books
Tips Mostly publishes dialect and slang books.

Academic Press
Linacre House, Jordan Hill, Oxford, OX2 8DP
01865 474010
01865 474011
authorsupport@elsevier.com
www.elsevier.com
Parent Company Elsevier Ltd (Science & Technology)
Established 1946
Insider Info Authors paid by royalty. Catalogue and author guidelines available online.
Non-Fiction Publishes Multimedia, Textbooks, Reference, Scholarly and Technical titles on the following subjects:
Education, Languages, Transport, Nature/Environment, Science, Social Sciences, Construction/Engineering
Submission Guidelines Accepts query with SAE. Submit proposal package (including outline and sample chapter if possible).
Recent Title(s) *Fiber Optic Measurement Techniques*, Hui and O'Sullivan (Reference)
Tips Academic Press publishes books, periodicals, online services and CD-ROMs (from single volumes to multi-volume reference works in the fields of physical, applied and life sciences). Titles are aimed at scientists, researchers, engineers, and other professionals in industry and academia. Authors' proposals for books are welcomed. The first step is to discuss the proposal with the relevant commissioning editor. Check the website for in-depth submission guidelines and a full list of editorial contacts. Elsevier recommend that prospective authors are as focused and specific as possible in their proposals, and that information on competitor titles is researched thoroughly.

Academy of Light
Unit 1c, Delta Centre, Mount Pleasant, Wembley, Middlesex, HA0 1UX
020 8795 2695
020 8903 3748
info@academyoflight.co.uk
www.academyoflight.co.uk
Contact Managing Director, Dr Yubraj Sharma
Established 2000
Non-Fiction Publishes Children's, Illustrated, Reference and Scholarly titles on the following subjects:
Alternative Lifestyles, Art/Architecture, Health/Medicine, New Age, Spirituality

Recent Title(s) *Spiritual Bioenergetics of Homeopathic Materia Medica Vol.1*, Dr. Yubraj Sharma (Medical/Spirituality)

Tips Academy of Light is a specialist book publisher on homoeopathy and spirituality. It aims to integrate the many fields of alternative medicine into a holistic system of new age medicine.

Acair Ltd

7 James Street, Stornoway, Isle of Lewis, HS1 2QN

☎ 01851 703020

☎ 01851 703294

✉ info@acairbooks.com

🌐 www.acairbooks.com

Established 1975

Insider Info Authors paid by royalty. Catalogue available online.

Non-Fiction Publishes Children's, General Non-Fiction, Illustrated, Reference and Scholarly titles on the following subjects:
History, Military/War, Regional

Fiction Publishes Children's, Young Adult and Gaelic (sometimes printed in Gaelic language) Fiction titles.

Poetry Publishes Poetry titles.

* See catalogue for more information on Acair poetry publishing.

Recent Title(s) *The Living Past*, Donald Macleod (Autobiography); *Aeolus*, Donald MacIntyre

Tips Acair is a bilingual publisher, printing books in both English and Gaelic languages, targeted mainly at Gaelic primary school education. At least 50 per cent of Acair publications will be in Gaelic.

Accent Press

The Old School, Upper High Street, Bedlinog, Mid-Glamorgan, CF46 6SA

☎ 01443 710930

☎ 01443 710940

✉ info@accentpress.co.uk

🌐 www.accentpress.co.uk

Contact Managing Director, Hazel Cushion (Fiction/Non-Fiction)

Established 2003

Imprint(s) Curriculum Concepts UK Ltd
Xcite Books

Insider Info Publishes roughly 36 titles per year. Receives approximately 500 queries and 750 manuscripts per year. Three per cent of books published are from first-time authors and ten per cent of books published are from unagented authors. Payment is via royalty (on retail price) with 0.1 (per £) maximum. Average lead time is six months, with simultaneous submissions not accepted. Submissions accompanied by SAE will be returned. Aims to respond to queries, proposals and manuscripts within six months, and all other enquiries within twelve months. A catalogue is free on request, and available online.

Non-Fiction Publishes Autobiography, Cookbooks, How-To and Self-Help titles on the following subjects:
Child Guidance/Parenting, Cooking/Foods/Nutrition, Gay/Lesbian, Literary Criticism, Memoirs

Submission Guidelines Accepts proposal package (including outline, three sample chapters, your publishing history, author biography, SAE and artworks/images (send digital files as jpegs).

Fiction Publishes Erotica (Short Stories), Historical, Literary, Mainstream/Contemporary, Romance, Crime and Thriller titles.

* Check the published titles catalogue to see what kind of fiction is of interest.

Submission Guidelines Accepts proposal package (including outline, with three sample chapters).

Recent Title(s) *The Death Pictures*, Simon Hall (Crime); *Successful Novel Plotting*, Jean Saunders (How To)

Tips Accent Press have a mainstream and mass market readership. They do not publish any poetry, or short story collections – with the exception of erotica – and have a limited production schedule. Curriculum Concepts is a new educational division which produces teacher resource materials.

Acorn Editions

PO Box 60, Cambridge, CB1 2NT

☎ 01223 350865

☎ 01225 366951

✉ publishing@lutterworth.com

🌐 www.lutterworth.com

Parent Company The Lutterworth Press

Insider Info Publishes 50 titles per year. Catalogue available online and on request.

Non-Fiction Publishes General Non-Fiction on the following subjects:
History, Memoirs, Regional, Local and Minority Interest

Submission Guidelines Submit proposal package (including outline and three sample chapters). No email submissions.

Recent Title(s) *From Anschluss to Albion: Memoirs of a Refugee Girl 1938–40*, Elizabeth Orsten (Memoir)

Tips Acorn Editions is a local and minority interest imprint of The Lutterworth Press, the UK's oldest independent publishing house. Unsolicited proposals are welcome, but read the guidelines on the website before submitting.

Acumen Publishing Limited

Stocksfield Hall, Stocksfield, NE43 7TN

☎ 01661 844865

☎ 01661 844865
✉ enquiries@acumenpublishing.co.uk
✉ tristanpalmereditor@yahoo.co.uk
✉ steven.gerrard@acumenpublishing.co.uk
🌐 www.acumenpublishing.co.uk
Contact Publisher, Steven Gerrard; Senior Editor, Tristan Palmer
Insider Info Catalogue and author guidelines available online.
Non-Fiction Publishes Scholarly titles and Academic journals on the following subjects:
Aesthetics, Classics, Epistemology, History, Language, Logic, Mathematics, Metaphysics, Mind, Philosophy, Social Theory
Submission Guidelines Submit proposal package (including outline, sample chapter(s) and author biography). Also submit a review of competing books and information about intended readership.
Recent Title(s) *The Self*, Stephen Burwood (Mind); *The Philosophy of Sartre*, Anthony Hatzimoysis (Philosophy)
Tips Acumen Publishing's books are read by a worldwide higher education audience; students, lecturers and researchers. There is good submission information for authors on the website, including information on style and indexing downloads.

Addison-Wesley
Edinburgh Gate, Harlow, Essex, CM20 2JE
☎ 01279 623623
☎ 0870 850 5255
🌐 www.pearsoned.co.uk/imprints/addison-wesley
Parent Company Pearson Education
Insider Info Catalogue and manuscript guidelines are available online.
Non-Fiction Publishes Reference, Scholarly, Technical and Academic titles on the following subjects:
Astronomy, Computers, Economics, Electronics, Finance, Mathematics, Physics
Submission Guidelines Accepts proposal package (including synopsis, sample chapters, market research, your publishing history and author biography).
Recent Title(s) *Flex on Rails*, Tony Hillerson and Daniel Wanja (Computing/Internet); *Securing PHP Web Applications*, Tricia Ballad and William Ballad (Computing/Internet)
Tips Addison-Wesley is a leading international technical publisher. The imprint specialises in the area of computer programming, producing high quality and up to date information for programmers, developers, engineers, and system administrators. It also focuses on astronomy and physics, computing, economics and finance, mathematics and statistics. See website for full list of submissions contacts.

Adlard Coles Nautical
38 Soho Square, London, W1D 3QY
☎ 020 7758 0200
☎ 020 7758 0333
✉ adlardcoles@acblack.com
🌐 www.acblack.com
Parent Company A&C Black Publishers Ltd
Contact Editorial Director, Janet Murphy
Established 1947
Imprint(s) Reeds Nautical Almanac (series) Thomas Reed Publications (list)
Insider Info Catalogue available online.
Non-Fiction Publishes How-To, Humour, Almanacs, Illustrated, Reference and Technical titles on the following subjects:
Hobbies, Marine Subjects, Sports, Travel, Nautical/ Sailing
Submission Guidelines Accepts query with SAE.
Recent Title(s) *Reeds Nautical Almanac 2009*, Neville Featherstone and Andy du Pont (eds.) (Technical Maritime); *Left for Dead*, Nick Ward and Sinead O'Brien
Tips Adlard Coles Nautical publishes practical and technical books on all manner of nautical, maritime and sailing topics. The Thomas Reed list publishes practical sailing books aimed at both professional merchant sailors and the practical boating leisure market. The *Nautical Almanac* series is a long running series of practical and general nautical interest. Subjects are generally practical or technical in nature, so some working experience in the field would be useful for a prospective contributor, but they also publish some general interest and humorous books.

African Books Collective
PO Box 721, Oxford, Ox1 9EN,
☎ 01869 349110
☎ 01869 349110
✉ orders@africanbookscollective.com
🌐 www.africanbookscollective.com
Contact CEO, Mary Jay
Established 1989
Insider Info Catalogue available online. Only accepts manuscripts from participating African publishers.
Non-Fiction Publishes Children's, General Non-Fiction, How-To, Scholarly and Self-Help titles on the following subjects:
African Literature, African Studies, Art & Culture, Children's Reference, Environmental Studies, Humanities & Social Sciences, Medicine, Policy & Development, Science & Technology
Fiction Publishes Children's, Multicultural, Short Story, Translation and Young Adult Fiction.

Recent Title(s) *Blackness: Culture, Ideology and Discourse*, Femi Abodunrin (African Studies); *Long Time Coming*, Jane Morris, ed. (Short Fiction Anthology)

Tips African Books Collective (ABC), founded, owned and governed by African publishers, seeks to strengthen indigenous African publishing through collective action, and to increase the visibility and accessibility of the wealth of African scholarship and culture. The collective is open to genuinely autonomous and independent African publishers, and ABC actively seeks suitable titles for distribution outside Africa.

Age Concern Books
1268 London Road, London, SW16 4ER
- 020 8765 7200
- 020 8765 7211
- books@ace.org.uk
- www.ace.org.uk

Contact Commissioning Editor, Becky Senior
Established 1973
Insider Info Catalogue available online.
Non-Fiction Publishes General Non-fiction, How-To, Reference and Self-Help titles on the following subjects:
Computers/Electronics, Counselling/Career, Health/Medicine, House and Home, Real Estate, Recreation, Geronotology
Submission Guidelines Accepts query with SAE. Submit proposal package (including outline and SAE).
Recent Title(s) *Feeling Good!*, Dr. Alan Maryon Davies; *Beat the Banks*, Paul Lewis
Tips Age Concern Books addresses the needs of older people, their families and professional carers, as well as business and voluntary organisations. The aim of their titles is to provide accurate and up to date information to improve quality of life and standards of care. Although fiction submissions are not accepted, Age Concern will consider ideas for new practical handbooks that are aimed at the elderly generation in tone and content.

Alastair Sawday Publishing
The Old Farmyard, Yanley Lane, Long Ashton, Bristol, BS41 9LR
- 01275 395433
- press@sawdays.co.uk
- www.sawdays.co.uk

Contact Publisher, Alastair Sawday
Established 1994
Insider Info Catalogue available online.
Non-Fiction Publishes Travel Guides under the *Special Places to Stay* and *Fragile Earth* series.

Recent Title(s) *Ban the Plastic Bag*, Rebecca Hoskins (ed.) (Fragile Earth)
Tips Alistair Sawday guides are aimed at discerning and interested travellers/holiday makers, who appreciate the vivid and honest style of the entries and are looking for unique and unusual places to stay.

Allen Lane
80 Strand, London, WC2R 0RL
- 020 7010 3000
- 020 7010 6060
- customer.service@penguin.co.uk
- www.penguin.co.uk

Parent Company Penguin Press
Contact Editorial Director, William Goodlad
Established 1967
Insider Info Catalogue is available online or by email.
Non-Fiction Publishes Autobiography, Biography, General Non-Fiction and Illustrated titles.
Submission Guidelines Agented submissions only.
Recent Title(s) *Travelling Heroes*, Robin Lane Fox (Literature); *Traffic*, Tom Vanderbilt (Popular Culture)
Tips Allen Lane is expanding steadily and aims to publish accessible and excellent non-fiction books of lasting value.

Alligator Books
Gadd House, Arcadia Avenue, London, N3 2JU
- 020 8371 6622
- 020 8371 6633
- sales@alligatorbooks.co.uk
- www.alligatorbooks.co.uk

Contact Publishing & Sales Director, Andrew H Rabin
Established 1999
Imprint(s) Pinwheel Limited (division)
Insider Info Catalogue available online.
Non-Fiction Publishes Children's Non-Fiction and Activity titles based on licensed characters.
Fiction Publishes Children's Fiction and Picture Books based on licensed brands.
* Brands include *Hannah Montana*, *High School Musical* and *Ben 10*.
Tips Specialises in film, television and magazine tie-ins. Produces activity packs, work books, stickers and other gifts, as well as more traditional picture books. Recently acquired Pinwheel Limited (see separate entry).

Allison & Busby Ltd
13 Charlotte Mews, London, W1T 4EJ
- 020 7580 1080
- 020 7580 1180
- susie@allisonandbusby.com

🌐 www.allisonandbusby.co.uk
Established 1969
Insider Info Catalogue is available online.
Non-Fiction Publishes Autobiography, Biography, General Non-Fiction, How-To, Encyclopedias and Reference titles on the following subjects: Computers/Electronics, Contemporary Culture, History, Language/Literature, Memoirs, Music/Dance, Psychology, Sex, Writing, Politics, Personalities, Crime, Film and Television
Submission Guidelines Agented submissions only.
Fiction Publishes Literary, Mainstream/Contemporary and Crime Fiction.
Submission Guidelines Agented submissions only.
Recent Title(s) *Envelopes*, Harriet Russell (Gift/Humour); *Above the Bright Blue Sky*, Margaret Thornton (Fiction)

Allyn & Bacon
Edinburgh Gate, Harlow, Essex, CM20 2JE
☎ 01279 623623
📠 01279 414130
🌐 www.pearsoned.co.uk/imprints/allynbacon
Parent Company Pearson Education
Insider Info Catalogue and manuscript guidelines are available online.
Non-Fiction Publishes Reference, Scholarly and Textbook titles on the following subjects: Education, Humanities, Social Sciences
Submission Guidelines Accepts proposal package (including synopsis, sample chapters, market research, your publishing history and author biography).
Recent Title(s) *The Allyn & Bacon Guide to Writing (5th Edition)*, John Ramage, John Bean and June Johnson (Reference)
Tips Allyn & Bacon is a leading publisher for higher education in the areas of education, humanities and the social sciences. See website for full list of submission contacts.

Alma Books Ltd
London House, 243–253 Lower Mortlake Road, Richmond, Surrey, TW9 2LL
☎ 020 8948 9550
📠 020 8948 5599
✉ info@almabooks.com
🌐 www.almabooks.com
Contact Publisher, Alessandro Gallenzi (Trade Fiction and Non-Fiction)
Established 2005
Imprint(s) Herla Publishing
Insider Info Publishes 25 titles per year. Receives 500 queries and 400 manuscripts per year. 30 per cent of books published are from first-time authors and 20 per cent are from unagented authors.

Payment is via royalty (on retail price) with 0.1 (per £) minimum and 0.12 (per £) maximum. Advance offered is from £1,000–£5,000. Average lead time is 12 months, with simultaneous submissions accepted. Submissions accompanied by SAE will be returned. Aims to respond to queries within one day, proposals within one week and manuscripts within one month. Catalogue is free on request, and available online or via email. Manuscript guidelines are available online.
Non-Fiction Publishes Biography, General Non-Fiction and Humour titles
Submission Guidelines Accepts query with SAE, or proposal package (including outline, two sample chapters, author biography and SAE) and artworks/images (send photocopies).
Fiction Publishes Humour, Literary, Mainstream/Contemporary, Short Story collections and Translation titles
Submission Guidelines Accepts query with SAE or proposal package (including outline, two sample chapters).
Poetry Publishes some poetry including European translations.
Submission Guidelines Accepts query or proposal package (including five sample poems).
Recent Title(s) *Men in Space* Tom McCarthy (Literary Fiction) *All Ears*, Michael Holden (Humour)

Amber Lane Press
Cheorl House, Church Street, Charlbury, OX7 3PR
☎ 01608 810024
📠 01608 810024
✉ info@amberlanepress.co.uk
🌐 www.amberlanepress.co.uk
Contact Managing Director, Judith Scott
Established 1979
Insider Info No longer actively publishing. Catalogue of titles still in print available online.
Non-Fiction Publishes Biography, General Non-Fiction, How-To, Reference and Scholarly titles on the following subjects: Art/Architecture, Drama/Theatre
Submission Guidelines No longer accepting submissions.
Fiction Publishes Plays.
Recent Title(s) *Kiss of the Spider Woman*, Manuel Puig, translated by Allan Baker (Play)

Andersen Press Ltd
20 Vauxhall Bridge Road, London, SW1V 2SA
☎ 020 7840 8701
📠 020 7233 6263
✉ andersoneditorial@randomhouse.co.uk
🌐 www.andersenpress.co.uk

Contact Fiction Editor, Liz Maude (Children's Fiction); Editorial Director, Rona Selby (Children's Books)
Established 1976
Insider Info Publishes roughly 60 titles per year. Receives approximately 200 queries and 500 manuscripts per year. 25 per cent of books published are from first-time authors and 30 per cent of books published are from unagented authors. Payment is via royalty (on retail price) with 0.075 (per £) minimum and 0.125 (per £) maximum. Advance offered is £2,000. Catalogue is free on request, and available online. Manuscript guidelines are free on request.
Non-Fiction Publishes Children's and Young Adult fiction and Picture Book titles.
* Publishes very little non-fiction.
Submission Guidelines Accepts proposal package (including outline, one sample chapter, author biography and SAE) and artworks/images (send digital files as jpegs or other formats).
Fiction Publishes Children's and Picture Book titles.
Submission Guidelines Accepts proposal package (including outline and three sample chapter). For picture book submissions include copies of artwork.
Recent Title(s) *Four Red Apples*, David McKee (Picture Book)
Tips Andersen Press' readership is children and young adults, between the ages of one and eighteen. They publish mainly picture books, for which the required text would be under 1,000 words. They also produce a series of early reader's fiction called *Tigers* which are about 3–5,000 words long. Older fiction texts are about 15–50,000 words. Books are sold in conjunction with Random House Children's Books.

Andre Deutsch
20 Mortimer Street, London, W1T 3JW
- 020 7612 0400
- 020 7612 0401
- enquiries@carltonbooks.co.uk
- www.carltonbooks.co.uk
Parent Company Carlton Publishing Group
Insider Info Publishes roughly four titles per year. Catalogue available online.
Non-Fiction Publishes Biography and General Non-Fiction on the following subjects: History, Travel, Current Affairs
Submission Guidelines Submit proposal package (including outline, the first 20 pages or two sample chapters – whichever is shorter). Submission details to: pmurrayhill@carltonbooks.co.uk
Tips Although Andre Deutsch was created to publish high end non-fiction, it does not accept proposals for academic books.

Andrew Brodie Publications
38 Soho Square, London, W1D 3HB
- 020 7758 0200
- 020 7758 0222
- childrens@acblack.com
- www.acblack.com
Parent Company A&C Black Publishers Ltd
Insider Info Publishes approximately 20 titles per year. Aims to respond to proposals within two months. Catalogue available online.
Non-Fiction Publishes Children's Illustrated Educational and Multimedia titles.
* Titles are aimed at primary and secondary schools.
Submission Guidelines Accepts postal submissions.
Recent Title(s) *Sentence Structure and Punctuation: Ages 4–5*, Andrew Brodie (Educational)
Tips Andrew Brodie Publications publishes reference and education material for children of all ages. Books are practical and educational in nature, but must also be easily photocopiable for use as teaching materials.

Andromeda Children's Books
Gadd House, Arcadia Avenue, London, N3 2JU
- 020 8371 6622
- 020 8371 6664
- www.pinwheel.co.uk
Parent Company Pinwheel Limited (division of Alligator Books)
Insider Info Catalogue available online.
Non-Fiction Publishes Children's, Cloth, Novelty, Gift and Illustrated titles on the following subjects: Children's and Baby's Early Learning
Fiction Publishes Children's, Picture Books and Illustrated Fiction titles.
Recent Title(s) *Secrets of the Master Magician* (Activity Pack); *The Beautiful Butterfly Book* (Illustrated Non-Fiction)
Tips As part of Pinwheel, specialist children's publishers, the Andromeda imprint focuses on the three to twelve year old age group. Typical titles include wipe clean books for pre-schoolers and novelty series such as *Beautiful Bugs*. Any picture book submissions should be directed to Gullane Children's Books (another imprint of Pinwheel) and not Andromeda.

The Angels Share
G/R 19 Netherton Avenue, Glasgow, Scotland, G13 1BQ
- 0141 954 8007
- 0560 150 4806
- info@nwp.co.uk
- www.nwp.co.uk
Parent Company Neil Wilson Publishing Ltd

Insider Info Catalogue and manuscript guidelines are available online.
Non-Fiction Publishes General Non-Fiction titles on the following subjects:
Cooking, Food and Drink, Scottish Cuisine, Whisky
Submission Guidelines Submit proposal package (including outline, synopsis, one sample chapter, author biography, CV and SAE). Will accept artworks/ images.
Recent Title(s) *A-Z Of Whisky, revised edition*, Gavin D Smith (Whisky)
Tips The Angels Share is an imprint of Neil Wilson Publishing and specialises in books on Scottish food and drink. It is the leading publisher of books on whisky and takes its name from the high amount of spirit that evaporates from Scotland's warehouses every year, the so called 'Angels Share'.

Anglo-Saxon Books

25 Brocks Road, EcoTech Business Park, Swaffham, Norfolk, PE37 7XG
- 0845 430 4200
- enq@asbooks.co.uk
- www.asbooks.co.uk

Contact Managing Editor, Tony Linsell
Established 1990
Insider Info Publishes five titles per year. Catalogue available online. No unsolicited manuscripts.
Non-Fiction Publishes General Non-Fiction, Illustrated, Reference and Scholarly titles on the following subjects:
History, Language/Literature, Tolkien Studies
Submission Guidelines Query by phone only.
Fiction Publishes Tolkien related fiction and Old English Fiction titles.
Poetry Publishes Poetry in Translation and Old English Poetry.
Submission Guidelines Query by phone only.
Recent Title(s) *Anglo-Saxon Burial Mounds*, Stephen Pollington
Tips Anglo-Saxon Books was created to promote a greater awareness of, and interest in early English history, language and culture. They aim to publish good books at a reasonable price. Phone with query before any submissions.

An Gúm

Foras na Gaeilge, 7 Merrion Square, Dublin 2, Republic of Ireland
- 00353 1 639 8400
- focloir@forasnagaeilge.ie
- www.forasnagaeilge.ie

Established 1926
Insider Info Has published around 2,500 books and 350 music pieces since its establishment.

Non-Fiction Publishes Dictionaries, Lexicograpy, Textbooks and General Readers for children and young people on the following subjects:
Education, Irish Language, Irish Literature, Music.
Recent Title(s) *Ar Thóir an Fhlaithis*, Vincent Foley
Tips An Gúm is the single largest Irish language publisher in the country. All books are in Irish language, guidelines for translators are available on the website.

Anness Publishing

Hermes House, 88–89 Blackfriars Road, London, SE1 8HA
- 020 7401 2077
- 020 7633 9499
- info@anness.com
- www.annesspublishing.com

Contact Chairman/Managing Director, Paul Anness; Publisher/Partner, Joanna Lorenz (Creative Issues)
Established 1988
Imprint(s) Lorenz Books
Southwater
Hermes House
Peony Press
Insider Info Publishes around 300 new titles per year. Catalogue available online. The company has embarked on a major forestry project by managing and planting trees to replace the ones used to produce its books.
Non-Fiction Publishes Children's, General Non-Fiction, Gift, Illustrated and Reference titles on the following subjects:
Art, Archaeology, Child Guidance/Parenting, Contemporary Culture, Cooking/Foods/Nutrition, Crafts, Gardening, Health/Medicine, History, Hobbies, House & Home, Memoirs, New Age, Sports, Food & Drink, Lifestyle, Pets
* The Lorenz Books and Southwater imprints publish traditionally across the range of non-fiction topics, whereas Hermes House and Peony Press deal with non-trade sales, promotional sales and customised publishing for major customers.
Recent Title(s) *Lavender: A Heritage Book of Creative Ideas*, Tessa Evelegh; *Practical Archaeology: a step-by-step guide to uncovering the past*, Christopher Catling
Tips Anness is the largest independent book publisher in the UK.

Anova Books Company Ltd

The Old Magistrates Court, 10 Southcombe Street, London, W14 0RA
- 020 7605 1400
- 020 7605 1401
- customerservices@anovabooks.com
- www.anovabooks.com

Contact Senior Editor, Emily Preece-Morrison; Commissioning Editor, Michelle Lo (Craft); Commissioning Editor, Victoria Alers-Hankey (Reference, Health); Commissioning Editor, Barbara Phelan (Biography, Popular Culture); Senior Editor, Nicola Birtwisle; Editor, Kristy Richardson

Established 2005

Imprint(s) Batsford
Chrysalis Children's Books
Collins & Brown
Conway Maritime Press
National Trust Books
Pavilion
Portico
Robson

Insider Info Publishes around 150 titles per year. Receives approximately 40 queries and 200 manuscripts per year. 50 per cent of books published are from first-time authors and 50 per cent of books published are from unagented authors. Payment is via royalty (on retail price), with 0.075 (per £) maximum, or outright purchase. Advance offered will be up to £10,000. Average lead time is seven months, with simultaneous submissions not accepted. Submissions accompanied by SAE will be returned. Aims to respond to queries within one week, proposals within two weeks, and manuscripts within five weeks. Catalogue is free on request, and available online.

Non-Fiction Publishes Biography, Children's and Coffee Table titles on the following subjects: Art/Architecture, Cooking/Foods/Nutrition, Crafts, Gardening, Health/Medicine, Memoirs, Military/War, Photography, Sports, Travel, Bridge/Chess, Fashion/Textiles, Popular Culture, History/Heritage, Lifestyle, Interiors Design, Maritime/Naval, Aviation, Mind, Body and Spirit

Submission Guidelines Accepts proposal package (including outline and one sample chapter).

Fiction Publishes Erotica, Fantasy, Military/War, Spiritual and Sports titles.

Submission Guidelines Accepts proposal package (including outline and one sample chapter).

Antique Collector's Club

Sandy Lane, Old Martlesham, Woodbridge, IP12 4SD

- 01394 389977
- 01394 389999
- info@antique-acc.com
- www.antique-acc.com

Contact Directors: D M Steel, D M Farrell, J Smith, M Jellinek, S Smye

Established 1966

Insider Info Catalogue free on request, or available online.

Non-Fiction Publishes Children's, General Non-Fiction, Gift and Illustrated titles on the following subjects:
Art/Architecture, Crafts, Gardening, Hobbies, Photography, Horology, Antiques/Collectables/Museums

Recent Title(s) *Debrett's Etiquette for Girls*, Fleur Britten; *The English Watch*, Terence Camerer Cuss

Tips Target audience is antiques/art collectors. Will consider synopses or ideas for books. Also publishes a journal, *Antique Collecting*, which may be more likely to accept article submissions.

Apex Publishing Ltd

PO Box 7086, Clacton on Sea, Essex, CO15 5WN

- 01255 428500
- mail@apexpublishing.co.uk
- www.apexpublishing.co.uk

Contact Production and Publishing Manager, Chris Cowlin; Marketing Manager, Jackie Bright

Established 2002

Insider Info Publishes 30 titles per year. Receives approximately 500 queries and 500 manuscripts per year. 60 per cent of books published are from first-time authors and 90 per cent of books published are from unagented authors. 50 per cent of books published are author subsidy published, based on potential sales. Payment is via royalty (on retail price). Average lead time is nine months, with simultaneous submissions accepted. Submissions accompanied by SAE will be returned. Aims to respond to queries within seven days, proposals within 14 days, manuscripts within 21 days, and any other enquiry within seven days. Catalogue and manuscript guidelines are free on request, and available online or by email.

Non-Fiction Publishes Autobiography, Biography, General Non-Fiction, Reference, True Crime, Young Adult and Self-Help titles on the following subjects: Animals, Cooking/Foods/Nutrition, Education, History, Hobbies, Military/War, New Age, Philosophy, Psychology, Regional, Religion, Science, Sex, Social Sciences, Sociology, Sports, Travel

Submission Guidelines Accepts query with SAE, or completed manuscript (including publishing history, clips, author biography and SAE), and artworks/images (send photocopies or digital files as jpegs).

Fiction Publishes Erotica, Fantasy, Horror, Humour, Regional, Science-Fiction, Children's and General Fiction titles

Submission Guidelines Accepts query with SAE, or completed manuscript (including publishing history, clips, author biography and SAE).

Apple Press

7 Greenland Street, London, NW1 0ND
- 020 7284 7168
- 020 7485 4902
- lianes@apple-press.com
- www.apple-press.com

Parent Company Quarto Group Inc
Contact Publisher, Liane Stark
Established 1984
Insider Info Catalogue free on request or available online.
Non-Fiction Publishes Illustrated titles on the following subjects:
Cooking, Crafts, Beauty, Food & Drink, Fashion, Gardening, General Interest, Gift, Home Decoration, Hobbies, House & Home, Lifestyle, Mind, Body & Spirit, Music Instruction.
Submission Guidelines Query with SAE.
Recent Title(s) *Handmade Breads*, Ciril Hitz (Cookery); *Spanish Cooking: Traditional Dishes and Regional Specialities*, Pepita Aris (Cookery)
Tips The hallmarks of Apple's books are clear, reliable and accessible content, with fresh, modern design. Any submissions need to be aware of this ethos.

Appletree Press Ltd

The Old Potato Station, 14 Howard Street South, Belfast, BT7 1AP
- 028 9024 3074
- 028 9024 6756
- reception@appletree.ie
- www.appletree.ie

Contact Managing Director, John Murphy
Established 1974
Insider Info Payment is via royalty. Catalogue and manuscript guidelines are available online.
Non-Fiction Publishes Biography, General Non-Fiction, Gift, How-To and Illustrated titles on the following subjects:
Art/Architecture, Cooking/Foods/Nutrition, Crafts, History, Music/Dance, Nature/Environment, Regional, Religion, Translation, Travel, Celtic
Submission Guidelines Accepts query with SAE and proposal package (including outline, synopsis and two-three sample capters).
Recent Title(s) *Keep Her Flying - Ireland's Rally Heroes*, Richard Young (Sport)
Tips Titles aimed at anyone Scottish, Irish or Celtic. Appletree Press does not accept unsolicited manuscripts, but will consider ideas or synopses for gift books or general interest Scottish or Irish non-fiction.

Arcadia Books

15–16 Nassau Street, London, W1W 7AB
- 020 7436 9898
- 020 7436 9898
- info@arcadiabooks.co.uk
- www.arcadiabooks.co.uk

Contact Managing Director, Gary Pulsifer; Associate Publisher, Daniela de Groote
Established 1996
Imprint(s) BlackAmber
Bliss Books
Eurocrime
Insider Info Catalogue available online.
Non-Fiction Publishes Autobiography, Biography and General Non-Fiction titles on the following subjects:
Memoirs, Travel.
Submission Guidelines Agented submissions only.
Fiction Publishes Ethnic, Gay/Lesbian, Literary, Mainstream/Contemporary, Multicultural, Short Story Collections, Suspense, Translation, European Crime Writing titles.
Submission Guidelines Agented submissions only.
Recent Title(s) *The Envoy*, Edward Wilson (Fiction, Arcadia Imprint); *Ken: The Ups and Downs of Ken Livingstone*, Andrew Hosken (Biography, Arcadia Imprint)
Tips Of the different imprints, Arcadia publishes fiction, translated world fiction, biography, memories, travel, and gay and gender studies. BlackAmber publishes multicultural literary fiction, non-fiction and translations. Bliss publishes popular best sellers, including biography and autobiography. Eurocrime publishes European crime writing. Arcadia Books does not consider poetry, plays, short stories, children's, teenage, science fiction, fantasy, horror, romance or self-help titles.

Architectural Press

Linacre House, Jordan Hill, Oxford, OX2 8DP
- 01865 474010
- 01865 474011
- authorsupport@elsevier.com
- www.elsevier.com

Parent Company Elsevier Ltd (Science & Technology)
Insider Info Payment is via royalties. Catalogue and manuscript guidelines available online.
Non-Fiction Publishes Reference, Scholarly and Technical titles on the following subjects:
Architecture, Building/Construction, Urban Design
Submission Guidelines Accepts query with SAE with proposal package (including outline).
Recent Title(s) *The Ecology of Building Materials*, Berge (Construction)

123

Tips Architectural Press publishes technical, theoretical and practical books written by experts from around the globe. The list of titles covers the full range of topics within architecture, from new theory through to practical design guides, breaking new ground and aiding work and study. They welcome authors' proposals for books. The first step is to discuss the proposal with the relevant publishing editor. Check the website for in-depth submission guidelines and a full list of editorial contacts.

Arcturus Publishers Ltd

26/27 Bickels Yard, 151–153 Bermondsey Street, London, SE1 3HA

📞 020 7407 9400
📠 020 7407 9444
✉ info@arcturuspublishing.com
🌐 www.arcturuspublishing.com

Parent Company Foulsham Publishers
Insider Info Catalogue is free on request and available online.
Non-Fiction Publishes Children's, General Non-Fiction, Illustrated, Reference and Self-Help titles on the following subjects:
Art/Architecture, Health/Medicine, History, Spirituality, Puzzles and Games, Practical Art and Manga, Real Crime
Submission Guidelines Accepts proposal package (including outline, author biography, SAE, information on the market position of the book, its competitors and its readership).
Recent Title(s) *The Nicotine Conspiracy* Allen Carr
Tips Will not accept emailed submissions.

The Arden Shakespeare

High Holborn House, 50–51 Bedford Row, London, WC1R 4LR

📞 020 7067 2500
📠 020 7067 2600
✉ margaret.bartley@thomson.com
🌐 www.ardenshakespeare.com

Parent Company Methuen Drama
Contact Editors: Richard Proudfoot, Ann Thompson, David Scott Kastan and Henry Woudhuysen
Insider Info Catalogue available online.
Non-Fiction Publishes Criticisms, Dictionaries of Quotations and Gift titles on Literary Criticism.
Fiction Publishes Plays.
Recent Title(s) *Shakespeare's Poems*, Katherine Duncan Jones and H.R. Woudhuysen
Tips Titles are aimed at teachers, scholars, students and general readers with an interest in Shakespeare's works. *The Arden Shakespeare* series was created by Methuen towards the end of the 19th Century. In 1995, The third series of *The Arden*

Shakespeare was launched as an imprint. The publishers focus largely on the works of Shakespeare.

Argentum

7 Greenland Street, London, NW1 0ND

📞 020 7284 7160
📠 020 7845 4902
✉ editorial@aurumpress.co.uk
🌐 www.aurumpress.co.uk

Parent Company Aurum Press (Quarto Group Inc.)
Contact Consultant Editor, Eddie Ephraums
Insider Info Catalogue is free on request and available online, or via an online request form. Manuscript guidelines are available by email.
Non-Fiction Publishes Coffee Table, General Non-Fiction, How-To and Technical titles on Photography.
Submission Guidelines Accepts email with brief proposal in the first instance.
Submission details to: onephraums@uk2.net
Recent Title(s) *Expression*, Paul Gallagher (Photography)
Tips Argentum publishes high quality practical photography titles and is now recognised as a leading publisher for photography books.

Arris Books

12 Main Street, Adlestrop, Moreton in Marsh, Gloucestershire, GL56 0YN

📞 01608 659328
📠 01608 659345
✉ info@arrisbooks.com
✉ victoriama.huxley@btinternet.com
🌐 www.arrisbooks.com

Contact Publishing Director, Victoria Huxley
Established 2003
Insider Info Submissions accompanied by SAE will be returned. Catalogue and manuscript guidelines available online.
Non-Fiction Publishes General Non-Fiction, Illustrated and Scholarly titles on the following subjects:
Culture, History, Politics & Current Affairs, Travel
Submission Guidelines Accepts query with SAE and proposal package (including outline and one sample chapter). Do not email submissions.
Fiction Publishes Multicultural and Translated Fiction titles.
Submission Guidelines Accepts query with SAE and proposal package (including outline and one sample chapter). Do not email submissions.
Recent Title(s) *Palestinian Costume*, Shelagh Weir (Culture); *Traveller's History of Bath*, Richard and Sheila Tames

Tips Titles aimed at travellers interested in world culture, not tourism. All submissions should reflect this principle.

Arrow

Random House, 20 Vauxhall Bridge Road, London, SW1V 2SA

- 020 7840 8518
- 020 7233 6127
- arroweditorial@randomhouse.co.uk
- www.randomhouse.co.uk

Parent Company The Random House Group Ltd
Contact Publishing Director, Kate Elton
Insider Info Catalogue available online.
Non-Fiction Publishes Autobiography, Biography and General Non-Fiction titles.
Submission Guidelines Agented submissions only.
Fiction Publishes mass market paperback Fiction titles.
Submission Guidelines Agented submissions only.
Recent Title(s) *Artistic Licence*, Katie Fforde (Fiction); *A Liverpool Lass*, Katie Flynn (Fiction)
Tips Writers are recommended to get a literary agent, as Arrow will not accept unagented submissions.

Artech House

16 Sussex Street, London, SW1V 4RW

- 020 7596 8750
- 020 7630 0166
- artech-uk@artechhouse.co.uk
- www.artechhouse.com

Parent Company Horizon House Publications Inc
Contact Senior Publishing Editor, Dr Simon Plumtree
Established 1969
Insider Info Publishes 65 titles per year. Payment is via royalty. Catalogue and manuscript guidelines available online.
Non-Fiction Publishes Reference, Scholarly, Technical and Textbook titles on the following subjects:
Agriculture/Horticulture, Communications, Computers/Electronics, Science, Software, Nanotechnology, Bioinformatics/Biomedical Engineering
Submission Guidelines Accepts query with SAE, or via email with proposal package (including outline, one sample chapter, reference forms and details of equations/figures and your publishing history). You may also fill in the online submission form, or submit a completed manuscript.
Submission details to: splumtree@artechhouse.co.uk
Recent Title(s) *Nano-Optics and Near-Field Optical Microscopy*, Anatoly Zayats (Technical/Reference)

Tips Artech House is a leading publisher of high quality professional books with titles aimed at engineers and managers, as well as high technology professionals and students internationally. They accept practical and informed proposals, ideally from academic or industry professionals in the specified subject areas.

Ashfield Press

30 Linden Grove, Blackrock, Co. Dublin, Republic of Ireland

- 00353 1 288 9808
- info@ashfieldpress.com
- www.ashfieldpress.com

Contact Director, Susan Waine
Imprint(s) Linden Press (Self Publishing)
Insider Info Catalogue available online.
Non-Fiction Publishes Autobiography, Biography, Cookbooks, General Non-Fiction, Scholarly and Self-Help titles on the following subjects:
Art/Architecture, Cooking/Foods/Nutrition, Culture, History, Military/War, Regional, Travel, Irish Folklore/Irish History.
Recent Title(s) *Faster, Higher, Stronger*, Lindie Naughton and Johnny Watterson (Sports); *Dublin's Magical Museums*, Muriel Bolger (Culture)
Tips Ashfield Press only publishes Irish non-fiction, but with sister company Linden Press, also offers various self publishing services in Ireland, including proofreading and editing.

Ashgate Publishing Group

Wey Court East, Union Road, Farnham, Surrey, GU9 7PT

- 01252 331551
- 01252 736736
- info@ashgate.com
- www.ashgate.com

Contact Publishers: Thomas Gray and John Smedley (History); Erika Gaffney (Art and Visual Culture, Literary Studies); Sarah Lloyd (Theology and Religious Studies); Alison Kirk (Law and Legal Studies); Kirstin Howgate (Politics); Publishing Director, Dymphna Evans (Social Sciences and Reference); Commissioning Editor, Guy Loft (Aviation); Publishing Director (Gower), Jonathan Norman
Established 1967
Imprint(s) Gower
Lund Humphries
Ashgate
Insider Info Publishes roughly 700 titles per year. Average lead time is between four and nine months. Catalogue and manuscript guidelines available online.

Non-Fiction Publishes Reference, Scholarly, Technical and Textbook titles on the following subjects:
Art/Architecture, Business/Economics, Education, Ethnic, Government/Politics, History, Humanities, Language/Literature, Law, Music/Dance, Philosophy, Social Sciences, Sociology, and Aviation
* The publishing programme is not centred around textbooks and journals but instead around ground breaking academic research publications, business practice guides and illustrated art books. Books published within the Ashgate programme are subject to peer review by recognised authorities in the field.
Submission Guidelines Accepts proposal package (including outline, table of contents, extent, illustration information, your publishing history, author biography, market research). Address proposals to the relevant commissioning editor (see contacts).
Tips Writers published within the Ashgate group are mostly experts in their fields and not necessarily career writers.

Ashley Drake Publishing Ltd
PO Box 733, Cardiff, Wales, CF14 7ZY
- 07803 940867
- 0870 705 2582
- post@ashleydrake.com
- www.ashleydrake.com

Contact Managing Director, Ashley Drake
Established 1994
Imprint(s) Welsh Academic Press
Scandinavian Academic Press
St David's Press
Welsh Educational Press
Y Ddraig Fach (The Little Dragon)
Insider Info Receives approximately ten queries per year and ten manuscripts per year. Three per cent of books published are from first-time authors and 100 per cent of books published are from unagented authors. Payment is via royalty on net receipts. Average lead time is one year, with simultaneous submissions not accepted. Submissions accompanied by SAE will be returned. Aims to respond to queries within five days, and proposals and manuscripts within one month. Catalogue is free on request, and available online or by email. Manuscript guidelines are available online.
Non-Fiction Publishes Autobiography, Biography, Scholarly and Textbook titles on the following subjects:
Business/Economics, Education, Government/Politics, History, Humanities, Language/Literature, Memoirs, Sports
* Welsh Academic Press and Scandinavian Academic Press focus on scholarly books; St David's press is a trade imprint; Welsh Educational Press publishes educational books; and Y Ddraig Fach has published children's books.
Submission Guidelines Not currently accepting any proposals or manuscripts.
Tips Ashley Drake is not currently commissioning any new material. Check website for any updates in commissioning status.

Ashmolean Museum Publications
Ashmolean Museum, Beaumont Street, Oxford, OX1 2PH
- 01865 278010
- 01865 278018
- publications@ashmus.ox.ac.uk
- www.ashmolean.org

Contact Publications Manager, Declan McCarthy; Publications Deputy Manager, Emily Jolliffe; Picture Library Manager, Amanda Turner
Insider Info Catalogue available online.
Non-Fiction Publishes Children's, Gift Books, Textbooks, Illustrated, Reference, Scholarly and Technical titles on the following subjects:
Anthropology/Archaeology, Art/Architecture, Crafts, Education, History, Photography, Science
Recent Title(s) *Watches in the Ashmolean Museum*, David Thomson; *The Alfred Jewel*, David Hinton; *Early Himalayan Art*, Amy Heller; *Chinese Prints 1950-2006*, Weimin He and Shelagh Vainker; *Sir John Evans 1823-1908*, Arthur MacGregor
Tips The publications department supports the Ashmolean's mission to disseminate information and educate the public through its collection. Only books directly concerned with the museum's own collections are published. Most of the authors are staff at the Ashmolean Museum, although sometimes an academic from another institution is appointed to write a book, if they are experts on the particular subject. Authors are not generally encouraged to submit manuscripts.

Atlantean Publishing
38 Pierrot Steps, 71 Kursaal Way, Southend on Sea, Essex, SS1 2UY
- atlanteanpublishing@hotmail.com
- www.geocities.com/dj_tyrer/atlantean_pub

Contact David John Tyrer
Insider Info Authors are paid with a free copy of the publication. Does not accept simultaneous submissions. Submissions accompanied by SAE will be returned. Aims to respond to proposals within six weeks. Catalogue and author guidelines available online.
Non-Fiction Publishes General Non-Fiction (Local Interest) and How-To (Particularly on writing and publishing with small presses) titles.

Submission Guidelines Submit proposal package by post or email. Will review artworks/photographs as part of the proposal package. Include as A4 or A5 photocopies, or digital files as jpegs. Text should be single sided.

Poetry Publishes Poetry Booklets and single poet broadsheet style papers, *The Bards*.

Submission Guidelines Accepts queries – submit sample poems or complete manuscript. Submissions should either be by email or post, single sided pages only.

Recent Title(s) *Grail* Ian O'Reilly and DJ Tyrer (Anthology)

Tips Atlantean Publishing also publishes five magazines; *Monomyth*, *The Supplement*, *BARD*, *AWEN*, and *Garbaj*. Submissions should be made to the company overall, and will be published in whatever medium the editors feel most suitable. The company prefers first British serial rights, but will consider previously published work as long as it is declared. SAEs are recommended if you wish your work to be returned, but if you do not need it back you may include a return email address instead.

Atlantic Books
26–27 Boswell Street, London, WC1N 3JZ
- 020 7269 1610
- 020 7430 0916
- enquiries@groveatlantic.co.uk
- www.groveatlantic.co.uk

Parent Company Grove/Atlantic Inc (see entry under European & International Publishers)
Contact Chairman & Publisher, Toby Mundy; Managing Director, Daniel Scott; Editor-in-Chief, Ravi Mirchandani
Established 2000
Insider Info Publishes roughly 90 titles per year. Publishing partner of *The Guardian* and *The Observer*.
Non-Fiction Publishes General Non-Fiction titles on the following subjects:
History, Current Affairs, Biography, Politics, Popular Sciecne and Reference.
Fiction Publishes Crime and Literary Fiction.
Tips No unsolicited submissions. Accepts agented submissions only.

Atlantic Europe Publishing Co. Ltd
Greys Court Farm, Grey's Court, Henley on Thames, Oxon, RG9 4PG
- 01491 628188
- 01491 628189
- enquiries@atlanticeurope.com
- www.atlanticeurope.com

Established 1990
Insider Info Accepts queries via email. Catalogues available online.

Non-Fiction Publishes Children's Educational and Reference titles on the following subjects:
Science, Maths, History, Technology, Geography, English, Spelling, Citizenship and R.E.
Submission Guidelines Accepts emailed submissions only.
Tips Prefers authors with relevant qualifications, such as teachers and other educational professionals.

Atom
100 Victoria Embankment, London, EC4Y 0DY
- 020 7911 8000
- 020 7911 8100
- atom@littlebrown.co.uk
- www.atombooks.co.uk

Parent Company Little, Brown Book Group
Contact Publishing Director, Tim Holman; Editorial Director, Darren Nash
Established 2002
Insider Info Submissions accompanied by SAE will be returned. Aims to respond to proposals within 12 weeks. Catalogue available online.
Fiction Publishes Fantasy and Science Fiction for Young Adults.
* Only able to read unsolicited submissions for novels in the science fiction genre. No other genres, short stories or poetry.
Submission Guidelines Send an outline and no more than 30 pages of double spaced text, and SAE.
Tips Prefers agented submissions. Does not accept email submissions.

Aureus Publishing Ltd
Castle Court, Castle upon Alun, St Brides Major, Vale of Glamorgan, CF32 0TN
- 01656 880033
- 01656 880033
- info@aureus.co.uk
- www.aureus.co.uk

Parent Company Quarto Group Inc.
Established 1993
Insider Info Publishes two titles per year. Receives approximately 50 queries and 20 manuscripts per year. 80 per cent of books published are from first-time authors and 100 per cent of books published are from unagented authors. Payment is via royalty (on wholesale price) with 0.01 (Per £) minimum. Average lead time is one year, with simultaneous submissions accepted. Submissions accompanied by SAE will be returned. Aims to respond to queries and proposals within three days, and manuscripts within one week. Catalogue and manuscript guidelines are available online.
Non-Fiction Publishes Celebrity Autobiography and Celebrity Biography titles on the following subjects:

Music/Dance, Sports, Entertainment.
Submission Guidelines Accepts query with SAE, or preferably by email, with proposal package (including outline and SAE) and artworks/images (send digital files as jpegs). Synopsis should be no more than 250 words. If Aureus Publishing is interested then further material will be requested.
Recent Title(s) *Born To Boogie*, Carl Ewens (Rock Biography)
Tips Readership is generally males in their 30s. Prospective authors are expected to thoroughly know their subject. If the book has little sales value, and the author is willing to take the risk, then Aureus Publishing will consider taking a subsidy published book.

Aurora Metro Publications
2 Oriel Court, The Green, Twickenham, TW2 5AG
- 020 8898 4488
- 020 8898 0735
- info@aurorametro.com
- www.aurorametro.com

Contact Publisher (Drama, Fiction, Biography), Cheryl Robson
Established 1989
Imprint(s) Amp Books
Insider Info Publishes eight titles per year. Receives approximately 100 queries and 25 manuscripts per year. Ten per cent of books published are from first-time authors and 50 per cent of books published are from unagented authors. 20 per cent of books published are author-subsidy published, based on funding available from the Arts Council. Payment is via royalty (on retail price), or outright purchase. Average lead time is one year, with simultaneous submissions accepted. Submissions will not be returned. Aims to respond to queries within ten days, proposals within four months, and manuscripts within six months. Catalogue is free on request, or available by email.
Non-Fiction Publishes Biography, Children's, Cookbooks, General Non-Fiction, Humour, Illustrated and Reference titles on the following subjects: Business/Economics, Contemporary Culture, Cooking/Foods/Nutrition, Creative Non-Fiction, Education, Ethnic, Gay/Lesbian, History, Humanities, Language/Literature, Multicultural, Music/Dance, Translation, Women's Issues/Studies, Young Adult
Submission Guidelines Accepts proposal package (including outline, synopsis, three sample chapters, author biography, reviews, your publishing history and clips) and artworks/images (send photocopies).
Fiction Publishes Adventure, Erotica, Ethnic, Experimental, Fantasy, Feminist, Gay/Lesbian, Gothic, Historical, Horror, Humour, Children's, Literary, Mainstream/Contemporary, Multicultural, Multimedia, Mystery, Plays, Regional, Romance,

Science Fiction, Suspense, Translation and Young Adult titles
Submission Guidelines Accepts proposal package (including outline, synopsis, three sample chapters, author biography and reviews).
Recent Title(s) *Sobiber*, Jean Molla (Young Adult)
Tips Aurora Metro specialises in theatre and play scripts, and often seeks subsidies from the Arts Council for projects that fall within their funding criteria, such as translations.

Aurum Press
7 Greenland Street, London, NW1 0ND
- 020 7284 7160
- 020 7485 4902
- editorial@aurumpress.co.uk
- www.aurumpress.co.uk

Contact Managing Director, Bill McCreadie; Editorial Director, Graham Coster; Consultant Editor (Photography), Eddie Ephraums
Established 1976
Imprint(s) Argentum
Jacqui Small
Insider Info Publishes roughly 75 titles per year. Catalogue and manuscript guidelines are available online.
Non-Fiction Publishes Biography, General Non-Fiction, Gift Books, Illustrated and Reference titles on the following subjects: Art/Architecture, Health, History, Military/War, Music, Sports, Travel, Current Affairs, Film, Walking Guides
Submission Guidelines Accepts queries by email.
Recent Title(s) *The Guardian Book of Rock and Roll*, Michael Hann, ed. (Music)
Tips Aurum Press is a medium sized independent publishing company that has built a reputation for topical, original and critically-acclaimed non-fiction. Aurum Press also publishes titles alongside alliances such as *Country Life* and the National Trust for Scotland, as well as successfully collaborating with *The Guardian* and the *Daily Telegraph*.

Australian Consolidated Press UK
10 Scirroco Close, Moulton Park Office Village, Northampton, NN3 6AP
- 01604 642200
- 01604 642300
- books@acpuk.com
- www.australian-womens-weekly.co.uk

Contact Director, Laura Bamford
Insider Info Catalogue is available online.
Non-Fiction Publishes General Non-Fiction and How-To titles on the following subjects: Cooking, Craft & Home, Foods, Gardening, Health & Nutrition, International Cuisine

Recent Title(s) *Tex Mex*, Australian Women's Weekly (Cooking); *Foods of the Mediterranean*, Australian Women's Weekly (Cooking)

Tips Specialists in innovative cooking and food preparation books. New titles are often commissioned in-house. Also publishes some craft, health and gardening titles for an international market. ACP Books UK distributes the *Australian Women's Weekly Cookbook* series throughout Europe and the Middle East.

Authentic Media
9 Holdom Avenue, Bletchley, Milton Keynes, MK1 1QR
- 01908 364213
- 01908 648952
- kath.williams@authenticmedia.co.uk
- www.authenticmedia.co.uk

Contact Publishing Co-ordinator, Kath Williams (Authentic); Robin Parry, Commissioning Editor (Paternoster)

Established 1962

Imprint(s) Authentic
Paternoster Press

Insider Info Publishes roughly 50 titles per year. Catalogue available online.

Non-Fiction Publishes Audio cassettes, Autobiography, Biography, Children's, General Non-Fiction, Gift Books, Illustrated Books, Multimedia, e-books/i-books and Scholarly titles on the following subjects:
Alternative Lifestyles, Child Guidance/Parenting, Religion, Spirituality

Fiction Publishes Children's, Multimedia, Religious, Spiritual and Young Adult titles.

Recent Title(s) *Breakout*, Stibbe and Williams

Tips Publishes Christian books to help all types of Christians, as well as music and other media content. Welcomes unsolicited manuscripts or synopsis submissions for fiction or non-fiction, sent by post or email to the editor. Does not publish poetry.

Autumn Publishing
Appledram Barns, Birdham Road, Chichester, West Sussex, PO20 7EQ
- 01243 531660
- 01243 538160
- autumn@autumnpublishing.co.uk
- www.autumnpublishing.net

Contact Editorial Director, Lyn Coutts

Established 1976

Imprint(s) Byeway Books

Insider Info Publishes around 200 titles per year. Submissions will not be not returned. Catalogue available online.

Non-Fiction Publishes Children's, Illustrated Books and Children's Activity Books.

Submission Guidelines Email submissions to anna@autumnpublishing.co.uk

Fiction Publishes Children's and Picture Books.

Recent Title(s) *All About Animals*, (Time to Shine series)

Tips All books are published under the Byeway Books imprint. Titles are aimed at giving children the chance to enjoy learning while they play. The creative teams work hard to ensure that the books are at the forefront of current trends and that the range is always fresh and vibrant. Focuses on younger children's and infant's activity books, which are often in high demand.

AVON
77–85 Fulham Palace Road, Hammersmith, London, W6 8JB
- 020 8741 7070
- 020 8307 4440
- uk.orders@harpercollins.co.uk
- www.avon-books.co.uk

Parent Company HarperCollins Publishers Ltd – General Books Division

Contact Publishing Director, Michael Doggart

Established 2007

Insider Info Catalogue available online.

Fiction Publishes Women's Fiction titles.

Submission Guidelines Agented submissions only.

Recent Title(s) *Love Struck*, Melanie Rose (Women's Fiction); *Desperate Measures*, Kitty Neale (Women's Fiction)

Tips AVON publishes a wide range of debut and established authors, both British and international, and aims to fast-track them to bestseller status.

Award Publications
The Old Riding School, The Welbeck Estate, Worksop, Nottinghamshire, S80 3LR
- 01909 478170
- 01909 484632
- info@awardpublications.co.uk
- www.awardpublications.co.uk

Established 1972

Insider Info Catalogue and manuscript guidelines are available online.

Non-Fiction Publishes Children's and Reference titles on the following subjects:
Crafts, Creative Non-Fiction, Education, Entertainment/Games

Submission Guidelines Accepts query with SAE/proposal package (including outline, one to two sample chapters and SAE) and artwork/images via email or post.

Fiction Publishes Children's, Picture Books, Religious, Short Story Collections and General Children's titles.
Submission Guidelines Accepts query with SAE/ proposal package (including outline, one to two sample chapters and SAE).
Recent Title(s) *Billy Brownmouse Won't Go to Sleep*, (Picutre Book)
Tips Titles are aimed at children and infants, and parents. Always on the lookout, particularly for new illustrators and designers. Send samples by post or email.

Badger Publishing
15 Wedgewood Gate, Pin Green Industrial Estate, Stevenage, Hertfordshire, SG1 4SU
- 01438 356907
- 01438 747015
- info@badger-publishing.co.uk
- www.badger-publishing.co.uk
Established 1989
Insider Info Catalogue available online.
Non-fiction Publishes Children's Educational and Reference titles on the following subjects:
All curriculum subjects from Foundation to Year 9.
Tips Badger Publishing started by selling educational books into schools, but over recent years has developed a publishing programme of its own. Books are aimed at both pupils and teachers.

Baillière Tindall
Linacre House, Jordan Hill, Oxford, OX2 8DP
- 01865 474010
- 01865 474011
- authorsupport@elsevier.com
- www.elsevierhealth.com/bt
Parent Company Elsevier Ltd (Health Sciences)
Established 1869
Insider Info Royalties paid. Catalogue available online. Manuscript guidelines available online.
Non-Fiction Publishes Multimedia, Scholarly, Technical, Textbook, Journal and Reference titles on the following subjects:
Education, Health/Medicine, Care/ Nursing, Midwifery
Submission Guidelines Fill in and return a proposal form, available on the website. Alternatively, authors may contact the publishing director or editor prior to submission to discuss the proposal.
Submission details to: c.makepeace@elsevier.com
Recent Title(s) *The Clinical Placement, A Nursing Survival Guide*, Levett-Jones and Bourgeois (Midwifery)
Tips The longest established publisher for all aspects of the nursing and midwifery professions. Baillière Tindall have always held the needs of nurses paramount, and have established a tradition of 'books for nurses, by nurses'. Baillière Tindall also publishes the renowned *Baillière's Best Practice & Research* series of journals.

Bantam Press
61–63 Uxbridge Road, London, W5 5SA
- 020 8579 2652
- 020 8579 5479
- info@transworld-publishers.co.uk
- www.booksattransworld.co.uk
Parent Company Transworld Publishers
Insider Info Catalogue available online. Manuscript guidelines not available.
Non-Fiction Publishes General Non-Fiction titles on the following subjects:
Diet and Healthy Eating
Submission Guidelines Agented submissions only.
Fiction Publishes Historical, Mainstream/ Contemporary, Military/War, Mystery, Romance and Suspense titles.
Submission Guidelines Agented submissions only.
Recent Title(s) *Twelve*, Jasper Kent (Military/Horror)
Tips Bantam Press publishes hardbacks only.

The Barddas Society
Pen-rhiw, 71 Ffordd Pentrepoeth, Treforys, Abertawe, Cymru, SA6 6AE
- 01792 772636
- 01792 792829
Non-fiction Publishes Biography and General Non-Fiction titles on the following subjects:
Literature, Literary Criticism, Literary History
* All titles are related to Welsh poetry.
Poetry Publishes Welsh Poetry Collections and Anthologies.
Tips The Barddas Society publishes an annual journal of poetry as well as books relating to Welsh poetry. It has produced over a hundred different titles, mainly focusing on poetry, literary criticism, literary history and biographies of well-known poets.

Bardfield Press
The Bardfield Centre, Great Bardfield, Essex, CM7 4SL
- 01371 811309
- 01371 811393
- info@mileskelly.net
- www.mileskelly.net
Contact Miles Kelly Publishing Ltd
Non-Fiction Publishes Children's titles.
Submission Guidelines Do not send any unsolicited manuscripts.
Fiction Publishes Children's titles.
Submission Guidelines Do not send any unsolicited manuscripts.

Tips An imprint of Miles Kelly Publishing focused specifically on children's books with a mass market appeal.

Barefoot Books Ltd
124 Walcot Street, Bath, Somerset, BA1 5BG
- 01225 322400
- 01225 322499
- info@barefootbooks.co.uk
- www.barefootbooks.com

Contact Editor in Chief, Tessa Strickland (Picture Books, Young Fiction)
Established 1993
Insider Info Publishes 16 titles per year, 15 per cent of books published are from first-time authors and 75 per cent of books published are from unagented authors. Payment is via royalty (on wholesale price) with 0.025 (per £) minimum and 0.05 (per £) maximum. Advance offered is variable. Average lead time is over 18 months, with simultaneous submissions accepted. Submissions will not be returned. Aims to respond to queries within eight weeks. Catalogue is free on request, and available online. Manuscript guidelines are available online.
Non-Fiction Publishes Children's Illustrated on the following subjects:
Multicultural, Nature/Environment, Spirituality, Travel
Submission Guidelines Accepts query with SAE, or send completed manuscript.
Fiction Publishes Illustrated Children's Fiction.
Submission Guidelines Accepts query with SAE, or send completed manuscript.

Barn Owl Books
157 Fortis Green Road, London, N10 3LX
- ann@barnowlbooks.com
- www.barnowlbooks.com

Contact Ann Jungman
Insider Info Catalogue available online.
Non-Fiction Publishes Out-of-print Children's titles.
Fiction Publishes Out-of-print Children's titles.
Tips Publishes reprints of out-of-print children's books only, no new titles.

Barny Books
The Cottage, Hough on the Mill, Grantham, Lincolnshire, NG32 2HL
- 01400 250246
- 01400 251737
- barnybooks@hotmail.co.uk
- www.barnybooks.biz

Contact Managing Director, Molly Burkett
Established 1980

Insider Info Catalogue available online. Too small to accept unsolicited manuscripts. Manuscript guidelines not available.
Non-Fiction Publishes Children's, Illustrated Books and General Non-Fiction titles on the following subjects:
Cooking/Foods/Nutrition, Health /Medicine, History, Hobbies, Military/War
Submission Guidelines Accepts query with SAE.
Fiction Publishes Historical, Children's, Military/War and Young Adult titles.
Submission Guidelines Accepts query with SAE.
Tips Barny Books offers professional critiquing and editing services, as well as some self publishing facilities. This process can also include translation when the author's first language is not English, and help for those who are dyslexic, handicapped or elderly. Be advised that services are fee-based and the minimum order for book printing is 300 copies.

Barrington Stoke
18 Walker Street, Edinburgh, EH3 7LP
- 0131 225 4113
- 0131 225 4140
- barrington@barringtonstoke.co.uk
- www.barringtonstoke.co.uk

Contact Publishing Administrator, Fiona Brown
Established 1998
Insider Info Catalogue available online or with SAE. Manuscript guidelines not available.
Non-Fiction Publishes Children's, How-To, Reference, Scholarly, Textbook and Self-Help titles for teachers or parents of struggling readers, on the following subjects:
Child Guidance/Parenting, Guidance, Education, Young Adult
Submission Guidelines Does not accept unsolicited manuscripts.
Fiction Publishes Children's Picture Books, Short Story collections, and Young Adult titles.
Submission Guidelines Does not accept unsolicited manuscripts.
Recent Title(s) *United Here I Come!*, Alan Combes; *One Mistake*, Joanna Hines
Tips Titles are aimed at children/young adults (struggling readers), and children with dyslexia or a learning difficulty. Texts must be subtly adapted, so that these children do not feel patronised or short changed. Accessible language, a fast moving and unambiguous plot and clear presentation are essential.

Batsford
10 Southcombe Street, London, W14 0RA
- 020 7605 1400
- 020 7605 1401

○ krichardson@anovabooks.com
ⓦ www.anovabooks.com/imprint/batsford
Parent Company Anova Books Company Ltd
Established 1843
Insider Info Catalogue available online.
Non-fiction Publishes General and Illustrated titles
on the following subjects:
Art, Embroidery & Textiles, Chess, Heritage,
Horticulture, Fashion & Design
Submission Guidelines Accepts proposal package
(including outline, synopsis and sample chapter) by
post, addressed to 'Publisher, Batsford'.
Recent Title(s) *Corsets*, Jill Salen (Fashion); *Free
Expression in Acrylics*, John Hammond (Art)
Tips Titles are aimed at serious enthusiasts and
professionals in many hobbyist areas.

BBC Active
Edinburgh Gate, Harlow, Essex, CM20 2JE
☏ 01279 623623
☏ 01279 414130
○ emma.shackleton@pearson.com
ⓦ www.bbcactive.com
Parent Company Pearson Education
Insider Info Catalogue and manuscript guidelines
are available online.
Non-Fiction Publishes Multimedia, Scholarly and
Textbooks titles on the following subjects:
Education, Home Learning, Languages
Submission Guidelines Accepts proposal package
(including synopsis, sample chapters, market
research, your publishing history and author
biography).
Tips BBC Active publishes learning resources for
children and adults, at home, school and college.
The imprint has developed a wide range of
innovative and interactive ways of learning to suit all
styles with DVDs, CD-ROMs and online products.
Resources cover the school curriculum and adult
learning across modern foreign languages, plus a
variety of other skills. Formerly known as BBC
Worldwide Learning.

BBC Books
**Random House, 20 Vauxhall Bridge Road,
London, SW1V 2SA**
☏ 020 7840 8400
☏ 020 7233 8791
○ emarketing@randomhouse.co.uk
ⓦ www.randomhouse.co.uk
Parent Company The Random House Group Ltd
Insider Info Catalogue available online.
Non-Fiction Publishes Cookbooks, Gift Books,
Illustrated Books, Television Tie-Ins and Reference
titles covering a wide range of subjects, including
Science Fiction.

Fiction Publishes Television Tie-In titles.
Recent Title(s) *It's Not Easy Being Green: One Family's
Journey Towards Eco-friendly Living*, Dick Strawbridge
(Eco-Living); *Doctor Who: Beautiful Chaos*, Gary
Russell (Sci-Fi/TV Tie-In)
Tips The vast majority of BBC Books are direct spin-
offs from BBC television programmes.

BBC Children's Books
80 Strand, London, WC2R 0RL
☏ 020 7010 3000
☏ 020 7010 6060
○ customer.service@penguin.co.uk
ⓦ www.penguin.co.uk
Parent Company Penguin Group UK
Established 2004
Insider Info Catalogue available online.
Non-Fiction Publishes Children's, General Non-
Fiction, Illustrated, Novelty and Television Tie-
In titles.
Submission Guidelines Agented submissions only.
Fiction Publishes Children's Television Tie-In titles.
Submission Guidelines Agented submissions only.
Recent Title(s) *Sarah Jane Adventures: Day of the
Clown*, Phil Ford (TV Tie-in)
Tips BBC Children's Books publishes illustrated titles
ranging from pre-school to older children. Most
books and products are linked to BBC children's
programmes. No unsolicited submissions.

Beautiful Books
36–38 Glasshouse Street, London, W1B 5DL
☏ 020 7734 4448
☏ 020 3070 0764
○ office@beautiful-books.co.uk
ⓦ www.beautiful-books.co.uk
Contact Publisher, Simon Petherick
Established 2005
Imprint(s) Bloody Books
Burning House
Insider Info Publishes 15 titles per year. Receives
500 queries and 300 manuscripts per year. 30 per
cent of books published are from first-time authors
and 30 per cent of books published are from
unagented authors. Payment via royalty (on
wholesale price) with 0.15 (per £) minimum and 0.20
(per £) maximum, or outright purchase. Advance
offered is from £1–£1,000. Average lead time is eight
months, with simultaneous submissions accepted.
Submissions accompanied by SAE will be returned.
Aims to respond to queries within seven days,
proposals within 18 days and manuscripts within
two months. Catalogue is free on request, and
available online, or by email. Manuscript guidelines
are available online.

Non-Fiction Publishes General Non-Fiction, Gift and Illustrated titles on the following subjects: Contemporary Culture, Current Affairs
Submission Guidelines Accepts query with SAE, or via email, and artworks/images (send photocopies or digital files as jpegs). All proposals will be considered on their merits.
Submission details to: submissions@beautiful-books.co.uk
Fiction Publishes Confession, Erotica, Gay/Lesbian, Horror, Humour, Literary, Mainstream/Contemporary, Picture Books and Translation titles.
* Horror fiction is published under the Bloody Books imprint, whilst contemporary fiction is published under the Burning House imprint.
Submission Guidelines Accepts query with SAE or via email.
Submission details to: submissions@beautiful-books.co.uk
Recent Title(s) *Will,* Christopher Rush (Literary Fiction); *Redress*, Adele Hartley (Psychological Thriller)
Tips When submitting to Beautiful Books be clear and patient, and give as much information about yourself as you can.

Benjamin Cummings
Edinburgh Gate, Harlow, Essex, CM20 2JE
☎ 01279 623623
☎ 01279 414130
🌐 www.pearsoned.co.uk/imprints/benjamincummings
Parent Company Pearson Education
Insider Info Catalogue and manuscript guidelines are available online.
Non-Fiction Publishes Reference, Scholarly and Textbook titles on the following subjects: Anatomy, Biology, Health, Physiology, Science
Submission Guidelines Accepts proposal package (including synopsis, sample chapters, market research, your publishing history and author biography).
Recent Title(s) *InterActive Physiology 10-System Suite CD-ROM*, Benjamin Cummings (Science)
Tips Benjamin Cummings specialises in the areas of anatomy and physiology, biology, health, kinesiology and microbiology. Work is published in both printed and electronic formats. See the website for a full list of submissions contacts.

Berghahn Books
3 Newtec Place, Magdalen Road, Oxford, OX4 1RE
☎ 01865 250011
☎ 01865 250056
✉ publisher@berghahnbooks.com
🌐 www.berghahnbooks.com
Contact Publisher/Editor-in-Chief, Marion Berghahn; Managing & Editorial Director (Journals), Vivian Berghahn; Editors: Mark Stanton (Film & Media), Penny Costley-White (Legal Studies).
Established 1994
Insider Info Publishes 90 titles per year. Catalogue and author guidelines available online. Prospective authors may download a copy of the 'New Book Outline' to be filled out and faxed, or emailed as an attachment to the New York or Oxford offices.
Non-Fiction Publishes General Non-Fiction, e-books and Scholarly titles on the following subjects: Anthropology/Archaeology, Economics, Education, Government/Politics, History, Nature/Environment, Regional, Travel, World Affairs, Migration Studies
Submission Guidelines Accept proposals in the form of a completed 'New Book Outline' form, available from the website. Fill this in and post it to the relevant editor along with a chapter summary.
Recent Title(s) *Taking Sides*, Heidi Armbruster and Anna Laerke, eds. (Anthropology); *All Tomorrows Culture*, Samuel Gerald Collins (Anthropology)
Tips Berghahn Books has a strong transatlantic position and close links to Continental Europe, and aims to further the dialogue between the European and the American scholar. Check the writers' guidelines on the website for style guides and publicity details.

Berg Publishers
1st Floor, Angel Court, 81 St Clements Street, Oxford, OX4 1AW
☎ 01865 245104
☎ 01865 791165
✉ enquiry@bergpublishers.com
🌐 www.bergpublishers.com
Contact Editorial Director, Tristan Palmer (Design/Visual Culture, Reference); Senior Commissioning Editor, Julia Hall (Fashion/Textiles, Journals); Assistant Commissioning Editor, Anna Wright (Anthropology, Fashion, General Queries)
Established 1983
Insider Info Simultaneous submissions not accepted. Submissions accompanied by SAE will be returned. Catalogue and manuscript guidelines available online.
Non-Fiction Publishes General Non-Fiction, Illustrated Book, Reference and Scholarly titles on the following subjects:
Agriculture/Horticulture, Alternative Lifestyles, Anthropology/Archaeology, Art/Architecture, Cooking/Foods/Nutrition, Crafts, Entertainment/Games, Gay/Lesbian, Government/Politics, History, Hobbies, House and Home, Humanities, Language/Literature, Literary Criticism, Philosophy, Sociology, Sports, Women's Issues/Studies, World Affairs

Submission Guidelines Accepts query with SAE/ proposal package (including outline, sample chapter(s), SAE, your publishing history, and author biography) and artworks/images (send transparencies, and digital files and other media as jpegs).

Recent Title(s) *Spirits with Scalpels*, Sidney M. Greenfield (Anthropology); *Underwater and Maritime Archaeology in Latin America and the Caribbean*, Margaret E. Leshikar-Denton and Pilar Luna Erreguerena (Archaeology)

Tips Berg is an international independent publisher committed to innovative ideas in visual and material culture, including fashion and textiles, cultural/ media studies, film, art and design, food, sport, and anthropology. Send submission proposals in the post to the relevant editor enclosing SAE. Be sure to be check the submission guidelines on the website thoroughly prior to posting a proposal.

Berlitz Publishing
APA Publications, 58 Borough High Street, London, SE1 1XF
- 020 7403 0284
- 020 7403 0290
- www.berlitzpublishing.com

Contact Apa Publications (The Langenscheidt Publishing Group)
Contact Managing Director, Jeremy Westwood (Apa Publications)
Established 1970
Insider Info Catalogue is available online.
Non-Fiction Publishes Audio cassettes, Guidebooks, Multimedia and Reference titles on the following subjects:
Travel Guides and Maps, Language Learning/Home Study, Phrasebooks, Travel Packs, Specialist Travel Books
Submission Guidelines Does not accept unsolicited material.
Recent Title(s) *Marrakesh*, Berlitz Pocket Guide (Travel Guide); *Caribbean Ports of Call*, Berlitz Pocket Guide (Travel Guide)

Bernard Babani (Publishing) Ltd
The Grampians, Shepherds Bush Road, London, W6 7NF
- enquiries@babanibooks.com
- www.babanibooks.com

Contact Company Director, Michael Babani
Established 1942
Insider Info Catalogue is available online.
Non-Fiction Publishes How-to, Reference, Technical titles on the following subjects:
Computing, Electronics, Radio, Robotics

Recent Title(s) *An Introduction to Excel Spreadsheets*, J. Gatenby (Computing)
Tips Bernard Babani has been specialising in computer books since 1980. The publisher only commissions specialist expert authors for its titles.

Between the Lines
The Cottage, 14 Lyncroft Gardens, Ewell, Surrey, KT17 1UR
- 020 8393 7055
- 020 8393 7055
- btluk@aol.com
- www.waywiser-press.com/imprints/ betweenthelines.html

Parent Company Waywiser Press
Contact Editor, Peter Dale; Editor, J.D. McClatchy; Editor, Philip Hoy; Editorial Assistant, Ryan Roberts
Established 1998
Insider Info Catalogue is available online.
Non-Fiction Publishes Literary Interviews.
* The subjects of these interviews are well-known contemporary poets, and they run from 20,000-40,000 words. They are typically accompanied by career sketches, bibliographies, poems, quotations from critics and reviewers, and in some cases are also accompanied by galleries of photographs.
Tips A list of past and present interviewers and interviewees is available on the website.

Beyond the Pale Publications Ltd
Unit 2.1.2, Conway Mill, 5-7 Conway Street, Belfast, BT13 2DE
- 028 9043 8630
- 028 9043 9707
- office@btpale.com
- www.btpale.com

Insider Info Catalogue available online. Author guidelines available online.
Non-Fiction Publishes Non-Fiction titles on the following subjects:
Irish Culture, Irish Politics.
Submission Guidelines Submit proposal package (including detailed outline and market research) by post.
Tips Beyond the Pale publishes 'high-quality books which mainstream publishers typically reject for being politically beyond the pale and of limited market potential.'

BFI Publishing
Porters South and Porters North, Crinan Street, London, N1 9XW
- 020 7843 4108
- 020 7843 4640
- r.barden@palgrave.com
- www.bfi.org.uk

Contact British Film Institute
Contact Head of Publishing, Rebecca Barden
Insider Info Catalogue and manuscript guidelines are available online.
Non-Fiction Publishes Illustrated Books, Reference and Scholarly titles on the following subjects: Film Classics, Modern Classics, Television Classics, Screen Classics, Film Criticism/History/Theory, Filmmakers, US Film and Television, British and Irish Film and Television, World Directors, Television Media and Cultural Studies, New Media, Teaching Resources, Understanding the Moving Image
Submission Guidelines Accepts proposal package (including outline, one to two sample chapters, author biography and market research).
Recent Title(s) *Sight & Sound: The Films of 2008*, BFI (Film)
Tips BFI Publishing is the publishing arm of the British Film Institute, publishing a wide range of books and educational materials on cinema/television, and related matters. Titles are aimed at primary and secondary school pupils, undergraduates and teachers, although many titles are also aimed at a broader audience with an informed interest in cinema and television.

Birlinn Ltd
West Newington House, 10 Newington Road, Edinburgh, EH9 1QS
☏ 0131 668 4371
☏ 0131 668 4466
✉ info@birlinn.co.uk
🖥 www.birlinn.co.uk
Contact Managing Editor, Hugh Andrew
Established 1992
Imprint(s) Birlinn Military and Adventure
John Donald Publishers
Polygon
Insider Info Publishes 90 titles per year. Receives approximately 50 queries and 25 manuscripts per year. Average lead time is 12 months, with simultaneous submissions accepted. Catalogue is available online.
Non-Fiction Publishes Biography, General Non-Fiction, Gift Books, Humour, Illustrated Books, Reference, Textbooks and Scholarly titles. Anthropology/Archaeology, Art/Architecture, Creative Non-Fiction, Education, History, Military/War, Nature/Environment, Regional, Religion, Sociology, Sports, Travel, Scottish Interest
Fiction Publishes Adventure, Crime/Detective, Historical, Humour, Military/War, Scottish Fiction and Gaelic Fiction titles.
Submission Guidelines Accepts unsolicited submissions.
Submission details to: submissions@birlinn.co.uk
Poetry Publishes Classic Scottish Poetry titles.

Submission Guidelines Accepts unsolicited submissions.
Submission details to: saraheream@googlemail.com
Recent Title(s) *Capital Caricatures*, Sheila Szatkowski (History/Scottish); *Shadow of the Serpent*, David Ashton (Fiction/Crime)
Tips Birlinn publishes a range of books of Scottish interest, including books on history, archaeology, customs and traditions, travel and folklore, and modern and classic Scottish poetry and fiction. Ideas or synopses for either fiction or non-fiction are welcomed, providing they relate to Scottish interest.

Biscuit Publishing
PO Box 123, Washington, Newcastle upon Tyne, NE37 2YW
✉ info@biscuitpublishing.com
🖥 www.biscuitpublishing.com
Contact Managing Director, Brian Lister
Established 2000
Insider Info Catalogue is available online.
Non-Fiction Publishes General Non-Fiction titles on the following subjects:
History, Regional, Local Interest
Fiction Publishes Adventure, Historical, Literary and Short Story Collection titles.
Poetry Publishes Poetry titles.
Recent Title(s) *Chasing Angels*, Sally Zigmond; *Full Fathom Five*, Mike Wilson
Tips All publications are by Biscuit prize winners, or by selected authors approached and commissioned by Biscuit. Therefore, it is best to enter one of Biscuit's many writing competitions, rather than sending unsolicited submissions.

BIS Publications
PO Box 14918, London, N17 8WJ
☏ 0845 226 4066
☏ 0845 226 4066
✉ info@bispublications.com
🖥 www.bispublications.com
Insider Info Catalogue available online.
Non-fiction Publishes Educational titles for children of African descent.
Recent Title(s) *Black Scientists and Inventors (Book 3)*, Michael Williams; *The Fight For Freedom Pack*, Kevin Des Robinson
Tips Titles need to inspire black children and many stories feature strong black characters overcoming difficulties.

Bitter Lemon Press
37 Arundel Gardens, London, W11 2LW
☏ 020 7727 7927
☏ 020 7460 2164
✉ books@bitterlemonpress.com

135

www.bitterlemonpress.com

Contact Managing Editors: Laurence Colchester and François von Hurte

Established 2003

Insider Info Publishes six to eight titles per year. Catalogue and manuscript guidelines are available online.

Fiction Publishes Crime, Thriller and Noir/Roman Noir titles.

* Must be foreign writers/fiction from abroad.

Submission Guidelines Only accepts agented submissions.

Submission details to: books@bitterlemonpress.com

Recent Title(s) *The Vampire*, Jacques Chessex

Tips Bitter Lemon Press aims to bring readers high quality thrillers and other contemporary fiction from abroad. The publisher is dedicated to the crime genre and publishes dark, sexy and often humorous novels that expose the seamier side of society. Bitter Lemon Press is pleased to receive submissions in the literary crime and thriller area, though submissions should be through a literary agent. Please include a synopsis and a sample chapter in the first submission.

Black & White Publishing
29 Ocean Drive, Edinburgh, EH6 6JL

☎ 0131 625 4500

☎ 0131 625 4501

✉ mail@blackandwhitepublishing.com

🌐 www.blackandwhitepublishing.com

Contact Managing Director, Campbell Brown

Established 1990

Imprint(s) Itchy Coo

Insider Info Submissions accompanied with SAE will be returned, but submissions by email are preferred. Aims to respond to queries and manuscript queries within three months. Catalogue and manuscript guidelines are available online.

Non-Fiction Publishes Biography, Cookbooks, General Non-Fiction, Sport, True Crime and Humour titles.

Submission Guidelines Accepts query with SAE/ proposal package (including outline, sample chapter(s), 30 pages maximum, contact details and SAE). Submission by email preferred.

Fiction Publishes General fiction, Historical, Children's, Crime, Children's Scottish Language and Scottish Interest titles.

Submission Guidelines Accepts query with SAE/ proposal package (including outline, sample chapter(s), 30 pages maximum, contact details and SAE). Submission by email preferred.

Recent Title(s) *The Good Mayor*, Andrew Nicoll (Fiction); *McGraw – The Incredible Untold Story of Tam 'The Licensee' McGraw*, Reg McKay (True Crime);

Graham Roberts – Hard As Nails, Graham Roberts with Colin Duncan (Sports Biography).

Tips Titles are aimed at anyone, especially children and Scottish language speakers. Unsolicited manuscripts are accepted, but please do not send complete manuscripts. For fiction and non-fiction submissions, please send a covering letter, a brief synopsis and sample chapters of no more than 30 pages and always include SAE. At present poetry submissions are not accepted.

Black Ace Books
PO Box 7547, Perth, Scotland, PH2 1AU

☎ 01821 642822

☎ 01821 642101

🌐 www.blackacebooks.com

Contact Publisher, Hunter Steele

Insider Info Catalogue and manuscript guidelines are available online.

Non-Fiction Publishes Biography, Anthologies and General Non-Fiction titles on the following subjects: Art/Architecture, History, Philosophy, Psychology.

Fiction Publishes Mainstream/Contemporary and Scottish Interest titles.

Recent Title(s) *The Broken Lyre*, Lorn Macintyre

Tips Black Ace Books are not currently accepting submissions from new authors. They also offer some self-publishing services, although they do not recommend this route for fiction titles.

Black Amber
15–16 Nassau Street, London, W1W 7AB

☎ 020 7436 9898

☎ 020 7436 9898

✉ info@arcadiabooks.co.uk

🌐 www.arcadiabooks.co.uk

Parent Company Arcadia Books

Contact Commissioning Editor, Rosemary Hudson

Insider Info Catalogue is available online.

Non-Fiction Publishes General Non-Fiction titles on Language/Literature.

Submission Guidelines Accepts agented submissions only.

Fiction Publishes Literary and Translation titles.

Submission Guidelines Accepts agented submissions only.

Recent Title(s) *Brixton Rock*, Alex Wheatle (Novel)

Tips Black Amber place strong emphasis on multicultural literary fiction and non-fiction.

Blackhall Publishing
33 Carysfort Avenue, Blackrock, Co. Dublin, Republic of Ireland

☎ 00 353 1 278 5090

☎ 00 353 1 278 4446

✉ editor@blackhallpublishing.com

🌐 www.blackhallpublishing.com
Contact Commissioning Editor, Elizabeth Brennan
Established 1997
Insider Info Publishes 15 titles per year. Receives approximately 30 queries and 20 manuscripts per year. 90 per cent of published books are from first-time authors and 100 per cent of published books are from unagented authors. 20 per cent of published books are author subsidy published. Payment is via royalty on net revenue. Average lead time is four months, with simultaneous submissions accepted. Submissions accompanied by SAE will be returned. Aims to respond to queries within 14 days, proposals within 31 days and manuscripts within six weeks. Catalogue is available online. Manuscript guidelines are available with SAE, or by email.
Non-Fiction Publishes General Non-Fiction, Scholarly, Self-Help, Textbook and Legal Statutes titles on the following subjects: Business/Economics, Communications, Computers/Electronics, Counselling/Career, Education, Government/Politics, Health/Medicine, Law, Money/Finance, Philosophy, Psychology, Religion, Social Sciences, Software
Submission Guidelines Accepts proposal package (including outline, synopsis, two sample chapters, author biography and and any artworks/images).
Recent Title(s) *The Men's Health Book*, Mark Rowe (Health); *How To Quit the Day Job ... and Remain Financially Healthy*, Ian Mitchell (Finance)
Tips Blackhall's readership consists of third level students, academics, businesses, management and marketing personnel, parents, and the general public.

Black Spring Press
Curtain House, 134–146 Curtain Road, London, EC2A 3AR
☎ 020 7613 3066
📠 020 7613 0028
📧 enquiries@blackspringpress.co.uk
🌐 www.blackspringpress.co.uk
Parent Company Dexter Haven Associates
Contact Publisher (Fiction, Biography, Film), Robert Hastings
Established 1985
Insider Info Publishes five titles per year. Receives approximately 100 queries and 80 manuscripts per year. 20 per cent of published books are from first-time authors and ten per cent of published books are from unagented authors. Payment is via royalty (on wholesale price). Average lead time is eight months, with simultaneous submissions accepted. Submission accompanied by SAE will be returned. Aims to respond to queries within two weeks, proposals and manuscripts within three months,

and all other enquiries within five weeks. Catalogue is free on request, and available online.
Non-Fiction Publishes Autobiography, Biography and General Non-Fiction titles.
Fiction Publishes Mainstream/Contemporary and Classic Fiction titles.
Poetry Publishes Contemporary and Classic Poetry titles.
Tips Specialises in contemporary, cutting edge literature as well as reviving classic works.

Blackstaff Press
4c Heron Wharf, Sydenham Business Park, Belfast, BT3 9LE
☎ 028 9045 5006
📠 028 9046 623
📧 info@blackstaffpress.com
🌐 www.blackstaffpress.com
Contact Managing Editor, Patsy Horton
Established 1971
Imprint(s) Beeline
Insider Info Publishes roughly 20 titles per year. Receives over 1,000 queries per year. Aims to respond to submissions within six months. Submissions accompanied by SAE will be returned. Catalogue is available online.
Non-Fiction Publishes Biography, Cookbooks, General Non-Fiction, How-To, Illustrated Books, Reference and Scholarly titles on the following subjects: Agriculture/Horticulture, Animals, Anthropology/Archaeology, Art/Architecture, Cooking/Foods/Nutrition, Crafts, Education, Government/Politics, Health/Medicine, History, Humanities, Music/Dance, Nature/Environment, Nostalgia, Photography, Religion, Sex, Travel, Women's Issues/Studies, Irish Interest, Northern Ireland
Submission Guidelines Accepts proposal package (including outline, synopsis, market report and three sample chapters). Will accept artwork/photos (send transparencies or digital files as jpegs).
Fiction Publishes Comic Books, Erotica, Romance, Short Story Collections and Irish Fiction titles.
Submission Guidelines Accepts proposal package (including outline, synopsis and three sample chapters) by post with SAE.
Poetry Publishes Poetry titles.
Recent Title(s) *Earth Voices Whispering*, Gerald Dawe (Poetry Anthology); *The North: A View from the Skies*, Esler Crawford (Photography)
Tips The publisher is always on the lookout for good new writing, but will only consider submissions of Northern Ireland/Irish interest.

Black Swan

61–63 Uxbridge Road, London, W5 5SA

- 020 8579 2652
- 020 8579 5479
- info@transworld-publishers.co.uk
- www.booksattransworld.co.uk

Parent Company Transworld Publishers
Insider Info Catalogue is available online. Manuscript guidelines are not available.
Fiction Publishes Historical, Humour, Mainstream/ Contemporary, Mystery, Romance, and Suspense titles.
Submission Guidelines Accepts agented submissions only.
Recent Title(s) *The White King*, Gyorgy Dragoman (Modern Fiction)
Tips Do not send any unsolicited manuscripts.

Bliss Books

15–16 Nassau Street, London, W1W 7AB

- 020 7436 9898
- 020 7436 9898
- info@arcadiabooks.co.uk
- www.arcadiabooks.co.uk

Parent Company Arcadia Books
Contact Managing Director, Gary Pulsifer
Insider Info Catalogue is available online.
Non-Fiction Publishes Biography, Memoir and General Non-Fiction titles.
Submission Guidelines Agented submissions only.
Recent Title(s) *The Real Diana*, Lady Colin Campell (Biography)
Tips Bliss Books publishes mainly popular bestsellers. Does not publish any poetry, plays, short stories, children's, teenage, science fiction, fantasy, horror, romance, spirituality or self-help titles.

Bloody Books

36–38 Glasshouse Street, London, W1B 5DL

- 020 7734 4448
- 020 3070 0764
- simon@beautiful-books.co.uk
- www.beautiful-books.co.uk

Parent Company Beautiful Books
Contact Publisher, Simon Petherick
Established 2006
Insider Info Publishes four titles per year. Catalogue is available online.
Fiction Publishes Horror Fiction titles.
Submission Guidelines Check website for latest submission guidelines.
Recent Title(s) *Dracula*, Luis Scafati; *Meat*, Joseph D'Lacey
Tips A proposal package should generally consist of a synopsis and the first three chapters.

Bloomsbury Academic

36 Soho Square, London, W1D 3QY

- 020 7494 2111
- 020 7434 0151
- frances_pinter@bloomsbury.com
- www.bloomsburyacademic.com

Parent Company Bloomsbury Publishing Plc
Contact Publisher, Dr Frances Pinter
Established 2008
Insider Info Payment is via royalties. Aims to respond to proposals within three months. Catalogue and manuscript guidelines are available online.
Non-Fiction Publishes Academic and Scholarly titles on the following subjects: Humanities, Social Sciences.
Submission Guidelines Accepts proposal package (including covering letter, outline and author CV) by post or email.
Recent Title(s) *Remix*, Lawrence Lessig (Copyright)
Tips Bloomsbury Academic is a new scholarly imprint that will publish simultaneously online, employing Creative Commons licences, and in print format, selling books around the world. The imprint is committed to working closely with the academic and library community to maximise the opportunities afforded by digital access to content. See the website for further details.

Bloomsbury Publishing Plc

36 Soho Square, London, W1D 3QY

- 020 7494 2111
- 020 7434 0151
- csm@bloomsbury.com
- www.bloomsbury.com

Contact Chairman/Chief Executive, Nigel Newton; Publishing Director (Book Division), Liz Calder (Fiction); Editorial Director, Sarah Odedina (Children's Books); Editor in Chief, Alexandra Pringle.
Established 1986
Imprint(s) A&C Black Publishers Ltd
Bloomsbury Academic
Berlin Verlag GmbH (German Division)
Bloomsbury USA (US Division)
Walker & Company (US Division)
Insider Info Payment is via royalties. Aims to respond to proposals within three months. Catalogue and manuscript guidelines are available online.
Non-Fiction Publishes Audio Cassettes, Autobiography, Biography, Children's, Cookbooks, General Non-Fiction, Gift Book, Humour, Illustrated Books, Multimedia and Reference titles on the following subjects: Art/Architecture, Gardening, Health/Medicine, History, House and Home,

Memoirs, Music/Dance, Photography, Psychology, Science, Sports, Travel, Exploration, Film
Submission Guidelines No unsolicted submissions.
Fiction Publishes Children's, Literary, Mainstream/Contemporary, Short Story collections, Translation, Young Adult and Classics titles.
Submission Guidelines No unsolicted submissions.
Poetry Publishes Poetry titles.
Recent Title(s) *Love Junkie*, Rachel Resnick (Memoir); *The Hot Topic: How to Tackle Global Warming*, David King and Gabrielle Walker (Current Affairs)
Tips Bloomsbury, and its various divisions, publishes a wide range of adult and children's books, both fiction and non-fiction. Bloomsbury is not currently accepting unsolicited submissions. Aside from its UK imprints, Bloomsbury also has a division in America and owns the American publisher Walker & Company and the German company Berlin Verlag GmbH.

Bluechrome
PO Box 109, Portishead, Bristol, BS20 7ZJ
☎ 07092 273360
🖷 07092 273357
✉ pr@bluechrome.co.uk
🌐 www.bluechrome.co.uk
Established 2002
Insider Info Publishes 20 titles per year. Receives approximately 2,000 queries per year. Submissions accompanied by SAE will be returned. Aims to respond to queries within 12 months. Catalogue available online.
Non-Fiction Publishes General Non-Fiction (often with a literary or writing connection) on the following subjects:
Creative Non-Fiction, Sports, Travel, Writing, Publishing and Poetry Guides.
Submission Guidelines No unsolicited manuscripts.
Fiction Publishes Experimental and Literary titles.
Submission Guidelines No unsolicited manuscripts.
Poetry Publishes Poetry titles.
Recent Title(s) *Another Man's World*, Joe Stein; *Dissonances*, Neil McLoughlin; *Stranger's Waiting*, Sally Spedding
Tips Bluechrome is not currently accepting submissions. Checking the website for current submission status.

Blue Door
77–85 Fulham Palace Road, Hammersmith, London, W6 8JB
☎ 020 8741 7070
🖷 020 8307 4440
✉ uk.orders@harpercollins.co.uk

🌐 www.harpercollins.co.uk
Parent Company HarperCollins Publishers Ltd – Press Books Division
Contact Publisher, Patrick Janson-Smith
Established 2008
Insider Info Publishes between 12 and 20 titles per year. Catalogue available online.
Fiction Publishes Commercial and Literary fiction titles.
Submission Guidelines Agented submissions only.
Recent Title(s) *The Hungry Ghosts*, Anne Berry (Family Saga); *Dead Spy Running*, Jon Stock (Thriller)
Tips Blue Door is a new imprint headed up by former Transworld publisher Patrick Janson-Smith, focusing primarily on fiction.

The Bodley Head
61–63 Uxbridge Road, London, W5 5SA
☎ 020 8231 6800
🖷 020 8231 6767
✉ childrenseditorial@randomhouse.co.uk
🌐 www.randomhouse.co.uk/childrens
Parent Company Random House Children's Books
Insider Info Catalogue available online.
Fiction Publishes Picture Books and Children's Fiction titles.
Submission Guidelines No unagented submissions.
Recent Title(s) *The Big Night-Night Book*, Georgie Birkett (Novelty Book); *Sebastian Darke: Prince of Explorers*, Philip Caveney (Fantasy)
Tips Publishes almost entirely in hardback.

The Book Castle
12 Church Street, Dunstable, Bedfordshire, LU5 4RU
☎ 01582 605670
🖷 01582 662431
✉ bc@book-castle.co.uk
🌐 www.book-castle.co.uk
Contact Managing Editors: Paul Bowes and Sally Siddons
Established 1986
Insider Info Publishes roughly ten titles per year. Payment is via royalties. Catalogue and manuscript guidelines available online.
Non-Fiction Publishes General Non-Fiction titles on the following subjects:
History and Regional
* The Book Castle publishes local interest and history books for the counties surrounding Bedfordshire.
Submission Guidelines Accepts query with SAE/proposal package (including outline). Mark for the attention of Paul Bowes or Sally Siddons and include any other relevant information.

Recent Title(s) *King of The 'Cali'*, Russ Sainty
(Memoir/Music)
Tips All publications must be of local interest,
particularly focusing upon the counties of
Bedfordshire, Buckinghamshire, Hertfordshire and
Oxfordshire.

Book Guild Publishing Ltd

**Pavilion View, 19 New Road, Brighton, East
Sussex, BN1 1UF**
- 01273 720900
- 01273 723122
- info@bookguild.co.uk
- www.bookguild.co.uk

Contact Managing Director, Carol Biss; Publishing
Manager, Lyn Parr; Managing Editor, Joanna Bentley
Established 1982
Insider Info Publishes 100 titles per year. 60 per cent
of books publishes are from first-time authors.
Payment is via royalties. Aims to respond to
proposals and manuscripts within one month.
Catalogue and manuscript guidelines are
available online.
Non-Fiction Publishes Biography, Children's and
General Non-Fiction titles on the following subjects:
History, Memoirs, World Affairs.
* Aims to publish vivid memoirs and biographies of
highly interesting people, past and present, and
timely books on current affairs.
Submission Guidelines Accepts query with SAE/
proposal package (including outline and synopsis).
Submission details to: joanna@bookguild.co.uk
Fiction Publishes General Fiction titles.
* Aims to publish engaging novels and stories for
adult and children readers.
Submission Guidelines Accepts query with SAE/
proposal package (including outline and synopsis).
Submission details to: joanna@bookguild.co.uk
Recent Title(s) *Tirolu*, June Lerina
Woodward (Romance)
Tips The Book Guild is an independent publisher
and most material is conventionally published, but
joint venture services – where the author
contributes costs – are offered, as well as other
production services. This option should be
researched thoroughly.

Book Guild Publishing Ltd

**Pavilion View, 19 New Road, Brighton, East
Sussex, BN1 1UF**
- 01273 720900
- 01273 723122
- info@bookguild.co.uk
- www.bookguild.co.uk

Contact Managing Director, Carol Biss; Managing
Editor, Joanna Bentley

Insider Info Offers a variety of publishing options for
authors, businesses and charities, including
conventional publishing, 'Partnership Publishing'
and production options. Publishes approximately
100 titles per year.
Non-fiction Subjects covered are varied and
include: Children's, Human Interest, Biography,
History and General Interest Non-Fiction titles
Fiction Produces Mainstream and Contemporary
Fiction titles
Submission Guidelines Ideas and manuscripts
welcome. Initially send a synopsis, covering letter
and CV. Submission details are on the website.
Tips Book Guild offers a range of different publishing
options, including subsidy publishing. Research all
fees carefully before you commit to anything.

Bookline & Thinker Ltd

Suite 231, 405 King's Road, London, SW10 0BB
- 0845 116 1476
- editor@booklinethinker.com
- www.booklinethinker.com

Non-Fiction Publishes General Non-Fiction
following subjects:
Biography, General History, Lifestyle.
Submission Guidelines Accepts proposal package
(including outline) by email.
Recent Title(s) *Not All Bonnets and Bustles*,
(Biograhpy/History)
Tips Bookline & Thinker is a small publisher and
member of the Independent Publishers Guild. They
also run a novel writing competition.

Bookmart Ltd

Blaby Road, Wigston, Leicester, LE18 4SE
- 0116 275 9060
- 0116 275 9090
- books@bookmart.co.uk
- www.bookmart.co.uk

Established 1989
Insider Info Catalogue available online. Accepts
queries via email or online form.
Non-Fiction Publishes Children's Educational,
Activity, Novelty and Adult's General Non-
Fiction titles.
Fiction Publishes Children's Fiction and
Picture Books.
Poetry Publishes Children's Poetry titles.
Recent Title(s) *The Encyclopaedia of Aircraft of WWII*,
Paul Eden (Adult Reference); *Messy Pig*, Jane Wolfe
(Children's Sound Book)
Tips Bookmart is one of the UK's leading distributors
and publishers of children's and adult illustrated
titles. It also provides a sales, marketing and
distribution service for international publishers who
require a presence in the UK.

BooksToListenTo

1 Royston Avenue, Sutton, Surrey, SM1 3PS
- 020 8641 2675
- submissions@bookstolistento.com
- www.bookstolistento.com

Parent Company House of Solomon Ltd
Contact Editorial Director, David Kessler; Editors: Derek Prior (Science Fiction and Fantasy); Mark Bentley (Thrillers); Nigel Farringdon (Literary Fiction); Philip Abrahams (Non-Fiction); Jane Ramsey (Romance, Chick-Lit, Historical Fiction)
Established 2007
Insider Info Publishes audiobooks from new and mid-list authors and sells them as digital downloads direct to customers through the website. All works are recorded in fully equipped recording studios and narrated by professional, trained actors. Advances from £500 to £2,500 for rights to publish in audio format, and for sale as digital downloads. Author retains all other rights including non-dowloadable rights. Royalties paid quarterly.
Non-Fiction Publishes a wide range of Autobiography, Biography, Business, Celebrity, Education, General Non-Fiction, Health, History, Human Interest, Language, Politics, Sport, True-Crime and other Non-Fiction topics.
Submission Guidelines Submit first 20 to 30 pages and synopsis. Email submissions welcome in MS Word or PDF formats. Postal submissions must include SAE if they are to be returned. Aims to respond to submissions within two to three weeks.
Fiction Publishes Action & Adventure, Children, Classics, Comedy, Crime & Thrillers, Erotica, Fantasy, Historical Fiction, Radio & Television, Science Fiction and Young Adult titles.
Submission Guidelines Submit first 20–30 pages and synopsis. Email submissions welcome in MS Word or PDF formats. Postal submissions must include SAE if they are to be returned. Aims to respond to submissions within two to three weeks.
Recent Title(s) *The Luddite Girls*, Karen Dee (Chick-Lit); *Ethan and the Web of Lies*, Dan Ryan (Childrens)
Tips Current areas of interest are: thrillers, chick-lit, romance, science fiction, historical fiction, true crime, political polemic and celebrity gossip. Being a small company BooksToListenTo only publishes a limited number of titles, but they also offer hosting on their site or other self-published audiobooks in return for a fixed fee per sale based on length. One of the conditions of this is that the author/publisher must agree to the issue of up to 12 free copies to randomly-selected regular customers for review purposes. This is done to ensure that self-published audiobooks will be fairly and impartially reviewed.

Booth-Clibborn Editions

Studio 83, 235 Earls Court Road, London, SW5 9FE
- 020 7565 0688
- 020 7244 1018
- info@booth-clibborn.com
- www.booth-clibborn.com

Established 1974
Insider Info Catalogue available online.
Non-Fiction Publishes General Non-Fiction, Illustrated titles and Multimedia on the following subjects:
Art/Architecture, Contemporary Culture, Photography
Recent Title(s) *The G Plan Revolution*, Basil Hyman & Stephen Braggs (Art/Design)
Tips Booth-Clibborn Editions was founded as a privately owned, wholly independent company publishing an outstanding list of books on the fine, media and decorative arts. Its policy is to commission first class creative work from the best of today's designers, whether they are renowned book specialists or innovative younger groups.

Bounty Books

2–4 Heron Quays, London, E14 4JP
- 020 7531 8400
- 020 7531 8607
- publisher@bounty.co.uk
- www.bountybooks.co.uk

Parent Company Octopus Publishing Group
Contact Publishing and International Sales Manager, Polly Manguel
Non-Fiction Publishes reprints of Non-Fiction titles.
Tips Bounty, the UK's first reprint company, is entirely based on reprints from across the Octopus Group's backlists.

Boxer Books

101 Turnmill Street, London, EC1M 5QP
- 020 7017 8980
- 020 7608 2314
- info@boxerbooks.com
- www.boxerbooksltd.co.uk

Insider Info Submissions accompanied by SAE will be returned. Catalogue available online.
Fiction Publishes Children's Picture Books.
Submission Guidelines Accepts entire manuscript and colour artwork by post to the Submissions Editor. Does not accept email submissions. All artwork and manuscripts must be copies, not originals.
Recent Title(s) *No More Blanket For Lambkin!*, Bernette Ford (Picture Books); *Big Noisy Book of Dinosaurs*, Britta Teckentrup (Picture Book/DVD)

Tips Boxer Books focuses on publishing new and established authors and illustrators and working with them to develop their personal style.

Boxtree
20 New Wharf Road, London, N1 9RR
- 020 7014 6000
- 020 7014 6001
- www.panmacmillan.com

Parent Company Pan Macmillan Publishers
Established 1990 (became an imprint of Pan Macmillan in 1996)
Insider Info Catalogue available online, as a downloadable pdf.
Non-Fiction Publishes Autobiography, Biography, General Non-Fiction, Gift Books, Humour and Illustrated titles on the following subjects: Entertainment, Film and Television Tie-Ins, Sport, Music
Submission Guidelines Accepts agented submissions only.
Recent Title(s) *Grandma's Dead: Breaking Bad News with Baby Animals*, Ben Schwartz (Humour); *This Diary Will Change Your Life 2009*, Benrik Ltd
Tips Specialises in quirky entertainment related and branded non-fiction. Do not send in any unsolicited manuscripts.

Boydell & Brewer Ltd
Whitwell House, St Audry's Park Road, Melton, Woodbridge, Suffolk, IP12 1SY
- 01394 610600
- 01394 610316
- editorial@boydell.co.uk
- www.boydell.co.uk

Established 1978
Insider Info Simultaneous submissions are not accepted. Catalogue is available free on request and online. Manuscript guidelines are available online.
Non-Fiction Publishes Autobiography, Biography, General Non-Fiction, Illustrated Books, Multimedia, Reference and Scholarly titles on the following subjects: Art/Architecture, Crafts, History, Hobbies, Humanities, Language/Literature, Literary Criticism, Military/War, Music/Dance, Philosophy, Photography, Religion
Submission Guidelines Use the downloadable submission form on the website.
Recent Title(s) *Elliott Carter*, Felix Meyer and Anne C. Shreffler (Biography); *The World of the Stonors*, Elizabeth Noble
Tips Boydell & Brewer is an independent publisher of scholarly works for the academic community. Titles cover humanities in all periods, up to and including the 19th Century. Prospective authors are asked to complete and return the submission form, available on the website.

BPS Blackwell Publishing
9600 Garsington Road, Oxford, OX4 2DQ
- andrew.mcaleer@blackwellpublishing.com
- www.bpsblackwell.co.uk

Contact Commissioning Editor, Andrew McAleer
Insider Info Publishes 12 titles per year. Receives approximately 30 queries and 15–20 manuscripts per year. 25 per cent of books published are from first-time authors and 95 per cent are from unagented authors. Payment via royalty (on retail price) with 0.07 (per £) minimum and 0.12 (per £) maximum. Average lead time is one year with simultaneous submissions not accepted. Book catalogue and manuscript guidelines are available online.
Non-fiction Publishes Multimedia, Reference, Scholarly and Reference titles on the following subjects: Education, Psychology, Sociology
Submission Guidelines Accepts proposal package (including outline, table of contents, market research and intended readership). Will accept initial query via email.
Submission details to: andrew.mcaleer@blackwellpublishing.com
Recent Title(s) *How to Write in Psychology: A Student Guide*, John Beech
Tips A unique partnership between The British Psychological Society and Wiley-Blackwell Publishers – whose titles are aimed at managers, teachers, medical and healthcare professionals, students and practising psychologists. They do not publish self-help, popular psychology or fiction. Authors should be able to provide evidence of qualifications that enable them to write titles with authority. All submissions will go through an editorial board.

Bradshaw Books
Civic Trust House, 50 Popes Quay, Co. Cork, Republic of Ireland
- 00353 21 421 5175
- 00353 21 455 1617
- info@tighfili.com
- www.tighfili.com

Contact Artistic Director, Maire Bradshaw; Literature Office, Paul Casey
Established 1985
Insider Info Publishes around eight titles per year. Submissions accompanied by SAE will be returned. Catalogue is available online.
Poetry Publishes Poetry titles.
* Concentrates on Irish poets. Also publishes the *Cork Literary Review* and the *Eurochild Anthologies*.

Tips Bradshaw encourages new and unknown Irish poets and welcomes unsolicited manuscripts, or proposal submissions. Also publishes the *Cork Literary Review* which has various poetry/prose competitions, some of which can also lead to publication by Bradshaw.

Bradt Travel Guides
23 High Street, Chalfont St Peter, Bucks, SL9 9QE
- 01753 893444
- 0753 892333
- info@bradtguides.com
- www.bradtguides.com

Contact Managing Director, Donald Greig; Editorial Director, Adrian Phillips
Established 1974
Insider Info Receives approximately 200 queries and 60 manuscripts per year. 30 per cent of books published are from first-time authors, 95 per cent of books published are from unagented authors. Payment is via royalty (on wholesale price). Advance is offered. Average lead time is eight months, with simultaneous submissions not accepted. Aims to respond to proposals and manuscripts within one month. Catalogue is available online. Manuscript guidelines are available by email.
Non-Fiction Publishes Guidebook and Reference titles on the following subjects:
Activity & Adventure, Ancient Sites & Cultures, City Guides, Cruising, Destinations, General Travel, Health, Islands and Beaches, Offbeat and Eccentric Travel, Wildlife
* Bradt's travel guides cover a range of subjects from general interest travel and city guides, to eccentric or remote destinations for the dedicated traveller.
Submission Guidelines Accepts proposal package (including outline, market research, CV and travelling history).
Recent Title(s) *Baltic Cities*, Neil Taylor (Travel); *Borneo: Sabah, Sarawak, Brunei*, Tamara Thiessen (Travel)
Tips Bradt's readership includes cultured, responsible travellers who are interested in destinations off the beaten track. They aim to publish guides to unusual destinations, or unusual guides to rather more mainstream places. Bradt does not publish standard travel narratives.

Brandon/Mount Eagle Publications
PO Box 32, Cooleen, Dingle, Co. Kerry, Republic of Ireland
- 00353 66 915 1463
- 00353 66 915 1234
- www.brandonbooks.com

Contact Publisher, Steve MacDonogh
Established 1997

Insider Info Publishes around 15 titles per year. Receives approximately 200 queries and 200 manuscripts per year. Submissions accompanied by SAE will be returned. Catalogue and manuscript guidelines are available online.
Non-Fiction Publishes Biography and General Non-Fiction titles on the following subjects: Government/Politics, History, Memoirs, Regional, World Affairs
Submission Guidelines Accepts query with SAE with proposal package (including outline, your publishing history, clips and author biography). Will accept artworks/images (send digital files as jpegs). No submissions by email or fax.
Fiction Publishes Crime/Thriller, Regional and Irish Fiction titles.
Submission Guidelines Accepts query with SAE with proposal package (including outline, synopsis and 40 sample pages, review quotes, author biography). No submissions by fax or email.
Recent Title(s) *Bloodstorm*, Sam Millar (Novel/Crime); *The Dramatist*, Ken Bruen (Novel/Thriller)
Tips Titles are aimed at a wide readership, generally with an Irish focus. The company is looking principally for biography, memoirs, popular history, current affairs and modern politics proposals.

Breedon Books Publishing
3 The Parker Centre, Mansfield Road, Derby, DE21 4SZ
- 01332 384235
- 01332 292755
- submissions@breedonpublishing.co.uk
- www.breedonbooks.co.uk

Contact Commissioning Editor, Susan Last
Established 1983
Insider Info Publishes 50 titles per year. Payment is via royalties (on retail price). Submissions accompanied by SAE will be returned. Catalogue is available online. Manuscript guidelines are available online via the website.
Non-Fiction Publishes Illustrated Books and General Non-Fiction titles on the following subjects: History, Photography and Sports
Submission Guidelines Accepts query with SAE and proposal package (including outline, sample chapter(s) and SAE). Will accept images (send transparencies/digital files as jpegs).
Recent Title(s) *The Hike and every damn thing else!*, Stephen Halliday
Tips Breedon Books is always looking for new authors in all our areas of publishing. Breedon concentrates on local history, motorsport and football titles, although there are always a few that fall outside these areas. Therefore, each submission will be looked at on its own merits.

Brewin Books Ltd

Doric House, 56 Alcester Road, Studley, Warwickshire, B80 7LG

☎ 01527 854228

🖷 01527 852746

✉ admin@brewinbooks.com

🌐 www.brewinbooks.com

Contact Managing Director, Alan Brewin (Non-Fiction); Editor, Alistair Brewin (Regional History Magazines)

Established 1976

Imprint(s) History Into Print

Brewin Junior

Insider Info Publishes 30 titles per year. Receives approximately 50 queries and 95 manuscripts per year. Payment is via royalty (on retail price). Average lead time is six months, with simultaneous submissions not accepted. Submissions accompanied by SAE will be returned. Catalogue is free on request, and available online or by email. Manuscript guidelines are free on request.

Non-Fiction Publishes Autobiography, Biography, Children's, General Non-Fiction, Humour, Illustrated, Reference and Scholarly titles on the following subjects:

Art/Architecture, Automotive, Communications, Cooking/Foods/Nutrition, Ethnic, Health/Medicine, History, Language/Literature, Memoirs, Military/War, Music/Dance, Nostalgia, Regional (Midlands), Social Sciences, Sports, Transportation, Travel

Submission Guidelines Accepts proposal package (including outline, sample chapters, your publishing history, author biography and SAE) and artworks/images.

Fiction Publishes Regional (Midlands) titles.

Submission Guidelines Accepts proposal package (including outline, sample chapters, your publishing history, author biography and SAE).

Recent Title(s) *All Change – Memories of a Trainspotter*, Bob Brueton (Transport); *Matthew Boulton – A Revolutionary Player*, Malcolm Dick and Richard Clay, eds. (Biography)

Tips Brewin Books publishes books with mass market appeal for a general readership.

Brilliant Publications

Unit 10, Sparrow Hall Farm, Edlesborough, Dunstable, Bedfordshire, LU6 2ES

☎ 01525 222292

🖷 01525 222720

✉ priscilla@brilliantpublications.co.uk

🌐 www.brilliantpublications.co.uk

Contact Publisher, Priscilla Hannaford

Established 1993

Insider Info Publishes 20 titles per year. Submissions accompanied by SAE will be returned. Catalogue

and manuscript guidelines are free on request, and available online.

Non-Fiction Publishes Children's, General Non-Fiction, Reference, Scholarly and Textbook titles on the following subjects:

Education, Teaching/Textbooks (all school subjects)

* Does not publish children's picture books.

Submission Guidelines Accepts query with SAE and proposal package (including outline, two sample chapters, author biography, market research, intended audience).

Recent Title(s) *J'aime Parler*, Ann May

Tips Specialises in producing high quality, well designed materials that make teaching and learning enjoyable and rewarding, for both teachers and pupils. Brilliant Publications are always looking for new book ideas, including book series. Writers should try to sell both themselves and their book strongly in the proposal, and include plenty of information on what makes their book, or series, distinct.

The British Academy

10 Carlton House Terrace, London, SW1Y 5AH

☎ 020 7969 5200

🖷 020 7969 5300

✉ pubs@britac.ac.uk

🌐 www.britac.ac.uk

Contact Chairman of the Publications Committee, Prof. David McKitterick

Established 1902

Insider Info Publishes 20 titles per year. Payment is via royalties. Catalogue available online.

Non-Fiction Publishes Reference, Scholarly and Technical titles on the following subjects:

Anthropology/Archaeology, Art/Architecture, Business/Economics, Ethnic, Government/Politics, History, Humanities, Language/Literature, Music/Dance, Philosophy, Psychology, Religion, Science, Social Sciences

* The Academy publishes a wide range of monographs, editions and catalogues, reflecting the breadth of its scholarly activities.

Submission Guidelines Accepts query with SAE.

Recent Title(s) *Becoming Muslim in Mainland Tanzania, 1890-2000*, Felicitas Becker

Tips The British Academy was established by Royal Charter under the full title of 'The British Academy for the Promotion of Historical, Philosophical and Philological Studies'. It is an independent and self-governing fellowship of scholars, elected for distinction and achievement in one or more branches of the academic disciplines, which make up the humanities and social sciences. The Academy's publishing programme is overseen by a Publications Committee and all new and recent titles are published worldwide by Oxford University

Press. The Academy mostly publishes work within its existing series', details of which are available on the website.

The British Computer Society
First Floor, Block D, North Star House, North Star Avenue, Swindon, SN2 1FA
- 01793 417674
- 01793 417444
- pubsenq@hq.bcs.org.uk
- www.bcs.org

Contact Commissioning Editor, Matthew Flynn (Business, IT)
Established 1957
Insider Info Publishes ten titles per year. Payment is via royalty (on wholesale price). Average lead time is five months, with simultaneous submissions accepted. Catalogue is free on request, and available online, or via email to matthew.flynn@hq.bcs.org.uk. Manuscript guidelines are free on request and available online.
Non-Fiction Publishes Reference, Scholarly, Technical and Textbook titles on the following subjects:
Business/Economics, Computers/Electronics
Submission Guidelines Accepts proposal package (including outline, sample chapter(s), your publishing history, author biography). Writers should download a book proposal form from the website. Submission details to: matthew.flynn@hq.bcs.org.uk
Tips The leading body for those working in IT, they aim to promote the study and practice of computing, and advance the knowledge of – and education in – IT for the benefit of the public. BCS is also a registered charity. Publications should support the professional, academic, and practical needs of both BCS members and the wider IT community. Readership includes students or those undertaking professional exams, IT managers, and senior directors wanting a greater understanding of their IT systems.

British Library
96 Euston Road, London, NW1 2BD
- 020 7412 7535
- 020 7412 7768
- blpublications@bl.uk
- www.bl.uk

Contact Head of Publishing, David Way; Publishing Manager, Catherine Britton; Managing Editor, Lara Speicher
Established 1973
Insider Info Publishes 50 titles per year. Receives approximately 500 queries per year. Average lead time is over 18 months. Catalogue is free on request, or by email.

Non-Fiction Publishes Biography, Illustrated, Reference and Scholarly titles on the following subjects:
Art/Architecture (Design), Typography, History (History of the Book), Humanities, Language/ Literature, Literary Criticism, Religion (History of Sacred texts), Cartography (History of Maps and Exploration), Bibliography, Biography
* Titles are linked to the collections of the British Library.
Submission Guidelines Accepts proposal package (including outline, sample chapters, your publishing history, author biography, and SAE).

The British Museum Press
38 Russell Square, London, WC1B 3DG
- 020 7323 1234
- 020 7436 7315
- customerservices@britishmuseum.co.uk
- www.britishmuseum.co.uk

Parent Company The British Museum
Contact Managing Director, Andrew Thatcher; Research Publications Editor, Joesephine Turquet
Established 1973
Insider Info Catalogue is available online.
Non-Fiction Publishes Biography, Children's, Coffee Table, Gift, Illustrated, Reference, Scholarly, and Anthology titles on the following subjects:
Exhibition Catalogues, Collection Guidebooks, Religion, History, Archaeology, Ethnography, Fine and Decorative Arts, Numismatics
Poetry Publishes some Classical Poetry titles.
Recent Title(s) *Chairman Mao Badges*, Helen Wang

Brooklands Books Ltd
PO Box 146, Cobham, Surrey, KT11 1LG
- 01932 865051
- 01932 868803
- sales@brookland-books.com
- www.brooklandsbooks.com

Contact Bryan Kennedy
Established 1954
Insider Info Catalogue is available online.
Non-Fiction Publishes General Non-Fiction, Reference and Technical titles on the following subjects: Automotive, History, Military/War, Aircraft
Recent Title(s) *Jaguar Service Manual 1946-1948 for 1.5, 2.5, 3.5 Litre Models*, (Service Manual)
Tips Brooklands Books are dedicated to preserving motoring literature for enthusiasts. They specialise in fully detailed motoring manuals – not to be confused with the much advertised 'condensed' manuals which are fine for servicing and small repair jobs, but often fall short when more detailed help is needed.

Brown, Son & Ferguson

4–10 Darnley Street, Glasgow, G41 2SD
☎ 0141 429 1234
☎ 0141 420 1694
✉ info@skipper.co.uk
🌐 www.skipper.co.uk
Contact Managing Director, T. Nigel Brown
Established 1832
Insider Info Catalogue available online.
Non-Fiction Publishes General Non-Fiction, Reference, and Technical titles on the following subjects:
Marine Subjects, Travel, and Nautical Reference
Fiction Publishes Plays and Regional Interest titles.
Recent Title(s) *Brown's Nautical Almanac 2009*, T. Nigel Brown (Nautical Reference); *Glenlee: The Life and Times of a Clyde-Built Cape Horner*, Colin Castle & Iain Macdonald (History); *Back From the Brink*, Webster & Walker
Tips Brown, Son & Ferguson have been nautical publishers, printers and ships' stationers since 1832. Their list ranges from nautical textbooks, both technical and non-technical, books about the sea, historical books, information on old sailing ships, and how to build model ships. Brown, Son & Ferguson publishes anything related to sailing or other nautical themes, plus Scottish interest plays and non-fiction.

Brown Skin Books

PO Box 57421, London, E5 0ZD
☎ 020 8986 1115
✉ info@brownskinbooks.co.uk
🌐 www.brownskinbooks.co.uk
Contact Managing Director, Vastiana Belfon
Established 2002
Insider Info Publishes roughly seven titles per year. 75 per cent of books published are from first-time authors and 80 per cent are from unagented authors. Payment is via royalty (on retail price), with £1,500 advance (for novels). Average lead time is ten months, with simultaneous submissions accepted. Submissions accompanied by SAE will be returned. Aims to respond to proposals and manuscripts within two months. Catalogue available online. Manuscript guidelines available online, by post or via email.
Fiction Publishes Erotica novels and short story titles.
* Does not publish any poetry.
Submission Guidelines Accepts query with proposal package (including outline, one sample chapter and SAE). Novels should be between 75,000 to 90,000 words. Short stories should be between 6,000 to 10,000 words.
Recent Title(s) *Sorcerer*, Tamzin Hall (Erotic Novel)

Tips Titles are primarily aimed at women of colour aged 18–50, living in the US, Canada, Europe, Africa and the Caribbean. There is a dedicated 'hints and tips' section published on the website that writers should read before submitting. Also, make sure there is a strong story with believable characters, as this is just as important as the sex in Brown Skin Books' publications.

Brown Watson

The Old Mill, 76 Fleckney Road, Kibworth Beauchamp, Leicestershire, LE8 0HG
☎ 0116 279 6333
✉ books@brownwatson.co.uk
🌐 www.brownwatson.co.uk
Non-Fiction Publishes Children's General Non-Fiction and Picture Book titles.
Fiction Publishes Children's titles.
Tips Brown Watson is a small, family owned, children's book publisher and distributor.

Bryntirion Press

Bryntirion, Bridgend, CF31 4DX
☎ 01656 655886
☎ 01656 665919
✉ office@emw.org.uk
🌐 www.emw.org.uk
Contact Press Manager, Huw Kinsey
Established 1955
Insider Info Catalogue free on request and online.
Non-Fiction Publishes Children's, General Non-Fiction, Illustrated Book, Reference and Scholarly titles on the following subjects:
Religion, Spirituality
Fiction Publishes Religious titles.
Recent Title(s) *On the Wings of the Dove*, Noel Gibbard (Religion/History); *Singing to the Lord*, Peter Trumper (Religion/Sermons)
Tips Titles aimed at the Evangelical/Welsh markets. Also publishes Christian books and magazines in the Welsh language, and Welsh language writers are in demand.

b small publishing

The Book Shed, 36 Leyborne Park, Kew, Richmond, Surrey, TW9 3HA
☎ 020 8948 2884
☎ 020 8948 6458
✉ info@bsmall.co.uk
🌐 www.bsmall.co.uk
Contact Managing Director & Publisher, Catherine Bruzzone; Editorial Contact, Susan Martineau
Insider Info Catalogue available online.
Non-fiction Publishes Children's Educational, Activity and Reference titles on the following subjects:

Languages, Activities, Animals, Art, Craft, History, Puzzles and Science.

Submission Guidelines No unsolicited proposals, as all books are created in-house.

Tips b small create most of their books with a small stable of writers and illustrators, details of whom appear on the website.

Bureau of Freelance Photographers
Focus House, 497 Green Lanes, London, N13 4BP
- 020 8882 3315
- 020 8886 3933
- info@thebfp.com
- www.thebfp.com

Insider Info Catalogue is available online.

Non-Fiction Publishes How-To and Reference titles on the following subjects:
Photography, Freelance Photography Market

Recent Title(s) *The Freelance Photographer's Project Book*, BFP Books (Handbook)

Tips The Bureau of Freelance Photographers publishes titles aimed at professional freelance photographers and keen amateurs.

Burning House
36–38 Glasshouse Street, London, W1B 5DL
- 020 7734 4448
- 020 3070 0764
- simon@beautiful-books.co.uk
- www.beautiful-books.co.uk

Parent Company Beautiful Books

Contact Publisher, Simon Petherick

Established 2007

Fiction Publishes Contemporary Fiction titles.

Submission Guidelines Accepts query with SAE or via email.
Submission details to: submissions@beautiful-books.co.uk

Recent Titles *The Turkish Diplomat's Daughter*, Deniz Goran

Tips Burning House is a new imprint focusing entirely on contemporary fiction.

Burns & Oates
The Tower Building, 11 York Road, London, SE1 7NX
- 020 7922 0880
- 020 7922 0881
- bhayes@continuumbooks.com
- www.continuumbooks.com

Parent Company The Continuum International Publishing Group

Contact Publishing Director, Robin Baird-Smith (General Trade and Religion); Editor, Ben Hayes (General Trade and Religion)

Established 1847

Insider Info Catalogue and manuscript guidelines are available online.

Non-Fiction Publishes General Non-Fiction of Roman Catholic interest, as well as official publications for the Catholic faith.

Submission Guidelines Accepts proposal package (including outline, your publishing history, published clips, author biography and market research). Send no more than four A4 sheets.

Tips Burns & Oates is the premier Roman Catholic publishing imprint in Great Britain and publishes traditional and contemporary titles from Catholic writers. Designated 'Publishers to the Holy See' by Pope Leo XIII, Burns & Oates has also maintained a strong tradition of publishing official works for the Catholic Church in England and Wales.

The Business Education Publishers Ltd
Cygnet Way, Rainton Bridge Business Centre, Houghton-le-Spring, Tyne and Wear, DH4 5QY
- 0191 305 5165
- 0191 305 5506
- info@bepl.com
- www.bepl.com

Insider Info Catalogue and manuscript guidelines are available online.

Non-Fiction Publishes titles on the following subjects:
Information Technology, Business, Education, Travel, Tourism and Leisure, Local Interest (Durham area)

Submission Guidelines Accepts proposal package (including outline, details of readership and competing titles and an electronic version).

Tips The Business Education Publishers are always interested in hearing from potential authors. As an independent publisher, they take a personal interest in each project and their staff work closely with authors to produce high quality work.

Buster Books
Michel O'Mara Books, 16 Lion Yard, Tremadoc Road, London, SW4 7NQ
- 020 7720 8643
- 020 7627 8953
- enquiries@mombooks.com
- www.mombooks.com/busterbooks

Parent Company Michael O'Mara Books

Contact Managing Director, Lesley O'Mara; Publishing Director, Philippa Wingate; Managing Editor, David Sinden

Established 1985

Insider Info Average lead time is six months, with simultaneous submissions accepted. Submissions accompanied by SAE will be returned. Catalogue is available with SAE. Manuscript guidelines are available online.

Non-Fiction Publishes Children's Educational and General Non-Fiction.

* Most educational non-fiction is aimed at children aged 8–12.

Submission Guidelines Accepts proposal package (including outline, two to three sample chapters, your publishing history, author biography and SAE) and artworks/images (send photocopies). Do not send original artworks or whole manuscripts.

Fiction Publishes Children's Board Books and Picture Book titles.

Submission Guidelines Does not accept fiction submissions.

Recent Title(s) *Christmas Doodles*, Piers Harper

Butterworth-Heinemann

Linacre House, Jordan Hill, Oxford, OX2 8DP

- 01865 474010
- 01865 474011
- authorsupport@elsevier.com
- www.elsevierhealth.com/bh

Parent Company Elsevier Ltd (Health Sciences)

Insider Info Royalties paid. Catalogue and manuscript guidelines available online.

Non-Fiction Publishes Illustrated Books, Multimedia, Reference, Scholarly, Textbook and Technical titles on the following subjects:
Education, Health/Medicine, Science, Veterinary Medicine, Optometry, Dentistry

Submission Guidelines See the online Proposal Form.
Submission details to: t.horne@elsevier.com

Recent Title(s) *Tourism Management, Managing for Change*, Page (Management)

Tips A leading international publisher of medical and health professions books, software and visual aids. Specialist areas include anesthesiology and intensive care, dentistry, neurology, ophthalmology, optometry, nursing, physiotherapy and veterinary. To submit a proposal to Butterworth-Heinmann, fill in and return a 'Proposal Form', available on the website. Alternatively authors may contact the publishing director or editor prior to submission, to discuss the proposal.

Cadogan Guides

New Holland Publishers, Garfield House, 86–88 Edgeware Road, London, W2 2EA

- 020 7724 7773
- 020 7258 1293
- cadogan@nhpub.co.uk
- www.cadoganguides.com

Parent Company New Holland Publishers

Insider Info Catalogue is available online.

Non-Fiction Publishes Children's, Guidebook and Reference titles on the following subjects:
Children's Travel books, Destinations, General Travel Guides, Life Writing (Travel Biography), Living Abroad, Property Buying, Short Breaks, Travel Literature

Tips Cadogan publishes a wide range of travel writing for both children and adults, including the *In The Footsteps* series which traces the travels of well known historical literary figures.

Cambridge Scholars Publishing

12 Back Chapman Street, Newcastle upon Tyne, NE6 2XX

- admin@c-s-p.org
- www.c-s-p.org

Established 2001

Insider Info Publishes roughly 120 titles per year. Receives approximately 1,200 manuscripts per year. 40 per cent of books published are from first-time authors and 100 per cent are from unagented authors. One per cent of books published are author subsidy published. Payment is via royalty (on wholesale price). Average lead time is four months, with simultaneous submissions accepted. Submissions will not be returned. Aims to respond to queries within seven days and proposals within one month. Catalogue is free on request, and available online. Manuscript guidelines are available online.

Non-Fiction Publishes Reference, Scholarly and Technical titles on the following subjects:
Anthropology/Archaeology, Art, Architecture, Business/Economics, Communications, Contemporary Culture, Education, Ethnic, Government/Politics, History, Humanities, Language, Literature, Literary Criticism, Multicultural, Music, Nature/Environment, Philosophy, Photography, Psychology, Religion, Science, Social Sciences, Translation, Travel, Women's Issues/Studies

Submission Guidelines Accepts proposal package (including outline, sample chapter and market survey).

Tips CSP has a policy of actively seeking and commissioning works in areas in which it has a publishing interest but at the same time invites and will consider unsolicited manuscripts in all of the areas in which it publishes. Does not publish textbooks or non-academic manuscripts.

Cambridge University Press

The Edinburgh Building, Shaftesbury Road, Cambridge, CB2 8RU

- 01223 312393
- 01223 315052
- editorial@cambridge.org

@ www.cambridge.org

Contact Chief Executive, Stephen R.R. Bourne; Managing Director (Europe, Middle East & Africa), Michael Holdsworth; Managing Director (Academic Publishing), Andrew Brown; Publishing Director (Humanities & Social Sciences), Richard Fisher; Publishing Director (Science, Technology & Medicine), Richard Barling

Established 1534

Insider Info Publishes around 1,200 titles per year. Payment is via royalties. Catalogue available online. Manuscript guidelines are available online.

Non-Fiction Publishes Reference, Scholarly and Technical titles on the following subjects: Anthropology/Archaeology, Business/Economics, Education, Government/Politics, Health/Medicine, History, Language/Literature, Law, Multicultural, Music/Dance, Nature/Environment, Philosophy, Psychology, Religion, Science, Transportation

Submission Guidelines Accepts query with SAE/ proposal package (including outline, two sample chapters, your publishing history, author biography, and SAE).

Recent Title(s) *The Conquests of Alexander the Great*, Waldemar Heckel

Tips CUP publishes academic and educational writing from around the world. As a department of the University of Cambridge, its purpose is to further the University's objective of advancing knowledge, education, learning, and research. They do not publish new fiction, poetry or other forms of creative writing, autobiography or memoir, overtly devotional or religious tracts (except for the Bible), political polemic, cookbooks, car handbooks or DIY manuals, or highly illustrated books for the general reader. Everything they do publish must have some educational and/or scholarly value.

Cameron & Hollis
PO Box 1, Moffat, Dumfriesshire, DG10 9SU
☏ 01683 220808
☏ 01683 220012
@ editorial@cameronbooks.co.uk
@ www.cameronbooks.co.uk
Contact Director, Ian A. Hamilton
Established 1976
Insider Info Catalogue available online.
Non-Fiction Publishes General Non-Fiction, Illustrated and Scholarly titles on the following subjects:
Art/Architecture, Crafts, Hobbies
Recent Title(s) *The Countryside Remembered*, Sadie Ward
Tips Specialises in creating books in the fields of contemporary art, film criticism, the decorative arts, architecture, social history and the environment for publishers in Britain, continental Europe and North

America. Operates abroad as well as in the UK, but only prints serious critical studies on the specified subject areas.

Campbell Books
20 New Wharf Road, London, N1 9RR
☏ 020 7014 6000
☏ 020 7014 6001
@ www.panmacmillan.com
Parent Company Pan Macmillan
Insider Info Catalogue available online.
Fiction Publishes Picture Books and Children's Interactive, Moving and Textured Books.
Submission Guidelines Agented submissions only.
Recent Title(s) *Honey Hill: Wipe-Clean Counting*, Dubravka Kolanovic (Wipe-Clean Book)
Tips Founded by Rod Campbell, creator of the toddler classic, *Dear Zoo*. The imprint is a front-runner in the specialist pre-school market. No unsolicited submissions.

Canongate Books Ltd
14 High Street, Edinburgh, EH1 1TE
☏ 0131 557 5111
☏ 0131 557 5211
@ info@canongate.co.uk
@ www.canongate.net
Contact Publisher, Jamie Byng; Managing Director, David Graham
Established 1973
Imprint(s) Canongate Classics
Canongate Crime
Canongate International
Insider Info Aims to respond to proposal within three months. Catalogue and manuscript guidelines available online.
Non-Fiction Publishes Biography, General Non-Fiction and Scholarly titles on the following subjects: History, Language/Literature, Music/Dance, Regional, Religion, Travel
Fiction Publishes Contemporary, Literary, Regional, Religious, Short Story Collections, Crime and Scottish titles.
Submission Guidelines Accepts proposal package (including outline, synopsis, sample chapters and an SAE) by post only.
Recent Titles *Eunoia*, Christian Bök (Contemporary Fiction); *Change We Can Believe In*, Barack Obama (Politics); *The Mighty Book of Boosh*, Noel Fielding (Humour/TV Tie-In)
Tips With a distinctly international outlook, Canongate Books continues to nurture and publish new talent from around the world, whilst retaining the essence of the Scottish Canon. They have no specific agenda other than to promote and publish

challenging, quality work from as broad a perspective as possible.

Canopus Publishing
15 Nelson Parade, Bristol, BS3 4HY
- 0117 963 3366
- robin@canopusbooks.com
- www.canopusbooks.com

Contact Managing Director, Robin Rees; Publishing Director, Tom Spicer; Commissioning Editor, Jim Revill

Insider Info Catalogue available online.

Non-Fiction Publishes General Non-Fiction, Reference, Scholarly, Textbook and Technical titles on the following subjects:
Science, Astronomy/Space

Recent Title(s) *Dark Side of the Universe*, Iain Nicolson

Tips Canopus publishes popular science titles, particularly in astronomy. Canopus also packages books for major publishing companies and institutions. Canopus has a new academic imprint, Canopus Academic Publishing, which publishes purely academic physics book through Springer Verlag.

Capall Bann Publishing
Auton Farm, Milverton, Somerset, TA4 1NE
- 01823 401528
- 01823 401529
- enquiries@capallbann.co.uk
- www.capallbann.co.uk

Contact Publisher (Alternative Health, Angels, Spiritual Living, Folklore, Animals and Lore, Fairies), Julia Day; Publisher (Magic, Witchcraft, Earth Magic, Sacred Sites, Shamanism), Jon Day

Established 1993

Insider Info Publishes 45 titles per year. Receives approximately 500 queries and 350 manuscripts per year. 50 per cent of books published are from first-time authors and 100 per cent of books published are from unagented authors. Five per cent of books published are author subsidy published, depending on whether the title has special requirements, such as colour pictures. Payment is via royalty (on wholesale price) at 0.1 (per £). Average lead time is six months, with simultaneous submissions accepted. Submissions accompanied by SAE will be returned. Catalogue is free on request, and available online or by email. Manuscript guidelines are available with SAE, or by email.

Non-Fiction Publishes Self-Help and General Non-Fiction titles on the following subjects:
Alternative Health, Animals, Astrology/Psychic, Cooking/Foods/Nutrition, Folklore, Gardening, Health/Medicine, Mind, Body and Spirit, Nature/

Environment, New Age, Philosophy, Religion (Pagan), Spirituality

Submission Guidelines Accepts query with SAE or by email, or proposal package (including outline, two sample chapters and SAE) and artworks/images (send photocopies or digital files as jpegs).

Tips Capall Bann Publishing does not require an author to make submissions through a literary agent.

Capstone Publishing
8 Newtec Place, Magdalen Road, Oxford, OX4 1RE
- 01865 798623
- 01865 240941
- info@wiley-capstone.co.uk
- www.capstoneideas.com

Parent Company John Wiley & Sons Inc

Contact Directors: Mark Allin and Richard Burton

Established 1997

Insider Info Catalogue is available online.

Non-Fiction Publishes General Non-Fiction, Humour, Multimedia and Scholarly titles on Business/Economics.

Submission Guidelines Query with SAE, or proposal package (including outline, sample chapter(s), author biography and SAE).

Tips Capstone is a business publisher, its mission is to make the ideas that are driving the new economy accessible and entertaining. The publisher, like the public, wants to find the right information quickly and easily, and start putting it into practice. Articles for submission must work towards understanding the key ideas and decisions that are influencing the way business is developing in the 21st Century.

Carcanet Press Ltd
4th Floor, Alliance House, 30 Cross Street, Manchester, M2 7AQ
- 0161 834 8730
- 0161 832 0084
- info@carcanet.co.uk
- www.carcanet.co.uk

Contact Editorial & Managing Director, Michael Schmidt; Managing Editor, Judith Wilson

Established 1969

Insider Info Aims to respond to queries and proposals within six weeks. Catalogue and manuscript guidelines are available online.

Non-Fiction Publishes Biography and Scholarly titles.

Fiction Publishes Classic, Contemporary and Translation titles.

Submission Guidelines Accepts query with SAE/proposal package (including outline, sample chapter(s)), or completed manuscript.

Poetry Publishes Poetry and Poetry Translation titles.

Submission Guidelines Accepts query/sample poems (6–10 pages) by post only with SAE.
Recent Title(s) *A Recipe for Water*, Gillian Clarke (Poetry); *Alphabets of Sand*, Khoury-Ghata (Author) and Marilyn Hacker (Translator) (Translated Poetry)
Tips Carcanet considers submissions and book proposals submitted in hard copy form only. No electronic submissions will be considered. Writers wishing to submit poetry should familiarise themselves with Carcanet's back list.

Cardiff Academic Press
St Fagans Road, Fairwater, Cardiff, CF5 3AE
☎ 029 2056 0333
🖷 029 2056 0313
✉ enquiries@cardiffacademicpress.com
🌐 www.cardiffacademicpress.com
Parent Company Drake Group
Non-Fiction Publishes Biography, Textbook and Scholarly titles on the following subjects: Cosmology, Education, Literature, Religious Studies, Women's Studies, Welsh History.
Fiction Publishes Literary titles.
Recent Title(s) *Can Darwinism Explain Morality?*, Daniel Oakey

Carlton Publishing Group
20 Mortimer Street, London, W1T 3JW
☎ 020 7612 0400
🖷 020 7612 0401
✉ enquiries@carltonbooks.co.uk
🌐 www.carltonbooks.co.uk
Contact Managing Director, Jonathan Goodman
Established 1992
Imprint(s) Carlton Books
Andre Deutsch
Prion
Insider Info Aims to respond to proposals within four weeks. Catalogue and manuscript guidelines are available online.
Non-Fiction Publishes Autobiography, Biography, Children's, Coffee Table Books, Gift Books, Humour, Illustrated Books, Arts Catalogues and Reference titles on the following subjects: Art/Architecture, Cooking/Foods/Nutrition, Entertainment/Games, Health/Medicine, Military/War, Music/Dance, Photography, Theatre and Drama, Mind, Body and Spirit, Criminology, and Erotica
* Does not consider proposals for academic books.
Submission Guidelines Accepts proposal package (including outline, author biography and two sample chapters, or 20 pages, whichever is shorter). Submission details to: pmurrayhill@carltonbooks.co.uk
Fiction Publishes Children's Illustrated Fiction.
Submission Guidelines Does not accept proposals.

Recent Title(s) *Vintage Shoes*, Caroline Cox (Fashion/Carlton Book); *Cat Nav*, Mike Mosedale (Humour/Prion)
Tips Does not consider proposals for fiction, poetry, children's or academic books.

Carlton Books
20 Mortimer Street, London, W1T 3JW
☎ 020 7612 0400
🖷 020 7612 0401
✉ enquiries@carltonbooks.co.uk
🌐 www.carltonbooks.co.uk
Parent Company Carlton Publishing Group
Insider Info Aims to respond to proposals within four weeks. Catalogue is available online.
Non-Fiction Publishes Humour, Illustrated Books and Reference titles on the following subjects: Entertainment/Games, History, Sports, Lifestyle, Humour
Submission Guidelines Accepts proposal package (including outline and the first 20 pages, or two chapters, whichever is shorter).
Recent Title(s) *The Treasures of Muhammad Ali*, Gavin Newsham and Muhammad Ali (Photography)
Tips Does not consider proposals for fiction, poetry, children's or academic books. Do not send a full manuscript other than via an agent.

Carroll & Brown Ltd
20 Lonsdale Road, London, NW6 6RD
☎ 020 7372 0900
🖷 020 7372 0460
✉ mail@carrollandbrown.co.uk
🌐 www.carrollandbrown.co.uk
Contact Editorial Director, Louise Dixon
Established 2000
Insider Info Catalogue is available online.
Non-Fiction Publishes How-To, Illustrated Books, Reference and Self-Help titles on the following subjects:
Pregnancy and Child Care, Medical Care, Alternative therapies, Fitness, Sex, Women's Health Issues, Pastimes, Crafts
Submission Guidelines Accepts queries by email. Manuscript submissions must be posted and accompanied by a stamped, self-addressed envelope.
Recent Title(s) *Beautiful Birth*, Suzanne Yates (Childcare); *A Dad's Guide to Babycare*, Colin Cooper (Childcare)

Cassell Illustrated
2–4 Heron Quays, London, E14 4JP
☎ 020 7531 8400
🖷 020 7537 0858
✉ publisher@cassell-illustrated.com

ⓦ www.cassell-illustrated.com

Parent Company Octopus Publishing Group
Contact Publishing Director, Iain MacGregor; Commissioning Editor, Laura Price
Insider Info Downloadable catalogue is available online.
Non-Fiction Publishes Coffee Table Books, Cookbooks, Gift Books, How-To, Humour, Illustrated Books, Reference and Self-Help titles on the following subjects: Art, Childcare/Parenting, Contemporary Culture, Crafts, Food & Drink, Gardening, Health/Medicine, History, House and Home, Psychology, Sex, Spirituality, Sports, Travel, Adventure, Television Tie-Ins
Submission Guidelines Accepts email or phone submission ideas in the first instance.
Submission details to: iain.macgregor@cassell-illustrated.co.uk
Recent Title(s) *1001 Movies You Must See Before You Die*, Steven Jay Schneider, ed. (Illustrated Reference); *The Wonder Book of Would You Believe It?* (Illustrated Reference)
Tips Cassell Illustrated's commissioning team will consider exciting new talent. Writers should make contact with the relevant commissioning editor.

Cassell Reference
Orion House, 5 Upper St Martin's Lane, London, WC2H 9EA
ⓞ 020 7240 3444
ⓕ 020 7240 4822
ⓦ www.orionbooks.co.uk
Parent Company Weidenfeld & Nicholson (Orion Publishing Group)
Insider Info Catalogue is available online and as a downloadable pdf.
Non-Fiction Publishes Illustrated and Reference titles.
Submission Guidelines Accepts agented submissions only.
Recent Title(s) *In Search of the Knights Templar*, Simon Brighton (Illustrated Reference)

Caterpillar Press
2 Coda Centre, 189 Munster Road, London, SW6 6AW
ⓞ 020 7386 6705
ⓕ 020 7610 3353
ⓔ jasher@caterpillarbooks.co.uk
ⓦ www.caterpillarbooks.com
Parent Company Magi Publications
Contact Publisher, Jamie Asher
Fiction Publishes Picture and Novelty Book titles for the 0–3 age group.
Tips Caterpillar specialises in novelty books such as board and cloth books for pre-schoolers only.

Contact Jamie Asher for more information. See Little Tiger Press for Magi Publications' imprint for slightly older children.

Catholic Truth Society
40–46 Harleyford Road, London, SE11 5AY
ⓞ 020 7640 0042
ⓕ 020 7640 0046
ⓔ p.finaldi@cts-online.org.uk
ⓦ www.cts-online.org.uk
Contact Publisher, Fergal Martin; Commissioning Editor, Pierpaolo Finaldi
Established 1868
Insider Info Catalogue is available online.
Non-Fiction Publishes Biography, General Non-Fiction, Gift Books and Reference titles on the following subjects: Alternative Lifestyles, History, Religion.
Fiction Publishes Religious titles.
Recent Title(s) *Fit for Mission? Church*, Patrick O'Donoghue; *Praying with Mary*, Juliette Levivier
Tips Publications appeal to many different age groups, to Catholic parishes and schools, and to the wider Christian community, as well as to a wide range of other enquirers. The principal goal of CTS publications is to explain the Catholic faith.

Catnip Publishing Ltd
14 Greville Street, London, EC1N 8SB
ⓞ 020 7138 3650
ⓕ 020 7138 3658
ⓔ andrea.reece@catnippublishing.co.uk
ⓦ www.catnippublishing.co.uk
Contact Editorial, Marketing & Publicity, Andrea Reece
Insider Info Catalogue available online. Accepts queries by email, phone or post
Fiction Publishes out-of-print Children's titles and New Children's Fiction.
* Publishes illustrated and non-illustrated books.
Recent Title(s) *Strange Hiding Place*, Graham Marks (Children's Novel); *Jake in Danger*, Annette Butterworth (Author) and Nick Butterworth (Illustrator) (Re-print)
Tips Although some new titles are published, the main emphasis of Catnip is on reprints.

CBD Research
Chancery House, 15 Wickham Road, Beckenham, Kent, BR3 5JS
ⓞ 0871 222 3440
ⓕ 020 8650 0768
ⓔ cbd@cbdresearch.com
ⓦ www.cbdresearch.com
Established 1961
Imprint(s) Chancery House Press

Insider Info Catalogue is available online.
Non-Fiction Publishes Multimedia, Directories and Reference titles.
Recent Title(s) *Directory of British Associations Edition 19*, (Directory)
Tips CBD Research is an independent publisher of high quality reference books and CD-ROMS. Titles are aimed at librarians, media researchers, journalists, PR, sales and marketing professionals, and career changers.

The Celtic Cross Press
Ovins Well House, Lastingham, York, YO62 6TJ
- 01751 417298
- 01751 417739
- books@celticcrosspress.com
- www.celticcrosspress.com

Non-Fiction Publishes short works of prose.
Fiction Publishes short works of prose fiction.
Poetry Publishes reprints of fine works.
Recent Title(s) *Butterflies*, David Burnett (Author) and Rosemary Roberts (Illustrator); *A Thrill of Pleasure*, William Wordsworth
Tips The Celtic Cross Press prints and publishes limited editions of fine books, hand-printed by letterpress and bound in full cloth covered boards. Every book is numbered and signed. All the original illustrations are printed from blocks cut in wood or lino, or from drawings made into metal line blocks. They are a member of the Fine Press Book Association.

Celtic Publications
16 Grove Lawn, Malahide, Co. Dublin, Republic of Ireland
- 00353 1 845 6860
- info@celticpublications.com
- www.celticpublications.com

Insider Info Catalogue available online.
Non-Fiction Publishes Education and Lexicography titles on the following subjects:
English as a Foreign Language, Art, Culture, Irish History, Music.
Recent Title(s) *Phonetics for Learners of English Pronunciation*; *Teaching English in Ireland*
Tips All writers must be qualified EFL teachers and/or experts in Irish history, music, art or culture.

Cengage Learning
High Holborn House, 50–51 Bedford Row, London, WC1R 4LR
- 020 7067 2500
- 020 7067 2600
- Online form.
- www.cengage.co.uk

Imprint(s) Arden Shakespeare

Insider Info Catalogue available online. Proposal guidelines and manuscript preparation, as well as a list of areas where Thomson Learning are actively seeking texts, are available on the website under 'Authors'.
Non-Fiction Publishes Multimedia, Reference, Scholarly, Technical and Textbook titles on the following subjects:
Business, Accounting, Economics, Psychology, Hair and Beauty, Shakespeare, and other diverse areas
Submission Guidelines Details on website. In the first instance email the editorial department or write to the Publishing Director at the address above.
Tips Formerly known as Thomson Learning EMEA, Cengage publishes titles for secondary, post-secondary and graduate level students, teachers, librarians and learning institutions in both traditional and distance-learning environments.

Century
Random House, 20 Vauxhall Bridge Road, London, SW1V 2SA
- 020 7840 8554
- 020 7233 6127
- centuryeditorial@randomhouse.co.uk
- www.randomhouse.co.uk

Parent Company The Random House Group Ltd
Contact Publishing Director, Mark Booth
Insider Info Catalogue is available online.
Non-Fiction Publishes Autobiography, Biography, General Non-Fiction and Self-Help titles on the following subjects: History, Spirituality, Parenting.
Submission Guidelines No unagented submissions.
Fiction Publishes Mystery, Romance, Suspense, General Fiction and 'Chick Lit' titles.
Submission Guidelines No unagented submissions.
Recent Title(s) *Eric Bristow: The Crafty Cockney*, Eric Bristow (Autobiography); *Cross Country*, James Patterson (Crime Fiction)
Tips View the Century section of the main Random House catalogue for examples of publishing lists.

CGP Books
Coordination Group Publications Ltd, Broughton House, Griffin Street, Broughton In Furness, Cumbria, LA20 6HH
- 01229 715714
- 0870 750 1292
- customerservices@cgpbooks.co.uk
- www.cgpbooks.co.uk

Insider Info Accept queries by email or phone. Catalogue available online.
Non-fiction Publishes Children's Educational titles and Revision guides on the following subjects:

All Curriculum subjects including Maths, English, Science, Technology, Languages and Humanities from Key Stage 1 to A2 level.

Recent Title(s) *GCSE Core & Additional Physics - Essential Formula Practice*

Tips CGP titles are written by educational professionals, and although they do not advertise for book proposals, they are on the look out for teachers who are interested in contributing to, or proofreading, their range of upcoming titles.

Chambers Harrap Publishers Ltd

7 Hopetoun Crescent, Edinburgh, EH7 4AY
- 0131 556 5929
- 0131 556 5313
- admin@chambers.co.uk
- www.chambersharrap.co.uk

Parent Company Hachette UK

Contact Managing Director & Publisher, Patrick White

Established 1819

Insider Info Catalogue is available online.

Non-Fiction Publishes Dictionary, Multimedia, Reference and Scholarly titles on the following subjects:
Biographical Reference, History, Factbooks, Language, Phrasebooks, Puzzles & Games, Quotations, Science, Thesaurus, Writing Guides

Recent Title(s) *The Chambers Dictionary (De luxe Edition)*

Chancery House Press

Chancery House, 15 Wickham Road, Beckenham, Kent, BR3 5JS
- 0871 222 3440
- 020 8650 0768
- cbd@cbdresearch.com
- www.cbdresearch.com/chanceryuk.htm

Parent Company CBD Research

Non-Fiction Publishes Esoteric, Specialist Non-Fiction and Reference titles.

Recent Title(s) *Alas, Poor Sherlock*, Joseph & Peter Ridgway Watt

Tips Chancery House titles are aimed at serious researchers and dedicated hobbyists. Publishes very specialist, niche books, often the products of detailed research or cataloguing exercises. Subjects have included records of hangings and wafer seals.

Channel 4 Books

61–63 Uxbridge Road, London, W5 5SA
- 020 8579 2652
- 020 8579 5479
- info@transworld-publishers.co.uk
- www.booksattransworld.co.uk

Parent Company Transworld Publishers

Insider Info Catalogue is available online.

Non-Fiction Publishes Illustrated Books, Television Tie-Ins and General Non-Fiction titles.

Submission Guidelines Accepts agented submissions only.

Tips Publishes mainly non-fiction books derived from popular Channel 4 television programmes.

Chapman Publishing

4 Broughton Place, Edinburgh, EH1 3RX
- 0131 557 2207
- chapman-pub@blueyonder.co.uk
- www.chapman-pub.co.uk

Contact General Editor (Poetry), Joy Hendry

Established 1986

Insider Info Publishes three titles per year. Receives approximately 200 queries and 80 manuscripts per year. 30 per cent of books published are from first-time authors, 100 per cent are from unagented authors. Payment is via royalty (on retail price).

Fiction Regional (Scottish) and Short Story titles

Poetry Scottish Poetry titles

Recent Title(s) *Winter Barley*, George Gunn (Poetry)

Tips Chapman publishes the *Chapman* literary magazines, as well as publishing new short-fiction and poetry with an emphasis on Scottish writing and Gaelic. Chapman books usually come under one of their various series, including the *Wild Women Series* and *New Writing Series*.

Charlewood Press

7 Weavers Place, Chandlers Ford, Eastleigh, Hampshire, SO53 1TU
- 023 8026 1192
- gponting@clara.net
- http://home.clara.net/gponting/index.html

Contact Managing Editors: Gerald Ponting and Anthony Light

Established 1987

Insider Info Catalogue is available online.

Non-Fiction Publishes General Non-Fiction titles on the following subjects: History, Regional, Local History, Local Walks.

Recent Title(s) *The History of Fordingbridge*, Anthony Light and Gerald Ponting (Local History); *Bournemouth Yesterday and Today*, Anthony Light and Gerald Ponting, (Local History)

Tips The publisher specialises in titles on guidebooks, local history, and archaeological sites.

Chatto & Windus

Random House, 20 Vauxhall Bridge Road, London, SW1V 2SA
- 020 7840 8745
- 020 7233 6117
- chattoeditorial@randomhouse.co.uk

W www.randomhouse.co.uk
Parent Company The Random House Group Ltd.
Contact Publishing Director, Alison Samuel
Established Founded in the 19th Century, part of
The Random House Group since 1987
Insider Info Catalogue is available online.
Non-Fiction Publishes General Non-Fiction titles on
the following subjects:
Government/Politics, History, Memoirs, Philosophy,
Biography.
Submission Guidelines No unagented
submissions.
Fiction Publishes Literary, Mainstream/
Contemporary and Translation titles.
Submission Guidelines No unagented
submissions.
Poetry Publishes Classic and Contemporary
Poetry titles.
Recent Title(s) *Once on a Moonless Night*, Dai Sijie
(Literary Fiction); *Called Out of Darkness: A Spiritual
Confession*, Anne Rice (Memoir/Religion)
Tips Look at the Chatto & Windus section of the
Random House catalogue to get a feel for the list
before submitting.

The Cherry on the Top Press
29 Vickers Road, Firth Park, Sheffield, S5 6UY
☏ 0114 244 1202
✉ dgk@kennedyd.fsworld.co.uk
W www.llpp.ms11.net/cherry.html
Contact Publisher, David Kennedy
Insider Info Catalogue available free on request. No
unsolicited manuscripts.
Non-Fiction Publishes Gift titles.
Fiction Publishes Short Story Collections.
Poetry Publishes Poetry titles.
Recent Title(s) *Four True Prophecies of the New State*,
David Kennedy; *A Walk Towards Spicer,* Stephen
Vincent (Contemporary Poetry)
Tips The press publishes artists' books, small run
pamphlets of innovative writing, and a magazine of
innovative poems in English called *The Paper*. The
press is unable to consider unsolicited submissions.

Chicken House Publishing
2 Palmer Street, Frome, Somerset, BA11 1DS
☏ 01373 454488
☏ 01373 454499
✉ chickenhouse@doublecluck.com
W www.doublecluck.com
Contact Publisher/Managing Director, Barry
Cunningham; Deputy Managing Director,
Rachel Hickman
Established 2000

Insider Info Aims to respond to proposals and
manuscripts within three months. Catalogue and
manuscript guidelines are available online.
Fiction Publishes Teenage, Picture Books, and
Children's titles.
Submission Guidelines Accepts query with SAE/
proposal package (including outline and three
sample chapters). No email submissions.
Recent Title(s) *Inkheart*, Cornelia Funke (Movie Tie-
in); *Numbers*, Rachel Ward (Teenage Novel)
Tips The Chicken House is a plucky, highly
individual, children's book publishing company with
an enthusiasm for finding new writers, artists and
ideas. Books are aimed at children, parents, teachers
and librarians.

Child's Play (International)
**Ashworth Road, Bridgemead, Swindon,
Wiltshire, SN5 7YD**
☏ 01793 616286
✉ Online form.
W www.childs-play.com
Contact Chief Executive, Neil Burden
Insider Info Catalogue is free on request and
available online or by email.
Non-Fiction Publishes Children's titles.
Fiction Publishes Picture Books, Board Books and
Children's titles.
Tips Child's Play is an independent publisher
specialising in learning through play with a range of
books, games, toys and other resources (aimed at
Key Stage 1 & 2). Company products also support
minority groups and languages.

Chimera
**Sheraton House, Castle Park, Cambridge,
CB3 OAX**
☏ 01223 370012
☏ 01223 370040
✉ editors@pegasuspublishers.com
W www.pegasuspublishers.com
Parent Company Pegasus Elliot MacKenzie
Publishers Ltd
Insider Info Catalogue and manuscript details are
available online.
Fiction Publishes Contemporary, Futuristic,
Historical and Relationship Erotica titles.
Submission Guidelines Accepts proposal package
(including outline and two sample chapters).
Tips Chimera publishes adult erotic fiction for over
18s and specialises in the work of 'previously
unpublished first time authors from all over the
world who have a good spanking tale to tell.'
Chimera accepts submissions of erotic fiction from
any author over the age of 18 as long as the content

does not 'contravene the law of the land or international law.'

Christian Education
1020 Bristol Road, Selly Oak, Birmingham, B29 6LB
- 0121 472 4242
- 0121 472 7575
- editorial@christianeducation.org.uk
- www.christianeducation.org.uk

Contact Publications Team Leader & Editor, Anstice Hughes
Insider Info Catalogue is available online.
Non-Fiction Publishes Textbook, Worship Resources and Scholarly titles on Religion.
Fiction Publishes Religious and Children's Religious titles.
Tips Christian Education (CE) provides advice, resources and opportunities for teaching and learning in the school, the church and the family group, carrying forward the work of the National Christian Education Council (NCEC, formerly the National Sunday School Union) and the Christian Education Movement (CEM). The two organisations are now joining together to maximise their delivery of high quality training and resources for Christian educators and for teachers of Religious Education in schools. Works must be aimed at academic usage either for schools or church groups.

Christian Focus Publications
Geanies House, Fearn, Tain, Ross-shire, IV20 1TW
- 01862 871011
- 01862 871699
- info@christianfocus.com
- www.christianfocus.com

Contact Editorial Manager, Willie Mackenzie
Established 1979
Imprint(s) CF4Kids
Christian Heritage
Mentor
Insider Info Catalogue and manuscript guidelines are available online.
Non-Fiction Publishes Biblical Studies, Biography, Children's Non-Fiction, Christian Life, Church Life, Inspirational, Ministry Resources, Pastoral Help, Seasonal and Theology & Doctrine titles.
Fiction Publishes Children's and Young Adult titles.
Submission Guidelines Query with SAE/Proposal package (including outline, two sample chapters, author biography and SAE).
Recent Title(s) *The Holy War*, John Bunyan (Allegorical Novel); *Morning & Evening*, C H Spurgeon (Biblical Teachings)
Tips Titles are aimed at all ages and abilities. Christian Focus Publications (CFP) is a conservative,

evangelical publishing house and comes from a non-denominational reformed background. Although it is not insisted that all authors call themselves reformed, anything that would be a polemic against the reformed faith would not be considered. CFP are committed to the historic foundations of the faith, the inerrancy of Scripture in its original manuscripts, the deity of Christ, his uniqueness as a means of salvation and the existence of hell.

Christopher Davies Publishers
PO Box 403, Swansea, SA1 4YF
- 01792 648825
- 01792 648825
- editor@cdaviesbookswales.com

Contact Director, Chris Talfan Davies; Editor; Morwenna Talfan Davies
Insider Info Catalogue is available online.
Non-Fiction Publishes General Non-Fiction on the following subjects: History, Regional, Sports, Travel, Welsh Interest.
Recent Title(s) *An A–Z of Wales and the Welsh*, Terry Breverton (Welsh Interest/Reference)
Tips Titles are aimed at anyone interested in books about Wales, its culture and its people. All books are of general Welsh interest, or concerning Welsh history.

Christopher Helm
38 Soho Square, London, W1D 3HB
- 020 7758 0200
- 020 7758 0222
- ornithology@acblack.com
- www.acblack.com

Parent Company A&C Black Publishers Ltd
Contact Department Head, Nigel Redman; Publishing Director, Jonathan Glasspool (Reference, Theatre and Ornithology)
Established 1983
Insider Info Catalogue is available online.
Non-Fiction Publishes General Non-Fiction, Illustrated Books and Reference titles on the following subjects: Nature/Environment, Ornithology
Recent Title(s) *Handbook of Western Palearctic Birds*, Hadoram Shirihai and Lars Svensson (Ornithology)
Tips Christopher Helm publishes taxonomic and geographic bird books, identification and field guides, and general interest nature books. Also publishes the *Where to Watch* series and books for the RSPB. Along with the other A&C Black nature imprints, Christopher Helm is the largest bird book publisher in the English language. They work with material from well known or celebrity naturalists, such as Bill Oddie, and produce books in

conjunction with companies such as the RSPB. They do not generally consider unsolicited material.

Chrysalis Children's Books
151 Freston Road, London, W10 6TH
☎ 020 7314 1400
☏ 020 7314 1401
🌐 www.anovabooks.com
Parent Company Anova Books Company Ltd
Contact Catalogue available online.
Non-fiction Publishes Children's Illustrated reference titles.
Fiction Publishes Children's Picture Book, Novelty and Classic titles.
Recent Title(s) *How to Cook Children*, Martin Howard (Author) and Colin Stimpson (Illustrator) (Picture Book)
Tips Chrysalis Children's Books are published within the Anova Books Company and are separated into five sub categories: Babies Books, Children's Fiction, Children's Non-Fiction, Children's Novelty Books. Picture Books. The age range covered is from infants to ten plus years.

Churchill Livingstone
Linacre House, Jordan Hill, Oxford, OX2 8DP
☎ 01865 474010
☏ 01865 474011
📧 authorsupport@elsevier.com
🌐 www.elsevierhealth.com/cl
Parent Company Elsevier Ltd (Health Sciences)
Established 1972
Insider Info Payment is via royalties. Catalogue and manuscript guidelines are available online.
Non-Fiction Publishes Multimedia, Reference, Scholarly, Textbook, Journals and Technical titles on the following subjects: Education, Health/Medicine, Science
Submission Guidelines Accepts submissions via online proposal form.
Submissions email: c.makepeace@elsevier.com
Recent Title(s) *Clinical Mycology with CD-ROM*, Anaissie, McGinnis and Pfaller (Medicine/Reference)
Tips Churchill Livingstone is a global publisher of health and medical books, journals and CD-ROMs, including medical reference for health professionals and textbooks for lecturers and students. To submit a proposal to Churchill Livingstone fill in and return a proposal form, available on the website. Alternatively authors may contact the publishing director or editor prior to submission to discuss the proposal.

Churchwarden Publications Ltd
PO Box 420, Warminster, BA12 9XB
☎ 01985 840189

☏ 01985 840243
Contact Managing Director, John Stidolph
Established 1974
Insider Info Publishes two titles per year.
Non-fiction Publishes books and stationery aimed at Churchwardens and Administrators.

Cicerone Press Ltd
2 Police Square, Milnthorpe, Cumbria, LA7 7PY
☎ 01539 562069
☏ 01539 563417
📧 info@cicerone.co.uk
🌐 www.cicerone.co.uk
Contact Director (all areas), Jonathan Williams
Established 1968
Imprint(s) Cicerone
Insider Info Publishes 20-30 titles per year. Receives 600 proposals and publishing enquiries per year, nearly all from unagented authors. Submissions accompanied by SAE will be returned. Payments by royalty, 10 per cent on retail/wholesale price. Catalogue and manuscript guidelines are available free on request and online.
Non-Fiction Publishes Walking Guidebooks and Non-Fiction titles on the following subjects: Guidance, Nature/Environment, Recreation, Travel, Walking
* Almost exclusively publishes guidebooks for walking, trekking, mountaineering and cycling.
Submission Guidelines Accepts proposal package (including outline, sample chapter(s), your publishing history, clips and author biography). Will accept artwork/photos (send digital files as jpegs). Submissions email: info@cicerone.co.uk
Recent Title(s) *Walking in Madeira*, Paddy Dillon (Walking)
Tips Titles are always aimed at adults.

Cico Books
1st Floor, 32 Great Sutton Street, London, EC1V ONB
☎ 020 7253 7960
☏ 020 7253 7967
Contact Managing Director, Mark Collins; Publisher, Lucinda Richards
Established 1999
Non-Fiction Publishes Illustrated Book and General Non-Fiction titles on the following subjects: Spirituality, Lifestyle/Interiors, Mind/Body/Spirit.
Submission Guidelines No unsolicited submissions.
Tips Cico Books publish stylish, highly illustrated non-fiction for the worldwide co-edition market. They specialise in design, interiors, craft, health, mind, body and spirit, magic, history and gift books.

Cinnamon Press

Ty Meirion, Glan yr afon, Tanygrisiau, Blaenau Ffestiniog, Gwynedd, LL41 3SU

- jan@cinnamonpress.com
- www.cinnamonpress.com

Contact Jan Fortune-Wood (Writers' Queries); Mike Fortune-Wood (Trade/Publicity/Payment Queries)

Insider Info Catalogue and manuscript guidelines are available online.

Non-Fiction Publishes limited Non-Fiction titles, no academic titles or local interest.

* Past non-fiction titles have focused on alternative parenting and memoirs.

Fiction Publishes all genres except Erotica, Crime and Horror.

* Wants full length novels that are unique and affecting. No children's novels, although well written work for older teenagers will be considered.

Poetry Publishes Contemporary Poetry titles.

* Poetry should be modern, have depth and an edge.

Submission Guidelines Not currently accepting submissions for the 2010 list. Check website for when submissions are being taken.

Tips Books should have a wide audience appeal and the publishers state that they are particularly interested in authors who can demonstrate a willingness to actively promote their work to the widest possible audience, particularly through local and national media. Submissions queries by email. Cinnamon Press publish authors from around the world, and also strongly promote the voice of Welsh writers. Check the website for any specific calls for anthology contributions.

CIPD Publishing

151 The Broadway, London, SW19 1JQ

- 020 8612 6562
- 020 8612 6201
- j.steventon@cipd.co.uk
- www.cipd.co.uk

Parent Company CIPD Enterprises Ltd (Chartered Institute of Personnel and Development)

Contact Commissioning Editor, Jenna Steventon (Student Textbooks); Commissioning Editor, Margaret Marriott (Professional Publications and Toolkits).

Insider Info Payment is via royalty (on wholesale price). Catalogue is available free on request and online. A hard copy catalogue/brochure can be ordered from the website.

Non-Fiction Publishes Textbooks, Subscription products, Toolkits, Electronic and General Non-Fiction titles on the following subjects:

Human Resources, Business Economics, Coaching, Learning and Development, General Management, Employment Law

Submission Guidelines Accepts proposal package (including outline, two sample chapters, author biography, competition analysis and market research).

Recent Title(s) *Coaching Skills for Line Managers*, Julia Lampshire (DVD)

Tips CIPD Publishing's readership consists of human resources practitioners, students and human resources training professionals. Author guidelines and instructions for initial proposal are available to download from the website.

Cisco Press

Edinburgh Gate, Harlow, Essex, CM20 2JE

- 01279 623623
- 01279 414130
- www.pearsoned.co.uk/imprints/ciscopress

Parent Company Pearson Education

Insider Info Catalogue and manuscript guidelines are available online.

Non-Fiction Publishes Reference, Textbooks and Scholarly titles on the following subjects: Computers, Computer Networking, Electronics, Server Mechanics.

Submission Guidelines Accepts proposal package (including synopsis, sample chapters, market research, your publishing history and author biography).

Recent Title(s) *The Power of IP Video* Jennifer Baker, Felicia Dalke, Mike Mitchell and Nader Nanjiani (Computing)

Tips Cisco Press is a partnership between Cisco Systems and Pearson Education. The books and software products are developed to enhance the online and instructor-led curriculum of the Cisco Networking Academies and contain programme materials for students and professionals.

CJ Fallon

Ground Floor, Block B, Liffey Valley Office Campus, Dublin 22, Republic of Ireland

- 00353 1 616 6400
- 00353 1 616 6499
- editorial@cjfallon.ie
- www.cjfallon.ie

Contact Managing Director, H.J. McNicholas; Editorial Director, N. White

Established 1927

Non-Fiction Publishes Textbooks and Educational titles.

Claire Publications

Unit 8, Tey Brook Craft Centre, Great Tey, Colchester, Essex, CO6 1JE
- 01206 211020
- 01206 212755
- mail@clairepublications.com
- www.clairepublications.com

Established 1980
Insider Info Catalogue available online
Non-Fiction Publishes Primary and Secondary Educational Resources on the following subjects:
Maths, English, PSHE, Science, Languages, Design and Technology
Submission Guidelines Will accept ideas for new products.
Tips As well as books, Claire Publications produce other classroom resources including games, activity packs and gifts. Products are mostly aimed at schools.

Clairview Books

Hillside House, The Square, Forest Row, East Sussex, RH18 5ES
- 0870 486 3526
- office@clairviewbooks.com
- www.clairviewbooks.com

Established 2000
Insider Info Catalogue is free on request or available online.
Non-Fiction Publishes General Non-Fiction titles on the following subjects:
Art, Current Affairs, Health and Healing, History, Politics, Spiritual Experience, World Affairs
Recent Title(s) *In the Belly of the Beast*, Sevak Edward Gulbekian (Cultural Studies)
Tips Clairview Books publishes non-fiction titles that engage with contemporary issues and challenge conventional thinking.

Co & Bear Productions

565 Fulham Road, London, SW6 1ES
- 020 7385 0888
- 020 7385 0101
- info@cobear.co.uk

Contact Publisher, Beatrice Vincenzini
Established 1996
Imprint(s) Scriptum Editions
Cartago
Non-Fiction Publishes Illustrated Books on the following subjects:
Alternative Lifestyles, Art/Architecture, Photography

Cois Life

62 Páirc na Rós, Ascaill na Cille, Dún Laoghaire, Co. Dublin, Republic of Ireland

- 00353 1 280 7951
- 00353 1 280 7951
- eolas@coislife.ie
- www.coislife.ie

Contact Directors: Dr Caoilfhionn Nic Pháidín and Dr Seán Ó Cearnaigh
Established 1995
Insider Info Catalogue available online.
Non-Fiction Publishes Academic and Research titles on the following subjects:
Irish Langauge and Culture
Fiction Publishes Irish language Fiction, Poetry and Plays.
Recent Title(s) *Canary Wharf*, Orna Ní Choileáin (Fiction); *Paidreacha na Gaeilge*, Donla uí Bhraonáin ed. (Poetry Anthology)
Tips Cois Life aims to publish literary and research works in the Irish language, for both young readers and learners of Irish.

Colin Smythe Limited

PO Box 6, Gerrards Cross, Buckinghamshire, SL9 8XA
- 01753 886000
- 01753 886469
- cs@colinsmythe.co.uk
- www.colinsmythe.co.uk

Contact Managing Director, Colin Smythe
Established 1966
Imprint(s) Dolmen Press
Van Duren Publishers
Insider Info Publishes four titles per year. No unsolicited submissions considered unless preceded by letter with synopsis.
Non-Fiction Publishes General Non-Fiction and Illustrated titles on the following subjects:
Irish Biography, Irish History, Irish Literature and Literary Criticism, Irish Theatre History, Parapsychology, Supernatural, Folklore, Heraldry, Mysticism
Fiction Publishes new editions of 19th and early 20th century Irish fiction.

Collins & Brown

The Old Magistrates Court, 10 Southcombe Street, London, W14 0RA
- 020 7605 1400
- 020 7605 1401
- customerservices@anovabooks.com
- www.anovabooks.com

Parent Company Anova Books Company Ltd
Contact Tom Stainer
Established 1989
Insider Info Catalogue is available online.
Non-Fiction Publishes How-To, IllustratedBbooks, Reference and Self-Help titles on the following

subjects: Art/Architecture, Cooking/Foods/Nutrition, Crafts, Gardening, Photography, Spirituality, Health, Lifestyle and Personal Development.
Submission Guidelines Accepts emailed synopses. Submission details to: tstainer@anovabooks.com
Recent Title(s) *The Harmony Guides: 101 Stitches to Crochet*, Erika Knight (Craft)
Tips The Collins & Brown imprint publishes high quality illustrated books that adopt a 'how-to' approach across a range of subjects. See Anova Books entry for more information about the company.

Collins
77–85 Fulham Palace Road, Hammersmith, London, W6 8JB
- 020 8741 7070
- 020 8307 4440
- customerservices@harpercollins.co.uk
- www.collins.co.uk

Parent Company HarperCollins Publishers Ltd
Contact Managing Director, Katie Fulford; Publishing Director, Denise Bates
Imprint(s) Collins Language/COBUILD
Collins Education
Collins Geo
Collins Maps & Atlases
Jane's
Times Books
Insider Info Catalogue available online.
Non-Fiction Publishes General & Popular Non-Fiction, Atlases, Dictionaries, Illustrated and Reference titles on the following subjects: Art/Architecture, Astrology/Psychic, Biography, Childcare/Parenting, Contemporary Culture, Cooking/Foods/Nutrition, DIY, Education, Gardening, House & Home, Language/Literature, Military, Natural History, Religion, Travel
Submission Guidelines Accepts agented submissions only.
Recent Title(s) *Collins – Speak Spanish* (Language); *Reggae Reggae Cookbook*, Levi Roots (Cooking)
Tips One of the UK's leading publishers of highly-illustrated non-fiction, dictionaries and world atlases. The Jane's imprint publishes military reference and guidebooks while Times Books publishes educational books, as well as books on astronomy and the *Times World Atlas* series. The HarperCollins group only accepts submissions from literary agents or previously published authors, but may consider submissions that are accompanied by a positive assessment from a manuscript assessment agency.

Collins Education
77–85 Fulham Palace Road, Hammersmith, London, W6 8JB
- 020 8741 7070
- 020 8307 4440
- editorial@collinseducation.com
- www.collinseducation.com

Parent Company Collins (HarperCollins Publishers Ltd)
Contact Managing Director, Nigel Ward
Insider Info Catalogue is available online.
Non-Fiction Publishes Children's, General Non-Fiction and Multimedia titles on Education.
Submission Guidelines Accepts queries and proposals from academic authors for educational books or materials. Contact by email with ideas in the first instance.
Recent Title(s) *Collins New Primary Maths Teacher's Guide 1*, Peter Clarke, ed. (Primary Education)
Tips Collins Education publishes books and electronic materials, including CD-ROMs and online resources, for schools, colleges and universities, as well as mature students and home learners.

Collins Language/COBUILD
77–85 Fulham Palace Road, Hammersmith, London, W6 8JB
- 020 8741 7070
- 020 8307 4440
- customerservices@harpercollins.co.uk
- www.collins.co.uk

Parent Company Collins (HarperCollins Publishers Ltd)
Contact Managing Director, Lorna Knight; Publishing Directors: Michela Clari, Helen Newstead
Insider Info Catalogue is available online.
Non-Fiction Publishes Multimedia, Dictionaries and Reference titles on the following subjects: Language/Literature, Translation.
Submission Guidelines Accepts agented submissions only.
Tips Publishes bilingual and English dictionaries, as well as the internationally successful Collins COBUILD series of dictionaries for foreign learners. Collins Dictionaries does not accept any submissions.

Collins Maps & Atlases
77–85 Fulham Palace Road, Hammersmith, London, W6 8JB
- 020 8741 7070
- 020 8307 4440
- customerservices@harpercollins.co.uk
- www.collins.co.uk

Parent Company Collins (HarperCollins Publishers Ltd)
Contact Managing Director, Mike Cottingham; Publishing Director, Helen Gordon
Insider Info Catalogue is available online.

Non-Fiction Publishes Maps, Atlases, Street Guides and Reference titles on the following subjects: History, Military, Nature, Travel.
Submission Guidelines Accepts agented submissions only.
Tips Collins Maps & Atlases publish illustrated maps, atlases, road and leisure travel guides. HarperCollins, as a group, only accepts submissions from literary agents or previously published authors, but may consider submissions that are accompanied by a positive assessment from a manuscript assessment agency.

Collins Geo
77–85 Fulham Palace Road, Hammersmith, London, W6 8JB
- 020 8741 7070
- 020 8307 4440
- customerservices@harpercollins.co.uk
- www.collins.co.uk

Parent Company Collins (HarperCollins Publishers Ltd)
Contact Managing Director, Sheena Barclay
Insider Info Catalogue is available online.
Non-Fiction Publishes Atlases, Illustrated, Reference and Digital titles on the following subjects: Cartography, Geography, Maps
Submission Guidelines Accepts agented submissions only.
Tips Aside from its published list, Collins Geo has a growing data and solutions business, counting Multimap, National Geographic, the World Bank, the United Nations and the defence sector among its customers.

The Collins Press
West Link Park, Doughcloyne, Wilton, Co. Cork, Republic of Ireland
- 00353 21 434 7717
- 00353 21 434 7720
- enquiries@collinspress.ie
- www.collinspress.ie

Contact Con Collins
Established 1989
Insider Info Catalogue and manuscript guidelines available online.
Non-Fiction Publishes Biography, General Non-Fiction, Illustrated and Reference titles on the following subjects:
Anthropology/Archaeology, Art/Architecture, Food & Drink, Health, History, Hobbies, Memoirs, Music, Nature/Environment, Regional, Spirituality, Sports, Travel
Submission Guidelines Accepts query with SAE/proposal package (including outline, three sample chapters, your publishing history and author

biography). Alternatively, submit completed manuscript.
Recent Title(s) *Arctic 2 Antarctic*, Michael Holland and Janet King (Sailing); *Birds of Ireland*, Glynn Anderson (Nature)
Tips The Collins Press's interests as a publisher are not limited to specific subject areas. Their assessment of a book's worth is based upon the quality of the writing, how well it engages the interest of the reader and whether it has new, interesting or original material. They do not publish poetry, short stories, drama or literary criticism and are discontinuing adult fiction for the present. Unsolicited material in any of these categories will not be returned.

Colourpoint Books
Colourpoint House, Jubilee Business Park, 21 Jubilee Road, Newtownards, Northern Ireland, BT23 4YH
- 028 9182 6339
- 028 9182 1900
- info@colourpoint.co.uk
- www.colourpoint.co.uk

Contact Partners: Sheila Johnston (Educational) and Norman Johnston (Transportation/General)
Established 1993
Insider Info Publishes 25 titles per year. Aims to respond to proposals and manuscripts within two months. Catalogue and submission details are available online.
Non-Fiction Publishes General Non-Fiction, Illustrated Books, Textbooks and Scholarly titles on the following subjects: Education, Regional, Travel, Irish Interest, Transport, Travel Maps (UK), School Textbooks
Submission Guidelines Accepts query with SAE/proposal package (including outline, sample chapter(s), your publishing history and SAE). Will accept emailed queries.
Submissions email: sheila@colourpoint.co.uk for educational submissions and norman@colourpoint.co.uk for transport submissions (write 'submissions query' as the subject line).
Recent Title(s) *Lough Swilly Buses*, G Irvine Millar (Transport)
Tips Titles are mainly aimed at students and teachers, or anyone involved with the education system. Before approaching the publisher with a proposal, be sure that it fits with the Colourpoint list, which focuses mainly on educational textbooks and transport subjects such as trains and buses.

The Columba Press
55a Spruce Avenue, Stillorgan Industrial Park, Blackrock, Co. Dublin, Republic of Ireland

☎ 00353 1 294 2556
🖶 00353 1 294 2564
✉ info@columba.ie
🌐 www.columba.ie
Contact Managing Director/Publisher, Sean O'Boyle
Established 1985
Imprint(s) Currach Press
Insider Info Publishes 35 titles per year. Payment is via royalties. Catalogue available online.
Non-Fiction Publishes General Non-Fiction titles on the following subjects:
Counselling/Career, Religion, Spirituality, Prayer Books/Hymnals
Submission Guidelines Accepts query with SAE or via email.
Submission details to: sean@columba.ie
Recent Title(s) *What was Mark at?*, Wilfrid Harrington; *Has God Logged Off?*, T. P. O'Mahony
Tips Columba publishes across a broad range of areas, including pastoral resources, spirituality, theology, the arts and history. They often publish seasonal themed books, such as hymns for Christmas or Easter. Proposals should be tagged to specific seasons, and submitted far enough in advance to be effective.

Comma Press
3rd Floor, 24 Lever Street, Manchester, M1 1DW
☎ 07792 564747
✉ commapublication@yahoo.co.uk
✉ ra.page@commapress.co.uk
🌐 www.commapress.co.uk
Contact Secretary & General Editor, Ra Page; Editor and New Writing Coordinator, Jim Hinks; Translation Editor, Maria Crossan
Established 2002
Insider Info Simultaneous submissions are not accepted. Submissions accompanied bySAE will be returned. Manuscript guidelines are available.
Fiction Publishes Short Story Collections (No stories on coming of age, student life, drug taking, splitting up with a partner, or anecdotes).
* Comma Press seek new writers to contribute to short story anthologies and any specific calls for submissions will be on the website.
Submission Guidelines Accepts proposal package (including story between 800 and 5,000 words and full contact details via email, or A4 one sided, double spaced hard copy via post). Alternatively, submit completed manuscript.
Poetry Publishes original, previously unpublished poetry from published writers.
* When submitting samples, try and be representative and include in the covering letter any magazine or anthology credits.
Submission Guidelines Submit six sample poems. Hard copies of the submission should be sent to:

Comma Poetry, 3 Vale Bower, Mytholmroyd, West Yorkshire, HX7 5EP.
Recent Title(s) *The Silence Room*, Sean O'Brien (Fiction); *The New Uncanny*, Sarah Eyre and Ra Page, eds. (Anthology)
Tips Comma Press is a not for profit publishing collective, with a particular focus on the short story. For potential contributors to anthologies, reading a sample of previously published short fiction is highly recommended. The website FAQ section contains detailed advice on what the editors do not like to see in new writing. Comma has recently begun to take on translations under the imprint Comma Translations. See website for translation guidelines. There may also be opportunities for scriptwriters through schemes run by Comma Films. For more details write to Tane Vayu, Comma Film, 5 Newhouse, Road, Wavertree, Livepool L1 OHL or email: tane.vayu@commapress.co.uk

Connections Book Publishing
St Chad's House, 148 King's Cross Road, London, WC1X 9DH
☎ 020 7837 1968
🖶 020 7837 2025
✉ info@connections-publishing.com
🌐 www.connections-publishing.com
Contact Publisher, Nick Eddison
Insider Info Catalogue is available online.
Non-Fiction Publishes Gift Books, Illustrated Books, Box Books and General Non-Fiction titles on the following subjects: New Age, Spirituality.
Recent Title(s) *Psychic Café Diary 2008*, (Calendar/Diary)
Tips Connections is a new imprint offering titles to meet the growing demands of the new age market. The list comprises interactive book, kits, and expertly written books in traditional areas. Specialises in gift book and curio titles such as 'books in a box'. Favours the unusual product.

Conran Octopus
2–4 Heron Quays, London, E14 4JP
☎ 020 7531 8400
🖶 020 7531 8627
✉ publisher@conran-octopus.co.uk
🌐 www.conran-octopus.co.uk
Parent Company Octopus Publishing Group
Contact Publishing Director, Lorraine Dickey; Art Director, Jonathan Christie
Established 1984
Insider Info Catalogue is available online.
Non-Fiction Publishes Illustrated titles on the following subjects:
Crafts, Food & Drink, Gardens, Interiors and Design, Living

Recent Title(s) *The Interior World of Tom Dixon*, Tom Dixon (Interior Design)

Tips Conran aims to publish books which combine authoritative and informed writing with cutting edge design and sumptuous photography.

Constable & Robinson Ltd
3 The Lanchesters, 162 Fulham Palace Road, London, W6 9ER
- 020 8741 3663
- 020 8748 7562
- enquiries@constablerobinson.com
- www.constablerobinson.com

Contact Publisher and Managing Director, Nick Robinson; Commissioning Editor (Non-Fiction, Literary Fiction), Becky Hardie; Editorial Director (True Crime, Crime Fiction), Krystyna Green; Editorial Director (Popular Science, Illustrated, Mammoth), Pete Duncan; Manager (Health and Psychology), Fritha Saunders; Commissioning Editor (Non-Fiction, History), Leo Hollis

Insider Info Publishes 160 titles per year. Receives approximately 3,000 queries and 1,000 manuscripts per year. Payment is via royalty and advance is offered. Average lead time is one year, with simultaneous submissions accepted. Aims to respond to proposals within one month and queries within three months. Catalogue is free on request.

Non-Fiction Publishes Autobiography, Biography, General Non-Fiction and Illustrated titles on the following subjects:
Current Affairs, World Politics, Military History, Health, Psychology, Travel, Photography
* Publishes across a wide range of non-fiction areas. Well known for the *Overcoming CBT* series, a series of consumer friendly psychology and behavioural therapy books, designed to help people overcome mental illnesses.

Submission Guidelines Accepts query with SAE, or proposal package (including outline, one sample chapter). Will accept artworks/images (send photocopies).

Fiction Publishes Mainstream/Contemporary, Mystery, Suspense and Crime Fiction titles

Submission Guidelines Accepts query with SAE, or proposal package (including outline, one sample chapter).

Tips Constable & Robinson does not accept email submissions, and does not accept children's fiction or any adult fiction other than crime.

Contact Publishing
Unit 346, 176 Finchley Road, London, NW3 6BT
- info@contact-publishing.co.uk
- www.contact-publishing.co.uk

Contact Anne Kontoyannis

Established 2003

Insider Info Aims to respond to proposals and manuscripts within one month. Catalogue and manuscript guidelines are available online.

Non-Fiction Publishes General Non-Fiction and Self-Help titles on the following subjects: Health/Medicine, Spirituality, Inspirational, Mind, Body & Spirit, Self-Help

Submission Guidelines Accepts query with SAE/proposal package (including outline, two sample chapter(s), author biography and SAE) or via email to: manuscripts@contact-publishing.co.uk

Fiction Publishes Short Story Collections and Spiritual titles.

Submission Guidelines Accepts query with SAE/proposal package (including outline, two sample chapter(s), author biography and SAE) or via email to: manuscripts@contact-publishing.co.uk.

Recent Title(s) *Sayonara, Dream-eater*, Ethne Ashizawa (Novel)

Tips Contact Publishing aims to highlight the diversity of new thought and perspective, whilst at the same time providing unknown and unpublished authors with an opportunity to reach the world with their stories and ideas. Every manuscript is read, and every effort is made to respond to submissions within one month of receipt, though periodic backlog can result in delays to response times. Contact regret that the quantity of submissions received prevents the possibility of entering into correspondence concerning individual submissions.

The Continuum International Publishing Group
The Tower Building, 11 York Road, London, SE1 7NX
- 020 7922 0880
- 020 7922 0881
- asandeman@continuumbooks.com
- www.continuumbooks.com

Contact Publishing Director, Robin Baird-Smith (General Trade and Religion); Associate Publisher, Anna Sandeman (Literary Studies and Humanities); Commissioning Editor, Joanne Allcock (Academic Division, Education)

Established 1999

Imprint(s) Burns & Oates
Thoemmes Continuum
T & T Clark
Network Continuum
Hambledon Continuum

Insider Info Publishes over 500 titles per year. Catalogue and manuscript guidelines are available online.

Non-Fiction Publishes General Non-Fiction, Reference and Scholarly titles on the following subjects:

Education, Government/Politics, History, Language, Literature, Philosophy, Religion, Biblical studies, Theology, Popular Culture

Submission Guidelines Accepts proposal package (including outline, your publishing history, author biography and market research). Send no more than four A4 sheets.

Tips Send submissions directly to the relevant editorial contact. See the company website for full contact details, downloads and submission guidelines. Also see individual imprint entries for more information.

Conway Maritime Press
The Old Magistrates Court, 10 Southcombe Street, London, W14 0RA
- 020 7605 1400
- 020 7605 1401
- customerservices@anovabooks.com
- www.anovabooks.com

Parent Company Anova Books Company Ltd
Contact Jon Lee
Non-fiction Publishes General Non-Fiction and Illustrated titles on the following subjects: History, Maritime, Military History, Transportation
Submission Guidelines Accepts emailed synopses. Submission details to: jlee@anovabooks.com
Recent Title(s) *Conway's Battleships*, Ian Sturton (ed.) (Maritime/History)
Tips Focuses entirely on maritime and shipping culture, including military elements.

Corgi
61–63 Uxbridge Road, London, W5 5SA
- 020 8579 2652
- 020 8579 5479
- info@transworld-publishers.co.uk
- www.booksattransworld.co.uk

Parent Company Transworld Publishers
Insider Info Catalogue is available online. Manuscript guidelines are not available.
Non-Fiction Publishes Biography and General Non-Fiction titles on the following subjects: Health, Sex, Relationships
Submission Guidelines Accepts agented submissions only.
Fiction Publishes Historical, Humour, Mainstream/Contemporary, Mystery, Romance and Suspense titles.
Submission Guidelines Accepts agented submissions only.
Recent Title(s) *The Survivor*, Tom Cain (Crime & Mystery)
Tips Do not send unsolicited submissions.

Corgi Children's Books
61–63 Uxbridge Road, London, W5 5SA
- 020 8231 6800
- 020 8231 6767
- childrenseditorial@randomhouse.co.uk
- www.kidsatrandomhouse.co.uk

Parent Company Random House Children's Books
Insider Info Catalogue is available online.
Fiction Publishes Children's and Teenage novels.
Recent Title(s) *The City Of Ember*, Jean Du Prau (Fantasy); *My Dad*, Anthony Brown (Gift Book)

Cork University Press
Youngline Industrial Estate, Pouladuff Road, Togher, Co. Cork, Republic of Ireland
- 00353 21 490 2980
- 00353 21 431 5329
- mike.collins@ucc.ie
- www.corkuniversitypress.com

Contact Publications Director, Mike Collins; Editor, Sophie Watson
Established 1925
Insider Info Publishes around 15 books per year. Catalogue and manuscript guidelines are available online.
Non-Fiction Publishes General Non-Fiction, Illustrated, Reference and Scholarly titles on the following subjects:
Art, Architecture, Government/Politics, History, Language, Literature, Law, Music/Dance, Philosophy, Travel, Women's Issues and Studies, Current Affairs, Film Studies
Submission Guidelines Downloadable proposal form and guidelines on website.
Recent Title(s) *Ireland Through the Looking-Glass: Flann O'Brien, Myles na gCopaleen and Irish Cultural Debate*; *Tuned Out: Traditional Music and Identity in Northern Ireland*

The Cosmic Elk
- cosmicelk@hotmail.com
- www.cosmicelk.co.uk

Contact Heather Hobden
Established 1988
Non-Fiction Publishes Multimedia, Reference, Scholarly and Technical titles on History and Science.
Recent Title(s) *The King of Siam's Eclipse*, Heather Hobden
Tips The Cosmic Elk is a small press that publishes books and booklets, and designs and maintains websites. The main topics are science, history and the history of science. All publications, print or web, are direct referrals or updates of previously published work. Cosmic Elk prefer not to disclose their address or phone number, and would ask that

all enquiries be made via their website or by email in the first instance.

Council for British Archaeology
St Mary's House, 66 Bootham, York, YO30 7BZ
- 01904 671417
- 01904 671384
- books@britarch.ac.uk
- www.britarch.ac.uk

Contact Publications Officer, Catrina Appleby
Established 1944
Insider Info Catalogue and manuscript guidelines are available online.
Non-Fiction Publishes Scholarly titles on the following subjects: Anthropology/Archaeology, History.
Submission Guidelines Contact publications@britarch.ac.uk to discuss proposals before submitting material.
Recent Title(s) *Londinium and Beyond*, Clark et al (Archaeology/Roman); *Laying the Foundations: A History and Archaeology of the Trent Valley Sand and Gravel Industry*, T Cooper (Social History/Industrial Archaeology)
Tips One of the main aims of the Council for British Archaeology (CBA) is to help facilitate communication between all those involved in archaeology in Britain. The CBA has a long established (but continuously developing) range of publications. The CBA 'Notes for Authors', available on the website, provides details of their latest recommendations on house style.

Country Publications Ltd
The Watermill, Broughton Hall, Skipton, BD23 3AG
- 01756 701381
- 01756 701326
- editorial@dalesman.co.uk
- www.dalesman.co.uk

Contact CEO, Matthew Townsend; Managing Director, Robert Flanagan
Insider Info Catalogue is available online.
Non-Fiction Publishes General Non-Fiction, Gift Books and Magazine titles on the following subjects: Agriculture, Countryside, Regional interest, Walking Guides, Humour, Country Crafts
Recent Title(s) *Little Book of Yorkshire Christmas*, compiled by Arnold Kellett (Gift Book)
Tips Country Publications are regional publishers of regional interest titles and magazines, including *The Dalesman* and *Down Your Way*. Subjects encompass walking, literature and art, people and dialect, humour, history and craft.

Countryside Books
Highfield House, 2 Highfield Avenue, Newbury, Berkshire, RG14 5DS
- 01635 43816
- 01635 551004
- info@countrysidebooks.co.uk
- www.countrysidebooks.co.uk

Contact Publisher, Nicholas Battle
Established 1976
Insider Info Publishes approximately 60 new titles per year. Catalogue and manuscript guidelines available online.
Non-Fiction Publishes General Non-Fiction titles on the following subjects: Hobbies, Regional, Travel.
Submission Guidelines Accepts query with SAE/proposal package (including outline, one sample chapter and SAE) by post or via email (see online form).
Recent Title(s) *A Rum Owd Dew!*, Charlie Haylock
Tips Countryside Books publishes books of regional interest, usually based upon English counties. Book subjects range from country walks and pub walks, to memories of second world war airfields. Two wider geographical series are aimed at people who want to discover more of England's living history, and at those researching their family tree. Book submissions are welcomed from new authors as long as the book covers a subject that fits into the existing list. Note in particular that Countryside Books only publishes non-fiction, and that most titles relate to English counties.

CRC Press
4th Floor, Albert House, 1–4 Singer Street, London, EC24 4BQ
- 020 7017 6000
- 020 7017 6747
- john.lavender@taylorandfrancis.com
- www.crcpress.com

Parent Company Taylor & Francis Group
Contact Senior Vice-President (Publishing), John Lavender
Established 1973
Insider Info Publishes roughly 350 titles per year, and 32 journals per year. Catalogue and manuscript guidelines are available online.
Non-Fiction Publishes Journals, Multimedia, Reference, Scholarly, Technical and Textbook titles on the following subjects:
Business and Management, Chemistry, Computer Science, Engineering, Environmental Science, Forensics & Criminal Justice, Food Science, Information Technology, Life Sciences, Mathematics, Nutrition, Pharmacology and Toxicology, Physics, Statistics, Electronic Publishing

Submission Guidelines Accepts proposal package (including outline, one sample chapter and CV).

Recent Title(s) *Vitamin K in Health and Disease*, John W. Suttie (Health); *Cyber Fraud: Tactics, Techniques and Procedures*, Rick Howard (Computer Science)

Tips CRC Press is a leading publisher of professional reference books and journals in the specialist areas of science, engineering and medicine. Detailed information on how to submit a proposal, or in some cases a camera ready manuscript, is available on the website. A full list of editors and their individual specialisms is also published on the website.

Crecy Publishing

1a Ringway Trading Estate, Shadowmoss Road, Manchester, M22 5LH

☎ 0161 499 0024

☎ 0161 499 0298

✉ enquiries@crecy.co.uk

🌐 www.crecy.co.uk

Contact Gillian Richardson (Sales and Editorial)

Established 1993

Imprint(s) Hikoki Publications

Flight Recorder Publications

Air Data Publications

Insider Info Publishes eight titles per year. Receives approximately 30 queries and 20 manuscripts per year. Eight per cent of books published are from first-time authors, 75 per cent of books published are from unagented authors. Payment is via royalty. Average lead time is one year, with simultaneous submissions accepted. Submissions accompanied by SAE will be returned. Aims to respond to queries within three days, proposals within two months and manuscripts within three months. Catalogue and manuscript guidelines are free on request.

Non-Fiction Publishes Autobiography, Biography, General Non-Fiction, Illustrated and Reference titles on the following subjects:

Aviation, History, Maritime (Naval), Military/War (WWII), Transportation

* Requires a number of photographs/illustrations with every submission.

Submission Guidelines Accepts proposal package (including outline, two sample chapters) or completed manuscript, and artworks/images (send photocopies or digital files as jpegs).

Recent Title(s) *Chinese Aircraft*, Yefim Gordon and Dmitrii Komissarov; *Faith, Hope and Malta GC*, Tony Spooner; *Stormbird*, Hermann Buchner

Tips Crecy publishes books for an adult readership only.

Creme de la Crime

PO Box 523, Chesterfield, S40 9AT

☎ 01246 520835

✉ info@cremedelacrime.com

🌐 www.cremedelacrime.com

Contact Managing Director (Debut Crime Fiction), Lynne Patrick

Established 2003

Insider Info Publishes six titles per year. Receives approximately 500 queries and 300 manuscripts per year. 60 per cent of books published are from first-time authors, 90 per cent of books published are from unagented authors. Payment is via royalty (on wholesale price). Average lead time is one year, with simultaneous submissions not accepted. Submissions accompanied by SAE will be returned. Aims to respond to queries within ten days and manuscripts within eight weeks. Catalogue is available online. Manuscript guidelines are available online, or by post for the cost of £2.50, with an A4 envelope and three first class stamps.

Fiction Publishes Crime, Mystery, Suspense and Thriller titles

* Creme de la Crime publishes crime fiction from both debut authors, and from a small stable of authors they have previously nurtured. All titles are 70–80,000 words in length.

Submission Guidelines Accepts proposal package (including a covering letter, an outline, a one page synopsis and three sample chapters – approximately 10,000 words).

Recent Title(s) *Dead Woman's Shoes*, Kaye C. Hill (Crime Fiction)

Tips Creme de la Crime stipulate that all prospective authors must follow their submission guidelines, available on the website, carefully when preparing a proposal.

Crescent Moon Publishing

PO Box 393, Maidstone, Kent, ME14 5XU

☎ 01622 729593

✉ cresmopub@yahoo.co.uk

🌐 www.crescentmoon.org.uk

Contact Director, Jeremy Robinson; Editor, C. Hughes; Editor, B.D. Barnacle

Established 1988

Insider Info Publishes 25 titles per year. Receives approximately 300 queries and 400 manuscripts per year. One per cent of books published are from first-time authors and one per cent are from unagented authors. Payment via royalty and an advance is offered. Average lead time is 18 months with simultaneous submissions accepted. Aims to respond to proposals and manuscripts within four months. Catalogue and manuscript guidelines are available online.

Non-Fiction Publishes Biography, General Non-Fiction, Illustrated Books, and Scholarly titles on the following subjects: Art, Architecture, History, Hobbies, Humanities, Literary Criticism, Philosophy,

Religion, Sociology, Translation, World Affairs, Politics.

Submission Guidelines Accepts query with SAE/ proposal package (including outline, one to two sample chapters, your publishing history, author biography and SAE). Will accept artworks/images (send photocopies).

Fiction Publishes Short Story Collections.

Submission Guidelines Accepts query with SAE/ proposal package (including outline, and one to two sample chapters and SAE).

Poetry Publishes Poetry titles.

* Prefers a very small selection of a writer's best work in the first instance, and tends to favour free or non-rhyming material.

Submission Guidelines Accepts query (including six sample poems).

Tips Crescent Moon publishes a number of critical subject studies, including painters and artists, literature, and art. All submissions are carefully reviewed.

Cressrelles Publishing Co. Ltd
10 Station Road Industrial Estate, Coldwall, Malvern, WR13 6RN
- 01684 540154
- 01684 540154
- simon@cressrelles.co.uk
- www.cressrelles.co.uk

Contact Simon Smith
Imprint(s) New Playwrights'
Anchorage
I. E. Clark
J. Garnet Miller
Kenyon-Deane
Insider Info Publishes 10–20 titles per year. Catalogue free on request.
Non-Fiction Publishes Drama/Plays.
Submission Guidelines Accepts completed manuscript.
Tips Visit the website for details on each individual imprint and the plays they publish.

Crocus Books
6 Mount Street, Manchester, M2 5NS
- 0161 832 3777
- 0161 832 2929
- crocus@commonword.org.uk
- www.commonword.org.uk

Parent Company Commonword/Cultureword
Insider Info Catalogue guidelines are available online.
Fiction Publishes Mainstream/Contemporary and Short Story Collection titles from writers in the North West of the UK.

Submission Guidelines Calls for submissions will posted on the website periodically.
Poetry Publishes Contemporary Poetry titles.
Recent Title(s) *Poems from a Northern Soul*, John Siddique (Poetry)
Tips Crocus is the publishing imprint of Commonword and Cultureword, two projects that coordinate a range of writing development and publishing projects. Cultureword was established in 1986 as a centre for Black creative writing in the North West of England, and Commonword is the virtual community of North West writers. Crocus Books often runs writing competitions offering cash prizes and publication – details will appear on the website.

Crombie Jardine Publishing Ltd
Office 2, 3 Edgar Buildings, George Street, Bath, BA1 2JF
- 01225 464445
- admin@crombiejardine.com
- www.crombiejardine.com

Contact Sales Director, David Crombie; Publishing Director, Catriona Jardine
Established 2004
Insider Info Publishes 12-24 titles per year. Catalogue is available online.
Non-Fiction Publishes Gift Books and Humour titles.
Submission Guidelines Accepts email queries. Do not send any proposals through the post.
Recent Title(s) *Stumped! The World's Funniest Cricket Quotes*, Charlie Croker
Tips Crombie Jardine specialise in impulse-buy humour titles.

Crossbridge Books
Tree Shadow, Berrow Green, Martley, WR6 6PL
- 01886 821128
- 01886 821128
- crossbridgebooks@btinternet.com
- www.crossbridgebooks.com

Contact Managing Director, Eileen Mohr
Established 1995
Imprint(s) Mohr Books
Insider Info Catalogue is available online.
Non-Fiction Publishes Children's, Illustrated Books and General Non-Fiction titles on Religion.
Submission Guidelines Currently not accepting submissions.
Fiction Publishes Religious titles.
Submission Guidelines Currently not accepting submissions.
Recent Title(s) *Saved by God*, Dave Bull (Christian Faith); *Mountains on the Moon*, Michael Arthern (Christian Faith)

Tips Titles are aimed at a predominantly Christian readership. Most books are inspirational or spiritual in nature and have a strong Christian focus.

Crown House Publishing Ltd
Crown Buildings, Bancyfelin, Carmarthen, SA33 5ND
- 01267 211345
- 01267 211882
- books@crownhouse.co.uk
- www.crownhouse.co.uk

Contact Managing Director, David Bowman; Marketing Director, Caroline Lenton
Established 1998
Insider Info Publishes 20 titles per year. Catalogue and manuscript guidelines are available online.
Non-Fiction Publishes Scholarly, Self-Help, and Technical titles on the following subjects: Neuro Linguistic Programming (NLP), Hypnosis, Counselling & Psychotherapy, Personal, Business & Life Coaching, Education, Accelerated Learning, Thinking Skills and Personalising Learning.
Submission Guidelines Accepts initial query and/or idea of no more than 200 words to: books@crownhouse.co.uk
Recent Title(s) *The Book of Thunks*, Ian Gilbert; *The Really Good Fun Cartoon Book of NLP*, Philip Miller; *Leadership with a Moral Purpose*, Will Ryan; *Imperfectly Natural Woman - the pocket book*, Janey Lee Grace
Tips Crown House Publishing is a rapidly growing publishing house specialising in the areas of neuro-linguistic programming (NLP), hypnosis, accelerated learning, stress management, health and well being, and personal growth. They have an established global distribution network.

The Crowood Press Ltd
The Stable Block, Crowood Lane, Ramsbury, Wiltshire, SN8 2HR
- 01672 520320
- 01672 520280
- enquiries@crowood.com
- www.crowoodpress.co.uk

Contact Chairman, John Dennis; Managing Director, Ken Hathway
Established 1982
Imprint(s) Farming Press
Airlife
Insider Info Publishes 70 titles per year. Payment is via royalties. Catalogue available free on request and online. Manuscript guidelines available online.
Non-Fiction Publishes Biography, General Non-Fiction, How-To, Illustrated and Reference titles on the following subjects:

Sport, Fishing, Equestrianism and Country Sports, Gardening, Farming, Dogs, Crafts, Motoring, Military History and Aviation.
Submission Guidelines Accepts written query with SAE.
Recent Title(s) *The Colour Book*, David Lloyd (Science/Art); *African Violets*, Hill Goodship (Gardening)
Tips The best approach for submissions is to send an initial query by letter, fax or email. Do not send complete manuscripts or photographs. More information will be requested if necessary.

CRW Publishing
69 Gloucester Crescent, London, NW1 7EG
- 020 7485 5764
- marcus@niche2002.fsnet.co.uk
- www.crw-publishing.co.uk

Contact Editorial Director, Marcus Clapham
Established 2003
Fiction Publishes reprints of Classic Fiction.
Recent Title(s) *Jane Austen: the Complete Works*; *Essential Thinkers: Aristotle*
Tips CRW publishes high quality hardback classics. Series produced by CRW Publishing include: *Book Blocks, Collector's Library, Essential Thinkers, Poetry Library, Myth and Legend,* and *Who? What? Where? When?* Note that CRW only publishes reprints, not new material.

Currach Press
55a Spruce Avenue, Stillorgan Industrial Park, Blackrock, Co. Dublin, Republic of Ireland
- 00353 1 294 2556
- 00353 1 294 3564
- info@currach.ie
- www.currach.ie

Contact Publisher (General Non-Fiction), Jo O'Donoghue
Established 2001
Insider Info Publishes 12 titles per year. Receives approximately 50 queries and 50 manuscripts per year. 20 per cent of books published are from first-time authors, 90 per cent of books published are from unagented authors. Payment is via royalty. Average lead time is six months, with simultaneous submissions not accepted. Submissions accompanied by SAE will be returned. Aims to respond to queries and proposals within eight weeks. Catalogue available with A5 SAE and an IRC (for outside of Ireland).
Non-Fiction Publishes Autobiography, Biography, Coffee Table Books, Cookbooks, General Non-Fiction, Gift, Illustrated, Reference and Self-Help titles on the following subjects: Alternative Lifestyles, Art/Architecture, Business/Economics, Contemporary

Culture, Cooking/Foods/Nutrition, Gay/Lesbian, Government/Politics, History, House and Home, Humanities, Memoirs, Money/Finance, Photography, Psychology, Regional, Travel

Submission Guidelines Accepts written proposal package (including outline, a sample chapter, market research, author biography, and SAE).

Recent Title(s) *Anyone Can Run*, Joan Geraghty (Fitness/Self-Help)

Tips Currach Press publishes books for a general interest adult readership. They have a detailed house style guide for use with new and existing authors, which is available by post, or to download from their website.

D&B Publishing
PO Box 18, Hassocks, West Sussex, BN6 9WR
- 01273 711443
- 01273 831629
- info@dandbpublishing.com
- www.dandbpublishing.com

Contact Editorial Director, Byron Jacobs (Poker, Puzzles, Games)

Established 2002

Insider Info Publishes eight titles per year. Receives approximately five queries per year. 20 per cent of books published are from first-time authors, 100 per cent of books published are from unagented authors. Also partakes in subsidy publishing. Payment is via royalty (on retail price). Average lead time is nine months, with simultaneous submissions accepted. Submissions accompanied by SAE will be returned. Aims to respond to queries within one day, and proposals and manuscripts within one week. Catalogue is free on request and available online, or by email. Manuscript guidelines are available by email.

Non-Fiction Publishes Games/Puzzles, How-To and Multimedia titles on the following subjects: Card Games, Casino Games, Entertainment/Games, Gambling, Poker, Puzzles

Submission Guidelines Accepts proposal package (including outline, two sample chapters and author biography).

Recent Title(s) *Limit Hold'em: Winning Short-handed Strategies*, Terry Borer, Lawrence Mak and Barry Tanenbaum (Poker)

Tips D&B publishes books for poker players and puzzle enthusiasts in general. They determine whether an author should be subsidy published by the quality of synopsis and sample chapters supplied.

Dalesman Publishing Co. Ltd
The Water Mill, Broughton Hall, Skipton, North Yorkshire, BD23 3AG
- 01756 701381
- 01756 701326
- editorial@dalesman.co.uk
- www.dalesman.co.uk

Contact Managing Director, Robert Flanagan; Editor in Chief, Terry Fletcher (Magazine)

Imprint(s) Country Publications

Insider Info Publishes ten titles per year. Catalogue is available online.

Non-Fiction Publishes Illustrated Books and General Non-Fiction titles on the following subjects: History, Hobbies, Regional, Travel, Local Interest (Northern UK), Northern Folklore

Tips Best known for publishing *The Dalesman* magazine. Dalesman Publishing acquired the Smith Settle publishing imprint in February 2003 and as a result hold the largest collection of Northern interest publications in the marketplace. See separate entry for Country Publications.

Darton Longman & Todd Ltd
1 Spencer Court, 140–142 Wandsworth High Street, London, SW18 4JJ
- 020 8875 0155
- 020 8875 0133
- editorial@darton-longman-todd.co.uk
- www.darton-longman-todd.co.uk

Contact Editorial Director, Brendan Walsh; Commissioning Editor, Virginia Hearn; Managing Editor, Helen Porter

Established 1959

Insider Info Publish 40 new titles per year. Catalogue and manuscript guidelines are available online.

Non-Fiction Publishes General Non-Fiction titles on the following subjects:
Religion, Spirituality, Prayer, Theology, Church Today, Personal Growth, Ministry, Counselling and Pastoral Care, Bereavement, Traditions of Christian Spirituality, Exploring Faith, Bibles

Submission Guidelines Accepts queries and completed manuscripts by post only.

Recent Title(s) *A Fallible Church*, Kenneth Stevenson (Essays)

Tips Darton Longman & Todd are the UK's leading independent publisher of high quality popular books on spirituality, religion and theology. They are not attached to a specific denomination, and their books come from many different backgrounds and traditions. Darton Longman & Todd are always looking for writers with freshness, inquisitiveness, faithfulness and passion.

David & Charles Publishers
Brunel House, Newton Abbot, Devon, TQ12 4PU
- 01626 323200

☎ 01626 364463
✉ postmaster@davidandcharles.co.uk
✉ firstname.lastname@davidandcharles.co.uk
🌐 www.davidandcharles.co.uk
Parent Company F+W Media (see European & International Publishers)
Contact President (F+W Media), Sara Domville; Managing Director & Publisher, Stephen Bateman; Director of Editorial and Design, Ali Myer; Senior Commissioning Editor, Freya Dangerfield (Practical & Fantasy Art); Commissioning Editor, Jane Trollope (Equestrian, Craft); Commissioning Editor, Neil Baber (General, History, Reference, Photography); Junior Commissioning Editor, Jennifer Fox-Proverbs (Craft); Editorial Manager, Emily Pitcher
Established 1960
Insider Info Publishes 70 new titles per year. Receives approximately 1,200–1,500 queries and 300–500 manuscripts per year. 30 per cent of books published are from first-time authors and 85 per cent of books published are from unagented authors. Payment is via royalty (on wholesale price), or outright purchase from £400–£10,000. Advance offered is from £2,000–£10,000. Average lead time is two years, with simultaneous submissions accepted. Submissions accompanied by SAE will be returned. Aims to respond to queries, proposals and manuscripts within two months. Catalogue available via A4 SAE.
Non-Fiction Publishes General Non-Fiction, Gift, How-To, Illustrated and Reference titles on the following subjects:
Agriculture/Horticulture (very broad interest), Animals (Equestrian and Pet Care), Archaeology, Art, Architecture, Astrology/Psychic (general titles only), Contemporary Culture, Cooking (mainly cakes and sugarcraft), Crafts, Creative Non-Fiction, Entertainment/Games, History, Hobbies (broad interest), House and Home, Military/War, Nature/Environment, Nostalgia (broad interest), Practical Photography, Sports, Transportation (mostly railways), Directories.
* As well as the areas mentioned above, David & Charles will always look at new ideas and new areas. Will consider brief and concise ideas.
Submission Guidelines Accepts query with SAE, or via email with proposal package (including outline, sample chapter(s), your publishing history, author biography), and artworks/images (send photocopies or digital files as jpegs).
Submission details to: ali.myer@davidandcharles.co.uk
Tips David & Charles publishes titles aimed at people with a strong interest and/or hobby. Submissions should be brief, concise and to the point. A short biography of the author is extremely helpful and you should note any previously published material, be it books or magazine articles. David & Charles will happily consider unagented authors. If your proposal is for a visual book e.g. art or photography, samples of your work should be included either as copies or on CD. Never send originals.

David Fickling Books
31 Beaumont Street, Oxford, OX1 2NP
☎ 01865 339000
☎ 01865 339009
✉ dfickling@randomhouse.co.uk
🌐 www.davidficklingbooks.co.uk
Parent Company Random House Children's Division
Contact Publisher, David Fickling; Senior Editor, Bella Pearson
Insider Info Catalogue available online.
Fiction Publishes Children's and Young Adult titles.
Submission Guidelines No unagented submissions.
Recent Title(s) *Solace of the Road*, Siobhan Dowd (Young Adult); *Eon: Rise of the Dragoneye*, Alison Goodman (Fantasy)
Tips David Fickling Books are a small imprint within Random House, but they publish some very commercially successful authors. They are the first bi-continental children's publisher, with books publishing simultaneously in the US and the UK.

David Fulton Publishers
2 Park Square, Milton Park, Abingdon, Oxford, OX14 4RN
☎ 020 7017 6000
☎ 020 7017 6699
✉ tf.enquiries@informa.com
🌐 www.routledgeeducation.com
Parent Company Routledge Education (Taylor & Francis Group)
Contact Commissioning Editor, Dr Monika Lee (Practical Teachers' Books – Early Years, Primary and Secondary Education); Senior Editor, Bruce Roberts (Practical Teachers' Books – Early Years, Primary and Secondary Education); Senior Editor, Alison Foyle (Special Educational Needs, Literacy, Early Years and Childhood Studies)
Insider Info Manuscript guidelines available online.
Non-fiction Publishes How-To, Reference, Scholarly and Textbook titles on the following subjects: Education, Teaching Resources
Submission Guidelines Accepts proposal package (including outline, sample chapters, market research, your publishing history and author biography). May also include draft manuscript for consideration.
Tips David Fulton publishes books for teacher training and continuing professional development,

as well as a comprehensive range of resources for SENCOs and teachers working with children with special educational needs.

David Porteous Editions

PO Box 5, Chudleigh, Newton Abbot, Devon, TQ13 0YZ
- 01626 853310
- 01626 853663
- editorial@davidporteous.com
- www.davidporteous.com

Non-Fiction Publishes How-To, Illustrated titles on the following subjects:
Arts and Crafts, Hobbies
Submission Guidelines Accepts proposal package (including outline and short synopsis) by post or email.
Recent Title(s) *The Dough Book*, Tone Bergli Joner (Craft)
Tips David Porteous are constantly seeking new ideas and welcome ideas from experienced artists or craftspeople.

Day Books

Orchard Piece, Crawborough, Charlbury, Oxfordshire, OX7 3TX
- 01608 811196
- 01608 811196
- lives@day-books.com
- www.day-books.com

Contact Managing Editor, James Sanderson
Established 1997
Imprint(s) Charlbury Press
Leo Children's Books
Insider Info Receives approximately 200 queries and 100 manuscripts per year. Ten per cent of books published are from first-time authors and 80 per cent are from unagented authors. Payment is via royalty (on wholesale price) with 0.1 (per £) maximum. Average lead time is one year, with simultaneous submissions accepted. Aims to respond to proposals and manuscripts within one month.
Non-Fiction Publishes Biography, General Non-Fiction, Diaries, and Local Interest (Oxfordshire) titles.
Submission Guidelines Accepts query with SAE.
Fiction Publishes Children's titles.
Submission Guidelines Accepts query with SAE.
Recent Title(s) *A Brief Jolly Change*, Henry Peerless (Diaries/Transport History)
Tips Day Books was originally established to publish a series of 'great diaries from around the world'. They have since branched out to include all kinds of personal writing, including biography, autobiography, and collections of letters in well edited and well produced editions. The company

can only respond to those who include return postage or provide an email address.

Debrett's Limited

18–20 Hill Rise, Richmond, Surrey, TW10 6UA
- 020 8939 2250
- 020 8939 2251
- publications@debretts.co.uk
- www.debretts.co.uk

Established 1769
Non-Fiction Publishes General Non-Fiction, Diary and Gift Books on the following subjects:
Etiquette/Culture
Submission Guidelines Query with SAE.
Recent Title(s) *Manners for Men*, Jane Dickson
Tips Debrett's is one of the oldest publishing brands in the world and remains the arbiter of taste, manners and correct form to this day. Publishes mainly on high culture and society, etiquette, and similar topics.

Dewi Lewis Publishing

8 Broomfield Road, Heaton Moor, Stockport, SK4 4ND
- 0161 442 9450
- 0161 442 9450
- mail@dewilewispublishing.com
- www.dewilewispublishing.com

Contact Director, Dewi Lewis
Established 1994
Insider Info Publishes 18 new titles per year. Average lead time is 12 months. Proposals will not be returned. Catalogue and manuscript guidelines are available online.
Non-Fiction Publishes Illustrated Book titles on Photography.
Submission Guidelines Accepts query with SAE/ proposal package (including outline, sample chapter(s), author biography) and artworks/images (send photocopies or digital files as jpegs). There are now specific periods in which proposals may be submitted, which are advertised on the website. Submissions received outside these dates will be held until the next period.
Recent Title(s) *Landscapes: 2001–03*, Richard Billingham (Photography); *As I Was Dying*, Paolo Pellegrin (Photography)
Tips Dewi Lewis Publishing is internationally known for its photography list. The aim of the company is to bring accessible but challenging contemporary photography, by both established and lesser known practitioners, to the attention of the wider public. They are looking for projects of quality, which are fresh, powerful, unique and aimed at an international audience. These points should be considered when proposing a project. They are

unlikely to be interested in something which is too specific to one country or geographical region.

Dionysia Press

127 Milton Road West, 7 Duddingston House, Edinburgh, EH15 1JG

☎ 0131 661 1156

☎ 0131 661 1156

Contact Director, Denise Smith

Established 1989

Fiction Publishes Short Stories, Translations and Novels.

Poetry Publishes Poetry Collections.

Tips Denise Smith is also the editor of *Understanding* magazine. Contact her directly for more information on her publications.

Discovery Walking Guides

21 Upper Priory Street, Northampton, NN1 2PT

✉ ask.discovery@ntlworld.com

🌐 www.walking.demon.co.uk

Contact Chairman, Rosamund C. Brawn

Established 1994

Insider Info Catalogue available online.

Non-Fiction Publishes General Non-Fiction and Technical titles on the following subjects:
Hobbies, Travel, Walking Guides, GPS Guides

Submission Guidelines Accepts query with SAE/proposal package (including outline, sample chapter(s))

Recent Titles *Walk! Exmoor*, David and Carol Hitt

Tips Titles are aimed at walking enthusiasts. Will accept proposals/ideas from experienced and technologically skilled walkers.

Diverta Ltd

Studio 208, 250 York Road, London, SW11 3SJ

☎ 020 7801 0411

✉ felicia@allegrapublishing.com

Contact Publisher, Felicia Law

Established 2004

Insider Info Catalogue available online.

Non-Fiction Publishes Children's Non-Fiction, Educational and Activity titles.

Fiction Publishes Children's Fiction and Picture Books.

Recent Title(s) *Bamboo, Velvet and Beak*, Felicia Law (Pre-school Children's Stories)

Tips Titles and resources are aimed at children between the ages of 0 and 14, with education and entertainment being the primary aims. Also produces audio visual products, gifts and activity packs alongside books and owns the copyright to a range of children's brands that are licensed out to worldwide media companies.

Donhead Publishing

Lower Coombe, Donhead St Mary, Shaftesbury, SP7 9LU

☎ 01747 828422

☎ 01747 828522

✉ jillpearce@donhead.com

🌐 www.donhead.com

Contact Managing Editor, Jill Pearce

Established 1990

Insider Info Publishes six titles per year. Catalogue is available online and by email to sales@donhead.com.

Non-Fiction Publishes General Non-Fiction, Illustrated Books and Scholarly titles on the following subjects:
Architecture, Building Conservation

Submission Guidelines Query with SAE.

Recent Title(s) *Windows: History, Repair and Conservation*, Michael Tutton and Elizabeth Hirst (eds.)

Tips Donhead is the leading independent publisher of building conservation, preservation and architecture books, specialising in publishing original material for professionals and academics. Welcomes unsolicited submissions from academic or technically experienced professionals. Also publishes the *Journal of Architectural Conservation*. Visit the website for details on how to contribute.

The Do-Not Press

16 The Woodlands, London, SE13 6TY

☎ 020 8698 7833

☎ 020 8698 7834

✉ info@thedonotpress.com

🌐 www.thedonotpress.com

Contact Editor in Chief, Jim Driver

Insider Info Publishes 12 titles per year. Catalogue and manuscript guidelines available online. Unsolicited submissions are no longer accepted.

Non-Fiction Publishes General Non-Fiction titles on the following subjects:
Art/Architecture, Music/Dance

Submission Guidelines No unsolicited manuscripts. Focuses on backlist only.

Fiction Publishes Erotica, Experimental, Mainstream/Contemporary, Mystery and Crime titles.

Submission Guidelines No unsolicited manuscripts. Focuses on backlist only.

Recent Title(s) *Write a Novel in 60 Days That Will Sell*, Mark Timlin

Tips The Do-Not Press is currently focusing on their backlist and is not accepting submissions of new material at this time.

Dorling Kindersley

80 Strand, London, WC2R 0RL

- 020 7010 3000
- 020 7010 6060
- adulteditorial@uk.dk.com
- childreneditorial@uk.dk.com
- travelguides@uk.dk.com
- www.dorlingkindersley-uk.co.uk

Parent Company Penguin Group (UK)
Contact CEO, Gary June; Global Managing Director, Andrew Welham
Established 1974
Insider Info Catalogue available as a pdf online.
Non-Fiction Publishes Children's, General Non-Fiction, Gift, How-To, Illustrated, Multimedia, Self-Help, Maps/Atlas, Guide, Dictionaries, Encyclopedias and Reference titles on the following subjects: Animals, Antiques & Collectibles, Architecture, Art & Crafts, Atlases, Business & Finance, Children's Books, Computing, Film, TV & Comics, Food & Drink, Gardening, Health & Fitness, History, House & Home, Humour, Languages, Music, Mythology & Astrology, Natural World, Photography, Politics, Society & Philosophy, Parenting, Relationships, Religion, Science, Sport, Travel, Video Games.
Submission Guidelines No unsolicited submissions, agented submissions only.
Recent Title(s) *Richard Hammond's Blast Lab*, Richard Hammond (TV Tie-in); *DK Illustrated Encyclopedia of the Universe*, Robert Dinwiddie (Science/Astrology)
Tips Dorling Kindersley is the world leader in illustrated reference books. Books aim to inspire and teach people of all ages by using design, illustration and photography to make ideas come alive.

Doubleday

61–63 Uxbridge Road, London, W5 5SA

- 020 8579 2652
- 020 8579 5479
- info@transworld-publishers.co.uk
- www.booksattransworld.co.uk

Parent Company Transworld Publishers
Non-Fiction Publishes General Non-Fiction titles on the following subjects:
Ethnic, Food & Drink, History, Humour, Military, Mind, Body & Spirit, Music, Science, True Life
Submission Guidelines Accepts agented submissions only.
Fiction Publishes Ethnic, Historical, Humour, Literary, Mainstream/Contemporary and Multicultural titles.
Submission Guidelines No unsolicited manuscripts, agented submissions only.
Recent Title(s) *The Spiders of Allah*, James Hider (Military/True Life)

Doubleday Children's Books

61–63 Uxbridge Road, London, W5 5SA

- 020 8231 6800
- 020 8231 6767
- childrenseditorial@randomhouse.co.uk
- www.kidsatrandomhouse.co.uk

Parent Company Random House Children's Books
Insider Info Catalogue is available online.
Non-Fiction Publishes Illustrated Non-Fiction titles.
Submission Guidelines No unagented submissions.
Fiction Publishes Picture Books and Children's Fiction.
Submission Guidelines No unagented submissions.
Recent Title(s) *Double Cross*, Malorie Blackman (Thriller); *A Really Short History of Nearly Everything*, Bill Bryson (Science)

Dovecote Press Ltd

Stanbridge, Wimborne Minster, Dorset, BH21 4JD

- 01258 840549
- 01258 840958
- online@dovecotepress.com
- www.dovecotepress.com

Contact Editorial Director, David Burnett
Established 1974
Insider Info Payment via royalties with a small advance offered. Catalogue available online. Manuscript guidelines available online.
Non-Fiction Publishes Autobiography, Biography, General Non-Fiction and Illustrated titles on the following subjects:
Art/Architecture, History, Hobbies, Nature/Environment, English Counties
Submission Guidelines Accepts proposal package (including detailed synopsis or outline and SAE) by post.
Recent Title(s) *Horses & Husbands: The Memoirs of Etti Plesch*, Hugo Vickers (ed.); *Lymington: An Illustrated History*, Jude James (Local Interest)
Tips The Dovecote Press specialises in high-quality local interest publishing. They pay royalties and are always willing to offer a small advance.

Drake Educational Associates

St Fagans Road, Fairwater, Cardiff, CF5 3AE

- 029 2056 0333
- 029 2055 4909
- info@drakeed.com
- www.drakeeducational.co.uk

Contact Managing Director, R.G. Drake
Established 1974
Non-Fiction Publishes Multimedia, Textbook and Educational titles.

Tips Also produces learning aids, study mats and audio products.

Dramatic Lines
PO Box 201, Twickenham, TW2 5RQ
- ☎ 020 8296 9502
- ☎ 020 8296 9503
- ✉ mail@dramaticlines.co.uk
- 🌐 www.dramaticlines.co.uk

Contact Managing Editor, John Nicholas
Non-Fiction Publishes General Non-Fiction, Reference and Scholarly titles on the following subjects:
Education, Drama
Submission Guidelines Query with SAE.
Fiction Publishes Plays and Theatre titles.
Submission Guidelines Query with SAE.
Tips Specialises in educational texts concerning varying aspects of drama and plays, as well as original works that have a wide variety of applications within the theatre.

Dref Wen
28 Church Road, Whitchurch, Cardiff, CFI4 2EA
- ☎ 029 2061 7860
- ☎ 029 2061 0507
- ✉ gwil-drefwen@btinternet.com

Established 1970
Non-Fiction Publishes General Non-Fiction, Scholarly, and Welsh Language titles on the following subjects:
Education, Translation, Welsh Language Educational
Fiction Publishes Children's (Welsh Language/ Bilingual) titles.
Tips Titles are aimed at Welsh language learners. Not seeking any English-only titles.

Drumlin Publications
Nure, Manorhamilton, Co. Leitrim, Republic of Ireland
- ☎ 00353 71 985 5237
- ☎ 00353 71 985 6063
- ✉ drumlin@eircom.net
- 🌐 www.drumlinpublications.com

Contact Founders: Prin and Betty Duignan
Established 1989
Insider Info Catalogue available online.
Non-Fiction Publishes General Non-Fiction titles on the following subjects:
Biography, History, Local Interest.
Recent Title(s) *The Scribe*, Caoimhin Mac Aoidh; *The Sharp and Gentle Side of an Irish Pen*, Declan Curneen
Tips Drumlin specialises in the production of history books and biographies by both local and national authors.

Dublar Scripts
204 Mercer Way, Romsey, Hampshire SO51 7QJ
- ☎ 01794 501377
- ☎ 01794 502538
- ✉ scripts@dublar.freeserve.co.uk
- 🌐 www.dublar.co.uk

Contact Managing Director, Bob Heather
Established 1994
Fiction Publishes Drama and Pantomime titles.
Recent Title(s) *Aladdin*, Bob Heather (Pantomime)
Tips Dublar has produced and published several pantomimes, performed all over Great Britain, Canada, Australia, and New Zealand, and a few in Malta, Poland, Spain and France. Publishes traditional family pantomimes only, written or co-authored by Bob Heather.

Duncan Baird Publishers
Castle House, 75–76 Wells Street, London, W1T 3QH
- ☎ 020 7323 2229
- ☎ 020 7580 5692
- ✉ enquiries@dbp.co.uk
- 🌐 www.dbponline.co.uk

Contact Publisher, Duncan Baird; Editorial Director, Bob Saxton
Established 1992
Imprint(s) Watkins Publishing
Insider Info Catalogue available online.
Non-Fiction Publishes General Non-Fiction, Illustrated Books and Self-Help titles on the following subjects:
Health/Medicine, Religion, Spirituality, Mind, Body and Spirit, World Culture/Civilisations
Tips Duncan Baird Publishers is the leading independent publisher of illustrated books in the fields of mind, body & spirit, health and well-being, culture and civilizations, and religion and faith. They are committed to innovation, design, editorial excellence and imagination, creating particularly unique books for a modern readership.

Duncan Petersen Publishing
31 Ceylon Road, London, W14 OPY
- ☎ 020 7371 2356
- ☎ 020 7371 2507
- ✉ dp@macunlimited.net

Contact Managing Director, Andrew Duncan; Editor, Fiona Duncan
Established 1986
Non-Fiction Publishes General Non-Fiction titles on the following subjects:
Antiques, Art/Architecture, Business, Childcare/ Parenting, Economics, Nature, Travel, Walking
Submission Guidelines Accepts query with SAE. Submit completed manuscript.

Recent Title(s) *Charming Small Hotel Guides*, Fiona Duncan (ed.) (Travel Guides)
Tips Duncan Petersen is a small co-edition publisher. Ideally seeking proposals for unbiased and totally objective travel texts, including detailed photographs.

Dunedin Academic Press Ltd
Hudson House, 8 Albany Street, Edinburgh, EH1 3QB
- 0131 473 2397
- 01250 870920
- mail@dunedinacademicpress.co.uk
- www.dunedinacademicpress.co.uk

Contact Director, Anthony Kinahan
Established 2000
Insider Info Publishes around 20 titles per year. 50 per cent of books published are from first-time authors, 100 per cent of books published are from unagented authors. Payment is via royalty (on wholesale price). Average lead time is six to nine months, with simultaneous submissions not accepted. Submissions accompanied by SAE will be returned. Aims to respond to queries within five days, proposals within ten days and manuscripts within two months. Catalogue and manuscript guidelines are free on request and available online.
Non-Fiction Publishes Scholarly titles on the following subjects:
Anthropology/Archaeology, Biology, Education Practice & Policy, Government/Politics, History, Music, Philosophy, Religion, Science (Earth Sciences), Social Sciences, Sociology, World Affairs.
Submission Guidelines See proposal guidelines on website.
Recent Title(s) *Mathematical Modelling for Earth Science*, Xin-She Yang (Earth Science); *A Passion for Justice - Social Ethics in the Celtic Tradition*, Johnston McMaster (Religion); *School Leadership 2nd Edition*, O'Brien et al (Education)
Tips Dunedin is an academic press and only publishes scholarly texts aimed at undergraduate level scholars upwards. Whilst based in Scotland the Press tackles subjects and authors from across the international academic world.

Earthscan Publications
8–12 Camden High Street, London, NW1 0JH
- 020 7387 8558
- 020 7387 8998
- earthinfo@earthscan.co.uk
- www.earthscan.co.uk

Contact Publishing Director, Jonathan Sinclair Wilson
Insider Info Catalogue free on request online or by email. Manuscript guidelines available online.

Non-Fiction Publishes Textbooks and Scholarly titles on the following subjects:
Business/Economics, Nature/Environment, Sustainable Development, Climate/Energy/Resource Management.
Submission Guidelines Accepts proposal package (including outline, sample chapter(s), publishing history, and author biography and SAE) and artworks/images (send photocopies or digital files as jpegs).
Submission details to: proposals@earthscan.co.uk
Recent Title(s) *The Sustainability Handbook*, William R. Blackburn (Economic/Environmental Management)
Tips Earthscan publishes a wide range of media, including books, magazines, journals, directories, CD-ROMs and other electronic products. They aim to increase understanding of environmental issues and their implications at all levels, and to influence opinion and policy towards sustainable forms of development. Earthscan also aims to promote the various businesses, industries and organisations that provide the infrastructure to make this happen. Readership of titles includes academics, professionals, business people, policy makers and general readers. They are always keen to work with new authors.

Ebury Press
Random House, 20 Vauxhall Bridge Road, London, SW1V 2SA
- 020 7840 8400
- 020 7840 8406
- eburyeditorial@randomhouse.co.uk
- www.randomhouse.co.uk

Parent Company The Random House Group Ltd
Contact Publishing Director, Hannah MacDonald (Non-Fiction); Publishing Director, Carey Smith (Illustrated)
Insider Info Catalogue available online.
Non-Fiction Publishes Autobiography, Biography, Cookbooks, General Non-Fiction, Gift Books, Humour, Illustrated Books, Reference and Television Tie-In titles.
Submission Guidelines No unagented submissions.
Recent Title(s) *A Home for Rose: How My Life Turned Upside Down for the Love of a Dog*, Jon Katz (Non-Fiction)
Tips Ebury only accepts submissions through a literary agent.

Economist Books
3a Exmouth House, Pine Street, Exmouth Market, London, EC1R 0JH
- 020 7841 6300

020 7833 3969
 stephen.brough@profilebooks.com
 www.profilebooks.co.uk
Parent Company Profile Books
Contact Editor, Stephen Brough
Insider Info Catalogue available online.
Non-Fiction Publishes General Non-Fiction, Reference and Scholarly title on the following subjects:
Business/Economics
* All books are published on economy issues and are linked with *The Economist* newspaper brand.
Submission Guidelines Accepts proposal package (including outline, two sample chapters, SAE).
Tips Economist Books mainly handles submissions through an agent or agency, but unsolicited proposals following the submission guidelines will be considered.

Edgewell Publishing
5a Front Street, Prudhoe, Northumberland, NE42 5HJ
 01661 835330
 01661 835330
 keith@tynedale-languages.co.uk
 www.tynedale-languages.co.uk
Contact Editor, Keith Minton
Established 2005
Insider Info Submissions accompanied by SAE will be returned. Manuscript guidelines available by email and online.
Non-Fiction Publishes Reference, Scholarly, Textbook and Self-Help titles on Education.
Submission Guidelines Accepts queries by phone or email.
Fiction Publishes Children's, Multicultural, Short Story Collections, Translation and Young Adult titles.
Submission Guidelines Accepts queries with SAE.
Poetry Publish Poetry titles.
Submission Guidelines Accepts queries by phone or email.
Recent Title(s) *LIVELY TALES Magazine*, (Short Story Magazine)
Tips Titles are aimed at foreign language students, immigrants and young or new writers. Edgewell Publishing also offers a basic critiquing service which can then lead to work being published in *LIVELY TALES Magazine* or as a stand alone book.

Edinburgh University Press
22 George Square, Edinburgh, Scotland, EH8 9LF
 0131 650 4218
 0131 662 0053
 jackie.jones@eup.ed.ac.uk
 www.eup.ed.ac.uk

Contact Deputy Chief Executive & Head of Publishing, Jackie Jones (Literary Studies); Senior Commissioning Editor, Nicola Ramsey (Politics, American Studies, Islamic Studies); Senior Commissioning Editor, Sarah Edwards (Language, Linguistics, Film & Media Studies); Commissioning Editor, Carol MacDonald (Classics, Philosophy, Ancient History); Commissioning Editor, Esme Watson (Scottish History); Journals Publishing Manager, Diana Spencer
Established 1946
Insider Info Publishes 105 titles per year. 15 per cent of books published are from first-time authors, 100 per cent of books published are from unagented authors. Five per cent of books published are author subsidy published, based on expected gross profit. Payment is via net receipts. Advance offered is from £100 to £1,500. Average lead time is eight months, with simultaneous submissions accepted. Submissions accompanied by SAE will be returned. Aims to respond to queries within 14 days, proposals within two months and manuscripts within three months. Catalogue is free on request. Manuscript guidelines are free on request and available online, or by email.
Non-Fiction Publishes Journals, and Reference, Scholarly and Textbook titles on the following subjects:
Ancient History, Anthropology/Archaeology, Contemporary Culture, Education, Film and Media Studies, Government/Politics, Humanities (Philosophy, Linguistics), Islamic Studies, English, Scottish and American Literature, Law, Literary Criticism, Military/War, Philosophy, Politics, Religion, Scottish History, Scottish Studies, Women's Issues/Studies
Submission Guidelines Accepts proposal package (including outline, one to three sample chapters, your publishing history, and author biography) and artworks/images (send photocopies, and digital files as jpegs).
Recent Title(s) *Clinical Linguistics*, Louise Cummings (Linguistics)
Tips Proposals should be prepared according to the EUP guidelines on the website and submitted as an email attachment.

The Educational Company of Ireland
Ballymount Road, Walkinstown, Dublin 12, Republic of Ireland
 00353 1 450 0611
 00353 1 450 0993
 info@edco.ie
 www.edco.ie
Contact Chief Executive, Frank Maguire; Publisher, Frank Fahy; Commissioning Editors, Robert Healy and Michelle Staunton

Established 1910
Insider Info Catalogue and manuscript guidelines available online.
Non-Fiction Publishes Reference, Scholarly and Textbook titles on the following subjects: Education, Language/Literature, Translation
Submission Guidelines Accepts proposal package (including outline, sample chapter and market report) by post.
Recent Title(s) *Living Life*, Ann Jones (Home Economics)
Tips Publishes educational books and teaching resources on all subjects, in both English and Irish. Prospective authors should bear in mind that educational publishers must keep an eye on the number of students taking a particular subject, in order to ensure that any publishing proposal is commercially viable.

Educational Heretics Press
113 Arundel Drive, Bramcote, Nottingham, NG9 3FQ
☎ 0115 925 7261
☎ 0115 925 7261
✉ www.gn.apc.org/edheretics
Contact Director, Janet Meighan; Director, Roland Meighan
Insider Info Catalogue available online.
Non-Fiction Publishes Scholarly titles on Education.
Tips Educational Heretics is a not for profit, research, writing and publishing company. Their main aim is to publish radical material that questions the education system, hopefully improving it. Any submissions must, 'ask necessary questions about the fundamental processes of schooling.'

Edward Elgar Publishing Ltd
Glensanda House, Montpellier Parade, Cheltenham, Gloucestershire, GL5O 1UA
☎ 01242 226934
☎ 01242 262111
✉ info@e-elgar.co.uk
✉ www.e-elgar.co.uk
Contact Managing Director, Edward Elgar
Established 1986
Insider Info Publishes over 250 titles per year. Catalogue available online. Submission guidelines available online.
Non-fiction Publishes General Non-Fiction and Scholarly titles in the following subjects: Business/Economics, Finance, Government/Politics, Law, Money, Nature/Environment
Submission Guidelines Accepts query with SAE and proposal package (including outline, sample chapter(s) or completed manuscript and author biography). See also the online proposal form.

Submissions email: submissions@e-elgar.co.uk
Recent Title(s) *Ageing Labour Forces*, Philip Taylor ed. (Economics)
Tips Edward Elgar are specialists in research monographs, reference books and upper-level textbooks. They are actively commissioning new titles and are always happy to consider and advise on ideas and proposals at any stage. If you would like to discuss your work, send a query by email.

Egg Box Publishing
25 Brian Avenue, Norwich, NR1 2PH
☎ 01603 470191
✉ mail@eggboxpublishing.com
✉ www.eggboxpublishing.com
Contact Managing Editor, Nathan Hamilton; Founder, Gordon Smith
Established 2001
Insider Info Receives approximately 5,000 manuscripts per year. Authors are paid around 30 per cent of the profits from their book.
Non-Fiction Publishes Non-Fiction by unpublished writers only.
Submission Guidelines Postal submissions only.
Fiction Publishes Fiction by unpublished writers only.
Submission Guidelines Accepts postal submissions only.
Poetry Publishes New Poetry from unpublished writers only.
Submission Guidelines Accepts postal submissions only.
Recent Title(s) *Donjong Heights*, Ben Borek
Tips Egg Box Publishing is completely self funded, and allows new writers the chance to be published and possibly picked up by a more mainstream publisher. Authors must not have had any poetry collections or novels previously published anywhere. There are no guidelines for manuscripts as the ethos of the company is to encourage writing outside the usual constraints of mainstream publishing.

Egmont Books
239 Kensington High Street, London, W8 6SA
☎ 020 7761 3500
☎ 020 7761 3510
✉ info@egmont.co.uk
✉ www.egmont.co.uk
Contact Publishing Director, David Riley
Established 1878
Insider Info Publishes roughly 500 titles per year. Catalogue available online. Manuscript guidelines available online.
Non-Fiction Publishes Gift Books and Children's titles.

Submission Guidelines No unsolicited manuscripts.
Fiction Picture Books and Children's titles.
Submission Guidelines No unsolicited manuscripts.
Recent Title(s) *Black Heart Jamaica*, Julia Golding (Adventure)
Tips Egmont Books' aim is to turn children into passionate readers, producing books that enrich and entertain. Due to a huge backlog, they are unable to accept unsolicited manuscripts and recommend seeking a literary agent.

Eilish Press

4 Collegiate Crescent, Broomhall Park, Sheffield, S10 2BA
07973 353964
eilishpress@hotmail.co.uk
http://eilishpress.tripod.com
Contact Dr. Suzi Kapadia (Women's Issues, Human Rights, Anti-Racism)
Established 2006
Insider Info Publishes five titles per year. Receives approximately 30 queries and five manuscripts per year. 100 per cent of books published are from unagented authors. Payment is via royalty (on wholesale price) or outright purchase. Catalogue available online or by email.
Non-Fiction Publishes Children's and Scholarly titles on the following subjects:
Ethnic, Health, History, Women's Issues/Studies, Young Adult
* Eilish Press only accepts email proposals for children's non-fiction titles with human rights or anti-racism themes.
Submission Guidelines Accepts query by email. All unsolicited manuscripts are returned unopened. Accepts artworks/images (send digital files as jpegs).
Fiction Publishes Ethnic, Feminist, Historical, Multicultural and Young Adult titles.
* All children's fiction proposals must contain human rights or anti-racism themes.
Recent Title(s) *Conception Diary: Thinking About Pregnancy & Childbirth*, Dr. Susan Hogan (Polemical Feminist, Humour)
Tips Eilish Press only publishes non-sexist, non-racist literature with humanitarian themes for children, or books on women's studies and childcare.

Eland Publishing Ltd

61 Exmouth Market, London, EC1R 4QL
020 7833 0762
020 7833 4434
info@travelbooks.co.uk
www.travelbooks.co.uk

Contact Directors: Rose Baring, John Hatt and Barnaby Rogerson
Established 1982
Imprint(s) Sickle Moon Books
Baring & Rogerson Books
Insider Info Catalogue available online.
Non-Fiction Publishes General Non-Fiction in the following subjects:
Regional, Travel.
Recent Title(s) *The Way of the World*, Nicolas Bouvier (Travel); *Bangkok*, Alec Waugh (Travel)
Tips Eland Publishing specialises in keeping the classics of travel literature in print and only tends to publish reprints. They aim to 'open out our understanding of other cultures, interpret the unknown and reveal different environments, as well as celebrate the humour and occasional horrors of travel.'

Elastic Press

85 Gertrude Road, Norwich, Norfolk, NR3 4SG
0845 398 3349
elasticpress@elasticpress.com
www.elasticpress.com
Contact Editor (Short Fiction), Andrew Hook
Established 2002
Insider Info Publishes five titles per year. Receives approximately 200 queries and 120 manuscripts per year. Ten per cent of books published are from first-time authors, 80 per cent of books published are from unagented authors. Payment is via royalty (on wholesale price). Average lead time is more than 18 months, with simultaneous submissions accepted. Submissions accompanied by SAE will be returned. Aims to respond to queries and proposals within two days, manuscripts within two months and all other enquiries within two days. Catalogue and manuscript guidelines are available with SAE, or available online or by email.
Fiction Publishes Experimental, Fantasy, Gothic, Horror, Literary, Mainstream/Contemporary, Science Fiction and Short Story collection titles.
* Elastic Press only publishes short stories and operates a reading window system for submissions. See website for full details.
Submission Guidelines Accepts query with SAE or via email, with a proposal package (including outline and synopsis).
Recent Title(s) *Subtle Edens: The Elastic Book of Slipstream*, Allen Ashely ed. (Short Story Anthology)
Tips Elastic Press is a small publishing house dedicated to showcasing the talents of previously published independent press writers. Elastic Press publishes four times per year; on the 1st of February, May, August and November.

11:9

19 Netherton Avenue, Glasgow, Scotland, G13 1BQ
- 0141 954 8007
- 0141 954 8007
- info@nwp.co.uk
- www.nwp.co.uk

Parent Company Neil Wilson Publishing Ltd
Insider Info Catalogue and manuscript guidelines are available online.
Fiction Publishes Contemporary Scottish Fiction and Anthologies.
Submission Guidelines Does not accept submissions.
Recent Title(s) *Saigon Tea*, Graham Reilly (Novel)
Tips 11:9 is the contemporary fiction imprint of Neil Wilson Publishing and specialises in Scottish fiction and regional anthologies. Due to the state of the market 11:9 is not currently commissioning any further titles.

Elliot Right Way Books

3 The Lanchesters, 162 Fulham Palace Road, London, W6 9ER
- 020 8741 3663
- 020 8748 7562
- enquiries@constablerobinson.com
- www.right-way.co.uk

Parent Company Constable & Robinson Ltd
Established 1946
Imprint(s) Right Way
Right Way Plus
Clarion
Insider Info Catalogue is available online. Manuscript guidelines are available online.
Non-Fiction Publishes General Non-Fiction, How-To, Reference and Scholarly titles on the following subjects: Business, Childcare/Parenting, Cooking, Counselling/Career, Economics, Education, Etiquette, Hobbies, House and Home, Law
Submission Guidelines Accepts query with SAE/proposal package (including outline, sample chapter(s)).
Recent Title(s) *Texas Hold 'Em Poker: Win Online*, Paul Mendelson (Gambling)
Tips Titles are aimed at general readers and are intended to be informative, helpful and reasonably priced guides on an ever widening range of subjects. Elliot Right Way Books seeks authors with specialist knowledge of their subjects. Editorial support is provided by in-house staff for authors whose spelling and grammar is not as good as it could be.

Elliott & Thompson

27 John Street, London, WC1N 2BX
- 020 7831 5013
- 020 7831 5011
- gmo73@dial.pipex.com
- www.elliottthompson.com

Contact Publishers: Brad Thompson and Lorne Forsythe
Established 2001
Imprint(s) Gold Edition
Spitfire
Spitfire Originals
Young Spitfire
Insider Info Catalogue is available online. Manuscript guidelines are available online.
Non-Fiction Publishes Biography and Belles-Lettres titles.
Submission Guidelines Accepts query with SAE/proposal package (including outline, sample chapter(s) and SAE).
Fiction Publishes Literary and Classic Male Writers titles.
Submission Guidelines Accepts query with SAE/proposal package (including outline, sample chapter(s) and SAE).
Recent Title(s) *A Captain's Mandate: Palestine 1946–1948*, Philip Brutton (History); *Dance to your Daddy*, Gail Levy (Novel)
Tips Elliott & Thompson publish within a specific area of writing, once classified by the more traditional bookshops as 'belles-lettres'. The list includes works in the areas of fiction, memoir, biography, history, art, politics and travel. Do not send unsolicited manuscripts, an outline with a sample chapter and SAE is sufficient.

Elm Publications/Training

Seaton House, Kings Ripton, Huntingdon, Cambridgeshire, PE28 2NJ
- 01487 773254
- 01487 773359
- elm@elm-training.co.uk
- www.elm-training.co.uk

Parent Company Elm Consulting Ltd
Contact Managing Director, Sheila Ritchie
Established 1977
Insider Info Publishes 30 titles per year. Catalogue is available online.
Non-Fiction Publishes Reference, Textbook and Technical titles on the following subjects: Business, Counselling/Career, Economics, Education, Finance, Management, Tourism
Submission Guidelines Accepts query with SAE/proposal package (including outline and SAE).
Recent Title(s) *Tourism and Leisure in the Countryside*, Richard Sharpley (Tourism)

Tips Titles are aimed at adults in education, training teams and businesses. Elm actively seeks high-quality, tested, training materials aimed at the public and private sectors, and at adults in employment. They are keen to hear from consultants and trainers who have tested materials and would like to extend their use through wider publication.

Elsevier Ltd
The Boulevard, Langford Lane, Kidlington, Oxford, OX5 1GB
- 01865 843000
- 01865 843010
- authorsupport@elsevier.com
- www.elsevier.com

Parent Company Reed Elsevier Group Plc
Contact CEO, Erik Engstrom; CEO (Science & Technology), Herman van Campenhout; CEO (Health Sciences), Michael Hansen
Established 1880
Imprint(s) Elsevier Ltd (Health Sciences) Elsevier Ltd (Science & Technology)
Insider Info Publishes 1,900 books per year. Authors paid by royalty. Catalogue and author guidelines available online.
Non-Fiction Publishes Journals/Monographs, Illustrated Books, Textbooks, Multimedia, Reference, Scholarly and Technical titles on the following subjects: Anthropology/Archaeology, Art/Architecture, Business/Economics, Communications, Computers/Electronics, Education, Government/Politics, Health/Medicine, Humanities, Language/Literature, Law, Money/Finance, Nature/Environment, Psychology Science, Social Sciences, Sociology, Sports, Transportation, Technology, Physics/Astronomy, Leisure/Tourism
Submission Guidelines Accepts query with SAE.
Tips Elsevier is the world's leading publisher of science and health information. The publishing operation is organised into two divisions: Science & Technology and Health Sciences. The company publishes various products and services, including electronic and print versions of journals, monographs, textbooks and reference works which cover the health, life, physical and social sciences. Elsevier welcomes authors' proposals for books. The first step is to discuss the proposal with the relevant publishing editor. Check the website for in-depth submission guidelines and a full list of editorial contacts. Note that most Elsevier publications are written by qualified academics.

Elsevier Ltd (Health Sciences)
Linacre House, Jordan Hill, Oxford, OX2 8DP
- 01865 474010
- 01865 474011
- authorsupport@elsevier.com
- www.elsevierhealth.com

Parent Company Elsevier Ltd
Contact CEO, Michael Hansen; Publishing Director, Caroline Makepeace (Health Professions); Publishing Manager, Timothy Horne (Medical Textbooks); Commissioning Editor, Michael Houston (Professional and Reference Medical Books)
Imprint(s) Baillière Tindall Butterworth-Heinemann Churchill Livingstone Hanley & Belfus Mosby Saunders
Insider Info Payment is via royalties. Catalogue available online. Manuscript guidelines available online.
Non-Fiction Publishes Illustrated Books, Multimedia, Reference, Scholarly, Textbook and Technical titles on the following subjects: Education, Health/Medicine, Psychology, Science, Social Sciences, Care, Veterinary Medicine, Midwifery, Complementary Therapies
Submission Guidelines Submissions accepted via online proposal form.
Tips A leading publisher of health science books and journals, including online material and CD-ROMs, Elsevier Health Sciences accepts unsolicited proposals in the relevant subject areas. To submit a proposal fill in a proposal form, available on the website, and return by email. Alternatively authors may contact the relevant editor prior to submission to discuss the proposal. Also see individual imprint entries.

Elsevier Ltd (Science & Technology)
Linacre House, Jordan Hill, Oxford, OX2 8DP
- 01865 474010
- 01865 474011
- authorsupport@elsevier.com
- www.elsevier.com

Parent Company Reed Elsevier Group Plc (Elsevier Ltd)
Contact CEO, Herman van Campenhout
Imprint(s) Academic Press Architectural Press Focal Press Gulf Professional Publishing Morgan Kauffman Newnes Pergamon Flexible Learning Syngress William Andrew
Insider Info Payment is via royalties. Catalogue and manuscript guidelines available online.

Non-Fiction Publishes Illustrated, Multimedia, Reference, Scholarly, Technical and Textbook titles on the following subjects:
Art/Architecture, Business/Economics, Communications, Computers/Electronics, Education, Government/Politics, Humanities, Language/Literature, Law, Money/Finance, Psychology, Science, Sports, Transportation, Technology, Construction/Engineering, Astronomy/Physics, Leisure and Tourism
Submission Guidelines Accepts query with SAE/proposal package (including outline and SAE).
Tips Elsevier Science & Technology is a division of Elsevier Ltd and publishes printed material and digital resources over a wide range of scientific, financial and construction related subjects. They welcome authors' proposals for books. The first step is to discuss the proposal with the relevant publishing editor. Check the website for in-depth submission guidelines and a full list of editorial contacts.

Emissary Publishing
PO Box 33, Bicester, OX26 4ZZ
- 01869 323447
- 01869 324096
- http://website.lineone.net/~selfpublishuk/Emissary_Publishing.htm
Contact Editorial Director, Val Miller
Established 1992
Insider Info Catalogue is available online at: http://website.lineone.net/~selfpublishuk/book_order_form.htm.
Fiction Publishes Humour titles.
Submission Guidelines Does not accept any unsolicited submissions.

Emma Treehouse Ltd
Little Orchard House, Mill Lane, Beckington, Somerset, BA11 6SN
- 01373 831215
- 01373 831216
- info@emmatreehouse.com
- www.emmatreehouse.com
Contact Director, David Bailey; Creative/Editorial Director, Richard Powell
Established 1992
Imprints Treehouse Children's Books
Insider Info Catalogue is available online.
Non-Fiction Publishes Gift Books and Children's titles.
Submission Guidelines Accepts query with SAE or via email.
Fiction Publishes Children's titles.
Submission Guidelines Accepts query with SAE or via email.

Recent Title(s) *Book-in-a-Book: Who Goes With Who?*, Ana Martin Larranaga (Illustrator)
Tips Emma Treehouse is a specialist creator of books for children from 0–7 years. Novelty, cloth, feel, flap and books with a sound concept are included in the company's list. Publishes in the UK as Treehouse Children's Books. Do not send unsolicited manuscript submissions, contact via email with ideas only.

Encyclopædia Britannica (UK) Ltd
2nd Floor, Unity Wharf, Mill Street, London, SE1 2BH
- 020 7500 7800
- 020 7500 7878
- http://info.britannica.co.uk
Contact Encyclopaedia Britannica Inc
Established 1768
Non-Fiction Publishes Multimedia and Reference titles on the following subjects:
Arts & Literature, The Earth, Geography, Health and Medicine, Philosophy, Religion, Sports & Recreation, Science, Mathematics, Life, Society, Technology, History
Tips Primarily publishes the Encyclopædia Britannica, a major reference guide.

English Heritage (Publishing)
Kemble Drive, Swindon, SN2 2GZ
- 01793 414497
- 01793 414769
- customers@english-heritage.org.uk
- www.english-heritage.org.uk
Contact Rob Richardson
Insider Info Catalogue is available online.
Non-Fiction Publishes General Non-Fiction, Illustrated Books, Scholarly Books and Reference titles.
Submission Guidelines No unsolicited submissions.
Tips English Heritage exists to protect and promote England's spectacular historic environment and ensure that its past is researched and understood. All titles relate directly to the work of the organisation, so unsolicited material is not accepted.

Enitharmon Press
26b Caversham Road, London, NW5 2DU
- 020 7482 5967
- 020 7284 1787
- books@enitharmon.co.uk
- www.enitharmon.co.uk
Contact Director, Stephen Stuart-Smith
Established 1967
Imprint(s) Enitharmon Editions
Insider Info Catalogue is available online.

Non-Fiction Publishes Illustrated and General Non-Fiction titles on the following subjects: Art/Architecture, Literary Criticism, Photography.
Submission Guidelines No unsolicited submissions.
Fiction Publishes Literary and Short Story collections.
Submission Guidelines No unsolicited submissions.
Poetry Publishes Poetry titles.
Submission Guidelines No unsolicited submissions.
Recent Title(s) *Out of the Blue*, Simon Armitage (Poetry Collection)
Tips Enitharmon commissions collaborations between distinguished artists and writers. These 'artists' books' have earned an international reputation for their exceptional quality.

Epworth Press
c/o Methodist Publishing House, 4 John Wesley Road, Werrington, Peterborough, PE4 6ZP
- 01733 325002
- 01733 384180
- customer.services@mph.org.uk
- www.mph.org.uk

Parent Company Methodist Publishing House
Contact Commissioning Editor, Dr. Natalie Watson
Established 1800
Insider Info Publishes ten titles per year. Payment is via royalties (annually). Catalogue and manuscript guidelines are available online.
Non-Fiction Publishes Illustrated books and General Non-Fiction titles on the following subjects: Religion, Methodist Faith
Submission Guidelines Accepts query with SAE submit proposal package (outline, two sample chapters, SAE).
Recent Title(s) *Five for Sorrow, Ten for Joy: A Consideration of the Rosary*, J. Neville Ward
Tips Epworth publishes titles on the Bible, worship, contemporary Christian issues and Methodism. Epworth is interested in hearing from new and aspiring authors who are writing, or have written something that might be of interest to a wider methodist readership.

The Erotic Print Society
1st Floor, 17 Harwood Road, London, SW6 4QP
- 020 7736 5800
- 020 7736 6330
- leadline@eroticprints.org
- www.eroticprints.org

Contact Managing Director, Jamie Maclean; Society Secretary, Tilly Johnson
Established 1994

Insider Info Publishes 20 titles per year. Catalogue available online.
Non-Fiction Publishes Illustrated and Multimedia titles on Sex.
Fiction Publishes Erotica and Multimedia titles.
Recent Title(s) *The Book Of Love*, James McConnachie (Biography)
Tips Titles are aimed at men and women who appreciate the best in erotic books, art, photography and literature. The Erotic Print Society is now established as the leading source of collectable erotica worldwide and publishes works such as pocket sized paperbacks and beautifully bound limited editions. They also publish several magazines, such as *SEx*, which can offer further publishing opportunities for shorter writing.

EuroCrime
15–16 Nassau Street, London, W1W 7AB
- 020 7436 9898
- 020 7436 9898
- info@arcadiabooks.co.uk
- www.arcadiabooks.co.uk

Parent Company Arcadia Books
Insider Info Catalogue available online.
Fiction Publishes Crime Fiction titles.
Submission Guidelines Accepts agented submissions only.
Recent Title(s) *Priest of Evil*, Matti Joensuu (Crime)
Tips Publishes European crime writing only (excluding the UK).

Euromonitor International
60–61 Britton Street, London, EC1M 5UX
- 020 7251 8024
- 020 7608 3149
- info@euromonitor.com
- www.euromonitor.com

Contact Chairman, R.N. Senior; Managing Director, T.J. Fenwick
Established 1972
Insider Info Publishes 1,000 titles per year. Author's work is purchased outright. Catalogue is available free on request, online and via email.
Non-Fiction Publishes Multimedia, Reference and Technical titles on the following subjects: Business/Economics, Market Reports/Analysis
Recent Title(s) *Consumer Asia*, Euromonitor (Market Analysis)
Tips Euromonitor International's mission is to be the best provider of quality international market intelligence on industries, countries and consumers. Prospective authors must be highly experienced with a background in technical market analysis, or similar.

Evans Brothers Ltd

2a Portman Mansions, Chiltern Street, London, W1M 1LE

☎ 020 7487 0920
☎ 020 7487 0921
✉ sales@evansbrothers.co.uk
🌐 www.evansbooks.co.uk

Contact Managing Director, Stephen Pawley; Publisher, Su Swallow
Established 1908
Imprint(s) Cherrytree Books
Zero to Ten
Insider Info Publishes roughly 120 titles per year. Payment is via royalties (annually). Catalogue is available online. Discounts are available for schools.
Non-Fiction Publishes Children's, Textbook and Scholarly titles on the following subjects: Education, Translation, Foreign Languages
Fiction Publishes Young Adult and Children's Fiction.
* Fiction published has an educational purpose.
Recent Title(s) *Enid Blyton's Nature Lover's Book*, Enid Blyton (Reference); *The Buckinghams at Ravenswyke*, Malcolm Saville (Young Adult Novel)
Tips Titles are aimed at a wide range of children, from early years to secondary school pupils. The publisher is committed to providing children, teachers and carers with books that help deliver key areas of the curriculum, whilst instilling a lifelong love of reading and learning in children and young people.

Everyman

Random House, 20 Vauxhall Bridge Road, London, SW1V 2SA

☎ 020 7840 8400
☎ 020 7840 8406
✉ sarah@everyman.uk.com
🌐 www.randomhouse.co.uk

Parent Company The Random House Group Ltd
Insider Info Catalogue is available online.
Non-Fiction Publishes Biography, Illustrated Books and General Non-Fiction titles on the following subjects:
Memoirs, Nostalgia
Submission Guidelines No unagented submissions.
Fiction Publishes reprints of Classic Novels.
Poetry Publishes reprinted Collections from established poets.
Recent Title(s) *Scottish Poems*, Gerard Carruthers, ed. (Poetry Collection)
Tips Everyman mainly handles reprints and doesn't often publish new works.

Everyman Classics

Orion House, 5 Upper St Martin's Lane, London, WC2H 9EA

☎ 020 7240 3444
☎ 020 7240 4822
🌐 www.orionbooks.co.uk

Parent Company Orion Publishing Group Ltd
Insider Info Catalogue is available online.
Non-Fiction Publishes General Non-Fiction titles on the following subjects: Creative Non-Fiction, History, Literary Criticism, Philosophy, Regional. All are reprints of classic works of non-fiction.
Fiction Publishes Literary, Plays and Poetry titles. All are reprints of classic fiction works.
Poetry Publishes reprints of Poetry Collections.
Tips Publishes reprints only, and therefore does not accept unsolicited submissions.

Everyman's Library

Northborough House, 10 Northborough Street, London, EC1V 0AT

☎ 020 7566 6350
☎ 020 7490 3708
✉ assistant@everyman.uk.com

Parent Company Everyman
Contact Publisher, David Campbell
Established 1906
Non-Fiction Publishes General Non-Fiction titles on the following subjects:
Travel.
* No new titles, only publishes classic reprints.
Fiction Publishes Children's, Literary, Poetry and Translation titles.
* No new titles, only publishes classic reprints.
Poetry Publishes new Poetry Anthologies.
Submission Guidelines Does not accept submissions.
Tips Titles are aimed at anyone interested in classic literary/world writing. Submissions cannot be accepted since titles are mainly reprints of 'classic' literature.

Exley Publications Ltd

16 Chalk Hill, Watford, Hertfordshire, WD19 4BG

☎ 01923 250505
☎ 01923 249795
✉ editorial@exleypublications.co.uk
🌐 www.helenexleygiftbooks.com

Contact Editorial Director, Helen Exley
Established 1976
Insider Info Catalogue is available online.
Non-Fiction Publishes Gift Books, Quotation Anthologies and Humour titles.
Submission Guidelines No submissions accepted.

Recent Title(s) *Utterly Adorable Cats*, Stuart and Linda Macfarlane eds. (Gift Book)
Tips Unsolicited material will not be accepted.

Faber & Faber Ltd
3 Queen Square, London, WC1N 3AU
- 020 7465 0045
- 020 7465 0034
- gapublicity@faber.co.uk
- www.faber.co.uk

Contact Chief Executive, Stephen Page; Publishing Director (Fiction), Lee Brackstone; Publishing Director (Non-Fiction), Julian Loose; Editor (Poetry), Paul Keegan; Editor (Crime), Angus Cargill; Editorial Director (Children's), Julia Wells
Established 1929
Insider Info Publishes roughly 300 titles per year. Payment is via royalty, along with varying advances. Submissions accompanied by SAE will be returned. Aim to respond to manuscripts within 12 weeks. Catalogue is available online and via email to: gacatalogue@faber.co.uk
Non-Fiction Publishes Biography, Children's, Coffee Table Books, Cookbooks, General Non-Fiction, Anthologies and Humour titles on the following subjects: Art, Architecture, Contemporary Culture, Cooking, Creative Non-Fiction, Entertainment/ Games, Food & Drink, Government/Politics, History, Humanities, Literary Criticism, Military/War, Multicultural, Music/Dance, Philosophy, Psychology, Recreation, Science, Sports, Travel, World Affairs, Young Adult, Film, Music
* Faber have rejuvenated their non-fiction lists in recent years and the film and drama books remain market leaders.
Submission Guidelines Accepts agented submissions only.
Fiction Publishes Adventure, Ethnic, Experimental, Historical, Literary, Mystery, Plays, Poetry, Short Story Collections, Sports, Suspense, Young Adult, Drama, Screenplays and Children's Fiction titles
Submission Guidelines Accepts agented submissions only.
Poetry Publishes Classic and Contemporary Poetry titles.
* Poetry is the only area where Faber & Faber will accept unsolicited submissions.
Submission Guidelines Submit up to six sample poems.
Recent Title(s) *The QI Annual 2009*, John Lloyd and John Mitchinson (Media Tie-In); *Somebody*, Stefan Kanfer (Drama).
Tips Faber & Faber will only accept submissions for poetry titles, and then only by post with accompanying SAE for return. If you have not heard anything 12 weeks after sending submissions you may then send a further query.

Fabian Society
11 Dartmouth Street, London, SW1H 9BN
- 020 7227 4900
- 020 7976 7153
- info@fabians.org.uk
- www.fabians.org.uk

Contact General Secretary, Sunder Katwala; Editorial Director, Tom Hampson
Established 1884
Insider Info Catalogue is available online.
Non-Fiction Publishes Booklets, General Non-Fiction, Reference, Policy Reports and Scholarly titles on the following subjects: Business/Economics, Community/Public Affairs, Contemporary Culture, Education, Finance, Government/Politics, Money, Social Sciences, Sociology, World Affairs
Submission Guidelines Submission details to: tom.hampson@fabian-society.org.uk
Recent Title(s) *Stopping the Far Right: How Progressive Politics Can Tackle Political Extremism*, Fred Grindrod and Mark Rusling (eds.) (Young Fabians)
Tips The Fabian Society has played a central role for more than a century in the development of political ideas and public policy on the left of centre. The Society's publishing programme aims to explore the political ideas and the policy reforms which will define progressive politics in the new century. The Society is affiliated to the Labour Party, but is editorially and organisationally independent. Through its publications, seminars and conferences, the Society provides an arena for open minded public debate. Proposals for publication must reflect this ethos.

Facet Publishing
7 Ridgemount Street, London, WC1E 7AE
- 020 7255 0590
- 020 7255 0591
- info@facetpublishing.co.uk
- www.facetpublishing.co.uk

Parent Company CILIP
Contact Publishing Director, Helen Carley; Commissioning Editor, Louise LeBas
Imprint(s) Library Association Publishing
Clive Bingley Books
Insider Info Publishes roughly 25 titles per year. Payment is via royalties. Catalogue and manuscript guidelines are available online.
Non-Fiction Publishes Scholarly, Textbook, Directories/Bibliographies and Reference titles on the following subjects: Library and Information Science, Information Technology
Submission Guidelines Accepts proposal package (including outline, two sample chapters, your

publishing history, author biography and SAE) by post or email.

Submissions details to: louise.lebas@facetpublishing.co.uk

Recent Title(s) *Librarianship: An Introduction*, G.G. Chowdhury, Paul F. Burton, David McMenemy and Alan Poulter (eds.) (Reference)

Tips A leading international publisher of books for the library and information profession. Facet provides dynamic, relevant and up-to-date books for information professionals wherever they may be, and acknowledges the need for high quality books that inform, instruct and inspire in the ever changing information world. The audiences of these books are industry professionals, so submissions need to reflect this.

Fal Publications

PO Box 74, Truro, Cornwall, TR1 1XS
- 07887 560018
- enquire@falpublications.co.uk
- www.falpublications.co.uk

Contact Publisher, Victoria Field (Poetry, Cornish Interest)

Established 2004

Insider Info Publishes three titles per year. Receives approximately 12 queries per year. 50 per cent of books published are from first-time authors, 80 per cent of books published are from unagented authors. Payment is via royalty (on wholesale price). Simultaneous submissions not accepted. Submissions accompanied by SAE will be returned. Aims to respond to queries within seven days. Catalogue available online.

Fiction Publishes Cornwall related Fiction titles.

Poetry Publishes Cornwall related Poetry titles.

Submission Guidelines Accepts query by email.

Recent Title(s) *The Gift*, Victoria Field (Illustrated story about Cornwall); *Knights of Love*, Jane Tozer

Tips Publishes general fiction and poetry aimed at those interested in Cornwall.

F.A. Thorpe (Publishing)

The Green, Bradgate Road, Anstey, LE7 7FU
- 0116 236 4325
- 0116 234 0205

Contact Group Chief Executive, Robert Thirlby

Established 1964

Imprint(s) Linford Mystery
Linford Romance
Linford Western

Insider Info Publishes 450 titles per year.

Non-Fiction Publishes General Non-Fiction titles in the form of large print books for libraries.

* No education, gardening, or any books unsuitable for large print.

Submission Guidelines Do not send any unsolicited submissions.

Fiction Publishes Mystery, Romance and Western titles.

* Large print books for libraries. No books unsuitable for large print.

Submission Guidelines Does not accept any unsolicited submissions.

Tips As part of the Ulverscroft Group, F.A. Thorpe supply large print books to libraries and other services. Unsolicited material cannot be accepted since only reprints (supplied to libraries) are published.

Fidra Books

219 Bruntsfield Place, Edinburgh, EH10 4DH
- 0131 447 1917
- info@fidrabooks.co.uk
- www.fidrabooks.co.uk

Contact Directors, Malcolm and Vanessa Robertson

Insider Info Catalogue is available online.

Fiction Publishes Children's and Young Adult titles.

* Reprints of children's fiction only.

Submission Guidelines Accepts query with SAE.

Recent Title(s) *The Team*, KM Peyton

Tips Fidra Books is a new publishing company, specialising in reprinting some of the best children's fiction from the 20th Century. Only approach Fidra if you are interested in reissuing a work of children's fiction. There is a definite policy of only publishing books which the publisher likes.

Fig Tree

80 Strand, London, WC2R 0RL
- 020 7010 3000
- 020 7010 6060
- customer.service@penguin.co.uk
- www.penguin.co.uk

Parent Company Penguin General

Contact Publishing Director, Juliet Annan

Established 2006

Insider Info Catalogue is available online.

Fiction Publishes Literary titles.

Submission Guidelines Agented submissions only.

Recent Title(s) *Mrs Woolf and the Servants*, Alison Light (Biography)

Tips Fig Tree is a new Penguin imprint that specialises in literary books with commercial appeal. Titles aim to be fresh, distinct, well written, clever, entertaining and sometimes funny.

Findhorn Press

305a The Park, Findhorn, Forres, Scotland, IV36 3TE
- 01309 690582
- 01309 690036

submissions@findhornpress.com
www.findhornpress.com
Contact Managing Director and Publisher, Thierry Bogliolo
Established 1971
Insider Info Publishes roughly 20 titles per year. Receives approximately 1,000 queries per year. 50 per cent of books published are from first-time authors. Average lead time is 12 months. Catalogue and manuscript guidelines are available online.
Non-Fiction Publishes General Non-Fiction, Gift Books and Self-Help titles in the following subjects: Alternative Lifestyles, Health, New Age, Spirituality, Mind, Body and Spirit
Submission Guidelines Accepts query with proposal package (including outline, two sample chapters, your publishing history, author biography and SAE). Will accept artwork/photos. Prefers submission by email.
Recent Title(s) *Fully Fertile: A 12–Week Plan for Optimal Fertility*, Quinn, Heller and Bussell (Holistics)
Tips Findhorn Press is a small publishing house that offers books, sets of cards and cds that cover a wide range of 'mind, body & spirit' topics such as nature, spirituality, alternative health (for both people and animals) and self-help. Before contacting the publisher take a good look at the type of books published to ensure your work is suitable. In particular, note that they do not publish poetry, fiction, short stories or autobiographies.

First & Best in Education
Earlstrees Court, Earlstrees Road, Corby, Northamptonshire, NN17 4HH
01536 399005
01536 399012
info@firstandbest.co.uk
www.firstandbest.co.uk
Contact Publisher, Tony Attwood; Editor, Anne Cockburn
Established 1992
Imprint(s) School Improvement Reports
Insider Info Payment via royalties. Catalogue and submission guidelines are available online.
Non-Fiction Publishes Reference, Textbook and Scholarly titles on Education.
* Books must be photocopiable.
Submission Guidelines Accepts query with SAE/proposal package (including outline, two to four sample chapters and SAE).
Recent Title(s) *Plays into Shakespeare*, William Harrison (Copiable book)
Tips Publishes photocopiable books and books on disk for teachers and parents. First & Best is interested in publishing the following types of educational books: materials for teachers, drama, history, DT, PSHE and religious studies lesson materials, special needs and behaviour management materials, and information for school administrators.

Fitness Trainers
38 Soho Square, London, W1D 3HB
020 7758 0200
020 7758 0222
rfoss@acblack.com
www.acblack.com
Parent Company A&C Black Publishers Ltd
Contact Department Head and Commissioning Editor, Robert Foss; Commissioning Editor, Charlotte Croft; Editor, Lucy Beevor; Editor, Alex Hazle
Established 2003
Insider Info Catalogue is available online.
Non-Fiction Publishes General Non-Fiction, Illustrated Books and Reference titles in the following subjects: Health/Medicine, Sports, Fitness Training
Recent Title(s) *101 Youth Athletics Drills*, John Shepherd (Fitness/Sport)
Tips Fitness Trainers publishes practical fitness and sports guides, training schedules, and general interest books on sports for all age ranges and abilities. Fitness Trainers specialises in comprehensive guides written by well known experts in their relevant fields.

Fitzgerald Publishing
89 Ermine Road, Ladywell, London, SE13 7JJ
020 8690 0597
fitzgeraldbooks@yahoo.co.uk
www.thebts.co.uk/fitzgerald_publishing.htm
Contact Managing Editor, Tim Fitzgerald; General Editor, Andrew Smith
Established 1974
Insider Info Publishes roughly two titles per year. Catalogue is available online.
Non-Fiction Publishes Illustrated Books and Scholarly titles on the following subjects: Nature/Environment, Spiders and Insects
Submission Guidelines Accepts query with SAE. Will accept artwork/photos.
Recent Title(s) *Scorpions Of Medical Importance*, Prof. Keegan
Tips Aimed at those who study arachnids and insects, titles are generally technical or academic in nature. Unsolicited submissions, or ideas for books are welcome, as are scripts for video documentaries (along with the video content).

Fitzwarren Publishing
2 Orchard Drive, Aston Clinton, Aylsebury, Buckinghamshire, HP22 5HR
01296 632627

☎ 01296 630028
✉ pen2paper@btopenworld.com
Contact Julie Stretton
Insider info Publishes roughly two titles per year. Payment is via royalties.
Non-Fiction Publishes Reference and Technical titles on Law.
* All books follow a rigid 128 page format. Books are all legal handbooks.
Submission Guidelines Accepts query with SAE/proposal package (including outline, sample chapter(s), author biography and SAE).
Tips Publishes mainly layman's handbooks on legal matters. Written approaches and synopses from prospective authors are welcome. Authors, although not necessarily legally qualified, are expected to know their subject as well as a lawyer would.

Flambard Press
Stable Cottage, East Fourstones, Hexham, Northumberland, NE47 5DX
☎ 01434 674360
☎ 01434 674178
✉ enquiries@flambardpress.co.uk
🌐 www.flambardpress.co.uk
Contact Managing Editor, Peter Lewis
Established 1990
Insider Info Publishes five titles per year. Authors are paid royalties. Catalogue and manuscript guidelines are available online.
Fiction Publishes Literary and Short Story Collections titles.
* No genre fiction.
Submission Guidelines Accepts query with SAE/proposal package (including outline and two sample chapters).
Poetry Publishes Poetry titles.
Submission Guidelines Accepts query with 15–20 sample poems.
Recent Title(s) *All Things Tire of Themselves*, Arnold Wesker (Poetry Collection); *The Sweet Track*, Avril Joy (Novel)
Tips Flambard Press is a small, independent publisher that aims to offer opportunities to new and neglected writers, especially in the North of England. Flambard is keen to nourish developing talent. Poetry is the backbone of the list, but Flambard now publishes a small amount of fiction as well. Authors are very carefully selected and only book length collections of poetry or short stories, and novels are considered. Children's books, science fiction, fantasy, romance, westerns, and horror are not published.

Flame Tree Publishing
Crabtree Hall, Crabtree Lane, London, SW6 6TY
☎ 020 7386 4700
☎ 020 7386 4701
✉ info@flametreepublishing.com
🌐 www.flametreepublishing.com
Parent Company The Foundry Creative Media Company Ltd
Contact CEO, Nick Wells
Established 1992
Insider Info Catalogue is available online.
Non-Fiction Children's, Gift Books and General Non-Fiction titles on the following subjects:
Art, Cooking, Education, History, Hobbies, Music
Recent Title(s) *The Wit and Wisdom of Cats & Kittens*, Ulysses Brave
Tips Flame Tree Publishing aims to create high quality books and stationery of great integrity and genuine value. Illustrated reference books are favoured above others.

Flicking Lizard
176c Hartfield Road, London, SW19 3TQ
☎ 020 8715 0072
✉ flickliz@googlemail.com
🌐 www.flickinglizard.co.uk
Contact Publisher, Mark Boccalatte
Established 2007
Insider Info Aims to publish 10 books per year. Accepts unagented submissions. Payment is via royalty (of net) with 0.1 (per £) minimum. Offers an advance. Aims to respond within three months for manuscripts.
Non-Fiction Publishes Autobiography, Biography and History titles.
Fiction Publishes Contemporary Fiction.
Submission Guidelines Accepts proposal package (including synopsis and first 40 pages) by post, with SAE, or by email.
Tips Flicking Lizard seeks fresh contemporary writing from quality authors that are often overlooked by the big publishing houses. They aim to give writers the opportunity to make themselves known to the public without having to resort to spending their own money on self-publishing or the vanity press.

Flicks Books
29 Bradford Road, Trowbridge, Wiltshire, BA14 9AN
☎ 01225 767728
☎ 01225 760418
✉ flicks.books@dial.pipex.com
Contact Publisher, Matthew Stevens
Established 1986

Non-Fiction Publishes General Non-Fiction titles on the following subjects:
Cinema, Entertainment, Media, Television

Flipped Eye Publishing Limited
PO Box 43771, Suite 13, London, W14 8ZY
- 0845 430 9517
- 0845 430 9518
- books@flippedeye.net
- www.flippedeye.net

Contact Editor (Literary Fiction), Sally Strong; Senior Editor (Poetry, Short Stories), Nii Ayikwei Parkes
Established 2001
Imprint(s) Lubin & Kleyner
Waterways
Mouthmark Poetry
Insider Info Publishes roughly ten titles per year. Receives approximately 200 queries and 140 manuscripts per year. 90 per cent of books published are from first-time authors, 95 per cent of books published are from unagented authors. Payment is via royalty (on retail price). Advance offered is from £50 to £1,000. Average lead time is nine months, with simultaneous submissions not accepted. Submissions will not be returned. Aims to respond to queries and proposals within three months, manuscripts within six months and all other enquiries within 14 days. Catalogue is free on request and available online. Manuscript guidelines are available online.
Fiction Publishes Erotica, Fantasy, Literary, Mainstream/Contemporary, Multicultural, Short Story Collections and Translation titles.
Submission Guidelines Accepts query with SAE/proposal package (including outline, three sample chapters and your publishing history).
Submission details to: newwork@flippedeye.net
Poetry Publishes Poetry (experience of reading to an audience required) and Poetry in Translation (short proposal must be sent first).
Submission Guidelines Accepts proposal package (including six sample poems).
Submission details to: newwork@flippedeye.net
Recent Title(s) *Black Angels with Sky Blue Feathers*, A. Burrows (Poetry Collection)

Floris Books
15 Harrison Gardens, Edinburgh, EH11 1SH
- 0131 337 2372
- 0131 347 9919
- floris@florisbooks.co.uk
- www.florisbooks.co.uk

Contact Managing Director, Christian Maclean; Editors, Gale Winskill and Christopher Moore
Established 1977
Imprint(s) Flyways (Young Adult's Fiction)

Kelpies (Scottish Children's Fiction)
Insider Info Payment via royalties. Catalogue and manuscript guidelines are available online.
Non-Fiction Publishes Children's, General Non-Fiction, Illustrated Books and Scholarly titles on the following subjects:
Art, Crafts, Education, Health, History, Religion, Science, Social Sciences, Spirituality, Celtic Studies
Submission Guidelines Accepts query with SAE/proposal package (including outline, three sample chapters and SAE). No email submissions.
Fiction Publishes Historical, Children's, Young Adult, Regional and Scottish titles.
Submission Guidelines Accepts query with SAE/proposal package (including outline, three sample chapters and SAE). No email submissions.
Recent Title(s) *Hox*, Annemarie Allan (Children's); *Colour: A Textbook for Anthroposophical Painting Groups*, Liane Collot D'Herbois (Art)
Tips Floris Books publishes books for children and adults, including fiction and non-fiction books in which the subject matter is predominantly Scottish in content. Floris primarily seeks books encompassing modern settings, with contemporary situations and characters to which today's children can relate. This does not rule out historical fiction, but more modern titles will be prioritised.

Flyleaf Press
4 Spencer Villas, Glenageary, Dublin, Republic of Ireland
- 00353 1 284 5906
- books@flyleaf.ie
- www.flyleaf.ie

Contact Managing Editor, Jim Ryan (Family History, Genealogy)
Established 1988
Insider Info Publishes three titles per year. Receives 20 queries and ten manuscripts per year. 75 per cent of books published are from first-time authors, 100 per cent of books published are from unagented authors. Payment is via royalty (on wholesale price) with 0.07 (per £) minimum and 0.1 (per £) maximum. Average lead time is eight months, with simultaneous submissions accepts. Submissions accompanied by SAE will be returned. Aims to respond to queries within five days, proposals within 30 days and manuscripts within six weeks. Catalogue available online and by email. Manuscript guidelines available by email.
Non-Fiction Publishes General Non-Fiction and Reference titles on the following subjects:
History (Irish Genealogical History), Hobbies, Family History and Genealogy (Irish family history and related local history).

* Flyleaf is interested in any works that will assist readers with interests in Irish family history. Flyleaf is not usually interested in histories of a single family.
Submission Guidelines Accepts proposal package (including outline, clips, author biography and SAE).
Recent Title(s) *Tracing your Roscommon Ancestors*, John Hamrock (Genealogy)
Tips Flyleaf's target readership is Irish family history and genealogy enthusiasts, and libraries and societies with genealogical interests.

Focal Press
Linacre House, Jordan Hill, Oxford, OX2 8DP
- 01865 474010
- 01865 474011
- authorsupport@elsevier.com
- www.elsevier.com

Parent Company Elsevier Ltd (Science & Technology)
Established 1946
Insider Info Payment via royalties. Catalogue available online.
Non-Fiction Publishes How-To, Illustrated, Textbook, Technical, and Reference titles on the following subjects:
Art, Architecture, Communications, Computers/ Electronics, Music/Dance, Photography, Digital Film/ Media, Cinematography, Computer Animation, Theatre Technology
Submission Guidelines Accepts query with SAE/ proposal package (including outline and SAE).
Recent Title(s) *After Effects Apprentice*, Meyer (Animation)
Tips Titles are aimed at professionals and students in many areas, including: film and digital video production, photography, digital imaging, graphics, animation and new media, broadcast and media distribution technologies, music recording and production, mass communications and theatre technology. Focal Press welcomes authors' proposals for books. The first step is to discuss the proposal with the relevant publishing editor. Check the website for in-depth submission guidelines and a full list of editorial contacts.

Fodor
Random House, 20 Vauxhall Bridge Road, London, SW1V 2SA
- 020 7840 8871
- 020 7840 8871
- www.randomhouse.co.uk

Parent Company The Random House Group Ltd
Insider Info Catalogue available online.
Contact Publishes General Non-Fiction and Guidebook titles on the following subjects:
Travel, Travel Destinations

Submission Guidelines No unagented submissions.
Recent Title(s) *Compass American Guides: Idaho, 3rd Edition* (Travel Guide)

Folens Ltd
Waterslade House, Thame Road, Haddenham, Buckinghamshire, HP17 8NT
- 0870 609 1235
- 0870 609 1236
- folens@folens.com
- www.folens.com

Contact Director of Publishing, Peter Burton
Established 1987
Imprint(s) Belair
Insider Info Publishes roughly 150 titles per year. Catalogue and manuscript guidelines available online.
Non-Fiction Publishes General Non-Fiction, Textbook and Scholarly titles on Education.
Submission Guidelines Accepts query with SAE, or via email, with proposal package (including outline, three sample chapters, market research, your author biography, and SAE)
Submission details to: pburton@folens.com
Recent Title(s) *Art Through Magic*, Belair (Textbook)
Tips Folens are one of the leading publishers of primary and secondary educational texts, classroom resources and software for both students and teaching professionals. They seek suggestions for publications from teachers or others involved in education. Check the website for manuscript submission guidelines.

Folens Publishers
Hibernian Industrial Estate, Greenhills Road, Tallaght, Dublin 24, Republic of Ireland
- 00353 1 413 7200
- 00353 1 413 7280
- info@folens.ie
- www.folens.ie

Contact Managing Director, John O'Connor
Established 1956
Imprint(s) Blackwater Press
Magic Emerald
Insider Info Catalogue available online.
Non-Fiction Publishes Children's Educational titles on the following subjects:
Irish Curriculum subjects.
Fiction Publishes Children's Irish Interest titles.
Recent Title(s) *Design and Communication Graphics*, Joseph Terry
Tips Publishes books and online resources for both primary and post primary Irish school children.

Footprint Handbooks

6 Riverside Court, Lower Bristol Road, Bath, BA2 3DZ

- ☎ 01225 469141
- ☎ 01225 469461
- ✉ webeditor@footprint.cix.co.uk
- 🌐 www.footprintbooks.com

Contact Managing Director, Andy Riddle; Managing Editor, Felicity Laughton

Insider Info Catalogue and manuscript guidelines available online.

Non-Fiction Publishes Travel Booklets and Travel Handbooks

Submission Guidelines Accepts query with SAE/ proposal package (including outline, your publishing history, clips and author biography with SAE). Will review artwork/photos as part of the manuscript package.

Recent Title(s) *Costa Rica, Nicaragua & Panama*, Peter Hutchinson and Richard Leonardi (Travel Handbook); *Ski Europe*, Matt Barr and Gabriella Le Breton (Sport/Travel)

Tips Footprint Handbooks aims to publish travel guides of the highest quality. The writing team comprises of over 30 authors and many contributors from around the globe. Authors all have first hand knowledge and prolonged experience of the regions they specialise in. CVs are welcome from potential authors, marked for the attention of the 'Office Manager', including a sample of travel writing and highlighting any areas of particular interest.

Forest Books

The New Building, Ellwood Road, Milkwall, Coleford, Gloucestershire, GL16 7LE

- ☎ 01594 833858
- ☎ 01594 833446
- ✉ Online form.
- 🌐 www.forestbooks.com

Contact Director, Doug McLean

Established 1989

Insider Info Catalogue available online and free on request.

Non-Fiction Publishes General Non-Fiction, Scholarly and Self-Help books on the following subjects:
Deafness/Disability, Education, Health/Medicine, Sign Language

Recent Title(s) *Children With Hearing Loss: A Family Guide*, David Luterman (ed.)

Tips Focuses on books, videos, DVDs, CD-ROMs and software specialising in sign language and deaf issues only.

Fort Publishing Ltd

Old Belmont House, 12 Robsland Avenue, Ayr, KA7 2RW

- ☎ 01292 880693
- ☎ 01292 270134
- ✉ fortpublishing@aol.com
- 🌐 www.fortpublishing.co.uk

Contact Director, James McCarroll

Established 1999

Insider Info Catalogue available online.

Non-Fiction Publishes Biography and General Non-Fiction titles on the following subjects:
History, Photography, Regional, Photography Sports, Local Interest, Scottish Interest and True Crime

Recent Title(s) *These Colours Don't Run*, Derek Dykes and Andy Colvin

Tips Specialises in Scottish books, but has also published books on Yorkshire, East Anglia and Surrey.

Foulsham Publishers (W Foulsham & Co Ltd)

The Publishing House, Bennetts Close, Slough, Berkshire, SL1 5AP

- ☎ 01753 526769
- ☎ 01753 535003
- ✉ marketing@foulsham.com
- 🌐 www.foulsham.com

Contact Publisher/Managing Director, B.A.R. Belasco

Established 1819

Imprint(s) Quantum
Arcturus

Insider Info Submissions accompanied by SAE will be returned. Catalogue available free on request and online. Manuscript guidelines available online (see 'Contact' for authors' information).

Non-Fiction Publishes Coffee Table Books, Cookbooks, General Non-Fiction, How-To, Humour, Illustrated Books, Reference, Self-Help, Children's titles and Textbooks on the following subjects:
Antiques and Collectables, Art/Architecture, Astrology, Childcare/Parenting, Contemporary Culture, Cooking, Counselling/Career, Diet, Dreams, Drinks and Cocktails, Guidance, Gardening, Gay/ Lesbian, Health, History, Hobbies, Languages, Letter Writing and e-matters, Mind Games and Puzzles, Mind, Body and Spirit, Money/Finance, Recreation, Self Development, Speeches and Toasts, Spirituality, Travel, Weddings, Young Adult

Submission Guidelines Accepts query with SAE/ proposal package addressed to the Editorial Department (including outline, sample chapter(s), chapter breakdown showing proposed structure, consumer profile defining target market, information on other books in same area, explaining how your title is different, and your author biography). No email submissions are accepted and material is not returned unless SAE is enclosed.

Recent Title(s) *Best Wines in the Supermarkets 2008*, Ned Halley

Fountain Press

Old Sawmills Road, Faringdon, SN7 7DS

- ☎ 01367 242411
- ☎ 01367 241124
- ✉ sales@newprouk.co.uk
- 🌐 www.newprouk.co.uk

Parent Company Newpro UK Ltd

Contact Publisher, C.J. Coleman

Established 1923

Insider Info Publishes five titles per year. Catalogue available online.

Non-Fiction Publishes General Non-Fiction, Illustrated Books, Reference and Technical titles on the following subjects:

Nature/Environment and Photography

Recent Title(s) *Digital Photographer's Guide to Photoshop Elements*, Barry Beckham

Tips Titles are aimed at photographers of any skill level or interest, who are seeking to learn technical skills and the history of their craft.

Four Courts Press

7 Malpas Street, Dublin 8, Republic of Ireland

- ☎ 00353 1 453 4668
- ☎ 00353 1 453 4672
- ✉ info@fourcourtspress.ie
- 🌐 www.fourcourtspress.ie

Contact Publisher, Michael Adams; Editor, Martin Fanning

Established 1970

Insider Info Publishes roughly 70 titles per year. Receives approximately 200 queries and 100 manuscripts per year. 30 per cent of books published are from first-time authors and 90 per cent are from unagented authors. Payment is via royalty (on wholesale price) of 0.1 (per £). Average lead time is six months, with simultaneous submissions not accepted. Aims to respond to manuscripts within two months. Catalogue and manuscript guidelines available online.

Non-Fiction Publishes General Non-Fiction and Scholarly titles on the following subjects:

Ancient History, Art, Education, Government/Politics, History, Language, Literature, Law, Music, Philosophy, Regional, Religion

Submission Guidelines Accepts query with SAE, or via email.

Recent Title(s) *On Literature and Science*, Philip Coleman

Tips Four Courts Press does not consider unsolicited manuscripts, therefore prospective authors should send a query by email before submitting anything. For more information concerning the Four Courts Press house style, consult the guidelines on their website.

Fourth Estate

77–85 Fulham Palace Road, Hammersmith, London, W6 8JB

- ☎ 020 8307 4149
- ☎ 020 8307 4440
- ✉ michelle.kane@harpercollins.co.uk
- 🌐 www.4thestate.co.uk

Parent Company HarperCollins Publishers Ltd – Press Books Division

Contact Publishing Director, Nick Pearson; Publicity Director, Michelle Kane

Insider Info Catalogue available online.

Non-Fiction Publishes Autobiography, Biography, General Non-Fiction and Humour titles on the following subjects:

Contemporary Culture, Government, Politics, Science, Social Sciences and World Affairs

Submission Guidelines Accepts agented submissions only.

Fiction Publishes Literary and Mainstream/Contemporary titles.

Submission Guidelines Accepts agented submissions only.

Recent Title(s) *The Shipping News, 25th Anniversary Edition*, Annie Proulx (Novel)

Tips Fourth Estate publishes cutting edge non-fiction and fiction, often with a controversial flavour. Editors only accept submissions from literary agents or previously published authors, but may consider submissions that are accompanied by a positive assessment from a manuscript assessment agency.

Frances Lincoln

4 Torriano Mews, Torriano Avenue, London, NW5 2RZ

- ☎ 020 7284 4009
- ☎ 020 7485 0490
- ✉ fl@frances-lincoln.com
- 🌐 www.franceslincoln.com

Contact Managing Director, John Nicoll

Established 1977

Insider Info Publishes roughly 100 titles per year, Catalogue available online.

Non-Fiction Publishes Illustrated Books and Children's titles on the following subjects:

Art/Architecture, Crafts, Gardening, Hobbies, Nature/Environment, Recreation and Walking

Submission Guidelines Submit completed manuscript. Will review artwork photos as part of the manuscript package.

Submission details to: michaelb@frances-lincoln.com

Fiction Publishes Children's Books and Young Adult titles.

Submission Guidelines Submit completed manuscript.

Submission details to: michaelb@frances-lincoln.com

Recent Title(s) *Toward an Architecture*, Le Corbusier (Architecture); *Catch That Crocodile!*, Anushka Ravishankar (Author) and Pulak Biswas (Illustrator)

Tips Frances Lincoln publishes high quality illustrated books, focusing mainly on gardening, walking and the outdoors, art, architecture, design and landscape titles. In 1983 they started to publish illustrated books for children and have since won many awards and prizes with both fiction and non-fiction children's books. Frances Lincoln do not have any submission guidelines as such - any submissions should be addressed to the attention of Mr John Nicoll (Managing Director).

Franklin Watts

338 Euston Road, London, NW1 3BH

✆ 020 7873 6000

✆ 020 7873 6024

🌐 www.orchardbooks.co.uk

Parent Company The Watts Publishing Group (Hachette Children's Books)

Established 1972

Insider Info Catalogue available online.

Non-Fiction Publishes Children's Educational titles, on the following subjects:

All aspects of the National Curriculum.

Submission Guidelines Agented submissions only.

Recent Title(s) *I Wish!*, Sue Graves (Author) and Shelagh McNicholas (Illustrator) (Picture Book)

Tips Publishes children's information books, designed to engage, stimulate and entertain the more reluctant reader, and generally encourage a positive response to discovering the world around us.

Free Association Books Ltd

PO Box 37664, London, NW7 2XU

✆ 020 8906 0396

✆ 020 8906 0006

✉ info@fabooks.com

🌐 www.fabooks.com

Contact Managing Director/Publisher, T.E. Brown

Established 1984

Insider Info Payment is via royalties. Catalogue available free on request and online.

Non-Fiction Publishes Scholarly, Self-Help, Textbook and Reference titles on the following subjects:

Contemporary Culture, Education, Psychology, Social Sciences, Sociology

Submission Guidelines Accepts query with SAE/proposal package (including outline).

Recent Title(s) *I Had a Mummy Too*, Maria Chiara Risoldi

Tips Titles are aimed at scholars and carers interested in the theoretical analysis and practical application of various social sciences, including psychotherapy, sexuality, gender studies, women's studies and psychoanalysis. Prospective writers should send a letter in the first instance, containing a brief outline of the project. Academic sources must be thoroughly referenced.

Free Press

1st Floor, 222 Gray's Inn Road, London, WC1X 8HB

✆ 020 7316 1900

✆ 020 7316 0332

✉ enquiries@simonandschuster.co.uk

🌐 www.simonsays.co.uk

Parent Company Simon & Schuster UK Ltd

Established 2003

Non-Fiction Publishes Biography/Autobiography and General Non-Fiction titles on the following subjects:

Business, Economics, Government/Politics, History, World Affairs and Current Affairs

Submission Guidelines Accepts agented submissions only.

Recent Title(s) *Infidel*, Ayaan Hirsi Ali (Memoir)

Tips Free Press is Simon & Schuster's 'serious' non-fiction imprint and publishes heavyweight works on subjects including business, politics and world affairs.

The Friday Project

142 Buckingham Palace Road, London, SW1W 9TR

✆ 020 3355 1490

✉ info@thefridayproject.co.uk

🌐 www.thefridayproject.co.uk

Parent Company HarperCollins Publishers Ltd – Press Books Division

Contact Managing Director, Clare Christian (Non-Fiction, Humour, Literary Fiction); Publisher, Scott Pack (Fiction, Humour, Non-Fiction); Managing Editor, Heather Smith

Established 2005

Insider Info Catalogue is available online.

Non-Fiction Publishes Autobiography, Biography, Coffee Table, Cookbook, General Non-Fiction, Gift and Humour titles on the following subjects:

Contemporary Culture, Cooking/Foods/Nutrition, Government/Politics, Memoirs, Sex, Travel

Submission Guidelines Accepts proposal package via email (including outline, sample chapters, your publishing history and author biography). Will not accept artworks/images.
Submission details to: authors@ thefridayproject.co.uk

Fiction Publishes Confession, Experimental, Gothic, Historical, Humour, Literary and Mainstream/ Contemporary titles.

Submission Guidelines Accepts proposal package via email (including outline, sample chapters, your publishing history and author biography).
Submission details to: authors@ thefridayproject.co.uk

Tips The Friday Project develops much of its publishing programme from the most exciting and innovative websites, properties and content already in existence, as well as from submissions. It is now owned by HarperCollins Publishers.

Frontier Publishing
Windetts, Kirstead, NR15 1EG
- 01508 558174
- contact@frontierpublishing.co.uk
- www.frontierpublishing.co.uk

Contact Managing Editor, John Black
Established 1983
Insider Info Publishes four titles per year. Payment is via royalties. Catalogue available online.
Non-Fiction Publishes Illustrated books and General Non-Fiction titles on the following subjects: Art/Architecture, History, Language/Literature and Travel
Submission Guidelines Accepts query with SAE.
Recent Title(s) *The Glorious Dead - Figurative Sculpture of British First World War Memorials*
Tips Frontier aims to publish books about history, travel, poetry and sculpture for a world market. The company is based on medium and smaller print runs of attractive volumes, which are publicised in the UK press and sold in UK bookshops. Authors must be passionate about their chosen subject.

FT Prentice Hall
Edinburgh Gate, Harlow, Essex, CM20 2JE
- 01279 623623
- 01279 414130
- tim_moore@prenhall.com
- www.pearsoned.co.uk/imprints/ftprenticehall

Parent Company Pearson Education
Contact Editor-in-Chief, Timothy C. Moore
Insider Info Catalogue and manuscript guidelines are available online.
Non-Fiction Publishes Reference, Scholarly and Textbook titles on the following subjects: Accountancy, Business, Finance, Management.

Submission Guidelines Accepts proposal package (including synopsis, sample chapters, market research, your publishing history and author biography).
Recent Title(s) *Changeability*, Michael Jarrett (Business); *Virtuoso Teams*, Andy Boynton and Bill Fischer (Management)
Tips FT Prentice Hall represents a powerful collaboration between the *Financial Times* and Pearson Education. Titles are aimed at both students and professionals. Authors are usually experts in their particular field.

Gaia Books
2–4 Heron Quays, London, E14 4JP
- 020 7531 8400
- 020 7531 8650
- publisher@gaiabooks.co.uk
- www.gaiabooks.co.uk

Parent Company Octopus Publishing Group
Contact Publisher, Jane Birch; Executive Editor, Jo Godfrey Wood
Established Joined Octopus Publishing Group in 2004.
Insider Info Catalogue available online.
Non-Fiction Publishes Illustrated Books on the following subjects:
Gardening, Health/Medicine, Natural Health, Personal Growth, Earth and Ecology
Recent Title(s) *Choosing and Keeping Ducks and Geese*, Liz Wright; *Inner Reiki*, Tanmaya Honervogt
Tips Gaia is the mind, body & spirit imprint of Octopus. Their vision is to see the relationship of people and the planet more clearly understood. One of its bestselling titles is an atlas of planet management.

Gairm Publications
29 Waterloo Street, Glasgow, G2 6BZ
- 0141 221 1971
- 0141 221 1971

Non-Fiction Publishes Biography, Children's, General Non-Fiction, Illustrated books, Reference, Scholarly and Gaelic titles on the following subjects:
Art/Architecture, Language, Literature, Music/Dance, Regional, Travel and Gaelic Language
* Texts are in Gaelic language only.
Fiction Publishes Adventure, Mainstream/ Contemporary, Short Story Collections, Suspense and Crime titles.
* Texts are in Gaelic language only.
Poetry Publishes Gaelic Language Poetry titles.
Tips Titles are aimed at fluent Gaelic readers and students.

Galactic Central Publications

25a Copgrove Road, Leeds, West Yorkshire, LS8 2SP

☎ 07968 851571

✉ gcp@philsp.com

🌐 www.philsp.com

Contact Publisher, Phil Stephensen-Payne (Science Fiction Author Bibliographies)

Established 1985

Insider Info Publishes two titles per year. Receives approximately four queries and two manuscripts per year. 100 per cent of books published are from unagented authors. Average lead time is three months, with simultaneous submissions not accepted. Submissions accompanied by SAE will be returned. Aims to respond to queries within one day, proposals and other enquiries within seven days, and manuscripts within one month. Catalogue available online.

Non-Fiction Publishes Bibliography titles on Science Fiction.

* Titles should be in keeping with the standard layout of GCP bibliographies.

Submission Guidelines Accepts queries by email.

Recent Title(s) *Anne McCaffrey: Dragon Lady and More: A Working Bibliography*, Phil Stephensen-Payne and Gordon Benson Jr (Bibliography)

Tips Galactic Central Publications target readership is science-fiction fans and collectors. GCP does not offer payment to authors as the business generally runs at a loss.

The Gallery Press

Loughcrew, Oldcastle, Co. Meath, Republic of Ireland

☎ 00353 49 854 1779

☎ 00353 49 854 1779

✉ contactus@gallerypress.com

🌐 www.gallerypress.com

Contact Editor and Publisher, Peter Fallon

Established 1970

Insider Info Offers advance, set against royalties on sales. Simultaneous submissions will be accepted. Submissions accompanied by SAE will be returned. Catalogue available online. Manuscript guidelines are available free on request and via email.

Fiction Publishes Plays (must have been professionally produced).

Submission Guidelines Submit completed manuscript.

Poetry Publishes Poetry titles.

* The Gallery Press was established to publish the work of young Irish poets in particular, so submissions are currently accepted from Irish writers only.

Submission Guidelines Submit complete manuscript. No email or fax submissions will be accepted.

Recent Title(s) *For All We Know*, Ciaran Carson (Poetry Collection)

Tips Although The Gallery Press is primarily a poetry publisher, it now accepts plays as long as they have received a professional production. It publishes some fiction but only from its own long-standing authors. Writers are advised to build up a publishing resume in magazines and newspapers before approaching the publisher with a collection of poems. The editor requests that you make it clear if your work is being simultaneously submitted elsewhere, as they generally prefer a clear option on it.

Galore Park

19–21 Sayers Lane, Tenterden, Kent, TN30 6BW

☎ 01580 764242

☎ 01580 764142

✉ info@galorepark.co.uk

🌐 www.galorepark.co.uk

Contact Managing Director, Nicholas Oulton (Classics, English, History, Languages); Director, Louise Martine (Science, Maths)

Established 1999

Insider Info Publishes 15 titles per year. Catalogue available free on request, online and via email.

Non-Fiction Publishes Textbooks on the following subjects:
Maths, Science, English, Spanish and French

* Galore Park's textbooks are tailored to the prep school market and are endorsed by the ISEB. Non-prep school material is not published.

Tips Galore Park titles must be aimed at prep school students.

Gardner Education

168e High Street, Egham, Surrey, TW20 9HP

☎ 01784 477470

✉ info@gardnereducation.com

🌐 www.gardnereducation.com

Insider Info Catalogue available online and in hard copy via an online form, or by a phone call to: 0845 230 0775.

Non-Fiction Publishes Children's Educational and Textbook titles.

Tips Formerly known as Horwitz Gardner, Gardner Education is an independent publisher of learning materials for both pupils and teachers. Most publications are linked to UK National Literacy Strategy and are designed to help children achieve results within the classroom in terms of literacy, as well as subject knowledge.

Garland Science

2 Park Square, Milton Park, Abingdon, Oxfordshire, OX14 4RN

- 020 7017 6000
- 020 7017 6699
- tf.enquiries@informa.com
- www.garlandscience.com

Parent Company Taylor & Francis Group
Contact Vice President (US), Denise Schanck.
Insider Info Catalogue and manuscript guidelines are available online and by email.
Non-Fiction Publishes Journals, Multimedia, Reference, Scholarly and Textbook titles on the following subjects:
Biology, Cell Biology, Immunology, Molecular Biology, Protein Science
Submission Guidelines Accepts proposal package (including outline, synopsis, one to two sample chapters, market research and CV).
Submission details to: denise.schanck@taylorandfrancis.com (US)
Recent Title(s) *Instant Notes in Human Physiology*, Daniel McLaughlin, Jonathan Stamford and David White (Biology)
Tips Garland Science has established itself as one of the leading textbook publishers in the fields of cell and molecular biology, immunology and protein science. Specific details of material to be included in your proposal are published on the website. It is useful to include a summary of a suitable competitor book.

Garnet Publishing Ltd

8 Southern Court, South Street, Reading, RG1 4QS

- 0118 959 7847
- 0118 959 7356
- enquiries@garnetpublishing.co.uk
- www.garnetpublishing.co.uk

Contact Editorial Manager, Dan Nunn
Established 1992
Imprint(s) Ithaca Press
Insider Info Publishes 20 titles per year. Payment is via royalties.
Non-Fiction Publishes General Non-Fiction, Illustrated Books and Scholarly titles on the following subjects:
Art/Architecture, Cooking/Foods/Nutrition, History, Photography, Religion, Translation, Travel, World Affairs and Islamic Culture
Submission Guidelines Accepts query with SAE/proposal package (including outline, publishing history, author biography and SAE).
Fiction Publishes Religious and Translation titles.
Submission Guidelines Accepts query with SAE/proposal package (including outline).

Tips Mostly publishes general interest or academic non-fiction relating to various aspects of Middle Eastern culture. Ensure you enclose an up to date CV with any submissions, including any relevant publishing history.

Geddes & Grosset

David Dale House, New Lanark, ML11 9DJ

- 01555 665000
- 01555 665694
- info@gandg.sol.co.uk
- www.geddesandgrosset.co.uk

Contact Publisher, Ron Grosset
Established 1989
Non-Fiction Publishes Children's and Reference titles.
Submission Guidelines Accepts query with SAE. Submit completed manuscript.
Fiction Publishes Children's titles.
Submission Guidelines Accepts query with SAE. Submit completed manuscript.
Tips Unsolicited submissions will be considered. Geddes & Grosset do not publish any adult fiction.

The Geological Society Publishing House

Unit 7, Brassmill Enterprise Centre, Brassmill Lane, Bath, BA1 3JN

- 01225 445046
- 01225 442836
- angharad.hills@geolsoc.org.uk
- www.geolsoc.org.uk

Contact Director, Neal Marriott; Commissioning Editor, Angharad Hills
Established 1998
Insider Info Publishes 30 titles per year. Author guidelines are available online. Catalogue is free on request, and available online or via email to: julie.webster@geolsoc.org.uk
julie.webster@geolsoc.org.uk
Non-Fiction Publishes Reference, Scholarly and Technical titles on the following subjects:
Nature/Environment, Geology, Science (mainly Earth Sciences).
Submission Guidelines Accepts query with SAE with proposal package (including outline, author biography, SAE). Will review artworks/images as part of proposal package.
Recent Title(s) *Fishes and the Break-up of Pangaea*, L. Calvin, A. Longbottom and M. Richter (eds.)
Tips The Geological Society is a major international earth science publisher and aims to provide a high-quality service to earth scientists throughout the world. Books are mainly published as part of a series, but occasionally some 'one off' titles are published.

George Ronald Publishers Ltd

3 Rosecroft Lane, Oaklands, Welwyn, Hertfordshire, AL6 0UB
- ☎ 01438 716062
- ☏ 0870 762 6242
- ✉ sales@grbooks.com
- 🌐 www.grbooks.com

Contact Director and Manager, Erica Leith; Director, May Hofman

Established 1943

Insider Info Publishes eight titles per year. Receives approximately 30 queries and 40 manuscripts per year. 60 per cent of books published are from first-time authors, 90 per cent of books published are from unagented authors. Payment is via royalty (on wholesale price), with 0.1 (per £). The advance offered is from £50 to £1,000. Simultaneous submissions are accepted. Submissions accompanied by SAE will be returned. Aims to respond to queries within two weeks and proposals and manuscripts within two months. Catalogue and manuscript guidelines are free on request, and available online, or by email.

Non-Fiction Publishes Autobiography, Biography, Children's, Coffee Table, General Non-Fiction, How-To, Illustrated, Reference, Scholarly and Self-Help titles on the following subjects:
Religion (Bahá'i Faith)
* George Ronald Publishers is only interested in manuscripts that have a connection with the Bahá'i Faith.

Submission Guidelines Accepts completed manuscripts.

Poetry Publishes some poetry titles that have a connection with the Bahá'i Faith.

Submission Guidelines Accepts complete manuscripts.

Recent Title(s) *Time and the Baha'i Era, A Study of the Badí' Calendar*, Gerald Keil (Scholarly); *The Art of Nesting*, Sandra Lynn Hutchison (Poetry Collection); *Immortal Heroines*, Jacqueline Mehrabi (Children's)

Tips Books are aimed at Bahá'is and those interested in the Bahá'i Faith. See the 'submitting a manuscript' section on their website for further details.

Gerald Duckworth & Co. Ltd

90–93 Cowcross Street, London, EC1M 6BF
- ☎ 020 7490 7300
- ☏ 020 7490 0080
- ✉ info@duckworth-publishers.co.uk
- 🌐 www.ducknet.co.uk

Established 1898

Imprint(s) Ardis
Bristol Classical Press
Duckworth Academic
Overlook

The Nonesuch Press

Insider Info Aims to respond to proposals within 12 weeks and manuscripts within 12 weeks. Catalogue and manuscript guidelines available online.

Non-Fiction Publishes titles on Anthropology/Archaeology, Art/Architecture, History, Language/Literature, Literary Criticism and Philosophy.

Submission Guidelines Non-fiction submissions should be via post only and include convering letter/proposal, three sample chapters and return postage. For further information see www.ducknet.co.uk.

Fiction Publishes Literary and Commercial fiction titles.

Submission Guidelines No unsolicited submissions.

Recent Title(s) *An Appeal to Reason*, Nigel Lawson; *Christopher's Ghosts*, Charles McCarry; *Britain at Play*, W. Heath Robinson

Tips Gerald Duckworth is an independent publisher with a general trade and academic list. Duckworth generally publishes literary and commercial fiction and non-fiction, including history, biography and memoir. They do not accept phone calls, or email submissions.

Gibson Square

47 Lonsdale Square, London, N1 1EW
- ☎ 020 7096 1100
- ☏ 020 7993 2214
- ✉ info@gibsonsquare.com
- 🌐 www.gibsonsquare.com

Contact Publisher, Martin Rynja (Serious Non-Fiction); Editorial Director, Dawn Schaefer (Women's Non-Fiction)

Established 2001

Insider Info Publishes 25 titles per year. Payment via royalties. Average lead time is six months, with simultaneous submissions not accepted. Submissions will not be returned. Catalogue available online. Manuscript guidelines are not available.

Non-Fiction Publishes Autobiography, Biography, Humour and General Non-Fiction titles on the following subjects:
Community/Public Affairs, Contemporary Culture, Creative Non-Fiction, Gay/Lesbian, History, Memoirs, Military/War, Philosophy, Psychology, Sex, Travel, Women's Issues/Studies, World Affairs

Submission Guidelines Accepts proposal package (including outline, the first few sample chapters, your publishing history and author biography). Will review photographs/artworks as part of the manuscript package (send photocopies).

Recent Title(s) *Ciao Bella*, Helena Frith Powell (Novel)

Tips Prospective authors should include details about any book(s) used as a model for their own, if appropriate. Due to the number of submissions received, only successful queries will receive a response.

Giles de la Mare Publishers Ltd
PO Box 25351, London, NW5 1ZT
- 020 7485 2533
- 020 7485 2534
- gilesdelamare@dial.pipex.com
- www.gilesdelamare.co.uk

Established 1995
Insider Info Publishes about two titles per year. Most books published are from unagented authors. Payment is via royalty (on retail price). Submissions accompanied by SAE will be returned.
Non-Fiction Publishes Art/Architecture, Biography, General Non-Fiction, History, Music and Travel titles.
Submission Guidelines Accepts queries by telephone initially. Artworks/images accepted with submission (send photocopies).

Gill & Macmillan Ltd
Hume Avenue, Park West, Dublin 12, Republic of Ireland
- 00353 1 500 9500
- 00353 1 500 9596
- info@gillmacmillan.ie
- www.gillmacmillan.ie

Contact Commissioning Editor, Fergal Tobin
Established 1968
Imprint(s) Tivoli
Insider Info Catalogue available free on request, online and via email.
Non-Fiction Publishes Biography, General Non-Fiction and Scholarly titles on the following subjects: Cooking/Foods/Nutrition, Education, History, Language/Literature, Memoirs, Travel, World Affairs
Submission Guidelines Accepts query with SAE/ proposal package (including outline, two to three sample chapters and author biography.
Submission details to: ftobin@gillmacmillan.ie
Fiction Publishes Mainstream/Contemporary titles.
Submission Guidelines Accepts query with SAE, or via email, with proposal package (including outline, two to three sample chapters and author biography).
Submission details to: ftobin@gillmacmillan.ie
Recent Title(s) *When Panic Attacks*, Dr. Aine Tubridy (Self-Help); *Grow and Cook*, Tom Doorley and Johann Doorley (Cookery)
Tips Gill & Macmillan is Ireland's leading publisher of further education, school textbooks and general books. First-time authors should check the website for tips on writing and submitting a book proposal

for educational, fiction and non-fiction texts, as well as detailed advice on how to get published.

Ginn & Co
Halley Court, Jordan Hill, Oxford, OX2 8EJ
- 01865 888000
- 01865 314091
- enquiries@pearson.com
- www.heinemann.co.uk

Parent Company Pearson Education
Non-Fiction Publishes Children's, Reference, Textbook and Scholarly titles.
Tips Ginn has a strong tradition for publishing quality educational resources, mainly for children aged three to twelve, including the UK's most successful maths scheme, *Abacus*, and the new *Abacus Evolve*. Its literacy and science materials are also popular with teachers internationally.

GL Assessment
The Chiswick Centre, 414 Chiswick High Road, London, W4 5TF
- 020 8996 8445
- 020 8996 3660
- www.gl-assessment.co.uk

Established 1981
Insider Info Catalogue available online and by email.
Non-fiction Publishes Educational and Scholarly materials.
Tips Formerly know as nferNelson, GL Assessment specialise in electronic and paper based tests and assessments for the educational market (largely focusing on ages up to 14, but also up to age 19), covering knowledge, understanding and progress, ability, special needs, personal development testing, and assessment.

GlassHouse Press
2 Park Square, Milton Park, Abingdon, Oxford, OX14 4RN
- 07833 930626
- 020 7017 6699Rules, Rubrics and Riches
- colin.perrin@informa.com
- www.routledgelaw.com/books/glasshouse

Parent Company Routledge-Cavendish (Taylor & Francis Group)
Contact Commissioning Editor, Colin Perrin
Established 2002
Insider Info Publishes roughly 30 titles per year. Catalogue and manuscript guidelines are available online.
Non-Fiction Publishes Scholarly and Technical titles on the following subjects:
Critical Legal Theory, Law/Legal, Socio-legal Studies

Submission Guidelines Accepts proposal package (including outline, synopsis, one to two sample chapters, market research and CV).

Recent Title(s) *Rules, Rubrics and Riches*, Shailaja Fennell (Law); *The Origins of Criminology*, Nicole H. Rafter, ed. (Criminology)

Tips GlassHouse Press is a leading publisher of texts in the areas of socio-legal studies and critical legal theory. They specialise in books that offer a fresh perspective on law and contemporary legal issues. Aside from individual titles GlassHouse also accepts proposals for titles for its six main book series': Critical Approaches to Law; Contemporary Issues in Public Policy; Nomikoi: Critical Legal Thinkers; Law, Science and Society; Discourses of Law; Law, Development and Globalisation. Names of series editors are available on the website.

Glosa Education Organisation
PO Box 18, Richmond, Surrey, TW9 2GE
- m001@glosa.org
- www.glosa.org

Contact Managing Editor, Wendy Ashby
Established 1981
Insider Info Catalogue available online.
Non-Fiction Publishes Booklets, Textbooks and Scholarly titles on the following subjects: Glosa Language/Literature and Translation
Submission Guidelines Accepts query with SAE/proposal package (including outline and SAE). Alternatively, submit completed manuscript.
Tips Publishes textbooks, dictionaries, guidebooks and translations for teachers and speakers of the Glosa language, an international auxiliary language. Also publishes a newsletter and journal dedicated to developments in Glosa. All books are either written in Glosa, or are written in English about the Glosa language.

Gloucester Publishers Plc
Northburgh House, 10 Northburgh Street, London, EC1V 0AT
- 020 7253 7887
- 020 7490 3708
- info@everymanchess.com
- www.everymanchess.com

Contact Managing Director, Mark Bicknall
Established 1998
Insider Info Publishes 30 titles per year. Payment is via royalties. Catalogue available online.
Non-Fiction Publishes Scholarly and Technical titles on Chess.
Submission Guidelines No unsolicited submissions are accepted.
Recent Title(s) *American Grandmaster: Four Decades of Chess Adventures*, Joel Benjamin

Tips Publishes academic and leisure books relating to the game of chess for medium to high level players. Gloucester does not use freelancers, or place any work outside their existing stable of collaborators.

Glowworm Books Ltd
Unit 4 Bishopsgate Business Park, Broxburn, EH52 5LH
- 01506 857570
- 01506 858100
- www.glowwormbooks.co.uk

Established 1999
Non-Fiction Publishes Children's titles.
Submission Guidelines Queries only, no unsolicited manuscripts.
Fiction Publishes Children's titles.
Submission Guidelines Queries only, no unsolicited manuscripts.
Recent Title(s) *The Ghost of Glenmellish*, Pat Gerber
Tips Formed by the merger of Glowworm Books and the Amaising Publishing house, known for its *Maisie* books. Glowworm continues to publish the *Maisie* titles, but has since branched out into other areas such as children's history.

Godsfield Press
2–4 Heron Quays, London, E14 4JP
- 020 7531 8400
- 020 7531 8650
- publisher@godsfieldpress.com
- www.godsfieldpress.com

Parent Company Octopus Publishing Group
Contact Publisher, Jane Birch; Executive Editor, Sandra Rigby
Established Joined Octopus Publishing Group in 2004
Insider Info Catalogue available online.
Non-Fiction Publishes Gift Books, Humour, Illustrated Books, Reference, Self-Help and Spiritual Development titles on the following subjects: Alternative Lifestyles, Astrology/Psychic, Health/Medicine, New Age, Religion, Sex, Spirituality, Magic and Witchcraft, Fortune Telling and Divination and the Bible
Recent Title(s) *Chinese Astrology Bible*, Derek Walters (Non-Fiction)
Tips Godsfield Press publishes books, packs and kits by highly regarded authors from the UK and the US. The publisher's aim is to promote and support spiritual growth.

Gollancz
Orion House, 5 Upper St Martin's Lane, London, WC2H 9EA
- 020 7240 3444

☎ 020 7240 4822
✉ info@orionbooks.co.uk
🌐 www.orionbooks.co.uk
Parent Company Orion Publishing Group Ltd
Contact Editorial Director, Simon Spanton; Editorial
Director, Jo Fletcher
Established 1927 (incorporated into Orion in 1998)
Imprint(s) Gollancz Manga
Insider Info Catalogue available online (as a
downloadable pdf or via the online catalogue
request form).
Fiction Publishes Fantasy, Science-Fiction
and Manga.
* Gollancz specialises in fantasy and science-fiction,
and also publishes the *Masterworks* series of reprints
of fantasy and science-fiction classics. Also publishes
illustrated books.
Submission Guidelines Accepts agented
submissions only.
Recent Title(s) *Absolution Gap*, Alastair Reynolds
(Sci-Fi); *Orcs, Bad Blood: Weapons of Magical
Destruction*, Stan Nicholls (Fantasy)

Gomer Press/Gwasg Gomer
**Llandysul Enterprise Park, Llandysul, Ceredigion,
SA44 4JL**
☎ 01559 362371
☎ 01559 363758
✉ gwasg@gomer.co.uk
🌐 www.gomer.co.uk
Contact Managing Director, Jonathan Lewis;
Publishing Director, Mairwen Prys Jones; Editor, Viv
Sayer (English Books for Children, Pont Books);
Editor, Ceri Wyn Jones (English Books for Adults);
Editor, Bethan Mair (Welsh Books for Adults); Editor,
Bryn James (Welsh Books for Adults); Editor, Sioned
Lleinau (Welsh Books for Primary School Children);
Editor, Helen Evans (Welsh Books for Secondary
School Children); Editor, Rhiannon Davies (Welsh
Educational Resources for Children)
Established 1892
Imprint(s) Gomer
Pont Books
Insider Info Publishes 120 titles per year. Aims to
respond to proposals and manuscripts within one
month. Catalogue and manuscript guidelines
available online.
Non-Fiction Publishes Biography, General Non-
Fiction, Textbooks and Scholarly titles on the
following subjects:
Art/Architecture, Cooking/Foods/Nutrition,
Education, History, Language/Literature and Travel
* Many texts are in Welsh language.
Submission Guidelines Accepts query with SAE, or
via email, with proposal package (including outline,
one sample chapter and your author biography).
Submission details to: ceri@gomer.co.uk

Fiction Publishes Children's, Young Adult and
Welsh titles.
Poetry Publishes Welsh Poetry Collections.
Submission Guidelines Accepts query with SAE, or
via email, with proposal package (including outline,
one sample chapter and your author biography).
Submission details to: firstname@gomer.co.uk (for
adult's book proposals); children@gomer.co.uk (for
children's book proposals).
Recent Title(s) *All Around Anglesey*, Terry Biggs
(Travel); *Here Comes the Doctor*, Viv Sayer (Illustrated
Children's Fiction)
Tips Gomer Press is Wales's largest independent
publisher, specialising in books from Wales, about
Wales. They work in Welsh and English language, for
children and adults. Do not send whole manuscripts
to an editor, a sample chapter and a synopsis will be
sufficient at first. It would also be useful to include a
CV and an outline of the sales strengths of the
proposal. As the publisher receives a large number
of manuscripts for consideration every week, they
advise authors to be patient. They aim to send an
acknowledgement of receipt for manuscripts within
one month.

The Good Web Guide Ltd
65 Bromfelde Road, London, SW4 6PP
☎ 020 7720 8919
☎ 020 7738 5717
✉ marketing@thegoodwebguide.com
🌐 www.thegoodwebguide.co.uk
Contact Managing Director, Sarah Mahaffy; Content
and Editorial Director, Arabella Dymoke;
Administrative Director, Nicky Granville
Established 1999
Insider Info Publishes five titles per year. Payment is
via royalties. Catalogue available online.
Non-Fiction Publishes Booklets, Multimedia and
Reference titles on the Internet.
Submission Guidelines Accepts query with SAE, or
via email, with proposal package (including outline,
clips and author biography).
Submission details to: a.dymoke@
thegoodwebguide.com
Tips The Good Web Guide publishes guidebooks to
the best sites on the internet. They aim to find out
what is best about life online, across a wide range of
lifestyle and consumer interests.

Government Supplies Agency
**Publications Division, Office of Public Works,
51 St Stephen's Green, Dublin 2, Republic of
Ireland**
☎ 00353 1 647 6000
☎ 00353 1 647 6843
✉ info@opw.ie

199

Non-fiction Publishes Irish government publications.

Gower Publishing Ltd

Gower House, Croft Road, Aldershot, Hampshire, GU11 3HR
- 01252 331551
- 01252 344405
- info@gowerpub.com
- www.gowerpub.com

Parent Company Ashgate Publishing Group
Contact Commissioning Editor, Jonathon Norman (Business and Management); Commissioning Editor, Martin West (Applied Academic Business Research)
Insider Info Publishes 70 titles per year. Catalogue available online.
Non-Fiction Publishes General Non-Fiction, Textbooks, How-To, and Scholarly titles on the following subjects:
Business/Economics, Education, Law, Money/Finance, Management, Marketing and Human Resources
* Gower Publishing Ltd is one of the world's leading publishers on management and business practice. They publish handbooks, popular paperbacks, training videos, activity manuals, and student skills materials, in conjunction with Ashgate Publishing.
Submission Guidelines Accepts proposal package (including outline, your publishing history, author biography, sample material in your proposed writing style and information about illustrations, the length of the book and the general appeal and purpose of the book).
Recent Title(s) *Activity-Based Training Design*, John Rodwell
Tips Writers tend to be experts in their fields.

Graffeg

2 Radnor Court, 256 Cowbridge Road East, Cardiff, CF5 1GZ
- 029 2037 7312
- info@graffeg.com
- www.graffeg.com

Contact Peter Gill
Insider Info Catalogue available online.
Non-Fiction General Non-Fiction and Illustrated Books on the following subjects:
Cooking/Foods/Nutrition, Crafts, Photography, Regional, Welsh Photography
Recent Title *Celtic Cuisine*, Gilli Davies (Cookery)
Tips Graffeg publishes illustrated books. Subjects include Welsh cities, towns, villages and travel, landscapes, food, where to eat and stay, festivals and events, culture, heritage and the arts, natural history and what to see and do. Publications are photography based, and submissions must therefore be accompanied by a range of suitable photographs.

Granta Books

12 Addison Avenue, London, W11 4QR
- 020 7605 1360
- 020 7605 1361
- info@granta.com
- www.granta.com

Parent Company Granta Publications
Contact Managing Director, David Graham; Editorial Director, Sara Holloway; Managing Editor, Christine Lo; Editor, Bella Shand
Established 1979
Insider Info Publishes 40 titles a year. Payment is via royalties. Catalogue and manuscript guidelines available via the website.
Non-Fiction Publishes General Non-Fiction and Scholarly titles on the following subjects:
Contemporary Culture, Government/Politics, History, Language/Literature, Literary Criticism, Memoirs, Social Sciences
Submission Guidelines Accepts query with SAE. Submit proposal package (including outline and 50 sample pages).
Fiction Publishes Literary titles.
* No genre fiction.
Submission Guidelines Accepts query with SAE/proposal package (including outline, 50 pages, or two sample chapters).
Recent Title(s) *The Rowing Lessons*, Anne Landsman (Novel); *Beslan*, Tim Phillips (Politics/Current Affairs)
Tips Granta Books is weighted more towards non-fiction publishing than fiction, with a ratio of about 70:30. The non-fiction tends to fall into the categories of serious cultural, political and social history, narrative history, or memoir. Granta rarely publishes straightforward biographies. Submissions should be made by post only. Granta does not accept faxes, emails or computer disc submissions. Due to the large numbers of submissions, it can take some time before they are able to respond.

Grant Books

The Coach House, New Road, Cutnall Green, Droitwich, Worcestershire, WR9 0PQ
- 01299 851588
- 01299 851446
- golf@grantbooks.co.uk
- www.grantbooks.co.uk

Contact Managing Editor, H.R.J. Grant
Established 1978
Insider Info Publishes six titles per year. Payment is via royalties. Catalogue available online via the website.

Non-Fiction Publishes Biography and General Non-Fiction on the following subjects:
Golf, Hobbies and Sports
Submission Guidelines Accepts query with SAE. Submit proposal package (including outline and sample chapter(s)). Also accepts completed manuscripts.
Recent Title(s) *Aspects of Golf Course Architecture*, Fred Hawtree
Tips Grant Books aims to publish the more unusual titles in the world of golf, whether new, old or out of print. Ideas and submissions welcome, but not for instructional material or fiction.

Great Northern Publishing

PO Box 202, Scarborough, North Yorkshire, YO11 3GE
☎ 01723 581329
☎ 01723 581329
✉ books@greatnorthernpublishing.co.uk
🌐 www.greatnorthernpublishing.co.uk
Contact Production Manager, Mark Marsay; Senior Editor, Diane Crowther
Established 1999
Insider Info Payment is via royalties. Catalogue and manuscript guidelines available via the website.
Non-Fiction Publishes General Non-Fiction titles on the following subjects:
History, Military/War
Submission Guidelines Accepts query with SAE.
Fiction Publishes Erotica, Humour and Crime titles.
Submission Guidelines Accepts query with SAE.
Recent Title(s) *The Drowning Man*, Gary Mortimer (Crime)
Tips Great Northern Publishing is a wholly independent, family owned, award winning small publishing and production company, who produce the bi-monthly magazines *The Great War* and *The Second World War*, and the international erotic art and literature magazine *Jade*. Book production is mainly done on contract terms with other publishers and organisations.

Green Books

Foxhole, Dartington, Totnes, Devon, TQ9 6EB
☎ 01803 863260
☎ 01803 863843
✉ edit@greenbooks.co.uk
🌐 www.greenbooks.co.uk
Contact Publisher, John Elford; Project Development (Green Lifestyle and Gardening), Amanda Cuthbert
Established 1986
Insider Info Publishes roughly 12 titles per year. Receives approximately 200–300 queries and 200–300 manuscripts per year. 15 per cent of books

published are from first-time authors, 100 per cent of books published are from unagented authors. Five per cent of books published are author subsidy published, and are usually produced in association with other green organisations, rather than being unsolicited submissions. Payment is via royalty (on wholesale price). Advance offered is up to £2,000. Average lead time is six months, with simultaneous submissions accepted. Submissions accompanied by SAE will be returned. Aims to respond to queries within one week, and proposals and manuscripts within two months. Catalogue is free on request, and available online. Manuscript guidelines are available online.
Non-Fiction Publishes Autobiography/Biography, How-To, Illustrated (full colour), Reference, Self-Help and Technical titles on the following subjects: Agriculture/Horticulture, Alternative Lifestyles, Art, Business/Economics, Community, Cooking (Organic), Crafts, Education, Gardening, Government/Politics, Health, House and Home, Language, Literature, Memoirs, Nature/Environment, Philosophy, Regional, Spirituality, World Affairs
Submission Guidelines Accepts email enquiries initially (including outline and one sample chapter), and artworks/images (send digital files as jpegs).
Recent Title(s) *Spiritual Compass: The Three Qualities of Life*, Satish Kumar (Spirituality)
Tips Green Books is an environmental publisher whose books are mainly aimed at the general reader interested in environmental issues.

Greenhill Books/Lionel Leventhal Ltd

Park House, 1 Russell Gardens, London, NW11 9NN
☎ 020 8458 6314
☎ 020 8905 5245
✉ info@greenhillbooks.com
🌐 www.greenhillbooks.com
Contact Director, Michael Leventhal
Established 1984
Insider Info Payment is via royalties. Catalogue and manuscript guidelines available via the website.
Non-Fiction Publishes General Non-Fiction and Reference titles on the following subjects:
Military/War
* Publishes military history or related subjects only.
Submission Guidelines Accepts query with SAE. Submit proposal package (including outline, one sample chapter, your publishing history, clips,and author biography).
Recent Title(s) *Napoleonic Uniforms*, John R. Elting (Military History)
Tips Greenhill specialises in reprinting and expanding the original text of military history books that have gone out of print. They also publish original military history titles. Prospective authors are

asked to follow the step by step 'Guidelines for Submission' on the website. It is important that you take note of these points, to ensure that your typescript is given proper assessment.

Grub Street Publishing
4 Rainham Close, London, SW11 6SS
- 020 7738 1008
- 020 7738 1009
- post@grubstreet.co.uk
- www.grubstreet.co.uk
Contact Managing Director, John B. Davies
Established 1982
Insider Info Publishes roughly 20 titles per year. Payment is via royalties. Aims to respond to proposals and manuscripts within three months. Catalogue is free on request and available online. Manuscript guidelines available online.
Non-Fiction Publishes General Non-Fiction and Reference titles on the following subjects: Cookery, Military Aviation History
Submission Guidelines Accepts query with SAE. Submit proposal package (including outline, one sample chapter and author biography).
Tips Grub Street publish a comprehensive range of food, wine and military aviation history titles, but are open to external book ideas.

GSSE
11 Malford Grove, Gilwern, Abergavenny, Monmouthshire, NP7 0RN
- 01873 830872
- gsse@zoo.co.uk
- www.gsse.org.uk/education
Contact Owner, Dr David P. Bosworth
Established 1987
Insider Info Receives approximately two queries and two manuscripts per year. One per cent of books published are from first-time writers, 100 per cent of books published are from unagented writers. Payment is via royalty (on retail price), with 0.05 (per £) minimum and 0.12 (per £) maximum. Average lead time is five months, with simultaneous submissions not accepted. Submissions accompanied by SAE will be returned. Aims to respond to queries and proposals within two weeks, and manuscripts within two months. Catalogue is free on request, or available by email.
Non-Fiction Publishes Booklets and How-To titles on the following subjects: Education, Application of Educational Technology in Higher/Further Education
Submission Guidelines Accepts query with SAE, and artworks/images (send digital files as jpegs).
Tips GSSE books are aimed at students and lecturers in higher/further education. Submissions should not

be written in an 'academic' style and instead should be easily accessible to students and readers of any level.

Guildhall Press
Unit 15, Rath Mor Business Park, Bligh's Lane, Creggan, Derry, BT48 0LZ
- 028 7136 4413
- 028 7137 2949
- info@ghpress.com
- www.ghpress.com
Contact Managing Editor, Paul Hippsley
Established 1979
Insider Info Catalogue available online.
Non-Fiction Publishes Biography, Scholarly and General Non-Fiction titles on the following subjects: Art, Education, Folklore, Irish History & Culture, Politics, Memoirs.
Fiction Publishes Historical, Literary, Humour and Young Readers fiction, poetry and plays.
Recent Title(s) *Derry: Through the Lens*, Willie Carson (Local History); *The Deep Green Pool*, Joyce Ann MacCafferty (Biography/Memoir)
Tips Guildhall Press is one of Northern Ireland's leading independent publishers.

Guild of Master Craftsman Publications Ltd
166 High Street, Lewes, East Sussex, BN7 1XU
- 01273 477374
- 01273 478606
- pubs@thegmcgroup.com
- www.thegmcgroup.com
Parent Company GMC Services Ltd
Established 1974
Imprint(s) Photographers' Institute Press (PIP)
Insider Info Publishes roughly 40 titles per year. Payment is via royalties. Catalogue is free on request and available online.
Non-Fiction Publishes General Non-fiction, Illustrated, Reference and Technical titles on the following subjects: Cooking, Construction, Crafts, Electronics, Gardening, Hobbies, Photography, Puzzles, Woodwork
Submission Guidelines Accepts query with SAE.
Recent Title(s) *Turning Green Wood*, Michael O'Donnell
Tips The Guild of Master Craftsman Publications is a publisher and distributor of over 1,000 books and magazines that are aimed at professional craftsmen and women, as well as keen amateurs. Titles cover photography, gardening, cookery, woodworking and related craft subjects such as toy making, dolls' houses, upholstery, furniture restoration, needlework

and cross stitch. Submissions and ideas are welcome.

Guinness World Records Ltd

3rd Floor, 184–192 Drummond Street, London, NW1 3HP

- 020 7891 4567
- 020 7891 4501
- info@guinnessrecords.com
- www.guinnessworldrecords.com

Contact Chief Operations Officer, Alistair Richards
Established 1954
Insider Info Publishes two to three titles per year.
Recent Title(s) *Guinness World Records: Gamer's Edition*, Guinness World Records Ltd (Reference)
Tips Company created to publish the *Guinness Book of World Records*, as well as the annual *British Hit Singles & Albums* book. Contact from prospective researchers is encouraged.

Gulf Professional Publishing

Linacre House, Jordan Hill, Oxford, OX2 8DP

- 01865 474010
- 01865 474011
- authorsupport@elsevier.com
- www.elsevier.com

Parent Company Elsevier Ltd (Science & Technology)
Insider Info Payment is via Royalties. Catalogue and manuscript guidelines available online.
Non-Fiction Publishes Reference, Scholarly and Technical titles on the following subjects: Business/Economics, Computers/Electronics, Regional, Science, Engineering, Oil/Petroleum/ Natural Gas and Oil Technologies
Submission Guidelines Accepts query with SAE. Submit proposal package (including outline).
Recent Title(s) *Natural Gas Hydrates, A Guide for Engineers*, Carroll (Science)
Tips Gulf Professional Publications publishes books and reports covering the oil and petroleum industry, natural gas, offshore drilling, carbon research, plastics research, resource engineering, facility operations, cosmetics industry reports and Gulf region resources. They welcome authors' proposals for books; the first step is to discuss the proposal with the relevant publishing editor. Check the website for in-depth submission guidelines and a full list of editorial contacts.

Gullane Children's Books

Winchester House, 259–269 Old Marylebone Road, London, NW1 5XJ

- 020 7616 7200
- 020 7616 7201
- claudia.holzer@pinwheel.co.uk

- www.pinwheel.co.uk

Parent Company Pinwheel Ltd
Insider Info Catalogue available online.
Non-Fiction Publishes Children's and Illustrated titles.
Submission Guidelines Accepts entire manuscript with SAE for children's picture books (up to 800 words).
Fiction Publishes Children's, Picture Book and Illustrated Fiction titles.
Submission Guidelines Accepts entire manuscript with SAE for children's picture books (up to 800 words).
Tips Within Pinwheel, a specialist children's publisher, the Gullane imprint publishes fairly traditional picture books. Titles submitted for consideration should be pitched at children aged seven or younger.

Gwasg Carreg Gwalch

6 Iard yr Orsaf, Llanrwst, Gwynedd, LL26 0EH

- 01492 642031
- 01492 641502
- llyfrau@carreg-gwalch.co.uk
- www.carreg-gwalch.co.uk

Contact Managing Editor, Myrddin ap Dafydd
Established 1980
Insider Info Publishes roughly 60 titles per year. Payment is via royalties. Catalogue available online.
Non-Fiction Publishes General Non-Fiction on the following subjects:
History, Language, Literature, Nature/Environment, Regional, Translation, Welsh Interest
* Publishes mainly in Welsh language.
Submission Guidelines Accepts query with SAE.
Tips Gwasg Carreg Gwalch is a productive printing house, which publishes a variety of Welsh books, and books of Welsh interest. Ideas and submissions are welcome.

Gwasg Pantycelyn

St Davids Road, Caernarfon, Gwynedd, LL55 1ER

- 01286 672018
- 01286 677823
- gwasgpantycelyn@ukonline.co.uk

Non-Fiction Publishes Welsh and English language books on the following subjects:
Literature Studies, History, Theology
Fiction Publishes Welsh and English Language Fiction titles.
Poetry Publishes Welsh and English Poetry titles.
Tips Gwasg Pantycelyn has previously published a collection of around 150 books for adults and children. The intended audience is general readers interested in a more analytical approach to literature,

as well as readers interested in the culture and social history of Wales.

Hachette UK
338 Euston Road, London, NW1 3BH
☎ 020 7873 6000
☎ 020 7873 6024
✉ www.hachettelivre.co.uk
Parent Company Hachette Livre Publishing Group
Contact CEO, Tim Hely Hutchinson; Commercial Director, Richard Kitson
Imprint(s) Hachette Children's Books
Hachette Australia
Hachette Ireland
Hachette Scotland
Headline
Hodder Education
Hodder & Stoughton General
Hodder & Stoughton Faith Books
John Murray
Little, Brown Book Group
Octopus Publishing Group
Orion Publishing Group Ltd
Chambers Harrap Publishers Ltd
Tips See individual division entries for more detailed information.

Hachette Children's Books
338 Euston Road, London, NW1 3BH
☎ 020 7873 6000
☎ 020 7873 6024
✉ www.hodderheadline.co.uk/ hachettechildrens.htm
Parent Company Hachette Livre UK
Contact Managing Director, Marlene Johnson
Established 2005
Imprint(s) Hodder Children's Books
Orchard Books
The Watts Publishing Group
Wayland
Insider Info Catalogue available online (see www.orchardbooks.co.uk for Franklin Watts and Orchard Books imprints).
Non-Fiction Publishes Children's titles, Gift and Children's information titles on the following subjects:
Animals, Crafts, History, Hobbies, Science, General Information, including Special Needs, Reading Development, Citizenship and PSHE
Submission Guidelines Agented submissions only.
Fiction Publishes Picture Book and Novelty titles.
Submission Guidelines Agented submissions only.
Tips Now reports directly to Hachette Livre UK, following the closure of Hodder Headline.

Hachette Ireland
8 Castlecourt, Castleknock, Dublin 15, Republic of Ireland
☎ 00353 1 824 6288
☎ 00353 1 824 6289
✉ info@hhireland.ie
✉ www.hodderheadline.co.uk
Parent Company Hachette UK
Contact Managing Director, Breda Purdue
Established 2003
Insider Info Catalogue available online on request. Manuscript guidelines available online via website.
Non-Fiction Publishes Autobiography, Biography, General Non-Fiction, Humour, Self-Help, Sports and Music titles on the following subjects:
Health/Medicine, History, Regional, Sports, Music
Submission Guidelines Accepts query with SAE/ proposal package (including outline, first 100 pages and SAE).
Fiction Publishes Literary and Mainstream/ Contemporary titles on the following subjects:
Crime, Irish Writing.
Submission Guidelines Accepts query with SAE/ proposal package (including outline, first 100 pages, SAE). Published writers only.
Tips Hachette Livre Ireland is not currently accepting unsolicited fiction from previously unpublished authors. Submission details for published authors and general non-fiction titles are available online. Now reports directly to Hachette Livre UK, following the closure of Hodder Headline.

Hachette Scotland
2a Christie Street, Paisley, PA1 1NB
✉ bob.mcdevitt@hodder.co.uk
✉ www.hodderheadline.co.uk
Parent Company Hachette UK
Contact Bob McDevitt
Insider Info Catalogue available from website on request.
Non-Fiction Publishes General Non-Fiction, Illustrated and Scottish Interest Books on the following subjects:
Contemporary Culture, History, Nature/Environment, Regional, Travel, Scotland
Submission Guidelines Accepts proposal package by post or email (including outline, first 50 pages, SAE if sending by post).
Fiction Publishes Literary, Mainstream/ Contemporary, Scottish Writing titles.
Submissions Guidelines Accepts proposal package by post or email (including outline, first 50 pages, SAE if sending by post). Address to Bob McDevitt.
Tips Seeking new Scottish writing and non-fiction books of general Scottish interest by Scottish writers.

Now reports directly to Hachette Livre UK, following the closure of Hodder Headline.

Halban Publishers Ltd
22 Golden Square, London, W1F 9JW
- 020 7437 9300
- 020 7437 9512
- books@halbanpublishers.com
- www.halbanpublishers.com

Contact Directors: Peter and Martine Halban
Established 1986
Insider Info Publishes eight titles per year. Payment is via royalties. Catalogue available online.
Non-Fiction Publishes Biography and General Non-Fiction titles on the following subjects: History, Memoirs, Religion, Jewish Interest
Submission Guidelines Accepts query with SAE.
Fiction Publishes Jewish Interest titles.
Submission Guidelines Accepts query with SAE.
Recent Title(s) *The Book of Q*, Jonathan Rabb (Thriller); *Once Upon A Country*, Sari Nusseibeh with Anthony David (Memoir)
Tips All titles should reflect Jewish interest. Welcomes proposals, but approach by letter first.

Haldane Mason Ltd
PO Box 34196, London, NW10 3YB
- 020 8459 2131
- 020 8728 1216
- info@haldanemason.com
- www.haldanemason.com

Contact Directors: Sydney Francis and Ron Samuel
Established 1995
Imprint(s) Red Kite Books
Non-Fiction Publishes Children's and Gift titles.
Submission Guidelines Accepts query with SAE. Submit proposal package (including outline, sample chapter(s)) by post addressed to Sydney Francis.
Tips Currently commissioning in the area of illustrated non-fiction for children. All submissions must be accompanied by SAE if material is to be returned.

Halsgrove
Halsgrove House, Ryelands Industrial Estate, Bagley Road, Wellington, Somerset, TA21 9PZ
- 01823 653777
- 01823 216796
- sales@halsgrove.com
- www.halsgrove.co.uk

Contact Publisher, Simon Butler
Established 1990
Insider Info Publishes roughly 150 titles per year. Payment is via royalties. Catalogue and manuscript guidelines are available online.

Non-Fiction Publishes Biography, General Non-Fiction and Illustrated titles on the following subjects: Art/Architecture, Cooking, Food and Drink, History, Regional and Local Interest.
* Mostly regional themed books.
Submission Guidelines Accepts query with SAE, or via email. Submit proposal package (including outline and sample chapter(s)).
Submission details to: simonb@halsgrove.com
Recent Title(s) *Ghost Fields of East Anglia*, Martin W. Bowman (Regional Interest)
Tips Halsgrove is England's leading regional publisher specialising in the varied history, art, heritage and life of England's regions, cities, towns and villages. Individual authors are welcome to submit works. Halsgrove also provides a complete publishing service to clients, from editorial, design and production through marketing, promotion and distribution. Contact the Publisher, Simon Butler, for further details of th editorial services.

Hamish Hamilton
80 Strand, London, WC2R 0RL
- 020 7010 3000
- 020 7010 6060
- customer.service@penguin.co.uk
- www.penguin.co.uk

Parent Company Penguin General
Contact Publishing Director, Simon Prosser
Established 1931
Insider Info Publishes no more than 20 titles per year. Catalogue is available online.
Non-Fiction Publishes Literary Non-Fiction titles.
Submission Guidelines Agented submissions only.
Fiction Publishes Literary Fiction titles.
Submission Guidelines Agented submissions only.
Recent Title(s) *The Idle Parent*, Tom Hodgkinson (Non-Fiction); *The Big Sleep*, Raymond Chandler (Fiction)
Tips The Hamish Hamilton list is a small section of the Penguin group and focuses entirely on distinct, often unusual, literary fiction and non-fiction from an exciting and eclectic group of authors.

Hamlyn
2–4 Heron Quays, London, E14 4JP
- 020 7531 8400
- 020 7531 8650
- publisher@hamlyn.co.uk
- www.octopusbooks.co.uk/hamlyn

Parent Company Octopus Publishing Group, Hachette UK
Contact Publisher, Jo Hemmings
Established 1950
Imprint(s) Gaia Books

Godsfield Press
Insider Info Catalogue available online.
Non-Fiction Publishes Coffee Table, Cookery, Gift, Illustrated, Reference and Self-Help titles on the following subjects:
Child Guidance/Parenting, Cooking/Foods/Nutrition, Crafts, Gardening, General Reference, Health/ Medicine, House & Home, Mind/ Body/Spirit, Popular Culture, Sex, Sports.
Recent Title(s) *Cooking for a Healthy Heart*, Jacqui Lynas (Cooking); *The Atlas of Lost Cults and Mystery Religions*, David Douglas (History)
Tips Two thirds of Hamlyn's business is in the international, US and export markets, therefore books may need to have a potentially international appeal.

Hammersmith Press Ltd
496 Fulham Palace Road, London, SW6 6JD
☏ 020 7736 9132
☏ 020 7348 7521
✉ gmb@hammersmithpress.co.uk
🌐 www.hammersmithpress.co.uk
Contact Publisher, Georgina Bentliff
Established 2004
Insider Info Publishes six titles per year. Receives approximately 40 queries and 30 manuscripts per year. 100 per cent of books published are from unagented authors. Payment is via royalty (on wholesale price). Average lead time is six months, with simultaneous submissions not accepted. Submissions accompanied by SAE will be returned. Aims to respond to queries within five days, proposals within two weeks and manuscripts within one month. Manuscript guidelines available by email.
Non-Fiction Publishes Self-Help titles on the following subjects:
Diet, Fitness, Health, Medicine, Nutrition
* Hammersmith books integrate conventional medicine with complementary/ alternative medicine.
Submission Guidelines Accepts query by email with brief outline initially. Will not accept artwork/ images.
Recent Title(s) *Trick and Treat - How 'Healthy Eating' is Making us Ill*, Barry Groves
Tips Books are targeted at members of the general public with specific health problems, and are generally written by specialists in the relevant area, rather than by general health writers.

Hanley & Belfus
Linacre House, Jordan Hill, Oxford, OX2 8DP
☏ 01865 474010
☏ 01865 474011

✉ authorsupport@elsevier.com
🌐 www.elsevierhealth.com/hb
Parent Company Elsevier Ltd (Health Sciences)
Insider Info Payment via royalty. Catalogue and manuscript guidelines are available online.
Non-Fiction Publishes Scholarly, Technical, Textbook and Reference titles on the following subjects:
Education, Health/Medicine, Science
Submission Guidelines Submit using an online proposal form.
Submission details to: t.horne@elsevier.com
Recent Title(s) *Hand Secrets*, Jebson and Kasdan (Reference)
Tips Hanley & Belfus publishes textbooks and reference books, specialising in carefully edited publications for medical students, residents, practising physicians, biomedical scientists and other healthcare professionals. These include a number of popular medical series, including the *Secrets* series. Authors may contact the publishing director or editor prior to making an online submission, to discuss the proposal.

Harlequin Mills & Boon Ltd
Eton House, 18–24 Paradise Road, Richmond, TW9 1SR
☏ 020 8288 2800
☏ 020 8288 2898
✉ andrea.grice@hmb.co.uk
🌐 www.millsandboon.co.uk
Contact Managing Director, Guy Hallowes; Editorial Director, Karin Stoecker; Senior Editor, Tessa Shapcott (Mills & Boon Modern Romance); Senior Editor, Kimberley Young (Mills & Boon Romance); Senior Editor, Sheila Hodgson (Mills & Boon Medical Romance); Senior Editor, Linda Fildew (Mills & Boon Historical Romance)
Established 1908
Imprint(s) Mills & Boon Modern Romance
Mills & Boon Romance
Mills & Boon Medical Romance
Mills & Boon Historical Romance
MIRA
Silhouette
Steeple Hill
Insider Info Publishes 600 titles per year. Receives approximately 2,000 manuscripts per year. Payment is via royalties. Simultaneous submissions not accepted. Submissions accompanied by SAE will be returned. Aims to respond to manuscripts within three months. Catalogue and manuscript guidelines available online. No non-fiction.
Fiction Publishes Erotica, Romance and Women's Fiction titles.
Submission Guidelines Accepts query with SAE. Submit proposal package (including outline).

Recent Title(s) *Count Maxime's Virgin*, Susan Stephens (Historical Romance); *Taken for Revenge, Bedded for Pleasure*, India Grey (Modern Romance)
Tips Harlequin Mills & Boon are a leading international publisher of romance fiction aimed at women. The Romance and Modern Romance imprints publish traditional romance novels, often set against a backdrop of luxury, wealth and international locations. Medical Romance publishes romance novels set in or around the medical professions. Historical Romance publishes romance novels set in historical eras and includes chivalrous knights, roguish rakes and rugged cattlemen as the main focus of interest. Steeple Hill publishes inspirational romance. Other imprints such as Silhouette and MIRA – which publish racier romance fiction and general women's fiction respectively – are available in the other international editorial offices. Harlequin Mills & Boon accept unsolicited submissions, and have substantial aspiring author information on their website, with detailed guidelines including word counts and proposal style guides, for each of their series.

Harley Books
Martins, Great Horkesley, Colchester, Essex, CO6 4AH
- 01206 271216
- 01206 271182
- harley@keme.co.uk
- www.harleybooks.com
Parent Company Apollo Books (Denmark)
Contact Managing Director, Basil Harley
Established 1983
Insider Info Payment is via royalties. Catalogue is available online.
Non-Fiction Publishes Reference and Scholarly titles on the following subjects:
Science, Botany/Entomoloy
Submission Guidelines Accepts query with SAE or via email.
Recent Title(s) *The Dragonflies of Europe*, R.R. Askew
Tips Harley Books is an independent publisher of natural history books, specialising in entomology and botany, with an established worldwide market. They aim to publish books of the highest editorial and production standards. Particular attention is paid to the quality of design, illustration, references and indexing.

Harold Starke Publishers Ltd
Pixey Green, Stadbroke, Eye, Suffolk, IP21 5NG
- 01379 388334
- 01379 388335
Contact Naomi Galinski

Non-Fiction Publishes Textbooks, Coffee Table and Scholarly titles on the following subjects:
Education, Health, Nature/Environment, Medicine
Tips Harold Starke publishing house specialises in high quality coffee table books but has also made innovative forays into educational publishing.

HarperCollins Publishers Ltd
77–85 Fulham Palace Road, Hammersmith, London, W6 8JB
- 020 8741 7070
- 020 8307 4440
- uk.orders@harpercollins.co.uk
- www.harpercollins.co.uk
Parent Company HarperCollins Worldwide (Division of News Corporation)
Contact CEO & Publisher, Victoria Barnsley; Managing Director, Amanda Ridout; Publishing Director, David Brawn
Established 1819
Imprint(s) Collins (division)
General Books (division)
Press Books (division)
Insider Info Publishes around 1,500 titles per year. Catalogue and manuscript guidelines available online.
Non-Fiction Publishes Audio cassettes, Autobiography, Biography, Children's, Cookery, General Non-Fiction, Gift, How-To, Humour, Illustrated, Multimedia, Reference, Scholarly, Self-Help, Textbooks, Maps and Atlases, and Guidebooks and Dictionaries on the following subjects: Alternative Lifestyles, Art/Architecture, Astrology/Psychic, Child Guidance/Parenting, Contemporary Culture, Cooking, Education, Entertainment/Games, Food & Drink, Health/Medicine, History, Hobbies, Humanities, Language, Literature, Memoirs, Military/War, Music, Nature/Environment, Philosophy, Psychology, Recreation, Science, Sex, Social Sciences, Spirituality, Sports, Travel, World Affairs, Young Adult, Film and Television Tie-Ins, Mind, Body and Spirit, Lifestyle, Relationships
Submission Guidelines Agented submissions only.
Fiction Publishes Adventure, Fantasy, Historical, Horror, Humour, Children's, Literary, Mainstream/Contemporary, Mystery, Romance, Science Fiction, Suspense, Young Adult and Thriller titles and Picture Books.
Submission Guidelines Agented submissions only.
Recent Title(s) *Cooking for Friends*, Gordon Ramsey (Cooking); *Dirty Game*, Jessie Keane (Thriller)
Tips HarperCollins Publishers UK is one of the leading English language publishers in the world, and publishes the widest range of books of any of Britain's publishing groups, in a variety of different genres and styles. In addition it also publishes the complete works of J.R.R. Tolkein, C.S. Lewis and

Agatha Christie. HarperCollins only accepts submissions from literary agents or previously published authors, but may also consider submissions that are accompanied by a positive assessment from a manuscript assessment agency.

HarperCollins Publishers Ltd – General Books Division

77–85 Fulham Palace Road, Hammersmith, London, W6 8JB

- 020 8741 7070
- 020 8307 4440
- uk.orders@harpercollins.co.uk
- www.harpercollins.co.uk

Parent Company HarperCollins Publishers Ltd
Contact Managing Director, Amanda Ridout
Imprint(s) AVON
HarperCollins Children's Books
HarperCollins Crime & Thrillers
HarperEntertainment
HarperEstates
HarperFiction
HarperThorsons/HarperElement
HarperSport
HarperTrue
HarperVoyager
Insider Info Catalogues available online at: www.harpercollins.co.uk, www.voyager-books.co.uk, www.thorsens.com, www.harpercollinschildrensbooks.co.uk, www.collins-crime.co.uk and www.tolkien.co.uk.
Non-Fiction Publishes Autobiography, Biography, Children's, General Non-Fiction, How-To, Humour, Illustrated, Reference, Self-Help, Television and Media Tie-In titles on the following subjects: Sports, Mind, Body and Spirit Lifestyle, Diet, Relationships, Work/Life Balance, Real life Issues, Film and Film Companions
Submission Guidelines Accepts agented submissions only.
Fiction Publishes Fantasy, Children's, Mainstream/Contemporary, Picture Book, Science Fiction, Young Adult, Crime and Thriller and Classic titles.
* Books published under license include: *Mary-Kate and Ashley, Noddy, The Hulk, Spiderman, The Simpsons, The Magic Roundabout, Dr Seuss* and *Paddington Bear.*
Submission Guidelines Agented submissions only.
Tips The General Books division of HarperCollins Publishers Ltd publishes some of the most high profile writers around under the HarperFiction imprint – from Josephine Cox and Tony Parsons, to Sidney Sheldon and Tracey Chavalier. The Voyager imprint is the UK's leading science-fiction and fantasy imprint. Non-fiction imprints include, HarperThorsons/HarperElement, with a list of well known brand name authors. HarperEntertainment

produces humour and media related books, while HarperSport is the country's top sports imprint. The list of HarperCollins Children's Books includes a wide range of children's fiction. See the individual entries for more details.

HarperTrue

77–85 Fulham Palace Road, Hammersmith, London, W6 8JB

- 020 8741 7070
- 020 8307 4440
- uk.orders@harpercollins.co.uk
- www.harpercollins.co.uk

Parent Company HarperCollins Publishers Ltd – General Books Division
Insider Info Catalogues available online.
Non-Fiction Publishes Autobiography, Biography and Memoir titles on the following subjects: True Life Stories
Submission Guidelines Accepts agented submissions only.
Recent Title(s) *Never Say Die*, Lynne Barrett-Lee (True Life)
Tips HarperTrue is a new imprint that publishes true life stories, including memoir, true crime and 'troubled lives' titles.

HarperCollins Publishers Ltd – Press Books Division

77–85 Fulham Palace Road, Hammersmith, London, W6 8JB

- 020 8741 7070
- 020 8307 4440
- uk.orders@harpercollins.co.uk
- www.harpercollins.co.uk

Parent Company HarperCollins Publishers Ltd
Contact Managing Director, John Bond
Imprint(s) Blue Door
Fourth Estate
The Friday Project
HarperPerennial
HarperPress
Insider Info Catalogue available online.
Non-Fiction Publishes Autobiography, Biography, General Non-Fiction and Humour on the following subjects: Contemporary Culture, Government/Politics, History, Memoirs, Science, Travel, World Affairs, Current Affairs.
Submission Guidelines Agented submissions only.
Fiction Publishes Humour, Literary, Mainstream/Contemporary, Romance, Translation, Crime and Genre Fiction titles
Submission Guidelines Agented submissions only.
Tips HarperCollins has acquired some of the assets of The Friday Project, the only publishing company

to specialise in sourcing the brightest talent from the web and developing it into great books, and also launched a new fiction imprint, Blue Dor, in 2008. Press Books is a large division within HarperCollins and it is best to direct enquiries to the relevant imprint, rather than to the division as a whole.

HarperCollins Children's Books
77–85 Fulham Palace Road, Hammersmith, London, W6 8JB
- 020 8741 7070
- 020 8307 4440
- enquiries@harpercollinschildrensbooks.co.uk
- www.harpercollinschildrensbooks.co.uk

Parent Company HarperCollins Publishers Ltd – General Books Division
Contact Publishing Director, Gillie Russel (Fiction); Publishing Director, Sue Buswell (Picture Books)
Insider Info Catalogue available online.
Non-Fiction Publishes Children's Non-Fiction books and Audiobooks.
Submission Guidelines Agented submissions only.
Fiction Publishes Picture Books and Children's and Young Adult fictiontitles.
Submission Guidelines Agented submissions only.
Recent Title(s) *Prince Caspian Movie Storybook*, C.S. Lewis (Film Tie-In); *Splat The Cat*, Rob Scotton (Picture Book); *Skulduggery Pleasant: Playing with Fire*, Derek Landy (Young Adult)
Tips HarperCollins Children's Books publishes fiction, picture books and audiobooks for children of all ages, including young adults. Various intellectual properties are also published under licence by the imprint, including *Spiderman, Paddington Bear* and *The Simpsons*. HarperCollins only accepts submissions from literary agents or previously published authors, but may consider submissions that are accompanied by a positive assessment from a manuscript assessment agency.

HarperCollins Crime & Thrillers
77–85 Fulham Palace Road, Hammersmith, London, W6 8JB
- 020 8741 7070
- 020 8307 4440
- uk.orders@harpercollins.co.uk
- www.collins-crime.co.uk

Parent Company HarperCollins Publishers Ltd – General Books Division
Contact Publishing Director, Julia Wisdom
Insider Info Catalogue available online.
Fiction Publishes Mystery, Suspense, Crime and Thriller titles.
Submission Guidelines Agented submissions only.
Recent Title(s) *They Do It With Mirrors*, Agatha Christie (Crime)

Tips HarperCollins Crime & Thrillers publishes the best in modern crime fiction from popular writers such as Val McDermid, Reginald Hill and Robert Wilson. HarperCollins only accepts submissions from literary agents or previously published authors, but may consider submissions that are accompanied by a positive assessment from a manuscript assessment agency.

HarperEntertainment
77–85 Fulham Palace Road, Hammersmith, London, W6 8JB
- 020 8741 7070
- 020 8307 4440
- uk.orders@harpercollins.co.uk
- www.harpercollins.co.uk

Parent Company HarperCollins Publishers Ltd – General Books Division
Contact Managing Director, Amanda Ridout
Imprint(s) HarperCollins Audio
Insider Info Catalogue available online.
Non-Fiction Publishes Audio cassettes, Autobiography, Biography, Children's, General Non-Fiction, Humour, Illustrated and Multimedia titles on the following subjects: Entertainment/Games, Memoirs, Sports, Film/Television Tie-Ins.
Submission Guidelines Agented submissions only.
Fiction Publishes Children's and Film/Television Tie-In titles and Comic Books and Audiobooks.
Submission Guidelines Agented submissions only.
Recent Title(s) *Attack of the Dinobots!* Transformers Animated series
Tips HarperEntertainment publishes humour and media related non-fiction books, from film companions and autobiographies, to various types of television and cinema tie-ins. HarperCollins Audio publishes recordings of HarperCollins fiction and non-fiction titles, for both children and adults. HarperCollins only accepts submissions from literary agents or previously published authors, but may consider submissions that are accompanied by a positive assessment from a manuscript assessment agency.

HarperEstates
77–85 Fulham Palace Road, Hammersmith, London, W6 8JB
- 020 8741 7070
- 020 8307 4440
- uk.orders@harpercollins.co.uk
- www.harpercollins.co.uk

Parent Company HarperCollins Publishers Ltd – General Books Division
Contact Publishing Director, David Brawn
Imprint(s) Tolkien

Insider Info Catalogue available online.
Fiction Publishes Classic reprints.
Tips HarperEstates publishes the complete works of J.R.R. Tolkien, along with the complete works of both Agatha Christie and C.S. Lewis. HarperEstates exists solely to print the works of Tolkien, Lewis and Christie, and therefore does not accept submissions.

HarperFiction

77–85 Fulham Palace Road, Hammersmith, London, W6 8JB

- 020 8741 7070
- 020 8307 4440
- uk.orders@harpercollins.co.uk
- www.harpercollins.co.uk

Parent Company HarperCollins Publishers Ltd – General Books Division
Contact Publisher, Lynne Drew
Insider Info Catalogue available online.
Fiction Publishes Fantasy, Historical, Horror, Literary, Mainstream/Contemporary, Romance, Science Fiction, Suspense, Women's Writing, and Crime/Thriller titles.
Submission Guidelines Agented submissions only.
Recent Title(s) *A Darker Domain*, Val McDermid (Crime)
Tips HarperFiction is the general fiction division under HarperCollins – General Books Division. HarperCollins only accepts submissions from literary agents or previously published authors, but may consider submissions that are accompanied by a positive assessment from a manuscript assessment agency.

HarperPerennial

77–85 Fulham Palace Road, Hammersmith, London, W6 8JB

- 020 8741 7070
- 020 8307 4440
- uk.orders@harpercollins.co.uk
- www.harperperennial.co.uk

Parent Company HarperCollins Publishers Ltd – Press Books Division
Contact Publishing Director, Paul Baggaley
Insider Info Catalogue available online.
Non-Fiction Publishes Autobiography, Biography and General Non-Fiction titles on the following subjects:
Contemporary Culture, Government/Politics, History, Memoirs, Science, Social Sciences, Travel
Submission Guidelines Agented submissions only.
Fiction Publishes Literary, Mainstream/Contemporary and Genre Fiction titles.
Submission Guidelines Agented submissions only.
Recent Title(s) *The Cat Sanctuary*, Patrick Gale (Novel); *Out At Night*, Susan Arnout Smith (Novel)

Tips HarperPerennial is the literary paperback imprint for all Press Books titles. The imprint only accepts submissions from literary agents or previously published authors, but may consider submissions that are accompanied by a positive assessment from a manuscript assessment agency.

HarperPress

77–85 Fulham Palace Road, Hammersmith, London, W6 8JB

- 020 8741 7070
- 020 8307 4440
- uk.orders@harpercollins.co.uk
- www.harpercollins.co.uk

Parent Company HarperCollins Publishers Ltd – Press Books Division
Contact Publishing Director, Michael Fishwick
Insider Info Catalogue available online.
Non-Fiction Publishes Biography and General Non-Fiction on the following subjects:
History, Memoirs, Travel
Submission Guidelines Agented submissions only.
Fiction Publishes Mainstream/Contemporary titles.
Submission Guidelines Agented submissions only.
Recent Title(s) *The Bitter Sea: The Struggle for Mastery in the Mediterranean 1935-1949*, Simon Ball (Military History)
Tips HarperPress publishes a wide range of award-winning non-fiction, including history, travel literature, biographies and memoirs, plus quality novels with real commercial potential. HarperCollins as a group only accepts submissions from literary agents or previously published authors, but may consider submissions that are accompanied by a positive assessment from a manuscript assessment agency.

HarperSport

77–85 Fulham Palace Road, Hammersmith, London, W6 8JB

- 020 8741 7070
- 020 8307 4440
- uk.orders@harpercollins.co.uk
- www.harpercollins.co.uk

Parent Company HarperCollins Publishers Ltd – General Books Division
Contact Publishing Director, Michael Doggart
Insider Info Catalogue available online.
Non-Fiction Publishes Autobiography, Biography, General Non-Fiction and Illustrated titles on Sports.
Submission Guidelines Agented submissions only.
Recent Title(s) *Hoggy: The Peculiar World of Matthew Hoggard*, Matthew Hoggard (Autobiography)
Tips HarperSports publishes biographies, guidebooks, history and general interest sporting titles. HarperCollins as a group only accepts

submissions from literary agents or previously published authors, but may consider submissions that are accompanied by a positive assessment from a manuscript assessment agency.

HarperThorsens/HarperElement
77–85 Fulham Palace Road, Hammersmith, London, W6 8JB
- 020 8741 7070
- 020 8307 4440
- uk.orders@harpercollins.co.uk
- www.thorsons.com

Parent Company HarperCollins Publishers Ltd – General Books Division
Contact Publishing Director, Carole Tonkinson (Mind, Body & Spirit); Publishing Director, Wanda Whiteley (Health)
Insider Info Catalogue available online.
Non-Fiction Publishes Biography, General Non-Fiction, Illustrated and Self-Help titles on: Alternative Lifestyles, Astrology/Psychic, Fashion, Food & Drink, Guidance, Health, Lifestyle, Sex, Spirituality, Mind, Body & Spirit, Relationships
Submission Guidelines Agented submissions only.
Recent Title(s) *Element Encyclopedia of Secret Signs and Symbols*, Adele Nozedar (Mind, Body & Spirit); *How to Dress: Your Complete Style Guide for Every Occasion*, Gok Wan (Fashion)
Tips HarperThorsons/HarperElement publishes a non-fiction list of promotable brand name authors, and has a 'quality meets populism' attitude. Subjects include sex, relationships, diet and nutrition, health, mind, body & spirit, psychic and self-help. HarperCollins as a group only accepts submissions from literary agents or previously published authors, but may consider submissions that are accompanied by a positive assessment from a manuscript assessment agency.

HarperVoyager
77–85 Fulham Palace Road, Hammersmith, London, W6 8JB
- 020 8741 7070
- 020 8307 4440
- uk.orders@harpercollins.co.uk
- www.voyager-books.co.uk

Parent Company HarperCollins Publishers Ltd – General Books Division
Contact Publishing Director, Jane Johnson
Insider Info Catalogue available online.
Fiction Publishes Fantasy, Gothic, Horror and Science-Fiction titles.
Submission Guidelines Agented submissions only.
Recent Title(s) *The Painted Man*, Peter V. Brett (Fantasy)

Tips HarperVoyager publishes modern fantasy, horror and science-fiction, with authors including Terry Goodkind, David Eddings, Raymond E. Feist, George R.R. Martin and Robin Hobb. HarperCollins as a group only accepts submissions from literary agents or previously published authors, but may consider submissions that are accompanied by a positive assessment from a manuscript assessment agency.

Harvard University Press
Fitzroy House, 11 Chenies Street, London, WC1E 7EY
- 020 7306 0603
- 020 7306 0604
- info@hup-mitpress.co.uk
- www.hup.harvard.edu

Contact General Manager, Ann Sexsmith
Established 1913
Insider Info Catalogue and manuscript guidelines available online.
Non-Fiction Publishes General, Reference and Scholarly titles on the following subjects: Classics, Economics, History, Literature, Literary Criticism, Music, Philosophy, Politics, Psychology, Science, Social Sciences, Sociology.
Submission Guidelines See website.
Tips The Harvard University Press website has very detailed submission guidelines. Please note that all manuscript submissions must be sent to the American office.

Harvill Secker
Random House, 20 Vauxhall Bridge Road, London, SW1V 2SA
- 020 7840 8893
- 020 7233 6117
- harvillseckereditorial@randomhouse.co.uk
- www.randomhouse.co.uk

Parent Company The Random House Group Ltd
Contact Publishing Director, Geoff Mulligan
Insider Info Catalogue available online.
Non-Fiction Publishes General Non-Fiction titles on the following subjects:
History, Literary Criticism and Memoirs
Submission Guidelines No unagented submissions.
Fiction Publishes Literary and Mainstream/Contemporary titles.
Submission Guidelines No unagented submissions.
Recent Title(s) *Novel 11, Book 18*, Dag Solstad (Novel); *Slumberland*, Paul Beatty (Novel)
Tips Does not accept unagented submissions. Research the Harvill Secker section of the Random

House catalogue for ideas about the types of titles published.

Haunted Library

36 Hamilton Street, Hoole, Chester, CH2 3JQ

☎ 01244 313685

✉ pardos@globalnet.co.uk

🌐 www.users.globalnet.co.uk/~pardos/GS.html

Contact Managing Editor, Rosemary Pardoe; Assistant Editor, David Rowlands; Assistant Editor, Steve Duffy

Established 1979

Tips Publishes the *Ghosts & Scholars M.R. James Newsletter* several times a year. Features various articles, reviews and literary criticism. No longer publishes fiction.

Haus Publishing

26 Cadogan Court, Draycott Avenue, London, SW3 3BX

☎ 020 7584 6738

☎ 020 7584 9501

✉ haus@hauspublishing.co.uk

🌐 www.hauspublishing.co.uk

Contact Managing Director, Barbara Schwepke

Established 2001

Imprint(s) Life & Times
Armchair Traveller
HBooks

Insider Info Publishes roughly 20 titles per year. Payment is via royalties. Catalogue available online. Manuscript guidelines available online.

Non-Fiction Publishes Biography and Scholarly titles on the following subjects:
Art, Biography, History, Music, Photography, Politics, Theatre and Film, Travel

Submission Guidelines Accepts query with SAE and proposal package (including outline, one sample chapter, author biography).

Recent Title(s) *The London Stage in the 20th Century*, Robert Tanitch (Theatre)

Tips Haus does accept unsolicited submissions direct from authors, as long as they follow the submission guidelines from the website. They also publish a literary travel series, *The Armchair Traveller*, which is travel literature of a personal nature and not a guidebook series.

Haynes Publishing

Sparkford, Yeovil, Somerset, BA22 7JJ

☎ 01963 440635

☎ 01963 440001

✉ info@haynes.co.uk

🌐 www.haynes.co.uk

Contact Chairman, John H. Haynes; Editorial Directors, Matthew Minter and Mark Hughes

Established 1960

Imprint(s) Haynes
Sutton Publishing Ltd

Insider Info Payment is via royalties. Catalogue available online.

Non-Fiction Publishes General Non-Fiction, Reference and Technical titles on the following subjects:
Hobbies, Leisure, Motoring/Engineering, Practical Manuals.

Submission Guidelines Accepts query with SAE and proposal package (including outline, sample chapters, author biography).

Recent Title(s) *Adventure Motorcycling*, Robert Wicks

Tips Alongside their world famous car and motorcycle manuals, Haynes also publishes a variety of books on many other motoring, transport, family and DIY related areas. These include; restoration, motor sport and maritime subjects, aviation, farm tractors, commercial vehicles, motorcycling, cycling, caravanning, camping, home decorating and DIY, health matters and American cars.

Headland Publications

York Avenue, West Kirby, Wirral, CH48 3JF

☎ 0151 625 9128

✉ headlandpublications@hotmail.co.uk

🌐 www.headlandpublications.co.uk

Contact Director and Editor, Gladys-Mary Coles

Established 1969

Fiction Publishes Short Story Collections and Mainstream/Contemporary titles.

Submission Guidelines Accepts query with SAE. No unsolicited manuscripts.

Poetry Publishes Poetry titles.

Submission Guidelines Accepts query with SAE. No unsolicited manuscripts.

Headline

338 Euston Road, London, NW1 3BH

☎ 020 7873 6000

☎ 020 7873 6024

✉ info@headline.co.uk

🌐 www.headline.co.uk

Parent Company Hachette UK

Contact Managing Director, Martin Neild; Publishing Director, Jane Morpeth (Fiction); Publishing Director, Val Hudson (Non-Fiction)

Established 1986

Insider Info Does not accept simultaneous submissions. Submissions accompanied by SAE will be returned. Aims to respond to proposals within three weeks. Catalogue and manuscript guidelines are available online on request.

Non-Fiction Publishes Autobiography, Biography, General Non-Fiction, Illustrated Books and Multimedia titles on the following subjects: Contemporary Culture, Entertainment/Games, History, Science, Sports, Film/Media
Submission Guidelines Accepts query with SAE and proposal package (including outline and first 100 pages).
Fiction Publishes Mainstream/Contemporary, Short Story Collections and Literary titles.
Submission Guidelines Accepts query with SAE and proposal package (including outline and first 100 pages).
Poetry Publishes Poetry titles.
Recent Title(s) *Evil Penguins*, Elia Anie (Humour); *The Rose Labyrinth*, Titania Hardie (Historical Fiction)
Tips Headline publishes best selling adult commercial and literary fiction, including romance. Its non-fiction list includes autobiographies and television tie-ins, humour and history titles. Headline will accept submissions of novels or non-fiction from first-time writers, as long as they follow the guidelines on the website. However, they will only accept submissions of novellas, poetry and short story collections from established authors. Now reports directly to Hachette UK, following the closure of Hodder Headline.

Headpress
Suite 306, The Colourworks, 2a Abbott Street, London, E8 3DP
- 020 7275 6001
- 020 7249 6395
- info@headpress.com
- www.headpress.com
Established 1991
Insider Info Publishes six titles per year. Receives approximately 50 queries and 50 manuscripts per year. 50 per cent of books published are from first-time authors, 100 per cent of books published are from unagented authors. Payment is via a flat fee. Catalogue available online.
Non-Fiction Publishes General Non-Fiction titles on the following subjects:
Alternative Lifestyles, Contemporary Culture, Creative Non-Fiction, Music, Film, True Crime
Recent Title(s) *No Focus: Punk on Film*, Chris Barber and Jack Sargeant (Music)

Heart of Albion
2 Cross Hill Close, Wymeswold, Loughborough, LE12 6UJ
- 01509 880725
- 01509 881715
- albion@indigogroup.co.uk
- www.hoap.co.uk

Contact Director, Bob Trubshaw
Established 1989
Imprint(s) Explore Books
Alternative Albion
Insider Info Publishes 12 titles per year. Receives approximately 200 queries and 20 manuscripts per year. Ten per cent of books published are from first-time authors, 90 per cent of books published are from unagented authors. Five per cent of books published are author subsidy published, depending on subject matter and estimates of realistic sales. Payment is via royalty (on retail price), with 0.15 (per £) maximum. Average lead time is six months, with simultaneous submissions accepted. Submissions accompanied by SAE will be returned. Aims to respond to queries within five days and proposals, manuscripts and all other enquiries within ten days. Catalogue and manuscript guidelines are free on request, and available online.
Non-Fiction Publishes General Non-Fiction, e-books and Multimedia titles on the following subjects: Cryptozoology, Emergence Theories, Folklore and Mythology, History, Medieval Carvings and Effigies, New Age, Non-Western Philosophy, Modern Pagan and Non-Western Religion
* Heart of Albion's overall aim is to popularise current 'academic' thinking in folklore, mythology, cultural studies and related disciplines.
Submission Guidelines Accepts proposal package (including outline, one sample chapter and your publishing history) by email preferably.
Recent Title(s) *Holy Wells in Britain: A Guide*, Janet Bord
Tips Heart of Albion's target readership is 'thinking' adults, especially those drawn to alternative ideas.

Heinemann Educational
Halley Court, Jordan Hill, Oxford, OX2 8EJ
- 01865 888000
- 01865 314091
- enquiries@pearson.com
- www.heinemann.co.uk
Parent Company Pearson Education
Non-fiction Publishes Children's, Reference, Scholarly and Textbook titles.
Tips Publishes educational titles aimed at primary and secondary school children, vocational and further education students, and library users and professionals. Publications need to fit within appropriate curriculum guidelines.

Helicon Publishing
RM Plc, 183 Milton Park, Abingdon, Oxfordshire, OX14 4SE
- 0845 070 0300
- 01235 826999

helicon@rm.com

www.helicon.co.uk

Contact General Manager, Caroline Dodds

Established 1992

Insider Info Catalogue available online.

Non-Fiction Publishes Reference titles.

Tips Helicon publishes reference material, such as the *Hutchinson Encyclopedia*, in print, on CD-ROM, and online. They specialise in electronic publishing however, and maintain databases containing over 21 million words, ranging from serious subject reference, to quizzes and memory joggers. As well as text, the databases contain thousands of maps, diagrams, illustrations, audio clips, and animations.

Helm Information

Crowham Manor, Main Road, Westfield, Hastings, TN35 4SR

01424 882422

01424 882817

amandahelm@helm-information.co.uk

www.helm-information.co.uk

Contact Proprietor, Amanda Helm

Established 1990

Insider Info Payment is via royalties. Catalogue available online.

Non-Fiction Publishes Reference, Scholarly and Textbook titles.

Submission Guidelines Any proposal must fit in with existing series.

Recent Title(s) *Joan of Arc*, John Flower (Icons of Modern Culture series); *Ned Kelly*, Lyn Innes (Icons of Modern Culture series)

Tips Since summer of 2008 Helm has been publishing two series only: The Dickens Companions Series and Icons of Modern Culture Series. Also offers publishing services and advice from manuscript to printer to writers and publishers.

Helter Skelter Publishing

18a Radbourne Road, Balham, London, SW12 0DZ

020 8673 6320

sales@helterskelterpublishing.com

www.helterskelterbooks.com

Contact Sean Body

Established 1995

Imprint(s) Firefly Publishing

Insider Info Publishes 15 titles per year. Receives approximately 50 queries and 30 manuscripts per year. 50 per cent of books published are from first-time authors and 60 per cent are from unagented authors. Payment is via royalty (on retail price) of 0.08 (per £) minimum and 0.125 (per £) maximum. Average lead time is six months with simultaneous submissions accepted. Catalogue available online.

Non-Fiction Publishes General Non-Fiction on Contemporary Culture, and Music/Dance.

Submission Guidelines Accepts query with SAE. Submit proposal package (including outline, sample chapter(s)). Will accept artworks/images (send photocopies).

Recent Title(s) *I'm With The Band*, Pamela Des Barres (Memoir); *Natural Born Man: The Life of Jack Johnson*, Marc Shapiro (Biography)

Tips Helter Skelter specialises in music titles, such as biographies and memoirs. Unsolicited submissions and ideas are welcome.

Herbert Press

36 Soho Square, London, W1D 3QY

020 7758 0320

020 7758 0222

llambert@acblack.com

www.acblack.com

Parent Company A&C Black Publishers Ltd

Contact Publisher (Visual Arts), Linda Lambert

Insider Info Catalogue available online.

Non-Fiction Publishes General Non-Fiction, How-To, Illustrated Books, Multimedia and Reference books on the following subjects: Art/Architecture, History, Photography, Visual Arts, Crafts, Ceramics, Printmaking, Jewellery Design and Calligraphy

Recent Title(s) *... isms: Understanding Fashion*, Mairi Mackenzie (Fashion)

Tips Herbert Press publishes practical and general interest handbooks on all aspects of art and design. It has recently redesigned its *Draw Books* series, which is a practical series offering tutorials and guidance for various art and craft techniques.

Hesperus Press

4 Rickett Street, London, SW6 1RU

020 7610 3331

020 7610 3337

info@hesperuspress.com

www.hesperuspress.com

Contact Managing Editor, Ellie Robins

Established 2001

Insider Info Publishes 50 titles per year. Payment via royalties. Catalogue available online or by post upon request.

Non-Fiction Publishes Literary Biographies and General Non-Fiction titles.

Fiction Publishes Literary, Translation and Classics titles.

Submission Guidelines Accepts query with SAE.

Recent Title(s) *The Maytrees*, Annie Dillard (Novel)

Tips Hesperus Press is committed to reprinting works that have been neglected or are simply little known in the English speaking world – making them accessible through new translations and a completely fresh editorial approach. They don't generally accept proposals for new fiction, as they mainly publish classic literary fiction. If you're proposing a translation, send it to Ellie Robins by post or email, with as many details as possible.

High Stakes Publishing

Oldcastle Books, PO Box 394, Harpenden, AL5 1XJ
☎ 01582 761264
☎ 01582 761264
🌐 www.highstakespublishing.co.uk
Parent Company Oldcastle Books
Established 2002
Insider Info Catalogue available online on request.
Non-Fiction Publishes Biography, Reference and How-To books on Gambling.
Recent Title(s) *The Punters Handbook: The Gambling Books Reference Guide*, John Newton

Hilltop Press

4 Nowell Place, Almondbury, Huddersfield, HD5 8PD
Contact Steve Sneyd
Insider Info Catalogue available with SAE.
Fiction Publishes Fantasy, Horror and Science-Fiction titles.
Poetry Publishes Dark Fantasy Poetry.
Tips All material falls within the speculative fiction category, which includes fantasy, horror and science-fiction. As well as by mail, a list of publications is available at www.bbr-online.com.

Hilmarton Manor Press

Hilmarton Manor Press, Calne, Wiltshire, SN11 8SB
☎ 01249 760208
☎ 01249 760379
✉ mailorder@hilmartonpress.co.uk
🌐 www.hilmartonpress.co.uk
Contact Managing Director, Charles Baile de Laperriere
Established 1964
Insider Info Payment via royalties. Catalogue available online.
Non-Fiction Publishes Reference titles on the following subjects:
Art
Tips Publishes art reference books and directories only, including *Who's Who In Art*.

Hobsons Publishing Plc

Challenger House, 42 Adler Street, London, E1 1EE
☎ 020 7958 5000
☎ 020 7958 5001
🌐 www.hobsons.com
Contact Chairman, Martin Morgan; Group Managing Director, Christopher Letcher
Established 1974
Non-Fiction Publishes Reference and Scholarly titles on Education.
Tips Publishes educational and careers information databases under licence to the Careers & Research Advisory Centre (CRAC). Hobsons enables schools to market their programs and opportunities to a large number of students, and also works with them to recruit a high quality, diverse student body. They aim to deliver both online and offline publications to help students learn more about the educational and career opportunities available to them.

Hodder Education

338 Euston Road, London, NW1 3BH
☎ 020 7873 6000
☎ 020 7873 6299
✉ educationenquiries@hodder.co.uk
🌐 www.hoddereducation.co.uk
Parent Company Hachette Livre UK
Contact Managing Director, Philip Walters; Publishing Director, Lis Tribe (School Textbooks and Learning Materials); Publishing Director, John Mitchell (Scottish School Textbooks and Learning Materials); Publishing Director, Alexia Chan (College and University Textbooks and Learning Materials, Reference); Publishing Director, Katie Roden (Self-Improvement and Home Learning Materials); Publishing Director, Joanna Koster (Health Sciences Textbooks, Reference and Other Learning Materials)
Established 2001
Imprint(s) Hodder Arnold
Hodder Murray
Hodder Gibson
Philip Allan Updates
Insider Info Catalogue available online, free on request.
Non-Fiction Publishes Audio Cassettes, How-To, Multimedia, Reference, Scholarly, Self-Help, Journals and Textbook titles on the following subjects: Computers/Electronics, Education, Health/Medicine, History, Humanities, Science, Home Learning, Self-Improvement
Submission Guidelines Accepts proposal package (including outline, sample chapter(s), market research, publishing history, author biography and SAE).
Tips Publishes books and digital materials for the Further Education, Higher Education, Health Sciences and Consumer Education markets. It comprises Hodder Arnold Further & Higher Education, Hodder Arnold Consumer Education, and

Hodder Arnold Health Sciences. It also publishes the popular *Teach Yourself* series. Hodder Murray publishes books, resources, digital materials and assessment for the schools market and is the second largest publisher for secondary education in the UK. Hodder Gibson publishes educational books and digital materials in Scotland. Philip Allan Updates runs conferences and courses, as well as publishing subject specific material for GCSE and A-Level studies across the UK. Hodder Education is always keen to hear from qualified writers with new educational books. Send a proposal along with market research and some personal information, including publishing history, to the relevant publishing contact (see website). Now reports directly to Hachette UK, following the closure of Hodder Headline.

Hodder & Stoughton General
338 Euston Road, London, NW1 3BH
- 020 7873 6000
- 020 7873 6024
- www.hodder.co.uk

Parent Company Hachette UK
Contact CEO, Martin Neild; Managing Director, Jamie Hodder-Williams
Established 1868
Imprint(s) Hodder Inspiration
Sceptre
Insider Info Catalogue available online.
Non-fiction Publishes Biography, General and Illustrated titles on the following subjects: Memoir, History, Sport, Entertainment and Lifestyle
Submission Guidelines Agented submissions only.
Fiction Publishes Mainstream/Contemporary Fiction.
Submission Guidelines Agented submissions only.
Recent Title(s) *Just After Sunset*, Stephen King (Fiction/Collection); *A Most Wanted Man*, John le Carré (Thriller)
Tips Hodder & Stoughton General publishes under three imprints: Hodder & Stoughton – which handles general fiction and non-fiction, including crime, thrillers and women's fiction; Hodder Inspiration – which publishes religious books for the general and Christian markets; and Sceptre – which publishes innovative non-fiction and prize-winning fiction author, such as Melvyn Bragg, Keri Hulme and David Mitchell. Hodder & Stoughton General now reports directly to Hachette UK, following the closure of Hodder Headline.

Hodder & Stoughton Faith Books
338 Euston Road, London, NW1 3BH
- 020 7873 6051
- 020 7873 6059

- hodderfaith-sales@hodder.co.uk
- www.hodderchristianbooks.co.uk

Parent Company Hachette UK
Contact Managing Director, Jamie Hodder-Williams; Publishing Director, Judith Longman
Established 1868
Imprint(s) Hodder Christian Books
Insider Info Catalogue available free online on request.
Non-Fiction Publishes Audio Cassettes, Autobiography, Biography, Children's, General Non-Fiction, Multimedia and Reference titles on the following subjects:
Guidance, Health/Medicine, Religion, Spirituality
Submission Guidelines Accepts proposal package (including outline, sample chapter(s), author biography, SAE and marketing and/or publicity information, if available).
Fiction Publishes Spiritual, Children's Religious titles.
Recent Title(s) *Rowan's Rule*, Rupert Shortt (Biography)
Tips Hodder Christian Books publishes various Christian books and bibles, as well as self-help and spirituality guides and religious teaching resources. Hodder & Stoughton Faith Books accepts unsolicited manuscripts, ideally with in-depth market research of similar titles and a brief author biography and publishing history. Full details are available on the website. Now reports directly to Hachette UK, following the closure of Hodder Headline.

Hodder Children's Books
338 Euston Road, London, NW1 3BH
- 020 7873 6000
- 020 7873 6024
- ad@hachettechildrens.co.uk
- www.hodderheadline.co.uk/hachettechildrens.htm

Parent Company Hachette Children's Books
Insider Info Catalogue available upon request.
Fiction Publishes Board books, Picture books, Novelty books, Children's fiction, Young Adult fiction, Poetry and Audiobooks.
Submission Guidelines No unsolicited manuscripts.
Tips Hodder Children's Books publishes successful brands, such as Enid Blyton's 'Famous Five' and 'Secret Seven', as well as bestselling writers and illustrators including David Almond, Lauren Child, Robert Muchamore and Guy Parker-Rees.

Honeyglen Publishing Ltd
56 Durrels House, Warwick Gardens, London, W14 8QB
- 020 7602 2876
- 020 7602 2876

Contact Director, N.S. Poderegin
Established 1983
Non-Fiction Publishes Biography and General Non-Fiction titles on the following subjects:
History, Philosophy.
Submission Guidelines Accepts query with SAE. Submit completed manuscript.
Fiction Publishes Literary titles.
* No science-fiction or children's fiction.
Submission Guidelines Accepts query with SAE. Submit completed manuscript.
Tips A small publishing house that handles biography, history and philosophy of history, as well as some literary fiction. Unsolicited submissions welcome, but due to the small size of the publisher, output is usually extremely limited.

Honno Welsh Women's Press
Canolfan Merched y Wawr, Vulcan Street, Aberystwyth, SY23 1JH
- 01970 623150
- 01970 623150
- post@honno.co.uk
- www.honno.co.uk
Contact Publishing Manager, Lindsay Ashford; Editor, Caroline Oakley
Established 1986
Insider Info Publishes eight titles per year. Payment is via royalties. Aims to respond to proposals and manuscripts within three months. Catalogue available online on request. Manuscript guidelines available online via website.
Fiction Publishes Children's, Mainstream/Contemporary, Regional, Short Story Collections, Translation, Young Adult and Welsh Fiction titles.
Submission Guidelines Accepts proposal package (including outline and 50 pages).
Poetry Publishes Poetry titles with a Welsh connection.
Submission Guidelines Accepts queries with complete manuscript.
Recent Title(s) *The Killer Inside*, Lindsay Ashford (Crime)
Tips Honno is an independent cooperative press run by women and committed to publishing the best in Welsh women's writing. Most of Honno's titles are novels, autobiographies and short story anthologies in English, but it also publishes poetry, children's and teenage titles and books in Welsh. Honno only considers for publication the work of women who are Welsh, living in Wales, or have a significant Welsh connection.

Hopscotch Educational Publishing Ltd
St Jude's Church, Dulwich Road, Herne Hill, London, SE24 0PB
- 020 7738 5454
- 020 7733 2325
- sales@hopscotchbooks.com
- www.hopscotchbooks.com
Contact Editorial Director, Margot O'Keeffe; Creative Director, Frances Mackay
Established 1997
Insider Info Catalogue available free on request and online. Manuscript guidelines are available online via the website.
Non-Fiction Publishes Reference, Scholarly and Textbook titles on the following subjects:
Literacy, Numeracy, Science, ICT, History, Geography, PSHE/Citizenship, Thinking Skills
Submission Guidelines Accepts query with SAE or by telephone. Alternatively, submit completed manuscript.
Recent Title(s) *Pick Up A Play: Plays for Primary Schools, Ages 7–8*; *Curriculum Focus – History KS1*
Tips Hopscotch exists to produce high quality, value for money resources that enable teachers to teach with confidence. The aim of the books is to enable children to have fun and success in their learning. They do accept manuscripts and ideas from first-time authors. The in-house team of experts will guide writers through the publishing process. Call the editorial department for further information or simply send in a manuscript.

House of Lochar
Isle of Colonsay, Argyll, PA61 7YR
- 01951 200323
- 01951 200323
- lochar@colonsay.org.uk
- www.houseoflochar.com
Contact Chairman, Kevin Byrne; Managing Director, Georgina Hobhouse
Established 1995
Imprint(s) Colonsay Books
West Highland Series
Insider Info Payment via royalties. Catalogue available online. Manuscript guidelines available on the website.
Non-Fiction Publishes General Non-Fiction titles on the following subjects:
History, Hobbies, Regional, Transportation, Walking Guides, Scottish Interest
Submission Guidelines Accepts query with SAE and proposal package (including outline and sample chapter(s)) addressed to the marketing agents at: Highland Media, Taigh na h-Alba, 35 High Street, South Queensferry, EH30 9HN, or tel. 0131 331 2700.

Fiction Publishes Mainstream/Contemporary, Children's, Regional and Scottish titles.
Submission Guidelines Accepts query with SAE and proposal package (including outline, sample chapter(s)) addressed to the marketing agents at: Highland Media, Taigh na h-Alba, 35 High Street, South Queensferry, EH30 9HN, or tel. 0131 331 2700.
Recent Title(s) *Yesterday Was Summer: The Marion Campbell Story*, Marian Pallister and David Adams McGilp (Biography)
Tips House of Lochar is a specialist Scottish publisher with a particular remit to print quality books on a number of subjects, including Scottish history, traditions and other titles of general Scottish interest in both fiction and non-fiction. They are always on the lookout for new material, and potential book ideas are welcome.

How To Books Ltd
Spring Hill House, Spring Hill Road, Begbroke, Oxford, OX5 1RX
- 01865 375794
- 01865 379162
- info@howtobooks.co.uk
- www.howtobooks.co.uk

Contact Publisher, Giles Lewis; Editorial Director, Nikki Read
Established 1991
Insider Info Publishes 100 titles per year. Receives approximately 200 queries and 100 manuscripts per year. 80 per cent of books are from first-time authors and 90 per cent are from unagented authors. Accepts simultaneous submissions. Aims to respond to proposals within one month and manuscripts within two months. Catalogue is free on request and available online. Manuscript guidelines are free on request.
Non-Fiction Publishes How-To, Reference and Self-Help titles.
Submission Guidelines Accepts query with SAE (include synopsis).
Recent Title(s) *How to Succeed at Interviews*, Rob Yeung
Tips How To Books has more than 250 titles in print, all of which aim to help readers achieve their dreams and their goals in their personal and working lives. They welcome proposals from authors with genuine experience of their subject.

Hurst & Co (Publishers) Ltd
41 Great Russell Street, London, WC1B 3PL
- 020 7255 2201
- 020 7255 2204
- hurst@atlas.co.uk
- www.hurstpub.co.uk

Contact Managing Director, Michael J. Dwyer

Established 1969
Insider Info Catalogue can be downloaded online.
Non-Fiction Publishes Biography, General Non-Fiction, Reference and Scholarly titles on the following subjects:
Anthropology/Archaeology, Current Affairs, Government/Politics, History, International Relations & Diplomacy, Islamic Studies, Memoirs, Religion
Submission Guidelines Accepts proposal package (including outline, sample chapters, market research and author biography). Do not send completed manuscripts.
Tips Hurst's authors include scholars, journalists and other authors who illuminate contemporary concerns and provide historical, cultural and religious background. Hurst also publishes books of wider public interest and two series, one in conjunction with CERI (Centre d'Etudes et de Recherches Internationales) in Paris, and the other, *Crises in World Politics*, with the Centre of International Studies, University of Cambridge.

Hutchinson
Random House, 20 Vauxhall Bridge Road, London, SW1V 2SA
- 020 7840 8564
- 020 7233 6127
- hutchinsoneditorial@randomhouse.co.uk
- www.randomhouse.co.uk

Parent Company The Random House Group Ltd
Contact Publishing Director, Sue Freestone
Non-Fiction Publishes Autobiography, Biography, Children's and History titles.
Submission Guidelines No unagented submissions.
Fiction Publishes General, Historical and Literary Fiction.
Submission Guidelines No unagented submissions.
Recent Title(s) *Land of Marvels*, Barry Unsworth (Historical Fiction); *The Time Traveller's Journal*, Prospero Hermes (Children's Non-Fiction)

Hutchinson Children's Books
61–63 Uxbridge Road, London, W5 5SA
- 020 7840 6848
- 020 7233 6058
- childrenseditorial@randomhouse.co.uk
- www.kidsatrandomhouse.co.uk

Parent Company Random House Children's Books
Insider Info Catalogue is available online.
Fiction Publishes Children's and Activity titles.
Submission Guidelines No unagented submissions.

Recent Title(s) *Little Red Train: Busy Day*, Benedict Blathwayt (Picture Book); *The Time Traveller's Journal*, Prospero Hermes (Pop-Up Book)
Tips Specialises in hardback children's books.

Hymns Ancient & Modern Ltd
St Mary's Works, St Mary's Plain, Norwich, Norfolk, NR3 3BH
- 01603 612914
- 01603 624483
- editorial@hymns-am.co.uk
- www.hymnsam.co.uk/hymnsam.asp
Contact CEO, Dominic Vaughan; Publisher, Christine Smith
Established 1975
Imprint(s) Canterbury Press
Hymns ancient & Modern
RMEP
SCM Press
Insider Info Publishes over 100 titles per year. Authors paid by royalty. Catalogue and author guidelines available online.
Non-Fiction Publishes Theology, Church Resources, Spirituality and Classroom Resources for religious education.
Submission Guidelines Accepts query with SAE. Submit proposal package (including outline, sample chapter(s), author biography and SAE).
Recent Title(s) *Tokens of Trust: an introduction to Christian belief*, Rowan Williams; *Happiness and Holiness: Thomas Traherne and his writings*, Denise Inge ed.; *Who or What is God?*, John Hick
Tips Hymns Ancient & Modern brings together distinct, but complementary religious publishing lists, including SCM Press, Canterbury Press and RMEP. It does not accept proposals for dissertations, fiction, poetry, drama, children's books, books of specialist local interest, or multi-authored collections of essays or symposium papers.

Ian Allan Publishing Ltd
Riverdene Business Park, Molesey Road, Hersham, Surrey, KT12 4RG
- 01932 266600
- 01932 266601
- peter.waller@ianallanpublishing.co.uk
- www.ianallanpublishing.com
Parent Company Ian Allan Group Ltd
Contact Publisher, Peter Waller
Established 1942
Imprint(s) Ian Allan Publishing
Lewis Masonic
Midland Publishing
Insider Info Publishes 150 titles per year. Receives approximately 300 queries and 50 manuscripts per year. Five per cent of books published are from first-time authors and 95 per cent are from unagented authors. Average lead time is six months, with simultaneous submissions accepted. Submissions accompanied by SAE will be returned. Aims to respond to queries, proposals, manuscripts and all other enquiries within seven days. Catalogue is free on request.
Non-Fiction Publishes General Non-Fiction and Illustrated titles on the following subjects: Aviation, Military/War, Sport and Leisure, Masonic, Hobbies, Transportation
Submission Guidelines Accepts query with SAE and artworks/images (send photocopies).
Tips Ian Allan Publishing's target readership is historians, enthusiasts, modellers and Freemasons. They do not publish books with a significant amount of personal reminiscence.

Ian Henry Publications Ltd
20 Park Drive, Romford, Essex, RM1 4LH
- 01708 749119
- 01708 736213
- info@ian-henry.com
- www.ian-henry.com
Established 1976
Insider Info Publishes roughly six titles per year. Authors paid by royalty. Catalogue available online.
Non-Fiction Publishes General Non-Fiction and Humour titles on the following subjects: Health and Well Being, History, Humour, Regional Interest (Essex), Sherlock Holmes, Transportation
Submission Guidelines Accepts query with SAE.
Fiction Publishes Sherlock Holmes pastiches.
Submission Guidelines Accepts query with SAE.
Recent Title(s) *The Past Revealed*, Ian Wilkes
Tips Ian Henry specialises in books on the history and topography of Essex, and is now recognised as the largest publisher of books on a single county in the country. A further specialism of Ian Henry Publications is books based on Sir Arthur Conan Doyle's *Sherlock Holmes*, both in pastiche form, novels, plays, television scripts, and factual titles on both Doyle himself, and his creations.

iBall Press
The Old Candlemakers, West Street, Lewes, East Sussex, BN7 2NZ
- 01273 487440
- 01273 487441
- hook@ivy-group.co.uk
- www.iballpress.co.uk
Parent Company The Ivy Group
Contact Publisher, Jason Hook
Insider Info Fees always paid for published work. Catalogue available online.

Non-Fiction Publishes Gift Books, Humour, Illustrated Books and Novelty titles on the following subjects:
Arts & Craft, Food & Drink, General Reference, Gift & Humour, Home & Garden, Mind, Body & Spirit, Pets, Popular Culture
* iBall is known as a quirky imprint of the Ivy Group that publishes novelty books on a huge range of subjects.
Submission Guidelines Accepts proposal package (including a table of contents and sample text and author biography).
Recent Title(s) *Towel Folding 101*, Deanna Campbell (Arts & Craft); *How To Live With a Unicorn*, Jane Moseley (Humour)
Tips Prospective authors should study the back catalogue to get a feel for the unusual, humorous subjects that iBall Press tends to publish.

I.B.Tauris & Co Ltd
6 Salem Road, London, W2 4BU
- 020 7243 1225
- 020 7243 1226
- mail@ibtauris.com
- www.ibtauris.com

Contact Chairman & Publisher, Iradj Bagherzade; Managing Director, Jonathan McDonnell; Publishing Director, Isabella Steer
Established 1984
Imprint(s) Tauris Parke Paperbacks
Tauris Academic Studies
Insider Info Publishes roughly 175 titles per year. Catalogue available free online, on request. Manuscript guidelines available online via website.
Non-Fiction Publishes Biography, General Non-Fiction and Scholarly titles on the following subjects:
Art & Architecture, Government/Politics, History, Religion, Travel, World Affairs, Film Studies, Middle Eastern Studies
Submission Guidelines Accepts query with SAE and proposal package (including outline, sample chapter(s), author biography and SAE).
Recent Title(s) *Defeat: Why They Lost Iraq*, Jonathan Steele
Tips I.B.Tauris is an independent publishing house that aims to publish books in the area of humanities and social sciences that appeal to academics, area specialists, students and researchers, as well as to general readers. They do not accept complete manuscripts, unless specifically requested. Unsolicited manuscripts will not be returned.

Icon Books Ltd
The Old Dairy, Brook Road, Thriplow, Cambridge, SG8 7RG
- 01763 208008
- 01763 208080
- info@iconbooks.co.uk
- www.iconbooks.co.uk

Contact Managing Director, Peter Pugh; Publishing Director, Simon Flynn; Editorial Director, Duncan Heath
Established 1992
Imprints Wizard Books
Non-Fiction Publishes Children's, General Non-Fiction, Reference, Scholarly, Technical and Young Adult titles on the following subjects:
Art/Architecture, Government/Politics, History, Philosophy, Psychology, Science
Submission Guidelines Query with SAE. Send submission proposals only, not full manuscripts.
Fiction Publishes Children's Fiction titles for ages seven and upwards.
* Children's books are largely published by Wizard Books (see separate entry).
Submission Guidelines Query with SAE.
Recent Title(s) *In the Red: The Diary of a Recovering Shopaholic*, Alexis Hall
Tips Icon Books is a small independent British publisher specialising in thought provoking books. Having previously tended to publish in series, such as the lists of *Postmodern Encounters*, *Ideas in Psychoanalysis* and *Revolutions in Science*, Icon is now publishing more and more individual titles.

ICSA Information & Training Ltd
16 Park Crescent, London, W1B 1AH
- 020 7612 7020
- 020 7612 7034
- publishing@icsa.co.uk
- www.icsainformationandtraining.co.uk

Contact Joint Managing Directors: Clare Grist Taylor and Susan Richards; Administration Assistant, Lindsay Maxey
Established 1981
Insider Info Catalogue and manuscript guidelines are available online.
Non-Fiction Publishes Reference and Technical titles on Business/Economics.
Submission Guidelines Accepts query with SAE, or via email and proposal package (including, outline, two sample chapters, your publishing history and author biography).
Submission details to: publishing@icsa.co.uk
Recent Title(s) *Boardroom Employment Law*, Julian Yew and Adam Grant; *The ICSA Company Secretary's Handbook, 7th edition*, Douglas Armour; *A Practical Guide to the UK Listing Regime*, Herbert Smith
Tips ICSA publishes a range of products in topic areas including corporate governance, company secretarial practice and law for business. ICSA is committed to providing high levels of support and advice to its authors. Potential authors are generally

invited to prepare a proposal only after initial discussions. Contact Clare Grist Taylor for further guidance.

Ignotus Press

BCM-Writer, London, WC1N 3XX
- 0845 230 2980
- info@ignotuspress.com
- www.ignotuspress.com

Contact Commissioning Editor, Suzanne Ruthven
Established 1994
Imprint(s) Moonraker (Fiction)
Past Tomes
Alphard (LifeStyle)
Insider Info Publishes 20 titles per year. Receives approximately 200 queries and 100 manuscripts per year. 50 per cent of books published are from first-time authors and 100 per cent are from unagented authors. Royalty (on retail price), is a maximum of £1 per book. Average lead time is 12 months. Simultaneous submissions accepted. Submissions accompanied by SAE will be returned. Aims to respond to queries within seven days, proposals two weeks and manuscripts within one month. Book catalogue available online.
Non-Fiction Publishes Autobiographies, How-To, Mind, Body and Spirit subjects, Humour, Pagan related humour, Self-Help, Metaphysical, and Reference titles with very specific guidelines, on the following subjects:
Alternative Lifestyles, Animals, Anthropology, Astrology/Psychic, Contemporary Culture, History, Nature, New Age, Nostalgia, Psychology, Religion, Spirituality
Submission Guidelines Accepts query with SAE. Will review artwork/photographs as part of the manuscript package.
Fiction Publishes Fiction on the following subjects:
Adventure, Gothic, Historical, Humour, Mystery, Occult, Regional, Spiritual
* All fiction proposals must be metaphysically based to appeal to the target audience.
Submission Guidelines Accepts query with SAE.
Recent Title(s) *Sea Witch: Practical Oceanic Magic*, Paul Holman (Withcraft); *The Google Tantra*, Alan Richardson (Fiction)
Tips Ignotus Press titles are aimed at those with an alternative lifestyle and an interest in genuine pagan/new age/metaphysical writing. Any prospective author should study the guidelines thoroughly before submission.

Ilex Press

The Old Candlemakers, West Street, Lewes, East Sussex, BN7 2NZ
- 01273 487440
- 01273 487441
- campbell@ilex-press.com
- www.ilex-press.com

Parent Company The Ivy Group
Contact Publisher, Alastair Campbell
Insider Info Always pays a fee for works published. Catalogue is free on request, or available via the website.
Non-Fiction Publishes Illustrated, Reference and Technical titles on the following subjects:
Art, Digital Art, Media Arts, Photography, Web Design.
Submission Guidelines Accepts queries with SAE or via email. Include a brief outline, table of contents and sample text and author biography. Submission details to: authors@ivy-group.co.uk
Recent Title(s) *Fantasy Art NOW!*, Martin McKenna; *The Photographer's Eye*, Michael Freeman
Tips Manuscripts should try to break down the technical and creative processes whilst avoiding jargon.

Immanion Press

8 Rowley Grove, Stafford, ST17 9BJ
- 01785 613299
- editorial@immanion-press.com
- www.immanion-press.com

Contact Managing Director and Commissioning Editor, Storm Constantine
Established 2003
Imprint(s) Megalithica
Insider Info Authors paid by royalty. Manuscript guidelines available online.
Non-Fiction Publishes Esoteric titles on the following subjects:
Magic, Paganism, Qabala, Tarot, Witchcraft
Submission Guidelines Accepts queries with SAE or via email. Include a brief outline, table of contents and sample text and author biography.
Fiction Publishes the following genres: Fantasy, Gothic, Horror, Science-Fiction, Slipstream.
Submission Guidelines Accepts query with SAE. Submit proposal package (including outline, synopsis, author biography and a sample of the first 30 pages).
Recent Title(s) *Angelglass*, David Barnett (Dark Fantasy); *Kink Magic: Sex Magic Beyond Vanilla*, Taylor Ellwood (Non-Fiction)
Tips Publishes mainly speculative fiction such as horror, fantasy and science-fiction. Also publishes esoteric non-fiction under the Megalithica imprint. Check the website for detailed submission guidelines before submitting by post or email.

I.M.P. Fiction Ltd

PO Box 69, Church Stretton, Shropshire, SY6 6WZ

- 01694 720049
- 01694 720049
- info@impbooks.com
- www.impbooks.com

Parent Company Independent Music Press
Contact Managing Director, Kaye Roach
Established 1998
Insider Info Authors paid by royalty. Catalogue and author guidelines available online.
Fiction Publishes Mainstream/ Contemporary Fiction.
* Does not publish science-fiction, horror, crime or novels about bands/music.
Submission Guidelines Accepts query with SAE. Submit proposal package (including outline, three sample chapters and author biography). Does not accept email submissions.
Recent Title(s) *The Peacock Manifesto*, Stuart David
Tips I.M.P. Fiction has a reputation for refreshing, innovative, cutting edge and original storytelling.

Imprint Academic

PO Box 200, Exeter, Devon, EX5 5YX

- 01392 851550
- 01392 851178
- keith@imprint.co.uk
- www.imprint-academic.com

Contact Anthony Freeman (Philosophy, Psychology, Religion); Keith Sutherland, (Politics, Cultural Studies)
Established 1980
Imprint(s) Imprint Arts
Societas
Insider Info Publishes roughly 30 titles per year. Receives approximately 200 queries and 200 manuscripts per year. Five per cent of books published are from first-time authors and 100 per cent of books are from unagented authors. Payment is via royalty (on wholesale price) with 0.35 (per £) minimum and 2.25 (per £) maximum. No advance offered. Average lead time is 12 months with simultaneous submissions accepted. Submissions accompanied by SAE will be returned. Aims to respond to queries within seven days, proposals within fourteen days and manuscripts within three months. Catalogue is free on request, and available online. Manuscript guidelines are available online, or via email.
Non-Fiction Publishes Booklets, General Non-Fiction and Scholarly titles on the following subjects: Anthropology, Government/Politics, Philosophy, Psychology, Religion, Social Sciences, Sociology, Spirituality, World Affairs

Submission Guidelines Accepts proposal package (including outline, one sample chapter, your publishing history, clips, author biography and SAE). Will not review artwork/images as part of the manuscript package.
Recent Title(s) *The Great Reading Disaster*, Mona McNee and Alice Coleman
Tips Titles are aimed at an educated and academic audience.

Independent Music Press

PO Box 69, Church Stretton, Shropshire, SY6 6WZ

- 01694 720049
- 01694 720049
- info@impbooks.com
- www.impbooks.com

Contact Managing Director, Martin Roach
Established 1992
Insider Info Authors paid by royalty. Catalogue and author guidelines available online.
Non-Fiction Publishes Biography, General Non-Fiction and Illustrated titles on the following subjects:
Alternative Lifestyles, Contemporary Culture, Music/ Dance
Submission Guidelines Accepts query with SAE. Submit proposal package (including outline, three sample chapters and author biography).
Recent Title(s) *Muse: Inside The Muscle Museum*, Ben Myers (Music Biography)
Tips Independent Music Press publishes high quality first biographies on popular bands such as Muse, Green Day, Beastie Boys, Foo Fighters, Prodigy and My Chemical Romance.

Infinite Ideas

36 St Giles, Oxford, OX1 3LD

- 01865 514888
- 01865 514777
- info@infideas.com
- www.infideas.com

Contact Co-Directors, David Grant and Richard Burton; Publishing Director, Katherine Hieronymus; Managing Editor, Rebecca Clare
Established 2004
Insider Info Publishes 40 titles per year. Always pays fees on published work. Catalogue and author guidelines are free on request, or available online.
Non-Fiction Publishes Self-Help titles on the following subjects:
Alternative Lifestyles, Art, Business, Careers, Entertainment/Games, Health, Hobbies, Language, Literature, Music/Dance, Sex, Sports
Submission Guidelines Accepts query with SAE or via email. Submit proposal package (including

outline and sample chapter(s)). Template available online.

Submission details to: richard@infideas.com

Tips Infinite Ideas are always open to new ideas, even if they don't appear to fit into the series. The editors state that if you think you've got a real best seller (strictly non-fiction) on your hands, get in touch. Study the author brief beforehand, available on the website.

Informa Law
4th Floor, Telephone House, 69-77 Paul Street, London, EC2A 4LQ
- 020 7017 5145
- victoria.ophield@informa.com
- www.informalaw.com

Parent Company Informa Plc
Contact Publishing Director, Victoria Ophield; Editorial: Laura Brown, Jessica Westwood, Gemma Avey, Timon Molloy, Leigh Stutter
Insider Info Catalogue available online.
Non-Fiction Publishes Books, Technical Titles and Online Services on Law.
Recent Title(s) *Arbitration Law Handbook*, Ben Horn and Roger Hopkins; *Time Charters, 6th Edition*, Terence Coghlin, Andrew Baker QC and Julian Kenny
Tips Informa Law publishes a wide range of books, loose leafs, newsletters, conferences, seminars, distance learning courses, law reporting services and strategic management reports for legal professionals. Publications are written and edited by independent experts, and read by senior legal professionals and executives in the legal fraternity worldwide. Parent company Informa Plc is the leading provider of specialist information to the global academic and scientific, professional communities.

Inner Sanctum Publications
75 Greenleaf Gardens, Polegate, BN26 6PQ
- 01323 484058
- mary@maryhession.com
- www.maryhession.com/innersanctumpublications.htm

Contact Managing Editor, Mary Hession
Established 1999
Insider Info Catalogue available online.
Poetry Publishes Spiritual Insights in the form of Inspirational Poetry.
Recent Title(s) *Beyond Words: Divine Inspirations Vol. 4*; *Journey Into Self: Divine Inspirations Vol. 5*

In Pinn
G/R 19 Netherton Avenue, Glasgow, G13 1BQ
- 0141 954 8007
- 0141 954 8007

- info@nwp.co.uk
- www.nwp.co.uk

Parent Company Neil Wilson Publishing Ltd
Insider Info Catalogue and manuscript guidelines are available online.
Non-Fiction Publishes General Non-Fiction titles on the following subjects:
Outdoor Pursuits, Travel, Wilderness Issues
Submission Guidelines Submit proposal package (including outline, synopsis, one sample chapter, author biography, CV and SAE). Will accept artworks/images.
Recent Title(s) *The Backpacker's Cookbook*, Dave Coustick (Outdoor Pursuits)
Tips In Pinn is the outdoor pursuits imprint of Neil Wilson Publishing. It publishes non-fiction titles about outdoor pursuits and travel in the Scotland area in particular.

Insight Guides
58 Borough High Street, London, SE1 1XF
- 020 7403 0284
- 020 7403 0290
- Online form.
- www.insightguides.com

Parent Company Apa Publications (The Langenscheidt Publishing Group)
Insider Info Catalogue is free on request or available online.
Non-Fiction Publishes Travel Guides, Maps and Atlases.
Recent Title(s) *Alaska Insight Guide*, Insight Guides (Travel/Nature)
Tips Insight Guides are not generally seeking aspiring travel writers. However, local updaters and researchers, to help maintain the topicality of titles, are always welcomed. As well as a detailed knowledge of a destination and its culture, an updater must know how to find information and fact check thoroughly and efficiently. Clear presentation of information is also important. Contact the Editorial Department with your CV and details of which destinations you know best, and include some short samples of your writing in the *Insight Guides* style.

Inspire
4 John Wesley Road, Werrington, Peterborough, PE4 6ZP
- 01733 325002
- 01733 384180
- customer.services@mph.org.uk
- www.mph.org.uk

Parent Company Methodist Publishing House
Contact Commissioning Editor, Natalie K. Watson

Insider Info Publishes 12 titles per year. Authors paid by royalty. Catalogue and author guidelines available online.
Non-Fiction Publishes General Non-Fiction titles on the following subjects:
Religion, Spirituality, Worship Resources
Submission Guidelines Accepts query with SAE. Submit proposal package (including, outline and two sample chapters).
Recent Title(s) *Walking the Story*, Jane Leach
Tips Before submitting your manuscript it is advisable to look at the Inspire back catalogue to ensure suitability. Inspire does not publish fiction or children's books.

Institute of Public Administration
Vergemount Hall, Clonskeagh, Dublin 4, Republic of Ireland
- 00353 1 240 3600
- 00353 1 269 8644
- information@ipa.ie
- www.ipa.ie
Contact Publisher, Declan McDonagh
Established 1957
Insider Info Catalogue available online.
Non-Fiction Publishes Reference, Scholarly and Technical titles on the following subjects:
Administrative History, Business, Economics, Government/Politics, Law, Public Management, Social Sciences
Recent Title(s) *Advisers or Advocates? The Impact of State Agencies on Social Policy*, Orlaigh Quinn
Tips The Institute of Public Administration is Ireland's only consultancy service focused exclusively on public sector development. It delivers its service through education and training, research and publishing, and direct consultancy. All publications relate directly to public administration.

Interpet Publishing
Interpet House, Vincent Lane, Dorking, Surrey, RH4 3YX
- customercare@interpet.co.uk
- www.interpet.co.uk
Established 1998
Non-Fiction Publishes General Non-Fiction, How-To and Reference titles on the following subjects:
Animals, Pet Care
Tips Interpet Publishing are market leaders in aquatic and pet publishing. Their philosophy is to provide both new and experienced pet keepers with the advice and information they need to care for their pets responsibly.

Inter-Varsity Press
Norton Street, Nottingham, NG7 3HR
- 0115 978 1054
- 0115 942 2694
- sales@ivpbooks.com
- www.ivpbooks.com
Contact Chief Executive, Brian Wilson; Commissioning Editor, Sandra Byatt; Senior Project Editor, Eleanor Trotter
Established 1930s
Imprint(s) IVP
Apollos
Crossway
Insider Info Publishes 50 titles per year. Authors paid by royalty. Aims to respond to proposals and manuscripts within three months. Catalogue and author guidelines are available online.
Non-Fiction Publishes General Non-Fiction and Scholarly titles on Religion and Spirituality.
Submission Guidelines Accepts query with SAE or via email. Submit proposal package (including, outline, two sample chapters and author biography). Submission details to: bookproposals@ivpbooks.com
Recent Title(s) *Planetwise*, Dave Bookless (Environment/Religion)
Tips Inter-Varsity Press (IVP) is the publishing arm of UCCF (Universities & Colleges Christian Fellowship). IVP publishes books that are true to the Bible and that communicate the gospel, develop discipleship and strengthen the church for its mission in the world. They welcome suggestions for new books and are happy to evaluate any proposals that are submitted. It is better to draft an overall plan and then talk to a commissioning editor at IVP, rather than writing the whole book, and then approaching one of the editors.

Irish Academic Press Ltd
44 Northumberland Road, Dublin 4, Republic of Ireland
- 020 8952 9526
- 020 8952 9242
- info@iap.ie
- www.irishacademicireland.com
Contact Editor, Lisa Hyde
Established 1974
Imprint Irish University Press
Insider Info Publishes 15 titles per year. Payment via royalty. Catalogue available online. Manuscript guidelines are free on request.
Non-Fiction Publishes Irish Interest Scholarly titles on the following subjects:
Art/Architecture, Contemporary Culture, History, Language, Literature, Military/War, Heritage, Women's Studies

Submission Guidelines Accepts query with SAE, or via email. Submit proposal package (including outline and sample chapter(s)).
Submission details to: lisa.hyde@vmbooks.com
Recent Title(s) *Founded on Fear*, Peter Tyrrell
Tips Irish Academic Press is a long established Dublin based publisher, producing high quality books of Irish interest. They welcome manuscript proposals and ideas in all publishing subject areas. These can be directed to the Editor, Lisa Hyde.

Irish Management Institue (IMI)
Sandyford Road, Dublin 16, Republic of Ireland
- 00353 1 207 8400
- 00353 1 295 5150
- reception@imi.ie
- www.imi.ie

Contact Dr Tom McCarthy
Non-Fiction Publishes General Non-Fiction, Reference and Technical titles on Business and Economics.
Tips Books are research led and business focused. Access to information, new thinking and best practice is a critical resource for organisations competing in a challenging business environment – IMI books reflect this.

Iron Press
5 Marden Terrace, Cullercoats, North Shields, Northumberland, NE30 4PD
- 0191 253 1901
- ironpress@blueyonder.co.uk
- www.ironpress.co.uk

Contact Peter Mortimer
Established 1973
Insider Info Submissions accompanied by SAE will be returned. Contact for catalogue.
Fiction Publishes Plays, Novels and Short Stories.
* Iron Press aims to publish fiction and poetry it likes, regardless of market potential.
Submission Guidelines Query with Peter Mortimer before submission.
Poetry Publishes Poetry titles.
Submission Guidelines Query with Peter Mortimer before submission.
Recent Title(s) *The Sara Poems*, Roy Cameron (Poetry Collection)
Tips Iron Press' policy is to seek new writers from the North of England, the rest of the country, and occasionally from overseas. It spurns literary competitions, prizes and mass market fiction.

Isis Publishing Ltd
7 Centremead, Osney Mead, Oxford, OX2 0ES
- 01865 250333
- 01865 790358
- sales@isis-publishing.co.uk
- www.isis-publishing.co.uk

Insider Info Authors paid by royalty. Catalogue available online.
Non-Fiction Publishes Audio books.
Fiction Publishes Audio books.
Recent Title(s) *The Dead Hour*, Denise Mina (Audio book)
Tips Isis is the world's leading publisher of unabridged audio books. Also publishes large print reprints, both fiction and non-fiction. Isis does not accept any submissions, as they do not undertake original titles.

The Islamic Foundation
Markfield Conference Centre, Ratby Lane, Markfield, Leicestershire, LE67 9SY
- 01530 244944
- 01530 244946
- i.foundation@islamic-foundation.org.uk
- www.islamic-foundation.org.uk

Insider Info Catalogue available online.
Non-Fiction Publishes Audio cassettes, Children's Non-Fiction, General Non-Fiction, Multimedia, Reference, Scholarly, Posters, Cards and Maps on Islam.
Tips The Islamic Foundation was established as a centre for education, training, research and publication. The foundation publishes titles on subjects relating to Islam, including history, economics, contemporary politics, women and family.

The Ivy Group
The Old Candlemakers, West Street, Lewes, East Sussex, BN7 2NZ
- 01273 487440
- 01273 487441
- surname@ivy-group.co.uk
- www.ivy-group.co.uk

Contact Group Managing Director, Stephen Paul; Group Creative Director, Peter Bridgewater
Imprint(s) iball Press
Ivy Press
Ixos Press
Ilex Press
Bridgewater Books
Insider Info Payment is via fees.
Non-Fiction Publishes General Non-Fiction, Illustrated and Reference titles on the following subjects:
Popular Culture, Art & Design, Digital Design, Photography, General Reference, Health & Parenting, Mind, Body & Spirit, Humour, Novelty

Submission Guidelines Accepts proposal package (including outline, table of contents, sample text, author biography).

Recent Title(s) *Breakthough Thinking*, Nick Souter (Ilex Press); *Foods for Mind and Body*, Michael van Straten (Ixos Press)

Tips The Ivy Group will consider proposals from both published and unpublished writers. They also occasionally have opportunities for freelance writers to work on specific projects. Send a biography, a list of published titles, and explain areas of interest and expertise.

Ivy Press
The Old Candlemakers, West Street, Lewes, East Sussex, BN7 2NZ
- 01273 487440
- 01273 487441
- hook@ivy-group.co.uk
- www.ivypress.co.uk

Parent Company The Ivy Group
Contact Publisher, Jason Hook
Insider Info Always pays fees for published work. Catalogue and author guidelines are available online.
Non-Fiction Publishes General Non-Fiction and Illustrated titles on the following subjects:
Arts & Crafts, Childcare/Parenting, Contemporary Culture, Cooking, Food & Drink, Health, House & Home, Lifestyle, Petcare
Submission Guidelines Accepts query with SAE or via email. Submit proposal package (including, outline, one sample chapter, your publishing history and an author biography).
Submission details to: authors@ivy-group.co.uk
Recent Title(s) *Artist's Materials*, Lorraine Harrison (Arts & Craft); *Get Fit With Your Dog*, Karen Sullivan (Health/Petcare)
Tips Ivy Press is a lifestyle and general reference imprint of the Ivy Group. They will consider any writer, published or unpublished. Ivy Press generally focuses on illustrated books for an international market, therefore submissions should have an international appeal.

Ixos Press
The Old Candlemakers, West Street, Lewes, East Sussex, BN7 2NZ
- 01273 403128
- 01273 487441
- hook@ixospress.com
- www.ixospress.com

Parent Company The Ivy Group
Contact Publisher, Jason Hook
Insider Info Always pays fees for published work. Catalogue available online.

Non-Fiction Publishes General Non-Fiction, How-To, Illustrated and Self-Help titles on the following subjects:
Counselling, Health, Holistic Medicine, New Age, Religion, Spirituality, Mind, Body & Spirit
Submission Guidelines Accepts query with SAE or via email. Submit proposal package (including outline, author biography, table of contents and some sample text).
Submission details to: authors@ivy-group.co.uk
Recent Titles *The Directory of Complementary Therapies*, C. Norman Shealy (Holistic Medicine)
Tips Works with both published and unpublished authors, and will read all proposals relating to the relevant subject areas.

J.A. Allen
Clerkenwell House, 45–47 Clerkenwell Green, London, EC1R 0HT
- 020 7251 2661
- 020 7490 4958
- allen@halebooks.com
- www.halebooks.com

Parent Company Robert Hale Ltd
Contact Publisher, Lesley Gowers
Established 1926
Insider Info Publishes 20 titles per year. Authors paid by royalty. Catalogue and author guidelines are available free on request, via email or online.
Non-Fiction Publishes General Non-Fiction, Reference and Technical titles on the following subjects:
Equine and Equestrian
Submission Guidelines Accepts query with SAE. Submit proposal package (including outline, and three sample chapters). No email submissions.
Tips Caters for beginners and experts in the equine world, publishing both academic and basic texts.

Jacqui Small
7 Greenland Street, London, NW1 0ND
- 020 7284 7160
- 020 7845 4902
- sales@jacquismallpub.com
- www.aurumpress.co.uk

Parent Company Aurum Press
Contact Managing Director, Bill McCreadie
Insider Info Catalogue and manuscript guidelines are free on request, or available online or by email.
Non-Fiction Publishes Coffee Table and Illustrated titles on the following subjects:
Cookery, Food and Drink, Crafts, Gardening, House and Home, Lifestyle
Submission Guidelines Email a brief proposal to editorial@aurumpress.co.uk.

Recent Title(s) *Cool Pools and Hot Tubs*, Vinny Lee (Interior Design)

Tips Jacqui Small publishes a range of upmarket illustrated lifestyle books. The books are written by the best authors in their field, therefore prospective authors should highlight any qualifications or achievements in their specialist area when proposing a book.

James Clarke & Co

PO Box 60, Cambridge, CB1 2NT

☎ 01223 350865

✆ 01223 366951

✉ publishing@jamesclarke.co.uk

🌐 www.jamesclarke.co.uk

Imprints The Lutterworth Press
Acorn Editions

Established 1859

Insider Info Catalogue available online and by request. Submission guidelines available online.

Non-Fiction Publishes Reference and Scholarly titles on the following subjects:
History & Biography, Philosophy & Ethics, Religion & Theology, Literary Criticism

Submission Guidelines Accepts query with SAE/proposal package (including outline, two sample chapters and contents list). No email submissions but email queries welcomed.

Recent Title(s) *Proof of the External World*, Steven M. Duncan; *Reading Bonhoefer*, Geffrey Kelly

Tips James Clarke only considers scholarly books on the humanities, focusing particularly on theology, history, or works of reference. They generally expect to take on books that offer some original scholarship, or alternatively present a well argued and authoritative case for a re-interpretation.

James Currey Publishers

73 Botley Road, Oxford, OX2 0BS

☎ 01865 244111

✆ 01865 246454

✉ editorial@jamescurrey.co.uk

🌐 www.jamescurrey.co.uk

Contact Chairman, James Currey; Managing Director and Editorial Director, Douglas H. Johnson; Editorial Manager, Lynn Taylor

Established 1985

Insider Info Authors paid by royalty. Catalogue and author guidelines available online.

Non-Fiction Publishes Scholarly titles on the following subjects:
Anthropology/Archaeology, Business, Economics, Government/Politics, History, Literary Criticism, Sociology.
* All books concern Africa and the Third World.

Submission Guidelines Accepts query with SAE or via email. Submit proposal package (including outline, author biography and SAE).
Submission details to: douglas.johnson@jamescurrey.co.uk

Recent Title(s) *The Resolution of African Conflicts*, Alfred Nhema and Paul Tiyambe Zeleza

Tips James Currey Publishers are leading academic publishers on Africa, specialising in archaeology, history, politics, development studies, economics, anthropology, gender studies, literary criticism, theatre and film studies. Do not send email attachments unless requested by the publisher.

Jane Nissen Books

Swan House, Chiswick Mall, London, W4 2PS

☎ 020 8994 8203

✆ 020 8742 8198

✉ jane@nissen.demon.co.uk

🌐 www.janenissenbooks.co.uk

Contact Jane Nissen

Insider Info Publishes approximately four titles per year. Catalogue available online.

Non-Fiction Publishes Out-of-print Children's titles.

Fiction Publishes Out-of-print Children's Fiction and Poetry titles.

Recent Title(s) *Johnny's Bad Day*, Edward Ardizzone; *Christmas with the Savages*, Mary Clive

Tips Publishes reprints of out-of-print children's books only, no new titles. Suggestions for 'forgotten classics' are welcome.

Jane's Information Group

Sentinel House, 163 Brighton Road, Coulsdon, Surrey, CR5 2YH

☎ 020 8700 3700

✆ 020 8763 1006

✉ customerservices.uk@janes.com

🌐 www.janes.com

Contact Managing Director, Alfred Rolington

Established 1898

Insider Info Authors paid by royalty. Catalogue available online.

Non-Fiction Publishes General Non-Fiction, Reference and Technical titles on Military/War.

Submission Guidelines Accepts query with SAE. Submit proposal package (including outline and sample chapter(s)).

Tips Jane's Information Group is a world leading provider of intelligence and analysis on national and international defence, security and risk developments.

Jarrold Publishing

4 Station Court, Station Lane, Hethersett, Norwich, NR9 3AX

☎ 01603 819420
🖷 01603 814325
✉ malcolm.crampton@jarrold-publishing.co.uk
🌐 www.jarrold-publishing.co.uk
Established 1770
Imprint(s) Pitkin
Unichrome
Insider Info Publishes 30 titles per year. Catalogue available online.
Non-Fiction Publishes Guidebooks and Illustrated titles on the following subjects:
History, Hobbies, Tourism, Travel, Walking
Submission Guidelines Accepts query with SAE.
Tips Jarrold Publishing has around 250 books currently in print, including walking and travel guides, history, biography and pictorial guides. Contact the editorial department before sending any submissions.

Jessica Kingsley Publishers Ltd
116 Pentonville Road, London, N1 9JB
☎ 020 7833 2307
🖷 020 7837 2917
✉ post@jkp.com
🌐 www.jkp.com
Contact Managing Director and Publisher, Jessica Kingsley; Senior Acquisitions Editor, Stephen Jones
Established 1987
Insider Info Publishes 100 titles per year. Receives approximately 500 queries and 30 manuscripts per year. 20 per cent of books published are from first-time authors and 99 per cent are from unagented authors. Authors are paid by royalty (on wholesale price), with an advance offered. Average lead time is five months, with simultaneous submissions not accepted. Aims to respond to proposals in one month and manuscripts within three months. Catalogue and author guidelines available online.
Non-Fiction Publishes General Non-Fiction, Reference, Scholarly and Technical titles on the following subjects:
Counselling/Careers, Disability, Health, Medicine, Mental Illness, Psychology
Submission Guidelines Accepts query with SAE. Submit proposal package (including outline, author biography, your CV/resume, and a completed copy of the 'New Book Proposals' form, available on the website).
Recent Title(s) *All Cats Have Asperger Syndrome*, Kathy Hoopmann
Tips Jessica Kingsley publishes books for professional and general readers on a range of subjects. It is well known for its long established lists on autism and mental illnesses. Ideas for new books in these areas are welcome.

John Blake Publishing Ltd
3 Bramber Court, 2 Bramber Road, London, W14 9PB
☎ 020 7381 0666
🖷 020 7381 6868
✉ words@blake.co.uk
🌐 www.jonblakepublishing.co.uk
Contact Managing Director, John Blake; Editor-in-Chief, Michelle Signore
Established 1991
Insider Info Publishes 100 titles per year. Authors paid by royalty. Aims to respond to proposals and manuscripts within three months. Catalogue and author guidelines are free on request, or available online.
Non-Fiction Publishes Autobiography, Biography and General Non-Fiction titles on the following subjects:
Celebrity Memoirs, Contemporary Culture, Cooking, Food & Drink, Government/Politics, Health, Spirituality
Submission Guidelines Accepts query with SAE. Submit proposal package (including outline, two sample chapters, your publishing history, author biography and SAE).
Recent Title(s) *Just Biggins*, Christopher Biggins (Biography)
Tips John Blake Publishing specialises in high profile, mass market non-fiction. The bulk of its output centres on the biography and true crime lists, and celebrity memoirs. If you would like to submit your work for consideration, check the submission guidelines on the website. The general commissioning criterion is: 'Could it be a bestseller?'.

John Donald Publishers Ltd
West Newington House, 10 Newington Road, Edinburgh, EH9 1QS
☎ 0131 668 4371
🖷 0131 668 4466
✉ info@birlinn.co.uk
🌐 www.john-donald.birlinn.co.uk
Contact Managing Director, Hugh Andrew
Established 1999
Insider Info Publishes 20 titles per year. Authors paid by royalty. Catalogue and author guidelines available online.
Non-Fiction Publishes General Non-Fiction, Reference and Scholarly titles on the following areas:
Archaeology, Architecture, Art, History, Scottish Interest, Social Sciences, Travel
Submission Guidelines No unsolicited submissions.
Recent Title(s) *The Wallace Book*, Edward J. Cowan (ed.) (History)

Tips John Donald specialises in academic books on Scottish subjects, and the local history of East coast Scotland. They do not accept any unsolicited submissions.

John Libbey Publishing
PO Box 276, Eastleigh, SO50 5YS
- 023 8065 0208
- 023 8065 0259
- libbeyj@asianet.co.th
- www.johnlibbey.com

Contact Publisher, John Libbey
Established 1979
Imprint(s) John Libbey Eurotext Ltd (France)
Insider Info Catalogue is free on request, or available online.
Non-Fiction Publishes General Non-fiction, Reference and Scholarly titles on the following subjects:
Animation, Art/Architecture, Cinema, Media, Medicine.
Submission Guidelines Accepts query with SAE.
Recent Title(s) *Hyperanimation: Digital Images and Virtual Worlds*, Robert Russett
Tips John Libbey publishes a range of books and journals aimed at researchers, academics, students and professionals in the fields of cinema, animation and media. They also publish the renowned series of *Media* books, formerly under the imprint of the University of Luton Press.

John Murray
338 Euston Road, London, NW1 3BH
- 020 7873 6000
- 020 7873 6024
- www.hodderheadline.co.uk/johnmurray.htm

Parent Company Hachette UK
Contact CEO, Martin Neild; Manging Director, Roland Philipps
Established 1768
Insider Info Catalogue available online.
Non-Fiction Publishes Biography and General Non-Fiction titles on the following subjects:
History, Memoirs, Travel and Current Affairs
Submission Guidelines Agented submissions only.
Fiction Publishes Literary Fiction.
Submission Guidelines Agented submissions only.
Tips A leading literary publisher. John Murray now reports directly to Hachette UK, following the closure of Hodder Headline.

Jolly Learning Ltd
Tailours House, High Road, Chigwell, Essex, IG7 6DL
- 020 8501 0405
- 020 8500 1696
- info@jollylearning.co.uk
- www.jollylearning.co.uk

Established 1987
Imprints Jolly Phonique
Jolly Phonics
Jolly Readers
Jolly Grammar
Insider Info Publishes approximately 25 titles per year. Catalogue available online.
Non-Fiction Publishes Children's Educational Resources on the following subjects:
Grammar, Langauge, Literacy, Reading
Submission Guidelines Will accept ideas for products that are add-ons to existing ranges. No unsolicited submissions or brand new ideas.
Tips Jolly Learning products are based around a teaching method called phonics, developed by the two primary authors Sue Lloyd and Sara Wernham, in which children are taught to hear and identify the sounds in words at the same time as they are being taught the letter sounds. As well as books, Jolly Learning produces activity packs, gifts and other learning materials, all highly illustrated. A more detailed explanation of the principles behind Jolly Learning is available on the website.

Jonathan Cape
Random House, 20 Vauxhall Bridge Road, London, SW1V 2SA
- 020 7840 8576
- 020 7233 6117
- capeeditorial@randomhouse.co.uk
- www.randomhouse.co.uk

Parent Company The Random House Group Ltd
Contact Publishing Director, Dan Franklin
Established 1921
Insider Info Catalogue available online.
Non-Fiction Publishes titles on the following subjects:
Government/Politics, History, Memoirs, Military/War, Photography, Travel, Current Affairs
Submission Guidelines No unagented submissions.
Fiction Publishes Literary, Picture Books and Children's Fiction.
Submission Guidelines No unagented submissions.
Poetry Publishes Poetry titles.
* Only publishes around four to six titles per year.
Recent Title(s) *The Bard*, Robert Crawford (Biography); *The Rescue Man*, Anthony Quinn (Literary Fiction)
Tips Jonathan Cape publishes poetry and poetry-related titles, but usually no more than six per year.

Jonathan Cape Children's Books
61–63 Uxbridge Road, London, W5 5SA

☎ 020 7840 8648

☎ 020 7233 6058

✉ childrenseditorial@randomhouse.co.uk

🌐 www.kidsatrandomhouse.co.uk

Parent Company Random House Children's Books

Insider Info Catalogue is available online.

Non-fiction Publishes Children's and Young Adult titles.

Submission Guidelines No unagented submissions.

Fiction Publishes Children's and Young Adult novels.

Submission Guidelines No unagented submissions.

Recent Title(s) *Box of Tricks*, Katie Cleminson (Picture Book); Grimble at Christmas, Clement Freud (Children's Fiction)

Jordan Publishing Ltd
21 St Thomas Street, Bristol, BS1 6JS

☎ 0117 923 0600

☎ 0117 925 0486

✉ achim.bosse@jordanpublishing.co.uk

🌐 www.jordanpublishing.co.uk

Contact Managing Director, Caroline Vandridge-Ames

Insider Info Catalogue available online.

Non-Fiction Publishes Reference and Technical titles on the subject of Law.

Recent Title(s) *Jordans Company Secretarial Precedents*, Cecile Gillard, Peter Van Duzer and HGM Leighton

Josef Weinberger Plays Ltd
12–14 Mortimer Street, London, W1T 3JJ

☎ 020 7580 2827

☎ 020 7436 9616

✉ general.info@jwmail.co.uk

🌐 www.josef-weinberger.com

Contact Editor, Christopher Moss

Established 1885

Insider Info Publishes 12 titles per year. Catalogue available online.

Fiction Publishes Plays.

Tips Josef Weinberger publishes musical and dramatic theatre from the West End, Broadway and Concert Hall. They will only consider acquiring rights to a new play in the event that a large scale professional production is planned or underway. They then publish the script to coincide with the opening performance, and handle subsidiary rights on future productions.

JR Books
10 Greenland Street, London, NW1 0ND

☎ 020 7284 7194

☎ 020 7485 4902

✉ jeremyr@jrbooks.com

🌐 www.jrbooks.com

Parent Company Quarto Group Inc.

Contact Publisher, Jeremy Robson; Publicity Director, Catherine Bailey

Established 2007

Insider Info Catalogue is available online.

Non-Fiction Publishes General Non-Fiction on the following subjects:
Biography, History, Humour, Music, Politics, Self-Help, Sport, Wildlife

Recent Title(s) *Billy Joel: THe Biography*, Mark Bego (Biography); *Whale Odyssey*, Michael Bright (Wildlife)

Tips JR Books is a new non-fiction imprint, backed by Quarto Publishing Group.

Karnak House
157 Dudden Hill Lane, London, NW10 1AU

✉ karnakhouse@aol.com

🌐 www.karnakhouse.co.uk

Contact Director, Amon Saba Saakana; Art Director, Seheri Sujai

Established 1979

Imprint(s) The Intef Institute

Insider Info Publishes seven titles per year. Receives approximately 30 queries and 20 manuscripts per year. 15 per cent of books published are from first-time authors, 100 per cent of books published are from unagented authors. Payment is via royalty (on wholesale price), with 0.08 (per £) minimum. Advance offered is from £200 to £500. Average lead time is more than 18 months, with simultaneous submissions accepted. Submissions accompanied by SAE will be returned. Aims to respond to queries within seven days, proposals within 14 days and manuscripts within four months. Catalogue is available online. Manuscript guidelines are available by email.

Non-Fiction Publishes General Non-Fiction titles on the following subjects:
Academic, Anthropology, Archaeology, Architecture, Art, Education, Egyptology, Health, History, Language, Literature, Literary Criticism, Music/Dance, Philosophy, Religion, Science, Sociology, Women's Issues/Studies

* Specialises in African and Caribbean Studies. All submissions must have an African/Caribbean connection.

Submission Guidelines Accepts query with SAE/proposal package (including outline, contents page, two sample chapters and SAE).

Fiction Publishes African/Caribbean and Children's Fiction titles.
Submission Guidelines Accepts query with SAE/ proposal package (including outline, contents page, two sample chapters and SAE).
Poetry Publishes African/Caribbean Poetry titles.

The Kates Hill Press
126 Watsons Green Road, Kates Hill, Dudley, West Midlands, DY2 7LG
- 01384 255973
- 01384 255973
- kateshillpress@blueyonder.co.uk
- www.kateshillpress.pwp.blueyonder.co.uk
Contact Greg Stokes
Established 1992
Insider Info Payment is via royalties.
Non-Fiction Publishes Social Histories of the West Midlands.
Submission Guidelines Accepts proposal package (including outline and sample chapter(s)).
Fiction Publishes Regional and Short Story Collections on a West Midlands theme, or by a West Midlands writer.
Submission Guidelines Accepts proposal package (including sample chapter(s)).
Poetry Publishes Poetry titles with a West Midlands connection.
Submission Guidelines Submit sample poems.
Recent Title(s) *The Book Cellar*, Barry Morris (Short Story Collection)
Tips Any work submitted should also be available in electronic format. Responses to proposals may take a while as the press is a part time venture.

Kenilworth Press
Wykey House, Wykey, Shrewsbury, Shropshire, SY4 1JA
- 01939 261616
- 01939 261606
- admin@quillerbooks.com
- www.kenilworthpress.co.uk
Parent Company Quiller Publishing Ltd
Contact Editorial, John Beaton
Established 1989
Insider Info Publishes around ten titles per year. Ten per cent of books published are from first-time authors and 95 percent of books published are from unagented authors. Approximately five per cent of books are author subsidy published. Payment is via royalty (on wholesale price or royalty on retail price). Average time between acceptance of book length manuscripts and publication is two months. Simultaneous submissions accepted, and submissions accompanied by SAE will be returned. Catalogue is free on request online and via email.

Non-Fiction Publishes General Non-Fiction and Illustrated titles on the following subjects: Dressage, Driving & Polo, Equestrian, Eventing, Horse Care (Health, Management & Alternative Care), Hunting, Lifestyle, Show Jumping, Young Riders
Submission Guidelines Accepts query with SAE/ proposal package (including, outline, sample chapter(s), publishing history, author biography) and artworks/images (send photocopies or digital files as jpegs).
Recent Title(s) *Correct Movement in Horses*, Klaus Schoneich and Gabriele Rachen-Schoneich
Tips Kenilworth will accept proposals, but only for horse or pony related material.

Kenneth Mason Publications Ltd
The Book Barn, Westbourne, Hampshire, PO10 8RS
- 01243 377977
- 01243 379136
- info@researchdisclosure.com
- www.researchdisclosure.com
Contact Chairman, Kenneth Mason; Managing Director, Piers Mason
Established 1958
Imprint(s) Boatswain Press
Research Disclosure
Insider Info Publishes 15 titles per year. Payment is via royalties. Catalogue available online.
Non-Fiction Publishes General Non-Fiction and Scholarly titles on the following subjects: Cooking, Food and Drink, Health, Fitness and Nutrition, Nautical
Submission Guidelines Accepts query with SAE/ proposal package (including outline).
Tips Kenneth Mason's main focus, rather than book publishing, is on the research disclosure arm of the business. Every month they publish details of many inventions, both in paper format in the *RD Journal* and in their RD electronic database. These details are then distributed to every major patent office, and many libraries worldwide. Those who would like details of their inventions published, should provide the disclosure text, along with any diagrams and illustrations, in either paper copy, or as an electronic file.

Kettillonia
Sidlaw House, South Street, Newtyle, Angus, PH12 8UQ
- 01828 650615
- james@kettillonia.co.uk
- www.kettillonia.co.uk
Contact James Robertson
Established 1999
Fiction Publishes Short Story Collections.

Poetry Publish a very diverse range of Prose and Poetry.

Tips Kettillonia's aim is to put 'original, adventurous, neglected and rare writing into print', mainly in pamphlet form. Their pamphlets are £3 each and vary tremendously in style and content.

Kevin Mayhew Publishers
Buxhall, Stowmarket, Suffolk, IP14 3BW
- 01449 737978
- 01449 737834
- sales@kevinmayhewltd.com
- www.kevinmayhewltd.com

Contact Chairman/Commissioning Editor, Kevin Mayhew
Established 1976
Imprint(s) Palmtree Press
Insider Info Payment is via royalties. Catalogue free on request, online. Manuscript guidelines available online.
Non-Fiction Publishes Audio cassettes, Children's, General Non-Fiction and Multimedia titles on the following subjects:
Music/Dance (Religious Music), Hymns, Religion
Submission Guidelines Accepts query with SAE/proposal package (including outline, one sample chapter, and SAE).
Recent Title(s) *Red Hot Recorder Songs*, Sarah Watts (Music)
Tips Kevin Mayhew products are targeted in equal measure to members of all Christian denominations. Email submissions are not accepted, and a hard copy of all manuscripts is required, together with a one page synopsis.

Kingfisher Publications Plc
New Penderel House, 283–288 High Holborn, London, WC1V 7HZ
- 020 7903 9999
- 020 7903 4979
- www.panmacmillan.com/imprints/kingfisher

Parent Company Pan Macmillan
Established 1973
Insider Info Catalogue available online or by email.
Non-Fiction Publishes Children's, Encyclopedias, Activity Books and Reference titles on the following subjects:
History, Language, Literature, Nature, Religion, Science, Maths, Technology
Fiction Publishes Humour, Children's Fiction, Picture Books, Pre-school, Toddler and Gift titles.
Poetry Publishes Children's Poetry.
Recent Title(s) *Darkness Slipped In*, Ella Burfoot (Picture Book); *The Pet Sitter: Tiger Taming*, Julie Sykes (Children's Fiction)

Tips Kingfisher is an award-winning publisher of non-fiction and fiction, particularly educational reference titles and picture books, for children of all ages. Does not accept unsolicited material.

Kinglake Publishing
Ashgrove House, Suite G8, Elland, Calderdale, HX5 9JB
- info@kinglakepublishing.co.uk
- www.kinglakepublishing.co.uk

Contact Managing Editor, Harry Taylor; Administrative Assistant, Jennifer Jackson
Established 2005
Imprint(s) Kinglake Non-Fiction
Kinglake Religion
Kinglake Fiction
Insider Info Publishes roughly 30 titles per year. Receives approximately 250 queries and 80 manuscripts per year. 30 per cent of books published are from first-time authors. Accepts work from unagented authors. Some books published are author subsidy published, based on an estimation of market reach. Payment is via annual royalty (on retail price), with 0.08 (per £) minimum and 0.12 (per £) maximum. Does not offer an advance. Catalogue is available with SAE, or by email.
Non-Fiction Publishes General Non-Fiction and Life History titles on the following subjects:
Cultural Studies, Education, History, Humour, New Age, Philosophy, Politics, Psychology, Religion, Science, Sociology, Travel.
Submission Guidelines Accepts initial queries by email only (including outline and short letter). Phone calls not welcome in the initial stages.
Fiction Publishes Novels in all genres. First novels welcome for consideration. No erotica unless there is a good narrative drive. Teen fiction welcome.
Submission Guidelines Accepts initial queries by email only (including outline and short letter). Phone calls not welcome in the initial stages.
Tips Kinglake publishes books for a popular/general readership, or a carefully worked out niche market.

Kingscourt/McGraw-Hill
Shoppenhangers Road, Maidenhead, Berkshire, SL6 2QL
- 0800 317457
- 0870 241 6398
- enquiries@kingscourt.co.uk
- www.mcgraw-hill.co.uk/kingscourt

Established 1988
Insider Info Catalogue and sales presentation available online.
Non-Fiction Publishes Children's Educational and Textbook titles for Key Stages 1–3 on the following subjects:

Literacy, Numeracy, Software/Interactive, Special Needs and PSHE

Tips Titles are aimed at schools in both the UK and Ireland and support The National Literacy and Numeracy Strategies, The Scottish Guidelines 5–14, The Northern Ireland Curriculum, and Curriculum 2000 in Wales.

The King's England Press
Cambertown House, Commercial Road, Goldthorpe, Rotherham, S63 9BL
- 01484 663790
- 01484 663790
- sales@kingsengland.com
- www.kingsengland.com

Established 1989

Insider Info Submissions accompanied by SAE will be returned. Catalogue and manuscript guidelines available online.

Non-Fiction Publishes Archaeology, History, Regional and Folklore titles.

Poetry Publishes Children's Poetry titles.

* Publishes the *Potty Poetry* series only (A5, 64-page books, illustrated by black and white line drawings for children).

Recent Title(s) *Don't Put Dave in the Microwave*, Chris White (Humour)

Kittiwake
3 Glantwymyn Village Workshops, Glantwymyn, Machynlleth, Montgomereyshire, SY20 8LY
- 01650 511314
- 01650 511314
- perrographics@btconnect.com
- www.kittiwake-books.com

Contact Director, David Perrott

Established 1984

Insider Info Publishes roughly six titles per year. Receives approximately two queries and six manuscripts per year. 40 per cent of books published are from first-time authors, 100 per cent of books published are from unagented authors. Payment is via royalty (on retail price), with 0.05 (per £) minimum and 0.10 (per £) maximum. Average lead time is six months, with simultaneous submissions not accepted. Submissions accompanied by SAE will be returned. Aims to respond to queries, proposals and all other enquiries within five days, and to manuscripts within four weeks. Catalogue is available with SAE, or by email. Manuscripts guidelines are available with SAE.

Non-Fiction Publishes General Non-Fiction titles on the following subjects:
Regional (Welsh), Welsh Walking Guides

Submission Guidelines Accepts queries with SAE, and artworks/images (send photocopies, and digital files as jpegs).

Kogan Page
120 Pentonville Road, London, N1 9JN
- 020 7278 0433
- 020 7837 6348
- kpinfo@kogan-page.co.uk
- www.kogan-page.co.uk

Contact Chairman, Philip Kogan; Managing Director, Helen Kogan; Publishing Services Director, Louise Cameron

Insider Info Publishes 130 titles per year. Catalogue and manuscript guidelines are available online.

Non-Fiction Publishes Reference and Technical titles on the following subjects:
Branding, Careers, Finance, General Reference, Human Resources, Logistics, Management, Marketing, Personal Development, Personal Finance, Property, Sales, Training, Transport

* Kogan Page publishes titles at every level, from basic skills to high level academic and professional texts.

Submission Guidelines Accepts proposal package (including outline, synopsis, one sample chapter, market research and author biography).

Recent Title(s) *Branded Male*, Mark Tungate (Marketing); *An UnAmerican Business*, Donald Kalff (Business)

Tips Kogan Page is Europe's largest independent publisher of business titles and has a global readership, selling in English and foreign language editions.

Kyle Cathie Ltd
122 Arlington Road, London, NW1 7HP
- 020 7692 7215
- 020 7692 7260
- general.enquiries@kyle-cathie.com
- www.kylecathie.co.uk

Contact Managing Director, Kyle Cathie

Established 1990

Insider Info Publishes 25 tiles per year. Receives approximately 300 queries per year. 15 per cent of books published are from first-time authors and ten per cent are from unagented authors. Payment is via royalties (on retail price), with 0.05 (per £) minimum and 0.125 (per £) maximum. An advance is offered. Average lead time is six months with simultaneous submissions accepted. Aims to respond to proposals within one month and manuscripts within two months. Catalogue available online. Manuscript guidelines available online.

Non-Fiction Publishes Cookbooks, General Non-Fiction and Illustrated titles in the following subjects:

Cooking, Food and Drink, Crafts, Gardening, Health, Hobbies, House and Home, Spirituality

Submission Guidelines Agented submissions only.

Recent Title(s) *Clarissa's Comfort Food*, Clarissa Dickson Wright; *Buonissimo!*, Gino D'Acampo; *Grow Your Own, Cook Your Own*, Bob Flowerdew; *The Thrifty Gardener*, Alys Fowler

Tips Kyle Cathie is particularly interested in books that will have a long life, which contribute something new to the marketplace and which have a strong publicity angle. It is generally best to submit your work via a literary agent, as they are not able to consider all the unsolicited manuscripts they are sent.

Ladybird Books

80 Strand, London, WC2R 0RL

☎ 020 7010 3000

☎ 020 7010 6060

✉ ladybird@uk.penguingroup.com

🌐 www.ladybird.co.uk

Parent Company Penguin Group (UK)

Insider Info Submissions accompanied by SAE will be returned. Catalogue and manuscript guidelines are available online.

Non-Fiction Publishes Children's Illustrated Books with an emphasis on Key Skills and Home Learning.

Submission Guidelines Accepts queries with SAE or completed manuscripts. Will accept artworks/images (send digital files as jpegs).

Fiction Publishes Children's and Picture Book titles, including Classic Tales.

* Most Ladybird story titles tend to be part of an already established series.

Submission Guidelines Accepts query with SAE or submit completed manuscript.

Recent Title(s) *Baby Touch: Playbook* (Board Book); *Gogo's Crazy Bones: Official Guide*, (Paperback)

Tips The well known Ladybird list covers illustrated books for Children aged 0–8 years old, with an emphasis on key skills and home learning. The list also encompasses classic children's stories and children's favourites, such as *Meg and Mog*, and *Angelina Ballerina*. Also, see www.vintageladybird.com for nostalgic adult titles.

Landmark Publishing Ltd

Ashbourne Hall, Cokayne Avenue, Ashbourne, DE6 1EJ

☎ 01335 347349

☎ 01335 347303

✉ Online form.

🌐 www.landmarkpublishing.co.uk

Contact Managing Director, Lindsey Porter

Established 1996

Insider Info Publishes 50 titles per year. Payment is via royalties. Catalogue available online.

Non-Fiction Publishes General Non-Fiction titles on the following subjects:
History, Local Interest, Nature/Environment, Regional, Travel

Recent Title(s) *Cromer Lifeboat*, Nicholas Leach and Paul Russell

Tips Specialises in itinerary based travel guidebooks and local interest books. Landmark also offers a bespoke self publishing service.

Laurence King Publishing

4th Floor, 361–373 City Road, London, EC1V 1LR

☎ 020 7841 6900

☎ 020 7841 6910

✉ enquiries@laurenceking.co.uk

🌐 www.laurenceking.co.uk

Contact Editorial Director (Architecture, Interior Design), Philip Cooper; Senior Commissioning Editor (Design, Graphics), Jo Lightfoot; Commissioning Editor (Design, Fashion), Helen Evans

Insider Info Publishes 50 titles per year. Catalogue is free on request.

Non-Fiction Publishes General Non-Fiction and Illustrated titles on the following subjects:
Art/Architecture, Contemporary Culture, Design, Fashion

Tips Laurence King publishes books for both business professionals and students, as well as for a more general readership.

Lawrence & Wishart Ltd

99a Wallis Road, London, E9 5LN

☎ 020 8533 2506

☎ 020 8533 7369

✉ info@lwbooks.co.uk

🌐 www.lwbooks.co.uk

Contact Managing Editor, Sally Davison

Established 1936

Insider Info Publishes ten titles per year. Payment is via royalties. Catalogue available online.

Non-Fiction Publishes General Non-Fiction titles on the following subjects:
Business, Economics, Education, Government/Politics, History, World Affairs

Submission Guidelines Accepts query with SAE or via email.
Submission details to: sally@lwbooks.co.uk

Recent Title(s) *Culture, Politics, Race & Diaspora: The Thought of Stuart Hall*, Brian Meeks (ed.) (Politics)

Tips Lawrence & Wishart believe that serious critical thought is a crucial, but often missing part of politics. Their titles aim to contribute to an understanding of the past, as well as reflect an engagement with the present and future. An aggressively independent publisher, L&W books have a reputation for being radically political.

Leaf Books
GTi Suite, Valleys Innovation Centre, Navigation Park, Abercynon, RCT, CF45 4SN

☎ 029 2081 0726

✉ contact@leafbooks.co.uk

🌐 www.leafbooks.co.uk

Insider Info Submissions accompanied by SAE will be returned. Aims to respond to manuscripts within three weeks.

Non-Fiction Publishes pocket sized Non-Fiction.

Submission Guidelines No unsolicited non-fiction at present.

Fiction Publishes Short Story Collections, Novellas, Children's Short Stories.

* Check the website for details of competitions for when fiction is periodically accepted.

Submission Guidelines Accepts query with SAE/proposal package (including first 50 pages of the novella, double spaced, with full contact details). Send a stamped addressed postcard if you require acknowledgement of the manuscript. No email submissions.

Poetry Publishes Poetry titles.

Submission Guidelines Check the website for details of competitions, when poetry submissions are periodically accepted.

Recent Title(s) *Naked Thighs and Cotton Frocks*, Various (Anthology)

Tips Leaf Books holds regular competitions for unpublished writers (including web publishing). Winners are often published in A5 sized anthologies and pocket sized A6 books. Entry guidelines are available on the website, as are the latest closing dates. They are generally for short stories of various genres, or poetry.

The Learning Institute
Overbrook Business Centre, Poolbridge Road, Blackford, Wedmore, BS28 4PA

☎ 0800 781 1715

🌐 www.inst.org

Contact Managing Director, Kit Sadgrove

Established 1994

Insider Info Payment is via royalties. Catalogue available online. Manuscript guidelines available via SAE.

Non-Fiction Publishes Multimedia and Scholarly titles on the following titles:

Catering, Complementary Therapies, Education, Garden Design & Horticulture, Writing

* The Learning Institute produces vocational home-study courses for people wanting to work from home, or change their career.

Recent Title(s) *Diploma in Private Investigation*, Learning Institute

Tips Printed materials are often supported by web-based resources. All written material must work towards the courses the company runs.

Learning Matters Ltd
33 Southernhay East, Exeter, EX1 1NX

☎ 01392 215560

☎ 01392 215561

✉ info@learningmatters.co.uk

🌐 www.learningmatters.co.uk

Contact Julia Morris (Education); Di Page (Social Work)

Insider Info Catalogue available online. Manuscript guidelines available online.

Non-Fiction Publishes Textbook and Scholarly titles on the following subjects:

Counselling/Career, Education, Law, Social Service

Submission Guidelines Accepts query with SAE, or via email, with a proposal package (including outline).

Submission details to: editor@learningmatters.co.uk

Recent Title(s) *Reflective Reader: Social Work and Mental Health*, John Archambeault (Educational)

Tips As publishers, particularly in the field of teacher training, Learning Matters primarily supply books for education and social services. They are keen to talk to authors with ideas for new books. Authors will be encouraged to help with the marketing of their book.

Leckie & Leckie
4 Queen Street, Edinburgh, EH2 1JF

☎ 0131 220 6831

☎ 0131 225 9987

✉ enquiries@leckieandleckie.co.uk

🌐 www.leckieandleckie.co.uk

Parent Company Huveaux

Contact Publishing Director, Martin Redfern; Publisher, Gillian Leslie; Publishing Assistant, Fiona McGlade

Established 1989

Insider Info Publishes 250 titles per year. Receives approximately 30 queries and 30 manuscripts per year. Five per cent of books published are from first-time authors, 100 per cent of books published are from unagented authors. Payment is via royalty (on wholesale price). Advance offered is from £500 to £2,000. Average lead time is nine months, with simultaneous submissions accepted. Submissions accompanied by SAE will be returned. Aims to respond to queries within five days and to proposals and manuscripts within four weeks. Catalogue is free on request and available online or by email.

Non-Fiction Publishes Scholarly and Textbook titles on the following subjects:
Education (Scottish), Scottish Secondary, Further Education
Submission Guidelines Accepts proposal package (including outline, one sample chapter, a proposal rationale, your publishing history and SAE), and artworks/images (send photocopies).
Submission details to: fiona.mcglade@ leckieandleckie.co.uk
Tips Submissions must be specifically tailored to fit with the Scottish education system. Readership will include Scottish secondary school teachers and students.

Legend Press Ltd
13a Northwold Road, London, N16 7HL
☎ 020 7249 6901
✉ info@legendpress.co.uk
🌐 www.legendpress.co.uk
Contact Managing Director, Tom Chalmers (Contemporary Fiction); Publishing Executive, Emma Howard (General Fiction)
Established 2005
Insider Info Publishes five titles per year. Receives approximately 500 queries and 300 manuscripts per year. 80 per cent of books published are from first-time authors, 80 per cent of books published are from unagented authors. Payment is via royalty (on wholesale price), with 0.08 (per £) minimum and 0.15 per cent (per £) maximum, or via royalty (on retail price), with 0.05 (per £) minimum and 0.09 (per £) maximum. Advance offered is from £1,000 to £5,000. Average lead time is six months, with simultaneous submissions accepted. Submissions will not be returned. Aims to respond to queries with five days, proposals within ten days and manuscripts withing six weeks. Catalogue is available with an A4 SAE, or by email. Manuscript guidelines are available online or by email.
Fiction Publishes Literary and Mainstream/ Contemporary titles, as well as Short Story collections (within the Legend Short Story series).
Submission Guidelines Accepts proposal package (including outline, three to four sample chapters and a full synopsis).
Recent Title(s) *Queer Fish In God's Waiting Room*, Lee Henshaw (Contemporary Fiction)
Tips Submissions are judged on a book by book basis, although they should generally be aimed at the mainstream, modern reader.

Leo Cooper
47 Church Street, Barnsley, South Yorkshire, S70 2AS
☎ 01226 734555

☎ 01226 734438
✉ enquiries@pen-and-sword.co.uk
🌐 www.pen-and-sword.co.uk
Parent Company Pen & Sword Books Ltd
Insider Info Catalogue available online.
Non-Fiction Publishes General Non-Fiction on the following subjects:
History, Military/War
Submission Guidelines Accepts query with SAE.
Submission details to: editorialoffice@pen-and-sword.co.uk
Tips Formerly run by Jilly Cooper's husband, Leo, Pen & Sword continue to publish military history books under the Leo Cooper imprint. No unsolicited manuscripts.

Letts Educational
4 Grosvenor Place, London, SW1X 7DL
☎ 01539 564911
✉ mail@lettsed.co.uk
🌐 www.lettsed.co.uk
Contact Publishing Director, Wayne Davies
Established 1979
Insider Info Catalogue available online, website http://shop.letts-successzone.com.
Non-Fiction Publishes Children's Textbook and Scholarly titles on the following subjects:
Education, Revision, Study Guides
Recent Title(s) *Alien Club Ten Minute Tests*, Letts (Primary Education Series); *Revise IGCSE Study Guides*, Letts (GCSE Revision Series)
Tips Letts Education is the UK's market leader in study and revision guides. Titles are aimed at all ages from pre-school to A-Level.

LexisNexis
Halsbury House, 35 Chancery Lane, London, WC2A 1EL
☎ 020 7400 2500
☎ 020 7400 2842
✉ customer.services@lexisnexis.co.uk
🌐 www.lexisnexis.co.uk
Parent Company Reed Elsevier Group Plc
Contact Managing Director, Josh Bottomley; Editorial & Publishing Director, Nicky Briggs
Insider Info Catalogue available online.
Non-Fiction Publishes General Non-Fiction, Scholarly, Textbook and Multimedia titles on the following subjects:
Law and Legal Information
Tips LexisNexis is a leading provider of information and services solutions. Products and publications are aimed at a wide range of professionals in the legal, risk management, corporate, government, law enforcement, accounting and academic markets.

Liberties Press

Guinness Enterprise Centre, Taylor's Lane, Dublin 8, Republic of Ireland

- 00353 1 415 1224
- sean@libertiespress.com
- www.libertiespress.com

Insider Info Aims to respond to submission within one month. Catalogue available online. Author guidelines available online.
Liberties Press is a member of CLÉ, the Irish Book Publishers' Association.

Non-Fiction Publishes Biography and General Non-Fiction titles on the following subjects:
Food & Drink, Irish Culture & Interest, Health, History, Memoirs, Music and Politics

Submission Guidelines Accepts proposal package (including outline, three sample chapters and SAE for return).

Recent Title(s) *Redemption Song: An Irish Reporter Inside the Obama Campaign*, Niall Stanage (Biography/Politics); *Stop Wasting Your Money*, Conor Pope (Finance)

Tips Liberties Press welcomes submissions of new work on any subject by both new and established authors but does not currently publish fiction, short stories or poetry.

LibraPharm Ltd

CMRO/Informa Healthcare, Telephone House, 69–77 Paul Street, London, EC2A 4LQ

- 020 7017 6457
- 020 7017 7831
- info@librapharm.com
- www.librapharm.com

Contact Managing Editor, Piers Allen; Deputy Managing Editor, Joanne Nicholl; Editorial and Production Manager, Richard Powell

Established 1995

Insider Info Catalogue available online. Manuscript guidelines available online.

Non-Fiction Publishes Journals on the following subjects:
Health/Medicine, Healthcare, Medical Research, Science

Submission Guidelines Submit completed manuscript and artworks/images (digital files as jpegs).
Submission details to: rmp@rpowell.co.uk

Recent Title(s) *Welcome to Paediatric and Perinatal Drug Therapy*, LibraPharm (Journal)

Tips LibraPharm is an independent publishing and communications company, offering innovative solutions to meet the information needs of professionals in the medical, pharmaceutical and biotechnology sectors. Manuscripts for publication should conform to the latest 'aims and scope' of the journal the piece is intended for. Details are available on the website.

Libris Ltd

26 Lady Margaret Road, London, NW5 2XL

- 020 7482 2390
- 020 7485 2730
- libris@onetel.com

Contact Directors: Nicholas Jacobs and S. A. Kitzinger

Established 1986

Insider Info Catalogue available online.

Non-Fiction Publishes Biography, General Non-Fiction and Scholarly titles on the following subjects: Language, Literature, Literary Criticism, Translation, German Studies

Fiction Publishes Literary, Translation and German Literature titles.

Poetry Publishes Bilingual Poetry titles.

Tips Libris specialises (though not exclusively) in publishing works of German literature for an international English language readership. The company does not have any special instructions for submissions.

The Liffey Press Ltd

Ashbrook House, 10 Main Street, Raheny, Dublin 5, Republic of Ireland

- 00353 1 851 1458
- 00353 1 851 1459
- info@theliffeypress.com
- www.theliffeypress.com

Contact Publisher, David Givens; Editorial, Brian Langan

Established 2001

Insider Info Publishes 20 titles per year. Payment is via royalties. Catalogue and manuscript guidelines available online.

Non-Fiction Publishes General Non-Fiction and Illustrated titles on the following subjects:
Art/Architecture, Business, Contemporary Culture, Economics, Education, Government/Politics, Language, Literature, Social Sciences, World Affairs
* Also welcomes proposals in the areas of Irish Culture, Social Policy, Arts and Literature, Current Events, Politics, Education, Economics and related fields.

Submission Guidelines Accepts query with SAE/proposal package (including outline, one sample chapter, market research, your publishing history and author biography).

Recent Title(s) *Ella Young, Irish Mystic and Rebel*, Rose Murphy

Tips The Liffey Press has a particular emphasis on contemporary Ireland. They will endeavour to respond promptly to all proposals received.

The Lilliput Press Ltd

62–63 Sitric Road, Arbour Hill, Dublin 7, Republic of Ireland

- 00353 1 671 1647
- 00353 1 671 1233
- info@lilliputpress.ie
- www.lilliputpress.com

Contact Publisher/Editor in Chief, Antony Farrell
Established 1984
Insider Info Publishes 18 titles per year. Receives approximately 300 queries and 200 manuscripts per year. 50 per cent of books published are from first-time authors and 50 per cent of books published are from unagented authors. Ten per cent of books are author subsidy published, and these are determined by integrity of subject and source of subvention. Payment is via royalty on wholesale price, with 0.1 (per £) minimum and 0.2 (per £) maximum, or royalty on retail price with 0.05 (per £) minimum and 0.15 (per £) maximum. Advance offered is from £300–£10,000. Simultaneous submissions are accepted. Submissions accompanied by SAE will be returned. Aims to respond to queries within five days, proposals within eight days, and manuscripts within ten months. Catalogue is free on request, and available online. Author guidelines are not available, although digital work is preferred.
Non-Fiction Publishes Autobiography, Irish Interest, Biography, General Non-Fiction, Illustrated, Reference, and Scholarly titles on the following subjects:
Art/Architecture, Contemporary Culture, History, Language/Literature, Literary Criticism, Memoirs, Nature/Environment, Philosophy, Travel, Literature
* Authors should have a familiarity with the Lilliput list and Irish culture in general.
Submission Guidelines Accepts proposal package (including two sample chapters, and author biography) and artworks/images.
Fiction Publishes Erotica and Literary Fiction.
Submission Guidelines Accepts proposal package (including outline, and two sample chapters).
Poetry Publishes Poetry titles, mostly with an Irish theme.
Submission Guidelines Submit sample poems.
Tips Most work published has a broadly Irish theme.

The Lindsey Press

Unitarian Headquarters, Essex Hall, 1–6 Essex Street, London, WC2R 3HY

- 020 7240 2384
- 020 7240 3089
- ga@unitarian.org.uk
- www.unitarian.org.uk/lindsey_press.htm

Contact Publications Panel Convenor, Kate Taylor
Insider Info Catalogue available online.

Non-Fiction Publishes General Non-Fiction, Multimedia and Scholarly titles on Religion.
Recent Title(s) *The Larger View: Unitarians and World Religions*, Vernon Marshall
Tips The Lindsey Press publishes works reflecting liberal religious thought, Unitarian history, and worship material.

Lion Hudson Plc

Wilkinson House, Jordan Hill Road, Oxford, OX2 8DR

- 01865 302750
- 01865 302757
- info@lionhudson.com
- www.lionhudson.com

Contact Commissioning Editor (Children's Books), Lois Rock; Commissioning Editor (Adult Books), Morag Reeve; Commissioning Editor (Children's Books), Carol Jones; Commissioning Editor (Adult Books), Tony Collins
Established 1971
Imprint(s) Lion Children's
Lion
Candle
Monarch
Insider Info Publishes 160 titles per year. Receives approximately 1,000 queries and 500 manuscripts per year. Three per cent of books published are from first-time authors, 90 per cent of books published are from unagented authors. Payment is via royalty (on wholesale price) or outright purchase. Average lead time is one year, with simultaneous submissions accepted. Submissions accompanied by SAE will be returned. Aims to respond to queries within one week, proposals within two months and manuscripts within three months. Catalogue is free on request and available online. Manuscript guidelines are available online.
Non-Fiction Publishes Autobiography, Biography, Children's, General Non-Fiction, Gift, Illustrated, Reference, Self-Help and Textbook titles on the following subjects:
Childcare/Parenting, Government/Politics, History, Memoirs, Nature, Religion, Young Adult
Submission Guidelines Submit a synopsis and covering letter by mail, clearly stating which imprint you are submitting to (details of which may be found on the website). Illustrators should send 72dpi colour jpegs or pdfs addressed to the Art Director, to: webmaster@lionhudson.com.
Tips The Lion and Lion Children's imprints publish Christian books for the general marketplace. Candle publishes bible adventure stories for children, and Monarch publishes world interest titles with a Christian outlook. All Lion Hudson books are written by people who are happy to be called Christians and reflect a Christian world view.

Little, Brown Book Group

100 Victoria Embankment, London, EC4Y 0DY
- 020 7911 8000
- 020 7911 8100
- info@littlebrown.co.uk
- www.littlebrown.co.uk

Parent Company Hachette UK
Contact CEO & Publisher, Ursula Mackenzie
Established 1988
Imprint(s) Abacus
Atom
Little, Brown
Orbit
Piatkus Books
Sphere
Virago Press
Insider Info Submissions accompanied by SAE will be returned. Aims to respond to proposals within eight weeks. Catalogue available online.
Non-Fiction Autobiography, Biography, General Non-Fiction.
* Publishes both literary and general non-fiction across its imprints.
Submission Guidelines Accepts query with SAE/proposal package (including outline, three sample chapters, covering letter and SAE).
Fiction Publishes Mainstream/Contemporary and General Fiction in most genres.
* Publishes literary and commercial fiction across various imprints.
Submission Guidelines Accepts query with SAE/proposal package (including outline, three sample chapters, covering letter and SAE).
Recent Title(s) *Testimony*, Anita Shreve (Novel); *Things Ain't What They Used to Be*, Philip Glenister (Humour/Nostalgia)
Tips Formerly known as The Time Warner Book Group, Little, Brown reverted to its original name following purchase by Hachette UK. The company publishes a wide range of paperback and hardcover fiction and non-fiction across its many imprints. See individual entries for more details.

Little, Brown

100 Victoria Embankment, London, EC4Y 0DY
- 020 7911 8000
- 020 7911 8100
- info@littlebrown.co.uk
- www.littlebrown.co.uk

Parent Company Little, Brown Book Group
Contact Publishing Director, Richard Beswick
Insider Info Submissions accompanied by SAE will be returned. Aims to respond to proposals within eight weeks. Catalogue available online.
Non-Fiction Publishes General and Literary Non-Fiction in the following subject areas:

History, Memoirs, Science, Travel
Submission Guidelines Accepts query with SAE/proposal package (including, outline, sample chapter(s), a covering letter and SAE).
Fiction Publishes Literary Fiction.
Submission Guidelines Accepts query with SAE/proposal package (including outline, sample chapter(s), a covering letter and SAE).
Tips Agented submissions are strongly preferred, but unagented proposals are accepted. All Little, Brown imprint books are published in hardback. Paperback versions are published by the Abacus imprint.

Little Books Ltd

48 Catherine Place, London, SW1E 6HL
- 020 7792 7929
- info@littlebooks.net
- www.littlebooks.net

Contact Publishers, Margaret Little and Max Hamilton Little
Established 2003
Imprint(s) Max Press
Insider Info Catalogue available online.
Non-Fiction Publishes Biography and General Non-Fiction titles in the following subjects: Cooking, Food and Drink, Health/Medicine, History, Language, Literature, Nature/Environment, Travel
Fiction Publishes Historical and Mainstream/Contemporary titles.
Recent Title(s) *All the Way Home*, Richard and Bookey Peek (Travel)
Tips Little Books publishes concise books to fit in pockets, by well known writers. Their philosophy is to bring books to those who are juggling busy lives, but are still passionate about reading, who want to be entertained as well as informed, without needing to devote huge chunks of time to reading. Each book needs to be about something important, something that makes the world a better place. Each is written by the leading writer in their field.

Little Tiger Press

1 The Coda Centre, 189 Munster Road, London, SW6 6AW
- 020 7385 6333
- 020 7385 7333
- info@littletiger.co.uk
- www.littletigerpress.com

Parent Company Magi Publications
Contact Editorial Jude Evans and Stefanie Stansbie
Insider Info Aims to respond to manuscripts within two months. Catalogue and manuscript guidelines are available online.
Fiction Publishes Picture and Novelty Book titles for the 0–7 age group.

Submission Guidelines Accepts completed manuscripts by post with SAE. Manuscripts must be no longer than 750 words. Accepts photocopied samples of illustrations/artworks.

Recent Title(s) *The Littlest Owl*, Caroline Pitcher and Tina Macnaughton (Picture Book)

Tips Little Tiger Books focuses on contemporary and innovative books for young children (Key Stage 1) that are also fun for adults. They publish board books, picture books, character books, gift books, home learning and books suitable for use in schools and pre-schools.

Liverpool University Press
4 Cambridge Street, Liverpool, L69 7ZU

- 0151 794 2233
- 0151 794 2235
- joanne.hart@liv.ac.uk
- www.liverpool-unipress.co.uk

Contact Publisher, Robin Bloxsidge (Art, Architecture, Public Space and Local Studies and all Journals); Editorial Director, Anthony Cond (Culture, Literature, History and Social Science); Production Manager, Andrew Kirk

Established 1899

Insider Info Publishes 40 titles per year. Payment is via royalties. Catalogue available online. Manuscript guidelines available online.

Non-Fiction Publishes General Non-Fiction, Reference, Scholarly and Technical titles in the following subjects:
Anthropology/Archaeology, Art, Architecture, Contemporary Culture, Government/Politics, History, Language, Literature, Literary Criticism, Music/Dance, Nature/Environment, Science, Sociology, Translation, Literary Criticism, Science Fiction

Submission Guidelines Would prefer to receive a proposal, rather than a completed manuscript in the first instance. Check website for submission guidelines. Accepts query with SAE/proposal package (including outline, two sample chapters, market research, publishing history, and author biography).

Recent Title(s) *Latin American Cyberculture and Cyberliterature*, Claire Taylor and Thea Pitman (eds.)

Tips Most books published by LUP are peer reviewed.

Logaston Press
Little Logaston, Woonton, Almeley, Herefordshire, HR3 6QH

- 01544 327344
- info@logastonpress.co.uk
- www.logastonpress.co.uk

Contact Managing Editors, Andy Johnson and Ron Shoesmith

Established 1985

Insider Info Publishes 15 titles per year. Payment is via royalties. Catalogue available online: www.members.lycos.co.uk/simonlogaston.

Non-Fiction Publishes Biography, General Non-Fiction and Reference titles on the following subjects:
Anthropology/Archaeology, Art, Architecture, History, Hobbies, Nature/Environment, Regional, Social Sciences, Touring/Walking guides, Folklore.
* Mostly local interest for Wales and West Midlands.

Submission Guidelines Query with SAE/proposal package (including outline, sample chapter(s)) and artworks/images.
The Pubs of Bromyard, Ledbury and East Herefordshire, John Eisel and Ron Shoesmith

Tips Logaston Press publishes books and guides on the history, archaeology and architecture of a region that encompasses the rural West Midlands, Central and South Wales. All book proposals should fall somewhere in those broad categories/locations.

Loki Books
38 Chalcot Crescent, London, NW1 8YD

- 020 7722 6718
- all@lokibooks.vianw.co.uk
- www.lokibooks.com

Established 1967

Fiction Publishes Full-length Fiction, Short Story Collections and Drama titles in translation.
* Often publishes work with women's voices in minority languages.

Poetry Publishes Poetry in Translation.

Recent Title(s) *Blue China*, Bamboo Hirst (Translation)

Tips One of Loki's main concerns is to promote women writers, who are dedicated to peace and the understanding of Arab–Israeli relations.

Lonely Planet Publications Ltd
2nd Floor, 186 City Road, London, EC1V 2NT

- 020 7106 2100
- 020 7106 2101
- go@lonelyplanet.co.uk
- www.lonelyplanet.com

Contact CEO, Matthew Goldberg; Editorial Head, Katherine Leck; Publishing Administrator (UK), Aaron Lamb

Established 1973

Insider Info Manuscript guidelines and catalogue available online.

Non-Fiction Publishes General Non-Fiction, Illustrated Books and Guidebooks on the following subjects:
Travel, Travel and Culture

Submission Guidelines Accepts query with SAE/proposal package (including outline, sample chapter(s), publishing history, clips, author biography) and artworks/images.
Submission details to: recruitingauthors@lonelyplanet.com.au
Recent Title(s) *France*, 7th Edition, Nicola Williams (Travel Guide)
Tips Lonely Planet publishes travel guidebooks for independent travellers. Lonely Planet does not accept travel literature submissions. However they do occasionally call for stories along a particular theme, for possible inclusion in their annual travel writing anthology.

Longman
Edinburgh Gate, Harlow, Essex, CM20 2JE
- 01279 623623
- 01279 414130
- schools@longman.co.uk
- www.longman.co.uk

Parent Company Pearson Education
Insider Info Catalogue and manuscript guidelines are available online
Non-Fiction Publishes Multimedia, Reference, Scholarly and Textbook titles on the following subjects:
Business, Citizenship, Design & Technology, Drama, Economics, English Language, English Literature, General Studies, Geography, History, ICT, Latin, Law, Maths, Politics, Psychology & Sociology, Religious Studies, Science, Travel & Tourism, Vocational.
Submission Guidelines Accepts proposal package (including synopsis, sample chapters, market research, your publishing history and author biography).
Recent Title(s) *Love That Dog*, S Creech (Education/Poetry); *Of Mice and Men* (without notes), J Steinbeck (Literature)
Tips Longman, the world's oldest commercial imprint, is a leading publisher of educational materials for schools and English Language Teaching (ELT) as well as for education. Target market includes primary and secondary pupils, adult learners and students taking English exams, as well as users of dictionaries and reference titles.

Lorenz Books
Hermes House, 88–89 Blackfriars Road, London, SE1 8HA
- 020 7401 2077
- 020 7633 9499
- info@anness.com
- www.lorenzbooks.com

Parent Company Anness Publishing

Contact Chairman/Managing Director, Paul Anness; Publisher, Joanna Lorenz
Established 1994
Insider Info Publishes 140 titles each year. Catalogue available online.
Non-Fiction Publishes Children's, General Non-Fiction, Gift Book and Illustrated titles on the following subjects:.
Cooking, Crafts, Food and Drink, Gardening, Health/Medicine, History, Nature/Environment, Recreation, Sports
Tips Lorenz Books is the trade sales imprint for new hardback titles at Anness Publishing Ltd. It includes the Aquamarine list of upmarket lifestyle directories.

Luath Press Ltd
543/2 Castlehill, The Royal Mile, Edinburgh, Lothian, EH1 2ND
- 0131 225 4326
- 0131 225 4324
- gavin.macdougall@luath.co.uk
- www.luath.co.uk

Contact Director, Gavin MacDougall
Established 1981
Insider Info Publishes 30 titles per year. Receives less than 1,000 queries and less than 1,000 manuscripts per year. 10–50 per cent of books published are from first-time authors, more than 90 per cent of books published are from unagented authors. Payment is via royalty. Submissions accompanied by SAE will be returned. Catalogue is free on request and available online. Manuscript guidelines are available online.
Non-Fiction Publishes Autobiography, Biography, Coffee Table, Cookbooks, Gift, How-To, Humour, Illustrated and Reference titles on the following subjects:
Animals, Art, Architecture, Cooking, Creative Non-Fiction, Food and Drink, Folklore, Gardening, History, Language, Literature, Literary Criticism, Memoirs, Military/War, Music/Dance, Photography, Religion, Spirituality, Sports, Travel, Women's Issues/Studies, World Affairs, Young Adult
Submission Guidelines Accepts queries with SAE and complete manuscripts (including your publishing history, clips, author biography and SAE).
Fiction Publishes Mainstream/Contemporary titles
Submission Guidelines Accepts queries with SAE and complete manuscripts (including your publishing history, clips, author biography and SAE).
Poetry Publishes Traditional and Contemporary Poetry
Submission Guidelines Accepts complete manuscripts.
Recent Title(s) *My Epileptic Lurcher*, Des Dillon (Humour); *The Bower Bird*, Ann Kelley (Children's)

Tips Most Luath Press books have a Scottish connection.

Lund Humphries
Ashgate Publishing Group, Wey Court East, Union Road, Farnham, Surrey, GU9 7PT
- ☎ 01252 331551
- ☎ 01252 736736
- ✉ info@lundhumphries.com
- 🌐 www.lundhumphries.com

Parent Company Ashgate Publishing Group
Contact Commissioning Editor, Lucy Clark
Insider Info Catalogue available online. Download PDF version, or fill in the online form.
Non-Fiction Publishes Coffee Table Books, Gift Books and Illustrated Books on the following subjects:
Architecture, Decorative Art, Design, Fine Arts, History of Art & Design, Museum Collections, Photography
Submission Guidelines Accepts proposal package (including outline, a sample list of competitor books, publishing history, author biography, information on the intended readership and all proposed illustrations).
For book proposals by post, do not use the main company address. Send to: Lucy Clark, Commissioning Editor, Lund Humphries, Sardinia House, 51–52 Lincoln's Inn Fields, London, WC2A 3LZ (Tel: 020 74440 7530)
Submission details to: lclark@lundhumphries.com
Recent Title(s) *London Transport Posters*, David Bownes and Oliver Green, eds.

The Lutterworth Press
PO Box 60, Cambridge, CB1 2NT
- ☎ 01223 350865
- ☎ 01223 366951
- ✉ publishing@lutterworth.com
- 🌐 www.lutterworth.com

Parent Company James Clarke & Co.
Insider Info Catalogue available online and by request. Manuscript guidelines available online.
Non-Fiction Publishes General Non-Fiction titles on the following subjects:
History & Biography, Literature & Criticism, Educational Titles, Biblical Studies, Religious History & Biography, Mission & Theology, Religious Education
* The Lutterworth Press specialises in adult and children's religious titles, alongside their general and scholarly non-fiction lists.
Submission Guidelines Accepts query with SAE/ proposal package (including outline, two sample chapters and contents list).

Recent Title(s) *Hanging a Rebel: The Life of C.R.W. Nevinson*, Michael Walsh; *The Philosophy of Religion: A Commentary and Sourcebook*, Michael Palmer
Tips The Lutterworth Press only accepts submissions for adult titles. Prospective authors are advised to thoroughly research the catalogue to ensure a book's suitability.

Lyfrow Trelyspen
The Roseland Institute, Gorran, St Austell, Cornwall, PL26 6NT
- ☎ 01726 843501
- ☎ 01726 843501
- ✉ trelispen@care4free.net

Contact Managing Editor, Dr James Whetter
Established 1975
Insider Info Publishes roughly two titles per year.
Non-Fiction Publishes Biography and General Non-Fiction titles in the following subjects:
History (Cornish History), Regional, Cornish Essays
Submission Guidelines Accepts query with SAE/ proposal package (including outline, sample chapter(s)). Accepts unsolicited submissions and ideas, providing they are of Cornish interest.

M&M Baldwin
24 High Street, Cleobury Mortimer, Kidderminster, DY14 8BY
- ☎ 01299 270110
- ✉ mb@mbaldwin.free-online.co.uk
- 🌐 www.enigmatixuk.com

Contact Proprietor, Dr. Mark Baldwin (Waterways, Intelligence)
Established 1974
Insider Info Publishes roughly three titles per year. Receives approximately 30 queries and 15 manuscripts per year. Ten per cent of books published are from first-time authors, 95 per cent of books published are from unagented authors. Payment is via royalty (on retail price). Average lead time is six months, with simultaneous submissions not accepted. Submissions accompanied by SAE will be returned. Aims to respond to queries, proposals and manuscripts within two days. Catalogue and manuscript guidelines are free on request.
Non-Fiction Publishes Biography, General Non-Fiction and Reference titles on the following subjects:
History, Marine Subjects, Military/War
Submission Guidelines Accepts query with SAE, and artworks/images (send photocopies).

Macmillan Publishers Ltd
The Macmillan Building, 4 Crinan Street, London, N1 9XW
- ☎ 020 7833 4000

☎ 020 7843 4640
✉ fiction@macmillan.co.uk
✉ nonfiction@macmillan.co.uk
🌐 www.macmillan.com
Parent Company Verlagsgruppe Georg von Holtzbrink GmbH
Contact CEO, Annette Thomas; Deputy Chairman, Michael Barnard
Established 1843
Imprint(s) Macmillan Education (division)
Palgrave Macmillan (division)
Pan Macmillan Publishers (division)
Nature Publishing (subsidiary)
Non-Fiction Publishes Biography, General Non-Fiction and Illustrated titles on the following subjects:
History, Memoirs, Sports, World Affairs, Politics and Current Affairs
Submission Guidelines Does not accept unsolicited or unagented submissions.
Fiction Publishes General Fiction from British and international writers.
Submission Guidelines Does not accept unsolicited or unagented submissions.
Tips The Macmillan Group and its divisions cover education publishing, including English language teaching (ELT), academic publishing, including reference science, technological and medical publishing, fiction and non-fiction book publishing, and publishing services including distribution and production. For more information, see the individual division entries. Authors should see the Macmillan New Writing imprint, under Pan Macmillan, for information about submitting manuscripts.

Macmillan Children's Books
20 New Wharf Road, London, N1 9RR
☎ 020 7014 6000
☎ 020 7014 6001
✉ children@macmillan.co.uk
🌐 www.panmacmillan.com
Parent Company Pan Macmillan Publishers (Macmillan Publishers Ltd)
Insider Info Catalogue available online.
Non-Fiction Publishes Children's titles.
Submission Guidelines Does not accept unsolicited submissions. Accepts agented submissions only.
Fiction Publishes Picture Books, Young Adult and Children's titles.
Submission Guidelines Accepts agented submissions only.
Poetry Publishes Children's Poetry titles.
Submission Guidelines Accepts agented submissions only.

Recent Title(s) *Changeling*, Steve Feasey (Novel); *Sparkle Street: LIzzie Ribbon's Hat Shop*, Vivian French (Children's/Pop-Up)
Tips Macmillan's Children's Books produces a diverse and quality list of fiction and non-fiction aimed at children aged 0–16 years.

Macmillan Education
Between Towns Road, Oxford, OX4 3PP
☎ 01865 405700
☎ 01865 405701
✉ elt@macmillan.com
🌐 www.macmillaneducation.com
Parent Company Macmillan Publishers Ltd
Contact CEO, Julian Drinkall
Insider Info Catalogue is available online.
Non-Fiction Publishes Text Books, Online Resources, Children's, Reference and Scholarly titles on the following subjects:
Language/Literature, English Language Teaching and Curriculum Materials for schools
Tips Macmillan Education operates in 40 countries, publishing school and learning materials. Most resources, both print and online, are developed in conjunction with teachers and other education professionals. Materials are always in line with the relevant curriculum. The three main areas are; Macmillan English (English language teaching), Macmillan Caribbean (books for and about the Caribbean) and Macmillan Africa (educational text books for African schools).

Macmillan New Writing
☎ 020 7014 6000
☎ 020 7014 6001
✉ Online form.
🌐 www.macmillannewwriting.com
Parent Company Pan Macmillan Publishers
Established 2006
Insider Info All books published are from first-time authors. No advances paid; instead an open ended royalty deal at a relatively high rate is offered.
Fiction Publishes General Fiction novels (all genres considered).
Submission Guidelines All submission must come through the website.
Recent Title(s) *The Hoard of Mhorrer*, M F W Curran (Supernatural)
Tips Macmillan New Writing is a fiction list set up specifically to publish first novels from new authors.

Magi Publications
1 The Coda Centre, 189 Munster Road, London, SW6 6AW
☎ 020 7385 6333
☎ 020 7385 7333

○ info@littletiger.co.uk

🌐 www.littletigerpress.com

Contact Editorial, Jude Evans and Stefanie Stansbie

Imprint(s) Little Tiger Press
Caterpillar Books

Insider Info Aims to respond to manuscripts within two months. Catalogue and manuscript guidelines are available online.

Fiction Publishes Picture and Novelty Book titles for the 0–7 age group.

Submission Guidelines Accepts completed manuscripts by post with SAE. Manuscripts must be no longer than 750 words. Accepts photocopied samples of artwork/illustrations.

Recent Title(s) *The Dark, Dark Night*, M. Christina Butler and Jane Chapman (Picture Book)

Tips Magi Press publish solely under their two imprints. Little Tiger focuses on books for children up to age seven, whereas Caterpillar mainly focuses on the 0–3 age group (see separate entries).

The Maia Press

82 Forest Road, Dalston, London, E8 3BH

○ 020 7249 3711

○ 020 7683 8141

○ maggie@maiapress.com

🌐 www.maiapress.com

Contact Founders, Maggie Hamand and Jane Havell

Established 2002

Insider Info Publishes six titles per year. Payment is via royalties. Aims to respond to proposals and manuscripts within six weeks. Catalogue and manuscript guidelines available online.

Fiction Publishes Literary and Mainstream/ Contemporary titles.

* The Maia Press aims to publish works by writers from diverse backgrounds, including works in translation, giving priority to writers whose work is censored in their country of origin.

Submission Guidelines Accepts query with SAE/ proposal package (including outline and three sample chapters).

Recent Title(s) *The Resurrection of the Body*, Maggie Hamand (Novel)

Tips The Maia Press is a young publishing house, dedicated to publishing new and established authors. They only publish a small number of books per year, so submissions should be carefully targeted, according to the guidelines on the website. Do not email submissions.

Mainstream

Random House, 20 Vauxhall Bridge Road, London, SW1V 2SA

○ 020 7840 8400

○ 020 7233 8791

○ emarketing@randomhouse.co.uk

🌐 www.randomhouse.co.uk

Parent Company The Random House Group Ltd

Insider Info Catalogue available online.

Non-Fiction Publishes Autobiography, Biography and General Non-Fiction on the following subjects: History, Memoirs, Music, Recreation, Sports and Drugs

Submission Guidelines No unagented submissions.

Recent Title *Talking Swing: The British Big Bands*, Sheila Tracy (Music); *Mrs Mills Solves All Your Problems*, Mrs Mills (Media Tie-In)

Mainstream Publishing Co. (Edinburgh) Ltd

7 Albany Street, Edinburgh, EH1 3UG

○ 0131 557 2959

○ 0131 556 8720

○ enquiries@mainstreampublishing.com

🌐 www.mainstreampublishing.com

Contact Directors, Bill Campbell and Peter Mackenzie; Editorial, Ailsa Bathgate

Established 1978

Insider Info Publishes roughly 80 titles per year. Authors paid by royalty. Catalogue and manuscript guidelines available online.

Non-Fiction Publishes Autobiography, Biography, Illustrated Books and General Non-Fiction titles on the following subjects:
Art, Architecture, Government/Politics, Health, History, Photography, Sports and World Affairs

Submission Guidelines Accepts query with SAE or via email. Submit proposal package (including outline and SAE).
Submission details to: graeme.blaikie@ mainstreampublishing.com

Fiction Publishes Mainstream/Contemporary titles.

Submission Guidelines Accepts query with SAE or via email. Submit proposal package (including outline).
Submission details to: graeme.blaikie@ mainstreampublishing.com

Recent Title *Falling*, Jeff Randall (Autobiography)

Tips Mainstream publishes various biographies, autobiographies, illustrated and general non-fiction. Random House currently owns a 50 per cent share in the company. To establish how the publishing process works at Mainstream, please see the website.

Mam Tor

PO Box 6785, Derby, DE22 1XT

○ info@mamtor.com

🌐 www.mamtor.com

Contact Editor-in-Chief, Liam Sharp; Prose Submissions Editor, Susan J. Boulton; Art Submissions Editors: Liam Sharp, John Bamber & Jason Harris
Established 2004
Insider Info Does not offer an advance or guarantee any payment as a result of sales. Due to being a small company Mam Tor may not be able to respond to failed submissions.
Fiction Publishes Science-fiction, Fantasy, Gothic/Horror and Comic content, in both prose and graphic novel format.
Recent Title(s) *The Enemy's Son*, James Johnson (Sci-fi/Fantasy)
Tips Mam Tor is a small company created not as a commercial venture, but as a forum for subcultural, underground, science fiction, horror or fantasy writers and artists. There are no fees for the work produced, nor are there the usual editorial restrictions. Mam Tor also accepts artwork submissions from fantasy artists and published the award-winning *Event Horizon* series.

Management Books 2000 Ltd
Forge House, Limes Road, Kemble, Cirencester, GL7 6AD
☎ 01285 771441
☎ 01285 771055
✉ info@mb2000.com
🌐 www.mb2000.com
Contact Publisher, Nicholas Dale-Harris
Established 1993
Insider Info Average lead time is 15 months. Catalogue available online.
Non-Fiction Publishes Reference titles on the following subjects:
Business, Management, Self-Development, Sales and Marketing
Submission Guidelines Accepts proposal package (including outline, two sample chapters, your publishing history and author biography).
Tips Management Books 2000 publishes books for executives and managers working in the modern business world. New ideas and synopses are welcome.

Manchester University Press
Oxford Road, Manchester, M13 9NR
☎ 0161 275 2310
☎ 0161 274 3346
✉ m.frost@manchester.ac.uk
🌐 www.manchesteruniversitypress.co.uk
Contact Chief Executive and Production Director, David Rodgers; Head of Editorial, Matthew Frost (Humanities); Commissioning Editor, Tony Mason (International Law and Economics); Commissioning

Editor, Emma Brennan (History, Art History and Design)
Established 1904
Insider Info Publishes roughly 120 titles per year. Authors paid by royalty. Catalogue free on request and available online. Manuscript guidelines available online.
Non-Fiction Publishes Textbooks, Reference and Scholarly titles on the following subjects:
Art, Architecture, Business/Economics, Government/Politics, History, Humanities, Language, Literature, Law, Literary Criticism and Media
Submission Guidelines Accepts query with SAE or via email. Submit proposal package (including outline, market research, your publishing history, author biography and SAE).
Submission details to: m.frost@manchester.ac.uk
Recent Title(s) *Public Issue Television*, Peter Goddard, John Corner and Kay Richardson
Tips Manchester University Press publishes work by authors from all over the world and its titles are generally aimed at the wider international academic community.

Mandrake of Oxford
PO Box 250, Oxford, OX1 1AP
☎ 01865 243671
✉ mandrake@mandrake.uk.net
🌐 www.mandrake.uk.net
Contact Directors: Mogg Morgan and Kym Morgan
Established 1986
Insider Info Catalogue and manuscript guidelines are available online.
Non-Fiction Publishes Biography, General Non-Fiction, Illustrated and Scholarly titles on the following subjects:
Art, Alternative Lifestyles, Astrology/Psychic, Contemporary Culture, Intellectual History, Magic/Witchcraft, Philosophy, Religion, Self-Help, Spirituality, True Crime
Submission Guidelines Accepts query with SAE. Submit proposal package (including outline, one sample chapter and SAE).
Fiction Publishes Crime, Occult and Spiritual fiction titles.
Submission Guidelines Accepts query with SAE. Submit proposal package (including outline, one sample chapter and SAE).
Poetry Publishes Poetry Collections.
* Sometimes publishes individual poems in a newsletter, which can be received by emailing mandrake-subscribe@yahoogroups.com.
Submission Guidelines Accepts query with SAE.
Recent Title(s) *Gateway to Hell*, Margaret Bingley (Occult); *Jack The Ripper in Fact and Fiction*, Robin Odell (True Crime); *The Camden Town Murder*, John Barber (True Crime); *Handbook for Rebels & Outlaws*,

Mark Mirabello (Intellectual History); *Bright from the Well*, Dave Lee (Northern Tradition); *Fire Child*, Maxine Sanders (Autobiography/Witchcraft/Occult)
Tips Mandrake of Oxford is a specialist independent press that is always happy to look at ideas for new books. The publishers urge that before potential authors submit their work they look at the catalogue, and a book in a similar category, to gauge whether a proposal fits their list.

Mango Publishing
PO Box 13378, London, SE27 0ZN
- 020 8480 7771
- 020 8480 7771
- info@mangoprint.com
- www.mangoprint.com
Established 1995
Insider Info Catalogue available online.
Non-Fiction Publishes Autobiography, Biography and General Non-Fiction titles in the following subjects:
Translation, Black African/Caribbean, Latin American
Fiction Publishes Mainstream/Contemporary, Short Story Collections, Translation, Black African/Caribbean and Latin American titles.
Poetry Publishes Black African/Caribbean Poetry titles.
Recent Title(s) *Havana: Between the Sky and Heaven*, Ruswel Piñeiro (Novel)
Tips Mango Publishing is committed to promoting and publishing the work of quality first-time and established writers. They focus on publishing and promoting literary works by writers from African, Caribbean, and Latin American literary traditions. The list includes translations of important works not originally written in English, such as poetry by leading contemporary authors, short and longer fiction, ranging from short story anthologies to novels, and autobiographical work.

Manson Publishing Ltd
73 Corringham Road, London, NW11 7DL
- 020 8905 5150
- 020 8201 9233
- manson@mansonpublishing.com
- www.mansonpublishing.com
Contact Managing Director, Michael Manson
Established 1992
Insider Info Publishes roughly ten titles per year. Payment is via royalties. Catalogue and manuscript guidelines available online.
Non-Fiction Publishes Scholarly, Technical, Textbook and Reference titles on the following subjects:
Health, Science, Veterinary, Agriculture, Microbiology

Submission Guidelines Accepts query with SAE. Welcomes proposals for highly illustrated books from authors in its main subject areas. Please contact Manson Publishing with an outline by email, post or fax.
Recent Title(s) *Fossil Ecosystems of North America*, John R. Nudds and Paul A. Selden
Tips Manson Publishing issues books for professionals and students in medicine, veterinary medicine and the sciences. They specialise in highly illustrated books for study and reference.

Mantra Lingua
Global House, 303 Ballards Lane, London, N12 8NP
- 020 8445 5123
- 020 8446 7745
- henrie@mantralingua.com
- www.mantralingua.com
Contact Managing Director, M. Chatterji; Commissioning Editor, Henriette Barkow
Established 1984
Insider Info Aims to respond to proposals and manuscripts within two months. Catalogue available online. Manuscript guidelines available online.
Non-Fiction Publishes Children's, Giftbooks and Multimedia titles.
Fiction Publishes Children's, Multimedia, Picture Books, Translation and Young Adult titles.
Submission Guidelines Accepts query with SAE or via email with proposal package (including a 250 word synopsis and sample chapter(s)), or completed manuscript. Manuscripts should be no longer than 1,200 words for picture books and 2,500 words for junior fiction.
Submission details to: mishti@mantralingua.com
Recent Title(s) *The Elves and the Shoemaker*, Henriette Barkow (Picture Book)
Tips Mantra Lingua is a UK based publishing house that supplies bilingual resources around the world focusing on connecting languages for children.

Mare's Nest
41 Addison Gardens, London, W14 0DP
- 020 7603 3969
- maresnest@tesco.net
- www.maresnest.co.uk
Contact Pamela Clunies-Ross
Non-Fiction Publishes Translated Non-Fiction titles.
Fiction Publishes Translation titles.
Poetry Publishes Translated Poetry titles.
Recent Title(s) *Z - a Love Story*, Vigdis Grimsdottir
Tips Publishes English translations of Icelandic poetry and fiction, as well as some Faroese fiction and Hungarian non-fiction.

Marion Boyars Publishers Ltd

24 Lacy Road, London, SW15 1NL

- 020 8788 9522
- 020 8789 8122
- catheryn@marionboyars.com
- www.marionboyars.co.uk

Contact Director, Catheryn Kilgarriff; Editor, Kit Maude (Non-Fiction); Editor, Rebecca Gillieron (Fiction)

Established 1960s

Insider Info Catalogue and manuscript guidelines available online.

Non-Fiction Publishes Biography, Children's, General Non-Fiction and Scholarly titles on the following subjects:
Contemporary Culture, Language, Literature, Literary Criticism, Memoirs, Music/Dance, Social Sciences, Theatre

Submission Guidelines Accepts complete manuscript by post with SAE.

Fiction Publishes Literary, Mainstream/ Contemporary, Translation, Black Writing and Women's titles.

Submission Guidelines Agented submissions only. Would prefer a synopsis and sample chapter in the first instance.

Recent Title(s) *Stolen Time*, Vangelis Hatziyannidis (Translation/Novel)

Tips Marion Boyars Publishers seek submissions for non-fiction in the areas of music, film and contemporary culture. Fiction submissions must be sent through an agent. Does not accept submissions by email.

Marshall Cavendish Ltd

5th Floor, 32/38 Saffron Hill, London, EC1N 8FH

- 020 7421 8120
- 020 7421 8121
- info@marshallcavendish.co.uk
- www.marshallcavendish.co.uk

Insider Info Catalogue available online.

Non-Fiction Publishes Children's, Gift Book, Part Works and General Non-Fiction titles on the following subjects:
Art, Architecture, Cooking, Education, Food and Drink, House and Home, Nature, Science, Sex, Supernatural

Submission Guidelines Accepts query with SAE.

Recent Title(s) *The Thai Table: A Celebration of Culinary Treasures*, Terry Tan (Cooking)

Tips Marshall Cavendish publishes titles in 13 languages and their publishing network spans Asia, Europe and the US. Marshall Cavendish's illustrated reference and non-fiction titles for schools and libraries are aimed at enhancing the educational experiences of students at all levels.

Martin Books

88 Regent Street, Cambridge, CB2 1DP

- 01223 448770
- 01223 448777
- martinbooks@simonandschuster.co.uk
- www.martinbooks.co.uk

Parent Company Simon & Schuster UK Ltd

Contact Director, Jane Coplestone; Business Development Manager, Katie Walsh; Business Development Executive, Deborah Ball

Non-Fiction Publishes General Non-Fiction and Illustrated titles on the following subject areas:
Childcare/Parenting, Cookery, Food & Drink, Gardening, Lifestyle

* Martin Books offers a bespoke publishing service to individual clients, rather than operating as a traditional commissioning publishing company. Books may be produced to a company's specifications under their own brand, or in partnership.

Submission Guidelines No book proposals from those looking to go down the traditional publishing route.

Tips Martin Books primarily functions as a bespoke publisher. Specialises in cookery book production.

Martin Breese International

19 Hanover Crescent, Brighton, BN2 9SB

- 01273 687555
- martin@abracadabra.co.uk
- www.abracadabra.co.uk

Contact Proprietor, Martin Breese

Established 1975

Non-Fiction Publishes books on Conjuring and the Allied Arts

Submission Guidelines No unsolicited manuscripts accepted as all titles are commissioned.

Recent Title(s) *Al Koran's Professional Presentations*, Hugh Miller

Tips Titles are aimed at professional magicians or anyone interested in magic and mentalism.

Maverick House Publishers

Office 19, Dunboyne Business Park, Dunboyne, Co. Meath, Republic of Ireland

- 00353 1 825 5717
- 00353 1 686 5036
- info@maverickhouse.com
- www.maverickhouse.com

Established 2001

Insider Info Aims to respond to proposals and manuscripts within eight weeks. Catalogue available online. Manuscript guidelines available online.

Non-Fiction Publishes Biography and General Non-Fiction titles on the following subjects:

Current Affairs, Memoirs, Sports, True Crime, Positive Living, Social Affairs, Politics
Submission Guidelines Accepts query with SAE/proposal package (including outline, sample chapter(s), author biography). Accept postal and emailed submissions.
Recent Title(s) *Miss Bangkok*, Bua Boonmee with Nicola Pierce
Tips Maverick House titles should be politically and socially relevant. They are now the fastest growing publisher of current affairs in the United Kingdom, Ireland and South East Asia.

Maypole Editions
22 Mayfair Avenue, Illford, Essex, IG1 3DQ
☎ 020 8252 3937
Fiction Publishes Plays.
Poetry Publishes Poetry titles.
* Poetry submissions are accepted for possible inclusion in themed anthologies. Previous themes have included social issues, ethnic minority issues, feminist themes, romance, travel and lyric rhyming verse. Generally no politics.
Submission Guidelines Submit sample poems. Poems should be around 30 lines.
Tips There could be a long delay in responding to submissions due to the volume received. Previously unpublished poets are welcome.

McGraw-Hill Education
McGraw-Hill House, Shoppenhangers Road, Maidenhead, Berkshire, SL6 2QL
☎ 01628 502500
☎ 01628 770224
✉ helpme@mcgraw-hill.com
🌐 www.mcgraw-hill.co.uk
Established 1909
Imprint(s) Open University Press
Insider Info Catalogue available online. Manuscript guidelines available online.
Non-Fiction Publishes Multimedia, Scholarly, Technical, Textbook and Reference titles on the following subjects:
Business, Computers/Electronics, Economics, Education, Engineering, Management
Submissions Guidelines Accepts queries and proposals for scholarly books or teaching resources. Check guidelines on website for further details.
Recent Title(s) *The Starbucks Experience: 5 Principles for Turning Ordinary into Extraordinary*, Joseph Michelli (Business)
Tips McGraw-Hill Education is a leading global provider of educational materials and professional information.

Meadow Books
35 Stonefield Way, Burgess Hill, RH15 8DW
☎ 01444 239044
✉ meadowbooks@hotmail.com
Contact Managing Director, C. O'Neill
Established 1990
Imprint(s) Diggory Press
Non-Fiction Publishes General Non-Fiction and Reference titles on the following subjects: Spirituality, Nursing History, Nursing Photo Reference Books, Folklore
Submission Guidelines Query with SAE. No telephone calls please.
Tips Be aware that Meadow Books also run self publishing services, mainly under the Diggory Press imprint – therefore all options should be researched thoroughly before committing to any services.

Meadowside Children's Books
185 Fleet Street, London, EC4A 2HS
☎ 0207400 1092
☎ 020 7400 1037
✉ info@meadowsidebooks.com
🌐 www.meadowsidebooks.com
Parent Company DC Thomson
Established 2003
Insider Info Publishes roughly 100 titles per year. Receives approximately 2,000 queries and 2,000 manuscripts per year. 50 per cent of books published are from first-time authors, 25 per cent of books published are from unagented authors. Payment is via royalty (on retail price). Average lead time is six months, with simultaneous submissions accepted. Submissions accompanied by SAE will be returned. Aims to respond to queries within three months. Catalogue is available with SAE, or by email. Manuscript guidelines are available online.
Fiction Publishes Children's and Young Adult titles.
Submission Guidelines Accepts proposal package (including outline, and three sample chapters).
Poetry Publishes Children's Poetry.
Submission Guidelines Accepts proposal package (including outline and three sample poems). Supply artworks/images digitally or photocopies by post.

The Medlar Press
The Grange, Ellesmere, Shropshire, SY12 9DE
☎ 01691 623225
✉ books@medlarpress.com
🌐 www.medlarpress.com
Contact Publishers, Jon Ward-Allen and Rosie Ward-Allen
Established 1994
Insider Info Submissions accompanied by SAE will be returned. Will accept unsolicited manuscripts and manuscripts from first-time or unagented authors.

Aims to respond to proposals within one month. Catalogue available online.

Non-Fiction Publishes General Non-Fiction and Illustrated Books on Fishing.

Submission Guidelines Submit proposal package (including outline, previous publishing history, market research, sample photographs/illustrations and a couple of sample chapters, if available) by post to Rosie Ward-Allen.

Submission Guidelines Accepts query with SAE. Submit proposal package (including outline, three sample chapters and a covering letter).

Tips Medlar Press suggests that prospective authors get in touch with a proposal before they start writing the book in full. Medlar Press also publishes the *Waterlog* fishing magazine.

Melrose Press Ltd
St Thomas Place, Ely, Cambridgeshire, CB7 4GG
- 01353 646600
- 01353 646601
- info@melrosepress.co.uk
- www.melrosepress.co.uk

Contact Managing Director, Nicholas S. Law
Established 1960
Imprint(s) International Biographical Centre Melrose Books
Insider Info Catalogue available online.
Non-Fiction Publishes Biography and Reference titles.
Recent Title(s) *The Cambridge Blue Book 2008/09* (Reference/Biography)
Tips Melrose Press is a world leader in biographical publishing, supplying biographical information to librarians, researchers and individuals worldwide, much of which is difficult to obtain elsewhere. Melrose Books is a new venture offering 'Commissioned Publishing' services where an author can commission Melrose to publish their book by sharing part of the cost. It is similar to subsidy publishing.

Menard Press
8 The Oaks, Woodside Avenue, London, N12 8AR
- 020 8446 5571
- Online form.
- www.menardpress.co.uk

Established 1969
Insider Info Catalogue available online.
Non-Fiction Publishes Autobiography, Biography, General Non-Fiction and Scholarly titles on the following subjects:
Art, Architecture, History, Literary Criticism, Memoirs, Translation.

Fiction Publishes Literary, Mainstream/Contemporary, Short Story Collections and Translation titles.
Poetry Publishes Translated Poetry titles.
Recent Title(s) *Flow Tide*, Claude Vigée and Rudolf Anthony
Tips Menard Press specialises in literary translation, mainly of poetry.

Mentor Books
43 Furze Road, Sandyford Industrial Estate, Dublin 18, Republic of Ireland
- 00353 1 295 2112
- 00353 1 295 2114
- admin@mentorbooks.ie
- www.mentorbooks.ie

Insider Info Catalogue is available online.
Non-Fiction Publishes Children's, General Non-Fiction, How-To, Humour, Illustrated, Textbook and Reference titles on the following subjects: Education, Humour, Irish History, Politics, Quiz, Trivia, True Crime
Fiction Publishes Children's titles.
Recent Title(s) *The Business World*, Enda Connolly (Business); *Planet and People Core Workbook*, Sue Honan and Sue Mulholland (Education)

Mercat Press Ltd
10 Coates Crescent, Edinburgh, EH3 7AL
- 0131 225 9774
- 0131 226 6632
- info@birlinn.co.uk
- www.birlinn.birlinn.co.uk

Parent Company Birlinn Ltd
Contact Managing Editors, Seán Costello and Tom Johnstone; Editorial and Marketing Assistant, Caroline Taylor
Established 1970
Imprint(s) Crescent Books
Insider Info Payment is via royalties. Aims to respond to proposals within two weeks. Catalogue free on request online and by email.
Non-Fiction Publishes Autobiography, Biography, and General Non-Fiction titles on the following subjects:
Art, Architecture, Contemporary Culture, Hobbies, Language, Literature, Literary Criticism, Nature/Environment, Regional, Sports, Travel, Walking guides.
* Most books are of Scottish interest.
Submission Guidelines Query with SAE, submit proposal package (including outline, two sample chapters and SAE).
Fiction Regional (Scottish Interest).

Submission Guidelines Accepts query with SAE/ proposal package (including outline, two sample chapters and SAE) sent to either Managing Editor.
Recent Title(s) *Edinburgh: A New Perspective*, Jason Baxter (Photography); *Blood in the Water*, Gillian Galbraith (Novel)
Tips Publishes books of predominantly Scottish interest.

Mercia Cinema Society
29 Blackbrook Court, Durham Road, Loughborough, LE11 5UA
- 01509 218393
- mervyn.gould@virgin.net
- www.merciacinema.org

Contact Managing Editors and Administrator, Mervyn Gould; Managing Editor, Paul Smith
Established 1980
Non-Fiction Publishes General Non-Fiction and Scholarly titles on the following subjects:
History, Regional, History of Cinema/Picture Houses
Submission Guidelines Accepts query with SAE.
Tips A national society for the promotion and publication of research into cinema history. Mercia Cinema are always interested in well written and thoroughly researched texts on cinema exhibition.

Mercier Press Ltd
Unit 3B, Oak House, Bessboro Road, Blackrock, Cork, Republic of Ireland
- 00353 21 461 4700
- 00353 21 461 4802
- info@mercierpress.ie
- www.mercierpress.ie

Contact Managing Director, Clodagh Feehan
Established 1944
Imprint(s) Marino Books
Insider Info Catalogue available online. Manuscript guidelines available online.
Non-Fiction Publishes Children's Fiction and General Non-Fiction, Humour, Scholarly and Irish interest titles on the following subjects:
Health/Medicine, History, Language, Literature, Regional, Sports, World Affairs
Submission Guidelines Accepts query with SAE or via email with proposal package (including outline, sample chapter(s), author biography). Submission details to: commissioning@ mercierpress.ie
Recent Title(s) *Great Irish Heroes*, Sean McMahon (History)
Tips Mercier Press is Ireland's oldest independent publishing house, based in Cork. They focus mainly on history, folklore and politics, although not exclusively, and their books are primarily aimed at the Irish market.

Meridian Books
40 Hadzor Road, Oldbury, West Midlands, B68 9LA
- 0121 429 4397
- meridian.books@btopenworld.com
- www.bestwalks.com/meridianbooks.htm

Contact Managing Editor, Peter Groves
Established 1985
Insider Info Publishes roughly five titles per year. Payment is via royalties. Catalogue available online.
Non-Fiction Publishes General Non-Fiction titles on the following subjects:
Regional Walking Guides
Submission Guidelines Accepts query with SAE/ proposal package (including outline and sample chapter(s)).
Recent Title(s) *The Elan Valley Way*, David Milton (Walking Guide)
Tips Meridian is a small, home based business publishing regional walking guidebooks. Relevant unsolicited submissions are welcomed.

Merlin Press
99b Wallis Road, London, E9 5LN
- 020 8533 5800
- info@merlinpress.co.uk
- www.merlinpress.co.uk

Established 1956
Insider Info Publishes 15 titles per year. Receives approximately 500 queries per year. Payment is via royalty (on wholesale price). Simultaneous submissions not accepted. Submissions accompanied by SAE will be returned. Aims to respond to queries within three months. Catalogue is free on request and available online. Manuscript guidelines are free on request.
Non-Fiction Publishes Autobiography, Biography and Scholarly titles on the following subjects:
Government/Politics, History, Humanities, Social Sciences, Women's Issues/Studies, World Affairs
Submission Guidelines Accepts proposal package (including outline, sample chapters and SAE).
Recent Title(s) *Confuse and Conceal*, Stewart Player and Colin Leys

Merlin Publishing
Newmarket Hall, Cork Street, Dublin 8, Republic of Ireland
- 00353 1 453 5866
- 00353 1 453 5930
- publishing@merlin.ie
- www.merlinwolfhound.com

Contact Editorial Manager, Aoife Barrett
Established 2000
Imprint(s) Wolfhound Press

Insider Info Publishes 15 titles per year. Catalogue available online.

Non-Fiction Publishes General Non-Fiction, Humour, Biography and Autobiography tiles on the following subjects:
Art, Architecture, Current Affairs, Health, Irish Interest, Lifestyle, Memoirs, Music/Dance, Politics, Sports, Travel, True Crime

Submission Guidelines Submissions by post or email accepted. Accepts outline, one sample chapter, author biography, SAE, list of unique selling points, artworks/images.
Submission details to: aoife@merlin.ie

Recent Title(s) *The Irish Scissor Sisters*, Mick McCaffrey (True Crime)

Tips Merlin Publishing and Wolfhound Press welcome submissions for non-fiction titles, particularly true crime, music, sports, lifestyle, politics, biography and Irish historical interest. No children's fiction or general fiction titles.

Merlin Unwin Books
Palmers House, 7 Corve Street, Ludlow, Shropshire, SY8 1DB
- 01584 877456
- 01584 877457
- books@merlinunwin.co.uk
- www.merlinunwin.co.uk

Contact Managing Director, Karen McCall (General Countryside, Country Crafts, Natural History); Chairman, Merlin Unwin (Fishing)

Established 1995

Insider Info Publishes 12 titles per year. Receives approximately 150 queries and 50 manuscripts per year. 50 per cent of books published are from first-time authors, 95 per cent of books are from unagented authors. Payment is via net receipts. Average lead time is one year, with simultaneous submissions not accepted. Submissions accompanied by SAE will be returned. Aims to respond to queries within three days, proposals within four weeks and manuscripts within four months. Catalogue is free on request and available online. Manuscripts guidelines are available with an SAE, or by email.

Non-Fiction Publishes Autobiography, Biography, Coffee Table Books, Cookbooks, General Non-Fiction, Gift, How-To, Humour, Illustrated, Reference and Textbook titles on the following subjects:
Agriculture/Horticulture, Alternative Lifestyles, Animals, Cooking, Crafts, Food and Drink, Hobbies, Memoirs, Nature/Environment, Recreation, Sports
* All submissions must have a UK countryside angle.

Submission Guidelines Accepts proposal package (including outline, three sample chapters, a brief synopsis, your publishing history, author biography and SAE) and artworks/images (send photocopies).

Tips Merlin Unwin Books prefer to work directly with their authors, not via an agent. Many of their titles are written by authors who are experts in their field, but not necessarily experienced or professional writers.

Merrell Publishers Ltd
81 Southwark Street, London, SE1 0HX
- 020 7928 8880
- 020 7928 1199
- jh@merrellpublishers.com
- www.merrellpublishers.com

Contact Publisher, Hugh Merrell; Editorial Director, Julian Honer; Art Director, Nicola Bailey

Established 1993

Insider Info Publishes 30 titles per year. Payment is via royalties. Catalogue free on request, online. Manuscript guidelines online.

Non-fiction Publishes General Non-Fiction, Gift book and Illustrated titles on the following subjects:
Art, Architecture, Cars and Motorcycles, Craft, Decorative Arts, Film, Gardening, History, House & Home, Photography, Science, Women's Issues/Studies

Submission Guidelines Query with SAE, submit completed manuscript and artwork/images. Address the package to Julian Honer. Will also accept informal telephone or email enquiries prior to a proposal being submitted.
Submission details to: jh@merrellpublishers.com

Recent Title(s) *Big-Eye Art*, Blonde Blythe (Art)

Tips Merrell is an independent publisher, specialising in illustrated art books, with offices in London and New York.

Methuen Drama
38 Soho Square, London, W1D 3HB
- 020 7758 0200
- 020 7758 0222
- performing@acblack.com
- www.acblack.com

Parent Company A&C Black Publishers Ltd

Imprints The Arden Shakespeare

Insider Info Catalogue available online.

Non-Fiction Publishes Illustrated, Reference, Technical and Anthology titles on the following subjects:
Music/Dance, Performing Arts, Classical Drama/Plays, Screen and Cinema, Theatre Studies

Recent Title(s) *Actors' Yearbook 2009*

Methuen Publishing Ltd
8 Artillery Road, London, SW1P 1RZ
- 020 7798 1600
- 020 7828 1244
- sales@methuen.co.uk

ⓦ www.methuen.co.uk
Contact Managing Director, Peter Tummons
Established 1889
Imprint(s) Politico's Publishing
Insider Info Publishes 60 titles per year. Receives approximately 200 queries and 100 manuscripts per year. Ten per cent of books published are from first-time authors, five per cent are from unagented authors and ten per cent are author subsidy published. Catalogue is available online.
Non-Fiction Publishes Autobiography, Biography, Humour, Diaries, Letters, Essay and Anthology titles on the following subjects:
Memoirs, Philosophy, Psychology, Sports, Travel, Cultural Studies, Writing Guides, Entertainment
Submission Guidelines Accepts query with SAE with proposal package (including synopsis). Prefers agented submissions.
Fiction Publishes Literary, Short Story Collections, Drama and and Stage Play titles.
Submission Guidelines Accepts query with SAE with proposal package (including synopsis). Prefers agented submissions.
Recent Title(s) *One Hundred Days: One Hundred Nights*, Christophtr Bigsby
Tips Does not encourage unagented submissions, but will accept short queries with SAE from unagented authors. Do not send any material via email.

Michael Joseph
80 Strand, London, WC2R 0RL
ⓞ 020 7010 3000
ⓞ 020 7010 6060
ⓔ customer.service@penguin.co.uk
ⓦ www.penguin.co.uk
Parent Company Penguin General
Contact Managing Director, Louise Moore; Editorial Director, Harriet Evans
Insider Info Catalogue is available online or by email.
Non-Fiction Publishes Autobiography, Biography, General Non-Fiction, How-To, Illustrated and Self-Help titles on the following subjects:
Celebrity Autobiography, Cookery, Current Affairs, Food & Drink, History, Humour, Mind, Body & Spirit, Showbiz, Sports, Travel, Television Tie-Ins
Submission Guidelines Agented submissions only.
Fiction Publishes Crime, Humour, Mainstream/Contemporary, Romance, Suspense, Thriller and Women's Interest titles.
Submission Guidelines Agented submissions only.
Recent Title(s) *Bleeding Heart Square*, Andrew Taylor (Crime); *Panic! The Story of Modern Financial Insanity*, Elise Lindsay (Economics)
Tips Michael Joseph publishes market focused popular fiction and non-fiction, and is primarily

focused on top-ten bestsellers from authors such as Tom Clancy, Jamie Oliver and Clive Cussler.

Michael O'Mara Books Ltd
16 Lion Yard, Tremadoc Road, London, SW4 7NQ
ⓞ 020 7720 8643
ⓞ 020 7627 8953
ⓔ enquiries@mombooks.com
ⓦ www.mombooks.com
Contact Editorial Directors, Lindsay Davies (General Non-Fiction, Biography, Humour) and Toby Buchan (General Non-Fiction, History, Military History)
Established 1985
Imprint(s) Buster Books (Children's)
Insider Info Publishes 70 titles per year. Average lead time is six months, with simultaneous submissions accepted. Submissions accompanied by SAE will be returned. Catalogue is available with SAE. Manuscript guidelines are available online.
Non-Fiction Publishes Autobiography, Biography, Children's, General Non-Fiction, Gift, How-To, Humour, Illustrated and Reference titles on the following subjects:
Animals, Contemporary Culture, Creative Non-Fiction, Entertainment/Games, Health/Medicine, History, Hobbies, Language/Literature, Memoirs, Military/War, Music/Dance, Nostalgia, Sex, Sports
* Michael O'Mara Books only publish commercial, mass market non-fiction.
Submission Guidelines Accepts proposal package (including outline, two to three sample chapters, your publishing history, author biography and SAE) and artworks/images (send photocopies).
Fiction Publishes Children's Board Books and Picture Book titles.
* Children's titles are published by Buster Books (see separate entry).
Submission Guidelines Does not accept fiction submissions.
Poetry Occasionally publishes humorous poetry from established authors.

Michelin Travel Publications
Hannay House, 39 Clarendon Road, Watford, Hertfordshire, WD17 IJA
ⓞ 01923 205240
ⓞ 01923 205241
ⓔ Online form.
ⓦ www.viamichelin.com
Established 1900
Non-Fiction Publishes General Non-Fiction and Illustrated titles on the following subjects:
Travel, Maps/Atlases
Tips A travel publisher specialising in maps, atlases and travel guides. Also offers an online route planning service.

Miles Kelly Publishing Ltd

The Bardfield Centre, Great Bardfield, Essex, CM7 4SL

- 01371 811309
- 01371 811393
- info@mileskelly.net
- www.mileskelly.net

Contact Publishers: Jim Miles and Gerard Kelly
Established 1996
Imprint(s) Miles Kelly
Bardfield Press
Insider Info Publishes 100 titles per year. Catalogue available online.
Non-Fiction Publishes Children's, Gift Book and Reference titles.
Submission Guidelines No unsolicited manuscripts.
Fiction Publishes Children's titles.
Recent Title(s) *The Miles Kelly Book of British History*, Miles Kelly Publishing (Children's Reference)
Tips Miles Kelly aims to publish high quality books that are enjoyable, attractive and useful, with fresh and innovative features that appeal to a wide readership.

Milestone Publications

62 Murray Road, Horndean, Waterlooville, PO8 9JL

- 023 9259 7440
- 023 9259 1975
- info@gosschinaclub.co.uk
- www.gosscrestedchina.co.uk

Contact Managing Director, Lynda Pine
Established 1967
Insider Info Catalogue available for a charge online, and via email.
Non-Fiction Publishes Reference titles on the following subjects:
Goss and Crested China
Recent Title(s) *The Price Guide to Crested China*, Nicholas Pine (Reference)
Tips The Goss and Crested China Club is the leading dealer in Goss and other crested china and is based in Horndean, Hampshire. Milestone Press is their publishing arm, specialising in titles to help collectors value their collections.

Millers Dale Publications

7 Weavers Place, Chandlers Ford, Eastleigh, Hampshire, S053 ITU

- 023 8026 1192
- gponting@clara.net

Contact Managing Editor, Gerald Ponting
Established 1990
Insider Info Catalogue available online.

Non-Fiction Publishes General Non-Fiction and Illustrated titles on the following subjects: Anthropology/Archaeology, Art, Architecture, History, Regional, Hampshire History/Guides
Submission Guidelines Proposals for local, Hampshire based, history books are welcomed.
Recent Title(s) *The Chandler's Ford Story*, Barbara Hillier and Gerald Ponting (Local History); *Shakespeare's Fantastic Garlands*, Gerald Ponting (Literature/Botany/Gardening)
Tips Millers Dale specialises in local history, particularly related to central Hampshire, and books about Gerald Ponting's historical slide presentations.

Mill Publishing

PO Box 120, 4 Balloo Avenue, Bangor, Co. Down, BT19 7PJ

- 02891 462226
- 02891 466474
- info@motivationinlearning.com

Parent Company Motivation in Learning Ltd
Imprint(s) Anglia Young Books
Insider Info Catalogue available online or via email to info@motivationinlearning.com
Non-Fiction Publishes Educational Resources on the following subjects:
National Curriculum (all stages)
Submission Guidelines Will accept ideas for new titles, particularly from teachers. Send a brief synopsis. Accept images/artworks.
Fiction Publishes Children's Historical titles.
* Fiction is published through the Anglia Young Books imprint (see separate entry). Historical fiction is aimed at Key Stage 2 children.
Tips Mill Publishing produces several series including *Skill Builder* and *Write into History*. These series have specific characteristics, details of which are on the website. See the Anglia Young Books entry for more information on this imprint.

Milo Books Ltd

The Old Weighbridge, Station Road, Wrea Green, Preston, PR4 2PH

- 01772 672900
- 01772 687727
- info@milobooks.com
- www.milobooks.com

Contact Publisher, Peter Walsh
Established 1997
Insider Info Publishes 12 titles per year. Receives approximately 200 manuscripts per year. 95 per cent of books published are from first-time authors, 90 per cent of books published are from unagented authors. Payment is via royalty (on retail price). Average lead time is six months, with simultaneous submissions accepted. Submissions accompanied

by SAE will be returned. Aims to respond to proposals within four weeks. Catalogue is available online. Manuscript guidelines are available by email.

Non-Fiction Publishes Autobiography, Biography and General Non-Fiction titles on the following subjects:
Contemporary Culture, Sports, True Crime

Submission Guidelines Accepts proposal package (including outline, two sample chapters, author biography and SAE).

Recent Title(s) *Hoods: The Gangs of Nottingham*

Tips Milo Books recommends that all prospective authors be familiar with their current list.

Mitchell Beazley
2–4 Heron Quays, London, E14 4JP
- 020 7531 8400
- 020 7531 8650
- publisher@mitchell-beazley.co.uk
- www.mitchell-beazley.co.uk

Parent Company Octopus Publishing Group

Contact Publisher, David Lamb

Imprint(s) Miller's Antiques

Insider Info Catalogue available online.

Non-Fiction Publishes Illustrated and Reference titles on the following subjects:
Art/Architecture, Crafts, Gardening, Health/Medicine, History, Sports, Antiques, Design, Interiors, Wine, Food and Drink, Health/Well Being

Recent Title(s) *The Gastropub Cookbook*, Diana Henry (Cookery); *Heard it Through the Grapevine*, Matt Skinner (Wine)

Tips Authors are often experts in their fields or well-known television personalities. Most antiques titles are published under the Miller's Antiques imprint, a leading name in antique publishing.

Morgan Kauffman
Linacre House, Jordan Hill, Oxford, OX2 8DP
- 01865 474010
- 01865 474011
- authorsupport@elsevier.com
- www.elsevier.com

Parent Company Elsevier Ltd (Science & Technology)

Established 1984

Insider Info Royalties paid. Catalogue is available online. Manuscript guidelines available online.

Non-Fiction Publishes Multimedia, Reference, Scholarly, Textbook and Technical titles on the following subjects:
Computers/Electronics, Computer Aided Design, Software Engineering, Artificial Intelligence, Databases

Submission Guidelines Accepts query with SAE/ Proposal package (including outline).

Submission Guidelines Morgan Kaufmann welcomes authors' proposals for books. The first step is to discuss the proposal with the relevant publishing editor. Check the website for in-depth submission guidelines and a full list of editorial contacts.

Recent Title(s) *Web Application Design Patterns*, Vora (Computing/Reference)

Tips Morgan Kaufmann publishes books and digital material in areas such as databases, computer networking, computer systems, human computer interaction, computer graphics, multimedia information and systems, artificial intelligence, and software engineering. Publications are aimed at the research and development communities, information technology (IS/IT) managers, and students in professional degree programmes.

Morning Star
19 Off Quay Building, Foundry Lane, Byker, Newcastle upon Tyne, NE6 1AF
- 0191 265 6699
- alecfinlay@yahoo.com
- www.alecfinlay.com

Contact Alec Finlay

Established 1990

Insider Info Catalogue available online.

Non-Fiction Publishes Regional and Travel titles.

Fiction Publishes Regional titles.

Poetry Publishes Poetry titles.

Tips Often co-publishes innovative projects that have included pocketbooks, folios and a small press series, combining poetry and other local accounts with art in unusual ways.

Mosby
Linacre House, Jordan Hill, Oxford, OX2 8DP
- 01865 474010
- 01865 474011
- authorsupport@elsevier.com
- www.elsevierhealth.com/mosby

Parent Company Elsevier Ltd (Health Sciences)

Established 1906

Insider Info Royalties paid. Catalogue available online. Manuscript guidelines available online.

Non-Fiction Publishes Booklets, Multimedia, Reference, Scholarly, Textbook, Journal and Technical titles on the following subjects:
Education, Health/Medicine, Science, Care

Submission Guidelines Use the online proposal form. Alternatively authors may contact the publishing director or editor prior to submission, to discuss the proposal.
Submission details to: c.makepeace@elsevier.com

Recent Title(s) *Modalities for Massage and Bodywork*, Stillerman (Reference)

Tips Mosby specialises in medicine, nursing, allied health and veterinary medicine, and publishes a wide range of textbooks, reference books and periodicals. Mosby's suite of healthcare resources includes newsletters, videos, posters, brochures, slides, CD-ROMs, seminars and conferences.

Motor Racing Publications
PO Box 1318, Croydon, Surrey, CR0 5YP
- 020 8654 2711
- 020 8407 0339
- john@mrpbooks.co.uk
- www.motorracingpublications.co.uk

Contact Editorial Head, John Blunsden
Insider Info Publishes five titles per year. Payment via royalties. Catalogue available online.
Non-Fiction Publishes General Non-Fiction, Reference and Technical titles on the following subjects:
Automotive History, Hobbies, Motor Racing, Motor Vehicles
Submission Guidelines Accepts query with SAE/ proposal package (including outline, sample chapter(s), and SAE).
Recent Title(s) *Powered By Jaguar*, Doug Nye
Tips Motor Racing Publications' titles are aimed at any motorsport or automotive enthusiast. They welcome synopses and ideas in the specified subject areas.

MQ Publications Ltd
12 The Ivories, 6–8 Northampton Street, London, N1 2HY
- 020 7359 2244
- 020 7359 1616
- mail@mqpublications.com
- www.mqpublications.com

Parent Company Octopus Publishing Group
Contact Publisher, Zaro Weil
Established 1992
Insider Info Publishes 70 titles per year. Catalogue free on request and available online.
Non-Fiction Publishes Biography, General Non-Fiction, Gift Book and Illustrated titles on the following subjects:
Contemporary Culture, Cooking, Food and Drink, Health, Photography, Spirituality
Recent Title(s) *Knitorama: 25 Great & Glam Things to Knit*, Rachael Matthews (Craft/Hobbies)
Tips MQ has become one of the UK's fastest growing and most respected publishers of illustrated non-fiction, specialising in books for the relatively niche craft market.

Mr & Mrs Smith
2nd Floor, 334 Chiswick High Road, London, W4 5TA
- 0845 034 0700
- www.mrandmrssmith.com

Contact Managing Director, James Lohan; Publishing Director, Andrew Grahame; Editor-in-Chief, Juliet Kinsman
Non-Fiction Publishes Guide Book and Travel titles.
Recent Title(s) *European Cities Hotel Collection*, Mr & Mrs Smith (Travel)
Tips Mr & Mrs Smith specialises in international lifestyle hotel and travel guides.

Mudfog Press
c/o Arts Development, The Stables, Stewart Park, The Grove, Marton, Middlesborough, TS7 8AR
- mudfog@hodgeon.demon.co.uk
- www.mudfog.co.uk

Established 1993
Insider Info Submissions accompanied by SAE will be returned. Aims to respond to manuscripts within three months.
Fiction Publishes Short Story Collections.
Submission Guidelines Manuscripts must be typed on white A4 paper, one side only, in plain font, and be accompanied by full return postage. No email submissions.
Poetry Publishes pamphlet length and occasionally full length collections of poetry and short stories.
Submission Guidelines Manuscripts must be typed on white A4 paper, one side only, in plain font, and be accompanied by full return postage. No email submissions.
Tips Mudfog showcases writers from the Tees Valley area only, and will not accept submissions from outside this region.

Multi-Sensory Learning Ltd
Highgate House, Creaton, Northamptonshire, NN6 8NN
- 01604 505000
- 01604 505001
- info@msl-online.net
- www.msl-online.net

Contact Senior Editor, Philippa Chudley
Established 1994
Insider Info Catalogue available free on request and online.
Non-Fiction Publishes Children's, General Non-Fiction, Self-Help, Textbook and Scholarly titles on Dyslexia.
Recent Title(s) *Dyslexia Pocketbook*, Julie Bennett
Tips MSL titles are aimed at schools, colleges, learning support centres, teachers, parents and

dyslexic adults. They are always seeking authors able to write materials for coping with, and overcoming dyslexia.

Murdoch Books UK Ltd

Erico House, 6th Floor, 93–99 Upper Richmond Road, London, SW15 2TG

- 020 8785 5995
- 020 8785 5985
- info@murdochbooks.co.uk
- www.murdochbooks.co.uk/mbuk.htm

Contact CEO (Australia), Juliet Rogers; Publishing Director (Australia), Kay Scarlett
Imprint(s) Pier 9
Insider Info Publishes 70 titles per year. Catalogue available online.
Non-Fiction Publishes General Non-Fiction titles on the following subjects:
Cooking, Crafts, Food & Drink, Gardening, Health, Hobbies, House & Home, Travel, Popular Science.
Submission Guidelines Accepts queries via email to Australia only.
Submission details to: inquiry@ murdochbooks.com.au
Recent Title(s) *Ripailles*, Stéphane Reynaud; *Venezia*, Tessa Kiros
Tips Murdoch Books have traditionally published high quality, illustrated non-fiction, in the leisure/ lifestyle categories – particularly cooking, DIY, gardening, health and craft. The Pier 9 imprint handles general narrative non-fiction. Murdoch Books is owned by an independent Australian company.

Myriad Editions

59 Lansdowne Place, Brighton, BN3 1FL

- 01273 720000
- 01273 720000
- info@myriadeditions.com
- www.myriadeditions.com

Contact Rights Manager, Sadie Mayne
Established 1993
Insider Info Catalogue available online.
Non-Fiction Publishes innovative Illustrated Books, Atlases and General Non-Fiction titles on the following subjects:
Business, Economics, Government/Politics, Military/ War, Regional, Social Sciences, Women's Issues/ Studies, World Affairs
Fiction Publishes Literary Fiction and Graphic titles.
Recent Title(s) *Rumble Strip*, Woodrow Phoenix (Graphic); *The Food of Love*, Kate Evans (Graphic); *365 Ways to Change the World*, Michael Norton (World Affairs); *The Cloths of Heaven*, Sue Eckstein (Fiction).
Tips Myriad Editions is committed to making global issues accessible for general readers, students and

professionals alike. They aim to combine clear analysis with creative graphics in order to illustrate human development and social concerns. Myriad has expanded its publishing programme to include edgy literary fiction, innovative non-fiction and documentary comic books.

N.A.G Press

Clerkenwell House, 45–47 Clerkenwell Green, London, EC1R 0HT

- 020 7251 2661
- 020 7490 4958
- submissions@halebooks.com
- www.halebooks.com

Parent Company Robert Hale Ltd
Insider Info Catalogue free on request via email.
Non-Fiction Publishes specialist Horological and Gemological titles.
Submission Guidelines Submit proposal package (including outline, three sample chapters, SAE).
Recent Title(s) *Artificial Gemstones*, Michael O'Donoghue (Gemology)
Tips N.A.G titles tend to be very niche and the target readership will generally be enthusiasts and collectors of gems or timepieces. No emailed submissions.

The National Archives

The National Archives, Kew, Richmond, Surrey, TW9 4DU

- 020 8876 3444
- 020 8487 1974
- catherine.bradley@nationalarchives.gov.uk
- www.nationalarchives.gov.uk

Insider Info Publishes 20 titles per year. Catalogue and author guidelines are free on request.
Non-Fiction Publishes Reference, Record, Directory and Archive Material titles on History and British History.
Tips The National Archives is a government department and an executive agency under the Secretary of State for Constitutional Affairs. Book titles are primarily aimed at history enthusiasts, genealogy researchers and military historians. Also publishes a wealth of record keeping documentation.

National Association for the Teaching of English (NATE)

50 Broadfield Road, Sheffield, South Yorkshire, S8 0XJ

- 0114 255 5419
- 0114 255 5296
- info@nate.org.uk
- www.nate.org.uk

Contact Publications Manager, Anne Fairhall; Publications Coordinator, Julie Selwood
Established 1963
Insider Info Publishes approximately four titles per year, as well as a journal.
Non-Fiction Publishes Primary, Secondary and Tertiary Educational and Teaching Resources on the following subjects:
English, Drama, Media
Submission Guidelines Will accept ideas for new publications from teachers.
Tips NATE is a voluntary association. All publication ideas will go through an editorial board.

National Library of Ireland
Kildare Street, Dublin 2, Republic of Ireland
- 00353 1 603 0213
- 00353 1 661 2523
- info@nli.ie
- www.nli.ie
Insider Info Catalogue available online.
Non-Fiction Publishes Booklets, Illustrated Books, Reference and Scholarly titles on the following subjects:
History, Irish Interest
Tips The National Library of Ireland is a cultural institution under the aegis of the Department of Arts, Sport and Tourism. Its mission is to collect, preserve, and make available, books, manuscripts and illustrative material of Irish interest.

National Trust Books
The Old Magistrates Court, 10 Southcombe Street, London, W14 0RA
- 020 7605 1400
- 020 7605 1401
- customerservices@anovabooks.com
- www.anovabooks.com
Parent Company Anova Books Company Ltd
Established 2005 (became an imprint of Anova)
Insider Info Catalogue available online.
Non-Fiction Publishes Children's, Coffee Table Books, Cookbooks, General Non-Fiction, Gift Books and Illustrated titles on the following subjects:
Heritage, Gardening, Craft, Cooking, Art, Architecture, History, Nature/Environment, Regional, Science, Social Sciences
Recent Title(s) *English Fairy Tales & Legends*, Rosalind Kerven
Tips National Trust books reflect work done by the trust to preserve and protect coastline, countryside and buildings, and aim to educate people about the importance of the environment and of preserving British heritage for future generations.

Natural History Museum Publishing
Natural History Museum, Cromwell Road, London, SW7 5BD
- 020 7942 5336
- 020 7942 6994
- publishing@nhm.ac.uk
- www.nhm.ac.uk
Contact Editorial Director, Trudy Brannan (Natural History/Science)
Established 1881
Insider Info Publishes roughly eight titles per year. Receives 40 queries and 40 manuscripts per year. 50 per cent of books published are from first-time authors, 100 per cent of books published are from unagented authors. Payment is via royalty (on wholesale price), or outright purchase. Simultaneous submissions are accepted. Submissions accompanied by SAE will be returned. Aims to respond to queries and proposals within 14 days and manuscripts within 28 days. Catalogue is free on request and available by email. Manuscript guidelines are free on request.
Non-Fiction Publishes Coffee Table, General Non-Fiction, Gift, Illustrated, Reference, Scholarly and Textbook titles on the following subjects:
Agriculture/Horticulture, Animals, Anthropology, Archaeology, Art, Architecture, Education, Gardening, History, Marine Subjects, Natural History, Nature/Environment, Photography, Popular Science
Submission Guidelines Accepts queries with SAE.
Recent Title(s) *Walter Rothschild: The Man, the Museum and the Menagerie*, Miriam Rothschild (Biography)
Tips Natural History Museum Publishing mainly publishes books for a general readership – although some titles are useful for students and academics. Most books are directly related to the museum or its contents. Some separate academic and specialist titles are published in association with external publishers.

Nature Publishing
The Macmillan Building, 4 Crinan Street, London, N1 9XW
- 020 7833 4000
- 020 7843 4640
- nature@nature.com
- www.nature.com
Parent Company Macmillan Publishers Ltd
Contact Managing Director, Steven Inchcoombe; Publishing Directors: David Swinbanks and Peter Collins; Senior Associate Director, Alison Mitchell; Editor in Chief, Philip Campbell
Insider Info Catalogue available online. Manuscript guidelines available online.

Non-Fiction Publishes Academic Journals and Online Resources on the following subjects:. Environment, Health, Medicine, Nature, Science
Submission Guidelines Academics should register on the website to allow the submission of their articles for particular journals.
Tips The scientific arm of the Macmillan Group, publishing mainly journals on health, science, medicine and technology. The 'Editorial Policy' section of the website gives authors information on how to submit their original research papers for consideration for particular journals. Publications are intended for academic and professional readerships.

Natzler Enterprises (Entertainments)
1 Wakeford Cottages, Selden Lane, Worthing, West Sussex, BN11 2LQ
- 01903 211785
- 01903 211519
- natzler@btinternet.com
- www.natzler.com

Contact Managing Editor, Paul Gordon
Established 1993
Insider Info Catalogue available online, at www.paulgordon.net/acatalog
Non-Fiction Publishes How-To, Multimedia and Reference titles on Magic Tricks.
Submission Guidelines No unsolicited manuscripts, but may consider ideas.
Tips Publishes magic trick books and equipment.

Nautical Data Ltd
The Book Barn, White Chimney Row, Westbourne, Hampshire, PO10 8RS
- 01243 389352
- 01243 379136
- enquiries@nauticaldata.com
- www.nauticaldata.com

Contact Managing Director, Piers Mason
Established 1999
Insider Info Publishes 20 titles per year. Payment is via royalties.
Non-Fiction Publishes Reference and Technical titles on the following subjects:
Nautical/Sailing
Submission Guidelines Accepts query with SAE/proposal package (including outline, sample chapter(s), and SAE).
Tips Publishes books on shipping and nautical reference. Will consider project ideas and proposals but not for fiction or non-nautical subjects.

NCVO Publications
The National Council for Voluntary Organisations, Regents Wharf, 8 All Saints Street, London, N1 9RL

- 020 7713 6161
- 020 7713 6300
- ncvo@ncvo-vol.org.uk
- www.ncvo-vol.org.uk/publications

Contact CEO, Stuart Etherington; Director of Services and Development, Ben Kernigha
Established 1919
Insider Info Catalogue available free on request and online.
Submission Guidelines No unsolicited manuscripts.
Recent Title(s) *Civil Society Almanac 2008*, NCVO
Tips NCVO mostly publishes directories and information on management, finance and employment.

Neate Publishing
Hedgerows, 33 Downside Road, Winchester, SO22 5LT
- 01962 841479
- 01962 841743
- bobbie@neatepublishing.co.uk
- www.neatepublishing.co.uk

Contact Managing Director, Bobbie Neate
Established 1999
Insider Info Catalogue available online.
Non-Fiction Publishes Children's, Textbook and Scholarly titles on Educational subjects.
Submission Guidelines The best way to get in touch is by post. Do not send emails with attachments, they will not be opened.
Recent Title(s) *Body Parts*, Bobbie Neate (Education/Reference)
Tips Neate specialises in non-fiction books, role play and the teaching of 'notemaking' and 'notetaking' for schools and pupils. All ideas for publishing are welcome. Of particular interest are titles for primary age children and ideas for new role play packs.

Neil Wilson Publishing Ltd
G/R 19 Netherton Avenue, Glasgow, G13 1BQ
- 0141 954 8007
- info@nwp.co.uk
- www.nwp.co.uk

Imprint(s) Vital Spark
In Pinn
The Angels Share
11:9
Insider Info Catalogue and manuscript guidelines are available online.
Non-Fiction Publishes Biography, General Non-Fiction and Reference titles on the following subjects:
General Reference, History, True Crime
Submission Guidelines Submit proposal package (including outline, synopsis, one sample chapter,

author biography, CV and SAE). Will accept artworks/images.

Recent Title(s) *Grape Britain: A Tour of Britain's Vineyards*, David Harvey (Food & Drink)

Tips Neil Wilson Publishing is one of Scotland's leading independent publishers. They specialise in non-fiction and fiction of Scottish, and sometimes Irish, interest and also offer some of their specialist titles on a 'Print on Demand' basis. See separate imprint entries for further details.

Nelson Thornes Ltd
Delta Place, 27 Bath Road, Cheltenham, Gloucestershire, GL53 7TH
- 01242 267100
- 01242 221914
- cservices@nelsonthornes.com
- www.nelsonthornes.com

Parent Company Infinitas Learning
Contact Managing Director, Mary O'Connor
Established Formed in 2000 with the merger of the Thomas Nelson and Stanley Thornes publishing companies
Insider Info Catalogue is free on request and available online, by email to, or by telephone, 01242 267382
Non-Fiction Publishes Illustrated, CD-ROM, Electronic Teaching and Learning Resource titles on the following subjects:
Education, Children's, Nursing, Health Sciences, Teacher Training, CPD
Tips Nelson Thornes is one of the UK's leading educational publishers.

New Beacon Books Ltd
76 Stroud Green Road, Finsbury Park, London, N4 3EN
- 020 7272 4889
- 020 7281 4662
- newbeaconbooks@btconnect.com
- www.newbeaconbooks.co.uk

Contact Editor in Chief, John La Rose; Managing Director, Sarah White
Established 1966
Insider Info Payment is via royalties.
Non-Fiction Publishes Children's, General Non-Fiction, Reference and Scholarly titles on the following subjects:
Education, Government/Politics, History, Language, Literature, Black Literature.
Fiction Publishes Black Literature titles.
Submission Guidelines No unsolicited material.
Tips New Beacon Books specialises in books that highlight Black life in Britain and their links in Europe, the Caribbean, Africa and African America.

New Cavendish Books
3 Denbigh Road, London, W11 2SJ
- 020 7229 6765
- 020 7792 0027
- sales@newcavendishbooks.co.uk
- www.newcavendishbooks.co.uk

Established 1973
Insider Info Catalogue available online, free on request.
Non-Fiction Publishes General Non-Fiction and Reference titles on the following subjects:
Hobbies, Collecting
Recent Title(s) *A Century of Deans Rag Books & Rag Dolls*, New Cavendish Books
Tips Specialises in books on toys, popular culture and collectibles of the 19th and 20th Centuries.

New Holland Publishers (UK) Ltd
Garfield House, 86–88 Edgware Road, London, W2 2EA
- 020 7724 7773
- 020 7724 6184
- enquiries@nhpub.co.uk
- www.newhollandpublishers.com

Contact Managing Director, Steve Connolly; Publishing Manager, Rosemary Wilkinson
Established 1956
Insider Info Publishes 100 titles per year. Catalogue available online.
Non-Fiction Publishes General Non-Fiction, How-To and Reference titles on the following subjects:
Cooking, Crafts, Food and Drink, Gardening, General Reference, Health/Medicine, History, Hobbies, House and Home, Nature/Environment, Science and Technology, Spirituality, Sports
Recent Title(s) *The New Home Buider*, Paul Hymers (House and Home)
Tips The publishing programme features new illustrated books from Australia, New Zealand and South Africa. With a large range of general and practical non-fiction books, New Holland are keen to expand their history book lists.

New Island
2 Brookside, Dundrum Road, Dublin 14, Republic of Ireland
- 00353 1 298 9937
- 00353 1 298 2783
- Online form.
- www.newisland.ie

Contact Publisher, Edwin Higel; Editorial Manager, Deirdre O'Neill
Insider Info Catalogue free on request online.
Non-Fiction Publishes Autobiography, Biography, General Non-Fiction, Humour and Illustrated titles on the following subjects:

Business, Community/Public Affairs, Economics, Finance, Government/Politics, History, Humanities, World Affairs

Fiction Publishes Plays and Mainstream/Contemporary titles.

Poetry Publishes Poetry titles.

Recent Title(s) *A Divided Paradise: An Irishman in the Holy Land*, David Lynch (World Affairs); *Drive Like a Woman, Shop Like a Man: Why Green is Cheaper*, Mary Mulvihill (Finance)

Tips New Island also publishes the *Open Doors* series of fiction novellas aimed at adults with literacy problems. *Open Doors* authors are advised to avoid sentences with multiple clauses, to keep vocabulary simple, using common and straightforward words, but to allow the occasional challenging word (where useful).

Newnes

Linacre House, Jordan Hill, Oxford, OX2 8DP

- 01865 474010
- 01865 474011
- authorsupport@elsevier.com
- www.elsevier.com

Parent Company Elsevier Ltd (Science & Technology)

Insider Info Royalties paid. Catalogue and manuscript guidelines available online.

Non-Fiction Publishes Reference, Scholarly, Textbook and Technical titles on the following subjects:
Communications, Computers/Electronics, Education, Power Engineering

Submission Guidelines Accepts query with SAE/proposal package (including outline). The first step is to discuss the proposal with the relevant publishing editor. Check the website for in-depth submission guidelines and a full list of editorial contacts.

Recent Title(s) *System Engineering for IMS Networks*, Handa (Computing/Networks)

Tips Newnes is a leading name in electronics and electrical engineering books, aimed at professional engineers and technicians, undergraduate and postgraduate students and electronics enthusiasts. Subjects include power engineering, telecommunications, consumer electronics, circuit design, computer engineering and embedded systems, plus vocational textbooks and the *Newnes Pocket Book* series.

New Riders

Edinburgh Gate, Harlow, Essex, CM20 2JE

- 01279 623623
- 01279 414130
- www.pearsoned.co.uk/imprints/newriders

Parent Company Pearson Education

Insider Info Catalogue and manuscript guidelines are available online.

Non-Fiction Publishes How-To, Illustrated, Multimedia and Reference titles on the following subjects:
Arts, Creative Technology, Design, Graphics, Visual Arts

Submission Guidelines Accepts proposal package (including synopsis, sample chapters, market research, your publishing history and author biography).

Recent Title(s) *Do Good Design*, David Bermans (Design)

Tips New Riders is a forum for leading voices in creative and information technologies. Titles are aimed at professionals in web development and design as well as networking and graphic design. See website for full list of submissions contacts.

New Theatre Publications/The Playwrights' Co-operative

2 Hereford Close, Woolston, Warrington, Cheshire, WA1 4HR

- 0845 331 3516/01925 485605
- 0845 331 3518
- info@plays4theatre.com
- www.plays4theatre.com

Contact Director, Ian Hornby

Established 1987

Insider Info Aims to respond to proposals and manuscripts within one month. Over 600 plays in catalogue, which is available free on request or on the website. Manuscript guidelines available online.

Fiction Publishes Plays.

Tips New Theatre Publications is the trading name of the publishing house that is owned by members of The Playwrights' Co-operative. They only accept play submissions from members of the Co-operative. See the website for details on how to join.

Nicholas Brealey Publishing

3–5 Spafield Street, Clerkenwell, London, EC1R 4QB

- 020 7239 0360
- 020 7239 0370
- sales@nicholasbrealey.com
- www.nicholasbrealey.com

Contact Managing Director, Nicholas Brealey

Established 1992

Insider Info Publishes 30 titles per year. Catalogue available online. Manuscript guidelines available online.

Non-Fiction Publishes General Non-Fiction, Reference, Self-Help and Technical titles on the following subjects:

Business, Economics, Government/Politics, Health, Medicine, Psychology, Travel

Submission Guidelines Accepts query with SAE or via email with proposal package (including outline, sample chapter(s), SAE).
Submission details to: editorial@ nicholasbrealey.com

Recent Title(s) *Get to the Top on Google*, David Viney

Tips An independent publisher of innovative books in business, economics, self-help, psychology, travel writing and crossing cultures, Nicholas Brealey Publishing welcomes fresh ideas and new insights.

Nick Hern Books

The Glasshouse, 49a Goldhawk Road, London, W12 8QP

- 020 8749 4953
- 020 8735 0250
- info@nickhernbooks.demon.co.uk
- www.nickhernbooks.co.uk

Established 1993

Insider Info Publishes 80 titles per year. Five per cent of books published are from first-time authors. Payment is via royalty (on retail price). Catalogue is free on request and available online. Manuscript guidelines are available online.

Non-Fiction Publishes General Non-Fiction and Practical titles on the following subjects: Drama, Plays, Theatre (Practical).

* Publishes books by practitioners of theatre, for practitioners of theatre, not historical/critical surveys.

Submission Guidelines Accepts proposal package (including outline, sample chapters, author biography and SAE).

Fiction Publishes Plays.

* Can only consider plays attached to significant professional productions in major theatres.

Submission Guidelines Submit completed manuscript.

Nightingale Books

Sheraton House, Castle Park, Cambridge, CB3 0AX

- 01223 370012
- 01223 370040
- editors@pegasuspublishers.com
- www.pegasuspublishers.com

Parent Company Pegasus Elliot MacKenzie Publishers Ltd

Insider Info Catalogue and manuscript guidelines available online.

Non-Fiction Publishes Children's, General Non-Fiction and Illustrated titles on Education.

Submission Guidelines Submit proposal package (including outline and two sample chapters).

Fiction Publishes Multimedia, Fables and Myths, Picture Books, Teenage Literature and 'Chick Lit'.

Submission Guidelines Submit proposal package (including two sample chapters).

Poetry Publishes Contemporary Poetry titles.

Submission Guidelines Accepts queries.

Tips Specialises in children's fiction and educational resources.

NMS Enterprises Limited-Publishing

National Museums Scotland, Chambers Street, Edinburgh, EH1 1JF

- 0131 247 4026
- 0131 247 4012
- publishing@nms.ac.uk
- www.nms.ac.uk

Contact Director of Publishing, Lesley A. Taylor; Publishing Administrator, Rajeev Jose

Established 1987

Insider Info Payment is via royalties.

Non-Fiction Publishes Children's, General Non-Fiction, Reference and Scholarly titles on the following subjects: Anthropology/Archaeology, Art, Architecture, History, Nature/Environment, Science

Submission Guidelines Accepts query with SAE/ proposal package (including outline, sample chapter(s) and SAE).

Recent Title(s) *Silver: Made in Scotland*, George Dalgleish and Henry Steuart Fothringham

Tips Books published by National Museums Scotland reflect the range and international importance of their collections. Publications vary from full colour exhibition catalogues, to children's books, academic monographs, biographies and souvenir booklets. The list of titles represents collections from all their museums and they are only interested in proposals that concern National Museum of Scotland collections.

No Exit Press

PO Box 394, Harpenden, AL5 1XJ

- 01582 761264
- 01582 7612264
- info@noexit.co.uk
- www.noexit.co.uk

Parent Company Oldcastle Books

Contact Managing Director, Ion Mills

Fiction Publishes Crime titles.

Submission Guidelines No unsolicited material. May not return unsolicited manuscripts.

Recent Title(s) *The Spare Change*, Robert B. Parker (Crime)

Nonsuch Publishing
73 Lower Leeson Street, Dublin 2, Republic of Ireland
- 00353 1 642 5672
- rcolgan@nonsuchireland.com
- www.nonsuchireland.com

Insider Info Aims to respond to submissions within four weeks. Catalogue available online. Author guidelines available online.
Non-Fiction Publishes Biography, Illustrated and General Non-Fiction titles on the following subjects: History, Humour, Local Interest, Maritime History, Military History, Photography, Sport.
Submission Guidelines Accepts proposal package (including outline, synopsis, details of images and one sample chapter).
Recent Title(s) *Boss Cat*, Nick Barnes (Sports); *Modern Images of Galway*, Paul Malone (Photography)
Tips Nonsuch is always happy to hear from authors, local history societies, photographers, schools and libraries interested in pursuing a local history publishing project.

Northcote House Publishers Ltd
Horndon House, Horndon, Tavistock, Devon, PL19 9NQ
- 01822 810066
- 01822 810034
- brian.hulme@virgin.net
- www.northcotehouse.co.uk

Contact Publisher, Brian Hulme
Established 1985
Insider Info Publishes 25 titles per year. Payment is via royalties. Catalogue available online.
Non-Fiction Publishes Scholarly titles on the following subjects:
Education, Language, Literature, Literary Criticism
Submission Guidelines Accepts query with SAE/proposal package (including outline, two sample chapters, market research and SAE). Will not read unsolicited manuscripts.
Recent Title(s) *Crime Fiction from Poe to the Present*, Martin Priestman
Tips Publishes brief but rigorous critical examinations of the works of distinguished writers and schools of writing. The series embraces the best of modern literary theory and criticism, and features studies of many popular late 20th Century writers, as well as the canonical figures of literature and important literary genres.

NorthernSky Press
PO Box 21548, Stirling, Scotland, FK8 1YY
- 07981 173819
- northernsky@hush.com
- www.northernskypress.co.uk

Contact Commissioning Editor, Sarah Young; Political Editor, Declan McCormick; Poetry Editor, Finn Brennan
Non-Fiction Publishes Political Writing.
Submission Guidelines Submit completed manuscript.
Poetry Publishes Poetry titles.
Submission Guidelines Submit sample poems.
Recent Title(s) *When the G8 Came to my Town*, Declan McCormick; *Photo-me*, Robin MacGregor
Tips Publishes new writing, including authors who do not come from an academic background and have no publishing history.

Norvik Press Ltd
LLT, University of East Anglia, Norwich, NR4 7TJ
- 01603 593356
- 01603 250599
- norvik.press@uea.ac.uk
- www.llt.uea.ac.uk/norvik_press

Contact Managing Editors, Janet Garton and Michael Robinson
Insider Info Publishes six titles per year. Payment is via royalties. Catalogue available online.
Non-Fiction Publishes Scholarly titles on the following subjects:
Language, Literary Criticism, Scandinavian Literature
Fiction Publishes Literary and Translation titles.
Submission Guidelines Query with SAE/proposal package (including outline, sample chapter(s) and SAE).
Recent Title(s) *Aspects of Modern Swedish Literature*, Irene Scobbie (ed.) (Literary Criticism)
Tips Norvik Press is a publishing house based at the University of East Anglia – specialising in Scandinavian literature. It also publishes the journals *Scandinavia* and *Swedish Book Review*. The press is only interested in submissions within the literary criticism and history fields of Scandinavian literature.

The Nostalgia Collection
Silver Link Publishing Ltd, The Trundle, Ringstead Road, Kettering, Northamptonshire, NN14 4BW
- 01832 734425
- 01832 734425
- wadams1907@aol.com
- www.nostalgiacollection.com

Contact Managing Editor, Will Adams
Established 1985
Imprint(s) Silverlink
Past & Present
Insider Info Payment is by royalty. Catalogue available online.

Non-Fiction Publishes General Non-Fiction, Illustrated, Reference and Technical titles on the following subjects:
General nostalgia including Regional Interest, Transport, Buses and Trams, Railways, History and Reminiscences.
Recent Title(s) *Rail Around Birmingham*, Andrew Doherty
Tips Publishes post-war nostalgia including 'then and now' titles under the Past & Present imprint; railways, road transport and maritime titles under the Silver Link imprint.

Nottingham University Press
Manor Farm, Church Lane, Thrumpton, Nottingham, NG11 0AX
- 0115 983 1011
- 0115 983 1003
- editor@nup.com
- www.nup.com

Insider Info Payment is via royalties. Catalogue available online.
Non-Fiction Publishes Reference and Scholarly titles on the following subjects:
Agriculture/Horticulture, Cooking, Food and Drink, Health, Medicine, Law, Social Sciences, Engineering
Recent Title(s) *The Magnetic Pulse Of Life*, Alan Cruice
Tips Nottingham University Press is a dynamic and rapidly expanding independent university press. It has gained international recognition as a publisher of high quality scientific and technical publications, particularly in the fields of animal and food science.

Nyala Publishing
4 Christian Fields, London, SW16 3JZ
- 020 8764 6292
- 020 8764 6292
- nyala.publishing@geo-group.co.uk
- www.geo-group.co.uk

Established 1980s
Non-Fiction Publishes Biography and General Non-Fiction titles on Travel.
* Nyala's publishing house is small and specialised in the areas of biographies, travel and other non-fiction. No fiction or poetry. The bulk of the work that Nyala do is providing publishing services to external clients.
Submission Guidelines No unsolicited manuscripts. Ideas and synopses only. Only submit book ideas that meet the required criteria of biography, travel, or non-fiction.
Tips Nyala is part of a larger company, the Geo Group. Explore the website to get a flavour for the company as a whole.

Oak Tree Press
19 Rutland Street, Cork, Republic of Ireland
- 00353 21 431 3855
- 00353 21 431 3496
- info@oaktreepress.com
- www.oaktreepress.com

Contact Managing Director, Brian O'Kane
Established 1991
Insider Info Catalogue is available online. Manuscript guidelines are available online.
Non-Fiction Publishes reference and technical titles on the following subjects:
Business, Small Business/Start-Up, Communications, Computers/Electronics, Economics, Law, Money/Finance and Management
Submission Guidelines Accepts initial queries via email. Following this, send a proposal package (including outline, chapter breakdown, sample chapters, market research, author biography and your publishing history). Alternatively send the completed manuscript.
Recent Title(s) *Grabbing the Oyster! Advice & Ancedotes from Icons of Irish Business*, Pearce Flannery; *STAR: Leadership Behaviours for Stellar SME Growth*, Will McKee & John McKee; *Work-Life Balance: Policies & Initiatives in Irish Organisations*, Geraldine Grady, Alma McCarthy, Colette Darcy & Melrona Kirrane
Tips Oak Tree Press aims to provide information, advice and resources to entrepreneurs and managers of SMEs, and those who support and educate them. Oak Tree Press is always interested in hearing from prospective authors and is happy to discuss submissions.

Oberon Books Ltd
521 Caledonian Road, London, N7 9RH
- 020 7607 3637
- 020 7607 3629
- info@oberonbooks.com
- www.oberonbooks.com

Contact Publisher, James Hogan; Managing Director, Charles Glanville
Insider Info Catalogue is available online.
Non-Fiction Publishes General Non-Fiction titles on the following subjects:
Dance, Opera and Theatre
* Also publishes play texts (modern and classics) and supporting material for teachers and students of the Young People's Theatre and the London Academy of Music & Dramatic Art (LAMDA).
Recent Title *Wesker's Love Plays*, Arnold Wesker

O Books
The Bothy, Deershot Lodge, Park Lane, Ropley, Hampshire, SO24 0BE

☎ 01962 773768
🖷 01962 773769
✉ office1@o-books.net
🌐 www.o-books.net

Parent Company John Hunt Publishing Ltd
Contact Publisher (MBS, Religion, History, Psychology), John Hunt
Established 2003
Insider Info Publishes 80 titles per year. Receives approximately 1,000 queries and 500 manuscripts per year. 20 per cent of books published are from first-time authors, 80 per cent of books published are from unagented authors. Five per cent of books published are author subsidy published, depending on sales prospects and category of publishing. Payment is via royalty (on wholesale price), with 0.1 (per £) minimum and 0.25 (per £) maximum. Average lead time is 14 months, with simultaneous submissions not accepted. Submissions accompanied by SAE will be returned. Aims to respond to queries, proposals and manuscripts within two weeks. Catalogue and manuscript guidelines are free on request.
Non-Fiction Publishes Autobiography, Biography, Children's, General Non-Fiction, Gift, How-To, Illustrated, Scholarly and Self-Help titles on the following subjects:
Alternative Lifestyles, Anthropology/Archaeology, Astrology/Psychic, Business, Contemporary Culture, Economics, Health, History, Medicine, Mind, Body & Spirit, Multicultural, Nature, New Age, Philosophy, Psychology, Religion, Science, Sex, Spirituality, Women's Issues/Studies, World Affairs
Submission Guidelines Accepts complete manuscripts (including outline, your publishing history and author biography) by email.
Fiction Publishes Religious and Spiritual titles
* O Books only publishes two or three fiction titles per year.
Submission Guidelines Query with SAE.
Tips O Books prefers all correspondence by email, as they are often unable to answer the phone or reply to postal queries.

The O'Brien Press
12 Terenure Road East, Rathgar, Dublin 6, Republic of Ireland
☎ 00353 1 492 3333
🖷 00353 1 492 2777
✉ books@obrien.ie
🌐 www.obrien.ie

Contact Managing Director, Michael O'Brien; Editorial Administrator, Sarah Bredin
Established 1974
Insider Info Payment is via royalties. Aims to respond to proposals and manuscripts within eight

weeks. Catalogue and manuscript guidelines available online.
Non-Fiction Publishes Biography, Children's, General Non-Fiction, Humour, Illustrated and Reference titles on the following subjects:
Art, Architecture, Business/Economics, Cooking, Crafts, Food & Drink, Government/Politics, History, Memoirs, Music, Sports, Travel
Submission Guidelines Accepts proposal package (including outline and two sample chapters) by post. Will review artwork/photos as part of the manuscript package. Send photocopies.
Fiction Publishes Children's and Young Adult titles.
Submission Guidelines Accepts proposal package (including outline and sample chapter(s)) by post.
Recent Title(s) *The Irish Bride's Survival Guide*, Natasha Mac a'Bháird
Tips The O'Brien Press is Ireland's leading general publisher of both adult and children's books. Their main focus is on children's fiction, children's non-fiction and adult non-fiction. They generally do not publish poetry, academic works, or adult fiction. Email submissions will not be considered. Due to the high level of submissions they receive, unsolicited manuscripts will not be returned.

Octagon Press Ltd
78 York Street, London, W1H 1DP
☎ 020 7193 6456
🖷 020 7117 3955
✉ admin@octagonpress.com
🌐 www.octagonpress.com

Contact Managing Director, Anna Murphy
Established 1960
Insider Info Payment is via royalties. Catalogue is available online.
Non-Fiction Publishes Autobiography, Biography, General Non-Fiction and Scholarly titles on the following subjects:
History, Language, Literature, Literary Criticism, Philosophy, Translation, Travel and Folklore
* Focuses mainly on East/West studies.
Submission Guidelines Send a one page summary of the book idea.
Poetry Publishes a small amount of Translated Poetry.
Recent Title *A Cat May Look at a King*, Ramsay Wood
Tips Octagon Press aims to connect the Orient to the occident, to provide accurate exposure and understanding of one tradition to the other. The press concentrates on works of travel, philosophy, poetry, humanities, folklore, cultural geography and traditional psychology. No unsolicited manuscripts.

Octopus Publishing Group

2–4 Heron Quays, London, E14 4JP

☎ 020 7531 8400

✉ info@octopus-publishing.co.uk

🌐 www.octopus-publishing.co.uk

Parent Company Hachette UK

Contact CEO, Alison Goff

Established Early 1970s

Imprint(s) Bounty Books

Cassell Illustrated

Conran Octopus

Gaia Books

Godsfield Press

Hamlyn

Mitchell Beazley

Philip's

Spruce

Insider Info Catalogue available online.

Non-Fiction Publishes General Non-Fiction, Illustrated, Multimedia, Children's and Educational titles on the following subjects:

Food and Drink, Maps and Cartography, Antiques, General Reference, Children's, Education, Health, Style, Art, Photography

Tips A major cross-platform illustrated publisher. See individual imprints for more detailed information.

Oldcastle Books

PO Box 394, Harpenden, AL5 1XJ

☎ 01582 761264

☎ 01582 761264

✉ Online form.

🌐 www.oldcastlebooks.co.uk

Imprint(s) No Exit Press

Pocket Essentials

High Stakes Publishing

Non-Fiction Publishes General Non-Fiction and Reference titles.

Fiction Publishes Suspense and Crime titles.

Recent Title(s) *Luca Antara*, Martin Edmond

Tips See separate imprint entries for more information.

The Old Stile Press

Catchmays Court, Llandogo, Monmouth, NP25 4TN

☎ 01291 689226

✉ oldstile@dircon.co.uk

🌐 www.oldstilepress.com

Contact 1979

Insider Info Publishes roughly three titles per year. Catalogue is free on request and available online.

Non-Fiction Publishes Illustrated and Hand-printed Artists' titles on the following subjects:

Art, Drama, Poetry

Submission Guidelines Does not accept unsolicited submissions.

Poetry Publishes Visual Poetry

Submission Guidelines Does not accept unsolicited submissions.

Tips The Old Stile Press is a small company that primarily works with artists and doesn't often respond to writer's submissions.

The Oleander Press Ltd

16 Orchard Street, Cambridge, CB1 1JT

☎ 01223 350898

✉ editor@oleanderpress.com

🌐 www.oleanderpress.com

Contact Managing Director, Dr Jane Doyle

Established 1960

Insider Info Catalogue available online.

Non-Fiction Publishes General Non-Fiction, Humour and Reference titles on the following subjects:

History, Language, Literature, Literary Criticism, Regional, Religion, Translation

Submission Guidelines Accepts query with SAE, or via email, with proposal package (including outline and sample chapter(s)).

Poetry Publishes Poetry titles.

Submission Guidelines Submit sample poems.

Recent Title(s) *The Night Climbers of Cambridge*, Whipplesnaith (History)

Tips Titles are aimed at the discerning, erudite and sometimes eccentric reader. Oleander publishes in a wide range of fields, including cultural travel guides, local history, biography, poetry, games, classics, language and literature. Potential authors are welcome to submit their material either by email or post.

OLM-Pavilion

Richmond House, Richmond Road, Brighton, East Sussex, BN2 3RL

☎ 01273 623222

☎ 01273 625526

✉ info@pavpub.com

🌐 www.pavpub.com

Contact Directors, Chris Parker, Julie Gibson and Loretta Harrison

Established 1987

Insider Info Catalogue available online.

Non-Fiction Publishes Reference, Health/Social Care and Training Resources titles on the following subjects:

Counselling/Career, Health, Medicine, Social Sciences

Tips Pavilion is the leading provider of social and healthcare training materials in the UK, publishing around 150 training packs, 17 journals and *Mental*

Health Today magazine. As well as publishing, Pavilion organises eight exhibitions and around 40 conferences each year for those working within the social, healthcare and housing fields, and offers publishing consultancy services.

Omnibus Press

Music Sales Ltd, 14–15 Berners Street, London, W1T 3LJ

- 020 7612 7400
- 020 7612 7545
- chris.charlesworth@musicsales.co.uk
- www.musicsales.co.uk

Parent Company Music Sales Group
Contact Editorial Head, Chris Charlesworth
Established 1971
Insider Info Payment is via royalties.
Non-Fiction Publishes Audio Cassettes, Biography/Autobiography, Photo Books and General Non-Fiction and Multimedia titles on the following subjects:
Music/Dance, Music Theory, Sheet Music
Submission Guidelines Submit query with SAE. Submit proposal package (including outline, sample chapter and SAE).
Tips Omnibus Press is a world leader in books about music, covering everything from grand opera to contemporary pop music. Titles range from high quality photo books on classic rock acts like Bob Dylan and Led Zeppelin to in-depth biographies on rock and pop stars both old, like Abba, The Beatles and Keith Moon, and new, like Morrissey, Amy Winehouse and Muse.

Oneworld Classics

London House, 243–253 Lower Mortlake Road, Richmond, Surrey, TW9 2LL

- 020 8948 9550
- 020 8948 5599
- info@oneworldclassics.com
- www.oneworldclassics.com

Established 2007
Insider Info Catalogue available online. Manuscript guidelines not available.
Non-Fiction Publishes Classic Autobiography, Biography, Booklets, Illustrated and Scholarly titles on the following subjects:
Art/Architecture, Contemporary Culture, Creative Non-Fiction, Government/Politics, History, Humanities, Language/Literature, Literary Criticism, Music/Dance, Philosophy, Sociology
Fiction Publishes Classic Literary Fiction and Short Story Collection titles.
Poetry Publishes Classic Poetry titles.
Recent Title(s) *Heart of Darkness*, Joseph Conrad (Fiction); *The Theatre and its Double*, Antonin Artaud

(Author) and Victor Corti (Translator) (Translated Non-Fiction)
Tips Oneworld Classics is an independent publisher, launched in 2007 by the directors of Oneworld Publications and Alma Books. Its aim is to expand the literary canon in the English-speaking world through a series of mainstream and lesser-known classics, often by commissioning new translations. Oneworld Classics has recently acquired the Calder Publications list.

Oneworld Publications

185 Banbury Road, Oxford, OX2 7AR

- 01865 310597
- 01865 310598
- info@oneworld-publications.com
- www.oneworld-publications.com

Contact Publishing Directors, Juliet Mabey and Novin Doostdar; Managing Director, Helen Coward
Established 1984
Insider Info Catalogue free on request online. Manuscript guidelines available online.
Non-Fiction Publishes Biography, General Non-Fiction, Gift and Self-Help titles on the following subjects:
Government/Politics, History, Philosophy, Psychology, Religion, Science
Submission Guidelines Accepts proposals via a submission form, which can be completed online or printed and sent by post.
Recent Title(s) *The Blue Death: Disease, Disaster, and the Water We Drink*, Robert D. Morris (Science)
Tips Oneworld welcomes proposals for new books in their core subject areas. They will only consider proposals sent using their submission form (on the website) and can not consider any materials that are not submitted in this way. Note that they do not publish fiction, children's books, or poetry.

Onlywomen Press

40d St Lawrence Terrace, London, W10 5ST

- 020 8354 0796
- onlywomenpress@btconnect.com
- www.onlywomenpress.com

Contact Lilian Mohin
Established 1974
Insider Info Publishes roughly four titles per year. 98 per cent of books published are from first-time authors, 100 per cent of books published are from unagented authors. Payment is via royalty (on retail price). Average lead time is one year, with simultaneous submissions not accepted. Submissions accompanied by SAE will be returned. Aims to respond to queries within one month and proposals and manuscripts within three months. Catalogue is free on request. Manuscript guidelines

are available with SAE, or available online or by email.

Non-Fiction Publishes Biography, Booklets, Children's and Scholarly titles on the following subjects:
Alternative Lifestyles, Contemporary Culture (Female), Gay/Lesbian, Language, Literature, Literary Criticism, Philosophy, Social Sciences, Sociology, Women's Issues/Studies, Young Adult

Submission Guidelines Accepts proposal package (including outline, first 60 pages, your publishing history, author biography and SAE).

Fiction Publishes Adventure, Children's, Fantasy, Feminist, Lesbian, Literary, Multicultural, Mystery, Picture Books, Science Fiction, Short Story Collections and Young Adult titles

Submission Guidelines Accepts proposal package (including outline, first 60 pages, your publishing history, author biography and SAE).

Poetry Publishes Women's Poetry

Submission Guidelines Submit sample poems (also include your publishing history, author biography, and SAE).

Tips Onlywomen Press publishes feminist fiction and non-fiction from female authors only. They will only accept postal submissions and tend to give priority to lesbian authors.

Onstream Publications

Currabaha, Cloghroe, Co. Cork, Republic of Ireland

- 00353 21 438 5798
- info@onstream.ie
- www.onstream.ie

Contact Founder and Managing Editor, Roz Crowley
Established 1992
Insider Info Publishes three titles per year. Receives 365 queries and five full manuscripts per year. 100 per cent of books published are from first-time authors, 100 per cent of books published are from unagented authors. 30 per cent of books published are author subsidy published, depending on how commercially viable the project is. Payment is via royalty (on retail price).
Non-Fiction Publishes General Non-Fiction titles on a wide variety of subjects.
Recent Title(s) *Stop Howling at the Moon*, Eamon O'Donnell (Management)

Open Gate Press

51 Achilles Road, London, NW6 1DZ

- 020 7431 4391
- 020 7431 5129
- books@opengatepress.co.uk
- www.opengatepress.co.uk

Established 1988

Insider Info Catalogue available online.
Non-Fiction Publishes Biography, Belles Lettres and Scholarly titles on the following subjects:
Psychoanalysis, Politics, Philosophy, Psychology
Recent Title(s) *The End of Abuse*, John Woods
Tips Open Gate Press publishes a series, *Psychoanalysis and Society,* as well as writings by experts in various fields of the social sciences. Their aim is to bring life to the increasingly moribund state of philosophy and psychology publishing.

Open University Press

McGraw-Hill Education, Shoppenhangers Road, Maidenhead, Berkshire, SL6 2QL

- 01628 502500
- 01628 635895
- enquiries@openup.co.uk
- www.openup.co.uk

Parent Company McGraw Hill Education
Contact Senior Commissioning Editor, Rachel Gear (Social Welfare and Management); Senior Commissioning Editor, Christopher Cudmore (Media, Film and Cultural Studies, Sociology and Criminology); Senior Commissioning Editor, Mark Kavanagh (Accounting, Finance and Economics)
Established 1977
Insider Info Publishes roughly 100 titles per year. Payment is via royalties. Catalogue and manuscript guidelines are available online.
Non-Fiction Publishes General Non-Fiction, Reference, Scholarly and Technical titles on the following subjects:
Counselling/Career, Education, Health, Humanities, Social Sciences, Sociology, Media, Film and Cultural Studies
Submission Guidelines Accepts query with SAE/proposal package (including outline, two sample chapters, author biography, SAE).
Recent Title(s) *Exceptional Students: Preparing Teachers for the 21st Century*, Ronald Taylor, Lydia Smiley and Stephen Richards
Tips Open University Press publishes books and resources for education, health, the social sciences, management and study skills. The majority of the books have no direct connection with Open University courses, so there is scope for more general scholarly publications from established academics.

Orbit

100 Victoria Embankment, London, EC4Y 0DY

- 020 7911 8000
- 020 7911 8100
- orbit@littlebrown.co.uk
- www.orbitbooks.net

Parent Company Little, Brown Book Group

Contact Publishing Director, Tim Holman

Insider Info Submissions accompanied by SAE will be returned. Aims to respond to proposals within 12 weeks. Catalogue available online.

Fiction Publishes Fantasy and Science Fiction titles. * Full length novels only, no short stories or poetry.

Submission Guidelines Accepts outline of up to 30 pages of double spaced text.

Recent Title(s) *The Riven Kingdom*, Karen Miller (Fantasy); *Orphan's Journey*, Robert Buettner (Sci-Fi)

Tips Orbit is the UK's leading science fiction and fantasy imprint, with a market share twice that of any other publisher. Orbit does not accept emailed submissions and prefers submissions from agented writers, although they will occasionally accept unsolicited material.

Orchard Books

338 Euston Road, London, NW1 3BH

☎ 020 7873 6000

☎ 020 7873 6024

🌐 www.orchardbooks.co.uk

Parent Company The Watts Publishing Group (Hachette Children's Books)

Insider Info Catalogue available online.

Fiction Publishes Children's Fiction, Picture Book and Young Adult titles.

Submission Guidelines Agented submissions only.

Recent Title(s) *Dr Miaow's Big Emergency*, Sam Lloyd (Picture Book)

Tips Titles are aimed at encouraging children of all ages to become avid readers.

Original Plus

17 High Street, Maryport, Cumbria, CA15 6BQ

☎ 01900 812194

☎ smithsssj@aol.com

🌐 www.freewebs.com/thesamsmith

Contact Publisher/Editor (Poetry), Sam Smith

Established 1995

Insider Info Publishes two titles per year. Receives approximately 100 queries and 12 manuscripts per year. 50 per cent of books published are from first-time authors, 100 per cent of books published are from unagented authors. Payment is via an agreed percentage of books for resale. Average lead time is one year, with simultaneous submissions not accepted. Submissions accompanied by SAE will be returned. Aims to respond to queries within two days and proposals and manuscripts within four weeks. Manuscript guidelines available with SAE, and available online or by email.

Non-Fiction Publishes Language, Literature and Literary Criticism titles.

Submission Guidelines Accepts queries with SAE (including your publishing history) and artworks/images (send photocopies).

Fiction Publishes Literary Fiction titles.

Poetry Publishes Poetry and Poetry in Translation titles.

* Original Plus seeks poetry written about contemporary subjects in contemporary idiom, preferably poems that are not obviously religious, that do not assume a shared religious knowledge, and that do not contain religious references.

Submission Guidelines Submit six to ten sample poems.

Recent Title(s) *Days of Fire and Flood*, Chrissy Banks

Tips Original Plus also publishes *The Journal*, a literary poetry journal that is open to single poem submissions.

Orion Publishing Group Ltd

Orion House, 5 Upper St Martin's Lane, London, WC2H 9EA

☎ 020 7240 3444

☎ 020 7240 4822

🌐 www.orionbooks.co.uk

Parent Company Hachette UK

Contact Chairman, Armand Nourry; Chief Executive, Peter Roche

Established 1992

Imprint(s) Everyman Classics

Orion

Gollancz

Weidenfeld & Nicholson

Insider Info Catalogue available online via downloadable pdf, online catalogue request form, or via email on request.

Non-Fiction Publishes Autobiography, Biography, Children's, General Non-Fiction, How-To, Illustrated, Reference, Scholarly, Dictionaries and Self-Help titles on the following subjects:

Child Guidance/Parenting, History, Literary Criticism, Philosophy, Religion, Sports, Drama

Submission Guidelines Accepts agented submissions only.

Fiction Publishes Fantasy, Humour, Children's, Literary, Mainstream/Contemporary, Picture books, Science Fiction, Crime, Thriller and Classics titles.

Submission Guidelines Accepts agented submissions only.

Poetry Publishes some Poetry titles.

Orion

Orion House, 5 Upper St Martin's Lane, London, WC2H 9EA

☎ 020 7240 3444

☎ 020 7240 4822

🌐 www.orionbooks.co.uk

Parent Company Orion Publishing Group Ltd
Contact Managing Director, Lisa Milton; Managing Director (Orion Paperback Division), Susan Lamb
Established 1992
Imprint(s) Orion Children's Books
Orion Paperback (division)
Insider Info Catalogue available online, download a pdf or use online request form. Also available via email on request.
Non-Fiction Publishes Autobiography, Biography, Children's, General Non-Fiction and Humour titles.
Submission Guidelines Accepts agented submissions only.
Fiction Publishes Crime and Thriller titles.
Submission Guidelines Accepts agented submissions only.
Recent Titles *Dexter by Design*, Jeff Lindsay (Crime/Thriller)

Orion Children's Books

Orion House, 5 Upper St Martin's Lane, London, WC2H 9EA
☎ 020 7240 3444
☎ 020 7240 4822
🌐 www.orionbooks.co.uk
Parent Company Orion
Contact Publisher, Fiona Kennedy
Established 1992
Insider Info Catalogue available online via request form or as a downloadable pdf.
Non-Fiction Publishes Children's, Multimedia and Illustrated titles on the following subjects: Children's, History
Submission Guidelines Accepts agented submissions only.
Fiction Publishes Children's, Multimedia, Picture Books, Young Adult and General Fiction titles. *Children's characters include *Asterix* and *Horrid Henry*.
Submission Guidelines Accepts agented submissions only.
Recent Title(s) *Horrid Henry's House of Horrors*, Francesca Simon (Picture Book)
Tips Orion Children's Books publishes fiction and non-fiction books for the children's and young adult markets, as well as audio and multimedia material. Orion Children's Books does not accept submissions from unknown authors unless they are submitted through a literary agent.

Orion Paperbacks

Orion House, 5 Upper St Martin's Lane, London, WC2H 9EA
☎ 020 7240 3444
☎ 020 7240 4822
🌐 www.orionbooks.co.uk

Parent Company Orion
Established 1993
Imprint(s) Phoenix
Everyman Classics
Insider Info Catalogue available online.
Non-fiction Publishes General Non-Fiction titles on a variety of subjects.
Submission Guidelines Accepts agented submissions only.
Fiction Publishes a variety of Fiction titles.
Submission Guidelines Accepts agented submissions only.
Tips All books are published in paperback. Everyman Classics' list is made up entirely of reprints.

Orpheus Publishing House

4 Dunsborough Park, Ripley Green, Guildford, Surrey, GU23 6AL
☎ 01483 225777
☎ 01483 225776
✉ orpheuspubl.ho@btinternet.com
Contact Managing Editor, J.S. Gordon
Established 1996
Insider Info Payment is via royalties.
Non-Fiction Publishes General Non-Fiction and Scholarly titles on the following subjects: Philosophy, Religion, Science, Occult Science, Esotericism
Submission Guidelines Accepts proposal package (including outline, three sample pages and SAE).
Tips Publishes well grounded and serious books about occult science, esotericism and comparative philosophy/religion. Will consider well researched and argued proposals from 'sensible' authors.

Osprey Publishing Ltd

Midland House, West Way, Botley, Oxford, OX2 0PH
☎ 01865 727022
☎ 01865 727017
✉ editorial@ospreypublishing.com
🌐 www.ospreypublishing.com
Contact Managing Director, William Shepherd
Established 1969
Insider Info Publishes roughly 130 titles per year. Payment by royalty. Catalogue available online.
Non-Fiction Publishes General Non-Fiction titles on the following subjects:
History, Military/War, Aviation
Submission Guidelines Accepts query with SAE with proposal package (including outline).
Recent Title(s) *Medieval Polish Armies 966–1500*, David Nicolle and Witold Sarnecki (Military History)
Tips Osprey Publishing is the world's leading publisher of illustrated military history and military aviation books. Series' span military history from the

ancient world to modern times and include *Men-at-Arms*, *Campaign*, *Fortress*, *New Vanguard*, *Warrior* and *Aircraft of the Ace*. They do not accept unsolicited manuscripts, but will consider carefully researched proposals.

Oxbow Books/Aris & Phillips

10 Hythe Bridge Street, Oxford, OX1 2EW

- 01865 241249
- 01865 794449
- oxbow@oxbowbooks.com
- www.oxbowbooks.com

Contact Publisher and Managing Director, John Hudson; Editor, Richard Purslow

Established 1983

Imprint(s) Aris & Phillips

Insider Info Catalogue is free on request and available online.

Non-Fiction Publishes Scholarly titles on the following subjects:
Anthropology, Archaeology, History (Ancient and Medieval History), Classics, Egyptology, Middle Eastern, Near Eastern and Hispanic Studies.
* Also publishes the titles of the Griffith Institute of the University of Oxford and the Australian Centre of Egyptology.

Recent Titles *An Atlas for Celtic Studies*, John T. Koch (Reference)

Tips Oxbow Books is Europe's largest specialist archaeological bookseller. The publishing programme takes place under the Aris & Phillips imprint. See www.arisandphillips.com for further details.

Oxford Education

Great Clarendon Street, Oxford, OX2 6DP

- 01865 556767
- 01865 556646
- webenquiry.uk@oup.com
- www.oup.com/oxed

Parent Company Oxford University Press

Contact Editorial Director, Antonia Owen; Managing Director (Education & Children's Division), Kate Harris; Children's Publisher (Fiction and Picture Books), Liz Cross; Publisher (Modern Foreign Languages), Dick Capel-Davies; Publisher (Science and Maths), Elspeth Boardley

Established 1907

Insider Info Payment is by royalties. Catalogue available online.

Non-Fiction Publishes General Non-Fiction, Reference, Scholarly and Textbook titles for Teenagers and Children on the following subjects:
National Curriculum subjects, Dictionaries, Atlases and General Reference topics.

Submission Guidelines Accepts query with SAE/proposal package (including outline, two sample chapters, author biography and SAE).

Fiction Publishes Children's Fiction and Picture Book titles.
* Key age ranges are 5–7, 8–12 and Teenage.

Poetry Publishes Children's Poetry.

Recent Title(s) *Pippi Longstocking*, Astrid Lindgren (Children's); *Read Write Inc*, Ruth Miskin (Primary Education – Phonics)

Tips Titles and materials are aimed at children from birth to teenage. Markets include primary schools, secondary schools, FE colleges, international schools and pre-school children.

Oxford University Press

Great Clarendon Street, Oxford, OX2 6DP

- 01865 556767
- 01865 556646
- webenquiry.uk@oup.com
- www.oup.co.uk

Contact Editorial Director, Antonia Owen; Commissioning Editor, David Musson (Academic and Professional Books)

Established 1478

Imprints Oxford Education (including Oxford Children's Books)

Insider Info Publishes roughly 6,000 titles per year. Payment is by royalties. Catalogue available online. Manuscript guidelines available online via the website.

Non-Fiction Publishes General Non-Fiction, Reference, Scholarly, Technical and Textbook titles for adults and children on the following subjects: Anthropology/Archaeology, Business, Economics, Education, Government/Politics, Health, History, Language, Literature, Law, Literary Criticism, Music/Dance, Philosophy, Religion, Science and Social Sciences, National Curriculum

Submission Guidelines Accepts query with SAE/proposal package (including outline, two sample chapters, author biography and SAE).

Fiction Publishes Children's Fiction titles.

Recent Title(s) *Saving Truth From Paradox*, Hartry Field (Philosophy)

Tips Oxford University Press (OUP) is a department of the University of Oxford. It furthers the University's objective of excellence in research, scholarship, and education by publishing worldwide. With the acquisition of Blackstone Press, OUP is now one of the leading law publishers. Please note that Oxford University Press is obliged by its charter to have all books published ratified by the University. As a rule, the press don't publish works of fiction, unless it forms part of an educational course or examination. The main criteria when evaluating a new title is its quality, and the contribution it will make to the furtherance of scholarship and education. Oxford Education (see separate entry) deals with all children's fiction, non-fiction and educational titles.

Packard Publishing Ltd
Forum House, Stirling Road, Chichester, West Sussex, PO19 7DN
- ☎ 01243 537977
- ☎ 01243 537977
- ✉ info@packardpublishing.co.uk
- 🌐 www.packardpublishing.com

Contact Managing Directors, Clare and Michael Packard
Established 1977
Insider Info Payment by royalties. Catalogue available online.
Non-Fiction Publishes Biography, General Non-Fiction, Reference, Scholarly and Technical titles on the following subjects:
Agriculture/Horticulture, Art, Architecture, Conservation, Ecology, Education, Environment, Gardening, History, Language, Literature, Music, Nature, Science, Translation
Submission Guidelines Accepts query with SAE.
Recent Title(s) *Specification Writing for Garden Design*, John Heather (Gardening)
Tips Packard Publishing is a low overhead publisher and distributor of books and journals aimed at university and professional levels, colleges and secondary schools. The company's subject specialisations are biology, especially ecology and nature conservation, land management - including agriculture, forestry and rural studies, and landscape design and its history. They also produce a small number of titles on languages, music and general knowledge.

Palgrave Macmillan
Houndmills, Basingstoke, Hampshire, RG21 6XS
- ☎ 01256 329242
- ☎ 01256 479476
- ✉ d.knight@palgrave.com
- 🌐 www.palgrave.com

Parent Company Macmillan Publishers Ltd
Contact Managing Director, Dominic Knight; Publishing Director (College Division), Margaret Hewinson; Publishing Director (Scholarly & Reference), Samantha Burridge; Director of Journals, David Bull
Established 2000
Insider Info Payment by royalties. Catalogue available online and via email on request. Manuscript guidelines available online via the website.
Non-Fiction Publishes Biography, Reference, Scholarly, Technical, Journals, Monographs, Online Publications and Textbook titles on the following subjects:
Archaeology, Business, Communications, Computing, Contemporary Culture, Counselling/Career, Education, Government/Politics, Health, History, Language, Law, Literature, Literary Criticism, Philosophy, Politics, Psychology, Religion, Science, Social Sciences, Sociology, Sports, Theatre and Performance, Nursing and Health, International Relations and Key Concepts
Submission Guidelines Accepts proposal package (including outline, chapter plan, author biography and information about the book's place in the market, i.e competition and potential readership). Proposals should be sent to the relevant editors, a long list of whom are published on the website. Emailed and postal submissions are welcomed. Alternatively, use the online proposal form to structure your submission.
Recent Titles *Morals and Markets*, Daniel Friedman (Economics); *India Express*, Daniel Lak (Economics)
Tips Palgrave Macmillan is a leading academic publisher whose authors are usually experts in their fields. Detailed author guides are downloadable from the website – they cover every stage, from proposals, to publicity of the finished book.

Palladour Books
23 Eldon Street, Southsea, Hampshire, PO5 4BS
- ☎ 023 9282 6935
- ☎ 023 9282 6395
- ✉ jeremy.powell@ntlworld.com

Contact Managing Editors, Anne and Jeremy Powell
Established 1986
Non-Fiction Publishes Scholarly titles on the following subjects:
Literary Criticism (World War Literature)
Fiction Publishes Military/War, World War(s) titles.
Poetry Publishes Historical Poetry titles.
Tips Palladour Books specialises in second hand and out of print books on the literature and poetry of the first world war. They produce catalogues twice a year in May and November. Unsolicited manuscripts or proposals are not accepted.

Pan
20 New Wharf Road, London, N1 9RR
- ☎ 020 7014 6000
- ☎ 020 7014 6001
- ✉ fiction@macmillan.co.uk
- ✉ nonfiction@macmillan.co.uk
- 🌐 www.panmacmillan.com

Parent Company Pan Macmillan Publishers
Established 1944
Insider Info Catalogue is available online.

Non-Fiction Publishes Biography and General Non-Fiction titles on the following subjects: Astrology/Psychic, Business, Economics, Finance, Health, History, Memoirs, Military/War, Puzzles and Travel

Submission Guidelines Accepts agented submissions only.

Fiction Publishes Mainstream/Contemporary and Popular Fiction titles.

Submission Guidelines Accepts agented submissions only.

Recent Titles *Life on the Refrigerator Door*, Alice Kuipers (Contemporary Fiction); *Daily Telegraph Book of Word Games*, Telegraph Group Limited (Puzzles)

Tips Has a strong reputation in history, military history and biography, as well as other areas of non-fiction and fiction. Publishes work by new writers, but will not accept unsolicited manuscripts. Pan is the market leader in puzzle books.

Panacea Press Ltd

86 North Gate, Prince Albert Road, London, NW8 7EJ

☎ 020 7722 8464

☎ 020 7586 8187

✉ ebrecher@panaceapress.net

🌐 www.panaceapress.net

Contact Managing Editor, Erwin Brecher

Established 2001

Insider Info Payment by royalties. Catalogue available online.

Non-Fiction Publishes General and Scholarly titles on the following subjects:

Games, Logic, Psychology & Science, Puzzles

Submission Guidelines Accepts query with SAE. Catalogue available online.

Recent Title(s) *One Move and You're Dead*, Erwin Brecher and Leonard Barden (Chess)

Tips Erwin Brecher formed Panacea Press to market his own books and those of other non-fiction authors. The press publishes scholarly articles related to science and psychology. They will consider academic material providing it has a wide audience and market. Approach by fax or letter, but not by telephone.

Pan Macmillan Publishers

20 New Wharf Road, London, N1 9RR

☎ 020 7014 6000

☎ 020 7014 6001

✉ nonfiction@macmillan.co.uk

✉ fiction@macmillan.co.uk

🌐 www.panmacmillan.com

Parent Company Macmillan Publishers Ltd

Contact Managing Director, Anthony Forbes Watson

Established 1843

Imprint(s) Boxtree
Campbell Books
Kingfisher Publications Plc
Macmillan Children's Books
Macmillan New Writing
Pan
Picador
Sidgwick & Jackson
Think Books
Tor
Young Picador

Insider Info Catalogue available online via downloadable pdf.

Non-Fiction Publishes Audio cassettes, Autobiography, Biography, Cookbook, General Non-Fiction, Gift Books, Humour, Illustrated Books, Reference and Self-Help titles on the following subjects:

Cookery, Entertainment/Games, Food & Drink, Gardening, Government/Politics, Health, History, Hobbies, Nature, Science, Sports, Travel, Poetry, Drama & Criticism and Writing

Submission Guidelines Accepts agented submissions only.

Fiction Publishes Fantasy, Historical, Humour, Mainstream/Contemporary, Mystery, Romance, Science Fiction, Short Story Collections, Suspense, Sagas, Thrillers, Anthologies, Children's, Young Adult and General Fiction titles.

Submission Guidelines Accepts agented submissions only.

Recent Title(s) *The Cradle Snatcher*, Tess Stimson (Thriller); *The Princess Diaries: Ten out of Ten*, Meg Cabot (Young Adult)

Tips Although Pan Macmillan does not accept unsolicited/unagented manuscripts there is still a good deal of information for aspiring authors on the website. See the separate entry for the Macmillan New Writing imprint, which does accept unsolicited manuscripts, or go to: www.macmillannewwriting.com.

PaperBooks Ltd

Neville House, Station Approach, Wendens Ambo, Essex, CB11 4LB

☎ 01799 544657

☎ 01799 541747

✉ submissions@paperbooks.co.uk

🌐 www.paperbooks.co.uk

Contact Keirston Clark

Established 2006

Insider Info Publishes roughly three titles per year. Catalogue available online. Manuscript guidelines available online via the website.

Fiction Publishes Mainstream/Contemporary titles.

Submission Guidelines Accepts query with SAE/proposal package (including three sample chapters, one page synopsis and a marketing brief detailing who the target reader is, a list of any authors similar in style, and any previous publishing history that may be relevant).

Recent Title(s) *Friday at the Nobody Inn*, Mark Hayhurst (Novel)

Tips PaperBooks is a small independent press, dedicated to promoting and enlivening the independent book publishing world.

Paper Tiger
10 Southcombe Street, London, W14 0RA
- 020 7314 1400
- 020 7314 1401
- www.anovabooks.com

Parent Company Anova Books Company Ltd
Insider Info Catalogue available online.
Non-fiction Publishes General and Illustrated Non-Fiction titles on the following subjects:
Science Fiction and Fantasy Art
Recent Title(s) *Imaginistix*, Boris Vallejo and Julie Bell (Fantasy Art)
Tips Paper Tiger is one of the leading publishers of science fiction and fantasy art in the UK.

Paradise Press
Unit 2, 9 Golden Square, London, W1F 9HZ
- 020 7734 4880
- enquiries@paradisepress.org.uk
- www.paradisepress.org.uk

Parent Company Gay Authors Self-Publishing Society
Established 1995
Insider Info Catalogue available online. Manuscript guidelines available online via website.
Fiction Publishes Gay/Lesbian fiction and Short Story Collections.
Poetry Publishes Gay/Lesbian Poetry titles.
Submission Guidelines Submissions from Gay Authors Workshop only. For membership details email eandk2@btinternet.com or write to GAW, BM Box 5700, London WC1N 3XX.
Recent Title(s) *Rid England of This Plague*, Rex Batten (Novel); *Slivers of Silver*, Jeffrey Doorn and Adrian Risdon, eds. (Poetry Collection); *Queer Haunts*, G. Abel-Watters, ed. (Short Story Collection)
Tips Paradise Press is the publishing arm of Gay Authors Workshop, a collective of lesbian and gay writers. Work is only published by members of this group after a process of collective discussion and review. To submit work, first read the guidelines on the website.

Parapress Ltd
The Basement, 9 Frant Road, Tunbridge Wells, Kent, TN2 5SD
- 01892 512118
- 01892 512118
- office@parapress.myzen.co.uk
- www.parapress.co.uk

Contact Managing Editor, Elizabeth Imlay
Established 1993
Insider Info Publishes roughly five titles per year. Catalogue available online.
Non-Fiction Publishes Autobiography, Biography, General Non-Fiction and Self-Help titles on the following subjects:
History, Hobbies, Literary Criticism, Military/War, Music/Dance and Nature
Recent Title(s) *The Knocknobbler: Or the Dog-catcher of Worcester*, Bernard Cartwright
Tips The press also facilitates some self-publishing, so research all options thoroughly before committing any money.

Parthian
The Old Surgery, Napier Street, Aberteifi, Cardigan, SA43 1ED
- 01239 612059
- 01239 612059
- info@parthianbooks.co.uk
- www.parthianbooks.co.uk

Contact Publishing Director, Richard Davies (Fiction); Poetry Editor, Jasmine Donahaye (Poetry)
Established 1993
Insider Info Payment by royalties. Aims to respond to proposals and manuscripts within 12 weeks. Catalogue available online. Manuscript guidelines available online via the website.
Fiction Publishes Literary, Mainstream/Contemporary, Plays, Short Story collections, Translation and Welsh writing in English titles.
Submission Guidelines Accepts query with SAE and proposal package (including outline and sample chapter(s)).
Poetry Publishes Welsh Poetry titles in English.
Submission Guidelines Submit sample poems (including 40 pages and SAE).
Recent Title(s) *Just Another Mzungu Passing Through*, Jim Bowen
Tips Publishes a range of new writing and is always available to read new material in the relevant subject areas.

Paupers' Press
37 Quayside Close, Trent Bridge, Nottingham, NG2 3BP
- 0115 986 3334
- 0115 986 3334

◉ books@pauperspress.com
ⓦ www.pauperspress.com
Contact Managing Editor, Colin Stanley (Literary Criticism, Philosophy)
Established 1983
Insider Info Publishes up to six titles per year. Receives approximately ten queries and ten manuscripts per year. 50 per cent of books published are from first-time authors, 100 per cent of books published are from unagented authors. Payment is via royalty (on retail price), with 0.1 (per £) maximum. Average lead time is six months, with simultaneous submissions not accepted. Submissions accompanied by SAE will be returned. Aims to respond to queries and proposals within seven days, and manuscripts within 31 days. Catalogue is free on request and available online or by email.
Non-Fiction Publishes Booklets, Essays and Scholarly titles on the following subjects: Humanities, Literary Criticism, Philosophy
Submission Guidelines Accepts query with SAE.
Recent Title(s) *Katherine Mansfield and Modernist Aesthetics*, Anthony Hendon (Literary Criticism); *'The Death of God' and other plays*, Colin Wilson (Literature); *McEwan's Only Childhood: development of a metaplot*, Bernie C. Byrnes (Literary Criticism); *Ian McEwan's 'Atonement' & 'Saturday'*, Bernie C. Byrnes (Literary Criticism)
Tips Paupers' Press is a semi-academic press and its books are written for an intelligent and scholarly readership.

Pavilion
10 Southcombe Street, London, W14 0RA
❶ 020 7314 1400
❶ 020 7314 1401
◉ jrajasingham@anovabooks.com
ⓦ www.anovabooks.com
Parent Company Anova Book Company Ltd
Contact Jeshuran Rajasingham
Established 1981
Insider Info Catalogue available online.
Non-Fiction Publishes Coffee Table Books, Cookbooks, General Non-Fiction, Gift Books, Illustrated Books, and Reference titles on the following subjects:
Cookery, Interiors, Food & Drink, Gardening, Popular Culture, Photography, Film and Inspirational Lifestyle Books
Submission Guidelines Accepts emailed synopses.
Recent Title(s) *The Story of Film*, Mark Cousins (Film)
Tips Focuses on 'glamorous' non-fiction and gift books.

Payne-Gallway
Halley Court, Jordan Hill, Oxford, 0X2 8EJ
❶ 01865 888118
❶ 01865 314029
◉ info@payne-gallway.co.uk
ⓦ www.payne-gallway.co.uk
Parent Company Pearson Education
Contact Editor in Chief, Pat Heathcote
Established 1998
Insider Info Catalogue available as a downloadable pdf online.
Non-Fiction Publishes Reference, Technical and Textbook titles on the following subjects: Computers/Electronics, IT Educational Solutions, Skills Development
Submission Guidelines Accept query via email with proposal package (including outline).
Tips Payne-Gallway specialises in computer and IT books, and resources for schools and colleges.

PCET Publishing
27 Kirchen Road, London, W13 0UD
❶ 020 8567 9206
❶ 020 8566 5120
◉ info@pcet.co.uk
ⓦ www.pcet.co.uk
Established 1964
Insider Info Catalogue available online or via an online form.
Non-fiction Publishes Children's Primary and Secondary Educational Resources and Activity Books.
Tips As well as books, PCET produce illustrated wallcharts and other classroom accessories based around key texts and aspects of the National Curriculum. Also provides funding and teaching resources for the developing world.

Peachpit Press
Edinburgh Gate, Harlow, Essex, CM20 2JE
❶ 01279 623623
❶ 01279 414130
ⓦ www.pearsoned.co.uk/imprints/peachpitpress
Parent Company Pearson Education
Established 1986
Insider Info Catalogue and manuscripts guidelines are available online.
Non-Fiction Publishes Reference, Technical and Textbook titles on the following subjects: Computing, Desktop Publishing, Graphic Design, Multimedia, Web Design, Web Development.
Submission Guidelines Accepts proposal package (including synopsis, sample chapters, market research, your publishing history and author biography).
Recent Title(s) *Apple Training Series: AppleScript 1-2-3*, Sal Soghoian, Bill Cheeseman (Computing)

Tips Peachpit Press specialises in the area of web development. Its award-winning books feature step-by-step explanations, timesaving techniques, excellent insider tips, and expert advice for computer users of all sorts. They are aimed at computer users of all levels. See the website for full list of submissions contacts.

Pearson Plc
80 Strand, London, WC2R 0RL
☎ 020 7010 2314
⊛ www.pearson.com
Contact Chairman (US), Glen Moreno; Chief Executive (US), Marjorie Scardino
Established 1844
Imprint(s) Financial Times Group
Pearson Education
Penguin Group
Insider Info Payment is via royalty.
Tips Pearson Plc is an international media company with market leading businesses in education, business information and consumer publishing. It is not a stand-alone publisher, therefore all publishing submissions or enquiries must be directed at the appropriate imprint within Pearson. The group's three main assets are: Pearson Education, which is a leading educational publishing group; Penguin Group, which is one of the largest consumer publishers in the world; and the Financial Times Group, which publishes a broad range of business information and multimedia services for a growing audience of internationally minded business people.

Pearson Education
Edinburgh Gate, Harlow, Essex, CM20 2JE
☎ 01279 623623
☎ 0870 850 5255
✇ Online form.
⊛ www.pearsoned.co.uk
Parent Company Pearson Plc
Contact CEO Pearson Education (Asia, Europe, Middle East & Africa), John Fallon
Established 1998
Imprint(s) Addison-Wesley
Allyn & Bacon
BBC Active
Benjamin Cummings
Cisco Press
FT Prentice Hall
Ginn & Co
Heinemann Education
Longman
New Riders
Payne-Gallway
Peachpit Press
Pengin Longman

Prentice Hall
QUE Publishing
Rigby
SAMS Publishing
Wharton School Publishing
York Notes
Insider Info Payment is via royalties. Catalogue and manuscript guidelines are available online.
Non-Fiction Publishes Academic, Multimedia, Reference, Scholarly, Technical and Textbook titles on the following subjects:
Business/Economics, Computer Science, Education, Humanities, Language/Literature, Law, Science, Technology
Submission Guidelines Accepts query with SAE or proposal package (including outline, sample chapters, market research, your publishing history author biography).
Tips Pearson Education is the world's leading educational and professional publisher. Pearson Education is always looking for exciting new projects to work on and new authors to work with. A project proposal can be submitted by post or email, check the website for a full list of editorial contacts and their interests. Alternatively contact one of Pearson Education's various imprints with suitable projects.

Peepal Tree Press
17 Kings Avenue, Leeds, LS6 1QS
☎ 0113 245 1703
✉ contact@peepalpress.com
⊛ www.peepaltreepress.com
Contact Founder and Managing Editor, Jeremy Poynting; Marketing Director, Hannah Bannister (Poetry); Editor, Kwame Dawes
Established 1985
Insider Info Publishes roughly 15 titles per year.
Non-Fiction Publishes Autobiography, General Non-Fiction and Academic titles.
Fiction Publishes Multicultural and Short Story Collection titles on the following subjects: Caribbean, Black British and South Asian Writing
Poetry Publishes Caribbean, Black British and South Asian Poetry titles.
Recent Title(s) *The Hangman's Game*, Karen King Aribisala (Novel)
Tips Peepal Tree Press publishes challenging and inspiring literature from the Caribbean and Black Britain. Its books aim to express the popular resources of transplanted and transforming cultures.

Pegasus
Sheraton House, Castle Park, Cambridge, CB3 0AX
☎ 01223 370012
☎ 01223 370040

editors@pegasuspublishers.com
www.pegasuspublishers.com
Parent Company Pegasus Elliot MacKenzie
Publishers Ltd
Insider Info Catalogue available online. Manuscript
guidelines available online via website.
Non-Fiction Publishes Biography, General Non-
Fiction, Reference and Scholarly titles on the
following subjects:
Contemporary Culture, Education and History
Submission Guidelines Accepts query with SAE.
Fiction Publishes Literary and Mainstream/
Contemporary titles.
Submission Guidelines Accepts query with SAE.
Tips Pegasus publishes fiction, non-fiction and
educational books from writers, agents and
educationalists. They very rarely accept submissions
from unknown or unpublished writers, but will
sometimes offer an advance for accepted work.

Pen & Sword Books Ltd

**47 Church Street, Barnsley, South Yorkshire,
S70 2AS**
01226 734555
01226 734438
editorialoffice@pen-and-sword.co.uk
www.pen-and-sword.co.uk
Contact Commissioning Editor, Peter Coles
(Aviation); Commissioning Editor, Henry Wilson
(Military and Maritime); Commissioning Editor,
Rupert Harding (History and Local Interest)
Imprint(s) Leo Cooper
Wharncliffe Books
Insider Info Publishes roughly 200 titles per year.
Payment is via royalties. Catalogue available online.
Fiction Publishes Autobiography, Biography,
General Non-Fiction, Reference and Scholarly titles
on the following subjects:
History and Military/War
Submission Guidelines Accepts query with SAE, or
via email.
Recent Title(s) *In the Service of the Sultan*, Ian
Gardiner (Military History)
Tips Pen & Sword Books is a leading military history
publisher, specialising primarily in aviation, naval and
world war history. They also publish books on the
Napoleonic war. Unsolicited manuscripts will not be
accepted, however queries and proposals within the
key interest areas will be considered.

Penguin Group (UK)

80 Strand, London, WC2R 0RL
020 7010 3000
020 7010 6060
customer.service@penguin.co.uk
www.penguin.co.uk

Parent Company Pearson Plc
Contact Group Chairman & Chief Executive, John
Makinson; Managing Director, Helen Fraser
Established 1936
Imprint(s) BBC Children's Books
Penguin General (division)
Penguin Press (division)
Penguin Ireland
Penguin Audiobooks
ePenguin
Dorling Kindersley
Puffin
Ladybird Books
Rough Guides
Warne
Insider Info Publishes approximately 4,000 titles per
year. Catalogue is available online.
Non-Fiction Publishes Autobiography, Biography,
Children's, Cookbook, General Non-Fiction, Gift,
How-To, Humour, Illustrated, Reference and Self-
Help titles on the following subjects:
Astrology/Psychic, Business, Childcare/Parenting,
Contemporary Culture, Cooking, Counselling/Career,
Entertainment, Government/Politics, Health, History,
Language, Law, Literature, Memoirs, Military/War,
Money/Finance, Nature, Recreation, Science, Social
Sciences, Sports, Travel, Film and Television Guides,
Children's Tie-Ins, Food and Drink Guides, Exercise
and Fitness, Lifestyle and Relationships
Submission Guidelines Accepts agented
submissions only.
Fiction Publishes Children's, Picture Books, Plays,
Short Story Collections, Young Adult, Crime and
Thriller, Classics, General Fiction, Literary Criticism,
Popular Fiction, Short Story and Anthology titles.
Submission Guidelines Accepts agented
submissions only.
Poetry Publishes a wide selection of children's and
adult poetry titles.
Submission Guidelines Accepts agented
submissions only.
Tips Although the Penguin Group does not accept
unagented submissions, it does have some good
information for authors on its website, including
advice for aspiring adult fiction and children's fiction
authors. Penguin Audiobooks, including the Puffin
Audiobooks imprint, publishes a diverse selection of
titles from across the Penguin range on both
cassette and CD. ePenguin, launched in 2001,
publishes a wide range of Penguin titles, including a
full selection of *Penguin Classics* and *Rough Guides*, in
digital e-book format. For all other imprints, see
individual entries.

Penguin General

80 Strand, London, WC2R 0RL
020 7010 3000

☎ 020 7010 6060
✉ customer.service@penguin.co.uk
🌐 www.penguin.co.uk
Parent Company Penguin Group (UK)
Contact Managing Director, Tom Weldon
Imprint(s) Penguin Paperbacks
Fig Tree
Hamish Hamilton
Michael Joseph
Viking
Insider Info Catalogue is available online.
Non-Fiction Publishes Autobiography, Biography,
General Non-Fiction and Self-Help titles on the
following subjects:
Celebrity Biography, Cookery, Comedy, Current
Affairs, History, Memoir, Military History, Mind, Body
& Spirit, Showbiz, Sport.
Submission Guidelines Accepts agented
submissions only.
Fiction Publishes Crime, Experimental, Humour,
Literary, Mainstream/Contemporary, Romance,
Thriller and Women's Interest titles.
Submission Guidelines Accepts agented
submissions only.

Penguin Press
80 Strand, London, WC2R 0RL
☎ 020 7010 3000
☎ 020 7010 6060
✉ customer.service@penguin.co.uk
🌐 www.penguin.co.uk
Parent Company Penguin Group (UK)
Contact Managing Director, Stefan McGrath
Imprint(s) Penguin Classics/Penguin
Modern Classics
Penguin Reference
Allen Lane
Insider Info Catalogues are available online
or by email.
Non-Fiction Publishes Autobiography, Biography,
General Non-Fiction, Illustrated and Reference titles.
* Publishes Non-fiction under the Allen Lane and
Penguin Reference imprints.
Submission Guidelines Accepts agented
submissions only.
Fiction Publishes reprints of Mainstream/
Contemporary, Classics and Modern Classic titles.
* Publishes reprints of classic and modern fiction
under the Penguin Classic/Penguin Modern
Classics imprints.
Submission Guidelines Agented submissions only.

Penguin Ireland
**25 St Stephen's Green, Dublin 2, Republic of
Ireland**
☎ 00353 1 661 7695

☎ 00353 1 661 7696
✉ info@penguin.ie
🌐 www.penguin.ie
Parent Company Penguin Group (UK)
Contact Editorial Officer, Patricia McVeigh
Established 2002
Insider Info Aims to respond to proposals within
three months. Catalogue is available online.
Non-Fiction Publishes Autobiography, Biography
and General Non-Fiction titles.
Submission Guidelines Accepts proposal package
(including outline, 20–40 sample pages and SAE).
Fiction Publishes Literary and Mainstream/
Contemporary titles.
Submission Guidelines Accepts proposal package
(including outline, 20–40 sample pages and SAE).
Recent Title(s) *Ronnie*, Ronnie Drew
(Autobiography); *Mr S and the Secrets of Andorra's
Box*, Ross O'Carroll Kelly (Humour)
Tips Penguin Ireland welcomes unsolicited
manuscripts and proposals. They're looking for
passion and excellence from their authors, with
books that are 'pitched towards that vast middle
ground between popular literature and high
literature,' and that get under the skin of
contemporary Ireland. Accepts typewritten
manuscripts only. Does not accept emailed
proposals or manuscripts.

Penguin Classics/Penguin Modern Classics
80 Strand, London, WC2R 0RL
☎ 020 7010 3000
☎ 020 7010 6060
✉ penguinclassics@penguin.co.uk
🌐 www.penguinclassics.co.uk
Parent Company Penguin Press
Established 1946
Insider Info Catalogue is available online.
Non-Fiction Publishes Classic Non-Fiction titles on
the following subjects:
Art/Architecture, Government/Politics, History,
Literary Criticism, Philosophy, Religion and Travel
* All titles are reprints of English, American,
European, Classical and Non-Western Literature.
Fiction Publishes Literary, Classic Fiction, British and
American Modern Classics titles.
* All titles are reprints.
Recent Title(s) *The Curious Case of Benjamin Button*,
F. Scott Fitzgerald (Short Story Collection)
Tips Penguin Classics/Penguin Modern Classics do
not accept submissions as they only publish reprints
of classic literature.

Penguin Longman

Edinburgh Gate, Harlow, Essex, CM20 2JE

☎ 01279 623623

☎ 01279 414130

🌐 www.pearsoned.co.uk/imprints/penguinlongman

Parent Company Pearson Education

Contact Series Editors (Penguin Readers): Andy Hopkins and Jocelyn Potter

Insider Info Catalogue and manuscript guidelines are available online.

Non-Fiction Publishes Reference and Textbook titles on the following subjects:
Education, English Language Teaching (ELT), Language, Literature, Teaching Guides.

Fiction Publishes Classic, Contemporary and Literary Fiction Readers.

Recent Title(s) *The Rainbow Serpent*, James V Marshall (Penguin Readers); *The Breathing Method*, Stephen King (Penguin English)

Tips Specialises in the fields of English Language Teaching and reading/supplementary materials for ELT students. The *Penguin Readers* series publishes reading guides of classic literary and popular fiction and media tie-ins. The *Penguin English* series provides teachers with guides and resources to supplement lessons.

Penguin Paperbacks

80 Strand, London, WC2R 0RL

☎ 020 7010 3000

☎ 020 7010 6060

✉ customer.service@penguin.co.uk

🌐 www.penguin.co.uk

Parent Company Penguin General

Contact Publishing Director, Venetia Butterfield

Established 1935

Insider Info Catalogue is available online.

Non-Fiction Publishes Biography, General Non-Fiction and History titles.

Submission Guidelines Accepts agented submissions only.

Fiction Publishes Literary and Mainstream/Contemporary titles.

Submission Guidelines Accepts agented submissions only.

Recent Title(s) *A New Earth*, Eckhart Tolle

Tips Penguin Paperbacks range from Booker Prize-winning contemporary authors, to mass market bestsellers, with successful history, biography and general non-fiction as well.

Penguin Reference

80 Strand, London, WC2R 0RL

☎ 020 7010 3000

☎ 020 7010 6060

✉ customer.service@penguin.co.uk

🌐 www.penguin.co.uk

Parent Company Penguin Press

Insider Info Catalogue is available online or by email.

Non-Fiction Publishes Illustrated and Reference titles on the following subjects:
Dictionaries, Guidebooks, Language, Literature

Submission Guidelines Accepts agented submissions only.

Recent Title(s) *The Penguin Book of Facts*, David Crystal (Reference)

Tips Penguin is one of the best known names in reference publishing, specialising in a wide range of dictionaries on subjects as diverse as psychology, science, symbols and saints.

Pennant Books

PO Box 5675, London, W1A 3FB

☎ 020 7287 1841

✉ info@pennantbooks.com

🌐 www.pennant-books.co.uk

Parent Company Pennant Publishing Ltd

Contact Managing Director, Cass Pennant; Editor, Paul A. Woods

Established 2004

Insider Info An independent publisher and producer of a wide-range of best-selling and highly illustrated non-fiction books.

Non-Fiction Publishes Autobiography, Biography, Humour, Lifestyle, Popular Fan Culture, Sports and True Crime titles.

Fiction Publishes select Literary Fiction.

Recent Title(s) *Lewis Hamilton: A Dream Comes True*, Brian Belton (Sports Biography)

Tips Pennant Books is primarily a popular sports publisher, although they also publish a growing true crime list.

Pennine Pens

32 Windsor Road, Hebden Bridge, West Yorkshire, HX7 8LF

☎ 01422 843724

✉ info@penninepens.co.uk

🌐 www.penninepens.co.uk

Established 1995

Insider Info Catalogue available online.

Non-Fiction Publishes Children's, General Non-Fiction and Humour titles on the following subjects: History, Regional/Local Interest

Fiction Publishes Historical, Humour, Children's and Mainstream/Contemporary titles.

Recent Title(s) *Gone Walkabout*, Anna Carlisle (Local Interest/Walking Guide)

Tips Pennine Pens started as a small press, and still publishes local interest books, or books on rural life, such as walking guides. Recently they have branched out into web design and development services.

Pergamon Flexible Learning
Linacre House, Jordan Hill, Oxford, OX2 8DP
- 01865 474010
- 01865 474011
- authorsupport@elsevier.com
- www.elsevier.com

Parent Company Elsevier Ltd (Science & Technology)
Insider Info Payment is via royalties. Catalogue and manuscript guidelines available online via the website.
Non-Fiction Publishes Audio cassettes, Multimedia, Reference, Scholarly, Technical and Textbook titles on the following subjects: Business/Economics, Counselling/Career, Education, Management Training
Submission Guidelines Accepts query with SAE and proposal package including (outline).
Recent Title(s) *Trainer's Workshop Series Bundle*, Kamin (Management)
Tips Pergamon publishes open learning materials for management training aimed at individuals, colleges and trainers. They are the publishing partner of the ILM (Institute of Leadership and Management) and jointly publish the *ILM Super Series*, a comprehensive set of 40 open learning workbooks on key management topics. Pergamon Flexible Learning welcomes authors' proposals for books. The first step is to discuss the proposal with the relevant publishing editor. Check the website for in-depth submission guidelines and a full list of editorial contacts.

Perjink Press
8a Leopold Place, Edinburgh, EH7 5JW
- 0131 478 1845
- djlawrenson@hotmail.com

Contact Dorothy Lawrenson
Established 2005
Fiction Publishes Short Story Collections.
Poetry Publishes Poetry Collections.
Tips Dorothy Lawrenson set up the press to publish her own work, and has since published two other collections in pamphlet form. It is a very small scale enterprise. Perjink Press is a member of the *Scottish Pamphlet Poetry* website.

Persephone Books Ltd
59 Lamb's Conduit Street, London, WC1N 3NB
- 020 7242 9292
- 020 7242 9272
- info@persephonebooks.co.uk
- www.persephonebooks.co.uk

Contact Managing Director, Nicola Beauman
Established 1999
Insider Info Publishes roughly eight titles per year. Payment is by royalties. Catalogue is available online.
Non-Fiction Publishes reprints of General Non-Fiction titles on the following subjects: Women's Issues/Studies.
Fiction Publishes reprints of Women's Literature titles.
Recent Title(s) *The Closed Door and Other Stories*, Dorothy Whipple (Short Story Collection)
Tips Persephone reprints forgotten fiction and non-fiction classics from 20th Century writers. The titles are chosen to appeal to busy women who rarely have time to spend in bookshops, and who would like to have access to a list of books designed to be neither too literary nor too commercial. Persephone only publishes reprinted women's literature from the mid 20th Century, therefore it will not print any new material or anything modern.

Peter Haddock Publishing Ltd
Pinfold Lane Industrial Estate, Bridlington, East Yorkshire, YO16 6BT
- 01262 678121
- 01262 400043
- pat.hornby@phpublishing.com
- www.phpublishing.co.uk

Contact Publisher, Pat Hornby; Creative Director, Jo Ross
Established 1952
Insider Info Catalogue and manuscript guidelines are available online via the website.
Non-Fiction Publishes Children's and Multimedia titles.
Submission Guidelines Send manuscript or ideas either via recorded delivery, addressed to the publisher, or via the online enquiry form as an attachment.
Fiction Publishes Picture Books and Children's titles.
Submission Guidelines Send manuscript or ideas either via recorded delivery, addressed to the publisher, or via the online enquiry form as an attachment.

Peter Owen Publishers
73 Kenway Road, London, SW5 0RE
- 020 7373 5628
- 020 7373 6760
- admin@peterowen.com
- www.peterowen.com

Contact Editorial Director, Antonia Owen (Non-Fiction and Literary Fiction)
Established 1951
Insider Info Publishes roughly 25 titles per year. Receives thousands of queries and several hundred

manuscripts per year. Twenty per cent of books published are from first-time authors, 50 per cent of books published are from unagented authors. Payment via royalty (on retail price). Average lead time is one year, with simultaneous submissions accepted. Submissions accompanied with SAE will be returned. Aims to respond to queries within four weeks, proposals within six weeks and manuscripts within eight weeks. Catalogue is free on request and available online. Manuscript guidelines are available online or by email.

Non-Fiction Publishes Biography and General Non-Fiction titles on the following subjects:
Art, Architecture, Contemporary Culture, History, Humanities, Language, Literature, Literary Criticism, Memoirs

Submission Guidelines Accepts proposal package (including outline, one to three sample chapters, your publishing history, author biography and SAE) and artworks/images (send photocopies).
Submission details to: antonia@peterowen.com

Fiction Publishes Literary Fiction and Translation titles.

* Peter Owen only publishes four or five fiction titles per year and hardly ever publishes first novels.

Submission Guidelines Accepts queries with SAE or proposal package (including outline and one to three sample chapters) ideally by email.
Submission details to: antonia@peterowen.com

Recent Title(s) *Wild and Fearless: The Life of Margaret Fountaine*, Natascha Scott-Stokes (Historical Biography); *Loving Mephistopheles*, Miranda Miller (Literary Fantasy)

Tips Peter Owen specialises in international literary fiction. They very rarely publish memoirs or fiction from previously unpublished authors, and prefer submissions through a literary agent.

Phaidon Press Ltd
Regent's Wharf, All Saints Street, London, N1 9PA
- 020 7843 1234
- 020 7843 1111
- enquiries@phaidon.com
- www.phaidon.com

Contact Group Chairman & Publisher, Richard Schlagman; Deputy Publisher, Amanda Renshaw (Photography); Managing Director, Christopher North

Established 1923

Insider Info Publishes roughly 100 titles per year. Payment is via royalties. Catalogue available online. Manuscript guidelines available online and via the website.

Non-Fiction Publishes Illustrated Books, Memoirs, Multimedia and Reference titles on the following subjects:

Art, Architecture, Contemporary Culture, Design, Fashion, Film, Photography

Submission Guidelines Accepts query with SAE and proposal package including (outline, sample chapter(s), author biography, CV and SAE). Will accept artworks/images (send photocopies/digital files as jpegs).

Recent Title(s) *The Curves of Time*, Oscar Niemeyer (Memoir)

Tips Phaidon Press is an international publisher of books on the visual arts, with offices in New York, London, Paris and Berlin. The books cover everything from art, architecture, photography, design, performing arts, and decorative arts, to contemporary culture, fashion and film. Phaidon Press welcomes submissions for books in the following topic areas: art, architecture, photography, design and the decorative arts.

Pharmaceutical Press
1 Lambeth High Street, London, SE1 7JN
- 020 7735 9141
- 020 7572 2509
- enquiries@rpsgb.org
- www.pharmpress.com

Parent Company RPS Publishing

Contact Director of Publications, Charles Fry; Publisher, Paul Weller; Senior Commissioning Editor, Christina de Bono

Insider Info Catalogue and author guidelines available online.

Non-Fiction Publishes Scholarly, Textbook, Professional Reference, Journal, Magazine and Online Resource titles on the following subjects: Pharmacy, Pharmacology, Pharmaceutical Sciences, Toxicology, Forensic Toxicology, Forensic Science

Submission Guidelines Accepts proposal package (including outline, sample chapter(s), your publishing history, author biography, tentative title, estimated length, proposed date for completion, information on competing books). Will accept completed manuscripts, but prefers an initial proposal.

Recent Title(s) *Community Pharmacy Handbook*, Jon Waterfield

Tips Titles are aimed at academics and professionals in the healthcare and pharmaceutical fields.

Philip's
2–4 Heron Quays, London, E14 4JP
- 020 7531 8400
- 020 7644 6986
- publisher@philips-maps.co.uk
- www.philips-maps.co.uk

Parent Company Octopus Publishing Group

Insider Info Catalogue is available online.

Non-Fiction Publish Illustrated, Reference, Maps, Atlases and Pocket Reference Guide titles on the following subjects:
History, Travel, Astronomy, Geography, Cycle Tours
Recent Title(s) *Philip's Stargazing 2009*, Philip's (Astronomy)
Tips Most Philip's products are created from existing electronic databases that are constantly updated to record changes as they happen, producing new and foreign editions of established titles.

Philip Wilson Publishers Limited
109 The Timber Yard, Drysdale Street, London, N1 6ND
- 020 7033 9900
- 020 7033 9922
- pwilson@philip-wilson.co.uk
- www.philip-wilson.co.uk

Contact Director, Philip Wilson; Commissioning Editors, Anne Jackson and Cangy Venables; Production Manager, Norman Turpin
Established 1977
Insider Info Publishes roughly 12 titles per year. Receives 200 queries and 30 manuscripts per year. Five per cent of books published are from first-time authors, 95 per cent of books published are from unagented authors. Payment is via royalty (on wholesale price). Advance offered up to £5,000. Average lead time is nine months, with simultaneous submissions accepted. Submissions accompanied by SAE will be returned. Aims to respond to proposal within two weeks. Catalogue is free on request and available by email.
Non-Fiction Publishes Illustrated titles on the following subjects:
Art, Collecting, Museum Collections, Galleries
Submission Guidelines Accepts proposal package (including outline and sample chapters).
Recent Title(s) *Carl Laubin Paintings*, David Watkin (Art)
Tips Potential titles should be aimed at art dealers, museum experts and art historians.

Phillimore & Co. Ltd
Madam Green Farm, Chichester, West Sussex, PO20 2DD
- 01243 787636
- 01243 787639
- publishing@phillimore.co.uk
- www.phillimore.co.uk

Contact Managing Director, Noel Osborne
Established 1897
Insider Info Publishes 70 titles per year. Payment is via royalties. Catalogue is free on request and available online.

Non-Fiction Publishes General Non-Fiction, How-To, Illustrated and Reference titles on the following subjects:
Local & Family History, Writing Guides
Recent Title(s) *Elgin's Love-gift*, John Barrett and Alastair Mitchell (Local History)
Tips Authors and editors in the fields of local and family history, archaeology and architectural history are invited to contact the editorial department at the earliest possible stage in the preparation of a manuscript for publication.

Phoenix
Orion House, 5 Upper St Martins Lane, London, WC2H 9EA
- 020 7240 3444
- 020 7240 4822
- www.orionbooks.co.uk

Parent Company Orion Paperbacks (Orion Publishing Group Ltd)
Insider Info Catalogue available online.
Non-Fiction Publishes Autobiography, Biography and General Non-Fiction titles.
* Publishes in paperback only.
Submission Guidelines Agented submissions only.
Fiction Publishes Mainstream/Contemporary titles.
* Publishes in paperback only.
Submission Guidelines Agented submissions only.
Recent Title(s) *Broken Bodies*, June Hampson (Crime/Thriller)
Tips Does not accept any unsolicited submissions.

Piatkus Books
Little, Brown Book Group, 100 Victoria Embankment, London, EC4Y 0DY
- 020 7911 8000
- info@littlebrown.co.uk
- www.piatkus.co.uk

Parent Company Little, Brown Book Group
Contact Publishing Director, Antonia Hodgson
Established 1979
Imprint(s) Piatkus
Portrait
Insider Info Publishes 150 titles per year. Payment is via royalties. Aims to respond to proposals and manuscripts within 12 weeks. Catalogue and manuscript guidelines available online.
Non-Fiction Publishes Autobiography, Biography, General Non-Fiction, Humour and Reference titles on the following subjects:
Business, Contemporary Culture, Counselling/Career, Economics, Health, History, Medicine, Memoirs, Music/Dance, Psychology, Spirituality
Submission Guidelines Accepts query/SAE with proposal package (including outline, three sample chapters, your publishing history).

Fiction Publishes Mainstream/Contemporary titles.

Submission Guidelines Accepts query/SAE with proposal package (including outline, chapter breakdown, one sample chapter, your publishing history and market research).

Recent Title(s) *Deadly Desire*, Keri Arthur

Tips When submitting be sure to include details of the target market and the need for your book, information about your previous publications and your credentials for writing the book.

Piatkus

Little, Brown Book Group, 100 Victoria Embankment, London, EC4Y 0DY

☎ 020 7911 8000

✉ info@littlebrown.co.uk

🌐 www.piatkus.co.uk

Parent Company Piatkus Books

Contact Publishing Director, Antonia Hodgson

Insider Info Payment via royalties. Aims to respond to proposals and manuscripts within 12 weeks. Book catalogue and manuscript guidelines available online.

Non-Fiction Publishes General Non-Fiction and Self-Help titles on the following subjects:
Business, Economics, Health, Medicine, Psychology, Spirituality, Mind, Body & Spirit

Submission Guidelines Accepts query with SAE, with proposal package (including outline, three sample chapters, your publishing history).

Fiction Publishes Mainstream/Contemporary titles.

Submission Guidelines Accepts query with SAE with proposal package (including outline, three sample chapters and your publishing history).

Tips The Piatkus imprint of Piatkus Books specialises in leading edge lifestyle titles, as well as bestselling commercial fiction.

Picador

20 New Wharf Road, London, N1 9RR

☎ 020 7014 6000

☎ 020 7014 6001

🌐 www.picador.com

Parent Company Pan Macmillan Publishers

Contact Publisher, Paul Baggaley; Editorial Director, Kate Harvey

Established 1972

Insider Info Catalogue available online as a downloadable pdf.

Non-Fiction Publishes Autobiography, Biography and General Non-Fiction titles on the following subjects:
Literary, Creative Non-Fiction, Memoir

Submission Guidelines Accepts agented submissions only.

Fiction Publishes General Fiction, Mainstream/Contemporary and Literary titles.

Submission Guidelines Accepts agented submissions only.

Poetry Publishes a range of Poetry titles.

Submissions Guidelines Accepts agented submissions only.

Recent Title(s) *A Beautiful Place to Die*, Malla Nunn (Crime); *Making an Elephant*, Graham Swift (Non-Fiction/Writing)

Tips Picador has a particular reputation for ground breaking non-fiction, reportage, literary biography and memoir, as well as poetry. Does not accept unsolicited manuscripts.

Pica Press

38 Soho Square, London, W1D 3HB

☎ 020 7758 0200

☎ 020 7758 0222

✉ ornithology@acblack.com

🌐 www.acblack.com

Parent Company A&C Black Publishers Ltd

Contact Department Head, Nigel Redman; Publishing Director, Jonathan Glasspool (Reference, Theatre and Ornithology)

Established 1995

Insider Info Catalogue available online.

Non-Fiction Publishes General Non-Fiction, Illustrated and Reference titles on the following subjects:
Nature/Environment, Natural History, Ornithology

Recent Title(s) *Birds By Colour*, Marc Duquet (Ornithology)

Tips Pica is the sister imprint of Christopher Helm at A&C Black, specialising in taxonomic and geographic bird books, field and identification guides, and general interest books on birds and nature. Pica authors are generally recognised scientists and academics, so a background in ornithological science would be useful for any would-be contributor.

Piccadilly Press

5 Castle Road, London, NW1 8PR

☎ 020 7267 4492

☎ 020 7267 4493

✉ books@piccadillypress.co.uk

🌐 www.piccadillypress.co.uk

Contact Publisher & Managing Director, Brenda Gardner

Established 1983

Insider Info Publishes 30 titles per year. Payment is via royalties. Catalogue and manuscript guidelines available online.

Non-Fiction Publishes Children's and General Non-Fiction titles on the following subjects:

Childcare/Parenting, Teenage Issues

Submission Guidelines Accepts query with SAE with proposal package (including outline and two sample chapters). Will accept artworks/images (send photocopies).

Fiction Publishes Picture Book, Children's and Young Adult titles.

Submission Guidelines Accepts query with SAE with proposal package (including outline and two sample chapters).

Recent Title(s) *Life Interrupted*, Damian Kelleher (Novel)

Tips Piccadilly Press is an independent publisher, specialising in teenage fiction and non–fiction, 'tween' fiction, picture books and parenting books by highly acclaimed authors and illustrators. They publish a range of titles, all of which can be seen on their website.

Picthall & Gunzi
21a Widmore Road, Bromley, Kent, BR1 1RW
- 020 8460 4032
- 020 8460 4021
- chris@picthallandgunzi.demon.co.uk
- www.picthallandgunzi.com

Contact Managing Director, Chez Picthall; Publisher & Editorial Director, Christiane Gunzi

Insider Info Catalogue available via email to sales@picthallandgunzi.com.

Non-Fiction Publishes Children's Activity, Board and Picture Books.

Recent Title(s) *In The Sea*, Baby Sees Series (Bath Book)

Tips All titles are aimed at pre-schoolers and are photographically illustrated.

Pigasus Press
13 Hazely Combe, Arreton, Isle of Wight, PO30 3AJ
- 01983 865668
- mail@pigasuspress.co.uk
- www.pigasuspress.co.uk

Contact Editor (Science Fiction, Fantasy, Horror), Tony Lee

Established 1989

Insider Info Publishes roughly two titles per year. Simultaneous submissions are not accepted. Submissions accompanied by SAE will be returned. Aims to respond to queries within seven days, proposals within ten days, and manuscripts and all other enquiries within six months. Catalogue and manuscript guideline are available with SAE, or online.

Non-Fiction Publishes General Non-Fiction (Interviews), Profiles, Essays, Top Ten listings, and

Reference and Scholarly titles on the following subjects:
Contemporary Culture, Entertainment/Games, Literary Criticism (Genre Fiction), Science

Submission Guidelines Accepts queries with SAE, or completed manuscripts. Also accepts artworks/images (send photocopies, and digital files as jpegs).

Fiction Publishes Experimental, Fantasy, Horror, Literary (Genre), Mystery, and Science Fiction titles

Submission Guidelines Accepts queries with SAE, or completed manuscripts.

Poetry Publishes some Contemporary Genre Poetry

Submission Guidelines Submit six sample poems.

Tips Pigasus Press is a genre publisher that specialises in speculative fiction of all kinds. They also publish *Premonitions* magazine which offers further publishing possibilities. Pigasus Press will not accept sword and sorcery fantasy submissions, or explicitly gory horror submissions.

Pimlico
Random House, 20 Vauxhall Bridge Road, London, SW1V 2SA
- 020 7840 8578
- 020 7233 6117
- pimlicoeditorial@randomhouse.co.uk
- www.randomhouse.co.uk

Parent Company The Random House Group Ltd

Contact Publisher, Will Sulkin

Insider Info Catalogue available online.

Non-Fiction Publishes Biography and General Non-Fiction on the following subjects:
Government/Politics, History, Philosophy, Adventure * Publishes entirely in paperback.

Submission Guidelines No unagented submissions.

Recent Title(s) *Under Two Dictators: Prisoner of Stalin and Hitler*, Nikolaus Wachsmann (Biography); *The Imperial Capitals of China: An Inside View of the Celestial Empire*, Arthur Cotterell (History)

Tips Specialises in historical biographies and accounts in paperback.

Pinwheel Ltd
Winchester House, 259–269 Old Marylebone Road, London, NW1 5XJ
- 020 7616 7200
- 020 7616 7201
- claudia.holzer@pinwheel.co.uk
- www.pinwheel.co.uk

Parent Company Alligator Books

Contact Managing Director, Andrew Flatt

Imprint(s) Pinwheel Children's Books
Andromeda Children's Books
Gullane Children's Books

Insider Info Catalogue available online.

Non-Fiction Publishes Children's, Cloth, Novelty, Gift, Illustrated, Reference, Dictionary and General Non-Fiction titles on the following subjects:
Baby & Child's Early Learning, Religion, Natural History
Submission Guidelines Accepts entire manuscript with SAE for children's non-fiction picture books (up to 800 words). Submissions should be addressed to: The Commissioning Editor, Gullane Children's Books.
Fiction Publishes Children's, Picture Book and Illustrated Fiction titles.
Submission Guidelines Accepts entire manuscript with SAE for children's fiction picture books (up to 800 words). Submissions should be addressed to: The Commissioning Editor, Gullane Children's Books.
Tips Specialises entirely in children's publishing. Within the company, The Pinwheel Children's imprint concentrates on packaging novelty books, Andromeda focuses on the 3–12 year old age group with gift books and Gullane publishes the more traditional picture books, for which submissions are sought. Titles submitted for consideration should be pitched at children aged seven or younger.

Pipers' Ash Ltd
Church Road, Christian Malford, Chippenham, Wiltshire, SN15 4BW
- 01249 720563
- 0870 056 8916
- pipersash@supamasu.com
- www.supamasu.com

Contact The Manuscript Evaluation Desk (All subjects)
Established 1976
Insider Info Publishes roughly 15 titles per year. Receives 1,200 queries and 800 manuscripts per year. 90 per cent of books published are from first-time authors and 100 per cent are from unagented authors. Payment is via royalty (on retail price) of 0.1 (per £). No advance is offered. Average lead time is six months, with simultaneous submissions not accepted. Submissions accompanied by SAE will be returned. Aims to respond to queries within seven days, proposals within five weeks, and manuscripts within two months. Catalogue and manuscript guidelines available online.
Non-Fiction Publishes Autobiography, Biography, Booklets, Children's, Coffee Table, General Non-Fiction, Gift, How-To, Scholarly, Self-Help and Textbook titles on the following subjects:
Creative Non-Fiction, History, Humanities, Language, Literature, Marine Subjects, Memoirs, Military/War, Multicultural, Philosophy, Psychology, Recreation, Regional, Sport, Translation (Classics), Young Adult, Local Histories, Stagecraft, True Life 'Problem' Stories
Submission Guidelines Accepts query with SAE, or via a telephone call. Will not accept artworks/images.

Fiction Publishes Adventure, Historical, Literary, Mainstream/Contemporary , Multicultural, Plays, Science Fiction, Short Story collections, Sports, Translation, Young Adult, Children's and Classics titles.
Submission Guidelines Accepts query with SAE, or via a telephone call.
Poetry Publishes Poetry Collections in the form of New Chapbooks and Pamphlets.
Submission Guidelines Accepts query with SAE or via a telephone call.
Recent Title(s) *My life in Mental Chains*, Ruth J Hartman (True Life/OCD); *Shrink in the Clink*, Dr Michael Haslam (Memoir); *Fancy All That*, Penny Fells (True Life/Epilepsy); *Jasmine*, Jasmine Maria Hill (Poetry)
Tips Pipers' Ash titles are aimed at a worldwide readership.

Planet
PO Box 44, Aberystwyth, Ceredigion, SY23 3ZZ
- 01970 611255
- 01970 611197
- planet.enquiries@planetmagazine.org.uk
- www.planetmagazine.org.uk

Contact Managing Editor, John Barnie
Established 1970
Insider Info Payment is via royalties. Catalogue and manuscript guidelines (for the magazine only) are available online.
Non-fiction Publishes Autobiography, Biography and General Non-Fiction titles on the following subjects:
Art, Architecture, History, Regional, World Affairs, Welsh Interest
* Also publishes *Planet: The Welsh Internationalist* magazine.
Fiction Publishes Mainstream/Contemporary, Regional, Short Story Collections, Translation, Welsh Fiction and World Writing titles.
Poetry Publishes Poetry with a particular slant towards Welsh Interest.
Recent Title(s) *O For A Gun*, Nigel Jenkins (Haiku)
Tips Planet mainly focuses on the arts and current affairs magazine *Planet: The Welsh Internationalist*. It expanded into book publishing in 1995, mostly of Welsh poetry and fiction, including short story collections, and also some translated fiction from around the world. Most articles, features and reviews in the magazine are commissioned, but if you have an idea for an article that you think might be relevant to the magazine, send a letter of enquiry with a brief synopsis.

The Playwrights Publishing Company

70 Nottingham Road, Burton Joyce, Nottingham, NG14 5AL

- 0115 931 3356
- playwrightspublishingco@yahoo.com
- www.geocities.com/playwrightspublishingco

Contact Partners: Tony and Elizabeth Breeze
Established 1990
Insider Info Publish 12 titles per year. Payment is via royalty (on retail price) and performance rights. Simultaneous submissions are not accepted. Submissions accompanied by SAE will be returned. Aims to respond to queries within one day and manuscripts within four weeks. Catalogue is free on request, and available via A4 SAE, online or email. Author guidelines are free on request and available via email.
Fiction Publishes Plays and Drama titles for theatre companies and schools.
Submission Guidelines Accepts proposal package (including SAE, reading fee of £15 for one act, £30 for full length). Submit completed manuscripts via email. Will not accept artwork/images.
Tips Titles should be aimed at general readers and drama groups.

Plexus Publishing Ltd

25 Mallinson Road, London, SW11 1BW

- 020 7924 4662
- 020 7924 5096
- info@plexusuk.demon.co.uk
- www.plexusbooks.com

Contact Managing Director, Terence Porter; Editorial Director, Sandra Wake
Established 1973
Insider Info Catalogue available online.
Non-Fiction Publish Biography and General Non-Fiction titles on the following subjects: Contemporary Culture, Music, Film/Television, Celebrity Culture
Submission Guidelines Accepts query with SAE along with the completed manuscript.
Recent Title(s) *Johnny Depp: A Modern Rebel*, Brian J. Robb (Biography)
Tips Plexus are publishers of high quality, illustrated non-fiction books, specialising in biography, popular culture, movies and music.

Pluto Publishing Ltd

345 Archway Road, London, N6 5AA

- 020 834 82724
- 020 834 89133
- pluto@plutobooks.com
- www.plutobooks.com

Contact Chairman, Roger van Zwanenberg; Managing Director, Anne Beech; Commissioning Editor, David Castle
Established 1970
Insider Info Publishes roughly 70 titles per year. Catalogue and manuscript guidelines available online.
Non-Fiction Publishes Scholarly titles on the following subjects: Anthropology/Archaeology, Contemporary Culture, Government/Politics, History, Regional, Social Sciences, World Affairs
Submission Guidelines Accepts query via email, with proposal package (including outline, table of contents, two sample chapters, author biography, market research).
Recent Title(s) *A Century of Spin*, David Miller and William Dinan (Politics)
Tips Pluto Press publishes the best in progressive, critical thinking across politics and the social sciences. Titles are aimed at an academic audience of students and professionals in higher education worldwide. The press is always interested in receiving proposals for new books that have a sharp critical edge and an intentionally political focus.

Pocket Books

1st Floor, 222 Gray's Inn Road, London, WC1X 8HB

- 020 7316 1900
- 020 7316 0332
- enquiries@simonandschuster.co.uk
- www.simonsays.co.uk

Parent Company Simon & Schuster UK Ltd
Insider Info Catalogue available online.
Non-Fiction Publishes Coffee Table, General Non-Fiction, Gift and Self-Help titles on the following subjects: Biography & True Stories, Crime, Current Affairs, Health, Humanities, Lifestyle, Spirituality, Television Tie-Ins, World Affairs.
Submission Guidelines Agented submissions only.
Fiction Publishes Fantasy, Science Fiction, Suspense, General Mass Market Fiction and Television Tie-In titles.
Submission Guidelines Agented submissions only.
Recent Title(s) *Beautiful Boy*, David Sheff (Novel); *Thirty Bullies: A History of the Rugby World Cup*, Alison Kervin (Sport)
Tips Pocket Books is Simon & Schuster's mass market fiction and non-fiction imprint. All books are published in paperback.

Pocket Essentials

PO Box 394, Harpenden, AL5 1XJ

- 01582 761264

☎ 01582 7612244
✉ info@pocketessentials.co.uk
🌐 www.pocketessentials.co.uk
Parent Company Oldcastle Books
Contact Editor, Mel McGinnis
Insider Info Average lead time is five months. Catalogue and manuscript guidelines available online.
Non-Fiction Publishes Reference titles on the following subjects:
Culture, Theory, Philosophy, Film, History, Literature, Science, Sport
Submission Guidelines Accepts proposal package via email (including outline and samples of writing). Read the very detailed author guidelines on the website before submitting.
Recent Title(s) *Saints*, Giles Morgan; *Superhero Movies*, Liam Burke
Tips Pocket Essentials (PEs) are cultural guides packed with facts, opinion, information, critical insights, trivia, bibliographies, plot summaries, biographies and essays by experts. The largest area of publishing is on film subjects, but PEs are also published on ideas and history. A limited number are published on television, sport, business, music and literature.

Pocket Mountains Ltd
6 Church Wynd, Bo'ness, West Lothian, EH51 0AN
☎ 01506 500404
✉ info@pocketmountains.com
🌐 www.pocketmountains.com
Contact Director, April Simmons; Director, Robbie Porteous
Established 2002
Insider Info Catalogue is available online. Manuscript guidelines are available online via the website.
Non-Fiction Publishes General Non-Fiction and Reference titles on the following subjects:
Hobbies, Nature/Environment, Regional, Sports, Travel and Hiking/Walking Guides
Submission Guidelines Accepts query with SAE and proposal package (including outline, one sample chapter and author biography).
Recent Title(s) *Edinburgh – 40 Town and Country Walks*, Kerry Nelson (Walking Guide)
Tips Pocket Mountains was set up by a group of outdoor enthusiasts who wanted to see books on the shelves that reflected the spirit of adventure and excitement that Scotland as an outdoor destination represents. From its roots as a mountain walking publisher, the company has now grown to include cycling, mountain biking and wildlife guides. Pocket Mountains is always on the lookout for new outdoor authors and welcomes ideas from non-established

authors with a sound knowledge of the particular subject area, plenty of enthusiasm, and an idea that excites.

The Policy Press
4th Floor, Beacon House, Queen's Road, Bristol, BS8 1QU
☎ 0117 331 4054
☎ 0117 331 4093
✉ tpp-info@bristol.ac.uk
🌐 www.policypress.org.uk
Parent Company University of Bristol
Contact Director, Alison Shaw (Social Policy); Assistant Director, Julia Mortimer (Social Work); Karen Bowler (Proposal Queries); Emily Watt (proposal queries)
Established 1996
Insider Info Publishes 60 titles per year. Receives approximately 150–200 queries and 80 manuscripts per year. 15 per cent of books published are by first-time authors and 100 per cent of books published are from unagented authors. Payment is based on net receipts. Average lead time is 18 months, with simultaneous submissions accepted. Submissions accompanied by SAE will be returned. Aims to respond to queries within two days, and proposals and manuscripts within six months. Catalogue and author guidelines are free on request, and available online.
Non-Fiction Publishes Scholarly and Textbook titles on the following subjects:
Community/Public Affairs, Education, Government/Politics, Health/Medicine, Social Sciences, Sociology, Women's Issues/Studies, World Affairs
* All publications are peer reviewed.
Submission Guidelines Accepts proposal package via email (including outline, sample chapter(s), your publishing history, author biography) and artworks/images (send digital files as jpegs).
Tips Titles are aimed at academics, students (all levels) and practitioners. Please follow the proposal guidelines on the website.

Policy Studios Institute
50 Hanson Street, London, W1W 6UP
☎ 020 7911 7500
☎ 020 7911 7501
✉ psi-admin@psi.org.uk
🌐 www.psi.org.uk
Contact Director, Malcolm Rigg
Established 1978
Insider Info Catalogue and manuscript guidelines available online.
Non-Fiction Publishes Reference, Scholarly and Technical titles on the following subjects:

Business/Economics, Community/Public Affairs, Contemporary Culture, Counselling/Career, Education, Government/Politics, Law, Money/ Finance, Nature/Environment, Social Sciences, Transportation, World Affairs

Tips PSI undertakes and publishes research studies relevant to social, economic and industrial policy. It takes a politically neutral stance on issues of public policy and has no connections with any political party, commercial interest or pressure group. Please note that PSI no longer publishes new material of its own. The remaining stock of PSI publications is handled by Central Books.

Politico's Publishing
8 Artillery Road, London, SW1P 1RZ
- 020 7798 1600
- 020 7828 1244
- methuenpubltd@btinternet.com
- www.politicospublishing.co.uk

Parent Company Methuen Publishing Limited
Contact Chairman/Managing Director, Peter Tummons; Publishing Director, Alan Gordon-Walker
Established 1998 (acquired by Methuen 2003)
Insider Info Catalogue available online.
Non-Fiction Publish Autobiography, Biography, Humour, Reference, Self-Help and Textbook titles on the following subjects:
Business/Economics, Education, Government/ Politics, History, Law, Military/War, Philosophy, Religion, Sociology, Travel, Communication Studies, Performing Arts, Literature, Europe, Asia
Submission Guidelines Accepts query with SAE/ proposal package (including synopsis). Prefers agented submissions.
Fiction Publishes Political Fiction titles.
Submission Guidelines Accepts query with SAE/ proposal package (including synopsis). Prefers agented submissions.
Recent Title(s) *Conflict of Loyalty*, Geoffrey Howe (Politics); *Iraq Endgame?: Surge, Suffering and the Politics of Denial*, Geoff Simons (Politics/ Current Affairs)
Tips Specialists in political publishing, particularly to do with Britain, Europe, USA and the Middle East. Unagented submissions are not encouraged. No submissions by email.

Polity Press
65 Bridge Street, Cambridge, CB2 1UR
- 01223 324315
- 01223 461385
- editorial@polity.co.uk
- www.polity.co.uk

Contact Editorial Director, Louise Knight (Politics, International Relations); Commissioning Editor,

Andrea Drugan (History, Literature, Media and Culture Studies); Commissioning Editor, Emma Longstaff (Sociology); Commissioning Editor, Emma Hutchinson (Philosophy); Commissioning Editor, Sarah Lambert (All Other Subjects)
Established 1983
Insider Info Catalogue and author guidelines available online.
Non-Fiction Publishes General Non-Fiction titles on the following subjects:
Anthropology/Archaeology, Government/Politics, History, Language/Literature, Literary Criticism, Philosophy, Psychology, Sex, Sociology, Women's Issues/Studies, Media and Cultural Studies.
Submission Guidelines Accepts query with SAE, or via email to the appropriate commissioning editor, with proposal package (including outline and sample chapter(s)).
Submission details to: firstname.lastname@ polity.co.uk (see contacts for commissioning editors).
Recent Title(s) *Gorbachev's Gamble*, Andrei Grachev
Tips Polity is a leading international publisher in the social sciences and humanities. Titles are aimed primarily at students and scholars in further and higher education. The list is particularly strong in the areas of sociology, politics, and social and political theory. They would like to hear from authors who have an idea for, or are currently writing an academic title in the appropriate subject areas.

Pomegranate Press
Dolphin House, 51 St Nicholas Lane, Lewes, Sussex, BN7 2JZ
- 01273 470100
- 01273 470100
- pomegranatepress@aol.com
- www.pomegranate-press.co.uk

Contact David Arscott (Self-Publishing; Sussex Themes)
Established 1992
Insider Info Publishes several titles per year, about half by first-time authors. Average lead time is three months. Aims to respond to queries and manuscripts within ten days. Catalogue available on the website.
Non-Fiction Publishes General Non-Fiction titles on any subject.
Submission Guidelines Accepts query with SAE, or via email.
Fiction Publishes Fiction for self-publishing authors.
Submission Guidelines Accepts query with SAE, or via email.
Recent Title(s) *A Sussex Kipling*, David Arscott; *City Streets to Sussex Lanes*, David Johnston (Memoir); *Out of the Shadows*, Adam Trimingham (Non-Fiction/ Mental Health); *Sandies in the Beach Huts*, Cathy

Watts (author) and Emma Ball (illustrator) (Children's Fiction)

Tips Pomegranate are a self-publishing company, with author/publisher David Arscott offering a one-to-one service.

Poolbeg Press

123 Grange Hill, Baldoyle Industrial Estate, Baldoyle, Dublin 13, Republic of Ireland
- 00353 1 832 1477
- 00353 1 832 1430
- info@poolbeg.com
- www.poolbeg.com

Contact Publishing Director, Paula Campbell; Managing Director, Kieran Devlin

Established 1976

Insider Info Catalogue available online.

Non-Fiction Publishes Biography, Children's and General Non-Fiction titles on the following subjects: Cooking, Food & Drink, Gardening, Government/Politics, Music, Regional Interest, Religion, World Affairs

Fiction Publishes Children's, Literary, Mainstream/Contemporary, Romance, Short Story Collections, Young Adult and Irish Interest titles.

Poetry Publish Irish Poetry.

Recent Title(s) *Nobody's Child*, Cora Coleman (Memoir)

Tips Poolbeg is Ireland's premier popular fiction publishing company and mainly publishes new Irish writers.

Portico

The Old Magistrates Court, 10 Southcombe Street, London, W14 0RA
- 020 7605 1400
- 020 7605 1594
- portico@anovabooks.com
- www.porticobooks.co.uk

Parent Company Anova Books Company Ltd

Contact Publisher, Tom Bromley

Established 2007

Insider Info Catalogue available online.

Non-Fiction Publishes General Non-Fiction, Humour and Reference titles on the following subjects:
Humour and Internet Books, Popular Culture, Reference, Sport, Narrative Non-Fiction

Recent Title(s) *Chateau Monty*, Monty Waldin (Wine)

Tips Portico is Anova's new imprint for non-fiction books with a 'fresh, funny and forthright' appeal.

Portland Press Ltd

3rd Floor, Eagle House, 16 Procter Street, London, WC1V 6NX

- 020 7280 4110
- 020 7280 4169
- editorial@portlandpress.com
- www.portlandpress.com

Contact Managing Director, Rhonda Oliver; Head of Editorial, Pauline Starley

Established 1990

Insider Info Publishes four titles per year. Payment is via royalties. Catalogue and manuscript guidelines available online.

Non-Fiction Publish Reference, Scholarly, Children's and Technical titles on Biomedical Sciences.

Submission Guidelines Accepts query with SAE.

Tips Portland Press is a not for profit publisher of journals and books on cellular and molecular life sciences. Titles are aimed largely at graduate, postgraduate and research students. The small book publishing programme falls within the biomedical sciences field, specifically the *Essays in Biochemistry* series and the Biochemical Society symposia. Children's titles are produced in the *Making Sense of Science Children's Books* series. They do not normally accept unsolicited proposals unless they could potentially form a volume of the *Essays* series.

Portobello Books Ltd

12 Addison Avenue, London, W11 4QR
- 020 7605 1380
- 020 7605 1361
- mail@portobellobooks.com
- www.portobellobooks.com

Established 2005

Insider Info Publishes 20 titles per year. Catalogue is free on request.

Non-Fiction Publishes General Non-Fiction on the following subjects:
Literary, History, Anthropology, Culture

Submission Guidelines Accepts emailed queries.

Fiction Publish Literary Fiction and Fiction in Translation.

Submission Guidelines Accepts emailed queries.

Tips As an independent publisher, Portobello is able to take more risks with unusual or new work than is common in contemporary publishing. Portobello does not consider unsolicited manuscripts, and will only accept queries by email.

Portrait

Little, Brown Book Group, 100 Victoria Embankment, London, EC4Y 0DY
- 020 7911 8000
- info@littlebrown.co.uk
- www.piatkus.co.uk

Parent Company Piatkus Books

Contact Publishing Director, Antonia Hodgson

Established 2004

Insider Info Submissions accompanied by SAE will be returned. Catalogue available online.
Non-Fiction Publishes Autobiography, Biography and General Non-Fiction titles on the following subjects:
Contemporary Culture, History, Music/Dance
Submission Guidelines Accepts query with SAE with proposal package (including outline, one sample chapter, and the introduction).
Tips Portrait is Piatkus Books' general non-fiction imprint, publishing history, memoirs, popular culture, music, humour and other subjects that appeal to the publishers and the market at the time. Emailed submissions are not accepted.

Praxis Books

Crossways Cottage, Walterstone, Herefordshire, HR2 0DX
- 01873 890695
- rebeccatope@btinternet.com
- www.rebeccatope.com/praxisbooks.asp
Contact Proprietor, Rebecca Smith
Established 1992
Insider Info Catalogue and manuscript guidelines available online.
Non-Fiction Publishes Autobiography, Children's and General Non-Fiction titles on the following subjects:
Memoirs, Philosophy, Walking Guides
Submission Guidelines Accepts query with SAE.
Fiction Publishes Contemporary Fiction and Sabine Baring-Gould reprints.
Submission Guidelines Accepts query with SAE.
Tips Praxis Books is a small press mainly dedicated to the reissue of the novels of Sabine Baring-Gould. They will also occasionally consider approaches from authors.

Prentice Hall

Edinburgh Gate, Harlow, Essex, CM20 2JE
- 01279 623623
- 01279 414130
- www.pearsoned.co.uk/Imprints/prenticehall
Parent Company Pearson Education
Insider Info Catalogue and manuscript guidelines are available online.
Non-Fiction Publishes Academic, Reference, Scholarly and Textbook titles on the following subjects:
Business, Computer Science, Engineering, Information Technology, Java.
Submission Guidelines Accepts proposal package (including synopsis, sample chapters, market research, your publishing history and author biography).

Recent Title(s) *Brilliant ITQ*, Nik Taylor and Catherine Jones (Information Technology)
Tips Prentice Hall has established itself as one of the leading professional and technical publishers within the industry. Using premier authors from around the globe, it offers computing professionals the information they need. Prentice Hall is also a leading authority on Java.

Prestel Publishing Ltd

4 Bloomsbury Place, London, WC1A 2QA
- 020 7323 5004
- 020 7636 8004
- sales@prestel-uk.co.uk
- www.prestel.com
Contact Commissioning Editor, Philippa Hurd
Established 1924
Insider Info Catalogue available online.
Non-Fiction Publishes Children's, Illustrated Books and General Non-Fiction titles on the following subjects:
Art, Architecture, Contemporary Culture, Ethnic, History, Photography and Ethnography
Submission Guidelines Accepts query with SAE/ proposal package (including outline, sample chapter(s) and SAE). Will accept artwork/images.
Recent Title(s) *Element*, Cecil Balmond (Architecture)
Tips Books published by Prestel range from museum guides, encyclopedic works, and monographs on artists and architects, to valuable facsimile editions and art books for children. Titles are published in both English and German.

Priddy Books

4 Crinan Street, London, N1 9XW
- 020 7418 5515
- 020 7418 85507
- website@priddybooks.com
- www.priddybooks.com
Contact Publisher, Roger Priddy
Insider Info Catalogue available online.
Non-fiction Publishes Illustrated Novelty Children's titles.
Fiction Publishes Picture Books and Young Children's Fiction.
Recent Title(s) *Slide and Find: Colours*
Tips Priddy Books specialises in novelty books, such as cloth books and board books, for young children. Books should be designed to stimulate a child's mind and raise awareness of the world around it.

Prim-Ed Publishing

PO Box 2840, Coventry, CV6 5ZY
- 0870 876 0151
- 0870 876 0152

○ authors@prim-ed.com

⊕ www.prim-ed.com

Insider Info Catalogue available online. Accept queries via email.

Non-Fiction Publishes Primary and Special Educational Needs Lower Secondary School Educational Resources.

Tips All texts are photocopiable and are called *Copymasters*. Although there is no official submissions policy, Prim-Ed are always looking for qualified teachers to undertake contract writing. Email for further details.

Princeton University Press

6 Oxford Street, Woodstock, Oxfordshire, OX20 1TW

○ 01993 814500

❶ 01993 814504

○ admin@pupress.co.uk

⊕ www.press.princeton.edu

Contact Publishing Director, Richard Baggaley; Senior Editor, Ian Malcolm

Insider Info Publish roughly 200 titles per year. Simultaneous submissions accepted. Submissions will not be returned. Catalogue is free on request and available online. Manuscript guidelines are free on request and available online, or via email.

Non-Fiction Publishes Biography, General Non-Fiction, Reference, Scholarly, Technical and Textbook titles on the following subjects: Anthropology/Archaeology, Art, Architecture, Astrology/Psychic, Business, Economics, Education, Environment, Government/Politics, History, Humanities, Law, Literary Criticism, Marine Subjects, Military/War, Money/Finance, Multicultural, Nature, Philosophy, Psychology, Religion, Science, Social Sciences, Sociology, Translation, World Affairs

Submission Guidelines Accepts proposal package (including outline, sample chapter(s), your publishing history, author biography).

Recent Title(s) *What Bugged the Dinosaurs? Insects, Disease, and Death in the Cretaceous*, George Poinar, Jr and Roberta Poinar (Natural History)

Tips Titles are aimed at university level students, as well as professional academics.

Prion Books

20 Mortimer Street, London, W1T 3JW

○ 020 7612 0400

❶ 020 7612 0401

○ enquiries@carltonbooks.co.uk

⊕ www.carltonbooks.co.uk

Parent Company Carlton Publishing Group

Insider Info Publishes four titles per year. Catalogue available online.

Non-Fiction Publishes Gift and Illustrated titles on the following subjects: Entertainment, Humour, Nostalgia, Photography

Submission Guidelines Accepts proposal package (including outline, 20 pages or two chapters – which ever is shorter).

Recent Title(s) *Every Boy's Book of Knowledge*, (Nostalgia)

Tips Specialises in humour and nostalgia. Do not send full manuscripts unless via an agent.

Profile Books

3a Exmouth House, Pine Street, Exmouth Market, London, EC1R 0JH

○ 020 7841 6300

❶ 020 7833 3969

○ info@profilebooks.com

⊕ www.profilebooks.co.uk

Contact Managing Director, Andrew Franklin; Editor & International Rights, Penny Daniel

Established 1996

Imprint(s) Profile Business
Economist Books
Serpents Tail

Insider Info Publishes 60 titles per year. Payment via royalties. Catalogue available online.

Non-Fiction Publishes General Non-Fiction and Scholarly titles on the following subjects: Business/Economics, Contemporary Culture, Government/Politics, History, Literary Criticism, Psychology, World Affairs

Submission Guidelines Accepts query with SAE, or via email, with proposal package (including outline and two sample chapters).

Recent Title(s) *The City: A Guide to London's Global Financial Centre*, Richard Roberts (Finance)

Tips Most books published by Profile are submitted through literary agents.

Profile Business

3a Exmouth House, Pine Street, Exmouth Market, London, EC1R 0JH

○ 020 7841 6300

❶ 020 7833 3969

○ stephen.brough@profilebooks.com

⊕ www.profilebooks.co.uk

Parent Company Profile Books

Contact Editor, Stephen Brough

Insider Info Catalogue available online.

Non-Fiction Publishes General Non-Fiction, Reference and Scholarly titles on the following subjects:
Business/Economics

Submission Guidelines Accepts proposal package including (outline, two sample chapters and SAE).

Recent Title(s) *Empires of Oil*, Duncan Clarke

Tips Most submissions are made by agents, although unsolicited proposals will be considered.

ProQuest Information & Learning Ltd
512 The Quorum, Barnwell Road, Cambridge, CB5 8SW

- 01223 215512
- 01223 215514
- marketing@proquest.co.uk
- www.proquest.co.uk

Contact General Manager, John Taylor
Established 1938
Non-Fiction Publish Reference, Scholarly and Technical titles.
Tips ProQuest Information & Learning provides access to information from periodicals, newspapers, out of print books, dissertations, and scholarly collections in various formats. They typically work in tandem with publishers to provide materials for academic institutions, libraries and classrooms.

PS Avalon
PO Box 1865, Glastonbury, Somerset, BA6 8YR

- 01458 833864
- info@psavalon.com
- www.psavalon.com

Contact Director, Will Parfitt
Established 2003
Insider Info Publishes roughly four titles per year. Receives approximately 50 queries per year. 50 per cent of books published are from first-time authors, 90 per cent of books published are from unagented authors. Payment is via royalty (on retail price), with 0.1 (per £) minimum and 0.25 (per £) maximum. Average lead time is six months, with simultaneous submissions accepted. Submissions accompanied by SAE will be returned. Aims to respond to queries and proposals within seven days and manuscripts within 28 days. Catalogue is free on request and available online. Manuscript guidelines are available online.
Non-Fiction Publishes Autobiography, Reference, Scholarly, Self-Help and Textbook titles on the following subjects:
Alternative Lifestyles, Astrology/Psychic, Contemporary Culture, Counselling/Career, Creative Non-Fiction, Education, Health/Medicine, New Age, Psychology, Spirituality
* All authors need to be active, willing and able to help promote their work.
Submission Guidelines Accepts query with SAE or by email, and artworks/images (send digital files as jpegs).
Fiction Publishes Occult, Religious and Spiritual titles

Submission Guidelines Accepts query with SAE, or by email.
Poetry Publishes Spiritually Orientated Poetry
* All authors must be willing to do public readings to promote their work.
Submission Guidelines Accepts query or proposal package (including two sample poems).
Recent Title(s) *Moonseanight*, Caeia March (Poetry); *The Something and Nothing of Death*, Will Parfitt (Self-Help)
Tips PS Avalon publishes for a general readership.

Psychology Press
Albert House, 1-4 Singer Street, London, EC2A 4BQ

- 020 7017 6000
- 020 7017 6701
- Online form.
- www.psypress.co.uk

Parent Company Taylor & Francis Group
Insider Info Catalogue and manuscript guideline are available online.
Non-Fiction Publishes Journals, Multimedia, Scholarly and Textbook titles on the following subjects:
Cognitive Psychology and Cognitive Neuroscience, Developmental Psychology, Industrial Psychology, Neuropsychology, Social Psychology
Submission Guidelines Uses an online form for proposal submissions. Hard copies accepted if no other option.
Recent Title(s) *Fundamentals of Psychology*, Michael W. Eysenck (Psychology)
Tips Psychology Press publishes in all areas of psychological science. Titles must be based on psychology in the broadest sense, and be written by credible experts.

Puffin
80 Strand, London, WC2R 0RL

- 020 7010 3000
- 020 7010 6060
- puffin@penguin.co.uk
- www.puffin.co.uk

Parent Company Penguin Group (UK)
Contact Managing Director, Francesca Dow; Publishing Director (Fiction), Sarah Hughes; Editorial Director (Picture Books), Louise Bolongaro; Senior Commissioning Editor (Fiction), Lindsey Heaven; Senior Editor (Picture Books), Janice Thompson
Established 1940
Insider Info Catalogue is available online.
Non-Fiction Publishes Children's, General Non-Fiction, Gift, Illustrated and Novelty titles on the following subjects:
Film, Popular Culture, Television Tie-Ins

Submission Guidelines Agented submissions only.
Fiction Publishes Children's, Humour, Mystery, Novelty, Picture, Teenage and Young Adult titles.
Submission Guidelines Agented submissions only.
Poetry Publishes collections of Poetry for Children and Young Adult readers.
Submission Guidelines Agented submissions only.
Recent Title(s) *Airman*, Eoin Colfer (Novel); *Monsterbook: Pongdollop and the School Stink*, Michael Broad (Picture Book)
Tips Puffin is the UK's leading publisher of children's books. Its titles are aimed at a range of age groups, from younger children through to young adult and teenage readers.

Pushkin Press
12 Chester Terrace, London, NW1 4ND
- 020 7730 0750
- 020 7730 1341
- books@pushkinpress.com
- www.pushkinpress.com

Contact Chairman, Melissa Ulfane
Fiction Publishes Classic and Contemporary Literary Fiction in Translation.
Recent Title(s) *Alphabet of the Night*, Jean-Euphèle Milcé (translated by Christopher Moncrieff)
Tips Most publications are European translations. Publishes both full-length novels and novellas, as well as short story collections.

QED Publishing
226 City Road, London, EC1V 2TT
- 020 7812 8600
- 020 7253 4370
- qedpublishing@quarto.com
- www.qed-publishing.co.uk

Parent Company The Quarto Group
Contact Publisher, Steve Evans; Editorial Director, Jean Coppendale; Editor, Hannah Ray
Established 2003
Insider Info Payment is via an outright fee. Catalogue free on request and available online.
Non-Fiction Publishes General Non-Fiction, Illustrated and Reference titles on the following subjects:
Children's, Childcare/Parenting, Education, History, Nature/Environment, Art & Design, ICT, Geography, Science, Maths and Literacy.
* Books are specially devised to support children's curriculum learning.
Submission Guidelines Accepts query with SAE.
Recent Title(s) *Animal Lives: Eagles*, Sally Morgan (Educational)
Tips Authors for children's educational books should be experts in their field.

Quadrille Publishing Ltd
5th Floor, Alhambra House, 27–31 Charing Cross Road, London, WC2H 0LS
- 020 7839 7117
- 020 7839 7118
- enquiries@quadrille.co.uk
- www.quadrille.co.uk

Contact Managing Director, Alison Cathie; Editorial Director, Jane O'Shea
Established 1994
Insider Info Authors paid by royalty. Catalogue available online.
Non-Fiction Publishes General Non-Fiction, Gift, Humour and Illustrated titles on the following subjects:
Automotive, Cooking, Crafts, Food & Drink, Gardening, Health/Medicine, House & Home, Nature/Environment, Photography, Spirituality
Recent Title(s) *Dinner in a Dash*, Lindsey Bareham (Cookery)
Tips Welcomes ideas or synopses for appropriate non-fiction books, but not fiction or children's books.

Quantum
The Publishing House, Bennetts Close, Cippenham, Slough, Berkshire, SL1 5AP
- 01753 526769
- 01753 535003
- marketing@foulsham.com
- www.foulsham.com

Parent Company Foulsham Publishers
Insider Info Catalogue available online.
Non-Fiction Publishes General Non-Fiction titles on the following subjects:
Astrology, Dreams, Health, Self-Help, Spirituality
Submission Guidelines Accepts query with proposal package (including outline, author biography and SAE). Address submissions to the 'Editorial Department'. No submissions accepted by email.

Quartet Books
27 Goodge Street, London, W1T 2LD
- 020 7636 3992
- 020 7637 1866
- quartetbooks@easynet.co.uk

Contact Managing Director, Jeremy Beale; Publishing Director, Stella Kane
Established 1972
Insider Info Authors paid by royalty.
Non-Fiction Publishes Biography, General Non-Fiction and Scholarly titles on the following subjects:
Contemporary Culture, Government/Politics, History, Music, Photography
Submission Guidelines Accepts query with SAE including outline and two sample chapters.

Fiction Publishes Literary, Mainstream/ Contemporary and Translation titles.
Submission Guidelines Accepts query with SAE including outline and two sample chapters. Submissions via email or on disk are not considered.
Tips No genre fiction is accepted.

The Quarto Group Inc
226 City Road, London, EC1V 2TT
- 020 7700 9000
- 020 7253 4437
- info@quarto.com
- www.quarto.com

Imprint(s) Apple Press
Argentum
Aurum Publishing
Non-fiction Publishes General and Illustrated titles on a wide variety of subjects.
Tips The UK based Quarto Group also has a presence in the US and Australia. Quarto undertakes co-edition publishing in the UK with companies including Design Eye, EYE, Jacqui Small, Marshall Editions, QED, Quantum Publishing, Quarto Publishing, Quarto Children's Books, Qu:id, Quintessence, and Quintet Publishing. See the separate imprint entries for the more traditional publishing arms of Quarto.

QueenSpark Books
Room 211, 10–11 Pavilion Parade, Brighton, BN2 1RA
- 01273 571710
- 01273 571710
- info@queensparkbooks.org.uk
- www.queensparkbooks.org.uk

Established 1974
Insider Info Catalogue available online.
Non-Fiction Publishes Biography and General Non-Fiction titles on the following subjects:
History and Regional Interest
Submission Guidelines No unsolicited manuscripts.
Recent Title(s) *The Deckchair Guide to Brighton & Hove*, QueenSpark Writers (Local Interest/Guide)
Tips QueenSpark is a non-profit community publishing and writing organisation, publishing books about local people's lives, running creative writing groups and facilitating oral history projects. Materials are sourced mainly from associated writing groups and no unsolicited manuscripts are accepted.

QUE Publishing
Edinburgh Gate, Harlow, Essex, CM20 2JE
- 01279 623623
- 01279 414130

- www.pearsoned.co.uk/imprints/quepublishing
Parent Company Pearson Education
Insider Info Catalogue and manuscript guidelines are available online.
Non-Fiction Publishes How-To, Reference and Technical titles on the following subjects:
Computers, Internet, Networking
Submission Guidelines Accepts proposal package (including synopsis, sample chapters, market research, your publishing history and author biography).
Recent Title(s) *MySpace Marketing*, Sean Percival (Internet)
Tips QUE specialises in the area of software applications and computing. It is one of the largest computer book publishers in the world and sets the standard for superior tutorial reference products, covering all major computer and internet applications at every user level. See the website for full list of submissions contacts.

Quercus Publishing Plc
21 Bloomsbury Square, London, WC1A 2NS
- 020 7291 7200
- 0870 730 1482
- mail@quercusbooks.co.uk
- www.quercusbooks.co.uk

Contact CEO/Managing Director, Mark Smith; Publishing Director, Wayne Davies; Consulting Editor, Otto Penzler (Crime Fiction)
Established 2004
Imprint(s) Quercus Editions (contract publishing) Quercus Books Limited (trade publishing)
Insider Info Catalogue available online.
Non-Fiction Publishes Biography, General Non-Fiction titles on the following subjects:
History, Hobbies and Science
Fiction Publishes Crime and Women's Fiction.
Recent Title(s) *The Girl with the Dragon Tattoo*, Stieg Larsson
Tips Quercus has both trade and contract publishing arms and is still largely driven by contract publishing, especially in the non-fiction areas. Their policy is to re-publish successful contract titles in trade editions, and establish a fiction list building on this trade presence.

Quiller Publishing Ltd
Wykey House, Wykey, Shrewsbury, , SY4 1JA
- 01939 261616
- 01939 261606
- info@quillerbooks.com
- www.countrybooksdirect.com

Contact Managing Director, Andrew Johnston (Country Sports); Editorial Director, John Beaton (Equestrian)

Established 2001

Imprint(s) Kenilworth Press
Sportsman's Press
Swan Hill Press

Insider Info Receives approximately 150 queries and 70 manuscripts per year. Ten per cent of books published are from first-time authors, 95 per cent are from unagented authors and five per cent are author subsidy published. Payment is via royalty (on wholesale price, or royalty on retail price). Average lead time is two months, with simultaneous submissions accepted. Submissions accompanied by SAE will be returned. Catalogue is free on request. Manuscript guidelines are free on request and available via email.

Non-Fiction Publishes Autobiography, Biography, Coffee Table Books, Cookbooks, General Non-Fiction, Gift, How-To, Humour, Illustrated, Reference and Technical titles on the following subjects: Agriculture/Horticulture, Animals, Cooking, Crafts, Food & Drink, Gardening, Hobbies, Military/War, Nature/Environment, Sports, Travel, Country Sports and Equestrianism

Submission Guidelines Accepts query with SAE, or via email with proposal package (including outline, sample chapter(s), publishing history, author biography). Will accept artworks/images (send photocopies or digital files as jpegs).

Tips Titles are mainly aimed at country sports and equestrian enthusiasts.

Quince Books Ltd
158 Hermon Hill, London, E18 1QH
- info@quincebooks.com
- www.quincebooks.com

Contact Simon Mitchell

Insider Info Catalogue available online.

Fiction Publishes Commercial Fiction titles.

Submission Guidelines Accepts query by email only with proposal package (including outline and three sample chapters).

Recent Title(s) *A God Named Joe*, Peter Jessop

Tips Welcomes new authors. The priority is entertainment and initial interest rather than quality of writing, which can be worked on collaboratively.

Radcliffe Publishing Ltd
18 Marcham Road, Abingdon, Oxfordshire, OX14 1AA
- 01235 528820
- 01235 528830
- contact.us@radcliffemed.com
- www.radcliffe-oxford.com

Contact Managing Director, Andrew Bax; Editorial Director, Gillian Nineham

Established 1987

Insider Info Payment is via royalties, catalogue available online

Non-Fiction Publishes Reference, Scholarly and Technical titles on the following subjects: Counselling/Career, Guidance, Health/Medicine, Science, General Practice, Health Service Management

Submission Guidelines Accepts query with SAE and proposal package (including outline and two sample chapters) Will accept artwork/images. Submission details to: gnineham@radcliffemed.com

Recent Title(s) *Parkinson's Disease in the Older Patient, Second Edition*, Jeremy Playfer and John Hindle eds. (Healthcare)

Tips Work submitted should be aimed at healthcare workers, as well as the general market.

Ragged Bears Publishing Ltd
Unit 14a Bennett's Field, Southgate Road, Wincanton, Somerset, BA9 9DT
- 01963 824184
- 01963 31147
- info@raggedbears.co.uk
- www.raggedbears.co.uk

Contact Managing Director, Henrietta Stickland; Submissions Editor, Barbara Lamb

Established 1994

Insider Info Publishes up to ten titles per year. Aims to respond to submissions within four months. Catalogue available online.

Non-fiction Publishes Illustrated Novelty Children's titles.

Submission Guidelines Accepts entire manuscript with SAE.

Fiction Publishes Children's Picture Books.

Submission Guidelines Accepts entire manuscript with SAE.

Recent Title(s) *Ten Terrible Dinosaurs*, Paul Stickland (Picture Book)

Tips Also publishes children's greetings cards, activity packs and other gift items.

The Random House Group Ltd
Random House, 20 Vauxhall Bridge Road, London, SW1V 2SA
- 020 7840 8400
- 020 7233 8719
- emarketing@randomhouse.co.uk
- www.randomhouse.co.uk

Parent Company Random House Inc US (Bertelsmann AG) (see entry under European & International Publishers)

Contact Chief Executive, Gail Rebuck

Imprint(s) Arrow
BBC Books
Century

Chatto & Windus
Ebury Press
Everyman
Fodor
Harvill Secker
Hutchinson
Jonathan Cape
Mainstream
Pimlico
Rider
Time Out Guides Ltd
Vermilion
Vintage
William Heinemann
Yellow Jersey
Random House Business Books
Random House Children's Books (division)
Transworld Publishers (division)

Insider Info Catalogue is available online (to search the catalogues of individual imprints go to 'advanced search').

Non-Fiction Publishes Autobiography, Biography, General Non-Fiction and Illustrated titles on a wide variety of subjects across its imprints.

Submission Guidelines No unagented submissions.

Fiction Publishes Mainstream/Contemporary, Literary and Classic Fiction across its imprints.

Submission Guidelines No unagented submissions.

Poetry Publishes a small amount of Poetry per year through the Jonathan Cape list.

Recent Title(s) *Heliopolis*, James Scudamore (Contemporary Fiction); *Chinese Cookery*, Ken Hom (Cookery)

Tips Random House is one of the largest general book publishing companies in the UK and has some of the world's best known authors on its lists. The Random House Group is an independently managed subsidiary of Bertelsmann AG. Will not accept unsolicited submissions, all submissions must come through a literary agent.

Random House Business Books
Random House, 20 Vauxhall Bridge Road, London, SW1V 2SA

❶ 020 7840 8451
❷ 020 7233 6127
📧 businesseditorial@randomhouse.co.uk
🌐 www.randomhouse.co.uk

Parent Company The Random House Group Ltd
Contact Publisher, Nigel Wilcockson
Insider Info Catalogue available online.
Non-Fiction Publishes General, Reference and Scholarly titles on the following subjects: Business, Economics, Finance, Management, Professional Development

Submission Guidelines No unagented submissions.

Recent Title(s) *The Crunch: How Greed and Incompetence Sparked the Credit Crisis*, Alex Brummer (Economics/Finance); *Buyology: How Everything We Believe About Why We Buy is Wrong*, Martin Lindstrom (Business)

Tips Publishes books mainly for a professional business readership. Does not accept emailed submissions.

Random House Children's Books
61–63 Uxbridge Road, London, W5 5SA

❶ 020 8231 6800
❷ 020 8231 6767
📧 childrenseditorial@randomhouse.co.uk
🌐 www.kidsatrandomhouse.co.uk

Parent Company The Random House Group Ltd
Contact Managing Director, Philippa Dickinson
Imprint(s) The Bodley Head
Corgi Children's Books
David Fickling Books
Doubleday Children's Books
Hutchinson Children's Books
Jonathan Cape Children's Books
Red Fox

Insider Info Catalogue available online.
Non-Fiction Publishes Children's and Young Adult titles.

Submission Guidelines Accepts agented submissions only.

Fiction Publishes Children's Fiction and Picture Book titles for children from 0 to 12 plus years.

Submission Guidelines Agented submissions only.
Poetry Publishes Children's Poetry.

Submission Guidelines Agented submissions only.

Recent Title(s) *Eon: Rise of the Dragoneye*, Alison Goodman (Young Adult); *Dog Biscuit*, Helen Cooper (Picture Book)

Tips Random House Children's Division merged with Transworld Publishers children's list in 2001, to form Random House Children's Books, and now ranks among the top five children's book publishers in the UK. Although unsolicited manuscripts are not accepted, there is some helpful submission advice on the children's division website.

Ransom Publishing
51 Southgate Street, Winchester, Hampshire, SO23 9EH

❶ 01962 862307
📧 ransom@ransom.co.uk
🌐 www.actinic.thwd.co.uk

Contact Managing Director, Jenny Ertle
Established 1995

Insider Info Publishes roughly 50 titles per year. Receives approximately 200 queries and 150 manuscripts per year. Ten per cent of books published are from first-time authors and 90 per cent are from unagented authors. Payment is via royalty (on retail price) with 0.1 (per £) minimum. Average lead time is six months, with simultaneous submissions accepted. Submissions accompanied by SAE will be returned. Catalogue and manuscript guidelines are free on request and available online.
Non-Fiction Publishes Children's titles on the following subjects:
Education (Literacy), General Non-Fiction, Young Adult (Easy Reads)
* Ransom specialise in books for reluctant and struggling readers.
Submission Guidelines Accept queries via email. Will accept artworks/images (send digital files as jpegs).
Fiction Publishes Fiction for reluctant and struggling readers.
* Ransom publish very little general children's fiction. They focus primarily on books for reluctant or very poor readers, ages six years up to adult.
Submission Guidelines Accepts queries via email. Will accept artworks/images (send digital files as jpegs).
Recent Title(s) *Boffin Boy and the Forest of the Ninja*, David Orme (Graphic Novel)
Tips Ransom titles are aimed at children and young adults who are reluctant, or struggling readers, as well as teachers of literacy and special educational needs teachers. Only submit proposals for books that suit these areas of interest. Email first to see if the proposal is of interest. Most projects are commissioned in-house with existing authors or selected freelancers.

Ravenhall Books
PO Box 357, Welwyn Garden City, AL6 6WJ
- 01707 371545
- 01707 325230
- info@ravenhallbooks.com
- www.ravenhallbooks.com
Contact Eugina North
Insider Info Catalogue available online.
Non-Fiction Publishes General Non-Fiction and Scholarly titles on the following subjects:
History, Military/War, Translation
Recent Title(s) *The Inquisitor's Guide: A Medieval Manual on Heretics*, Bernard Gui (History/Translation)
Tips Ravenhall is an independent publisher specialising in historical accounts, translations and guides.

Reader's Digest Association
11 Westferry Circus, Canary Wharf, London, E14 4HE
- 020 7715 8000
- 020 7715 8181
- Online form
- www.readersdigest.co.uk
Insider Info Catalogue available online.
Non-Fiction Publishes Children's, General Non-Fiction, Humour, Illustrated and Reference titles on the following subjects:
Cooking, Crafts, Food & Drink, Gardening, Health/Medicine, History, Photography, Travel, Computing, DIY, General Knowledge.
* Also publishes Magazines, Videos and CDs.
Tips The main editorial office for Reader's Digest is based in the US.

Reaktion Books Ltd
33 Great Sutton Street, London, EC1V 0DX
- 020 7253 1071
- 020 7253 1208
- info@reaktionbooks.co.uk
- www.reaktionbooks.co.uk
Contact Managing Director, Michael R. Leaman
Established 1985
Insider Info Publishes roughly 30 titles per year. Payment is via royalties. Catalogue available online. Manuscript guidelines available online via the website.
Non-Fiction Publishes General Non-Fiction, Illustrated Books, Reference and Scholarly titles on the following subjects:
Art, Architecture, History, Nature/Environment, Photography, Travel, Art History, Asian Studies, Natural History, Geography
Submission Guidelines Accepts query with SAE and proposal package (including outline, CV, two sample chapters, market research and SAE). Submission details to: sophie@reaktionbooks.co.uk
Recent Title(s) *Anatomy Museum: Death and the Body Displayed*, Elizabeth Hallam
Tips When submitting a manuscript be sure to refer to the submission guidelines on the website.

Reality Street Editions
63 All Saints Street, Hastings, East Sussex, TN34 3BN
- 01424 431271
- info@realitystreet.co.uk
- www.realitystreet.co.uk
Contact Ken Edwards
Established 1993
Fiction Publishes Mainstream/Contemporary and Translation titles.

Submission Guidelines No unsolicited manuscripts.
Poetry Publishes Poetry titles.
* The majority of Reality Street Editions' output is poetry.
Submission Guidelines No unsolicited manuscripts.
Tips Reality Street often publishes poetry anthologies. Publishing programmes are announced on the website up to two years in advance.

Reardon Publishing
PO Box 919, Cheltenham, Gloucestershire, GL50 9AN
- 01242 231800
- reardon@bigfoot.com
- www.reardon.co.uk
Contact Director, Nicholas Reardon
Established 1976
Insider Info Publish roughly 15 titles per year. Receives approximately 20 queries and ten manuscripts per year. 75 per cent of books published are by first-time authors, 100 per cent are by unagented authors and 50 per cent are author subsidy published. Payment is via royalty (on retail price). Average lead time is six months, with simultaneous submissions accepted. Submissions accompanied by SAE will be returned. Aims to respond to queries, proposals and manuscripts within two weeks. Catalogue available online. Manuscript guidelines available via email.
Non-Fiction Publishes Booklets, Children's and Guidebook titles on the following subjects: Animals, Folklore, General Interest, Hiking, History, Hobbies, Nature/Environment, Regional Interest (Cotswolds), Walking Guides
Submission Guidelines Accepts query with SAE. Will accept artworks/images (send photocopies or digital files as jpegs).
Fiction Publishes Children's and Young Adult titles.
Submission Guidelines Accepts query with SAE.
Poetry Publishes Poetry titles.
Submission Guidelines Accepts query with sample poems.
Recent Title(s) *Cotswold Driveabout: The Northern Cotswolds*, Peter Reardon (Guidebook); *The Vegetable Lovers Guide*, Chris Evans (Booklet)

Red Bird Press
Kiln Farm, Brighlingsea, Colchester, Essex, C07 0SX
- 01206 303525
- 01206 304545
- info@red-bird.co.uk
- www.red-bird.co.uk
Insider Info Catalogue available online.

Fiction Publishes Picture Books and Children's Illustrated Fiction titles.
Tips Red Bird specialises in distinctive children's formats featuring 3D vision, glow in the dark, hidden pictures and other special effects. Books are often based on international licensed characters, including those from Disney, Hasbro, Mirage and Fox Kids.

Red Fox
61–63 Uxbridge Road, London, W5 5SA
- 020 7840 8640
- 020 7233 6058
- childrenseditorial@randomhouse.co.uk
- www.kidsatrandomhouse.co.uk
Parent Company Random House Children's Books
Insider Info Catalogue available online.
Fiction Publishes Picture Books and Children's Fiction titles.
Submission Guidelines No unagented submissions.
Recent Title(s) *Follow That String*, Deborah Brown and Kathy Bacovitch (Novelty Book); *The Lady Grace Mysteries: Keys*, Grace Cavendish (Children's Fiction)
Tips The focus of Red Fox tends to be on illustrated books for young children.

Reed Elsevier Group Plc
1–3 Strand, London, WC2N 5JR
- 020 7930 7077
- 020 7166 5799
- www.reedelsevier.com
Contact CEO, Sir Crispin Davis
Established 1993
Imprint(s) Elsevier Ltd (division)
LexisNexis (division)
Reed Business (division)
Non-Fiction Publishes General Non-Fiction, CD-ROM, Multimedia, Reference and Scholarly, and Technical titles on the following subjects: Accounting, Corporate Business, Education, Government, Health, Law & Legal, Medicine, Risk Management, Science, Technology
Tips Reed Elsevier is a world leading publisher of information and solutions aimed at professional users in the fields of science and medical, legal, education and business.

Reed Business
Quadrant House, The Quadrant, Sutton, Surrey, SM2 5AS
- 020 8652 3500
- webmaster@rbi.co.uk
- www.reedbusiness.co.uk
Parent Company Reed Elsevier Group Plc
Contact CEO, Gerard van de Aast

Non-Fiction Publishes General Non-Fiction, CD-ROM, Multimedia, Reference, Scholarly and Technical titles on the following subjects:
Business and Management
Tips Titles and products are aimed at professional global business markets.

Regency House Publishing Ltd
Niall House, 24–26 Boulton Road, Stevenage, Hertfordshire, SG1 4QX
- 01438 314488
- 01438 311303
- regency-house@btconnect.com
- www.regencyhousepublishing.com
Contact Managing Director, Nicolette Trodd
Established 1991
Insider Info Catalogue available online.
Non-Fiction Publishes General Non-Fiction and Illustrated titles on the following subjects:
Art, Architecture, Cooking, Crafts, Food & Drink, Hobbies, Nature/Environment, Regional, Sports, Transportation, Equestrianism
Tips Bear in mind that Regency House produces a large list of titles for the international and co-edition markets. They also offer services as a book packager for other publishers.

Revenge Ink
1 Roger Close, Rommely, Stockport, Cheshire, SK6 3DJ
- Online form.
- www.revengeink.com
Contact Founders: Amita Mukerjee and Gopal Mukerjee
Established 2008
Insider Info Aims to respond within six to eight weeks.
Recent Title(s) *Ugly Duckling*, Amita Mukerjee; *The Armageddon Mandala*, Gopal Mukerjee
Tips Prospective authors may submit proposals by email, using the online form, or by post. If submitting by post ensure that you use the alternative postal address listed on the website.

Reverb
PO Box 615, Oxford, OX1 9AL
- mail@readreverb.com
- www.readreverb.com
Parent Company Osiris Press Ltd
Insider Info Catalogue available online.
Fiction Publishes Mainstream/Contemporary and Literary Fiction.
Submission Guidelines Does not accept unsolicited submissions.
Recent Title(s) *Who Needs Cleopatra?*, Steve Redwood

Tips Reverb publishes contemporary literary fiction with an edge and is committed to publishing new writers (and supporting independent bookshops). The Reverb website contains an informative writer's guide for prospective authors.

Reynolds & Hearn Ltd
61a Priory Road, Kew Gardens, Richmond, Surrey, TW9 3DH
- 020 8940 5198
- 020 8940 7679
- enquiries@rhbooks.com
- www.rhbooks.com
Contact Managing Director, Richard Reynolds; Editorial Director, Marcus Hearn
Established 1999
Insider Info Catalogue is available online.
Non-Fiction Publishes Biography and General Non-Fiction titles on the following subjects:
Contemporary Culture, Film, Television and Music
Recent Title(s) *The Complete Iggy Pop*, Richard Adams (Biography)
Tips Reynolds & Hearn specialises in media publishing, with an emphasis on subjects from the film, television and music industries.

Richard Dennis Publications
The Old Chapel, Shepton Beauchamp, Ilminster, Somerset, TA19 0LE
- 01460 240044
- 01460 242009
- books@richarddennispublications.com
- www.richarddennispublications.com
Established 1976
Insider Info Catalogue available online.
Non-Fiction Publishes Autobiography, Biography, Illustrated and Reference titles on the following subjects:
Art, Architecture, Hobbies, Memoirs
Recent Title(s) *Highland Stoneware*, Malcolm Haslam (Art)
Tips Publishes books for collectors specialising in ceramics, glass, illustration, sculpture and facsimile editions of early catalogues. The books are often unique, in that no other title is available on that subject.

Richmond House Publishing Company Ltd
70–76 Bell Street, Marylebone, London, NW1 6SP
- 020 7224 9666
- 020 7224 9688
- sales@rhpco.co.uk
- www.rhpco.co.uk

Contact Managing Directors, Gloria Gordan and Spencer Block
Insider Info Publishes three titles per year. Catalogue available online.
Non-Fiction Publishes Reference titles on the following subjects:
Theatre and Entertainment Directories
Submission Guidelines Accepts query with SAE.
Recent Title(s) *The Original British Theatre Directory* (Directory)
Tips Richmond House publishes directory books, and online resources for the theatre and entertainment industry. Synopses and ideas for further theatre related projects are welcome.

Rider
Random House, 20 Vauxhall Bridge Road, London, SW1V 2SA
- 020 7840 8400
- 020 7840 8406
- ridereditorial@randomhouse.co.uk
- www.randomhouse.co.uk

Parent Company The Random House Group Ltd
Contact Publishing Director, Judith Kendra
Insider Info Catalogue available online.
Non-Fiction Publishes Biography and General Non-Fiction titles on the following subjects:
Astrology/Psychic, History, Memoirs, Philosophy, Psychology, Spirituality, Travel, Personal Development
Submission Guidelines No unagented submissions.
Recent Title(s) *Becoming Enlightened*, Dalai Lama (Self-Help); *Last Night I Dreamed of Peace: An extraordinary diary of courage from the Vietnam War*, Dang Thuy Tram (Biography)
Tips Read the Rider section of the Random House catalogue for a detailed guide to the types of books published.

Rigby
Halley Court, Jordan Hill, Oxford, OX2 8EJ
- 01865 888000
- 01865 314091
- enquiries@pearson.com
- www.heinemann.co.uk

Parent Company Pearson Education
Non-Fiction Publishes Children's, Reference, Scholarly, and Textbook titles.
Tips Rigby publishes titles that are designed to provide flexible support for teachers, and challenging materials for school pupils, mainly aged from three to twelve years.

Rivers Oram Press
144 Hemingford Road, London, N1 1DE
- 020 7607 0823
- 020 7609 2776
- ro@riversoram.demon.co.uk
- www.riversoram.com

Contact Managing Director, Elizabeth Rivers Fidlon
Established 1991
Imprint(s) Pandora Press
Non-Fiction Publishes Biography, General Non-Fiction, Illustrated and Reference titles on the following subjects:
Art, Architecture, Contemporary Culture, Government/Politics, Health, History, Medicine, Photography, Sex, Social Sciences, Women's Issues/Studies, World Affairs, Media
Tips Rivers Oram is a non-fiction publisher specialising in social and political sciences with a feminist slant. All proposals must conform to these elements.

Robert Hale Ltd
Clerkenwell House, 45–47 Clerkenwell Green, London, EC1R 0HT
- 020 7251 2661
- 020 7490 4958
- submissions@halebooks.com
- www.halebooks.com

Contact Managing Director, John Hale
Established 1936
Imprint(s) J.A. Allen
N.A.G. Press
Insider Info Publishes roughly 250 titles per year. Receives approximately 3,000 queries and 1,000 manuscripts per year. 15 per cent of books published are from first-time authors and 15 per cent are from unagented authors. Payment is via royalty (on retail price). Average lead time is 12 months, with simultaneous submissions accepted. Aims to respond to queries within seven days, proposals within ten days, and manuscripts within two weeks. Catalogue is free on request. Manuscript guidelines are not available.
Non-Fiction Publishes Biography, Cookbook, General Non-Fiction, Illustrated and Self-Help titles on the following subjects:
Agriculture/Horticulture, Animals, Crafts, Gardening, Health, History, Hobbies, Law, Medicine, Memoirs, Mind, Body and Spirit, Military/War, Music, New Age, Photography, Regional, Spirituality, Sports Travel
Submission Guidelines Accepts query with SAE/proposal package (including outline, and three sample chapters). Will accept artworks/images (send photocopies).
Fiction Publishes Adventure, Historical, Literary, Mainstream/Contemporary, Military/War, Mystery,

Crime, Regional, Romance, Suspense and Western titles.

Submission Guidelines Accepts query with SAE/proposal package (including outline, and three sample chapters).

Recent Title(s) *The Cat Trap*, K.T. McCaffrey (Crime); *Fly Fisher's Logbook*, Terry Lawton (Fishing)

Tips Robert Hale specialises in general hardcover fiction. See the website for submission guidelines, and details of subjects they are currently looking to receive submissions on.

Robinswood Press Ltd
South Avenue, Stourbridge, West Midlands, DY8 3XY
- 01384 397475
- 01384 440443
- publishing@robinswoodpress.com
- www.robinswoodpress.com

Contact Publishing & Marketing, Sally Connolly

Established 1985

Insider Info Publishes 15 titles per year. Payment via royalties. Catalogue and manuscript guidelines available online.

Non-Fiction Publishes Children's, General Non-Fiction, Illustrated, Multimedia and Scholarly titles on the following subjects:
Childcare/Parenting, Education, Teaching Resources
* Books should contribute to a particular objective, to foster a love of reading and writing, especially where students need to overcome difficulties with words and literacy.

Submission Guidelines Accepts query with SAE/proposal package (including outline, one sample chapter, your publishing history, and author biography).

Fiction Publishes Picture Books and Children's Educational titles.

Submission Guidelines Accepts query with SAE/proposal package (including outline, one sample chapter, your publishing history, and author biography).

Recent Title(s) *Ghost House*, Paul Kropp (High Interest series); *The Lifeboat Read and Spell Scheme*, Sula Ellis, Tony Ellis, Jackie Davison and Mick Davison (Literacy)

Tips Authors usually have an established reputation in some aspect of teaching or work with children. Books should fit into the Robinswood objectives of encouraging reading and writing, and helping overcome difficulties in these areas.

Robson Books
The Old Magistrates Court, 10 Southcombe Street, London, W14 0RA
- 020 7605 1400

- 020 7605 1401
- customerservices@anovabooks.com
- www.anovabooks.com

Parent Company Anova Books Company Ltd

Contact Malcolm Croft

Insider Info Catalogue available online.

Non-Fiction Publishes Autobiography, Biography, General Non-Fiction, Humour and Anthology titles on the following subjects:
Celebrity, Memoirs, Sex, Adventure, Sports, Education, Theatre, Cinema

Submission Guidelines Accepts emailed synopses. Submission details to: mcroft@anovabooks.com

Recent Title(s) *The Boys of Everest*, Clint Willis (Adventure/Biography)

Tips Robson mainly focuses on celebrity autobiographies or biographies.

Rockingham Press
11 Musley Lane, Ware, Hertfordshire, SG12 7EN
- 01920 467868
- 01920 467868
- david@rockpress.freeserve.co.uk
- www.rockingham-press.co.uk

Contact David Perman

Established 1991

Insider Info Submissions accompanied by SAE will be returned.

Non-Fiction Publishes Biography and General Non-Fiction titles on the following subjects:
History, Memoirs and Regional Interest (Hertfordshire)

Submission Guidelines No unsolicited manuscripts are accepted.

Poetry Publishes Poetry titles.

Submission Guidelines No unsolicited manuscripts are accepted.

Recent Title(s) *Enclosures and Disclosures*, Mercer Simpson (Poetry)

Tips Rockingham Press have little funding and a long backlog of writers whose projects are already in the pipeline. Therefore they very rarely consider manuscripts from new writers.

Rockpool Children's Books
15 North Street, Marton, CV23 9RJ
- 01926 633114
- info@rockpoolchildrensbooks.com
- www.rockpoolchildrensbooks.com

Contact Creative Director, Stuart Trotter

Established 2006

Insider Info Catalogue available online.

Fiction Publishes Picture Book titles.

Recent Title(s) *Scaredy Cat*, Stuart Trotter

Tips Rockpool is still a fairly new company and as such only has a small number of books on its current list, most by Creative Director Stuart Trotter. More books are planned for the future.

RotoVision

Sheridan House, 112–116A Western Road, Hove, East Sussex, BN3 1DD

☎ 01273 727268

✆ 01273 727269

✉ sales@rotovision.com

🌐 www.rotovision.com

Contact Publisher, April Sankey; Senior Project Editor, Lindy Dunlop; Project Editor, Jane Roe

Established 1996

Insider Info Payment via outright purchase. Catalogue available online.

Non-Fiction Publishes General Non-Fiction, Illustrated and Reference titles on the following subjects:
Art, Architecture, Photography, Design, Digital Media and Film & Cinema

Submission Guidelines Accepts query with SAE. Will review artworks/photos as part of the manuscript package.
Submission details to: aprils@rotovision.com

Recent Title(s) *Secrets of Digital Illustration*, Lawrence Zeegen (Art)

Tips RotoVision specialises in all aspects of design, media, photography and the performing arts. Book proposals must be pinned to the latest techniques and developments in film and digital media.

Rough Guides

80 Strand, London, WC2R 0RL

☎ 020 7010 3000

✆ 020 7010 6060

✉ customer.service@penguin.co.uk

🌐 www.roughguides.com

Parent Company Penguin Group (UK)

Established 1982

Insider Info Catalogue is available online and by email.

Non-Fiction Publishes Dictionaries, Phrasebooks, General Non-Fiction, Gift, Illustrated and Reference titles on the following subjects:
Contemporary Culture, History, Hobbies, Internet, Music/Dance, Pregnancy, Sports, Travel, Maps and Unexplained Phenomena

Submission Guidelines Accepts proposal package (including outline, chapter breakdown, sample chapter, author biography and market research). Submission details to: write@roughguides.com

Recent Title(s) *The Rough Guide to Men's Health*, Lloyd Bradley (Health/Fitness); *The Rough Guide to The Dominican Republic*, Sean Harvey (Travel)

Tips Rough Guides is known for its travel guides, which combine a journalistic, critical approach with practical information. Rough Guides also publishes reference and guidebooks on a range of other subjects including film and media, health issues, music and contemporary culture. To apply to join their database of contributors/writers, send a CV and samples of writing with 1,000 words on any location, written in the Rough Guides style. Otherwise, submit a book proposal directly in the usual manner.

Round Hall

43 Fitzwilliam Place, Dublin 2, Republic of Ireland

☎ 00353 1 662 5301

✆ 00353 1 662 5302

✉ info@roundhall.ie

🌐 www.roundhall.ie

Parent Company Sweet & Maxwell Group

Contact Publisher, Catherine Dolan; Editorial Manager, Martin McCann

Established 1980

Insider Info Catalogue available online.

Non-Fiction Publishes Reference, Journals, Periodicals, Loose leaf services, CD-ROMs, Online services, Textbooks and Scholarly titles on the following subjects:
Law, Irish Law, Legal Systems

Recent Title(s) *Planning and Development Law, 2nd Edition*, Garrett Simons

Tips Potential readership of Round Hall books includes members of the judiciary, legal practitioners, academics, law students and other professionals, both in Ireland and abroad.

Routledge

2 Park Square, Milton Park, Abingdon, Oxford, OX14 4RN

☎ 020 7017 6000

✆ 020 7017 6699

✉ Online form.

🌐 www.routledge.com

Parent Company Taylor & Francis Group

Contact Managing Editor, Jon Manley; Publishing Editor, Louise Glenn (Journals); Editor, Andrew Humphreys (Military & Strategic Studies); Commissioning Editor, Samantha Grant (Sport & Leisure Studies)

Established 1836

Imprint(s) Routledge-Cavendish
Routledge Education

Insider Info Publishes over 1,000 new titles per year. Catalogue and manuscript guidelines are available online. Routledge maintains the following lists: Routledge Asian & Middle East Studies; Routledge Classics; Routledge Mental Health; Routledge Politics & International Relations; Routledge Reference;

Routledge Sport; Routledge Military & Strategic Studies.

Non-Fiction Publishes Journals, Reference, Scholarly and Textbook titles on the following subjects: Anthropology, Art, Counselling/Guidance, Cultural Theory, Ethnic Studies, History, Leisure, Literature/Language, Mental Health, Military/War, Philosophy, Politics, Psychology, Religion, Science, Social Sciences, Sport

Submission Guidelines Accepts proposal package (including outline, synopsis, one to two sample chapters, market research and CV).

Recent Title(s) *Female Terrorism and Militancy*, Cindy D. Ness, ed. (Gender Studies); *Routledge Companion to Britain in the Twentieth Century*, Mark Clapson (Reference)

Tips Routledge is a multi-disciplinary publisher of leading academic and reference titles. Submissions should be directed towards the appropriate list/series; full editorial contacts are available on the website.

Routledge-Cavendish

2 Park Square, Milton Park, Abingdon, Oxford, OX14 4RN

- 020 7017 6004
- 020 7017 6699
- fiona.kinnear@tandf.co.uk
- www.routledgelaw.com

Parent Company Routledge (Taylor & Francis Group)

Contact Publisher, Fiona Kinnear; Associate Editor, Katie Carpenter

Imprint(s) Glasshouse Press
Routledge Criminology (series)

Insider Info Catalogue and manuscript guidelines are available online.

Non-Fiction Publishes Scholarly and Technical titles on the following subjects:
Academic Law, Criminology, Law/Legal, Policy & Practice

Submission Guidelines Accepts Proposal package (including outline, synopsis, one to two sample chapters, market research, and CV).

Recent Title(s) *Risk and the Law*, Gordon Woodman and Diethelm Klippel, eds. (Law/Legal)

Tips Routledge-Cavendish specialises in academic law publishing, and also publishes titles on criminology under the Routledge Criminology series.

Routledge Education

2 Park Square, Milton Park, Abingdon, Oxford, OX14 4RN

- 020 7017 6248
- 020 7017 6699
- anna.clarkson@tandf.co.uk

- www.routledgeeducation.com

Parent Company Routledge (Taylor & Francis Group)

Contact Senior Publisher, Anna Clarkson (Education); Publisher, Philip Mudd (Adult Education); Senior Editors: Alison Foyle (Special Education Needs and Literacy) and Bruce Roberts (Education and Psychology); Commissioning Editor, Dr Monika Lee (David Fulton Practical Teachers' Books)

Imprint(s) David Fulton Publishers
Lawrence Erlbaum Associates

Insider Info Catalogue and manuscript guidelines are available online.

Non-Fiction Publishes Practical, Reference, Scholarly and Textbook titles on the following subjects: Education (Primary, Secondary and Higher), Open and Distance Learning, Psychology, Special Needs Education, Teacher Training, Teaching Resources

Submission Guidelines Accepts Proposal package (including outline, synopsis, one to two sample chapters, market research and CV).

Recent Title(s) *Observing, Assessing and Planning for Children in the Early Years*, Sandra Smidt (Education)

Tips Routledge Education publishes books aimed at professionals at any level, including textbooks for trainee teachers, books for classroom practitioners and research books for international academics. The Routledge Education list now includes David Fulton Publishers (see seperate entry), and also Lawrence Erlbaum Associates, an international academic publisher of books and journals in education and psychology.

Royal Collection Enterprises

York House, St James's Palace, Lonon, SW1A 1BQ

- 020 7839 1377
- 020 7839 8168
- press@royalcollection.org.uk
- www.royalcollection.org.uk

Contact Publisher, Jacky Colliss Harvey; Commissioning Editor, Marie Leahy

Established 1993

Insider Info Publishes roughly 12 titles per year. Catalogue available online at: www.the-royal-collection.com/UK/shop

Non-Fiction Publishes General Non-Fiction, Gift, Illustrated and Reference titles on the following subjects:
Art, Architecture, History, Guidebooks and the Royal Family

* Royal Collection Publications produces guidebooks, exhibition catalogues, scholarly catalogues and stand alone books about the collection and the royal palaces and residences.

Tips All Royal Collection publications are written solely by, or in consultation with its own curators.

Royal Irish Academy
19 Dawson Street, Dublin 2, Republic of Ireland
- 00353 1 676 2570
- 00353 1 676 2346
- publications@ria.ie
- www.ria.ie

Established 1787
Insider Info Catalogue available online.
Non-Fiction Publishes Reference and Scholarly titles on the following subjects:
Mathematics, Biological and Environmental Sciences, History, Archaeology
* Also publishes journals on Irish philology and literature – the *Irish Journal of Earth Sciences* and *Irish Studies in International Affairs*.
Recent Title(s) *Irish Agriculture: A Price History from the Mid-Eighteenth Century to the Eve of the First World War*, Liam Kennedy and Peter M. Solar
Tips The Academy is the largest publisher of scholarly journals in Ireland and also has an extensive list of series and monographs.

Royal National Institute of the Blind Publications
RNIB Corporate Publishing, 105 Judd Street, London, WC1H 9NE
- 020 7388 1266
- 020 7388 2034
- cippub@rnib.org.uk
- www.rnib.org.uk

Established 1868
Insider Info Catalogue available online.
Non-Fiction Publishes Audio cassettes, General Non-Fiction, Multimedia, Braille and Large Print titles on the following subjects:
Counselling/Career, Education, Health, Hobbies, House & Home, Practical Books
* RNIB publications aim to help people understand and cope with sight problems, assisting them in living independent lives.
Tips Most titles are published in multiple formats, including braille and large print, in addition to audio cassettes and CDs. Potential readership includes parents, teachers, and health, rehabilitation and employment service professionals.

Rudolf Steiner Press
Hillside House, The Square, Forest Row, East Sussex, RH18 5ES
- 01342 824433
- 01342 826437
- office@rudolfsteinerpress.com
- www.rudolfsteinerpress.com

Contact Chairman, P. Martyn; Manager, S. Gulbekian
Established 1925
Imprint(s) Sophia Books
Insider Info Publishes 15 titles per year. Payment is via royalties. Catalogue available free on request and online.
Non-Fiction Publishes General Non-Fiction and Scholarly titles on the following subjects:
Education, Philosophy, Spirituality
Submission Guidelines No unsolicited manuscripts.
Recent Title(s) *Anthroposophy (A Fragment)*, Rudolf Steiner
Tips Publishes the work of Rudolf Steiner and any other related materials. Titles focus on philosophy, spirituality and the Steiner education system.

RYA (Royal Yachting Association)
RYA House, Ensign Way, Hamble, Southampton, Hampshire, SO31 4YA
- 023 8060 4100
- 023 8060 4299
- phil.williamsellis@rya.org.uk
- www.rya.org.uk

Contact CEO, Rod Carr; Publications Manager, Phil Williams-Ellis
Established 1875
Insider Info Publishes ten titles per year. Payment is via royalties.
Non-Fiction Publishes General Non-Fiction, Reference and Technical titles on the following subjects:
Yachting, Sailing and Boating
Submission Guidelines Accepts proposal package (including outline).
Recent Title(s) *Sail for Gold*, Skandia Team GBR
Tips RYA titles contain expert information on a full range of boating related subjects, including training courses, handbooks, and technical and legal boating advice.

Sage Publications
1 Oliver's Yard, 55 City Road, London, EC1Y 1SP
- 020 7324 8500
- 020 7324 8600
- info@sagepub.co.uk
- www.sagepub.co.uk

Contact Publisher, Sara Miller McCune; Managing Director, Stephen Barr; Editorial Director, Ziyad Marar
Established 1965
Insider Info Payment is via royalties. Catalogue available free on request and online. Manuscript guidelines available online.
Non-Fiction Publishes Textbooks, Journals, Reference and Scholarly titles on the following subjects:

Anthropology/Archaeology, Business, Criminology, Economics, Education, Engineering, History, Humanities, Nature/Environment, Psychology, Science, Social Sciences and Sociology

Submission Guidelines Accepts proposal package (including outline, sample chapter(s), competing texts, a sample of your writing style, pedagogical features and author biography).

Recent Title(s) *The Practitioner's Handbook*, Stephen Palmer and Robert Bor (eds.)

Tips Sage publishes upper level and graduate textbooks and handbooks, and professional books. A full list of commissioning editors in every subject is published on the website. It would be useful to read the detailed proposal guidelines published on the website before submitting a manuscript.

Saint Andrew Press

121 George Street, Edinburgh, EH2 4YN

- ☎ 0131 225 5722
- 🖷 0131 220 3113
- ✉ standrewpress@cofscotland.org.uk
- 🌐 www.churchofscotland.org.uk/standrewpress

Contact Head of Publishing, Ann Crawford; Editorial Manager, Richard Allen

Established 1954

Insider Info Publishes 20 titles per year. Payment is via royalties.

Non-Fiction Publishes Children's, General Non-Fiction and Reference titles on Religion.

Submission Guidelines Accepts query with SAE.

Tips Saint Andrew Press is owned by the Church of Scotland and publishes books on religion and general faith. Also publishes a range of reference and children's books, aimed at both local and international trade markets.

Salariya Book Company Ltd

Book House, 25 Marlborough Place, Brighton, BN1 1UB

- ☎ 01273 603306
- 🖷 01273 693857
- ✉ salariya@salariya.com
- ✉ david.salariya@salariya.com
- 🌐 www.salariya.com

Contact Director, David Salariya

Established 1989

Imprint(s) Book House

Insider Info Catalogue available online.

Non-Fiction Publishes Children's and Illustrated titles.

Recent Title(s) *Scary Creatures: Sharks*, Penny Clarke

Tips Specialises in illustrated information books with a unique appeal for the younger reader. Many Salariya books are aimed at the international market and translated into multiple languages. New titles for the UK are published under the Book House imprint. Most titles are commissioned.

Salt Publishing

PO Box 937, Great Wilbraham, Cambridge, CB21 5JX

- ☎ 01223 882220
- 🖷 01223 882260
- ✉ chris@saltpublishing.com
- 🌐 www.saltpublishing.com

Contact Directors, Linda Bennett, Chris Hamilton-Emery, Linda Hamilton-Emery and John Skelton; Commissioning Editor, Chris Hamilton-Emery (Poetry and Literary Studies); Commissioning Editor, Jen Hamilton-Emery (Fiction and Non-Fiction); Commissioning Editor, Katherine M. Hedeen (Latin American Poetry); Commissioning Editor, John Kinsella (Australian and International Poetry); Commissioning Editor, Janet McAdams (Native American Writing); Commissioning Editor, Victor Rodríguez-Núñez (Latin American Poetry)

Established 1999

Insider Info Publishes 40 titles per year. Submissions accompanied by SAE will be returned. Aims to respond to manuscripts within six months. Catalogue available online.

Non-Fiction Publishes Biography, Textbooks (From UK and US authors) and Scholarly titles on the following subjects:
Literary Criticism and Interviews

Fiction Publishes Short Story Collections.

Submission Guidelines Accepts proposal package (including up to three short stories, addressed to Jen Hamilton Emery). Aims to respond to submissions within three months.

Poetry Publishes Contemporary and Mainstream Poetry Collections.

Submission Guidelines Accepts proposal package (including six to ten sample poems), addressed to Chris Hamilton Emery. Will aim to respond to submissions within six months.

Recent Title(s) *Body Parts*, Richard Bardsley; *Los Alamos Mon Amour*, Simon Barraclough

Tips Authors should refer to submission guidelines on the website when preparing a manuscript. Queries about how to submit work, or advice on writing, will go unanswered.

SAMS Publishing

Edinburgh Gate, Harlow, Essex, CM20 2JE

- ☎ 01279 623623
- 🖷 01279 414130
- 🌐 www.pearsoned.co.uk/imprints/samspublishing

Parent Company Pearson Education

Insider Info Catalogue and manuscript guidelines are available online.

Non-Fiction Publishes How-to, Reference and Technical titles on the following subjects: Computers, Computer Programming/Developing, Internet, Networking, System Administration.
Submission Guidelines Accepts proposal package (including synopsis, sample chapters, market research, your publishing history and author biography).
Recent Title(s) *Xcelsius 2008 Dashboard Best Practices*, Loren Abdulezer (Computing)
Tips SAMS publishes professional reference books for programmers and developers, web developers, designers, networking and system administrators.

Samuel French Ltd
52 Fitzroy Street, London, W1T 5JR
020 7387 9373
020 7387 2161
theatre@samuelfrench-london.co.uk
www.samuelfrench-london.co.uk
Contact Chairman, Leon F Embry; Managing Director, Vivien Goodwin
Established 1830
Insider Info Publishes roughly 35 titles per year. Payment is via royalties. Hardcopy catalogue available.
Fiction Publishes Plays.
* Samuel French have over 2,000 published plays available, covering all genres of performing theatre including Comedies, Tragedies, Sketches and full scale Musicals. Most plays are staged prior to publication.
Submission Guidelines Accepts query with SAE.
Recent Title(s) *I Dreamt I Dwelt in Marble Halls*, Ade Morris (Play)
Tips New writers are advised to try one act plays, as these are the most in demand.

Sangam Books Ltd
57 London Fruit Exchange, Brushfield Street, London, E1 6EP
020 7377 6399
020 7375 1230
sangambks@aol.com
Contact Executive Director, Anthony de Souza
Non-Fiction Publishes General Non-Fiction, Textbooks and Scholarly titles on the following subjects:
Art, Architecture, Education, Ethnic, Health/ Medicine, Religion, Science, Social Sciences and Technology
Fiction Publishes Literary and Mainstream/ Contemporary titles.
Tips Sangam Books specialises in school and college textbooks and other educational publishing. They also publish fiction and non-fiction titles on

technology, science, medicine, India, social sciences, art, and religion.

Saqi Books
26 Westbourne Grove, London, W2 5RH
020 7221 9347
020 7229 7492
enquiries@saqibooks.com
www.saqibooks.com
Contact Publisher, Andre Gaspard; Editorial Manager, Lara Frankena
Established 1981
Insider Info Publishes 20 titles per year. Payment is via royalties. Aims to respond to manuscripts within ten weeks and manuscripts within ten weeks. Catalogue available online and free on request. Manuscript guidelines available online and via the website.
Non-Fiction Publishes Biography, General Non-Fiction, Illustrated and Scholarly titles on the following subjects:
Art, Architecture, Contemporary Culture, Cooking, Food & Drink, Government/Politics, History, Philosophy, Religion, World Affairs and Middle-East/ Asia
Submission Guidelines Accepts query with SAE/ proposal package (including outline and two sample chapters). Will review artworks/photos as part of the manuscript package (send photocopies only).
Fiction Publishes Literary and Mainstream/ Contemporary titles.
Submission Guidelines Accepts query with SAE/ proposal package (including outline and two sample chapters).
Recent Title(s) *New York: States of Mind*, Shaheen Meral (World Affairs)
Tips Saqi books does not accept submissions by fax, email or on disk. Never send the original photographs or manuscript.

Saunders
Linacre House, Jordan Hill, Oxford, OX2 8DP
01865 474010
01865 474011
authorsupport@elsevier.com
www.elsevierhealth.com/saunders
Parent Company Elsevier Ltd (Health Sciences)
Established 1888
Insider Info Payment is via royalties. Catalogue available online. Manuscript guidelines available online and via the website.
Non-Fiction Publishes Illustrated, Multimedia, Reference, Scholarly, Textbooks and Technical titles on the following subjects:

Education, Health/Medicine, Science, Care/Nursing, Veterinary Medicine, Medical Drugs and Medical Technology
Submission Guidelines Accepts submissions via the online proposal form.
Submission details to: c.makepeace@elsevier.com
Recent Title(s) *Medical Assisting PDQ*, Fuqua and Zonderman (Reference)
Tips Saunders publishes books and multimedia specialising in health and clinical medicine, veterinary medicine, care and nursing, laboratory equipment and pharmaceuticals, amongst other medical subjects. Each title is written by experts in the field and edited to reflect the latest research. Titles will be organised and indexed to enable readers to find urgent information immediately. Authors may contact the publishing director or editor prior to submission, to discuss the proposal.

S.B. Publications
14 Bishopstone Road, Seaford, East Sussex, BN25 2UB
01323 893498
01323 893860
sbpublications@tiscali.co.uk
www.sbpublications.co.uk
Contact Lindsay Woods
Established 1987
Insider Info Publishes roughly 20 titles per year. Payment is via royalties. Catalogue available online.
Non-Fiction Publishes Illustrated and General Non-Fiction titles on the following subjects:
History, Hobbies, Regional, Transportation, Travel, Walking Guides, Folklore, Transportation (Railway)
* Main focus is on local and regional titles.
Recent Title(s) *Vital Signs*, Andy Thomas
Tips S.B. Publications also offers marketing and distribution services for local authors.

Scala Publishers
Northburgh House, Northburgh Street, London, EC1V 0AT
020 7490 9900
020 7336 6870
jmckinley@scalapublishers.com
www.scalapublishers.com
Contact Chairman, David Campbell; Commissioning Editor, Jenny McKinley
Established 1992
Non-Fiction Publishes General Non-Fiction and Reference titles on the following subjects:
Art, Architecture, Antiques and Museum/Gallery Guides
Tips Most material published is written by the museum or gallery curators.

Schofield & Sims Ltd
Dogley Mill, Fenay Bridge, Huddersfield, HD8 0NQ
01484 607080
01484 606815
post@schofieldandsims.co.uk
www.schofieldandsims.co.uk
Contact Chairman, C.N. Platts
Established 1901
Insider Info Catalogue available online and free on request.
Non-Fiction Publishes Multimedia, Scholarly, Textbook, Dictionaries, Posters, Educational Workbooks and Children's titles on the following subjects:
Childcare/Parenting, Counselling/Career and Education
Recent Title(s) *Understanding Maths*, Steve Mills and Hilary Koll (Textbook Series)
Tips Titles are aimed at home tutors, schools, nurseries and playgroups. Most products are created by classroom teachers.

Scholastic Ltd
FREEPOST (SCE 2665), Windrush Park, Range Road, Witney, Oxfordshire, OX29 0YV
0845 603 9091
0845 603 9092
enquiries@scholastic.co.uk
www.scholastic.co.uk
Parent Company Scholastic Inc (see entry under European & International Publishers)
Contact Chairman and Chief Executive Officer (USA), Richard Robinson; Manging Director, Miles Stevens-Hoare (Book Fair Division and Book Clubs); Publishing Director, Anne Peel (Education)
Established 1920
Imprint(s) Scholastic Children's Books
Scholastic Educational Publishing
Insider Info Catalogue available online.
Non-Fiction Publishes Children's, Illustrated, Multimedia, Reference and Scholarly titles on the following subjects:
Contemporary Culture, Education, Geography, History, Literature/Literacy, Nature/Environment, Science and Teaching Materials
Submission Guidelines Accepts proposal package (including outline, synopsis, author biography and SAE) by post only.
Fiction Publishes Children's Books, Picture Books and Young Adult titles.
Submission Guidelines Accepts proposal package (including outline, synopsis, author biography and SAE) by post only.
Recent Title(s) *Adrift in Space: Space Sports Zone 3*, Sally Odgers (Guided Reading)

Tips Scholastic Ltd publishes fiction, non-fiction and picture books for children and young adults under the Children's division, which includes Scholastic Children's Books. The Educational division publishes a wide range of educational and teaching material for primary school teachers, in addition to related magazines. The Direct Marketing division handles Scholastic book fairs and the children's book clubs. Scholastic welcomes manuscripts for either its Educational Publishing or its Children's Books divisions.

Scholastic Children's Books
Euston House, 24 Eversholt Street, London, NW1 1DB
- 020 7756 7756
- scbenquiries@scholastic.co.uk
- www.scholastic.co.uk/zone

Parent Company Scholastic Ltd
Contact Editorial Director, Caroline Gott (Pre-School); Editorial Director, Charlie Cousins (Non-Fiction); Editorial Director, Kristen Skidmore (Fiction)
Imprint(s) Hippo
Point
Scholastic Fiction
Scholastic Non-Fiction
Scholastic Press
Insider Info Payment is via royalties. Aims to respond to proposals within six months. Catalogue available online.
Non-Fiction Publishes Children's, Illustrated, Multimedia and Reference titles on the following subjects:
Contemporary Culture, Education, History, Nature/Environment, Science, Sports and Television/Film Tie-Ins.
Submission Guidelines Accepts hard copy manuscripts sent to the Editorial Department.
Fiction Publishes Children's, Picture Books, Television/Film Tie-Ins and Young Adult titles.
Submission Guidelines Accepts hard copy manuscripts sent to the Editorial Department.
Recent Title(s) *The Hunger Games*, Suzanne Collins (Young Adult); *The 39 Clues: One False Note*, Gordan Korman (Interactive)
Tips Scholastic Children's Books publishes a wide range of fiction, non-fiction, picture and activity books for children of all ages. The Hippo imprint publishes paperback fiction for younger children, whereas the Point imprint specialises in paperback fiction for older children and young adults, including the work of Philip Pullman. Scholastic Press is a specialist hardback imprint.

Scholastic Educational Publishing
Villiers House, Clarendon Avenue, Leamington Spa, Warwickshire, CV32 5PR
- 01926 887799
- 01926 883881
- www.scholastic.co.uk

Parent Company Scholastic Ltd
Contact Managing Director, Denise Cripps
Insider Info Payment is via royalties. Catalogue available online. Aims to respond to proposals within six months.
Non-Fiction Publishes Educational Resources and Classroom Materials for schools.
* Focuses on primary education.
Submission Guidelines Accepts proposal package (including synopsis, sample sections, author biography and SAE). Outline should be no longer than one side of A4 paper and should be typed.
Tips Does not accept proposals via email or on disk. Including any relevant teaching qualifications and experience in your author biography may help. Also publishes the magazines *Child Education, Junior Education, Nursery Education, Literacy Time, Junior Focus* and *Child Education Topics*.

Science Navigation Group
Middlesex House, 34–42 Cleveland Street, London, W1T 4LB
- 020 7323 0323
- 020 7580 1938
- info@sciencenavigation.com
- www.sciencenavigation.com

Contact Group Chairman, Vitek Tracz; Group Managing Director, Anne Greenwood
Insider Info Catalogue available online.
Non-Fiction Publishes Journals, Websites, Databases, Maps, Audio Visuals and Multimedia, Reference, Scholarly, and Technical titles on the following subjects:
Health, Medicine, Science, Bio-Medicine
Tips Titles are aimed at the professional biomedical community, as well as more general audiences. Clients include physicians, scientists, pharmaceutical companies, patients, students and the general public.

SCM-Canterbury Press Ltd
13–17 Long Lane, London, EC1A 9PN
- 020 7776 7540
- 020 7776 7556
- admin@scm-canterburypress.co.uk
- www.scm-canterburypress.co.uk

Parent Company Hymns Ancient & Modern Ltd
Contact Publishing Director, Christine Smith; Senior Commissioning Editor, Natalie Watson
Established 1986

Imprint(s) Canterbury Press
SCM Press
Religious & Moral Education Press (RMEP)
Epworth Press
Insider Info Catalogue available free on request
and online.
Non-Fiction Publishes Autobiography, Biography,
Booklets, Children's, General Non-Fiction, Illustrated,
Multimedia, Reference, Textbooks, Dictionaries,
Translations, Popular Religious, Hymn Books and
Scholarly titles on the following subjects:
Religion, Spirituality, Translation, Lifestyle,
Contemporary Issues, History, Philosophy, Theology,
Academic Theology, Poetry, Science, World
Religions, Jewish Studies
Submission Guidelines Will accept proposal
package (including contents page, synopsis and one
sample chapter) by post.
Recent Title(s) *Controversies in Body Theology*,
Marcella Althaus Reid and Lisa Isherwood (eds.)
(SCM Press)
Tips SCM Press is the UK's best known publisher of
academic theology and provides text books,
reference books and other resources aimed at
students and clergy. Canterbury Press is a supplier of
popular religious books, resources and gift stationery
for the general, religious and church markets. Recent
publications include high quality liturgical books, as
well as general market non-fiction with a
religious angle.

Scottish Cultural Press & Scottish Children's Press

**Unit 6, Newbattle Abbey Business Park,
Newbattle Road, Dalkeith, EH22 3LJ**
- 0131 660 4666
- 0131 660 4666
- info@scottishbooks.com
- www.scottishbooks.com

Contact Directors, Avril Gray and Brian Pugh
Established 1992
Insider Info Payment is via royalties. Aims to
respond to proposals within six months. Catalogue
and manuscript guidelines available online.
Non-Fiction Publishes Children's and General Non-
Fiction titles on the following subjects:
Anthropology/Archaeology, Art, Architecture,
Contemporary Culture, History, Language, Literature,
Literary Criticism, Regional and Scottish Interest.
Submission Guidelines Accepts query with SAE/
proposal package (including outline, one sample
chapter, intended market and readership). Will
accept artworks/images (send photocopies).
Fiction Publishes Children's, Literary, Mainstream/
Contemporary, and Young Adult titles.
Submission Guidelines No unsolicited
manuscripts.

Poetry Publishes Poetry titles.
Submission Guidelines No unsolicited
manuscripts.
Recent Title(s) *Argyll: Land of Blood and Beauty*,
Mary McGrigor (Guidebook); *Moray the Dolphin's
Adventure in Loch Ness*, Marit Brunskill (Picture Book)
Tips Scottish Cultural Press is one of the foremost
publishers in Scotland, specialising in quality books
with a Scottish interest. Scottish Children's Press
publishes quality Scottish interest books for children
of all ages, from graded readers to teacher's resource
books, and fun and games, to young fiction. Titles
are written for, about and by Scottish children and
they aim to encompass Scots, English and Gaelic. As
the publishers receive a great quantity of
manuscripts, they recommend that prospective
authors should phone first to discuss the suitability
of the manuscript before sending any work.

Scribner

**1st Floor, 222 Gray's Inn Road, London,
WC1X 8HB**
- 020 7316 1900
- 020 7316 0332
- enquiries@simonandschuster.co.uk
- www.simonsays.co.uk

Parent Company Simon & Schuster UK Ltd
Established 1999
Non-Fiction Publishes Biography and General Non-
Fiction titles on the following subjects:
Art, Contemporary Culture, Creative Non-Fiction,
Humanities, Lifestyle, Memoirs, Society, Sports
and Travel.
Submission Guidelines Accepts agented
submissions only.
Fiction Publishes Contemporary and Literary titles.
Submission Guidelines Accepts agented
submissions only.
Tips Scribner is designed specifically to be Simon &
Schuster's 'literary' imprint, publishing high-quality
non-fiction and literary fiction.

Scripture Union

**Queensway House, 207–209 Queensway,
Bletchley, Milton Keynes, Buckinghamshire,
MK2 2EB**
- 01908 856000
- 01908 856111
- info@scriptureunion.org.uk
- www.scriptureunion.org.uk

Contact Publishing Director, Terry Clutterham
Established 1867
Insider Info Catalogue and manuscript guidelines
available online.

Non-Fiction Publishes Children's, General Non-Fiction, Multimedia, Reference and Scholarly titles on the following subjects:
Religion (including Christian Faith Resources) and Spirituality.
Submission Guidelines Accepts query with SAE/proposal package (including outline and one sample chapter).
Fiction Publishes Children's, Religious (including Bible Stories) and Young Adult titles.
Tips Scripture Union is a non-denominational, international movement, working in partnership with individuals and churches across the world. All books must be sympathetic to the Christian faith. Scripture Union publish very few unsolicited manuscripts.

Seafarer Books Ltd
102 Redwald Road, Rendlesham, Woodbridge, Suffolk, IP12 2TE
☎ 01394 420789
☎ 01394 461314
✉ info@seafarerbooks.com
🌐 www.seafarerbooks.com
Contact Managing Director, Patricia Eve
Established 1998
Insider Info Publishes four titles per year. Receives approximately 100 queries and 200 manuscripts per year. Ten per cent of books published are from first-time authors and 90 per cent are from unagented authors. Payment is via royalty (on retail price).
Non-Fiction Publishes Autobiography, Biography, Humour and General Non-Fiction titles on the following subjects:
Classic Sailing Narratives, Commercial Sailing, Maritime Archaeology and History, Voyaging, Guides to Practical Seamanship, Boat Building/Yacht Design, Arts, Literature
Fiction Publishes General and Classic Maritime titles.
Recent Title(s) *Walking on Water*, Geoff Holt

Search Press
Wellwood, North Farm Road, Tunbridge Wells, Kent, TN2 3DR
☎ 01892 510850
☎ 01892 515903
✉ searchpress@searchpress.com
✉ roz_d@searchpress.com
🌐 www.searchpress.com
Contact Managing Director, Martin de la Bedoyere; Commissioning Editor, Rosalind Dace; Managing Editor, Sophie Kersey
Established 1970
Insider Info Publishes 30 titles per year. Receives approximately 200 queries and 100 manuscripts per year. 50 per cent of books published are from first-

time authors and 100 per cent are from unagented authors. Payment is via royalty (on retail price). Simultaneous submissions are accepted and submissions accompanied with SAE will be returned. Aim to respond to queries, proposals and manuscripts within 14 days. Catalogue is free on request and available online.
Non-Fiction Publish How-To, Practical, Colour Illustrated and Reference titles on the following subjects:
Art, Architecture, Crafts, Hobbies
Submission Guidelines Accept queries with SAE or via email. Will review artworks/images (send photocopies, transparencies, and digital files as jpegs)
Recent Title(s) *Money Folding*, Jannie van Schuylenburg-Dekker (Papercraft)
Tips Titles are aimed at hobby and professional artists and crafters. Authors are usually experts in their field, and should send images of their art/craft works in the first instance.

Seren
57 Nolton Street, Bridgend, CF31 3AE
☎ 01656 663018
☎ 01656 649226
✉ seren@seren-books.com
🌐 www.seren-books.com
Contact Chairman, Cary Archard; Managing Director, Mick Felton; Fiction Editor, Penny Thomas
Established 1981
Insider Info Publishes roughly 25 titles per year. Payment is via royalties. Catalogue and manuscript guidelines available online.
Non-Fiction Publishes Biography and General Non-Fiction titles on the following subjects:
Art, Architecture, History, Language, Literature, Literary Criticism, Photography, Sports, Translation and World Affairs
Submission Guidelines Accepts query with SAE/proposal package (including outline and three sample chapters).
Fiction Publishes Literary, Mainstream/Contemporary, Plays, Translation and Welsh Writing titles.
* Seren only publishes around five works of fiction a year.
Submission Guidelines Accepts query with SAE/proposal package (including outline and three sample chapters).
Poetry Publish Poetry titles.
Submission Guidelines Submit sample poems.
Recent Title(s) *Blue Sky July*, Nia Wyn (Novel); *At Arm's Length*, Geraint Talfan Davies (Autobiography/Politics)
Tips Seren specialises in English language writing from Wales. Authors considering submitting a

manuscript should be aware that fiction and poetry lists are often full at least two years in advance.

Serif

47 Strahan Road, London, E3 5DA
- 020 8981 3990
- 020 8981 3990
- info@serifbooks.co.uk
- www.serifbooks.co.uk

Contact Managing Editor, Stephen Hayward
Established 1993
Insider Info Payment is via royalties. Catalogue available online.
Non-Fiction Publishes General Non-Fiction titles on the following subjects:
Cooking, Food & Drink, History, Travel, Irish Studies, African Studies
Submission Guidelines Accepts query with SAE.
Fiction Publishes Literary and Mainstream/Contemporary titles. Does not publish any new fiction titles.
Submission Guidelines Accepts query with SAE.
Tips Serif welcomes ideas and proposals for non-fiction publications, but does not accept unsolicited manuscripts.

Serpent's Tail

3a Exmouth House, Pine Street, London, EC1R 0JH
- 020 7841 6300
- info@serpentstail.com
- www.serpentstail.com

Parent Company Profile Books Ltd
Established 1987
Insider Info Catalogue available online.
Non-Fiction Publishes Autobiography, Biography, Illustrated and General Non-Fiction titles on the following subjects:
Contemporary Culture, Music/Dance, Travel, Cult Books, Black Writing, Gay/Lesbian, Race, Sex/Gender, Politics/Current Affairs, Philosophy, Cultural Criticism, World Literature.
Submission Guidelines Accepts agented submissions only.
Fiction Publishes Short Story Collections, Translation, Women's Writing, Classics, Debuts, Crime Fiction and Anthology titles.
Submission Guidelines Accepts agented submissions only.
Poetry Publishes Poetry titles.
Submission Guidelines Accepts agented submissions only.
Recent Title(s) *Old Devil Moon*, Christopher Fowler (Horror)
Tips Serpent's Tail is a renowned publisher of international fiction and non-fiction, founded with a commitment to publishing authors 'neglected by the mainstream'.

Severn House Publishers Ltd

9–15 High Street, Sutton, Surrey, SM1 1DF
- 020 8770 3930
- 020 8770 3850
- sales@severnhouse.com
- www.severnhouse.com

Contact Chairman, Edwin Buckhalter; Editorial, Amanda Stewart
Established 1974
Insider Info Publishes roughly 150 titles per year. Payment is via royalties. Catalogue and manuscript guidelines available online.
Fiction Publishes Historical, Horror, Literary, Mainstream/Contemporary, Military/War, Mystery, Romance, Science Fiction, Suspense and Crime titles. * Severn House publishes various kinds of genre and general fiction in large and regular print sizes. Most books are hardback and aimed at fiction libraries, however some titles are produced as paperbacks.
Submission Guidelines Accepts agented submissions only. Will not accept unsolicited manuscripts.
Recent Title(s) *Fathers and Sins*, Jo Bannister (Crime)
Tips As publications are aimed at the UK and US fiction library markets, they are unable to add authors to the list who do not have a significant background in this market.

Shanway Press

3 Eia Street, Belfast, BT14 6BT
- 028 9022 2070
- 028 9022 2077
- info@shanway.com
- www.shanway.com

Contact Managing Director, Micheal McKernon
Insider Info Catalogue available online.
Non-Fiction Publishes Books, Booklet and Misallette titles on the following subjects:
Church Information, Parish History, Culture.
Recent Title(s) *Secrets of Cistercian Music in Ireland*, Geraldine Carville; *The Shakespeare Conspiracies*, Brian McClinton
Tips Shanway specialises in publishing and multimedia projects. Much of Shanway's work has been with churches, specialising in parish histories.

Shearsman Books Ltd

58 Velwell Road, Exeter, Devon, EX4 4LD
- 01392 434511
- 01392 434511
- editor@shearsman.com
- www.shearsman.com

Contact Publisher, Tony Frazer

Established 1981
Insider Info Publishes 50 titles per year. Receives 3,000 queries and 500 manuscripts per year. 15 per cent of books published are from first-time authors, 90 per cent of books published are from unagented authors. Payment is via royalty (on retail price), with 0.1 (per £) maximum; this rate applies after 150 copies have been sold – the first 150 copies are royalty free. Average lead time is one year, with simultaneous submissions accepted. Submissions accompanied by SAE will be returned. Electronic submissions of initial samples are permitted, by PDF or in the body of an email message. Aims to respond to queries and proposals withing six weeks, and manuscripts within four months. Catalogue and manuscript guidelines are free on request and available online or by email.
Non-Fiction Publishes Literature, Memoir and Journal titles
* Shearsman Books does not publish non-fiction other than journals and memoirs by poets, and then very infrequently. Send an initial query if intending to submit such work.
Submission Guidelines Accepts proposal package (including sample chapters, your publishing history, author biography and SAE).
Poetry Publishes Contemporary Poetry Collections and Anthologies, Poetry in Translation and new editions of Classic Poetry.
Submission Guidelines Accepts proposal package (including six to ten pages of sample poems, your publishing history, author biography and SAE).
Recent Title(s) *Collected Poems*, John Welch (Poetry)

Sheldon Press
36 Causton Street, London, SW1P 4ST
- director@sheldonpress.co.uk
- www.sheldonpress.co.uk
Parent Company Society for Promoting Christian Knowledge
Contact Editor, Fiona Marshall
Established 1973
Insider Info Catalogue available online
Non-Fiction Publishes Self-Help titles on the following subjects:
Major Illnesses & Health, Mental Health Issues, Healthy Eating Issues, Life Challenges (Trauma and Bereavement), Life Skills, Guides for Parents & Children, Business & Work
Submission Guidelines Accepts proposal package (including outline, chapter one and introduction, author biography and market information). Send by post to the Editorial Director at the address above. Submission details to: director@sheldonpress.co.uk
Recent Title(s) *How to Get the Best from Your Doctor*, Dr Tom Smith

Tips Sheldon Press is always interested in commissioning new authors and ideas. They specialise in books on medical and emotional subjects, aimed at the general reader.

Sheldrake Press
188 Cavendish Road, London, SW12 0DA
- 020 8675 1767
- 020 8675 7736
- mail@sheldrakepress.demon.co.uk
- www.sheldrakepress.demon.co.uk
Contact Publisher, Simon Rigge; Assistant Editor, Nicholas Lim
Established 1979
Insider Info Catalogue available online.
Non-Fiction Publishes General Non-Fiction and Multimedia titles on the following subjects: Cooking, Food & Drink, History, House & Home, Travel and Stationary Books
Submission Guidelines Accepts query with SAE/ proposal package (including outline) Submission details to: jsr@ sheldrakepress.demon.co.uk
Recent Title(s) *The The Victorian House Book*, Robin Guild
Tips Welcomes synopses for non-fiction books, but will not accept any fiction titles.

Shepheard-Walwyn (Publishers) Ltd
15 Alder Road, London, SW14 8ER
- 020 8241 5927
- books@shepheard-walwyn.co.uk
- www.shepheard-walwyn.co.uk
Contact Managing Director, Anthony Werner
Established 1972
Insider Info Publishes five titles per year. Payment is via royalties. Catalogue available free on request and online.
Non-Fiction Publishes Biography, Gift, Illustrated and General Non-Fiction titles on the following subjects:
Business, Economics, Government/Politics, History, Law, Philosophy, Calligraphy, Shakespeare Studies and Scottish Interest
Submission Guidelines Accepts query with SAE/ proposal package (including outline and author biography).
Poetry Publishes a variety of Classic and Contemporary Poetry titles.
Submission Guidelines Accepts query with SAE.
Recent Title(s) *There's No More Dying Then*, Stephanie Wilson
Tips Before submitting a proposal, check the website to assess whether your title is suitable, then submit your synopsis and CV.

The Shetland Times Ltd

Gremista, Lerwick, Shetland, ZE1 0PX
- ☎ 01595 693622
- ☎ 01595 694637
- ✉ publishing@shetland-times.co.uk
- 🌐 www.shetlandtoday.co.uk

Contact Managing Director, June Wishart; Publications Manager, Charlotte Black
Established 1872
Insider Info Payment is via royalties. Catalogue available online.
Non-Fiction Publishes General Non-Fiction titles on the following subjects:
Regional, Shetland Interest
Recent Title(s) *Birds of Shetland*, Mike Pennington
Tips Much of the available literature about Shetland is printed and published by The Shetland Times, including Shetland's only weekly magazine *The Shetland Times*, and the monthly magazine *Shetland Life*. All material must be of local Shetland interest.

Shire Publications Ltd

Midland House, West Way, Botley, Oxford, OX2 0PH
- ☎ 01865 811306
- ☎ 01865 242009
- ✉ shire@shirebooks.co.uk
- 🌐 www.shirebooks.co.uk

Contact General Manager, Sue Ross
Established 1962
Insider Info Publishes 25 titles per year. Payment is via royalties. Catalogue available free on request and online.
Non-Fiction Publishes Illustrated, Biography and General Non-Fiction titles on the following subjects: Anthropology/Archaeology, Art, Architecture, Crafts, Ethnic, History, Hobbies, House and Home, Humanities, Photography, Regional, Transportation, Collectables and Ephemera, Regional Interest, Folklore and Legends, Egyptology, and Walking
Submission Guidelines Accepts query with SAE.
Recent Title(s) *Discovering Churches and Churchyards*, Mark Child
Tips Because each book is numbered within its series (except for a few miscellaneous titles), Shire books have become 'collectables' with readers seeking full sets. Prospective authors must be aware of the various Shire series' on offer.

Short Books

3a Exmouth House, Pine Street, London, EC1R 0JH
- ☎ 020 7833 9429
- ☎ 020 7833 9500
- ✉ info@shortbooks.co.uk
- 🌐 www.shortbooks.co.uk

Contact Editorial Directors, Aurea Carpenter and Rebecca Nicholson
Established 2000
Insider Info Catalogue and manuscript guidelines available online.
Non-Fiction Publishes Biography, Children's, General Non-Fiction and Humour titles on the following subjects:
Education, Government/Politics, History and Teaching Resources
Submission Guidelines No unsolicited manuscripts.
Fiction Publishes Children's Novels.
Recent Title(s) *One to Nine*, Andrew Hodges
Tips Shortbooks strives to bridge the gap between publishing and journalism. They publish general non-fiction titles for adults and children and offer teaching resources to support classroom orientated books.

Sidgwick & Jackson

20 New Wharf Road, London, N1 9RR
- ☎ 020 7014 6000
- ☎ 020 7014 6001
- ✉ nonfiction@macmillan.co.uk
- 🌐 www.panmacmillan.com

Parent Company Pan Macmillan Publishers
Established 1908
Insider Info Catalogue available online (downloadable pdf catalogue available on the website).
Non-Fiction Publishes Autobiography, Biography and General Non-Fiction titles on the following subjects:
Contemporary Culture, History, Memoirs and Military/War
Submission Guidelines Agented submissions only (no unsolicited manuscripts).
Recent Title(s) *Kate Moss*, Laura Collins (Biography); *Dunkirk*, Julian Thompson (Military History)
Tips Sidgwick & Jackson are specialists in commercial and popular non-fiction, including high-profile biographies, popular culture and military history. They do not publish fiction titles.

Sigma Press

5 Alton Road, Wilmslow, Cheshire, SK9 5DY
- ☎ 01625 531035
- ☎ 01625 531035
- ✉ info@sigmapress.co.uk
- 🌐 www.sigmapress.co.uk

Contact Senior Partner, Graham Beech
Established 1980
Insider Info Publishes 12 titles per year. Receives approximately 100 queries and 15 manuscripts per year. 90 per cent of books published are from first-

time authors and 100 per cent are from unagented authors. Payment is via royalty (on wholesale price). Average lead time is four months, with simultaneous submissions not accepted. Submissions accompanied by SAE will be returned. Aims to respond to queries within two days, proposals within two weeks and manuscripts within one month. Catalogue is free on request and available online. Manuscript guidelines are free on request.
Non-Fiction Publish Guidebook titles on the following subjects:
Outdoor Pursuits, Nature/Environment, Travel, Walking/Hiking
Submission Guidelines Accepts query with SAE, or via email. Will accept artworks/images (send digital files as jpegs).
Recent Title(s) *Cornish Place Names and Language*, Craig Weatherhill (Guidebook)
Tips Titles are aimed at walkers, or their friends and family.

Simon & Schuster UK Ltd
1st Floor, 222 Gray's Inn Road, London, WC1X 8HB
☎ 020 7316 1900
☎ 020 7316 0332
✉ enquiries@simonandschuster.co.uk
❂ www.simonsays.co.uk
Contact CEO/Managing Director, Ian Stewart Chapman
Established 1924
Imprint(s) Free Press
Martin Books
Pocket Books
Scribner
Simon & Schuster Children's Books (division)
Insider Info Catalogue available online.
Non-Fiction Publishes Audio cassettes, Autobiography, Biography, Children's, Cookbooks, General Non-Fiction, Gift, Humour, Illustrated, Reference, Self-Help and Media Tie-In titles on the following subjects:
Alternative Lifestyles, Art, Biography/Autobiography, Business/Economics, Contemporary Culture, Cooking/Foods/Nutrition, Creative Non-fiction, Government/Politics, Health/Medicine, History, Language/Literature, Memoirs, Psychology, Science, Social Sciences, Spirituality, Sports, Translation, Travel, World Affairs and Popular Culture.
Submission Guidelines Accepts agented submissions only.
Fiction Publishes Fantasy, Historical, Horror, Humour, Children's, Mainstream/Contemporary, Mystery, Picture Books, Romance, Science Fiction, Spiritual, Sports, Suspense, Media Tie-Ins and Translation titles.

Submission Guidelines Accepts agented submissions only.
Recent Title(s) *Appetite for Self-Destruction*, Steve Knopper (Music); *The Thirteen Treasures*, Michelle Harrison (Young Adult)
Tips Simon & Schuster publishes a broad range of non-fiction and fiction, from popular bestsellers, to heavyweight literary and non-fiction titles. No unsolicited manuscripts are accepted.

Simon & Schuster Children's Books
1st Floor, Gray's Inn Road, London, WC1X 8HB
☎ 020 7316 1900
☎ 020 7316 0332
✉ editorial.enquiries@simonandschuster.co.uk
❂ www.simonsays.co.uk
Parent Company Simon & Schuster UK Ltd
Contact Publishing Director, Ingrid Selberg
Established 1998
Non-fiction Publishes Children's, Illustrated, Media Tie-In and Young Adult titles.
Submission Guidelines Accepts agented submissions only.
Fiction Publishes Children's Fiction, Picture Book and Young Adult titles.
Submissions Guidelines Accepts agented submissions only.
Recent Title(s) *Hotel for Dogs Movie Storybook*, (Media Tie-In); *Dragon Orb: Shadow*, Mark Robson (Novel)

Sixties Press
89 Connaught Road, Sutton, SM1 3PJ
☎ 020 8286 0419
✉ info@sixtiespress.co.uk
✉ sixtiespress@blueyonder.co.uk
❂ www.sixtiespress.co.uk
Contact Publisher, Barry Tebb
Insider Info Catalogue available online.
Non-Fiction Publishes guides for - and memoirs of - the mentally ill and their carers.
Fiction Publishes Novels and Novellas.
Poetry Publishes Poetry titles.
Tips The website contains free samples of poetry, which the Sixties Press publish.

Smart Learning
PO Box 321, Cambridge, CB1 2XU
☎ 01223 477550
☎ 01223 477551
✉ admin@smart-learning.co.uk
❂ www.smart-learning.co.uk
Contact Sarah Baron (Foundation to Key Stage 2); Sam Watkins (Key Stage 3)
Insider Info Catalogue available online. Accept queries via email.

Non-Fiction Publishes Classroom Resources, Activity Books, Educational Packs and Photocopiable Resources on the following subjects:
ICT, PSHE, English, UK Citizenship, Literacy
Submission Guidelines Accepts query via email from people interested in authoring or evaluating products.
Recent Title(s) *Inspiring Primary Teaching*, Denis Hayes (Educational)
Tips Products are aimed at either Foundation, or Key Stages 1, 2 or 3. Smart Learning works with teachers, freelance writers and designers in creating books and packs.

Snowbooks Ltd
120 Pentonville Road, London, N1 9JN
- 020 7837 6482
- 020 7837 6348
- info@snowbooks.com
- www.snowbooks.com

Contact Director, Rob Jones; Managing Director, Emma Barnes; Publisher, James Bridle; Publisher (Memoir, Handicrafts), Anna Torborg; Publisher, Gilly Barnard
Established 2003
Insider Info Publishes ten titles per year. Payment is via royalties. Catalogue and manuscript guidelines available online.
Non-Fiction Publishes Biography, Illustrated and General Non-Fiction titles on the following subjects: Business/Economics, Crafts, Government/Politics, Hobbies, Memoirs, Social Sciences, and Sports
Submission Guidelines Accepts proposal package (including outline, two sample chapters and author biography). Submissions must be emailed.
Submission details to: submissions@snowbooks.com
Fiction Publishes Mainstream/Contemporary, Short Story Collections, Thrillers and Women's Fiction titles.
Submission Guidelines Accepts proposal package (including outline and sample chapter(s)). Submissions must be emailed.
Submission details to: submissions@snowbooks.com
Recent Title(s) *God's End: The Fall*, Michael McBride (Modern Fiction); *Drugs Are Nice*, Lisa Crystal Carver (Memoir)
Tips Snowbooks are happy to look at excellent works of fiction and non-fiction. They do not specify particular genres as they believe it is the writing that matters, not the category. Prospective authors must email submissions straight away (there is no need to send an initial email to check if the novel is appropriate). Postal submissions will not be accepted.

The Society for Promoting Christian Knowledge (SPCK)
36 Causton Street, London, SW1P 4ST
- 020 7592 3900
- 020 7592 3939
- spck@spck.org.uk
- www.spck.org.uk

Imprint(s) Azure
Sheldon Press
Insider Info Catalogue available online.
Non-Fiction Publishes Biography, Children's, Gift Book, Humour, Illustrated Book, Reference, Scholarly, Textbook, Music Hymn Books and Self-Help titles on the following subjects:
Art, Architecture, Christianity, Education, History, Language, Literature, Music/Dance, Religion, Spirituality, Travel, Women's Issues/Studies, Biblical Studies, Church History, Family Life, Relationships, Comparative Religion, Liturgical Studies, Pastoral Care, Poetry, Commentaries, Devotional
Submission Guidelines Accepts proposal package (including outline and two sample chapters). Address to Editorial Department (Submissions).
Recent Title(s) *The Dawkins Delusion?*, Alister McGrath
Tips Publishes work for students and teachers of theology, lay Christians, spiritual seekers, and a general readership with an interest in Christianity. The list covers a wide range of Christian traditions from the Evangelical to the Catholic, the conservative to the liberal. Azure books explore a range of subjects and styles, from travel literature to illustrated gift books, each one with an implicit Christian understanding. See the Sheldon Press entry for more details.

Society of Genealogists Enterprises Ltd
14 Charterhouse Buildings, Goswell Road, London, EC1M 7BA
- 020 7251 8799
- 020 7250 1800
- sales@sog.org.uk
- www.sog.org.uk

Contact Acting Director, June Perrin
Insider Info Catalogue available online.
Non-Fiction Publishes Multimedia, Reference and Scholarly titles on Genealogy.
Recent Title(s) *First Steps in Family History*
Tips The Society of Genealogists publishes research material (including books, finding aids, indexes, CDs and software) for those interested in family history and the lives of earlier generations. Any resource proposed should be designed to aid research into this area.

Southwater

Hermes House, 88–89 Blackfriars Road, London, SE1 8HA

☎ 020 7401 2077

🖷 020 7633 9499

✉ info@anness.com

🌐 www.annesspublishing.com

Parent Company Anness Publishing Ltd

Contact Chairman/Managing Director, Paul Anness; Publisher/Partner, Joanna Lorenz

Established 1999

Insider Info Publishes 150 titles per year. Catalogue available online.

Non-Fiction Publishes Children's, Illustrated and General Non-Fiction titles on the following subjects: Cooking, Crafts, Food and Drink, Gardening, History, House and Home, Recreation, Spirituality and Sports

Recent Title(s) *Life in the Ancient World: A History of People and How they Lived*, Charlotte Hurdman, Fiona Macdonald, John Haywood, Philip Steele and Richard Tames (History)

Tips Southwater is the trade paperback imprint for Anness Publishing Ltd.

Souvenir Press Ltd

43 Great Russell Street, London, WC1B 3PD

☎ 020 7580 9307

🖷 020 7580 5064

✉ sp.trade@ukonline.co.uk

Contact Managing Director, Ernest Hecht

Imprint(s) Condor

Insider Info Publishes 50 titles per year. Payment is via royalties. Catalogue available free on request and via email.

Non-Fiction Publishes Autobiography, Biography, Children's, General Non-Fiction, Humour, Illustrated and Scholarly titles on the following subjects: Anthropology/Archaeology, Art, Architecture, Astrology/Psychic, Business, Cooking, Crafts, Food & Drink, Economics, Education, Gardening, Health/Medicine, History, Hobbies, Military/War, Music, Nature/Environment, Philosophy, Psychology, Religion, Sociology, Spirituality, Sports, Women's Issues/Studies, Theatre and Magic and the Occult

Submission Guidelines Accepts query with SAE/proposal package (including outline and two sample chapters).

Fiction Publishes Children's, Humour, Literary, Mainstream/Contemporary, and Crime titles.

Submission Guidelines Accepts query with SAE/proposal package (including outline and two sample chapters).

Poetry Publishes Poetry titles.

Submission Guidelines Submit sample poems.

Recent Title(s) *Kangaroo Babies*, Nathalie Charpak (Childcare)

Tips Souvenir Press covers a wide range of academic and general non-fiction topics, specialising in spiritual and mystical titles. Fiction and poetry lists are limited in comparison to the non-fiction list.

Spacelink Books

115 Hollybush Lane, Hampton, Middlesex, TW12 2QY

☎ 020 8979 3148

🌐 www.spacelink.fsworld.co.uk

Contact Managing Director, Lionel Beer

Established 1967

Insider Info Payment is according to contract. Catalogue available online.

Non-Fiction Publishes Booklets, General Non-Fiction and Scholarly titles on the following subjects: New Age, Spirituality, UFO's and the Paranormal

Submission Guidelines Accepts query with SAE (including outline).

Tips Spacelink is named after a UFO magazine from the 1960s/1970s and publishes general non-fiction titles on the subject of UFOs, fortean phenomena and paranormal events. They also handle distribution of a wide range of magazines and related titles. No unsolicited manuscripts are accepted, however prospective authors are encouraged to send in a synopsis.

Special Interests Model Books

Stanley House, 3 Fleets Lane, Poole, Dorset, BH15 3AJ

☎ 01202 649930

🖷 01202 649950

✉ chrlloyd@globalnet.co.uk

🌐 www.specialinterestmodelbooks.co.uk

Contact Chris Lloyd

Insider Info Payment is via royalties. Catalogue available online.

Non-Fiction Publishes General Non-Fiction titles on the following subjects: Computers/Electronics, Cooking, Food & Drink, Hobbies, Transportation, Modelling/Collecting, Engineering, Wine & Beer and Engineering

* Specialists in hobbyist and collectables publishing.

Recent Title(s) *Parkflyer*, Hinrik Schulte (Model Aircraft)

Speechmark

70 Alston Drive, Bradwell Abbey, Milton Keynes, MK13 9HG

☎ 01908 326944

🖷 01908 326960

✉ info@speechmark.net

🌐 www.speechmark.net

Contact Managing Director, Liz Lane; Senior Publishing Coordinator, Tanya Dean

Insider Info Publish 25 titles per year. Receives approximately 250 queries and 40 manuscripts per year. Five per cent of books published are from first-time authors and 25 per cent are from unagented authors. Payment is via royalty (on retail price) with 0.1 (per £) maximum. Average lead time is nine months, with simultaneous submissions accepted. Submissions accompanied by SAE will be returned. Aims to respond to queries within seven days, proposals within six weeks, and manuscripts within six months. Catalogue and manuscript guidelines are free on request and available online.

Non-Fiction Publishes Books, Manuals, Card Packs, Games, CD-ROM Resources and Assessment titles on the following subjects:
Speech & Language, Social & Emotional Development, Education (for all ages), Autism, Learning Disabilities, Groupwork & Creative Activities, Mental Health, Personal Development and Elderly Care. Speechmark also publishes ColorCards - the world's leading photographic language cards - designed to help develop both language and social skills.

Submission Guidelines Accepts proposal package via post or email (including outline, one sample chapter, your publishing history, author biography, SAE). Will accept artworks/images (send photocopies).

Tips Speechmark publications are designed by professionals for health and educational professionals.

Sphere
100 Victoria Embankment, London, EC4Y 0DY
- 020 7911 8000
- 020 7911 8100
- info@littlebrown.co.uk
- www.littlebrown.co.uk

Parent Company Little, Brown Book Group
Contact Publishing Director, Antonia Hodgson (Commercial); Publishing Director, David Shelley (Digital)
Insider Info Submissions accompanied by SAE will be returned. Aims to respond to proposals within eight weeks. Catalogue available online.
Non-Fiction Publishes Autobiography, Biography, Commercial Non-Fiction, General Non-Fiction, Memoirs and Humour titles.
Submission Guidelines Accepts query with SAE/proposal package (including outline, three sample chapters and covering letter). No email submissions are accepted.
Fiction Publishes Humour, Mainstream/Contemporary, Romance and Commercial Fiction titles.
Submission Guidelines Accepts query with SAE/proposal package (including outline, three sample

chapters and covering letter). No email submissions are accepted.

SportsBooks Ltd
PO Box 422, Cheltenham, GL50 2YN
- 01242 256755
- 0560 3108126
- info@sportsbooks.ltd.uk
- www.sportsbooks.ltd.uk

Contact Chairman/Managing Director, Randall Northam
Established 1995
Imprint(s) BMM
SportsBooks
Insider Info Publishes twelve titles per year. Catalogue and manuscript guidelines available online.
Non-Fiction Publishes Biography, General Non-Fiction, Practical Guides, How-To and Reference titles on a wide range of Sports.
Submission Guidelines Accepts query with SAE/proposal package (including outline, three sample chapters). Submissions should be sent by post. Do not send full manuscripts unless requested.
Recent Title(s) *The Lion and the Eagle*; *Sporting Justice*

The Sportsman's Press
Wykey House, Wykey, Shrewsbury, Shropshire, SY4 1JA
- 01939 261616
- 01939 261606
- admin@quillerbooks.com
- www.countrybooksdirect.com

Parent Company Quiller Publishing Ltd
Insider Info Publishes five titles per year. Ten per cent of book published are from first-time authors, 95 per cent of books published are from unagented authors and approximately five per cent of books are author subsidy published. Payment is via royalty on wholesale or retail price. Average lead time is two months. Simultaneous submissions accepted. Submissions accompanied by SAE will be returned. Catalogue free on request, online.
Non-Fiction General Non-Fiction, Countryside Pursuits.
Submission Guidelines Accepts proposal package (including outline, sample chapter(s), your publishing history, author biography) and artworks/images (send photocopies or digital files as jpegs). Submission details to: john@beaton.org.uk
Tips Postal submissions preferred.

Spruce
2–4 Heron Quays, London, E14 4JP
- 020 7531 8400

0 020 7531 8650

@ info@octopus-publishing.co.uk

🌐 www.octopusbooks.co.uk/spruce

Parent Company Octopus Publishing Group

Insider Info Catalogue available online.

Non-Fiction Publishes Illustrated Books on the following subjects:
Biography, Cooking, Gift, Mind, Body & Spirit

Recent Title(s) *A Thousand Paths to Happiness*, David Baird; *Good Kitchen Magic*, Carol Tennant

Tips Spruce is known for its innovative design and beautiful books across a range of areas including cookery, biography, mind, body & spirit and gift books. It has a great reputation for publishing well-defined, distinct series which become backlist classics.

Stacey International
128 Kensington Church Street, London, W8 4BH

0 020 7221 7166

0 0207 792 9288

@ info@stacey-international.co.uk

🌐 www.stacey-international.co.uk

Contact Editor, Christopher Ind

Established 1973

Insider Info Catalogue available online.

Non-Fiction Publishes Biography, Children's, General Non-Fiction, Illustrated and Scholarly titles on the following subjects:
Anthropology/Archaeology, Cooking, Food & Drink, History, Language, Literature, Memoirs, Multicultural, Nature/Environment, Photography, Religion and Travel

* Stacey International also publishes academic reference sources, ranging from *The Encyclopaedia of Islam* to *The Concise Dictionary of Foreign Quotations*.

Submission Guidelines Accept proposal package via post or email (including sample chapter, covering letter, market research, intended book specifications and proposed schedule and SAE).

Fiction Publish Mainstream/Contemporary titles.

Submission Guidelines Accepts proposal package via post or email (including sample chapter, covering letter, market research, intended book specifications and proposed schedule and SAE).

Recent Title(s) *An A to Z of Places and Things Saudi*, Kathy Cuddihy

Tips Titles are orientated towards a niche readership and must fulfil a specific practical use.

Stanley Gibbons Publications
7 Parkside, Ringwood, Hampshire, BH24 3SH

0 01425 472363

0 01425 470247

@ ahalligan@stanleygibbons.co.uk

🌐 www.stanleygibbons.com

Contact Chairman, M. Hall; Editorial Head, A. Halligan

Established 1856

Insider Info Publishes approximately 30 titles per year. Payment is via royalties or fees. Catalogue available online.

Non-Fiction Publishes General Non-Fiction and Reference titles on the following subjects:
Collecting, Hobbies, Philately

* Stanley Gibbons also publishes many international catalogues and magazines, including *Gibbons Stamp Monthly*.

Submission Guidelines Accepts queries and proposals via email.

Tips Most material concerns philately, however solid proposals on other areas of collecting may be considered.

Stenlake Publishing
54–58 Mill Square, Catrine, Ayrshire, KA5 6RD

0 01290 552233

0 01290 551122

@ info@stenlake.co.uk

🌐 www.stenlake.co.uk

Contact Managing Director, Richard Stenlake

Established 1997

Insider Info Publishes 40 titles per year. Payment is via royalties or a flat fee. Catalogue and manuscript guidelines available online.

Non-Fiction Publishes illustrated and General Non-Fiction titles on the following subjects:
Sports, Transportation (Railways, Aviation & Canals), Local Interest, Towns & Suburbs, Rural Areas, and Industry

* Stenlake Publishing produces books of local interest illustrated with old photographs and accompanied by an informative and interesting narrative. Proposals or ideas in the local history range will also be considered.

Submission Guidelines Accepts query with SAE/proposal package (including outline).

Recent Title(s) *Memories of East Sutherland*, Christopher J. Uncles (Local History)

Tips Stenlake is often looking for freelance writers for commissioned works. Check the 'writers' section on their website.

The Stinging Fly Press
PO Box 6016, Dublin 8, Republic of Ireland

@ stingingfly@gmail.com

🌐 www.stingingfly.org

Contact Editor, Declan Meade

Established 2005

Fiction Publishes Short Story Collections.

* Stinging Fly seeks to promote the best in new Irish and international writing. Plans are to build up the press over the coming years, with a small number of titles.

Poetry Publishes Poetry titles.

Recent Title(s) *There Are Little Kingdoms*, Kevin Barry (Short Story Collection)

Tips Also publishes *The Stinging Fly* magazine. Not seeking submissions.

St James Publishing

Suite 213 Parkway House, Sheen Lane, East Sheen, London, SW14 8LS

- 0870 870 8797
- 0870 870 8798
- stjamespublishing@stjamesschools.co.uk
- www.stjamespublishing.co.uk

Contact Managing Editors, David and Linda Smith
Established 1995
Insider Info Catalogue available online.
Non-Fiction Publishes Textbooks, Reference and Scholarly titles on the following subjects: Education, Religion and Spirituality
Recent Title(s) *St James Reading Scheme Level 3*, St James Junior School English Department (Educational Series)
Tips St James Publishing is a registered educational charity and its publications are produced on a non-profit making basis for purchase by pupils/parents. They source most of their material internally and do not accept submissions or proposals.

Storysack

Resource House, Kay Street, Bury, BL9 6BU

- 0161 763 6232
- 0161 763 5366
- hello@resourcehouse.co.uk
- www.storysack.com

Established 1999
Insider Info Catalogue available via online form.
Fiction Publishes Picture Books with accompanying Fact Books, Parent's Guides and Games.
Tips The packages of books and games are highly illustrated and presented in cloth sacks (called 'Storysacks'). Titles are aimed at children aged three and above.

St Pauls Publishing

187 Battersea Bridge Road, London, SW11 3AS

- 020 7978 4300
- 020 7978 4370
- editorial@stpaulspublishing.com
- www.stpaulspublishing.com

Contact Publisher, Fr. Celso Godilano
Established 1914
Insider Info Publishes 20 titles per year. Catalogue available online.

Non-Fiction Publishes Biography, General Non-Fiction, Children's Picture Books and Multimedia titles on the following subjects: Religion, Spirituality and Prayer
Submission Guidelines Accepts query with SAE/proposal package (including outline) or submit completed manuscript.
Recent Title(s) *Who Was John?*; *Sister Wendy Contemplates Saint Paul in Art*; *Saint Paul Friend of Jesus* (Children's)
Tips All proposals should relate to the Catholic faith.

Straightline Publishing Ltd

29 Main Street, Bothwell, Glasgow, G71 8RD

- 01698 853000
- 01698 854208
- Online form
- www.straightlinepublishing.com

Contact Director, Patrick Bellew; Editor, Colin Calder
Established 1989
Insider Info Payment is via royalties.
Non-Fiction Publishes Directories, General Non-Fiction, Multimedia and Reference titles on the following subjects: Business/Economics and Regional Interest
Recent Title(s) *Enterprising Glasgow* (Journal/Directory)
Tips Straightline Publishing offers professional assistance in journalism, photography, design, print and advertising sales as a contract publisher. It also works as an independent publisher, producing newsletters, newspapers, magazines, directories, annual reports and prospectuses. Straightline Publishing works mainly on a contractual basis and does not accept unsolicited material.

Studymates

PO Box 225, Abergele, Conwy County, LL18 9AY

- 01745 832863
- 01745 826606
- info@studymates.co.uk
- www.studymates.co.uk

Contact Managing Director, Dr Graham Lawler; Senior Editor, Edward James
Established 1999
Insider Info Publishes 40 titles per year. Receives approximately 200 queries and 50 manuscripts per year. 25 per cent of books published are from first-time authors and 95 per cent are from unagented authors. Payment is via royalty (on wholesale price) with 0.37 (per £) minimum and 0.5 (per £) maximum. Average lead time is 12 months with simultaneous submissions not accepted. Submissions accompanied by SAE will be returned. Aims to respond to queries within one day, proposals within ten days, and manuscripts within 21 days. Catalogue

is free on request, via an A5 SAE with two first class stamps, online, or by email. Manuscript guidelines free on request with an A5 SAE, or by email.

Non-Fiction Publishes Scholarly and Textbook titles on the following subjects:

Business, Economics, Education, History, Humanities, Language, Literature, Literary Criticism, Religion, Science, Social Sciences, Translation.

* Studymates also publishes writer's guides.

Submission Guidelines Accepts query with SAE, or via email, (including author biography) but no unsolited manuscripts. Will review artworks/images (send photocopies or digital files as jpegs).

Recent Title(s) *Statistics for Social Sciences*, Ian Hosker

Tips Titles are mainly aimed at post 16 students. All authors must be, or have been recently, teaching the subject of their book and have been successfully published in their genre. Do not send full manuscripts as they will be returned unopened.

Summersdale Publishers Ltd
46 West Street, Chichester, West Sussex, PO19 1RP
- 01243 771107
- 01243 786300
- enquiries@summersdale.com
- www.summersdale.com

Contact Editorial and Rights Director, Jennifer Barclay
Established 1990
Insider Info Publishes 85 titles per year. Some of the books acquired are from first-time authors and unagented authors. Payment is via a royalty based on net receipts, or outright purchase. Average lead time is twelve months, with simultaneous submissions accepted. Submissions accompanied by SAE will be returned; responses are generally by email. Aims to respond to proposals within 2 months depending on time of year. Catalogue and submissions guidelines available on the website.

Non-Fiction Publishes General Non-Fiction and Gift titles on the following subjects:

Humour, Military, Travel, True Crime, Self-Help.

Submission Guidelines Accepts query with SAE, or via email, with proposal package (including outline, three sample chapters, your publishing history, author biography, and SAE). Will review artworks/images (send digital files as jpegs).

Submission details to: submissions@summersdale.com

Tips Titles are mainly aimed at a general readership. Summersdale will consider authors without agents.

Summertown Publishing
Aristotle House, Aristotle Lane, Oxford, OX2 6TR
- 01865 454130
- 01865 454131
- info@summertown.co.uk
- www.summertown.co.uk

Contact Managing Director, Louis Garnade
Established 1998
Insider Info Catalogue available online.
Non-Fiction Publishes Reference, Scholarly and Textbook titles on the following subjects:

Business, Communications, Education, Language, Literature, Teaching resources

Recent Title(s) *50 Ways to Improve your Telephoning and Teleconferencing Skills*, Summertown Publishing
Tips Summertown Publishing relies on a team of practising teachers who aim to provide solutions to the problems many teachers face in everyday classroom situations. Therefore, any proposals should be reinforced with academic experience.

Sunflower Books
PO Box 36160, London, SW7 3HG
- 020 7589 1862
- 020 7589 1862
- mail@sunflowerbooks.co.uk
- www.sunflowerbooks.co.uk

Parent Company P A Underwood Ltd
Contact Joint Managing Director, Patricia Underwood
Established 1982
Insider Info Publishes roughly 12 titles per year. Receives approximately 50–60 queries per year and 20 manuscripts. 50 per cent of books published are from first-time authors and 100 per cent are from unagented authors. Payment is via royalty (on wholesale price) by arrangement. The advance offered is undisclosed. Average lead time is four months, with simultaneous submissions not accepted. Submissions accompanied by SAE will not be returned. Aims to respond to queries within three days and proposals within 14 days. Catalogue is free on request. Manuscript guidelines are available online.

Non-Fiction Publishes Illustrated and Guidebook titles on the following subjects:

Travel, Walking

* All publications have to match an existing style, extent and format.

Submission Guidelines Accepts proposal package (including outline). Will review artworks/images (send digital files as jpegs).

Submission details to: mail@sunflowerbooks.co.uk

Tips Authors submitting proposals should study existing publications, check which destinations are already covered, and focus on regions with which they are 100 per cent familiar - 'armchair-researched' books will not be considered.

Superscript
The Publishing House, 404 Robin Square, Newtown, Powys, SY16 1HP
☎ 01686 610883
✉ drjbford@yahoo.co.uk
🌐 www.dubsolution.org
Contact Editor-in-Chief, Max Fuller; Prof. Ray Pahl (Social Sciences, Politics, Community); Prof. Bernard Burgoyne (Lacanian Analysis Mathematics, Logic, Philosophy); Dr Bronwen Martin (Semiotics, Literary Fiction); Prof. Geoff Dench (Community Studies, Family); Dr Julie Ford (Revolution, Deontology, Epistemology, Education)
Established 2002
Insider Info Publish roughly four titles per year. Receives approximately 85 queries and ten manuscripts per year. Ten per cent of books published are from first-time authors, 100 per cent are from unagented authors and 20 per cent are author subsidy published. These are decided by a system where each title is assessed by the Editorial Board who vote on three ways forward: will not publish, will subsidy publish, or will publish traditionally. The eight members base their decision on the proposal and the comparative state of the company's and author's finances at the time the contract is negotiated. Payment is via royalty (on retail price) with 0.1 (per £) standard. Average lead time is nine months, with simultaneous submissions accepted. Submissions accompanied by SAE will be returned. Aims to respond to queries within two days, proposals within five days, and manuscripts within 21 days. Catalogue is free on request. Manuscript guidelines are available via email.
Non-Fiction Publishes Biography, Illustrated and Scholarly titles on the following subjects: Alternative Lifestyles, Community/Public Affairs, Contemporary Culture, Government/Politics, History, Humanities, Multicultural, Nature/Environment, Philosophy, Psychology, Religion, Social Sciences, Sociology, Spirituality and World Affairs
* Books are para-academic in that, while not academic books, they are intended mainly for academics, students and other 'bookish' readers. All books are required to include an appropriate bibliography.
Submission Guidelines Accepts query with SAE, or via email, with proposal package (including outline, two sample chapters, contents page, your publishing history, author biography, and SAE). Will not review artworks/images.
Fiction Publishes Ethnic, Experimental, Historical, Literary, Mainstream/Contemporary, Multicultural, Mystery, Science Fiction, Suspense, Political, Faction (20th Century), Spy Fiction.
* Books should not include racism, sexism or vengeance as themes. The question must be asked of all proposals, 'What is the point of this book?'
Submission Guidelines Accepts query with SAE, or via email.
Recent Title(s) *Never Point at a Rainbow: Dialectical Universalism: An Introduction to Radical Logic*, Julienne Ford
Tips Titles are aimed at a readership that is university educated and/or streetwise. Potential authors should realise that the company aims to spread excellent ideas, not to make writers famous or rich.

Sussex Academic Press
PO Box 139, Eastbourne, East Sussex, BN24 9BP
☎ 01323 479220
✉ edit@sussex-academic.co.uk
🌐 www.sussex-academic.co.uk
Contact Editorial Director, Anthony V.P. Grahame
Established 1994
Imprint(s) Alpha Press
Insider Info Publishes 40 titles per year. Payment is via royalties. Catalogue available free on request and online. Manuscript guidelines available online.
Non-Fiction Publishes Reference and Scholarly titles on the following subjects:
Archaeology, Art History, Biography, Economics, Management/Investment, Education, Geography, History, Jewish Studies, Latin American Studies, Library Studies, Literary Criticism & Linguistics, Middle East Studies, Musicology, Philosophy, Politics, Psychology, Psychotherapy, Social Anthropology, Social Studies, Theatre & Drama, Theology & Religion, Women's Studies
Submission Guidelines A 'Book proposal form' can be downloaded from the Press website by clicking on the 'Authors' section.
Recent Title(s) *Jeanie, an 'Army of One'*, Sybil Oldfield (Biography)
Tips Publishes titles for the international academic community. Books cover all academic subject disciplines, from original research to scholarly reference. The Press continues to commission actively, and new proposals are always welcome. All books submitted to the Press are refereed by external advisers.

Sutton Publishing
Phoenix Mill, Thrupp, Stroud, Gloucestershire, GL5 2BU
☎ 01453 731114
☎ 01453 731117
✉ publishing@sutton-publishing.co.uk
🌐 www.sutton-publishing.co.uk

Contact Managing Director, Jeremy Yates-Round; Senior Commissioning Editor, Jonathan Falconer (Military History); Senior Commissioning Editor, Christopher Feeney (General History); Senior Commissioning Editor, Simon Fletcher (Local History); Senior Commissioning Editor; Jaqueline Mitchell (Biography)
Established 1979
Insider Info Publishes around 200 titles per year. Payment is via royalties. Catalogue and manuscript guidelines available online.
Non-Fiction Publishes Autobiography, Biography, General Non-fFiction, Illustrated, Reference and Scholarly titles on the following subjects: Agriculture/Horticulture, Anthropology/Archaeology, History, Hobbies, Military/War, Aviation, Pre-History, Photography, Regional and Transportation
* The company's core focus remains on local interest books.
Submission Guidelines Accepts query with SAE/proposal package (including outline, two to three sample chapters, your publishing history and author biography).
Recent Title(s) *Battles for the Three Kingdoms*, John Barratt (History)
Tips Many of Sutton's books are illustrated and it is generally the author's responsibility to provide illustrations. Writers should investigate illustrations, cost and copyright prior to making contact. No proposals will be accepted via email.

Swan Hill Press

Wykey House, Wykey, Shrewsbury, Shropshire, SY4 1JA
- 01939 261616
- 01939 261606
- admin@quillerbooks.com
- john@beaton.org.uk
- www.countrybooksdirect.com

Parent Company Quiller Publishing Ltd
Contact Managing Director, Andrew Johnston; Editorial Director, John Beaton (Equestrianism)
Insider Info Publishes 15 titles per year. Ten per cent of books published are from first-time authors, 95 per cent are from unagented authors and approximately five per cent are author subsidy published. Payment is via royalties (on wholesale price and on retail price). Average lead time is two months with simultaneous submissions accepted. Submissions accompanied by SAE will be returned. Catalogue available free on request, online and via email.
Non-Fiction Publishes Coffee Table and General Non-Fiction titles on the following subjects: Countryside Pursuits, Shooting, Fishing

Submission Guidelines Accepts proposal package (including outline, sample chapter(s), your publishing history, author biography and SAE).
Tips Accepts postal submissions only. No novels or poetry titles will be considered.

Sweet & Maxwell Group

100 Avenue Road, Swiss Cottage, London, NW3 3PF
- 020 7393 7000
- 020 7393 7020
- sweetandmaxwell.customer.services@thomson.com
- www.sweetandmaxwell.co.uk

Contact Managing Director, Peter Lake; Editorial Manager, Linda Casbolt (Aviation, Banking, Construction, Entertainment & Media, Insurance Law); Editorial Manager, Tania Quan (Company Law, International Law, IT); Editorial Manager, Victoria Giblin (Academic)
Established 1799
Imprint(s) W. Green
Round Hall
Insider Info Publishes 200 titles per year. Payment is via royalties. Catalogue and manuscript guidelines available online.
Non-Fiction Publishes Multimedia, Reference, Scholarly and Technical titles on Law.
* There are no plans to publish in any areas other than law and the legal system.
Submission Guidelines Accepts query with SAE/proposal package (including outline and author biography).
Submission details to: firstname.lastname@thomson.com
Recent Title(s) *Renewal of Business Tenancies*, Kirk Reynolds and Wayne Clark (eds.)
Tips Sweet & Maxwell publishes in a variety of media for law students and legal and regulatory professionals. Products include books, journals, periodicals, looseleafs, CD-ROMs and online services. The group will consider proposals, but will not accept complete manuscripts with the proposal package. The website lists relevant managers and their interests to enable a more targeted submission.

Syngress

Linacre House, Jordan Hill, Oxford, OX2 8DP
- 01865 474010
- 01865 474011
- authorsupport@elsevier.com
- www.elsevier.com

Parent Company Elsevier Ltd (Science & Technology)
Insider Info Royalties paid. Catalogue is available online. Manuscript guidelines available online.

Non-Fiction Publishes Multimedia, Reference, Scholarly, Textbook and Technical titles on the following subjects:
Computers/Electronics, Computer Aided Design, Software Engineering, Artificial Intelligence, Databases
Submission Guidelines Accepts query with SAE/ Proposal package (including outline).
Recent Title(s) *The Real Citrix CCA Exam Preparation Kit, Prepare for XenApp 5.0*, Tooley (Computing/ Reference)
Tips Syngress is dedicated to producing high quality reference works for IT professionals. Focuses on the hottest topics and latest technologies to bring expert information to network administrators, engineers, developers and consultants.

T&D Poyser
38 Soho Square, London, W1D 3HB
- 020 7758 0200
- 020 7758 0222
- ornithology@acblack.com
- www.acblack.com
Parent Company A&C Black Publishers Ltd
Contact Department Head, Nigel Redman; Publishing Director, Jonathan Glasspool (Reference, Theatre and Ornithology)
Established 1973
Insider Info Catalogue available online.
Non-Fiction Publishes General Non-Fiction, Illustrated and Reference titles on the following subjects:
Nature/Environment, Natural History
Recent Title(s) *The Encyclopedia of Sharks*, Steve Parker (Reference)
Tips T&D Poyser publishes a range of ornithology and natural history titles for a general readership, specialising in ornithological atlases and natural history reference material.

T&T Clark
The Tower Building, 11 York Road, London, SE1 7NX
- 020 7922 0880
- 020 7922 0881
- tkraft@continuumbooks.com
- www.continuumbooks.com
Parent Company The Continuum International Publishing Group
Contact Associate Publisher, Thomas Kraft (Theology); Senior Editor, Haaris Naqvi (Biblical Studies, Philosophy of Religion); Editorial Assistant, Dominic Mattos
Established 1821
Insider Info Catalogue and manuscript guidelines are available online.

Non-Fiction Publishes Reference and Scholarly titles on the following subjects:
Biblical Studies, Theology, Church History
Submission Guidelines Accepts proposal package (including outline, one sample chapter, your publishing history, published clips, author biography and market research).
Recent Title(s) *Anglican Covenant*, Mark Chapman (Theology)

Tamarind Ltd
61–63 Uxbridge Road, Ealing, London, W5 5SA
- 020 8231 6800
- 020 8231 6737
- info@tamarindbooks.co.uk
- www.tamarindbooks.co.uk
Contact Publisher, Verna Allette Wilkins
Established 1987
Insider Info Catalogue is available free on request, online, or via email to: catalogues@ tamarindbooks.co.uk
Non-Fiction Publishes Children's Illustrated History and Biography.
Fiction Publishes Children's Board Books, Picture Books and Illustrated Fiction titles.
Recent Title(s) *Big Eyes, Scary Voice*, Edel Wignell (Author), Carl Pearce (Illustrator); *The Dragon Kite*, Kenneth Steven (Author), Karin Littlewood (Illustrator); *Malorie Blackman*, Verna Wilkins (Author), Virginia Gray (Illustrator)
Tips Tamarind publishes multicultural children's books, both fiction and non-fiction. Books are typically picture books with an age range of 0–12 years. Books are published for both the trade and educational markets, and scope exists for teaching reference material or classroom aids promoting a positive multicultural image.

Tango Books Ltd
PO Box 32595, London, W4 5YD
- 020 8996 9970
- 020 8996 9977
- sales@tangobooks.co.uk
- www.tangobooks.co.uk
Contact Director, Sheri Safran
Established 1982
Insider Info Publishes roughly 20 titles per year. Receives approximately 500 queries and 200 manuscripts per year. 80 per cent of books published are from first-time authors and 90 per cent are from unagented authors. Payment is via royalty (on retail price), or via outright purchase. Average lead time is nine moths, with simultaneous submissions accepted. Submissions accompanied by SAE will be returned. Aims to respond to queries within 14 days, proposals within 21 days, and

manuscripts within 30 days. Catalogue is available free on request and online. Manuscript guidelines are free on request, and available online or via email.

Non-Fiction Publishes Children's titles on a wide variety of subjects.

* Books must be suitable for quality novelty book publication.

Submission Guidelines Accepts query with SAE or via email. Will accept artworks/images (send digital files as jpegs).

Fiction Publishes Novelty titles.

* No poetry or rhyming stories. Strong stories are the most important element, novelty elements can be created at a later stage if the book lends itself to them.

Submission Guidelines Accepts query with SAE or via email. Also accepts completed manuscripts.

Tips Titles are aimed at children aged 0–12 years, as well as schools and specialist markets (particularly in diverse and multicultural areas).

Tarquin Publications
99 Hatfield Road, St Albans, Hertfordshire, AL1 4JL

- 01727 833866
- 0845 456 6385
- info@tarquinbooks.com
- www.tarquinbooks.com

Contact Managing Editor, Andrew Griffin
Established 1970
Insider Info Publishes five titles per year. Payment is via royalties. Catalogue available free on request and online.
Non-Fiction Publishes Multimedia and Scholarly titles on the following subjects:
Crafts, Hobbies, Science, Optical Illusions, Mirror Reflections, Costume, History and Paper Engineering.
* Also publishes DIY pop-up books, and collections of colourful mobiles and gift boxes.
Submission Guidelines Accepts query with SAE/proposal package (including outline).
Recent Title(s) *Automata Too!*, Magdalen Bear (Papercraft)
Tips Tarquin specialises in papercraft and modelling, but will consider publishing in other areas if there is a strong connection to papercraft.

Tartarus Press
Coverley House, Carlton, Leyburn, North Yorkshire, DL8 4AY

- 01969 640399
- 01969 640399
- tartarus@pavilion.co.uk
- www.tartaruspress.com

Contact Manager, Raymond Russell; Editor, Rosalie Parker
Established 1987
Insider Info Publishes 12 titles per year. Catalogue and manuscript guidelines available online.
Fiction Publishes Reprints of Classic texts and Fantasy, Gothic, Horror, Mystery, the Occult, and Supernatural titles.
* Tartarus titles cross various genres and are often of an unusual nature, meaning that they may have been overlooked by mainstream publishers. All should evoke a sense of wonder at the supernatural, in well written prose.
Submission Guidelines Accepts query via email with a synopsis.
Recent Title(s) *The Triumph of Night*, Edith Wharton (Reprint)
Tips Authors or editors who wish to submit a typescript should make sure that the subject matter of the book is relevant before emailing a synopsis. The manuscript, or a sample of it, may then be requested.

Taschen UK
5th Floor, 1 Heathcock Court, 415 Strand, London, WC2R 0NS

- 020 7845 8585
- 020 7836 3696
- contact-uk@taschen.com
- www.taschen.com

Insider Info Catalogue available free on request and online.
Non-Fiction Publishes Autobiography, Biography, General Non-Fiction and Illustrated titles on the following subjects:
Art, Architecture, Design, Photography
Recent Title(s) *Diego Rivera: The Complete Murals*, Luis-Martín Lozano and Juan Coronel Rivera (Art/Photography)
Tips Taschen's editorial offices are located in Germany at the main Taschen office. Any editorial queries must be sent to the main office: Hohenzollernring 53, D–50672 Köln, Deutschland.

Tate Publishing
Millbank, London, SW1P 4RG

- 020 7887 8869
- 020 788 78878
- tgpl@tate.org.uk
- www.tate.org.uk/publishing

Contact Publishing Director, Roger Thorpe
Established 1932
Insider Info Catalogue available online.
Non-Fiction Publishes General Non-Fiction, Illustrated, Multimedia, Reference, Catalogues and Scholarly titles on the following subjects:

Art, Architecture, Art History

* As well as producing exhibition catalogues, Tate galleries also publish a number of series on different aspects of art and art history. The series often require material from established academics.

Recent Title(s) *The Life and Death of Images: Ethics and Aesthetics*, Diarmuid Costello and Dominic Willsdon (eds.) (Art)

Tips Tate Publishing, part of the Tate Gallery, is one of the world's leading publishers on the visual arts, aiming to bring the best new writing on art, and the highest quality reproductions to the widest possible range of readers. Authors are generally experts in the fields of art and art history.

Taylor & Francis Group
2 Park Square, Milton Park, Abingdon, Oxford, OX14 4RN
- 020 7017 6000
- 020 7017 6699
- tf.enquiries@tfinforma.com
- www.taylorandfrancis.com

Parent Company T&F Informa Plc
Contact CEO, Roger Horton
Established 1936
Imprint(s) Taylor & Francis
CRC Press
Garland Science
Psychology Press
Routledge
Insider Info Publishes around 1,800 titles per year, and over 1,000 journals per year. Catalogue and manuscript guidelines are available online.
Non-Fiction Publishes Multimedia, Reference, Scholarly, Technical and Textbook titles.
* Imprints under the Taylor & Francis Group publish academic titles in a broad range of science and humanities subject areas, from Biotechnology to Ergonomics, Earth Sciences, Physical Sciences, Psychology and Social Studies.
Submission Guidelines Accepts proposal package (including outline, synopsis, one to two sample chapters, market research and CV).
Tips Taylor & Francis Group is the academic publishing division of T&F Informa Plc (formerly Informa Plc). Taylor & Francis mainly publishes at university level and readership includes researchers, students, academics and increasingly, professionals. See the individual imprint entries for more details.

Taylor & Francis
2 Park Square, Milton Park, Abingdon, Oxford, OX14 4RN
- 020 7017 6000
- 020 7017 6699
- tf.enquiries@tfinforma.com
- www.taylorandfrancis.com

Parent Company Taylor & Francis Group
Contact CEO, Roger Horton
Established 1936
Insider Info Catalogue and manuscript guidelines are available online.
Non-Fiction Publishes Multimedia, Reference, Scholarly, Technical and Textbook titles on the following subjects:
Biotechnology, Built Environment, Engineering, Ergonomics, Geographical Information Systems, Medicine, Science
Submission Guidelines Accepts proposal package (including outline, synopsis, one to two sample chapters, market research and CV).
Tips Taylor & Francis is best known for its scientific and reference books and specialises in niche areas such as biotechnology and ergonomics. Taylor & Francis now includes the former imprints Martin Dunitz and Spon Press.

Telegram Books
26 Westbourne Grove, London, W2 5RH
- 020 7229 2911
- 020 7229 7492
- info@telegrambooks.com
- www.telegrambooks.com

Contact Publisher, André Gaspard; Director, Mai Ghoussoub; Commissioning Editor, Rebecca O'Connor
Established 2005
Insider Info Aims to respond to proposals and manuscripts within ten weeks. Catalogue is free on request and available online or via email to catalogues@telegrambooks.com. Manuscript guidelines are available online.
Fiction Publishes Mainstream/Contemporary, Short Story Collections, Translation, and International Fiction titles.
Submission Guidelines Accepts query with SAE, or via email, with proposal package (including outline and two sample chapters).
Recent Title(s) *Cairo Stories*, Anne-Marie Drosso
Tips Telegram Books publish new international writing, in the areas of fiction and literary memoir. Telegram do not accept unsolicited manuscripts, but may do so in the future. Keep on eye on the 'Submissions' section of their website for current status.

Telegraph Books
1 Canada Square, Canary Wharf, London, E14 5DT
- 020 7538 6826
- 020 7538 6064
- support@books.telegraph.co.uk

@ www.telegraphbooksdirect.co.uk
Parent Company Telegraph Group Ltd
Contact Publisher, Morven Knowles
Established 1920
Insider Info Publishes 50 titles per year. Payment is via royalties. Catalogue available online.
Non-Fiction Publishes Biography, General Non-Fiction, Humour, Multimedia and Scholarly titles on the following subjects:
Business/Economics, Cooking, Food & Drink, Gardening, History, House & Home, Language, Literature, Law, Science, Sports, and Travel
Recent Title(s) *Change in the Weather*, Philip Eden
Tips Telegraph Books primarily publishes books under the *Telegraph* newspaper name, but also offers bookselling services to other publishers. Books published at Telegraph Books will usually have some kind of link to the Telegraph newspaper.

Templar Publishing
The Granary, North Street, Dorking, RH4 1DN
@ 01306 876361
@ 01306 889097
@ info@templarco.co.uk
@ www.templarpublishing.co.uk
Contact Publishing Manager, Rebecca Elliott; Creative Administrator (Unsolicited Manuscripts), Rebecca Beves; Art Director, Mike Jolly
Insider Info Catalogue available online.
Non-Fiction Publishes Children's, Illustrated and Multimedia titles.
* Templar publishes illustrated and interactive books for children of all ages, including the hugely successful *Ologies* series.
Fiction Publishes Children's, Multimedia and Picture titles.
* Many of Templar's books have interactive elements such as puppets, pop-outs and unconventional design.
Recent Title(s) *Varmints*, Helen Ward (Author), Marc Craste (Illustrator)
Tips Virtually all of Templar's books are highly illustrated or interactive in some way, and many are concept driven. For prospective authors, a background in art and design would be helpful.

Temple Lodge Publishing
Hillside House, The Square, Forest Row, East Sussex, RH18 5ES
@ 01342 824000
@ 01342 824367
@ office@templelodge.com
@ www.templelodge.com
Imprint(s) Clairview Books
Insider Info Catalogue is available online, or by email through an online form.

Non-Fiction Publishes Biography, Reference, Illustrated and Self-Help titles on the following subjects:
Esoteric Studies, Religion, Spirituality, Mind, Body and Spirit
Fiction Publishes some Children's Fiction.
Recent Title(s) *Thinkers, Saints, Heretics*, Virginia Sease and Manfred Schmidt-Brabant

Tempus Publishing Ltd
The Mill, Brimscombe Port, Stroud, Gloucestershire, GL5 2QG
@ 01453 883300
@ 01453 883233
@ info@tempus-publishing.com
@ www.tempus-publishing.com
Parent Company The History Press
Established 1993
Non-Fiction Publishes General Non-Fiction titles on Anthropology/Archaeology, Art, Architecture, Creative Non-Fiction, History, Language, Literature, Recreation, Regional, Sociology, Sports, Transportation and Travel
Submission Guidelines Accepts book proposals via email.
Submission details to: submissions@tempus-publishing.com
Tips Tempus Publishing are specialists in local history that have branched out into other non-fiction areas, largely history and nostalgia.

Thalamus Publishing
4 Attorney's Walk, Bull Ring, Ludlow, Shropshire, SY8 1AA
@ 01584 874977
@ 01584 872125
@ sales@thalamus-books.com
@ www.thalamus-books.com
Parent Company International Media Solutions Ltd
Contact Oliver Frey
Insider Info Catalogue available online.
Non-Fiction Publishes General Non-Fiction, Illustrated, Reference and Scholarly titles on the following subjects:
Art, Architecture, Entertainment/Games, History, Science, Fantasy Art, Pet Care, Aviation, Space Exploration and Knot Tying
* The majority of the publishing output is comprised of illustrated historical reference titles.
Recent Title(s) *The Ottomans - Empire of Faith*, Dr David Nicolle; *Exploring Ancient Egypt*, Roger Michael Kean
Tips Titles tend to originate from in-house interests, or are started by specific requests from foreign publishing partners.

Thames & Hudson

181a High Holborn, London, WC1V 7QX
- 020 7845 5000
- 020 7845 5050
- editorial@thameshudson.co.uk
- www.thameshudson.co.uk

Contact Chairman, Thomas Neurath; Deputy Chairman, Constance Kaine; Managing Director, Jamie Camplin
Established 1949
Insider Info Publishes around 180 titles per year. Book catalogue and manuscript guidelines available online.
Non-Fiction Publishes Illustrated and Reference titles on the following subjects: Anthropology/Archaeology, Architecture, Art, Contemporary Culture, Decorative Arts, Design, Ethnic Arts, Fashion, Gardening, Graphics, History, Jewelry, Mythology, Nature/Environment, Philosophy, Photography, Religion, Science, Style and Interiors, Textiles, Trave
Submission Guidelines Accepts a brief proposal and CV via email (with no attachments). Submission details to: editorial@ thameshudson.co.uk
Recent Title(s) *Magnum Magnum* (Photography); *Paintings in Proust* (Art); *World Architecture: The Masterworks* (Architecture); *The Seventy Great Mysteries of the Natural World* (Science); *The Atlas of the Real World* (World Affairs)
Tips One of the company's best known ventures is its *World of Art* series, which currently has well over 200 titles. Do not send submissions by post and do not submit fiction.

Think Books

20 New Wharf Road, London, N1 9RR
- 020 7014 6000
- 020 7014 6001
- www.panmacmillan.com

Parent Company Pan Macmillan Publishers
Established 1999
Insider Info Catalogue is available online.
Non-Fiction Publishes Coffee Table, General Non-Fiction, Gift Books, Illustrated and Reference titles on the following subjects: Animals, Cooking/Foods/Nutrition, Gardening, History, Nature/Environment, Travel
Submission Guidelines No unagented submissions.
Recent Title(s) *Make a Difference at Work*, Adharanand Finn (Careers); *The RSPCA Animal Action Annual 2009*, Sarah Evans (Animals)
Tips Think Books is a young publisher of accessible and informative books on topics such as wildlife, natural history, gardening and the environment.

Third Millennium Information

2–5 Benjamin Street, London, EC1M 5QL
- 020 7336 0144
- 020 7608 1188
- info@tmiltd.com
- www.tmiltd.com

Contact Managing Director, Julian Platt
Established 1999
Insider Info Publishes 15 titles per year. Payment is via royalties. Catalogue available free on request, online.
Non-Fiction Publishes Coffee Table Books, General Non-Fiction, Illustrated Books, Multimedia, Catalogues, Guidebooks, Magazines/Newsletters.
Recent Title(s) *Clare through the Twentieth Century: Portrait of a Cambridge College*, Lindsey Shaw-Miller (Photography)
Tips Works mainly with cultural and educational institutions in the museum, heritage and art gallery markets. Products include illustrated books, catalogues, guidebooks, magazines, newsletters, bespoke merchandise and a variety of multimedia support activities. Also offers a wide range of contract publishing services. Unsolicited proposals are welcome providing they are supported by in-depth market research.

Thoemmes Continuum

The Tower Building, 11 York Road, London, SE1 7NX
- 020 7922 0880
- 020 7922 0881
- david@continuum-books.com
- www.continuumbooks.com

Parent Company The Continuum International Publishing Group
Contact Vice President & Senior Editor, Evander Lomke; Managing Editor, Merilyn Holm
Established 1989
Insider Info Catalogue and manuscript guidelines are available online.
Non-Fiction Publishes Bibliography, Dictionary, Encyclopedia, Reference and Scholarly titles on the following subjects: Antiques, Biographical Dictionaries, Intellectual History, Philosophy
Submission Guidelines Accepts proposal package (including outline, your publishing history, author biography and market research).
Recent Title(s) *Philosophy of History*, Mark Day (Philosophy)
Tips Thoemmes specialises in philosophy and is well known for its biographical dictionaries. For detailed submission information and a list of editorial contacts see the company website.

Thomas Cook Publishing

PO Box 227, Peterborough, PE3 8SB

☎ 01733 416477
☎ 01733 416688
✉ publishing-sales@thomascook.com
🌐 www.thomascookpublishing.com

Established 1873

Insider Info Publishes roughly 165 titles per year. Payment is via outright purchase.

Non-Fiction Publishes General Non-Fiction and Illustrated titles on the following subjects: Travel Guides, Holidays, Maps, Timetables, City Guides

Recent Title(s) *Europe by Rail* (Independent Travellers)

Ticktock

Unit 2 Orchard Business Centre, North Farm Road, Tunbridge Wells, Kent, TN2 3XF

☎ 01892 509400
✉ editorial@ticktock.co.uk
🌐 www.ticktock.co.uk

Contact Managing Director, John Twiggs; Publishing Director, Ruth Owen; Managing Editor, Sophie Furse; Creative Manager, Emma Randall

Established 2002

Imprints Little Ticktock

Insider Info Catalogue available free on request, online and via email to info@ticktock.co.uk.

Non-Fiction Publishes Children's Illustrated Books and Educational titles on a variety of National Curriculum and General Interest subjects.

Fiction Publishes Children's Picture Books and Novelty Books.

Recent Title(s) *If Dinosaurs Were Alive Today*, Dougal Dixon

Tips All Ticktock books are produced in-house but the team do work with freelance authors and editors. Most titles are aimed at either the trade or school markets. The Little Ticktock imprint was launched in 2007 and deals with books for pre-schoolers.

Time Out Guides Ltd

Random House, 20 Vauxhall Bridge Road, London, SW1V 2SA

☎ 020 7840 8400
☎ 020 7840 8791
🌐 www.randomhouse.co.uk

Parent Company The Random House Group Ltd

Insider Info Catalogue available online.

Non-Fiction Publishes City Guides.

Recent Title(s) *Morocco: Perfect places to stay, eat and explore*; *Time Out Costa Rica - 1st edition*

Tips The imprint solely publishes *Time Out Guides*, no other travel writing is published.

Timewell Press

10 Porchester Terrace, London, W2 3TL

☎ 0870 760 5250
☎ 0870 760 5250
✉ info@timewellpress.com
🌐 www.timewellpress.com

Contact Andreas Campomar

Insider Info Catalogue available online.

Non-Fiction Publishes Autobiography, Biography and General Non-Fiction titles on the following subjects: Business/Economics, Contemporary Culture, Government/Politics, History, Regional

Fiction Publishes Literary and Mainstream/Contemporary titles and Short Story Collections.

Recent Title(s) *Happy Hair Days*, Philip Kingsley

Tips Timewell Press specialises in contemporary life writing and cultural writing, either concerning current affairs, or popular celebrities. Queries are welcome using the online form on the website.

Tindal Street Press Ltd

217 The Custard Factory, Gibb Street, Birmingham, B9 4AA

☎ 0121 773 8157
☎ 0121 693 5525
✉ info@tindalstreet.co.uk
🌐 www.tindalstreet.co.uk

Contact Managing Editor, Emma Hargrave; Assistant Editor, Luke Brown; Publishing Director, Alan Mahar

Established 1998

Insider Info Publishes six titles per year. Payment is via royalties. Catalogue and manuscript guidelines available online.

Fiction Publishes Mainstream/Contemporary and Regional titles and Short Story Collections.

Submission Guidelines Accepts query with SAE. Submit proposal package (including outline and three sample chapters).

Submission details to: emma@tindalstreet.co.uk

Recent Title(s) *What Was Lost*, Catherine O'Flynn (Novel)

Tips Tindal Street Press publishes contemporary fiction from the English regions – which means the manuscripts that interest them mostly have a centre of gravity outside of London and the South East. They welcome unsolicited manuscripts, but will not consider poetry, children's, teenage, science fiction, fantasy or romance.

Tír Eolas

Newtownlynch, Doorus, Kinvara, Co. Galway, Republic of Ireland

☎ 00353 91 637452
☎ 00353 91 637452
✉ info@tireolas.com

www.tireolas.com
Contact Managing Director, Anne Korff
Established 1985
Insider Info Payment is via royalties. Catalogue available online.
Non-Fiction Publishes General Non-Fiction and Illustrated titles on the following subjects: Anthropology/Archaeology, Contemporary Culture, History, Hobbies, Nature/Environment, Walking Guides, Irish Culture/Folklore
Submission Guidelines Accepts query with SAE.
Recent Title(s) *The Shannon Valley: A Rambler's Guide and Map*, Stephen Heery
Tips Tír Eolas, literally translated as 'knowledge of the land', is an independent publisher specialising in producing books, walking guides and maps on Irish history, archaeology, landscape, culture and tradition. They will consider proposal submissions providing they are accompanied by high quality illustrations and are not scholarly or technical in tone.

Titan Books
Titan Books, 144 Southwark Street, London, SE1 0UP
 020 7620 0200
 020 7803 1990
 editorial@titanmail.com
 www.titanbooks.com
Parent Company Titan Publishing Group
Contact Editorial Director, Katy Wild
Established 1981
Insider Info Publishes around 220 titles per year. Receives approximately 100 queries and 50 manuscripts per year. 15 per cent of books published are from first-time authors. Payment is via royalty (on retail price) or an outright purchase. Simultaneous submissions are accepted. Submissions accompanied by SAE will be returned. Aims to respond in one week to queries, one month to proposals, and three months to manuscripts. Catalogue and author guidelines are free on request.
Non-Fiction Publishes Coffee Table, General Non-Fiction and Illustrated titles on the following subjects: Entertainment/Games, Media, Film, Television
* Will only work with writers who have proven experience and contacts in the field.
Submission Guidelines Submit proposal package (including outline, sample chapter(s), author biography, and SAE) Will not review artworks/images as part of the manuscript package. Submission details to: editorial@titanmail.com
Fiction Publishes Comic Books and Graphic Novel titles
Submission Guidelines No fiction or comic book proposals accepted.

Recent Title(s) *Heroes*, Michael Turner, Tim Sale and Phil Jimenez (Graphic Novel); *My Boring-Ass Life*, Kevin Smith (Biography)
Tips Titles are aimed at film and television fans.

Top That! Publishing Plc
Marine House, Tide Mill Way, Woodbridge, Suffolk, IP12 1AP
 01394 386651
 01394 386011
 info@topthatpublishing.com
 www.topthatpublishing.com
Contact Managing Director, Barrie Henderson; Creative Director, Simon Couchman
Established 1999
Imprint(s) Top That! Kids
KUDOS
Tide Mill Press
Insider info Catalogue available online.
Non-Fiction Publishes Children's, General Non-Fiction, Gift, Humour and Illustrated titles on the following subjects:
Cooking, Crafts, Creative Non-Fiction, Food & Drink, Entertainment/Games, Hobbies, House & Home, Sex
Submission Guidelines Accepts query via phone before sending in any material.
Fiction Publishes Children's and Multimedia titles and Picture Books.
Submission Guidelines Accepts query via phone before sending in any material.
Recent Title(s) *A Bright New Star*, Erin Ranson (Author), Dan Crisp (Illustrator)
Tips Titles are designed to challenge and stimulate young minds. The Tide Mill imprint publishes children's books. KUDOS publishes craft, entertainment, hobbies, lifestyle and gift books for the adult market. The Imagine That! imprint offers bespoke packaging services to other market leading companies. Most books in the children's ranges are highly illustrated, so it is important to send sample illustrations with any submission.

Tor
20 New Wharf Road, London, N1 9RR
 020 7014 6000
 020 7014 6001
 fiction@macmillan.co.uk
 questions@tor.com
 www.tor.com
Parent Company Pan Macmillan Publishers
Established 2003
Insider Info Downloadable pdf version of catalogue available online.
Fiction Publishes Fantasy and Science Fiction titles.
Submission Guidelines Agented submissions only.

Recent Title(s) *Busted Flush*, George R.R. Martin (Science Fiction); *Winterstrike*, Liz Williams (Science Fiction)
Tips Tor does not accept unsolicited submissions.

TownHouse Dublin

Mountpleasant Business Centre, Mountpleasant Avenue, Ranelagh, Dublin 6, Republic of Ireland
☎ 00353 1 497 2399
☎ 00353 1 499 5150
✉ books@townhouse.ie
🖰 www.townhouse.ie
Contact Managing Director & Publisher, Treasa Coady; Editors, Deirdre O Neill and Marie Heaney
Established 1980
Imprint(s) Simon & Schuster/TownHouse
Insider Info Publishes 25 titles per year. Payment via royalties. Aims to respond to proposals and manuscripts within eight weeks. Catalogue and manuscript guidelines available online.
Non-Fiction Publishes Biography, General Non-Fiction, Illustrated and Reference titles on the following subjects:
Anthropology/Archaeology, Art, Architecture, Contemporary Culture, Government/Politics, Health, History, Language, Literature, Literary Criticism, Memoirs, Music, Nature, Photography, Science, Sport, Travel, Genealogy, Irish Folklore
Submission Guidelines Accepts query with SAE. Submit proposal package (including outline, three to four sample chapter(s) and author biography).
Fiction Publishes Literary and Mainstream/Contemporary titles.
Submission Guidelines Accepts query with SAE/proposal package (including outline, three to four sample chapter(s)).
Poetry Publishes Poetry titles.
Recent Title(s) *Viking Age Dublin*, Ruth Johnson (History)
Tips TownHouse has become a leader in the production of Irish interest non-fiction books. The joint venture, Simon & Schuster/TownHouse, publishes fiction from both emerging and established Irish writers and is committed to the ongoing task of publishing great storytelling. Those interested in submitting manuscripts for consideration are invited to send proposals in the form of an outline in the case of non-fiction, or a synopsis in the case of fiction. A short autobiographical note and details of previous publications are also encouraged.

Transita Ltd

Spring Hill House, Spring Hill Road, Begbroke, OX5 1RX
☎ 01865 375794
☎ 01865 379162
✉ info@transita.co.uk
🖰 www.transita.co.uk
Contact Managing Director, Giles Lewis; Editorial Director, Nikki Read
Insider Info Catalogue is available free on request. Manuscript guidelines available online.
Fiction Publishes Mainstream/Contemporary titles.
Submission Guidelines Submit completed manuscript.
Submission details to: nikki@transita.co.uk
Recent Title(s) *The Gardener*, Prue Leith (Novel)
Tips Transita primarily publishes contemporary women's fiction that reflects the lives of women aged 45–75. Due to the high volume of submissions received, they do not acknowledge individual manuscripts.

Transworld Publishers

61–63 Uxbridge Road, London, W5 5SA
☎ 020 8579 2652
☎ 020 8579 5479
✉ info@transworld-publishers.co.uk
🖰 www.booksattransworld.co.uk
Parent Company The Random House Group Ltd
Contact Publisher, Bill Scott-Kerr
Established 1950
Imprint(s) Bantam Press
Black Swan
Channel 4 Books
Corgi
Doubleday
Insider Info Catalogue available online. Imprints do not have individual websites; for imprint catalogues go to 'search catalogue by imprint'.
Non-Fiction Publishes Autobiography, Biography, Coffee Table, Cookery, General Non-Fiction, Gift, How-To, Humour, Illustrated, Reference and Self-Help titles on the following subjects:
Art, Business, Cookery, Finance, Food & Drink, Gardening, Health, History, Humour, Money, Music, Science, Sport, Travel, Television Tie-Ins
Submission Guidelines Agented submissions only.
Fiction Publishes Crime, Fantasy, Historical, Literary, Mainstream/Contemporary, Mystery, Romance, Science Fiction and Suspense titles.
Submission Guidelines Agented submissions only.
Recent Title(s) *Dragon Harper*, Anne & Todd McCaffrey (Fantasy); *I Can Make You Sleep*, Paul McKenna (Self-Help)
Tips Does not accept unsolicited manuscripts. Hardbacks are published under the Doubleday or Bantam Press imprints. Paperbacks are published by Black Swan, Bantam and Corgi. Transworld also publishes books for the Eden Project, in Cornwall.

Travel Publishing Ltd

7a Apollo House, Calleva Park, Aldermaston, Berkshire, RG7 8TN

☎ 0118 981 7777

☎ 0118 982 0077

✉ info@travelpublishing.co.uk

🌐 www.travelpublishing.co.uk

Contact Directors, Chris Day and Peter Robinson

Established 1997

Insider Info Payment is via royalties. Catalogue is available free on request and online.

Non-Fiction Publishes Travel Guides on the following subjects:

Cooking, Food & Drink, Regional Interest, Travel

Tips Travel Publishing's major series include *The Hidden Places, The Hidden Inns, Country Living Rural Guides* and *Off the Motorway*. Writers are advised to try and write for one of these series, rather than writing a stand alone piece.

Trentham Books Ltd

Westview House, 734 London Road, Stoke on Trent, ST4 5NP

☎ 01782 745567

☎ 01782 745553

✉ tb@trentham-books.co.uk

🌐 www.trentham-books.co.uk

Contact Editorial Director, Dr. Gillian Klein; Executive Director, Barbara Wiggins

Established 1978

Insider Info Publishes 30 titles per year. Payment is via royalties. Aims to respond to proposals and manuscripts within one month. Catalogue and manuscript guidelines available online.

Non-Fiction Publishes Reference, Scholarly and Technical titles on the following subjects: Education, Law, Social Sciences, Cultural/Gender Studies

Submission Guidelines Accepts query with SAE. Submit proposal package (including outline, two sample chapters, publishing history and author biography). Will accept artworks/images.

Recent Title(s) *The Way We See It*, Sandra Richards

Tips Trentham publishes a wide range of titles, plus five professional journals, mainly in the fields of education and social policy. Titles are aimed at professional readers and teachers, not children or parents. Trentham accepts book proposals providing they follow the guidelines from their website. All new titles must conform to the company's ethical stance and commitment to equality, academic rigour and readability.

Trident Press Ltd

175 Piccadilly, Mayfair, London, WIJ 9TB

☎ 020 7491 8770

☎ 020 7491 8664

✉ admin@tridentpress.com

🌐 www.tridentpress.com

Contact Managing Director, Peter Vine

Established 1997

Imprint(s) Trident Media

Insider Info Payment via royalties. Catalogue available online.

Non-Fiction Publishes General Non-fiction, Illustrated, Multimedia and Reference titles on the following subjects:

Anthropology/Archaeology, Contemporary Culture, History, Nature/Environment, Photography, Translation, World Affairs, Irish Interest

Submission Guidelines Accepts query with SAE.

Fiction Publishes Irish Interest titles.

Recent Title(s) *The Emirates - A Natural History*, Mohammed Al Bowardi

Tips Trident Press publishes in a wide range of languages, including French and Arabic. Trident Media is a sister company based in Ireland that handles all the pre-press work for the main press. Trident Press will not accept unsolicited submissions, but will respond to brief email or phone contact.

Trotman & Co. Ltd

c/o Crimson Publishing, Westminster House, Kew Road, Richmond, Surrey, TW9 2ND

☎ 020 8334 1600

☎ 020 8334 1601

✉ enquiries@trotman.co.uk

🌐 www.trotman.co.uk

Contact Managing Director, Toby Trotman; Editorial Director, Mina Patria; Commissioning Editor, Rachel Lockhart

Established 1970

Insider Info Publishes roughly 60 titles per year. Payment is via royalties. Catalogue available online.

Non-Fiction Publishes Multimedia and Reference titles on the following subjects:

Business, Counselling/Career, Economics, Education, Training Courses

Submission Guidelines Accepts submissions via online form.

Submission details to: editorial@trotman.co.uk

Recent Title(s) *Gap Year Guidebook 2008*, Alison Withers

Tips Trotman publishes products in a wide range of media, including books, photocopiable packs, videos, the internet and CD-ROMs, which cover the areas of higher education, careers information, teaching resources, employment and training.

TSO (The Stationary Office)

Mandela Way, Southwark, London, SE1 5SS

☎ 020 7394 4284

○ parlypubs@tso.co.uk
ⓦ www.tso.co.uk
Parent Company Williams Lea Holdings Plc
Contact Director of Parliamentary & Statutory Publishing, Richard South; Production Manager, Pete Christopher; Parliamentary & Statutory Publishing Manager, Kanta Craigen-Straughn
Established 1996
Insider Info Publishes around 15,000 titles per year. Catalogue and manuscript guidelines available.
Non-Fiction Publishes Multimedia, Reference and Technical titles on the following subjects: Business/Economics, Community/Public Affairs, Education, Government/Politics, Law, Nature/Environment, Transportation
Tips TSO manages print and publishing services for public and private sector clients. They specialise in the creation, production and distribution of information in print, online and electronic formats, including print management and design services. They mainly publish material sponsored by the government and other official bodies, as well as some commercial publishing in the fields of business, law, education, transportation and the environment. TSO is the largest publisher in the UK by volume, but this mostly consists of government sponsored books and reports. They do not publish general books.

Twenty First Century Publishers Ltd
Braunton Barn, Kiln Lane, Isfield, TN22 5UE
○ 01892 522802
○ tfcp@btinternet.com
ⓦ www.twentyfirstcenturypublishers.com
Contact Chairman, Fred Piechoczek
Established 2002
Insider Info Payment is via royalties. Catalogue and manuscripts guidelines available online.
Fiction Publishes Literary, Mainstream/Contemporary and Financial Thriller titles.
Submission Guidelines Accepts proposal package (including outline and three sample chapters) by email. Send fictional writing in English, French or German. The outline should be in the body of the email and the manuscript, or sample chapters should be sent as a file attachment.
Recent Title(s) *Celebrate Myself*, James Buckley (Novel)
Tips TFCP concentrates on developing new authors whom they wish to bring to the market, and they use the latest technology, including e-books, to achieve publication in minimum times. They publish general fiction, plot-driven original works and knowledgeably written financial thrillers.

Two Rivers Press
35–39 London Street, Reading, Berkshire, RG1 4PS
○ 0118 966 2345
○ tworiverspress@virgin.net
ⓦ www.tworiverspress.com
Contact Publisher, John Froy
Established 1994
Insider Info Catalogue and manuscript guidelines available online.
Non-Fiction Publishes General Non-Fiction and Illustrated titles on the following subjects: Local Interest (Thames Valley)
Submission Guidelines Accepts query with SAE. Submit proposal package (including outline and sample chapter(s)). Will accept artworks/images (send photocopies).
Fiction Publishes Short Story Collections.
Submission Guidelines Accepts query with SAE. Submit proposal package (including outline and sample chapter(s)).
Poetry Publishes Poetry titles.
Submission Guidelines Submit six sample poems.
Recent Title(s) *A Thames Bestiary*, Peter Hay and Geoff Sawers; *Hearthstone*, Joseph Butler (Collection)
Tips Two Rivers is a small co-operative run press, publishing general interest non-fiction, poetry and prose from the Thames Valley area. They are a very small press, with two part-time workers and a number of freelancers and volunteers, and receive limited funding to produce books within a well-defined remit: books about the local area, and literature (mainly poetry). Only rarely do they deviate from these areas.

UKUnpublished
23 Mapledene Avenue, Hullbridge, Hockley, Essex, SS5 6JB
○ 01702 780840
○ 01702 260102
○ david@ukunpublished.co.uk
ⓦ www.ukunpublished.co.uk
Contact Proprietor, David Buttle
Insider Info UKUnpublished is a brand new publisher looking to offer the benefits of both Traditional and Self Publishing – Full Publishing, Printing, and Distribution throughout the UK and the US, but paying up to 44 per cent higher royalties. Editing/Proofreading services are not available. Will publish all categories of books, from Children's Fiction to Adult/Erotica, and Technical Non-Fiction to Cookery. Aims to respond to queries and manuscripts within six weeks, however this is considered to be an outside timescale. Visit the website to find out more about the service, or email/write/fax to request a brochure. Prefers to deal

UK & IRISH BOOKS

PUBLISHERS

LISTINGS

331

directly with the author, instead of through an agent.

Non-Fiction Publishes all categories of Non-Fiction.

Fiction Publishes all Fiction genres, including Children's, Adult and Short Stories.

Submission Guidelines Visit the website to find out full details about the service and the company, and email David Buttle directly to ask any questions you may have.

Tips UKUnpublished is dedicated to giving as many authors as possible an outlet, to 'Let the World Share Your Imagination', while providing a quality and personal service. UKUnpublished also offers Accounting and Tax Services provided by qualified Accountants, ensuring that you can concentrate on writing. All royalties are paid regularly.

Ulric Publishing Ltd
PO Box 55, Church Stretton, Shropshire, SY6 6WR
- 01694 781354
- 01694 781372
- books@ulric-publishing.com
- www.ulric-publishing.com

Contact Director, Ulric Woodhams; Director, Elizabeth Oakes

Established 1992

Insider Info Catalogue available online.

Non-Fiction Publishes General Non-Fiction and Illustrated titles on the following subjects: Automotive, Military/War, Transportation

Submission Guidelines No unsolicited material.

Recent Title(s) *Cromwell's Deputy*, Dame Joan Fleetwood Vairey DBE

Tips Ulric Publishing is a small press specialising in military and political history, automotive, classic cars, transportation and other forms of travel.

Ulster Historical Foundation
Cotton Court, 30–42 Waring Street, Belfast, BT1 2ED
- 028 9033 2288
- 028 9023 9885
- enquiry@uhf.org.uk
- www.booksireland.org.uk

Insider Info Catalogue available online.

Non-Fiction Publishes General Non-Fiction, Guidebooks and Map titles on the following subjects:
Church History, Education, Family History, Gaelic Culture, Genealogy, Irish History, Local Interest, Ordnance Survey, Ulster.

Recent Title(s) *Linen Houses of the Bann Valley*, Kathleen Rankin; *Clergy of Waterford, Lismore and Ferns*, Iain Knox .ed

Tips Ulster Historical Foundation specialises in historical titles and family history guides relating to the province of Ulster.

University College Dublin Press
Newman House, 86 St Stephen's Green, Dublin 2, Republic of Ireland
- 00353 1 477 9812/9813
- 00353 1 477 9821
- ucdpress@ucd.ie
- www.ucdpress.ie

Contact Executive Editor, Barbara Mennell

Insider Info Catalogue and manuscript guidelines available online.

Non-Fiction Publishes Reference and Scholarly titles on the following subjects:
Government/Politics, History, Language, Literature, Literary Criticism, Music, Nature/Environment, Science, Social Sciences, Study Guides

Submission Guidelines Accepts query with SAE. Submit proposal package (including outline, three sample chapters, market research, publishing history, clips and author biography).

Recent Title(s) *The Sea of Disappointment*, Andrew Fitzsimons

Tips UCD Press is the publishing imprint of Ireland's largest university, University College Dublin, publishing a diversity of academic titles. In particular UCD Press is a market leader in research relating to historic and contemporary Ireland, and is committed to enhancing further its dynamic profile in this area. Check the website for full submission guidelines.

University of Exeter Press
Reed Hall, Streatham Drive, Exeter, EX4 4QR
- 01392 263066
- 01392 263064
- uep@ex.ac.uk
- www.exeterpress.co.uk

Contact Publisher, Simon Baker

Insider Info Catalogue available online.

Non-Fiction Publishes General Non-Fiction, Reference and Scholarly titles on the following subjects:
Archaeology, Classics, History, Literature, Literary Criticism, Medieval Studies, Film History, Performance Studies, Regional Interest.

Submission Guidelines Accepts query with SAE. Editorial enquiries, including short publishing proposals, are welcome and authors should address them to Simon Baker, Publisher.

Tips Exeter's main subject areas are medieval studies, classical studies, history, film history, performance studies, archaeology, landscape history and South West studies.

University of Hertfordshire Press
University of Hertfordshire, College Lane, Hatfield, Hertfordshire, AL10 9AB
- 01707 284654
- 01707 281354
- uhpress@herts.ac.uk
- www.herts.ac.uk/uhpress

Contact Press Manager, Jane Housham
Established 1992
Imprint(s) University of Hertfordshire Press
Hertfordshire Publications
Insider Info Payment is via royalties. Catalogue and manuscript guidelines available online.
Non-Fiction Publishes Reference and Scholarly titles on:
Education, History, Language, Literature, Psychology, Science, Romani Studies
Submission Guidelines Accepts query with SAE. Submission details to: j.j.housham@herts.ac.uk
Recent Title(s) *Gypsy Dialects*, Edward Proctor
Tips The Hertfordshire Publications imprint publishes local interest and Hertfordshire history books.

University of Plymouth Press
Room M12, Scott Building, University of Plymouth, Drake Circus, Plymouth, Devon, PL4 8AA
- phoneywill@plymouth.ac.uk
- www.uppress.co.uk

Contact Publisher, Paul Honeywill
Established 2005
Insider Info Catalogue and manuscript guidelines available online.
Non-Fiction Publishes Illustrated and Multimedia titles on the following subjects:
Art, Architecture, Design, Media Art, Music/Dance, Photography
Submission Guidelines Form available online for new writers.
Recent Title(s) *Last Paintings of London*, John Virtue (Photography)
Tips Publishes works that aim to extend the intellectual reach of scholarship, while helping to define new areas of knowledge and learning. In keeping with the University of Plymouth's mission, the Press fosters an understanding and partnership between communities to enrich the cultural life of the region. See website for new author form.

University of Wales Press
10 Columbus Walk, Brigantine Place, Cardiff, CF10 4UP
- 029 2049 6899
- 029 2049 6108
- press@press.wales.ac.uk
- www.uwp.co.uk

Contact Director, Ashley Drake; Commissioning Editor, Sarah Lewis; Editors, Elin Lewis and Nia Peris
Established 1922
Imprint(s) University of Wales Press
Insider Info Publishes roughly 60 titles per year. Payment is via royalties. Catalogue available free on request and online. Manuscript guidelines available online.
Non-Fiction Publishes General Non-Fiction, Scholarly and Welsh Non-Fiction titles on the following subjects:
Contemporary Culture, Government/Politics, History, Language, Literature, Law, Literary Criticism, Nature/Environment, Philosophy, Religion, Translation, Welsh Studies
Submission Guidelines Accepts query with SAE. Proposal questionnaire available on website. Authors should submit a detailed proposal at an early stage, preferably before the book is written. Proposals should be structured around the proposal questionnaire (on the website). Please note that they will not give detailed consideration to your proposal until the questionnaire is received, preferably by email.
Submission details to: s.lewis@press.wales.ac.uk
Tips Concentrates on six main subject areas of history, political philosophy, religious studies, Welsh & Celtic studies, literary studies, European studies and Medieval studies.

University Presses of California, Columbia & Princeton Ltd
1 Oldlands Way, Bognor Regis, West Sussex, PO22 95A
- 01243 842165
- 01243 842167
- lois@upccp.demon.co.uk

Non-Fiction Publishes Reference and Scholarly titles and Textbooks on the following subjects:
Business/Economics, Education, History, Humanities, Literary Criticism, Science
Submission Guidelines Accepts query with SAE.
Tips The UK based enquiries office for the California, Columbia and Princeton Universities. The editorial departments of the three universities are based in the US at the corresponding universities.

Usborne Publishing Ltd
Usborne House, 83–85 Saffron Hill, London, EC1N 8RT
- 020 7430 2800
- 020 8636 3758
- mail@usborne.co.uk
- www.usborne.co.uk

Contact Managing Director, Peter Usborne; Director, Robert Jones

Established 1975

Insider Info Publishes around 250 titles per year. Payment via royalty. Aims to respond to manuscripts within six months. Catalogue and manuscript guidelines available online.

Non-Fiction Publishes Illustrated Children's Reference titles on the following subjects:
Art, Crafts, Entertainment/Games, Hobbies, Language, Literature, Music, Sports, Puzzle Books

Submission Guidelines All unsolicited manuscripts returned unopened.

Fiction Publishes Babies, Children's and Early Years titles and Picture Books.

Submission Guidelines Submit proposal package (including outline and three sample chapters) for fiction for children up to 12. Address to 'Fiction Submissions'. See detailed manuscript guidelines, available to download from the website, for specific age ranges. Will not accept picture book proposals or manuscripts.

Recent Title(s) *First Book of Art*, Usborne (Art); *The Vietnam War*, Katie Daynes (History)

Tips Usborne is a major independent UK publishing company. Their list includes almost every type of children's book, from babies to young adult, and covering a wide range of topics. Usborne will only accept submissions for new children's fiction, not for picture books or non-fiction, as they are commissioned in-house.

Vallentine Mitchell Publishers Ltd
Suite 314 Premier House, 112–114 Station Road, Edgware, Middlesex, HA8 7BJ

- 020 8952 9526
- 020 8952 9242
- info@vmbooks.com
- www.vmbooks.com

Insider Info Publishes 30 titles per year. 80 per cent of books published are from unagented authors. Advance offered is from £250. Simultaneous submissions accepted. Submissions accompanies by SAE will be returned. Catalogue and author guidelines are free on request.

Non-Fiction Publishes Autobiography, Biography, Reference and Scholarly titles on the following subjects:
Anthropology/Archaeology, Contemporary Culture, Government/Politics, History, Humanities, Literary Criticism, Memoirs, Military/War, Philosophy, Religion.

* All titles must be of Jewish interest.

Submission Guidelines Accepts proposal package (including outline, sample chapter(s), your publishing history, author biography), and artworks/images.

Recent Title(s) *A Life in Israel's Intelligence Service*, Meir Amit (Autobiography)

Tips Make sure your book fits in with the Jewish interest of the list, and do not send entire manuscripts.

Vanguard Press
Sheraton House, Castle Park, Cambridge, CB3 0AX

- 01223 370012
- 01223 370040
- editors@pegasuspublishers.com
- www.pegasuspublishers.com

Parent Company Pegasus Elliot MacKenzie Publishers Ltd

Insider Info Catalogue and manuscript guidelines available online.

Non-Fiction Publishes Autobiography, Biography and General Non-Fiction titles on the following subjects:
Cooking, Food & Drink, Government/Politics, History, Memoirs, Military/War, Sports, Travel, Women's Issues/Studies

Submission Guidelines Accepts proposal package (including outline, two sample chapters and SAE).

Fiction Publishes Adventure, Historical, Humour, Mainstream/Contemporary, Romance, Science Fiction and Crime titles.

Submission Guidelines Accepts proposal package (including outline, two sample chapters).

Poetry Publishes Poetry titles.

Tips Vanguard Press encourages submissions from new and untested authors.

Veritas
7–8 Lower Abbey Street, Dublin 1, Republic of Ireland

- 00353 1 878 8177
- 00353 1 878 6507
- sales@veritas.ie
- www.veritas.ie

Parent Company Veritas Communications

Contact Managing Editor, Ruth Garvey; Commissioning Editor, Donna Doherty

Established 1969

Insider Info Publishes 30 titles per year. Payment via royalty. Aims to respond to proposals and manuscripts within six weeks. Catalogue and manuscript guidelines available online.

Non-Fiction Publishes Audio cassettes, Biography, Textbooks, Children's, General Non-Fiction, Gift, Multimedia and Self-Help titles on the following subjects:
Child Guidance/Parenting, Health/Medicine, Philosophy, Psychology, Religion, Social Sciences,

Spirituality, Christian Resources, Social Issues, Bible Study, Parish and Church Resources
Submission Guidelines Accepts query with SAE. Submit proposal package (including outline, three sample chapters and author biography). Accepts either printed proposals, or those saved on disk, addressed to Donna Doherty.
Fiction Publishes Illustrated Children's Fiction, often linked to Christianity or Christian values.
Submission Guidelines Accepts query with SAE. Submit proposal package (including outline, three sample chapters and author biography). Accepts either printed proposals, or those saved on disk, addressed to Donna Doherty.
Recent Title(s) *Epiphanies: Moments of Grace in Daily Life*, Mary Murphy
Tips Vertitas' market is Christian based and is an ever growing entity. It is not restricted to the parameters of Ireland and the UK. Titles are published for companies and groups such as churches, schools and other organisations, and also for retail customers, including students and parents.

Vermilion

Random House, 20 Vauxhall Bridge Road, London, SW1V 2SA
- 020 7840 8400
- 020 7840 8406
- vermilioneditorial@randomhouse.co.uk
- www.randomhouse.co.uk

Parent Company The Random House Group Ltd
Contact Publishing Director, Clare Hulton
Insider Info Catalogue available online.
Non-Fiction Publishes Autobiography, Biography, General Non-Fiction and How-To titles on the following subjects:
Food & Nutrition, Health & Diet, Parenting, Personal Development, Relationships
Submission Guidelines No unagented submissions.
Recent Title(s) *Quantum Wellness: A Step-by-Step Guide to Health and Happiness*, Kathy Freston (Health); *The Diet Delusion*, Gary Taubes (Health)

Verso Ltd

6 Meard Street, London, W1F 0EG
- 020 7437 3546
- 020 7734 0059
- enquiries@verso.co.uk
- www.versobooks.com

Contact Managing Director, Guy Bentham
Established 1970
Insider Info Catalogue and manuscript guidelines available online.
Non-Fiction Publishes General Non-Fiction and Scholarly titles on the following subjects:

Business/Economics, Contemporary Culture, Government/Politics, History, Philosophy, Sociology
Submission Guidelines Accepts query with SAE. Submit proposal package (including outline, market research, publishing history and author biography).
Recent Title(s) *Political Interventions: Social Science and Political Action*, Pierre Bourdieu
Tips Verso is a radical publisher specialising in intelligent, critical works located at the intersection of the academic and trade markets. Verso's list of writers in English includes many key authors in the social sciences and humanities, with particular strength in politics, cultural studies, history, philosophy, sociology and literary criticism. Submission guidelines for Verso are available on the website. All proposals must include information on market research and target audience for the book.

Viking

80 Strand, London, WC2R 0RL
- 020 7010 3000
- 020 7010 6060
- customer.service@penguin.co.uk
- www.penguin.co.uk

Parent Company Penguin General
Contact Publisher, Venetia Butterfield; Editorial Director, Joel Rickett
Insider Info Catalogue is available online.
Non-Fiction Publishes Biography and General Non-Fiction on the following subjects:
History, Sports, Travel, Current Affairs, Belles Lettres
Submission Guidelines Agented submissions only.
Fiction Publishes Experimental, Literary and Mainstream/Contemporary titles.
Submission Guidelines Agented submissions only.
Recent Title(s) *Operation Snakebite: The Explosive True Story of an Afghan Desert Siege*, (Military/ True Story)
Tips Viking publishes the widest possible range of literary fiction and non-fiction. This varies from the highly literary and sometimes experimental, to more commercial titles.

Vintage

Random House, 20 Vauxhall Bridge Road, London, SW1V 2SA
- 020 7840 8608
- 020 7233 6117
- vintageeditorial@randomhouse.co.uk
- www.randomhouse.co.uk/vintage

Parent Company The Random House Group Ltd
Contact Publisher, Rachel Cugnoni
Established 1990
Imprint(s) Vintage Books
Vintage Classics
Vintage Originals

Insider Info Catalogue available online.
Non-Fiction Publishes Autobiography, Biography, General Non-Fiction and Reference titles on the following subjects:
Contemporary Culture, Crime, Film & TV Tie-In, History, Literary Criticism, Music, Psychology, Science, Travel
Submission Guidelines No unagented submissions.
Fiction Publishes Literary and Mainstream/Contemporary titles and Classics.
Submission Guidelines No unagented submissions.
Recent Title(s) *Revolutionary Road*, Richard Yates (Novel/Film Tie-In); *Too Far From Home*, Chris Jones (Biography)
Tips Vintage publishes entirely in paperback and places itself at the cutting edge of contemporary fiction and non-fiction publishing. Vintage Classics publishes re-prints of 'classic books that changed the world'.

Virago Press
100 Victoria Embankment, London, EC4Y 0DY
- 020 7911 8000
- 020 7911 8100
- virago.press@littlebrown.co.uk
- www.virago.co.uk
Parent Company Little, Brown Book Group
Contact Publishing Director, Lennie Goodings
Established 1973
Insider Info Catalogue available online.
Non-Fiction Publishes Autobiography, Biography and Illustrated titles on the following subjects:
Memoirs, Travel, Women's Issues/Studies
Submission Guidelines Agented submissions preferred.
Fiction Publishes Women's Literary Fiction titles.
Submission Guidelines Agented submissions preferred.
Poetry Publishes Poetry by female writers.
Submission Guidelines Agented submissions preferred.
Recent Title(s) *Apology for the Woman Writing*, Jenny Diski (Novel)
Tips Virago, founded by Carmen Callil, has grown into the largest women's imprint in the world. The Virago VS list publishes the best young female writers with an eclectic mix of subject matter and style. Virago Modern Classics incorporates a large backlist of female fiction. They are not currently accepting unsolicited manuscripts.

Virgin Books Ltd
Thames Wharf Studios, Rainville Road, London, W6 9HT

- 020 7386 3300
- 020 7836 3360
- info@virgin-books.co.uk
- www.virginbooks.com
Established 1991 (following a merger with publisher WH Allen)
Imprint(s) Black Lace
Nexus
Cheek
Virgin
Insider Info Catalogue available online.
Non-Fiction Publishes Autobiography, Biography, Cookery, General Non-Fiction, Gift, Humour, Illustrated, Multimedia, Reference and Self-Help titles on the following subjects:
Animals, Business/Economics, Cooking/Foods/Nutrition, Entertainment/Games, Health/Medicine, Memoirs, Music/Dance, Nature/Environment, Sex, Sport, Food and Drink/Wine, Fitness and Exercise, Health and Beauty, Leisure Books, Mind, Body and Spirit, Paranormal, Theatre and Drama, Cult Writing, Crime, Television and Film.
Fiction Publishes Erotica, Romance and General Adult Fiction.
Recent Title(s) *Max Clifford: Read All About It*, Max Clifford and Angela Levin

Virtue Books Ltd
Edward House, Tenter Street, Rotherham, S60 1LB
- 01709 365005
- 01709 829982
- info@russums.co.uk
- www.russums-shop.co.uk/virtuebooks.asp
Contact Director, Peter E. Russum; Editorial, Karen Harrison
Insider Info Catalogue available free on request and online.
Non-Fiction Publishes General Non-Fiction, How-To and Illustrated titles on the following subjects:
Cooking, Food & Drink, Nutrition
Tips Virtue has a reputation for publishing, supplying and recommending good cookery books to professional chefs and catering schools, students, cookery shops and leading department stores. Apart from occasional historical titles, Virtue Books no longer publish books, and are mainly involved with distribution.

Vital Spark
19 Netherton Avenue, Glasgow, Scotland, G13 1BQ
- 0141 954 8007
- 0141 954 8007
- info@nwp.co.uk
- www.nwp.co.uk

Parent Company Neil Wilson Publishing Ltd
Insider Info Catalogue and manuscript guidelines are available online.
Non-Fiction Publishes Illustrated Humour titles.
Submission Guidelines Submit proposal package (including outline, synopsis, one sample chapter, author biography, CV and SAE). Will accept artworks/images.
Fiction Publishes Illustrated Humour and Cartoon titles.
Recent Title(s) *Auld Lang Syne!*, Allan Morrison (Humour)
Tips Vital Spark is the humour imprint of Neil Wilson Publishing and will accept non-fiction humour submissions. They mostly publish cartoon illustrated titles, so submissions should include sample illustrations.

Wakefield Historical Publications
19 Pinder's Grove, Wakefield, West Yorkshire, WF1 4AH
- 01924 372748
- kate@airtime.co.uk
- www.wakefieldhistoricalsoc.org.uk
Parent Company Wakefield Historical Society
Contact President, Kate Taylor
Established 1977
Insider Info Publishes roughly two titles per year. Catalogue available online.
Non-Fiction Publishes Scholarly titles on the following subjects:
History, Regional Interest (West Riding)
Submission Guidelines Accepts query with SAE.
Recent Title(s) *The Castleford Pottery*, Diane Edwards Roussel
Tips Wakefield Historical Publications is the publishing arm of Wakefield Historical Society and handles scholarly non-fiction of regional and historical interest, mostly about the West Riding of Yorkshire. Unsolicited proposals are welcome, but only a small amount of work is published in any given year.

Walker Books
87 Vauxhall Walk, London, SE11 5HJ
- 020 7793 0909
- editorial@walker.co.uk
- www.walkerbooks.co.uk
Contact Publisher, Jane Winterbotham
Established 1978
Insider Info Catalogue available online.
Non-Fiction Publishes Audio cassettes, Children's, Young Adult, Gift, Illustrated and Reference titles and Big Books, Board Books, Character Books, Novelty and Activity Books on the following subjects:

Early Learning, Activity, Hobby and Craft, Biography, History, Arts, Life Issues, Animals, Environment and Conservation, Feelings, Language, Football, First Concepts
Submission Guidelines Approach with query in first instance. Mainly accepts agented submissions.
Fiction Publishes Adventure, Humour, Children's and Young Adult titles. Also publish Short Story Collections, Anthologies and Traditional Tales.
Submission Guidelines No fiction or picture book submissions. Agented submissions only.
Poetry Publishes Poetry titles.
Recent Title(s) *The Tale of Despereaux*, Kate Di Camillo (Novel); *Sweet Dreams, Maisy*, Lucy Cousins (Picture Book)
Tips In 1983 Walker became an independent company and is now a leading publisher of children's books in the UK. Titles are aimed at a wide age range, from babies to teenagers. Walker Books is happy to accept artwork samples and illustrated stories; see the website for submission details.

Wallflower Press
6 Market Place, London, W1W 8AF
- 020 7436 9494
- 020 7690 4333
- info@wallflowerpress.co.uk
- www.wallflowerpress.co.uk
Contact Commissioning Editor & Editorial Director, Yoram Allon
Established 1999
Insider Info Publishes 30 titles per year. Payment is via royalties. Catalogue available online.
Non-Fiction Publishes General Non-Fiction and Scholarly titles on the following subjects:
Contemporary Culture, Education, Film & Media Studies
Submission Guidelines Accepts query by email to Yoram Allon.
Submission details to: yoram@wallflowerpress.co.uk
Recent Title(s) *Dark Carnival: The Cinema of Neil Jordan*, Carole Zucker (ed.)
Tips Wallflower Press is an independent publishing house specialising in cinema and the moving image. They are devoted to the publication of the highest quality academic and popular literature in film, television and media studies, as well as related areas of the visual arts. Contact Yoram Allon, Commissioning Editor, to discuss proposals. You may then be invited to submit a full book proposal for further consideration.

The Warburg Institute
University of London, Woburn Square, London, WC1H 0AB
- 020 7862 8949

☎ 020 7862 8955
✉ warburg@sas.ac.uk
🌐 http://warburg.sas.ac.uk/publications/publications_index.htm
Contact Publications Assistant, Jenny Boyle; Editors (Warburg Journal), Jill Kraye and Elizabeth McGrath
Insider Info Catalogue available online.
Non-Fiction Publishes Scholarly titles on the following subject areas:
Art, Architecture, History, Philosophy, Science
Tips The Warburg Institute of the University of London exists principally to further the study of the classical tradition. It publishes books and journals on cultural and intellectual history, with reference to the classical tradition. The Institute also publishes its own journal, which does not solicit contributions.

Ward Lock Educational Co. Ltd
BIC Ling Kee House, 1 Christopher Road, East Grinstead, West Sussex, RH19 3BT
☎ 01342 318980
☎ 01342 410980
✉ wle@lingkee.com
🌐 www.wardlockeducational.com
Established 1952
Insider Info Catalogue available online or on request.
Non-Fiction Publishes Primary and Secondary Educational Resources on the following subjects:
English, Reading, Drama, Science, Music, Teaching, Maths
Tips Titles are mainly aimed at Key Stages 1–4. Also publishes resource materials for the Numeracy Hour and the Literacy Hour.

Warne
80 Strand, London, WC2R 0RL
☎ 020 7010 3000
☎ 020 7010 6060
✉ customer.service@penguin.co.uk
🌐 www.penguin.co.uk
Parent Company Penguin Group (UK)
Established 1865 (acquired by Penguin in 1983)
Insider Info Catalogue is available online. Manages character licences from classic children's literature. Does not publish new titles.
Fiction Publishes Children's, Illustrated and Picture Book titles.
Recent Title(s) *Spot's Playbook*, Eric Hill (Picture Book)
Tips Warne specialises in book-based children's character properties, including the *Beatrix Potter* titles and other classic children's titles such as the *Flower Fairies* and *Orlando the Marmalade Cat*. As such, they cannot accept unsolicited proposals.

For the main children's publishing programme at Penguin, see the entries for Puffin and Ladybird Books.

Watling Street
33 Hatherop, Near Cirencester, Gloucestershire, GL7 3NA
☎ 01285 750212
✉ chris.mclaren@saltwaypublishing.co.uk
Contact Editorial Director, Christine Kidney
Established 2000
Insider Info Publishes roughly 12 titles per year. Payment is via outright purchase. Simultaneous submissions are not accepted. Submissions will not be returned. Catalogue is available online. Author guidelines are not available.
Non-Fiction Publishes Children's and General Non-Fiction titles on the following subjects:
Gardening, History, Nature/Environment
Submission Guidelines Agented submissions only. Submission details to: chris.mclaren@saltwaypublishing.co.uk
Recent Title(s) *London's Gardens*, Lorna Parker (Guidebook)
Tips All unsolicited manuscripts will be returned unopened.

The Watts Publishing Group
338 Euston Road, London, NW1 3BH
☎ 020 7873 6000
☎ 020 7873 6024
🌐 www.orchardbooks.co.uk
Parent Company Hachette Children's Books
Established 1972
Imprint(s) Franklin Watts
Orchard Books
Cat's Whiskers
Insider Info Catalogue available online.
Non-Fiction Publishes Teacher Resources, Young Adult, Big Books and Children's titles on the following subjects:
Citizenship and PHSE, Special Needs, Religious Education, Geography - People and Environment, History through Story, Social History, Science, Technology, Art, Craft and Music, Hobbies and Pets
Submission Guidelines Agented submissions only.
Fiction Publishes Children's Picture Books, Gift Books, Novelty Books, Board Books, Graded Reading Books and Children's Classics.
Submission Guidelines Agented submissions only.
Poetry Publishes Children's Poetry titles.

Wayland
338 Euston Road, London, NW1 3BH
☎ 020 7873 6000
☎ 020 7873 6024

ad@hachettechildrens.co.uk
www.waylandbooks.co.uk
Parent Company Hachette Children's Books
Established 1972
Insider Info Catalogue available online.
Non-Fiction Publishes Children's Fiction, and Illustrated titles on Information and Education.
Submission Guidelines Agented submissions only.
Recent Title(s) *Grains and Cereals*, Good For Me series
Tips Titles must have quality educational content, and an up to date, appealing, child friendly approach to design.

The Waywiser Press
The Cottage, 14 Lyncroft Gardens, Ewell, KT17 1UR
020 8393 7055
020 8393 7055
waywiserpress@aol.com
www.waywiser-press.com
Contact Dr Philip Hoy (Poetry, Fiction, Memoir, Criticism)
Established 2001
Imprint(s) Between The Lines
Insider Info Publishes five or six titles per year. Receives approximately 500 queries and 1,000 manuscripts per year. 40 per cent of books published are from first-time authors, 85 per cent of books published are from unagented authors. Poetry submissions from people with no more than one previous collection must be entered for the annual Anthony Hecht Poetry Prize, deadline December 1st, with an entry fee of £15, and a prize to the winner of £1,750 plus publication in UK and USA. Payment is via royalty. Average lead time is nine months, with simultaneous submissions accepted. Aims to respond to queries and proposals within two weeks and manuscripts within twelve weeks. Catalogue and manuscript guidelines are available online.
Non-Fiction Publishes Autobiography, Biography, Illustrated and Scholarly titles on the following subjects:
History, Literary Criticism, Literary History, Memoirs, Poetry, Fiction
Submission Guidelines Accepts proposal package (including one to two sample chapters, your publishing history, author biography and SAE), and artworks/images (send photocopies). For full details, see www.waywiser-press.com/authors.html.
Fiction Publishes Novels and Short Story collection titles.
Submission Guidelines Accepts proposal package (including outline, one to two sample chapters, author biography and SAE). For full details, see www.waywiser-press.com/authors.html.

Poetry Publishes Contemporary Poetry collections.
Submission Guidelines Accepts complete manuscript. If author has no more than one previous collection published, submission must be via the annual Anthony Hecht Poetry Prize, whose deadline is December 1st. For full details, see www.waywiser-press.com/authors.html.
Recent Title(s) *Bundle o' Tinder*, Rose Kelleher; *Shuffle and Breakdown*, Cody Walker; *Seven American Poets in Conversation*, Between The Lines Paperback; *Identity Theft*, Joseph Harrison; *A Most Marvelous Piece of Luck*, Greg Williamson
Tips Waywiser Press titles are aimed at a general literary readership. The press is currently seeking submissions for poetry, fiction, literary history and criticism, memoir and biography. See the website for further details, at: www.waywiser-press.com/authors.html.

WBI Media & Entertainment
Paulton House, 8 Sheperdess Walk, London, , N1 7LB
020 7549 8666
020 7549 8666
orders@wbime.com
www.wbime.com
Contact Managing Director, Les Kelly
Established 1967
Insider Info Catalogue available online via website.
Non-Fiction Publishes Reference titles and Directories.
Recent Title(s) *Press Gazette*; *Hollis UK PR Annual*; *Hollis Europe Hollis Sponsorship & Donations Yearbook*; *Benn's Media Guide*; *Advertisers Annual*; *Showcase Music Directory*; *CES - Corporate Event Services*; *ASK Hollis*
Tips WBI Media & Entertainment is the leading publisher of directories and online information for public relations, media, advertising, sponsorship and marketing.

Weidenfeld & Nicholson
Orion House, 5 Upper St Martin's Lane, London, WC2H 9EA
020 7240 3444
020 7240 4822
www.orionbooks.co.uk
Parent Company Orion Publishing Group Ltd
Contact Managing Director, Malcolm Edwards; Publisher, Alan Samson
Established 1949
Imprint(s) Weidenfeld Illustrated
Weidenfeld General
Weidenfeld Fiction
Cassell Reference

Insider Info Catalogue available online, or via an online form.

Non-Fiction Publishes Autobiography, Biography, Cookbook, General Non-Fiction, Gift, How-To, Illustrated, Reference, Self-Help, Diaries and Letters, Television Tie-Ins, Dictionaries and Guide titles on the following subjects:
Child Guidance/Parenting, Cooking/Foods/Nutrition, History, Memoirs, Military/War, Science

Submission Guidelines Agented submissions only.

Fiction Publishes Literary, Mainstream/Contemporary and Translation titles.

Submission Guidelines Agented submissions only.

Recent Title(s) *Robert Pattinson: True Love Never Dies*, Josie Rusher (Biography); *Demi Lovato: Me And You*, Posy Edwards (Biography)

Tips Weidenfeld & Nicholson publishes a range of titles under its various imprints: Weidenfeld Illustrated publishes high-quality illustrated non-fiction on subjects such as arts & craft, gardening, lifestyle and history; Weidenfeld General covers general non-fiction including military history; and Weidenfeld Fiction publishes a range of literary and commercial fiction. For more information on Cassell Reference see the individual entry.

Wendy Webb Books

9 Walnut Close, Taverham, Norwich, NR8 6YN

☎ 07989 174076

✉ wwbuk@yahoo.co.uk

🌐 www.webbw.freeserve.co.uk

Contact Wendy Webb

Fiction Publishes Children's Fiction titles.

Poetry Publishes Poetry titles.

* Wendy Webb has invented a new poetry form, the 'Davidian'. Writers are encouraged to try it out.

Tips Contact from writers is invited by email.

WF Graham

2 Pondwood Close, Moulton Park, Northampton, NN3 6RT

☎ 01604 645537

☎ 01604 648414

✉ books@wfgraham.co.uk

🌐 www.wfgraham.co.uk

Non-Fiction Publishes Children's Colouring and Activity titles.

Recent Title(s) *Countryside to Colour; Magic Painting Book*

Tips WF Graham only publish colouring books and related items, therefore will not accept submissions from children's writers.

W. Green

21 Alva Street, Edinburgh, EH2 4PS

☎ 0131 225 4879

☎ 0131 225 2104

✉ wgreen.enquiries@thomson.com

🌐 www.wgreen.co.uk

Parent Company Sweet & Maxwell Group

Contact Publisher, Jill Hyslop; Director, Gilly Grant; Head of Editorial Operations, Rebecca Standing

Insider Info Catalogue and manuscript guidelines available online.

Non-Fiction Publishes Textbooks, Multimedia, Reference and Scholarly titles on the following subjects:
Law, and Scottish Law

* The aim of the company is to provide the Scottish legal profession with practical, quality information. Welcomes new proposals that share the same goal.

Submission Guidelines Fill out the online proposal form and send it to Jill Hyslop.
Submission details to: jill.hyslop@thomson.com

Tips New writers welcome. They regularly publish first-time authors and can give advice and support where required.

Wharncliffe Publishing

47 Church Street, Barnsley, S70 2AS

☎ 01226 734639

☎ 01226 734478

✉ editorial@wharncliffepublishing.co.uk

🌐 www.wharncliffepublishing.co.uk

Parent Company Pen & Sword Books, Acredula Group

Non-Fiction Publishes General Non-Fiction titles on the following subjects:
History and Regional.

Submission Guidelines Accepts query with SAE.

Tips Publishes local history books in conjunction with Pen & Sword. Also publishes niche magazines, newspapers and business to business materials. No unsolicited manuscripts.

Wharton School Publishing

Edinburgh Gate, Harlow, Essex, CM20 2JE

☎ 01279 623623

☎ 01279 414130

✉ gydeb@wharton.upenn.edu

🌐 www.pearsoned.co.uk/imprints/wharton

Parent Company Pearson Education

Contact Managing Director, Barbara Gyde; Chair of the Editorial Board, David C. Scmittlein; Editor-in-Chief, Timothy C. Moore

Insider Info Catalogue and manuscripts guidelines are available online.

Non-Fiction Publishes Multimedia, Reference and Scholarly titles on the following subjects:
Business, Economics, Finance, Management Practices, Policy.

Submission Guidelines Accepts proposal package (including synopsis, sample chapters, market research, your publishing history and author biography).

Recent Title(s) *Key Marketing Metrics*, Paul Farris, Neil Bendle, Phillip Pfeifer and David Reibstein (Business)

Tips A joint venture between Pearson Education and The Wharton School of the University of Pennsylvania, Wharton publishes books and management tools in a range of formats, including print, audio and electronic titles. By publishing many of the world's leading business authors Wharton School Publishing aims to provide practical knowledge that can be applied by business people and policy makers. See the website for full list of editorial contacts.

Which? Books

2 Marylebone Road, London, NW1 4DF

- 020 7770 7000
- 020 7770 7600
- which@which.co.uk
- www.which.net

Contact Editorial Director, Helen Parker

Established 1957

Insider Info Publishes 30 titles per year. Payment is via royalties. Catalogue available online.

Non-Fiction Publishes General Non-Fiction, Multimedia and Reference titles: Business/Economics, Cooking/Foods/Nutrition, Counselling/Career, Guidance, Education, Health/Medicine, House and Home, Law, Money/Finance, Housing, Technology

Submission Guidelines Accepts query with SAE.

Recent Title(s) *The Good Food Guide 2008*, Which?

Tips Which? Books are packed with independent and unbiased research, to help you make informed choices about what brand or service to buy. Which? also publishes *Which? Magazine*. Unsolicited manuscripts are not accepted, but Which? is open to queries and ideas for new topics.

White Ladder Press

Great Ambrook, Near Ipplepen, Devon, TQ12 5UL

- 01803 813343
- 01803 813928
- enquiries@whiteladderpress.com
- www.whiteladderpress.com

Contact Publisher, Roni Jay

Established 2003

Insider Info Publishes 12 titles per year. Payment is via royalties. Catalogue and manuscript guidelines available online.

Non-Fiction Publishes General Non-Fiction, How-To and Reference titles on the following subjects:

Child Guidance/Parenting, Gardening, Health/Medicine, House and Home, Miscellaneous/Practical

Submission Guidelines Accepts query with SAE. Submit proposal package (including outline and market research).

Recent Title(s) *Sneaky Parenting*, Jo Wiltshire

Tips White Ladder Press publishes practical lifestyle books with a broad appeal and a quirky angle. Their mission statement says, 'We want to teach old dogs new tricks, by presenting a new angle on everyday living. We want to intrigue, entertain and be useful at the same time'. They are very clear about precisely what constitutes a White Ladder book and reject plenty of their own ideas because they don't fit the bill. Consequently they will be as brutal with you as they are with themselves. All White Ladder titles must be quirky in some way, be practical, have plenty of obvious marketing channels outside the book trade, and must attract media interest.

Whittet Books

South House, Yatesbury Manor, Yatesbury, SN11 8YE

- 01672 539004
- 01672 555555
- info@whittetbooks.com
- www.whittetbooks.com

Parent Company A Whittet & Co Ltd

Contact Annabel Whittet (Natural History, Horses, Horticulture)

Established 1976

Insider Info Publishes six titles per year. 40 per cent of books published are from first-time authors and 95 per cent of books published are from unagented authors. Payment is via royalty (on retail price) with 0.1 (per £) minimum and 0.15 (per £) maximum, outright purchase is from £500. Average lead time is six months, with simultaneous submissions accepted. Submissions accompanied by SAE will be returned. Aims to respond to queries in ten days, proposals in 14 days and manuscripts in eight weeks. Catalogue is free on request. Author guidelines are not available.

Non-Fiction Publishes General Non-Fiction and Illustrated titles on the following subjects: Agriculture/Horticulture, Animals (reference books, not anecdotal), Gardening, Nature/Environment (reference books).

* Memoirs are not published

Submission Guidelines Accepts query with SAE, or via email, and artworks/images (send photocopies). Submission details to: annabel@whittet.dircon.co.uk

Recent Title(s) *The New Hedgehog Book*, Pat Morris

Tips Titles are aimed at a broad, general readership.

Whittles Publishing

Dunbeath Mains Cottages, Dunbeath, Caithness, KW6 6EY

☎ 01593 731333

☎ 01593 731400

✉ info@whittlespublishing.com

🌐 www.whittlespublishing.com

Contact Publisher, Keith Whittles

Insider Info Payment is via royalties. Catalogue and manuscript guidelines available online

Non-Fiction Publishes General Non-Fiction, Reference, Scholarly and Technical titles on the following subjects:

History, Marine Subjects, Military/War, Nature/Environment, Civil/Structural Engineering

Submission Guidelines Accepts query with SAE. Submit proposal package (including outline, two sample chapter(s) and SAE).

Fiction Publishes Classic Fiction titles

Recent Title(s) *Tooth & Claw, living with Britain's predators*, Peter Cairns and Mark Hamblin

Tips Whittles have particular specialisms in the following subjects; geomatics, civil and structural engineering, and applied science. They are also developing new lists in specific disciplines, including engineering geomorphology and geotechnics. Whittles are always pleased to receive ideas or proposals for new technical books within the spheres of interest, whether authors are in academia or industry. Suggestions for new non-technical books within topics such as pharology, military history, and nature writing are also very welcome. An initial telephone call may prove constructive to discuss a proposal.

Wiley-Blackwell

The Atrium, Southern Gate, Chichester, West Sussex, PO19 8SQ

☎ 01243 779777

☎ 01243 775878

🌐 www.wiley.com

Parent Company John Wiley & Sons Inc (see entry under European & International Publishers)

Established 2001

Imprint(s) BMJ Books

Blackwell Futura

Insider Info Publishes 650 titles per year, and 805 Journals per year. Catalogue and manuscript guidelines are available online.

Non-Fiction Publishes Journals, Multimedia, Reference, Scholarly and Textbook titles on the following subjects:

Agriculture and Aquaculture, Animal Science, Applied Arts, Architecture, Art History and Theory, Business, Construction, Economics, Finance and Accounting, Humanities, Property, Engineering and Technology, Law and Criminology, Life and Physical Sciences, Mathematics and Statistics, Medicine, Music, Nursing Health and Dentistry, Performing Arts, Social and Behavioural Studies, Veterinary Medicine

Submission Guidelines Accepts proposal package (including outline, sample chapters, your publishing history and author biography) by email to the relevant editorial contact, details of which may be found on the website.

Recent Title(s) *Online Marketing Heroes: Interviews with 25 Successful Online Marketing Gurus*, Michael Miller (Computing); *Guitar Exercises For Dummies*, Mark Phillips and Jon Chappell (Music/How-To)

Tips Wiley-Blackwell was created in 2007 when Blackwell Publishing merged with Wiley's Global Scientific, Technical, and Medical business, and is now one of the world's foremost academic and professional publishers and the largest society publisher. There is an extensive list of departmental editorial contacts published on the website, which potential authors should consult in order to direct their email to the appropriate department. There is also detailed information on how to prepare proposals and how books and authors are dealt with at Wiley-Blackwell.

Wiley Nautical

The Atrium, Southern Gate, Chichester, West Sussex, PO19 8SQ

☎ 01243 770372

☎ 01243 770481

✉ nautical@wiley.co.uk

🌐 www.wileynautical.com

Parent Company John Wiley & Sons Inc (see entry under European & International Publishers)

Contact Publisher, Simon Davison; Commissioning Editor, David Palmer

Established 1979

Insider Info Publishes 12 titles per year. Receives approximately 30 queries per year. 50 per cent of books published are from first-time authors and 90 per cent are from unagented authors. Payment via royalty with 0.1 (per £) maximum. An advance is offered. Average lead time is one year with simultaneous submissions not accepted. Catalogue is available online.

Non-Fiction Publishes General Non-Fiction, How-To, Reference and Technical titles on the following subjects:

Hobbies, Marine Subjects, Recreation, Sports, Transportation

Recent Title(s) *Be Your Own Sailing Coach: 20 Goals for Racing Success*, Jon Emmett (Yachting)

Tips Formerly know as Fernhurst Books. Titles are aimed at nautical sports/watersports/sailing enthusiasts and professional sailors.

William Andrew

Linacre House, Jordan Hill, Oxford, OX2 8DP

☎ 01865 474010

☎ 01865 474011

✉ authorsupport@elsevier.com

🌐 www.elsevier.com

Parent Company Elsevier Ltd (Science & Technology)

Insider Info Authors paid by royalty. Catalogue and author guidelines available online.

Non-Fiction Publishes Multimedia, Textbooks, Reference, Scholarly and Technical titles on the following subjects:
Cosmetics & Pharmaceuticals, Electrical & Electronics Engineering, Energy, Environmental Engineering, Industrial Chemicals, Materials, Micro & Nanotechnology, Safety, Surface Engineering, Emerging Technologies.

Submission Guidelines Accepts query with SAE. Submit proposal package (including outline and sample chapter if possible).

Recent Title(s) *Global Regulatory Issues for the Cosmetics Industry*, Lintner (Reference)

Tips William Andrew is dedicated to publishing world class technical and scientific materials, both books and databases, that promote knowledge, technology, and productivity. William Andrew is also know for the *Noyes* publications and the *Plastics Design Library Series*.

William Heinemann

Random House, 20 Vauxhall Bridge Road, London, SW1V 2SA

☎ 020 7840 8707

☎ 020 7233 6127

✉ heinemanneditorial@randomhouse.co.uk

🌐 www.randomhouse.co.uk

Parent Company The Random House Group Ltd

Contact Publishing Director, Ravi Mirchandani

Insider Info Catalogue available online.

Non-Fiction Publishes General Non-Fiction titles.

Submission Guidelines No unagented submissions.

Fiction Publishes General, Women's Fiction, Crime and Thriller titles.

Submission Guidelines No unagented submissions.

Recent Title(s) *The Last Watch*, Sergei Lukyanenko (Novel); *Bad Vibes: Britpop and my part in its downfall*, Luke Haines (Non-Fiction)

Willow Bank Publishers Ltd

E-Space North, 181 Wisbech Road, Littleport, Ely, CB8 8X 1RA

☎ 0800 731 5258

✉ editorial@willowbankpublishers.co.uk

🌐 www.willowbankpublishers.co.uk

Contact Christopher Sims

Imprint(s) Willow Books
Derringer Books
Butterfly Books
Fen Books

Insider Info Payment is via royalties. Catalogue and manuscript guidelines available online.

Non-Fiction Publishes Children's and General Non-Fiction titles.

Submission Guidelines Accepts query with SAE. Submit proposal package (including outline, two sample chapters and SAE).

Fiction Publishes Children's, Mainstream/ Contemporary, Mystery and Crime titles.

Submission Guidelines Accepts query with SAE. Submit proposal package (including outline and two sample chapters).

Recent Title(s) *White Roads to Akyab*, James Meridew

Tips Willow Bank publishes general fiction and non-fiction, as well as crime fiction under thier Derringer imprint. The Butterfly Books imprint publishes children's non-fiction, fiction and poetry. The newly established Fen Books imprint is a mainstream publisher of literary fiction from authors with a proven writing history. Any book accepted by Fen Books will be funded entirely by the company and may also receive an advance. Willow Bank Publishers may choose to offer either a traditional or author-funded publishing agreement for authors whose work meets the required standard set by their publishing panel, but whose commercial viability is not quite strong enough.

Windhorse Publications

38 Newmarket Road, Cambridge, CB5 8DT

☎ 01223 911997

✉ info@windhorsepublications.com

🌐 www.windhorsepublications.com

Contact General Manager, Caroline Jestaz

Established 1972

Insider Info Publishes six titles per year. Receives approximately 100 queries and 50 manuscripts from writers each year. 20 per cent of books published are from first-time authors and 100 per cent of books published are from unagented authors. Payment is via royalty with 0.08 (per £) minimum and 0.1 (per £) maximum. Average lead time is 18 months with simultaneous submissions accepted. Submissions accompanied by SAE will be returned. Aims to respond to queries within 28 days, and proposals and manuscripts within three months. Catalogue is free on request, and available online or via email.

Non-Fiction Publishes books on Buddhism, from introductory guides to translations and commentaries on traditional texts, as well as guides to help develop or deepen meditation practices and titles offering a Buddhist perspective on a range of prevalent topics.

* Windhorse Publications are a charity, so can only accept books in the field of Buddhism and Buddhist meditation.

Submission Guidelines Accepts a proposal package (including outline, three sample chapters, author biography and SAE). Will not review artwork/images as part of the manuscript package. Submission details to: sarah.ryan@ windhorsepublications.com

Recent Title(s) *A Guide to the Buddhas*, Vessantara; *A Guide to the Bodhisattvas*, Vessantara; *A Guide to the Deities of the Tantra*, Vessantara

Tips Potential audiences are those interested in Buddhism, exploring Buddhism or practitioners of Buddhism. Also those interested in awakening and self development more generally, and in discovering a Buddhist perspective on this.

Witan Books

Cherry Tree House, 8 Nelson Crescent, Cotes Heath, Stafford, Staffordshire, ST21 6ST
- 01782 791673
- witan@mail.com

Contact Director, Jeff Kent
Established 1980
Insider Info Publishes one title per year on average. Payment is via royalty (on retail price). Simultaneous submissions are accepted. Submissions accompanied by SAE will be returned. Aims to respond to queries, proposals and manuscripts within 14 days. Catalogue not available. Author guidelines available via SAE.

Non-Fiction Publishes Autobiography, Biography, Booklets, Coffee Table, General Non-Fiction, Illustrated, Reference and Scholarly titles on the following subjects:
Alternative Lifestyles, Animals, Business/Economics, Community/Public Affairs, Creative Non-Fiction, Education, Government/Politics, History, Humanities, Marine Subjects, Music/Dance, Nature/Environment, New Age, Philosophy, Recreation, Science, Social Sciences, Sociology, Spirituality, Sports, Transportation, Travel, World Affairs

Submission Guidelines Accepts query with SAE (including A4 synopsis and potential readership) and artworks/images (send photocopies).

Recent Title(s) *The Constitution of Mercia*, The Mercian Constitutional Convention; *The Mysterious Double Sunset*, Jeff Kent

Tips Titles are aimed at a general non-fiction market. The company began life as a self-publisher, but now publishes other authors' work.

WIT Press

Ashurst Lodge, Ashurst, Southampton, SO40 7AA
- 023 8029 3223
- 023 8029 2853
- witpress@witpress.com
- www.witpress.com

Contact Chairman, Prof. Carlos Brebbia
Established 1980
Insider Info Publishes 50 titles per year. Payment is via royalties. Catalogue and manuscript guidelines are available online.

Non-Fiction Publishes Reference, Scholarly and Technical titles on the following subjects: Art/Architecture, Computers/Electronics, Science, Technology, Civil/Electrical Engineering

Submission Guidelines Submission sheets are available on the website.

Recent Title(s) *Eco-Architecture II*, M.A. Atherton (Hardback)

Tips All books are aimed at postgraduate level and above. To assist authors and contributors with the keying of their work to the standard required, they have made available 'Instructions for Authors' and 'Example Sheets' on the website. It is important that you use the correct set of instructions, as there are four, each pertaining to a different size of book.

Wizard Books

The Old Dairy, Brook Road, Thriplow, Cambridge, SG8 7RG
- 01763 208008
- 01763 208080
- wizard@iconbooks.co.uk
- www.iconbooks.co.uk/wizard

Parent Company Icon Books
Contact Managing Director, Peter Pugh; Publishing Director, Simon Flynn; Editorial Director, Duncan Heath
Established 2002
Insider Info Publishes around four titles per year.
Non-Fiction Publishes Illustrated Children's titles for ages eight to thirteen.

Submission Guidelines Query with SAE. Include a detailed proposal (for what to include in this section, see the website), synopsis, table of contents, sample of writing and CV (listing any relevant previous publications) or author biography.

Fiction Publishes Children's Fiction titles for ages eight to thirteen.

Submission Guidelines Query with SAE. Include a detailed proposal (for what to include in this section, see the website), synopsis, table of contents, sample of writing and CV (listing any relevant previous publications) or author biography.

Recent Title(s) *The Toxic Toadburger Conspiracy*,
Ian Hills
Tips Specialises in children's fantasy gaming books.
For detailed submission guidelines, visit the website.
The current emphasis is on books aimed at children
aged nine and older.

Wolfhound Press
Newmarket Hall, Cork Street, Dublin 8, Republic of Ireland
- 00353 1 453 5866
- 00353 1 453 5930
- publishing@merlin.ie
- www.merlinwolfhound.com

Parent Company Merlin Publishing
Contact Editorial Manager, Aoife Barrett
Established 1974
Insider Info Catalogue and manuscript guidelines
are available online.
Non-Fiction Publishes Children's and General Non-
Fiction (Irish Interest) titles.
Submission Guidelines Accepts proposal package
(including outline, synopsis, one sample chapter,
marketing information, author biography and SAE or
IRC for overseas replies). Will accept artworks/images
(send photocopies or digital files as jpegs). Send
submissions by post or email.
Submission details to: aoife@merlin.ie
Fiction Publishes the Liam O'Flaherty backlist of Irish
novels and story collections as well as
children's fiction.
Submission Guidelines Will not be publishing any
new fiction for the near future.
Recent Title(s) *Run with the Wind*, Tom McCaughren
(Children's)
Tips Wolfhound Press has a well-known reputation
for producing high quality books of Irish interest,
along with a range of children's books. Wolfhound
also publishes the collected fiction of Irish author
Liam O'Flaherty, but will not accept any further
fiction submissions.

Wolters Kluwer (UK) Ltd
145 London Road, Kingston upon Thames, Surrey, KT2 6SR
- 020 8547 3333
- 020 8547 2637
- info@croner.co.uk
- www.wolterskluwer.co.uk

Established 1948
Non-Fiction Publishes Multimedia, Reference and
Technical titles on the following subjects:
Business/Economics, Law, Money/Finance,
Insurance, Taxation
Recent Title(s) *British Master Tax Guide 2007/2008*

Tips CCH is a trading name of Wolters Kluwer (UK)
Limited. They are a leading supplier of information
for accountants, tax practitioners and financial
professionals, whether in practice or in business,
both in the UK and globally. CCH publishes a wide
variety of products – from reference books, CD-
ROMs and online information services, to software
packages, professional development programmes
and fee protection services. As CCH is an information
supplier, any publications must be on top of the
latest developments and regulatory changes in the
accountancy world.

The Women's Press
27 Goodge Street, London, W1T 2LD
- 020 763 63992
- 020 763 71866
- david@the-womens-press.com
- www.the-womens-press.com

Contact Managing Director, Stella Kane
Established 1978
Imprint(s) Women's Press Classics
Livewire Books for Teenagers
Insider Info Publishes 50 titles per year. Payment is
via royalties. Catalogue available online.
Non-Fiction Publishes Autobiography, Biography
and General Non-Fiction titles on the
following subjects:
Contemporary Culture, Government/Politics, Health/
Medicine, History, Psychology, Sex, Women's Issues/
Studies
Submission Guidelines Agented submissions only.
Fiction Publishes Literary, Mainstream/
Contemporary and Young Adult titles.
Submission Guidelines Agented submissions only.
Recent Title(s) *Soul Kiss*, Shay Youngblood; *Mud
Puppy*, Erica Wooff
Tips The Women's Press is dedicated to publishing
incisive feminist fiction and non-fiction by
outstanding women writers from all round the
world. They will only publish books written by
women and even then, only if there is a female
protagonist (for fiction) or the book deals with
women's issues (for non-fiction). A series of up-front,
contemporary, issue driven works of fiction and non-
fiction for young women are published in the
Livewire list. A series of classic works by women are
published through the Women's Press Classics list.

Wooden Books
The Walkmill, Cascob, Presteigne, Powys, LD8 2NT
- 01547 560251
- 01547 560113
- info@woodenbooks.com
- www.woodenbooks.com

Contact Managing Director, John Martineau
Established 1996
Insider Info Catalogue available online.
Non-Fiction Publishes General Non-Fiction, Illustrated and Scholarly titles on the following subjects:
Science, Spirituality, Magic, Mathematics, Folklore, Ancient Sciences
Recent Title(s) *Ancient British Rock Art*, Chris Mansell
Tips Wooden Books is a series of small, beautifully produced introductions to the liberal arts, aimed at scientists and artists alike. The books are produced with exquisite illustrations, superfine printing, and the finest quality recycled papers. Wooden Books is actively seeking illustrators and cartoonists to work on the Wooden Books series.

The Woodfield Press
17 Jamestown Square, Dublin 8, Republic of Ireland
● 00353 1 454 7991
● terri.mcdonnell@ireland.com
● www.woodfield-press.com
Contact Director, Terri McDonnell
Established 1995
Insider Info Catalogue available online.
Non-Fiction Publishes General Non-Fiction and Scholarly titles on the following subjects:
Biography, Gaelic Culture, Local History, Social History, Women's Studies
Recent Title(s) *From the Margins to the Centre - A History of the Irish Times*, Dermot James
Tips The Woodfield Press is a Dublin-based publisher of books which conform to academic standards but are accessible in style and written, generally, with the non-academic in mind.

Woodhead Publishing Ltd
Abington Hall, Abington, Cambridge, CB1 6AH
● 01223 891358
● 01223 893694
● wp@woodheadpublishing.com
● www.woodheadpublishing.com
Contact Editorial Director, Francis Dodds
Established 1989
Insider Info Publishes 50 titles per year. Payment is via royalties. Catalogue available free on request and online. Manuscript guidelines available online.
Non-Fiction Publishes Reference and Technical titles on the following subjects:
Cooking/Foods/Nutrition, Money/Finance, Science, Technology, Engineering and Construction, Environmental Technology
Submission Guidelines Accepts query with SAE. Submit proposal package (including outline and two sample chapters)

Recent Title(s) *Environmentally PCompatible Food ackaging*, E. Cheillini
Tips A leading independent international publishing company. Following initial success in the materials engineering area, they have expanded substantially and now also publish on food science, technology and nutrition, welding and metallurgy, textile technology, environmental technology, finance, commodities, and investment. Woodhead is always pleased to hear proposals from authors for new books. If there is a subject that doesn't appear in the catalogue, or you can't find the book you want, or think you could write a book, or contribute a chapter, contact the editorial staff.

Wordsonthestreet
Six San Antonio Park, Salthill, Co. Galway, Republic of Ireland
● publisher@wordsonthestreet.com
● www.wordsonthestreet.com
Contact Directors: Gerardine Burke and Tony O'Dwyer; Editorial Assistant, Judith Gannon
Imprint(s) 6th House
Insider Info Catalogue available online. Author guidelines available online.
Member of CLÉ, The Irish Book Publishers' Association.
Non-Fiction Publishes General Non-Fiction titles on the following subjects:
Biography, History, Irish Interest, Memoir.
Fiction Publishes Novels/Novellas, Drama, Poetry and Short Story Collections.
Submission Guidelines Accepts proposal package (including synopsis, author biography and three sample chapters) by post only. For collections include three sample short stories or ten sample poems.
Recent Title(s) *Eclipsed*, Patricia Burke Brogan (Drama); *Liar, Liar*, Alan McMonagle (Short Story Collection)
Tips Only accepts submissions by post, but include an email address for reply. The 6th House imprint handles general non-fiction.

Wordsworth Editions Ltd
8b East Street, Ware, Hertfordshire, SG12 9HJ
● 01920 465167
● 01920 462267
● enquiries@wordsworth-editions.com
● www.wordsworth-editions.com
Contact Managing Director (Sales), Helen Trayler; Derek Wright (Finance, Marketing), Avril Strange (Customer Orders)
Established 1986
Insider Info Publishes 20 titles per year. Receives approximately five to ten queries and six

manuscripts from writers each year. 100 per cent of books are from unagented authors. Payment is via outright purchase. Submissions accompanied by SAE will be returned. Catalogue is free on request, online and via email. Manuscript guidelines are not available.

Non-Fiction Publishes Reference titles on the following subjects:
Language Dictionaries and Guides to Language, Dictionaries of History and Dates, Quotations, Drink, Medical Facts, Sexuality, Symbols, Opera and Folklore (Out of Copyright)
* Most reference works are written by specialists in their field.
Submission Guidelines No submissions, all work is specially commissioned. Will not review artwork/images as part of a manuscript package.
Fiction Publishes Gothic, Horror, Classic Fiction, Children's and Mystery titles
* Does not publish living authors of fiction.
Poetry Publishes some Poetry
* No living authors.
Recent Title(s) *Labour & the London Poor*, Henry Mayhew (Reference); *The Complete Illustrated Lewis Carroll*, Lewis Carroll (Children's)
Tips Typical audiences are those with a general interest in fiction, and students. Do not send in any submissions, any new non-fiction works are always commissioned, while the rest of the publishing programme is made up of reprints.

Wordwell Books
Media House, South County Business Park, Leopardstown, Dublin 18, Republic of Ireland
- 00353 1 294 7860
- 00353 1 294 7861
- helen@wordwellbooks.com
- www.wordwellbooks.com
Established 1986
Imprint(s) Rathdown Press
Insider Info Catalogue available online.
Non-Fiction Publishes General Non-Fiction and Scholarly titles on the following subjects:
Archaeology, Crafts, Disability, Health & Health Care, Irish History, Maps.
Recent Title(s) *The Light of Other Days*, Sam Hutchison; *The Ballyhoura Hills Project*, Martin Doody
Tips Wordwell is best known as the publisher of *Excavations* and as a key partner in Archaeology Ireland and History Ireland. The Rathdown Press imprint publishes titles on health and health care, disability and related subjects.

Working White Ltd
Chancery Court, Lincolns Inn, Lincoln Road, High Wycombe, Buckinghamshire, HP12 3RE
- 01494 429318
- 01494 429317
- info@workingwhite.co.uk
- www.workingwhite.co.uk
Contact Erica Filler
Imprint(s) Poppy Red
Insider Info Catalogue is available free on request and via email: sales@workingwhite.co.uk
Non-Fiction Publishes Children's and Illustrated titles.
Fiction Publishes Children's titles.
Tips Working White is an independent publisher of co-edition children's books for the international market. Titles are aimed at children of pre-school age through to young teenagers. Poppy Red is the sister company, which publishes and distributes the books solely in the UK. Working White children's books are always illustrated and informative, and usually have an extra 'interactive' component such as pop-up, touch and feel sections, or kit-books.

Worple Press
Achill Sound, 2B Dry Hill Road, Tonbridge, TN9 IJE
- 01732 368958
- 01732 352057
- theworpleco.@aol.com
- www.worplepress.com
Contact Director, Peter Carpenter; Director, Amanda Carpenter
Established 1997
Insider Info Publishes five titles per year. Payment is via royalties. Catalogue available free on request.
Non-Fiction Publishes General Non-Fiction titles on Art/Architecture.
Poetry Publishes Poetry titles.
Tips Worple Press is an independent publisher of poetry and art books.

Wrecking Ball Press
24 Cavendish Square, Hull, East Yorkshire, HU3 1SS
- editor@wreckingballpress.com
- www.wreckingballpress.com
Contact Managing Editor, Shane Rhodes
Insider Info Catalogue and manuscript guidelines available online.
Fiction Publishes Mainstream/Contemporary titles and Short story collections.
Submission Guidelines Submit completed manuscript.
Poetry Publishes poetry titles.
Submission Guidelines Submit complete manuscript.
Recent Title(s) *Stranger in the House*, Brendan Cleary (Poetry); *Digging the Vein*, Tony O'Neill (Novel)

Tips Wrecking Ball Press is an independent press specialising in poetry and contemporary fiction. It also publishes a poetry journal, *The Reater*, and specialises in 'blunt, hammered-home words'. If you wish to submit any poems or stories for inclusion in *The Reater* there is a limit of six poems and two stories per person. Illustrations and photographs will also be accepted for consideration and manuscripts can also be submitted. If possible all submissions should be on a disk, as well as paper.

Xcite Books
PO Box 26, Treharris, Cardiff, CF46 9AG
- 01443 710930
- 01443 710940
- info@accentpress.co.uk
- www.xcitebooks.moonfruit.com

Parent Company Accent Press
Contact Editor, Miranda Forbes
Insider Info Catalogue is free on request, and available online. Manuscript guidelines are available via email: editor@xcitebooks.com
Fiction Publishes Erotica titles.
Submission Guidelines Email Miranda Forbes for more information.
Submission details to: editor@xcitebooks.com
Poetry Publishes Erotic Poetry.
Submission Guidelines Email Miranda Forbes for more information.
Submission details to: editor@xcitebooks.com
Recent Title(s) *Spank Me: 20 Erotic Stories*, Cathryn Cooper (ed.) (Short Story Collection); *The First Deadly Sin*, Gwen Masters
Tips Short story collections are published mainly in three series; *Sex and Seduction; Sex and Submission*; and *Sex and Satisfaction*.

The X Press
PO Box 25694, London, N17 6FP
- 020 8801 2100
- 020 8885 1322
- vibes@xpress.co.uk
- www.xpress.co.uk

Contact Editorial Director, Dotun Adebayo; Publisher, Steve Pope
Established 1992
Imprint(s) Black Classics
Nia
20/20
Insider Info Publishes 25 titles per year. Catalogue available online.
Fiction Publishes Children's/Teenage, Literary, Mainstream/Contemporary and Black interest titles.
Submission Guidelines Submit completed manuscript.
Recent Title(s) *Black Rising Star*, Peter Kalu (Novel)

Tips The X Press has grown into Europe's largest publisher of black interest books. The Nia imprint publishes literary black fiction, 20/20 publishes contemporary black fiction, and the Black Classics series re-prints classic novels by black writers. The X Press also publishes general black fiction aimed at a younger audience, and aims to take black writing into a new era. Prefers full manuscript submissions rather than proposals, preferably black interest popular fiction from black writers.

Yale University Press (London)
47 Bedford Square, London, WC1B 3DP
- 020 7079 4900
- 020 7079 4901
- sales@yaleup.co.uk
- www.yalebooks.co.uk

Established 1961
Insider Info Publishes 300 titles per year. Payment is via royalties. Catalogue available free on request and online.
Non-Fiction Publishes Autobiography, Biography, General Non-Fiction, Reference and Scholarly titles on the following subjects:
Art/Architecture, Business/Economics, Education, Government/Politics, Health/Medicine, History, Language/Literature, Law, Literary Criticism, Music/Dance, Nature/Environment, Philosophy, Psychology, Religion
Submission Guidelines Accepts query with SAE.
Recent Title(s) *After Iraq*, Gywnne Dyer
Tips The London office of Yale University Press was established in 1961 as a marketing base, and in 1973 commenced publishing its own list. It has several book series, including *Yale Nota Bene* paperbacks, the *Pevsner Architectural Guides*, and books for the National Gallery. Yale London publishes scholarly books on a range of subjects, including life writing, but always with a wide appeal that may appeal to the general reader.

Yellow Jersey Press
Random House, 20 Vauxhall Bridge Road, London, SW1V 2SA
- 020 7840 8621
- 020 7233 6117
- yellowjerseyeditorial@randomhouse.co.uk
- www.randomhouse.co.uk

Parent Company The Random House Group Ltd
Contact Editorial Director, Tristan Jones
Insider Info Catalogue available online.
Non-Fiction Publishes General Non-Fiction, Sports and Leisure Narratives, Television Tie-Ins and Memoirs on the following subjects:
Recreation, Sports

Submission Guidelines No unagented submissions.
Recent Title(s) *Not a Proper Journalist*, Bob Humphrys (Memoir); *Fight the Good Fight: From Vicar's Wife to Killing Machine*, Catherine Fox (Sport/Biography)

Y Lolfa Cyf
Talybont, Ceredigion, SY24 5AP
- 01970 832304
- 01970 832782
- ylolfa@ylolfa.com
- www.ylolfa.com

Contact Managing Director, Garmon Gruffudd; Chief Editor, Lefi Gruffudd
Established 1967
Imprint(s) Dinas
Insider Info Publishes 50 titles per year. Payment is via royalties. Catalogue available online.
Non-Fiction Publishes Biography, Children's, General Non-Fiction and Humour titles on the following subjects:
Art/Architecture, Cookery, Food & Drink, Education, Government/Politics, History, Language, Literature, Translation
Fiction Publishes Mainstream/Contemporary and Translation titles.
Poetry Publishes Poetry titles.
Recent Title(s) *Welsh Folk Tales in a Flash*, Y Lolfa (Children's)
Tips Y Lolfa is an independent Welsh publisher specialising in fiction and non-fiction from, or about Wales. They print in both Welsh and English and also offer services as a commercial print company. The Dinas imprint is a part-author subsidised press for unusual and non-mainstream Welsh interest books. Its aim is to produce interesting and original books, which enhance the variety of books published in Wales.

York Notes
Edinburgh Gate, Harlow, Essex, CM20 2JE
- 01279 623623
- 01279 414130
- www.pearsoned.co.uk/imprints/yorknotes

Parent Company Pearson Education
Insider Info Catalogue and manuscript guidelines are available online.
Non-Fiction Publishes Study Guide titles on the following subjects:
Film, Language, Literature, Literary Criticism
* York Notes provides three main series, catering for different ages groups: 11–14 years, 14–16 years and 16–18 years & undergraduates. Each series covers the main curriculum texts studied at that level.

Submission Guidelines Accepts proposal package (including synopsis, sample chapters, market research, your publishing history and author biography).
Recent Title(s) *Hamlet*, William Shakespeare (Study Guide)
Tips York Notes publishes comprehensive literature guides to help students gain a better understanding of a curriculum text. Each title aims to help students form their own ideas and opinions, and help them to success in examinations. See the website for full list of submissions contacts.

Young Picador
20 New Wharf Road, London, N1 9RR
- 020 7014 6000
- 020 7014 6001
- www.panmacmillan.com

Parent Company Pan Macmillan Publishers
Established 2002
Insider Info Downloadable pdf of catalogue available online.
Non-Fiction Young Adult and Teenage non-fiction titles.
Fiction Publishes Young Adult fiction.
Poetry Publishes a small amount of Poetry.
Submission Guidelines Agented submissions only.
Recent Title(s) *The Witness*, James Jauncey (Thriller); *The Spell Book of Listen Taylor*, Jaclyn Moriarty (Teenage)
Tips Concentrates mainly on teenage fiction. The non-fiction and poetry sections of the list are extremely small. No unsolicited submissions.

Zambezi Publishing Ltd
PO Box 221, Plymouth, PL2 2YJ
- 01752 367300
- 01752 350453
- info@zampub.com
- www.zampub.com

Contact Chair, Sasha Fenton; Managing Director, Jan Budkowski
Established 1999
Imprint(s) ESP (Exclusive Self-Publishing)
Insider Info Publishes 12 titles per year. Payment is via royalties. Catalogue and manuscript guidelines available online.
Non-Fiction Publishes General Non-Fiction and Self-Help titles on the following subjects:
Business, Economics, Health/Medicine, Money/Finance, Spirituality, Mind, Body and Spirit
Submission Guidelines Accepts query with SAE/proposal package (including outline, one sample chapter, your publishing history, author biography, SAE).
Submission details to: sasha@zampub.com

Recent Title(s) *End the Food Confusion!*, Sonia Jones
Tips Zambezi publishes general non-fiction books. Their ESP imprint also offers 'assisted self-publishing' services and they are keen to push self-publishing as the ideal publishing method. They will consider unsolicited proposals, but thorough market research is needed with every proposal.

Zed Books Ltd
7 Cynthia Street, London, N1 9JF
- 020 7837 0384
- 020 7833 3960
- editorial@zedbooks.net
- www.zedbooks.co.uk

Contact Commissioning Editor, Ellen McKinlay (Current Affairs, Economics, African Studies, Latin American Studies); Commissioning Editor, Tamsine O'Riordan (Development Studies, Gender Studies, African Studies, Middle East Studies, Asian Studies)
Established 1976
Insider Info Publishes around 60 titles per year. Payment is via royalties. Catalogue available free on request, online. Manuscript guidelines available online.
Non-Fiction Publishes Reference, Scholarly and Technical titles on the following subjects: Business/Economics, Government/Politics, Multicultural, Regional, Women's Issues, International Relations, Cultural/Development Studies
Submission Guidelines Accepts query with SAE/proposal package (including outline, your publishing history, author biography, SAE). Submission details to: firstname.lastname@zedbooks.net
Recent Title(s) *The Enemy of Nature*, Joel Kovel (Sociology)
Tips Zed Books is an independent scholarly publishing house, catering predominantly to the needs of academics and students, and occasionally to a wider audience of activists and policy makers. They aim for books to reach the broadest possible audience, and therefore only publish those likely to have a substantial market, in hardback and paperback.

ZooBooKoo
4 Gurdon Road, Grundisburgh, Woodbridge, Suffolk, IP13 6XA
- 01473 735346
- 01206 212755
- sales@zoobookoo.com
- www.zoobookoo.com

Insider Info Catalogue available online.
Non-Fiction Publishes Illustrated, Educational folding 'Book Cubes' and Mats.

Tips ZooBooKoo products are all highly illustrated and are aimed at making education fun for children by changing the traditional book format into a 3D folding cube, or an activity mat.

Zymurgy Publishing
Hoults Estate, Walker Road, Newcastle upon Tyne, NE6 2HL
- 0191 276 2425
- 0191 276 2425
- martin.ellis@ablibris.com

Contact Chairman, Martin Ellis
Established 2000
Insider Info Payment is via royalties.
Non-Fiction Publishes General Non-Fiction and Illustrated titles.
Submission Guidelines Accept proposal package with SAE.
Tips Zymurgy publishes illustrated adult non-fiction on a range of subjects. Proposals welcome, but no unsolicited manuscripts. Zymurgy does not have a website.

UK & IRISH POETRY PUBLISHERS

Aard Press
(See entry under UK & Irish Book Publishers)

Abbey Press
(See entry under UK & Irish Book Publishers)

Acair Ltd
(See entry under UK & Irish Book Publishers)

Agenda Editions
The Wheelwrights, Fletching Street, Mayfield, East Sussex, TN20 6TL
- 01435 873703
- editor@agendapoetry.co.uk
- www.agendapoetry.co.uk

Contact Editor, Patricia McCarthy; Admin, Marcus Frederick
Insider Info Catalogue available online.
Poetry Agenda Editions is the book publishing arm of *Agenda* magazine. It publishes limited editions of an individual's poems.
Submission Guidelines Submit six sample poems.
Recent Title(s) *The Madness of Amadis and other poems*, Jean Cassou (Author and Timothy Adès (Translator)
Tips Read copies of *Agenda* magazine to get a feel for the types of poetry published. The editor wants

less cliché ridden poetry and more well crafted and deeply felt writing. Being published in the magazine is more likely to be a step towards getting a book published, rather than approaching the editor with an entire collection.

Akros Publications
(See entry under UK & Irish Book Publishers)

Alison Allison
Double Dykes, Elm Row, Galashiels, TD1 3HT
- 01896 753728
- alisonallisondouble@yahoo.co.uk
Poetry Publishes poetry books and pamphlets.
Tips Make contact by email for more information on current activities.

Alma Books Ltd
(See entry under UK & Irish Book Publishers)

Anchor Books
Forward Press, Remus House, Woodston, Peterborough, PE2 9JX
- 01733 898101
- 01733 313524
- anchorbooks@forwardpress.co.uk
- www.forwardpress.co.uk
Parent Company Forward Press
Established 1992
Poetry Publishes Poetry titles.
* Almost all material is traditional, rhyming poetry, which is suitable for all the family to read. It should be uncomplicated and accessible.
Submission Guidelines Submit two sample poems. Submission details to: inbox@forwardpress.co.uk
Tips Anchor Books authors are from a variety of age ranges and backgrounds. Popular subjects tend to be those from everyday life, such as interesting anecdotes, stories and tales to give readers inspiration. Bear in mind that this imprint is very much designed to publish poetry for the whole family. The Forward Press website has details of any current calls for submission.

Anglo-Saxon Books
(See entry under UK & Irish Book Publishers)

Anvil Press Poetry Ltd
Neptune House, 70 Royal Hill, London, SE10 8RF
- 020 8469 3033
- 020 8469 3363
- info@anvilpresspoetry.com
- www.anvilpresspoetry.com
Contact Editorial Director, Peter Jay

Established 1968
Insider Info Publishes around 12 titles per year. Receives approximately 2,000 queries and 600 manuscripts per year. Five per cent of books published are from first-time authors and 60 per cent of books published are from unagented authors. Payment is via royalty (on retail or wholesale price) with 0.07 (per £) minimum and 0.1 (per £) maximum. Advance offered is from £2,000–£5,000. Average lead time is 15 months, with simultaneous submissions accepted. Submissions accompanied by SAE will be returned. Aims to respond to queries with seven days and proposals within four weeks. Catalogue is free on request, and available online or by email.
Poetry Publishes book-length poetry manuscripts, or single poems in anthologies.
Submission Guidelines Accepts complete manuscripts by post.
Tips Does not accept submissions by email. Anvil advises new authors that 'if you haven't published poems in poetry magazines, you should be aiming to do so before approaching book publishers'.

Arrowhead Press
70 Clifton Road, Darlington, Co. Durham, DL1 5DX
- editor@arrowheadpress.co.uk
- www.arrowheadpress.co.uk
Contact Managing Editor, Roger Collett; Poetry Editor, Joanna Boulter
Established 2001
Insider Info Catalogue and manuscript guidelines available online.
Poetry Publishes books and pamphlets of Contemporary Poetry.
Submission Guidelines Accepts proposal package (including brief biography, publishing history and SAE) by post only.
Recent Title(s) *Home Field*, Ann Pilling (Poetry Collection)
Tips The editor states that it is a waste of time and money submitting to Arrowhead if you have not already been published in reputable magazines and possibly already had a pamphlet published (excluding self published works).

Atlantean Publishing
(See entry under UK & Irish Book Publishers)

The Barddas Society
(See entry under UK & Irish Book Publishers)

Barque Press

c/o Andrea Brady, 26 Allerton Road, London, N16 5UJ

☎ 020 8809 9652

✉ a.brady@qmul.ac.uk

🌐 www.barquepress.com

Contact Publisher, Andrea Brady; Publisher, Keston Sutherland

Established 1995

Poetry Barque Press publishes poetry chapbooks, perfect bound books and media anthologies.
* The press is not currently accepting any new manuscripts for publication.

Submission Guidelines Does not accept unsolicited submissions.

BB Books

Spring Bank, Longsight Road, Copster Green, Blackburn, BB1 9EU

☎ 01254 249128

Contact Dave Cunliffe

Poetry Publishes Poetry titles.

Tips BB Books is the publisher for poetry magazine *Global Tapestry Journal*.

Beyond the Cloister Publications

14 Lewes Crescent, Brighton, BN2 1FH

☎ 01273 687053

✉ sales@www.beyondthecloister.com

🌐 www.beyondthecloister.com

Contact Editor, Hugh Hellicar

Established 1994

Poetry Specialises in single poet volumes, as well as anthologies.

Submission Guidelines Accepts sample poems.

Tips Sample poems are welcomed by either mail or email. Please address them to the editor.

Big Little Poem Books

3 Park Avenue, Melton Mowbray, Leicestershire, LE13 0JB

Contact Publisher & Editor, Robert Richardson

Established 1987

Poetry The *Big Little Poem* series, a set of poems printed on cards, was discontinued in 1992. The editorial policy was to focus on consciousness of form and precision of language, and to promote effective contemporary approaches to the lyric and epigram. The book imprint may occasionally still publish.

Tips Submissions are limited to those poets who have already been published in the *Big Little Poem* series.

Birlinn Ltd

(See entry under UK & Irish Book Publishers)

Biscuit Publishing

(See entry under UK & Irish Book Publishers)

Black Spring Press

(See entry under UK & Irish Book Publishers)

Blackstaff Press

(See entry under UK & Irish Book Publishers)

Bloodaxe Books

Highgreen, Tarset, Northumberland, NE48 1RP

☎ 01434 240500

☎ 01434 240505

✉ editor@bloodaxebooks.com

🌐 www.bloodaxebooks.com

Contact Editor, Neil Astley

Established 1978

Insider Info Publishes 30-35 titles per year. Receives approximately 5,000 submissions per year. Submissions accompanied by SAE will be returned. Aims to respond to queries within four months. Catalogue available via email to: sales@bloodaxebooks.com. Manuscript guidelines available online.

Poetry Publishes Contemporary Poetry titles.
* Bloodaxe currently have a large backlog of submissions to review and may not be able to read new submissions in the short or medium term. Much of their publishing programme is filled by authors they already publish.

Submission Guidelines Submit up to 12 sample poems from a book-length collection by post with SAE.

Recent Title(s) *In Person: 30 Poets*, Pamela Robertson-Pearce (director) and Neil Astley (editor) (DVD-book); *The Sinking Road*, Paul Batchelor (First Collection); *The Hidden River*, Stephanie Norgate (First Collection)

Tips Bloodaxe do have a policy for publishing new writers, although they state that 'new writers' often means those that have built up extensive publishing history through literary or poetry magazines, and have a collection of poems large enough to fill a book. Do not submit a manuscript if your poetry has not already been extensively published.

Bloomsbury Publishing Plc

(See entry under UK & Irish Book Publishers)

Blue Butterfly Publishers
13 Irvine Way, Inverurie, Aberdeenshire, Scotland, AB51 4ZR
- 01467 625986
- blue7butterfly@which.net
- www.madill.prodigynet.co.uk/bbp

Contact Editor, Betty Madill
Insider Info Payment is a free copy of the publication.
Poetry Publishes anthologies of Christian poetry, the contents largely consisting of the winning entries from annual competitions.
Tips Details of competitions and guidelines for the types of poetry required change with each new round, so check the website for the latest opportunities.

Bluechrome
(See entry under UK & Irish Book Publishers)

The Boho Press
PO Box 109, Portishead, Bristol, BS20 7ZJ
- 07092 273360
- 07092 273357
- info@bohopress.co.uk
- www.bohopress.co.uk

Insider Info Catalogue available online.
Poetry Publishes Poetry titles.
* The Boho Press is interested in writers' groups who may be interested in publishing an anthology. The publishers welcome emails containing an outline of the book in the first instance.
Tips The Boho Press is a 'sister' imprint of Bluechrome. Email communication is preferred over postal contact.

Bradshaw Books
(See entry under UK & Irish Book Publishers)

Bridge Pamphlets
PO Box 309, Aylsham, Norwich, NR11 6LN
- mail@therialto.co.uk
- www.therialto.co.uk

Contact Editor, Mike Mackmin; Creative Director, Nick Stone
Insider Info Submissions accompanied by SAE will be returned. Aims to respond to proposals within ten weeks. Catalogue available online.
Poetry Bridge Pamphlets, associated with the *Rialto Poetry Magazine*, publishes collections in pamphlet format, from poets who are not ready for a full first collection but deserve to be published in a single author volume.
Submission Guidelines Submit six sample poems.

Recent Title(s) *Developing the Negative*, Emily Wills (Collection); *The Magnolia*, Richard Lambert (Collection)
Tips Submitting poems to the magazine may be advisable to start with, rather than approaching Bridge Pamphlets with a collection that has had no prior publication.

The British Museum Press
(See entry under UK & Irish Book Publishers)

The Brodie Press
c/o Dept. of English, University of Bristol, 3/5 Woodland Road, Bristol, BS8 1TB
- thebrodiepress@hotmail.com
- www.brodiepress.co.uk

Contact Editors: Hannah Sheppard, Tom Sperlinger and Penny Price
Established 2002
Insider Info Catalogue available online.
Poetry Publishes Poetry titles.
Submission Guidelines No unsolicited submissions are accepted.
Recent Title(s) *Letters North*, Julie-Ann Rowell (Collections)
Tips The Brodie Press is a not-for-profit organisation, staffed by volunteers. They publish new writers and established authors who wish to undertake experimental or unusual projects.

Bullseye Publications
5 Camptoun, North Berwick, East Lothian, Scotland, EH39 5BA
- 01620 880311
- alancharlesgay@aol.com

Contact Alan Gay
Poetry Currently publishes the poetry of Alan Gay in book and pamphlet form.

Calder Publications
(See entry under UK & Irish Book Publishers)

Calder Wood Press
1 Beachmont Court, Dunbar, East Lothian, EH42 1YF
- colin.will@zen.co.uk
- www.calderwoodpress.co.uk

Contact Director, Colin Will
Poetry Calder Wood Press is a small poetry publisher, focusing mainly on chapbooks in English and Scots. It also publishes poetry cards, books and occasional short story collections.
Submission Guidelines No unsolicited submissions.

Tips Calder Wood Press only publishes work from authors they know personally.

Carcanet Press Ltd
(See entry under UK & Irish Book Publishers)

The Celtic Cross Press
(See entry under UK & Irish Book Publishers)

Chapman Publishing
(See entry under UK & Irish Book Publishers)

Chatto & Windus
(See entry under UK & Irish Book Publishers)

The Cherry on the Top Press
(See entry under UK & Irish Book Publishers)

Cinnamon Press
(See entry under UK & Irish Book Publishers)

Clutag Press
PO Box 154, Thame, OX9 3RQ
❍ Online form.
⦿ www.clutagpress.com
Contact Andrew McNeillie
Established 2000
Insider Info Submissions will not be returned. Catalogue is available online.
Non-Fiction Publishes Memoirs.
* Only two memoirs have been published.
Submission Guidelines No unsolicited manuscripts.
Poetry Publishes Leaflets and Pamphlet Collections from well known poets, including Seamus Heany and John Fuller.
Tips Please note that absolutely no unsolicited manuscripts will be read or returned. If you wish to make contact, use the form on the website.

The Collective Press
Penlanlas Farm, Llantilio Pertholey, Y-Fenni, Gwent, NP7 7HN
❶ 01873 856350
❶ 01873 859559
⦿ jj@jojowales.co.uk
⦿ www.welshwriters.com
Contact Coordinator, John Jones; Chief Editor, Frank Olding; Events Manager, Ric Hool
Established 1990
Insider Info Submissions accompanied by SAE will be returned.
Poetry Publishes poetry collections.

* Poets are welcomed from around the world and from any background.
Submission Guidelines Submit complete manuscript. No email submissions are accepted.
Tips The Collective Press is a not-for-profit organisation. They recommend that writers who are seeking publication read a few existing Collective Press titles to get a feel for what they do. Replies to submissions may take a while due to the voluntary nature of the organisation, but manuscript submissions with enclosed SAEs should receive a reply.

Comma Press
(See entry under UK & Irish Book Publishers)

Crescent Moon Publishing
(See entry under UK & Irish Book Publishers)

Dagger Press
1 Portland Street, Worcester, WR1 2NL
⦿ dagger.press@tiscali.co.uk
Contact Editor, Brian Morse
Poetry Publishes 32 page pamphlets written by adult poets.
Tips The idea behind Dagger Press is to showcase poets which the publisher feels should be more widely read. Editor, Brian Morse, is himself a published children's author and poet. Three poets who have been published by Dagger have gone on to publish with larger presses.

Dedalus Press
13 Moyclare Road, Baldoyle, Dublin 13, Republic of Ireland
❶ 00353 1 839 2034
❶ 0870 127 2089
⦿ office@dedaluspress.com
⦿ www.dedaluspress.com
Contact Publisher & Editor, Pat Boran
Established 1985
Insider Info Publishes 8-10 titles per year. 100 per cent of books published are from unagented authors. Payment is via royalty (on retail price). Simultaneous submissions are not accepted. Submissions accompanied by SAE will be returned. Aims to respond to manuscripts within three months. Catalogue is available online. Manuscript guidelines are available online, or by email.
Poetry Publishes a small number of Contemporary Poetry collections every year.
Submission Guidelines Accepts query with SAE or complete manuscript (including covering letter and your publishing history).

Recent Title(s) *Even So: New & Selected Poems*, Mark Roper; *Music for Dogs: Work for Radio*, Paula Meehan
Tips Dedalus Press advises prospective authors to read some previous Dedalus publications before submitting to get an accurate feel of what the company is interested in publishing.

Diehard
91–93 Main Street, Callander, Scotland, FK17 8BQ
☎ 01877 339449
✉ sally.king4@btinternet.com
🌐 www.poetryscotland.co.uk
Contact Editor, Sally Evans (Poetry Scotland)
Insider Info Catalogue and manuscript guidelines available online.
Poetry Publishes Poetry titles as well as the poetry magazine, *Poetry Scotland*.
Recent Title(s) *The Bees*, Sally Evans
Tips Authors are advised to subscribe to the *Poetry Scotland* magazine to get a feel for the types of poetry published. This will cost £5 per year and details are on the website. Do not approach Diehard if you are not currently being published by *Poetry Scotland*.

Dionysia Press
(See entry under UK & Irish Book Publishers)

Donut Press
PO Box 45093, London, N4 1UZ
✉ donutchops@yahoo.co.uk
🌐 www.donutpress.co.uk
Contact Andy Ching
Established 2001
Poetry Publishes Poetry titles.
Recent Title(s) *Super Try Again*, Roddy Lumsden
Tips Donut Press is a small, independent publisher of poetry collections. Queries about Donut Press are invited by email.

Dreadful Night Press
82 Kelvin Court, Glasgow, G12 0AQ
☎ 0141 339 9150
✉ dreadfulnight1@aol.com
Insider Info Publishes booklets and pamphlets only.
Poetry Publishes poetry by a range of writers in both black and white, and colour booklet form.
Recent Title(s) *The Boy Who Came Ashore*, Alan Gay (Poetry)
Tips A member of the *Scottish Pamphlet Poetry* website, whose pamphlets usually have some kind of Scottish connection.

Driftwood Publications
5 Timms Lane, Formby, Merseyside, L37 9DW
☎ 01704 833911
☎ 0151 524 0216
✉ janet.speedy@tesco.net
Contact Editor, Brian Wake (Poetry); Editor, Tony Dash (Poetry); Coordinator, Janet Speedy (Poetry)
Established 1972
Insider Info Publishes ten titles per year. Receives 750 queries and 200 manuscripts per year. 75 per cent of books published are from first-time authors, 100 per cent of books published are from unagented authors. Payment is via complimentary copies. Average lead time is nine months, with simultaneous submissions accepted. Submissions accompanied by SAE will be returned. Aims to respond to queries within two weeks, proposals within 12 weeks and manuscripts within three months. Manuscript guidelines available with SAE.
Poetry Publishes poetry collections and poetry in performance, ideally from unknown or neglected poets.
Recent Title(s) *Raining Upwards*, Brian Wake
Tips Driftwood is a non-profit making organisation that promotes poetry in performance and poetry publications.

Edgewell Publishing
(See entry under UK & Irish Book Publishers)

Egg Box Publishing
(See entry under UK & Irish Book Publishers)

Enitharmon Press
(See entry under UK & Irish Book Publishers)

Erran Publishing
43 Willow Road, Carlton, Nottingham, NG4 3BH
✉ erranpublishing@hotmail.com
🌐 www.poetichours.homestead.com
Contact Editor, Nick Clark (Poetry, Articles)
Established 1993
Imprints Poetic Hours
Insider Info Receives approximately 400 queries and 400 manuscripts per year. Accepts simultaneous submissions. Submissions accompanied by SAE will be returned. Aim to respond to queries within one week and manuscripts within three weeks. Manuscript guidelines are available with SAE, and available online or by email.
Poetry Publishes general contemporary poetry in the *Poetic Hours Magazine*.
* Does not publish extremist or political poetry.
Submission Guidelines Accepts complete manuscripts.

Tips Erran Publishing only publishes the *Poetic Hours Magazine*. Aspiring authors should submit work to the magazine rather than direct to the publisher.

Essence Press
8 Craiglea Drive, Edinburgh, EH10 5PA
- editor@essencepress.co.uk
- www.essencepress.co.uk

Contact Editor, Julie Johnstone
Insider Info Submissions accompanied by SAE will be returned. Aim to respond to manuscripts within 12 weeks.
Poetry Publishes small hand bound poetry pamphlets and postcards, bookmarks and cards.
Submission Guidelines Submit five sample poems.
Recent Title(s) *Aves*, Gerry Cambridge
Tips The publisher will accept unsolicited submissions, although many works are commissioned. Queries will be accepted by email, but emails with unsolicited attachments will not be opened. Include all information in the body of the email. The subject line of the email should be very direct; emails with vague subject lines are unlikely to be opened.

Etruscan Books
Stowe Lane, Exbourne, West Devon, EX20 3RY
- 01364 643128
- atetruscan@aol.com
- www.e-truscan.co.uk

Contact Nicholas Johnson
Poetry Publishes poetry from both UK and US poets, with distribution outlets in both countries.
Tips Etruscan also runs a book club, the products of which give a good indication of the company's style.

Everyman
(See entry under UK & Irish Book Publishers)

Everyman Classics
(See entry under UK & Irish Book Publishers)

Everyman's Library
(See entry under UK & Irish Book Publishers)

Faber & Faber Ltd
(See entry under UK & Irish Book Publishers)

Fal Publications
(See entry under UK & Irish Book Publishers)

Flambard Press
(See entry under UK & Irish Book Publishers)

Flarestack Publishing
8 Abbot's Way, Pilton, Somerset, BA4 4BN
- 01749 890019
- tarotqua@madasafish.com
- www.flarestack.co.uk

Contact Editor (Obsessed with Pipework), Charles Johnson; Editors (Flarestack Poets): Meredith Andrea and Jacqui Rowe
Established 1995
Imprint(s) Flarestack Poets
Insider Info Publishes around eight titles per year. Receives approximately 30 queries and 25 manuscripts per year. 60 per cent of books published are from first-time authors, 95 per cent of books published are from unagented authors. Payment is via percentage discount on sales. Simultaneous submissions are not accepted. Submissions accompanied by SAE will be returned. Aims to respond to queries and other enquiries within three weeks, proposals within one month and manuscripts within three months. Catalogue is free on request. Manuscript guidelines are free on request, and available online or by email.
Poetry Publishes original Contemporary Poetry titles.
Submission Guidelines Accepts query/proposal package (including outline, six sample poems and author biography and SAE).
Tips From Autumn 2009 Flarestack Publishing will continue to publish their poetry magazine, *Obsessed with Pipework*, but all new poetry pamphlets will be published by new imprint Flarestack Poets. They are looking for encouraging work from new and established voices, especially if it dares outside current trends. See their new website for more information, at: www.flarestackpoets.co.uk

Flipped Eye Publishing Limited
(See entry under UK & Irish Book Publishers)

Forward Press
Remus House, Woodston, Peterborough, PE2 9JX
- 01733 890099
- 01733 313524
- info@forwardpress.co.uk
- www.forwardpress.co.uk

Contact Managing Director, Ian Walton
Established 1989
Imprint(s) Anchor Books
Poetry Now
Pond View
Need2Know
New Fiction
Spotlight Poets
Triumph House

Writers' Bookshop
Insider Info Average lead time is three months.
Poetry Publishes a wide variety of poetry titles.
* The website details specific calls for submissions under particular themes. These change regularly.
Submission Guidelines Submit two sample poems by email. Poems submitted for the monthly themes may be sent by post or email. If posting, write your name and address on each piece separately. If emailing, enter the theme name in the subject box.
Recent Title(s) *Child Obesity - A Parent's Guide*, Judith Manson (Need2Know)
Tips Forward Press are the largest publisher of new poetry in the world. All poets published by Forward Press, or any of its imprints, are automatically entered into the Top 100 Poets of the Year competition. Forward Press also publishes short stories (under the New Fiction imprint), biographies, children's titles, educational titles, general non-fiction (under the Pond View Books imprint), books for writers, and a series of books which address the problems/situations that ordinary people encounter in their everyday lives (under the Need2Know imprint).

Four Quarters Press
7 The Towers, Stevenage, Hertfordshire, SG1 1HE
✉ octillion@ntlworld.com
Poetry Publishes Poetry titles.
Tips Four Quarters Press produce not for profit publications (mainly poetry), for charity purposes only.

Gairm Publications
(See entry under UK & Irish Book Publishers)

The Galdragon Press
10 Citadel Drive, Stromness, Orkney, KW16 3EJ
✉ galdragon@virgin.net
Contact Anne Thomson
Insider Info Submissions will not be returned. Catalogue available free on request and via email. Email with your postal address for a printed list.
Poetry Publishes Poetry titles.
Recent Title(s) *The Shortest Days*, Elizabeth Burns (Pamphlet)
Tips Publishes small, hand-set, letterpress editions of poetry and some pamphlet poetry. No unsolicited manuscripts or email attachments will be accepted.

The Gallery Press
(See entry under UK & Irish Book Publishers)

George Ronald Publishers Ltd
(See entry under UK & Irish Book Publishers)

Gomer Press/Gwasg Gomer
(See entry under UK & Irish Book Publishers)

Gwasg Pantycelyn
(See entry under UK & Irish Book Publishers)

Hands Up Books
1 New Cottages, Spout Hill, Brantingham, East Yorkshire, HU15 1QW
✉ handsup@handsup.karoo.co.uk
🌐 www.handsupbooks.co.uk
Contact Founder/Editor, Graham Denton
Established 2002
Insider Info Accepts queries by email. Catalogue available online.
Poetry Publishes Children's Poetry titles.
Recent Title(s) *A Stegosaurus is For Life and Other Animal Poems*, Trevor Millum (Poetry Collection); *Mrs Pringle's Jolly Jingles*, Linda Knaus (Poetry Collection)
Tips A very small press that is focused solely on publishing poetry for children, mainly 7-11 years.

HappenStance Press
21 Hatton Green, Glenrothes, Fife, Scotland, KY7 4SD
✉ nell@happenstancepress.com
🌐 www.happenstancepress.com
Contact Editor, Helena Nelson
Established 2005
Insider Info Catalogue and submission guidelines are available online.
Poetry Publishes mainly first collection Poetry Pamphlet titles.
Submission Guidelines Welcomes unsolicited submissions (8-20 poems) along with a brief publishing history and SAE. No email submissions. Poems may have been previously published.
Recent Title(s) *The Two-Coat Man*, Martin Reed
Tips Download for free the 'Bluffer's Guide to Getting Your Chapbook Published' and 'Dos and Don'ts' from the website, for detailed explanations as to what HappenStance Press expects from potential authors. HappenStance also publishes *Sphinx* magazine, covering the world of independent poetry publishing.

hardPressed Poetry
Shanbally Road, Annacotty, Co. Limerick, Republic of Ireland
✉ bmills@netg.ie
🌐 http://gofree.indigo.ie/~hpp

Established 1997
Poetry Publishes Poetry titles.
* Prefers poetry that you won't find in average bookshops.
Recent Title(s) *City West*, Catherine Walsh
Tips hardPressed has also published poetry cards, journals and anthologies in the past. There is an enquiry form on the website for more information.

Harpercroft Publications
Old Bank House, 24 Castle Street, Crail, Fife, KY10 3SH
☎ 01333 451744
Contact Founder, Gordon Jarvie
Poetry Publishes poetry pamphlets to showcase the work of owner Gordon Jarvie.
Recent Title(s) *The Tale of the Crail Whale*, Gordon Jarvie
Tips Member of the *Scottish Pamphlet Poetry* website, where recent titles can also be viewed and ordered.

Headland Publications
(See entry under UK & Irish Book Publishers)

Headline
(See entry under UK & Irish Book Publishers)

Hearing Eye Publications
99 Torriano Avenue, London, NW5 2RX
☎ 020 7267 2751
✉ hearing_eye@torriano.org
🌐 www.hearingeye.org
Contact John Rety
Established 1987
Insider Info Catalogue available online.
Poetry Publishes Poetry titles.
Recent Title(s) *On the LookoutKingston*, Jeremy Kingston
Tips Primarily publishes poetry collections, but also some other literature, and have recently produced a CD of poetry readings. Attend the poetry readings at the Torriano Avenue address (check website for details) to get a flavour of their poetry, as well as browsing their catalogue. Hearing Eye also runs an annual poetry competition every January.

Heaventree Press
Koco Building, The Arches, Spon End, Coventry, CV1 3JQ
☎ 024 7671 3555
✉ admin@heaventreepress.com
🌐 www.heaventreepress.co.uk
Contact Director, Jonathan Morley

Insider Info Submissions accompanied by SAE will be returned. Catalogue available online.
Poetry Publishes Anthologies and Pamphlets of New Literature.
Submission Guidelines Submit complete manuscript.
Tips Heaventree is a non-profit organisation, set up by local poets to help encourage and promote arts in the Coventry area. Also publishes *Avocado* magazine.

Hilltop Press
(See entry under UK & Irish Book Publishers)

Honno Welsh Women's Press
(See entry under UK & Irish Book Publishers)

Hub Editions
Longholm, Eastbank, Wingland, Sutton Bridge, Spalding, Lincolnshire, PE12 9YS
✉ coljo@metronet.co.uk
🌐 www.colinblundell.co.uk/publishing
Contact Director, Colin Blundell
Poetry Publishes small collections of Poetry and Poetry Anthologies, especially Haiku.
Tips Hub Editions is a subsidy press, which means that they charge authors a fee to publish their work as if it were a service. See the website for further details.

Inner Sanctum Publications
(See entry under UK & Irish Book Publishers)

Iron Press
(See entry under UK & Irish Book Publishers)

Jonathan Cape
(See entry under UK & Irish Book Publishers)

Karnak House
(See entry under UK & Irish Book Publishers)

Katabasis
10 St Martin's Close, London, NW1 0HR
☎ 020 7485 3830
✉ katabasis@katabasis.co.uk
🌐 www.katabasis.co.uk
Contact Director, Dinah Livingstone
Established 1967
Insider Info Catalogue available online.
Poetry Publishes Poetry book and Pamphlet titles.
Submission Guidelines No unsolicited manuscripts

Recent Title(s) *Kindness*, Dinah Livingstone (Collection)

Tips Katabasis has a strong international flavour, and publishes a lot of south american bi-lingual poetry, particularly from Nicaragua. They seek down to earth poetry that is rooted in a particular place and history, but also speaks beyond them.

The Kates Hill Press
(See entry under UK & Irish Book Publishers)

Kettillonia
(See entry under UK & Irish Book Publishers)

Kingfisher Publications Plc
(See entry under UK & Irish Book Publishers)

KT Publications
16 Fane Close, Stamford, PE9 1HG
❶ 01780 754193
Contact Kevin Troop
Poetry Publishes Poetry titles.
Tips Publishes the *Kite Modern Poetry* series as well as *The Third Half* magazine. Contact Kevin Troop for more information.

Landfill Press
17 Waldeck Road, Norwich, NR4 7PG
✉ sales@landfillpress.co.uk
🌐 www.landfillpress.co.uk
Poetry Publishes Poetry titles.
Recent Title(s) *I Haven't Been Anywhere, Man*, Linh Dinh
Tips Publishes pocket-sized poem sequences. No unsolicited manuscripts.

Lapwing Publications
1 Ballysillan Drive, Belfast, Northern Ireland, BT14 8HQ
❶ 028 9039 1240
❶ 028 9039 1240
✉ catherine.greig1@ntlworld.com
Contact Dennis Greig
Poetry Publishes small, first-edition Poetry Collections.
Tips Lapwing started off as a not for profit organisation to serve the needs of emerging Northern Irish writers, although it quickly extended its reach to the Republic of Ireland. It now publishes poets who make their home in Ireland, Irish poets who now live elsewhere, and occasionally poets who have no connection to Ireland.

Laurel Books
282 The Common, Holt, BA14 6QJ
❶ 01225 782874
✉ mail@laurelbooks.co.uk
🌐 www.laurelbooks.co.uk
Contact Patrick Ingram
Insider Info Catalogue available online.
Poetry Publishes small Poetry Collections.
Recent Title(s) *The Blackbird Inspector*, Pamela Coren (Poetry Collection)
Tips A small press who often commission their titles.

Leaf Books
(See entry under UK & Irish Book Publishers)

Leafe Press
4 Cohen Close, Chilwell, Nottingham, NG9 6RW
✉ leafepress@hotmail.com
🌐 www.leafepress.com
Poetry Publishes Pamphlets and Contemporary Poetry titles.
Submission Guidelines Submissions are by invitation only. No unsolicited manuscripts. Leafe Press also publishes *Litter* magazine.

Libris Ltd
(See entry under UK & Irish Book Publishers)

The Lilliput Press Ltd
(See entry under UK & Irish Book Publishers)

Littoral Press
10 Prail Court, Vesta Close, Coggeshall, Essex, CO6 1QG
Contact Mervyn Linford
Insider Info Publishes a small number of Poetry Collections every year.
Recent Title(s) *Chorus and Coda*, Adrian Green (Poetry)
Tips Past publications are available to order from the website and will give an indication of the type of poetry Littoral Press is interested in.

Loki Books
(See entry under UK & Irish Book Publishers)

Luath Press Ltd
(See entry under UK & Irish Book Publishers)

Ludovic Press
3rd Floor, 65 Glassford Street, Glasgow, G1 1UB
❶ 01415 525239
Poetry Publishes Poetry titles.

Recent Title(s) *High Auchensale*, Jim Carruth
Tips Member of the *Scottish Pamphlet Poetry* website, where their publications can be ordered.

Macmillan Children's Books
(See entry under UK & Irish Book Publishers)

Malfunction Press
Rose Cottage, 3 Tram Lane, Flintshire, CH7 3JB
❶ 01244 5438209
✉ rosecot@presford.freeserve.co.uk
Contact Editor, Peter E. Presford
Established 1969
Poetry Publishes Poetry booklets on the following subjects: Science Fiction, Fantasy and Horror.
* Publishes very infrequently.
Submission Guidelines Accepts email submissions.
Tips Favours poetry with Italian connections. Also publishes *Postern* magazine, which covers castle studies and travels.

Mandrake of Oxford
(See entry under UK & Irish Book Publishers)

Mango Publishing
(See entry under UK & Irish Book Publishers)

Mare's Nest
(See entry under UK & Irish Book Publishers)

Mariscat Press
10 Bell Place, Stockbridge, Edinburgh, EH3 5HT
❶ 0131 343 1070
✉ hamish.whyte@btinternet.com
Contact Hamish Whyte
Poetry Publishes Poetry Collections and Pamphlets.
Recent Title(s) *Paper Run*, Jim C. Wilson; *Kept In The Dark*, Donald Mackay
Tips Member of the *Scottish Pamphlet Poetry* website, where previous publications can be ordered.

Maypole Editions
(See entry under UK & Irish Book Publishers)

Meadowside Children's Books
(See entry under UK & Irish Book Publishers)

Menard Press
(See entry under UK & Irish Book Publishers)

Mews Press
English Department, Sheffield Hallam University, Collegiate Crescent, Sheffield, S10 2BP
❶ 0114 225 2241
✉ s.l.earnshaw@shu.ac.uk
🌐 http://extra.shu.ac.uk/mews-press
Contact Dr Steven Earnshaw
Established 2000
Insider Info Catalogue available online.
Poetry The press exists solely to publish poetry from students of the MA Writing course at Sheffield Hallam. No external submissions.
Tips Also publishes a magazine, *Matter*, showcasing fiction, scriptwriting and poetry talent from the course, and the *Ictus* pamphlet.

Michael O'Mara Books Ltd
(See entry under UK & Irish Book Publishers)

Morning Star
(See entry under UK & Irish Book Publishers)

Mudfog Press
(See entry under UK & Irish Book Publishers)

New Island Books
(See entry under UK & Irish Book Publishers)

Nightingale Books
(See entry under UK & Irish Book Publishers)

NorthernSky Press
(See entry under UK & Irish Book Publishers)

Object Permanence
1st Floor, 16 Ruskin Terrace, Glasgow, G12 8DY
✉ undigest@hotmail.com
✉ robinpurves@yahoo.co.uk
🌐 www.objectpermanence.co.uk
Contact Editors: Peter Mason and Robin Purves
Poetry Publish Pamphlet and Poetry Collection titles.
Submission Guidelines No unsolicited manuscripts. Accepts queries by email.
Tips Object Permanence was once a poetry magazine and is now a small poetry press.

Octagon Press Ltd
(See entry under UK & Irish Book Publishers)

Odyssey Poets

Coleridge Cottage, Nether Stowey, Somerset, TA5 1NQ

☎ 01278 732662

Contact Derrick Woolf

Poetry Publishes Poetry titles.

Tips A small press publishing poetry, prose, first collections, interim booklets and full collections.

The Old Stile Press

(See entry under UK & Irish Book Publishers)

The Oleander Press Ltd

(See entry under UK & Irish Book Publishers)

The Once Orange Badge Poetry Press

PO Box 184, South Ockendon, RM15 5WT

☎ 01708 852827

✉ orangebadge@poetry.fsworld.co.uk

Contact DM Heath

Poetry Publishes first-edition Pamphlets and Collections.

Tips The Press prefers enquiries and submissions via email.

The One Time Press

Model Farm, Linstead Magna, Halesworth, Suffolk, IP19 0DT

☎ 01986 785422

🌐 www.onetimepress.com

Contact Director, Peter Wells

Poetry Publishes Classic Poetry titles.

Tips The One Time Press publishes fine editions of poetry by 1940s writers. No contemporary poetry will be considered.

Onlywomen Press

(See entry under UK & Irish Book Publishers)

Original Plus

(See entry under UK & Irish Book Publishers)

Orion Publishing Group Ltd

(See entry under UK & Irish Book Publishers)

The Other Press

19 Marriot Road, London, N4 3QN

☎ 020 7272 9023

✉ fpresley@compuserve.com

🌐 www.llpp.ms11.net/other.html

Poetry Publishes Poetry titles.

Tips A very small poetry press based in London.

Palladour Books

(See entry under UK & Irish Book Publishers)

Paradise Press

(See entry under UK & Irish Book Publishers)

Parthian

(See entry under UK & Irish Book Publishers)

The Patchwork Press

PO Box 109, Portishead, Bristol, BS20 7ZJ

✉ info@patchworkpress.co.uk

🌐 www.patchworkpress.co.uk

Contact Editor, Beth Morgan

Established 2006

Poetry Publishes Themed Anthologies.

Submission Guidelines Submit one to two sample poems. Welcomes submissions from poets who would like to be included in the Anthologies. Poems should be no longer than 32 lines long and may be posted or emailed.

Tips The Patchwork Press specialises in themed anthologies. They will issue a call for submissions under a particular theme, such as *Poems of Love* or *My Hometown*. For up to the minute information, sign up to the newsletter via the website.

Peepal Tree Press

(See entry under UK & Irish Book Publishers)

Penguin Group (UK)

(See entry under UK & Irish Book Publishers)

Perjink Press

(See entry under UK & Irish Book Publishers)

Picador

(See entry under UK & Irish Book Publishers)

Pigasus Press

(See entry under UK & Irish Book Publishers)

Pikestaff Press

Ellon House, Harpford, Sidmouth, Devon, EX10 0NH

☎ 01395 568941

Contact Robert Robertson

Poetry Publish Poetry Collections and Pamphlets.

Recent Title(s) *Green Eyes,* Adrian Blackledge

Tips Pikestaff is a very small press concentrating on publishing poetry collections in booklet or pamphlet form only.

Pipers' Ash Ltd
(See entry under UK & Irish Book Publishers)

Planet
(See entry under UK & Irish Book Publishers)

Poems in the Waiting Room
PO Box 488, Richmond, Surrey, TW9 4SW
- 020 8876 4379
- pitwr@blueyonder.co.uk
- www.poemsinthewaitingroom.org

Contact Chair, Michael Lee; Editor, Isobel Montgomery Campbell; Executive Editor, Cynthia Turner Roberts
Established 1995
Insider Info An arts in health charity which supplies short collections of poems for patients to read while waiting to see their doctor. Poems in the Waiting Room Poetry Cards are published quarterly in March, May, September and November. Manuscript guidelines are available with SAE, online or by email.
Poetry Publishes Poetry Pamphlets.
Submission Guidelines Submit short poems (20-30 lines) by post or email.
Recent Title(s) *Poems in the Waiting Room*, Collection (Pamphlet)
Tips Poems in the Waiting Room publishes poetry cards expressly for the waiting rooms of hospitals and clinics. Poems should be suitable for patients and relatives.

Poetry Now
Remus House, Woodston, Peterborough, PE2 9JX
- 01733 898101
- 01733 313524
- poetrynow@forwardpress.co.uk
- www.forwardpress.co.uk

Parent Company Forward Press
Contact Steve Twelvetree
Established 1989
Poetry Publishes Poetry Anthologies and Collections with a wide appeal.
Submission Guidelines Accepts one to two sample poems. Check the website for specific calls for submissions, particularly for themed anthologies. Send submissions via email or post.
Tips All work that is published by Poetry Now is considered for Forward Press poetry competitions, see the website for up to date details. Also publishes the *Poetry Now* magazine.

Poetry Press Ltd
26 Park Grove, Edgware, Middlesex, HA8 7SJ
- 020 8958 6499
- poetrypress@yahoo.co.uk

Contact Commissioning Editor, Judy Karbritz (Poetry)
Established 2005
Insider Info Publishes three titles per year. Receives approximately 100 queries and 70 manuscripts per year. 100 per cent of books published are from first-time authors, 100 per cent of books published are from unagented authors. 30 per cent of books published are author subsidy published based on merit. Simultaneous submissions are accepted. Submissions accompanied by SAE will be returned. Aims to respond to queries, proposals and manuscripts within four weeks.
Poetry Publishes Anthologies of both Traditional and Contemporary Poetry – often with mental health themes.
Submission Guidelines Accepts proposal package (including outline, author biography and three sample poems).
Recent Title(s) *Get Out Of My Head!*, Alison Islin; *Have I Got A Poem For You!*, Judy Karbritz; *The Vital Spark*, Michael Igoe
Tips Poetry Press titles are mainly aimed at women and sufferers of mental health problems, particularly OCD and Epilepsy.

Poets Anonymous
70 Aveling Close, Purley, CR8 4DW
- poets@poetsanon.org.uk
- www.poetsanon.org.uk

Poetry Poets Anonymous exists to publish the individual collections and anthologies emerging from the writers' group of the same name. They also publish the *Poetic Licence* magazine, which features new poetry from around the world.

Poolbeg Press
(See entry under UK & Irish Book Publishers)

PS Avalon
(See entry under UK & Irish Book Publishers)

Puffin
(See entry under UK & Irish Book Publishers)

Puppet State Press
40/1 Woodhall Road, Edinburgh, EH13 0DU
- 0131 441 9693
- richard@puppetstate.com
- www.puppetstate.com

Contact Editors: Richard Medrington and Rhona Matheson
Poetry Publishes Poetry Booklets and Pamphlets.

Tips Member of the *Scottish Pamphlet Poetry* website. Puppet State also runs performance poetry and writing workshops for primary and secondary schools.

QQ Press
York House, 15 Argyle Terrace, Rothesay, Isle of Bute, PA20 0BD
Contact Alan Carter
Poetry Publishes a small number of poetry collections and anthologies.

Rack Press
The Rack, Kinnerton, Presteigne, Powys, Wales, LD8 2PF
✆ 01547 560411
✉ rackpress@nicholasmurray.co.uk
🌐 www.nicholasmurray.co.uk/RackPress.html
Contact Nicholas Murray
Insider Info Catalogue available online.
Poetry Publishes Poetry and Translated Poetry in Booklet and Pamphlet format.
Recent Title(s) *Cuffs*, Byron Beynon; *Landing*, Steve Griffiths
Tips Based in Wales, Rack Press has an international vision. It hopes to combine translations and versions with new work by established and new talents from all sources. The company also has a blog available at: www.rackpress.blogspot.com

Ragged Raven Press
1 Lodge Farm, Snitterfield, Stratford-on-Avon, Warwickshire, CV37 0LR
✆ 01789 730320
✉ raggedravenpress@aol.com
🌐 www.raggedraven.co.uk
Contact Editors: Bob Mee and Janet Murch
Established 1998
Insider Info Publishes around two titles per year. Receives 150 queries and 100 manuscripts per year. 100 per cent of books published are from first-time authors, 100 per cent of books published are from unagented authors. Payment is via royalty (on retail price). An advance is offered. Average lead time is nine months, with simultaneous submissions not accepted. Submissions accompanied by SAE will be returned. Catalogue is available online. Manuscript guidelines are available by email.
Poetry Publishes Poetry Anthologies and Collections.
* Only one or two individual collections are published each year, usually by a poet whose work has appeared in Ragged Raven's magazine, *Iota*, or through their annual anthology linked to a competition.

Submission Guidelines Submit six sample poems. Check the website to make sure they are open for submissions.
Tips Ragged Raven also publishes the *Iota* poetry magazine and runs various poetry competitions, including the Annual International Poetry Competition, all of which offer publication in anthologies.

Random House Children's Books
(See entry under UK & Irish Book Publishers)

The Random House Group Ltd
(See entry under UK & Irish Book Publishers)

Raunchland Publications
26 Aldergrove, Dunfermline, KY12 8RP
✉ raunchland@hotmail.com
🌐 www.raunchland.co.uk
Contact John Mingay
Poetry Publishes Poetry titles.
* Raunchland has two online outlets for publication as well as publishing limited edition poetry pamphlets. The first, *Eternal Anthology*, requires a maximum of five short poems in any form. The second, *Repository*, requires sequence poems or linked series.
Submission Guidelines Accepts between one and five sample poems. Email submissions but do not send attachments.
Tips No payment is made for online publication, although the poet retains all rights to their work. Read through the site to get a flavour of the different areas.

Reality Street Editions
(See entry under UK & Irish Book Publishers)

Reardon Publishing
(See entry under UK & Irish Book Publishers)

Redbeck Press
24 Aireville Road, Frizinghall, Bradford, West Yorkshire, BD9 4HH
Contact David Tipton
Poetry Publishes Poetry Collections.
Tips Redbeck are a small independent publisher who publish a few poetry collections a year. Some Redbeck poets are; Debjani Chatterjee, Barry Tebb, Michael Curtis, Terry Gifford, Jane Tipton, Tulio Mora and David Gill.

The Red Candle Press

1 Chatsworth Court, Outram Road, Southsea, Hampshire, PO5 1RA

- 023 9275 3696
- rosecottage@poetry7.fsnet.co.uk
- www.members.tripod.com/redcandlepress

Established 1970

Insider Info Payment is a complimentary copy. Does not accept simultaneous submissions.

Poetry Publishes Poetry books and Pamphlet titles.
* The Red Candle Press primarily publishes the twice yearly magazine *Candelabrum*, and brings out books very occasionally. It is a formalist press, i.e. metrical and rhymed poetry has preference. It does not publish collections on behalf of authors.

Submission Guidelines Accepts proposal package (including outline, three to six sample poems and SAE) by post only.

Tips Red Candle's readership is people who are interested in modern formalist poetry.

Rockingham Press

(See entry under UK & Irish Book Publishers)

Salmon Poetry

Knockevan, Cliffs of Moher, Co. Clare, Republic of Ireland

- 00353 0 65 708 1941
- info@salmonpoetry.com
- www.salmonpoetry.com

Contact Editor, Jessie Lendennie

Established 1981

Insider Info Has published over 200 books. Aims to respond to queries, proposals and manuscript submissions within four months. Catalogue available online.

Poetry Publishes Irish and Contemporary Poetry.

Recent Title(s) *Thornfield: Poems by the Thornfield Poets*, Andrew Carpenter .ed (Anthology); *I Live by the Invisible*, Ray Bradbury (Collection)

Tips One of the largest poetry publishers in Ireland. Salmon is not currently accepting submissions but will post guidelines on their website whenever they are next open for submissions.

Salt Publishing

(See entry under UK & Irish Book Publishers)

Scottish Cultural Press & Scottish Children's Press

(See entry under UK & Irish Book Publishers)

The Seer Press

PO Box 29313, Glasgow, G20 2AE

- 07743 307808
- admin@theseerpress.com

Poetry Publishes Poetry titles.

Recent Title(s) *A Glass of Pure Water*, Suzanne Muir Scott

Tips Publishes poetry collections in pamphlet form. Member of the *Scottish Pamphlet Poetry* website.

Seren

(See entry under UK & Irish Book Publishers)

Serpent's Tail

(See entry under UK & Irish Book Publishers)

Shearsman Books Ltd

(See entry under UK & Irish Book Publishers)

Shepheard-Walwyn (Publishers) Ltd

(See entry under UK & Irish Book Publishers)

Shoestring Press

19 Devonshire Avenue, Beeston, Nottingham, NG9 1BS

- 0115 925 1827
- info@shoestringpress.co.uk
- www.shoestringpress.co.uk

Contact Publisher, John Lucas

Poetry Publishes Poetry titles.

Recent Title(s) *About Love and About Nothing Else*, Toon Tellegen (Collection)

Tips Shoestring Press specialise in sequences and collections by established British poets, or poets from overseas that are unknown to a British audience. Many of the publications use innovative layouts and visual art to enhance them.

Sixties Press

(See entry under UK & Irish Book Publishers)

Smith/Doorstop

Bank Street Arts, 32–40 Bank Street, Sheffield, , S1 2DS

- 0114 346 3037
- Online form.
- www.poetrybusiness.co.uk

Parent Company The Poetry Business

Contact Publisher/Editors: Peter Sansom and Ann Sansom

Established 1986

Poetry Publishes Poetry Books and Pamphlet titles.

Recent Title(s) *Lip*, Catherine Smith

Tips Smith/Doorstop is a small independent publisher of contemporary poetry in book, pamphlet and audio cassette formats. They also publish the winners of *The Poetry Business* competitions (up to date details of which can be found on their website) and *the North* literary magazine. An entry fee is charged. No email entries are accepted.

Smokestack Books
PO Box 408, Middlesbrough, TS5 6WA
☎ 01642 813997
✉ info@smokestack-books.co.uk
🌐 www.smokestack-books.co.uk
Contact Founder/Editor, Andy Croft
Established 2004
Insider Info Publishes six titles per year. Receives 80 queries and 60 manuscripts per year. 25 per cent of books published are from first-time authors, seven per cent of books published are from unagented authors. Payment consists of a standard £500 fee on publication. Average lead time is six months, with simultaneous submissions accepted. Submissions accompanied by SAE will be returned. Aims to respond to queries within two weeks and proposals and manuscripts within four weeks. Catalogue is available with an SAE and available online. Manuscript guidelines are available online.
Poetry Publishes new Contemporary and Traditional Poetry.
Submission Guidelines Submit complete manuscript of at least 45 pages.
Recent Title(s) *Crucifixion in the Plaza de Armas*, Martín Espada
Tips According to their website, Smokestack champions poets who are unconventional, unfashionable, radical or left-field and who are working a long way from the metropolitan centres of cultural authority. Smokestack does not think 'difficulty' in poetry is a virtue, or that poetry is a place in which to hide, but argues that if poetry does not belong to everyone it is not poetry. They do not usually publish first collections.

Souvenier Press Ltd
(See entry under UK & Irish Book Publishers)

Spectacular Diseases
83b London Road, Peterborough, PE2 9BS
Contact Paul Green
Poetry Publishes Poetry titles.
Recent Title(s) *Bird Migration in the 21st Century*, Ken Edwards
Tips Spectacular Diseases started as a magazine and has developed into a small poetry press. All contact must be made by post.

The Stinging Fly Press
(See entry under UK & Irish Book Publishers)

Stride
(See entry under UK & Irish Book Publishers)

Superscript
(See entry under UK & Irish Book Publishers)

Tall Lighthouse Press
Stark Gallery, 384 Lee High Road, Lee Green, London, SE12 8RW
✉ info@tall-lighthouse.co.uk
🌐 www.tall-lighthouse.co.uk
Established 2000
Poetry Publishes Poetry titles.
Recent Title(s) *Turn the Clocks Upside Down*, Aoife Mannix; *But Black & White is Better*, Ken Champion
Tips Tall Lighthouse is an independent literary organisation with a small publishing programme of books and pamphlets. They also organise events, workshops and readings around London and the South East, details of which are on the website.

Tarantula Publications
14 Vine Street, Salford, Manchester, M7 3PG
☎ 0161 792 4593
☎ 0161 792 4593
Contact Sean Brody
Poetry Publishes Poetry titles.
Tips Tarantula Publications are a small publisher of poetry collections.

Templar Poetry
PO Box 7082, Bakewell, Derbyshire, DE45 9AF
☎ 01629 582500
✉ info@templarpoetry.co.uk
🌐 www.templarpoetry.co.uk
Contact Managing Editor, Alex McMillen
Poetry Publishes Poetry titles.
Tips Submissions to the press are not accepted due to time constraints, but poets looking for a route to publication are advised to enter the annual pamphlet and first collection competition. Three winners will see their small collections published in pamphlet form and will be invited to submit a full collection for publication. Other single poems will be published in an anthology. Details of each competition are available on the website.

Terra Firma Press
11 Sinclair Drive, Glasgow, G42 9PR
Contact Anne Murray
Poetry Publishes Poetry titles.

Recent Title(s) *Who Cares, Writes!* Various (Anthology)

Tips Terra Firma Press publishes poetry collections in pamphlet form. They are a member of the *Scottish Pamphlet Poetry* website.

Touch the Earth Publications

39 McKenzie Crescent, Lochgelly, Fife, KY5 9LT

Contact William Hershaw

Poetry Publishes Poetry titles.

Recent Title(s) *The Faerie Walk*, William Hershaw

Tips Publishes William Hershaw's poetry in pamphlet form. All proceeds go to the CHAS (Children's Hospice Association Scotland). Member of the *Scottish Pamphlet Poetry* website.

TownHouse Dublin

(See entry under UK & Irish Book Publishers)

Triumph House

Remus House, Woodston, Peterborough, PE2 9JX

🕿 01733 898101

🕿 01733 313524

🖂 triumphhouse@forwardpress.co.uk

🌐 www.forwardpress.co.uk

Parent Company Forward Press

Established 1994

Insider Info Submissions accompanied by SAE will be returned. Catalogue available online.

Poetry Publishes Religious Poetry titles, in both Traditional and Modern Verse.

* Check the website for specific calls for submissions, particularly for themed anthologies.

Submission Guidelines Submit one to two sample poems.

Submission details to: inbox@forwardpress.co.uk

Tips Triumph House is a Christian poetry imprint. Book themes are either directly about religion and faith, or cover current topics from a Christian point of view.

Tuba Press

Tunley Cottage, Tunley, Near Cirencester, Gloucestershire, GL7 6LW

🕿 01285 760424

🖂 tubapress@mac.com

🌐 www.tubapress.eu

Contact Partners: Peter Ellson and Charles Graham

Insider Info Accepts written requests for full catalogue.

Poetry Publishes 20th and 21st Century Poetry and Prose titles.

Two Rivers Press

(See entry under UK & Irish Book Publishers)

Vane Women Press

c/o Darlington Arts Centre, Vane Terrace, Darlington, DL3 7AX

🕿 01325 348843

🌐 www.vanewomen.co.uk

Poetry Publishes Poetry titles.

Recent Title(s) *Stripping the Blackthorn*, Lindsay Balderson (Collection)

Tips Vane Women is a writers' collective from the North of England that runs a small poetry press. Members also perform their poetry regularly. For more information on existing writers in the collective, there are biographies and many sample poems on the website.

Vanguard Press

(See entry under UK & Irish Book Publishers)

Virago Press

(See entry under UK & Irish Book Publishers)

Walker Books

(See entry under UK & Irish Book Publishers)

Waterloo Press

95 Wick Hall, Furze Hill, Hove, BN3 1NG

🕿 01273 202876

🖂 Online form.

🌐 www.waterloopresshove.com

Contact Founder, Sonja Ctvrtecka; Director, Judy Anderson; Editors: David Kendall, Andrew Duncan, Dr David Pollard and Alan Morrison

Poetry Publishes Poetry titles.

Recent Title(s) *Dandy Lady*, Beryl Fenton (Collection); *Uncaged Sea*, John Goodby (Collection)

Tips Waterloo Press is a not for profit publisher that aims to promote regional poets to a national and international audience, and to publish established, or long neglected modern and modernist poets. There is strong editorial input from previous Waterloo Press poets, who recommend new authors. Also publishes the poetry journal *Eratica*.

The Watts Publishing Group

(See entry under UK & Irish Book Publishers)

The Waywiser Press

(See entry under UK & Irish Book Publishers)

Wendy Webb Books
(See entry under UK & Irish Book Publishers)

West House Books
40 Crescent Road, Sheffield, S7 1HN
- 0114 258 6035
- info@westhousebooks.co.uk
- www.westhousebooks.co.uk
Contact Founder, Alan Halsey; Partner, Geraldine Monk
Established 1994
Insider Info Catalogue available online.
Poetry Publishes Poetry Books and Pamphlets.
* The current focus is on late modernist poetry. Pamphlets are often seen as the quickest and most effective way of publishing brand new work.
Recent Title(s) *Escafeld Hangings*, Geraldine Monk
Tips West House involves its authors in all aspects of book production, including design and layout. They also publish some poetry-related work, such as non-fiction.

Wild Honey Press
16a Ballyman Road, Bray, Co. Wicklow, Republic of Ireland
- 00353 71 985 5237
- 00353 71 985 6063
- poetry@wildhoneypress.com
- www.wildhoneypress.com
Contact Founders: Prin and Betty Duignan
Established 1989
Insider Info Catalogue available online.
Poetry Publishes Contemporary and Irish poetry.
Recent Title(s) *Nelson & the Huruburu Bird*, Mairéad Byrne; *Livelihood*, Maurice Scully
Tips Wild Honey is a small, independent publisher and is often unable to accept submissions. Check the website submissions status.

Wild Women Press
Flat 10, The Common, Windermere, LA23 1JH
- vik@wildwomenpress.com
- adam@wildwomenpress.com
- www.wildwomenpress.com
Contact Director, Victoria Bennett; Design, Adam Clarke
Established 1999
Poetry Publishes Poetry titles.
* Publishes unique poetry by women only, particularly writers at the start of their careers who deserve to be published.
Submission Guidelines Unsolicited manuscripts are not being accepted at present.
Tips Wild Women Press are a not for profit collective of writers who aim to bring a 'wild' attitude to poetry

publishing. As well as commissioning books, the press organises poetry events and competitions, details of which are on the website.

Woodburn Press
Kendalmere, Caledonian Road, Peebles, EH45 9DL
Poetry Publishes Poetry Books and Pamphlets.
Recent Title(s) *Garden Party*, Gill McConnell
Tips Member of the *Scottish Pamphlet Poetry* website.

Wordsonthestreet
(See entry under UK & Irish Book Publishers)

Wordsworth Editions Ltd
(See entry under UK & Irish Book Publishers)

Worple Press
(See entry under UK & Irish Book Publishers)

Wrecking Ball Press
(See entry under UK & Irish Book Publishers)

Xcite Books
(See entry under UK & Irish Book Publishers)

Y Lolfa Cyf
(See entry under UK & Irish Book Publishers)

Young Picador
(See entry under UK & Irish Book Publishers)

UK & IRISH PACKAGERS

Aladdin Books
2/3 Fitzroy Mews, London, W1T 6DF
- 020 7383 2084
- 020 7388 6391
- alexandra.mew@aladdinbooks.co.uk
- www.aladdinbooks.co.uk
Contact Managing Director, Charles Nicholas
Established 1979
Insider Info Aladdin Books Ltd creates highly illustrated non-fiction books for children aged from one to sixteen. The company focuses on reading schemes, and social, environmental and world issues.
Non-fiction Subjects covered include: Maths, Science and Technology, Natural History, Arts, Crafts & Hobbies, Geography and Environment, General Interest and Novelty

The Albion Press Ltd

Spring Hill, Idbury, Oxfordshire, OX7 6RU
- 01993 831094
- 01993 831982

Contact Managing Director, Emma Bradford
Established 1984
Insider Info Specialises in children's books.
Submission Guidelines No unsolicited manuscripts or synopses.

Amber Books Ltd

Bradley's Close, 74–77 White Lion Street, London, N1 9PF
- 020 7520 7600
- 020 7520 7606/7607
- editorial@amberbooks.co.uk
- www.amberbooks.co.uk

Contact Managing Director, Stasz Gynch
Insider Info Amber Books presents a broad range of illustrated non-fiction for adults and children.
Non-fiction Subjects include: Military History, Military Technology, Aviation, Transport, Children's, Combat and Survival Techniques, Games and Pastimes, Music, Mind, Body and Spirit, Crime, Detection and Punishment, Science and Nature, Health and Medicine, Social History and Cookery
Submission Guidelines Send a synopsis, contents list, a sample chapter or two, and a single page CV or resume addressed to the 'Publishing Manager'.
Tips Amber Books are particularly interested in submissions on military topics, but also welcome good ideas on any non-fiction subject suitable for an illustrated book. No fiction, biography or poetry. The children's imprint, Tiptoe Books, was launched at Bologna Book Fair in 2008.

BCS Publishing Ltd

2nd Floor, Temple Court, 109 Oxford Road, Cowley, Oxford, OX4 2ER
- 01865 770099
- 01865 770050
- bcs-publishing@dcl.pipex.com

Contact Managing Director, Steve McCurdy
Non-fiction Produces General Interest, Illustrated Non-Fiction

Bender Richardson White

c/o Lionel Bender, 10 Chelmsford Square, London, NW10 3AR
- 020 8459 0453
- 020 8451 3681
- lionel@brw.co.uk
- www.brw.co.uk

Contact Partner (Editorial), Lionel Bender

Insider Info BRW is a UK-based editorial, design and production team producing books for publishers around the world. It specialises in illustrated non-fiction for children and adults, educational and home learning materials. Also see: www.nibweb.co.uk/lionelbender.htm
Non-fiction Subjects covered include: Educational Resources, Home Learning Materials, Dictionaries, Encyclopedias, Computers, Science, History, Maths, English, Religion, Reference titles, Natural History and Activity Books

Bookwork Ltd

Unit 17, Piccadilly Mill, Lower Street, Stroud, Gloucester, GL5 2HT
- 01453 752521
- bookwork@compuserve.com

Contact Director, Louise Pritchard (Editorial); Director, Alan Plank (Production); Editor, Annabel Blackledge; Art Editor, Kate Mullins
Insider Info Produces activity, board, novelty and reference books for children. Also packages under the Pangolin imprint.

Brainwaves Ltd

Epson House, 31 Chart Lane, Reigate, Surrey, RH2 7DY
- 01737 224444
- 01737 225777

Contact Keith Faulkner
Insider Info Packages children's activity, board, novelty, picture and gift books.

Breslich & Foss Ltd

2a Union Court, 20–22 Union Road, London, SW4 6JP
- 020 7819 3990
- 020 7819 3998
- www.breslichfoss.co.uk

Contact Managing Director, Paula Breslich
Established 1978
Insider Info Breslich & Foss are well-established, independent packagers of co-edition books for the international market.
Non-fiction Specialises in Crafts, Interior Design, Gardening, Health & Beauty, Children's Non-Fiction and Picture Books
Submission Guidelines Does not accept unsolicited manuscripts.

The Bridgewater Book Company Ltd

c/o Clark Browncombe, 33 Cliffe High Street, Lewes, East Sussex, BN7 2AN
- 01273 403120
- 01273 487441

- bailey@bridgewaterbooks.co.uk
- www.bridgewaterbooks.co.uk

Contact Operations Manager, Jonathan Bailey
Insider Info Bridgewater Books is the contract publishing arm of the Ivy Publishing Group. They produce illustrated books in all subject areas, and offer design and publishing services.
Tips Details of freelance opportunities are given on the website.

Brown Reference Group (BRG)
1st Floor, 9–17 St Albans Place, London, N1 0NX
- 020 7424 5640
- 020 7424 5641
- info@brownreference.com
- www.brownreference.com

Contact Managing Director, Sharon hutton; Children's Publisher, Anne O'Daly; Editorial Director, Lindsey Lowe
Established 1995
Insider Info The Brown Reference Group (BRG) is a leading packager of high quality reference books and encyclopedias for all age groups. The company now has clients worldwide. BRG has produced more than 100 major reference encyclopedias, and is also leading supplier of part works.

Brown Wells & Jacobs Ltd
Foresters Hall, 25–27 Westow Street, London, SE19 3RY
- 020 8771 5115
- 020 8771 9994
- graham@bwj-ltd.com
- www.bwj.org

Contact Managing Director, Graham Brown
Established 1978
Insider Info Produces high quality non-fiction children's books, including novelty and pop-up books. Offers a wide range of services from creating original formats for the trade and licensed character markets to producing special projects.

Cambridge Publishing Management Ltd
Burr Elm Court, Main Street, Caldecote, Cambridge, CB23 7NU
- 01954 214000
- 01954 214002
- www.cambridgepm.co.uk

Contact Managing Editor, Jackie Dobbyne; Production Manager, Tim Newton
Insider Info A creative book production company, offering a comprehensive service to publishers. Specialises in the complete project management of trade, travel, educational and ELT titles.

Cameron & Hollis
PO Box 1, Moffat, Dumfriesshire, DG10 9SU
- 01683 220808
- 01683 220012
- editorial@cameronbooks.co.uk
- www.cameronbooks.co.uk

Contact Directors, Ian A. Cameron and Jill Hollis
Insider Info Cameron & Hollis, the publishing imprint of Cameron Books, specialises in creating non-fiction books with publishers in Britain, continental Europe and North America.
Non-fiction Subjects covered include: Contemporary Art, Film Criticism, Decorative Arts, Architecture, Social History, and the Environment

Canopus Publishing
15 Nelson Parade, Bristol, BS3 4HY
- 0117 963 3366
- robin@canopusbooks.com
- www.canopusbooks.com

Contact Managing Director, Robin Rees; Publishing Director, Tom Spicer; Commissioning Editor, Jim Revill
Insider Info Canopus is a book packager and publisher.
Non-fiction Specialises in Popular Science and Astronomy titles.

Carroll & Brown Ltd
20 Lonsdale Road, London, NW6 6RD
- 020 7372 0900
- 020 7372 0460
- mail@carrollandbrown.co.uk
- www.carrollandbrown.co.uk

Contact Editorial Director, Amy Carroll
Insider Info Carroll & Brown has been a book packager for more than fifty years and has been publishing under its own imprint for more than five years.
Non-fiction Specialises in Health, Craft, Mind, Body & Spirit, Lifestyle and Pregnancy & Childcare titles for the UK and international markets.

Cowley Hunter Publishing
8 Belmont, Bath, BA1 5DZ
- 01225 339999
- 01225 339995
- info@cowleyrobinson.com
- www.cowleyrobinson.com

Contact Publishing Director, Stewart Cowley
Insider Info Produces children's novelty titles for the co-edition market, specialising in paper engineering and licensed character publishing.

D & N Publishing
3c Lowesden Works, Lambourn Woodlands, Hungerford, Berkshire, RG17 7RU
- ☎ 01488 73657
- ✉ d@dnpublishing.co.uk

Contact Partners, David Price-Goodfellow and Namrita Price-Goodfellow
Established 1991
Insider Info Offers complete project management, including some or all of the following (depending on project): commissioning, editing, picture research, illustration and design, page layout, proofreading, indexing and printing. Each stage is managed in-house and produced on Apple Macs running the latest software. All subjects are covered, with natural history a speciality. 40–50 titles are produced per year. Clients include HarperCollins Publishers and The Crowood Press.
Tips No unsolicited manuscripts accepted, but there are opportunities for freelancers with a proven track record, and several years' experience (would need experience of book publishing).

David West Children's Books
7 Princeton Court, 55 Felsham Road, London, SW15 1AZ
- ☎ 020 8780 3836
- ☎ 020 8780 9313
- ✉ dww@btinternet.com
- 🌐 www.davidwestchildrensbooks.com

Insider Info Produces highly illustrated children's information books, designed for translation, specifically for the international market.
Non-fiction Children's subjects covered include: Mysteries, Ancient Civilisations, Animals, Cinema, History, Science, Aviation, Sports, Machines and Fashion

Design Eye Ltd
226 City Road, London, EC1V 2TT
- ☎ 020 7812 8601
- ☎ 020 7253 4370
- ✉ info@designeye.co.uk
- 🌐 www.quarto.com

Parent Company The Quarto Group Inc
Contact Publisher, Sue Grabham
Insider Info Design Eye publishes innovative interactive kit books for adults and children, often incorporating extras such as craft materials, moulded figures or working models.

Diagram Visual Information Ltd
34 Elaine Grove, London, NW5 4QH
- ☎ 020 7485 5941
- ☎ 020 7482 4932

Contact Managing Director, Bruce Robertson
Established 1967
Insider Info Produces reference books for trade, library, school and academic markets.

Eddison Sadd Editions Ltd
St Chad's House, 148 King's Cross Road, London, WC1X 9DH
- ☎ 020 7837 1968
- ☎ 020 7837 2025
- ✉ info@eddisonsadd.com
- 🌐 www.eddisonsadd.com

Contact Managing Director, Nick Eddison; Editorial Director, Ian Jackson
Established 1982
Insider Info Eddison Sadd is one of the world's leading co-edition packagers. The company produces non-fiction books, including gift and reference books.
Non-fiction Publishes Non-Fiction titles, with an emphasis on Health and Mind, Body & Spirit titles

Focus Publishing (Sevenoaks) Ltd
The Courtyard, 26 London Road, Sevenoaks, TN13 1AP
- ☎ 01732 742456
- ☎ 01732 743381
- ✉ focus-publishing@netway.co.uk
- 🌐 www.focus-publishing.co.uk

Contact Managing Director, Guy Croton; Publishing Manager & Editor, Caroline Watson
Insider Info Offers a complete Direct To Print book packaging service and produces its own illustrated concepts in a range of subjects.
Non-fiction Subjects covered include: Gardening, DIY, Food & Drink, Photography, Sports, Transport and Health

Graham-Cameron Publishing & Illustration
The Studio, 23 Holt Road, Sheringham, Norfolk, NR26 8NB
- ☎ 01263 821333
- ☎ 01263 821334
- ✉ enquiry@graham-cameron-illustration.com
- 🌐 www.graham-cameron-illustration.com

Contact Partners, Mike Graham-Cameron, Helen Graham-Cameron and Duncan Graham-Cameron
Established 1985
Insider Info As well as being an illustration agency, Graham Cameron also packages illustrated books, both fiction and non-fiction, for children.
Non-fiction Deals with Educational, Reference, Activity and Picture Books.
Fiction Deals with Picture Books and Activity Books.

Haldane Mason Ltd

PO Box 34196, London, NW10 3YB
- 020 8459 2131
- 020 8728 1216
- info@haldanemason.com
- www.haldanemason.com

Contact Editorial Director, Samuel Francis
Established 1984
Insider Info Haldane Mason Ltd primarily produces children's illustrated non-fiction. Their adult list consists mainly of mind, body and spirit titles.

Hart McLeod Ltd

14 Greenside, Waterbeach, Cambridge, CB25 9HP
- 01223 861495
- 01223 862902
- inhouse@hartmcleod.co.uk
- www.hartmcleod.co.uk

Contact Partners: Graham Hart, Chris McLeod and Joanne Barker
Insider Info A leading supplier of editorial, design and production services in the UK. The company is at the forefront of developments in interactive publishing for UK schools. It produces around 200 titles a year.

Hawcock Books

Grafton House, High Street, Norton St Philip, Bath, BA2 7LG
- 01373 834055
- 01373 834622
- Online form
- www.hawcockbooks.co.uk

Insider Info Packager specialising solely in pop-up, novelty and paper engineering designs for the publishing industry.

HL Studios Ltd

17 Fenlock Court, Blenheim Office Park, Long Hanborough, Oxford, OX29 8LN
- 01993 881010
- 01993 882713
- info@hlstudios.eu.com
- www.hlstudios.eu.com

Contact Managing Director, Robin Hickey
Established 1985
Insider Info HL Studios Ltd specialises in educational titles, general non-fiction co-editions and multimedia.
Non-fiction Subjects include: Travel Guides, Gardening, and Cookery

Hutton & Partners

Borough House, 32 West Borough, Wimborne Minster, Dorset, BH21 1NF
- 01202 849976
- info2@huttonpartners.com
- www.huttonpartners.com

Contact Founder & Director, Steve Hutton
Insider Info A graphic design company that offers creative solutions for packaging design, websites and product branding. Hutton & Partners has designed packaging and branding logos for toy and craft clients such as Humbrol, Hazel Mill Toys and The Toy & Hobby Association.

The Ilex Press Ltd

The Old Candlemakers, West Street, Lewes, BN7 2NZ
- 01273 487440
- 01273 487441
- name@ilex-press.com
- www.ilex-press.com

Contact Managing Director, Stephen Paul
Insider Info Ilex Press is a sister company to The Ivy Press Ltd. It produces titles on the digital arts, design, popular culture, website design, graphics software, photography and e-books.

Inky Press

- info@inkypress.com
- www.inkypress.com

Parent Company Creations for Children International
Insider Info Produces children's paper-engineered non-fiction and illustration-led picture book titles for readers aged up to nine.
Submission Guidelines Appreciates brief intro addressed to info@inkypress.com. Do not send hard copies, any texts, illustrations or design concepts (and certainly not originals) before established email exchange with Inky Press.

Interpretation

84a Hough Green, Chester, CH4 8JW
- 01244 676741
- tony@heritageinterpretation.co.uk
- www.heritageinterpretation.co.uk

Contact Tony Bowerman, Chris Bullock
Insider Info Among other things, Interpretation conceive, write and develop publications for organisations and publishers, including guidebooks, teaching packs and work sheets.
Tips The company centres its business on visitor attractions at countryside and heritage sites. Primary products are interpretation panels, leaflets, and guidebooks for exhibits.

The Ivy Press Ltd

The Old Candlemakers, West Street, Lewes, East Sussex, BN7 2NZ

- ☎ 01273 487440
- ☎ 01273 487441
- ✉ name@ivy-group.com
- 🌐 www.ivypress.co.uk

Contact Managing Director, Stephen Paul; Creative Director, Peter Bridgewater; Publisher, Jason Hook
Established 1996
Insider Info The Ivy Press Ltd is part of The Ivy Group and produces various non-fiction illustrated titles.
Non-fiction Subjects include: Arts and Crafts, Art and Design, Children's, Food and Drink, General Interest, Health, Home and Garden, Humour, Mind, Body and Spirit, Parenting, Pets and Popular Culture titles
Submission Guidelines Welcomes unsolicited ideas and manuscripts. Please send a synopsis and your CV, a table of contents, and sample text.
Tips Project ideas should be topical and suitable for the international market. Also, see entry under UK & Irish Book Publishers. Ivy Press are also keen to hear from freelance writers; send a biography, list of published titles, and areas of interest and expertise by post or email.

John Brown

136–142 Bramley Road, London, W10 6SR

- ☎ 020 7565 3000
- ☎ 020 7565 3060
- ✉ andrew.hirsch@johnbrownmedia.com
- 🌐 www.jbcp.co.uk

Contact Director, Andrew Jarvis
Insider Info As well as being a well-known magazine publisher and PR firm, John Brown also packages children's part works and educational titles.

Julian Holland

1st Floor, 64 High Street, Glastonbury, Somerset, BA6 9DY

- ☎ 01458 832222
- ✉ jules@julesholland.com
- 🌐 www.julesholland.com

Contact Proprietor, Julian Holland
Insider Info Julian Holland is an experienced book packager, author and photographer, specialising in travel and transport titles.
Submission Guidelines No unsolicited manuscripts or synopses.

Lexus Ltd

60 Brook Street, Glasgow, G40 2AB

- ☎ 0141 556 0440
- ☎ 0141 556 2202
- ✉ peterterrell@lexusforlanguages.co.uk
- 🌐 www.lexusforlanguages.co.uk

Contact Editorial Director, Peter Terrell
Established 1980
Insider Info Lexus compiles bilingual dictionaries, phrasebooks and text books spanning 29 languages. They publish the *Travelmates* series and *The Chinese Classroom* (a beginner's course in Mandarin Chinese). They offer a range of publishing services, including text processing, type setting, translation and project management.

Market House Books Ltd

Suite B, Elsinore House, 43 Buckingham Street, Aylesbury, Buckinghamshire, HP20 2NQ

- ☎ 01296 484911
- ☎ 01296 338934
- ✉ books@mhbref.com
- 🌐 www.mhbref.com

Contact Managing Director, John Daintith; Managing Editor, Elizabeth Martin; Production Editor, Anne Kerr
Insider Info A book producer and packager specialising in reference books, with a list that ranges from small pocket dictionaries to large, multi-volume colour encyclopedias. Major reference works include the *Collins English Dictionary*, the *Macmillan Encyclopedia*, and the *Grolier Library of Women's Biographies*.

Marshall Editions Ltd

The Old Brewery, 6 Blundell Street, London, N7 9BH

- ☎ 020 7700 6764
- ☎ 020 7700 4191
- ✉ info@www.marshalleditions.com
- 🌐 www.marshalleditions.com

Parent Company The Quarto Group Inc
Contact Publisher, Jenni Johns
Insider Info Marshall Editions publishes highly illustrated non-fiction books in co-edition for adults and children.
Non-fiction Subjects include titles on: Culture, Health, History, Gardening, Interiors, Natural History and Popular Science

Mathew Price Ltd

Albury Court, Albury, Thame, Oxon, OX9 2LP

- ☎ 01844 337000
- ✉ mathewp@mathewprice.com
- 🌐 www.mathewprice.com

Contact Managing Director, Mathew Price
Insider Info Produces novelty and picture books, educational titles, and fiction for children up to eleven years old.

Monkey Puzzle Media Ltd
Little Manor Farm, The Street, Brundish, Woodbridge, Suffolk, IP13 8BL
- 01379 388990
- info@monkeypuzzlemedia.com

Contact Managing Director, Roger Goddard-Coote
Established 1998
Insider Info Packager of non-fiction for trade, school, library and mass markets. Publishes about 80 titles a year.

Nicola Baxter
PO Box 215, Framingham Earl, Yelverton, Norwich, NR14 7UR
- 01508 491111

Contact Proprietor & Commissioning Editor, Nicola Baxter; Submissions, Sally Delaney
Insider Info Deals with the packaging of children's books, from concept to production.

Orpheus Books Ltd
6 Church Green, Witney, Oxfordshire, OX28 4AW
- 01993 774949
- 01993 700330
- info@orpheusbooks.com
- www.orpheusbooks.com

Contact Executive Director, Nicholas Harris
Established 1992
Insider Info Orpheus Books are specialists in children's non-fiction for the international co-edition market. They are known for their unique concepts and use of die cuts, flaps and foldouts. The company list has a wide ranging subject matter, for children from three to twelve years. Orpheus also produces high quality encyclopedias and atlases.
Submission Guidelines Freelance writers should send their CVs. Illustrators should send sample copies.

OutHouse Publishing
9 Fairmount, Shalbourne, Marlborough, Wiltshire, SN8 3JQ
- 01672 871387
- 01672 870350
- sales@outhousepublishing.co.uk

Contact Partners, Sue Gordon and Elizabeth Mallard-Shaw
Established 1996
Insider Info OutHouse specialises in illustrated non-fiction. They offer project management, copyediting, design and layout, cartography, proofreading and indexing, and can provide a full packaging service from concept to warehouse. All members of the OutHouse team are traditionally trained and highly experienced. Clients include The Crowood Press, New Holland Publishing, and AA Publishing.
Non-fiction Subjects include: Gardening, Biography, Animals, Walking and Hiking, and British History
Submission Guidelines No unsolicited ideas or manuscripts.

Quantum Publishing Ltd
The Old Brewery, 6 Blundell Street, London, N7 9BH
- 020 7700 6700
- 020 7700 4191
- quantum@quarto.com
- www.quarto.com

Parent Company The Quarto Group Inc
Contact Publisher, Anastasia Cavouras
Established 1995
Insider Info Quantum is Quarto Publishing Plc's specialist backlist division. It focuses on repackaging successful titles for worldwide distribution.

Quarto Publishing Plc
The Old Brewery, 6 Blundell Street, London, N7 9BH
- 020 7700 6700
- 020 7700 4191
- quarto@quarto.com
- www.quartobooks.com

Parent Company The Quarto Group Inc
Contact Publisher, Paul Carslake
Insider Info Quarto Publishing is the original co-edition list in the Quarto Group, and produces illustrated non-fiction books.
Non-fiction Subjects include: Arts & Crafts, Gardening, Lifestyle and Reference

Quintet Publishing Ltd
The Old Brewery, 6 Blundell Street, London, N7 9BH
- 020 7700 2001
- 020 7700 4191
- jamet@quarto.com
- www.quarto.com

Parent Company The Quarto Group Inc
Contact Publisher, James Tavendale
Insider Info Quintet publishes highly illustrated non-fiction co-edition books for international markets.
Non-fiction Subjects include: Arts & Crafts, Interior Design, Gardening, Health & Well-Being, Cookery and Illustrated Reference

Salariya Book Company Ltd
Book House, 25 Marlborough Place, Brighton, East Sussex, BN1 1UB

☎ 01273 603306
🖷 01273 693857
✉ salariya@salariya.com
🌐 www.salariya.com

Contact Managing Director, David Salariya; Editorial: Karen Barker Smith and Michael Ford

Insider Info The Salariya Book Company is an award winning publisher specialising in illustrated information books for children. In the UK it publishes under its own imprint, Book House, which was founded in 2002.

Non-fiction Topics include: Animals, Earth and the Environment, History, Science and Technology

Savitri Books Ltd
25 Lisle Lane, Ely, Cambridgeshire, CB7 4AS
☎ 01353 654327
✉ munni@savitribooks.demon.co.uk

Contact Director, Mrinalini S. Srivastava
Established 1983

Insider Info Savitri Books Ltd commissions illustrated non-fiction, including biography, history and travel.

Small World Design
72a Pope Lane, Penwortham, Preston, Lancashire, PR1 9DA
☎ 01772 750885
🖷 01772 750885
✉ Online form.
🌐 www.smallworlddesign.co.uk

Contact Partners: David Peet and Sue Chadwick
Established 1995

About A freelance design company who write, illustrate, design and package all manner of children's material and merchandise. Customers include children's book publishers, packagers, wholesalers, toy and game manufacturers and educational suppliers across the UK, Europe and worldwide. They also offer product licensing for their designs.

Non-fiction Topics include: Pre-school Resources, Novelty Books, Big Books, Games, Jigsaw Puzzles, Activity Packs and Licenced Products

Southbank Design
11 Millbridge Street, Romsey, Hampshire, SO51 8HJ
☎ 01794 513338
✉ enquiries@southbank-design.co.uk
🌐 www.southbank-design.co.uk

About A graphic design company that creates design solutions for a number of clients in many business sectors, from individual traders to multinationals. Provides solutions for packaging,

illustrations and artworks, and other services such as website design.

Tips For enquiries about designer and illustrator jobs, send a query letter and CV by email.

Stonecastle Graphics Ltd
Highlands Lodge, Chartway Street, Sutton Valence, Kent, ME17 3HZ
☎ 01622 844414
🖷 01622 844414
✉ info@stonecastle-graphics.co.uk
🌐 www.stonecastle-graphics.com

Contact Partners: Paul Turner and Sue Pressley

Insider Info Offers a complete book design, photography, editorial, illustration and packaging service. Illustrated general non-fiction is commissioned for adults and children across a range of subjects. In 2003 Stonecastle Graphics founded Touchstone Books Ltd, their own imprint, which publishes high quality, highly illustrated non-fiction adult titles.

Studio Cactus Ltd
13 Southgate Street, Winchester, Hampshire, SO23 9DZ
☎ 01962 878600
✉ mail@studiocactus.co.uk
🌐 www.studiocactus.co.uk

Contact Editorial Director, Damien Moore
Established 1998

Insider Info Produces high quality, illustrated books for international publishers including Dorling Kindersley and David & Charles. Projects range from illustrated reference to children's educational titles.

Tips Opportunities exist for designers and editorial freelancers with a proven track record.

Tangerine Designs Ltd
2 High Street, Freshford, Bath, BA2 7WE
☎ 01225 720001
✉ tangerinedesign@btinternet.com

Contact Managing Director, Christine Swift
Established 2000

Insider Info Packagers and co-edition publishers of children's books.

Submission Guidelines Accepts submissions with SAE.

Thomas Bohm: Graphic Communication Design & Illustration
Based in London
☎ 07790 924159
✉ email@tbohm.info
🌐 www.tbohm.info

Contact Director, Thomas Bohm

Insider Info Offers graphic communication design (book design, corporate communications, document design, form design, graphic design, information design, instruction manual design, textbook design, typesetting, typography, and website design) and an illustration service (freehand, technical), across print, web and interactive medias. Also offers a large, giant, and clear print transcription service for people with visual impairments. Specialises in educational, medical, scientific and children's books.

Tony Potter Publishing Ltd
1 Stairbridge Court, Bolney Grange Business Park, Haywards Heath, West Sussex, RH17 5PA
- 01444 232889
- 01444 232142
- info@tonypotter.com
- www.tonypotter.com

Contact Managing and Creative Director, Tony Potter

Insider Info Tony Potter Publishing creates innovative paper based products and high quality books for the international co-edition market. Specialising in interactive books for children (from one to twelve years old), the company also publishes custom and own brand books for adults and children. Adult titles now come under The Teapot Press Imprint (www.teapotpress.com) and a small list is published under the Over the Moon imprint.

Submission Guidelines Tony Potter Publishing Ltd is happy to consider unsolicited ideas (although most of their work is generated in-house). Send ideas in hard copy form only and enclose SAE. They are particularly looking for pre-school level interactive education/novelty books, and chapter book fiction for nine to twelve year olds.

Toucan Books Ltd
3rd Floor, 89 Charterhouse Street, London, EC1M 6HR
- 020 7250 3388
- 020 7250 3123
- info@toucanbooks.co.uk
- www.toucanbooks.co.uk

Contact Director, Robert Sackville West; Managing Director, Ellen Dupont

Established 1985

Insider Info Toucan Books has a reputation as a leading packager of illustrated reference titles. Specialising in international co-editions, Toucan commissions illustrated non-fiction for children and adults. The company client list includes Reader's Digest and the BBC.

Tucker Slingsby Ltd
Regal House, 70 London Road, Twickenham, TW1 3QS
- 020 8744 1007
- 020 8744 0041
- sales@tuckerslingsby.co.uk
- www.tuckerslingsby.co.uk

Insider Info A packager specialising in preschool early learning books, children's non-fiction, anthologies, religious and activity books. They also produce health and beauty titles for adults.

Working Partners Ltd
Stanley House, St Chad's Place, London, WC1X 9HH
- 020 7841 3939
- 020 7841 3940
- enquiries@workingpartnersltd.co.uk
- www.workingpartnersltd.co.uk

Contact Managing Director, Chris Snowdon; Editorial, Charles Nettleton

Established 1995

Insider Info A creative team dedicated to the development of quality commercial fiction, contracted to supply fully edited texts to publishers. Working Partners has created many highly popular series' in children's fiction, such as the classic *Animal Ark* series. Working Partners Two was founded in 2006 to create novels across most adult genres, and aims to recreate the successes of the children's list in the adult market.

Submission Guidelines Will accept queries from agents and writers. Adult Fiction queries should be sent to: charlesn@workingpartnersltd.co.uk

Zoe Books Ltd
15 Worthy Lane, Winchester, Hampshire, SO23 7AB
- 01962 851318
- enquiries@zoebooks.co.uk

Contact Managing Director, Imogen Dawson

Insider Info Zoe Books creates and publishes quality full colour reference books, for children and young adults, and for trade and educational markets worldwide. The company specialises in series co-editions for the school and library markets.

Non-fiction Subjects include: Arts and Crafts, Clothing, Food and Drink, Geography, History, Science, Sports, Travel, and World Habitats

EUROPEAN & INTERNATIONAL PUBLISHERS

Abingdon Press

201 Eighth Avenue South, PO Box 801, Nashville, Tennessee, 37202, USA

- 001 615 749 6290
- 001 615 749 6128
- publicity@abingdonpress.com
- www.abingdonpress.com

Parent Company The United Methodist Publishing House

Contact President/Publisher, Neil M. Alexander; Senior Editor, Robert Ratcliff; Senior Editor, Ron Kidd

Imprint(s) Abingdon Press
Cokesbury
Dimensions for Living

Categories Publishes Non-Fiction on the following subjects: Children's, Biography, Education, General Interest, Reference, Religion, Scholarly, Sociology, Textbook, Theology

Insider Info Publishes 120 titles per year. Pays 7.5 per cent royalty on retail price. Receives 3,000 queries per year. Receives 250 manuscripts per year. Does not accept simultaneous submissions. Average lead time is two years. Book catalogue available free on request.

Submission Guidelines Accepts unsolicited manuscripts and proposals.

Recent Title(s) *The Unshuttered Heart*, Ann Belford Ulanov

Tips Abingdon is a religious publisher and produces various multimedia products, including audiobooks and computer software.

ACER Press

19 Prospect Hill Road, Camberwell, Victoria, 3124, Australia

- 0061 3 9277 5555
- 0061 3 9277 5500
- info@acer.edu.au
- www.acer.edu.au

Parent Company Australian Council for Educational Research (ACER)

Contact Chief Executive Officer, Geoff Masters; General Manager (ACER Press), Ralph Saubern

Categories Publishes Non-Fiction on the following subjects: Academic, Counselling, Education, Human Resources, Multimedia, Psychology, Reference, Teaching Resources

Submission Guidelines Accepts unsolicited manuscripts and proposals.

Recent Title(s) *Play Matters: Engaging Children in Learning*, Kathy Walker

Tips ACER Press accepts evidence or research-based submissions as long as they are sent using the ACER Publishing Proposal Form - available on the website.

Adams Media

57 Littlefield Street, Avon, Massachusetts, 02322, USA

- 001 508 427 7100
- 001 800 872 5628
- submissions@adamsmedia.com
- www.adamsmedia.com

Parent Company F+W Media Inc

Contact Executive Publishing Director, Gary M. Krebs; Senior Editor, Jill Alexander

Categories Publishes Non-Fiction on the following subject areas: Self-Help, Inspiration, Women's Issues, Pop Psychology, Relationships, Business, Careers, Parenting, New Age, Gift Books, Cookbooks, How-To and Reference titles.

Insider Info Publishes 230 titles per year. Receives 5,000 queries and 1,500 manuscripts per year. Receives 40 per cent of books from first-time authors. 40 per cent of books are from unagented writers. Average lead time is 12–18 months. Accepts simultaneous submissions.

Submission Guidelines Accepts unsolicited manuscripts and proposals.

Recent Title(s) *Kncok 'Em Dead 2008: The Ultimate Job Search Guide*, Martin Yate

Tips Adams Media will only accept proposals by post and they should include relevant market research, along with SAE or IRC (for international submissions).

Adriano Salani Publisher S.p.A.

Via Gherardini 10 – 20145, Milan, Italy

- 0039 2 3459 7624
- 0039 2 3459 7206
- info@salani.it
- www.salani.it

Contact President, Luigi Spagnol; General Executive Manager, Guglielmo Tognetti; Publisher, Maria Mazzitelli

Parent Company Group Mauri Spagnol

Categories Publishes Children's Fiction, Picture Books, How-To Books, Comics, Gift Books, Film/Television Tie-Ins in all genres including; Fantasy, Fairy Tales, Action/Adventure, Animals, and Poetry

Insider Info Adriano Salani publishes bestselling children's book translations such as *Harry Potter* and the *His Dark Materials* trilogy.

Recent Titles *La Bussola D'oro*, Phillip Pullman (Film Tie-In); *Ogni Gatto E' Illuminato*, Laura De Tomasi and Yoshitaka Masumi

Albert Bonniers Förlag

PO Box 3159, S-103 63, Stockholm, Sweden

- 0046 8 696 8620
- 0046 8 696 8369
- info@abforlag.bonnier.se
- www.albertbonniersforlag.se

Contact Publisher, Albert Bonnier; Editor, Åsa Ernflo; Editor, Susanna Höijer; Editor (Fiction, Poetry, Biography), Sophie Sällström; Editor (Non-Fiction), Thomas Lundvall

Imprint(s) Bonnierpocket
Bonnier Fakta
Bonnier Impact
Panache

Categories Publishes Non-Fiction, Fiction and Children's on the following subject areas: Biography, Essays, General Interest, Literary Fiction, Mainstream Fiction, Memoir, Poetry

Insider Info Publishes 150 titles per year.

Submission Guidelines Accepts unsolicited manuscripts and proposals.

Recent Title(s) *Supermat*, Helena Nyblom

Tips Submissions to Albert Bonniers Förlag must be directed to either the fiction or non-fiction editor, as appropriate.

Allen & Unwin (Pty) Ltd

PO Box 8500, St Leonards, New South Wales, 1590, Australia

- 0061 2 8425 0100
- 0061 2 9906 2218
- info@allenandunwin.com
- www.allenandunwin.com

Contact Publishers: Sue Hines; Patrick Gallagher; Jane Palfreyman; Annette Bowring; Elizabeth Weiss (Academic); Rebecca Kaiser; Maggie Hamilton (Inspired Living); Louise Egerton (Natural History); Ian Bowring (Military History, Business); Erica Wagner (Children); Louise Thurtell (Arena)

Imprint(s) Arena

Categories Publishes Non-Fiction, Fiction, and Children's books on the following subjects: Academic, Biography, Business, Children's Fiction, Commercial Fiction, Crime Fiction, General Interest, Health, History, Humour, Illustrated Books, Literary Fiction, Military History, Politics & Current Affairs, Young Adult

Insider Info Publishes 220 titles per year. Responds to proposals in three-six months.

Submission Guidelines Accepts unsolicited manuscripts and proposals for all areas except children's fiction.
Submission details to: submissions@allenandunwin.com

Recent Title(s) *The Guernsey Literary and Potato Peel Pie Society*, Mary Ann Shaffer; *A Thousand Splendid Suns*, Khaled Hosseini; *Eat, Pray, Love*, Elizabeth Gilbert

Tips Allen & Unwin accepts submissions for their main subjects areas. For adult fiction submissions that fall outside of the main areas, Louise Thurtell runs the 'Friday Pitch' – where she will review any kind of submission as long as she receives it on a Friday.

Arcade Publishing

116 John Street, Suite 2810, New York, 10038, USA

- 001 212 475 2633
- 001 212 353 8148
- info@arcadepub.com
- www.arcadepub.com

Contact President/Editor in Chief, Richard Seaver; Publisher, Jeannette Seaver; Senior Vice President/General Manager/Senior Editor, Calvert Barksdale

Categories Publishes Non-Fiction and Fiction titles on the following subjects: Biography, General Interest, History, Literary Fiction, Mainstream Fiction, Memoirs, Nature, Science, Short Story Collections, Translation, Travel

Insider Info Publishes 35 titles per year. Authors are paid by royalty on retail price, and an advance is also offered. Authors also receive ten copies of their title. Five per cent of books published are from first-time authors. Aims to respond to manuscripts within four months. Average lead time is 18 months. Catalogue and author guidelines are available free on request by sending SAE.

Submission Guidelines Does not accept unsolicited manuscripts or proposals.

Recent Title(s) *A Field Guide to Demons, Fairies, Fallen Angels, and Other Subversive Spirits*, Carol & Dinah Mack

Tips Publishes top quality non-fiction and fiction, with a special interest in foreign translations. Arcade does not accept unagented submissions or proposals.

Arena

83 Alexander Street, Crows Nest, New South Wales, 2065, Australia

- 0061 2 8425 0100
- 0061 2 9906 2218
- louiset@allenandunwin.com
- www.allenandunwin.com

Contact Publisher (Fiction), Louise Thurtell; Publisher (Non-Fiction), Jade McGee

Parent Company Allen & Unwin (Pty) Ltd

Categories Publishes Adult Non-Fiction and Fiction on the following subjects: Crime, Thrillers, Fantasy, Chick Lit, Lad Lit, Science Fiction, Popular Culture,

Health, Popular Science, Memoir, Travel, Self-Help, Gift and Personal Finance.

Submission Guidelines Accepts proposal package (including synopsis and first chapter) but only as part of the 'Friday Pitch'.
Submission details to: fridaypitch@ allenandunwin.com

Tips Louise Thurtell runs the 'Friday Pitch' – where she will review any kind of submission as long as she receives it on a Friday.

Arnoldo Mondadori Editore S.p.A.
via Mondadori 1, 20090 Segrate, Milan, Italy
- 0039 2 7542 3215
- 0039 2 7542 2302
- infolibri@mondadori.it
- www.mondadori.it

Parent Company The Mondadori Group
Contact Chairman, Marina Berlusconi
Imprint(s) Harlequin
Mondadori Books
Mondadori Illustrati
Random House Mondadori
Categories Publishes Non-Fiction, Fiction and Children's titles on the following subjects: Autobiography, Biography, Children's Fiction, Classics, Contemporary Fiction, Education, General Interest, Literary Fiction, Local Interest, Magazines, Mainstream Fiction, Media, Professional, Tourist Guides
Insider Info Publishes 2,500 titles per year.
Recent Title(s) *Le Benevole*, Jonathan Littell
Tips Mondadori is Italy's largest publisher, also publishing magazines and offering printing services. They are mostly interested in contemporary adult or children's fiction, and reprints of classics.

Ballantine Publishing Group
1745 Broadway, 18th Floor, New York, 10019, USA
- 001 212 782 9000
- 001 212 782 9700
- bfi@randomhouse.com
- www.randomhouse.com/rhpg

Parent Company Random House Inc
Contact President/Publisher, Gina Centrello
Imprint(s) Ballantine Books
Del Rey/Lucas Books
Fawcett
Ivy
One World
Wellspring
Categories Publishes Non-Fiction and Fiction on the following subjects: General Interest, Health, Mainstream Fiction, Mystery, Science Fiction/ Fantasy, Western

Insider Info Authors paid by royalty, with advance offered.
Submission Guidelines Does not accept unsolicited manuscripts or proposals.
Recent Title(s) *Shadow Music*, Julie Garwood
Tips Ballantine has a wide scope but generally specialises in science fiction, fantasy, westerns, and mystery novels. They do not accept any unagented submissions or proposals.

Bantam Dell Publishing Group
1745 Broadway, 18th Floor, New York, 10019, USA
- 001 212 782 9000
- 001 212 782 9700
- bdpublicity@randomhouse.com
- www.bantamdell.com

Parent Company Random House Inc
Contact Irwyn Applebaum
Imprint(s) Bantam Hardcover/Mass Market/ Trade Paperback
Crimeline
Delacorte Press
Dell, Delta, The Dial Press
Domain, DTP, Fanfare, Island
Spectra
Categories Publishes Non-Fiction and Fiction on the following subjects: General Interest, Health, Mainstream Fiction, Mystery, Science Fiction/ Fantasy, Suspense, Women's Fiction
Insider Info Authors paid by royalty, with advance offered. Accepts simultaneous submissions.
Submission Guidelines Does not accept simultaneous proposals or manuscripts.
Recent Title(s) *Blood Dreams*, Kay Hooper
Tips Bantam Dell does not accept any unagented submissions or proposals.

Barron's Educational Series Inc
250 Wireless Boulevard, Hauppage, New York, 11788, USA
- 001 800 645 3476
- 001 631 434 3723
- fbrown@barronseduc.com
- www.barronseduc.com

Contact Acquisitions Editor, Wayne Barr
Categories Publishes Non-Fiction and Children's titles on the following subjects: Art Books, Business & Finance, Children's Books, Cooking, Crafts & Hobbies, Employment/Careers, English Language Arts, Family & Health, Foreign Languages, Gift Books, History/ Biography, Mind Body & Spirit, Pets, School Guides, Spanish Language, Sports & Recreation, Study Guides, Test Preparation
Insider Info Publishes 300 titles per year. Pays 12–14 per cent royalty on net receipts, with advance

offered. Receives 2,000 queries per year. Receives 75 per cent of books from unagented writers, and 25 per cent of books from first-time authors. Aims to respond to proposals within eight months. Accepts simultaneous submissions. Average lead time is 18 months.

Submission Guidelines Accepts unsolicited manuscripts and proposals.

Recent Title(s) *Painless French*, Carol Chaitkin and Lynn Gore (Painless Series)

Tips Barron's books usually fit within one of several different series, such as the Painless Series. Children's titles are less likely to be successful due to the high volume of submissions.

Berlin Verlag

Greifswalder Strasse 207, D-10405, Berlin, Germany

- 0049 30 443 8450
- 0049 30 4438 4595
- info@berlinverlag.de
- www.berlinverlag.de

Parent Company Bloomsbury Publishing Plc (see entry under UK & Irish Book Publishers)

Contact Managing Director, Kathy Rooney

Categories Publishes Non-Fiction, Fiction and Children's titles on the following subjects: Children's Books, Contemporary Fiction, General Interest, History, Literary Fiction, Mainstream Fiction, Translation

Insider Info Publishes 102 titles per year.

Recent Title(s) *Hand Werk*, Richard Sennett

Tips Berlin Verlag, owned by Bloomsbury Publishing Plc, is one of the leading literary publishers in Germany and focuses mainly on literary fiction for the adult market. Berlin Verlag will accept proposals in either German or English language.

Bertelsmann

Verlagsgruppe Random House, Neumarkter Strasse 28, D-81673, Munich, Germany

- 0049 89 41360
- 0049 89 4136 3333
- kundenservice@randomhouse.de
- www.randomhouse.de

Parent Company Random House Group Inc

Categories Publishes Non-Fiction, Fiction and Children's titles on the following subjects: Biography, Children's Fiction, Contemporary Fiction, Education, General Interest, How-To, Literary Fiction, Local Interest, Mainstream Fiction, Politics, Reference, Self-Help, Travel

Insider Info Average lead time is six months.

Submission Guidelines Accepts unsolicited manuscripts and proposals.

Recent Title(s) *Das Speck-weg-Programm*, India Knight and Neris Thomas

Tips Bertelsmann accepts unsolicited submissions by post only, not by email.

Bloomsbury USA

175 Fifth Avenue, Suite 300, New York, 10010, USA

- 001 212 780 0115
- 001 646 727 8300
- info@bloomsburyusa.com
- www.bloomsburyusa.com

Parent Company Bloomsbury Publishing Plc

Contact Publisher/Editorial Director, Karen Rinaldi

Imprint(s) Bloomsbury Adult Books
Bloomsbury Children's Books

Categories Publishes Non-Fiction, Fiction and Children's titles on the following subjects: Biography, Children's Fiction, General Interest, Literary Fiction, Mainstream Fiction, Picture Books, Reference, Self-Help

Insider Info Authors are paid by royalty, with an advance offered. Simultaneous submissions accepted.

Submission Guidelines Accepts unsolicited manuscripts and proposals for children's books only.

Recent Title(s) *The Gum Thief*, Douglas Coupland

Tips Bloomsbury does not accept unagented submissions to its adult division, but will accept proposals for new children's fiction or non-fiction. See website for guidelines.

Bloomsbury USA Children

175 Fifth Avenue, 8th Floor, New York, 10011, USA

- 001 646 307 5151
- 001 212 727 0984
- bloomsbury.kids@bloomsburyusa.com
- www.bloomsburyusa.com

Parent Company Bloomsbury Publishing Plc

Contact Executive Editor, Jill Davis; Editorial Director, Melanie Cecka; Editor, Sarah Odedina; Editor, Ele Fountain

Established 1998

Categories Publishes Children's Fiction, Picture Books, Young Novels, Series Fiction, Poetry, Fantasy, Easy Reads, and some Non-Fiction

Insider Info Publishes 40 titles per year and has 80 in print.

Submission Guidelines Accepts unsolicited manuscripts, but they will only respond if they are interested in pursuing the manuscript. Do not send SAE. They welcome picture book manuscripts and queries for longer works, whether fiction or non-fiction. Send illustration samples to the art department. Does not accept simultaneous submissions.

Recent Title(s) *Peiling and the Chicken-Fried Christmas*, Pauline Chen; *Big Fat Manifesto*, Susan Vaught (Young Adult)

Tips Offers reading group guides available to download from their website - which accompanies their successful books.

Brepols Publishers NV
Begijnhof 67, B-2300, Turnhout, Belgium
- 0032 14 448020
- 0032 14 428919
- info@brepols.net
- www.brepols.net

Contact General Manager, Paul De Jongh; Publishing Manager, Christophe Lebbe; Publishing Manager, Chris VandenBorre; Publishing Manager, Johan Van der Beke; Publishing Manager, Luc Jocque; Publishing Manager, Simon Forde

Categories Publishes Non-Fiction titles on the following subjects: Academic, Archaeology, Architecture, Art History, Bible Studies, Design, Electronic, Essays, Language, Linguistics, Literature, Middle Ages, Online, Religious History, Scholarly

Recent Title(s) *Frauen-Kloster-Kunst*, J. Hamburger (ed.)

Tips Brepols specialises in publishing academic books and essays from leading scholars. They also publish electronic material.

Cambridge University Press (US)
32 Avenue of the Americas, New York, 10013, USA
- 001 212 924 3900
- 001 212 691 3239
- newyork@cambridge.org
- www.cambridge.org/us

Contact Director, Richard L. Ziemacki

Categories Publishes Non-Fiction titles on the following subjects: Academic, Biography, General Interest, Higher Education, Journals, Literary Criticism, Online Products, Popular Non-Fiction, Reference, Scholarly, Textbook

Insider Info Authors are paid by royalty, with an advance offered.

Submission Guidelines Accepts unsolicited manuscripts and proposals.

Recent Title(s) *Our Changing Planet*, Michael D. King (ed.)

Tips Cambridge University Press has a dedicated online service for its authors called 'Authornet'. Authornet contains in-depth submission details, as well as listing the relevant editors and their fields of interest.

The Caxton Press
113 Victoria Street, Christchurch, New Zealand
- 0064 3 366 8516
- 0064 3 365 7840
- print.design@caxton.co.nz
- www.caxton.co.nz

Contact Managing Director, Bruce Bascand; General Manager, Peter Watson; Print & Production Manager, Murray Craig

Categories Publishes Non-Fiction titles on the following subjects: Art, Calendars, Craft, General Interest, History, Local Interest

Recent Title(s) *New Zealand Alpine Calendar 2008*

Tips The Caxton Press specialises in graphic design and printing, and also offers a wide range of self-publishing and printing services.

The Charlton Press
PO Box 820, Station Willowdale B, North York, Ontario, M2K 2R1, Canada
- 001 416 488 1418
- 001 416 488 4656
- chpress@charltonpress.com
- www.charltonpress.com

Contact President, W.K. Cross

Categories Publishes Catalogues on Canadiana, Collectibles, Numismatics, Sports Cards

Recent Title(s) *Coalport Collectables*, Jean Dale

Tips The Charlton Press publishes collectibles catalogues only and does not accept unsolicited submissions.

Columbia University Press
61 West 62nd Street, New York, 10023, USA
- 001 212 459 0600
- 001 212 459 3678
- jc373@columbia.edu
- www.columbia.edu/cu/cup

Contact Associate Director/Editorial Director, Jennifer Crewe (Asian Humanities, Film); Senior Executive Editors: Peter Dimock (History, Middle East Studies) and Wendy Lochner (Religion, Philosophy); Publisher for Life Sciences, Patrick Fitzgerald; Publisher for Finance and Economics, Myles Thompson; Executive Editor, Lauren Docket (Social Work, Criminology), Editors: Anne Routon (Asian History, International Relations) and Philip Leventhal (Literary Studies)

Categories Publishes Non-Fiction and Translation titles on the following subjects: Academic, Asian Translations (Fiction/Poetry), Biography, Finance & Economics, General Interest, History, Journals, Literary Criticism, Philosophy, Politics, Reference, Religion, Scholarly, Science, Textbook.

Insider Info Authors are paid by royalty, with advance offered. Aims to respond to submissions in four weeks.

Submission Guidelines Accepts unsolicited manuscripts and proposals.

Recent Title(s) *Strategic Intuition*, William Duggan

Tips Columbia welcomes submissions for academic non-fiction, directed to the appropriate editor. Columbia also publishes poetry and fiction translations from Asian languages.

The Continuum International Publishing Group

80 Maiden Lane, Suite 704, New York, 10038, USA

- 001 212 953 5858
- 001 212 953 5944
- david@continuum-books.com
- www.continuumbooks.com

Contact Editorial Director (US), David Barker; Vice President/Senior Editor, Frank Oveis

Imprint(s) Burns & Oates
Continuum
Thoemmes Continuum
T&T Clark

Categories Publishes Non-Fiction on the following subjects: Academic, Biblical Studies, Education, History, Linguistics, Literature, Philosophy, Politics, Religious Studies, Theology, General Religion, Popular Culture

Insider Info Publishes 500 titles per year. Authors paid by royalty, with advance offered. Catalogue available free on request. Does not accept simultaneous submissions.

Submission Guidelines Accepts unsolicited manuscripts and proposals.

Recent Title(s) *Reflective Language Teaching*, Thomas Farrell

Tips The Continuum International Publishing Group only publish in areas they are already strong in, so make sure that all submissions are in keeping with guidelines on the website.

Cornell University Press

Sage House, 512 East State Street, Ithaca, New York, 14850, USA

- 001 607 277 2338
- 001 607 277 2374
- cupressinfo@cornell.edu
- www.cornellpress.cornell.edu

Contact Director, John G. Ackerman; Editor in Chief, Peter J. Potter

Imprint(s) Comstock
ILR Press

Categories Publishes Non-Fiction on the following subjects: Academic, Anthropology, Asian Studies, Biological Sciences, Classics, History, Industrial Relations, Literary Criticism and Theory, Natural History, Philosophy, Politics, Scholarly, Veterinary Science, Women's Studies

Insider Info Publishes 150 titles per year. Authors paid by royalty, with advance offered. Accepts simultaneous submissions. Average lead time is one year.

Submission Guidelines Accepts unsolicited manuscripts and proposals.

Recent Title(s) *Winners Without Losers*, Edward J. Lincoln

Tips Cornell welcomes academic submissions in their fields of interest, ideally addressed to the correct acquisitions editor.

Crown Publishing Group

1745 Broadway, New York, 10019, USA

- 001 212 782 9000
- 001 212 782 9700
- crownbiz@randomhouse.com
- www.randomhouse.com/crown

Parent Company Random House Inc

Contact President/Publisher, Jenny Frost

Imprint(s) Bell Tower
Clarkson Potter
Crown Business/Forum
Harmony Books
Shaye Arehart Books
Three Rivers Press

Categories Publishes Non-Fiction and Fiction titles on the following subjects: General Interest, Illustrated Books, Literary Fiction, Mainstream Fiction

Insider Info Authors paid by royalty with advance offered.

Submission Guidelines Does not accept unsolicited manuscripts or proposals.

Recent Title(s) *The Art of Simple Food*, Alice Waters

Tips Crown Publishing does not accept any unagented submissions or proposals.

David Bateman Ltd

Tarndale Grove, Albany Business Park, Bush Road, Auckland, 1330, New Zealand

- 0064 9 415 7664
- 0064 9 415 8892
- bateman@bateman.co.nz
- www.bateman.co.nz

Contact Chairman/Publisher, David Bateman

Categories Publishes Non-Fiction, Fiction and Children's titles on the following subjects: Adult Books, Architecture, Art, Biography, Business, Children's Fiction, Craft, Education, General Interest, History, How-To, Literary Fiction, Local Interest, Mainstream Fiction, Reference, Science, Self-Help, Travel, Ufology

Recent Title(s) *Big Resource Book Australia*, R. Naumann

David R. Godine, Publisher Inc

9 Hamilton Place, Boston, Massachusetts, 02108, USA
- 001 617 451 9600
- 001 617 350 0250
- info@godine.com
- www.godine.com

Contact President, David Godine
Imprint(s) Black Sparrow Books
Categories Publishes Non-Fiction, Fiction and Children's Books on the following subjects: Americana, Art/Architecture, Biography, Children's Books, Coffee Table Books, Cooking, Gardening, Historical Fiction, Illustrated Books, Literary Criticism, Literary Fiction, Nature, Photography, Translation, Typography
Insider Info Publishes 30 titles per year. Authors are paid by royalty on retail price. Average lead time of three years.
Submission Guidelines Does not accept unsolicited manuscripts or proposals. Agented submissions only.
Recent Title(s) *In the Blood: A Memoir of My Childhood*, Andrew Motion

DAW Books Inc

375 Hudson Street, New York, 10014, USA
- 001 212 366 2096
- 001 212 366 2090
- daw@penguinputnam.com
- www.dawbooks.com

Parent Company Penguin Group (USA) Inc
Contact Publisher, Elizabeth R. Wollheim; Publisher, Sheila E. Gilbert; Submissions Editor, Peter Stampfel
Categories Publishes Fiction on the following subjects: Fantasy, Horror, Science Fiction
Insider Info Publishes 80 titles per year. Aims to respond to manuscripts within three months. Does not accept simultaneous submissions.
Submission Guidelines Accepts unsolicited manuscripts and proposals.
Recent Title(s) *The Name of the Wind*, Patrick Rothfuss
Tips DAW Books publishes fantasy and science fiction, they welcome submissions of first novels if they are of professional quality.

DK Publishing Inc

375 Hudson Street, New York, 10014, USA
- 001 800 631 8571
- 001 201 256 0000
- info@dk.com
- www.dk.com

Parent Company Pearson Plc
Contact Publisher, Christopher Davis
Categories Publishes Non-Fiction and Children's titles on the following subjects: Adult Reference, Children's Reference, Disney/Pixar, Encyclopedias, Multimedia, Picture Books.
Insider Info Authors are paid by royalty, with advance offered.
Submission Guidelines Does not accept unsolicited manuscripts or proposals.
Recent Title(s) *Do Not Open*, John Farndon (Children's)

Doubleday Broadway Publishing Group

1745 Broadway, New York, 10019, USA
- 001 212 782 9000
- 001 212 782 9700
- ddaypub@randomhouse.com
- www.randomhouse.com/doubleday

Parent Company Random House Inc
Imprint(s) Broadway Books
Currency
Doubleday
Main Street Books
Nan A. Talese
Categories Publishes Non-Fiction and Fiction titles on the following subjects: Americana, Biography, Society and Culture, General Interest, Genre Fiction, Politics, Literary Fiction, Mainstream Fiction
Insider Info Authors are paid by royalty, with advance offered. Receives thousands of manuscripts per year.
Submission Guidelines Does not accepts unsolicited manuscripts or proposals. Agented submissions only.
Recent Title(s) *Liberal Facism*, Jonah Glodberg

Douglas & McIntyre Publishing Group

2323 Quebec Street, Suite 201, Vancouver, British Columbia, V5T 4S7, Canada
- 001 604 254 7191
- 001 604 254 9099
- dm@douglas-mcintyre.com
- www.douglas-mcintyre.com

Imprint(s) Douglas & McIntyre
Greystone Books
Categories Publishes Non-Fiction and Fiction titles on the following subjects: Architecture, Art, Canadian Interest, Celebrity Biography, Environment, Food & Drink, Health, Literary Fiction, Natural History, Popular Culture, Science, Sports
Insider Info Publishes 75 titles per year.
Submission Guidelines Accepts unsolicited manuscripts and proposals.

Recent Title(s) *City Making In Paradise*, Ken Cameron and Mike Harcourt

Tips Douglas & McIntyre accepts proposals and manuscript submissions but very rarely publishes unsolicited work. Check the website to see which subjects they are currently accepting.

Dover Publications Inc

31 East 2nd Street, Mineola, New York, 11501, USA

- 001 516 294 7000
- 001 516 873 1401
- info@doverpublications.com
- www.doverpublications.com

Contact Editor in Chief, Paul Negri; Editor (Math/Science Reprints), John Grafton

Categories Publishes Non-Fiction and Children's titles on the following subjects: Art, Biography, Children's, Cookbooks, General Interest, History, How-To, Humour, Illustrated Books, Science, Textbooks

Insider Info Publishes 660 titles per year. Accepts simultaneous submissions.

Submission Guidelines Accepts unsolicited manuscripts and proposals.

Recent Title(s) *Rackham's Fairies, Elves and Goblins*, Jeff A. Menges

Tips Dover publishes mostly reprints, but will accept unsolicited proposals for non-fiction.

The Dundurn Group

3 Church Street, Suite 500, Toronto, Ontario, M5E 1M2, Canada

- 001 416 214 5544
- 001 416 214 5556
- info@dundurn.com
- www.dundurn.com

Imprint(s) Boardwalk Books
Dundurn Press
Hounslow Press
Simon & Pierre
Natural Heritage
XYZ Publishing (the Quest Library)

Categories Publishes Non-Fiction and Fiction titles on the following subjects: Art Criticism, Biography, History, Illustrated Books, Literary Criticism, Literary Fiction, Military History, Nature, Outdoors, Politics, Popular Non-Fiction, Regional History, Young Adult

Insider Info Pays 8-10 percent royalty on net receipts, with advance offered. Receives 600 queries per year. 50 per cent of books come from unagented writers, and 25 per cent of books from first-time authors. Accepts simultaneous submissions. Average lead time of one year.

Submission Guidelines Accepts unsolicited manuscripts and proposals.

Recent Title(s) *Forever Dead*, Suzanne F. Kingsmill (Mystery)

Tips Dundurn does not accept submissions by email and all postal submissions must be addressed simply to the 'Acquisitions Editor' - otherwise they may not get recorded in the submission system.

Dunmore Press Ltd

PO Box 25080, Wellington, 6146, New Zealand

- 0064 4 472 2705
- 0064 4 471 0604
- books@dunmore.co.nz
- www.dunmore.co.nz

Categories Publishes Non-Fiction titles on the following subjects: Business, Economics, Education, Environment, General Interest, Health, History, Law, Media, Politics, Society

Insider Info Publishes 30 titles per year. Pays ten per cent royalty on retail price. Aims to respond to proposals within three weeks. Average lead time is three months. Authors receive ten free copies of their publication.

Submission Guidelines Accepts unsolicited manuscripts and proposals.

Recent Title(s) *The Problems of Prisons*, Greg Newbold

Tips Dunmore Press publishes New Zealand themed non-fiction only.

ECW Press Ltd

2120 Queen Street East, Suite 200, Toronto, Ontario, M4E 1E2, Canada

- 001 416 694 3348
- 001 416 698 9906
- info@ecwpress.com
- www.ecwpress.com

Contact Publisher, Jack David; Associate Publisher, David Caron; Managing Editor, Chrissy Boylan; Senior Editor, Michael Holmes; Senior Editor, Jennifer Hale

Categories Publishes Non-Fiction, Fiction and Poetry titles on the following subjects: Biography, Business, Creative Non-Fiction, Economics, Finance, Gay/Lesbian, General Interest, Health/Medicine, History, Literary Fiction, Memoirs, Mystery Fiction, Poetry, Politics, Regional, Sex, Short-Stories, Sports, Women's Issues/Studies, Contemporary Culture, Wicca, Gambling, Television and Movie Stars

Insider Info Publishes 70 titles per year. Pays 8–12 per cent royalty on net receipts, with advance offered. Receives 1,500 manuscripts per year. 30 per cent of books come from first-time authors. Aims to respond to manuscripts within four months. Accepts simultaneous submissions. Average lead time of 18 months.

Submission Guidelines Accepts unsolicited manuscripts and proposals.

Recent Title(s) *From the Flight Deck: Plane Talk and Sky Science*, Doug Morris
Tips ECW Press does not accept fiction or poetry submissions from writers outside of Canada.

Editions Larousse
21 rue de Montparnasse, F-75283 Paris, Cedex 6, France
- ☎ 0033 1 44 39 44 00
- ☎ 0033 1 44 39 43 43
- ✉ Online form
- 🌐 www.larousse.fr

Parent Company Hachette Livre
Imprint(s) Petit Larousse
Petits Classiques
Categories Publishes Non-Fiction and Children's titles on the following subjects: Bilingual Dictionaries, Children's, Culture, Dictionaries, Encyclopedias, General Interest, Practical, Translations, Young Adult
Submission Guidelines Accepts unsolicited manuscripts and proposals.
Recent Title(s) *Le Boys' Book*, Con and Hal Iggulden
Tips Larousse is a subsidiary of Hachette Livre and publishes practical non-fiction books and dictionaries, including bilingual dictionaries. See the Hachette website for submission details.

Egmont
Vognmagergade 11, DK-1148, Copenhagen, K, Denmark
- ☎ 0045 33 305550
- ☎ 0045 33 321902
- ✉ egmont@egmont.com
- 🌐 www.egmont.com

Parent Company Egmont International Holdings A/S
Contact President/Chief Executive Officer, Steffen Kragh; Executive Vice President (Egmont Group)/ Managing Director (Egmont Books), Tom Harald Jenssen; Editor (Aschehoug), Jeppe Markers
Imprint(s) Aschehoug
Categories Publishes Non-Fiction, Fiction and Children's titles on the following subjects: Audio Books, Children's Fiction, Education, General Interest, Literary Fiction, Mainstream Fiction
Submission Guidelines Egmont accept submissions for fiction or non-fiction directed at Aschehoug publishers. See www.aschehoug.dk for details (only available in Danish).
Tips Egmont publishes books, magazines and multimedia, and also distributes films and computer games.

Elsevier Australia
30–52 Smidmore Street, Marrickville, New South Wales, 2204, Australia
- ☎ 0061 2 9517 8999
- ☎ 0061 2 9517 2249
- ✉ s.kaliniecki@elsevier.com
- 🌐 www.elsevier.com.au

Parent Company Reed Elsevier Group Plc
Contact Publisher, Debra Gooley; Publisher, Heidi Allen; Publishing Editor, Sophie Kaliniecki
Imprint(s) Balliere Tindall
Butterworth-Heinemann
Churchill Livingstone
Mosby
Saunders
Categories Publishes Non-Fiction on the following subjects: Academic, Health, Medicine, Psychology, Reference, Science, Technology, Textbook
Insider Info Author paid by royalty, with advance offered.
Submission Guidelines Accepts unsolicited manuscripts and proposals.
Recent Title(s) *Community Pharmacy*, Newby & Rutter
Tips Elsevier Australia is the leading health and science publisher for Australia and New Zealand. Elsevier Australia accepts submissions and proposals from Australian writers, as well as for adaptations of international books.

Engineers Media
PO Box 588, 2 Ernest Place, Crows Nest, New South Wales, 1585, Australia
- ☎ 0061 2 9438 1533
- ☎ 0061 2 9438 5934
- ✉ dgeorg@engineersmedia.com.au
- 🌐 www.engineersmedia.com.au

Parent Company Institution of Engineers Australia
Contact General Manager, Bruce Roff; Managing Editor, Dietrich Georg; Editor, Bob Jackson; Editor, Danny Cameron; Editor, Justin Liew
Imprint(s) EA Books
Categories Publishes Non-Fiction on the following subjects: Construction, Engineering, Journals, Magazines, Multimedia, Technical
Submission Guidelines Accepts unsolicited manuscripts and proposals.
Recent Title(s) *New Railway Environment*, Various
Tips Engineers Media publishes many magazines and journals, as well as technical books - submissions can be aimed exclusively at these publications.

Evan-Moor Educational Publishers
18 Lower Ragsdale Drive, Monterey, California, 93940, USA

○ 001 800 714 0971
🖷 001 831 649 6256
🌐 www.evan-moor.com

Contact President, Linda Hanger; Senior Editor, Marilyn Evans; Art Director, Cheryl Pucket

Established 1979

Categories Publishes Educational Materials (such as Activity Books, Textbooks, How-To Books, and CD-ROMs) on all school subjects including: Maths, Science, Social Studies, English, Arts & Craft Books (for children and teachers)

Insider Info Publishes 50 titles per year with 450 in print.

Submission Guidelines Less than ten per cent of books are by first-time authors. Visit website for submission guidelines.

Recent Title(s) *Look, Listen, & Speak: Grades K-3* (English/Education)

F+W Media Inc

4700 East Galbraith Road, Cincinnati, Ohio, 45236, USA

○ 001 513 531 2690
○ Online form.
🌐 www.fwpublications.com

Contact President (Book Division), Sara Domville; Editorial Director (Writer's Digest), Jane Friedman; Publisher (North Light), Jamie Markle

Imprint(s) Adams Media
David & Charles Publishers
Krause Publications
Memory Makers
North Light Books
Writer's Digest Books

Categories Publishes Non-Fiction on the following subjects: General Interest, How-To, Antiques and Collectibles, Art, Crafts, Equestrian, Sports, Automotive, Outdoors, Military, Firearms, Writing Reference, Woodworking

Insider Info Authors are paid by royalty with advance offered.

Submission Guidelines Accepts unsolicited manuscripts and proposals.

Recent Title(s) *Design Essentials Index*, Jim Krause (Graphic Design)

Tips See website or individual listings for specific submission guidelines on the company's imprints.

Facts On File Inc

132 West 31st Street, New York, 10001, USA

○ 001 800 322 8755
🖷 001 800 678 3633
○ editorial@factsonfile.com
🌐 www.factsonfile.com

Contact Editorial Director (Science, Fashion, Natural History), Laurie Likoff; Senior Editor (Science and

Technology, Nature, Reference), Frank Darmstadt; Senior Editor (American History, Women's Studies, Young Adult Reference), Nicole Bowen; Trade Editor (Health, Pop Culture, True Crime, Sports), James Chambers; Acquisitions Editor (Language/Literature), Jeff Soloway

Imprint(s) Checkmark Books

Categories Publishes Non-Fiction on the following subjects: Careers, Contemporary Culture, Education, Education, Entertainment, Health/Medicine, History, Language/Literature, Multicultural, Natural History, Popular Culture, Recreation, Reference, Religion, Sociology, Sports

Insider Info Publishes 150 titles per year. Pays ten per cent royalty on retail price, with advance offered. 25 per cent of books come from unagented writers. Accepts simultaneous submissions. Book catalogue available free on request.

Recent Title(s) *Immigration*, Dennis Wepman

Tips Facts On File publishes educational reference material aimed mostly at schools and libraries. Submissions must be directed to the appropriate editor.

Fernwood Press

3 Victory Close, Simonskloof, Simon's Town, Cape, 7975, South Africa

○ 0027 21 786 2460
🖷 0027 21 786 2478
○ ferpress@iafrica.com
🌐 www.fernwoodpress.co.za

Contact Director, Pam Struik; Director, Pieter Struik

Categories Publishes Non-Fiction on the following subjects: Catalogues, Culture, History, Illustrated Non-Fiction, Local Interest, South African Non-Fiction, Travel

Recent Title(s) *African Basketry: Grassroots Art from Southern Africa*, Anthony B. Cunningham and M. Elizabeth Terry

Tips Fernwood specialises in illustrated non-fiction books from, or about South Africa.

Fitzhenry & Whiteside Ltd

195 Allstate Parkway, Markham, Ontario, L3R 4T8, Canada

○ 001 800 387 9776
🖷 001 800 260 9777
○ godwit@fitzhenry.ca
🌐 www.fitzhenry.ca

Contact President, Sharon Fitzhenry; Publisher (Children's Books), Gail Winskill; Managing Editor (Adult Books), Richard Dionne

Imprint(s) Fifth House
Fitzhenry & Whiteside
Stoddart Kids
Red Deer

Categories Publishes Non-Fiction, Poetry and Children's titles on the following subjects: Children's Books, Education, General Interest, Poetry, Social Studies, Young Adult
Submission Guidelines Accepts unsolicited manuscripts and proposals. Will only accept submissions for adult trade titles by email, in the body of the email rather than as an attachment.
Recent Title(s) *A Bumble Bee Sweater*, Betty Waterton
Tips Fitzhenry & Whiteside do not accept submissions for children's books.

Flux
2143 Wooddale Drive, Woodbury, Minnesota, 55125 USA
- 001 800 843 6666
- 001 651 291 1908
- submissions@fluxnow.com
- www.fluxnow.com

Parent Company Llewellyn Worldwide Ltd
Contact Acquisitions Editor, Brian Farrey
Categories Publishes edgy, strongly written fiction for teenagers across the genres.
Insider Info Publishes books in most genres for children aged 12 and upwards.
Submission Guidelines Accepts unsolicited manuscripts and proposals. Will accept manuscripts and queries by email. Aims to respond in six months.
Recent Title(s) *The Dust of 100 Dogs*, A.S. King; *Lament: The Faerie Queen's Deception*, Maggie Stiefvater; *The Shape of Water*, Anne Spollen
Tips Submissions to Flux should be no less than 35,000 words. Visit website for full submission guidelines.

Free Press
1230 Avenue of the Americas, New York, 10020, USA
- 001 212 698 7000
- 001 212 698 7007
- Online form
- www.simonsays.com

Parent Company Simon & Schuster Adult Publishing Group
Contact Publisher, Martha Levin; Vice President/ Senior Editor (History/Serious Non-Fiction), Bruce Nichols; Vice President/Senior Editor (Psychology/ Spirituality/Self-Help), Leslie Meredith; Vice President/Editorial Director (Self-Help/Serious Non-Fiction), Dominick Anfuso; Senior Editor (Literary Fiction), Amy Scheibe; Senior Editor (History, Current Events, Biography, Memoir), Elizabeth Stein
Categories Publishes Non-Fiction and Fiction titles on the following subjects: Faith, General Interest,
How-To, Literary Fiction, Self-Help, Spirituality, Politics
Insider Info Publishes 85 titles per year. Authors paid by royalty, with advance offered. 15 per cent of books come from first-time authors. Average lead time of one year.
Submission Guidelines Does not accept unsolicited manuscripts or proposals.
Recent Title(s) *Comeback Season: How I Learned to Play the Game of Love*, Cathy Day (Contemporary Fiction)
Tips Despite Simon & Schuster's policy of not accepting unagented submissions, ten per cent of Free Press' publications are from unagented writers.

Free Spirit Publishing
217 Fifth Avenue North, Suite 200, Minneapolis, 55401, USA
- 001 612 338 2068
- 001 612 337 5050
- help4kids@freespirit.com
- www.freespirit.com

Contact President, Judy Galbraith
Established 1983
Categories Publishes learning materials and educational resources for children, teachers, parents and the medical profession. Produces audio and posters, and self-help titles for teenagers, tackling subjects from bullying to grief.
Insider Info Free Spirit is the leading publisher of learning tools that support young people's social and emotional health. Publishes approximately 18–22 new books per year, with a backlist of over 100 books.
Submission Guidelines They advise authors to read their author guidelines before submitting any work as the books published are highly specialised and many authors are expert educators or heath professionals. Visit the website for author guidelines. Aims to respond to proposals in two to six months.
Recent Title(s) *The Complete Guide to Service Learning*, Cathryn Berger Kaye

Front Street Books
815 Church Street, Honesdale, Pennsylvania, 18431, USA
- 001 800 490 5111
- 001 501 372 5579
- contactus@frontstreetbooks.com
- www.frontstreetbooks.com

Parent Company Boyds Mill Press
Contact President, Stephen Roxburgh
Established 1994
Categories Publishes Children's Fiction, Young Novels and unique Picture Books

Insider Info Publishes high quality fiction for children and young adults and sophisticated picture books from here and abroad. They strive to expose young readers to the best literature available in other countries, cultures, and languages.

Submission Guidelines Accepts unsolicited manuscripts or queries. They are interested in imaginative picture books send entire manuscript. For fiction submit three sample chapters. For non-fiction send a detailed synopsis outlining what the books is about.

Recent Title(s) *The Book of Jude*, Kimberely Heuston (Young Adult); *Naked Bunyip Dancing*, Steven Herrick (Young Adult)

Tips Front Street Books address important and sensitive issues that face some young adults, such as child abuse and depression. Through their publications, they aim to offer hope and encouragement.

The Galago Publishing Company
PO Box 1645, Alberton, 1450, South Africa
- 0027 11 907 2029
- 0027 11 869 0890
- lemur@mweb.co.za
- www.galago.co.za

Contact Managing Director, Francis Stiff; Publisher, Peter Stiff

Categories Publishes Non-Fiction on the following subjects: Biographies, Hunting, Local Interest, Military History, Political, South African Non-Fiction

Recent Title(s) *Executive Outcomes: Against All Odds*, Eeben Barlow

Tips Galago publishes books on military history, and anything relating to South Africa.

Giunti Editore S.p.A
Via Bolognese 165, 50139, Florence, Italy
- 0039 55 50621
- 0039 55 506 2298
- segreteriaeditoriale@giunti.it
- www.giunti.it

Parent Company Giunti Gruppo Editoriale

Contact Chairman, Sergio Giunti; Managing Director/Chief Executive Officer, Martino Montanarini; Editorial Manager, Bruno Mari

Imprint(s) Dami
Giunti
Giunti Demetra
Giunti Junior
Giunti Kids

Categories Publishes Non-Fiction and Children's titles on the following subjects: Art, Crafts, Education, Essays, Grandi Opere, Guidebooks, History, Multimedia, Practical, Science, School Journals, Teaching Resources, Tourism

Insider Info Publishes 481 titles per year. Catalogue available online.

Tips Giunti primarily publishes books and educational materials for children and students, including electronic resources.

The Globe Pequot Press Inc
246 Goose Lane, PO Box 480, Guilford, Connecticut, 06437, USA
- 001 203 458 4500
- 001 203 458 4604
- info@globepequot.com
- www.globepequot.com

Contact President/Publisher, Linda Kennedy; Submissions Editor, Shelley Wolf

Imprint(s) Lyons Press

Categories Publishes Non-Fiction titles on the following subjects: Cooking, History, Local Interest, Natural History Field Guides, Nature, Outdoor Recreation Guides, Popular Western and Women's History, Regional Travel Guides, Sports, Travel

Insider Info Publishes 600 titles per year. Advance offered. 70 per cent of books come from unagented writers, and 30 per cent of books from first-time authors. Aims to respond to proposals within eight weeks. Accepts simultaneous submissions. Average lead time of one year.

Submission Guidelines Accepts unsolicited manuscripts and proposals.

Recent Title(s) *The Cult of Perfection*, Cooper Lawrence

Tips Globe Pequot is the largest publisher of regional travel books, local interest titles and outdoor recreation guides in America. They welcome proposals for travel and guide books.

Grand Central Publishing
Time & Life Building, 1271 Avenue of the Americas, New York, NY 10020, USA
- 001 212 522 7200
- 001 212 522 7993
- info@hbgusa.co.uk
- www.hachettebookgroupusa.com

Parent Company Hachette Book Group USA

Contact Publisher, Maureen Egen; Senior Vice President/Publisher, Jamie Raab; Associate Publisher, Les Pockell; Vice President/Editorial Director (Trade Paperback), Amy Einhorn; Editorial Director (Mass Market Paperback), Beth de Guzman

Imprint(s) Aspect
Mysterious Press
Walk Worthy Press
Business Plus
Warner Faith
Warner Vision

Categories Publishes Non-Fiction, Fiction and Children's titles on the following subjects: Biography, Business, Children's, Cooking, Economics, Education, Fantasy, General Interest, Historical, Horror, Mainstream/Contemporary Fiction, Reference, Romance, Science Fiction, Self-Help, Sports

Insider Info Publishes 250 titles per year. Authors are paid by royalty, with advance offered. Average lead time of two years.

Submission Guidelines Does not accept unsolicited manuscripts and proposals.

Recent Title(s) *The Geography of Bliss: One Grump's Search for the Happiest Places in the World*, Eric Weiner

Tips Grand Central publishes a diverse range of material, but does not accept unagented submissions or proposals. Formerly known as Warner Books.

Graphia

222 Berkeley Street, Boston, Massachusetts, 02116, USA

☎ 001 617 351 5000

🌐 www.hmco.com

Contact Editorial Director, Judy O'Mailey; Executive Editor, Margaret Raymo; Paperback Director, Julia Richardson; Senior Editor, Ann Rider; Submissions Coordinator, Hannah Rodgers; Editor, Amy Flynn; Assistant Editor, Kate O'Sullivan

Parent Company Houghton Mifflin Inc

Insider Info Publishes both paperback originals and reprints in fiction and non-fiction, poetry and graphic novels. Graphia is recognised for its quality and unique books.

Submission Guidelines No unsolicited queries, manuscripts only via literary agents.

Recent Title(s) *The Fragile Edge*, Julia Whitty

Graywolf Press

2402 University Avenue, Suite 203, St Paul, Minnesota, 55114, USA

📧 wolves@graywolfpress.org

🌐 www.graywolfpress.org

Contact Director/Publisher, Fiona McCrae; Executive Editor/Art Director, Anne Czarniecki; Editorial Manager, Katie Dublinski; Poetry Editor, Jeffrey Shotts

Categories Publishes Non-Fiction, Fiction and Poetry titles on the following subjects: Contemporary Culture, Contemporary Poetry, Gay and Lesbian Literature, Literary Criticism, Literary Fiction, Mainstream Fiction, Memoirs, Short Story Collections

Insider Info Publishes 25 titles per year. Royalty paid on retail price, with advance offered. Receives 3,000 queries per year. 50 per cent of books come from unagented writers and 20 per cent of books from first-time authors. Average lead time of 18 months. Catalogue available free on request.

Submission Guidelines Accepts unsolicited manuscripts and proposals.

Recent Title(s) *A Wake for the Living*, Charles Simic and Radmila Lazic

Tips Graywolf welcomes submissions for poetry and fiction, but does not publish genre fiction. They will publish single-author collections of poetry or short stories, as well as novels and non-fiction.

Grove/Atlantic Inc

841 Broadway, 4th Floor, New York, 10003, USA

☎ 001 212 614 7850

📠 001 212 614 7886

📧 info@groveatlantic.com

🌐 www.groveatlantic.com

Imprint(s) Atlantic Monthly Press
Black Cat
Grove Press
Atlantic Books (UK)

Categories Publishes Non-Fiction, Fiction and Poetry titles on the following subjects: Biography, General Interest, History, Literary Fiction, Poetry, Politics, Translation

Insider Info Publishes 70 titles per year. Pays 7.5–15 per cent royalty on retail price, with advance offered. 10–15 per cent of books come from first-time authors. Book catalogue available free on request.

Submission Guidelines Does not accept unsolicited manuscripts or proposals.

Recent Title(s) *The Delivery Man*, Joe McGinniss Jr.

Tips Grove/Atlantic does not accept unagented submissions or proposals.

Gyldendal

Klareboderne 3, DK-1001, Copenhagen, K, Denmark

☎ 0045 33 755555

📠 0045 33 755556

📧 gyldendal@gyldendal.dk

🌐 www.gyldendal.dk

Imprint(s) Forlaget Forum
Forlaget Fremad
Hans Reitzels Forlag
Høst & Søns Forlag
Rosinante
Samlerens Forlag

Categories Publishes Non-Fiction, Fiction and Children's titles on the following subjects: Art, Biography, Children's Fiction, Directories, Education, General Interest, How-To, Literary Fiction, Local Interest, Mainstream Fiction, Politics, Reference, Young Adult

Recent Title(s) *Skoven*, Tana French

Tips Gyldendal publishes various types of fiction and non-fiction through its many imprints. Check the individual imprint's website for submission guidelines.

Hachette Livre Publishing Group
43 Quai de Grenelle, F-75905, Paris, Cedex 15, France
- 0033 1 43 92 30 00
- 0033 1 43 92 30 30
- info@hachette-livre.fr
- www.hachette.com

Contact Editor, Catherine Rouyer
Imprint(s) Hachette Education/Istra
Hachette Littératures
Hachette Pratique
Hachette Tourisme
Larousse
Hachette UK

Categories Publishes Non-Fiction, Fiction and Children's titles on the following subjects: Biography, Children's Fiction, Contemporary Fiction, Directories, Education, General Interest, History, How-To, Language/Literature, Literary Fiction, Local Interest, Mainstream Fiction, Politics, Practical, Reference, Science, Self-Help, Textbooks, Travel
Insider Info Publishes 5,000 titles per year. Authors paid by royalty, with advance offered.
Submission Guidelines Accepts unsolicited manuscripts and proposals.
Recent Title(s) *Toubib or not Toubib*, Agnès Abécassis
Tips A major French publisher with many varied imprints. See website for editorial details and submission guidelines for each imprint.

Hachette Australia
Level 17, 207 Kent Street, Sydney, New South Wales, 2000, Australia
- 0061 2 8248 0800
- 0061 2 8248 0810
- auspub@hachette.com.au
- www.hha.com.au

Parent Company Hachette UK
Contact Managing Director, Malcolm Edwards; Publishing Director, Fiona Hazard; Publisher, Bernadette Foley; Publisher, Vanessa Radnidge; Non-Fiction Publisher, Matthew Kelly
Imprint(s) Hachette Children's Books (AUS)
Hodder Headline Australia
Little, Brown (AUS)
Orion (AUS)
Categories Publishes Non-Fiction, Fiction and Children's titles on the following subjects: Australiana, Autobiography, Biography, Children's, Cookbooks, Current Affairs, General Interest, Health,

History, Humour, Lifestyle, Literary Fiction, Mainstream Fiction, Self-Help, Sport, Travel
Insider Info Authors paid by royalty, with advance offered. Aims to respond to proposals within three to six months.
Submission Guidelines Does not accept unsolicited proposals.
Recent Title(s) *The Low GI Handbook*, Jennie Brand-Miller, Stephen Colagiuri and Kaye Foster-Powell
Tips Hachette Livre Australia specialises in publishing Australian writers, but does not accept unagented submissions or proposals.

Harcourt Children's Book
525 B Street, Suite 1900, San Diego, California, 92101, USA
- 001 619 699 6560
- 001 619 699 5555
- www.harcourtbooks.com

Parent Company Harcourt Trade Publishers
Imprint(s) Gulliver Books
Silver Whistle
Red Wagon Books
Harcourt Young Classics
Green Light Readers
Voyager Books/Libros Viajeros
Harcourt Paperbacks
Odyssey Classics
Magic Carpet Books.
Contact Editor in Chief, Allyn Johnston; Editors, Michael Sterns & Karen Grove; Executive Editor, Jeanette Larson; Editorial Director, Elizabeth Van Doren; Associate Editorial Director, Kathy Dawson
Categories Publishes Picture Books, Board and Novelty Books, Gift Items, Contemporary and Historical Fiction for Teenagers, and Non-Fiction for Children
Insider Info Pays 6–15 per cent royalty on retail price, with advance offered.
Submission Guidelines Does not accept unsolicited manuscripts or proposals, only accepted via literary agents.
Recent Title(s) *Grayson*, Lynne Cox
Tips Harcourt is a major educational and children's publisher, and will not accept unagented submissions or proposals.

Harcourt Inc
525 B Street, Suite 1900, San Diego, California, 92101, USA
- 001 619 699 6560
- 001 619 699 5555
- www.harcourtbooks.com

Parent Company Reed Elsevier Group Plc
Contact Editor in Chief, Rebecca Saletan; Managing Editor, David Hough

Imprint(s) Harcourt School Publishers
Holt, Rinehart and Winston
Harcourt Achieve
Harcourt Trade Publishers
Harcourt Children's Books
Categories Publishes Non-Fiction, Fiction and
Children's titles on the following subjects: Biography,
Children's, Education, General Interest, Multimedia,
Reference, Technical, Textbooks
Insider Info Pays 6–15 per cent royalty on retail
price, with advance offered.
Submission Guidelines Does not accept
unsolicited manuscripts or proposals.
Recent Title(s) *My Enemies Cradle*, Sara Young
Tips Harcourt is a major educational and children's
publisher, and will not accept unagented
submissions or proposals.

Harlequin Enterprises Ltd (Canada)
225 Duncan Mill Road, Don Mills, Ontario,
M3B 3K9, Canada
☎ 001 416 445 5860
☎ 001 416 445 5865
🌐 www.eharlequin.com
Contact President/Publisher, Donna Hayes; Vice
President (Editorial), Isabel Swift
Imprint(s) Harlequin Books Division
Mills & Boon
Categories Publishes Fiction titles on the following
subjects: Mainstream Fiction, Romance,
Women's Fiction
Insider Info Publishes 1,500 titles per year. Authors
paid by royalty, with advance offered. Average lead
time of 18 months. Aims to respond to manuscripts
within three months.
Submission Guidelines Accepts unsolicited
manuscripts and proposals.
Recent Title(s) *A Mother in a Million*, Melissa James
Tips Harlequin is Canada's largest publisher, with
scores of international imprints. They support new
writers, and will accept unsolicited manuscripts and
proposals. Check the website for details on which
imprints are currently seeking submissions.

Harlequin Enterprises Ltd (US)
233 Broadway, Suite 1001, New York, 10279,
USA
☎ 001 212 553 4200
🌐 www.eharlequin.com
Imprint(s) Harlequin Books/Mills and Boon
Silhouette
Luna
Steeple Hill Books
Red Dress Ink

Categories Publishes Fiction titles on the following
subjects: Mainstream Fiction, Romance,
Women's Fiction
Insider Info Publishes 1,500 titles per year. Authors
are paid by royalty, with advance offered. Average
lead time is 18 months. Aims to respond to
manuscripts within three months of receipt.
Submission Guidelines Accepts unsolicited
manuscripts and proposals.
Recent Title(s) *The Rancher's Doorstep Baby*,
Patricia Thayer
Tips The American office of the Canadian publisher,
Harlequin. They are often open to unsolicited
manuscripts. Check the website for details on which
imprints are currently seeking submissions.

HarperCollins
10 East 53rd Street, New York, 10022, USA
☎ 001 212 207 7000
☎ 001 212 207 7633
🌐 www.harpercollins.com
Parent Company News Corporation
Contact President & Publisher, Michael Morrison;
CEO, Brian Murray
Imprint(s) HarperCollins Australia/New Zealand
HarperCollins Canada
HarperCollins Children's Books Group
HarperCollins General Books Group
HarperCollins UK
Zondervan
Categories Publishes Non-Fiction, Fiction and
Children's titles on the following subjects: Academic,
Business, Children's, Educational, General Interest,
Genre Fiction, Mainstream Fiction, Multimedia,
Professional, Religious, Spiritual
Insider Info Authors paid by royalty, with
advance offered.
Submission Guidelines Generally only accepts
agented submissions, check the website for
further details.
Recent Title(s) *Sharp Teeth*, Toby Barlow
Tips HarperCollins generally only accepts agented
submissions.

HarperCollins Canada Ltd
2 Bloor Street East, 20th Floor, Toronto, Ontario,
M4W 1A8, Canada
☎ 001 416 975 9334
☎ 001 416 975 5223
🌐 www.harpercollins.ca
Parent Company News Corporation
Contact President & Publisher, Michael Morrison
Imprint(s) HarperCollins Publishers
HarperPerennial Canada
HarperTrophy Canada
Phyllis Bruce Books

Categories Publishes Non-Fiction, Fiction and Children's titles on the following subjects: Business, Children's, Cookbooks, Educational, General Interest, Genre Fiction, Literary Fiction, Mainstream Fiction, Multimedia, Professional, Reference, Spiritual
Insider Info Authors paid by royalty, advance offered.
Submission Guidelines Does not accept unsolicited manuscripts or proposals.
Recent Title(s) *Lords of the Bow*, Conn Iggulden

HarperCollins Children's Books (Canada)
2 Bloor Street East, 20th Floor, Toronto, Ontario, M4W 1A8, Canada
- 001 416 975 9334
- 001 416 975 5223
- www.harpercollins.ca
Parent Company HarperCollins Canada Ltd
Contact President, David Kent
Categories Publishes Children's Fiction and Non-Fiction, Picture Books, General Interest, Series Books, Teenage Fiction, Middle Grade Books, Beginner Books, Film/Television Tie-Ins and Seasonal Books
Insider Info HarperCollins is home to many of the classics of children's literature including; *Goodnight Moon*, *Where the Wild Things Are*, *The Giving Tree*, and *Charlotte's Web*. Authors are paid by royalty, with advance offered.
Submission Guidelines Does not accept unsolicited manuscripts or proposals.
Recent Title(s) *Alone on a Wide Wide Sea*, Michael Morpurgo

HarperCollinsPublishers Australia
PO Box 321, 25 Ryde Road, Pymble, New South Wales, 2073, Australia
- 0061 2 9952 5000
- 0061 2 9952 5555
- www.harpercollins.com.au
Parent Company News Corporation
Contact CEO & Publisher, Victoria Barnsley; Publishing Director, Shona Martyn; Managing Editor, Belinda Yuille
Imprint(s) Angus & Robertson
Fourth Estate
HarperCollins/Collins
HarperSports
HarperPerennial
Voyager
Categories Publishes Non-Fiction, Fiction and Children's titles on the following subjects: Academic, Business, Children's, Educational, General Interest, Genre Fiction, Mainstream Fiction, Multimedia, Professional, Religious, Spiritual

Insider Info Authors paid by royalty, with advance offered.
Submission Guidelines Does not accept unsolicited manuscripts or proposals.
Recent Title(s) *People of the Book*, Geraldine Brooks

HarperCollinsPublishers New Zealand
31 View Road, Glenfield, Auckland, New Zealand
- 0064 9 443 9400
- 0064 9 443 9403
- editors@harpercollins.co.nz
- www.harpercollins.co.nz
Parent Company News Corporation
Contact CEO & Publisher, Victoria Barnsley; Managing Director, Tony Fisk; Publishing Manager, Lorain Day; Commissioning Editor (Non-Fiction), Tracey Wogan
Imprint(s) Flamingo
HarperCollins
HarperSports
Perennial
Voyager
Categories Publishes Non-Fiction, Fiction and Children's titles on the following subjects: Autobiography, Biography, Business, Children's, Cookbooks, Educational, General Interest, Genre Fiction, Health, History, Literary Fiction, Mainstream Fiction, Multimedia, Professional, Reference, Spiritual, Travel, True Crime.
Insider Info Authors paid by royalty, with advance offered. Aims to respond to proposals within six weeks.
Submission Guidelines Accepts unsolicited manuscripts or proposals.
Recent Title(s) *Confessor*, Terry Goodkind; *The Dastardly Book for Dogs*, Rex and Sparky
Tips HarperCollins New Zealand does accept unsolicited submissions of non-fiction or fiction, but only from New Zealand writers.

Harry N. Abrams Inc
115 West 18th Street, New York, 10011, USA
- 001 212 206 7715
- 001 212 519 1210
- submissions@abramsbooks.com
- www.abramsbooks.com
Parent Company La Martiniere Groupe
Contact Chief Executive Officer, Michael Jacobs
Imprint(s) Abrams Books
Abrams Books for Young Readers
Abrams Image
Stewart, Tabori & Chang
Categories Publishes Non-Fiction and Children's titles on the following subjects: Art, Art History,

Children's Books, Illustrated Non-Fiction, Picture Books, Scholarly
Insider Info Publishes 250 titles per year. Does not accept simultaneous submissions. Aims to respond to proposals within six months (if interested).
Submission Guidelines Accepts unsolicited manuscripts and proposals.
Recent Title(s) *Beneath the Roses*, Russell Banks
Tips Abrams specialises in illustrated books for the adult trade market. Any sample artwork included with submissions must be in printed form rather than digital.

Harvard University Press
79 Garden Street, Cambridge, Massachusetts, 02138, USA
- 001 401 531 2800
- 001 401 531 2801
- contact_hup@harvard.edu
- www.hup.harvard.edu

Contact Editor in Chief, Michael Fisher
Categories Publishes Non-Fiction titles on the following subjects: American Literature, Economics, Education, History, History of Science, Law, Natural Science, Philosophy, Psychology, Public Policy, Reference, Scholarly
Insider Info Authors are paid by royalty, with advance offered.
Submission Guidelines Accepts unsolicited manuscripts and proposals.
Recent Title(s) *A Secular Age*, Charles Taylor
Tips Harvard University Press will accept scholarly proposals in its specialist areas. See website for editorial contact details.

H. Aschehoug & Co (W.Nygaard) AS
Postboks 363, Sentrum, N-0102, Oslo, Norway
- 0047 22 400400
- 0047 22 206395
- epost@aschehoug.no
- www.aschehoug.no

Contact Editor, Jeppe Markers
Imprint(s) Forlaget Oktober AS
Kirkelig Kulturverksted AS
Universitetsforlaget AS
Categories Publishes Non-Fiction, Fiction and Children's titles on the following subjects: Education, Fantasy, General Interest, Genre Fiction, History, Literary Fiction, Mainstream Fiction, Mystery, Practical, Romance, Science Fiction, Teaching Resources, Textbooks, Translation
Insider Info Publishes 500 titles per year. Aims to respond to manuscripts within six months.
Submission Guidelines Accepts unsolicited manuscripts and proposals.
Recent Title(s) *Straff*, Birger Baug

Tips Aschehoug accepts submissions in any area, as long as they are directed to the correct imprint. See website for details.

Hastings House/Daytrips Publishers
PO Box 908, Winter Park, Florida, 32790, USA
- 001 407 339 3600
- 001 407 339 5900
- hastings_daytrips@earthlink.net
- www.hastingshousebooks.com

Parent Company Lini Llc
Contact Publisher, Peter Leers; Senior Travel Editor (Daytrips Series), Earl Steinbicker
Categories Publishes Non-Fiction on the following subjects: Tourist Information, Travel, Travel Guides
Insider Info Publishes 20 titles per year. Pays eight to ten per cent royalty on net receipts. Receives 600 queries per year and 900 manuscripts per year. 40 per cent of books are from unagented writers, and ten per cent are from first-time authors. Average lead time of six to ten months.
Recent Title(s) *Daytrips London*, Early Steinbicker
Tips Hastings House/Daytrips Publishers is currently focusing on the *Daytrips Travel Series* and is seeking material from both local and international contributors.

Houghton Mifflin Co.
222 Berkeley Street, Boston, Massachusetts, 02116, USA
- 001 617 351 5000
- www.hmco.com

Contact Chairman/President/Chief Executive Officer, Anthony Lucki; Executive Vice President, Stephen Richards
Imprint(s) Great Source
Houghton Mifflin College Division
Houghton Mifflin School Division
Houghton Mifflin Trade and Reference Division
McDougal Littell
Riverside
Categories Publishes Non-Fiction, Fiction, Poetry and Children's titles on the following subjects: Biography, Children's, Education, General Interest, How-To, Literary Fiction, Reference, Self-Help, Textbooks
Insider Info Authors are paid by royalty, with advance offered. Accepts simultaneous submissions.
Submission Guidelines Accepts unsolicited manuscripts and proposals.
Recent Title(s) *How Doctors Think*, Jerome Groopman
Tips Houghton Mifflin are not a mass market publisher. They do practical self-help, but not pop psychology. The main focus is on serious non-fiction and their audience is a high-end literary one.

Houghton Mifflin Trade & Reference Division
222 Berkeley Street, Boston, Massachusetts, 02116, USA

🕿 001 617 351 5000

🌐 www.hmco.com

Contact Editorial Director, Judy O'Mailey; Executive Editor, Magaret Raymo; Paperback Director, Julia Richardson; Senior Editor, Ann Rider; Submissions Coordinator, Hannah Rodgers, Editor, Amy Flynn; Assistant Editor, Kate O'Sullivan

Imprint(s) Clarion Books

Houghton Mifflin Books for Children

Graphia

Walter Lorraine Books

Categories Publishes Children's Fiction and Non-Fiction, Poetry, and Reference

Insider Info Publishes approximately 400 books annually. Authors are paid by royalty, with an advance offered. Accepts simultaneous submissions.

Submission Guidelines See individual imprints for submission guidelines.

Recent Title(s) *How to Pick a Peach*, Russ Parsons

Indiana University Press
601 North Morton Street, Bloomington, Indiana, 47404, USA

🕿 001 812 855 8817

🖷 001 812 855 8507

✉ iupress@indiana.edu

🌐 www.iupress.indiana.edu

Contact Director (Russian & East European Studies, United Nations, Jewish & Holocaust Studies, Art), Janet Rabinowitch; Editorial Director (American History, African American Studies, Bioethics, Military History, Paleontology, Philanthropy), Robert Sloan; Sponsoring Editor (African Studies, Philosophy, Religion), Dee Mortensen; Sponsoring Editor (Regional Trade, Regional Natural History, Railroads Past & Present), Linda Oblack; Sponsoring Editor (Music, Cinema, Media Studies), Jane Quinet; Sponsoring Editor (Anthropology, Asian Studies, Middle East Studies, Political Science/International Relations, Folklore), Rebecca Tolen

Categories Publishes Non-Fiction and Journals on the following subjects: Academic, African, African American, Anthropology, Asian, Classical and Ancient, Cultural Studies, Gender Studies, Jewish, Middle East, Russian and East European Studies, Film, Folklore, History, Bio-ethics, Music, Paleontology, Philanthropy, Philosophy, Reference, Religion, Scholarly, Women's Studies

Insider Info Publishes 200 titles per year. Offers an advance. Aims to respond to proposals within four months.

Submission Guidelines Accepts unsolicited manuscripts and proposals.

Recent Title(s) *The Unknown Black Book*, Joshua Rubenstein and Ilya Altman (eds.)

Tips Indiana University Press is the second largest public university press in America, it specialises mainly in humanities and social sciences.

The Johns Hopkins University Press
2715 North Charles Street, Baltimore, Maryland, 21218, USA

🕿 001 410 516 6900

🖷 001 410 516 6968

✉ tcl@press.jhu.edu

🌐 www.press.jhu.edu

Contact Director, Kathleen Keane; Editor in Chief (Mathematics, Physics, Astronomy), Trevor C. Lipscombe; Senior Acquisitions Editor (Clinical Medicine, Public Health, Health Policy), Wendy Harris; Senior Acquisitions Editor (American History, History of Science & Technology, Regional Books), Robert J. Brugger; Senior Acquisitions Editor (Biology & Life Sciences), Vincent J. Burke

Categories Publishes Non-Fiction on the following subjects: Academic, Biography, General Interest, History, Journals, Literary Criticism, Politics, Reference, Religion, Scholarly, Science, Textbook

Insider Info Publishes 140 titles per year. Authors paid by royalty. Average lead time is one year.

Submission Guidelines Accepts unsolicited manuscripts and proposals.

Recent Title(s) *Beyond the Black Box: The Forensics of Airplane Crashes*, George Bibel

Tips Johns Hopkins welcomes academic proposals providing they are sent to the correct editor. Check the website for further details.

John Wiley & Sons Australia Ltd
PO Box 1226, 42 McDougall Street, Milton, Queensland, 4064, Australia

🕿 0061 7 3859 9755

🖷 0061 7 3859 9715

✉ brisbane@johnwiley.com.au

🌐 www.johnwiley.com.au

Parent Company John Wiley & Sons Inc

Contact Managing Director, Peter Donoughue

Imprint(s) Higher Education Division

Jacaranda

Categories Publishes Non-Fiction and Children's titles on the following subjects: Academic, Business, Children's Education, Education, Engineering, Multimedia, Online, Psychology, Reference, Science, Sociology, Teacher Resources, Technology, Textbooks

Insider Info Authors paid by royalty, with advance offered.

Submission Guidelines Accepts unsolicited manuscripts and proposals.
Recent Title(s) *Australian Shopaholic's Guide to Buying Online*, Annie Fox and Patricia Davidson
Tips John Wiley Australia accepts submissions using a downloadable submission form. See website for further details and downloads.

John Wiley & Sons Inc
111 River Street, Hoboken, New Jersey, 07030, USA
- 001 201 748 6000
- 001 201 748 6088
- info@wiley.com
- www.wiley.com

Contact President/Chief Executive Officer, William J. Pesce; Chairman, Peter B. Wiley
Imprint(s) Jossey-Bass
Wiley-Blackwell (UK)
Wiley Nautical (UK)
Categories Publishes Non-Fiction titles on the following subjects: Biography, Children's, Education, Health, History, Medical, Psychology, Reference, Science, Technology, Textbooks
Insider Info Offers an advance. Accepts simultaneous submissions.
Submission Guidelines Accepts unsolicited unsolicited proposals and manuscripts. A detailed set of submission guidelines for each division are published on the website.
Recent Title(s) *Windows Vista Secrets*, Brian Livingston and Paul Thurrott

Jonathan Ball Publishers
PO Box 33977, Jeppestown, Cape Town, 2043, South Africa
- 0027 11 622 2900
- 0027 11 601 8183
- jball@jonathanball.co.za
- www.jonathanball.co.za

Contact Managing Director, Jonathan Ball; Publishing Director, Jeremy Boraine; Editor, Jane Rogers; Editor (Sunbird), Natanya Mulholland
Imprint(s) Jonathan Ball
Sunbird
Categories Publishes Non-Fiction and Fiction titles on the following subjects: Biography, History, Maps, Literary Fiction, Politics, South African Non-Fiction, Tourism, Travel
Submission Guidelines Accepts unsolicited manuscripts and proposals.
Recent Title(s) *Notes from a Fractured Country*, Jonny Steinberg
Tips Jonathan Ball accepts submissions from international writers but will only publish non-fiction

relating to South Africa, and a limited amount of fiction.

Juta & Company Ltd
PO Box 14373, Lansdowne, Cape Town, 7779, South Africa
- 0027 21 763 3500
- 0027 21 761 5861
- cserv@juta.co.za
- www.juta.co.za

Contact Chief Executive Officer, Lynne du Toit; Publisher (Juta Law), Chipo Chipidza; Publisher (Juta Academic), Glenda Younge
Imprint(s) Double Storey
Juta Academic
Juta Law
Juta Learning
Categories Publishes Non-Fiction on the following subjects: Academic, Art, Biography, Business, Education, Health, Law, Legal Interest, Local Interest, Memoirs, Multimedia, Music, Psychology, Science, South African Non-Fiction, Spirituality, Teacher Resources, Tourism
Recent Title(s) *A Guide to Managing Research*, William Fox and Mohamed Saheed Bayat eds.
Tips Juta specialises mainly in law and legal matters, or education titles, but also publishes more mainstream South African interest titles through the Double Storey imprint.

Kensington Publishing Corp.
850 3rd Avenue, 16th Floor, New York, 10022, USA
- 001 212 407 1500
- 001 212 935 0699
- jscognamiglio@kensingtonbooks.com
- www.kensingtonbooks.com

Contact President/CEO, Steven Zacharius; Editor in Chief, John Scognamiglio; Editorial Director (Romance), Kate Duffy; Editorial Director, Audrey LaFehr
Imprint(s) Kensington Books
Brava Books
Citadel Press
Dafina Books
Pinnacle Books
Zebra Books
Categories Publishes Non-Fiction and Fiction titles on the following subjects: African-American, Biography, Gay/Lesbian, General Interest, Health, How-To, Mainstream Fiction, Mystery, Reference, Romance, Self-Help, Wiccan
Insider Info Publishes 600 titles per year. Pays 6–15 per cent royalty on retail price, with advance offered. Receives 5,000 queries per year and 2,000 manuscripts per year. Ten per cent of books come

from first-time authors. Aims to respond to proposals within one month and manuscripts within three months. Accepts simultaneous submissions. Average lead time is one year.

Submission Guidelines Accepts unsolicited manuscripts and proposals.

Recent Title(s) *Hide and Seek*, Fern Michaels

Tips Kensington is a major independent US publisher of trade and mass market books. They will accept submissions as long as they are addressed to the relevant editor and accompanied by SAE. Check website for list of editors and their fields of interest.

Key Porter Books Ltd
6 Adelaide Street East, 10th Floor, Toronto, Ontario, M5C 1H6, Canada

- 001 416 862 7777
- 001 416 862 2304
- info@keyporter.com
- www.keyporter.com

Contact Publisher, Jordan Fenn

Imprint(s) Key Porter Kids

Categories Publishes Non-Fiction and Children's titles on the following subjects: Art, Autobiography, Biography, Business, Children's, Cookbooks, Gift Books, Health, History, How-To, Humour, Illustrated Books, Politics, Science, Self-Help, Translation, Travel, Young Adult

Insider Info Publishes 100 titles per year. Authors paid by royalty, with advance offered. Receives 1,000 queries per year and 500 manuscripts per year. Aims to respond to proposals within six months.

Submission Guidelines Does not accept unsolicited manuscripts, but will usually respond to proposals or queries.

Recent Title(s) *Happiness and Other Disorders*, Ahmad Saidullah

Kids Can Press
29 Birch Avenue, Toronto, Ontario, M4V 1E2, Canada

- 001 800 265 0884
- 001 416 960 5437
- webmaster@kidscan.com
- www.kidscan.com

Contact Publisher Valerie Hussey, Karen Boersma

Categories Publishes Children's Fiction and Non-Fiction, Poetry, Picture Books, Novelty Books, Craft Books, Activity Books, Hands-On Science Experiment Books, How-To Books (Children's), Nature Books, General Non-Fiction

Insider Info Publishes approximately 50 children's books per year. Famous children's book characters are *Franklin the Turtle* and *Eloise Moose*.

Submission Guidelines For fiction send in plot synopsis and three chapter samples. For picture

books send the entire manuscript, and include SAE. All manuscripts must be typed and doubled spaced. Aims to respond within six months. Address the envelope to 'Acquisitions Editor'. Send illustration samples and resume to the 'Art Director'.

Recent Title(s) *123 I Can Paint!*, Irene Luxbacher (Craft); *The Faceless Fiend*, Howard Whitehouse (Author), Bill Slavin (Illustrator)

Tips The company does not accept unsolicited submissions from authors outside of Canada, or from teenagers or children.

Kingfisher
222 Berkeley Street, Boston, Massachusetts, 02116, USA

- 001 617 351 5000
- www.hmco.com

Contact Editor, Eden Edwards

Parent Houghton Mifflin Inc

Insider Info Kingfisher is an imprint company that specialises in non-fiction for children of all ages. Known around the world for its informative and engaging reference books, activity books, and early learning books, classic anthologies and original picture books.

Submission Guidelines No unsolicited manuscripts, only via literary agents.

Recent Title(s) *Kingfisher Knowledge Series*

Knopf Publishing Group
1745 Broadway, New York, 10019, USA

- 001 212 572 2600
- 001 212 572 8700
- knopfwebmaster@randomhouse.com
- www.randomhouse.com/knopf

Parent Company Random House Inc

Contact President, Sonny Metha

Imprint(s) Alfred A. Knopf
Everyman's Library
Pantheon Books
Schocken Books
Vintage Anchor Publishing

Categories Publishes Non-Fiction, Fiction and Children's titles on the following subjects: Biography, Children's, Education, General Interest, Literary Fiction, Mainstream Fiction, Reference

Insider Info Authors paid by royalty with advance offered. Accepts simultaneous submissions. Catalogue available by sending SAE.

Submission Guidelines Does not accept unsolicited proposals or manuscripts.

Recent Title(s) *This Republic of Suffering*, Drew Gilpin Faust

Krause Publications

700 East State Street, Iola, Wisconsin, 54990, USA

- 001 715 445 2214
- 001 715 445 4087
- info@krause.com
- www.krause.com

Parent Company F+W Media Inc

Contact Editorial Director, Paul Kennedy; Editor (Soft Crafts), Candy Wiza; Editor (Firearms and Knives), Derrek Sigler; Editor (Antique and Collectibles), Joe Kertzman; Editor (Transportation), John Gunnell

Categories Publishes Non-Fiction titles on the following subjects: Antiques andCollectibles, Crafts, Coins and Paper Money, Comics and Games, Construction, Firearms, Knives, Militaria, Old Cars, Outdoors, Records and CDs, Sports, Toys

Insider Info Publishes 170 titles per year. Receives 400 queries and 40 manuscripts per year. Ten per cent of books come from first-time authors, and 90 per cent of books from unagented writers. Average lead time is 18 months. Does not accept simultaneous submissions. Aims to respond to proposals and manuscripts within two months.

Submission Guidelines Accepts unsolicited manuscripts and proposals.

Recent Title(s) *Quilt as Desired*, Charlene C. Frable

Tips Krause's audience consists of serious hobbyists so proposals should provide a unique contribution to the special interest. Submission guidelines available by post.

Langenscheidt KG

Mies van der Rohe Straße 1, D-80807, Munich, Germany

- 0049 89 360960
- 0049 89 3609 6222
- redaktion.wb@langenscheidt.de
- www.langenscheidt.de

Parent Company The Langenscheidt Publishing Group

Contact President, Andreas Langensheidt

Imprint(s) Axel Juncker Verlag

Berlitz

Langenscheidt Fachverlag

Mentor

Polyglott

Categories Publishes Non-Fiction titles on the following subjects: Atlases, Bilingual Dictionaries, Dictionaries, Encyclopedias, Language Books, Road Maps, Translations, Travel Guides

Recent Title(s) *Langenscheidt Vokabeltrainer*

Tips Langenscheidt primarily publishes dictionaries and linguistic reference material.

Learning Media Ltd

PO Box 3293, Wellington, 6001, New Zealand

- 0064 4 472 5522
- 0064 4 472 6444
- info@learningmedia.co.nz
- www.learningmedia.co.nz

Contact Chief Executive Officer, Gillian Candler; Manager (Sales Publishing), Michelle Kelly; Manager (Curriculum Publishing), Kirsty Farquharson; Manager (Mori Publishing), Huhana Rokx

Categories Publishes Non-Fiction, Fiction and Children's titles on the following subjects: Academic, Children's Fiction, Education, Language, Literacy, Multimedia, Pasifika Language, Student Resources, Teacher Resources, Translation, Young Adult

Insider Info Aims to respond to proposals within 12 weeks. Manuscript guidelines are available online.

Submission Guidelines Accepts unsolicited manuscripts/proposals.

Recent Title(s) *A Nest of Singing Birds*, Gregory O'Brien

Tips Learning Media publishes educational material for a specific region and prints in many different Pasifika languages. Learning Media recommends that submissions be written for a particular series, and are currently seeking submissions for the Tupu series in particular.

Les Presses de la Cité

12 avenue d'Italie, F-75627, Paris, Cedex 13 France

- 0033 1 44 16 05 00
- 0033 1 44 16 05 05
- edito_fr_pressesdelacite@placedesediteurs.com
- www.pressesdelacite.com

Parent Company Editions Belfond

Contact Editorial Director, Jean Arcache

Categories Non-Fiction, Fiction, Biography, Fantasy, General Interest, Genre Fiction, History, Literary Fiction, Mainstream Fiction, Mystery, Romance, Science Fiction

Insider Info Responds to manuscripts in two months. Manuscript guidelines are available online.

Submission Guidelines Accepts unsolicited manuscripts.

Recent Title(s) *La Mémoire du Sang*, Greg Iles

Tips Presses de la Cité accepts submissions by post, but not email. Enclose SAE for return of manuscript.

LexisNexis Canada Inc

123 Commerce Valley Drive East, Suite 700, Markham, Ontario, L3T 7W8 Canada

- 001 905 479 2665
- 001 905 479 2826
- info@lexisnexis.ca
- www.lexisnexis.ca

Parent Company LexisNexis Group
Imprint(s) Butterworths
LexisNexis
Quicklaw
Categories Non-Fiction, Academic, Business, Finance, Law/Legal, Multimedia, Online, Reference, Technology, Textbooks
Insider Info Publishes 100 titles per year. Pays 5–15 per cent royalty on wholesale price. Receives 100 per cent of its books from unagented writers. Receives 50 per cent of books from first-time authors. Accepts simultaneous submissions. Publishes manuscript four months after acceptance. Book catalogue free on request.
Submission Guidelines Accepts unsolicited manuscripts/proposals.
Recent Title(s) *Alcohol and Drugs in the Canadian Workplace*, Norm Keith and Ailsa Wiggins
Tips LexisNexis Canada accepts submissions for law and legal material in both print and electronic formats.

LexisNexis New Zealand
PO Box 472, 205–207 Victoria Street, Wellington, New Zealand
- 0064 4 385 1479
- 0064 4 385 1598
- customer.service@lexisnexis.co.nz
- www.lexisnexis.co.nz

Parent Company LexisNexis Group
Contact Executive Director, Sharon Bennett; Editorial, Helen Scott
Categories Non-Fiction, Academic, Business, Finance, Law/Legal, Multimedia, Online, Reference, Technology, Textbook
Insider Info Pays royalty, advance offered. Manuscript guidelines are available online.
Submission Guidelines Accepts unsolicited manuscripts and proposals.
Recent Title(s) *Electoral Law in New Zealand: Practice and Policy*, Andrew Geddis
Tips LexisNexis New Zealand is always looking for submissions of law and legal related material. See website for editorial contact details.

Llewellyn Publications
2143 Wooddale Drive, Woodbury, Minnesota, 55125 USA
- 001 800 843 6666
- 001 651 291 1908
- lwlpc@llewellyn.com
- www.llewellyn.com

Parent Company Llewellyn Worldwide Ltd
Contact Acquisitions Editor, Nancy J. Mostad
Categories Publishes Non-Fiction and Fiction titles on the following subjects: Astrology, Cooking/ Foods/Nutrition, Health/Medicine, How-To, Metaphysical Fiction, Multimedia, Nature, New Age, Occult, Pagan, Psychology, Self-Help, Women's Issues/Studies
Insider Info Publishes 100 titles per year. Pays ten per cent royalty on wholesale price. 90 per cent of books come from unagented writers and 30 per cent of books from first-time authors. Accepts simultaneous submissions.
Submission Guidelines Accepts unsolicited manuscripts and proposals. Manuscripts must be posted rather than emailed.
Recent Title(s) *Dancing with Dragons: Invoke Their Ageless Wisdom & Power*, D.J. Conway
Tips Submissions to Llewellyn should be of a practical or how-to nature, but content should remain accessible to the average reader.

Lonely Planet Publications
90 Maribyrnong Street, Footscray, Victoria, 3011, Australia
- 0061 3 8379 8000
- 0061 3 8379 8111
- talk2us@lonelyplanet.com.au
- www.lonelyplanet.com

Contact Director, Maureen Wheeler; Director, Tony Wheeler
Categories Publishes Non-Fiction on the following subjects: Tourist Guides and Travel.
Insider Info Advance offered. Accepts simultaneous submissions.
Submission Guidelines Accepts unsolicited manuscripts and proposals.
Recent Title(s) *Lonely Planet Bluelist 2008*
Tips Lonely Planet accepts queries and submissions, but read something from their catalogue first to get an idea of their writing style.

Lone Pine Publishing
10145–81 Avenue, Edmonton, Alberta, T6E 1W9, Canada
- 001 780 433 9333
- 001 780 433 9646
- info@lonepinepublishing.com
- www.lonepinepublishing.com

Contact Chairman, Grant Kennedy; Managing Director, Shane Kennedy; Editorial Director, Nancy Foulds
Imprint(s) Ghost House Books
Home World
Lone Pine
Pine Candle
Pine Cone
Categories Publishes Non-Fiction titles on the following subjects: Canadian Interest, Environment, Food and Drink, Ghost Short Stories, Health, Local

Interest, Natural History, Nature, Outdoors, Paranormal, Popular History, Regional Interest, Science, Travel/Tourist Guides

Insider Info Publishes 40 titles per year. Authors are paid by royalty, with advance offered. 95 per cent of books come from unagented writers, and 75 per cent of books from first-time authors. Does not accept simultaneous submissions. Catalogue available free on request.

Submission Guidelines Accepts unsolicited manuscripts and proposals.

Recent Title(s) *O'ahu Hikes*, Yvonne Harris

Tips Lone Pine only publishes non-fiction books of regional interest, the exception being its Ghost House imprint, which is often interested in ghost stories as well as non-fiction.

Macmillan South Africa
PO Box 32484, Braamfontein, 2017, South Africa
- 0027 11 731 3300
- 0027 11 731 3500
- info@macmillan.co.za
- www.macmillan.co.za

Parent Company Boleswa
Imprint(s) Clever Books
Guidelines

Categories Publishes Non-Fiction, Fiction and Children's titles on the following subjects: African Literature, Education, General Interest, How-To, Literacy, Mainstream Fiction, Reference, Science, Scholarly, Self-Help, Teaching Guides

Insider Info Authors paid by royalty, with advance offered.

Tips Macmillan South Africa is interested in educational non-fiction about literacy, numeracy and similar subjects. They are currently developing their website, so check back frequently for possible submission guidelines.

McClelland & Stewart Ltd
75 Sherbourne Street, 5th Floor, Toronto, Ontario, M5A 2P9, Canada
- 001 416 598 1114
- 001 416 598 7764
- editorial@mcclelland.com
- www.mcclelland.com

Contact Chairman/Publisher, Douglas Pepper
Imprint(s) Douglas Gibson Books
Emblem Editions
New Canadian Library
McClelland & Stewart

Categories Publishes Non-Fiction and Fiction titles on the following subjects: Art, Canadiana, General Interest, Historical Fiction, Literary Interest, Mainstream Interest, Military Interest, Nature,

Photography, Short Story Collections, Sports, Translation, Travel, Women's Issues

Insider Info Publishes 80 titles per year. Advance offered. Receives 1,500 queries per year. 30 per cent of books come from unagented writers, and ten per cent from first-time authors. Aims to respond to proposals within three months. Average lead time is one year.

Submission Guidelines Does not accept unsolicited submissions or proposals.

Recent Title(s) *Late Nights on Air*, Elizabeth Hay

McGraw-Hill Professional
2 Penn Plaza, 11th Floor, New York, 10121, USA
- 001 609 426 5793
- 001 609 426 7917
- international_cs@mcgraw-hill.com
- www.books.mcgraw-hill.com

Parent Company The McGraw Hill Companies
Contact Publisher, Philip Ruppel; Editor in Chief, Jeffrey Krames

Imprint(s) McGraw-Hill Business
McGraw-Hill Medical
McGraw-Hill Education
McGraw-Hill Technical
McGraw-Hill Consumer

Categories Publishes Non-Fiction titles on the following subjects: How-To, Reference, Self-Help, Technical, Management, Finance, Business, Careers, Health, Medicine, Education, Study Guides, Science, Engineering, Computing, Parenting, Sports, Outdoors, General Interest

Submission Guidelines Accepts unsolicited manuscripts and proposals. All submissions must be as in-depth as possible and include relevant market research, including information about similar products, and a recent CV. It is advisable to send any illustrations along with the proposal and a list of potential reviewers with experience and knowledge of the subject covered.

Recent Title(s) *Getting Sober*, Kelly Madigan Erlandson (Self-Help)

Melbourne University Publishing Ltd
187 Grattan Street, Carlton, Victoria, 3053, Australia
- 0061 3 9342 0300
- 0061 3 9342 0399
- mup-info@unimelb.edu.au
- www.mup.com.au

Contact Chairman, Alan Kohler; CEO/Publisher-in-Chief, Louise Adler; Managing Editor, Felicity Edge/ Cinzia Cavallaro

Imprint(s) Melbourne University Press
Miegunyah Press

Categories Publishes Non-Fiction titles on the following subjects: Aboriginal Studies, Architecture, Art, Biography, Cultural Studies, Current Affairs, Environmental Studies, Food & Wine, Gardening, Gender Studies, Journals, Literary Criticism, Media Studies, Natural History, Philosophy, Politics, Scholarly, Social Sciences, Travel.
Insider Info Publishes 70-80 titles per year. Aims to respond to proposals within four months.
Submission Guidelines Accepts unsolicited manuscripts and proposals. See website for submission details.
Recent Title(s) *The Costello Memoirs*, Peter Costello with Peter Coleman

Michelle Anderson Publishing (Pty) Ltd
PO Box 6032, Chapel Street North, South Yarra, Victoria, 3141, Australia
- 0061 3 9826 9028
- 0061 3 9826 8552
- info@michelleandersonpublishing.com
- www.michelleandersonpublishing.com

Categories Publishes Non-Fiction and Children's titles on the following subjects: Children's Non-Fiction, Guidance, Health, Local Interest, Mind and Body, Parenting, Self-Help, Spirituality, Travel
Submission Guidelines Michelle Anderson will accept queries, as long as SAE is included for a response.
Recent Title(s) *Secrets of Cancer Survivors*, Elizabeth Gould

Michigan State University Press
Suite 25, 1405 South Harrison Road, East Lansing, Michigan, 48823, USA
- 001 517 355 9543
- 001 517 432 2611
- msupress@msu.edu
- www.msupress.msu.edu

Contact Director, Fredric C. Bohm; Assistant Director and Editor in Chief, Julie L. Loehr; Acquisitions Editor, Martha A. Bates; Managing Editor (Journals Division), Margot Landa Kielhorn
Imprint(s) MSU Press Book Division
MSU Press Journals Division
Categories Publishes Non-Fiction, Fiction, Poetry and Journals on the following subjects: Academic, American History, Art/Architecture, Cultural Studies, Environmental Affairs, History, Human Ecology, Literary Criticism, Literary Fiction, Multicultural Studies, Native American Studies, Philosophy, Poetry, Political Sciences, Reference, Regional (Upper Midwest, Great Lakes, Canada), Rhetoric, Sciences, Scholarly, Short Stories, Social Sciences, Women's Studies

Submission Guidelines Accepts proposals, not full manuscripts. Email submissions must be included in the body of the email, and not sent as an attached file.
Recent Title(s) *Judging the Supreme Court*, Clarine Rountree

Milkweed Editions
1011 Washington Avenue South, Suite 300, Minneapolis, Minnesota, 55415, USA
- 001 612 332 3192
- 001 612 215 2550
- www.milkweed.org

Contact Editor in Chief, Daniel Slager
Imprint(s) Milkweeds for Young Readers
Categories Publishes Non-Fiction, Fiction, Poetry and Children's titles on the following subjects: Children's Fiction, Culture, General Interest, Literary Fiction, Nature, Poetry, Social Studies, Young Adult
Insider Info Publishes 20 titles per year. Pays six per cent royalty on retail price, with advance offered. 70 per cent of books come from unagented writers and 30 per cent from first-time authors. Aims to respond to manuscripts within six months. Accepts simultaneous submissions. Average lead time of 18 months.
Submission Guidelines Accepts unsolicited manuscripts and proposals.
Recent Title(s) *The Windows of Brimnes*, Bill Holm
Tips Milkweed only reads poetry submissions in January and June, but non-fiction and fiction can be submitted at any time.

Morehouse Publishing
4775 Linglestown Road, Harrisburg, Pennsylvania, 17112, USA
- 001 212 592 1800
- 001 717 541 8136
- nfitzgerald@cpg.org
- www.churchpublishing.org

Parent Company Church Publishing Inc
Contact Executive Editor, Nancy Fitzgerald
Categories Publishes Non-Fiction on the following subjects: Bible Studies, Church History, Education, Ethics, Liturgy, Marriage and Family, Multimedia, Prayer Books, Religion, Social Issues, Women's Studies.
Insider Info Publishes 35 titles per year for Episcopalians and other Christians from liturgical traditions. Pays ten per cent royalty on net receipts, with advance offered. 50 per cent of books come from first-time authors. Accepts simultaneous submissions. Average lead time is 18 months. Please allow 3 months for a response.

Recent Title(s) *In the Eye of the Storm*, Gene Robinson; *A Wing and a Prayer*, Katharine Jefferts Schori

Tips Morehouse Publishing focuses on books and teaching resources for a mainline/liturgical Christian readership. Prefers to receive proposals by regular post.

Napoleon Publishing/RendezVous Press

178 Willowdale Avenue, Suite 201, Toronto, Ontario, M2N 4Y8, Canada
- 001 416 730 9052
- 001 416 730 8096
- editorial@transmedia95.com
- www.rendezvouspress.com

Contact Editor, Allister Thompson

Imprint(s) Dark Star Fiction
Napoleon Publishing
RendezVous Crime
RendezVous Press

Categories Publishes Fiction and Children's titles on the following subjects: Canadian Literature, Children's Fiction, Contemporary Fiction, Crime Fiction, Literary Fiction, Mainstream Fiction, Mystery Fiction

Insider Info Publishes 20 titles per year. Receives 200 queries and 100 manuscripts per year. 80 per cent of books come from unagented writers, and 50 per cent from first-time authors. Aims to respond to manuscripts within six months. Accepts simultaneous submissions. Average lead time is 18 months.

Submission Guidelines Accepts unsolicited manuscripts and proposals.

Recent Title(s) *Lucky Strike*, Pat Wilson and Kris Wood

Tips Napoleon/RendezVous Press usually only accept work from Canadian writers. See the website to check which imprints are accepting submissions at any given time.

National Archives of Australia

PO Box 7425, Canberra Business Centre, Canberra, Australian Capital Territory, 2610, Australia
- 0061 2 6212 3900
- 0061 2 6212 3999
- archives@naa.gov.au
- www.naa.gov.au

Categories Publishes Non-Fiction on the following subjects: Australian History, Biography, Catalogues, Genealogy, History, Multimedia, Reference, Teaching Resources

Tips The National Archives mainly publish books on Australian history, genealogy and record-keeping,

but they also produce various types of multimedia material.

NB Publisher (Pty) Ltd

PO Box 879, Cape Town, 8000, South Africa
- 0027 21 406 3033
- 0027 21 406 3812
- nb@nb.co.za
- www.nb.co.za

Contact Publisher (Non-Fiction), Danita van Romburgh

Imprint(s) Human & Rousseau
Kwela
Pharos
Tafelberg

Categories Publishes Non-Fiction, Fiction and Children's titles on the following subjects: Afrikaans Novels, Children's Fiction, Children's Non-Fiction, Cookery, Craft, Dictionaries, General Interest, Health, Literary Fiction, Local Interest, Mainstream Fiction, Picture Books, Spirituality, Young Adult

Insider Info Aims to respond to manuscripts within three months.

Submission Guidelines Accepts unsolicited manuscripts and proposals.

Recent Title(s) *Formula Three, Two, One!*, Franci Greyling (Children's)

Tips Accepts submissions either by post or email, providing they are sent to the correct imprint.

NeWest Press

201, 8540 109th Street, Edmonton, Alberta, T6G 1E6, Canada
- 001 780 432 9427
- 001 780 433 3179
- info@newestpress.com
- www.newestpress.com

Contact General Manager, Amber Rider

Categories Publishes Non-Fiction, Fiction, Poetry and Drama titles on the following subjects: Western Canadiana, History, Literary Fiction, Mainstream Fiction, Mystery Fiction, Nature, Play Scripts, Poetry Collections, Politics

Insider Info Publishes 20 titles per year. Pays ten per cent royalty, with advance offered. Receives 800 manuscripts per year. 85 per cent of books come from unagented writers and 40 per cent from first-time authors. Accepts simultaneous submissions. Average lead time is two and a half years.

Submission Guidelines Accepts unsolicited manuscripts and proposals.

Recent Title(s) *Icefields*, Thomas Wharton

Tips NeWest Press only accepts submissions from Canadian writers.

New York University Press
838 Broadway, 3rd Floor, New York, 10003, USA
- ☎ 001 212 998 2575
- ☎ 001 212 995 3833
- ✉ information@nyupress.org
- 🌐 www.nyupress.org

Contact Director, Steve Maikowski; Editor in Chief (Literary, Cultural, and Media Studies, American History), Eric Zinner; Executive Editor (Sociology, Politics, Anthropology), Ilene Kalish; Senior Editor (Law, American History to 1900, Military History), Deborah Gershenowitz; Editor (Religion, Psychology), Jennifer Hammer

Categories Publishes Non-Fiction and Art titles on the following subjects: Art, Biography, Cultural and Media Studies, General Interest, History, Journals, Law, Literary Criticism, Politics, Reference, Religion, Scholarly, Textbook

Insider Info Publishes 100 titles per year. Pays royalty on net receipts. Receives 800–1,000 queries per year. 90 per cent of books come from unagented writers, and 30 per cent of books from first-time authors. Aims to respond to queries within four months (peer reviewed). Accepts simultaneous submissions. Average lead time of one year.

Submission Guidelines Accepts unsolicited manuscripts and proposals.

Recent Title(s) *How the University Works*, Marc Bousquet

Tips New York University Press welcomes submissions in their fields of interest. Make sure submission is sent to the correct editor.

Norstedts Förlag
PO Box 2052, S-103 12, Stockholm, Sweden
- ☎ 0046 8 769 8850
- ☎ 0046 8 769 8864
- ✉ info@panorstedt.se
- 🌐 www.panorstedt.se

Parent Company Norstedts Förlagsgrupp
Contact Publishing Chief, Ekelund Viveca; Publishing Chief, Bladh Annika; Publishing Chief, Eva Gedin; Editor in Chief, Enochsson Birgitta

Categories Non-Fiction, Fiction, Children's Classics, Contemporary Culture, General Interest, History, Literary Fiction, Mainstream Fiction, Swedish Fiction

Insider Info Publishes 100 titles per year. Responds to manuscripts in two months. Manuscript guidelines are available online at: www.panorstedt.se/templates/Norstedts/Page.aspx?id=28829

Submission Guidelines Accepts unsolicited manuscripts and proposals

Recent Title(s) *Rötter Smälter*, Sara Hallström

Tips Norstedts accepts submissions by post only, not by email. Include SAE for return of manuscript.

Otava Publishing Company Ltd
Uudenmaankatu 10, SF-00120, Helsinki, Finland
- ☎ 00358 9 19961
- ☎ 00358 9 199 6560
- ✉ name.surname@otava.fi
- 🌐 www.otava.fi

Parent Company Otava Books and Magazines Group Ltd
Contact Managing Director, Antti Reenpää; Publishing Director (Otava General Literature), Leena Majander; Publishing Director (Otava Education), Jukka Vahtola

Imprint(s) Otava Education
Otava General Literature

Categories Non-Fiction, Fiction, Architecture, Art, Children's Books, Cuisine, Dictionaries, Education, General Interest, History, Mainstream Fiction, Scholarly, Teaching Resources, Textbooks, Translation, Young Adult

Insider Info Publishes 600 titles per year.
Recent Title(s) *Tuhat Loistavaa Aurinkoa*, Khaled Hosseini

Tips Otava supports new writers and has an 'open-minded, yet resolute' approach to publishing.

The Overlook Press
141 Wooster Street, New York, 10012, USA
- ☎ 001 212 673 2210
- ☎ 001 212 673 2296
- ✉ sales@overlookpress.com
- 🌐 www.overlookpress.com

Parent Company Peter Mayer Publishers Inc
Contact Publisher, Peter Mayer
Imprint(s) Ardis
Duckworth

Categories Publishes Non-Fiction, Fiction and Children's titles on the following subjects: Art/Architecture, Biography, Children's Books, Design, Health/Fitness, History, How-To, Lifestyle, Literary Fiction, Mainstream Fiction, Martial Arts, Picture Books, Regional (New York State), Translation

Insider Info Publishes 100 titles per year. Does not accept simultaneous submissions. Catalogue available free on request.

Submission Guidelines Does not accept unsolicited manuscripts or proposals.

Recent Title(s) *The Secret History of the World*, Mark Booth

Tips The Overlook Press does not accept unagented submissions.

Oxford University Press (US)
198 Madison Avenue, New York, 10016, USA
- ☎ 001 212 726 6000
- 🌐 www.oup.com/us

Contact Vice President/Editorial Director, Joan Bossert; President, Laura Brown
Categories Publishes Non-Fiction titles on the following subjects: Academic, Biography, General Interest, Higher Education, Journals, Literary Criticism, Popular Non-Fiction, Reference, Scholarly, Textbook
Insider Info Publishes 1,500 titles per year. Pays 0–15 per cent royalty on retail price, with an advance offered. 80 per cent of books come from unagented writers, and 40 per cent from first-time authors. Aims to respond to proposals within three months. Accepts simultaneous submissions. Average lead time of ten months. Catalogue available free on request.
Submission Guidelines Accepts unsolicited manuscripts and proposals.
Recent Title(s) *Desperate Passage*, Ethan Rarick
Tips Oxford University Press welcomes academic proposals, but they must be sent to the correct editor. See the website for a list of editorial contacts.

Pan Macmillan Australia Pty Ltd
Level 25, 1 Market Street, Sydney, New South Wales, 2000, Australia
☎ 0061 2 9285 9100
🖷 0061 2 9285 9190
✉ panpublishing@macmillan.com.au
🌐 www.panmacmillan.com.au
Contact Publishing Director, James Fraser; Publishing Director, Roxanne Burns
Imprint(s) Macmillan Australia Group
Pan Australia Group
Picador Australia
Categories Publishes Non-Fiction, Fiction and Children's titles on the following subjects: Adventure, Autobiography, Biography, Children's Picture Books, Crime Fiction, Current Affairs, Fantasy, General Interest, Health, History, Horror, Humour, Literary Fiction, Mainstream Fiction, Memoir, Science Fiction, Self-Help, Thrillers, Travel, True Crime
Insider Info Authors paid by royalty, with advance offered. Aims to respond to proposals within 10–12 weeks.
Submission Guidelines Accepts unsolicited manuscripts and proposals.
Recent Title(s) *The Almost Moon*, Alice Sebold
Tips Pan Macmillan Australia will accept submissions for non-fiction and fiction, but they are currently cutting back on their publishing programme, so unsolicited material has little chance of being accepted unless it is uniquely appealing and original.

Paragon House
1925 Oakcrest Avenue, Suite 7, St Paul, Minnesota, 55113-2619, USA
☎ 001 651 644 3087
🖷 001 651 644 0997
✉ paragon@paragonhouse.com
🌐 www.paragonhouse.com
Contact Acquisitions Editor, Rosemary Yokoi
Imprint(s) New Era Books
Omega Books
Categories Publishes Non-Fiction titles on the following subjects: Education, Government/Politics, History, Multicultural, Philosophy, Reference, Religion, Science, Scholarly, Textbook, Women's Issues/Studies, World Affairs
Insider Info Publishes 8-12 titles per year. Advance offered. Receives 1,500 queries and 150 manuscripts per year. 90 per cent of books come from unagented writers and seven per cent from first-time authors. Accepts simultaneous submissions. Average lead time is 12-18 months.
Submission Guidelines Accepts unsolicited manuscripts and proposals.
Recent Title(s) *Digital Game-Based Learning*, Marc Prensky
Tips Paragon House accepts submission of scholarly or reference books either by post, or as an email attachment. If submitting by post always include SAE for reply.

Paul Zsolnay Verlag GmbH
Prinz-Eugen-Straße 30, A-1040, Vienna, Austria
☎ 0043 1 505 76610
🖷 0043 1 505 766110
✉ info@zsolnay.at
🌐 www.zsolnay.at
Contact Publisher, Michael Krüger
Categories Non-Fiction, Fiction, Children's, Biography, Children's, Crime Fiction, General Interest, History, Literary Fiction, Mainstream Fiction, Poetry, Translation
Recent Title(s) *Maestro*, Peter Goldsworthy
Tips Zsolnay focuses mainly on fiction submissions from new and established Austrian writers.

Peachtree Publishers
1700 Chattahoochee Avenue, Atlanta, Georgia, 30318, USA
☎ 001 404 876 8761
🖷 001 404 875 2578
✉ hello@peachtree-online.com
🌐 www.peachtree-online.com
Contact Submissions Editor, Helen Harriss
Imprint(s) Peachtree Children's Books
Categories Publishes Non-Fiction, Fiction and Children's titles on the following subjects: American

South Guidebooks, Children's Fiction, Education, Health, Outdoor Pursuits, Parenting, Picture Books, Psychology, Self-Help, Young Adult

Insider Info Publishes 30 titles per year. Authors paid by royalty, with an advance offered. 75 per cent of books come from unagented writers, and 25 per cent from first-time authors. Aims to respond to manuscripts within six months. Accepts simultaneous submissions. Average lead time is one year. Catalogue available free on request – send SAE.

Submission Guidelines Accepts unsolicited manuscripts and proposals for both adult and children's non-fiction, but only accepts fiction submissions for children's books.

Recent Title(s) *Martine the Beautiful Cockroach*, Carmen Agra Deedy (Author), Michael Austin (Illustrator); *The Boy Who Was Raised by Librarians*, Carla Morris (Author), Brad Sneed (Illustrator); *The Real Question*, Adrian Fogelin; *Gabriel's Horses*, Alison Hart

Pearson Education Australia
Locked Bag 507, Unit 4, Level 3, 14 Aquatic Drive, Frenchs Forest, New South Wales, 2086, Australia
- 0061 2 9454 2200
- 0061 2 9453 0089
- alison.green@pearsoned.com.au
- www.pearsoned.com.au

Parent Company Pearson Plc

Contact Editor in Chief (Higher Education), Paul Petrulis; Senior Acquisitions Editor and Development Manager (Higher Education), Alison Green; Publisher (Professional and Vocational Education), Diane Gee-Clough; Senior Acquisitions Editor (Professional and Vocational Education), Natalie Muir

Imprint(s) Addison Wesley
Allyn & Bacon
Benjamin Cummings
Longman
Prentice Hall

Categories Publishes Non-Fiction and Children's titles on the following subjects: Academic, Children's Education, Education, Multimedia, Online, Reference, Science, Sociology, Teacher Resources, Technology, Textbooks

Insider Info Authors paid by royalty, with advance offered.

Submission Guidelines Accepts unsolicited manuscripts and proposals.

Recent Title(s) *Australian Business Law*, Roger Vickery and Wayne Pendleton

Tips Pearson Education Australia accepts submissions of educational non-fiction or reference material. See website for a full list of acquisitions editors and their interests.

Pearson Education Canada
26 Prince Andrew Place, Toronto, Ontario, M3C 2T8, Canada
- 001 416 447 5101
- 001 416 443 0948
- samantha.scully@pearsoncanada.ca
- www.pearsoncanada.ca

Parent Company Pearson Plc

Contact Executive Acquisitions Editor (Accounting, Decision Science, Finance), Samantha Scully; Executive Acquisitions Editor (Anthropology, History, Linguistics, Modern Languages, Political Science), Laura Forbes; Executive Acquisitions Editor (Engineering, Science, Math, Geography, Health, Nursing), Michelle Sartor

Imprint(s) Addison-Wesley
Allyn & Bacon
Copp Clark
Longman
Prentice Hall

Categories Publishes Non-Fiction and Children's titles on the following subjects: Academic, Children's Education, Education, Multimedia, Online, Reference, Science, Sociology, Teacher Resources, Technology, Textbooks

Insider Info Authors paid by royalty, with advance offered.

Submission Guidelines Accepts unsolicited manuscripts and proposals.

Tips Pearson Education Canada accepts submissions of educational non-fiction or reference material. See website for a full list of acquisitions editors and their interests.

Pearson Education New Zealand
PO Box 102902, North Shore, North Shore City, Auckland, 0745, New Zealand
- 0064 9 442 7400
- 0064 9 442 7401
- bronwen.nicholson@pearsoned.co.nz
- www.pearsoned.co.nz

Parent Company Pearson Plc

Contact Publisher (Higher Education), Bronwen Nicholson; Publisher (Higher Education), Norman Mailer; Publisher (Schools), Ken Harrop

Imprint(s) Addison-Wesley
Allyn & Bacon
Benjamin Cummings
Longman
Prentice Hall

Categories Publishes Non-Fiction and Children's titles on the following subjects: Academic, Children's Education, Education, Multimedia, Online, Reference, Science, Sociology, Teacher Resources, Technology, Textbooks

Insider Info Authors paid by royalty, with advance offered.

Submission Guidelines Accepts unsolicited manuscripts and proposals.

Recent Title(s) *Sigma Mathematics: NCEA Level 3 Statistics and Modelling*, David Barton

Tips Pearson Education New Zealand accepts submissions of educational non-fiction or reference material. See website for a full list of acquisitions editors and their interests.

Pearson Education South Africa
PO Box 396, Cape Town, 8000, South Africa
- 0027 21 532 6000
- 0027 021 532 2303
- info@pearsoned.co.za
- www.pearsoned.co.za

Parent Company Maskew Miller Longman

Imprint(s) Addison-Wesley

Allyn & Bacon

Benjamin Cummings

Macmillan Lifestyle/Technical Publishing

Maskew Miller Longman

Prentice Hall

Categories Publishes Non-Fiction and Children's titles on the following subjects: Academic, Children's Education, Education, Multimedia, Online, Reference, Science, Sociology, Teacher Resources, Technology, Textbooks

Tips Pearson Education South Africa is a subsidiary of Maskew Miller Longman, which is the country's largest educational publisher. They mainly publish educational material, but also maintain a local list, including some fiction.

Penguin Group (Australia)
250 Camberwell Road, Camberwell, Victoria, 3124, Australia
- 0061 3 9811 2400
- 0061 3 9811 2620
- adult.publishing@au.penguingroup.com
- www.penguin.com.au

Parent Company Pearson Plc

Contact Managing Director, Gabrielle Coyne; Publishing Director, Robert Sessions

Imprint(s) Penguin Books

Lantern

Viking

Categories Publishes Non-Fiction, Fiction and Children's titles on the following subjects: Children's Fiction, Contemporary Fiction, Education, General Interest, How-To, Mainstream Fiction, Reference, Self-Help

Insider Info Authors paid by royalty, with advance offered.

Submission Guidelines Does not generally accept unsolicited manuscripts or proposals.

Recent Title(s) *Sylvia*, Bryce Courtenay

Tips Penguin Australia does not except unagented submissions for adult non-fiction and fiction, but is occasionally open for submissions for children's books. See the website for details.

Penguin Group (Canada)
90 Eglinton Avenue East, Suite 700, Toronto, Ontario, M4P 2Y3, Canada
- 001 416 925 2249
- 001 416 925 0068
- info@penguin.ca
- www.penguin.ca

Parent Company Pearson Plc

Contact President, Ed Carson

Imprint(s) Penguin Canada

Puffin Canada

Viking Canada

Categories Publishes Non-Fiction, Fiction and Children's titles on the following subjects: Canadian Interest, Children's Fiction, Contemporary Fiction, Education, General Interest, How-To, Mainstream Fiction, Reference, Self-Help

Insider Info Authors paid by royalty, with advance offered.

Submission Guidelines Does not accept unsolicited manuscripts or proposals.

Recent Title(s) *Betrayal*, John Lescroart

Tips Penguin Canada specialises in writing about Canada, and the work of Canadian writers. Penguin Canada does not except unagented submissions or proposals.

Penguin Group (NZ)
67 Apollo Drive, Albany, Auckland, 10, New Zealand
- 0064 9 442 7400
- 0064 9 442 7401
- info@penguin.co.nz
- www.penguin.co.nz

Parent Company Pearson Plc

Categories Publishes Non-Fiction, Fiction and Children's titles on the following subjects: Children's Fiction, Contemporary Fiction, Education, General Interest, How-To, Local Interest, Mainstream Fiction, Reference, Self-Help

Insider Info Authors paid by royalty, with advance offered. Aims to respond to queries within two months.

Submission Guidelines Accepts unsolicited manuscripts and proposals.

Recent Title(s) *Invisible Wounds*, Kay Douglas (Non-Fiction); *In The Evil Day*, Philip Temple (Contemporary Fiction)

Tips Penguin New Zealand recommends submissions be directed through a literary agent, but they will also accept unsolicited proposals, although the odds of them being accepted are very low.

Penguin Group (South Africa)
24 Sturdee Avenue, Rosebank, 2196, South Africa
- 0027 11 327 3550
- 0027 11 327 3660
- info@za.penguingroup.com
- www.penguinbooks.co.za

Parent Company Pearson Plc
Categories Publishes Non-Fiction and Fiction titles on the following subjects: African Literature, Business, Contemporary Fiction, Current Affairs, Education, General Interest, How-To, Literary Fiction, Local Interest, Mainstream Fiction, Politics, Sports, Travel
Insider Info Publishes 30 titles per year. Authors paid by royalty, with advance offered. Aims to respond to manuscripts within three months.
Submission Guidelines Accepts unsolicited manuscripts and proposals.
Recent Title(s) *The Blade Itself*, Marcus Sakey
Tips Penguin South Africa accepts proposals for adult non-fiction and fiction, although they warn that 'it is rare for unsolicited manuscripts or proposals to be accepted for publication.' Follow the guidelines on the website for more effective submissions.

Penguin Group (USA) Inc
375 Hudson Street, New York, 10014, USA
- 001 212 366 2000
- www.penguin.com

Parent Company Pearson Plc
Contact Chief Executive Officer, David Shanks; President, Susan Petersen Kennedy; President (Books for Young Readers), Doug Whiteman
Imprint(s) Penguin Adult Division
Penguin Children's Division
Categories Publishes Non-Fiction, Fiction and Children's titles on the following subjects: General Interest, Mainstream, Contemporary, How-To, Self-Help, Reference, Education, Children's
Insider Info Authors paid by royalty, with advance offered.
Submission Guidelines Does not accept unsolicited manuscripts or proposals.
Recent Title(s) *Eat, Pray, Love*, Elizabeth Gilbert
Tips Penguin does not generally except unagented submissions, except for on rare occasions when an imprint may be seeking new titles. Penguin's

website has current details of which imprints are open for submission.

Picador
175 Fifth Avenue, New York, 10010, USA
- 001 646 307 5629
- 001 212 253 9627
- webmaster@picadorusa.com
- www.picadorusa.com

Parent Company Holtzbrinck Publishers Holdings LLC
Categories Publishes Non-Fiction and Fiction titles on the following subjects: Autobiography, Biography, General Interest, Literary Fiction, Mainstream Fiction, Women's Fiction
Insider Info Authors paid by royalty, with advance offered.
Submission Guidelines Does not accept unsolicited manuscripts or proposals.
Recent Title(s) *Travels in the Scriptorium*, Paul Auster
Tips Picador specialises in trade paperbacks and reprints. It does not accept any unagented submissions or proposals.

Pippin Publishing Corporation
PO Box 242, Don Mills, Ontario, M3C 2S2, Canada
- 001 416 510 2918
- 001 416 510 3359
- cynthia@pippinpub.com
- www.pippinpub.com

Categories Publishes Non-Fiction titles on the following subjects: Art, Autobiography, Biography, Canadian Interest, Education, History, Humanities, Literacy, Memoir, Numeracy, Science, Teaching Resources
Recent Title(s) *A Leg Up: Enhancing Your Child's Reading and Writing*, Lenore H. Ringler and Carole S. Rhodes
Tips Pippin Publishing is an educational publisher, and prints books written by teachers or similarly qualified academics.

Princeton University Press
41 William Street, Princeton, New Jersey, 08540, USA
- 001 609 258 4900
- 001 609 258 6305
- elizabeth_byrd@pupress.princeton.edu
- www.pup.princeton.edu

Contact Managing Editor, Elizabeth Byrd
Categories Publishes Non-Fiction titles on the following subjects: Academic, Biography, General Interest, Journals, Literary Criticism, Reference, Religion, Scholarly, Science, Textbook

Insider Info Authors paid by royalty, with advance offered.
Submission Guidelines Accepts unsolicited manuscripts and proposals. Hard-copy manuscripts must be accompanied by an electronic form, available on the website.
Recent Title(s) *What Bugged the Dinosaurs?*, George Poinar Jr. and Roberta Poinar

Random House Australia Pty Ltd

Level 3, 100 Pacific Highway, North Sydney, New South Wales, 2060, Australia
☎ 0061 2 9954 9966
☎ 0061 2 9954 4562
✉ random@randomhouse.com.au
⊕ www.randomhouse.com.au
Parent Company Bertelsmann Book Group
Contact Managing Director, Margaret Seale; Head of Publishing, Jane Palfreyman
Imprint(s) Random House Division
Transworld Division
Categories Publishes Non-Fiction, Fiction and Children's titles on the following subjects: Biography, Children's Fiction, Contemporary Fiction, Education, General Interest, How-To, Literary Fiction, Local Interest, Mainstream Fiction, Reference, Self-Help, Travel
Insider Info Authors paid by royalty, with advance offered. Aims to respond to manuscripts within nine months.
Submission Guidelines Accepts unsolicited manuscripts and proposals.
Recent Title(s) *His Illegal Self*, Peter Carey
Tips Random House Australia accepts adult fiction submissions from previously published authors. It will only accept submissions from new writers if they come through an agent.

Random House Inc

1745 Broadway, 10th Floor, New York, 10019, USA
☎ 001 212 782 9000
✉ customerservice@randomhouse.com
⊕ www.randomhouse.com
Parent Company Bertelsmann Book Group
Contact See individual imprint listings for their contact details
Imprint(s) Ballantine Publishing Group
Bantam Dell Publishing Group
Crown Publishing Group
Doubleday Broadway Publishing Group
Knopf Publishing Group
Random House Publishing Group
Categories Publishes Non-Fiction, Fiction and Children's titles. See individual imprint listings.

Insider Info Authors paid by royalty, with advance offered.
Submission Guidelines Does not accept unsolicited manuscripts or proposals.
Recent Title(s) *The Senator's Wife*, Sue Miller
Tips Random House is the world's largest English language publisher, and will not accept unagented submissions or proposals.

Random House New Zealand

18 Poland Road, Glenfield, Auckland, 10, New Zealand
☎ 0064 9 444 7197
☎ 0064 9 444 7524
✉ editor@randomhouse.co.nz
⊕ www.randomhouse.co.nz
Parent Company Bertelsmann Book Group
Contact Laura Sanders
Imprint(s) Black Swan
Godwit
Random House
Vintage
Categories Publishes Non-Fiction, Fiction and Children's titles on the following subjects: Art, Autobiography, Biography, Children's Picture Books, Cookery, Gardening, Health, Human Interest, Lifestyle, Literary Fiction, Local Interest, Mainstream Fiction, New Zealand Fiction, Social History, Tourism
Insider Info Publishes 80 titles per year. Authors paid by royalty, with advance offered.
Submission Guidelines Accepts unsolicited manuscripts and proposals.
Recent Title(s) *7th Heaven*, James Patterson
Tips Random House New Zealand does accept non-fiction and fiction submissions, but only of work with New Zealand based content, or from New Zealand writers.

Random House of Canada Ltd

1 Toronto Street, Unit 300, Toronto, Ontario, M5C 2V6, Canada
☎ 001 416 364 4449
☎ 001 416 364 6863
⊕ www.randomhouse.ca
Parent Company Bertelsmann Book Group
Contact Chairman, John Neale
Imprint(s) Anchor Canada
Doubleday Canada Group
Knopf Canada
Random House Canada
Seal Books
Vintage
Categories Publishes Non-Fiction, Fiction and Children's titles on the following subjects: Biography, Children's Fiction, Contemporary Fiction, Education, General Interest, How-To, Literary Fiction, Local

Interest, Mainstream Fiction, Reference, Self-Help, Travel

Insider Info Authors paid by royalty, with advance offered.

Submission Guidelines Does not accept unsolicited manuscripts or proposals.

Recent Title(s) *The Anatomy of Deception*, Lawrence Goldstone

Random House South Africa
Endulini, 5A Jubilee Road, Parktown, 2193, South Africa
- 0027 11 484 3538
- 0027 11 484 6180
- www.randomhouse.co.za

Parent Company Bertelsmann Book Group

Imprint(s) Umuzi

Categories Publishes Non-Fiction, Fiction and Children's titles.

Insider Info Authors paid by royalty, with advance offered.

Submission Guidelines Does not accept unsolicited manuscripts or proposals.

Reed Publishing (New Zealand) Ltd
PO Box 34901, 39 Rawene Road, Birkenhead, Auckland 10, New Zealand
- 0064 9 441 2960
- 0064 9 480 4999
- info@reed.co.nz
- www.reed.co.nz

Parent Company Reed Elsevier Group Plc

Contact Managing Director, Alan Smith; Publishing Manager, Peter Janssen

Imprint(s) Heinemann Education
Reed Books
Reed Children's Books

Categories Publishes Non-Fiction and Children's titles on the following subjects: Biography, Children's Fiction, Cooking, Education, General Interest, History, Humour, Language, Mainstream Fiction, Maori Culture, New Zealand Interest, Outdoor, Picture Books, Tourism

Submission Guidelines Accepts unsolicited manuscripts and proposals.

Recent Title(s) *Active Kids Cookbook*, Jeni Pearce

Tips Reed Publishing mainly publish non-fiction of New Zealand interest, and mass market children's books. They publish very little adult fiction.

Rodale Books
33 East Minor Street, Emmaus, Pennsylvania, 18098, USA
- 001 610 967 5171
- 001 610 967 8963
- customer_service@rodale.com
- www.rodale.com

Parent Company Rodale Book Group

Contact Chairman, Ardath Rodale; President/Chief Executive Officer, Steve Murphy; Vice President/Publisher (Rodale Trade Books), Liz Perl

Categories Publishes Non-Fiction titles on the following subjects: Cooking, Current Affairs, Gardening, General Interest, Health/Fitness, Magazines, Nature, Pet Care, Reference, Social Studies, Spirituality, Women's Studies

Tips Rodale is primarily a health and spirituality publisher, but also publishes topical material of global or social interest. Publishing opportunities are also available through Rodale's many magazines.

Routledge
270 Madison Avenue, New York, 10016, USA
- 001 212 216 7800
- 001 212 563 7854
- www.routledge.com

Parent Company Taylor and Francis LLC

Contact Vice President/Publisher, Mary MacInnes

Imprint(s) Theatre Arts Books

Categories Publishes Non-Fiction titles on the following subjects: Education, History, Politics, Psychology, Reference, Science, Sociology, Technology, Textbook

Insider Info Publishes 2,000 titles per year. Authors paid by royalty, with advance offered. Nine per cent of books come from unagented writers, and ten per cent from first-time authors. Accepts simultaneous submissions. Average lead time of one year.

Submission Guidelines Accepts unsolicited manuscripts and proposals.

Tips Routledge accepts unsolicited proposals for academic reference and educational books. The proposal must include detailed market research, including details on any relevant competitor books.

RSVP Publishing Company Ltd
PO Box 47–166, Ponsonby, Auckland, New Zealand
- 0064 9 372 8480
- 0064 9 372 8480
- rsvppub@iconz.co.nz
- www.rsvp-publishing.co.nz

Contact Publisher, Stephen Picard; Editorial Manager, Rosie Parkes

Categories Publishes Non-Fiction and Fiction titles on the following subjects: Contemporary Fiction, General Interest, Local Interest, New Zealand Metaphysical Books

Insider Info Publishes six titles per year.

Submission Guidelines Accepts unsolicited manuscripts and proposals.

Recent Title(s) *Arrive Alive*, Michael Furniss; *Vision of Maui*, Joyce Paraone Hemana

Tips RSVP primarily publish New Zealand metaphysical books but are also willing to accept other forms of innovative non-fiction or fiction.

Rutgers University Press
100 Joyce Kilmer Avenue, Piscataway, New Jersey, 08854, USA
- 001 732 445 7762
- 001 732 445 7039
- lmitch@rutgers.edu
- http://rutgerspress.rutgers.edu

Contact Director, Marlie Wasserman; Editor in Chief/Associate Director, Leslie Mitchner

Categories Publishes Non-Fiction titles on the following subjects: Academic, Biography, General Interest, History, Journals, Literary Criticism, Politics, Reference, Scholarly, Science, Textbook

Insider Info Publishes 90 titles per year. Pays 7.5–15 per cent royalty, with advance offered. Receives 1,500 queries and 300 manuscripts per year. 70 per cent of books come from unagented writers, and 30 per cent from first-time authors. Aims to respond to proposals within one month. Average lead time of one year. Catalogue available online or by sending SAE.

Submission Guidelines Accepts unsolicited manuscripts and proposals.

Recent Title(s) *Justice and Science*, George Clarke

Tips Rutgers prefers submissions by post rather than by email, and all submissions must be addressed to the relevant editor. See website for list of editorial contacts.

SanomaWSOY Education and Books
PO Box 222, SF-00121, Helsinki, Finland
- 00358 9 61681
- 00358 9 6168 3560
- www.wsoy.fi

Parent Company Werner Söderström Corporation

Contact President/Chairman, Hannu Syrjänen; Literary Director (General Literature), Touko Siltala

Imprint(s) Bertmark Media AB
General Literature
WSOYpro
WSOY Educational Corporation

Categories Publishes Non-Fiction, Fiction and Children's titles on the following subjects: Children's Fiction, Contemporary Fiction, Dictionaries, Directories, Education, Finnish Fiction, General Interest, Language/Literature, Literary Fiction, Local Interest, Mainstream Fiction, Practical, Reference, Teaching Resources, Textbooks, Translated Foreign Fiction, Young Adult

Insider Info Publishes 800 titles per year.

Recent Title(s) *Neljä Kvartettoa: Four Quartets*, T.S. Eliot

Tips One of Finland's largest book publishers, mostly specialising in educational resources for all age ranges and abilities

Scholastic Australia Pty Ltd
76–80 Railway Crescent, Lisarow, New South Wales, 2250, Australia
- 0061 2 4328 3555
- 0061 2 4323 3827
- customer_service@scholastic.com.au
- www.scholastic.com.au

Parent Company Scholastic Inc

Contact General Manager (Publishing), Andrew Berkhut

Imprint(s) Omnibus Books
Scholastic Australia
Scholastic Press

Categories Publishes Non-Fiction, Fiction and Children's titles on the following subjects: Children's Fiction, Children's Non-Fiction, Picture Books.

Insider Info Authors paid by royalty, with advance offered. Receives 1,000+ manuscripts per year. Aims to respond to manuscripts within three months.

Submission Guidelines Accepts submissions of full manuscripts for children's non-fiction, fiction, and picture books from Australian writers.

Recent Title(s) *Alpha Quest*, Bruce Whatley and Rosie Smith (Children's)

Tips Scholastic Australia is also always seeking illustrators for picture books.

Scholastic Canada Ltd
175 Hillmount Road, Markham, Ontario, ML6C 1Z7, Canada
- 001 416 915 3500
- 001 416 849 7912
- www.scholastic.ca

Parent Company Scholastic Inc

Imprint(s) Les Editions Scholastic
North Winds Press

Categories Publishes Non-Fiction, Fiction and Children's titles, Picture Books, and Young Adult titles.

Insider Info Publishes 40 titles per year. Pays 5–10 per cent royalty on retail price, with advance offered. 50 per cent of books come from unagented writers, and three per cent of books from first-time authors. Aims to respond to proposals within six months. Does not accept simultaneous submissions. Average lead time of one year. Catalogue available free with SAE.

Recent Title(s) *The Invention of Hugo Cabret*, Brian Selznick

Tips Scholastic Canada publishes books for children and young adults, generally from Canadian authors only. To check if Scholastic Canada is open to submissions, phone their publishing status line on: 001 905 887 7323, extension 4308, or check their website.

Scholastic Inc

557 Broadway, New York, 10012, USA

- 001 212 343 6100
- 001 212 343 4713
- info@scholastic.com
- www.scholastic.com

Contact Editorial Director, Elizabeth Szabla; Executive Editor, Kara LaReau; Senior Editor, Lauren Thompson

Imprint(s) Scholastic Education
Scholastic Library Publishing
Scholastic Media
Scholastic Trade Books

Categories Publishes Non-Fiction, Fiction and Children's titles on the following subjects: Education, General Interest, Multimedia, Picture Books, Reference, Textbooks

Insider Info Pays royalty on retail price, with advance offered. Average lead time is two years.

Submission Guidelines Does not generally accept unsolicited manuscripts or proposals.

Recent Title(s) *Spiders*, Nic Bishop (Non-Fiction)

Tips Scholastic is major publisher of children's education and fiction books. They only accept unagented proposals for professional education books.

Scholastic New Zealand Ltd

21 Lady Ruby Drive, East Tamaki, Auckland, New Zealand

- 0064 9 274 8112
- 0064 9 274 8114
- publishing@scholastic.co.nz
- www.scholastic.co.nz

Parent Company Scholastic Inc

Contact Publishing Manager, Christine Dale

Categories Publishes Non-Fiction, Fiction, Children's Fiction, Children's Non-Fiction, Picture Books and Young Adult titles.

Insider Info Authors paid by royalty, with advance offered. Aims to respond to manuscripts within three months.

Submission Guidelines Accepts unsolicited manuscripts and proposals.

Recent Title(s) *Baby Bear's Big Dreams*, Jane Yolen

Tips Scholastic New Zealand accepts submissions for their 'Survive!' and 'My Story' series from New Zealand writers. See website for guidelines.

Scribner

1230 Avenue of the Americas, New York, 10020, USA

- 001 212 698 7000
- 001 212 698 7007
- Online form
- www.simonsays.com

Parent Company Simon & Schuster Adult Publishing Group

Contact Nan Graham; Sarah McGrath

Imprint(s) Lisa Drew Books
Scribner Classics (reprints)
Scribner Poetry

Categories Publishes Non-Fiction, Fiction and Poetry titles on the following subjects: General Interest, Literary Fiction, Mainstream Fiction, Politics, Reprints

Insider Info Publishes 75 titles per year. Pays 7.5–15 per cent royalty, with advance offered. Receives thousands of queries per year. 20 per cent of books come from first-time authors. Accepts simultaneous submissions. Average lead time is nine months.

Submission Guidelines Does not accept unsolicited manuscripts or proposals.

Recent Title(s) *The Scribner Anthology of Contemporary Short Fiction*, Michael Martone

Tips Scribner often seeks biography, but will not accept unagented submissions or proposals.

Shuter & Shooter Publishers (Pty) Ltd

21c Cascades Crescent, Pietermaritzburg, KwaZulu-Natal, 3201, South Africa

- 0027 33 347 6100
- 0027 33 347 6120
- dryder@shuter.co.za
- www.shuter.co.za

Contact Managing Director, Dave Ryder

Imprint(s) Ziptales

Categories Publishes Non-Fiction, Fiction and Children's titles on the following subjects: Afrikaans Literature, Art, Craft, Education, General Interest, History, How-To, Literacy, Local Interest, Mainstream Fiction, Poetry, Reference, Science, Scholarly, Teaching Guides, Textbooks

Recent Title(s) *Crazy World: A Tribute to Lucky Dube (Revised Edition)*, Guy Henderson

Tips Shuter & Shooter primarily publishes Zulu fiction and poetry, as well as educational material for the whole of South Africa.

Simon & Schuster Inc

1230 Avenue of the Americas, New York, 10020, USA

- 001 212 698 7000
- 001 212 698 7007
- Online form

⊕ www.simonsays.com

Parent Company Viacom Entertainment Group

Contact President, Jack Romanos; Chief Executive Officer, Carolyn Reidy

Imprint(s) Simon & Schuster Adult Publishing Group
Simon & Schuster Audio/Online
Simon & Schuster Australia
Simon & Schuster Canada
Simon & Schuster Children's Publishing
Simon & Schuster UK

Categories Publishes Non-Fiction, Fiction and Children's titles on the following subjects: Autobiography, Biography, Children's, Entertainment, General Interest, Genre Fiction, Mainstream Fiction, Multimedia

Insider Info Authors paid by royalty, with advance offered.

Submission Guidelines Does not accept unsolicited manuscripts or proposals.

Recent Title(s) *The Watchman*, Robert Crais (Thriller)

Tips Simon & Schuster is run alongside Paramount Studios and focuses on entertainment and media.

Simon & Schuster Australia
Suite 2, Lower Ground Floor, 14–16 Suakin Street, Pymble, New South Wales, 2073, Australia

☎ 0061 2 9983 6600

☎ 0061 2 9988 4293

✉ info@simonandschuster.au

⊕ www.simonsaysaustralia.com

Parent Company Simon & Schuster Inc

Contact Managing Director, Jon Attenborough

Imprint(s) Kangaroo Press
Simon & Schuster Australia

Categories Publishes Non-Fiction, Fiction and Children's titles on the following subjects: Children's Fiction, Contemporary Fiction, Education, General Interest, How-To, Literary Fiction, Mainstream Fiction, Practical, Reference, Self-Help

Insider Info Authors paid by royalty, with advance offered.

Submission Guidelines Does not accept unsolicited manuscripts or proposals.

Recent Title(s) *The Ex-Boyfriend's Handbook*, Matt Dunn

Tips Simon & Schuster Australia specialises in general interest non-fiction books by Australian writers, and do not accept submissions from unagented authors.

Simon & Schuster Canada
625 Cochrane Drive, Suite 600, Markham, Ontario, L3R 9R9, Canada

☎ 001 905 943 9942

☎ 001 905 943 9026

✉ info@simonandschuster.ca

⊕ www.simonsayscanada.com

Parent Company Simon & Schuster Inc

Imprint(s) Simon & Schuster
Simon & Schuster Audio
Simon & Schuster Books for Young Readers

Categories Publishes Non-Fiction, Fiction and Children's titles on the following subjects: Children's Fiction, Contemporary Fiction, Computers, Education, General Interest, How-To, Literary Fiction, Mainstream Fiction, Multimedia, Practical, Reference, Self-Help, Study Aids, Travel

Insider Info Authors paid by royalty, with advance offered.

Submission Guidelines Does not accept unsolicited manuscripts or proposals.

Recent Title(s) *Duma Key*, Stephen King

Tips Simon & Schuster Canada does not accept submissions or proposals from unagented authors.

Soho Press
853 Broadway, New York, 10003, USA

☎ 001 212 260 1900

☎ 001 212 260 1902

✉ soho@sohopress.com

⊕ www.sohopress.com

Contact Editor in Chief, Laura Hruska; Editor, Katie Herman

Imprint(s) Soho Crime

Categories Publishes Non-Fiction and Fiction titles on the following subjects: Biography, Contemporary/Modern Fiction, Contemporary Crime Fiction, Cultural History Studies, Literary Fiction

Insider Info Authors paid by royalty, with advance offered. Accepts simultaneous submissions.

Submission Guidelines Accepts unsolicited manuscripts and proposals.

Recent Title(s) *Prayer of the Dragon*, Eliot Pattison

Tips Soho Press places a high priority on publishing 'quality unsolicited materials from new writers'. They look for adult literary fiction that breaks away from traditional formulas and explores new avenues.

Springer Science+Business Media GmbH
Heidelberger Platz 3, D-14197, Berlin, Germany

☎ 0049 6221 4870

☎ 0049 6221 487 8366

✉ ilka.holzinger@springer.com

⊕ www.springer.de

Parent Company Springer Science+Business Media

Contact Managing Director, Derk Haank; Editorial Director, Ilka Holzinger

Categories Publishes Non-Fiction titles on the following subjects: Academic, Architecture,

Construction, Economics, Engineering, Medicine, Reference, Science, Technology, Traffic

Insider Info Publishes 5,500 titles per year.

Recent Title(s) *Wissen Hoch 12*, Harald Frater, Nadja Podbregar & Dieter Lohmann

Tips Springer is a major global publisher of science, technology and medical material, and only publishes work from leading academics in these fields.

Springer-Verlag GmbH
Postfach 89, 1201, A-Vienna, Austria
- 0043 1 330 2415
- 0043 1 330 2426
- springer@springer.at
- www.springer.at

Parent Company Springer Science+Business Media

Contact Managing Director, Sven Fund; Head of Production, Franz Schaffer; Editor, Renate Eichhorn; Editor, Franziska Brugger

Categories Publishes Non-Fiction titles on the following subjects: Academic, Architecture, Construction, Economics, Education, Engineering, Law/Legal, Medicine, Reference, Science, Technology

Insider Info Publishes 220 titles per year.

Submission Guidelines Accepts unsolicited manuscripts and proposals.

Recent Title(s) *Jähzorn*, T. Itten

Tips Submissions to Springer must follow the detailed guidelines on their website.

Stackpole Books
5067 Ritter Road, Mechanicsburg, Pennsylvania, 17055, USA
- 001 717 796 0411
- 001 717 796 0412
- jschnell@stackpolebooks.com
- www.stackpolebooks.com

Contact Acquisitions Editor (Outdoor Sports, Fly Fishing, Military Reference), Judith Schnell; Acquisitions Editor (Nature), Mark Allison; Acquisitions Editor (History), Christopher Evans; Acquisitions Editor (Regional, Travel), Kyle Weaver; Acquisitions Editor (Military, Reference), Dave Reisch

Categories Publishes Non-Fiction and Fiction titles on the following subjects: Fishing, History, Military/War, Mainstream Fiction, Nature, Outdoors, Pets, Recreation, Reference, Regional, Sports, Travel, Wildlife

Insider Info Publishes 100 titles per year. Does not accept simultaneous submissions. Average lead time of one year,

Submission Guidelines Accepts unsolicited proposals. Prefer queries to full submissions, along

with market research and any relevant publishing history.

Recent Title(s) *Creating Candles*, Luisa Sacchi (Craft)

Stanford University Press
1450 Page Mill Road, Palo Alto, California, 94304, USA
- 001 650 723 9434
- 001 650 725 3457
- info@www.sup.org
- www.sup.org

Contact Associate Director/Editor in Chief, Alan Harvey; Acquisitions Editor (Asian Studies, US Foreign Policy, Asian American Studies), Muriel Bell; Acquisitions Editor (Law, Political Science, Public Policy), Amanda Moran; Acquisitions Editor (Sociology, Anthropology, Education, Middle Eastern Studies), Kate Wahl; Acquisitions Editor (Economics & Organizational Studies), Margo Beth Crouppen

Categories Publishes Non-Fiction on the following subjects: Academic, Professional, Reference, Regional Interest, Scholarly, Textbook

Insider Info Offers advance. Does not accept simultaneous submissions.

Submission Guidelines Accepts unsolicited manuscripts and proposals. All submissions must be posted, not emailed.

Recent Title(s) *Geography of Hope*, Pierre Birnbaum

Tips Stanford University Press accepts submissions for academic and professional books, textbooks for upper-level undergraduate students, and regional interest books.

St Martin's Press
175 Fifth Avenue, New York, 10010, USA
- 001 212 674 5151
- 001 212 420 9314
- www.stmartins.com

Parent Company Holtzbrinck Publishers Holdings LLC

Contact President, John Sargent

Imprint(s) Griffin
Minotaur
Palgrave Macmillan
Picador
Thomas Dunne Books

Categories Publishes Non-Fiction, Fiction and Children's titles on the following subjects: Biography, Business, Children's, Cooking, Economics, Education, Fantasy, General Interest, Historical, Horror, Mainstream/Contemporary Fiction, Reference, Science Fiction, Self-Help, Sports

Insider Info Publishes 1,500 titles per year. Authors paid by royalty, with advance offered.

Submission Guidelines Does not accept unsolicited manuscripts or proposals.

Recent Title(s) *Tom Cruise*, Andrew Morton (Biography)

Tips St Martin's Press is the American arm of UK publisher Macmillan and is one of the ten largest publishers in America. St Martin's will not accept unagented submissions or proposals.

Struik New Holland Publishers
PO Box 1144, Cape Town, 8000, South Africa
- 0027 21 462 4360
- 0027 21 462 4377
- info@struik.co.za
- www.struik.co.za

Parent Company Johnnic Publishing Limited
Contact Publishing Manager (Struik Lifestyle), Linda de Villiers; Publishing Manager (Struik Natural History), Pippa Parker; Publishing Manager (Struik Travel & Tourism), Dominique le Roux; Publishing Manager (Zebra Press), Marlene Fryer; Publishing Manager (Oshun Books), Michelle Matthews; Publishing Manager (Two Dogs), Tim Richman
Imprint(s) Oshun
Struik Christian Books
Struik Lifestyle/Natural History/People, Art & Culture/Travel & Tourism
Two Dogs
Zebra

Categories Publishes Non-Fiction, Fiction and Children's titles on the following subjects: Afrikaans Literature, General Interest, Illustrated Books, Lifestyle, Local Interest, Mainstream Fiction, Memoirs, Natural History, Religion, South African Men's Literature, South African Women's Literature, Spirituality, Travel, Tourism
Submission Guidelines Accepts unsolicited manuscripts and proposals.
Tips Struik accepts submissions for non-fiction and fiction, as long as they addressed to the correct imprint and publishing manager.

Taschen GmbH
Hohenzollernring 53, D-50672, Cologne, Germany
- 0049 221 201800
- 0049 221 254919
- contact@taschen.com
- www.taschen.com

Contact Editor, Dian Hanson; Editor, Eric Kroll
Categories Publishes Non-Fiction titles on the following subject: Architecture, Art, Artist's Editions, Classics, Design, Film, Lifestyle, Photography, Pop Culture, Sex/Erotica
Recent Title(s) *Jeff Koons*, Hans Werner Holzwarth ed.
Tips Taschen is a global publisher of art and design, renowned for their stylish and often raunchy

approach to publishing. Taschen also publish various magazines.

Tor Books
175 Fifth Avenue, New York, 10010, USA
- 001 212 388 0100
- 001 212 388 0191
- www.tor-forge.com

Parent Company Tom Doherty Associates Llc
Imprint(s) Forge Books
Orb Books
Starscape Books
Tor Books
Tor Teen Books

Categories Publishes Non-Fiction, Fiction and Children's titles on the following subjects: Autobiography, Biography, Children's Fiction, Contemporary Fantasy, Crime Fiction, Dark Fantasy, Epic Fantasy, General Interest, Genre Fiction, Graphic Novels, Historical Fiction, History, Horror, Humour, Memoir, Science, Science Fiction, Short Stories, Space Opera, Westerns, Young Adult
Insider Info Authors paid by royalty, with advance offered. Aims to respond to manuscripts within six months.
Submission Guidelines Accepts unsolicited manuscripts and proposals.
Recent Title(s) *Halo: Contact Harvest*, Joseph Staten; *Inside Straight*, George R.R. Martin (ed.) (Wild Cards Series)
Tips Tor publishes all types of genre fiction and maintains an open submissions policy, meaning that they will accept proposal packages from absolutely anyone. See website for further details.

Tundra Books
75 Sherbourne Street, 5th Floor, Toronto, Ontario, M5A 2P9, Canada
- tundra@mcclelland.com
- www.tundrabooks.com

Parent Company McClelland & Stewart Ltd
Contact Publisher, Kathy Lowinger
Categories Publishes Fiction and Children's titles on the following subjects: Art, Children's Literature, Contemporary Fiction, Picture Books
Submission Guidelines Accepts unsolicited manuscripts and proposals.
Recent Title(s) *Eats*, Marthe Jocelyn (Author), Tom Slaughter (Illustrator)
Tips Tundra Books does not accept many unsolicited manuscripts and will not accept art submissions at all, unless of gallery standard.

Uitgeverij Lannoo Groep
Kasteelstraat 97, B-8700, Tielt, Belgium
- 0032 51 424211

☎ 0032 51 401152
✉ lannoo@lannoo.be
🌐 www.lannoo.be
Imprint(s) DistriMedia nv
Editions Racine
LannooCampus
Lannoo Graphics
Uitgeverij Lannoo nv
Uitgeverij Terra Lannoo bv
Categories Publishes Non-Fiction titles on the following subjects: Business, Economics, Education, General Interest, Health, History, How-To, Local Interest, Politics, Practical, Reference, Science, Self-Help, Textbooks, Travel
Recent Title(s) *Magnum Magnum*, Brigitte Lardinois
Tips Lannoo is a general non-fiction publisher that specialises mainly in business and management material.

Umuzi
3rd Floor, Safmarine House, 22 Riebeek Street, Cape Town, 8001, South Africa
☎ 0027 21 410 8785
☎ 0027 21 410 8711
✉ jeanne.umuzi@randomhouse.co.za
🌐 www.umuzi-randomhouse.co.za
Parent Company Random House South Africa
Contact Publishing Director, Annari van der Merwe; Submissions Editor, Jeanne Hromnik
Categories Publishes Non-Fiction, Fiction, Poetry and Children's titles on the following subjects: Afrikaans Writing, Biography, Children's Fiction, Contemporary Fiction, Education, General Interest, How-To, Literary Fiction, Local Interest, Mainstream Fiction, Reference, Self-Help, Travel
Insider Info Authors paid by royalty, with advance offered.
Recent Title(s) *Emily Green and Me*, Kathryn White
Tips Umuzi is an imprint of Random House South Africa and publishes mainly in English, but also some African language translations. They accept submissions for adult fiction and non-fiction that has a South African flavour.

University of Alabama Press
PO Box 870380, 20 Research Drive, Tuscaloosa, Alabama, 35487, USA
☎ 001 205 348 5180
☎ 001 205 348 9201
✉ danross@uapress.ua.edu
🌐 www.uapress.ua.edu
Contact Director, Daniel J.J. Ross; Senior Acquisitions Editor, Judith Knight; Acquisitions Editor (Humanities), Dan Waterman; Associate Editor (Digital and Electronic Publishing), Claire Evans; Managing Editor, Suzette Griffith

Categories Publishes Non-Fiction titles on the following subjects: Academic, African-American Studies, Biography, Anthropology/Archaeology, Government/Politics, History, Jewish Studies, Language/Literature, Literary Criticism, Religion, Rhetoric, Southern History, Translation
Insider Info Publishes 60 titles per year. Offers advance. 95 per cent of books come from unagented writers, and 70 per cent from first-time authors. Catalogue free on request.
Submission Guidelines Accepts unsolicited manuscripts and proposals.
Recent Title(s) *Survival Pending Revolution*, Paul Alkebulan
Tips University of Alabama Press specialises in American South history, and ethnic and religious studies, but will consider any relevant academic book for publication. Submissions must be directed to the appropriate editor, full details can be found on the website.

University of Arkansas Press
McIlroy House, 201 Ozark Avenue, Fayetteville, Arkansas, 72701, USA
☎ 001 479 575 3246
☎ 001 479 575 6044
✉ uapress@uark.edu
🌐 www.uapress.com
Contact Director and Acquisitions Editor, Lawrence J. Malley; Editorial and Production Manager, Brian King; Project Editor, Sarah White; Acquisitions Assistant, Julie Watkins; Series Editor (Poetry Series), Enid Shomer
Imprint(s) The University of Arkansas Press
Poetry Series
Categories Publishes Non-Fiction and Poetry titles on the following subjects: Academic, African-American History, Arkansas & Regional Studies, Civil War Studies, Government/Politics, History, Literary Criticism, Middle East Studies, Nature, Regional, Scholarly, Southern History, Translated Fiction
Insider Info Publishes 20 titles per year. Royalty paid on net receipts. 95 per cent of books come from unagented writers, and 30 per cent from first-time authors. Aims to respond to proposals within three months. Average lead time of one year. Catalogue and author guidelines available free on request.
Submission Guidelines Accepts unsolicited manuscripts and proposals.
Recent Title(s) *Outlaw Style*, R.T. Smith (Poetry)
Tips University of Arkansas Press publishes academic books on a range of American South and social interest subjects, and also publishes an annual poetry series which is run in a similar fashion to a poetry competition. Details and instructions for submitting to the poetry series are available on the website.

University of Chicago Press

1427 East 60th Street, Chicago, Illinois, 60637, USA

☎ 001 773 702 7700

☎ 001 773 702 9756

✉ agt@press.uchicago.edu

🌐 www.press.uchicago.edu

Contact Director (Books Division), Robert Lynch; Editorial Director (Humanities, Sciences), Alan G. Thomas; Editorial Director (Social Sciences, Paperback Publishing), John Tryneski; Executive Editor (Art, Architecture, Ancient Archeology, Classics, Film Studies), Susan Bielstein; Executive Editor (Anthropology, Paleoanthropology, Philosophy, Psychology), T. David Brent

Categories Publishes Non-Fiction and Journals on the following subjects: Academic, Art/Architecture, Dictionaries, History, Humanities, Journals, Law/Legal, Multimedia, Reference, Scholarly, Science, Social Sciences

Submission Guidelines Accepts unsolicited manuscripts and proposals. Electronic submissions are supported with 'Electronic Manuscript Preparation Guidelines for Authors', also available on the website.

Recent Title(s) *On the Make: The Hustle of Urban Nightlife*, David Grazian

Tips University of Chicago Press welcomes unsolicited submissions as long as they are sent to the correct editor. Check website for full details of editorial contacts and interests.

University of Illinois Press

1325 South Oak Street, Champaign, Illinois, 61820, USA

☎ 001 217 333 0950

☎ 001 217 244 8082

✉ uipress@uillinois.edu

🌐 www.press.uillinois.edu

Contact Director (Literature, Classics, Classical Music, Sports History), Willis Regier; Associate Director and Editor in Chief (Women's Studies, Film, African-American Studies), Joan Catapano; Acquisitions Editor (American History, Labor History, American Music, American Studies), Laurie Matheson; Poetry Editor, Laurence Lieberman

Categories Publishes Non-Fiction and Poetry titles on the following subjects: Academic, Americana, Animals, Biography, Cooking/Foods/Nutrition, Education, Government/Politics, History (American History), Language/Literature, Military/War, Music/Dance (American Music), Poetry, Philosophy, Reference, Regional, Scholarly, Sports, Translation, Women's Studies

Insider Info Publishes 150 titles per year. Pays 0–10 per cent royalty on net receipts, with advance offered. 95 per cent of books come from unagented writers and 35 per cent from first-time authors. Average lead time of one year.

Submission Guidelines Accepts unsolicited manuscripts and proposals.

Recent Title(s) *Women for President: Media Bias in Eight Campaigns*, Erika Falk

Tips University of Illinois Press (UIP) prefers proposals rather than full manuscript submissions, directed to the appropriate editor. UIP also publishes a poetry series which accepts submissions every February.

University of Massachusetts Press

671 North Pleasant Street, East Experiment Station, Amherst, Massachusetts, 01003, USA

☎ 001 413 545 2217

☎ 001 413 545 1226

✉ info@umpress.umass.edu

🌐 www.umass.edu/umpress

Contact Director, Bruce Wilcox; Senior Editor, Clark Dougan; Managing Editor, Carol Betsch

Categories Publishes Non-Fiction titles on the following subjects: Academic, American History, Art/Architecture, Black & Ethnic Studies, Cultural History, Literary Criticism, Philosophy, Political Sciences, Reference, Scholarly, Women's Studies. The press only publishes works of Fiction and Poetry once a year under the auspices of the Juniper Prize competitions.

Insider Info Publishes 40 titles per year.

Submission Guidelines Accepts unsolicited manuscripts and proposals. Submission guidelines available online, at: www.umass.edu/umpress/authinfo.html

Tips The University of Massachusetts Press holds annual competitions – the Juniper Prize for Fiction and Poetry. Each prize carries a $1,500 cash award plus publication. The press also publishes the annual winner of the Association of Writers & Writing Programs (AWP) Grace Paley Prize for short fiction.

University of Michigan Press

839 Greene Street, Ann Arbor, Michigan, 48104, USA

☎ 001 734 764 4388

☎ 001 734 615 1540

✉ ducsaya@umich.edu

🌐 www.press.umich.edu

Contact Director (American History), Phil Pochoda; Senior Executive Editor (American Studies, Theatre and Performance Studies, Literature), LeAnn Fields; Acquisitions Editor (Regional Interest: Michigan and Great Lakes), Mary Erwin; Acquisitions Editor (Music, Fiction, Classics and Archaeology, Early Modern History, German Studies), Christopher J. Hebert; Acquisitions Editor (New Media Studies, Cultural

Studies), Alison MacKeen; Acquisitions Editor (Politics, Law, Economics), James F. Reische

Imprint(s) Sweetwater Fiction

Categories Publishes Non-Fiction and Fiction titles on the following subjects: American History, American Studies, Anthropology, Applied Linguistics, Classical Archaeology, Classics, Cultural Studies, Economics, English as a Second Language, Fiction, Gender Studies, German Studies, Great Lakes Regional Interest, Law, Literary Criticism and Theory, Medieval Studies, Music, Poetics, Political Science, Renaissance Studies, Theatre and Performance, Women's Studies

Submission Guidelines Accepts unsolicited manuscripts and proposals.

Recent Title(s) *Points of Contact*, Susan Crutchfield and Marcy Epstein, eds.

Tips Apart from academic non-fiction, the University of Michigan Press also publishes literary fiction, novels, and collections of short stories which are set within the Great Lakes region.

University of New South Wales Press
University of New South Wales, Sydney, New South Wales, 2052, Australia

❶ 0061 2 9664 0900

❷ 0061 2 9664 5420

📧 frontdesk.press@unsw.edu.au

🌐 www.unswpress.com.au

Categories Publishes Non-Fiction titles on the following subjects: Anthropology, Art, Australian Society, Biography, Cultural Studies, Journals, Environmental Studies, Medicine, Multimedia, Natural History, Philosophy, Politics, Practical Guides, Psychiatry, Reference, Scholarly, Science, Social Sciences, Teaching Resources, Textbooks

Insider Info Publishes 40 titles per year. Pays royalty on wholesale price.

Submission Guidelines Accepts unsolicited manuscripts and proposals.

Recent Title(s) *T Visionarium: A User's Guide*, Jill Bennett

Tips UNSW Press is a leading publisher in Australian studies and natural history. Many of its publications are aimed at students and teachers as teaching resources.

University Of Queensland Press
PO Box 6042, Staff House Road, St Lucia, Queensland, 4067, Australia

❶ 0061 7 3365 2127

❷ 0061 7 3365 7579

📧 uqp@uqp.uq.edu.au

🌐 www.uqp.uq.edu.au

Categories Publishes Non-Fiction, Fiction, Poetry and Children's titles on the following subjects:

Australian History, Biography, Children's Fiction, Current Affairs, Indigenous Issues, Literary Fiction, Poetry, Politics, Social Studies, Young Adult

Insider Info Aims to respond to proposals within six months.

Submission Guidelines Accepts unsolicited manuscripts and proposals.

Recent Title(s) *Just Words? Australian Authors Writing for Justice*, Bernadette Brennan ed.

Tips University of Queensland Press accepts unsolicited non-fiction submissions, but will only accept fiction submissions through a literary agent.

University of Western Australia Press
University of Western Australia, M419, 35 Stirling Highway, Crawley, Western Australia, 6009, Australia

❶ 0061 8 6488 3670

❷ 0061 8 6488 1027

📧 admin@uwapress.uwa.edu.au

🌐 www.uwapress.uwa.edu.au

Contact Director, Terri-Ann White; Business Manager, Emma Smith; Editorial Manager, Kate McCleod; Marketing Manager, Jade Knight

Imprint(s) Staples

Tuart House

UWA Press

Categories Publishes Non-Fiction and Fiction titles on the following subjects: Academic, Contemporary Issues, Critical Studies, General Interest, History, Literary Studies, Maritime History, Natural History and Scholarly.

Submission Guidelines Accepts unsolicited manuscripts and proposals.

Recent Title(s) *Socialism is Great!*, Lijia Zhang; *Conversations with the Mob*, Megan Lewis

University Press of Kansas
2502 Westbrooke Circle, Lawrence, Kansas, 66045, USA

❶ 001 785 864 4154

❷ 001 785 864 4586

📧 upress@ku.edu

🌐 www.kansaspress.ku.edu

Contact Director (American Government and Public Policy, Presidential Studies, Urban Politics, Kansas and Regional Studies), Fred M. Woodward; Editor in Chief (Military History and Intelligence Studies, Law and Legal History, Political Science), Michael Briggs; Acquisitions Editor (Western History, Native American Studies, Environmental Studies, American Studies, Women's Studies), Kalyani Fernando

Categories Publishes Non-Fiction titles on the following subjects: Academic, American History, Cultural Studies, Government, History, Law, Political Science, Reference, Scholarly

Insider Info Publishes 55 titles per year. Pays 5–10 per cent royalty on net receipts, with advance offered. Receives 600 queries per year. 98 per cent of books come from unagented writers, and 20 per cent from first-time authors. Aims to respond to proposals within one month. Does not accept simultaneous submissions. Average lead time is nine months.

Submission Guidelines Prefers proposals over manuscripts, and is willing to accept them by email, as well as by post.

Recent Title(s) *Wolfram von Richthofen*, James Corum; *The Constitution and 9/11*, Louis Fisher; *Electing FDR*, Donald Ritchie; *Weather Matters*, Bernard Mergen

Vanderbilt University Press
VU Station B 351813, Nashville, Tennessee, 37235, USA
- 001 615 322 3585
- 001 615 343 8823
- vupress@vanderbilt.edu
- www.vanderbilt.edu/vupress

Contact Director, Michael Ames

Categories Publishes Non-Fiction titles on the following subjects: Academic, Biography, Education, General Interest, Health, Humanities, Practical, Reference, Scholarly, Social Sciences, Textbook

Insider Info Publishes 25 titles per year. Pays eight per cent royalty on net receipts, with advance offered. Receives 500 queries per year. 90 per cent of books come from unagented writers and 25 per cent from first-time authors. Aims to respond to proposals within two weeks. Accepts simultaneous submissions. Average lead time of ten months. Catalogue available free on request.

Submission Guidelines Accepts unsolicited manuscripts and proposals.

Recent Title(s) *A Shot in the Dark: Making Records in Nashville*, Martin Hawkins

Tips Vanderbilt University Press looks for interdisciplinary intellectual works that 'blend scholarly and practical concerns.'

Walker & Company
104 Fifth Avenue, 7th Floor, New York, 10011, USA
- 001 212 727 8300
- 001 212 727 0984
- www.walkerbooks.com

Parent Company Bloomsbury Publishing Plc (see entry under UK & Irish Book Publishers)

Contact Managing Editor, Karen Rinaldi; Publisher, George Gibson

Categories Publishes Non-Fiction, Fiction and Children's titles on the following subjects: Biography, Business/Economics, Children's Books, Health/Medicine, History, Literary Fiction, Mystery Fiction, Nature, Picture Books, Science, Sports, Technology, Young Adult

Insider Info Does not accept simultaneous submissions.

Submission Guidelines Accepts unsolicited manuscripts and proposals.

Recent Title(s) *Salt River*, James Sallis

Tips Walker will consider material from new or unagented writers, but they are currently only accepting submissions for children's and young adult books - particularly young adult novels and high-quality picture books.

Whitecap Books Ltd
351 Lynn Avenue, North Vancouver, British Columbia, V7J 2C4, Canada
- 001 416 469 1555
- 001 416 537 0588
- www.whitecap.ca

Contact President, Michael E.Burch; Publisher, Robert McCullough

Established 1977

Categories Publishes Cookery, Craft, Gardening, Health, History, Travel, Children's Fiction and Non-Fiction, Picture Books and Young Adult titles

Insider Info Whitecap is one of the top ten Canadian owned publishers and distributors. Picture books like *Gilbert de la Frogponde* and *Dog Tales* have become standards for library reading programmes across Canada and the United States. Authors are paid by royalty, with advance offered.

Submission Guidelines For picture books send the whole manuscript. For other submissions send a synopsis and three chapter samples, plus any publishing credits to date. Send illustration and photograph samples with SAE. If you are submitting from outside of Canada, please include an international postal voucher.

Recent Title(s) *Deconstructing the Dish*, David Adjey (Cookery); *Mountainboard Maniacs*, Pam Withers (Children's)

Women's Press
180 Bloor Street West, Suite 801, Toronto, Ontario, M5S 2V6, Canada
- 001 416 929 2774
- 001 416 929 1926
- info@womenspress.ca
- www.womenspress.ca

Parent Company Canadian Scholars' Press Inc

Contact Publishing Manager, Rebecca Conolly; Editorial Director, Megan Mueller

Categories Publishes Non-Fiction, Fiction and Children's titles on the following subjects:

Autobiography, Biography, Children's Literature, Contemporary Fiction, Creative Non-Fiction, Literary Fiction, Memoirs, Plays, Poetry, Women's Writing
Submission Guidelines Accepts unsolicited manuscripts and proposals.
Recent Title(s) *Sons of the Movement*, Jean Bobby Noble
Tips Women's Press now only accepts a select few manuscripts per year and no longer accepts any children's material. Most Women's Press titles are aimed at students of women's studies, gender studies and social studies.

Workman Publishing Co.
225 Varick Street, New York, 10014, USA
- 001 212 254 5900
- 001 212 254 8098
- info@workman.com
- www.workman.com

Contact Editor in Chief, Susan Bolotin; Executive Editor, Suzanne Rafer; Senior Editor, Ruth Sullivan; Senior Editor, Margot Herrera; Senior Editor, Richard Rosen; Senior Editor (Children's), Raquel Jaramillo
Imprint(s) Algonquin
Artisan
Greenwich Workshop Press
Storey
Timber
Categories Publishes Non-Fiction, Children's and Calendars on the following subjects: Business, Cookbooks, Economics, General Interest, Guidance, Health, How-To, Humour, Self-Help
Insider Info Publishes 40 titles per year. Authors paid by royalty, with advance offered. Receives thousands of queries per year. Accepts simultaneous submissions. Average lead time of one year.
Submission Guidelines Accepts unsolicited manuscripts and proposals.
Recent Title(s) *How Come? In The Neighbourhood*, Kathy Wollard (Author), Debra Solomon (Illustrator)
Tips Workman welcomes unsolicited manuscript submission by post only, no email submissions. Workman also publishes various types of calendars.

W.W. Norton & Company Inc
500 Fifth Avenue, New York, 10110, USA
- 001 212 354 5500
- 001 212 869 0856
- manuscripts@wwnorton.com
- www.wwnorton.com

Contact Editor in Chief, Starling Lawrence; Executive Editor, Robert Weil
Imprint(s) Backcountry Publication
Berkshire House Press
Countryman Press
Norton Professional Books
W.W. Norton
Categories Publishes Non-Fiction, Fiction and Poetry titles on the following subjects: Gardening, Art, Biography, Business/Economics, Parenting, Computers/Electronics, Cooking, Politics, Health, History, Hobbies, Language, Literature, Law, Literary Fiction, Memoirs, Music/Dance, Nature, Poetry, Photography, Psychology, Reference, Religion, Science, Self-Help, Sports, Translation, Travel
Insider Info Publishes 400 titles per year. Authors paid by royalty, with advance offered. Does not accept simultaneous submissions.
Submission Guidelines Accepts unsolicited manuscripts and proposals.
Recent Title(s) *The Age of Shiva*, Manil Suri
Tips W.W. Norton will not accept submissions by post or as an email attachment. Submit a proposal only in the body of an email, or telephone with queries.

Yale University Press
302 Temple Street, New Haven, Connecticut, 06511, USA
- 001 203 432 0960
- 001 203 432 0948
- jonathan.brent@yale.edu
- www.yale.edu/yup

Contact Editorial Director, Jonathan Brent; Publisher, Mary Jane Peluso; Senior Editor, Jean E. Thomson Black; Senior Editor, John Kulka
Categories Publishes Non-Fiction and Poetry (Competition) titles on the following subjects: Academic, Biography, General Interest, History, Journals, Literary Criticism, Literature, Poetry, Politics, Reference, Religion, Scholarly, Science, Textbook
Insider Info Accepts simultaneous submissions. Book catalogue available online.
Submission Guidelines Accepts unsolicited manuscripts and proposals.
Recent Title(s) *Election 2008: A Voter's Guide*, Franklin Foer ed.
Tips Aside from academic publishing, Yale University Press also runs the Yale Series of Younger Poets competition, where one previously unpublished poet can have their book published by Yale.

SHEET MUSIC

ABRSM Publishing
24 Portland Place, London, W1B 1LU
- 020 7636 5400
- rholey@abrsm.ac.uk
- www.abrsmpublishing.com

About ABRSM Publishing is the publishing company of the Associated Board of the Royal Schools of Music. They produce repertoire volumes for a variety of instruments, and for voice, and also publish materials used in exams, including theory papers and student textbooks.

Bardic Edition
6 Fairfax Crescent, Aylesbury, Buckinghamshire, HP20 2ES
- 01296 428609
- 01296 581185
- info@bardic-music.com
- www.bardic-music.com

About Publishes sheet music and repertoire in all genres, by a wide variety of composers.

Boosey & Hawkes
Aldwych House, 71–91 Aldwych, London, WC2B 4HN
- 020 7054 7260
- 020 7054 7290
- composers@boosey.com
- www.boosey.com

Contact Chief Executive, John Minch; Head of Publishing, David Bray

About Boosey & Hawkes is the largest specialist classical music publishing company in the world. They publish a wide range of material for professionals, students and hobbyists.

Brass Wind Publications
4 St Mary's Road, Manton, Oakham, Rutland, LE15 8SU
- 01572 737210
- deliatriggel@brasswindpublications.co.uk
- www.brasswindpublications.co.uk

About Publishes music primarily for brass and wind instruments, but also for ensembles.

Broadbent & Dunn Ltd
66 Nursery Lane, Dover, Kent, CT16 3EX
- 01304 825604
- 0870 135 3567
- music@broadbent-dunn.com
- www.broadbent-dunn.com

About Publishes music for a variety of instruments and ensembles including strings, brass, woodwind and piano.

Chester Music and Novello & Co.
14–15 Berners Street, London, W1T 3LJ
- 020 7612 7400
- 020 7612 7545
- howard.friend@musicsales.com
- www.chesternovello.com

Contact Managing Director, James Rushton; Managing Editor, Howard Friend

About A large music publisher, part of the Music Sales Group. Will accept unsolicited submissions. Send scores of up to three pieces, preferably with recordings, to the Managing Editor. Response time may be several months.

Edition Peters
Hinrichsen House, 10–12 Baches Street, London, N1 6DN
- 020 7553 4000
- 020 7490 4921
- Online form.
- www.edition-peters.com

Established 1800

About Publishes a wide range of compositions through a cutting-edge publishing and composer promotion programme. Has four publishing centres around the world, in Frankfurt, London, Leipzig and New York.

Faber Music Ltd
Bloomsbury House, 74-77 Great Russell Street, London, WC1B 3DA
- 020 7833 7900
- 020 7833 7939
- information@fabermusic.com
- www.fabermusic.com

About Publishes repertory works by well known composers, but also seeks to discover new talent. Unsolicited submissions for performance and concert works are accepted by post only. Alongside the submission send your performance history, biography, recordings and reviews. Unsolicited print publication submissions are rarely accepted for either scores or textbooks, check the website for details. Average response time is within six weeks.

Fand Music Press

Glenelg, 10 Avon Close, Petersfield, Hampshire, GU31 4LG

- ☎ 01730 267341
- ☎ 01730 267341
- ✉ contact@fandmusic.com
- 🌐 www.fandmusic.com

Contact Peter Thompson

About First edition publisher of scores for a range of instruments, as well as educational music and CDs. Fand Music Press also publishes fiction and non-fiction books about music, or by musicians.

Fraser-Enoch Pubilcations

64 Tremaine Road, London, SE20 7TZ

- ☎ 020 8778 4670
- ☎ 020 8659 7716

About Publishes sheet music for piano teachers.

Good Music Publishing

PO Box 100, Tewkesbury, GL20 7YQ

- ☎ 01684 773883
- ☎ 01684 773884
- ✉ sales@goodmusicpublishing.co.uk
- 🌐 www.goodmusicpublishing.co.uk

About Publishes sheet music for a variety of instruments.

G. Ricordi & Co.

20 Fulham Broadway, London, SW6 1AH

- ☎ 020 7835 5380
- ☎ 020 7835 5384
- ✉ miranda.jackson@umusic.com
- 🌐 www.ricordi.co.uk

Contact General Manager, Miranda Jackson

About Commissions and publishes music from in-house composers. Current print focus is on choral music by living British composers.

Guildhall School of Music

Silk Street, Barbican, London, EC2Y 8DT

- ☎ 020 7628 2571
- ☎ 020 7256 9438
- ✉ music@gsmd.ac.uk
- 🌐 www.gsmd.ac.uk

About Publishes CDs and research reports with the Guildhall School Press. Also has a co-publishing arrangement with Ashgate Publishing Ltd.

Kevin Mayhew Publishers

Buxhall, Stowmarket, Suffolk, IP14 3BW

- ☎ 01449 737978
- ✉ sales@kevinmayhewltd.com
- 🌐 www.kevinmayhew.com

Established 1976

About Specialists in Christian music and associated products, for both beginners and experts. Publishes existing recordings, books and original recordings on its own record label. Hard copy submissions are accepted.

Music Sales

14–15 Berners Street, London, W1T 3LJ

- ☎ 020 7612 7400
- ☎ 020 7612 7545
- ✉ Online form.
- 🌐 www.musicsales.com

Contact Chairman and Managing Director, Robert Wise

About Publishes sheet music and other print products under its international imprints. They also handle the copyright for over 200,000 music titles. Submissions are rarely accepted but they will occasionally review manuscripts. Please send a comprehensive outline, sample pages and an assessment of market interest and placement. Music Sales also owns the Chester Music and Novello & Co. publishers.

Oxford University Press

Music Department, Oxford University Press, 37a St Giles, Oxford, OX1 3LD

- ☎ 01865 355067
- ☎ 01865 355060
- ✉ music.submissions.uk@oup.com
- 🌐 www.oup.co.uk/music

Contact Head of Music Publishing, David Blackwell

About Oxford University Press is one of the largest and longest-established music publishers in the world. They publish musical scores and books covering the professional, educational and recreational markets. Unsolicited submissions. are accepted. Include a copy of the score, the text and a recording if appropriate. Responses may take several weeks.

Stainer & Bell

PO Box 110, Victoria House, 23 Gruneisen Road, London, N3 1DZ

- ☎ 020 8343 3303
- ☎ 020 8343 3024
- ✉ post@stainer.co.uk
- 🌐 www.stainer.co.uk

Contact Publishing Director, Nicholas Williams; Sales Manager & Music Editor, Jeremy Aknai

About An independent, family run business, specialising in the publication of quality printed music and books. Also runs an archive and hire department.

Studio Music

Cadence House, Eaton Green Road, Luton, Bedfordshire, LU2 9LD

☎ 01582 432139
🖶 01582 731989
✉ info@studio-music.co.uk
🌐 www.studio-music.co.uk

About Publishes a variety of different music styles, particularly orchestral and band music.

United Music Publishers

33 Lea Road, Waltham Abbey, Essex, EN9 1ES

☎ 01992 703110
🖶 01992 703189
✉ info@ump.co.uk
🌐 www.ump.co.uk

Contact Shirley Ranger, Shirley Ranger

About UMP is well known as the representative in the UK and Ireland for all the major French classical sheet music catalogues and a selection of international catalogues. They also publish their own British-based catalogue of works by innovative contemporary composers.

Universal Edition

48 Great Marlborough Street, London, W1F 7BB

☎ 020 7292 9173
✉ uelondon@universaledition.com
🌐 www.universaledition.com/london

Established 1901

About Founded in Vienna, Universal Edition has over 30,000 items in its catalogue of works. It publishes performance materials, music and literature for learners and performers.

Warwick Music Ltd

1 Broomfield Road, Coventry, CV5 6JW

☎ 024 7671 2081
🖶 024 7671 2550
✉ sales@warwickmusic.com
🌐 www.warwickmusic.com

About Publishes music for brass and wind, as well as books on music.

Yorke Edition

Grove Cottage, Southgate, South Creake, Fakenham, Norfolk, NR21 9PA

☎ 01328 823501
🖶 01328 823502
✉ info@yorkedition.co.uk
🌐 www.yorkedition.co.uk

Contact Founder, Rodney Slatford

About Publishes graded music and materials for students and children.

MUSIC PUBLISHERS

Big Life

67–69 Chalton Street, London, NW1 1HY

☎ 020 7554 2126
☎ 020 7554 2101
✉ reception@biglifemanagement.com
🌐 www.biglifemanagement.com

About Holds over 2,000 copyrights including artists such a Lisa Stansfield. Manages a number of modern bands and artists, including Snow Patrol, The Verve and Badly Drawn Boy.

Bucks Music

Onward House, 11 Uxbridge Street, London, W8 7TQ

☎ 020 7221 4275
🖶 020 7229 6893
✉ info@bucksmusicgroup.co.uk
🌐 www.bucksmusicgroup.com

About International and independent music publisher. No longer accepts submissions or demos by post. Send a covering letter with links to your music online to: demos@bucksmusicgroup.co.uk. Please allow several weeks for a response.

Carlin Music

Iron Bridge House, 3 Bridge Approach, London, NW1 8BD

☎ 020 7734 3251
✉ info@carlinmusic.com
🌐 www.carlinmusic.com

Contact CEO, David Japp

About Publishes a catalogue spanning a hundred years of music, including jazz, soul, blues, country, pop, motown, dance, rap and rock. Carlin also publishes the scores to many well-known and much loved stage musicals such as 'Fiddler on the Roof' and 'Cabaret', while many of its titles have featured in blockbuster motion pictures such as 'Oh Brother Where Art Thou' and 'Titanic'.

Chrysalis Music Publishing

The Chrysalis Building, 13 Bramley Road, London, W10 6SP

☎ 020 7221 2213
✉ info@chrysalismusic.co.uk
🌐 www.chrysalismusic.co.uk

Contact Creative Director, Sophie Urquhart; A&R Scout, Craig Michie

About A leading independent publisher of music, with a particular focus on contemporary, unsigned artists. Send no more than three demos on a CD by post, addressed to the A&R Scout.

EMI Music Publishing Ltd
27 Wrights Lane, London, W8 5SW
- 020 3059 3059
- 020 3059 2059
- webmaster@emimusicpub.com
- www.emimusicpub.com

Contact President, Guy Moot; Senior Vice-President (A&R), Fran Malyan
About Publishes a wide range of music, including two catalogues; KPM (www.playkpm.com) and Music House (www.playmusichouse.com). Does not accept unsolicited submissions.

Independent Music Group
3 York House, Langston Road, Loughton, Essex, IG10 3TQ
- 0845 371 1113
- 0845 371 1114
- jbrown@independentmusicgroup.com
- www.independentmusicgroup.com

Contact CEO, Ellis Rich; Director of A&R, Andy Bailey; Director of Creative, Jacqui Brown
About Independent music publisher of thousands of classic and modern pop songs. Send up to four songs in CD format with a short biography. Initial enquiry can be done by phone, then follow up a submission ten days after posting with another call.

Kobalt Music Group
4 Valentine Place, London, SE1 8QH
- 020 7401 5500
- 020 7401 5501
- info@kobaltmusic.com
- www.kobaltmusic.com

Contact Founder & CEO, Willard Ahdritz; Executive Vice President (Creative), Sas Metcalfe
About Independent and international music publisher. Clients include Gwen Stefani, Kid Rock and Wet Wet Wet. No unsolicited submissions.

Notting Hill Music
Bedford House, 8b Berkeley Gardens, London, W8 4AP
- 020 7243 2921
- 020 7243 2894
- leo@nottinghillmusic.com
- www.nottinghillmusic.com

Contact Chairman, Andy McQueen; Managing Director, Dave Loader; Head of Creative/A&R, Leo Whiteley

About International publishers based in London and Los Angeles, they represent over 25,000 copyrights. Artists include Britney Spears, Snoop Dogg and Machinehead.

Sony/ATV Music Publishing
30 Golden Square, London, W1F 9LD
- 020 3206 2501
- 020 3206 2596
- rachel.iver@uk.sonymusic.com
- www.sonyatv.com/en-uk

Contact Head of A&R, Ian Ramage
About Publishes a large selection of music covering a wide variety of genres. Unsolicited submissions will be accepted. Send short CDs, plus press cuttings, gig lists and biography package to the A&R department. A response is not guaranteed, although packages including SAEs will be returned.

Sony BMG Music Entertainment
9 Derry Street, London, W8 5HY
- 020 7384 7500
- www.bmg.com

Contact CEO, Rolf Schmidt-Holtz
About A record label that publishes thousands of titles across a wide range of music, including modern pop and rock, hip-hop, dance, christian and classical music.

Universal Music Publishing
136–144 New Kings Road, London, SW6 4FX
- 020 8752 2600
- 020 8752 2601
- ukpublishing@umusic.com
- www.universalmusicpublishing.com

Contact Chairman and CEO (US based), David Renzer
About Owns or administers of over 1,000,000 copyrights. No unsolicited submissions. Universal also owns the Sanctuary Music Group.

Warner/Chappell UK
Griffin House, 161 Hammersmith Road, London, W6 8BS
- 020 8563 5800
- 020 8563 5801
- webmaster@warnerchappell.com
- www.warnerchappell.co.uk

Contact Head Of UK Administration, Barry McKee
About Large, international publisher of music in all genres. Does not accept unsolicited submissions.

UK & IRISH MAGAZINES

A470 – What's on in Literary Wales

3ydd Llawr, Ty Mount Stuart, Sgwar Mount
Stuart, Cardiff, CF10 5FQ

- 029 2047 2266
- 029 2049 2930
- post@academi.org
- www.academi.org

Parent Company Academi
Editor Petra Bennett
Established 1998
Insider Info A quarterly literary consumer magazine
aimed at a Welsh literary audience. Present
circulation is roughly 5,000. Accept queries by
mail or email.
Non-fiction Publishes interviews/profiles, reviews,
general interest, news and event listings articles.
Submission Guidelines Accepts queries.
Fiction Publishes short fiction.
Tips Publishes articles in both English and Welsh. It is
aimed at professional writers in Wales, and seeks the
latest information and event listings for the Welsh
literary scene.

Able

15–39 Durham Street, Kinning Park, Glasgow,
G41 1BS

- 0141 419 0044
- 0141 419 0077
- melissa@cravenpublishing.co.uk
- www.ablemagazine.co.uk

Parent Company Craven Publishing Ltd
Editor Emily Rodway
Contact Features Writer, Melissa Holmes
Established 1994
Insider Info A bi-monthly consumer magazine
covering lifestyle and general interest, aimed at
disabled people. Present circulation is 31,127.
Non-fiction Publishes news, features, interviews,
profiles and event listings.
Tips *Able* covers lifestyle and general interest issues
affecting disabled people. Features include art,
politics, health, leisure and travel.

Abraxas

57 Eastbourne Road, St Austell, Cornwall,
PL25 4SU

- lordcrashingbore@btinternet.com
- www.abraxasmagazine.com

Editor Paul Newman

Established 1991
Insider Info A quarterly literary consumer magazine,
aimed at a general interest literary audience. Byline is
given. Accepts queries by mail or email. Writer's
guidelines are available online.
Non-fiction Publishes essays, poetry articles,
features and reviews on psychology and
existentialism.
Submission Guidelines Accepts queries.
Fiction Publishes intellectual short stories.
Submission Guidelines Accepts queries for articles
of up to 2,000 words.
Poetry Publishes avant-garde, free verse and light
verse poetry.
* Poetry tends to be used as fillers.
Tips *Abraxas* incorporates the *Colin Wilson Newsletter*
and publishes poetry, fiction and articles on
philosophy and metaphysics. It is focused on the
work of Colin Wilson, particularly scholarly articles on
psychology and existentialism. Short stories are
welcome as long as they are suitably intellectual,
and in keeping with tone of the rest of the content.

Accountancy

145 London Road, Kingston upon Thames,
Surrey, KT2 6SR

- 020 8247 1387
- 020 8247 1424
- accountancynews@cch.co.uk
- www.accountancymagazine.com

Parent Company Wolters Kluwer (UK) Ltd
Editor Chris Quick
Established 1889
Insider Info A monthly consumer magazine that
covers accounting, finance, legal and taxation
subjects. Accepts queries by mail or email. Present
circulation is 150,456.
Tips *Accountancy* is aimed at professional
accountants in practice or industry.

Action Man A.T.O.M.

Brockbourne House, Mount Ephrain, Tunbridge
Wells, TN4 8BS

- 01892 500100
- 01892 500146
- paninicomics@panini.co.uk
- www.paninicomics.co.uk

Parent Company Panini UK Ltd
Editor Ed Caruana
Contact Managing Editor, Alan O'Keefe
Established 2006
Insider Info A consumer magazine published every
three weeks. The magazine is aimed at children and

fans of *Action Man*. Present circulation is roughly 100,000. 50 per cent of the publication is written by freelance writers. A media pack is available online.

Non-fiction Publishes reviews and information on *Action Man* products.

Fiction Publishes comic strip stories based around *Action Man*.

Images Publishes cartoon illustrations of the *Action Man* stories.

Tips The magazine is specifically aimed at 6–12 year old readers and contains collectible features and fact files on the heroes, villains and hi-tech gadgets of the A.T.O.M. world and lots of puzzles and competitions. The ethos is that a mixture of imaginative editorial, modern, urban design, and cool, aspirational heroes will attract a broad range of readers.

Acumen

6 The Mount, Higher Furzeham Road, Brixham, Devon, TQ5 8QY

- 01803 851098
- 01803 851098
- patricia@acumen-poetry.co.uk
- www.acumen-poetry.co.uk

Parent Company Ember Press/Acumen Publications Ltd

Editor Patricia Oxley

Insider Info A literary consumer journal, published three times per year (in January, May and September), aimed at a general interest and literary audience. Present circulation is roughly 800. Receives approximately 10–15,000 queries per year. Aims to respond to submissions within between one and six weeks. Accepts queries by mail or email. Writer's guidelines are available online.

Non-fiction Publishes articles on poetry and literary criticism.

Submission Guidelines Accepts completed manuscript of between 1,500 and 3,500 words. No emailed submissions.

Poetry Publishes avant-garde, free verse, light verse and traditional poetry.

* Buys approximately 150 poems per year.

Submission Guidelines Accepts sample poems. No emailed submissions.

Tips *Acumen* places an emphasis on publishing a wide range of poetry both in style and in its poets. Work is considered from both established and talented newcomers, on an equal basis. It publishes around 50 poems per issue as well as reviews, poetry comment, and reader feedback. Besides poetry, *Acumen* also prints articles of high quality prose on poetry or poetry related subjects. These can be literary criticism, techniques and poetics, poetry reviews, or anything similar providing they are relevant and interesting.

Aeroplane Monthly

Blue Fin Building, 110 Southwark Street, London, SE1 0SU

- 020 3148 4100
- editoraero@ipcmedia.com
- www.aeroplanemonthly.com

Parent Company IPC Media Ltd

Editor Mick Oakey

Contact Publishing Director, Alex Robb; Features Editor, Nick Stroud

Established 1973

Insider Info A monthly consumer magazine, covering aviation history. Present circulation is 35,704. Media pack available online.

Non-fiction Publishes aviation history, event listings, letters, aircraft preservation and personal recollection articles.

Submission Guidelines Accepts queries and manuscripts by email.

Images Publishes aviation imagery. Send photos with submission.

Tips *Aeroplane Monthly* is an illustrated magazine that covers all aspects of aviation history and related event listings. The magazine regularly publishes personal recollections from military aeroplane ground-crews and will accept enquiries or contributions by email, a full list of email contacts is available on the website.

Aesthetica

PO Box 371, York, YO23 1WL

- 01904 527560
- info@aestheticamagazine.com
- www.aestheticamagazine.com

Editor Cherie Federico

Established 2003

Insider Info A quarterly literary consumer magazine aimed at a general interest and literary audience. A byline is given. Accepts queries by mail or email. Writer's guidelines are available online.

Non-fiction Publishes articles on poetry, features, reviews and general interest articles on music and film.

Submission Guidelines Accepts queries via email or post.
Submission details to: submissions@aestheticamagazine.com

Fiction Publishes prose and mainstream fiction.
* Payment is via contributor copy.

Submission Guidelines Accepts a complete manuscript of between 300 and 2,000 words via email.
Submission details to: submissions@aestheticamagazine.com

Poetry Publishes avant-garde, free verse, light verse and traditional poetry.

Submission Guidelines Submit five sample poems. Submission details to: submissions@ aestheticamagazine.com

Tips *Aesthetica* is a cultural arts magazine that publishes contemporary poetry and prose fiction, art, and articles on music and film. They do not accept postal submissions, instead send all submissions as word document attachments. Be sure to include your name and the title of your work within the email subject header.

Agenda

The Wheelwrights, Fletching Street, Mayfield, East Sussex, TN20 6TL
- 01435 873703
- editor@agendapoetry.co.uk
- www.agendapoetry.co.uk

Editor Patricia McCarthy
Established 1959
Insider Info A quarterly literary consumer journal, aimed at a general interest literary audience. Accepts queries by mail or email. Writer's guidelines available online.
Non-fiction Publishes articles on poetry, features, book reviews, essays and literary criticism.
* Buys approximately 80 non-fiction manuscripts from writers per year.
Submission Guidelines Accepts complete manuscript.
Poetry Publishes avant-garde, free verse, light verse and traditional poetry.
* Buys approximately 200 poems per year.
Submission Guidelines Submit six sample poems. Avoid clichèd poetry, the overly sentimental, poems with forced rhymes, and poetry that does not come from the heart.
Tips Sometimes publishes special issues which focus on a well-known poet alive or dead, and international issues. Each issue contains a general selection of poetry and articles including foreign language translations. Agenda aims to promote young, talented new voices, as well as previously neglected voices and work by established poets. Another of the chief aims of *Agenda* is to provide foreign language poetry to an English speaking audience.

Aireings

Dean Head Farm, Scotland Lane, Leeds, LS18 5HU
- editors@aireings.co.uk
- www.aireings.co.uk

Editor Lesley Quayle; Linda Marshall
Established 1980
Insider Info A quarterly literary consumer magazine, aimed at a general interest and literary audience.

Non-fiction Publishes articles on poetry.
Poetry Publishes free verse and traditional poetry (mostly women's poetry).
Submission Guidelines All submissions must be sent by email, in the body of the text, not as an attachment.
Submission details to: submissions@aireings.co.uk
Tips *Aireings* has become an online magazine, focusing on poetry, prose and short stories. Print issues were discontinued in early 2008.

Airliner World

PO Box 100, Stamford, PE9 1XQ
- 01780 755131
- 01780 757261
- tony.dixon@keypublishing.com
- www.airlinerworld.com

Parent Company Key Publishing Ltd
Editor Tony Dixon
Contact Deputy Editor, Richard Maslen
Established 1999
Insider Info A monthly consumer magazine covering commercial aviation. Present circulation is 33,638.
Non-fiction Publishes news, features, reviews, interviews and profiles.
Tips *Airliner World* focuses on commercial aviation and airliners. It publishes the latest industry news and reviews and is aimed at both enthusiasts and professionals working in the aviation industry.

Air Mail

Unit 3, 5 Sybron Way, Millbrook Industrial Estate, Crowborough, TN6 3DZ
- 01892 600192
- 01892 665375
- colin.pullen@rafatrad.co.uk
- www.rafatrad.co.uk

Parent Company RAFATRAD Ltd
Editor Colin Pullen
Established 1940
Insider Info A quarterly journal covering the RAF Association (RAFA). Present circulation is 63,999.
Non-fiction Publishes features, news and historical articles linked to the RAF.
Tips *Air Mail* is the official trade magazine of the RAF Association (RAFA) and is aimed at both serving and ex-RAF members.

Albedo One

2 Post Road, Lusk, Co. Dublin, Republic of Ireland
- 01353 777931
- bobn@yellowbrickroad.ie
- www.albedo1.com

Parent Company Aeon Press

Editor Editors: John Kenny, Bob Neilson, David Murphy, Frank Ludlow and Roelof Goudriaan.
Established 1993
Insider Info A quarterly consumer magazine, covering genre fiction writing. Payment is upon acceptance of manuscript. A byline is given. Does not accept previously published or simultaneous submissions. Accepts queries by mail or email. Writer's guidelines are available online.
Fiction Publishes horror, science-fiction, experimental, fantasy and slipstream.
* Pays 3 euros per 1,000 words, plus one contributor copy.
Submission Guidelines Send complete manuscript of between 2,500 to 8,000 words) by post or in the body of an email.
Tips *Albedo One* is always looking for thoughtful, well written fiction. Thier definition of what constitutes SF, horror and fantasy is extremely broad and they hope to see material which pushes at the boundaries.

All Out Cricket

c/o Trinorth Ltd, The Brit Oval, Kennington, London, SE11 5SS
☎ 020 7820 4190
☎ 020 7953 8329
✉ comments@alloutcricket.co.uk
🌐 www.alloutcricket.co.uk
Parent Company Professional Cricketers Association
Editor Andy Afford
Established 2004
Insider Info A monthly consumer magazine, covering sports and cricket in particular. Present circulation is roughly 30,000.
Non-fiction Publishes photo features, features and interviews/profiles.
Tips *All Out Cricket* (AOC) magazine is a contemporary lifestyle publication with a young, lively approach to cricket. It has a markedly less formal style than other cricket and sporting publications and looks for articles relating to the contemporary lifestyle choice of cricketers.

Altitude

7A Hithercroft Court, Lupton Road, Wallingford, OX10 9BT
☎ 01491 837117
✉ info@theadplain.com
🌐 www.altitudemagazine.com
Parent Company The Ad Plain Ltd
Contact Editorial Director, Charlotte Ricca-Smith; Publisher, Duncan Murray-Clarke
Established 2001

Insider Info A consumer in-flight magazine, with two issues per year, covering general lifestyle features. Present circulation is 92,500.
Non-fiction Publishes features, celebrity profiles and travel articles. Topics covered include property, wine, food, health, beauty, gadgets and sports
Tips *Altitude* is a lifestyle magazine that is distributed to passengers on Excel Airways. It is designed to compete with similar high-street lifestyle and travel brands.

Amateur Gardening

Westover House, West Quay Road, Poole, BH15 1JG
☎ 01202 440840
☎ 01202 440860
✉ amateurgardening@ipcmedia.com
🌐 www.amateurgardening.co.uk
Parent Company IPC Media Ltd
Editor Tim Rumball
Established 1884
Insider Info A weekly consumer magazine, covering gardening topics. Present circulation of 46,128.
Non-fiction Publishes how-to, features, general interest and news articles.
Submission Guidelines Accepts articles of up to 1,200 words.
Images Accepts photos with submissions.
Tips The editorial mix includes practical hints and tips, topical news and features and advice, mainly from celebrity names in gardening. The magazine is looking for 'topical, practical, or newsy articles', ideally supported by colour pictures.

Amateur Photographer

Blue Fin Building, 110 Southwark Street, London, SE1 0SU
☎ 020 3148 5000
☎ 020 3148 8123
✉ amateurphotographer@ipcmedia.com
🌐 www.amateurphotographer.co.uk
Parent Company IPC Media Ltd
Editor Damien Demolder
Contact Features Editor, Bob Aylott
Established 1884
Insider Info A weekly consumer magazine covering photography subjects. Present circulation of 24,567.
Non-fiction Publishes photo features, features, reviews, new products and technical articles.
Submission Guidelines Accepts queries.
Images Send photos with submission.
Tips *Amateur Photographer* is designed to appeal to those interested in buying photographic equipment or wanting advice about improving their picture taking. Contact the Editor with ideas first, and

remember that in general, all articles must be accompanied by photos.

Amateur Stage
Hampden House, 2 Weymouth Street, London, SW1W 5BT
- 020 7636 4343
- 020 7636 2323
- editor@asmagazine.co.uk
- www.amateurstagemagazine.co.uk

Parent Company Platform Publications Ltd
Editor Doug Mayo
Established 1946
Insider Info A monthly consumer magazine that covers all aspects of amateur theatre and performance. Accepts queries by mail or email.
Non-fiction Interested in factual and practical articles related to theatre.
Submission Guidelines Accepts queries and completed manuscript submissions of between 600 to 2,000 words.

Ambit
17 Priory Gardens, London, N6 5QY
- 020 8340 3566
- info@ambitmagazine.co.uk
- www.ambitmagazine.co.uk

Editor Martin Bax
Established 1959
Insider Info A quarterly literary consumer magazine, covering general literary topics. 100 per cent of the publication is written by freelancers. A byline is given. Accepts queries by mail or email. Aims to respond to queries and manuscripts within four months. Sample copy and writer's guidelines available online.
Fiction Publishes humorous, erotica, mainstream and experimental short fiction.
Submission Guidelines Accepts complete manuscript of up to 10,000 words. Does not accept genre fiction, horror, fantasy or science fiction unless suitably subverted. No stories about domestic boredom/bliss, school, or stories that end with 'it was all a dream'. No emailed submissions.
Poetry Publishes avant-garde, free verse, light verse and traditional poetry.
Submission Guidelines Accepts six sample poems with SAE. Does not want cliched, parochial, overly self-conscious or generalised poetry. No emailed submissions.
Tips *Ambit* publishes both new and established writers. It does not print articles, essays, interviews, memoirs or biography, and does not accept unsolicited submissions for book reviews. Ambit does not work by email and SAE must be included with any submissions.

Ancestors Magazine
Ruskin Avenue, Richmond, Surrey, TW9 4DU
- 020 8392 5370
- 020 8392 5266
- ancestors@nationalarchives.gov.uk
- www.ancestorsmagazine.co.uk

Parent Company The National Archives
Editor Simon Fowler
Established 2001
Insider Info A monthly consumer magazine, covering genealogy, family history, social history (medieval to the 1950s), military history, archives and libraries. It is the monthly family history magazine of The National Archives. Present circulation of roughly 22,000. 60 per cent of the publication is written by freelancers. It takes on average four months to publish a manuscript after acceptance. Payment is upon publication, sometimes via a contributor copy, although this is by prior agreement. A byline will be given. The publication is copyrighted and buys first UK serial rights from writers. Editorial lead time is two months and seasonal material must be submitted three months in advance. Accepts queries via mail, email, fax or phone. Aims to respond to queries and manuscripts within five days. Will not pay the expenses of writers on assignments. Sample copy and writer's guidelines are free on request.
Non-fiction Publishes how-to, research (particularly tracing ancestors using particular archives or records) and historical articles.
* Buys approximately 60 non-fiction manuscripts per year. Pays between £50 and £180 for assigned articles. Unsolicited articles are rarely accepted.
Submission Guidelines Contact the Editor to discuss ideas before submission. Articles should be between 1,000 and 3,000 words. Does not publish nostalgia articles.
Images Accepts images with submission.
* Negotiates payment individually. Buys one time rights.
Submission Guidelines Accepts gif/jpeg files with captions. State availability of photos with submission.
Columns Regular columns include *Off the Record,* a history column of around 700 words.
* Buys 12 columns per year. Payment is between £30 and £50.
Tips Writing should be in clear, concise English and only relevant articles should be submitted. The audience of *Ancestors Magazine* is considered more 'advanced' than that of rival publications. Contact the Editor to discuss any ideas.

Angler's Mail
Blue Fin Building, 110 Southwark Street, London, SE1 0SU

- 020 3148 5000
- 020 3148 8129
- anglersmail@ipcmedia.com
- www.anglersmail.com

Parent Company IPC Media Ltd
Editor Tim Knight
Contact Publishing Director, Hamish Dawson; Features Editor, Richard Howard; Art Editor, Kaith Chambers
Insider Info A weekly consumer magazine, covering angling and coarse fishing. Present circulation is 32,400. Media pack available online.
Non-fiction Publishes angling news, reviews, instruction features and advice articles.
Tips Aimed at the leisure angler. Regularly prints articles on where the best fishing is available.

Angling Times
Bushfield House, Orton Centre, Peterborough, PE2 5UW
- 01733 232600
- 01733 465658
- rich.lee@bauer.com
- www.anglingtimes.co.uk

Parent Company Bauer Consumer Media
Editor Richard Lee
Contact Publishing Director, Aran Beesley; Features Editor, Steven Partner; News Editor, Stephen Stones
Established 1953
Insider Info A weekly consumer magazine covering angling and coarse and sea fishing. Present circulation is 51,006.
Non-fiction Publishes photo features, news, product reviews and match result articles.

AN Magazine
1st Floor, 7-15 Pink Lane, Newcastle-upon-Tyne, NE1 5DW
- 0191 241 8000
- 0191 241 8001
- edit@a-n.co.uk
- www.a-n.co.uk

Parent Company AN: The Artists Information Company
Editor Gillian Nicol
Established 1980
Insider Info A monthly consumer magazine that covers all aspects of visual and applies arts. Accepts queries by mail or email.
Non-fiction Interested in news, interviews, reviews and feature articles.
Submission Guidelines Accepts queries and completed manuscript submissions of up to 1,000 words.

Annual Bulletin of Historical Literature
Department of History, University of Huddersfield, Queensgate, Huddersfield, HD1 3DH
- 01484 422288
- 01484 472655
- k.laybourn@hud.ac.uk
- www.history.org.uk

Parent Company The Historical Association
Editor Keith Laybourn and Kathleen Thompson
Established 1916
Insider Info An annual literary consumer magazine covering reviews of historical books and journals. Present circulation of 1,000. A byline is given. Accepts queries by mail or email.
Non-fiction Publishes essays, features, reviews and historical/nostalgic articles.
Submission Guidelines Accepts queries.
Tips The *Annual Bulletin of Historical Literature* publishes critical reviews of new historical books and journals, but only from recognised history scholars. It is published on behalf of the Historical Association.

Anon
67 Learmonth Grove, Edinburgh, EH4 1BL
- 0131 332 2398
- mike@volta1.fsworld.co.uk
- www.blanko.org.uk/anon

Editor Mike Stocks
Established 2005
Insider Info A consumer literary journal with three issues per year, covering poetry and other literature. 100 per cent of the publication is written by freelancers. A byline is given. Accepts queries by mail or email. Aims to respond to manuscripts within three months. Writer's guidelines available online.
Non-fiction Publishes articles on poetry.
Submission Guidelines Accepts queries.
Poetry Publishes avant-garde, free verse, light verse and traditional poetry.
* 90 per cent of submissions to *Anon* are free verse, so formal verse submissions, or interesting hybrids, are in high demand.
Submission Guidelines Submit three sample poems.
Tips *Anon* is a poetry journal to which poems are submitted anonymously and assessed 'blind' – using procedures similar to those used by poetry competitions. The selected poems are then published under their author's name. In this way *Anon* publishes any type of poetry from any type of writer, new, established or otherwise, and also prints some articles on poetry or related subjects. Please note that when submitting to *Anon*, name and

address details should be included separately to the poems.

A Place in the Sun

Westgate, 120–128 Station Road, Redhill, RH1 1ET

- 01737 786800
- 01737 786801
- richard.way@brooklandsgroup.com

Parent Company Brooklands Group Ltd
Editor Richard Way
Contact Features Editor, Amy Carroll
Established 2004
Insider Info A monthly consumer magazine covering international property buying. Present circulation is 33,386.
Non-fiction Publishes features, property news, case studies and advice.
Tips *A Place in the Sun* is the sister publication of the television programme of the same name. It covers the international property market with news, features and advice articles. It is aimed at people who wish to live abroad, or purchase a second home abroad.

Apollo

The International Magazine of Arts and Antiques
20 Old Queen Street, London, WC1X 8PF

- 020 7961 0150
- editorial@apollomagazine.com
- www.apollo-magazine.com

Parent Company The Spectator Ltd
Editor Michael Hall
Contact Assistant Editor, Annie Blinkhorn; Art Editor, Jessica Chaney
Established 1925
Insider Info A monthly consumer magazine covering arts and antiques.
Non-fiction Publishes essays, features, reviews, and general interest articles
Submission Guidelines Accepts queries for articles of up to 3,000 words.
Tips The publishers are most interested in research, ideally new, or otherwise ground breaking, on fine arts, architecture, and antiques. A specialist knowledge would be more than useful.

Aquarius

Flat 4, Room B, 116 Sutherland Avenue, London, W9 2QP

- 020 7289 4338
- www.geocities.com/eddielinden

Editor Eddie Linden
Insider Info A literary consumer magazine covering mainly short fiction and poetry.
Non-fiction Publishes articles on poetry.

Submission Guidelines Accepts queries.
Fiction Publishes mainstream short fiction.
Poetry Publishes free verse and traditional poetry.
Tips *Aquarius* is a small literary magazine that publishes prose and poetry from new and established writers. Bear in mind that although it is fairly well known in literary circles, its publication dates can be sporadic.

AQUILA

Studio 2, Willowfield Studios, 67a Willowfield Road, Eastbourne, BN22 8AP

- 01323 431313
- 01323 731136
- info@aquila.co.uk
- www.aquila.co.uk

Parent Company New Leaf Publishing
Editor Jackie Berry
Contact Publisher, Ron Bryant-Funnell
Established 1993
Insider Info A monthly consumer magazine for children aged 8-11, covering a different topic each month. Present circulation of roughly 8,000. Sample copy is available for a cost.
Non-fiction Publishes photo features, features and general interest articles.
Submission Guidelines Accepts queries for articles of roughly 800 words.
Fiction Publishes short fiction.
* Pays between £80 and £90 for fiction articles.
Submission Guidelines Guidelines available by email.
Tips The magazine takes a non-denominational approach, and is not restricted in any way, or limited by school curriculum requirements. It aims to provide quality ideals and to encourage children to develop caring and thoughtful attitudes towards others and their environment.

The Architect's Journal

Greater London House, Hampstead Road, London, NW1 7EJ

- 020 7728 5000
- 020 7728 4666
- kieran.long@emap.com
- www.ajplus.co.uk

Parent Company EMAP Plc
Editor Kieran Long
Contact News Editor, Max Thompson; Art Editor, Cecilia Lindgren
Established 1895
Insider Info A weekly trade journal covering the architecture and construction industry. Present circulation is 9,999. Media pack is available online.
Non-fiction Publishes news, features and industry information on building techniques and practices.

The Architectural Review

Greater London House, Hampstead Road, London, NW1 7EJ

- 020 7728 4589
- paul.finch@emap.com
- www.arplus.com

Parent Company EMAP Plc

Editor Paul Finch

Contact Publishing Director, Jonathan Stock; Managing Editor, Catherine Slessor; Art Editor, Michael Hardaker

Established 1896

Insider Info A monthly trade journal covering the architecture industry. Present circulation is 18,180.

Non-fiction Publishes news, features, reviews and industry information.

Tips *The Architectural Review* covers architecture, but also interior design, landscape and process.

Arena

Mappin House, 4 Winsley Street, London, W1W 8HF

- 020 7182 8000
- arenamag@emap.com
- www.arenamagazine.co.uk

Parent Company EMAP Plc

Contact Editor-in-Chief, Anthony Noquera; Creative Director, Balwant Ahira; Features Editor, Simon Kurs

Established 1986

Insider Info A monthly consumer magazine covering men's lifestyle interest. Present circulation is 30,896.

Non-fiction Publishes photo features, news, interviews, reviews and general interest articles on sport, fashion, lifestyle, politics, television and cinema, music, celebrities and general men's interest subjects.

Tips *Arena* is aimed at men of all ages.

Areopagus

48 Cornwall Road, Plympton, Plymouth, Devon, PL7 1AL

- editor@areopagus.org.uk
- www.areopagus.org.uk

Parent Company Areopagus Publications

Editor Julian Barritt

Established 1990

Insider Info A quarterly consumer literary magazine, aimed at Christian writers. Byline is given. Accepts queries by mail or email. Payment may be via a contributor copy, in lieu of cash. Writer's guidelines and sample copy are available online.

Non-fiction Publishes how-to articles on creative writing, and poetry, religious articles and features.

* Payment is via a contributor copy.

Submission Guidelines Send complete manuscript. Length should be between 300 and 1,800 words.

Fiction Publishes religious fiction.

* Payment is via contributor copy.

Submission Guidelines Send complete manuscript. Length should be between 300 and 1,800 words.

Poetry Publishes free verse and traditional poetry.

Tips *Areopagus* magazine is a special interest publication for Christian writers, which is run voluntarily by editorial teams based in both the UK and US. Due to low funding, *Areopagus* can only accept submissions from subscribers, and is therefore not interested in any unsolicited manuscripts from other sources. It is preferred that subscribers submit their work by email. All articles have a Christian basis.

Areté

8 New College Lane, Oxford, OX1 3BN

- 01865 289193
- 01865 289194
- craigraine@aretemagazine.com
- www.aretemagazine.com

Editor Craig Raine

Established 1999

Insider Info A consumer publication with three issues per year, covering literature, poetry and fiction. Byline is given. Queries accepted by mail or email. Writer's guidelines available online.

Non-fiction Publishes articles on poetry, features, interview/profiles, reviews and news/reportage.

Submission Guidelines Accepts complete manuscript with SAE.

Fiction Publishes mainstream fiction and short stories.

Poetry Publishes avant-garde, free verse, light verse and traditional poetry.

Tips Focuses on poetry, fiction, reportage and book reviews. Its major emphasis is on poetry, articles relating to poetry, and poetics and many of its contributors are famous authors in their own right. *Arete* does not accept email submissions, so send work as hard copy only. All submissions must also include SAE for return or reply.

Army Families Journal

Trenchard Lines, Upavon, Pewsey, Wiltshire, SN9 6BE

- 01980 615518
- 01980 615526
- editor@afj.org.uk
- www.afj.org.uk

Parent Company Method Publishing

Editor Charlotte Eadie

Contact Deputy Editor, Claire Gill
Established 1996
Insider Info Quarterly magazine publication representing the registered charity The Army Families Federation (AFF). Present circulation of roughly 64,000. Five per cent of the magazine is written by freelance writers. Submissions are published approximately three months after acceptance. Articles are written for free, as the *AFF Families Journal* is a charity. Publication is copyrighted. Editorial lead time is six weeks. Seasonal material must be submitted three months in advance. Queries accepted by mail, email, fax and telephone. Accepts simultaneous and previously published submissions. Aims to respond to queries within one day, manuscripts and other enquiries within two days. Sample copy available online or via email. Writer's guidelines available online. Editorial calendars available free on request.
Non-fiction Publishes articles on experiences of British Army life and issues that affect Army families in the UK and around the world.
Submission Guidelines Articles must be 1,000–1,500 words in length.
Images Accepts high-res images with submissions. * Does not offer payment for images.
Submission Guidelines Send as gif/jpeg files, including captions and identification of subjects.
Columns Publishes columns on 'Family Life', 'Education', 'Army and You', 'Workplace', 'Housing', 'Money and You', 'Foreign and Commonwealth', 'Territorial Army Families' and 'Special Needs'.
Fillers Publishes News, Information and Letters as fillers.
Tips The *Army Families Journal* is a quarterly publication that is distributed to all Army families based within the UK and across the world. The magazine is free, funded by its advertising, and is supported by the Army Families Federation. The magazine also has pages which cover life in Cyprus, Northern Ireland and Germany, where Army families are based, as well as a strong 'Postbag' section where letters can be published and views aired.

The Art Book
Laughton Cottage, Brickhurst Lane, Laughton, Lewes, BN8 6DD
- 01323 811759
- 01323 811756
- ed-exec-theartbook@aah.org.uk
- www.blackwellpublishing.com/journals/artbook
Parent Company The Association of Art Historians
Editor Sue Ward
Established 1993
Insider Info A quarterly scholarly journal covering art issues. Present circulation of roughly 9,000. Byline is given. Accepts queries by mail and email. Sample copy and writer's guidelines are available online.
Non-fiction Publishes articles on the history of art, architecture, design, the latest exhibitions, reviews and new media.
Submission Guidelines Accepts query with published clips. Articles must be 800–2,000 words.
Tips *The Art Book* is aimed at academics, students and anyone working with art or history, and anyone interested in new interpretations of arts histories. They are always looking for reviewers of the latest art history books or related subjects. All submissions must be written in a scholarly manner, but with direct and accessible language and little jargon or technical terms.

Art Business Today
The Fine Art Trade Guild, 16–18 Empress Place, London, SW6 1TT
- 020 7381 6616
- 020 7381 2596
- abt@fineart.co.uk
- www.artbusinesstoday.co.uk
Parent Company The Fine Art Trade Guild
Editor Mike Sims
Established 1905
Insider Info A consumer magazine, with five issues per year, that covers the fine art and framing industry. Payment by arrangement. Accepts queries by mail or email.
Non-fiction Interested in industry news, new products, market and business analysis, research and technology articles related to the fine art industry.
Submission Guidelines Accepts queries and completed manuscript submissions of between 800 to 1,600 words, with colour photos.

The Artist
Caxton House, 63–65 High Street, Tenterden, Kent, TN30 6BD
- 01580 763673
Parent Company The Artist's Publishing Co. Ltd
Editor Sally Bulgin
Established 1931
Insider Info A monthly consumer magazine that covers practical art. Accepts queries by mail or email.
Non-fiction Interested in practical, how-to, reviews and new product articles related to art.
Tips *The Artist* is aimed at both amateur and professional artists.

Artists & Illustrators
226 City Road, London, EC1V 2TT
- 020 7700 8500
- 020 7700 4985
- info@artistsandillustrators.co.uk

◎ www.artistsandillustrators.co.uk
Editor John Swinfield
Established 1986
Insider Info A monthly consumer magazine that covers practical art and illustration. Accepts queries by mail or email.
Non-fiction Interested in practical, how-to, new product, reviews and inspirational articles related to art.
Submission Guidelines Accepts queries and completed manuscript submissions of between 1,000 to 1,500 words.
Tips *Artists & Illustrators* focuses on practical articles and is aimed at both amateur and professional artists.

Art Monthly
4th Floor, 28 Charing Cross Road, London, WC2H 0DB
◎ 020 7240 0389
◎ 020 7497 0726
◎ info@artmonthly.co.uk
◎ www.artmonthly.co.uk
Parent Company Britannia Art Publications
Editor Patricia Bickers
Contact Managing Editor, Letty Mooring; Deputy Editor, Ian Hunt; Assistant Editor, Frederika Whitehead
Established 1976
Insider Info A monthly trade magazine covering contemporary visual arts, museums and galleries, curating, collecting, related book and exhibition reviews, and legal and business advice. Present circulation of roughly 6,000. 100 per cent of the publication is written by freelance writers. Payment upon publication, with byline given. Publication is copyrighted. Queries accepted by email or phone.
Non-fiction Publishes exhibition reviews and features on contemporary art.
Submission Guidelines Phone or email the Editorial Assistant to discuss any possible ideas.
Images Accepts images with submission.
Submission Guidelines Send photos (gif/jpeg files) with submission. Contact person for images is Frederika Whitehead.
Tips The magazine's audience is made up of art world insiders be they students, artists, collectors, dealers or historians. It focuses on writing about art, rather than printing reproductions of art itself, therefore all freelancers require a very high level of art world knowledge. Read sample articles on the website first to check that you have sufficient background knowledge in contemporary visual art.

Art Quarterly
Millais House, 7 Cromwell Place, London, SW7 2JN
◎ 020 7225 4800
◎ 020 7225 4807
◎ cbugler@artfund.org
◎ www.artfund.org
Parent Company The Art Fund
Editor Caroline Bugler
Established 1990
Insider Info A quarterly consumer magazine covering art. Present circulation is 49,068.
Non-fiction Publishes news, features and reviews on classic and modern art, design, sculpture and photography.

Art Review
23–24 Smithfield Street, London, EC1R 0BE
◎ 020 7107 2760
◎ 020 7075 6001
◎ office@artreview.com
◎ www.artreview.com
Editor Mark Rappolt
Established 1949
Insider Info A monthly consumer magazine that covers all aspects of modern and contemporary art. Payment is £350 per 1,000 words. Accepts queries by mail or email.
Non-fiction Interested in general interest, style features and review articles related to art.
Submission Guidelines Accepts queries and completed manuscript submissions.

ASDA Magazine
23 Howland Street, London, W1T 4AQ
◎ 020 7462 7891
◎ 020 7462 7931
◎ info@publicis-blueprint.co.uk
◎ www.publicis-blueprint.co.uk
Parent Company Publicis Blueprint (Magazine Publishers) and Asda
Editor Melanie Leyshon
Established 1999
Insider Info A monthly consumer magazine for the customers of Asda supermarket, covering food, drink and retail issues. Present circulation of 2,907,325.
Non-fiction Publishes general interest, interviews, reviews and photo features on food, wine, new products, parenting, cookery, fashion, beauty, health and lifestyle.
Tips The magazine is aimed at women (mothers in particular) aged 25-44.

Asian Times

Unit 2, 65 Whitechapel Road, London, E1 1DU

☎ 020 7650 2000

☎ 020 7650 2001

✉ asiantimes@ethnicmedia.co.uk

🌐 www.asiantimesonline.co.uk

Parent Company Ethnic Media Group

Editor Hamant Verma

Established 1981

Insider Info A weekly consumer newspaper covering news and current affairs in the Asian community. Present circulation of 28,525.

Non-fiction Publishes features, interviews/profiles, general interest, and news/current affairs.

Submission Guidelines Accepts written queries.

Tips The *Asian Times* newspaper aims to be the most reliable source for creating awareness in the Asian community. The Editor is interested in relevant articles on public affairs, international issues and politics, as well as general interest and local issues affecting the British Asian community. Approach in writing with ideas before submission.

Athletics Weekly

83 Park Road, Peterborough, PE1 2TN

☎ 01733 898440

☎ 01733 898441

✉ jason.henderson@athletics-weekly.co.uk

🌐 www.athleticsweekly.com

Parent Company Descartes Publishing Ltd

Editor Jason Henderson

Established 1945

Insider Info A weekly consumer magazine covering the sport of athletics. Present circulation of roughly 14,000. Approximately 50 per cent of the publication is written by freelance writers. It takes on average one month from acceptance of manuscript to publication. Payment upon publication, sometimes with contributor copies. A byline is given and publication is copyrighted. Editorial lead time is one week and seasonal material must be submitted one month in advance. Queries accepted by mail or email. Simultaneous submissions are accepted. Aims to respond to queries in one week, and manuscripts within one month. Expenses of writers on assignment will sometimes be paid, with a limit agreed upon in advance. Sample copy available for £3. Writer's guidelines and editorial calendars are available via email: officemanager@athletics-weekly.co.uk

Non-fiction Publishes athletics articles.

* Pays £70 per 1,000 words.

Submission Guidelines Accepts queries.

Images Uses sports images.

* Pays £15 per photo published.

Submission Guidelines Send images and captions.

Submission details to: pictures@athletics-weekly.co.uk

Tips As well as covering the latest happenings in athletics, the magazine also includes features, letters, fixtures and comment articles.

Attitude

Northern Shell Tower, City Harbour, London, E14 9GL

☎ 020 7308 5090

☎ 020 7308 5384

✉ attitude@nasnet.co.uk

🌐 www.attitude.co.uk

Parent Company Remnant Media

Editor Adam Mattera

Established 1994

Insider Info A monthly consumer magazine that covers men's lifestyle. Accepts queries by mail or email.

Non-fiction Interested in health, beauty, fashion, reviews, interviews, news, humour and celebrity articles.

Tips *Attitude* is a men's lifestyle magazine aimed primarily at gay men.

Audio Visual

Communications for Business

174 Hammersmith Rd, London, W6 7JP

☎ 020 8267 8005

☎ 0208 267 8008

✉ anthony.clark@haymarket.com

🌐 www.avinteractive.co.uk

Parent Company Haymarket

Established 1972

Insider Info A monthly trade magazine covering B2B communications. Present circulation of roughly 15,000. 40 per cent of the publication is written by freelance writers. Takes on average six weeks to publish a manuscript after it is accepted. Payment is upon publication and never with contributor copies instead of cash. Kill fee for articles not published is 100 per cent. Byline is given and publication is copyrighted. Purchases all rights. Average editorial lead time is eight weeks, whilst seasonal material must be submitted three months in advance. Queries accepted by email. Aims to respond to queries and manuscripts within two months. Will sometimes pay the fees of writers on assignment with a limit agreed upon in advance. Sample copy, editorial calendar and writer's guidelines are free on request.

Non-fiction Publishes features, interview/profiles, reviews, new product, opinion (excluding letters to Editor) and personal experience articles.

* Buys 24 non-fiction manuscripts per year. Pays £250 per 1,000 words for assigned articles. Unsolicited articles are not usually accepted.

Submission Guidelines Contact with synopsis, for articles of between 500 and 2,000 words. No reprints. Call Peter Lloyd to discuss in the first instance.

Images Uses images with articles.

* Buys all rights to images.

Tips The magazine is devoted to B2B communications and the use of content and technology. Research the website to gain a fuller understanding of content and issues covered.

Australia & NZ magazine

3–4 Riverside Court, Lower Bristol Road, Bath, Somerset, BA2 3DZ
- 01225 786882
- 01225 789801
- anna.scrivenger@merricksmedia.co.uk
- www.merricksmedia.co.uk

Parent Company Merricks Media Ltd
Editor Anna Scrivenger
Contact Art Editor, Becky Johnson
Established 2005

Insider Info A monthly consumer magazine covering travel, lifestyle and migration with an Australia and New Zealand regional focus. Present circulation of roughly 18,000. 30 per cent of the publication is written by freelance writers. Takes on average two months between acceptance and publication of manuscript. Payment is issued 30 days after publication. Junior writers/students may receive a free subscription instead of cash, subject to negotiation. A byline is given and publication is copyrighted. First UK serial rights, first rights, second serial (reprint) rights, and electronic rights are all purchased. Average editorial lead time is three months. Seasonal material must be submitted three months in advance. Queries accepted by mail or email. Simultaneous submissions and previously published submissions are accepted. Aims to respond to queries within one week and manuscripts within one month. Do not pay the expenses of writers on assignments. A sample copy and writer's guidelines are free on request and available via email.

Non-fiction Publishes book excerpts and articles on interiors, recipes, travel writing, how-to, migration, relocation, property, humour, personal experience, migrant diaries, real-life stories and real holidays.

* Buys 40 non-fiction manuscripts from writers per year. Pays between £200 and £300 for assigned articles and between £100 and £250 for unsolicited articles.

Submission Guidelines Accepts query with synopsis and intro paragraph for an article of between 1,300 and 2,000 words. Send a typed manuscript to the editor. Email submissions are preferred.

Tips The tone of the magazine is upbeat, friendly, with bright, lively design. Read the magazine to get an idea of its content, then email initial ideas to the Editor and they'll take it from there. Email submissions are preferred, but everything is considered.

The Author

84 Drayton Gardens, London, SW10 9SB
- 020 7373 6642
- 020 7373 5768
- editor@societyofauthors.org
- www.societyofauthors.org

Parent Company The Society of Authors
Editor Andrew Taylor
Established 1890

Insider Info The quarterly journal of the Society of Authors, an organisation that serves the interests of all types of professional writers. Present circulation of roughly 8,500. Accepts queries by mail and email.

Non-fiction Publishes articles and features related to professional writing, reviews, and the latest news and events from the writing world.

Submission Guidelines *The Author* is the journal of The Society of Authors and writers must be members of the society before they can contribute anything to the journal.

Tips The Society of Authors itself offers various prizes and grants for professional writers (see Competitions & Prizes and Bursaries, Fellowships & Grants).

Autocar

Teddington Studios, Broom Road, Teddington, Middlesex, TW11 9BE
- 020 8267 5630
- 020 8267 5759
- autocar@haymarket.com
- www.autocar.co.uk

Parent Company Haymarket Business Media Ltd
Editor Charles Hallett
Established 1895

Insider Info A weekly consumer magazine covering motoring subjects. Present circulation of 58,091. Accepts queries by mail or email.

Non-fiction Publishes photo features, features, interviews/profiles and reviews.

Submission Guidelines Submit completed manuscript.

Images Send photos with submission.

Fillers Publishes newsbreaks, and hints and tips as fillers.

Tips The oldest surviving car magazine in the world, dealing with all aspects of cars, motoring, and the motoring industry. The magazine will be looking for articles with a strong technical understanding, but also with a friendly and approachable tone. Check previous issues for style.

Auto Express

30 Cleveland Street, London, W1T 4JD
- 020 7907 6200
- 020 7907 6234
- editorial@autoexpress.co.uk
- www.autoexpress.co.uk

Parent Company Dennis Publishing Ltd
Editor David Johns
Established 1988
Insider Info A weekly consumer magazine covering motoring subjects. Present circulation of 77,587. Queries accepted by email.
Non-fiction Publishes photo features, features, interviews/profiles, reviews and technical articles.
* Pays £350 per 1,000 words for unsolicited articles.
Submission Guidelines Accepts queries by email for articles of up to 2,000 words. Do not send full manuscript.
Images Send photos with submission.
Fillers Publishes newsbreaks, hints and tips as fillers of between 50 and 300 words.
Tips Specialises in car news and reviews with car specification, photos, videos rating and price. Proposals for features are welcome, but not fully-written articles. Articles will be commissioned if they are appropriate and up to the magazine's standards.

Autosport

Teddington Studios, Broom Road, Teddington, TW11 9BE
- 020 8267 5998
- 020 8267 5922
- autosport.editorial@haynet.com
- www.autosport.com

Parent Company Haymarket Autosport & Classic Publications
Contact Editor in Chief, Damien Smith; Editor, Andrew Van De Burgt; Deputy Editor, Gemma Briggs; Art Editor, Phill Fields
Established 1950
Insider Info A weekly consumer magazine covering motorsports. Present circulation is 38,324.
Non-fiction Publishes news, features, events listings, race reports, and analysis of all types of motorsport.

Avocado

Koco Building, The Arches, Spon End, Coventry, CV1 3JQ
- 024 7671 3555
- avocado@heaventreepress.com
- www.heaventreepress.co.uk/Avocado/avocado.htm

Parent Company The Heaventree Press
Editor Loveday Why
Established 2002
Insider Info A quarterly consumer journal covering literature, poetry and arts. Byline is given. Accepts queries by mail or email.
Non-fiction Publishes photo features, features, interviews/profiles and literary criticism articles.
Submission Guidelines Accepts completed manuscript of up to 1,250 words with SAE.
Fiction Publishes short fiction.
Submission Guidelines Accepts completed manuscript of up to 1,250 words with SAE.
Poetry Publishes avant-garde, free verse, light verse and traditional poetry.
Submission Guidelines Submit sample poems of up to 40 lines with SAE.
Images Send photos with submission.
Tips *Avocado* is the literary journal of The Heaventree Press and prints new poetry, prose, fiction and artwork that is fresh, innovative and culturally aware. It seeks work that is diverse, musical, politically aware and free thinking in terms of subject matter and ideology, and that shows an understanding of writing as a craft, and contemporary art forms. Note that *Avocado* does not accept email submissions and all submissions must include SAE for reply.

Awen

38 Pierrot Steps, 71 Kursaal Way, Southend on Sea, Essex, SS1 2UY
- atlanteanpublishing@hotmail.com
- www.geocities.com/dj_tyrer/awen.html

Parent Company Atlantean Publishing
Editor David-John Tyrer
Insider Info A literary consumer magazine, covering poetry and short fiction. Buys first UK serial rights. Accepts queries by mail or email. Previously published submissions are accepted.
Non-fiction Publishes articles on poetry.
Fiction Publishes flash fiction.
Submission Guidelines Submit complete manuscript of up to 500 words.
Poetry Publishes avant-garde, free verse, light verse and traditional poetry.
Submission Guidelines Submit poetry of up to 40 lines.
Tips *Awen* is a small poetry and flash-fiction magazine that prints poetry and vignette length fiction of any style or genre. Submissions to *Awen* magazine may also be considered for other titles published by Atlantean.

Back Brain Recluse

PO Box 625, Sheffield, S1 3GY

○ backbrainrecluse@bbr-online.com
ⓦ www.bbr-online.com/backbrainrecluse

Parent Company BBR Solutions Ltd

Editor Chris Reed

Insider Info A consumer literary magazine covering science fiction writing. Byline is given. Accepts queries by mail and email.

Fiction Publishes science fiction.

Submission Guidelines Accepts queries.

Tips *Back Brain Recluse* is a popular literary magazine with international standing. It publishes original science fiction writing and has built up a cult following amongst its readers. It has a policy of publishing the most experimental and uncommercial types of science fiction.

Back Street Heroes

19th Floor, 1 Canada Square, Canary Wharf, London, E14 5AP

○ 020 7772 8300
○ 020 7772 8585

Editor Stu Garland

Established 1983

Insider Info A monthly consumer magazine that covers motorcycling and motorbike lifestyle.

Ballista

Flapjack Press, 6 Chiffon Way, Trinity Riverside, Greater Manchester, M3 6AB

○ flapjackpress@live.co.uk
ⓦ www.mucusart.co.uk/ballista.htm

Parent Company Flapjack Press

Editor Paul Neads and Andrew Myers

Established 2006

Insider Info A bi-annual literary magazine covering speculative fiction. Payment is £5 plus one free copy per story. Accepts queries by mail or email.

Fiction Publishes science-fiction, fantasy and horror stories with supernatural or psychological themes.

Submission Guidelines Accepts submissions of short stories of up to 3,500 by email.

Tips *Ballista* also runs an open story competition with prizes of £60, £30 and £20. Winning stories will also be published in the magazine.

Banipal

Magazine of Modern Arab Literature, PO Box 22300, London, W13 8ZQ

○ 020 8569 9747
○ 020 8568 8509
○ editor@banipal.co.uk
ⓦ www.banipal.co.uk

Parent Company Banipal Publishing

Editor Margaret Obank

Established 1998

Insider Info A tri annual independent literary magazine covering contemporary literature from the Arab world. Present circulation of roughly 1,200. 90 per cent of the publication is written by freelance writers. Takes on average four months from acceptance of manuscript to publication. Payment is upon publication and a byline is given. Publication is copyrighted. Accepts queries by email. Accepts previously published submissions. Aims to respond to queries within four weeks and manuscripts within three months. A sample copy is free on request. Writers guidelines and a media pack are available online.

Non-fiction Publishes photo features, articles on poetry, features, interviews/profiles, reviews and general interest literary articles.

Submission Guidelines Send completed manuscript via post or email, but do not send any email attachments.

Fiction Publishes fiction in translation from Arab writers.

Poetry Publishes avant-garde, free verse, light verse and traditional poetry.

Images Each issue is fully illustrated with author photographs, and the full colour covers feature prominent Arab artists.

Tips An independent literary magazine publishing contemporary authors from all over the Arab world in English translation. Publishes poems, short stories or excerpts of novels, as well as author interviews, profiles and book reviews. It is aimed at lovers of world literature, educators, professionals, academics, and all those interested in dialogue with other cultures and the relevance of cultural exchange in today's world. See the website for detailed submission methods.

Bard

38 Pierrot Steps, 71 Kursaal Way, Southend On Sea, Essex, SS1 2UY

○ atlanteanpublishing@hotmail.com
ⓦ www.geocities.com/dj_tyrer/bard.html

Parent Company Atlantean Publishing

Editor David-John Tyler

Insider Info A monthly consumer newsletter style magazine covering literature and poetry. Byline is given. Buys first UK serial rights. Accepts queries by mail or email. Previously published submissions are accepted. Writer's guidelines are available online.

Poetry Publishes avant-garde, free verse, light verse and traditional poetry.

Submission Guidelines Accepts poems of up to 40 lines.

Tips *Bard* is a flyer-style broadsheet of poetry that is provided free of charge to subscribers to Atlantean

Publishing magazines. It contains short poetry from new and unpublished writers, but is a very small publication, designed to complement Atlantean's existing set of literary magazines.

Barddas
Pen-rhiw, 71 Ffordd Pentrepoeth, Treforys, Abertawe, SA6 6AE
- 01792 792829
- 01792 792829
- alanllwyd@barddas.freeserve.co.uk
- www.barddas.com

Editor Alan Llwyd
Established 1976
Insider Info A consumer publication covering Welsh literature and poetry. Byline is given. Accepts queries by mail or email.
Poetry Specialises in Welsh poetry.
Tips Barddas is published solely in Welsh language, so will only accept Welsh language submissions.

BBC Good Food
Room AG170, Woodlands, 80 Wood Lane, London, W12 0TT
- 020 8433 2000
- 020 8433 3931
- goodfoodrs@bbc.co.uk
- www.bbcgoodfood.com

Parent Company BBC Worldwide Publishing
Editor Gillian Carter
Contact Editorial Assistant, Sarah Sysum
Established 1989
Insider Info A monthly consumer magazine covering food, drink and cooking topics. Present circulation of 340,057.
Non-fiction Publishes general interest articles, reviews, features and photo features on food, wine and cookery.
Tips The magazine is aimed at food and wine enthusiasts.

BBC Good Homes
Woodlands, 80 Wood Lane, London, W12 0TT
- 020 8433 2391
- 020 8433 2691
- deargoodhomes@bbc.co.uk
- www.bbcgoodhomes.com

Parent Company BBC Worldwide Publishing
Editor Bernie Herlihy
Contact Home Editor, Diana Civil; Art Editor, Heather Heward
Established 1998
Insider Info A monthly consumer magazine covering homes and decorating topics. Present circulation of 117,466.

Non-fiction Publishes general interest features and photo features on houses, style, crafts and decorating.
Tips The titles is aimed specifically at home owners aged 20–50.

BBC History Magazine
(incorporating Living World)
Tower House, Fairfax Street, Bristol, BS1 3BN
- 0117 933 8048
- 0117 933 8032
- historymagazine@bbcmagazinesbristol.co.uk
- www.bbchistorymagazine.com

Parent Company Bristol Magazines Ltd
Editor Dave Musgrove
Established 2000
Insider Info A monthly consumer magazine, covering general history topics. Present circulation of 58,530. Accepts queries by mail or email.
Non-fiction Publishes photo features, features and historical/nostalgic articles.
Submission Guidelines Accepts queries for articles between 750 and 3,000 words. Only accepts submissions from academic or expert historians/archaeologists, and occasionally historically literate journalists.
Tips Aimed at history enthusiasts of all levels of knowledge and interest. Being a British publication, the magazine focuses particularly on British history, but its remit is worldwide. Will only consider submissions providing expert analysis and information. Features should be pegged to historical anniversaries, forthcoming books/television programmes, or current affairs topics.

BBC Homes & Antiques
9th Floor, Tower House, Fairfax Street, Bristol, BS1 3BN
- 0117 927 9009
- 0117 927 9008
- angelalinforth@bbcmagazinesbristol.com
- www.homesandantiques.com

Parent Company Bristol Magazines Ltd
Editor Angela Linforth
Contact Features Editor, Natasha Goodfellow
Established 1993
Insider Info A monthly consumer magazine covering homes, antiques and lifestyle topics. Present circulation of 85,121.
Non-fiction Publishes general interest features and photo features on houses, heritage and antiques.
Tips The title is aimed specifically at antiques enthusiasts.

BBC Music Magazine

Tower House, Fairfax Street, Bristol, BS1 3BN
- ☎ 0117 927 9009
- ☎ 0117 933 8032
- ✉ music@bbcmagazinesbristol.com
- 🌐 www.bbcmusicmagazine.com

Parent Company Bristol Magazines Ltd
Editor Oliver Condy
Established 1992
Insider Info A monthly consumer magazine covering classical music topics. Present circulation of 47,104. Accepts queries by email or fax.
Non-fiction Publishes articles on classical music and the music industry.
Submission Guidelines Accepts outline ideas by email or fax, but not entire manuscripts.

BBC Sky At Night Magazine

Tower House, Fairfax Street, Bristol, BS1 3BN
- ☎ 0117 927 9009
- ☎ 0117 934 9008
- ✉ inbox@skyatnightmagazine.com
- 🌐 www.skyatnightmagazine.com

Parent Company BBC Magazines Bristol
Editor Graham Southorn
Established 2005
Insider Info A monthly consumer magazine covering astronomy subjects. Accepts queries by email and phone.
Non-fiction Publishes articles on astronomy and related subjects.
Submission Guidelines Contact by phone or email with idea. Do not send in unsolicited manuscripts.
Tips Features contributions from world leading astronomers and writers. With articles covering the latest discoveries in astrophysics, to observing guides and equipment reviews, the title is aimed at both the experienced and amateur astronomer. Articles should concern the latest in astronomical science, so a technical or academic background is necessary.

BBC Wildlife Magazine

Tower House, Fairfax Street, Bristol, BS1 3BN
- ☎ 0117 927 9009
- ☎ 0117 934 9008
- ✉ wildlifemagazine@bbcmagazinesbristol.com
- 🌐 www.bbcwildlifemagazine.com

Parent Company BBC Bristol Magazines
Editor Sophie Stafford
Established 1963
Insider Info A monthly consumer magazine covering wildlife topics. Present circulation of 45,033. Accepts queries by email or phone.

Non-fiction Publishes photo features, animal behaviour and conservation features, travel and news articles.
* Fee subject to word count, £450 for full-length features.
Submission Guidelines Submit brief pitch by email first. Only successful pitches will be followed up. If successful, word counts and full commission will follow.
Tips Most articles are illustrated with world class wildlife photography. Articles focus on the latest discoveries, views and news on wildlife, conservation and environmental issues, and trusted further information sources. The magazine is aimed at a broad readership, encompassing anyone with a passion for wildlife. Features are generally only commissioned from experts in wildlife or conservation. In-depth knowledge is essential in the first instance.

The Beano

2 Albert Square, Dundee, DD1 9QJ
- ☎ 01382 223131
- ☎ 01382 322214
- ✉ beano@dcthomson.co.uk
- 🌐 www.dcthomson.co.uk

Parent Company D.C. Thomson & Co. Ltd
Editor Alan Dogby
Insider Info A weekly comic for 7–12 year old boys, covering Beano characters. Present circulation is 61,931.
Fiction Publishes comic strips and stories.
Tips The Beano is an established comic for young and teenage boys. Regular characters include Dennis the Menace and Ivy the Terrible.

Beat Scene

27 Court Leet, Binley Woods, Coventry, CV3 2JQ
- ☎ 024 7654 3604
- ✉ kev@beatscene.freeserve.co.uk
- 🌐 www.beatscene.net

Editor Kevin Ring
Established 1988
Insider Info A consumer magazine with four issues per year, covering the poets of the 'Beat generation.' Present circulation of roughly 4,000.
Non-fiction Publishes photo features, essays, poetry articles, features, interviews/profiles and reviews.
Submission Guidelines Accepts queries.
Tips Beat Scene is an 'information magazine' devoted to the poets of the Beat Generation, including Jack Kerouac, Allen Ginsberg and William Burroughs. The magazine does not publish any fiction or poetry, only articles or news in the relevant subject areas.

Bella

Academic House, 24–28 Oval Road, London, NW1 7DT

☎ 020 7241 8000
🖷 020 7241 8056
🌐 www.bauer.co.uk

Parent Company H. Bauer Publishing
Editor Jayne Marsden
Contact Deputy Editor, Eleanor Levy
Established 1987
Insider Info A weekly consumer magazine covering women's lifestyle topics. Present circulation of 191,547.
Non-fiction Publishes general interest features, interviews and photo features on real life, fashion, beauty, food, home, competitions and travel.
Fiction Publishes short fiction of less than 1,000 words.
Tips The title is aimed specifically at women aged 25–54, with children.

Best

National Magazine House, 33 Broadwick Street, London, W1F 0DQ

☎ 020 7339 4500
🖷 020 7339 4580
📧 best@natmag.co.uk
🌐 www.natmags.co.uk

Parent Company National Magazine Company Ltd
Editor Michelle Hather
Contact Deputy Editor, Andrew Flemming; Features Editor, Charlotte Seligman; Fiction & Travel Editor, Pat Richardson; Books Editor, Josie Merrell
Established 1987
Insider Info A weekly consumer magazine covering women's interest. Present circulation is 301,437. Media pack available online.
Non-fiction Publishes news, interviews, profiles, features and true-life stories. Subjects include celebrities, fashion, health and beauty.
Fiction Publishes short stories.
Tips Best covers all aspects of women's interest. The magazine also publishes short fiction from readers, usually of a general interest style.

The Big Issue

1–5 Wandsworth Road, London, SW8 2LN

☎ 020 7526 3200
🖷 020 7526 3201
📧 editorialinfo@bigissue.com
🌐 www.bigissue.com

Parent Company Big Issue Ltd
Editor Charles Howgego
Contact Publisher, Lisa Woodman; Deputy Editor, Judy Kerr; Art Director, Sam Freeman; Book Reviews Editor, Emma Rubach

Established 1991
Insider Info A weekly consumer magazine covering current affairs and entertainment. Present circulation is 67,641.
Non-fiction Publishes news, current affairs and features.
Tips The Big Issue covers news and current affairs, as well as features on the arts and media. It is aimed at socially aware young people and is by no means solely focused on homelessness as a subject matter, despite being distributed by authorised homeless people.

The Big Issue Cymru

55 Charles Street, Cardiff, CF10 2GD

☎ 029 2025 5670
🖷 029 2025 5673
📧 editorial@bigissuecymru.com
🌐 www.bigissue.com

Parent Company Big Issue Ltd
Editor Rachel Howells
Established 1994
Insider Info A weekly consumer magazine covering current affairs, entertainment and local interest. Present circulation is 8,451.
Non-fiction Publishes news, current affairs, features and local interest (Wales) articles.
Tips The Welsh edition of The Big Issue covers news, current affairs, arts and lifestyle, as well as local interest pieces about Wales. It welcomes ideas for new articles or features.

The Big Issue in Scotland

71 Oxford Street, Glasgow, G5 9EP

☎ 0141 418 7000
🖷 0141 418 7061
📧 editorial@bigissuescotland.com
🌐 www.bigissuescotland.com

Parent Company Big Issue Ltd
Editor Clare Harris
Established 1993
Insider Info A weekly consumer magazine covering current affairs, entertainment, environment, news and local interest. Present circulation is 22,210.
Non-fiction Publishes news, current affairs, features and local interest (Scotland) articles.
Tips The Big Issue in Scotland will also publish international news stories or features.

The Big Issue in the North

135–141 Oldham Street, Manchester, M4 1LL

☎ 0161 834 6300
🖷 0161 819 5000
🌐 www.bigissueinthenorth.com

Parent Company Big Issue Ltd
Editor Matt Baker

Established 1992
Insider Info A weekly consumer magazine covering current affairs, entertainment and local interest. Present circulation is 23,572.
Non-fiction Publishes news, current affairs, features and local interest (Wales) articles.
Tips *The Big Issue in the North* will also publish short stories or poetry, but only from homeless people.

The Big Issue South West
5 Brunswick Court, Brunswick Square, Bristol, BS2 8PE
☎ 0117 916 6593
✉ 0117 916 6599
✉ editorial@bigissuesouthwest.co.uk
🌐 www.bigissuesouthwest.co.uk
Parent Company Big Issue Ltd
Editor Rachel Howells
Established 1991
Insider Info A weekly consumer magazine covering current affairs, entertainment, news and local interest. Present circulation is 12,582.
Non-fiction Publishes news, current affairs, features, arts coverage and local interest (South West) articles.
Tips *The Big Issue South West* will consider unsolicited material.

Bike
Media House, Lynchwood, Peterborough Business Park, Peterborough, PE2 6EA
☎ 01733 468181
✉ 01733 468196
✉ bike@bauer.com
🌐 www.bikemagazine.co.uk
Parent Company Bauer Consumer Media
Editor Steve Rose
Contact Deputy Editor, Ben Miller; Senior Art Editor, Garry Mears
Established 1971
Insider Info A monthly consumer magazine covering motorcycling. Present circulation is 81,579.
Non-fiction Publishes photo features, news, profiles, product reviews, events listings and road test articles.
Tips *Bike* covers all aspects of motorcycling including sports bikes.

Birding World
Sea Lawn, Coast Road, Cley next the Sea, Holt, Norfolk, NR25 7RZ
☎ 01263 740913
✉ 01263 741173
✉ steve@birdingworld.co.uk
🌐 www.birdingworld.co.uk
Editor Steve Gantlett
Established 1987

Insider Info A monthly consumer magazine, covering birds and birdwatching topics. Present circulation is roughly 6,000. Accepts queries by mail or email. Writer's guidelines and sample copies are free on request and available with SAE.
Non-fiction Publishes photo features and other features on birds.
Submission Guidelines Accepts queries to the Editor before submitting completed manuscript.
Images Good quality bird photographs are always welcomed. Lesser quality photographs are also welcomed when they depict particularly rare birds.
* Pays between £5 and £30 per photo.
Submission Guidelines Accepts gif/jpeg files with captions. Send photos with submissions to the Editor, Steve Gantlett.
Tips Aimed at keen birdwatchers in Britain and throughout Europe, as well as North American and Worldwide birders.

Birds
The Lodge, Sandy, Bedfordshire, SG19 2DL
☎ 01767 680551
✉ 01767 683262
✉ rob.hume@rspb.org.uk
🌐 www.rspb.org.uk
Parent Company The RSPB
Editor Rob Hume
Established 1900
Insider Info A quarterly, RSPB members only consumer magazine, covering wild birds (not captive or pets, nor welfare of sick and injured birds), other wildlife and habitat conservation. Present circulation of 616,197. 25 per cent of the publication is written by freelance writers. Takes on average six months between acceptance of a manuscript and publication. Payment is upon publication, never with contributor copies instead of cash. A byline is given. Publication is copyrighted and all rights are purchased. Average editorial lead time is three months and seasonal material must be submitted six months in advance. Accepts queries by mail, phone or email. Aims to respond to queries and manuscripts within two weeks. Sometimes pays the expenses of writers on assignment, with a limit agreed upon in advance. Sample copies and writer's guidelines are free on request.
Non-fiction Publishes photo features, essays, features and personal experience articles.
* Payment for assigned and unsolicited articles is by negotiation.
Submission Guidelines Accepts query with published clips for articles between 750 and 2,000 words. Approach Rob Hume, Editor. Ideas are welcome but space limited – good writers are always required but 'RSPB led' subject matter and regular features inevitably dominate and leave little

flexibility for other material. Do not send entire manuscript.

Images Uses images within features.

* Pays standard fees and buys one-time rights.

Submission Guidelines Identification of subjects is required, as is a statement regarding captive subjects. Send photos with submission to Picture Researcher, Lisa Fell.

Tips The magazine is essentially about the RSPB and what it does and why, with members' support; however, within that, evocation of wildlife experiences and features on conservation issues are also published. Articles need to be accurate and reliable but readable and enjoyable. Email or phone the Editor, with specific ideas, to discuss possibilities. There are no formal writer's guidelines, but information will be given when applicable.

Bird Watching

Media House, Peterborough Business Park, Lynch Wood, Peterborough, PE2 6EA

- 01733 468000
- 01733 468387
- kevin.wilmot@bauer.com
- www.birdwatching.co.uk

Parent Company Bauer Consumer Media
Editor Kevin Wilmot
Contact Reviews Editor, Carol Debney
Established 1986
Insider Info A monthly consumer magazine covering birdwatching. Present circulation is 19,763.
Non-fiction Publishes photo features, walking guides, spotting news, activities and product review articles.
Images Publishes wildlife photography, with a strong focus on birds.
Submission Guidelines Accepts query to the editor before submitting.
Tips *Bird Watching* contains articles about bird sightings in the UK, walking guides, expert tips and product reviews.

Bizarre

30 Cleveland Street, London, W1T 4JD

- 020 7907 6000
- 020 7907 6020
- bizarre@dennis.co.uk
- www.bizarremag.com

Parent Company Dennis Publishing Ltd
Editor David McComb
Established 1997
Insider Info A monthly consumer magazine covering men's lifestyle topics. Present circulation of 50,132. Accepts queries by mail or email.
Non-fiction Publishes articles on events from around the world, drug culture and news, interviews with famous counter culture figures and showcases of cult directors, musicians and authors.

* Pays £80 per 1,000 words.

Submission Guidelines Accepts queries with outlines for articles of between 800 and 2,000 words. No unsolicited manuscripts.

Images Accepts images with submission.

* Pays a variable fee per photo.

Submission Guidelines Accepts transparencies and prints. State availability of photos with submission.

Tips The magazine features tend to concern unusual news on many different types of fetishistic and deviant behaviour that the mainstream media would most likely stereotype as bizarre. Does not accept unsolicited manuscripts, but does appreciate ideas for features. Study the magazine for style and content before submitting synopsis via post or email.

Black Static

5 Martins Lane, Witcham, Ely, CB6 2LB

- 01353 777931
- andy@ttapress.demon.co.uk
- www.ttapress.com

Parent Company TTA Press
Editor Andy Cox
Established 1993
Insider Info A bi-monthly consumer magazine, covering genre fiction writing. Present circulation is roughly 10,000. 100 per cent of the publication is written by freelance writers. Payment is upon acceptance of manuscript. A byline is given. Accepts queries by mail or email. Writer's guidelines are available online.
Fiction Publishes horror, science fiction, experimental, fantasy and slipstream.

* Pays £30 per 1,000 words.

Submission Guidelines Send complete manuscript. Does not want general fiction/romance/etc.

Tips Contains a mix of new fiction, artwork, interesting features and provocative comment. It often transcends the genre divide between science fiction/fantasy/horror and mainstream literature. It is strongly recommended that you study the magazine before submitting as this will greatly improve your chances of acceptance. Story content often goes against the grain of 'traditional' genre writing. Formerly known as *The Third Alternative*.

Bliss

Brockbourne House, Mount Ephrain, Tunbridge Wells, TN4 8BS

- 01892 500100
- 01892 546666
- bliss@panini.co.uk

🐦 www.mybliss.co.uk
Parent Company Panini UK Ltd
Editor Leslie Sinoway
Contact Features Editor, Angeli Milburn; Features
Writer, Rebecca Davies
Established 1995
Insider Info A monthly consumer magazine
covering teenage girls' lifestyle topics. Present
Circulation of 107,112. A media pack is
available online.
Non-fiction Publishes general interest features,
interviews and photo features on television, real life,
fashion, beauty, celebrities, health and
entertainment.
Tips The magazine's target audience is girls aged 12
to 18. The website gives a good idea as to the
magazine's style, and has its own editorial content.

Blithe Spirit
12 Eliot Vale, Blackheath, London, SE3 0UW
☎ 01547 528542
☎ 01547 520685
🐦 www.britishhaikusociety.org
Parent Company British Haiku Society
Editor Graham High
Established 1990
Insider Info A quarterly consumer literary journal,
specialising in British haiku. Present circulation of
roughly 300. A byline is given. Queries accepted by
mail. Sample copy and writer's guidelines
available online.
Non-fiction Publishes articles on poetry (haiku in
particular), features, reviews and interviews/profiles.
Submission Guidelines Accepts submissions from
subscribers only.
Poetry Publishes haiku poetry.
Tips Regularly contains original poems, articles
about the writing and appreciation of haiku and
related forms, book reviews, letters to the editor, and
announcements of haiku awards and news. The
editorial policy is to encourage new writing, value a
diversity of approaches to haiku, and promote
excellence. The magazine operates as a membership
magazine, and as such, only accepts submissions
from subscribers. However, non-members may be
invited to contribute as featured writers.

Bonmarché
**Victory House, 14 Leicester Place, Leicester
Square, London, WC2H 7BZ**
☎ 020 7306 0304
☎ 020 7306 0314
✉ jdavis@riverltd.co.uk
🐦 www.bonmarche.co.uk/magazine.php
Parent Company River Publishing Ltd
Editor Sarah Touquet

Contact Sub-Editor, Jassy Davis
Established 2003
Insider Info A quarterly consumer magazine
covering fashion and shopping. Present circulation
is 127,206.
Non-fiction Publishes features, interviews, profiles,
product reviews, puzzles and travel articles.
Tips *Bonmarché* is the official magazine of the
Bonmarché clothes shop, whose customer base is
made up of women aged 45 plus.

Book & Magazine Collector
**Unit 101, 140 Wales Farm Road, London,
W3 6UG**
☎ 020 8752 8172
☎ 020 8752 8185
✉ chris.peachment@metropolis.co.uk
Parent Company Diamond Publishing Ltd
Editor Chris Peachment
Established 1984
Insider Info A journal, with 13 issues per year, that
covers all aspects of collecting books and
magazines. Accepts queries by mail or email.
Non-fiction Interested in bibliographical articles
related to collectible authors, books or magazines.
Tips Articles must be bibliographical in nature and
include a full bibliography and price guide.

The Book Collector
PO Box 12426, London, W11 3GW
☎ 020 7792 3492
☎ 020 7792 3492
✉ nicolasb@nixnet.clara.co.uk
Parent Company The Collector Ltd
Editor Nicolas Barker
Established 1952
Insider Info A quarterly journal that covers all
aspects of studying and collecting books. Accepts
queries by mail or email.
Non-fiction Interested in biographical and
bibliographical articles related to book collecting.
Tips Also incorporates the journal *Bibliographical
Notes & Queries*.

The Book Magazine
PO Box 37, Southrop, Lechlade, GL7 3ZX
☎ 01285 750212
✉ christine.kidney@thebookmagazine.co.uk
🐦 www.thebookmagazine.co.uk
Parent Company The Book Magazine
Editor Christine Kidney
Established 2006
Insider Info A quarterly consumer magazine,
covering literary and book related subjects. Present
circulation 50,000. Accepts queries by mail
and email.

Non-fiction Publishes articles, book reviews, author interviews, opinion (excluding letters to the Editor) and features on book-related subjects. Regular features include 'Bookworld', 'Reading Group' and 'Writer Revisited'.

Submission Guidelines Send query before sending submissions.

Fiction Publishes book excerpts and poetry.

Tips Articles in *The Book Magazine* are generally privately commissioned by the Editor, although they are willing to accept ideas for future articles by email.

The Bookseller

5th Floor, Endeavour House, 189 Shaftesbury Avenue, London, WC2H 8TJ
- 020 7420 6006
- 020 7420 6103
- philip.jones@bookseller.co.uk
- www.thebookseller.com

Parent Company VNU Entertainment Media
Contact Editor-in-Chief, Neil Denny; Managing Editor, Philip Jones; Children's Books Staff Writer, Caroline Horn; Features Editor, Tom Tivnan
Established 1858
Insider Info A trade magazine, issued weekly, covering the book trade.
Non-fiction Publishes news, features, interviews, bestseller charts and information on the book publishing trade.
Tips *The Bookseller* covers the whole of the book publishing industry, and also publishes a regular *Children's Bookseller* supplement that focuses exclusively on the children's book trade. Book trade news and articles are also available on the website, which is updated daily.

Books for Keeps

1 Effingham Road, London, SE12 8NZ
- 020 8852 4953
- 020 8318 7580
- enquiries@booksforkeeps.co.uk
- www.booksforkeeps.co.uk

Parent Company School Bookshop Association Ltd
Editor Rosemary Stones
Established 1980
Insider Info A bi-monthly consumer magazine covering the children's book industry. Present circulation of roughly 8,500. Accepts queries by mail or email. Sample copy is available online.
Non-fiction Publishes articles on children's poetry, features, interviews/profiles, reviews, general interest articles and opinions (excluding letters to the Editor).
Submission Guidelines Accepts queries.
Fiction Publishes some children's fiction.
Tips Aimed at adults, mostly teachers, librarians and parents. It contains articles about the latest

developments in children's books, interviews and reviews, excerpts and critical essays. Articles tend to lean towards an academic and critically informative style.

Books Ireland

11 Newgrove Avenue, Dublin 4, Republic of Ireland
- 00353 1 269 2185
- booksi@eircom.net

Editor Jeremy Addis
Established 1976
Insider Info A trade and consumer magazine with nine issues per year, covering Irish interest books and Irish publishing. 65 per cent of the publication is written by freelance writers. It takes on average, two months to publish a manuscript after acceptance. Payment is upon publication, and never with a sample copy instead of cash. A byline is given. Publication is copyrighted and first rights are purchased. Editorial lead time is one month. Seasonal material should be submitted six weeks in advance. Accepts queries by email. Aims to respond to queries in three days and manuscripts within two weeks. Will not pay the expenses of writers on assignments. Sample copy available for £3. Writer's guidelines are available via email.
Non-fiction Publishes Interviews and Profiles by prior arrangement, about new books of Irish interest. Also publishes commissioned book reviews.
* Buys 126 non-fiction manuscripts per year. Payment (in Euros) is agreed by arrangement for assigned articles. Does not pay for unsolicited articles.
Submission Guidelines Accepts queries, with published clips, for articles of between 1,000 and 3,000 words.
Tips Particularly interested in interviews with Irish authors and publishers.

Book Talk

115 Anglesea Road, Ipswich, IP1 3PJ
- 01473 250949
- sblbooktalk@btinternet.com
- www.sbl.org.uk

Parent Company The Suffolk Book League
Editor Kay McElhinney
Established 1982
Insider Info A quarterly consumer newsletter covering The Sussex Book League's news and events as well as more general literature topics. Present circulation of roughly 200.
Non-fiction Publishes features, interviews/profiles, reviews and news articles.
Tips Due to the nature of the newsletter, much of the content is sourced internally.

Book World Magazine

2 Caversham Street, London, SW3 4AH

- 020 7351 4995
- 020 7351 4995
- leonard.holdsworth@btopenworld.com

Parent Company Christchurch Publishers Ltd
Editor Leonard Holdsworth
Contact Features Editor, James Hughes
Established 1972

Insider Info A monthly trade journal covering the world of books. Present circulation of roughly 6,000. 50 per cent of the publication is written by freelance writers. Takes on average two months between a manuscript's acceptance and its publication. Payment is upon publication, never with contributor copies instead of cash. Byline is given. Publication is copyrighted and all rights are purchased. Average editorial lead time is two months. Seasonal material should be submitted three months in advance. Accepts queries by mail, email and fax. Aims to respond to queries and manuscripts within two weeks. Does not pay the expenses of writers on assignment. Sample copy available for £2. Media pack available on request.
Non-fiction Publishes essays, features, interviews/profiles and general interest articles.
* Payment for assigned and unsolicited articles is by negotiation.
Submission Guidelines Accepts queries for articles of up to 5,000 words. No reprints. Contact James Hughes.
Images Contact James Hughes for images submissions.
Tips Aimed at serious book collectors, librarians and booksellers. The magazine's emphasis is on more erudite and literary books.

Boots Health & Beauty

7 St Martin's Place, London, WC2N 4HA

- 020 7747 0700
- 020 7747 0649
- www.redwoodgroup.net

Parent Company Redwood
Editor Jane Druker
Contact Deputy Editor, Lisa Reich' Chief Sub-Editor, Charlotte Price
Established 1999

Insider Info A bi-monthly consumer magazine covering healthcare. Present circulation is roughly 1,800,000.
Non-fiction Publishes features, product reviews and advice articles.
Tips Boots Health & Beauty is the magazine of Boots the Chemist and publishes a wide range of product reviews and health and beauty tips focusing on Boots' product ranges.

Borderlines

Nant y Brithyll, Llangynyw, Welshpool, Powys, SY21 0JS

- 01938 810263

Parent Company Anglo-Welsh Poetry Society
Editor Kevin Bamford
Established 1986

Insider Info A consumer magazine with two issues per year, covering poetry and poetry related topics. Present circulation is 200. Byline is given. Accepts queries by mail or phone. Will pay the expenses of writers on assignment. Writer's guidelines and sample copy available online.
Non-fiction Publishes articles on poetry.
Poetry Publishes avant-garde, free verse, haiku, light verse and traditional poetry.
Tips Borderlines is a long-running general literary magazine that publishes any kind of poetry from anyone, anywhere. It is open to any kind of poetry submission but the editors generally do not accept long poems.

Brand Strategy Magazine

Strategic Thinking for Today's Marketing Professional
St Giles House, 50 Poland Street, London, W1F 7AX

- 020 7970 4000
- ruth.mortimer@centaur.co.uk
- www.brandstrategy.co.uk

Parent Company Centaur Media Plc
Editor Ruth Mortimer
Established 2005

Insider Info A monthly trade magazine with a daily blog and monthly newsletter. Covers the global branding industry, advertising, marketing and new trends in the business world. Present circulation is roughly 1,000. Ten per cent of the publication is written by freelance writers. Takes on average one month between acceptance of manuscript, to publication. Payment is upon publication and a byline is given. Publication is copyrighted. Average editorial lead time is one month. Seasonal material must be submitted one month in advance. Accepts queries by mail or email. Writer's guidelines and sample copy are available online. Editorial calendar is not available as they do not produce forward features.
Non-fiction Publishes business articles.
Submission Guidelines Accepts queries to Ruth Mortimer, Editor.
Images Accepts images with submission.
* Negotiates payment individually for images. Purchases all rights.
Tips A global marketing and business publication, whose audience is Chief Marketing Officers and other Senior Executives. All articles aim to help

British Journalism Review

Sage Publications, 1 Oliver's Yard, 55 City Road, London, EC1Y 1SP

- 📞 020 7324 8500
- 📠 020 7324 8600
- ✉ info@sagepub.co.uk
- 🌐 www.bjr.org.uk

Parent Company Sage Publications
Editor Bill Hagerty
Established 1989
Insider Info A quarterly consumer magazine that covers journalism and the media. Accepts queries by mail or email.
Non-fiction Interested in comment, criticism, general interest and review articles related to the media.
Submission Guidelines Accepts queries and completed manuscript submissions of between 1,500 to 3,000 words.

British Journal of Photography

The Professionals' Weekly

32–34 Broadwick Street, London, W1A 2HG

- 📞 020 7316 9376
- 📠 020 7316 9003
- ✉ bjp.features@bjphoto.co.uk
- 🌐 www.bjp-online.com

Parent Company Incisive Media Publications
Editor Simon Bainbridge
Contact Deputy Editor, Diane Smyth
Established 1854
Insider Info A weekly trade journal covering professional photography; technical reviews and issues, business matters relating to the industry, interviews with photographers, and in-depth pieces on specialist areas of the market. Present circulation of 5,592. 30 per cent of the publication is written by freelance writers. Takes on average three weeks between the acceptance of a manuscript, to its publication. Payment is made approximately 30 days after publication and never with a free contributor copy instead of cash. Byline is given. Average editorial lead time is eight weeks. Accepts queries by email. Will not pay the expenses of writers on assignment. Writer's guidelines and editorial calendars are free on request.
Non-fiction Publishes book excerpts (occasionally) how-to (only if high-end technical), photo features (often, but unpaid), essays, (occasionally), features, interviews/profiles (usually assigned rather than suggested), reviews (limited opportunities), new product articles (two per issue), technical articles (freelancers must have specialist knowledge), opinions (around ten a year; writer must have some relevant position in photography), and market reports on specialist areas such as fashion, or architecture.
* Purchases 120 Non-fiction manuscripts per year. Payment is negotiable, but between approximately £150 and £1,000.
Submission Guidelines Accepts queries, with published clips, for articles of between 500 and 2,000 words.
Tips Aimed at everyone involved in the professional photography market in the UK, including photographers, picture editors, trade, students and aspiring professionals. Aims to inform them of the latest news, trends, technologies and issues in contemporary photography. They tend to find their own photographers to interview, and are more interested in ideas for specialist areas or issue-based material from freelancers. Be aware that they focus on contemporary photographers and issues and look at photography in a way that is very distinct from most other (amateur oriented) photo publications. Think about what professional photographers already assume, and what they need to learn from an article. It must be tightly focused on their needs and aspirations.

British Medical Journal

BMA House, Tavistock Square, London, WC1H 9JR

- 📞 020 7387 4499
- 📠 020 7383 6418
- ✉ editor@bmj.com
- 🌐 www.bmj.com

Parent Company BMJ Publishing Group
Editor Dr. Fiona Godlee
Established 1840
Insider Info A weekly consumer magazine covering medicine and hospital science. Accepts queries by mail or email. Present circulation is 120,606.
Tips The *BMJ* is aimed at professionals working in medicine or the health sector.

Brittle Star

PO Box 56108, London, E17 0AY

- ✉ magazine@brittlestar.org.uk
- 🌐 www.brittlestar.org.uk

Contact Editors: Louisa Hooper, Jacqueline Gabbitas, David Floyd, Martin Parker
Established 1999
Insider Info A consumer magazine with three issues per year, covering poetry and fiction. Present circulation of 200. 100 per cent of the publication is written by freelance writers. Byline is given. Accepts queries by mail or email. Aims to respond to queries

clients and agencies understand branding, trends and business philosophy in a detailed way that benefits the bottom line.

and manuscripts within six weeks after the relevant submission deadline. Writer's guidelines are available online.

Non-fiction Publishes articles on poetry, features, interviews/profiles and general interest articles.

Submission Guidelines Accepts queries by post with published clips.

Fiction Publishes short fiction.

Submission Guidelines Send complete manuscript of up to 1,200 words by post.

Poetry Publishes avant-garde, free verse, light verse and traditional poetry.

Submission Guidelines Accepts up to four sample poems by post.

Tips *Brittle Star* is a small literary magazine which contains new poems, stories and interviews with authors. It is especially committed to giving new writers a chance to get their poetry published, but also has some space for more established writers. The magazine prefers to have submissions by post. Also, authors should include a short biography of no more than 40 words, for use if the piece is selected.

Broadcast
Greater London House, Hampstead Road, London, NW1 7EJ
- 020 7728 5542
- 020 7728 5555
- lisa.campbell@emap.com
- www.broadcastnow.co.uk

Parent Company EMAP Plc
Editor Lisa Campbell
Contact Features Editor, Emily Booth; News Editor, Chris Curtis
Insider Info A weekly trade journal covering broadcast media. Present circulation is 9,702.
Non-fiction Publishes industry news, profiles, special reports and ratings.
Tips *Broadcast* is a business publication aimed at decision makers within the broadcasting industry. It contains articles on the latest developments within television, radio, cable and satellite.

Buckinghamshire Countryside
PO Box 5, Hitchin, Hertfordshire, SG5 1GJ
- 01462 431237
- 01462 422015
- martin_small@btconnect.com

Parent Company Beaumonde Publications Ltd
Editor Sandra Small
Established 1995
Insider Info A bi-monthly consumer magazine covering Buckinghamshire. Accepts queries by mail or email.
Non-fiction Interested in local interest articles related to Buckinghamshire.

Submission Guidelines Accepts queries and completed manuscript submissions of up to 1,000 words.

Bunkered
50 High Craighill Road, Glasgow, G4 9UD
- 0141 353 2222
- 0141 332 3811
- mdempster@bunkered.co.uk
- www.bunkered.co.uk

Parent Company Pro-Sports Promotions Ltd
Editor Martin Dempster
Contact Publisher, Paul Grant
Established 1996
Insider Info A bi-monthly consumer magazine covering golf. Present circulation is 26,858.
Non-fiction Publishes features, interviews, profiles, product reviews and instruction articles.
Tips *Bunkered* covers all aspects of golf including reviews of the latest products, player profiles and practical instruction articles. It is aimed at golfers of all skill levels.

The Burlington Magazine
14–16 Duke's Road, London, WC1H 9SZ
- 020 7388 8157
- 020 7388 1230
- editorial@burlington.org.uk
- www.burlington.org.uk

Editor Richard Shone
Contact Deputy Editor, Bart Cornelis
Established 1903
Insider Info An academic periodical, issued monthly. Founded in 1903 by a group of eminent art critics and historians, *The Burlington Magazine* is the world's leading monthly art periodical. 75 per cent of the publication is written by freelance writers. Submissions are published up to ten months after acceptance. Publication is copyrighted and a byline is given. Seasonal material must be submitted 12 months in advance. Accepts queries by mail and email. Accepts simultaneous submissions. Aims to respond to queries within one day and manuscripts within three months. Assignment expenses are sometimes paid (limit agreed upon in advance). Sample copy is available for £14.40. Writer's guidelines are available free on request. Editorial calendars are available via email. Media packs are available online.
Non-fiction Interested in essays, historical writing and unpublished fine art research of the highest quality.
Submission Guidelines Articles must be 1,000–5,000. Address submissions to Editorial Assistant, Helen Oakden.
Images Accepts images with submission.

* Negotiates payment for images individually.
Submission Guidelines State the availability of photos with submission. Send as transparencies or gif/jpeg files, with captions. Contact Editorial Assistant, Helen Oakden.

Tips Covers all aspects of the fine and decorative arts, from ancient times to the present day. They only accept contributors who have a fine arts degree at a very high level, and whose writings conclude extensive archival research.

The Burns Chronicle

1 Cairnsmore Road, Castle Douglas, DG7 1BN
- 01556 504448
- 01556 504448
- admin@worldburnsclub.com
- www.worldburnsclub.com

Parent Company The Robert Burns World Federation Ltd
Editor Peter J. Westwood
Established 1892
Insider Info The annual publication of The Robert Burns World Federation, which prints historical articles about Scotland and Robert Burns, as well as previously unpublished fiction and poetry from Burns and his contemporaries. *The Burns Chronicle* publishes up to date articles and news from the Burns Club, and more contemporary fiction and poetry. Present circulation is roughly 1,200. Byline is given. Accepts queries by mail and email.
Non-fiction Publishes essays, poetry, interviews/profiles, general interest and historical articles.
Submission Guidelines Send query before sending submissions.
Fiction Publishes fiction.
Tips *The Burns Chronicle* generally prints articles and writing from Burns Federation members, but unsolicited submissions with new or ground breaking writing, or research on Robert Burns may be well received.

Business Life

Pegasus House, 37–43 Sackville Street, London, W1S 3EH
- 020 7534 2400
- 020 7534 2401
- businesslife@cedarcom.co.uk
- www.cedarcom.co.uk/business_life.html

Parent Company Cedar Communications
Editor Tim Hulse
Contact Deputy Editor, Bryony Coleman; Art Editor, Belinda Tighe
Established 1986
Insider Info An in-flight monthly consumer magazine, covering business and lifestyle. Present circulation is 96,184. Media pack is available online.

Non-fiction Publishes news, features and travel articles.
Tips *Business Life* is a lifestyle magazine distributed to British Airways business passengers travelling on the UK and continental European routes. It covers a range of subjects including business, travel, fashion, film and sport and aims to 'put a business twist on lifestyle subjects'.

Business Traveller

Cardinal House, 39–40 Albemarle Street, London, W1S 4TE
- 020 7647 6330
- 020 7647 6331
- editorial@businesstraveller.com
- www.businesstraveller.com

Parent Company Perry Publications Ltd
Editor Tom Otley
Established 1976
Insider Info A monthly consumer magazine covering all aspects of business travel. Present circulation of 57,394. Accepts queries by mail.
Non-fiction Publishes features and articles on business travel.
Submission Guidelines Accepts queries by post with published clips, plus CV.
Images State availability of photos with submission.
Tips Specialises in articles, features and news aimed at individual, frequent, international business travellers. Submit ideas via post, but please ensure that the topic is firmly business travel only, rather than leisure.

Business Travel World

Greater London House, Hampstead Road, London, NW1 7EJ
- 020 7728 3642
- 020 7505 8573
- btw.editorial@emap.com
- www.businesstravelworld.com

Parent Company EMAP Plc
Contact Editorial Director, Betty Low; Deputy Editor, Ian Morgan; Publisher, Tessa Cook
Established 1993
Insider Info A monthly trade journal covering business travel. Present circulation is 7,943.
Non-fiction Publishes news, views, forecast and feature articles on the international business travel market.

Cadenza

Broadlea House, Heron Way, Hickling, Norfolk, NR12 0YQ
- eds@cadenza-magazine.co.uk
- www.cadenza-magazine.co.uk

Editor Zoe King

Established 2000

Insider Info A consumer magazine with two issues per year, focusing on poetry and short fiction. Payment is upon publication and a byline is given. Accepts queries by mail or email. Previously published submissions are accepted. Writer's guidelines are available online.

Non-fiction Publishes articles on poetry and all other aspects of creative writing.

Submission Guidelines Send complete manuscript of up to 2,000 words by email only.

Fiction Publishes mainstream and experimental fiction.

Submission Guidelines Send complete manuscript pf up to 3,000 words by email only.

Poetry Publishes avant-garde, free verse, light verse and traditional poetry.

Submission Guidelines Accepts poems of up to 40 lines. Submit to Poetry Editor, William Conelly, by email only.

Tips *Cadenza* is an independent literary magazine that publishes new poetry and short fiction, articles, interviews with published authors, and market information for fiction and poetry writers. It is looking for fiction writers with unique voices to produce 'crackling, vibrant work' and those who are prepared to take some risks with their writing. For poetry, *Cadenza* has in-depth submissions guidelines on their website.

Caduceus
9 Nine Acres, Midhurst, West Sussex, GU29 9EP
- 01730 816799
- 01730 816799
- caduceus@caduceus.info
- www.caduceus.info

Editor Simon Best

Established 1987

Insider Info A quarterly consumer journal covering health and healing, holistic medicine, ecology, science and spirituality.

Non-fiction Publishes photo features, inspirational articles, features, technical and general interest articles.

Tips *Caduceus* is an independent journal, which investigates 'critical issues ahead of mainstream media, searches out pioneers who are lighting the way for humanity, and keeps readers up to date with developments worldwide.' Tends to publish articles from academics and experienced workers from the healing and spirituality community.

Caduta Arts Review
23 Southgate Road, Tenterden, Kent, TN30 7BS
- caduta@hotmail.co.uk
- www.caduta.org.uk

Established 2006

Insider Info A consumer magazine with three issues per year, covering arts subjects such as photography, painting, poetry, prose, and drama. Byline is given. Queries accepted by mail or email. Writer's guidelines are available online.

Non-fiction Publishes photo feature, articles on poetry, and features.

Submission Guidelines Send complete manuscript.

Fiction Publishes mainstream short fiction.

Submission Guidelines Send complete manuscript of up to ten pages.

Poetry Publishes avant-garde, free verse, light verse and traditional poetry.

Submission Guidelines Accepts up to six sample poems.

Tips A new magazine that aims to promote new and diverse talent in the arts. Accepts submissions from a wide range of arts categories, which will be published on the website as competition entries. The best selected pieces will then be printed in the magazine. *Caduta Arts Review* does not pay for work, but offers a prize of £50 for the best selected entry.

Cage & Aviary Birds
Blue Fin Building, 110 Southwark Road, London, SE1 0SU
- 020 3148 4171
- 020 3148 8129
- birds@ipcmedia.com
- www.ipcmedia.com

Parent Company IPC Media Ltd

Editor Kim Forrester

Established 1902

Insider Info A weekly consumer magazine, covering bird keeping. Circulation is 16,045. Media pack available online.

Non-fiction Publishes bird keeping, product reviews, news and technical tips articles.

Tips *Cage & Aviary Birds* is the UK's only bird keeping magazine and publishes the latest news, reviews and tips from the aviculture community. The magazine also has a detailed classified section.

Cambridgeshire Agenda
Alexander House, 1 Milton Road, Cambridge, CB4 1UY
- 01223 309227
- 01223 309226
- editorial@thecambridgeagenda.co.uk
- www.thecambridgeagenda.co.uk

Parent Company Life Publishing Ltd

Editor Justin Coleman

Contact Associate Publisher, Claire Curran

Insider Info A monthly, regional, consumer magazine covering lifestyle topics in the Cambridgeshire area. Present circulation of roughly 30,000. 100 per cent of the publication is written by freelance writers. Manuscripts are published four weeks after acceptance. Payment is upon acceptance. Byline given and publication is copyrighted. Editorial lead time is two months and seasonal material must be submitted two months in advance. Accepts queries by mail or email.

Non-fiction Publishes articles on beauty/health, fashion, travel, interiors and arts.

Tips All topics must be related to the Cambridgeshire area and be relevant to its residents.

Cambridgeshire Journal
Winship Road, Milton, Cambridge, CB4 6PP
- 01223 434434
- 01223 434415

Parent Company Cambridge Newspapers Ltd
Editor Debbie Tweedie
Established 1994
Insider Info A monthly consumer magazine covering Cambridgeshire. Accepts queries by mail or email.
Non-fiction Interested in local interest and lifestyle articles related to Cambridgeshire.
Submission Guidelines Accepts queries and completed manuscript submissions of up to 1,500 words.

Campaign
161 Hammersmith Road, London, W6 8SD
- campaign@haymarket.com
- www.brandrepublic.com/campaign

Parent Company Haymarket Publishing
Editor Claire Beale
Established 1968
Insider Info A weekly trade magazine covering the world of advertising. Present circulation of 10,112. Accepts queries by mail or email. Editorial calendar is available online.
Non-fiction Publishes feature articles.
Submission Guidelines Accepts queries for articles of up to 2,000 words.
Fillers Uses newsbreaks of up to 320 words.
Tips Aimed at media moguls and advertising addicts, which makes it a good way to influence key opinion formers. Articles featuring insider knowledge and the latest scoops are ideal, but propose ideas in writing first as *Campaign* is not keen on unsolicited submissions.

Camping & Caravanning
Greenfields House, Westwood Way, Coventry, CV4 8JH
- 024 7647 5300
- 024 7647 5413
- magazine@thefriendlyclub.co.uk
- www.campingandcaravanningclub.co.uk

Parent Company Camping & Caravanning Club
Editor Simon McGrath
Contact Features Editor, Sue Taylor; News Editor, Laura Rainbow
Established 1905
Insider Info A monthly consumer magazine covering camping and caravanning. Present circulation is 209,042.
Non-fiction Publishes features, road tests, product and equipment reviews, tips and travel articles.
Tips *Camping & Caravanning* is the official publication of the Camping & Caravanning Club and is distributed to members on a monthly basis.

Candelabrum Poetry Magazine
1 Chatsworth Court, Outram Road, Southsea, PO5 1RA
- rcp@poetry7.fsnet.co.uk
- www.members.tripod.com/redcandlepress

Parent Company Red Candle Press
Editor Len McCarthy
Established 1970
Insider Info A consumer poetry magazine with two issues per year. Present circulation of 900. Byline is given.
Non-fiction Publishes articles and features on poetry.
Submission Guidelines Accepts queries.
Poetry Publishes haiku and traditional poetry.
Tips Interested primarily in formalist poetry with traditional metrical and rhymed forms. The magazine prints articles and poems from new and established formalist poets. While *Candelabrum* specialises in formalist poetry, it doesn't disregard free verse or other forms, although they are less likely to be successful if they are submitted.

Candis
Newhall Lane, Hoylake, Wirral, CH47 4BQ
- 0151 632 7641
- 0870 745 3003
- debbie@candis.co.uk
- www.candis.co.uk

Parent Company Newhall Publications Ltd
Editor Debbie Attewell
Contact Senior Sub-Editor, Lucy Higgins; Art Director, Becky Haslam
Established 1962
Insider Info A monthly consumer magazine covering women's interest. Present circulation is 296,103. Sample copy is free on request or available online.

Non-fiction Publishes features, profiles, practical articles, advice and true-life stories. Subjects covered include health, beauty, fashion and relationship advice.

Fiction Publishes short stories.

Tips *Candis* is a subscription-only magazine that covers a wide range of general and women's interest topics, competitions and stories. It is aimed primarily at women with families. *Candis* does publish true-life stories and the occasional piece of short fiction.

The Cannon's Mouth

22 Margaret Grove, Harborne, Birmingham, B17 9JH

- ☏ 0121 426 6413
- ☏ info@cannonpoets.co.uk
- ☏ www.cannonpoets.co.uk

Parent Company Cannon Poets Group

Editor Greg Cox

Established 1983

Insider Info The quarterly journal of the Cannon Poets group. Prints new poetry and articles from subscribers and non-subscribers alike, and aims to stimulate interest in the writing of poetry and its presentation to the public. Byline is given. Queries accepted by mail and email.

Non-fiction Publishes poetry features.

Submission Guidelines Send query before sending submissions.

Poetry Publishes free verse, light verse and traditional verse.

Tips *Cannon's Mouth* now accepts submissions from non-subscribers, but the standard of poetry printed may vary, as the journal focuses on improving writing in progress through peer assessment.

Car

Media House, Lynchwood, Peterborough Business Park, Peterborough, PE2 6EA

- ☏ 01733 468379
- ☏ 01733 468660
- ☏ car@emap.com
- ☏ www.carmagazine.co.uk

Parent Company EMAP Plc

Editor Phil McNamara

Contact Publisher, Mark Frost; Associate Editor, Tim Pollard; Art Director, Andy Thomas

Established 1962

Insider Info A monthly consumer magazine covering cars. Present circulation is 68,126.

Non-fiction Publishes news, features, technical and review articles.

Tips Covers the new car market and developments in the industry. Articles focus on the latest performance cars, new car and product reviews, and expert advice on any motoring or car owning issues.

The Caravan Club Magazine

East Grinstead House, Wood Street, East Grinstead, RH19 1UA

- ☏ 01342 336804
- ☏ 01342 410258
- ☏ enquiries@caravanclub.co.uk
- ☏ www.caravanclub.co.uk

Parent Company Caravan Club

Editor Gary Martin

Contact Deputy Editor, George Hinton

Established 1964

Insider Info A monthly consumer magazine covering caravanning. Present circulation is 365,048.

Non-fiction Publishes features, news, reviews, travel and technical articles.

Tips *The Caravan Club* covers the latest news and products from the caravanning world. It publishes features on the latest caravans and products, travel camp site guides and technical legal matters related to caravanning.

Caravan Magazine

Leon House, 233 High Street, Croydon, CR9 1HZ

- ☏ 020 8726 8245
- ☏ 020 8726 8299
- ☏ caravan@ipcmedia.com
- ☏ www.caravanmagazine.co.uk

Parent Company IPC Media Ltd

Editor Victoria Heath

Contact Publisher, Joanna Pieters; Art Editor, Sarah Collins

Established 1933

Insider Info A monthly consumer magazine, covering caravanning. Circulation is 15,774. Media pack available online.

Non-fiction Publishes advice, news, reviews, travel and practical articles.

Tips *Caravan Magazine* is a monthly publication that covers all aspects of caravans and caravanning, including site guides and practical advice articles.

Card Making & Papercraft

14th Floor, Tower House, Fairfax Street, Bristol, BS1 3BN

- ☏ 0117 927 9009
- ☏ 0117 937 9008
- ☏ writetous@cardmakingandpapercraft.com
- ☏ www.cardmakingandpapercraft.com

Parent Company Origin Publishing Ltd

Editor Kirstie Sleight

Contact Deputy Editor, Diane Hollands; Art Editor, Esther Curtis

Established 2004

Insider Info A monthly consumer magazine covering craft. Present circulation is 31,882.

Non-fiction Publishes features, reviews, event listings and practical, how-to advice.
Tips *Card Making & Papercraft* covers all aspects of papercrafts, including events listings and practical guides. The magazine runs regular competitions and is aimed at card makers of any skill level.

Carillon
19 Godric Drive, Brinsworth, Rotherham, South Yorkshire, S60 5AN
- editor@carillonmag.org.uk
- www.carillonmag.org.uk

Editor Graham Rippon
Established 2001
Insider Info A consumer magazine with three issues per year (February, June, October), covering poetry, prose and literary topics. Present circulation is 100. Manuscripts are published three months after acceptance. Payment is upon publication, with contributor copies for non-subscribers instead of cash. Byline is given. Accepts queries by mail or email. Aims to respond to queries and manuscripts within two weeks. Writer's guidelines are available online.
Non-fiction Publishes articles on poetry, features and reviews.
* Pays between £1 and £3 for unsolicited articles (with contributor copies for non-subscribers).
Submission Guidelines Accepts queries.
Fiction Publishes mainstream short fiction.
* Pays between £1 and £3 for unsolicited articles (with contributor copies for non-subscribers).
Submission Guidelines Send complete manuscript of up to 1,200 words. Does not accept 'bad' language, pornography, anything socially or culturally offensive, or clichéd writing or overtly political texts.
Poetry Publishes free verse, light verse and traditional poetry.
* Pays between £1 and £2 per poem (with contributor copies for non-subscribers).
Submission Guidelines Accepts poetry of up to 40 lines.
Tips *Carillon* magazine publishes new poetry and prose from contributors across the world, and also contains book reviews, articles on writing and reader competitions. It is an eclectic magazine and publishes newcomers and 'old hands' in both traditional and modern forms. They prefer hard copies, and will give preference to subscriber submissions.

Carousel
The Guide to Children's Books
The Saturn Centre, 54–76 Bissell Street, Birmingham, B5 7HX
- 0121 622 7458
- carousel.guide@virgin.net
- www.carouselguide.co.uk

Editor Jenny Blanch
Established 1995
Insider Info A consumer magazine with three issues per year (March, June, October) covering children's books and stories. Present circulation of 10,000. Accepts queries by mail or email. Sample copy is available online.
Non-fiction Publishes features, interviews/profiles, reviews, and opinion (excluding letters to the Editor).
Tips *Carousel* publishes reviews of all children's and young adult fiction books, as well as poetry and non fiction books. Each issue includes interviews with children's authors and illustrators and, occasionally, articles about the children's book world. Be aware its articles are aimed at adults, teachers and parents, rather than at children.

Celebrity Diet Now
Blue Fin Building, 110 Southwark Street, London, SE1 0AU
- 020 3148 5000
- 020 3148 8173
- karen_cross@ipcmedia.com
- www.ipcmedia.com

Parent Company IPC Media Ltd
Editor Karen Cross
Established 2000
Insider Info A consumer magazine, with three issues per year, covering celebrity dieting and health. Present circulation is roughly 250,000. Media pack available online.
Non-fiction Publishes celebrity interviews, diet techniques and fitness articles.
Tips Celebrity Diet Now is aimed at women of between 18 and 44 years of age, and covers all aspects of celebrity dieting and fitness.

Cencrastus
Unit 1, Abbeymount Techbase, 2 Easter Road, Abbeymount, Edinburgh, EH8 8EJ
- 0131 661 5687
- cencrastus1@hotmail.com

Editor Raymond Ross
Established 1979
Insider Info A consumer literary magazine covering Scottish literary topics. Present circulation of roughly 2,000. Accepts queries by mail or email.
Non-fiction Publishes essays, poetry articles, features and reviews on Scottish literature.
Submission Guidelines Accepts queries.
Fiction Publishes Scottish short fiction.
Poetry Publishes Scottish poetry.

Tips *Cencrastus* is a Scottish literary magazine that publishes new poetry and short fiction, articles and literary criticism, as well as line illustrations. Although it focuses on Scottish literature and arts, the magazine will also accept international submissions.

CFUK
105b Fidlas Road, Cardiff, CF14 0LY
- 07786 988836
- cfuk@hotmail.co.uk
- www.cfukmagazine.net

Editor Dylan Moore
Insider Info A quarterly consumer magazine covering prose, poetry and other literature. Byline is given. Accepts queries by mail and email.
Non-fiction Publishes poetry articles and features.
Submission Guidelines Accepts queries.
Fiction Publishes mainstream fiction.
Submission Guidelines Send complete manuscript of up to 3,000 words.
Poetry Publishes free verse and traditional poetry.
Tips *CFUK*'s aim is to provide an exciting an independent outlet for writers in Cardiff, Wales and beyond. It publishes prose, poetry and articles relating to writing. It will sometimes consider well-written articles not directly related to writing, but which are related to Cardiff or events in Cardiff.

Champions
Teddington Studios, Broom Road, Teddington, TW11 9BE
- 020 8267 5876
- 020 8267 5194
- champion@haymarket.com

Parent Company Haymarket Customer Publishing
Editor Paul Simpson
Contact Chief Sub-Editor, Martin Rosser; Deputy Editor, Stephanie Jones; Art Editor, Steve Hopkins
Established 2003
Insider Info A bi-monthly consumer magazine covering champions league football. Present circulation is 24,775.
Non-fiction Publishes news, features, interviews, profiles, statistics, match reports and analysis of UEFA Champion's League football.

Chapman
Scotland's Quality Literary Magazine
4 Broughton Place, Edinburgh, EH1 3RX
- 0131 557 2207
- chapman-pub@blueyonder.co.uk
- www.chapman-pub.co.uk

Parent Company Chapman Publishing Ltd.
Editor Joy Hendry
Established 1970

Insider Info A consumer magazine with three issues per year (April, August, December) covering the best in Scottish and international writing. Present circulation of roughly 2,000. 95 per cent of the publication is written by freelance writers. Manuscripts are published 12 months after acceptance. Payment is upon publication and may be by contributor copies instead of cash, if the writer prefers. Byline is given. Publication is copyrighted and the magazine purchases first UK serial rights. Editorial lead time is six months. Seasonal material should be submitted six months in advance. Accepts queries by mail, email or phone. Aims to respond to queries within five days and manuscripts within three months. Does not pay the expenses of writers on assignment. A sample copy is available for £6.50 (£5.50 with SAE and four first class stamps). Writer's guidelines are free on request, send SAE with two first class stamps, or by email.
Non-fiction Publishes articles on poetry, and literary/cultural criticism.
* Payment for articles is by negotiation.
Submission Guidelines Accepts query with outline. No reprints.
Fiction Publishes short stories.
* Buys 40 fiction manuscripts from writers per year. Payment is by negotiation.
Submission Guidelines Accepts articles of up to 5,000 words. Anything longer than this is unlikely to be accepted. No more than two short stories per submission. Please enclose SAE for reply or supply email address for email reply. Does not accept submissions by email or simultaneous submissions.
Poetry Publishes avant-garde, free verse, haiku, light verse and traditional poetry.
* Buys 500 poems per year.
Submission Guidelines Submit up to ten sample poems. Please enclose SAE for reply or supply email address for email reply. Does not accept submissions by email or simultaneous submissions.
Images Accepts images with submission.
* Pays a varied fee per photo. Purchases one-time rights.
Submission Guidelines Accepts photocopies and transparencies sized 6x4 inches. Also accepts gif/jpeg files with captions. State availability of photos with submission.
Tips *Chapman* publishes the best in Scottish and international writing – new work by both well-known and new writers, and readable, enlightening critical discussion. They promote energetic ideas and approaches, always with an eye to the future. While their central commitment is to Scottish literature, *Chapman* is increasingly international. English, Scots and Gaelic appear in every issue, reflecting the linguistic diversity of Scotland. They do not accept any emailed or faxed submissions.

Chat

Blue Fin Building, 110 Southwark Street, London, SE1 0SU
- 020 3148 5000
- 020 7261 6534
- chat_magazine@ipcmedia.com
- www.ipcmedia.com

Parent Company IPC Media Ltd
Editor Gilly Sinclair
Contact Publishing Director, Sandy Gale; Deputy Feature Editor, Devinder Bains
Established 1985
Insider Info A weekly consumer magazine, covering women's interest. Circulation is 489,682. Media pack available online.
Non-fiction Publishes beauty, cooking, house & home, photo features, fashion, news and story articles.
Tips *Chat* is a popular women's weekly magazine that aims to be 'irreverent, gritty and funny.' It covers all aspects of women's fashion, beauty and health, as well as true-life stories. Please note that the beauty section is now being written entirely in-house.

Child Education

Villiers House, Clarendon Avenue, Leamington Spa, CV32 5PR
- 0845 850 4411
- childed@scholastic.co.uk
- www.scholastic.co.uk

Parent Company Scholastic UK Ltd
Editor Michael Ward
Contact Deputy Editor, Charlotte Ronalds
Established 1923
Insider Info A trade journal, issued monthly, covering practical education and lesson plans. Present circulation is 13,895.
Non-fiction Publishes features, practical activities, lesson plans and resources.
Submission Guidelines Accepts articles from specialists of between 600–1,200 words. Payment by arrangement.
Tips *Child Education* is a teaching magazine from the book publisher Scholastic. It is primarily concerned with practical articles and resources from specialist writers covering Key Stage 1. The magazine is fully illustrated and comes with an A1 size picture poster.

Child Education Topics

Villiers House, Clarendon Avenue, Leamington Spa, CV32 5PR
- 0845 850 4411
- childed@scholastic.co.uk
- www.scholastic.co.uk

Parent Company Scholastic UK Ltd

Editor Michael Ward
Established 1978
Insider Info A trade journal, issued bi-monthly, covering project activities.
Non-fiction Publishes features and ideas for classroom project activities.
Submission Guidelines Accepts articles from specialists of between 500–1,000 words. Payment by arrangement. Most material is specially commissioned.
Tips *Child Education Topics* is the sister magazine to *Child Education*. It contains suggestions and plans for classroom based teaching activities.

Chimera

118 Nayland Road, Mile End, Colchester, C04 5ET
- 01206 751887
- poetry@chimeramagazine.co.uk
- prose@chimeramagazine.co.uk
- www.chimeramagazine.co.uk

Contact Poetry Editor, Robert Cole; Prose Editor, Susie Reynolds
Established 2004
Insider Info A consumer magazine with two issues per year covering new prose and poetry. Byline is given. Accepts queries by mail or email. Writer's guidelines available online.
Non-fiction Publishes articles on poetry and literature.
Submission Guidelines Accepts queries.
Fiction Publishes short fiction.
* Payment via contributor copy.
Submission Guidelines Send complete manuscript of up to 1,500 words.
Poetry Publishes avant-garde, free verse and light verse poetry.
* Payment via contributor copy.
Tips An award-winning small press magazine, which publishes well-written contemporary prose and poetry from both new and established writers. Chimera is open to submissions from any writer, either local or international, and often has a theme for the forthcoming issues. Check the website for further details.

Choice

First Floor, 2 King Street, Peterborough, PE1 1LT
- 01733 555123
- 01733 427500
- editorial@choicemag.co.uk
- www.choicemag.co.uk

Editor Norman Wright
Contact Editorial Assistant, Kim Rule
Insider Info A monthly consumer magazine covering all aspects of retirement and retired life. Present circulation is roughly 85,000. Editorial lead

time is eight weeks. Seasonal material should be submitted three months in advance. Accepts queries by mail, email or phone. Sample copy available for £2.70.

Non-fiction Publishes how-to, interviews/profiles, new product, general interest, travel, and historical/nostalgic articles on retirement issues.

Tips Aimed at a readership aged over fifty.

Church Music Quarterly
19 The Close, Salisbury, Wiltshire, SP1 2EB
- 01722 424848
- 01722 424849
- cmq@rscm.com
- www.rscm.com/publications/cmq.php

Parent Company The Royal School of Church Music
Editor Esther Jones
Contact Review Editor, Julian Elloway
Established 1977

Insider Info A quarterly consumer magazine covering all aspects of church music. Present circulation of 15,500. Accepts queries by email. Writer's guidelines are free on request and available via email.

Non-fiction Publishes religious, interviews/profile, review and general interest articles.

* Payment for assigned articles is £60 per page (maximum).

Submission Guidelines Accepts queries with published clips, for articles of up to 1,400 words.

Tips Available exclusively to members of the RSCM, *Church Music Quarterly* (CMQ) offers a wide range of articles and interviews by distinguished musicians, theologians and scholars, and provides expert advice, information and inspiration for readers. Any reports, press releases, letters, classified advertisements or reviews should be sent to the Editor at least two months before publication. CMQ does not pay for unsolicited articles, only for commissioned ones.

Church Times
13–17 Long Lane, London, EC1A 9PN
- 020 7776 1060
- news@churchtimes.co.uk
- features@churchtimes.co.uk
- www.churchtimes.co.uk

Parent Company Hymns Ancient & Modern
Editor Paul Handley
Contact Features Editor, Christine Miles; Books Coordinator, Sally Fraser; News Editor, Helen Saxbee; Comment Editor, Rachel Boulding
Established 1863

Insider Info A weekly specialist religious newspaper. Present circulation of 28,000. 40 per cent of the publication is written by freelance writers. Payment

is at the beginning of the month after publication. Byline is given. Editorial lead time for features is four weeks. Queries accepted by mail, email, fax, or phone. For an editorial calendar, request an advertising features list by email.

Non-fiction Publishes news, comment, faith pages, book excerpts and reviews, photo features, features, interviews/profile, historical articles, arts pages and reviews, topical features (especially social, environmental, ethical, religious and cultural issues), eduation supplements and an annual travel supplement.

* Pays between £10–£15 per 100 words for unsolicited which are accepted for publication.

Submission Guidelines Established writers may submit articles/outlines to the appropriate section editor. For features, established writers may submit an article (1,200-2,000 words) or outline to Christine Miles, Features Editor.

Fiction Publishes reviews of religious fiction.

Submission Guidelines The Church Times commission book reviews of between 350-500 words. Contact Sally Fraser, Books Coordinator.

Columns Publishes eight columns per week.

Submission Guidelines For topical opinion pieces, speculative articles accepted of between 800-1,200 words. Contact Comment Editor, Rachel Boulding.

Tips The *Church Times* (CT) is the UK's bestselling independent religious newspaper. It serves a largely Anglican readership and covers UK and international news, lifestyle features, faith and devotional pages, comment, books, arts, media, news from diocese and worldwide church. For new writers to the features pages, it is best to write the piece first and send it on speculative basis. If CT would like to use the piece, they will inform the writer. After the first piece is accepted on spec, it is easier to get commissioned. CT would never commission an unknown writer except on this basis.

Citizen32
PO Box 219, Manchester, M23 9XZ
- editor@citizen32.co.uk
- www.citizen32.co.uk

Editor John G. Hall
Contact Co-Editor, Dave Toomer
Insider Info A consumer literary magazine with three issues per year, covering poetry and prose. Byline is given. Accepts queries by mail or email.

Non-fiction Publishes articles on poetry, features, interviews/profiles, reviews and opinion (excluding letters to the Editor).

Submission Guidelines Accepts queries.

Fiction Publishes mainstream fiction.

Poetry Publishes avant-garde, free verse and light verse poetry.

Tips *Citizen32* is a politically charged literary magazine that publishes contemporary poetry and prose from new and established writers, plus articles, reviews and interviews with popular authors. The magazine has a different theme for every issue, and often uses a guest editor, so prospective contributors must bear this in mind when submitting. Check the website for the current theme.

Classic & Sports Car

Teddington Studios, Broom Road, Teddington, Middlesex, TW11 9BE
- 020 8267 5000
- 020 8267 5725
- letters.classicandsportscar.haynet.com
- www.classicandsportscar.com

Parent Company Haymarket Publishing
Editor James Elliott
Established 1982
Insider Info A monthly consumer magazine, covering motoring and car related topics. Present circulation of 76,508. Accepts queries by email.
Non-fiction Publishes photo features and features.
* Pays £250 per 1,000 words for unsolicited articles.
Submission Guidelines Send complete manuscript
Fillers Uses newsbreaks.
Tips *Classic & Sports Car* is aimed at enthusiasts who wish to buy, maintain, restore or dream about classic cars. When submitting feature ideas be patient as hundreds of unsolicited submissions are received monthly.

The Classical Review

The Edinburgh Building, Shaftesbury Road, Cambridge, CB2 2RU
- 01223 326070
- 01223 325150
- journals@cambridge.org
- www.journals.cambridge.org

Parent Company Cambridge University Press
Editor Neil Hopkinson
Established 1886
Insider Info An academic journal that publishes scholarly articles on the classical civilisations, twice yearly. Present circulation is 1,800. Byline is given. Queries accepted by mail and email.
Non-fiction Publishes essays, features and historical articles.
* Purchases 150 manuscripts per year from freelance writers.
Submission Guidelines Send query before sending submissions.
Tips *The Classical Review* only publishes articles from leading scholars in the classical field.

Classic Bike

Media House, Lynchwood, Peterborough Business Park, Peterborough, PE2 6EA
- 01733 468188
- 01733 468466
- classic.bike@emap.com

Parent Company EMAP Plc
Editor Hugo Wilson
Contact Associate Editor, Brain Crichton
Established 1978
Insider Info A monthly consumer magazine covering classic motorcycles. Present circulation is 41,285.
Non-fiction Publishes news, features and review articles.
Tips *Classic Bike* covers classic motorcycles from the 1950s to the 1980s, including Japanese motorcycles. Articles consist mainly of the latest news, photo features, reviews and road tests.

Classic Boat Magazine

Leon House, 233 High Street, Croydon, CR9 1HZ
- 020 8726 8000
- 020 8726 8195
- cb@ipcmedia.com
- www.classicboat.co.uk

Parent Company IPC Media Ltd
Editor Dan Houston
Contact Publishing Director, Nick Hopkinson; Editorial Assistant, Annette Turner
Established 1987
Insider Info A monthly consumer magazine, covering classic boats and yachting. Circulation is 12,505. Payment is upon publication. Does not pay a kill fee. Between 50 to 66 per cent of the magazine is written by freelancers. Purchases first British serial rights and, occasionally, second rights. Accepts previously published work (if published abroad). Average lead time is four months. Aims to respond to queries and manuscripts within one months. Manuscripts guidelines and media pack are available online.
Non-fiction Interested in historical or technical boat photo features, features on successful restoration projects, construction tutorials and cruising/seamanship articles.
* Payment is £100 per 1,000 words for text articles and between £75 to £90 per page for words and photo articles.
Submission Guidelines Accepts queries by post for articles of between 1,500 to 3,000 words.
Tips *Classic Boats* welcomes submissions but recommends that prospective contributors read several copies of the magazine first and then purchase the *'Classic Boats' Index* for £10 which has details of all articles published since the magazines

launch. Prefers a query in the first instance and will then request a full manuscript if interested.

Classic Cars
Media House, Lynchwood, Peterborough Business Park, Peterborough, PE2 6EA
- 01733 468000
- 01733 468888
- classic.cars@emap.com
- www.classiccarsmagazine.co.uk

Parent Company EMAP Plc
Editor Philip Bell
Contact Deputy Editor, Mike Goodbun; Art Editor, Tracy Radnell; Features Editor, Tim Nevinson
Established 1973
Insider Info A monthly consumer magazine covering classic cars. Present circulation is 34,589.
Non-fiction Publishes news, historical features, events listings, road tests and review articles.
Tips The magazine is aimed at classic car enthusiasts between 15 and 55 years old.

Classic FM
Teddington Studios, Broom Road, Teddington, TW11 9BE
- 020 8267 5180
- 020 8267 5150
- classicfm@haynet.com
- www.classicfm.com

Parent Company Haymarket Consumer Publications Ltd
Editor John Evans
Contact Publishing Director, Bob McDowell; Art Editor, Sandra Marques
Established 1995
Insider Info A monthly consumer magazine covering classical music and lifestyle. Present circulation is 41,412.
Non-fiction Publishes feature, news and reviews.
Tips *Classic FM* is the official magazine of the Classic FM radio station and covers the latest classical music, composers and artists with an overarching lifestyle feel.

Classic Ford
30 Monmouth Street, Bath, BA1 2BW
- 01225 442244
- 01225 446019
- simon.woolley@futurenet.co.uk
- www.classicfordmag.co.uk

Parent Company Future Publishing Ltd
Editor Simon Woolley
Contact Publisher, Helen Richmond; Art Editor, Rob Crossland; Features Editor, Gareth Charlton
Established 1997

Insider Info A monthly consumer magazine covering classic Ford cars. Present circulation is roughly 33,000.
Non-fiction Publishes event and show listings, historical, photo features, restoration and technical articles.
Tips *Classic Ford* is aimed at men aged between 18 to 65 years old and covers all aspects of classic Ford restoration, maintenance and modification, as well as event and show listings.

Classic Rock
2 Balcombe Street, London, NW1 6NW
- 020 7042 4000
- sian.llewellyn@futurenet.co.uk
- www.classicrockmagazine.com

Parent Company Future Publishing Ltd
Editor Sian Llewellyn
Contact Editor in Chief, Scott Rowley; Art Editor, Brad Merrett; Reviews Editor, Ian Fortnam
Established 1998
Insider Info A monthly consumer magazine covering classic rock music. Present circulation is 66,632.
Non-fiction Publishes features, interviews, profiles, news, tour date listings, reviews and retrospective articles.
Tips *Classic Rock* is aimed at rock music lovers of any age and covers classic rock music in general, including hard rock and the heavy metal scene. Focus is on 'classic' rock such as Iron Maiden or Metallica, rather than contemporary rock music trends.

Classics Monthly
30 Monmouth Street, Bath, BA1 2BW
- 01225 442244
- 01689 876438
- classicsmonthly@futurenet.co.uk
- www.futurenet.co.uk

Parent Company Future Publishing Ltd
Editor Gary Stretton
Contact Art Editor, Mark Field
Established 1997
Insider Info A monthly consumer magazine covering classic cars. Present circulation is roughly 55,000.
Non-fiction Publishes car restoration, group test, comparison, driving, reviews, news and photo feature articles.
Tips *Classics Monthly* is aimed at owners and enthusiasts of classic cars and covers restoration and maintenance as well as road tests and event listings. The magazine also has a photo classifieds section which is free to readers.

Classic Stitches Magazine

80 Kingsway East, Dundee, DD4 8SL
☎ 01382 223131
☎ 01382 452491
✉ editorial@classicstitches.com
🌐 www.classicstitches.com
Parent Company D.C. Thomson & Co. Ltd
Editor Bea Neilson
Contact Managing Editor, Irene Duncan; Deputy Editor, Liz O'Rourke
Established 1994
Insider Info A bi-monthly specialist hobby magazine that also appears online, covering embroidery and needlecrafts. Present circulation of 10,790. 60 per cent of the publication is written by freelance writers. Payment is upon acceptance with no kill fees. Payment is never made with contributor copies instead of cash. Byline is given. Publication is copyrighted and all rights are purchased. Editorial lead time is three months. Seasonal materials should be submitted six months in advance. Accepts queries by mail, email, fax or phone. Simultaneous submissions are accepted. Aims to respond to queries within two weeks and manuscripts within four weeks. Sometimes pays the expenses of writers on assignment (limit agreed upon in advance). Sample copy and writer's guidelines are free on request. Although they are seasonal, they do not have a calendar as such.
Non-fiction Publishes book excerpts (usually stitching books), how-to (detailed stitching techniques), features (stitching, embroidery related), interviews/profiles, (stitching and embroidery related) and technical (stitching and embroidery related) articles.
* Purchases approximately 18 non-fiction manuscripts per year. Payment is by negotiation for assigned and unsolicited articles.
Submission Guidelines Accepts query with published clips for articles or between 800 and 2,000 words. No reprints. Contact Bea Neilson, Editor.
Images Accepts images with submission.
* Negotiates payment individually for images. Purchases all rights.
Submission Guidelines Accepts contact sheets, negatives, prints and transparencies of various sizes and gif/jpeg files. Identification of subjects is required. State availability of photos with submission. Contact Deputy Editor, Liz O'Rourke.
Tips The magazine is aimed at stitchers who want to explore new media and experiment. Features tend to be about designers and embroidery related exhibitions. Study the magazine and the website, it is really the only way to get to know what the magazine requires from an article.

Closer

Endeavour House, 189 Shaftesbury Avenue, London, WC2H 8JG
☎ 020 7437 9011
☎ 020 7437 8600
✉ closer@emap.com
🌐 www.closeronline.co.uk
Parent Company EMAP Plc
Editor Lisa Burrow
Contact Deputy Editor, Sophie Barton; Features Editor, Helen Morgan; Lifestyle Editor, Juliet Blank
Established 2002
Insider Info A weekly consumer magazine covering women's lifestyle topics. Present circulation of 527,325.
Non-fiction Publishes general interest, expose, interviews, reviews and photo features on celebrities, fashion, beauty, music, television, film and real-life.
Tips The magazine is aimed at women aged 25 to 35.

CNN Traveller

141–143 Shoreditch High Street, London, E1 6JE
☎ 020 7613 8777
☎ 020 7613 8776
✉ dan.hayes@ink-publishing.com
🌐 www.cnntraveller.com
Parent Company Ink Publishing
Editor Daniel Hayes
Established 1998
Insider Info A bi-monthly consumer magazine covering travel journalism and holidays. Present circulation of roughly 106,000. 50 per cent of the publication is written by freelance writers. Manuscripts are published three months after acceptance. Offers a 50 per cent kill fee for unpublished articles. Byline is given. Publication is copyrighted and all rights are purchased. Editorial lead time is six months. Seasonal material should be submitted four months in advance. Queries will be accepted by mail and fax. Will not pay the expenses of writers on assignment. Sample copy available online. Writer's guidelines are free on request.
Non-fiction Publishes book excerpts and travel articles.
* Buys 50 non-fiction manuscripts per year.
Submission Guidelines Accepts queries with outline and published clips, for articles between 600 and 2,000 words.
Images Accepts images with submission.
* Negotiates payment individually for images. Purchases one-time rights.
Submission Guidelines Accepts gif/jpeg files with captions. State availability of photos with submission.

Columns Purchases ten columns per year.
* Pays between £100 and £200 per column.
Submission Guidelines Accepts queries with a 150 word outline and published clips. Address queries to the Editor.
Tips *CNN Traveller* aims to marry the best in travel journalism and photography, with the news values of CNN. The magazines takes an issues led view of travel, getting behind the headlines with articles that need to be intriguing and thought provoking. The magazine considers work only by published, professional photographers and journalists. Features should have a solid news, or issue led angle.

Coast

National Magazine House, 72 Broadwick Street, London, W1F 9EP
- 020 7439 5000
- 020 7437 5077
- enquiries.coast@natmags.co.uk
- www.coastmagazine.co.uk

Parent Company National Magazine Company Ltd
Contact Editor in Chief, Susy Smith; Editor, Clare Gogerty, Deputy Editor (Features), Alex Reece, Art Director, Joe McIntyre
Established 2004
Insider Info A monthly consumer magazine covering coastal living and lifestyle. Present circulation is 41,116.
Non-fiction Publishes news, photo features, profiles and accommodation guides.
Tips *Coast* covers all aspects of living on and visiting the British coastline. Features include house, hotel and restaurant guides, as well as lifestyle features such as cooking, health, beauty and fashion.

The Coffee House

31 Granby Street, Loughborough, Leicestershire, LE11 3DU
- 01509 822558
- 01509 822559
- info@charnwood-arts.org.uk
- www.charnwoodarts.com

Parent Company Charnwood Arts
Editor Deborah Tyler-Bennett
Established 1998
Insider Info A poetry, prose and visual arts magazine published twice yearly. Present circulation is 300. Publication is copyrighted and a byline is given. Queries accepted by mail and email.
Fiction Publishes mainstream fiction and short stories.
Submission Guidelines Send complete manuscript. Articles must be 2,500 words.
Poetry Publishes avant-garde poetry, free verse, haiku, light verse and traditional verse.

Tips *The Coffee House* serves as a literary meeting place for writers and artists of all types, and prints new poetry, prose and art from local, national and international artists. It was founded primarily to serve the local arts and literature scene in Charnwood, but has outlets in New York and across the UK, and will consider submissions from further afield. Accepts submissions of any kind of writing from ghost stories, to sonnets and villanelles.

Coffee House Poetry

Meirion House, Tanygrisiau, Blaenau Ffestiniog, Gwynedd, LL41 3SU
- 01766 832112
- jan@coffeehousepoetry.co.uk
- www.coffeehousepoetry.co.uk

Parent Company Cinnamon Press
Editor Jan Fortune-Wood
Established 2003
Insider Info A consumer poetry journal with three issues per year (January, May, September). Byline is given. Accepts queries by mail or email. Aims to respond to queries and manuscripts within six weeks. Writer's guidelines are available online.
Poetry Publishes avant-garde, free verse, haiku, light verse and traditional poetry.
Submission Guidelines Accepts up to six poems, each up to 40 lines.
Tips A literary journal for quality contemporary poetry, which aims to provide a platform for innovative new work that has 'edge and depth'. Welcomes poetry submissions in any style, and also runs an annual competition with cash prizes, where the prize winners will also receive publication in the magazine.

Company

National Magazine House, 72 Broadwick Street, London, W1F 9EP
- 020 7439 5000
- 020 7312 3797
- company.mail@natmags.co.uk
- www.getlippy.com

Parent Company National Magazine Company Ltd
Editor Victoria White
Contact Deputy Editor, Claire Askew; Features Editor, Emma Justice
Established 1978
Insider Info A monthly consumer magazine covering women's lifestyle topics. Present circulation of 240,078.
Non-fiction Publishes general interest, interviews, reviews and photo features on celebrities, fashion, beauty, music, television, film and real-life.
Tips The magazine is aimed at young, working women and articles must reflect this.

Compass Sport

Glenmore House, 6 Glenmore Park, Tunbridge Wells, Kent, TN2 5NZ

- 07720 952241
- nick@compasssport.co.uk
- www.compasssport.co.uk

Editor Nick Barrable
Established 1979
Insider Info A bi-monthly national sports magazine covering the sport of orienteering. Present circulation of roughly 2,000. 50 per cent of the publication is written by freelance writers. Manuscripts are published two weeks after acceptance. Contributors are not paid, although some may receive a free copy of the magazine. Byline is given. Publication is copyrighted. Editorial lead time is four weeks. Seasonal material should be submitted six weeks in advance. Accepts queries by mail, email or phone. Aims to respond to queries within one week and manuscripts within two weeks. Will not pay the expenses of writers on assignment. Sample copy available for £2. Writer's guidelines and editorial calendars available via email.
Non-fiction Publishes features on orienteering.
Submission Guidelines Send manuscripts by email.
Images Publish photographs and maps.
Submission Guidelines Email photographs or maps as digital files.
Tips A niche orienteering magazine, which covers foot/trail/ski/MTBO and radio topics.

Computeractive

VNU House, 32–34 Broadwick Street, Leicester, W1A 2HG

- 020 7316 9000
- 020 7316 9520
- news@computeractive.co.uk
- www.computeractive.co.uk

Parent Company Incisive Media Publications
Editor Paul Allen
Contact Editor in Chief, Dylan Armbrust; Deputy Editor, Tom Royal; News Editor, Dinah Greek
Established 1998
Insider Info A bi-weekly consumer magazine covering computing. Present circulation is 200,307.
Non-fiction Publishes features, news, advice and practical articles.
Tips *Computeractive* covers practical computer use at home and in the office. The magazine publishes practical features and tips on computing and aims to keep jargon to a minimum.

Computer Arts

30 Monmouth Street, Bath, BA1 2BW

- 01225 442244
- 01225 732295
- ca.mail@futurenet.co.uk
- www.computerarts.co.uk

Parent Company Future Publishing Ltd
Editor Garrick Webster
Established 1995
Insider Info A monthly consumer magazine covering computer computers and digital arts subjects. Present circulation of 21,452.
Non-fiction Publishes how-to, features, reviews, new product and technical articles.
Submission Guidelines No unsolicited manuscripts. Queries only.
Tips *Computer Arts* aims to give professional advice on creating digital art and illustrations. They won't accept unsolicited manuscripts, so approach by post or email first. Practical tips and tutorials for unusual techniques, or similar, are most useful.

Computer Buyer

30 Cleveland Street, London, W1T 4JD

- 020 7907 6000
- 020 7907 6282
- editor@computerbuyer.co.uk
- www.computerbuyer.co.uk

Parent Company Dennis Publishing Ltd
Editor Adam Banks
Contact Publisher, John Garewal
Insider Info A monthly consumer magazine covering the computer industry and market. Present circulation is 9,477.
Non-fiction Publishes industry and market news, features, reviews, product tests, advice and technical articles.

Computer Music

30 Monmouth Street, Bath, BA1 2BW

- 01225 442244
- 01225 822793
- ronan.macdonald@futurenet.co.uk
- www.computermusic.co.uk

Parent Company Future Publishing Ltd
Editor Ronan MacDonald
Contact Deputy Editor, Lee Du-Caine; Art Editor, Stuart Radcliffe; Multimedia Editor, Tim Cant
Established 1998
Insider Info A monthly consumer magazine covering classic computer music. Present circulation is 18,762.
Non-fiction Publishes news, reviews and tutorial articles on all aspects of musical computer software.

Computer Shopper

30 Cleveland Street, London, W1T 4JD

- 020 7907 6000
- 020 7907 6304
- david@computershopper.co.uk

☻ www.computershopper.co.uk
Parent Company Dennis Publishing Ltd
Editor David Ludlow
Contact Publisher, John Garewal; Commissioning Editor, Lynley Oram
Insider Info A monthly consumer magazine covering computing. Present circulation is 68,171.
Non-fiction Publishes news, features, product reviews and buying guides.
Tips *Computer Shopper* covers personal computers, the internet and any related products, mainly from a consumer angle

Computer Weekly
Quadrant House, The Quadrant, Sutton, Surrey, SM2 5AS
☎ 020 8652 8642
☎ 020 8652 8979
☻ www.computerweekly.com
Parent Company Reed Business Information Ltd
Editor Hooman Bassirian
Established 1966
Insider Info A weekly consumer magazine that covers all aspects of IT and computing. Accepts queries by mail or email.
Non-fiction Interested in general interest, new products and business articles related to IT/Computing.
Submission Guidelines Accepts queries and completed manuscript submissions of up to 1,200 words.
Tips Primarily aimed at business/industry users rather than general computer users.

Condé Nast Traveller
Vogue House, Hanover Square, London, W1S 1JU
☎ 020 7499 9080
☎ 020 7493 3758
☻ cntraveller@condenast.com
☻ www.cntraveller.com
Parent Company Condé Nast Publications UK Ltd
Editor Sarah Miller
Established 1997
Insider Info A monthly consumer magazine that covers travel and holidays. Accepts queries by mail or email. Present circulation is 85,262.
Non-fiction Interested in food & drink, health, lifestyle, review and guide articles related to travel.
Tips Generally, all articles will be accompanied by several high-quality photographs.

Construction News
Greater London House, Hampstead Road, London, NW1 7EJ
☎ 020 7728 4632
☎ 020 7728 4400
☻ cneditorial@emap.com
☻ www.cnplus.co.uk
Parent Company EMAP Plc
Editor Nick Edwards
Contact Features Editor, Emma Crates; News Editor, David Rogers
Established 1871
Insider Info A weekly trade journal covering the construction industry. Present circulation is 19,776.
Non-fiction Publishes industry news, materials and equipment market listings and reviews and feature articles.
Tips *Construction News* is a business publication aimed at contractors, materials manufacturers and suppliers, and plant hire services in the construction industry.

Contemporary
Suite K101, Tower Bridge Business Complex, 100 Clements Road, London, SE16 4DG
☎ 020 7740 1704
☎ 020 7252 3510
☻ info@contemporary-magazine.com
☻ www.contemporary-magazine.com
Editor Deborah Basckin
Established 1997
Insider Info A monthly consumer magazine that covers contemporary architecture, fashion, film, photography, music, dance and visual arts. Accepts queries by mail or email.
Non-fiction Interested in news, interviews, profiles and feature articles.

Cosmopolitan
National Magazine House, 72 Broadwick Street, London, W1F 9EP
☎ 020 7439 5000
☎ 020 7439 5016
☻ info@cosmopolitan.co.uk
☻ www.cosmopolitan.co.uk
Parent Company The National Magazine Company
Editor Louise Court
Established 1886
Insider Info A monthly consumer magazine covering women's lifestyle and fashion topics. Present circulation of 470,735.
Non-fiction Publishes photo feature, exposé, features, interviews/profile and general interest articles.
Tips *Cosmopolitan* has traditionally been a women's magazine discussing such topics as sex, health, fitness and fashion. Recently the magazine is sharing their focus with men's issues as well. "Cosmo for your guy" is featured in every issue with exclusive advice for men. *Cosmopolitan* also recruit men as a part of

their staff, to answer their female readers' burning questions. The magazine is always on the lookout for new writers with original and relevant ideas, and a strong voice.

Cotswold Life

Cumberland House, Oriel Road, Cheltenham, Gloucestershire, GL50 1BB

☎ 01242 216050

☎ 01242 255116

Parent Company Archant Life South

Editor Mike Lowe

Insider Info A monthly consumer magazine covering the Cotswolds. Accepts queries by mail or email. Present circulation is 14,948.

Non-fiction Interested in local interest and event listings related to the Cotswolds.

Submission Guidelines Accepts queries and completed manuscript submissions.

Country

Chalke House, Station Road, Codford, Warminster, BA12 0JX

☎ 01985 850706

☎ 01985 850378

🌐 www.thecga.co.uk

Parent Company Country Gentleman's Association

Editor Simon Moss

Established 1893

Insider Info A consumer magazine, with eight issues per year, covering the countryside and rural life. Accepts queries by mail or email.

Non-fiction Interested in news, features, rural event reviews, leisure, heritage and lifestyle articles related to the countryside and rural life.

Country Homes & Interiors

Blue Fin Building, 110 Southwark Street, London, SE1 0SU

☎ 020 3148 5000

✉ countryhomes@ipcmedia.com

🌐 www.countryhomesandinteriors.co.uk

Parent Company IPC Media Ltd

Editor Rhoda Parry

Contact Features Editor, Jean Carr

Established 1986

Insider Info A monthly consumer magazine aimed at women, and covering countryside house and home topics. Present circulation of 87,056. Accepts queries by mail.

Non-fiction Publishes photo features, features and interviews/profiles.

* Pays up to £250 per 1,000 words for unsolicited articles.

Submission Guidelines Accepts queries for articles of up to 1,200 words.

Tips *Country Homes & Interiors* magazine shows readers how to buy, decorate and enjoy their dream country home. They seek features on country style properties, or interviews of relevance to the target readership.

Country Life

Blue Fin Building, 110 Southwark Street, London, SE1 0SU

☎ 020 3148 5000

✉ mark_hedges@ipcmedia.com

🌐 www.countrylife.co.uk

Parent Company IPC Media Ltd

Editor Mark Hedges

Established 1897

Insider Info A weekly consumer magazine covering countryside topics. Present circulation of 40,821.

Non-fiction Publishes photo features, features, interviews/profiles and general interest articles.

Submission Guidelines Accepts queries for articles of between 1,000 and 1,300 words.

Tips *Country Life* covers the pleasures and joys of rural life, as well as the concerns of rural people. It is primarily concerned with the lifestyle and concerns of landowners and other rich country dwellers, but it has many readers who do not belong to those categories. Unsolicited material is rarely accepted. The magazine seeks strong informed material, rather than amateur enthusiasm.

Country Living

National Magazine House, 72 Broadwick Street, London, W1F 9EP

☎ 020 7439 5000

☎ 020 7439 5093

✉ kitty.corrigan@natmags.co.uk

🌐 www.countryliving.co.uk

Parent Company National Magazine Company Ltd

Editor Susy Smith

Contact Deputy Editor, Kitty Corrigan; Acting Art Director, Alex Breuer; Features Editor, Lisa Sykes

Established 1985

Insider Info A monthly consumer magazine covering country lifestyle. Present circulation is 199,510.

Non-fiction Publishes photo features, inspiration, design and lifestyle articles.

Tips *Country Living* covers country style homes and gardens, wildlife stories and rural issues. Also publishes features on arts and craft, health, beauty, fashion and travel. It is mainly aimed at people living in, or wishing to move to, rural areas.

The Countryman

The Water Mill, Broughton Hall, Skipton, BD23 3AG

☎ 01756 701381
🖷 01756 701326
✉ editorial@thecountryman.co.uk
🌐 www.countrymanmagazine.co.uk
Parent Company Country Publications Ltd
Editor Paul Jackson
Established 1927
Insider Info A monthly consumer magazine covering countryside and rural issues. Present circulation of 19,817. Accepts queries by email.
Non-fiction Publishes photo features, features, interviews/profiles and general interest articles.
* Pays £70 per 1,000 words for unsolicited articles.
Submission Guidelines Accepts queries, or complete manuscripts for articles of up to 1,200 words.
Images Send images with submission.
Tips *The Countryman* is read by people throughout Britain and overseas, who share its concerns for the countryside, the people who live and work in it, and its wildlife. The magazine focuses on the rural issues of today, and tomorrow, as well as including features on the people, places, history and wildlife of the British countryside. Articles supplied with good quality illustrations are far more likely to be accepted.

Countryside Tales
14 The Park, Stow on the Wold, Cheltenham, Gloucestershire, GL54 1DX
☎ 01451 831053
✉ sales@parkpublications.co.uk
🌐 www.parkpublications.co.uk
Parent Company Park Publications Ltd
Editor David Howath
Established 2000
Insider Info A quarterly consumer magazine covering literature with a countryside theme. Byline is given. Accepts queries by mail. Writers' guidelines available online.
Non-fiction Publishes articles on poetry and features.
* Payment is via contributor copy (plus a credit voucher for subscription).
Submission Guidelines Accepts queries for articles of between 400 and 1,500 words.
Fiction Publishes rural/countryside fiction.
* Payment is via contributor copy (plus a credit voucher for subscription).
Submission Guidelines Send complete manuscripts for stories of up to 2,000 words.
Poetry Publishes avant-garde, free verse, light verse and traditional poetry.
* Payment is via contributor copy (plus a credit voucher for subscription).
Submission Guidelines Accepts poetry of up to 40 lines.

Tips In each issue, *Countryside Tales* offers cash prizes for the best selected stories in the categories of poetry, fiction, and non-fiction.

Country Smallholding
Fair Oak Close, Exeter Airport Business Park, Clyst Honiton, Exeter, EX5 2UL
☎ 01392 888481
🖷 01392 888550
✉ editorial.csh@archant.co.uk
🌐 www.countrysmallholding.com
Parent Company Archant South West
Editor Diane Cowgill
Established 1975
Insider Info A monthly consumer magazine covering smallholdings and associated lifestyle. Present circulation is 18,372.
Non-fiction Publishes features, advice, technical and lifestyle articles on topics such as smallholdings, hobby farming, poultry, smallholding animals, organic gardening, alternative lifestyle and organic living.

Country Walking
Media House, Peterborough Business Park, Lynch Wood, Peterborough, PE2 6EA
☎ 01733 468000
🖷 01733 468387
✉ jonathan.manning@emap.com
🌐 www.countrywalking.co.uk
Parent Company EMAP Plc
Editor Jonathan Manning
Contact Publisher, Rob Croxall; Gear Editor, Michelle Daniel
Established 1987
Insider Info A monthly consumer magazine covering walking and hiking. Present circulation is 44,549.
Non-fiction Publishes photo features, walking guides, product reviews and travel articles.
Tips The magazine is aimed at walkers between 30 and 65 years old.

Crime Time
PO Box 394, Harpenden, AL5 1XJ
☎ 01582 761264
🖷 01582 712244
✉ crimetime@blueyonder.co.uk
🌐 www.crimetime.co.uk
Parent Company Oldcastle Books Ltd
Editor Barry Forshaw
Established 1999
Insider Info A bi-monthly consumer magazine covering crime fiction topics. Accepts queries by mail or email.

Non-fiction Publishes features, interviews/profiles, reviews and general interest articles on crime writing.

Submission Guidelines Accepts queries.

Fiction Publishes mystery, suspense and crime fiction.

Tips *Crime Time* is a literary magazine that publishes crime fiction stories from new and established authors, as well as articles on crime writing, film and cinema, and book reviews. It mostly uses regular contributors, rather than occasional freelancers.

Crimewave

5 Martins Lane, Witcham, Ely, CB6 2LB

📧 andy@ttapress.demon.co.uk

🌐 www.ttapress.com

Parent Company TTA Press

Editor Andy Cox

Established 1998

Insider Info A quarterly consumer magazine covering new crime writing. 100 per cent of the publication is written by freelance writers. A byline is given. Accepts queries by mail. Aims to respond to queries and manuscripts within two months. Writer's guidelines available online.

Fiction Publishes mystery, suspense, experimental and crime fiction.

Submission Guidelines Send complete manuscripts. Do not send any general fiction or non-crime fiction.

Tips *Crimewave's* mission is to totally re-create crime fiction. They aim to publish something entirely different to whatever people have read before. They hope to help people discover a new universe of fiction in which morality is real but fluid, the story is central but skewed, and the traditions of the genre are neither dumped nor subverted, but rather viewed through fresh eyes, from a new hill. The magazine is looking for outstanding modern stories of crime, mystery and suspense, as well as borderline material which uses genre elements in a new way. It is strongly recommended that you study at least one volume of *Crimewave* before submitting.

Critical Quarterly

School of English, University of Exeter, Queen's Building, The Queen's Drive, Exeter, Devon, EX4 4QH

☎ 01392 264257

📠 01392 264361

📧 ink201@exeter.ac.uk

🌐 www.criticalquarterly.com

Parent Company Blackwell Publishing

Editor Colin MacCabe

Contact Managing Editor, Kate Mellor; Editorial Assistant, Luke Kennard

Established 1959

Insider Info A quarterly consumer literary journal covering all aspects of the arts and literature. Byline is given. Accepts queries by mail or phone. Writer's guidelines available online.

Non-fiction Publishes essays, articles on poetry, features, interviews/profiles, reviews and opinion (excluding letters to the Editor) on arts subjects.

Submission Guidelines Send complete manuscripts.

Fiction Publishes some fiction.

Tips *Critical Quarterly* publishes informative and scholarly criticism on all aspects of cultural studies, including literature, the arts, media, film and cinema. The journal encourages articles from both new and international writers, as well as regular contributors. It is mostly scholarly in its approach and has a detailed style guide for submissions available through the Blackwell website. Contributors must ensure that any quotations or references are accurate.

Cross Stitch Collection

30 Monmouth Street, Bath, BA1 2BW

☎ 01225 442244

📠 01225 822793

📧 csc@futurenet.co.uk

🌐 www.futurenet.co.uk

Parent Company Future Publishing Ltd

Editor Catherine Hood

Contact Publisher, Ursula Morgan; Art Editor, Patricia Ball

Insider Info A monthly consumer magazine covering cross stitch.

Non-fiction Publishes news, letters, product reviews, advice, designer interviews, features and technical articles.

Tips *Cross Stitch Collection* is aimed at women between 35 and 45 years old who are interested in cross stitch. Technical or how-to articles should be written for an intermediate to advanced skill level.

Cross Stitch Crazy

9th Floor, Tower House, Fairfax Street, Bristol, BS1 3BN

☎ 0117 927 9009

📠 0117 934 9008

📧 emmaroberts@originpublishing.co.uk

🌐 www.cross-stitching.com

Parent Company Origin Publishing Ltd

Editor Emma Roberts

Established 1999

Insider Info A monthly consumer magazine covering cross stitching. Present circulation is 21,805.

Non-fiction Publishes features, news, technical articles, designs, and puzzles on cross stitching.

Cross Stitcher

30 Monmouth Street, Bath, BA1 2BW

☏ 01225 442244

☏ 01225 822793

✉ cathy.lewis@futurenet.co.uk

🌐 www.futurenet.co.uk

Parent Company Future Publishing Ltd

Editor Cathy Lewis

Contact Publisher, Ursula Morgan

Insider Info A monthly consumer magazine covering cross stitch. Present circulation is 63,365.

Non-fiction Publishes features, news, reviews, true life stories and technical articles.

Tips *Cross Stitcher* is aimed at anyone interested in cross stitch. Articles cover a wide range of tastes and skill levels, from beginner to expert.

Curlew

Hare Cottage, Kettlesing, Harrogate, HG3 2LB

Editor Jocelyn Precious

Established 1975

Insider Info A consumer magazine, covering poetry subjects.

Non-fiction Publishes articles on poetry.

Submission Guidelines Accepts queries.

Fiction Publishes some fiction.

Poetry Publishes free verse, light verse and traditional poetry.

Images Publishes images to accompany articles.

Tips *Curlew* is a small independent poetry magazine that publishes poetry of all types, as well as some fiction and articles. It is often illustrated and will accept submissions of art and graphics for inclusion in the magazine.

Current Accounts

16–18 Mill Lane, Horwich, Bolton, Lancashire, BL6 6AT

☏ 01204 669858

✉ bswscribe@aol.com

Editor Rod Riesco

Established 1995

Insider Info A semi-annual creative writing magazine, covering the literary interests of the Bank Street Writer's Group. Present circulation of 70. 100 per cent of the publication is written by freelance writers. Manuscripts are published four months after acceptance. Payment is one complimentary copy. Byline is given. Publication is not copyrighted, but one time rights are bought. Editorial lead time is six months. Accepts queries by mail, email or phone. Aims to respond to queries and manuscripts within two months. Sample copy available for £3. Writer's guidelines are free on request.

Non-fiction Publishes articles on poetry, features, essays and reviews.

Fiction Publishes short fiction.

Submission Guidelines Accepts queries for fiction of up to 2,000 words. No gratuitously offensive language is accepted.

Poetry Publishes free verse, light verse and traditional poetry.

Submission Guidelines Accepts up to six sample poems.

Tips Produced by Bank Street Writers *Current Accounts* mostly features work from members of the group, but sometimes accepts contributions from other writers worldwide. Prefers work from subscribers to the magazine. Poetry, fiction, reviews and essays are welcome.

Cutting Teeth

1–2, 15 Granville Street, Glasgow, G3 7EE

✉ info@cuttingteeth.org

🌐 www.cuttingteeth.org

Editor Lynne Mackenzie

Established 1994

Insider Info A consumer literary magazine with two issues per year, covering new Scottish writing. Byline is given. Accepts queries by mail or email. Writer's guidelines available online.

Non-fiction Publishes articles on poetry and features.

Submission Guidelines Accepts queries.

Fiction Publishes short fiction.

Submission Guidelines Send complete manuscripts for fiction, of up to 2,500 words.

Poetry Publishes avant-garde, free verse and light verse poetry.

Submission Guidelines Accepts up to six sample poems.

Tips *Cutting Teeth* is a small literary magazine dedicated to promoting new Scottish writing. It publishes both poetry and prose, as well as some articles, but only accepts submissions by post. Currently redeveloping their website, check back frequently for updates.

Cycle Sport

Leon House, 233 High Street, Croydon, CR9 1HZ

☏ 020 8726 8462

☏ 020 8726 8499

✉ cyclesport@ipcmedia.com

🌐 www.cyclesport.co.uk

Parent Company IPC Media Ltd

Editor Robert Garbutt

Contact Deputy Editor, Nigel Wynn

Established 1991

Insider Info A monthly consumer magazine covering cycle sports subjects. Present circulation of 18,165. Accepts queries by mail and email,

Non-fiction Publishes photo features and features.

* Pays £120 per 1,000 words for unsolicited articles.
Submission Guidelines Send complete manuscripts for articles between 1,500 and 2,000 words.
Images Send photos with submission.
Tips Prints comprehensive coverage of the world's leading professional events, like the Tour de France. It also has big interviews and action photography. Will consider unsolicited manuscripts, but articles with accompanying illustrations are preferred.

Cycling Plus
30 Monmouth Street, Bath, BA1 2BW
- 01225 442244
- 01225 822793
- cyclingplus@futurenet.co.uk
- www.cyclingplus.co.uk

Parent Company Future Publishing Ltd
Editor Rob Spedding
Contact Deputy Editor, Neil Pedoe; Art Editor, Warren Rossiter
Established 1992
Insider Info A monthly consumer magazine covering cycling. Present circulation is 31,704.
Non-fiction Publishes bike repair & maintenance, cycling & route guides, fitness, health, product test, tips and technique articles.
Tips *Cycling Plus* covers every aspect of sport and leisure road cycling. The magazine is aimed at beginner and expert cyclists of between 25 to 40 years of age.

Cycling Weekly
Leon House, 233 High Street, Croydon, CR9 1HZ
- 020 8726 8462
- 020 8726 8499
- cycling@ipcmedia.com
- www.cyclingweekly.co.uk

Parent Company IPC Media Ltd
Editor Robert Garbutt
Established 1891
Insider Info A weekly consumer magazine covering cycling topics. Present circulation of 27,609. Accepts queries by mail.
Non-fiction Publishes features, interviews/profiles, reviews, and new product articles.
* Purchases 60 non-fiction manuscripts per year. Pays between £60 and £120 per 1,000 words for unsolicited articles.
Submission Guidelines Accepts queries or complete manuscripts of up to 2,000 words.
Fillers Uses newsbreaks of up to 300 words.
* Pays a maximum of £15 per filler.
Tips Covers a mix of fitness advice, bike tests, product reviews, news and ride guides, as well as coverage of the national and international racing

scene. Most work is commissioned privately, but they are interested in seeing unsolicited manuscripts and ideas. Writers with a strong technical knowledge, or a background in cycle sport will have an advantage.

Cyphers
3 Selskar Terrace, Ranelagh, Dublin 6, Republic of Ireland
- 00353 1 497 8866
- www.cyphersmagazine.org

Editor Eilean Ní Chuilleanain
Established 1975
Insider Info A consumer literary magazine covering Irish writing. Accepts queries by mail or fax.
Non-fiction Publishes critical articles on poetry.
Fiction Publishes new Irish fiction.
Poetry Publishes free verse, light verse and traditional Irish language poetry.
Tips *Cyphers* is Ireland's longest running literary magazine and publishes Irish poetry – in Irish and English – and poetry in translation, as well as some prose fiction and criticism and graphic art. The major focus however, remains on Irish poetry.

Daemon
2/R West Bank Quadrant, Glasgow, G12 8NT
- 0141 334 0310
- 0141 586 3027
- dharma46@hotmail.com

Parent Company Survivors' Poetry Scotland
Editor Gerry Loose
Insider Info A bi-monthly consumer literary magazine focusing on Scottish poetry from the survivors of abuse of various kinds.
Tips *Daemon* will usually only publish work from within the Survivors' Poetry Scotland group.

Dalesman
The Water Mill, Broughton Hall, Skipton, BD23 3AG
- 01756 701381
- 01756 701326
- editorial@dalesman.co.uk
- www.dalesman.co.uk

Parent Company Country Publications Ltd
Editor Terry Fletcher
Established 1939
Insider Info A monthly consumer magazine covering countryside pursuits in Yorkshire. Present circulation of 37,687. Accepts queries by mail, email or phone.
Non-fiction Publishes photo features, features, interviews/profile and historical/nostalgic articles on Yorkshire.

Submission Guidelines Accepts queries for articles of between 1,000 and 1,500 words.
Images Send photos with submission.
Tips Each issue contains stories about the people and places that make Yorkshire unique, articles on history and nature, and colour photography. Submissions must be of specific Yorkshire interest. It is the largest local interest magazine in the UK.

Dandelion Arts Magazine
24 Frosty Hollow, East Hunsbury, Northamptonshire, NN4 0SY
- 01604 701730
- 01604 701730

Editor Joaquina Gonzales-Marina
Insider Info A consumer literary and arts magazine.
Non-fiction Publishes articles on poetry, features and interviews/profiles on artists and arts topics.
Submission Guidelines Accepts queries.
Fiction Publishes short stories.
Poetry Publishes free verse and traditional poetry.
Tips An international magazine of arts and writing, which publishes new poetry, short stories, articles and interviews. As an arts magazine, it does not solely focus on writing. Will also consider submissions from abroad.

The Dark Horse
c/o 3–B Blantyre Mill Road, Bothwell, South Lanarkshire, G71 8DD
- 01698 850410
- gjctdh@freenetname.co.uk
- www.star.ac.uk/darkhorse.html

Parent Company The Dark Horse
Editor Gerry Cambridge
Established 1995
Insider Info An international literary magazine committed to British and American poetry, published in Scotland annually. Queries are accepted by mail and email. Aims to respond to queries and manuscripts within ten weeks. Writer's guidelines are available online.
Non-fiction Publish a mix of essays, reviews, and interviews
Submission Guidelines Submissions should include sufficient return postage or international reply coupons, and SAE if contributors wish unused submissions to be returned. Prefers to respond by email to all work submitted, and to recycle unused typescripts. Unsolicited submissions by email are not accepted. Send hard copy only in the first instance.
Poetry Publishes free verse and traditional verse.
Tips *Dark Horse* are proud of discovering new writers and poets, so publishing history is not necessarily important.

Dark Tales
7 Offley Street, Worcester, WR3 8BH
- sean@darktales.co.uk
- darktales.co.uk

Editor Sean Jeffery
Established 2003
Insider Info A consumer magazine publication, issued quarterly, covering horror, science fiction, speculative fiction and dark fantasy short stories. Payment is upon publication. 100 per cent of the magazine is written by freelancers. Submissions are published approximately six months after acceptance. Publication is copyrighted, and a byline is given. Publishes first UK serial rights and electronic rights. Average lead time is three months. Seasonal material must be submitted three months in advance. Queries accepted by mail and email. Aims to respond to queries within one month and manuscripts within three months. Payment is via cash and a complimentary copy. Sample copy, a 'best of' issue, is available by post for £1.50. Manuscript guidelines are available online or by email.
Fiction Interested in horror (psychological horror preferred), science fiction, dark fantasy and speculative fiction.
* Buys roughly 48 fiction manuscripts per year. Payment is £2.50 per thousand words, plus one contributor copy.
Tips Dark Tales is looking for well-written, entertaining speculative fiction, horror and dark fantasy stories, with believable characters and page turning plot. Think of the work of authors such as Douglas Adams, Orson Scott Card, Stephen King, Dean Koontz and Michael Marshall Smith and you're somewhere along the right lines. There must be an emotional heart to a story, no matter how dark. Stories also published from regular short story contest with prize money of £250 for the winner, £50 and £25 for the runners-up, and £5 for all other shortlisted entrants.

The David Jones Journal
22 Gower Road, Sketty, Swansea, SA2 9BY
- 01792 206144
- 01792 470385
- anne.price-owen@davidjonessociety.org
- www.davidjonessociety.org

Contact The David Jones Society
Editor Anne Price-Owen
Established 1997
Insider Info The annual publication of The David Jones Society. Present circulation 400.
Non-fiction Publishes articles on poetry, features, interviews/profiles, reviews and news relating to David Jones the poet.

Submission Guidelines Send query before sending submissions.
Fiction Publishes short fiction.
Tips Submissions should relate to the painter/poet, David Jones, his life, work and themes.

Debenhams Desire
23 Howland Street, London, W1A 1AQ
- 020 7462 7913
- 020 7462 7467
- www.publicis-blueprint.co.uk
Parent Company Publicis Blueprint Ltd (Publishers) and Debenhams
Editor Amanda Morgan
Contact Art Director, Dale Walker
Established 2004
Insider Info A bi-monthly consumer magazine covering Debenhams' product ranges and general lifestyle. Present circulation is 747,251.
Non-fiction Publishes features and product review articles.
Tips *Debenhams Desire* is available to customers of the department store. It covers the designer clothing ranges at Debenhams and include articles on beauty, fashion and homes. It is primarily aimed at women aged between 25 and 55 years old.

Decanter
Blue Fin Building, 110 Southwark Street, London, SE1 0SU
- 020 7261 5000
- 020 3148 8524
- editor@decanter.com
- www.decanter.com
Parent Company IPC Media Ltd
Editor Guy Woodward
Established 1975
Insider Info A monthly consumer magazine covering the world of wine. Present circulation of roughly 40,000.
Non-fiction Publishes illustrated features on wine.
* Pays £230 per 1,000 words for unsolicited articles.
Submission Guidelines Accepts articles of between 1,000 and 1,800 words by hard copy.
Tips *Decanter* aims to be the 'wine bible'. As Britain's leading wine magazine, it is aimed at both experts and enthusiasts in over 90 countries. The Editor does not like email submissions, so please send feature ideas via post or fax.

Decanto
PO Box 3257, Littlehampton, BN16 9AF
- masque_pub@tiscali.co.uk
- myweb.tiscali.co.uk/masquepublishing/decanto.html
Parent Company Masque Publishing

Editor Lisa Stewart
Established 2002
Insider Info A bi-monthly consumer poetry magazine. Accepts queries by mail or email. Aims to respond to queries and manuscripts within six weeks. Writer's guidelines are available online.
Poetry Publishes avant-garde, free verse, haiku, light verse and traditional poetry.
Submission Guidelines Accepts up to six sample poems.
Tips *Decanto* is an independent self-funded poetry magazine, which aims to offer poets the freedom to write in whatever style they wish. It includes new poetry from new and established writers, as well as articles on poetics and reviews. The magazine will accept any kind of poetry submission, but unfortunately, being entirely self-funded, cannot offer payment or contributor copies for accepted submissions.

delicious
Sea Containers House, 20 Upper Ground, London, SE1 9PD
- 020 7775 7775
- 020 7775 7705
- info@deliciousmagazine.co.uk
- www.deliciousmagazine.co.uk
Parent Company Seven Publishing
Editor Matthew Drennan
Established 2003
Insider Info A monthly consumer magazine covering cookery and kitchen topics. Present circulation of 103,041. Accepts queries by email.
Non-fiction Publishes recipes and features on food.
Tips Aims to appeal to food lovers with well packaged and unusual features and food ideas. Seeks recipes, either simple or sophisticated, as well as features on food and where it comes from.

Derbyshire Life & Countryside
61 Friar Gate, Derby, DE1 1DJ
- 01332 227850
- 01332 227860
- joy.hales@archant.co.uk
- www.derbyshirelife.co.uk
Parent Company Archant Life
Editor Joy Hales
Contact Features, Penny Oldham
Insider Info A monthly consumer magazine covering the Derbyshire area. Present circulation of 15,793. Accepts queries by mail or email.
Non-fiction Interested in local interest articles, event listings and information on products and services across Derbyshire.
Submission Guidelines Accepts queries and completed manuscript submissions.

Descent

PO Box 100, Abergavenny, NP7 9WY

- 01873 737707
- descent@wildplaces.co.uk
- www.caving.uk.com

Parent Company Wild Places Publishing
Editor Chris Howes
Established 1969
Insider Info A bi-monthly consumer magazine that covers caving and mine exploration. Accepts queries by mail or email.
Non-fiction Interested in exploration news, reviews and general articles on caves and caving written by those taking part.
Submission Guidelines Accepts queries and completed manuscript submissions of up to 2,000 words.

Devon Life

Archant House, Babbage Road, Totnes, Devon, TQ9 5JA

- 01803 860916
- 01803 860926
- devonlife@archant.co.uk
- www.devonlife.co.uk

Parent Company Archant Life
Editor Jane Fitzgerald
Established 1996
Insider Info A monthly consumer magazine covering lifestyle topics in the county of Devon. Present circulation of 16,217. Accepts queries by mail or email. Sample copy available online. Writer's guidelines are free on request. Media pack is available online.
Non-fiction Publishes photo features, features, interviews/profiles and general interest articles.
Submission Guidelines Accepts queries, with published clips, for articles between 600 and 2,000 words.
Images Accepts transparencies. Send photos with submission.
Tips *Devon Life* includes photo features, articles, regional food and drink guides, property, and general regional interest. 'It is wise to submit a synopsis that indicates why the article would appeal to *Devon Life*. Include clips and your publishing history. You can attach the complete manuscript, but there is no guarantee it will be used.'

Dial 174

21 Mill Road, Watlington, Norfolk, PE33 0HH

- 01533 811949
- apoet@globalnet.co.uk

Editor Josephine Hemmings
Insider Info A quarterly consumer literary magazine.

Non-fiction Publishes articles on poetry, features and reviews.
Submission Guidelines Accepts queries.
Fiction Publishes short fiction.
Poetry Publishes a mixture of poetry.
Tips *Dial 174* publishes short stories and poetry, reviews, articles on writing, news and artwork. It also runs various writing competitions, where the winners can be published in the magazine.

The Dickensian

The Dickens Fellowship, Dickens House, 48 Doughty Street, London, WC1N 2LX

- 01227 827001
- m.y.andrews@ukc.ac.uk

Parent Company The Dickens Fellowship
Editor Prof Malcolm Andrews
Insider Info A journal, with three issues per year, covering the life and work of Charles Dickens. Accepts queries by mail or email.
Non-fiction Interested in articles related to Charles Dickens.
Submission Guidelines Accepts completed manuscript submissions by post (with SAE) to the editor at: School of English, Rutherford College, University of Kent, Canterbury, Kent, CT2 7NX.
Tips *The Dickensian* welcomes articles about any aspect of Dickens' life, work or characters, but cannot offer any payment.

Digital Camera Magazine

30 Monmouth Street, Bath, BA1 2BW

- 01225 442244
- 01225 732295
- digital.camera@futurenet.co.uk
- www.digitalcameramagazine.co.uk

Parent Company Future Publishing Ltd
Editor Marcus Hawkins
Insider Info A consumer magazine with 13 issues per year, covering digital photography topics. Present circulation of 55,525.
Non-fiction Publishes photo features and features.
Submission Guidelines Accepts queries.
Tips The magazine looks for inspirational images, expert techniques and essential tips. It also aims to keep up to date with the latest cameras, accessories and software. Contact the Editor with feature ideas. Technical knowledge or practical experience is necessary.

Digital Photo

Media House, Peterborough Business Park, Peterborough, PE2 6EA

- 01733 468000
- 01733 468397
- dp@emap.com

@ www.dpmag.co.uk
Parent Company EMAP Plc
Editor Jon Adams
Contact Deputy Editor, Kingsley Singleton; Creative Editor, Chris Robinson; Technical Editor, Phil Hall
Established 1997
Insider Info A monthly consumer magazine covering digital photography. Present circulation is 70,039.
Non-fiction Publishes photo features, expert advice and tutorials, software tutorials, buying and selling guides and product reviews.
Tips *Digital Photo* covers all aspects of buying and selling digital cameras, practical digital photography and printing or downloading images to a computer.

Digital Video
2 Balcombe Street, London, NW1 6NW
@ 020 7042 4000
@ jamie.ewbank@futurenet.co.uk
@ www.camuser.co.uk
Parent Company Future Publishing Ltd
Editor Robert Hull
Contact Publisher, Kelly Corten; Deputy Editor, Jamie Ewbank
Established 1988
Insider Info A monthly consumer magazine covering digital video making. Present circulation is 14,380.
Non-fiction Publishes photo features, news, product reviews and technical articles.
Tips *Digital Video* covers all aspects of using and creating high quality digital videos. The magazine is aimed at amateur digital video makers of any skill level.

Director
116 Pall Mall, London, SW1Y 5ED
@ 020 7766 8950
@ 020 7766 8840
@ director-ed@iod.com
@ www.director.co.uk
Parent Company Director Publications Ltd
Editor Richard Cree
Contact Managing Editor, Amy Duff
Established 1947
Insider Info A monthly trade magazine covering business management topics. Present circulation of 58,404. 65 per cent of the publication is written by freelance writers. Manuscript is published eight weeks after acceptance. A kill fee of 50 per cent is offered and a byline is sometimes given. Purchases all rights. Editorial lead time is 12 weeks. Seasonal material should be submitted three months in advance. Aims to respond to queries within two weeks and manuscripts within one week. Accepts queries by mail. Sample copy is free on request.
Non-fiction Publishes features, interviews/profile and reviews.
Submission Guidelines Accepts query with published clips, plus CV, for articles between 500 and 2,000 words.
Tips *Director's* readers are members of the UK based business organisation, the Institute of Directors (IoD). The magazine reflects the real issues and interests of this influential group, while maintaining editorial independence from the IoD. It generally only uses work from regular contributors rather than unsolicited submissions. Send a letter with feature ideas and examples of printed work to the Editor.

Dirtbike Rider
Victoria Street, Morecombe, Lancashire, LA4 4AG
@ 01524 834030
@ 01524 423469
@ sean.lawless@dirtbikerider.co.uk
@ www.dirtbikerider.co.uk
Parent Company Lancaster & Morecombe Newspapers Ltd
Editor Sean Lawless
Established 1981
Insider Info A monthly consumer magazine covering motoring and specialising in dirtbiking. Accepts queries by email.
Non-fiction Publishes features, interviews/profiles, reviews, new product and technical articles.
Submission Guidelines Accepts queries for articles of up to 2,000 words.
Tips Publishes stories on motocross, supercross and the rest of the off-road motorcycle world. A high level of interest and experience in dirt bikes is essential for any article.

Disability Arts in London (DAIL) Magazine
20–22 Waterson Street, London, E2 8HE
@ 020 7739 1133
@ dailmagazine@gmail.com
@ www.ldaf.org
Parent Company London Disability Arts Forum (LDAF)
Established 1986
Insider Info A consumer magazine focusing on the world of disabled artists. Accepts queries by mail or email. Sample copy available online.
Non-fiction Publishes photo features, inspirational articles, features, interviews/profiles and reviews.
Submission Guidelines Accepts queries.
Tips DAIL publishes news, previews, reviews and articles about the work of disabled artists. It also

prints interviews and general information about coping with disability. The magazine runs various short fiction and poetry competitions, that are open to disabled artists and writers. Prizewinners are often published in the magazine.

Disability Now (DN)
6 Market Road, London, N7 9PW

📞 020 7619 7323
📠 020 7619 7331
📧 editor@disabilitynow.org.uk
🌐 www.disabilitynow.org.uk
Parent Company Scope
Editor Ian Macrae
Contact Deputy Editor, John Pring
Established 1984
Insider Info A monthly consumer magazine covering all aspects of disability, including news, features, profiles, arts, sport, holidays and equipment. Present circulation of 20,735. 30 per cent of the publication is written by freelance writers. Payment is upon publication and never with contributor copies instead of cash. A byline is given. Publication is copyrighted. Accepts queries by mail, email, fax or phone. Will pay the expenses of writers on assignment. Sample copy, writer's guidelines and editorial calendar are free on request.
Non-fiction Publishes photo features, interviews/ profiles, reviews, new product, general interest, travel and personal experience articles.
Submission Guidelines Accepts queries for articles of up to 800 words.
Images State availability of photos with submission.
* Pays a variable fee per photo.

Diva
Unit M, Spectrum House, 32–34 Gordon House Road, London, NW5 1LP

📞 020 7424 7400
📠 020 7424 7401
📧 edit@divamag.co.uk
🌐 www.divamag.co.uk
Parent Company Millivres-Prowler Ltd
Editor Jane Czyzselska
Established 1994
Insider Info A monthly consumer magazine covering the gay and lesbian lifestyle. Present circulation is roughly 50,000. Accepts queries by email.
Non-fiction Publishes photo features, interviews, illustrations and features of gay and lesbian interest.
* Pays £15 per 100 words for unsolicited articles.
Submission Guidelines Accepts queries or complete manuscripts for articles of between 800 and 1,500 words. Please send samples of writing with any new pitches.

Images Send photos with submission.
Tips *Diva* welcomes unsolicited news and features – ideally supported by photographs, and in keeping with the overall tone of the magazine. Will occasionally accept short stories. Check the magazine prior to submitting, for a style guide.

Dive Magazine
1 Victoria Villas, Richmond, TW9 2GW

📞 020 8332 9995
📠 020 8332 9307
📧 simon@dive.uk.com
🌐 www.divemagazine.co.uk
Parent Company Circle Publishing
Editor Simon Rogerson
Contact Publisher, Paul Critcher; News Editor, Charlotte Boan
Established 1999
Insider Info A monthly consumer magazine covering scuba diving. Present circulation is 39,307.
Non-fiction Publishes news, features, profiles, product reviews and practical articles on diving.
Tips Examples of regularly published articles are industry news, new product reviews, advice articles, and dive location guides.

Dorset Life
7 The Leanne, Sandford Lane, Wareham, Dorset, BH20 4DY

📞 01929 551264
📠 01929 552099
Editor John Newth
Established 1967
Insider Info A monthly consumer magazine covering Dorset. Accepts queries by mail or email.
Non-fiction Interested in local interest and lifestyle articles related to Dorset.
Submission Guidelines Accepts queries and completed manuscript submissions.

Drapers
Greater London House, Hampstead Road, London, NW1 7EJ

📞 020 7728 5000
📠 020 7812 3760
📧 lauretta.roberts@emap.com
🌐 www.drapersonline.com
Parent Company EMAP Retail Ltd
Editor Lauretta Roberts
Contact Executive Editor, Lorna Hall
Established 1887
Insider Info A weekly trade journal covering fashion and clothing. Present circulation of 12,672. Accepts queries by email.
Non-fiction Publishes photo features and features.
Submission Guidelines Accepts queries.

Images Send photos with submission.
Tips The business editorial content is aimed primarily at fashion retailers. Contains articles on fashion, recruitment, current vacancies in the industry, and the latest trends. Check previous issues for tone and content.

Dream Catcher
Jasmine Cottage, 4 Church Street, Market Rasen, Lincolnshire, LN8 3ET
01673 844325
paulsuther@hotmail.com
Parent Company Dream Catcher Books
Editor Paul Sutherland
Established 1995
Insider Info A consumer literary journal with two issues per year. Present circulation of 600. A byline is given.
Non-fiction Publishes articles on poetry, features, interviews/profiles and reviews.
Submission Guidelines Accepts queries.
Fiction Publishes mainstream short fiction.
Submission Guidelines Accepts queries for short fiction of up to 2,000 words.
Poetry Publishes free verse and traditional poetry.
Tips *Dream Catcher* is a national literary journal that publishes the latest stories, poems and artwork, as well as reviews and biographies of the new and established contributors. The magazine often has submissions from well-known authors, and is large enough to be able to accept many submissions per issue. The Editor looks for diversity in submissions and welcomes poetry, short stories, literary articles and reviews from either new, or established authors. *Dream Catcher* will accept longer submissions for short stories if they are of exceptional quality.

The Drouth
PO Box 7419, Glasgow, G5 9WB
0141 554 1071
0141 429 1805
thedrouth@yahoo.co.uk
www.thedrouth.com
Editor Mitchell Miller
Established 2001
Insider Info A quarterly consumer magazine offering informed critique, satire and prose and covering film and theatre. Queries accepted by mail and email. Writer's guidelines are available online.
Non-fiction Publishes book excerpts, poetry, features and literary criticism.
Submission Guidelines Send complete manuscript via email. Articles may be of any length.
Fiction Publishes mainstream fiction, short stories and novellas.

Submission Guidelines Send complete manuscript via email. Submissions may be of any length.
Poetry Publishes free verse and traditional verse.
Submission Guidelines Send complete manuscript via email.
Tips *The Drouth* is also a forum, its format providing structure for continuing debate and dialogue. Although they have no explicit political or social agenda, each issue tends to be loosely set around an underlying satirical theme or debate. They also have a strong commitment to theatre, publishing full or extracted original plays. There is no editorial control over the views of contributors, and *The Drouth* welcomes work from a wide range of viewpoints and of any length. The editors are keen to make contact with potential writers and discuss ideas for pieces. The best way to contact them is by email.

DVD & Blu-ray Review
2 Balcombe Street, London, NW1 6NW
020 7042 4000
020 7042 4389
dvdreview@futurenet.co.uk
Parent Company Future Publishing Ltd
Editor Alastair Upham
Contact Deputy Editor, Michael Carhart-Harris; Features Editor, Richard Matthews
Insider Info A monthly consumer magazine covering DVD reviews. Present circulation is 24,957.
Non-fiction Publishes news, features and review articles.
Tips *DVD Review* covers all the latest film, television and music DVD releases.

Earth Love
PO Box 11219, Paisley, PA1 2WH
earth.love@ntlworld.com
Editor Tracy Patrick
Established 2001
Insider Info A consumer literary magazine issued three times a year, covering general interest literary subjects with a particular focus on the environment. A byline is given. Writer's guidelines are available online.
Non-fiction Interested in photo features, poetry articles, features, interviews/profiles, and general interest pieces.
Submission Guidelines Send complete manuscript.
Poetry Interested in free verse, light verse and traditional poetry.
Tips *Earth Love* is a small poetry magazine with a conservation and nature theme. It is dedicated to helping the environment and all proceeds go to animal welfare and environmental charities. The magazine contains poetry, articles on books, music

and people, black and white photography, and articles about conservation and nature. *Earth Love* also publishes anthologies and booklets on the same theme as the magazine, and is generally seeking articles for their 'Inspirations' feature. Articles should be about conservation or nature themes, or about important people working in conservation.

Eastern Art Report
PO Box 13666, London, SW14 8WF
- 020 8392 1122
- 020 8392 1422
- ear@eapgroup.com
- www.eapgroup.com

Parent Company EAPGroup International Media
Contact Editor in Chief, Sajid Rizvi
Established 1989
Insider Info A consumer magazine publication issued bi-weekly, covering Asian and African leisure interests and art. Present circulation of roughly 14,600. Accepts queries by mail, email and fax. Sample copy is available free on request. Writer's guidelines and media packs are available on the website.
Non-fiction Interested in reviews, art market reports and general interest pieces.
Submission Guidelines Accepts queries.
Tips *Eastern Art Report* (EAR) is an international magazine focused on the arts of Asia and Africa and the arts practised by the people of Asian and African origin in North America, Europe and elsewhere. EAR includes scholarly articles, exclusive interviews, exhibition and book reviews and news stories. Contributions to EAR are welcomed (on a wholly voluntary basis) from curators, historians, journalists and readers – provided such submissions satisfy the general guidelines on the website.

Eastern Rainbow
17 Farrow Road, Whaplode Drove, Spalding, PE12 0TS
- p_rance@yahoo.co.uk
- http://uk.geocities.com/p_rance/pandf.htm

Parent Company Peace & Freedom Press
Editor Paul Rance
Established 1992
Insider Info A consumer magazine issued twice a year, which covers general literary subjects with a particular focus on 20th Century arts and culture. Present circulation of 500. A byline is given.
Non-fiction Interested in photo features, poetry, features, interviews/profile, and general interest pieces.
Submission Guidelines Please send complete manuscript. Articles should be a maximum of 500 words.

Fiction Publishes short, genre fiction.
Submission Guidelines Accepts submissions from subscribers only.
Poetry Accepts free verse, light verse and traditional poetry.
Submission Guidelines Poems should be a maximum of 23 lines. Accepts submissions from subscribers only.
Tips *Eastern Rainbow* accepts any kind of genre fiction, including science fiction, fantasy and horror, and often prints articles on famous 20th Century icons, such as David Bowie or George Orwell.

East Lothian Life
1 Beveridge Row, Belhaven, Dunbar, East Lothian, EH42 1TP
- 01368 863593
- 01368 863593
- info@east-lothian-life.co.uk
- www.eastlothianlife.co.uk

Parent Company PJ Design
Editor Pauline Jaffray
Established 1988
Insider Info A consumer magazine publication issued quarterly, covering life in East Lothian. Present circulation of roughly 3,500. Payment is upon publication. 50 per cent of the magazine is written by freelancers. Publication is copyrighted and a byline is given. Submissions are published approximately four months after publication, with an editorial lead time of 12 weeks. Seasonal material must be submitted 16 weeks in advance. Queries accepted by mail. Simultaneous submissions and previously published submissions accepted. Aims to respond to queries and manuscripts within ten days and other issues within 17 days. A sample copy and writer's guidelines are available free on request. Payment is not made with contributor copies or other premiums.
Non-fiction Interested in features, general interest, travel and historical/nostalgic pieces.
Submission Guidelines Articles should be between 650 and 1,300 words. Contact Pauline Jaffray.
Tips All articles must have an East Lothian slant.

Easy Living
6–8 Old Bond Street, London, W1S 4PH
- 020 7499 9080
- 020 7399 2625
- easylivingeditorial@condenast.co.uk
- www.easylivingmagazine.com

Parent Company Condè Nast Publications Ltd
Editor Susie Forbes
Contact Features Director, Andreina Cordani
Established 2005

Insider Info A monthly consumer magazine covering women's interest and lifestyle. Present circulation is 201,147.

Non-fiction Publishes features, interviews, profiles, product reviews and advice articles on fashion, health, beauty, house & home, entertainment and the arts.

Tips *Easy Living* is aimed at women between the ages of 30 and 59.

ECM

European Cosmetic Markets
6–14 Underwood Street, London, N1 7JQ
- 020 7549 8626
- 020 7549 8622
- ecm@wilmington.co.uk
- www.cosmeticsbusiness.com

Parent Company Wilmington Media
Contact Managing Editor, Clare Henderson; Assistant Editor, Georgina Caldwell
Established 1983

Insider Info A trade journal magazine issued monthly covering the cosmetics industry and market research. Present circulation of 500. Payment upon publication. 25 per cent of publication is written by freelancers. Submissions published approximately 30 days after acceptance with an editorial lead time of 30 days. Publication is copyrighted and a byline is sometimes given. Seasonal material must be submitted 30 days in advance. Purchases all rights. Queries accepted by email. A sample copy is available online. Editorial calendars are available free on request. Media packs are available on the website.

Non-fiction Publishes news and features.

Tips *ECM* occupies a unique niche in the C&T industry. Its detailed market reports must give up to date statistics, market trends and product information from France, Germany, Italy, Spain and the UK. Also publishes columns from the US, Russia and Brazil.

The Ecologist

Unit 102D Lana House Studios, 116–118 Commercial Street, Spitalfields, London, E1 6NF
- 020 7422 8100
- 020 7422 8101
- editorial@theecologist.org
- www.theecologist.org

Parent Company Ecosystems Ltd
Editor Pat Thomas
Contact Deputy Editor, Jon Hughes
Established 1970

Insider Info A monthly consumer magazine, covering science related news and current affairs.

Present circulation of roughly 30,000. Queries accepted by email.

Non-fiction Publishes social, economic and ecologic features and articles.

Submission Guidelines Send query with published clips, plus CV. Articles must be 500–3,000 words.

Tips *The Ecologist* aims to help set environmental and political agendas around the world by focusing on the root causes, not just the after-effects, of current events. Each month they examine the connection between a wide range of subjects including food, war, politics, pharmaceuticals, farming, toxic chemicals, corporate fraud, mass media and supermarkets. Articles for *The Ecologist* must challenge conventional thinking, and empower readers to tackle global issues on a local scale. Any submitted work must be supported by deep and accurate scientific or political knowledge, but at the same time fit in with the strong political ideology of *The Economist*.

The Economist

25 St James's Street, London, SW1A 1HG
- 020 7830 7000
- 020 7839 2968
- letters@economist.com
- www.economist.com

Parent Company The Economist Newspaper Ltd
Editor John Micklethwait
Established 1843

Insider Info A weekly consumer magazine, covering news, international affairs, business and finance. Present circulation 182,539. All articles published anonymously. Queries accepted by mail.

Non-fiction Publishes features, interviews/profiles and opinion (excluding letters to the Editor) on politics/current affairs/economy, science and technology.

Submission Guidelines Send query before sending submissions.

Tips According to its contents page, *The Economist's* goal is to 'take part in a severe contest between intelligence, which presses forward, and an unworthy, timid ignorance obstructing our progress.' Subjects covered include international news, economics, politics, business, finance, science and technology and the arts, but not sports (though articles about the business of sports are occasionally published). The publication is targeted at the high-end 'prestige' segment of the market. If submissions are as close to *The Economist's* political style as possible (prior to editing), and also have an edge of wry humour, they may have a better chance.

Edge

30 Monmouth Street, Bath, BA1 2BW
- 01225 442244
- 01225 732275
- edge-online@futurenet.co.uk
- www.edge-online.co.uk

Parent Company Future Publishing
Editor Tony Mott
Established 1993
Insider Info A consumer magazine publication issued monthly covering computing and gaming consoles. Present circulation of 30,164.
Non-fiction Interested in features, interviews/profiles, reviews, new products, and technical pieces.
Tips *Edge* is known for its harsh editorial stance and its controversial grading of popular games. Check the magazine for style and tone before contacting the Editor with ideas.

The Edge

65 Guinness Buildings, Hammersmith, London, W6 8BD
- davec@theedge.abelgratis.co.uk
- www.theedge.abelgratis.co.uk

Editor Dave Clark
Insider Info A literary magazine, priced at £5 per issue, covering speculative fiction. Payment is negotiable up to £50 per 1,000 words, plus one free copy. Accepts queries by mail or email.
Non-fiction Publishes reviews (books, films and graphic novels), interviews/profiles and feature articles of between 2,000 to 20,000 words.
Submission Guidelines Write with samples of written work, either published or unpublished, by post.
Fiction Publishes science-fiction, fantasy, horror, erotica and slipstream stories, often with an urban theme.
Submission Guidelines Accepts submissions of short stories of over 2,000 words by post.
Tips *The Edge* often includes fiction and articles from well-known authors, such as Michael Moorcock. Experimental fiction is from new or previously published writers is welcome but note that The Edge has never published an unsolicited non-fiction article - always write with samples in the first instance.

Edinburgh Review

22a Buccleuch Place, Edinburgh, EH8 9LN
- 0131 651 1415
- 0131 651 1415
- edinburgh.review@ed.ac.uk
- www.englit.ed.ac.uk/edinburghreview

Parent Company Centre for the History of Ideas in Scotland

Contact Managing editor, Brian McCabe
Established 1802
Insider Info A consumer journal publication issued three times per year, covering general interest, literary subjects. Queries accepted by mail and email. A sample copy and writer's guidelines are available online.
Non-fiction Interested in reviews and literary criticism.
Submission Guidelines Accepts query with published clips.
Fiction Interested in novel excerpts and short fiction pieces.
Submission Guidelines Please send complete manuscript. Articles should be a maximum of 3,000 words.
Poetry Interested in free verse and traditional poetry.
Submission Guidelines Submit a maximum of 12 poems at a time.
Tips Scotland's leading journal of ideas, the *Edinburgh Review* publishes essays, short fiction, poetry and reviews aimed at an educated reading public with an interest in critical thought. The journal welcomes unsolicited submissions of short fiction, novel extracts, poetry, and critical material. The *Edinburgh Review* is also keen to hear from people interested in reviewing contemporary Scottish literature and critical monographs.

Education Journal

Devonia House, 4 Union Terrace, Crediton, Exeter, EX17 3DY
- 01363 774455
- 01363 776592
- www.educationpublishing.com

Editor Demitri Coryton
Established 1903
Insider Info A journal, with 11 issues per year, covering all aspects of education. Accepts queries by mail or email.
Non-fiction Interested in development, management, policy, reference, research and statistical articles related to the education industry.
Submission Guidelines Accepts queries and completed manuscript submissions of up to 1,000 words.

The Eildon Tree

Library Headquarters, St Mary's Mill, Selkirk, TD7 5EW
- 01750 724901
- artservice@scotborders.gov.uk
- www.eildontree.org.uk

Parent Company Scottish Borders Council

Insider Info A literary magazine published by the Scottish Borders Council. Queries accepted by mail and telephone.
Non-fiction Publishes articles and information about writing in Scotland.
Fiction Publishes mainstream fiction.
Submission Guidelines Send query before sending submissions. Submissions should be 3,000 words in length.
Poetry Publishes free verse, light verse and traditional verse.
Submission Guidelines Send query before sending submissions. Poems should be up to 40 lines in length.
Tips Publishes poetry and prose from writers in, or around, the Scottish Borders region, as well as some writing from further afield. Runs various themed writing competitions, which offer publication in the magazine as a prize.

Elle
64 North Row, London, W1K 7LL
- 020 7150 7000
- 020 7150 7670
- www.elle.com

Parent Company Hachette Filipacchi Media
Editor Lorraine Candy
Contact Entertainment Director/Executive Editor, Tom Macklin; Features Editor, Anna Pursglove; Features Assistant, Sarah Lowden
Established 1985
Insider Info A consumer magazine publication issued monthly, covering women's interests, lifestyle and fashion. Present circulation of 203,471. Accepts query by mail.
Non-fiction Interested in exposés, features, interviews/profiles and general interest pieces.
Submission Guidelines Articles should be between 500 and 2,000 words. Contact the Features Editor by post with ideas for articles, and be sure to include clippings.
Tips *Elle* is the world's largest fashion magazine for the women. The style of the magazine is designed to be a mix of culture, controversy and cool.

Elle Decoration
64 North Row, London, W1K 7LL
- 020 7150 7000
- 020 7150 7671
- amybradford@hf-uk.com

Parent Company Hachette Filipacchi (UK) Ltd
Editor Michelle Ogundehin
Contact Features Editor, Amy Bradford; Art Editor, Brian Sasser
Established 1989

Insider Info A monthly consumer magazine covering interior design and decoration. Present circulation is 64,030.
Non-fiction Publishes features, reviews and showcase articles.
Tips *Elle Decoration* focuses mainly on contemporary design.

Emma's Diary
1 Globeside Business Park, Field House Lane, Marlow, SL7 1HY
- 01628 891644
- 01628 816883
- enquiries@emmasdiary.co.uk
- www.emmasdiary.co.uk

Parent Company Lifecycle Marketing Ltd
Contact Editor in Chief, Alison Mackonochie
Insider Info A consumer magazine, with two issues per year, covering pregnancy and childbirth. Present circulation is 414,240.
Non-fiction Publishes features, true-life stories, advice and technical articles.
Tips Emma's Diary is available at surgeries around the UK and is given to women on confirmation of their pregnancy. It contains features and medical advice on pregnancy and childbirth, as well as real-life stories and experience features.

Empire
Mappin House, 4 Winsley Street, London, W1W 8HF
- 020 7182 8000
- 020 7182 8703
- empire@emap.com
- www.empireonline.co.uk

Parent Company EMAP
Editor Mark Dinning
Contact Editor-at-Large, Nev Pierce; Features Editor, Dan Jolin
Established 1989
Insider Info A consumer magazine publication issued monthly, covering leisure interests, film and video reviews. Present circulation of 187,202.
Non-fiction Interested in features and reviews.
* Payment for unsolicited articles is £300 per 1000 words.
Submission Guidelines Accepts written queries.
Images Send photos with submission.
Tips *Empire* is a guide to the movies, it aims to cover the world of films in a 'comprehensive, adult, intelligent, and witty package'. The majority of the magazine is devoted to mainstream cinema, but it also looks at art house movies, as well as the technology behind television and DVD and other media forms. *Empire* does accept submissions, but it is best to contact in writing first with a synopsis and

covering letter. Well-written reviews are most commonly accepted.

Employee Benefits
50 Poland Street, London, W1F 7AX
- 020 7970 4000
- 020 7943 8095
- amanda.wilkinson@centaur.co.uk
- www.employeebenefits.co.uk

Parent Company Centaur Media Plc
Editor Amanda Wilkinson
Contact Editorial Director, Debi O'Donovan
Established 1996
Insider Info A trade journal magazine issued monthly, covering employee benefits and human resources. Present circulation of 9,892. Payment is made upon acceptance and a byline is given. The percentage of the magazine written by freelancers varies. Queries are accepted via email.
Tips *Employee Benefits* is written for human resources practitioners and compensation and reward specialists.

The Engineer
50 Poland Street, London, W1F 7AX
- 020 7970 4000
- 020 7970 4189
- andrew.lee@centaur.co.uk
- www.theengineer.co.uk

Parent Company Centaur Holdings Plc
Editor Andrew Lee
Contact Features Editor, Jon Excell
Established 1856
Insider Info Fortnightly consumer magazine, covering engineering. Present circulation is 31,469. Queries accepted by mail and email.
Non-fiction Publishes features, interviews/profiles, technical articles and engineering news.
Submission Guidelines Send query before sending submissions. Articles must be 2,000 words.
Fillers Publishes newsbreaks as fillers. Maximum of 500 words in length.
Tips There is no demand for long features but the magazine is actively seeking national freelancers, for news and specialist technology coverage.

The English Garden
Jubilee House, 2 Jubilee Place, King's Road, London, SW3 3TQ
- 020 7751 4800
- 020 7751 4848
- theenglishgarden@archant.co.uk
- www.theenglishgarden.co.uk

Parent Company Archant Specialist
Editor Janine Wookey
Contact Deputy Editor, Jackie Bennett

Established 1996
Insider Info A monthly consumer magazine about gardening. Present circulation is 32,850. Queries accepted by mail and email.
Non-fiction Publishes photo features, features, interviews/profiles, technical and how-to articles.
Submission Guidelines Send a synopsis of 150 words along with any images. Final articles must be 1,000–1,200 words. Address to the Features Editor.
Tips Articles should contain inspiration and design ideas to help readers create the 'English' look in their own garden.

The English Home
Jubilee House, 2 Jubilee Place, King's Road, London, SW3 3TQ
- 020 7751 4800
- 020 7751 4848
- theenglishhome@archant.co.uk
- www.theenglishhome.co.uk

Parent Company Archant Specialist (London)
Editor Sharon Parsons
Contact Deputy Editor, Philippa Howard; Features Editor, Harriet Paige
Established 2000
Insider Info A bi-monthly consumer magazine covering homes and furniture. Present circulation is 70,133.
Non-fiction Publishes features, reviews, practical articles, showcase articles and buying and selling guides.
Tips Articles are largely on the subject of 'traditionally English' homes.

Envoi
44 Rudyard Road, Biddulph Moor, Stoke on Trent, ST8 7JN
- 01782 517892

Editor Roger Elkin
Established 1957
Insider Info A consumer journal publication issued three times per year in February, June and October covering general interest, poetry subjects. Present circulation of 800. A byline is given. Accepts queries by mail.
Non-fiction Interested in poetry articles, features, interviews/profiles, reviews, opinion (excluding letters to the Editor) pieces.
Submission Guidelines Accepts queries.
Poetry Interested in avant-garde, free verse, light verse and traditional poetry.
Submission Guidelines Submit a maximum of six poems at one time.
Tips Prints modern poetry from new and established writers, as well as articles on poetry, reviews, letters and competition results. All writers

featured in *Envoi* will have more than poem included, so multiple submissions are necessary. *Envoi* will usually only publish work from relatively well-known or up and coming poets. The magazine also runs various poetry competitions in each issue, with publication as a prize.

EOS magazine

Exploring the world of EOS photography
The Old Barn, Ball Lane, Tackley, Kidlington, Oxfordshire, OX5 3AG
☏ 01869 331741
☏ 01869 331641
✉ editorial@eos-magazine.com
🌐 www.eos-magazine.com
Parent Company Robert Scott Publishing
Editor Angela August
Established 1996
Insider Info A consumer magazine covering photography. The publication is issued quarterly and has a present circulation of roughly 22,000. Payment upon acceptance. Ten per cent of the magazine is written by freelancers. Submissions are published approximately three months after acceptance with an editorial lead time of two months. Publication is copyrighted and a byline is given. Purchases first UK serial rights. Seasonal work must be submitted three months in advance. Queries are accepted via email and phone. Aims to respond to queries, manuscripts and other issues within one week. For a sample copy send SAE (32mm long by 23mm), with four first class stamps. Writer's guidelines and editorial calendars are free on request.
Non-fiction Publishes how-to and technical articles on photography.
Images Accepts images with submission.
* Pays a varied fee per photo between £15 and £250. Purchases one time rights.
Submission Guidelines Submit gif/jpeg files with captions and model releases. Identification of subjects, camera, lens and exposure details are required. Send photos with submission. Contact Angela August.
Tips The magazine is dedicated to Canon EOS camera users. Articles must be technical and very specifically targeted to EOS users, and not the sort of general article you could read in other photographic press.

Equinox

134b Joy Lane, Whitstable, Kent, CT5 4ES
Editor Barbara Dordi
Insider A small consumer magazine publication, published twice a year covering general literary subjects, particularly poetry.
Poetry Interested in contemporary poetry.

Submissions Guidelines Accepts query with SAE. Poems should have lines of no more than 40 words.
Tips The magazine only accepts hard copy submissions, so always enclose SAE when sending work in.

Eratica

51 Waterloo Street, Hove, BN3 1AN
☏ 01273 302876
🌐 www.waterloopresshove.co.uk
Parent Company Waterloo Press
Editor Alan Morrison
Contact Co-Editor, Simon Jenner
Established 2001
Insider Info A consumer journal publication issued semi annually, covering literary subjects.
Non-fiction Interested in poetry, features and general interest pieces.
Poetry Interested in free verse, light verse and traditional poetry.
Tips *Eratica* poetry journal is published by Waterloo Press and prints contemporary poetry from new and established writers, as well as articles on art and music. *Erratica*'s name was formed from a crossing of 'erratic' with 'erotica' and its aim is to 'sell poetry sexily'. The magazine prefers to publish original, often disreputable poetry.

Erbacce

5 Farrell Close, Liverpool, L31 1BU
✉ erbacce@hotmail.com
🌐 www.erbacce.com
Editor Andrew Taylor
Established 2004
Insider Info A consumer journal publication issued quarterly, covering radical literary subjects. A byline is given. Queries accepted by mail and email. A sample copy is available online.
Non-fiction Interested in essays, poetry, features and reviews.
Submission Guidelines Please send complete manuscript.
Poetry Interested in avant-garde, free verse and light verse.
Submission Guidelines Submit a maximum of six poems at one time.
Tips *Erbacce* is a print and online literary journal, which publishes radical poetry from new and established writers, as well as articles, essays and reviews. The magazine aims to 'interfere with the 'normal' and 'formal' gardens of poetry.' They claim that they will publish any poetry submission from anyone, so long as it is radical and non-conformist in either content or layout, even if they disagree with the content personally.

Esquire

National Magazine House, 72 Broadwick Street, London, W1F 9EP

- 020 7439 5000
- 020 7439 5675
- esquireeditors@esquire.co.uk
- www.esquire.co.uk

Parent Company National Magazine Company Ltd
Editor Jeremy Langmead
Established 1991
Insider Info A consumer magazine publication issued monthly covering men's lifestyle. Present circulation of 58,136.
Non-fiction Publishes photo features, features, reviews, interviews/profiles and general lifestyle articles.
Tips *Esquire*'s target reader is the 'well educated, career-minded and successful' man of about 30 to 40 years of age.

Essentially America

55 Hereford Road, London, W2 5BB

- 020 7243 6954
- 020 7243 2047
- marymooremason@phoenixip.com
- www.essentiallyamerica.com

Parent Company Phoenix International Publishing
Editor Mary Moore Mason
Established 1994
Insider Info A consumer magazine publication issued quarterly covering travel to North America (USA, Canada, occasionally Mexico) for frequent British travellers. Present circulation of roughly 50,000. Payment is upon publication and is not made with contributor copies or other premiums. Assignment expenses are not paid. 90 per cent of magazine is written by freelancers. Submissions published approximately three months after acceptance with an editorial lead time of two months. Commissioning is undertaken very carefully and kill fees are very rarely required. Purchases all rights. Seasonal material must be submitted three months in advance. Accepts queries via email. Aims to respond to queries within one week. A sample copy is a available for £2.95 plus postage, which can be considerable as some issues of the magazine are more than 200 pages.
Non-fiction Interested in photo features (photos are occasionally bought in to accompany articles), humour about travel within North America and features on food, drink, film and literary sites. Also interviews/profiles (occasionally publish celebrity interviews if they are destination related), reviews (there is a book review in most issues), travel (the majority of the publication is travel), historical/nostalgic (occasional features on iconic American figures such as Elvis, or Muhammad Ali, and also on great events in North American history) and personal experience (amusing, unusual experiences in North America).
* Receives approximately 40 manuscripts from freelancers per year. Payment for assigned and unsolicited articles is negotiated upon commission.
Submission Guidelines Accepts query by email including a brief synopsis of the article. Final articles should be between 500 and 2,000 words. Send a photocopy for reprint submissions.
Images Occasionally accepts images.
* Pays a varied fee per photo that is negotiated on the few occasions photos are bought in. Purchases one time rights.
Submission Guidelines Submit gif/jpeg files with captions.
Tips Exclusively covers travel to – and the lifestyle within – the USA, Canada and, to a lesser degree, Mexico. It is aimed at well-informed frequent British travellers to these destinations. Therefore writers must be both skilled and experienced – although young talent is welcomed – and extremely knowledgeable about North America. Potential contributors should study back issues of the magazine and then send the Editor a brief email stating in one paragraph the concept of the feature, and in a second your qualifications to write the feature.

Essentials

Blue Fin Building, 110 Southwark Street, London, SE1 0SU

- 020 3148 5000
- 020 7261 5262
- essentials_feedback@ipcmedia.com
- www.essentialsmagazine.com

Parent Company IPC Media Ltd
Editor Julie Barton-Breck
Contact Editorial Assistant, Fiona Galley
Established 1988
Insider Info A consumer magazine publication issued monthly, covering women's interests and women's lifestyle/fashion. Present circulation of 100,214. Accepts query by mail.
Non-fiction Interested in inspirational articles, features, general interest and personal experience pieces.
Submission Guidelines Accepts query with complete manuscript and include SAE. Final articles should be a maximum of 2,000 words.
Tips *Essentials* tends to focus fairly heavily on health and weight loss issues, although it does cover many other aspects of lifestyle. Prospective contributors should study the magazine thoroughly before submitting anything.

Essex Life

PO Box 1099, Colchester, CO1 9DE
☎ 01772 722022
Editor Robyn Bechelet
Established 1952
Insider Info A monthly consumer magazine that covers Essex. Accepts queries by mail or email.
Non-fiction Interested in local interest and lifestyle articles related to Essex.

European Boatbuilder

Grove Farm, Botany Lane, Stratford St Andrew, Saxmundham, IP17 1LT
☎ 01728 604641
✉ phil_draper@ipcmedia.com
🌐 www.europeanboatbuilder.com
Parent Company IPC Media Ltd
Editor Phil Draper
Insider Info A trade journal, with six issues per year, covering boat construction. Circulation is ghly 6,000. Media pack available online.
Non-fiction Publishes boat construction and design articles.
Tips *European Boatbuilder* is a business publication aimed at professionals involved with the design and construction of pleasure boats and small commercial craft. Articles tend to be technical or practical in nature.

eve

174 Hammersmith Road, London, W6 7JP
☎ 020 8267 8223
☎ 020 8267 8222
✉ evemagazine@haymarket.com
🌐 www.evemagazine.co.uk
Parent Company Haymarket Publishing
Editor Nic McCarthy
Contact Features Editor, Linda Gray
Established 2000
Insider Info A consumer magazine publication issued monthly covering women's interests, women's lifestyle/fashion. Present circulation of 163,415. Queries accepted by mail.
Non-fiction Interested in features, interviews/profiles and general interest pieces.
Submission Guidelines Accepts postal queries with published clips.
Tips Contact via post with ideas aimed at specific features for the magazine, and be sure to include recent examples of writing.

Eventing

Blue Fin Building, 110 Southwark Street, London, SE1 0SU
☎ 020 3148 5000
☎ 020 3148 8127
✉ julie_harding@ipcmedia.com
Parent Company IPC Media Ltd
Editor Julie Harding
Established 1985
Insider Info A consumer magazine publication issued monthly, covering equestrian interests. Present circulation of roughly 12,000.
Non-fiction Covers news, results, features, opinions and instructional articles.
Tips The international voice and only magazine for the sport of horse trials. There are also commentaries and results from all major events, together with training features and profiles. The magazine is focused solely on the sport of horse trials and events, unrelated subjects would be covered in the sister publication, *Horse & Hound*.

Evergreen & This England

PO Box 52, Cheltenham, Gloucester, GL50 1YQ
☎ 01242 537900
☎ 01242 537901
Editor Stephen Garnett
Established 1985
Insider Info A quarterly consumer magazine that covers British lifestyle and history. Accepts queries by mail or email.
Non-fiction Interested in history, nostalgia, traditions, lifestyle and media articles related to British culture.
Tips *Evergreen* is a nostalgia magazine that celebrates British culture over the years.

evo

The Thrill of Driving
5 Tower Court, Irchester Road, Wollaston, Wellingborough, NN29 7PJ
☎ 020 7907 6310
☎ 01933 663367
✉ harrym@evo.co.uk
🌐 www.evo.co.uk
Parent Company Dennis Publishing Ltd
Editor Harrison Metcalfe
Contact Managing Editor, Janet Mills; Editor at Large, Richard Meaden
Established 1998
Insider Info A consumer magazine publication issued monthly covering motoring and motorcycling. Present circulation of 74,201.
Tips *evo* is devoted exclusively to the world's fastest and most desirable cars. It has a definite editorial slant towards the feel of a car – the 'emotive drive' – rather than its performance, this must be reflected in submitted articles.

Executive PA

Alpha House, 100 Borough High Street, London, SE1 1LB

- ☎ 020 7863 3333
- ☎ 020 7173 5101
- ✉ michael@executivepa.net
- 🌐 www.executivepa.net

Parent Company Solutions Publish Ltd

Editor Mike Dingle

Insider Info A trade journal magazine issued quarterly covering personal assistants – venues, office, business travel and legislation. Present circulation is roughly 15,000. 75 per cent of the magazine is written by freelancers. A byline is given. Seasonal material must be submitted three months in advance. Queries accepted via email. A sample copy and writer's guidelines are available via email.

Non-fiction Publishes general interest and real life articles on the Personal Assistant profession.

Executive Woman

2 Chantry Place, Harrow, Middlesex, HA3 6NY

- ☎ 020 8420 1210
- ☎ 020 8420 1691
- ✉ info@execwoman.com
- 🌐 www.execwoman.com

Parent Company Saleworld Ltd

Editor Angela Giveon

Established 1987

Insider Info A bi-monthly consumer magazine that covers all aspects of women in business. Accepts queries by mail or email.

Non-fiction Interested in business features, management, networking, personnel and mentoring articles.

Submission Guidelines Accepts queries and completed manuscript submissions of between 500 to 1,000 words.

Tips *Executive Woman* is aimed at successful working women in business and upper-management roles. Its features often take a holistic approach.

Exile

A Poetry Magazine For New Poets

1 Armstrong Close, Hundon, Suffolk, CO10 8HD

- ✉ exile@2from.com
- 🌐 www.2from.com/exile/poetry.htm

Editor Ann Elliott-Marr, John Marr

Established 1988

Insider Info A consumer magazine publication issued quarterly, covering literary subjects, with a particular focus on poetry. A byline is given. Queries accepted by mail and email. A sample copy and writer's guidelines are available online.

Non-fiction Interested in poetry articles and features.

Submission Guidelines Please send complete manuscript.

Poetry Interested in free verse, light verse and traditional poetry.

* Payment for assigned poetry is with a contributor copy.

Submission Guidelines Poetry should have a maximum line length of 40 words.

Tips *Exile* is a small literary magazine that aims to encourage new poets and poetry. Many back issues of the magazine are available as pdfs on the website. *Exile* was founded specifically to help new poets achieve publication, so submissions from first-time writers on any subject, or in any style, are more than welcome.

F1 Racing

Teddington Studios, Broom Road, Teddington, TW11 9BE

- ☎ 020 8267 5806
- ☎ 020 8267 5022
- ✉ editorial@f1racing.co.uk
- 🌐 www.f1racing.co.uk

Parent Company Haymarket Autosport & Classic Publications

Editor Hans Seeburg

Contact Publishing Director, Peter Higham; Deputy Editor, Stuart Codling; Features Editor, Bradley Lord; News Editor, James Roberts; Art Editor, Frank Foster; Picture Editor, Jonathan Reynolds

Established 1996

Insider Info A monthly consumer magazine covering Formula 1 motor racing. Present circulation is 64,405.

Non-fiction Publishes news, features, information, interviews, driver profiles, track profiles and race result analysis.

Families North (London)

PO Box 14965, London, NW3 5WA

- ☎ 020 7794 5690
- ☎ 020 7794 0951
- ✉ cathy@familiesnorth.com
- 🌐 www.familiesnorth.com

Parent Company Families Magazines Group

Editor Kathy Watson

Contact Managing Editor, Cathy Youd

Established 1997

Insider Info A consumer magazine publication issued bi-monthly, covering local life for young families. Present circulation of 19,000. Payment is not given for articles. Between zero and five per cent of the magazine is written by freelancers. Publication is not copyrighted and a byline is given. Submissions published approximately six weeks after acceptance with an editorial lead time of two months. Seasonal material should be submitted three months in advance. Queries accepted by mail, email and phone. Accepts previously published submissions. A sample copy is available free on request.

Non-fiction Publishes general interest articles with a local theme.

Tips *Families North* is designed to be an extremely useful resource for families with young children living in North London. It provides information on all the things young parents need to know about, for example, local nurseries, children's entertainers, activities, places to go, things to do, childcare, and so on.

Farmers Weekly
Quadrant House, The Quadrant, Sutton, Surrey, SM2 5AS
- 020 8652 4911
- 020 8652 4005
- farmers.weekly@rbi.co.uk
- www.fwi.co.uk

Parent Company Reed Business Information
Editor Jane King
Established 1934
Insider Info A weekly consumer magazine that covers all aspects of farming and agriculture. Accepts queries by mail or email. Present circulation is 68,897.

Fast Bikes
30 Monmouth Street, Bath, BA1 2BW
- 01225 442244
- 01225 446019
- fastbikes@futurenet.co.uk
- www.fastbikesmag.com

Parent Company Future Publishing Ltd
Editor Richard Newland
Contact Publisher, Paul Sloggett
Insider Info A monthly consumer magazine covering sport motorbikes. Present circulation is 33,085.

Non-fiction Publishes interviews, news, photo features, road tests and product review articles.

Tips *Fast Bikes* covers all aspects of owning, maintaining and riding sports motorbikes. The magazine is aimed mainly at men over the age of 35 with high disposable incomes.

Fast Car Magazine
30 Monmouth Street, Bath, BA1 2BW
- 01225 442244
- 01225 446019
- steve.chalmers@futurenet.co.uk
- www.fastcar.co.uk

Parent Company Future Publishing Ltd
Editor Steve Chalmers
Contact Publisher, Gez Jones; Deputy Editor, Jules Truss; Art Editor, Mark Thomas; Reviews Editor, Ben Chandler; Online Editor, Glenn Rowswell
Insider Info A monthly consumer magazine covering car modifications. Present circulation is 49,298.

Non-fiction Publishes news, photo features, interviews, reviews and technical articles.

Tips *Fast Car Magazine* covers all aspects of the car modification community. It is aimed at men between the ages of 18 and 35 years old. Articles cover performance tuning, practical modification tutorials and reader reviews.

Fast Ford
30 Monmouth Street, Bath, BA1 2BW
- 01225 442244
- 01225 446019
- fastford@futurenet.co.uk
- www.fastfordmag.co.uk

Parent Company Future Publishing Ltd
Editor Dan White
Established 1987
Insider Info A monthly consumer magazine covering modified Ford cars. Present circulation is roughly 40,000.

Non-fiction Publishes advice, photo features, news, reviews, road test and modification tutorial articles.

Tips *Fast Ford* covers modifications and performance upgrades of Ford cars. The magazine is aimed at men aged between 17 and 35 years old.

Federation Magazine
Burslem School of Art, Queen Street, Stoke on Trent, Staffordshire, ST6 3EJ
- 01782 822327
- fwwcp@tiscali.co.uk
- www.fedonline.org.uk/fed

Parent Company The Federation of Worker Writers & Community Publishers
Editor Tim Diggles
Insider Info A consumer magazine publication issued erratically (often three times per year), covering general interest, literary subjects.

Non-fiction Interested in poetry articles, features, interviews/profiles, reviews, opinion (excluding letters to the Editor), news and events pieces.

Submission Guidelines Accepts queries.
Fiction Interested in fiction pieces.
Poetry Publishes poetry.

Tips *Federation* is the magazine of The Federation of Worker Writers & Community Publishers, which is an umbrella organisation for writers' groups and community publishers. The magazine publishes new poetry and fiction from members of the federation, and also news, events and articles of interest to the writing groups. Publication of *Federation* is erratic at best, ranging from two to four issues per year. It is best to join the federation before approaching them with any submissions.

The Feminist Review

Houndsmill, Basingstoke, Hampshire, RG21 6XS
- 01256 329242
- 01256 354018
- www.feminist-review.com

Parent Company Palgrave Macmillan Ltd
Established 1979
Insider Info A journal, with three issues per year, that covers all aspects of feminism and feminist theory. Accepts queries by mail or email.
Non-fiction Interested in politics, research, statistical and theory articles related to feminism.
Tips Each issue will be themed around a specific debate and articles will reflect this.

FHM

Mappin House, 4 Winsley Street, London, W1W 8HF
- 020 7182 8000
- 020 7182 8021
- general@fhm.com
- www.fhm.com

Parent Company EMAP Plc
Editor Anthony Noquera
Contact Deputy Editor, Chris Bell; Associate Editor, Justin Quirk; Production Editor, Alan Kindell
Established 1986
Insider Info A consumer magazine publication issued monthly, covering men's lifestyle. Present circulation of 280,392. Accepts queries via email.
Non-fiction Interested in photo features, humour, exposés, features, interviews/profiles and general interest articles.
Submission Guidelines Accepts very short queries in the first instance. Final articles should be between 1,200 and 2,000 words.
Tips 'Lads' magazine featuring the latest in men's fashion, sports, and reviews, as well as provocative pictures of women. Don't submit finished articles – a brief two line description and bullet points is more than enough, but bear in mind it is extremely unlikely that any unsolicited material will ever appear in the magazine.

The Field

Blue Fin Building, 110 Southwark Street, London, SE1 0SU
- 020 3148 5000
- 020 3148 8179
- jonathan_young@ipcmedia.com
- www.thefield.co.uk

Parent Company IPC Media Ltd
Editor Jonathan Young
Contact Features Editor, Sarah Fitzpatrick
Established 1853
Insider Info Monthly consumer magazine, covering countryside life, gun sports and hunting. Present circulation of 32,366. Queries accepted by phone. Media packs available online.
Non-fiction Publishes hunting/shooting related photo features, features, interviews/profiles, general interest and how-to articles.
Submission Guidelines Accepts queries and complete manuscripts.
Tips Although positioned as a countryside magazine, rather than covering all countryside issues *The Field* is more or less focused on gun sports and hunting.

Film Ireland

Filmbase, Curved Street, Temple Bar, Dublin 2, Republic of Ireland
- 00353 1 671 1303
- 00353 1 679 6717
- editor@filmbase.ie
- www.filmireland.net

Editor Lir Mac Cárthaigh
Established 1987
Insider Info A bi-monthly consumer magazine that covers all aspects of film making and cinema. Accepts queries by mail or email.
Non-fiction Interested in features, interviews, reviews and practical articles related to films.
Tips Covers both Irish and international movie-making and cinema.

Film Review

9 Blades Court, Deodar Road, Lonon, SW15 2NU
- 020 8875 1520
- 020 8875 1588
- www.visimag.com

Parent Company Visual Imagination Ltd
Editor Grant Kempster
Established 1950
Insider Info A four-weekly consumer magazine that covers films and cinema. Accepts queries by mail or email.
Non-fiction Interested in features, interviews and review articles related to contemporary cinema.
Submission Guidelines Accepts queries and completed manuscript submissions of between 1,000 to 3,000 words.

Financial World

5 Derby Street, London, W1J 7AB

📞 020 7493 0173
📞 020 7493 0190
✉ editor@financialworld.co.uk
🌐 www.financialworld.co.uk

Parent Company Institute of Financial Services
Editor James Elwes
Established 2004

Insider Info A monthly management magazine, also available online, covering worldwide financial services. Present circulation of 30,590. Payment is upon acceptance and is not made with contributor copies or other premiums. Assignment expenses are not paid. 100 per cent of the magazine is written by freelancers, Submissions are published approximately two months after acceptance, with an editorial lead time of two months. Publication is copyrighted and a byline is given. Seasonal material must be submitted two months in advance. Queries are accepted by email. Simultaneous submissions are accepted. Aims to respond to queries, manuscripts and other issues within two weeks. A sample copy is available online. Writer's guidelines are available free on request, via email and online. Editorial calendars are available free on request, via email and online. Media packs are available on the website.

Non-fiction Interested in features on financial services topics, interview/profiles with financial services personnel, and opinion (excluding letters to the Editor) on financial services topics.

Submission Guidelines Articles should be between 600 and 800 words. Contact Denise Smith, Online Editor and Advertising Executive.

Tips *Financial World,* along with its online version, is aimed at financial services professionals. Submissions, especially for the website, need to be short and punchy, and have a strict relevance to the industry. *Financial World Online* is the web-based version of *Financial World.*

FIRE

Field Cottage, Old Whitehill, Tackley, Kidlington, Oxfordshire, OX5 3AB

✉ firejhilton@talk21.com
🌐 www.poetical.org

Editor Jeremy Hilton
Established 1997

Insider Info A consumer magazine publication issued twice a year and covering general interest, literary subjects. A byline is given. Accepts query by mail.

Non-fiction Interested in poetry articles.
Fiction Interested in fiction pieces.

Poetry Interested in avant-garde, free verse and experimental poetry.

Tips *FIRE* is a poetry magazine that prints imaginative contemporary poetry. It aims to 'promote unpublished, unknown, and unfashionable writers, including young writers and those just starting out.' *FIRE* also actively solicits submissions from selected poets and therefore leaves little space in the magazine for work from previously published writers. The magazine favours inventive, experimental and alternative poetry from new writers anywhere in the world, but discourages submissions from published writers. *FIRE* prefers all correspondence in writing by post, rather than email.

The Firing Squad

25 Griffiths Road, West Bromwich, B71 2EH

✉ firingsquad@purplepatchpoetry.co.uk
🌐 www.purplepatchpoetry.co.uk/firingsquad

Parent Company Purple Patch Poetry
Editor Geoff Stevens
Contact Alex Barzdo
Established 1989

Insider Info Sister publication to *Purple Patch* magazine. Specialises in complaint or protest poetry, often of a strong and controversial nature. *The Firing Squad* is issued when the themes included are topical, and will soon be relying on the internet for publication. A byline is given. Accepts queries by mail and email.

Poetry Publishes political complaint/protest poetry.

Tips *The Firing Squad* aims to publish any political views, providing they are poetic and have some literary merit, as well as a protest element.

First Offense

Sails Field, Mare Hill Road, Pulborough, West Sussex, RH20 2DS

✉ tim@firstoffense.co.uk
🌐 www.firstoffense.co.uk

Editor Tim Fletcher

Insider Info A consumer magazine publication issued annually, covering literary subjects, particularly poetry. Present circulation of 300. A byline is given.

Poetry Interested in avant-garde, experimental and modernist poetry.

* No traditional poetry.

Submission Guidelines Accepts sample poems with SAE.

Tips *First Offense* is a small poetry magazine that specialises in ground breaking and inventive contemporary poetry. Modernist poetry and language based texts are good examples of the types of writing favoured. The magazine does not accept traditional forms of poetry. Submissions must be in hard copy and must include SAE, otherwise they will be rejected.

First Time

The Snoring Cat, 194 Downs Road, Hastings, East Sussex, TN34 2DZ

- 01424 423105
- 01424 428855
- josephinepoetry@btinternet.com
- www.josephineaustin.co.uk

Editor Josephine Austin

Insider Info A consumer magazine publication issued twice a year, covering general interest, literary subjects. Present circulation of 1,000. A byline is given.

Poetry Interested in free verse, light verse and traditional poetry.

Submissions Guidelines Poetry should have maximum line length of 30 words.

Tips *First Time* is a poetry magazine that aims to encourage first-time poetry writers. Generally publishes traditional and mainstream poetry on the subjects of love, the countryside and social issues. *First Time* welcomes submissions from international writers. The magazine is geared towards helping new writers get their first poems published, and most poems are traditional in style, or otherwise mainstream, rather than experimental.

Fleet News

Media House, Lynchwood, Peterborough Business Park, Peterborough, PE2 6EA

- 01733 468306
- 01733 468296
- martyn.moore@emap.com
- www.fleetnewsnet.co.uk

Parent Company EMAP Plc

Editor Martyn Moore

Contact Deputy Editor, Julian Kirk

Established 1978

Insider Info A weekly trade journal covering the company car and van market. Present circulation is 19,334.

Non-fiction Publishes industry news, features and running cost tables.

Tips *Fleet News* is aimed at businesses that run a fleet of ten or more vehicles. Prints articles on the latest industry news and vehicle reviews, vehicle finance, accident management and running cost tables for over 1,500 new cars.

Flight International

Quadrant House, The Quadrant, Sutton, SM2 5AS

- 020 8652 3842
- 020 8652 3840
- murdo.morrison@flightglobal.com
- www.flightglobal.com

Parent Company Reed Business Information

Editor Murdo Morrison

Established 1909

Insider Info A trade journal magazine issued weekly, covering business travel. Present circulation of 42,817. Accepts query by phone.

Non-fiction Interested in features, interview/profile pieces on defence, general aviation, business aviation, and technology and spaceflight sectors.

Submission Guidelines Accepts queries or complete manuscripts. Articles should be a maximum of 1,800 words.

Tips *Flight International* usually only uses commissioned work, but does consider unsolicited manuscripts. Analytical, in-depth coverage is required, preferably supported by interviews.

The Fly

59–61 Worship Street, London, EC2A 2DU

- 020 7688 9000
- will.kinsman@channelfly.com
- www.the-fly.co.uk

Parent Company Channelfly Plc

Editor Niall Doherty

Established 1999

Insider Info A monthly consumer magazine covering music. Present circulation is 105,212.

Non-fiction Publishes features, profiles, interviews, reviews, event listings and gig guides.

Tips *The Fly* covers all the latest new and live music in the UK. A large portion of the magazine is given over to event and gig listings.

FlyPast

PO Box 100, Stamford, PE9 1XQ

- 01780 755131
- 01780 757261
- flypast@keypublishing.com
- www.flypast.com

Parent Company Key Publishing Ltd

Editor Ken Ellis

Contact Publisher, Ann Saundry; Deputy Editor, Jarod Cotter; Assistant Editor, Nigel Price

Established 1981

Insider Info A monthly consumer magazine covering aviation. Present circulation is 39,620.

Non-fiction Publishes news, features, profiles, historic articles and event listings.

Tips *FlyPast* covers all aspects of aviation including features on vintage aircraft and restoration, and modern airshows.

Focus

8th Floor, Tower House, Fairfax Street, Bristol, BS1 3BN

- 0117 314 8776
- 0117 934 9008
- jheniosman@bbcmagazinesbristol.com
- www.focusmag.co.uk

Parent Company Origin Publishing
Editor Jheni Osman
Contact Deputy Editor, Ian Taylor; News Editor, Andy Ridgway
Established 1992
Insider Info A consumer magazine publication issued monthly, covering science topics. Present circulation of 58,272. Accepts query via email.
Non-fiction Interested in features and technical pieces.
* Pays £200 per 1,000 words for unsolicited articles.
Submission Guidelines Articles should be between 1,000 and 3,000 words.
Tips Covers all aspects of science and technology for general readers, as well as for people with a more in-depth knowledge of science. Articles that coincide with recent BBC television programmes are often used, so peg submissions to upcoming show content.

Folio

64–65 North Road, St Andrews, Bristol, BS6 5AQ

- 0117 942 8491
- 0117 942 0369
- editor@venue.co.uk
- www.venue.co.uk

Editor Dave Higgitt
Established 1994
Insider Info A monthly consumer magazine that covers news and local interest in the Bath, Bristol and Cheltenham area. Accepts queries by mail or email.
Non-fiction Interested in news, features, interviews, lifestyle, event listings and local interest articles.
Submission Guidelines Accepts queries and completed manuscript submissions of between 600 to 2,000 words.
Tips Folio is the sister publication of Venue. It does not publish fiction or poetry.

Fortean Times

The World of Strange Phenomena
30 Cleveland Street, London, W1T 4JD

- 020 7907 6235
- 020 7907 6406
- david_sutton@dennis.co.uk
- www.forteantimes.com

Parent Company Dennis Publishing
Editor David Sutton
Established 1973
Insider Info A consumer magazine publication issued 13 times per year, covering science fiction and the supernatural. Present circulation of 21,529.
Non-fiction Interested in photo features, features, general interest and news pieces.
Submission Guidelines Accepts written queries. Final articles should be between 500 and 5,000 words.
Images Send photos with submission.
Tips Fortean Times is a monthly magazine of news, reviews and research on strange phenomena and experiences, curiosities, prodigies and portents. Seeks 'well-researched and referenced material on current or historical mysteries, or first hand accounts of oddities.' Approach in writing first with ideas.

Fortune

Blue Fin Building, 110 Southwark Street, London, SE1 0SU

- 020 3148 3000
- peter_gumbel@fortunemail.com
- www.fortune.com

Parent Company Time Inc
Contact Europe Editor, Peter Gumbel
Established 1930
Insider Info A bi-weekly consumer magazine covering business and finance. Present circulation is 105,937.
Non-fiction Publishes news, features, analysis, profiles and technical articles.
Tips Fortune is an American magazine that covers business and finance. The European version focuses on investment trends, updates on the management behind the trends, and analysis of the effects of current events on the business world.

For Women

4 Selson Way, London, E14 9GL

- 020 7308 5090
- 020 7308 5377

Editor Karen Denman
Established 1992
Insider Info A 6-weekly consumer magazine that covers women's lifestyle and sex. Payment is £150 per story. Accepts queries by mail or email.
Non-fiction Interested in lifestyle, sex and health articles.
Fiction Interested in erotic fiction and illustrated fiction.
Submission Guidelines Accepts queries and completed manuscript submissions. of between 2,000 to 3,000 words.
Tips For Women publishes articles and stories with an erotic focus. It will accept unsolicited fiction submissions.

4x4 Magazine

Leon House, 233 High Street, Croydon, CR9 1HZ

- 020 8726 8374
- 020 8726 8398
- 4x4.ed@kelsey.co.uk
- www.4x4i.com

Parent Company Kelsey Publishing Ltd
Editor John Carroll
Contact Publisher, Richard Marcroft
Established 1997
Insider Info A monthly consumer magazine, covering four wheel drive and off road motoring. Circulation is roughly 32,000. Media pack available online.
Non-fiction Publishes road tests, reviews, photo features and motoring articles.
Tips *4x4 Magazine* covers a wide range of subjects concerning 4x4 vehicles and motoring, including reviews of the latest products and vehicles, road tests and driving tips. It also features worldwide off-road driving travel features.

FourFourTwo

Teddington Studios, Broom Road, Teddington, TW11 9BE

- 020 8267 5848
- 020 8267 5354
- louis.massarella@haymarket.com
- www.fourfourtwo.com

Parent Company Haymarket Consumer Publications Ltd
Editor Hugh Sleight
Contact Publisher, Martyn Jones; Deputy Editor, Matthew Weiner; Features Editor, Louis Massarella
Established 1994
Insider Info A monthly consumer magazine covering football. Present circulation is 110,968.
Non-fiction Publishes features, interviews, profiles, match reports and reader letters.
Tips *FourFourTwo* is aimed at football fans over the age of 16.

Freelance Market News

An Essential Guide for Freelance Writers

Sevendale House, 7 Dale Street, Manchester, M1 1JB

- 0161 228 2362
- 0161 228 3533
- fmn@writersbureau.com
- www.freelancemarketnews.com

Parent Company The Writers Bureau
Editor Angela Cox
Established 1968
Insider Info A subscription only newsletter issued monthly covering freelance writing. Payment is upon acceptance and is not made with contributor copies, or other premiums. Assignment expenses are not paid. 25 per cent of publication is written by freelancers. Submissions published approximately three months after acceptance with an editorial leda time of three months. Publication is copyrighted and a byline is given. Purchases first UK serial rights. Seasonal material should be submitted three months in advance. Accepts queries by mail, email and fax. Aims to respond to queries, manuscripts and other issues within one month. A sample copy and writer's guidelines are available with SAE (230mm long, 160mm wide) and one first class stamp, or alternatively online. Media packs are available online.
Non-fiction Interested in how-to pieces on 'improving your writing' and features on writing for a specific market.
* Receives approximately 12 manuscripts from freelancers per year.
Submission Guidelines Please send complete manuscript. Articles should be between 700 and 1,500 words. Please do no submit any previously published material. Contact Angela Cox.
Tips *Freelance Market News* is aimed at freelance writers of all levels and gives news, views and advice about new publications. It also publishes information on trends and developments in established markets, both in the UK and overseas.

The Friend

173 Euston Road, London, NW1 2BJ

- 020 7663 1010
- 020 7663 1182
- editorial@thefriend.org
- www.thefriend.org

Parent Company The Friend Publications Ltd
Editor Judy Kirby
Established 1843
Insider Info A weekly consumer magazine, covering news and views from a Quaker perspective. Present circulation of 4,500, Byline is given. Accepts queries by mail, email and phone. Sample copy and media packs are available online.
Non-fiction Publishes News, Comment & Analysis, Features and General Interest articles.
Submission Guidelines Send query before sending submissions. Articles must be 300–1,200 words.
Images Send photos with submission.
Tips Completely independent, *The Friend* publishes news and views from a Quaker perspective, as well as articles from a wide range of authors whose writings are of interest to Quakers and non-Quakers alike. To save wasting time, the Editor prefers to give responses to ideas before they are written. Send an initial outline by email or post, or give the office a ring. Writers are welcome to chase up their queries.

The Frogmore Papers

18 Nevill Road, Lewes, East Sussex, BN7 1PF
ⓦ www.frogmorepress.co.uk
Parent Company The Frogmore Press
Editor Jeremy Page
Established 1983
Insider Info A consumer journal, issued twice a year, publishing poetry, prose and artwork from new and established authors. Byline is given. Queries accepted by mail. Sample copy is available online.
Fiction Publishes novel excerpts and short stories.
Submission Guidelines Send complete manuscript. Submissions must be 2,000 words. Will not accept anything too experimental or too traditional.
Poetry Publishes free verse and light verse.
Submission Guidelines Submit a maximum of six poems. Poems must be 20–80 lines.
Tips *The Frogmore Papers* tries to publish work that finds a happy medium between traditional and experimental. Poetry submissions must be driven by meaning rather than form, and anything too traditional will be rejected. Prose submissions should not be too experimental, but not too traditional either.

Frontier

The Business Magazine for Travel Retail
Central House, 27 Park Street, Croydon, Surrey, CR0 1YD
ⓞ 0870 049 4444
ⓞ 0870 049 4400
ⓔ marek.kolasinski@metropolis.co.uk
ⓦ www.frontiermagazine.co.uk
Parent Company Metropolis Business Publishing
Editor Marek Kolasinski
Established 1983
Insider Info A trade journal magazine issued eight times per year covering the travel retail industry and all its related products. These include, fashion, cosmetics, accessories, wine and spirits, jewellery, electronics, etc. Present circulation of 2,859. Payment is upon acceptance and is not made with contributor copies or other premiums. Assignment expenses are not paid. 15 per cent of the publication is written by freelancers. Submissions will be published approximately one month after acceptance, with an editorial lead time of three weeks. Publication is copyrighted and a byline is given. Purchases all rights. Accepts queries by email. Aims to respond to queries within one week, manuscripts within four weeks and other issues within two weeks. Sample copy and editorial calendars are available free on request. Media packs are available on the website.

Non-fiction Interested in features and interviews/profiles.
* Payment for assigned and unsolicited articles is between £100 and £400.
Submission Guidelines Accepts query with published clips. Articles should be between 500 and 2,000 words. Please do not submit any reprint material. Contact Marek Kolasinski.
Images Accepts images with submission.
* Offers no additional payment for photos accepted with a manuscript. Purchases one time rights.
Submission Guidelines Submit gif/jpeg files, with model releases and identification of subjects. State availability of photos with submission. Contact Marek Kolasinski.
Tips *Frontier* is the only ABC audited publication in the industry. The magazine is feature led and the articles are based on first-hand interviews with executives – be it retailers, operators, or suppliers. The writing is informational and targeted at business readers and executives around the world. There is no marketing slant to the articles and the writing itself is as objective as possible. Style is not as important as subject matter and content. If the feature is a new take on a subject, or something that has not been published yet, then it will be considered more than articles which rehash well-known subjects. Originality and quality are the key.

Full House

The Tower, Phoenix Square, Wyncolls Road, Severalls Industrial Estate, Colchester, CO4 9HU
ⓞ 01206 851117
ⓞ 01206 849078
ⓔ features@fullhousemagazine.co.uk
ⓦ www.fullhousemagazine.co.uk
Parent Company Hubert Burda Media UK
Editor Dave Claridge
Insider Info A weekly consumer magazine covering women's interests. Present circulation is 135,725. Media pack is available online.
Non-fiction Publishes features, interviews, profiles, true-life stories, puzzles and competitions.
* Payment for stories is £500.
Submission Guidelines Accepts complete manuscripts for true-life stories by post, email or online form.
Tips *Full House* focuses heavily on true-life stories. They will pay for a true-life story providing it isn't offered anywhere else and will also offer editorial support for the submission.

Future Music

30 Monmouth Street, Bath, BA1 2BW
ⓞ 01225 442244
ⓞ 01225 446019

○ futuremusic@futurenet.co.uk
⊛ www.futuremusic.co.uk
Parent Company Future Publishing Ltd
Editor Daniel Griffiths
Established 1992
Insider Info A monthly consumer magazine covering music and technology. Present circulation is 9,787.
Non-fiction Publishes news, features, reviews and technical articles.
Tips *Future Music* is aimed at musicians using the latest music technology. It covers reviews and guides for musical equipment, software and hardware.

Gairm
29 Waterloo Street, Glasgow, G2 6BZ
○ 0141 221 1971
Parent Company Gairm Publications
Editor Derick Thomson
Established 1951
Insider Info A consumer magazine publication issued quarterly covering general interest, literary subjects. Present circulation of 2,000.
Non-fiction Interested in poetry articles and pieces on writing.
Submission Guidelines Accepts queries.
Fiction Publishes Gaelic fiction.
Poetry Publishes Gaelic poetry.
Tips *Gairm* is a Scottish Gaelic literary magazine published by one of the largest Gaelic publishing houses, Gairm Publications. It prints poetry and fiction in the Gaelic language, as well as articles about writing. The magazine itself does not have a website but Gairm Publications can be contacted for further details and submission guidelines.

Galleries Magazine
54 Uxbridge Road, London, W12 8LP
○ 020 8740 7020
○ ed@artefact.co.uk
⊛ www.galleries.co.uk
Parent Company Barrington Publications
Editor Andrew Aitken
Insider Info A consumer magazine publication issued monthly, covering galleries and art exhibitions. Accepts queries by mail and email.
Non-fiction Interested in photo features, features, interviews/profiles, reviews, general interest and opinion (excluding letters to the Editor) pieces.
Submission Guidelines Accepts queries.
Tips *Galleries Magazine* prints articles about galleries and art exhibitions in Britain, including previews of upcoming events, interviews, book and gallery reviews, opinions and features. Also has an in-depth art listings section. Articles should contain insider or

advance information of important shows nationwide.

GamesMaster
30 Monmouth Street, Bath, BA1 2BW
○ 01225 442244
○ 01225 446019
○ gamesmaster@futurenet.co.uk
⊛ www.futurenet.co.uk
Parent Company Future Publishing Ltd
Editor Robin Alway
Established 1993
Insider Info A monthly consumer magazine covering computer games. Present circulation is 47,719.
Non-fiction Publishes features, letters, news, reviews and preview articles.
Tips *GamesMaster* is the official magazine of the *GamesMaster* television programme and covers the latest multi-format computer game releases.

The Garden
4th Floor, Churchgate, New Road, Peterborough, PE1 1TT
○ 01733 775775
○ 01733 775819
○ thegarden@rhs.org.uk
⊛ www.rhs.org.uk
Parent Company RHS Publications Ltd
Editor Ian Hodgson
Contact Deputy Editor, Chris Young; Features Editor, John Ardle; News Editor, Anisa Gress
Established 1866
Insider Info A monthly consumer magazine covering gardening. Present circulation is 350,817.
Non-fiction Publishes features, news, reviews and practical advice articles.
Tips *The Garden* is the monthly magazine of the Royal Horticulture Society and covers gardening news and reviews, as well as practical gardening articles and photo features.

Garden Answers
Bauer Media, Bushfield House, Orton Centre, Peterborough, PE2 5UW
○ 01733 237111
○ 01773 465779
○ gardenanswers@bauermedia.co.uk
⊛ www.gardeningmags.co.uk
Parent Company Bauer Media
Editor Geoff Stebbings
Established 1986
Insider Info A monthly consumer magazine covering gardening. Present circulation is 28,018.

Non-fiction Publishes features, interviews, practical and how-to, products, profiles, show and event information and review articles.

Tips *Garden Answers* is aimed at gardening enthusiasts of all levels.

Gardeners' World Magazine

2D1 The Media Centre, 201 Wood Lane, London, W12 7TQ

☏ 020 8433 3959

☏ 020 8433 3986

✉ gweditorial@bbc.co.uk

🌐 www.gardenersworld.com

Parent Company BBC Worldwide Publishing

Editor Adam Pasco

Established 2005

Insider Info A consumer magazine publication issued monthly, covering home interest and gardening subjects. Present circulation of 303,623.

Non-fiction Publishes general interest articles, photo features, features and how-to articles on gardening, garden design and new products for the garden.

Tips The magazine already has many regular features, so unusual articles are more likely to succeed, ideally of a seasonal nature, or pegged to upcoming events in the gardening world.

Garden News

Bushfield House, Orton Centre, Peterborough, PE2 5UW

☏ 01733 237111

✉ neil.pope@emap.com

🌐 www.gardennews-mag.com

Parent Company EMAP Plc

Editor Neil Pope

Contact Sub Editor, Jane Blackford; News Editor, Carol Warters

Established 1958

Insider Info A weekly consumer magazine covering gardening. Present circulation is 36,248.

Non-fiction Publishes features, interviews, news, practical and how-to, showcase and review articles on gardens and gardeners.

Gardens Illustrated

14th Floor, Tower House, Fairfax Street, Bristol, BS1 3BN

☏ 0117 314 8774

✉ gardens@bbcmagazinesbristol.com

🌐 www.gardensillustrated.com

Parent Company BBC Worldwide Publishing

Editor Juliet Roberts

Established 1993

Insider Info A consumer magazine publication issued ten times per year, covering gardening.

Present circulation of 30,753. Accepts queries by mail.

Submission Guidelines Accepts queries.

Tips The titles is aimed at the 'discerning gardener'. Ideas must focus on garden design specifically, ideally with international appeal, and will be strengthened by including full colour photographs.

Gath

Martins Printworks, Main Street, Pittal, Berwick upon Tweed, TD15 1RS

☏ 01289 306006

Insider Info A consumer magazine publication issued quarterly, covering general interest, literary subjects.

Tips *Gath* magazine is a Gaelic periodical which aims to stimulate contemporary Gaelic writing. Being a Gaelic magazine, *Gath* only accepts submissions in the Gaelic language.

Gay Times

Spectrum House, 32–34 Gordon House Road, London, NW5 1LP

☏ 020 7424 7400

☏ 020 7424 7401

✉ edit@gaytimes.co.uk

🌐 www.gaytimes.co.uk

Editor Joseph Galliano

Established 1984

Insider Info A monthly consumer magazine that covers gay life and lifestyle. Accepts queries by mail or email.

Non-fiction Interested in lifestyle, news, reviews, health, beauty and style articles related to gay life.

Submission Guidelines Accepts queries and completed manuscript submissions of up to 2,000 words.

Geographical

1 Victoria Villas, Richmond, Surrey, TW9 2GW

☏ 020 8332 2713

☏ 020 8332 9307

✉ magazine@geographical.co.uk

🌐 www.geographical.co.uk

Parent Company Royal Geographic Society

Editor Geordie Torr

Contact Features Editor, Natalie Hoare

Established 1935

Insider Info A consumer magazine publication issued monthly, covering the interests of the Royal Geographic Society. Present circulation of 21,217.

Non-fiction Publishes articles on people, places, cultures, adventure, responsible travel, history, science and environmental issues.

Tips *Geographical* 'takes pride in its high quality editorial and photographic content', so all submissions must be well crafted and fully researched. Supplying accompanying photographs is a must.

Geographical Journal
Royal Geographical Society, Kensington Gore, London, SW7 2AR
- 020 7591 3026
- 020 7591 3001
- journals@rgs.org

Parent Company Royal Geographical Society
Editor Prof John Briggs
Established 1893
Insider Info A quarterly journal that covers all aspects of geography and earth science. Accepts queries by mail or email.
Non-fiction Interested in research, theory, current interest, reviews and development articles related to geography.

Geological Magazine
Department of Earth Sciences, Downing Street, Cambridge, CB2 3EQ
- 01223 313393
- 01702 588434
- gael@yachtsandyachting.com
- www.yachtsandyachting.com

Established 1864
Insider Info A bi-monthly consumer magazine that covers all aspects of earth science. Accepts queries by mail or email.
Non-fiction Interested in reviews, notices and research articles related to geology and the earth sciences.
Tips Most articles in *Geological Magazine* are taken from independent research by experts, all authors must be experts in their field.

Glamour
6–8 Old Bond Street, London, W1S 4PH
- 020 7499 9080
- 020 7491 2551
- letters@glamourmagazine.co.uk
- corrie.jackson@condenast.co.uk
- www.glamourmagazine.co.uk

Parent Company Conde Nast Publications Ltd
Editor Jo Elvin
Contact Sub-Editor, Lyndsey Heffernan; Features Editor, Corrie Jackson
Established 2001
Insider Info A monthly consumer magazine covering women's lifestyle topics. Present circulation of 551,351. Media pack available online: www.condenast.co.uk/mediapacks.

Non-fiction Publishes general interest, interviews, reviews and photo features on celebrities, fashion, beauty, music, television, film and real-life.
Tips The magazine is aimed at women aged 18–35 and is published in a small, 'handbag-sized' format.

Global Tapestry Journal
Spring Bank, Longsight Road, Copster Green, Blackburn, Lancashire, BB1 9EU
Parent Company BB Books Press
Editor Dave Cunliffe
Established 1961
Insider Info A consumer journal publication issued quarterly, covering general interest, literary subjects. Present circulation of 1,000. A byline is given.
Non-fiction Interested in poetry articles, features, interviews/profiles, reviews, and opinion (excluding letters to the Editor) pieces.
Submission Guidelines Accepts query with SAE.
Fiction Interested in mainstream fiction, novel excerpts and short stories.
Submission Guidelines Please send complete manuscript with SAE.
Poetry Accepts avant-garde, free verse, light verse and traditional poetry.
Submission Guidelines Please send complete manuscript with SAE.
Tips *Global Tapestry Journal* publishes global poetry and prose with a cultural orientation, as well as articles about writing, reviews, interviews, artwork and opinion columns. *Global Tapestry Journal* will publish both short and longer submissions of prose or poetry. An SAE must be enclosed with all submissions, for reply.

Go Belfast
Penton House, 38 Heron Road, Sydenham Business Park, Belfast, BT3 9LE
- 028 9045 7457
- tara.craig@pentonpublications.co.uk

Parent Company Penton Publications Ltd
Editor Tara Craig
Established 2006
Insider Info A bi-monthly consumer magazine covering lifestyle and events in Belfast. Present circulation is 24,850.
Non-fiction Publishes features, interviews, profiles, accommodation reviews and event listings. Topics include fashion, music, dining, culture and activities.
Tips *Go Belfast* is aimed at both residents of and visitors to the city.

Going for Golf
71 St Stephen's Road, Canterbury, CT2 7JW
- 01227 457948
- 01227 763384

○ admin@goingforgolf.com
ⓦ www.goingforgolf.com
Parent Company Going For Golf Ltd
Editor Neil Webber
Established 1994
Insider Info A quarterly consumer magazine covering golf abroad. Present circulation is 29,411.
Non-fiction Publishes news, features, travel and golf course review articles.
Tips *Going for Golf* is distributed in golf clubs across the UK. It publishes features on golf holiday destinations and packages.

Golf International

10 Buckingham Place, London, SW1E 6HX
○ 020 7828 3003
○ 020 7828 6999
○ richard@golfinternationalmag.com
ⓦ www.golfinternationalmag.com
Parent Company Golf International Services
Contact Editor in Chief, Robert Green; Editor, Richard Simmons
Established 1997
Insider Info A monthly consumer magazine covering golf. Present circulation is 31,396. Media pack is available online.
Non-fiction Publishes news, features, reviews, profiles and instruction articles.
Tips Many of the advice articles tend to be written by golfing professionals.

Golf Monthly

Blue Fin Building, 110 Southwark Street, London, SE1 0SU
○ 020 3148 5000
○ michael_harris@ipcmedia.com
ⓦ www.golf-monthly.co.uk
Parent Company IPC Media Ltd
Editor Michael Harris
Contact Deputy Editor, Neil Tappin
Established 1911
Insider Info A consumer magazine publication issued monthly, covering golf. Present circulation of 82,264. Accepts queries by mail and email.
Non-fiction Interested in how-to, features, interviews/profiles, reviews, new products and general interest pieces.
Submission Guidelines Accepts query or complete manuscript. Articles should be between 1,500 and 2,000 words.
Tips *Golf Monthly* is aimed at good golfers who are regular players. The magazine is Britain's most widely read golfing magazine. It aims to represent the 'real voice of golf' with leading columnists, top players and detailed coverage of equipment and instruction. The editors are not interested in instruction articles

from outside contributors – try something else such as unusual kit reviews or player profiles.

Golf World

Media House, Lynch Wood, Peterborough Business Park, Peterborough, PE2 6EA
○ 01733 468000
○ golf.world@emap.com
Parent Company EMAP Plc
Editor Chris Jones
Contact Deputy Editor, Peter Masters; Art Director, Paul Ridley
Insider Info A monthly consumer magazine covering golf. Present circulation is 35,014.
Non-fiction Publishes event listings and coverage, interviews, fashion, practical advice, tips and product reviews.
Tips *Golf World* is aimed at experienced golfers or club members. It covers all the major tours and events as well as providing tips and tutorial articles and product reviews.

The Good Book Guide

29–30 Monument Business Park, Chalgrove, Oxfordshire, OX44 7RW
○ 01865 893434
○ 01865 893430
○ enquiries@gbgdirect.com
ⓦ www.thegoodbookguide.com
Editor Hilary Foakes
Insider Info A monthly consumer magazine that covers book reviews. Accepts queries by mail or email.

Good Housekeeping

National Magazine House, 72 Broadwick Street, London, W1F 9EP
○ 020 7439 5000
○ 020 7439 5616
○ jo.adnitt@natmags.co.uk
ⓦ www.goodhousekeeping.co.uk
Parent Company National Magazine Company
Editor Louise Chunn
Contact Features Editor, Lucy Moore; Features Assistant, Jo Adnitt; Picture Editor, Laura McIff
Established 1922
Insider Info A consumer magazine publication issued monthly covering women's interests and women's lifestyle. Circulation of 430,930. Accepts queries by mail.
Non-fiction Interested in general interest lifestyle and housekeeping pieces.
Submission Guidelines Accepts query with outline and published clips.
Tips *Good Housekeeping* is the UK's most popular consumer magazine for women over 35. Most work

is commissioned, but send ideas via post including a synopsis of your idea, relevant cuttings in support of the idea, and examples of previously printed work.

GQ

Vogue House, 1 Hanover Square, London, W1S 1JU

- 020 7499 9080
- 020 7495 1679
- andy.morris@condenast.co.uk
- www.gqmagazine.co.uk

Parent Company Conde Nast Publications
Editor Dylan Jones
Contact Features Director, Alex Bilmes; Literary Editor, Andy Morris
Established 1988
Insider Info A consumer magazine publication issued monthly covering men's lifestyle. Present circulation of 130,008. Accepts queries by mail and fax.
Non-fiction Publishes articles on men's fashion and style as well as feature articles on food, movies, fitness, sex, music, toys, and books.
Tips GQ (originally called Gentlemen's Quarterly) is generally perceived as more upscale than so-called 'lad mags'. GQ's readership is older, and has more expendable income than that of other men's magazines, so any submitted ideas should be targeted accordingly. Reviews of expensive high-end gadgets are popular.

Gramophone

Teddington Studios, Broom Road, Teddington, TW11 9BE

- 020 8267 5050
- 020 8267 5854
- info@gramophone.co.uk
- www.gramophone.co.uk

Parent Company Haymarket Consumer Publications Ltd
Contact Editor in Chief, James Jolly; Editor, James Inverne; Publishing Director, Bob McDowell; Deputy Editor, Martin Cullingford; Art Editor, Ben Martin
Established 1923
Insider Info A monthly consumer magazine covering classical music and instruments. Present circulation is 36,817.
Non-fiction Publishes news, features, reviews and concert listings related to classical music.

Grand Designs Magazine

National House, 121–123 High Street, Epping, Essex, CM16 4BD

- 01992 563422
- yasmine@granddesignsmagazine.com
- www.granddesignsmagazine.com

Parent Company Media 10
Editor Claire Barrett
Contact Deputy Editor, Beth Myers; Chief Sub Editor, Morag Bruce; Features Editor, Luke Tebbutt; Editorial Assistant, Anya Pope
Established 2004
Insider Info A consumer magazine publication issued monthly covering interiors and architecture. Present circulation of 38,000. 50 per cent of the magazine is written by freelancers. Submissions are published approximately two months after acceptance, with an editorial lead time of two months. Publication is copyrighted and a byline is given. All rights are purchased. Seasonal material must be submitted approximately two months in advance. Queries accepted by mail, email and phone. Simultaneous submissions and previously published submissions are accepted. Aims to respond to queries and manuscripts within four days. Payment is upon acceptance and is not made with contributor copies, or other premiums. Assignment expenses are paid. A sample copy and writer's guidelines are available free on request. Media packs are available on the website.
Non-fiction Interested in how-to, photo features inspirational, features, interviews/profiles and technical pieces.
* Receives approximately 50 manuscripts from freelancers per year. Payment for assigned articles is between £300 and £500. Payment for unsolicited articles is between £250 and £500.
Submission Guidelines Accepts emailed ideas. Final articles should be between 800 and 1,200 words. Please do not send any material for reprints. Contact Fiona Sibley.
Images Accepts images with submission.
* Negotiates payment individually. Purchases all rights.
Submission Guidelines State availability of photos with submission. Contact Claire Limpus.
Tips The readership for Grand Designs Magazine is a 50:50 male/female ratio, covering those who watch Grand Designs with Kevin McLeod, and those interested in home improvement. Potential contributors should contact the Deputy Editor with their idea, and then call a couple of days later to chase it up.

Granta

2/3 Hanover Yard, Noel Road, London, N1 8BE

- 020 7704 9776
- 020 7704 0474
- info@granta.com
- www.granta.com

Parent Company Granta Publications
Editor Alex Clark
Established 1889

Insider Info A consumer magazine publication issued quarterly, covering new writing and documentary photography. Present circulation of 46,831. Publication is copyrighted and a byline is given. Editorial lead time is three months. Queries are accepted by mail and email. Aims to respond to manuscripts within three months. Writer's guidelines and media packs are available on the website.
Non-fiction Interested in photo features, features, travel and historical/nostalgic pieces.
Submission Guidelines Send completed manuscript.
Fiction Interested in novel excerpts and new writing pieces.
* Payment for fiction is between £75 and £5,000.
Submission Guidelines Send complete manuscript. Please do not submit genre fiction, i.e. no romance, crime, science fiction, fantasy fiction, or historical/poetry.
Images State availability of photos with submission. Contact Liz Jobey.
Tips *Granta* magazine publishes new writing, fiction, personal history, reportage and inquiring journalism, four times a year. It also publishes documentary photography. *Granta* does not have a political or literary manifesto, but it does have a belief in the power and urgency of the story, both in fiction and non-fiction, and the story's supreme ability to describe, illuminate and make real. 'The main guideline for submitting work to *Granta* is simply to read the magazine thoroughly and ask yourself honestly if you feel your piece meets our criteria. We receive many submissions every day, many of which are completely unsuitable for *Granta* (however well written).'

Grazia
Endeavour House, 189 Shaftesbury Avenue, London, WC2H 8JG
☎ 020 7437 9011
☎ 020 7520 6599
✉ siam.goorwich@emap.com
🌐 www.graziamagazine.co.uk
Parent Company EMAP Plc
Editor Jane Bruton
Contact Health & Lifestyle Editor, Maria Casey; Editorial Assistant, Siam Goorwich
Established 2005
Insider Info A weekly glossy consumer magazine covering women's lifestyle topics. Present circulation of 227,102.
Non-fiction Publishes general interest features, interviews and photo features on real life, fashion, beauty, food, home and travel.
Tips The title is aimed specifically at women aged 25–45 and aims to bridge the gap between monthly glossies and weekly titles, by being Britain's first weekly glossy.

Green Futures
Overseas House, 19-23 Ironmonger Row, London, EC1V 3QN
☎ 020 7324 3660
✉ post@greenfutures.org.uk
🌐 www.greenfutures.org.uk
Editor Editor-in-Chief, Martin Wright
Established 1996
Insider Info A quarterly trade journal that covers environmental issues. Accepts queries by mail or email.
Non-fiction Interested in articles related to the environment and sustainable development futures.
Submission Guidelines Accepts article pitches.
Tips *Green Futures* is aimed mainly at businesses and organisations. Most material is specially commissioned.

Grow Your Own
The Best for Kitchen Gardeners
25 Phoenix Court, Hawkins Road, Colchester, Essex, CO2 8JY
☎ 01206 505979
✉ craig.drever@aceville.co.uk
🌐 www.growfruitandveg.co.uk
Parent Company Aceville Publications
Editor Craig Drever
Established 2005
Insider Info A consumer magazine publication issued monthly covering growing fruit, vegetables and herbs in gardens and allotments. Present circulation of 40,000. Payment upon publication and assignment expenses are sometimes paid (limit agreed upon in advance). 50 per cent of the magazine is written by freelancers. Submissions are published approximately one month after acceptance. Publication is copyrighted and a byline is given. Seasonal material must be submitted two months in advance. Queries are accepted by mail, email, and phone. Simultaneous submissions and previously published submissions are accepted.
Non-fiction Interested in book excerpts, how-to, photo features and technical pieces.
Submission Guidelines Articles should be between 400 and 2,000 words. Contact Craig Drever.
Images Accepts images with submission.
* Pays a varied fee per photo.
Submission Guidelines Submit contact sheets, prints, gif/jpeg files. Contact Craig Drever.

Guitar & Bass
Leon House, 233 High Street, Croydon, CR9 1HZ
☎ 020 8726 8000

- 020 8726 8397
- guitar@ipcmedia.com
- www.guitarmagazine.co.uk

Parent Company IPC Media Ltd
Editor Marcus Leadley
Contact Publisher, Richard Marcroft; Features Editor, John Callaghan; Art Editor, Steve Bailey
Insider Info A monthly consumer magazine, covering guitar owning and playing. Circulation is 10,883. Media pack available online.
Non-fiction Publishes interviews, features, reviews and practical playing articles.
Tips *Guitar & Bass* publishes the latest product and equipment reviews, as well as practical playing articles and interviews and advice from celebrity guitarists. The magazine is generally aimed at practising guitarists and focuses more on playing than buying.

Guitarist
The Guitar Player's Bible
30 Monmouth Street, Bath, BA1 2BW
- 01225 442244
- 01225 732285
- guitarist@futurenet.co.uk
- www.guitarist.co.uk

Parent Company Future Publishing
Editor Mick Taylor
Established 1984
Insider Info A magazine consumer publication issued 13 times per year, covering guitar music and playing. Present circulation of 29,419.
Non-fiction Publishes photo features, how-to, reviews, interviews/profiles and technical articles on guitars.
Submission Guidelines Ideas for articles are welcome, particularly tutorial, lessons or practical techniques, so contact the Editor with a synopsis via post or email.
Tips *Guitarist* is the longest established guitar magazine in Europe, aimed at players who are serious about their art and craft. An in-depth knowledge of guitar is essential for contributors.

Guitar Techniques
30 Monmouth Street, Bath, BA1 2BW
- 01225 442244
- 01225 732398
- guitar.tech@futurenet.co.uk
- www.guitartechniques.com

Parent Company Future Publishing
Editor Neville Marten
Insider Info A consumer magazine publication issued monthly, covering guitar music and playing. Present circulation of 20,924.

Non-fiction Published technical, feature, how-to and review articles on guitars and guitar music.
Tips *Guitar Techniques* takes the UK's foremost guitar teachers and players, and transfers their finesse and passion for music into a magazine, therefore all contributors are highly skilled and experienced. The magazine includes UK focused reports on new bands and gigs, plus kit reviews and tutorials.

The Haiku Quarterly (HQ)
39 Exmouth Street, Swindon, Wiltshire, SN1 3PU
- 01793 523927
- www.noggs.dsl.pipex.com/hq

Parent Company HQ Poetry Magazine
Editor Kevin Bailey
Established 1990
Insider Info Quarterly consumer magazine that specialises in publishing Haiku or Haiku-esque poetry from new or established writers. A byline is given. Accepts queries by mail. Aims to respond to manuscripts within six months. Sample copy is available online.
Non-fiction Publishes features and reviews on haiku poetry.
Submission Guidelines Send query before sending submissions.
Poetry Publishes free verse, haiku and light verse.
* Payment via contributor copy for poetry.
Tips At least a third of every issue is given over to Haiku, the rest is filled with mainstream contemporary poetry, articles, reviews and some more experimental types of poetry. *HQ* mostly publishes work from established writers, but will also accept submissions from new writers, especially experimental or developmental poetry.

Hair
Blue Fin Building, 110 Southwark Street, London, SE1 0SU
- 020 7261 6975/020 3148 5000
- 020 7261 7382
- leanne_hutchinson@ipcmedia.com
- www.ipcmedia.com

Parent Company IPC Media Ltd
Editor Louise White
Contact Publisher, Lynsey Bushell; Art Editor, Sue Wilkins
Insider Info A monthly consumer magazine, covering hair and beauty. Circulation is 80,319. Media pack available online.
Non-fiction Publishes expert advice, beauty and practical hair styling articles.
Tips *Hair* is aimed at women aged between 18 and 30 and covers all aspects of hair styling and beauty. Articles include fashion trends, expert advice and practical step-by-step styling guides.

Hairflair & Beauty

Freebournes House, Freebournes Road, Witham, CM8 3US

- 01376 534534
- 01376 534546
- laura.webb@hairmags.co.uk
- www.hairflairandbeauty.co.uk

Parent Company Haversham Publications Ltd
Editor Ruth Page
Contact Deputy Editor, Claire Muffett; Assistant Editor, Laura Webb
Established 1983
Insider Info A bi-monthly consumer magazine covering hair and fashion. Present circulation is 16,537.
Non-fiction Publishes features, photo features and how-to articles, as well as advice on hair care, fashion and beauty.

Hair Ideas

9th Floor, Tower House, Fairfax Street, Bristol, BS1 3BN

- 0117 927 9009
- 0117 934 9008
- michelletiernan@originpublishing.co.uk

Parent Company Origin Publishing Ltd
Contact Editor, Michelle Tiernan; Commissioning Editor, Sophie Jordan; Art Editor, Neil Donnelly
Established 2003
Insider Info A monthly consumer magazine covering hairstyles. Present circulation is 76,426.
Non-fiction Publishes features, advice and review articles.
Tips *Hair Ideas* covers hairstyles, hair advice, product tests and make-overs. It is aimed at women aged between 18 and 40 years old.

Hairstyles Only

Freebournes House, Freebournes Road, Witham, CM8 3US

- 01376 534534
- 01376 534546
- info@hairstylesonly.co.uk
- www.hairstylesonly.co.uk

Parent Company Haversham Publications Ltd
Editor Claire Muffett
Contact Assistant Editor, Laura Webb
Established 1998
Insider Info A bi-monthly consumer magazine covering hairstyles and fashion. Present circulation is 114,290.
Non-fiction Publishes features and practical advice articles on hairstyles and fashion.

HALI

Carpet, Textile & Islamic Art

50 Poland Street, London, W1F 7AX

- 020 7970 4600
- 020 7578 7221
- hali@centaur.co.uk
- hali.com

Parent Company Hali Publications/Centaur Media
Editor Ben Evans
Contact Managing Editor, Daniel Shaffer
Established 1978
Insider Info A special interest magazine issued bi-monthly at present, soon to return to quarterly. *HALI* covers antique and modern oriental and European carpets, tapestry, world textile art, tribal art, Asian art and Islamic art. Present circulation of 4,000. 80 per cent of magazine is written by freelancers. Payment is upon publication. Publication is copyrighted and a byline is given. Purchases one time rights and electronic rights. Average lead time is ten weeks. Seasonal material must be submitted ten weeks in advance. Queries accepted by mail, email and fax. Previously published submissions are accepted.
Non-fiction Publishes features and technical articles.
Tips *HALI* is a special interest magazine with a small circulation, and a loyal and very involved core readership. The magazine is mainly supported by the oriental carpet trade, but covers all aspects of the arts with textile artefacts of all kinds from all places being the starting point and unifying theme. Specialist writers need to be extremely knowledgeable.

Hampshire

Jesses Farm, Snow Hill, Dinton, Wiltshire, SP3 5HN

- 01722 716996

Parent Company A&D Media Ltd
Editor Philip Wettingsteel
Established 1960
Insider Info A monthly consumer magazine that covers Hampshire. Accepts queries by mail or email.
Non-fiction Interested in local interest and lifestyle articles related to Hampshire.
Submission Guidelines Accepts queries and completed manuscript submissions of between 600 to 1,500 words.

Handshake

5 Cross Farm, Station Road North, Fearnhead, Warrington, WA2 0QG

- www.waldeneast.fsnet.co.uk/handshakeinfo.htm

Parent Company The Eight Hand Gang
Editor John Francis Haines

Insider Info A consumer newsletter publication issued irregularly, covering science fiction literary subjects.

Non-fiction Interested in poetry articles and market news.

Poetry Interested in science fiction poetry.

Submission Guidelines Send sample poetry with SAE.

Tips *Handshake* is the irregular newsletter of The Eight Hand Gang, an association of UK science fiction poets. It is only one sheet of A4, a side of which contains association news and market information for science fiction poets, the other containing short science fiction poetry from contributors. *Handshake* accepts submissions of science fiction poetry, providing they are short, due to the limited space available. All submissions must be accompanied by SAE.

Harlequin
PO Box 23392, Edinburgh, EH8 7YZ

- 01506 510002
- columbine@harlequinmagazine.com
- www.harlequinmagazine.com

Editor Jim Sinclair

Established 2001

Insider Info A consumer magazine publication issued three times per year covering new-age literary subjects. Present circulation of 100.

Poetry Interested in avant-garde, free verse, light verse and post-modern poetry.

Tips *Harlequin* is a poetry magazine that combines art and poetry with a mystic, new-age theme. The magazine has a very strong sense of theme and style, so it is advantageous to study back issues of the magazine carefully, to check the suitability of your work.

Harper's Bazaar
National Magazine House, 72 Broadwick Street, London, W1F 9EP

- 020 7439 5000
- 020 7437 6886
- lucy.yeomans@natmags.co.uk
- www.harpersbazaar.co.uk

Parent Company National Magazine Company Ltd

Editor Lucy Yeomans

Contact Deputy Editor, Sarah Bailey; Contributing Editor, Rachel Meddowes; Art Director, Tom Usher; Features Director, Francesca Martin; Deputy Travel Editor, Lydia Bell

Established 1970

Insider Info A monthly consumer magazine covering lifestyle. Present circulation is 109,146.

Non-fiction Publishes news and features. Topics covered include health, beauty, fashion, arts, house & home, gardening, food, restaurants and travel.

Tips *Harper's Bazaar* is a high-end magazine aimed at adults. It covers a wide range of lifestyle subjects.

Health & Fitness Magazine
The Tower, Phoenix Square, Colchester, Essex, CO4 9HU

- 01206 851117
- 01206 849079
- www.healthandfitnessonline.co.uk

Parent Company Hubert Burda Media UK

Editor Mary Comber

Contact Deputy Editor, Margaret Bartlett; Fitness Editor, Antonia Kanczula

Established 1981

Insider Info A monthly consumer magazine covering health and fitness. Present circulation is 31,260.

Non-fiction Publishes beauty, exercise, fitness, health and news articles.

Tips *Health & Fitness Magazine* is aimed at health conscious women and prints a wide range of health and beauty tips, including product reviews.

Health Service Journal
Greater London House, Hampstead Road, London, NW1 7EJ

- 020 7874 0253
- 020 7874 0265
- hsjnews@emap.com
- www.hsj.co.uk

Parent Company EMAP Plc

Editor Richard Vize

Contact Features Editor, Alexis Nolan; News Editor, Rebecca Evans; Art Editor, Jonathan Dawson

Established 1892

Insider Info A weekly trade journal covering the health services. Present circulation is 17,861.

Non-fiction Publishes industry news, features, special reports and policy.

Tips *Health Service Journal* is mainly aimed at managers working in the NHS. Articles focus on health policy and management.

Healthy
Victory House, 14 Leicester Place, Leicester Square, London, WC2H 7BZ

- 020 7306 0304
- 020 7306 0303
- healthy@riverltd.co.uk
- www.healthy-magazine.co.uk

Parent Company River Publishing Ltd

Established 1999

Insider Info A bi-monthly consumer magazine covering health and lifestyle. Present circulation is 180,134. Media pack is available online.

Non-fiction Publishes features, product reviews and advice articles.

Tips *Healthy* is published on behalf of Holland & Barrett, covering health and dieting, vegetarianism and alternative therapies. It is aimed at both men and women interested in healthy lifestyles.

Heat
Endeavour House, 189 Shaftesbury Avenue, London, WC2H 8JG
- 020 7437 9011
- 020 7859 8670
- heat@emap.com
- www.emap.com

Parent Company EMAP Plc
Editor Julian Linley
Contact Features Editor, Lucie Cave
Established 1999
Insider Info A weekly consumer magazine covering celebrity gossip and women's lifestyle. Present circulation of 470,129.

Non-fiction Publishes general interest, expose, reviews and photo features on celebrities, fashion, beauty, music, television, film and real-life.

Tips The magazine is aimed at women aged 18–40, although it also has a substantial gay male following. The publication is mainly image based and any text heavy articles tend to be celebrity interviews.

Hello!
Wellington House, 69–71 Upper Ground, London, SE1 9PQ
- 020 7667 8700
- 020 7667 8716
- www.hellomagazine.com

Contact Editorial Assistant, Megan Conway
Established 1988
Insider Info A weekly consumer magazine covering celebrity gossip and women's lifestyle topics. Present circulation of 427,054.

Non-fiction Publishes general interest features, interviews and photo features on celebrities and international royalty.

Tips The title is aimed specifically at women aged 25 to 44 years old.

Heritage
Archant House, Oriel Road, Cheltenham, , GL50 1BB
- 020 7751 4800
- 020 7751 4848
- editorial@heritagemagazine.co.uk
- www.heritagemagazine.co.uk

Parent Company Archant Specialist (London)
Editor Matt Havercroft
Contact Art Editor, Steve Rayner; Editorial Assistant, Katy Green
Established 1984
Insider Info A bi-monthly consumer magazine covering British heritage and history. Present circulation is 48,167.

Non-fiction Publishes photo features, news, site reviews and historical articles.

Tips *Heritage* is an illustrated magazine that covers all aspects of British heritage sites and history, including site reviews and illustrated features. Half of its subscribers live overseas but the magazine has a distinctly British style.

Heritage Today
15 Prescott Place, London, SW4 6BS
- 020 7819 1111
- 020 7819 1122
- customers@english-heritage.org.uk
- www.english-heritage.org.uk/server/show/nav.898

Parent Company Square One Group Ltd
Editor Mark Palmer
Established 1999
Insider Info A quarterly consumer magazine covering English heritage and history. Present circulation is 270,739.

Non-fiction Publishes news and feature articles.

Tips *Heritage Today* is available exclusively to English Heritage members. It focuses on historic English buildings, architecture and monuments of national importance.

Hertfordshire Countryside
PO Box 5, Hitchin, Hertfordshire, SG5 1GJ
- 01462 431237
- 01462 422015
- martin_small@btconnect.com

Parent Company Beaumonde Publications Ltd
Editor Sandra Small
Established 1946
Insider Info A monthly consumer magazine that covers Hertfordshire. Accepts queries by mail or email.

Non-fiction Interested in local interest and lifestyle articles related to Hampshire.

Submission Guidelines Accepts queries and completed manuscript submissions of up to 1,000 words.

Hi-Fi Choice
2 Balcombe Street, London, NW1 6NW
- 020 7317 2600
- tim.bowern@futurenet.co.uk

🌐 www.hifichoice.co.uk
Parent Company Future Publishing Ltd
Editor Dan George
Contact Publisher, Andy Ford; Art Editor, Benjamin Benson
Established 1975
Insider Info A monthly consumer magazine covering the hi-fi market. Present circulation is 10,013.
Non-fiction Publishes features, news, product tests and review articles.
Tips Hi-Fi Choice prints reviews, tests and comparisons of the latest hi-fi and home audio technology.

Hi-Fi News
10th Floor, Leon House, 233 High Street, Croydon, Surrey, CR9 1HZ
☎ 020 8726 8311
☎ 020 8726 8397
✉ hi-finews@ipcmedia.com
🌐 www.hifinews.co.uk
Parent Company IPC Media Ltd
Editor Paul Miller; Steve Fairclough
Contact Managing Editor, Andrew Harrison; Editorial Assistant, Marie Ek
Established 1956
Insider Info A consumer magazine publication issued monthly covering high end audio equipment. Present circulation of 11,353. 40 per cent of the magazine is written by freelancers. It takes three weeks from manuscript acceptance, to publication. Publication is copyrighted and a byline is not given. First rights are purchased. Queries will be accepted by mail, email, fax and phone. Accepts simultaneous submissions. Aims to respond to queries and manuscripts within five days. Sample copy is available free on request. Writer's guidelines are available via email. Payment is upon publication and writer's are not paid with contributor copies or other premiums. Assignment expenses are sometimes paid (limit agreed upon in advance).
Non-fiction Interested in photo features, features, reviews, new products and technical articles.
* Payment is made for assigned articles on agreement.
Submission Guidelines Accepts query. Articles should be between 2,000 and 3,000 words. Please do not submit any reprint material. Contact Marie Ek.
Images Send photos with submission.
Tips The leading audio journal in the UK. Hi Fi News review, test and provide information on audio equipment. They are passionate about all things audio, from vintage gear to iPods. Writers should have a passion for audio, and expert technical knowledge. They should be dedicated to meeting

deadlines and be able to give objective views on high-end audio kit. Love for music and sound is vital.

High Life
Pegasus House, 37–43 Sackville Street, London, W1S 3EH
☎ 020 7534 2400
☎ 020 7534 2553
✉ high.life@cedarcom.co.uk
🌐 www.cedarcom.co.uk/high_life.html
Parent Company Cedar Communications (Publishers)
Editor Kerry Smith
Contact Deputy Editor, Harriet Cooper; Art Director, Jamie Macpherson
Established 1973
Insider Info A monthly consumer magazine covering general lifestyle and travel. Present circulation is 188,673.
Non-fiction Publishes features, celebrity profiles and travel articles.
Tips High Life is a lifestyle magazine distributed to British Airways passengers.

History Today
20 Old Compton Street, London, W1D 4TW
☎ 020 7534 8000
✉ editorial@historytoday.com
🌐 www.historytoday.com
Parent Company History Today Trust for the Advancement of Education
Editor Paul Lay
Established 1951
Insider Info A consumer magazine publication issued monthly, covering domestic news and current affairs. Present circulation of 25,274. Accepts queries by mail. Please do not send any unsolicited manuscripts.
Non-fiction Interested in photo features, features and historical/nostalgic pieces.
Submission Guidelines Accepts query including SAE. Articles should be a maximum of 3,500 words.
Tips History Today publishes essays on all periods, regions and themes of history, many of them by the world's leading scholars. All are carefully edited and illustrated. The publication will only accept freelance contributions from academic scholars, or equivalent, concerning new developments in history or archaeology.

Holiday
Kettering Parkway, Kettering, NN15 6EY
☎ 01536 310101
☎ 01536 314682
✉ holiday@europe.rci.com
🌐 www.rci.com

Parent Company RCI Europe
Contact Managing Editor, Sarah Davies
Insider Info A consumer magazine, with three issues per year, covering travel and timeshares. Present circulation is 184,531.
Non-fiction Publishes features, advice and travel articles.
Tips *Holiday* is the official magazine of RCI, the timeshare company. It publishes features and advice articles on travel and timeshare around the world.

Homebase Ideas
23 Howland Street, London, W1T 4AY
- 020 7462 7777
- 020 7462 7931
- ward.hellwell@publicis-blueprint.co.uk
- www.publicis-blueprint.co.uk
Parent Company Publicis Blueprint Ltd (Publishers) and Homebase
Editor Ward Hellwell
Contact Editorial Director, Penny MacDonald
Established 2002
Insider Info A quarterly consumer magazine covering Homebase department store products. Present circulation is 426,855.
Non-fiction Publishes inspirational features and product reviews.
Tips Homebase sells largely home and garden design products.

Homebuilding & Renovating
2 Sugar Brook Court, Aston Road, Bromsgrove, B60 3EX
- 01527 834420
- 01527 834497
- homebuilding@centaur.co.uk
- www.homebuilding.co.uk
Parent Company Ascent Publishing Ltd
Contact Editor in Chief, Michael Holmes; Editor, Jason Orme; Publishing Director, Peter Harris; Deputy Editor, Natasha Brinsmead
Established 1990
Insider Info A monthly consumer magazine covering home building and construction. Present circulation is 41,602.
Non-fiction Publishes features, showcases and practical articles.
Tips *Homebuilding & Renovating* covers every aspect of building, renovating, converting and extending. It is aimed at self-builders and industry professionals alike.

Home Cinema Choice
30 Monmouth Street, Bath, BA1 2BW
- 01225 224422
- 01225 732275

- www.homecinemachoice.com
Parent Company Future Publishing
Editor Steve May
Insider Info A consumer magazine publication issued monthly, covering home entertainment subjects. Present circulation of 12,420.
Non-fiction Publishes technical, feature and review articles on home cinema.
Tips *Home Cinema Choice* is the UK's best-selling home cinema enthusiasts magazine. It covers news and reviews of the latest home cinema equipment, including amplifiers, receivers, processors, power amps, DVD recorders, speakers, projectors and flat panel TVs. Writers should check regular features and develop an article that covers unusual topics around the magazine's interests.

Homes & Gardens
Blue Fin Building, 110 Southwark Street, London, SE1 0SU
- 020 3148 5000
- homesandgardens@ipcmedia.com
- www.homesandgardens.com
Parent Company IPC Media Ltd
Editor Deborah Baker
Contact Managing Editor, Fiona Surfleet; Features Editor, Helen Stone
Established 1919
Insider Info A consumer magazine publication issued monthly, covering women's and home interests. Present circulation of 143,900. Accepts query by mail and email.
Non-fiction Interested in photo features, features, interview/profile pieces on classic British homes and gardens.
Submission Guidelines Accepts query. Articles should be between 900 and 1,000 words long.
Images Send photos with submission.
Tips Most material is specially commissioned. Submissions must be supported by suitable photographs where appropriate, include as many as possible.

Homes Overseas
The UK's leading international property magazine
1st floor, 1 East Poultry Avenue, West Smithfield, London, EC1A 9PT
- 020 7002 8300
- 020 7002 8310
- info@blendoncom.com
- www.homesoverseas.co.uk
Parent Company Globespan Media Ltd
Editor Kate Hamilton
Established 1965
Insider Info A consumer magazine publication issued 13 times a year, covering overseas residential

property. Present circulation of 50,842. 75 per cent of the magazine is written by freelancers. Submissions are published approximately three months after acceptance, with an editorial lead time of two weeks. 50 per cent kill fee is paid for not published assigned manuscripts. Publication is copyrighted and all rights are purchased. Seasonal material must be submitted four weeks in advance. Accepts query by mail, email and phone. Aims to respond to queries and manuscripts within two weeks. Payment is upon publication, and is not given via contributor copies or other premiums. Assignment expenses are sometimes paid (limit agreed upon in advance), Sample copy is available with SAE. Writer's guidelines are available free on request. Limited forward features will be made available upon request. Media packs are available on the website.

Non-fiction Interested in how-tos, photo features, features with generally no fewer than three property or property buying examples, personal experience of buying overseas property, destination (including at least three detailed property examples) and case studies (including buying process).

* Approximately 130 non-fiction manuscripts are purchased from freelancers each year. Assigned and unsolicited articles are paid at approximately 25p per word.

Submission Guidelines Accepts query with published clips. Articles should be between 1,200 and 3,000 words.

Tips The magazine is largely aimed at potential buyers, be they holiday homers, retirees or pure investors. The readership generally falls into the ABC1 category.

Honda Dream
Victory House, 14 Leicester Place, Leicester Square, London, WC2H 7BZ
- 020 7306 0304
- dream@riverltd.co.uk
- www.honda.co.uk/dreamonline
Parent Company River Publishing Ltd
Editor Chris Hatherill
Established 2004
Insider Info A quarterly consumer magazine covering Honda products and technology. Present circulation is 207,636. Media pack is available online.
Non-fiction Publishes features, news, profiles, interviews, product reviews and technical articles.

Horse & Hound
Blue Fin Building, 110 Southwark Street, London, SE1 0SU
- 020 3148 5000
- 020 7401 6009
- jaki_bell@ipcmedia.com
- www.horseandhound.co.uk
Parent Company IPC Media Ltd
Contact Acting Editor, Jaki Bell
Established 1884
Insider Info A consumer magazine publication issued weekly, covering leisure interests and equestrianism. Present circulation of 65,631. Accepts queries by mail and email.
Non-fiction Publishes features, photo features, news and reviews on equine and countryside subjects.
Tips Regarded as the 'bible' of the equestrian world and aimed at horse lovers and professionals alike. As the only equestrian weekly, *Horse & Hound* provides reportage covering all disciplines, together with the latest news and views from around the country. Specialist information is in high demand, particularly veterinary information relating to the health and care of horses.

Horse
Inspiration for Riders
Blue Fin Building, 110 Southwark Street, London, SE1 0SU
- 020 3148 5000
- joanna_pyatt@ipcmedia.com
- www.horsemagazine.co.uk
Parent Company IPC Media Ltd
Editor Joanna Pyatt
Established 1997
Insider Info A consumer magazine publication issued monthly, covering leisure interests and equestrianism. Present circulation of 20,062.
Non-fiction Interested in horse related how-to features, i.e. 'hints and tips', 'techniques', 'grooming', exposés, interviews/profiles and general interest articles.
Submission Guidelines Accepts query with published clips and a CV.
Tips *Horse* magazine aims to help reader get more out of their time with their horse, whether readers ride as a hobby, or are a keen competitors looking for expert tips on how to move up to the next level. The magazine is mostly interested in articles on leading equestrian celebrities.

Horticulture Week
Teddington Studios, Broom Road, Teddington, Middlesex, TW11 9BE
- 020 8267 4977
- 020 8267 4987
- kate.lowe@haymarket.com
- www.hortweek.com
Parent Company Haymarket Publications
Editor Kate Lowe

Insider Info A trade journal magazine issued weekly, covering horticulture. Present circulation of 9,579.
Non-fiction Publishes business news, reviews and features on horticulture topics.
Tips *Horticulture Week* is aimed at all horticulture professionals, whatever sector they work in. Writers should have insider knowledge about the horticulture industry, concerning the latest developments, or knowledge of a related subject that is in demand.

Hospital Doctor
15th Floor Quadrant House, The Quadrant, Sutton, Surrey, SM2 5BR
- 020 8652 8763
- 020 8652 8946
- hospital.doctor@rbi.co.uk
- www.hospital-doctor.net
Parent Company Reed Elsevier
Insider Info A trade journal tabloid publication issued weekly, covering NHS and private medicine for all junior, consultant and staff and associate grade hospital doctors. Present circulation of 38,800. Payment upon publication. 15 per cent of the publication is written by freelancers. Average lead time of two weeks. Publication is copyrighted and a byline is given. Seasonal material must be submitted two weeks in advance. Queries are accepted by email. Aims to respond to queries and manuscripts within three days. Sample copy is available online and via email. Writer's guidelines are available free on request and via email.
Non-fiction Interested in opinion (excluding letters to the Editor) on medical, financial and political issues.
Tips *Hospital Doctor* is aimed at busy doctors.

Hotline
Victory House, 14 Leicester Place, Leicester Square, London, WC2H 7BZ
- 020 7306 0304
- 020 7306 0303
- arayner@riverltd.co.uk
- www.riverltd.co.uk
Parent Company Ink Publishing (Publishers) and Virgin
Editor Alex Rayner
Contact Art Director, John Bailey
Established 1998
Insider Info A monthly consumer magazine covering lifestyle and entertainment. Present circulation is 172,938.
Non-fiction Publishes features, profiles, interviews, book excerpts and event listings. Topics covered include political and social issues, celebrity profiles, sports, music, movies, theatre, and cinema reviews.

Tips *Hotline* is distributed free to Virgin Trains passengers. Articles tend to have some sort of broad connection to rail travel.

Hot Press
13 Trinity Street, Dublin 2, Republic of Ireland
- 00353 1 241 1500
- 00353 1 241 1539
- info@hotpress.com
- www.hotpress.com
Editor Niall Stokes
Established 1977
Insider Info A bi-weekly consumer magazine that covers news and lifestyle. Accepts queries by mail or email. Present circulation is 19,215.
Non-fiction Interested in news, features, politics, music, media, sport, sex, local interest (Ireland) and event listings.
Tips Most articles in *Hot Press* are related to Ireland or events in Ireland.

House & Garden
Vogue House, Hanover Square, London, W1S 1JU
- 020 7499 9080
- 020 7629 2907
- harriet.milward@condenast.co.uk
- www.houseandgarden.co.uk
Parent Company Conde Nast Publications
Editor Susan Crewe
Established 1947
Insider Info A consumer magazine publication issued monthly, covering women's and home interests. Present circulation of 142,511.
Non-fiction Publishes general interest articles on house and garden, along with business directories.
Tips Most material is produced in-house and other material will usually only come from qualified freelancers with specialised knowledge.

House & Home
PO Box 29, 76–86 Walmgate, York, YO1 9YN
- 01904 653051
- 01904 612853
- lynne.martin@ycp.co.uk
Parent Company Newsquest (York) Ltd
Editor Lynne Martin
Insider Info A consumer magazine, with three issues per year, covering homes and gardens. Present circulation is roughly 22,442.
Non-fiction Publishes features, profiles, practical guides, how-to and showcase articles.
Tips *House & Home* covers all aspects of home and garden renovation, including photo features and how-to articles.

House Beautiful

National Magazine House, 72 Broadwick Street, London, W1F 9EP

☎ 020 7439 5000

☎ 020 7439 5141

✉ houseb.mail@natmags.co.uk

🌐 www.housebeautiful.co.uk

Parent Company National Magazine Company

Editor Julia Goodwin

Established 1989

Insider Info A consumer magazine publication issued monthly covering women's home interests. Present circulation of 173,129. Queries are accepted by mail.

Non-fiction Interested in photo features, features and interviews/profiles on decorating and shopping for the home.

Submission Guidelines Accepts queries. Do not send any unsolicited manuscripts.

Tips *House Beautiful* is only looking for contributions from freelancers with specialist knowledge and examples of similar previously published articles.

IBI (International Boat Industry)

Leon House, 233 High Street, Croydon, CR9 1HZ

☎ 020 8726 8134

☎ 020 87268196

✉ ed_slack@ipcmedia.com

🌐 www.ibinews.com

Parent Company IPC Media Ltd

Editor Ed Slack

Contact Publishing Director, Nick Hopkinson

Established 1968

Insider Info A trade journal, with eight issues per year, covering the international marine leisure industry. Circulation is 10,800. Media pack available online.

Non-fiction Publishes company profiles, industry news, managerial and marketing articles.

Tips *IBI* is aimed at the business market and covers managerial, marketing and retail aspects of the boat building industry.

Ideal Home

Blue Fin Building, 110 Southwark Street, London, SE1 0SU

☎ 020 3148 5000

☎ 020 3148 8121

✉ ideal_home@ipcmedia.com

🌐 www.idealhomemagazine.co.uk

Parent Company IPC Media Ltd

Contact Editorial Director, Isobel McKenzie-Price; Executive Editor, Sarah Warwick; Deputy Editor, Jennifer Morgan

Established 1920

Insider Info Consumer magazine publication issued monthly, covering women's and home interests. Present circulation of 221,080. Queries accepted by mail.

Non-fiction Interested in photo features and features on the home.

Submission Guidelines Accepts query.

Tips The magazine is aimed at creative homeowners. Most features are privately commissioned. Check the latest trends in interior design and plan articles to work ahead of them if possible to catch the latest new, or unusual developments.

Illustration

39 Elmsleigh Road, Twickenham, Middlesex, TW2 5EF

✉ ruth.prickett@illustration-mag.com

🌐 www.illustration-mag.com

Editor Ruth Prickett

Established 2004

Insider Info A consumer magazine publication issued quarterly covering art. Present circulation of 2,000. Queries accepted via mail and email.

Non-fiction Interested in photo features, features, interviews/profiles, reviews, general interest, historical/nostalgic articles and news and events pieces on artists, collectors and collections, exhibitions, the history of art, art philosophy and any important events relating to the art world.

Submission Guidelines Accepts query.

Tips *Illustration* often has many articles about the latest news and events in the art world, and is always seeking interesting news breaks.

ImagineFX

30 Monmouth Street, Bath, BA1 2BW

☎ 01225 442244

☎ 01225 446019

✉ rob@imaginefx.com

🌐 www.imaginefx.com

Parent Company Future Publishing Ltd

Editor Rob Carney

Contact Book Reviewer, Tom Rudderham

Established 2006

Insider Info A monthly consumer magazine covering fantasy and science fiction digital art. Present circulation is 15,752.

Non-fiction Publishes community news, features, interviews, reviews, tips and workshop articles.

Tips *ImagineFX* covers all aspects of fantasy and science fiction digital art, including comics, graphic novels and computer games. The magazine often contains how-to workshop articles, and the website offers a service where members can upload their digital art portfolios for free.

Improve Your Coarse Fishing
Bushfield House, Orton Centre, Peterborough, PE2 5UW
- ☎ 01773 237111
- ✆ 01773 465810
- ✉ kevin.green@emap.com

Parent Company EMAP Plc
Editor Kevin Green
Established 1991
Insider Info A monthly consumer magazine covering coarse fishing. Present circulation is 52,594.
Non-fiction Publishes equipment advice and reviews and fishing locations.
Tips *Improve Your Coarse Fishing* focuses on features and advice on tackle and equipment, as well as guides to the best fishing spots.

In Britain
Jubilee House, 2 Jubilee Place, King's Road, London, SW3 3TQ
- ☎ 020 7751 4800
- ✆ 020 7751 4848
- ✉ inbritain@archant.co.uk
- ⊕ www.inbritain.co.uk

Parent Company Archant Specialist (London)
Editor Andrea Spain
Established 1932
Insider Info A bi-monthly consumer magazine covering travel and tourism in Britain. Present circulation is 27,882.
Non-fiction Publishes features and travel articles.
Tips *In Britain* is published on behalf of Visit Britain and covers travel and tourism within Britain. It is aimed at foreign visitors to the country and features include accommodation showcases, travel options and destination advice.

Incentive & Motivation
3rd Floor, Broadway House, 2–6 Fulham Broadway, London, SW6 1AA
- ☎ 020 7610 3001
- ✆ 020 7610 3566
- ✉ mark.ludmon@emap.com
- ⊕ www.incentiveandmotivation.com

Parent Company EMAP Plc
Editor Mark Ludmon
Contact Publisher, David Metcalfe; Deputy Editor, Anna Czerny
Established 1985
Insider Info A monthly trade journal covering promotional marketing. Present circulation is 15,050.
Non-fiction Publishes features, reviews and analysis.
Tips *Incentive & Motivation* is aimed at managers of promotional marketing or motivation campaigns and related activities. Features, reviews and analysis

cover promotional marketing, motivation and incentive techniques.

IN London
233 High Holborn, London, WC1V 7DN
- ☎ 020 7242 5222
- ✆ 020 7242 4184
- ✉ johnson@morriseurope.com
- ⊕ www.morriseurope.com

Parent Company MVP Europe
Contact Editorial Director, Chris Johnson; Publisher, Chris Manning; Art Director, John Barker; Deputy Editor, Johanna Agerman
Insider Info A quarterly consumer magazine covering London lifestyle and events. Present circulation is 54,570.
Non-fiction Publishes features, news, reviews and event listings.
Tips *IN London* publishes news and reviews on events in London, including art, theatre, fairs, business, property, shopping and restaurants. It is available to buy in Harrods' Bookshop and in Selfridges, therefore the target customers of these shops are the target customer of the magazine.

Inside Soap
64 North Row, London, W1K 7LL
- ☎ 020 7150 7000
- ✆ 020 7150 7683
- ✉ katymoon@insidesoap.co.uk
- ⊕ www.insidesoap.co.uk

Parent Company Hachette Filipacchi (UK) Ltd
Editor Steven Murphy
Contact Deputy Editor, Gary Gillatt; Publisher, Grace Stewart; Features Editor, Allison Maund
Established 1992
Insider Info A weekly consumer magazine covering television soap operas. Present circulation is 195,125.
Non-fiction Publishes features, interviews, profiles, news and television listings.

Inspire
Garcia Estate, Canterbury Road, Worthing, West Sussex, BN13 1BW
- ☎ 01903 264556
- ✆ 01903 537321
- ✉ editor@inspiremagazine.org.uk
- ⊕ www.inspiremagazine.org.uk

Editor Russ Bravo
Insider Info A monthly magazine that covers Christian news and lifestyle. Accepts queries by mail or email.
Tips Available in churches, *Inspire* magazine publishes inspirational 'good news' stories related to the Christian faith. It rarely accepts features.

InStyle

Blue Fin Building, 110 Southwark Street, London, SE1 0SU

- 020 3148 5000
- 020 3148 8166
- eilidh.macaskill@instyleuk.com
- www.instyle.com

Parent Company IPC Media Ltd

Editor Eilidh MacAskill

Contact Deputy Editor, Charlotte Moore; Senior Editor (Features), Kate O'Donnel

Established 2001

Insider Info A consumer magazine publication issued monthly, covering women's interests and women's lifestyle/fashion. Present circulation is 180,879. Accepts queries via email.

Non-fiction Publishes articles on beauty, fashion, home, entertaining, and the charitable endeavours of well known people.

Submission Guidelines Accepts query.

Tips Target readership is women aged 25–44. Ideas for features or articles aimed at the target audience are welcome.

Interlude

Limehouse Town Hall, 646 Commercial Road, London, E14 7HA

- submissions@interludemagazine.co.uk
- www.interludemagazine.co.uk

Editor Francesca Ricci; Helen Nodding; Becky Philp

Insider Info A consumer magazine publication, covering general interest, literary subjects. Queries accepted by mail and email. Sample copy is available online.

Non-fiction Interested in poetry articles, features and visual art pieces.

Submission Guidelines Submit complete manuscript.

Fiction Interested in fiction pieces.

Poetry Publishes poetry.

Tips *Interlude* is a multi-disciplinary magazine, which publishes poetry, fiction, visual art, and anything in between. Each page is designed and formatted by the contributor of the work appearing on it. *Interlude*'s editors take a back seat on the design process, making it very much a 'writers magazine'. The magazine has no particular theme and will accept any type of submission, but content in the magazine does tend to be very visually or conceptually driven.

International Homes

3 St Johns Court, Moulsham Street, Chelmsford, CM2 0JD

- 01245 358877
- 01245 357767
- jill@international-homes.com
- www.international-homes.com

Parent Company PPASS Ltd

Contact Editor in Chief, Helen Shield; Publisher, Stuart Shield; Editor, Jill Keene; Deputy Editor, Ben Bouckley

Established 1990

Insider Info A monthly consumer magazine covering the international property market. Present circulation is 28,340.

Non-fiction Publishes news, advice and market listings.

Tips Articles must cover an aspect of buying or selling a home abroad.

The Interpreter's House

19 The Paddox, Oxford, OX2 7PN

- www.interpretershouse.org.uk

Parent Company The Interpreter's House

Editor Merryn Williams

Established 1996

Insider Info A consumer magazine, issued three times a year, covering poetry and prose. Present circulation of 350. A byline is given. Sample copy is available online.

Fiction Publishes mainstream fiction, mystery and short stories.

Submission Guidelines Send complete manuscript.

Poetry Publishes free verse, light verse and traditional poetry.

Tips *The Interpreter's House* is a poetry and prose magazine, which prints writing that blends mystery and simplicity. Each issue contains new short stories and poems from contributors, as well as various writing competitions. Any poems that are published in the magazine may also appear on the website and be submitted for the Forward Prize.

Interzone

5 Martins Lane, Witcham, Ely, CB6 2LB

- andy@ttapress.demon.co.uk
- www.ttapress.com

Parent Company TTA Press

Editor Andy Cox

Established 1982

Insider Info A consumer magazine publication issued bi-monthly, covering new genre writing. Present circulation is 10,000. A byline is given. Queries are accepted by mail and email. Writer's guidelines are available online.

Non-fiction Interested in interviews/profiles and reviews relating to literary subjects.

Submission Guidelines Accepts query. Send complete manuscript.

Fiction Interested in science fiction and fantasy pieces.
* Payment is £30 per 1000 words.
Submission Guidelines Accepts queries or complete manuscript of a maximum of 10,000 words.
Tips *Interzone* has published short stories by many of the big names in the fantasy and science fiction fields, from Brian Aldiss and J.G. Ballard, to Ian Watson and Gene Wolfe, but its particular strength has been in the nurturing of newer writers. Unsolicited manuscripts are welcome 'from writers who have a knowledge of the magazine and its contents'. *Interzone* is an established magazine and submitted stories must fit into its preferred style. The magazine only accepts email submissions during certain months, so make sure you check the details on the submissions section of the website.

Iota

1 Lodge Farm, Snitterfield, Stratford upon Avon, Warwickshire, CV37 0LR
- 01789 730320
- iotapoetry@aol.com
- www.iotapoetry.co.uk

Parent Company Ragged Raven Press
Contact Editors: Bob Mee and Janet Murch
Established 1987
Insider Info A consumer magazine publication issued quarterly, covering general interest, literary subjects, with poetry a particular focus. Present circulation is 300. A byline is given. Queries by mail are accepted and previously published submissions are accepted.
Poetry Interested in contemporary, fresh, unpublished poetry
Submission Guidelines Maximum of six poems to be submitted at a time. *Iota* prefers submissions of poetry by post, but will accept submissions by email as well, providing that the poetry is printed in the body text of the email, rather than as an attachment.
Tips *Iota* publishes poetry from new and established authors, along with poetry reviews and profiles.

Irish Arts Review

State Apartments, Dublin Castle, Dublin 2, Republic of Ireland
- 00353 1 679 3525
- 00353 1 633 4417
- www.irishartsreview.com

Editor John Mulcahy
Insider Info A quarterly consumer magazine that covers Irish art and heritage. Accepts queries by mail or email.

Non-fiction Interested in art, heritage, culture, design, architecture, photography and media arts articles related to Ireland.

The Irish Books Review

Ashbrook House, 10 Main Street, Raheny, Dublin 5, Republic of Ireland
- 00353 1 851 1459
- info@irishbookreview.com
- www.irishbookreview.com

Insider Info A quarterly literary journal that covers Irish Literature. Accepts queries by mail or email. Reviews high quality, upmarket books of Irish interest, i.e. written by Irish authors, or where the subject has some specific interest to an Irish audience. Is particularly interested in literature and fiction, poetry, drama, visual arts and film, music, criticism, biography, autobiography and memoir, current events, history, politics, Irish culture and society, religion and business tiltes. Does not tend to review mass market literature.
Submission Guidelines Authors and publishers send review copies of titles by post, including press release or advance information sheet.

Irish Pages

A Journal of Contemporary Writing
The Linen Hall Library, 17 Donegall Square North, Belfast, BT1 5GB
- irishpages@yahoo.co.uk
- www.irishpages.org

Parent Company Irish Pages
Editor Chris Agee
Contact Managing Editor, Sean Mac Aindreasa; Irish Language Editor, Cathal Ó Searcaigh
Established 2002
Insider Info A consumer journal publication issued twice a year, covering general interest, literary subjects. A byline is given.
Non-fiction Interested in photo features, poetry articles, features, interviews/profiles, general interest and travel pieces.
Submission Guidelines Accepts query.
Fiction Interested in mainstream and Irish language pieces.
Submission Guidelines Send complete manuscript.
Poetry Interested in free verse, light verse and traditional poetry.
Submission Guidelines A maximum of six poems to be submitted at a time.
Tips *Irish Pages* is a literary journal, based in Belfast, that publishes English and Irish fiction and poetry, articles, photography features, and general Irish interest articles. It likes to remain unbiased in its editorial policy and will be as likely to accept

submissions from unknown, unsupported authors, as it is from popular writers, or writing organisations.

Irish Printer

52 Glasthule Road, Sandycove, Co. Dublin, Republic of Ireland

- 00353 1 280 0000
- 00353 1 280 1818
- f.venturini@jemma.ie

Parent Company Jemma Publications Ltd
Editor Fabio Venturini
Established 1974
Insider Info A monthly consumer magazine covering the printing industry. Accepts queries by mail or email. Present circulation is 1,472.
Non-fiction Interested in news, reviews and technical articles related to the Irish printing industry.
Submission Guidelines Accepts queries and completed manuscript submissions of between 800 to 1,000 words.

Irish Tatler

Rosemount House, Dundrum Road, Dublin 14, , Republic of Ireland

- 00353 1 240 5367
- 00353 1 661 9757
- www.harmonia.com

Parent Company Harmonia Ltd
Editor Elaine Prendeville
Insider Info A monthly consumer magazine that covers women's interest and lifestyle. Accepts queries by mail or email. Present circulation is 26,427.
Non-fiction Interested in beauty, celebrity news, cookery, current affairs, design, fashion, house & home and lifestyle articles.
Submission Guidelines Accepts queries and completed manuscript submissions of between 2,000 to 4,000 words.

Is This Music?

PO Box 13516, Linlithgow, EH49 6WB

- 01506 840063
- editor@isthismusic.com
- www.isthismusic.com

Editor Stuart McHugh
Established 2002
Insider Info A consumer magazine publication issued bi-monthly, covering music in Scotland.
Non-fiction Interested in photo features, features, interviews/profiles, reviews and general interest articles on Scottish music.
Submission Guidelines Accepts query.
Tips Is This Music? is an independent contemporary music magazine dedicated to reporting on, and supporting, the music scene all over Scotland. The

magazine runs lots of news and review articles on all aspects of the Scottish music scene, including smaller groups and gigs, and unsigned artists.

Italy Magazine

Middle Farm, Middle Farm Way, Dorchester, Dorset, DT1 3RS

- 01305 266360
- 01305 262760
- editor@italymag.co.uk
- www.italymag.co.uk

Parent Company Poundbury Publishing
Editor Melissa Ormiston
Established 2001
Insider Info A monthly consumer magazine, covering all things Italian. It is the bestselling glossy magazine about Italy published in the UK. Present circulation of 20,000. 80 per cent of the publication is written by freelance writers. Submissions are published up to six months after acceptance. Payment is upon publication. Writers may be paid with advertising space if they prefer. Publication is copyrighted. A byline is given. Purchases first UK serial rights, second serial (reprint) rights and electronic rights. Editorial lead time is three months and seasonal material must be submitted six months in advance. Queries are accepted by email. Aims to respond to queries within one week, and manuscripts within four weeks. Will not pay the expenses of writers on assignment. Sample copy and media pack available online. Writer's guidelines available via email.
Non-fiction Interested in photo features, features, and travel pieces. Publish special supplements bi-monthly, which focus on Italian themes such as winter holidays and language courses. Also publishes a weddings magazine four times a year, which is distributed with the magazine.
* Payment for assigned articles is between £60 and £300.
Submission Guidelines Accepts email synopsis for articles of between 500 and 1,500 words. Of particular interest are tutorial, lessons or practical techniques. Images must also be sent to the Art Editor to check before any submission is made. Does not accept reprints. Contact Melissa Ormiston, Editor.
Images Accepts images with submission.
* Payment for two images are included in the text fee and then additional images are paid at £35 each. Buys one time rights.
Submission Guidelines Submit gif/jpeg files and captions. Identification of subjects is required. Send photos with submission. Contact Art Editor, Paul Tutill.
Tips Italy Magazine magazine covers all aspects of Italian life: food, wine, sport, fashion, house interiors,

gardens, arts, culture, holidays, destination guides and property. There are also popular case studies and business pages. Once writers have heard back about their submission (which could take several weeks) and the Editor likes the idea, they will be asked to send images to accompany the feature to be checked by the Art Editor. Due to the overwhelming number of submissions, the whole process could take up to three months.

Jewish Chronicle
25 Furnival Street, London, EC4A 1JT
- 020 7415 1500
- 020 7405 9040
- editorial@thejc.com
- www.thejc.com

Parent Company Kessler Foundation
Editor Stephen Pollard
Contact Features Editor, Gerald Jacobs
Established 1841
Insider Info Consumer newspaper publication issued covering general interest religion. Present circulation of 32,875. Queries accepted by mail.
Non-fiction Interested in Jewish interest features.
Submission Guidelines Accepts query. Articles should be a maximum of 1,500 words.
Tips The world's oldest and most influential Jewish newspaper, the London based *Jewish Chronicle* has a 164 year history of editorial independence. Its news and opinion pages reflect the entire spectrum of Jewish religious, social and political thought, from left to right, orthodox to secular. The arts and lifestyle coverage includes film, theatre, travel, cookery and youth, and singles events. News articles are appreciated, especially when linked to upcoming community events.

Jewish Quarterly
PO Box 37645, London, NW7 1WB
- 020 8830 5367
- editor@jewquart.freeserve.co.uk
- www.jewishquarterly.org

Editor Matthew Reisz
Established 1953
Insider Info A consumer magazine publication issued quarterly covering general interest, literary topics. Present circulation of 2,000. A byline is given. Queries accepted by mail and email.
Non-fiction Interested in religious features, interviews/profiles, reviews, general interest and opinion (excluding letters to the Editor) pieces.
Submission Guidelines Accepts query.
Fiction Interested in Jewish fiction pieces.
Submission Guidelines Accepts query.
Tips *Jewish Quarterly* publishes news, reviews, interviews and articles from the Jewish community,

as well as new Jewish fiction. *Jewish Quarterly* holds an annual writing competition called the 'Wingate Literary Prize' which is Britain's only major literary award for Jewish interest books. The prize recognizes work that stimulates an interest in, and awareness of themes of Jewish concern, among a wider reading public and offers a prize of £5,000, along with publication in the *Jewish Quarterly*.

Jewish Renaissance
PO Box 28849, London, SW13 0WA
- 020 8876 1891
- 020 8392 1339
- editor@jewishrenaissance.org.uk
- www.jewishrenaissance.org.uk

Parent Company Renaissance Publishing Ltd
Editor Janet Levin
Contact Poetry Editor, Liz Cashdan
Insider Info A qaurterly consumer magazine covering Jewish culture.
Non-fiction Publishes news, photo features, features, poetry and cultural events listings.
Submission Guidelines Welcomes full details of all cultural events of Jewish interest, in UK, Europe or major cities elsewhere, by email, as early as possible or at least by the third week of the month preceding publication. Publication dates: mid January, mid April, mid July, mid October.
Tips *Jewish Renaissance* aims to encourage and intensify the current renaissance in Jewish culture. All articles are of the highest standards of writing, editing and presentation.

The Journal
17 High Street, Maryport, Cumbria, CA15 6BQ
- 01900 812194
- smithsssj@aol.com
- www.freewebs.com/thesamsmith

Parent Company Original Plus
Editor Sam Smith
Established 1994
Insider Info Poetry magazine, issued three times a year. Present circulation of 150. 100 per cent of the publication is written by freelance writers. Submissions are published approximately five months after acceptance. Contributors receive a complimentary copy of the magazine as payment. Publication is copyrighted and a byline is given. Acquires first UK serial rights on accepted submissions. Editorial lead time is five months. Queries accepted by mail and email. Accepts simultaneous and previously published submissions. Aims to respond to queries and manuscripts within three weeks. Assignment expenses are not paid. Sample copy is available for 1.50. Writer's guidelines are available free on request.

Non-fiction Publishes reviews of poetry collections and articles on the poetry scene. The Journal does not have special issues.

* Payment for unsolicited manuscripts is a complimentary copy of the magazine.

Submission Guidelines Send complete, typed manuscript to the Editor, Sam Smith. Submissions must be 1,000 words.

Fictions Publishes mainstream fiction.

Submission Guidelines Send complete manuscript.

Poetry Publishes free verse, haiku, traditional and avant-garde poetry and poetry in translation.

Submission Guidelines Submit a maximum of six poems. There is no limit on line length. Will not accept end rhyming poems or anything with religious content.

Tips The editorial policy is to try to publish poems written with thought as to what the poem is saying, and to how it is being said. Also welcomed are poems that can travel, that can cross boundaries and do not assume in their readers a shared knowledge, or a shared set of beliefs. Aside from poetry and prose submissions *The Journal* is also interested in interviews with poets, reviews, and appraisals of the current poetry scene.

Journal of Hellenic Studies
Senate House, Malet Street, London, WC1E 7HU
- 020 7862 8730
- 020 7862 8731
- office@hellenicsociety.org.uk
- www.hellenicsociety.org.uk

Parent Company The Society for the Promotion of Hellenic Studies
Editor Angus Bowie
Established 1880
Insider Info A trade journal published annually, covering Hellenic studies. Present circulation of 3,500. A byline is given. Queries accepted by mail and email. Writer's guidelines are available online.
Non-fiction Interested in academic articles, reviews, technical and historical/nostalgic pieces.
Submission Guidelines Send complete manuscript.
Tips The *Journal of Hellenic Studies* is an academic journal that publishes articles on the research and study of Greek language, literature, art and history. It also prints reviews of books relating to Hellenic studies. The *Journal of Hellenic Studies* will only consider article submissions from recognised scholars in the field of Hellenic studies, and then only if they follow the detailed guidelines on the website.

Junior
15–18 White Lion Street, Islington, London, N1 7PD
- 020 7042 4000
- editorial@juniormagazine.co.uk
- www.juniormagazine.co.uk

Parent Company Magicalia Ltd
Editor Catherine O'Dolan
Contact Commissioning Editor, Suzanne Milne
Established 1998
Insider Info A monthly consumer magazine covering child care and parenting. Present circulation is 16,978.
Non-fiction Publishes children's health and development, food & nutrition, education, lifestyle and travel articles.
Tips Junior is aimed at parents of children up to eight years old. The magazine covers all aspects of parenting and childcare, including children's fashion, lifestyle and travel.

Junior Education
Villiers House, Clarendon Avenue, Leamington Spa, CV32 5PR
- 01926 887799
- 01926 883331
- juniored@scholastic.co.uk
- www.scholastic.co.uk

Parent Company Scholastic UK Ltd
Editor Michelle Guy
Contact Deputy Editor, Victoria Paley
Established 1977
Insider Info A trade journal, issued monthly, covering primary education news and practical teaching. Present circulation is 9,654.
Non-Fiction Publishes news, practical teaching articles, product reviews, study packs and resources.
Submission Guidelines Accepts practical teaching articles of between 800–1,000 words. Payment by arrangement.
Tips *Junior Education* is aimed at teachers of 7–11 year olds and covers primary education news. It also publishes practical teaching articles and resources. All articles are photocopiable for use in the classroom.

Junior Education Topics
Villiers House, Clarendon Avenue, Leamington Spa, CV32 5PR
- 01926 887799
- 01926 883331
- jet@scholastic.co.uk
- www.scholastic.co.uk

Parent Company Scholastic UK Ltd
Editor Michelle Guy
Established 1982

Insider Info A trade journal, issued monthly, covering teaching resources.

Non-fiction Publishes themed teaching supplements, articles and resources.

Tips *Junior Education Topics* is the sister publication of *Junior Education*. Each issue is based on a theme that ties in with the National Curriculum. The majority of the journal consists of photocopiable teaching resources, with A1 and A3 full colour posters.

KAL

57 Poland Street, London, W1F 7NW

- 020 7439 9100
- 020 7439 9101
- media@arberrypink.co.uk
- www.kalmagazine.com

Parent Company Arberry Pink Ltd

Editor Laura Sheed

Established 1994

Insider Info Student and graduate careers/recruitment magazine and online publication issued bi-anually, covering career opportunities for black and minority ethnic students and graduates. Present circulation of 10,000. 75 per cent of the publication is written by freelancers. Publication is copyrighted and a byline is given. Purchases all rights. Editorial lead time is four weeks. Queries accepted by mail and email. Aims to respond to queries within three days, manuscripts within one week and other issues within three days. A sample copy is available for a cost of £3, online and via email. Writer's guidelines are available free on request, online and via email.

Non-fiction Interested in how-tos, photo features, essays, humour, inspirational, features, interviews/profiles, reviews, new products, general interest, opinion (excluding letters to the Editor), travel, historical/nostalgic and personal experience pieces.

Submission Guidelines Articles should be between 400 and 1,200 words.

Tips A contemporary careers magazine written to inspire and inform students and graduates from ethnic minority backgrounds. Written by students, for students. Material is provided through work experience and free contributions.

Kent Life

25a Pudding Lane, Maidstone, Kent, ME14 1PA

- 01622 762818
- 01622 663294
- sarah.sturt@kent-life.co.uk
- www.kent-life.co.uk

Editor Sarah Sturt

Insider Info A monthly consumer magazine covering Kent. Accepts queries by mail or email.

Non-fiction Interested in local interest, heritage, event listings and feature articles related to Kent.

Submission Guidelines Accepts queries and completed manuscript submissions of up to 1,000 words.

Kerrang!

Mappin House, 4 Winsley Street, London, W1W 8HF

- 020 7182 8000
- 020 7312 8910
- kerrang@emap.com
- www.kerrang.com

Parent Company EMAP Plc

Editor Paul Brannigan

Contact Editor in Chief, Phil Alexander; Features Editor, Nichola Browne; Reviews Editor, Nick Ruskell; Art Editor, Caroline Fish

Established 1981

Insider Info A weekly consumer magazine covering rock music. Present circulation is 60,290.

Non-fiction Publishes features, gig guides, interviews, news and reviews.

Tips *Kerrang!* covers all kinds of rock, metal and punk music. The magazine usually contains many reviews of the latest music and music DVD releases.

Keystone

53 Arcadia Court, 45 Old Castle Street, London, E1 7NY

- 020 7375 0258
- info@pennedinthemargins.co.uk
- www.pennedinthemargins.co.uk

Parent Company Penned in the Margins

Editor Tom Chivers

Insider Info A consumer magazine publication covering general interest, literary subjects. Queries accepted by mail and email.

Poetry Publishes contemporary poetry.

Tips An eclectic literary magazine that publishes contemporary and visual poetry from both known and unknown writers. *Keystone* is currently dormant and not accepting any further submissions. Check the website frequently for new developments.

Kick

Unit 1.08 Clerkenwell Workshops, 27–31 Clerkenwell Close, London, EC1R 0AT

- 020 7014 3762
- monique@atticmedianetwork.com

Parent Company Attic Media Network

Editor Ian Pollard

Contact Consultant Editor, Monique Webber

Established 2006

Insider Info A monthly consumer magazine covering football. Present circulation is 62,339.

Non-fiction Publishes features, profiles, interviews and competitions.

Tips *Kick* is aimed at boys aged 6 to 13 years old. It covers both premiership and championship football and articles include player and team profiles, interviews, match reports and football news.

Koi

Tower House, Fairfax Street, Bristol, BS1 3BN
- 0117 927 9009
- 0117 934 9008
- beckierodgers@originpublishing.co.uk
- www.koimag.co.uk

Parent Company Origin Publishing
Editor Beckie Rodgers
Established 1999
Insider Info A consumer magazine publication issued every four weeks, covering the Koi keeping hobby, including Koi health and pond construction. Present circulation is 15,000. 80 per cent of publication is written by freelancers. Submissions are published approximately two months after acceptance, with an editorial lead time of three months. A byline is given. Seasonal material must be submitted three months in advance. Queries are accepted by email and phone. Payment is not made with contributor copies or other premiums. A sample copy and writer's guidelines are available free on request.
Non-fiction Interested in how-tos, practical articles, photo features, interviews/profiles, reviews, new products, press releases, opinions and personal experience pieces.
Images Accepts images with submission.
* Negotiates payment individually for images.
Submission Guidelines Submit transparencies, print or gif/jpeg files. Contact Beckie Rodgers.
Tips The magazine is aimed at every kind of hobbyist, from the beginner to the more advanced.

Krax

63 Dixon Lane, Leeds, LS12 4RR
Editor Andy Robson
Established 1971
Insider Info A consumer magazine publication issued annually, covering general interest, literary subjects. Present circulation of 400. A byline is given. Payment is always made with contributor copies or other premiums.
Non-fiction Interested in poetry articles.
Submission Guidelines Submit query.
Fiction Interested in short fiction pieces.
Submission Guidelines Send complete manuscript.
Poetry Interested in contemporary poetry.

Tips *Krax* is a literary magazine that publishes contemporary poetry, prose and artwork – whose contents are generally whimsical or humorous in nature. *Krax* often has a large amount of submissions, so publication of accepted stories may often take a long time.

Kudos

17 Greenhow Avenue, West Kirby, Wirral, Cheshire, CH48 5EL
- carolebaldock@hotmail.com
- www.kudoswriting.wordpress.com

Editor Carole Baldock
Established 1998
Insider Info A bi-monthly consumer bulletin covering news and information on literary competitions. Present circulation around 500. Subs: £18/6 pa; single issue, £3.
Tips Kudos provides details and other information about UK and international writing competitions. It is purely an information service for writing competitions and does not publish features.

The Lady

39–40 Bedford Street, London, WC2E 9ER
- 020 7379 4717
- 020 7379 4620
- editors@lady.co.uk
- www.lady.co.uk

Editor Arline Usden
Established 1885
Insider Info A weekly consumer magazine, covering women's interests. Present circulation of 29,095. Queries accepted by mail.
Non-fiction Publishes photo features, features, interviews, general interest, travel and how-to articles on culture, travel, gardening, art and antiques, books, finance, history, fashion, cookery and beauty.
Submission Guidelines Accepts queries and completed manuscripts. Articles should be 1,200 words.
Images State availability of photos with submission.
Tips Ideally looking for well-researched pieces on local or foreign travel, historical subjects, or events. The magazine has regular staff writer for features.

Lallans

Blackford Lodge, Blackford, Perthshire, PH4 1QP
- 01764 682315
- 01764 682465
- mail@lallans.co.uk
- www.lallans.co.uk

Parent Company The Scots Language Society
Editor Kenneth Farrow and Elaine Morton
Established 1972

Insider Info Semi annual consumer journal for the Scots Language Society.

Non-fiction Publishes features, reviews and literary articles.

Submission Guidelines Queries accepted by mail and email.

Fiction Publishes short stories.

Submission Guidelines Writers should query before any submission.

Poetry Publishes free verse and traditional poetry.

Tips Publishes poetry, short fiction, reviews and articles printed in the Scottish dialect. *Lallans* welcomes short story and poetry submissions, providing they are written in Scottish dialect.

Lancashire Life
3 Tustin Court, Port Way, Ashton on Ribble, Preston, PR2 2YQ

- 01772 722022
- 01772 736496
- roger.borrell@lancashirelife.co.uk
- www.lancashirelife.co.uk

Parent Company Archant Life (North) Plc
Editor Roger Borrell
Contact Publisher, Andy Phelan
Established 1947
Insider Info A monthly consumer magazine covering Lancashire lifestyles. Present circulation is 23,455. Media pack is available online.

Non-fiction Publishes news, features, historical and lifestyle articles. Topics include heritage, life in the county, property, antiques, fashion, interior design, gardening, food and wine and motoring, and Lancashire's society scene.

Tips Articles must be directly linked to a Lancashire town or village, or the surrounding countryside.

Lancashire Magazine
Unit 200, Oyston Mill, The Strand, Preston, PR1 8UR

- info@lancashiremagazine.co.uk
- www.lancashiremagazine.co.uk

Editor Brian Hargreaves
Established 1977
Insider Info A bi-monthly consumer magazine covering Lancashire. Accepts queries by mail or email. Present circulation is 20,299.

Non-fiction Interested in local interest and lifestyle articles related to Lancashire.

Submission Guidelines Accepts queries and completed manuscript submissions. of between 700 to 1,000 words.

Lancet
32 Jamestown Road, London, NW1 7BY

- 020 7424 4910

- 020 7424 4911
- www.thelancet.com

Editor Richard Horton
Established 1823
Insider Info A weekly journal that covers all aspects of health and medical science. Accepts queries by mail or email.

Non-fiction Interested in commentaries, policy, research papers, reviews and editorial articles related to international medicine.

Submission Guidelines Contact the editor with proposal before submitting a manuscript.

Land Rover Owner International
Media House, Lynchwood, Peterborough Business Park, Peterborough, PE2 6EA

- 01733 468000
- 01733 468888
- john.pearson@emap.com
- www.lro.com

Parent Company EMAP Plc
Contact Editor in Chief, John Pearson; Production Editor, Rob McCabe; Features Editor, Mark Saville; Art Editor, Karen Elliot
Established 1987
Insider Info A monthly consumer magazine covering land rover vehicles. Present circulation is 43,021.

Non-fiction Publishes features, news and reviews.

Tips *Land Rover Owner International* is aimed at Land Rover and 4x4 enthusiasts around the world. It covers reviews and off-road tests of the latest Land Rover vehicles.

Land Rover World
Leon House, 233 High Street, Croydon, CR9 1HZ

- 020 8726 8374
- 020 8726 8398
- lrw.ed@kelsey.co.uk
- www.landroverworld.co.uk

Parent Company Kelsey Publishing Ltd
Editor John Carroll
Established 1993
Insider Info Monthly consumer magazine covering motoring, motorcycling and motoring 4x4. Present circulation of roughly 30,000. Queries accepted by mail and email. Media packs available at: www.ipcmedia.com/magazines/landroverworld

Non-fiction Publishes photo features, features, reviews, new product and technical articles.

Submission Guidelines Accepts queries. Send complete manuscript.

Images Send photos with submission.

Tips *Land Rover World* has a growing circulation among enthusiasts and professionals. Include high quality illustrations in support of any submissions.

Language Travel Magazine

11–15 Emerald Street, London, WC1N 3QL

- 020 7440 4020
- 020 7440 4033
- mail@hothousemedia.com
- www.hothousemedia.com

Parent Company Hothouse Media
Editor Amy Baker
Established 1991
Insider Info A monthly B2B magazine, covering education and travel. Present circulation is 12,000. Queries accepted by email. Media packs available on the website.
Non-fiction Publish news and features relating to language education and travel.
Tips *Language Travel Magazine* is the only B2B publication written for, and read by, students, recruiters and educational consultants in over 100 countries every month.

Legal Week

Level 3, 32-34 Broadwick Street, London, W1A 2HG

- 020 7316 9000
- 020 7316 9278
- john.malpas@legalweek.com
- www.legalweek.com

Parent Company Incisive Media Ltd
Editor Alex Novarese
Established 1999
Insider Info A weekly consumer magazine that covers law and legal practice. Accepts queries by mail or email. Present circulation is 28,697.
Non-fiction Interested in news and feature articles related to law.
Submission Guidelines Accepts queries and completed manuscript submissions of between 750 to 1,000 words.
Tips *Legal Week* is aimed at lawyers and professionals in the legal industry. It welcomes unsolicited submissions and ideas for new features.

Legion

17 Britton Street, London, EC1M 5TP

- 020 7880 6200
- 020 7324 2791
- editorial@legion-magazine.co.uk
- www.legion-magazine.co.uk

Parent Company Redactive Publishing Ltd
Editor Claire Townley-Jones
Contact Publisher, Jason Grant; Art Director, Mark Parry
Insider Info A quarterly consumer magazine covering the Royal British Legion. Present circulation is 389,183.
Non-fiction Publishes news, features and event information.
Tips *Legion* is the official publication of the Royal British Legion. All articles focus on the ex-service community.

Leisure Report

Broadfield House, Broadfield Park, Crawley, Sussex, RH11 9RT

- 01293 846500
- duncan.rowe@william-reed.co.uk
- www.wr-bi.com

Parent Company William Reed
Editor Duncan Rowe
Established 2000
Insider Info A monthly journal covering the business aspects of the UK leisure sector; health and fitness, betting and gaming, tourism, entertainment, attractions, cinema, tenpin, and food. Present circulation is approximately 450. Ten per cent of the publication is written by freelance writers. Takes one week to publish manuscripts after acceptance. Payment on publication. Kill fee for assigned manuscripts not published is negotiable. A byline is given and simultaneous rights are purchased. Editorial lead time is five weeks. Seasonal material must be submitted one month in advance. Queries are accepted via email. Aims to report back on queries within three days. No payment other than cash. Payment of assignment expenses will occasionally be made. Sample copy and writer's guidelines are free on request. Don't carry advertising, or compile a 'Forward Features' list. Editorial decides monthly which features to run, based on what is newsworthy. Will always listen to relevant ideas for submission. Media packs available online.
Non-fiction Articles include, book excerpts, interviews/profiles, new products and technical pieces, all of which are linked to the UK leisure market.
* Negotiable payment for assigned articles.
Submission Guidelines Accepts queries from writers. Articles should be a 1,300 words minimum, 2,500 words maximum. No reprints accepted.
Tips The magazine is aimed at a high level readership and contributors require in-depth sector and business knowledge. They consider themselves the 'FT' of the UK leisure sector. Writers should have a strong understanding of current events and trends in the UK leisure market, and use this knowledge in their work.

The Liberal

208–210a High Road, London, N2 9AY

- 020 8444 5413

☎ 020 8444 1944
✉ editor@theliberal.co.uk
🌐 www.theliberal.co.uk
Editor Benjamin Ramm
Established 2004
Insider Info A consumer magazine, issued every two months, covering literary/political subjects. Present circulation of 35,000. Queries accepted by mail and email.
Non-fiction Publishes photo features, features, interviews/profiles, reviews, opinion (excluding letters to the Editor) and travel articles.
Submission Guidelines Send query before sending submission.
Fiction Publishes fiction.
Poetry Publishes poetry.
Tips *The Liberal* is a literary political magazine that publishes newsy articles, interviews, book reviews and some fiction and art. Currently in the process of re-launching their website. Check the website in the future for updated submission guidelines.

Lighting
19th Floor, Leon House, 233 High Street, Croydon, CR0 9XT
☎ 020 8277 5622
☎ 020 8277 5622
✉ lighting@emap.com
Parent Company EMAP Plc
Editor Ray Molony
Contact Publishing Director, Rowan Crowley
Established 1967
Insider Info A monthly trade journal covering the lighting industry. Present circulation is 9,962. Media pack available online.
Non-fiction Publishes design features and analysis, industry news, product reviews and technical information, job opportunities listings and a lighting directory.
Tips *Lighting* is a business publication that covers all aspects of commercial, industrial, public, decorative and architectural lighting.

Lincolnshire Life
County House, 9 Checkpoint Court, Sadler Road, Lincoln, LN6 3PW
☎ 01522 527127
☎ 01522 842000
✉ editorial@lincolnshirelife.co.uk
🌐 www.lincolnshirelife.co.uk
Editor Judy Theobald
Established 1961
Insider Info A monthly consumer magazine covering Lincolnshire. Accepts queries by mail or email.

Non-fiction Interested in local interest and lifestyle articles related to Lincolnshire.
Submission Guidelines Accepts queries and completed manuscript submissions of up to 1,500 words.

The Linguist
Saxon House, 48 Southwark Street, London, SE1 1UN
☎ 020 8292 3196
✉ linguist.editor@gogglemail.com
🌐 www.iol.org.uk/linguistmagazine
Parent Company The Chartered Institute of Linguists
Editor Miranda Moore
Insider Info A bi-monthly consumer magazine that covers language and translation. Accepts queries by mail or email.
Submission Guidelines Accepts queries and completed manuscript submissions of between 1,500 to 2,000 words.
Tips *The Linguist* is aimed at professional linguists and translators. Most articles are contributed, authors must be experts in their field.

Linkway Magazine
The Shieling, The Links, Burry Port, Carmarthenshire, SA16 0HU
☎ 01554 834486
☎ 01554 834486
Editor Fay Davies
Established 1999
Insider Info Consumer magazine covering literary subjects. A byline is given. Accepts queries by mail. Sample copy is available via SAE (include two first class stamps).
Non-fiction Articles include articles on poetry and features about creative writing.
Submission Guidelines Accepts queries.
Fiction Articles include mainstream short fiction.
Submission Guidelines Accepts queries.
Poetry Articles include free verse, light verse and traditional poetry.
Submission Guidelines Accepts queries.
Tips *Linkway Magazine* publishes new short stories, poetry and articles on creative writing for a general readership. The magazine runs various writing competitions, offering publication in the magazine as prizes. Also accepts unsolicited submissions, but it is advisable to read the magazine first to ensure suitability.

Linux Format
(DVD Edition)
30 Monmouth Street, Bath, BA1 2BW
☎ 01225 442244

☎ 01225 732275
✉ lfx.letters@futurenet.co.uk
✉ nick.veitch@futurenet.co.uk
🌐 www.linuxformat.co.uk
Parent Company Future Publishing
Editor Nick Veitch
Established 2000
Insider Info Consumer magazine publishing 13 issues per year, covering the Linux computer operating system. Present circulation is 25,353. Accepts queries by mail and email. Sample copy is available via website. Writer's guidelines available at: paul.hudson@futurenet.co.uk
Non-fiction Publishes how-tos, features, reviews, technical articles and new product pieces. Contact Paul Hudson.
Submission Guidelines Accepts queries, submission guidelines online.
Tips *Linux Format* actively encourages submissions from freelancers who know their subject. Check out their website for full submission guidelines.

The List
14 High Street, Edinburgh, EH1 1TE
☎ 0131 550 3050
☎ 0131 557 8500
✉ mail@list.co.uk
🌐 www.list.co.uk
Parent Company The List Ltd
Editor Claire Prentice
Established 1985
Insider Info A fortnightly consumer magazine, covering arts and entertainment listings in Glasgow and Edinburgh. Present circulation of 9,686. 25 per cent of the magazine is written by freelance writers. Submissions are published approximately two weeks after acceptance. Payment is made on publication of material. Publication is copyrighted and a byline is given. Kill fee for articles not published is 100 per cent of the original fee. Purchases first rights and second serial (reprint) rights. Editorial lead time is one month. Seasonal material must be submitted one month in advance. Queries accepted by mail and email. Accepts simultaneous submissions. Assignment expenses sometimes paid (limit agreed upon in advance). Media packs available online.
Non-fiction Publishes interviews/profiles, opinion (excluding letters to the Editor) and travel articles.
Submission Guidelines Send query with published clips. Articles must be 300 words.
Columns Publishes reviews (50–650 words), book reviews (150 words), comic reviews (100 words), television/video reviews (100 words) and record reviews (100 words).
* Payment for columns is between £10 and £35.
Submission Guidelines Query with published clips.

Tips *The List* was originally founded to publicise and promote the wide range of arts and entertainment taking place throughout the year in Glasgow and Edinburgh. The company now produces a series of additional titles and supplements and is at the forefront of gathering and collating events information for a wide variety of publications, organisations and new media. *The List* is pitched at educated 18–35 year olds. Any articles or features that are included in each issue usually preview forthcoming events in greater detail.

Literary Review
44 Lexington Street, London, W1F 0LW
☎ 020 7437 9392
☎ 020 7734 1844
✉ editorial@literaryreview.co.uk
🌐 www.literaryreview.co.uk
Editor Nancy Sladek
Established 1979
Insider Info A monthly consumer journal covering literary interests. Circulation is presently roughly 15,000. Accepts queries by mail and email.
Non-fiction Publishes features, interviews/profiles, and reviews on literature topics.
Submission Guidelines Accepts queries.
Tips *The Literary Review* publishes reviews of the best new books, along with author interviews and articles about writing. *The Literary Review* aims to be an 'intelligent literary magazine for people who love reading, but hate academic and intellectual jargon.' The magazine tries to keep jargon and academic styles to a minimum. Reviews are usually sourced from professional authors rather than critics.

Livewire
Sea Containers House, 20 Upper Ground, London, SE1 9PF
☎ 020 7805 5555
☎ 020 7805 5911
✉ laura.richardson@iln.co.uk
🌐 www.gner.co.uk/gner/livewire
Parent Company Illustrated London News Group and GNER
Editor Claire Roberts
Contact Acting Editor, Laura Richardson; Art Director, Adrian Hulf
Insider Info A quarterly consumer magazine for rail passengers covering travel and lifestyle. Present circulation is 108,894.
Non-fiction Publishes news, features, information and event listings.
Tips *Livewire* is distributed to GNER rail passengers. It covers the latest GNER industry news and information, general railway news and rail travel

articles, as well as news and current affairs features, event listings and general features.

Living etc

Blue Fin Building, 110 Southwark Street, London, SE1 0SU
- 020 3148 5000
- livingetc@ipcmedia.com
- www.livingetc.com

Parent Company IPC Media Ltd
Editor Suzanne Imre
Contact Publishing Director, Yvonne Ramsden; Publisher, Chris Kelly; Art Director, David Dowding; Chief Sub-Editor, Sarah Alcroft
Established 1998
Insider Info A monthly consumer magazine, covering homes and modern living. Circulation is 98,395. Media pack available online.
Non-fiction Publishes food, home furnishing, interior design, lifestyle, shopping and travel articles.
Tips *Living etc* is a home and lifestyle magazine with a relaxed, contemporary outlook aimed at 30-something urbanites. Articles cover all aspects of modern living as well as interior design and furnishing showcases.

Loaded

Blue Fin Building, 110 Southwark Street, London, SE1 0SU
- 020 3148 5000
- 020 3148 8107
- www.loaded.co.uk

Parent Company IPC Media Ltd
Editor Martin Daubney
Contact Commissioning Editor, Andy Sherwood
Established 1994
Insider Info A monthly consumer magazine covering men's lifestyle topics. Present circulation of 95,371.
Non-fiction Publishes general men's interest articles, interviews, reviews and photo features on celebrities, fashion, sport, humour, sex, music, television, film and real-life.
Tips The magazine is aimed at young men aged 18–30 and contains some mild adult content.

LOGOS

5 Beechwood Drive, Marlow, Buckinghamshire, SL7 2DH
- 01628 483371
- 01628 477577
- logos-marlow@dial.pipex.com
- www.logos-journal.org

Editor Gordon Graham
Established 1990

Insider Info A quarterly consumer magazine that covers publishing, libraries and bookselling. Accepts queries by mail or email.
Submission Guidelines Accepts queries and completed manuscript submissions of between 3,500 to 7,000 words.
Tips Articles in *LOGOS* tend to be very in-depth and industry specific, so insider knowledge is essential in any submission.

The London Magazine

A Review of Literature and the Arts

70 Wargrave Avenue, Stamford Hill, London, N15 6UB
- 020 8802 6686
- 020 8994 1713
- editor@thelondonmagazine.net
- www.thelondonmagazine.net

Parent Company The London Magazine
Editor Sebastian Barker
Established 1732
Insider Info A consumer magazine, published every two months, covering poetry, fiction, features about all the arts, and critical reviews of literature and the arts. Present circulation of 1,200. 100 per cent of the magazine is written by freelance writers. Submissions are published approximately three months after acceptance. Payment is made on publication of material. Copyright is held by contributors. Queries are accepted by mail. Aims to respond to manuscripts within six weeks. Sample copy, writer's guidelines and editorial calendars are available online.
Non-fiction Publishes photo features, essays, humour, exposé, features, interviews/profiles, reviews on travel, history, inspirational topics and religious subjects, as well as pieces on music, film, satire, science, painting, dance, archaeology, drama, translation, sculpture and biography. No special issues.
* Purchases 18 non-fiction manuscripts from freelance writers per year. Payment for articles is between £30 and £175.
Submission Guidelines Send complete manuscript with SAE. Articles must be 250–5,000 words. Submissions must be of high quality. Address submissions to the Editor.
Fiction Publishes adventure, erotica, fantasy, historical, humorous, mainstream, ethnic and experimental fiction.
Purchases 18 fiction manuscripts per year. Payment is between £50 and £75.
Submission Guidelines Send complete manuscript with SAE. Submissions must be 250–5,000 words. Will not accept fiction that lacks literary merit. Address submissions to the Editor.

Poetry Publishes free verse, haiku, light verse, avant-garde and traditional poetry.

* Purchases 100 poems per year. Payment for poetry is between £30 and £175.

Submission Guidelines Submit a maximum of six poems with SAE. Poems should be 10–4,500 lines in length. Poetry must be of quality. Address submissions to the Editor.

Images Accepts images with submission.

* Varied fee per photo. Rights stay with photographer.

Submission Guidelines Send transparencies, prints or gif/jpeg files with submission.

Tips Committed to publishing established, young, and unknown talents – writers, artists, and critics – from all backgrounds around the world. Writers should send in well-produced manuscripts with SAE or International Reply Coupon (IRC) if abroad. The SAE or IRC must cover return postage for a reply only, or for return of the manuscript, whichever is applicable.

London Review of Books
28 Little Russell Street, London, WC1A 2HN
- 020 7209 1101
- 020 7209 1102
- edit@lrb.co.uk
- www.lrb.co.uk

Parent Company LRB Ltd
Editor Mary-Kay Wilmers
Contact Deputy Editor, Jean McNicol
Established 1979
Insider Info Bi-weekly consumer journal covering literary general interest. Present circulation of 45,905. A byline is given. Accepts queries by mail and email.
Non-fiction Publishes essays, features, interviews/profiles and reviews.
Submission Guidelines Queries accepted.
Tips *The London Review of Books* is an old fashioned literary journal, that publishes critical essays from leading writers and critics, as well as interviews and the latest book reviews. It sources most of its content from regular contributing editors, including leading writers and literary critics.

Look
Blue Fin Building, 110 Southwark Street, London, SE1 0SU
- 020 3148 5000
- look.editorial@ipcmedia.com
- www.look.co.uk

Parent Company IPC Media Ltd
Editor Alison Hall
Contact Features Editor, Zoe Oliver; Managing Editor, Duncan Baizley; Deputy Chief Sub Editor, Rachael Sanderson

Established 2007
Insider Info A weekly consumer magazine covering women's lifestyle and celebrity topics. A preview sample of an issue is available online. Present circulation is 307,274.
Non-fiction Publishes general interest features, interviews and photo features on celebrities, real life, fashion and beauty.
Tips The title is aimed specifically at women aged 18 to 30. Its main focus is celebrity gossip and style advice for young women.

Lothian Life
Larick House, Whitehouse, Tarbert, Argyll, PA29 6XR
- 07734 699607
- editor@lothianlife.co.uk
- www.lothianlife.co.uk

Editor Susan Coon
Established 1995
Insider Info A consumer magazine that covers the Lothian area. Accepts queries by mail or email.
Non-fiction Interested in lifestyle and local interest articles.
Tips *Lothian Life* only publishes online.

Love It!
2 Chelsea Manor Gardens, London, SW3 5PN
- 020 7198 3020
- any.brookbanks@newsmagazines.co.uk

Parent Company News Group Newspapers Ltd
Editor Karen Pasquali-Jones
Contact Deputy Editor, Joely Carey; Commissioning Editor, Karen Lester; Features Director, Steve Tooze; Features Writer, Sarah Whiteley
Established 2006
Insider Info A weekly consumer magazine covering women's interest and lifestyle. Present circulation is 372,247.
Non-fiction Publishes features, interviews, profiles, true-life stories and celebrity gossip articles.
Tips *Love It!* is aimed at women of between 18 and 35 years of age.

MacFormat
30 Monmouth Street, Bath, BA1 2BW
- 01225 442244
- 01225 732275
- graham.barlow@futurenet.co.uk
- www.macformat.co.uk

Parent Company Future Publishing
Editor Graham Barlow
Insider Info Monthly consumer magazine covering Mac computing. Present circulation of 18,722.
Non-fiction Publishes technical, how-to and feature articles on Mac computers and related accessories.

Tips As well as dealing with Mac computers, it also handles all Mac/Apple accessories including iPods and iPod related gadgets. Also interested in music and the downloading of music for use on Macs and iPods.

MacUser
30 Cleveland Street, London, W1T 4JD
- 020 7907 6000
- mailbox@macuser.co.uk
- www.macuser.co.uk

Parent Company Dennis Publishing
Editor Nik Rawlinson
Established 1985
Insider Info A fortnightly consumer magazine covering Mac computing. Present circulation of 14,502.
Non-fiction Publishes how-to, feature and technical articles.
Tips *MacUser* is a magazine focused at the professional and creative markets with its core readers working in graphics, design and publishing, video and audio. With in-house testing, *MacUser*'s reviews are rigorous and extensive. The magazine also features many articles completely unrelated to Mac computers, such as the latest gadget trends, or news from the electronic industry. As long as it is Mac compatible, for example the latest digital video camcorder, then it is possible to write a feature about it.

Macworld
IDG Media, 4th Floor, 101 Euston Road, London, NW1 2RA
- 020 7756 2877
- editor@macworld.co.uk
- www.macworld.co.uk

Parent Company IDG Media
Editor Karen Haslam
Established 1989
Insider Info A consumer magazine, with 14 issues per year, that covers all aspects of Mac computing. Accepts queries by mail or email. Present circulation is 23,457.
Non-fiction Interested in how-tos, new product articles, general interest reviews, news and feature articles related to Apple Mac computers.
Tips Most articles are specially commissioned but *Macworld* will accept queries or ideas for new features.

Magma
43 Keslake Road, London, NW6 6DH
- 020 7975 5236
- 020 8980 6533
- magmapoetry@ntlworld.com
- www.magmapoetry.com

Editor David Boll
Contact Editor, David Boll
Established 1994
Insider Info Consumer magazine publishing three issues per year (Spring, Autumn, Winter). Covers literary interests and poetry. Present circulation of 700. 100 per cent of the publication is written by freelance writers. Accepts queries by mail and email. Sample copy is available online at www.magmapoetry.com/submission.php, or by email to contributions@magmapoetry.com.
Non-fiction Publishes articles on poetry, features, interviews/profiles and reviews.
Submission Guidelines Accepts queries.
Poetry Publishes free verse, light verse and traditional poetry.
Submission Guidelines No more than six poems to be submitted at one time. Send poems via email within the body of the text, not as attachments.
Tips *Magma* is a literary magazine that prints poetry and articles about poetry, as well as a range of features, reviews and interviews. It is run by a group of editors who take turns to edit the magazine. Magma looks for well-crafted poems 'which give a direct sense of what it is to live today - honest about feelings, alert about the world, sometimes funny.'

Marie Claire
Blue Fin Building, 110 Southwark Street, London, SE1 0SU
- 020 3148 5000
- 020 3148 8120
- marieclaire@ipcmedia.com
- www.marieclaire.co.uk

Parent Company IPC Media Ltd
Editor Trish Halpin
Contact Deputy Editor, Vanessa Thompson; Assistant Commissioning Editor, Emma Sibbles
Established 1988
Insider Info Monthly consumer magazine covering women's interests, lifestyle and fashion. Present circulation is 316,765. Queries by mail and email.
Non-fiction Publishes features and articles on women's lifestyle, fashion, beauty, real life, career and health.
Submission Guidelines Accepts queries with published clips. Address to 'Features Editor'. No unsolicited manuscripts.

Marketing Week
St Giles House, 50 Poland Street, London, W1F 7AX
- 020 7970 6328
- 020 7970 6721
- stuart.smith@centaur.co.uk

🌐 www.marketingweek.co.uk
Parent Company Centaur Communications
Editor Stuart Smith
Contact Deputy Editor, Sonoo Singh; Features Editor, Catherine Turner; Digital Editor, Rufus Jay
Established 1978
Insider Info Weekly trade journal magazine, covering marketing. Present circulation is 39,063. Accepts queries by mail and email.
Non-fiction Publishes features, interviews/profiles and news/analysis from the marketing profession. * Pays £200 per 1,000 words.
Submission Guidelines Accepts queries. Send complete manuscript of 1,000 words minimum and 2,000 words maximum.
Tips *Marketing Week* is aimed at professionals working in marketing, marketing services and media. The magazine also publishes a range of supplements and yearbooks, including design, market research, conferences and exhibitions, and search marketing. As the magazine is aimed at marketing management, any article submissions must include relevant data and statistical analysis.

Markings
44 High Street, Gatehouse of Fleet, Dumfries and Galloway, DG7 2HP
☎ 01557 814196
🖷 01557 332339
✉ johnhudson@markings.org.uk
🌐 www.markings.org.uk
Parent Company The Bakehouse
Editor John Hudson
Established 1995
Insider Info Bi-annual consumer magazine covering Scottish literary interests.
Non-fiction Publishes poetry articles and literary criticism.
Submission Guidelines Send complete manuscript.
Fiction Publishes short stories.
Submission Guidelines Send complete manuscript.
Poetry Publishes free verse and traditional poetry.
Submission Guidelines Send complete manuscript.
Tips *Markings* is a bi-annual arts magazine in its eleventh year offering a synergy between the written word and performance, and is now one of Scotland's most popular literary magazines. They invite unsolicited submissions of poetry, fiction, artwork and criticism in any language, providing they are accompanied by either an English or Scots translation.

Match
Bushfield House, Orton Centre, Peterborough, PE2 5UW
☎ 01733 237111
🖷 01733 288150
✉ match.magazine@emap.com
🌐 www.matchmag.co.uk
Parent Company EMAP Plc
Editor Ian Foster
Contact Publisher, Alan Morrison; Deputy Editor, James Bandy
Insider Info A weekly children's consumer magazine covering football. Present circulation is 113,049.
Non-fiction Publishes features, interviews, match reports and football news.
Tips *Match* is aimed at boys aged between 9 and 15 and often contains a lot of interactive content, such as puzzles and quizzes.

Matchbox
87 Thornton Road, Fallowfield, Manchester, M14 7NT
✉ matchbox@matchbox.org.uk
🌐 www.matchbox.org.uk
Editor James Davies
Insider Info Consumer poetry publication in the 'matchbox' format, publishing three editions per year.
Poetry Publishes poetry collections in a unique 'matchbox' form.
Tips Each *Matchbox* publication consists of a decorated matchbox (a real matchbox) containing selected poetry by a single writer, usually well-established, and a free gift. They are available from certain shops in Manchester, as well as from the *Matchbox* website. *Matchbox* issues are always dedicated to selected well-known writers, therefore they do not accept submissions of any kind. General queries are welcome by email.

Maxim
30 Cleveland Street, London, W1T 4JD
☎ 020 7907 6000
🖷 020 7907 6439
✉ editorial@maxim-magazine.co.uk
✉ derek_harbinson@dennis.co.uk
🌐 www.maxim-magazine.co.uk
Parent Company Dennis Publishing
Editor Editorial Director, Ben Raworth
Contact Deputy Editor and Reviews Editor, Stuart Messham; Features Editor, Nick Leftley; Picture Editor, Joanna Moran
Established 1995

517

Insider Info Monthly consumer magazine covering men's lifestyle. Present circulation is 43,542. Accepts queries by mail.

Non-fiction Publishes features, interviews/profiles, reviews and travel pieces.

Submission Guidelines Accepts query with published clips of 1,500 words minimum and 2,500 words maximum.

Tips *Maxim* addresses the real life needs of intelligent, professional men in an entertaining as well as informative way. They set out to reach men in their late 20s rather than out and out 'lads', producing a magazine that readers can grow into rather than out of. Research confirms that their mean average age is 28.

Max Power

Media House, Lynchwood, Peterborough Business Park, Peterborough, PE2 6EA

- 01733 468000
- 01733 468217
- maxpowereditor@emap.com
- www.maxpower.co.uk

Parent Company EMAP Plc

Editor Simon Penson

Contact Deputy Editor, Rich Beach; Features Editor, Dan Sherwood; Art Editor, Mark Guest

Insider Info A monthly consumer magazine covering car modification. Present circulation is 45,806.

Non-fiction Publishes photo features, interviews, profiles, reviews and practical how-to articles.

Tips *Max Power* covers street-legal car modifications and performance boosting. It is aimed at men between 15 and 25 years old.

MBR (Mountain Bike Rider)

Leon House, 233 High Street, Croydon, CR9 1HZ

- 020 8726 8000
- 020 8726 8499
- mbr@ipcmedia.com
- www.mountainbikerider.co.uk

Parent Company IPC Media Ltd

Editor John Kitchiner

Contact Publishing Director, Keith Foster; Features Editor, Tom Locke; Technical Editor, Paul Burwell

Established 1997

Insider Info A monthly consumer magazine, covering mountain biking. Circulation is 35,653. Media pack available online.

Non-fiction Publishes practical articles, reviews, route guides and technical articles.

Submission Guidelines Send completed manuscript.

Images State availability of photos with submission.

MCN (Motor Cycle News)

Media House, Lynchwood, Peterborough Business Park, Peterborough, PE2 6EA

- 01733 468000
- 01733 468028
- marc.potter@motorcyclenews.com
- www.motorcyclenews.com

Parent Company Bauer Consumer Media

Editor Marc Potter

Contact Publisher, Will Hattam; Deputy Editor, Peter Baker

Insider Info A weekly consumer magazine covering motorcycling. Present circulation is 128,801.

Non-fiction Publishes event listings and coverage, news, equipment and vehicle reviews, road tests and community feature articles on the international motorcycling community.

Media Week

174 Hammersmith Road, London, W6 7JP

- 020 8267 8032
- 020 82678020
- mwnewsdesk@haynet.com
- steve.barrett@haymarket.com
- www.mediaweek.co.uk

Parent Company Haymarket Publishing

Editor Steve Barrett

Contact Features Editor, Julia Martin; News Editor, Ellen Bennett

Established 1985

Insider Info Weekly trade journal magazine covering advertising. Present circulation is 11,494. Accepts queries by mail and email.

Non-fiction Publishes feature articles and news on the media industry.

Tips *Media Week* is a trade journal, so any submitted articles will be expected to contain relevant information, evidence and possibly statistical analysis.

Men's Fitness

30 Cleveland Street, London, W1T 4JD

- 020 7907 6000
- 020 7907 6516
- mensfitness@dennis.co.uk
- www.mensfitness.com

Parent Company Dennis Publishing Ltd

Editor Peter Muir

Contact Publisher, Simon Clark; Art Director, Donovan Walker; Deputy Editor, Jon Lipsey; Features Editor, Nick Hutchings

Established 1999

Insider Info A monthly consumer magazine covering lifestyle and fitness. Present circulation is 65,626.

Non-fiction Publishes news, features, product reviews and advice articles. Subjects include sex and relationships, dieting and exercise plans, health, grooming and travel.

Tips *Men's Fitness* is aimed at men in their early 30s, covering mental, physical and sexual health.

Men's Health

33 Broadwick Street, London, W1F 0DQ
- 020 7339 4400
- 020 7339 4455
- nicky.williams@natmag-rodale.co.uk
- www.menshealth.co.uk

Parent Company NatMag Rodale Ltd
Editor Morgan Rees
Contact Commissioning Editor, Jonathan Thompson; Art Director, Gary Cadogan; Features Editor, Toby Wiseman
Established 1995
Insider Info A monthly consumer magazine covering health and lifestyle. Present circulation is 245,212.
Non-fiction Publishes features, profiles and product reviews.
Submission Guidelines Accepts proposal package (including outline, CV and details of publishing history) by post or email.
Tips *Men's Health* covers health, fitness, fashion and relationship issues. It is aimed at men aged between 25 and 45 years old. *Men's Health* rarely publishes unsolicited articles, get in touch first with a CV and details of publishing history.

Metal Hammer

1 Balcombe Street, London, NW1 6NA
- 0870 444 8649
- jamie.hibbard@futurenet.co.uk
- www.metalhammer.co.uk

Parent Company Future Publishing
Editor Jamie Hibbard
Contact Managing Editor, Alex Burrows
Established 1983
Insider Info Monthly consumer magazine covering rock music. Present circulation is 48,540.
Non-fiction Publishes features, interviews/profiles, reviews, gig reports and alternative lifestyle features.
Tips Britain's only monthly music magazine which covers both traditional and contemporary metal bands, hardcore, gothic rock, punk and alternative. Reports on the burgeoning British scene, as well as all the latest bands Stateside, and around the world. Most reviews and interview material is commissioned from regular contributors or staff, so focus on alternative lifestyle features, or possibly local interest articles.

Micro Mart

30 Cleveland Street, London, W1T 4JD
- 020 7907 6000
- 020 7907 6020
- simon_brew@dennis.co.uk
- www.micromart.co.uk

Parent Company Dennis Publishing Ltd
Contact Managing Editor, Simon Brew
Insider Info A weekly consumer magazine covering the computer market. Present circulation is 20,316.
Non-fiction Publishes news, features, advice and product reviews.
Tips *Micro Mart* covers all aspects of buying a computer or computing peripherals. It is aimed at the intermediate home or business computer user.

Microsoft Windows XP: The Offical Magazine

30 Monmouth Street, Bath, BA1 2BW
- 01225 442244
- geoff.harris@futurenet.co.uk
- www.windowsxpmagazine.co.uk

Parent Company Future Publishing Ltd
Editor Geoff Harris
Contact Publisher, Richard Keith; Production Editor, Charlie Coles
Established 2001
Insider Info A monthly consumer magazine covering computing and Windows XP. Present circulation is 20,309.
Non-fiction Publishes news, reviews, technical and tutorial articles.
Tips *Microsoft Windows XP* is the official magazine covering the XP operating system. It publishes reviews, features and technical articles on improving readers' PCs and adding components.

Military Modelling

Berwick House, 8–10 Knoll Rise, Orpington, Kent, BR8 0PS
- 01689 899200
- 01689 899240
- editor@militarymodelling.com
- www.militarymodelling.com

Editor Ken Jones
Established 1970
Insider Info Monthly consumer magazine covering military model collecting.
Non-fiction Publishes feature and photo features about collecting/modelling.
Submission Guidelines Submissions should be 2,000 words maximum.
Tips Written by leading experts, many of whom are well known modellers in their own right. Articles should contain both illustrations and historical context in support of the models in question.

Miniature Wargames

Strelley hall, Nottingham, NG8 6PE

☎ 0115 906 1218
☎ 0115 906 1251
✉ andrew@miniwargames.com
🌐 www.miniwargames.com

Parent Company Pireme Publishing Ltd
Editor/Publisher Andrew Hubback
Established 1983

Insider Info Monthly consumer magazine covering gaming military history from all periods of history and all theatres of the world. Present circulation is 5,000. 80 per cent of the publication written by freelancers. Manuscripts are published four months after acceptance. Payment is on publication and no payment other than cash is offered. Expenses are paid sometimes (limit agreed upon in advance). A byline is given and publication copyrighted. First UK serial rights are purchased. Editorial lead time is seven weeks. Seasonal material should be submitted three months in advance. Accepts queries by mail and email. Aim to respond to queries and manuscripts within two weeks, and anything else within three days. Sample copy available for cost of £4.10. Writer's guidelines are free on request via email, media packs are available on request. Editorial calendar not available.

Non-fiction Publishes articles about new products (figures and rule reviews), gaming and tactical issues, translating military history into a tabletop game, and Wargaming (battle game reports).
* 60+ Non-fiction manuscripts per year are bought from freelancers. Pays £20 per published page.

Submission Guidelines Send complete manuscripts between 1,700 and 5,400 words. No reprints accepted.

Fiction Publishes historical, science fiction, western and fantasy fiction pieces.

Images Accepts images with submission.
* Negotiates payment individually and purchases one time rights.

Submission Guidelines Reviews gif/jpeg files; identification of subjects is required. State availability of photos with submission.

Columns Columns featured include book, figure and gaming reviews, each an average of 150 words.
* 120 columns bought every year for £10 each. Accepts queries.

Fillers Publishes letters.

Tips The articles convert an historical scenario into a tabletop game. At least half of any article should be on gaming rather than history. Phone or email queries first.

Mini Magazine

30 Monmouth Street, Bath, BA1 2BW

☎ 01225 442244
☎ 01225 446019
✉ mark.robinson@futurenet.co.uk
🌐 www.minimag.co.uk

Parent Company Future Publishing Ltd
Editor Mark Robinson
Contact Art Editor, Julian Jefferson; Staff Writer, Jeff Ruggles
Established 1996

Insider Info A monthly consumer magazine covering Mini cars. Present circulation is 30,000.

Non-fiction Publishes photo features, event listings, news, product reviews and technical articles.

Tips *Mini Magazine* is aimed at 'the Mini community'. Articles include technical advice on restoration.

MiniWorld Magazine

Blue Fin Building, 110 Southwark Street, London, SE1 0SU

☎ 020 3148 5000
✉ monty_watkins@ipcmedia.com
✉ miniworld@ipcmedia.com
🌐 www.miniworld.co.uk

Parent Company IPC Media Ltd
Editor Monty Watkins
Established 1991

Insider Info Monthly consumer magazine covering motoring with a particular focus on Minis. Present circulation is 37,000. Accepts queries by mail and email.

Non-fiction Publishes features, interviews/profiles, technical and general interest articles on minis.

Submission Guidelines Accepts queries.

Tips Ideal articles should cover unusual minis owned by the reader; a review and full details of the work carried out on the car would be ideal.

Mixmag

90–92 Pentonville Road, London, N1 9HS

☎ 020 7078 8417
☎ 020 7833 9900
✉ mixmag@mixmag.net
🌐 www.mixmag.net

Parent Company Development Hell Ltd
Editor Nick de Cosemo
Contact Editor in Chief, Andrew Harrison; Art Editor, Hayden Russel; Features Editor, Duncan Dick

Insider Info A monthly consumer magazine covering dance music. Present circulation is 34,073. Media pack available online.

Non-fiction Publishes news, features, reviews and lifestyle articles.

Tips *Mixmag* covers dance music and clubbing. Features include reviews of the latest releases, celebrity profiles and dance lifestyle features.

Mizz

Brockbourne House, 77 Mount Ephrain, Tunbridge Wells, TN4 8BS

☎ 01892 500100

☎ 01892 545666

✉ info@mizz.com

🌐 www.mizz.com

Parent Company Panini UK Ltd

Editor Karen O'Brien

Contact Deputy Editor, Julie Rolling; Features Editor, Lucy Saxton

Established 1985

Insider Info A bi-weekly consumer magazine covering pre-teenge/teenage female interests. Present circulation is 65,609.

Non-fiction Publishes fashion advice, features, problem pages, a career orientated section and gossip articles.

Tips *Mizz* is aimed at girls aged between ten and 14.

Model Collector

Leon House, 233 High street, Croydon, CR9 1HZ

☎ 020 8726 8000

✉ lindsey_amrani@ipcmedia.com

🌐 www.modelcollector.co.uk

Parent Company IPC Media Ltd

Editor Lindsey Amrani

Established 1987

Insider Info Consumer magazine publishing 13 issues per year, covering model collecting. Present circulation of 10,254. Media pack is available online.

Non-fiction Publishes new product and historical/ nostalgic articles as well as news, reviews, special reports, features, interviews, and details of forthcoming events and dates of interest to model collectors.

Submission Guidelines Queries accepted.

Images State availability of photos with submission.

Tips Contact the Editor with ideas for articles, particularly historical pieces about particular models or ranges.

Model Rail

Bretton Court, Bretton, Peterborough, PE3 8DZ

☎ 01733 264666

☎ 01733 282720

✉ chris.leigh@emap.com

🌐 www.model-rail.com

Parent Company EMAP Plc

Editor Chris Leigh

Contact Deputy Editor, Ben Jones

Established 1997

Insider Info A monthly consumer magazine covering model railways. Present circulation is 30,228

Non-fiction Publishes photo features, showcases, product reviews, how-to and design layout articles on model railway construction.

Tips Articles consist of practical design and layout guidelines, construction tips and new product reviews, along with showcases of readers' model railways and exhibitions.

Modern Language Review

c/o Money Publishing, Suite 1c, Joseph's Well, Hanover Walk, Leeds, LS3 1AB

Parent Company Modern Humanities Research Association

Established 1905

Insider Info A quarterly journal that covers modern languages and literature. Accepts queries by mail or email.

Non-fiction Interested in articles and reviews related to English, Germanic or Slavic language and literature.

Tips Articles are typically of a scholarly nature.

Modern Poetry in Translation

The Queens College, Oxford, OX1 4AW

☎ 01865 244701

✉ Online form

🌐 www.mptmagazine.com

Editor David Constantine

Contact Co-Editor, Helen Constantine

Established 1966

Insider Info Consumer magazine published twice a year, publishing poetry in translation. Accepts queries by mail. Writer's guidelines are available online.

Non-fiction Publishes essays and poetry/ translation articles.

Submission Guidelines Send complete manuscript.

Poetry Publishes free verse, light verse, traditional poetry and translation.

Submission Guidelines Submit sample poems.

Tips Modern Poetry in Translation *(MPT)* is an international magazine that specialises in the translation of poetry into English. It prints the latest translated foreign language poetry, as well as articles on poetry and poets, and articles on translation. *MPT* will accept submissions of good translated poetry from anywhere in the world, as well as poems and short essays that 'address such characteristic signs of our times as exile, the movement of peoples, the search for asylum, and the speaking of languages outside their native home.'

Mojo

Mappin House, 4 Winsley Street, London, W1W 8HF

- 020 7182 8616
- 020 7182 8596
- mojo@bauerconsumer.co.uk
- www.mojo4music.com

Parent Company Bauer Consumer Media
Contact Editor in Chief, Phil Alexander; Deputy Editor, Andrew Male; News Editor, Ian Harrison; Reviews Editor, Jenny Bulley
Established 1993
Insider Info A monthly consumer magazine covering popular music. Present circulation is 106,367.
Non-fiction Publishes features, gig guides, interviews, news and reviews.
Tips *Mojo* is a monthly music magazine that covers all kinds of new and old popular music, although the emphasis is on rock and indie music. Articles largely consist of new music reviews and event details.

Money Marketing

St Giles House, 50 Poland Street, London, W1T 3QN

- 020 7970 4000
- 020 7943 8097
- www.moneymarketing.co.uk

Parent Company Centaur Communications
Editor John Lappin
Established 1985
Insider Info Weekly trade newspaper journal, covering finance and investment. Present circulation of 30,770. Accepts queries by mail, fax and phone.
Non-fiction Publishes features, interviews/profiles and technical articles on finance.
Submission Guidelines Articles should be 900 words minimum.
Tips *Money Marketing* is the number one weekly newspaper for the Independent Financial Adviser (IFA). As it is a business journal, subjects covered must be breaking news/latest developments, and articles must contain a degree of in-depth knowledge and factual analysis.

Money Week

7th Floor, Sea Containers House, 20 Upper Ground, London, SE1 9JD

- 020 7633 3729
- 020 7633 3740
- editor@moneyweek.com
- www.moneyweek.com

Parent Company Fleet Street Publications Ltd
Editor Merryn Somerset-Webb
Contact Publisher, Bill Bonner; Deputy Editor, John Stepek; Art Director, Kevin Cook

Established 2000
Insider Info A weekly trade journal covering business and finance. Present circulation is 35,794.
Non-fiction Publishes financial and investment news.
Tips *Money Week* covers a wide range of financial and investment news taken from the British and international media, newsletters and websites. It is aimed at private investors and industry professionals.

Moneywise

1st Floor, Standon House, 21 Mansell Street, London, E1 8AA

- 020 7680 3600
- 020 7702 0710
- news@moneywise.co.uk
- www.moneywise.co.uk

Parent Company Moneywise Publishing
Editor Rachel Lacey
Contact Publisher, Jeremy King; Art Editor, Mark Stammers
Established 1990
Insider Info A monthly consumer magazine covering personal finance. Present circulation is 25,399.
Non-fiction Publishes news, features and advice articles.
Tips *Moneywise* covers all aspects of personal finance including features on the stock market, pensions, insurance, investments, banking, borrowing and tax.

Monkey Kettle

- monkeykettle@hotmail.com
- www.monkeykettle.co.uk

Editor Matthew Michael Taylor
Established 1998
Insider Info Consumer magazine published bi-annually, concerning literary interests. Present circulation is 100. 100 per cent of the publication is written by freelancers. Accepts queries by email.
Non-fiction Publishes articles on poetry, features, interviews/profiles and reviews.
Submission Guidelines Accepts queries.
Fiction Publishes short stories.
Submission Guidelines Send complete manuscript of up to four pages maximum.
Poetry Publishes free verse, light verse and traditional poetry.
Submission Guidelines A maximum of ten poems may be submitted at one time.
Tips *Monkey Kettle* is a small, black and white printed poetry and fiction magazine. It contains new poetry and short stories from contributors and also has a website that runs news stories, interviews and articles related to writing. *Monkey Kettle* doesn't have

any concrete submission guidelines, and are willing to consider anything, but the preference is for funny, surreal, dark, poignant or political work.

Monomyth

38 Pierrot Steps, 71 Kursaal Way, Southend on Sea, Essex, SS1 2UY

- ○ atlanteanpublishing@hotmail.com
- ⓦ www.geocities.com/dj_tyrer/monomyth.html

Parent Company Atlantean Publishing
Editor David-John Tyrer
Insider Info Quarterly consumer magazine covering literary topics. A byline is given. First UK serial rights are bought. Accepts queries by mail and email. Accepts previously published submissions. Writer's guidelines available online.
Non-fiction Publishes articles on poetry and general writing.
Submission Guidelines Send complete manuscript.
Fiction Publishes short fiction.
Submission Guidelines Send complete manuscript.
Poetry Publishes avant-garde, free verse, light verse and traditional poetry.
Submission Guidelines Submit sample poems.
Tips *Monomyth* is a quarterly literary magazine from Atlantean Publishing that specialises in printing longer short fiction and poetry. Welcomes new and unpublished writers, and will print stories in any genre or style. Also prints articles on fiction or poetry writing. Submissions to *Monomyth* will also be considered for Atlantean's other literary publications.

More!

Endeavour House, 189 Shaftesbury Avenue, London, WC2H 8JG

- ○ 020 7208 3165
- ○ 020 7379 4936
- ○ emma.ledger@moremagazine.co.uk
- ⓦ www.moremagazine.co.uk

Parent Company Bauer Consumer Media
Editor Lisa Smosarski
Contact Features Editor, Susan Riley; Editorial Assistant, Emma Ledger
Established 1988
Insider Info A weekly consumer magazine covering young women's lifestyle and celebrity topics. Present Circulation of 162,544.
Non-fiction Publishes general interest features, interviews and photo features on television, real life, fashion, sex, beauty, celebrities, health and entertainment.
Tips The magazine's target audience is girls aged 18 to 25 – the style and content bridges a gap between teenage magazines and the classic women's

glossies. The website gives a good idea as to the magazine's content.

Mortgage Finance Gazette

6th Floor, Davis House, 2 Robert Street, Croydon, CR0 1QQ

- ○ 020 8253 8618
- ○ 020 8253 4603
- ○ joanne.atkin@metropolis.co.uk
- ⓦ www.mfgonline.co.uk

Parent Company Metropolis Business Publishing
Editor Joanne Atkin
Established 1869
Insider Info Monthly trade journal magazine covering the mortgage lending industry. Present circulation of 5,500. Ten percent of the publication is written by freelancers. Takes five weeks to publish a manuscript after acceptance. Payment is on publication and a byline is given. Publication is copyrighted and all rights are purchased. Editorial lead time is three months. Queries accepted by mail, email and phone. Expenses will not be paid. Sample copy and editorial calendar available free on request. Media pack available online.
Submission Guidelines Manuscripts should be between 1,500 and 2,000 words.
Images Accepts images with submission.
* Offers no additional payment for photos accepted with manuscript.
Tips Aimed at mortgage lenders and associated industries such as legal, insurance, and IT.

Mother & Baby

Endeavour House, 189 Shaftsbury Avenue, London, WC2H 8JG

- ○ 020 7295 5560
- ○ 020 7347 1888
- ○ mother&baby@bauerconsumer.co.uk
- ⓦ www.motherandbabymagazine.com

Parent Company Bauer Consumer Media
Editor Miranda Levy
Contact Publishing Director, Dani Zur; Deputy Editor, Kathryn Blundell; Features Editor, Wendy Golledge; Art Editor, Emma Sayers; Associate Editor (Parenting), Katy Holland; Editorial Assistant, Lucy Quick
Insider Info A monthly consumer magazine covering pregnancy, birth and childcare. Present circulation is 65,996.
Non-fiction Publishes features, tips and advice articles on health, fitness, baby care and consumer issues related to childbirth.

Motor Boat & Yachting

IPC Media, Blue Fin Building, 110 Southwark Street, London, SE1 0SU

☎ 020 3148 4643
✉ mby@ipcmedia.com
🌐 www.mby.com
Parent Company IPC Media Ltd
Editor Hugo Andreae
Established 1904
Insider Info Monthly consumer magazine covering boating leisure interests. Present circulation of 17,504. Accepts queries by mail and email. Media pack available at: www.ipcmedia.com/magazines/mby
Non-fiction Publishes features, interviews/profiles, reviews, new products and photo features on sea-faring/nautical subjects.
* Pays average of £120 per 1,000 words.
Submission Guidelines Contact editor with synopsis of feature idea.
Tips Core editorial coverage focuses on boats up to 80ft, while four times a year *MBY* also carries 'Custom Yachting', a special focus on 80ft plus boats. Although a good deal of technical knowledge is useful, the editors will look at articles on general (sea-faring) interest, as well as specialist motor boating subjects.

Motor Boats Monthly

Blue Fin Building, 110 Southwark Street, London, SE1 0SU
☎ 020 3148 5000
✉ mbm@ipcmedia.com
✉ carl_richardson@ipcmedia.com
🌐 www.mbmclub.com
Parent Company IPC Media Ltd
Editor Carl Richardson
Established 1982
Insider Info Monthly consumer magazine covering motorboats. Present circulation of 16,246. 30 per cent of publication written by freelancers. Payment is upon publication and only in cash. Expenses are paid sometimes (limit agreed upon in advance). A byline is given and publication is copyrighted. Accepts queries by mail and email. Accepts simultaneous and previously published submissions. Aims to respond to queries and manuscripts within one day. A sample copy is free on request via email and website. Writer's guidelines available free on request via email.
Non-fiction Publishes humour, features, interviews/profiles, new products, travel, historical/nostalgic and personal experience articles.
Submission Guidelines Contact Claire Frew, Editorial Assistant, at: claire_frew@ipcmedia.com
Images Accepts images with submission.
* Pays varied fee per photo.
Submission Guidelines Reviews contact sheets, transparencies, gif/jpeg files with identification of

subjects required. Send photos with submission to Editorial Assistant, Claire Frew.
Tips Editorial coverage ranges from the sports boat markets right up to 40-foot cruisers and beyond. The magazine often includes anecdotal stories pertaining to motor boating, so travel writers may have an edge. Ideally submissions should also include relevant photos/illustrations.

Motorcaravan & Motorhome Monthly

PO Box 88, Tiverton, Devon, EX16 7ZN
☎ 01778 391181
✉ mmmeditor@warnersgroup.co.uk
🌐 www.mmmonline.co.uk
Parent Company Warners Group Publications
Editor Mike Jago and Jane Jago
Established 1966
Insider Info Monthly consumer magazine covering motorhomes and caravanning. Present circulation of 40,408. Accepts queries by mail.
Non-fiction Publishes features, technical articles and travel articles related to caravanning.
Submission Guidelines Accepts queries with a synopsis, addressed to the Editor. Final articles should be 2,000 words, maximum.

Motor Caravan

Blue Fin Building, 110 Southwark Street, London, SE1 0SU
☎ 020 3148 5000
✉ helen_avery@ipcmedia.com
🌐 www.motorcaravanmagazine.co.uk
Parent Company IPC Media Ltd
Editor Helen Avery
Established 1986
Insider Info Monthly consumer magazine covering motoring caravanning. Present circulation of 15,000. Accepts queries by email and phone. Media packs available at: www.ipcmedia.com/magazines/motorcaravan/
Non-fiction Publishes photo features, features, and travel articles relating to caravanning.
* Pays £60 per page.
Submission Guidelines Accepts queries in writing or via the telephone to discuss ideas. Final articles should be 2,500 words maximum.
Tips Mostly interested in holiday reports, interesting or unusual caravans, and practical caravanning features.

Motorhome Monthly

Andrew House, Granville Road, Sidcup, DA14 4BN
☎ 020 8302 6069
☎ 020 8300 2315
✉ mhm@stoneleisure.com

www.stoneleisure.com/motorhome_monthly
Parent Company Stone Leisure Ltd
Editor Bob Griffiths
Insider Info A monthly consumer magazine covering motor caravanning. Present circulation is 38,595.
Non-fiction Publishes news, features, reviews and touring guides.
Tips *Motorhome Monthly* covers all aspects of motor caravanning, including news, vehicle reviews and touring guides. It is aimed at first-time buyers and motor home enthusiasts, as well as at organisers of motor home events.

Motoring & Leisure
Britannia House, 21 Station Street, Brighton, BN1 4DE
01273 744757
01273 744761
magazineenquiries@csma.uk.com
www.csma.uk.com
Parent Company CSMA Ltd
Contact Managing Editor, David Arnold; Deputy Editor, Lisa Jackson; Travel Editor, Anna Hyman; Motoring Projects Editor, Sean McGreevy
Established 1985
Insider Info A consumer magazine, with ten issues per year, covering motoring and leisure interests. Present circulation is 294,107.
Non-fiction Publishes news, features, road tests, offers and travel articles.
Tips *Motoring & Leisure* is the magazine of the CSMA (Civil Service Motoring Association) and covers all aspects of motoring features and road tests, as well as general features on leisure and travel.

Motorsport News
Teddington Studios, Broom Road, Teddington, TW11 9BE
020 8267 5385
020 8267 5322
mn.letters@haymarket.com
www.motorsport-news.co.uk
Parent Company Haymarket Autosport & Classic Publications
Editor Jim Holder
Contact Publishing Director, Andrew Goldby; Deputy Editor, James Attwood; Art Editor, Mike Stokoe
Established 1955
Insider Info A weekly consumer magazine covering international motorsport. Present circulation is 21,679.
Non-fiction Publishes industry news, race reports and track reviews.

Tips *Motorsport News* includes Formula 1, touring car, and rallying.

Mountain Biking UK
30 Monmouth Street, Bath, BA1 2BW
01225 442244
01225 822793
mbuk@futurenet.co.uk
www.mbuk.com
Parent Company Future Publishing Ltd
Editor Danny Walter
Contact Publisher, Richard Schofield; Art Editor, James Blackwell; Reviews Editor, Ian Collins
Established 1988
Insider Info A monthly consumer magazine covering mountain biking. Present circulation is 45,681.
Non-fiction Publishes photo features, event listings, news, product reviews and technical articles.
Tips The magazine is always looking for freelance writers or photographers, contact by email in the first instance.

Moving Worlds
School of English, University of Leeds, Leeds, LS2 9JT
mworlds@leeds.ac.uk
www.movingworlds.net
Editor Shirley Chew
Contact Susan Burns
Insider Info Bi-annual consumer journal covering literary interests. Accepts queries by mail and email.
Non-fiction Publishes essays, literary criticism and articles on poetry/general fiction.
Submission Guidelines Send complete manuscript.
Fiction Publishes fiction.
Poetry Publishes poetry.
Tips *Moving Worlds* is an international literary journal that publishes creative, critical, literary and visual texts. Particularly encourages submission from new writers – from any cultural background – and aims to be as diverse as possible with its content. Publishes a wide range of material and is looking for scholarly critical work from international writers, as much as fiction or poetry.

Mslexia
PO Box 656, Newcastle upon Tyne, NE99 1PZ
0191 261 6656
0191 261 6636
postbag@mslexia.demon.co.uk
daneet@mslexia.demon.co.uk
www.mslexia.co.uk
Parent Company Mslexia Publications Ltd
Editor Daneet Steffens

Established 1999

Insider Info Quarterly consumer magazine covering literary subjects. Present circulation of 20,000. 60 per cent of the publication is written by freelancers. Payment is on publication. There is a 50 per cent kill fee for assigned manuscripts not published. A byline is given. Editorial lead time is three months. Seasonal material must be submitted three months in advance. Accepts queries by mail, email and phone. Accepts simultaneous submissions; aims to report back on manuscripts within three months. Sample copy free on request online. Writer's guidelines, editorial calendar and media pack available online.

Non-fiction Publishes how-to, interviews/profiles, opinion (excluding letters to the Editor) and personal experience articles, mainly covering literary topics.

* 40 manuscripts are bought from freelance writers every year.

Submission Guidelines Accepts query with published clips. Articles should be between 500 and 2,000 words.

Fiction Publishes mainstream and literary fiction.

* 30 manuscripts are bought from freelance writers per year. Will pay £15 per 1,000 words.

Submission Guidelines Send complete manuscript, which should be between 50 and 3,000 words.

Poetry Publishes avant-garde, free verse, haiku and traditional poetry.

* 40 poems are bought per year. Pays £25 per poem.

Submission Guidelines Submit a maximum of four poems at once.

Columns Uses columns in the publication.

* 12 columns bought per year.

Submission Guidelines Accepts written query with published clips.

Tips *Mslexia* is a national magazine for woman writers, it prints a substantial section of poetry and prose by published and unpublished authors. The title is aimed at top authors and absolute beginners. The editors welcome submissions for every part of the magazine. They commission work by prominent authors and artists, as well as talented newcomers and aim to publish some new voices in every copy of the magazine. The majority of readers live in the UK, so any feature pitches should be aware of this. Also, please note that they only accept email submissions from overseas writers.

Musical Opinion
50 Collinswood Drive, St Leonards on Sea, East Sussex, TN38 0NX
- 01424 715167
- 01424 712214
- musicalopinion2@aol.com
- www.musicalopinion.com

Editor Denby Richards

Contact Managing Editor, Judith Monk

Established 1877

Insider Info Bi-monthly consumer magazine covering musical opinion. A specialist magazine for classical music lovers, which offers many years of expertise in presenting in-depth information for concerts, operas, festivals, instruments and musical education. Present circulation of 8,500. 50 per cent is written by freelancers. Takes three months to publish a manuscript after acceptance. Payment is on publication. A byline is given and publication is copyrighted. There is an editorial lead time of six weeks. Seasonal material should be submitted eight weeks in advance. Accepts queries by email. Aims to respond to queries within two weeks. Expenses are not paid. Sample copy available for cost of £5.50. Writer's guidelines available by email.

Non-fiction Publishes features and interviews/profiles (well written and relevant to the classical music field).

Submission Guidelines Accepts queries. Contact Judith Monk, Managing Editor.

Tips *Musical Opinion* has a strong and loyal following of all age groups in the UK and abroad, in over 38 countries. It is read by musicians, teachers, students, artist management agents, concert hall managers and many professionals in the music world.

Musician
60–62 Clapham Road, London, SW9 0JJ
- 020 7840 5531
- 020 7582 9805
- keith.ames@musiciansunion.org.uk
- www.musiciansunion.org.uk

Parent Company Future Publishing Ltd

Contact Communications Official, Keith Ames

Established 1950

Insider Info A quarterly trade journal for the Musicians Union. Present circulation is 35,000.

Non-fiction Publishes news, reviews, events listing and coverage and current issues of concern to Musicians Union members.

myBOOKSmag
4 Froxfield Close, Winchester, SO22 6JW
- 01962 620320
- guy@newbooksmag.com
- www.newbooksmag.com

Parent Company New Books

Editor Guy Pringle

Established 2002

Insider Info Quarterly consumer magazine covering children's literary interests. Present circulation is 5,000.

Non-fiction Publishes photo features, features, interviews/profiles and reviews.
Submission Guidelines Accepts queries.
Fiction Publishes fiction and children's book excerpts.
Submission Guidelines Accepts queries.
Tips *myBOOKSmag* is a literary magazine aimed at five to seven year olds. It contains extracts from children's books, as well as activities, author and illustrator information, reviews and directories. Often requires reviews of current children's books, especially with a seasonal theme.

My Weekly
80 Kingsway East, Dundee, DD4 8SL
- 01382 223131
- 01382 452491
- myweekly@dcthomson.co.uk
Parent Company D.C. Thomson & Co Ltd
Editor Sally Hampton
Established 1910
Insider Info Weekly consumer magazine covering women's interests. Present circulation of 155,087. Seasonal material should be submitted three months in advance. Accepts queries by mail and email. Writer's guidelines free on request by email.
Non-fiction Publishes Celebrity, Cookery, Diet, Health, Lifestyle and Travel articles aimed mainly at women.
Submission Guidelines Pitch ideas via email.
Fiction Publishes short stories and 3-part serials. Email for current submission guidelines (updated every 3 months).
Tips *My Weekly* is aimed at women of all ages; stories deal with real, down to earth themes that are related to the lives of readers.

NADFAS Review
8 Guilford Street, London, WC1N 1DA
- 020 7430 0730
- 020 7242 0686
- nadfasreview@nadfas.org.uk
- www.nadfas.org.uk
Parent Company NADFAS Enterprises Ltd
Editor Danielle Green
Contact Publisher, Judith Quiney
Insider Info A quarterly consumer magazine covering decorative and fine arts. Present circulation is 77,886.
Non-fiction Publishes artwork, course information, event listings and features.
Tips *NADFAS Review* is distributed to members of the National Association of Decorative and Fine Arts Societies. It showcases artwork and articles from members of the group, as well as supplying information on courses and upcoming events. It is

particularly focussed on NADFAS, rather than being a general arts title.

Nasty Piece of Work
20 Drum Mead, Petersfield, Hampshire, GU32 3AQ
Editor David Green
Insider Info Quarterly consumer magazine covering horror literature.
Fiction Publishes horror.
Poetry Publishes poetry with a horror theme.
Tips A genre magazine, dedicated to publishing horror fiction and poetry. The content is often extreme in nature, even by typical horror fiction standards. The stories and poetry are often extremely graphic or violent, and otherwise controversial, but must still be considered intelligent contemporary horror.

The National Trust Magazine
Heelies, Kemble Drive, Swindon, SN2 2NA
- 01793 817716
- 01793 817401
- magazine@nationaltrust.org.uk
- www.nationaltrust.org.uk
Parent Company National Trust
Editor Sue Herdman
Contact Assistant Editor Debbie Schrieber
Established 1968
Insider Info A consumer magazine, with three issues per-year, covering National Trust sites and issues. Present circulation is 1,821,846.
Non-fiction Publishes photo features, features, news, global and environmental issue articles.
Tips Every member of the National Trust receives a copy. Articles cover all environmental, conservation and restoration issues effecting National Trust sites across the UK.

The Naturalist
Department of Environmental Science, University of Bradford, Bradford, Yorkshire, BD7 1DP
- 01274 234212
- 01274 234231
- m.r.d.seaward@bradford.ac.uk
Parent Company Yorkshire Naturalists' Union
Editor Professor Mark R.D. Seaward
Contact Professor Mark R.D. Seaward
Established 1876
Insider Info Quarterly scientific journal, covering biological sciences and natural history, particularly relating to the North of England. Present circulation of 1,000. Features peer reviewed articles for an amateur and professional scientific readership. Submissions are published approximately ten weeks

after acceptance. No payment is made for submissions. Publication is copyrighted and queries are accepted by mail, email, fax and telephone. Aims to respond to queries with one week, and manuscripts within four weeks. Assignment expenses are not paid. Sample copy is available on receipt of SAE (230mm x 160mm). Writer's guidelines are available free on request.

Non-fiction Publishes articles on natural history and biological sciences.

Natural World
The Pall Mall Deposit, 124-128 Barlby Road, London, W10 6BL
- 020 8962 3020
- 020 8962 8689

Parent Company Think Publishing Ltd
Editor Rupert Paul
Established 1981

Insider Info A consumer magazine, with three issues per year, covering the UK's wildlife trusts. Accepts queries by mail or email.

Tips The national magazine of the UK's 47 wildlife trusts. Does not accept unsolicited submissions.

Nature
The Macmillan Building, 4 Crinan Street, London, N1 9XW
- 020 7833 4000
- 020 7843 4596
- nature@nature.com
- www.nature.com

Parent Company Nature Publishing Group
Editor Philip Campbell
Established 1869

Insider Info Weekly trade journal, covering science news and current affairs. Present circulation of roughly 65,000. Byline is given. Publication is copyrighted. Aims to respond to queries and manuscripts within one week. Writer's guidelines are available online.

Non-fiction Publishes technical and science/research articles.

Submission Guidelines Accepts queries. Send complete manuscript.

Images Send photos with submission.

Tips *Nature* is one of the oldest scientific journals. Although most scientific journals are now highly specialised, *Nature* is idiosyncratic in still publishing original research articles across a wide range of scientific fields. In most fields of scientific research, many of the most important new advances each year are published as articles or letters. Articles must be considered ground breaking as well as being scientifically relevant and contemporary. They must

also be from a specialist with an advanced knowledge of their field.

The Nautical Magazine
4–10 Darnley Street, Glasgow, G41 2SD
- 0141 429 1234
- 0141 420 1694
- info@skipper.co.uk
- www.skipper.co.uk

Parent Company Brown, Son & Ferguson Ltd
Editor Leslie Ingram-Brown
Established 1832

Insider Info Monthly consumer journal covering nautical and maritime interest. Present circulation is 800. 100 per cent of the publication is written by freelance writers. Submissions are published up to three months after acceptance. Payment is on publication. Publication is copyrighted and first rights are purchased. Average lead time is four weeks. Seasonal material must be submitted three months in advance. Queries accepted by mail, email and fax. Accepts simultaneous submissions. Aims to respond to queries and manuscripts within four weeks. Sample copy, manuscript guidelines and editorial calendars are free on request. Media pack is available online.

Non-fiction Interested in features, reviews of nautical books, technical, general interest, historical/nostalgic and personal experience articles.
* Purchases approximately 200 non-fiction manuscripts per year.

Submission Guidelines Accepts complete manuscripts of between 100 and 1,000 words. Does not publish reprints.

Fiction Publishes historical and nautical short fiction.
* Purchases 50 fiction manuscripts per year.

Submission Guidelines Accepts complete manuscripts.

Fillers Publishes facts, newsbreaks and letters of up to 500 words.

Tips *The Nautical Magazine* is aimed at anyone interested in nautical or maritime subjects. Articles can be technical or general interest in tone.

Neon Highway
37 Grinshill Close, Liverpool, L8 8LD
- 0151 727 5129
- poetshideout@yahoo.com
- www.geocities.com/poetshideout/Neon.html

Editor Alice Lenkiewicz
Established 2002

Insider Info Annual consumer magazine covering literary and poetry interests. Byline is given.

Poetry Publishes avant-garde, free verse, light verse and experimental poetry.

Tips *Neon Highway* publishes original and experimental poetry and also organises public poetry reading events in the North West. It commissions all poetry content and does not accept unsolicited submissions.

.net
30 Monmouth Street, Bath, BA1 2BW
- 01225 442244
- 01225 732295
- mailus@netmag.co.uk
- www.netmag.co.uk

Parent Company Future Publishing
Editor Dan Oliver
Established 1994
Insider Info Monthly consumer magazine covering internet computing. Present circulation of 18,001. Accepts queries by mail and email.
Non-fiction Publishes features and technical articles on design, development, sales, marketing, usability and accessibility, information architecture, security, copywriting and advertising on the internet.
Submission Guidelines Send complete manuscript between 1,000 and 3,000 words.
Tips Aimed at people who are serious about the commercial application of the internet, therefore an amount of technical or business expertise relating to the internet is invaluable.

New!
The Northern & Shell Building, 10 Lower Thames Street, London, EC3R 6EN
- 0871 520 7016
- 0871 434 2763
- kirsty.mouatt@express.co.uk

Parent Company Express Newspapers Ltd
Editor Kirsty Mouatt
Contact Deputy Editor, Lebby Eyres; Commissioning Editor, Clare Thorp; Features Director, Patrick Strudwick
Established 2003
Insider Info A weekly consumer magazine covering women's interest, celebrity features and lifestyle. Present circulation is 434,218.
Non-fiction Publishes celebrity gossip, features, interviews, real-life stories, profiles, product reviews and news on fashion, beauty and entertainment.
Tips *New!* is aimed primarily at women aged between 18 and 30.

newBOOKS
4 Froxfield Close, Winchester, SO22 6JW
- 01962 620320
- guy@newbooksmag.com
- www.newbooksmag.com

Editor Guy Pringle

Established 2000
Insider Info Bi-monthly consumer magazine covering literary topics for readers' and writers' groups. Present circulation of 17,000. Accepts queries by mail and email. Sample copy free on request, online.
Non-fiction Publishes features, interviews/profiles, reviews, general interest and news articles.
Submission Guidelines Accepts queries.
Tips *newBOOKS* has in-depth interviews with the latest authors, book related articles and insider knowledge. It also offers the opportunity to apply for free books to read. The editors are interested in any genre or type of book and are always seeking reviews of the latest releases.

New Civil Engineer
151 Roseberry Avenue, London, EC1R 4GB
- 020 7505 6666
- 020 7505 6667
- antony.oliver@emap.com
- www.nceplus.co.uk

Parent Company EMAP Plc
Editor Antony Oliver
Contact Deputy Editor, Jackie Whitelaw; Features Editor, Mark Hansford; News Editor, Bernadette Redfern
Established 1972
Insider Info A weekly trade journal covering engineering. Present circulation is 55,143.
Non-fiction Publishes industry news and features.
Tips *New Civil Engineer* is aimed at engineers working in all areas of the construction industry. The magazine also publishes a diary of the Institution of Civil Engineers.

New Day
Goldhay Way, Orton Goldhay, Peterborough, Cambridgeshire PE2 5GZ
- 01733 370505
- 01733 404880
- post@tlmew.org.uk
- www.leprosymission.org.uk

Parent Company The Leprosy Mission
Editor Karen du Plessis
Contact Managing Editor, Jean Jones; Communications Officer, Karen du Plessis
Established 1896
Insider Info A free charity magazine with two issues per year. It covers the Leprosy Mission's work to eradicate the causes and consequences of leprosy, and looks at healthcare, fighting stigma and poverty. Present circulation of 150,000. A byline is given. Editorial lead time is 13 weeks. Seasonal material should be submitted 13 weeks in advance. Accepts queries by mail, email, fax or phone. Accepts

previously published submissions. Aims to respond to queries within five days and manuscripts within four months. Will not pay the expenses of writers on assignments. Sample copy is free on request and available online or by email. Writer's guidelines and editorial calendars are available via email.

Non-fiction Publishes features with a focus on leprosy.

Submission Guidelines Accepts email queries for articles of between 350 and 850 words. No reprints. Contact Karen du Plessis, Communications Officer.

Images Accepts images with submission.

* Pays a variable fee per photo up to a maximum of £100. Buys one time rights.

Submission Guidelines Accepts gif/jpeg files and identification of subjects is required. Send photos with submission to Communications Officer, Karen du Plessis.

Tips *New Day* is a free magazine mailed twice a year to supporters in England, Wales, the Channel Islands and the Isle of Man. It covers the Leprosy Mission's work around the world with people affected by leprosy. The Leprosy Mission is a Christian charity but helps people from all faiths and their supporters come from a wide cross section of society. Writers are advised to email first to ask what kind of article is needed. The magazine does not pay for submissions

New Internationalist

55 Rectory Road, Oxford, OX4 1BW
- 01865 811400
- 01865 793152
- ni@newint.org
- www.newint.org

Parent Company New Internationalist Trust
Contact Co-Editors: Vanessa Baird; Chris Bozier; Adam Ma'amit; David Ransom
Established 1973
Insider Info A monthly consumer magazine covering international news and current affairs. Present circulation of roughly 40,000. Accepts queries by mail or email. Writer's guidelines, editorial calendar and media pack available online.
Non-fiction Publishes features, opinion (excluding letters to the Editor) and world affairs/politics articles.
* Pays £80 per 1,000 words for unsolicited articles
Submission Guidelines Send complete manuscript.
Tips The *New Internationalist* is renowned for its radical, campaigning stance on a range of world issues. Please note that the format of the *New Internationalist* magazine always has the main body of the magazine dedicated to the theme of the month. This means that in general, all pieces are commissioned for that particular theme. However, if you have a local perspective on a social event that

occurred recently (e.g. a rally, protest, or other significant social change event) perhaps it may be suitable for the 'NI Special Features' section of their website. If so, email the editorial team with your suggestion.

New Nation

Unit 2, 65 Whitechapel Road, London, E1 1DU
- 020 7650 2000
- 020 7650 2001
- general@ethnicmedia.co.uk
- www.newnation.co.uk

Parent Company Ethnic Media Group
Editor Michael Eboda
Established 1996
Insider Info Weekly consumer magazine covering news and current affairs. Present circulation is 6,189. Accepts queries by mail.
Non-fiction Interested in general interest and political articles.
Submission Guidelines Accepts queries in the first instance.
Tips Aimed at young, educated black Britons and the wider African and Caribbean communities. The magazine covers a mix of news, sport, social and political issues, recruitment and contact pages. Relevant current affairs, especially local interest pieces, are appreciated.

New Scientist

Lacon House, 84 Theobalds Road, London, WC1X 8NS
- 020 7611 1200
- 020 7611 1250
- news@newscientist.com
- www.newscientist.com

Parent Company Reed Business Information Ltd
Editor Roger Highfield
Contact Editor-in-Chief, Jeremy Webb
Established 1956
Insider Info Weekly consumer magazine covering scientific news and current affairs. Present circulation is 173,820 worldwide. Accepts queries by email.
Non-fiction Interested in photo features, features and technical articles.
Submission Guidelines Accepts queries in the first instance.
Tips *New Scientist* aims to keep its readers up to date with the latest science and technology news from around the world. Although *New Scientist* rarely uses unsolicited work, they do run an internship program for any budding scientific journalists, which can lead to publication in the magazine. Further details can be found on their website.

New Statesman

3rd Floor, 52 Grosvenor Gardens, London, SW1W 0AU

- ☎ 020 7730 3444
- ☎ 020 7259 0181
- ✉ info@newstatesman.co.uk
- 🌐 www.newstatesman.co.uk

Editor Jason Cowley
Contact Deputy Editor, Sue Matthias
Established 1913
Insider Info Weekly consumer magazine covering news and current affairs. Present circulation is 26,208. Accepts queries by mail.
Non-fiction Interested in features, interviews/ profiles, reviews and general interest articles.
Submission Guidelines Accepts queries (including SAE).
Tips The *New Statesman* is a British left of centre political magazine published weekly in London. The magazine is committed to 'development, human rights and the environment, global issues the mainstream press often ignores'. *New Statesman* has a very well defined writing style and political bias. Be aware of these things before submitting.

New Stitches

Well Oast, Brenley Lane, Faversham, Kent, ME13 9LY

- ☎ 01227 750215
- ☎ 01227 750813
- ✉ janice@ccpuk.co.uk
- 🌐 www.newstitches.co.uk

Parent Company Creative Crafts Publishing
Editor Janice Broadstock
Established 1992
Insider Info A consumer embroidery magazine publication issued monthly. Present circulation of 25,000. Payment is upon publication. 30 per cent of the publication is written by freelancers. Submissions are published approximately one month after acceptance, with an editorial lead time of two months. Publication is copyrighted and first UK serial rights are purchased. Seasonal material must be submitted two months in advance. Accepts queries by mail, email and fax. Aims to respond to queries within two days.
Non-fiction Publishes how-to, technical and general interest articles on needlecraft.
Tips *New Stitches* is aimed at the discerning embroiderer with emphasis on high quality designs covering cross stitch, hardanger, blackwork and many other embroidery techniques.

New Theatre Quarterly

Oldstairs, Kingsdown, Deal, Kent, CT14 8ES

- ✉ simontrussler@btinternet.com

Editor Simon Trussler
Established 1985
Insider Info A quarterly consumer magazine covering theatre. Accepts queries by mail or email.
Non-fiction Interested in reviews, interviews and reference articles related to live theatre.
Tips Articles should take a serious, scholarly approach and be supported by factual information.

New Welsh Review

PO Box 170, Aberystwyth, Ceredigion, SY23 1WZ

- ☎ 01970 628410
- ✉ editor@newwelshreview.com
- 🌐 www.newwelshreview.com

Editor Francesca Rhydderch
Established 1988
Insider Info A quarterly consumer literary journal focusing on Welsh writing in English. Present circulation of 3,500. Payment is upon publication. A byline is given. Queries are accepted by mail or email. Aims to respond to queries and manuscripts within three months. Writer's guidelines are available online.
Non-fiction Publishes articles on poetry, features, interview/profiles, reviews and general interest articles relating to the Welsh literary scene.
* Pays between £100 and £150 for unsolicited articles.
Submission Guidelines Accepts queries with outlines.
Fiction Publishes short stories.
* Pays between £60 and £75 for fiction.
Submission Guidelines Submit complete manuscript by post.
Poetry Publishes free verse, light verse and traditional poetry.
* Pays £25 maximum for poems.
Submission Guidelines Submit complete manuscript by post.
Tips The *New Welsh Review* maintains a cosmopolitan outlook to appeal to international markets. It accepts postal submissions for poetry and fiction, but most non-fiction articles are commissioned privately, so only submit a query for these. The magazine is always looking for freelance reviewers, either send a CV or check the website for further detail.

The New Writer

PO Box 60, Cranbrook, Kent, TN17 2RE

- ☎ 01580 212626
- ✉ admin@thenewwriter.com
- 🌐 www.thenewwriter.com

Editor Suzanne Ruthven
Contact Publisher, Merric Davidson
Established 1996

Insider Info Bi-monthly magazine covering literature and creative writing. Present circulation is 3,000. 80 per cent of the publication is written by freelance writers. Submissions published approximately four months after acceptance. Payment is on publication. A byline is given. Publication is copyrighted and first UK serial rights are purchased. Average lead time is four months. Accepts queries by mail and email. Aims to respond to queries within three weeks and manuscripts within six months. Payment to writers includes contributor copy. Sample copy is available with SAE. Manuscript guidelines are free on request. Media pack is available by email.

Non-fiction Interested in how-to, features, interviews/profiles and articles on poetry and prose writing.

* Payment for non-fiction is £20 per 1,000 words.

Submission Guidelines Accepts complete manuscript of between 500 and 2,000 words.

Fiction Publishes mainstream short fiction.

Submission Guidelines Accepts complete manuscript up to 4,000 words. Only accepts fiction from prizewinners/subscribers.

Poetry Publishes contemporary, free verse and traditional poetry.

Submission Guidelines Submit up to three poems. Do not submit therapeutic/confessional poetry, or poems that meander without rhyme or reason.

Tips *The New Writer* is a forward looking magazine with a range of expert contributors. Every issue contains original short stories, a showcase for new poetry, articles, book reviews, market information, news and readers' views. *The New Writer* accepts article and poetry submissions, but only accepts fiction submissions from prizewinners or subscribers. All submissions should be posted to the Editor. The magazine also runs annual poetry and prose competitions, details of which can be found at www.thenewwriter.com/prizes.

New Writing Scotland

7 University Gardens, University of Glasgow, Glasgow, Strathclyde, G12 8QH
- 0141 330 5309
- 0141 330 5309
- nws@asls.org.uk
- www.asls.org.uk

Parent Company ASLS
Editor Liz Niven and Brian Whittingham
Contact Managing Editor, Duncan Jones
Established 1982
Insider Info An annual anthology of short fiction, poetry and other creative prose, written in any of the languages of Scotland. Present circulation of 600. 100 per cent of the publication is written by freelance writers. Manuscripts are published six

months after acceptance. Payment is upon publication and never with contributor copies instead of cash. A byline is given. Purchases first serial rights, and copyright reverts to the individual authors after publication. Accepts queries by mail, email, fax or phone. Aims to respond to queries within two months and manuscripts within six months. A sample copy is available for cost. Writer's guidelines are free on request and available online.

Fiction Publishes adventure, historical, romance, horror, science fiction, confession, humour, erotica, slice of life vignettes, ethnic, mystery, suspense, experimental, novel excerpts, western, fantasy, and religious fiction.

* Purchases 50 fiction manuscripts per year. Pays £20 per published page.

Submission Guidelines Send complete manuscripts for fiction of up to, 3,500 words. No previously published material. Contact Managing Editor, Duncan Jones.

Poetry Publishes avant-garde, free verse, haiku, light verse, traditional and concrete poetry.

* Purchases 40 poems per year. Pays £20 per published page

Submission Guidelines Accepts up to four sample poems. No previously published material. Contact Managing Editor, Duncan Jones.

Tips *New Writing Scotland* publishes new short fiction and poetry, in any of the languages of Scotland, from writers resident in Scotland or Scots by birth, upbringing or inclination. Style and subject matter are unimportant, the quality of writing is what counts. There is no need to be consciously Scottish, nor any penalty for being so.

NME

(New Musical Express)
Blue Fin Building, 110 Southwark Street, London, SE1 0SU
- 020 3148 5000
- 020 3148 8107
- news@nme.com
- www.nme.com

Parent Company IPC Media Ltd
Editor Conor McNicholas
Established 1952
Insider Info A weekly consumer magazine covering the world of rock and alternative music. Present circulation of 56,284. Accepts queries by mail. Media pack available online.

Non-fiction Publishes features, interviews/profiles and reviews.

Submission Guidelines Accepts queries

Tips *NME* is the biggest selling and most respected music weekly in the world. Freelancers are often used, but usually for reviews.

The North

The Studio, Byram Arcade, Westgate, Huddersfield, HD1 1ND

☎ 01484 434840

☎ 01484 426566

🌐 www.poetrybusiness.co.uk

Parent Company The Poetry Business Ltd

Editor Peter Sansom

Contact Co-Editor, Janet Fisher

Established 1986

Insider Info A consumer magazine, with two issues per year, covering contemporary poetry. Present circulation is 500. Payment on publication. A byline is given. Accepts queries by mail. Aims to respond to queries and manuscripts within six weeks. Manuscript guidelines are available online.

Non-fiction Interested in essays, features, interviews/profiles, book reviews, critical articles, autobiographies and guides.

Submission Guidelines Accepts queries in the first instance.

Poetry Publishes contemporary poetry.

Submission Guidelines Submit up to six poems. Accepts postal submissions.

Tips *The North* is an independent magazine that publishes contemporary poetry from new and established writers. The magazine accepts submissions for contemporary poetry in any style and is always seeking synopses for good critical articles, as well as reviews concerning contemporary poetry.

North West Business Insider

Boulton House, 17–21 Chorlton Street, Manchester, M1 3HY

☎ 0161 907 9711

☎ 0161 236 9862

✉ insider@newsco.com

🌐 www.insidermagazine.co.uk

Parent Company Insider Media

Editor Michael Taylor

Contact Deputy Editor, Lisa Miles

Established 1991

Insider Info A monthly regional business magazine covering business issues in the North West of England. Present circulation of 17,025. 50 per cent of the publication is written by freelance writers. Manuscripts are published one month after acceptance. Payment is upon publication. A byline is given. Publication is copyrighted and all rights are purchased. Editorial lead time is one month. Seasonal material should be submitted one month in advance. Queries are accepted by email. Sample copy, media pack and editorial calendar available online. Writer's guidelines are free on request.

Non-fiction Publishes feature articles on business topics.

Tips Aimed at business owners and company directors. The editors recommend reading the magazine and understanding the target audience, before submitting original ideas they won't have thought of.

Notes & Queries

Pembroke College, Oxford, OX1 1DW

☎ 01865 276463

✉ notes.queries@oup.com

🌐 www.nq.oxfordjournals.org

Parent Company Oxford University Press

Editor L. Glenn Black, J. Bernard O'Donoghue

Established 1849

Insider Info A quarterly consumer literary journal. Present circulation of 1,475. A byline is given. Queries accepted by mail and email. Writer's guidelines are available online.

Non-fiction Publishes features, reviews and letters/queries on literary subjects.

Submission Guidelines Accepts complete manuscripts.

Tips *Notes & Queries* is a literary journal that aims to answer readers queries about various language and literature subjects. Each issue focuses on works of a specific period and prints factual notes, book reviews, readers queries and replies. The articles published are often quite short, and any submission should be as factually informative as possible, rather than speculative.

Now

Blue Fin Building, 110 Southwark Street, London, SE1 0SU

☎ 020 3148 5000

✉ karen_cross@ipcmedia.com

🌐 www.nowmagazine.co.uk

Parent Company IPC Media Ltd

Contact Deputy Editor, Jeremy Mark; Health Editor, Ali Agnew; Assistant Editor, Karen Cross

Established 1996

Insider Info A weekly consumer magazine covering celebrity gossip and women's lifestyle. Present circulation of 447,094.

Non-fiction Publishes exposé, general interest and celebrity culture articles.

Tips *Now's* target readership is, 'young, independent urbanites with a high disposable income, aged between 16 and 34'. Write a celebrity article aimed at this audience, but contact the Editor first with a synopsis.

Nursery World

174 Hammersmith Road, London, W6 7JP
- ☎ 020 8267 8409
- ✉ liz.roberts@haymarket.com
- 🌐 www.nurseryworld.co.uk

Parent Company Haymarket Business Publications Ltd
Editor Liz Roberts
Insider Info A weekly trade magazine covering nursery level education. Present circulation of 18,096. Accepts queries by mail or email.
Non-fiction Publishes how-to, features and childcare articles.
Submission Guidelines Send complete manuscript for articles of between 800 and 1,300 words.
Images Send photos with submission.
Tips The leading magazine for early years and childcare practitioners, aiming to offer in-depth coverage in specific areas of the early years and childcare sector. Guides for managers and practitioners, all written by early years experts, provide clear, accessible information and advice on key issues such as behaviour, additional learning needs, planning, working with under threes, and nursery food. Articles should be as practical and informal as possible, so an academic or practical background in early years studies would be useful. Include any relevant photographs.

Nursing Times

Greater London House, Hampstead Road, London, NW1 7EJ
- ☎ 020 7874 0502
- ☎ 020 7874 0505
- ✉ nt@emap.com
- 🌐 www.nursingtimes.net

Parent Company EMAP Healthcare
Editor Rachel Downey
Established 1905
Insider Info A weekly trade magazine focussing on nursing topics. Present circulation of 35,754. Accepts queries by mail.
Non-fiction Publishes how-to, feature and technical articles on nursing.
Submission Guidelines Accepts completed manuscripts.
Tips The UK's best selling weekly magazine for nurses, publishing news, clinical features and educational material. *Nursing Times* makes ready use of unsolicited content, but it is a trade orientated publication, so expert clinical knowledge and insider knowledge of the nursing industry and new developments is essential.

Nuts

Blue Fin Building, 110 Southwark Street, London, SE1 0SU
- ☎ 020 3148 5000
- ✉ nutsmagazine@ipcmedia.com
- 🌐 www.nuts.co.uk

Parent Company IPC Media Ltd
Editor Dominic Smith
Established 2004
Insider Info A weekly consumer magazine covering young men's lifestyle topics. Present circulation of 250,061. Accepts queries by email.
Non-fiction Publishes photo features, humour, exposé, features, interviews/profiles, reviews and general interest articles.
Submission Guidelines Accepts queries.
Tips The magazine's mix of humour, sport, news, television, women, and true stories is aimed a target readership of 16–45 year old men. Will not accept fashion, health, or grooming articles.

Obsessed With Pipework

8 Abbot's Way, Pilton, Somerset, BA4 4BN
- ☎ 01749 890019
- ✉ cannula.dementia@virgin.net
- 🌐 www.flarestack.co.uk/obsessedwithpipework.htm

Parent Company Flarestack Publishing
Editor Charles Johnson
Established 1997
Insider Info A small, quarterly, consumer literary magazine focusing on poetry. Accepts queries by mail or email.
Poetry Publishes avant-garde and free verse poetry.
Tips *Obsessed With Pipework* publishes new poetry from both new and established writers. They tend to prefer modern, non-conformist poetry, which takes risks and attempts to 'make it new.' They do not want safe poems that are about what the author knows, but poems in which the author tries to write about something new to themselves.

Occupational Health Journal

Quadrant House, The Quadrant, Sutton, Surrey, SM2 5AS
- ☎ 020 8652 4669
- ☎ 020 8652 8805
- ✉ oh.editor@rbi.co.uk
- ✉ noel.oreilly@rbi.co.uk
- 🌐 www.ohmagazine.co.uk

Parent Company Reed Business Information
Editor Noel O'Reilly
Insider Info A monthly trade magazine covering aspects of occupational health. Present circulation of 5,000. 50 per cent of the publication is written by freelance writers. Manuscripts are published eight months after acceptance. Payment is upon

publication, never with contributor copies instead of cash, with no formal kill fee offered. The expenses of writers on assignments will sometimes be paid (limit agreed upon in advance). A byline is given. Publication is copyrighted and all rights are purchased. Editorial lead time is three months. Seasonal material should be submitted four months in advance. Queries are accepted by mail, email or phone. Sample copies are available for £99 per year. Writer's guidelines and editorial calendar are free on request.

Non-fiction Publishes features and technical articles on occupational health.

Submission Guidelines Accepts queries with published clips, for articles of between 700 and 2,200 words.

Tips The magazine is read by occupational health nurse practitioners and others with responsibility for health at work. It covers workplace health and well-being issues for a professional audience.

Octane
1 Tower Court, Irchester Road, Wollaston, Wellingborough, NN29 7PJ
- 020 7907 6000
- info@octane-magazine.com, david@octane-magazine.com
- www.octane-magazine.com

Parent Company Dennis Publishing
Contact Managing Editor, David Lilywhite
Established 2003
Insider Info A monthly consumer magazine covering classic and performance cars. Present circulation is 33,039.
Non-fiction Publishes news, features, reviews, technical articles, event listings and classified directories.

Official Nintendo Magazine
2 Balcombe Street, London, NW1 6NW
- 020 7042 4000
- lee.nutter@futurenet.co.uk
- www.officialnintendomagazine.co.uk

Parent Company Future Publishing Ltd
Editor Lee Nutter
Established 1992
Insider Info A monthly consumer magazine covering Nintendo computer games. Present circulation is 61,159.
Non-fiction Publishes photo feature, news, reviews and walkthrough articles.
Tips *Official Nintendo Magazine* covers the latest Nintendo computer games. The website also has an active online forum.

Official PlayStation 2 Magazine
30 Monmouth Street, Bath, BA1 2BW
- 01225 442244
- 01225 732275
- ps2postal@futurenet.co.uk

Parent Company Future Publishing Ltd
Editor Nick Ellis
Contact Publisher, Matt Pierce
Established 2000
Insider Info A monthly consumer magazine covering PlayStation 2 computer games. Present circulation is 76,351.
Non-fiction Publishes photo feature, news, reviews and walkthrough articles.
Tips *Official PlayStation 2 Magazine* covers news and new-releases for PlayStation 2 consoles, as well as information and reviews for PlayStation 3.

Official Xbox 360
2 Balcombe Street, London, NW1 6NW
- 01225 442244
- 01225 732285
- jon.hicks@futurenet.co.uk
- www.oxm.co.uk

Parent Company Future Publishing
Editor Jon Hicks
Contact Community Editor, Ben Talbot
Insider Info A monthly consumer magazine focusing on the Xbox games console. Present circulation of 67,097.
Non-fiction Publishes features and technical articles directly relating to the Xbox, its capabilities and its games.
Tips The magazine is linked to a playable demo disc and website. Game coverage is done internally by staff writers, but there is scope for detailed articles concerning Xbox 360's external capabilities as a media centre. Hardware reviews and pieces on unusual console uses would be the most likely to succeed.

OK!
10 Lower Thames Street, London, EC3R 6EN
- 0871 434 1010
- lisa.byrne@express.co.uk
- www.ok-magazine.com

Parent Company Northern & Shell Plc
Editor Lisa Byrne
Contact Features Editor, Marcia Moody
Established 1923
Insider Info A weekly consumer magazine covering celebrity gossip and women's lifestyle topics. Present circulation of 607,048.
Non-fiction Publishes general interest features, interviews and photo features on celebrities.

Tips The title is aimed specifically at women and articles tend to be aspirational and based around the rich and famous. Also includes the sister magazine, *Hot Stars*.

The Oldie

65 Newman Street, London, W1T 3EG

☎ 020 7436 8801

☎ 020 7436 8804

✉ theoldie@theoldie.co.uk

🌐 www.theoldie.co.uk

Parent Company Oldie Publications Ltd

Editor Richard Ingrams

Established 1992

Insider Info Monthly consumer magazine covering news, current affairs and lifestyle topics for the older generation. Present circulation is 28,862. Accepts queries by mail and email. Sample copy is free on request and available by email. Manuscript guidelines are available online.

Non-fiction Interested in humour and general interest articles.

Submission Guidelines Accepts complete manuscripts (including SAE) of between 600 to 1,800 words.

Tips *The Oldie* is a tongue in cheek, general interest news and lifestyle magazine, aimed at the older generation. The magazine will not commission articles from ideas or treatments, so always send them completed articles for consideration. Detailed submission guidelines are available on their website.

Olive

80 Wood Lane, London, W12 0TT

☎ 020 8433 1828

✉ letters@olivemag.co.uk

🌐 www.olivemagazine.co.uk

Parent Company BBC Worldwide Publishing Ltd

Editor Christine Haynes

Contact Features Editor, Jenny McIvor

Established 2003

Insider Info A monthly consumer magazine covering cookery and kitchen topics. Present circulation of 85,196.

Non-fiction Publishes photo features and features on food and cooking.

Tips Olive generally only uses regular freelancers for its features. It is impossible for them to respond to all the proposals that they receive.

The Once Orange Badge Poetry Supplement

PO Box 184, South Ockendon, Essex, RM15 5WT

☎ 01708 852827

✉ onceorangebadge@poetry.fsworld.co.uk

Editor D. Martyn Heath

Established 2003

Insider Info A consumer supplement, with two issues per year, covering poetry. A byline is given. Accepts queries by mail and email. Sample copy is free on request, or available by email.

Poetry Publishes contemporary, free verse, light verse and traditional poetry.

Submission Guidelines Send sample poems with SAE.

Tips *The Once Orange Badge Poetry Supplement* is a free supplement for everyone who has been touched by disability in some way, or at some time. It prints modern poetry of any type or style. The supplement is usually seeking regular contributors rather than single submissions, so there is plenty of scope for multiple publications.

Open Wide Magazine

40 Wingfield Road, Lankenheath, Suffolk, , IP27 9HR

✉ contact@openwidemagazine.co.uk

🌐 www.openwidemagazine.co.uk

Parent Company Open Wide Books

Editor Elizabeth Roberts

Contact Managing Editor, James Quinton

Established 2001

Insider Info A quarterly consumer literary magazine showcasing new poetry and prose. Open Wide is Christian in outloo and aims to support new writers. Writer's guidelines are free on request and available online or via email.

Non-fiction Publishes literary features, reviews and interviews.

Fiction Publishes short fiction.

Poetry Publishes a mixture of poetry forms.

Submission Guidelines Accepts completed manuscripts for fiction stories of between 500 and 2,000 words, or queries with published clips for non-fiction. Accepts any length of poetry. Submission details to: submissions@openwidemagazine.co.uk (as a Word attachment).

Tips Welcomes submissions from new writers. Tends to favour submissions that go against literary traditions.

Orbis

Quarterly International Literary Journal

17 Greenhow Avenue, West Kirby, Wirral, CH48 5EL

☎ 0151 625 1446

✉ carolebaldock@hotmail.com

🌐 www.poetrymagazines.org.uk

Editor Carole Baldock

Established 1969

Insider Info A quarterly literary journal with 84 pages of news, reviews, views, letters, features, prose and quite a lot of poetry. 100 per cent of the publication is written by freelance writers. Manuscripts are published three months after acceptance. Payment is via a Readers' Award of £50, plus £50 for four runners up. All contributors are paid with contributor copies. A byline is given. Contributors retain copyright, but the magazine purchases first UK serial rights. Editorial lead time is three months and seasonal material should be submitted six months in advance. Accepts queries by mail, email or phone. Simultaneous submissions are accepted. Aims to respond to queries within seven days and manuscripts within 14 days. Will not pay the expenses of writers on assignment. Sample copy available for £4 or £15 for four, send SAE. Writer's guidelines available by post, with SAE, via email, or online.

Non-fiction Publishes book excerpts, how-to, essays, humour, inspirational articles, features, interviews/profiles and reviews.
* Accepts around eight non-fiction manuscripts per year.
Submission Guidelines Accepts queries with outline and published clips for articles of between 500 and 1,000 words. No reprints. Contact Carole Baldock, Editor, or Nessa O'Mahony, Reviews Editor (for reviews only).
Fiction Publishes adventure, historical, romance, condensed novels, horror, science fiction, humorous, mainstream, ethnic, mystery, suspense, experimental, novel excerpts and fantasy fiction.
* Accepts around 12 fiction manuscripts per year.
Submission Guidelines Send complete manuscripts for stories of between 500 and 1,000 words, with SAE.
Poetry Publishes avant-garde, free verse, haiku, light verse, traditional and rhyming poetry.
* Purchases 200 poems per year.
Submission Guidelines Accepts up to four sample poems with SAE.
Tips Besides poems, *Orbis* welcomes prose, 500 to 1,000 words, suggestions for cover artwork and features, e.g. the 'Past Master Section'. Do not send in the entire manuscript for non-fiction before discussing the idea first. The Editor has been involved for some time with social inclusion projects and encouraging access to the arts, for example, the South Asian Showcase for Liverpool. She is interested in work from all such communities, especially young people, under 20s and 20 somethings. Also, the editor is particularly interested in women writers, because although magazine subscriptions are around 50 per cent each, male and female, submissions from women are still a good third less than those from men. Writers are recommended to study the guidelines, and stick to them. Always enclose SAE, with sufficient postage.

Orient Express
The Best of Contemporary Writing
Wythgreen House, Coleshill, Swindon, SN6 7PS
⊙ oemagazine@yahoo.co.uk
⊛ www.writersartists.net/oexpress/orientex.htm
Editor Fiona Sampson
Established 2002
Insider Info A consumer book length journal with two issues per year, covering European literature. Queries accepted by mail or email. Present circulation is 74,697.
Non-fiction Publishes essays, articles on poetry and features.
Fiction Publishes short fiction.
Tips *Orient Express* specialises in publishing literature, both fiction and non-fiction, from the entire European region. The magazine is particularly interested in submissions from the European enlargement area, with countries such as Croatia, Lithuania and Ukraine.

The Orphan Leaf Review
26 Grove Park Terrace, Bristol, BS16 2BN
⊙ orphanleaf@jpwallis.co.uk
⊛ www.jpwallis.co.uk/orphanleaf/index.htm
Parent Company The Orphan Leaf
Editor James Paul Wallis
Established 2004
Insider Info A consumer magazine, with two issues per year, covering literature. A byline is given. Accepts queries by mail and email. Manuscript guidelines are available online.
Non-fiction Interested in 'Orphan Leaf' non-fiction (see Tips) as well as author information and interviews/profiles.
Fiction Publishes 'Orphan Leaf' fiction (see Tips).
Tips An orphan leaf is a single page of text taken from within a longer work, such as a novel, which may or may not exist. *The Orphan Leaf Review* publishes these orphan leaves from international writers. Each magazine consists of the leaves, which are each individual, often being printed in different styles and on different paper, and information about their authors. *The Orphan Leaf Review* has very detailed submission guidelines on their website, including a template for submissions. Leaves can be in any style, or 'from' any type of book, as long as they test the boundaries of the genre.

OS Magazine
Office Secretary Magazine
15 Grangers Place, Witney, Oxfordshire, OX28 4BS
☎ 01993 775545
📠 01993 778884
⊙ paul.ormond@peeblesmedia.com

www.peeblesmedia.com
Parent Company Peebles Media
Editor Michelle Crawley
Contact Managing Editor, Mike Travers; Sponsorship and Promotions Manager, Paul Ormond
Established 1976
Insider Info A bi-monthly trade magazine aimed at secretaries. Present circulation of 24,977. Ten per cent of the publication is written by freelance writers. Payment is upon acceptance and a byline is given. Simultaneous submissions are accepted. A sample copy is free on request.
Non-fiction Publishes features and news articles on office and secretarial topics.
Tips *OS Magazine* is aimed at PAs, office managers, and senior and executive secretaries.

Other Poetry
29 Western Hill, Durham, DH1 4RL
editors@otherpoetry.com
www.otherpoetry.com
Editor Michael Standen
Established 1979
Insider Info A consumer literary magazine with three issues per year, focusing mainly on poetry. Present circulation of 250. 100 per cent of the publication is written by freelance writers. A byline is given. Queries are accepted by mail or email. Aims to respond to queries and manuscripts within six weeks. Sample copy available, send SAE with three first class stamps.
Non-fiction Publishes articles on poetry.
Poetry Publishes avant-garde, free verse, light verse and traditional poetry.
Submission Guidelines Accepts up to six sample poems with SAE.
Tips *Other Poetry* is a small magazine that publishes 'good poetry in all its forms'. It prints any kind of poetry, from any kind of writer and its main aim is to publish those poems which do not conform to modern trends. They request that SAEs be included with every postal submission.

Outposts Poetry Quarterly
22 Whitewell Road, Frome, Somerset, BA11 4EL
01373 466653
01373 466657
rjhippopress@aol.com
Editor Roland John
Established 1943
Insider Info A quarterly journal that covers poetry and literature. Accepts queries by mail or email.
Non-fiction Interested in essays, poetry and poetry criticism.

Panda Poetry
46 First Avenue, Clase, Swansea, SA6 7LL
www.geocities.com/slap_dash/quarterly_poetry.html
Editor Esmond Jones
Established 2000
Insider Info A consumer magazine, published quarterly, covering poetic and literary interests.
Poetry Publishes free verse, light verse and traditional poetry.
Submission Guidelines Accepts sample poetry via email or by post with SAE.
Tips *Panda* is a small magazine that publishes general, mainstream poetry from new writers. Panda will accept submissions of any type of poetry.

Papercraft Inspirations
30 Monmouth Street, Bath, BA1 2BW
01225 442244
papercraft@futurenet.co.uk
www.papercraftinspirationsmagazine.co.uk
Parent Company Future Publishing Ltd
Editor Jenny Dixon
Contact Deputy Editor, Zoe Beer; Art Editor, Jo Chivers
Established 2004
Insider Info A monthly consumer magazine covering papercraft. Present circulation is 35,062.
Non-fiction Publishes photo features, how-to, event listings, news and product review articles.
Tips *Papercraft Inspirations* is a monthly magazine that covers cards, papercraft and scrapbooking. The magazine contains practical how-to articles as well as photo features and product reviews, and is aimed primarily at women aged between 35 and 55.

Park Home & Holiday Caravan
Blue Fin Building, 110 Southwark Street, London, SE1 0SU
020 3148 5000
em_bartlett@ipcmedia.com
www.phhc.co.uk
Parent Company IPC Media Ltd
Editor Emma Bartlett
Established 1960
Insider Info A consumer magazine, publishing 13 issues per year. Covers caravanning and mobile home topics.
Non-fiction Publishes features, reviews, new product and technical articles on caravans and park homes.
Submission Guidelines Send complete manuscripts.
Tips The magazine will take anything directly, so there will be a higher than average volume of submissions. To be more noticeable than other

submissions, writers should focus on style, more than content. Any 'hooks', such as specialist or insider knowledge would also be helpful in the long run.

Parking Review

Quadrant House, 250 Kennington Lane, London, SE11 5RD

☎ 0845 270 7871

✉ ed.pr@landor.co.uk

🌐 www.landor.co.uk/parkingreview

Parent Company Landor Publishing

Editor Mark Moran

Established 1989

Insider Info A trade magazine, published monthly and covering motoring and motorcycling parking issues.

Non-fiction Publishes news and features coverage of the on-street and off-street parking sectors.

Tips The magazine also runs the popular and sought after 'British Parking Awards', which are announced each February. Article submissions would have to contain a good deal of industry related knowledge, although there is scope for more humanised articles to run alongside the 'Special Focus' section.

Passion

PO Box 393, Maidstone, Kent, ME14 5XU

☎ 01622 729593

✉ cresmopub@yahoo.co.uk

🌐 www.crescentmoon.org.uk

Parent Company Crescent Moon Publishing

Editor Jeremy Robinson

Established 1994

Insider Info A consumer magazine, published quarterly and covering general literary interest. Present circulation is 200. Byline is given. Accepts queries by mail and email. Writer's guidelines available online.

Non-fiction Publishes essays, poetry, features, reviews and opinion (excluding letters to the Editor) on the media, politics and literary criticism from around the world.

Submission Guidelines Accepts queries.

Fiction Publishes mainstream fiction.

Submission Guidelines Accepts queries.

Poetry Publishes avant-garde, free verse and light verse.

Submission Guidelines A maximum of six poems are to be submitted at one time.

Tips Passion publishes work from both new and established writers, and is dedicated to passionate and emotional writing. Editors are looking for submissions of book reviews on a wide range of subjects, critical essays on politics, philosophy, ideologies and media and submissions of fiction of poetry. Check the website for further details and full submission guidelines.

PC Advisor

4th Floor, Clifton House, 101 Euston Road, London, NW1 2RA

☎ 020 7071 3615

☎ 020 7071 3658

✉ letters@pcadvisor.co.uk

🌐 www.pcadvisor.co.uk

Parent Company International Data Group

Editor Paul Trotter

Contact Deputy Editor, Rosemary Haworth; Reviews Editor, Andrew Harrison

Established 1995

Insider Info A consumer magazine, published monthly and covering computing and business. Current circulation of 52,504. Accepts queries by mail and email.

Non-fiction Publishes how-to, features, interviews/profiles, new product and technical articles.
* Will pay £200 per 1,000 words for unsolicited articles.

Submission Guidelines Accepts queries along with complete manuscript. Articles must be between 1,500 and 3,000 words.

Images Send photos with submission.

Tips Aimed at business and home PC users. Articles pegged on upcoming releases, i.e. reviews, comparisons and tutorials, are least in demand. There may be scope for more practical advice, such as articles on physical computer repair.

PC Answers

30 Monmouth Street, Bath, BA1 2BW

☎ 01225 442244

☎ 01225 732295

✉ pca.experts@futurenet.co.uk

🌐 www.pcanswers.co.uk

Parent Company Future Publishing

Editor Simon Pickstock

Established 1991

Insider Info A consumer magazine, publishing 13 issues per year, covering computing and PC leisure. Current circulation is 19,505.

Non-fiction Publishes how-to, features, reviews, new product and technical articles.

Submission Guidelines Maximum length for articles is 2,500 words.

Tips PC Answers targets an audience of dedicated PC enthusiasts. The magazine contains practical articles and 'how-to advice' and most articles are system or software based. There may be scope for pieces on computer DIY, i.e. articles on the physical repair or upgrading of damaged or flagging computers.

PC Format

30 Monmouth Street, Bath, BA1 2BW
- ☎ 01225 442244
- ☎ 01225 732295
- ⊙ pcfmail@futurenet.co.uk
- ⊛ www.pcformat.co.uk

Parent Company Future Publishing
Editor Adam Evans
Contact Deputy Editor, Alan Dexter
Established 1991
Insider Info A consumer magazine, issued four weekly, covering computing and PC leisure. Current circulation is 23,764.
Non-fiction Publishes features, interviews/profiles and technical articles.
Submission Guidelines Accepts queries by phone, email or writing. No unsolicited manuscripts.
Tips *PC Format (PCF)* is a computer magazine which includes articles about games, entertainment and how to get the most out of the platform. Aimed at a reader with an average age of around 30, *PCF* tends to be more irreverent and opinionated than other, similar magazines, edging towards being a lifestyle magazine as well as a computing one. It is open to new ideas but does not like unsolicited work.

PC Gamer

30 Monmouth Street, Bath, BA1 2BW
- ☎ 01225 442244
- ☎ 01225 732275
- ⊙ pcgamer@futurenet.co.uk
- ⊛ www.pcgamer.co.uk

Parent Company Future Publishing Ltd
Editor Ross Atherton
Contact Publisher, James Binns; Deputy Editor, Tim Edward; Art Editor, Daniel Vincent
Insider Info A monthly consumer magazine covering PC computer games. Present circulation is 38,654.
Non-fiction Publishes news, review and preview articles.
Tips *PC Gamer* covers all aspects of PC computer games and related products, including online gaming.

PC Plus

30 Monmouth Street, Bath, BA1 2BW
- ☎ 01225 442244
- ☎ 01225 732295
- ⊙ pcplus@futurenet.co.uk
- ⊛ www.pcplus.co.uk

Parent Company Future Publishing Ltd
Editor Martin Cooper
Contact Publisher, Stuart Anderton; Features Editor, Richard Cobbett
Established 1986
Insider Info A monthly consumer magazine covering computing. Present circulation is 27,931.
Non-fiction Publishes how-to, photo features, news, reviews and technical articles.
Tips *PC Plus* covers all aspects of computing. It is aimed at home users and enthusiasts, as well as small businesses, and contains practical computing articles and the latest product and online reviews.

PC Pro

30 Cleveland Street, London, W1T 4JD
- ☎ 020 7907 6000
- ☎ 020 7907 6282
- ⊙ editor@pcpro.co.uk
- ⊛ www.pcpro.co.uk

Parent Company Dennis Publishing Ltd
Editor Tim Danton
Contact Deputy Editor, David Fearon; News & Features Editor, Barry Collins
Insider Info A monthly consumer magazine covering computing. Present circulation is 83,204.
Non-fiction Publishes news, features, product reviews and lab-test articles.
Tips *PC Pro* covers personal computers at home or in the workplace, and publishes articles in both areas.

PC Zone

2 Balcombe Street, London, NW1 6NW
- ☎ 020 7317 2600
- ⊙ jamie.sefton@futurenet.co.uk
- ⊛ www.pczone.co.uk

Parent Company Future Publishing Ltd
Contact Deputy Editor, Steve Hogarty; Art Editor, Matthew Kendall; Reviews Editor, Suzy Wallace
Established 1993
Insider Info A monthly consumer magazine covering PC computer games. Present circulation is 22,297.
Non-fiction Publishes news, review and preview articles.
Tips *PC Zone* covers the latest developments in PC and online computer gaming. The magazine is aimed at PC games and leisure enthusiasts aged 20 to 30 years old.

Pennine Ink

The Gallery, Yorke Street, Haslingden, BB11 1HD
- ☎ 01282 703657
- ⊙ sheridans@casanostra.p3online.net

Parent Company Mid Pennine Arts
Editor Laura Sheridan
Established 1983
Insider Info An annual consumer magazine covering general literary interest. Current circulation of 400.

Non-fiction Publishes poetry articles, features and reviews.
Submission Guidelines Accepts queries.
Fiction Publishes short fiction.
Submission Guidelines Accepts queries.
Poetry Publishes avant-garde, free verse, light verse and traditional poetry.
* Purchases 50 poems per year.
Submission Guidelines Maximum length for poems is 40 lines.
Tips *Pennine Ink* magazine publishes contemporary poetry and related articles, usually featuring work from workshops held at the Mid Pennine Arts Gallery. *Pennine Ink* is in the process of developing a website which will include submission details for the magazine. Until then they are willing to accept submission for any type of modern poetry and also some short fiction.

Pennine Platform
Frizingley Hall, Frizinghall Road, Bradford, BD9 4LD
☏ 01274 541015
✉ nicholas.bielby@virgin.net
🌐 www.pennineplatform.co.uk
Editor Nicholas Bielby
Established 1973
Insider Info A twice-yearly consumer magazine covering general literary interest. Present circulation of 300. 100 per cent of the publication is written by freelance writers. A byline is given. Accepts queries by mail.
Non-fiction Publishes poetry articles, features and reviews.
Submission Guidelines Accepts queries with SAE.
Poetry Publishes light verse and traditional poetry.
Submission Guidelines Accepts sample poems with SAE.
Tips *Pennine Platform* is a long running independent literary magazine that publishes new poetry, book reviews and articles. It is supported by the Leeds Philosophical and Literary Society. *Pennine Platform* prefers traditionally influenced poetry over 'free verse' and the Editor will respond with feedback to every submission sent. This does mean, however, that response and publication times can often be quite long. Always include SAE with your submission.

Pensions World
LexisNexis, 2 Addiscombe Road, Croydon, CR9 5AF
☏ 020 8686 9141
☏ 020 8212 1920
✉ stephanie.hawthorne@lexisnexis.co.uk
🌐 www.pensionsworld.co.uk
Parent Company LexisNexis
Editor Stephanie Hawthorne
Established 1972
Insider Info A monthly trade magazine, covering finance and investment. Current circulation is 7,483.
Non-fiction Publishes features and news on pensions.
Submission Guidelines Accepts an emailed synopsis, along with CV and published clips. No unsolicited manuscripts.
Tips Aimed at pensions professionals and it is distributed to all members of the NAPF (National Association of Pension Funds). A degree of expertise in the field would be an advantage.

People Management
17–18 Britton Street, London, EC1M 5TP
☏ 020 7324 2729
☏ 020 7324 2791
✉ editorial@peoplemanagement.co.uk
🌐 www.peoplemanagement.co.uk
Parent Company Chartered Institute of Personnel and Development
Editor Steve Crabb
Contact Managing Editor, Rima Evans; Commissioning Editor, Claire Warren
Established 1995
Insider Info A bi-weekly trade magazine, covering personnel management. Current circulation of 128,904. Editorial lead time is two months. Accepts queries by email and phone. Writer's guidelines available online.
Non-fiction Publishes how-to and general interest articles.
Submission Guidelines Accepts a two-page query (include outline, published clips and author biography). Final articles must be between 1,000 and 2,500 words.
Columns Publishes the following columns: Indicator (business-related research/analysis slant, maximum 400 words), Learning centre/Viewpoint (training and development matters/opinions slant, 350–600 words), Research (academic research slant, maximum 500 words), Troubleshooter (problems/solution slant, 350–400 words).
Submission Guidelines Accepts queries with published clips.
Tips *People Management* publishes articles on all aspects of managing and developing people at work. It is the official magazine of the Chartered Institute of Personnel and Development and publishes articles about best practice and leading edge ideas, as well as acting as a forum for debate on topical issues. They do not normally accept articles that have been published elsewhere, that promote a particular product or service, or are purely promotional copy for the organisation involved.

People's Friend

80 Kingsway East, Dundee, DD4 8SL

☎ 01382 223131

🖷 01382 452491

Parent Company D.C. Thomson & Co Ltd

Established 1869

Insider Info A weekly consumer magazine that covers fiction and women's lifestyle. Accepts queries by mail or email. Present circulation is 330,093.

Non-fiction Interested in women's lifestyle, cookery and craft articles.

Fiction Interested in romantic short stories, serials and children's fiction.

Submission Guidelines Accepts completed manuscript submissions of between 1,500 to 3,000 words for short stories and between 60,000 to 70,000 words for serials.

Tips *People's Friend* publish a wide range of fiction, all of which is aimed predominantly at women.

Performance Bikes

Media House, Lynchwood, Peterborough Business Park, Peterborough, PE2 6EA

☎ 01733 468099

🖷 01733 468104

📧 perf.bikes@bauermedia.com

🌐 www.performancebikes.co.uk

Parent Company Bauer Consumer Media

Editor Tim Thompson

Contact Publisher, Charley Davies; Features Editor, Matt Wildee

Insider Info A monthly consumer magazine covering high performance bikes. Present circulation is 28,011.

Non-fiction Publishes photo features, interviews, profiles, reviews, road-tests and practical how-to articles.

Period Living

St Giles House, 50 Poland Street, London, W1F 7AX

☎ 020 7970 4433

🖷 020 7970 4438

📧 period.living@centaur.co.uk

🌐 www.periodliving.co.uk

Parent Company Centaur Communications Ltd

Contact Editor in Chief, Michael Holmes; Editor, Sarah Whelan; Features Editor, Naomi Jones; Editorial Assistant, Katharine Clemow

Insider Info A monthly consumer magazine covering homes and furnishing. Present circulation is 52,834.

Non-fiction Publishes features, reviews, showcase and practical articles.

Tips *Period Living* covers homes and furnishing with a period style, including articles on traditional restoration, antiques and buying guides.

Personal Computer World

Tower House, Sovereign Park, Market Harborough, Leicester, LE16 9EF

☎ 01858 438881

🖷 01858 468969

📧 letters@pcw.co.uk

🌐 www.pcw.co.uk

Parent Company Incisive Media Ltd

Editor Kelvyn Taylor

Contact Deputy Editor, Will Stapley

Established 1979

Insider Info A monthly consumer magazine, covering computing and PC business. Current circulation of 60,081.

Non-fiction Publishes news, reviews, photo features and features on PCs.

Tips Aimed at an audience of technology enthusiasts and IT business professionals, although it tends to lean towards a consumer angle in its reporting. Any article submitted must be thorough and accurate in its reporting or analysis, and must also remain unbiased as far as possible.

The Pharmaceutical Journal

1 Lambeth High Street, London, SE1 7JN

☎ 020 7572 2414

🖷 020 7572 2405

📧 editor@pharmj.org.uk

🌐 www.pjonline.com

Parent Company RPS Publishing

Editor Olivia Timbs

Contact Managing Editor, Graeme Smith; News Editor, Harriet Adcock

Established 1841

Insider Info Weekly trade journal covering pharmaceutical subjects and trade information. Present circulation is 56,322. One per cent of the publication is written by freelance writers. Submissions are published up to two months after acceptance. Payment is on publication and sometimes pays by contributor copies. The expenses of writers on assignment are sometimes paid (limit agreed upon in advance). A byline is given for features only. Publication is copyrighted. Average lead time is two days. Accepts queries by mail, email, fax and telephone. Aims to respond to queries within two days and manuscripts within six days. Sample copy is free on request and available online. Manuscript guidelines are available online.

Non-fiction Interested in pharmacy related features, new product reviews and news features.

* Payment for assigned articles is £0.0955 per word. Payment for unsolicited articles is £0.04775 per word.

Images Accepts images with submission.

* Negotiates payment individually.

Submission Guidelines Send contact sheets, negatives, transparencies, prints or gif/jpeg files with captions, model releases and identification of subjects to News Editor, Harriet Adcock. State the availability of photos with submission.

Columns Publishes news and broad spectrum columns.

Tips *The Pharmaceutical Journal* is the official journal of the Royal Pharmaceutical Society of Great Britain, and is aimed at professionals within the pharmaceutical industries.

The Photographer

Fox Talbot House, 2 Amwell End, Ware, Hertfordshire, SG12 9HN

- 01920 487268
- 01920 487056
- info@bipp.com
- www.bipp.com

Parent Company The British Institute of Professional Photography
Editor Steve Hynes
Established 1947
Insider Info A monthly journal covering all aspects of photography. Accepts queries by mail or email.
Non-fiction Interested in new product reviews, news, practical guides and features articles related to traditional and digital photography.

Photography Monthly

The Mill, Bearwalden Business Park, Wendens Ambo, Saffron Walden, CB11 4GB

- 0845 650 1065
- 01733 558623
- photography.monthly@ photographymonthly.co.uk
- www.photographymonthly.co.uk

Parent Company Archant Specialist (London)
Contact Editorial Director, William Cheung; Features Editor, Adam Scorey
Established 2001
Insider Info A monthly consumer magazine covering photography. Present circulation is 36,028.
Non-fiction Publishes news, photo features, product reviews, interviews, profiles and technical advice articles.
Images Check the website for latest details on images needed.
Tips The magazine is always looking for photo submissions from readers to illustrate forthcoming

features. See website for details of current submission needs.

Pick Me Up

Blue Fin Building, 110 Southwark Street, London, SE1 0SU

- 020 3148 5000
- pickmeup@ipcmedia.com
- www.pickmeupmagazine.com

Parent Company IPC Media Ltd
Editor June Smith-Shepphard
Contact Features Editor, Heather Bishop
Established 2005
Insider Info A weekly consumer magazine covering real life stories and women's lifestyle topics. Present Circulation of 409,112. Media pack is available online.
Non-fiction Publishes general interest features, interviews and photo features on real life, fashion and beauty.
Tips The magazine's main focus is on real life experiences and its editorial style is described as bringing the feel of a celebrity weekly to the real life market.

Pilot

The Mill, Bearwalden Business Park, Saffron Walden, CB11 4GB

- 01799 544200
- 01799 544201
- nick.bloom@pilotweb.aero
- www.pilotweb.co.uk

Parent Company Archant Specialist
Editor Nick Bloom
Established 1968
Insider Info A monthly consumer magazine, covering aviation. Current circulation of 19,181. Will pay on publication and all rights are purchased. Byline given and the publication is copyrighted. Accepts queries via mail and email. Writer's guidelines available online.
Non-fiction Publishes how-to, photo features, interviews/profiles, technical, travel and private aviation based articles.

* Pays between £150 and £400, or more for longer features.

Submission Guidelines Send complete manuscript (including SAE). Maximum length of 1,200 words.
Images Accepts images with submission.

* Will pay a varied fee per photo and will purchase all rights.

Submission Guidelines Reviews prints, gif/jpeg files, and captions. Send photos with submission.
Tips The magazine works in tandem with the website work to offer an enhanced and interactive service to *Pilot* readers and subscribers. Submit a straightforward account, preferably on a subject of

widespread, rather than purely personal, interest. Humour is particularly welcome. See the website for further submission guidelines.

Planet – The New Welsh Internationalist

PO Box 44, Aberystwyth, Ceredigion, SY23 3ZZ
- 01970 611255
- 01970 611197
- planet.enquiries@planetmagazine.org.uk
- www.planetmagazine.org.uk

Editor Helle Michelsen
Established 1970
Insider Info A bi-monthly consumer publication, covering the arts, culture and politics in Wales and beyond. Current circulation of 1,500. Will pay on publication. Sample copies available, costing £4. Writer's guidelines available online. Will accept queries by mail, or via email to: helle.michelsen@planetmagazine.org.uk
Fiction Publishes mainstream fiction.
* Will pay £50 per 1,000 words.
Submission Guidelines Accepts queries. Word length for articles should be between 1,500 and 4,000 words. Will not consider magical realism, horror or science fiction.
Poetry Publishes traditional poetry.
Tips In addition to features on, and interviews with contemporary Welsh artists and writers, *Planet* includes political analysis, both of Welsh affairs and international issues. *Planet* also prints several poems and one short story in every issue of the magazine. They do not look for fiction which necessarily has a 'Welsh' connection, which some writers might assume from the title.

Play

Richmond House, 33 Richmond Hill, Bournemouth, BH2 6EQ
- 01202 586216
- nick.jones@imagine-publishing.co.uk
- www.play-mag.co.uk

Parent Company Imagine Publishing
Contact Editor in Chief, Nick Jones
Established 1996
Insider Info A monthly consumer magazine covering PlayStation computer games. Present circulation is 24,007.
Non-fiction Publishes news, features, reviews and tips articles.
Tips *Play* covers Sony PlayStation games consoles and their games. Features should cover the latest releases, walkthroughs and game guides.

PN Review

4th Floor, Alliance House, Cross Street, Manchester, M2 7AP
- 0161 834 8730
- 0161 832 0084
- info@carcanet.co.uk
- www.pnreview.co.uk

Parent Company Carcanet Press Ltd
Editor Michael Schmidt
Established 1973
Insider Info A bi-monthly consumer magazine, covering literary interests, particularly poetry. Bylines are given. Accepts queries by mail. Writer's guidelines available online.
Non-fiction Publishes articles on poetry, features, interviews/profiles, reviews and opinions (excluding letters to the Editor).
Submission Guidelines Accepts queries.
Poetry Publishes avant-garde, free verse and light verse poetry.
Submission Guidelines Accepts sample poems by post with SAE
Tips *PN Review* has an international focus and is a champion of modernist and experimental writing. It does not publish short stories or any non-poetry related articles, and is not considering fiction in English, or in translation at the moment. Proposals for poetry submission must be posted rather than emailed.

Poetic Hours

43 Willow Road, Carlton, Nottingham, NG4 3BH
- erranpublishing@hotmail.com
- www.poetichours.homestead.com

Parent Company Erran Publishing
Editor Nick Clark
Insider Info A twice-yearly consumer magazine, covering literary – particularly poetry – interests. A byline is given. Accepts queries by email.
Non-fiction Publishes poetry articles.
Poetry Publishes free verse, light verse and traditional articles.
Submission Guidelines Maximum of four poems to be submitted at any one time.
Tips *Poetic Hours* is a small, not for profit poetry magazine that donates all of its proceeds to charity. Its main aims are firstly, to raise money for charity, and secondly, to provide an opening for amateur poets to publish their work. The magazine is for charity, so contributors can donate their poetry on a 'single use' basis but will not be paid. *Poetic Hours* will not accept any work that attacks the position of any other person, group or belief.

The Poetry Church

Eldwick Crag Farm, High Eldwick, Bingley,, West Yorkshire, BD16 3BB

- 01743 872177
- 01743 872177
- reavill@globalnet.co.uk

Parent Company Moorside Words and Music
Editor Tony Reavill
Established 1995
Insider Info Quarterly consumer magazine covering poetry with particular religious slants.
Non-fiction Interested in religious and poetry related articles.
Submission Guidelines Accepts queries in the first instance.
Poetry Publishes free verse, light verse and traditional religious poetry.
Tips *The Poetry Church* is a religious poetry magazine that prints new poetry and articles with a Christian slant. *The Poetry Church* generally only accepts manuscripts from subscribers, and offers no payment for contributions.

Poetry Combination Module

196 High Road, London, N22 8HH

- page84direct@yahoo.co.uk
- www.geocities.com/andyfloydplease

Parent Company P.E.F Productions
Contact Managing Editor, Andy Floyd
Established 1999
Insider Info A poetry magazine in A5 format, publishing Winter, Spring and Autumn Issues. Publishes articles on poetry, anti-poetry, art and artwork. 100 per cent of the magazine is written by freelance writers. Lead time is approximately five months. The magazine does not offer payment, but sends writers two free issues which are printable online. Bylines are given and the magazine is copyrighted. Seasonal material must be submitted five days in advance. Accepts queries by mail and email, and will accept simultaneous submissions and previously published submissions. Aims to report back to queries within five weeks. Writer's guidelines are available free on request, with SAE, or online. Writer's guidelines and editorial guidelines are also available online.
Non-fiction Publishes photo features, humour, poetry articles, personal experience, anti-poetry, aphorism and graphic art articles, as well as cartoons. Forthcoming issues for which freelance material will be needed in the next few months are *PCM* 27 (The Family Issue), poetry on Family Matters, *PCM 28* (The British Shorthair Issue) – poetry on British Shorthair (cat breed), Cats, Hair and Hairy matters and for *PCM 29*, Poetry on Benignant Issues. Aphorism on topics is also welcome.

Submission Guidelines Send a sample of work via email.
Fiction Publishes adventure, historical, romance, humorous, mainstream, ethnic, mystery, suspense, experimental, fantasy, societal and environmental fiction.
Poetry Publishes avant-garde, free verse, light verse and traditional poetry.
Submission Guidelines Accepts sample poetry via email. Include the words 'PCM Submission' in email message. Clearly state the writer and where you live (e.g. London) after each poem.
Images Accepts images with submission.
* Will not offer payment for photos accepted.
Fillers Publishes anecdotes, facts, jokes (to be illustrated by a cartoonist), short humour, hints and tips and strange but true fillers.

Poetry Cornwall

1 Station Hill, Redruth, Cornwall, TR15 2PP

- poetrycornwall@yahoo.com
- www.poetrycornwall.freeservers.com

Editor Les Merton
Established 2002
Insider Info A consumer magazine, publishing three times per year, covering literary interests, particularly poetry. A byline is given. Accepts queries by mail and email. Sample copy available, with SAE and two first class stamps. Writer's guidelines available online.
Non-fiction Publishes poetry articles and features.
Submission Guidelines Accepts queries.
Poetry Accepts free verse, traditional and translation/dialect poetry.
Submission Guidelines A maximum of three poems can be submitted at one time, and poems must be a maximum of 36 lines. Subscribers are allowed to send poetry submissions by email. Non-subscribers must use standard post and include SAE.
Tips *Poetry Cornwall* publishes new and established poets from around the world, as well as poetry in various dialects; from Jamaica to regions such as Cornwall, Devon, and Norfolk. Apart from poetry, the magazine is also interested in short articles on related subjects.

Poetry Express

Diorama Arts Centre, 34 Osnaburgh Street, London, NW1 3ND

- 020 7916 5317
- survivor@survivorspoetry.org.uk

Parent Company Survivor's Poetry Group
Established 1997
Insider Info A consumer newsletter, issued quarterly and covering general literary interest. Current circulation of 2,500. Byline is given. Accepts

query by mail and email. Will always pay writers with a contributor copy.

Non-fiction Publishes articles on poetry and news/events related to the Survivor's Group.

Submission Guidelines Accepts queries.

Fiction Publishes short fiction.

Poetry Publishes avant-garde, free verse, light verse and traditional titles.

Submission Guidelines Maximum of four poems to be submitted at one time.

Tips The Survivor's Poetry Group is an arts charity dedicated to promoting poetry by, and for survivors of mental distress. The *Poetry Express* is the quarterly newsletter of the group and publishes the latest news and events concerning the group, as well as new poetry and prose articles of interest to survivors. Any submissions must be of interest to survivors of mental distress.

Poetry Ireland Review

2 Prouds Lane, St Stephen's Green, Dublin 2, Republic of Ireland

- 00353 1 478 9974
- 00353 1 478 0205
- poetry@iol.ie
- www.poetryireland.ie

Parent Company Poetry Ireland/Éigse Éireann

Insider Info A quarterly consumer journal, covering poetic interests. A byline is given. Accepts queries by mail and email. Reports back on queries and manuscripts within six months. Writer's guidelines available online.

Non-fiction Publishes poetry articles, features and reviews.

* Maximum pay for assigned and unsolicited articles is €50, plus one contributor copy.

Submission Guidelines Accepts proposals but not complete manuscripts.

Poetry Publishes avant-garde, free verse, light verse and traditional poetry.

* Maximum pay for poems is €32, plus one contributor copy.

Submission Guidelines Maximum of six poems to be submitted at one time. Poems advocating sexism or racism will not be accepted.

Tips *Poetry Ireland Review* publishes poetry from new and established writers from both Ireland and abroad. In order to keep the review progressive, a new editor is appointed every four issues. Articles and reviews are mostly commissioned privately but the Editor will accept unsolicited proposals for articles, not full manuscripts.

Poetry London

1a Jewel Road, London, E17 4QU

- 020 8521 0776

- 020 8521 0776
- editors@poetrylondon.co.uk
- www.poetrylondon.co.uk

Editor Maurice Riordan

Established 1988

Insider Info A consumer journal, publishing three issues per year (March, June, October) and covering general literary interest, particularly poetry. Current circulation of 800. A byline is given. Accepts queries by mail and email. Aims to report back on queries and manuscripts within two months.

Non-fiction Publishes poetry articles, features, interviews/profiles, reviews and news/event listings.

Submission Guidelines Accepts query.

Poetry Publishes avant-garde, free verse, light verse and traditional poetry.

Submission Guidelines Submit a maximum of six poems. No email submissions. Address poetry submissions to: Maurice Riordan, 6 Daniels Road, London, SE15 3LR

Tips *Poetry London* publishes new poetry from new and established writers, as well as selected poetry from competition winners. It also publishes a wide range of event listings, reviews, feature articles, interviews and general information from the poetry world. Submissions for book reviews must be directed to a separate address (see the website for details). *Poetry London* will often print translated poetry, as well as the regular submissions.

Poetry Nottingham

11 Orkney Close, Stenson Fields, Derbyshire, DE24 3LW

- info@nottinghampoetrysociety.co.uk

Parent Company Nottingham Poetry Society

Editor Adrian Buckner

Established 1947

Insider Info A quarterly consumer magazine, covering the interests of the Nottingham Poetry Society. Current circulation of 250. Bylines are given. Accepts query via mail or email.

Non-fiction Publishes poetry articles, features and reviews.

Submission Guidelines Accepts queries.

Poetry Publishes avant garde, free verse, light verse and traditional titles.

Submission Guidelines Accepts postal submissions accompanied by SAE.

Tips *Poetry Nottingham* publishes new poetry, articles and reviews and has an international outlook, accepting submissions from anywhere in the world.

Poetry Now

Remus House, Woodston, Peterborough, PE2 9JX

- ☎ 01733 898101
- 🖷 01733 313524
- ✉ poetrynow@forwardpress.co.uk
- 🌐 www.forwardpress.co.uk

Parent Company Forward Press
Editor Heather Killingray
Established 1989
Insider Info Consumer monthly magazine, covering general literary and poetry interests. Bylines are given. Accepts query via mail and email.
Non-fiction Publishes poetry articles.
Submission Guidelines Accepts queries.
Poetry Publishes avant-garde, free verse, light verse and traditional poetry.
Tips *Poetry Now* aims to publish poetry for the simple pleasure of reading, rather than for academic reasons, and actively supports new writers that wish to see their work in print. It prints poetry of any style or form, as long as it is relevant to everyday life. *Poetry Now* also publishes books and anthologies, to place new writers alongside established writers. The magazine has a different theme each month for poetry submissions, as well as regular features and competitions. The theme of the month can be found on the website, but the magazine also offers a monthly email, which details the theme and all relevant submission guidelines for the forthcoming issue.

Poetry Review
22 Betterton Street, London, WC2H 9BX
- ☎ 020 7420 9880
- 🖷 020 7240 4818
- ✉ poetryreview@poetrysociety.org.uk
- 🌐 www.poetrysociety.org.uk

Parent Company The Poetry Society
Editor Fiona Sampson
Established 1912
Insider Info Publishes a quarterly consumer journal, covering general literary interests with a particular emphasis on poetry. Current circulation of roughly 4,000. A byline is given. Accepts query via mail and email. Writer's guidelines are available online.
Non-fiction Publishes poetry articles, features and reviews.
Submission Guidelines Accepts queries.
Poetry Publishes avant-garde, free verse, light verse and traditional titles.
Submission Guidelines A maximum of six poems can be submitted at one time.
Tips *The Poetry Review* prints articles and reviews of the latest poetry. Its aim is to help poets and poetry thrive in Britain today. *The Poetry Review* is very popular and receives between 30,000 to 50,000 poetry submissions every year, but prints only 200 at most. However, they do support new poets and

actively encourage submissions from first-time writers.

Poetry Scotland
91–93 Main Street, Callander, FK17 8BQ
- ✉ sally.king4@btinternet.com
- 🌐 www.poetryscotland.co.uk

Parent Company Diehard Publishers
Editor Sally Evans
Insider Info A quarterly consumer poetry broadsheet, publishing nothing but new poetry, from new and established writers. Accepts query by mail and email.
Poetry Publishes avant-garde, free verse, light verse and traditional poetry.
Tips *Poetry Scotland* generally runs a Scottish theme for submissions, but will also accept submissions from, or about, other places.

Poetry Wales
57 Nolton Street, Bridgend, CF31 3AE
- ☎ 01656 663018
- 🖷 01656 649226
- ✉ poetrywales@seren-books.com
- 🌐 www.poetrywales.co.uk

Editor Robert Minhinnick
Established 1965
Insider Info A quarterly consumer magazine, covering poetry. Current circulation is roughly 800. Byline is given. Accepts queries via mail or email.
Non-fiction Publishes poetry articles, features and reviews.
Submission Guidelines Accepts queries.
Poetry Publishes avant-garde, free verse, light verse and traditional poetry.
Tips *Poetry Wales* is a literary magazine that publishes the best new poetry from both Wales and abroad. The magazine supports new poetry and publishes work from new and established writers. Although it will accept poetry submissions from international writers, one of its main aims is to help new writers in Welsh achieve publication.

Poet's Letter Magazine
75 Cannon Street, London, EC4N 5BN
- ☎ 020 7556 7052
- 🖷 020 7556 7511
- ✉ editor@poetsletter.com
- 🌐 www.poetsletter.com

Editor Munayem Mayenin
Established 2006
Insider Info A monthly consumer magazine, covering general literary and poetry interests. Current circulation of 90,000. Byline is given. Accepts queries via mail and email.

Non-fiction Publishes photo features, poetry articles, religious pieces, features, interviews/profiles, reviews, general interest and travel articles.
Submission Guidelines Send complete manuscripts.
Fiction Publishes mainstream short fiction.
Submission Guidelines Send complete manuscripts.
Poetry Publishes free verse, light verse and traditional poetry.
Submission Guidelines A maximum of three poems can be submitted at one time.
Tips *Poet's Letter* accepts submissions for poetry, short stories, novel excerpts, book reviews, interviews and articles on philosophy, psychology, sociology, politics and the arts.

The Political Quarterly
9600 Garsington Road, Oxford, Ox4 2DQ
- 01865 776868
- 01865 714591
- www.blackwellpublishing.com
Parent Company Blackwell Publishing
Editor Tony Wright
Established 1930
Insider Info A quarterly journal that covers all aspects of national and international politics. Accepts queries by mail or email.
Tips The Political Quarterly covers national and international politics with a progressive, but neutral point of view. Address all submissions to the 'Assistant Editor'.

Pop
Endeavour House, 189 Shaftesbury Avenue, London, WC2H 8JG
- 020 7520 6400
- 020 7520 6440
- info@popmagazine.co.uk
Parent Company EMAP Plc
Contact Editor in Chief, Katie Grand; Executive Editor, Murray Healy; Art Director, Stuart Spalding; Fashion Editor, Victoria Young
Established 2000
Insider Info A consumer magazine, with two issues per year, covering popular culture. Present circulation is 80,000.
Non-fiction Publishes features and news on art, fashion, music and popular culture.

Porsche Post
Cornbury House, Cotswold Business Village, London Road, Moreton in Marsh, Gloucestershire, GL56 0JQ
- 01608 652911
- 01608 652944

- publications@porscheclubgb.com
- www.porscheclubgb.com
Parent Company Porsche Club GB
Editor Stephen Mummery
Established 1962
Insider Info A monthly consumer magazine, about Porsche cars. Present circulation of 16,000. Ten to twenty percent of the magazine is written by freelance writers. Payment is on publication. A byline is given and the publication is copyrighted. Purchases first UK serial rights on accepted material. Accepts queries by mail, email and phone. Will accept previously published submissions. A sample copy is free on request.
Non-fiction Publishes articles about Porsche and related topics.

Portfolio
43 Candlemaker Row, Edinburgh, EH1 2QB
- 0131 220 1911
- 0131 226 4287
- info@portfoliocatalogue.com
- www.portfoliocatalogue.com
Editor Gloria Chalmers
Insider Info A consumer magazine, publishing two issues per year (June and December), covering photography. Accepts queries via mail and email.
Non-fiction Publishes photo features, essays, features, interviews/profiles, reviews, technical pieces and general interest articles on visual arts.
Submission Guidelines Send complete manuscript.
Images Publishes photographic art.
Tips *Portfolio* is an art magazine with very high production values. It publishes innovative photographic art from established artists, as well as articles and essays on photography and visual arts, and a series of portfolios by up and coming artists. *Portfolio* is a visual arts magazine only, and as such only accepts submissions of visual arts. The magazine is especially keen to see proposals from new artists with a ready portfolio of work that might be suitable for the magazine.

Portuguese Studies
1 Carlton House Terrace, London, SW1Y 5DB
- 020 7848 2507
- 020 7848 2787
- portuguese@mhra.org.uk
- www.mhra.org.uk/Publications/Journals/Portuguese.html
Parent Company Modern Humanities Research Association
Editor David Treece
Established 1985

Insider Info A consumer journal, publishing two issues per year, covering Portuguese studies. Byline is given.

Non-fiction Publishes photo features, features, technical and historical/nostalgic articles.

Submission Guidelines Send complete manuscripts.

Tips *Portuguese Studies* is an academic journal dedicated to research on the culture and history of Portuguese society. It welcomes scholarly contributions on all aspects of the literature, culture and history of the Portuguese societies.

Practical Boat Owner

Westover House, West Quay Road, Poole, BH15 1JG
- 01202 440820
- 01202 440860
- pbo@ipcmedia.com
- www.pbo.co.uk

Parent Company IPC Media Ltd
Editor Sarah Norbury
Contact PA to Editor, Roz Jones
Established 1967
Insider Info A monthly consumer magazine, covering boating. Present circulation of 48,202. Accepts query via mail and email.
Non-fiction Publishes how-to, photo features, features and technical articles on boating.
Submission Guidelines Accepts query with SAE and synopsis.
Tips Aimed at boat owners, both power and sail, who tend to be affluent but practically minded consumers. The magazine is interested in hard facts about gear, equipment, pilotage and renovation from experienced yachtsman.

Practical Caravan

Teddington Studios, Broom Road, Teddington, TW11 9BE
- 020 8267 5629
- 020 8267 5725
- practical.caravan@haynet.com
- www.practicalcaravan.com

Parent Company Haymarket Publishing
Editor Nigel Donelly
Established 1967
Insider Info A monthly consumer magazine, covering caravanning. Present circulation is 45,158. Accepts query via mail and email.
Non-fiction Publishes photo features, features, reviews and technical articles.
Submission Guidelines Send complete manuscript. Maximum length for articles is 2,000 words.
Images Send photos with submission.

Tips Regularly publishes 'Great Escape' holiday features. Article submissions must be relevant to the caravanning hobby and include a good depth of detail, but must also be written in a chatty and friendly manner. The inclusion of photos is essential.

Practical Classics

Media House, Lynchwood, Peterborough Business Park, Peterborough, PE2 6EA
- 01733 468000
- 01733 468397
- practical.classics@bauermedia.com
- www.practicalclassics.co.uk

Parent Company Bauer Consumer Media
Editor Matt Wright
Contact Deputy Editor, Gervais Seymour; Art Editor, Tracey Radnall
Established 1980
Insider Info A monthly consumer magazine covering classic cars. Present circulation is 59,011.
Non-fiction Publishes news, features, events listings, road tests and review articles.
Tips The magazine covers all classic cars between the 1930s to the 1980s.

Practical Fishkeeping

Bretton Court, Bretton, Peterborough, PE3 8DZ
- 01733 264666
- 01733 465246
- karen.youngs@bauermedia.com
- www.practicalfishkeeping.co.uk

Parent Company Bauer Consumer Media
Editor Karen Young
Contact Sub-Editor, Sandra Pearce; Art Editor, Rachel Thickpenny
Established 1981
Insider Info A four-weekly consumer magazine covering fishkeeping. Present circulation is 15,466.
Non-fiction Publishes news, photo features and how-to articles.
Tips *Practical Fishkeeping* covers all aspects of keeping fish, both inside and outside, including tropical fish, marine fish, cold water fish, pond fish, reefkeeping and water gardening.

Practical Parenting

15–18 White Lion Street, Islington, London, N1 7PD
- 020 3148 5000
- 020 7261 6542
- www.practicalparenting.co.uk

Parent Company Magicalia Ltd
Editor Susie Boon
Contact Features Assistant, Cassandra Roberts
Established 1987

Insider Info A monthly consumer magazine, covering parenthood. Present circulation of 35,844. Accepts query via mail and email. Media packs available online.
Non-fiction Publishes how-to, features and parenting/childcare articles.
Submission Guidelines Accepts query with complete manuscript. Articles must be between 750 and 3,000 words.
Tips Aimed at pregnant women and mums with children aged 0–5. Interested in long feature articles or shorter viewpoint pieces, written in the existing style of the magazine.

Practical Photography
Bretton Court, Bretton, Peterborough, PE3 8DZ
- 01733 264666
- 01733 465246
- practical.photography@bauermedia.com
- www.practicalphotography.co.uk

Parent Company Bauer Consumer Media
Editor Andrew James
Contact Deputy Editor, Shane Collins; Features Editor, Ben Hawkins; Techniques Editor, Chris Rutter; Art Editor, Rob Holmes
Insider Info A monthly consumer magazine covering photography. Present circulation is 62,303.
Non-fiction Publishes photo features, how-to, tutorials, buying and selling guides and product reviews.
Tips *Practical Photography* is a monthly magazine that covers all aspects of photography, including equipment tests and reviews, showcase articles, and tutorials and guidance.

Prediction
Blue Fin Building, 110 Southwark Street, London, SE1 0SU
- 020 3148 5000
- marion_williamson@ipcmedia.com
- predictionfeatures@ipcmedia.com
- www.predictionmagazine.com

Parent Company IPC Media Ltd
Editor Marion Williamson
Established 1936
Insider Info A monthly consumer magazine, covering astrology. Present circulation of 13,718. Average lead time is four months and payment is on publication. A byline is given and the publication is copyrighted. All rights are purchased on accepted material. Seasonal material must be submitted four months in advance. Accepts queries via mail or email. Aims to report back on manuscripts within six weeks. Writer's guidelines available with SAE, or online. Media packs available online.

Non-fiction Publishes features, general interest, astrology and mind/body/spirit articles.
Submission Guidelines Accepts query with complete manuscript. Maximum length for articles is 3,000 words.
Tips *Prediction* is Britain's original mind, body and spirit magazine, and contains information on angels, the meaning of dreams, the tarot, holistic healing and more. Articles should be aimed at benefiting women, and should be optimistic, light, practical or problem solving, with a humorous tone where it suits. Articles must be written in the second person if possible, as the magazine likes to talk to its readers directly.

Pregnancy & Birth
Endeavour House, 189 Shaftesbury Avenue, London, WC2H 8JG
- 020 7295 5563
- sarah.hart@bauermedia.com
- www.askamum.co.uk

Parent Company Bauer Consumer Media
Editor Katy Holland (Acting Editor)
Contact Acting Deputy Editor, Anne-Marie O'Leary; Picture Editor, Deborah Roberts
Insider Info A monthly consumer magazine covering pregnancy, birth and childcare. Present circulation is 44,466.
Non-fiction Publishes features, tips, product reviews and advice articles.
Tips Prints articles on maternity fashion, health and products that are aimed at expectant mothers.

Premonitions
13 Hazely Combe, Arreton, Isle of Wight, PO30 3AJ
- 01983 865668
- mail@pigasuspress.co.uk
- www.pigasuspress.co.uk

Parent Company Pigasus Press
Editor Tony Lee
Established 1992
Insider Info An annual consumer magazine, covering science fiction, fantasy and horror. 100 per cent of the magazine is written by freelance writers. Average lead time is eighteen months. Payment is on publication. A byline is given and the publication is copyrighted. Purchases first UK serial rights on accepted material. Accepts query by mail and email. Aims to report back on queries within two weeks and manuscripts within six weeks. The company does not pay with contributor copies, or other premiums and will pay the expenses of the writer on assignment. A sample copy and writer's guidelines are available to order from the website.

Fiction Publishes fiction, horror, science fiction and fantasy pieces.

* Purchases twelve manuscripts per year. Will pay £5 per 1,000 words, plus one contributor copy.

Submission Guidelines Send complete manuscript. Special instructions are as follows: for horror writing, there must be no serial killers; mystery writing must have science fiction content; and fantasy writing must contain no sorcery.

Poetry Publishes avant-garde, free verse, light verse and science fiction poetry.

Submission Guidelines A maximum of six poems can be submitted at one time and poems must be between five and 100 lines. Not interested in non-genre poetry.

Tips *Premonitions* is genre writing magazine that publishes horror, fantasy and science fiction short stories, genre poetry and artwork. Also publishes graphic poetry, in a graphic novel style. The main aim of *Premonitions* is to bridge the British horror and science fiction fields, without compromising the quality of the writing.

Press Gazette
14–16 Underwood Street, London, N1 7JQ

- 020 7324 2385
- 020 7566 5777
- www.pressgazette.co.uk

Parent Company Wilmington Media
Editor Dominic Ponsford
Established 1965

Insider Info A weekly consumer magazine that covers journalism and the media. Accepts queries by mail or email.

Non-fiction Interested in news and feature articles related to the media and journalism industry.

Submission Guidelines Accepts queries and completed manuscript submissions of up to 1,200 words.

Pretext
School of Literature and Creative Writing, University of East Anglia, Norwich, Norfolk, NR4 7TJ

- 01603 592783
- 01603 507728
- info@penandinc.co.uk

Parent Company Pen & Inc Press
Editor Katri Skala
Established 1999

Insider Info A consumer magazine, publishing two issues per year and covering general literary interest. Current circulation of 800. A byline is given. Accepts queries via mail and email, and reports back on queries and manuscripts within two months. Writer's guidelines available online.

Non-fiction Publishes essays, poetry articles and features.

Submission Guidelines Accepts queries.

Fiction Publishes mainstream short stories.

* Will pay a maximum of £50 for fiction.

Submission Guidelines Send complete manuscript with SAE. Maximum word length for articles is 6,000 words.

Poetry Publishes avant-garde, free verse and light verse poetry.

Submission Guidelines A maximum of five poems can be submitted at one time. Accepts postal submissions with SAE.

Tips *Pretext* is an international literary magazine that publishes new fiction, poetry and literary essays from new and established writers. The magazine aims to encourage new writers by championing the best of contemporary literature and opening new channels for short stories.

Prima
National Magazine House, 72 Broadwick Street, London, W1F 9EP

- 020 7312 4114
- 020 7439 4100
- prima@natmags.co.uk
- www.prima.co.uk

Parent Company National Magazine Company Ltd
Editor Maire Fahey
Established 1986

Insider Info A monthly consumer magazine covering women's lifestyle topics. Present Circulation of 282,544. Media pack available online.

Non-fiction Publishes general interest features, interviews and photo features on television, real life, fashion, beauty, craft, celebrities, food, cookery, travel, home, health and entertainment.

Tips Aimed at women aged 25–45 with a warm, supportive tone, and what is described as a 'modern' point of view.

Printing World
174 Hammersmith Road, London, W6 7JP

- 020 8267 4552
- 020 8267 4455
- printingworld.editorial@haymarket.com
- www.dotprint.com

Parent Company Haymarket Publishing
Editor Barney Cox
Established 1878

Insider Info A monthly consumer magazine that covers all aspects of the global printing industry. Accepts queries by mail or email. Present circulation is 10,142.

Tips Articles are generally fairly business orientated.

Private Eye

6 Carlisle Street, London, W1D 3BN

- 020 7437 4017
- 020 7347 0705
- strobes@private-eye.co.uk
- www.private-eye.co.uk

Parent Company Pressdram Ltd
Editor Ian Hislop
Established 1961
Insider Info A bi-weekly consumer magazine covering current affairs and political satire. Present circulation is 205,231.
Non-fiction Publishes news, political satire, investigative journalism, gossip and jokes.
Tips *Private Eye* covers current affairs and politics with a well-known satirical slant.

Procycling

2 Balcombe Street, London, NW1 6NW

- 020 7042 4000
- procycling@futurenet.co.uk
- www.procycling.com

Parent Company Future Publishing Ltd
Editor Peter Cossins
Contact Deputy Editor, Ellis Bacon
Insider Info A monthly consumer magazine covering international cycling. Present circulation is 30,000.
Non-fiction Publishes features, interviews, news and product reviews.
Tips *Procycling* covers all aspects of professional cycling sports, both in the UK and overseas. The magazine is aimed at enthusiasts and regularly publishes readers' letters.

Product

PO Box 23071, Edinburgh, EH7 5GT

- 0141 332 3738
- 0141 332 3738
- info@productmagazine.co.uk
- www.productmagazine.co.uk

Parent Company Red Herring Arts and Media Ltd
Editor Chris Small
Established 1999
Insider Info A quarterly consumer magazine, covering Scottish literary interests.
Non-fiction Publishes photo features, poetry articles, features, general interest articles, opinions (excluding letters to the Editor) and literary criticism.
Fiction Publishes mainstream short stories.
Submission Guidelines Accepts queries.
Poetry Publishes free verse and traditional poetry.
Tips *Product* is an independent magazine established to promote the work of Scottish writers and artists. It aims to cover ground breaking ideas missed by the mainstream media. They accept submissions for fiction and poetry, as well as feature articles about counter-culture, or other ideas and events.

Professional Electrician

The Business Magazine for the Electrical Trade
Regal House, Regal Way, Watford, Hertfordshire, WD24 4YF

- 01923 237799
- 01923 246901
- pe@hamerville.co.uk
- www.hamerville.co.uk

Parent Company Hamerville Magazines
Editor Jonathan Cole
Contact Managing Editor, Terry Smith; Editor, Jonathan Cole
Established 1984
Insider Info A monthly trade magazine. Present circulation of 68,600. Five per cent of the publication is written by freelance writers. Will pay on publication. A byline is sometimes given. Editorial lead time is two months. Accepts queries by mail, and editorial catalogues are free on request.
Non-fiction Publishes features and technical articles on electrics and electricians.

Prospect

2 Bloomsbury Place, London, WC1A 2QA

- 020 7255 1281
- 020 7255 1279
- editorial@prospect-magazine.co.uk
- www.prospect-magazine.co.uk

Parent Company Prospect Publishing Ltd
Editor David Goodhart
Contact Senior Editor, James Crabtree; Arts & Books Editor, Tom Chatfield; Assistant Editor, Mary Fitzgerald
Established 1995
Insider Info A monthly consumer magazine, covering domestic news and current affairs, with a current circulation of 27,522. Will pay up to six weeks after publication. The publication will sometimes pay pay the expenses of writers on assignment (limit agreed upon in advance). A byline is given and the magazine is copyrighted. Will accept simultaneous submissions and aims to report on manuscripts within three months. Accepts query by mail, fax and email. For writer's guidelines or email queries, email: submissions@prospect-magazine.co.uk
Non-fiction Publishes book excerpts, essays, humour, exposé, features, interviews/profiles, reviews, general interest, opinions (excluding letters to the Editor) and personal experience articles.
Submission Guidelines Contact submissions@prospect-magazine.co.uk for submission guidelines. Articles should be between 3,000 and 6,000 words

Fiction Publishes short fiction.

Tips *Prospect* aims to be 'more readable than the *Economist*, more relevant than the *Spectator*, more romantic than the *New Statesman*.' The short story content is generally specially commissioned from well-known authors such as Margaret Atwood, Michel Faber and Ali Smith, therefore the fiction side of the magazine can be very tough get in to.

PSM 3
30 Monmouth Street, Bath, BA1 2BW

📞 01225 442244

📠 01225 732384

📧 daniel.dawkins@futurenet.co.uk

🌐 www.computerandvideogames.com/sites/psm

Parent Company Future Publishing Ltd

Editor Daniel Dawkins

Insider Info A monthly consumer magazine covering PlayStation gaming. Present circulation is 31,235.

Non-fiction Publishes photo feature, news, reviews and walkthrough articles.

Tips *PSM 3* covers the latest developments in PlayStation gaming. Formerly *PSM 2*, the magazine has evolved with the recent release of the PlayStation 3 and now almost exclusively covers this particular console.

Pulsar Poetry Magazine
34 Lineacre, Grange Park, Swindon, Wiltshire, SN5 6DA

📧 pulsar.ed@btopenworld.com

🌐 www.pulsarpoetry.com

Editor David Pike

Established 1994

Insider Info A consumer magazine, publishing two issues per year (in March and September) and covering general poetry interests. Present circulation of 400. A byline is given. Accepts queries via mail and email.

Non-fiction Publishes poetry articles, features and reviews.

Submission Guidelines Accepts queries.

Poetry Publishes avant-garde, free verse, light verse and traditional poetry.

* Will pay for assigned poetry with a contributor copy.

Submission Guidelines A maximum of six poems can be submitted at any one time.

Tips *Pulsar* is a small literary magazine that publishes new poetry from anyone and anywhere in the world. It also prints book and event reviews and is often fully illustrated. *Pulsar* looks for well-written submissions, which are 'thought provoking and hard-hitting poems which have something interesting to say.'

Pulse
Ludgate House, 245 Blackfriars Road, London, SE1 9UY

📞 020 7921 8102

📠 020 7921 8133

📧 pulse@cmpmedica.com

🌐 www.pulse-i.co.uk

Parent Company CMPMedica

Editor Jo Haynes

Contact Publisher, Phil Johnson; News Editor, Ian Quinn

Insider Info A weekly consumer newspaper, covering medical information. Present circulation is 41,000. Two per cent of the publication is written by freelance writers. Will take up to 12 months to publish a manuscript after it has been accepted. Will pay on publication, sometimes pays the expenses of writers on assignment (limit agreed upon in advance). A byline is given and the publication is copyrighted. Will purchase all rights on accepted material. Editorial lead time is six months and seasonal material must be submitted six months in advance. Accepts queries by mail, email, fax and phone. Simultaneous submissions and previously published submissions will be accepted. Sample copies and writer's guidelines are available free on request. For an editorial calender, contact Julia Mcnamara on 020 7921 8120.

Non-fiction Publishes photo features, inspirational, features, interviews/profiles, reviews, technical, general interest and personal experience articles.

Submission Guidelines Contact John Robinson, News Editor, for more information.

Images Contact Picture Editor, Marie-Louise Collard for photos.

* Negotiates payment individually on photos and all rights will be purchased.

Tips *Pulse* is the leading GPs' newspaper.

Purple Patch
25 Griffiths Road, West Bromwich, B71 2EH

📧 geoff@purplepatchpoetry.co.uk

🌐 www.purplepatchpoetry.co.uk

Editor Geoff Stevens

Established 1976

Insider Info A consumer magazine, publishing three issues per year, and covering literary and poetry interests. A byline is given. Accepts queries via mail and email.

Poetry Publishes avant-garde, free verse, haiku, light verse and traditional poetry.

Tips *Purple Patch* is a long running literary magazine that publishes poetry from anyone, anywhere in the world. The magazine usually accepts open submissions of any kind of poetry, but will occasionally have a themed issue, which would be announced in the previous issue.

Q

Mappin House, 4 Winsley Street, London, W1W 8HF
☎ 020 7436 1515
📠 020 7182 5457
✉ paul.rees@qthemusic.com
🌐 www.qthemusic.com
Parent Company Bauer Consumer Media
Editor Paul Rees
Contact Senior Editor, Matt Mason; Deputy Editor, Gareth Grundy; Associate Editor (Features), Dave Everley; Associate Editor (News), Luke Lewis; Associate Editor (Reviews), Ted Kessler; Picture Director, Russ O'Connell; Picture Editor, Stephen Peck; Editorial Assistant, Nasarene Asghar
Established 1986
Insider Info A monthly consumer magazine covering contemporary music. Present circulation is 113,174.
Non-fiction Publishes news, interviews, features, tour dates, and event listings and reviews.

Quattrocento

'Bodnant', 10 Llwynnon Gardens, Llandudno, Conwy, LL30 2HP
✉ peter@quattrocento.co.uk
🌐 www.quattrocento.co.uk
Editor Malcolm Bradley
Established 2004
Insider Info A consumer magazine, publishing two issues per year (April and October), covering poetry and the arts. 100 per cent of the publication is written by freelance writers. A byline is given. Accepts queries via mail and email. Writer's guidelines available online and free on request. Sample copies and editorial calenders available free on request.
Non-fiction Publishes photo features, essays, memoirs and poetry.
Submission Guidelines Send complete manuscript. Articles should be between 2,000 and 3,000 words.
Fiction Publishes mainstream fiction.
Submission Guidelines Send complete manuscript.
Submission Guidelines Short stories must be a maximum of 3,000 words. For fiction, contact Editor, Malcolm Bradley.
Poetry Publishes avant-garde, free verse, light verse, experimental, haiku and traditional poetry.
* Will pay for assigned poetry with a contributor copy.

Submission Guidelines Poems should be a maximum of 150 lines. Contact Editor, Malcolm Bradley.
Tips *Quattrocento* is Welsh literary magazine with an international readership. The magazine publishes poetry and prose writing with a particular interest in supporting new writers and experimental writing. The magazine is is keen to receive submissions of risk taking, experimental poetry, providing they are artistically successful and are suitable for small-press production.

Quick & Easy Stitch & Craft

30 Monmouth Street, Bath, BA1 2BW
☎ 01225 442244
📠 01225 822793
✉ quickandeasy@futurenet.co.uk
Parent Company Future Publishing Ltd
Editor Ruth Spolton
Contact Publisher, Ursula Morgan; Art Editor, Sarah Doe; Technical Editor, Angela Poole
Established 1995
Insider Info A monthly consumer magazine covering cross stitch. Present circulation is 22,280.
Non-fiction Publishes cross stitch charts, crosswords, features, puzzles, tips and stories.
Tips *Quick & Easy Stitch & Craft* is aimed at cross stitch enthusiasts. The magazine publishes a range of practical cross stitch articles, as well as crosswords and puzzles. It also publishes occasional stories from contributors.

Quid

70a Cranwich Road, London, N16 5JD
☎ 020 7502 0906
✉ info@barquepress.com
🌐 www.barquepress.com
Parent Company Barque Press
Editor Dr. Keston Sutherland
Established 1995
Insider Info A consumer journal, covering literary interests, particularly poetry. Frequency of publication varies. A byline is given. Accepts queries via mail and email.
Non-fiction Publishes essays, poetry articles, features, reviews and opinions (excluding letters to the Editor).
Poetry Publishes avant-garde, free verse and light verse poetry.
Tips *Quid* is an occasional journal that publishes poetry, criticism, opinions, reviews and articles on poetics and writing. *Quid* has a largely modernist/post-modernist outlook. The magazine is not currently accepting unsolicited submissions and most content is sourced internally.

The Quiet Feather
St Mary's Cottage, Church Street, Dalton in Furness, Cumbria, LA15 8BA
- editors@thequietfeather.co.uk
- www.thequietfeather.co.uk

Editor Dominic Hall

Insider Info A consumer magazine covering literature. A byline is given. Accepts queries by mail and email. Manuscript guidelines are available online.

Non-fiction Interested in photo features, features, interviews/profiles, reviews, opinion, and general interest articles on poetry and prose.

Submission Guidelines Accepts complete manuscripts of up to 1,500 words.

Fiction Publishes mainstream short fiction.

Poetry Publishes contemporary, avant-garde, free verse and light verse poetry.

Images Send photos with submission, including captions.

Tips *The Quiet Feather* is an eclectic literary magazine that, as well as publishing new poetry and prose, also prints various articles and features on practically anything including music, local interest and activities so long as it is well-written, interesting and informative. The magazine is always looking for photographers, cartoonists and illustrators to tell their stories in pictures, but is often unable to reply directly to all submissions.

Racecar Engineering
Blue Fin Building, 110 Southwark Street, London, SE1 0SU
- 020 3148 5000
- racecar@ipcmedia.com
- www.racecar-engineering.com

Parent Company IPC Media Ltd
Editor Charles Armstrong-Wilson
Established 1990

Insider Info A monthly consumer magazine, covering race cars and associated sports. Present circulation of 22,000.

Non-fiction Publishes reviews, new product and technical articles.

Submission Guidelines Maximum length for articles is 3,000 words. Contact by phone or email to discuss ideas.

Tips Aims to keep pace with the latest technologies and expand the readers' knowledge of race car design and operation. Articles must contain specialist or insider knowledge about race car engineering only, no road cars.

Radio Times
Room A1179, 80 Woodlane, London, W12 0TT
- 020 8433 3400
- 020 8433 3160
- radio.times@bbc.co.uk
- www.radiotimes.com

Parent Company BBC Worldwide
Editor Gill Hudson
Contact Commissioning Editor, Terry Payne; Features Editor, Kim Newson
Established 1923

Insider Info A weekly consumer magazine covering television and radio listings and related topics. Present circulation of 1,009,028.

Non-fiction Publishes general interest features and photo features on current happenings in television and radio programmes, as well as other media.

Submission Guidelines Query with ideas for feature articles of around 600–2,500 words. Do not send entire manuscript.

Rail
Bretton Court, Bretton, Peterborough, PE3 8DZ
- 01733 264666
- 01733 282720
- rail@bauermedia.com

Parent Company Bauer Consumer Media
Contact Managing Editor, Nigel Harris

Insider Info A bi-weekly consumer magazine covering rail travel and railways. Present circulation is 21,369.

Non-fiction Publishes news, features, interviews and industry information.

Tips *Rail* covers all the latest news and information from the railway industry. It is aimed at both railway professionals and enthusiasts.

Railway Gazette International
Quadrant House, Sutton, SM2 5AS
- 020 8652 8608
- 020 8652 3738
- railway.gazette@rbl.co.uk
- www.railwaygazette.com

Parent Company Reed Business Information
Editor Chris Jackson
Established 1835

Insider Info A monthly trade magazine, covering railways. Present circulation is 9,945. Accepts queries via mail or phone.

Non-fiction Publishes photo features, features, technical and general interest articles on the railway, metro, light rail, and tram industries worldwide.

Submission Guidelines Accepts queries via post or phone before submitting ideas.

Images Send photos with submission.

Tips Features a mix of technical, commercial and geographical feature articles, plus the regular monthly news pages, covering developments in all aspects of the rail industry, including infrastructure, operations, rolling stock and signalling. Articles of a practical or technical nature are required, rather than 'material for railway enthusiast publications.'

The Railway Magazine
Blue Fin Building, 110 Southwark Street, London, SE1 0SU
- 020 3148 5000
- nick_pigott@ipcmedia.com
- www.railwaymagazine.co.uk

Parent Company IPC Media Ltd
Editor Nick Pigott
Established 1897
Insider Info Monthly consumer magazine covering railways. Present circulation is 34,661. Accepts queries by mail and email.
Non-fiction Interested in photo features, interviews/profiles, technical, general interest and historical/nostalgic articles.
Submission Guidelines Accepts complete manuscripts up to 2,000 words.
Tips Covers all aspects of the scene from steam through to modern rail developments. It seeks articles, ideally with photos, covering modern railways, or steam preservation and railway history.

Railway Modeller
Underleys, Beer, Seaton, EX12 3NA
- 01297 20580
- 01297 20229
- railway-modeller@btconnect.com
- www.peco-uk.com

Parent Company Peco Publications & Publicity Ltd
Editor Steve Flint
Contact Production Editor, Tim Rayner
Established 1949
Insider Info A monthly consumer magazine covering railway models. Present circulation is 44,607.
Non-fiction Publishes features, reviews, trade reports, design and historical articles.
Tips *Railway Modeller* covers mainly small-scale railway modelling for the hobbyist.

Rain Dog
PO Box 68, Manchester, M19 2XD
- rd_poetry@yahoo.com
- www.panshinepress.co.uk

Parent Company Panshine Press
Editor Suzanne Batty, Jan Whalen
Established 2000
Insider Info A consumer magazine, publishing two issues per year and covering literary interests, particularly poetry. 100 per cent of the publication is written by freelance writers. A byline is given.

Accepts query via mail and email. Writer's guidelines are available online.
Poetry Publishes avant-garde, free verse, light verse and traditional poetry.
* Will pay for assigned poetry with a contributor copy.
Submission Guidelines A maximum of five poems can be submitted at one time.
Tips *Rain Dog* is a creative writing magazine that publishes contemporary poetry from both new and established writers. It offers book vouchers as prizes for the top selected poems each issue. The magazine welcomes submissions of poetry that are exciting, moving, inspiring or honest, and in particular are looking for submissions from women poets whom they feel to be generally under-represented in the small press poetry world.

Rare Book Review
24 Maddox Street, London, W1S 1PP
- 020 7495 9499
- 020 7529 4229
- editor@rarebookreview.com
- www.rarebookreview.com

Parent Company Countrywide Editions Ltd
Editor Jeff Hudson
Established 1974
Insider Info A bimonthly trade journal covering literary and book collecting topics. Accepts queries via mail and email.
Non-fiction Publishes photo features, features, interviews/profiles, reviews and general interest and historical/nostalgic articles on rare book collecting.
Submission Guidelines Accepts queries.
Tips The magazine plans to increase coverage of the book collecting scene in Europe, Asia and the United States. Articles about collections, or collectors abroad may be advisable.

Raw Edge
PO Box 4867, Birmingham, B3 3HD
- raw_edgemag@yahoo.co.uk
- www.lit-net.org/remhp.htm

Parent Company The Moving Finger Press
Editor Dave Reeves
Established 1995
Insider Info A consumer magazine, publishing two issues per year and covering literary interests in the West Midlands. A byline is given. Accepts queries via mail and email. Sample copy available online.
Non-fiction Publishes poetry articles, features, interviews/profiles, reviews and news articles.
Submission Guidelines Accepts queries.
Fiction Publishes mainstream fiction.
Poetry Publishes avant-garde, free verse, light verse and traditional poetry.

Tips *Raw Edge* is distributed through libraries and arts outlets, as well as by post, for the West Midlands. As such it only excepts submissions from writers in this area.

Raw Vision
International Journal of Outsider Art
1 Watford Road, Radlett, Hertfordshire, WD7 8LA
- 01923 856644
- 01923 859897
- info@rawvision.com
- rawvision.com

Parent Company Raw Vision Ltd
Editor John Maizels
Insider Info A quarterly magazine, covering outsider art, visionary art and contemporary folk art. Present circulation is 10,000. 50 per cent of the publication is written by freelance writers. Editorial lead time is three months and seasonal material must be submitted two months in advance. Will pay on publication. A byline is given and the publication is not copyrighted. Will buy one time rights on accepted material. Accepts queries via mail, email, fax, and phone. Simultaneous submissions and previously published submissions will be accepted. Aims to report back on queries within two weeks, on manuscripts within one months. Sample copies available with SAE, and writer's guidelines available free on request and via email. Editorial calendars are available via email.
Non-fiction Publishes articles, news and reviews on 'outsider art'.
Tips The 'outsider art' school consists of people untrained and uninfluenced by the art world who invent their own forms, techniques and create private worlds. This is a fairly niche area and writers should have in depth knowledge of this unusual topic.

The Reader
19 Abercromby Square, Liverpool, L69 7ZG
- 0151 794 2830
- readers@liv.ac.uk
- www.thereader.co.uk

Editor Jane Davis
Established 1997
Insider Info Quarterly consumer magazine covering poetry and literature. Byline is given. Accepts queries by mail and email. Manuscript guidelines are available online.
Non-fiction Interested in literary essays, features, interviews/profiles, reviews and articles on poetry and prose.
Submission Guidelines Accepts complete manuscript of between 1,500 and 4,000 words by post only.

Fiction Publishes mainstream short fiction.
Submission Guidelines Accepts complete manuscript of between 2,000 and 2,500 words by post only.
Poetry Publishes contemporary, free verse, light verse and traditional poetry.
Submission Guidelines Accepts sample poems by post only.
Tips *The Reader* publishes some new poetry and short fiction, along with book reviews, interviews and articles on writers, writing, and reading. It welcomes submissions for short fiction and poetry, as well as for non-fiction articles. Submissions for short fiction greatly outnumber those of non-fiction, despite only making up 25 per cent of the magazine.

Reader's Digest
11 Westferry Circus, Canary Wharf, London, E14 4HE
- 020 7715 8000
- 020 7715 8716
- theeditor@readersdigest.co.uk
- www.readersdigest.co.uk

Parent Company Reader's Digest Association Ltd
Contact Acting Editor in Chief, Simon Hartley; Publisher, Victoria Scott; Books Editor, Rachel Warren Chad
Established 1938
Insider Info A monthly consumer magazine covering general interest and lifestyle issues. Present circulation is 638,693. All rights purchased. Does not accept previously published submissions.
Non-fiction Publishes features, advice, reviews and real life stories.
* Payment for fiction is £100.
Submission Guidelines Send complete manuscript by post or email.
Fillers Publishes end-of-article fillers as well as regular sections 'Laughter' and 'The Best Medicine' for which short contributions are sought.
* Pays up to £60 for filler articles.
Submission Guidelines Send complete manuscript by post or email.
Tips *Reader's Digest* covers universal interest topics and advice such as articles on health, beauty, dieting, finance, entertainment, science and inspiration. Any true-life submissions should be previously unpublished stories that deal with adult human nature, ideally humorous in tone.

Read The Music
25 Griffiths Road, West Bromwich, B71 2EH
- 0121 556 9304
- admin@poetrywednesbury.co.uk
- www.poetrywednesbury.co.uk

Parent Company Poetry Wednesbury

Editor Brendan Hawthorne
Insider Info A consumer magazine, featuring poetry influenced by music.
Poetry Publishes free verse, light verse and traditional poetry.
Submission Guidelines Accepts sample poems with SAE.
Tips *Read The Music* publishes poetry submissions inspired by music and its influences. The magazine is always looking for submissions of music themed poetry.

Real
The Tower, Phoenix Square, Colchester, Essex, CO4 9HU
- 01206 851117
- 01206 849079

Parent Company Essential Publishing
Editor David Claridge
Established 2001
Insider Info A monthly consumer magazine that covers women's health and lifestyle. Accepts queries by mail or email.
Non-fiction Interested in health, beauty, fashion, relationships, celebrity interest and lifestyle articles.
Submission Guidelines Accepts queries and proposals.
Tips *Real* is aimed at women aged between 25 and 40.

Real Business Magazine
198 King's Road, London, SW3 5XP
- 020 7368 7189
- editors@realbusiness.co.uk
- www.realbusiness.co.uk

Parent Company Caspian Publishing
Contact Managing Editor, Kate Pritchard, Deputy Editor, Charles Orton-Jones
Established 1997
Insider Info A B2B monthly magazine, covering entrepreneurs and fast-growth SMEs. Ten per cent of the publication is written by freelance writers. A byline is given and the publication is copyrighted. Accepts queries via email and phone. Sample copies and writer's guidelines are available free on request. Present circulation is 40,982.
Non-fiction Publishes how-to, interviews/profiles and opinion articles (excluding letters to the Editor).
Submission Guidelines Contact Online Editor, Dan Matthews, for information.
Images State availability of photos with submission.
Submission Guidelines Contact Art Director, Erroll Jones for photos.

Real Homes
64 North Row, London, W1K 7LL
- 020 7150 7000
- 020 7150 7001
- lisa.mcfarlane@hf-uk.com
- www.hf-uk.com

Parent Company Hachette Filipacchi (UK) Ltd
Editor Ben Spriggs
Contact Picture Editor, Claire Riordan
Established 1998
Insider Info A monthly consumer magazine covering homes and lifestyle. Present circulation is 70,559.
Non-fiction Publishes features and showcase articles on real-life homes, interior design, decorating and renovating, homes abroad, and general lifestyle tips.

Real People
33 Broadwick Street, London, W1F 0DQ
- 020 7339 4570
- 020 7339 4527
- features@realpeoplemag.co.uk
- www.realpeoplemag.co.uk

Parent Company ACP-NatMag
Editor Sam Taylor
Contact Art Director, Barry Nunn; Features Editor, Lucy Welsh
Established 2006
Insider Info A weekly consumer magazine covering women's interests and real-life stories. Present circulation is 230,135.
Non-fiction Publishes features, profiles, interviews, advice and true-life stories.
* Payment for true-life stories is up to £500.
Submission Guidelines Accepts complete manuscripts for true-life stories by post or email.
Tips *Real People* is a weekly women's interest magazine that specialises in true-life stories from real readers. The stories can be happy, sad, funny or shocking as long as they are based on real events. It also publishes features on health, beauty, fashion and advice.

The Reater
24 Cavendish Square, Hull, East Yorkshire, HU3 1SS
- 01430 424346
- editor@wreckingballpress.com
- www.wreckingballpress.com/html/reater.php

Parent Company Wrecking Ball Press
Editor Shane Rhodes
Established 1997
Insider Info Annual consumer magazine covering contemporary poetry, prose and photography.

Present circulation is 800. Byline is given. Accepts queries by mail and email.

Non-fiction Interested in features and articles on poetry and literature.

Submission Guidelines Accepts queries in the first instance.

Fiction Publishes contemporary short fiction.

Poetry Publishes contemporary, avant-garde, free verse and light verse poetry.

Submission Guidelines Submit up to six poems.

Tips *The Reater* publishes new poetry and prose, primarily from Yorkshire writers, but also from further afield. The magazine also prints illustrations and photographs. *The Reater's* editorial stance is as follows: 'Strictly no flowers, just blunt hammered-home words.' Submissions should be hard-hitting and direct.

Record Collector

Serious About Music

Room 101, The Perfume Factory, 140 Wales Farm Road, London, W3 6UG

📞 0870 732 8080

📠 0870 737 6060

✉ alan.lewis@metropolis.co.uk

🌐 www.recordcollectormag.com

Parent Company Diamond Publishing Ltd

Editor Alan Lewis

Established 1979

Insider Info A monthly consumer magazine, covering popular music from 1950 to the present, especially focusing on classic, rare and reissued records. Present circulation is over 30,000. *Record Collector* is the longest established monthly music magazine in the UK and is respected worldwide by serious collectors of popular music across all genres. 80 per cent of the publication is written by freelance writers. Editorial lead time is one month and seasonal material must be submitted two months in advance. Will pay on publication and the kill fee for for assigned manuscripts not published is 50 per cent. A byline is given and the publication is copyrighted. Will purchase all rights on accepted material. Accepts queries via email. Simultaneous submissions and previously published submissions will be accepted. Aims to report back on queries within two days and manuscripts within one week. The publication will not pay writers with contributor copies or other premiums other than a cash payment. They will sometimes pay the advances of writers on assignment (limit agreed upon in advance). They send out sample copies to selected contacts via email. Writer's guidelines and editorial calenders available via email. Media packs available on www.recordcollectormag.com

Non-fiction Publishes book excerpts, how-to, essays, humour, features, interviews/profiles,

reviews, new product, technical, opinion (excluding letters to the Editor), personal experience, illustrated discographies articles, and items about rare records and interesting sales of records on eBay.

* Purchases 100 non-fiction articles from freelance writers every year. Will pay between £50 and £1,000 for assigned articles and approximately 8p per word for unsolicited articles.

Submission Guidelines Accepts query (including published clips). Articles can be up to 10,000 words in length (send photocopies). Contact Alan Lewis, Editor, for more information.

Images Accepts images with submission.

* Will negotiate payment individually and will purchase one-time rights on photos.

Submission Guidelines Reviews gif/jpeg files and requires identification of subjects. Freelancers must state availability of photos with submission. Contact Editor, Alan Lewis, for more information.

Columns Regularly publishes reviews of CDs, DVDs and books.

* Purchases 2,000 columns per year and pays between £10 and £50.

Submission Guidelines Accepts query (including published clips). Contact Reviews Editor, Jason Draper for columns.

Tips *Record Collector* covers popular music of all genres from 1950 to the present. In particular it celebrates collectable, rare and classic records with in-depth interviews, discographies and coverage of reissued albums on CD, vinyl and download.

Red

64 North Row, London, W1K 7LL

📞 020 7150 7600

📠 020 7150 7684

✉ gabriellenathan@hf-uk.com

🌐 www.redmagazine.co.uk

Parent Company Hachette Filipacchi

Editor Sam Baker

Contact Health Director, Brigid Moss; Features Assistant, Gabrielle Nathan

Established 1998

Insider Info A monthly consumer magazine covering women's interests, lifestyle and fashion. Present circulation of 220,804. Accepts queries via mail.

Non-fiction Publishes humour, features and interviews/profile articles on fashion, beauty, real life and other women's lifestyle topics.

Submission Guidelines Send complete manuscript. Maximum length for articles is 1,500 words.

Images Send photos with submission.

Tips *Red* is aimed at thirty-something women. Articles should be written in a witty and intelligent manner and targeted at stylish and independent readers with a youthful spirit.

Redline

30 Monmouth Street, Bath, BS1 2BW
- 01225 442244
- redline@futurenet.co.uk
- www.redlinemag.com

Parent Company Future Publishing Ltd
Editor Dan Lewis
Insider Info A four-weekly consumer magazine, covering tuned/modified performance cars. 40 per cent of the publication is written by freelance writers. Editorial lead time is four months and seasonal material must be submitted four months in advance. Will pay on publication. A byline is given and the magazine is copyrighted. Rights purchased can be negotiated. Accepts query via mail and email. Present circulation is 24,272.
Non-fiction Publishes photo features and technical articles on performance vehicles.

The Red Wheelbarrow

School of English, University of St Andrews, Castle House, The Scores, St Andrews, Fife, KY16 9AL
- 01334 462666
- redwheelbarrow@st-and.ac.uk
- www.st-andrews.ac.uk/~redbarrow

Established 1999
Insider Info A consumer magazine, with two issues per year, covering mainly poetry. Byline is given. Accepts queries by mail and email.
Non-fiction Interested in literary essays, features, opinions and articles on poetry.
Submission Guidelines Accepts queries in the first instance.
Poetry Publishes contemporary, free verse, light verse and traditional poetry.
Submission Guidelines Accepts sample poetry.
Tips The Red Wheelbarrow publishes poetry and opinion from both amateur and professional writers, as well as articles, essays and writing related to poetry. The Red Wheelbarrow is looking for international submissions, either of contemporary poetry or related non-fiction.

reFRESH Magazine

22a Iliffe Yard, Kennington, London, SE17 3QA
- 020 7277 4517
- 020 7703 8718
- david@wildpublishing.com
- www.refreshmag.co.uk

Parent Company Wild Publishing Limited
Editor David Tickner
Contact Editorial Assistant, Dione Van Heer

Established 2002
Insider Info A bi-monthly consumer magazine, covering gay lifestyle – culture, arts, fashion, style, travel, homes and interiors, general features, business and topical issues. Present circulation of 40,000. 65 per cent of the publication is written by freelance writers. A manuscript will be published six months after it is accepted. Payment will be on publication and kill fee for assigned manuscripts not used is 50 per cent. A byline is given and the publication is copyrighted. Will purchase first rights on accepted material. Editorial lead time is eight weeks and seasonal material must be submitted ten months in advance of publication. Accepts queries via mail and email. Simultaneous submissions will be accepted. Will aim to report on queries, manuscripts and any other information within four days. The publication will not pay writers with contributor copies or other premiums other than a cash payment. They will sometimes pay the expenses of a writer on assignment (limit agreed upon in advance). Sample copies available with SAE (envelope must be 340mm length and 240mm width, and postage cost will be £3). Writer's guidelines and editorial catalogues are available free on request and media packs are available from www.refreshmag.co.uk
Non-fiction Publishes how-to, photo features, exposé, features, interviews/profiles, reviews, general interest, opinion (excluding letters to the Editor) and travel articles.
* Will pay a minimum of £200 for assigned articles.
Submission Guidelines Articles must be between 500 and 1,500 words in length. Contact Editor in Chief, David Tickner, for more information.
Images Accepts images with submission.
* Offers no additional payment for photos accepted with manuscripts. Will negotiate payment individually, depending on the situation.
Submission Guidelines Requires captions and model releases and freelancers must state availability of photos with submission. Contact Editor in Chief, David Tickner for photos.
Tips Presented in a coffee table style format, reFRESH is the only gay lifestyle magazine on the newsstand that does not contain any adult content. The magazine's core audience ranges from 18 to 55.

The Renault Magazine

Westgate, 120–128 Station Road, Redhill, RH1 1ET
- 01737 786800
- 01737 786801
- ann.wallace@brooklandsgroup.com
- www.brooklandsgroup.com/magazines/renault-magazine/index.html

Parent Company Brooklands Group Ltd (Publishers)

Contact Editorial Director, Ann Wallace; Creative Director, Kevin Ingles; Publishing Editor, Darren Styles
Established 1962
Insider Info A consumer magazine, with three issues per year, covering Renault vehicles. Present circulation is 212,117. Media pack is available online.
Non-fiction Publishes features, product and part reviews and technical articles.
Tips *Renault Magazine* covers all aspects of owning and maintaining Renault cars and commercial vehicles. It covers a range of subjects, including practical and technical maintenance articles, as well as travel, lifestyle and leisure activity features.

Resurgence
Ford House, Hartland, Bideford, Devon, EX39 6EE
- 01237 441293
- 01237 441203
- editorial@resurgence.org
- www.resurgence.org
Editor Satish Kumar
Contact Co-Editor, Lorna Howarth
Established 1966
Insider Info A bi-monthly consumer magazine, covering ecology, the environment, the arts and spirituality with a literary slant. Present circulation of 30,000. Accepts queries via mail and email. Aims to report back on queries and manuscripts within one month. Writer's guidelines available online.
Non-fiction Publishes photo features, essays, humour, poetry, features, interviews/profiles, reviews, general interest, opinion (excluding letters to the Editor), travel and historical/nostalgic articles.
Submission Guidelines Accepts queries.
Poetry Publishes free verse, light verse and traditional poetry.
Submission Guidelines Accepts sample poems.
Tips As well as the ecological content, the magazine also prints social commentaries and political articles, humour and more general articles from writers. *Resurgence* has a regular poetry page, and welcomes submissions of poetry that are in keeping with the style and content of the magazine in general.

Retail Jeweller
33–39 Bowling Green Lane, London, EC1R 0TD
- 020 7812 3725
- 020 7812 3720
- jenni.middleton@emap.com
- retail-jeweller.com
Parent Company Emap Retail Ltd
Contact Deputy Editor, Marie Dill
Established 1965

Insider Info A monthly trade magazine, covering jewellery and watches. Present circulation of 4,207. 30 per cent of the publication is written by freelance writers. Manuscripts will be published two months after they are accepted. Payment on publication. A byline is sometimes given and the publication is copyrighted. All rights will be purchased on accepted material. Editorial lead time is four months and seasonal material must be submitted three months before it is published. Accepts queries by mail, phone, fax and email to rj@fashion.emap.co.uk. Simultaneous submissions will be accepted. Aims to report back to queries within one week, and manuscripts within two weeks. Sample copies are free on request and they do not have written writer's guidelines. Editorial calendars are on a person-by-person basis.
Non-fiction Publishes how-to, features, interviews/profiles, reviews and new product articles.
Tips *Retail Jeweller* is a monthly B2B magazine published by Emap for retailers in the jewellery and watch industry. Its mission is to help retailers sell more watches and jewellery.

Retail Week
Greater London House, Hampstead Road, London, NW1 7EJ
- 020 7728 5000
- tim.danaher@emap.com
- www.retail-week.com
Parent Company EMAP Retail Ltd
Editor Tim Danaher
Contact Features Editor, Charlotte Dennis-Jones
Established 1988
Insider Info A weekly trade magazine covering retailing, with a present circulation of 10,197.
Non-fiction Publishes features and business news.
Submission Guidelines Maximum length for articles is 1,000 words.
Images Send photos with submission.
Tips *Retail Week* is very clearly focused on the marketing and retail management industry, and therefore insider or specialist knowledge is definitely required in any submitted article.

Retail World
33–39 Bowling Green Lane, London, EC1R 0DA
- 020 7505 8000
- 020 7520 3503
- tim.danager@emap.com
- www.retail-world.com
Parent Company EMAP Plc
Editor Tim Danaher
Contact Publisher, Tessa Cook; Art Editor, Michael Sullivan
Established 2003

Insider Info A quarterly trade journal covering the retail industry. Present circulation is 15,500.

Non-fiction Publishes news, features and industry information.

Tips *Retail World* is the sister publication to *Retail Week* and covers international retail strategy. It is aimed at leading European retailers.

Reveal

National Magazine House, 33 Broadwick Street, London, W1F 0DQ

- 020 7339 4534
- 020 7339 4529
- jennifer.dunkerley@natmag.co.uk
- www.natmags.co.uk

Parent Company National Magazine Company Ltd

Editor Michael Butcher

Contact Features Editor, Ashling McCoy; Deputy Features Editor, Su Karney; Editorial Assistant/Work Experience Liason, Jennifer Dunkerley

Established 2004

Insider Info A weekly consumer magazine covering celebrity gossip and women's lifestyle topics. Present Circulation of 277,002. Media pack is available online.

Non-fiction Publishes general interest features, exposes, interviews and photo features on celebrities, television, real life, fashion, home, food, cookery and beauty.

Tips The title is aimed specifically at women between 25 and 45, although the readership can be younger. Most lead articles relate directly to celebrity interviews and gossip. Articles should be instantly involving, and suitable for the intended readership.

The Review

4 Algar House, Webber Row, London, SE1 8QT

- 020 7261 1134
- editor@thereview.freeserve.co.uk
- www.thereviewmagazine.com

Editor Raúl Peschiera

Established 1995

Insider Info Annual consumer magazine contemporary poetry and literature. Byline is given. Accepts queries by mail and email.

Non-fiction Interested in features, interviews/ profiles, reviews and articles on poetry and literature.

Submission Guidelines Accepts query in the first instance.

Fiction Publishes contemporary short fiction.

Submission Guidelines Accepts query in the first instance.

Poetry Publishes contemporary and translated poetry.

Submission Guidelines Accepts sample poems.

Tips *The Review* was originally based in America and Canada, but moved to the UK following publication of its fourth issue. It will accept submissions from anywhere in the world and is especially interested in literary translations and contemporary poetry.

Rhythm

30 Monmouth Street, Bath, BA1 2BW

- 01225 442244
- 01225 732353
- phil.ascott@futurenet.co.uk
- www.rhythmmag.co.uk

Parent Company Future Publishing Ltd

Editor Phil Ascott

Contact Art Editor, Kevin Lowery; Features Editor, Chris Barnes

Established 1985

Insider Info A monthly consumer magazine covering drums and percussion. Present circulation is 9,914.

Non-fiction Publishes feature, how-to, news and reviews articles.

Tips Focuses on drumming, percussion and drum programming. Articles include features on, and technique advice from, celebrity drummers.

The Rialto

PO Box 309, Aylsham, Norwich, NR11 6LN

- 01603 666455
- mail@therialto.co.uk
- www.therialto.co.uk

Editor Michael Mackmin

Established 1984

Insider Info A consumer magazine, with three issues per year, covering contemporary poetry. Present circulation is 1,500. Byline is given. Accepts queries by mail and email. Aims to respond to queries and manuscripts within ten weeks. Manuscript guidelines are available online.

Non-fiction Interested in features, reviews and articles on poetry.

Poetry Publishes contemporary, avant-garde, free verse, light verse and traditional poetry.

Submission Guidelines Submit up to six poems.

Tips *The Rialto* is a respected literary magazine that publishes the best contemporary poetry from new or established writers, as well as some literary articles and reviews. *The Rialto* receives many poetry submissions every week and it can take some time for a reply to be sent. At present they commission all articles and review content internally, and are only accepting unsolicited submissions for poetry.

RiDE

Media House, Lynchwood, Peterborough Business Park, Peterborough, PE2 6EA

☎ 01733 468081
🖷 01733 468092
✉ ride@bauermedia.com
🌐 www.ride.co.uk
Parent Company Bauer Consumer Media
Editor Colin Overland
Contact Publishing Director, Charley Davies;
Features Editor, Ben Wilkins
Established 1995
Insider Info A monthly consumer magazine
covering motorcycling. Present circulation is 50,598.
Non-fiction Publishes news, photo features,
interviews, reviews and technical articles.
Tips *RiDE* covers all aspects of motorcycling, from
product reviews and technical maintenance and
repair articles, to event reports, classified ads and a
directory of dealers and parts suppliers.

Rock Sound

**Unit 22, Jack's Place, 6 Corbet Place, London,
E1 6NN**
☎ 020 7877 8770
🖷 020 7377 0455
✉ darren.taylor@rock-sound.net
🌐 www.rock-sound.net
Parent Company Rock Sound Ltd
Editor Darren Taylor
Contact Publisher, Patrick Napier; News & Features
Editor, Darren Sadler; Reviews Editor, Rachel Kellehar
Established 1999
Insider Info A monthly consumer magazine
covering rock music. Present circulation is 22,527.
Non-fiction Publishes news, features, reviews,
interviews, profiles and event listings.
Tips *Rock Sound* covers rock, metal, indie and
alternative music. Features include the latest album
and gig reviews, interviews and insider information.
It is aimed at 15 to 25 year olds.

Rowing & Regatta

6 Lower Mall, Hammersmith, London, W6 9DJ
☎ 0870 060 7100
🖷 0870 060 7101
✉ sarah.chapman@ara-rowing.org
🌐 www.ara-rowing.org
Parent Company Amateur Rowing Association
Editor Wendy Kewley
Established 1987
Insider Info A monthly consumer magazine
covering rowing topics. Present circulation is 22,131.
Non-fiction Publishes news, features and reviews.
Tips *Rowing & Regatta* is the official magazine of the
Amateur Rowing Association and covers all aspects
of rowing news and reviews from both the UK and
internationally.

Rugby World

**Blue Fin Building, 110 Southwark Street,
London, SE1 0SU**
☎ 020 3148 5000
✉ paul_morgan@ipcmedia.com
🌐 www.rugbyworld.com
Parent Company IPC Media Ltd
Editor Paul Morgan
Established 1960
Insider Info A monthly consumer magazine,
covering rugby. Present circulation of 48,381.
Accepts query via mail and phone and media packs
available on www.ipcmedia.com/magazines/rugby.
Non-fiction Publishes features on rugby.
* Will pay a maximum of £120 for unsolicited articles.
Submission Guidelines Accepts query. Send
complete manuscript. Maximum length for articles is
1,200 words.
Images Send photos with submission.
Tips *Rugby World* is the voice of global rugby and
the biggest selling rugby magazine anywhere. Find
unusual rugby based subjects for articles, rather than
just match reports, etc. Quality photographs are also
essential.

Runner's World

33 Broadwick Street, London, W1F 0DQ
☎ 020 7339 4400
🖷 020 7339 4220
✉ editor@runnersworld.co.uk
🌐 www.runnersworld.co.uk
Parent Company Rodale Press
Editor Andy Dixon
Established 1979
Insider Info A monthly consumer magazine
covering athletics. Present circulation is 88,567.
Accepts queries by mail.
Non-fiction Publishes features, interviews/profiles,
reviews, new products and running articles.
Submission Guidelines Accepts query with
complete manuscript.
Tips *Runner's World* is the UK's largest running
magazine. It is seeking articles on famous non-
sportspeople who run, personal running articles, or
'off-beat travel articles'.

RYA Magazine

Ensign Way, Hamble, Southampton, SO31 4YA
☎ 023 8060 4100
🖷 023 8060 4293
✉ deborah.cornick@rya.org.uk
🌐 www.rya.org.uk
Parent Company Royal Yachting Association
Editor Deborah Cornick
Insider Info A quarterly consumer magazine
covering yachting. Present circulation is 90,186.

Non-fiction Publishes news, features, events and articles on regulations.

Tips *RYA Magazine* is the official magazine of the Royal Yachting Association and covers news and information from the association, as well as features on cruising, yachting, training and racing.

Sable

PO Box 33504, London, E9 7YE

● 020 8985 9419

● editorial@sablelitmag.org

● www.sablelitmag.org

Parent Company S.A.K.S. Media

Editor Dorothea Smartt

Contact Kadija Sesay

Established 2000

Insider Info A quarterly consumer magazine, covering literary interests for writers of colour. A byline is given. Accepts query by mail and email. Writer's guidelines and sample copy available online.

Non-fiction Publishes poetry articles, features, interviews/profiles and reviews.

Submission Guidelines Send complete manuscript. Maximum length for articles is 3,000 words.

Fiction Publishes mainstream fiction and novel excerpts.

Submission Guidelines No unsolicited submissions.

Submission Guidelines Accepts query. Maximum length for articles is 5,000 words.

Poetry Publishes free verse, light verse and traditional poetry.

Submission Guidelines Accepts sample poetry. A maximum of 15 poems can be submitted at one time.

Tips *Sable* is a literary magazine for writers of colour and publishes new fiction and poetry, including translations, as well as articles, interviews, reviews and information. *Sable* is not currently accepting submissions for fiction, but they are looking for poetry submissions, and reviews and essays on historical or contemporary aspects of literature/culture. Check the guidelines on the website for further details.

Saga Magazine

Saga Building, Enbrook Park, Folkestone, CT20 3SE

● 01303 771111

● 01303 776699

● editor@saga.co.uk

● www.saga.co.uk/magazine

Parent Company Saga Publishing Ltd

Editor Katy Bravery

Established 1984

Insider Info A monthly consumer magazine, covering retirement and associated lifestyle, with a present circulation of 653,657.

Submission Guidelines Articles must be between 1,000 and 1,200 words.

Non-fiction Publishes general interest non-fiction articles aimed at older readers.

Tips *Saga Magazine* sets out to celebrate the role of older people in society, reflecting their achievements, promoting their skills, protecting their interests and campaigning on their behalf. Most material is commissioned in-house. Exclusive celebrity interviews with a warm, personal approach are well received, if relevant – ideally with photos.

Sailing Today

Swanwick Marina, Lower Swanwick, Southampton, SO31 1ZL

● 01489 585225

● 01489 565054

● editor@sailingtoday.co.uk

● www.sailingtoday.co.uk

Parent Company Boat International Media Ltd

Editor Duncan Kent

Established 1997

Insider Info A monthly consumer magazine, covering sailing topics. Accepts queries via email and phone. Writer's guidelines available online.

Non-fiction Publishes photo features, features, reviews, new product, technical and travel articles.

Submission Guidelines Accepts queries.

Tips Articles cover relevant, up to date information in a concise, authoritative, yet entertaining way. The magazine would like to hear from writers who would like to share how they tackled a practical maintenance or upgrade project, have an interesting account of cruising their own boat (even if it's a small one), or an out of the ordinary tale to tell about their charter/flotilla trip.

Sainsbury's Magazine

Sea Containers House, 20 Upper Ground, London, SE1 9PD

● 020 7633 0266

● 020 7401 9423

● edit@7publishing.co.uk

● www.sainsburysmagazine.co.uk

Parent Company Seven Squared

Editor Sue Robinson

Contact Deputy Editor, Gillian Rhys

Established 1993

Insider Info A monthly consumer magazine for the customers of Sainsbury's supermarket, covering food, drink and retail issues. Present circulation of 308,175.

Non-fiction Publishes general interest articles, interviews, reviews and photo features on food, wine, new products, parenting, cookery, fashion, beauty, health and lifestyle.
Tips The magazine's readership is split roughly 70:30, women to men. A large proportion of these readers are women aged 35–44. The editorial content of the magazine is split evenly between food and drink articles and lifestyle articles.

Saltire Magazine
9 Fountain Close, 22 High Street, Edinburgh, EH1 1TF
✆ 0131 556 1836
✉ saltire@saltiresociety.org.uk
🌐 www.saltiresociety.org.uk
Parent Company The Saltire Society
Editor Michael Hance
Insider Info A consumer magazine, publishing two issues per year, covering the literary interests of the Saltire Society.
Non-fiction Publishes features, general interest and opinion articles (excluding letters to the Editor).
Tips *Saltire magazine* is published by The Saltire Society to encourage debate and discussion about cultural issues. *Saltire* does not publish any fiction or poetry, only the latest news, views and interviews from the Saltire Society.

Scarlet
Unit 503, Erico House, 93-99 Richmond Road, London, SW15 2TG
✆ 020 7835 5554
✉ editor@scarletmagazine.co.uk
🌐 www.scarletmagazine.co.uk
Parent Company Scarlet Publishing
Editor Sarah Hedley
Contact Assistant Editor, Linda McCormick; Picture Editor, Sophie Palmer
Established 2003
Insider Info A monthly middle-shelf, glossy, consumer magazine for women, with a present circulation of roughly 40,000. 70 per cent of the the publication is written by freelance writers. It takes one month to publish a manuscript after it has been accepted. Payment occurs 30 days after publication and the kill fee is 50 per cent. A byline is given and the publication is copyrighted. All rights will be purchased on accepted material. Editorial lead time is two months and seasonal material must be submitted two months in advance. Accepts queries via mail, email and phone. Simultaneous submissions will be accepted. Aims to report back on queries within two months. Sample copies are available at £2.50 per issue. Writer's guidelines are available free on request. Editorial calenders are

available for cost and media packs are available online.
Non-fiction Publishes how-to, photo features, humour, exposé, inspirational pieces, features, interviews/profiles, new product pieces, general interest lifestyle articles, opinion (excluding letters to the Editor), historical/nostalgic and personal experience articles.
Submission Guidelines Contact Assistant Editor, Linda McCormick, for more information.
Fiction Publishes erotica.
Submission Guidelines Contact Deputy Editor, Alyson Fixter, for fiction.
Tips *Scarlet* is aimed at women aged 20 to 40.

The School Librarian
Unit 2, Lotmead Business Village, Wanborough, Swindon, SN4 0UY
✆ 0870 777 0979
✆ 0870 777 0987
✉ info@sla.org.uk
🌐 www.sla.org.uk
Parent Company School Library Association
Editor Steve Hird
Established 1937
Insider Info A trade journal, issued quarterly, covering school library services and the children's book trade. Present circulation is roughly 4,000. Accepts queries by email.
Non-fiction Publishes News, Articles, Features and Reviews of Children's Fiction, Non-fiction, Multimedia and Websites.
Submission Guidelines Accepts queries by email to: sleditor@sla.org.uk
Tips *The School Librarian* is the official journal of the School Library Association. It covers both school library services and every aspect of the children's book trade. *The School Librarian* is always keen to receive contributors articles or reviews. Contact the Editor for further information.

Scintilla
Little Wentwood Farm, Llantrisant, Usk, NP5 1ND
✉ anne.cluysenaar@virgin.net
🌐 www.cf.ac.uk/encap/scintilla
Parent Company Usk Valley Vaughan Association (UVVA)
Editor Dr. Peter Thomas, Anne Cluysenaar
Established 1995
Insider Info A consumer journal publication, issued annually, covering the literature of Henry and Thomas Vaughan. Byline is given.
Non-fiction Publishes essays on themes related to the Breconshire writers Henry and Thomas Vaughan.
Submission Guidelines Accepts queries.

Fiction Publishes prose fiction and drama on themes related to Henry and Thomas Vaughan.
Poetry Publishes poetry relating to Henry and Thomas Vaughan
Tips Articles in *Scintilla* must engage in some way with Henry and Thomas Vaughan, famous for poetry, medical practice and alchemy.

Scotland in Trust
91 East London Street, Edinburgh, Midlothian, EH7 4BQ
- 0131 556 2220
- 0131 556 3300
- editor@scotlandintrust.co.uk
- www.scotlandintrust.co.uk

Parent Company National Trust for Scotland
Editor Iain Gale
Established 2002
Insider Info A membership magazine publication, issued three times a year, covering historical, conservation and wildlife issues surrounding the National Trust for Scotland. Present circulation is 179,082. 70 per cent of the magazine is written by freelance writers. Average lead time is one month and payment is on publication. The kill fee for manuscripts not published is 50 per cent of original fee. It takes two months to publish a manuscript once it is accepted. Publication is copyrighted, and a byline is given. Purchases one-time rights. Seasonal material must be submitted three months in advance. Accepts queries by mail and email, and aims to respond to queries within five days. Assignment expenses are sometimes paid (limit agreed upon in advance). Sample copy is available with SAE (320mm x 230mm and three first class stamps), and writer's guidelines and editorial calendars are available via email request.
Non-fiction Interested in new product articles, features, general interest articles, opinions (excluding letters to the Editor), travel and historical/nostalgic articles.
Submission Guidelines Query with published clips. Does not accept unsolicited manuscripts.
Images Accepts images with submission.
* Negotiates payment individually. One-time rights purchased.
Submission Guidelines Send photos with submission to Art Director, Neil Braidwood. Supply captions and identify subjects.
Tips The magazine is sent by direct mail to households who are members of The National Trust for Scotland, Scotland's leading conservation charity. With a circulation of 158,000 throughout the world, the readership is very broad and aged from early 20s to over 100. Research shows that the readership enjoys taking holidays at home and abroad, gardening, wine, theatre and visiting museums and galleries. Readers are also moving with the times, 55 per cent regularly use a personal computer and 42 per cent regularly use the internet. Above all, and as a common denominator, readers have an interest in, or passion for Scotland – its heritage, gardens, buildings, countryside and culture.

Scottish Home & Country
42 Heriot Row, Edinburgh, EH3 6ES
- 0131 225 1724
- 0131 225 8129
- magazine@swri.demon.co.uk
- www.swri.org.uk

Parent Company Scottish Women's Rural Institutes
Editor Liz Ferguson
Established 1924
Insider Info A voluntary organisation magazine publication issued monthly, covering issues faced by members of Scottish Women's Rural Institutes. Present circulation of 10,000. Payment upon publication. 50 percent of magazine is written by freelancers. A byline is given. Editorial lead time is four weeks. Accepts query by mail, email, fax and phone. Aims to respond to queries, manuscripts and other issues within one week. Payment is not made with contributor copies or other premiums. Assignment expenses are not paid. Sample copy and writer's guidelines are free on request.
Non-fiction Interested in humour, inspirational pieces, features, interviews/profiles, general interest articles, opinion (excluding letters to the Editor), travel writing, historical/nostalgic pieces, personal experiences, and articles on health, cookery, crafts, rural issues and women's issues.
* Receives approximately 50 manuscripts per year. Pays between £20 and £60 for unsolicited articles.
Submission Guidelines Please send complete manuscript. Articles should be between 500 and 1,000 words. Contact Liz Ferguson.
Images Accepts images with submission.
* Pays a varied fee per photo. Purchases one-time rights.
Submission Guidelines Submit high-res jpegs/tiffs. Contact Liz Ferguson.
Fillers Interested in facts, short humour, hints and tips and strange but true pieces.
Tips Readership is mainly women, aged 50 and upwards, who live largely in rural Scotland. Illustrated articles always have an advantage, as do seasonal features.

Scrapbook Inspirations
30 Monmouth Street, Bath, BA1 2BW
- 01225 442244
- scrapbookinspirations@futurenet.co.uk
- www.scrapbookinspirationsmagazine.co.uk

Parent Company Future Publishing Ltd
Editor Joanne Mullen
Contact Creative Editor, Cara Medus
Established 2005
Insider Info A monthly consumer magazine covering scrapbooking. Present circulation is 17,481.
Non-fiction Publishes design advice, how-to, layouts, practical guides, product reviews and celebrity tips.

Screen International

The International Voice Of The Film Business
33–39 Bowling Green Lane, London, EC1R 0DA
☎ 020 7505 8000
✉ michael.gubbins@emap.com
🌐 www.screendaily.com
Parent Company EMAP Plc
Editor Michael Gubbins
Established 1976
Insider Info A trade journal magazine, issued weekly, covering the film industry. Present circulation is 6,828. 60 per cent of the magazine is written by freelancers. It takes three months to publish a manuscript after it is accepted. Payment is upon publication. 30 per cent kill fee (of original fee) for manuscripts not published. Publication is copyrighted, and a byline given. Purchases first UK serial rights, first rights, second serial (reprint) rights and electronic rights. Average lead time is three weeks. Seasonal material must be submitted four weeks in advance. Accepts queries by mail, email, fax and phone. Accepts simultaneous submissions. Aims to respond to queries within one day and manuscripts within three days. Never pays writers with contributor copies or other premiums. Payment is via cash, with assignment expenses sometimes paid (limit agreed upon in advance). Writer's guidelines and editorial calendars are free on request. Sample copy is available with SAE.
Non-fiction Publishes book excerpts, features, interviews/profiles and technical articles, as well as articles on new films.
* Minimum payment for assigned and unsolicited articles is £250 per 1,000 words.
Submission Guidelines Articles must be 250–3,000 words.
Images Accepts images with submission.
* *Screen International* negotiates payment individually. One-time rights purchased.
Submission Guidelines Send images as gif/jpeg files, with captions, and identification of subjects to Art Editor, Alan Bingle.
Tips Target audience is anyone involved in the international film business, who has special interest in any area of the film industry, and that travels globally.

ScriptWriter Magazine

2 Elliott Square, London, NW3 3SU
☎ 020 7586 4853
☎ 020 7284 0442
✉ julian@scriptwritermagazine.com
🌐 www.scriptwritermagazine.com
Parent Company Scriptease Ltd
Editor Julian Friedmann
Established 2001
Insider Info A creative writing skills magazine, issued bi-monthly, covering scriptwriting and script development, and film and television from a creative point of view. A magazine for professional scriptwriters, or those wanting to be professional. Also relevant to script editors, development executives, producers and directors - anyone who works with writers. Present circulation of 5,000. 50 per cent of the magazine is written by freelancers. Manuscripts are published within eight weeks of being accepted. Payment is on publication. Publication is copyrighted, and a byline given. Purchases one time rights (sometimes repeated). Average lead time of ten weeks. Seasonal material must be submitted eight weeks in advance. Accepts queries by mail, email and fax. Aims to respond to queries and manuscripts within two weeks. Sometimes pays writers with contributor copies or other premium other than cash if contributor asks. Assignment expenses sometimes paid (limit agreed upon in advance). Sample copy available: £7 per copy; £36 for subscription of six issues. Writer's guidelines are available via email on request.
Non-fiction Publishes book excerpts, how-to and humour articles, features, interviews/profiles, opinion (excluding letters to the Editor), and an annual on audiences – demographic and psychological profile and analysis of who watches what.
* Buys 50 manuscripts from freelancers each year. Pays £20 per 1,000 words (it is a non-profit making magazine) for both assigned and unsolicited articles.
Submission Guidelines Accepts query with published clips and sample of writing. Final articles should be 1,500 words (two page articles) or 4,000 words for (five page articles).
Images Accepts images with submission.
* Offers no additional payment for photos accepted with the manuscript.
Columns Publishes a humorous column about being a writer.
* Pays £20 per 1,000 words.
Submission Guidelines Accepts query with published clips.
Tips A pragmatic magazine about how professional writers work; useful to beginners but not specifically for beginners. Read the magazine first. Send an

example of writing together with a proposal for an article.

SeaAngler
Bushfield House, Orton Centre, Peterborough, PE2 5UW
- 01733 465702
- 01733 465658
- mel.russ@bauermedia.com
- www.seaangler.co.uk

Parent Company Bauer Consumer Media
Editor Mel Russ
Contact Deputy Editor, Cliff Brown
Insider Info A monthly consumer magazine covering sea fishing. Present circulation is 41,668.
Non-fiction Publishes features, how-to, product reviews and location guides.
Tips *Sea Angler* covers all aspects of sea fishing, including equipment reviews and location reports for the best fishing.

Seam
PO Box 1051, Sawston, Cambridge, CB22 3WT
- seam.magazine@googlemail.com
- www.seampoetry.co.uk

Editor Anne Berkeley, Frank Dullaghan
Established 1994
Insider Info A consumer magazine publication, issued twice yearly, covering general literary/poetry interests. A byline is given. Accepts queries by mail and email. Writer's guidelines are available online.
Non-fiction Publishes poetry articles, features, interviews/profiles, essay and reviews.
Submission Guidelines Send query before sending submissions.
Poetry Publishes avant-garde, free verse and light Verse.
Submission Guidelines Accepts sample poems with SAE.
Tips *Seam* publishes the latest contemporary poetry from new and established writers, along with reviews, interviews and essays. *Seam* is interested in exploration and experimental poetry, as well as translated literature. The magazine does not accept email submissions, and will only accept proposals for essays, not full manuscripts.

SelfBuild & Design
151 Station Street, Burton on Trent, DE14 1BG
- 01584 841417
- 01584 841417
- ross.stokes@sbdonline.co.uk
- www.selfbuildanddesign.com

Parent Company Waterways World Ltd
Editor Ross Stokes
Established 1997

Insider Info A consumer magazine publication, issued monthly, covering home building and renovating. Accepts queries by email.
Non-fiction Interested in how-to, photo and technical features and articles.
* Pays £100–£200 per 1000 words.
Submission Guidelines Send complete manuscript via email.
Tips Welcomes tips and advice from readers wanting to share their knowledge, and articles from people nearing completion of their home. Email article and details to the Editor.

The Sentinel Quarterly
The Journal of African and World Literature
60 Titmuss Avenue, London, SE28 8DJ
- 0870 127 1967
- 07812 755751
- thequarterly@sentinelpoetry.org.uk
- www.sentinelpoetry.org.uk

Parent Company Sentinel Poetry Movement
Editor Afam Akeh
Established 2004
Insider Info Quarterly literary journal covering poetry and short fiction. Byline is given. Accepts queries by mail and email. Aims to respond to queries and manuscripts within eight weeks. Manuscript guidelines are available online.
Non-fiction Interested in essays, features, interviews/profiles, literary criticism, reviews and articles on poetry and literature.
* Payment is via a contributor copy.
Submission Guidelines Accepts complete manuscripts of up to 8,000 words.
Fiction Publishes short fiction.
Poetry Publishes contemporary, avant-garde, free verse, light verse and traditional poetry.
Submission Guidelines Submit up to six poems of 40 lines in length.
Tips *The Sentinel Quarterly* is the literary journal of The Sentinel Poetry Movement. It also has a sister website, which is independent from the printed journal. *The Sentinel* publishes work from any background, but its main focus is on literature of the African diaspora.

Seventh Quarry
The Swansea Poetry Quarterly
Dan-y-bryn, 74 Cwm Level Road, Brynhyfryd, Swansea, SA5 9DY
Editor Peter Thabit Jones
Insider Info A regional South Wales consumer magazine publication, covering poetry and prose interests.
Fiction Publishes new writing.
Poetry Publishes new poetry.

Tips *Seventh Quarry* is an established literary magazine in Swansea that publishes poetry and new writing, mainly from Swansea but also from outside the area. The magazine often organizes poetry readings and events in the Swansea area in conjunction with the local arts councils. Contact the Editor for submission details.

SFX

30 Monmouth Street, Bath, BA1 2BW
- 01225 442244
- 01225 822793
- sfx@futurenet.co.uk
- www.sfx.co.uk

Parent Company Future Publishing
Editor David Bradley
Established 1995
Insider Info A consumer magazine publication, issued monthly, covering science fiction. Present circulation is 31,634. Payment is on acceptance.
Non-fiction Publishes general and technical articles on science fiction.
Submission Guidelines Email a CV and samples of work for consideration (word documents are best).
Tips *SFX* is a science fiction and fantasy magazine covering all aspects of science fiction and fantasy, including television, films, DVDs, books, comics, games, collectables and more. *SFX* generally do not accept speculative submissions.

She

National Magazine House, 72 Broadwick Street, London, W1F 9EP
- 020 7439 5000
- 020 7312 3940
- editor@shemagazine.co.uk
- www.allaboutyou.com

Parent Company National Magazine Company
Editor Sian Rees
Established 1955
Insider Info A consumer magazine publication, issued monthly, covering women's interests and women's lifestyle/fashion. Present circulation of 173,377. Accepts queries by mail and email.
Non-fiction Publishes features and general interest articles on women's lifestyle, fashion, beauty, childcare and health.
Submission Guidelines Send query before sending submissions. Articles should be a maximum of 1,200 words.
Tips The readership tends towards middle class, affluent women, with or without children.

Shearsman

58 Velwell Road, Exeter, Devon, EX4 4LD
- 01392 434511
- 01392 434511
- editor@shearsman.com
- www.shearsman.com

Parent Company Shearsman Books Ltd
Editor Tony Frazer
Established 1981
Insider Info A magazine, issued twice yearly, devoted to poetry. Publication is copyrighted. Accepts queries by mail and email. Writer's guidelines available online.
Submission Guidelines Submissions may be made by mail or by email during the magazine's reading windows. If submitting by email, attachments are unacceptable other than PDF files.
Poetry Publishes poetry of all styles but more daring, exploratory work is preferred. Either original English work or translations.
Tips Shearsman publishes contemporary poetry in the modernist tradition. The magazine operates a 'reading window' system for dealing with submissions, whereby there will be a one month 'window' for each issue, when writers can submit their manuscripts. These are in March and September of each year. Further details are on the website.

Ships Monthly

222 Branston Road, Burton on Trent, DE14 3BT
- 01283 542721
- 01283 546436
- shipsmonthly@ipcmedia.com
- www.shipsmonthly.com

Parent Company IPC Media Ltd
Editor Ian Wakefield
Contact Publishing Director, Nick Hopkinson; Deputy Editor, Nicholas Leach
Established 1966
Insider Info A monthly trade journal, covering ships and shipping. Circulation is 21,000. Media pack available online.
Non-fiction Publishes features, photo features, news and review articles covering all aspects of sea shipping including cruising, tug boats and ferries.
Tips *Ships Monthly* is a business magazine aimed at professionals in the shipping trade.

The Shooting Gazette

Blue Fin Building, 110 Southwark Street, London, SE1 0SU
- 020 3148 5000
- will_hetherington@ipcmedia.com
- www.ipcmedia.com

Parent Company IPC Media Ltd
Editor William Hetherington

Contact Publishing Director, Hamish Dawson; Publisher, Fiona Mercer; Assistant Editor, Martin Puddifer
Established 1989
Insider Info A monthly consumer magazine, covering game and shooting. Circulation is 17,200. Media pack available online.
Non-fiction Publishes agricultural, game & rough shooting, gun dog training, product reviews, news and topical articles.
Tips *The Shooting Gazette* covers all aspects of game and rough shooting, as well as reviews of the latest equipment and clothing. The magazine is aimed at shooting enthusiasts with high disposable incomes. Its emphasis is on quality of writing and topical feature material.

Shooting Times & Country Magazine
Blue Fin Building, 110 Southwark Street, London, SE1 0SU
- 020 3148 5000
- steditorial@ipcmedia.com
- www.shootingtimes.co.uk

Parent Company IPC Media Ltd
Editor Camilla Clark
Contact Publishing Director, Hamish Dawson; Publisher, Fiona Mercer; Art Editor, Harriot Osbourne; News Editor, Selena Masson
Insider Info A weekly consumer magazine, covering shooting and rural issues. Circulation is 26,614. Media pack available online.
Non-fiction Publishes game, rough & stalking, features, product reviews, news and conservation articles.
Tips *Shooting Times & Country Magazine* has been published for over 100 years and covers all aspects of shooting and hunting, as well as dealing with relevant agricultural and conservation issues.

The Shop
Skeagh, Schull, Co. Cork, Republic of Ireland
- hilary.wakeman@gmail.com
- theshop@theshop-poetry-magazine.ie
- ww.theshop-poetry-magazine.ie

Contact Editors: John and Hilary Wakeman
Established 1999
Insider Info A consumer magazine, with three issues per year, covering poetry. Accepts queries by mail or email.
Tips *The Shop* publishes poetry, particularly Irish poetry, but will also publish occasional essays about poetry. They do not accept submissions by email.

Shots
Greater London House, Hampstead Road, London, NW1 7EJ
- 020 7728 5000
- 020 7713 1374
- lyndy@shots.net
- www.shots.net

Parent Company EMAP Plc
Editor Lyndy Stout
Contact Deputy Editor, Danny Edwards; Art Director, Sarah Watson
Insider Info A bi-monthly trade journal covering the advertising and creativity industry. Present circulation is 4,000.
Non-fiction Publishes news, features and reviews.
Tips Articles include full reviews of television commercials, film effects, and press and poster campaigns.

Shout
2 Albert Square, Dundee, DD1 9QJ
- 01382 223131
- 01382 200880
- mwelch@shoutmag.co.uk
- www.shoutmag.co.uk

Parent Company D.C. Thomson & Co. Ltd
Editor Maria Welch
Contact Assistant Editor, Michael Stirling; Problem Page Editor, Laura Brown
Established 1993
Insider Info A bi-weekly consumer magazine covering teenage girls' interests. Present circulation is 84,937.
Non-fiction Publishes features, interviews, profiles, reviews and true-life stories.
* Pays £50 for true-life stories.
Submission Guidelines For true-life stories fill in the online form.
Tips *Shout* is aimed at younger teenage girls, covering health, beauty, fashion, celebrity gossip, boys and relationship advice. *Shout* is always looking for embarrassing or shocking true-life stories from readers.

Shropshire Magazine
Ketley, Telford, TF1 5HU
- 01952 242424
- 01952 222451
- www.shropshiremagazine.com

Parent Company Shropshire Newspapers
Editor Neil Thomas
Established 1950
Insider Info A monthly consumer magazine covering Shropshire. Accepts queries by mail or email.
Non-fiction Interested in local interest and lifestyle articles related to Shropshire.

Submission Guidelines Accepts queries and completed manuscript submissions of up to 1,500 words.

Sight & Sound
21 Stephen Street, London, W1T 1LN
- 020 7255 1444
- 020 7436 2327
- s&s@bfi.org.uk
- www.bfi.org.uk/sightandsound

Parent Company British Film Institute
Editor Nick James
Contact Publisher, Rob Winter; Deputy Editor, Kieron Corless
Established 1932
Insider Info A monthly consumer magazine covering film and cinema. Present circulation is 20,283.
Non-fiction Publishes news, features, commentaries, interviews, profiles and reviews.
Tips *Sight & Sound* is the official magazine of the British Film Institute. It covers the latest film releases as well as articles on the old classics, and is aimed at both enthusiasts and professionals in the media industry. It is also widely read by film and media studies students.

Simply Knitting
30 Monmouth Street, Bath, BA1 2BW
- 01225 442244
- 01225 822793
- simplyknitting@futurenet.co.uk
- www.simplyknitting.co.uk

Parent Company Future Publishing
Editor Debora Bradley
Established 2005
Insider Info A monthly consumer magazine covering knitting. Present circulation of 42,463. Ten per cent of the magazine is written by freelance writers. Submissions are published approximately six months after acceptance. Payment is made on publication of material. Kill fee for commissioned articles that are not published is 50 per cent of original fee. Publication is copyrighted and a byline is given. Purchases all rights. Editorial lead time is six weeks. Seasonal material must be submitted six months in advance. Queries accepted by mail and email to debora.bradley@futurenet.co.uk. Aims to respond to queries within one week and manuscripts within three months. If writers submit features which are to do with their own business, then the publicity is considered to be the 'fee'. Assignment expenses are sometimes paid (limit agreed upon in advance). Editorial calendars are available free on request. Media packs are available by email to amanda.haughey@futurenet.co.uk.

Non-fiction Publishes features and photo features on knitting.
Submission Guidelines Send query before sending submissions. Articles must be 300–1,000 words. No reprints.
Tips The magazine covers the best new products, interviews, club news, competitions and technical advice. The audience is largely female, with an average age of 48, and most are dedicated enthusiasts. Writing, or submitted knitwear designs, should reflect the gender and age of reader, recognising there are readers from 8 to 80. The tone should be friendly and non-patronising, and knitwear design must be modern, but mainstream.

Skald
6 Hill Street, Menai Bridge, Anglesey, LL59 5AG
- 01248 716343
- editors@skald.co.uk
- www.skald.co.uk

Editor Zoe Skoulding
Contact Co-Editor, Ian Davidson
Established 1994
Insider Info A consumer magazine, with two issues per year, covering literary and arts topics. Byline is given. Accepts queries by mail and email.
Non-fiction Interested in photo features and literary articles.
Submission Guidelines Accepts queries in the first instance.
Fiction Publishes short fiction.
Poetry Publishes contemporary, avant-garde, free verse and light verse poetry.
Tips *Skald* is a small magazine that publishes new poetry and short fiction, as well as some visual art in black and white. It prints work in both the English and Welsh language and is interested in representing both local and international writers.

Ski & Board
The White House, 57–63 Church Road, Wimbledon, London, SW19 5SB
- 020 8410 2000
- 0845 458 0781
- editor@skiclub.co.uk
- www.skiclub.co.uk

Parent Company Ski Club of Great Britain
Editor Arnie Wilson
Contact Assistant Editor, Ben Letham
Insider Info A quarterly consumer magazine covering snow sports. Present circulation is 20,821.
Non-fiction Publishes news, features, profiles and product and resort reviews.
Tips *Ski & Board* is the official magazine of the Ski Club of Great Britain and is distributed to all members. It covers the latest product and resort

reviews, ski and snowboard news, celebrity gossip and practical articles on health, fitness and fashion. Be aware that the readership are likely to be already very well informed about skiing and able to ski at a fairly advanced level.

Slightly Foxed

67 Dickinson Court, 15 Brewhouse Yard, London, EC1V 4JX
- 020 7549 2121/2111
- 0870 1991245
- all@foxedquarterly.com
- www.foxedquarterly.com

Contact Publisher and Co-Editor, Gail Pirkis; Co-Editor, Hazel Wood
Insider Info A quarterly literary magazine, at £8 per issue. Accepts queries by mail or email.
Non-fiction Publishes book reviews and articles.
Tips Slightly Foxed aims to provide informal and independent-minded book reviews of al kinds of books, not just bestseller from the big publishers.

Slim at Home

No gyms, no meetings, no problem
25 Phoenix Court, Hawkins Road, Colchester, Essex, CO2 8JY
- 01206 505987
- naomi@aceville.co.uk

Parent Company Aceville Publications Ltd
Editor Naomi Abeykoon
Established 2007
Insider Info A consumer publication magazine, issued monthly, covering weight loss. Present circulation of 100,000. Zero to ten per cent of articles are written by freelancers. Manuscripts are published two months after they are accepted. Payment is on publication. A byline is sometimes given. Publication is copyrighted. Average lead time of one month. Seasonal material must be submitted two months in advance. Accepts queries by email and phone. Does not pay the expenses of writers on assignment.
Non-fiction Publishes features and photo features on slimming.
* Buys two to three manuscripts from freelancers per year.
Submission Guidelines Send query with published clips before sending submissions.
Images Send photos with submission.
* Negotiates payment for individual photos.

Slimming World

Clover Nook Road, Somercotes, Alfreton, DE55 4RF
- 01773 546071
- 0870 442 9935
- editorial@slimming-world.com

- www.slimmingworldmagazine.co.uk

Parent Company Miles-Bramwell Executive Services Ltd
Editor Elise Wells
Contact Assistant Editor, Sarah Davison; Creative Director, Lynn Hayes; Contributing Features Editor, Sara Niven
Established 1998
Insider Info A bi-monthly consumer magazine covering slimming and lifestyle. Present circulation is 286,032.
Non-fiction Publishes features, profiles and advice articles on weight loss.
Tips Slimming World covers all aspects of slimming and healthy dieting, particularly the Slimming World regime. Articles include dieting plans and advice, recipes, fashion and fitness. The magazine is primarily aimed at Slimming World members but also anyone else who is interested in healthy eating.

Smallholder

Hook House, Hook Road, Wimblington, March, PE15 0QL
- 01354 741538
- 01354 741182
- liz.wright1@btconnect.com
- www.smallholder.co.uk

Parent Company Newsquest Plc
Editor Liz Wright
Established 1975
Insider Info Monthly consumer magazine covering agriculture, farming and smallholdings. Present circulation is roughly 20,000. 75 per cent of the publication is written by freelance writers. Submissions published up to eight weeks after acceptance. Payment on publication. Byline is given. Publication is copyrighted. Purchases first UK serial rights. Average lead time is two months. Seasonal material must be submitted three months in advance. Accepts queries by email. Aims to respond to queries within one week and manuscripts within four months. Sample copy, manuscript guidelines and editorial calendar are free on request.
Non-fiction Interested in book excerpts, how-tos, photo features, inspirational pieces, features, interviews/profiles, reviews, new product pieces, technical articles, opinions and travel articles.
Submission Guidelines Accepts queries for articles of between 500 and 2,000 words.
Images Accepts images with submission.
* Negotiates payment individually for photos.
Submission Guidelines State availability of photos with submission. Include contact sheets, captions and identification of subjects. Please email for further details before sending contributions.
Tips Smallholder is a practical magazine for smallholders in country or town situations.

Smiths Knoll

Goldings, Goldings Lane, Leiston, Suffolk, IP16 4EB

- 01728 830631
- michael.laskey@ukonline.co.uk

Editor Michael Laskey

Contact Co-Editor, Joanna Cutts

Established 1991

Insider Info A consumer magazine, with three issues per year, focusing on poetry. Present circulation is 500. Submissions are published up to four months after acceptance. Payment is on publication. A byline is given. Accepts queries by mail and email. Aims to respond to queries and manuscripts within two weeks.

Poetry Publishes contemporary, avant-garde, free verse, light verse and traditional poetry.

Tips *Smiths Knoll* is a small magazine with high production values that publishes any type of poetry from new and established writers. Roughly 40 per cent of the poetry in each issue is from new contributors, and the magazine has a history of nurturing new poets. *Smiths Knoll* will give critical feedback on any submission that interests them, they also offer weekend writing courses for subscribers.

Smoke

Liver House, 96 Bold Street, Liverpool, L1 4HY

- 0151 709 3688
- 0151 707 8722
- windows@windowsproject.demon.co.uk
- www.windowsproject.demon.co.uk

Parent Company The Windows Projects Trust

Editor Dave Ward

Contact Co-Editor, Dave Calder

Established 1974

Insider Info A consumer magazine, with two issues per year, covering poetry topics. Present circulation is 700. Byline is given. Accepts queries by mail and email. Sample copy is available online.

Poetry Publishes contemporary, avant-garde, free verse, light verse and traditional poetry.

Submission Guidelines Accepts sample poems.

Tips *Smoke* magazine publishes new poetry, artwork and some short fiction. Although not aimed at young readers, *Smoke* is published by the Windows Project which is a charity that aims to help children get involved with poetry. The magazine accepts submissions of any kinds of poetry, usually contemporary poems aimed at an adult readership.

Snow

Thompson House, 42–44 Dolben Street, Blackfriars, London, SE1 0UQ

- 020 7261 9111
- 020 7261 0990
- info@altitudemedia.co.uk
- www.snowmagazine.com

Parent Company Altitude Media

Editor Anton Strack

Established 2003

Insider Info A bi-monthly consumer magazine covering snow sports and lifestyle. Present circulation is 26,250.

Non-fiction Publishes news, features and product reviews. Topics include skiing, snowboarding and the mountain lifestyle.

Soaplife

Blue Fin Building, 110 Southwark Street, London, SE1 0SU

- 020 3148 5000
- 2hellen_gardner@ipcmedia.com
- www.ipcmedia.com

Parent Company IPC Media Ltd

Editor Hellen Gardner

Contact Publishing Director, Angela O'Farrell; Publisher, Richard Coles; Art Editor, Brian Hawthorne; Deputy Editor, Di Hollingsworth

Established 1999

Insider Info A bi-weekly consumer magazine, covering television soap operas. Circulation is 109,493. Media pack available online.

Non-fiction Publishes celebrity gossip, interviews, profiles, soap news and storyline information, and television listings articles.

Tips *Soaplife* is a bi-weekly magazine aimed at soap opera lovers. It covers every aspect of soaps including insider info, plot spoilers, and interviews and profiles of the actors on and off the screen.

Solicitors Journal

6–14 Underwood Street, London, N1 7JQ

- 020 7566 8210
- 020 7566 8238
- clientservices@solicitorsjournal.co.uk
- www.solicitorsjournal.com

Parent Company Waterlow Legal & Regulatory Ltd

Editor Jean-Yves Gilg

Established 1856

Insider Info Weekly trade journal covering the legal trade. Present circulation is 5,000.

Non-fiction Publishes a round up of the weeks legal news, and intelligent and analytical articles covering the latest developments in the legal profession. Case reports and changes to legislation also covered.

Tips *Solicitors Journal* is aimed at professionals within the legal trade.

Sol Magazine

PO Box 5828, Southend on Sea, SS1 9FA

◉ solmag@solpubs.freeserve.co.uk
◉ www.solpubs.freeserve.co.uk/solmagazine.htm
Parent Company Sol Publications
Editor Malcolm E. Wright
Established 1969
Insider Info A consumer magazine, with two issues per year, covering poetry and fiction. Byline is given. Accepts queries by mail and email. Manuscript guidelines are available online.
Non-fiction Interested in features, reviews and articles on poetry and prose writing.
Submission Guidelines Accepts queries in the first instance.
Fiction Publishes short fiction.
* Contributors receive one year's free subscription to the magazine.
Submission Guidelines Accepts complete manuscripts of between 500 and 5,000 words.
Poetry Publishes contemporary, free verse, light verse and traditional poetry.
Submission Guidelines Submit up to six poems.
Tips *Sol Magazine* publishes short stories, poetry, book reviews and articles about literature, music and philosophy. The magazine publishes any kind of poetry or fiction as long as they are original. Longer works of fiction may be considered for individual publication as a booklet, instead of in the magazine.

Solo Survivors

37 Micklehill Drive, Shirley, Solihull, West Midlands, B90 2PU

◉ 0121 743 4381
◉ johnalanhirst@ukonline.co.uk
◉ www.johnalanhirst.com/solo_survivors_mag.shtml
Parent Company Survivor's Poetry Group
Editor John Hirst
Established 2002
Insider Info Quarterly consumer magazine covering poetry and fiction. Byline is given. Accepts queries by mail and email. Manuscript guidelines are available online.
Non-fiction Interested in features, interviews/profiles, opinion, self-help and poetry articles.
Submission Guidelines Accepts complete manuscript.
Fiction Publishes short fiction.
Poetry Publishes contemporary, free verse, light verse and traditional poetry.
Submission Guidelines Submit up to three poems of 30 lines in length.
Tips *Solo Survivors* is a small magazine published in accordance with the Survivor's Poetry Group, a group for survivors of mental or physical distress. The

magazine focuses on publishing poetry from new and established contributors, and also prints short fiction, self-help articles, artwork and a 'guest poet' slot. *Solo Survivors* will accept any kind of submission, including self-help articles, but will focus mostly on poetry. Submissions should ideally come from members of the Survivor's Group.

Somerfield Magazine

The Mill House, Redcliff Backs, Bristol, BS1 6LY

◉ 0117 989 7800
◉ hsmith@rarepublishing.co.uk
Parent Company PSP Rare Publishing and Somerfield
Editor Hannah Smith
Insider Info Monthly consumer magazine covering customer information and products for Somerfield Stores. Present circulation is 1,173,303. Ten per cent of the publication is written by freelance writers. Payment is on publication. Publication is copyrighted and the publisher purchases all rights. Average lead time is four months. Seasonal material must be submitted four weeks in advance. Accepts queries by email.
Non-fiction Publishes general interest articles and photo features.
Tips Customer magazine free to Somerfield shoppers, deals mainly with food and food related issues, but also health and lifestyle.

South

PO Box 5369, Poole, Dorset, BH14 0XN

◉ south@martinblyth.co.uk
Editor Martin Blyth
Established 1990
Insider Info A consumer magazine, with two issues per year, covering literature and writing. Present circulation is 350. Byline is given.
Non-fiction Interested in features, book reviews and articles on poetry and prose.
Fiction Publishes short fiction.
Poetry Publishes contemporary, free verse, light verse and traditional poetry.
Tips *South* is a literary magazine that focuses on writers and work from the southern counties of England, including Berkshire, Dorset, Hampshire and Sussex. *South* has a 'rolling editorial' where each issue has a new editor, or editorial team. This allows *South* to use a completely anonymous selection process and give every contributor the same chance of publication.

Spanner

14 Hopton Road, Hereford, HR1 1BE

◉ kaa45@dial.pipex.com
◉ www.shadoof.net/spanner

Editor Allen Fisher
Insider Info A consumer magazine, publishing three issues per year, covering literary interests.
Tips *Spanner* is a literary magazine that focuses on specific authors or subjects in each issue. The magazine publishes examples and reproductions of the work in question, and articles about the subject. *Spanner* does not accept contributions in any form.

The Spectator
22 Old Queen Street, London, SW1H 9HP
☎ 020 7961 2000
✉ editor@spectator.co.uk
🌐 www.spectator.co.uk
Parent Company The Spectator Ltd
Editor Matthew d'Ancona
Established 1828
Insider Info Weekly consumer magazine covering news and current affairs. Present circulation is 76,952. Accepts queries by mail and email.
Non-fiction Interested in book excerpts, essays, features, interviews/profiles, reviews and general interest articles on current affairs, news and politics.
Submission Guidelines Accepts complete manuscripts.
Tips Controversy is important to *The Spectator,* so submissions should cover breaking, or forthcoming current affairs that will cause a stir. The quality of writing is also of high priority, so ensure your article is submitted in clear, elegant prose.

Spirit & Destiny
10 Jamestown Road, London, NW1 7BY
☎ 020 7424 7050
☎ 020 7424 7081
✉ spirit.destiny@bauer.co.uk
🌐 www.spiritanddestiny.co.uk
Parent Company H. Bauer Publishing
Editor Rhiannon Powell
Contact Deputy Editor, Helen Saunders
Established 2002
Insider Info A monthly consumer magazine covering astrology and spirituality. Present circulation is 66,097. Media pack available online.
Non-fiction Publishes features and inspirational articles.
Tips *Spirit & Destiny* covers astrology, alternative therapies, holistic therapies, self discovery and spiritual self improvement, along with more traditional women's monthly features.

Sport
3rd Floor, Courtyard Building, 11 Curtain Road, London, EC2A 3LT
☎ 020 7375 3175
✉ simoncaney@myfreesport.co.uk

🌐 www.myfreesport.co.uk
Parent Company Sport Media & Strategy Ltd
Contact Editor in Chief, Simon Caney; Deputy Editor, Kevin Hughes; Features Editor, Nick Harper
Established 2006
Insider Info A weekly consumer magazine covering sports and lifestyle. Present circulation is 313,274.
Non-fiction Publishes features, news, reviews, events coverage and advice articles.
Tips *Sport* is a free weekly magazine that covers forthcoming sporting events, features and advice on sports, news and lifestyle articles. It is distributed by hand at 'commuter hotspots' throughout the UK.

Sporting Gun
Blue Fin Building, 110 Southwark Street, London, SE1 0SU
☎ 020 3148 5000
✉ sportinggun@ipcmedia.com
🌐 www.ipcmedia.com
Parent Company IPC Media Ltd
Editor Robin Scott
Contact Publishing Director, Hamish Dawsonn; Publisher, Fiona Mercer
Established 1978
Insider Info A monthly consumer magazine, covering shooting and gun sports. Circulation is 33,799. Media pack available online.
Non-fiction Publishes clay, game and rough shooting, gun dog training, news, practical advice, reviews and tutorial articles.
Tips *Sporting Gun* prints features on gun dog training, shooting techniques and equipment reviews and is aimed at enthusiasts of any skill level.

Springboard
Corrimbla, Ballina, Co. Mayo, Republic of Ireland
✉ bobgroom@eircom.net
Editor Robert Groom
Established 1990
Insider Info A quarterly consumer magazine that covers short stories, poetry and articles. Accepts queries by mail or email.
Tips *Springboard* is a not-for-profit magazine that runs four different writing competitions: Short Story, Poetry, Children's Short Story and Articles. The winner and runner-up in each competition will be published in the following issue of *Springbaord*. Other than competition entries they do not accept submissions.

Square Meal
5th Floor, Quadrant House, 250 Kennington Lane, London, SE11 5RD
☎ 020 7582 0222
☎ 020 7582 5444

o editor@squaremeal.co.uk
w www.squaremeal.co.uk
Parent Company Monomax Ltd
Editor Ben McCormack
Contact Publisher, Mark de Wesselow
Established 1990
Insider Info A quarterly consumer magazine covering food and restaurant news. Present circulation is 101,393.
Non-fiction Publishes news, features and review articles.
Tips *Square Meal* covers restaurant and dining news, including openings and closures, reviews, showcase articles, profiles and general features on food and dining.

Staffordshire Life
The Publishing Centre, Derby Street, Stafford, ST16 2DT
o 01785 257700
o 01785 253287
o editor@staffordshirelife.co.uk
w www.staffordshirelife.co.uk
Parent Company Staffordshire Newspapers Ltd
Editor Philip Thurlow-Craig
Established 1948
Insider Info A monthly consumer magazine covering Staffordshire. Accepts queries by mail or email.
Non-fiction Interested in lifestyle, history and local interest articles related to Staffordshire.
Submission Guidelines Accepts queries and completed manuscript submissions of between 50 to 800 words.

The Stage
Stage House, 47 Bermondsey Street, London, SE1 3XT
o 020 7403 1818
o 020 7357 9287
o editor@thestage.co.uk
w www.thestage.co.uk
Editor Brian Attwood
Established 1880
Insider Info A weekly consumer magazine that covers all aspects of theatre and broadcast stagecraft. Payment is £100 per 1,000 words. Accepts queries by mail or email. Present circulation is 21,362.
Non-fiction Interested in practical and technical articles related to stagecraft.
Submission Guidelines Accepts queries and completed manuscript submissions of between 500-900 words.

Stamp Lover
107 Charterhouse Street, London, EC1M 6PT
o 020 7490 9610
o nps@ukphilately.org.uk
w www.ukphilately.org.uk/nps
Parent Company The National Philatelic Society
Editor D. Alford
Established 1908
Insider Info Bi-monthly society journal covering stamp collecting and history. Present circulation is 700. Submissions are published up to three months after acceptance. No payment is offered for contributions. Byline is given. Publication is copyrighted. Average lead time is one month. Seasonal material must be submitted two months in advance. Accepts queries by mail.
Non-fiction Publishes general articles on stamps.
Tips *Stamp Lover* is the journal of the National Philatelic Society and covers all aspects of stamp collecting, including history, collection reviews, and markets.

Stamp Magazine
Leon House, 233 High Street, Croydon, CR9 1HZ
o 020 8726 8000
o 020 8726 8299
o guy_thomas@ipcmedia.com
w www.stampmagazine.co.uk
Parent Company IPC Media Ltd
Editor Guy Thomas
Contact Publishing Director, Joanna Pieters; Art Editor, Heather Peters; Assistant Editor, Julia Lee
Insider Info A monthly consumer magazine, covering stamp collecting. Circulation is 23,000. Media pack available online.
Non-fiction Publishes auction features, exhibition reviews, historical and news articles.
Tips *Stamp Magazine* is a monthly publication that covers all aspects of philately, or stamp collecting.

Stand Magazine
School of English, Leeds University, Leeds, LS2 9JT
o 0113 343 4794
o stand@leeds.ac.uk
w www.standmagazine.org
Editor John Whale
Contact Managing Editor, Jon Glover
Established 1952
Insider Info Quarterly consumer magazine covering literature. Payment is on publication. Accepts queries by mail. Manuscript guidelines are available online.
Fiction Publishes mainstream and literary short fiction.

* Payments is £20 for the first 1,000 words, £5 for additional words.

Submission Guidelines Accepts complete manuscripts with SAE. No email submissions.

Poetry Publishes traditional poetry.

Submission Guidelines Accepts sample poems with SAE. No email submissions.

Tips *Stand* publishes poetry, prose and various literary articles. *Stand* can only consider previously unpublished material, including that sent in by literary agents. Please note that email submissions are not accepted.

Staple

74 Rangeley Road, Walkley, Sheffield, S6 5DW

- 0114 233 6946
- 0870 054 7400
- e.barrett@shu.ac.uk

Editor Elizabeth Barrett

Contact Co-Editor, Ann Atkinson

Established 1983

Insider Info A consumer magazine, with three issues per year (March, July, November), covering literary topics. Byline is given. Accepts queries by mail and email.

Fiction Publishes contemporary and experimental short fiction.

Poetry Publishes contemporary, avant-garde and free verse poetry.

Tips *Staple* is a small press magazine that publishes contemporary, often experimental, poetry, and short stories which are more likely to subvert the norms of fiction narratives, rather than to conform. *Staple* looks for submissions from abroad, as well as in the UK. It is proud of its small press heritage and always looks for submissions with an independent spirit, experimental stories and poems that work against the accepted norm.

Star

10 Lower Thames Street, London, EC3R 6EN

- 0871 434 1010
- 0871 434 7505
- starmagazine@express.co.uk
- www.starmagazine.com

Parent Company Northern & Shell Plc

Editor Busola Odulate

Contact Deputy Editor, Anna Pointer; Features Editor, Lisa Pollen

Established 2003

Insider Info A weekly consumer magazine covering women's lifestyle and celebrity gossip. Present circulation is 287,368.

Non-fiction Publishes features, celebrity news, interviews, profiles, product reviews and television listings.

Tips *Star* is aimed at women between 25 and 35 years old.

Steam Railway

Bretton Court, Bretton, Peterborough, PE3 8DZ

- 01733 282719
- 01733 282720
- steam.railway@bauermedia.com
- www.steamrailway.co.uk

Parent Company Bauer Consumer Media

Editor Danny Hopkins

Contact Assistant Editor, Richard Foster; News Editor, David Wilcox

Established 1979

Insider Info A monthly consumer magazine focussing on steam engines. Present circulation is 32,889.

Non-fiction Publishes features, news, technical and historical articles.

Tips *Steam Railway* covers all aspects of steam engines, railways and the history of steam.

The Stinging Fly

Dublin's Literary Magazine

PO Box 6016, Dublin 8, Republic of Ireland

- stingingfly@gmail.com
- www.stingingfly.org

Parent Company The Stinging Fly Press

Editor Declan Meade

Contact Poetry Editor, Eabhan Ní Shúileabháin

Established 1997

Insider Info A consumer literary magazine, with three issues per year, covering Irish and international literature. Byline is given. Accepts queries by mail and email. Manuscript guidelines are available online.

Non-fiction Interested in features, reviews and articles on poetry and literature.

Submission Guidelines Accepts queries in the first instance.

Fiction Publish mainstream and contemporary short fiction.

* Payment is two contributor copies.

Submission Guidelines Accepts complete manuscripts of up to 3,000 words.

Poetry Publishes contemporary, avant-garde, free verse, light verse and traditional poetry.

Tips *The Stinging Fly* is an Irish literary magazine that publishes short fiction, poetry and book reviews. The magazine welcomes submissions from Irish and international writers and has a particular interest in new writers and promoting the short story form. *The Stinging Fly* operates a 'reading window', so submissions will only be accepted during the first three months of the year.

The Strad

Newsquest Specialist Media, 30 Cannon Street, London, SEC4M 6YJ

☎ 020 7618 3456

☎ 020 7618 3483

✉ thestrad@orpheuspublications.com

🌐 www.thestrad.com

Parent Company Newsquest Magazines

Editor Ariane Todes

Established 1890

Insider Info A monthly consumer magazine that covers music and stringed instruments. Accepts queries by mail or email.

Non-fiction Interested in product reviews, news and feature articles related to stringed instruments.

Submission Guidelines Accepts queries and completed manuscript submissions of between 1,000 to 2,000 words.

Tips *The Strad* is aimed at both professional and amateur music enthusiasts.

Streetfighters

19th Floor, 1 Canada Square, Canary Wharf, London, E14 5AP

✉ dave.manning@oceanmedia.co.uk

🌐 www.streetfightersmag.com

Parent Company Ocean Media

Editor Dave Manning

Contact Managing Editor, Stu Garland

Established 1991

Insider Info Monthly consumer magazine covering motorcycle riding and modification. Present circulation is 25,000. 50 per cent of the publication is written by freelance writers. Submissions are published up to six weeks after acceptance. Payment is on publication and the publication will be copyrighted. Average lead time is six weeks and seasonal material must be submitted six weeks in advance. Accepts queries by mail, email and fax. Simultaneous submissions are accepted, as are previously published submissions. Aims to respond to queries within two days and manuscripts within ten days.

Non-fiction Interested in how-tos, motorcycle modification articles, photo features, humour, inspirational pieces, features, interviews/profiles, new product reviews, technical and personal experience articles.

Submission Guidelines Accepts manuscripts of between 800 and 3,000 words.

Stuff

Teddington Studios, Broom Road, Teddington, TW11 9BE

☎ 020 8267 5036

☎ 020 8267 5019

✉ stuff@haymarket.com

🌐 www.stuffmag.co.uk

Parent Company Haymarket Consumer Publications Ltd

Editor Fraser Macdonald

Contact Deputy Editor, Simon Osborne-Walker; Commissioning Editor, Will Findlater

Insider Info A monthly consumer magazine covering gadgets and innovation. Present circulation is 88,081.

Non-fiction Publishes news, features and product reviews.

Tips *Stuff* is aimed at men between 25 and 34 years of age.

The Suffolk Journal

Winship Road, Milton, Cambridge, CB4 6PP

☎ 01223 434434

☎ 01223 434415

🌐 http://magazines.cambridge-news.co.uk

Editor Alexandra Fedoruk

Established 1994

Insider Info A monthly consumer magazine covering Suffolk. Present circulation is roughly 25,000. Accepts queries by mail or email.

Non-fiction Interested in interviews, restaurant reviews, cooking, fashion, beauty, lifestyle and local interest articles related to Suffolk.

Suffolk Norfolk Life

The Publishing House, Station Road, Framlingham, Suffolk, IP13 9EE

☎ 01728 622030

☎ 01728 622031

🌐 www.suffolknorfolklife.com

Parent Company Today Magazines Ltd

Editor William Locks

Established 1989

Insider Info A monthly consumer magazine covering Suffolk and Norfolk counties. Accepts queries by mail or email.

Non-fiction Interested in lifestyle, art, history, leisure and local interest articles related to Suffolk and Norfolk.

Submission Guidelines Accepts queries and completed manuscript submissions of between 900 to 1,500 words by email.

Sugar

64 North Row, London, W1K 7LL

☎ 020 7150 7087

☎ 020 7150 7678

✉ sugarreaders@sugarmagazine.co.uk

🌐 www.sugarmagazine.co.uk

Parent Company Hacette Filipacchi

Editor Annabel Brog

Contact Features Editor, Diane Leeming
Established 1994
Insider Info A monthly consumer magazine for teenage girls. Present circulation of 158,835. Queries accepted by mail.
Tips The magazine's content concentrates mainly on the opposite sex, fashion, celebrities, and real stories about teenagers. *Sugar* helps solve 'female' issues by publishing articles that offer helpful advice. *Sugar* seeks real life stories, but also practical articles of help dealing with teenage issues. Experience as either a guidance counsellor, or a previously troubled teenager, would add to any article idea.

SuperBike
Blue Fin Building, 110 Southwark Street, London, SE1 0SU
- 020 3148 5000
- kenny_pryde@ipcmedia.com
- www.superbike.co.uk

Parent Company IPC Media Ltd
Editor Kenny Pryde
Established 1977
Insider Info A monthly consumer magazine covering motoring and motorcycling. Present circulation of 47,511. Queries accepted by mail and email.
Non-fiction Publishes features, reviews, new product profiles and technical articles.
Submission Guidelines Accepts queries and complete manuscripts.
Tips Britain's best selling sports bike magazine. Focuses on serious testing, technical features and in-depth bike reviews. Mostly publishes articles on road testing of high performance bikes or technical features, so any expertise in these areas – especially technical bike maintenance/modification – would be favourable.

Surrey Life
Holmesdale House, 46 Croydon Road, Reigate, Surrey, RH2 0NH
- 01737 248802
- 01737 246596
- editor@surreylife.co.uk
- www.surreylife.co.uk

Editor Caroline Harrap
Established 1970
Insider Info A monthly consumer magazine covering Surrey. Accepts queries by mail or email.
Non-fiction Interested in lifestyle, arts, history, interviews, cooking, event listings and local interest articles related to Surrey.

T3
2 Balcombe Street, London, NW1 6NW
- 020 7042 4000
- t3@futurenet.co.uk
- www.t3.co.uk

Parent Company Future Publishing Ltd
Editor James Beechinor-Collins
Contact Deputy Editor, Luke Peters; Commissioning Editor, Nigel Brown; Art Editor, Stuart James
Established 1997
Insider Info A monthly consumer magazine covering gadgets and technology. Present circulation is 60,028.
Non-fiction Publishes news, reviews and feature articles.
Tips Gadgets covered include digital cameras, computers, hi-fis, home cinema equipment and PDAs. The magazine is aimed primarily at men aged between 25 and 45 years old.

Take A Break
Academic House, 24–28 Oval Road, London, NW1 7DT
- 020 7241 8000
- 020 7241 8052
- tab.features@bauer.co.uk
- www.bauer.co.uk

Parent Company H. Bauer Publishing
Editor John Dale
Contact Fiction Editor, Norah McGrath; Features Writer, Tina Campanella; Editorial Assistant, Katie Slater
Established 1990
Insider Info A weekly consumer magazine covering women's lifestyle topics. Present circulation of 981,504.
Non-fiction Publishes general interest features, interviews and photo features on real life, fashion, beauty, food, home, travel and competitions.
Fiction Publishes women's short fiction.
Tips The title is aimed specifically at women aged 25 to 55, with children. It has been the UK's biggest selling women's weekly for more than 14 years.

Taliesin
Ty Mount Stuart, Sgwâr Mount Stuart, Cardiff, CF10 5FQ
- 029 2047 2266
- 029 2049 2930
- taliesin@academi.org
- www.academi.org/taliesin

Parent Company Yr Academi Gymreig
Editor Manon Rhys
Established 1959
Insider Info Welsh language literary journal, published three times per year (March, July,

December) by the Academi, which is the Welsh National Literature Promotion Agency and Society for Authors. Present circulation of 1,000. Queries accepted by mail and email.

Non-fiction Publishes features, interviews/profiles and reviews on all subjects to do with Welsh literature.

Fiction Publishes fiction.

Tips *Taliesin* is written purely in the Welsh language and will only accept submissions related to Welsh literature.

TATE ETC
20 John Islip Street, London, SW1P 4RG
- 020 7887 8724
- 020 7887 3940
- tateetc@tate.org.uk
- www.tate.org.uk/tateetc

Editor Simon Grant

Insider Info A consumer magazine, with three issues per year, that covers visual arts and galleris. Accepts queries by mail or email.

Non-fiction Interested in reviews, previews, interviews, opinion and feature articles.

Submission Guidelines No unsolicited manuscripts.

Tips *TATE ETC* is published the Tate art gallery. All articles are commissioned privately so the magazine does not accept unsolicited manuscripts.

Tatler
Vogue House, 1 Hanover Square, London, W1S 1JU
- 020 7499 9080
- 020 7409 0451
- fiona.kent@condenast.co.uk
- www.tatler.co.uk

Parent Company Conde Nast Publications Ltd
Editor Geordie Greig
Established 1707

Insider Info A monthly consumer magazine, covering contemporary British society/lifestyle/fashion. Present circulation of 90,128. Queries accepted by mail.

Non-fiction Publishes features, interviews/profiles and general interest articles.

Submission Guidelines Send query with published clips and CV.

Tips Carries articles on a broad number of topics, but its primary focus is on social trends amongst the very wealthy and aristocratic. Previous Editor Geordie Greig said that reading *Tatler* should be 'like a fabulous journey in an incredible sports car... It should be a journey of speed and surprises.'

Taxation
2 Addiscombe Road, Croydon, Surrey, CR9 5AF
- 020 8212 1949
- 020 8212 1970
- mike.truman@lexisnexis.co.uk
- www.taxation.co.uk

Parent Company LexisNexis
Editor Mike Truman
Contact Feature Editor, Allison Plager
Established 1927

Insider Info A weekly trade journal covering accountancy. Present circulation of 8,358. Queries accepted by mail and email.

Non-fiction Publishes technical and legal articles on taxation.

* Payment for unsolicited articles is £100 per 800 words.

Submission Guidelines Accepts queries and complete manuscripts. Articles must be 2,000 words.

Tips The magazine provides its readership with news and comment on legal decisions for all those engaged in tax work, as well as information on changes in legislation, and items affecting tax practice. There are practical solutions to problems, lively debate, and commentary from leading experts every week. Professional expertise in tax law or similar is a pre-requisite for submissions. Articles – ideally about upcoming changes in UK tax law – should examine the legal issues thoroughly and also present solutions to any problems.

tBkmag
4 Froxfield Close, Winchester, SO22 6JW
- 01962 620320
- www.newbooksmag.com

Parent Company New Books
Editor Guy Pringle

Insider Info A quarterly book magazine for pre-teenage readers (the sister publication of *myBOOKSmag*). Present circulation of 10,000.

Non-fiction Publishes features, interviews/profiles, reviews, general interest articles and event news.

Submission Guidelines Send query before submitting.

Fiction Publishes book excerpts.

Submission Guidelines Send query before submitting.

Tips Publishes book reviews, information on children's and young adult books, book excerpts, interviews, and reports on events for young readers. *tBkmag* often requires reviews and book excerpts from the latest children's and young people's books.

The Teacher
Hamilton House, Mabledon Place, London, WC1H 9BD

☎ 020 7380 4708
⊜ 020 7383 7230
Parent Company National Union of Teachers
Editor Elyssa Campbell-Barr
Established 1872
Insider Info A magazine, with eight issues per year, that covers education and teaching. Accepts queries by mail or email.
Non-fiction Interested in news and feature articles related to teaching.
Submission Guidelines Accepts queries and completed manuscript submissions of up to 750 words.

Tears in the Fence
38 Hod View, Stourpaine, Blandford Forum, Dorset, DT11 8TN
☎ 01258 456803
⊜ 01258 454026
Editor David Caddy
Contact Associate Editor, Sarah Hopkins
Established 1984
Insider Info An international literary journal, published three times a year, covering poetry, fiction, translations, reviews and essays from new and established writers around the world. 100 per cent of the publication is written by freelance writers. Byline is given. Queries are accepted by mail and email. Sample copy is available online.
Non-fiction Publishes features and reviews.
Submission Guidelines Send query with SAE before submitting.
Fiction Publishes mainstream and experimental fiction.
Submission Guidelines Send complete manuscript with SAE. Submissions must be 100–25,000 words.
Poetry Publishes free verse, light verse and avant-garde poetry.
Submission Guidelines Accepts sample poems with SAE.
Tips *Tears in the Fence* focuses on political and socio-economic themes and is keen to keep up to date with the latest trends in world poetry. The magazine does not have a set theme for poetry and fiction submissions, but is looking for work that is unexpected and takes the reader on a journey.

10th Muse
33 Hartington Road, Southampton, SO14 0EW
⊜ a.jordan@surfree.co.uk
Editor Andrew Jordan
Insider Info An occasional consumer magazine, at £3.50 per issue, aimed at a literary audience. Focuses on poetry, short fiction and some artwork. Aims to respond to queries and manuscripts within 12 weeks.

Fiction Publishes short fiction articles.
Submission Guidelines Accepts queries with SAE for articles of up to 2,000 words.
Poetry Publishes avant-garde and free verse poetry.
Submission Guidelines Accepts queries with SAE and up to six sample poems.
Tips *10th Muse* is a small magazine that focuses particularly on innovative contemporary poetry.

Tesco: The Magazine
Pegasus House, 37–43 Sackville Street, London, W1S 3EH
☎ 020 7534 2400
⊜ 020 7534 2555
⊜ emma.oliver@cedarcom.co.uk
⊕ www.tescomagazine.co.uk
Parent Company Cedar Communications Ltd and Tesco
Editor Dawn Alford
Contact Editorial Assistant, Emma Oliver
Established 1993
Insider Info A bi-monthly consumer magazine for the customers of Tesco supermarket, covering food, drink and retail issues. Present circulation of 1,951,020.
Non-fiction Publishes general interest articles, interviews, reviews and photo features on food, wine, new products, parenting, cookery, fashion, beauty, health and lifestyle.
Tips The magazine is aimed at women aged 25 to 45. The editorial content of the magazine accounts for roughly 70 per cent, the rest is advertising.

Textualities
8 Lauriston Street, Edinburgh, EH3 9EU
☎ 0131 228 4837
⊜ 0131 228 4837
⊜ the.editor@textualities.net
⊕ www.textualities.net
Editor Jennie Renton
Insider Info The annual printed journal of textualities.net, an online literature and writing magazine.
Non-fiction Publishes interviews/profiles, literary criticism, bibliography and general interest articles.
Submission Guidelines Send complete manuscript. Accepts email submissions.
Fiction Publishes mainstream fiction.
Submission Guidelines Send complete manuscript. Accepts email submissions.
Poetry Publishes free verse and traditional poetry.
Submission Guidelines Submit sample poetry. Accepts email submissions.
Tips The journal includes new fiction and poetry, literary criticism, interviews and bibliography. To submit an article to textualities.net or *Textualities*

print edition, email the Editor with your proposal. All submitted articles must relate in some way to books and writing.

That's Life!

24–28 Oval Road, London, NW1 7DT

- 020 7241 8000
- 020 7241 8008
- jo.checkley@bauer.co.uk
- www.bauer.co.uk/our-magazines/thats-life

Parent Company H. Bauer Publishing
Editor Jo Checkley
Established 1995
Insider Info A weekly consumer magazine, covering women's interests and lifestyle. Present circulation of 433,921. Seasonal material must be submitted three months in advance. Queries accepted by mail and email. Aims to respond to manuscripts with six weeks. Writer's guidelines are available free on request and by email.
Fiction Publishes romance, humorous and mainstream short fiction.
* Maximum payment for accepted submissions is £400.
Submission Guidelines Send complete manuscript. Submissions must be 700 words. Will not accept straightforward romance, historical, science fiction, animal or children's stories. No stories about gratuitous violence or sex crimes.
Tips Short stories should have a strong plot and a good twist. A sexy relationship/scene can feature strongly, but isn't essential – the plot twist is much more important. The writing should be chronological and fast moving, with a maximum of four characters.

This Is...

PO Box 16185, Writing Space Publications, London, NW1 8ZH

- writingspace@btinternet.com
- www.btinternet.com/~writingspace/thisis/

Parent Company Writing Space Publications
Editor Carol Cornish
Insider Info Quarterly consumer literary magazine covering short fiction and poetry. Byline is given. Accepts queries by mail and email. Manuscript guidelines are available online.
Non-fiction Interested in features and articles on poetry.
Submission Guidelines Accepts queries in the first instance.
Fiction Publishes mainstream and experimental short fiction and works in progress.
Submission Guidelines Accepts complete manuscripts.

Poetry Publishes avant-garde, contemporary and free verse poetry.
Tips *This Is...* looks for extreme writing with a 'sharp cutting edge', that is non-conformist and will force a reaction from the reader. The magazine has a theme for every issue and submissions must be written with the theme in my mind. Forthcoming themes will be detailed on the website, along with submission guidelines.

3D World

30 Monmouth Street, Bath, BA1 2BW

- 01225 442244
- jim.thacker@futurenet.co.uk
- www.3dworldmag.com

Parent Company Future Publishing
Editor Jim Thacker
Insider Info A consumer magazine published every four weeks, specialising in computing. Every issue of *3D World* comes with a CD containing 3D resources, including full software, exclusive trial and learning editions, models, textures, HDRI files, mocap data and architectural content. Present circulation is 15,069.
Non-fiction Publishes general, technical and how-to articles on computers and 3D design.
Tips A strong technical knowledge base is required in every article. Tutorials and 'how to' guides are the main focus of the magazine.

Time

Brettenham House, Lancaster Place, London, WC2E 7TL

- 020 7499 4080
- edit_office@timemagazine.com
- www.timeeurope.com

Parent Company Time Inc
Editor Eric Pooley
Established 1923
Insider Info Weekly consumer magazine covering international news and current affairs. Present circulation is 136,164.
Non-fiction Publishes news and features on world affairs.
Tips *Time* offers very little opportunity for freelance work, as nearly all of its material is produced internally in its various international bureaus.

Time Out London

Universal House, 251 Tottenham Court Road, London, W1T 7AB

- 020 7813 3000
- 020 7813 6001
- editorial@timeout.com
- www.timeout.com

Parent Company Time Out Group Ltd

Editor Gordon Thompson
Contact Publisher, Mark Elliot; Deputy Editor, Rachel Halliburton; Features Editor, Nina Caplan
Established 1968
Insider Info Weekly consumer magazine covering consumer lifestyle and culture in London. Present circulation is 87,308. Accepts queries by mail.
Non-fiction Interested in interviews/profiles, reviews, general interest articles on London entertainment and events listings.
Submission Guidelines Accepts proposals for articles up to 2,000 words in length.
Tips *Time Out London* is the Time Out Group's flagship publication. It was the first listings magazine to cover all aspects of cultural and consumer life in London. The magazine is always looking for ideas for relevant articles, but a detailed local knowledge of the entertainment scene is required.

The Times Educational Supplement
26 Red Lion Square, London, WC1R 4HQ
- 020 3194 3000
- 020 3194 3200
- features@tes.co.uk
- www.tes.co.uk

Parent Company TSL Education Ltd
Editor Jo Faragher
Established 1910
Insider Info Weekly consumer magazine covering education. Present circulation is 57,714. Accepts queries by mail.
Non-fiction Interested in features, reviews and general interest articles on education.
Submission Guidelines Accepts queries (including published clips and CV) for articles of between 1,000 to 2,000 words.
Tips *The Times Educational Supplement* is Britain's leading publication covering the world of primary, secondary and further education, as well as the market leader for teaching job vacancies. Specialist knowledge in the teaching industry is required for all submissions, but a sense of humour is also important.

The Times Educational Supplement Cymru
Sophia House, 28 Cathedral Road, Cardiff, CF11 9LJ
- 02920 660201
- 02920 660207
- cymru@tes.co.uk
- www.tes.co.uk/cymru

Parent Company TSL Education Ltd
Editor Nicola Porter
Established 2004

Insider Info Weekly consumer magazine covering education in Wales. Accepts queries by mail.
Non-fiction Interested in features, interviews/profiles and technical or general interest articles on Welsh education.
Submission Guidelines Accepts queries (including published clips and CV) for articles of between 1,000 to 2,000 words.
Tips *The Times Educational Supplement Cymru* is the sister magazine to *The Times Educational Supplement*. It covers primary, secondary and further education in Wales.

The Times Educational Supplement Scotland
21–23 Thistle Street, Edinburgh, EH2 1DF
- 0131 624 8333
- 0131 624 8350
- scoted@tes.co.uk
- www.tes.co.uk/scotland

Parent Company TSL Education Ltd
Editor Neil Munro
Established 1965
Insider Info Weekly consumer magazine covering Scottish education. Present circulation is roughly 7,062. Accepts queries by mail.
Non-fiction Interested in features, interviews/profiles and technical or general interest articles on Scottish education.
Submission Guidelines Accepts queries (including published clips and CV) for articles of between 1,000 to 2,000 words.
Tips *The Times Educational Supplement Scotland* is the sister magazine to *The Times Educational Supplement*. It covers the world of primary, secondary and further education in Scotland, and is the market leader for Scottish teaching job vacancies. Specialist knowledge in the teaching industry is required for all submissions, but a sense of humour is also important.

The Times Higher Education Supplement
26 Red Lion Square, London, WC1R 4HQ
- 020 3194 3000
- 020 3194 3300
- gerard.kelly@tsleducation.com
- www.thes.co.uk

Parent Company TSL Education Ltd
Established 1971
Insider Info Weekly consumer magazine covering higher education. Accepts queries by mail. Present circulation is 21,140.
Non-fiction Interested in features, reviews, statistics and general interest articles on higher education.

Submission Guidelines Accepts queries (including published clips and CV) for articles of between 1,000 to 2,000 words.

Tips *The Times Higher Education Supplement* is Britain's leading publication covering the world of higher education. Specialist knowledge or experience of the teaching industry is required for all submissions.

The Times Literary Supplement

Times House, 1 Pennington Street, London, E98 1BS

- 020 7782 5000
- 020 7782 4966
- letters@the-tls.co.uk
- www.the-tls.co.uk

Parent Company TSL Education Ltd
Editor Peter Stothard
Established 1902
Insider Info Weekly consumer literary magazine covering literature, literary criticism and literary markets. Present circulation is 36,535. Accepts queries by mail.
Non-fiction Interested in essays, features, reviews and articles on poetry, current affairs and literature.
Submission Guidelines Accepts queries in the first instance.
Fiction Publishes book excerpts.
Poetry Publishes poetry.
Submission Guidelines Accepts sample poems.
Tips Since 1902, *The Times Literary Supplement* has followed the work of the twentieth century's leading writers and thinkers. The supplement covers developments in literature, politics, scholarship and the arts, and will consider poems, literary discoveries and current affairs articles for publication.

Today's Golfer

Bushfield House, Orton Centre, Peterborough, PE2 5UW

- 01733 288016
- 01733 288014
- editorial@todaysgolfer.co.uk
- www.todaysgolfer.co.uk

Parent Company Bauer Consumer Media
Editor Andy Calton
Contact Deputy Editor, Chris Jones; Course Editor, Kevin Brown; Equipment Editor, Simon Daddow
Established 1988
Insider Info A monthly consumer magazine covering golf. Present circulation is 86,428.
Non-fiction Publishes features, interviews, equipment reviews, tips and course guides.
Tips *Today's Golfer* is aimed generally at the amateur leisure golfer.

Toni & Guy Magazine

58–60 Stamford Street, London, SE1 9LX

- 020 7921 9018
- mfitzgerald@fstcomms.com
- www.toniandguy.com

Parent Company Fitzgerald Shurey Tarbuck
Contact Editorial, Mark Fitzgerald
Established 2003
Insider Info A quarterly consumer magazine covering hairstyles and fashion. Present circulation is 100,000.
Non-fiction Publishes features and product review articles on hair care.
Tips *Toni & Guy Magazine* is distributed to customers of their hair salons across the UK. It covers a range of hair, fashion and beauty articles as well as the latest Toni & Guy news and product reviews.

TopGear

Woodlands, 80 Wood Lane, London, W12 0TT

- 020 8433 2313
- 020 8433 3754
- sarah.bold@bbc.co.uk
- www.topgear.com

Parent Company BBC Worldwide Publishing
Editor Michael Harvey
Contact Deputy Editor, Peter Grunert; Editorial Assistant, Sarah Martin
Insider Info A monthly consumer magazine covering new cars and car buying. Present circulation is 182,706.
Non-fiction Publishes photo features, road tests, reviews, buying guides and technical articles.
Tips *TopGear* is the official magazine of the BBC television programme of the same name and maintains a similar editorial style.

Top of the Pops Magazine

Media Centre, 201 Wood Lane, London, W12 7TQ

- 020 8433 3910
- peter.hart@bbc.com
- www.totpmag.com

Parent Company BBC Worldwide Publishing
Editor Peter Hart
Contact Publisher, Duncan Gray; Art Director, Terry Hewitt; Deputy Editor, Lara Hutcheson
Insider Info A monthly consumer magazine covering popular music. Present circulation is 130,174.
Non-fiction Publishes features, interviews, profiles, reviews and event listings.
Tips *Top of the Pops* magazine is aimed at teenagers.

Top Santé Health & Beauty

Greater London House, Hampstead Road, London, NW1 7EJ

● 020 7874 0200

● 020 7391 3333

● www.emap.co.uk

Parent Company Bauer Consumer Media

Editor Lauren Libbert

Contact Features Writer, Fiona Embleton; Editorial Assistant, Victoria Joy

Established 1993

Insider Info A monthly consumer magazine covering health and beauty topics. Present circulation of 92,981.

Non-fiction Publishes general interest features, and photo features on health, fitness and beauty.

Tips Aimed at women of all ages. As well as general health and beauty features, the magazine also publishes details of medical reports and specific health issues.

Total Carp

2 Stephenson Close, Drayton Fields Industrial Estate, Daventry, NN11 8RF

● 01327 311999

● 01327 311190

● marccoulson@dhpub.co.uk

● www.total-fishing.com

Parent Company David Hall Publishing Ltd

Editor Marc Coulson

Contact Publisher, David Hall; Deputy Editor, Jonathan Bones

Established 1999

Insider Info A monthly consumer magazine covering carp fishing. Present circulation is 22,524.

Non-fiction Publishes news, features, product reviews, advice and how-to articles.

Total Film

2 Balcombe Street, London, NW1 6NW

● 020 7317 2600

● 020 7042 4839

● totalfilm@futurenet.co.uk

● www.totalfilm.com

Parent Company Future Publishing

Editor Nev Pierce

Contact Associate Editor (Film), Jamie Graham; Associate Editor (Art), Andy Lowe

Established 1996

Insider Info Monthly consumer magazine covering film and video reviews. Present circulation is 84,520. Payment is on acceptance.

Non-fiction Interested in features, reviews and general interest articles on film.

Submission Guidelines Accepts queries in the first instance.

Tips *Total Film* covers all the latest releases, exclusive news and DVD reviews, plus interviews, features and competitions. Short review material will be published, but longer features are generally privately commissioned.

Total Guitar

30 Monmouth Street, Bath, BA1 2BW

● 01225 442244

● totalguitar@futurenet.co.uk

● www.totalguitar.co.uk

Parent Company Future Publishing

Editor Stephen Lawson

Contact News Editor, Nick Cracknell

Insider Info Monthly consumer magazine covering practical guitar playing and reviews. Present circulation is 48,673.

Non-fiction Publishes product reviews, artist profiles and interviews as well as techniques and tutorial pages.

Tips Aimed at guitarists and guitar enthusiasts of all abilities, but leans heavily towards novices, with more tutorial content than features.

Total Sea Fishing

2 Stephenson Close, Drayton Fields Industrial Estate, Daventry, NN11 8RF

● 01327 311999

● 01327 311190

● barney.wright@dhpub.co.uk

● www.total-fishing.com

Parent Company David Hall Publishing Ltd

Editor Barney Wright

Contact Publisher, David Hall; Deputy Editor, Roger Mortimore

Established 1998

Insider Info A monthly consumer magazine covering sea fishing.

Non-fiction Publishes news, features, product reviews, advice and how-to articles.

Total Vauxhall

30 Monmouth Street, Bath, BA1 2BW

● 01225 442244

● 01225 732275

● drankine@futurenet.co.uk

● www.totalvauxhall.co.uk

Parent Company Future Publishing Ltd

Editor Barton Brisland

Contact Features Editor, Dougie Rankine

Established 2001

Insider Info A monthly consumer magazine covering Vauxhall cars. Present circulation is 28,000.

Non-fiction Publishes photo features, product reviews, technical advice and how-to articles.

Tips *Total Vauxhall* covers buying and selling of Vauxhall cars, and practical advice on repair and modification.

Toybox
Room A1130, Woodlands, 80 Wood Lane, London, W12 0TT
- 020 8433 2000
- 020 8433 2941
- divinia.fleary@bbc.co.uk

Parent Company BBC Children's Magazines
Editor Paddy Kempshall
Contact Divinia Fleary, Editorial Assistant
Insider Info A monthly consumer magazine covering toys and puzzles. Present circulation is 73,290.
Non-fiction Publishes stories, puzzles, games, colouring and competitions.
Tips *Toybox* is aimed at children aged between three and five years old.

Traction
The Maltings, West Street, Bourne, Lincolnshire, PE10 9PH
- 01778 391160
- 01778 425437
- davidb@warnersgroup.co.uk
- www.traction.co.uk

Parent Company Warners Group Publications
Contact Managing Editor, David Brown
Established 1993
Insider Info Monthly consumer magazine covering diesel and electric railway nostalgia. Present circulation is 8,000. 90 per cent of the publication is written by freelance writers. Manuscripts are published 14 days after acceptance. Payment is on publication and a byline is given. Publication is not copyrighted and first UK serial rights will be purchased. Average lead time is two days. Seasonal material must be submitted one month in advance. Accepts queries by mail and email. Aims to respond to queries within two weeks and manuscripts within five weeks. Sample copy and manuscript guidelines are free on request.
Non-fiction Interested in photo features, features, reviews and technical articles.
* Purchases over 100 manuscripts per year. Payment is £50 per published page.
Submission Guidelines Accepts proposals or complete manuscripts of between 750 and 8,500 words. Does not publish reprints. Send submissions to Managing Editor, David Brown.
Images Accepts images with submission.
* Payment varies from between £15 to £50 per photo. Purchases one-time rights.

Submission Guidelines Send transparencies, prints or gif/jpeg files, with captions and identification of subjects to, Managing Editor, David Brown. Send photos with submissions.
Tips *Traction* is devoted to classic diesel and electric trains, past and present. Ideas for potential articles can be sent to the Managing Editor for approval. Submissions require a good knowledge and/or enthusiasm of railway operation.

Tractor & Machinery
Cudham Tithe Barn, Berrys Hill, Berrys Green, Westerham, TN16 3AG
- 01323 833125
- 01323 833125
- peter.love@kelsey.co.uk

Parent Company Kelsey Publishing Ltd
Editor Peter Love
Contact Publisher, Stephen Wright
Established 1994
Insider Info A monthly consumer magazine covering tractors and other machinery. Present circulation is 48,012.
Non-fiction Publishes features, news, practical and historical articles.
Tips *Tractor & Machinery* covers all aspects of antique, classic and modern tractors and other machinery from around the world. Features of particular interest are history and restoration projects, vintage news, sales, models and pricing guides.

Trail
Bretton Court, Bretton, Peterborough, PE3 8DZ
- 01733 264666
- 01733 282653
- trail@bauermedia.com
- www.trailroutes.com

Parent Company Bauer Consumer Media
Editor Matt Swaine
Contact Publisher, Mel Bagnall; Editor in Chief, Guy Proctor; Features Editor, Simon Ingram; Art Editor, Louise Parker
Established 1990
Insider Info A monthly consumer magazine covering trail walking, climbing and cycling. Present circulation is 39,349.
Non-fiction Publishes features, profiles, advice and review articles on all aspects of trail sports, including walking, running, climbing and mountain biking.
Tips Articles contain clothing and equipment reviews, as well as fitness advice and techniques.

Translation & Literature
Edinburgh University Press Ltd, 22 George Square, Edinburgh, EH8 9LF

- ☎ 0131 650 4218
- ☏ 0131 662 0053
- ✉ editorial@eup.ed.ac.uk
- 🌐 www.eup.ed.ac.uk

Parent Company Edinburgh University Press Ltd
Editor Stuart Gillespie
Established 1992
Insider Info A consumer literary journal, with two issues per year, covering literary translation. Present circulation is 500.
Non-fiction Interested in essays, features, technical articles, opinions and historical/nostalgic articles.
Submission Guidelines Accepts queries in the first instance.
Tips *Translation and Literature* is an academic journal that prints articles on translations of classic texts into English language, translation theory and techniques, and the history of translation in literature. Will consider articles on any theme related to translation in literature, but they must be from established academics in the field.

Traveller

Traveller/Wexas, 45–49 Brompton Road, London, SW3 1DE

- ☎ 020 7589 3315
- ☏ 020 7589 8418
- ✉ traveller@wexas.com
- ✉ duncanmills@wexas.com
- 🌐 www.traveller.org.uk

Parent Company WEXAS Ltd
Editor Amy Sohanpaul
Contact Deputy Editor, Duncan Mills
Established 1970
Insider Info Quarterly consumer magazine covering travel. Present circulation is 23,817. 50 per cent of the publication is written by freelance writers. Submissions are published up to three months after acceptance. Payment is on publication and a byline is given. Publication is copyrighted and one time rights are purchased. Average lead time is three months. Seasonal material must be submitted four months in advance. Accepts queries by mail, email, fax and telephone. Manuscript guidelines are free on request and available online or by email.
Non-fiction Interested in features, travel and personal experience articles.
* Pay for unsolicited articles ranges from £100 to £200.
Submission Guidelines Accepts manuscripts of between 800 and 1,000 words.
Images Accepts images with submission.
* Negotiates payment individually. Purchases one-time rights.
Submission Guidelines Send contact sheets, transparencies and gif/jpeg files, to Deputy Editor, Duncan Mills. Send images with submissions.

Tips *Traveller* is the UK's oldest travel magazine and reports on the real experience of travelling the world, especially to 'off the beaten track' destinations.

Tremblestone

Stowford House, 43 Seymour Avenue, St Judes, Plymouth, PL4 8RB

- 🌐 www.tremblestone.co.uk

Editor Kenny Knight
Established 1999
Insider Info A literary journal covering contemporary poetry as well as literature reviews. Byline is given. Accepts queries by mail. Aims to respond to queries and manuscripts within two months.
Non-fiction Interested in articles on poetry and literary reviews.
Submission Guidelines Accepts queries in the first instance.
Poetry Publishes contemporary, avant-garde, free verse and light verse poetry.
Submission Guidelines Submit up to six poems at a time.
Tips *Tremblestone* is a literary journal with an international outlook, which publishes new contemporary poetry, as well as book and magazine reviews. It is open to 'surprising' poetry and is looking for the more unusual side of contemporary poetry, including submissions from abroad.

Trout & Salmon

Bushfield House, Orton Centre, Peterborough, PE2 5UW

- ☎ 01733 237111
- ☏ 01733 465820
- ✉ andrew.flitcroft@bauermedia.com
- 🌐 www.trout-and-salmon.com

Parent Company Bauer Consumer Media
Editor Andrew Flitcroft
Contact Deputy Editor, Richard Baker; Features Editor, Henry Giles; Art Editor, October Ward
Established 1955
Insider Info A monthly consumer magazine covering game fishing. Present circulation is 33,183.
Non-fiction Publishes photo features, product reviews and practical advice articles.
Tips *Trout & Salmon* covers all aspects of salmon and trout fishing. Publishes articles from angling writers or photographers, anecdotes, and advice on tackle, tactics and location. Also publishes regular 'Fishing Reports'.

Trout Fisherman

Bushfield House, Orton Centre, Peterborough, PE2 5UW

- ☎ 01733 237111
- ✆ 01733 465820
- ✉ russell.hill@bauermedia.com
- 🌐 www.troutfisherman.co.uk

Parent Company Bauer Consumer Media
Editor Russell Hill
Contact Publisher, Steve Windsor; Features Editor, Jeffrey Prest; Art Editor, Hakan Simsek
Insider Info A monthly consumer magazine covering fishing. Present circulation is 25,673.
Non-fiction Publishes photo features, product reviews and practical advice articles.
Tips Articles include technique advice, fly tying, tackle reviews and also a guide to day ticket fisheries in the UK. The magazine is aimed at stillwater trout fishermen, and novice and experienced fly anglers.

Trucking

30 Monmouth Street, Bath, BA1 2BW
- ☎ 01225 442244
- ✆ 01225 446019
- ✉ steev.hayes@futurenet.co.uk

Parent Company Future Publishing Ltd
Editor Steve Hayes
Established 1983
Insider Info A monthly trade journal covering trucking. Present circulation is 20,032.
Non-fiction Publishes legal advice, news, product tests and profiles.
Tips *Trucking* is aimed at professionals within the trucking industry.

25 Beautiful Homes

Blue Fin Building, 110 Southwark Street, London, SE1 0SU
- ☎ 020 3148 5000
- ✆ 020 7261 6680
- ✉ 25_beautiful_homes@ipcmedia.com
- 🌐 www.ipcmedia.com

Parent Company IPC Media Ltd
Editor John Smigielski
Contact Publishing Director, Yvonne Ramsden; Publisher, Chris Kelly
Established 1997
Insider Info A consumer magazine, with 13 issues per year, covering homes and decorating. Circulation is 118,373. Media pack available online.
Non-fiction Publishes construction, interior design and home showcase articles.
Tips *25 Beautiful Homes* showcases 25 real homes every issue, covering aspects of their construction, design and decoration.

25 Beautiful Kitchens

Blue Fin Building, 110 Southwark Street, London, SE1 0SU

- ☎ 020 3148 5000
- ✆ 020 7261 6680
- ✉ ysanne_brooks@ipcmedia.com
- 🌐 www.ipcmedia.com

Parent Company IPC Media Ltd
Editor Ysanne Brooks
Contact Publishing Director, Yvonne Ramsden; Publisher, Belinda Cooper; Chief Sub Editor, Rachel Ogden
Established 1997
Insider Info A consumer magazine, with ten issues per year, covering kitchen design and decorating. Circulation is 30,375. Media pack available online.
Non-fiction Publishes construction, interior design and kitchen showcase articles.
Tips *25 Beautiful Kitchens,* sister magazine of *25 Beautiful Homes*, showcases 25 real kitchens every issue and covers aspects of their construction, design and decoration.

247 Magazine

Grosvenor House, Belgrave Lane, Plymouth, Devon, PL4 7DA
- ☎ 01752 294130
- ✆ 01752 601199
- ✉ 247@outofhand.co.uk
- 🌐 www.247magazine.co.uk

Parent Company Out of Hand Ltd
Contact Managing Editor, Nigel Muntz
Established 2000
Insider Info A consumer magazine publication, issued monthly, covering music and lifestyle in the South West of England. Present circulation of 30,000. 50 per cent of the magazine is written by freelancers. Average lead time of one month. Publication is copyrighted, and a byline is given. Purchases simultaneous, electronic and regional rights. Seasonal material must be submitted two months in advance. Aims to respond to queries within a day, manuscripts and other issues within five days. Payment is on publication, via cash, with assignment expenses sometimes paid (limit agreed upon in advance). Sample copy and writer's guidelines are available free on request, online or via email. Editorial calendars are free on request.
Non-fiction Interested in photo features, new products and travel writing.
* Maximum payment for both assigned and unsolicited articles is £200.
Submission Guidelines Send query before sending submissions. Articles must be 1,000–1,500 words.
Images Accepts images with submission.
* Offers no additional payment for photos accepted with manuscripts. One time rights are purchased.
Submission Guidelines Send images as gif/jpeg files, with captions, model releases and identification of subjects.

Tips Target audience are 18–35 year olds living in, or visiting, South West England. Includes music, lifestyle and listings guides for all suitable events taking place in the region.

U
1 Mabledon Place, London, WC1H 9AJ
☎ 0845 355 0845
🌐 www.unison.org.uk/news/umagazine.asp
Parent Company UNISON
Insider Info A quarterly consumer magazine covering UNISON issues. Present circulation is 1,476,877. Sample copy is free on request.
Non-fiction Publishes news, interviews, profiles, features and current affairs articles.
Tips *U* is the magazine of UNISON trade union. It is quarterly and distributed only to UNISON members. It covers any issues that affect UNISON members at work and at home, and also publishes interviews and profiles of prominent UNISON members.

The Ugly Tree
6 Chiffon Way, Trinity, Greater Manchester, M3 6AB
✉ flapjackpress@live.co.uk
🌐 www.mucusart.co.uk/theuglytree.htm
Parent Company Mucusart Publications
Editor Paul Neads
Insider Info A consumer magazine, with three issues per year (February, June, October), covering print and performance poetry. Byline is given. Accepts queries by mail and email. Manuscript guidelines are available online.
Non-fiction Interested in articles on poetry and reviews.
Submission Guidelines Accepts queries in the first instance.
Poetry Publishes contemporary, avant-garde, free verse, light verse and spoken/performance poetry.
Submission Guidelines Submit up to five poems of 40 lines in length.
Tips *The Ugly Tree* specialises in the relationship of spoken and performance poetry with the printed page, but will often publish any type or style of poetry. *The Ugly Tree* also prints some interviews, reviews and articles related to poetry and runs poetry writing competitions that offer cash prizes, as well as publication in the magazine.

Ulster Grocer
5b Edgewater Business Park, Edgewater Road, Belfast Harbour Estate, Belfast, Antrim, BT3 9JQ
☎ 028 9078 3200
☎ 028 9078 3210
✉ kathyj@writenow.prestel.co.uk
🌐 www.greerpublications.com

Parent Company Greer Publications
Editor Kathy Jensen
Established 1972
Insider Info Monthly trade journal covering issues relevant to the grocery retail trade in Northern Ireland. Present circulation is 4,287. Five per cent of the publication is written by freelance writers. Submissions are published up to four weeks after acceptance. Payment completed 30 days after publication. Publication is copyrighted. Average lead time is four weeks. Seasonal material must be submitted four weeks in advances. Accepts queries by email. Aims to respond to queries within five days and manuscripts within seven days. Sometimes pays expenses of writers on assignment (limit agreed upon in advance). Sample copy is free on request. Editorial calendar and manuscript guidelines are free on request and available by email. Media pack is available online.
Non-fiction Interested in photo features, relevant news stories, features, interviews/profiles, technical and relevant general interest articles.
* Freelance articles are by commission only. Fee is by agreement beforehand.
Submission Guidelines Accepts queries in the first instance. Articles are between 700 and 2,000 words.
Tips *Ulster Grocer* is ABC audited and is distributed to multiple, symbol and independent retailers; confectionery, tobacconists and newsagents, buyers, wholesalers, FMCG manufacturers, agents and distributors, and others involved in the grocery trade. *Ulster Grocer* is designed to be the key medium to reach the independent retail sector, which continues to account for a significant share of overall Northern Irish grocery spend.

Uncut
Music and Movies With Something To Say
Blue Fin Building, 110 Southwark Street, London, SE1 0SU
☎ 020 3148 5000
✉ farah_ishaq@ipcmedia.com
🌐 www.uncut.co.uk
Parent Company IPC Media Ltd
Editor Allan Jones
Insider Info Monthly consumer magazine covering music and film. Present circulation is 68,925. 75 per cent of the publication is written by freelance writers. Payment is on publication. The kill fee for assigned manuscripts not published is between 50 and 100 per cent. Byline is given. Publication is copyrighted and all rights are purchased. Aims to respond to queries within two months and manuscripts within three months. Accepts queries by mail and email. Manuscript guidelines are free on request.

Non-fiction Interested in features, interviews and reviews.
Images Accepts images with submission.
* Negotiates payment individually. Purchases one-time rights.
Submission Guidelines Send images (contact sheets, negatives, transparencies, prints, gif/jpeg files) to Picture Editor, May Starey. State availability of photos with your submission.

Understanding
20a Montgomery Street, Edinburgh, EH7 5JS
- 0131 478 0680
- 0131 478 0680
Parent Company Dionysia Press
Editor Denise Smith
Established 1989
Insider Info Annual consumer literary magazine covering new poetry, prose and drama. Present circulation is 500.
Non-fiction Interested in essays, literary articles, features and reviews.
Submission Guidelines Accepts queries in the first instance.
Fiction Publishes short fiction and play excerpts.
Submission Guidelines Accepts short fiction with SAE.
Poetry Publishes contemporary and traditional poetry.
Submission Guidelines Accepts sample poetry with SAE.
Tips *Understanding* accepts submissions for general poetry and short fiction, as well as more academic submissions of literary criticism, ideally by post with SAE.

Unlimited
14th Floor, Tower House, Fairfax Street, Bristol, BS1 3BN
- 0117 314 8333
- 0117 934 9008
- patreid@bbccustomerpublishing.com
- www.bbccustomerpublishing.com
Parent Company Bristol Magazines Ltd
Editor Pat Reid
Established 2003
Insider Info A consumer magazine, with ten issues per year, covering film and cinema. Present circulation is 500,500.
Non-fiction Publishes features, interviews, profiles and reviews.
Tips *Unlimited* is a film magazine available from Cineworld cinemas. It covers the latest movie news and reviews, as well as star profiles and interviews.

Urthona Magazine
Old Abbey House, Abbey Road, Cambridge, CB5 8HQ
- 01223 362513
- urthonamag@onetel.com
- www.urthona.com
Parent Company FWBO Arts
Established 1992
Insider Info A consumer magazine, with two issues per year, covering international Buddhist arts and culture. Present circulation is 1,100. Accepts queries by mail and email.
Non-fiction Interested in features, interviews/profiles and reviews linked to Buddhist culture.
Tips *Urthona* is a Buddhist arts and world culture magazine, publishing articles on the arts, including interviews with artists, historical articles, reviews and events news. In particular *Urthona* often publishes Buddhist readings, and interpretations of famous artists or literary works.

Utility Week
Quadrant House, The Quadrant, Sutton, Surrey, SM2 5AS
- 020 8652 8678
- 020 8652 8906
- steve.hobson@rbi.co.uk
- www.utilityweek.co.uk
Parent Company RBI
Editor Steve Hobson
Established 1994
Insider Info Weekly trade journal covering business issues relating to UK utilities (gas, water and electricity). Present circulation is 3,524. 25 per cent of the publication is written by freelance writers. Submissions are published up to six weeks after acceptance. Payment is on acceptance. A byline is given. Publication is copyrighted and all rights are purchased. Average lead time is six weeks. Accepts queries by email and telephone. Simultaneous submissions will be accepted. Aims to respond to queries and manuscripts within one week. Sometimes pays the expenses of writers on assignment. Sample copy, editorial calendars and manuscript guidelines are free on request. Media pack is available online.
Non-fiction Interested in features, new product reviews and technical articles.
* Payment is £220 per 1,000 words.
Submission Guidelines Accepts manuscripts of between 800 and 1,500 words.
Images Accepts images with submission.
* Payment varies per photo. Purchases all rights.
Submission Guidelines Include captions, model releases and identification of subjects. State availability of photos with submission.

Tips *Utility Week* is aimed at managers and directors working for UK utilities companies. Major issues covered include regulation, competitive environment, customer service and asset management. Queries by phone call are preferred.

Vanity Fair
Vogue House, 1 Hanover Square, London, W1S 1JU
- 020 7499 9080
- 020 7409 0783
- www.vanityfair.com

Parent Company Conde Nast Publications
Editor Henry Porter
Established 1914
Insider Info Monthly consumer magazine covering women's interests, lifestyle and fashion. Present circulation is 101,166. Editorial calendars and media pack are available online.
Non-fiction Publishes photo features and general articles on fashion and culture.
Submission Guidelines No unsolicited manuscripts.
Tips *Vanity Fair* is an intellectual and visually orientated magazine that aims to cover the people, places, and ideas that are defining modern culture. *Vanity Fair* does not accept unsolicited manuscripts and commissions all work internally.

Variant
1/2 189b Maryhill Road, Glasgow, G20 7XJ
- 0141 333 9522
- 0141 333 9522
- variantmag@btinternet.com
- www.variant.org.uk

Editor Leigh French
Established 1996
Insider Info A consumer literary magazine, with three issues per year (February, June, October), covering literature, arts and culture. Present circulation is 15,000. Accepts queries by mail and email. Sometimes pays writers with contributor copies. Media pack and manuscript guidelines are available online.
Non-fiction Interested in features, interviews/profiles, reviews and general interest articles.
Submission Guidelines Accepts queries of between 750 and 4,000 words.
Tips Based in Glasgow and Belfast, *Variant* is the UK and Ireland's only free international arts and culture magazine. *Variant* welcomes contributions in the form of news, previews, articles, interviews, polemical pieces and artists pages. It aims to include writing which is constructive and thought provoking, and which provides a context in which younger writers can find a platform for their work.

Vauxhall Magazine
Westgate, 120–128 Station Road, Redhill, RH1 1ET
- 01737 786800
- 01737 786801
- vmeditor@vauxhall.co.uk
- www.vmonline.co.uk

Parent Company Brooklands Group Ltd
Editor Nina San
Contact Publishing Editor, Brian Laban
Established 1996
Insider Info A consumer magazine, with three issues per year, covering Vauxhall cars. Present circulation is 396,294.
Non-fiction Publishes photo features, news, product reviews, lifestyle features and road test articles.
Tips *Vauxhall Magazine* covers the latest news and models of Vauxhall cars and publishes features on new ranges, road tests and maintenance tips. Articles are not always directly related to the cars themselves and may take a more general lifestyle approach.

Vertigo
4th Floor, 26 Shacklewell Lane, London, E8 2EZ
- 020 7690 0124
- editor@vertigomagazine.co.uk
- www.vertigomagazine.co.uk

Editor Holly Aylett
Contact Co-Editor, Gareth Evans
Established 1994
Insider Info Quarterly consumer magazine covering independent film and media. Present circulation is 7,000. Accepts queries by mail and email. Manuscript guidelines are available by email.
Non-fiction Publishes essays, features, interviews/profiles, reviews and opinions.
Submission Guidelines Accepts queries in the first instance.
Tips *Vertigo* magazine is published as both a print and online magazine, and publishes articles, interviews and critical debate about independent and artists' filmmaking. The magazine encourages submission of articles on a voluntary basis. Email the Editor for full submission guidelines.

Village
Ireland's weekly current affairs magazine
44 Westland Row, Dublin 2, Republic of Ireland
- 00353 1 642 5050
- 00353 1 642 5001
- editor@villagemagazine.ie
- www.village.ie

Parent Company Village Communications Ltd
Editor Vincent Browne

Established 2004

Insider Info Weekly consumer magazine covering current affairs, including politics, media, arts, books and technology. Present circulation is 9,467. 30 per cent of the publication is written by freelance writers. Submissions are published up to one week after acceptance. Payment is completed 30 days after publication. A byline is given. Publication is copyrighted and first rights are purchased. Average lead time is three days. Seasonal material must be submitted 14 days in advance. Accepts queries by email. Simultaneous submissions will be accepted. Aims to respond to queries and manuscripts within three days. Sometimes pays expenses of writers on assignment (limit agreed upon in advance). Sample copy and editorial calendars are available online. Manuscript guidelines are free on request.

Non-fiction Publishes nook excerpts (non-fiction), photo features (related to social issues), exposés, religious pieces, features, interviews/profiles, general interest and historical/nostalgic articles.
* Payment is from €100 to €400.

Submission Guidelines Accepts complete manuscripts of between 500 and 2,000 words. Does not publish reprints.

Images Accepts images with submissions.
* Offers no additional payment for photos accepted with manuscripts. Purchases one time rights.

Submission Guidelines Send contact sheets and gif/jpeg files, with captions, to News Editor, John Byrne.

Tips *Village* has a left of centre political viewpoint and all submissions must be written accordingly.

Viz

30 Cleveland Street, London, W1T 4JD

- 020 7907 6000
- 020 7907 6020
- viz@viz.co.uk
- www.viz.co.uk

Parent Company Dennis Publishing
Editor Simon Donald
Established 1979
Insider Info A consumer magazine, with ten issues per year, covering adult humour, satire and cartoons. Present circulation is 88,165.
Fiction Publishes comic-style illustrated fiction.
Tips *Viz* is an adult comic with recurring characters such as 'the Fat Slags', 'Roger Mellie' and 'Sid the Sexist'. It tends to contain lewd content and explicit language. It is mostly an illustrated comic and there is little scope for written contribution, but a high quality satirical article or a spoof newspaper feature may be considered.

Vogue

Vogue House, 1 Hanover Square, London, W1S 1JU

- 020 7499 9080
- 020 7408 0559
- voguemagazine@condenast.co.uk
- www.vogue.co.uk

Parent Company Conde Nast Publications
Editor Alexandra Shulman
Contact Deputy Editor, Emily Sheffield; Features Assistant, Aimee Farrell
Established 1916
Insider Info Monthly consumer magazine covering women's interests, lifestyle and fashion. Present circulation is 221,090.
Non-fiction Publishes photo features on culture, the fashion industry and high-end lifestyle.
Tips *Vogue* is a fashion and lifestyle magazine published in several countries around the world. *Vogue Paris* and *Vogue Italia* are possibly the most influential magazines of the modern fashion world. The magazine tends to use commissioned work, or submissions from well-known writers only, so good internal contacts are important. It's best to focus on upmarket general interest such as highbrow art and literary articles, as well as reviews, home interest, and cuisine.

Volkswagon Golf+

Leon House, 233 High Street, Croydon, CR9 1HZ

- 020 8726 8354
- 020 8726 8399
- golf.ed@kelsey.co.uk
- www.thegolf.co.uk

Parent Company Kelsey Publishing Ltd
Editor Fabian Cotter
Contact Publisher, Gavin De Carle; Art Editor, Justin Smith; Deputy Editor, James Wallace
Established 1995
Insider Info A monthly consumer magazine, covering the Volkswagon Golf community. Circulation is 3,000. Media pack available online.
Non-fiction Publishes photo features, reviews and technical articles.
Tips *Volkswagon Golf+* is a monthly magazine that covers all aspects of the VW Golf community, including car modification, reviews, showcases and technical advice.

VolksWorld

Leon House, 233 High Street, Croydon, CR9 1HZ

- 020 7261 5015
- 020 7261 6680
- volksworld@ipcmedia.com
- www.volksworld.com

Parent Company IPC Media Ltd

Editor Ivan McCutcheon
Contact Publisher, Gavin De Carle
Established 1987
Insider Info A consumer magazine, with 13 issues per year, covering the Volkswagon Beetle community. Circulation is 36,000. Media pack available online.
Non-fiction Publishes news, photo features, reviews and technical articles.
Tips *VolksWorld* covers all aspects of the Volkswagon Beetle community including car modification, reviews, showcases and event and exhibition listings. It also contains a detailed classified section.

Waitrose Food Illustrated

The New Boathouse, 136–142 New Bramley Road, London, W10 6SR
- 020 7565 3000
- 020 7565 3076
- food@jbcp.co.uk
- www.waitrose.com/wfi

Parent Company John Brown Citrus Publishing
Editor William Sitwell
Contact Publisher, Sarah Arthur; Deputy Editor, Paul Dring; Art Director, Brian Saffer; Acting Commissioning Editor, Katy Salter; Features Assistant/Restaurant Editor, Heidi Ruge
Established 1999
Insider Info A monthly consumer magazine covering food and other Waitrose products. Present circulation is 320,006.
Non-fiction Publishes features, reviews, profiles and practical articles.
Tips *Waitrose Food Illustrated* covers all aspects of food, including articles on restaurants, chefs, farmers and producers. Most articles are connected to the Waitrose product range in some way.

Walk

2nd Floor, Camelford House, 87–90 Albert Embankment, London, SE1 7TW
- 020 7339 8500
- 020 7339 8501
- chriso@ramblers.org.uk
- www.ramblers.org.uk

Parent Company The Ramblers Association
Editor Chris Ord
Established 2003
Insider Info Quarterly consumer magazine covering camping, walking, climbing and outdoor interests. Present circulation is 105,168. Payment is on publication. Average lead time is six months. Accepts queries by mail. Sample copy is available with SAE. Manuscript guidelines are free on request or available by email.

Non-fiction Interested in photo features, features and travel articles.
Submission Guidelines Accepts queries of between 500 and 800 words, with published clips.
Images Accepts images with submissions.
* Negotiates payment individually.
Submission Guidelines Send photos with captions
Tips Formerly known as *The Rambler*, *Walk* contains photography, engaging issue-based articles, editorial opinion, reviews, competitions and inspirational walking guides. Articles are normally written in-house. Feature articles should promote an interest in walking, but should not just profile a location. Articles should describe why a particular walk is special to the writer.

Wallpaper*

Brettenham House, Lancaster Place, London, WC2E 7TL
- 020 7322 1177
- 020 7322 1171
- editor@wallpaper.com
- www.wallpaper.com

Parent Company IPC Media Ltd
Editor Tony Chambers
Contact Publishing Director, Gord Ray
Established 1996
Insider Info A consumer magazine, with ten issues per year, covering contemporary interior design and lifestyle. Present circulation is 112,847.
Non-fiction Publishes photo features and general interest articles on contemporary design.
Tips *Wallpaper** prides itself on having 'consistently been one of the most influential design magazines, as well as the most beautiful.' Therefore any submitted articles or ideas must be well-designed and attractive, as well as being on the cutting edge of the latest trends in design.

Wanderlust

PO Box 1832, Windsor, SL4 1YT
- 01753 620426
- www.wanderlust.co.uk

Editor Dan Linstead
Established 1993
Insider Info A consumer magazine, with eight issues per year, covering travel. Accepts queries by mail or email.
Non-fiction Interested in guide, review and feature articles related to travel.
Submission Guidelines Accepts queries and completed manuscript submissions of up to 2,500 words.
Tips *Wanderlust* focuses on independent, adventure and special interest travel.

Wasafiri

The Magazine Of International Contemporary Writing

The Open University, 1–11 Hawley Crescent, Camden Town, London, NW1 8NP

- 020 7556 6110
- 020 7556 6187
- wasafiri@open.ac.uk
- www.wasafiri.org

Editor Susheila Nasta

Contact Editorial Manager, Teresa Palmiero

Established 1984

Insider Info A consumer magazine, with three issues per year (March, July, November), covering all aspects of international writing. Present circulation is 6,000. Byline is given. Accepts queries by mail and email. Manuscript guidelines are available online.

Non-fiction Interested in poetry and prose articles, features, interviews/profiles and reviews.

Submission Guidelines Accepts complete manuscripts of between 1,000 and 2,500 words. Include two hard copies, one for reference, and also an electronic submission.

Fiction Publishes international fiction and translated/foreign language fiction.

Submission Guidelines Accepts complete manuscripts of between 5,000 and 6,000 words. Include two hard copies, one for reference, and also an electronic submission.

Poetry Publishes international poetry.

Tips *Wasafiri* is a literary magazine that focuses on writing as a 'form of cultural travelling'. It prints contemporary international literature, both fiction and poetry, and also various articles on contemporary art and book reviews. *Wasafiri's* website has a very extensive style guide for article submissions.

Waterlog

The Grange, Ellesmere, Shropshire, SY12 9DE

- 01691 623225
- books@medlarpress.com
- www.waterlogmagazine.com

Parent Company The Medlar Press

Editor Co-Editor, Chris Yates

Established 1855

Insider Info A quarterly consumer magazine covering angling.

Non-fiction Publishes news, features, interviews, profiles, event listings and anecdotes related to angling.

Tips *Waterlog* is run by fishing specialists The Medlar Press and is the world's longest-running angling magazine. Approach the publisher with possible contributions.

Waterstone's Books Quarterly

Seven Squared, Sea Containers House, 20 Upper Ground, London, SE1 9PD

- 020 7775 5777
- 020 7775 5711
- ed@sevensquared.co.uk
- www.wbqonline.com

Parent Company Seven Squared

Editor Ed Wood

Established 2001

Insider Info Quarterly consumer magazine covering new books and literary markets at Waterstone's the retailer. Present circulation is 144,350.

Non-fiction Publishes book excerpts, features, interviews/profiles and reviews.

Tips *Waterstone's Books Quarterly* is published to promote new book releases and unknown authors to Waterstone's customer base. The magazine prints book reviews, interviews and articles about the latest developments in the book trade. The majority of content in *Waterstone's Books Quarterly* is made up of reviews of the latest books, many of which are commissioned from freelance writers.

Waterways World

151 Station Street, Burton on Trent, Staffordshire, DE14 1BG

- 01283 742951
- 01283 742957
- richard.fairhurst@wwonline.co.uk

Editor Richard Fairhurst

Established 1972

Insider Info Monthly consumer magazine covering boating and UK waterways. Present circulation is 16,602. Payment is on publication. Average lead time is two months. Accepts queries by mail and email. Manuscript guidelines are free on request or available by email.

Non-fiction Interested in photo features and general interest articles on waterways.

Submission Guidelines Accepts complete manuscripts.

Images Accepts images with submissions.

Submission Guidelines Send transparencies.

Tips *Waterways World* covers all aspects of inland waterways in Britain, and also limited aspects of waterways abroad. It is interested in all canals and navigable rivers, whether operational or derelict, and suggested topics for feature articles include waterways, boats and boating, waterway history and current waterway affairs.

Web User

Blue Fin Building, 110 Southwark Street, London, SE1 0SU

- 020 3148 5000

- editor@web-user.co.uk
- www.webuser.co.uk

Parent Company IPC Media Ltd
Editor Claire Woffenden
Established 2001
Insider Info Bi-weekly consumer magazine covering computing and the internet. Present circulation is 35,279. Accepts queries by mail and email. Media pack is available online.
Non-fiction Publishes general interest article and features on the internet and its uses.
Tips *Web User* is approved by the 'Plain English Campaign' which means that they keep technical jargon to a minimum. Articles must be informative, but clear and easy to read and understand.

Wedding

Blue Fin Building, 110 Southwark Street, London, SE1 0SU
- 020 3148 5000
- 020 7261 7459
- wedding@ipcmedia.com
- www.ipcmedia.com

Parent Company IPC Media Ltd
Editor Catherine Westwood
Contact Publisher, Lynne Bushell; Art Editor, Julia Peter
Established 1997
Insider Info A bi-monthly consumer magazine, covering wedding planning. Circulation is 38,026. Media pack available online.
Non-fiction Publishes beauty, catering, fashion and general wedding planning articles.
Tips Topics covered include beauty tips, fashion and dress shopping, honeymoon travelling, reception and catering, and general wedding ideas. The magazine is aimed women in their mid 20s to early 30s.

Wedding Ideas

8 Hammet Street, Taunton, TA1 1RZ
- 01823 288344
- 01823 288239
- rachelm@weddingideasmagazine.co.uk
- www.weddingideasmagazine.co.uk

Parent Company Giraffe Media Ltd
Editor Rachel Moschke
Contact Deputy Editor, Suzi Dixon
Established 2004
Insider Info A monthly consumer magazine covering marriage and weddings. Present circulation is 29,476.
Non-fiction Publishes features, practical and advice articles on all aspects of getting married, including planning the wedding service and reception, honeymoon ideas, advice on dresses, caterers, venues, flowers, and hair and beauty.
Tips *Wedding Ideas* is aimed at women between the ages of 25 and 35 who are getting married for the first time.

The Weekly News

2 Albert Square, Dundee, Tayside, DD1 9QJ
- 01382 223131
- 01382 201390
- weeklynews@dcthomson.co.uk
- www.dcthomson.co.uk

Parent Company D.C. Thomson & Co. Ltd
Editor David Burness
Contact Deputy Editor, Rod Cameron
Established 1855
Insider Info Weekly consumer newspaper covering news, culture and lifestyle. Present circulation is 64,358. Five per cent of the publication is written by freelance writers. Payment is on acceptance and a byline is given. Publication is copyrighted, with first UK serial rights purchased. Average lead time is two weeks. Seasonal material should be submitted four weeks in advance. Accepts queries by mail and email. Aims to respond to queries within five days and manuscripts within two weeks. Sample copy and manuscript guidelines are free on request. Media pack is available online.
Non-fiction Interested in photo features and personal experience articles in the first person.
* Purchases approximately 200 non-fiction manuscripts per year. Payment is by arrangement.
Submission Guidelines Accepts complete manuscripts of up to 1,200 words. Send submissions to Deputy Editor, Rod Cameron.
Fiction Publishes adventure, humorous, mainstream, mystery and suspense short fiction.
* Purchases approximately 150 fiction manuscripts per year. Payment is by arrangement.
Submission Guidelines Accepts complete manuscripts of between 600 to 1,200 words. Send submissions to Fiction Editor, Jill Finlay.
Tips *The Weekly News* targets both men and women, mainly in the 50 plus age group. There is a wide mix of subject matter, including real-life human interest, celebrity interviews, health, leisure (including travel and gardening), royalty, fiction and sport. Fiction submissions must be general interest rather than overly romantic, and must appeal to both sexes.

Welsh Country

Aberbanc, Llandysul, Ceredigion, SA44 5NP
- 01559 372010
- 01559 371995
- kath@welshcountry.co.uk
- www.welshcountry.co.uk

Parent Company Equine Marketing Ltd
Editor Kath Rhodes
Established 2004
Insider Info Bi-monthly consumer magazine covering Welsh interest subjects. Present circulation is 19,408. 20 per cent of the publication is written by freelance writers. Submissions are published approximately three months after acceptance. Payment is on publication Sometimes the expenses of writers on assignment are paid (limit agreed upon in advance). Publication is copyrighted and one time rights are purchased. A byline is sometimes given. Average lead time is two months, seasonal material must be submitted four months in advance. Accepts queries by email and telephone. Aims to respond to queries within five days and manuscripts within three months. Sample copy is available for £2.95. Editorial calendars are available by email. Media pack is available online.
Non-fiction Interested in photo features, poetry articles, historical/nostalgic articles and features about Welsh people living abroad.
* All articles must be of Welsh interest.
Submission Guidelines Accepts queries of between 700 and 1,200 words by email, with published clips.
Images Accepts images with submission.
* Purchases one time rights. Offers no additional payment for photos accepted with manuscripts.
Submission Guidelines Send gif/jpeg files with captions and credit name to the Artistic Designer, Tony Brindley.
Columns Publishes motoring and wine & beer columns, depending on advertising, of 600 words each.
* Buys approximately eight column pieces per year.
Fillers Publishes letters and star letters.
Tips *Welsh Country* covers an eclectic mix of articles about Welsh culture, interests and general information about Wales. The magazine sources much of its material from a pool of regular freelancers.

Weyfarers

1 Mountside, Guildford, Surrey, GU2 4JD
- admin@weyfarers.com
- www.weyfarers.com
Parent Company Guildford Poets Press
Editor Martin Jones, Stella Stocker, Jeffery Wheatley
Established 1972
Insider Info A consumer magazine, with three issues per year, covering contemporary and traditional international poetry. A byline is given. Accepts queries by mail.
Non-fiction Interested in articles on international poetry and literary reviews.

Submission Guidelines All submissions should be made by post and include SAE.
Poetry Publishes international, contemporary, free verse, light verse and traditional poetry.
* Payment is by contributor copies.
Submission Guidelines Accepts queries by email only. All submission of material should be by post and include SAE.
Tips *Weyfarers* is an international poetry magazine, which publishes modern and traditional poetry from new and established writers, including translations of foreign language poetry. The magazine also prints book and magazine reviews.

What Bike?

Media House, Lynchwood, Peterborough Business Park, Peterborough, PE2 6EA
- 01733 468000
- 01733 468092
- whatbike@emap.com
- www.emap.com
Parent Company EMAP Plc
Contact Managing Editor, Stefan Bartlett
Established 1985
Insider Info A quarterly consumer magazine covering motorcycling. Media pack available online.
Non-fiction Publishes features, road tests, reviews and buying guides.
Tips Aside from articles and reviews the magazine also publishes a comprehensive buyers guide for new bikes.

What Car?

Teddington Studios, Broom Road, Teddington, TW11 9BE
- 020 8267 5688
- 020 8267 5750
- editorial@whatcar.com
- www.whatcar.com
Parent Company Haymarket Autosport & Classic Publications
Contact Group Editor, Steve Fowler; Associate Editor, Roger Stansfield; Art Editor, Steve Moore
Established 1973
Insider Info A monthly consumer magazine covering car buying and selling. Present circulation is 108,028.
Non-fiction Publishes features, reviews, road tests and buying and selling guides.

What Digital Camera

Blue Fin Building, 110 Southwark Street, London, SE1 0SU
- 020 3148 5000
- wdc@ipcmedia.com
- www.whatdigitalcamera.com

Parent Company IPC Media Ltd
Editor Nigel Atherton
Contact Publishing Director, Alex Robb; Publisher, Angela O'Farrell
Established 1997
Insider Info A monthly consumer magazine, covering digital cameras. Circulation is 25,195. Media pack available online.
Non-fiction Publishes how-tos, practical articles, reviews and technical articles.
Tips *What Digital Camera* is a monthly magazine that covers all aspects of buying and using digital cameras and other imaging technology, including software techniques. The magazine encourages submissions of letters, photos and images from readers for the regular sections.

What HD TV
2 Balcombe Street, London, NW1 6NW
- 020 7042 4000
- rob.lane@futurenet.co.uk
Parent Company Future Publishing Ltd
Editor Rob Lane
Contact Deputy Editor, Jamie Carter
Established 2000
Insider Info A bi-monthly consumer magazine covering the high-definition television market. Present circulation is 15,000.
Non-fiction Publishes features, news, reviews and product tests.
Tips *What HD TV* covers all aspects of buying a high-definition television, including reviews and comparison tests.

What Hi-FI? Sound & Vision
Teddington Studios, Broom Road, Teddington, Middlesex, TW11 9BE
- 020 8267 5000
- 020 8267 5019
- whathifi@haynet.com
- www.whathifi.com
Parent Company Haymarket Publishing
Editor Claire Newsome
Established 1976
Insider Info A consumer magazine, published 13 times per year, covering hi-fi and home cinema equipment and markets. Present circulation is 59,147.
Non-fiction Publishes photo features, reviews and general articles on music systems.
Tips *What Hi-Fi? Sound & Vision* positions itself as an independent guide to buying and owning hi-fi and home cinema products. Freelance writing for reviews is no longer accepted, but they will consider ideas for general or specific features on hi-fi or home cinema.

What Home Cinema
2 Balcombe Street, London, NW1 6NW
- 020 7042 4940
- 020 7042 4949
- adrian.justins@futurenet.co.uk
- www.whathomecinemamag.com
Parent Company Future Publishing Ltd
Editor Adrian Justins
Contact Publisher, Andy Ford; Deputy Editor, Richard Holliss
Established 2002
Insider Info A monthly consumer magazine covering the home cinema market. Present circulation is 20,000.
Non-fiction Publishes features, news, reviews and product tests.
Tips *What Home Cinema* covers all aspects of home cinema systems, including DVD players and recorders, projectors, speakers and high-definition sets. The magazine is aimed at the regular consumer and avoids overly technical jargon.

What Investment
Octavia House, 50 Banner Street, London, EC1Y 8ST
- 020 7250 7026
- 020 7250 7011
- keiron.root@vitessemedia.co.uk
- www.whatinvestment.co.uk
Parent Company Vitesse Media Plc
Contact Editor in Chief, Keiron Root; Editorial Director, Leslie Copeland; Publisher, Darren Griffin; Deputy Editor, Jenny Lowe
Established 1982
Insider Info A monthly consumer magazine covering personal finance and investment. Present circulation is 21,446.
Non-fiction Publishes retail investment news, features, analysis and technical articles.
Tips *What Investment* covers all aspects of investment and finance and is aimed at the individual investor.

What Laptop
2 Balcombe Street, London, NW1 6NW
- 020 7317 2429
- michael.browne@futurenet.co.uk
- www.whatlaptop.co.uk
Parent Company Future Publishing Ltd
Editor Michael Browne
Contact Reviews Editor, Alex Bentley
Established 1999
Insider Info A monthly consumer magazine covering the laptop computer market. Present circulation is 13,900.

Non-fiction Publishes features, news, reviews and product tests.
Submission Guidelines Freelance writers should contact the editor by email with ideas for features or reviews.

What Mountain Bike
30 Monmouth Street, Bath, BA1 2BW
- 01225 442244
- 01225 822793
- jane.bentley@futurenet.co.uk

Parent Company Future Publishing Ltd
Editor Matt Skinner
Contact Publisher, Richard Schofield; Product Editor, Justin Loretz
Established 2000
Insider Info A monthly consumer magazine covering the mountain bike market. Present circulation is 16,970.
Non-fiction Publishes features, news and reviews on buying mountain bikes or equipment, as well as product tests.

What Satellite & Digital TV
2 Balcombe Street, London, NW1 6NW
- 020 7042 4000
- wotsat@futurenet.co.uk
- www.wotsat.com

Parent Company Future Publishing Ltd
Editor Alex Lane
Contact Publisher, Andy Ford; TV Editor, Stephen Graves
Established 1986
Insider Info A monthly consumer magazine covering the digital and satellite television market. Present circulation is 20,000.
Non-fiction Publishes features, news, reviews and product tests.
Tips *What Satellite & Digital TV* covers all aspects of buying digital televisions, set-top boxes, sky installation and freeview.

Which Motorcaravan?
The Maltings, West Street, Bourne, Lincolnshire, PE10 9NS
- 01778 391000
- marks@warnersgroup.co.uk
- www.whichcaravan.co.uk

Parent Company Warners Group Publications
Editor Sally Pepper
Contact Managing Editor, Mark Sutcliffe
Established 1987
Insider Info Monthly consumer magazine covering new and used caravans. Present circulation is 8,319. 70 per cent of the publication is written by freelance writers. Payment is on publication. Byline given.

Publication is copyrighted and all rights are purchased. Accepts queries by mail and email.
Non-fiction Publishes features, photo features and reviews on caravans.
Tips *Which Caravan* is the only magazine dedicated solely to reviewing and rating new and used caravans in the UK.

WI Life
104 New King's Road, London, SW6 4LY
- 020 7731 5777
- 020 7736 4061

Parent Company National Federation of Women's Institutes
Editor Joanna Gray
Insider Info A magazine, with eight issues per year, that covers all aspects of the Women's Institute. Accepts queries by mail or email. Present circulation is 202,399.
Non-fiction Interested in news, current affairs, events and feature articles of interest to WI members.
Tips Most articles are sourced internally or contributed by WI members.

Windows Vista: The Official Magazine
30 Monmouth Street, Bath, BA1 2BW
- 01225 442244
- windowsvistamagazine@futurenet.co.uk
- www.windowsvistamagazine.com

Parent Company Future Publishing Ltd
Editor Paul Douglas
Contact Deputy Editor, Jon Hicks
Established 2006
Insider Info A monthly consumer magazine covering Microsoft Windows Vista. Present circulation is 28,274.
Non-fiction Publishes news, reviews, technical and tutorial articles on on installing, using and getting the most out of Windows Vista.

The Wisden Cricketer
1.4 Shepherds Buildings, Charecroft Way, London, W14 0EH
- 020 7471 6900
- 020 7471 6901
- www.cricinfo.com/wisdencricketer

Parent Company BSkyB Publications
Editor John Stern
Contact Publishing Director, Lynda Wheeler; Deputy Editor, Edward Craig; Features Editor, Paul Coupar
Established 2003
Insider Info A monthly consumer magazine covering cricket. Present circulation is 34,559. Media pack is available online.

Non-fiction Publishes news, features, interviews, profiles, statistics, match reports and analysis.
Tips Covers both domestic and international cricket. It includes statistics and analysis, as well as full events and cricket-related television listings.

The Wolf
April Heights, Fagnal Lane, Winchmore Hill, Amersham, HP7 0PG
- editor@wolfmagazine.co.uk
- www.wolfmagazine.co.uk
Editor James Byrne
Established 2002
Insider Info A consumer literary magazine with three issues per year, covering contemporary poetry and photography. A byline is given. Accepts queries by mail and email. Manuscript guidelines are available online.
Non-fiction Interested in photo features, essays (on poetry subjects), interviews/profiles and reviews.
Submission Guidelines Accepts queries in the first instance, for articles between 500 and 1,500 words.
Poetry Publishes contemporary, avant-garde, free verse and light verse poetry.
Submission Guidelines Submit up to five poems.
Images Send photos with submission.
Tips *The Wolf* is a literary magazine that publishes interviews with leading contemporary poets as well as poetry from contributors and the latest in contemporary photography. *The Wolf* is open to submissions of contemporary poetry from new and established authors, however, it is a relatively new, self-funded magazine and so cannot offer any payment or contributor copies for accepted contributions.

Woman & Home
Blue Fin Building, 110 Southwark Street, London, SE1 0SU
- 020 3148 5000
- sue_james@ipcmedia.com
- www.womanandhome.com
Parent Company IPC Media Ltd
Editor Sue James
Contact Deputy Editor, Gaby Huddart
Established 1926
Insider Info Monthly consumer magazine covering women's lifestyle and fashion. Present circulation is 336,888. Accepts queries by mail.
Non-fiction Interested in general interest articles on home and garden, health, beauty and fashion.
Submission Guidelines Does not accept unsolicited submissions.
Fiction Publishes commissioned short stories only.
Tips *Woman & Home* magazine aims to reflect the way women live and work today. There is not much

scope for freelance work, as most material is specially commissioned.

Woman
Blue Fin Building, 110 Southwark Street, London, SE1 0SU
- 020 3148 5000
- woman@ipcmedia.com
- www.ipcmedia.com
Parent Company IPC Media Ltd
Editor Jackie Hatton
Contact Publishing Director, Oswin Grady; Editorial Manager, Tracey Baldwin; Features Editor, Jenny Vereker
Established 1937
Insider Info A weekly consumer magazine, covering women's interests and lifestyle. Circulation is 370,289. Media pack available online.
Non-fiction Publishes advice, beauty, celebrity gossip, health, fashion, news, practical and real life articles.
Tips Also publishes the occasional piece of women's interest short fiction.

Woman Alive
Garcia Estate, Canterbury Road, Worthing, West Sussex, BN13 1BW
- 01903 264556
- 01903 821081
- womanalive@cpo.org.uk
- www.womanalive.co.uk
Parent Company Christian Publishing & Outreach
Editor Jackie Stead
Established 1982
Insider Info Monthly consumer magazine covering Christian women's issues. Present circulation is 10,000. 65 per cent of the publication is written by freelance writers. Payment on is publication and a byline given. Purchases first UK serial rights. Average lead time is three months. Seasonal material must be submitted three months on advance. Accepts queries by mail and email. Accepts simultaneous submissions. Aims to respond to queries within three days and manuscripts within seven days. Sometimes pays writers with contributor copies for promotional reasons. Sometimes pays the expenses of writers on assignment (limit agreed upon in advance). Sample copy is available for £2.20. Manuscript guidelines are available with SAE, or by email.
Non-fiction Interested in how-tos, inspirational pieces, religious articles, features, interviews/profiles, new product articles, general interest and personal experience articles.
* Payment for assigned articles ranges from £70 to £125.

Submission Guidelines Accepts complete manuscripts of between 750 and 1,600 words.
Tips The majority of *Woman Alive* readers are aged between 35 and 50.

Woman's Own
Blue Fin Building, 110 Southwark Street, London, SE1 0SU
- 020 3148 5000
- karen_livermore@ipcmedia.com
- www.ipcmedia.com/brands/womansown

Parent Company IPC Media Ltd
Editor Karen Livermore
Contact Publishing Director, Sandy Gale; Publisher, Sally Gray; Deputy Editor, Natasha Cook
Established 1932
Insider Info A weekly consumer magazine, covering women's interest. Circulation is 339,138. Media pack available online.
Non-fiction Publishes advice, beauty, celebrity gossip, health, fashion, news, practical, lifestyle and real life articles.
Fiction Publishes short fiction.
Submission Guidelines Contact Fiction Editor, Sarah Jacob
Tips *Woman's Own* is a weekly magazine aimed at women over 35 years old. It covers general women's interest and also prints regular short stories from contributors. Fiction submissions must be of general women's interest, nothing too explicit.

Woman's Weekly
Blue Fin Building, 110 Southwark Street, London, SE1 0SU
- 020 3148 5000
- womansweeklypostbag@ipcmedia.com
- www.ipcmedia.com

Parent Company IPC Media Ltd
Editor Diane Kenwood
Contact Fiction Editor, Gaynor Davies; Features Editor, Sue Pilkington
Established 1993
Insider Info A weekly consumer magazine covering women's lifestyle and hobby topics. Present circulation of 346,540. Media pack available online.
Non-fiction Publishes general interest features, practical articles and photo features on crafts, food, cookery, fashion, lifestyle and leisure.
Fiction Publishes women's short fiction, including several fiction special editions. Contact the Fiction Editor for more details.
Tips Aimed at mature women, the average age of the reader is 55. The magazine takes a practical stance on many issues, designed to have a real impact on women's lives, particularly domestically.

The Woman Writer
31 Eaton Court, Eaton Gardens, Hove, East Sussex, BN3 3PL
- swwjnews@morrisdancer.fsnet.co.uk
- www.swwj.co.uk

Parent Company Society of Women Writers & Journailsts
Editor Ann Hamilton
Established 1894
Insider Info A bi-monthly consumer magazine that covers women's writing. Accepts queries by mail or email.
Tips *The Woman Writer* is the official magazine of the Society of Women Writers & Journailsts.

Women & Golf
Blue Fin Building, 110 Southwark Street, London, SE1 0SU
- 020 3148 5000
- women&golf@ipcmedia.com
- www.ipcmedia.com

Parent Company IPC Media Ltd
Editor Michael Harris
Contact Publishing Director, Hamish Dawson; Travel & Lifestyle Editor, Alicia Harney
Established 1991
Insider Info A monthly consumer magazine, covering women's golf. Circulation is 15,000. Media pack available online.
Non-fiction Publishes celebrity profiles, golf fashion, reviews and practical tutorial articles.
Tips Covers all aspects of women's golf including the latest trends in golfing fashion, tutorial and technique advice and event news.

The World of Cross Stitching
14th Floor, Tower House, Fairfax Street, Bristol, BS1 3BN
- 0117 927 9009
- 0117 934 9008
- hannahbellis@originpublishing.co.uk
- www.cross-stitching.com

Parent Company Origin Publishing Ltd
Editor Hannah Bellis
Established 1977
Insider Info A monthly consumer magazine covering cross stitching. Present circulation is 44,277.
Non-fiction Publishes features, designs and practical how-to articles.
Tips *The World of Cross Stitching* is aimed at cross stitchers of all skill levels.

The World of Interiors
Vogue House, 1 Hanover Square, London, W1S 1JU

☎ 020 7499 9080

🖶 020 7493 4013

✉ woi-editorial@condenast.co.uk

🌐 www.worldofinteriors.co.uk

Parent Company Condè Nast Publications Ltd

Editor Rupert Thomas

Contact Publisher, Emma Redmayne; Creative Director, Jessica Hayns; Art Director, Mark Lazenby

Established 1981

Insider Info A monthly consumer magazine covering interior design and gardens. Present circulation is 67,575.

Non-fiction Publishes features, showcases and event reviews based around interior design topics.

World Poker Tour - The Official Magazine
30 Monmouth Street, Bath, BA1 2BW

☎ 01225 442244

✉ ian.harris@futurenet.co.uk

Parent Company Future Publishing Ltd

Editor Ian Harris

Contact Art Editor, Carlton Hibbert

Established 2006

Insider Info A monthly consumer magazine covering poker. Present circulation is 50,000.

Non-fiction Publishes event news, interviews and tutorial articles.

Tips *World Poker Tour* contains practical articles on playing both live and online poker.

World Soccer
Blue Fin Building, 110 Southwark Street, London, SE1 0SU

☎ 020 3148 5000

✉ jamie_rainbow@ipcmedia.com

🌐 www.worldsoccer.com

Parent Company IPC Media Ltd

Editor Jamie Rainbow

Established 1960

Insider Info Monthly consumer magazine covering international football. Present circulation is 44,020. Accepts queries by email.

Non-fiction Interested in articles on football and football culture.

Submission Guidelines Accepts complete manuscripts of between 600 and 2,000 words.

Tips *World Soccer* is very much focused on international football, and is aimed at an adult audience only.

Writers' Forum
PO Box 3229, Bournemouth, BH1 1ZS

☎ 01202 589828

🖶 01202 587758

✉ editorial@writers-forum.com

🌐 www.writers-forum.com

Parent Company Writers International Ltd

Editor John Jenkins

Established 1995

Insider Info Monthly consumer literary magazine covering short stories, magazine features, novels, plays, film scripts and poetry. Present circulation is 25,000.

Non-fiction Interested in how-to (craft of writing) articles.

Submission Guidelines Accepts queries between 800 and 1,500 words.

Fiction

Publishes short stories, book excerpts and drama.

Submission Guidelines Accept short fiction through monthly competitions, see website for details. There is a reading fee charged and prize money offered.

Poetry

Publishes poetry.

Submission Guidelines Accept poetry through monthly competitions, see website for details. There is a reading fee charged and prize money offered.

Tips *Writers' Forum* is dedicated to providing encouragement and inspiration to those who want to write and see their work published. The majority of writing published in the magazine is from competitions.

Writers' News
5th Floor, 31–32 Park Row, Leeds, LS1 5JD

☎ 0113 200 2929

🖶 0113 200 2928

✉ jonathan.telfer@writersnews.co.uk

🌐 www.writersnews.co.uk

Parent Company Warners Group Publications

Editor Jonathan Telfer

Established 1989

Insider Info Monthly literary magazine covering all the latest news, insider information, market leads and research from the world of writing, as well as directory listings and help columns. Payment is on publication and a byline given. Accepts queries by mail or email. Manuscript guidelines are available online.

Non-fiction Interested in features, interviews/profiles, reviews, personal experience and news articles.

Submission Guidelines Accepts query in the first instance.

Tips *Writers' News* is a guide to what's going on in the world of writing. *Writers' News* is mostly interested in articles and market news reports, but also runs writing competitions, which offer cash prizes and publication in the magazine.

Writing Magazine

5th Floor, 31–32 Park Row, Leeds, LS1 5JD

- 0113 200 2929
- 0113 200 2928
- derek.hudson@writersnews.co.uk
- www.writersnews.co.uk

Parent Company Warners Group Publications
Editor Derek Hudson
Established 1992
Insider Info Monthly literary journal covering every genre of writing with regular how-to guides, columns, interviews and articles. Payment on publication. Byline is given. Accepts queries by mail and email. Manuscript guidelines are available online.
Non-fiction Interested in how-to articles, features, interviews/profiles and reviews.
Submission Guidelines Accepts queries in the first instance.
Fiction Publishes adventure, historical, romance, horror, science fiction, confession, humorous, erotica, mainstream, ethnic, mystery, suspense, experimental, western, fantasy and religious short stories.
* Only publishes fiction from competition winners.
Poetry Publishes avant-garde, contemporary, free verse, light verse and traditional poetry.
* Only publishes poetry from competition winners.
Tips *Writing Magazine* is the sister publication to *Writers' News* and covers every genre of writing, both prose and poetry. *Writing Magazine* runs runs various writing competitions with the winners being published in the magazine. Always contact with a proposal first, rather than submitting an unsolicited article.

X360

Richmond House, 33 Richmond Hill, Bournemouth, BH2 6EQ

- 01202 586200
- x360@imagine-publishing.co.uk
- www.360magazine.co.uk

Parent Company Imagine Publishing
Contact Editor in Chief, Simon Philips; Deputy Editor, Ryan King
Established 2005
Insider Info A monthly consumer magazine covering the Xbox 360 games console. Present circulation is 30,203. Sample copy available online.
Non-fiction Publishes news, features, reviews, letters and walkthrough articles.

Xbox World 360

30 Monmouth Street, Bath, BA1 2BW

- 01225 442244
- xbw@futurenet.co.uk

Parent Company Future Publishing Ltd
Editor Tim Weaver
Contact Publisher, James Binns; Art Editor, Richard Hood
Established 2003
Insider Info A monthly consumer magazine covering the Xbox 360 console. Present circulation is 29,135.
Non-fiction Publishes game events, news, previews, reviews and walkthrough articles on the latest developments and releases for the Microsoft Xbox 360 games console.

X Magazine

PO Box 43771, London, W14 8ZY

- 0845 430 9517
- 0845 430 9518
- submissions@x-bout.com
- www.flippedeye.net/xmag

Parent Company Flipped Eye Press
Editor Sally Strong
Established 2002
Insider Info A consumer literary magazine covering poetry and fiction, experimental writing, interviews, feature articles and competition listings. 100 per cent of the publication is written by freelance writers. Byline is given. Accepts queries by mail and email. Manuscript guidelines are available online.
Non-fiction Interested in cover art, features, interviews/profiles and reviews.
Fiction Publishes contemporary and experimental short fiction.
Submission Guidelines Accepts completed manuscripts of no more than 5,000 words via email.
Poetry Publishes avant-garde, contemporary, free verse and light verse.
Submission Guidelines Submit a maximum of five poems via email.
Tips *X Magazine* only considers submissions from live performance writers who read their work in public at least once every other month, and prefers to take submissions from writers' groups, or regular events, in order to feature a few writers from one group/event at a time. They only accept submissions by email, and then only during reading periods in February, May, August and November. Work submitted outside of these months is likely to be deleted unread.

Yachting Monthly

Blue Fin Building, 110 Southwark Street, London, SE1 0SU

- 020 3148 5000
- yachting_monthly@ipcmedia.com
- www.yachtingmonthly.com

Parent Company IPC Media Ltd

Editor Paul Gelder
Contact Production Editor, Kieran Flatt; News & Features Editor, Dick Durham; Art Editor, Steve Trodd
Established 1906
Insider Info A monthly consumer magazine, covering yachting. Circulation is 34,402. Media pack available online.
Non-fiction Publishes cruising narratives, design & construction, photo features, reviews and technical articles.
Submission Guidelines Accepts proposal package (including synopsis and CV) for articles of up to 1,800 words in length.
Tips *Yachting Monthly* covers all aspects of British yachting and is aimed at people who actively sail their boats. The magazine encourages submissions of cruising narratives, practical or technical articles and carefully researched pilotage articles on anchorages and cruising areas, particularly if accompanied by relevant illustrations.

Yachting World
Blue Fin Building, 110 Southwark Street, London, SE1 0SU
- 020 3148 5000
- yachting_world@ipcmedia.com
- www.yachtingworld.com
Parent Company IPC Media Ltd
Editor Andrew Bray
Contact Deputy Editor, David Glenn
Established 1894
Insider Info Monthly consumer magazine covering yachting, blue water cruising, global sailing epics, international yacht racing, super yachting, international events and charters. Present circulation is 27,430. Accepts queries by mail and email. Manuscript guidelines are free on request and available by email to andrew_bray@ipcmedia.com.
Non-fiction Interested in photo features, features, reviews and technical articles.
Submission Guidelines Accepts queries with published clips, or completed manuscripts of between 2,500 and 3,000 words.
Tips *Yachting World* is the world's oldest sailing magazine. Over 50 per cent of the circulation is outside of the UK. The editorial emphasis is on quality of writing, photography, and the topics covered.

Yachts & Yachting
196 Eastern Esplanade, Southend on Sea, Essex, SS1 3AB
- 01702 582245
- 01702 588434
- gael@yachtsandyachting.com
- www.yachtsandyachting.com

Parent Company Yachts & Yachting Ltd
Editor Gael Pawson
Established 1947
Insider Info A bi-weekly consumer magazine that covers all aspects of yachting, from sport and race meets, to buying and restoring boats. Accepts queries by mail or email.
Non-fiction Interested in how-tos, new product articles, general interest and personal experience articles related to yachting.
Submission Guidelines Accepts queries and completed manuscript submissions.
Tips *Yachts & Yachting* will accept short, technically correct articles.

The Yellow Crane
20 Princes Court, The Walk, Roath, Cardiff, CF24 3AU
Editor Jonathan Brookes
Insider Info A consumer literary magazine covering Welsh poetry.
Poetry Publishes contemporary, free verse, light verse and traditional poetry from Welsh and International writers.
Submission Guidelines Accepts complete manuscripts by post.
Tips *The Yellow Crane* is a Welsh literary magazine that publishes mainstream poetry from new and established writers. Although it is based in South Wales, the magazine will accept poetry submissions from outside the region, including from international writers.

Yorkshire Life
1200 Century Way, Thorpe Park, Leeds, LS15 8ZA
- 01772 722022
- 01772 736496
- esther.leach@yorkshirelife.co.uk
- www.yorkshirelife.co.uk
Parent Company Archant Norfolk
Editor Esther Leach
Contact Publisher, Trevor Lee
Established 1946
Insider Info A monthly consumer magazine covering Yorkshire interest. Present circulation is 22,531. Media pack is available online.
Non-fiction Publishes news, features and lifestyle articles.
Tips *Yorkshire Life* covers lifestyle and general interest articles from the county of Yorkshire, including features on personalities, food and drink, gardening, property, the arts and town and village profiles.

Yorkshire Ridings

Unit 200, Oyston Mill, The Strand, Preston, PR1 8UR

☎ 01772 761277

Editor Anthony Skinner

Established 1964

Insider Info A bi-monthly consumer magazine that covers the three Ridings of Yorkshire. Accepts queries by mail or email. Present circulation is 18,042.

Non-fiction Interested in lifestyle, interviews and local interest articles.

Submission Guidelines Accepts queries and completed manuscript submissions of up to 1,000 words.

Yorkshire Women's Life Magazine

PO Box 113, Leeds, West Yorkshire, LS8 2WX

☻ ywlmagenquiries@btinternet.com

✇ www.yorkshirewomenslife.co.uk

Editor Dawn-Maria France

Contact Editorial Assistant, India Jones

Established 2001

Insider Info A consumer magazine, published three time per year. Covers women's lifestyle, news, art and fashion. Present circulation is over 15,000. Ten per cent of the magazine is written by freelance writers. Submissions are published approximately two months after acceptance, payment is on publication. Byline is given and publication is copyrighted. Average lead time is four months and seasonal material must be submitted four months in advance. Accepts queries by post. Accepts simultaneous submissions. Aims to respond to queries and manuscripts within two months. Sample copy is available for £9.25. Manuscript guidelines and editorial calendars are available with SAE and two first-class stamps.

Non-fiction Interested in interviews/profiles, reviews of new beauty and lifestyle products, and articles on personal experience.

* Payment for articles is negotiable.

Submission Guidelines Accepts queries with published clips for articles between 180 and 250 words. Does not publish reprints.

Fillers Interested in jokes (to be illustrated by cartoonist) and newsbreak fillers between 55 and 80 words.

* Payment for fillers is negotiable.

Tips *Yorkshire Women's Life* is an independent, handbag sized women's magazine aimed at career minded women; managers and working professional women. *Yorkshire Women's Life* works with subscribers in order to get their work on the pages of the title, wherever possible.

You & Your Wedding

National Magazine House, 72 Broadwick Street, London, W1F 9EP

☎ 020 7439 5000

☎ 020 7439 2985

☻ yywinfo@natmags.co.uk

✇ www.youandyourwedding.co.uk

Parent Company National Magazine Company Ltd

Editor Colette Harris

Contact Publisher, Meribeth Parker; Art Director, Lisa Collins; Associate Editor, Debbie Codd

Insider Info A bi-monthly consumer magazine covering weddings. Present circulation is 60,024.

Non-fiction Publishes features, travel and practical articles on every aspect of wedding planning including honeymoon destinations, wedding outfits and home buying.

Tips *You & Your Wedding* is aimed at brides to be, aged between 25 and 34 years old.

Young People Now

174 Hammersmith Road, London, W6 7JP

☎ 020 8267 4793

☎ 020 8267 4728

☻ ypn.editorial@haynet.com

✇ www.ypnmagazine.com

Parent Company Haymarket Publishing

Editor Ravi Chandiramani

Contact Features Editor, Andy Hillier

Established 1989

Insider Info Weekly trade journal covering social services and welfare for young people. Present circulation is 14,688.

Non-fiction Publishes news and features.

Tips *Young People Now* is the only weekly title for those who work with young people between the ages of 11 to 25. It is an industry publication, so a specialist knowledge in the field of child care/youth guidance is essential for contributors.

Your Dog

33 Broad Street, Lincolnshire, PE9 1RB

☎ 01780 766199

☎ 01780 766416

☻ s.wright@bournepublishinggroup.co.uk

✇ www.yourdog.co.uk

Parent Company Bourne Publishing Group Ltd

Editor Sarah Wright

Contact Publisher, Alison Queenborough; Art Editor, Shaun Smith; Assistant Editor, Emma Hawkins

Established 1995

Insider Info A monthly consumer magazine covering dogs. Present circulation is 31,299.

Non-fiction Publishes news, features and advice articles on owning and caring for a dog.

Your Family

7 St Martin's Place, London, WC2N 4HA
- 020 7747 0834
- your.family@redwoodgroup.net
- www.yourfamily.org.uk

Parent Company Redwood (Publishers) and NSPCC
Editor Susannah Pearce
Contact Deputy Editor, Claire Sargent; Sub-Editor, Gemma Rollason; Editorial Assistant, Erin Smith
Established 2005
Insider Info A bi-monthly consumer magazine covering parenting and lifestyle. Present circulation is 394,307.
Non-fiction Publishes features, advice and product reviews on parenting, children's fashion, cooking, lifestyle and celebrity parents.
Tips *Your Family* is the parenting magazine from the NSPCC. Articles must be sympathetic to its aims.

Your Family Tree

30 Monmouth Street, Bath, BA1 2BW
- 01225 442244
- aylene.rogers@futurenet.co.uk
- www.yourfamilytreemag.co.uk

Parent Company Future Publishing Ltd
Editor Garrick Webster
Contact Art Editor, Andy McGregor
Established 2003
Insider Info A monthly consumer magazine covering genealogy. Present circulation is 20,384.
Non-fiction Publishes expert tips, how-to and case study articles.
Tips *Your Family Tree* covers a wide range of genealogy subjects, including tips from well-known researchers, news, guidance and case studies. The magazine is aimed at general enthusiasts and experts alike.

Your Hair

14th Floor, Tower House, Fairfax Street, Bristol, BS1 3BN
- 0117 927 9009
- 0117 934 9008
- sophiejordan@originpublishing.co.uk
- www.yourhair.co.uk

Parent Company Origin Publishing Ltd
Contact Commissioning Editor, Sophie Jordan; Picture Editor, Katherine Hallett; Editorial Assistant, Nicola Clare
Insider Info A monthly consumer magazine covering hairstyles and fashion. Present circulation is 38,206.
Non-fiction Publishes features and advice articles on hair care, fashion and styling.

Your Home

The Tower, Wyncolls Road, Severalls Industrial Park, Colchester, CO4 9HU
- 01206 851117
- 01206 849078
- yourhome@essentialpublishing.co.uk

Parent Company Essential Publishing Ltd
Editor Anna-Lisa De'Ath
Contact Deputy Editor, Helen Jones; Features Editor, Lisa Hibberd; Editorial Assistant, Alison Lovett
Established 1997
Insider Info A monthly consumer magazine covering house and home. Present circulation is 122,402.
Non-fiction Publishes photo features, profiles and practical advice articles.
Tips *Your Home* covers interior design and decoration, DIY, renovation and gardening. It is aimed at homeowners between the age of 25 and 45 years old. Regularly prints features on real homes with interesting qualities.

Your Horse

Bretton Court, Bretton, Peterborough, PE3 8DZ
- 01733 264666
- 01733 465200
- nicola.dela-croix@bauermedia.com
- www.yourhorse.co.uk

Parent Company Bauer Consumer Media
Editor Nicola Dela-Croix
Contact Deputy Editor, Jo Fobbester; Art Editor, Carolyn Maile; Creative Editor, Amanda Rigby
Established 1983
Insider Info A monthly consumer magazine covering horses. Present circulation is 40,006.
Non-fiction Publishes features, product reviews and practical advice.
Tips *Your Horse* covers all aspects of horse owning and riding, from riding techniques to advice, and articles on horse health care and accommodation.

Yours

Media House, Lynchwood Business Park, Peterborough, PE2 6EA
- 01733 468000
- 01733 465266
- yours@bauermedia.co.uk
- www.yours.co.uk

Parent Company Bauer Consumer Media
Editor Valery McConnell
Contact Managing Director, Sam Fitz-Gibbon; Deputy Editor, Sharon Reid; Features Editor, Rebecca Speechley
Established 1974

Insider Info A fortnightly consumer magazine covering general women's interest and lifestyle. Present circulation is 337,639.

Non-fiction Publishes features, interviews, profiles and news articles on a wide range of subjects including health, beauty, lifestyle, cooking, finance, society, gardening and retirement.

Fiction Publishes general interest short fiction.

Tips *Yours* is aimed at women over 50 years old.

Zest

National Magazine House, 72 Broadwick Street, London, W1F 9EP

- 020 7439 5000
- 020 7437 6886
- zest.mail@natmags.co.uk
- www.zest.co.uk

Parent Company National Magazine Company

Editor Mandie Gower

Contact Features Assistant, Zoe McDonald

Established 1994

Insider Info A monthly consumer magazine covering women's interests, health, beauty, diet and fitness. Present circulation of 104,636.

Non-fiction Publishes general interest articles aimed at women's lifestyle.

Fiction Publishes short stories and articles of 50–2,000 words in length.

Tips *Zest* is targeted firmly at a female readership, and any story or article submissions must be written with this in mind, as well as being generally uplifting in tone.

Zoo

Mappin House, 4 Winsley Street, London, W1W 8HF

- 020 7182 8355
- 020 7182 8300
- info@zooweekly.co.uk
- www.zooweekly.co.uk

Parent Company Bauer Consumer Media

Editor Ben Todd

Contact Deputy Editor, Damien McSorley; Editorial Assistant, Natalie Cornish

Established 2004

Insider Info A weekly consumer magazine covering men's lifestyle topics. Present circulation of 161,331.

Non-fiction Publishes general interest, interviews, reviews and photo features on celebrities, fashion, sport, humour, sex, music, television, film and real-life.

Tips The magazine is aimed at young men aged 16–30 and may contain mild adult content.

UK & IRISH NATIONAL NEWSPAPERS

The Art Newspaper

70 South Lambeth Road, London, SW8 1RL

- 020 7735 3331
- 020 7735 3332
- contact@theartnewspaper.com
- www.theartnewspaper.com

Contact Editor, Christina Ruiz

Established 1990

Insider Info An international newspaper, 11 issues per year, covering art and visual arts. Aimed primarily at practising artists and industry professionals. Publishes a mixture of short news stories, exhibition reviews and features of between 200 to 1,000 words. Payment is generally £120 per 1,000 words.

The Business

Sir David & Sir Frederick Barclay

22 Old Queen Street, London, SW1H 9HP

- 020 7961 0000
- 020 7961 0101
- newsdesk@thebusiness.co.uk
- www.thebusiness.co.uk

Contact Editor, Allister Heath; Deputy Editor, Abigail Townsend

Established 1998

Insider Info A Sunday national newspaper which focuses on different aspects of business. Present circulation of 43,383. Aimed primarily at business people and entrepreneurs aged 35 plus who work in London. Publishes a mixture of short news stories of 200 plus words, and features – which are considerably longer. Payment varies from job to job.

Submission Guidelines Contact firstly with ideas. Do not send unsolicited articles.

Tips Browse their website for a breakdown of topics and features that *The Business* consider topical business news.

Daily Express

Northern & Shell Media/Richard Desmond

The Northern & Shell Building, 10 Lower Thames Street, London, EC3R 6EN

- 0871 434 1010
- 0871 520 7702
- news.desk@express.co.uk
- www.express.co.uk

Contact Editor, Peter Hill; Deputy Editor, Hugh Whittow; News Editor, Allister Hagger; Features Editor, Fergus Kelly; Literary Editor, Caroline Jowett; Picture Editor, Neil McCarthy

Established 1900

Insider Info A daily tabloid. National and international news is covered, along with features on business and finance, entertainment and sport. Circulation of around 752,181. Publishes features and news stories. Also publishes feature articles in its supplements.

Submission Guidelines For features, write to the relevant department editor with an outline. There are also quick links on the website to send ideas in. If you have a news story, call 0871 202982. If you have a photograph relevant to a news story, call 0871 520 7171. Send mobile phone pictures by texting EXPRESS to 07843 500911. Email to expresspix@express.co.uk.

Tips Although ideas are welcome, be aware that at a national newspaper outlines from unknown writers will stand little chance of being commissioned.

Daily Mail

Associated Newspapers Ltd/Lord Rothermere
Northcliffe House, 2 Derry Street, London, W8 5TT
- 020 7938 6000
- 020 7937 4463
- news@dailymail.co.uk
- www.dailymail.co.uk

Contact Editor, Paul Dacre; News Editor, Keith Poole; Features Editor, Jim Gillespie; Commissioning Editor (Features), Maureen O'Donnell; Literary Editor, Sandra Parsons; Fiction Editor, Amber Pearson; Travel Editor, Mark Palmer; Picture Editor, Paul Silva

Established 1896

Insider Info The *Daily Mail* now has a circulation of over two million. Its readership is primarily ABC1. Produced from Monday to Saturday. Most material is written by known freelancers, or in-house staff. Publishes breaking news stories. There are also regular columns on sport, showbiz, health, travel and money. Present circulation is 2,193,715.

Submission Guidelines Phone or email with exclusive news. Photographs relating to current news stories are welcome.

Tips The *Daily Mail* has a large readership and often takes a very particular stance on issues. Read several copies of the paper to get an idea of its style.

Daily Mirror

Trinity Mirror plc
1 Canada Square, Canary Wharf, London, E14 5AP
- 020 7293 3000
- 020 7293 3409
- mirrornews@mirror.co.uk
- www.mirror.co.uk

Contact Editor, Richard Wallace; Deputy Editor, Conor Hanna; Head of News, Gary Jones; News

Editor, Anthony Harwood; Head of Features, Carole Watson; Literary Editor, Henry Sutton; Books Editor, Andrea Henry; Commissioning Editor, Gary Quinn; Picture Editor, Ian Down

Established 1903

Insider Info Daily tabloid. Covers national and international news stories, with particular emphasis on entertainment, showbiz and sport. Publishes from Monday to Saturday. Unknown feature writers are unlikely to be published. Regularly features celebrity and gossip columns. Present circulation is 1,400,206.

Submission Guidelines For current news stories, call 0800 282591. Call the 3am pages on 020 7293 3950 for showbiz stories. For general news pictures email picturedesk@mirror.co.uk.

Tips The news stories can be heavily influenced by celebrity stories. Known tabloid freelancers stand a much better chance of being published than new writers.

Daily Record

Trinity Mirror plc
1 Central Quay, Glasgow, G3 8DA
- 0141 309 3000
- 0141 309 3340
- reporters@dailyrecord.co.uk
- www.dailyrecord.co.uk

Contact Editor, Bruce Waddell; Deputy Editor, Murray Foote; Digital Editorial Director, Ewan Watt; Head of News, Andy Lines; Deputy News Editor, Kevin Mansi; Features Editor, Melanie Harvey; Picture Editor, Alistair Baird

Established 1895

Insider Info A Scottish tabloid. Present circulation is 361,857. It publishes from Monday to Saturday. Publishes some freelance material. Publishes a mixture of news and features.

Tips Articles of Scottish relevance are of particular interest.

Daily Sport

Sport Newspapers Ltd
19 Great Ancoats Street, Manchester, M60 4BT
- 0161 236 4466
- 0161 236 4535
- murray.morse@sportnewspapers.co.uk
- www.dailysport.co.uk

Contact Editor-in-Chief, Murray Morse; Editor, Pam McVitie; Deputy Editor, Gary Doran; News Editor, Neil Goodwin; Picture Editor, Paul Currie

Established 1986

Insider Info A daily tabloid with a sister title, *The Sunday Sport*. The content tends to centre around female celebrities and models, humour, scandal and sports. Circulation of around 300,000. Publishes fairly short articles, both news and features, often less than 1,000 words.

Submission Guidelines Unsolicited material, which is relevant to the style of the paper will be reviewed.

Tips The content and style of the paper is very specifically aimed at young men, so check the suitability of your work before submission.

Daily Star

Northern & Shell Media/Richard Desmond
The Northern & Shell Building, 10 Lower Thames Street, London, EC3R 6EN
- 0871 434 1010
- 020 8612 7401
- news@dailystar.co.uk
- www.dailystar.co.uk

Contact Editor, Dawn Neesom; Deputy Editor, Ben Knowles; Associate Editor, Ian Trueman; Acting Features Editor, Ted Thornhill; Picture Editor, Rob Greener

Established 1978

Insider Info The *Daily Star* is published from Monday to Saturday. Stories tend to revolve around celebrities, sport, news and gossip. Present circulation is 714,192. Freelance payment can range from less than £100 for short articles, to upwards of £500 for double page spreads. Even more is paid for leading exclusives. Publishes big news exclusives, often celebrity interviews, and picture features. The stance of the newspaper leans towards right wing.

Tips The content and style of the paper is very specifically aimed at young men, so check the suitability of your work before submission.

Daily Star Sunday

Northern & Shell Media/Richard Desmond
The Northern & Shell Building, 10 Lower Thames Street, London, EC3R 6EN
- 0871 520 7424
- 0871 434 7967
- news@dailystar.co.uk
- www.dailystarsunday.co.uk

Contact Editor, Gareth Morgan; Deputy Editor, Ella Buchan; News Editor, Michael Booker; Picture Editor, Tomasina Brittain

Insider Info Similar to the *Daily Star*, it is aimed at a young male readership. It offers sports, quirky stories and celebrity gossip. There are opportunities for freelance workers. Present circulation is 346,942.

Tips Aim articles specifically towards the male target audience.

The Daily Telegraph

Sir David & Sir Frederick Barclay
111 Buckingham Palace Road, London, SW1W 0DT

- 020 7931 2000
- 020 7931 2938
- dtnews@telegraph.co.uk
- www.telegraph.co.uk

Contact Editor in Chief, William Lewis; Deputy Editor, Tony Gallagher; Executive Head of News, Chris Evans; News Editor, Matthew Bayley; Commissioning Editor (Features), Robert Colvile; Arts Editor, Sarah Crompton; Commissioning Editor (Arts), Ben Secher; Review Editor, Tom Horan; Picture Editor, Stefanie Hart; Assistant Editor (Books), Brian MacArthur

Established 1855

Insider Info A broadsheet, containing in-depth national and international news, political and financial coverage, social issues, media, IT, jobs, travel, sport, arts and entertainment. Publication is from Monday to Saturday. Present circulation is 835,497. The *Sunday Telegraph* is its sister newspaper. Articles on a wide range of subjects are considered, however, few outside contributors are ever published.

Tips Writers must be extremely well informed on the subject area they are writing about.

The Financial Times

Pearson PLC
1 Southwark Bridge, London, SE1 9HL
- 020 7873 3000
- 020 7873 3076
- news.desk@ft.com
- www.ft.com

Contact Editor, Lionel Barber; Deputy Editor, Martin Dickson; News Editor, Robert Shrimsley; Arts Editor, Jan Dalley; Picture Editor, Marcus Cotton

Established 1888

Insider Info The *Financial Times* (FT) is a broadsheet newspaper providing UK and international coverage of finance and business news. It also includes features on IT, national and international news, sport, and entertainment. Readers tend to be high achievers in business and politics. Present circulation is around 448,523. Accepts articles of financial, commercial, industrial and economic interest.

Tips It is worth bearing in mind that the FT uses fewer unsolicited contributions than any other national newspaper.

The Guardian

The Scott Trust
Kings Place, 90 York Way, London, N1 9GU
- 020 7278 2332
- 020 7837 2114
- national@guardian.co.uk
- www.guardian.co.uk

Contact Editor, Alan Rusbridger; Senior Commissioning Editor, Rob Fearn; National News Editor, Nick Hopkins; Features Editor, Katharine Viner; Commissiong Editor (Features), Homa Khaleeli; Literary Editor, Claire Armitstead; Reviews Editor, Imogen Tilden; Sports Editor, Ian Prior; Arts Editor, Melissa Denes; Commissioning Editor (Arts), Laura Barnett; Picture Editor, Fiona Shields
Established 1821
Insider Info Published from Monday to Friday, it has a circulation of 358,379. Because of the specialised pages, freelancers have greater opportunities to get their work published.
Submission Guidelines Ideas should be emailed in to the paper.
Tips Research their specialised pages thoroughly, as this is where freelancers stand the best chance. There is a detailed freelance guide on the website with the necessary information.

The Herald
Gannet UK Ltd
200 Renfield Street, Glasgow, G2 3QB
- 0141 302 7000
- 0141 302 7007
- news@theherald.co.uk
- www.theherald.co.uk
Contact Deputy Editor, Janette Harkiss; News Editor, Calum MacDonald; Features Editor, Mark Smith; Literary Editor, Rosemary Goring; Arts Editor, Keith Bruce; Acting Picture Editor, Deborah Keeping
Insider Info Quality broadsheet, focused on Scottish news. Present circulation is 62,749.

The Independent
Independent News & Media (UK) Ltd
Northcliffe House, 2 Derry Street, London, W8 5TT
- 020 7005 2000
- 020 7005 2999
- newseditor@independent.co.uk
- www.independent.co.uk
Contact Managing Director, Simon Kelner; Editor, Roger Alton; Deputy Editor, Ian Birrell; News Editor, Oliver Wright; Executive Editor (Features), Adam Leigh; Features Editor, Nicole Mowbray; Literary Editor, Boyd Tonkin; Arts Editor, David Lister; Picture Editor, Lynn Cullen; Deputy Literary Editor, Katy Guest
Insider Info The paper is mainly aimed at an intelligent ABC1 readership. Likes to focus on the arts and culture. Appears to encourage freelance contributions however, a fee will not always be paid for published work. Has regular features on the arts, lifestyle, motoring, education and book reviews. Present circulation is 201,113.

Tips *The Independent* likes to receive work in hard copy form. Further information for freelance writers is on the website.

The Independent on Sunday
Independent News & Media (UK) Ltd
Northcliffe House, 2 Derry Street, London, W8 5TT
- 020 7005 2000
- 020 7005 2047
- sundaynews@independent.co.uk
- www.independent.co.uk
Contact Managing Director, Simon Kelner; Acting Editor, John Mullin; Executive Editor (News), Peter Victor; Arts Editor, Mike Higgins; Literary Editor, Suzi Feay; Reviews Editor, Jenny Gilbert; Picture Editor, Hannah Brenchley
Insider Info Quality Sunday paper, similar readership to *The Independent*. Present circulation is 166,071.
Tips *The Independent on Sunday* like to receive work in hard copy form. Further information for freelance writers is on the website.

Irish Daily Star
Independent News & Media/Express Newspapers Ltd
Star House, 62a Terenure Road North, Dublin 6W, Republic of Ireland
- 00353 1 490 1228
- 00353 1 490 2193
- info@therstar.ie
- www.thestar.ie
Contact Editor, Gerard Colleran
Insider Info A sports based paper, aimed at young male readers.
Submission GUidelines Call 00353 1 490 1228, if you have a story (this line is used for tip-offs and not always for written or planned articles).
Tips When writing, bear in mind the large male readership of the paper.

Irish Examiner
Thomas Crosbie Holdings
The Irish Examiner, City Quarter, Lapps Quay, Cork
- 00353 21 427 2722
- 00353 21 427 5477
- name.surname@examiner.ie
- www.irishexaminer.com
Contact Editor, Tim Vaughn; Sports Editor, Tony Leen; News Editor, John O'Mahony; Features Editor, Joe Dermody
Insider Info A broadsheet covering national and international news in Ireland. In-depth coverage of sport, but also has regular features on politics,

health, business, finance, and general topics of interest. Present circulation is 54,191.

Tips Any correspondence should be via email.

Irish Independent
Independent House, 27–32 Talbot Street, Dublin 1, Republic of Ireland
- 00353 1 705 5333
- 00353 1 872 0304
- info@independent.ie
- independent.letters@independent.ie
- www.independent.ie

Contact Editor, Gerard O'Regan; Business Editor, Richard Curran; Deputy Editor, Michael Wolsey; Features Editor, Peter Carvosso

Insider Info Focuses on topical news. Present circulation is 159,363.

Tips Letters (for publication) can be sent to the editor, via independent.letters@independent.ie.

Irish Mail on Sunday
Associated Newspapers Ltd, Embassy House, Ballsbridge, Dublin 4, Republic of Ireland
- 00353 1 637 5800
- 00353 1 637 5880
- news@irelandonsunday.com

Contact Editor, Paul Drury; Assistant Editor, John Cooper

Irish Times
11–15 D'Olier Street, Dublin 2, Republic of Ireland
- 00353 1 675 8000
- 00353 1 675 8035
- gkennedy@irish-times.ie
- www.ireland.com

Contact Editor, Geraldine Kennedy; Features Editor, Sheila Wayman; News Editor, Miriam Donohoe; Literary Editor, Caroline Walsh

Mail on Sunday
Associated Newspapers/Lord Rothermere
Northcliffe House, 2 Derry Street, London, W8 5TT
- 020 7938 6000
- 020 7937 3829
- news@mailonsunday.co.uk
- www.mailonsunday.co.uk

Contact Editor, Peter Wright; Deputy Editor, Eric Bailey; News Editor, David Dillon; Commissioning Editor, James Mannion; Features Editor, Sian James; Literary Editor, Neil Armstrong; Books Editor, Marilyn Warnick; Picture Editor, Liz Cox

Insider Info Deals with news media and current affairs. Feature writers are frequently used. Recurring features include articles on travel, women's interest, health and entertainment. Has a colour supplement called *You*. Present circulation is 2,211,029.

Tips Take advantage by researching their regular, recurring features.

Morning Star
People's Press Printing Society
William Rust House, 52 Beachey Road, London, E3 2NS
- 020 8510 0815
- 020 8986 5694
- newsed@peoples-press.com
- www.morningstaronline.co.uk

Contact Editor, John Haylett; News Editor, Daniel Coysh; Features Editor, Richard Bagley; Arts Editor, Katie Gilmore

Insider Info Circulation is around 25,000. A socialist paper aimed at Labour supporters. There are opportunities for freelance writers, but to be considered stories need to take a left wing stance. Focuses on current affairs, politics and the Labour Party.

Tips Take into account the potential left wing views of the readership.

News of the World
News Group Newspapers Ltd
1 Virginia Street, London, E98 1NW
- 020 7782 4000
- 020 7583 9504
- newsdesk@notw.co.uk
- www.newsoftheworld.co.uk

Contact Editor, Colin Myler; News Editor, James Mellor; Deputy Editor, Jane Johnson; Features Editor, Matthew Nixson

Insider Info The paper was first published in 1843. It covers news, media and current affairs. Celebrity exposés are appreciated. Payment for stories varies according to importance and the position printed in the paper. Has regular celebrity gossip columns in their *Sunday* magazine. Photographs are welcome. Present circulation of 3,153,521.

Tips Stories from outside the paper are welcome, but bear in mind the target audience enjoys celebrity gossip and breaking news. For more information on how to sell a story, see the website.

The Observer
Guardian Newspapers Ltd
3–7 Herbal Hill, London, EC15 5EJ
- 020 7278 2332
- 020 7837 7817
- reader@observer.co.uk
- www.observer.co.uk

Contact Arts Editor, Sarah Donaldson; Books Editor, William Skidelsky; Assistant Editor, Books, Robert McCrum

Insider Info The longest running Sunday national. Focuses in-depth on national and international news. It has a large readership of working women. Unusual for the paper to except freelance work. Includes special interest supplements, such as *Observer Food Monthly*, *Observer Women*, *Observer Sport Monthly*. Present circulation is 443,975.

Tips Expertise in any of the supplement subjects will be an advantage.

The People

Trinity Mirror plc

1 Canada Square, Canary Wharf, London, E14 5AP

☎ 020 7293 3000

🖷 020 7293 3517

✉ peoplenews@people.co.uk

🌐 www.people.co.uk

Contact Editor, Lloyd Embley; Deputy Editor, Ben Proctor; Head of News, Lee Harpin; Features Editor, Chris Bucktin; Picture Editor, Paula Berry

Insider Info Focuses on exclusives and celebrity stories. Uses investigative journalism. Has in-depth sports features. Stories can fetch high prices. Exclusives very welcome. Present circulation is 595,795.

Submission Guidelines If you have a story, call 020 7293 3202. This number is used for tip-offs and not always for planned or written articles. Photographs are welcome, either send to pictures@people.co.uk, or ring 020 7293 3901.

Tips It is worth bearing in mind that popular stories are based around high profile celebrity gossip. Advice on selling stories can be found on the website.

Scotland on Sunday

Scotsman Publications Ltd

Barclay House, 108 Holyrood Road, Edinburgh, EH8 8AS

☎ 0131 620 8620

🖷 0131 020 8491

✉ newssos@scotlandonsunday.com

🌐 www.scotlandonsunday.com

Contact Editor, Les Snowdon; Deputy Editor, Tom Little; Literary Editor, Peter Laing; Arts Editor, Fiona Leith; Picture Editor, Alan MacDonald

Established 1988

Insider Info A popular Sunday broadsheet. Features national and international news, and current affairs. Articles appear on politics, finance, business and health. Has regular features such as reviews. Present circulation is 62,399.

Tips The paper is aimed at a fairly intellectual reader. Scottish related work is welcomed.

The Scotsman

Scotsman Publications Ltd

Barclay House, 108 Holyrood Road, Edinburgh, EH8 8AS

☎ 0131 620 8620

🖷 0131 620 8616

✉ newsdesk_ts@scotsman.com

🌐 www.scotsman.com

Contact Editor, Mike Gilson; Deputy Editor, Ian Stewart; News Editor, Frank O'Donnell; Features Editor, Jackie Hunter; Literary Editor, David Robinson; Arts Editor, Andrew Eaton; Picture Editor, Andy O'Brien; Senior Assistant Editor, David Lee

Established 1817

Insider Info A quality paper focusing on news and current affairs. There may be a better chance of freelance work being published, than at other similar papers. Publishes regular articles on education, business, sport, and UK news, as well as Scottish news. Present circulation is 50,205.

Tips Stories on topical issues are encouraged.

Star Sunday

Independent News & Media/Express Newspapers Ltd

Star House, 62a Terenure Road North, Dublin 6, Republic of Ireland

☎ 00353 1 490 1228

🖷 00353 1 490 1538

✉ news.sunday@thestar.ie

🌐 www.thestar.ie

Contact Editor, Des Gibson

Insider Info Sports-based Sunday paper, aimed predominantly at young male readers. Present circulation is 346,942.

The Sun

News International plc

1 Virginia Street, London, E98 1SN

☎ 020 7782 4000

🖷 020 7782 4095

✉ news@the-sun.co.uk

🌐 www.thesun.co.uk

Contact Editor, Rebekah Wade; Publishing Director, Steve Waring; Deputy Editor, Dominic Mohan; Head of News, Chris Pharo; Head of Features & Entertainment, Victoria Newton; Features Editor, Ben Jackson; Picture Editor, John Edwards

Insider Info Daily paper focusing on celebrity culture and popular news. The readership is fairly young. Freelance ideas and stories are accepted. Exposés can be highly paid. Large sports section and regular 'Page 3' feature aimed at male readers. Present circulation is 3,045,899.

Tips *The Sun* tends to look for investigative journalism pieces. The information on how to send in a story is on the website.

The Sunday Business Post
80 Harcourt Street, Dublin 2, Republic of Ireland
- ☎ 00353 1 602 6000
- ☎ 00353 1 679 6496
- ✉ sbpost@iol.ie
- ⊕ www.thepost.ie

Contact Editor, Cliff Taylor

Insider Info Sunday newspaper focusing on financial, political and economical news. Readership is largely those involved in making key business decisions. Freelance work is considered. Features articles on motoring and computers. Present circulation is 55,971.

Tips It is important to show a thorough understanding of the area your article focuses on.

Sunday Express
Northern & Shell Media/Richard Desmond
Northern & Shell Building, 10 Lower Thames Street, London, EC3R 6EN
- ☎ 0871 434 1010
- ☎ 0871 434 7300
- ✉ news.desk@express.com
- ⊕ www.express.co.uk

Contact Editor, Martin Townsend; Deputy Editor, Richard Dismore; News Editor, Stephen Rigley; Features Editor, Giulia Rhodes; Literary Editor, Caroline Jowett; Arts & Entertainment Editor, Rachel Jane; Picture Editor, Terry Evans

Insider Info Tabloid-style Sunday paper. Likes to feature stories on celebrities. Regularly features celebrity exclusives and gossip columns. Present circulation is 670,486.

Tips You will find links to sell stories through the website. The paper is interested in fresh spins on popular culture and exposes. An investigative style of journalism is popular.

Sunday Herald
Newsquest Sunday Herald Ltd
200 Renfield Street, Glasgow, G2 3QB
- ☎ 0141 302 7800
- ☎ 0141 302 7863
- ✉ news@sundayherald.com
- ⊕ www.sundayherald.com

Contact Editor, Richard Walker; Deputy Editor, Stephen Penman; Online Editor, David Milne; Head of News, Bill Mackintosh; Acting Arts Editor, Barry Didcock; Picture Editor, Elaine Livingstone

Insider Info An award winning independent newspaper. Features national and international news. Favours stories of Scottish interest. Present circulation is 43,518.

Tips Links to specific contacts are on the website.

Sunday Independent
27–32 Talbot Street, Dublin 1, Republic of Ireland
- ☎ 00353 1 705 5333
- ☎ 00353 1 872 0304
- ✉ info@independent.ie
- ✉ sunday.letters@unison.independent.ie
- ⊕ www.independent.ie

Contact Editor, Aengus Fanning; Business Editor, Shane Ross

Insider Info Popular Irish Sunday newspaper. Freelance work is considered. Published in five sections: News, Sport, Business, Property, and Living. Present circulation is 283,024.

Sunday Mail
Scottish Daily Record & Sunday Mail Ltd
1 Central Quay, Glasgow, G3 8DA
- ☎ 0141 309 3000
- ☎ 0141 309 3587
- ✉ mailbox@sundaymail.co.uk
- ⊕ www.sundaymail.co.uk

Contact Editor, Allan Rennie; Deputy Editor, Jim Wilson; Digital Editorial Director, Ewan Watt; News Editor, Brendan McGinty; Picture Editor, Andrew Hosie

Insider Info Scottish Sunday tabloid, which combines news, showbiz and current affairs. Payment for exclusives can be generous. Publishes a mixture of news and features. Has a supplement magazine called *7-Days*, edited by Liz Cowan. Present circulation is 452,031.

Tips Exclusives or articles of Scottish relevance are favoured.

Sunday Mirror
Trinity Mirror plc
1 Canada Square, Canary Wharf, London, E14 5AP
- ☎ 020 7293 3000
- ☎ 020 7293 3587
- ✉ news@sundaymirror.co.uk
- ⊕ www.sundaymirror.co.uk

Contact Editor, Tina Weaver; Deputy Editor, James Scott; Head of News, Nick Buckley; News Editor, James Saville; Features Editor, Jill Main; Picture Editor, Ivor Game

Insider Info Sunday tabloid, which likes to cover big news scoops. Tip-offs and freelance work on exclusives can be highly paid. Articles on breaking news, entertainment, current affairs and sports. Photograph exclusives are welcome. Present circulation is 1,255,150.

Submission Guidelines Stories, photographs and videos can be submitted via an online form.

Tips Stories are only welcome if they fit closely with the style of the newspaper. A good knowledge of the paper and their readership is essential.

Sunday Post

D.C. Thompson & Co. Ltd
144 Port Dundas Road, Glasgow, G4 0HZ
- 0141 332 9933
- 0141 331 1595
- newsdesk@sundaypost.com
- www.sundaypost.com

Contact Editor, David Pollington; News Editor, Colin Grant

Insider Info A Sunday paper, which focuses on news and topical interests. Freelance writers are considered. Articles include those on health and sport. A pull out magazine is also available. Present circulation is 378,639.

Tips In order to be considered, you need to have proven knowledge on the subject you are writing about.

Sunday Telegraph

Telegraph Media Group Ltd
111 Buckingham Palace Road, London, SW1W 0DT
- 020 7931 2000
- 020 7513 2504
- stnews@telegraph.co.uk
- www.telegraph.co.uk

Contact Editor-in-Chief, William Lewis; Editor, Ian MacGregor; Deputy Editor, Tim Jotischky; Sunday Editor, Maggie O'Sullivan, Executive Editor (Features), Anna Murphy; Literary Editor, Michael Prodger; News Editor, James Hall; Arts Editor, Peter Reed; Assistant Editor (News & Features), Olga Craig; Picture Editor, Mike Spillard

Insider Info Traditional quality broadsheet. Tends to have a slightly older readership. Freelance work is considered. Publish features on politics, national and international news, lifestyle and sports. Produces colour supplements. Present circulation is 622,260.

Tips In order to be considered, writers need should be able to prove their knowledge of the subject they are writing about.

The Sunday Times

Times Newspapers Ltd
1 Pennington Street, London, E98 1XY
- 020 7782 5000
- 020 7782 5046
- letters@sunday-times.co.uk
- www.sunday-times.co.uk

Contact Managing Editor, Richard Caseby; Editor, John Witherow; Deputy Editor, Martin Ivens; Deputy Editor (News Review), Margarette Driscoll; News Editor, Charles Hymas; Commissioning Editor, Pip McCormack; Features Editor, Jessica Brinton; Literary Editor, Andrew Holgate; Picture Editor, Ray Wells; Assistant Editor, Jessica Jonzen

Insider Info Quality broadsheet known for its investigative journalism and sometimes controversial stance on issues. Aimed at an educated readership. Exclusives can reach high prices. Has a colour supplement containing lifestyle features. Present circulation is 1,223,577.

Tips Writers need an in-depth knowledge of their subject matter.

The Sunday Times Scotland

News International (Scotland) Ltd
57 Queen Street, Glasgow, G1 3EN
- 0141 420 5100
- 0141 420 5262
- scotland@sunday-times.co.uk
- www.timesonline.co.uk

Contact Editor, Carlos Alba; Deputy Editor, Camillo Fracassini; Features Editor, Joan McAlpine; Picture Editor, Jeremy Bayston

Insider Info Scottish national broadsheet. Present circulation is roughly 89,000.

The Times

Times Newspapers Ltd
1 Pennington Street, London, E98 1TT
- 020 7782 5000
- 020 7782 5988
- home.news@thetimes.co.uk
- www.thetimes.co.uk

Contact Managing Editor, David Chappell; Editor, James Harding; Executive Editor, Alex O'Connell; Head of Features, Sandra Parsons; Deputy Editor, Keith Blackmore; News Editor, Anne Barrowclough; Features Editor, Michael Harvey; Associate Features Editor, Shaun Philips; Arts & Entertainment Editor, Tim Teeman; Online Editor, Brigid Callaghan; Picture Editor, Paul Sanders

Insider Info A broadsheet for 200 years, it recently switched to a more compact size in order to appeal to a younger audience. Readership consists largely of professionals. *The Times* is considered to have a right wing stance, but it has supported New Labour. All contact to be addressed to relevant desks. Has in-depth articles on national and international news, sport, finance and lifestyle. Present circulation is 621,831.

Tips Take into account the paper's desire to appeal to a younger audience.

Wales on Sunday

Thomson House, Havelock Street, Cardiff, CF10 1XR
- 029 2058 3583
- 029 2058 3725
- wosmail@mediawales.co.uk
- www.icwales.co.uk

Contact Editor, Tim Gordon; Deputy Editor, Wayne Davies; Head of Content, Laura Kemp; News Editor, Nick Rippington; Features Editor, Sarah Manners; Picture Editor, Rob Watkins

Insider Info National Welsh Sunday newspaper covering news, sports and entertainment, mainly of Welsh importance. Present circulation is 42,763.

Submission Guidelines To contact the paper with a story, call 029 2058 3733.

Tips Welsh interest stories are preferable.

UK & IRISH LOCAL NEWSPAPERS

The Argus

Argus House, Crowhurst Road, Hollingbury, Brighton, BN1 8AR
- 01273 544544
- 01273 505703
- news@theargus.co.uk
- www.theargus.co.uk

Contact Editor, Micheal Beard; News Editor, Frankie Taggart; Features Editor, Jakki Philips; Literary Editor, Anne Hill

Insider Info Covers Brighton, Hove and the rest of Sussex. Publishes features on local homes, business, cars and lifestyle. Present circulation is 11,477.

The Bath Chronicle

Western Newspapers Ltd
Windsor House, Windsor Bridge, Bath, Somerset, BA2 3AU
- 01225 322322
- 01225 322291
- news@bathchron.co.uk
- www.bathchronicle.co.uk

Contact Editor, Sam Holliday; News Editor, Paul Wiltshire; Features Editor, Jackie Chappell; Picture Editor, Kevin Bates; Sports Editor, Julie Riegal; Arts Editor, Christopher Hansford

Established 1760

Insider Info Covers Bath. Present circulation is 20,275.

Tips News and stories of local Bath interest are favoured.

Belfast Telegraph

Independent News & Media (UK) Ltd
124–144 Royal Avenue, Belfast, BT1 1EB, Northern Ireland
- 028 9026 4000
- 028 9055 4506
- newseditor@belfasttelegraph.co.uk
- www.belfasttelegraph.co.uk

Contact Editor, Martin Lindsay; News Editor, Ronan Henry; Deputy Editor, Paul Connolly; Features Editor, Gail Walker

Insider Info A widely read daily paper, covering local, national and international news. Freelance work is considered. Has a wide ranging editorial coverage. Regular features appear on recruitment, property, motoring and business. Present circulation is 75,964. For the *Community Telegraph* – focusing on localised news and events, contact m.reilly@belfasttelegraph.co.uk.

Tips Ideally work should be connected with Northern Ireland.

Birmingham Mail

PO Box 78, Weaman Street, Birmingham, B4 6AY
- 0121 236 3366
- 0121 233 0271
- www.birminghammail.net

Contact Editor, Steve Dyson; Head of News, Andy Richards; Deputy Editor, Carole Cole; Features Editor, Paul Fulford; Literary Editor, Alf Bennett; Picture Editor, Steve Murphy

Established 1870

Insider Info Covers Birmingham Present circulation is 66,166.

Submission Guidelines Contact the editor, steve_dyson@mrn.co.uk with ideas.

The Birmingham Post

PO Box 78, Weaman Street, Birmingham, B4 6AY
- 0121 236 3366
- 0121 625 1105
- postnewsdesk@mrn.co.uk
- www.birminghampost.net

Contact Editor, Marc Reeves; News Editor, Mo Ilyas; Features Editor, Sarah Probert; Picture Editor, Simon Hadley

Insider Info Quality paper covering news in the Midlands. Features on business and industry. Present circulation is 12,795.

Tips An in-depth knowledge of relevant subject areas in relation to the Birmingham region is required.

Blackpool Gazette

Blackpool Gazette & Herald Ltd

Avroe House, Avroe Crescent, Blackpool Business Park, Blackpool, FY4 2DP

- 01253 400888
- alison.bott@blackpoolgazette.co.uk
- www.blackpooltoday.co.uk

Contact Assistant Editor, Alison Bott

Insider Info Covers local news, sport and entertainment. Photographs are accepted. Present circulation is 28,340.

Bolton News

Newspaper House, Churchgate, Bolton, Lancashire, BL1 1DE

- 01204 522345
- 01204 365068
- newsdesk@theboltonnews.co.uk
- www.thisisbolton.co.uk

Contact Editor in Chief, Ian Savage; Assistant Editor, Lynn Ashwell; Deputy News Editor, Dave Crookes; Features Editor, Andrew Mosley; Picture Editor, Richard Rollon

Established 1867

Insider Info Has pages on business, leisure, homes and jobs. Present circulation is 28,835.

Submission Guidelines Contact the relevant editor with ideas (see above).

Bristol Evening Post

Temple Way, Bristol, BS99 7HD

- 0117 934 3000
- 0117 934 3575
- epnews@bepp.co.uk
- www.thisisbristol.co.uk

Contact Editor in Chief, Mike Norton; Deputy News Editor, Ian Onions; Features Editor, David Webb; Picture Editor, Rachel Profit

Established 1932

Insider Info Covers the Bristol area with articles on local news and sport. Present circulation is 49,386.

Burton Mail

Staffordshire Newspapers Ltd

65–68 High Street, Burton on Trent, DE14 1LE

- 01283 512345
- 01283 515351
- editorial@burtonmail.co.uk
- www.burtonmail.co.uk

Contact Editor, Paul Hazeldine; News Editor, Steve Doohan; Features Editor, Louise Elliot; Picture Editor, Neil Barker

Insider Info Daily paper with a circulation of 14,509. Has features on jobs, property and motors as well as entertainment and lifestyle.

Cambridge Evening News

Cambridge Newspapers Ltd

Winship Road, Milton, Cambridge, CB24 6PP

- 01223 434434
- 01223 434415
- newsdesk@cambridge-news.co.uk
- www.cambridge-news.co.uk

Contact Editor, Paul Brackley; News Editor, Paul Holland; Features Editor, Paul Kirkley; Picture Editor, Dave Harwood

Insider Info Covers local news, sports and entertainment. Present circulation is 26,462. Magazine supplements include, *Style* magazine and *Our Time* magazine. Contact the magazine editor on 01223 434309.

Camden New Journal

New Journal Enterprises Ltd

40 Camden Road, Camden Town, London, NW1 9DR

- 020 7419 9000
- 020 7209 1322
- editorial@camdennewjournal.co.uk
- www.thecnj.com

Contact Editor, Eric Gordon; Deputy Editor, Andrew Johnson

Insider Info A free, independent newspaper covering the London Borough of Camden. Articles cover local and national news, health, events and sport.

Tips The newspaper is known for its investigative journalism and high news content, both local and national.

Chester Chronicle

Trinity Mirror Cheshire

Chronicle House, Commonhall Street, Chester, CH1 2AA

- 01244 606425
- 01244 606498
- newsroom@cheshirenews.co.uk
- http://iccheshireonline.icnetwork.co.uk/chesterchronicle

Contact Editor, Eric Langton; Deputy Editor, Michael Green; News Editor, Barry Ellams

Established 1775

Insider Info There are localised versions of the paper for separate areas, these include: *Chester City & Country* editions, and *'Chronicles* for Wirral, Frodsham and Helsby, Deeside, Flint and Holywell, and Mold and Buckley. Articles include local news, sport and events. *The Guide*, a supplement, contains features on arts and entertainment. Present circulation is 24,642.

Chronicle & Echo (Northampton)
Northamptonshire Newspapers Ltd
Upper Mounts, Northampton, NN1 3HR
- 01604 467000
- 01604 467190
- editor@northantsnews.co.uk
- www.northamptonchron.co.uk

Contact Editor, David Summers; News Editor, Richard Edmondson; Features Editor, Lily Canter; Literary Editor, Vaughan Tucker; Picture Editor, Tracey Chambers
Established 1931
Insider Info Covers the Northampton area with local news and sport. Present circulation is 19,827. Supplements include *Sport on Monday*, *Term Time*, *Property Today*, *Jobs Today*, *The Guide* and *Weekend Life*.
Email photographs to, editor@northantsnews.co.uk.

The Citizen
6–8 The Oxebode, Gloucester, GL1 1RZ
- 01452 420621
- 01452 420664
- citizen.news@glosmedia.co.uk
- www.thisisgloucestershire.co.uk

Contact Editor, Ian Mean; Assistant Editor, Matt Holmes; Features Editor, Tanya Gledhill; Picture Editor, Mikal Ludlow
Insider Info A daily paper which covers the western side of Gloucester. Present circulation is 25,681.

Cornish Guardian Series
Cornwall & Devon Media Ltd
3 Fore Street, St Austell, Cornwall, PL25 5PX
- 01276 76815
- 01726 69694
- cgedit@c-dm.co.uk
- www.thisiscornwall.co.uk

Contact Editor in Chief, Andy Cooper; Community Editor, Oscar Morse; Community Editor, Richard Whitehouse; Book Review/Local News Editor, Julia Bryan
Established 1901
Insider Info Publishes eight weekly editions, covering St Austell, Newquay, Lostwithiel & Fowey, Bodmin, Wadebridge, Camelford, Launceston & Bude, and Liskeard. Combined circulation is 32,384. Articles focus on local and regional news, sport and features.
Submission Guidelines Email the news or sports desk with stories.
Tips For contact details of individual local editions, visit the website. Bear in mind that a majority of the readership will live in rural or semi-rural locations.

The Courier & Advertiser
D.C. Thompson & Co. Ltd
80 Kingsway East, Dundee, DD4 8SL
- 01382 223131
- 01382 454590
- courier@dcthomson.co.uk
- www.thecourier.co.uk

Contact Editor, William Hutcheon; Deputy Editor, Jim Allison; News Editor, Mike Alexander; Features Editor, Catriona MacInnes
Insider Info Covers local news and sport across Tayside and Fife. Regular feature pages include those on health, fashion, motors and art. Present circulation is 72,527.

Coventry Telegraph
Corporation Street, Coventry, CV1 1FP
- 024 7663 3633
- 024 7655 0869
- news@coventrytelegraph.co.uk
- www.go2coventry.co.uk

Contact Editor, Alan Kirby; News Manager, Steve Williams; Features Editor, Tara Cain; Literary Editor, John West; Picture Editor, Pete Roberts
Insider Info Local tabloid paper for Coventry. Supplements include *What's On*, a weekly entertainment guide. Present circulation is 46,297.

Daily Echo
Richmond Hill, Bournemouth, Dorset, BH2 6HH
- 01202 554601
- 01202 551246
- newsdesk@bournemouthecho.co.uk
- www.bournemouthecho.co.uk

Contact Editor, Neal Butterworth; Deputy Editor, Ed Perkins; News Editor, Andy Martin; Features Editor, Kevin Nash
Insider Info Circulation of 32,085 in the Bournemouth area. Freelance news and feature articles are considered.

Derby Evening Telegraph
Derby Daily Telegraph Ltd
Northcliffe House, Meadow Road, Derby, DE1 2BH
- 01332 291111
- newsdesk@derbytelegraph.co.uk
- www.thisisderbyshire.co.uk

Contact Editor, Steve Hall; Deputy Editor, Neil White; News Editor, Emma Slee; Features Editor, Jill Gallone; Picture Editor, Victoria Wilcox
Insider Info Circulation of 41,799 in the Derbyshire area.

Dorset Echo

Fleet House, Hampshire Road, Granby Industrial Estate, Weymouth, DT4 9XD

- ☎ 01305 830930
- ☎ 01305 830956
- ✉ newsdesk@dorsetecho.co.uk
- 🌐 www.dorsetecho.co.uk

Contact Editor, David Murdock; News Editor, Paul Thomas; Features Editor, Diarmuid MacDonagh; Arts Editor, Ruth Meech; Picture Editor, Finnbarr Webster

Insider Info A local evening paper covering Dorset, with a circulation of 18,702.

Submission Guidelines Contact the news desk on 01305 830999 if you have a story.

Dundee Evening Telegraph & Post

D.C. Thompson & Co. Ltd

80 Kingsway East, Dundee, DD4 8SL

- ☎ 01382 223131
- ☎ 01382 454590
- ✉ newsdesk@eveningtelegraph.co.uk
- ✉ features@eveningtelegraph.co.uk
- 🌐 www.eveningtelegraph.co.uk

Contact Editor, Gordon Wishart; Deputy & Features Editor, Philip Smith; News Editor, Elaine Harrison

Insider Info Local news and sport coverage for Tayside, Dundee and Fife. Present circulation is 24,533.

East Anglian Daily Times

Press House, 30 Lower Brook Street, Ipswich, IP4 1AN

- ☎ 01473 230023
- ☎ 01473 324776
- ✉ news@eadt.co.uk
- 🌐 www.eadt.co.uk

Contact Editor, Terry Hunt; News Editor, Brad Jones; Features Editor, Julian Ford; Book Review Editor, Steve Russell; Arts Editor, Andrew Clarke

Established 1884

Insider Info Covers a wide range of local, national, and international news and sport. Features regular lifestyle and entertainment supplements. Photographs will be considered. Circulation is 34,055.

Submission Guidelines News stories should be sent to the news desk via email, or text to 84070 starting the message with EADT.

Tips Local interest stories are well received.

Eastern Daily Press

Archant Norfolk

Prospect House, Rouen Road, Norwich, NR1 1RE

- ☎ 01603 628311
- ☎ 01603 623872
- ✉ edpnewsdesk@archant.co.uk
- 🌐 www.edp24.co.uk

Contact Editor, Peter Franzen OBE; Deputy Editor, Peter Waters; News Editor, Paul Durrant; Content Editor, Sarah Hardy; Picture Editor, Nolan Lincoln

Insider Info A daily paper, which likes to focus on the local community. Covers news, business, lifestyle and entertainment. Circulation os 63,508.

Tips Information on getting started in journalism can be found on the website, which has good key advice.

The Echo

Newspaper House, Chester Hall Lane, Basildon, Essex, SS14 3BL

- ☎ 0844 4774 512
- ☎ 0844 477 4286
- ✉ echo.editor@nqe.com
- 🌐 www.echo-news.co.uk

Contact Editor, Martin McNeill; News Editor, Christina Ongley; Features Editor, Claire Borley; Picture Editor, Luan Marshall

Established 1969

Insider Info Published daily, covering the Basildon area of Essex. Present circulation is 9,263.

Evening Chronicle

Newcastle Chronicle & Journal Ltd

Groat Market, Newcastle upon Tyne, NE1 1ED

- ☎ 0191 232 7500
- ☎ 0191 232 2256
- ✉ ec.news@ncjmedia.co.uk
- 🌐 www.icnewcastle.co.uk

Contact Editor, Paul Robertson; News Editor, James Marley; Features Editor, Jennifer Bradbury; Picture Editor, Rod Wilson

Insider Info Covers a mix of local news, sport and entertainment in the wider Newcastle area. Present circulation of 71,878.

Evening Courier

PO Box 19, King Cross Street, Halifax, HX1 2SF

- ☎ 01422 260200
- ☎ 01422 260341
- ✉ newsdesk@halifaxcourier.co.uk
- 🌐 www.halifaxcourier.co.uk

Contact Editor, John Furbisher; Deputy Editor, John Kenealy; News Editor, Sophie McCandlish; Features Editor, Tim Worsnop; Arts Editor, Pauline Hawkins

Established 1937

Insider Info Publishes local Halifax news and sport, as well as guides to local entertainment and events. Present circulation is 19,681.

Tips Local interest stories will be considered.

Evening Echo (Cork)

Evening Echo Publications Ltd

The City Quarter, Lapps Quay, Cork, Republic of Ireland

- 00353 21 427 2722
- 00353 21 480 2135
- maruice.gubbins@eecho.ie
- www.eveningecho.ie

Contact Editor, Maurice Gubbins; News & Fashion Editor, Emma Connolly; Features Editor, John Dolan; Pictures Editor, Brian Lougheed

Insider Info Covers in-depth local news, national news and sports. Regular features on local community news. Present circulation is 25,829.

Tips Individual staff contact details can be found on the website.

Evening Express

Aberdeen Journals Ltd

PO Box 43, Lang Stracht, Mastrick, Aberdeen, AB15 6DF

- 01224 690222
- 01224 699575
- ee.news@ajl.co.uk
- www.thisisaberdeen.co.uk

Contact Editor, Damien Bates; Deputy Editor, Richard Prest; News Editor, Louise Redvers; Picture Editor, Alan Paterson

Insider Info Covers local, national and international news. Additional contacts are on the website. Present circulation is 53,130.

Submission Guidelines If you have a news story, call 01224 344150.

Evening Gazette

Gazette Media Company Ltd

Gazette Buildings, 105–111 Borough Road, Middlesborough, TS1 3AZ

- 01642 245401
- 01642 232014
- news@eveninggazette.co.uk
- www.gazettelive.co.uk

Contact Editor, Darren Thwaites; News Editor, Jim Horsley; Head of Features, Karen McLauchlan; Arts Editor, Keith Newton

Insider Info Popular daily paper providing coverage for the Tees Valley area. Freelance work is considered. Present circulation is 50,431.

Tips Work of specific local interest is popular.

Evening Gazette (Colchester)

Newsquest Ltd

43 North Hill, Colchester, Essex, CO1 1TZ

- 01206 506000
- 01206 508274
- gazette_newsdesk@nqe.com
- www.evening-gazette.co.uk

Contact Editor in Chief, Irene Kettle; Group News Editor, Sally Teatheredge; Head of Features, Iris Clapp; Picture Editor, Steve Brading

Established 1970

Insider Info A paid for local paper, with a circulation of 21,194. Covers north Essex including the towns of Colchester, Harwich and Clacton. Articles focus on regional news, current affairs and features, as well as entertainment and sport.

Evening Herald

Independent News & Media

27–32 Talbot Street, Dublin 1, Republic of Ireland

- 00353 1 705 5333
- herald.news@independent.ie
- herald.features@independent.ie
- www.evening-herald.ie

Insider Info Covers the Dublin area of Ireland. Payment will be made by arrangement for each article accepted. Present circulation is 79,447. Phone 'Your Letters' on freephone 1800 733 733. Name, address and telephone must be supplied for verification.

Evening News

Archant Norfolk

Prospect House, Rouen Road, Norwich, NR1 1RE

- 01603 628311
- 01603 219060
- eveningnews@archant.co.uk
- www.eveningnews24.co.uk

Contact Editor, James Foster; News Editor, Tim Hawkins; Features Editor, Derek James; Picture Editor, Nolan Lincoln

Insider Info Combines a mix of news and information on the local area. Present circulation is 22,250.

Submission Guidelines If you have a story call the News Editor on 01603 772443.

Tips Interested in news and features about local communities or individuals.

Evening News (Edinburgh)

108 Holyrood Road, Edingburgh, EH8 8AS

- 0131 620 8620
- 0131 620 8696
- news_en@scotsman.com
- www.edinburghnews.com

Contact Editor, John McLellan; Assistant & News Editor, Euan McGrory; Deputy Features Editor, Judy Vickers; Arts & Entertainment Editor, Liam Rudden; Picture Editor, Roger Johnathan

Insider Info Covers local, national, and international news. Regular features on business, health, politics and entertainment. Present circulation is 49,208.

Evening Standard

Associated Newspapers Ltd
Northcliffe House, 2 Derry Street, London, W8 5TT
- 020 7938 6000
- features@standard.co.uk
- www.thisislondon.co.uk

Contact Editor, Veronica Wadley; Deputy Editor, Andrew Bordiss; News Editor, Hugh Dougherty; Features Editor, Charlotte Ross; Arts Editor, Fiona Hughes; Literary Editor, David Sexton; Commissioning Editor (Features), Christina Madden; Picture Editor, Luke Brighty; Deputy Arts Editor, Richard Godwin

Insider Info A tabloid sized paper delivering people in London coverage of city news, sport and lifestyle. National and international news is also covered. Publishes regular guides to what's on in London, arts and reviews. Weekly colour supplements are *ES Magazine* and *Homes and Property*. Present circulation is 303,049.

Tips Writers stand a better chance of getting published if the work is of direct local importance.

Express & Echo

South West Media Group Ltd
Heron Road, Sowton Industrial Estate, Exeter, Devon, EX2 7NF
- 01392 442211
- 01392 442294
- echonews@expressandecho.co.uk
- www.thisisexeter.co.uk

Contact Editor, Marc Astley; Deputy Editor, Andrew Howard; Head of Content, Lynne Turner; News Editor, Rob Sims; Features Editor, Becky Moran; Picture Editor, James Millar

Insider Info Daily paper covering local news and sport for Exeter and the surrounding areas in East Devon. Includes regular supplements on property, jobs, business and motoring. Present circulation is 20,625.

Express & Star

Midland News Association
51–53 Queen Street, Wolverhampton, WV1 1ES
- 01902 313131
- 01902 319721
- newsdesk@expressandstar.co.uk
- www.expressandstar.co.uk

Contact Editor, Adrian Faber; Deputy Editor, Keith Harrison; Head of News; Mark Drew; Features Editor, Emma Farmer; Picture Editor, Stephen Derry

Established 1880s

Insider Info The *Express & Star* is the biggest selling regional evening newspaper, covering Wolverhampton and the surrounding areas in the Midlands. Covers local news and events. Present circulation is 138,116. Send photographs to: internet@expressandstar.co.uk.

Glasgow Evening Times

Newsquest Herald & Times Ltd
200 Renfield Street, Glasgow, G2 3QB
- 0141 302 7000
- 0141 302 6600
- times@eveningtimes.co.uk
- www.eveningtimes.co.uk

Contact Editor, Donald Martin; Deputy Editor, Tony Carlin; Head of News, Yvonne Fylnn; News Editor, Hugh Boaq; Features Editor, Garry Scott; Group Multimedia Editor, John Young

Insider Info One of Scotland's best selling newspapers. It provides in-depth coverage of local news and sport for the Glasgow area. Present circulation is 72,535.

Gloucestershire Echo

Cheltenham Newspaper Company Ltd
1 Clarence Parade, Cheltenham, Gloucestershire, GL50 3NY
- 01242 271900
- 01242 271848
- editor@glosecho.co.uk
- www.thisisgloucestershire.co.uk

Contact Editor, Paul Kennedy; Deputy Editor, Marianne Sweet; News Editor, Sam Shepherd; Features Editor, Tanya Gledhill; Picture Editor, Michael Swift

Established 1873

Insider Info Local stories for the county of Gloucestershire will be considered. Other newspapers covered by the same website include *The Citizen* and *The Forester*. Present circulation is 20,613.

Grimsby Telegraph

Grimsby & Scunthorpe Media Group
80 Cleethorpe Road, Grimsby, Lincolnshire, DN31 3EH
- 01472 360360
- 01472 372257
- newsdesk@grimsbytelegraph.co.uk
- www.thisisgrimsby.co.uk

Contact Editor, Michelle Lalor; Deputy Editor, Michelle Hurst; News Editor, Lucy Wood

Established 1897

Insider Infor Covers local news and sport for the Grimsby area. Present circulation is 33,678.

Guernsey Press & Star

Guernsey Press Co. Ltd

**PO Box 57, Braye Road, Vale, Guernsey,
GY1 3BW**

- 01481 240240
- 01481 240235
- newseditor@guernsey-press.co.uk
- www.guernseypress.co.uk

Contact Editor, Richard Digard; Content Editor, Suzanne Heneghan; News Editor, Paul Baker; Features Editor, Di Digard

Insider Info A popular tabloid paper, which covers local news and sport, as well as in-depth coverage of local commercial and financial news. The main readership is aged between 35 to 64. Supplements include motoring, property, finance, personal finance, leisure, boating and Christmas specials. Letters and commentaries about local issues are invited. Present circulation is 16,023.

Hartlepool Mail

Northeast Press Ltd

**New Clarence House, Wesley Square, Hartlepool,
TS24 8BX**

- 01429 239333
- 01429 869024
- mail.news@northeast-press.co.uk
- www.hartlepooltoday.co.uk

Contact Editor, Joy Yates; Deputy Editor, Gavin Foster; News Editor, Paul Watson

Established 1849

Insider Info Delivers local news and sport to Hartlepool and the surrounding area. Further contact links can be found on the website. Present circulation is 17,773.

Herald Express

South West Media Group Ltd

**Harmsworth House, Barton Hill Road, Torquay,
Devon, TQ2 8JN**

- 01803 676000
- 01803 676223
- newsdesk@heraldexpress.co.uk
- www.thisissouthdevon.co.uk

Contact Editor, Andy Phelan; Deputy Editor, Jim Parker; Head of Content, Guy Henderson; Picture Editor, John Whitehead

Insider Info Present circulation is 23,992. The paper covers local news and sport for Torquay and surrounding areas.

Tips Interested in work that reflects the life of the local communities.

The Herald (Plymouth)

South West Media Group Ltd

**17 Brest Road, Derriford Business Park,
Plymouth, Devon, PL6 5AA**

- 01752 765500
- 01752 765527
- newsdesk@eveningherald.co.uk
- www.thisisplymouth.co.uk

Contact Editor, Bill Martin; News Editor, James Garnett; Executive Features Editor, Su Carroll; Picture Editor, Peter Holdgate

Insider Info Covers local news, sports and general interest stories. Present circulation is 36,236.

The Huddersfield Daily Examiner

**PO Box A26, Queen Street South, Huddersfield,
HD1 2DT**

- 01484 430000
- 01484 437789
- editorial@examiner.co.uk
- www.examiner.co.uk

Contact Editor, Roy Wright; Deputy Editor, Michael O'Connell; News Editor, Neil Atkinson; Features Editor, Andrew Flynn

Established 1871

Insider Info Covers the Huddersfield area, publishing local features, news and sport. Present circulation is 24,853.

Hull Daily Mail

Mail News & Media Ltd

Blundell's Corner, Beverley Road, Hull, HU3 1XS

- 01482 327111
- 01482 315353
- news@mailnewsmedia.co.uk
- www.thisishullandeastriding.co.uk

Contact Editor, John Meehan; Deputy Editor, Mel Cook; News Editor, Paul Baxter; Features Editor, Bryan Marshall

Insider Info Local sport and news for Hull and the surrounding areas. Present circulation is 56,287.

Inverness Courier

Scottish Provincial Press

**New Century House, Stadium Road, Inverness,
IV1 1FF**

- 01463 233059
- 01463 243439
- editorial@inverness-courier.co.uk
- www.inverness-courier.co.uk

Contact Editor, Robert Taylor; Editorial Director, Nick Hunter; News Editor, Olivia Bell; Arts & Features Editor, Callum Macloud

Insider Info Local paper covering much of the Highlands. Present circulation is 30,383.

Tips Welcomes stories of local public interest, and current or historical features.

The Irish News
Irish News Ltd
113–117 Donegall Street, Belfast, BT1 2GE
- 028 9032 2226
- 028 9033 7505
- newsdesk@irishnews.com
- www.irishnews.com

Contact Editor, Noel Doran; News Editor, Billy Foley; Features Editor, Joanna Braniff; Picture Editor, Ann McManus

Established 1891

Insider Info Regarded as a quality paper, it covers local and national news and sport, with in-depth coverage of traditional Gaelic sport. Freelance work is considered. Supplements include, *Jobs on Thursday*, *Scene*, *Business Insight*, *Women Talk*, *Weekend* and *Drive*. Present circulation is 47,911.

Tips Work should be sent directly to the appropriate department, details are on the website.

Jersey Evening Post
PO Box 582, Five Oaks, St Saviour, Jersey, JE4 8XQ
- 01534 611611
- 01534 611622
- editorial@jerseyeveningpost.com
- www.thisisjersey.com

Contact Editor, Chris Bright; New Editor, Carl Walker; Features Editor, Anna Plunkett-Cole; Pictures Editor, Peter Mourant;

Established 1890

Insider Info The Jersey Evening Post has 73 per cent of Jersey's adult newspaper readership. Regular features include, property, business, food and drink, farming and careers. Present circulation is 21,098.

The Journal
Groat Market, Newcastle upon Tyne, NE1 1ED
- 0191 232 7500
- 0191 201 6044
- jnl.newsdesk@ncjmedia.co.uk
- www.icnewcastle.co.uk

Insider Info Covers the Newcastle area. Correspondence is welcomed, email the editor at letters@nwemail.co.uk. Features regular articles on local jobs, property and entertainment. Present circulation is 34,189.

Kent Messenger
Kent Messenger Group
6–7 Middle Row, Maidstone, Kent, ME14 1TG
- 01622 695666
- 01622 757227
- messengernews@thekmgroup.co.uk
- www.kentmessenger.co.uk

Contact Editor, Bob Bounds; Senior News Editor, Nikki White

Insider Info Covers Kent with County, Weald, Malling, Maidstone, Medway and Sittingbourne editions. Published weekly (Friday). Circulation of 49,834.

Lancashire Evening Post
Olivers Place, Eastway, Fulwood, Preston, Lancashire, PR2 9ZA
- 01772 254841
- 01772 880173
- lep.newsdesk@lep.co.uk
- www.lep.co.uk

Contact Editor, Simon Reynolds; Head of Content, Blaise Tapp; Deputy News Editor, Nicola Adam; Features Editor, Peter Richardson; Picture Editor, Iain Lynn

Insider Info Covers local news, sports and entertainment for Lancashire. Present circulation is 29,716.

Lancashire Telegraph
Newsquest Ltd
Newspaper House, High Street, Blackburn, Lancashire, BB1 1HT
- 01254 678678
- 01254 680429
- let_editorial@lancashire.newsquest.co.uk
- www.lancashiretelegraph.co.uk

Contact Editor, Kevin Young; Deputy News Editor, Ian Singleton; Arts & Features Editor, John Anson; Picture Editor, Neil Johnson

Insider Info A well established tabloid, which provides local and national news to East Lancashire. Present circulation is 29,753.

Tips Although the paper does cover national news, local news is strongly favoured.

The Leicester Mercury
Leicester Mercury Media Group Ltd
St George Street, Leicester, LE1 9FQ
- 0116 251 2512
- 0116 253 0645
- newsdesk@leicestermercury.co.uk
- www.thisisleicestershire.co.uk

Contact Editor, Nick Carter; Deputy Editor, Richard Bettsworth; News Editor, Mark Charlton; Features Editor, Alex Dawson; Picture Editor, Jason Senior

Insider Info Covers local news, sports and entertainment. Present circulation is 69,069.

Lincolnshire Echo

Brayford Wharf East, Lincoln, Lincolnshire, LN5 7AT
- 01522 820000
- 01522 804493
- news@lincolnshiremedia.co.uk
- www.thisislincolnshire.co.uk

Contact Editor, Jon Grubb; Deputy Editor, Martin Mammatt; News Editor, Mel West; Features Editor, Sarah Overton

Insider Info Covers local news, events and sports. Present circulation is 21,565.

Tips The specific target areas for this newspaper are Lincoln, Scunthorpe, Barton upon Humber, Brigg, Epworth, Crowle and Messingham.

Liverpool Daily Post

PO Box 48, Old Hall Street, Liverpool, L69 3EB
- 0151 227 2000
- 0151 472 2474
- andykelly@dailypost.co.uk
- www.liverpooldailypost.co.uk

Contact Editor, Mark Thomas; Deputy Editor, Alison Gow; News Editor, Andrew Kelly; Features Editor, Emma Johnson; Arts Editor, Philip Key; Picture Editor, Stephen Shakeshaft

Insider Info Covers local news and sport for Liverpool. Publishes regular features on local lifestyle and entertainment. Present circulation is 14,266.

Liverpool Echo

PO Box 48, Old Hall Street, Liverpool, L69 3EB
- 0151 227 2000
- 0151 272 2474
- www.liverpoolecho.co.uk

Contact Editor, Alastair Machray; News Editor, Maria Breslin; Features Editor, Jane Haase; Arts Editor, Joe Riley; Picture Editor, Stephen Shakeshaft

Insider Info A popular local paper with a high circulation, consisting of local news and sport. Circulation is around 102,488.

Submission Guidelines Contact the editor on 0151 472 2507, but send ideas in writing first.

Manchester Evening News

1 Scott Place, Hardman Street, Manchester, M3 3RN
- 0161 832 7200
- 0161 211 2034
- newsdesk@men-news.co.uk
- features@men-news.co.uk
- www.manchestereveningnews.co.uk

Contact Editor, Paul Horrocks; Deputy Editor, Maria McGeoghan; News Editor, Ian Wood; Features Editor, Deanna Delamotta; Literary Editor, David Graham; Picture Editor, John Jeffay

Insider Info A leading regional paper with over half its readers between the ages of 15 to 44. Publishes regular features such as: *Property World*, *Lifestyle*, *Go*, *Go Family* and *Business*. Present circulation is 161,545.

Submission Guidelines Stories can be sent to the appropriate email addresses. These can all be found on the website and above. Articles should really be no more than 1,000 words.

Medway Messenger

North Kent Media Centre, 4 Ambley Green, Gillingham Business Park, Gillingham, ME8 0NJ
- 01634 236320
- 01634 715256
- newdesk.medway@krnmedia.co.uk
- www.kentonline.co.uk

Contact Senior Editor, Bob Bounds; News Editor, Sarah Clarke; Picture Editor, Barry Hollis

Insider Info A twice weekly paper, which publishes local news and sport for the east Kent costal area. Present circulation is 12,362.

News Letter

2 Esky Drive, Carn Industrial Area, Portadown, Craigavon, Belfast, BT63 5YY
- 028 3839 5577
- 028 3839 5599
- newsdesk@newsletter.co.uk
- www.newsletter.co.uk

Contact Editor, Darwin Templeton; News Editor, Karen Grimason; Features Editor, Geoff Hill; Literary Editor, Billy Kennedy

Established 1737

Insider Info A well established paper covering national (Northern Irish) and international news. Publishes regular colour supplements. Features include, lifestyle, motoring and health. Present circulation is 26,199.

Submission Guidelines The paper can be approached with ideas and comments through its website.

The News (Portsmouth)

The News Centre, Hilsea, Portsmouth, PO2 9SX
- 023 9266 4488
- 023 9267 3363
- newsdesk@thenews.co.uk
- www.thenews.co.uk

Contact Editor, Mark Waldron; Deputy Editor, Mark Acheson; News Editor, Graeme Patfield; Pictures Editor, Dean Kedward; Acting Features Editor, Simon Toft

Established 1877

Insider Info The paper is designed to appeal to a cross section of the communities in the Portsmouth area. It has in-depth coverage of local news. Present circulation is approximately 53,159.
Tips Changed from broadsheet to tabloid last year, in order to appeal to a younger audience.

The Northern Echo
PO Box 14, Priestgate, Darlington, Co. Durham, DL1 1NF
- 01325 381313
- 01325 380539
- newsdesk@nne.co.uk
- picturedesk@nne.co.uk
- www.thenorthernecho.co.uk

Contact Editor, Peter Barron; Deputy Editor, Chris Lloyd; News Editor, Nigel Burton; Literary Editor, Jenny Needham
Insider Info Covers local news and sport for the North East of England. Present circulation is 50,427.
Submission Guidelines Accepts email enquiries for both news and pictures (see above for email addresses).
Tips The publication has two editions: *The Northern Echo* (Darlington, Tees Valley & North Yorkshire) and *The Northern Echo* (County Durham).

North-West Evening Mail
Newspaper House, Abbey Road, Barrow in Furness, LA14 5QS
- 01229 821835
- 01229 840164
- news@nwemail.co.uk
- www.nwemail.co.uk

Contact Editor, Steve Brauner; News Editor, Robert Johnson; Features Editor, Peter Leach
Insider Info Covers sport and news for the North West region of England. Present circulation is 18,386.
Submission Guidelines Stories are welcomed, contact the news desk.
Tips The paper will consider stories relevant to the wider North West area.

Nottingham Evening Post
Nottingham Post Group Ltd
Castle Wharf House, Nottingham, NG1 7EU
- 0115 948 2000
- 0115 964 4032
- newsdesk@nottinghameveningpost.co.uk
- www.thisisnottingham.co.uk

Contact Editor, Malcolm Pheby; Deputy Editor, Martin Done; News Editor, Steven Fletcher; Features Editor, Claire Catlow; Picture Editor, Steve Mitchell
Established 1778
Insider Info The paper now has a circulation of 55,507.

Submission Guidelines Send stories or ideas to the news desk.
Tips Focus on local interests directly related to Nottingham.

Oldham Evening Chronicle
PO Box 47, 172 Union Street, Oldham, Lancashire, OL1 1EQ
- 0161 633 2121
- 0161 652 2111
- editorial@oldham-chronicle.co.uk
- www.oldham-chronicle.co.uk

Contact Editor, Jim Williams; Deputy Editor, David Whaley; News Editor, Mike Attenborough; Picture Editor, Vincent Brown
Insider Info Family owned newspaper, covering news in Oldham. Present circulation is 20,149.

Oxford Mail
Newspaper House, Osney Mead, Oxford, OX2 0EJ
- 01865 425262
- 01865 425554
- nqonews@nqo.com
- www.oxfordmail.net

Contact Editor, Simon O'Neil; Deputy Editor, Toby Granville; News Editor, Jason Collie; Picture Editor, Jessica Mann
Insider Info Published daily, covering local news and sport for Oxford. Present circulation is 20,149.

Paisley Daily Express
Scottish & Universal Newspapers Ltd
14 New Street, Paisley, Renfrewshire, PA1 1YA
- 0141 887 7911
- 0141 887 6254
- pde@s-un.co.uk
- http://icrenfrewshire.icnetwork.co.uk/pde

Contact Editor, Anne Dalrymple; News Editor, Gavin Pennie; Picture Editor, Tom Nicol
Insider Info Local coverage of news, sports and features. Freelance material is considered. Present circulation is 9,289.
Tips Material tends to only be considered if work is about local interests, or communities.

Peterborough Evening Telegraph
New Priestgate House, 57 Priestgate, Peterborough, PE1 1JW
- 01733 555111
- 01733 313417
- news@peterboroughtoday.co.uk
- www.peterboroughtoday.co.uk

Contact Editor, Mark Edwards; News Editor, Rose Taylor; Features Editor, Julia Ogden; Picture Editor, Rowland Hobson
Insider Info Peterborough's number one newspaper, covers local news, sport and community. Photographs are welcome. Present circulation is 18,051.
Submission Guidelines To contact with a story, call 01733 588713 or send an email.

The Press & Journal
Aberdeen Journals Ltd
PO Box 43, Lang Stracht, Mastrick, Aberdeen, AB15 6DF
☎ 01224 690222
☎ 01224 663575
✉ pj.features@ajl.co.uk
🌐 www.thisisnorthscotland.co.uk
Contact Editor, Derek Tucker; Deputy Editor, Richard Neville; News Editor, Andrew Hebden; Features Editor, Sonja Cox
Insider Info Covers a large area of Northern Scotland. Monthly supplements include *Your Car*, *Your Job*, *Your Home*. Also publish weekly lifestyle magazine, *Your Life*. Present circulation is 80,136.
Tips Interesting, quirky local stories or ideas are well received.

The Press
PO Box 29, 76–86 Walmgate, York, Yorkshire, YO1 9YN
☎ 01904 653051
☎ 01904 612853
✉ newsdesk@ycp.co.uk
✉ features@ycp.co.uk
✉ ron.godfrey@ycp.co.uk
🌐 www.yorkpress.co.uk
Contact Editor, Kevin Booth; Deputy Editor, Bill Hearld; Head of Content, Scott Armstrong; Picture Editor, Martin Oates
Insider Info Covers a large area of North and East Yorkshire, based around York. Known as a campaigning, community newspaper. Strong coverage of business and commerce in York, as well as around North and East Yorkshire. Present circulation is 32,856.
Submission Guidelines For photographs, contact the picture desk at photographers@ycp.co.uk
Tips Readers letters are always welcome, but those under 300 words are more likely to be published. Email letters@ycp.co.uk and include your full postal address.

Reading Evening Post
8 Tessa Road, Reading, Berkshire, RG1 8NS
☎ 0118 918 3000

☎ 0118 959 9363
✉ editorial@reading-epost.co.uk
🌐 www.getreading.co.uk
Contact Editor, Andy Murril; Deputy Editor, Hilary Scott; News Editor, Sarah Dave; Features Editor, Phil Creighton; Picture Editor, Steve Templeman
Insider Info The only daily paper to cover Reading and the surrounding areas. Very much a community paper. Special features include business, community, entertainment, recruitment, motoring and sport. Present circulation is 13,549.
Tips Local life makes up the main content of the paper.

Scarborough Evening News
17–23 Aberdeen Walk, Scarborough, Yorkshire, YO11 1BB
☎ 01723 363636
✉ editorial@yrnltd.co.uk
🌐 www.scarboroughtheveningnews.co.uk
Contact Editor, Ed Asquith; Deputy Editor, Sue Wilkinson; News Editor, Stephen Hartley
Insider Info Covers local news and sport for Scarborough and North Yorkshire. Accepts news enquiries by email or via the form on the website. Present circulation is 13,382.

The Scottish Sun
Guildhall, 57 Queen Street, Glasgow, G1 3EN
☎ 0141 420 5200
☎ 0141 420 5248
✉ scoop@thesun.co.uk
Contact Editor, David Dinsmore; Deputy Editor, Paul McLaren; News Editor, Alan Muir; Features Editor, Gill Smith; Picture Editor, Mark Sweeny
Insider Info A tabloid paper aimed at a young demographic. It publishes showbiz news and exposes, as well as current affairs. Photographs are welcome.

Scunthorpe Telegraph
4–5 Park Square, Laneham Street, Scunthorpe, DN15 6JH
☎ 01724 273273
☎ 01724 273101
✉ newsdesk@scunthorpetelegraph.co.uk
🌐 www.thisisscunthorpe.co.uk
Contact Editor, Jane Manning; Deputy Editor, David Atkin; News Editor, Vicky Cottam; Features Editor, Christopher Horan
Insider Info A paid for local newspaper covering the Scunthorpe area. Present circulation is 20,132. Publishes six days a week.
Submission Guidelines For news stories relating to the Scunthorpe area, email the news desk. For

photographs, email: pictures@
grimsbytelegraph.co.uk.

The Sentinel
Sentinel House, Etruria, Stoke on Trent, ST1 5SS
- 01782 602525
- 01732 201167
- newsdesk@thesentinel.co.uk
- www.thesentinel.co.uk

Contact Editor in Chief, Mike Sassi; Deputy Editor,
Richard Bowyer; News Editor, Rob Cotterill; Features
Editor, Richard Bramwell
Insider Info Covers news, sport and entertainment
in the Stoke on Trent area. Present circulation
is 60,776.
Tips Also publishes a sunday edition, *The Sentinel
Sunday*, where articles are not restricted in length.
The Editor is Steven Houghton.

Sheffield Star
York Street, Sheffield, S1 1PU
- 0114 276 7676
- 0114 272 5978
- starnews@sheffieldnewspapers.co.uk
- www.thestar.co.uk

Contact Editor, Alan Powell; Deputy Editor, Paul
License; News Editor, Charles Smith; Features Editor,
Martin Smith; Picture Editor, Dennis Lound
Established 1870
Insider Info Publishes regular features on
entertainment, as well as local news and sport for
Sheffield. Present circulation is 50,285.
Tips Community interest articles are favoured.

Shropshire Star
**Waterloo Road, Ketley, Telford, Shropshire,
TF1 5HU**
- 01952 242424
- 01952 254605
- newsroom@shropshirestar.co.uk
- www.shropshirestar.com

Contact Editor, Sarah-Jane Smith; News Editor, Jon
Simock; Head of Features, Carl Jones; Arts Editor,
Sharon Walters; Picture Editor, Paul Morstatt
Insider Info Evening paper which covers Shropshire
and Mid Wales. Publishes regular features on
business, lifestyle, community, motors and jobs.
Fiction work is not accepted. Present circulation is
roughly 70,574.

Somerset Standard & Guardian Series
Western Newspapers Ltd
Westpoint, James St West, Bath, BA1 2DA
- 01225 322322
- 01225 322297

- editor@somersetguardian.co.uk
- www.somersetguardian.co.uk

Contact Editor, Sam Holliday; Assistant Editor,
Stephanie Feldwicke
Insider Info A series of local paid for, weekly
newspapers for the Somerset area. These include,
the *Warminster and Westbury Standard*, *The Somerset
Guardian* and the *Frome and Somerset Standard*. The
combined circulation of these papers is roughly
15,500. Articles tend to focus on regional and local
news, and sport.
Tips The newspapers have a high rural and semi-
rural readership.

Southend Echo
Newsquest Ltd
**Newspaper House, Chester Hall Lane, Basildon,
Essex, SS14 3BL**
- 0844 477 4512
- 0844 477 4286
- echonews@nqe.com
- www.echo-news.co.uk

Contact Editor, Martin McNeill; Assistant Editor, Chris
Hatton; Picture Editor, Nick Ansell
Insider Info Part of the Echo group of newspapers
covering Essex. A paid for local paper for Southend –
previously known as the *Southend Evening Echo*.
Circulation of just under 34,692. Articles focus on
local news, sport and events.
Submission Guidelines Email or call the news desk
with stories.

The Southern Daily Echo
**Newspaper House, Test Lane, Redbridge,
Southampton, SO16 9JX**
- 023 8042 4777
- 023 8042 4545
- newsdesk@dailyecho.co.uk
- www.dailyecho.co.uk

Contact Editor, Ian Murrey; News Editor, Gordon
Sutter; Features Editor, Andy Bissell; Picture Editor,
Paul Collins
Insider Info Popular daily newspaper. Outsider
writers are rarely used, but they will be considered.
Also publish a weekend magazine, containing
features on lifestyle, fashion, entertainment and
food. Present circulation is 38,974.

South Wales Argus
**Cardiff Road, Maesglas, Newport, Gwent,
NP20 3QN**
- 01633 772201
- 01633 777202
- newsdesk@gwent-wales.co.uk
- www.southwalesargus.co.uk

Contact Editor, Gerry Keighley; Deputy Editor, Nicole Garnon; News Editor, Maria Williams; Picture Editor, Chris Tinsley
Insider Info Covers news and sport, in and around the Gwent area. Present circulation is 28,236.

South Wales Echo
Thomson House, Havelock Street, Cardiff, CF10 1XR
- 029 2058 3583
- 029 2058 3624
- echo.newsdesk@mediawales.co.uk
- www.icwales.co.uk

Contact Acting Editor, Mike Hill; Deputy Head of Content, Rohdri Evans; Head of Features, Margaret O'Reilly; Picture Editor, Colin Robertson
Insider Info Covers news, sport, features and entertainment. Outside work or input from freelancers will be considered. Present circulation is 44,624.

South Wales Evening Post
PO Box 14, Adelaide Street, Swansea, SA1 1QT
- 01792 510000
- 01792 514697
- postnews@swwmedia.co.uk
- www.thisissouthwales.co.uk

Contact Editor in Chief, Spencer Feeney; News Editor, Peter Slee; Features Editor, Cathryn Ings
Established 1897
Insider Info Publishes regular features on health, business, property and the environment, as well as local news and sport from South Wales. Present circulation is 51,269.

Sunday Independent
The Tindle Suite, Webbs House, The Parade, Liskeard, Cornwall, PL14 6AH
- 01579 342174
- newsdesk@sundayindependent.co.uk
- www.sundayindependent.co.uk

Contact Editor, John Noble
Insider Info Covers West Country news and sport, as well as features relating to themes such as tourism and nostalgia, with a direct bearing on the area. Present circulation is roughly 32,000.

Sunday Life
124–144 Royal Avenue, Belfast, BT1 1EB
- 028 9026 4000
- 028 9055 4507
- mhill@belfasttelegraph.co.uk
- www.sundaylife.co.uk

Contact Editor, Jim Flanagan; Deputy & News Editor, Martin Hill; Features Editor, Audrey Watson; Photographic Editor, Mark McCormack
Insider Info Published weekly, covering news and features for Belfast and Northern Ireland. Present circulation is 66,763.

Sunday Mercury
PO Box 78, Weaman Street, Birmingham, B4 6AY
- 0121 236 3366
- 0121 234 5877
- sundaymercury@mrn.co.uk
- www.sundaymercury.co.uk

Contact Editor, David Brookes; Deputy Editor, Paul Cole; Head of Content & News Editor, Tony Larner; Picture Editor, Adam Fradgley
Insider Info Sunday tabloid focusing on exclusive news, sport and entertainment. Present circulation is 57,470.
Tips Keen on investigative writing.

Sunday Sun
Newcastle Chronicle & Journal Ltd
Groat Market, Newcastle upon Tyne, NE1 1ED
- 0191 201 6201
- 0191 201 6180
- scoop.sundaysun@ncjmedia.co.uk
- www.sundaysun.co.uk

Contact Editor, Colin Patterson; Deputy Editor, Ken Oxley; News Editor, Mike Kelly
Established 1919
Insider Info Sunday tabloid covering local news and sport, as well as international news. Present circulation is 63,953.
Submission Guidelines Contact the editor on 0191 201 6299.
Tips Local interest stories are favoured.

The Sunday Tribune
Tribune Publications Plc
15 Lower Baggot Street, Dublin 2, Republic of Ireland
- 00353 1 631 4300
- 00353 1 661 5302
- newsdesk@tribune.ie
- www.tribune.ie

Contact Editor, Noirin Hegarty; Magazine Editor, Fionnuala McCarthy
Insider Info Sunday paper covering local and international news. *The Tribune Review* includes articles on books, health, jobs, motoring and finance. *The Tribune Magazine* contains features on fashion and lifestyle. Present circulation is 65,717.
Submission Guidelines Where possible contact the editor via email: nhegarty@tribune.ie.

Sunderland Echo
Echo House, Pennywell, Sunderland, SR4 9ER
- 0191 501 5800
- 0191 534 5975
- echo.news@northeast-press.co.uk
- www.sunderlandtoday.co.uk

Contact Editor, Rob Lawson; Deputy Editor, Richard Ord; News Editor, Peter Jeffrey; Features Editor, Steve Sharpe
Established 1873
Insider Info Covers local news, sport and entertainment in Sunderland. Publishes regular columns on cooking, lifestyle, and local community issues. Present circulation is 44,198.

Swindon Advertiser
100 Victoria Road, Swindon, Wiltshire, SN1 3BE
- 01793 528144
- 01793 501888
- newsdesk@newswilts.co.uk
- www.swindonadvertiser.co.uk

Contact Editor, Dave King; Deputy Editor, Pauline Leighton; News Editor, Kevin Burchall; Features Editor, Jaine Blackman; Arts Editor, Flicky Harrison; Picture Editor, Dave Evans
Established 1854
Insider Info Covers the Swindon area. Present circulation is 21,828.
Tips Only local interest stories for Swindon are considered.

Telegraph & Argus
Hall Ings, Bradford, Yorkshire, BD1 1JR
- 01274 729511
- 01274 723634
- newsdesk@bradford.newsquest.co.uk
- www.thetelegraphandargus.co.uk

Contact Editor, Perry Austin-Clarke; News Editor, Gareth Duggan; Deputy Editor, Brian Nuttney
Insider Info An award winning tabloid, with a present circulation of 35,592.
Submission Guidelines Approach the editor with ideas via telephone.

Western Daily Press
Temple Way, Bristol, BS99 7HD
- 0117 934 3000
- 0117 934 3574
- wdnews@bepp.co.uk
- www.westpress.co.uk

Contact Editor, Andy Wright; Deputy Editor, Stephen White; News Editor, Cathy Ellis; Features Editor, David Webb; Books Editor, Geoff Ward
Established 1858

Insider Info Publishes regular features on education, finance, business and industry, as well as local news and sport from the Bristol area. Present circulation is 40,432.

The Western Mail
6 Park Street, Cardiff, CF10 1XR
- 029 2058 3654
- 029 2058 3652
- newsdesk@mediawales.co.uk
- www.icwales.co.uk

Contact Editor, Alan Edmunds; Deputy Editor, Ceri Gould; News Editor, Catrin Pascoe; Features Editor, Peter Morrell; Arts Editor, Karen Price
Established 1869
Insider Info Freelance work is considered, but the payment for articles may vary. Present circulation is 37,152.
Tips Local Welsh interest stories are preferred.

Western Morning News
South West Media Group Ltd
17 Brest Road, Derriford Business Park, Plymouth, Devon, PL6 5AA
- 01752 765538
- 01752 765535
- wmnnewsdesk@westernmorningnews.co.uk
- www.westernmorningnews.co.uk

Contact Editor, Alan Qualtrough; Deputy Editor, Philip Bowern; News Editor, Steve Grant; Features Editor, Su Carol; Picture Editor, Mike Cranmer
Insider Info Coverage of local, national and international news for Devon, Cornwall, West Somerset and West Dorset. Unsolicited work is welcome. Present circulation is 39,561.
Tips Local news and features are favoured.

Wigan Evening Post
Lancashire Evening Post Ltd
Martland Mill, Martland Mill Lane, Wigan, WN5 0LX
- 01942 506221
- 01942 221223
- fistname.lastname@lancspublications.co.uk
- www.wigantoday.net

Contact Editor, Simon Reynolds; Deputy Editor, John Thompson; Head of Content, Gillian Gray; Features Editor, Peter Richardson
Established 1950s
Insider Info Circulated six nights a week to the Wigan area. Formerly the *Wigan Post and Chronicle*. Features news, sport, competitions, entertainment and gossip. Regular columns include *Talking Sport, Music Scene* and one written by Charles Graham. Present circulation is 8,549.

Worcester News

Berrows House, Hylton Road, Worcester, Worcestershire, WR2 5JX

☎ 01905 748200

🖷 01905 742277

✉ wenedit@thisisworcester.co.uk

🌐 www.worcesternews.co.uk

Contact Editor, Kevin Ward; Deputy Editor, John Wilson; News Editor, Stephanie Preece; Features Editor, David Chapman

Established 1937

Insider Info Covers the wider Worcester area. Outside contributions are considered. Content is made up of local and national news articles. Present circulation is 17,573.

Yorkshire Evening Post

PO Box 168, Wellington Street, Leeds, Yorkshire, LS1 1RF

☎ 0113 243 2701

🖷 0113 238 8536

✉ eped@ypn.co.uk

🌐 www.ypn.co.uk

Contact Editor, Paul Napier; Deputy Editor, Nicola Megson; News Editor, Gillian Haworth; Features Editor, Jayne Dawson; Arts Editor, Rod McPhee; Picture Editor, Andy Manning

Established 1890

Insider Info Covers local news and sport in the wider Yorkshire area. Present circulation is 53,262.

Yorkshire Post

PO Box 168, Wellington Street, Leeds, Yorkshire, LS1 1RF

☎ 0113 243 2701

🖷 0113 238 8521

✉ yp.newsdesk@ypn.co.uk

🌐 www.yorkshirepost.co.uk

Contact Editor, Peter Charlton; Deputy Editor, Duncan Hamilton; Head of Content, Andrew Vine; News Editor, Hannah Start; Picture Editor, Ian Day; Features Editor, Sarah Freeman; Picture Editor, Ian Day

Established 1734

Insider Info A daily newspaper covering the wider Yorkshire area. Also publishes the weekly Yorkshire Post Magazine. Present circulation is 47,760.

BBC

The BBC as a whole is split into five areas: Radio and Music; Drama, Entertainment and Children's; Factual and Learning; Sport; and News. All information on commissioning in each of these areas can be found at: www.bbc.co.uk/commissioning. Proposals from members of the public to BBC national programming may only be submitted in these three areas: Drama and comedy scripts, via Writers Room (see entry); Entertainment formats, including quiz and game shows, sent to: Format Entertainment Development Team, Room 4010, BBC Television Centre; and Factual entertainment treatments sent to: Factual Entertainment Development, Room 4010 BBC Television Centre. All other areas of programming are commissioned through independent production companies. Submissions for these must be made through the RAP system. For access, contact Gerardina Carbone on 020 7765 4901. BBC local programming may be interested in ideas with a regional flavour. All proposals are stored in a confidential database.

The BBC
BBC Television Centre, Wood Lane, London, W12 7RJ
- 020 8743 8000
- www.bbc.co.uk

Contact Director General, Mark Thompson; Deputy Director General, Mark Byford; Director, BBC Vision, Jana Bennett; Director of Sport, Roger Mosey; Director of BBC Future Media and Technology, Ashley Highfield; Creative Director, Alan Yentob

BBC TV CHANNELS

BBC One
BBC Television Centre, Wood Lane, London, W12 7RJ
- 020 8576 8000
- roly.keating@bbc.co.uk
- www.bbc.co.uk/bbcone

Contact Controller, BBC One, Roly Keating
About A terrestrial channel that aims to be the favourite channel for most people, most of the time.

It broadcasts flagship events such as Live 8, weddings and funerals, as well as a mix of comedy, drama and entertainment. There are also slots for historical, factual, educational and learning programming, as well as regular news and sport. BBC One is regarded as the shop window to all other BBC channels and its audience is massively wide ranging.

BBC Two
BBC Television Centre, Wood Lane, London, W12 7RJ
- 020 8576 8000
- roly.keating@bbc.co.uk
- www.bbc.co.uk/bbctwo

Contact Controller, BBC Two, Roly Keating
About A terrestrial channel that aims to broadcast entertaining programmes with depth and substance. Factual programmes are the core of the schedules, although drama is present, along with documentary and light entertainment formats. The channel's audience is broad but tends towards an older audience of 35–54.

BBC Three
BBC Television Centre, Wood Lane, London, W12 7RJ
- 020 8576 8000
- danny.cohen@bbc.co.uk
- www.bbc.co.uk/bbcthree

Contact Controller, BBC Three, Danny Cohen
About A digital channel with mixed programming aimed at a young audience, mainly 25–30 year olds. It often acts as a laboratory for BBC One and Two in its comedy and entertainment content. The channel also broadcasts drama, current affairs and factual programming and incorporates repeats from BBC One and Two. The tone of the channel is fun, cheeky and unconventional, whilst remaining appealing to a wider audience.

BBC Four
BBC Television Centre, Wood Lane, London, W12 7RJ
- 020 8576 8000
- janice.hadlow@bbc.co.uk

🌐 www.bbc.co.uk/bbcfour

Contact Controller, BBC Four, Janice Hadlow; Editorial Executive, David Okuesuna

About A digital channel that aims to be a place to think 'unashamedly intelligent' thoughts and to provide an alternative to the mainstream channels. The content will begin to move towards series based programming, rather than the current one offs, seasons and theme nights. It will still retain the diversity of the programming. The channel's audience is not distinguished by age, but rather by the fact that television is likely to compete with radio, print journalism and other interests. This attitude means television watching must be time well spent, so these viewers need authoritative and sharp content.

BBC News 24

BBC Television Centre, Wood Lane, London, W12 7RJ

☎ 020 8576 8000

✉ kevin.bakhurst@bbc.co.uk

🌐 www.bbc.co.uk/bbcnews24

Contact Controller, BBC News 24, Kevin Bakhurst

About A 24 hour digital news and weather channel.

BBC Parliament

4 Millbank, London, SW1P 3JA

☎ 0870 010 0123

✉ parliament@bbc.co.uk

🌐 www.bbc.co.uk/bbcparliament

About A 24 hour digital channel dedicated to political coverage, supplemented by live footage from the Houses of Parliament.

BBC World

BBC Television Centre, Wood Lane, London, W12 7RJ

☎ 020 8576 8000

🌐 www.bbcworld.com

Contact News Editor, Eleanor Montague

About A commercially funded 24 hour news channel, which broadcasts around the world from its base in London.

CBBC Channel

BBC Television Centre, Wood Lane, London, W12 7RJ

☎ 020 8576 8000

✉ anne.gilchrist@bbc.co.uk

🌐 www.bbc.co.uk/cbbc

Contact Controller, BBC Children's, Richard Deverell; Controller, CBBC, Anne Gilchrist; Head of Factual, Learning & Entertainment, Joe Godwin

About A digital channel aimed primarily at children aged 6–12, aiming to offer children a breadth of multi-platform content. The channel runs from 7am–7pm, but its output is also broadcast on BBC One and Two at peak times. Programming includes drama, animation, comedy, news, factual programming and events.

Cbeebies Channel

BBC Television Centre, Wood Lane, London, W12 7RJ

☎ 020 8576 8000

✉ richard.deverell@bbc.co.uk

🌐 www.bbc.co.uk/cbeebies

Contact Controller, BBC Children's, Richard Deverell; Creative Director, Cbeebies, Michael Carrington; Producer & News Editor, Angela Young

About A digital channel aimed at pre-school children. Cbeebies is designed to be a brand, rather than simply a channel, and as such offers content across many media platforms. The channel airs from 6am–7pm and content is sometimes simultaneously broadcast on BBC Two. Content aims to inspire play, creativity and imagination.

BBC RADIO & MUSIC STATIONS

BBC Radio and Music is responsible for commissioning content for all national BBC analogue and digital radio stations. It also deals with much of the music and dance content on BBC television channels, as well as music content on the BBC World Service. Radio entertainment is one of the few areas that will accept unsolicited proposals from writers not already attached to a production company. www.bbc.co.uk/writersroom/writing/submissions.shtml for submission guidelines.

BBC Radio & Music

BBC Broadcasting House, Portland Place, London, W1A 1AA

☎ 020 7580 4468

✉ sue.lynas@bbc.co.uk

Contact Director of BBC Audio and Music, Jenny Abramsky CBE; Head of Compliance, Susan Binney; Finance Director, Jo Brindley; Head of Press and Publicity, Sue Lynas; Head of Radio Drama, Alison Hindell; Head of Radio Entertainment, Paul Schlesinger; Head of BBC Radio News, Stephen Mitchell; Head of Radio Current Affairs, Gwyneth Williams; Head of BBC Radio Sport, Gordon Turnball; Controller, BBC Popular Music, Lesley Douglas

BBC 1xtra

BBC Broadcasting House, Portland Place,
London, W1A 1AA

☎ 020 7580 4468

✉ andy.parfitt@bbc.co.uk

🌐 www.bbc.co.uk/1xtra

Contact Controller Radio 1, Andy Parfitt; Managing Editor, Tarrant Steele; Commissioning Editor, Documentaries, Russell Crewe; News Editor, Angela Clark

About A digital station whose target audience is 16–24 year old fans of black music. Development priorities can be viewed at www.bbc.co.uk/commissioning, most content is made in-house, although documentaries are made by a combination of freelancers, in-house producers and independent production companies. Documentaries are preferred in the first person narrative and must be of direct relevance to the target audience. Commissioning rounds take place through the year, but a short synopsis may be submitted to Russell Crewe on 020 7765 5551 or by email, as an initial query before submitting through the RAP system.

BBC Radio Five Live

BBC Broadcasting House, Portland Place,
London, W1A 1AA

☎ 020 8624 8945

✉ michael.hill@bbc.co.uk

🌐 www.bbc.co.uk/fivelive

Contact Commissioning Editor, Moz Dee; Head of News, Matt Morris; News Editor, Robin Britten

About Five Live is a 24-hour rolling sports and news service, and much of the content is live. There are no formal commissioning rounds, however treatments will be looked at throughout the year. Submissions to Moz Dee by email or phone, 020 8624 8948.

BBC 6 Music

BBC Broadcasting House, Portland Place,
London, W1A 1AA

☎ 020 7580 4468

✉ ric.blaxill@bbc.co.uk

🌐 www.bbc.co.uk/6music

Contact Head of Programmes, Ric Blaxill; Managing Editor and News Editor, Antony Bellekom

About A digital radio station aimed at 25–44 year old music fans. Strands that are open for independent production companies are announced on www.bbc.co.uk/commissioning, in the 6 Music section.

BBC 7

BBC Broadcasting House, Portland Place,
London, W1A 1AA

☎ 020 7580 4468

✉ mary.kalemkerian@bbc.co.uk

🌐 www.bbc.co.uk/bbc7

Contact Head of Programmes and News Editor, Mary Kalemkerian

About A digital radio station for comedy and drama. Commissions through the BBC Writer's Room website.

BBC Asian Network

The Mailbox, Birmingham, B1 1RF

☎ 0121 567 6767

✉ vijay.sharma@bbc.co.uk

🌐 www.bbc.co.uk/asiannetwork

Contact Managing Editor, Asian Network, Vijay Sharma; Network Manager, Michael Hill; Head of News, Husain Husaini; News Editor, Neerja Sood; Head of Music, Mark Strippel

About The target audience is British Asians under 35, in major cities and towns throughout the UK. Approximately ten per cent of content is commissioned from independent producers. Music and journalism is predominantly Asian with an 'urban' feel. Details of specific commissioning rounds are posted on www.bbc.co.uk/commissioning in the Asian Network section. Short synopses may be also be submitted to Michael Hill by email or phone, 020 8624 8945, before submitting through the RAP system.

BBC Radio 1

BBC Broadcasting House, Portland Place,
London, W1A 1AA

☎ 020 7580 4468

✉ andy.parfitt@bbc.co.uk

🌐 www.bbc.co.uk/radio1

Contact Controller, Radio 1, Andy Parfitt; Head of Programmes, Ben Cooper; Executive Producer, Speech and Campaigns, Sam Steele; Head of Music, Radio 1, George Ergatoudis

About Radio 1 mostly broadcasts long running strands, which are commissioned by Ben Cooper. All documentaries are commissioned by Sam Steele - enquiries from independent production companies or established programme makers about submitting documentary ideas should be directed to her, by email or phone, 020 7765 3827. Commissioning rounds for this are usually twice yearly, the current one being for March to September, and beyond. Commissioning briefs are downloadable from www.bbc.co.uk/commissioning.

BBC Radio 2

BBC Broadcasting House, Portland Place, London, W1A 1AA

☎ 020 7580 4468

✉ julian.grundy@bbc.co.uk

🌐 www.bbc.co.uk/radio2

Contact Head of Live Music, Events & Talent, Lewis Carnie; Editor, Planning and Station Sound, Robert Gallacher; Manager, Commissions and Schedules, Julian Grundy

About Radio 2 mostly consists of long running strands, however commissioning rounds take place twice yearly for additional content, and are open to submissions from independent producers or production companies. Initial enquiries about submissions should be directed by email, or phone to Robert Gallacher, 020 7765 4373, or Lewis Carnie. Development priorities can be viewed at www.bbc.co.uk/commissioning.

BBC Radio 3

BBC Broadcasting House, Portland Place, London, W1A 1AA

☎ 020 7580 4468

✉ roger.wright@bbc.co.uk

🌐 www.bbc.co.uk/radio3

Contact Controller, Radio 3, Roger Wright; Head of Speech Programming and Presentation, Abigail Appleton; Commissions and Schedules Manager, David Ireland; Music Editors, Edward Blakeman, Tony Cheevers, Adam Gatehouse, Andrew Kurowski, Edwina Wolstencroft

About Radio 3 is aimed at listeners of any age and its current priorities are classical music, jazz, drama, world music and speech programmes. As well as broadcasting long-running strands, Radio 3 holds commissioning rounds for both drama and non-drama content. These usually open in April to May, for the following year. Details of these rounds are on www.bbc.co.uk/commissioning, initial enquiries should be directed to David Ireland by email, or phone, 020 7765 4943.

BBC Radio 4

BBC Broadcasting House, Portland Place, London, W1A 1AA

☎ 020 7580 4468

✉ mark.damazer@bbc.co.uk

🌐 www.bbc.co.uk/radio4

Contact Controller, BBC Radio 4, Mark Damazer; Commissioning Editor, Comedy and Entertainment, Caroline Raphael; Commissioning Editor, Specialist Factual Programmes, Andrew Caspari; Commissioning Editor, General Factual Programmes, Jane Ellison; Commissioning Editor, Drama, Jeremy Howe; Creative Director, New Writing, Kate Rowland

About Radio 4 do not accept any proposals, unless through an in-house production department or a registered independent production company. Submission forms are downloadable from www.bbc.co.uk/commissioning, in the Radio 4 section.

BBC World Service

Bush House, The Strand, London, WC2B 4PH

☎ 020 7240 3456

☎ 020 7557 1900

✉ nigel.chapman@bbc.co.uk

🌐 www.bbc.co.uk/worldservice

Contact Director BBC World Service, Nigel Chapman; Editor, News and Current Affairs, Liliane Landor; News Editor, Peter Burdin; Business Editor, Martin Webber

About The World Service commissions a wide range of content through its 'Invitation to Bid' scheme, details of which come out in May/June each year. The invitation to bid gets automatically sent to a list of suppliers. If you wish to join this list, contact Karen Howe by email or post (Room 828).

BBC REGIONAL & LOCAL RADIO STATIONS

There are 40 BBC radio stations throughout the UK, some transmitting on AM and some on FM. They are mainly news and sport based, however some transmit other content relevant to their area.

BBC Coventry & Warwickshire

Priory Place, Coventry, CV1 5SQ

☎ 024 7655 1000

✉ coventry@bbc.co.uk

✉ warwickshire@bbc.co.uk

🌐 www.bbc.co.uk/coventry/local_radio

Contact Editor, David Clargo; Assistant Editor, Duncan Jones; News Editor, Tim Atkinson; Rugby Correspondent, Sue Curtis

About First came on air in 1990 under the name CWR. Broadcasts on 94.8, 104 and 103.7 FM and DAB digital radio.

BBC Essex

PO Box 765, Chelmsford, Essex, CM2 9XB

☎ 01245 616000

☎ 01245 492983

✉ essex.online@bbc.co.uk

🌐 www.bbc.co.uk/essex/local_radio

Contact Managing Editor, Margaret Hyde; Head of Music, Steve Scruton; Programme Editor, Tim Gillet
About Broadcasts on 103.5 and 95.3 FM and DAB digital radio.

BBC Guernsey
Bulwer Avenue, St Sampson's, Guernsey, GY2 4LA
- 01481 200600
- 01481 200361
- guernsey@bbc.co.uk
- www.bbc.co.uk/guernsey/local_radio
Contact Managing Editor, David Martin; Assistant Editor, Kay Langlois
About First came on air in 1982. Broadcasts on 93.2 and 99 FM, and 1116 MW.

BBC Hereford & Worcester
Hylton Road, Worcester, WR2 5WW
- 01905 748485
- 01905 748446
- worcester@bbc.co.uk
- hereford@bbc.co.uk
- www.bbc.co.uk/herefordworcester/localradio
Contact Managing Editor, James Coghill; Assistant Editor, Mark Hellings; Head of Music, Max Thomas; News Editor, Joe Baldwin; Sports Editor, Trevor Owens
About Broadcasts on 104, 104.4, 104.6 and 94.7 FM, and 738 and 1584 MW.

BBC London
PO Box 94.9, Marylebone High Street, London, W1A 6FL
- 020 7224 2424
- 020 7224 2424
- yourlondon@bbc.co.uk
- www.bbc.co.uk/london/radio
Contact Managing Editor, David Robey; News Editor, Lorraine Maguire; Sports Editor, Pete Stevens
About Covers Greater London and the Home Counties. Broadcasts on 94.9 FM and DAB digital radio.

BBC Oxford
269 Banbury Road, Oxford, OX2 7DW
- 0845 931 1444
- 0845 931 1555
- oxford@bbc.co.uk
- www.bbc.co.uk/oxford
Contact Executive Editor, Steve Taschini; Assistant Editor, Will Banks; Sports Editor, Jerome Sale
About Formerly known as BBC Thames Valley and BBC Radio Berkshire. Broadcasts on 95.2 FM.

BBC Radio Berkshire
PO Box 104.4, Reading, RG4 8FH
- 0845 900 1044/0118 946 4200
- 0118 946 4555
- radio.berkshire.news@bbc.co.uk
- www.bbc.co.uk/berkshire/local_radio
Contact Station Manager, Lizz Loxam; News Editor, Patrick O'Hagan; Sports Editor, Joel Hufford
About Broadcasts on 104.1, 104.4, 95.4 and 94.6 FM, DAB digital radio and online.

BBC Radio Bristol
PO Box 194, Bristol, BS99 7QT
- 0117 974 1111
- 0117 923 8323
- radio.bristol@bbc.co.uk
- www.bbc.co.uk/bristol/local_radio
Contact Station Manager, Tim Pemberton; News Editor, Charlotte Callen; Sports Editor, Geoff Twentyman
About Broadcasts on 94.9, 103.6 and 104.6 FM and 1548 AM and DAB digital radio.

BBC Radio Cambridegshire
104 Hills Road, Cambridge, CB2 1LQ
- 01223 259696
- 01223 460832
- cambs@bbc.co.uk
- www.bbc.co.uk/cambridge/local_radio
Contact Managing Editor, Jason Horton; Assistant Editor, Alison Dawes; News Editor, Louise Gosling; Sport Editor, Tom Williams; Trustline Producer, Jan Reynolds; CSV Action Desk Producer, Pamela Mungroo
About First came on air in 1982. Broadcasts on 96 and 95.7 FM and DAB digital radio.

BBC Radio Cornwall
Phoenix Wharf, Truro, TR1 1UA
- 01872 275421
- radio.cornwall@bbc.co.uk
- www.bbc.co.uk/radiocornwall
Contact Editor, Pauline Causey; Assistant Editor, Daphne Skinnard; News Editor, Ed Goodridge; Sports Editor, Matt Sandoz
About Covers Cornwall and the Isle of Scilly. Broadcasts on 103.9 and 95.2 FM and DAB digital radio.

BBC Radio Cumbria
Annetwell Street, Carlisle, CA3 8BB
- 01228 592444
- 01228 511195
- cumbria@bbc.co.uk
- www.bbc.co.uk/cumbria/local_radio

Contact Managing Editor, Nigel Dyson; News Editor, Neil Smith; Assistant Editor, Graham Moss
About Broadcasts on 95.6, 96.1 and 104.1 FM.

BBC Radio Cymru
Broadcasting House, Llandaff, Cardiff, CF5 2YQ
- 029 2032 2018
- 029 2032 2473
- radio.cymru@bbc.co.uk
- www.bbc.co.uk/cymru/radiocymru

Contact Deputy Editor, Orwain Arfon Williams; News Editor, Bethan Roberts; Political Editor, Ashok Ahir
About A Welsh language station. Broadcasts a daily soap, *Rhydeglwys* and other drama and comedy, as well as music, news, sport and features. Broadcasts on 92–105 FM.

BBC Radio Derby
PO Box 1045, St Helen's Street, Derby, DE1 3HL
- 01332 361111
- 01332 290794
- radio.derby@bbc.co.uk
- www.bbc.co.uk/derby/local_radio

Contact Editor, Simon Cornes; News and Sports Editor, John Atkin
About Broadcasts on 104.5, 95.3 and 96 FM and 1116 AM.

BBC Radio Devon
Broadcasting House, Seymour Road, Plymouth, PL3 5BD
- 01752 260323
- 01752 234564
- radio.devon@bbc.co.uk
- www.bbc.co.uk/devon/local_radio

Contact Managing Editor, Robert Wallace; Head of Programmes, Ian Timms; News Editor, Emma Clements; Sports Editor, Richard Green
About First came on air in 1983. Broadcasts on 94.8, 95.7 and 95.8, 96, 103.4 and 104.3 FM and DAB digital radio.

BBC Radio Foyle
8 Northland Road, Londonderry, Northern Ireland, BT48 7GD
- 028 7137 8600
- 028 7137 8666
- radio.foyle@bbc.co.uk
- www.bbc.co.uk/northernireland/radiofoyle

Contact Managing Editor, Stephen McCauley; Head of News, Eimear O'Callaghan
About Broadcasts on 93.1 FM and 792 MW. Some programmes are transmitted simultaneously on BBC Radio Ulster.

BBC Radio Gloucestershire
London Road, Gloucester, GL1 1SW
- 01452 308585
- 01452 309491
- radio.gloucestershire@bbc.co.uk
- www.bbc.co.uk/gloucestershire/local_radio

Contact Managing Editor, Mark Hurrell; News Editor, Graham Day; Sports Editor, Ian Randall
About Broadcasts on 104.7, 95 (Stroud) and 95.8 (Cirencester) FM and 1413 AM.

BBC Radio Humberside
Queen's Court, Hull, HU1 3RH
- 01482 323232
- 01482 621403
- radio.humberside@bbc.co.uk
- www.bbc.co.uk/radiohumberside

Contact Managing Editor, Derrick McGill; Head of Programmes, Carl Wheatley; News Editor, Kate Slade; Sports Editor, David Burns
About First came on air in 1971. Broadcast on 95.9 FM and DAB digital radio.

BBC Radio Jersey
18–21 Parade Road, St Helier, Jersey, JE2 3PL
- 01534 870000
- 01534 732569
- radiojersey@bbc.co.uk
- www.bbc.co.uk/jersey/bbc_in_jersey

Contact Managing Editor, Denzil Dudley; Editor, Denzil Dudley; Assistant Editor, Matthew Price; News Editor, Hamish Marret-Crosby
About Broadcasts on 88.8 FM and 1026 AM.

BBC Radio Kent
The Great Hall, Mount Pleasant Road, Tunbridge Wells, TN1 1QQ
- 01892 670000
- 01892 549118
- radio.kent@bbc.co.uk
- www.bbc.co.uk/kent/local_radio

Contact Managing Editor, Paul Leaper; Assistant Editor, Will Roffey; News Editor, Simon Long-Price; Sport Editor, Matt Davison
About Broadcasts on 96.7, 97.6 and 104.2 FM, 774 AM and DAB digital radio.

BBC Radio Lancashire
20–26 Darwen Street, Blackburn, BB2 2EA
- 01254 262411
- lancashire@bbc.co.uk
- www.bbc.co.uk/lancashire/local_radio

Contact Editor, John Clayton; Head of Programming, Alison Brown; News Editor, Chris Rider; Sports Editor, Gary Hickson

About Broadcasts on 95.5, 103.9 and 104.5 FM and DAB digital radio.

BBC Radio Leeds
2 St Peter's Square, Leeds, LS9 8AH
- 0113 244 2131
- 0113 224 7316
- radioleeds@bbc.co.uk
- www.bbc.co.uk/radioleeds

Contact Managing Editor, Phil Roberts; Assistant Editor and News Editor, Phil Squire; Sports Editor, Derm Tanner
About Broadcasts on 92.4 and 95.3 FM, 774 AM and DAB digital radio. Covers most of West Yorkshire.

BBC Radio Leicester
9 St Nicholas Place, Leicester, LE1 5LB
- 0116 251 6688
- 0116 251 1463
- radioleicester@bbc.co.uk
- www.bbc.co.uk/leicester/local_radio

Contact Managing Editor, Kate Squire; News Editor, Lucy Collins
About Britain's first local radio station, aired in 1967. Broadcasts on 104.9 FM and DAB digital radio.

BBC Radio Lincolnshire
PO Box 219, Newport, Lincoln, LN1 3XY
- 01522 511411
- 01522 511058
- radio.lincolnshire@bbc.co.uk
- www.bbc.co.uk/radiolincolnshire

Contact Managing Editor, Charlie Partridge; Assistant Editor, Andy Farrant; News Editor, Maggie Curtis; Sports Editor, Michael Hortin
About Broadcasts on 94.9 and 104.7 FM, 1368 AM and DAB digital radio.

BBC Radio Manchester
PO Box 951, Oxford Road, Manchester, M60 1SD
- 0161 200 2000
- 0161 228 6110
- radio.manchester@bbc.co.uk
- www.bbc.co.uk/manchester

Contact Managing Editor, John Ryan; Head of Programmes, Lawrence Mann; News Editor, Mark Elliott; Sports Editor, Andy Buckley
About First aired in 1970. Covers the Greater Manchester area. Broadcasts on 95.1 FM and DAB digital radio.

BBC Radio Merseyside
PO Box 95.8, Liverpool, L69 1ZJ
- 0151 708 5500
- 0151 794 0988
- radio.merseyside@bbc.co.uk
- www.bbc.co.uk/radiomerseyside

Contact Editor, Mick Ord; News Editor, Andy Ball; Arts Editor, Angela Heslop; Sports Editor, Ian Kennedy
About Broadcasts on 95.8 FM and 1485 AM.

BBC Radio nan Gaidheal
Rosebank, Church Street, Stornoway, Isle of Lewis, HS1 2LS
- 01851 705000
- www.bbc.co.uk/scotland/alba/radio

Contact Editor, Marion Mackinnon
About A Gaelic language service. Broadcast on 103.5 and 105 FM and DAB digital radio.

BBC Radio Newcastle
Broadcasting Centre, Barrack Road, Newcastle upon Tyne, NE99 1RN
- 0191 232 4141
- radionewcastle.news@bbc.co.uk
- www.bbc.co.uk/tyne/local_radio

Contact Managing Editor, Graham Moss; Assistant Managing Editor, Doug Morris; News Editor, Rik Martin; Editor, Andrew Robson
About First aired in 1971. Broadcasts on 95.4 FM and DAB digital radio. Alternative website: www.bbc.co.uk/wear/local_radio

BBC Radio Norfolk
The Forum, Millennium Plain, Norwich, NR2 1BH
- 01603 617411
- 01603 633692
- radionorfolk@bbc.co.uk
- www.bbc.co.uk/radionorfolk

Contact Managing Editor, David Clayton; Assistant Editor, Graham Barnard; News Editor, Sarah Kings; Sports Editor, Matthew Gudgin
About Broadcasts on 95.1, 95.6 and 104.4 FM and DAB digital radio.

BBC Radio Northampton
Broadcasting House, Abington Street, Northampton, NN1 2BH
- 01604 239100
- 01604 230709
- northampton@bbc.co.uk
- www.bbc.co.uk/northampton/local_radio

Contact Editor, Laura Moss; Assistant Editor, Louise Daw; Sports Editor, Geoff Doyle
About Broadcasts on 104.2 and 103.6 FM.

BBC Radio Nottingham
London Road, Nottingham, NG2 4UU
- 0115 955 0500

☎ 0115 902 1983
✉ radio.nottingham@bbc.co.uk
🌐 www.bbc.co.uk/radionottingham
Contact News Editor, Aeneas Rotsos; Sports Editor, Colin Fray
About Broadcasts on 95.5 and 103.8 FM and DAB digital radio.

BBC Radio Orkney
Castle Street, Kirkwall, Orkney, KW15 1DF
☎ 01856 873939
☎ 01856 872908
✉ radio.orkney@bbc.co.uk
🌐 www.bbc.co.uk/northeastscotlandnorthernisles
Contact Editor & News Editor, John Ferguson
About A BBC community radio station. All content is produced in the Orkney Islands. Broadcast on 92.4 and 94.7 FM, 810 MW and DAB digital radio.

BBC Radio Scotland
BBC Broadcasting House, Queen Margaret Drive, Glasgow, GL12 8DG
☎ 0141 339 8844
✉ hops@bbc.co.uk
🌐 www.bbc.co.uk/scotland/radioscotland
Contact Head of BBC Radio Scotland, Jeff Zycinski; Art Editor, Pauline McLean; Editor of Radio Drama, Bruce Young
About Broadcasts throughout Scotland on 92–95 FM and 810 MW (585 Dumfries).

BBC Radio Scotland (Aberdeen)
Beechgrove Terrace, Beechgrove House, Aberdeen, AB15 5ZT
☎ 01224 384888
✉ news.aberdeen@bbc.co.uk
🌐 www.bbc.co.uk/scotland/radioscotland
Contact Head of Programmes, Andrew Jones; Head of News, Sandy Bremner; Radio Bulletin Editor, Fiona Stalker
About Broadcasts news bulletins across the North East of Scotland on BBC Radio Scotland.

BBC Radio Scotland (Dumfries)
Elmbank, Lover's Walk, Dumfries, DG1 1NZ
☎ 01387 268008
☎ 01387 252568
✉ dumfries@bbc.co.uk
🌐 www.bbc.co.uk/scotland/radioscotland
Contact Senior Broadcast Journalist, Sports and News Editor, Willie Johnston
About Mainly news bulletins, which are broadcast four times a day on BBC Radio Scotland.

BBC Radio Scotland (Inverness)
7 Culduthel Road, Inverness, IV2A 4AD
☎ 01463 720720
✉ inverness.news@bbc.co.uk
🌐 www.bbc.co.uk/scotland/radioscotland
Contact News Editor, Craig Swan; Sports Editor, Charles Bannerman
About Mainly news bulletins, which are broadcast four times a day, on BBC Radio Scotland.

BBC Radio Scotland (Selkirk)
Unit 1, Ettrick Riverside, Dunsdale Road, Selkirk, TD7 5EB
☎ 01750 724567
☎ 01750 724555
✉ selkirk@bbc.co.uk
🌐 www.bbc.co.uk/scotland/radioscotland
Contact Senior Broadcaster and News Editor, Cameron Battle; Sports Editor, Grahame MacGregor
About Mainly news bulletins, which are broadcast four times a day, on BBC Radio Scotland.

BBC Radio Sheffield
54 Shoreham Street, Sheffield, S1 4RS
☎ 0114 273 1177
☎ 0114 267 5454
✉ radio.sheffield@bbc.co.uk
🌐 www.bbc.co.uk/southyorkshire/community/radio_sheffield
Contact Managing Editor, Gary Keown; Head of News, Mark Woodcock; Sports Editor, Paul Walker
About Broadcasts on 88.6, 94.7 and 104.1 FM and DAB digital radio.

BBC Radio Shetland
Pitt Lane, Lerwick, ZE1 0DW
☎ 01595 694747
☎ 01595 694307
✉ radio.shetland@bbc.co.uk
🌐 www.bbc.co.uk/scotland
Contact News & Sports Editor, Caroline Moyes
About Broadcasts regular news bulletins and programmes such as *Good Evening Shetland*.

BBC Radio Shropshire
2–4 Boscobel Drive, Shrewsbury, SY1 3TT
☎ 01743 248484
☎ 01743 237018
✉ radio.shropshire@bbc.co.uk
🌐 www.bbc.co.uk/shropshire/local_radio
Contact Managing Editor, Tim Beech; News and Environment Editor, Sharon Simcock
About Broadcasts on 96 FM and DAB digital radio. First came on air in 1985.

BBC Radio Solent

Broadcasting House, 10 Havelock Road,
Southampton, SO14 7PW

- 023 8063 2811
- 023 8033 9648
- radio.solent@bbc.co.uk
- www.bbc.co.uk/radiosolent

Contact Managing Editor, Mia Costello
About Broadcasts on 96.1 and 103.8 FM, and DAB
digital radio.

BBC Radio Stoke

Cheapside, Hanley, Stoke on Trent,
Staffordshire, ST1 1JJ

- 01782 208080
- 01782 289115
- radio.stoke@bbc.co.uk
- www.bbc.co.uk/radiostoke

Contact Managing Editor, Sue Owen; Programme
Organiser, Mary Fox; News Editor, James O' Hara;
Sports Editor, Graham McGarry
About First came on air in 1968. Broadcasts on 64.6
and 104.1 FM, and DAB digital radio.

BBC Radio Suffolk

Broadcasting House, St Matthew's Street,
Ipswich, IP1 3EP

- 01473 250000
- 01473 210887
- radiosuffolk@bbc.co.uk
- www.bbc.co.uk/radiosuffolk

Contact Managing Editor, Gerald Main; News Editor,
Lis Henderson; Sports Editor, Mark Matthews
About Broadcasts on 95.5, 95.9, 103.9 and 104.6 FM.
Email the Editor with any local programme ideas
or queries.

BBC Radio Swindon

BBC Broadcasting House, Prospect Place,
Swindon, Wiltshire, SN1 3RW

- 01793 513626
- 01793 513650
- radio.swindon@bbc.co.uk
- www.bbc.co.uk/wiltshire/local_radio/
radio_swindon

Contact Managing Editor, Tony Worgan; News
Editor, Jillian Moody
About Broadcasts on 103.6 FM and DAB
digital radio.

BBC Radio Ulster

Broadcasting House, Ormeau Avenue, Belfast,
Northern Ireland, BT2 8HQ

- 028 9033 8000
- peter.johnston@bbc.co.uk
- www.bbc.co.uk/northernireland/radioulster

Contact Controller, Peter Johnston; Head of News,
Andrew Colman; News Editor, Kathleen Carragher;
Art/Entertainment Editor, Maggie Taggart; Sports
Editor, Edward Smith
About Broadcasts on 92–95 FM.

BBC Radio Wales

Broadcasting House, Llandaff, Cardiff, CF5 2YQ

- 0870 010 0110
- 029 2032 2674
- radio.wales@bbc.co.uk
- www.bbc.co.uk/radiowales

Contact Editor, Sali Collins; Editor, Ruth Sally; Head
of News, Mark O'Callaghan
About Broadcasts 19 hours a day in the English
language, for an audience living west of Offa's Dyke.

BBC Radio Wiltshire

BBC Broadcasting House, 56–58 Prospect Place,
Swindon, SN1 3RW

- 01793 513626
- 01793 513650
- radio.wiltshire@bbc.co.uk
- www.bbc.co.uk/wiltshire/local_radio

Contact Managing Editor, Tony Worgan; News
Editor, Kirsty Ward; Sports Editor, Ed Hadwin
About Closely linked with BBC Radio Swindon.
Broadcasts on 103.5, 104.3 and 104.9 FM and DAB
digital radio.

BBC Radio York

20 Bootham Row, York, YO30 7BR

- 01904 641351
- 01904 610937
- radio.york@bbc.co.uk
- www.bbc.co.uk/northyorkshire

Contact Managing Editor, Sarah Drummond; News
Editor, Anna Evans
About Broadcasts on 103.7, 104.3 and 95.5 FM.

BBC Somerset

Broadcasting House, Park Street, Taunton,
Somerset, TA1 4DA

- 01823 323956
- 01823 332539
- somerset.sound@bbc.co.uk
- www.bbc.co.uk/somerset/local_radio

Contact Managing Editor & News Editor,
Simon Clifford
About Broadcasts on 95.5 FM and 1566 AM
across Somerset.

BBC Southern Counties Radio

Broadcasting House, 40–42 Queens Road, Brighton, East Sussex, BN1 3XB
- 01273 320400/01483 306306
- southerncounties@bbc.co.uk
- www.bbc.co.uk/southerncounties/local_radio

Contact Managing Editor, Nicci Holliday; Programme Editor, Mark Carter; Sports Editor, Tim Durrans

About Also has a base at Broadcasting Centre, Guildford, GU2 7AP. Broadcasts on 104–104.8 and 95–95.3 FM, 1161, 1368 and 1485 AM, and DAB digital radio.

BBC Tees

Broadcasting House, Newport Road, Middlesborough, TS1 5DG
- 01642 225211
- 01642 211356
- tees.studio@bbc.co.uk
- tees.programmes@bbc.co.uk
- tees.news@bbc.co.uk
- www.bbc.co.uk/tees/local_radio

Contact Managing Editor, Peter Cook; Head of Programmes, Will Davies; News Editor, Peter Harris; Sport Editor, Paul Addison

About Covers Teesside, County Durham and North Yorkshire. Broadcasts on 95 FM and DAB digital radio.

BBC Three Counties Radio

1 Hastings Street, Luton, LU1 5XL
- 01582 637400
- 01582 401467
- threecounties@bbc.co.uk
- www.bbc.co.uk/threecounties/local_radio

Contact Station Editor, Mark Norman; Sports Editor, Simon Oxley

About Covers Bedfordshire, Hertfordshire and Buckinghamshire. Broadcasts on 90.4, 92.1, 94.7, 95.5, 98, 103.8 and 104.5 FM.

BBC WM

The Mailbox, Birmingham, B1 1RF
- 0121 567 6000
- 0121 567 6025
- bbcwm@bbc.co.uk
- www.bbc.co.uk/radiowm

Contact Managing Editor, Keith Beech; News Editor, Chris Kowalik

About Broadcasts on 95.6 FM and DAB digital radio. Covers the West Midlands, South Staffordshire and North Worcestershire.

BBC DRAMA, ENTERTAINMENT & CHILDREN'S

BBC Drama, Entertainment and Children's is responsible for commissioning content in these areas, across television, radio and film.

BBC Drama, Entertainment & Children's

BBC Television Centre, Wood Lane, London, W12 7RJ
- 020 8743 8000
- nicolas.brown@bbc.co.uk

Contact Director, Drama Production, Nicolas Brown; Creative Director, Drama, Sally Woodward Gentle; Controller, Drama Production Studios, John Yorke; Controller, BBC Fiction, Jane Tranter; Controller, Entertainment Group, BBC Vision Studios, Jon Beazley; Creative Director, Entertainment Production, BBC Vision Studios, Karen Smith; Head of Drama Series and Serials, Kate Harwood; Controller, BBC Children's, Richard Deverell

BBC Comedy

BBC Television Centre, Wood Lane, London, W12 7RJ
- 020 8743 8000
- lucy.lumsden@bbc.co.uk
- www.bbc.co.uk/comedy

Contact Controller, Comedy Commissioning, Lucy Lumsden; Executive Editors, Cheryl Taylor, Simon Wilson and John Rolph; Development Co-ordinator, Comedy, Michael Buchanan-Dunne; Comedy contact, Scotland, Alan Tyler; Comedy contact, Northern Ireland, Mike Edgar; Comedy contact, Wales, Gareth Gwenlan

About Responsible for commissioning comedy (sitcom and sketch) across all BBC channels. Check www.bbc.co.uk/commissioning for current development focus. Proposals from independent producers may be submitted at any time. For the London team, contact Michael Buchanan-Dunne. For the nations and regions, approach the relevant comedy/entertainment contact.

BBC Daytime

BBC Television Centre, Wood Lane, London, W12 7RJ
- 020 8743 8000
- jay.huny@bbc.co.uk

Contact Controller of Daytime, Jay Hunt; Executive Producer (Independent Producers), Alison Kirkham;

Commissioning Editor, Entertainment and Out of London, Sumi Coonock; Executive Editor, Lindsay Bradbury

About Commissioning covers daytime drama, entertainment and factual entertainment. Development priorities can be viewed at www.bbc.co.uk/commissioning. Proposals from outside of London go to Sumi Connock. All other proposals go to Lindsay Bradbury. Proposals from independent producers may be submitted at any time.

BBC Drama
BBC Television Centre, Wood Lane, London, W12 7RJ

- 020 8743 8000
- julie.gardner@bbc.co.uk
- www.bbc.co.uk/drama

Contact Head of Series and Serials, Kate Harwood; Head of Drama Serials, Laura Mackie; Head of Independent Drama, Lucy Richer; Head of Drama, BBC Wales and Head of Drama Commissioning, Julie Gardner; Head of Drama, BBC Northern Ireland, Patrick Spence

About Check www.bbc.co.uk/commissioning for the latest development priorities. Proposals may be submitted from independent producers at any time to the editorial heads: Julie Gardner; Sarah Brandist; Polly Hill; Patrick Spence; and Anne Mensah. There are three possible outcomes to a submission: input into paid development; unpaid development; or rejection. This will be announced within four weeks.

BBC Entertainment
BBC Television Centre, Wood Lane, London, W12 7RJ

- 020 8743 8000
- elaine.bedell@bbc.co.uk
- www.bbc.co.uk/entertainment

Contact Controller, Entertainment Commissioning, BBC Vision, Elaine Bedell; Executive Editors, Jo Wallace, Katie Taylor and Suzanne Gilfillan; Executive Producer (Independent Producers), Gilly Hall; Development Co-ordinator, Pinki Chambers; Entertainment contact, Scotland, Alan Tyler; Entertainment contact, Northern Ireland, Mike Edgar; Entertainment contact, Wales, David Jackson; Head of Genre Management, Claire Evans

About Responsible for commissioning entertainment formats, light entertainment, quizzes and panel shows, and entertainment/celebrity documentaries. Check www.bbc.co.uk/commissioning for the latest development priorities. Independent producers/companies wishing to submit proposals may do so at any time. For nationwide proposals, contact Pinki Chambers and

for the nations and regions, submit via the contact for that area. A decision will be made within six weeks of receipt.

BBC Films
First Floor, Grafton House, 379–381 Euston Road, London, NW1 3AU

- 020 7765 0251
- 020 7765 0278
- www.bbc.co.uk/bbcfilms

Contact Head of BBC Films, David Thompson; Development Editor, Beth Richards

About The feature film arm of the BBC. No unsolicited scripts. Submit via Writers' Room, www.bbc.co.uk/writersroom. Independent producers may submit scripts by post to Beth Richards.

BBC WritersRoom
1st Floor, Grafton House, 379–381 Euston Road, London, NW1 3AU

- writersroom@bbc.co.uk
- www.bbc.co.uk/writersroom

About A route for the public to submit scripts for radio drama, television drama, CBBC, television/radio comedy, film and theatre. There are detailed guidelines online about what to submit and what not to submit, as well as links to other BBC departments that will also accept unsolicited material from the public. Send hard copies only and include SAE. Read all guidelines thoroughly before submitting.

CBBC
BBC Television Centre, Wood Lane, London, W12 7RJ

- 020 8743 8000
- anne.gilchrist@bbc.co.uk
- cbbcanimation.submissions@bbc.co.uk
- www.bbc.co.uk/cbbc

Contact Creative Director, CBBC, Anne Gilchrist; Head of CBBC Drama & Animation, Jon East; Head of CBBC Co-productions and Acquisitions, Jesse Cleverly

About Aimed at children and young people, CBBC runs two commissioning rounds a year. Details of closing dates are posted on www.bbc.co.uk/commissioning. CBBC is a self commissioning, self scheduling department. Independent producers may submit proposals to Anne Gilchrist, or Jon East for drama. Acquisitions and animation enquiries should be directed to Jesse Cleverly. A final decision will be given no longer than 20 weeks after receipt of the proposal. Children's drama is one of a few departments that accept unsolicited proposals from writers. See www.bbc.co.uk/writersroom/writing/submissions.shtml for submission guidelines.

CBeebies

BBC Television Centre, Wood Lane, London, W12 7RJ

☎ 020 8743 8000

✉ michael.carrington@bbc.co.uk

🌐 www.bbc.co.uk/cbeebies

Contact Creative Director, CBeebies, Michael Carrington; Head of CBeebies Acquisitions and Animation, Kay Benbow

About Aimed at a very young audience, content includes entertainment, drama, comedy and factual programming. Cbeebies runs two commissioning rounds a year, details of which appear on www.bbc.co.uk/commissioning. Independent producers may send proposals in to Michael Carrington, or direct animation or acquisition enquiries to Kay Benbow. Replies to proposals should be within five weeks. The department is one of few that still accept unsolicited proposals from writers themselves. For submission guidelines see: www.bbc.co.uk/writersroom/writing/submissions.shtml.

BBC FACTUAL & LEARNING

The Factual and Learning division is responsible for content across many platforms including television, radio and interactive. The academic revision guides, such as GSCE Bitesize, are part of its remit, as well as campaigns and technology awareness.

BBC Factual & Learning

BBC Television Centre, Wood Lane, London, W12 7RJ

☎ 020 8743 8000

✉ glenwyn.benson@bbc.co.uk

Contact Controller, Knowledge, BBC Vision, Glenwyn Benson

BBC Arts, Music, Performance & Religion

BBC Television Centre, Wood Lane, London, W12 7RJ

☎ 020 8743 8000

✉ arts.proposals@bbc.co.uk

Contact Commissioning Editor (Arts, Performance & Religion), Adam Kemp; Executive Producer (Independents), Jaquie Hughes; Factual and CA Network & Commissions, Northern Ireland, Jeremy Adams; Head of Factual Programmes, Scotland, Andrea Miller; Series Producer, Imagine, Janet Lee; Series Editor, Arena, Anthony Wall; Executive Producer, BBC Religion & Ethics (Songs of Praise), Hugh Faupel; Religion, Northern Ireland, Bert Tosh; Arts, Northern Ireland, Mike Edgar; Music, Northern Ireland, Declan McGovern

About Commissions across all media platforms, in the areas of arts, music and religion. The aim is to produce programming with depth, ambition and style. Development priorities are posted on www.bbc.co.uk/commissioning for each commissioning round. Independent proposals should be sent to Adam Kemp, preferably by email, or by post to: Room 6051, BBC Television Centre. Strand proposals may be sent straight to the strand editor or producer, and proposals from the nations may be sent directly to the relevant contact. An initial decision is made within six weeks.

BBC Documentaries

BBC Television Centre, Wood Lane, London, W12 7RJ

☎ 020 8743 8000

✉ docs.proposals@bbc.co.uk

Contact Commissioning Editor (Documentaries), Richard Klein; Executive Producer (Independents), Charlotte Moore, Ben Gale (BBC3), Maxine Wilson, and Emma Willis; Head of Factual Programmes, Scotland, Andrea Miller; Head of Factual Programmes, Wales, Adrian Davies; Commissioning Editor, Documentaries (One Life), Todd Austin; Commissioning Editor, Storyville, Nick Fraser

About Commissions documentaries across all content platforms as singles or series. Development priorities are posted on www.bbc.co.uk/commissioning. Independent proposals should be sent to Richard Klein preferably by email, or by post to: Room 6060, BBC Television Centre. For One Life documentaries, send a one page proposal including possible producers or directors to Todd Austin, preferably by email to onelife.documentaries@bbc.co.uk, or by post to: Room 5503, BBC White City, Wood Lane, London, W12 7TS. To speak with Todd, call 020 8752 6608 or fax 020 8752 6117. One Life films must reflect contemporary British Life. For the Storyville strand, send proposals to Nick Fraser, preferably by email to storyville@bbc.co.uk or by post to: Room 202, 1 Mortimer Street, London, W1T 3JA. To speak with Nick Fraser call 020 7765 5211 or fax 020 7765 5210. Proposals from the nations may be sent directly to the contact in that country. An initial decision is available in six weeks.

BBC Features & Factual Entertainment

BBC Television Centre, Wood Lane, London, W12 7RJ

☎ 020 8743 8000

✉ features.proposals@bbc.co.uk

Contact Controller, Entertainment Commissioning, BBC Vision, Elaine Bedell; Executive Producers (Independents), Mirella Breda, Ben Gale (BBC3); Factual and CA Network Commissions, Northern Ireland, Jeremy Adams; Head of Programme Production, Northern Ireland, Mike Edgar; Head of Factual Programmes, Wales, Adrian Davies; Head of Factual Programmes, Scotland, Andrea Miller

About Feature and factual entertainment commission all video content across television, radio, mobile, interactive and 'red button' platforms. They deal with the 'lighter' side of factual programming. Development priorities are updated for every commissioning round on www.bbc.co.uk/commissioning. Proposals from independent production companies should be sent to Elaine Bedell, preferably by email, or by post to: Room 6060, BBC Television Centre. An announcement from the website will let the public know if they are accepting proposals not linked to production companies. Independent producers in the nations may submit to the relevant contact in their area. An initial decision should be available within six weeks.

BBC Specialist Factual

BBC Television Centre, Wood Lane, London, W12 7RJ

☎ 020 8743 8000

✉ specfact.proposals@bbc.co.uk

Contact Head of In-House Knowledge Commissioning, Emma Swain; Executive Producer (Independents), Martin Davidson; Factual and CA Network and Commissions, Northern Ireland, Jeremy Adams; Head of Factual Programmes, BBC Wales, Adrian Davies; Creative Director, Specialist Factual, Scotland, Neil McDonald; Editor, Horizon, Andrew Cohen; Executive Producer, Money Programme, Clive Edwards; Editor, Timewatch, John Farren; Executive Editor, Wild, Vyv Simson; Series Editor, Natural World, Tim Martin

About Commissions across all media platforms, in the areas of science, history, business, and natural history. Detailed development plans and editorial needs are posted on www.bbc.co.uk/commissioning. Independent proposals should be sent to Emma Swain, preferably by email, or by post to: Room 6051, BBC Television Centre. Independent proposals for specific strands may be sent directly to the strand editor, and independent proposals from the nations may be sent straight to the appropriate

contact. An initial decision will be made within six weeks.

BBC NEWS

BBC News is responsible for national daily news, business, political and current affairs programmes on BBC television and radio. It also produces the continuous news channels BBC News 24, BBC Parliament, BBC World, interactive services, Ceefax and the BBC News website.

BBC News

BBC Television Centre, Wood Lane, London, W12 7RJ

☎ 020 8743 8000

✉ helen.boaden@bbc.co.uk

🌐 www.bbc.co.uk/news

Contact Director, News, Helen Boaden; Head of BBC Radio News, Stephen Mitchell; Head of Television News, Peter Horrocks; Deputy Director, News and Controller, News Production, Adrian Van Klaveren; Head of Political Programmes, Sue Inglish; Economics Editor, Evan Davis; Editor, Economics & Business Centre, Daniel Dodd; Controller, Editorial Policy, David Jordan; Political Editor, Nick Robinson; Head of BBC Newsgathering, Francesca Unsworth

BBC Current Affairs & Investigations

BBC White City, 201 Wood Lane, London, W12 7TQ

☎ 020 8743 8000

✉ george.entwistle@bbc.co.uk

✉ curraffairs.proposals@bbc.co.uk

Contact Head of Television Current Affairs, George Entwistle; Executive Producers (Independents), Eamon Hardy and Lucy Hetherington; Head of Programme Production, Northern Ireland, Mike Edgar; Head of Factual Programmes, Scotland, Andrea Miller; Head of Factual Programmes, Wales, Adrian Davies; Editor, Panorama, Sandy Smith; Editor, This World, Karen O'Connor; Executive Editor, Network Current Affairs, Manchester (Real Story), Dave Stanford

About Commissions across all platforms, aiming to open viewers' eyes to world issues. Development priorities are updated on www.bbc.co.uk/commissioning, independent proposals should be sent to George Entwistle preferably by email, or by post to: Room 1172, BBC White City. Strand proposals may be sent directly to the strand editor, and proposals from the nations may be sent to the relevant contact in that country. An initial decision will be made within six weeks.

BBC News Interactive

BBC Television Centre, Wood Lane, London, W12 7RJ

☎ 020 8576 8000

🌐 www.bbc.co.uk/news

Contact Editor, BBC News Website, Steve Hermann; Deputy Editor, BBC News Website, Paul Brannan; Editor, Interactivity, Vicky Taylor; UK Editor, BBC News Website, Gary Duffy; World Editor, BBC News Website, Adam Curtis

About Covers interactive mediums, including websites and Ceefax.

BBC Radio News Programmes

BBC Television Centre, Wood Lane, London, W12 7RJ

☎ 020 8743 8000

Contact Editor, Today, Kevin Marsh; Editor, World at One and The World This Weekend, Colin Hancock; Editor, PM and Broadcasting House, Peter Rippon

About Covers all news content on analogue and digital radio stations.

BBC Television News Programmes

BBC Television Centre, Wood Lane, London, W12 7RJ

☎ 020 8743 8000

🌐 www.bbc.co.uk/news

Contact Daytime News Editor, Amanda Farnsworth; Editor, Newsnight, Peter Barron; Science Editor, Newsnight, Susan Watts; Editor, Sunday AM, Barney Jones; Editor, Breakfast, David Kermode; Controller, BBC Parliament, Peter Knowles; Controller, News 24, Kevin Bakhurst; Editorial Director, BBC News 24, Mark Popescu

About Covers all news content on terrestrial and digital television channels.

BBC SPORT

BBC Sport

BBC Television Centre, Wood Lane, London, W12 7RJ

☎ 020 8576 8000

✉ roger.mosey@bbc.co.uk

🌐 www.bbc.co.uk/sport

Contact Director of Sport, Roger Mosey; Head of Major Events, BBC Sport, Dave Gordon; Editor, BBC Sport Interactive, Ben Gallop; Head of Radio Sport, Gordon Turnbull; Sports Editor, Interactive, Alex Gubbay; Head of BBC Football, Niall Sloane

About Responsible for sports coverage across the full range of BBC media platforms.

BBC NATIONS & REGIONS

This sector of the BBC is responsible for a large proportion of the corporation's output across television and radio. BBC Scotland, Northern Ireland and Wales produce content for their national networks, while the 12 BBC regions produce regular news and current affairs programming for television and local radio. National and regional BBC websites are also part of the remit.

BBC Nations & Regions

BBC Media Centre, 201 Wood Lane, London, W12 7TQ

☎ 020 8743 8000

✉ pat.loughrey@bbc.co.uk

Contact Director, Nations & Regions, Pat Loughrey; Controller, English Regions, Andy Griffee

BBC Birmingham

The Mailbox, Birmingham, B1 1RF

☎ 0121 567 6767

☎ 0121 567 6875

✉ david.holdsworth@bbc.co.uk

🌐 www.bbc.co.uk/birmingham

Contact Head of Regional & Local Programmes, BBC West Midlands and Deputy Controller, BBC English Regions, David Holdsworth; Head of Studio, Factual and Learning, Birmingham, Tessa Finch

About BBC Birmingham's main headquarters contains the Documentaries and Contemporary Factual Department. They produce content for all BBC channels. It also acts as the headquarters for all BBC regions.

BBC Birmingham Drama Village

Archibald House, 1059 Bristol Road, Selly Oak, Birmingham, B29 6LT

☎ 0121 567 7350

About BBC Drama Village is based on the Selly Oak campus of the University of Birmingham, and is used as a set for BBC dramas.

BBC Bristol Natural History Unit

BBC Broadcasting House, Whiteladies Road, Bristol, BS28 2LR

☎ 0117 973 2211

✉ neil.nightingale@bbc.co.uk

🌐 www.bbc.co.uk/bristol

Contact Head of Programmes, Leisure & Factual Entertainment, Tom Archer; Head of BBC Natural History Unit, Neil Nightingale
About Home of the BBC's Natural History Unit, producing programmes for all major BBC channels.

BBC East
The Forum, Millennium Plain, Norwich, NR2 1BH
- 01603 619331
- 01603 284399
- tim.bishop@bbc.co.uk
- www.bbc.co.uk/norfolk

Contact Head of Regional Programming, Tim Bishop; Planning & News Editor, Jackie Leggett

BBC East Midlands
East Midlands Broadcasting Centre, London Road, Nottingham, NG2 4UU
- 0115 955 0500
- aziz.rashid@bbc.co.uk
- www.bbc.co.uk/nottingham

Contact Head of Regional & Local Programmes, BBC East Midlands, Aziz Rashid; TV & News Editor, Emma Agnew; Assistant Editor, Kevin Hill

BBC London
35c Marylebone High Street, London, W1H 4QA
- 020 7224 2424
- michael.macfarlane@bbc.co.uk
- www.bbc.co.uk/london

Contact Head of BBC London, Michael MacFarlane; Head of News & Sport, Pete Stevens; Assistant Editor, Duncan Williamson
About Responsible for BBC London News, BBC London 94.9FM and the BBC London website.

BBC North East & Cumbria
Broadcasting Centre, Barrack Road, Newcastle upon Tyne, NE99 1RN
- 0191 232 1313
- wendy.pilmer@bbc.co.uk

Contact Head of Local & Regional Programmes, Wendy Pilmer; TV Editor, Andy Cooper; News Editor, John Lawrence; Sports Editor, Jeff Brown

BBC Northern Ireland
Broadcasting House, Ormeau Avenue, Belfast, Northern Ireland, BT2 8QH
- 028 9033 8000
- fistname.lastname@bbc.co.uk
- www.bbc.co.uk/northernireland

Contact Controller, BBC Northern Ireland, Peter Johnstone; Head of Arts & Entertainment, Mike Edgar; Head of Programmes, Ailsa Orr; Head of Drama, Patrick Spence; News Editor, Tom Coulter

About Produces a wide variety of content for both main BBC platforms and regional channels. Programming includes drama, documentaries, current affairs, news, sports and entertainment, often relating to Irish and Ulster Scots. Scripts for dramas, via agents only, may be sent to: Susan Carson, Programme Development Executive (Television), or Anne Simpson, Manager (Radio), Radio Drama, BBC Northern Ireland Drama, Room 3.07, Blackstaff House, Great Victoria Street, Belfast, BT2 7BB. Alternatively email: tvdrama.ni@bbc.co.uk. The latest writing opportunities and competitions are posted on the website.

BBC North West
New Broadcasting House, Oxford Road, Manchester, M60 1SJ
- 0161 200 2020
- jim.clarke@bbc.co.uk

Contact News Assistant Editor, Jim Clarke
About Responsible for BBC Radio Manchester, North West Tonight, and all online content across the region.

BBC Scotland
BBC Broadcasting House, 40 Pacific Quay, Glasgow, G51 1DA
- 0141 422 6000
- ken.macquarrie@bbc.co.uk
- www.bbc.co.uk/scotland

Contact Controller, BBC Scotland, Ken MacQuarrie; Head of New Media, Learning & Communities, BBC Scotland, Julie Adair; Commissioning Editor, Television, BBC Scotland, Ewan Angus; Head of Programmes & Services, BBC Scotland, Maggie Cunningham; Editor, BBC Scotland News Interactive (News Online & Ceefax), Mark Coyle; Editor, Features & Religion, BBC Scotland, Jane Fowler; Executive Editor of News & Current Affairs, Alasdair MacLeod; Head of Drama, BBC Scotland, Anne Mensah; Head of Factual, BBC Scotland, Andrea Miller; Head of Gaelic, BBC Scotland, Margaret Mary Murray; Head of Talent, BBC Scotland, Donald-Iain Brown

About One of the largest production centres outside of London. Produces a variety of content for both regional (BBC One and Two Scotland) and nationwide networks. These include drama, entertainment formats, current affairs, news, sports, documentary, arts, religion and music. There are several production centres in Scotland other than the headquarters. The BBC Scotland website announces any competitions, or calls for writing submissions from the public - although these are rare.

BBC South

Broadcasting House, Havelock Road, Southampton, SO14 7PW
☎ 023 8022 6201
✉ mike.hapgood@bbc.co.uk
Contact Head of Local & Regional Programming, Mike Hapgood; News Editor, Liesel Smith; TV Editor, Lee Desty; Sports Editor, Roger Johnson
About Responsible for BBC Radio Berkshire, BBC Radio Oxford, BBC South TV, BBC Radio Solent, and all online content across the region.

BBC South East

The Great Hall, Mount Pleasant Road, Tunbridge Wells, TN1 1QQ
☎ 01892 670000
✉ mike.hapgood@bbc.co.uk
Contact Head of Local & Regional Programming, Mike Hapgood; Sports Editor, Neil Bell
About Covers BBC South East (Television), BBC Radio Kent, and BBC Southern Counties Radio.

BBC South West

Broadcasting House, Seymour Road, Mannamead, Plymouth, PL3 5BD
☎ 01752 229201
✉ john.lilley@bbc.co.uk
Contact Head of BBC South West, John Lilley; News Editor, Simon Read; Political Editor, Chris Rogers
About Responsible for BBC South West TV, BBC Spotlight, Inside Out, The Politics Show South West, BBC Radio Devon, BBC Radio Cornwall, BBC Radio Guernsey, BBC Radio Jersey, and all regional websites.

BBC Wales

Broadcasting House, Llantrissant Road, Llandaff, Cardiff, CF5 2YQ
☎ 029 2032 2222
☎ 029 2055 2973
✉ menna.richards@bbc.co.uk
🌐 www.bbc.co.uk/wales
Contact Controller, BBC Wales, Menna Richards; Head of Programmes, English, Clare Hudson; Head of Programmes, Welsh & New Media, Keith Jones; Head of Broadcast Development, Cathryn Allen; Head of News & Current Affairs, Mark O'Callaghan; Head of Sport, Nigel Walker; Head of Comedy, Gareth Gwenlan; Head of Music, David Jackson; Head of Drama, BBC Wales, Julie Gardner
About Provides content in both Welsh and English for a wide range of platforms including regional Welsh channels BBC One and Two Wales, BBC2W and S4C, as well as mainstream BBC channels. There are detailed guidelines on commissioning at:

www.bbc.co.uk/wales/info/commissioning, however this mainly applies to independent production companies or in-house producers. The BBC Wales writers unit undertakes to read unsolicited scripts and give brief feedback on them, in rare cases this may lead to script development opportunities. For more information, visit: www.bbc.co.uk/wales/info/commissioning/content/writers or email: writerswales@bbc.co.uk.

BBC West

BBC Broadcasting House, Whiteladies Road, Bristol, BS28 2LR
☎ 0117 973 2211
✉ lucio.mesquita@bbc.co.uk
🌐 www.bbc.co.uk/bristol
Contact Head of Regional & Local Programmes, BBC West, Lucio Mesquita; News Editor, Caroline Le Marachel
About The West region broadly covers Bristol, Wiltshire, Somerset and Gloucestershire.

BBC Yorkshire

Broadcasting Centre, 2 St Peter's Square, Leeds, LS9 8AH
☎ 0113 244 1188
✉ helen.thomas@bbc.co.uk
🌐 www.bbc.co.uk/leeds
Contact Head of BBC Yorkshire, Helen Thomas
About Responsible for BBC Radio Leeds, Look North, and all online content across the region.

BBC WORLDWIDE

BBC Worldwide Ltd is a subsidiary of the BBC, dealing with the BBC's commercial activities. Its seven areas of business are: television channels; television sales; content and production; magazines; digital media; home entertainment; and children's.

BBC Worldwide

Woodlands, 80 Wood Lane, London, W12 0TT
☎ 020 8433 2000
☎ 020 8749 0538
🌐 www.bbcworldwide.com
Contact Chief Executive, John Smith; Managing Director (Global Channels), Darren Childs; Chief Operating Officer, Sarah Cooper; Director of Content & Production, Wayne Garvie; Managing Director (Digital Media) & Director (Strategy & Business Development), David Moody; Managing Director (BBC Magazines), Peter Phippen; Managing Director (Home Entertainment), Chris Weller; Managing Director (Global Television Sales), Steve Macallister

COMMERCIAL NATIONAL TV

Channel 4
124 Horseferry Road, London, SW1P 2TX
- 020 7396 4444
- 020 7306 8356
- www.channel4.com

Contact Chief Executive, Andy Duncan; Director, Nations & Regions, Stewart Cosgrove; Director of Content, Kevin Lygo; Head of Programmes, Julian Bellamy; Head of News & Current Affairs, Dorothy Byrne

About Channel 4 first broadcast in 1981. It now broadcasts across the UK, except to parts of Wales covered by S4C. It is a free to air, public service channel, funded entirely by advertising revenue and sponsorship. Along with Channel 4 itself, there are also the free digital channels, E4 (teenage/young adult audiences), More4 (a lifestyle and current affairs channel for older audiences), FilmFour (independent, contemporary cinema) and the broadband services FourDocs and 4OD.
All content is commissioned through independent production companies or producers. For up to date names and contact details of the entire Channel 4 commissioning structure, visit www.channel4.com/corporate/4producers where there are downloadable documents. For opportunities to showcase your talent to the channel, visit the website www.channel4.com/corporate/4talent, where you will find details of schemes, competitions and opportunities for members of the public.

Five
22 Long Acre, London, WC2E 9LY
- 020 7550 5555/0845 705 0505
- 020 7550 5554
- customerservices@five.tv
- www.five.tv

Contact Chief Executive, Jane Lighting; Managing Director, Lisa Opie; Director of Programmes, Jay Hunt; Controller of News & Current Affairs, Chris Shaw

About Five is the final terrestrial free to view channel, which launched in 1997. For details of submitting programme ideas (mainly for independent producers/companies) visit www.five.tv/aboutfive/producersnotes.
The site contains controller level contacts and development priorities in all areas of programming.

Each controller specifies how to submit ideas in their area. Response time is around four weeks.

GMTV
London Television Centre, Upper Ground, London, SE1 9TT
- 020 7827 7000
- 020 7827 7249
- john.scammell@gm.tv
- www.gm.tv

Contact Acting Managing Director, Clive Crouch; Director of Programmes, Peter McHugh; Editorial Manager, John Scammell

About GMTV owns ITV1's breakfast franchise and has been broadcasting since 1993. It is owned by ITV Plc and Disney. GMTV2 is broadcast on ITV2, the network's digital channel. Programming is a mixture of news, sports, entertainment, current affairs, travel and lifestyle.

ITN
200 Grays Inn Road, London, WC1X 8XZ
- 020 7833 3000
- 020 7430 4305
- itvplanning@itn.co.uk
- newsdesk@itvlondon.com
- c4home@itn.co.uk
- www.itn.co.uk

Contact Chief Executive, Mark Wood; Programme Editor, Alex Chandler; News Editor, Emma Hoskyns

About ITN is made up of five business areas; ITN News, ITN Source, ITN On, ITN Factual and Visual Voodoo.
ITN News produces the ITV News, Channel 4 News, More 4 News, London Tonight and International distributing news worldwide. ITN Source is a large moving image library. ITN On delivers content via mobile, radio and broadband. ITN Factual is a production house, and Visual Voodoo is another production company under the ITN umbrella.

ITV Network
200 Grays Inn Road, London, WC1V 8HF
- 0844 881 8000
- 0844 881 6355
- info@itv.com
- www.itv.com

Contact Director of Television, Simon Shaps; Director of Programme Strategy, David Bergg; Director of Factual and Daytime, Alison Sharman; Director of Drama, Nick Elliott; Director of Entertainment and Comedy, Paul Jackson

About ITV is Britain's most watched commercial television channel; it broadcasts across 15 regional licences and has three digital channels; ITV2, ITV3 and ITV4. At least 25 per cent of the output is commissioned through independent producers and production companies. For details on the procedure, visit the 'producer's page' on the ITV website.

Radio Telef's Éireann (RTÉ)
Donnybrook, Dublin 4, Republic of Ireland
- 00353 1 208 3111
- 00353 1 208 3080
- info@rte.ie
- www.rte.ie

Contact Director General, Cathal Goan; Managing Director of Television, Noel Curran; Managing Director of Radio, Adrian Moynes; Managing Director of News, Ed Mulhall; Managing Director of Publishing, Muirne Laffan

About Ireland's public service broadcaster, which outputs content on television, radio and the internet. For full details on commissioning for independent producers, including commissioning rounds and contact details, visit the website.

S4C
Parc Ty Glas, Llanishen, Cardiff, CF14 5DU
- 029 2074 7444
- 029 2075 4444
- s4c@s4c.co.uk
- www.s4c.co.uk

Contact Chief Executive, Iona Jones; Director of Commissioning, Rhian Gibson

About Currently a channel broadcast in Wales, in place of Channel 4. As such, rescheduled Channel 4 content makes up some of the programming, as do outputs from ITV Wales and the BBC. The majority of programmes are commissioned from independent producers. In 2009, at the time of the digital switchover, S4C will cease showing Channel 4 programmes, as Channel 4 will then be available in Wales. To contact Rhian Gibson, Director of Commissioning, approach Gwerfyl Griffiths at rhaglennide@s4c.co.uk, or on 029 2074 1422. For details on the commissioning procedures for independent producers, visit www.s4c.co.uk/production.

COMMERCIAL REGIONAL TV

Channel Television Ltd
Television Centre, La Pouquelaye, St Helier, Jersey, Channel Islands, JE1 3ZD

- 01534 816816
- 01534 816817
- production@channeltv.co.uk
- www.channeltv.co.uk

Contact Managing Director, Michael Lucas; Director of Programmes, Karen Rankine; Director of Resources & Transmission, Kevin Banner

About The smallest ITV regional company, which only broadcasts in the Channel Islands. Launched in 1962, it produces television commercials and corporate productions for Channel Island and UK companies.

ITV Anglia
Anglia Television, Anglia House, Norwich, NR1 3JG
- 01603 615151
- 01603 623081
- anglia@itvlocal.com
- www.itvlocal.com/anglia

Contact Managing Director, Neil Thompson; Channel Manager, Rob Halden-Pratt

About First broadcast in 1959, it is now one of the largest ITV regional stations. Also incorporates Anglia Factual, a production house which makes content for UK and US audiences, and Commercial Breaks, an advertisement production house.

ITV Border
The Television Centre, Carlisle, CA1 3NT
- 01228 525101
- 01228 541384
- border@itvlocal.com
- btvnews@itv.com
- www.itvlocal.com/border

Contact Managing Director, Douglas Merrall; Head of News, Catherine Houlihan; Literary/Arts Editor, Jack Johnstone

About ITV Border encompasses three different cultures; English, Scottish and Manx. It broadcasts across the region surrounding the English/Scottish border.

ITV Central
Gas Street, Birmingham, B1 2JT
- 0844 881 4150
- 0844 881 4198
- central@itvlocal.com
- centralnews@itv.com
- www.itvlocal.com/central

Contact Channels Manager, Dan Barton; Head of News (East Midlands), Alan Rook; Acting Head of News (West Midlands), Steve Lambden

About ITV Central covers a large area, stretching from the Welsh border, to the Peak District and down to the Home Counties. It is divided into three sub regions, West, South and East. Each has its own news service. News for the West is based at the administrative headquarters in Birmingham, East is based in Nottingham and South is in Abingdon near Oxford.

ITV Granada
Quay Street, Manchester, M60 9EA
- 0161 832 7211
- 0161 827 2180
- granada.reports@itv.com
- www.itvlocal.com/granada

Contact Managing Director, Susan Woodward; Head of Regional Programmes, Duncan Rycroft; Head of News, Richard Frediani
About Established in 1959, Granada is the longest running ITV regional station. As well as regional programming covering the North West of England and North Wales, its studios produce national content, such as *Coronation Street* and *A Question of Sport*.

ITV London
London Television Centre, Upper Ground, London, SE1 9LT
- 020 7261 8162
- 020 7261 8163
- london@itvlocal.com
- newsdesk@itvlondon.com
- www.itvregions.com/london

Contact Managing Director, Christy Swords
About Formerly LWT and Carlton, ITV London was formed in 2004. Broadcasts to the Greater London Area.

ITV Meridian & Thames Valley
Forum One, Solent Business Park, Whiteley, PO15 7PA
- 0844 881 2000
- 01622 674010
- yournews@itv.com
- thamesvalley@itv.com
- meridiannewssouth@itv.com
- www.itvlocal.com/meridian

Contact Managing Director, Lindsay Charlton; Regional Editor, Nick Myers
About Covers the region along the south coast, from Weymouth to Southend on Sea, as well as stretching up to the Thames Valley area. The area is split into three, with each having a separate news bulletin.

ITV Tyne Tees
Television House, The Watermark, Gateshead, NE11 9SZ
- 0844 881 5000
- 0844 881 5010
- tynetees@itvlocal.com
- news@tynetees.tv
- www.itvregions.com/tyne_tees

Contact Managing Director & Controller of Programmes, Graeme Thompson; Head of New Media, Malcolm Wright; Head of News, Andrew Friend
About Covers the North East of England and North Yorkshire. Tyne Tees Television is now part of the Granada group of companies.

ITV Wales
The Television Centre, Culverhouse Cross, Cardiff, CF5 6XJ
- 029 2059 0590
- 029 2059 7183
- wales@itvlocal.com
- news@itvwales.com
- www.itvlocal.com/wales

Contact Managing Director & Controller of Programmes, Elis Owen; Head of News, Phil Henfrey; Carmarthen Office, Giles Smith; Colwyn Bay Office, Carole Green & Ian Lang; Newtown Office, Rob Shelley; Wrexham Office, Paul Mewies
About Formerly HTV Wales, ITV Wales now broadcasts regional programming for Welsh viewers. There are several regional centres across Wales. Programming is a mix of news, current affairs, features, comedy and music.

ITV West
The Television Centre, 470 Bath Road, Bristol, BS4 3HG
- 0117 972 2722
- 0117 971 7685
- west@itvlocal.com
- itvwestnews@itv.com
- www.itvlocal.com/west

Contact Managing Director, Mark Haskell; Director of Programmes, Jane McCloskey; Head of News, Liz Hannam; Head of Features & Current Affairs, James Garrett
About Formerly HTV, ITV West now broadcasts regional programming for the West of England.

ITV Westcountry
Langage Science Park, Western Wood Way, Plymouth, PL7 5BQ
- 0844 881 4900
- 0844 881 4901
- westcountry@itvlocal.com
- www.itvregions.com/westcountry

Contact Managing Director, Mark Haskell; Director of Programmes, Jane McCloskey; Head of News, Phil Carrodus; Head of Features, Jane Blanchard
About Based in Plymouth, but with regional offices in Exeter, Weymouth, Taunton, Barnstaple, Truro and Penzance. ITV Westcountry broadcasts to Cornwall and Devon, as well as much of Somerset and Dorset.

ITV Yorkshire
The Television Centre, 104 Kirkstall Road, Leeds, LS3 1JS
- 0113 243 8283
- 0113 244 5107
- calendar@yorkshiretv.com
- www.itvlocal.com/yorkshire

Contact Managing Director, David Croft; Controller of Regional Programmes, Neil Thompson; Features Producer, Mark Witty; News Editor, Chris Ward
About Established in 1968, ITV Yorkshire is now one of the biggest ITV regional companies. Broadcasts a mixture of programming, including 'Calendar News' bulletins. As well as local programming, ITV Yorkshire also produces drama and entertainment shows such as *A Touch of Frost* and *Countdown*.

STV
Pacific Quay, Glasgow, G51 1PQ
- 0141 300 3704
- yourview@stv.tv
- scotlandtoday@stv.tv
- www.stv.co.uk

Contact Managing Director, Bobby Hain; Head of News, Gordan McMillan; Head of Features, Linda Grimes
About STV, owned by SMG, holds the current licence for Northern and Southern Scotland. There are separate news bulletins for the Scottish regions, along with fifteen hours of other regional programming for Scotland. SMG also owns Ginger Productions.

UTV
Ormeau Road, Belfast, Northern Ireland, BT7 1EB
- 028 9032 8122
- 028 9024 6695
- info@u.tv
- www.u.tv

Contact Managing Director, Michael Wilson; Managing Director (UTV Radio Great Britain), Scott Taunton; Managing Director (UTV Radio Ireland), Ronan McManamy; Head of News & Current Affairs, Rob Morrison
About UTV broadcasts across television, radio and new media. It covers Northern Ireland and around 70 per cent of the Republic of Ireland. UTV is part of the ITV network.

DIGITAL, SATELLITE AND CABLE

4Music
Channel 4 Enquiries, PO Box 1058, Belfast, BT1 9DU
- 0845 076 0191
- Online form.
- http://4music.channel4.com

Contact Programme Director, David Young; Programme Controller, Phil Poole; Director of Music, Simon Sadler
About Formerly known as THe Hits. A 24-hour urban and popular music video channel.

African Movie Channel
Devlin House, 36 St George Street, Mayfair, London, W1S 2FW
- 0870 622 0858
- info@africanmoviechannel.com
- www.africanmoviechannel.tv

About The African Movie Channel is a video on demand channel launched in the UK in April 2006. It is dedicated to top quality African movies from Nollywood and other major African motion picture houses.

Alpha ETC Punjabi
Unit 7, Belvue Business Centre, Belvue Road, Northolt, Middlesex, UB5 5QQ
- 020 8839 4000
- 020 8841 9950
- www.zeetv.co.uk

Contact News Editor, Sumant Dahl; Communications Manager, Kevin Rego
About A Punjabi language channel, which broadcasts a mixture of entertainment, drama and music.

Animal Planet
Discovery House, Chiswick Park, Building 2, 566 Chiswick High Road, London, W4 5YB
- 0870 050 6939
- www.animalplanet.co.uk

Contact News Editor and Press Officer, Delyth Hughes
About A sister channel to the Discovery Channel. Programming centres on wildlife. For submissions from independent producers visit http://producers.discovery.com and register.

At The Races

James House, 18–21 Corsham Street, London, N1 6DR

☎ 020 7954 3000

🌐 www.attheraces.com

Contact International Director, Nigel Roddis; News Editor & Office Manager, Julie Phelps

About A horse racing channel that shows many live races and related shows.

B4

37 Harwood Road, London, SW6 4QP

☎ 020 7371 5999

☎ 020 7384 2026

🌐 www.chartshow.com

Contact Chief Executive, Gail Screene; Head of Music, Sarah Gaughan

About New music channel, owned by Chart Show Television.

B4U Music & Movies

19 Heather Park Drive/Transputec House, Wembley, Middlesex, HA0 1SS

☎ 020 8795 7171

☎ 020 8795 7181

✉ enquiries@b4unetwork.com

🌐 www.b4utv.com

Contact Chief Executive, Sunil Rohra; News Editor, Kevin Rego

About B4U, a leading Bollywood network, launched B4U Music and B4U Movies in the UK, in 1999.

The Baby Channel

1st Floor, Bentima House, 168–172 Old Street, London, EC1V 9BP

☎ 0870 787 7351

✉ info@babychanneltv.com

🌐 www.babychanneltv.com

Contact Chief Executive, Leon Hawthorne

About A digital channel aimed at pregnant women and parents of children aged under five years old. Topics for programmes include pregnancy, child health, early learning, first aid, safety and cooking for children.

BabyTV

Baby Network Limited, PO Box 63107, London, W14 4AA

✉ info@babytvchannel.com

🌐 www.babytvchannel.com

About A channel aimed at providing 24-hour programming for the under threes.

Bangla TV (Worldwide) Ltd

67 Rothbury Road, Hackney Wick, London, , E9 5HA

☎ 020 8985 1450

☎ 020 8985 3794

✉ info@banglatv.co.uk

🌐 www.banglatv.co.uk

Contact Head of News & Current Affairs, M Shamsul Alam Liton

About A digital channel aimed at Bengali speaking audiences. Broadcasts entertainment, news and current affairs programmes. Audience size approximately 2 million people in the UK and EU.

BEN (Bright Entertainment Network)

25 Ashley Road, Tottenham Hale, London, N17 9LJ

☎ 07050 202460

✉ admin@bentelevision.com

🌐 www.bentelevision.com

Contact Director, Alistair Prince

About A British channel aimed at expatriate Africans living in Europe. It broadcasts home grown programming, Nollywood films and several hours of programming from African Independent Television. Free to air on sky digital.

Bid TV

sit-up Ltd, PO Box 45981, London, W3 0WJ

☎ 020 8600 9700

☎ 020 8746 0299

🌐 www.bid.tv

Contact Chief Executive

About An auction shopping channel, owned by sit-up TV.

Bio.

Grant Way, Isleworth, Middlesex, TW7 5QD

☎ 0870 240 3000

☎ 0870 240 3060

✉ contact@thebiographychannel.co.uk

🌐 www.thebiographychannel.co.uk

Contact Managing Director, Geoff Metzger; Head of Programming, Richard Melman; Head of New Media, Emily Lloyd; Head of On Air, Richard Morgan; New Media Editor, Paul Armstrong

About Formerly known as the Biography Channel. Features the latest showbiz news, profiles and biographical movies.

BLISS

37 Harwood Road, London, SW6 4QP

☎ 020 7371 5999

☎ 020 7384 2026

🌐 www.welovebliss.com

Contact Chief Executive, Gail Screene; Head of Music, Sarah Gaughan
About A continuous music channel.

Bloomberg
City Gate House, 39–45 Finsbury Square, London, EC2A 1PQ
- 020 7330 7797
- newsalert@bloomberg.net
- www.bloomberg.com

Contact News Editor, Laura Chapman
About A 24-hour digital channel with a multi-screen format. Bloomberg delivers news, data, financial market updates and weather reports.

Boomerang
Turner House, 16 Great Marlborough Street, London, W1W 8HF
- 020 7693 1000
- 020 7693 1001
- www.boomerangtv.co.uk

About A 24-hour cartoon channel, it broadcasts mainly from Warner Brothers and Hanna-Barbera archives.

The Box
Mappin House, 4 Winsley Street, London, W1W 8HF
- 020 7182 8000
- 020 7376 1313
- tvfeedbackmusic@emap.com
- www.thebox.co.uk

Contact Communications Director, Vikki Timmons; Commercial Manager, Programme Director, David Young; Head of Marketing, Melissa Pine
About A 24-hour viewer requested music channel.

Bravo
160 Great Portland Street, London, W1W 5QA
- 0870 043 4029
- 020 7299 5516
- enquiries@bravo.co.uk
- www.bravo.co.uk

Contact Senior Commissioning Editor (Entertainment), Rebecca Johnson; Senior Commissioning Editor (Factual), Lucy Pilkington
About An entertainment channel aimed at men aged 16–44. Programming includes crime documentaries, factual entertainment, comedy, and drama. Submissions are only accepted from independent production companies, for commissioning needs, visit www.virginmediatv.co.uk/commissioning/bravo.

British Eurosport (1&2)
Eurosport TV, Heathrow West Business Park, Heron Drive, Langley, SL3 8XP
- 020 7468 7777
- ukcomms@eurosport.com
- ukfeedback@eurosport.com
- www.eurosport.co.uk

Contact Director, David Kerr; Managing Editor, Adam Marshall; News Editor, Louise Moss
About Live and recorded sports programming broadcast across Europe.

BSkyB
Grant Way, Isleworth, TW7 5QD
- 0870 240 3000
- 0870 240 3060
- www.sky.com

Contact Chief Executive, James Murdoch
About The UK's biggest digital provider. Also broadcasts a number of Sky channels.

Cartoon Network
Turner House, 16 Great Marlborough Street, London, W1F 7HS
- 020 7693 1000
- 020 7693 1001
- www.cartoon-network.co.uk

About A cartoon channel owned by Turner Entertainment, a division of Time Warner.

Cartoon Network Too
Turner House, 16 Great Marlborough Street, London, W1F 7HS
- 020 7693 1000
- 020 7693 1001
- www.cartoon-network.co.uk

About A spin off channel from Cartoon Network, broadcasting a mixture of archived cartoons and identical programming to its sister channel.

Celtic TV
Building 5, Chiswick Business Park, Chiswick High Road, London, W4 5YF
- 020 7766 8484
- 020 7766 8485
- stantauk@setanta.com
- www.setanta.com

Contact Contact, Helena O'Sullivan
About A paid for digital channel on Celtic Football Club.

Challenge
160 Great Portland Street, London, W1W 5QA
- 0870 043 4030

○ enquiries@challenge.co.uk
◍ www.challenge.co.uk
Contact Editor, Kate Barnes; PR Manager, Jakki Lewis
About A gameshow and quiz channel, showing both repeats and original broadcasting. For commissioning needs, visit www.virginmediatv.co.uk/commissioning/ challenge. All proposals must come via independent production companies.

Channel U
Video Interactive Television Plc, PO Box 50239, London, EC1V 3YF
○ 020 7054 9010
○ 020 7054 9011
○ info@vitv.co.uk
○ production@vitv.co.uk
◍ www.channelu.tv
Contact Director, Darren Platt; News Editor, Nick Dereka
About An urban music video channel. Video submissions by post only, with a £20 fee to cover administrative costs. Read the submissions section on the website for full guidelines.

Chart Show TV
8 Chelsea Gate Studios, 115 Harwood Road, London, SW6 4QP
○ 020 7371 5999
○ 020 7384 9003
○ reception@chartshow.com
◍ www.chartshow.com
Contact Head of Music, Sarah Gaughan
About Chart music video channel.

Chelsea TV
Chelsea Football Club, Stamford Bridge, Fulham Road, London, SW6 1HS
○ 020 7915 1980
○ 020 7915 2902
○ chelseatv@chelseavillage.com
◍ www.tv.chelseafc.com
About Programming centring on Chelsea football club, mainly previous matches and features.

Classic FM TV
30 Leicester Square, London, WC2H 7LA
○ 020 7343 9000
○ classicfmtv@classicfm.com
◍ www.classicfm.co.uk
Contact Managing Director, Darren Henley
About 24-hour classical music channel.

CNBC Europe
10 Fleet Place, London, EC4M 7QS
○ 020 7653 9427
○ 020 7653 9393
◍ www.cnbceurope.com
Contact Producer, Helen Alexander; Director of Programmes, Barbara Stelzner-Large
About The leading pan European business and financial television channel. Broadcasts real time coverage of financial markets and international business news.

CNN International
Turner House, 16 Great Marlborough Street, London, W1F 7HS
○ 020 7693 1000
○ 020 7693 1001
◍ www.europe.cnn.com
Contact International Managing Editor (CNN Europe), Nick Wrenn
About An international news channel.

Community Channel
3–7 Euston Centre, Regent's Place, London, NW1 3JG
○ 0870 850 5500
○ info@communitychannel.org
◍ www.communitychannel.org
About A 24-hour channel dedicated to highlighting issues from both local and international communities, as well as the voluntary and charitable sectors. It broadcasts original shows, as well as repeats from terrestrial television, and showcases the work of new directors and community programme makers. The Film Makers' Guide on the website details how to submit your film to the channel.

Create & Craft
Ideal Home House, Newark Road, Peterborough, PE1 5WF
○ 0870 077 7002
○ 0870 078 0739
◍ www.createandcraft.com
About A demonstration and shopping channel entirely about crafts.

Dating Channel
130 City Road, London, EC1V 2NW
○ 020 7748 1500
○ info@thedatingchannel.com
◍ www.thedatingchannel.com
About An interactive dating channel.

Dave

2nd Floor, 160 Great Portland Street, London, W1W 5QA

- ☎ 020 7299 6200
- ☎ 020 7299 5412
- ✉ zoec.clap@uktv.co.uk
- 🌐 http://dave.uktv.co.uk

Contact Publicist, Zoe Clapp

About Incorporates the former UKTV G2 and UKTV Bright Ideas channels under a new name. Dave is a digital channel broadcasting contemporary entertainment, often with a satirical edge. Mostly archive content.

Discovery Channel

Discovery House, Chiswick Park Building 2, 566 Chiswick High Road, London, W4 5YB

- ☎ 020 8811 3000
- ☎ 020 8811 3100
- ✉ rebecca_vase@discovery-europe.com
- 🌐 www.discoverychannel.co.uk

Contact Press Officer, Rebecca Vase

About Broadcasts programmes on technological and natural knowledge, and investigations. Programme ideas should be registered at http://producers.discovery.com or sent to 'The Commissioning Editor, Commissioning Department'.

Discovery Home & Health

Discovery House, Chiswick Park Building 2, 566 Chiswick High Road, London, W4 5YB

- ☎ 020 8811 3000
- ☎ 020 8811 3100
- 🌐 www.homeandhealthtv.co.uk

About Programming on health and lifestyle. Programme ideas should be registered at http://producers.discovery.com or sent to 'The Commissioning Editor, Commissioning Department'.

Discovery Kids

Discovery House, Chiswick Park Building 2, 566 Chiswick High Road, London, W4 5YB

- ☎ 020 8811 3000
- ☎ 020 8811 3100
- 🌐 www.discoverykids.co.uk

About Television which encourages children to 'find out' and 'discover', whilst having fun. It is primarily an educational channel. Programme ideas should be registered at http://producers.discovery.com or sent to 'The Commissioning Editor, Commissioning Department'.

Discovery Knowledge

Discovery House, Chiswick Park Building 2, 566 Chiswick High Road, London, W4 5YB

- ☎ 020 8811 3000
- ☎ 020 8811 3100
- ✉ kate_buddle@discovery-europe.com
- 🌐 www.discoveryknowledge.co.uk

Contact Press Officer, Kate Buddle

About Documentaries and features about people and events that have shaped the world. Programme ideas should be registered at http://producers.discovery.com or sent to 'The Commissioning Editor, Commissioning Department'.

Discovery Real Time

Discovery House, Chiswick Park Building 2, 566 Chiswick High Road, London, W4 5YB

- ☎ 020 8811 3000
- ☎ 020 8811 3100
- ✉ caroline_watt@discovery-europe.com
- 🌐 www.realtimetv.co.uk

Contact Senior Press Officer, Caroline Watt

About Programming aimed primarily at male viewers. Covers property, DIY, mechanics, cars, gardening and sports, as well as true-life features. Programme ideas should be registered at http://producers.discovery.com or sent to 'The Commissioning Editor, Commissioning Department'.

Discovery Science

Discovery House, Chiswick Park Building 2, 566 Chiswick High Road, London, W4 5YB

- ☎ 020 8811 3000
- ☎ 020 8811 3100
- ✉ kate_buddle@discovery-europe.com
- 🌐 www.discoveryscience.co.uk

Contact Press Officer, Kate Buddle

About Broadcasts educational programmes based around scientific knowledge and investigations. Programme ideas should be registered at http://producers.discovery.com or sent to 'The Commissioning Editor, Commissioning Department'.

Discovery Travel & Living

Discovery House, Chiswick Park Building 2, 566 Chiswick High Road, London, W4 5YB

- ☎ 020 8811 3000
- ☎ 020 8811 3100
- ✉ caroline_watt@discovery-europe.com
- 🌐 www.travelandliving.co.uk

Contact Senior Press Officer, Caroline Watt

About Programmes cover travelling and living abroad, lifestyle features and documentaries. Programme ideas should be registered at http://producers.discovery.com or sent to 'The Commissioning Editor, Commissioning Department'.

Discovery Turbo

Discovery House, Chiswick Park Building, 566 Chiswick High Road, London, W4 5YB

☎ 020 8811 3000

☎ 020 8811 3100

✉ kate_buddle@discovery-europe.com

🌐 www.discoverywings.co.uk

Contact Press Officer, Kate Buddle

About A 24-hour channel dedicated to speed and motors. Formerly known as Discovery Wings. Programme ideas should be registered at http://producers.discovery.com or sent to 'The Commissioning Editor, Commissioning Department'.

Disney Channel

Building 12, 566 Chiswick High Road, London, W4 5AN

☎ 020 8636 2000

☎ 020 8636 2200

✉ studio@disneychannel.co.uk

🌐 www.disneychannel.co.uk

Contact Managing Director (Disney TV Europe), John Hardie; Executive Producer, Jonathan Bosely

About A children's channel aimed at seven to 14 year olds. Programmes include live action shows, animations and original films.

Disney Cinemagic

Building 12, 566 Chiswick High Road, London, W4 5AN

☎ 020 8636 2000

☎ 020 8636 2200

✉ studio@disneychannel.co.uk

🌐 www.disney.co.uk/disneychannel/cinemagic

Contact Managing Director (Disney TV Europe), John Hardie

About Broadcasts live action and animated Disney films.

DM Digital

Television House, 33–35 Turner Street, Manchester, M4 1DW

☎ 0161 833 1555

☎ 0161 833 0391

✉ info@dmdigitaltv.co.uk

🌐 www.dmdigitaltv.co.uk

Contact Chairman, Dr Liaqat Malik; Head of Music, Irfan Malik

About A 24-hour Pakistani business and general entertainment channel, available via cable and satellite in the UK, Europe, Middle East, Africa and Asia.

DM Islam

33–35 Turner Street, Manchester, M4 1DW

☎ 0161 833 1555

☎ 0161 833 0391

✉ info@dmdigitaltv.co.uk

🌐 www.dmdigitaltv.co.uk

Contact Chairman, Dr Liaqat Malik; Head of Music, Irfan Malik

About An Islamic channel broadcasting in Urdu, Punjabi, English, Arabic, Sindhi, Kashmiri and Pushto languages.

E!

141 Wardour Street, London, W1F 0UT

☎ 020 7297 5050

☎ 020 7297 5060

🌐 www.eonline.com

About Showbiz and entertainment programming, mainly from the US.

E4

124 Horseferry Road, London, SW1P 2TX

☎ 020 7396 4444

🌐 www.e4.com

Contact Head of E4, Danny Cohen; Editor, Ruby Kuraishe

About A digital station from Channel 4, which screens repeats from terrestrial television, as well as original programming and first broadcasts of US programmes. For all commissioning details for independent producers, visit www.channel4.com/corporate/4producers.

eeZee TV

JML House, Regis Road, London, NW5 3EG

☎ 020 7691 3814

🌐 www.jmldirect.com

Contact Direct Marketing Manager, Max Way

About A shopping channel with next day delivery. Now owned by the JML group.

Extreme Sports Channel

105–109 Salisbury Road, London, NW6 6RG

☎ 020 7328 8808

☎ 020 7624 3652

ben.hobson@chellozone.com

🌐 www.extreme.com

About An extreme sports channel covering urban, board, water and snow sports.

Fame TV

PO Box 249, Radlett, WD7 0BH

☎ 01923 857004

✉ info@fametv.com

www.fametv.com
Contact Development Manager, John Hayes
About A viewer generated content channel. Clips, pictures, texts and shorts are uploaded, via email or SMS. There is a charge for uploading.

Fashion Music TV
271 Regent Street, London, W1B 6ES
020 3178 4156
info@fashionmusic.tv
www.fashionmusic.tv
About A 24-hour channel broadcasting a mixture of music, fashion, lifestyle, celebrity gossip, showbiz, art and entertainment.

FilmFour
124 Horseferry Road, London, SW1P 2TX
020 7396 4444
020 7306 8366
editorialissues@filmfour.com
www.filmfour.co.uk
Contact Director of Acquisitions & Film Four, Jeff Ford; News Editor & Press Office, Steve Pinder
About A digital channel, owned by Channel 4. It broadcasts contemporary and independent films.

Five Life
22 Long Acre, London, WC2E 9LY
0845 705 0505
020 7421 7270
customerservices@five.tv
www.five.tv/fiver
Contact Senior Programme Controller, Chris Shaw; Director of Children's Programmes, Nick Wilson
About Broadcasts films, drama, soaps and lifestyle shows, as well as some children's programming, geared mainly towards women. Sister channel of Five. Five Life accepts programme ideas, see www2.five.tv/aboutfive/producersnotes for more details.

Five US
22 Long Acre, London, WC2E 9LY
0845 705 0505
020 7421 7270
customerservices@five.tv
www.five.tv/us
Contact Senior Programme Controller, Chris Shaw
About Broadcasts drama, comedy, films, sports and youth programming from the US. Sister channel of Five.

Fizz
Video Interactive Television, Studio 4, 3 Lever Street, London, EC1V 3QU
020 7054 9010
020 7054 9011
www.fizzmusic.com
Contact Channel Manager, Cat Park
About Music video channel. Fizz also accepts video submissions, see the website for submission guidelines.

Flaunt
115 Harwood Road, 8 Chelsea Gate Studios, London, SW6 4QL
020 7371 5999
020 7384 2026
contact@flaunt.tv
www.loveflaunt.com
Contact Production Co-ordinator, Rick Clapp
About A popular music channel aimed at 16–34 year olds.

FX
Unit 2.5, Shepherd's Studios, Richmond Way, London, W14 0DQ
020 7751 7602
020 7751 7601
www.fxuk.com
About A drama and comedy channel, with much of its content from the US network, Fox.

Gala TV
New Castle House, Castle Boulevard, Nottingham, NG7 1FT
0800 294 7294
01483 747097
customer.services@galabingo.co.uk
www.galatv.co.uk
About An interactive live bingo and gaming channel.

Gay Date TV
Room 101, Coppergate House, 16 Brune Street, London, E1 7NJ
020 7748 1500
020 7748 1501
www.gaydatetv.co.uk
About A gay dating channel.

Gems.TV & Gems.TV2
Unit 306, 3rd Floor, Fort Dunlop, Fort Parkway, Birmingham, B24 9FD
01527 406100
01527 406128
customercare@gemstv.com
www.gemstv.co.uk
About A gem set jewellery shopping channel.

Genesis - Revelation TV

Suite 16, Pegaxis House, 61 Victoria Road, Surbiton, Surrey, KT6 4JX

- 020 8972 1400
- info@revelationtv.com
- www.revelationtv.com

Contact Founders, Lesley and Howard Conder; Operations Manager & News Editor, William George
About A Christian television channel.

God TV

Angel House, Borough Road, Sunderland, SR1 1HW

- 0191 568 0800
- 0191 568 0808
- info@god.tv
- www.god.tv

Contact Regional Director for UK & Ireland, Chris Cole; Head of Production, Graeme Spencer
About A digital channel broadcasting religious programmes.

The Golf Channel UK

Martland Park, Challenge Way, Wigan, Lancashire, WN5 0LD

- 01942 210987
- 01942 210997
- press@golftvinfo.co.uk
- www.thegolfchannel.com

About Programmes include golf tournaments, reports, highlights and special features.

Golf TV Pro Shop

Martland Park, Challenge Way, Wigan, WN5 0LD

- 0870 005 3380
- lee.kenny@golftvgroup.com
- www.golftvproshop.com

Contact Senior Vice President, Lee Kenny
About A golf equipment shopping channel, broadcasts daily.

Hallmark Channel

234a Kings Road, London, SW3 5UA

- 020 7368 9100
- 020 7368 9101
- www.hallmarkchannel.com

Contact Senior Director, Jaime Saberito; PR Manager, Jane Muirhead
About Broadcasts original films, and comedy and drama series, as well as a variety of classic television series. Films are always acquired through major production companies, although if scripts are sent directly to Hallmark from individuals or smaller production companies they will endeavour to pass them on to suitable larger organisations.

Hellenic TV

50 Clarendon Road, London, N8 0DJ

- 020 8292 7037
- 020 8292 7042
- info@hellenictv.net
- www.hellenictv.net

Contact Channel Manager, Myroula Fellas; Managing Director, Chris Fellas
About A Greek language channel broadcasting 24-hours a day. They will consider Greek language programme ideas.

History Channel

Grant Way, Isleworth, Middlesex, TW7 5QD

- 020 7705 3000
- 020 7941 5187
- feedback@thehistorychannel.co.uk
- www.thehistorychannel.co.uk

Contact Channel Director, Richard Melman; News Editor & PR Manager, Joannna Mitchell
About Broadcasts historical programming, mainly documentaries and features.

Hollywood Classics Network

PO Box 7777, Brixworth, Northamptonshire, NN6 9YJ

- 01604 882581
- shaneknock@hollywoodclassics.co.uk
- www.openaccess.tv

About A free to air film and comedy channel, with a large archive of classic US content.

Hometime TV

32 Ludgate Hill, Birmingham, B3 1EH

- 0121 200 2444
- 0121 200 3002
- info@hometimetv.com
- www.hometimetv.com

Contact Managing Director, Stuart Roberts; Programme Director, Trevor Bedford
About Due to go on air in late autumn 2008, Hometime TV offers estate agents and property sellers an effective method of using digital media to market properties. It also broadcasts quality generic programming with property related content.

Horse & Country TV

Stoneleigh Park, Kenilworth, Warwickshire, CV8 2LG

- 024 7669 2269
- info@horseandcountry.tv
- www.horseandcountry.tv

Contact Founder/Director of Programming, Nick Ludlow; Head of Production & Programme

Acquisition, Teresa Watts; Executive Producer, Nigel Mercer

About An relatively new digital and online channel that broadcasts programmes related to countryside subjects, particularly equestrian features and events.

Ideal Vitality Channel

Ideal Home House, Newark Road, Peterborough, PE1 5WG

- 0870 077 7002
- 0870 077 7003
- customer.services@idealshoppingdirect.co.uk
- www.idealvitality.tv

About A television shopping channel owned by Ideal Shopping Direct Plc.

Ideal World

Ideal Home House, Newark Road, Peterborough, PE1 5WG

- 0870 077 7002
- 0870 070 0803
- customer.services@idealshoppingdirect.co.uk
- www.idealworld.tv

About A television shopping channel owned by Ideal Shopping Direct Plc. Specialises in innovative products with a story to tell, across the categories of fashion, health and beauty, jewellery, leisure, craft, homewares and technology.

Information TV

1 Stephen Street, London, W1T 1AL

- 020 7131 6693
- 020 7131 6698
- info@information.tv
- www.information.tv

Contact CEO, Fred Perkins; Production Manager, Paul Nicholson

About Broadcasts in-depth public service programming on topics of interest to various sectors of the community. Public bodies use Information TV to broadcast their own video material in the form of sponsored television programming. Programmes may be one-off broadcasts, or regularly repeated, and can be as short as five minutes. The sponsor of each programme will be clearly credited so that viewers know who has enabled the broadcast.

Islam Channel

14 Bonhill Street, London, EC2A 4BX

- 020 7374 4511
- 020 7374 4602
- pr@islamchannel.tv
- www.islamchannel.tv

About An English digital channel broadcasting internationally. Programming aims to represent and reinforce true Islamic values.

ITV2

17th Floor, London Television Centre, Upper Ground, London, SE1 9LT

- 020 8528 2000
- 0844 881 3060
- itv2@itv.com
- www.itv.com/itv2

Contact Channel Controller, Zai Bennett; Director, Jonathan Lewis

About A younger, entertainment based sister channel to ITV1. Broadcasts drama, comedy, sport, films and events including original commissions, high profile ITV1 programming and brand extensions of ITV1 shows. At least 25 per cent of the output is commissioned through independent producers and production companies. For details on the procedure, visit the 'producer's page' on the ITV website.

ITV3

20th Floor, London Television Centre, Upper Ground, London, SE1 9LT

- 0844 881 3038
- emma.tennant@itv.com
- www.itv.com/itv3

Contact Channel Controller, Emma Tennant; Director, Jonathan Lewis

About Broadcasts the best of ITV drama, with programmes from ITV1 and ITV2. At least 25 per cent of the output is commissioned through independent producers and production companies. For details on the procedure, visit the 'producer's page' on the ITV website.

ITV4

17th Floor, London Television Centre, Upper Ground, London, SE1 9LT

- 020 7620 1620
- 020 7261 3307
- david.fewings@itv.com
- www.itv.com/itv4

Contact Channel Controller, David Fewings

About Broadcasts programmes from 6pm each day. These include live sport and new cutting edge drama. At least 25 per cent of the output is commissioned through independent producers and production companies. For details on the procedure, visit the 'producer's page' on the ITV website.

Jetix

Chiswick Park, Building 12, 566 Chiswick High Road, London, W4 5AN

- webmaster_uk@jetixeurope.net
- www.jetix.co.uk

Contact UK Managing Director, Boel Ferguson
About Digital channel dedicated to animated children's programming. The Walt Disney Company owns a 75 per cent share.

The Jewellery Channel

Teddington Studios, Broom Road, Teddington, Middlesex, TW11 9NT

- 0844 412 2222
- www.thejewellerychannel.tv

About A digital shopping channel for jewellery.

Kerrang!

Mappin House, 4 Winsley Street, London, W1W 8HF

- 020 7436 1515
- 020 7376 1313
- tvfeedbackmusic@emap.com
- www.kerrang-tv.co.uk

Contact Programme Director, David Young; Director of Music, Simon Sadler
About A music video channel focused on rock, metal and alternative music.

Kiss TV

Mappin House, 4 Winsley Street, London, W1W 8HF

- 020 7182 8000
- tvfeedbackmusic@emap.com
- www.totalkiss.com

Contact Brand & Communications Director, Vikki Timmons; News Editor & Programme Director, David Young
About A commercial music television channel owned by Emap. It plays mainstream urban music and is based on the format of the London radio station Kiss 100.

Konta Music Television

9 Ilex Close, Hampton Hargate, Peterborough, PE7 8AD

- 0845 051 9998
- 0871 666 3074
- info@kontamtv.com
- www.kontamtv.com

About A channel combining a mix of programmes, including cultural heritage, news, current affairs, folk music, chat shows and comedy. Aimed at African and Caribbean audiences in Europe and across the

world. To submit music videos, download the form from the website.

Legal TV

Unit 3 Avenue Road, Aston, Birmingham, B6 4DY

- 0121 380 1050
- 0121 359 8839
- info@legaltv.co.uk
- www.legaltv.co.uk

Contact Production Manager, Simon Harland
About A digital channel featuring fiction and non-fiction legal programmes, designed to inform viewers about the legal system.

Life Television

Maidstone Studios, Vinters Park, New Cut Road, Maidstone, Kent, ME14 5NZ

- 01622 684444
- 01622 684445
- info@lifetvmedia.com
- www.lifetvmedia.com

Contact Chairman, James Braithwaite; Operations Manager, Jonathan Murphy
About A digital channel combining reality tv, lifestyle and factual formats.

LIVING

160 Great Portland Street, London, W1W 5QA

- 0870 043 4028
- enquiries@livingtv.co.uk
- livingcommissions@virginmediatv.co.uk
- clare.hollywood@virginmediatv.co.uk
- www.livingtv.co.uk

Contact Head of Commissioning, Clare Hollywood; Commissioning Editors, Sophie Morgan and Mark Sammon
About Broadcasts a mixture of high end factual entertainment, premiere dramas, groundbreaking comedy, pre-school programmes and reality television. All programme ideas must be submitted via an independent production company. For commissioning needs, visit www.virginmediatv.co.uk/commissioning/livingtv.

LoveWorld Christian Network

10 Henley Road, Standard Industrial Estate, Woolwich, Docklands, E16 2ES

- www.loveworldchristiannetwork.org

About A 24-hour digital channel broadcasting Christian faith based programmes. Also offers video on demand from their website.

Magic

Mappin House, 4 Winsley Street, London, W1W 8HF

- 020 7436 1515
- 020 7376 1313
- tvfeedbackmusic@emap.com
- www.magic.fm

Contact Managing Director, Shirley Renwick; Programme Controller, Phil Poole; Music & Programme Director, Simon Sadler; Programme Director, David Young

About A music video channel which broadcasts classic pop hits. Also a radio station, Magic FM.

MATV
Combine House, 7 Woodboy Street, Leicester, LE1 3NJ
- 0116 253 2288
- 0116 253 8900
- info@matv.co.uk
- localprograme@matv.co.uk
- www.matv.co.uk

Contact Chief Executive, Vinod Popat; News Editor, Sandi Shidhu

About A free to air 'sixth terrestrial channel' available to over 180,000 homes in Leicestershire. Also available nationally as a digital channel. Aimed at the Asian market, the channel has links with Bollywood and Indian broadcaster SAB. Programmes include drama, current affairs, comedy, cookery and local interest.

Max TV
Brooms Road, Stone Business Park, Stone, Staffordshire, ST15 0SH
- 0845 070 2571
- support@max.tv
- www.max.tv

About A shopping channel dedicated to video game accessories, innovative gadgets and boys toys.

Men & Motors
200 Grays Inn Road, London, WC1X 8HF
- 020 7843 8000
- men@itv.com
- www.menandmotors.co.uk

Contact Press Officer & News Editor, Mirinda Dawkins; Commissioning Editor, Joe Talbot

About A mixture of adult programming, factual, and motor sports content, heavily targeted towards men.

More4
124 Horseferry Road, London, SW1P 2TX
- 020 7306 3636
- 020 7340 9733
- hmykura@channel4.co.uk,
- www.channel4.com/more4

Contact Head of More4, Hamish Mykura; Editor, Katie Speight; Editorial Manager, Peter Wildash

About A digital channel from Channel 4, it broadcasts repeated Channel 4 content and original lifestyle programming. Aimed at a middle aged audience.

Movies4Men & Movies4Men2
Dolphin Broadcast Services Ltd, 3rd Floor, 114 St Martin's Lane, London, WC2N 4BE
- 020 7420 8290
- info@dolphintv.com
- press@dolphintv.com
- www.movies4men.co.uk

About Two digital film channels aimed specifically at men. Movies4Men broadcasts classic western, war, film noir, and detective films. Movies4Men2 broadcasts contemporary films, such as gangster, drama, and martial arts movies.

Movies 24 & Movies 24+
234a Kings Road, London, SW3 5UA
- 020 7368 9100
- 020 7368 9101
- www.tvmovies24.com

About A channel totally dedicated to made for television films. Movies 24+ is a sister channel that broadcasts the same movies as Movies 24 but on a completely different schedule. Neither channel produces films and they do not accept script submissions.

MTV
180 Oxford Street, London, W1D 1DS
- 020 7478 6000
- 020 7478 6007
- contact@mtvne.com
- www.mtv.co.uk

Contact Executive Vice President & Managing Director, David Lynn; Executive Vice President, Content & Creative, Music & Comedy, and Director of Television, Heather Jones

About A music television channel aimed at teenagers and young adults, broadcasting music videos, documentaries, comedy and celebrity related programming. Also broadcasts live studio programmes.

MTV2
180 Oxford Street, London, W1D 1DS
- 020 7478 6000
- 020 7478 6007
- contact@mtvne.com
- www.mtv.co.uk/channel/mtv2

Contact Executive Vice President & Managing Director, David Lynn; Executive Vice President, Content & Creative, Music & Comedy, and Director of Television, Heather Jones

About A music television channel focused around rock and alternative music. Aimed at teenagers and young adults.

MTV Base
180 Oxford Street, London, W1D 1DS
- 020 7478 6000
- 020 7478 6007
- contact@mtvne.com
- www.mtv.co.uk/mtvbase

Contact Executive Vice President & Managing Director, David Lynn; Executive Vice President, Content & Creative, Music & Comedy, and Director of Television, Heather Jones

About A music television channel focused on urban music, aimed at teenagers and young people.

MTV Dance
180 Oxford Street, London, W1D 1DS
- 020 7478 6000
- 020 7478 6007
- contact@mtvne.com
- www.mtv.co.uk/channel/mtvdance

Contact Executive Vice President & Managing Director, David Lynn; Executive Vice President, Content & Creative, Music & Comedy, and Director of Television, Heather Jones

About A music television channel focused on dance music, aimed at teenagers and young people.

MTV Flux
180 Oxford Street, London, W1D 1DS
- 020 7478 6000
- 020 7478 6007
- contact@mtvne.com
- www.mtv.co.uk/channel/flux

Contact Executive Vice President & Managing Director, David Lynn; Executive Vice President, Content & Creative, Music & Comedy, and Director of Television, Heather Jones

About A music video channel that allows viewers to publish messages and video content, via mobile phone or the internet. These then play alongside music videos of the viewers' choice. The channel is aimed at teenagers and young adults.

MTV Hits
180 Oxford Street, London, W1D 1DS
- 020 7478 6000
- 020 7478 6007
- contact@mtvne.com

- www.mtv.co.uk/hits

Contact Executive Vice President & Managing Director, David Lynn; Executive Vice President, Content & Creative, Music & Comedy, and Director of Television, Heather Jones

About A chart music channel. Features requests, competitions, features, a forum and charts. Aimed at teenagers and young people.

MUTV
274 Deansgate, Manchester, M3 4JB
- 0161 834 1111
- 0161 827 1190
- mark.pearson@manutd.co.uk
- www.manutd.com/mutv

Contact Head of Programming & Production, Mark Pearson

About A digital channel broadcasting matches, news and features about Manchester United Football Club.

National Geographic Channel
4th Floor, Shepherds Building East, Richmond Way, London, W14 0DQ
- 020 7751 7681
- 020 7751 7699
- natgeoweb@bskyb.com
- www.nationalgeographic.co.uk

Contact Publicity Manager, Emma Murphy

About A digital channel covering science, history, nature and geography. It is normally included in the free packages by most digital television providers. All commissioning for the channel is done electronically through the website, www.ngcideas.com

National Geographic Wild
3rd Floor, Shepherds Building East, Richmond Way, W14 0DQ
- natgeoweb@bskyb.com
- www.natgeowild.co.uk

About A sister channel to the National Geographic Channel, launched in March 2007, in place of Adventure One. Content comes from co-productions and international acquisitions, and is mainly related to wildlife and nature. The National Geographic channels have gone paper free; so all commissioning is done through www.ngcideas.com, where interested parties can register their ideas.

Nepali TV
Westec House, Westgate, Ealing, London, W5 1YY
- 020 8728 6470
- 020 8728 6479

○ info@nepalitv.com
ⓦ www.nepalitv.com
Contact Contact, Bijaya Thapa
About A Nepalese satellite channel broadcasting the latest news, current affairs, films, music and television series from Nepal, to over 58 countries.

Nick Jr.
15–18 Rathbone Place, London, W1T 1HU
❶ 020 7462 1000
❶ 020 7462 1040
○ howard.litton@nickelodeon.co.uk
ⓦ www.nickjr.co.uk
Contact Director of Channels, Howard Litton
About A digital channel for pre-school children, which aims to combine entertainment with learning and development. Much of the programming is produced in collaboration with child development experts.

Nickleodeon
15–18 Rathbone Place, London, W1T 1HU
❶ 020 7462 1000
❶ 020 7462 1040
○ howard.litton@nickelodeon.co.uk
ⓦ www.nicktv.co.uk
Contact Director of Channels, Howard Litton
About A digital channel for children, broadcasting a mixture of live studio programmes, comedy dramas and animations.

Nicktoons
15–18 Rathbone Place, London, W1T 1HU
❶ 020 7462 1000
❶ 020 7462 1040
○ howard.litton@nickelodeon.co.uk
ⓦ www.nick.co.uk/nicktoons
Contact Director of Channels, Howard Litton
About A digital channel for children broadcasting entirely animated shows.

Noor TV
14 Victoria Road, Aston, Birmingham, B6 5HA
❶ 0121 551 5700
❶ 0121 551 1119
○ info@noortv.co.uk
ⓦ www.noortv.co.uk
Contact Contact, Tahir Riaz
About Launched in 2007, Noor TV is a new Islamic entertainment channel, broadcasting programs in Urdu, Punjabi, Arabic and English.

Open View
6 Hoxton Square, London, N1 6NU
❶ 020 7012 1200

❶ 020 7729 9540
○ info@openaccess.tv
○ freelancers@openaccess.tv
ⓦ www.openaccess.tv
Contact Channel Manager, Matthew Andrew
About A digital channel broadcasting at Friday 11.30pm and Sunday 7.00pm, where freelance film makers may submit their films for broadcast, and peers can vote for their favourites via a forum. The channel is interactive and allows viewers to vote on the films. It acts as a competition and showcase channel. To join the database, freelancers should download an application form from the website.

Overseas Property TV
Church Studios, 50 Church Road, London, NW10 9PY
❶ 020 8965 6694
❶ 020 8181 4542
○ wendy@macanthonyrealty.com
ⓦ www.overseasproperty.tv
Contact Managing Director, Wendy MacAnthony
About A digital channel broadcasting features about buying properties abroad.

Paramount Comedy
180 Oxford Street, London, W1D 1DS
❶ 020 7478 5300
❶ 020 7478 5442
○ press@paramountcomedy.com
ⓦ www.paramountcomedy.com
Contact General Manager, Jill Offman; Head of Programming & Development, Sarah Mahoney; Marketing & Communications Manager, Zoe Diver
About A digital channel broadcasting mainly US comedy series' with a few British re-runs. Also produces some original comedy content with Five.

Passion TV
2nd Floor, Unit 28, 34 Bowater Road, Woolwich, London, SE18 5TF
❶ 020 8855 5010
❶ 020 8855 5949
○ info@passiontv.co.uk
ⓦ www.passiontv.co.uk
About A digital channel aimed at meeting the audience needs of British Afro-Caribbeans. It seeks to broadcast challenging, thought provoking programming, on difficult and taboo issues.

Pitch TV
13 Station Road, Finchley, London, N3 2SB
❶ 0871 225 3946
❶ 020 8438 6445
○ customerservice@pitchwell.com

🌐 www.pitchwell.com
About A digital shopping channel where products are demonstrated by experts, not presenters.

Playhouse Disney
Building 12, 2nd Floor, 566 Chiswick High Road, London, W4 5AN
☎ 0870 880 7080
📧 studio@disneychannel.co.uk
🌐 www.disney.co.uk/disneychannel/playhouse
Contact Managing Director (Disney TV Europe), John Hardie; Channel Manager, Jonathan Boseley
About Disney programmes for younger children.

Play Jam
Block C, Morelands, 5 Old Street, London, EC1V 9HL
☎ 0870 333 3146
📧 customerservices@playjam.com
🌐 www.playjam.com
Contact Channel Head, Jeff Zie; Head of Operations, Matt Wilson; Executive Producer, Graham Sidwell
About The world's leading interactive television channel, broadcasting interactive games and other media across Europe, South Africa, Malaysia and North America.

The Poker Channel
Queen's Wharf, Queen Caroline Street, London, W6 9RJ
☎ 020 8600 2698
☎ 020 8600 2501
📧 info@thepokerchannel.co.uk
🌐 www.pokerchannel.co.uk
Contact Chief Executive, Crispin Nieboer; Director of Broadcasting, Angus Gairdner; Head of Programming, James Hopkins
About Live programmes and features dedicated to poker.

Pokerzone
Northumberland House, 155–157 Great Portland Street, London, W1W 6QP
☎ 020 7942 7942
☎ 020 7942 7943
🌐 www.pokerzone.tv
Contact Managing Director, Jim Sibcy; Creative Director, Sam Ormas
About Broadcasts casino and poker programming.

Pop
115 Harwood Road, London, SW6 4QL
☎ 020 7371 5999
☎ 020 7384 9003
📧 francesca@chartshow.com

🌐 www.chartshow.com
Contact Brand Manager, Francesca Newington
About A mixture of cartoons and pop music for children.

Price Drop TV
sit-up House, 179–181 The Vale, London, W3 7RW
☎ 020 8600 9700
☎ 020 8746 0299
🌐 www.price-drop.tv
Contact Chief Executive, Ian Percival
About An auction shopping channel where the price drops until the product is sold out. Owned by sit-up TV.

Prime TV
Crown House, North Circular Road, London, NW16 7PN
☎ 020 8965 0333
☎ 020 8965 5723
📧 info@primetv.tv
🌐 www.primetv.tv
Contact Managing Director, Haroon Kahn
About A Pakistani family entertainment channel, broadcasting a mixture of religious, music, current affairs and entertainment programmes.

Propeller
46 The Calls, Leeds, LS2 7EY
☎ 0113 236 8240
📧 filmfirst@propellertv.co.uk
📧 redcarpet@propellertv.co.uk
🌐 www.propellertv.co.uk
About Working with the Skills Set organisation and wholly owned by the Grimsby Institute, Propeller is a digital channel set up to showcase new talent in film and television. The scheme 'Red Carpet' is an arena for students to air their work and 'Film First' is for independents and community groups to display their shorts or feature films. The channel also broadcasts news programmes and industry features. To submit content, visit the website and read through the online PDF files before sending films by post to either John Offord (Film First), or Dawn Simpson (Red Carpet). Films must have a minimum technical specification, but Propeller is always looking for new approaches to animation, comedy, drama, music and documentary making.

Psychic Interactive
16 Hanover Square, Mayfair, London, W1S 1HT
☎ 020 7408 9475
☎ 020 7408 9414
🌐 www.psychic-tv.com

Contact Contact, Steve Fishwick
About A live phone in channel for psychic readings.

The Pub Channel
Grant Way, Isleworth, Middesex, TW7 5QD
- 020 7941 5084
- 020 7941 5123
- pubchannel@bskyb.com
- www.pubchannel.com

Contact Head of Editorial & Broadcasting, Kate Oppenheim; Producer, Alison Clarke
About A digital channel aimed at the pub trade. It broadcasts a mixture of features, entertainment, and documentaries about the food and drink trade and licensing industry.

Q
Mappin House, 4 Winsley Street, London, W1W 8HF
- 0845 053 1052
- qtv@q4music.com
- www.q4music.com

Contact Press Contact, Jo Pinkney
About A music video channel linked with Q magazine.

QVC
Marco Polo House, Chelsea Bridge, 346 Queenstown Road, London, SW8 4NQ
- 0800 514131
- www.qvcuk.com

About A digital shopping channel.

Racing UK
Third Floor, Gillingham House, 38–44 Gillingham Street, London, SW1V 1HU
- 0870 735 9150
- 0870 735 9151
- info@racingtv.uk
- www.racinguk.tv

Contact Executive Assistant, Zenia Wright
About A horse racing channel, broadcasting live racing from 31 racecourses across the UK. It is a subscription based digital channel.

Racing World
Third Floor, Gillingham House, 38–44 Gillingham Street, London, SW1V 1HU
- 0870 735 9150
- 0870 735 9151
- info@racinguk.tv
- www.racinguk.tv

Contact Executive Assistant, Zenia Wright

About The sister channel to Racing UK, broadcasting programming from the world of US Horse Racing. Free to Racing UK and Setanta subscribers.

Raj TV
150–152 Wharfside Street, The Mailbox, Birmingham, B1 1RQ
- 0121 632 1011
- 0121 632 1482
- info@rajtvnet.in
- www.rajtvnet.in

Contact Contact, Iris Farley
About A free to air Asian digital channel aimed at 16–35 year olds.

Rangers TV
4th Floor, 8 Waterloo Place, London, SW1Y 4BE
- 020 7766 8484
- 020 7766 8485
- setantauk@setanta.com
- www.rangerstv.info

Contact Managing Director (Setanta), Leonard Ryan
About A paid for digital channel about Glasgow Rangers Football Club, available to Setanta subscribers.

Rapture
79 Brewer Street, London, W1F 9UU
- 07808 444583
- info@rapturetv.com
- www.rapturetv.com

Contact Managing Director/Head of Programming, David Henry
About A general entertainment digital channel which broadcasts gaming, music and current affairs shows.

Real Estate TV
3rd Floor, 1–6 Falconberg Court, London, W1D 3AB
- 020 7440 1070
- 020 7440 1077
- info@realestatetv.tv
- mark@realestatetv.tv
- www.realestatetv.tv

Contact Head of Channels, Mark Dodd
About A digital channel broadcasting property programmes from the UK and abroad. As well as commissioned programmes, it also broadcasts long advertisements for estate agents and property developers.

SCI FI
Oxford House, 76 Oxford Street, London, W1D 1BS

☎ 020 7307 6600
🖷 020 7307 6644
✉ scifipressoffice@nbcuni.com
🌐 www.scifi.co.uk
Contact Head of Marketing & Communications, Faye Harcourt
About The UK's only TV channel dedicated to science-fiction and fantasy.

Screenshop
sit-up House, 179–181 The Vale, London, W3 7RW
☎ 020 8600 9700
🖷 020 8746 2606
🌐 www.sit-up.tv
Contact Chief Executive, Ian Percival
About A shopping channel owned by sit-up TV.

Scuzz
115 Harwood Road, 8 Chelsea Gate Studios, London, SW6 4QL
☎ 020 7371 5999
🖷 020 7384 2026
✉ moshpit@scuzz.tv
🌐 www.scuzz.com
Contact Production Co-ordinator, Keeley Gray
About A music channel focused on rock, metal, alternative and indie music.

Setanta Golf
4th Floor, 8 Waterloo Place, London, SW1Y 4BE
☎ 020 7766 8484
🖷 020 7766 8485
✉ setantauk@setanta.com
🌐 www.setanta.com
Contact Managing Director (Setanta), Leonard Ryan; Programme Planner, Darren Lochead
About A subscription based golf channel, available through Setanta.

Setanta Ireland
George's Quay House, 43 Townsend Street, Dublin 2, Republic of Ireland
✉ setanta.irl@setanta.com
🌐 www.setanta.com
Contact Press Contact, Julianne McKeigue
About A paid for digital channel broadcasting Irish sports, including football and rugby. Also broadcasts a daily magazine show, 'The Hub'. Available through Setanta.

Setanta Sports 1 & 2
4th Floor, 8 Waterloo Place, London, SW1Y 4BE
☎ 020 7766 8484
🖷 020 7766 8485
✉ setantauk@setanta.com
🌐 www.setanta.com
Contact Managing Director, Leonard Ryan
About Paid for digital sports channels. Setanta Sports 1 shows Scottish Premier League matches, and Setanta Sports 2 broadcasts European League football matches.

Simply Ideas
1st Floor, Bentima House, 168–172 Old Street, London, EC1V 9BP
☎ 020 7608 8650
✉ info@simplymedia.tv
🌐 www.simplymedia.tv
Contact Chief Executive, Henry Scott
About A 24-hour digital shopping channel.

Simply Shopping
1st Floor, Bentima House, 168–172 Old Street, London, EC1V 9BP
☎ 020 7608 8650
✉ info@simplymedia.tv
🌐 www.simplymedia.tv
Contact Chief Executive, Henry Scott
About A 24-hour digital shopping channel.

sit-up TV
sit-up House, 179–181 The Vale, London, W3 7RW
☎ 020 8600 9700
🖷 020 8746 0299
🌐 www.sit-up.tv
Contact Chief Executive, Ian Percival
About Television retail channels, including Bid TV, Price Drop TV, Speed Auction TV and Screenshop TV.

Sky Arts
BSkyB, Grant Way, Isleworth, TW7 5QD
☎ 08702 404040
✉ tv@artsworld.com
🌐 www.skyarts.co.uk
Contact Press Enquiries, Samantha Jones; Head of Acquisitions, Phil Barnsdall-Thompson; Producer/ Director, Daniel Bougourd
About A digital channel dedicated to the arts, featuring live performances, documentaries and films.

Sky Bet
Central House, Beckwith Knowle, Otley Road, Harrogate, North Yorkshire, HG3 1WA
☎ 0800 0724 777
🖷 01423 720578
🌐 www.skybet.com

Contact Entertainment Consultant, Helen Jacobs; PR Coordinator, Tim Reynolds

About An interactive betting channel.

Sky Box Office
Grant Way, Isleworth, TW7 5QD
- 0870 240 3000
- 0870 240 3060
- www.skymovies.com

Contact Head of Production (Sky Movies), Mark Aldridge

About A pay-per-view film service.

Sky Movies 1-10
Grant Way, Isleworth, TW7 5QD
- 0870 240 3000
- 0870 240 3060
- www.skymovies.com

Contact Head of Production (Sky Movies), Mark Aldridge

About Continuous films across ten channels.

Sky Movies Cinema
Grant Way, Isleworth, TW7 5QD
- 0870 240 3000
- 0870 240 3060
- www.skymovies.com

Contact Head of Production (Sky Movies), Mark Aldridge

About Broadcasts film repeats.

Sky News
Grant Way, Isleworth, TW7 5QD
- 0870 240 3000
- 020 7705 2966
- news@sky.com
- www.sky.com/news

Contact Viewer's Editor, Paul Bromley; Head of News, John Ryley; Entertainment Editor, Jonathan Bennett

About A continuous news coverage channel.

Sky One
Grant Way, Isleworth, TW7 5QD
- 0870 240 3000
- 0870 240 3060
- www.skyone.co.uk

Contact Head of Sky 1, 2 & 3, Richard Woolfe; Commissioning Editor (Specialist Factual & Factual Entertainment), Emma Read; Commissioning Editor (Entertainment), Andrea Hamilton; Commissioning Editor (Drama), Elaine Pyke; Commissioning Editor (Entertainment & Features), Donna Taberer; Commissioning Editor (Factual), Andrew O'Connell; Commissioning Editor (Entertainment & Factual Entertainment), Steve Jones; Commissioning Editor (Drama), Sarah Conroy

About The UK's leading non-terrestrial channel, broadcasting a mixture of drama, factual, and entertainment programming, including shows for children and teenagers. For independent production companies, all details of commissioning routes can be found at www.skyone.co.uk/commissioning, where the specific needs of individual commissioning editors are displayed.

Sky Two
Grant Way, Isleworth, TW7 5QD
- 0870 240 3000
- 0870 240 3060
- www.skyone.co.uk

Contact Head of Sky 1, 2 & 3, Richard Woolfe

About Sister channel of Sky One, it broadcasts the same content at alternative times.

Sky Three
Grant Way, Isleworth, TW7 5QD
- 0870 240 3000
- 0870 240 3060
- www.skyone.co.uk/skythree

Contact Head of Sky 1, 2 & 3, Richard Woolfe

About Sky's first freeview digital entertainment channel. It showcases programming from Sky One, Sky Travel, and Artsworld. It also broadcasts news and reviews from Sky Movies and Sky Sports.

Sky Sports 1, 2, 3 & Extra
Grant Way, Isleworth, TW7 5QD
- 0870 240 3000
- 0870 240 3060
- www.skysports.co.uk

Contact Managing Director, Vic Wakeling

About Broadcasts news, features and live action from a wide variety of international sports. Some pay per view programming.

Sky Sports News
Grant Way, Isleworth, TW7 5QD
- 0870 240 3000
- 0870 240 3060
- snn-planning@bskyb.com
- www.skysports.co.uk

Contact Managing Director, Vic Wakeling; News Editor, Nick Seymour

About A digital channel showing only sports news.

Sky Travel, Sky Travel+1, Sky Travel Extra & Sky Travel Shop
Grant Way, Isleworth, TW7 5QD
- 0870 240 3000

0870 240 3060

www.skytravel.co.uk

Contact Head of Communications, Andrea Weselby; Channel Manager, Barbara Gibbons

About Sky Travel Shop is a 24-hour interactive holiday shop channel. Sky Travel, Sky Travel+1 and Sky Travel Extra are travel related entertainment channels, featuring a wide range of programming formats.

Sky Vegas Live
Central House, Beckwith Knowle, Otley Road, Harrogate, North Yorkshire, HG3 1WA

08000 720882

www.skyvegas.com

About A Las Vegas casino style gambling channel.

Smash Hits
Mappin House, 4 Winsley Street, London, W1W 8HF

020 7182 8767

020 7376 1313

smashhits@emap.com

www.smashhits-tv.co.uk

Contact Director of Music, Simon Sadler; Programme Controller, Phil Poole; Programme Director, David Young

About A pop music video channel based on the same brand as the former teenage magazine.

Speed Auction
sit-up House, 179–181 The Vale, London, W3 7RW

020 8600 9700

020 8746 0299

www.speedauction.tv

Contact Chief Executive, Ian Percival

About An auction shopping channel owned by sit-up TV.

Sumo TV
148–150 Great Portland Street, London, W1W 6QD

0871 200 0211

info@sumo.tv

www.sumo.tv

About A digital and online channel broadcasting short, user generated film clips. Users can earn money each time their clip is broadcast or downloaded.

Superstore TV
1st Floor, Bentima House, 168–172 Old Street, London, EC1V 9BP

020 7608 8650

020 7608 8651

info@superstore.tv

www.superstore.tv

About A digital shopping channel.

TCM
Turner House, 16 Great Marlborough Street, London, W1F 7HS

020 7693 1000

020 7693 1001

tcmmailuk@turner.com

www.tcmonline.co.uk

About A 24-hour digital channel broadcasting 20th Century Hollywood films, from classics to more contemporary pieces. Also runs an annual short film competition in association with the London Film Festival.

TCM 2
Turner House, 16 Great Marlborough Street, London, W1F 7HS

020 7693 1000

020 7693 1001

tcmmailuk@turner.com

www.tcm2.co.uk

Contact News Editor, Ann Rosen

About A sister channel to TCM, which broadcasts from 7pm–3am. It concentrates on core films and shows the same films every night for a week. Programming changes every Sunday.

Teachers TV
16–18 Berners Street, London, W1T 3LN

020 7182 7430

020 7580 3656

info@teachers.tv

news@teachers.tv

www.teachers.tv

Contact Chief Executive & Creative Director, Andrew Bethell; Head of Scheduling & Acquisitions, Alison Martin; Director of Educational Content, David Libbert; Commissioning Editor, Paul Ashton

About A 24-hour digital, satellite and web based channel aimed at teachers and all those in the education industry. Programming includes educational features and special features from inside the classroom and is designed to help improve teaching throughout the country. Programme ideas are best submitted through a teaching or educational organisation, e.g. DCSF. Most of these organisations will have a nominated person who deals with the channel and it is recommended that you go through them. Individuals may approach the channel directly but are less likely to receive a response. Do not send full programmes, only a brief proposal. There are three commissioning rounds per year: March, June and November, with a deadline two months before each one. Programmes usually take six to nine months between commissioning and broadcast, so if a piece is directly related to current news, use the 'news' email address.

Teletext Holidays
Building 10 Chiswick Park, 566 Chiswick High Road, London, W4 5TS
- 0870 731 3000
- 0870 731 3001
- webmaster@teletext.co.uk
- www.teletextholidays.co.uk
About A holiday shopping channel.

TG4
Baile na hAbhann, Co. na Gaillimhe, Republic of Ireland
- 00353 91 505050
- 00353 91 505021
- eolas@tg4.ie
- www.tg4.ie
Contact Director of Television, Alan Esslemont; Commissioning Editor, Proinsias Ni Ghrainne; Commissioning Editor, Maire Ni Chonlain
About An Irish digital channel celebrating Irish storytelling, sport, music, drama and culture. Programmes are often in the Irish language. For submission information, visit www.tg4.ie/bearla/fais/fais.htm. Submissions from independent companies are invited for documentaries, music, comedy, drama, soaps, lifestyle and travel. All submissions must be via the form, downloadable from the website.

Tiny Pop
115 Harwood Road, London, SW6 4QL
- 020 7371 5999
- 020 7384 9003
- francesca@chartshow.com
- www.chartshow.com
Contact Brand Manager, Francesca Newington
About A mixture of cartoons and pop music for very young children. Formerly known as Pop Plus.

TMF
17–29 Hawley Crescent, London, NW1 8TT
- 020 7284 7777
- 020 7284 6466
- lastname.firstname@mtvne.com
- www.mtv.co.uk/tmf
Contact Controller of Programmes, Michael Barry; Programme Director, Jed Mahoney
About A digital music channel broadcasting music videos, entertainment and features on popular music. Aimed at teenagers and young adults.

Travel Channel
64 Newman Street, London, W1T 3EF
- 020 7636 5401
- 020 7636 6424
- Online form.
- www.travelchannel.co.uk
Contact Press Contact & Head of Research, Petra Shepherd
About A digital channel broadcasting travel and holiday features from around the world.

Trouble
160 Great Portland Street, London, W1W 5QA
- 0870 043 4027
- 020 7299 5516
- enquiries@trouble.co.uk
- www.trouble.co.uk
Contact Director of Programmes, Jonathan Webb; Channel Editor, Celia Taylor; Senior Commissioning Assistant, Ellie Di Martino
About A young adult digital channel broadcasting mainly teenage/young adult drama and comedies from the US. All programme ideas must be submitted via an independent production company. For commissioning needs, visit www.virginmediatv.co.uk/commissioning/trouble.

UKTV Documentary
2nd Floor, 160 Great Portland Street, London, W1W 5QA
- 020 7299 5000
- 020 7299 5412
- danielle.kimble@uktv.co.uk
- www.uktvdocumentary.co.uk
Contact Press Officer, Danielle Kimble
About A digital channel broadcasting documentaries on a variety of topics. Also has occasional themed days and evenings.

UKTV Drama
2nd Floor, 160 Great Portland Street, London, W1W 5QA
- 020 7299 5000
- 020 7299 5412
- zoe.clapp@uktv.co.uk
- www.uktvdrama.co.uk
Contact Publicist, Zoe Clapp
About A digital channel broadcasting drama and films, mainly archive content.

UKTV Food
2nd Floor, 160 Great Portland Street, London, W1W 5QA
- 020 7299 5000
- 020 7299 5412

○ tamsin.zietsman@uktv.co.uk
⊕ www.ukfood.tv
Contact News Editor & PR Manager,
Tamsin Zietsman
About A digital channel focused entirely on food
and cooking. It shows a mixture of archive and
original programming, including magazine
style shows.

UKTV Gardens
**2nd Floor, 160 Great Portland Street, London,
W1W 5QA**
○ 020 7299 5000
○ 020 7299 5412
○ tamsin.zietsman@uktv.co.uk
⊕ www.uktvgardens.co.uk
Contact Publicity Manager, Tamsin Zietsman
About A digital channel, which specialises in
gardening features. It mainly broadcasts
archive material.

UKTV Gold
**2nd Floor, 160 Great Portland Street, London,
W1W 5QA**
○ 020 7299 5000
○ 020 7299 5412
⊕ www.uktvgold.co.uk
About A digital channel broadcasting comedy and
entertainment, mainly from the archives of terrestrial
television channels.

UKTV History
**2nd Floor, 160 Great Portland Street, London,
W1W 5QA**
○ 020 7299 5000
○ 020 7299 5412
○ danielle.kimble@uktv.co.uk
⊕ www.ukhistory.tv
Contact Publicist, Danielle Kimble; Press Officer,
Chris Masters
About A digital channel broadcasting a mixture of
newly commissioned and archived history
programmes.

UKTV People
**2nd Floor, 160 Great Portland Street, London,
W1W 5QA**
○ 020 7299 5000
○ 020 7299 5412
○ danielle.kimble@uktv.co.uk
⊕ www.uktvpeople.co.uk
Contact Publicist, Danielle Kimble
About A digital channel specialising in real life
stories. Programming includes a range of docusoaps
and biographical features.

UKTV Style
**2nd Floor, 160 Great Portland Street, London,
W1W 5QA**
○ 020 7299 5000
○ 020 7299 5412
○ tamsin.zietsman@uktv.co.uk
⊕ www.ukstyle.tv
Contact PR Manager, Tamsin Zietsman
About A digital lifestyle channel broadcasting
programmes from the UK and US. Subjects include
homes, property, fashion, makeovers and self
improvement.

The Vault
37 Harwood Road, London, SW6 4QP
○ 020 7371 5999
○ 020 7384 2026
○ help@vaultclassics.co.uk
⊕ www.vaultclassics.co.uk
Contact Chief Executive, Gail Screene; Head of
Music, Sarah Gaughan
About A music video channel broadcasting music
mainly from the 70s, 80s and 90s.

VH1
17–29 Hawley Crescent, London, NW1 8TT
○ 020 7284 7777
○ 020 7284 6466
○ lastname.firstname@mtvne.com
⊕ www.mtv.co.uk/channel/vh1
Contact Controller of Programmes, Steve Shannon;
Publicity Manager, Mandy Hershon
About A music video channel broadcasting features,
documentaries and popular music. Aimed at viewers
between the ages of 25 and 44.

VH1 Classic
17–29 Hawley Crescent, London, NW1 8TT
○ 020 7284 7777
○ 020 7284 6466
○ lastname.firstname@mtvne.com
⊕ www.mtv.co.uk/channel/vh1
Contact Controller of Programmes, Steve Shannon;
Publicity Manager, Mandy Hershon
About A music video channel broadcasting features
and classic music tracks from the 80s and 90s. It is
aimed at ages 35 to 45.

Virgin 1
160 Great Portland Street, London, W1W 5QA
○ 0870 043 4141
○ haveaword@virgin1.co.uk
⊕ http://virgin1.virginmedia.com
About Formerly known as FTN. The channel
broadcasts programmes from LivingTV, Bravo,

Trouble and Challenge, as well as some original programming. Airs from 6pm to 6am. For commissioning needs visit www.virginmediatv.co.uk/commissioning/virgin1. Only accepts programme proposals via independent production companies.

Wedding TV
44 Clipstone Street, London, W1W 5JT
- 020 7255 6240
- 020 7255 6241
- info@weddingtv.com
- www.weddingtv.com

Contact Programming Director, Tony Prince
About A digital channel based entirely around weddings. Broadcasts a mixture of entertainment, documentaries, reality television and gameshows.

Zee Cinema
Unit 8 Belvue Business Centre, Belvue Road, Northolt, UB5 5QQ
- 020 8839 4000
- 020 8841 6123
- www.zeetelevision.com

Contact News Editor, Sangraam Marathe
About A digital channel focusing on Asian cinema.

Zee Music
Unit 8 Belvue Business Centre, Belvue Road, Northolt, UB5 5QQ
- 020 8839 4000
- 020 8841 6123
- www.zeetelevision.com

Contact News Editor, Sangraam Marathe
About A digital channel featuring Asian music programming.

Zee TV
Unit 8 Belvue Business Centre, Belvue Road, Northolt, UB5 5QQ
- 020 8839 4000
- 020 8841 6123
- www.zeetelevision.com

Contact Controller of Programmes, Shaney Burney; News Editor, Sangraam Marathe
About A digital channel aimed at an Asian audience. Broadcasts entertainment, news, drama and music.

Zone Club
105–109 Salisbury Road, London, NW6 6RG
- 020 7328 8808
- 020 7624 3652
- george.hills@zonevision.com
- www.zoneclub.tv

Contact Press Contact, George Hills
About A digital lifestyle television channel broadcasting dramas, chat, DIY and documentaries. Aimed at women viewers.

Zone Fantasy
105–109 Salisbury Road, London, NW6 6RG
- 020 7328 8808
- 020 7624 3652
- www.zonefantasy.tv

Contact Press Contact, George Hills
About A digital channel dedicated entirely to fantasy movies and television shows.

Zone Horror
105–109 Salisbury Road, London, NW6 6RG
- 020 7328 8808
- 020 7624 3652
- george.hills@zonevision.com
- www.zonehorror.tv

Contact Press Contact, George Hills
About A digital channel dedicated to horror films, and features about the making of them.

Zone Reality
105–109 Salisbury Road, London, NW6 6RG
- 020 7328 8808
- 020 7624 3652
- george.hills@zonevision.com
- www.zonereality.tv

Contact Press Contact, George Hills
About A 24-hour digital channel dedicated entirely to reality television.

Zone Romanctica
105–109 Salisbury Road, London, NW6 6RG
- 020 7328 8808
- 020 7624 3652
- www.zoneromantica.tv

Contact Press Contact, George Hills
About A digital channel dedicated entirely to romantic movies and television shows, such as Ally McBeal and Chicago Hope.

Zone Thriller
105–109 Salisbury Road, London, NW6 6RG
- 020 7328 8808
- 020 7624 3652
- www.zonethriller.tv

Contact Press Contact, George Hills
About A digital channel dedicated entirely to thriller movies and 'making of' documentaries.

Absolute Radio
1 Golden Square, London, W1F 9DJ
- 020 7434 1215
- 020 7434 1197
- newsroom@absoluteradio.co.uk
- www.absoluteradio.co.uk

Contact Programme Director, Paul Jackson; Head of News, Andrew Bailey; Head of Music, James Curran; Head of Sport, Dominic Johnson
About Formerly known as Virgin Radio. An analogue and digital station playing contemporary music, along with classic rock and pop music. Part of the TIML Radio Ltd network.

Capital Life
30 Leicester Square, London, WC2H 7LA
- 020 7766 6000
- 020 7766 6601
- kevin.palmer@qcapmedia.com
- www.ukcapitallife.com

Contact Programme Director, Kevin Palmer
About A national digital radio station broadcasting a mixture of classic and contemporary pop music for listeners aged 25 plus.

Classic FM
30 Leicester Square, London, WC2H 7LA
- 020 7343 9000
- 020 7766 6100
- darren.henley@classicfm.com
- www.classicfm.com

Contact Station Manager, Darren Henley; News Manager, Ann-Marie Minhall
About A national station which is available on analogue and digital radios. It broadcasts classical music, features, interviews and news programmes.

Core
30 Leicester Square, London, WC2H 7LA
- 0117 984 3200
- fresh@corefreshhits.com
- www.corefreshhits.com

Contact Station Manager, Bern Leckie
About Part of the Digital One network. A digital radio station broadcasting contemporary pop music and news, for a young adult audience.

Fun Kids
One Passage Street, Bristol, BS2 0JF
- 020 7739 7879
- matt@foldermedia.co.uk
- www.funkidslive.com

Contact Creative Director, Matt Deegan
About A radio station entirely for children, available on Sky Digital 0162 and Virgin Media, as well as DAB digital radio in the following parts of the country: London, Essex, Berkshire, Wiltshire, Bristol, Cardiff, Kent, Sussex, and Bournemouth.

Newstalk
Warrington House, Mount Street Crescent, Dublin 2, Republic of Ireland
- 00353 1 644 5100
- 00353 1 661 1602
- info@newstalk.ie
- www.newstalk.ie

Contact Station Editor, Garett Harte; News Director, John Keogh; Sports Editor, Jerry O'Sullivan
About A national station for Ireland, which broadcasts a variety of programmes; mainly news, sport, discussion and entertainment.

OneWord Radio
50 Lisson Street, London, NW1 5DF
- 020 7453 1600
- 020 7723 6132
- simon.blackmore@oneword.co.uk
- www.oneword.co.uk

Contact Managing Director and News Editor, Simon Blackmore
About A national digital radio station, broadcasting a mixture of features on books, comedy, drama and discussion. Part of the Digital One network. There is currently no budget for producing new shows and therefore scripts are not being accepted. According to the website the future of the radio station is uncertain.

Planet Rock
30 Leicester Square, London, WC2H 7LA
- 0845 000 7625
- jon@planetrock.com
- www.planetrock.com

Contact Executive Producer, Trevor White; Marketing Manager, Jon Norman
About A national digital radio station, part of the Digital One network. Broadcasts rock music mainly from the 60s, 70s and 80s, as well as live music, interviews and features on rock music.

RTÉ 2FM
Donnybrook, Dublin 4, Republic of Ireland
- 01850 715922
- 00353 1 208 3080

info@rte.ie
www.rte.ie/2fm
About A national public service radio station for Ireland, broadcasting a variety of music and entertainment features.

RTÉ Lyric FM
Cornmarket Square, Limerick, Republic of Ireland
00353 61 207300
00353 61 207390
lyric@rte.ie
www.rte.ie/lyricfm
About A national public service radio station for Ireland, it broadcasts a mixture of programmes on opera, musicals, jazz, new music, arts and the theatre.

RTÉ Radio 1
Donnybrook, Dublin 4, Republic of Ireland
00353 1 208 3111
info@rte.ie
www.rte.ie/radio1
Contact Head of Radio, Adrian Moynes; Head of RTÉ Radio 1, Ana Leddy
About A national public service broadcast radio station for Ireland. A mixture of news, current affairs, drama, music, entertainment features and arts.

RTÉ Raidió na Gaeltachta
Casla, Conamara, Co. na Gaillimhe, Republic of Ireland
00353 91 506677
00353 91 506666
rnag@rte.ie
www.rte.ie/rnag
About An Irish language radio station, with regional headquarters.

talkSport
18 Hatfields, London, SE1 8DJ
020 7959 7800
020 7959 7806
customer.services@talksport.co.uk
www2.talksport.net/index.asp
Contact Programme Manager, Matt Smith; Programme Director, Bill Ridley; Sports Editor, Andrew McKenna
About Part of the Digital One network. A talk based radio station concentrating mainly on sports programmes, but also broadcasting news, current affairs and entertainment content.

theJazz
30 Leicester Square, London, WC2H 7LA
020 7054 9000
020 7344 2703
www.thejazz.com
Contact Station Manager, Darren Henley
About A national digital radio station, part of the Digital One network and sister station to Classic FM. Broadcasts jazz music and features.

Today FM
124 Upper Abbey Street, Dublin 1, Republic of Ireland
00353 1 804 9000
www.todayfm.com
About Ireland's main independent national radio station.

COMMERCIAL UK & IRISH LOCAL RADIO

Capital Radio
30 Leicester Square, London, WC2H 7LA
020 7766 6155
020 7766 6012
newsdesk@capitalradio.com
www.capitalradio.com
Contact Music & Film Editor, Sarah Ward; Entertainment Reporter, Jodie Ross
About A London station broadcasting a mixture of popular music, celebrity features and news.

Central FM
201–203 High Street, Falkirk, FK1 1DU
01324 611164
01324 611168
news@centralfm.co.uk
www.centralfm.co.uk
Contact Controller of Programmes, Tom Bell; Sports Editor, Tadek Kopszywa
About Broadcasts to central Scotland on the FM wavelength. Programmes include music, sports, news, and local events and information.

Clare FM
Francis Street, Ennis, Co. Clare, Republic of Ireland
00353 65 682 8888
00353 65 682 3366
info@clarefm.ie
www.clarefm.ie

Contact Managing Director, Liam O'Shea; News Editor, John Cooke
About A station broadcasting to County Clare and the surrounding areas. A mixture of music, news and talk.

Clyde 1
3 South Avenue, Clydebank Business Park, Glasgow, G81 2RX
- 0141 565 2200
- 0141 565 2265
- clydenews@radioclyde.com
- www.clyde1.com

Contact Managing Director, Tracey McNellan; News Editor, Lorraine Herbison; Sports Editor, Peter Martin
About A Glasgow radio station aimed at older teenagers and young adults. Broadcasts a mixture of music, news, sport, competitions and entertainment features. Most content is produced in-house, or commissioned by invitation.

Clyde 2
3 South Avenue, Clydebank Business Park, Glasgow, G81 2RX
- 0141 565 2200
- 0141 565 2265
- clydenews@radioclyde.com
- www.clyde2.com

Contact Head of News & Sport, Russel Walker
About A sister station to Clyde 1, it is aimed at an older audience of 35 plus. Programmes include music, news, sport and competitions. Most content is produced in-house, or commissioned by invitation.

Cork's 96 FM & 103 FM
Broadcasting House, Patrick's Place, Cork, Republic of Ireland
- info@96fm.ie
- news@96fm.ie
- www.96fm.ie

About A station for Cork, broadcasting mainly music and light entertainment features.

Downtown Radio
Newtownards, Co. Down, BT23 4ES
- 028 9181 5555
- 028 9181 5252
- news@downtown.co.uk
- programmes@downtown.co.uk
- www.downtown.co.uk

Contact Managing Director, David Sloan; Features Coordinator, Florence Ambrose; Head of Music, Eddie West

About A radio station for Northern Ireland, which broadcasts music, news, sport and entertainment features. The station runs an annual short story competition for previously unpublished work. Entrants must live in the Downtown area. The prize is £250 in cash and £100 in gift vouchers. There are four categories. For details of closing dates and categories, go to www.downtown.co.uk/article.asp?id=170750.

Dublin's Q102
Glengeary Office Park, Glengeary, Co. Dublin, Republic of Ireland
- 00353 1 662 1022
- 00353 1 662 9974
- comments@q102.ie
- news@q102.ie
- admin@q102.ie
- www.q102.ie

About A station for the Dublin area, broadcasting mainly music and news, it is aimed at a 30 plus audience.

Forth 1
Forth House, Forth Street, Edinburgh, EH1 3LE
- 0131 556 9255
- 0131 557 8489
- forth-news@radioforth.com
- www.forthone.com

Contact Managing Director, Adam Finlay; Programme Director, Luke McCullough; Head of News, Paul Robertson
About A Scottish radio station aimed at young adults. Broadcasts music, news, sport and entertainment features.

Forth 2
Forth House, Forth Street, Edinburgh, EH1 3LE
- 0131 557 1005
- 0131 557 8489
- forth-news@srh.co.uk
- www.forth2.com

Contact Station Director, Cathy Kirk; Head of News, Paul Robertson
About A sister station to Forth 1, aimed at a slightly older audience aged 35 plus. Content includes music, sport, and a range of interesting features relevant to the people of Scotland.

Heart FM
1 The Square, 111 Broad Street, Birmingham, B15 1AS
- 0121 695 0000
- 0121 696 1007
- news@heartfm.co.uk

www.heartfm.co.uk
Contact Managing Director, Anita Wright; News Editor, Dave McMullen
About A regional West Midlands station with a newer sister station in London. Broadcasts female friendly music, news and entertainment features.

Isle of Wight Radio
Dodnor Park, Newport, Isle of Wight, PO30 5XE
01983 822557
01983 822109
hello@iwradio.co.uk
www.iwradio.co.uk
Contact Station Manager, Amy Stroud; Controller of Programmes, Tom Stroud
About A station for the Isle of Wight that also reaches parts of Hampshire, Dorset and Sussex. The audience is primarily middle aged, and programmes are a mixture of music, news, sport, and general entertainment and community features.

KCLR 96 FM
1st Floor, Exchequer House, Potato Market, Carlow, Republic of Ireland
00353 59 913 9696
00353 59 913 7912
info@kclr96fm.com
news@kclr96fm.com
www.kclr96fm.com
Contact Programme Coordinator, Mags Murphy
About A station broadcasting to Kilkenny and Carlow. Content is a mixture of music, news, sport, and local community features. For any news, documentary or local feature enquiries, contact Mags Murphy.

KMfm
34–36 North Street, Ashford, Kent, TN24 8JR
01233 623232
radams@kmfm.co.uk
www.kmfm.co.uk
About A group of local stations for Kent, with the head office in Ashford and other studios in Medway, Canterbury, Thanet, Folkestone and West Kent. Broadcasts local news and sport, as well as music and general entertainment features.

LBC
13 Bramley Road, London, W10 6SP
020 7314 7300
020 7314 7317
jonathan.richards@lbc.co.uk
www.lbc.co.uk

Contact Programme Director & Editorial Director (News), Jonathan Richards; Marketing Manager, Sam Walker
About Broadcasts news, current affairs and features for London. Submit interesting news stories through the online form on the website.

LMFM Radio
Rathmullan Road, Drogheda, Co. Louth, Republic of Ireland
00353 41 983 2000
00353 41 983 2957
www.lmfm.ie
Contact Production, Maria Harman
About The largest local radio station for Ireland outside of Dublin and Cork. Broadcasts to Counties Meath and Louth. A mix of music, news, and local programmes.

Midlands 103
The Mall, William Street, Tullamore, Co. Offaly, Republic of Ireland
00353 57 935 1333
00353 57 935 2444
info@midlandsradio.fm
www.midlandsradio.fm
Contact Managing Director, Albert FitzGerald; Director of Programming, William Faulkner
About A radio service broadcasting to Counties Laois, Offaly and Westmeath. A mixture of news, music and local events.

98FM
Level 3, The Malthouse, Grand Canal Quay, Dublin 2, Republic of Ireland
00353 1 670 8970
00353 1 670 8969
dublinnewscentre@98fm.ie
www.98fm.ie
Contact Managing Director, Ciaran Davis
About A station for Dublin and the surrounding area, broadcasting mainly music programming.

Northsound One
Abbotswell Road, West Tullos, Aberdeen, Scotland, AB12 3AJ
01224 337000
01224 633282
news@northsound.co.uk
www.northsound1.com
Contact Managing Director, Ken Massie; Programme Director, Chris Thompson; Head of News, Sarah Campbell; Sports Editor, David Ridd
About A station for Aberdeen and the surrounding area, aimed at teenagers and young adults.

Broadcasts a mixture of contemporary music, news, sport, and entertainment.

Northsound Two
Abbotswell Road, West Tullos, Aberdeen, AB12 3AJ
- 01224 337000
- 01224 400003
- news@northsound.co.uk
- www.northsound2.com

Contact Managing Director, Ken Massie; Programme Director, Chris Thompson; Head of News, Sarah Campbell; Sports Editor, David Ridd
About A sister station of Northsound One, aimed at an older audience of over 30s. Broadcasts music, news and general interest features. Also features live local sport.

Premier Christian Radio
Premier Media Group, PO Box 13000, London, SW1P 4NP
- 020 7316 1300
- 020 7316 1371
- studio@premier.org.uk
- www.premier.org.uk

Contact Chief Executive, Peter Kerridge; Programme Controller, Charmaine Noble-McLean; News Editor, Victoria Lawrence
About A Christian station broadcasting to the London area, featuring music and speech in a Christian vein. The station is run by a team of volunteers. Contact eventsteam@premier.org.uk to find out more information.

Radio Kerry
Maine Street, Tralee, Co. Kerry, Republic of Ireland
- 00353 66 712 3666
- info@radiokerry.ie
- www.radiokerry.ie

About A station broadcasting throughout County Kerry. A mixture of discussion, features, news and music.

Radio XL
KMS House, Bradford Street, Birmingham, West Midlands, B12 0JD
- 0121 753 5353
- 0121 753 3111
- news@radioxl.net
- info@radioxl.net
- www.radioxl.net

Contact Managing Director, Arun Bajaj
About A West Midlands radio station aimed at the Asian community. The target audience is young

people aged 15 and over. Programmes are broadcast mainly in Hindi and English. Specialist programmes are in other languages such as Urdu, Gujarati, Punjabi and Bengali.

Real Radio Scotland
PO Box 101, Unit 1130, Parkway Court, Glasgow Business Park, Glasgow, G69 6GA
- 0141 781 1011
- 0141 781 1112
- www.realradiofm.com

About A station for Scotland, which broadcasts phone-ins, discussions, news, sport and music.

Real Radio Wales
1 Ty Nant Court, Morganstown, Cardiff, CF15 8YF
- 029 2031 5100
- 029 2031 5150
- www.realradiofm.com

Contact Managing Director, Billy Andersen; Programme Director, Jay Crawford
About A station for Wales, which broadcasts phone-ins, discussions, news, sport and music.

Real Radio Yorkshire
1 Sterling Court, Capitol Business Park, Tingley, Wakefield, WF3 1EL
- 0113 238 1114
- 0113 238 1191
- www.realradiofm.com

Contact Programme Director, Terry Underhill
About A station for Yorkshire, which broadcasts phone-ins, discussions, news, sport, and music.

Sabras Radio
Radio House, 63 Melton Road, Leicester, LE4 6PN
- 0116 261 0666
- 0116 266 7776
- studio@sabrasradio.com
- www.sabrasradio.com

Contact Managing Director, Don Kotak
About An Asian radio station broadcasting to Greater London, parts of the South and South East, and to the East Midlands. Programmes are a mixture of music, news and discussion.

Saga FM
3rd Floor Crown House, 123 Hagley Road, Birmingham, B16 8LD
- 0121 452 1057
- 0121 452 3222
- www.saga.co.uk

About A radio station broadcasting to the West Midlands and aimed exclusively at the over 50s.

Programmes are a mixture of music, news, features and talk shows. The station has many resident experts for a variety of topics.

Shannonside FM
MasterTech Business Park, Athlone Road, Co. Longford, Republic of Ireland
- 00353 43 47777
- 00353 43 49384
- info@shannonside.ie
- news@shannonside.ie
- www.shannonside.ie

Contact Head of Programmes, Jon Finnegan; Head of News, Ann Norris; Head of Sport, John Lynch
About A station broadcasting to Counties Longford, Roscommon, South Leitrim, Cavan and Monaghan. There is a strong bias towards speech based programming, with news, community events, and sport, although there is also some music programming.

Spectrum Radio
International Radio Centre, 4 Ingate Place, Battersea, London, SW8 3NS
- 020 7627 4433
- 020 7627 3409
- enquiries@spectrumradio.net
- www.spectrumradio.net

Contact General Manager, Paul Hogan
About A radio station aimed at London and the South East's ethnic population. It broadcasts a variety of programmes for the different nationalities living in the UK. Content includes music, news and features.

Spire FM
City Hall Studios, Malthouse Lane, Salisbury, SP2 7QQ
- 01722 416644
- 01722 416688
- hello@spirefm.co.uk
- www.spirefm.co.uk

Contact Station Manager, Karen Boseley; Programme Controller, Stuart McGinley
About A station for Salisbury and the surrounding areas in Wiltshire and parts of Hampshire. Broadcasts a mixture of music, news, and sport.

Sunrise Radio (Yorkshire)
Sunrise House, 55 Leeds Road, Little Germany, Bradford, BD1 5AF
- 01274 735043
- 01274 728534
- news@sunriseradio.fm
- info@sunriseradio.fm
- www.sunriseradio.fm

Contact Chief Executive, Usha Parmar; News Editor, Gail Papworth
About A radio station aimed at Yorkshire's Asian community. Broadcasts a mixture of music, news and information features.

Swansea Sound
Radio House, Victoria Road, Gowerton, Swansea, SA4 3AB
- 01792 511170
- 01792 511171
- newsroom@swanseasound.co.uk
- reception@swanseasound.co.uk
- www.swanseasound.co.uk

Contact Station Director, Carrie Mosley; Programme Director, Steve Barnes; Head of News, Emma Thomas; Sports Editor, Wyn Evans
About An AM frequency station for Swansea and South Wales, it broadcasts a mixture of music, news and regional programming.

Talk 107
9 South Gyle Crescent, Edinburgh Park, Edinburgh, EH12 9EB
- 0131 316 3107
- 0131 316 3136
- news@talk107.co.uk
- studio@talk107.co.uk
- www.talk107.co.uk

Contact Programme Director, Mike Graham; News Editor, Gwen Lawrie; Head of Sport, Mark Donaldson
About A station broadcasting to Edinburgh, Fife and the Lothians. Content includes local news, opinions and discussion, and sport.

The Wave
Victoria Road, Gowerton, Swansea, SA4 3AB
- 01792 511964
- 01792 511964
- news@thewave.co.uk
- reception@thewave.co.uk
- www.thewave.co.uk

Contact Station Director, Carrie Mosley; Programme Director, Steve Barnes; Head of News, Emma Thomas
About An FM sister station to Swansea Sound, broadcasting mainly popular music, as well as local news for Swansea and the surrounding areas.

Aardman Animations
Gas Ferry Road, Bristol, BS1 6UN
- 0117 984 8485
- 0117 984 8486

Contact Creative Director of Features, Sarah Smith
Established 1972
Insider Info Produces material for film and television. Specialists in animation, traditionally using models, but more recently using CGI. Well known characters include *Wallace and Gromit* and *Angry Kid*. Will not accept previously published material. Submissions will not be returned.
Submission Guidelines No unsolicited manuscripts.

Above the Title
Level 2, 10–11 St George's Mews, London, NW1 8XE
- 020 7916 1984
- 020 7722 5706
- mail@abovethetitle.com
- www.abovethetitle.com

Contact Head of Development, Jo Wheeler
Insider Info Productions include radio programming on music, the arts, comedy, drama, and factual subjects. BBC Radio 2 and 4 are frequent recipients of the shows. Submissions accompanied by SAE will be returned. Catalogue available online.
Submission Guidelines Send a one paragraph synopsis to Jo Wheeler. Email or postal submissions are accepted.
Tips Read the extensive back catalogue of productions on the website and note where each show was broadcast, for an idea of style and potential audience groups.

Absolutely Productions Ltd
Unit 19, 77 Beak Street, London, W1F 9DB
- 020 7644 5575
- www.absolutely.biz

Established 1988
Insider Info Produces programming for national television and radio stations, particularly comedy and drama. Recent productions include *Welcome to Strathmuir* for Channel 4 and *Baggage (Series 3)* for Radio 4. Catalogue available online.
Submission Guidelines No unsolicited manuscripts.

Abstract Images
117 Willoughby House, Barbican, London, EC2Y 8BL
- 020 7638 5123
- productions@abstract-images.co.uk

Insider Info A producer of factual and dramatic programmes for television. Includes some Christian programmes.
Submission Guidelines Contact the company by email for more information on submitting scripts. If in doubt, send a synopsis and your contact details.

Acacia Productions Ltd
80 Weston Park, London, N8 9TB
- 020 8341 9392
- 020 8341 4879
- em@acaciaproductions.co.uk
- projects@acaciaproductions.co.uk
- www.acaciaproductions.co.uk

Contact Managing Director, J. Edward Milner
Established 1984
Insider Info Produces material for television and video and DVD (non-broadcast). Produces documentaries and features, predominantly on environmental and third world issues, as well as current affairs in general. Broadcast outlets have included the BBC.
Submission Guidelines No unsolicited manuscripts.

ACP Television & Crosshands Ltd
Crosshands, Coreley, Ludlow, Shropshire, SY8 3AR
- 01584 890893
- 01584 890893
- webmaster@acptv.com
- www.acptv.com

Contact Richard Uridge
Insider Info A producer of television and radio documentaries. Work has previously been broadcast on satellite channels such as UKTV Style.
Tips Contact Richard Uridge for more information on the company. Does not produce drama or other fictional programming.

Acrobat Television
107 Wellington Road North, Stockport, Cheshire, SK4 2LP
- 0161 477 9090
- 0161 477 9191
- info@acrobat-tv.co.uk
- www.acrobat-tv.co.uk

Established 1986
Insider Info Provides production services both for broadcast television and corporate videos.

Specialises in sports and action filming. Also draws from an extensive footage library.
Submission Guidelines No unsolicited manuscripts.

Actaeon Films
50 Gracefield Gardens, London, SW16 2ST
- 020 8769 3339
- 0870 134 7980
- info@actaeonfilms.com
- www.actaeonfilms.com
Contact Founder, Daniel Cormack
Established 2004
Insider Info Produces feature length and short films, typically with commercial elements that are given a new, innovative twist. A recent example of a feature film is the award winning *A Fitting Tribute*. Submissions accompanied by SAE will be returned. Aims to respond to submissions within one month.
Tips A young company who are interested in new writing, but will not necessarily be able to respond in full to all unsolicited manuscripts.

All3Media
Berkshire House, 168–173 High Holborn, London, WC1V 7AA
- 020 7845 4377
- 020 7845 4399
- information@all3media.com
- www.all3media.com
Contact Chief Executive, Steve Morrison; Creative Director, David Liddiment
Established 2003
Insider Info Produces material for film and television. All3Media group encompasses a range of production companies: ARG; Bentley Productions; Cactus TV; Company Pictures; IdtV Productions; Lion Television; Lime Pictures; North One Television; and Pacific Pictures. Among them they produce high-profile programming nationally and internationally.
Tips All3Media's output is varied depending on the subsidiary company involved. Visit each company's section of the website for further details, but be aware that much of the programming is commercially very high-profile. Examples include *Midsomer Murders* and *Richard & Judy*.

All Out Films
50 Copperas Street, Manchester, M4 1HS
- 0161 834 9955
- 0161 834 6978
- mail@allout.co.uk
- www.allout.co.uk
Contact Founders: David Cook, David Prosser and Nigel Wrench

Insider Info Produces news, factual features, documentaries and current affairs programming, predominantly for BBC radio. Catalogue available online.
Submission Guidelines Accepts query with synopsis.
Tips No unsolicited full manuscripts. Bear in mind that productions are usually commissioned for broadcast on BBC radio stations and their various audiences.

Angel Eye Media
9 Rudolf Place, Miles Street, London, SW8 1RP
- 0845 230 0062
- 0845 230 9562
- ideas@angeleye.co.uk
- www.angeleye.co.uk
Contact Company Director, James Harding; Creative Director, John O'Callaghan
Insider Info Produces material for film, television, radio, the web and new media. Produces programming for various media platforms, including comedy, entertainment, documentary, education and drama. Clients have included the BBC, Channel 4, Channel Five and numerous corporate clients. Submissions will not be returned.
Submission Guidelines Email submissions only. Send proposal as an attachment.
Tips Read the 'Ideas' page on the website carefully before submitting treatments.

Anglo-Fortunato Films Ltd
170 Popes Lane, London, W5 4NJ
- 020 8932 7676
- 020 8932 7491
Contact Luciano Celentino
Insider Info Produces material for film and television. The genres worked with tend to be dramas, both action thriller and comedy.
Submission Guidelines No unsolicited manuscripts.

Arlington Productions Ltd
Cippenham Court, Cippenham Lane, Cippenham, Slough, SL1 5AU
- 01753 516767
- 01753 691785
Insider Info Produces dramas and documentaries for television audiences.
Submission Guidelines Agented submissions only.
Tips Arlington do commission new writers, but will not accept unsolicited scripts. Approach agents in the first instance.

Art & Adventure Ltd

5 Darling Road, London, SE4 1QY

☎ 020 8692 0145

📠 020 8692 0145

✉ roger@artandadventure.org

🌐 www.artandadventure.org

Contact Creative Directors: Roger Elsgood and Willi Richards

Established 1996

Insider Info Produces material for film, radio and the web. Credits include *The Two Gentlemen of Valasna*, *The Mrichhakatikaa*, *Occasional Offices* and *Berlin Project* for BBC Radio 3, and *King Trash*, *The Last Time I Saw Richard* and *Beau Geste* for BBC Radio 4. Works with about 30 writers per year. Purchases all rights on accepted material. Will accept previously published material. Aims to respond to queries within two weeks and submissions within one month. Payment is via outright purchase. Catalogue available by email.

Submission Guidelines Produces films, radio and audio. Accepts query with synopsis and CV.

Tips Needs good, relevant, drama scripts for BBC Radio 4. Writers should know BBC Audio commissioning requirements, published at www.bbc.co.uk/commissioning.

Art & Training Films Ltd

PO Box 3459, Stratford upon Avon, CV37 6ZJ

✉ andrew.haynes@atf.org.uk

🌐 www.atf.org.uk

Contact Andrew Haynes

Insider Info Produces material for film and television and video content for theatre productions. Previous output has included history documentaries, corporate training videos and short films. Projects in development include a sitcom and a dramatic adaption of a novel.

Submission Guidelines Agented submissions only.

Ashford Entertainment

20 The Chase, Coulsdon, Surrey, CR5 2EG

☎ 0844 357 6393

📠 0870 116 4142

✉ info@ashford-entertainment.co.uk

🌐 www.ashford-entertainment.co.uk

Contact Founder, Frazer Ashford

Established 1996

Insider Info Produces dramatic film and television programming as well as documentaries. Most output has been broadcast on satellite channels and some on terrestrial television. Recent examples include *Serial Killers* for The Crime Network Channel, and *Hands Up*, with Gangway Films. Submissions accompanied by SAE will be returned. Aims to respond to queries within four weeks.

Submission Guidelines Accepts query with synopsis.

Tips Submit succinct documentary treatments by post.

Athena Media

The Digital Depot, The Digital Hub, Thomas Street, Dublin 8, Republic of Ireland

☎ 00353 1 488 5850

✉ info@athenamedia.ie

🌐 www.athenamedia.ie

Contact Helen Shaw

Established 2003

Insider Info Produces radio and television documentaries, as well as multimedia projects for various broadcast and corporate clients such as *The Irish Times* and SABC (South African Broadcast Commission).

Tips Does not produce drama. A major broadcast client is BBC Radio 4. Non-broadcast clients are very varied and range from publishers, to newspapers, to health agencies. Recent projects include an audio visual awareness video for the Crisis Pregnancy Agency. The aim of the company is to add value to other businesses or organisations through digital products.

At IT Productions Ltd

68–70 Salisbury Road, Queens Park, London, NW6 6NU

☎ 020 7644 0000

📠 020 7644 0001

✉ reception@eyeworks.tv

🌐 www.eyeworks.tv

Contact Managing Director, Martin Cunning; Managing Director, Chris Fouracre; Executive Consultant, Tamsin Summers; Executive Producer, Richard Cook

Established 1997

Insider Info Producers of television programmes for Channel 4, Channel Five, BBC, ITV, Sky One and the US channels TLC and The Discovery Channel. Genres include documentaries, travel, pop music, films, quiz shows and children's television. An example of current output is the teenage brand, *T4*, currently showing on Channel 4.

Tips For a feel of the style and production values of the company, view the digital showreel available on the website. At IT is now part of Eyeworks UK.

Attaboy TV

Unit 1, 23a Blue Anchor Lane, London, SE16 3UL

☎ 020 7740 3000

📠 020 7740 3008

✉ business@attaboytv.com

🌐 www.attaboytv.com

Contact Directors, Michael Wood and Daniel Allum
Established 1997
Insider Info Produces factual entertainment series'
and documentaries, as well as interactive
programmes and commercials. Credits include *Road
Movies* for Channel 4, and *Life at the Sport* for Five.
Submission Guidelines Individuals and companies
are welcome to make contact with
programme ideas.
Tips Ideas should be able to entertain a large
television audience on terrestrial or satellite
television, and must be factual. No drama.

Available Light Productions Ltd
**The Victorian Arcade, 3a Boyce's Avenue,
Clifton, Bristol, BS8 4AA**
- 0117 908 4433
- info@availablelight.tv
- www.availablelight.tv

Contact Managing Director/Producer, David Parker;
Co-Director, Wendy MacLean; Production Manager,
Sue Bennett
Established 1994
Insider Info Available Light Productions produces
documentary and factual programmes for network
television, as well as interactive media including
web, CD and DVD projects. Clients include the BBC,
Channel 4, Grid Club, ITV and Teachers TV. Credits
include *Johnny's New Kingdom* for BBC 2, and *Skills
For Life* for Teachers TV.
Tips Aside from factual documentaries, Available
Light also specialises in producing Flash based e-
learning websites for major broadcasters, including
Teachers TV. *Brunel's Britain*, a Teachers TV/Grid Club
project, was nominated for a Children's BAFTA in the
interactive category at the 2006 awards.

Baby Cow Productions Ltd
77 Oxford Street, London, W1D 2ES
- 020 7399 1267
- 020 7399 126
- john@babycow.co.uk

Established 1999
Insider Info Founded by Steve Coogan and Henry
Normal. Produces comedy programming for a range
of UK and international broadcasters, including the
BBC and ITV. The company have recently added
Baby Cow Radio, Films and Animations to their
profile, producing comedy output in these genres. A
recent example of a Baby Cow Film production is *A
Cock & Bull Story*, starring Steve Coogan. Submissions
accompanied by SAE will be returned. Catalogue
available online.
Submission Guidelines Accepts query with
synopsis. Include a ten page sample and a DVD or
VHS sample if possible. Send by post or email.

Tips Work should be cutting edge comedy with
widespread broadcast potential. A dedicated team
will look at all unsolicited manuscripts, but there
may be delays in response due to the volume of
material received.

Beckmann International
**Milntown Lodge, Lezayre Road, Ramsey, Isle of
Man, IM8 2TG**
- 01624 816585
- 01624 816589
- sales@beckmanngroup.co.uk
- www.beckmanngroup.co.uk

Contact Managing Director, Jo White
Established 1983
Insider Info Distributors of factual documentary
programming for a variety of television broadcasters
and DVD/VHS output. Catalogue available online.
Tips For producers of documentaries and factual
programming, fill in the online submissions form to
apply for distribution through Beckmann.

Big Heart Media
Flat 4, 6 Pear Tree Court, London, EC1R 0DW
- 020 7608 0352
- 020 7250 1138
- info@bigheartmedia.com
- www.bigheartmedia.com

Contact Director/Producer, Colin Izod
Established 1998
Insider Info Producers of educational, factual and
dramatic programming for television, radio and the
web. Clients include the BBC, Pearson Education,
Teacher's TV and Channel 4.
Submission Guidelines Accepts query with
synopsis by email only. No unsolicited manuscripts.
Tips Although the full catalogue is not available on
the website, samples and clips of work across all
media platforms give a sense of the style and
content of the company's productions.

Big Umbrella Media Ltd
**The Oracle Building, Blythe Valley Park, Solihull,
B90 8AD**
- 0121 506 9620
- 0121 506 9621
- production@bigumbrellamedia.co.uk
- www.bigumbrellamedia.co.uk

Contact Managing Director, Martin Head; Head of
Development, Claire Campbell; Editor/Graphic
Designer, Bim Ajadi
Established 1998
Insider Info Develops and produces formats, one-
offs and series for UK and international television
broadcasters. Focuses on factual entertainment and
documentaries.

Submission Guidelines Agented submissions welcome, as are collaborative ideas from other production companies.

Tips Check the broadcast news section of the website for upcoming projects and chances to become involved in programmes.

Blue-zoo Productions

Chesterfield House, 385 Euston Road, London, NW1 3AU

- 020 7434 4111
- info@blue-zoo.co.uk
- www.blue-zoo.co.uk

Contact Executive Producer, Daniel Isman
Established 2000
Insider Info Blue-zoo produces computer animations for television. Clients include the BBC and Nickelodeon. Also produces original material. Credits include *Blue Cow* and *Those Scurvy Rascals*, which received a BAFTA nomination for Best Children's Animation, and also received British Animation Awards for Best Children's Series, and the Children's Choice Award.

Bona Broadcasting Ltd

Second Floor, 9 Gayfield Square, Edinburgh, EH1 3NT

- 0131 558 1696
- 0131 558 1694
- enquiries@bonabroadcasting.com
- www.bonabroadcasting.com

Contact Director, Turan Ali
Insider Info Produces material for film, television and Radio. Producers of drama, comedy, magazine shows and documentary output for clients such as the BBC and Scottish Screen.
Submission Guidelines Send a one paragraph synopsis to: ideas@bonabroadcasting.com.
Tips No unsolicited manuscripts. Individuals whose ideas are commissioned and who have the appropriate professional experience will be guaranteed a role on the production team.

Brook Lapping Productions

6 Anglers Lane, London, NW5 3DG

- 020 7428 3100
- 020 7284 0626
- info@brooklapping.com
- www.brooklapping.com

Contact Lesley Calmels
Established 1982
Insider Info A producer of current affairs television and radio programming for broadcasters such as BBC, ITV, Channel 4 and international broadcasters.
Tips The website section on past productions gives a flavour of the high-profile nature of previous programmes. These include *The Rise and Fall of Tony Blair* for Channel 4, and *Ocean Of Fear* for the Discovery Channel (US).

Cactus TV

373 Kennington Road, London, SE11 4PS

- 020 7091 4900
- 020 7091 4901
- touch.us@cactustv.co.uk
- www.cactustv.co.uk

Contact Managing Directors: Amanda Ross and Simon Ross; Head of Entertainment, Sinead Oldnall
Established 1994
Insider Info Produces popular light entertainment programmes for television. Catalogue available online.
Tips Check the online catalogue for the nature of programmes produced. Recent examples include *Richard & Judy* for Channel 4, and *Saturday Kitchen* for the BBC. Does not make drama or other fictional television.

Caledonia TV

147 Bath Street, Glasgow, G2 4SQ

- 0141 564 9100
- 0141 564 9200
- info@caledonia.tv
- lcumming@caledonia.tv
- www.caledonia.tv

Contact Creative Director, Les Wilson
Established 1992
Insider Info Producers of documentaries, factual entertainment formats, and children's programmes for television. Subjects include history, science, current affairs, arts and education.
Submission Guidelines Proposals are welcome from experienced producers, directors, or researchers of factual programming. No drama scripts.

Calon Ltd

3 Mount Stuart Square, Butetown, Cardiff, CF10 5EE

- 029 2048 8400
- 029 2048 5962
- enquiries@calon.tv
- www.calon.tv

Contact Head of Development, Andrew Offiler
Insider Info Produces material for television – live action and animated drama and entertainment for children.
Submission Guidelines Accepts query with synopsis. No unsolicited manuscripts.
Tips Formerly Siriol Productions, the focus has traditionally been on animated series' such as *SuperTed* and *Under Milk Wood*. Calon is now moving

into live action programming. View clips in the production section of their website for programmes in development.

Campbell Davison Media
110 Gloucester Avenue, London, NW1 8HX
- 020 7209 3740
- 020 7483 4541
- clare@campbelldavison.com
- www.campbelldavison.com

Contact Clare Davison
Established 1991
Insider Info Produces news, features, live sport, documentaries and entertainment programming for the BBC, and commercial radio and television. Credits include *606* and *The Rumour Mill* for BBC Radio Five Live. Catalogue available.
Tips All programming is factually based. Radio productions are much more prevalent than television programmes. Much of the live radio has a sports topic, but the documentaries for BBC Radio 4 are more varied in terms of themes. For BBC commissioning information (which Campbell Davison will use themselves), see www.bbc.co.uk/commissioning.

Carbon Princess
First Floor, Trowbray House, The Leathermarket, 108 Weston Street, London, SE1 3ER
- 020 7378 7217
- 020 7407 0260
- the.mikes@carbonhq.com
- www.carbonhq.com

Contact Director, Mike Christie; Executive Producer, Mike Smith
Established 2004
Insider Info Works with Princess TV. Produces television documentaries and material for film. Carbon Princess is the exclusive UK production partner of Lonely Planet Television.
Tips For editorial queries, contact either of the 'Mikes' by email. Be aware that the main broadcast route so far for Carbon Princess has been Channel 4, typically an 8pm weekday slot.

Carnival Films & Television Ltd
47 Marylebone Lane, London, W1U 2NT
- 020 7317 1370
- 020 7317 1380
- info@carnivalfilms.co.uk
- www.carnivalfilms.co.uk

Contact Managing Director, Gareth Neame; Creative Director, Sally Woodward Gentle
Established 1978
Insider Info Producers of popular drama for theatre, television and film. Productions are commissioned by all major terrestrial UK networks and feature films have been nominated for awards such as Oscars and BAFTAs. Recent output includes *Hotel Babylon* for BBC One and *As If* for Channel 4.
Submission Guidelines No unsolicited manuscripts.
Tips Although Carnival are committed to new writing, connections are made through known drama commissioners.

Cartwn Cymru
12 Queens Road, Mumbles, Swansea, SA3 4AN
- 01792 363600 / 07771 640400
- production@cartwn-cymru.com

Contact Producer, Naomi Jones
Insider Info An animation production company producing both drawn and 3D animation for film and television.
Tips Contact Naomi Jones for more information on this company. Previous productions include feature films such as *The Miracle Maker* (written by Murray Watts) and *Otherworld* (written by Martin Lamb and Penelope Middelboe)

Celador Films
39 Long Acre, London, WC2E 9LG
- 020 7845 6800
- 020 7845 6980
- www.celadorfilms.com

Contact Head of Development, Ivana MacKinnon
Insider Info Produces commercial feature films. Previous productions include *The Descent* and *Dirty Pretty Things*.
Submission Guidelines Agented submissions only.
Tips Films produced by Celador must be commercially viable and commissions are usually made through script agents, or collaborations with other production companies.

Celador Productions
39 Long Acre, London, WC2E 9LG
- 020 7240 8101
- 020 7845 6976
- info@celador.co.uk
- www.celadorproductions.com

Contact Managing Director, Danielle Lux; Director of Production, Heather Hampson; Head of Entertainment, Ruth Wrigley; Head of Factual Entertainment, Murray Boland; Head of Radio, Liz Anstee
Established 1983
Insider Info Produces quizzes, comedy, drama, factual entertainment and daytime game shows for television, as well as radio. Output includes *Who Wants to be a Millionaire* for ITV1, and *You Are What You Eat: Gillian Moves In*, for Channel 4. Commissions

for BBC Radio 2 and 4. Submissions accompanied by SAE will be returned.
Submission Guidelines Accepts unsolicited submissions for radio programmes only. Post to Liz Anstee, Head of Radio.
Tips No unsolicited manuscripts for television formats.

Celtic Films Entertainment Ltd
Lodge House, 69 Beaufort Street, London, SW3 5AH
- 020 7351 0909
- 020 7351 4139
- info@celticfilms.co.uk
- www.celticfilms.co.uk

Contact Producer/Chairman, Muir Sutherland
Established 1986
Insider Info Specialist producers of television drama and feature films. Well known productions include *Sharpe* for the BBC, and *Hornblower* for ITV. Submissions accompanied by SAE will be returned.
Submission Guidelines Read submissions guidelines and agreement documents, downloadable from the website, before submitting.
Tips Unsolicited material is welcome but bear in mind that the company produces mainly one-off drama features or drama series. For series, prepare a pilot episode.

Chameleon TV
Great Minster House, Lister Hill, Horsforth, Leeds, LS18 5DL
- 0113 205 0040
- 0113 281 9454
- allen@chameleontv.com
- www.chameleontv.com

Contact Managing Director, Allen Jewhurst; Head of Production, Richard Everiss; Development Producer, Alice Welch
Insider Info Produces television documentaries, current affairs, drama and factual programmes for broadcasters such as the BBC and Channel 4. Previous subject matters have included docusoaps, religion, arts, and wildlife.
Submission Guidelines Agented submissions only.

Charles Dunstan Communications
42 Wolseley Gardens, London, W4 3LS
- 020 8994 2328
- 020 8994 2328

Insider Info Produces material for film, television and corporate video - mainly factual material for documentaries.
Submission Guidelines No unsolicited manuscripts.

Children's Film & Television Foundation
Ealing Studios, Ealing Green, London, W5 5EP
- 07887 573479
- info@cftf.org.uk
- www.cftf.org.uk

Contact Chief Executive, Anna Home
Established 1951
Insider Info Has produced films and television content for children such as classic shows *The Borrowers* and *The Queen's Nose*, both for the BBC. The production archive is administered by Granada International.
Tips The most recent source of funding has stopped, therefore the Foundation are no longer undertaking new projects.

Childsplay Productions
8 Lonsdale Road, London, NW6 6RD
- 0831 600400

Contact Producer, Peter Tabern
Insider Info Childsplay Productions produces children's and family drama programmes for television. Clients include the BBC. Credits include *Feather Boy* and *Johnny and the Bomb*.
Tips Childsplay Productions specialises in high-profile adaptations of popular children's books, such as *Stig of the Dump* and Terry Pratchett's *Johnny and the Bomb*. These are often produced for the BBC, sometimes under the name Childsplay Television.

Cinécosse
Lethenty Mill, Inverurie, AB51 0HQ
- 01467 670707
- 01467 670071
- info@cinecosse.co.uk
- admin@cinecosse.co.uk
- www.cinecosse.co.uk

Established 1978
Insider Info Produces corporate videos, educational training packs and some documentaries and features for television broadcast. Productions include work for BBC Scotland's Gaelic language programme *Eorpa*, and BBC One's *Tomorrow's World* and *Watchdog*. Also undertakes graphic design projects, media training and a range of other services.
Submission Guidelines No unsolicited manuscripts.

Classic Arts
The Old Rectory, Hampton Lovett, Droitwich, Worcestershire, WR9 0LY
- 01299 851563
- 01299 851728

- wendy@classicarts.co.uk
- www.classicarts.co.uk

Contact Executive Director, Wendy Thompson
Established 1993
Insider Info Producers of music and arts programmes, mainly for BBC Radio. Content is live music, as well as documentary style programmes. They also offer podcasting services.
Tips Specialists in classical music. Major broadcast routes are BBC Radio 3 for music, and BBC Radio 4 for speech based programming. Their commissioning needs can be found at www.bbc.co.uk/commissioning.

Collingwood O'Hare Entertainment
10–14 Crown Street, London, W3 8SB
- 020 8993 3666
- 020 8993 9595
- info@crownstreet.co.uk
- www.collingwoodohare.com

Contact Managing Director & Producer, Christopher O'Hare; Writer & Director, Tony Collingwood; Head of Development, Helen Stroud
Established 1988
Insider Info A leading animation studio for children's television. Productions include *The Magic Key* for BBC, and *Animal Stories* for ITV.
Submission Guidelines No unsolicited submissions.
Tips Interested in new writing, although it is normally sourced through industry contacts or agents.

The Comedy Unit
6th Floor, 53 Bothwell Street, Glasgow, G2 6TS
- 0141 305 6400
- 0141 305 6600
- info@comedyunit.co.uk
- www.comedyunit.co.uk

Contact Managing Directors: April Chamberlain and Colin Gilbert
Established 1996
Insider Info The Comedy Unit produces comedy programmes for network and satellite television, radio and websites. Credits include *Still Game* and *The Karen Dunbar Show*. The company works with 20 to 50 writers and performers per year and will accept previously published material. Submissions accompanied by SAE will be returned, although they will not send a catalogue to writers on request. The company aim to report on queries within two days, and submissions within 25 days. Payment is in accordance with industry standards.
Submission Guidelines Submit completed script. Email or postal submissions are welcome (email:

scripts@comedyunit.co.uk). Scripts themselves should be emailed as an attachment.

Company Pictures
Suffolk House, 1–8 Whitfield Place, London, W1T 5JU
- 020 7380 3900
- 020 7380 1166
- enquiries@companypictures.co.uk
- www.companypictures.co.uk

Contact Managing Directors, George Faber and Charles Pattinson; Executive Producer, Suzan Harrison
Established 1998
Insider Info Produces television drama series' and features, as well as some feature films. Productions include Jimmy McGovern's *The Palace* for BBC One, and *Wild at Heart: Series 3* for ITV1.
Submission Guidelines Agented submissions only.
Tips For those writers that do have agents, be aware that the television drama produced by Company Pictures is often for prime time terrestrial television and must have widespread appeal. The feature films are relatively less high profile.

Cosgrove Hall Films
8 Albany Road, Chorlton cum Hardy, Manchester, M21 0AW
- 0161 882 2500
- 0161 882 2555
- animation@cosgrovehall.com
- www.cosgrovehall.com

Parent Company Granada Media
Contact Managing Director, Anthony Utley
Established 1976
Insider Info Specialists in animation of all kinds for film and television. Develops mainly children's programmes, although animation for adults is also produced.
Tips Cosgrove Hall has produced both series' – such as *Roary the Racing Car* for CBeebies – and feature films – such as *Roald Dahl's BFG*. Co-productions are becoming increasingly popular, as are series that have an international audience without alienating British audiences.

The Creative Partnership
13 Bateman Street, London, W1D 3AF
- 020 7439 7762
- 020 7437 1467
- nic.ost@thecreativepartnership.co.uk
- www.thecreativepartnership.co.uk

Contact Audio Visual/Home Entertainment, Nic Ost; Audio Visual/Theatrical, Sarah Fforde; Print, Mia Matson

Insider Info The Creative Partnership are a film marketing agency who write campaigns to go alongside both feature films and television projects.
Tips Experienced writers interested in writing marketing copy and campaigns for films and television should submit their CVs.

CSA Word
6a Archway Mews, London, SW15 2PE
- 020 8871 0220
- 020 8877 0712
- info@csaword.co.uk
- www.csaword.co.uk

Contact Managing Director, Clive Stanhope; Audio Commissioning Editor, Victoria Williams
Established 1989
Insider Info Produces radio drama series for the BBC, as well as making audio books.
Submission Guidelines Post or email submissions.
Tips The audiences for radio dramas are exclusively BBC Radio 2 and 4, therefore it is a good idea to research these stations thoroughly.

Cutting Edge Productions
27 Erpingham Road, London, SW15 1BE
- 020 8780 1476
- 020 8780 0102
- juliannorridge@btconnect.com

Contact Director, Julian Norridge
Insider Info Produces television documentaries as well as some corporate videos.
Submission Guidelines No unsolicited submissions.
Tips The company has no official website. Contact Julian Norridge for the latest information. Documentary ideas are usually commissioned directly through existing contacts.

Darrall MacQueen
17 Park Street, Borough Market, London, SE1 9AB
- 020 7407 2322
- info@darrallmacqueen.com
- www.darrallmacqueen.com

Contact Development, Maddy Darrall
Insider Info Produces material for television, the web, mobiles and interactive media. A large independent producer of children's television. Third largest supplier of programmes for the BBC.
Tips Produces both presenter led live shows, as well as original children's drama series for CBBC. For the BBC children's commissioning needs, visit www.bbc.co.uk/commissioning.

Diverse Production
6–12 Gorleston Street, London, W14 8XS
- 020 7603 4567
- 020 7603 2148
- www.diverse.tv

Contact Creative Director, Roy Ackerman
Insider Info Produces factual television and drama documentary for major broadcasters. Much of the output is for prime time slots in terrestrial television channels. Subject matters include religion, the arts, current affairs and investigative journalism. Previous productions include *Codex: Series 2* for Channel 4, and *Badger or Bust?* for Sky One. Catalogue available online.
Submission Guidelines Strictly no unsolicited manuscripts.

DMS Films Ltd
89 Sevington Road, London, NW4 3RU
- 020 8203 5540
- 0870 762 5671
- danny@dmsfilms.co.uk
- www.dmsfilms.co.uk

Contact Daniel San
Insider Info Produces feature films, shorts, retail video films and television content, including documentaries. A recent project is the British teenage comedy *Popcorn*.
Submission Guidelines Post or email a short synopsis only to begin with.
Tips No unsolicited manuscripts. Read the 'credits' section of the website to view the full breadth of projects undertaken by DMS films.

DoubleBand Films
3 Crescent Gardens, Belfast, Northern Ireland, BT7 1NS
- 028 90 24 3331
- 028 90 23 6980
- mhewitt@doublebandfilms.com
- www.doublebandfilms.com

Contact Directors: Michael Hewitt and Dermot Lavery
Established 1985
Insider Info A producer of documentaries, mainly on sports, medical and social topics. Also produces occasional drama features. Credits include *George Best's Body* for Channel 4, and *Unfinished Business* for the BBC.
Tips The company's back catalogue is available online, which shows the types of documentaries previously made. Their three major clients are the BBC, Channel 4 and RTE.

Ecosse Films

Brigade House, 8 Parsons Green, London, SW6 4TN

- 020 7371 0290
- 020 7736 3436
- info@ecossefilms.com
- www.ecossefilms.com

Contact Managing Director & Executive Producer, Douglas Rae; Company Director & Executive Producer, Robert Bernstein

Insider Info Produces television dramas and feature films. Recent productions include the feature film *Becoming Jane*, written by Kevin Hood and Sarah Williams, and *My Boy Jack* for ITV1. Catalogue available online.

Tips Agented submissions only, no unsolicited manuscripts.

The Elstree Company

Room 960, Shepperton Studios, Studios Road, Shepperton, TW17 0QD

- 01932 592680
- 01932 592682
- enquiries@elsprod.com
- www.elsprod.com

Contact Producer, Greg Smith

Insider Info The Elstree Company produces entertainment, drama and factual programming for television, as well as theatre productions. Catalogue available online.

Tips Clients tend to include many satellite channels such as TNT and Hallmark, as well as terrestrial television. Formats include full length television films, documentaries, sit-coms and dramatic adaptions of well known novels.

Endemol UK

Shepherd's Studios – Central, Charecroft Way, Shepherds Bush, London, W14 0EE

- 0870 333 1700
- 0870 333 1800
- info@endemoluk.com
- www.endemoluk.com

Contact Creative Director, Richard Osman

Insider Info Produces material for television and online, and also produces digital content. A leading producer of factual and entertainment formats for television including *Big Brother* for Channel 4, and *Restoration Village* for BBC 2. Endemol UK companies include Brighter Pictures, Cheetah Television, Endemol Gaming, Endemol Mobile, Hawkshead, Initial, Showrunner, Victoria Real, Zeppotron.

Tips Endemol's productions are largely very high profile and they are unlikely to commission unsolicited manuscripts. They do not tend to produce straight drama, although the Endemol

company Zeppotron does produce comedy programming.

Entertainment Rights

Colet Court, 100 Hammersmith Road, London, W6 7JP

- 020 8762 6200
- 020 8762 6299
- info@entertainmentrights.com
- www.entertainmentrights.com

Contact CEO, Michael Heap; Head of Creative Services, Sarah Slatter; Producer, Annika Bluhm

Established 1999

Insider Info Entertainment Rights produces animated and live-action children's and family television. Clients include the BBC, Cartoon Network, Hasbro, Mattel, Nickelodeon and Scholastic. Credits include *3-2-1 Penguins!*, *Clifford the Big Red Dog*, and *The Tweenies*.

Tips Entertainment Rights is one of the UK's leading specialist media companies. They own the rights to approximately 2,000 hours of programming, including characters such as *He-Man*, *Postman Pat* and *Rupert the Bear*. The company mainly focuses on purchasing rights to existing characters or shows, and unsolicited material is not likely to be successful.

Fairline Productions

Kirk Burn Lodge, South Lanarkshire, Biggar Road, Symington Road, M12 6FT

- 0141 331 0077
- 0141 331 0066
- fairlineteam@aol.com

Insider Info A producer of corporate and broadcast television. An extended showreel of Fairline Productions' work can be ordered from the website.

Submission Guidelines No unsolicited manuscripts.

Farnham Film Company

34 Burnt Hill Road, Lower Bourne, Farnham, GU10 3LZ

- 01252 710313
- 01252 725855
- info@farnfilm.com
- www.farnfilm.com

Contact Company Directors: Ian Lewis and Melloney Roffe

Established 1985

Insider Info Producers of television programmes and occasional low budget feature films. Credits include the feature film *Children of the Lake* and *Mona the Vampire*, an animated children's series. Submissions accompanied by SAE will be returned.

Submission Guidelines No longer accepting unsolicited submissions. Query by post or email with outline/synopsis first. Will look at intelligent, low-budget feature films with international legs. No 'Golden Geezers'.

Tips The company exists primarily to produce its own projects, but nobody wants to miss the next 'Big Thing'. No longer looking at television ideas. No unpublished or self-published novels, handwritten scripts, or short films.

Feelgood Fiction Ltd
49 Goldhawk Road, London, W12 8QP
- 020 8746 2535
- 020 8740 6177
- feelgood@feelgoodfiction.co.uk
- www.feelgoodfiction.co.uk

Contact Managing Directors: Philip Clarke and Lawrence Bowen
Established 1996
Insider Info Producers of film and television comedy and drama. Credits include *Suburban Shootout: Series 2* for Five, and *The Nathan Caton Show* for Paramount Comedy.
Tips Feelgood Fiction also has a feature film arm, Feelgood Films, which has produced the film *Miranda*. The company as a whole are committed to developing new writers and many of their projects – although high profile – are the first credits of the writers. A list of the new writers they are currently working with is published on their website.

Festival Productions
PO Box 70, Brighton, BN1 1YJ
- 01273 669595
- 01273 669596
- info@festivalradio.com
- www.festivalradio.com

Contact Director, Steve Strak
Established 1989
Insider Info Produces drama features and series, as well as documentaries, mainly for BBC Radio. Also creates music based programming for commercial radio stations.
Tips The writing opportunities are likely to come in the dramas and documentaries which are almost entirely made for BBC Radio 3 and 4. For their programme needs see www.bbc.co.uk/commissioning.

Film & General Productions Ltd
4 Bradbrook House, Studio Place, London, SW1X 8EL
- 020 7235 4495
- 020 7245 9853
- cparsons@filmgen.co.uk

Contact Producer, Clive Parsons
Established 1971

Insider Info Produces film and television drama for general audiences and children. Credits include *The Queen's Nose* for the BBC and the feature film, *Tea with Mussolini*. Works with three scripts and writers per year and purchases film and television rights on accepted material. Will accept previously published material and submissions accompanied by SAE. Aims to respond to queries within three days and submissions within two weeks. Writers will be paid for their work in accordance with industry standards. Will not send catalogues.
Submission Guidelines Accepts query with synopsis.
Tips Do not send full scripts without querying first.

The First Film Company Ltd
3 Bourlet Close, London, W1W 7BQ
- 020 7436 9490
- 020 7637 1290
- info@firstfilmcompany.com
- www.firstfilmcompany.com

Contact Producers: Robert Randall-Cutler and Robert Cheeck
Established 1984
Insider Info The First Film Company produces UK feature films for cinema and television.
Submission Guidelines Accepts agented submissions only.

First Writes Radio
Lime Kiln Cottage, High Starlings, Banham, Norwich, NR16 2BS
- 01953 888525
- 01953 888974
- info@firstwrites.co.uk
- www.first-writes.co.uk

Contact Executive Producer, Richard Blake
Established 1995
Insider Info First Writes are a specialist radio drama producer for BBC Radio 2 and 4. Credits include *The Ghost of Thomas Kempe*, and *Walking to Africa*.
Tips First Writes are unlikely to be able to develop first time writers. Productions are generally made with particular attention paid to careful casting, and highlighting the atmospheric nature of the piece. Audiences are that of BBC Radio 2 and 4.

Flashback Television Ltd
9–11 Bowling Green Lane, London, EC1R 0BG
- 020 7490 8996
- 020 7490 5610
- mailbox@flashbacktv.co.uk
- www.flashbacktelevision.com

Contact Creative Director, David Edgar
Established 1982

Insider Info Producers of factual entertainment television programmes for broadcasters both in the UK and internationally. Clients include the BBC, Channel 4 and The Discovery Network. They have recently branched out into drama for the first time.
Tips An extensive list of current and past productions is published on the website, and gives an idea of the scope of Flashback. Recent credits include *The Brink of Apocalypse* for The Discovery Channel/Channel 4, and *The Lost Evidence* for The History Channel.

Focus Films Ltd
The Rotunda Studio, Rear of 116–118 Finchley Road, London, NW3 5HT
- 020 7435 9004
- 020 7431 3562
- focus@focusfilms.co.uk
- www.focusfilms.co.uk
Contact Company Founder/ Director, Marsha Levin; Executive Producer/ CEO, David Pupkewitz; Producer/ Head of Development, Malcolm Kohll
Established 1982
Insider Info Focus Films is a feature film production company that also finances and develops films in collaboration with other production companies. Credits include *Heaven & Earth* and *Houseboat*.
Submission Guidelines No unsolicited manuscripts will be accepted. Agents of writers should email Malcolm Kohll at: malcolm@focusfilms.co.uk with script ideas.
Tips The company is in the process of setting up Chilla Productions, an imprint created to make low-budget (under $5 million) thriller films.

The Foundation TV Productions Ltd
The Maidstone Studios, Maidstone, Kent, ME14 5NZ
- 01622 691111
- 01622 684421
- www.foundationtv.co.uk
Insider Info Foundation TV Productions produces educational and animated television and website content. Clients include the BBC. Credits include *The Basil Brush Show*, *Brilliant Creatures* and *Tricky TV*.
Tips Focuses mainly on web-based content, including Flash animation.

Fox Television Studios UK
Lamb House, Church Street, London, Greater London, W4 2PD
- 020 8995 8255
- 020 8995 8456
- info@foxtvstudios.co.uk
- www.foxtvstudios.co.uk
Contact Office Manager, Caroline Christierson

Established 2001
Insider Info Fox Television Studios produce television programming for a wide, general audience (both terrestrial and satellite channels). Accepts previously published material, and submissions accompanied by SAE will be returned. Aims to report on queries and submissions within two weeks. Will not send a catalogue to writers on request. Writers are paid for their work in accordance with industry standards.
Submission Guidelines Accepts query with synopsis.
Tips Do not send entire scripts unless invited after querying.

FREE@LAST TV
2nd Floor, 47 Farringdon Road, London, EC1M 3JB
- 020 7242 4333
- 020 7242 7910
- info@freeatlasttv.co.uk
- www.freeatlasttv.co.uk
Established 2000
Insider Info Producers of mainly factual television programming, including music-based programmes, documentaries and reality formats. Recent credits include *The Punk Years* for Play UK, and *Spandau Ballet Live* for ITV1.
Submission Guidelines Accepts query with synopsis. Send ideas by email only.
Tips Much of the programming tends to focus on celebrity, music and light entertainment. Clients include ITV1, ITV3 and ITV4, Channel 4, Five, The Sci Fi Channel, UKTV Gold and Play UK.

FremantleMedia Ltd
1 Stephen Street, London, W1T 1AL
- 020 7691 6000
- 020 7691 6100
- www.fremantlemedia.com
Contact CEO, Tony Cohen
Established 1993
Insider Info Formerly Pearson Television, Fremantle are major producers of prime time television drama, serial drama, entertainment and factual entertainment programmes. Companies under the Fremantle umbrella include, UFA, Blu, teamWorx, talkbackThames, Grundy, Blue Circle and Crackerjack.
Tips Many productions have been big-budget, international successes, and include *X Factor* and *American Idol*. Dramas include *The Bill* and *Neighbours*. Shows generally have an international appeal and need to be commercially successful.

Fulcrum TV

3rd Floor, Bramah House, 65–71 Bermondsey Street, London, SE1 3XF

- ☎ 020 7939 3160
- 🖷 020 7403 2260
- ✉ team@fulcrumtv.com
- 🌐 www.fulcrumtv.com

Contact Head of Production, Sandra Leeming

Insider Info Produces factual television programming, including light entertainment, investigative journalism, and programmes to mark major events. Subjects include history, politics, archaeology, and memoirs. Credits include *Don't Worry* for UKTV History and *Revealed: When M&S Lost its Billions* for Channel Five.

Tips Fulcrum works in both live action and animation formats. Part of the company's ethos is to bring new ideas and talent to the screen, they are committed to finding new funding streams in order to do so.

Gaia Communications

20 Pevensey Road, Eastbourne, East Sussex, BN21 3HP

- ☎ 01323 727183
- 🖷 01323 734809
- ✉ production@gaiacommunications.co.uk
- 🌐 www.gaiacommunications.co.uk

Contact Directors, Robert Armstrong and Loni von Grüner

Insider Info Produces tourist and local heritage television programmes, as well as a range of videos and audio books on holistic subjects.

Submission Guidelines Produces videotapes, DVDs and audio books.

Tips Gaia are specialists on the South East counties. Previous projects have included writers' views and musings on their surroundings, in a narrated documentary format.

Ginger Productions

1st Floor, 3 Waterhouse Square, 138–142 Holborn, London, EC1N 2NY

- ☎ 020 7882 1020
- 🖷 020 7882 1040
- ✉ production@ginger.com
- 🌐 www.ginger.tv

Contact Executive Producer, Ed Stobart; Creative Director, Stephen Joel

Insider Info Produces factual entertainment and light entertainment television formats. Credits include *Jack Osbourne: Adrenaline Junkie 2*, and *Solve Your Murder*. Owned by SMG productions.

Tips Ginger's style tends to be light hearted, humorous and aimed at a fairly young teenage/ adult audience.

Goldcrest Films

65–66 Dean Street, London, W1D 4PL

- ☎ 020 7437 8696
- 🖷 020 7437 4448
- ✉ mailbox@goldcrestfilms.com
- 🌐 www.goldcrestfilms.com

Contact Director of Acquisitions & Development, Wayne Godfrey

Established 1977

Insider Info Goldcrest finances, produces and distributes feature films.

Submission Guidelines Accepts agented submissions only.

The Good Film Company Ltd

The Studio, 5–6 Eton Garages, Lambolle Place, London, NW3 4PE

- ☎ 020 7794 6222
- 🖷 020 7794 4651
- ✉ info@goodfilms.co.uk
- 🌐 www.goodfilms.co.uk

Contact Producer, Yanina Barry

Established 1988

Insider Info The Good Film Company produces film, video and multimedia pieces, including documentaries, music videos and commercials. Credits include Justin Timberlake Promo for Home Box Office Creative Services, New York, and Alicia Keys Web episode for Dove.

Submission Guidelines No unsolicited manuscripts.

Granada Kids

The London Television Centre, Upper Ground, London, SE1 9LT

- ☎ 020 7620 1620
- 🌐 www.granadamedia.com

Insider Info Granada Kids produces documentary, factual, drama and gameshow programmes, as well as some animation. Clients include the BBC, Channel 4, Five and Sky. Credits include *The Illustrated Mum*, and *My Parents are Aliens*.

Tips Granada Kids is one of the largest commercial producers of children's television in the UK. Cosgrove Hall Films (see separate entry) is the animation house that produces all animated programming for Granada Kids.

Green Umbrella

59 Cotham Hill, Cotham, Bristol, BS6 6JR

- ☎ 0117 906 4336
- 🖷 0117 923 7003
- ✉ info@green-umbrella.co.uk
- 🌐 www.green-umbrella.co.uk

Contact Managing Director, Nigel Ashcroft; Producer & Director, Saxon Logan
Established 1991
Insider Info Green Umbrella originally produced science and natural history television programmes. The company has since moved into other areas, including lifestyle, history and earth sciences. Credits include *Seeing in the Dark* for PBS, and *Dirty Weekend* for ITV1. Submissions accompanied by SAE will be returned.
Tips Material submitted must directly relate to the company's specialist subject areas, in particular science, wildlife, history and lifestyle.

Greenwich Village Productions & The Fiction Factory

14 Greenwich Church Street, London, SE10 9BJ
- 020 8853 5100
- 020 8293 3001
- gvproductions@fictionfactory.co.uk
- radio@fictionfactory.co.uk
- www.fictionfactory.co.uk

Insider Info GVT produces television documentaries and short films. Recent productions include *In Search of Lost Time* for BBC Radio 4. Fiction Factory supplies radio and television productions for the BBC.
Submission Guidelines Accepts postal submissions of radio scripts by established writers, or through agents.
Tips Although Greenwich Village and The Fiction Factory will only read scripts by experienced writers, they employ the services of Brian Miller Script Reading to deal with unsolicited manuscripts from new writers. Brian can be contacted via email at: brianmiller19@yahoo.co.uk. There is a fee for this service and the company are currently only accepting radio scripts (no television or stage work will be accepted).

Hat Trick Productions Ltd

10 Livonia Street, London, W1F 8AF
- 020 7434 2451
- 020 7287 9791
- info@hattrick.com
- www.hattrick.com

Contact Managing Director, Jimmy Mulville; Head of Production, Laura Djanogly
Established 1986
Insider Info Produces mainstream comedy, drama and entertainment for most major television broadcasters. Recent credits include *Have I Got News for You* for the BBC, and *Fonejacker* for Channel 4.
Submission Guidelines Accepts agented submissions only.
Tips No unsolicited manuscripts will be accepted.

Heavy Entertainment Ltd

111 Wardour Street, London, W1F 0UH
- 020 7494 1000
- 020 7494 1100
- info@heavy-entertainment.com
- www.heavy-entertainment.com

Contact Director, David Roper; Head of Production, David Nougarede
Established 1992
Insider Info Heavy Entertainment produces material for television, radio, websites, videos, DVDs, CD-ROMs and audiobooks. They produce corporate videos and news releases, as well as programmes for broadcast radio. They also produce radio advertising. Programmes range from high end documentaries, to light entertainment formats and quizzes.
Tips In terms of broadcast radio, Heavy Entertainment work with all BBC stations, meaning their content and formats are extremely varied. Drama productions are likely to be limited to BBC Radio 4.

Heritage Theatre Ltd

Unit 1, 8 Clanricarde Gardens, London, W2 4NA
- 020 7243 2750
- 020 7792 8584
- rm@heritagetheatre.com
- www.heritagetheatre.com

Contact Managing Director, Robert Marshall
Established 2000
Insider Info Heritage produces recordings of live stage productions on DVD and VHS, for lovers of great live theatre productions, arts and theatre viewers, teachers, and students. Aims to report on queries within two days. Purchases rights on broadcast and DVD distribution of live productions. Will accept previously published material, and submissions accompanied by SAE will be returned. Payment is via royalty. Catalogue available with SAE, online or via email.
Submission Guidelines Heritage do not work from a script, but from live productions.
Tips Heritage produce recordings of important live stage productions for distribution to broadcasters and on their DVD label. They do not accept submissions from writers.

Hi8us Projects Ltd

Ground Floor West, Towpath House, Limehouse Court, 3–11 Dod Street, London, E14 7EQ
- 020 7538 8080
- 020 7987 4522
- julia@hi8us.co.uk
- www.hi8us.co.uk

Contact Executive Director, Mark Dunford

Insider Info Hi8us produces television programmes, short films, websites and DVD media projects. Clients include Channel 4 and Carlton Television. Credits include *L8R* and *Projecting Stoke*. Hi8us is a network organisation and has offices in London, Cornwall, the Midlands, the North and the South. Contact information for each office is available on the website.

Tips Hi8us gives young people across the UK the opportunity to gain experience of innovative media production. Projects are often aimed at a teenage audience.

HIT Entertainment Ltd
5th Floor, Maple House, 149 Tottenham Court Road, London, W1T 7NF
- 020 7554 2500
- Online form
- www.hitentertainment.com

Contact CEO, Bruce Steinberg; Executive Vice President, Production & Programming, Lenora Hume
Established 1989
Insider Info HIT Entertainment produces children's entertainment programmes and animated series for network television. Clients include BBC2, Cbeebies and Nick Jr. Credits include *Angelina Ballerina, Barney & Friends, Bob the Builder, Pingu* and *Thomas & Friends*.
Submission Guidelines HIT Entertainment will only accept submissions through an agent, publisher, or other content provider.
Tips HIT Entertainment is the world's leading independent children's producer and rights owner. The company is open to a wide range of ideas but is primarily interested in material aimed at pre-school children, with long running series potential and a global appeal. Submission guidelines are available on the website, but HIT will only accept submissions through an agent, or other similar representative.

Hourglass Productions
27 Prince's Road, Wimbledon, London, SW19 8RA
- 020 8540 8786
- 020 8543 8396
- productions@hourglass.co.uk
- www.hourglass.co.uk

Contact Director, Martin Chilcott; Head of Production, Jacqueline Chilcott
Established 1984
Insider Info Produces documentaries and factual features for film and television on scientific, educational and current affairs. Clients include the BBC, Channel 4 and The Discovery Network. Past productions include *Fruity Stories* for Channel 4 and an episode of *Horizon* for BBC 2. Hourglass is one of the world's leading producers of pharmaceutical and medical videos.

Tips Recent production styles have included the use of technology to explain or investigate detailed subjects, such as medical or environmental matters. The programmes tend to offer an air of authority on important issues.

Icon Films
1–2 Fitzroy Terrace, Bristol, BS6 6TF
- 0117 317 1717
- 0117 973 3890
- info@iconfilms.co.uk
- www.iconfilms.co.uk

Contact Creative Director, Harry Marshall
Insider Info Producers of documentaries for UK and international television. Specialist subjects include natural history (particularly the Indian subcontinent), history, science, travel, anthropology, and religion. Recent productions include *Nick Baker's Weird Creatures* for Animal Planet and *Tiger Diaries* for the BBC.
Submission Guidelines Accepts query with synopsis.
Tips Ideas must be documentaries, broadly within the subject areas that Icon are familiar with. Possible broadcast outlets include the BBC, Channel 4 and the Discovery Network of channels.

Ignition Films
4 Somerset Street, Bristol, BS2 8NB
- 0117 909 9941
- alison@ignitionfilms.org
- www.ignitionfilms.org

Contact Alison Sterling
Established 1999
Insider Info Ignition Films are producers of television, cinema, internet, home DVD and digital installations. They are specialists in high definition television and programmes produced include feature films, drama and documentaries. Credits include *Botanical Wonders* for ITV and the feature film *Human Remains*.
Submission Guidelines Accepts agented submissions only.
Tips Although unsolicited scripts are not accepted Ignition have a commitment to new writing, particularly from South West based writers. A feature film has previously been commissioned from the winner of a South West Script Award.

Illuminations
19–20 Rheidol Mews, Rheidol Terrace, Islington, London, N1 8NU
- 020 7288 8400
- 020 7288 8488

seb@illuminationsmedia.co.uk
www.illuminationsmedia.co.uk
Contact Head of Production, Seb Grant
Established 1982
Insider Info Illuminations produce material for television, websites, video and DVD. Television and multimedia programming is in the fields of the arts, culture, science and innovation. Clients include the BBC, Channel 4, Channel Five, and Artsworld. Catalogue available online.
Tips Programmes are not only made for broadcast television, but for corporate clients, educational institutions and arts organisations. They usually have an arts or cultural theme at their core.

Imari Entertainment
PO Box 158, Beaconsfield, Buckinghamshire, HP9 1AY
01494 677147
01494 677147
info@imarientertainment.com
www.imarientertainment.com
Established 1999
Insider Info Mainly known for corporate video production, Imari has also developed and produced content for presentation to television commissioning editors. Areas include light entertainment, documentaries, sit-coms, and children's and adult's drama.
Tips The corporate side of the business is the most developed, therefore unsolicited manuscripts for television pilots are unlikely to be taken on. However, a recent television project – children's drama, *Operation Fox* – was developed in conjunction with a local published writer.

Isis Productions
106 Hammersmith Grove, London, W6 7HB
020 8748 3042
020 8748 3046
isis@isis-productions.com
www.isisproductions.co.uk
Contact Directors: Nick de Grunwald and Jamie Rugge-Price
Established 1991
Insider Info Produces mainly documentary and factual entertainment television programmes, largely centred on music. Programmes have been shown on ITV1, Channel Five and the BBC.
Tips A popular style of programming has been biography type documentaries on particular musical artists with a colourful life story.

ITV Productions (Granada)
The London Television Centre, Upper Ground, London, SE1 9LT

020 7620 1620
www.granadamedia.com
Contact Directors, John Whiston
Insider Info Produces a wide range of television programming, including drama, children's, arts, factual, entertainment, sport, daytime and lifestyle content. Acts as the main provider of content for the ITV channels, but also produces programming for the BBC, Channel 4, Sky One, Channel Five and many satellite channels.
Tips Much of the content is made up of entertainment formats, factual programming, drama and comedy series and dramatic adaptions of established novels, such as those of Agatha Christie. Although original drama is produced, there is unlikely to be any opportunities for unknown writers.

IWC
St George's Studio, 93–97 St George's Road, Glasgow, G3 6JA
0141 353 3222
0141 353 3221
mailglasgow@iwcmedia.co.uk
www.iwcmedia.co.uk
Contact Head of Production, Jonathan Warne
Insider Info Owned by the RDF Media group, IWC produces prime time television programming including drama, documentaries, history, reality TV and features. Credits include *Root of all Evil* for Channel 4 and *Fallen Angel* for ITV.
Tips Writers with an established record but no prime time television credits may apply to the 'Coming Up' scheme, in association with Channel 4. Eight winners get a 30 minute slot on Channel 4 for a piece of drama and £3,000. Submission guidelines are on the website, where details will appear each year for the annual scheme. Multicultural and regional film makers are particularly encouraged to apply. The scheme is not for complete beginners.

Jam Creative
18 Soho Square, London, W1D 3QL
020 7439 1600
mail@jamcreative.com
www.jamcreative.com
Contact Jon Harvey; Eddie Marshall
Insider Info Jam Creative produces branded entertainment, commercials, programme sponsorships, and television idents, as well as short films for website and DVD media. Clients include The Discovery Channel, Nick Jr, Penguin and Persil. Credits include *Little Green Fingers*, and the *Be My Coach* campaign for Persil.
Tips Jam Creative's core business is on-air marketing for broadcasters and blue chip clients, but they also

create material that is suitable for different types of media.

JAM Pictures & Jane Walmsley Productions

8 Hanover Street, London, W1S 1YE

☎ 020 7290 2676

☎ 020 7256 6818

✉ producers@jampix.com

Contact Producer, Jane Walmsley

Insider Info JAM pictures produces drama for various media, including television films, feature films and some theatre pieces. Jane Walmsley Productions produces features and documentaries mainly for broadcast television.

Submission Guidelines Accepts query with synopsis.

Tips Do not send the full scripts in the first instance. A writing CV, or a list of credits will help in establishing your quality and experience.

Jane Marshall Productions

The Coach House, Westhill Road, Blackdown, Leamington Spa, CV32 6RA

☎ 01926 831680

✉ jane@jmproductions.freeserve.co.uk

Contact Jane Marshall

Insider Info Produces radio programmes from book readings. Will accept previously published material.

Tips Readings must be taken from formally published books.

Justice Entertainment

PO Box 4377, London, W1A 5SX

☎ 020 7467 5450

☎ 020 7467 5451

✉ info@timwestwood.com

🌐 www.timwestwood.com

Contact CEO, Tim Westwood

Insider Info Produces programmes for BBC Radio 1 specialising in black and urban music. Credits include the Radio 1 Rap show, *In New Music We Trust* and *Reggae Dancehall*.

Submission Guidelines No unsolicited manuscripts will be accepted.

KEO Films

101 St John Street, London, EC1M 4AS

☎ 020 7490 3580

☎ 020 7490 8419

✉ keo@keofilms.com

🌐 www.keofilms.com

Contact Head of Development, Jaimie D'Cruz; Head of Production, Katherine Perry; Director/Editor/Producer, Zam Baring

Insider Info KEO Films produces material for television, websites and digital output. They are producers of light entertainment formats, documentaries and interactive content for a variety of media. Credits include *Save Lullingstone Castle: Series 2* for BBC2 and *The River Cottage Treatment* for Channel 4.

Submission Guidelines Accepts query with synopsis, via email only. Mark emails 'Development'.

Tips No unsolicited manuscripts will be accepted. A major area of business for the company is producing documentaries, both features and series, to be broadcast on Channel 4.

Kickback Media

Silverlocks, Cradducks Lane, Staplehurst, Kent, TN12 0DN

☎ 01580 890107

✉ john@kickbackmedia.com

🌐 www.kickbackmedia.com

Contact Managing Director, John Bullivant

Established 2002

Insider Info Kickback Media produces character and design-based animated intellectual property for the children's and teenage market. Clients include Granada Media and Lego. Characters include *Missy Miss* and *Surfin' Turkeys*.

Tips Specialises in both 2D and 3D animation.

Kingfisher Television

Martindale House, The Green, Ruddington, Nottingham, NG11 6HH

☎ 0115 945 6581

✉ info@kingfishertv.co.uk

🌐 www.kingfishertv.co.uk

Contact Managing Director, Tony Francis; Producer/Director, Laura Francis

Established 1988

Insider Info Produces factual content for television broadcast outlets, such as the BBC, ITV, Channel 4, Animal Planet and Discovery. Subjects have included sports, the environment and wildlife. Recent productions include the rural series *Saving Planet Earth* for the BBC and *Safari Park: Series 2* for ITV.

Submission Guidelines Email or post ideas for programmes or features

Tips Bear in mind the topics and styles of programmes previously worked with. View the website for examples, as well as details of upcoming programmes.

Kudos Film & Television Ltd

12–14 Amwell Street, London, EC1R 1UQ

☎ 020 7812 3270

☎ 020 7812 3271

✉ info@kudosfilmandtv.com

⊕ www.kudosfilmandtv.com

Contact Managing Directors, Stephen Garrett and Jane Featherstone; Head of Production, Alison Barnett; Creative Recruitment, Oona O'Beirn

Established 1992

Insider Info Producers of drama and documentaries for television and feature films. Recent productions include *Spooks: Series 4* for BBC1 and *Pleasureland* for Channel 4.

Submission Guidelines Accepts agented submissions only.

Tips No unsolicited manuscripts will be accepted. For those writers with agents, view the production archive to get a feel for previous productions. Their style tends to be sharp and edgy, yet deals with both controversial subject matters and lighter entertainment.

Ladbroke Radio (Electric Airwaves)

Essel House, 29 Foley Street, London, W1W 7JW

⊕ 020 7323 2770

⊕ 020 7079 2080

⊖ andrew@electricairwaves.com

⊕ www.electricairwaves.com

Contact Managing Director, Andrew Caesar-Gordon

Insider Info Ladbroke is an independent radio production company, producing content for the BBC and Channel 4 radio. They also cater for corporate clients.

Tips Ladbroke Radio, owned by Electric Airwaves, was the first independent radio production company to be commissioned by the BBC and continues to work within the BBC's commissioning needs.

Lagan Pictures Ltd

21 Tullaghbrow, Tullaghgarley, Ballymena, BT42 2LY Northern Ireland

⊕ 028 2563 9479

⊕ 028 2563 9479

⊖ laganpictures@tullaghbrow.freeserve.co.uk

Contact Producer, Stephen Butcher

Insider Info Producers of factual, drama, and corporate programming for film and television. Credits include *A Force Under Fire* for Ulster TV.

Submission Guidelines Accepts query with synopsis.

Tips Writers from Northern Ireland, or pieces to do with the region, are of particular interest.

Landseer Films

140 Royal College Street, London, NW1 0TA

⊕ 020 7485 7333

⊖ mail@landseerfilms.com

⊖ db@landseerfilms.com

⊖ ken@landseerfilms.com

⊕ www.landseerfilms.com

Contact Directors: Derek Bailey and Ken Howard

Established 1977

Insider Info Producers of television broadcasts, including dance, drama, children's television, opera, documentaries and music. Programmes are regularly made for prime time slots across international networks. Credits include *LSO: Awakening St Luke's* for the BBC. Catalogue available online.

Tips Potential writers should bear in mind the heavy bias towards culture and arts based programming. View the website for a full list of productions.

Leopard Films

1–3 St Peters Street, Islington, London, N1 8JD

⊕ 0870 420 4232

⊕ 0870 443 6099

⊖ enquiry@leopardfilms.com

⊕ www.leopardfilms.com

Contact CEO, James Burstall; Managing Director, Susie Field; Head of Development, Jenny Coyle; Head of Production, Verity Sutton Barrow

Insider Info Produces a broad range of programming for major terrestrial and satellite television channels across the world. Productions range from drama and documentary, to light entertainment series. Credits include *Crash Scene Investigators* for ITV and *Farm of Fussy Eaters* for UKTV Style. A sister company of Leopard Films USA.

Submission Guidelines No unsolicited manuscripts will be accepted.

Libra Television Ltd

4th Floor, 22 Lever Street, The Northern Quarter, Manchester, M1 1EA

⊕ 0161 236 5599

⊕ 0161 236 6877

⊖ hq@libratelevision.com

⊕ www.libratelevision.com

Contact Managing Directors: Louise Lynch and Madeline Wiltshire; Development Executive, Kate Pickering

Established 1999

Insider Info Producers of children's television and educational programming. Credits include *Sorted: Series 2* for Sky, and *Road Safety* for the Greater Manchester Police.

Tips Broadcast outlets include Teacher's TV, the BBC, Discovery Kids, 4Learning, Channel 4, CITV and Sky Digital. People wishing to work or gain experience with children's television production should research the company carefully before sending their CV to the Managing Directors.

Lilyville Screen Entertainment Ltd

7 Lilyville Road, Fulham, London, SW6 5DP

☎ 020 7471 8989

✉ tony.cash@btclick.com

Contact Managing Director, Tony Cash

Established 1983

Insider Info Produces television programmes, radio dramas and documentaries for a general audience. Credits include *Poetry in Motion* for Channel 4, and *Landscape and Memory* for the BBC. Accepts previously published material and submissions accompanied by SAE will be returned. Aims to report on queries and submissions within two weeks. Payment will be in accordance with industry standards. Will not send a catalogue to a writer on request.

Submission Guidelines Accepts query with synopsis.

Tips Lilyville is currently looking for religious, arts, music and historical documentaries as well as dramas.

Lime Pictures Ltd

Campus Manor, Childwall Abbey Road, Childwall, Liverpool, L16 OJP

☎ 0151 722 9122

☎ 0151 722 1969

✉ twood@limepictures.com

🌐 www.limepictures.com

Contact CEO, Carolyn Reynolds; Managing Director, Sean Marley; Creative Director, Tony Wood

Established 1982

Insider Info Formerly known as Mersey TV, Lime Pictures produces drama content for broadcast television. Long running productions include *Living On The Edge* for MTV and *Hollyoaks* for Channel 4.

Tips Much of Lime Pictures' output is made up of long running series' and its newer drama developments are usually high profile productions for prime time terrestrial television. Unsolicited scripts are unlikely to be taken further within this environment.

Lion Television

Lion House, 26 Paddenswick Road, London, W6 0UB

☎ 020 8846 2000

☎ 020 8846 2001

✉ ideas@liontv.co.uk

🌐 www.liontv.co.uk

Contact Company Director, Shahana Meer; Head of Production, Patsy Blades

Established 1997

Insider Info Produces documentaries, entertainment, factual and history programming for most major television broadcasters in the UK and US.

Credits include *Spartans* for Channel 4 and *Whose Wedding Is It Anyway?* for the BBC.

Submission Guidelines Accepts query with synopsis, via email.

Tips Explore the website to get an idea of the breadth of past projects undertaken by Lion. Detailed information on brand new commissions is also published.

Little Bird

9 Grafton Mews, London, W1T 5HZ

☎ 020 7380 3980

☎ 020 7380 3981

✉ info@littlebird.ie

🌐 www.littlebird.ie

Contact Directors: James Mitchell and Jonathan Cavendish

Established 1982

Insider Info An independent producer of television and film with offices in Dublin, London and Johannesburg. Credits include *Bridget Jones' Diary* and *Bridget Jones: The Edge of Reason*, both in association with Working Title Films. Submissions will not be returned.

Submission Guidelines Unsolicited scripts are not accepted and will not be read.

Tips The company states that they are free to use any ideas or material contained in unsolicited communications they receive from the public.

Loftus Audio

2a Aldine Street, Shepherd's Bush, London, W12 8AN

☎ 020 8740 4666

☎ 020 8740 4777

✉ ask@loftusaudio.co.uk

🌐 www.loftusaudio.co.uk

Contact Producer, Jo Coombs

Established 1996

Insider Info Produces documentaries and features for radio. Credits include *Something Understood* and *Book of the Week* for BBC Radio 4 and *Between the Ears* and *The Sunday Documentary* for BBC Radio 3. Also produces audio guides for museums and galleries.

Submission Guidelines Accepts query with synopsis, via email.

Tips A major broadcast outlet for radio productions is BBC Radio 4. Check the BBC website, www.bbc.co.uk/commissioning for commissioning needs. Loftus are also interested in developing scripts already commissioned for the station.

London Scientific Films Ltd

Dassels House, Dassels, Braughing, Ware, Hertfordshire, SG11 2RW
☎ 01763 289905
✉ lsf@londonscientificfilms.co.uk
⊕ www.londonscientificfilms.co.uk
Contact Mike Vockburn
Insider Info Producers of integrated media output on scientific and medical subjects.
Submission Guidelines No unsolicited manuscripts will be accepted.

Loonland UK Ltd
3rd Floor, Royalty House, 72–74 Dean Street, London, W1D 3SG
☎ 020 7434 2377
☎ 020 7434 1578
✉ bparker@loonland.com
⊕ www.loonland.com
Contact President/CEO, Simon Flamank; Managing Director, Olivier Dumont; Head of Production of TV-Loonland & Managing Director of Telemagination, Beth Parker
Insider Info Loonland UK produces animated children's and youth programming for television. Credits include *Cramp Twins, Jem, My Little Pony* and *Transformers*.
Tips Loonland UK is owned by German company TV-Loonland, which has offices all over the world. Loonland UK also incorporates the Telemagination studio, its main production arm (see separate entry).

Lupus Films
Studio 212, Black Bull Yard, 24–28 Hatton Wall, London, EC1N 8JH
☎ 020 7419 0997
☎ 020 7404 9474
✉ info@lupusfilms.net
⊕ www.lupusfilms.net
Contact Directors, Camilla Deakin and Ruth Fielding
Established 2002
Insider Info Lupus Films produces animated features, shorts, and series, mainly for television. They work with puppetry and 2D techniques. Credits include *Combat Club: Series 2* for Channel Five, and *Meerkats Luuvies* for UKTV Documentaries.
Tips The vast majority of programming is aimed at young children and families. New projects in development are published on the website and give an idea as to current priorities.

Malone Gill Productions Ltd
27 Campden Hill Road, London, SE21 8BN
☎ 020 7937 0557
☎ 020 7376 1727
✉ malonegill@aol.com
Contact Producer, Georgina Denison
Established 1978
Insider Info A production company making documentaries and drama for television. Credits include *The Feast of Christmas* for Channel 4 and *Highlanders* for ITV.
Submission Guidelines Accepts query with synopsis.
Tips Approach in writing for more information on the company and its future projects.

Marchmont Films
24 Three Cups Yard, Sandland Street, London, WC1R 4PZ
✉ office@marchmontfilms.com
⊕ www.marchmontfilms.com
Contact Executive Producer, Mark Tuffey
Insider Info Marchmont Films produce short films and features. Credits include Andrew Cussens' *Out in the Cold* and Terry Newman's *The Green Wave*.
Submission Guidelines Use the online form to submit script ideas. Specific deadlines are published on the site.
Tips Within the specified calls for submissions, Marchmont are keen to hear from both new and established writers of short and feature length drama. Productions tend to be low budget, but are not restricted to any particular genres. They also offer a writers feedback service.

Maverick Television
Progress Works, Heath Mill Lane, Birmingham, B9 4AL
☎ 0121 771 1812
☎ 0121 771 1550
✉ mail@mavericktv.co.uk
⊕ www.mavericktv.co.uk
Contact Managing Director, Jim Sayer; Creative Director, Alexandra Fraser
Established 1994
Insider Info Producers of broadcast television, digital media and printed books for television, DVD and websites. Credits include *10 Years Younger: Series 4* and *How to Look Good Naked: Series 2* for Channel 4, and *One Life: Gail Porter Laid Bare* for BBC One.
Submission Guidelines Accepts query with synopsis. Email queries relating to factual, entertainment or documentary programmes, websites or books. No unsolicited scripts for drama or unagented submissions will be considered.
Tips Bear in mind that Maverick produces projects for television, websites and books, and they welcome project ideas that combine all three medias.

Maya Vision International
6 Kinghorn Street, London, EC1A 7HW
- 020 7796 4842
- 020 7796 4580
- info@mayavisionint.com
- www.mayavisionint.com

Contact Producer & Director, Rebecca Dobbs
Established 1983
Insider Info Producers of history documentaries, and other factual programming for film and television, including archaeology, the arts and current affairs. Maya Vision International also produces low budget features films and experimental dramas.
Submission Guidelines No unsolicited manuscripts will be accepted.

Melendez Films
Julia House, 44 Newman Street, London, W1T 1QD
- 020 7323 5273
- 020 7323 5373
- stevemelendez@billmelendez.tv
- www.billmelendez.tv

Contact Steve Melendez
Established 1963
Insider Info Melendez Films produces material for film and television, it is also the London office of Bill Melendez, an American animator. The company as a whole produces television series and commercials. Credits include *Babar*, *The Lion, The Witch & The Wardrobe* and numerous *Snoopy* and *Charlie Brown* series' and specials. Submissions accompanied by SAE will be accepted.
Submission Guidelines Accepts query with synopsis.
Tips All programming is aimed at children and often has a strong American feel, due to the organisation of the company.

Mendoza
3–5 Barrett Street, London, W1U 1AY
- 020 7935 4674
- 020 7935 4417
- office@mendozafilms.com
- www.mendozafilms.com

Contact Executive Producer, Debby Mendoza
Insider Info Mendoza are a production company specialising in television commercials, producing material for film and television. They also produce title sequences and are moving into the development of feature films – comedies in particular. Submissions accompanied by SAE will be returned.
Submission Guidelines Submit completed manuscript, enclosing SAE.

Tips Only send comedy scripts that may be suitable for future development. The company's main business remains the production of television commercials.

Mentorn
Elsinore House, 77 Fulham Palace Road, London, W6 8JA
- 020 7258 6700
- 020 7258 6888
- factual@mentorn.tv
- entertainment@mentorn.tv
- currentaffairs@mentorn.tv
- www.mentorn.co.uk

Established 1985
Insider Info Producers of drama, current affairs, factual and entertainment programming for major television broadcasters in the UK and internationally. Past productions include the political dramatisations, *A Very Social Secretary* and *The Government Inspector*, as well as the documentary *The Boy Who Gave Birth to His Twin*, and ITV's entertainment show *Take My Mother-in-Law*.
Submission Guidelines Accepts query with synopsis. Email the relevant department (factual, entertainment, or current affairs).
Tips Mentorn's output is extremely varied in style and content. The company recommend that ideas are focused on either factual, entertainment or current affairs categories in order to help direct them to to the right person within the company. Explore the website for past programmes that fall within these three categories to help guide your submission.

Mint Productions
205 Lower Rathmines Road, Dublin 6, Republic of Ireland
- 00353 1 491 3333
- 00353 1 491 3334
- info@mint.ie
- www.mint.ie

Contact Head of Production, Dhruba Banerjee
Insider Info Producers of documentaries for UK and Irish television. Productions include *Junior Doctors* for RTE and *Heir Hunters* for BBC One.
Tips Mint Productions are specialists in historical and observational documentaries.

Moonstone Films
5 Linkenholt Mansions, Stamford Brook Avenue, London, W6 0YA
- 020 7870 7180
- 0870 005 6839
- info@moonstonefilms.co.uk
- www.moonstonefilms.co.uk

Contact Executive Producer, Tony Stark

Insider Info Produces documentaries for television, both in historical and investigative, presenter led formats. Credits include *Arafat Investigated* for BBC 2 and *Muslim Survey* for Channel 4. Submissions accompanied by SAE will be returned.

Submission Guidelines Accepts unsolicited manuscripts.

Tips Documentary ideas should fall into the very broad remits of 'current affairs' or 'historical'.

Mute Marmalade Ltd
23 Prince Albert Road, London, NW1 7ST
- 020 7449 2552
- 020 7449 2662

Contact Jonathan Bentata

Insider Info Mute Marmalade are producers of films including *Black Soles* and *Making Mistakes*. Will report on queries within one week. Catalogue available online.

Submission Guidelines Produces films (35mm). Send a beat sheet (short sentences arranged in columns that break down a screenplay to its narrative core), a one page synopsis, and a signed submissions sheet, available from the website.

Tips Do not send full manuscript. Selected writers who submit will win a paid for course at The Script Factory.

Neon
Studio 2, 19 Marine Crescent, Kinning Park, Glasgow, G51 1HD
- 0141 429 6366
- 0141 429 6377
- mail@go2neon.com
- www.go2neon.com

Contact Managing Directors, Stephanie Pordage and Robert Noakes

Established 1995

Insider Info Neon produces material for film and radio. They are producers of weekly programmes, short series, stand alone features and music videos. Specialist areas include drama, arts, music and documentary production. The company also runs a record label and a music publishing business.

Submission Guidelines Query first, before sending any manuscripts.

Tips Much of the radio output in particular is for BBC Scotland's regional stations, as well as BBC national stations. Content with a Scottish connection has featured heavily in their back catalogue.

Nexus Productions Ltd
113–114 Shoreditch High Street, London, E1 6JN
- 020 7749 7500
- 020 7749 7501

- info@nexusproductions.com
- www.nexusproductions.com

Established 1997

Insider Info Nexus produces animated programmes. They work with 2D, 3D, puppetry, live-action and flash animations.

Tips Nexus works with creative professionals, including writers from all over the world. The main bulk of its output is animation for television, commercials, music videos and films.

Noel Gay Television
19 Denmark Street, London, WC2H 8NA
- 020 7836 3941
- info@noelgay.com
- www.noelgay.com

Established 1987

Insider Info Producers of comedy, entertainment and drama formats for television. Credits include Rob Grant and Doug Naylor's *Red Dwarf*, and *The Weakest Link*.

Submission Guidelines Accepts query with synopsis.

Tips Strictly no unsolicited manuscripts will be accepted.

Number 9 Films
Linton House, 24 Wells Street, London, W1T 3PH
- 020 7323 4060
- 020 7323 0456
- info@number9films.co.uk

Contact Stephen Wooley and Elizabeth Karlsen

Established 2002

Insider Info Number 9 are producers of feature films including *Stoned* and *Breakfast on Pluto*. The company recently entered a funding agreement with the UK Film Council, Film 4, Intandem Films and the Irish Film Board; one of several partnerships designed to build the profile of British cinema.

Submission Guidelines No unsolicited manuscripts will be accepted.

Odyssey Productions Ltd
72 Tay Street, Newport on Tay, Fife, Scotland, DD6 8AP
- 01382 542070
- 01382 542070
- billykay@sol.co.uk
- www.sol.co.uk/b/billykay

Contact Directors, Billy Kay and Maria João Kay

Established 1994

Insider Info Odyssey produces radio features, as well as corporate audio visual packages. Previous productions have been broadcast on BBC Radio 2 and 4, as well as BBC Radio Scotland.

Submission Guidelines Accepts query
with synopsis.
Tips Many past productions have had a
Scottish theme.

Omnivision Ltd
**Pinewood Studios, Iver Heath, Buckinghamshire,
SL0 0NH**
- 01753 656329
- 01753 421045
- info@omnivision.co.uk
- www.omnivision.co.uk

Contact Managing Director, Christopher Morris;
Senior Editor, Nick Long
Insider Info Omnivision produces material for
television, video and DVDs. This includes broadcast
and corporate television productions, including
documentaries, news, current affairs, sports and
outside broadcasts.
Submission Guidelines Accepts query with
synopsis. Email programme ideas or fill in the online
contact form, including your full contact details.
Tips In terms of ideas for broadcast television, the
areas to aim for are; documentary, news, features
and lifestyle programmes.

Orlando Media
**Up the Steps, Little Tew, Chipping Norton,
Oxfordshire, OX7 4JB**
- 01608 683218
- 01608 683364
- info@orlandomedia.co.uk
- www.orlandodigital.co.uk

Contact Creative Director, Mike Tomlinson
Insider Info Orlando Media produces material for
television, web and digital media, including factual
programming for broadcast television and video.
Subject areas include science, nature and
technology. Credits include *The Planets* for the BBC
and *Peak Performance* for the ITV network.
Tips The Creative Director, Mike Tomlinson, also acts
as a writer for much of the programming. Therefore
proposals from other writers are usually with a view
to collaborating.

Oxford Scientific (OSF)
**Network House, Station Yard, Thame,
Oxfordshire, OX9 3UH**
- 01844 262370
- 01844 262380
- uksales@osf.co.uk
- www.osf.co.uk

Insider Info Oxford Scientific have a large image
library (still and moving) on worldwide wildlife.
Images are sold on for television and film
production.

Tips If you have existing footage or photography,
there is information on the website on how to
submit your images to the library.

Parallax Independent Ltd
7 Denmark Street, London, WC2H 8LZ
- 020 7836 1478
- 020 7497 8062
- www.parallaxindependent.co.uk

Insider Info A co-operative of producers and
directors of feature films, short films and
documentaries for television. Credits include *The
Navigators* and *Bread & Roses*.
Tips Parallax state they have 'an open door policy'
for new writers and directors. Current members
include film makers Les Blair and Sarah Curtis.

Passion Pictures
**County House, 33–34 Rathbone Place, London,
W1T 1JN**
- 020 7323 9933
- 020 7323 9030
- info@passion-pictures.com
- www.passion-pictures.com

Contact Associate Producer, Andrew Ruhemann
Insider Info Produces material for film and
television, including animated and live action work
for feature films, short films, music videos and
commercials. Credits include videos for the
animated pop band *Gorillaz* and the Vodafone
Mayfly advert.
Tips Although the company is best known for its
animation, particularly in music videos and
advertisements, it has recently developed some
award winning documentaries for broadcast
television. A list of development projects are
published on the website give an idea of where the
company might be heading.

Pathé Productions Ltd
**Kent House, 14–17 Market Place, Great Titchfield
Street, London, W1W 8AR**
- 020 7323 5151
- 020 7631 5368
- www.pathe.co.uk

Insider Info A feature film production and
distribution company. Recent production credits
include *The Queen* and *Big Nothing*.
Submission Guidelines Agented submissions or
proposals from independent production
companies only.
Tips Pathé's output is extremely varied in genre and
subject matter. Its own productions are reasonably
high profile, and normally achieve a general
cinema release.

Pennine Productions

Kilmagadwood Cottage, Scotlandwell, Kinross, KY13 9HY

- 01560 472247
- clare@pennine.biz
- www.pennine.biz

Contact Producers: Clare Jenkins, Janet Graves, Mike Hally and Mark Whitaker

Established 2000

Insider Info Producers for BBC Radio. Programmes include documentaries, features and readings.

Submission Guidelines Accepts queries with a brief email summarising the idea.

Tips No unsolicited manuscripts will be accepted. Send a short query by email. Be aware that BBC Radio listeners will be the eventual audience. Programmes that deal with stories from interesting, worldwide locations are preferred.

Pesky Ltd

11 Morecambe Street, London, SE17 1DX

- 020 7703 2080
- hodge@pesky.com
- www.pesky.com

Contact Creative Director, David Hodgson; Animation Director, Claire Underwood

Established 1997

Insider Info Pesky produces Flash animation and cross platform media for television and the internet. Clients include the BBC, Channel 4, Cartoon Network, Philips and Nestle. Credits include *The Amazing Adrenalini Brothers*, *MissyMiss* and *Stress Maniacs*.

Tips Pesky do not have any submission guidelines available, but are always interested in meeting new animators and scriptwriters.

Photoplay Productions Ltd

21 Princess Road, London, NW1 8JR

- 020 7722 2500
- 020 7722 6662
- info@photoplay.co.uk
- www.photoplay.co.uk

Contact Patrick Stanbury

Insider Info Producers of documentaries and restorers of silent films and theatrical work for film and television. Past work has been broadcast on Channel 4. Credits include *The Iron Mask* and *The Phantom of the Opera*.

Submission Guidelines No unsolicited manuscripts will be accepted.

Tips Due to the nature of work undertaken by Photoplay, works are written, developed, or restored in-house.

Picardy Media & Communication

Dalintober Hall, 40 Dalintober Street, Glasgow, G5 8NW

- 0141 420 0909
- 0141 429 3723
- info@picardy.co.uk
- www.picardy.co.uk

Contact Head of Production, John Rocchiccioli; Producers, Sharon Fullarton and Sarah Gill

Established 1993

Insider Info Produces material for television, websites, interactive CDs and DVDs, including screen-based projects, mainly for corporate clients. Areas of expertise include sales and marketing, health and safety, human resources, and training and communications. They also provide editing, graphics and sound recording services.

Submission Guidelines Accepts queries via direct email to a staff member.

Tips A showreel is published on the website, from which writers can get a sense of the projects undertaken. Picardy aims to entertain people whilst training, educating or informing them in some way, according to the needs of the client.

Picture Palace Films

13 Egbert Street, London, NW1 8LJ

- 020 7586 8763
- 020 7586 9048
- info@picturepalace.com
- www.picturepalace.com

Contact Producer & CEO, Malcolm Craddock

Established 1972

Insider Info Produces film and television material for UK adult audiences. The London base, headed by Malcolm Craddock, produces television drama such as *Sharpe's Challenge* and *Frances Tuesday* for ITV. Picture Palace North, the Manchester base headed by Alex Usbourne, produces controversial films and dramas set in the north, such as *F***ing Sheffield* and *Large*. The company purchases three to five scripts per year and works with three to five writers accordingly. They purchase all rights on accepted material. Picture Palace will accept previously published material, and submissions accompanied by SAE will be returned. They aim to report on queries within two weeks and submissions within six weeks. They will not send a catalogue to a writer on request. Writers are paid for their work in accordance with industry standards.

Submission Guidelines Produces films (16 or 35mm) and videotapes (in digibeta format). Accepts query with synopsis.

Tips Bear in mind that although the broadcast drama is fairly high profile, the feature film productions tend to be low budget and deal with difficult, gritty subjects.

Pier Productions

Lower Ground Floor, 1 Marlborough Place, Brighton, BN1 1TU

- 01273 691401
- 01273 693658
- pierprod@mistral.co.uk

Contact Managing Director, Peter Hoare

Insider Info Produces drama and documentaries for film, television and radio (particularly prevalent in radio). Credits include Neville Smith's *Dear Doctor Goebbels* for BBC Radio 4.

Tips For radio drama scripts, BBC Radio 4 is the most likely commissioner of Pier's work.

Plantaganet Films Ltd

Ard-Daraich Studio B, Ardgour, Near Fort William, PH33 7AB

- 01588 841384
- 01855 841384
- plantaganetfilms@aol.com

Contact Norrie Maclaren

Established 1949

Insider Info Produces factual and drama programming for broadcast television and film. Credits include episodes of *Dispatches* for Channel 4.

Tips Contact Norrie Maclaren for more information on how to submit manuscripts. Will potentially work with new writing.

Portobello Pictures

12 Addison Avenue, Holland Park, London, W11 4QR

- 020 7605 1396
- 020 7605 1391
- mail@portobellopictures.com
- www.portobellopictures.com

Established 1987

Insider Info Producers of feature films and television dramas. Credits include the film *Birthday Girl* and the long running series *Dalziel and Pascoe* for ITV. The company has also moved into theatre productions.

Tips The company states that as well as developing film and television projects with established writers, they are keen to develop new talent. In 2006 they set up a base in South Africa and have begun producing new drama using South African writers, stories and actors. This is part of a commitment to bring the country's creative output onto an international level.

Pozzitive Television

Paramount House, 162–170 Wardour Street, London, W1F 8AB

- 020 7734 3258
- 020 7437 3130
- david@pozzitive.co.uk

Contact David Tyler

Insider Info Produces comedy and entertainment for major radio and television broadcasters including the BBC. Productions include *Dinnerladies* for BBC 1 and *The Very World of Milton Jones* for Radio 4.

Submission Guidelines Submit completed manuscript. Accepts postal submissions only, no email submissions will be considered.

Tips Pozzitive focuses strongly on comedy. The BBC is a regular client and it may be useful to bear in mind their commissioning strategies, published at: www.bbc.co.uk/commissioning.

Praxis Films Ltd

Suite 3N, Leroy House, 436 Essex Road, London, N1 3QP

- 020 7682 1865
- 020 7682 1868
- inquiries@praxisfilms.co.uk
- www.praxisfilms.co.uk

Contact Tony Cook

Established 1985

Insider Info Produces documentaries, current affairs and factual programming for broadcast television. Also produces material for videos, DVDs and CDs, including non-broadcast products, such as educational and training titles.

Tips Praxis offer training in various areas of media production. For those interested in the styles of their production output and writers they have previously worked with, credits are published on the website.

Princess Productions

Whiteley's Centre, 151 Queensway, London, W2 4YN

- 020 7985 1985
- 020 7985 1986
- formatsales@princeestv.com
- www.princesstv.com

Established 1996

Insider Info Produces entertainment programming for UK television broadcasters. Recent credits include *The Friday Night Project* and *The Big Art Project,* both for Channel 4. Catalogue available online.

Tips Formats tend to be light entertainment, with a satirical or comedic edge. View the catalogue published online for more details.

Promenade Enterprises Ltd

6 Russell Grove, London, SW9 6HS

- 020 7582 9354
- 020 7564 3026
- nnewton@promenadeproductions.com

⊕ www.promenadeproductions.com
Contact Producer, Nicholas Newton
Established 1994
Insider Info Producers of drama, primarily for BBC Radio, but also for television and theatre. Previous radio productions include *Afternoon Romancers* and *The Pickwick Papers*.
Submission Guidelines Only agented submissions will be accepted.
Tips No unsolicited manuscripts will be considered. For those with agents, BBC Radio 4 is a regular broadcaster of productions from Promenade, both for new writing and adaptions of established books and plays.

Prospect Pictures
13 Wandsworth Plain, London, SW18 1ET
☎ 020 7636 1234
☎ 020 7636 1236
✉ info@prospect-uk.com
⊕ www.prospect-uk.com
Contact Managing Director, Liam Hamilton; Creative Director, Todd Austin; Head of Production, Louise Doffman
Insider Info Produces lifestyle television programming, as well as factual entertainment and entertainment formats. Credits include *Saturday Cooks* and *Call Me A Cabbie*. Catalogue available online.
Tips Light entertainment programmes dealing with food and cooking are a particular speciality of Prospect, although programmes are also produced on a wide range of other topics, including sport, music, comedy, gardening, health and travel.

Ragdoll Ltd
Timothy's Bridge Road, Stratford upon Avon, CV37 9NQ
☎ 01789 404100
☎ 01789 404136
✉ info@ragdoll.co.uk
⊕ www.ragdoll.co.uk
Contact Founder & Creative Director, Anne Wood
Established 1984
Insider Info Ragdoll produces live action, animated, and puppetry programmes for young children. Clients include the BBC, Channel 4 and ITV. Credits include *Brum, In The Night Garden, Rosie & Jim, The Teletubbies* and *Tots TV*.
Tips Ragdoll specialises in producing programs for pre-school children, and aims to have an international appeal.

Raw Charm Ltd
Ty Cefn, Rectory Road, Cardiff, CF5 1QL
☎ 029 2064 1511

☎ 029 2066 8220
✉ enquiries@rawcharm.tv
✉ ian@rawcharm.co.uk
⊕ www.rawcharm.tv
Contact Managing Director, Kate Jones-Davies; Development Producer, Ian Brown; Commissioning Executive, Jane McCloskey
Established 1990
Insider Info Producers of documentary and factual programming for broadcast television and radio, both national and regional. Credits include *War Stories* for BBC Wales, and *Grave Detectives* for HTV West.
Tips Currently seeking international collaborations and co-productions. A particular area of interest to the development producer is programming for digital and satellite channels.

RDF Television
The Gloucester Building, Kensington Village, Avonmore Road, London, W14 8RF
☎ 020 7013 4000
☎ 020 7013 4001
✉ contactus@rdftelevision.com
⊕ www.rdftelevision.com
Contact Managing Director, Grant Mansfield; Director of Production, Jane Wilson; Creative Director - Development, Teresa Watkins
Established 1993
Insider Info The largest television company within the RDF Media Group. Produces a wide range of television programmes including entertainment formats, reality, documentaries and features. Credits include *Shipwrecked: Battle of the Islands* for Channel 4, and *Oz & James's Big Wine Adventure* for BBC 2. Catalogue available online.
Tips No unsolicited showreels will be accepted. The programmes produced at RDF are high profile, prime time entertainment shows and unsolicited manuscripts are unlikely to be taken further.

Red Kite Animations
89 Giles Street, Edinburgh, EH6 6BZ
☎ 0131 554 0060
☎ 0131 553 6007
✉ info@redkite-animations.com
⊕ www.redkite-animation.com
Contact Managing Director, Ken Anderson; Head of Production, Sueann Smith
Established 1997
Insider Info Produces animated content for broadcast television and film in the UK and internationally, as well as commercials. Clients include the BBC, S4C, Cartoon Network US, The Family Channel and Disney Japan. Previous productions include *The Imp* and *The Puddleducks*.

Submission Guidelines No unsolicited showreels will be considered.

Tips Red Kite runs workshops in animation throughout Scotland. For more information, email: studio@redkite-animation.com.

RS Productions
191 Trewhitt Road, Heaton, Newcastle upon Tyne, NE6 5DY
- 0191 224 4301
- info@rsproductions.co.uk
- www.rsproductions.co.uk

Contact Managing Director & Producer, Mark Lavender
Established 1993
Insider Info Produces material for film, television, websites and new media. They produce documentaries and factual programmes, as well as feature films. Co-productions are developing with companies from the UK, USA, Germany, Denmark and Hungary. Submissions accompanied by SAE will be returned.
Submission Guidelines For television proposals, send a one or two page synopsis with any relevant background information. For feature films, send a one or two page synopsis with details of where the films has been sent before, and what the response was, as well as an author biography. No unsolicited manuscripts will be accepted, unless from agents, publishers or industry lawyers.
Tips Ideas should be fresh and original. Be aware that hard copy materials will not be returned.

Rubber Duck Entertainment
120 New Cavendish Street, London, W1W 6XX
- 020 7909 3773
- 020 7907 3777
- info@rde.co.uk
- www.rde.co.uk

Contact Producer, Alexi Wheeler; Production Assistant, Gemma Church
Insider Info Rubber Duck Entertainment produces animated programs for children. Clients include CITV, Five and Nickleodeon. Credits include *Peppa Pig*, *Tractor Tom* and *Bzots*. Part of the Contender Entertainment Group.
Submission Guidelines Submissions should be sent to Gemma Church, at: gchurch@rde.co.uk (please do not send original artwork)
Tips At present, Rubber Duck Entertainment is focused on producing animated children's programming. They are especially interested in project ideas for children in the 6-9/8-12 age ranges with a comedy or action skew.

Ruth Evans Productions Ltd
4 Offlands Cottages, Moulsford, Oxfordshire, OX10 9HP
- 01491 651331
- ruth@ruthevans.com

Contact Ruth Evans
Established 2002
Insider Info An independent radio producer. Programmes include factual features and documentaries.
Tips Main clients are BBC Radio 4 and BBC World Service. For more information on their programming needs, see www.bbc.co.uk/commissioning.

Scala Productions
4th Floor Portland House, 4 Great Portland Street, London, W1W 8QJ
- 020 7612 0060
- 020 7612 0031
- scalaprods@aol.com

Contact Chairman and Director, Nik Powell
Established 1983
Insider Info Previously known as Palace Productions, Scala are producers of feature films, including *Little Voice* and *Ladies in Lavender*.
Tips There is often a strong British theme in Scala films; many have starred well known British actors and have been set in Britain.

Scope Productions Ltd
180 West Regent Street, Glasgow, G2 4RW
- 0141 221 4312
- 0141 332 1049
- laurakingwell@scopeproductions.co.uk
- www.scopeproductions.co.uk

Established 1984
Insider Info Scope are producers of corporate videos, DVDs and multimedia projects. They also create some broadcast documentaries and television commercials.
Tips Bear in mind a major part of the business is corporate work. No full length dramas will be considered.

Screen First Ltd
The Studios, Funnells Farm, Down Street, Nutley, TN22 3LG
- 01825 712034
- paul.madden@virgin.net

Contact Paul Madden
Insider Info Produces children's animations, dramas and documentaries for broadcast television. Credits include Raymond Briggs' *Ivor the Invisible* for Channel 4.

Submission Guidelines No unsolicited manuscripts will be accepted.

Screenhouse Productions Ltd
Chapel Allerton House, 114 Harrogate Road, Leeds, LS7 4NY
- 0113 266 8881
- 0113 266 8882
- info@screenhouse.co.uk
- paul.bader@screenhouse.co.uk
- www.screenhouse.co.uk

Contact Creative Director, Paul Bader; Head of Production, Catherine Mounsey
Established 1991
Insider Info Producers of science and history television programmes and websites. Also produces props and machinery for scientific television content. Credits include *Stardate* and *Hart-Davis on History* for the BBC.
Submission Guidelines Accepts query with synopsis. Contact Paul Bader with ideas.
Tips Screenhouse goes beyond television production to develop projects with websites, books, props and events. Much of the content is conceived and developed in-house, therefore unsolicited ideas are unlikely to be taken further. Keep ideas within science or history topic areas.

ScreenProjex
13 Manette Street, London, W1D 4AW
- 020 7287 1170
- 020 7287 1123
- info@screenprojex.com
- www.screenprojex.com

Contact Managing Director, Julia Vickers
Insider Info ScreenProjex are a distribution company created to acquire and promote independent British films. Their portfolio includes Simon Rumley's *Club Le Monde* and *The Truth Game*.
Tips Accepts finished films only, and only from British producers. Any genre will be considered as long as it has an engaging narrative and strong production values.

Screen Ventures
49 Goodge Street, London, W1T 1TE
- 020 7580 7448
- 020 7631 1265
- info@screenventures.com
- www.screenventures.com

Contact Managing Director, Christopher Mould; Head of Development, David Chambers; Development Producer, Naima Mould
Established 1978
Insider Info Screen Ventures produces, markets and sells television programmes and films. In-house production credits include *Mojo Working: The Making of Modern Music* for Channel 4 and *The South Bank Show* for ITV.
Tips Incoming scripts and ideas are assessed initially by Naima Mould.

September Films
Glen House, 22 Glenthorne Road, London, W6 0NG
- 020 8563 9393
- 020 8741 7214
- september@septemberfilms.com
- www.septemberfilms.com

Contact Director of Programmes, Peter Davey
Established 1992
Insider Info Produces factual entertainment, features, reality programming and entertainment formats for broadcast television. Recent credits include *Beauty and the Geek* for Channel 4 and E4, and *Aircrash Unsolved: The Mystery of Helios* for Discovery (Europe).
Tips Productions are often aimed at both the UK and US market. The majority of September's output remains focused on popular light entertainment. Dramatic writing is largely restricted to a small list of television dramas and feature films.

Shell Like Radio Production
81 Whitfield Street, London, W1T 4HG
- 020 7255 5204
- enquiries@shelllike.com
- www.shelllike.com

Contact Senior Producer, Anna Pollard; Production Assistant, Richard Donaghue
Insider Info Producers of radio material, particularly commercials. Clients include Toyota, Breakthrough Breast Cancer, and Carling.
Submission Guidelines Send all ideas by email to Richard Donaghue.

Sianco Cyf
Pen-y-graig, Llanfaglan, Caernarfon, Gwynedd, LL54 5RF
- 01286 676100
- sian@sianco.tv

Contact Managing Director, Siân Teifi
Insider Info Specialises in children's television programming, but also produces adult entertainment, factual, and documentary programmes.
Submission Guidelines No unsolicited manuscripts will be accepted.

Silent Sound Films Ltd

Cambridge Court, Cambridge Road, Frinton on Sea, CO13 9HN
- 01255 676381
- 01255 676381
- thj@silentsoundfilms.co.uk
- www.silentsoundfilms.co.uk

Contact Managing Director, Timothy Foster
Established 1997
Insider Info Silent Sound Films are producers of films and musical scores for silent films. They also aim to develop the awareness of the arts through documentaries. Does not accept previously published material. Aims to respond to queries within two weeks and submissions within two months. Writers are paid in accordance with WGA standards, or the UK 'pact' agreement, if it is a British production.
Submission Guidelines Produces material for films (35mm). Accepts query with synopsis by email only (including a one page synopsis, eight pages of scenario and a writer biography). No images, complete plays, or other large attachments will be accepted.
Tips Silent Sound Films are interested in excellent writing (specifically musicals, art house and stage plays) with well developed plot themes and original characters. They seek material that may well include a good 'pitchable idea' but also one that goes a lot deeper. Definitely not interested in the broad spectrum of commercial cinema.

Skyline Productions

10 Scotland Street, Edinburgh, EH3 6PS
- 0131 557 4580
- 0131 556 4377
- admin@skyline.uk.com
- www.skyline.uk.com

Contact Leslie Hills
Established 1974
Insider Info Skyline produces features films, documentaries, music, arts and comedy programming for television. Broadcasters worked with include major UK terrestrial channels and stations across Europe and the US. Credits include *Living Lightly* and *The Holocaust Tourist*.
Tips For enquiries about projects past, present and future, email Leslie Hill at: leslie@skyline.uk.com.

SMG Productions

Pacific Quay, Glasgow, G51 1PQ
- 0141 300 3000
- website@smgproductions.tv
- www.smgproductions.tv

Contact Managing Director, Elizabeth Partyka
Insider Info Produces adult and children's television programming, including drama, documentaries, factual entertainment and entertainment formats. Credits include *Rebus* for ITV1 and *Nick Hancock's Fishing School* for Discovery Realtime. SMG Productions also incorporates Ginger Productions.
Tips SMG's range of programming is varied in style, however most output is broadcast on major terrestrial and satellite channels, often in prime time slots. Unsolicited manuscripts from new writers are unlikely to be picked up, due to the high profile needed for the shows.

Smooth Operations

PO Box 286, Cambridge, CB1 7XW
- 01223 244544
- 01223 244384
- info@smoothoperations.com
- www.smoothoperations.com

Insider Info Smooth Operations are producers of music programming and content for BBC television and radio. Credits include *My Country Jukebox* for BBC Radio 2, and *Border Blaster - In Search Of Wolfman Jack* for BBC Radio 4. They also operate from a base in Oldham, headed up by John Leonard. Catalogue available online.
Tips All content is for BBC television, and radio and music is the sole focus of all productions.

Somethin' Else

20–26 Brunswick Place, London, N1 6DZ
- 020 7250 5500
- 020 7250 0937
- info@somethinelse.com
- www.somethinelse.com

Contact Managing Director, Steve Ackerman; Creative Director, Jez Nelson
Established 1992
Insider Info Somethin' Else is the largest UK independent radio producer and also produces television entertainment formats. As well as television and radio, content is made for interactive media such as the web, games and mobile television. Credits include *Buzz* for Playstation 2 and *MyTv: Homegrown* for Trouble.
Submission Guidelines Accepts query with synopsis. Send ideas by post.
Tips Much of the content produced across all media is based around light entertainment, music and pop culture. For more information on the various media output contact samb@somethinelse.com for radio, leo.burley@somethinelse.com for television, and simon.hopkins@somethinelse.com for interactive.

So Television

18 Hatfields, London, SE1 8GN

☎ 020 7960 2000

☎ 020 7960 2095

✉ info@sotelevision.co.uk

🌐 www.sotelevision.co.uk

Contact Founders: Graham Norton and Graham Stuart

Established 2000

Insider Info So Television also incorporates So Radio and produces entertainment formats for broadcast television. Credits include *The Graham Norton Show: Series 2* for the BBC, and *Sketchy* for CBBC.

Submission Guidelines No unsolicited manuscripts will be accepted.

Soundplay

17 Gleneagles Drive, Henbury, Bristol, BS10 7PS

☎ 07818 271659

✉ enquiries@soundplay.co.uk

🌐 www.soundplay.co.uk

Contact Shaun MacLoughlin, Tom Bennett, Vanessa Dodd

Established 1998

Insider Info Soundplay are producers of radio dramas, podcasts and features. They aim to bring attention to the media through working with schools, community groups and prison groups. Productions include *Brave Georgina* by Matthew Friday, and in *In Search of the Picturesque*. Most output is designed to be broadcast across the internet. Catalogue available online.

Tips Bear in mind that Soundplay do not produce radio for broadcast. They undertake community projects, often culminating in radio productions that can be listened to through their website. Information on upcoming projects will be published on their website, where there is also a discussion board.

Specific Films

25 Rathbone Street, London, W1T 1NQ

☎ 020 7580 7476

☎ 020 7494 2676

✉ info@specificfilms.com

Contact Managing Director, Michael Hamlyn

Established 1991

Insider Info Produces feature films and material for television. Credits include *The Adventures of Priscilla, Queen of the Desert*.

Tips Specific Films also produce music videos for very high profile artists.

Spellbound Entertainment Ltd

6 Primrose Mews, Sharpleshall Street, Primrose Hill, London, NW1 8YL

☎ 020 7483 2172

☎ 020 7483 2059

✉ info@spellbound.uk.com

🌐 www.spellbound.uk.com

Contact Managing Director & Creative Director, Peter Curtis

Established 2001

Insider Info Spellbound Entertainment produces animated programming for international clients. Clients include the BBC, Disney Channel and ABC. Credits include *The Koala Brothers*.

Tips Primarily a rights holding company, specialising in the ownership, creative management, distribution and merchandising of high quality children's and family programming.

Spice Factory UK

14 Regent Hill, Brighton, East Sussex, BN1 3ED

☎ 01273 739182

☎ 01273 749122

✉ info@spicefactory.co.uk

🌐 www.spicefactory.co.uk

Contact Head of Development, Lucy Shuttleworth

Established 1995

Insider Info Produces feature films. Credits include *Beowulf and Grendel* and *The Merchant of Venice*.

Submission Guidelines No unsolicited manuscripts will be accepted.

Tips Despite not accepting any unsolicited material, Spice Factory's development department is active in seeking new writing talent. Previous features have come about after the successful production of short films from new writers.

Spire Films

7 High Street, Kidlington, Oxford, OX5 2DH

☎ 01865 371979

☎ 01865 371962

✉ proposals@spirefilms.co.uk

🌐 www.spirefilms.co.uk

Contact Head of Development, Bernadette O'Farrell

Established 1997

Insider Info Produces factual television programming for terrestrial and satellite channels in the UK and US. Subjects include history, the arts, leisure and entertainment. Productions include *Delia's How to Cook* for the BBC, and *The Worst Jobs in History* for Channel 4 and Discovery.

Submission Guidelines Accepts query with synopsis, via email.

Tips Spire Films does not produce any drama.

Stampede Ltd

The Hat Factory, 65–67 Bute Street, Luton, Bedfordshire, LU1 2EY

❶ 01582 727330
❷ 01582 726910
📧 dave@stampede.co.uk
🌐 www.stampede.co.uk

Contact Managing Director, Mike Chamberlain; Head of Production, Dave Allison

Established 1996

Insider Info Stampede produces film and television documentaries for a wide British and international audience. Credits include *My Sister the Geisha* and *Global Protest* for BBC World. Purchases first rights on accepted material. Will accept previously published material and submissions accompanied by SAE will be returned. Aims to respond to queries within two weeks, and submissions within five weeks. Payment will be in accordance with industry standards. Catalogue available online or via email.

Submission Guidelines Accepts queries.

Tips Stampede Limited produce documentaries only. Work should be challenging, and go beyond being formulaic.

Stirling Film & Television Productions Ltd

137 University Street, Belfast, Northern Ireland, BT7 1HP

❶ 028 9033 3848
❷ 028 9043 8644
📧 anne@stirlingtelevision.co.uk
🌐 www.stirlingtelevision.co.uk

Contact Anne Stirling

Established 1994

Insider Info Produces factual programming for broadcast television. Clients include BBC, Channel 4, Five, Discovery and RTÈ. Stirling works across a range of subject areas, although their specialism is in Irish music and dance.

Tips A major broadcast outlet for Stirling is the Irish station RTÈ. Much of the content for this station has a specifically Irish theme, subject, or feel.

Straight Forward Film and Productions Ltd

Building 2, Lesley Office Park, 393 Holywood Road, Belfast, Northern Ireland, BT4 2LS

❶ 028 9065 1010
❷ 028 9065 1012
📧 enquiries@straightforwardltd.co.uk
🌐 www.straightforwardltd.co.uk

Contact Head of Production, Joy Hines

Established 1992

Insider Info Produces factual television programmes for broadcasters including BBC Northern Ireland, Ulster Television, RTÈ, TG4, Channel 4, Five, Living, PBS (US), and NHK (Japan). Subject matters covered includes news and current affairs, light entertainment, arts, sport, history, and lifestyle. Catalogue available online.

Tips The company state that they are always looking out for new talent and ideas, and frequently use freelancers along with their core staff.

Sunset+Vine Productions

Elsinore House, 77 Fulham Palace Road, London, W6 8JA

❶ 020 7478 7400
❷ 020 7478 7412
📧 enquiries@sunsetvine.co.uk
🌐 www.sunsetvine.co.uk

Established 1983

Insider Info Produces sports television programming, including both live coverage, and features for major broadcasters and entertainment formats. Credits include *The Tour de France* for ITV and *Gillette World Sport*.

Submission Guidelines No unsolicited manuscripts will be considered. Accepts commissions only.

Table Top Productions

1 The Orchard, Chiswick, London, W4 1JZ

❶ 020 8742 0507
❷ 020 8742 0507
📧 top@tabletopproductions.com
🌐 www.tabletopproductions.com

Contact Production Manager, Ben Berry

Established 1989

Insider Info Producers of feature films and drama for television. Film credits include *On Friday At Eleven* and *City On Fire*.

Submission Guidelines No unsolicited manuscripts will be accepted.

Talent Television Ltd

Lion House, 72–75 Red Lion Street, London, WC1R 4NA

❶ 020 7421 7800
❷ 020 7421 7811
📧 entertainment@talenttv.com
🌐 www.talenttv.com

Contact Managing Director, Anthony Humphreys; Creative Director, John Kaye Cooper

Established 2002

Insider Info Produces entertainment and factual television programmes for UK and international broadcasters. Credits include *Test the Nation* for the BBC, and *Mr Miss Pageant*.

Tips No drama or fictional output will be accepted. A full back catalogue is published on the website.

Talisman Films Ltd

5 Addison Place, London, W11 4RJ

- 020 7603 7474
- 020 7602 7422
- email@talismanfilms.com
- www.talismanfilms.com

Contact Director of Programmes, Richard Jackson
Established 1991
Insider Info Creates screenplays for film and television dramas. Credits include *Complicity*, and *The Secret Adventures of Jules Verne*.
Submission Guidelines Synopses should be sent via agents. No unsolicited manuscripts will be accepted.

talkbackThames

20–21 Newman Street, London, W1T 1PG

- 020 7861 8000
- 020 7861 8001
- www.talkbackthames.tv

Contact CEO, Lorraine Heggessey; Director of Production, Joanna Beresford
Established 2003
Insider Info talkbackThames is the UK arm of Fremantle Media. The company produce drama, comedy, entertainment, features, documentaries, and factual entertainment programming for major television broadcasters. Credits include *The X-Factor* and *How Clean Is Your House?*.
Submission Guidelines Strictly no unsolicited comedy manuscripts.
Tips Shows are very high profile and often fill prime time slots on national television channels.

Talking Heads Productions

2–4 Noel Street, London, W1F 8GB

- 020 729 27575
- 020 7292 7576
- johnsachs@talkingheadsproductions.com
- www.talkingheadsproductions.com

Contact John Sachs
Established 1992
Insider Info Talking Heads Productions historically produced trailers and commercials for corporate clients, and now project manages films and television projects. Credits include the management of aspects of *The Merchant of Venice* film.
Tips Contact John Sachs by email for more information on possible projects.

Tandem TV & Film Ltd

Charleston House, 13 High Street, Hemel Hempstead, HP1 3AA

- 01442 261576
- 01442 219250

- info@tandem.tv
- www.tandem.tv

Insider Info Produces content for corporate and broadcast television. Specialisms in the corporate area are in construction, civil engineering, tunnelling and charities. Tandem deal with both factual and dramatic content.
Tips Tandem provide services to help people or companies achieve their audio visual projects. Contact them for more details on the services provided, from scripting to foreign versions, and to get more information on pricing.

Taylor Made Broadcasts

3B Cromwell Park, Chipping Norton, OX7 5SR

- 01608 646444
- 01608 646461
- post@tmtv.co.uk

Contact Trevor Taylor
Insider Info Taylor Made produces broadcast and corporate television, and video and radio material, specialising in documentaries and factual programmes.
Submission Guidelines No unsolicited manuscripts will be accepted.

Telemagination

Royalty House, 72–74 Dean Street, London, W1D 3SG

- 020 7434 1551
- 020 7434 3344
- mail@tmation.co.uk
- www.telemagination.co.uk

Parent Company Loonland UK Ltd
Contact Managing Director/Head of Studio, Beth Parker
Established 1983
Insider Info Telemagination is a 2D animation studio, mainly producing content for children's television and occasionally producing feature films. Credits include *Heidi* (feature film) and *The Cramp Twins II* (series).
Submission Guidelines Animators, designers, storyboarders and digital artists should send in their CVs, a covering letter and samples of work if interested in working with Telemagination.
Tips Programmes tend to be aimed specifically at young children. View the filmography on the website for examples.

Television Junction

Waterside House, 46 Gas Street, Birmingham, B1 2JT

- 0121 248 4466
- 0121 248 4477
- info@televisionjunction.co.uk

🌐 www.televisionjunction.co.uk
Contact Managing Directors, Yvonne Davies and Paul Davies
Established 1997
Insider Info Produces material for television, websites, DVD, CD-ROM, and print - including educational programming for television. Credits include *What's So Good About Jacqueline Wilson?* and *Reading Aloud with Michael Rosen Christmas Special*.
Submission Guidelines Television Junction is happy to receive and review programme ideas.
Tips Programmes should be educational. Productions include documentaries, animation, drama, training films and corporate videos. Two main broadcast routes are Teachers' TV and Channel 4 daytime.

Tern Television Productions Ltd
73 Crown Street, Aberdeen, AB11 6EX
☎ 01224 211123
☎ 01224 211199
✉ aberdeen@terntv.com
🌐 www.terntv.com
Contact Managing Directors, David Strachan and Gwyneth Hardy
Insider Info Produces mainly factual content for broadcast television. Clients include BBC, ITV, Channel 4 and UKTV. Credits include *The Spa Of Embarrassing Illnesses* for UKTV Style, and *Great British Journeys* for BBC 2. Also has offices in Glasgow and Belfast.
Tips Tern Television produces both regional (for BBC regional channels) and national programming. An overarching theme is 'lifestyle'. Potential writers should explore the back catalogue for a feel of previous style and subject matter.

Testimony Films
12 Great George Street, Bristol, BS1 5RH
☎ 0117 925 8589
✉ steve.humphries@testimonyfilms
🌐 www.testimonyfilms.com
Contact Executive Producer/Producer & Director, Steve Humphreys; Head of Development, David Long
Established 1992
Insider Info Producers of social history and life story programmes for television. Credits include *Little Kinsey* for BBC 4's 'Lost Decade' series and *Timewatch: Children of the Doomed Voyage* for BBC 2.
Submission Guidelines Fill in the online form in the 'Tell us your Story' area of the website. All programme ideas are read.
Tips Ideas should be based around biographies, autobiographies, or historical topics in general. Sex histories have recently been particularly successful.

Tiger Aspect Productions
7 Soho Street, London, W1D 3DQ
☎ 020 7434 6700
☎ 020 7434 1798
✉ general@tigeraspect.co.uk
🌐 www.tigeraspect.co.uk
Contact Managing Director, Andrew Zein
Insider Info Producers of children's, comedy, drama, entertainment, factual, animation and wildlife programming for television, alongside feature films. Credits include *Drugs: A Young Person's Guide* for Channel 4, and *Robin Hood: Series 2* for BBC One.
Submission Guidelines Accepts agented submissions only.
Tips No unsolicited manuscripts, programme ideas or showreels will be considered.

Torpedo Ltd
Llantrisant House, Llantrisant, Cardiff, CF72 8BS
☎ 01443 231989
☎ 01443 231664
✉ info@torpedoltd.co.uk
🌐 www.torpedoltd.co.uk
Contact Head of Production, Jill Jones; Producer, Ceri Wyn Richards
Insider Info Produces factual entertainment and documentaries for radio and television for a variety of clients, including the BBC, ITV and S4C.
Tips Much of the television production in particular has been made for broadcast on regional Welsh stations, and has consisted of documentaries with a strong Welsh element.

Touch Productions
18 Queen Square, Bath, BA1 2HN
☎ 01225 484666
☎ 01225 483620
✉ ideas@touchproductions.co.uk
🌐 www.touchproductions.co.uk
Contact CEO, Malcolm Brinkworth; Creative Director, Nic Jeune
Insider Info Touch produce factual content for broadcast television. Subjects include science, history, current affairs, documentaries, medicine, social history and the arts. Styles range from landmark features to Saturday night entertainment formats. Credits include *Building Britain* for BBC One, and *Human Footprint* for Channel 4.
Submission Guidelines Accepts query with synopsis (email a one page proposal).
Tips Touch Productions welcomes ideas for features or series.

TransAtlantic Films

Studio 1, 3 Brackenbury Road, London, W6 0BE
- 020 8735 0505
- 020 8735 0605

Contact Managing Director, Corisande Albert
Established 1968
Insider Info Produce television documentaries and series, particularly in the areas of travel, music, the arts, science and history. Catalogue available online.
Submission Guidelines No unsolicited scripts will be accepted.

TV Choice

PO Box 597, Bromley, Kent, BR2 0YB
- 020 8464 7402
- 020 8464 7845
- tvchoice@aol.com
- www.tvchoice.uk.com

Contact Norman Thomas
Established 1982
Insider Info Produces material for television, video and DVD. The company produces and distributes educational films for school, libraries, colleges and universities.
Submission Guidelines Accepts query with synopsis.
Tips The productions and distribution library are not primarily for broadcast, but rather for publishing on removable media. Subject matters are wide ranging, but are always educational.

12 Yard Productions

10 Livonia Street, London, W1F 8AF
- 020 7432 2929
- 020 7439 2037
- contact@12yardproductions.com
- www.12yard.com

Established 2001
Insider Info Produces television shows, mainly quiz show formats and innovative factual entertainment. Recent productions include *Eggheads* for BBC 2 and *Without Prejudice* for Channel 4.
Tips The company run a creative trainee scheme for those interested in developing programme ideas. Contact trainees@12yard.com, for details.

Twentieth Century Fox Productions Ltd

Twentieth Century House, 31–32 Soho Square, London, W1D 3AP
- 020 7437 7766
- 020 7434 2170
- www.fox.co.uk

Insider Info The UK arm of the US feature film company. Recent credits include *Die Hard 4.0* and *Alvin and the Chipmunks*.
Submission Guidelines Accepts agented submissions only.

Twofour

Twofour Studios, Estover, Plymouth, PL6 7RG
- 01752 727400
- 01752 727450
- enq@twofour.co.uk
- www.twofour.co.uk

Contact Creative Director & Executive Producer, Stuart Murphy
Established 1988
Insider Info Twofour produces factual entertainment for UK and international terrestrial and satellite television channels. Credits include *The Hotel Inspector* for Five and *Are You Smarter Than A 10 Year Old?* for Sky 1.
Tips Although Twofour is predominantly known for factual and light entertainment, it has recently opened a new drama department, headed by Jo Wright, and is also moving into comedy.

Two Hand Productions

Unit 7, The Old Power Station, 121 Mortlake High Street, London, SW14 8SN
- 020 8878 9777
- 020 8878 9801
- info@twohandproductions.com
- www.twohandproductions.com

Contact Managing Directors, Jonathan Frisby and Luke Gallie
Established 1996
Insider Info Two Hand Productions produces documentary, educational and light entertainment programming for children and adults. Clients include The Discovery Channel, and Five. Credits include *Animal Families* and *No Girls Allowed*, both for Five Children's.
Tips In 2006 Two Hand Productions was the sixth largest supplier of programmes to Channel Five.

UBA Ltd

21 Alderville Road, London, SW6 2EE
- 01984 623619
- 01984 623733
- peterjshaw@btinternet.com

Contact Peter Shaw, Joanna Shaw
Insider Info UBA produces feature films with an international flavour. Credits include *Turtle Diary* and *Castaway*.
Tips UBA will consider new writers. Films should have appeal to an international market.

UBC Media Group

50 Lisson Street, London, NW1 5DF

- 020 7453 1600
- 020 7723 6132
- info1@ubcmedia.com
- www.ubcmedia.com

Insider Info UBC Media owns the radio stations Classic Gold Digital, and One Word Radio. They also produce content for many UK commercial radio stations, as well as the BBC. The group encompasses the Unique and Smooth Operations production companies. Programming ranges from factual entertainment to documentaries, specialist music shows, and comedy.

Tips UBC does not tend to produce straight drama. Most content is factual and varies depending on the radio audience, which in UBC's case stretches across both commercial and public service broadcasters.

Vera Productions

66–68 Margaret Street, London, W1W 8SR

- 020 7436 6116
- 020 7436 6117

Contact Vivienne Clore, Geoff Atkinson
Established 1994

Insider Info Vera produce television comedy. Credits include *Bremner, Bird & Fortune*. A recent link up with Hanrahan Media means a move towards documentary making, alongside the comedy.

Tips Vera Productions have recently been working on developing a successful sit-com type show, particularly for ITV1. As well as traditional broadcasting, Vera also explore viral methods such as internet publishing and podcasting.

VIP Broadcasting

8 Banbury Way, Epsom, KT17 4JP

- 01372 721196
- 01372 726697
- info@vipbroadcasting.co.uk
- www.vipbroadcasting.co.uk

Contact Founder, Chris Vezey
Established 1998

Insider Info Produces features, series and concerts for radio broadcasters.

Submission Guidelines Accepts query with synopsis. No unsolicited manuscripts will be accepted

Tips Programmes are mainly music based. VIP also publish CDs (both live recordings and information based productions).

Waddell Media

Strand Studios, 5–7 Shore Road, Holywood, County Down, Northern Ireland, BT18 9HX

- 028 9042 7646
- 028 9042 7922
- info@waddellmedia.com
- davidc@waddellmedia.com
- www.waddellmedia.com

Contact Head of Development, David Cumming; Creative Director, Jon-Barrie Waddell
Established 1988

Insider Info Waddell Media produces factual and documentary programming for broadcast television. Subjects include lifestyle, leisure, entertainment and music. Credits include *FutureWeapons: Series 3* for Discovery US, and *How Long Will You Live? Series 3* for RTÈ.

Tips Waddell Media do not produce any drama. Waddell's market includes the US, as well as the UK and its regions.

WAGtv

2D Leroy House, 436 Essex Road, London, N1 3QP

- 020 7688 1711
- 020 7688 1702
- info@wagtv.com
- www.wagtv.com

Contact Head of Development, Eliya Arman

Insider Info WAGtv produces factual television programmes and documentaries across a range of subjects. Clients include the BBC, Channel 4, Channel Five, Discovery Networks and PBS.

Tips Copies of past productions are available from the website, and will give a feel for previously successful styles and subject matters.

Wall to Wall

8–9 Spring Place, Kentish Town, London, NW5 3ER

- 020 7485 7424
- 020 7267 5292
- mail@walltowall.co.uk
- development@walltowall.co.uk
- www.walltowall.co.uk

Contact Head of Development, Gavin Rota

Insider Info Produces factual and drama programming for broadcast television. Credits include *Who Do You Think You Are? Series 4* for the BBC, and *Underworld Histories* for the National Geographic Channel. Submissions accompanied by SAE will not be returned. Catalogue available online.

Submission Guidelines Accepts queries by email, or through an agent first.

Tips No unsolicited manuscripts will be accepted, read or stored. Most development is done using in-house writers.

Walsh Bros Ltd
4 The Heights, London, SE7 8JH
- 020 8854 5557
- development@walshbros.co.uk
- www.walshbros.co.uk

Contact John Walsh, David Walsh
Insider Info Produces high-end documentaries, television drama, and feature films. Credits include *Don't Make Me Angry: Series 3*, and the feature film *The Sleeper*.
Submission Guidelines Accepts query via email.
Tips Particular needs for submissions are published on the website.

Walt Disney Company Ltd
3 Queen Caroline Street, London, W6 9PE
- 020 8222 1000
- 020 8222 2795
- customer.support.london@disney.co.uk
- www.disney.co.uk

Insider Info The London offices of the Disney Corporation, producing live action and animated feature films and television, primarily for children and families.
Submission Guidelines No unsolicited manuscripts.
Tips All Disney's commissioning takes place in the US Office, and is through script and film agents only.

Warner Bros. Studios
Warner House, 98 Theobald's Road, London, WC1X 8WB
- 020 7984 5000
- www.warnerbros.co.uk

Insider Info The UK office of the major US production company. Produce feature films and television series, including *The Polar Express* and *Friends*.
Submission Guidelines Accepts agented writers only.

Whistledown Productions Ltd
8a Ayres Street, London, SE1 1ES
- 020 7407 8001
- 020 7261 0939
- info@whistledown.net
- www.whistledown.net

Established 1998
Insider Info Produces features, documentaries, podcasts and adverts for radio. Credits include *The Climate Train* for the BBC World Service and *The Sound of Flanders* for BBC Radio 4.
Submission Guidelines Accepts queries. No unsolicited manuscripts will be accepted without prior arrangement.

Tips The main broadcast route for Whistledown Productions is BBC Radio 4.

Wild Rover Productions
112–114 Lisburn Road, Belfast, Northern Ireland, BT9 6AH
- 028 9050 0980
- 028 9050 0970
- enquiries@wild-rover.com
- www.wild-rover.com

Contact Managing Director, Philip Morrow; Head of Development, John Fitzgerald
Insider Info Produces factual, comedy and entertainment programmes for broadcast television. Credits include *Just for Laughs* for BBC1, and *Nolan Live* for UTV.
Tips Previous programmes have included documentaries and live shows specifically relevant to Northern Ireland, as well as entertainment shows with an international appeal.

Wise Buddah
74 Great Titchfield Street, London, W1W 7QP
- 020 7307 1600
- 020 7307 1601
- info@wisebuddah.com
- www.wisebuddah.com

Contact Paul Plant, Mark Goodier
Established 1994
Insider Info Produces radio programmes, as well as providing post production facilities, talent management, and jingles and music remix production facilities. Productions include *The Johnnie Walker Show* for BBC Radio 2, and *Send In The Clones* for BBC Radio 4.

Working Title Films
Oxford House, 76 Oxford Street, London, W1D 1BS
- 020 7307 3000
- 020 7307 3001
- www.workingtitlefilms.com

Contact Chairmen, Tim Bevan and Eric Fellner
Insider Info Produces feature films and drama, family entertainment and comedy for television. Credits include the films *Pride and Prejudice* and *Atonement*, as well as the television series *Randall and Hopkirk*, and *The Borrowers*.
Submission Guidelines No unsolicited manuscripts will be accepted.

World Productions Ltd
16 Dufours Place, London, W1F 7SP
- 020 7734 3536
- 020 7758 7000

○ jemma@world-productions.com

○ www.world-productions.com

Contact Executive Producer, Tony Garnett;
Development Producer, Tim Baker

Established 1990

Insider Info Produces British television drama.
Recent credits include *Saddam's Tribe* for E4 and
Never Better for BBC2. Purchases around 100 hours of
scripts per year and purchases all rights on accepted
material. Will accept previously published material,
and submissions accompanied with SAE will be
returned. Catalogue available online.

Tips World Productions produces drama for all of
the main UK television broadcasters.

Wortman UK/Polestar

48 Chiswick Staithe, Hounslow, London, W4 3TP

○ 020 8994 8886

○ nevillewortman@beeb.net

Contact Producer (Development), Neville Wortman

Established 1989

Insider Info Film and television. Produces drama,
entertainment, documentaries and corporate
content for mainstream audiences.

Submission Guidelines For films, submit resume,
writing samples and include a short example
of dialogue.

Tips Always look ahead and don't follow
current trends.

WT2

**Oxford House, 76 Oxford Street, London,
W1D 1BS**

○ 020 7307 3000

○ 020 7307 3004

○ www.workingtitlefilms.com

Insider Info A sister company of Working Title Films,
developing lower budget feature films. Credits
include *Billy Elliot* and *Shaun of the Dead*.

Submission Guidelines No unsolicited
manuscripts.

Abbey Theatre

26 Lower Abbey Street, Dublin 1, Republic of Ireland

- 00353 1 887 2000
- 00353 1 872 9177
- info@abbeytheatre.ie
- www.abbeytheatre.ie

Artistic/Editorial Director Fiach Mac Conghail
Contact Literary Director, Aideen Howard; Literary Assistant, Aoife Habenicht
Established 1904
Insider Info Also known as the National Theatre of Ireland.
Submission Guidelines Submit a complete script, but do not write your name on the script itself, only on the covering letter, which should include contact details, background information on the play and your writing experience to date. Submissions accompanied by SAE will be returned. There is no particular style of genre of writing needed, only original, theatrical scripts. Will not accept television or radio scripts, previously published or produced plays, handwritten or emailed scripts, or incomplete scripts.
Tips Presently concentrating on Irish writing only. Check the website for changes to this policy.

Actual Theatre

25 Hamilton Drive, Glasgow, G12 8DN

- 0141 339 0654
- 0141 339 0654
- susan.triesman@strath.ac.uk

Artistic/Editorial Director Susan Triesman
Established 1980
Insider Info Previous plays have been produced in conjunction with the Ramshorn Theatre at the University of Strathclyde.
Tips Past productions have tackled difficult and sensitive subject areas. Send synopsis and sample scene, not whole script.

Almeida Theatre

Almeida Street, Islington, London, N1 1TA

- 020 7288 4900
- 020 7288 4901
- info@almeida.co.uk
- www.almeida.co.uk

Artistic/Editorial Director Michael Attenborough
Established 1837
Insider Info A theatre that produces classic British, Irish and international plays, as well as newly commissioned material. Also hosts an annual opera season. The theatre has a distinctive rounded back wall.
Submission Guidelines No unsolicited scripts.
Tips Freelance directors, assistant directors and freelance actors are used for various productions. Queries about upcoming vacancies are accepted by email.

ATC (Actors Touring Company)

Malvern House, 15–16 Nassau Street, London, W1W 7AB

- 020 7580 7723
- 020 7580 7724
- info@atc-online.com
- www.atc-online.com

Artistic/Editorial Director Gordon Anderson
Established 1980
Insider Info The ATC is a company that produces and tours innovative new work from both the UK and abroad. Plays are performed in small theatres throughout the country.
Tips ATC place great importance on adaptions and translations of international plays, as well as innovative pieces from the UK, and have forged links with companies and playwrights from other countries.

Belgrade Theatre

Belgrade Square, Coventry, CV1 1GS

- 024 7625 6431
- admin@belgrade.co.uk
- www.belgrade.co.uk

Artistic/Editorial Director Hamish Glen
Established 1958
Insider Info Since opening, the Belgrade has produced more than 800 shows including musicals, comedies and drama, seen by over four million people.
Tips The Belgrade Theatre has recently been completely renovated and now has a reputation as one of Britain's most daring theatres.

Bill Kenwright Ltd

BKL House, 106 Harrow Road, London, W2 1RR

- 020 7446 6200
- 020 7446 6222
- www.kenwright.com

Artistic/Editorial Director Bill Kenwright
Insider Info The UK's largest independent theatre production company, producing major plays and musicals for the West End, Broadway and touring companies.

Submission Guidelines Submit script and covering letter by post. Submissions accompanied by SAE will be returned.

Tips Most of the plays produced are by established writers and past productions include hits such as Willy Russel's *Blood Brothers*. Unsolicited scripts are unlikely to be commissioned.

Birmingham Repertory Theatre

Centenary Square, Broad Street, Birmingham, B1 2EP

📞 0121 245 2000

✉ info@birmingham-rep.co.uk

🌐 www.birmingham-rep.co.uk

Artistic/Editorial Director Rachel Kavanaugh

Established 1913

Insider Info The Rep has produced many new UK and foreign plays – many of which have transferred to London theatres. Emphasis is placed upon encouraging a young audience and this is helped by 'Transmissions', a young writers' festival; 'The Young Rep' youth theatre; and 'Page to Stage', a project during which young people can experience the processes involved in producing a new play.

Submission Guidelines No unsolicited scripts.

Tips Although the theatre no longer accepts unsolicited submissions, scripts will be read as part of the 'attachment' scheme with the aim of developing new pieces for production by the company, and to give the writer creative support. First-time writers are eligible, as are established writers who want to develop a brand new play with no pressure. For more information, contact the literary department on 0121 245 2045.

Bootleg Theatre Company

23 Burgess Green, Bishopdown, Salisbury, Wiltshire, SP1 3EL

📞 01722 421476

✉ colin281@btinternet.com

🌐 www.bootlegtheatre.co.uk

Artistic/Editorial Director Colin Burden

Contact Colin Burden

Established 1991

Insider Info Bootleg Theatre Company produces new writing with socially relevant themes for as wide an audience as possible. Produces two professional small scale productions per year, which tour briefly before running on the London Fringe. Aims to respond to manuscript submissions within four weeks. Obtains sole performing rights during the time of production on accepted manuscripts. Payment for accepted manuscripts is a minimum of £500. The maximum depends on funding but can be the Arts Council recommendation payment.

Submission Guidelines Submit complete manuscript. Submissions accompanied by SAE will be returned. Usually produces comedy dramas in the vein of Barrie Keeffe, Tony Marchant etc., which are between 60 and 100 minutes in length. They are simple, yet effective, with fairly minimalistic staging and no more than four cast members. Will not consider any physical theatre, 'Greek style' tragedy or 'Agatha Christie style' pieces with large casts.

Tips Bootleg avoids predictable new work that does not challenge an audience or provoke any thought whatsoever. It produces pieces that are thoughtful, as well as entertaining.

Borderline Theatre Company

North Harbour Street, Ayr, KA8 8AA

📞 01292 281010

📞 01292 263825

✉ enquiries@borderlinetheatre.co.uk

🌐 www.borderlinetheatre.co.uk

Contact Producer, Eddie Jackson

Established 1974

Insider Info One of Scotland's oldest touring companies. Also runs a Lifelong Learning Programme and over 1,400 drama workshops each year, in schools and local communities.

Submission Guidelines Recent plays include *Passing Places* by Stephen Greenhorn; *Good Things* by Liz Lochhead; and *Dead Funny* by Terry Johnson

Tips As well as the adult touring company, Borderline are also involved in youth theatre and work with new plays. Contact emma@borderlinetheatre.co.uk for more details on the youth theatre in general.

Bristol Old Vic Theatre

King Street, Bristol, BS1 4ED

📞 0117 949 3993

📞 0117 949 3996

✉ admin@bristol-old-vic.co.uk

🌐 www.bristol-old-vic.co.uk

Artistic/Editorial Director Simon Reade

Contact Assistant to the Directors, Jane Totney

Established 1776

Insider Info The Main House theatre is set in a Georgian auditorium and is the oldest continuously working theatre in the country. The Studio is a smaller space in the same complex.

Submission Guidelines Submit query to Jane Totney.

Tips The theatre is keen on commissioning new work for the Main House and Studio, as well as for a basement space they have available for development of new pieces. Be aware however, that there is no formal script reading service and it is not exclusively new work that they produce.

Bruce James Productions

68 St George's Park Avenue, Westcliff on Sea, Essex, SS0 9UD

☎ 01702 335970

✉ info@brucejamesproductions.co.uk

🌐 www.brucejamesproductions.co.uk

Artistic/Editorial Director Bruce James

Established 1995

Insider Info The company has produced over 100 musicals, comedies, thrillers, dramas and pantomimes for a number of venues across the country.

Tips Already has an extensive portfolio of shows – see website for details.

Bush Theatre

Shepherd's Bush Green, London, W12 8QD

☎ 020 8743 3584

☎ 020 8743 5443

✉ playsadmin@bushtheatre.co.uk

🌐 www.bushtheatre.co.uk

Artistic/Editorial Director Josie Rourke

Contact Artists Administrator, Tara Wilkinson

Established 1972

Insider Info A London theatre that both commissions pieces and hosts guest productions throughout the year. Produces eight plays per year. Aims to respond to manuscript submissions within four months.

Submission Guidelines Send full manuscript of plays, which are at least 80 minutes in length, by post. Also include a short covering letter and an email address. Submissions accompanied by SAE will be returned.

Tips Of the eight new plays produced per year, around five or six of these are commissioned from new writers through the script reading service. This is a tiny proportion of the 1,000s of scripts received, but the reading team will attempt to give some feedback to each writer that submits their work, even if they are unsuccessful.

The Byre Theatre of St Andrews

Abbey Street, St Andrews, Fife, KY16 9LA

☎ 01334 475000

☎ 01334 475370

✉ enquiries@byetheatre.com

🌐 www.byretheatre.com

Artistic/Editorial Director Stephen Wrentmore

Established 1933

Insider Info The theatre puts on a programme of drama, dance and music. It also runs an active education programme, including groups and projects for the young and old.

Tips The theatre runs a playwrights group, 'Byrewriters'. This is a good source of support for new

writing – previous group members have gone on to be successful playwrights and screenwriters. For more information on joining this group, telephone or write to Elsie Lindsay.

Cheeky Maggot Productions

PO Box 273, 2–3 Bedford Street, London, WC2E 9HH

✉ info@cheekymaggot.co.uk

🌐 www.cheekymaggot.co.uk

Artistic/Editorial Director Amber Agar

Established 2002

Insider Info Cheeky Maggot's aim is to support new writing talent for stage and screen, including the development of first-time writers. Writers who come from minority groups and those who write about subjects that are not typically dealt with in mainstream theatre and film are welcomed. Plays have been performed at the Hampstead Theatre and the Soho Theatre.

Submission Guidelines Submit CV, a description of what you want to work on (new play, workshop, rewrites, etc), and full script if applicable, to: writers@cheekymaggot.co.uk. Plays should have an edge, a passion, and a message that will stimulate an audience. This includes politically or socially aware works. The maximum cast number is usually eight. Prefers not to see previously performed work, although rewrites are considered.

Tips No postal submissions. Actors and directors are also invited to join the company. The company has recently branched out into film development.

Chichester Festival Theatre

Oaklands Park, Chichester, West Sussex, PO19 6AP

☎ 01243 784437

✉ productions@cft.org.uk

🌐 www.cft.org.uk

Artistic/Editorial Director Jonathan Church

Established 1962

Insider Info The theatre presents major productions for audiences both from the UK and internationally. A highlight of the theatre's programme is the Summer Festival, which runs from April to September and showcases both new and classic pieces of theatre. The smaller Minerva Theatre is a later addition to the theatre in a separate building.

Tips Each month, the website publishes an interview with a key member of the theatre's staff. This can be a good source of information on future plans and directions for the theatre. Writers may also email: marketing@cft.org.uk with a review of one of the shows (250 words maximum). Those selected will gain free entry to a future show and the review published on the website. The subject line for this email should read 'Community Critic'.

Citizens Theatre
119 Gorbals Street, Glasgow, G5 9DS
- 0141 429 0022
- 0141 429 7374
- info@citz.co.uk
- www.citz.co.uk

Artistic/Editorial Director Jeremy Raison
Established 1943
Insider Info Citizens Theatre is both a company and a theatre building. As well as the 600 seat Citizens Theatre, there are the Circle Studio, which seats 120 and the Stalls Studio, seating 60. The company largely focuses on classic plays, both British and international, and has presented 288 productions since it began.
Tips Anyone wishing to become involved in the Citizens Community Company, an amateur theatre group, should contact Martin Travers by email: martin@citz.co.uk.

Clwyd Theatr Cymru
Mold, Flintshire, CH7 1YA
- 01352 756331
- 01352 701558
- admin@clwyd-theatr-cymru.co.uk
- www.clwyd-theatr-cymru.co.uk

Artistic/Editorial Director Terry Hands
Established 1976
Insider Info Clywd Theatr Cymru is Wales' most prominent drama production outlet, and houses a production company that tours throughout Wales and the UK, performing mainly in English, but also in Welsh. The Theatre for Young People department uses the same performers, technicians and creative staff when developing productions as the main company does. Hosts drama, dance, music and a community festival in the summer.
Submission Guidelines Plays are a mixture of classics, contemporary pieces and new writing.
Tips Plays from Welsh writers, or about Wales, are of particular interest.

Compass Theatre Company
St Jude's Parish Hall, 175 Gibraltar Street, Sheffield, S3 8UA
- 0114 275 5328
- 0114 278 6931
- neil@compasstheatrecompany.com
- www.compasstheatrecompany.com

Artistic/Editorial Director Neil Sissons
Established 1981
Insider Info A touring company mainly focused on performing classical and modern classic theatre, and classic children's plays.
Tips Although the company are mainly dedicated to producing established plays, part of their artistic policy is to develop some new work that fits well with their classical focus.

Concordance
Finborough Theatre, 118 Finborough Road, London, SW10 9ED
- admin@concordance.org.uk
- www.concordance.org.uk

Artistic/Editorial Director Neil McPherson
Established 1981
Insider Info Theatrical production company resident at the Finborough Theatre, London. Produces six plays per year. Aims to respond to manuscript submissions within three months. Rights obtained on accepted manuscripts are negotiable. Payment is via royalty.
Submission Guidelines Read the literary policy at www.finboroughtheatre.co.uk/literary.htm. Submissions accompanied by SAE will be returned. Produces plays with political and social themes, musical theatre and adaptations of novels. Will not consider adaptations of famous novels, or those on any literary figure prior to 1850.
Tips Concordance also runs a resident assistant director programme. See the website for details of current vacancies.

Contact Theatre Company
Oxford Road, Manchester, M15 6JA
- 0161 274 0642
- 0161 274 0640
- info@contact-theatre.org.uk
- www.contact-theatre.org

Artistic/Editorial Director John E. McGrath
Insider Info An innovative theatre comprising: Space 1, a 350 seat theatre; Space 2, an 80 seat studio; and Space 3, a rehearsal, workshop and performance space. Performances are also put on in the lounge/bar area. Most audiences and participants are aged between 13 and 30, although all ages are welcome. Participation and community outreach is a major part of the theatre's work. Payment for full commissions is in accordance with Writers' Guild of Great Britain rates.
Submission Guidelines Submit an outline summary, a sample of work, and background information on the writer(s) in the form of a covering letter to: RAW@contact-theatre.org.uk, or by post. RAW (Rhythm and Words) is the theatre's new writing scheme. It commissions to various stages, plays, poetry, rap, dance and visual arts pieces.

Anyone with a performance idea that could work in a theatre, whatever its form, is welcome to get in touch.

Tips RAW guidelines are available to download from the website. Ideas go through initial script development (Seed Commission), then onto 'Flip the Script' night, whereby actors perform a small section of the play to a live audience who vote for their favourite. The next stage is a development workshop (this can be the first stage for some ideas). Ideas that are deemed ready are then considered for a full commission.

Crucible Theatre
55 Norfolk Street, Sheffield, S1 1DA
- 0114 249 5999
- 0114 249 6003
- www.sheffieldtheatres.co.uk

Artistic/Editorial Director Samuel West
Contact Literary Associate, Matthew Byam Shaw
Established 1971
Insider Info The Crucible is the main venue in the Sheffield Theatres group for producing theatre works. It also hosts touring productions and famously, the annual World Snooker Championships.
Submission Guidelines Productions tend to use minimal scenery, to avoid blocking the audience's view.
Tips Although few unsolicited scripts are commissioned for the Crucible, the Literary Associate's role is to source and read new scripts and pass promising works on to the Associate Director.

CV Productions
Hampden House, 2 Weymouth Street, London, W1N 3FD
- 020 7636 4343
- 020 7636 2323
- info@cvtheatre.co.uk
- www.cvtheatre.co.uk

Artistic/Editorial Director Charles Vance
Established 1960
Insider Info Presents quality productions in theatres throughout the UK, including adaptations, classic drama and weekly repertory, musicals and pantomime.
Tips Very rarely commissions new works.

Derby Playhouse
Eagle Centre, Theatre Walk, Derby, DE1 2NF
- 01332 363275
- 01332 547200
- info@derbyplayhouse.co.uk
- www.derbyplayhouse.co.uk

Artistic/Editorial Director Stephen Edwards and Karen Louise Hebden
Established 1975
Insider Info Produces new and classic plays. Recent productions include *The Importance of Being Earnest* and *Merrily We Roll Along*. The theatre has a strong reputation outside of the UK.
Tips No longer able to accept unsolicited scripts.

Druid Theatre Company
Flood Street, Galway, Republic of Ireland
- 00353 91 568660
- 00353 91 563109
- info@druidtheatre.com
- www.druidtheatre.com

Artistic/Editorial Director Garry Hynes
Contact New Writing Manager, Thomas Conway
Established 1975
Insider Info Druid was the first professional theatre company in Ireland outside of Dublin. Productions are performed at its home theatre in Galway, as well as being toured nationally and internationally.
Submission Guidelines Submit complete manuscript, with a covering letter. All pages should be A4, single-sided, numbered and bound. Postal submissions only. Submissions accompanied by SAE will be returned. Will not accept plays that have been professionally produced before, or unfinished plays. Cannot produce one act plays, children's plays or musicals, although they can be considered as an introduction to a writer's work.
Tips Although Druid is committed to nurturing new Irish writing, writers from any location are welcome to submit their scripts. Those submitting from outside Ireland must include International Reply Coupons if the manuscript is to be returned.

The Dukes
Moor Lane, Lancaster, LA1 1QE
- 01524 598505
- 01524 598519
- info@dukes-lancaster.org
- www.dukes-lancaster.org

Artistic/Editorial Director Ian Hastings
Contact Theatre Secretary, Jacqui Wilson
Established 1971
Insider Info The Dukes is an independent producing theatre with an integrated programme of participatory activities. The company produces approximately six plays per year. There are five professional productions at The Dukes, and one site specific production at Williamson Park, Lancaster. Plays for, and by young people are presented, specifically at DT3, a dedicated space for this work. Payment is via royalties (eight per cent).

Submission Guidelines Accepts query and synopsis.

Dundee Repertory Theatre
Tay Square, Dundee, DD1 1PB
- 01382 227684
- 01382 228609
- enquiries@dundeereptheatre.co.uk
- www.dundeereptheatre.co.uk

Artistic/Editorial Director James Brining and Dominic Hill
Established 1939
Insider Info The Rep acts as a production house, producing around six new plays a year, as well as receiving touring productions. Works range from drama and comedy, to dance.
Tips The Rep also commissions new works and seeks to translate and adapt classical texts, giving them relevance to the Scotland of today.

Eastern Angles Theatre Company
Sir John Mills Theatre, Gatacre Road, Ipswich, Suffolk, IP1 2LQ
- 01473 218202
- box1@eaternangels.co.uk
- ivan@easternangels.co.uk
- www.easternangles.co.uk

Artistic/Editorial Director Ivan Cutting
Insider Info Produces new plays, mostly with a direct link to East Anglia, either through the writer or subject matter. Plays are performed in theatres throughout the East of England, as well as other venues that can be adapted for the purposes of individual plays.
Tips Eastern Angles focus exclusively on new writing and welcome script submissions, but bear in mind the necessary connection to East Anglia and the types of rural venues that plays are likely to be performed in.

English Touring Theatre
25 Short Street, London, SE1 8LJ
- 020 7450 1990
- 020 7633 0188
- sunwin@ett.org.uk
- www.ett.org.uk

Artistic/Editorial Director Stephen Unwin
Established 1993
Insider Info The company usually spends a part of each season in London, as well as touring the rest of the country. It has a repertoire of around 40 productions of both European classics and new works. Plays are usually performed in medium-sized theatres throughout the UK.
Submission Guidelines No unsolicited submissions.

Tips Although the company does not accept scripts, they do offer some work experience places and a fast track professional development programme, for black, asian and minority ethnic trainee arts managers.

Everyman Theatre
Regent Street, Cheltenham, Gloucestershire, GL50 1HQ
- 01242 512515
- 01242 224305
- admin@everymantheatre.org.uk
- www.everymantheatre.org.uk

Artistic/Editorial Director Sue Colverd
Established 1891
Insider Info Produces and hosts ballet, opera, drama, dance, comedy, musical performances and Christmas pantomimes. As well as the main theatre seating 684, there is also space for 66 people in the Other Space studio theatre, a flexible performance space.
Tips Everyman Reachout is a community scheme designed to involve the young, through youth theatre, right through to older people with the lifelong learning scheme. Part of Reachout's remit is to work with and develop new writers. For more information on any Reachout scheme, contact: reachout@everymantheatre.org.uk.

Finborough Theatre
118 Finborough Road, London, SW10 9ED
- admin@finboroughtheatre.co.uk
- www.finboroughtheatre.co.uk

Artistic/Editorial Director Neil McPherson
Contact Literary Manager, Jane Fallowfield
Established 1980
Insider Info One of London's leading off West End venues, well known for new writing. Produces 15 plays per year, which are performed at the Finborough Theatre, although a number also transfer to other venues - including those in the West End. Aims to respond to manuscript submissions within three months. Rights obtained on commissioned plays are negotiable. Payment is via royalty.
Submission Guidelines Please read and submit according to the literary policy on website. Submissions accompanied by SAE will be returned. Produces new plays, usually on political and social themes. See website for details of what will not be accepted, including plays about the 'relationships or emotional problems of twenty-somethings' and historical and biographical plays set before 1850.
Tips Strongly prefers plays that can only be produced for the stage, and are not just television or

radio scripts by any other name. Please read the literary policy on the website.

Focus Theatre Company

School House, Down Hatherley, Gloucester, GL2 9QB

- 01452 731099
- info@focustheatre.co.uk
- www.focustheatre.co.uk

Artistic/Editorial Director Sheila Mander

Insider Info A company of young people who produce and perform mainly musical theatre at a range of venues.

Tips The website lists the existing portfolio of shows and songs.

Full Circle Theatre Company

16 Hagden Lane, Watford, Hertfordshire, WD18 0HE

- 01923 499 549
- info@fullcircletheatre.co.uk
- scripts@fullcircletheatre.co.uk
- www.fullcircletheatre.co.uk

Established 2002

Insider Info Produces an entire show from script to production. Encourages new writing and the philosophy is to involve members in all aspects of the creative process. Also runs workshops in theatre production and writing skills. Produces two plays per year. Previous performance venues have included the Harrow Arts Centre. Copyright remains with the author. Writers are not paid, but are given full acknowledgement.

Submission Guidelines Submit complete manuscript. All material must be typed. Include contact details on a separate page. Scripts can be in any genre and of any style. One act plays running from 30 to 45 minutes, and short plays which can range from 5 to 20 minutes are considered. Will not accept previously published plays.

Tips Any number of scripts can be submitted by one writer at any time. Those interested in volunteering to become involved in any aspect of the productions are advised to make contact by email.

Gate Theatre Company

11 Pembridge Road, London, W11 3HQ

- 020 7229 5387
- 020 7221 6055
- gate@gatetheatre.co.uk
- www.gatetheatre.co.uk

Artistic/Editorial Director Thea Sharrock

Contact Literary Manager, Claire Lovett

Established 1979

Insider Info The Gate is London's only theatre dedicated to producing international work on a British stage. It has a capacity of around 70.

Submission Guidelines Submit complete manuscript. Submissions accompanied by SAE will be returned. Produces English language plays from non-British writers, including those from North America, Canada, New Zealand, Australia and the Republic of Ireland. Also seeks plays from any country, translated from any language. Will not accept plays by British writers, except foreign adaptions.

Tips Particular attention is paid to lesser known plays in translation. Rights for translation and adaption must be checked thoroughly. Details are usually found within the publication of the play.

Graeae Theatre Company

LVS Resource Centre, 356 Holloway Road, London, N7 6PA

- 020 7700 2455
- 020 7609 7324
- info@graeae.org
- www.graeae.org

Artistic/Editorial Director Jenny Sealey

Established 1980

Insider Info A theatre company staffed and run by disabled people. Productions are a mixture of new interpretations of established plays and newly commissioned pieces. Produces one to three plays per year.

Submission Guidelines Submit complete manuscript. Submissions accompanied by SAE will be returned. Plays must be suitable for disabled performers.

Tips Only interested in plays in English from disabled writers. Although unsolicited scripts are welcomed, there is no official reading service and most plays are commissioned based on previous writing credits.

Hampstead Theatre

Eton Avenue, Swiss Cottage, London, NW3 3EU

- 020 7449 4200
- 020 7449 4201
- info@hampsteadtheatre.com
- literary@hampsteadtheatre.com
- www.hampsteadtheatre.com

Artistic/Editorial Director Anthony Clark

Contact Literary and Education Assistant, Holly Hughes

Insider Info Aims to be a leading theatre for new writing. Rarely produces previously performed plays unless there is a good enough artistic reason to do so. Presents both British and international work. The main auditorium seats 325.

Submission Guidelines Submit complete manuscript. Include a short synopsis and covering letter, as well as an equal opportunities form, available from the website. All pages must be typed, double spaced and A4-sized. Submissions accompanied by SAE will be returned. Will not accept musicals or genre plays.

Tips The theatre is unlikely to produce a play that has been performed before, even at a fringe venue (although it is still worth sending, as an example of your work). All writers who submit work will be given feedback but this is limited to once per play. Only writers who are being developed will be given further assistance, therefore submitting a play before it is ready is unadvisable.

Harrogate Theatre
Oxford Street, Harrogate, North Yorkshire, HG1 1QF
- 01423 502710
- 01423 563205
- info@harrogatetheatre.co.uk
- www.harrogatetheatre.co.uk
Established 1900
Insider Info The theatre and company focus on high quality professional productions, alongside community and outreach work.
Tips The 107 year old Harrogate Theatre has recently been fully refurbished.

Headlong Theatre
Chertsey Chambers, 12 Mercer Street, London, WC2H 9QD
- 020 7438 9940
- 020 7438 9941
- info@headlongtheatre.co.uk
- www.headlongtheatre.co.uk
Artistic/Editorial Director Rupert Goold
Insider Info A touring company interested in exploring new and established writers. The Headlong Theatre likes to commission new work from a wide range of sources. Previously known as the Oxford Stage Company.
Submission Guidelines No unsolicited submissions due to the lack of a dedicated literary department.

Hiss & Boo Theatre Company
1 Nyes Hill, Wineham Lane, Bolney, Sussex, RH17 5SD
- 01444 881707
- 01444 882057
- ian@hissboo.co.uk
- www.hissboo.co.uk
Artistic/Editorial Director Ian Liston
Established 1977

Insider Info A company specialising in music hall, pantomimes, children's theatre, light entertainment and variety. Also provides corporate entertainment and has had some success overseas. Productions are performed in theatres and other venues of all sizes across the UK and abroad. Some productions have been housed in the West End.
Submission Guidelines Accepts query and synopsis by post only (no phone calls). Submissions accompanied by SAE will be returned. Interested in fresh approaches to pantomimes, comedies, thrillers, compilation musicals, children's theatre and revue-style shows.
Tips Hiss & Boo do not usually have the resources to develop new projects, but will read synopses of suitable pieces as detailed above.

Hull Truck Theatre Company
Spring Street, Hull, HU2 8RW
- 01482 224800
- 01482 581182
- admin@hulltruck.co.uk
- literary@hulltruck.co.uk
- www.hulltruck.co.uk
Artistic/Editorial Director John Godber and Gareth Tudor Price
Contact Literary Development Manager, Steven Jon Atkinson
Established 1971
Insider Info One of only six producing theatres in Yorkshire, committed to producing popular and accessible plays. In the past, the works of John Godber have dominated the theatre's programmes.
Submission Guidelines Submit complete manuscript. Script must be bound and typed in single spacing on A4 paper. Also include a covering letter and a half page synopsis. Submissions accompanied by SAE will be returned.
Tips As well as the opportunity to submit unsolicited scripts, Hull Truck also offer the PlayWrite scheme, a ten week course during which students will be encouraged to write a play whilst learning about the craft. Application details and the latest course dates are available on the website. The course is free of charge with the exception of a small admin fee.

Kali Theatre Company
18 Rupert Street, London, W1D 6DE
- 020 7494 9100
- info@kalitheatre.co.uk
- www.kalitheatre.co.uk
Artistic/Editorial Director Janet Steel
Established 1995
Insider Info A company focusing on the writing of Asian women, seeking to give them a voice and to

tackle difficult subjects. Presents full touring productions.

Tips Kali Shorts is a programme that seeks first-time Asian women writers and gives those chosen the chance to go through basic script development, workshops and produce a short piece of their script for audience feedback. Kali Futures gives those successful in Kali Shorts further one to one support, working towards a public reading at the Soho Theatre and Writers Centre. For more information on these schemes, sign up for the newsletter and state that you are a writer.

Kings Head Theatre
115 Upper Street, Islington, London, N1 1QN
- 020 7226 1916
- 020 7226 8507
- info@kingsheadtheatre.org
- www.kingsheadtheatre.org

Artistic/Editorial Director Stephanie Sinclaire
Insider Info One of London's oldest fringe theatres. Produces new works, musicals, classic plays, British contemporary pieces and revues. Performance venue is situated above a bar.
Submission Guidelines No unsolicited scripts.
Tips Although it does not accept unsolicited manuscripts, the King's Head runs a 'Trainee Assistant Director Programme' and an 'Intern programme'. Details are on the website.

Library Theatre Company
Central Library, St Peters Square, Manchester, M2 5PD
- 0161 234 1913
- 0161 228 6481
- ltc@libraries.manchester.gov.uk
- www.librarytheatre.com

Artistic/Editorial Director Chris Honer
Established 1934
Insider Info Produces modern classics, contemporary work and children's theatre.
Tips The theatre is a producing theatre and commissions many new plays, although rarely from unsolicited manuscripts.

Liverpool Everyman and Playhouse
13 Hope Street, Liverpool, L1 9BH
- 0151 708 3700
- 0151 708 3701
- info@everymanplayhouse.com
- www.everymanplayhouse.com

Artistic/Editorial Director Gemma Bodinetz
Contact Literary Manager, Suzanne Bell
Established 1964

Insider Info A producing theatre with a strong new writing element. Aims to respond to manuscript submissions within three months.
Submission Guidelines Submit complete manuscript. All pages must be typed on A4 paper and numbered. Include covering letter, a title page and a list of characters. Submissions accompanied by SAE will be returned. There are no set styles, subjects or genre for plays, but the theatre look for writers who have a genuine passion for storytelling and a willingness to learn, develop and challenge themselves.
Tips No email or faxed scripts. All scripts received with incorrect return postage will be recycled.

Live Theatre Company
Broad Chare, Quayside, Newcastle upon Tyne, NE1 3DQ
- 0191 232 1232
- max@live.org.uk
- www.live.org.uk

Artistic/Editorial Director Max Roberts
Contact Associate Director – New Writing, Jeremy Herrin
Established 1973
Insider Info A theatre company based in a small venue in Newcastle, whose main emphasis is on developing and performing new writing. Works in radio, television and film, as well as theatre. Offers a free script reading service to encourage new writing. Aims to respond to manuscript submissions within two months.
Submission Guidelines Submit complete manuscript. Send two copies, double-spaced on A4 paper, loosely bound. Include a covering letter, a title page and a list of characters. Number all pages and include all contact details on the first page. Submissions will not be returned. Will not accept handwritten manuscripts, email submissions, incomplete scripts, synopses, pantomimes, autobiographies, novels or poetry.
Tips As well as the script reading service in which work is read by a specialist reader and possibly the artistic director, Live Theatre run a scheme called 'Short Cuts'. Email a five minute play or excerpt along with contact details, a synopsis and a character list to degna@live.org.uk and it will be posted on the website for peer review and discussion. The scheme is designed for writers in the Newcastle/North East region, to gain support and constructive feedback.

London Bubble Theatre Company
5 Elephant Lane, London, SE16 4JD
- 020 7237 4434
- 020 7231 2366
- admin@londonbubble.org.uk

www.londonbubble.org.uk
Artistic/Editorial Director Jonathan Petherbridge
Insider Info The company exists to promote theatre arts to both existing fans and first-time theatre goers. Particular emphasis is placed on involving those for whom theatre is not usually accessible because of financial, cultural or geographical barriers. Produces between one and five plays per year. Pieces are performed in small theatres and other venues around London.
Tips London Bubble like to tackle subjects that challenge bigotry and celebrate diversity, whilst remaining accessible and open to those unfamiliar with theatre and the arts.

Lyric Hammersmith
Lyric Square, King Street, London, W6 0QL
- 020 8741 6819
- 020 8741 5965
- enquiries@lyric.co.uk
- www.lyric.co.uk
Artistic/Editorial Director David Farr
Insider Info The Lyric's main auditorium seats 550 whilst The Lyric Studio is a 100 seat 'black box'. The theatre both produces and receives pieces from Britain and abroad.
Tips Productions made in-house are very rarely the result of unsolicited scripts. New pieces are far more likely to come out of an ongoing relationship with a promising writer.

M6 Theatre Company
Studio Theatre, Hamer CP School, Albert Royds Street, Rochdale, Lancashire, OL16 2SU
- 01706 355898
- 01706 712601
- info@m6theatre.co.uk
- www.m6theatre.co.uk
Artistic/Editorial Director Dot Wood
Insider Info A touring company, designed to encourage the development of theatre for young people. Tours schools, community centres and arts centres, mainly in the North West.
Tips The audiences of M6's productions range from very young children to teenagers.

mac
Cannon Hill Park, Birmingham, B12 9QH
- 0121 440 3838
- 0121 446 4372
- info@macarts.co.uk
- www.macarts.co.uk
Artistic/Editorial Director Dorothy Wilson
Established 1963
Insider Info An arts centre offering a wide range of activities and performances, including live theatre,

literary events and children's shows. Spaces include a theatre, cinemas and a variety of other creative studios.
Tips mac Productions is the centre's in-house production company. Opportunities to become involved will be advertised on the website.

Mercury Theatre
Balkerne Gate, Colchester, Essex, CO1 1PT
- 01206 577006
- 01206 769607
- info@mercurytheatre.co.uk
- www.mercurytheatre.co.uk
Artistic/Editorial Director Greg Floy
Contact Administration Assistant, Sam Leppard
Established 1972
Insider Info The Mercury Theatre Company is a highly respected ensemble company producing classic plays and working extensively in the community. Although it focuses predominantly on classic work, there is some scope for producing new writing. Professional productions take place in Mercury's main house or studio theatre. On occasion these productions may subsequently tour.
Submission Guidelines Submit complete manuscript. Manuscripts accompanied by SAE will be returned. Mercury are interested in plays that at some level address significant contemporary questions.
Tips Although there are opportunities for new work to be staged in Mercury's main house, it is more likely to consider work that is suitable for its studio theatre. The website displays Mercury's current season, which should give an idea of the kind of work produced. Although Mercury are fond of farce and light hearted drama, this type of work is generally brought in from commercial producers.

Michael Codron Plays
Aldwych Theatre Offices, Aldwych, London, WC2B 4DF
- 020 7240 8291
- 020 7240 8467
Artistic/Editorial Director Michael Codron
Insider Info A renowned theatre producer, whose company also manages the Aldwych Theatre in London. Not all plays are performed at the Adlwych; many are performed at other venues throughout London, and are toured throughout the UK.
Tips Plays produced tend to be larger productions and are usually straight dramas rather than musicals.

Moral Support
Studio 2, Greville House, 35 Greville Street, London, EC1N 8TB
- 020 7430 9324

moralsupportadmin@gmail.com
www.moralsupport.org.uk
Artistic/Editorial Director Elizabeth Barber and Zoe Klinger
Established 1993
Insider Info Moral Support is a multimedia performance company, which also runs an education programme. Performances are usually staged in fringe theatres and other small arts venues across London and the UK.
Tips All productions are innovative and make use of various media elements. Previous performances have included visual art, dance, sign language and electronic music.

Neal Street Productions
26–28 Neal Street, London, WC2H 9QQ
020 7240 8890
020 7240 7099
post@nealstreetproductions.com
www.nealstreetproductions.com
Artistic/Editorial Director Caro Newling
Insider Info Neal Street are a large scale independent theatre and film production company set up by Sam Mendes, Pippa Harris and Caro Newling. Performances take place in a range of venues, from Broadway to major UK theatres. Previous productions include *Shrek: The Musical*.
Submission Guidelines For legal reasons, unsolicited submissions will not be accepted. All scripts with SAE will be returned unread.

Net Curtains Theatre Company
The Bath House, 96 Dean Street, London, W1D 3TD
07968 564687
claire@netcurtains.org
newplays@netcurtains.org
www.netcurtains.org
Artistic/Editorial Director Claire Farrington
Contact Lorraine Coady
Established 2001
Insider Info Net Curtains is a company of actors that produce and develop new writing for the theatre. They produce two to three plays per year. The company mainly perform in small theatres and other arts venues around London.
Submission Guidelines Submit complete manuscript by post (including synopsis and SAE). Submissions accompanied by SAE will be returned. There are no specific styles or genres required, however pieces on social issues that capture the imagination of the company are preferred.
Tips The company meet once a week to review scripts that have either been commissioned or submitted. They also welcome applications from workshop leaders and directors who are interested in working in partnership with them. Email for further details.

Newpalm Productions
20 Cavendish Avenue, London, N3 3QN
020 8349 0802
020 8346 8257
Artistic/Editorial Director John Newman
Established 1970
Insider Info Newpalm Productions has produced hundreds of touring productions for the UK (including the West End) and internationally. Previous shows have included *The Blue Angel* and *Peter Pan – The Musical*, both in the West End.
Tips Newpalm Productions very rarely produce new writing, although new pieces have been produced in the past.

New Perspectives Theatre Company
Park Lane Business Centre, Park Lane, Basford, Nottingham, NG6 0DW
0115 927 2334
0115 927 1612
info@newperspectives.co.uk
www.newperspectives.co.uk
Artistic/Editorial Director Daniel Buckroyd
Insider Info New Perspectives is a touring company that aims to bring theatre to new and existing audiences around the villages, market towns and more prominent venues. Three to four plays are produced per year.
Tips The company offers trainee schemes and other opportunities to get involved. Subscribe to the e-newsletter for news on the latest commissions and opportunities for new talent.

The New Theatre
43 East Essex Street, Temple Bar, Dublin 2, Republic of Ireland
00353 1 670 3361
info@thenewtheatre.com
www.thenewtheatre.com
Artistic/Editorial Director Anthony Fox, Leanne Willars, Robert Lane, and Ronan Wilmot
Insider Info The New Theatre presents and produces new work, established plays and other theatre mainly dealing with Irish social issues. It is also available to youth theatre companies and can offer them the chance to work with theatre professionals.
Tips Prospective writers must bear in mind the Irish slant on most new work produced.

The New Vic Theatre

Etruria Road, Newcastle under Lyme, Staffordshire, ST5 0JG

☎ 01782 717954

✆ 01782 712885

✉ admin@newvictheatre.org.uk

🌐 www.newvictheatre.org.uk

Artistic/Editorial Director Theresa Heskins

Established 1986

Insider Info The New Vic is Staffordshire's regional producing theatre. It also tours productions and receives a number of shows and exhibitions. Ten new plays are produced per year.

Submission Guidelines Submissions accompanied by SAE will be returned.

Tips Most new plays are produced through commissions, and there is no official script reading service for writers unknown to the theatre.

The New Wolsey Theatre

Civic Drive, Ipswich, Suffolk, IP1 2AS

☎ 01473 295911

✆ 01473 295910

✉ info@wolseytheatre.co.uk

✉ ekidd@wolseytheatre.co.uk

🌐 www.wolseytheatre.co.uk

Artistic/Editorial Director Peter Rowe

Established 2001

Insider Info The New Wolsey opened in 2001, following the closure of the original Wolsey Theatre. The main theatre seats 400 and hosts in-house productions, as well as those from touring companies. Performances include drama, music, comedy, poetry, dance and children's shows.

Tips The theatre runs a variety of workshops and competitions for playwrights wishing to develop their scripts.

NITRO

6 Brewery Road, London, N7 9NH

☎ 020 7609 1331

✆ 020 7609 1221

✉ info@nitro.co.uk

🌐 www.nitro.co.uk

Artistic/Editorial Director Felix Cross

Established 1978

Insider Info Previously known as The Black Theatre Cooperative, Nitro is Europe's oldest black theatre company and produces mainly musical theatre from new black writers.

Tips New writing should reflect the experiences of black people in contemporary society.

Northcott Theatre

Stocker Road, Exeter, Devon, EX4 4QB

☎ 01392 223999

✆ 01392 223996

✉ artisticdirector@northcott-theatre.co.uk

🌐 www.northcott-theatre.co.uk

Artistic/Editorial Director Ben Crocker

Established 1967

Insider Info Northcott Theatre is the South West's leading producing theatre, opening around 44 weeks per year. The theatre also hosts a limited number of touring productions. Produces approximately ten productions per year.

Tips Email marketing@northcott-theatre.co.uk to sign up for their newsletter and keep updated with the news surrounding future programmes.

Northern Stage

Barras Bridge, Newcastle upon Tyne, NE1 7RH

☎ 0191 230 5151

✆ 0191 261 8093

✉ info@northernstage.co.uk

🌐 www.northernstage.co.uk

Artistic/Editorial Director Erica Whyman

Insider Info Northern Stage is the largest producing theatre company in the North East. They also tour throughout the UK and Europe and seek to continue forging links with theatre groups in South Africa.

Tips The theatre's audience is very varied. Past shows have included modern dance, Shakespeare, children's theatre, musicals, comedy, poetry and international drama.

Northumberland Theatre Company (NTC)

The Playhouse, Bondgate Without, Alnwick, NE66 1PQ

☎ 01665 602586

✆ 01665 605837

✉ admin@ntc-touringtheatre.co.uk

🌐 www.ntc-touringtheatre.co.uk

Artistic/Editorial Director Gillian Hambleton

Established 1978

Insider Info NTC is a professional small scale touring company that aims to provide theatre to rural areas, where access to live performance is scarce.

Tips Unsolicited scripts are unlikely to be commissioned. However, this contact may lead to a future relationship in the case of promising writers.

Norwich Puppet Theatre

St James, Whitefriars, Norwich, Norfolk, NR3 1TN

☎ 01603 615564

✆ 01603 617578

✉ luisboy@puppettheatre.co.uk

www.puppettheatre.co.uk
Artistic/Editorial Director Luis Boy
Established 1980
Insider Info Norwich Puppet Theatre produces puppetry and animation theatre, primarily for a family centred audience. The touring company performs at their home base in Norwich and also to schools, venues in the UK, and festivals abroad. The aims of the company are to develop and promote the art form of puppetry/theatre of animation to wider audiences. If they are selected to go to festivals, productions can travel through Europe and beyond. The company produce one play per year and aim to report back to writers within four weeks. Most NPT productions are created in a workshop environment, so often a script is the starting point from which the production will be created. The rights agreement and subsequent payment will depend on the resulting production and payment will be via royalties (three per cent).
Submission Guidelines Accepts query and synopsis. Submissions accompanied by SAE will be returned.

Nottingham Playhouse
Wellington Circus, Nottingham, NG1 5AF
- 0115 947 4361
- 0115 947 5759
- www.nottinghamplayhouse.co.uk
Artistic/Editorial Director Giles Croft
Established 1963
Insider Info Nottingham Playhouse is a 750 seat theatre that produces new pieces, as well as receiving productions and touring.
Tips Nottingham Playhouse is part of the Theatre Writing Partnership scheme, along with Derby Playhouse, Leicester Haymarket, New Perspectives and Royal and Derngate Theatres, Northampton. The scheme is designed to develop new theatre writing in the region. For more information, visit www.theatrewritingpartnership.com.

Nottingham Playhouse Roundabout
Wellington Circus, Nottingham, NG1 5AF
- 0115 947 4361
- 0115 947 5759
- www.nottinghamplayhouse.co.uk
Established 1973
Insider Info Nottingham Playhouse Roundabout is a theatre in education company, working as part of Nottingham Playhouse Theatre. It produces plays and workshops for children and young people, as well as training and support for teachers. It mainly works within schools, colleges, universities, community and youth groups, small theatre venues, conferences and festivals around Nottingham,

although it occasionally tours around the UK and internationally.
Tips For information for new writers, visit the Theatre Writing Partnership, www.theatrewritingpartnership.com, of which the Roundabout Theatre company is a member. Bear in mind that scripts must have an educational value and be aimed at children.

Nuffield Theatre
University Road, Southampton, SO17 1TR
- 023 8031 5500
- 023 8031 5511
- info@nuffieldtheatre.co.uk
- www.nuffieldtheatre.co.uk
Artistic/Editorial Director Patrick Sandford
Contact Assistant to the Directors, Alison Thurley
Established 1964
Insider Info The Nuffield Theatre produces plays for adults and children in the main house and studio. It also tours nationally and internationally to theatres, schools and other arts venues. Productions include new writing and classics.
Tips New writers wishing to work with the theatre are invited to apply for The Nuffield Theatre Writers' Group, which meets fortnightly on Thursday evenings. Each cycle runs for two years and members produce a ten minute play, a 40 minute radio play and a full length piece for the theatre. For details for the next round of applications email: alison.thurley@nuffieldtheatre.co.uk.

The Octagon Theatre
Howell Croft South, Bolton, BL1 1SB
- 01204 529407
- 01204 556502
- info@octagonbolton.co.uk
- www.octagonbolton.co.uk
Artistic/Editorial Director Mark Babych
Established 1967
Insider Info Octagon Theatre is a production and receiving theatre company with two seasons of shows per year; January to July, and September to January. Shows include musical theatre, classic drama, contemporary classics and comedies.
Tips There are many community and education projects linked with the theatre that can help develop script writing skills, as well as an established youth theatre. There is no literary department and therefore they have no official reading scheme for unsolicited scripts.

Oldham Coliseum Theatre
Fairbottom Street, Oldham, OL1 3SW
- 0161 624 1731
- 0161 624 2829

mail@coliseum.org.uk
www.coliseum.org.uk
Artistic/Editorial Director Kevin Shaw
Contact Production Manager, Mark Alexander
Insider Info The Coliseum Theatre hosts touring productions and commissions new work. Aims to respond to submissions within four months.
Submission Guidelines Submit complete script, typed on single-sided A4 sheets (including a synopsis and a list of casting requirements). Submissions accompanied with SAE will be returned.
Tips The Coliseum runs playwrights courses, and workshops as well as industry sessions and playwriting competitions. Check the website for details, or email: insideout@coliseum.org.uk.

Old Red Lion Theatre
418 St John Street, London, EC1V 4NJ
020 7833 3053
helenoldredlion@yahoo.co.uk
www.oldredliontheatre.co.uk
Artistic/Editorial Director Helen Devine
Established 1979
Insider Info The Old Red Lion theatre is mainly a receiving theatre for innovative and contemporary work.
Tips Theatre companies that are producing new writing and interested in hiring the venue should post a script to the Artistic Director, including some information about the company and a production proposal.

Operating Theatre Company
22 Burghley Road, Kentish Town, London, NW5 1UE
020 7419 2476
info@operating-theatre.co.uk
operating-theatre.co.uk
Artistic/Editorial Director Ken Christiansen
Contact Literary Manager, Mali Tudno Jones
Established 2002
Insider Info Operating Theatre Company is a new writing theatre network. The company offers opportunities and developmental training to all manner of writers. From established names through to novices and first-time playwrights, they provide dramaturgical services and run regular workshops to improve skills and test ideas. Since 2002 the company has strived to generate the sharpest and most original new writing in the UK, and has created a community of enthusiastic and busy artists. Approximately 14 plays aimed at all audiences are produced every year, at various venues. The company aims to respond to writers within six weeks. No rights are obtained on accepted

manuscripts and payment is via outright purchase (minimum £1,500, maximum £6,000).
Submission Guidelines Submissions accompanied by SAE will be returned. Email copies are preferred on request. Plays produced focus upon new writing and there are no limitations in terms of cast, props or staging.

Orange Tree Theatre
1 Clarence Street, Richmond, Surrey, TW9 2SA
020 8940 0141
020 8332 0369
admin@orange-tree.demon.co.uk
www.orangetreetheatre.co.uk
Artistic/Editorial Director Sam Walters
Established 1971
Insider Info Orange Tree Theatre is an off West End theatre, in the round, producing new plays, adaptations, foreign pieces and musicals.
Submission Guidelines No unsolicited manuscripts will be accepted. Send an initial query before submitting material.
Tips All productions must be suitable for a theatre in the round.

Out of Joint
7 Thane Works, Thane Villas, London, N7 7NU
020 7609 0207
020 7609 0203
ojo@outofjoint.co.uk
www.outofjoint.co.uk
Artistic/Editorial Director Max Stafford-Clark
Contact Literary Manager, Alex Roberts
Insider Info Out of Joint is a national and international touring company focused on the development and production of new writing. The company performs in various venues throughout the UK and abroad. Frequent venues include the Royal Court and the National Theatre. They aim to report back to writers within three months.
Submission Guidelines Submit complete manuscript, by post only, to Alex Roberts. Submissions accompanied by SAE will be returned. Email submissions will not be accepted.
Tips View www.outofjoint.co.uk/education/readinglist.html for an extensive list of writers that Out of Joint have previously worked with.

Ovation Theatres
Upstairs at the Gatehouse, Highgate Village, London, N6 4BD
020 8340 4256
020 8340 3466
events@ovationproductions.com
www.ovationtheatres.com
Established 1985

Insider Info Ovation Theatres is the company responsible for running Upstairs at the Gatehouse, a 140 seat fringe theatre in Highgate, North London. It also stages productions for events such as the Edinburgh Fringe festival.

Tips Upstairs at the Gatehouse's artistic policy is to encourage new writers and directors. They will give preference to the hire of theatre space for theatre companies who wish to revive established plays.

Paines Plough
4th Floo, 43 Aldwych, London, WC2A 4DN
- 020 7240 4533
- 020 7240 4534
- office@painesplough.com
- www.painesplough.com

Artistic/Editorial Director Roxana Silbert
Contact Literary Manager, Pippa Ellis
Insider Info Paines Plough is a touring company, specialising in developing new and contemporary writers and the production of their work. They also offer a script reading service. Aims to respond to writers within three months.

Submission Guidelines Submit complete manuscript. Postal submissions only will be accepted. Submissions accompanied by SAE will be returned. Will not accept musicals, pantomimes, TIE plays or performance art pieces, or any scripts from writers outside the UK.

Tips Other than the script reading facility, Paines Plough offer other services to new writers such as 'Wild Lunches' where 45 minute scripts are developed in conjunction with the theatre and then performed to the public. Check their website for other upcoming calls for submissions and competitions.

Perth Theatre and Horsecross
185 High Street, Perth, PH1 5UW
- 0845 612 6324
- info@horsecross.co.uk
- www.horsecross.co.uk

Artistic/Editorial Director Ian Grieve
Insider Info The theatre hosts performances produced by Horsecross, an organisation borne out of the Perth Theatre. Horsecross produce a varied programme of theatre, dance, drama, comedy and music in this and other venues.

Tips 'Horsecross' is the brand name for the Perth Concert Hall, the Perth Theatre, Horsecross conferences and Horsecross events. As a brand, they place great emphasis on new technologies and experimental performances, as represented by Threshold, the new media digital art exhibition space in Perth Concert Hall foyer.

Polka Theatre for Children
240 The Broadway, Wimbledon, London, SW19 1SB
- 020 8545 8320
- 020 8545 8365
- admin@polkatheatre.com
- richardmashannon@polkatheatre.com
- www.polkatheatre.com

Artistic/Editorial Director Jonathan Lloyd
Contact Associate Director (New Writing), Richard Shannon
Established 1967
Insider Info The Polka Theatre is a specialist theatre for young people and children, exploring new writing and classics. It is a registered charity, open to a local and international audience.

Submission Guidelines Submit a five page sample and a synopsis in the first instance, then a full script may be requested. Submissions accompanied by SAE will be returned.

Tips There are extremely detailed guidelines on the website as to what makes a good piece of children's theatre. The theatre also runs the scheme, 'Playgrounding', through which writers can develop through workshops, one to one sessions and mentoring. For further details of the scheme and how to apply, email: frauke@polkatheatre.com.

Popular Productions Ltd
18b Hornsey High Street, London, N8 7PB
- 020 8347 0221
- info@popularproductions.co.uk
- www.popularproductions.co.uk

Contact Producers: John Payton and Lucy Blakeman
Insider Info The company produces a range of theatre, from musical comedies to straight drama and thrillers. Recent productions have included *Teachers*, by John Godber, and *Look Back in Anger*, by John Osbourne, at the Madinat Theatre in Dubai. Most plays are performed at prominent theatrical venues across the world.

Tips Although the company tend to put on well established, popular works, they state that new writing is something that they develop alongside their more commercial shows.

Proteus Theatre Company
Queen Mary's College, Cliddesden Road, Basingstoke, Hampshire, RG21 3HF
- 01256 354541
- 01256 356186
- info@proteustheatre.com
- www.proteustheatre.com

Artistic/Editorial Director Mary Swan
Established 1979

Insider Info Proteus is a touring company with an audience across the South East of England, producing approximately three plays per year. Many shows are inter-disciplinary, including photography, film, dance, music and visual arts. Touring venues are mainly village halls and community spaces.

Submission Guidelines No unsolicited manuscripts will be accepted. Proposals must include a synopsis, cast breakdown and a CV. A cast of approximately four actors is normally employed, although there can be more than four characters in the play.

Tips The subject matter of the plays must appeal to families.

Queen's Theatre
Billet Lane, Hornchurch, RM11 1QT
- 01708 462362
- 01708 462363
- info@queens-theatre.co.uk
- www.queens-theatre.co.uk

Artistic/Editorial Director Bob Carlton

Established 1953

Insider Info The Queen's Theatre is a producing theatre for Essex and Outer London. The main theatre seats 503 people.

Submission Guidelines Accepts submissions via query and synopsis. No unsolicited scripts will be considered. Queen's Theatre produces a mixture of musical theatre, comedy and straight drama.

Tips The theatre runs an established new writing programme, including an awards scheme, a playwright's festival, a writers' group and playwriting courses. Details and dates of events are advertised on the website.

The Questor's Theatre
12 Mattock Lane, Ealing, London, W5 5BQ
- 020 8567 0011
- enquiries@questors.org.uk
- www.questors.org.uk

Artistic/Editorial Director Peter Field

Established 1929

Insider Info The Questor is Europe's largest community theatre, producing both classic theatre and new writing, as well as reviving little known plays. The complex has a 400 seat main theatre and a 100 seat studio space. Recent productions include J.M. Barrie's *Peter Pan* and Shakespeare's *As You Like It*.

Submission Guidelines No unsolicited manuscripts will be accepted.

Quicksilver Theatre
4 Enfield Road, London, N1 5AZ
- 020 7241 2942
- 020 7254 3119
- talktous@quicksilvertheatre.org
- www.quicksilvertheatre.org

Artistic/Editorial Director Guy Holland and Carey English

Established 1977

Insider Info Quicksilver is a touring company specialising in new writing for children. An emphasis is placed on bold visual style and strong narratives, to produce exciting and educational theatre for young audiences.

Tips Quicksilver usually split their audience into two groups; three to five year olds who like small productions in intimate venues, based on things that matter to their lives; and older children who require challenging plays with thought provoking storylines.

The Ramshorn Theatre
University of Strathclyde Drama Centre, 98 Ingram Street, Glasgow, G1 1ES
- 0141 552 3489
- 0141 553 2036
- ramshorn.theatre@strath.ac.uk
- www.strath.ac.uk/culture/ramshorn

Artistic/Editorial Director Susan Triesman

Established 1992

Insider Info The Ramshorn Theatre is based around an 80 seat studio space with a movable seating system. It has a very close relationship with the Strathclyde Theatre Group.

Tips The Ramshorn New Playwrights Initiative encourages new playwriting through readings, courses and productions. The idea is to give a voice to those writers not normally heard in Scottish theatre. Contact the theatre for details on how to become involved.

The Really Useful Group Ltd
22 Tower Street, London, WC2H 9TW
- 020 7240 0880
- 020 7240 1204
- online_team@reallyuseful.co.uk
- www.reallyuseful.com

Artistic/Editorial Director Andrew Lloyd Webber

Established 1977

Insider Info The Really Useful Group is an international entertainment company whose activities include theatre, film, television, video and concert productions, merchandising, records and music publishing. Performances are usually for the West End or Broadway initially, and have resulting tours. Theatre productions tend to be large scale musical productions or dramas. Recent productions include *The Sound of Music* and *The Woman in White*

Submission Guidelines The Really Useful Group is owned and run by Andrew Lloyd Webber and tends to focus on productions of his work. No unsolicited manuscripts will be accepted and all scripts will be returned unopened.

Real People Theatre Company
37 Curlew Glebe, Dunnington, Yorkshire, YO19 5PQ
- 01904 488870
- realpeople@totalserve.co.uk

Artistic/Editorial Director Sue Lister
Established 1999
Insider Info Real People Theatre Company is a touring company of women.
Tips Contact Sue Lister for details of current and future work. Writing and productions are by women only.

Red Ladder Theatre Company
3 St Peter's Buildings, York Street, Leeds, LS9 8AJ
- 0113 245 5311
- 0113 245 5351
- rod@redladder.co.uk
- www.redladder.co.uk

Artistic/Editorial Director Rod Dixon
Established 1969
Insider Info The company produces approximately three performances per year and aims to produce high quality theatre, new writing and educational works. Performances tend to take place in small community venues, youth clubs and small-scale theatres, where theatre is not normally available to young people. Aims to respond back to writers within six months and offers ITC/Equity writer's contract rights on accepted manuscripts.
Submission Guidelines Accepts query and synopsis. Produces one-hour plays for a cast of no more than five actors. The work should aim to connect with a youth audience and both challenge them and offer them new insights. The company considers a range of styles and seeks originality. No single issue dramas will be considered.
Tips Upcoming trends to be aware of include the uses of new technologies in production (DVD, video projection), which appeal to sophisticated young audiences. The company request that full length plays are not submitted and that prospective writers get in contact before submitting any material, with details about yourself, why you would like to write for Red Ladder and any ideas you have. For young people aged 18–25 who want to become involved in the company in any capacity, email Leyla Asadi for more information. For young, Northern Asian people who wish to attend drama workshops in Bradford as part of Red Ladder's ATC (Asian Theatre School), email Madani Younis.

Red Shift Theatre Company
TRG2 Trowbray House, 108 Weston Street, London, SE1 3QB
- 020 7378 9787
- 020 7378 9789
- mail@redshifttheatreco.co.uk
- www.redshifttheatreco.co.uk

Artistic/Editorial Director Jonathan Holloway
Established 1982
Insider Info The Red Shift Theatre Company is a touring company. Produces one or two performances per year. Performances usually take place in unusual venues, both rural and urban, throughout the UK.
Submission Guidelines No unsolicited scripts will be accepted. The company produce adaptions of classic works, in addition to some new writing.
Tips Although Red Shift do not read unsolicited scripts, they do have occasional placements for directing and administration staff for particular productions. Visit the jobs section of the website for details.

Ridiculusmus
BAC, Lavender Hill, London, SW11 5TN
- 020 7223 9959
- 020 7978 5207
- enquiries@ridiculusmus.com
- www.ridiculusmus.com

Artistic/Editorial Director David Hough and John Woods
Established 1992
Insider Info Ridiculusmus is a touring company that produces new plays and adaptions.
Submission Guidelines Ridiculusmus does not accept unsolicited scripts.
Tips Plays tend to be produced spontaneously rather than to adhere to an artistic policy.

Robert Fox Ltd
6 Beauchamp Place, London, SW3 1NG
- 020 7584 6855
- 020 7225 1638
- info@robertfoxltd.com
- www.robertfoxlimited.com

Artistic/Editorial Director Robert Fox
Established 1980
Insider Info Robert Fox is a producer of high profile theatre and films. Stage productions are mainly for the West End. Recent venues have included the Theatre Royal, Haymarket and the Wyndhams Theatre.
Submission Guidelines Either fill out the online form, or send a one page synopsis by mail. No full manuscripts will be accepted, Plays must appeal to audiences in the West End, on Broadway and at

other major receiving theatres throughout the UK, the US and Australia.

Tips Read through the extensive list of previous productions on the website to check that your work is on a similar scale.

Royal Court Theatre
Sloane Square, London, SW1W 8AS
- 020 6565 5050
- 020 7565 5001
- info@royalcourttheatre.com
- www.royalcourttheatre.com

Artistic/Editorial Director Domonic Cooke
Established 1956
Insider Info Royal Court Theatre is a leading national theatre company focussed on new writing from the UK and abroad. The theatre has strong links with many countries across the world and runs a very active international education programme. As well as at its home in London, productions are staged in the US and Australia.
Submission Guidelines Submit complete manuscript, by mail only, addressed to the Literary Department (including a half page synopsis and SAE). Strictly no email or fax submissions will be accepted. Submissions accompanied with SAE will be returned.
Tips The theatre also runs a Young Writer's Programme for people aged 13–25 who want to become involved in contemporary drama production. The scheme involves courses, workshops and much more. Young people are welcome to submit their scripts for feedback. For more information, contact: ywp@ royalcourttheatre.com.

Royal Exchange Theatre Company
St Ann's Square, Manchester, M2 7DH
- 0161 833 9333
- 0161 832 0881
- marketing@royalexchange.co.uk
- www.royalexchange.co.uk

Artistic/Editorial Director Braham Murray and Greg Hersov
Established 1976
Insider Info The Royal Exchange Theatre Company is committed to developing and producing new writing. Since the opening of a 90 seat studio in 2002, performances have included international pieces, commissions by writers from the North West and plays for young people.
Tips In recent years writers have been invited to enter the Bruntwood Playwriting Competition as a way of submitting scripts to the theatre. They have also been offered the opportunity to propose short pieces for performance in summer festivals. Check

the website for ongoing schemes such as this, as the theatre is dedicated to new writing.

Royal Lyceum Theatre Company
Grindlay Street, Edinburgh, EH3 9AX
- 0131 248 4800
- 0131 228 3955
- info@lyceum.org.uk
- www.lyceum.org.uk

Artistic/Editorial Director Mark Thomson
Established 1965
Insider Info The Royal Lyceum Theatre Company produces classic British and international plays. They are also keen on developing new writing, particularly by Scottish writers. The theatre itself has a well developed range of educational programmes.
Tips New Scottish writing is always of interest, but there is no official script reading policy in place.

Royal National Theatre
South Bank, London, SE1 9PX
- 020 7452 3333
- 020 7452 3030
- info@nationaltheatre.org.uk
- www.nationaltheatre.org.uk

Artistic/Editorial Director Nicholas Hytner
Contact Literary Manager, Jack Bradley
Established 1963
Insider Info The National Theatre's complex houses three theatres and has up to eight productions in repertory at any one time. As well as productions, the theatre offers other events and services, including short early evening performances, children's and educational work, exhibitions, live music and outdoor events.
Submission Guidelines The theatre will accept postal submissions only of entire scripts. Submissions accompanied by SAE will be returned.
Tips Although the National Theatre is dedicated to producing new writing, the pieces are usually directly commissioned. They do state however, that unsolicited scripts will get read and responded to individually, although there may be a delay due to the sheer volume of scripts received.

Royal Shakespeare Company
The Courtyard Theatre, Southern Lane, Stratford upon Avon, Warwickshire, CV37 6BB
- 01789 403444
- 01789 262341
- www.rsc.org.uk

Artistic/Editorial Director Michael Boyd
Insider Info The Royal Shakespeare Company is a national theatre company who perform both at home in Stratford upon Avon and in venues throughout the UK. Productions include the works of

Shakespeare, other classic English plays, and new writing.

Tips The vast majority of productions are Shakespeare plays and although the RSC do produce some new plays, these are usually directly commissioned by well known writers.

Salisbury Playhouse
Malthouse Lane, Salisbury, Wiltshire, SP2 7RA
- 01722 320117
- 01722 421991
- info@salisburyplayhouse.com
- www.salisburyplayhouse.com

Artistic/Editorial Director Joanna Read
Insider Info Salisbury Playhouse is a producing theatre for audiences in Salisbury, Wiltshire, Hampshire and Dorset. The company aims for a mixture of local, national and international theatre, and stages both new and classic productions.
Tips Co-productions are an emerging trend in the theatre's output, including collaborations with the Young Vic and the Chester Gateway. Plays staged at the Playhouse need to appeal to a largely semi-rural audience.

7:84 Theatre Company (Scotland) Ltd
4 Summertwon Road, Glasgow, G51 2LY
- 0141 445 7245
- admin@784theatre.com
- www.784theatre.com

Artistic/Editorial Director Lorenzo Mele
Established 1970
Insider Info A prominent Scottish touring company whose focus is on political theatre and its ability to affect policy making decisions. Performances are hosted at theatres and other arts venues throughout Scotland.
Submission Guidelines No unsolicited manuscripts.
Tips Although 7:84 cannot accept scripts from new writers, it does take part in Fuse, a national script search project in association with Playwrights' Studio, Scotland and NTS Workshop. For more information on submitting your script to Fuse, visit www.playwrightsstudio.co.uk/fuse.html.

Sgript Cymru
Chapter, Market Road, Canton, Cardiff, CF5 1QE
- 029 2023 6650
- 029 2023 6651
- sgriptcymru@sgriptcymru.com
- www.sgriptcymru.com

Artistic/Editorial Director Simon Harris
Contact Literary Manager, Arwel Gruffydd
Established 2000

Insider Info Sgript Cymru is Wales' national company for contemporary theatre, dedicated to developing new writing. Plays are produced in both Welsh and English.
Submission Guidelines Submit complete manuscript. All pages should be single sided, typed, loosely bound and accompanied by SAE. No email submissions will be accepted. Submissions accompanied by SAE will be returned. No film, television or radio scripts will be accepted.
Tips Writers must either be Welsh or living in Wales. Although Welsh themes are important, scripts do not have to reflect these directly and the writer's Welsh connection is more important than the story's. Plays should be broadly placed in the contemporary drama genre.

Shared Experience
The Soho Laundry, 9 Dufour's Place, London, W1F 7SJ
- 020 7434 9248
- 020 7287 8763
- admin@sharedexperience.org.uk
- www.sharedexperience.org.uk

Artistic/Editorial Director Nancy Meckler and Polly Teale
Established 1975
Insider Info Shared Experience is a touring company whose aim is to explore the physical and emotional relationship between the actor and the audience. Recent productions have included Diane Samuels' *Kindertransport*.
Submission Guidelines No unsolicited manuscripts will be accepted.
Tips Shared Experience are not a new writing company and although they produce some new adaptions, these are always directly commissioned.

Sherman Theatre Company
Senghennydd Road, Cardiff, CF24 4YE
- 029 2064 6901
- 029 2064 6902
- admin@shermantheatre.co.uk
- www.shermantheatre.co.uk

Artistic/Editorial Director Chris Ricketts
Insider Info The Sherman Theatre Company houses a producing and receiving theatre, a touring company, and a well developed youth theatre. Performances are primarily aimed at young audiences. Plays are performed at the Sherman theatre and toured nationally and internationally.
Tips The Sherman Theatre is in the process of merging with Sgript Cymru. The new company, called Sherman Cymru, is due to launch at the end of the year.

Show of Strength

74 Chessel Street, Bedminster, Bristol, BS3 3DN

- ☎ 0117 902 0235
- ☎ 0117 902 0196
- ✉ info@showofstrength.org.uk
- 🌐 www.showofstrength.org.uk

Contact Creative Producer, Sheila Hannon; Associate Producer, Gill Loats

Established 1986

Insider Info Show of Strength is a company that focuses on contemporary drama in unusual spaces, from conventional theatres to railway stations. The company is mainly based in South West England.

Tips Recent productions have included short pieces on railway platforms at commuter times, demonstrating the innovative nature of the company. Staffing and time issues mean there may be a long delay in reading any unsolicited scripts.

Soho Theatre

21 Dean Street, London, W1D 3NE

- ☎ 020 7287 5060
- ☎ 020 7287 5061
- ✉ writers@sohotheatre.com
- 🌐 www.sohotheatre.com

Artistic/Editorial Director Lisa Goldman

Contact Literary Assistant, Dale Heinan

Established 1969

Insider Info Soho Theatre is a London producing theatre whose productions include drama, comedy and cabaret, appealing to a wide ranging audience. The theatre has a well developed new writing programme. Aims to report back to writers within three months.

Submission Guidelines Submit complete manuscript (including a brief covering letter and SAE). No email submissions will be accepted. Submissions accompanied by SAE will be returned. No excerpts, incomplete scripts, pieces for radio, television or film, novels, or poetry that is not specifically for performance will be considered.

Tips As well as the script reading service, the theatre's new writing programme offers writing attachments, competitions, awards and seed commissions, all open to new playwrights. Visit the website for full details.

Solent People's Theatre

Bedhampton Arts Centre, Bedhampton Road, Havant, PO9 3ET

- ☎ 023 9242 3399
- ☎ 023 9242 3401
- ✉ info@solentpeoplestheatre.com
- 🌐 www.solentpeoplestheatre.com

Established 1976

Insider Info Solent People's Theatre is a touring company that aims not only to entertain audiences, but to forge communities through cultural participation. An example of the theatre's work is the current three year project, 'Critical Engagement' that aims to encourage participation in democracy, especially by young people. Performances include a short piece of drama followed by the use of electronic voting systems and democratic discussion.

Tips Bear in mind the theatre's aim to engage people and communities in wider social issues that directly affect them.

Sphinx Theatre Company

25 Short Street, London, SE1 8LJ

- ☎ 020 7401 9993/4
- ☎ 020 7401 9995
- ✉ info@sphinxtheatre.co.uk
- 🌐 www.sphinxtheatre.co.uk

Artistic/Editorial Director Sue Parrish

Established 1973

Insider Info The Sphinx Theatre Company is touring company focused on women's experiences. Writers and directors are predominantly women, although men are involved as actors and other collaborators. The company usually tours small or mid-sized venues throughout the UK and sometimes internationally.

Submission Guidelines Submit complete manuscript (hard copies only, including SAE) addressed to the Artistic Director. Submissions accompanied by SAE will be returned.

Tips Writers are advised to contact the Artistic Director before submitting a script, to establish if there is any initial interest. Productions are predominantly written by women, but men are invited to submit scripts for the Brave New Roles scriptwriting award, details of which will appear on the website.

Steven Joseph Theatre

Westborough, Scarborough, YO11 1JW

- ☎ 01723 370540
- ☎ 01723 360506
- ✉ enquiries@sjt.uk.com
- 🌐 www.sjt.uk.com

Artistic/Editorial Director Alan Ayckbourn

Established 1955

Insider Info The Steven Joseph Theatre as it exists now, was opened in 1996. It houses The Round, a 404 seat auditorium, and The McCarthy, a 165 seat end stage. Most resources are put into first productions of new plays. Produces appropriately ten plays per year.

Submission Guidelines Check the website to see if unsolicited submissions are being accepted at this time

Tips Many of the plays produced are the work of Alan Ayckbourn, however a new writing programme does exist to ensure other writers are given opportunities. In usual circumstances, scripts will be read and assessed by a team of readers. It is rare for an unsolicited script to be produced, but it can be a way of starting a relationship with the theatre.

Tabard Theatre

2 Bath Road, London, W4 1LW
- 020 8995 6035
- info@tabardtheatre.co.uk
- www.tabardtheatre.co.uk

Established 1985

Insider Info Located above a pub, the theatre has traditionally been known for new writing, but now has a broader programme of entertainment and theatre.

Tips New writing is less of a focus for the theatre now, as it becomes a more prominent receiving venue.

TEG Productions

Third Floor, 73 Great Titchfield Street, London, W1W 6RD
- 020 7379 1066
- enquiries@tegproductions.com
- www.jeremymeadow.com

Artistic/Editorial Director Jeremy Meadow

Established 1997

Insider Info TEG productions is a producer of large scale musicals and straight theatre.

Submission Guidelines Recent productions include Alan Plater's *Blonde Bombshells of 1944* at the Hampstead Theatre and Bolton Octagon.

Tips TEG Productions only produces plays with good commercial potential, and is not likely to commission unknown writers.

Theatre Absolute

57–61 Corporation Street, Coventry, CV1 1GQ
- 024 7625 7380
- 024 7655 0680
- chris@theatreabsolute.co.uk
- www.theatreabsolute.co.uk

Artistic/Editorial Director Chris O'Connell

Established 1992

Insider Info Theatre Absolute is a touring company dedicated to developing and producing new writing. Performance venues tend to be small and mid-sized theatres and arts centres across the UK.

Submission Guidelines Submit complete manuscript.

Tips Plays are invited for submission to The Writing House, a scheme whereby plays are given real, in-depth development over a long period, with no time or commissioning pressures. An example of a play developed in this way is Chris O'Connell's *Street Trilogy*.

Theatre Centre

Shoreditch Town Hall, 380 Old Street, London, EC1V 9LT
- 020 7729 3066
- 020 7739 9741
- admin@theatre-centre.co.uk
- www.theatre-centre.co.uk

Artistic/Editorial Director Natalie Wilson

Established 1953

Insider Info Theatre Centre is a touring company that aims to produce exciting new theatre for young people. The company produces approximately four new productions per year. Performance sites include schools, theatres and other arts venues that are accessible for young people.

Tips The company has a strong new writing policy. An example of a recent production is Sarah Woods' *Walking on Water*, a piece about exclusion using playground games, music and strong visuals to convey a message. As part of its equal opportunities philosophy, new writing from women, black, asian, gay, disabled and young people is welcomed. The theatre currently commissions plays by firstly approaching writers of whom they have been made aware.

Theatre of Comedy Company

210 Shaftesbury Avenue, London, WC2H 8DP
- 020 7379 3345
- 020 7836 8181

Insider Info The Theatre of Comedy Company produces new comedy and adapts established and classic works.

Tips The company reviews scripts for film and television as well as theatre. All submissions must be comedic in the broadest sense.

The Theatre Royal and Drum Theatre

Royal Parade, Plymouth, PL1 2TR
- 01752 668282
- info@theatreroyal.com
- www.theatreroyal.com

Artistic/Editorial Director Simon Stokes

Insider Info A producing and receiving theatre with two auditoriums. The main theatre seats between 787 and 1,315 (with its adjustable seating), and the Drum Theatre seats 200. Presents a mixture of musical theatre and drama by local, national and international companies.

Submission Guidelines No unsolicited manuscripts will be accepted.

Tips Although the theatre does produce original material, this is normally commissioned via known agents or scriptwriters' societies.

Theatre Royal Stratford East
Gerry Raffles Square, London, E15 1BN

- 020 8534 7374
- 020 8534 8381
- theatreroyal@stratfordeast.com
- rmishra@stratfordeast.com
- www.stratfordeast.com

Artistic/Editorial Director Kerry Michael

Contact New Writing c/o Karen Fisher; Assistant to Artistic Director, Ritra Mishra

Established 1884

Insider Info Located in a very culturally mixed community, the theatre is committed to developing new writing that reflects and appeals to a diverse audience.

Submission Guidelines No unsolicited manuscripts will be accepted, but proposals are welcome (including a synopsis, ten page sample and a short writer's biography).

Tips Be very aware of the local community and potential audience, as the area contains very deprived communities and is extremely culturally diverse. Plays that bring out these themes through drama are welcomed, although quality pieces on a variety of other themes will also be considered. Check the website for up to date details of courses and workshops that are regularly offered.

Theatre Royal Windsor
Thames Street, Windsor, Berkshire, SL4 1PS

- 01753 863444
- 01753 831673
- info@theatreroyalwindsor.co.uk
- www.theatreroyalwindsor.co.uk

Artistic/Editorial Director Angela Edwards

Established 1793

Insider Info The Theatre Royal Windsor is a producing theatre, with productions including classics, drama, comedy, pantomime and new work.

Tips The theatre has produced several plays that have been transferred to the West End. Productions tend to be reasonably commercial; comedies, thrillers and dramas are most popular.

Theatre Workshop
34 Hamilton Place, Edinburgh, EH3 5AX

- 0131 225 7942
- 0131 220 0112
- info@theatre-workshop.com
- www.theatre-workshop.com

Artistic/Editorial Director Robert Rae

Established 1965

Insider Info Theatre Workshop is a producing theatre that includes disabled actors in its main productions, paying special attention to access and inclusion issues. The theatre itself seats 155.

Tips Theatre Workshop regularly commissions new writing. As the theatre is located in Scotland, Scottish writers or pieces relevant to modern Scottish life are popular. Scripts should take into account that actors and others involved may be disabled, as well as able bodied. The theatre enjoys working with organisations of minority groups.

The Torch Theatre
St Peter's Road, Milford Haven, Pembrokeshire, SA73 2BU

- 01646 694192
- 01646 698919
- info@torchtheatre.co.uk
- www.torchtheatre.co.uk

Artistic/Editorial Director Peter Doran

Established 1977

Insider Info The Torch Theatre produces pieces for in-house performances and touring. Recent productions include the farce piece *Noises Off*.

Tips The Torch Theatre is a registered charity and is unlikely to have the funding to produce work with new writers. However, this does not mean that scripts will not be read, time permitting.

Traverse Theatre
10 Cambridge Street, Edinburgh, EH1 2ED

- 0131 228 3223
- philip@traverse.co.uk
- www.traverse.co.uk

Artistic/Editorial Director Philip Howard

Contact Literary Assistant, Louise Stephens

Established 1963

Insider Info Scotland's theatre of new writing, with two performance spaces – 100 and 250 seats respectively. Produces six plays per year. Aims to respond to manuscript submissions within six months. Only retains rights on play texts at the point at which they are produced, unless they are commissioned scripts.

Submission Guidelines Submit complete manuscript. Submissions accompanied by SAE will be returned.

Tips Produces some international work but rarely from unsolicited sources. Focuses on producing contemporary Scottish plays, plays by writers based in Scotland and plays with a strong and clear connection to Scottish culture.

Trestle Theatre Company

Trestle Arts Base, Russet Drive, St Albans, Hertfordshire, AL4 0JQ

- 01727 850950
- 01727 855558
- admin@trestle.org.uk
- www.trestle.org.uk

Artistic/Editorial Director Emily Gray
Established 1981
Insider Info A touring company producing storytelling, mask-based theatre from its Hertfordshire base. Offers a range of educational and community drama activities. Produces two to three plays per year. Performances take place at a variety of venues including small and medium sized theatres and arts centres across the UK. A recent production was *Little India*, a reworking of *Shakuntala*, involving the physicalities of martial arts, rhythmic patterns and hand gestures.
Submission Guidelines Unsolicited scripts are unlikely to be accepted.

Tricycle Theatre

269 Kilburn High Road, London, NW6 7JR

- 020 7372 6611
- 020 7328 0795
- info@tricycle.co.uk
- www.tricycle.co.uk

Artistic/Editorial Director Nicholas Kent
Established 1980
Insider Info A theatre, cinema and exhibition centre within a culturally diverse community.
Submission Guidelines Submissions accompanied by SAE will be returned.
Tips The local community includes such diverse cultural groups as Irish, Afro-Caribbean, Jewish and Asian, and the choice of writers and writing tends to reflect this. A fee may be charged for unsolicited scripts. Please phone or email for details.

Tron Theatre Company

63 Trongate, Glasgow, G1 5HB

- 0141 552 3748
- 0141 552 6657
- casting@tron.co.uk
- www.tron.co.uk

Artistic/Editorial Director Gregory Thompson
Established 1981
Insider Info A producing and receiving theatre committed to producing new work from Scottish writers, as well as hosting drama, music and comedy events. Although the theatre itself houses most of the home grown productions, some pieces are toured internationally.
Submission Guidelines No unsolicited manuscripts.

Unicorn Theatre

147 Tooley Street, More London, Southwark, London, SE1 2HZ

- 020 7645 0500
- 020 7645 0550
- artistic@unicorntheatre.com
- www.unicorntheatre.com

Artistic/Editorial Director Tony Graham
Contact Associate Artistic Director, Rosamunde Hutt; Associate Director (Literary), Carl Miller; Assistant to the Artistic Team, Ruth Weyman
Established 1947
Insider Info A professional theatre producing and programming work for a young and family audience. Produces four plays per year, which are performed at the Unicorn Theatre, London. Aims to respond to manuscript submissions within one month.
Submission Guidelines Query by email for information on the way in which they work with writers. Submissions accompanied by SAE will be returned. Must have a maximum cast of eight.

Warehouse Theatre

Dingwall Road, Croydon, CR0 2NF

- 020 8681 1257
- 020 8688 6699
- info@warehousetheatre.co.uk
- www.warehousetheatre.co.uk

Artistic/Editorial Director Ted Craig
Contact Literary Associate, Richard Vincent; Writers Workshop Leader, Ken Christiansen
Established 1977
Insider Info A producing theatre focused on new writing. The theatre itself seats around 100. Also runs the annual International Playwriting Festival.
Submission Guidelines Read the guidelines on the website for information on how to submit plays for the International Playwriting Festival and to download an application form. Postal submissions only.
Tips The best way to submit a script is via the festival (see above). Entries must not have been published or performed before (amateur productions notwithstanding), but may be translations. Full length plays only, on any topic. Firstly the judges select the shortlist of ten plays, then four of these plays are selected to be performed during the festival itself. Full details are published on the website, or contact ted@warehousetheatre.co.uk.

Watford Palace Theatre

Clarendon Road, Watford, WD17 1JZ

- 01923 235455
- 01923 819664
- enquiries@watfordpalacetheatre.co.uk
- www.watfordtheatre.co.uk

Artistic/Editorial Director Brigid Larmour
Established 1908
Insider Info A regional producing theatre presenting modern works, comedy, adaptations, classics, and pantomimes. Also acts as a receiving theatre to touring productions.
Submission Guidelines Although unsolicited scripts will be read, writers are advised to send a synopsis in the first instance. Submissions accompanied by SAE will be returned.
Tips The theatre runs a playwright's group, WPT Playwrights, designed to provide script development and support. Group plays are sometimes performed at the theatre. There is a separate group for young playwrights.

West Yorkshire Playhouse
Playhouse Square, Quarry Hill, Leeds, LS2 7UP
☎ 0113 213 7800
☎ 0113 213 7250
✉ info@wyp.org.uk
🌐 www.wyp.org.uk
Artistic/Editorial Director Ian Brown
Contact Literary Manager, Alex Chisholm
Established 1990
Insider Info A community producing theatre comprising of the 750 seat Quarry Theatre, and the Courtyard Theatre, which seats 350. Has a strong new writing emphasis. Productions include classic British and international drama, contemporary work, and new plays with particular focus on writers from the North of England.
Submission Guidelines Only send the first ten pages in the first instance – promising scripts will be requested in full. Address to Alex Chisholm. Submissions accompanied by SAE will be returned.
Tips As well as a script reading service, the Playhouse offer a range of schemes designed to foster new writing, including performances of developing plays with after show discussions, workshops, and the chance to apply for script development grants.

Whirligig Theatre
14 Belvedere Drive, Wimbledon, London, SW19 7BY
☎ 020 8947 1732
☎ 020 8947 1732
✉ whirligig-theatre@virgin.net
🌐 www.davidwood.org.uk
Artistic/Editorial Director David Wood
Insider Info Occasionally produces theatre for young children, both from new writing and adaptions of existing plays and children's books. Performance venues range from primary schools to theatres.

Tips David Wood's back catalogue of plays is available on his website. He also answers script queries from new writers through a forum on the site.

White Bear Theatre Club
138 Kennington Park Road, London, SE11 4DJ
☎ 020 7793 9193
🌐 www.whitebeartheatre.co.uk
Artistic/Editorial Director Michael Kingsbury
Insider Info A company producing new writing and reviving classic plays. Has previously had productions transferred to the West End.
Tips Scripts should fit with the contemporary, risk-taking ethos of the company. View the recent productions on the website, as well as the website of their associated company, Box of Tricks, at www.boxoftrickstheatre.co.uk.

York Theatre Royal
St Leonard's Place, York, YO1 7HD
☎ 01904 658162
☎ 01904 550164
✉ marketing@yorktheatreroyal.co.uk
🌐 www.yorktheatreroyal.co.uk
Artistic/Editorial Director Damien Cruden
Established 1744
Insider Info Primarily a receiving theatre, presenting drama and musical theatre, including West End shows.
Tips The theatre runs youth projects and community education projects. There is no official new writing scheme.

The Young Vic
66 The Cut, London, SE1 8LZ
☎ 020 7922 2800
☎ 200 7922 2802
✉ info@youngvic.org
🌐 www.youngvic.org
Artistic/Editorial Director David Lan
Established 1970
Insider Info A leading theatre for young talent, particularly directors. These productions are presented alongside those by more established artists. Recent productions include Tarell Alvin McCraney's *The Brothers Size,* and Peter Weiss's *The Investigation.*
Tips There are extensive opportunities for young people and adults to become involved with the theatre in many capacities. Visit the website for details of schemes such as work experience and training projects. The productions tend to be fairly high profile, so unsolicited scripts are unlikely to be commissioned.

Y Touring Theatre Company

One KX, 120 Cromer Street, London, WC1H 8BS

- 020 7520 3090
- 020 7520 3099
- info@ytouring.org.uk
- www.ytouring.org.uk

Artistic/Editorial Director Nigel Townsend
Contact Associate Director, Jenny May While
Established 1989
Insider Info The touring theatre arm of the YMCA, which aims to explore issues that are pertinent for young people in contemporary society. Many productions deal with difficult subjects. Recently, the company has moved into performances for adults.
Submission Guidelines Submit complete manuscript. Include a CV and covering letter. Email or postal submissions are accepted.
Tips The company advise that responses to scripts may be subject to lengthy delays due to time and staffing constraints. It is also recommended that writers join the mailing list, so they can be kept up to date with productions in their area.

Yvonne Arnaud Theatre

Millbrook, Guildford, Surrey, GU1 3UX

- 01483 440077
- 01483 564071
- yat@yvonne-arnaud.co.uk
- www.yvonne-arnaud.co.uk

Artistic/Editorial Director James Barber
Established 1965
Insider Info A theatre complex with a main stage hosting pantomimes, touring productions and plays commissioned in-house, and the smaller Mill Studio – showcasing smaller, experimental productions, and dance shows.
Tips The website details the many community projects and courses that those interested in the theatre may become involved in, including production groups, outreach projects and classes.

UK & IRISH LITERARY AGENTS

A&B Personal Management Ltd
Suite 330 Linen Hall, 162–168 Regent Street, London, W1B 5TD
- 020 7434 4262
- 020 7038 3699
- billellis@aandb.co.uk

Contact R.W. Ellis
Established 1982
Insider Info Currently handles non-fiction and fiction writing, as well as scripts. No unsolicited manuscripts. Please submit query email first. Rejected work will be destroyed with no rejection slip sent. Commission rates of 12.5 per cent for domestic sales, 15 per cent for foreign sales and 12.5 per cent for film sales. Charges a reading fee for full length book manuscripts.
Non-fiction Accepts General non-fiction books.
Fiction Deals with Novels.
Scripts Handles Television and Film scripts, Stage plays, Episodic dramas, and Sitcoms.
Tips Enquire about fees before submitting proposal. No unsolicited manuscripts considered.

Abner Stein
10 Roland Gardens, London, SW7 3PH
- 020 7373 0456
- 020 7370 6316

Contact Abner Stein
Established 1971
Insider Info Not currently seeking new clients. Handles non-fiction books and novels. Submissions by query letter first. Commission rates of ten per cent for domestic sales, 20 per cent for foreign sales.
Non-fiction Deals with General non-fiction books.
Fiction Handles General fiction and Novels.
Tips Represents mainly US authors and agents.

The Agency (London) Ltd
24 Pottery Lane, Holland Park, London, W11 4LZ
- 020 7727 1346
- 020 7727 9037
- info@theagency.co.uk
- www.theagency.co.uk

Contact Stephen Durbridge, Leah Schmidt, Julia Kreitman, Bethan Evans, Norman North, Hilary Delamere, Katie Haines (Children's Authors/Illustrators), Nick Quinn, Faye Webber, Fay Davies, Ian Benson (Film & Television), Jago Irwin; Royalty Manager, Natalicio Barretto
Established 1995
Insider Info Currently handles writers and authors for television, film, theatre and radio, as well as directors, producers and composers. Also represents children's authors and illustrators. Commission rates of ten per cent for domestic sales, with foreign sale commission by arrangement. Does not charge a reading fee.
Fiction Will consider Children's and Adult's fiction.
Scripts Will consider Film, Television, Radio and Theatre scripts.
Submission Guidelines Does not accept unsolicited material.
Recent Sale(s) *Bog Child*, Siobhan Dowd (David Fickling Books); *Yes Man*, Danny Wallace (Heyday Films/Warner Brothers)
Client(s) Andy Armitage, Steve Barlow, Janet Burchett, Alan Durant, Amanda Swift, Fiona Dunbar, Michael Bond, Heather Dyer, Tom Macrae, Andrew Norris, Malorie Blackman, Neil Arksey
Tips Adult fiction is accepted from existing clients only. Unsolicited manuscripts will not be accepted.

Aitken Alexander Associates
18–21 Cavaye Place, London, SW10 9PT
- 020 7373 8672
- 020 7373 6002
- reception@aitkenalexander.co.uk
- www.aitkenalexander.co.uk

Contact Gillon Aitken; Clare Alexander (New Fiction Writers, History, Biography, Memoir and Science); Kate Shaw (Literary and Popular Fiction for Adult's and Children's Authors); Lesley Thorne (Screenplays, Literary Fiction, Crime Thrillers, Memoir, Travelogue/Adventure, Biography and Popular Culture); Ayesha Karim (Memoir, Travelogue, History and Current Affairs); Matthew Hamilton (Literary Fiction, Thrillers and Popular Culture); Andrew Kidd (Literary and Contemporary Fiction)
Established 1976
Insider Info Actively seeking clients. Currently handles non-fiction books, novels, children's books, television scripts and movie scripts. Aims to respond to queries and proposals within eight weeks. Unsuccessful submissions are returned with SAE.

Commission rates are ten per cent for domestic sales, 20 per cent for foreign sales and ten per cent for film sales. Does not charge a reading fee.

* The agents have mainly come from publishing and editorial backgrounds.

Non-fiction Considers Biography/Autobiography, History, Memoirs, Popular culture, Science/Technology and Travel books.

Fiction Consider General, Literary and Children's fiction titles.

Scripts Considers General scripts.

Submission Guidelines Send query letter with outline, biography and a 30 page sample of writing. All pages should be single-sided and double-spaced.

Client(s) Josephine Cox, Sebastian Faulks, Helen Fielding, Germaine Greer, J.D. Salinger, Tom Shakespeare and Andrew Wilson

Tips Formerly known as Gillon Aitken Associates. Aitken Alexander Associates are unable to answer queries by email. Postal queries and submissions only. A list of writing credits (in any genre) would be useful to include with the submission.

Alan Brodie Representation Ltd

6th Floor, Fairgate House, 78 New Oxford Street, London, WC1A 1HB

- 020 7079 7990
- 020 7079 7999
- info@alanbrodie.com
- www.alanbrodie.com

Contact Managing Director (and Agent), Alan Brodie; Director (and Agent), Sarah McNair; Director, Alison Lee (Finance); Agent, Lisa Foster (New Writing); PA to Alan Brodie, Harriet Pennington Legh (Amateur Licensing)

Established 1989

Insider Info Specialises in stage, screen and radio. Seeking both new and established writers for television scripts, film scripts, stage plays and radio scripts. Queries responded to within three months. Manuscripts returned only if accompanied by SAE. Does not charge a reading fee. Clients usually obtained through recommendation. Commission rates of ten per cent for domestic sales, and 15 per cent for foreign sales.

Scripts Will consider Television, Film, Stage Play and Radio scripts.

Submission Guidelines Accepts query letter with CV and letter of recommendation. Sample work will be requested if interested.

* No book proposals considered.

Recent Sale(s) *Confessions of a Shopaholic*, Tim Firth; *My Family Christmas Special*, Brian Leveson and Paul Minett (BBC1)

Client(s) Paul Mendelson, Penny Black, Roger Crane, John Godber, Tom McGrath, Gordon Steel, Malcolm McGee, C.P.Taylor, Sharon Foster, Nell Dunn, Alistair McGowan, Moby Pomerance, James Stock, Mark Tuohy, Morna Regan, Bill Morrison, Michael Wilcox, Abi Zakarian, Thornton Wilder, Corin Redgrave, Bertolt Brecht

Tips Initial contact must include a recommendation from an industry professional. No unsolicited manuscripts accepted.

Alexandra Nye

'Craigower', 6 Kinnoull Avenue, Dunblane, Perthshire, FK15 9JG

- 01786 825114

Contact Director, Alexandra Nye

Established 1991

Insider Info Actively seeking clients. Currently handles fiction and non-fiction books and novels. Submissions accompanied by SAE will be returned. Clients usually obtained through queries/submissions. Commission rates of ten per cent for domestic sales, 20 per cent for foreign sales. Reading fee will be charged for a detailed report on manuscripts.

Non-fiction Will consider Biography/Autobiography and History.

Fiction Will consider General and Literary fiction.

Submission Guidelines Accepts query with SAE and synopsis.

* No telephone enquiries. Poetry or plays not considered.

Client(s) Dr Tom Gallagher, Harry Mehta

Tips The agency is known for its interest in Scottish history and literary fiction.

A.M. Heath

6 Warwick Court, Holborn, London, WC1R 5DJ

- 020 7242 2811
- 020 7242 2711
- www.amheath.com

Contact Bill Hamilton, (Literary and Commercial Fiction and Non-fiction); Sara Fisher (Translation Rights, Client Representation); Sarah Molloy (Children's Writers); Victoria Hobbs (Literary and Commercial Fiction and Non-fiction); Euan Thorneycroft (Literary and Commercial Fiction and Non-fiction)

Established 1919

Insider Info Actively seeking clients. Currently handles non-fiction books, children's books and novels. Aims to respond within four months. Proposals returned if accompanied by SAE. Commission rates of 15 per cent for domestic sales, 20 per cent for foreign sales, 15 per cent for film sales. Does not charge a reading fee.

Non-fiction Will consider Biography/Autobiography and History.

Fiction Will consider Literary, Commercial and Children's fiction.

Submission Guidelines Send query letter with SAE, synopsis and three sample chapters. Submission should be double spaced on single-sided A4 paper.

Client(s) Christopher Andrew, Rosemary Ashton, David Conn, Kate Ellis, William Horwood and Helena McEwan

Tips No young children's fiction, scripts or poetry accepted. Manuscripts or queries will not be accepted via email.

The Ampersand Agency
Ryman's Cottages, Little Tew, Chipping Norton, Oxfordshire, OX7 4JJ

- 01608 683677/683898
- 01608 683449
- peter@theampersandagency.co.uk
- www.theampersandagency.co.uk

Contact Peter Buckman (All types of submissions); Anne-Marie Doulton (Literary Fiction, Women's Fiction)

Established 2003

Insider Info Seeking both new and established writers. Considers literary and commercial fiction and non-fiction books, and children's books aimed at 8 year-olds and above. No poetry, fantasy or science fiction. Represents more than 35 clients, 85 per cent of whom are new or previously unpublished writers. Will consider simultaneous submissions. Aims to respond to queries within two weeks and manuscripts within four weeks. Unsuccessful proposals will be returned with SAE. The Ampersand Agency obtains new clients through recommendations from others and through queries and submissions. Will also sometimes approach writers with ideas. Has seen 17 book projects through publication in the past year. Commission rates of 12.5–15 per cent for domestic sales, 20 per cent for foreign sales and 15 per cent for film sales. Offers a written contract that may be terminated at any time. Does not charge a reading fee or offer a criticism service.

* The agency specialises in good story-telling, whether in fiction or non-fiction, and is made distinct by its candour and rapid responses. Before becoming an agent, Peter Buckman was a publisher and then a full-time writer. Anne-Marie Doulton was an editor and a literary scout.

Non-fiction Will consider Biography/Autobiography, Children's, Cooking/Food, Education, History, Memoirs, Politics/Current Affairs, Popular Culture, True Crime/Investigative and Women's non-fiction.

Fiction Will consider Children's Fiction, Detective/Police/Crime, Family saga, Historical, Literary, Mainstream, Mystery, Romance, Thriller/Espionage, Women's/'Chick lit' and Young Adult fiction.

Scripts Only handles scripts from existing book author clients.

Submission Guidelines Send query letter with outline, one or two sample chapters and author biography. Also accepts queries via email. Actively seeking good stories, commercial and literary fiction and non-fiction, for adults and young people. Does not want poetry, science fiction, fantasy or political satires set in the future.

Recent Sale(s) *Taking the Medicine*, Druin Burch (Chatto); *Zelah Green: Queen of Clean*, Vanessa Curtis (Egmont); *Dream Machine*, Will Davis (Bloomsbury); *Double Cross*, Tracy Gilpin (Black Star); *Sting of Justice*, Cora Harrison (Macmillan); *Octavia's War*, Beryl Kingston (Allison & Busby); *Smart/Casual*, Niamh Shaw (Headline)

Client(s) Client(s) include: Helen Black, S.J. Bolton, Martin Conway, Druin Burch, Anna Crosbie, Andrew Cullen, Vanessa Curtis, Will Davis, Catherine Deveney, Tracy Gilpin, Cora Harrison, Georgette Heyer, Michael Hutchinson, Beryl Kingston, Miriam Morrison, Philip Purser, Richard Piers Rayner, Niamh Shaw, P . Robert Smith, Georgina Sowerby & Brian Luff, Ivo Stourton, Vikas Swarup, Nick Van Bloss, Michael Walters.

Andrew Lownie Literary Agency Ltd
36 Great Smith Street, London, SW1P 3BU

- 020 7222 7574
- 020 7222 7576
- mail@andrewlownie.co.uk
- www.andrewlownie.co.uk

Contact Managing Director, Andrew Lownie (History and Biography)

Established 1988

Insider Info Actively seeking clients. Currently handles non-fiction books. Has approximately 100 clients, of which 20 per cent are new or unpublished writers. Simultaneous submissions are accepted. Aims to respond to queries within two days and proposals within 14 days. Submissions accompanied by SAE will be returned. Clients are usually acquired through recommendation or queries/submissions. 40 books were sold in the last year. Commission rates of 15 per cent for domestic sales, 15 per cent for foreign sales and 15 per cent for film sales. A written contract is offered.

* The agency specialises in non-fiction, in particular history and biography. All clients are handled by Andrew Lownie. Prior to becoming an agent, Andrew Lownie was a journalist, bookseller, writer and law student.

Non-fiction Will consider Biography/Autobiography, Childcare/Parenting, Current affairs, History, Humour, Memoirs, Military and True crime.

Submission Guidelines Send proposal with SAE, synopsis, one sample chapter and biography.
Recent Sale(s) *An Ordinary Soldier*, Doug Beattie; *Outcast*, Cathy Glass; *Apache Dawn*, Damien Lewis
Client(s) Richard Aldrich, Juliet Barker, Joyce Cary Estate, Roger Crowley, Tom Devine, Patrick Dillon, Peter Forbes, Laurence Gardner, Timothy Good, David Hasselhoff, Lawrence James, Damien Lewis, Julian Maclaren-Ross Estate, Peter Padfield, Tom Pocock, David Roberts, Norman Rose, Michael Schuster, David Stafford, Daniel Tammet, Peter Thompson, Adrian Weale, Christian Wolmar, Simon Young, Charlotte Zeepvat
Tips Seeking published writers, journalists, young academics and celebrities. Fiction will not be considered.

Andrew Mann Ltd
1 Old Compton Street, London, W1D 5JA
- 020 7734 4751
- 020 7287 9264
- manuscript@onetel.com

Contact Anne Dewe, Tina Betts, Sacha Elliot
Established 1975
Insider Info Actively seeking clients. Considers non-fiction books, children's books, novels, television scripts, film scripts and stage plays. Submissions accompanied by an SAE will be returned. Clients usually acquired through queries/submissions. Commission rates of 15 per cent for domestic sales, 20 per cent for foreign sales. No reading fees charged.
Non-fiction Will consider General non-fiction.
Fiction Will consider Children's and Adult fiction.
Scripts Will consider scripts for Film, Television and Radio plays.
Submission Guidelines Send submissions with SAE, synopsis and three sample chapters. Queries accepted by email. No poetry considered.
Tips Manuscripts sent by email will not be accepted, send a synopsis only. Unsolicited manuscripts will only be accepted with an accompanying letter.

Andrew Nurnberg Associates Ltd
Clerkenwell House, 45–47 Clerkenwell Green, London, EC1R 0QX
- 020 7417 8800
- 020 7417 8812
- all@nurnberg.co.uk

Contact Director, Andrew Nurnberg
Established 1970s
Insider Info Seeking both new and established writers. Considers non-fiction books and novels. Clients usually acquired through queries/submissions. Commission rates of 15 per cent for domestic sales and 20 per cent for foreign sales.
Non-fiction Will consider General non-fiction.
Fiction Will consider Novels.
Tips Represents established authors and agents. Specialises in foreign rights.

Annette Green Authors' Agency
1 East Cliff Road, Tunbridge Wells, Kent, TN4 9AD
- 01892 514275
- 01892 518124
- david@annettegreenagency.co.uk
- www.annettegreenagency.co.uk

Contact Annette Green, David Smith
Established 1998
Insider Info Actively seeking clients. Considers non-fiction books, children's books and novels. Simultaneous submissions are accepted. Aims to respond to queries/proposals within four weeks. Submissions accompanied by SAE will be returned. Clients usually acquired through queries/submissions. Commission rates of 15 per cent for domestic sales and 20 per cent for foreign sales. Does not charge a reading fee.
* Annette Green established her own literary agency in 1998 after working at A.M. Heath & Co. Ltd. for several years. David Smith joined as a partner in 2001.
Non-fiction Will consider Biography/Autobiography, Current Affairs, History, Children's, Music, Dance, Theatre, Film, Popular culture and Science/Technology.
Fiction Will consider Novels.
Submission Guidelines Send query letter with SAE, synopsis and 5,000–10,000 words of the opening chapters. No dramatic scripts, poetry, science fiction or fantasy considered.
Recent Sale(s) *Duncan Bannatyne: Anyone Can Do It*, Duncan Bannatyne (Autobiography); *Mummy Said the F-Word*, Fiona Gibson (Novel)
Client(s) Meg Cabot, Fiona Gibson, Justin Hill, J.B. Aspinall, Ian Marchant, Anvar Khan, Bernadette Strachan
Tips Specialises in discovering new, exciting talent.

Anthony Sheil
18–21 Cavaye Place, London, SW10 9PT
- 020 7373 8672
- 020 7373 6002
- anthony@gillonaitken.co.uk
- www.aitkenalexander.co.uk/asheil.php

Contact Anthony Sheil
Established 1998
Insider Info Actively seeking clients. Considers non-fiction books and novels. Aims to respond to

queries/proposals within eight weeks. Submissions accompanied by SAE will be returned. Clients usually acquired through queries/submissions. Commission rates of ten per cent for domestic sales and 20 per cent for foreign sales. Does not charge a reading fee.
* Anthony Sheil became an independent agent in association with Gillon Aitken Associates in 1998, after running Anthony Sheil Associates and being Chairman of Sheil Land Associates.
Non-fiction Will consider General non-fiction.
Fiction Will consider Novels.
Submission Guidelines Send query letter with SAE, synopsis and sample chapters consisting of the first 30 pages of continuous text. Submission should be double spaced, single-sided A4.
Client(s) Caroline Alexander, Paul Arden, Rosalind Belben, Catrine Clay, Piers Dudgeon, John Fowles, Diarmuid Jeffreys, John Keegan, Maurice Keen, Patrick Leigh-Fermor, Robert Wilson, Benjamin Woolley
Tips Qualifications must be included when submitting non-fiction.

Antony Harwood Ltd
103 Walton Street, Oxford, OX2 6EB
☎ 01865 559615
🖷 01865 310660
✉ mail@antonyharwood.com
🌐 www.antonyharwood.com
Contact Antony Harwood, James MacDonald Lockhart
Established 2000
Insider Info Actively seeking clients. Considers non-fiction books and novels. Submissions accompanied by SAE will be returned. Clients usually acquired through queries/submissions. Does not charge a reading fee.
* Before establishing the agency in 2000, Antony Harwood began in publishing at Chatto & Windus in 1978, then became an agent at Gillon Aitken. In 1990 he joined the Curtis Brown Group as a director, before returning for a period to Gillon Aitken. James MacDonald Lockhart was with Hodder Headline before going to Gillon Aitken in 1998. Two years later he joined Antony Harwood to set up their own independent agency.
Non-fiction Will consider all genres except books for young children.
Fiction Will consider Novels.
Submission Guidelines Send query letter with SAE, synopsis and three sample chapters. Queries accepted by email. No material for children under ten. Screenwriting or poetry considered.
Recent Sale(s) *The Temporal Void*, Peter F Hamilton (Tor); *The Woman in the Fifth*, Douglas Kennedy (Arrow Books)

Client(s) Peter F Hamilton, Douglas Kennedy, Malcolm Knox, Deborah Levy, Roger Levy, Mark Lynas

Anubis Literary Agency
6 Birdhaven Close, Lighthorne, Warwick, CV35 0BE
☎ 01926 642588
🖷 01926 642588
Contact Steve Calcutt
Established 1994
Insider Info Specialise in fiction. Submissions accompanied by SAE will be returned. Commission rates of 15 per cent for domestic sales, 20 per cent for foreign sales. Does not charge a reading fee.
Fiction Will consider Fantasy, Horror and Science-Fiction.
Submission Guidelines Send submission with SAE, a one-page synopsis and the first 50 pages only. Queries are not accepted by telephone.
Tips No manuscripts accepted other than fiction from the genres listed above.

A.P. Watt Ltd
20 John Street, London, WC1N 2DR
☎ 020 7405 6774
🖷 020 7831 2154
✉ apw@apwatt.co.uk
🌐 www.apwatt.co.uk
Contact Books: Caradoc King, Derek Johns, Linda Shaughnessy, Georgia Garrett, Natasha Fairweather Jon Elek, Juliet Pickering, Elinor Cooper; Foreign Rights: Linda Shaughnessy, Teresa Nicholls, Homa Driver; Media: Rob Kraitt, Christine Glover, Yasmin McDonald
Established 1875
Insider Info Considers non-fiction books, children's books, novels, television scripts, movie scripts, stage plays. Commission rates of 15 per cent for domestic sales, 20 per cent for foreign sales. No reading fee charged.
Non-fiction Will consider General non-fiction.
Fiction Will consider Literary, Commercial and Children's fiction.
Scripts Will consider Television and Film scripts and Stage plays.
Submission Guidelines Send query letter to the relevant agent. Does not accept poetry or any unsolicited manuscripts.
Recent Sale(s) *The Secret Scripture*, Sebastian Barry (Literary Fiction)
Client(s) Tony Parsons, Dame Ellen MacArthur, Rudyard Kipling, John Creed, Michael Innes and Camille Griffin, Robert Heller, Mick Jackson, James Robertson, Elaine Showalter and Zadie Smith

Tips No unsolicited manuscripts accepted. No responsibility accepted for submitted materials.

Artellus Ltd
30 Dorset House, Gloucester Place, London, NW1 5AD
- 020 7935 6972
- 020 8609 0347
- leslie@artellusltd.co.uk
- www.artellusltd.co.uk

Contact Chairperson/Agent/Consultant, Gabriele Pantucci; Director/Agent, Leslie Gardner (Film Rights); Associate Agent/Company Secretary, Darryl Samaraweera (Foreign and Theatrical rights); Associate Agent/Administrator/Picture Researcher, Liz Mallett

Established 1986

Insider Info Actively seeking clients. Considers non-fiction books, scholarly books, textbooks, children's books, novels, and novellas. Submissions accompanied by SAE will be returned. Clients are usually acquired through recommendation or queries/submissions. Commission rate of ten per cent for domestic sales, 15 per cent for foreign sales. Fee charged for a selective reading service, by invitation.

Non-fiction Will consider Art, Biography/Autobiography, Current Affairs, History, Military, Popular Culture, Science/Technology, Fashion and Celebrity non-fiction.

Fiction Will consider Crime, Fantasy, Literary fiction and Science-fiction.

Submission Guidelines Send query letter with SAE, synopsis, three sample chapters and a biography by post only. Film or television scripts will not be considered.

Recent Sale(s) *A Visible Darkness*, Michael Gregorio; *The Valley*, J.D. Landis

Client(s) Anthony Burgess, Lois McMaster Bujold, Sir John Pope-Hennessy, Roger Lewis, Martin van Creveld, Robert Hazen, Robert Gallo and Salma Samar Damluji

Tips The agency has a worldwide client list, and is established in the handling of all exploitation of book rights through to periodicals, film, television and radio. Enquire thoroughly about the reading fee before submitting work.

Author Literary Agents
53 Talbot Road, Highgate, London, N64QX
- 020 8341 0442
- 020 8341 0442
- agile@authors.co.uk

Contact John Havergal

Established 1997

Insider Info Actively seeking clients. Considers non-fiction books, children's books, novels, television scripts, movie scripts, animation and thrillers. Prefers to receive exclusive submissions. Aims to respond to queries within seven days. Submissions accompanied by SAE will be returned. Clients usually acquired through recommendation or queries/submissions. Does not charge a reading fee.

Non-fiction Will consider Agriculture, Animals, Anthropology, Archaeology, Art, Biography/Autobiography, Business, Childcare/Parenting, Computers/Electronics, Cookery, Crafts & Hobbies, Education, Film, History, Psychology, Humour, Language, Literature, Finance/Economics, Music, Nature, Religion Science/Technology, Sociology and True Crime.

Fiction Will consider Action/Adventure, Confessional, Crime, Experimental, Family saga, Fantasy, Historical, Children's, Literary, Mainstream, Mystery, Picture book, Religious/Inspirational, Romance, Science-fiction, Thriller and Young adult fiction.

Scripts Will consider Action/Adventure, Animation, Biography/Autobiography, Cartoon, Contemporary issues, Crime, Experimental and Family saga.

Submission Guidelines Send query letter with SAE, synopsis, biography and first chapter. Queries accepted by fax, email and telephone.

Barbara Levy Literary Agency
64 Greenhill, Hampstead High Street, London, NW3 5TZ
- 020 7435 9046
- 020 7431 2063

Contact Director, Barbara Levy; Associate and Solicitor, John Selby

Established 1986

Insider Info Actively seeking clients. Considers non-fiction books and novels. Unsuccessful proposals will be returned if accompanied by SAE. Obtains new clients by queries and submissions. Commission rates of ten per cent for domestic sales, with rates for foreign sales by arrangement. Does not charge a reading fee.

Non-fiction Will consider General non-fiction books.

Fiction Will consider General fiction, mainly full length novels.

Submission Guidelines Send query letter with synopsis and SAE.

Tips Do not send entire manuscripts.

Barrie James Literary Agency
Rivendell, Kingsgate Close, Torquay, Devon, TQ2 8QA
- 01803 326617
- mail@newauthors.org.uk

www.new-writer.co.uk
Contact Barrie James
Established 1997
Insider Info Actively seeking clients. Considers novels, non-fiction books and poetry. Will consider simultaneous submissions. Unsuccessful proposals will be returned if accompanied by SAE. Obtains new clients through queries and submissions.
Non-fiction Will consider General non-fiction.
Fiction Will consider Mainstream fiction and poetry.
Submission Guidelines Accepts query letter with SAE or queries via email.
Tips Also operates a website for unpublished authors to display their work for a fee: www.newauthors.org.uk. See website for full submission guidelines, costs and new author listings - please research costs and benefits thoroughly before committing.

The Bell Lomax Agency
James House, 1 Babmaes Street, London, SW1Y 6HF
020 7930 4447
020 7925 0118
agency@bell-lomax.co.uk
Contact Executives; Eddie Bell, Pat Lomax, Paul Moreton, June Bell
Established 2000
Insider Info Actively seeking clients. Considers non-fiction books, children's books, and novels. Unsuccessful proposals will be returned with SAE. Obtains new clients through queries and submissions. Does not charge a reading fee.
Non-fiction Considers Biography/Autobiography, Business, Children's and Sports non-fiction titles.
Fiction Considers General and Children's fiction.
Submission Guidelines Send query letter. Will not accept scripts.
Tips Do not send any manuscripts before first approaching with a query letter.

Bill McLean Personal Management Ltd
23b Deodar Road, London, SW15 2NP
020 8789 8191
Contact Bill McLean
Established 1972
Insider Info Seeking both new and established writers. Considers television scripts, film scripts, stage plays and radio scripts. Unsuccessful proposals will be returned if accompanied by SAE. Obtains new clients through queries and submissions. Commission rates of ten per cent for domestic sales. Does not charge a reading fee.
Scripts Considers scripts for Television, Film, Radio and Theatre.

Submission Guidelines Send query letter with SAE, or query over the phone. Does not accept any books.
Tips Will not accept any unsolicited manuscripts.

Binnacle Press
4 The Avenue, Compass Quay, Kinsale, Co. Cork, Republic of Ireland
info@binnaclepress.com
www.binnaclepress.com
Contact Agent, Deborah Lysaght
Insider Info Currently handles fiction and poetry. Obtains new clients through queries and submissions. Does not accept simultaneous submissions. Commission upon arrangement. Does not charge a reading fee. Also offers a fee-based review service.
Fiction Will consider thought provoking and intelligent fiction and poetry.
Submission Guidelines Accepts proposal package (including covering letter, synopsis and author biography) by post or email. Email submissions must use 'Enquiry for Binnacle Press' as the subject line.
Tips Binnacle Press is not interested in non-fiction, scripts or 'Chick-Lit'.

Blake Friedmann Literary, Film & TV Agency
122 Arlington Road, London, NW1 7HP
020 7284 0408
020 7284 0442
info@blakefriedmann.co.uk
www.blakefriedmann.co.uk
Contact Carole Blake, Oliver Munson (Books); Julian Friedmann (Film/TV); Conrad Williams (Original Scripts/Radio); Isobel Dixon (Foreign Titles); Katie Williams
Established 1977
Insider Info Actively seeking clients. Considers non-fiction books, novels, television scripts, short story collections, film scripts, and radio scripts. Unsuccessful proposals will be returned if accompanied by SAE. Obtains new clients through queries and submissions. Commission rates of 15 per cent for domestic sales and 20 per cent for foreign sales. Does not charge a reading fee.
* Specialises in film and television rights.
Non-fiction Considers Biography/Autobiography, Crime and Travel titles.
Fiction Considers General fiction, Genre fiction, Literary and Commercial titles.
Scripts Considers scripts for Television, Film and Radio.
Submission Guidelines Send query letter with a synopsis and three sample chapters. Do not send any science fiction or poetry.

Client(s) Jane Asher, Elizabeth Chadwick, Maeve Haran, Ken Hom, Bookey Peek, Craig Russell, Peter James

Tips Short stories are only accepted from existing clients. Caters for a large overseas market. All ranges of fiction - from genre to literary - are accepted.

BookBlast Ltd
PO Box 20184, London, W10 5AU
- 020 8968 3089
- 020 8932 4087
- gen@bookblast.com
- www.bookblast.com

Contact Georgia de Chamberet; Andrea Prezens
Established 1997
Insider Info Not seeking new clients at present. Considers non-fiction and novels. Initiates in-house projects. Commission rates of 12 per cent for domestic sales and 20 per cent for foreign sales.
* Before founding BookBlast Georgia de Chamberet was an editor at Quartet Books.

Non-fiction Considers Literary non-fiction, Memoir, Travel, Popular Culture and Multicultural writing.
Fiction Considers Literary and Mainstream Adult fiction.
Submission Guidelines Send query letter. Does not accept scripts, horror, crime, science fiction and fantasy, poetry, children's books, health, cookery, gardening, short stories or articles.
Recent Sale(s) *Britain's Slave Trade,* S.I. Martin; *Daybreak & Darkness,* Rupert Bogarde; *The Demented Dance,* Mounsi; *The Mad Mosaic,* Gael Elton Mayo (Japanese Rights)
Client(s) Jamika Ajalon, Rupert Bogarde, Charlie Caselton, M.V. Diboll, Luis Domingues, Samara Hain, Nikola Lashley, Onyekachi Wambu.
Tips Always write before sending any manuscripts. Email enquiries are accepted as body text only, no attachments.

The Book Bureau Literary Agency
7 Duncairn Avenue, Bray, Co. Wicklow, Republic of Ireland
- 00353 1 276 4996
- 00353 1 276 4834
- thebookbureau@oceanfree.net

Contact Geraldine Nichol
Insider Info Actively seeking clients. Considers novels. Unsuccessful proposals will be returned if accompanied by SAE, Obtains new clients through queries and submissions. Commission rates of ten per cent on domestic sales and 20 per cent on foreign sales. Does not charge a reading fee.
Fiction Consider Crime, Literary, Thriller, Women's/ 'Chick lit' and General commercial fiction.

Submission Guidelines Send query letter with a synopsis, three to five sample chapters and SAE. Does not accept science fiction, horror, poetry or children's titles.
Tips Writers may usually expect a prompt response to proposals, and may be offered editorial support.

Brie Burkeman
14 Neville Court, Abbey Road, London, NW8 9DD
- 0870 199 5002
- 0870 199 1029
- brie.burkeman@mail.com

Contact Brie Burkman
Established 2000
Insider Info Both new and established writers considered but taking on few new clients except by recommendation. Considers fiction and non-fiction books, full length scripts for stage and film. Prefers to receive exclusive submissions. Unsuccessful proposals will only be returned with SSAE. Does not charge a reading fee or offer a criticism service.
Non-fiction Considers Biography/Autobiography, Food & Drink, History, Memoirs, Mind, Body & Spirit, Popular Culture, Popular Science, Scoail Commentary and True Crime.
Fiction Considers Action/Adventure, Children's, Crime, Ethnic, Historical, Literary, Mainstream, Mystery, Thriller and Young Adult fiction.
Scripts Considers full length commercial scripts in most genres.
Submission Guidelines Send query letter or email in first instance. Do not send attachments (which will be automatically deleted) or enclosures until invited. Do not send any poetry, musicals, textbooks or academic titles, as they are not handled.

Bryan Drew Ltd
Quadrant House, 80–82 Regent Street, London, W1B 5AU
- 020 7437 2293
- 020 7437 0561
- bryan@bryandrewltd.com

Contact Literary Manager, Bryan Drew
Established 1962
Insider Info Seeking both new and established writers. Considers non-fiction books, novels, television scripts, film scripts, and stage plays. Unsuccessful proposals will be returned if accompanied by SAE. Obtains new clients through queries and submissions. Commission rates of 12.5 per cent for domestic sales and 15 per cent for foreign sales. Does not charge a reading fee.
Non-fiction Considers Biography/Autobiography titles.

Fiction Considers Crime, Thriller and General fiction titles.
Scripts Considers scripts for Television, Film and Theatre.
Submission Guidelines Send query letter with synopsis, two to three sample chapters and SAE.
Tips SAE is essential.

The Buckman Agency
Ryman's Cottages, Little Trew, OX7 4JJ
- 01608 683677
- 01608 683449
- r.buckman@talk21.com
- j.buckman@talk21.com

Contact Rosie Buckman, Jessica Buckman
Established Early 1970s
Insider Info Seeking mostly established writers through referrals. Commission rates of 20 per cent for domestic and foreign sales.
* Specialises in foreign rights.
Tips Represents established authors and agents from the UK and USA.

Campbell, Thomson & McLaughlin Ltd
11–12 Dover Street, London, W1S 4LJ
- 020 7399 2808/2800
- 020 7399 2801
- submissions@ctmcl.co.uk

Contact Charlotte Bruton
Established 1931
Insider Info Seeking both new and established writers. Considers non-fiction books and novels. Unsuccessful proposals will be returned if accompanied by SAE. Obtains new clients through queries and submissions. Commission rates of ten per cent for domestic sales and up to 20 per cent for foreign sales. Does not charge a reading fee.
Non-fiction Considers General non-fiction.
Fiction Considers General fiction.
Submission Guidelines Send query letter with SAE, or query via email. Do not send scripts, poetry or children's titles.
Tips Do not send entire manuscript before first sending a query letter.

Capel & Land Ltd
29 Wardour Street, London, W1D 6PS
- 020 7734 2414
- 020 7734 8101
- georgina@capelland.co.uk
- www.capelland.com

Contact Directors: Georgina Capel (Literary) and Anita Land (TV & Radio); Agents: Phillipa Brewster, Abi Fellows and Rosie Apponyi (Literary); Joscelyn Evans (Television and Radio)

Established 2000
Insider Info Actively seeking clients. Considers non-fiction books, novels, television scripts and film scripts. Obtain new clients through queries and submissions. Commission rates of 15 per cent for domestic and foreign sales. Does not charge a reading fee.
Non-fiction Considers Biography/Autobiography, General non-fiction and History titles.
Fiction Considers General and Literary fiction.
Scripts Considers Film and Television scripts.
Submission Guidelines Send query letter with a synopsis, three sample chapters and SAE.
Client(s) Kohn Bew, Matthew Dennison, Julie Burchill, Andrew Greig, Eammon Holmes, Liz Jones, Dr. Tristram Hunt, Stella Rimington, Jeremy Paxman, Fay Weldon and Greg Woolf
Tips In some instances revision to proposals or manuscripts may be suggested.

Caroline Davidson Literary Agency
5 Queen Anne's Gardens, London, W4 1TU
- 020 8995 5768
- 020 8994 2770
- caroline@cdla.co.uk
- www.cdla.co.uk

Contact Founder, Caroline Davidson
Established 1988
Insider Info Actively seeking clients. Considers non-fiction books and novels. Represents around 30 clients. Aims to respond to queries and proposals with four weeks. Obtains new clients through queries and submissions. Commission rates of 12.5 per cent for domestic sales and foreign sales (20 per cent for foreign sales if sub-agents are involved). Does not charge a reading fee.
* Caroline Davidson was has been a journalist for Reuters in London and BBC television in the USA, and has wide experience of the international market. She has been the author of five books including *A Woman's Work is Never Done*.
Non-fiction Considers Agriculture, Animals, Art, Biography/Autobiography, Gardening, Health, History, Medicine, Nature and Science/Technology titles.
Fiction Considers Literary fiction.
Submission Guidelines Send query letter with a synopsis, the first 50 pages for fiction writing, author biography and SAE. Do not send fantasy, thrillers, crime, occult, children's, scripts or poetry titles.
Client(s) Perter Barham, Nigel Barlow, Emma Donoghue, Paul Luff, Malachi McIntosh, Simon Unwin, Helena Whitbread
Tips A CV must accompany the preliminary letter and submission. The agency will endeavour to reply to submissions as quickly as possible. No response will be given to submissions by fax or email.

Caroline Sheldon Literary Agency

71 Hillgate Place, London, W8 7SS
☎ 020 7727 9102
✉ carolinesheldon@carolinesheldon.co.uk
✉ pennyholroyde@carolinesheldon.co.uk
🌐 www.carolinesheldon.co.uk
Contact Caroline Sheldon, Penny Holroyde
Established 1985
Insider Info Actively seeking clients. Considers non-fiction books, children's books and novels. Aims to respond to proposals within four weeks. Unsuccessful proposals will be returned with SAE. Obtains new clients through queries and submissions. Commission rates of 10–15 per cent for domestic sales and 20 per cent for foreign sales. Does not charge a reading fee.
* Before establishing her agency, Caroline Sheldon was a publisher at Hutchinson/Arrow, specialising in women's and children's books. Penny Holroyde has worked at Walker Books and as a rights director for Candlewick Press in the USA. She joined Caroline Sheldon in 2004.
Non-fiction Considers Memoirs and Human interest titles.
Fiction Considers Adult's and Children's fiction.
Submission Guidelines Send query letter with a synopsis, three sample chapters and SAE. Pages should be double-spaced and single-sided A4. No staples or bound manuscripts. Do not send scripts.
Tips The Caroline Sheldon Literary Agency is always looking out for exciting projects by debut authors in both adult and children's books, but out of the enormous amount they see, only a few are selected. There are occasions when they make detailed editorial suggestions and comments but only when they see real promise in the work. Caroline Sheldon does not charge a reading fee.

Casarotto Ramsay & Associates Ltd

Waverley House, 7–12 Noel Street, London, W1F 8GQ
☎ 020 7287 4450
☎ 020 7287 9128
✉ info@casarotto.co.uk
🌐 www.casarotto.co.uk
Contact Head of Film & TV, Jenne Casarotto; Agents (Film & TV): Rachel Holroyd, Charlotte Kelly (Dublin), Jodi Shields, Elinor Burns, Lucinda Prain, Miriam James, Mark Casarotto and Abby Singer (Comedy); Head of Theatrical, Tom Erhardt and Mel Kenyon; Agents (Theatrical): Mel Kenyon, (Theatrical); Ruth Arnaud (Amateurs and Stock Rights); Kirsty Coombs (Stage Directors)
Established 1989
Insider Info Actively seeking clients. Considers television scripts, film scripts, stage plays and radio scripts. Unsuccessful proposals will be returned if accompanied by SAE. Obtains new clients through queries and submissions. Commission rates of ten per cent for domestic sales. Does not charge a reading fee.
Scripts Considers scripts for Film, Television, Radio and Stage.
Submission Guidelines Send query letter with SAE.
Client(s) Howard Brenton, Simon Callow, Caryl Churchill, David Hare, Nick Hornby, Bob Hoskins, Terry Jones, Dominic Minghella, Frank McGuinness, Ian Hislop, Nick Newman
Tips Do not send any book manuscripts, only scripts. A preliminary letter is essential.

Cat Ledger Literary Agency

20–21 Newman Street, London, W1T 1PG
☎ 020 7861 8226
☎ 020 7861 8001
Contact Cat Ledger
Insider Info Seeking both new and established writers. Considers non-fiction books and novels. Unsuccessful proposals will be returned with SAE.
Non-fiction Considers Art, Biography/ Autobiography, Politics, Humour, Music, Sports, Theatre, True Crime, Lifestyle, Travel, Academia and Journalism titles
Fiction Considers General adult fiction.
Submission Guidelines Send query letter with SAE. Do not send poetry, science fiction, fantasy, romance, scripts or children's titles.
Tips Mostly deals with non-fiction titles.

Cecily Ware Literary Agents

19C John Spencer Square, London, N1 2LZ
☎ 020 7359 3787
☎ 020 7226 9828
✉ info@cecilyware.com
Contact Cecily Ware, Warren Sherman, Gilly Schuster
Established 1972
Insider Info Seeking both new and established writers. Considers television scripts and film scripts. Unsuccessful proposals are returned if accompanied by SAE. Obtains new clients through queries and submissions. Commission rates of ten per cent for domestic sales and 10–20 per cent for foreign sales. Does not charge a reading fee.
Scripts Considers Comedy, Family saga, Adaptations, Drama, Series/Serials, and Children's scripts.
Submission Guidelines Send query letter with SAE.
Tips Never send entire manuscript unless requested.

Celia Catchpole

56 Gilpin Avenue, London, SW14 8QY

☎ 020 8255 4835

🌐 www.celiacatchpole.co.uk

Contact Celia Catchpole

Established 1996

Insider Info Seeking both new and established writers. Considers children's books and novels. Simultaneous submissions are accepted. Unsuccessful proposals will be returned if accompanied by SAE. Obtains new clients through queries and submissions. Commission rates of ten per cent for domestic sales (15 per cent for illustrators) and 20 per cent on foreign sales.
* Specialises in children's authors and illustrators.
Fiction Considers General Children's and Picture book titles.
Submission Guidelines Send query letter with SAE. Do not accept scripts or poetry.
Client(s) Laura Adkins, Pedro de Alcantara, Sheila M Bird, Dinah Capparucci, Matt Chamings, Rob Childs, Jane Clarke, Malachy Doyle, Polly Dunbar, Lesley Ely, Alan Fraser, Tim Hopgood, Sandra Ann Horn, Ursula Jones, Tim Kennemore, Lucy Micklethwait, Charlotte Middleton, Trish Phillips, Josephine Poole, Daniel Postgate, Julia Rawlinson, SF Said, Jane Simmons, Sean Taylor, Joseph Theobald, Peter Utton, Fernando Vilela, Jennie Walters, Hannah Webb, Carrie Weston
Tips Does not accept unsolicited manuscripts.

Chapman & Vincent

The Mount, Sun Hill, Royston, Hertfordshire, SG8 9AT

☎ 01763 245005

☎ 01763 243033

✉ info@chapmanvincent.co.uk

Contact Directors, Jennifer Chapman and Gilly Vincent

Established 1992

Insider Info Seeking mostly established writers through referrals. Consider non-fiction books and novels. Simultaneous submissions are accepted. Unsuccessful proposals will be returned with SAE. Obtains new clients through recommendations from others as well as queries and submissions. Commission rates of 15 per cent for domestic sales and 20 per cent for foreign sales. Does not charge a reading fee.
Non-fiction Considers General non-fiction titles.
Fiction Considers upmarket Adult fiction titles.
Submission Guidelines Send query letter with two sample chapters and SAE. No thrillers, adventure, poetry, scripts or children's books.
Client(s) George Carter, Leslie Geddes-Brown, Rowley Leigh, Eve Pollard

Tips The agency does not accept telephone calls, or any proposals by fax or email.

Christine Green Authors' Agent

6 Whitehorse Mews, Westminster Bridge Road, London, SE1 7QD

☎ 020 7401 8844

☎ 020 7401 8860

✉ info@christinegreen.co.uk

🌐 www.christinegreen.co.uk

Contact Christine Green

Established 1984

Insider Info Actively seeking clients. Considers non-fiction books and novels. Prefers to receive exclusive submissions. Aims to respond to queries and proposals within four weeks. Unsuccessful proposals will be returned with SAE. Obtains new clients through queries and submissions. Commission rates of 10 per cent for domestic sales and 20 per cent for foreign sales. Does not charge a reading fee.
Non-fiction Considers General non-fiction titles.
Fiction Considers General fiction titles.
Submission Guidelines Send a query letter with the first three chapters, a synopsis and SAE. Pages should be double-spaced, single sided, numbered and A4 in size. Do not send scripts, science fiction, fantasy, children's books or poetry.
Recent Sale(s) *Heart and Soul*, Maeve Binchy; *Bitter Chocolate*, Lesley Lokko
Client(s) Mary Beckett, Meave Binchy, Allie Cresswell, Ita Daly, Winston Fletcher, Carl Gibeily, Sylvian Hamilton, Marilyn Heward Mills, Mary Joyce, Leslie Lokko, Gaile Parkin

The Christopher Little Literary Agency

Eel Brook Studios, 125 Moore Park Road, London, SW6 4PS

☎ 020 7736 4455

☎ 020 7736 4490

✉ info@christopherlittle.net

🌐 www.christopherlittle.net

Contact Christopher Little

Established 1979

Insider Info Actively seeking clients. Considers non-fiction books, novels, children's books, television scripts and film scripts. Aims to respond to queries and manuscripts within six weeks. Unsuccessful proposals will be returned with SAE. Obtains new clients through queries and submissions. Commission rates of 15 per cent for domestic sales, and 20 per cent for foreign sales and film rights. Does not charge a reading fee.
Non-fiction Considers Mainstream and Literary non-fiction.

Fiction Considers Mainstream and Literary full length fiction.

Scripts Mainly considers scripts from existing clients only.

Submission Guidelines Check the website for submission status. No poetry, plays, science fiction, illustrated material, fantasy, textbooks or short stories.

Client(s) Paul Bajoria, A.J. Butcher, Janet Gleeson, Gorillaz, Christopher Hale, Pete Howells, Carol Hughes, General Sir Mike Jackson, Lauren Liebenberg, Alistair MacNeill, Christopher Matthew, Robert Mawson, Haydn Middleton, Shiromi Pinto, Robert Radcliffe, Dr Nicholas Reeves, J.K. Rowling, Darren Shan, Wladyslaw Szpilman, Shayne Ward, Pip Vaughn-Hughes, John Watson and Anne Zouroudi

Tips The agency also handles merchandising, in-house legal matters, contract affairs, royalties and accounting for their clients, as well as offering a high level of personal, hands-on representation.

Conville & Walsh Ltd
2 Ganton Street, Westminster, London, W1F 7QL
- 020 7287 3030
- 020 7287 4545
- info@convilleandwalsh.com
- www.convilleandwalsh.com

Contact Directors, Clare Conville and Patrick Walsh; Agents: Jake Smith-Bosanquet (Foreign Rights), Susan Armstrong (Debut Fiction), Ben Mason, Jo Unwin,

Established 2000

Insider Info Seeking both new and established writers. Considers non-fiction books, children's books and novels. Unsuccessful proposals will be returned if accompanied by SAE. Obtains new clients through queries and submissions. Commission rates of 15 per cent for domestic sales and 20 per cent for foreign sales. Aims to respond to submissions within two months. Does not charge a reading fee.

Non-fiction Considers Children's non-fiction, History, Science/Technology and Journalism titles.

Fiction Considers Children's fiction, Literary and Commercial fiction.

Submission Guidelines Accepts query letter with a synopsis, three sample chapters and SAE. No scripts, short stories, or poetry.

Client(s) John Burningham, Helen Castor, Mike Dash, Professor John Emsley, Dermot Healy, Manjit Kumar, Patrick Redmond

Tips Has an interest in first-time novelists.

Coombs Moylett Literary Agency
3 Askew Road, London, W12 9AA
- 020 8740 0454
- 020 8354 3065

Contact Lisa Moylett

Insider Info Seeking both new and established writers. Considers non-fiction books and novels. Aims to respond to queries and proposals within one week. Unsuccessful proposals will be returned if accompanied by SAE. Obtains new clients through queries and submissions. Commission rates of 15 per cent for domestic sales, foreign sales and film rights. Does not charge a reading fee.

Non-fiction Considers Biography/Autobiography, Current affairs and History titles.

Fiction Considers Crime, Literary fiction, Thriller, Women's/'Chick lit' and Contemporary fiction.

Submission Guidelines Send query letter with SAE, synopsis, and three sample chapters.

Tips The agency is known for its speed in responding to submissions. No electronic submissions.

Crawford & Pearlstine Associates Ltd
31 Ashley Gardens, Ambrosden Avenue, London, SW1P 1QE
- 0845 262 4212
- 0845 262 5546

Contact Jamie Crawford, Maggie Pearlstine

Established 1989

Insider Info Seeking both new and established writers. Considers non-fiction books and novels. Commission rates are variable for domestic sales and 20 per cent for foreign sales and film rights. Does not charge reading fee.

Non-fiction Considers Biography/Autobiography, Current affairs, Health, History, Medicine, Sports and General non-fiction titles.

Fiction Considers General fiction.

Submission Guidelines Send query letter with SAE, and sample chapters. No poetry, science fiction, short stories, horror, scripts or children's books.

Tips No fax or email submissions, and no submissions from outside the UK.

Curtis Brown Group Ltd
Haymarket House, 28–29 Haymarket, London, SW1Y 4SP
- 020 7393 4400
- 020 7393 4401
- cb@curtisbrown.co.uk
- www.curtisbrown.co.uk

Contact CEO, Jonathan Lloyd (Fiction, Autobiographies); Managing Director, Jonny Geller (Book Division); Gordon Wise, (History, Lifestyle, Literary Estate of Winston Churchill); Camilla Hornby/Vivienne Schuster/Jonathan Pegg (Non-fiction, Literary Estates, Literary Commercial Fiction, Biographies, Memoirs, History and Travel); Elizabeth Sheinkman/Janice Swanson/Stephanie Thwaite

(Debut Novelists, Journalism, Memoirs, Culture and History, Children's Authors, Author Illustrators, Literary Estates) Kate Cooper/Carol Jackson/Betsy Robbins (Foreign Rights)

Established 1899

Insider Info Actively seeking clients. Considers non-fiction books, children's books, novels, television scripts, film scripts, stage plays, multimedia and radio scripts. Simultaneous submissions are accepted. Aims to respond to queries and proposals within eight weeks. Unsuccessful proposals are returned if accompanied by SAE. Obtains new clients by queries and submissions. Does not charge a reading fee.

* Jonathan Lloyd was with HarperCollins before joining the Curtis Brown Group Ltd. in 1994. He was also President of the Association of Author's Agents (AAA) from 1999–2002. Jonny Geller originally trained as a actor, but joined the group in 1993 as a book agent.

Non-fiction Considers Biography/Autobiography, History, Humour, Memoirs and Popular culture titles.

Fiction Considers Humour, Literary, Women's Fiction /'Chick lit' titles.

Scripts Considers scripts for Television, Radio, Film and Theatre.

Submission Guidelines Send query letter with SAE, a synopsis, and three sample chapters. Pages should be double-spaced, single-sided and A4 sized.

Recent Sale(s) *Child 44*, Tom Rob Smith (Simon & Schuster); *The Painter of Shanghai*, Jennifer Cody (Penguin)

Client(s) Jake Arnott, Barbara Davies, Jane Fallon, Jane Harris, David Hewson, F.E. Higgins, Cathy Kelly, Marion Keyes, Josie Lloyd, Emlyn Rees, David Mitchell and Christopher Skidmore

Tips When submitting sample chapters make sure your name, contact number and email address are clearly written on the cover. No stapled, bound or emailed manuscripts.

Darley Anderson Literary, TV & Film Agency

Estelle House, 11 Eustace Road, London, SW6 1JB

- 020 7385 6652
- 020 7386 5571
- enquiries@darleyanderson.com
- www.darleyanderson.com

Contact Darley Anderson (Crime and Thrillers); Becky Stradwick (Children's); Ella Andrews (Women's Fiction); Zoe King (Non-fiction); Camilla Bolton (Crime and Thrillers)

Established 1988

Insider Info Actively seeking clients. Considers non-fiction books, children's books, novels, television scripts and film scripts. 95 per cent of clients are new or previously unpublished writers. Simultaneous

submissions are accepted. Aims to respond to queries, proposals and manuscripts within one month. Unsuccessful proposals will be returned if accompanied by SAE. Obtains new clients through recommendations from others, queries and submissions.

Non-fiction Considers Animals, Biography/Autobiography, Childcare/Parenting, Children's non-fiction, Food & Drink, Memoirs, Finance, Popular Culture, Religion Self-help and Sports titles.

Fiction Considers Action/Adventure, Confessional, Crime, Erotica, Ethnic, Family saga, Fantasy, Gay/Lesbian, Glitz, Historical, Horror, Children's, Mainstream, Mystery, Picture book, Psychic/Supernatural, Regional, Religious, Romance, Science-fiction, Sports, Thriller, Women's/'Chick lit' and Young Adult titles.

Scripts Considers Action/Adventure, Animation, Biography/Autobiography, Cartoon, Comedy, Contemporary issues, Crime, Ethnic, Sitcom and Family saga scripts.

Submission Guidelines Send query letter with SAE, synopsis and the first three chapters. Also accepts queries by email or phone.

David Grossman Literary Agency Ltd

118b Holland Park Avenue, London, W11 4UA

- 020 7221 2770
- 020 7221 1445

Established 1976

Insider Info Actively seeking clients. Considers novels. Simultaneous submissions are accepted. Unsuccessful manuscripts are returned if accompanied by SAE. Obtains new clients through queries and submissions. Commission rates are variable for domestic sales and 20 per cent for foreign sales. Does not charge a reading fee.

Fiction Considers Literary and General fiction.

Submission Guidelines Send query letter with SAE, synopsis, and the first 50 pages. No poetry, textbooks or scripts.

Tips No faxes or emailed submissions will be accepted. Debut novelists' well written, original works will be considered.

David Higham Associates Ltd

5–8 Lower John Street, Golden Square, London, W1F 9HA

- 020 7434 5900
- 020 7437 1072
- dha@davidhigham.co.uk
- www.davidhigham.co.uk

Contact Books: Veronique Baxter, Georgia Glover, Anthony Goff, Andrew Gordon, Bruce Hunter, Lizzy Kremer, Caroline Walsh, Alice Williams; Script Writing

& Drama: Georgia Ruffhead, Nicky Lund; Translation: Ania Corless, Tine Nielsen

Established 1935

Insider Info Seeking both new and established writers. Considers non-fiction, fiction, film scripts, television scripts, stage plays and children's books. Simultaneous submissions are accepted. Unsuccessful proposals will be returned with SAE. Obtains new clients through recommendations from others, queries and submissions. Commission rates of 15 per cent for domestic sales, 20 per cent for foreign sales and 15 per cent for film rights (scripts ten per cent). Offers a written contract until it is terminated by either party. Does not charge a reading fee or offer a criticism service.

Non-fiction Considers General non-fiction titles.

Fiction Considers Adult's and Children's fiction.

Scripts Considers scripts for Film, Television and Theatre.

Submission Guidelines Send query letter with SAE, outline, synopsis, three sample chapters and an author biography. The agency is actively seeking good commercial and literary fiction, and general non-fiction.

Client(s) Lauren Child, J.M. Coetzee, Roald Dahl, Anne Fine, Jane Green, James Herbert, Penelope Lively, Michael Morpurgo, Alexander McCall Smith, Alice Sebold, Lynne Truss, Jacqueline Wilson

Tips Postal submissions only.

David O'Leary Literary Agency

10 Lansdowne Court, Lansdowne Rise, London, W11 2NR

🕿 020 7229 1623

🕿 020 7229 1623

✉ d.o'leary@virgin.net

Contact David O'Leary

Established 1988

Insider Info Seeking both new and established writers. Considers non-fiction books and novels. Simultaneous submissions are accepted. Unsuccessful proposals will be returned if accompanied by SAE. Obtains new clients through queries and submissions. Commission rates of ten per cent for domestic and foreign sales. Does not charge a reading fee.

Non-fiction Considers History and Popular science titles.

Fiction Considers Literary and Thriller/Espionage fiction titles.

Submission Guidelines Send query letter with SAE and outline proposal. Also accepts queries by email and phone. No science fiction or poetry.

Client(s) Nick Kochan, Jim Lusby, Derek Malcolm, Ken Russell

Tips The agency are happy to discuss proposals, but do not accept unsolicited manuscripts.

Deborah Owen Ltd

78 Narrow Street, London, E14 8BP

🕿 020 7987 5119/5441

🕿 020 7538 4004

Contact Deborah Owen

Established 1971

Insider Info Not currently seeking new clients. Represents non-fiction books.

* A small agency which represents two authors only.

Client(s) Delia Smith, Amos Oz

The Dench Arnold Agency

10 Newburgh Street, London, W1F 7RN

🕿 020 7437 4551

🕿 020 7439 1355

✉ contact@dencharnold.co.uk

🌐 www.dencharnold.co.uk

Contact Elizabeth Dench, Michelle Arnold, Matthew Dench, Fiona Grant and Davinia Andrew-Lynch

Established 1972

Insider Info Seeking both new and established writers. Considers television scripts, movie scripts, directors, and non-fiction and fiction. Unsuccessful proposals will be returned if accompanied by SAE. Obtains new clients through queries and submissions. Commission rates of 10–15 per cent on domestic sales.

Non-fiction Considers General non-fiction titles.

Fiction Considers General fiction titles.

Scripts Considers scripts for Television and Film.

Submission Guidelines Send query letter with SAE, author biography and a sample of work for scripts.

Client(s) Karen Brown, Lucy Flannery, Jeff Gross, Michael Hines, Phil O'Shea and Julian Kemp

DGA Ltd

55 Monmouth Street, London, WC2H 9DG

🕿 020 7240 9992

🕿 020 7395 6110

✉ assistant@davidgodwinassociates.co.uk

🌐 www.davidgodwinassociates.co.uk

Contact Director, David Godwin; Director, Heather Godwin; Sophie Hoult, Charlotte Knight (Publicity & Client Enquiries); Kerry Glencorse (Foreign Rights); Kirsty McLachan (Film/TV rights)

Established 1995

Insider Info Considers non-fiction books and novels. Aims to respond to queries within three weeks. Unsuccessful proposals will be returned if accompanied by SAE.

* Specialises in film and television rights worldwide.

Non-fiction General non-fiction.

Fiction Considers Literary fiction.

Submission Guidelines Send query letter with SAE, synopsis, three sample chapters and an author biography. No children's books, science fiction, graphic or illustrated novels.

Client(s) Diane Atkinson, Arundhati Roy, Aiden Hartley, Jim Crace, Brian Lara, Michael Pye, Simon Armitage, Ronan Bennett, William Dalrymple, Joe Lovejoy, Clare Tomalin, Donald Sassoon, Ben Rice and Alan Warner

Tips Does not accept submissions by email.

Diane Banks Associates

submissions@dianebanks.co.uk

Contact Diane Banks

Established 2006

Insider Info Seeking both new and established writers. Considers non-fiction books and novels. Simultaneous submissions will be accepted. Aims to respond to queries within two weeks. Obtains new clients through queries and submissions. Commission rates of 15 per cent for domestic sales and 20 per cent for foreign sales. Does not charge a reading fee.

Non-fiction Considers Biography/Autobiography, Fashion & Beauty, Health, History, Medicine, Memoir, Psychology, Self-help and Science titles.

Fiction Considers Crime, Literary fiction, Thriller/Espionage and Women's/'Chick lit' titles.

Submission Guidelines Send a synopsis, two to three sample chapters, and an author biography. Also accepts queries by email. No short stories, poetry, scripts, academic, science fiction or children's titles.

Tips Will only accept submissions via email.

Dinah Wiener Ltd

12 Cornwall Grove, London, W4 2LB

020 8994 6011

020 8994 6044

Contact Dinah Wiener

Established 1985

Insider Info Actively seeking clients. Considers non-fiction books and novels. Simultaneous submissions are accepted. Unsuccessful submissions will be returned with SAE. Obtains new clients through queries and submissions. Commission rates of 15 per cent for domestic sales and 20 per cent for foreign sales.

Non-fiction Considers Biography/Autobiography, Food & Drink, Lifestyle, Popular Culture and Science/Technology titles.

Fiction Considers General fiction titles.

Submission Guidelines Send query letter, SAE, two sample chapters and a CV giving information on past work and future plans. No scripts, poetry or children's books.

Tips All submitted manuscripts must be double-spaced, single-sided and A4 sized.

Don Baker Associates

25 Eley Drive, Rottingdean, East Sussex, BN2 7FH

01273 386842

01273 386842

Contact Director, Donald Baker; Director, Katy Quayle

Established 1996

Insider Info Seeking both new and established writers. Considers television scripts, film scripts and stage plays. Simultaneous submissions are accepted. Obtains new clients through queries and submissions. Commission rates of 12.5 per cent for domestic sales and 15 for foreign sales. Does not charge a reading fee.

Scripts Considers scripts for Television, Film and Stage.

Submission Guidelines Send a query letter with SAE.

Tips No unsolicited submissions.

Dorian Literary Agency (DLA)

Upper Thornehill, 27 Church Road, St Marychurch, Torquay, Devon, TQ1 4QY

01803 312095

01803 312095

Contact Proprietor, Dorothy Lumley

Established 1986

Insider Info Actively seeking clients. Considers non-fiction and novels. Simultaneous submissions are accepted. Unsuccessful proposals will be returned if accompanied by SAE. Obtains new clients through queries and submissions. Commission rates are variable for domestic sales and 15 per cent for foreign sales. Does not charge a reading fee.

Non-fiction Considers Popular culture titles.

Fiction Considers Crime, Family saga, Fantasy, Historical, Horror, Romance, Science-fiction, Thriller/Espionage and Women's/'Chick lit' titles.

Submission Guidelines Send query letter with SAE, synopsis and three sample chapters. No poetry, drama, or children's books for children aged under ten.

Client(s) Gillian Bradshaw, Brian Lumley, Rosemary Rowe, Lyndon Stacey

Tips No enquiries via telephone, or manuscripts via email or fax.

Dorie Simmonds Agency

Riverbank House, 1 Putney Bridge Approach, London, SW6 3JD

020 7736 0002

dhsimmonds@aol.com

Contact Dorie Simmonds

Insider Info Seeking both new and established writers. Considers non-fiction and fiction books as well as children's books. Unsuccessful proposals will be returned if accompanied by SAE. Obtains new clients through queries and submissions. Commission rates of 15 per cent for domestic and North American sales; commission rate of 20 per cent for foreign translations Does not charge a reading fee.

Non-fiction Considers Biography/Autobiography, General Non-Fiction, History, Humour, Popular Science and Psychology titles.

Fiction Considers Commercial, Crime/Thriller, General, Historical and Women's fiction titles, as well as Children's novels.

Submission Guidelines Send a query letter with SAE, synopsis, and two to three sample chapters. Include any publishing history in the letter.

Tips Authors of non-fiction are to submit only an outline with the preliminary letter.

Duncan McAra

28 Beresford Gardens, Edinburgh, EH5 3ES
- 0131 552 1558
- 0131 552 1558
- duncanmcara@hotmail.com

Contact Duncan McAra
Established 1988
Insider Info Actively seeking clients. Considers non-fiction books and novels. Commission rates of ten per cent on domestic sales and 20 per cent on foreign sales. Does not charge a reading fee.

Non-fiction Considers Art, Biography/Autobiography, Military, Travel, Local Interest, Scottish and Academic titles.

Fiction Considers Literary fiction.

Submission Guidelines Send query letter with SAE, synopsis, and sample chapters.

Eddison Pearson Ltd

West Hill House, 6 Swains Lane, London, N6 6QS
- 020 7700 7763
- 020 7700 7866
- submissions@eddisonpearson.com

Contact Clare Pearson
Established 1996
Insider Info Considers non-fiction books, poetry, children's books, and novels. Simultaneous submissions are accepted. Aims to respond to queries and proposals within four weeks. Obtains new clients through queries and submissions. Commission rates of ten per cent for domestic sales and 15–20 per cent for foreign sales. Does not charge a reading fee.

Non-fiction Considers Literary and General non-fiction.

Fiction Considers Literary and Children's fiction.

Submission Guidelines Send query letter and outline by email only.

Client(s) Valerie Bloom, Sue Heap, Robert Muchamore
Tips Query by email for up-to-date submission guidelines. The agency endeavours to reply promptly to all submissions.

Ed Victor Ltd

6 Bayley Street, Bedford Square, London, WC1B 3HE
- 020 7304 4100
- 020 7304 4111

Contact Executive Chairman, Ed Victor; Director, Sophie Hicks; Director, Margaret Phillips
Established 1976
Insider Info Considers non-fiction books, children's books and novels. Obtains new clients through queries and submissions. Commission rates of 15 per cent on domestic and foreign sales. Does not charge a reading fee.

Non-fiction Considers General non-fiction.

Fiction Considers Action/Adventure, Children's, Mystery, Romance, Thriller/Espionage, and Women's/'Chick lit' titles.

Submission Guidelines Send query letter with SAE and synopsis. No scripts, academic, or poetry titles.

Client(s) John Banville, Herbie Brennan, Eoin Colfer, Frederick Forsyth, A.A. Gill, Josephine Hart, Jack Higgins, Nigella Lawson, Kathy Lette, Allan Mallinson, Andrew Marr and Janet Street-Porter

Tips Ed Victor does not accept unsolicited manuscripts. The agency also represents the estates of Douglas Adams, Raymond Chandler, Dame Iris Murdoch, Sir Stephen Spender and Irving Wallace.

Edwards Fuglewicz

49 Great Ormond Street, London, WC1N 3HZ
- 020 7405 6725
- 020 7405 6726

Contact Partners: Ros Edwards, Helenca Fuglewiscz
Established 1996
Insider Info Actively seeking clients. Considers non-fiction books, novels, and scholarly books. Simultaneous submissions are accepted. Unsuccessful submissions will be returned if accompanied by SAE. Obtains new clients through queries and submissions. Commission rates of 15 per cent on domestic sales and 20 per cent on foreign sales. Does not charge a reading fee.

Non-fiction Considers Biography/Autobiography, History and Popular culture titles.

Fiction Considers Literary and Commercial fiction.

Submission Guidelines Send query letter with SAE, three sample chapters and a brief CV. No science fiction, fantasy, horror, or scripts.

Tips No unsolicited submissions or electronic manuscripts.

Elaine Steel

110 Gloucester Avenue, London, NW1 8HX
- 020 8348 0918
- 020 8341 9807
- ecmsteel@aol.com

Contact Elaine Steel
Established 1986
Insider Info Seeking both new and established writers. Considers non-fiction books, novels, television scripts, film scripts and stage plays. Unsuccessful proposals will be returned if accompanied by SAE. Obtains new clients through queries and submissions. Commission rates of ten per cent for domestic sales, and 20 per cent for foreign sales.
Non-fiction Considers General non-fiction.
Fiction Considers General fiction.
Scripts Considers Scripts for Film, Television and Theatre.
Submission Guidelines Send query letter with SAE. No academic or technical titles.
Tips First contact by telephone is preferred.

Elisabeth Wilson

24 Thornhill Square, London, N1 1BQ
- 020 7609 6045

Established 1979
Insider Info Seeking both new and established writers. Considers illustrated books for children only. Simultaneous submissions are accepted. Unsuccessful proposals will be returned if accompanied by SAE. Obtains new clients through queries and submissions.
Non-fiction Does not consider Children's non-fiction.
Tips Mainly acts as a rights agent and consultant, rather than a traditional agent.

Elizabeth Roy Literary Agency

White Cottage, Greatford, Nr. Stamford, Lincolnshire, PE9 4PR
- 01778 560672
- 01778 560672

Established 1990
Insider Info Seeking both new and established writers. Considers non-fiction books, children's books and novels. Simultaneous submissions are accepted. Unsuccessful proposals will be returned if accompanied by SAE. Obtains new clients through queries and submissions. Commission rates of 15 per cent for domestic sales and 20 per cent on foreign sales. Does not charge a reading fee.
* Specialises in children's books, both writers and illustrators.
Non-fiction Considers Children's non-fiction titles.

Fiction Considers Children's and Picture book fiction titles.
Submission Guidelines Send query letter with SAE, synopsis, and two to three sample chapters.
Tips Writers should declare all the agents and publishers that the proposal has already been submitted to.

Elspeth Cochrane Personal Management

16 Old Town, Clapham, London, SW4 0JY
- 020 7819 6256
- 020 7819 4297
- elspeth@elspethcochrane.co.uk

Contact Elspeth Cochrane
Established 1960
Insider Info Actively seeking clients. Considers non-fiction books, novels, television scripts, film scripts, stage plays, and radio scripts. Obtains new clients through queries and submissions. Commission rates are variable on domestic sales. Does not charge a reading fee.
Non-fiction Considers Biography/Autobiography and General non-fiction titles.
Fiction Considers General Adult's fiction titles.
Scripts Considers scripts for Film, Television, Radio and Theatre.
Submission Guidelines Send query letter with SAE and synopsis. Telephone in the first instance before submitting any proposal. No self-help, memoirs, poetry or children's fiction.
Client(s) Alex Jones, Dominic Leyton, Royce Ryton, F.E. Smith and Robert Tannitch

Eric Glass Ltd

25 Ladbroke Crescent, London, W11 1PS
- 020 7229 9500
- 020 7229 6220
- eglassltd@aol.com

Contact Janet Glass
Established 1932
Insider Info Actively seeking clients. Considers non-fiction books, novels, television scripts, film scripts, stage plays and radio scripts. Simultaneous submissions are accepted. Unsuccessful proposals will be returned if accompanied by SAE. Obtains new clients through queries and submissions. Commission rates of 15 per cent for domestic sales and 20 per cent for foreign sales. Does not charge a reading fee.
Non-fiction Considers General non-fiction.
Fiction Considers General fiction.
Scripts Considers scripts for Television, Film, Radio and Theatre.

Submission Guidelines Send query letter with SAE and the entire manuscript if requested. No short stories, poetry, or children's titles.

Client(s) Herbert Appleman, Henry Fleet and Alan Melville

Tips No unsolicited manuscripts.

Eunice McMullen Children's Literary Agent Ltd

Low Ibbotsholme Cottage, Off Bridge Lane, Troutbeck Bridge, Windermere, Cumbria, LA23 1HU

- ☎ 01539 448551
- 🖷 01539 442289
- ✉ eunice@eunicemcmullen.co.uk
- 🌐 www.eunicemcmullen.co.uk

Contact Director, Eunice McMullen

Established 1992

Insider Info Actively seeking clients. Considers children's books and novels. Unsuccessful proposals will be returned if accompanied by SAE. Obtains new clients through telephone queries. Commission rates of ten per cent on domestic sales and 15 per cent on foreign sales.

* Eunice had worked in publishing, including for the Puffin imprint of Penguin, before beginning work as an agent. In 1992 she established her own agency.

Non-fiction Considers Children's titles.

Fiction Considers Children's and Picture book titles.

Submission Guidelines Query via phone.

Recent Sale(s) *Septimus Heap Book 1 'Magyk'*, Angie Sage

Client(s) Wayne Anderson, Sam Childs, Ross Collins, Charles Fuge, Angie Sage, Gillian Shields and Susan Winter

Tips Telephone enquiries only before submission, no unsolicited manuscripts.

Eve White

1a High Street, Kintbury, Berkshire, RG17 9TJ

- ☎ 01488 657656
- 🖷 01488 657656
- ✉ eve@evewhite.co.uk
- 🌐 www.evewhite.co.uk

Contact Eve White

Established 2003

Insider Info Seeking both new and established writers. Considers non-fiction books, children's books and novels. Receives 150 manuscripts per month. Represents 40 clients, 25 of whom are new or previously unpublished writers. Prospective clients must see the website for submission requirements. Aims to respond to manuscripts within two months. Unsuccessful proposals will be returned if accompanied by SAE. Obtains new clients through recommendations from others, queries and submissions. Commission rates of 15 per cent on domestic sales and 20 per cent on foreign sales and film rights. Does not charge a reading fee or offer a criticism service. They will sometimes suggest a literary consultancy or a specific editor where work looks promising but not right for them at the time. Eve White Literary Agency is a member of The Association of Authors' Agents.

* Eve White has a degree in Education (with English and Drama). She worked as a teacher and then as a writer, director and actress in theatre and television. The agency will frequently get involved in the PR side of an author's career.

Non-fiction Considers General Non-fiction for adults but always check the website as requirements may change.

Fiction Considers Literary and Commercial fiction, Children's fiction (for ages seven and up only) but always check the website as requirements may change.

Submission Guidelines For Adult and Children's submissions, authors must see www.evewhite.co.uk for up-to-date requirements.

Faith Evans Associates

27 Park Avenue North, London, N8 7RU

- ☎ 020 8340 9920
- 🖷 020 8340 9410

Contact Faith Evans

Established 1987

Insider Info Actively seeking clients. Currently handles non-fiction books and novels. Considers non-fiction and fiction. Obtains commissions through recommendations from others. Commission rates of 15 per cent for domestic sales and 20 per cent for foreign sales.

Non-fiction Considers General non-fiction titles

Fiction Considers General fiction titles.

Submission Guidelines Does not accept scripts.

Client(s) Melissa Benn, Shyam Bhatia, Cherie Booth, Carolyn Cassady, Caroline Conran, Alicia Foster, Helena Kennedy, Seumas Milne and Jim Kelly

Tips Does not accept telephone queries. Manuscripts are only accepted by recommendation.

Felicity Bryan Literary Agency

2a North Parade Avenue, Oxford, OX2 6LX

- ☎ 01865 513816
- 🖷 01865 310055
- ✉ agency@felicitybryan.com
- 🌐 www.felicitybryan.com

Established 1988

Insider Info Seeking both new and established writers. Currently handles non-fiction books, novels and children's books. Simultaneous submissions are accepted. Aims to respond to queries and manuscripts within eight weeks. Unsuccessful proposals are returned if accompanied by SAE. Obtains new clients through recommendations from others and queries/submissions. Written contract offered. Does not charge a reading fee, or offer a criticism service.

Non-fiction Considers Biography, History, Current Affairs, Philosophy and Popular Culture titles.

Fiction Considers Children's Fiction (9-12 years), Crime, Literary Fiction, Thriller/Espionage and Young Adult titles.

Submission Guidelines Send query letter with SAE, outline, synopsis, sample chapters, biography and a proposal. Does not accept poetry, film, television and play scripts, science fiction, horror, fantasy, light romance, illustrated children's books, autobiography, self-help or how-to books.

Client(s) Authors include Roy Strong, John Julius Norwich, A.C. Grayling, Meg Rosoff, Iain Pears, Miriam Stoppard, Karen Armstrong, John Dickie, Simon Blackburn, Katherine Langrish, Eleanor Updale, Matthew Skelton, Jenny Downham, Sadie Jones, Tim Harford and James Naughtie

Tips Does not accept authors from North America for practical reasons.

Felix De Wolfe

Kingsway House, 103 Kingsway, London, WC2B 6QX

- 020 7242 5066
- 020 7242 8119
- info@felixdewolfe.com
- www.felixdewolfe.com

Insider Info Seeking both new and established writers. Currently handles non-fiction books, novels, television scripts, film scripts, stage plays and sound broadcasting scripts. Considers non-fiction, fiction, film scripts, television scripts, stage plays and sound broadcasting. Obtains new clients by queries/submissions. Commission rates of 10–15 per cent for domestic sales and 20 per cent for foreign sales. Does not charge a reading fee.

Non-fiction Considers General non-fiction.

Fiction Considers General fiction.

Scripts Considers General scripts.

Tips Approach first by telephone.

Film Rights Ltd

Mezzanine, Quadrant House, 80–82 Regent Street, London, W1B 5AU

- 020 7734 9911
- 020 7734 0044
- information@filmrights.ltd.uk
- www.filmrights.ltd.uk

Contact Director, Brendan Davis; Director, Joan Potts

Established 1932

Insider Info Seeking both new and established writers. Currently handles television scripts, film scripts, stage plays, radio broadcasting. Considers non-fiction, fiction, film scripts, television scripts, stage plays, and radio broadcasting. Unsuccessful proposals are returned if accompanied by SAE. Obtains new clients by queries/submissions. Commission rate of ten per cent for domestic sales, and 15 per cent for foreign sales. Does not charge a reading fee.

Scripts Considers scripts for Adults and Children.

Submission Guidelines Send query letter with SAE.

Tips Works in association with Laurence Fitch Ltd.

Font Literary Agency

Hollyville House, Hollybrook House, Clontarf, Dublin 3, Republic of Ireland

- 00353 1 853 2365
- info@fontlitagency.com
- www.fontlitagency.com

Contact Agents: Ita O'Driscoll (Direcotr) and Orna Ross (Founder)

Established 2003

Insider Info Currently handles fiction and non-fiction internationally. Obtains new clients through queries and submissions. Does not accept simultaneous submissions. Commission rate of 15 per cent for domestic sales. Does not charge a reading fee.

Fiction Will consider commercial fiction novels, but does not handle short stories, scripts, sci-fi, poetry or children's writing.

Non-Fiction Will consider general non-fiction titles, but does not handle articles, textbooks or academic work.

Submission Guidelines As an initial contact send a query by email outlining the subject matter of the book, its title and purpose, as well as proposed length and target readership.

Recent Sale(s) *Champagne Kisses*, Amanda Brunker (Novel); *Ruinair*, Paul Kilduff (Non-Fiction)

Client(s) Amanda Brunker, Evelyn Cosgrave, Cornucopia Creative Team, Garbhan Downey, Paul Kilduff, Karen Lotter, Paul Lynch, Susanne O'Leary, Dearbhail McDonald, Donal Maguire, Orna Ross, Audrey Talbot.

Tips Authors are asked to submit an email query in the first instance, but only if they have completed their manuscript (for fiction) or have a proposal package ready (for non-fiction). Font will then request a full submission if they are interested. See the website for further details.

Fox & Howard Literary Agency

4 Bramerton Street, London, SW3 5JX

☎ 020 7352 8691

✆ 020 7352 8691

Contact Chelsey Fox; Charlotte Howard

Established 1992

Insider Info Actively seeking clients. Currently handles non-fiction books. Unsuccessful proposals are returned if accompanied by SAE. Obtains new clients by queries and submissions. Commission rates of 15 per cent for domestic sales and 20 per cent for foreign sales. Does not charge a reading fee.

Non-fiction Considers Academia, Biography/Autobiography, Health, Lifestyle, Mind, Body & Spirit, Popular Culture and Self-help titles.

Submission Guidelines Send query letter with SAE and a synopsis.

Tips Please do not send any unsolicited manuscripts.

Frances Kelly

111 Clifton Road, Kingston upon Thames, Surrey, KT2 6PL

☎ 020 8549 7830

✆ 020 8547 0051

Contact Frances Kelly

Established 1978

Insider Info Actively seeking clients. Currently handles non-fiction, and illustrated books. Unsuccessful proposals are returned if accompanied by SAE. Obtains new clients with queries/submissions. Commission rates of ten per cent for domestic sales and 20 per cent for foreign sales. Does not charge a reading fee.

Non-fiction Considers Academic, Art, Biography/Autobiography, Business, Food & Drink, Finance, Health, History, Lifestyle, Medicine and Self-help titles.

Submission Guidelines Send query letter with SAE, synopsis and a biography. Will not accept scripts, except from existing clients.

Tips Please do not send any unsolicited manuscripts.

Fraser Ross Associates

6 Wellington Place, Edinburgh, EH6 7EQ

☎ 0131 657 4412/0131 553 2759

✉ kjross@tiscali.co.uk

✉ lindsey.fraser@tiscali.co.uk

🌐 www.fraserross.co.uk

Contact Linsey Fraser; Kathryn Ross

Established 2002

Insider Info Actively seeking clients. Currently handles children's books, and non-fiction and novels for adults. Unsuccessful proposals are returned if accompanied by SAE. Obtains new clients by queries/submissions. Commission rates of 12.5 per cent for domestic sales and 20 per cent for foreign sales. Does not charge a reading fee.

* Both partners had careers in readership development, book-selling and teaching before establishing their own agency, and they also ran the Scottish Book Trust from 1991–2002. They have been judges on panels for such prizes as the Whitbread, Blue Peter, Smarties and Fidler, and have addressed conferences on readership development worldwide. Presently they run the Pushkin Prizes (www.pushkinprizes.net) and offer readership development workshops and training to teachers and librarians.

Fiction Considers Children's Fiction and Picture Books, Commercial and Literary Fiction.

Submission Guidelines Send query letter with SAE for return of material, synopsis, three sample chapters and a short biography. Pages should be one-sided, double-spaced, numbered and A4 sized. Please do not send any unfinished work. General information and full submission guidelines are on the website.

Client(s) Gill Arbuthnott, Erica Blaney, Tom Bloor, John Cresswell, Samantha David, Robert Dodds, Lari Don, Jane Eagland, Richard Edwards, Anne Forbes, Vivian French, Edward Hardy, Chris Higgins, Barry Hutchison, Janey Louise Jones, Ann Kelley, Joan Lennon, Joan Lingard, Tanya Landman, Jack McLean, Helena Pielichaty, Sue Purkiss, Lynne Rickards, Jamie Rix, Dugald Steer, Linda Strachan, Chae Strathie and Matilda Webb. Illustrators: Ella Burfoot, Sally Collins, Teresa Flavin, Shona Grant, Iain McIntosh, Moira Munro, Katie Pamment.

Tips When submitting picture books send complete manuscript; illustrators should send two to three samples of artwork (colour, and black & white), plus a rough storyboard of sketches with complete story. If acknowledgement is required of submitted material, a paid reply postcard must be included with manuscript. Material will only be returned if a SAE is enclosed.

Futerman, Rose & Associates (FRA)

91 St Leonards Road, London, SW14 7BL

☎ 020 8255 7755

✆ 020 8286 4860

✉ enquiries@futermanrose.co.uk

🌐 www.futermanrose.co.uk

Contact Partner, Guy Rose (Non-fiction, Autobiographical/Biographical, Film, Television, Client & Business Development); Betty Schwartz (Commercial and Literary Fiction); Barnaby Fisher-Turner (Screenplays and Telelvision); Alexandra Green (Teenage Fiction)

Established 1984

Insider Info Actively seeking clients. Currently handles non-fiction books, novels, television scripts and movie scripts. Unsuccessful proposals are returned with SAE. Obtains new clients by queries and submissions. Commission rates of ten per cent for domestic sales and 20 per cent for foreign sales. Does not charge a reading fee. Affiliated to the Authors' Agents Association and the Personal Managers Association.

Non-fiction Considers Biography/Autobiography and Popular Culture titles.

Fiction Considers Commercial, Literary and Young Adult fiction titles.

Scripts Considers General scripts

Submission Guidelines Send query letter with SAE, synopsis, three sample chapters and a biography. Does not accept science fiction, poetry, young children's, or textbooks.

Recent Sale(s) *Fading with the Limelight*, Peter Sallis (Autobiogrphy); *Jumping to Confusions*, Liz Rettig (Young Adult)

Client(s) Paul Hendy, Ciaran O'Keeffe, Sue Lenier, David Brett, Kenneth Branagh, Susan George, Stephen Griffin, Yvette Fielding, Iain Duncan Smith, Peter Sallis, Elizabeth Taylor, Tom Conti, Toyah Wilcox, Paul Marx and Philip Dart

Tips The agency is especially interested in political, music and show business autobiographies.

Graham Maw Christie Literary Agency

19 Thornhill Crescent, London, N1 4LD
- ☎ 020 7737 4766
- ✉ enquiries@grahammawchristie.com
- 🌐 www.grahammawchristie.com

Contact Jane Graham Maw; Jennifer Christie
Established 2005
Insider Info Seeking mostly established writers through referrals. Currently handles non-fiction books, television tie-ins and blog to book projects. Obtains new clients through recommendations from others. Commission rates of 15 per cent for domestic sales and 20 per cent for foreign sales. Does not charge a reading fee.

Non-fiction Considers Biography/Autobiography, Business, Childcare/Parenting, Gift Books, Health, History, Humour, Lifestyle, Memoirs, Popular Culture and Psychology titles.

Submission Guidelines Submissions should include a one-page summary and a paragraph on the content of each chapter, the qualification one has for writing upon the subject, ideas for promotion of the material, plus full contact details. Does not accept fiction, children's or poetry titles.

Tips Graham Maw Christie are always looking to hear from experienced ghostwriters. Email ghostwriters@grahammawchristie.com for further information.

Greene & Heaton Ltd

37 Goldhawk Road, London, W12 8QQ
- ☎ 020 8749 0315
- ☎ 020 8749 0318
- ✉ info@greeneheaton.co.uk
- 🌐 www.greeneheaton.co.uk

Contact Director, Carol Heaton (Authors); Judith Murray (Authors); Antony Topping (Authors); Nick Harrop (Authors); Linda Davis (Children's Authors); Ellie Glason (Translations and Subsidiary rights); Belou Charlaff (Authors)
Established 1963
Insider Info Actively seeking clients. Currently handles non-fiction books, children's books and novels. Simultaneous submissions are accepted. Aims to respond to queries and proposals within six weeks. Unsuccessful submissions returned with SAE. Obtains new clients by queries and submissions. Commission rates of 10–15 per cent for domestic sales and 20 per cent for foreign sales. Does not charge a reading fee.

Non-fiction Considers Agriculture/Horticulture, History, Humour, Children's, Science/Technology, Travel and General non-fiction titles.

Fiction Considers Children's fiction, Literary fiction, Mainstream fiction, Science fiction, Fantasy, Crime and Graphic novel titles.

Submission Guidelines Send query letter with SAE, synopsis and three sample chapters. Does not accept scripts.

Recent Sale(s) *Urban Sanctuaries*, Stephen Anderton; *How to be Cool*, Will Smith; *Unknown Soldiers*, Matthew Carr; *Voyaging the Pacific*, Miles Hordern

Client(s) Michael Frayn, P.D. James, William Shawcross, Mark Barrowcliffe, Bill Bryson, Hugh Fearnley-Whittingstall, C.J. Sansom, Marcus du Sautoy, Sarah Waters, Kathryn Hymen, Tom Ryan, Russell Davis and Tabitha Suzuma

Tips The agency has a very diverse list of clientele, handling all types of fiction and non-fiction. Greene & Heaton are also the first literary agency to open an office in 'Second Life', the online virtual world.

The Greenhouse Literary Agency Ltd

Stanley House, St Chad's Place, London, WC1X 9HH
- ✉ submissions@greenhouseliterary.com
- 🌐 www.greenhouseliterary.com

Contact Julia Churchill; Sarah Davies
Established 2008
Insider Info Represents children's and teenage fiction, from young high-concept series through to

sophisticated young-adult novels. Welcomes submissions (email only) from debut authors. The Greenhouse's trademark is in working editorially and creatively with writers to achieve their potential, where outstanding promise is evident. A uniquely transatlantic literary agency that represents UK and US authors directly to both markets (taking same commission, 15%, for each). Foreign rights sold by sister company Rights People (www.rightspeople.com) – commission 25%. Does not charge a reading fee.

Fiction Will consider Children's and Young Adult fiction titles. Greenhouse is not currently seeking picture book texts or illustrators, non-fiction, short stories, very short single young novels under 10,000 words or work for adults.

Scripts No scripts. Film/TV rights sold only when book rights have been placed with a publisher.

Submission Guidelines Email queries only (no postal queries). Up to five (the first five) pages of the story should be pasted into the body of the email. See website for full details, at: www.greenhouseliterary.com

Recent Sale(s) *The Devil's Kiss*, Sarwat Chadda (Puffin); *Princess for Hire*, Lindsey Leavitt (Egmont)

Client(s) A building client list of British and American authors.

Gregory & Company Authors' Agents
3 Barb Mews, Hammersmith, London, W6 7PA
- 020 7610 4676
- 020 7610 4686
- info@gregoryandcompany.co.uk
- www.gregoryandcompany.co.uk

Contact Director, Jane Gregory; Agent, Emma Dunford (Editorial); Rights Manager, Claire Morris (Foreign & Audio Rights); Rights Executive, Jemma McDonagh (Publicity)

Established 1987

Insider Info Actively seeking clients. Currently handles non-fiction books and novels. Accepts simultaneous submissions. Unsuccessful manuscripts will be returned if accompanied by SAE. Clients usually obtained through queries and submissions. Commission of 15 per cent for domestic sales, 20 per cent for foreign sales. Does not charge a reading fee.

Non-fiction Will consider Biography/Autobiography and General non-fiction.

Fiction Will consider Crime, Family saga, Historical, Literary, and Thriller/Espionage.

Submission Guidelines Authors should include query letter, SAE, synopsis and three sample chapters as double-spaced, one-sided A4. Accepts queries by email. Children's, 'chick lit', science fiction, fantasy, poetry, short stories, and scripts will not be considered.

Recent Sale(s) *Singing to the Dead*, Caro Ramsay (W.F. Howes); *Mad Dogs and an Englishwoman*, Polly Evans (Oakhill)

Client(s) Julian Thompson, John Ryan, Eileen Dewhurst, Betty Boothroyd, Jo Bannister, Minette Walters, Robert Barnard, Gladys Mitchell, Sarah Diamond, Val McDermid

Tips If submission is by email, send a brief letter with a synopsis, but no more than ten pages. When entering the book title also write 'Submission' in subject line. Do not send an entire manuscript without prior authorisation.

Gunn Media Associates
50 Albemarle Street, London, W1S 4BD
- 020 7529 3745
- ali@gunnmedia.co.uk

Contact Ali Gunn

Established 2005

Insider Info Seeking both new and established writers. Considers non-fiction books and novels. Does not accept simultaneous submissions. Unsuccessful proposals will be returned with SAE. Obtains new clients through queries and submissions. Commission rates of 15 per cent on domestic sales and 20 per cent on foreign sales. Does not charge a reading fee.

Non-fiction Considers Commercial non-fiction.

Fiction Considers Commercial fiction.

Submission Guidelines Send a query letter with SAE, synopsis, and two to three sample chapters. No scripts.

Tips Unsolicited proposals are welcome by post only.

Henser Literary Agency
174 Pennant Road, Llanelli, Wales, SA4 8HN
- 01554 753520
- henserliteraryagency@btopenworld.com

Contact Steve Henser

Established 2002

Insider Info Seeking both new and established writers. Considers novels, television scripts, film scripts, stage plays and radio scripts. Simultaneous submissions are accepted. Obtains new clients through queries and submissions. Commission rates of 15 per cent on domestic sales and 20 per cent on foreign sales.

Fiction Considers Fantasy, Literary, Mainstream, Mystery and Science fiction titles.

Scripts Considers scripts for Television, Film, Radio and Theatre.

Submission Guidelines Send query letter with SAE and synopsis. No horror.

Tips Does not accept unsolicited manuscripts.

hhb agency ltd

122 Arlington Road, London, NW1 7HP

☎ 020 7485 0044

✉ heather@hhbagency.com

🌐 www.hhbagency.com

Contact Heather Holden-Brown

Established 2005

Insider Info Contact by telephone or email before sending through submissions. Commission rates of 15 per cent on domestic sales. Does not charge a reading fee.

Non-fiction Considers Biography/Autobiography, Family Memoirs, Cookery/Food, Current Affairs, Politics, Business, History, Humour and Journalism titles.

Tips hhb agency ltd does not accept unsolicited fiction without prior discussion.

ICM Books

61 Frith Street, London, W1D 3JL

☎ 020 7851 4853

☎ 020 7432 0808

✉ books@icmtalent.com

🌐 www.icmtalent.com

Contact Margaret Halton

Insider Info Handles non-fiction books, novels and screenplays. Obtains new clients through queries. Does not charge a reading fee.

Non-fiction Considers General non-fiction and Journalism titles.

Fiction Considers General Commercial fiction titles.

Submission Guidelines No unsolicited submissions.

Tips ICM have a very strict policy of not accepting unsolicited materials of any kind.

IMG UK Ltd

McCormack House, Hogarth Business Park, Burlington Lane, Chiswick, London, W4 2TH

☎ 020 8233 5300

☎ 020 8233 5301

🌐 www.imgworld.com

Contact Joint CEOs: Bob Kain and Alastair Johnston

Established 1960

Insider Info Considers non-fiction books and celebrity and sports related material. Unsuccessful proposals will be returned with SAE. Obtains new clients through queries and submissions. Commission rates of 15 per cent for domestic sales and 20–25 per cent for foreign sales. Does not charge a reading fee.

* IMG are a specialist sports and entertainment media company.

Non-fiction Consider Music, Dance, Theatre, Film, Sports and Celebrity titles.

Submission Guidelines Send query letter with SAE.

Tips Represents television properties, celebrities, entertainers, artists, musicians, sports personalities, organisations and events, as well as writers.

Intercontinental Literary Agency

Centric House, 390–391 Strand, London, WC2R 0LT

☎ 020 7379 6611

☎ 020 7240 4724

✉ ila@ila-agency.co.uk

🌐 www.ila-agency.co.uk

Contact Nicki Kennedy (Rights in France, Germany, Italy, Spain and Japan); Sam Edenborough, (Rights in Denmark, Finland, Sweden, Norway, Holland, Greece, Iceland, Portugal and Brazil); Mary Esdaile (Arabic and Indonesian rights, works with co-agents in Bulgaria, Hungary, Lithuania, Romania, Estonia, Croatia, the Czech Republic, Latvia, Serbia, Slovakia, Slovenia, Turkey, China, Korea, Thailand and Israel); Tessa Girvan (Rights for Children's and Young Adult titles Worldwide, including work with co-agents in Poland and Russia); Jenny Robson (Indonesian and Arabic rights); Katherine West (Handles rights in Greece, Poland and Portugal)

Established 1965

Insider Info Considers non-fiction, fiction, children's books and young adult titles. Works with other agents and publishers exclusively.

* Specialises in translation rights for authors from Britain, USA and Australia.

Client(s) Elyse Cheney Literary Associates, Lucas Alexander Whitley Ltd, Luigi Bonomi Associates, Mulcahy & Viney Ltd, PDF, Turnbull Agency (John Irving), and Wade & Doherty Literary Agency

Tips As a specialist translation rights agency ILA does not deal directly with writers, only other agents and publishers.

International Scripts

1a Kidbrooke Park Road, London, SE3 0LR

☎ 020 8319 8666

☎ 020 8319 0801

✉ internationalscripts@btinternet.com

Contact H.P. Tanner; J. Lawson

Established 1979

Insider Info Actively seeking clients. Considers non-fiction books, novels, television scripts and film scripts. Simultaneous submissions are accepted. Unsuccessful proposals will be returned with SAE. Obtains new clients through queries and submissions. Commission rates of 15 per cent on domestic sales and 20 per cent on foreign sales. May charge reading fees.

Non-fiction Considers Biography/Autobiography, Business and General non-fiction titles.

Fiction Considers Detective/Police/Crime, Women's/'Chick lit' and General Contemporary fiction titles.

Scripts Considers scripts for Television and Film.

Submission Guidelines Send query letter with SAE. No short stories, poetry or articles.

Client(s) Jane Adams, Ashleigh Bingham, Dr James Fleming, Trevor Lummis, Chris Pascoe, Anne Spencer

Tips If a full manuscript is requested, an editorial financial contribution may be required along with SAE.

Jane Conway-Gordon Ltd

1 Old Compton Street, London, W1D 5JA

- 020 7494 0148
- 020 7287 9264

Contact Jane Conway-Gordon

Established 1982

Insider Info Actively seeking clients. Currently handles general fiction and non-fiction books and novels. Accepts simultaneous submissions. Manuscripts returned with SAE. Clients usually obtained through queries/submissions. Commission rate of 15 per cent for domestic sales, 20 per cent for foreign sales. Does not charge a reading fee.

Submission Guidelines Authors should include query letter and SAE with submissions. No short stories, poetry, ccience fiction or children's books considered.

Tips The agency is represented worldwide.

Jane Judd Literary Agency

18 Belitha Villas, London, N1 1PD

- 020 7607 0273
- 020 7607 0623

Contact Jane Judd

Established 1986

Insider Info Actively seeking clients. Currently handles non-fiction books and novels. Accepts simultaneous submissions. Manuscripts returned with SAE. Clients usually obtained through queries/submissions. Commission rates of ten per cent for domestic sales, 20 per cent for foreign sales. Does not charge a reading fee.

Non-fiction Will consider Biography/Autobiography, Health/Medicine, Humour, Travel, Lifestyle and General.

Fiction Will consider Detective/Police/Crime, Thriller/Espionage, Women's/'Chick lit' and Literary fiction.

Submission Guidelines Authors should include query letter, SAE, synopsis, one sample chapter and complete contact details and an email address with their submission. No academia, scripts, DIY or gardening considered.

Janet Fillingham Associates

52 Lowther Road, London, SW13 9NU

- 020 8748 5594
- 020 8748 7374
- info@janetfillingham.com
- www.janetfillingham.com

Contact Director, Janet Fillingham

Established 1992

Insider Info Seeking mostly established writers through referrals. Currently handles television scripts, film scripts and stage plays. Clients are usually obtained through recommendations from others. Commission rates of ten per cent for domestic sales, 15–20 per cent for foreign sales.

Scripts Considers scripts for Television, Theatre and Film.

Recent Sale(s) *Bye Bye Harry*, Graham Alborough; *Casualty*, Ray Brooking; *Doctors*, Michael Chappell & Richard Stevens; *Dream Team*, Eddy Marshall

Client(s) Esther May Campbell, Clive Endersby, Nick Gleaves, Christopher Green, Steve Griffiths, Charles McKeown, Dale Overton, Tina Pepler, Allan Plenderleith, Robert Rigby, Robert Rohrer and Frances Tomelty

Tips JFA runs a bespoke service and has no immediate requirement for new writers and/or directors, although potential clients are invited to register via the website. JFA does not represent book authors.

Jane Turnbull

Barn Cottage, Veryan, Truro, TR2 5QA

- 01872 501317/020 7727 9409
- jane.turnbull@btinternet.com

Contact Jane Turnbull

Established 1986

Insider Info Actively seeking clients. Currently handles non-fiction books and some fiction. Manuscripts returned with SAE. Clients usually obtained through personal recommendation or queries/submissions. Commission rates of 15 per cent for domestic sales, 20 per cent for foreign sales. Works with specialised sub-agents for sale of film/TV, and translation rights. Does not charge a reading fee.

Non-fiction Will consider any well researched and original material including Biography/Autobiography, Current affairs/Politics, Health/Medicine, History, Lifestyle/Design and Humour.

Fiction Considers General fiction.

Submission Guidelines Authors should include query letter and SAE with submissions. Science fiction and fiction for young children will not be considered.

Tips Jane Turnbull does not accept unsolicited submissions of full manuscripts, always send a query letter first.

Janklow & Nesbit (UK) Ltd

33 Drayson Mews, London, W8 4LY

☏ 020 7376 2733

☏ 020 7376 2915

✉ queries@janklow.co.uk

Contact Tif Loehnis, Claire Paterson, Jenny McVeigh

Established 2000

Insider Info Seeking both new and established writers. Currently handles non-fiction books, scholarly books and novels. Accepts simultaneous submissions. Manuscripts returned with SAE. Does not charge reading or office fees, and does not offer a criticism service. Does not refer to an editing service.

Non-fiction Considers Academic and General non-fiction.

Fiction Considers General fiction.

Submission Guidelines Authors should include query letter, SAE, outline, synopsis, three sample chapters, author biography and proposal with submissions. Actively seeking commercial and literary fiction and non-fiction. Email submissions are not accepted.

Jeffrey Simmons

15 Penn House, Mallory Street, London, NW8 8SX

☏ 020 7224 8917

✉ jasimmons@unicombox.com

Contact Jeffrey Simmons

Insider Info Currently handles non-fiction books and novels. Manuscripts returned with SAE. Clients usually obtained through recommendations and direct submissions. Commission rate for new clients, 15 percent. Does not charge a reading fee.

Non-fiction Will consider Biography/ Autobiography, Current affairs, Government/Politics/ Law, History, Sports, True crime/Investigative, Academia, Parapsychology, Quality commercial writing, and Writing on the Arts.

Fiction Will consider quality Commercial fiction.

Submission Guidelines Authors should include query letter, SAE, synopsis, two or three sample chapters (not with email submissions), author biography, brief publishing history - including list of manuscripts with submission. No hobbies, science fiction, fantasy, horror, children's, cookery or gardening titles considered.

Tips Genuinely interested in new, exciting young writers. Will suggest revisions. Include any publishing history and a list of agents/publishers that the manuscript has been submitted to.

Jennifer Luithlen Agency

88 Holmfield, Leicester, LE2 1SB

☏ 0116 273 8863

☏ 0116 273 5697

Contact Agent, Jennifer Luithlen; Agent, Penny Luithlen

Established 1986

Insider Info Not currently seeking new clients. Currently handles children's books and adult fiction. Commission rate is 15 per cent for domestic sales, 20 per cent for foreign sales.

Fiction Will consider Detective/Police/Crime, Family saga, Historical, Children's, Literary and General.

Tips No unsolicited manuscripts.

Jenny Brown Associates

33 Argyle Place, Edinburgh, EH9 1JT

☏ 0131 229 5334

✉ info@jennybrownassociates.com

🌐 www.jennybrownassociates.com

Contact Jenny Brown (Literary Fiction & Non-fiction); Mark Stanton (Non-fiction - Sports & Music); Allan Guthrie (Novels); Lucy Juckes (Children's Books); Kevin Pocklington (Rights)

Established 2002

Insider Info Actively seeking clients. Currently handles non-fiction books, children's books and novels. Accepts simultaneous submissions. Aims to respond to queries/proposals withing six weeks. Manuscripts returned with SAE. Clients usually obtained through queries/submissions. Commissions rate of 12.5 per cent for domestic sales, 20 per cent for foreign sales. Does not charge a reading fee.

* Before establishing the agency, Jenny Brown was formerly Director of the Edinburgh International Book Festival and Head of Literature at the Scottish Arts Council.

Non-fiction Considers Biography/Autobiography, History, Music/Dance/Theatre/Film, Popular culture and Sports.

Fiction Considers Detective/Police/Crime, Children's and Literary fiction.

Submission Guidelines Authors should include SAE, synopsis, sample chapters (30 pages), author biography, one page synopsis and brief CV with submission. No poetry, science fiction, fantasy, sagas or academia considered.

Recent Sale(s) *Enchanted Forests*, Sara Maitland (Granta); *Easy Kill*, Lin Anderson (Hodder)

Client(s) Lin Anderson, Richard Blandford, Linda Cracknell, David White, Patrick Lambe, Esther Woolfson, Dennis O'Donnell, Erica Munro, Alex Gray, Diana Hendry, David Barnes, Catherine De Courcy, Neil Drysdale, Guy Kennaway, Richard Moore, and Aidan Smith

Tips Any non-fiction manuscripts should be accompanied by ideas for possible promotion and outlets, plus any notes on comparable or competing literature.

Jill Foster Ltd

9 Barb Mews, Brook Green, London, W6 7PA
- 020 7602 1263
- 020 7602 9336
- agents@jfagency.com

Contact Jill Foster, Alison Finch, Simon Williamson, Dominic Lord, Gary Wild
Established 1976
Insider Info Actively seeking clients. Currently handles television scripts, film scripts and stage plays. Accepts simultaneous submissions. Clients usually obtained through queries/submissions. Commission rate of 12.5 per cent for domestic sales, 15 per cent for foreign sales. Does not charge a reading fee.
Scripts Considers scripts for Television, Film and Theatre.
Submission Guidelines Authors should include query letter with submission. No books, poetry or short stories considered.
Tips No submissions by email. A preliminary letter is essential in the first instance.

JMLA

The Basement, 94 Goldhurst Terrace, London, NW6 3HS
- 020 7372 8422/3140
- 020 7372 8423

Contact Managing Director, Judy Martin
Established 1990
Insider Info Actively seeking clients. Currently handles non-fiction books. Manuscripts returned with SAE. Clients usually obtained through queries/submissions Commission rate of 15 per cent for domestic sales, 20 per cent for foreign sales. Does not charge reading fee.
Non-fiction Will consider Biography/Autobiography, Jazz origins/History, American, Art/Surrealism.
Submission Guidelines Authors should include query letter, SAE, synopsis, two to three sample chapters, and publishing history with submission. No cookery, gardening, poetry or children's considered.
Tips Specialises in jazz material.

J.M.Thurley Management

Archery House, 33 Archery Square, Walmer, Deal, Kent, CT14 7JA
- 01304 371421
- 01304 371416
- JMThurley@aol.com

Contact Jon Thurley
Established 1976
Insider Info Seeking both new and established writers. Currently handling novels, television scripts and film scripts. Accepts simultaneous submissions.

Manuscripts returned with SAE. Clients usually obtained through queries/submissions. Commission of 15 per cent for domestic sales, 20 per cent for trade sales. Does not charge a reading fee.
Fiction Will consider Literary and Commercial fiction.
Scripts Will consider General/Commercial scripts.
Submission Guidelines Authors should include query letter and SAE with submissions. No short stories, poetry, articles, fantasy or play scripts considered.
Tips The agency provides editorial and creative assistance to new, exciting writers and constructive revision advice to authorised manuscripts that are rejected.

John Pawsey

60 High Street, Tarring, Worthing, Essex, BN14 7NR
- 01903 205167
- 01903 205167

Contact John Pawsey
Established 1981
Insider Info Actively seeking clients. Currently handles non-fiction books and novels. Accepts simultaneous submissions. Manuscript return with SAE. Clients usually obtained through queries/submissions. Commission for domestic and foreign sales variable. Does not charge a reading fee.
Non-fiction Will consider Art/Architecture/Design, Biography/Autobiography, Business, Current affairs, Ethnic/Cultural interests, Music/Dance/Theatre/Film, Popular culture, Sports, Lifestyle, Travel and Politics.
Fiction Will consider Detective/Police/Crime, Mystery and Thriller/Espionage.
Submission Guidelines Authors should submit query letter, SAE, synopsis and three sample chapters with submission. No science fiction, fantasy, horror, poetry, children's, short stories, journalism, scripts or drama considered.
Client(s) Jennie Bond, David Ashforth, William Fotheringham, Don Hale, Patricia Hall, Dr. David Lewis and Anne Mustoe
Tips Has a strong list of established clients, but is always looking to meet bright new talent.

Johnson & Alcock Ltd

Clerkenwell House, 45–47 Clerkenwell Green, London, EC1R 0HT
- 020 7251 0125
- 020 7251 2172
- info@johnsonandalcock.co.uk

Contact Michael Alcock, Anna Power, Andrew Hewson, Ed Wilson
Established 1956

Insider Info Actively seeking clients. Currently handles non-fiction books, children's books and novels. Accepts simultaneous submissions. Manuscripts returned with SAE. Clients usually obtained through queries/submissions. Commission of 15 per cent on domestic sales, 20 per cent on foreign sales. Does not charge a reading fee.

Non-fiction Will consider Biography/Autobiography, Current Affairs, Health/Medicine, History, Memoirs, Self-help/Personal improvement and Lifestyle.

Fiction Will consider Children's, Literary and Commercial fiction.

Submission Guidelines Authors should include query letter, SAE, synopsis, and author biography with submissions. Include details of media/writing experience. No scripts, poetry, science fiction, academia or technical writing considered.

Tips No unsolicited manuscripts, but fiction writers may submit the first three chapters with first contact. No email submissions.

John Welch, Literary Consultant & Agent

Mill Cottage, Calf Lane, Chipping Camden, GL55 6JQ

☎ 01387 840237

✆ 01386 840568

Contact John Welch

Established 1992

Insider Info Not currently seeking new clients. Currently handles non-fiction books. Commission of ten per cent on domestic sales.

Non-fiction Will consider Biography/Autobiography, History, Military/War, Sports, Aviation and Naval history and Travel.

Submission Guidelines Authors should submit query letter and SAE with submissions. However, no new authors are being considered at this time. No fiction, poetry, scripts, or children's writing considered.

Tips No unsolicited manuscripts whatsoever.

Jonathan Clowes Ltd

10 Iron Bridge Road, Bridge Approach, London, NW1 8BD

☎ 020 7722 7674

✆ 020 7722 7677

Contact Jonathan Clowes

Established 1960

Insider Info Actively seeking clients. Currently handles non-fiction books, novels, television scripts, film scripts, and stage plays. Manuscripts returned with SAE. Clients usually obtained through recommendations from others and queries/submissions. Commission rate of 15 per cent for

domestic sales, variable for foreign sales. Does not charge a reading fee.

Non-fiction Considers General non-fiction.

Fiction Will consider Literary fiction.

Scripts Will consider Comedy scripts in particular.

Submission Guidelines Authors should include a query letter and SAE with submissions. No textbooks or children's considered.

Tips No unsolicited manuscripts. Always contact with a query letter in the first instance.

Jonathan Williams Literary Agency

Rosney Mews, Upper Glenageary Road, Glenageary, Co. Dublin, Republic of Ireland

☎ 00353 1 280 3482

✆ 00353 1 280 3482

Contact Director, Jonathan Williams

Established 1981

Insider Info Seeking both new and established writers. Currently handles non-fiction books and novels. Manuscripts returned with SAE. Clients usually obtained through queries/submissions. Commission rate of ten per cent on domestic sales. Does not charge reading fee (see Tips).

Non-fiction Considers General non-fiction.

Fiction Considers General fiction.

Submission Guidelines Authors should include query letter, SAE, synopsis, and two to three sample chapters.

Tips Reading fees will be charged if a quick response is required. Include IRCs with submissions, instead of UK stamps.

Josef Weinberger Plays

12–14 Mortimer Street, London, W1T 3JJ

☎ 020 7580 2827

✆ 020 7436 9616

✉ general.info@jwmail.co.uk

🌐 www.josef-weinberger.com

Contact Michael Callahan, (Stage Licensing - Plays); John Schofield, Sally Irwin, Sean Gray (Stage Licensing - Musicals); Lewis Mitchell (Concert & Educational Music Promotion); Rupert Sharp, Ian Reeder, Emma Dolan, Caroline Moore (Stage Licensing - Amateur Musicals & Plays); Stephanie Parker (Perusal Requests - Amateur)

Established 1938

Insider Info Actively seeking clients. Currently handles stage plays, ballet, musicals and operas and operettas. Accepts simultaneous submissions. Clients usually obtained through queries/submissions.

Scripts Considers scripts for the theatre, including musical scripts.

Submission Guidelines Submit query letter.

Tips The agency specialises in stage plays on an international scale. No unsolicited manuscripts.

Judith Chilcote Agency
8 Wentworth Mansions, Keats Grove, London, NW3 2RL
☎ 020 7794 3717
✉ judybks@aol.com
Contact Judith Chilcote
Established 1990
Insider Info Actively seeking clients. Currently handles non-fiction books and novels. Accepts simultaneous submissions. Manuscripts returned with SAE. Clients usually obtained through queries/submissions. Does not charge a reading fee.
Non-fiction Will consider Art, Biography/Autobiography, Current Affairs, Food & Drink, Health, Lifestyle, Popular Culture, Psychology, Self-help and Sports.
Fiction Will consider Commercial fiction.
Submission Guidelines Authors should include query letter, SAE, three sample chapters and biography with submission. No poetry, scripts, short stories, academia or children's considered.
Tips A CV is essential with submissions. The agency is primarily interested in cinema/television tie-ins for its clients.

Judith Murdoch Literary Agency
19 Chalcot Square, London, NW1 8YA
☎ 020 7722 4197
Contact Judith Murdoch
Established 1993
Insider Info Commission rate of 15 per cent for domestic sales, 20 per cent for foreign sales. Editorial advice is given and the agency does not charge a reading fee. Translation rights are handled by the Marsh Agency Ltd.
Fiction Will consider full-length Fiction only, particularly accessible Literary and Commercial Women's fiction.
Submission Guidelines Author should include synopsis and two sample chapters with submission, including an SAE for return. No science fiction/fantasy, children's, short stories or poetry considered. Does not accept queries by telephone or email.
Client(s) Alison Bond, Anne Bennett, Meg Hutchinson, Lisa Jewell, Pamela Jooste, Eve Makis

Judy Daish Associates Ltd
2 St Charles Place, London, W10 6EG
☎ 020 8964 8811
☎ 020 8964 8966
Contact Judy Daish; Howard Gooding; Tracey Elliston
Established 1978

Insider Info Actively seeking clients. Currently handling television scripts, film scripts, stage plays and radio scripts. Accepts simultaneous submissions. Manuscripts returned with SAE. Clients usually obtained through queries/submissions. Commission rated on domestic and foreign sales by negotiation. Does not charge a reading fee.
Scripts Considers scripts for Broadcast, Film and Theatre.
Submission Guidelines Authors should submit a query letter. Books will not be considered.
Tips No unsolicited manuscripts.

Juliet Burton Literary Agency
2 Clifton Avenue, London, W12 9DR
☎ 020 8762 0148
☎ 020 8743 8765
✉ juliet.burton@btinternet.com
Contact Juliet Burton
Established 1999
Insider Info Seeking both new and established writers. Currently handles non-fiction books and novels. Manuscripts returned with SAE. Clients usually obtained through queries/submissions. Commission rate of 15 per cent for domestic sales, 20 per cent for foreign sales. Does not charge a reading fee.
Non-fiction Will consider True crime/Investigative.
Fiction Will consider Crime, Detective and Women's fiction.
Submission Guidelines Authors should include query letter, SAE, synopsis, and two or three sample chapters with submission. No scripts, academia, poetry or articles considered.
Tips No unsolicited or emailed manuscripts.

Juri Gabriel
35 Camberwell Grove, London, SE5 8JA
☎ 020 7703 6186
☎ 020 7703 6186
Contact Juri Gabriel
Insider Info Actively seeking clients. Currently handles novels. Simultaneous submissions accepted. Manuscripts returned with SAE. Clients usually obtained through queries/submissions. Commission rate of ten percent for domestic sales, 20 per cent for foreign sales. Does not charge a reading fee.
* Juri Gabriel worked in television for many years and is the author of several books. He is also chairman of Dedalus Publishers.
Fiction Will consider Literary fiction.
Submission Guidelines Authors should include query letter, SAE, three sample chapters, biography and written query with submissions. No poetry, short stories, articles or children's considered.

Client(s) Maurice Caldera, Diana Constance, Miriam Dunne, Richard Mankiewicz, Karina Mellinger, Dr Terence White

Tips Juri Gabriel handles mainly established clients, and insists on a high quality of manuscript. Mainly focuses on television, film and radio rights.

Kate Hordern Literary Agency
18 Mortimer Road, Clifton, Bristol, BS8 4EY
- 0117 923 9368
- 0117 973 1941
- katehordern@blueyonder.co.uk

Contact Kate Hordern
Established 1999
Insider Info Actively seeking clients. Currently looking for non-fiction books and novels. Considers non-fiction and fiction. Will consider simultaneous submissions, and unsuccessful proposals will be returned with SAE. Obtain new clients via queries/submissions. Commission rates of 15 per cent by domestic sales and 20 per cent by foreign sales. Does not charge a reading fee.
Non-fiction Will consider quality General non-fiction titles.
Fiction Will consider quality General fiction titles.
Submission Guidelines Send proposal package with query letter, SAE and synopsis.
Tips Sample chapters for fiction upon request only. For non-fiction, submit only a proposal and chapter breakdown. No unsolicited manuscripts will be accepted.

Knight Features (Peter Knight Agency)
20 Crescent Grove, London, SW4 7AH
- 020 7622 1467
- 020 7622 1522
- peter@knightfeatures.co.uk
- www.knightfeatures.co.uk

Contact Director, Peter Knight; Associate, Andrew Knight; Associate, Gaby Martin; Associate, Samantha Ferris
Established 1985
Insider Info Actively seeking clients. Will consider non-fiction and syndicated material. Will consider simultaneous submissions and unsuccessful proposals will be returned with SAE. Obtains new clients via queries/submissions.
Non-fiction Will consider Academic, Biography/Autobiography, Business, History, Humour, Motor sport, Puzzles and Well-being titles.
Fiction Will consider Cartoons/Comic titles.
Submission Guidelines Send proposal package with query letter, SAE, synopsis and author biography. Will not consider science fiction, poetry or cookery titles.

Client(s) Simon Shuker, Frank Dickens, Gray Jolliffe, Angus Mcgill, Chris Maslanka, Barbara Minto
Tips No emailed or unsolicited submissions will be accepted.

Laura Morris Literary Agency
21 Highshore Road, London, SE15 5AA
- 020 7732 0153
- 020 7732 9022
- laura.morris@btconnect.com

Contact Laura Morris
Established 1998
Insider Info Actively seeking clients. Currently handles non-fiction books and novels. Will consider simultaneous submissions, and unsuccessful proposals will be returned with SAE. Obtains new clients via queries/submissions. Commission rates of ten per cent by domestic sales and 20 per cent by foreign sales. Does not charge a reading fee.
Non-fiction Will consider Biography/Autobiography, Food & Drink, Humour, Popular Culture and Film/Media studies titles.
Fiction Will consider Literary titles.
Submission Guidelines Send proposal package with query letter and SAE. No children's books will be considered.
Tips No unsolicited manuscripts will be accepted.

Lavinia Trevor
The Glasshouse, 49a Goldhawk Road, London, W12 8QP
- 020 8749 8481
- 020 8749 7377

Contact Lavinia Trevor
Established 1993
Insider Info Actively seeking clients. Currently handles novels and general non-fiction titles. Will consider simultaneous submissions. Unsuccessful proposals will be returned with SAE. Obtains clients via queries/submissions. Commissions paid for domestic and foreign sales by agreement. Does not charge a reading fee.
Non-fiction Will consider Popular Science titles.
Fiction Will consider Literary and Commercial titles.
Submission Guidelines Send proposal package with query letter, SAE, synopsis, sample chapters, brief biography and the first 50–60 pages only. No scripts, poetry, science fiction, fantasy, academia, technical or children's titles will be considered.
Tips Concentrates mainly on literary and commercial fiction/non-fiction.

LAW Ltd
14 Vernon Street, London, W14 0RJ
- 020 7471 7900
- 020 7471 7910

ⓦ www.lawagency.co.uk

Contact Mark Lucas, Julian Alexander, Araminta Whiteley (Fiction and Non-fiction); Lucinda Cook (Translation Rights & Literary Estates); Philippa Milnes-Smith (Children's & Young Adults); Alice Saunders, (Audio Rights & Speaker Engagements)
Established 1996
Insider Info Actively seeking clients. Currently handles non-fiction books, children's books and novels. Will consider simultaneous submissions. Aims to respond to queries/proposals within eight weeks. Unsuccessful proposals will be returned with SAE. Obtains new clients via queries/submissions. Commission rates are 15 per cent by domestic sales and 20 per cent by domestic sales. Does not charge a reading fee.
Non-fiction Will consider Commercial non-fiction.
Fiction Will consider Children's, Literary and Young adult.
Submission Guidelines Send proposal package with query letter, SAE, synopsis, and two sample chapters, or up to 30 pages in single-sided, double-spaced A4 format. No scripts, poetry or textbooks will be accepted. Recent Sale(s)
The Accident Man, Tom Cain; *The Ultimate Teen Book Guide*, Daniel Hahn
Client(s) Tracy Edwards, Gene Kemp, Felicity Kendall, Sophie Kinsella, Andy McNab, Livi Michael, Philip Reeve, John Sergeant, Nigel Slater
Tips LAW are happy to consider material from potential new clients although it should be noted that they take on very few of those projects submitted to them. Submissions by email, fax, or disk will not be accepted.

Limelight Management
33 Newman Street, London, W1T 1PY
ⓣ 020 7637 2529
ⓕ 020 7637 2538
ⓔ mary@limelightmanagement.com
ⓦ www.limelightmanagement.com
Contact Managing Director and Literary Agent, Fiona Lindsay; Partner and Agent, Linda Shanks
Established 1991
Insider Info The company's speciality is celebrity management and literary sales. Actively seeking clients. Currently handles non-fiction books and novels. Will consider simultaneous submissions. Obtains new clients via queries/submissions. Commission rate is 15 per cent by domestic sales and 20 per cent by foreign sales. Does not charge a reading fee.
Non-fiction Will consider Beauty, Business, Design, Food & Drink, Gardening, Health and Lifestyle titles.
Fiction Will consider Women's fiction and 'Chick lit'.

Submission Guidelines Send proposal package with query letter and proposal. Accepts queries by email.
Client(s) Antony Worrall Thompson, Linda Barker, Oz Clarke, James Martin, Paul Rankin, Mary Berry, Paul Gaylor, Alastair Hendy, Orlando Murrin, Jo Glanville-Blackburn, Fumi Odulate, Fay Goodman, Richard Koch, Jill Billington, Barbara Griggs, Pat Chapman and Ariana Bundy
Tips The agency will respond only if interested in the proposal email. They will not accept large attachments, and if any are received they are automatically deleted. Currently there is an interest in women's fiction. Note that Limelight Management is a celebrity agency and only represents television, literary, or media personalities.

Lisa Eveleigh Literary Agency
c/o Pollinger Ltd, 9 Staple Inn, London, WC1V 7QH
ⓣ 020 7404 0342
ⓕ 020 7242 5737
ⓔ lisaeveleigh@dial.pipex.com
Contact Lisa Eveleigh
Established 1996
Insider Info Actively seeking clients. Currently handles non-fiction books, novels and children's books. Unsuccessful submissions will be returned with SAE. Obtains new clients via queries/submissions. Commission rate is 15 per cent by domestic sales and 20 per cent by foreign sales. Does not charge a reading fee.
Non-fiction Will consider Astrology, Biography/Autobiography, General Interest and Health titles.
Fiction Will consider Children's, Literary, Young adult and Commercial fiction titles.
Submission Guidelines Send proposal package with query letter, SAE, synopsis, two to three sample chapters, and author biography. Accepts queries by email. No scripts, children's picture books, horror, science fiction or poetry titles will be accepted.
Tips Send preliminary letter only, via email (no manuscripts).

The Lisa Richards Agency
108 Upper Leeson Street, Dublin 4, Republic of Ireland
ⓣ 00353 1 637 5000
ⓕ 00353 1 667 1256
ⓔ info@lisarichards.ie
ⓦ www.lisarichards.ie
Contact Literary Agent, Faith O'Grady; Actors Agents: Lisa Cook, Richard Cook, Jonathan Shankey, Lorraine Cummins; Comedy Agentss: Carolyn Lee, Christina Dwyer
Established 1998

Insider Info Seeking both new and established writers. Currently handles non-fiction books and novels for both adults and children. Unsuccessful proposals will be returned with SAE. Obtains new clients via queries/submissions. Commission rates are 10–15 per cent by domestic sales, 20 per cent by foreign sales and 15 per cent by film sales. Does not charge a reading fee.

Non-fiction Will consider Biography/Autobiography, Current Affairs, History, Memoirs, Politics, Popular Culture and Travel titles.

Fiction Will consider General fiction titles for both adults and children.

Submission Guidelines Send proposal package with query letter, SAE, synopsis, and two to three sample chapters.

Client(s) Helena Close, Susan Connolly, Matt Cooper, Denise Deegan, Christine Dwyer Hickey, Robert Fannin, Karen Gillece, Paul Howard aka Ross O'Carroll-Kelly, Arlene Hunt, Roisin Ingle, Alison Jameson, George Lee, Declan Lynch, Anna McPartlin, Pauline McLynn, Roisin Meaney, David O'Doherty, Jarlath Regan.

Tips Non-fiction submissions should include a detailed proposal and one sample chapter only.

London Independent Books
26 Chalcot Crescent, London, NW1 8YD
- 020 7706 0486
- 020 7724 3122

Contact Carolyn Whitaker
Established 1971

Insider Info Actively seeking clients. Currently handles Non-fiction books and Novels. Will consider Non-fiction and Fiction titles. Simultaneous submissions will be accepted. Unsuccessful proposals will be returned with SAE. Obtains new clients via queries/submissions. No reading fee.

Non-fiction Will consider Travelogues.

Fiction Consider Fantasy, Young Adult and Commercial fiction.

Submission Guidelines Send proposal package with query letter, SAE, synopsis, two sample chapters or up to 30 pages. No young children's or computer books.

Tips The agent will suggest revision and offer constructive criticism.

Lorella Belli Literary Agency (LBLA)
54 Hartford House, 35 Tavistock Crescent, Notting Hill, London, W11 1AY
- 020 7727 8547
- 0870 787 4194
- info@lorellabelliagency.com
- www.lorellabelliagency.com

Contact Lorella Belli

Established 2002

Insider Info A small agency seeking both new and established writers. Currently handles non-fiction books and novels. Aims to respond to queries/proposals within one week and manuscripts within one month. Manuscripts will be returned with SAE. Clients are usually obtained through recommendations from others, queries/submissions and conferences. Commission rate of 15 per cent for domestic sales, 20 per cent for foreign sales and 20 per cent for film sales. Offers a written contract that is binding until terminated by either party, 60 days notice must be given to terminate. Does not charge a reading fee, or offer a criticism service.

Non-fiction Will consider Art, Biography/Autobiography, Business, Childcare/Parenting, Current Affairs, Finance, Food & Drink, Gay/Lesbian, History, How-to, Humour, Memoirs, Military, Music, Politics, Nature, Popular Culture, Science/Technology, Self-help, Sociology, Sports, True Crime and Women's issues.

Fiction Will consider Adventure, Confessional, Crime, Erotica, Ethnic, Experimental, Family saga, Feminist, Gay/Lesbian, Glitz, Historical, Humour/Satire, Literary, Mainstream, Mystery, Supernatural, Romance, Sports, Thriller and Women's fiction titles.

Submission Guidelines Authors should include query letter, SAE, outline, synopsis, sample chapters (initial three for fiction, two for non-fiction), biography, and proposal with submission. Accepts queries by fax, email, and phone. Actively seeking first novelists, journalists, international and multicultural writing, non-fiction proposals, and books on Italy/with an Italian connection. Does not accept children's books, fantasy and science fiction, poetry, scripts, plays, academic books or short stories.

Client(s) Michael Bess, Zoe Bran, Sean Bidder, Annalisa Coppolaro-Nowell, Dario Fo, Emily Giffin, Rick Mofina, Paul Martin, Nisha Minhas, Alanna Mitchell, Angela Murrills, Jennifer Ouellette, Robert Ray, Grace Saunders, Dave Singleton, Rupert Steiner, Diana Winston.

Tips Lorella Belli also represents a number of US, Canadian, Australian and European agencies in the UK.

Louise Greenberg Books Ltd
The End House, Church Crescent, London, N3 1BG
- 020 8349 1179
- 020 8343 4559
- louisegreenberg@msn.com

Contact Louise Greenberg
Established 1997

Insider Info Actively seeking clients. Currently handles non-fiction books and novels. Manuscripts returned with SAE. Clients usually obtained through queries/submissions. Commission rate of 15 per cent for domestic sales, 20 per cent for foreign sales. Does not charge a reading fee.

Non-fiction Will consider Serious non-fiction.

Fiction Will consider Literary fiction.

Submission Guidelines Author should submit query letter, SAE, and three sample chapters with submissions.

Tips No telephone enquiries.

Lucy Luck Associates
18–21 Cavaye Place, London, SW10 9PT
- lucy@lucyluck.com
- www.lucyluck.com

Contact Lucy Luck

Established 2006

Insider Info Seeking both new and established writers. Currently handles non-fiction books, novels, novellas and short story collections. Currently represents 20 clients, 50 per cent of which are new/ previously unpublished writers. Accepts simultaneous submissions. Aims to respond to queries/proposals and manuscripts within three months. Manuscript returned with SAE. Clients usually obtained through recommendations from others. 60 days notice required to terminate contract. Does not charge reading or office fees, and also offers a criticism service.

* Lucy Luck has worked as an agent since 1997 and specialises in edgy, thoughtful literary fiction and quirky, narrative non-fiction. The agency works with young writers to establish a writing career, in the first instance forming a relationship with a publisher, but then working on related areas such as journalism. Their experience ranges from working with first-time novelists to established writers, and their stated strength is their commitment to personal relationships and a belief that books matter.

Non-fiction Will consider Current Affairs, History and Popular Culture.

Fiction Will consider Action/Adventure, Crime, Historical, Literary, Mystery, Thriller and Young Adult fiction.

Submission Guidelines Authors should include query letter, SAE, sample chapters and biography with submission. Accepts queries by email. Actively seeking writers of ability, both fiction and non-fiction, who are looking to build a career through their writing. Illustrated books or one-off books, anything too technical or academic, or anything too derivative will not be considered.

Recent Sale(s) *Hodd*, Adam Thorpe (Cape); *Menage*, Ewan Morrison (Cape); *What Was Lost*, Catherine O'Flynn (Tindal Street Press); *Black Rock*, Amanda Smyth (Serpent's Tail); *The Years of the Locust*, Jon

Hotten (Yellow Jersey); *Take Me To The Source*, Rupert Wright (Harvill Secker)

Client(s) Ewan Morrison, Doug Johnstone, Philip O Ceallaigh, Jon Hotten, Lorelei Matthias, Tom Chesshyre, J. A. Henderson and Catherine O'Flynn

Tips The website has a secure online form for submissions.

Luigi Bonomi Associates Ltd
91 Great Russell Street, London, WC1B 3PS
- 020 7637 1234
- 020 7637 2111
- info@bonomiassociates.co.uk

Contact Luigi Bonomi, Amanda Preston

Established 2005

Insider Info Actively seeking clients. Currently handles non-fiction books and novels. Manuscripts are returned with SAE. Clients usually obtained through queries/submissions. Commission rate of 15 per cent for domestic sales, 20 per cent for foreign sales and 15 per cent for film sales. Does not charge a reading fee.

Non-fiction Will consider Childcare/Parenting, Food & Drink, Gardening, Health, History, Journalism, Lifestyle, Mind, Body & Spirit Science/Technology and Sports titles.

Fiction Will consider Crime, Literary, Thriller, Women's and Young adult fiction.

Submission Guidelines Authors should submit query letter, SAE, synopsis, and three sample chapters with submission. No poetry, science fiction, fantasy, scripts, or children's will be considered.

Client(s) James Barrington, John Humphreys, Nick Foulkes, Eamonn Holmes, James May, Richard Madeley and Judy Finnigan, Esther Rantzen, Professor Bryan Sykes, Alan Titchmarsh, Kim Woodburn and Aggie MacKenzie, Sir Terry Wogan

Tips Interested in new authors and television tie-ins.

Lutyens & Rubinstein
231 Westbourne Park Road, London, W11 1EB
- susannah@lutyensrubinstein.co.uk

Contact Susannah Godman

Established 1991

Insider Info Currently handles non-fiction books, children's books and novels. Accepts simultaneous submissions. Aims to respond to queries/proposals and within six week. Manuscripts returned with SAE.

Non-fiction Considers General non-fiction titles.

Fiction Considers Children's and Adult's fiction.

Submission Guidelines Authors should include query letter, SAE, synopsis and sample chapters with submissions. Queries accepted by email.

Manuscript ReSearch

PO Box 33, Bicester, Oxfordshire, OX26 4ZZ

☎ 01869 322552

Contact Graham Jenkins

Insider Info Seeking both new and established writers. Currently handles television and film scripts. Proposals accompanied by SAE will be returned.

Scripts Considers General Television and Film scripts.

Submission Guidelines Send a query letter, including SAE.

Tips Only interested in books from existing clients, but will accept unsolicited script submissions.

Margaret Hanbury Literary Agency

27 Walcot Square, London, SE11 4UB

☎ 020 7735 7680

☎ 020 7793 0316

Contact Margaret Hanbury

Established 1983

Insider Info Actively seeking clients. Currently handles novels. Proposals returned if accompanied by SAE. Commission rates of 15 per cent for domestic sales and 20 per cent for foreign sales.

Fiction Considers Literary fiction.

Submission Guidelines Send query, including SAE, before sending submission. Will not accept scripts, children's fiction, poetry, fantasy or horror.

Client(s) George Alagiah, J.G. Ballard, Simon Callow and Judith Lennox

Tips No unsolicited manuscripts.

Marianne Gunn O'Connor Literary Agency

Morrison Chambers, Suite 17, 32 Nassau Street, Dublin 2, Republic of Ireland

☎ magoclitagency@eircom.net

Contact Marianne Gunn O'Connor

Established 1996

Insider Info Seeking both new and established writers. Currently handles non-fiction books, children's books and adult novels. Proposals accompanied by SAE will be returned. Commission rates are 15 per cent for domestic sales, 20 per cent for foreign sales and 20 per cent for films.

Non-fiction Will consider Biography/Autobiography and Commercial non-fiction.

Fiction Will consider Children's, Literary and Commercial fiction.

Submission Guidelines Send proposal package including a brief synopsis, and two or three sample chapters.

Tips No unsolicited manuscripts.

Marjacq Scripts Ltd

34 Devonshire Place, London, W1G 6JW

☎ 020 7935 9499

☎ 020 7935 9115

☎ enquiries@marjacq.com

🌐 www.marjacq.com

Contact CEO, Jacqui Lyons; Literary Agent, Philip Patterson; Film and TV Agent, Luke Speed

Established 1974

Insider Info Actively seeking clients. Currently handles non-fiction books, novels, fiction, television scripts, radio scripts, film scripts. Will consider simultaneous submissions. Aims to respond to queries/proposals within six weeks. Commission rates are ten per cent for domestic sales and 20 per cent for foreign sales. Does not charge a reading fee.

Non-fiction Will consider Biography/Autobiography, Children's, Health, History, Sports and Travel titles.

Fiction Will consider Commercial and Literary fiction.

Scripts Considers scripts for Film and Broadcast.

Submission Guidelines Send proposal package with synopsis and three sample chapters (typed, single-side and double-spaced on A4 paper). Will not accept stage plays or poetry. For screenplay submissions send a letter, your CV and a sample film/showreel. DVDs and VHS tapes are both acceptable.

Recent Sale(s) *Magda's Daughter*, Catrin Collier; *The Church Mouse*, Graham Oakley (Templar)

Client(s) Anita Anderson, Bill Brown, David Evans and Scott Michaels, James Follett, Ian Pryor, Richard Templar, Stuart Macbride, Jeannie Johnson

Tips Will not accept handwritten/illegible material or queries without submission. Submissions are usually shredded. The agency does not discuss manuscripts unless the author becomes a client.

The Marsh Agency Ltd

50 Albemarle Street, London, W1S 4BD

☎ 020 7493 4361

☎ 020 7495 8961

☎ Online form.

🌐 www.marsh-agency.co.uk

Contact Managing Director, Paul Marsh (Serious Non-fiction, Literary Fiction, Client Development, Business Development & Client Account Management); Rights Director, Camilla Ferrier; Agents: Charlotte Bruton, Geraldine Cooke, Hannah Ferguson, Piers Russell-Cobb, Jessica Woollard, Stephanie Ebdon (Translation), Caroline Hardman (Translation)

Established 1994

Insider Info Seeking both new and established writers. Currently handles non-fiction, children's books, novels, fiction and short story collections. Proposals accompanied by SAE will be returned. Commission rates are 15 per cent for domestic sales and 20 per cent for foreign sales.

* Paul Marsh worked for Anthony Sheil Associates Ltd, from 1977 and became their Foreign Rights Director in 1979. He left in 1993 and went on to establish The Marsh Agency in 1994 with his wife. Camilla Ferrier worked for HarperCollins prior to joining the agency in 2002, and Geraldine Cooke was an Editor for many years at Penguin before joining in 2004. She also founded the Headline Review List. Jessica Woollard was a Director for Toby Eady Associates before joining the agency in 2006, and Leyla Moghadam worked for some time at the European Commission. Leyla is multi-lingual, speaking English, German, French and Farsi.

Non-fiction Will consider Biography/Autobiography, Business, Childcare/Parenting, Children's, Current Affairs, Health, History, Humour, Psychology, Memoirs, Nature/Environment, Philosophy, Popular Culture, Religion, Self-help, Travel and Quiz titles.

Fiction Will consider Action/Adventure, Children's fiction, Crime, Fantasy, Historical, Literary, Mystery, Romance, Science-fiction, Thriller and Young adult titles.

Submission Guidelines Send proposal package with SAE, synopsis, three sample chapters and author biography (double-spaced, numbered A4 pages). Can also submit via an online form. Will not accept scripts, poetry, or children's picture books.

Recent Sale(s) *The Drop Edge of Yonder*, Rudolph Wurlitzer (Novel); *The Good Thief*, Hannah Tinti (First Novel)

Client(s) Monica Ali, Kate Atkinson, Jonathan Safran Foer, Meg Cabot, Toby Litt, Vikram Seth, Bill Bryson

Tips When submitting manuscripts print your name, address and contact number on the front, and your name and the title on all pages.

Mary Clemmy Literary Agency
6 Dunollie Road, London, NW5 2XP
- 020 7267 12990
- 020 7482 7360

Contact Mary Clemmy
Established 1992
Insider Info Actively seeking both new and established clients. Currently handles non-fiction and fiction titles. Proposals returned with SAE. Commission rates of ten per cent for domestic sales and 20 per cent for foreign sales. Usually obtains new clients through queries and submissions. Does not charge a reading fee.

Non-fiction Will consider General non-fiction titles.
Fiction Will consider General fiction titles.

Submission Guidelines Accepts proposal package with query letter, SAE and outline.

Tips Accepts scripts from existing clients only. Does not deal with science fiction, fantasy or children's titles.

MayerBenham Ltd
55 Athenlay Road, London, SE15 3EN
- 020 7277 8560
- 020 7277 8560
- simon@mayerbenham.co.uk

Contact Director & Agent, Simon Benham; Director, Agent & Film Rights, Jo Mayer
Established 2002
Insider Info Actively seeking both new and established clients. Deals with general non-fiction titles. Unwanted material will be returned with SAE. New clients are usually obtained through queries and submissions. Commission rates of ten per cent for domestic sales. Does not charge a reading fee.

Non-fiction Will consider Business, History, Humour, Music and Popular Culture titles.

Submission Guidelines Accepts submission with query letter and SAE.

Tips Will not accept unsolicited manuscripts. MayerBenham may suggest revisions to manuscripts.

MBA Literary Agents Ltd
62 Grafton Way, London, W1T 5DW
- 020 7387 2076
- 020 7387 2042
- diana@mbalit.co.uk
- www.mbalit.co.uk

Contact Managing Director and Literary Agent, Diana Tyler; Director, Meg Davis (Scriptwriters/Authors all genres); Director, Laura Longrigg (Fiction/Non-fiction); Agents: Sophie Gorell Barnes, Susan Smith, Stella Kane, David Riding, Jean Kitson
Established 1971
Insider Info Actively seeking clients. Deals with non-fiction, novels, television scripts, film scripts, stage plays and radio scripts. Will consider simultaneous submissions. Unwanted material will be returned with SAE. New clients are usually obtained through queries and submissions. Commission rates of 15 per cent for domestic sales, 20 per cent for foreign sales and 10–20 per cent for firm sales.

Non-fiction Will consider Biography/Autobiography, History, Memoirs, Popular Culture, Self-help and Travel titles.

Fiction Will consider Fantasy, Literary, Commercial and Science-fiction titles.

Scripts Considers scripts for Film, Broadcast and Theatre.

Submission Guidelines See submission details for each individual agent on the website.

Recent Sale(s) *A Mile of River*, Judith Allnatt (Fiction); *We're British, Innit*, Iain Aitch (Humour); *Flight Into Darkness*, Sarah Ash (Fantasy)

Client(s) Robert Jones, Nick Angel, Dr. Mark Atkinson, Anila Baig, Rob Bailey, Ed Hurst, Christopher Bird, Vivienne Bolton, Audrey and Sophie Boss, Martin Buckley, Debbie Cash, Vic Darkwood, Sarah Ash, Michael Cobley, Murray Davis, Alan Dunn and Stef Penney

Tips Authors are advised to check the submission details and email address of the relevant agent before sending a submission.

McKernan Agency
5 Gayfield Square, Edinburgh, EH1 3NW
- 0131 557 1771
- maggie@mckernanagency.co.uk
- www.mckernanagency.co.uk

Contact Maggie McKernan
Established 2005
Insider Info Actively seeking both new and established clients. Deals with non-fiction, fiction and young adult fiction. Currently working with 20 clients, around 50 per cent of whom are previously unpublished writers. Accepts queries by email. Will accept simultaneous submissions. Will return unwanted material with SAE. Usually obtains new clients through recommendations from others, queries and submissions.

* A small agency, therefore clients receive very individual attention. During Maggie McKernan's career she edited many prize winning authors, including Jim Crace, Ben Okri and Vikram Seth.

Non-fiction Will consider Biography/Autobiography, Current Affairs, Food & Drink, Gardening, History, Memoirs, Military, Politics, Popular Culture, Religion, Women's titles.

Fiction Will consider Crime, Ethnic, Experimental, Family Saga, Fantasy, Feminist, Gay/Lesbian, Glitz, Historical, Horror, Humour/Satire, Literary, Mainstream, Mystery, Supernatural, Thriller, Women's and Young adult.

Submission Guidelines Accepts queries by email, no attachments. Prefers initial contact by letter without attachments.

Tips Seeks novels of all kinds, both commercial and literary, quality non-fiction, biography and history.

Mic Cheetham Literary Agency
50 Albemarle Street, London, W1S 4BD
- 020 7495 2002
- 020 7399 2801
- info@miccheetham.com
- www.miccheetham.com

Contact Director, Mic Cheetham
Established 1994
Insider Info Actively seeking both new and established clients. Deals with fiction titles. Unwanted material will be returned with SAE. Obtains new clients mostly through queries and submissions. Commission rates of 10–15 per cent for domestic sales, 10–15 per cent for foreign sales and 10–20 per cent for film sales. Does not charge a reading fee.

Fiction Will consider Fantasy, Genre, Mainstream, Literary, Science fiction, Crime and Historical fiction titles.

Submission Guidelines Accepts proposal with SAE, one page synopsis, three sample chapters, by post only. Will not accept poetry or illustrated books.

Recent Sale(s) *The Temporal Void*, Ian M. Banks (Science-Fiction)

Client(s) Ian M. Banks, Simon Beckett, Mark Behr, John Binias, Carol Birch, NM Browne, Stuart Browne, Anita Burgh, Alan Campbell, Paul Cornell, Barbara Ewing, Laurie Graham, David Gunn, Jon Courtenay Grimwood, M. John Harrison, Toby Litt, Ken MacLeod, Graham McCann, China Mieville, Sharon Penman, Anthony Sher, Harry Shapiro, Peter Smalley, Veronica Stallwood, Tricia Sullivan, Steph Swainston.

Tips Will not accept entire manuscripts, except from existing clients.

Michael Motley Ltd
The Old Vicarage, Tredington, Tewkesbury, Gloucestershire, GL20 7BP
- 01684 276390
- 01684 297355

Contact Michael Motley
Established 1973
Insider Info Seeking mostly established writers through referrals. Currently handles fiction. Commission rate of ten per cent for domestic sales, 15 per cent for foreign sales. Does not charge a reading fee.

Fiction Considers General fiction.
Submission Guidelines No science fiction, poetry, horror, short stories or journalism will be considered.
Tips All submissions by referral. No unsolicited manuscripts.

Micheline Steinberg Associates
104 Great Portland Street, London, W1W 6PE
- 020 7631 1310
- 020 7631 1146
- info@steinplays.com
- www.steinplays.com

Contact Agents: Micheline Steinberg and Matt Connell; Assistant, Helen MacAuley
Established 1985

Insider Info Actively seeking clients. Currently handles television scripts, film scripts, stage plays, radio scripts, animation, soap opera and mini series scripts. Manuscripts returned with SAE. Clients usually obtained through recommendations from others and queries/submissions. Commission rate of ten per cent for domestic sales, 15–20 per cent for foreign sales. Does not charge a reading fee.
Scripts Will consider all areas.
Submission Guidelines Include SAE.
Recent Sale(s) *Coming Up For Air*, Laura Stevens (Drama)
Client(s) Ed Harris, Tim Green, Matt Evans, Polly Wiseman, David Hermanstein, Jennifer Farmer, Sarah Woods, Diane Samuels, Stephen Starkey and Jack Shepherd
Tips Contact by email for submission details. Specialises in stage, television, film and radio plays, and animation.

Michelle Kass Associates
85 Charing Cross Road, London, WC2H 0AA
- 020 7439 1624
- 020 7734 3394
- office@michellekass.co.uk
Contact Michelle Kass
Established 1991
Insider Info Seeking both new and established writers. Currently handles movie scripts. Clients usually obtained through queries/submissions. Commission rate of ten per cent for domestic sales, 15–20 per cent for foreign sales. Does not charge a reading fee. No email submissions.
Scripts Will consider Drama and Literary fiction.
Submission Guidelines Contact by telephone before submitting manuscripts. No unsolicited manuscripts.

Mulcahy Conway Associates
15 Canning Passage, Kensington, London, W8 5AA
- Online form.
- www.mca-agency.com
Contact Ivan Mulcahy, Jonathan Conway, Laetitia Rutherford, Stephanie Cohen
Established 2008
Insider Info Seeking both new and established writers. Currently handles non-fiction books, novels and children's books. The agents' backgrounds include periods in journalism, publishing, printing, business and research. Does not charge a reading fee.
Non-fiction Will consider Biography/Autobiography, Current Affairs, Food & Drink, History, Journalism and Politics.
Fiction Deals Children's and Adult fiction.

Submission Guidelines Accepts proposal package (including query letter, outline, synopsis, 50-100 sample pages, biography and a summary of competitor books in the market).
Recent Sale(s) *I Think There's Something Wrong With Me*, Nigel Smith (Non-Fiction); *War Child*, Emmanuel Jal (Film)
Client(s) Catherine Arnold, Tony Allan, Michelle Dewberry, David Hencke, Shrabani Basu, Ian Kelly, Leslie Ash, Emmanuel Jal, Nigel Smith
Tips Formerly part of the Mulcahy & Viney agency.

The Narrow Road Company
182 Brighton Road, Coulsden, Surrey, CR2 2NF
- 020 8763 9695
- narrowroad@freeuk.com
- www.narrowroad.co.uk
Insider Info Actively seeking clients. Currently handles television scripts, stage plays, radio scripts - non-fiction and fiction. Manuscripts returned with SAE. Clients usually obtained through queries/submissions.
Scripts Will consider General scripts for Broadcast and Theatre.
Submission Guidelines Authors should include query letter, SAE and biography. No novels or poetry considered.

Paterson Marsh Ltd
50 Albemarle Street, London, W1S 4BD
- 020 7493 4361
- 020 7495 8961
- Online form.
- www.patersonmarsh.co.uk
Contact Mark Paterson, Stephanie Ebdon
Established 1961
Insider Info Seeking both new and established writers. Currently handles non-fiction books. Manuscripts returned with SAE. Clients usually obtained through queries/submissions. Commission rate is 20 per cent for domestic and foreign sales. Does not charge a reading fee.
* Represents world rights for estates, authors and publishers specialising in psychoanalysis, psychotherapy and related subjects.
Non-fiction Will consider Childcare/Parenting, Education, Health, History, Psychology and Neuroscience.
Submission Guidelines Authors should include query letter, SAE, synopsis and sample chapters with submission. No fiction, poetry, children's, scripts, articles or short stories considered.
Recent Sale(s) *Breakfast with Socrates*, Robert Rowland Smith (Philosophy)

Client(s) The estates of Anna Freud, Sigmund Freud, Sandor Ferenczi, Donald Winnicott, Michael Ballint and Wilfred R. Bion

Tips Paterson Marsh is run alongside The Marsh Agency. Articles are only accepted from existing clients.

Peake Associates

14 Grafton Crescent, London, NW1 8SL

- 020 7482 0609
- 0870 141 0447
- tony@tonypeake.com
- www.tonypeake.com

Contact Tony Peake

Insider Info Not currently seeking new clients. Currently handles non-fiction books, poetry and novels, television scripts and movie scripts.

* Tony has spent time as a theatre production manager, model, actor and film distributor.

Non-fiction Deals with General non-fiction.

Fiction Deals with General fiction and Poetry.

Scripts Deals with Television and Film scripts.

Client(s) Johnathon Coe, Steven Kelly, David Reynolds and Alison Fell

Tips Not currently taking on new clients.

PFD (Peters, Fraser & Dunlop)

Drury House, 34–43 Russell Street, London, WC2B 5HA

- 020 7344 1000
- 020 7836 9543
- info@pfd.co.uk
- www.pfd.co.uk

Contact CEO, Caroline Michel; Managing Director, Lesley Davey; Book Agents: Marcella Edwards; Annabel Merullo; Caroline Michel; Michael Sissons; Suzy Jenvey (Children's); Zoe Pagnamenta (US Authors/US Rights); Louisa Pritchard (Foreign Rights); Theatre, Film & Television Agents: Michelle Archer (Film & Television only); Jessica Cooper; Kenneth Ewing; Gemma Hirst; Nicki Stoddart

Insider Info Currently handles non-fiction books, novels, television scripts and film scripts. Will consider all genres of work. Prefers to receive exclusive submissions. Commission rates of ten per cent for domestic sales, and 20 for foreign sales.

Non-fiction Will consider all genres.

Fiction Will consider all genres.

Scripts Will consider all genres.

Submission Guidelines Send query letter, SAE, synopsis, two to three sample chapters, and author biography. Submission should be double-spaced, on single-sided A4. Do not bind or staple. Include a brief CV.

Recent Sale(s) *Archibald Wavell: The Life and Times of An Imperial Servant*, Adrian Fort (Jonathan Cape); *Passion*, Louise Bagshawe (Headline)

Client(s) Sandy Gall CBE, Mary Alexander, Paul Arnott, Hilaire Belloc (Estate), Michael Collins, Lucy Diamond, Rick Parfitt, Richard Pitman, Robery Uhlig, Ann Widdecombe, Barbara Vine, Clive james and Rt. Hon. William Hague MP

Tips PFD has a vast worldwide client list. Writers of non-fiction, children's books, scripts and illustrators should visit the website before submitting material, as submission details may vary.

Pollinger Ltd

9 Staple Inn, Holborn, London, WC1V 7QH

- 020 7404 0342
- 020 7242 5737
- info@pollingerltd.com
- www.pollingerltd.com

Contact Managing Director/Agent, Lesley Pollinger; Agent, Joanna Devereux; Agent, Tim Bates; Agent (Film & TV), Ruth Needham; Consultant, Leigh Pollinger; Consultant, Joan Deitch

Established 1935

Insider Info Currently handles non-fiction books, children's books, novels, television scripts and film scripts. Manuscripts will be returned with SAE. Clients usually obtained through queries/submissions. Commission rate of 15 per cent for domestic sales, 20 per cent for foreign sales.

* The agency has always been a family business.

Non-fiction Will consider most subjects including Children's and Photography.

Fiction Will consider all genres.

Scripts Will consider all genres for Television and Film.

Submission Guidelines Authors should include query letter, SAE, synopsis, three sample chapters and biography with submissions, which should be in black type, double-spaced, on one-sided A4. No poetry or academia considered.

Recent Sale(s) *Billie Jo*, Kimberley Chambers (Random House); *Roger Moore: My Word Is My Bond*, Roger Moore (Michael O'Mara)

Client(s) Max Allen, Peter Clover, Michael Coleman, Laura Denham, Teresa Driscoll, Jacqui Farley, Catherine Fisher, Helen Macgee, Anne Miller, Gareth Owen, Roger Forsdyke, Philip Cross, Bruce Hobson, Alan Wilkinson, Peter Walker, Mark Stay and Robert Sellers

Tips Manuscripts will not be accepted by email or fax.

Puttick Agency

46 Brookfield Mansions, Highgate West Hill, London, N6 6AT

○ 020 8340 6383
○ 0870 751 8098
○ enquiries@puttick.com
🌐 www.puttick.com
Contact Elizabeth Puttick, Robin Puttick
Established 1995
Insider Info Currently handles non-fiction books and television tie-ins. Accepts simultaneous submissions. Proposals returned if accompanied by SAE. Obtains new clients by queries or submissions. Commission rates of 15 per cent for domestic sales and 20 per cent for foreign sales. Does not charge a reading fee.
* Elizabeth Puttick has experience in publishing, including time as an Editorial Director for HarperCollins. She has also written two books and many articles. Robin Puttick has worked in adult education and training, IT management and programming, and international sales.
Non-fiction Will consider titles (especially television tie-ins) on Art, Beauty, Biography/Autobiography, Business, Childcare/Parenting, Current Affairs, Food & Drink, Health, History, Humour, Lifestyle, Memoirs, Nature, Politics, Popular Culture, Psychology, Science/Technology, Self-help, Travel and Women's titles.
Submission Guidelines No unsolicited submissions.
Recent Sale(s) *The Philosopher Wolf*, Mark Rowlands (Granta)
Client(s) Al Avlicino, Karen Bali, Cornel Chin, Nicki Defago, Mike Fisher, Sue Kay, Bonnie Macmillan, Sarah Modlock, Steve Nobel, Emma Restall-Or, Ed & Deb Shapiro, Margot Sutherland, Lorraine Thomas, John Timperley and William Young
Tips Puttick Agency is not currently accepting new clients. Check the website for further updates on their list status.

PVA Management
Hallow Park, Worcester, WR2 6PG
○ 01905 640663
○ 01905 641842
○ books@pva.co.uk
Contact Managing Director, Paul Vaughan
Established 1978
Insider Info Actively seeking clients. Currently handles non-fiction books. Accepts simultaneous submissions. Obtains new clients by queries or submissions. Commission rates of 15 per cent for domestic sales and 20 per cent for foreign sales.
Non-fiction Will consider General non-fiction titles.
Submission Guidelines Send proposal package with SAE, synopsis, and three sample chapters.
Tips PVA Management handles non-fiction only.

Real Creatives Worldwide
14 Dean Street, London, W1D 3RS
○ 020 7437 4188
○ malcolm.rasala@realcreatives.com
Contact Malcolm Rasala; Mark Maco
Established 1984
Insider Info Seeking established writers. Currently handles books, television and movie scripts. Obtains new clients by queries or submissions. Does not charge a reading fee.
Fiction Will consider General and Commercial fiction.
Non-Fiction Will consider General and Commercial non-fiction.
Scripts Will consider Drama, Factual and General entertainment scripts.
Submission Guidelines Send query letter by post with SAE.
Tips Real Creatives Worldwide specialises in literature, film and television scripts. The initial contact should be to request a writer's submission agreement. The agency also has a production interest; see their website at: www.tvmyworld.com

Rebecca Winfield Literary Agency
84 Cowper Road, London, W7 1EJ
○ 020 8567 6738
○ rebecca.winfield@btopenworld.com
Contact Proprietor, Rebecca Winfield
Established 2003
Insider Info Actively seeking clients. Currently handles non-fiction books and novels. Accepts simultaneous submissions. Proposals will be returned if accompanied by SAE. Obtains new clients by queries or submissions. Commission rates of 15 per cent for domestic sales and 20 per cent for foreign sales. Does not charge a reading fee.
Non-fiction Will consider History, Memoirs, Politics, Popular Culture, Science/Technology and Sociology titles.
Fiction Will consider Literary fiction.
Submission Guidelines Send query letter with SAE, three sample chapters and publishing history. No science fiction, fantasy, children's books, poetry or scripts.
Tips Rebecca Winfield Literary Agency will not accept submissions by email.

Redhammer Management Ltd
186 Bickenhall Mansions, London, W1U 6BX
○ 020 7224 1748
○ 020 7224 1802
○ info@redhammer.info
🌐 www.redhammer.info
Contact Managing Director, Peter Cox

Insider Info Seeking both new and established writers. Currently handles non-fiction books, fiction novels, children's books, television scripts and film scripts. Accepts simultaneous submissions. Aims to respond to queries, proposals and manuscripts within six weeks. Proposals will be returned if accompanied by SAE. Obtains new clients by queries or submissions. Commission rates of 17.5 per cent for domestic sales and 20 per cent for foreign sales. Does not charge a reading fee.

Non-fiction Will consider Biography/Autobiography, Business, Current Affairs, Finance, Gay/Lesbian, Health, History, How-to, Humour, Language/Literature, Memoirs, Military, Music, Nature, Politics, Popular Culture, Psychology, Religion, Science/Technology, Self-help, Sociology, Sports and True crime titles.

Fiction Will consider Action/Adventure, Children's fiction, Erotica, Family saga, Feminist, Gay/Lesbian, Historical, Horror, Humour/Satire, Literary, Mainstream, Mystery, Romance, Science-fiction, Sports, Thriller, Women's and Young adult fiction.

Scripts Will consider Action/Adventure, Biography/Autobiography, Comedy, Contemporary Issues, Crime, Fantasy, Glitz, Historical, Children's, Mainstream, Mystery, Romantic Comedy, Science-fiction and Thriller scripts.

Recent Sale(s) *The Joshua Files* MG Harris (Scholastic Children's Books)

Client(s) Martin Bell, Nicholas Booth, Brian Clegg, Joe Donnelly, Amanda Lees, Michelle Paver, Carole Stone and Justin Wintle.

Tips Redhammer Management only accepts submissions from previously published writers. A limited number of unpublished writers may be approached by the agency through Litopia Writers' Colony, an internet writing community, at www.litopia.com.

Robert Dudley Agency
8 Abbotstone Road, London, SW15 1QR
- 020 8788 0938
- 020 8780 3586
- info@robertdudleyagency.co.uk
- www.robertdudleyagency.co.uk

Contact Proprietor, Robert Dudlley
Established 2000
Insider Info Seeking both new and established writers. Represents around 40 authors. Currently handles non-fiction books. 60 per cent of their clients are new, or previously unpublished authors. Proposals will be returned if accompanied by SAE. Obtains new clients by queries or submissions. Commission rates of 15 per cent for domestic sales, 15 per cent for foreign sales and 15–20 per cent for film sales. Does not charge a reading fee.

Non-fiction Will consider Biography/Autobiography, Business, Current Affairs, Health, History, Memoirs, Military and Sports titles.

Submission Guidelines Send proposal package with SAE, synopsis, three sample chapters and author biography. No film or television scripts unless derived from book sales.

Recent Sale(s) *Living with Schizophrenia*, Neel Burton and Phil Davison (Sheldon Press); *Hearts and Minds*, Rosy Thornton (Headline)

Client(s) Robert Ashton, Ian Baxter, Professor Paul Cornish, Jim Drury, Paul Gannon, Solomom Hughes, Duncan Martin, Ian Pont, Rosy Thornton, David Tweedie

Tips When submitting to Robert Dudley, keep the synopsis and author biography fairly brief.

Robert Smith Literary Agency Ltd
12 Bridge Wharf, 156 Caledonian Road, London, N1 9UU
- 020 7278 2444
- 020 7833 5680
- robertsmith.literaryagency@virgin.net

Contact Robert Smith
Established 1997
Insider Info Actively seeking clients. Currently handles non-fiction books. Obtains new clients by queries or submissions. Commission rates of 15 per cent for domestic sales and 20 per cent for foreign sales. Does not charge a reading fee.

Non-fiction Will consider Art, Biography/Autobiography, Entertainment, Food & Drink, Health, Lifestyle and True Crime titles.

Submission Guidelines Send proposal package including synopsis. No fiction, scripts, poetry or children's books considered.

Client(s) Kate Adie (serialisations), Martin Allen, Richard Baker, Peta Bee, Martyn and Michelle Compton, Judy Cook, Stewart Evans, Neil and Christine Hamilton, James Haspiel, Bob Harris, Albert Jack, Roberta Kray, Mark Lawrenson, Ann Ming, Michelle Morgan, Theo Paphitis, Frances Reilly, Keith Skinner and Jayne Sterne.

Tips Robert Smith does not accept unsolicited manuscripts, but will suggest revisions if needed, in the cases where full manuscripts are requested.

Robin Jones Literary Agency
6b Marmora Road, East Dulwich, London, SE22 0RX
- 020 8693 6062
- robijones@gmail.com

Contact Robin Jones
Established 2008
Insider Info Actively seeking clients, both new and established authors. Adult fiction and non-fiction,

literary and commercial. Commission rates of 15 per cent for domestic sales, 20 per cent for foreign sales, 15 per cent for film. Does not charge a reading fee. Specialises in personal contact, fast response and detailed feedback.

Non-fiction Accepts Adult non-fiction books.

Fiction Deals with Commercial and Literary fiction.

Submission Guidelines Will accept unsolicited material. Send query letter with SAE, synopsis and three sample chapters.

Recent Sale(s) *F—K It – The Ultimate Spiritual Way*, John Parkin (Hay House)

Client(s) John Parkin, Fred Nath, Sara Mendes da Costa, Ashley Stokes, Geoffrey Newsome, Paul Lyons

Tips Does offer a criticism service. Robin has worked at four literary agencies, been an international literary scout for seven years, and an editorial consultant for five. Very keen on ideas and philosophy, thrillers, journalism and zeitgeist books, history, history, biography and autobiography.

Robinson Literary Agency

Block A511, The Jam Factory, 27 Green Walk, London, SE11 4TT

- 020 7096 1460
- 020 7245 6326
- info@rlabooks.co.uk

Contact Managing Director, Peter Robinson

Established 2005

Insider Info Seeking both new and established writers. Currently handles non-fiction books, fiction novels and documentary scripts. Commission rates vary for domestic sales and are 20 per cent for foreign sales. Does not charge a reading fee.

Non-fiction Will consider Popular Culture and General Non-fiction titles.

Fiction Will consider General Mainstream/Contemporary fiction.

Scripts Will consider scripts for Documentaries.

Submission Guidelines Send query letter with SAE.

Tips Robinson Literary Agency will suggest revisions for any submitted work.

Rochelle Stevens & Co.

2 Terretts Place, Upper Street, London, N1 1QZ

- 020 7359 3900
- 020 7354 5729
- info@rochellestevens.com

Contact Founder, Rochelle Stevens; Agents: Frances Arnold, Lucy Fawcett

Established 1984

Insider Info Actively seeking clients. Currently handles scripts. Obtains new clients by queries or submissions. Commission rates of ten per cent for domestic sales and 15 per cent for foreign sales. Does not charge a reading fee.

Scripts Will consider Television, Film and Radio scripts, as well as Drama and Stage plays.

Submission Guidelines Send query letter with SAE and author biography.

Tips Rochelle Stevens & Co. does not accept unsolicited manuscripts.

The Rod Hall Agency

6th Floor, Fairgate House, 78 New Oxford Street, London, WC1A 1HB

- 020 7079 7987
- 0845 638 4094
- office@rodhallagency.com
- www.rodhallagency.com

Contact Company Director, Charlotte Mann; Tanya Tillet (Submissions, Amateur & Play Leasings, Foreign Rights, General Enquiries); Emily Hayward (Film, Television & Theatre)

Established 1997

Insider Info Not currently seeking new clients. Currently handles television scripts, film scripts, stage plays and radio scripts. Does not accept simultaneous submissions. Proposals returned if accompanied by SAE. Obtains new clients by queries or submissions. Commission rates of ten per cent for domestic sales and 15 per cent for foreign sales. Does not charge a reading fee.

* Charlotte Mann has worked extensively in theatre, whilst Tanya Tillet's experience lies in film and television development and production. Emily Hayward studied drama before working as an agent at both PFD and Sheil Land Associates.

Scripts Deals with most categories of scripts and screenplays.

Submission Guidelines Send query with SAE, outline, author biography and CV. No writing partnerships or soap writers considered.

Recent Sale(s) *Driving Lessons,* Jeremy Brock; *Men Behaving Badly,* Simon Nye; *Flush,* David Dipper

Client(s) Sean Buckley, Clare Duffy, Tom Farrelly, Patrick Gale, Bettina Gracias, Simon Nye, Mike Packer and Mike Wheatley

Tips The Rod Hall Agency is only interested in career writers who also direct, although the agency will sometimes sell books for existing clients.

Roger Hancock Ltd

4 Water Lane, London, NW1 8NZ

- 020 7267 4418
- 020 7267 0705
- info@rogerhancock.com
- www.rogerhancock.com

Established 1960

Insider Info Actively seeking clients. Currently handles television and film scripts. Obtains new clients by queries or submissions. Commission rates of ten per cent for domestic sales and 15 per cent for foreign sales.

Scripts Will consider Comedy, Drama and Light entertainment scripts.

Tips Roger Hancock specialises in comedy, drama and light entertainment. First contact should be by telephone.

Rogers, Coleridge & White Ltd
20 Powis Mews, London, W11 1JN

- ☎ 020 7221 3717
- 📠 020 7229 9084
- ✉ info@rcwlitagency.co.uk
- 🌐 www.rcwlitagency.co.uk

Contact Deborah Rogers (Illustrated, Children's); Gill Coleridge (Illustrated, Children's); Pat White (Illustrated, Children's); Peter Straus (Fiction, Biography, Current Affairs, Narrative, History); David Miller (Fiction, Biography, Current Affairs, Narrative, History); Zoë Waldie (Fiction, Biography, Current Affairs, Narrative, History); Catherine Pellegrino (Children's, Young Adult); Hannah Westland (Debut Fiction, Non-Fiction); Laurence Laluyaux (Foreign Rights)

Established 1987

Insider Info Seeking both new and established writers. Currently handles non-fiction books, novels and children's books. Aims to respond to queries and proposals within eight weeks. Proposals will be returned if accompanied by SAE. Obtains new clients by recommendation, conferences and queries or submissions. Commission rates of 15 per cent for domestic sales and 20 per cent for foreign sales.

* Prior to opening the agency Deborah Rogers was an agent and also worked in publishing. Gill Coleridge worked at Anthony Sheil Associates and is also President of the Association of Author's Agents. Pat White was an editor and rights director for Simon Schuster. Peter Straus worked at Hodder & Stroughton, Hamish Hamilton and Macmillan.

Non-fiction Will consider Biography/Autobiography, Current Affairs, Food & Drink, History, Humour, Satire and Sports titles.

Fiction Will consider most categories of fiction.

Submission Guidelines Send proposal package with SAE, synopsis, three sample chapters and author biography. No plays, screenplays, technical or educational books considered.

Recent Sale(s) *The Suspicions of My Whicher*, Kate Summerscale (Bloomsbury); *Netherland*, Joseph O'Neill (Fourth Estate); *The Bolter*, Frances Osborne (Little, Brown)

Tips Rogers, Coleridge & White does not accept submissions by fax or email.

Rosemary Sandberg Ltd
6b Bayley Street, London, N4 2EE

- ☎ 020 7304 4110
- 📠 020 7304 4109
- ✉ rosemary@sandberg.demon.co.uk

Contact Director, Rosemary Sandberg

Established 1991

Insider Info Not currently seeking new clients. Currently handles children's books.

Fiction Will consider Children's fiction, Picture books and Children's illustrated titles.

Tips Rosemary Sandberg's client list is full at present, and the agency is not currently accepting unsolicited submissions of any kind.

Rosica Colin Ltd
1 Clareville Grove Mews, London, SW7 5AH

- ☎ 020 7370 1080
- 📠 020 7244 6441

Contact Director, Joanna Marston

Established 1949

Insider Info Actively seeking clients. Currently handles scripts. Aims to respond to queries and proposals within four months. Proposals will be returned if accompanied by SAE. Obtains new clients by queries or submissions. commission rates of ten per cent for domestic sales and 10–20 per cent for foreign sales. Does not charge a reading fee.

Scripts Will consider Television, Film and Radio scripts, as well as Stage plays.

Submission Guidelines Send query letter with SAE and synopsis.

Tips Covering letter should include details of any previous writing credits, and whether the manuscript has been submitted previously to any other agents or publishers.

Rupert Crew Ltd
1a King's Mews, London, WC1N 2JA

- ☎ 020 7242 8586
- 📠 020 7831 7914
- ✉ info@rupertcrew.co.uk
- 🌐 www.rupertcrew.co.uk

Contact Chairman and Joint Managing Director, Doreen Montgomery; Join Managing Director, Caroline Montgomery (Fiction)

Established 1927

Insider Info Not actively seeking clients. Currently handles non-fiction books and novels. Proposals will only be returned if accompanied by SAE bearing sufficient postage. Obtains new clients by recommendations, queries or submissions. Commission rates of 15 per cent for domestic sales and 20 per cent for foreign sales, film and TV. Does not charge a reading fee.

Non-fiction Will consider Biography/ Autobiography, Food & Drink, Health, History, Memoirs, Mind, Body & Spirit, Natural History, Popular Culture, Travel and True Crime titles.
Fiction Will consider Crime, Literary Fiction, Thriller, Women's and Young adult fiction.
Submission Guidelines Accepts query letter with SAE. No screenplays, poetry, short stories, journalism, horror, science fiction or fantasy considered.
Client(s) Represents the estates of Sir Cecil Beaton, Patience Strong, Ida Cook (aka Mary Burchell) and Dame Barbara Cartland.
Tips Rupert Crew independently acts as a publisher/ consultant for various literary estates. As agents, they look for mainstream fiction or non-fiction projects.

Rupert Heath Literary Agency
177a Old Winton Road, Andover, SP10 2DR
- 020 7788 7807
- 020 7691 9331
- emailagency@rupertheath.com
Contact Rupert Heath
Established 2000
Insider Info Actively seeking clients. Currently handles non-fiction books and novels. Accepts simultaneous submissions. Proposals will be returned if accompanied by SAE. Obtains new clients by queries or submissions. Commission rates of 15 per cent for domestic sales and 20 per cent for foreign sales. Does not charge a reading fee.
Non-fiction Will consider Art, Biography/ Autobiography, Current Affairs, History, Popular Culture and Science titles.
Fiction Will consider General Mainstream/ Contemporary fiction.
Submission Guidelines Send query letter with SAE, and one sample chapter by email. No poetry or scripts considered.
Tips Rupert Heath prefers to receive submissions by email.

Sarah Manson Literary Agent
6 Totnes Walk, London, N2 0AD
- 020 8442 0396
- info@sarahmanson.com
- www.sarahmanson.com
Contact Sarah Manson
Established 2002
Insider Info Currently handles children's and young adult fiction titles. Does not accept simultaneous submissions. Does not charge a reading fee.
Fiction Will consider Children's fiction and Young adult titles.
Submission Guidelines Send proposal package with SAE, synopsis, three sample chapters and author biography.

Tips Sarah Manson does not handle poetry or picture books.

Sayle Screen Ltd
11 Jubilee Place, London, SW3 3TD
- 020 7823 3883
- 020 7823 3363
- info@saylescreen.com
- www.saylescreen.com
Contact Toby Moorcroft, Jane Villiers, Matthew Bates
Established 1952
Insider Info Seeking both new and established writers. Currently handles television scripts and film scripts. Aims to respond to queries, proposals and manuscripts within three months. Proposals will be returned if accompanied by SAE. Obtains new clients by recommendation. Commission rates of ten per cent for domestic sales and 15 per cent for foreign sales. Does not charge a reading fee.
Scripts Will consider Action/Adventure, Comedy, Crime, Ethnic, Experimental, Fantasy, Glitz, Historical, Mainstream/Contemporary, Mystery, Romantic Comedy, Science-fiction and Thriller scripts.
Submission Guidelines Send query letter with CV, showreel or sample pages, and SAE.
Recent Sale(s) *I Know You Know*, Justin Kerrigan (Film); *Girl With A Pearl Earring*, David Joss Buckley (Stage)
Tips Sayle Screen does not accept submissions by email.

The Science Factory Ltd
2 Twyford Place, Tiverton, Devon, EX16 6AP
- 020 7193 7296
- info@sciencefactory.co.uk
- www.sciencefactory.co.uk
Contact Director, Peter Tallack
Established 2008
Insider Info Seeking both new and established writers. Specialises in serious popular non-fiction, particularly science. Obtains new clients through queries, recommendations and submissions. Commission rates of 15 per cent for domestic sales and 20 per cent for foreign sales. Does not charge a reading fee.
Non-fiction Considers General Non-fiction for adults and children, especially when dealing with important, controversial and original ideas.
Fiction Considers occasional Children's fiction and Literary and Commercial fiction, especially if related to science.
Submission Guidelines Initial query letters only, describing the author's project, background and credentials, preferably sent by email (emails with unsolicited attachments will be deleted unread). No

sample chapter for first contact. SAE for hard-copy reply.

Client(s) Anil Ananthaswamy, Jim Baggott, David Bainbridge, Jesse Bering, Piers Bizony, Dennis Bray, Ken Bray, Michael Brooks, Warwick Cairns, Rita Carter, Stuart Clark, Matthew Cobb, Donna Dickenson, Clare Dudman, Nicholas Dunbar, John Duncan, Kevin Dutton, Georgina Ferry, Christine Garwood, Simon Ings, Manjit Kumar, Peter Lamont, Jo Marchant, Paul Mason, Arthur I. Miller, Ted Nield, Paul Parsons, Aarathi Prasad, Nicholas J. Saunders, P.D. Smith, Ian Stewart, Geerat Vermeij, Adam Zeman

Tips Has an interest in young university academics and research scientists who want to write for a broader public.

Scott Ferris Associates
Brynfield, Reynoldston, Swansea, SA3 1AE
- 01792 390009
- scottferris@macunlimited.net

Contact Gloria Ferris, Rivers Scott
Established 1981
Insider Info Currently handles non-fiction books and novels. Commission rates of 15 per cent for domestic sales and 20 per cent for foreign sales. Charges an arranged reading fee.
Non-fiction Will consider General non-fiction titles.
Fiction Will consider General fiction.
Submission Guidelines Send query letter with SAE.
Tips Scott Ferris does not accept unsolicited manuscripts.

Seven Towers
4 St Mura's Terrace, Strangford Road, East Wall, Dublin 3, Republic of Ireland
- info@seventowers.ie
- www.seventowers.ie

Contact Directors: Sarah Lundberg and Colm Lundberg
Insider Info Currently handles non-fiction, fiction and poetry for both children and adults, as well as scripts, music and graphics works. No unsolicited manuscripts. Catalogue available online.
Non-fiction Accepts Children's and General non-fiction books.
Fiction Deals with Children's and Adult fiction and poetry, as well as graphic works.
Scripts Handles Stage plays and Drama.
Submission Guidelines Accepts proposal package (including outline, synopsis and three sample chapters). In the case of drama, submissions must contain a first act and a final act, or a description of the final act.
Clients Oran Ryan, Ross Hattaway, Conor Farrell, Noel Ó Briain.

Tips Seven Towers is also a small press and publishes limited editions of works of merit, where Seven Towers does not act as agent to the author, for instance works which may have specified areas of interest but which deserve publication, as well as some collections of poetry and short stories to help showcase new writers.

The Sharland Organisation Ltd
The Manor House, Manor Street, Raunds, Northamptonshire, NN9 6JW
- 01933 626600
- 01933 624860
- info@sharlandorganisation.co.uk
- www.sharlandorganisation.co.uk

Contact Managing Director, Mike Sharland; Director, Alice Sharland
Established 1988
Insider Info Seeking both new and established writers. Currently handles television scripts, film scripts, stage plays and radio scripts. Does not accept simultaneous submissions. Proposals will be returned if accompanied by SAE. Obtains new clients by queries or submissions. Commission rates of 15 per cent for domestic sales and 20 per cent for foreign sales. Does not charge a reading fee.
Scripts Will consider most categories of script writing, including Documentary, Soap Opera and Mini-series.
Submission Guidelines Send a query letter with SAE. No scientific, technical or poetry titles considered.
Tips The Sharland Organisation works in conjunction with overseas agents and specialises in international rights.

Sheila Ableman Literary Agency
48–56 Bayham Place, London, NW1 0EU
- 020 7388 7222
- sheila@sheilaableman.co.uk

Contact Sheila Ableman
Established 1999
Insider Info Always seeking new clients. Currently handles non-fiction books. Proposals will be returned if accompanied by SAE. Obtains new clients by queries or submissions. Commission rates of 15 per cent for domestic sales and 20 per cent for foreign sales.
Non-fiction Will consider General Non-Fiction, including Biography/Autobiography, Cookery, History, Science and TV tie-in titles.
Submission Guidelines Unsolicited manuscripts welcome. Send proposal package (including synopsis, three sample chapters, CV and publishing history) by post with SAE. No gardening, poetry, sports or children's titles considered.

Tips Sheila Ableman Literary Agency specialises in television tie-ins and in ghost-writing. No reading fee.

Sheil Land Associates Ltd

(incorporating Richard Scott Simon Ltd 1971 and Christy & Moore Ltd 1912)

52 Doughty Street, London, WC1N 2LS

❶ 020 7405 9351

❶ 020 7831 2127

✉ info@sheilland.co.uk

Contact Agents UK & US: Sonia Land, Vivien Green, Piers Blofeld, Ian Drury; Film/Theatre/TV: Sophie Janson, Lucy Fawcett; Foreign: Gaia Banks, Emily Dyson

Established 1962

Insider Info Currently handles full length, literary and commercial fiction and non-fiction. Proposals will be returned if accompanied by SAE. Obtains new clients by queries or submissions. Commission rates of 15 per cent for domestic sales and 20 per cent for foreign sales. Does not charge a reading fee.

Non-fiction Will consider Biography/ Autobiography, Business, Cookery, Gardening, History, Memoirs, Military History, Politics, Science and Travel titles.

Fiction Will consider Literary and Commercial Fiction, Crime/Thrillers, Drama, Humour, Romance, Science-Fiction and Fantasy fiction.

Scripts Deals with scripts for Theatre, Film Radio and Television.

Submission Guidelines Send proposal package with SAE, synopsis, two to three sample chapters and author biography. No science fiction, fantasy children's or poetry considered.

Client(s) Peter Ackroyd, Benedict Allen, Charles Allen, Pam Ayres, Melvyn Bragg, Steven Carroll, David Cohen, Anna del Conte, Judy Corbalis, Elizabeth Corley, Seamus Deane, Greg Dyke, Rosie Goodwin, Chris Ewan, Jean Goodhind, Robert Green, Susan Hill, Richard Holmes, HRH The Prince of Wales, Ian Johnstone, Irene Karafilly, Richard Mabey, Graham Rice, Robert Rigby, Steve Rider, Martin Riley, Diane Setterfield, Tom Sharpe, Martin Stephen, Jeffrey Tayler, Andrew Taylor, Rose Tremain, Barry Unsworth, Kevin Wells, Prof. Stanley Wells, Neil White, John Wilsher, Paul Wilson and the Estates of Catherine Cookson, Patrick O'Brian, Penelope Mortimer, Jean Rhys and F.A. Wesley.

Tips Sheil Land Associates welcomes new writers and aims to help in the development of their careers.

Shelley Power Literary Agency

13 rue du Pre Saint Gervais, Paris, 75019, France

❶ 0033 1 42 38 36 49

❶ 0033 1 40 40 70 08

✉ shelley.power@wanadoo.fr

Contact Shelley Power

Established 1977

Insider Info Seeking both new and established writers. Currently handles non-fiction books and novels. Currently represents 35 clients. Does not accept simultaneous submissions. Aims to respond to queries and proposals within one week, and manuscripts within three weeks. Proposals will be returned if accompanied by SAE. Obtains new clients by recommendation and by queries or submissions. Commission rates of 12.5 per cent for domestic sales, 20 per cent for foreign sales and 20 per cent for film sales. Offers an open-ended written contract with 60 days notice for termination. Does not charge a reading fee.

Non-fiction Will consider Architecture, Biography/ Autobiography, Business, Current Affairs, Health, Memoirs, Popular Culture, Psychology, Self-help, True Crime and Women's Issues titles.

Fiction Will consider Crime, Family Saga, Feminist, Glitz, Historical, Literary, Mainstream, Thriller and Women's/'Chick lit' fiction.

Submission Guidelines Send query letter with SAE, outline, three sample chapters and author biography by email. No children's books, poetry, plays, scripts, short stories, science fiction or fantasy considered.

Tips Shelley Power is a British agent who lives in, and therefore works from, Paris. She represents only English language authors.

Shirley Stewart Literary Agency

3rd Floor, 21 Denmark Street, London, WC2H 8NA

❶ 020 7836 4440

❶ 020 7836 3482

Contact Director, Shirley Stewart (Literary)

Established 1993

Insider Info Actively seeking clients. Currently handles non-fiction books and fiction novels. Proposals will be returned if accompanied by SAE. Obtains new clients by queries or submissions. Commission rates of 10–15 per cent for domestic sales and 20 per cent for foreign sales. Does not charge a reading fee.

Non-fiction Will consider General non-fiction titles.

Fiction Will consider Literary fiction.

Submission Guidelines Send query letter with SAE, synopsis, and three sample chapters. No scripts, poetry, science fiction, fantasy or children's titles.

Tips Shirley Stewart Literary Agency does not accept submissions by fax, or on disk.

Sinclair-Stevenson

3 South Terrace, London, SW7 2TB

☎ 020 7581 2550

☎ 020 7581 2550

Contact Director, Christopher Sinclair-Stevenson; Director, Deborah Sinclair-Stevenson

Established 1995

Insider Info Seeking both new and established writers. Currently handles non-fiction books and novels. Accepts simultaneous submissions. Proposals will be returned if accompanied by SAE. Obtains new clients by queries or submissions. Commission rates of ten per cent for domestic sales and 15 per cent for foreign sales. Does not charge a reading fee.

Non-fiction Will consider Art, Biography/Autobiography, Current Affairs, History, Popular Culture and Travel titles.

Fiction Will consider General fiction.

Submission Guidelines Send query letter with SAE and synopsis. No science fiction, fantasy, academia, scripts or children's titles.

Tips Sinclair-Stevenson also handles estates, and will suggest revisions on authorised submissions.

The Standen Literary Agency

53 Hardwicke Road, London, N13 4SL

☎ 020 8889 1167

☎ 020 8889 1167

✉ yasmin@standenliteraryagency.com

🌐 www.standenliteraryagency.com

Contact Yasmin Standen

Established 2004

Insider Info Not currently seeking new clients. Currently handles non-fiction books, novels and children's books. Aims to respond to queries and proposals within four months. Proposals will be returned if accompanied by SAE. Obtains new clients by queries or submissions. Commission rates of 15 per cent for domestic sales and 20 per cent for foreign sales. Does not charge a reading fee.

Non-fiction Will consider General interest and Children's titles.

Fiction Will consider Literary and Children's fiction.

Submission Guidelines Send proposal packaged with SAE, synopsis and three sample chapters. For children's books of 500 words or less send the entire manuscripts. No illustrated or science fiction titles, or scripts considered.

Recent Sale(s) *Daughter of the Flames*, Zoe Marriott (Young Adult); *Ghost Rescue*, Andrew Murray (Children's Fiction)

Client(s) Kara Kane, Zoe Marriott, Andrew Murray and J.Y. Bee

Tips Does not accept submissions by recorded/special delivery, or electronic submissions of any form. Overseas submissions will not be returned, but include an email address for response.

Sunflower Literary Agency

BP 14, Lauzerte, 82110, France

✉ submission@sunflowerliteraryagency.com

🌐 www.sunflowerliteraryagency.com

Contact David Sherriff (Submissions and Correspondence); Senior Editor and Agent, Phillip Adams (Action, Psychological and Techno thrillers); Mss Stone (Literary Novels and Social Satire)

Established 2003

Insider Info Seeking new writers. Currently handles novels. Does not accept simultaneous submissions. Proposals will be returned if accompanied by SAE. Obtains new clients by queries or submissions. Commission rates are variable.

Fiction Will consider Crime, Erotic, Literary, Thriller, Psychological/Techno Thrillers, Satirical and Social Satire fiction.

Submission Guidelines Send a brief query by email, conforming to the guidelines on the website. No scripts, romance, 'who done it', or spirit world titles considered.

Tips See website for submission process, as the agency has very strict submission rules. Sunflower is only interested in new authors, or established authors who are changing genre. The agency does not accept unsolicited manuscripts and is usually closed to all submissions in January and February.

The Susie Adams Agency

PO Box 3820, Bath, BA2 4WY

☎ 01225 445777

✉ susieara@aol.com

Contact Susie Adams

Established 1998

Insider Info Seeking both new and established clients.

Tips The Susie Adams Agency is a rights consultancy and subsidiary rights agent. Handles literary agents, packagers and publishers.

The Susijn Agency Ltd

3rd Floor, 64 Great Titchfield Street, London, W1W 7QH

☎ 020 7580 6341

☎ 020 7580 8626

✉ info@thesusijnagency.com

🌐 www.thesusijnagency.com

Contact Founder & Agent, Laura Susijn; Agent, Nicola Barr

Established 1998

Insider Info Actively seeking clients. Currently handles non-fiction books and novels. Aims to respond to queries and proposals within eight weeks. Proposals will be returned if accompanied by SAE. Obtains new clients by queries or submissions. Commission rates of 15 per cent for domestic sales, 20 per cent for foreign sales and 15 per cent for film sales. Does not charge a reading fee.

Non-fiction Will consider Ethnic/Cultural interest and General non-fiction titles.

Fiction Will consider Literary fiction.

Submission Guidelines Send proposal package with SAE, synopsis and two sample chapters. No self-help, romance, sagas, science fiction, fantasy, computer, business, military, screenplay, children's or illustrated titles.

Client(s) Peter Ackroyd, Robin Baker, Jon Butler & Bruno Vincent, Gwynne Dyer, Travis Elborough, Bi Feiyu, Radhika Jha, Kluun, Kolton Lee, Christine Leunens, Yan Lianke, Tessa De Loo, Karel van Loon, Jeffrey Moore, Tor Norretranders, Mineke Schipper, Rowan Simons, Paul Sussman, Shimon Tzabar, Dubravka Ugresic, Alex Wheatle, Simone van der Vlugt, Henk Van Woerden, and Adam Zameenzad.

Tips The Susijn Agency are specialists in English and foreign language world rights and are interested in authors from various cultures with cross-cultural themes. Does not accept submissions by email, but include an email address with manuscripts for a quick reply.

Talent Media Group t/a ICM
Oxford House, 76 Oxford Street, London, W1D 1BS
- 020 7636 6565
- 020 7323 0101
- writers@icmlondon.co.uk

Contact Director, Lyndsey Posner; Director, Sally Long-Innes; Director and Agent, Duncan Heath; Director and Agent, Susan Rodgers; Director and Agent, Paul Lyon-Maris; Jessica Sykes, Catherine King, Greg Hunt, Hugo Young, Michael McCoy

Insider Info Seeking both new and established writers. Currently handles television scripts, film scripts, stage plays and radio scripts. Commission rates of ten per cent for domestic sales, and ten per cent for foreign sales.

Scripts Will consider general scripts for Television, Film and Radio, as well as Stage plays.

Tamar Karat Literary Agency
56 Priory Road, London, N8 7EX
- 020 8340 6460
- tamar.karat.agent@btinternet.com

Contact Tamar Karat

Insider Info Actively seeking clients. Currently handles non-fiction books and novels. Accepts simultaneous submissions. Proposal will be returned if accompanied by SAE. Obtains new clients by queries or submissions. Commission rates of 15 per cent for domestic sales, and 20 per cent for foreign sales.

Non-fiction Will consider Biography/Autobiography, History, Leisure, Politics, Sociology and Travel titles.

Fiction Will consider Literary fiction.

Submission Guidelines Send proposal package with SAE, synopsis, and two to three sample chapters. No science fiction, academia, poetry, horror, military or children's titles considered.

Tips Tamar Karat does not accept submissions by email, but include an email address with manuscripts for a quick reply.

Tanja Howarth Literary Agency
19 New Row, London, WC2N 4LA
- 020 7240 5553
- 020 7379 0969
- tanja.howarth@btinternet.com

Established 1970

Insider Info Actively seeking clients. Currently handles novels. Accepts simultaneous submissions. Proposals will be returned if accompanied by SAE. Commission rates of 15 per cent for domestic sales, and 20 per cent for foreign sales. Does not charge a reading fee.

Fiction Will consider General fiction.

Submission Guidelines Send query letter with SAE. No scripts, poetry or children's titles considered.

Tips Tanja Howarth Literary Agency specialises in German translation rights. Does not accept unsolicited manuscripts.

Teresa Chris Literary Agency
43 Musard Road, London, W6 8NR
- 020 7386 0633

Contact Director, Teresa Chris

Established 1988

Insider Info Actively seeking clients. Currently handles non-fiction books and novels. Accepts simultaneous submissions. Proposals will be returned if accompanied by SAE. Obtains new clients by queries or submissions. Commission rates of ten per cent for domestic sales and 20 per cent for foreign sales. Does not charge a reading fee.

Non-fiction Will consider Biography/Autobiography, Fitness, Food & Drink, Gardening, Health, History, Lifestyle, Popular Culture, Sports, True Crime and Women's Issues titles.

Fiction Will consider Crime, Literary and Women's/'Chick lit' fiction.

Submission Guidelines Send query letter with SAE, synopsis, and two to three sample chapters. No scripts, poetry, academia, short stories or genre fiction considered.

Tips Teresa Chris Literary Agency welcomes unsolicited proposals.

Toby Eady Associates

3rd Floor, 9 Orme Court, London, W2 4RL

☎ 020 7792 0092

🖷 020 7792 0879

✉ jamie@tobyeady.demon.co.uk

🌐 www.tobyeadyassociates.co.uk

Contact Managing Director, Toby Eady; Directors: Samar Hammam and Jamie Coleman; Assistant, Pamela Hunt

Established 1968

Insider Info Seeking both new and established writers. Currently handles non-fiction books, fiction, novels, novellas, short story collections and anthologies. Proposals will be returned if accompanied by SAE. Obtains new clients from recommendation, conferences and queries or submissions. Commission rates of 15 per cent for domestic sales and 20 for film/scripts and foreign sales. Written contract is offered, with three months notice required for termination.

* Representatives attend the City Literature Writer's Festival, in Winchester.

Non-fiction Will consider Art, Current Affairs, Ethnic/Cultural Interests, Food & Drink, Health, History, Memoirs, Politics and Popular culture titles.

Fiction Will consider Action/Adventure, Confessional, Historical, Literary, Mainstream and Contemporary fiction.

Submission Guidelines Send proposal package with SAE, outline, synopsis, short author biography and 50 sample pages. No poetry, children's books or screenplays considered.

Recent Sale(s) *Sword Song*, Bernard Cornwell (HarperCollins)

Client(s) Bernard Cornwell, Chris Cleave, Rana Dasgupta, Julia Lovell, Rachel Sieffert

Tips Top quality research is essential in any submitted material.

UKUnpublished

23 Mapledene Avenue, Hullbridge, Hockley, Essex, SS5 6JB

☎ 01702 780840

🖷 01702 260102

✉ david@ukunpublished.co.uk

🌐 www.ukunpublished.co.uk

Contact Proprietor, David Buttle

Insider Info UKUnpublished is a brand new publisher/agent looking to offer the benefits of both Traditional and Self Publishing – Full Publishing, Printing, and Distribution throughout the UK and the US, but paying up to 44 per cent higher royalties. Editing/Proofreading services are not available. Will publish all categories of books, from Children's Fiction to Adult/Erotica, and Technical Non-Fiction to Cookery. Aims to respond to queries and manuscripts within six weeks, however this is

considered to be an outside timescale. Visit the website to find out more about the service, or email/write/fax to request a brochure. Prefers to deal directly with the author, instead of through an agent.

Non-Fiction Will consider all categories of Non-Fiction.

Fiction Will consider all Fiction genres, including Children's, Adult and Short Stories.

Submission Guidelines Visit the website to find out full details about the service and the company, and email David Buttle directly to ask any questions you may have.

Tips UKUnpublished is dedicated to giving as many authors as possible an outlet, to 'Let the World Share Your Imagination', while providing a quality and personal service. UKUnpublished also offers Accounting and Tax Services provided by qualified Accountants, ensuring that you can concentrate on writing. All royalties are paid regularly.

Uli Rushby-Smith Literary Agency

72 Plimsoll Road, London, WN4 2EE

☎ 020 7354 2718

🖷 020 7354 2718

Contact Uli Rushby-Smith

Established 1993

Insider Info Seeking both new and established writers. Currently handles non-fiction books, fiction, novels and children's books. Will consider simultaneous submissions. Proposals will be returned if accompanied by SAE. Commission rates of 15 per cent for domestic sales and 20 per cent for foreign sales. Does not charge a reading fee.

Non-fiction Will consider General non-fiction and Children's titles.

Fiction Will consider Literary, General and Commercial fiction.

Submission Guidelines Send query letter with SAE, outline, and two to three sample chapters. No scripts or poetry considered.

Tips Uli Rushby-Smith does not accept submissions on disk.

United Agents

12–26 Lexington Street, London, W1F 0LE

☎ 020 3214 0800

🖷 020 3214 0801

✉ info@unitedagents.co.uk

🌐 www.unitedagents.co.uk

Contact Chair, Lindy King; Managing Director, St John Donald; Head of Books: Caroline Dawnay and Simon Trewin; Agents (Books): Pat Kavanagh, Robert Kirby, Charles Walker, Rosemary Canter, Rosemary Scoular, James Gill, Anna Webber, Sarah Ballard, Jessica Craig (Adult Foreign Rights) and Jane Willis (Children's Foreign Rights); Agents (Theatre, Film &

Television): Hannah Begbie, Duncan Millership, Olivia Homan, Dallas Smith, Lindy King, Maureen Vincent, Ruth Young, Lisa Toogood, Duncan Hayes, Kirk Whelan-Foran

Insider Info Currently handles non-fiction books, novels, television scripts and film scripts. Will consider all genres of work. Aims to respond to proposals within 4 to 6 weeks. Submission guidelines available online.

Non-fiction Will consider all genres.

Fiction Will consider all genres.

Scripts Will consider all genres.

Submission Guidelines For books send proposal package (including synopsis, two to three sample chapters and author biography) by email. Does not accept unsolicited submissions for film & television scripts.
Submission details to: looking@unitedagents.co.uk

Recent Sale(s) *The IT Crowd*, Graham Linehan (Script); *Happy-Go-Lucky*, Mike Leigh (Film)

Client(s) Nick Hornby, Anthony Horowitz, John Boyne, Julian Barnes, Justin Cartwright, Scarlett Thomas, Joanna Trollope, Ruth Rendell, Nicki French, Ewan MacGregor, Keira Knightly.

Tips UA receives over 200 submissions per week across all areas and responds only to those of interest. Note that they have very detailed submission guidelines on their website, covering each of their departments.

United Authors Ltd
11–15 Betterton Street, London, WC2H 9BP
- 020 7470 8886
- 020 7470 8887
- editorial@unitedauthors.co.uk
Established 1998

Insider Info Seeking both new and established writers. Currently handles non-fiction, fiction and children's books. Will consider simultaneous submissions. Proposals will be returned if accompanied by SAE. Obtains new clients by queries or submissions. Commission rates of 12 per cent for domestic sales, 20 per cent for foreign sales and 15–20 per cent for film (and radio) sales. Does not charge a reading fee.

Non-fiction Will consider Biography/Autobiography, Children's, General non-fiction and Travel titles.

Fiction Will consider General fiction, Novels and Children's fiction.

Submission Guidelines Send query letter with SAE.

Client(s) Terence Brady, Peter Willet, Charlotte Bingham, the estate of John Bingham

Tips Will suggest revision on any solicited manuscripts.

Valerie Hoskins Associates Ltd
20 Charlotte Street, London, W1T 2NA
- 020 7637 4490
- 020 7637 4493
- vha@vhassociates.co.uk
Contact Valerie Hoskins, Rebecca Watson
Established 1983

Insider Info Seeking both new and established writers. Currently interested in scripts. Will consider simultaneous submissions. Proposals will be returned if accompanied by SAE. Obtains new clients by queries or submissions. Commission rates of 12.5 per cent for domestic sales, and 20 per cent for foreign sales. Does not charge a reading fee.

Scripts Will consider General non-fiction and Animation scripts for Television, Film and Radio.

Submission Guidelines Send query letter with SAE.

Tips Valerie Hoskins specialises in feature films, television and animation. Does not accept unsolicited manuscripts.

Vanessa Holt Ltd
59 Crescent Road, Leigh on Sea, Essex, SS9 2PF
- 01702 473787
- 01702 471890
- vanessa@holtlimited.freeserve.co.uk
Contact Director, Vanessa Holt
Established 1989

Insider Info Actively seeking clients. Currently handles non-fiction books, fiction, novels, and children's books. Will consider simultaneous submissions. Proposals will be returned if accompanied by SAE. Obtains new clients by queries or submissions. Commission rates of 15 per cent for domestic sales, 20 per cent for foreign sales and 15 per cent for film sales. Does not charge a reading fee.

Non-fiction Will consider General non-fiction and Children's titles.

Fiction Will consider Crime, Children's, Literary, Young Adult and General fiction.

Submission Guidelines Send query letter with SAE. No children's illustrated books, scripts, poetry, academia, or technical books considered.

Tips Vanessa Holt is interested in books with potential film, television or radio tie-ins. Does not accept unsolicited manuscripts.

The Viney Agency
23 Erlanger Road, Telegraph Hill, London, SE14 5TF
- charlie@thevineyagency.com
- www.thevineyagency.comm
Contact Charlie Viney, Pippa Le Quesne
Established 2008

Insider Info Seeking both new and established writers. Currently handles non-fiction books, novels and children's books, representing around 60 clients.

The agents' backgrounds include periods in journalism, publishing, printing, business and research. Does not charge a reading fee.

Non-fiction Will consider Biography/Autobiography, History and Politics.

Fiction Deals with Novels and Children's books from previously published writers.

Submission Guidelines Accepts proposal package (including synopsis, author biography and sample pages) by post. No unsolicited fiction submissions.

Client(s) David Ambrose, David Andress, Chris Blackhurst, Kirk Buttermore, Adam Edwards, Tim FitzHigham, Janet Hoggarth, Mike Hobbs, Robin Ince, Michael Jones, Robert Kershaw, John Lazenby, Maureen Lipman, Tamara Macfarlane, Emily Maguire, Angela McCourt, Clare Peake, Helen Rappaport, Mark Stevenson, David Whitley, Kit Williams, Duncan Wu

Tips Only accepts unsolicited submissions for adult non-fiction. Unsolicited fiction proposals or children's books must be by previously published writers. Formerly part of the Mulcahy & Viney agency.

Wade & Doherty Literary Agency Ltd
33 Cormorant Lodge, Thomas More Street, London, E1W 1AU
- 020 7488 4171
- 020 7488 4172
- rw@rwla.com
- www.rwla.com

Contact Robin Wade (General Fiction, Non-fiction and Children's Books); Broo Doherty (General Fiction, Non-fiction, Commercial Women's Fiction and Crime Novels)

Established 2001

Insider Info Actively seeking clients. Currently handles non-fiction books, scholarly books, fiction, novels, children's books and anthologies. Currently represents around 30 clients, half of whom are new or previously unpublished writers. Will consider simultaneous submissions. Aims to respond to queries and proposals within seven days, and manuscripts within 30 days. Proposals returned if accompanied by SAE. Obtains new clients by recommendation, conferences and queries or submissions. Commission rates of ten per cent for domestic sales, 20 per cent for foreign sales and 20 for film sales. Written contract offered for extent of publishing, with 30 days notice required for termination. Does not charge a reading fee, and does not offer a criticism service.

* Attends the annual Crime Writers Association conference, in Harrogate, and the Romantic Novelists Association conference, in London.

Non-fiction Will consider Biography/Autobiography, Business, Children's, Current Affairs, History, How-to, Humour, Memoirs, Military, Nature,

Politics, Popular Culture, Science/Technology, Self-help, Sports, and True Crime titles.

Fiction Will consider Action/Adventure, Confessional, Crime, Erotica, Ethnic, Experimental, Family Saga, Fantasy, Feminist, Gay/Lesbian, Glitz, Historical, Horror, Humour, Children's, Literary, Mainstream, Mystery, Picture book, Regional, Religion, Romance, Science-fiction, Sports, Supernatural, Thriller, Women's/'Chick lit', and Young Adult fiction.

Submission Guidelines Send proposal package with synopsis, author biography and first 10,000 words of sample material, by email or post.

Recent Sale(s) *Dragon Horse,* Peter Ward (Doubleday); *The Secret of Excalibur,* Andy McDermott (Headline)

Client(s) Philippa Ashley, Marion Husband, Caroline Kington, Ray Connolly, Georgina Harding, Helen Oyeyemi, Lance Price, Rachel Trezise, Caroline Carver, Angela Dracup, Steve Hague, Eve Isherwood, Andy McDermott, Paul Johnston, Louise Cooper, Kimberly Greene, Adam Guillain, Steve Alton, Andrea Shavick, Peter Ward, Sameem Ali, Alison Bruce, Steuart Campbell, Sheila Hardy, Neil Hegarty, Brenda James, Prof. W.D. Rubinstein, Mike Newlands, Lance Price, Ewen Southby-Tailyour and Ayowa Taylor

Watson, Little Ltd
48–56 Bayham Place, London, NW1 0EU
- 020 7388 7529
- 020 7388 8501
- office@watsonlittle.com
- www.watsonlittle.com

Contact Managing Director, Mandy Little; Senior Agent, James Wills

Insider Info Actively seeking clients. Currently handles non-fiction books, fiction, novels and children's books. Will consider simultaneous submissions. Proposals returned if accompanied by SAE. Obtains new clients by queries or submissions. Commission rates of 15 per cent for domestic sales, 20 per cent for foreign sales and 15 per cent for film sales. Overseas Associates are The Marsh Agency Ltd; Film & TV Associates are The Sharland Organisation Ltd and MBA Literary Agents Ltd; USA Associates are Howard Morhaim Literary Agency (Adult) and The Chudney Organisation (Children's). Does not charge a reading fee.

Non-fiction Special interests include Children's books, History, Leisure, Popular Psychology, Science and Self-help books.

Fiction Will consider Women's fiction, Crime, Children's and Literary fiction.

Submission Guidelines Send query letter with SAE and synopsis. No scripts, poetry, short stories or pure academia considered.

Recent Sale(s) *Football Dynamo*, Marc Bennetts (Virgin); *Shooting the Moon*, V.M. Jones (Andersen Press)

Client(s) Helen Armstrong, Adrian Bloom, Robin Cohen, Mark Hanson, Deborah Jaffe, Michael Jordan, Alice Muir, Ian Palmer, Mark Ronan, Rosie Swale, Edward Craig, Robert Giddings, Mukul Patel, Stewart Ross, Wayne Talbot, Henning Wehn, Duncan Cameron, Nicola Hill, Ann Kramer, Karen Saunders and Jane Wright

Tips Watson, Little does not accept email queries or full-length unsolicited manuscripts. The agency also represents illustrators.

The Whispering Buffalo Literary Agency Ltd
97 Chesson Road, London, W14 9QS
- 020 7565 4737
- mariam@whisperingbuffalo.com
- www.whisperingbuffalo.com

Contact Mariam Keen
Established 2008
Insider Info Actively seeking clients. Handles commercial/literary fiction/non-fiction & children's/ Young Adult fiction with special interest in book to film adaptations. Commission rates of 12.5 per cent for domestic sales, 20 per cent for foreign sales & film rights. Does not charge a reading fee.
Non-fiction Will consider Non-fiction.
Fiction Will consider Commercial/Literary, Children's and Young Adult fiction.
Scripts Handles scripts for existing clients only.
Submission Guidelines Accepts query letter with synopsis, three sample chapters and SAE to ensure return of hardcopy material. Pages should be double-spaced, single-sided and A4. No Poetry, plays or academic/textbooks.
Tips The agency provides a high level of personal representation and also handles merchandising.

William Morris Agency (UK) Ltd
Centre Point, 103 New Oxford Street, London, WC1A 1DD
- 020 7534 6800
- 020 7534 6900
- www.wma.com

Contact CEO, Jim Wiatt; Chairman, Norman Brokaw
Established 1965
Insider Info Seeking both new and established writers. Currently handles non-fiction books, fiction, novels, television scripts and film scripts. Will consider simultaneous submissions. Proposals returned if accompanied by SAE. Obtains new clients by queries or submissions. Commission rates of 15 per cent for domestic sales, 20 per cent for foreign sales, and ten per cent for film sales. Does not charge a reading fee.

Non-fiction Will consider General non-fiction.
Fiction Will consider General fiction and Novels.
Scripts Will consider Television and Film scripts.
Submission Guidelines Send query letter with SAE, synopsis and up to 50 sample pages.
Tips William Morris has worldwide offices and represents both entertainment talent and literary clients. Contact by telephone first for television or film scripts.

The Wylie Agency (UK) Ltd
17 Bedford Square, London, WC1B 3JA
- 020 7908 5900
- 020 7908 5901
- mail@wylieagency.co.uk
- www.wylieagency.com

Contact President, Andrew Wylie
Established 1996
Insider Info Currently handles novels. Considers simultaneous submissions. Proposals returned if accompanied by SAE. Obtains new clients by queries or submissions. Commission rates of ten per cent for domestic sales, and between 15 and 20 per cent for foreign sales. Does not charge a reading fee.
Fiction Will consider Novels and General fiction.
Submission Guidelines Send query letter with SAE, or query by email. No scripts or children's fiction considered.
Client(s) Chinua Achebe, Ken Adam, Chimamanda N. Adichie, Arthur Allen, Martin Amis, Laurie Anderson, Matt Bai, Philip Bobbitt, Patricia Bosworth, Paul Collier, Ian Frazier, Al Gore, Tipper Gore, Dennis Hopper, Michael Kantor, Annie Leibovitz, Norman Mailer, Jon McGregor, Louis Menand, Miyuki Miyabe, Thom Mount, Michael O'Brien, Paul Preston, Lou Reed, Salman Rushdie, Jeffrey D.Sachs and Robert Schlesinger
Tips The Wylie Agency does not accept unsolicited manuscripts.

Zebra Agency
Broadland House, 1 Broadland, Shevington, Lancashire, WN6 8DH
- 07949 584758
- Online form.
- www.zebraagency.co.uk

Insider Info Seeking mostly established writers through referrals. Currently handles non-fiction books, novels, television scripts, movie scripts, stage plays and radio scripts. Considers simultaneous submissions. Obtains new clients by queries or submissions.
Tips Zebra Agency only represents professional writers. Especially interested in 15-minute comedy scripts and ghost writers for celebrities.

Adventures in Fiction

14 Grosvenor Avenue, London, N5 2NR

☎ 020 7354 2598

✉ enquiries@adventuresinfiction.co.uk

🌐 www.adventuresinfiction.co.uk

About A consultancy that works with writers at all stages in their careers, offering appraisal services for individual manuscripts, as well as a range of ongoing 'mentoring' programmes.

Andrew Crofts

☎ 01403 864518

✉ croftsa@aol.com

🌐 www.andrewcrofts.com

About A professional, best selling ghost writer, dealing in fiction and non-fiction.

Anne Barclay Enterprises

The Old Farmhouse, Hexworthy, Yelverton, Devon, PL20 6SD

☎ 01364 631405

☎ 01364 631112

✉ amb@theswiftgroup.co.uk

🌐 www.theswiftgroup.co.uk

About Provides editorial services to both published and unpublished authors. Packages include ghost writing, editing, copyediting and assessment of manuscripts.

Book Production Consultants

25–27 High Street, Chesterton, Cambridge, CB4 1ND

☎ 01223 352790

☎ 01223 460718

✉ enquiries@bpccam.co.uk

🌐 www.bpccam.co.uk

About Businesses are taken through the complete publishing processes including writing, editing, production and distribution. Books, manuals, catalogues, leaflets, electronic publishing and reports are all dealt with.

BookType

17 Yeoford Meadows, Yeoford, Crediton, Devon, EX17 5PW

✉ info@booktype.co.uk

🌐 www.booktype.co.uk

About A typesetting service for publishers.

Brackley Proofreading Services

PO Box 5920, Brackley, Northamptonshire, NN13 6YB

☎ 01280 703355

✉ brackleyproof@lineone.net

About Proofreading services from John Skermer.

Cambridge Publishing Management

Burr Elm Court, Main Street, Caldecote, Cambridge, CB23 7NU

☎ 01954 214000

☎ 01954 214002

✉ j.dobbyne@cambridgepm.co.uk

🌐 www.cambridgepm.co.uk

Contact Managing Director, Jackie Dobbyne

About Provides full editing and production services for publishers of business, educational, travel and illustrated non-fiction titles.

Chapter One Promotions

19–35 Sylvan Grove, London, SE15 1PD

☎ 0845 456 5364

✉ info@chapteronepromotions.com

🌐 www.chapteronepromotions.com

About Chapter One Promotions runs annual short story, poetry and novel competitions, plus children's story and young illustrator's competitions. They provide creative workshops and literary events as well as a critique and proofreading service.

Christine Foley Secretarial Services

Glynedwydd, Login, Whitland, Carmarthenshire, SA34 0TN

☎ 01994 448414

☎ 01994 448414

✉ foley@glyndedwydd.freeserve.co.uk

About Manuscript preparation service, from handwritten or typed notes and audio transcription (cassette tapes, CDs and digital sound files). Est. 1991.

Christopher Pick

41 Chestnut Road, London, SE27 9EZ

☎ 020 8761 2585

✉ christopher@the-picks.co.uk

About Writer of promotional material, as well as fiction, non-fiction and children's books. Editorial, or ghost writing services are provided. Member of the Society of Authors.

College-on-the-Net
81 Warwick Road, Sutton, Surrey, SM1 4BL
- 020 8642 1063
- 07092 194837
- info@college-on-the-net.co.uk
- www.college-on-the-net.co.uk

About Mainly offers tutorial courses on a wide range of subjects but also offers an author's appraisal service, where specialists will provide various levels of critique on a manuscript. Clients may use the service as an ongoing course, or as a one off. They deal with novels, short stories, poetry, journalism, writing for children and scriptwriting.

Cornerstones
Milk Studios, 34 Southern Row, London, W10 5AN
- 020 8968 0777
- 020 8969 8677
- kathryn@cornerstones.co.uk
- www.cornerstones.co.uk

Contact Director, Helen Corner; Managing Editor, Kathryn Robinson

About Cornerstones offers a manuscript assessment and advisory service for both children's and adult fiction, and non-fiction. They also scout for literary agencies such as Annette Green, Conville & Walsh, LAW, United Agents, and others. Authors are asked to ring or email with a query before submitting their complete manuscript.

Creative Plus Publishing
2nd Floor, 151 High Street, Billericay, Essex, CM12 9AB
- 01277 633005
- 01277 633003
- enquiries@creative-plus.co.uk
- www.creative-plus.co.uk

About Editorial and design services offered for books, part works and magazines. They are specialists in crafts, home and garden, cookery, art, literature, children's books, and adaptations.

The Cutting Edge
Archery House, 33 Archery Square, Walmer, Deal, Kent, CT14 7JA
- 01304 371721
- 01304 371416
- jmthurley@aol.com
- www.thecuttingedge.biz

About Cutting Edge offers many services, including manuscript assessment, editorial input, constructive criticism and creative advice, re-writing, presentation for the market, and contractual and business advice. Authors are asked to submit a hardcopy of their completed manuscript along with a cheque for the fees. See the website for details about fees.

Daniel Goldsmith Associates
Unit 17, Percival Lane, Runcorn, Cheshire, WA7 4UX
- 01928 440012
- lorena@danielgoldsmith.co.uk
- www.danielgoldsmith.co.uk

About Book editors and literary consultants. Fiction and non-fiction only, no fantasy, sci-fi, children's literature, scripts or poetry. Assessment reports from £125. Market assessment for foreign published authors. Free submission and recommendation to agents and publishers.

David Price
Acupunctuation Ltd, 4 Harbidges Lane, Long Buckby, Northampton, NN6 7QL
- 01327 844119
- acuedit@fireflyuk.net
- www.acuedit.co.uk

About Proofreading and editing services available, particularly in the areas of travel, dance, arts, popular culture and European history.

David Winpenny Public Relations Ltd
Victoria Villa, Princess Road, Ripon, North Yorkshire, HG4 1HW
- 01765 607641
- 01765 608320
- info@winpennypr.co.uk
- www.winpennypr.co.uk

About A public relations and media agency that provides editorial services, including ghost writing, feature writing, copyediting and proofreading.

Duncan McAra
28 Beresford Gardens, Edinburgh, EH5 3ES
- 0131 552 1558
- 0131 552 1558
- duncanmcara@hotmail.com

About Provides a full range of editorial services for publishers, and other businesses and institutions. These include editing, re-writing, copyediting and proofreading. Specialises in Scottish literature, art, architecture, travel, military history and archaeology. Also acts as a literary agent.

Editorial Solutions
537 Antrim Road, Belfast, Northern Ireland, BT15 3BU
- 028 9077 2300
- info@editorialsolutions.com
- www.editorialsolutions.com

About Writing and editing services, primarily for business documents, marketing and public relations material, as well as websites. Packages include copywriting, copyediting, proofreading, page design and complete project management.

1st Call Editorial
19 Albermarle Road, Gorleston, Norfolk, NR31 7AR
- 01493 444556
- 01493 444556
- eldo@1stcalleditorial.com
- www.1stcalleditorial.com

About On-screen proofreading and copyediting from Eldo Barkhuizen, an advanced member of the SfEP.

First Editing
17 West Winter Park Street, Orlando, Florida 32804, , USA
- questions@firstediting.com
- www.firstediting.com

About US based editing service that will edit anything from a full length manuscript to a business speech. A team of professional editors review all documents. They offer an initial free sample; email them part of your writing and they will proofread, revise, and edit a small section of it and provide you with a precise price quote.

First Edition Translations
6 Wellington Court, Wellington Street, Cambridge, CB1 1HZ
- 01223 356733
- 01223 316232
- info@firstedit.co.uk
- www.firstedit.co.uk

About A translations service for non-fiction books, covering all subject areas. Additional services include proofreading, copyediting, typesetting, Americanisation and indexing.

Fish Publishing
Durras, Bantry, Co. Cork, Republic of Ireland
- info@fishpublishing.com
- www.fishpublishing.com

About Fish Publishing runs the annual Fish Short Story Prize with prizes from €300 to €3000. They also provide a full editorial consultancy service designed to provide writers with one-on-one, on-going, constructive feedback on their work, whether it is a complete novel or a proposal package. All enquires regarding the editorial consultancy should be sent to Katie Gould at: kgould@fishpublishing.com

Florence Productions
Stoodleigh Court, Stoodleigh, Devon, EX16 9PN
- 01398 351556
- 01398 351388
- info@florenceproduction.co.uk
- www.florenceproduction.co.uk

About An out of house desk editing and typesetting service for publishers. Individual services can be provided, or they can project manage the entire process.

Freelance Editing Services
60 Norman Road, Tunbridge Wells, Kent, TN1 2RP
- 01892 671066
- fes.editor@gmail.com
- www.freelanceediting.co.uk

About Comprehensive copyediting, proofreading and developmental editing services at competitive rates. Also offers: interim editorial management; advice on preparing and submitting work to publishers and journal editors; help with style and content guidelines; and commissioning, research and project support. Specialist areas include health care, medicine, nursing, academic subjects and US/UK English.

Good Writing Matters
2 The Island, Thames Ditton, Surrey, KT7 0SH
- 020 8339 0945
- 020 8339 0945
- mruswords@aol.com

About Provides copyediting and proofreading services for businesses and individual clients. Also runs a small publishing imprint, Riverside Press.

Hans Zell Publishing Consultants
Glais Bheinn, Lochcarron, Ross-shire, IV54 8YB
- 01520 722951
- 01520 722953
- hanszell@hanszell.co.uk
- www.hanszell.co.uk

About Academic, reference and journal publishing management is offered, as are marketing and training services for businesses and individuals. Specialists in providing internet training for publishers in developing countries in the third world, particularly in Africa. Also publishers of reference resources (print and online) on Africa and African studies.

The Hilary Johnson Authors' Advisory Service
1 Beechwood Court, Syderstone, Norfolk, PE31 8TR

☎ 01485 578594
✉ enquiries@hilaryjohnson.com
🌐 www.hilaryjohnson.com
About Offers professional appraisals of authors' typescripts: novels (all genres), literary fiction, children's books, full-length non-fiction, short stories, TV/radio/screenplays and poetry. General writing-related advice also given. Also acts as a scout for a well-know literary agency.

IB Editorial Services
16 Hipkin Road, Dersingham, near Kings Lynn, Norfolk, PE31 6XX
☎ 01485 543746
✉ boston@ibss.fsnet.co.uk
🌐 www.ibedit.fsnet.co.uk
About Editorial services offered by Irene Boston. Copyediting, proofreading, indexing and technical writing are among the packages. Assistance is also provided for students and academics with reports and theses.

Indexing Specialists (UK) Ltd
Indexing House, 360a Portland Road, Hove, East Sussex, BN3 5LP
☎ 01273 416777
☎ 01273 424411
✉ indexers@indexing.co.uk
🌐 www.indexing.co.uk
About Offers specialist, comprehensive indexing services, as well as copyediting, conference document management, and website management.

Jacqui Bennett Writers Bureau
87 Home Orchard, Yate, South Gloucestershire, BS37 5XH
☎ 01454 324717
✉ jenny@jbwb.co.uk
🌐 www.jbwb.co.uk
About Can either read and critique a sample of work, or edit a full manuscript. Fees vary depending on the service required and length of the manuscript.

Jan Henley Manuscript Appraisal Service
☎ 01903 235508/07979 280697
✉ jan.henley@sky.com
🌐 www.janhenley.co.uk
About Published writer Jan Henley (also writing as Anna Cheska and Juliet Hall) offers a personal manuscript appraisal service, with links to a leading literary agent.

Jeremy Lockyer
☎ 01884 243261
✉ jeremy@jeremylockyer.co.uk
🌐 www.jeremylockyer.co.uk
About A freelancer, providing proofreading, editing, re-writing and photography services for writers and publishers.

Leda Sammarco
☎ 07930 568516
✉ info@ledasammarco.com
🌐 www.ledasammarco.com
About Leda Sammarco provides coaching services for writers at every stage, from the creative process all the way through to publication. She works in the following genres: personal development, popular psychology, health and wellbeing, spirituality and inspirational memoir.

Linda Acaster
✉ lindaacaster@yahoo.co.uk
🌐 www.linda.acaster.btinternet.co.uk
About In-depth critique of fiction offered by a published novelist and short story writer, and former tutor at the Arvon Foundation and the Open College of Arts. No poetry or drama.

The Literary Consultancy
The Crypt Centre, Munster Square, London, NW1 3PL
☎ 020 7813 4330
✉ info@literaryconsultancy.co.uk
🌐 www.literaryconsultancy.co.uk
About Fiction, non-fiction, autobiography and children's books are critiqued, as are film, television, theatre and radio scripts, and poetry. They also scout for leading agencies.

New Writers Consultancy
35a Lower Park Road, Brightlingsea, Colchester, Essex, CO7 0JX
☎ 01206 303607
✉ submissions@new-writers-consultancy.com
About Offers a variety of packages including appraisals, critiques and editing. Services are provided by Diana Hayden, an ex BBC worker, editor and proofreader, and Karen Scott, a published author. Submissions are accepted by post or email.

Nyala Publishing (Geo Group)
4 Christian Fields, London, SW16 3JZ
☎ 020 8764 6292
☎ 020 8764 6292
✉ nyala.publishing@geo-group.co.uk

www.geo-group.co.uk
About Offers a range of services including copyediting, proofreading, manuscript appraisal and research. Promotional material can also be designed and produced.

Oxford Designers & Illustrators
Aristotle Lane, Oxford, OX2 6TR
- 01865 512331
- 01865 517999
- pete@odi-design.co.uk
- www.o-d-i.com

About A creative design and illustration company. All aspects of pre-press production are covered, including proof-reading, project management and art buying. A specialist area is illustrated educational texts.

Oxford Literary Consultancy
191 The Slade, Headington, Oxford, OX3 7HR
- 01865 751004
- oxfordwriters@mac.com
- www.oxfordwriters.com

About Offers manuscript assessment and editing, proofreading, copyediting and mentoring services, as well as acting as a scout for leading literary agents. They have had a number of previous successes in placing first-time writers with literary agents or publishers.

Pen Friends UK
7 Lane Close, Horley, Oxfordshire, OX15 6BH
- penfriendsUK@btinternet.com
- www.pefruk.co.uk

About Pen Friends UK is an editing, proofreading and critique service, specialising in self-publishing and print-on-demand publishers. Contact Carlie Lee or James Malvern for further information.

Reading & Righting
618b Finchley Road, London, NW11 7RR
- 020 8455 4564
- lambhorn@gmail.com
- www.readingandrighting.netfirms.com

About A script/manuscript reading and assessment service, that also offers advice on agents and publishers. Fiction, plays, screenplays and non-fiction are dealt with. One-to-one follow up tuition and mentoring can also be provided, as well as editing of complete manuscripts, websites and blogs. Other services include workshops and lectures. Specialist interests include the performing arts, popular culture, psychotherapy, social issues and current affairs.

Real Writers
PO Box 170, Chesterfield, Derbyshire, S40 1FE
- info@real-writers.com
- www.real-writers.com

About Offers a manuscript appraisal service by correspondence or email, on either a one-off or an ongoing basis. Readers are specialists in fiction, poetry, journalism, writing for children, and scriptwriting.

The Right Bookseller
CBXII, West Wing, 382–390 Midsummer Boulevard, Office 329, Milton Keynes, MK9 2RG
- 0845 652 9637
- 01525 636085
- info@therightbookseller.com
- www.therightbookseller.com

About Offers proofreading and editing services, as well as typesetting, printing books in bulk quantity, and promotional services. Deals with manuscripts from all genres.

Sandhurst Editorial Consultants
36 Albion Road, Sandhurst, Berkshire, GU47 9BP
- 01252 877645
- 01252 890508
- mail@sand-con.demon.co.uk
- www.sand-con.demon.co.uk

About Editorial services for both writers and publishers. Packages include manuscript appraisal, proofreading, copyediting, writing, re-writing, and, if desired, complete project management.

Sarah Sutton Consulting
PO Box 134, Shaftesbury, Dorset, SP7 8WS
- 01747 850100
- info@sarahsutton.co.uk
- www.sarahsutton.co.uk

About Sarah Sutton offers freelance editorial services to publishers, as well as being a writer specialising in business, lifestyle, parenting and television tie-ins. She also offers ghost writing services.

Script Centre
13 Wingfield Street, London, SE15 4LN
- 020 7358 8216
- info@scriptcentre.co.uk
- www.scriptcentre.co.uk

About Offers either initial comments, standard feedback or an extensive report on scripts for film, television, radio or theatre. Cheaper rates can be offered for treatments or partial scripts.

Small Print

The Old School House, 74 High Street, Swavesey, Cambridge, CB24 4QU

- 01954 231713
- 01954 205061
- info@smallprint.co.uk
- www.smallprint.co.uk

About Provides project management packages for publishers, including commissioning writers and illustrators, translations, research, proofreading, copyediting, page design and layout. Specialists in non-fiction, particularly foreign language course books, training materials, guidebooks, dictionaries, and audio packages. Print, online and audio visual media are all dealt with.

Special Edition Pre-Press Services

2 Caledonian Wharf, London, E14 3EW

- 020 7987 9600/07930 997535
- c.orde@btinternet.com
- www.special-edition.co.uk

About Provides a range of services including editing and proofreading, typesetting and design, and services for self publishers. Works with both individual and corporate clients.

S. Ribeiro, Literary Consultant

42 West Heath Court, North End Road, London, NW11 7RR

- 020 8458 9082
- sribeiroeditor@aol.com

About Freelance services include copywriting and jacket information, editing to publication standards, and detailed manuscript appraisal. Works with writers, small presses and self published writers.

StorytrackS

16 St Briac Way, Exmouth, Devon, EX8 5RN

- 01395 279659
- mail@margaretjames.com
- www.storytracks.net

About Provides manuscript appraisal services on fiction, non-fiction and children's writing, but not for poetry. Also offers a ghost writing service, can run workshops, and may act as a scout for a literary agency.

Susan Wallace

PO Box 95, Liverpool, L17 8WY

- 0151 233 3689/07801 055556
- susan@storieswanted.com
- www.novelsediting services.com

About Journalist and writer. Provides authors with sensitive, but stern editing, copy-editing and proofreading to help lift and crystallize manuscripts

with a significant, professional polish. Understanding, confidential, thorough and loyal; aims to help bring your work to fruition. Fee for entire manuscript agreed after a test example. Fast turnaround available.

Welsh Books Council

Castell Brychan, Aberystwyth, Ceredigion, SY23 2JB

- 01970 624151
- 01970 625385
- castellbrychan@wbc.org.uk
- www.wbc.org.uk

Contact Director, Gwerfyl Pierce Jones; Head of Children's Books, Menna Lloyd Williams

About The Welsh Books Council is a national body, funded by the Welsh Assembly Government, which provides a focus for the publishing industry in Wales. It provides a number of specialist services, including editing, design, marketing and distribution, with a view to improving standards of book production and publication in both Welsh and English. Writers in Welsh and English are welcome to approach the Editorial Department for advice on how to get their manuscripts published. See the website for further details.

WordsRU

2 High Ridge, Tiptree Road, Great Braxted, Essex, CM8 3EE

- 07789 495922
- admin@wordsru.com
- www.wordsru.com

About Offers proofreading and editing services across a wide range of formats, including novels, articles, screenplays, business and academic documents, application forms, letters, and much more. Individual editors are assigned to each project. Visit the website for details of fees and services.

Writers' Workshop

Pritchards Cottage, Steeple Barton, Oxfordshire, OX25 4QP

- 01869 347040
- info@writersworkshop.co.uk
- www.writersworkshop.co.uk

About The team will appraise manuscripts and produce reports, as well as entering into dialogue over the findings of the appraisal. Most types of manuscript are dealt with, including fiction, poetry, scripts and writing for children. The editors are a team of published writers, most of whom have taught creative writing at university level and/or have won or been shortlisted for major literary awards. They can also provide help in finding agents. Check the website to view their credentials.

The Writing Coach

⊙ Online form.

ⓦ www.thewritingcoach.co.uk

About Run by published novelist Jacqui Lofthouse. Can provide either a reader's report or a full critique of both fiction and non-fiction. No poetry or screenplays.

Writing Literary Consultants

Neville House, Station Approach, Wendens Ambo, Essex, CB11 4LB

⊙ 01799 544659

⊙ info@writing.co.uk

ⓦ www.writing.co.uk

About Provides a range of services from assisting with submissions to publishers, to manuscript appraisals. Books, poetry, screenplays and even illustrations are dealt with. They also act as scouts for leading literary agents.

CONSULTANCIES

LISTINGS

ORGANISATIONS

ABC

🌐 www.abc.org.uk

Contact Chief Executive, Jerry Wright

About ABC (the Audit Bureau of Circulation) is the UK's leading source of information and statistics for newspapers, magazines and periodicals. The website includes lots of information, such as circulation figures and which magazines are the UK's bestsellers. ABC is an independent not-for-profit organisation.

Academi

Main Office: 3rd floor, Mount Stuart House, Mount Stuart Square, Cardiff, CF10 5FQ

☎ 029 2047 2266

☎ 029 2049 2930

✉ post@academi.org

🌐 www.academi.org

Contact Chief Executive, Peter Finch; Literature Officer, Hollie Aldridge

About Academi is the Welsh National Literature Promotion Agency and Society for Authors. It works to promote the literature of Wales, both in Wales and elsewhere. It hosts literary events and competitions, including the Cardiff International Poetry Competition and the Wales Book of the Year awards. It also provides bursaries and grants.

ALCS

The Writers' House, 13 Haydon Street, London, EC3N 1DB

☎ 020 7264 5700

☎ 020 7264 5755

✉ alcs@alcs.co.uk

🌐 www.alcs.co.uk

Contact Chief Executive, Owen Atkinson

About ALCS (the Author's Licensing and Collecting Society) is dedicated to protecting and promoting authors' rights and aims to ensure that writers are fairly compensated for any works that are copied, broadcast or recorded, particularly with regard to secondary rights in such usage as photocopying, repeat broadcasts and digital use. It distributes millions of pounds to authors every year. It is also an internationally known centre of expertise on copyright generally.

Alliance of Literary Societies

59 Bryony Road, Birmingham, B29 4BY

✉ l.j.curry@bham.ac.uk

🌐 www.allianceofliterarysocieties.org.uk

Contact Chair, Linda Curry; Treasurer and Membership Secretary, Julie Shorland

About The ALS is the umbrella organisation for literary societies/groups in the UK. It aims to provide support and advice on a variety of literary subjects, as well as promoting cooperation between member societies. ALS was formed in 1973 and currently has over one hundred members.

An Comunn Gàidhealach

109 Church Street, Inverness, IV1 1EY

☎ 01463 231226

☎ 01463 715557

✉ info@ancomunn.co.uk

🌐 www.ancomunn.co.uk

Contact Chief Executive, Calum Iain MacLeod

About An Comunn Gàidhealach is a voluntary membership organisation, with charitable status, founded in 1891 as a vehicle for the preservation and development of the Gaelic language. It actively encourages the teaching, learning and use of the Gaelic language and the study and cultivation of Gaelic literature, history, music and art.

Apples & Snakes

The Albany, Douglas Way, London, SE8 4AG

☎ 0845 521 3460

✉ info@applesandsnakes.org

🌐 www.applesandsnakes.org

Contact Director, Geraldine Collinge; See website for Regional Co-ordinators

About Apples & Snakes is a poetry performance organisation covering all of England. It focuses on working with emerging artists and commissions and produces new work. It regularly curates, hosts and acts as a partner to facilitate and promote performance poetry through live events. With education at the core of its mission, it works with schools, prisons, libraries and more, to use performance poetry to develop literacy and communication skills, motivation and self-esteem.

ASLIB
Holywell Centre, 1 Phipp Street, London, EC2A 4PS
- 020 7613 3031
- 020 7613 5080
- aslib@aslib.com
- www.aslib.co.uk

About ASLIB (The Association for Information Management) will be of interest primarily to writers and information specialists who are seeking knowledge about managing information in large and corporate environments. One of its roles is to represent and lobby for the interests of the information sector on matters which are of national and international importance, varying from copyright and data protection, to the role of scientific journals. See also www.managinginformation.com

ASLS
c/o Department of Scottish Literature, University of Glasgow, 7 University Gardens, Glasgow, G12 8QH
- 0141 330 5309
- 0141 330 5309
- d.jones@scothist.arts.gla.ac.uk
- www.asls.org.uk

Contact General Manager, Duncan Jones
About ASLS (The Association for Scottish Literary Studies) aims to promote the study, teaching and writing of Scottish literature, and to further the study of the languages of Scotland. To that end, it publishes various collections of Scottish writing and poetry, and also publishes the *International Journal of Scottish Literature*.

Association of Authors Agents
c/o Philippa Milnes-Smith, Lucas Alexander Whiteley, 14 Vernon Street, London, W14 0RJ
- 020 7471 7900
- philippa@lawagency.co.uk
- www.agentsassoc.co.uk

Contact President, Philippa Milnes-Smith; Secretary, Penny Holroyde
About Exists to provide a forum for member agents to discuss industry matters, to represent the interests of agents and their clients, and to uphold a code of good practice. The majority of established agencies in the UK belong to the Association. Most writers will never need to have direct contact with the Association, but all receive indirect benefits.

Association of British Science Writers
Wellcome Wolfson Building, 165 Queen's Gate, London, SW7 5HD
- 0870 770 3361
- absw@absw.org.uk
- www.absw.org.uk

About The ABSW exists to help those who write about science and technology, and to improve the standard of science journalism in the UK. They also run the ABSW Science Writers' Awards, which seek to set standards of excellence in science writing across eight categories.

Association of Christian Writers
- www.christianwriters.org.uk

About The aim of the Association of Christian Writers is to see quality writing in every area of the media – whether it be overtly Christian, or shaped by a Christian perspective – and to reach the widest possible range of people throughout the UK and beyond.

Association of Freelance Editors, Proofreaders & Indexers (Ireland)
c/o Winifred Power, Friar's Walk, Abbeyside, Dungarven, Co. Waterford
- 00353 058 48458
- 00353 058 48458
- powerediting@eircom.net
- www.afepi.ie

Contact Co-chairperson, Winifred Power; Co-chairperson, Brenda O'Hanlon
About The Irish Association of Freelance Editors, Proofreaders & Indexers (AFEPI) was established to provide information to publishers on professional freelancers, and to protect the interests of those freelancers. All members are expected to have professional experience.

The Association of Learned & Professional Society Publishers (ALPSP)
Blenheim House, 120 Church Street, Brighton, BN1 1AU
- 01235 847776
- 0870 706 0332
- ian.russell@alpsp.org
- www.alpsp.org.uk

Contact Chief Executive, Ian Russell
About The Association of Learned & Professional Society Publishers (ALPSP), founded in 1972, is the international trade association for not-for-profit publishers and those who work with them. It provides information, education, representation, co-operative initiatives and guidelines for good practice.

The Audiobook Publishing Association

- ☎ 07531 902975
- ✉ info@theapa.net
- 🌐 www.theapa.net

Contact Chair, Alison Muirden; Administrator, Laura Briscall

About The APA is the UK trade association for the audiobook industry, with membership open to all those involved in the publishing of spoken word audio, including publishers, producers, abridgers, agents, actors and studios.

The Bibliographical Society

c/o Institute of English Studies, University of London, Senate House, Malet Street, London, WC1E 7HU

- ✉ secretary@bibsoc.org.uk
- 🌐 www.bibsoc.org.uk

Contact President, John Barnard; Hon. Secretary, Meg Ford

About The Bibliographical Society deals with the study of the book and its history. Its objectives are to promote and encourage study and research in the fields of historical, analytical, descriptive and textual bibliography, and the history of printing, publishing, bookselling, bookbinding and collecting. It holds meetings at which papers are read and discussed; publishes its journal, *The Library*, and books concerned with bibliography; maintains a bibliographical library; and awards a medal for services to bibliography. It supports bibliographical research by awarding grants and bursaries. Full details of meetings are on the website.

Book Marketing Ltd

39 Store Street, London, WC1E 7DS

- ☎ 0870 870 2345
- ✉ bml@bookmarketing.co.uk
- 🌐 www.bookmarketing.co.uk

Contact Managing Director, Jo Henry; Research Directors: Steve Bohme and Leslie Henry

About BML is the UK's premier source of information and research on the book industry, undertaking a wide range of research projects and publishing a variety of market research. It is best known for its *Books and the Consumer* survey, accessed on subscription via the website.

The Bookseller

Endeavour House, 189 Shaftesbury Avenue, London, WC2H 8TJ

- ☎ 020 7420 6006
- ☎ 020 7420 6103
- ✉ philip.jones@bookseller.co.uk

- 🌐 www.thebookseller.com

Contact Editor-in-Chief, Neill Denny; Managing Editor, Philip Jones; Book Editor, Alice O'Keeffe; Features Editor, Tom Tivnan

About *The Bookseller* is the UK's leading journal for book publishing professionals, covering every aspect of the book publishing industry. It provides news, in-depth articles, book industry statistics and bestseller charts.

The Booksellers Association

Minster House, 272 Vauxhall Bridge Road, London, SW1V 1BA

- ☎ 020 7802 0802
- ☎ 020 7802 0803
- ✉ mail@booksellers.org.uk
- 🌐 www.booksellers.org.uk

Contact President, Graham Rand; Chief Executive, Tim Godfray

About The Booksellers Association represents over 95 per cent of booksellers in the UK and Ireland. It also operates the Boo Tokens scheme. Its website will be of interest to writers for information and statistics on the book trade and publishing industry.

Booktrust

Book House, 45 East Hill, London, SW18 2QZ

- ☎ 020 8516 2977
- ☎ 020 8516 2978
- ✉ query@booktrust.org.uk
- 🌐 www.booktrust.org.uk

Contact Chief Executive, Viv Bird

About Booktrust is an independent national charity that encourages people of all ages and cultures to engage with book and the written word. It administers seven book prizes, including the Orange Prize for Fiction. It has many ongoing projects that promote reading, including the Children's Laureate.

BRAD

- ☎ 020 7728 4326
- ☎ 020 7728 4800
- ✉ info@brad.co.uk
- 🌐 www.brad.co.uk

About BRAD is available in both print and online versions, and is one of the UK's leading media databases, providing statistics for newspapers, consumer and business press, radio, television, and new media.

BRAW

Scottish Book Trust, Sandeman House, Trunks Close, 55 High Street, Edinburgh, EH1 1SR

- ☎ 0131 524 0160
- ☎ 0131 524 0161

⊛ www.scottishbooktrust.com/info-about-braw-network

About BRAW (Books, Reading And Writing) is the national children's book network in Scotland. It aims to promote books, reading and writing, by authors and illustrators living in Scotland, to Scottish children and young people – whatever their particular circumstances may be. BRAW's priority is to reach children and young people in areas of social deprivation, with the aim of increasing their literacy skills.

The British Academy
10 Carlton House Terrace, London, SW1Y 5AH
- 020 7969 5200
- 020 7969 5300
- r.jackson@britac.ac.uk
- www.britac.ac.uk

Contact Chief Executive & Secretary, Robin Jackson
About The British Academy is the national academy for the humanities and the social sciences. It represents the interests of scholarship nationally and internationally, and promotes and supports research. It seeks to make research and scholarship more widely understood and appreciated. Every year it awards eight medals and prizes in specialist areas of learning and research.

The British Academy of Composers & Songwriters
26 Berners Street, London, W1T 3LR
- 020 7636 2929
- 020 7636 2212
- Online form.
- www.britishacademy.com

Contact CEO, Patrick Rackow; Membership Manager, Vicky Hunt
About The 'voice' of all UK composers and songwriters, the BAC&S campaigns to protect the value of copyright, and to create a better environment in which music writers can flourish. It is the home of the prestigious Ivor Novello and British Composer Awards, celebrating excellence in contemporary songwriting and composing.

British Association of Communicators in Business
Suite GA2, Oak House, Woodlands Business Park, Linford Wood, Milton Keynes, MK14 6EY
- 01908 313755
- 01908 313661
- enquiries@cib.uk.com
- www.cib.uk.com

Contact Chief Executive, Kathie Jones; Membership Manager, Tim Beynon

About The British Association of Communicators in Business (CiB) is a professional body for in-house, freelance and agency staff involved in internal and corporate communications.

The British Association of Journalists
89 Fleet Street, London, EC4Y 1DH
- 020 7353 3003
- 020 7353 2310
- office@bajunion.org.uk
- www.bajunion.org.uk

Contact General Secretary, Steve Turner
About A non-political, industrial union for journalists which seeks to protect and improve pay, conditions, pensions and fees for its members. It seeks to defend and promote freedom of information.

The British Comparative Literature Association
c/o Penny Brown, Department of French Studies, University of Manchester, Oxford Road, Manchester, M13 9PL
- penny.brown@manchester.ac.uk
- www.bcla.org

Contact President, Gillian Beer; Secretary, Penny Brown
About The British Comparative Literature Association (BCLA) aims to promote the scholarly study of literature without confinement to national and linguistic boundaries, and in relation to other disciplines. The BCLA's primary interests are in literature, the contexts of literature and the interaction between literatures. It is primarily an academic organisation, one of its aims being to foster and make possible links between people involved in similar research areas.

The British Copyright Council
29–33 Berners Street, London, W1T 3AB
- 01986 788122
- 01986 788847
- secretary@britishcopyright.org
- www.britishcopyright.org

Contact Chairman, Paul Mitchell
About The British Copyright Council is an umbrella organisation bringing together organisations which represent those who create, or hold rights in literary, dramatic, musical and artistic works, and those who perform such works. It functions principally as a liaison committee for its member associations, providing them with a forum for the discussion of matters of copyright interest.

The British Council

10 Spring Gardens, London, SW1A 2BN

☎ 0161 957 7755

☎ 0161 957 7762

✉ general.enquiries@britishcouncil.org

🌐 www.britishcouncil.org

Contact Director General, Sir David Green

About The British Council is the UK's international organisation for educational opportunities and cultural relations. Its purpose is to build mutually beneficial relationships between people in the UK and other countries, and to increase appreciation of the UK's creative ideas and achievements. For writers, this might mean your book or ideas being promoted, perhaps in one of the Council's exhibitions or publications, or in one of its libraries. See the website for details.

The British Fantasy Society

23 Mayne Street, Hanford, Stoke on Trent, ST4 4RF

🌐 www.britishfantasysociety.org.uk

Contact President, Ramsey Campbell; Chair, Guy Adams

About The British Fantasy Society exists to promote the genres of fantasy, science fiction and horror in all their forms. It has an active and enthusiastic membership, and runs a number of well-respected awards.

British Guild of Beer Writers

Woodcote, 2 Jury Road, Dulverton, Somerset, TA22 9DU

☎ 01398 324314

✉ tierneyjones@btinternet.com

🌐 www.beerwriters.co.uk

Contact Chairman, Tim Hampson; Hon. Secretary, Adrian Tierney-Jones

About The British Guild of Beer Writers was formed in 1988 to improve standards of beer writing and extend the public knowledge of beer. Its 130 members cover every aspect of beer, from making to drinking; their details can be found on the website.

British Guild of Travel Writers

5 Berwick Courtyard, Berwick St Leonard, Salisbury, Wiltshire, SP3 5UA

☎ 1747 820455

☎ 020 8975 2801

✉ info@bgtw.org

🌐 www.bgtw.org

Contact Chairman, John Carter

About Founded in 1960, The Guild of Travel Writers is an association of nearly 300 writers, editors, photographers, producers, radio and television presenters involved in the world of travel. Their Yearbook – available via the website – is an invaluable tool for all involved in travel writing and travel publishing.

The British Haiku Society

38 Wayside Avenue, Hornchurch, Essex, RM12 4LL

🌐 www.haikusoc.ndo.co.uk

Contact Membership Secretary, Stanley Pelter

About The BHS seeks to promote and encourage haiku in as many ways and in as many places as possible, including in education. The society has a journal which members can contribute to, and it has several prizes for haiku. Its 300 members are linked to similar organisations throughout the world.

British Society of Magazine Editors

137 Hale Lane, Edgware, Middlesex, HA8 9QP

☎ 020 8906 4664

✉ admin@bsme.com

🌐 www.bsme.com

Contact Administrator, Gill Branston

About The BSME aims to represent the needs and views of all UK magazine editors, and enhance their status, acting as a voice for the industry.

Broadcasting Press Guild

☎ 01483 764895

☎ 01483 765882

✉ sc@broadcastingpressguild.org

🌐 www.broadcastingpressguild.org

Contact Chairman, Neil Midgley; Membership Secretary, Steve Clarke

About The Broadcasting Press Guild is an association of journalists who specialise in writing and broadcasting about television, radio and the media generally. Membership is by invitation only.

Broadcast Journalism Training Council

18 Miller's Close, Rippingale, Nr. Bourne, Lincolnshire, PE10 0TH

☎ 01778 440025

✉ sec@bjtc.org.uk

🌐 www.bjtc.org.uk

Contact Secretary, Jim Latham

About The BJTC is a partnership of all the main employers in the UK broadcast industry - three departments of the BBC (News, Nations and Regions and Training), ITV News Group, ITN, IRN, Sky News, C4, Reuters, GCap Media News, RadioCentre, the NUJ and Skillset, the Sector Skills Council for the audio-visual industries. The BJTC exists to improve the skills and knowledge across the Broadcast Journalism industry. They set the criteria for course accreditation and then send teams of professional journalists and tutors to inspect courses and provide advice.

Campaign for Press & Broadcasting Freedom
2nd Floor, Vi & Garner Smith House, 23 Orford Road, Walthamstow, London, E17 9NL
- 020 8521 5932
- freepress@cpbf.org.uk
- www.cpbf.org.uk

Contact National Organiser, Barry White
About The CPBF campaigns to defend the principles of public service broadcasting, and to argue for democratically accountable forms of broadcasting regulation, which actively promote and encourage high programme standards and genuine cultural diversity.

Careers Writers' Association
16 Caewal Road, Llandaff, Cardiff, CF5 2BT
- 029 2056 3444
- 029 2065 8190
- helen.scott@btinternet.com
- www.careerswriting.co.uk

Contact Adminstrator, Alison Dixon
About The Careers Writers' Association works to achieve high standards of careers writing, to improve access to sources of such information, to forge links with organisations sharing related interests, and to provide a network for members to exchange information and experience. Membership is only open to writers with an established reputation for providing objective and up to date careers information. Many members draw on expertise gained as specialist information providers in careers services, as employment researchers, or as careers consultants to the national press.

Centerprise Literature Development Project
136–138 Kingsland High Street, London, E8 2NS
- 020 7254 9632
- literature@centerprisetrust.org.uk
- www.centerprisetrust.org.uk

Contact Administrator, Susan Yearwood
About Centerprise Literature is an arts development agency for the promotion of access to, and enjoyment of, literature in all its forms, through local and community based initiatives. Centerprise Literature serves North and North East London with two parallel programmes of work. Its core programme focuses on providing a through-line of support for writers by offering courses, specialist groups, and one-on-one support. Their magazine, *Calabash*, has a high reputation, focusing on Black and Asian literature. They also run the Hackney Word Festival.

Chartered Institute of Journalists
2 Dock Offices, Surrey Quays Road, London, SE16 2XU
- 020 7252 1187
- 020 7232 2302
- memberservices@cioj.co.uk
- www.cioj.co.uk

Contact President, John Thorpe; General Secretary, Dominic Cooper
About The Chartered Institute of Journalists combines the role of professional society with that of a trade union – known as the IoJ (TU). The Institute's union section protects its members' interests in the workplace and campaigns for better conditions for working journalists. The Institute's professional side is concerned with the standards and ethics of the media, the protection of journalistic freedom, and training, and also administers the Institute's many charities.

CILIP
7 Ridgmount Street, London, WC1E 7AE
- 020 7255 0500
- 020 7255 0501
- info@cilip.org.uk
- www.cilip.org.uk

Contact Chief Executive, Bob McKee
About CILIP (the Chartered Institute of Library & Information Professionals) is the leading professional body for librarians, information specialists and knowledge managers. CILIP provides practical support for members throughout their entire careers, helping them with their academic education, professional qualifications, job hunting and continuing professional development.

Circle of Wine Writers
c/o Scots Firs, 70 Joiners Lane, Chalfont St Peter, Buckinghamshire, SL9 0AU
- 01753 882320
- 01753 882320
- administrator@winewriters.org
- www.winewriters.org

Contact President, Steven Spurrier; Circle Administrator, Andrea Warren
About The Circle of Wine Writers is an association of authors, broadcasters, journalists, photographers and lecturers who are professionally engaged in communicating about wines and spirits. It aims to improve the standard of communication about wines, spirits and beers, and to contribute to the growing knowledge and interest in wine.

Classical Association

Senate House, Malet Street, London, WC1E 7HU
- 020 7862 8706
- 020 7862 8729
- office@classicalassociation.org
- www.classicalassociation.org

Contact Secretary, Clare Roberts
About The Classical Association is the largest classical organisation in Great Britain. It has a worldwide membership, and unites the interests of all who value the study of the languages, literature and civilisation of ancient Greece and Rome. The CA website has a database of all classicists in UK universities.

Copyright Licensing Agency (CLA)

Saffron House, 6–10 Kirby Street, London, EC1N 8TS
- 020 7400 3100
- 020 7400 3101
- cla@cla.co.uk
- www.cla.co.uk

Contact Chief Executive & Company Secretary, Peter F. Shepherd
About The CLA (Copyright Licensing Agency) is the pivotal organisation in the UK for the licensing of re-use, reproduction and copying of copyrighted materials in books, journals, magazines and periodicals. It pays authors and publishers for such use through ALCS, DACS and PLS (see relevant entries). The CLA's website explains its various roles in depth, and has a valuable section on copyright that will be of use to all writers.

Crime Writer's Association

- 07780 693144 (press only)
- info@thecwa.co.uk
- www.thecwa.co.uk

Contact Chair, Lesley Horton; Membership Secretary, Rebecca Tope
About The Crime Writer's Association has over 450 members. The minimum qualification for membership is to have at least one published book with a crime theme. The CWA is best known for its various 'Dagger' awards for crime fiction.

The Critics Circle

c/o William Russell, 50 Finland Road, Brockley, London, SE4 2JH
- 020 7732 9636
- williamfinland@gmail.com
- www.criticscircle.org.uk

Contact President, Charles Spencer; Hon. General Secretary, William Russell

About The Critics Circle aims to promote the art of criticism, to uphold its integrity in practice, to foster and safeguard members' professional interests, to provide opportunities to meet, and to support the advancement of the arts. Membership to the Circle is by invitation only. It give awards in five categories each year; Dance, Art & Architecture, Drama, Film and Music, as well as the prestigious Critics Circle Annual Award.

Data Publishers Association

Queens House, 28 Kingsway, London, WC2B 6JR
- 020 7405 0836
- 020 7404 4167
- info@dpa.org.uk
- www.dpa.org.uk

Contact Chairman, Jerry Gosney
About The Data Publishers Association (DPA) is the industry body representing data and directory publishers in the UK. Its role is to protect and promote the interests of the industry, both in print and electronic media.

Digital Content Forum

131–151 Great Titchfield Street, London, W1W 5BB
- 020 7665 8440
- info@dcf.org.uk
- www.dcf.org.uk

Contact Chairman, Michael Rawlinson; Policy & Communications Manager, Simon Sauntson
About The DCF's own mission statement says: 'The DCF forms a two-way conduit between industry and government to gather views and input into policy-making processes. It goes further to broker relationships, develop shared knowledge and undertake activities to promote innovation and excellence in the content sector.' For writers, its main use will be the news, reports and information on all aspects of digital content on its website. The site also has useful links to official bodies and quangos.

EBU

L'Ancienne-Route 17A, CH-1218 Grand-Saconnex, Switzerland
- 0041 22 717 2111
- 0041 22 747 4000
- ebu@ebu.ch
- www.ebu.ch

Contact Secretary General, Jean Réveillon
About The European Broadcasting Union (EBU) is the largest professional association of national broadcasters in the world. Working on behalf of its members in the European area, it negotiates broadcasting rights for major sports events, operates the Eurovision and Euroradio networks, organises

programme exchanges, stimulates and co-ordinates co-productions, and provides a full range of other operational, commercial, technical, legal and strategic services.

English Association
University of Leicester, University Road, Leicester, LE1 7RH, UK
- 0116 252 3982
- 0116 252 2301
- engassoc@le.ac.uk
- www.le.ac.uk/engassoc

Contact President, Professor Peter J. Kitson; Chair, Professor Maureen Moran; Administrator, Julia Hughes

About The aim of the English Association is to further knowledge, understanding and enjoyment of the English language and its literatures, and to foster good practice in its teaching and learning at all levels. Based at the University of Leicester, the Association awards four prizes a year in specialist areas, and organises and participates in academic conferences.

English PEN
6–8 Amwell Street, London, EC1R 1UQ
- 020 7713 0023
- 020 7837 7838
- enquiries@englishpen.org
- www.englishpen.org

Contact President, Lisa Appignanesi; Director, Jonathan Heawood

About English PEN exists to work with, and fight for, the rights of writers throughout the world who are persecuted or imprisoned because of their writing. In the UK, English PEN campaigns to improve the understanding of freedom of expression as a fundamental human right.

The English-Speaking Union
Dartmouth House, 37 Charles Street, London, W1J 5ED
- 020 7529 1550
- 020 7495 6108
- esu@esu.org
- www.esu.org

Contact Director General, Valerie Mitchell; Secretarial Assistant, Anne Hamilton

About The English-Speaking Union is an international educational charity founded in 1918 to promote 'international understanding and friendship through the use of the English language.' With almost 40 branches in the UK, and over 50 international branches in countries in every part of the world, the ESU's mission is to bring people together and share their experiences. It is this network that writers may find of value.

The Fabian Society
11 Dartmouth Street, London, SW1H 9BN
- 020 7227 4900
- info@fabians.org.uk
- www.fabian-society.org.uk

Contact Editorial Director, Tom Hampson

About The Fabian Society plays an important role in the development of political ideas and public policy on the left of centre. Analysing the challenges facing the UK and the rest of the industrialised world in a changing society and global economy, the Society's programme aims to explore the political ideas and the policy reforms which will define progressive politics in the new century. The Fabian Society is a democratically constituted membership organisation. It is affiliated to the Labour Party but is editorially and organisationally independent. Through its publications, seminars and conferences, the Society provides an arena for open-minded public debate.

FACT
Europa House, Church Street, Old Isleworth, Middlesex, TW7 6DA
- 020 8568 6646
- 020 8560 6364
- contact@fact-uk.org.uk
- www.fact-uk.org.uk

About The Federation Against Copyright Theft is the leading UK representative trade body committed to protecting the interests of the industry in the fight against pirate film and DVDs, and the increasing threat from online piracy.

Fellowship of Authors & Artists
PO Box 158, Hertford, SG13 8FA
- 01992 511697
- 0870 116 3398
- Online form.
- www.author-fellowship.co.uk

Contact Graham Irwin

About The stated aims of the Fellowship are to promote and encourage the use of writing and all art forms as a means of therapy and self-healing, and to publish as web pages or ebooks any suitable works that may help to support or promote these aims. They also have a list of useful online information and links to websites for authors and artists.

The Folklore Society

The Warburg Institute, Woburn Square, London, WC1H 0AB
- ☎ 020 7862 8564
- ✉ enquiries@folklore-society.com
- 🌐 www.folklore-society.com

Contact President, Dr Eddie Cass; Secretary, Prof. James H. Grayson

About The Folklore Society's interest and expertise covers topics such as traditional music, song, dance and drama, narrative, arts and crafts, customs and belief. It is also interested in popular religion, traditional and regional food, folk medicine, children's folklore, traditional sayings, proverbs rhymes and jingles. It aims to foster folklore research and recording worldwide, and to make the results of such study available to all, whether members of the Society or not. The Society publishes a journal, *Folklore*, and the links to other folklore sites on its website are essential for anyone interested in this area of research.

The Football Writers' Association

- 🌐 www.footballwriters.co.uk

About The FWA aims to obtain higher standards of facilities for football correspondents and journalists. Membership is by invitation only for working journalists who are accredited football correspondents for newspapers or agencies. Contact via the website.

The Garden Media Guild

Katepwa House, Ashfield Park Avenue, Ross-on-Wye, Herefordshire, HR9 5AX
- ☎ 01989 567393
- ✉ info@gardenmediaguild.co.uk
- 🌐 www.gardenmediaguild.co.uk

Contact Membership Administrator, Gill Hinton

About The Garden Media Guild's aims are to raise the quality of garden writing, photography broadcasting and editing, and keep members up-to-date with what's going on in the world of gardening and horticulture. Its awards, presented at an annual lunch, are the 'Oscars' of the UK's gardening communication industry.

Guild of Agricultural Journalists

c/o Woodcote Communications, 14 Clarice Way, Wallington, Surrey, SM6 9LD
- ☎ 020 8669 0686
- ☎ 020 8669 3678
- ✉ lindym@woodcote-communications.co.uk
- 🌐 www.gaj.org.uk

Contact Chairman, Joe Watson; General Secretary, Don Gomery; Membership Secretary, Lindy Margach

About The Guild of Agricultural Journalists represents more than 500 journalists and media specialists working in the agricultural industry. Members range from agricultural and environmental correspondents, to specialists writing for industry magazines, plus the in-house and agency PR and marketing managers of companies and organisations supporting British agriculture.

Guild of Food Writers

255 Kent House Road, Beckenham, Kent, BR3 1JQ
- ☎ 020 8659 0422
- ✉ guild@gfw.co.uk
- 🌐 www.gfw.co.uk

Contact Administrator, Jonathan Woods

About The Guild represents professional food writers and broadcasters in the UK. It has over 370 authors, columnists, freelance journalists and broadcasters amongst its members.

Guild of Health Writers

Dale Lodge, 88 Wensleydale Road, Hampton, Middlesex, TW12 2LX
- ☎ 020 8941 2977
- ✉ admin@healthwriters.com
- 🌐 www.healthwriters.com

Contact Acting Chair, Paul Dinsdale; Hon. Secretary, Judy Hobson

About The Guild of Health Writers is a national, independent membership organisation representing Britain's leading health journalists and writers. It was founded to encourage the provision of readable and accurate health information to the public. Members write on every aspect of health and well-being, from innovative medical science, to complementary therapies and lifestyle issues. Membership of the Guild brings access to training, networking opportunities and a forum for balanced debate.

Guild of Motoring Writers

40 Baring Road, Bournemouth, Dorset, BH6 4DT
- ☎ 01202 422424
- ☎ 01202 422424
- ✉ generalsec@gomw.co.uk
- 🌐 www.guildofmotoringwriters.co.uk

Contact General Secretary, Patricia Lodge

About The UK's professional body for motoring journalists and writers. It has over 400 members, including daily and regional newspaper correspondents, magazine writers, book publishers, photographers, and radio and television broadcasters.

Harleian Society

College of Arms, Queen Victoria Street, London, EC4V 4BT

- info@harleian.co.uk
- www.harleian.co.uk

Contact Chairman, Thomas Woodcock; Hon. Secretary & Treasurer, Timothy Duke

About The Society's official objectives are 'the transcribing, printing and publishing of the heraldic visitations of counties, parish registers or any manuscripts relating to genealogy, family history and heraldry'. The Society is unable to provide any services, apart from the sale of volumes either by annual subscription or individual purchase. It cannot help with research queries. It does, however, have a useful links page.

Historical Novel Society

- richard@historicalnovelsociety.org
- www.historicalnovelsociety.org

Contact Founder/Publisher, Richard Lee

About The Historical Novel Society promotes all aspects of historical fiction. It provides support and opportunities for new writers, information for students, booksellers and librarians, as well as a community for authors, readers, agents and publishers. The society publishes the quarterly *Historical Novels Review* magazine.

HoldtheFrontPage

AN Digital, Northcliffe House, Meadow Road, Derby, Derby, DE1 2BH

- 01332 228020
- editor.htfp@and.co.uk
- www.holdthefrontpage.co.uk

Contact Acting Publisher, Paul Linford; Reporter, Tamlyn Jones

About A website for journalists and journalism students. HoldtheFrontPage is editorially independent and all-inclusive, writing about the smallest free weekly papers and the biggest regional dailies. For those who are working, or want to work, in the regional press, this is a place to find out more about the industry. It offers news stories about what is happening in the regional press, information on campaigning journalism, and updates on breaking news. It has full details of job vacancies in the industry and a range of articles about breaking into journalism.

Horror Writers Association UK

- hwa@horror.org
- www.horror.org/uk

About The Horror Writers Association UK is the UK chapter of the Horror Writers Association, a worldwide organisation of writers and publishing professionals. The Society is dedicated to the pursuit of professional conduct within the industry, and to creating quality horror literature. Please note that the email contact given is to the HWA central US site.

Institute of Copywriting

Overbrook Business Centre, Poolbridge Road, Blackford, Wedmore, Somerset, BS28 4PA

- 0800 781 1715
- 01934 713492
- copy@inst.org
- www.inst.org/copy

About In operation since 1998, the Institute serves the needs of people who are, or who want to become, copywriters. It also offers courses and qualifications in copywriting.

The Institute of Linguists

Saxon House, 48 Southwark Street, London, SE1 1UN

- 020 7940 3100
- 020 7940 3101
- info@iol.org.uk
- www.iol.org.uk

Contact Chief Executive, John Hammond; Director of Membership, Alan Peacock

About The Chartered Institute of Linguists serves the interests of professional linguists throughout the world, and acts as a language assessment and accredited awarding body. It aims to promote the learning and use of modern languages, improve the status of all professional linguists, and ensure professional standards among language practitioners through its code of conduct. Founded in 1910, the Institute now has around 6,500 Fellows, Members and Associate Members.

The Institute of Translators & Interpreting

Fortuna House, South Fifth Street, Milton Keynes, MK9 2EU

- 01908 325250
- 01908 325259
- info@iti.org.uk
- www.iti.org.uk

Contact Administration, Madeline Stewart

About The ITI was founded in 1986 as the only independent professional association of practising translators and interpreters in the United Kingdom. It is now one of the primary sources of information on these services to government, industry, the media and the general public. ITI aims to promote the highest standards in the profession, and serves as a meeting place for all those who understand the importance of translation and interpreting to the economy and society. It also offers guidance to those entering the profession and advice to those who offer language services.

International Publishers Association
3 Ave. de Miremont, 1206 Geneva, Switzerland
- ☎ 0041 22 346 3018
- ☎ 0041 22 347 5717
- ✉ secretariat@internationalpublishers.org
- ⊕ www.internationalpublishers.org

Contact Secretary General, Jens Bammel; Director, Freedom to Publish, Alexis Krikorian

About The IPA's aims are to uphold and defend the right of publishers to produce and distribute the works of the mind in complete freedom. It promotes and protects the principles of copyright, and works to overcome illiteracy and the lack of books and other education materials in the community. It has links to many other publishing organisations and international governing bodies and governments. Writers will find its website links useful in research.

International Travel Writers Alliance
Hampton House, 77 The Ridgeway, North Chingford, London, E4 6QW
- ☎ 020 8524 4089
- ✉ ashley@itwalliance.com
- ⊕ www.internationaltravelwritersalliance.com

Contact Director General, Ashley Gibbins

About The Alliance provides key information in a no frills format for professionals who travel to write, broadcast or create images. They also establish links between their members and publishing editors, agencies and other industry bodies.

Irish Book Publishers' Association
Guinness Enterprise Centre, Taylor's Lane, Dublin 8, Republic of Ireland
- ☎ 00353 1 415 1210
- ✉ info@publishingireland.com
- ⊕ www.publishingireland.com

Contact President, Seán Ó'Cearnaigh; Treasurer, Marie Maguire

About Cumann Leabharfhoilsitheoirí Éireann (CLÉ), the Irish Book Publisher's Association, is a cross-border organisation representing all publishers in Ireland. Its website is useful for writers as it provides information and links to Irish publishers, agents and publishing freelancers, and information about copyright and other issues.

The Irish Copyright Licensing Agency
25 Denzille Lane, Dublin 2, Republic of Ireland
- ☎ 00353 1 662 4211
- ☎ 00353 1 662 4213

- ✉ info@icla.ie
- ⊕ www.icla.ie

About The ICLA licenses the copying of extracts from books, journals and magazines protected by copyright in Ireland, the UK and 17 other countries.

Irish Playwrights & Screenwriters Guild
Art House, Curved Street, Temple Bar, Dublin 2, Republic of Ireland
- ☎ 00353 1 670 9970
- ✉ info@script.ie
- ⊕ www.script.ie

Contact Chair, Audrey O'Reilly; Chief Executive, David Kavanagh

About The Irish Playwrights & Screenwriters Guild is the representative body in Ireland for writers for the stage and screen. Full membership of the Guild is available to any writer who has contracted to write for payment in Ireland for the stage for screen including radio and the new media. Associate membership is also available for those who have not yet contracted.

Irish Translators & Interpreters Association
c/o Irish Writers' Centre, 19 Parnell Square, Dublin 1, Republic of Ireland
- ☎ 00353 87 673 8386
- ☎ 00353 1 872 6282
- ✉ itiasecretary@gmail.com
- ⊕ www.translatorsassociation.ie

Contact Chairperson, Annette Schiller; Secretary, Alison Boardman

About The Irish Translators & Interpreters Association (Cumann Aistritheoir' agus Teangair' na hÉireann) represents the interests of translators and interpreters in Ireland. It aims to promote the highest professional and ethical standards in translation and interpreting.

Irish Writers' Union
19 Parnell Square, Dublin 1, Republic of Ireland
- ☎ 00353 1 872 1302
- ✉ iwu@ireland-writers.com
- ⊕ www.ireland-writers.com

Contact Chair, Helen Dwyer; Secretary, Brid Quinn

About The Irish Writers' Union represents the interests of all Irish writers, whether they were born in Ireland or elsewhere. Writers who are Irish by attachment, inclination or persuasion, are also welcome to join. The Union offers a model contract for guidance to members, and assists in disputes if, or when, things go wrong. It also acts as a watchdog, on both contract and royalty payments, for members, or for their estate.

Kid's Own Publishing Partnership
Carrigeens, Ballinful, Co. Sligo, Republic of Ireland
- 00353 71 912 4945
- Online form.
- www.kidsown.ie

About Kids' Own is a non-profit arts organisation dedicated to raising the status of children's work as writers and artists to a wider audience. Kids' Own Publishing Partnership is Ireland's leading specialist in facilitating children to publish books through collaborative projects in partnership with schools, festivals, arts centres and other organisations. Does not accept manuscript submissions.

literaturetraining
PO Box 23595, Edinburgh, EH6 7YX
- 0131 553 2210
- info@literaturetraining.com
- www.literaturetraining.com

Contact Director, Philippa Johnston

About literaturetraining is the UK's only dedicated provider of free information and advice on professional development for the literature sector. It aims to help writers and literature professionals – at every stage of their career – to invest in themselves and their professional development, so that they can realise their full potential. Writers, and those involved in some way with creating or supporting new writing and literature, will find information on training and professional development opportunities on the website. If advice is needed on how to move forward professionally, literaturetraining can offer various forms of help.

The MCPS-PRS Alliance
Copyright House, 29–33 Berners Street, London, W1T 3AB
- 020 7580 5544
- 020 7306 4455
- publisherquery@mcps-prs-alliance.co.uk
- www.mcps-prs-alliance.co.uk

About The MCPS-PRS Alliance is a not-for-profit organisation which currently represents a community of over 50,000 composers, songwriters and music publishers. Its essential function is to collect and distribute royalties. It acts on behalf of its members by negotiating agreements with those who wish to record and distribute product containing copyright musical works, and collecting licence fees for this use. The money is subsequently distributed to its members as mechanical royalties. Also see the Performing Rights Society.

The Media Society
66 Lincoln's Inn Field, London, WC2A 3LH
- dorothy@themediasociety.co.uk
- www.themediasociety.co.uk

Contact President, Geraldine Sharpe-Newton; Administrator, Dorothy Josem

About The Media Society stands for freedom of expression and the encouragement of high standards in journalism. It is unique in bringing together people working in all branches of the media – radio, television production and broadcasting, newspapers and magazines, new media, academia and media law. Its membership includes both senior figures and those at the beginning of their careers.

mediawatch-uk
3 Willow House, Kennington Road, Ashford, Kent, TN24 0NR
- 01233 633936
- 01233 633836
- info@mediawatchuk.org
- www.mediawatchuk.org

Contact Director, John C. Beyer

About mediawatch-uk provides an independent voice for those concerned about issues of taste and decency in the media. It publishes newsletters and reports on the portrayal of violence, bad language and sexual conduct, briefings on film classification, content regulation, and the public interest.

Medical Journalists' Association
Red Door Communications, The Limes, 123 Mortlake High Street, London, SW14 8SN
- secretary@mja-uk.org
- www.mja-uk.org

Contact Membership Secretary, Rachel Vrettos

About The MJA exists to support and encourage its members and enable them to work efficiently and at high levels of accuracy. More than 400 of the UK's medical and health journalists belong to the MJA, making its website a point of contact for anyone wanting to employ a writer with specific expertise, or alert medical journalists to events or achievements that deserve publicity.

Music Publishers' Association
6th Floor, British Music House, 26 Berners Street, London, W1T 3LR
- 020 7580 0126
- 020 7637 3929
- info@mpaonline.org.uk
- www.mpaonline.org.uk

Contact Chief Executive, Stephen Navin; Administrator/PA, Mikki Francis

About The Music Publishers Association (MPA) looks after the interest of all music publishers based or working in the UK, and exists to safeguard and improve the business and legal environment within which its members are operating.

National Association for Literature Development
PO Box 49657, London, N8 7YZ
- 01753 714033
- director@nald.org
- www.nald.org

Contact Director, Melanie Abrahams; Administrator, Catherine McInerney
About NALD is the UK's largest membership organisation for literature professionals. It is the only national body for all those involved in developing writers, readers and literature audiences. It exists so that literature professionals can communicate with each other.

National Association of Press Agencies
c/o Mercury Press Agency, Unit 218, Century Buildings, Tower Street, Liverpool, L3 4BJ
- 0870 609 1935
- enquiries@napa.org.uk
- www.napa.org.uk

About NAPA is an umbrella organisation covering press agencies throughout the UK. Its members adhere to a code of conduct. Its website provides links by region and field of interest for those who may wish to contact them with a story.

National Association of Writers in Education (NAWE)
PO Box 1, Sheriff Hutton, York, YO60 7YU
- 01653 618429
- paul@nawe.co.uk
- www.nawe.co.uk

Contact Director, Paul Munden
About NAWE aims to support the development of creative writing of all genres and in all educational and community settings throughout the UK. The website provides extensive information and links for all interested in this field, including a database of funding opportunities, and as part of its Higher Education Network, a list of all writing courses in UK higher education.

National Centre for Research in Childern's Literature
School of Arts, Digby Stuart College, Roehampton University, Roehampton Lane, London, SW15 5PH
- 020 8392 3008
- 020 8392 3000
- ncrcl@roehampton.ac.uk
- www.ncrcl.ac.uk

About A research centre within the School of Arts at Roehampton University, the NCRCL works to research the whole area of children's literature. It has PhD students, runs an MA, and holds conferences. Writers will find the links on its website of use.

National Literacy Trust
68 South Lambeth Road, London, SW8 1RL
- 020 7587 1842
- 020 7931 9986
- sam.brookes@literacytrust.org.uk
- www.literacytrust.org.uk

Contact Director, Jonathan Douglas; Trust Administrator, Jacky Taylor
About The National Literacy Trust is an independent charity that changes lives through literacy. It has a vision of a society in which everyone has the reading, writing, speaking and listening skills that they need to fulfil their own and, ultimately, the nation's potential. The National Literacy Trust links home, school and the wider community to inspire learners and create opportunities for everyone. It supports those who work with learners through innovative programmes, information and research and brings together key organisations to lead literacy promotion in the UK. Among its campaigns are: Reading is Fundamental UK, the National Reading Campaign, Talk to Your Baby, Reading the Game, Reading Connects, and the Vital Link. Results of research into specific areas of concern to do with literacy can be found on the website. The site also provides a rich range of resources to help with reading, and it also links to many other organisations.

National Union of Journalists
Headland House, 308–312 Gray's Inn Road, London, WC1X 8DP
- 020 7278 7916
- 020 7837 8143
- info@nuj.org.uk
- www.nuj.org.uk

Contact General Secretary, Jeremy Dear
About The NUJ has been Britain and Ireland's leading trades union for journalists of all sorts since 1907. Members cover a wide range of editorial work – staff and freelance, writers and reporters, editors and sub-editors, photographers and illustrators, working in broadcasting, newspapers, magazines, books, on the internet and in public relations. See the website for a full list of regional staff contacts.

The Newspaper Society

8th Floor, St Andrew's House, 18–20 St Andrew Street, London, EC4A 3AY

● 020 7632 7400

● 020 7632 7401

● ns@newspapersoc.org.uk

● www.newspapersoc.org.uk

Contact Director, David Newell

About The Newspaper Society represents and promotes the interests of Britain's regional and local press, who between them own over 1,300 daily and weekly, paid-for and free newspaper titles. It was founded in 1836 and is believed to be the oldest publishers' association in the world. Its services are split into three broad areas: lobbying, marketing and communications. It provides legal advice and lobbying services to regional newspaper publishers and their staff, and also to the national newspaper, magazine and distribution industries. It promotes the regional press as a medium to national advertisers and agencies. It holds a series of conferences and seminars and runs the annual Local Newspaper Week.

New Writing North

Culture Lab, Grand Assembly Rooms, Newcastle University, King's Walk, Newcastle upon Tyne, NE1 7RU

● 0191 222 1332

● 0191 222 1372

● mail@newwritingnorth.com

● www.newwritingnorth.com

About New Writing North (NWN) is the writing development agency for the North East of England (the area covered by Arts Council England North East). It aims to create an environment in which new writing in all genres can flourish and develop. It merges individual development work from writers across all media, with educational work and the production of creative projects. It works with writers from different genres and forms to develop career opportunities, new commissions, projects, residencies, publications and live events. NWN manage the Northern Writers' Awards and the Northern Rock Foundation Writer's Award, and also aims to support writers at all stages of their careers through mentoring programmes and the creation of professional development training initiatives and projects.

New Writing South

9 Jew Street, Brighton, East Sussex, BN1 1UT

● 01273 735353

● enquiries@newwritingsouth.com

● www.newwritingsouth.com

About A writing organisation open to all creative writers in the South East of England, and also for those seeking creative writers and for other creative writing agencies, including all producers of dramatic writing. Sister organisation of New Writing North.

New Zealand Book Council

Level 7, Alan Burns Insurances House, 69 Boulcott Street, Wellington 6011, New Zealand

● 0064 4 499 1569

● 0064 4 499 1424

● admin@bookcouncil.org.nz

● www.bookcouncil.org.nz

Contact Chief Executive, Noel Murphy

About The New Zealand Book Council is a not-for-profit organisation that presents a wide range of programmes promoting a love of books and reading. They run a comprehensive website and publish a quarterly magazine called *Booknotes*. The Book Council also runs educational projects with children in schools and has the largest online database of New Zealand writers, which is used by researchers, journalists, students and publishers.

Northern Ireland Publications Resource

Belfast Central Library, Royal Avenue, Belfast, BT1 1EA

● 028 9024 2740

● 028 9033 2819

● info@nibooks.org

● www.nibooks.org

● Contact

● Project Manager, Monica McErlane

About NIPR is an initiative sponsored by the Library & Information Services Council (Northern Ireland) with funding from the Department of Culture, Arts and Leisure (DCAL). It aims to acquire and preserve every book, pamphlet, periodical and report published in Northern Ireland since January 2000 and create an accompanying bibliography.

Outdoor Writers' Guild

PO Box 520, Bamber Bridge, Preston, Lancashire, PR5 8LF

● 01772 321243

● 0870 137 8888

● secretary@owg.org.uk

● www.owg.org.uk

About The Outdoor Writers' Guild is open to writers, journalists, photographers, illustrators, broadcasters, film-makers, artists, publishers and editors who are actively and professionally involved in sustainable activities in any outdoor setting. The Guild is an important link between the outdoor trade and the public, and offers a wide range of services to meet the needs of editors, publishers, public relations companies and picture researchers.

Pact
3rd Floor, Fitzrovia House, 153-157 Cleveland Street, London, W1T 6QR
- 020 7067 4367
- 020 7067 4377
- enquiries@pact.co.uk
- www.pact.co.uk

Contact Chief Executive, John McVay
About Pact is the UK trade association that represents and promotes the commercial interests of independent feature film, television, animation, and interactive media companies. It negotiates terms of trade with all public service broadcasters in the UK and supports members in their business dealings with cable and satellite channels.

Periodical Publishers Association
Queens House, 28 Kingsway, London, WC2B 6JR
- 020 7404 4166
- 020 7404 4167
- www.ppa.co.uk

Contact Chief Executive, Jonathan Shephard; Chief Executive PPA Ireland, Grace Aungier
About PPA is the association for publishers and providers of consumer, customer and business media in the UK. PPA's role is to promote and protect the interests of the industry in general, and member companies in particular.

The Personal Managers' Association Ltd
PO Box 63819, London, N1P 1HL
- 0845 602 7191
- info@thepma.com
- www.thepma.com

About The PMA is the professional association of agents representing UK based actors, writers, producers, directors, designers and technicians in the film, television and theatre industries.

Press Complaints Commission
Halton House, 20–23 Holborn, London, EC1N 2JD
- 020 7831 0022
- 020 7831 0025
- complaints@pcc.org.uk
- www.pcc.org.uk

About If you have a complaint about a newspaper or magazine in the UK, this is the place to register that complaint. Visit the website to learn more.

Public Lending Right
Richard House, Sorbonne Close, Stockton-on-Tees, TS17 6DA
- 01642 604699
- 01642 615641
- www.plr.uk.com

About Under the United Kingdom's PLR Scheme authors receive payments from government funds for the free borrowing of their books from public libraries. To qualify for payment, authors must apply to register their books with the PLR organisation. Payments are made annually on the basis of loans data collected from a sample of public libraries in the UK. All authors can benefit from this; indeed, books that may not necessarily have been successes in the high street might earn pleasant fees from library borrowing over time. Most writers would be advised to register their titles for PLR.

The Publishers Association
29b Montague Street, London, WC1B 5BW
- 020 7691 9191
- 020 7691 9199
- mail@publishers.org.uk
- www.publishers.org.uk

Contact Chief Executive, Simon Juden; Director of Educational, Academic & Professional Publishing, Graham Taylor
About The Publishers Association is the leading organisation working on behalf of book, journal and electronic publishers based in the UK. It brings publishers together to discuss the issues facing the industry, and to define the practical policies which will drive lobbying and campaigns in the UK and internationally. The aim of The Publishers Association is to ensure a secure future for the UK publishing industry.

Publishers Licensing Society Ltd (PLS)
37–41 Gower Street, London, WC1E 6HH
- 020 7299 7730
- 020 7299 7780
- pls@pls.org.uk
- www.pls.org.uk

Contact Chief Executive, Alicia Wise
About Together with ALCS and CLA (see entries) PLS manages the collective licensing of reprography in the UK. To do this, PLS needs agreement from publisher rights owners to authorise CLA to operate its licensing schemes. CLA offers licences to institutions and individuals who want to photocopy parts of copyright works. The money collected from these licences, after deduction of costs, is shared between PLS and ALCS. These societies then have a responsibility for distributing that share fairly to their rights owner members. CLA licenses educational,

business and government sectors to copy parts of works. Most of the licences are blanket licences. Users pay an annual fee determined on the basis of the number of full time equivalent students, or employees, that are in the organisation.

Publisher's Publicity Circle
65 Airedale Avenue, London, W4 2NN
- 020 8994 1881
- ppc-@lineone.net
- www.publisherspublicitycircle.co.uk

About The Publisher's Publicity Circle exists to enable all book publicists from publishing houses and freelance PR agencies to gather and share information on a regular basis. Monthly meetings are held in central London to provide a forum for press journalists, television and radio researchers, and producers to meet publicists collectively. Representatives from the media are invited to speak about the ways in which they can feature authors and their books, and how book publicists can most effectively provide relevant information and material. The PPC website has a directory of publicists, both in publishing houses and freelance.

Publishing Scotland
Scottish Book Centre, 137 Dundee Street, Edinburgh, EH11 1BG
- 0131 228 6866
- 0131 228 3220
- enquiries@publishingscotland.org
- www.publishingscotland.co.uk

Contact Director, Marion Sinclair; Information & Professional Development, Joan Lyle
About Publishing Scotland, previously The Scottish Publishers Association, is the network, trade and development body representing over 100 Scottish publishers and individuals allied to the industry. It does not publish books, but works to help its members with training, seminars, events, book fair support and the marketing of their books to the widest possible readership within the UK and overseas.

The Radio Academy
5 Market Place, London, W1W 8AE
- 020 7927 9920
- 020 7636 8924
- trevor@radioacademy.org
- www.radioacademy.org

Contact Director, Trevor Dann
About The Radio Academy is dedicated to the encouragement, recognition and promotion of excellence in UK broadcasting and audio production. It represents the radio industry to outside bodies including the government, and offers neutral ground where everyone - from the national networks to individual podcasters - is encouraged to discuss the broadcasting, production, marketing and promotion of radio and audio.

The Romantic Novelists' Association
Venue: Regular meetings held at The New Cavendish Club, 44 Great Cumberland Place, London, W1H 8BS
- 01342 323991
- eabailey@tiscali.co.uk
- www.rna-uk.org

Contact President, Diane Pearson; Hon. Secretary, Evelyn Ryle; Chairman, Catherine Jones; Press Officer, Liz Bailey
About The RNA works to enhance and promote the various types of romantic and historical fiction, to encourage good writing in all its many varieties, to learn more about the craft and help readers enjoy it. Membership of the association now stands at almost 700. A scheme for appraisal of manuscripts (see website), is an important element in helping unpublished writers to achieve first publication. See the RNA website for details, dates and contact information.

The Royal Literary Fund
3 Johnson's Court, off Fleet Street, London, EC4A 3EA
- 020 7353 7159
- egunnrlf@globalnet.co.uk
- www.rlf.org.uk

Contact General Secretary, Eileen Gunn
About The Royal Literary Fund is a benevolent fund for professional, published authors in financial difficulties. It has been continuously helping authors since it was set up in 1790. It is funded by bequests and donations from writers who wish to help other writers. Its committee members come from all walks of literary life and include novelists, biographers, poets, publishers, lawyers and agents. Help is given to writers in many different situations where personal or professional setbacks have resulted in loss of income. Pensions are considered for older writers who have seen their earnings decrease. The RLF also runs a Fellowship scheme for writers in partnership with British universities and colleges. Writers are appointed as Fellows based on their literary merit and aptitude for the role, irrespective of their financial circumstances.

The Royal Society of Literature
Somerset House, Strand, London, WC2R 1LA
- 020 7845 4676
- info@rslit.org
- www.rslit.org

Contact President, Michael Holroyd; Chair, Anne Chisholm

About The Royal Society of Literature is entirely devoted to the promotion and enjoyment of excellence in British writing. Founded in 1820, past and present Fellows (who are elected) include some of the most eminent names in British literature. Membership is open to all. Regular meetings with speakers from the world of literature are held at Somerset House; and members of the public are welcome. The society also has major annual awards for both fiction and non-fiction. It supports the work of writers in many ways, including campaigning for libraries to remain providers of good books above all else, and to keep English literature at the heart of the learning curriculum.

Royal Television Society

5th Floor, Kildare House, 3 Dorset Rise, London, EC4Y 8EN

- 020 7822 2810
- 020 7822 2811
- info@rts.org.uk
- www.rts.org.uk

Contact Chief Executive, Simon Albury; Office Administrator/Receptionist, Lucy Martin

About The Royal Television Society is the leading forum for discussion and debate on all aspects of the television community. With a full calendar of events, dinners, meetings, talks, awards and ceremonies, it provides unrivalled opportunities for learning and getting in contact with people at all levels across the television community.

Science Fiction Foundation

75 Rosslyn Avenue, Harold Wood, Essex, RM3 0RG

- www.sf-foundation.org

Contact Roger Robinson

About The aim of the SFF is to promote science fiction and bring together those who read, write, study, teach, research or archive science fiction in Britain and the rest of the world. It also supports science fiction at conventions, at conferences and at other events which bring those interested in science fiction together. The four main objectives of the SFF are: to provide research facilities for anyone wishing to study science fiction; to investigate and promote the usefulness of science fiction in education; to disseminate information about science fiction; and to promote a discriminating understanding of the nature of science fiction. Its main activities include publication of the journal *Foundation: The International Review of Science Fiction*, and supporting the research library The Science Fiction Foundation Collection, at the University of Liverpool.

Scottish Book Trust

Sandeman House, Trunk's Close, 55 High Street, Edinburgh, EH1 1SR

- 0131 524 0160
- 0131 524 0161
- info@scottishbooktrust.com
- www.scottishbooktrust.com

Contact CEO Marc Lambert; General Manager, Jeanette Harris

About Scottish Book Trust is Scotland's national agency for reading and writing. It promotes reading and books. Under its umbrella is Live Literature Scotland, a national initiative that enables Scottish citizens to engage with the nation's authors, playwrights, poets, storytellers and illustrators. It is the only writer bursary scheme of its kind in the UK, subsidising the cost of 1,200 community visits by writers in all areas of Scotland, and is extremely popular. More than 500 writers who are available to conduct readings and literary events in Scotland are listed and searchable on the SBT database.

Scottish Newspaper Publishers Association

48 Palmerston Places, Edinburgh, EH12 5DE

- 0131 220 4353
- 0131 220 4344
- info@snpa.org.uk
- www.snpa.org.uk

About The Scottish Newspaper Publishers Association (SNPA) is the trade association representing publishers of 100 weekly and bi-weekly newspapers, and a further 30 free distribution newspapers. Its website is particularly useful for links to Scottish local paper groups.

Scottish Screen

249 West George Street, Glasgow, G2 4QE

- 0845 300 7300
- info@scottishscreen.com
- www.scottishscreen.com

Contact Chair, Dr Richard Holloway; CEO, Ken Hay; Chief Operating Officer & Company Secretary, Alyson Hagan

About Scottish Screen is the national screen agency for Scotland with responsibility for developing all aspects of screen culture and industry across the country. Its work includes: production company growth; short and feature film development and production; freelancer and company skills development; experimental, alternative and interactive digital screen content, formats and platforms; the development and production of television drama pilots; and audience and market development and distribution initiatives.

The Society for Editors & Proofreaders (SfEP)

Erico House, 93–99 Upper Richmond Road, London, SW15 2TG
- 020 8785 5617
- 020 8785 5618
- administration@sfep.org.uk
- www.sfep.org.uk

Contact Honorary President, Judith Butcher

About The Society for Editors & Proofreaders (SfEP) is a professional organisation for editors and proofreaders. Its aims are to promote high editorial standards and to achieve recognition of the professional status of its members and associates.

Society for Storytelling (SfS)

PO Box 2344, Reading, RG6 7FG
- 0118 935 1381
- admin@sfs.org.uk
- www.sfs.org.uk

Contact Chair, Martin Manasse; Treasurer, Administrator & Newsletter Editor, Tina Bilbé

About The SfS is an open organisation which welcomes anyone with an interest in oral storytelling. It aims to provide an information network for oral storytelling, stories, storytellers and storytelling clubs, and organises storytelling events, such as storytelling festivals. The SfS publishes *Storylines* magazine and the quarterly *Directory of Storytellers*.

The Society for Theatre Research

PO Box 53971, London, SW15 6UL
- contact@str.org.uk
- www.str.org.uk

Contact Eileen Cottis

About The Society for Theatre Research provides a meeting point for all those interested in the history and technique of the British theatre. It acts as an advisory body on theatrical matters, puts on occasional study days on particular aspects of theatre, publishes new books and reprints texts chosen to illustrate aspects of theatre history (members receive a free book every year). Research grants are awarded by the Society to encourage work on theatrical subjects – especially those connected with live theatre – and there is an annual theatre book prize for original research into any aspect of the history and technique of British theatre. The Society also distributes *Theatre Notebook*, an illustrated journal devoted to the history and technique of the British theatre, hosts lectures in London on topics of theatrical interest, and holds an annual festival in memory of William Poel.

The Society of Authors

84 Drayton Gardens, London, SW10 9SB
- 020 7373 6642
- 020 7373 5768
- info@societyofauthors.org
- www.societyofauthors.org

Contact Chair, Tracy Chevalier; General Secretary, Mark Le Fanu

About The Society of Authors is a non-profit organisation, founded to protect the rights and further the interests of authors. The society offers grants to previously published writers who are British by birth and under the age of 40, to benefit them in research and travel. The twice-yearly grants, awarded in April and September, are normally between £1,000 and £2,000 and rarely exceed £4,000. Authors must submit: a copy of their latest published book; a brief history of their writing career; details of their current work; size of advance (if any); names of publishers already approached or working with; overall financial position and why the grant is needed; details of past grants; confirmation of their eligibility to enter; and copies of past reviews (if any). Full application details are available on the website. See entries under Bursaries, Fellowships and Grants and Competitions and Prizes for more information. See the website for details of regional groups, including The Society of Authors, Scotland.

The Society of Authors in Scotland

(See The Society of Authors)

Society of Children's Book Writers & Illustrators

56 Ackroyd Road, Forest Hill, London, SE23 1DL
- Online form.
- www.britishscbwi.jimdo.com

Contact Regional Advisor, Natascha Biebow

About The British arm of the SCBWI is part of an international organisation offering a variety of services to people who write, illustrate or share an interest in children's literature. SCBWI acts as a network for the exchange of knowledge between writers, illustrators, editors, publishers, agents, librarians, educators, booksellers and others involved with literature for young people. There are currently more than 12,000 members worldwide, in over 70 regions, making it the largest children's writing organisation in the world. The organisation also offers members support, information and education at a local level.

The British SCBWI runs two annual conferences – an illustrator's day in the spring, and a writer's day in the autumn. They also publish a quarterly newsletter, *Words and Pictures*, which includes up to date events and marketing information for UK and American publishers. See website for local regional contacts.

The Society of Civil & Public Service Writers
c/o Membership Secretary, 17 The Green, Corby Glen, Grantham, NG33 4NP

- membership@scpsw.co.uk
- www.scpsw.co.uk

Contact Chairman, Terry Rickson; Membership Secretary, Joan M. Lewis

About The society encourages authorship by present and past members of the Civil Service, Armed Forces and certain other public service bodies. It also provides opportunities for social and cultural activities. There is an annual poetry weekend at Birmingham University and the society supports and encourages writers' weekend meetings in any part of the country.

Society of Editors
University Centre, Granta Place, Mill Lane, Cambridge, CB2 1RU

- 01223 304080
- 01223 304090
- info@societyofeditors.org
- www.societyofeditors.co.uk

Contact Executive Director & Company Secretary, Bob Satchwell; Administrator, Angela Varley

About The society campaigns and lobbies to fight for media freedom. It has more than 400 members made up of editors, managing editors, editorial directors, training editors, editors-in-chief and deputy editors, in national, regional and local newspapers, magazines, radio, television and new media, plus lawyers and academics in journalism education. Its values are: the promotion of press and broadcasting freedom and the public's 'right to know'; the universal right to freedom of expression; the vitality of the news media in a democratic society; the commitment to high editorial standards. The society influences debate on press and broadcasting freedom, ethics and the culture and business of news media.

Society of Indexers
Woodbourn Business Centre, 10 Jessell Street, Sheffield, S9 3HY

- 0114 244 9561
- admin@indexers.org.uk
- www.indexers.org.uk

Contact Chairman, Ann Kingdom; Secretary, Judith Menes

About The Society exists to promote indexing, the quality of indexes and the profession of indexing.

The website contains a wealth of information and resources for indexers.

The Society of Medical Writers
c/o Dr R Cutler, 30 Dollis Hill Lane, London, NW2 6JE

- raymond.hume@btinternet.com
- www.somw.org.uk

Contact Chairman, Dr Raymond Hume

About Membership of the Society of Medical Writers is open to anyone who publishes or aspires to publish written work – fact or fiction, prose or poetry – as long as it is medically based or themed. The association aims to be enjoyable, stimulating and educational, so that writing from medical practice, including general practice, is improved and encouraged. See the website for various committee, activity and competition names, contacts and addresses.

Society of Women Writers & Journalists
c/o Jean Morris, 31 Eaton Court, Eaton Gardens, Hove, BN3 3PL

- j.morris031@btinternet.com
- www.swwj.co.uk

Contact Chair, Jean Morris; Membership Secretary, Wendy Hughes

About The UK's longest established organisation for professional women writers. The aims of the SWWJ include the encouragement of literary achievement, the upholding of professional standards, and social contact with fellow writers and others in the field, including editors, publishers, broadcasters, and agents. It is an international association, and is affiliated to women's associations across the world. The society has been accepting male writers as associate members since 2004. See the website for regional contacts and activities. Many of the London meetings are held at The New Cavendish Club, 44 Great Cumberland Place, London W1.

Society of Young Publishers
c/o The Bookseller, Endeavour House, 189 Shaftesbury Avenue, London, WC2H 8TJ

- membersec@thesyp.org.uk
- www.thesyp.org.uk

Contact Chair, Doug Wallace; Membership Secretary, Claire Morrison

About The Society of Young Publishers is open to anyone in publishing or a related trade (in any capacity) – or who is hoping to be soon. Anyone interested or working in the publishing industry is welcome to join. The only exception is that those who have been in the industry for more than ten years are not able to stand on the committee. There are two branches, in London and Oxford. Both branches have regular events and meetings, and both are run by volunteers.

Sports Journalists' Association
c/o Start2Finish Event Management, Unit 92, Capital Business Centre, 22 Carlton Road, Surrey, CR2 0BS
- 020 8916 2234
- 020 8916 2235
- stevenwdownes@btinternet.com
- www.sportsjournalists.co.uk

Contact Chairman, Barry Newcombe; Secretary, Steven Downes

About The SJA is an association for British-based professional sports journalists, whether writers or photographers, editors or broadcasters.

The Translators Association
(See The Society of Authors)

Voice of the Listener & Viewer Ltd (VLV)
PO Box 401, Gravesend, Kent, DA12 9FY
- 01474 352835
- 01474 351112
- info@vlv.org.uk
- www.vlv.org.uk

Contact Chairman, Richard Lindley; Membership Secretary, Sue Washbrook

About Voice of the Listener & Viewer (VLV) represents the consumer interest in broadcasting. It campaigns for high quality radio and television programmes, and in particular for the principles of public service broadcasting. It is influential, and attracts big names as speakers and contributors to its conferences and events. It represents the interests of listeners, viewers, citizens and consumers, and works to keep them informed about current developments in British broadcasting. These include proposed new legislation, public consultation on broadcasting policy and the likely impact of digital technology.

WATCH
c/o David Sutton, University of Reading Library, PO Box 223, Whiteknights, Reading, RG6 6AE
- 0118 931 8783
- d.c.sutton@reading.ac.uk
- www.watch-file.com

Contact Director of Research Projects, David Sutton

About WATCH is an online database of authors and artists that enables users to search for contact details of rights holders. This is primarily of use when looking for contacts of those holding or administering the rights of deceased persons. Searches are free. The database is managed jointly by the University of Reading and the University of Texas.

Welsh Books Council
Castell Brychan, Aberystwyth, Ceredigion, SY23 2JB
- 01970 624151
- 01970 625385
- castellbrychan@wbc.org.uk
- www.wbc.org.uk

Contact Director, Gwerfyl Pierce Jones; Personal Secretary, Menai Lloyd Williams

About The Welsh Books Council is a national body, funded by the Welsh Assembly Government, which provides a focus for the publishing industry in Wales. It provides a number of specialist services, including editing, design, marketing and distribution, with a view to improving standards of book production and publication in both Welsh and English. For writers, its main interest may be that it aims to assist and support them by providing services and by awarding grants/commissions which are channelled through publishers. See the website for further details.

Women in Publishing
c/o Multilingual Matters, Frankfurt Lodge, Clevedon Hall, Victoria Road, Clevedon, BS21 7HH
- info@wipub.org.uk
- www.womeninpublishing.org.uk

Contact PR, Matina Grebener

About Women in Publishing works to promote the status of women working in publishing and related trades by helping them to develop their careers. Its aims are to provide a forum for the discussion of ideas, trends and subjects of interest to women in the publishing trades, to encourage networking and mutual support, to provide opportunities for sharing information and expertise, to support and publicise women's achievements and successes, and to promote the status of women within publishing. Monthly meetings are a key part of what WiP does. See website for the location of monthly meetings.

Women Writers Network
Venue: Conway Hall, 25 Red Lion Square, Holborn, London
- info@womenwriters.org.uk
- www.womenwriters.org.uk

About WWN is a networking group for professional women writers. Most are freelance, some are salaried, and together they represent a wide range of writing interests. WWN is not a writers' circle, but a group formed to help women further their professional development. The usual venue is Conway Hall, on the 2nd Monday of every month – see the website for further details.

Writers' Advice Centre for Children's Books
16 Smiths Yard, Summerley Street, London, SW18 4HR
☎ 07979 905353
✉ info@writersadvice.co.uk
🌐 www.writersadvice.co.uk
Contact Managing Editor, Louise Jordan
About A literary consultancy service offering professional editorial and marketing advice to new and published children's writers, on a fee basis. The Writers Advice Centre for Children's Books is the only manuscript agency in the UK specialising solely in children's publishing. Its manuscript assessment service provides new, and published, children's writers with critical feedback that can increase chances of publication. The Writers Advice Centre is open to everyone writing for children whether they be complete beginners or published authors. It will look at all types of writing for children. This could include picture books, early readers, short stories, novels for older children, non-fiction, and poetry. They have now also expanded their services to include an online correspondence course, a mentoring scheme and workshop days.

The Writers' Guild of Great Britain
40 Rosebery Avenue, London, EC1R 4RX
☎ 020 7833 0777
☎ 020 7833 4777
✉ erik@writersguild.org.uk
🌐 www.writersguild.org.uk
Contact President, David Edgar; Chair, Katharine Way; General Secretary, Bernie Corbett; Admin Assistant, Erik Pohl
About The Writers' Guild of Great Britain is the trade union representing writers in television, radio, theatre, books, poetry, film and video games. In television, film, radio and theatre, the Guild is the recognised body for negotiating minimum terms and practice agreements for writers. It campaigns and lobbies on behalf of all writers, and is influential up to government level. Its voice is listened to and its views are respected. Any writer who has received payment under a contract in terms at or above the Writers' Guild minimum terms for at least one piece of work is entitled to become a full member.

Yachting Journalists' Association
36 Church Lane, Lymington, Hampshire, SO41 3RB
☎ 01590 673894
✉ sec@yja.co.uk
🌐 www.yja.co.uk
Contact Chairman, Bob Fisher; Honorary Membership Secretary, Rachel Nuding
About The aim of the Association is to promote greater awareness of a wide range of leisure boating activities through the professional services offered by its members.

WRITER'S GROUPS

Aberdeen Writers' Circle
Aberdeen Arts Centre, 33 King Street, Aberdeen, AB24 5AA
✉ awcwrite@aol.com
Contact Moira Brown
Meetings Meeting time: 10.30am–12.30pm, every Wednesday
About New members are welcome, either make contact or go along. Meetings take the form of readings and constructive feedback. There are sometimes written exercises, guest speakers and workshops throughout the year. Fees are £2 per meeting.

Anderida Writers
The Lansdowne Hotel, Grand Parade, Eastbourne, East Sussex
☎ 01323 725174
✉ pjesampson@tiscali.co.uk
Contact Mrs Ann Botha (japann@talktalk.net)
7 Fraser Avenue
Eastbourne
East Sussex
BN23 6BB
News Editor, Harry Pope (harry.pope@sky.com)
10/6 Queens Gardens
Eastbourne
BN21 3EF

Meetings Meeting time: 8pm, second Tuesday of each month

About New members are welcome; please contact Ann Botha for details. Covers fiction, non-fiction, short stories, poetry, children's and travel writing, and members are encouraged to eventually produce a piece of publishable standard work. Current members are both published and unpublished. The group holds an annual short story competition and a Christmas dinner. A voluntary fee of £1 per meeting is expected from attendees.

Armagh Writers' Group
Windmill House, Windmill Hill, Armagh, Northern Ireland, BT60 4BR

🌐 kevin@abcwritersnetwork.co.uk
🌐 www.abcwritersnetwork.co.uk
Contact Kevin Hart
Meetings Meeting time: Every Tuesday 7:30pm-9:00pm
About One of five writers groups operating in and around County Armagh, Northern Ireland. The groups are located in Armagh, Banbridge and Craigavon - contact Kevin at the ABC Writers Network for more information.

Ashburton Writers' Group
Members' homes, Ashburton area

☎ 01364 653177 (Jean Clegg)
🌐 ianroyce@tesco.net
Contact Ian Chamberlain
Meetings Meeting time: 9.30am, alternate Tuesdays
About New members welcome. The informal meetings, based on a set theme and led by different members each week, include an hour of actual writing, followed by critiques of previously circulated members' work. A range of writing is covered, from biography and journalism to historical writing, and current members include award winning poets. There are no fees.

Ayr Writers' Club
Prestwick Community Centre, 25 Caerlaverlock Road, Prestwick, Ayrshire, KA9 1HP

☎ 01294 214641
🌐 fiona@webwrite.eclipse.co.uk
🌐 www.ayrwritersclub.co.uk
Contact Catherine Lang
Meetings Meeting time: 7.30–9.30pm, Wednesday evenings
About New members over the age of 16 are welcome. Either make contact or go to a meeting. Meetings are workshops, informal club nights, or based around guest speakers. The group also runs competitions, which are judged by guest speakers. Check the website for up to date programmes. Fees are £20 per annum, or £10 per annum for postal membership. Non-members may attend twice for free before joining.

Ballea Writers Club Ireland
c/o Ballea Castle, Carrigaline, Co. Cork, Republic of Ireland

🌐 balleawriters@gmail.com
🌐 www.balleawriters.com
Contact Elaine Rhys-Davies
Meetings Meeting time: Fiction workshops on the 2nd and 4th Mondays of each month from 7.30pm-9.30pm. Other workshops are also available.
About Ballea Writers Club formed in March 2006 and achieved over 200 publications in their first two years. The writing group operates on four arms: fiction, non-fiction, poetry and journalism, and publishes extensively in each. They also have a youth writing group. The Club welcomes new members. Enquiries can be made through balleawriters@gmail.com. Novice writers are as welcome and supported as professional writers. The club does not stipulate that prospective members take a course in creative writing before joining the group but encourage that a parallel evening class be started as soon as possible thereafter. Membership costs €40 per year, plus €5 per workshop.

Ballycastle Writers
Rathmoyle Recreation Centre, Mary Street, Ballycastle, Co. Antrim, Republic of Ireland

🌐 www.ballycastlewritersnews.blogspot.com
Contact Heather Newcombe
Meetings Meeting time: 7.30pm, every Wednesday
About Group currently has 12 to 15 members, although membership is on a casual basis.

Ballymena Writers' Group
The Showgrounds, Warden Street, Ballymena, BT43 7DR

☎ 028 2564 3904
🌐 r.doherty2@ukonline.co.uk
Contact Mary Higgins; Secretary, Rita Doherty
Meetings Meeting time: 7.30pm–9.30pm, every Monday
About New members are welcome, the only requirement is an interest in writing. There is full disabled access. The group has tutors that cover every genre of writing.

Bank Street Writers
16–18 Mill Lane, Horwich, Bolton, BL6 6AT

☎ 01204 669858
🌐 bswscribe@aol.com

ⓦ http://hometown.aol.co.uk/bswscribe/
myhomepage/writing.html
Contact Secretary, Rod Riesco
Meetings Meeting time: Monthly, first Wednesday
About Meets at venues around Bolton. New
members of any level and experience are welcome.
Covers all types of writing including fiction, non-
fiction, poetry and drama. The group also produces a
magazine, 'Current Accounts' and runs a writing
competition. Fees are £10 per annum but new
members are welcome to attend for free on a
trial basis.

Basingstoke Writers' Circle
**United Reform Church, 20 London Road,
Basingstoke, Hampshire, RG21 7NU**
ⓞ 01256 326453
ⓦ www.communigate.co.uk/hants/bwc
Meetings Meeting time: 8pm–10pm, fourth
Tuesday of each month
About New members welcome, but are
recommended to make contact to confirm the
venue first. All levels of experience are catered for
and meeting structures vary from week to week.
Fees are £2.50 per meeting and £10 per annum, but
new members can try the group for free before
committing.

Battersea Writers' Group
**Family Room, Battersea Arts Centre, Lavender
Hill, London, SW11 5TN**
ⓔ jasonyoung72@yahoo.com
ⓦ http://thebatterseawritersgroup.blogspot.com
Contact Jason Young
Meetings Meeting time: 7.30pm, one
Wednesday a month
About An informal forum to workshop new
material. Contact Jason Young for details.

The Birmingham Writers
**Birmingham Central Library, Chamberlain
Square, Birmingham, B3 3HQ**
ⓞ 0121 711 2166
ⓔ isabella.self@bluyonder.co.uk
ⓦ www.scorpiopsc.pwp.blueyonder.co.uk/bw
Meetings Meeting time: 6pm–8pm, first and third
Wednesday of each month (excluding August)
About New members should call or email for more
details. The group organise a structured programme
of meetings for the year, including themes,
competitions and workshops. Members have the
opportunity to receive feedback on their work. Fees
are £1 each for the first two sessions and if accepted,
an undisclosed annual membership fee.

Blackheath Poetry Society
Members' homes around Blackheath, London
ⓞ 020 8852 9608
ⓔ gps5@tutor.open.ac.uk
Contact Gill Stoker
38 Lee Road
London
SE3 9RU
Meetings Meeting time: Second Monday of every
other month
About New members welcome, please call or email
Gill Stoker. The group is mainly based around poetry
appreciation rather than creative writing, although
members do write their own pieces. A theme is
usually set for the evening and poetry read and
discussed. There are no fees, but a small contribution
is required towards the cost of refreshments.

Brentwood Writers' Circle
**Fairview Room, Ursuline Convent School,
Queens Road, Brentwood, Essex**
ⓔ christine_easter@yahoo.co.uk
Contact Secretary, Christine Easter
Jubilee
Mill Lane
Hook End
Brentwood
Essex
CM15 0PP
Meetings Meeting time: 2.30–4.30pm, first Saturday
of the month
About New members are welcome, but there may
be a waiting list as membership is restricted to 60.
Applications should be made to the secretary,
Christine Easter. All genres of writing are covered,
except poetry. Alternate meetings involve guest
speakers. Most other meetings are workshops, with a
special writers day taking place on the first Saturday
in June. The December meeting is a Christmas party
and an awards ceremony.

Bridgend Writers Circle
**Coed Parc, Library Headquarters, Park Street,
Bridgend, CF31 4BA**
ⓔ kirsten@barrettpianos.co.uk
Contact Kirsten Barrett
Meetings Meeting time: 7.15pm, second Friday of
each month
About New members are welcome. Any type of
creative writing and level of experience are covered
as the group is not tutored, but it is designed to be
stimulating. Fees are £6 per year, but new members
may attend for free initially.

Bridgnorth Writers' Group

Cinnamon Coffee & Meeting House, Cartway, Bridgnorth, WV16 4EG

☎ 01746 761246

✉ phelps_jeff@tiscali.co.uk

Contact Jeff Phelps

18 Pineway

Bridgnorth

Shropshire

WV15 5DT

Meetings Meeting time: 7.30pm–10pm, third Tuesday of each month

About New members welcome, any level of experience. Current members range from published writers and hobbyists, to beginners. Writing tends to be poetry, short stories, plays and novels, although other types of writing are encouraged and welcomed. Meetings are usually based around reading of members' work and feedback, but there is no obligation to read or write anything every month. The group organises occasional social events and has run a number of imaginative and lively writing, publishing and performing projects. Fees are either £15 per annum, or £2 per session – the first visit is free.

Brighton Nightwriters

The Pub With No Name, 58 Southover Street, Brighton, BN2 2UF

☎ 01273 505642

Contact Tim Shelton-Jones

Meetings Meeting time: 7.30pm every Wednesday

About New members welcome, just turn up to a meeting, or call for details. All types of writing covered. A friendly, informal group with both regular and irregular members.

Bristol & Kingswood Writers Ink-Corporated

Kingswood Library, High Street, Kingswood, Bristol, BS15 4AR

☎ 0117 986 9322

✉ alanbyrom@blueyonder.co.uk

Contact Alan Byrom

37 Gaston Avenue

Keynsham

Bristol

BS31 1LR

Meetings Meeting time: 7.30pm, second and fourth wednesday of each month

About Kingswood Writers Ink-Corporated has been going for around 15 years and meets twice-monthly at Kingswood Library, near Bristol. They are a friendly mixed group of all ages, interested in creative writing in all genres. The group aims to encourage each other in a non-competitive, non-threatening environment. Meetings generally last around 2 hours with a break for coffee and chat. Meetings on the 2nd Wednesday of the month are to share writing. The Winter meetings on 4th Wednesdays are usually led by a member of the group and are themed to encourage members to take their writings further and hopefully to publication. During the summer the 4th Wednesday meeting takes the form of a minibus inspirational ride which usually involves a pub stop.

Bristol Writers' Group

Members' homes, Bristol

✉ organiser@bristolwritersgroup.net

🌐 www.bristolwritersgroup.net

Contact Louise Gethin

Meetings Meeting time: 7.30pm–9.30pm every Wednesday

About Predominantly a fiction writing group, although sometimes members bring travel writing, poetry or scripts. Meetings are focused around one piece of a member's work, which is emailed around in advance, on a rota basis. The group also organises social events. There are no fees.

Bute Writers

Orissor House, Craigmore Road, Rothesay, Isle of Bute

✉ steve@butewriters.co.uk

🌐 www.butewriters.co.uk

Contact Jenny Campbell

Meetings Meeting time: 7.30pm every second Wednesday

About Meetings usually take the form of business meetings, a pre-assigned project or assignment, or a workshop. The group also arranges visits and guest speakers, and welcomes contact with other writers' groups.

Café Writers

Jurnet's Bar, Wensum Lodge, King Street, Norwich, NR1 1QW

✉ tom@cafewriters.org.uk

🌐 www.cafewriters.org.uk

Meetings Meeting time: 7.15pm, second Monday of each month

About The main meeting is based around reading of poetry; however there are two off-shoot writers groups, one for poetry and one for other writing. The poetry group meets 7.30pm–9.30pm every other Monday. Contact dstreet@streetview.co.uk for details. The Voices Writers meet on the first and third Tuesday of each month, in the BBC Voices room, first floor of The Forum, Norwich. Contact Nic Rigby, nic.rigby@bbc.co.uk, for details. Please make contact before turning up, as groups may be full or venues may have changed.

Cannon Poets

Moseley Community Development Trust, The Post Office Building, 149-153 Alcester Road, Moseley, Birmingham, B13 8JP

- martin@cannonpoets.co.uk
- www.cannonpoets.co.uk

Contact Secretary/Treasurer, Martin Underwood
c/o 22 Margaret Grove
Harbourne
Birmingham
B17 9JH

Meetings Meeting time: 2pm, Sundays, monthly

About Group revolves around poetry workshops run by members, or visitors. Members can be published in the quarterly journal, *Cannon's Mouth*, which can be subscribed to for £10.50 per annum. The group also runs poetry competitions. Full membership (group and journal) is £30 per annum, £20 for concessions, and families may pay the cost of two adults less the cost of one subscription to the journal. Associate membership is £15 and meeting attendance is £3, or £2 for concessions.

Cardiff Writers' Circle

62 Park Place, Cardiff, CF10 3AS

- niva@nivapete.freeserve.co.uk

Meetings Meeting time: 7pm every Monday (term time only)

About New writers of all genres welcome. The aim of the group is to promote good writing for publication and members are published writers as well as beginners. Membership costs £10 per annum, plus £1.50 for each meeting attended (hot drink included). The group holds three annual competitions for articles, poetry and short stories, with professional adjudicators.

Cheltenham Writer's Circle

Parmoor House, 13 Lypiatt Terrace, Lypiatt Road, Cheltenham, GL50 2SX

- 01242 578109
- carol.sandiford@blueyonder.co.uk

Contact Carol Sandiford
4 Battledown Cottages
Harp Hill
Cheltenham
GL53 6QG

Meetings Meeting time: 7.30pm–10pm, first and third Monday of each month

About New members are welcome and can simply turn up, or make prior contact if they wish. The circle covers all genres of writing at all levels of experience and most meetings provide the chance to present work and receive constructive feedback. Occasionally there will be a guest speaker, a workshop or an outing. Fees are £12 per year, plus £1 for each meeting attended. New members may attend one meeting for free, and another at £1 before committing to the annual fee.

Chirk Writers' Circle

The Bungalow, Church of the Sacred Heart, Station Road, Chirk, Wrexham, Wales

- 01691 777390
- melodyrobinson@btinternet.com

Contact Melody Robinson

Meetings Meeting time: 10am–12pm, first Wednesday of every month

About New members welcome, apply by phone to the secretary. The group deals with all types of writing and levels of experience. Each meeting has a tutor and the group arranges outings to the theatre, workshops and participates in local events. Fees are £3, and £2 for concessions.

Conway Mill Writers Group

Conway Mill, 5/7 Conway Street, Belfast, Northern Ireland, BT13 2DE

- info@conwaymill.org
- www.conwaymill.org

Contact Liam Donnelly

Meetings Meeting time: 10am-1pm, every Monday

About A writers group that meets at the Conway Mill community and culture centre, in Belfast.

Deal Writers

Dealability, 43 Victoria Road, Deal, Kent, CT14 7AY

- 01304 379886
- dealwriters@hotmail.co.uk
- www.dealwriters.co.uk

Contact Bettine Walters

Meetings Meeting time: First Thursday of each month

About New members are welcome to turn up, or contact Bettine Walters. Meetings usually alternate between guest speakers and critique of members' work. Fees are £15 per annum to cover the expenses of guest speakers, plus £1 each month for the room hire.

The Deeside Writers

Burnett Arms Hotel, Banchory, Scotland

- 01330 850691
- mslaven@aol.com

Contact Marion Slaven
Adendale
Strachan

Aberdeenshire
AB31 6NP
Meetings Meeting time: 10am–12pm and 7.30pm–9.30pm (alternate weeks) every Thursday during term time
About New members of any age and any level of experience are welcome. People can go to the morning, evening or both sessions, depending on their availability. Current members include poets, budding novelists and those who submit articles for publication. Fees are £10 per annum, plus £2 per session – which includes hot drinks.

Denny Writers
Community Education Centre, 40 Duke Street, Denny, FK6 6NW
☎ 01324 504260
✉ jimturpie@hotmail.com
🌐 www.fdacc.org.uk/dennywriters.htm
Contact Jim Turpie
Meetings Meeting time: 1.30pm–2.45pm, every Thursday
About New members welcome. Group includes hobby writers and professionals of all ages and genders, working under the guidance of a tutor.

Dereham & District Writers' Group
Members' homes around Norfolk
☎ 01362 850433
✉ william.english@virgin.net
Contact William English
Wisteria Cottage
South Green
Mattishall
Norfolk
NR20 3JZ
Meetings Meeting time: 7.30pm–9.30pm
About New members are welcome, numbers permitting. Please contact William English in the first instance. The group deals mainly with fiction in all genres, although there is flexibility if a poet joins. The group works to a four week cycle: week one is submissions for review; week two is writing exercises; week three is short story writing; and week four is the review session where members critique the submitted work based on set guidelines. The group roughly follows the academic terms and costs £2 per meeting, saved by the treasurer for an end of term meal.

Devizes Writers' Group
The Crown Centre, St John's Street, Devizes
Contact Chairman, Paul Snook
Ridgeway House
20 White Street
Easterton

Devizes
SN10 4NZ
Meetings Meeting time: 7.30pm, fourth Tuesday of each month
About The group is very informal, with some on the spot writing and some 'homework' on a pre-allocated theme. There is an email form on the website for contact.

Fire River Poets
Private houses around Taunton and Somerset
☎ 01823 252486
✉ enquiry@fireriverpoets.org.uk
🌐 www.fireriverpoets.org.uk
Contact John Stuart
2 Deane View
Bishops Hull Road
Bishops Hull
Taunton
Somerset
TA1 5EG
Meetings Meeting time: Monthly, no fixed venue
About New members are always welcome, but as the meeting places are private houses there are sometimes limits to group size. Prospective members should approach John Stuart with a sample of their work. The group is restricted to practising poets only, and beginners are referred to local writing courses. Meetings usually focus around reading and criticising the poetry of fellow members, however consideration is sometimes given to other published poets and once every few months meetings take the form of a workshop where poetry is written during the meeting to a given specification. Members pay £2 per meeting attended.

4Words Media Group/ Interchange4Words
Bradford, West Yorkshire and Online.
✉ joedot@blueyonder.co.uk
🌐 http://uk.groups.yahoo.com/group/hear4words
Contact Joe Ogden
Meetings Meeting time: Online 24/7 and occasionally on Fridays in Bradford
About What started as the Interchange Writers' Network has now become the 4Words Media Group, an online writing community. New members are welcome as long as they have internet access. They should contact Joe Ogden by email. The group mainly deals with poetry, writing, plays and screenplays, although they can put you in contact with other groups in and around the Bradford area. There are no fees.

Free Spirit Writers

40 Burstall Hill, Bridlington, East Yorkshire, YO16 7GA

- freespiritwriters@tesco.net
- www.freespiritwriters.me.uk

Contact Mike and Diane Wilson

About Free Spirit Writers is an informal group consisting of husband and wife Mike and Diane Wilson. They are not seeking new members, although anyone interested in their extensive catalogue of poetry, novels, dramas and numerous other projects should contact them, or visit their website. Mike and Diane are available to give talks and workshops on their historical novels and dramas and have in the past worked within schools.

Fresh Start Writers

Horsefair Paddock, Brigg, North Lincolnshire

- stansfield522@btinternet.com
- www.freshstartnorthlincs.com

Contact David Stansfield

Meetings Meeting time: Monthly

About A group for the over 50s, backed by the Fresh Start organisation. Led by journalist and author David Stansfield, the group often works on collections of short stories or poetry for adults and children. Current member ages vary from 51 to 83.

The Glass Mountain Writers

Crystal Peaks Library, 1–3 Peak Square, Crystal Peaks Complex, Waterthorpe, Sheffield, S20 7PH

- 0114 293 0612
- 0114 293 0611
- crystalpeaks.library@sheffield.gov.uk

Contact John Gosnell/Margaret Lambert

Meetings Meeting time: 2pm–3.30pm, every Thursday

About New members welcome, either turn up, or phone in advance. Covers every type of writing, including fiction, song writing, poetry and plays. Meetings are usually based around listening and commenting on members' work and set exercises, although there are occasional workshops and visiting writers. Fees are 50 pence to cover tea, coffee and biscuits.

Hampshire Writers

Bird in Hand, Gosport Road, Fareham, Hampshire, PO16 0PZ

- joe@joe-jenkins.com

Contact Joe Jenkins

Meetings Meeting time: 7.30pm on the first Thursday of every month

About Hampshire Writers is open to all writers, of all genres, lengths and styles including short stories,

novels, poems and scripts. They are an informal gathering of writers, providing support and friendship. Organiser Joe Jenkins is an author of non-fiction paranormal and horror/science fiction short stories. He runs a small Fareham based production company, in the role of writer/producer/director. His first book is to be published in 2008.

Havering Writers' Circle

Fairkytes Arts Centre, 53 Billet Lane, Hornchurch, Essex, RM11 1AX

- 01708 375549
- hamiltonmike@hotmail.co.uk

Contact Mike Hamilton
36 Tindall Close
Harold Wood
Romford
Essex
RM3 0PD

Meetings Meeting time: 7.30pm–10pm, first Monday of each month

About New members are welcome and should contact Mike Hamilton. Membership costs £25 per annum, concessions £20. Consists of published and unpublished writers, mainly of prose (little poetry).

Hertsmere Writers' Circle

Bushey Grove Leisure Centre, Aldenham Road, Bushey, Hertfordshire, WD23 2TD

- 01923 247329
- srilekharach@hotmail.com

Contact Coordinator, Mrs R.A. Rach

Meetings Meeting time: 1pm–3pm every Wednesday

About Welcomes new members, particularly poets, novelists and short story writers of all genres. Please phone or email the Coordinator or Assistant Coordinator. As well as opportunities to give and receive constructive feedback on your writing, the circle also runs brief workshops and organise set projects designed to encourage creativity. Members are required to take an active part.

Hornsea Writers

The Bowls Club, Atwick Road, Hornsea, East Yorkshire, HU18 1EJ

- lindaacaster@yahoo.co.uk

Contact Linda Acaster

Meetings Meeting time: 7.30pm every Wednesday

About New members welcome if they're willing to accept constructive criticism. Full disabled access. All prose writing is covered, including short fiction and novels, scripts, non-fiction and memoirs. No poetry. The group is geared towards writers with a professional attitude towards honing their skills. Most members are published and the emphasis is on gaining feedback on individual pieces, not on group projects.

Identity Workshop
Commonword, 6 Mount Street, Manchester, M2 5NS
- 0161 832 3777
- 0161 832 2929
- cultureword@commonword.org.uk
- www.commonword.org.uk

Contact Pete Kalu
Meetings Meeting time: 7pm–9pm, every Wednesday
About New members welcome. The group is for Asian, African Caribbean and Chinese writers of all levels. Contact Commonword for further details.

Irish Writers' Centre
19 Parnell Square, Dublin 1, Republic of Ireland
- 00353 1 872 1302
- 00353 1 872 6282
- info@writerscentre.ie
- www.writerscentre.ie

Contact Anthony Anatoly Kudryavitsky
Meetings Meeting time: Monthly or fortnightly
About A new writers group at the writers' centre aimed at refugees, asylum seekers, migrant workers and members of other language communities in the Dublin area. Its function will be to develop writing skills and creativity in these categories of people, introduce them to Irish literature and encourage their wider participation in local cultural activities. No fee. Please contact tutor Anthony Anatoly Kudryavitsky for more information.

Johnstone Writers' Group
Johnstone Central Library, Ludovic Square, Johnstone, Renfrewshire
- 0141 552 5239
- ihunter24601@hotmail.com
- www.johnstonewritersgroup.com

Contact Ian Hunter
Meetings Meeting time: 7pm–9pm, every Thursday
About Potential members should contact Ian Hunter, Chair. The group is over 20 years old and has around 18 members, some of whom are published. Everything from poetry to novels is covered. The group also has its own publishing imprint, Ludovic Press, which publishes members' poetry and books. There are special events, around once a month, which include visiting writers. There are no fees.

Kent & Sussex Poetry Society
The Camden Centre, Market Square, Tunbridge Wells, Kent, TN1 2SW

- info@kentandsussexpoetrysociety.org
- www.kentandsussexpoetrysociety.org

Contact Keith Francis
Broomhill
Benenden
Kent
TN17 4JT
Meetings Meeting time: 8pm, Tuesdays, two per month
About New members are welcome, email for details. Poetry only. The group holds two meetings a month with readings, special guests and workshops. There is an annual fee of £15. Non-members may attend the meetings for £3 (£2 concessions). The society also runs a competition, extra workshops and organises a retreat.

King's Lynn Writers' Circle
The Friend's Meeting House, 38 Bridge Street, King's Lynn, Norfolk, PE30 5AB
- enquiries@lynnwriters.org.uk
- www.lynnwriters.org.uk

Contact Secretary, Alison Carter (01553 849951)
Gables End
1 Burman Mews
Lynn Road
East Winch
King's Lynn
Norfolk
PE32 1NP
Meetings Meeting time: 7.30pm, second Thursday of each month
About New members welcome, either contact Alison Carter or come along to a meeting. All types of writing covered, occasional group anthologies produced and competitions run.

Lampeter Writers' Group
Lecture Room 7, Canterbury Building, University of Wales, Lampeter, SA48 7ED
- k.miles@lamp.ac.uk
- gillian@gillianclarke.co.uk

Contact Gillian Clarke (contact via Kathy Miles)
c/o Library, University of Wales
Lampeter
Ceredigion
SA48 7ED
Meetings Meeting time: 7pm–9pm (contact for days, term time only)
About New members are welcome to attend at any time. All forms of writing are covered, but the main emphasis is on poetry. There is a charge of £20 per term, however students at the university may attend for free.

Llantrisant Ready Writers

19 Davids Court, Pontyclun, Rhondda Cynon Taff, CF72 9AY

☎ 01443 239868

✉ readywritersllan@aol.com

Contact Judith Sly

Meetings Meeting time: 7.30pm, second Thursday of each month

About New members welcome, please apply by post, phone or email. Any types of creative writing are covered as long as they do not conflict with the Christian ethos of the group. The group also meets at an annual gathering in the autumn with other Christian writers' groups where they invite a guest speaker and enjoy a three course lunch for no more than £15 inclusive. Group annual membership fees are currently £17.50 per year.

Lucht Focail Irish Writer's Group

Leeds Irish Centre, York Road, Leeds, LS9 9NT

☎ 0113 242 9765

✉ bill.fitzsimons@lfha.co.uk

Contact Bill Fitzsimons

32 Alexandra Grove

Hyde Park

Leeds

LS6 1QX

Meetings Meeting time: 8pm, second and fourth Thursday of each month

About New members welcome, any level of experience. Either come along for a taster session, or contact Bill Fitzsimons. The group is principally poetry, but prose is encouraged too. Work tends to reflect the ethnic background of members, which is mostly Irish, but not exclusively so. No fees.

Marsh Ink Writers' Group

Southlands Comprehensive School, Station Road, New Romney, Kent

☎ 01797 366621

✉ bridget@fowkes16.fsnet.co.uk

Contact Bridget Fowkes

Meetings Meeting time: 7.30pm–9.30pm, two Wednsdays a month during term time

About New members are welcome, either contact Bridget Fowkes or simply turn up. Covers all types of fiction and non-fiction writing. The group's president is novelist Pamela Oldfield. It has frequent guest speakers and runs workshops. Previous guests have included Jane Wenham-Jones and Simon Brett. Fees are £12 per year, plus £1 per meeting, £1.50 when a guest speaker is present and £3 for non-members. The first meeting is free for prospective new members.

Mayo Writers' Block

IRD Building, Ballyhaunis Road, Claremorris, Co. Mayo, Republic of Ireland

☎ 00353 87 984 3900

✉ info@mayowriters.org

🌐 www.mayowriters.org

Meetings Meeting time: Second and fourth Wednesday of the month

About New members welcome, please contact by phone or email. The group aims to encourage creative writing of all kinds and its members range for beginners, to those who have more experience.

Medway Mermaids

The Sunlight Centre, 105 Richmond Road, Gillingham, Kent, ME7 1LX

✉ medwaymermaids@yahoo.co.uk

🌐 www.medwaymermaids.btik.com

Contact Chair

Meetings Meeting time: 7.30pm–9.30pm, one Monday a month

About Welcomes new members, who must apply with a sample of their writing to be reviewed by the group. Will also meet prospective members for an informal chat. All types of writing are covered including poetry, prose, factual and plays. Fees are £18 per annum, or £9 for six months. Members need to attend regularly and be prepared to comment on the work of others.

The Memoir Writing Club (Worldwide)

PO Box 1, Kinvara, Co. Galway, Republic of Ireland

✉ office@thememoirwritingclub.com

🌐 www.thememoirwritingclub.com

Contact Irene Graham

Meetings Meeting time: Visit the website to find a Memoir Writing Club in your area.

About The Memoir Writing Club provides a platform for memoir writers to initiate Memoir Writing Clubs throughout the world. The Memoir Writing Club will provide each club member with The Memoir Writing Workbook, an innovative workbook created and written by Irene Graham, founder of The Creative Writer's Workshop in 1991. The workbook (which includes blank pages for your writings) is based upon 36 right-brain/left-brain exercises and techniques that will show you how to creatively write your Memoir. See the website for further details.

New Edinburgh Writers

Fountainbridge Library, Dundee Street, Edinburgh, Scotland, EH11 1BG

☎ 0131 466 2384
✉ edinnick272@hotmail.com
🖥
www.newedinburghwriters.pwp.blueyonder.co.uk
Contact Nick Morrison
7/4 Weir Court
3 Sighthill Bank
Edinburgh
EH11 4BB
Meetings Meeting time: 6pm–7.45pm
every Wednesday
About New members welcome, although numbers
are limited by room size. Most current members are
writers of poetry and short stories, although novels
and screenplays are also familiar to some members.
The meetings usually consist of members reading
their work and receiving feedback, the aim of which,
is to get work to competition standard. Fees are £2
per month which covers refreshments,
competitions, trips out and magazines.

North Camden & Belsize Writers' Group
Members' homes
✉ simeon.shoul@virgin.net
Contact Simeon Shoul
Meetings Meeting time: Approximately once every
four weeks, each member hosts in turn
About New members should make initial contact by
email. Please be aware that there is often a waiting
list. Covers fiction only, but all genres welcome.
There are no fees charged.

Northern Gay Writers
6 Mount Street, Manchester, M2 5NS
☎ 0161 832 3777
☎ 0161 832 2929
✉ cathy@commonword.org.uk
🖥 www.commonword.org.uk
Meetings Meeting time: 2pm–4pm, Saturdays
About Open to lesbian, gay and bisexual writers.
Contact for details of meeting dates.

Northwest Highland Writers
Durness Village Hall, Durness, Sutherland, IV27 4PN
☎ 01571 844020
✉ branchis@dsl.pipex.com
Contact Irene Brandt
Meetings Meeting time: Second Saturday of each
month, venues rotate.
About New members welcome; either get in touch
or go along to a meeting. Any creative writing is
covered, however the members must live in
Northwest Sutherland or Wester Ross. Fees are £5

per annum, plus £1 per meeting to cover the cost of
the venue.

Octoprose
Various locations around Guildford
☎ 07810 505035
Contact Roger Kendall
6 Princes Gardens
Worplesdon
Guildford
Surrey
GU3 3RY
Meetings Meeting time: Every other Thursday,
term time only
About New members are welcome, contact Roger
Kendall for more information. All types of writing are
covered, although they currently do not deal with a
lot of poetry. Fees are £3.50 per meeting, which
covers room hire and refreshments, with any excess
going towards group meals out.

The Original Writers' Group
The Battersea Library, 265 Lavender Hill, London, SW11 1JB
✉ info@theoriginalwriter.com
🖥 www.theoriginalwriter.com
Contact Rupert Davies-Cooke
Meetings Meeting time: 7pm–9pm every first and
third Wednesday of each month
About Has many members: poets, novelists,
playwrights, scriptwriters, historians, philosophers.
Welcomes writers from all walks of life as everyone
has a point of view, and the more varied these
opinions the richer the experience. Even if you are
just starting out and are interested in writing, but
don't have anything to bring, come along and just
experience the evening.

Ormskirk Writers & Literary Society (OWLS)
New Church House, Park Road, Ormskirk,
☎ 01695 423141
✉ judy.ingman@gmail.com
Contact Hon. Secretary, Judy Ingman
Meetings Meeting time: 7.30pm–10pm, first and
third Monday of each month
About New members welcome. Covers stories,
plays, sketches, verse and other types of writing.
Members suggest topics for meetings including
manuscript readings, writing workshops,
competitions and guest speakers. Fees are £20 per
annum, but new members may attend three
sessions for free.

Oxford Writer's Group

Member's Homes, Oxford

ⓦ www.oxfordwritersgroup.blogspot.com

Contact Jane Gordon-Cumming

Meetings Meeting time: Every other Tuesday

About The Oxford Writer's Group has been going strong for over 25 years. They are focused primarily on fiction, but also cover non-fiction and poetry. Past members include Veronica Stallwood, Linda Taylor and Catherine Fox. They are unable to accept new members at present, due to numbers, but keep an eye on their blog for any upcoming events.

Penicuik Writers' Group

Penicuik Library, The Penicuik Centre, Carlops Road, Penicuik, EH26 9EP

ⓞ 0131 440 1051

ⓔ davidcpurdie@aol.com

Contact David Purdie

12 Mayburn Vale

Loanhead

Midlothian

EH20 9HH

Meetings Meeting time: TBA

About New members welcome, just turn up to the meetings. All types of creative writing covered, no fees.

Pennine Ink Writers' Workshop

The Woodman Inn, 129 Todmorden Road, Burnley, Lancashire, BB11 3EX

ⓔ sheridansand1@yahoo.co.uk

Contact Laura Sheridan

Mid Pennine Arts

The Gallery

Yorke Street

Burnley

Lancashire

Meetings Meeting time: 8pm–10pm every Monday

About New members are always welcome, as long as they are willing to listen to constructive criticism. Please contact Laura Sheridan. Covers all types of writing. Fees are £1 per session.

The Pennine Poets Group

Private homes around West Yorkshire

ⓔ pmk@pkirk304.force9.co.uk

ⓦ www.penninepoets.co.uk

About Welcomes new members. First point of contact should be through the website. Please check the site for up to date details of meetings and who to contact. Poetry is the main focus of the group and readings, sometimes to music, are held regularly. The group also takes part in literary festivals and is associated with the journal 'Pennine

Platform'. Their small press, 'Pennine Poets Publications', also occasionally publishes members' work, and anthologies are published by Fighting Cock Press.

Phrase Writers

Hillingdon Park Baptist Church, Hercies Road, Hillingdon, Uxbridge, UB10 9LS

ⓔ rosemarysheath@hotmail.com

Contact Mrs Kath Lewis (Chairman)

Tel: 0208 573 3504

48 Hughes Road

Hayes

Middlesex

UB3 3AP

Meetings Meeting time: 1pm–3pm on alternate Thursdays

About Not actively seeking new members, however the group do welcome enquiries from suitable local writers of all abilities. Current members are mainly over retirement age and writing fiction, some non-fiction and plays. Fees are payable annually or monthly, equivalent to £2.50 per meeting.

Player-Playwrights

Venue: Horse and Groom, Great Portland Street, London, W1W 6PX

ⓞ 020 8883 0371

ⓔ playerplaywrights@groups.msn.com

ⓦ http://groups.msn.com/playerplaywrights

About A networking group where actual and aspiring playwrights discuss their work, and where links are made to potential producers and actors. Meetings take place at the Horse and Groom pub - see website for more details.

Plymouth Writers' Circle

Plymstock Community Centre, Plymstock, Plymouth, Devon, PL9 9DA

ⓞ 01752 491616

ⓔ edward.cartner@lineone.net

Contact Edward Cartner

66 Mount Batten Way

Plymstock

Plymouth

PL9 9EB

Meetings Meeting time: 7.30pm–9.30pm, every Tuesday

About New members from all backgrounds and levels of experience are welcome, just turn up on the night. Current members range from published writers to beginners. The group covers all types of fiction and non-fiction. The group does not adopt a teaching style and members can take what they want from the informal, friendly meetings. The group also stage an annual short story and verse competition. Fees are £1 per session.

The Poetry Society of Cheltenham
Venues around Montpellier, Cheltenham
☎ 01242 515595
✉ rturner@asvr.freeserve.co.uk
Contact Roger Turner
Meetings Meeting time: Last Tuesday of each month
About New poets are welcome and should contact Roger Turner (Chair) or Michael Newman (01242 675028). You will be asked to send a sample of writing to ensure a match of expectations. There is also a reading group that meets on the third Thursday of the month to read and discuss poetry.

Porthcawl Ready Writers
12 Hawkhurst Court, Porthcawl, Wales, CF36 3NU
☎ 01656 783873
✉ jopalewis@aol.com
Contact Pauline Lewis
c/o Library, University of Wales
Lampeter
Ceredigion
SA48 7ED
Meetings Meeting time: 7.30pm, first Tuesday of each month
About New members welcome, but please make contact first. The writing covered is mostly Christian and devotional, although all types are possible. The group joins other Christian writers groups for an annual day with a guest speaker, around £14 for the day.

Portway Writers
Adult Learning & Leisure Centre, Portway Annexe, Portway, Wells, Somerset, BA5 2QF
☎ 01749 676441
✉ jmthom@tiscali.co.uk
Contact Judith Thomas
11 Chapman's Close
Wookey
Wells
BA5 1LU
Meetings Meeting time: 10.30am–12.30pm, Tuesdays
About New members should contact Judith Thomas in the first instance, but will have to enrol at the leisure centre by phone. Beginners are welcome and the building has full disabled access. The group is a tutored class, as well as a writers' circle. Poetry, prose and drama writing are covered at the moment, although any other genres could be

catered for. There are several social events and members also take part in the Bath Festival in March.

Rathmine Writers' Workshop
Christ Church, Rathgar, Republic of Ireland
☎ 00353 86 402 5578
✉ info@rathmineswritersworkshop.com
🌐 www.rathmineswritersworkshop.com
Contact James Conway
Meetings Meeting time: 7.30pm–10pm, every other Thursday
About The focus is around readings of members' work and group feedback. Members currently write both poetry and prose, however there are additional prose only meetings every third Monday. Fees are €5 per person, €3 for concessions.

Redcar Writers
Coatham Memorial Hall, Coatham Road, Redcar
☎ 01642 478699
✉ writers@redpark.co.uk
🌐 www.communigate.co.uk/ne/redcarwritersgroup
Contact Brian Morton
Meetings Meeting time: 7pm–9pm every second Tuesday
About New members are welcome and there are no fees. Current members are writers of poetry, short stories, plays and novels.

Redwell Writers
Church House, Church Street, off Redwell Street, Norwich
✉ elasticpress@elasticpress.com
Contact Andrew Hook
85 Gertrude Road
Norwich
NR3 4SG
Meetings Meeting time: 7pm–9pm every Wednesday
About New members welcome, apply by email in the first instance. The group covers short story and novel writing of any genre, but not poetry. The fees are £5 per meeting.

Salisbury Writers
The United Reformed Church, Fisherton Street, Salisbury, Dorset
☎ 01980 629440
✉ susandown@aol.com
Contact Susan Down
4 Rosedale
Cholderton Road
Newton Toney
Salisbury
SP4 0EU

Meetings Meeting time: 7pm–9pm, first Thursday of every month

About New members welcome, with any level of experience. Current interests include poetry, short stories, novels, crime, romance and biography. The group also have a 'buddy system' for members to exchange longer pieces of work outside of the group. This is usually a pair that has found each other's comments helpful. Fees are £3 per session, plus £28 per annum.

Scarborough Writers' Circle
Allatt House, West Parade Road, Scarborough, YO12 5ED
- 01723 30535
- carol@newby.btinternet.com

Contact Carol Stockill
16 Fieldstead Crescent
Newby
Scarborough
North Yorkshire
YO12 6TH

Meetings Meeting time: 7.30pm every other Tuesday

About New members are welcome and can attend meetings as guests. Anyone wishing to join must submit a piece of writing to the president. The group encourages and shares all kinds of writing. Fees are £18 per annum, plus £1 per meeting. Guests can pay £3 per meeting.

ScribesRus
Brynaman Community Centre, Cwmgarw Road, Brynaman, SA18 1BU
- scribesrus1@aol.com

Contact Jan Slade

Meetings Meeting time: 2pm–4pm, every Monday

About New members are welcome, either make contact or go along. The group has been running for four years so far. Usual activities include producing stories and poems on a theme chosen by the members each week, which are given feedback and comments, producing anthologies and working on collaborative projects. Internet access and a café are available in the centre, and free parking is available in a car park directly opposite. Fees are £2.50 per meeting.

Speakeasy, Milton Keynes Writers' Group
The Quaker Centre, 1 Oakley Gardens, Downhead Park, Milton Keynes, MK15 9BH
- 01908 663860
- speakeasy@writerbrock.co.uk
- www.mkweb.co.uk/speakeasy

Contact The Secretary

Speakeasy
PO Box 5948
Stoke Hammond
Milton Keynes
MK10 1GX

Meetings Meeting time: 8pm–10.15pm, first Friday of each month

About New members are welcome to turn up and introduce themselves at any meeting. All genres of writing are covered, but members must write in English. Fees will be around £4 per session and £6 for a visiting guest night.

Stortford Scribblers
Apton Road Day Centre, Apton Road, Bishop's Stortford, Hertfordshire
- 01279 503582
- leo@applecroft.freeserve.co.uk

Contact Lesley Mace
29 Zambesi Road
Bishop's Stortford
Hertfordshire
CM23 3JR

Meetings Meeting time: 8pm, every other Thursday

About New members welcome. Either make contact or turn up to a meeting. Any type of writing in any genre is also welcome. Fees are £12 per annum, plus £3 per meeting.

Stort Valley Writers Group
Members' homes around Essex
- 01376 551379
- liberato@talktalk.net

Contact Maureen Blundell
16 Middle King
Braintree
Essex
CM7 3XY

Meetings Meeting time: Every second Monday

About New members welcome, please contact Maureen Blundell for information. Fiction, autobiography, poetry and article writing are covered. Members are encouraged to read their work and receive feedback from the group, but this is not compulsory. Trips are organised around once a year, as well as an annual Christmas dinner that is not always at Christmas. Fees are 50 pence per session.

Sutton Writers
Meeting Room 2 or 3, Civic Offices, St Nicholas Way, Sutton, Surrey, SM1 1EA
- teresa.tipping@tesco.net
- www.suttonwriters.info

Contact Teresa Tipping
24 Twickenham Close

Beddington
Croydon
CR0 4SZ
Meetings Meeting time: 8pm–10pm, second Friday of each month
About New members with any level of experience are welcome, whether writing for pleasure or for profit. All types of creative writing are covered, including poetry, non-fiction, drama, short stories, writing for children and novels. Various workshops for fully paid up members are hosted by members in their homes. Annual fee for full membership is £20. This includes entry to the main monthly meetings, workshops, in-house competitions and our newsletter. For country members who cannot attend the meetings but wish to enter competitions and receive the newsletter, the annual cost is £10. To hear a particular speaker or find out what we are about, visitors can pay £3 on the door at a monthly meeting.

Tavistock Writers' Group
11 Watts Road, Tavistock, Devon, PL19 8LF
- simon.c.baker@googlemail.co.uk
Contact Simon Baker
Meetings Meeting time: 7pm, Wednesday evenings
About An informal but critical group reading poetry, drama and fiction. Prospective members should submit a writing sample and enquiry in the first instance.

Tenbury Writers' Group
Tenbury Library, 24 Teme Street, Tenbury Wells, Worcestershire, WR15 8AA
- 01584 810493
- sallytenbury@yahoo.com
Contact Sally Matthews
Meetings Meeting time: 7.30pm, second Tuesday of each month
About All types of writing are tried and reviewed. Current members range from 16–70, so anyone is welcome to make contact. There are no fees, except for coffee at 50 pence.

Thames Valley Writers' Circle
St Joseph's Church Hall, Berkshire Drive, Tilehurst, Reading, RG31 5JJ
- sawdonsmith@hotmail.com
- www.thamesvalleywriterscircle.org
Contact Dick Sawdon Smith
Meetings Meeting time: 7.30pm–9.30pm every Tuesday
About New members are welcome. Novels, articles, short stories and poetry are all covered. Meetings usually revolve around constructive feedback after

members' readings of the work. Longer work may be dissected before the meeting. The group also organises workshops, outings and guest speakers, a notable past guest speaker being Colin Dexter. Fees are £3 per session, or £2 for concessions.

Toddington Poetry Society
Hightown Community Centre, Concorde Street, Luton, Bedfordshire, LU2 0JD
- 01234 822230
- toddington.poetry@tiscali.co.uk
- www.toddingtonpoetrysociety.co.uk
Contact Peter Stileman
Meetings Meeting time: 8pm, second and fourth Tuesday of each month
About New members welcome. Either turn up or make contact. Focused entirely on poetry, with either guest speakers (previous guests have included Andrew Motion and Simon Armitage) or more informal evenings.

The T Party Writers' Group
Venues around central London
- 020 8773 3566
- enquiries@t-party.org.uk
- www.t-party.org.uk
Contact Sara Townsend
8 Wrythe Green
Carshalton
Surrey
SM5 2QR
Meetings Meeting time: Monthly, Saturday afternoons
About Specialist group focusing mainly on science fiction, fantasy and horror. New members welcome, make email contact in the first instance. Members should have had something published prior to joining, as the group is serious and professional in its criticisms of work and not suitable for beginners. New members are advised to sit in on a couple of meetings first, before committing to join. Special guest speaker events are run alongside the monthly meetings, with input from writers, editors and agents. Fees are £10 per annum.

The University of Liverpool Creative Writing Society for Lifelong Learning
Room 102, The Alastair Pilkington Building, University of Liverpool, Liverpool, L69 3BX
- 0151 291 6942
- thomas.mcbride2@btopenworld.com
Contact Tommy McBride
Meetings Meeting time: 7pm–9pm every Monday
About New members welcome, any level of experience. The group is informal and friendly, and meets to discuss the theory and practice of creative

writing. All genres of creative writing are covered and members can bring their work to be criticised. Each week a theme is put forward to offer the writers a challenge, but this aspect, as with all aspects of the group, is entirely optional.

Ver Poets
St Michael's Church Hall, St Michael's Street, St Albans, Hertfordshire
- ☎ 01727 864898
- ✉ daphne.schiller@virgin.net
- 🌐 www.verpoets.org.uk
Contact Daphne Schiller
15 Brampton Road
St Albans
Hertfordshire
AL1 4PP
Meetings Meeting time: 8pm, monthly on a Friday
About Membership enquiries welcome from people with a love of poetry. Day workshops for members only are held fortnightly in members' homes, although anyone can attend the evening meetings. The group runs two members' competitions, as well as an annual open competition. Fees are £3 per meeting for non-members and £2 for members.

Verulam' Writers Circle
St Michael's Church Hall, St Michael's Street, St Albans, Hertfordshire, AL3 4SL
and
The Goat Pub, Sopwell Lane, St Albans
- ☎ 07713 515868
- ✉ info@verulamwriterscircle.org.uk
- 🌐 www.verulamwriterscircle.org.uk
Contact Kevin
Meetings Meeting time: 8pm (see website for programme)
About The group holds regular manuscript evenings, workshops and meetings at both venues. Writers of any level of experience and any type of writing are welcome. The group run competitions and they have a very active and full website. Fees are £30 per year for membership but guests can 'pay as you go' for £3 per meeting, or £5 for a guest speaker. Manuscript evenings at The Goat Pub are £1 for members and non-members.

Walsall Writers' Circle
Park Hall Community School, Park Hall Road, Walsall, WS5 3HF
- ☎ 01922 458595
- ✉ walsallwriterscircle@mereed.co.uk
- 🌐 www.wwc.mereed.co.uk
Contact Secretary, Mrs A.R. Reed
Meetings Meeting time: 7.30pm, second Thursday of each month (except August)

About New members with any level of experience are welcome. The meetings are varied and can be based around members' manuscripts, workshops, special events and competitions. Fees are £8 per annum. Postal members and families may subscribe for £12 per annum. Visitors pay £1 which is refunded if they join.

Watford Writers
The Cha Cha Cha Café, Cassiobury Park, Shepherd Road, Watford, Hertfordshire
- ☎ 01923 227054
- ✉ watfordwriters@gmail.com
- 🌐 www.watfordwriters.co.uk
Contact Lynne Motijoane
2 Howard Close
Watford
WD24 5JB
Meetings Meeting time: 7.30pm–9.30pm every Monday
About New members should contact Lynne Motijoane. The group organises guest speakers, workshops and manuscript evenings. Fees are £3 per session.

The Western Writers' Centre
34 Nun's Island, Galway, Republic of Ireland
- ☎ 00353 91 533594
- ✉ westernwriters@eircom.net
- 🌐 www.twwc.ie
Meetings Meeting time: 2pm every Wednesday or Thursday
About The centre runs a 'Diverse Writers Group' which is free of charge, as well as a general writers group on a Wednesday, also at 2pm.

West Sussex Writers' Club
The Pavillion, Field Place, The Boulevard, Worthing
- ☎ 01273 701235
Contact Heather Reay
131 Bevendan Crescent
Brighton
BN2 4RE
Meetings Meeting time: 7.30pm, second Thursday of each month
About New members of any experience level welcome. The group covers every genre of writing from scriptwriting and journalism, to novels and non-fiction. There is a guest speaker each month, and the group runs various workshops and competitions. It is a large group, with over 130 members.

Wimpole Street Writers

1a Upper Wimpole Street, Westminster, London, W1G 6LA

- 020 7486 6128
- jschary@mac.com
- www.wimpolestreetwriters.com

Contact Jill Robinson

Meetings Meeting time: 6.30pm–9.30pm, every Tuesday and Thursday

About New members who are committed to writing are welcome, subject to space, and are advised to contact Jill Robinson for an informal interview. Workshops are held in Jill's dining room where she makes dinner for the writers. The group covers fiction, non-fiction, memoirs, plays, screenplays and poetry. An annual literary event is also held in January where members read their work to invited members of the press. Jill is also involved in meeting with agents and publishers. Fees are £20 per session (including dinner).

Wirral Writers

Joseph Meyer Rooms, Bebington Civic Centre, Civic Way, Bebington, Wirral, CH63 7PN

- 01352 750708
- clang5454@aol.com
- www.communigate.co.uk/chesh/wirralwritersgroup

Contact Cheryl Lang
8 Llys Gwynant
Bryn Road, Byn y Baal
Mold
Flintshire
CH7 6NL

Meetings Meeting time: 7.30pm–10pm, first and third Friday of each month

About New members welcome. Either go along, or contact beforehand for an informal chat. Members range from beginners to the more experienced, and all types of writing are encouraged. Meetings are usually informal feedback sessions and throughout the year the group hold competitions, workshops and special discussions. They also occasionally organise social meals or walks. Fees are £20 per annum, but new members can trial before they commit.

Woking Writers' Circle

Strollers Drop-in Centre, Goldsworth Park, Woking, Surrey

- info@wokingwriterscircle.org.uk
- www.wokingwriterscircle.org.uk

Contact Sharyn Owen

Meetings Meeting time: 7.30pm–10pm, third Thursday of each month

About The group is for people who write for pleasure but would also like to be published. Current members are very mixed in terms of age, gender and ethnic background. The main focus of each meeting is to receive constructive feedback on your work, although there are sometimes exercises and 'homework' set. The group also runs an informal breakfast meeting on the first Sunday of each month, at 10am in the Cafe Giardino, 41 Wolsey Walk, Woking. Fees are £20 per annum, although new members can attend twice for free.

Womanswrite

6 Mount Street, Manchester, M2 5NS

- 0161 832 3777
- 0161 832 2929
- cathy@commonword.org.uk
- www.commonword.org.uk

Meetings Meeting time: 11am–1pm every Tuesday

About Open to women to meet and discuss different aspects of writing and publishing every week. Sometimes use practical exercises to stimulate creativity.

Wood Green Group

Wood Green Library, High Road, Wood Green, London, N22 6XD

- word4wordwoodgreen@hotmail.co.uk
- www.wforw.org.uk

Contact Richard Jones

Meetings Meeting time: 11am–1pm every Saturday

About This group is an offshoot of Word for Word (see their separate entries).

Worcester Writers' Circle

Dancox House Club Room, St Clements Close, St John's, Worcester

- 01905 619062

Contact Sue Round

Meetings Meeting time: 7.30pm–9.30pm, every other Tuesday

About New members welcome. For more information contact Susan Round. Meetings usually consist of readings, feedback and discussions. Current members range from hobbyists to published writers.

Word for Word Novel Writing Group

Hornsey Library, Haringey Park, Crouch End, London, N8 9JA

- info@wforw.org.uk
- www.wforw.org.uk

Meetings Meeting time: 3.15pm–5.15pm alternate Wednesdays

About New members welcome, numbers permitting. Please make contact in the first instance. Writers of every kind are welcome as long as they are beginning, or working on a novel, and are committed to participating in feedback sessions.

Word for Word Poetry Group
Hornsey Library, Haringey Park, Crouch End, London, N8 9JA
- poetic@btinternet.com
- www.wforw.org.uk

Contact Laurence Scott
Meetings Meeting time: 1pm–3pm every Wednesday during term time
About New members welcome, contact tutor and published poet, Laurence Scott. Designed for beginning and improving poets. Fees range from £4–£6 per meeting, the first meeting is free.

Word Weavers
South Moor Branch Library
and
Oxhill Workingmen's Club, Stanley, County Durham
- www.wordweavers.org.uk

Contact Marjorie Briggs
Meetings Meeting time: 6pm–8pm, first Thursday of each month (South Moor Branch Library). Every other Thursday 7pm–9pm (Oxhill Workingmen's Club)
About New members welcome, visit website for details. Small, friendly group.

WordWrights
The Abbey Room, Titchfield Community Centre, Mill Street, Titchfield, Hampshire
- 01329 846480
- liza.look@btinternet.com

Contact Rosa Johnson
Little Oak
293a Titchfield Road
Titchfield
Hampshire
PO14 3ER
Meetings Meeting time: 1.30pm, first and third Thursday of every month
About New members welcome as long as the maximum limit of 22 members isn't exceeded. Please call Rosa Johnson in the first instance. Most types of writing are covered and members are expected to take part in giving mutual support. The group does not organise its own special events, but does help with other community projects. Fees are £10 per annum, plus £1.50 per meeting.

Wrekin Writers
29 Christine Avenue, Wellington, Shropshire, TF1 2DX
- 01952 299232
- admin@wrekinwriters.co.uk
- www.wrekinwriters.co.uk

Meetings Meeting time: 10am–12pm, third Saturday of each month
About Welcomes new members. 'Just come along to any meeting and try us out for a few months to see if you like us.' Covers all types of novels, poetry, short stories and articles. Runs an open writing workshop in October each year, in conjunction with Wellington Literary Festival, as well as an annual retreat.

Writability
Carnegie Library, Main Street, Ayr, Scotland
- webmaster@writability.co.uk

Meetings Meeting time: 7pm–9pm, Mondays from October–May
About A readers and writers group, with a strong emphasis on books and writing book reviews. Able bodied and disabled members are welcome. Run by Writeability, an educational charity.

Write Now!
Venues in and around Bury St Edmonds, Suffolk
- george@wickerswork.co.uk
- www.writenow.wickerswork.co.uk

Meetings Meeting time: 7.30pm–10pm every other Tuesday
About New members can be nominated by existing members or make contact directly. Meetings are focused around a set theme, with readings and constructive criticism. Writers are expected to fully participate, with guidelines and information available on the website. Fees are £10 annual subscription and £2 per meeting

Write Out Loud
Venues in Bolton, Wigan, Oldham and Rochdale, and irregularly in Bordeaux
- 01204 398148
- editor@writeoutloud.net
- www.writeoutloud.net

Contact Julian Jordan, Dave Morgan
Meetings Meeting time: Write Out Loud organises scores of public events every month. Check the Gig Guide on the website for more details.
About Write Out Loud encourages ordinary folks who write poetry to share their words with others in friendly, welcoming open-floor read-around and open-mic events. They also support individual poets, organisations and groups across the country, via

their website, which contains community pages, poetry galleries and an in-depth event guide.

Writers Against Writing
Venues around Edinburgh
- ✉ writersagainstwriting@yahoo.co.uk
- ⊕ www.writersagainstwriting.co.uk

Meetings Meeting time: Irregular meetings
About New members are always welcome, email for details. The group is mainly web based and face to face meetings are irregular and sporadic. The group's ethic is strongly against writing to get published, or writing within constraints. It encourages not for profit writing that will never be bought or sold. Prose is the main focus, although there is occasional poetry.

Writers in Glasgow
Glasgow
- ✉ anmshrestha@gmail.com

Contact Mahima Shrestha
Meetings Meeting time: 2.00pm–4.00pm, every Friday
About The primary aim of the group is to encourage members to find/develop their own voice in thier writing. The program is very flexible - the group has several prompts and discussions for each meeting but members are free to explore other ideas or topics, whatever inspires them that day. Members range from students, to writers with dyslexia, beginners to experienced. Fees are £2 per meeting.

Writers' Meet
Clevedon Community Centre, Princes Hall, Sunhill Park, Clevedon
- ☎ 01275 873452
- ✉ snake@ukgateway.net

Contact David Robinson
Meetings Meeting time: 10.30am–12.30pm, every second Thursday
About Potential new members should phone or email in the first instance. They should be currently engaged in writing, and producing results in any genre. The group's primary function is help and support, although they also organise member led workshops and regular guest speakers.

Writers of our Age
Venues around Brockley, South East London
- ☎ 07748 185325
- ✉ pjbruce@ukonline.co.uk

Contact Pamela Bruce
Meetings Meeting time: Fortnightly
About New members welcome. Call or email for details of the next meeting. The group deals with all types of fiction, but primarily novels of any genre. Once a year the group organises a weekend away.

York Novelist Society
Room W/035A, Wentworth College, York University, York
- ⊕ www.yorknovelistsociety.bravehost.com

Contact Kaitlyn Kernek
Meetings Meeting time: 7pm, every Wednesday
About New members are welcome; post in the forum on the website with a brief description of your writing experience and a short synopsis of your novel. All genre of novels are accepted, but no short stories or poetry. This is a workshopping group and all members are working toward producing a piece of publishable standard work. Current members are both published and unpublished. There is no cost to join.

York Writers
The Golden Fleece, 16 Pavement, York, YO1 9UP
- ✉ clintwastling@aol.com
- ⊕ www.yorkwriters.org.uk

Contact Clint Wastling
Meetings Meeting time: 8pm, alternate Wednesdays
About Meetings are held in the function room of The Golden Fleece from 8–10pm. The first Wednesday meeting of the month is a manuscript meeting and the last is usually a speaker, with a discussion or readings. All types of creative writing are covered. The entry fee is £2.50 for guests and £1 for members. More information can be found at on the website.

Artists' Choice

PO Box 3, Huntingdon, Cambridgeshire, PE28 0QX

☎ 01832 710201

🖷 01832 710488

🌐 www.artists-choice.co.uk

About An independent book club for practising artists with a quarterly magazine. They also created and co-sponsor the Practical Art Book of The Year Award.

Baker Books

Manfield Park, Cranleigh, Surrey, GU6 8NU

☎ 01483 267888

🖷 01483 267409

📧 bakerbooks@dial.pipex.com

🌐 www.bakerbooks.co.uk

About An independent school book club, for children aged between three and sixteen.

BCA

Hargreaves Road, Swindon, Wiltshire, SN99 9NX

☎ 0844 499 0000

📧 e-support@booksdirect.co.uk

🌐 www.bca.co.uk

About BCA is a wholly owned subsidiary of Bertelsmann. Its clubs include: World Books; Mango; World of Mystery & Thriller; History Guild; Ancient History; Arts; Fantasy & Science Fiction; Railway; Books for Children; Military & Aviation; Escape Fiction; Quality Paperbacks Direct (QPD) and The Softback Preview (TSP).

Bibliophile

Unit 5, Thomas Road, London, E14 7BN

☎ 020 7515 9222

🖷 020 7538 4115

📧 customercare@bibliophilebooks.com

🌐 www.bibliophilebooks.com

Contact Annie Quigley

About A discount postal club with around 4,000 titles available in a wide range of genres. Request the free catalogue, or order directly from the website.

The Book People Ltd

Catteshall Manor, Catteshall Lane, Godalming, Surrey, GU7 1UU

☎ 0845 602 3030

🖷 0845 606 4242

📧 feedback@thebookpeople.co.uk

🌐 www.thebookpeople.co.uk

About The Book People is not a traditional book club, as there is no obligation to buy more than once. Members can receive a free monthly catalogue.

Cygnus Book Club

PO Box 15, Llandeilo, Carmarthenshire, SA19 6YX

☎ 01550 777701

🖷 01550 777569

📧 enquiries@cygnus-books.co.uk

🌐 www.cygnus-books.co.uk

About A book club catering for those interested in mind, body and spirit titles. They also publish a monthly magazine The Cygnus Review.

David Arscott's Sussex Book Club

Dolphin House, 51 St Nicholas Lane, Lewes, Sussex, BN7 2JZ

☎ 01273 470100

🖷 01273 470100

📧 sussexbooks@aol.com

🌐 www.pomegranate-press.co.uk

Contact David Arscott

About Founded by David Arscott, publisher of Pomegranate Press. The club caters for those interested in books on Sussex and Sussex life.

The Folio Society

44 Eagle Street, London, WC1R 4FS

☎ 020 7400 4200

🖷 020 7400 4242

🌐 www.foliosociety.com

About Catering for those interested in classic literature.

Letterbox Library

71–73 Allen Road, Stoke Newington, London, N16 8RY

☎ 020 7503 4801

🖷 020 7503 4800

📧 info@letterboxlibrary.com

🌐 www.letterboxlibrary.com

About A not for profit workers cooperative, which specialises in multicultural, non-sexist, children's books.

The Poetry Book Society

4th Floor, 2 Tavistock Place, London, WC1H 9RA

☎ 020 7833 9247

🖷 020 7833 5990

@ info@poetrybooks.co.uk
🌐 www.poetrybooks.co.uk
About A poetry book club, which also has a children's poetry book club and a niche online poetry store.

Readers' Union
Brunel House, Forde Close, Newton Abbot, Devon, TQ12 4PU
☎ 01626 323200
☎ 01626 323318
@ comments@readersunion.co.uk
🌐 www.readersunion.co.uk
About Reader's Union book clubs will cease operations from June 2009. Ran ten different clubs including: The Craft Club; Needlecrafts with Cross Stitch; Painting for Pleasure; Craftsman's Book Club; The Equestrian Book Society and Photographers' Book Club.

Red House
PO Box 142, Bangor, Wales, LL57 4ZP
☎ 0845 606 4280
☎ 0845 606 4242
@ Online form.
🌐 www.redhouse.co.uk
About Red House isn't a traditional book club as there is no obligation to buy. It sells children's books through a free monthly catalogue.

Scholastic Book Clubs
FREEPOST, Windrush Park, Range Road, Witney, Oxon, OX29 0YZ
☎ 01993 893475
☎ 01993 893424
@ sbcenquiries@scholastic.co.uk
🌐 www.scholastic.co.uk
About Two age specific school book clubs for children including: Early Years and Primary (Ages 0-13) and C2C (Ages 11+).

Writers' Bookshelf
5th Floor, 31-32 Park Row, Leeds, LS1 5JD
☎ 0113 200 2929
☎ 0113 200 2928
@ castlehills@yorkshirebooks.com
🌐 www.writersnews.co.uk
About Writers' News magazine compiles a selection of books for writers.

BOOK CLUBS

ORGS, GROUPS & CLUBS

LISTINGS

REFERENCE & SPECIALIST LIBRARIES

The Ancell Library
King Charles Street, London, SW1A 2AH
- 020 7008 3925
- 020 7008 3270
- library.enquiries@fco.gov.uk
- www.fco.gov.uk

About The Ancell Library has a collection of books, journals, pamphlets and papers on international affairs, diplomacy, defence and security issues, countries and regions, politics, parliamentary issues, maps and geographical information. The historical collection includes material of the former Foreign Office, Colonial Office and Commonwealth Relations Office, and includes many rare volumes and early works on travel. Much of the historical collection is in the process of being transferred to King's College London - see the website for details.

Although it is primarily a resource for Foreign & Commonwealth Office (FCO) staff, access to The Ancell Library is available to the general public, if publications are not available elsewhere. An application form must be submitted by post. See the website for further details.

Armitt Gallery, Museum & Library
Rydal Road, Ambleside, Cumbria, LA22 9BL
- 01539 431212
- 01539 431313
- info@armitt.com
- www.armitt.com

About The Armitt Gallery, Museum & Library houses a collection of art, archaeology, archives, books, geology and photography. There is also a local history collection, which includes over 400 water colours by Beatrix Potter. The library has over 10,000 titles relating to the Lake District and the people who lived, worked and visited there, plus an extensive collection of early guidebooks.

Atheneum Liverpool
Church Alley, Liverpool, L1 3DD
- 0151 709 7770
- 0151 709 7770
- library@theathenaeum.org.uk
- www.theathenaeum.org.uk

About Liverpool's renowned Athenaeum Library, founded in 1797, is one of the most important regional history resources in the country. The library has some 60,000 items in stock. The collection is particularly strong in classical and other literature, and theology, history, biography and travel. The local history section includes manuscripts, maps, playbills, prints and drawings. There are also books from the library of William Roscoe, 17th Century grammars of South American Indian languages, and 18th Century plays. Other collections include bound volumes of economic pamphlets and local directories. See the website for access details for non-members.

Barbican Library
Barbican Centre, Silk Street, London, EC2Y 8DS
- 020 7638 0569
- 020 7638 2249
- barbicanlib@cityoflondon.gov.uk
- www.cityoflondon.gov.uk

About The largest of the City of London's public lending libraries, the Barbican Library has specialist sections on conservation, crime, and fiction, and finance, the history of London, natural resources and socialism. The Barbican Music Library has one of the largest recorded music collections in London that is available to the public. The Barbican Children's Library has a large collection of children's fiction and non-fiction books and also organises regular free events.

Bath Royal Literary & Scientific Institution
6–18 Queen Square, Bath, BA1 2HN
- 01225 312084
- admin@brlsi.org
- www.brlsi.org

About The Bath Royal Literary & Scientific Institution (BRLSI) was founded in 1824. Its antiquarian library now contains over 7,000 volumes, notably from the Jenyns and Broome natural history libraries. Smaller collections cover local history, theology, travel and government. Archives contain bound volumes of letters from eminent naturalists and scientists, including Charles Darwin, Sir Joseph Hooker and Professor J.S. Henslow. Open to members (new members welcome) and to researchers by appointment. There are frequent lectures, special events and exhibitions, and specialist discussion groups on literature, science and the arts, plus scientific demonstrations for young people.

BFI National Archive
21 Stephen Street, London, W1T 1LN
- 020 7255 1444
- 020 7436 0165
- library@bfi.org.uk
- www.bfi.org.uk

About Holding the world's largest collection of film and television information, the BFI National Archive is a major national research collection of documentation and information on film and television. The archive contains more than 50,000 fiction films, over 100,000 non-fiction titles and around 625,000 television programmes. The library specialises in British film and television, but it also has international scope. There is an online catalogue.

The Birmingham & Midland Institute
9 Margaret Street, Birmingham, B3 3BS
- 0121 236 3591
- 0121 212 4577
- admin@bmi.org.uk
- www.bmi.org.uk

About A private lending library for Institute members, specialising in humanities. Some of the local history books can be purchased as copies on a CD. The BMI also includes The Birmingham Library, founded in 1779.

Birmingham Library Services
Birmingham Central Library, Chamberlain Square, Birmingham, B3 3HQ
- 0121 303 4511
- 0121 233 4458
- central.library@birmingham.gov.uk
- www.birmingham.gov.uk/libraries

About Birmingham Central Library holds one of the national collections of photography. Materials held include prints, lantern slides and books illustrated with photographic prints. There are also numerous other special collections. The website acts as a portal page, containing a range of information about libraries within the Birmingham area.

Bishopsgate Library
230 Bishopsgate, London, EC2M 4QH
- 020 7392 9270
- 020 7392 9275
- library@bishopsgate.org.uk
- www.bishopsgate.org.uk

About Free public access to world renowned collections on London, Labour, Freethought and Co-operation. The extensive London history section includes the personal library and papers of George Howell; publications and papers of George Jacob Holyoake; the Raphael Samuel archive; and the London Co-operative Society collection. In addition, the library holds research materials for local and family historians, general reference materials, and current national and local newspapers. Bishopsgate Library does not allow their books to be borrowed.

The Bodleian Library
Broad Street, Oxford, Oxfordshire, OX1 3BG
- 01865 277000
- Online form.
- www.ouls.ox.ac.uk/bodley

About The Bodleian Library is situated at the heart of the University of Oxford in a group of buildings spanning over 500 years of history. It is one of the five national copyright libraries, the principal library for Oxford University, and an international resource for scholarship and research worldwide. Being the second largest library in the UK (after the British Library), the Bodleian has 30 reading rooms – with 2,482 places – in ten buildings in central Oxford. With annual acquisitions of over 300,000 items (including foreign purchases), there are over 7 million volumes held by the Library on over 190km (118 miles) of shelving.

Admission to read in the Library is by card. For external readers and visitors a card can be obtained at the Admissions Office.

British Architectural Library
Royal Institute of British Architects, 66 Portland Place, London, W1B 1AD
- 020 5480 5533
- 020 7251 1541
- info@inst.riba.org
- www.architecture.com

About The largest and most comprehensive resource in Britain for research and information on all aspects of architecture. The library collections (close to four million objects) include books, periodicals, manuscripts, archives, drawings, photographs, models, paintings, medals and artefacts. Books, periodicals and photographs are held at the Royal Institute of British Architects (RIBA) headquarters, and drawings and archives are located at the Victoria and Albert Museum (V&A). Library services include a cutting edge information centre, available to both the public and RIBA members. The library is open to members, and to non-members buying day tickets.

The British Library

St Pancras, 96 Euston Road, London, NW1 2DB

☎ 020 7412 7676

✉ reader-services-enquiries@bl.uk

🌐 www.bl.uk

About The British Library is the national library of the United Kingdom. The collections include such items as the Magna Carta, Lindisfarne Gospels and Leonardo da Vinci's notebook. The British Library serves business and industry, researchers, students and academics in the UK and worldwide. The collection includes 150 million items in most known languages, with three million new items being incorporated each year. There is space at the library for over 1,200 readers. Collections include: Americas, Asia, Pacific & Africa, East European, Modern British, Modern Irish, and West European. There are also collections on early printed manuscripts, maps, music, newspapers, patents, trademarks and designs. Alongside this, there are also reports, conferences and theses, philatelic, science, technology, and the business and sound archive.

British Library Newspapers

Colindale Avenue, London, NW9 5HE

☎ 020 7412 7353

☎ 020 7412 7379

✉ newspaper@bl.uk

🌐 www.bl.uk

About British Library Newspapers contains the national archive collection of British and overseas newspapers. The collection also includes popular magazines and periodicals, and is available in hard copy, microform or CD-ROM. The library has over 52,000 newspaper and periodical titles within its web catalogue. There is an online search function for selected issues of *London's Daily News, The News of the World, The Weekly Dispatch* and *The Manchester Guardian*.

British Organ Archive

Birmingham Central Library (Archives Department), Birmingham, B3 3HQ

☎ 0121 303 4217

🌐 www.bios.org.uk

About Material held at the library is mainly the property of the British Institute of Organ Studies. The collections held relate to all aspects of these instruments, their history and conservation.

Bromley House Library/Nottingham Subscription Library

Bromley House, Angel Row, Nottingham, NG1 6HL

☎ 0115 947 3134

✉ enquiries@bromleyhouse.org

🌐 www.bromleyhouse.org

About Founded in 1816, the Nottingham Subscription Library collection has approximately 35,000 books. These include local history, many topographical works and a wide selection of 19th and early 20th Century novels. In recent years the collection's emphasis has been on biographies, travel books and new novels.

CAA Library & Information Centre

Aviation House, Gatwick Airport South, Gatwick, RH6 0YR

☎ 01293 573725

☎ 01293 573181

✉ infoservices@caa.co.uk

🌐 www.caa.co.uk

About The CAA Library & Information Centre is open to the public and contains a collection of books, reports, directories, statistics, videos, and periodicals on most aspects of civil aviation and related subjects.

The Caird Library

National Maritime Museum, Park Row, Greenwich, London, SE10 9NF

☎ 020 8312 6516

✉ library@nmm.ac.uk

🌐 www.nmm.ac.uk

About Named after the Museum's principal founder and benefactor, Sir James Caird, the National Maritime Museum Library holds over 100,000 books, 20,000 pamphlets, 20,000 bound periodicals and 8,000 rare books, dating from 1474 to 1850. The library's contents cover every aspect of maritime history, including emigration, navigation, piracy, astronomy, shipping companies, shipwrecks, biographies, the two world wars, and the merchant and royal navies. There are special collections for researching family history, merchant shipping and warships. The manuscripts collection is the largest and most important dedicated archive for the study of maritime history in the world. The library is open to anyone over 18 years of age with a research query. There is an online catalogue and an on site e-library.

Catholic Central Library

St Michael's Abbey, Farnborough Road, Farnborough, Hampshire, GU14 7NQ

☎ 01252 543818

✉ library@catholic-library.org.uk

🌐 www.catholic-library.org.uk

About The Catholic Central Library has 70,000 books and periodicals, including subjects on theology, spirituality, biography, and history - including Catholic Family History.

Chetham's Library
Long Millgate, Manchester, M3 1SB
- 0161 834 7961
- 0161 839 5797
- librarian@chethams.org.uk
- www.chethams.org.uk

About Founded in 1653, Chetham's Library is the oldest public library in the English speaking world. The library holds more than 100,000 volumes of printed books, of which 60,000 were published before 1851. It houses renowned collections of 16th and 17th Century printed works, periodicals and journals, and a wide ranging collection of images and photographs. Specialises in the history of Northwest England.

City Business Library
1 Brewers' Hall Garden (off Aldermanbury Square), London, EC2V 5BX
- 020 7332 1812
- 020 7332 1847
- www.cityoflondon.gov.uk

About The City Business Library is a public reference library specialising in current business information of practical use. The library has a major collection of sources of business information, including market research, and UK and international directories, in both print and electronic format. No membership required – email enquiry service is via an online form on the website.

Commonwealth Secretariat Library
Marlborough House, Pall Mall, London, SW1Y 5HX
- 020 7747 6253
- 020 7747 6168
- library@commonwealth.int
- www.thecommonwealth.org

About The Commonwealth Secretariat is the main intergovernmental agency of the Commonwealth. The Library has a collection of documentation covering a subject range that includes politics and international relations, economics, education, health, gender, environment, science and technology, and management. Much of the collection consists of government publications, conference reports, discussion and working papers, with a wide range of publications from international organisations. Most of the materials have been published within the last ten years. The library is also the official repository for the Secretariat's own publications and holds more than 3,000 separate items. Open to members of the public by prior appointment.

Copac
- www.copac.ac.uk

About The Copac library catalogue gives free access to the merged online catalogues of major university and national libraries in the UK and Ireland, including the British Library.

The Devon & Exeter Institution Library
7 The Close, Exeter, Devon, EX1 1EZ
- 01392 251017
- www.library.ex.ac.uk/dei

About The Devon & Exeter Institution is an independent subscription library founded in 1813. The library collections, of around 34,000 volumes, are included in the University of Exeter's library catalogue. They are particularly strong in West Country materials, and 18th and 19th Century books. For access please contact the Institution.

Directory of Local Councils
- www.direct.gov.uk/en/dl1/directories/localcouncils/index.htm

About Lists local councils by region. Users can find public library information from the local authority websites.

Dr William's Library
14 Gordon Square, London, WC1H 0AR
- 020 7387 3727
- 020 7388 1142
- enquiries@dwlib.co.uk

About Dr William's Library is primarily a theological library, although collections also include philosophy, history and literature. The library has a large collection of Byzantine history and culture, and considerable holdings of pre 19th Century works relating to English Non-conformity. The library contains approximately 20,000 items.

Dublin City Public Libraries
Dublin City Council, Civic Offices, Wood Quay, Dublin 8, Republic of Ireland
- 00353 1 222 2222
- customerservices@dublincity.ie
- www.dublincitypubliclibraries.ie

About The Dublin City Public Libraries website provides a network of twenty-one branch libraries, a number of specialist information services and a mobile library service to meet the information needs of the citizens of Dublin. The site also has further information on library events and services in Dublin.

Family Records Centre

1 Myddelton Street, Islington, London, EC1R 1UW

- 020 8392 5300
- 020 8487 9214
- frc@nationalarchives.gov.uk
- www.familyrecords.gov.uk

About The Family Records Office is part of The National Archive. It holds census records, records of births, marriages and deaths, adoptions, religious records, wills, immigration, emigration, and military records.

French Institute Library (Institut Français)

17 Queensberry Place, London, SW7 2DT

- 020 7073 1354
- 020 7073 1355
- library@ambafrance.org.uk
- www.institut-francais.org.uk

About The French Institute Library has wide and varied documentation on all aspects of France, especially the works of French and French speaking authors. There are books, comics, CDs, videos and DVDs, CD-ROMs, talking books, French newspapers and periodicals, press cutting files, archival audio material, specialist resources for French language learners and a children's library. Loans are restricted to members, but the library is open to the general public for reference.

Goethe Institute Library

50 Princes Gate, Exhibition Road, London, SW7 2PH

- 020 7596 4000
- 020 7594 0240
- info@london-goethe.org
- www.goethe.de/london

About The German Cultural Centre library has an up to date collection of German language books, English translations, reference works and dictionaries. There are also German newspapers and journals, databases and language resources. The library houses specialist collections on contemporary literature, film and theatre, fine arts and photography.

The Guildford Institute Library

Ward Street, Guildford, Surrey, GU1 4LH

- 01483 562142
- 01483 451034
- library@guildford-institute.org.uk
- www.guildford-institute.org.uk/library.htm

About The Institute (originally the Guildford Mechanics Institute) was founded in 1834. It holds over 14,000 volumes, of which many pre-date the First World War. They hold up to date fiction, and non-fiction, plus newspapers and periodicals. Books, photographs, prints and drawings are held, which relate to the history, people, antiquities and topography of Guildford and the county of Surrey. Research appointments should be made in advance. The Surrey History Service holds the institutional archive.

Guildhall Library

Aldermanbury, London, EC2V 7HH

- 020 7332 1868
- printedbooks.guildhall@cityoflondon.gov.uk
- manuscripts.guildhall@cityoflondon.gov.uk
- www.cityoflondon.gov.uk/guildhalllibrary

About A major public reference library, founded in the early 15th Century, specialising in the history of London. Specialist collections in the printed books department include; the Gardeners' Company Collection (historic books on gardening), the Fletchers' Company Collection (archery), the Gresham College Collection (17th and 18th Century music, and early travel and exploration), the Cock Collection (material on Sir Thomas More), the Charles Lamb Society Collection, the Chapman Bequest (19th Century plays), the Hamilton Bequest (18th and 19th Century plays), and the Pepys Collection. There are also collections on marine history, clocks and clockmakers, wine and food, English law and business.

HERO (Higher Education Research Organisation)

- www.hero.ac.uk

About HERO is the official gateway to universities, colleges and research organisations in the UK. It links to the online library catalogues of higher education institutions.

Highgate Literary & Scientific Institution Library

11 South Grove, Highgate, London, N6 6BS

- 020 8340 3343
- 020 8340 5632
- admin@hlsi.net
- www.hlsi.net

About Established in 1839, the Highgate Literary & Scientific Institution Library has extensive local archives and special collections on London, and local poets Coleridge and Betjeman. There is also a general fiction and non-fiction section and a children's section.

Imperial College & Science Museum Libraries
Imperial College Road, South Kensington, London, SW7 5NH
- 020 7942 4242
- 020 7942 4243
- smlinfo@sciencemuseum.org.uk
- www.sciencemuseum.org.uk/library

About Founded in 1883, the Science Museum Library is a research library for the history and public understanding of the physical sciences and all branches of engineering. Since 1992 it has been linked with the Central Library of Imperial College London, which is open to all for reference use. The collection of rare books includes major classics in the history of science and technology. There are sections on astronomy, biology, chemistry, physics, medicine and engineering. More general works on history and languages, and accounts of voyages of discovery are also housed.

The Imperial War Museum
Lambeth Road, London, SE1 6HZ
- 020 7416 5342
- 020 7416 5344
- books@iwm.org.uk
- http://collections.iwm.org.uk

About Books, pamphlets, periodicals, maps, technical drawings, propaganda leaflets, song sheets and army forms are among the items that can be viewed in the Reading Room of the Imperial War Museum, a major national gallery and archive. Open to any member of the public.

Innerpeffray Library
Crieff, Perthshire, PH7 3RF
- 01764 652819
- info@innerpeffraylibrary.co.uk
- www.innerpeffraylibrary.co.uk

About The collection at Innerpeffray Library was founded before 1680 and includes some 3,800 titles printed between 1502 and 1920, many of which are rare, specialising in religious titles. The library is open to the general public (there is a small admission charge).

Institute of Commonwealth Studies
University of London, 28 Russell Square, London, WC1B 5DS
- 020 7862 8844
- 020 7862 8820
- icommlib@sas.ac.uk
- www.commonwealth.sas.ac.uk

About A major resource on the Commonwealth and its member states. Subjects include history, politics and international relations, agriculture, education, the environment and social questions. They specialise in providing material that is unavailable elsewhere in the UK.

The Institute of Contemporary History & Wiener Library
4 Devonshire Street, London, W1W 5BH
- 020 7636 7247
- 020 7436 6428
- info@wienerlibrary.co.uk
- www.wienerlibrary.co.uk

About Founded in 1933, the Wiener Library is the world's oldest Holocaust memorial institution. Its multi-language collections relate to the Holocaust, its causes and legacies, and include published and unpublished works, press cuttings, photographs and eyewitness testimonies. The library is open to the general public, but users must bring proof of address and photo ID, and undergraduate students need a letter of introduction from their tutor. Only members of the library may borrow books.

The Institute of Historical Research
Senate House, Malet Street, London, WC1E 7HU
- 020 7862 8760
- 020 7862 8762
- ihr.library@sas.ac.uk
- www.history.ac.uk/library

About The best open access collection of printed historical sources in the United Kingdom; the Institute of Historical Research holds around 169,000 items. Central to the collection are primary sources for the medieval and modern history of the British Isles and Western Europe, the history of North and South America, international relations, and war. There is also a large collection of the most essential historical periodicals, microforms and electronic resources. Most of the holdings are open access; membership is free for staff and postgraduate students of all UK and EU universities.

Ipswich Institute Reading Room & Library
15 Tavern Street, Ipswich, Suffolk, IP1 3AA
- 01473 253992
- library@ipswichinstitute.org.uk
- www.ipswichinstitute.org.uk

About The library of the Ipswich Institute has around 9,000 books, including an impressive collection of large print books, talking books and music CDs, as well as a reference section including many volumes of local history.

Italian Institute, Eugenio Montale Library
39 Belgrave Square, London, SW1X 8NX
- ☎ 020 7235 1461
- 🖷 020 7235 4618
- ✉ icilondon@esteri.it
- 🌐 www.italcultur.org.uk

About The Eugenio Montale Library is open to the general public and has around 25,000 books in Italian, with a large reference section on Italian culture and history. Major Italian newspapers are delivered to the Institute daily.

Kew Library
Library, Arts & Archives, Royal Botanic Gardens, Kew, Surrey, TW9 3AE
- ☎ 020 8332 5414
- 🖷 020 8332 5430
- ✉ library@kew.org
- 🌐 www.rbgkew.org.uk/library

About One of the most important botanical reference sources in the world, the library at Kew is open to researchers by appointment, although a written application (by fax, email or letter) is usually required. The library and archives contain more than half a million items, including books, botanical illustrations, photographs, letters and manuscripts.

Lambeth Palace Library
Lambeth Palace, London, SE1 7JU
- ☎ 020 7898 1400
- 🖷 020 7928 7932
- ✉ lpl.staff@c-of-e.org.uk
- 🌐 www.lambethpalacelibrary.org

About Lambeth Palace Library is one of Britain's oldest public libraries, it is the historic library of the Archbishops of Canterbury and the principal library and record office for the history of the Church of England. Specialising in ecclesiastical history, collections include the history of art and architecture, and colonial and commonwealth history. The library is also a resource for local history and genealogy, and many aspects of English social, political and economic history. Founded in 1610, it contains an immense quantity of important historical books and documents. It houses over 4,000 manuscripts and almost 200,000 printed books, with around 20,000 items printed before 1700. In 1996 the Library acquired the Sion College collection of books and manuscripts. Those wishing to use the library must obtain a readers' ticket – further details are given on the website.

The Langholm Library
3 Walter Street, Langholm, Dumfriesshire, DG13 0AX
- 🌐 www.langholm-online.co.uk

About The Langholm Library was founded in 1800 and in 1834 it received a substantial bequest in the will of Thomas Telford, the engineer. In 1853 it absorbed the Langholm Trades Library. The collection consists of 5,000 books, representing stock typical of a Scottish community library at the turn of the century.

The Leeds Library
18 Commercial Street, Leeds, LS1 6AL
- ☎ 0113 245 3071
- 🖷 0113 245 1191
- ✉ enquiries@leedslibrary.co.uk
- 🌐 www.theleedslibrary.org.uk

About The Leeds Library – the oldest surviving proprietary subscription library in the UK – has a stock of over 135,000 books. The library is particularly strong in travel, biography, history and literature. Special collections include Civil war pamphlets and Reformation tracts. Access by prior appointment only, researchers will require a letter of reference from an appropriate institution, or a professional person. About 1,000 new books and audio titles are added annually.

Library of the Religious Society of Friends in Britain
Friends House, 173–177 Euston Road, London, NW1 2BJ
- ☎ 020 7663 1135
- 🖷 020 7663 1001
- ✉ Online form.
- 🌐 www.quaker.org.uk

About The library holds one of the most important collections relating to Quakers in the world. The library has over 80,000 books and pamphlets, including a unique collection of 17th Century Quaker and anti-Quaker material. It has collections relating to areas in which Quakers have been active, including peace, anti-slavery, and relief work. Quakers and non-Quakers from all around the world use the library, although all are welcome. Researchers must register on their first visit.

Linen Hall Library
17 Donegall Square North, Belfast, BT1 5GB, Northern Ireland
- ☎ 028 9032 1707
- 🖷 028 9043 8586
- ✉ info@linenhall.com
- 🌐 www.linenhall.com

About Founded in 1788, Belfast's Linen Hall Library is renowned for its unparalleled Irish and Local Studies Collection, including more than 250,000 items in the Northern Ireland Political Collection. It also contains a noted theatre and performing arts archive, a significant genealogy and heraldry collection and one of the largest collections of Burnsiana outside Scotland.

The Literary & Philosophical Society
23 Westgate Road, Newcastle upon Tyne, NE1 1SE
- 0191 232 0192
- 0191 261 4494
- library@litandphil.org.uk
- www.litandphil.org.uk

About The Literary & Philosophical Society, founded in 1793 as a learned society, took on the role of a university in the city. It is the largest independent library outside of London, housing over 150,000 books (including many rare items). Alongside the wide selection of current fiction and non-fiction, are historical collections covering every field of interest. Specialist areas include 19th Century science and technology, exploration and travel, history, biography, literature, music, and local history. The music library is unequalled in the North of England, including 6,000 CDs and 10,000 LPs. Non-members should apply to the Librarian.

The London Library
14 St James's Square, London, SW1Y 4LG
- 020 7930 7705
- 020 7766 4766
- enquiries@londonlibrary.co.uk
- www.londonlibrary.co.uk

About Founded by Thomas Carlyle in 1841. The library was set up with the aim of advancing education, learning and knowledge, and is now the largest independent lending library in the world, serving readers, writers, researchers and scholars. There are over one million volumes in the collection, covering every aspect of the humanities in all major (and many minor) European languages, dating from the 16th Century to the present. The library specialises in history, literature, biography, art, religion, bibliography, travel and topography. Over 95 per cent of the collection is housed on open access shelves, and over 97 per cent is available for loan. Membership is open to all; temporary reference tickets are also available.

London Metropolitan Archives
40 Northampton Road, Clerkenwell, London, EC1R 0HB
- 020 7332 3820
- 020 7833 9136
- ask.lma@cityoflondon.gov.uk
- www.cityoflondon.gov.uk

About London Metropolitan Archives (LMA) is the largest local authority record office in the UK. Material dates from 1067 to 2006 and is part of the History of London Collection. The City of London archive is one of the oldest, most complete, and wide ranging civic archives in the world. Collections include topics that range from the built environment, migration and settlement, to education, justice and social activities. Downloadable factsheets on a wide range of topics are available from the website.

Marsh's Library
St Patrick's Close, Dublin 8, Republic of Ireland
- 00353 1 454 3511
- 00353 1 454 3511
- keeper@marshlibrary.ie
- www.marshlibrary.ie

About Built in 1701 by Archbishop Narcissus Marsh, Marsh's Library was the first public library in Ireland. The library houses four main collections, many of which are still kept on the shelves allocated to them when the library first opened. The main collections consist of 25,000 books relating to the 16th, 17th and the early part of the 18th Centuries. Works include liturgical works, missals, breviaries, bibles printed in almost every language, theology and religious controversy. There are also collections on medicine, law, science, travel, navigation, mathematics, music, surveying, and classical literature. A separate room is reserved for books and periodicals relating to Irish history printed in the last hundred years. A full catalogue is available online. Students and scholars are admitted free, but there is a charge for visitors.

The Mitchell Library
North Street, Glasgow, G3 7DN
- 0141 287 2999
- 0141 287 2815
- lil@csglasgow.org
- www.glasgow.gov.uk

About Glasgow's Mitchell Library, which opened in 1877, is one of Europe's largest public reference libraries. From its earliest years it established two main collections, the Scottish Poetry Collection and the Glasgow Collection. The library holds the world's largest Robert Burns collection, and the Jeffrey Library; which contains illustrated volumes on travel, literature, art, architecture and natural history, including the extremely valuable Birds of America series of prints, by J.J. Audubon. The Baillie's Institution Library is also housed in the Mitchell (Baillie was an early pioneer of 'adult education'), as is the Henry Dyer Collection, which includes unique Japanese scrolls and albums acquired by the Glasgow engineer and educationalist.

The Morrab Library
Morrab Gardens, Penzance, Cornwall, TR18 4DA
- 01736 364474
- 01736 364474
- morrablibrary@hotmail.co.uk
- www.morrablibrary.co.uk

About The Morrab Library, founded in 1818, is the sixth largest independent library in the country, with more than 40,000 volumes. It is strong in literature, history, biography, antiquities, topography and travel and religion. The Jenner Room houses an extensive Cornish collection and holdings on other Celtic countries. There is also a collection of 3,000 Napoleonic memorabilia. The library's photographic archive has a catalogue of over 10,000 prints and negatives of antiquities, places, people and events in West Cornwall. It has recently acquired a further 15,000 transparencies of buildings, industrial archaeology and related interests.

Museum of the History of Science
Broad Street, Oxford, OX1 3AZ
- 01865 277278
- 01865 277288
- library@mhs.ox.ac.uk
- www.mhs.ox.ac.uk

About The museum library holds approximately 20,000 items with a main theme of scientific instruments. However, it also has strong collections in other fields, including zoology, botany, the medical sciences, Oxford science and the history of museums. The library holds rare early pamphlets and runs of old scientific periodicals. The museum also holds important collections of printed ephemera, prints, photographs, and manuscripts. The library is mainly a research and reference source for academics, researchers and students, but also welcomes members of the public with an interest in its collections (by prior appointment). An online catalogue is also available, and most of the holdings can be found on the University of Oxford library catalogue at http://solo.ouls.ox.ac.uk.

The National Archives
Ruskin Avenue, Kew, Richmond, Surrey, TW9 4DU
- 020 8876 3444
- Online form.
- www.nationalarchives.gov.uk

About The National Archives is the official archive for England, Wales and the central UK government. It holds 900 years of history from the Domesday Book, to the most recent government papers. The collection covers the British Isles, territories that formed the British Empire, and the countries of the Commonwealth. There is also a museum, which is free of charge. There is an online catalogue and certain documents are downloadable.

The National Archives (Ireland)
Bishop Street, Dublin 8, Republic of Ireland
- 00353 1 407 2300
- 00353 1 407 2333
- mail@nationalarchives.ie
- www.nationalarchives.ie

About The Irish National Archives holds the records of the modern Irish state and documents its historical evolution. It holds many of the records relevant to Irish genealogy and local history.

National Art Library
V&A South Kensington, Cromwell Road, London, SW7 2RL
- 020 7942 2400
- 020 7942 2401
- nal.enquiries@vam.ac.uk
- www.vam.ac.uk/nal

About The National Art Library is a major public reference library, as well as being the Victoria and Albert Museum's curatorial department for the art, craft and design of the book. The library is accessible to the public as a reference library. All material must be consulted in one of the library's reading rooms.

National Library for the Blind (NLB)
RNIB National Library Service, PO Box 173, Peterborough, PE2 6WS
- 0845 762 6843
- cservices@rnib.org.uk
- www.rnib.org.uk

About The National Library for the Blind is a leading agency in the provision of library and information services for visually impaired people. The library holds Europe's largest collection of Braille and Moon books, and provides a free postal library service to blind and partially sighted people worldwide. It also has a large collection of Braille music scores, giant print books, e-resources and reference materials. The NLB was merged with the RNIBs library services in 2007.

National Library of Ireland
Kildare Street, Dublin 2, Republic of Ireland
- 00353 1 603 0200
- 00353 1 676 6690
- info@nli.ie
- www.nli.ie

About The National Library of Ireland has the world's largest collection of Irish documentary material, including books and periodicals, newspapers, photographs, prints and drawings, and manuscripts.

National Library of Scotland
George IV Bridge, Edinburgh, EH1 1EW
- 0131 623 3700
- 0131 623 3701
- enquiries@nls.uk
- www.nls.uk

About The National Library of Scotland contains more than 13 million printed items about Scotland. It holds collections of books, manuscripts and maps, which cover the nation's history and culture. There are a number of online catalogues and a digital library service on the website.

National Library of Wales
The National Library of Wales, Aberystwyth, Ceredigion, Wales, SY23 3BU
- 01970 632800
- 01970 615709
- Online form.
- www.llgc.org.uk

About The National Library of Wales contains over six million printed volumes, including books, periodicals, newspapers, official publications and maps from many countries. For catalogue comments or questions, email cat@llgc.org.uk. The National Screen and Sound Archive of Wales is also part of the library (tel. 01972 632828, or email agssc@llgc.org.uk).

National Meteorological Library & Archive
Met Office, FitzRoy Road, Exeter, Devon, EX1 3PB
- 01392 884841
- metlib@metoffice.gov.uk
- www.metoffice.gov.uk/corporate/library

About Open to any member of the public with an interest in weather and climate, the library's holdings include the majority of published writing on meteorology in the UK over the last 150 years. There are weather reports for the UK, from 1 January 1869, to the present. The collection of historical meteorological literature contains all the great early writings on meteorology; these are maintained in cooperation with the Royal Meteorological Society.

Natural History Museum, Library & Archives
Library Information Services, Cromwell Road, London, SW7 5BD
- 020 7942 5000
- Online form.
- www.nhm.ac.uk/research-curation/library

About The Natural History Museum Library & Archives holds the world's premier collections of literature, original drawings and manuscripts relating to natural history. The library is a reference source for the biological and earth sciences and is comprised of over one million books dating from 1469. It holds 25,000 periodical titles and half a million artworks, together with extensive map, manuscript and photographic collections. Much of the library catalogue is online. Visits by appointment only – researchers should contact the relevant subject department. Contact details are given on the website.

Northern Poetry Library
County Library, The Willows, Morpeth, Northumberland, NE61 1TA
- 01670 534524
- www.northumberland.gov.uk/services/libraries.htm

About Established in 1968, the Northern Poetry Library aims to collect all poetry published from the area, as well as UK wide contemporary poetry. A postal lending service is available for members.

Office for National Statistics
Cardiff Road, Newport, South Wales, NP10 8XG
- 01633 456582
- library.enquiries@ons.gsi.gov.uk
- www.ons.gov.uk

About Provides information on 200 years of government statistical publishing. A unique collection of publications produced by the Office for National Statistics (ONS) and its predecessors (Central Statistical Office and the Office of Population Censuses and Surveys). Visits are by appointment only. There are online catalogues, and many of the resources will be accessible through local libraries.

People's Network
c/o Museums, Libraries & Archives Council (MLA), Victoria House, Southampton Row, London, WC1B 4EA
- 020 7273 1444
- 020 7273 1404
- info@peoplesnetwork.gov.uk
- www.peoplesnetwork.gov.uk

About People's Network is a national online resource, managed by the Museums, Libraries & Archives Council. To find your nearest public library click on 'Discover' (where there is a searchable database by postcode). There is also an online enquiry service.

The Poetry Library
Level 5, Royal Festival Hall, London, SE1 8XX
- 020 7921 0943/0664
- www.poetrylibrary.org.uk

About Founded in 1953, The Poetry Library is the major library for modern and contemporary poetry, with the most comprehensive collection of poetry in the UK. They aim to stock all poetry titles published in the UK, plus a representation of work from other countries, including work in parallel text and English translation. The library's holdings date back to 1912; it currently has around 90,000 items.

The Portico Library & Gallery
57 Mosley Street, Manchester, M2 3HY
- 0161 236 6785
- 0161 236 6803
- librarian@theportico.org.uk
- www.theportico.org.uk

About The Portico Library & Gallery was founded in 1806 and still occupies its original site. Its collection reflects the literary and intellectual interests of the 19th Century. There is a wide selection of travel literature, novels, biographies and history, with a good representative selection of fiction, including a number of first editions. The strong travel section covers the voyages of Captain Cook, many Victorian women travellers, and Victorian continental exploration. The topography section includes 18th Century antiquarian surveys of English counties, as well as contemporary accounts. Students and researchers wishing to access the library should contact the Librarian.

Royal Geographical Society
1 Kensington Gore, London, SW7 2AR
- 020 7591 3000
- 020 7591 3001
- Online form.
- www.rgs.org

About The library collection of the Royal Geographical Society (RGS), holds over 150,000 bound volumes. These date primarily from the foundation of the Society in 1830 onwards, and focus on the history and geography of places across the world. The society also has one of the largest private map collections in the world and a collection of historical travel guides. The Society's Foyle Reading Room is open to members of the public (identification needed for registering), but there is a charge for non-members.

Royal Observatory Edinburgh
The Library, Royal Observatory, Blackford Hill, Edinburgh, EH9 3HJ
- 0131 668 8395
- 0131 668 8264
- library@roe.ac.uk
- www.roe.ac.uk/roe/library

About The Royal Observatory holds one of the most comprehensive collections of astronomical literature in existence. The Crawford Collection of books and manuscripts in particular is one of the most valuable astronomical libraries in the world. Donated by James Ludovic Lindsay, 26th Earl of Crawford in 1888, it consists of around 15,000 books, pamphlets and manuscripts dating from the 13th Century to the end of the 19th Century. Bona fide researchers only - most publications can be searched via the online catalogue.

The Royal Society
Library & Information Services, 6–9 Carlton House Terrace, London, SW1Y 5AG
- 020 7451 2606
- 020 7930 2170
- www.royalsoc.ac.uk

About The Royal Society is the independent scientific academy of the UK and the Commonwealth. Its library is open on a reference basis to visitors from all over the world, and the library catalogue includes books and journals dating back to the foundation of the Society in 1660.

Royal Society of Chemistry, Library & Information Centre
Burlington House, Piccadilly, London, W1J 0BA
- 020 7440 3373
- 020 7287 9798
- Online form.
- www.rsc.org/library

About The Library & Information Centre (LIC) has been a focus for research for over 160 years, first as part of the Chemical Society from 1841, and now as part of the Royal Society of Chemistry. RSC Virtual Library is a free of charge, searchable resource, for premium chemical sciences and business information.

Saffron Walden Town Library
2 King Street, Saffron Walden, Essex, CB10 1ES
- 01799 523178
- 01799 513642
- saffronwalden.library@essexcc.gov.uk
- www.townlib.org.uk

About Formerly the Saffron Walden Literary & Scientific Institution, the Town Library collection has more than 25,000 volumes. Although the earliest material dates back to the middle of the 14th Century, it is a major resource for the study of the Victorian and Edwardian periods.

SCONUL Access

ⓦ www.access.sconul.ac.uk

About SCONUL Access is a co-operative venture between most of the higher education libraries of the UK and Ireland. It enables staff, research students, full time postgraduates and part-time, distance learning, and placement students to borrow material from other libraries. It was created from two existing schemes, SCONUL Research Extra and UK Libraries Plus.

The Scottish Poetry Library

5 Crichton's Close, Canongate, Edinburgh, EH8 8DT

ⓣ 0131 557 2876

ⓕ 0131 557 8393

ⓔ reception@spl.org.uk

ⓦ www.spl.org.uk

About The emphasis of the library is on contemporary poetry written in Scotland, in Scots, Gaelic and English. It also houses historic Scottish poetry and international contemporary works. Postal borrowing is available, plus an outreach loan service. There is a reading room for members.

Society of Antiquaries of London

Burlington House, Piccadilly, London, W1J 0BE

ⓣ 020 7479 7084

ⓕ 020 7287 6967

ⓔ library@sal.org.uk

ⓦ www.sal.org.uk/library

About The foremost and oldest archaeological research library in the UK. The library's present holdings number more than 100,000 books and around 800 currently received periodical titles. The Society of Antiquaries library collection includes British county histories, 18th and 19th Century books on the antiquities of Britain and other countries, plus a wide collection of international periodicals. The collection includes a collection of prints and drawings. Access to the general public is available for a limited period, after application.

Society of Genealogists, Library & Education Centre

14 Charterhouse Buildings, Goswell Road, London, EC1M 7BA

ⓣ 020 7251 8799

ⓕ 020 7250 1800

ⓔ library@sog.org.uk

ⓦ www.sog.org.uk

About A large collection of family histories, civil registration and census material. Over 9,000 county sources are held, including local histories, poll books, directories and other topographical material.

Membership is open to anyone with an interest in family and social history. Non-members may use the library on payment of a search fee.

St Bride Library

Bride Lane, Fleet Street, London, EC4Y 8EE

ⓣ 020 7353 4660

ⓦ www.stbride.org

About St Bride Library is the world's premier printing and graphic arts library. There are about 50,000 books and pamphlets in the general collection, as well as 200 special collections. These include cover printing and related subjects, including paper and binding, graphic design and typography, typefaces and calligraphy, illustration and printmaking. They also hold collections on publishing and book selling, and the social and economic aspects of the printing, book, newspaper and magazine trades. Open to the public free of charge, no registration required.

St Deiniol's Library

Church Lane, Hawarden, Flintshire, CH5 3DF

ⓣ 01244 532350

ⓕ 01244 520643

ⓔ deiniol.librarian@btconnect.com

ⓦ www.st-deiniols.org

About The St Deiniol's collection, although now holding around 250,000 printed items, is based around Gladstone's own collection of over 30,000 volumes (many of them annotated by Gladstone). With particular strengths in theology and 19th Century studies, the library has been recognised as the most important Welsh research library and collection, after the National Library of Wales. The purpose built library buildings also house an exhibition on Gladstone and offer overnight accommodation, as well as being a venue for conferences and other events.

Tennyson Research Centre

Lincoln Central Library, Free School Lane, Lincoln, LN2 1EZ

ⓣ 01522 782040

ⓕ 01522 575011

ⓔ grace.timmins@lincolnshire.gov.uk

ⓦ http://microsites.lincolnshire.gov.uk/tennyson

About The Tennyson Research Centre at Lincoln Central Library is a world renowned collection on Alfred, Lord Tennyson, his family, and the Victorian era. The collection includes letters, over 3,000 books from Tennyson's own library, and around 700 volumes from his father's library. There are also proofs of Tennyson's poetry and manuscripts.

UK Public Libraries on the Web

ⓦ www.dspace.dial.pipex.com/town/square/ac940/weblibs.html

About A–Z and regional listing of UK public libraries.

Vaughan Williams Memorial Library

Cecil Sharp House, 2 Regents Park Road, London, NW1 7AY

ⓣ 020 7485 2206

ⓕ 020 7284 0534

ⓔ library@efdss.org

ⓦ www.efdss.org

About The multimedia library of the English Folk Dance & Song Society has collections relating to British folk culture and British based cultures in other countries, particularly North America and Ireland. There is also information about other world cultures, as well as important works on social history and folklore. Reference only for non-members, who will be charged a daily fee.

The Waterways Trust

7th Floor, Llanthony Warehouse, Gloucester Docks, Gloucester, GL1 2EH

ⓣ 01452 318220

ⓕ 01452 318202

ⓔ bwarchive@thewaterwaystrust.net

ⓦ www.thewaterwaystrust.org.uk

About The UK's largest collection of inland waterways information, with around 78,000 records. Its archive can be searched online at www.virtualwaterways.co.uk. Access to the archive is by appointment only.

Wellcome Library

183 Euston Road, London, NW1 2BE

ⓣ 020 7611 8722

ⓕ 020 7611 8369

ⓔ library@wellcome.ac.uk

ⓦ http://library.wellcome.ac.uk

About With over 750,000 books and journals, an extensive range of manuscripts, archives and films, and more than 250,000 pictures, the Wellcome Library is one of the world's major resources for the study of medical history. The library also holds a growing collection of contemporary biomedical information resources, relating to consumer health, popular science, biomedical ethics and public understanding of science. Membership of the library is open to all.

Westminster Reference Library

35 St Martin's Street, London, WC2H 7HP

ⓣ 020 7641 1300

ⓕ 020 7641 4606

ⓔ referencelibrarywc2@westminster.gov.uk

ⓦ www.westminster.gov.uk/libraries/findalibrary/westref.cfm

About Specialist public reference library, with key subject collections on business, art & design and performing arts.

The Women's Library

London Metropolitan University, 25 Old Castle Street, London, E1 7NT

ⓣ 020 7320 2222

ⓕ 020 7320 2333

ⓔ moreinfo@thewomenslibrary.ac.uk

ⓦ www.londonmet.ac.uk/thewomenslibrary

About The Women's Library contains the most extensive women's history archive in the UK. A variety of topics are covered, including women's rights, suffrage, sexuality, health, education and employment, reproductive rights, the family, and the home. Some international material is included. Access is open to all.

The Zoological Society of London

Regent's Park, London, NW1 4RY

ⓣ 020 7449 6293

ⓔ library@zsl.org

ⓦ www.zsl.org/info/library

About Founded in 1826, The Zoological Society of London's library is one of the world's major zoological libraries, with more than 200,000 volumes and 5,000 journal titles on zoology and animal conservation. Books date from the 16th Century. The library is open to the general public (reference only for non-members), but bring identification on your first visit. Applications to consult rare books should be made in advance - consult the online catalogue in the first instance.

WRITER'S SITES

ABC Writers Network
ⓦ www.abcwritersnetwork.co.uk
About A free, international writer's forum, originating from Ireland.

All Books Review
ⓦ www.allbookreviews.com
About A review site, largely for self published books.

Ascriber/Writers Eyes
ⓦ www.writerseyes.org
About A showcase site for unpublished or self published writers. For a small fee you may display your work on the site, which the team claim to actively promote. The site also has sections for news, competitions and events, all of which are free to post in.

Ask About Writing
ⓦ www.askaboutwriting.net
About A site containing information on writer's awards and competitions. There is also advice on aspects of writing, and advertisements for other services of use to writers.

Ask Oxford
ⓦ www.askoxford.com
About A spin-off from the Oxford English Dictionary. Includes tips on spelling, grammar and producing better writing, as well as stories of interest from around the globe.

Authonomy.com
ⓦ www.authonomy.com
About A peer review site, run by HarperCollins, where the top rated authors for each month receive a free critique from a HarperCollins editor. Several authors have secured publishing deals through Authonomy.com.

Authorbank
ⓦ www.authorbank.com
About Members can upload a synopsis to be viewed by publishers who are also registered. Publishers can then approach the writer through Authorbank, who can act as literary agents.

Authorbank is currently offering this service free of charge to writers.

Author Network
ⓦ www.author-network.com
About A site with articles, tips and resources for writers.

Author's Den
ⓦ www.authorsden.com
About A free community site. Content includes book reviews, articles, e-books and more. Members get a free biography page.

BBC WritersRoom
ⓦ www.bbc.co.uk/writersroom
About Offers advice on writing for the BBC. Potential BBC writers can submit scripts for consideration.

Booktribes
ⓦ www.booktribes.com
About Booktribes is an online community for book lovers, where they can share their passion for books they already know and discover books that they don't know through recommendation.

Chapter One Promotions
ⓦ www.chapteronepromotions.com
About A writer's site, which is also a literary agency and consultancy. Authors and illustrators may display their work on the site for a fee. There are details of events and competitions, as well as a section on resources for children.

Characterisation Tool for Novelists
ⓦ www.synergise.com/p4
About A process and tool, available for a fee, that helps novelists to quickly and intuitively create realistic characters based upon accepted psychological types. Works both online and offline.

Classic Short Stories
ⓦ www.classicreader.com/short-stories.php
About An online resource containing complete short stories from a wide range of authors spanning several centuries, including authors such as Honore de Balzac, Anton Chekhov, Edgar Allan Poe, and many others.

ONLINE · RESOURCES · LISTINGS

East of the Web

ⓦ www.eastoftheweb.com/short-stories

About East of the Web is a British site dedicated to new, previously unpublished fiction, as well as to classic short stories from well-known authors. Genres include Children's, Crime, General Fiction, Horror, Humour, Non-Fiction, Romance, Science-Fiction and Hyperfiction. See the website for full submission details.

Film Angel

ⓦ www.filmangel.co.uk

About A site for screenwriters, developed in conjunction with Hammerwood Films. Writers may post synopses of their work on the site for a fee and potential investors – or 'angels' – can request further information. Clients may also commission tailor made films, for a substantial fee, that may act as showcases for their writing or acting talents.

Freelance Writing Organization International

ⓦ www.fwointl.com

About A Canadian based members site, which is free to join. Contains many resources for writers, including forums, markets, research resources and more.

The Frontlist

ⓦ www.thefrontlist.com

About A site where users can upload samples of their work, and in turn provide several critiques of others' work. Once the critiques have been done, their own work will be put up for critique. Pieces scoring above a certain threshold will be put forward to specialist editors and agents. The Friday Project has published recent high scoring additions to this site in print. A £10 charge is made to view the critiques of your own work. You do not have to view them if you do not wish to, but they will still be sent forward if they score highly enough.

Great Writing

ⓦ www.greatwriting.co.uk

About Great Writing is a volunteer-run online community that was formed after the closure of the BBCs 'Get Writing' service. It is free to join and offers members a chance to submit their own writing to the site for peer review, as well as providing writing forums and chat areas, articles, news and the occasional competition.

Hackwriters

ⓦ www.hackwriters.com

About A free internet magazine which accepts submissions of travel writing, fiction, lifestyle and social comment, but does not pay any fees.

Horror Writers UK

ⓦ www.horrorwriters.net

About HorrorWriters.net was specially set up for all writers of horror fiction and screenplays. As well as giving writers the opportunity to post their work and receive valuable and constructive feedback, the site also features many other topics of interest relating to the whole craft of horror writing, such as book reviews, articles and much more. Membership is free.

JBWB Writing Competitions

ⓦ www.jbwb.co.uk/writingcomps.htm

About A detailed list of writing competitions, compiled by the Jacqui Bennett Writers Bureau.

Journalism.co.uk

ⓦ www.journalism.co.uk

About Journalism.co.uk is a community-based news and recruitment site aimed at journalists around the world, running independently since 1999. It is run by Editor/Publisher John Thompson and provides industry specific news, the latest journalism jobs, training information and a comprehensive events and awards guide for journalists and media professionals. It also publishes a daily e-bulletin, containing news and job alerts, which is free to subscribe to at: www.journalism.co.uk/listsub.shtml. To contact journalism.co.uk email: info@ mousetrapmedia.co.uk.

Journalism UK

ⓦ www.journalismuk.co.uk

About A small directory site of interest to UK journalists working in print.

Market List

ⓦ www.marketlist.com

About A detailed site aimed at genre fiction writers, with directories of US markets, articles and interviews, as well as the space to start your own blog.

Merriam Webster

ⓦ www.m-w.com

About A US dictionary site with added features such as 'word of the day' and word games.

National Novel Writing Month
ⓦ www.nanowrimo.com
About US site which challenges people to write a 50,000 word novel between the 1st and 30th of November each year. If you make the deadline, you are a 'winner'. The idea is to encourage fast writing and not necessarily to focus on quality.

Novelists Inc.
ⓦ www.ninc.com
About US based membership site with advice and practical help for fiction writers. Members' only sections include an agent guide and an email list.

nthPosition
ⓦ www.nthposition.com
About A free online magazine/e-zine with politics and opinion, travel writing, fiction and poetry, reviews and interviews.

One of Us
ⓦ www.oneofus.co.uk
About A resource site with articles, writing tips and a discussion forum. Free to access.

Plays on the Net
ⓦ www.playsonthenet.com
About An online shop, specialising in the sale of books, plays and audio books. The site advertises writing competitions and has the facility for new playwrights to submit their work for public view.

The Poetry Archive
ⓦ www.poetryarchive.org
About A site for poetry readings by well known poets. Users can download audio clips, read poems and also purchase poetry CDs.

Preditors & Editors
ⓦ www.anotherealm.com/prededitors
About Preditors & Editors' sole purpose is to provide writers, artists, composers and game designers with information and contacts for the purpose of seeking publication of their work. P&E also maintains a 'Warnings' page, listing known scam artists, vanity publishers and literary fraudsters. They are always seeking information from writers who have been badly treated by agents, publishers, or the like.

Prize Magic
ⓦ www.prizemagic.co.uk
About A site which contains a useful directory of writing competitions and links to them.

Proof Postive Writing Contests
ⓦ www.proofpositive.com/contests/writecontests.php
About A US site advertising many writing contests, including those that are open to UK residents.

Publisher's Lunch
ⓦ www.caderbooks.com
About A subscription-based free daily newsletter of news and events in publishing (US based). Publishing professionals may sign up to the deluxe service for a fee.

The Publishing Law Center
ⓦ www.publaw.com
About US site containing useful information for publishers, editors, agents and writers on all aspects of publishing and its legal issues. They also offer a free newsletter.

Pulp.net
ⓦ www.pulp.net
About Pulp.net is a not-for-profit organisation that aims to advance the art and practice of literature, promote the art of literature for the public benefit, and encourage greater participation in literature creation. Pulp.net functions in a similar way to a monthly e-zine, but also hosts a variety of talks, literary events and workshops at venues such as courses, writing conferences and festivals. Pulp.net accepts open submissions of short fiction and will publish as many as three new short stories per issue, from both established and first-time authors.

Reactive Writing
ⓦ www.reactivewriting.co.uk
About A site dedicated to exploring creative writing on the internet.

Screenwriters Online
ⓦ www.screenwriter.com
About A US site with input from major Hollywood screenwriters. Offers a newsletter, industry analysis, master classes and links to other services.

Shaw Guides
ⓦ www.writing.shawguides.com
About This US based portal site allows users to search for writers, conferences and workshops, including those based in the UK.

ONLINE

RESOURCES

LISTINGS

Six Sentences

www.sixsentences.blogspot.com

About Six Sentences is a flash-fiction site where each story is told in six sentences. The editor publishes everything that is submitted, and usually publishes six new stories per day.

Slush Pile Reader

questions@slushpilereader.com

www.slushpilereader.com

About A site that showcases authors manuscripts to an audience of online readers. The readers vote upon whether or not the manuscript should be published, and give reviews and criticism. Slush Pile Reader will also publish the most popular submissions.

Story

www.theshortstory.org.uk

About Home of the 'Save Our Short Story' campaign, Story provides a wealth of information, event listings, advice, articles, reviews and features for short fiction writers. It also runs competitions and prizes and hosts the *Endangered Species* online anthology.

Trace

http://tracearchive.ntu.ac.uk

About A free online resource linked to Nottingham Trent University. Trace provides a space for writers to meet, communicate, discuss work and be creative. Also offered through the site are courses, a consultancy service and a children's area.

UK Children's Books

www.ukchildrensbooks.co.uk

About A large site containing links to many publishers and authors of children's books, as well as other helpful organisations. The site is affiliated with Word Pool, a resource site centred on children's books.

Whisper from the Heart Poetry Club

www.whisperpoetry.com

About An online club/community site that covers the full spectrum of the arts, including poetry, music, art, literature and photography. It has member's forums and blogs, as well as a monthly newsletter, and runs a number of different writing competitions. The site also maintains an online book store.

Winning Writers

www.winningwriters.com

About Winning Writers is an award-winning website that finds and creates resources for poets and writers. The free newsletter provides details of over 150 quality poetry contests, while the larger premium database, Poetry Contest Insider, profiles over 750 poetry contests.

WordCounter

www.wordcounter.com

About A site that allows you to copy and paste text into a field and check for repetitions. In a separate field you may also check your writing for political leanings.

The Workhouse

www.fictionworkhouse.com

About An online literary writer's forum. Registration (free) is required to use the forum.

Write4Kids

www.write4kids.com

About US site, with many free resources and advice on writing for children. The site also has a free newsletter.

Write A Book Now

www.writeabooknow.com

About US site with a free email course on the various aspects of getting published. There is a strong emphasis on shortcuts and speediness. You may sign up for email newsletters or read articles directly from the site.

Write Away

www.writeaway.co.uk

About A membership site, which offers a writers' community forum, access to editors and library information staff, plus the option of paying for appraisal services. The team can also advise on self publishing and sell your books through the site. Lifetime membership costs from £27.45.

Write Link

www.writelink.co.uk

About A membership site where work in progress is rated by other members. Once the work is at a certain level it gets linked to the resources area, which contains information on paying markets. Each piece published in the resources area earns £20. There is a discussion forum and subscription is free, although if you want the chance to submit work for review you must pay a fee.

Writer Beware
ⓦ www.sfwa.org/beware
About Writer Beware is the public face of the Science Fiction & Fantasy Writers of America's Committee on Writing Scams. The site contains discussions of a variety of literary schemes and deceptions, information on how to identify them, advice on how to avoid them, and links to useful online resources. It has been designed so that it can be used by any writer, regardless of subject, style, genre or nationality.

The Writer Gazette
ⓦ www.writergazette.com
About Provides free writer-related articles, job listings, contests, resources, tips, and more – all of which are designed to help improve and promote your writing career. Updated on a weekly basis.

Writernet
ⓦ www.writernet.co.uk
About A site dedicated to writers of drama, designed to act as a networking and resource site.

Writers' Circles
ⓦ www.writers-circles.com
About A directory of writers' circles across the country that is also available to buy in print. The site links to other resources, such as writing competitions, and contains small market directory sections, including agents and magazines.

Writers Free Reference
ⓦ www.writers-free-reference.com
About A free portal site containing links to many other sites, resources and articles of interest to writers.

Writer's Market UK
ⓦ www.writersmarket.co.uk
About The sister site to this book, updated daily, packed with hundreds of extra directory listings that we couldn't fit in the book. Also contains writers' resources, articles, community features and current writing and publishing news, plus much more.

Writer's Market US
ⓦ www.writersmarket.com
About A subscription based site with access to thousands of frequently updated US writing markets, plus advice, tips and resources.

Writers Net
ⓦ www.writers.net
About A US site containing information for writers, editors, agents and publishers. The site contains lists of US contacts and has a discussion forum.

WritersReign
ⓦ www.writersreign.co.uk
About A website of useful resources for writers, including: regularly updated lists of competitions for short stories, poetry, rolling competitions, non-fiction and creative arts; listings of publishers and self-publishing links; writing for children; research and markets. There is also a comprehensive blog of articles on the writing craft.

WritersServices
ⓦ www.writersservices.com
About A very full site with information, services and advice for writers.

Writers Write
ⓦ www.writerswrite.com
About US resource site, which contains articles and links of interest to writers.

Write This Moment
ⓦ www.writethismoment.net
About An established writing jobs and opportunities board that aims to help writers find freelance writing jobs, magazine commissions, staff writing vacancies, writing residencies, publishers requirements, creative writing markets and other paying writing opportunities. Membership costs £8 for three months or £24 for one year.

Writing World
ⓦ www.writing-world.com
About A US site full of articles on writing and publishing. There are also links to freelance job opportunities and a book shop.

YouWriteOn.com
ⓦ www.youwriteon.com
About A peer review site where the top five authors for each month receive a free, Arts Council-funded critique from top editors at leading literary agents and publishers, including Curtis Brown, Orion and Bloomsbury. The site aims to help new writers develop, and to help talented writers get noticed and published.

RESEARCH & LANGUAGE SITES

4 Talent
🌐 www.channel4.com/4talent/national
About A site full of resources for those interested in the media, with a specific section on writing. Contains interviews, articles, videos and advice.

AbeBooks
🌐 www.abebooks.co.uk
About An online marketplace for books, particularly rare and out of print editions. Useful for research material and information on the independent bookselling world.

Access to Archives (A2A)
🌐 www.nationalarchives.gov.uk/a2a/default.aspx
About Access to Archives (A2A) contains catalogues describing archives held throughout England and dating from the 900s to the present day.

Alt-X
🌐 www.altx.com
About A site dedicated to the various forms of online publishing. As well as the opportunity to buy e-books, the site contains comments and discussion on aspects of the online world, in particular how it meets the world of literature and publishing.

Ananova
🌐 www.ananova.com
About A good resource for journalists; the site contains all the latest UK news headlines, as well as 'quirkies' – a selection of more unusual stories.

Ancestry
🌐 www.ancestry.co.uk
About A site offering genealogical data. Potentially useful for historical fiction and non-fiction writers.

Bartleby
🌐 www.bartleby.com
About A site containing many free resources, book extracts and quotations. Users can search through texts from fiction, non-fiction, verse and reference. Includes an online version of Roget's Thesaurus.

Bible Gateway
🌐 www.biblegateway.com
About A site which allows you to search for extracts from the Bible.

Bibliomania
🌐 www.bibliomania.com
About A research site featuring many free book extracts, study guides, articles, interviews and reference texts.

British Library
🌐 www.bl.uk
About The British Library's vast site contains information about the Library and its various collections, as well as thousands of images and hundreds of sound samples. It offers free searches of major reference and document collections, and has areas for researchers and students.

CIA World Fact Book
🌐 www.cia.gov/cia/publications/factbook
About A useful, searchable resource, with information and statistics on individual countries. The publication is also available to download.

The Complete Works of William Shakespeare
🌐 www-tech.mit.edu/shakespeare
About A fairly static site that contains full text versions of Shakespeare's complete works.

Corsinet
🌐 www.corsinet.com
About A site full of supposedly 'useless' information, including famous deathbed quotes, 'Brain Candy' and general trivia.

CrossRef
🌐 www.crossref.org
About A membership website that allows users to gain access to primary research sources and citations by cross referencing with other people's work.

Dictionary of Slang
🌐 www.dictionaryofslang.co.uk
About A searchable dictionary of slang words.

Encyclopaedia Britannica
🌐 www.britannica.com
About A searchable encyclopedia site full of general knowledge and specialist resources. Some parts of

the site are free and others require a subscription. A free trial is offered.

The English Server
ⓦ www.eserver.org
About A collection of online literary work. Also has a community support element.

Frankfurt Book Fair
ⓦ www.frankfurt-book-fair.com
About The site that accompanies the Frankfurt Book Fair.

FreePint
ⓦ www.freepint.com
About FreePint is a global network of almost 80,000 researchers who find, use, manage and share work-related information. Members receive a free newsletter with news and tips on researching and information sources. The FreePint Bar is a facility where specific questions can be posted. A good resource for those wanting to conduct large amounts of research or information gathering.

The Good Web Guide
ⓦ www.thegoodwebguide.co.uk
About A review site, which lists thousands of websites and their ratings. A good starting place to check the reliability of websites for research.

Guide to Grammar and Style
ⓦ www.andromeda.rutgers.edu/~jlynch/writing
About A US site, which contains many tips and resources on correct grammar and good writing style.

Ingenta
ⓦ www.ingentaconnect.com
About A bibliographic database site for academic research. Membership is required, although access is often free through educational institutions if you are a student. Users may then search journals and articles and, depending on level of membership, gain access to either the abstract or the full text.

Internet Archive
ⓦ www.archive.org
About A massive archive of texts, music and moving images from the Internet.

Internet Classics Archive
ⓦ http://classics.mit.edu
About A database of classical writing in Greek, Latin, Chinese and Peruvian. All are translated into English, although many of the originals are available.

Internet Movie Database
ⓦ www.imdb.com
About An enormous searchable database of actors, films, television programmes and other entertainment. Enter a search term and the site will pull up all references across all genres, and provide detailed information such as an actor's entire biography, or a film's entire credits. All are cross referenced.

Internet Public Library
ⓦ www.ipl.org
About Started by students at the University of Michigan, the site has grown into a large set of resources for researchers. Users can search by topics, categories or keywords. Sections include magazines, encyclopedias, dictionaries and blogs.

Internet Writing Journal
ⓦ www.internetwritingjournal.com
About A US online journal for writers, including many articles on writing itself. Other sections of the site include news, blogs and many links.

Location Register of 20th Century English Literary Manuscripts and Letters
ⓦ www.reading.ac.uk/library/about-us/projects/lib-location-register.asp
About A searchable site detailing the current homes of many literary manuscripts in Britain, as well as recordings and letters. The database includes small museums, as well as large institutions and is not only limited to well known pieces of work.

London Book Fair
ⓦ www.londonbookfair.co.uk
About Information on all aspects of Britain's largest trade book fair.

Murder Files
ⓦ www.murderfiles.com
About A site detailing murders, both past and present. Users can pay for information on crimes they want to know more about. Particularly good for historical fiction and crime writers. The website also provides links to other useful sites.

Oxford Text Archive

🌐 www.ota.ahds.ac.uk

About A collection of online texts in literature, arts and humanities. This site is not updated regularly.

Ref Desk

🌐 www.refdesk.com

About A large reference site full of weird and wonderful facts, trivia and links to other interesting sites.

Rhyme Zone

🌐 www.rhymezone.com

About Type in a word and the site will come back with a list of words that rhyme with it.

Rimbaud

🌐 www.rimbaud.org.uk

About Dee Rimbaud's site for writers looking to get their work published. Articles, advice, resources and listings are all part of the content.

The Science Fiction Hub

🌐 www.sfhub.ac.uk

About A portal site for readers, writers and students of science fiction. The SF Hub is based on the wealth of research resources in the Science Fiction Collections of The University of Liverpool's Special Collections and Archives, including the renowned Science Fiction Foundation Collection.

Shakespeare at eNotes

🌐 www.enotes.com/william-shakespeare

About A portal to many Shakespeare resources, including notes and study guides.

Sourcewire

🌐 www.sourcewire.com

About A site for business and technology journalists, featuring up to the minute press releases and other resources such as industry events and jobs.

TheyWorkForYou.com

🌐 www.theyworkforyou.com

About A site containing a vast amount of political information, including Hansard debates (House of Commons), and a searchable database of MPs and Lords. Good for providing general contextual information, as well as for specific research to inform political writing.

United Kingdom Parliament

🌐 www.parliament.uk

About The site contains access to many research reports and general information on parliament.

Virtual Perpetual Calendars

🌐 www.vpcalendar.net

About A site for checking dates and their corresponding days of the week, from 1900 onwards. Great for historical accuracy.

WATCH

🌐 http://tyler.hrc.utexas.edu

About A limited site, which features a searchable database of who to contact if using particular copyrighted material. Hosted in the UK by the University of Reading, and in the US by the University of Texas.

What's on When

🌐 www.whatsonwhen.com

About An international events calendar, possibly useful for journalists, reviewers or for general research.

World Wide Words

🌐 www.worldwidewords.org

About A site exploring the worldwide use of the English language, looked at from a British viewpoint. Contains definitions, language information and other resources.

Write Brain

🌐 www.write-brain.com

About As well as selling software, the website links to many other useful sites for researchers and writers. Users may search by research category.

WRITING SOFTWARE

ADM (Advanced Data Manager)

🌐 www.adm21.net

About An 'advanced data management' tool from the US, that could be of use to research heavy projects, such as academic writing, non-fiction, or historical fiction. Costs $129.99.

Book Writer

🌐 www.yadudigital.com

About A downloadable piece of software, designed to simplify and organise the process of writing a book. A free trial is granted for 30 days, after which you may buy a single user licence for $89.95.

Dramatica
🌐 www.dramatica.com
About A site selling the Dramatica Pro screenwriting software. Costs $269.95.

DreamaScript
🌐 www.dreamascript.com
About DreamaScript Screenwriting Software is a tool that helps writers create and sell their scripts. Costs £120.

Final Draft
🌐 www.finaldraft.com
About Downloadable, professional scriptwriting software, as used by Hollywood director Michael Bay. Costs $229.

Idea Tracker
🌐 www.intellectusenterprises.com/ideatracker.html
About An online application designed to help sort, organise and track ideas. A license can be bought for £16.84.

New Novelist
🌐 www.newnovelist.com
About A software package, which provides help with novel writing including editing, structure, characterisation, and plot. Costs around £29.99.

Screenforge
🌐 www.apotheosispictures.com
About A downloadable software package for scriptwriters that works with Microsoft Word. An initial 45 day trial period is offered, after which the software must be registered for $45.

Storycraft Pro
🌐 www.writerspage.com
About A series of software packages, based around the Jarvis method of fiction writing. Prices range from $49–$129 and software is available as a CD or download.

StyleWriter
🌐 www.editorsoftware.com
About A word processor add on package that checks writing against a large database of style and usage issues, picking up on any inconsistencies or poor practice in writing style. Costs £110 plus VAT.

Synergise P4 Characterisation Tool
🌐 www.synergise.com/p4
About A process and tool that helps novelists to quickly and intuitively create realistic characters based upon accepted psychological types. Works both online and offline.

Write it Now
🌐 www.ravensheadservices.com
About A downloadable package designed to help write and store complete novels. The registration fee is from £35, which also allows users to download add-ons from the website. Offers a free trial.

Writer's Blocks
🌐 www.writersblocks.com
About A software package that allows writers to organise their notes, research and writing into 'blocks'. These can then be easily manipulated and amalgamated. A free trial is available. The newest version is currently available to buy for $149.

Writer's Café
🌐 www.writerscafe.co.uk
About A story writing software package, available as a CD or a download. Costs £32.20.

Z-Write
🌐 www.stonetablesoftware.com
About A writing package solely for Macs, combining the functions of a word processor with a project manager. You may download Z-Write free of charge, but after two weeks it reverts to a demo version and you must pay to upgrade.

GENERAL STUDENT WEBSITES

British Universities Sports Association
🌐 www.busa.org.uk
About Website of the British Universities Sports Association (BUSA). Includes news, fixtures and results from UK universities with BUSA membership.

Fresh Direction
🌐 www.freshdirection.com
About General student information, news and discussion.

HERO
🌐 www.hero.ac.uk
About Official gateway to universities, colleges and research organisations in the UK. The site is full of higher education information and links, including a comprehensive section on study skills.

Lazy Student
🌐 www.lazystudent.co.uk
About Lazystudent is the UK's most comprehensive student website. It links to hundreds of other sites, with commentary and star ratings.

National Union of Students
🌐 www.nusonline.co.uk
About Information about student campaigns, student life and discounts for NUS cardholders.

NewStudent
🌐 www.newstudent.org
About Advice for new and prospective students.

One Life
🌐 www.bbc.co.uk/radio1/onelife
About BBC Radio One's online guide to life and key issues for young people. The site includes advice on health, relationships, sex, drugs, travel, work and education.

Push Online
🌐 www.push.co.uk
About A website that gives information on UK universities and advice about life as a student. Includes an excellent jargon buster.

The Site
🌐 www.thesite.org
About Owned and run by YouthNet UK, this website offers support and guidance for young adults (age 16–24). It provides fact sheets and articles on the key issues they face. There is also an online community, offering peer to peer discussion and support.

Student Accommodation UK
🌐 www.studentpad.co.uk
About A site that helps students find accommodation. It also includes advice and a comprehensive housing guide.

Studentastic
🌐 www.studentastic.co.uk
About Founded in 2005 to offer a reference point on how to survive as a student. The site features articles written by experts on accommodation, work, relationships, and exams.

Student Hampers
🌐 www.studenthampers.com
About A site offering student food and stationary parcels, delivered straight to the door.

Student Health
🌐 www.studenthealth.co.uk
About Dedicated health site for students.

StudentUK.com
🌐 www.studentuk.com
About Help and advice for students on many topics, including studying, jobs, health, accommodation and travel. There are also chat forums and a guide to UK universities and colleges.

Studentzone
🌐 www.studentzone.org.uk
About All round site offering information and links on studying, careers, legal issues and finance, health, sport and entertainment.

Support4learning
ⓦ www.support4learning.org.uk
About Resource links for advisers and students, or anyone involved in education and training. The site has information about finance and supporting education, training, career planning and job searching.

Universities and Colleges Admissions Service for the UK
ⓦ www.ucas.co.uk
About Comprehensive information about getting into higher education, full course listings and other student issues. Includes a selection of information for parents.

Woman Student
ⓦ www.womanstudent.co.uk
About A site covering student and lifestyle issues, from a female perspective.

LEARNING RESOURCES

AskOxford.com
ⓦ www.askoxford.com
About The site allows you to search the compact Oxford English Dictionary, ask a grammar question, or get spelling and grammar tips. It also offers a section where you can find out the meaning of your name, and get help with CV and job applications.

Atlapedia Online
ⓦ www.atlapedia.com
About Maps, key facts and statistics on countries of the world.

Cambridge Dictionaries Online
ⓦ www.dictionary.cambridge.org
About Choose the dictionary you require and look up words and phrases.

Foreignword.com
ⓦ www.foreignword.com
About A global dictionary, which searches in 275 dictionaries on the internet. The site translates from 69 source languages, into 73 target languages.

How to get a First
ⓦ www.howtogetafirst.co.uk
About Advice from a student who achieved a first class degree, and advice about degrees and higher education in general.

The Internet Public Library
ⓦ www.ipl.org
About A site founded by the University of Michigan School of Information. Extensive resources are available, including the 'Ask a Question' reference service.

Intute:virtual training suite
ⓦ www.vts.intute.ac.uk
About The site offers free, subject specific online tutorials, which are designed to improve internet information literacy.

Presenters University
ⓦ www.presentersuniversity.com
About Tips and downloads for better presentations. The site is designed for businesses, but is useful for students too.

Researchtogether.com
ⓦ www.researchtogether.com
About A useful site for researchers. Allows users to search for others doing similar work and compare notes.

Skills4study
ⓦ www.palgrave.com/skills4study/index.asp
About Practical advice for studying more effectively in higher education, from one of the leading academic publishers.

Thesaurus.com
ⓦ http://thesaurus.reference.com
About Offers a thesaurus, dictionary, encyclopedia and general online reference.

The UK Grad Programme
ⓦ www.grad.ac.uk
About Support and advice for postgraduates. The 'Just for Postgrads' section on the site gives information on managing research and careers.

Using English for Academic Purposes
ⓦ www.uefap.com
About Advice for UK and international students, on writing and related study skills.

VARK - a guide to learning styles
ⓦ www.vark-learn.com
About Allows you to find out your preferred learning style with its online questionnaire.

Yourdictionary.com
🌐 www.yourdictionary.com
About Free online dictionary and thesaurus, with definitions, audio pronunciation and correct grammar usage.

STUDENTS WITH DISABILITIES

Department for Work and Pensions (DWP)
🌐 www.disability.gov.uk
About Information for disabled people and carers.

Ouch
🌐 www.bbc.co.uk/ouch/lifefiles/student
About A BBC website about life as a student with disabilities. It has regular columns, features, quizzes, a monthly podcast, blogs and a community messageboard.

Skill: National Bureau for Students with Disabilities
🌐 www.skill.org.uk
About A national charity promoting opportunities for young people with any kind of impairment in 16 plus education, training, or employment. The website offers comprehensive information, profiles and a series of free downloadable booklets.

MONEY

DfES: Higher Education Student Support
🌐 www.dfes.gov.uk/studentsupport
About Financial information for students in higher education, including a section for parents.

Discounts for Students
🌐 www.discounts4students.net
About An online directory for students, with offers, services and discounts.

HM Revenue & Customs
🌐 www.hmrc.gov.uk/taxandu
About Accessible information about student tax matters and loans.

S-k-i-n-t
🌐 www.s-k-i-n-t.co.uk
About Money savers, discounts, quizzes and competitions for students.

Student Awards Agency for Scotland
🌐 www.student-support-saas.gov.uk
About Financial support and advice for Scottish students.

Student Finance Direct
🌐 www.studentsupportdirect.co.uk
About Information about financial support for students in further, or higher education in England.

Student Finance NI
🌐 www.studentfinanceni.co.uk
About Information about financial support for students in further, or higher education in Northern Ireland.

Student Finance Wales
🌐 www.studentfinancewales.co.uk
About Information about financial support for students in further, or higher education in Wales.

Student Free Stuff
🌐 www.studentfreestuff.com
About A site offering free deals for students. Also includes a student guide and lots of links to other student sites.

Student Loans Company Ltd
🌐 www.slc.co.uk
About Access to key information about student loans and the Student Loans Company UK.

BOOKS & MAGAZINES

Student Subscription Service
🌐 www.student-subscription-service.co.uk
About Offers cheap magazine subscriptions for students and teachers.

Student Subscription Service (Ireland)
🌐 www.student-subscription-service.ie
About Offers cheap magazine subscriptions for students in Ireland.

Study Bookshop

ⓦ www.studybookshop.com
About A second hand textbook website.

INTERNATIONAL STUDENTS

British Council

ⓦ www.britishcouncil.org
About Information on teaching English worldwide. The website also includes information about studying in the UK.

Hobsons Study UK

ⓦ www.studyuk.hobsons.com
About Information and advice for international students about living and studying in the UK.

HOST UK

ⓦ www.hostuk.org.uk
About HOST UK is a registered charity that works with international students studying at UK institutions. It gives them the opportunity to have a day or a weekend visit in a British home.

International Students Union

ⓦ www.isu.org.uk
About Founded in 2002 by a group of international students from several London universities, ISU is run by students and open to students all over the world. It provides free advice on UK education, and a range of other information regarding studying in the UK.

Okey Dokey

ⓦ www.okey-dokey.co.uk
About A free website for students learning English.

Studystay.com

ⓦ www.studystay.com
About An online study guide for international students, with comprehensive information on every aspect of student life in the UK.

UKCISA: UK Council for International Student Affairs

ⓦ www.ukcosa.org.uk
About Advice and guidance for international students (and their families) planning to study in the UK. The site also has information for UK students thinking about studying abroad.

UK Student Life

ⓦ www.ukstudentlife.com
About A comprehensive guide to student life in the UK (aimed at international students). Also has a large list of links covering student life in the UK.

CAREERS & QUALIFICATIONS

Everything You Wanted To Know

ⓦ www.everythingyouwantedtoknow.com
About Everything you wanted to know about university, sponsorship, placements and graduate opportunities. Offers advice on student finance, careers and how to make the most of university.

Foundation Degree Forward

ⓦ www.fdf.ac.uk
About Foundation Degree Forward (fdf) is a national body that supports the development of high quality Foundation degrees. Includes a student guide to this relatively new qualification.

Graduate Prospects

ⓦ www.prospects.ac.uk
About The UK's official graduate careers website. Excellent, comprehensive careers advice and information on postgraduate studies.

Mind Tools

ⓦ www.mindtools.com
About A site with learning tools, and life, career training, and management training advice.

WORKING STUDENTS

Department for Education and Skills

ⓦ www.dcsf.gov.uk/index.htm
About Information for international students about working in the UK.

Morethanwork

ⓦ www.morethanwork.worksmart.org.uk
About A website for all working students. Enables you to identify your skills, build a CV and find out about employment rights.

Trouble at Work
ⓦ www.troubleatwork.org.uk
About A website with up to date information and advice for working students with job problems.

Work Smart
ⓦ www.worksmart.org.uk
About Guide to working, from the TUC. The site has a page of information for working students.

TRAVEL

Foreign & Commonwealth Office
ⓦ www.fco.gov.uk
About This site has a country by country travel advice section, including a risk assessment of threats from terrorism. The FCO runs the 'Know Before You Go' campaign.

Go Gap Year
ⓦ www.gogapyear.com
About Advice, tips and useful hints on planning your gap year travels.

Intern Abroad
ⓦ www.internabroad.com
About Lists overseas internship opportunities.

Lonely Planet
ⓦ www.lonelyplanet.com
About Travel advice, guidebooks and information for the independent traveller including Thorntree, the worldwide message board.

Rough Guides
ⓦ www.roughguides.com
About Online information and travel guides.

Tours4students
ⓦ www.tours4students.co.uk
About Specialist student tour operator, for large or small groups.

Travellers Worldwide
ⓦ www.travellersworldwide.com
About Contains details of voluntary work placements overseas.

Travel Line
ⓦ www.traveline.org.uk
About UK public transport information.

Working Travel Directory
ⓦ www.workingtravel.co.uk
About An online working travel directory, free to use.

SECONDHAND BOOKS

AbeBooks
AbeBooks Europe GmbH, Ronsdorfer Strasse 77a, 40233 Düsseldorf, Germany
ⓔ content@abebooks.co.uk
ⓦ www.abebooks.co.uk
About The world's largest site for new, second hand, rare, and out of print books. Over 100,000,000 titles listed.

A Book for All Reasons
Rockville House, 6 Pakefield Road, Lowestoft, Suffolk, NR33 0HS
ⓦ www.2nd-hand-books.co.uk
Contact G. A. Michael Sims
About A resource site for booksellers and book collectors. Includes information on databases, repair services, book prizes and book searches.

Alibris
1250 45th Street, Suite 100, Emeryville, California, 94608, USA
ⓦ www.alibris.co.uk
About A large international database of second hand, new, out of print, foreign language and hard to find titles. There are over 60,000,000 titles in the database.

Amazon
ⓦ www.amazon.co.uk
About The online retailer. As well as selling new books, Amazon also acts as a marketplace for used books worldwide.

Barter Books
Alnwick Station, Northumberland, NE66 2NP
ⓣ 01665 604888

bb@barterbooks.co.uk

www.barterbooks.co.uk

About A Northumberland based independent bookshop, with a large online catalogue and purchase facility. Sells both fiction and non-fiction books.

Biblio Inc
PO Box 1211, Asheville, North Carolina, 28802, USA

www.biblio.com

About A US based service, allowing users to search for used, rare, and out of print books from booksellers around the world. The list contains more than 45,000,000 books.

Biblion
Biblion Mayfair, 1–7 Davies Mews, London, W1K 5AB

www.biblion.co.uk

About A London bookshop with an online facility that allows users to find dealers for second hand and rare books.

Book Lovers
c/o David Gower Spence, BookLovers.co.uk, The Post Office, 12 Bath Road, Peasedown St John, BA2 8DH

0845 009 4455

0845 009 1876

dgs@booklovers.co.uk

www.booklovers.co.uk

About Lists over 350,000 books from independent dealers. Also sells bibliographies and runs a book valuation service.

The Bookshop
17 North Main Street, Wigtown, DG8 9HL

01988 402499

mail@the-bookshop.com

www.the-bookshop.com

About A secondhand bookshop located in the Scottish national book town, Wigtown.

Byre Books
24 South Main Street, Wigtown, DG8 9EH

0845 458 3813

enquiries@byrebooks.co.uk

www.byrebooks.co.uk

About Based in Wigtown – the Scottish national book town. Byre Books specialises in books on folklore and mythology, theatre, film and television, and books of Scottish interest. The website can take secure orders, and contains a large online catalogue.

Discovery Bookshop
52 Cwmamman Road, Garnant, Ammanford, South Wales, SA18 1LT

01269 823839

www.discoverybookshop.co.uk

About A shop in South Wales, with an online store in conjunction with AbeBooks. The site sells second hand books, records, CDs, sheet music, videos, cassettes and reel to reel tapes.

Dusty Books
The Old Woollen Mill, Shortbridge Street, Llanidloes, Powys, SY18 6AD

01686 411247

01686 411248

scribe@dustybooks.co.uk

www.dustybooks.co.uk

About A searchable online shop of used, rare and out of print books.

eBay Inc
2145 Hamilton Avenue, San Jose, California, 95125, USA

www.ebay.co.uk

About An online auction site containing a category for books, comics and magazines, both new and used.

Fullerton's Booksearch
The Dukes House, Moorgate Road, Hindringham, Fakenham, Norfolk, NR21 0PT

01328 878781

01328 878782

fullertons.books@virgin.net

www.glavenvalley.co.uk/fullertons

About An international out of print book searching service, dealing with English language titles. Three out of four books tend to be found within ten days. There is no obligation to purchase. Fullerton's website provides further information.

Hay-on-Wye Bookshops
www.hay-on-wye.co.uk/bookshops/default.asp

About A directory of the many second hand bookshops and booksellers in Hay-on-Wye, Hereford.

Inprint/The Book Guide
31 High Street, Stroud, Gloucestershire, GL5 1AJ

01453 759731

enquiries@inprint.co.uk

www.inprint.co.uk

About A bookshop selling second hand and out of print books, it also has a full online catalogue and purchase facility. They are specialists in out of print books about cinema. The Book Guide is a resource area with a searchable database of second hand bookshops in the UK by region. Also contains information on book fairs and auctions.

Mary Ward Books
Blyford, Halesworth, Suffolk, IP19 9JR
- 01986 875543
- sales@marywardbooks.com
- www.marywardbooks.com

About An independent online bookstore specialising in second hand books, out of print books and used books. As well as the online search facility, there are many titles offline that can be requested.

Read Ireland
392 Clontarf Road, Clontarf, Dublin 3, Republic of Ireland
- 00353 1 853 2063
- 00353 1 853 2063
- ri-info@readireland.ie
- www.readireland.ie

About An Internet bookstore dedicated exclusively to Irish interest books, both fiction and non-fiction.

UK Book World
- www.ukbookworld.com

About Allows users to search the databases of booksellers across the UK, containing over a million old and out of print books.

UK Christian Bookshops Directory
- ukcbd.enquiries@christianbookshops.org.uk
- www.christianbookshops.org.uk

Contact Phil Groom

About A directory of UK Christian bookshops, including a list of those who stock second hand, rare and out of print books.

Used Book Search
- contact@usedbooksearch.co.uk
- www.usedbooksearch.co.uk

About A large search facility, allowing users to locate second hand books from databases including AbeBooks, WH Smith, Amazon and Biblion.

Word Power Bookshop
43 West Nicolson Street, Edinburgh, EH8 9DB
- 0131 662 9112
- 0131 662 9112
- books@word-power.co.uk
- www.word-power.co.uk

About An independent bookshop in Scotland with a fully developed online service that can source and deliver any book in print. They maintain a core list of literature outside the mainstream and aim to increase the profile of small presses and new writers by fostering debate and selling radical books.

Zardoz Books
20 Whitecroft, Dilton Marsh, Westbury, Wiltshire, BA13 4DJ
- 01373 865371
- 01373 303984
- mflanagan@zardozbooks.co.uk
- www.zardozbooks.co.uk

Contact Maurice Flanagan

About A collectible and out of print book dealer. Also sells books via auction on eBay.

BURSARIES, FELLOWSHIPS & GRANTS

ABSW Student Journalism Bursaries

Association of British Science Writers, Wellcome Wolfson Building, 165 Queen's Gate, London, SW7 5HD

☎ 0870 770 3361

✉ absw@absw.org.uk

🌐 www.absw.org.uk

About Nine bursaries are offered to students taking a science communication course (seven for full time courses, two for part time). Bursaries are designed to cover course fees and living expenses. Candidates must be able to demonstrate a background in science, an aptitude for communication and a lack of alternative sources for funding. Applications should consist of a CV, a 500 word stated case for the bursary, and completion of a set exercise. An application form is available on the website.

The Airey Neave Trust

PO Box 36800, 40 Bernard Street, London, WC1N 1WJ

☎ 020 7833 4440

✉ info@aireyneavetrust.org.uk

🌐 www.aireyneavetrust.org.uk

Contact Mrs Hannah Scott

About Offers fellowships for scholars wishing to undertake research in the field of 'human freedom'. Masters and PhD students are discouraged from applying. There is no application form and applicants should submit a research plan for either one or two years – of not more than 500 words – giving a synopsis of the planned research and a more detailed account suitable for an expert referee's judgment.

Alfred Bradley Bursary Award

BBC Radio Drama Room, Room 2129, New Broadcasting House, Oxford Road, Manchester, M60 1SJ

About A biennial radio drama award in memory of Alfred Bradley, a distinguished BBC radio writer. The winner is awarded a bursary of up to £6,000 and a commission for an afternoon play on BBC Radio 4. Applicants must have been born in the North of England, been bought up there, or currently live in the region. Applicants cannot have had a play produced by the BBC in the past. To apply, send a hard copy of an original 45 minute play of around 7,000 words. Closing date generally around November. Previous winners include Julia Copus and Katie Douglas.

The Authors' Foundation

The Society of Authors, 84 Drayton Gardens, London, SW10 9SB

☎ 020 7373 6642

📠 020 7373 5768

✉ info@societyofauthors.org

🌐 www.societyofauthors.org

About Grants are available for writers who are already commissioned by a British publisher to write a full length work of fiction, poetry or non-fiction. There are also grants for those that have been previously published and can demonstrate a strong likelihood they will be published in Britain again. Money is designed to assist with the research, travel and living costs that a publisher's advance may not cover. The twice-yearly grants, awarded in April and September, are normally between £1,000 and £2,000, and rarely exceed £4,000. Applicants should include: a brief history of their writing career; details of their current work; size of advance (if any); names of publishers already approached, or working with; overall financial position and why the grant is needed; details of past grants; and copies of past reviews (if any). Full application details are available on the website.

British Academy Research Funding

10 Carlton House Terrace, London, SW1Y 5AH

☎ 020 7969 5217

📠 020 7969 5414

✉ grants@britac.ac.uk

🌐 www.britac.ac.uk

About Research grants are awarded at postdoctoral or equivalent level, for researchers in the humanities and social sciences fields. Application forms are available for both small (up to £7,500) and large (up to £100,000) awards, reflecting the size and scope of different research proposals.

Charles Pick Fellowship

School of Literature and Creative Writing, University of East Anglia, University Plain, Norwich, NR4 7TJ

- ☏ 01603 592810
- ☏ 01603 507728
- ✉ charlespickfellowship@uea.ac.uk
- 🌐 www1.uea.ac.uk/lit/awards/pick

About A six month bursary of £10,000 in memory of Charles Pick, a publisher and literary agent. Applicants must be unpublished writers of fictional or non-fictional prose (excluding reports from academic research). Winners will be picked on the strength of their writing proposal and references from editors, agents or accredited creative writing teachers. Fellows must reside at the University of East Anglia. Shared office space and computer facilities will be made available for the Fellow in the School of Literature and Creative Writing. The Fellow will be required to submit written work to a nominated mentor and take part in creative writing research seminars, however there are no teaching duties.

David T. K. Wong Fellowship

School of Literature and Creative Writing, University of East Anglia, University Plain, Norwich, NR4 7TJ

- ☏ 01603 592810
- ☏ 01603 507728
- ✉ davidtkwongfellowship@uea.ac.uk
- 🌐 www1.uea.ac.uk/lit/awards/wong

About An annual grant of around £26,000 to enable a writer to spend a year based at the University of East Anglia writing a work of fiction incorporating an aspect of life in the Far East as a subject matter. Applicants may be of any nationality, and can be a published or an unpublished writer.

European Jewish Publication Society

PO Box 19948, London, N3 3ZL

- ☏ 020 8346 1668
- ☏ 020 8346 1776
- ✉ cs@ejps.org.uk
- 🌐 www.ejps.org.uk

Contact Dr Colin Shindler

About The society supplies grants of up to £3,000 to publishers seeking assistance in the publication of Jewish interest books, both fiction and non-fiction (£1,000 for poetry). Assistance is also given with the marketing and promotion of the title once published. Potential applicants must first approach a publisher, and then the publisher must contact the society. Recent examples of books include; *Photographing the Holocaust* by Janina Struck and *The Arab-Israeli Cookbook* by Robin Soans.

Fulbright Awards

The Fulbright Commission, Fulbright House, 62 Doughty Street, London, WC1N 2JZ

- ☏ 020 7404 6880
- ☏ 020 7404 6834
- ✉ programmes@fulbright.co.uk
- 🌐 www.fulbright.co.uk

Contact British Programme Manager

About A set of postgraduate awards, with one in journalism, to fund British students undertaking courses at American universities (first year only). Students must research and apply to each university course themselves. Either apply on the website, or send SAE with enough postage to cover 100g. Include a covering letter stating which award you require information on.

The George Viner Memorial Fund Trust

Headland House, 308–312 Grays Inn Road, London, WC1X 8DP

- ☏ 020 7843 3708
- ☏ 020 7278 1812
- ✉ georgeviner@nuj.org.uk
- 🌐 www.georgeviner.org.uk

About Sponsorship opportunities facilitated by the National Union of Journalists. They are granted once a year for potential students from ethnic minority backgrounds who have been accepted onto a course, but cannot accept for financial reasons. Check website for application details. Deadlines are normally in August.

Guardian Research Fellowship

Nuffield College, Oxford, OX1 1NF

- ☏ 01865 278542
- ☏ 01865 278666

Contact Academic Administrator, S. Wright

About A year long fellowship, endowed by the Scott Trust and the *Guardian* newspaper. The fellowship enables a media professional to put their experiences into a published report and give a lecture. Applicants include journalists, managers and broadcasters. The research proposals must be linked to working in the media.

Hawthornden Literary Institute

Hawthornden International Retreat for Writers, Lasswade, EH18 1EG

- ☏ 0131 440 2180
- ☏ 0131 440 1989

About Hawthornden provides a quiet retreat for up to six writers to concentrate on their work. Writers who win access to this facility are known as Hawthornden Fellows. They become guests of the retreat once they have arrived, but no travel expenses are paid. Application forms can be requested by telephone or fax and must be returned by the end of November for retreats the following year.

Jerwood Awards
The Royal Society of Literature, Somerset House, Strand, London, WC2R 1LA
- 020 7845 4676
- paulaj@rslit.org
- www.rslit.org

Contact Paula Johnson
About Offers three annual awards, one of £10,000 and two of £5,000, to authors engaged on their first major commissioned works of non-fiction. Open to first time writers resident in the UK or Ireland for at least three years, and who have been firmly contracted to write a piece of non-fiction. Applicants should send: a covering letter explaining the piece; a copy of the contract with the publisher; a synopsis of the book; and a letter of recommendation from the editor confirming that the piece is the author's first, and is of literary merit.

Journalists' Charity
Dickens House, 35 Wathen Road, Dorking, Surrey, RH4 1JY
- 01306 887511
- 01306 888212
- enquiries@journalistscharity.org.uk
- www.journalistscharity.org.uk

About A charity providing grants, bursaries and other financial assistance to journalists and their dependants. The charity also runs retirement homes and can provide nursing care. Originally established in 1860. Charles Dickens was a founding member.

Laurence Stern Fellowship
Department of Journalism, City University, Northampton Square, London, EC1V 0HB
- 020 7040 4036
- a.r.mckane@city.ac.uk
- www.city.ac.uk/journalism

Contact Anna McKane
About An opportunity for a journalist with experience of working on national stories to intern at the *Washington Post* in the US, for three months during the summer. Applicants may be working in print, radio, television, or web, but should demonstrate relevant experience in print particularly. The intention is to send a young journalist, although there is no age limit. Applicants should attach a CV, no more than three samples of their work, and two references (the candidate must obtain the references and include them with the application). Television or radio journalists may submit scripts, or cite examples of their recent achievements. The fellowships normally start in July and the deadline is the previous February, check the website for more details.

The Nico Colchester Journalism Fellowship
1 Southwark Bridge, London, SE1 9HL
- 020 7873 3000
- 020 7873 3076
- ncprize@economist.com
- www.ft.com/nicocolchester

About Two internships are available, each for three months. One is for a British journalist at an *Economist* office in Europe, and one for a European journalist at the *Financial Times* in London. Both winners receive a £4,000 bursary. Submit a 1,000 word article on the topic 'How can national economic interests be protected in this era of globalisation?' in English, together with a CV and covering letter.

North East Literary Fellowship
Arts Council England North East, Central Square, Forth Street, Newcastle upon Tyne, NE1 3PJ
- 0191 255 8542
- 0191 230 1020
- www.artscouncil.org.uk/funding

About A fellowship in association with the University of Durham and the University of Newcastle. Contact the North East branch of Arts Council England for more details, and how to apply.

PAWS (Public Awareness of Science) Drama Fund
PAWS and Omni Communications, First Floor, 155 Regents Park Road, London, NW1 8BB
- 020 7483 4545
- pawsomni@btconnect.com
- www.pawsdrama.com

About Two levels of grants for dramatic writers in the field of science and technology. The first, at around £5,000 is for top writers whose ideas feature engineers in leading roles or women scientists. The second level, around £1,000 to £2,000, is for writers who already have some interest in their work from a producer or broadcaster. There is no competitive element for the top grants. Any writer in these fields may approach PAWS directly about the application process.

Pearson Playwrights' Scheme
c/o Pearson Plc, 80 Strand, London, WC2R 0RL
- playwrightsscheme@tiscali.co.uk

Contact Jack Andrews MBE

About Five bursaries of £6,500 are awarded annually to scriptwriters. A theatre must make nominations in October each year, and winners then gain a year's attachment with that theatre. An additional prize is awarded the following year for the best play emerging from the five winners.

Peggy Ramsay Foundation
Hanover House, 14 Hanover Square, London, W1S 1HP
- 020 7667 5000
- 020 7667 5100
- laurence.harbottle@harbottle.com
- www.peggyramsayfoundation.org

Contact G. Laurence Harbottle
About A foundation borne out of the will of Peggy Ramsay, a play agent. Grants totalling around £200,000 per year are made directly to writers. The writer must show that they have had at least one full length play produced professionally for an adult audience, need time to write again for the stage, and cannot otherwise afford to do so. Also considered from time to time, are organisations whose projects and awards may help new writing for the stage. Writers must be resident in Britain, but of no particular nationality. The trustees meet four to five times a year. Applications should be brief, made by the writer concerned, preferably in a simple letter stating the need and the amount requested. A full CV of the applicant must be enclosed. Scripts and previous publicity should not be sent.

Peter Martin Fellowship
1 Southwark Bridge, London, SE1 9HL
- 020 7873 3000
- 020 7873 3076
- pmfellow@ft.com
- www.ft.com/petermartin

About A three month internship in memory of Peter Martin, a former chief business columnist and deputy editor of the Financial Times. A bursary of £4,000 will be made to cover living expenses. Candidates must have a thorough grounding in economics, a first degree and possibly a postgraduate qualification. They must demonstrate an interest in the areas that interested Peter, particularly the impact of technology on the economy. Submit a CV and draft editorial piece of up to 5,000 words.

The Richard Casement Internship
The Economist, 25 St James's Street, London, SW1A 1HG
- 020 7830 7000
- casement2007@economist.com
- www.economist.com

Contact Science Editor, Geoffrey Carr
About A summer internship for a young person to spend three months working as a journalist in the science and technology section. Applicants should be under 25 and are more likely to succeed if they're a science student who wants to develop writing skills, rather than a writer who wants to learn about science. Details usually appear in the magazine, and on the website in January or February.

Robert Louis Stevenson Memorial Fellowship
The National Library of Scotland, George IV Bridge, Edinburgh, EH1 1EW
- 07748 782058
- morrisongraham@tiscali.co.uk
- www.scottisharts.org.uk

Contact Fiona Morrison Graham
About Winners receive a two-month residency at Grez-sur-Loing, Fontainbleu, France, where Stevenson first met his wife Fanny Osborne, funded by the Scottish Arts Council and the National Library of Scotland. Applicants must be writers living in Scotland, or be Scottish by birth. Submit no more than 3,000 words of original work (in progress or recently published), along with a brief statement of how the fellowship would be useful, and a short career history. An application form is downloadable from the website.

The Royal Literary Fund
3 Johnson's Court, London, EC4A 3EA
- 020 7353 7160
- rlitfund@btconnect.com
- www.rlf.org.uk

Contact General Secretary, Eileen Gunn
About The Royal Literary Fund has been continuously helping authors since it was set up in 1790. It is funded by bequests and donations from writers who wish to help other writers. Its committee members come from all walks of literary life and include novelists, biographers, poets, publishers, lawyers and agents. Help is given to writers in many different situations, where personal or professional setbacks have resulted in loss of income. Grants cannot be made for works in progress. Pensions are considered for older writers who have seen their earnings decrease. To apply, contact Eileen Gunn providing a list of your work, including names of publishers, dates, and whether sole author. Of special interest to all involved in writing in higher edcucation is Writing Matters, the RLF report on student writing in higher education. It examines the difficulties many students face in writing effectively, and proposes a range of measures to address these. The report argues that much greater attention

should be paid to helping students adjust to the demands of writing at university, and that writing development is a key factor for progress in the higher education sector.

The Royal Literary Fund Fellowship Scheme
3 Johnson's Court, off Fleet Street, London, EC4A 3EA

- 020 7353 7160
- rlitfund@btconnect.com
- www.rlf.org.uk

Contact Fellowship and Education Officer, Stephen Cook

About A fellowship scheme for professional, published writers of literary merit, with at least two (sole-authored) books published of any genre, mainstream theatre works performed, or scripts broadcast. Applicants must be native English speakers and the resident of a commonwealth country. Citizens of other countries may apply if they have been resident in the UK for at least three years. Fellows will be attached to a British university and will be paid a fee of around £14,000 for one academic year. There are two recruitment rounds per year. Contact Stephen Cook for an application pack (not usually available between April and November).

Sander Thoenes Award
1 Southwark Bridge, London, SE1 9HL

- 020 7873 3000
- 020 7873 3076
- www.ft.com/sanderthoenes

About An annual award in memory of the former Jakarta correspondent for the *Financial Times*, who was killed in East Timor in September 1999. The winner is offered a three month internship at the FT's headquarters in London, and a bursary of £5,250 to cover accommodation and living expenses. Applicants are welcomed from all over the world, but must be fluent in written English and have no more than five years journalistic experience. Submit a CV, two references, an unpublished original article of 900 words max. on an issue relevant to emerging democracies, plus copies of two published articles, or an academic essay. Also send a covering letter of no more than 400 words explaining how you would benefit from winning.

Scottish Arts Council Bursaries
Grants Administration Department, 12 Manor Place, Edinburgh, EH3 7DD

- 0131 226 6051
- 0131 225 9833
- help.desk@scottisharts.org.uk

- www.scottisharts.org.uk

About A range of grants, which are available for professionals working in the arts, including some in the literature and drama fields. Check the website for details of current offers and application procedures. Applicants should normally live in Scotland, or work in Scotland.

Scott Trust Bursaries
60 Farringdon Road, London, EC1R 3GA

- 020 7278 2332

About The Scott Trust, owners of the Guardian Media Group plc, offer four annual bursary places on the Postgraduate Diploma course in Newspaper Journalism at City University, London. The bursaries cover course fees and a contribution towards living expenses, plus work experience with the Guardian Media Group. Preference is given to those who already have some work experience within newspapers. Ethnic minorities, disabled applicants and applicants with varied experience since graduating are encouraged to apply. The trust is also open to application for charitable donations.

The Society of Authors Charitable Trusts
The Society of Authors, 84 Drayton Gardens, London, SW10 9SB

- 020 7373 6642
- 020 7373 5768
- info@societyofauthors.org
- www.societyofauthors.org

Contact Dorothy Sim

About There are currently three funds available for professional freelance writers who experience sudden, or temporary financial difficulty. The Francis Head Bequest is open to all writers, particularly those with unexpected health problems. The Authors' Contingency Fund is open to writers (or their dependents) who are in extreme financial difficulty. The John Masefield Memorial Trust is open to poets (or their dependents) who face sudden financial problems. Applications for all three may be made using the form available on the website.

Tony Doyle Bursary for New Writing
BBC NI Drama Department, Broadcasting House, Ormeau Avenue, Belfast, BT2 8HQ

- 028 9033 8845
- tvdrama.ni@bbc.co.uk
- www.bbc.co.uk/northernireland/drama/writing_opps/tony_doyle04.shtml

About A bursary which encourages new scriptwriters to produce television drama about Ireland. The winner will receive £2,000 and an invitation to attend a residential seminar. This will consist of a series of intensive sessions with the BBC Northern Ireland development team and experienced practitioners – producers, directors, actors and fellow writers. Two runners up will also receive invitations. Submit a 60 or 90 minute script for a television drama, either a single piece, the first part of a series, serial or a two part show. For anything other than a one off, also attach a synopsis of future storylines. Writers who have been produced for television or feature film are not eligible. Independent films that have subsequently been broadcast are eligible. Check the website for deadlines. In 2007 the deadline was the end of January.

Tony Godwin Memorial Trust
c/o 38 Lyttelton Court, Lyttelton Road, London, N2 0EB
- 020 8209 1613
- info@tgmt.org.uk
- www.tgmt.org.uk

Contact Iain Brown
About A biennial award (odd years) commemorating the life of Tony Godwin, a distinguished publisher from the 1960s and 70s. A grant of up to $5,000 allows the winner to spend at least a month working at an American publishing house and learning about international publishing.

The Travelling Scholarships
The Society of Authors, 84 Drayton Gardens, London, SW10 9SB
- 020 7373 6642
- 020 7373 5768
- info@societyofauthors.org
- www.societyofauthors.org

About Honorary grants awarded to established writers nominated by the Society of Authors' committee of management. No submissions are accepted.

WRITING & PUBLISHING COURSES

FULL-TIME COURSES

Anglia Ruskin University
East Road, Cambridge, CB1 1PT
- 0845 271 3333
- answers@anglia.ac.uk
- www.anglia.ac.uk

Courses BA Writing
BA Writing and Drama, English or Film Studies

Bath Spa University
School of English & Creative Studies, Bath Spa University, Newton Park Campus, Newton St Loe, Bath, BA2 9BN
- 01225 875875
- 01225 875444
- www.bathspa.ac.uk

Courses BA Creative Writing (Single or Joint). Contact Richard Kerridge, r.kerridge@bathspa.ac.uk
MA Creative Writing. Contact Richard Kerridge, r.kerridge@bathspa.ac.uk
MA Writing for Young People. Contact Julia Green, j.a.green@bathspa.ac.uk
PhD Creative Writing. Contact Dr. Tracey Brain, t.brain@bathspa.ac.uk

Birkbeck College
Malet Street, Bloomsbury, London, WC1E 7HX
- 020 7631 6000
- 020 7631 6270
- info@bbk.ac.uk
- www.bbk.ac.uk

Courses MA Creative Writing. Contact office@eng.bbk.ac.uk

Blackpool & The Fylde College
Ashfield Road, Bispham, Blackpool, FY2 0HB
- 01253 504343
- 01253 356127
- visitors@blackpool.ac.uk
- www.blackpool.ac.uk

Courses BA English Language, Literature and Writing

Bournemouth University
Fern Barrow, Talbot Campus, Poole, Dorset, BH12 5BB
- 01202 524111
- 01202 962736
- enquiries@bournemouth.ac.uk
- www.bournemouth.ac.uk

Courses BA Scriptwriting for Film and Television. Contact kking@bournemouth.ac.uk
BA Multimedia Journalism. Contact Kread@bournemouth.ac.uk
MA Journalism (International), Multimedia Journalism, or Magazine Journalism. Contact sbrownlee@bournemouth.ac.uk

Brunel University
Uxbridge, Middlesex, UB8 3PH
- ☎ 01895 274000
- ☎ 01895 232806
- ✉ admissions@brunel.ac.uk
- 🌐 www.brunel.ac.uk

Courses BA Creative Writing. Contact Rose Atfield, english.admissions@brunel.ac.uk
BA English with Creative Writing. Contact Rose Atfield, english.admissions@brunel.ac.uk
MA Creative and Professional Writing. Contact Donna White, donna.white@brunel.ac.uk
MA Creative Writing (The Novel). Contact Donna White, donna.white@brunel.ac.uk
MA Journalism. Contact Donna White, donna.white@brunel.ac.uk

Buckinghamshire Chilterns University College
Queen Alexandra Road, High Wycombe, Buckinghamshire, HP11 2JZ
- ☎ 01494 522141
- ☎ 01494 524392
- ✉ advice@bucks.ac.uk
- 🌐 www.bcuc.ac.uk

Courses BA Creative Writing with Film Studies, Drama, English Literature, Media Studies, or Digital Video Production (or combinations)

Canterbury Christchurch University
North Holmes Road, Canterbury, Kent, CT1 1QU
- ☎ 01227 767700
- ☎ 01227 470442
- ✉ admissions@canterbury.ac.uk
- 🌐 www.canterbury.ac.uk

Courses MA Creative Writing. Contact Dr. Andrew Palmer
MA Journalism. Contact Kate Handley, kk23@canterbury.ac.uk

Cardiff University
Park Place, Cardiff, Wales, CF10 3AT
- ☎ 029 2087 4000
- 🌐 www.cardiff.ac.uk

Courses MA Journalism Studies. Contact Karin Wahl-Jorgensen, wahl-jorgensenK@cardiff.ac.uk
MA International Journalism. Contact Sara Hadwin, hadwins@cardiff.ac.uk
MA Teaching & Practice of Creative Writing. Contact encap@cardiff.ac.uk

Central School of Speech and Drama
Embassy Theatre, Eton Avenue, London, NW3 3HY
- ☎ 020 7722 8183
- ✉ enquiries@cssd.ac.uk
- 🌐 www.cssd.ac.uk

Courses MA Writing for Stage & Broadcast Media. MA Writing for Performance.

City University
Northampton Square, London, EC1V 0HB
- ☎ 020 7040 5060
- ☎ 020 7040 5070
- ✉ enquiries@city.ac.uk
- ✉ journalism@city.ac.uk
- 🌐 www.city.ac.uk

Courses BA Journalism
BA Journalism & Contemporary History
BA Journalism & Social Science
MA Broadcast Journalism
MA Creative Writing (Novels)
MA Creative Writing (Non-fiction)
MA Creative Writing (Plays & Scripts)
MA Magazine, Newspaper or International Journalism
MA Publishing Studies

Coventry University
Priory Street, Coventry, CV1 5FB
- ☎ 024 7688 7688
- ✉ studentenquiries@coventry.ac.uk
- 🌐 www.coventry.ac.uk

Courses BA Journalism with English (Joint)
BA Journalism and Media
MA Journalism (Automotive/Global/Health). Contact postgraduate@coventry.ac.uk

Cumbria Institute of Arts
Brampton Road, Carlisle, Cumbria, CA3 9AY
- ☎ 01228 400300
- ☎ 01228 514491
- ✉ info@cumbria.ac.uk
- 🌐 www.cumbria.ac.uk

Courses BA Creative Writing. Contact Nick Pemberton
BA Journalism
MA Scriptwriting. Contact Dr. Fiona Powley, fiona.powley@cumbria.ac.uk

Dartington College of Arts
Dartington Hall Estate, Totnes, Devon, TQ9 6EJ
- ☎ 01803 862224
- ☎ 01803 861666
- ✉ enquiries@dartington.ac.uk
- 🌐 www.dartington.ac.uk

Courses BA Writing, Writing (Scripted Media) or Writing (Contemporary Practices)
MA Performance Writing

De Montfort University
The Gateway, Leicester, LE1 9BH
- ☎ 0116 255 1551
- ☎ 0116 257 7533
- ✉ enquiry@dmu.ac.uk
- 🌐 www.dmu.ac.uk

Courses BA Creative Writing (Joint). Contact huadmiss@dmu.ac.uk
BA Journalism (Joint). Contact huadmiss@dmu.ac.uk
MA Creative Writing and New Media. Contact Sue Thomas, hsspgrad@dmu.ac.uk
PGDip Journalism. Contact hsspgrad@dmu.ac.uk
MA Television Scriptwriting. Contact hsspgrad@dmu.ac.uk

Doncaster College
The Hub, Chappell Drive, Doncaster, DN1 2RF
- ☎ 01302 553553
- ☎ 01302 553559
- ✉ infocentre@don.ac.uk
- 🌐 www.don.ac.uk

Courses BA Scriptwriting

Dublin City University
The Registry, Dublin City University, Dublin 9, Republic of Ireland
- ☎ 00353 1 700 5566
- ☎ 00353 1 836 0830
- ✉ registry@dcu.ie
- 🌐 www.dcu.ie

Courses BA Journalism. Contact Martin Molony, martin.molony@dcu.ie
MA Journalism. Contact John O'Sullivan, john.osullivan@dcu.ie

Dublin Institute of Technology, School of Languages
Kevin Street, Dublin 8, Republic of Ireland
- ☎ 00353 1 402 4609
- ✉ helene.conway@dit.ie
- 🌐 www.dit.ie

Courses BA Journalism

Edge Hill University
St Helen's Road, Ormskirk, Lancashire, L39 4QP
- ☎ 01695 575171
- ☎ 01695 579997
- ✉ enquiries@edgehill.ac.uk
- 🌐 www.edgehill.ac.uk

Courses BA Creative Writing. Contact Dr. Ailsa Cox, coxa@edgehill.ac.uk
BA Creative Writing & English. Contact Dr. Ailsa Cox, coxa@edgehill.ac.uk
BA Journalism. Contact Angela Birchall, birchala@edgehill.ac.uk
MA Writing Studies. Contact Prof. Robert Sheppard

Goldsmiths College
University of London, New Cross, London, SE14 6NW
- ☎ 020 7919 7171
- ✉ admissions@gold.ac.uk
- 🌐 www.gold.ac.uk

Courses MA Creative & Life Writing. Contact english@gold.ac.uk
MA Creative Writing. Contact english@gold.ac.uk
MA Writing for Performance. Contact drama@gold.ac.uk
MA Journalism. Contact media-comms@gold.ac.uk
MA Scriptwriting. Contact media-comms@gold.ac.uk
MA Feature Film. Contact media-comms@gold.ac.uk
MA Radio. Contact media-comms@gold.ac.uk
MA Filmmaking. Contact media-comms@gold.ac.uk
MA Screen Documentary. Contact media-comms@gold.ac.uk

Griffith College
Wellington House, 9/11 Patrick's Hill, Cork, Republic of Ireland
- ☎ 00353 21 450 7027
- ☎ 00353 21 450 7659
- ✉ day@gcc.ie
- 🌐 www.griffithcollegecork.ie

Courses BA Journalism

Grimsby Institute of Further & Higher Education
Nuns Corner, Grimsby, North East Lincolnshire, DN34 5BQ
- ☎ 01472 311222
- ☎ 01472 879924
- ✉ infocent@grimsby.ac.uk
- 🌐 www.grimsby.ac.uk

Courses BA Journalism
BA Professional Writing

King's College London
Strand, London, WC2R 2LS
- ☎ 020 7836 5454
- ✉ ceu@kcl.ac.uk
- 🌐 www.kcl.ac.uk

Courses MA Text & Performance Studies. Contact helene.hokland@kcl.ac.uk

Kingston University
River House, 53–57 High Street, Kingston upon Thames, Surrey, KT1 1LQ
- ☎ 020 8547 2000

admissions-info@kingston.ac.uk
www.kingston.ac.uk
Courses BA Journalism. Contact hsundergrad-info@
kingston.ac.uk
MA Creative, Fiction or Travel Writing. Contact Susan
Henry, fasspostgrad-info@kingston.ac.uk
MA Writing for Children. Contact Susan Henry,
hsundergrad-info@kingston.ac.uk
MA Poetry. Contact Susan Henry, hsundergrad-info@
kingston.ac.uk
MA Publishing Studies. Contact Susan Henry,
hsundergrad-info@kingston.ac.uk
MA Making Plays: Writing & Devising for the Stage.
Contact Susan Henry, hsundergrad-info@
kingston.ac.uk
MA The Creative Economy & Creative Writing,
Publishing, Journalism, Film and Video, or Digital
Media. Contact creativeindustries@kingston.ac.uk

Lancaster University
Bailrigg, Lancaster, LA1 4YW
01524 65201
www.lancaster.ac.uk
Courses BA English Language with Creative Writing.
Contact l.williams5@lancaster.ac.uk
BA English Literature with Creative Writing. Contact
k.elliott@lancaster.ac.uk
BA English Literature, Creative Writing and Practice.
Contact k.elliott@lancaster.ac.uk
MA Creative Writing. Contact englishpg@
lancaster.ac.uk

Leeds Metropolitan University
Civic Quarter, Leeds, LS1 3HE
0113 283 3113
0113 283 3148
www.lmu.ac.uk
Courses MA Screenwriting: Fiction. Contact Chris
Pugh, c.j.pugh@leedsmet.ac.uk

Liverpool John Moores University
**Faculty of Media, Arts & Social Science, Dean
Walters Building, Upper Duke Street, Liverpool,
L1 7BT**
0151 231 5090
recruitment@ljmu.ac.uk
www.ljmu.ac.uk
Courses BA Journalism. Contact Lynne Gilbertson,
l.gilbertson@ljmu.ac.uk or lssadmissions@ljmu.ac.uk
MA International Journalism. Contact Lynne
Gilbertson, l.gilbertson@ljmu.ac.uk or lssadmissions@
ljmu.ac.uk
MA Journalism. Contact Lynne Gilbertson,
l.gilbertson@ljmu.ac.uk or lssadmissions@ljmu.ac.uk

BA Creative Writing. Contact Julie Quine-Yankson,
j.quine-yankson@ljmu.ac.uk or mcaadmissions@
ljmu.ac.uk
MA Writing. Contact Julie Quine-Yankson, j.quine-
yankson@ljmu.ac.uk or mcaadmissions@ljmu.ac.uk
MA Screenwriting. Contact Julie Quine-Yankson,
j.quine-yankson@ljmu.ac.uk or mcaadmissions@
ljmu.ac.uk

London Metropolitan University
166–220 Holloway Road, London, N7 8DB
020 7133 4200/020 7133 4202
admissions@londonmet.ac.uk
www.londonmet.ac.uk
Courses BA Creative Writing (Single or Joint)
BA Creative Writing & English Literature
BA Journalism Studies
MA Professional Writing. Contact humanities@
londonmet.ac.uk
MA Screenwriting. Contact Brian Dunnigan,
b.dunnigan@lfs.org.uk

London South Bank University
90 London Road, London, SE1 6EN
020 7815 7815
enquiry@lsbu.ac.uk
www.lsbu.ac.uk
Courses BA Writing for Media Arts. Contact Colin
Harvey, harveycb@lsbu.ac.uk
BA Creative Writing. Contact Margaret Kinsman,
kinsmam@lsbu.ac.uk
MA Writing for Media. Contact Dr. Anna Reading,
readinam@lsbu.ac.uk

Loughborough University
Loughborough, Leicestershire, LE11 3TU
01509 263171
postmaster@lboro.ac.uk
www.lboro.ac.uk
Courses BA Publishing with English. Contact
j.harrison@lboro.ac.uk
MA Creative Writing. Contact Dr. Jonathan Taylor,
j.p.taylor1@lboro.ac.uk
MA Modern & Contemporary Writing. Contact Dr.
Brian Jarvis, b.jarvis@lboro.ac.uk

Manchester Metropolitan University
**All Saints Building, All Saints, Manchester,
M15 6BH**
0161 247 2000
0161 247 6390
enquiries@mmu.ac.uk
www.mmu.ac.uk
Courses BA Creative Writing (Single and Joint).
Contact adm.cheshire@mmu.ac.uk

BA English & Creative Writing. Contact english-hums@
mmu.ac.uk
PgDip/MA Creative Writing. Contact Heather Beck,
h.beck@mmu.ac.uk

Marjon
University College Plymouth, St Mark & St John,
Derriford Road, Plymouth, Devon, PL6 8BH
- 01752 636700
- admissions@marjon.ac.uk
- www.marjon.ac.uk
Courses BA Creative Writing (Joint)
BA Writing for the Media

Napier University
Craiglockhart Campus, Edinburgh, EH14 1DJ
- 0845 260 6040
- info@napier.ac.uk
- www.napier.ac.uk
Courses BA Journalism
BA Publishing Media
MSc Journalism
MSc Publishing

National Film & Television School
Beaconsfield Studios, Station Road,
Beaconsfield, Buckinghamshire, HP9 1LG
- 01494 671234
- 01494 674042
- info@nfts.co.uk
- www.nftsfilm-tv.ac.uk
Courses MA Screenwriting

National University of Ireland, Galway
University Road, Galway, Republic of Ireland
- 00353 91 524411
- info@imagenuigalway.ie
- www.nuigalway.ie
Courses MA Literature & Publishing. Contact Julia
Kilroy, julia.kilroy@nuigalway.ie
MA Journalism. Contact Bernadette O'Sullivan,
bernadette.osullivan@nuigalway.ie
MA Writing. Contact Adrian Frazier, adrian.frazier@
nuigalway.ie
MA Screenwriting. Contact Rod Stoneman,
rod.stoneman@nuigalway.ie

Newcastle University
Newcastle upon Tyne, NE1 7RU
- 0191 222 6000
- enquiries@ncl.ac.uk
- www.ncl.ac.uk
Courses MA Creative Writing

Newman College of Higher Education
Genners Lane, Bartley Green, Birmingham,
B32 3NT
- 0121 476 1181
- 0121 476 1196
- registry@newman.ac.uk
- www.newman.ac.uk
Courses Creative Writing (Combined Honours
Programmes). Contact Jenny Daniels, english@
newman.ac.uk

Northumbria University
Ellison Place, Newcastle upon Tyne, NE1 8ST
- 0191 232 6002
- 0191 227 3903
- er.admissions@northumbria.ac.uk
- www.northumbria.ac.uk
Courses BA English & Creative Writing
BA Journalism
MA Creative Writing

North Wales School of Art & Design
North East Wales Institute of Higher Education,
Plas Coch Campus, Mold Road, Wrexham,
LL11 2AW
- 01978 293439
- sid@newi.ac.uk
- www.newi.ac.uk
Courses BA Illustration for Children's Publishing.
BA Illustration for Graphic Novels.

The Norwich School of Art & Design
Francis House, 3–7 Redwell Street, Norwich,
Norfolk, NR2 4SN
- 01603 610561
- 01603 615728
- info@nsad.ac.uk
- www.nsad.ac.uk
Courses MA Writing the Visual. Contact postgrad@
nsad.ac.uk

Nottingham Trent University
Burton Street, Nottingham, NG1 4BU
- 0115 941 8418
- hum.undergrad@ntu.ac.uk
- hum.postgrad@ntu.ac.uk
- www.ntu.ac.uk
Courses BA English with Creative Writing
BA Print Journalism
BA Broadcast Journalism
MA Creative Writing
MA Newspaper Journalism
MA Radio Journalism
MA Television Journalism
MA Online Journalism

Oxford Brookes University
Gipsy Lane, Oxford, OX3 0BP
- ☎ 01865 741111
- ✉ query@brookes.ac.uk
- 🌐 www.brookes.ac.uk

Courses BA/BSc Publishing. Contact Lisa Atkinson, lisa.atkinson@brookes.ac.uk
MA Publishing. Contact pgah@brookes.ac.uk
MA Publishing & Language. Contact pgah@brookes.ac.uk
MA Publishing, Interactive Media. Contact pgah@brookes.ac.uk

Queen Mary, University of London
Department of History, Mile End Road, London, E1 4NS
- ☎ 020 7882 8351
- ☎ 020 8980 8400
- ✉ history@qmul.ac.uk
- 🌐 www.qmul.ac.uk

Courses BA Journalism & Contemporary History

Queen's University Belfast
University Road, Belfast, Northern Ireland, BT7 1NN
- ☎ 028 9024 5133
- ☎ 028 9097 5137
- ✉ admissions@qub.ac.uk
- 🌐 www.qub.ac.uk

Courses MA English (Creative Writing)

The Robert Gordon University
Schoolhill, Aberdeen, Scotland, AB10 1FR
- ☎ 01224 262728
- ☎ 01224 262728
- ✉ admissions@rgu.ac.uk
- 🌐 www.rgu.ac.uk

Courses BA Publishing with Journalism
MSc Publishing with Journalism. Contact Dr. Sarah Pedersen, s.pedersen@rgu.ac.uk
MSc Publishing Studies. Contact Dr. Sarah Pedersen, s.pedersen@rgu.ac.uk

Roehampton University
Erasmus House, Roehampton Lane, London, SW15 5PU
- ☎ 020 8392 3232
- ☎ 020 8392 3470
- ✉ enquiries@roehampton.ac.uk
- 🌐 www.roehampton.ac.uk

Courses BA Creative Writing (Single or Joint)
BA Journalism & News Media (Joint)
MA Creative & Professional Writing. Contact Jeff Hilson, j.hilson@roehampton.ac.uk

MA Children's Literature. Contact Lisa Sainsbury, l.sainsbury@roehampton.ac.uk

Royal Holloway, University of London
Egham Hill, Egham, Surrey, TW20 0EX
- ☎ 01784 434455
- ☎ 01784 437520
- ✉ admissions@rhul.ac.uk
- 🌐 www.rhul.ac.uk

Courses BA English & Creative Writing
BA Drama & Creative Writing
MA Creative Writing. Contact Prof. Andrew Motion, andrew.motion@rhul.ac.uk
MA Feature Film Screenwriting. Contact mediaarts@rhul.ac.uk
MA Screenwriting for Television & Film. Contact mediaarts@rhul.ac.uk

Ruskin College, Oxford
Walton Street, Oxford, OX1 2HE
- ☎ 01865 310713
- ☎ 01865 554372
- ✉ enquiries@ruskin.ac.uk
- 🌐 www.ruskin.ac.uk

Courses BA English Studies (Creative Writing & Critical Practice)

Sheffield Hallam University
City Campus, Howard Street, Sheffield, S1 1WB
- ☎ 0114 225 5555
- ☎ 0114 225 4449
- ✉ enquiries@shu.ac.uk
- 🌐 www.shu.ac.uk

Courses BA Journalism Studies
MA Writing. Contact dsenquiry@shu.ac.uk
MA Broadcast Journalism. Contact aces-info@shu.ac.uk
MA International Broadcast Journalism. Contact aces-info@shu.ac.uk

Southampton Solent University
East Park Terrace, Southampton, Hampshire, SO14 0YN
- ☎ 023 8031 9000
- ☎ 023 8022 2259
- ✉ enquiries@solent.ac.uk
- 🌐 www.ssu.ac.uk

Courses BA Journalism
BA Magazine Journalism & Feature Writing
BA Media Writing
BA Online Journalism
BA Screenwriting
BA Writing Fashion & Culture
BA Writing Popular Fiction
MA Media Writing

South East Essex College
Luker Road, Southend on Sea, Essex, SS1 1ND
- 01702 220400
- admissions@southend.ac.uk
- www.southend.ac.uk
Courses BA Journalism

Staffordshire University
Stoke on Trent, Staffordshire, ST4 2DE
- 01782 294000
- admissions@staffs.ac.uk
- www.staffs.ac.uk
Courses BA Creative Writing
BA Journalism (Single or Joint)
BA Broadcast Journalism
BA Sports Journalism

St Martin's College
Lancaster Campus, Bowerham Road, Lancaster, LA1 3JD
- 01524 384384
- 01524 384385
- admissions@ucsm.ac.uk
- www.stmartins.ac.uk
Courses BA Drama & Creative Writing
BA English & Creative Writing
MA Creative Writing

St Mary's College
Waldegrave Road, Strawberry Hill, Twickenham, TW1 4SX
- 020 8240 4000
- 020 8240 4255
- admit@smuc.ac.uk
- www.smuc.ac.uk
Courses BA Professional & Creative Writing. Contact Peter Dewar, dewarp@smuc.ac.uk

Trinity & All Saints
Brownberrie Lane, Horsforth, Leeds, LS18 5HD
- 0113 283 7100
- 0113 283 7200
- enquiries@leedstrinity.ac.uk
- www.leedstrinity.ac.uk
Courses BA English & Writing
BA Journalism
MA Bi-media, Radio, or Print Journalism. Contact Graham Greer, g.greer@leedstrinity.ac.uk

Trinity College, Carmarthen
Carmarthen, Wales, SA31 3EP
- 01267 676767
- 01267 676766
- registry@trinity-cm.ac.uk
- www.trinity-cm.ac.uk
Courses BA Creative Writing with English, Film Studies or Media Studies. Contact Paul Wright, p.wright@trinity-cm.ac.uk
MA Creative Writing. Contact Paul Wright, p.wright@trinity-cm.ac.uk

Trinity College, Dublin
College Green, Dublin 2, Republic of Ireland
- 00353 1 896 1000
- oscar@tcd.ie
- www.tcd.ie
Courses M.Phil Creative Writing

University College, Falmouth
Woodlane, Falmouth, Cornwall, TR11 4RH
- 01326 211077
- 01326 213880
- admissions@falmouth.ac.uk
- www.falmouth.ac.uk
Courses BA English with Creative Writing. Contact 01326 214358
BA Journalism. Contact 01326 214370
MA/PgDip Professional Writing. Contact 01326 214374
MA International Journalism. Contact 01326 214389
MA/PgDip Broadcast Journalism. Contact 01326 214386

University College for the Creative Arts
Ashley Road, Epsom, Surrey, KT18 5BE
- 01372 728811
- 01372 747050
- info@ucreative.ac.uk
- www.ucreative.ac.uk
Courses BA Fashion Journalism
BA Journalism

University College London
Gower Street, London, WC1E 6BT
- 020 7679 2000
- admissions@ucl.ac.uk
- www.ucl.ac.uk
Courses MA Publishing
MA Electronic Communication & Publishing

University of Bedfordshire
Park Square, Luton, Bedfordshire, LU1 3JU
- 01234 400400
- www.beds.ac.uk
Courses BA Creative Writing
BA Journalism
BA Journalism & Public Relations
BA Sport Journalism

MA Creative Writing (by research)
To find out more about these courses contact Keith Jebb, keith.jebb@beds.ac.uk.

University of Birmingham
Edgbaston, Birmingham, B15 2TT
- 0121 414 3344
- 0121 414 3971
- english@bham.ac.uk
- www.bham.ac.uk

Courses BA English with Creative Writing. Contact english@bham.ac.uk
M.Phil (B) Playwriting Studies. Contact Steve Waters, dramapg@contacts.bham.ac.uk

University of Bolton
Deane Road, Bolton, BL3 5AB
- 01204 900600
- enquiries@bolton.ac.uk
- www.bolton.ac.uk

Courses BA Creative Writing (Single or Joint). Contact Matthew Welton, mw7@bolton.ac.uk
BA Media, Writing & Production. Contact Jenny Shepherd, jms3@bolton.ac.uk
MA Creative Writing (Part time). Contact Jon Glover, jg5@bolton.ac.uk

University of Central England
Perry Barr, Birmingham, B42 2SU
- 0121 331 5595
- 0121 331 7994
- choices@bcu.ac.uk
- www.uce.ac.uk

Courses BA Media & Communication (Journalism)
MA Broadcast Journalism. Contact Diane Kemp, diane.kemp@uce.ac.uk
MA International Broadcast Journalism. Contact Diane Kemp, diane.kemp@uce.ac.uk

University of Central Lancashire
Preston, PR1 2HE
- 01772 201201
- www.uclan.ac.uk

Courses Combined Honours Creative Writing. Contact chonours@uclan.ac.uk
BA Journalism (Single or Joint). Contact Andrea Walker, alwalker1@uclan.ac.uk
BA Journalism & English Literature. Contact Andrea Walker, alwalker1@uclan.ac.uk
BA Sports or International Journalism. Contact Andrea Walker, alwalker1@uclan.ac.uk

University of Chester
Parkgate Road, Chester, CH1 4BJ
- 01244 511000
- 01244 511300
- enquiries@chester.ac.uk
- www.chester.ac.uk

Courses BA Creative Writing (Joint Honours). Contact Jen Mawson, j.mawson@chester.ac.uk
MA Creative & Critical Writing. Contact Dr. Ashley Chantler, a.chantler@chester.ac.uk

University of Chichester
Bishop Otter Campus, College Lane, Chichester, West Sussex, PO19 6PE
- 01243 816000
- admissions@chi.ac.uk
- www.chiuni.ac.uk

Courses BA English & Creative Writing. Contact english.chiuni.ac.uk
MA Creative Writing. Contact english.chiuni.ac.uk

University of Derby
Kedleston Road, Derby, DE22 1GB
- 01332 590500
- 01332 294861
- askadmissions@derby.ac.uk
- www.derby.ac.uk

Courses BA Creative Writing (Single and Joint). Contact adtenquiry@derby.ac.uk
BA Media Writing (Joint). Contact adtenquiry@derby.ac.uk.

University of Dundee
Nethergate, Dundee, DD1 4HN
- 01382 383000
- 01382 201604
- university@dundee.ac.uk
- www.dundee.ac.uk

Courses MA Writing Culture. Contact Dr. K.B. Williams, k.b.williams@dundee.ac.uk

University of East Anglia
Norwich, NR4 7TJ
- 01603 456161
- 01603 458553
- www.uea.ac.uk

Courses BA English Literature with Creative Writing. Contact Dr. P Magrs, p.magrs@uea.ac.uk
MA Creative Writing (Prose). Contact Prof. Michele Roberts, m.roberts@uea.ac.uk
MA Creative Writing (Poetry). Contact Prof. Denise Riley, d.riley@uea.ac.uk
MA Creative Writing (Scriptwriting). Contact Val Taylor, v.taylor@uea.ac.uk
MA Life Writing. Contact Prof Janet Garton, j.garton@uea.ac.uk

University of East London
Docklands Campus, 4–6 University Way, London, E16 2RD
- 020 8223 3000
- 020 8590 7799
- admiss@uel.ac.uk
- www.uel.ac.uk

Courses BA Creative & Professional Writing. Contact Tessa McWatt, t.mcwatt@uel.ac.uk
MA Journalism & Society. Contact Dr. Andrew Calcutt, a.calcultt@uel.ac.uk
MA Magazines. Contact Dr. Andrew Calcutt, a.calcultt@uel.ac.uk
MA Writing (Imaginative Practice). Contact Tessa McWatt, t.a.mcwatt@uel.ac.uk

University of Edinburgh
Old College, South Bridge, Edinburgh, EH8 9YL
- 0131 650 1000
- 0131 650 2147
- communications.office@ed.ac.uk
- www.ed.ac.uk

Courses MSc Creative Writing. Contact rajamieso@staffmail.ed.ac.uk

University of Essex
Wivenhoe Park, Colchester, CO4 3SQ
- 01206 873333
- 01206 873598
- admit@essex.ac.uk
- pgadmit@essex.ac.uk
- www.essex.ac.uk

Courses BA Journalism
BA Creative Writing
MA Literature, Creative Writing
MA/Diploma in Professional Theatre (Writing, Directing, Pedagogy)

University of Exeter
The Queen's Drive, Exeter, Devon, EX4 4QJ
- 01392 661000
- admissions@exeter.ac.uk
- www.exeter.ac.uk

Courses MA Creative Writing. Contact soe.pgoffice@exeter.ac.uk

University of Glamorgan
Pontypridd, Wales, CF37 1DL
- 0800 716925
- 01443 654050
- www.glam.ac.uk

Courses BA Creative & Professional Writing
MA Scriptwriting
MPhil Writing

University of Glasgow
University Avenue, Glasgow, G12 8QQ
- 0141 330 2000
- pgadmissions@admin.gla.ac.uk
- www.glasgow.ac.uk

Courses MA Creative Writing. Contact Prof. Michael Schmidt, m.schmidt@englit.arts.gla.ac.uk
MA Film Journalism. Contact Dr. Dimitris Eleftheriotis, tfts.office@arts.gla.ac.uk
MA Writing. Contact Tom Powell, t.pow@crichton.gla.ac.uk

University of Gloucestershire
Albert Road, Cheltenham, GL52 3JG
- 0870 720 1100
- 01242 714827
- admissions@glos.ac.uk
- www.glos.ac.uk

Courses BA Creative Writing
BA Broadcast Journalism
BA Print Journalism
BA Publishing
MA Creative & Critical Writing. Contact Dr. Nigel McLoughlin, humanities@glos.ac.uk
MA Broadcast Journalism. Contact Claire Simmons, csimmons@glos.ac.uk

University of Greenwich
Old Royal Navy College, Park Row, Greenwich, London, SE10 9LS
- 020 8331 8000
- 020 8331 8145
- courseinfo@greenwich.ac.uk
- www.gre.ac.uk

Courses BA Creative Writing
BA Media Writing
PgDip Journalism

University of Hertfordshire
College Lane, Hatfield, Hertfordshire, AL10 9AB
- 01707 284000
- 01707 284115
- admissions@herts.ac.uk
- www.herts.ac.uk

Courses BA Film and Television Documentary, Fiction or Entertainment. Contact Prof. Alan Horrox, a.horrox@herts.ac.uk
BA Journalism (Humanities)
BA Digital Publishing (Humanities)
BA Creative Writing (Humanities)
MA Film and Television Screenwriting. Contact Prof. A Horrox, a.horrox@herts.ac.uk

University of Huddersfield
Queensgate, Huddersfield, HD1 3DH
- 01484 422288
- admissions@hud.ac.uk
- www.huddersfield.ac.uk

Courses English Literature with Creative Writing BA(Hons), englishadmissions@hud.ac.uk
English Language with Creative Writing BA(Hons), englishadmissions@hud.ac.uk
English with Creative Writing BA(Hons),englishadmissions@hud.ac.uk
English Language BA(Hons), englishadmissions@hud.ac.uk
English Language with Journalism BA(Hons),englishadmissions@hud.ac.uk
English Literature BA(Hons), englishadmissions@hud.ac.uk
English Literature with a Modern Language BA(Hons), englishadmissions@hud.ac.uk
English Literature with Journalism BA(Hons),englishadmissions@hud.ac.uk
English Studies BA(Hons), englishadmissions@hud.ac.uk
English with Journalism BA(Hons),englishadmissions@hud.ac.uk
English and Media BA(Hons), englishadmissions@hud.ac.uk
English with a Modern Language BA(Hons),englishadmissions@hud.ac.uk
History with Journalism BA(Hons),historyadmissions@hud.ac.uk
Television Production and Media BA (Hons),mediaadmissions@hud.ac.uk
Journalism and Media BA (Hons), mediaadmissions@hud.ac.uk
Radio Journalism and Media BA (Hons),mediaadmissions@hud.ac.uk
Sports Journalism and Media BA (Hons), mediaadmissions@hud.ac.uk
Music Journalism and Media BA (Hons), mediaadmissions@hud.ac.uk
Film Journalism and Media BA (Hons), mediaadmissions@hud.ac.uk

University of Hull
Hull, HU6 7RX
- 01482 346311
- www.hull.ac.uk

Courses BA Creative Writing (Joint Honours)
MA Creative Writing

University of Kent
Department of English, Rutherford College, University of Kent, Canterbury, CT2 7NX
- 01227 823054
- 01227 827001
- english@kent.ac.uk
- www.kent.ac.uk

Courses BA English with American Literature and Creative Writing
MA Creative Writing. Contact english-office@kent.ac.uk

University of Leeds
Leeds, LS2 9JT
- 0113 243 1751
- 0113 244 3923
- enquiry@leeds.ac.uk
- www.leeds.ac.uk

Courses MA Writing for Performance and Publication. Contact admissions-pci@leeds.ac.uk

University of Manchester
Oxford Road, Manchester, M13 9PL
- 0161 306 6000
- pg.admissions@manchester.ac.uk
- www.manchester.ac.uk

Courses MA Creative Writing. Contact pg-english@manchester.ac.uk

University of Middlesex
Bramely Road, London, N14 4YZ
- 020 8411 5555
- admissions@mdx.ac.uk
- www.mdx.ac.uk

Courses BA Film and Creative Writing
BA Publishing and Media
BA Creative and Media Writing
BA Television Journalism
BA Publishing, Journalism and Media
BA Publishing, Media and Cultural Studies
BA Publishing, Writing and Media
BA Writing and Publishing
BA Creative Writing and English Literature
BA Publishing, Media and English
BA Media and Cultural Studies with Journalism, or Journalism with Media and Cultural Studies
BA Journalism, Publishing and Media
BA Media, Publishing and Cultural Studies
BA Journalism and Communication
MA Writing

University of Northampton
Park Campus, Boughton Green Road, Northampton, NN2 7AL
- 01604 735500
- study@northampton.ac.uk
- www.northampton.ac.uk

Courses BA Creative Writing (Joint)
BA Journalism

University of Oxford
Wellington Square, Oxford, OX1 2JD
- 01865 270000
- 01865 270708
- www.ox.ac.uk

Courses MSc Creative Writing. Contact Dr. Clare Morgan, clare.morgan@conted.ox.ac.uk

University of Plymouth
Drake Circus, Plymouth, PL4 8AA
- 01752 600600
- www.plymouth.ac.uk

Courses BA English and Creative Writing. Contact arts.admissions@plymouth.ac.uk
MA Creative Writing. Contact artspostgrad@plymouth.ac.uk
MA Publishing. Contact artspostgrad@plymouth.ac.uk

University of Portsmouth
University House, Winston Churchill Avenue, Portsmouth, Hampshire, PO1 2UP
- 023 9284 8484
- 023 9284 3082
- info.centre@port.ac.uk
- www.port.ac.uk

Courses BA Creative Writing and Drama. Contact humanities.admissions@port.ac.uk
BA Films Studies and Creative Writing. Contact create.admissions@port.ac.uk
BA Creative Writing (Joint). Contact create.admissions@port.ac.uk
MA Creative Writing. Contact create.admissions@port.ac.uk

University of Salford
Salford, Greater Manchester, M5 4WT
- 0161 295 5000
- 0161 295 5999
- course-enquiries@salford.ac.uk
- www.salford.ac.uk

Courses BA English and Creative Writing. Contact Alex Farrell, a.l.farrell@salford.ac.uk
BA Journalism and English (Joint). Contact l.a.harris@salford.ac.uk
MA Journalism. Contact Tom Gill, t.gill@salford.ac.uk
MA Creative Writing. Contact Beryl Pluples, b.pluples@salford.ac.uk

University of Sheffield
Western Bank, Sheffield, S10 2TN
- 0114 222 2000
- 0114 222 2000
- www.sheffield.ac.uk

Courses BA Journalism Studies. Contact Celia Harvey, c.e.harvey@sheffield.ac.uk
BA Journalism (Joint). Contact Celia Harvey, c.e.harvey@sheffield.ac.uk
MA Print, Magazine, Broadcast or Web Journalism
MA Journalism Studies (Broadcast or Web)

University of St Andrews
St Andrews, Fife, KY16 9AJ
- 01334 476161
- admissions@st-andrews.ac.uk
- www.st-andrews.ac.uk

Courses M.Litt Creative Writing. Contact Prof. Douglas Dunn, ded@st-andrews.ac.uk

University of Stirling
Stirling, FK9 4LA
- 01786 473171
- infocentre@stir.ac.uk
- www.stir.ac.uk

Courses MLitt Publishing Studies. Contact english-pg@stir.ac.uk

University of Strathclyde
16 Richmond Street, Glasgow, G1 1XQ
- 0141 552 4400
- 0141 552 0775
- contact-facultyofarts@strath.ac.uk
- www.strath.ac.uk

Courses BA Journalism & Creative Writing
M.Litt Journalism Studies

University of Sunderland
Edinburgh Building, City Campus, Chester Road, Sunderland, SR1 3SD
- 0191 515 2000
- admissions@sunderland.ac.uk
- www.sunderland.ac.uk

Courses BA Broadcast Journalism. Contact Ian Blackhall, ian.blackhall@sunderland.ac.uk
BA Journalism. Contact Ian Blackhall, ian.blackhall@sunderland.ac.uk
MA Journalism. Contact Ian Blackhall, ian.blackhall@sunderland.ac.uk

University of Sussex
Sussex House, Brighton, BN1 9RH
- 01273 606755
- 01273 678335
- pg.admissions@sussex.ac.uk
- www.sussex.ac.uk

Courses MA Creative Writing and Authorship. Contact Dr. Sue Roe, s.m.roe@sussex.ac.uk
MA Creative Writing and Personal Development. Contact Dr. Celia Hunt, c.m.hunt@sussex.ac.uk

MA Dramatic Writing. Contact Richard Crane, r.a.crane@sussex.ac.uk

University of Teeside
Middlesbrough, Tees Valley, TS1 3BA
- 01642 218121
- 01642 342067
- hotline@tees.ac.uk
- arts@tees.ac.uk
- www.tees.ac.uk

Courses BA Journalism and News Practice (Top-up award)
BA Multimedia Journalism Professional Practice

University of the Arts, London
65 Davies Street, London, W1K 5DA
- 020 7514 6000
- info@arts.ac.uk
- www.lcc.arts.ac.uk

Courses BA Magazine Publishing with Public Relations, Media and Cultural Studies, or Marketing and Advertising. Contact info@lcc.arts.ac.uk
BA Journalism. Contact info@lcc.arts.ac.uk
BA Fashion Journalism. Contact enquiries@fashion.arts.ac.uk
MA Journalism. Contact info@lcc.arts.ac.uk
MA Fashion Journalism. Contact enquiries@fashion.arts.ac.uk
MA Critical Writing and Curatorial Practice. Contact enquiries@chelsea.arts.ac.uk
MA Screenwriting. Contact info@lcc.arts.ac.uk
MA Publishing. Contact Tina Stennet, t.stennett@lcc.arts.ac.uk

University of Ulster
Coleraine Campus, Cromore Road, Coleraine, Co. Londonderry, Northern Ireland, BT52 1SA
- 0870 040 0700
- www.ulster.ac.uk

Courses BA Journalism with English
MA Journalism. Contact Colm Murphy, c.murphy@ulster.ac.uk

University of Wales, Aberystwyth
Department of English, Hugh Owen Building, Aberystwyth, SY23 3DY
- 01970 622534
- 01970 622530
- mjb@aber.ac.uk
- www.aber.ac.uk/english

Courses BA English & Creative Writing. Contact Dr. Sarah Prescott, scp@aber.ac.uk
MA Creative Writing. Contact Dr. Rhys Williams, pg-admissions@aber.ac.uk

University of Wales, Bangor
University of Wales, Bangor, Gwynedd, LL57 2DG
- 01248 351151
- enquiries@bangor.ac.uk
- www.bangor.ac.uk

Courses BA English Language with Creative Writing. Contact Prof. Jenny Thomas, e.price@bangor.ac.uk
BA English with Creative Writing. Contact Dr. Tony Brown, els015@bangor.ac.uk
BA English with Journalism. Contact Dr. Tony Brown, els015@bangor.ac.uk
BA Journalism and Media Studies. Contact mediastudies@bangor.ac.uk
BA Literature and Creative Writing (Part time). Contact doll@bangor.ac.uk
MA Creative Writing. Contact Dr. Ian Gregson, i.gregson@bangor.ac.uk
PhD/MPhil Creative and Critical Writing. Contact Dr. Ian Gregson, i.gregson@bangor.ac.uk

University of Wales, Lampeter
Ceredigion, Wales, SA48 7ED
- 01570 422351
- 01570 423423
- www.lamp.ac.uk

Courses BA English with Creative Writing. Contact Beryl Doyle, b.doyle@lamp.ac.uk
MA Creative and Scriptwriting. Contact Dic Edwards, d.edwards@lamp.ac.uk
MA Screenwriting

University of Wales, Newport
Information Centre, Caerleon Campus, PO Box 101, Newport, NP18 3YH
- 01633 432432
- 01633 432046
- uic@newport.ac.uk
- www.newport.ac.uk

Courses BA Creative Writing (Joint)
BA Cinema Studies and Scriptwriting
BA Publishing Design

University of Wales, Swansea
Singleton Park, Swansea, SA2 8PP
- 01792 205678
- 01792 295157
- www.swansea.ac.uk

Courses MA Creative and Media Writing. Contact Dr. Stevie Davis, stephanie.davies@swansea.ac.uk
MA Professional Writing
MA Comparative Journalism. Contact Mala Jagmohan, r.m.jagmohan@swan.ac.uk

University of Wales Institute, Cardiff
Howard Gardens, Cardiff, CF24 0SP
- 029 2041 6070
- 029 2041 6286
- uwicinfo@uwic.ac.uk
- www.uwic.ac.uk

Courses BA Art and Creative Writing. Contact Dr. Clive Cazeaux, ccazeaux@uwic.ac.uk
BA Writing for Media and the Arts. Contact Andrea Williams, abwilliams@uwic.ac.uk

University of Warwick
Coventry, CV4 7AL
- 024 7652 3523
- 024 7646 1606
- ugadmissions@warwick.ac.uk
- pgadmissions@warwick.ac.uk
- www.warwick.ac.uk

Courses BA English Literature and Creative Writing
MA Writing
MA Translation, Writing and Cultural Difference

University of Westminster
35 Marylebone Road, London, NW1 5LS
- 020 7915 5511
- 020 7911 5858
- course-enquiries@wmin.ac.uk
- www.wmin.ac.uk

Courses BA English Literature and Creative Writing. Contact Paul O'Hanlon, ohanlop@wmin.ac.uk
BA Linguistics and Creative Writing. Contact Paul O'Hanlon, ohanlop@wmin.ac.uk
BA Media Studies (Journalism). Contact Alan Greere, a.geere@westminster.ac.uk
BA Medical Journalism
MA Journalism
MA Screenwriting and Producing for Film and Television. Contact Steve May, mays@westminster.ac.uk

University of Winchester
West Hill, Winchester, SO22 4NR
- 01962 841515
- 01962 842280
- course.enquiries@winchester.ac.uk
- www.winchester.ac.uk

Courses BA Creative Writing
BA Journalism
MA Creative and Critical Writing
MA Writing for Children

University of Wolverhampton
Millennium City Building, City Campus South, Wulfruna Street, Wolverhampton, WV1 1SB
- 01902 322222

- enquiries@wlv.ac.uk
- www.wlv.ac.uk

Courses BA Creative and Professional Writing (Joint)
BA Journalism and Editorial Design

PART-TIME COURSES

The Academy of Children's Writers
PO Box 95, Huntingdon, Cambridgeshire, PE28 5RL
- 01487 832752
- 01487 832752
- enquiries@childrens-writers.co.uk
- www.childrens-writers.co.uk

Courses Writing for Children
About The Academy of Writers offers a correspondence course package, either fully tutored or untutored. The Academy of Writers is the trading name of Per Ardua Ltd.

ACS Distance Education
PO Box 4171, Stourbridge, DY8 2WZ
- 0800 328 4723
- 020 7681 2702
- info@acsedu.co.uk
- www.acsedu.co.uk

About Writing, publishing and journalism courses by correspondence.

AD Services (Scotland) Ltd
Suite 15, The Beckford Business Centre, 28 Beckford Street, Hamilton, ML3 0BT
- 01698 307171
- 01698 307140
- info@ad-services-scotland.co.uk
- www.ad-services-scotland.co.uk

About Distance learning courses in fiction writing and journalism.

Adult College, Lancaster
White Cross Education Centre, Quarry Road, Lancaster, LA1 3SE
- 01524 60141
- 01524 581137
- adcollege.info@ed.lancscc.gov.uk
- www.theadultcollege.org

About Part time creative writing courses.

Alston Hall
Alston Lane, Longridge, Preston, PR3 3BP
- 01772 784661
- 01772 785835
- alston.hall@ed.lancscc.gov.uk
- www.alstonhall.com

About A range of day, evening and weekly courses on writing and literature.

Ammerdown Conference & Retreat Centre
Ammerdown Park, Radstock, Bath, BA3 5SW
- 01761 433709
- 01761 433094
- centre@ammerdown.org.uk
- www.ammerdown.org

About Various day and residential writing courses.

Arts Institute at Bournemouth
Wallisdown, Poole, Bournemouth, BH12 5HH
- 01202 533011
- 01202 537729
- general@aib.ac.uk
- www.aib.ac.uk

About Short courses in copywriting, editing and journalism.

The Arvon Foundation
42a Buckingham Palace Road, London, SW1 0RE
- 020 7931 7611
- www.arvonfoundation.org

About Residential writing courses across four properties in Devon, Scotland, Shropshire and West Yorkshire.

Aspiring Writers
47 Old Exeter Road, Tavistock, Devon, PL19 0JE
- 01822 615610
- info@aspiringwriters.co.uk
- www.aspiringwriters.co.uk

About Courses and workshops on every aspect of writing with a creative and practical approach. Residential weekends can also be arranged.

Ballsbridge College of Further Education
Shelbourne Road, Ballsbridge, Dublin 4, Republic of Ireland
- 00353 1 668 4806
- 00353 1 668 2361
- info@ballsbridge.cdvec.ie
- www.ballsbridgecollege.com

About Creative writing evening course.

Ballyfermot College of Further Education
Ballyfermot Road, Ballyfermot, Dublin 10, Republic of Ireland
- 00353 1 626 9421
- 00353 1 626 6754

- info@bcfe.cdvec.ie
- www.bcfe.ie

About Evening classes in creative writing, journalism and screenwriting.

Barry College of Further Education
Colcot Road, Barry, CF62 8YJ
- 01446 725000
- 01446 732667
- enquiries@barry.ac.uk
- www.barry.ac.uk

About Journalism and media access course.

Beginning to Write
United Reform Church, 30 Fisherton Street, Salisbury, SP2 7RG
- susandown5@aol.com

About Beginner's writing course. Wednesday evenings from 7–9pm, throughout October and November. Contact Susan Down.

Belfast Institute
Belfast Metropolitan College, Brunswick Street, Belfast, Northern Ireland, BT2 7GX
- 028 9026 5265
- central_admissions@belfastmet.ac.uk
- www.belfastmet.ac.uk

About Adult learning and vocational courses in writing, media and journalism. Formed by the merger of the Belfast Institute and Castlereagh College on 1st August 2007.

Belstead House Education & Conference Centre
Belstead House, Sprites Lane, Ipswich, Suffolk, IP8 3NA
- belstead.house@educ.suffolkcc.gov.uk

About Offers a range of residential courses.

Birkbeck College
Birkbeck College, University of London, Malet Street, Bloomsbury, London, WC1E 7HX
- 0845 601 0174
- 020 7079 0641
- info@bbk.ac.uk
- www.bbk.ac.uk

About Short courses and adult learning classes for various types of writing.

Blackpool & The Fylde College
Ashfield Road, Bispham, Blackpool, Lancashire, FY2 0HB
- 01253 504343
- 01253 356127

visitors@blackpool.ac.uk
www.blackpool.ac.uk
About Adult community learning, and access courses in creative writing.

Bournemouth Adult Learning
Ensbury Avenue, Bournemouth, Dorest, BH10 4HG
01202 451950
01202 451989
bal.enquiries@bournemouth.gov.uk
About Various adult learning courses.

Bournville College
Bristol Road South, Northfield, Birmingham, B31 2AJ
0121 483 1111
0121 411 2231
info@bournville.ac.uk
www.bournville.ac.uk
About Offers a range of media courses.

Brighton Writers' Workshop
Varndean College, Surrenden Road, Brighton, East Sussex, BN1 6WQ
01273 546604
01273 542950
commed@varndean.ac.uk
www.varndean.ac.uk
About Writing courses for adults.

Brockenhurst College
Lyndhurst Road, Brockenhurst, Hampshire, SO42 7ZE
01590 625555
adulteducation@brock.ac.uk
www.brock.ac.uk
About Wide range of adult courses, including an open college certificate in creative writing.

Brooklands College
Heath Road, Weybridge, Surrey, KT13 8TT
info@brooklands.ac.uk
www.brooklands.ac.uk
About Diploma in publishing and journalism.

BSY Group
Stanhope Square, Holsworthy, Devon, EX22 6DF
0800 731 9271
info@bsygroup.co.uk
www.bsygroup.co.uk
About Distance learning courses, including creative writing.

Buckingham Adult Learning
Data Centre, Evreham, Swallow Street, Iver, SL0 0HS
0845 045 4040
01753 783756
studentenquiries@buckscc.gov.uk
www.adultlearningbcc.ac.uk
About Adult creative writing courses.

Burnley College
Shorey Bank, off Ormerod Road, Burnley, Lancashire, BB11 2RX
01282 711222
01282 711200
student.services@burnley.ac.uk
www.burnley.ac.uk
About Adult creative writing courses.

Burton Manor
The Village, Burton, Neston, Cheshire, CH64 5SJ
0151 336 5172
0151 336 6586
enquiry@burtonmanor.com
www.burtonmanor.com
About Variety of short residential and non-residential writing courses.

Bury Adult & Community Learning Service
Bury Adult Education Centre, 18 Haymarket Street, Bury, BL9 0AQ
0161 253 7501
student.services@bury.gov.uk
About Community courses in creative writing.

Caboodle Retreats
Caboodle Cottage, 69 Southwold Road, Wrentham, Beccles, Suffolk, NR34 8JE
01502 676136
01502 676136
About Runs various courses and writing holidays.

Cambridge Institute of Continuing Education
Institute of Continuing Education, University of Cambridge, Madingley Hall, Madingley, Cambridge, CB3 8AQ
01954 280218
01954 280200
registration@cont-ed.cam.ac.uk
www.cont-ed.cam.ac.uk
About Offers a wide variety of creative writing courses.

Cambridge Women's Resources Centre

Hooper Street, Cambridge, CB1 2NZ
- 01223 321148
- admin@cwrc.org.uk
- www.cwrc.co.uk

About Offers English, English Literature, and English as a second language courses for women.

Carlow College

College Street, Carlow, Republic of Ireland
- 00353 59 915 3200
- 00353 59 914 0258
- catherinecarey@carlowcollege.ie
- www.carlowcollege.ie

About Offers creative writing, and drama and theatre evening courses.

Castle College Nottingham

Maid Marian Way, Nottingham, NG1 6AB
- 0845 845 0500
- learn@castlecollege.ac.uk
- www.castlecollege.ac.uk

About Wide range of writing and journalism courses.

Central Saint Martins College of Art & Design

Southampton Row, London, WC1B 4AP
- 020 7514 7015
- shortcourse@csm.arts.ac.uk
- www.csm.arts.ac.uk

About Evening and weekend courses on all types of writing.

Chapter Centre

Market Road, Cardiff, CF5 1QE
- 029 2031 1050
- enquiry@chapter.org
- www.chapter.org

About Offers writing workshops and competitions.

Charles Street Community Education Centre

16 Charles Street, Newport, NP20 1JU
- 01633 656656

About Short courses in writing.

Cheadle & Marple Sixth Form College

Cheadle Road, Cheadle Hulme, Stockport, Cheshire, SK8 5HA
- 0161 486 4602
- 0161 482 8129
- info@camsfc.ac.uk
- www.camsfc.ac.uk

About Adult learning courses in creative writing.

Chesterfield College

Infirmary Road, Chesterfield, S41 7NG
- 01246 500500
- 01246 500587
- advice@chesterfield.ac.uk
- www.chesterfield.ac.uk

About Part time, adult and community courses.

City College Brighton & Hove

Pelham Street, Brighton, East Sussex, BN1 4FA
- 01273 667788
- 01273 667703
- info@ccb.ac.uk
- www.ccb.ac.uk

About Full and part time certificates and diplomas in writing and journalism.

City Lit

Keeley Street, Covent Garden, London, WC2B 4BA
- 020 7492 2600
- 020 7492 2735
- humanities@citylit.ac.uk
- www.citylit.ac.uk

About A wide range of writing and journalism short courses. New courses are added on a regular basis.

City of Bath College

Avon Street, Bath, BA1 1UP
- 01225 312191
- 01225 444213
- courses@citybathcoll.ac.uk
- www.citybathcoll.ac.uk

About Part time creative writing courses.

City of Bristol College

College Green Centre, St George's Road, Bristol, BS1 5UA
- 0117 312 5000
- 0117 312 5053
- enquiries@cityofbristol.ac.uk
- www.cityofbristol.ac.uk

About Part time adult courses in various types of writing, and diplomas in journalism.

City of Wolverhampton College

Paget Road Campus, Paget Road, Wolverhampton, West Midlands, WV6 0DU
- 01902 836000
- 01902 423070
- mail@wolvcoll.ac.uk

ⓦ www.wolverhamptoncollege.ac.uk
About Offers full and part time journalism courses.

City University Courses for Adults
Northampton Square, London, EC1V 0HB
ⓞ 020 7040 8268
ⓞ 020 7040 5070
ⓔ ell@city.ac.uk
ⓦ www.city.ac.uk/conted/cfa.htm
About Courses for adults in writing and journalism.

Clydebank College
College Square, 2 Aurora Avenue, Queen's Quay, Clydebank, G81 1BF
ⓞ 0141 951 7400
ⓞ 0141 951 7401
ⓔ info@clydebank.ac.uk
ⓦ www.clydebank.ac.uk
About Offers part time journalism courses.

Coleg Powys
Llanidloes Road, Newtown, Powys, Wales, SY16 4HU
ⓞ 0845 408 6200
ⓞ 01686 622246
ⓔ enquiries@coleg-powys.ac.uk
ⓦ www.coleg-powys.ac.uk
About Access courses in writing and literature.

The College of Technical Authorship
PO Box 7, Cheadle, Stockport, Cheshire, SK8 3BY
ⓞ 0161 437 4235
ⓞ 0161 437 4235
ⓔ crossley@coltecha.com
ⓦ www.coltecha.com
About Technical authorship distance learning course.

Comberton Village College
West Street, Comberton, Cambridgeshire, CB23 7DU
ⓞ 01223 262503
ⓞ 01223 264116
ⓔ thecollege@comberton.cambs.sch.uk
ⓦ www.combertonvc.org
About Offers various community courses.

The Complete Creative Writing Course
The Groucho Club, 45 Dean Street, Soho, London, W1D 4QB
ⓔ maggie@writingcourses.org.uk
ⓦ www.writingcourses.org.uk/home.php

About Original, advanced residential writing courses.

Conway Education Centre
Conway Mill, 5–7 Conway Street, Belfast, Northern Ireland, BT13 2DE
ⓞ 028 9024 8543
About Various writing courses.

The Creative Writers Workshop
PO Box 1, Kinvara, Co. Galway, Republic of Ireland
ⓞ 00353 86 252 3428
ⓔ creativewriting@ireland.com
ⓦ www.thecreativewritersworkshop.com
About Creative writing workshops and retreats using right-brain/left-brain techniques in locations across Ireland. Contact Irene Graham.

CTJT
Forum House, Stirling Road, Chichester, West Sussex, PO19 7DN
ⓞ 01243 381998
ⓔ e-courses@ctjt.biz
ⓦ www.ctjt.biz
About Online courses in most spheres of writing, journalism, proofreading and editing.

Darlington College of Technology
Darlington College, Central Park, Haughton Road, Darlington, DL1 1DR
ⓞ 01325 503050
ⓞ 01325 503000
ⓔ enquire@darlington.ac.uk
ⓦ www.darlington.ac.uk
About Journalism short courses.

Dillington House
Dillington House, Illminster, Somerset, TA19 9DT
ⓞ 01460 52427
ⓞ 01460 52433
ⓔ dillington@somerset.gov.uk
ⓦ www.dillington.co.uk
About Residential and day courses in literature and creative writing.

Dingle Writing Courses
Ballintlea, Ventry, Co. Kerry, Republic of Ireland
ⓞ 00353 66 915 9815
ⓞ 00353 66 915 9815
ⓔ info@dinglewritingcourses.ie
ⓦ www.dinglewritingcourses.ie
About Various weekend writing courses for all levels of experience.

Doncaster College

The Hub, Chappell Drive, Doncaster, DN1 2RF
- 01302 553553
- 01302 553559
- infocentre@don.ac.uk
- www.don.ac.uk

About Introduction to creative writing course.

Dublin College of Management & IT

College House, 10 Southern Cross Business Park, Bray, Co. Wicklow, Republic of Ireland
- 00353 1 286 5783
- 00353 1 633 5544
- info@cmit.ie
- www.cmit.ie

About Distance learning courses in journalism and fiction writing.

Dunstable College

Dubstable College, Kingsway, Dunstable, Bedfordshire, LU5 4HG
- 01582 477776
- 01582 478801
- enquiries@dunstable.ac.uk
- www.dunstable.ac.uk

About Creative writing examination courses.

The Earnley Concourse

Earnley Concourse, Earnley, Chichester, West Sussex, PO20 7JN
- 01243 670392
- 01243 670832
- info@earnley.co.uk
- www.earnley.co.uk

About Various residential writing courses.

Eastleigh College

Chestnut Avenue, Eastleigh, SO50 5SF
- 023 8091 1299
- 023 8032 2133
- goplaces@eastleigh.ac.uk
- www.eastleigh.ac.uk

About Part time creative writing course.

Eastmoors Community Education Centre

Sanquahar Street, Splott, Cardiff, CE24 2AD
- 029 2046 2858
- eastmoorsac@cardiff.gov.uk

About Various community courses.

East Surrey College

Gatton Point North, Claremont Road, Redhill, Surrey, RH1 2JX

- 01737 772611
- 01737 788444
- studentservices@esc.ac.uk
- www.esc.ac.uk

About Part time creative writing workshops.

Edinburgh University

Office of Lifelong Learning, University of Edinburgh, 11 Buccleuch Place, Edinburgh, EH8 9LW
- 0131 650 4400
- 0131 662 0783
- oll@ed.ac.uk
- www.lifelong.ed.ac.uk

About Wide variety of adult learning courses, including aspects of creative writing.

Emerson College

Emerson College, Forest Row, East Sussex, RH18 5JX
- 01342 822238
- 01342 826055
- info@emerson.org.uk
- www.emerson.org.uk

About Various weekend and short courses in literature and creative writing.

Essex Live Literature Courses

Essex Libraries, Goldlay Gardens, Chelmsford, Essex, CM2 6WN
- 01245 436759
- malcolm.burgess@essexcc.gov.uk

About Various literature events, including writing courses. Contact Malcolm Burgess.

Euroscript

64 Hemingford Road, London, N1 1DB
- 07958 244656
- enquiries@euroscript.co.uk
- www.euroscript.co.uk

About A range of scriptwriting and development workshops. Also provides a consultancy service.

Exeter College

Victoria House, 33/36 Queen Street, Exeter, EX4 3SR
- 01392 205223
- 01392 205225
- info@exe-coll.ac.uk
- www.exe-coll.ac.uk

About Courses in 'writing for fun and publication' and creative writing. Print journalism certification course.

Exeter Phoenix

Exeter Phoenix Centre, Bradninch Place, Gandy Street, Exeter, EX4 3LS

- 01392 667080
- programming@exeterphoenix.org.uk
- www.exeterphoenix.org.uk

About Various community classes and workshops.

Falmouth College of Arts

Woodlane, Falmouth, Cornwall, TR11 4RH

- 01326 211077
- 01326 213880
- admissions@falmouth.ac.uk
- www.falmouth.ac.uk

About Summer schools on novel writing and writing for children.

Farncombe Estate

Farncombe Estate Centre, Broadway, Cotswolds, Worcestershire, WR12 7LJ

- 01386 854100
- 01386 854350
- enquiries@farncombeestate.co.uk
- www.farncombeestate.co.uk

About Weekend courses on various types of writing and literature.

Far West

23 Chapel Street, Penzance, Cornwall, TR18 4AP

- angela@farwest.co.uk
- www.farwest.co.uk

About Writing for connection course, focusing on writing as a connection to dreams, adventure, healing and strength. Contact Angela Stoner.

Fire in the Head

PO Box 17, Yelverton, Devon, PL20 6YF

- 01822 841081
- roselle.angwin@internet-today.co.uk
- www.fire-in-the-head.co.uk

About Various residential and day courses for writers at locations across the south of England.

Galway Arts Centre

47 Dominick Street, Co. Galway, Republic of Ireland

- 00353 91 565886
- 00353 91 568642
- info@galwayartscentre.ie
- www.galwayartscentre.ie

About Various writing courses and events, as part of the literature and arts programme.

Grimsby Institute of Further Education

Nuns Corner, Grimsby, North East Lincolnshire, DN34 5BQ

- 0800 315002
- 01472 879924
- infocent@grimsby.ac.uk
- www.grimsby.ac.uk

About Offers a range of journalism courses.

Guildford Institute

Ward Street, Guildford, Surrey, GU1 4LH

- 01483 562142
- info@guildford-institute.org.uk
- www.guildford-institute.org.uk

About A range of part time writing courses.

Harrow College

Harrow on the Hill Campus, Lowlands Road, Harrow, HA1 3AQ

- 020 8909 6000
- enquiries@harrow.ac.uk
- www.harrow.ac.uk

About Part time creative writing courses.

Havering Adult College

23 Scimitar House, Eastern Road, Romford, Essex, RM1 3NH

- 01708 433790
- 01708 379569
- enquiries-adultcollege@havering.gov.uk
- www.havering.gov.uk

About Adult learning courses in creative writing.

Hereward College

Bramston Crescent, Tile Hill, Coventry, CV4 9SW

- 024 7646 1231
- 024 7669 4305
- enquiries@hereward.ac.uk
- www.hereward.ac.uk

About Full and part time courses in media and creative studies. The college has a particularly well developed programme for disabled students.

Higham Hall

Higham Hall College, Bassenthwaite Lake, Cockermouth, Cumbria, CA13 9SH

- 01768 776276
- 01768 776013
- admin@highamhall.com
- www.highamhall.com

About Day and residential courses in literature and writing.

Highbury College Portsmouth
Dovercourt Road, Portsmouth, Hampshire, PO6 2SA
- 023 9231 3373
- 023 9232 5551
- info@highbury.ac.uk
- www.highbury.ac.uk
About Adult learning and full time certification courses in journalism, media, and publishing.

Hull College
Part Time Provision Office, Larkin Building, University of Hull, Hull, HU6 7RX
- 01482 466605
- v.j.magee@hull.ac.uk
- www.hull.ac.uk
About Creative writing evening course.

Indian King Arts
Garmoe Cottage, 2 Trefrew Road, Camelford, Cornwall, PL32 9TP
- indianking@btconnect.com
About One-day and half-day poetry workshops.

The Institute of Copywriting
Overbrook Business Centre, Poolbridge Road, Blackford, Wedmore, BS28 4PA
- 0800 781 1715
- 01934 713492
- copy@inst.org
- www.inst.org/copy
About Distance learning copywriting courses, for beginners and professionals.

The Institute of Creative Writing
Overbrook Business Centre, Poolbrook Road, Blackford, Wedmore, BS28 4PA
- 0800 781 1715
- 01934 713492
- creative_writing_main_index_page_uk@inst.org.uk
- www.inst.org/authors
About Distance course on creative writing and getting published.

Irish Academy
Academy House, 1 Newtown Park, Blackrock, Co. Dublin, Republic of Ireland
- 00353 1 278 0802
- 00353 1 278 0251
- info@irishacademy.com
- www.irishacademy.com
About Diploma and higher diploma in journalism. Also runs distance learning journalism courses.

Irish Writers Centre
19 Parnell Square, Dublin 1, Republic of Ireland
- 00353 1 872 1302
- 00353 1 872 6282
- info@writerscentre.ie
- www.writerscentre.ie
About Wide range of part time courses on writing.

Itchen College
Middle Road, Bitterne, Southampton, SO19 7TB
- 023 8043 5636
- 023 8042 1911
- info@itchen.ac.uk
- www.itchen.ac.uk
About Journalism diplomas and short courses.

Josiah Mason College
Slade Road, Erdington, Birmingham, B23 7JH
- 0121 603 4757
- 0121 377 6076
- enquiries@jmc.ac.uk
- www.jmc.ac.uk
About Full time adult courses in journalism and media.

Journalism School
PO Box 380, Grimsby, DN32 8XR
- 07951 815885
- info@thejournalismschool.co.uk
- www.thejournalismschool.co.uk
About Distance learning courses in journalism.

Keele University
Centre for Continuing & Professional Education, Keele University, Freepost ST1666, Newcastle, Staffordshire, ST5 5BR
- 01782 583436
- enquiries@cpe.keele.ac.uk
- www.keele.ac.uk/courses/cpe
About Creative writing courses at a range of centres within the Staffordshire area.

Killaloe Hedge-School of Writing
4 Riverview, Ballina, Killaloe, Co. Clare, Republic of Ireland
- 00353 61 375217
- 00353 61 375487
- www.killaloe.ie/khs/index.html
About Various weekend writing courses and workshops. Contact David Rice.

Kilroy's College
26 York Street, London, W1U 6PZ
- 0845 300 4259

homestudy@kilroyscollege.ac.uk
www.kilroyscollege.co.uk
About Distance learning courses in creative writing and journalism.

Knowsley Community College
Roby Centre, Robert Road, Roby, Liverpool, L36 9TD
0845 155 1055
info@knowsleycollege.ac.uk
www.knowsleycollege.ac.uk
About A-level enhancement course on an 'Introduction to Journalism'.

Knuston Hall Residential College
Irchester, Wellingborough, Northamptonshire, NN29 7EU
01933 312104
01933 357596
enquiries@knustonhall.org.uk
www.knustonhall.org.uk
About Residential college running various short writing courses.

Lambeth College
Brixton Centre, 56 Brixton Hill, Lambeth, London, SW2 1QS
020 7501 5000
courses@lambethcollege.ac.uk
www.lambeth.ac.uk
About Pre-entry, foundation degrees and certification courses in journalism. A short, part time, creative writing course is also available.

Lancaster University
Department of Continuing Education, Lancaster University, Ash House, Lancaster, LA1 4YT
01524 592623
01524 592448
conted@lancaster.ac.uk
www.lancs.ac.uk/users/conted/index.htm
About Offers a variety of creative writing courses and holidays for all levels of experience.

Learning Curve Home Study Ltd
Leader Cottage, Blainslie, Galashiels, TD1 2PR
01896 860661
edesk@learningcurve.uk.com
www.learningcurve-uk.com
About Various correspondence courses in writing and copywriting.

Leicester City Council
New Walk Centre, Welford Place, LE1 6ZG
0116 229 4367
lifelonglearning@leicester.gov.uk
www.leicester.gov.uk
About Community classes in creative writing.

Leicestershire County Council
County Hall, Glenfield, Leicester, LE3 8RA
0116 265 6387
0116 265 6398
communityed@leics.gov.uk
www.leics.gov.uk
About Creative writing classes at various locations around Leicestershire. Contact Louise Robinson.

Liberato
16 Middle King, Braintree, Essex, CM7 3XY
01376 551379
liberato@talktalk.net
www.liberato.co.uk
About Writing retreats and courses in Suffolk and Greece. Also provides editorial services.

Liverpool Community College
The Arts Centre, Myrtle Street, Liverpool, L7 7JA
0151 252 4360
peter.dutton@liv-coll.ac.uk
www.liv-coll.ac.uk
About Foundation diplomas in journalism disciplines. Contact Peter Dutton.

London Academy of Radio, Film & TV
1 Lancing Street, London, NW1 1NA
0871 566 1631
www.media-courses.com
About Vocational part time and short courses for all broadcast and audio media, including scriptwriting.

London College of Communication
Elephant and Castle, London, SE1 6SB
020 7514 6569
shourtcourses@lcc.arts.ac.uk
www.lcc.arts.ac.uk/training
About Wide range of short courses in writing and journalism.

London School of Journalism
126 Shirland Road, Maida Vale, London, W9 2BT
020 7289 7777
020 7432 8141
ltw@lsjournalism.org
www.learntowrite.org

About Distance learning and short courses in journalism and creative writing, including short stories, novel writing and writing for children.

The Lotus Foundation
16 Lancaster Grove, Swiss Cottage, London, NW3 4PB
- 020 7794 8880
- info@lotusfoundation.org.uk
- www.lotusfoundation.org.uk
About Courses, workshops, therapy and poetry groups.

Manchester Adult Education Service
Chorlton Park Adult Learning Centre, Mauldeth Road West, Manchester, M21 7HH
- 0800 083 2121
- adult-education@manchester.gov.uk
- www.manchester.gov.uk/education
About Community creative writing courses across Manchester.

Marlborough College Summer School
Marlborough College, Marlborough, Wiltshire, SN8 1PA
- 01672 892388
- 01672 892476
- admin@mcsummerschool.org.uk
- www.mcsummerschool.org.uk
About July summer school with adult courses and workshops in creative writing disciplines.

Mary Immaculate College, University of Limerick
Department of English and Literature, Mary Immaculate College, University of Limerick, Republic of Ireland
- maeve.tynan@mic.ul.ie
- www.mic.ul.ie/creativewriting/creativewriting3.htm
About A creative writing course based around a series of workshops. Contact Maeve Tynan.

Middlesex University Summer School
Summer School Office, Middlesex University, Trent Park, Bramley Road, London, N14 4YZ
- 020 8411 5782
- 020 8411 2297
- sschool@mdx.ac.uk
- www.mdx.ac.uk/summer
About Summer school runs from June to August and includes several courses on writing for different types of media.

Morley College
61 Westminster Bridge, London, SE1 7HT
- 020 7928 8501
- 020 7928 4074
- enquiries@morleycollege.ac.uk
- www.morleycollege.ac.uk
About Part time creative writing courses, for beginners.

National Academy of Writing
School of English, University of Central England, Perry Barr, Birmingham, B42 2SU
- 0121 331 5471
- nicola.monaghan@uce.ac.uk
- www.thenationalacademyofwriting.org.uk
About Diploma in writing, covering various genres. There is a strict application process to be followed before being accepted onto the full diploma course. Contact Nicola Monaghan.

National Council for the Training of Journalists
The New Granary, Station Road, Newport, Saffron Walden, Essex, CB11 3PL
- 01799 544014
- 01799 544015
- info@nctj.com
- www.nctj.com
About Accredits journalism courses at many different centres. Runs distance learning courses in magazine and newspaper journalism, and editing.

National Extension College
The Michael Young Centre, Purbeck Road, Cambridge, CB2 8HN
- info@nec.ac.uk
- www.nec.ac.uk
About Distance learning courses on creative writing, writing for money, writing short stories and writing humour.

National Film & Television School
Beaconsfield Studios, Station Road, Beaconsfield, Buckinghamshire, HP9 1LG
- 01494 677903
- 01494 674042
- shortcourses@nfts.co.uk
- www.nftsfilm-tv.ac.uk
About Many short courses on film and television writing and producing.

National Home Study College
5 High Street, Pinner, HA5 5PJ
- 0870 242 7141

☎ 020 8868 7125
✉ enquiries@nationalhomestudy.co.uk
🌐 www.homestudynet.com
About Distance learning journalism, television and film production courses.

Newcastle under Lyme College
Liverpool Road, Newcastle under Lyme, Staffordshire, ST5 2DF
☎ 01782 715111
✉ info@nulc.ac.uk
🌐 www.nulc.ac.uk
About Diploma in media techniques, with radio and journalism.

Nightcourses
🌐 www.nightcourses.com
About Search facility for courses of various types, including part time and evening courses in the Republic of Ireland.

North Warwickshire & Hinckley College
Hinckley Road, Nuneaton, Warwickshire, CV11 6BH
☎ 024 7624 3000
☎ 024 7632 9056
✉ the.college@nwhc.ac.uk
🌐 www.nwhc.ac.uk
About A range of certificated writing courses.

North West Kent College
Oakfield Lane, Dartford, DA1 2JT
☎ 01322 629400
☎ 01332 629468
✉ course.enquiries@nwkcollege.ac.uk
🌐 www.nwkcollege.ac.uk
About Part time and full time foundation degree in professional writing. Contact Neil Nixon.

North West Regional College
Strand Road, Londonderry, Northern Ireland, BT48 7AL
☎ 028 7127 6000
☎ 028 7126 0520
✉ info@nwrc.ac.uk
🌐 www.nwrc.ac.uk
About Journalism GCSE (part time), and radio journalism certificate.

noSWeat Journalism Training
16/17 Clerkenwell Close, London, EC1R 0AN
☎ 020 7490 2006
✉ info@nosweatjt.co.uk

🌐 www.nosweatjt.co.uk
About Newspaper, magazine and broadcast journalism, also editing courses. Contact Stephen Ward.

Oaklands College
St Albans Smallford Campus, Hatfield Road, St Albans, Hertfordshire, AL4 0JA
☎ 01727 737080
✉ advice.centre@oaklands.ac.uk
🌐 www.oaklands.ac.uk
About Journalism and media studies A-Level, and part time courses in fiction writing.

Open College of the Arts
Open College of the Arts, Freepost SF10678
☎ 0800 731 2116
☎ 01226 730838
✉ open.arts@ukonline.co.uk
🌐 www.oca-uk.com/courses
About A range of beginner and advanced creative writing courses.

Open University
Literature Department (Faculty of Arts), The Open University, Walton Hall, Milton Keynes, MK7 6AA
☎ 0845 300 6090
☎ 01908 654806
✉ general-enquiries@open.ac.uk
🌐 www.open.ac.uk/arts/literature/creative-writing.htm
About Short beginners courses in creative writing.

Oxford University Department for Continuing Education
Rewley House, 1 Wellington Square, Oxford, OX1 2JA
☎ 01865 270360
✉ enquiries@conted.ox.ac.uk
🌐 www.conted.ox.ac.uk
Courses MSt Creative Writing: two years part-time
Undergraduate Diploma Creative Writing: two years part-time
Summer Programme in Creative Writing: three week residential course
Summer School: Several one-week residential courses in creative writing
Online course in Creative Writing: Ten online sessions

Oxford University Summer School
Oxford University Department for Continuing Education, Rewley House, 1 Wellington Square, Oxford, OX1 2JA

- 01865 270360
- 01865 270309
- oussa@conted.ox.ac.uk
- www.conted.ox.ac.uk/oussa

About July summer school, running a variety of writing courses and workshops.

Periodical Publishers Association
Queens House, 28 Kings Way, London, WC2B 6JR
- 020 7404 4166
- 020 7404 4167
- www.ppa.co.uk

About Full day, half day and two day courses in every aspect of periodical publishing, writing and marketing.

Perth College
Crieff Road, Perth, PH1 2NX
- 01738 877000
- 01738 877001
- pc.enquiries@perth.uhi.ac.uk
- www.perth.ac.uk

About Creative writing leisure courses.

Peterborough Regional College
Park Crescent, Peterborough, PE1 4DZ
- 0845 872 8722
- 01733 767986
- info@peterborough.ac.uk
- www.peterborough.ac.uk

About Part time journalism and creative writing courses.

Pitman Training Centre
- 0800 220454
- www.pitman-training.com

About Journalism courses at centres around the country.

Plunket College
Swords Road, Whitehall, Dublin 9, Republic of Ireland
- 00353 1 837 1689
- 00353 1 836 8066
- info@plunketcollege.ie
- www.plunketcollege.ie

About Short evening course in creative writing.

PMA Training
PMA House, Free Church Passage, St Ives, Cambridgeshire, PE27 5AY
- 01480 300653
- 01480 496022
- training@pma-group.com

- www.pma-group.com

About Training courses in journalism, media, and communications – from beginner to postgraduate level. Courses are run at their centre in central London, or as in-house training sessions throughout the UK.

Queens University, Belfast School of Education
Lifelong Learning, School of Education, Queen's University Belfast, Northern Ireland, BT7 1LN
- 028 9097 3323/3539
- 028 9023 9263
- education@qub.ac.uk
- www.qub.ac.uk/edu

About Open learning courses in creative writing.

Regent Academy
Lyne Akres, Brandis Corner, Devon, EX22 7YH
- 0800 378281/01409 220415
- 01409 220416
- info@regentacademy.com
- www.regentacademy.com

About Distance learning courses in many aspects of writing, publishing and the media.

Reid Kerr College
Renfrew Road, Paisley, Renfrewshire, PA3 4DR
- 0800 052 7343
- 0141 581 2204
- sservices@reidkerr.ac.uk
- www.reidkerr.ac.uk

About Runs a creative writing course.

Richmond Adult Community College
Parkshot, Richmond, TW9 2RE
- 020 8843 7997
- 020 8332 6560
- enquiries@racc.ac.uk
- www.racc.ac.uk

About Range of part time writing courses including screenwriting, creative writing and comedy writing.

Rotherham College of Arts & Technology
Town Centre Campus, Eastwood Lane, Rotherham, S65 1EG
- 08080 722777
- info@rotherham.ac.uk
- www.rotherham.ac.uk

About Offers a part time advanced creative writing course.

Scottish Universities International Summer School
21 Buccleuch Place, Edinburgh, EH8 9LN
- 0131 650 4369
- 0131 662 0275
- suiss@ed.ac.uk
- www.llc.ed.ac.uk/suiss

About An annual summer school, which includes a Creative Writing course in cooperation with the Edinburgh International Book Festival (in August).

Screenwriters' Workshop
NPA Film Centre, 1.07 Tea Building, 56 Shoreditch High Street, London, E1 6JJ
- 020 7613 0440
- 020 7729 1852
- queries@npa.org.uk
- www.npa.org.uk

About Training and events for producers and film makers.

The Script Factory
Welbeck House, 66/67 Wells Street, London, W1T 3PY
- 020 7323 1414
- general@scriptfactory.co.uk
- www.scriptfactory.co.uk

About Training, masterclasses and workshops on scriptwriting and development.

Sheffield College
Norton College Site, Dyche Lane, Sheffield, S20 8LY
- 0114 260 3603
- 0114 260 3655
- www.sheffcol.ac.uk

About Full time accredited journalism courses.

Somerset College of Arts & Technology
Wellington Road, Taunton, Somerset, TA1 5AX
- 01823 366366
- 01823 366418
- enquiries@somerset.ac.uk
- www.somerset.ac.uk

About Access to higher education courses in teaching, history and journalism.

South East Essex College
Luker Road, Southend on Sea, Essex, SS1 1ND
- 01702 220400
- 01702 432320
- admissions@southend.ac.uk
- www.southend.ac.uk

About Diploma in advanced publishing, and weekend courses in creative writing and writing novels.

South Nottingham College
West Bridgford Centre, Greythorn Drive, West Bridgford, Nottingham, NG2 7GA
- 0115 914 6400
- 0115 914 6444
- enquiries@snc.ac.uk
- www.snc.ac.uk

About Part time creative writing courses.

South Tyneside College
St George's Avenue, South Shields, Tyne & Wear, NE34 6ET
- 0191 427 3500
- www.stc.ac.uk

About Foundation degree in media design.

Spread the Word
77 Lambeth Walk, London, SE11 6DX
- 020 7735 3111
- 020 7735 2666
- info@spreadtheword.org.uk
- www.spreadtheword.org.uk

About Courses, workshops and advice for London writers.

Stevenson College Edinburgh
Bankhead Avenue, Edinburgh, EH11 4DE
- 0131 535 4600
- 0131 535 4708
- info@stevenson.ac.uk
- www.stevenson.ac.uk

About Open access creative writing courses.

St Helens College
Town Centre Campus, Water Street, St Helens, Merseyside, WA10 1PP
- 01744 733766
- 01744 623400
- enquire@sthelens.ac.uk
- www.sthelens.ac.uk

About Adult workshops in creative writing and radio journalism.

Stonebridge Associated Colleges
Stonebridge House, Ocean View Road, Bude, Cornwall, EX23 8ST
- 0845 230 6880
- 01288 355799
- enquiries@stonebridge.uk.com
- www.stonebridge.uk.com

About Wide range of short distance courses in writing and journalism.

Strode College
Strode College, Church Road, Street, Somerset, BA16 0AB
- 01458 844400
- 01458 844411
- courseinfo@strode-college.ac.uk
- www.strode-college.ac.uk

About Part time creative writing course.

Study House
Writers College, 8 Hillswood Avenue, Kendal, Cumbria, LA9 5BT
- 01539 724622
- info@study-house.com
- www.study-house.com/Writers%20College/writer_college.htm

About Certificates in fiction writing and journalism.

St Vincent's College
Mill Lane, Gosport, Hampshire, PO12 4QA
- 023 9258 8311
- 023 9251 1186
- info@stvincent.ac.uk
- www.stvincent.ac.uk

About Diploma in media techniques (journalism and radio).

Sutton Coldfield College
Lichfield Road, Sutton Coldfield, West Midlands, B74 2NW
- 0121 355 5671
- 0121 355 0799
- infoc@sutcol.ac.uk
- www.sutcol.ac.uk

About Full and part time adult courses in journalism, media and publishing. Pre-entry certificate in journalism.

Swanwick Writers' Summer School
Hayes Conference Centre, Alfreton, Swanwick, Derbyshire, DE55 1UY
- swanwick@neteireann.com
- www.wss.org.uk

About Two week summer school in August, dedicated to writing courses. For all levels of experience.

Swarthmore Education Centre
2–7 Woodhouse Square, Leeds, West Yorkshire, LS3 1AD
- 0113 243 2210
- 0113 243 2210
- info@swarthmore.org.uk
- www.swarthmore.org.uk

About Creative writing courses.

Training & Performance Showcase
Shepperton Studios, Studios Road, Shepperton, Middlesex, TW17 0QD
- 01932 592151
- 01932 592233
- jill@tapsnet.org
- www.tapsnet.org

About Masterclasses and workshops for British television and film scriptwriters.

Travellers' Tales
92 Hillfield Road, London, NW6 1QA
- info@travellerstales.org
- www.travellerstales.org

About Residential courses, retreats, holidays and masterclasses in travel writing.

Ty Newydd
Llanystumdwy, Cricieth, Gwynedd, LL52 0LW
- 01766 522811
- post@tynewyyd.org
- www.tynewydd.org

About Residential writing courses.

UCD Adult Education Centre
Library Building, University College Dublin, Belfield, Dublin 4, Republic of Ireland
- 00353 1 716 7123
- 00353 1 716 7500
- adult.education@ucd.ie
- www.ucd.ie/adulted/courses

About Adult courses in creative writing.

UK Open Learning
31 Chapel Street, Bigrigg, Egremont, Cumbria, CA22 2UU
- 0800 043 4288
- sales@uk-open-learning.com
- www.uk-open-learning.com

About Distance learning courses in writing, journalism and editing.

University Centre Hastings
Havelock Road, Hastings, East Sussex, TN34 1DQ
- 0845 602 0607
- information@uch.ac.uk
- www.uch.ac.uk

About Print and radio journalism certification course, as well as short courses in writing, poetry and screenwriting.

University of Bristol
Senate House, Tyndall Avenue, Bristol, BS8 1TH
- 0117 928 9000
- admissions@bristol.ac.uk
- www.bris.ac.uk

About Short courses and day courses in creative writing, contact Tom Sperlinger, tom.sperlinger@bris.ac.uk.
Part time diploma in creative writing, contact Hilary Betts, hilary.betts@bristol.ac.uk.

University of Derby
1 Devonshire Road, Buxton, Derbyshire, SK17 6RY
- 01298 71100
- 01298 27261
- adultedbuxton@derby.ac.uk
- www.derby.ac.uk

About Introduction to creative writing, part time adult course.

University of Dundee
Continuing Education, University of Dundee, Nethergate, Dundee, DD1 4HN
- 01382 383000
- 01382 201604
- university@dundee.ac.uk
- www.dundee.ac.uk/learning/conted

About Adult creative writing courses.

University of East Anglia
Continuing Education, Faculty of Social Sciences, University of East Anglia, Norwich, NR4 7TJ
- 01603 591451
- 01603 451999
- cont.ed@uea.ac.uk
- www.uea.ac.uk/contedu

About Certificates and diplomas in creative writing, screenwriting, fiction and poetry. Also runs creative writing and literature day schools.

University of Glasgow
Department of Adult and Continuing Education, St Andrew's Building, 11 Eldon Street, Glasgow, G3 6NH
- 0141 330 1835
- 0141 330 1821
- dace-query@educ.gla.ac.uk
- www.glasgow.ac.uk/dace

About Creative writing part time courses.

University of Hull
Part Time Provision Office, Larkin Building, University of Hull, Hull, HU6 7RX
- 01482 466605
- p.robinson@hull.ac.uk
- v.j.magee@hull.ac.uk
- j.ayres@hull.ac.uk
- www.hull.ac.uk

About Certificate and diploma in creative writing.

University of Kent
School of English, Rutherford College, University of Kent, Canterbury, Kent, CT2 7NZ
- 01227 823054
- 01227 827001
- part-time@kent.ac.uk
- www.kent.ac.uk

About Part time certificates and diplomas in creative writing subjects. Run at a range of locations across Kent.

University of Liverpool
Continuing Education, University of Liverpool, 126 Mount Pleasant, Liverpool, L69 3GR
- 0151 794 2538
- conted@liv.ac.uk
- www.liv.ac.uk/conted

About Part time courses in creative writing and getting published. Contact Joan Squires.

University of Newcastle
School of English Literature, Percy Building, Newcastle upon Tyne, NE1 7RU
- 0191 222 7625
- 0191 222 8708
- j.hampson@ncl.ac.uk
- www.ncl.ac.uk/elll/creative

About Short courses in various types of creative writing. Also runs spring and summer schools on creative writing, and host many other writing events – such as readings.

University of Reading
The School of Continuing Education, University of Reading, London Road, Reading, RG1 5AQ
- 0118 378 8347
- continuing-education@reading.ac.uk
- www.reading.ac.uk/conted

About Day courses on writing for radio, screenwriting, picture writing and other writing topics.

University of Sheffield

Institute for Lifelong Learning, University of Sheffield, 196–198 West Street, Sheffield, S1 4ET
- 0114 222 7000
- 0114 222 7001
- till@sheffield.ac.uk
- www.sheffield.ac.uk/till

About Certificate in creative writing. Contact Dr Sandra Courtman, s.courtman@sheffield.ac.uk. Also runs a range of creative writing and general interest courses.

University of St Andrews

University of St Andrews Creative Writing Summer Program, St Katharine's West, 16 The Scores, St Andrews, Fife, KY16 9AX
- 01334 462238
- 01334 462158
- crsp@st-andrews.ac.uk
- www.st-andrews.ac.uk/~adweb/cwspweb.htm

About Summer school for creative writing. Contact Dr M.I.S. Hunter.

University of Strathclyde

Centre for Lifelong Learning, 7th Floor, Graham Hills Building, 40 George Street, Glasgow, G1 1QE
- 0141 548 4287
- 0141 553 1270
- learn@strath.ac.uk
- www.cll.strath.ac.uk

About Evening and weekend classes in many types of writing. Contact Janice MacWhirter.

University of Sunderland

Centre for Lifelong Learning, Joseph Cowen House, St Thomas Street, Newcastle upon Tyne, NE1 7RU
- 0191 515 2800
- 0191 515 2890
- lifelong.learning@sunderland.ac.uk
- www.cll.sunderland.ac.uk

About Wide range of adult education courses in literature, writing and getting published.

University of Sussex

Centre for Continuing Education, The Sussex Institute, Essex House, University of Sussex, Falmer, Brighton, BN1 9QQ
- 01273 877888
- 01273 877534
- si-enquiries@sussex.ac.uk
- www.sussex.ac.uk/cce

About Open courses in creative writing. Also teach a certificate in creative writing.

University of the Arts, London

65 Davies Street, London, W1K 5DA
- 020 7514 6000
- info@arts.ac.uk
- www.arts.ac.uk

About Many short courses on writing, editing, journalism and publishing, at various centres in London.

University of Warwick

Centre for Lifelong Learning, Westwood Campus, University of Warwick, Coventry, CV4 7AL
- 024 7652 4617
- 024 7652 4223
- cll@warwick.ac.uk
- www.warwick.ac.uk/cll/openstudies

About Adult short courses in creative writing, journalism and publishing.

Urchfont Manor College

Urchfont, Devizes, Wiltshire, SN10 4RG
- 01380 840495
- 01380 840005
- urchfontmanor@wiltshire.gov.uk
- www.urchfontmanor.co.uk

About Residential courses, day courses and study tours on creative writing topics.

Wakefield Adult & Community Education Service

Manygates Education Centre, Manygates Lane, Sandal, Wakefield, WF2 7DQ
- 01924 303302
- aces@wakefield.gov.uk
- www.wakefieldaes.org.uk

About Creative writing community course. Contact Andrea Benson.

Waterford Institute of Technology

Adult & Continuing Education Office, WIT, St Dominics, College Street Campus, Waterford, Republic of Ireland
- 00353 51 302000
- info@wit.ie
- www.wit.ie

About Creative writing evening class.

The Watermill at Posara

The Mill, Posara, Fivizzano, MS Italy
- Online form.
- www.watermill.net

About Wide range of residential creative writing courses.

Wedgewood Memorial College
Station Road, Barlaston, Stoke-on-Trent, ST12 9DG
- 01782 373427
- 01782 372393
- wedgewood.memorial@swann.stoke.gov.uk
- extwww.sgfl.org.uk/ghumphrey/wmc/home.asp

About Residential and day courses on various writing topics.

Weston College
Knightsone Road, Weston Super Mare, BS23 2AL
- 01934 411411
- 01934 411410
- enquiries@weston.ac.uk
- www.weston.ac.uk

About Part time creative writing courses.

Workers Educational Association
3rd Floor, 70 Clifton Street, London, EC2A 4HB
- 020 7426 3450
- 020 7426 3451
- national@wea.org.uk
- www.wea.org.uk

About Voluntary provider of adult learning, including courses in creative writing, publishing and journalism. Search the website by location to find the nearest course.

Write Away
Arts Training Central, 16 New Street, Leicester, LE1 5NR
- 0116 242 5202
- info@artstrainingcentral.co.uk
- www.artstrainingcentral.co.uk

About Residential courses on writing, from Friday to Sunday afternoon. Held at Leicester University.

The Write Coach
12 Kidderpore Gardens, London, NW3 7SR
- 020 7794 0288
- susangrossman@tiscali.co.uk
- www.susangrossman.co.uk

About Individual mentoring, 'Life's a Pitch' workshops, and distance learning, on all aspects of getting published, from writing book or feature proposals to how to be a successful journalist or travel writer. Inside information offered by an experienced magazine editor, journalist and BBC broadcaster, currently a visiting lecturer in journalism at two London universities.

Writers Academy
Carrig on Bannow, Co. Wexford, Republic of Ireland
- 00353 51 561789
- thewritersacademy@eircom.net
- www.thewritersacademy.net

About Correspondence courses in short story writing and freelance article writing. Also offers editorial services for writers of all abilities.

Writers Bureau
Sevendale House, 7 Dale Street, Manchester, M1 1JB
- 0845 345 5995
- 0161 236 9440
- advisory@writersbureau.com
- www.writersbureau.com

About The Writers Bureau offers home study creative writing courses, with individual guidance from expert tutors and flexible tuition. Courses cover style, presentation, copyright and how to sell your writing in different markets. They cater for a wide range of skill levels, including beginners, and cover articles, short stories, journalism, novels, romances, historicals, writing for children, writing for television, and writing for radio and theatre, among other subjects. Details are free on request and a 15 day trial period is available, as well as the option for a full refund if not successful.

Writers' News Home Study
5th Floor, 31–32 Park Row, Leeds, LS1 5JD
- 0113 200 2917
- 0113 200 2928
- homestudy@writersnews.co.uk
- www.writersnews.co.uk

About Nine home based writing courses. Contact the Home Study Coordinator for a free prospectus.

WritersReign
Fortress Publishing, 1 Delta Road, Hutton, Brentwood, Essex, CM13 1NG
- 01277 226840
- editor@writersreign.co.uk
- www.writersreign.co.uk

About The WritersReign website is for all aspiring writers. It has a comprehensive pool of articles covering many interesting and exciting topics, as well as frequently updated writing and poetry competition listings. It also has an impressive array of links to other writers' websites and a software page with details about some useful products you may not know about. WritersReign also offers a free article writing e-course.

WriteWords
PO Box 850, St Albans, AL1 9BE
- admin@writewords.org.uk
- www.writewords.org.uk

About Range of email correspondence courses on different types of writing and publishing.

The Writing College
16 Magdalen Road, Exeter, EX2 4SY
- 01392 499488
- 01392 498008
- enquiries@writingcollege.com
- www.writingcollege.com

About Offers a creative writing correspondence course.

Writing Holidays, Writers' Seminars & Workshops
F*F Productions, 39 Ranelagh Road, Sandown, PO36 8NT
- contact@writeplot.co.uk
- www.learnwriting.co.uk

About Organises writers' retreats and conferences. Also runs screenwriting courses. For these contact: admin@cityeye.co.uk

Written Words
5 Queen Elisabeth Close, London, N16 0HL
- henrietta@writtenwords.net
- www.writtenwords.net

About Intensive workshops for fiction writers. Also offers private tutorials for novels/short stories. Full mss. welcomed.

Wye Valley Arts Centre
Hephzibah Gallery, Llandogo, Monmouthshire, NP25 4TW
- 01594 530214
- 01594 530321
- wyearts@cwc.net
- www.wyeart.cwc.net

About Workshops and residential courses on various types of writing.

Yorkshire Art Circus
School Lane, Glasshoughton, Castleford, West Yorkshire, WF10 4QH
- 01977 550401
- 01977 512819
- admin@artcircus.org.uk
- www.artcircus.org.uk

About Courses and workshops in creative writing and publishing for writers throughout Yorkshire. Also runs a young writer development programme. Contact beccy@artcircus.org.uk.

COMPETITIONS & PRIZES

Academi Cardiff International Poetry Competition
Academi, 3rd Floor, Mount Stuart House, Mount Stuart Square, Cardiff, CF10 5FQ
- 029 2047 2266
- 029 2049 2930
- post@academi.org
- www.academi.org

Competition/Award Director Chief Executive, Peter Finch
Established 1986
Insider Info The competition is administered by Academi with the financial assistance of Cardiff Council. The competition takes place annually, with a first prize of £5,000; second prize of £500; third prize of £250; and five runner up prizes of £50 each. The competition is judged by three established poets, with one acting as a filter judge. Copyright will remain with the competitor, but Academi reserves the right to arrange the first publication or broadcast of selected poems as it sees fit. The competition is open to poets of all nationalities, they do not have to be resident in Wales.
Genres Poetry
Submission Guidelines Submissions should be received before January 29 each year and must be previously unpublished, in English and no more than 50 lines in length. Guidelines and entry forms are available by post with an SAE or on the website, at: www.academi.org/cipc/. There is an entry fee of £6 per poem.

Aeon Award
8 Bachelor's Walk, Dublin 1, Republic of Ireland
- fraslaw@yahoo.co.uk
- www.albedo1.com

Insider Info The Aeon Award is for the best submitted short story in the Science Fiction, Horror or Fantasy genres. Submissions are invited for four closing dates (end of March, June, September and November each year) and the shortlist is added to after each round is complete. The competition takes place annually, and the overall winner, chosen from the shortlist compiled after four rounds of submissions, wins €1,000. Second prize is €200. The top four entrants will be published in *Albedo One* magazine and writer Ian Watson will judge the overall winner.
Genres Short Stories
Submission Guidelines Submission guidelines are available on the website. There is an entry fee of €5 per entry and stories must be previously unpublished. Email and postal submissions are welcome.
Tips Entries must be no longer than 8,000 words and be typed with double spacing.

The Alexander Prize
University College London, Gower Street, London, WC1E 6BT
- 020 7387 7532
- 020 7387 7532
- royalhistsoc@ucl.ac.uk
- www.royalhistoricalsociety.org

Contact Executive Secretary
Established 1897
Insider Info Sponsored by the Royal Historical Society. Awarded annually for a published scholarly journal article or an essay based on original historical research. The award recognises the accomplishments of doctoral candidates and fledgling historians. The prize consists of £250 or a silver medal. Entrants must be doctoral students in history in a UK institution, or be within two years of having graduated from a doctoral degree course in history in a UK institution.
Genres Essays, Articles
Submission Guidelines Deadline for entries is the end of December. Previously published entries must have been published in an academic journal or an edited collection between January 1 and December 31 the current year.
Tips Submit two hard copies of the published item (not manuscript copies) with full information on the journal or volume in which it was published. Candidates must be doctoral students in history in a UK institution, or be within two years of having completed a doctorate in history in a UK institution.

The Alfred Fagon Award
The Royal Court Theatre, Sloane Square, London, SW1W 8AS
- www.talawa.com/afa

Established 1997
Insider Info An award in memory of playwright Alfred Fagon designed to recognise a variety of writing talents in people of Caribbean descent, particularly playwrights. Awarded annually, winners receive £5,000. Writers must be of Caribbean descent and living in the UK.
Genres Scripts
Submission Guidelines The play need not have been produced. Deadline for entries is the 31st of August.

Tips To apply send two copies of a script along with an author biography and covering letter by post before the deadline. Closing dates will be published on the website.

ALPSP Awards & ALPSP/Charlesworth Awards

Blenheim House, 120 Church Street, Brighton, BN1 1AU

- 01245 260571
- 01245 260935
- events@alpsp.org
- www.alpsp.org

Competition/Award Director Events Coordinator, Lesley Ogg

Insider Info Awards for achievements in learning and professional publishing. The awards ceremony is held annually and takes place in September. Entries are judged by a panel of independent experts.

Tips The ALPSP Awards are open to publishers, societies and journals, either UK or internationally-based. Includes commercial and not-for-profit organisations. Full details available on the website.

The Amaury Talbot Prize for African Anthropology

50 Fitzroy Street, London, W1T 5BT

- 020 7387 0455
- 020 7388 8817
- admin@therai.org.uk
- www.therai.org.uk

Contact Amaury Talbot, Prize Coordinator

Insider Info Sponsored by the Royal Anthropological Institute. An award for non-fiction on anthropological research relating to Africa. Awarded annually, prize money is £500. Judges are appointed by the RAI Council.

Genres Non-Fiction

Submission Guidelines Deadline for entries is end of March each year. Work should be published previously, between April 1 and March 31.

Tips Preference is given firstly to work relating to Nigeria and secondly to another part of West Africa, or West Africa in general. Submit three copies of the book, work or article.

The André Simon Memorial Book Awards

1 Westbourne Gardens, Glasgow, G12 9XE

- 0141 342 4929
- katie@andresimon.co.uk
- www.andresimon.co.uk

Competition/Award Director Katie Lander

Established 1975

Insider Info Awards for Best Food Book and Drink Book, which may include recipe books, biographies, guides, polemical works or reference books that focus from some angle on food and drink. Awarded annually, the winners in each category receive £2,000 with special commendations receiving £1,000.

Genres Non-Fiction, Food & Drink Books

Submission Guidelines Deadline for entries is November; books must have been published in the previous year.

Tips Nominations are usually invited from publishers from April onwards, although all books within the remit of the award will be considered.

Angus Book Award

Educational Resources Service, Angus Council, Bruce House, Wellgate, Arbroath, DD11 3TL

- 01241 435008
- hoodm@angus.gov.uk
- www.angus.gov.uk/bookaward

Competition/Award Director Educational Resources Librarian, Moyra Hood

Established 1996

Insider Info A shortlist of four new paperback novels for teenagers are voted for by Angus secondary school children. This award is designed to encourage older children to take an active interest in books and is held annually. Sponsored by Angus Council. The winner receives a replica of the Pictish Aberlemno Serpent stone and a cheque for £500.

Genres Teenage Fiction.

Submission Guidelines Titles must be published for the first time in paperback between July and June of the preceding year.

Tips To be eligible for this award, books must have been written by a UK author.

The Anthony Hecht Poetry Prize

The Waywiser Press, The Cottage, 14 Lyncroft Gardens, Ewell, Surrey, KT17 1UR

- 020 8374 5526
- 020 8374 5736
- waywiserpress@aol.com
- www.waywiser-press.com/hechtprize.html

Competition/Award Director Philip Hoy

Established 2005

Insider Info Sponsored by the Waywiser Press. The prize is awarded annually to the best collection of poems in English submitted by an author who has no more than one previous collection of poems published. The purpose is to reward the author of the best collection with a cash prize of £1,750 or $3,000, as well as publication of his/her collection by the Waywiser Press in the UK and USA. The prize winner will be offered a publishing contract with a standard set of royalties specified. Entrants must be 18 or over. They may not have published more than one previous collection of poems (though they may have published books belonging to other genres, and individual poems from the submission may have been published in magazines, journals, anthologies and chapbooks of 32 pages or less, or self-published books of 46 pages or less). No author who has a book published by, or forthcoming from Waywiser may enter. Manuscripts must be in English, though as much as one third of the poems they contain can consist of public domain or permission-secured translations.

Genres Poetry

Submission Guidelines Deadline for entry is December 1st – some small changes are possible and potential entrants are advised to consult the guidelines (available with entry forms via SAE). Entry fee is £15 or $25. Work should be unpublished. Manuscripts should be between 50 and 100 pages in length.

Tips Waywiser features poems from each of the people who get as far as the semi-finals on its website; the work is very diverse, but some idea of the standard required can be seen there.

Arthur C. Clarke Award for Science Fiction

60 Bournemouth Road, Folkestone, Kent, CT19 5AZ

☎ 01303 252939

✉ chairofjudges.clarkeaward@gmail.com

🌐 www.clarkeaward.com

Competition/Award Director Paul Billinger

Established 1986

Insider Info The Arthur C. Clarke Award for Science Fiction is presented for the best science fiction novel of the year, as selected from a shortlist. The award is presented annually and the prize consists of a trophy and £2,009 (for the 2009 award and increasing by £1 annually). The winning book is picked by a jury panel. This competition is open to writers from any nationality, provided their book is in English and published in the UK.

Genres Science Fiction

Submission Guidelines Titles must be previously published in the UK between January 1 and December 31 in the current year.

Tips Novellas (less than 30,000 words) and short story collections are not eligible for this award. Entries should be made by the book's publishers.

Arundel Theatre Trails Writers Competitions

Drip Action Theatre, 1 Norfolk House, 28 High Street, Arundel, BN18 9AB

☎ 01903 885250

✉ dripactioninfo@btinternet.com

Established 2000

Insider Info Entries are invited to fill the slots designated for eight short plays at The Arundel Festival. Competition takes place annually. Eight winning plays will be performed at the festival and the overall winner will receive the Joy Gaun award (£200). Each writer will also receive a £150 fee.

Genres Scripts

Submission Guidelines Submissions should be received before January 31 each year. There is no entry fee.

Scripts need to be 30–40 minutes long and suitable to be performed in the day with limited props and cast. Submit a hard copy by post, restricted to one play per entrant.

Arvon Foundation International Poetry Competition

2nd Floor, 42a Buckingham Palace Road, London, SW1W 0RE

☎ 020 7931 7611

☎ 020 7963 0961

✉ comps@arvonfoundation.org

🌐 www.arvonfoundation.org

Competition/Award Director Director, Ariane Koek

Established 1980

Insider Info This is a competition for unpublished poems in the English language. The competition is held annually with a first prize of £5,000, second prize of £2,500, third prize of £1,000 and three runner up prizes of £500 each. Worldwide copyright remains with the poets but Arvon may publish the poem or produce reading in all media platforms within 12 months of the prize-giving.

Genres Poetry

Submission Guidelines Submissions should be received between May and the middle or August each year. Submission guidelines are available on the website. Entry fee is £6 per poem. Poems must be previously unpublished.

Tips Submit two hard copies of each poem on single-sided sheets, along with an entry form which is available on the website.

Asham Award

Lewes Town Hall, High Street, Lewes, East Sussex, BN7 2QS

☎ 01273 483159

✉ carole.buchan@btinternet.com

🌐 www.ashamaward.com

Contact Administrator, Carole Buchan

Established 1995

Insider Info The Asham award is a short story competition open to women of any nationality, providing they have not previously had any short or full length fiction published. The award is designed to allow new women writers the same platform as more well-known authors. The competition is held every two years (odd years). Winners are published in an anthology of short stories and receive a share of £3,000 prize money. Winners also get advice from novelist Kate Pullinger and are given the chance to take part in writing workshops. The competition is open to female writers only, over the age of 18.

Genres Short Stories

Submission Guidelines Submissions must be previously unpublished.

Tips There is no set theme or genre for the stories. There are normally between 700 and 950 entries for the award every year.

Authors' Club First Novel Award
40 Dover Street, London, W1S 4NP

- 020 7499 8581
- 020 7409 0913
- authors@theartsclub.co.uk

Competition/Award Director Stella Kane
Established 1954

Insider Info The Authors' Club award is presented to a promising work of fiction written by a British author and published in the UK. The award is presented annually, with prize money of £1,000.

Genres Novels

Submission Guidelines Submissions must be previously published full-length novels by first-time authors.

Tips Entries are usually nominated by publishers.

BAAL Book Prize
Department of Linguistics & English Language, Lancaster University, Lancaster, LA1 4YT

- c.dembry@lancs.ac.uk
- www.baal.org.uk

Contact Claire Dembry

Insider Info This prize is awarded to a book in the field of Applied Linguistics. This prize is offered annually and is open to any writer worldwide.

Genres Non-Fiction and Linguistics

Submission Guidelines Submissions should be received before December 13 each year. Guidelines are available on the website. There is a fee of £35 per title submitted. Titles must be previously published. Nominations must be made by the book's publishers and be accompanied by four hard copies of the book itself. Post to Claire Dembry at the above address.

Tips Linguistics is a broad term and can include sociolinguistics, discourse analysis, communication studies and education. If unsure about the work's eligibility, contact Veronika Koller, Publications Secretary, at v.koller@lancaster.ac.uk.

BA/Nielsen BookData Author of the Year
The Booksellers Association of the UK & Ireland, 272 Vauxhall Bridge Road, London, SW1V 1BA

- 020 7802 0802
- 020 7802 0803
- naomi.gane@booksellers.org.uk
- www.booksellers.org.uk

Competition/Award Director Naomi Gane
Established 1993

Insider Info Booksellers Association members vote for the writer who has made the biggest impact on their business in that year. This can be in a sales context or could reflect their personal tastes. This award is presented annually and consists of £1,000 and a trophy.

Submission Guidelines The title must be published within the preceding year.

Tips There are no entries invited as the winner is voted for entirely by BA members.

BBC Four Samuel Johnson Prize for Non-Fiction
28 Windmill Street, London, W1T 2JJ

- 020 7631 2666
- 020 7631 2699
- lois@colmangettypr.co.uk
- www.thesamueljohnsonprize.co.uk

Established 1999

Insider Info Celebrates the best work of non-fiction published in the previous year. Competition takes place annually. The prize consists of £30,000 for the winner and smaller cash prizes for shortlisted books.

Genres Non-Fiction

Submission Guidelines Work should be previously published, having appeared between May 1 of the previous year and April 30 of the year of entry.

Tips Entries should be submitted by publishers only and can include non-fiction books on a wide range of topics.

The BBC National Short Story Award
Booktrust, Book House, 45 East Hill, London, SW18 2QZ

- story@booktrust.org.uk
- www.theshortstory.org.uk

Established 2005

Insider Info Sponsored by the National Endowment for Science, Technology and the Arts (NESTA) and BBC Radio 4. The BBC National Short Story Award is the biggest single short story award in the world, designed to bring attention to the short story form. Stories should be a maximum of 8,000 words. The prize is awarded annually. Prizes consist of: £15,000 for the winner; £3,000 for 2nd place; and £500 for three shortlisted stories.

Genres Short Stories

Submission Guidelines Submissions should be received by January 22. Submissions should be published previously having appeared between January 1 and December 31 of the previous year, or should be unpublished.

Tips Entrants are advised that they should have some history of creative writing and their work (although not necessarily the piece they are submitting) should have been published in book or magazine form. Formerly known as the National Short Story Prize.

Ben Pimlott Prize for Political Writing

The Fabian Society, 11 Dartmouth Street, London, SW1H 9BN

❶ 020 7227 4900

❶ 020 7676 7153

⊚ www.guardian.co.uk/benpimlottprize

Established 2005

Insider Info This competition is sponsored by The Fabian Society and *The Guardian*. The Ben Pimlott Prize for Political Writing is an open competition for political essays on a particular theme and using a given title. The competition was started in memory of Ben Pimlott, political writer and regular contributor to *The Guardian*. The competition is held annually. The winner receives £3,000 and the essay is published in *The Guardian Review*.

Genres Political Essays

Submission Guidelines Submissions must be received by the end of March each year. Essays must be previously unpublished.

Tips Essays should be no longer than 3,000 words. Because the winning entry will be published in *The Guardian*, it may be useful to follow *The Guardian* style guide, available at www.guardian.co.uk/styleguide although this is not mandatory.

The Bernard Levin Award

Woodbourn Business Centre, 10 Jessell Street, Sheffield, S9 3HY

❶ 0114 244 9561

⊚ admin@indexers.org.uk

⊚ www.indexers.org.uk

Established 2000

Insider Info Sponsored by The Society of Indexers. Awarded to an individual for outstanding services to The Society of Indexers. Competition held every one to two years.

Tips Does not accept submissions outside of the Society.

Betty Trask Awards

84 Drayton Gardens, London, SW10 9SB

❶ 020 7373 6642

❶ 020 7373 5768

⊚ info@societyofauthors.org

⊚ www.societyofauthors.org

Insider Info These awards are sponsored by the Society of Authors and presented for the best debut, due to be published, or unpublished novel by a writer under the age of 35. Novels should be romantic or traditional and the prize will not be awarded to experimental fiction. Several prizes may be presented in one year and prize money totals £25,000 and should be used for periods of foreign travel.

Genres Fiction, Novels

Submission Guidelines Submissions must be received by the end of January each year. Guidelines/entry forms are available on the website. Writers should be Commonwealth citizens and must not have had work published other than the novel submitted. Unpublished writers should submit a copy of the manuscript. Published writers should send a book, proof or manuscript via their publisher. Mark for the attention of Dorothy Sym.

Bill Naughton Short Story Competition

Box No 2006, Aghamore, Ballyhaunis, County Mayo, Republic of Ireland

❶ 00353 94 936 7019

⊚ www.aghamoreireland.com/kennynaughton/shortstory.htm

Insider Info This is an open short story competition for stories of up to 2,500 words on any subject matter or theme. The competition is held annually and €200 is awarded for 1st prize, €130 for 2nd prize and €65 for 3rd prize.

Genres Short Stories

Submission Guidelines Submissions must be received by the end of September each year. There is a £5 fee per story or £10 for three stories. Stories must be previously unpublished. There is no entry form, but all entries must be postal.

The Biographer's Club Prize

119a Fordwych Road, London, NW2, 3NJ

❶ 020 8452 4993

⊚ anna@annaswan.co.uk

⊚ www.biographersclub.co.uk

Contact Prize Administrator, Anna Swan

Established 1999

Insider Info Sponsored by the *Daily Mail*. Created to finance and encourage new writers researching a biography. Awarded annually, with prize money of £2,000. Entrants must be previously unpublished and uncommissioned. Entry fee is £10 (cheques payable to The Biographers' Club).

Genres Biographies

Submission Guidelines Deadline for entries is 1 August. Work should be previously unpublished.

Tips Submit a 20-page proposal to Anna Swan, prize administrator. Include a synopsis and 10-page sample chapter (both double-spaced), CV and a note on sources and market competition.

Biscuit Poetry & Short Story Prizes
PO Box 123, Washington, Newcastle upon Tyne, NE37 2YW
- info@biscuitpublishing.com
- www.biscuitpublishing.com

Insider Info Biscuit Publishing run a variety of competitions that may change from year to year. The winners of each category (short fiction or poetry) win £1,000 cash. Runners up win a writer's retreat at Flanders Talbot House.

Genres Poetry, Short Stories and Story Collections

Submission Guidelines Submissions must be received by October 1 each year. Guidelines are available on the website. There is a fee of £12 per portfolio. Submit either three short stories of 1,000–5,000 words, or six poems along with a cover sheet. Writers can enter in both categories if they wish and can win in both. State on the cover sheet if the poetry or stories are intended for children, and what ages. Sheets should be single sided and double spaced. Include SAE for results and a postcard if acknowledgement is required. No email entries accepted.

Boardman Tasker Prize
Pound House, Llangennith, Swansea, West Glamorgan, SA3 1JQ
- 01792 386215
- 01792 386215
- margaretbody@lineone.net
- www.boardmantasker.co.uk

Contact Secretary, Margaret Body

Established 1983

Insider Info This prize is sponsored by Boardman Tasker Charitable Trust and is for an original work in book form. Given in memory of climbers Peter Boardman and Joe Tasker, the prize honours the best literary work, whether fiction or non-fiction, the central theme of which is concerned with the mountain environment (not necessarily mountaineering). The competition is held annually with a prize of £3,000 and is judged by a panel of three different people each year. Any published writer may enter via their publisher.

Genres Fiction, Non-Fiction, Poetry, Essays, Novels, Story Collections.

Submission Guidelines Submissions must be received by August 16 each year. Entry should be via publisher. The submitted work must be previously published between November 1 of the previous year and October 31 in the current year.

The Bollinger Everyman Wodehouse Prize for Comic Fiction
c/o Colman Getty PR, Middlesex House, 32–42 Cleveland Street, London, W1T 4JE
- 020 7631 2666
- 020 7631 2699
- info@colmangettypr.co.uk
- lois@colmangetty.co.uk

Established 2000

Insider Info A celebration of comic writing in the memory of P.G. Wodehouse. Awarded annually, the winner receives a bottle of Bollinger champagne, and a rare breed of pig is named after the novel.

Genres Comic Fiction

Submission Guidelines Work should be published previously.

Tips Enquiries about nominating books should be directed to Colman Getty PR.

The Booktrust Early Years Awards
Book House, 45 East Hill, Wandsworth, London, SW18 2QZ
- 020 8516 2972
- 020 8516 2978
- query@booktrust.org.uk
- www.booktrust.org.uk

Established 2004

Insider Info Sponsored by Booktrust. This annual award has three categories: Best Book for Babies under one year old; Best Picture Book for pre-school children up to five years of age; and Best New Illustrator, again up to five years old, for the illustrator's first ever published pre-school picture book. The winners will each receive a cheque for £2,000 (to be shared between author & illustrator if appropriate) and a crystal ornament, and in addition the Best New Illustrator will receive a specially commissioned award. Also, the publishers of the winning titles will be presented with an award naming them as one of the Booktrust Early Years Awards Publishers of the Year. The aim of the prize is to celebrate, publicise and reward the exciting range of books being published today for babies, toddlers and pre-school children. Also to promote and make these books accessible to as wide an audience as possible. The publishers of all three books will also receive a crystal ornament pronouncing them as one of the Booktrust Early Years Awards Publishers of the Year. There is a panel of five, chaired by Wendy Cooling, Children's Book Consultant. She is joined each year by a representative from the library service, the health service, a parent from the National Bookstart programme and a children's illustrator. The prize is only open to UK citizens, but other nationalities are eligible to enter as long as they have been in the British Isles for at least five years.

Genres Children's, Baby Books

Submission Guidelines Deadline for entry is June; this date may change. There is no entry fee. Work should be published previously, between September 1 and August 31.

Tips Entries are invited from publishers only.

Book Trust Teenage Prize
Book House, 45 East Hill, London, SW18 2QZ
- ☎ 020 8516 2986
- ☎ 020 8516 2978
- ✉ query@booktrust.org.uk
- 🌐 www.bookheads.org.uk

Established 2003

Insider Info Recognises the best works of Teenage Fiction in the UK in the preceding year. The competition is held annually and the winner receives £2,500. It is open to residents of the UK as well as citizens of the UK. Works must be in English but can be in any genre, providing they are aimed at teenagers.

Genres Story Collections and Fiction for 13–16 year olds

Submission Guidelines Submissions must be received by the end of March each year. They must be previously published between July 1 of the previous year and June 30 of the current year.

Tips Entries are invited from publishers only.

Bookworms Short Story Competition
3 Yeomanry Road, Battlefield Enterprise Park, Shrewsbury, Shropshire, SY1 3EH
- ☎ 01743 360573
- ☎ 01743 443388
- ✉ kazbamail-fern@yahoo.co.uk
- 🌐 www.beanpolebooks.co.uk

Competition/Award Director Karen Lowe

Established 2006

Insider Info This competition is sponsored by Beanpole Books and involves submitting a 1,500 word short story suitable for general reading on a public website. The title is chosen from the crossword titles in *50 Bookworms Crosswords*, to give an opportunity to a new or little-published writer to share their work with a wider public. This competition takes place annually and the prize is £100 and publication on the Beanpole Books website for a year. Entries are judged by Karen Lowe and a guest judge (will vary each year). Entry to the competition assumes Beanpole Books has the right to publish the winning story on its website for

twelve months. This competition is open to any UK based writer.

Genres Fiction and Short Stories

Submission Guidelines Submissions must be received by October 30. Entry form is included with purchase of *50 Bookworms Crosswords*, £3.99. Short stories must be previously unpublished.

Tips View the website to see previous winners. The story should be suitable for general viewing on a public website which may be accessed by children. No science fiction, violence, explicit sex, or strong language. This is a new competition. Details may vary in future years.

The Branford Boase Award
Library & Information HQ, 81 North Walls, Winchester, SO23 8BY
- ☎ 01962 826658
- ✉ anne.marley@tiscali.co.uk
- 🌐 www.branfordboaseaward.org.uk

Insider Info Annually awarded for the most promising first novel by a new writer of a book for young people. The winner receives £1,000 and a handcrafted box. Writers may have been published before in other fields but must enter their first, unpublished, book for children.

Genres Fiction, Novels for young people aged 7+

Submission Guidelines Entry deadline is December. Guidelines available on website. Work should be published previously, between January 1 and December 31.

Tips Entries are invited from publishers, who may submit up to five books. No short story collections by multiple authors, poetry, or picture books.

Brian MacMahon Short Story Award
Writer's Week, 24 the Square, Listowel, Co. Kerry, Republic of Ireland
- ☎ 00353 682 1074
- ☎ 00353 682 2893
- ✉ info@writersweek.ie
- 🌐 www.writersweek.ie

Insider Info This award is sponsored by The American Ireland Funds and is an open short story competition for stories of up to 3,000 words. The competition takes place annually and the winner receives €2,000. *Writer's Week* reserves the right to withhold or publish winning entries in the publication the *Winners Anthology*.

Genres Short Stories

Submission Guidelines Submissions must be received by the end of March. There is a fee of €10 per entry and the short stories must be previously unpublished.

Tips Entries must be either in English or Irish. Entrants may enter as many stories as they wish with the appropriate fees.

Brian Way Award
Theatre Centre, Shoreditch Town Hall, 380 Old Street, London, EC1V 9LT
- 020 7729 3066
- 020 7739 9741
- admin@theatre-centre.co.uk
- www.theatre-centre.co.uk

Established 2000

Insider Info Formerly the Arts Council Children's Award. Named after the late Brian Way, founder of the Theatre Centre, and designed to celebrate the achievements and raise the profile of playwrights who write specifically for young people. The competition takes place annually and offers a first prize of £6,000, with a runner-up prize of £1,000 for a production of a play written within the last decade. Writers must either be resident in the UK or Republic of Ireland, or have had a writing association with a UK theatre company or group.

Genres Plays for young people up to the age of 18.

Submission Guidelines Submissions must be received by December 1 each year and the play itself must be performed between September 1 the previous year and September 30 the current year. Postal submissions of scripts may come from agents or writers themselves. Also include details of where and when performances have taken place.

Tips Judges look for plays that demonstrate a special quality in the writing, that stimulate the imagination and use innovative languages and forms.

The Bridport Prize
PO Box 6910, Bridport, Dorset, DT6 9BQ
- frances@bridportprize.org.uk
- www.bridportprize.org.uk

Insider Info An international creative writing competition for poetry of up to 42 lines and short stories of up to 5,000 words. Awarded annually, prizes consist of: 1st £5,000; 2nd £1,000; 3rd £500; and ten runner up prizes of £50 each. The poetry judge for 2009 is Jackie Kay; for short stories it is Ali Smith. Copyright remains with the author but the administration retains unrestricted rights to publish winning entries in the Bridport Anthology. Open to any writer over the age of 18 and resident in the UK.

Genres Poetry, Short Stories

Submission Guidelines Deadline for entry is the 30th of June. Guidelines available on the website. Entry fee is £6 per poem or £7 per story. Work should be previously unpublished.

Tips Submit as many entries as you wish, either by post or online. Entry forms are available online. The judges' criteria for winning entries are published on the website.

Bristol Short Story Prize
7 Exeter Buildings, Redland, Bristol, BS6 6TH
- 0117 923 8891
- enquiries@bristolprize.co.uk
- www.bristolprize.co.uk

Competition/Award Director Prize Coordinator, Joe Melia

Established 2008

Insider Info An offshoot of *Bristol Review of Books* magazine. The competition takes place annually, with a first prize of £500, second prize of £350 and third prize of £200. Winners will also receive additional Waterstone's gift cards as part of their prizes, and 17 runners-up will receive £50 each. The top 20 entries selected by the judging panel will be published in the annual *Bristol Short Story Prize Anthology*. The anthology will then go on general release at an RRP of £8. The first, second and third prize winning stories will also be published in *Bristol Review of Books* magazine. The competition is open to writers of all ages and nationalities. Entries must be previously unpublished and may be on any subject or theme.

Genres Short Fiction

Submission Guidelines Submit stories of up to 3,000 words via the website or by post along with an entry form, which is downloadable from the website. The deadline for submissions is the 31st of March. There is an entry fee of £7 per story.

Tips One of the major aims of the prize is to get undiscovered, talented writers into print and on to the high street shelves.

British Book Awards
7 John Street, London, WC1N 2ES
- 0870 870 2345
- 0870 870 0385
- www.britishbookawards.co.uk

Established 1990

Insider Info These awards are sponsored by Galaxy and are known as 'The Nibbies'. They are the publishing industry's equivalent of the BAFTAs, where awards in various categories are handed out at a televised awards ceremony. This takes place annually and trophies are awarded at the ceremony.

Submission Guidelines Submissions must be previously published.

Tips Each category is voted for by various groups based on books published in the previous year, therefore there is no opportunity for writers to submit unpublished works for consideration.

British Czech & Slovak Association Writing Competition

BCSA Prize Administrator, 24 Ferndale, Tunbridge Wells, Kent, TN2 3NS

- 01892 543206
- 020 8795 4875
- prize@bcsa.co.uk
- www.bcsa.co.uk

Contact Edward Peacock, Prize Administrator

Established 2002

Insider Info This competition is sponsored by the British Czech & Slovak Association. It is open to all, regardless of age, nationality or educational background. Fiction or non-fiction is welcome, based on the links between Britain and the Czech and Slovak Republics, or on society in transition in those Republics since the Velvet Revolution in 1989. The competition is firstly for fun, and secondly to advance the BCSA's purpose in encouraging links between Britain and the Czech & Slovak Republics. The competition takes place annually offering £300 for the first prize, presented at BCSA Annual Dinner; £100 for the second prize and winning entries are published in *British Czech & Slovak Review*. A panel of expert judges is recruited each year. By entering, authors allow the BCSA to publish entries in their publications, but entrants retain the copyright to their entries. Submissions are invited from individuals of any age, nationality or educational background.

Genres Fiction, Non-Fiction, Essays and Short Stories

Submission Guidelines Submissions must be received by June 30 each year. There is no entry fee. Guidelines and entry forms are available for self-addressed SAE. Submissions must be previously unpublished.

Tips Entries should be in English and should not exceed 2,000 words in length.

British Fantasy Awards

201 Reddish Road, South Reddish, Stockport, SK5 7HR

- 0161 476 5368
- info@britishfantasysociety.org.uk
- www.britishfantasysociety.org.uk

Contact British Fantasy Awards Administrator, David Sutton

Insider Info Sponsored by the British Fantasy Society. The awards are presented at an annual conference to recognise achievement in the fantasy genre. Categories include best novel, best novella and best artist.

Genres Fantasy

Submission Guidelines Titles must be previously published. Submission deadline is the 28th of February.

Tips The awards are not an open competition for writers.

British Press Awards

Press Gazette, 10 Old Bailey, London, EC4M 7NG

- 020 7038 1469
- 020 7038 1155
- www.britishpressawards.com

Insider Info A ceremony to award UK newspapers and journalists in various categories. Winners are voted for by industry professionals. The awards take place annually. Judges include 80 established journalists and a smaller grand jury from each of the national newspaper groups.

Tips Visit the website for details on how to enter the newspapers, journalists and articles categories.

British Science Fiction Association Awards

16 Napier Road, Oxford, OX4 3JA

- 01865 749378
- bsfamail@gmail.com
- www.bsfa.co.uk

Established 1970

Insider Info These awards are presented at The British National Science Fiction Convention to recognise excellence in various categories within the genre. The awards take place annually and winners are voted for by BSFA members and members of the British National Science Fiction Convention (Eastercon).

Genres Science Fiction Writing and Artwork

Submission Guidelines Writing and artwork must be previously published. See website for details of how to nominate.

Tips Entry is by nomination only.

British Sports Book Awards

Café Royal, 68 Regent Street, London, W1B 5EL

- 020 7437 0144
- 020 7437 5441
- david@nationalsportingclub.co.uk
- www.nationalsportingclub.co.uk

Competition/Award Director David Wilis

Established 2003

Insider Info The British Sports Book Awards is sponsored by the National Sporting Club. It is an awards ceremony to celebrate the best in Sports publishing. Categories include Best Autobiography, Best Biography, Best New Writer, Best Illustrated Title, Best Cricket Book, Best Football Book, and Outstanding Contribution to Sports Publishing. The awards take place annually and judges are a panel made up of sports journalists and publishing professionals.

Genres Non-Fiction, Sports Non-Fiction and Biography
Submission Guidelines Submissions must be received by the end of November each year. Titles must be previously published.
Tips Entry is by nomination only.

The Caine Prize for African Writing
Menier Chocolate Factory, 51 Southwark Street, London, SE1 1RU
- 020 7378 6234
- 020 7378 6234
- info@caineprize.com
- www.caineprize.com
Competition/Award Director Nick Elam
Established 2000
Insider Info Sponsored by The Menier Gallery. An annual short story competition for African writers, designed to highlight African work that has dealt with African sensibilities. Awarded annually, prize money is £10,000 for the winner and a travel award for up to five shortlisted entrants. Writers must be from Africa, an African resident or have African parents. Work must be in English, or have been published in English translation.
Genres Short Stories
Submission Guidelines Deadline for submission is end January each year. Work should be published previously, between February 1 (five years previously) and January 31 (year of the prize giving).
Tips Stories of over 3,000 words must be submitted by publishers. Submit six hard copies. Internet publications are eligible.

Calvin & Rose G Hoffman Prize
Kings School Canterbury, 25 The Precincts, Canterbury, Kent, CT1 2ES
- 01227 595544
- 01227 595589
Insider Info Awarded to the best piece of written work on Christopher Marlowe and his relationship with William Shakespeare. The competition is held annually and the prize consists of £5,000.
Genres Non-Fiction
Submission Guidelines Submissions must be received by September 1 each year. The scholarly work must be previously unpublished.
Tips This award is normally awarded to scholarly works of up to 5,000 words. Contact the administrator at the above address for more information.

Carey Award
Woodbourn Business Centre, 10 Jessell Street, Sheffield, S9 3HY
- 0114 244 9561

- info@indexers.org.uk
- www.indexers.org.uk
Established 1977
Insider Info This award is sponsored by the Society of Indexers. It is an award presented occasionally by the Society to individuals who are deemed to have made a significant contribution to indexing. The award consists of a framed, illuminated parchment.
Tips This award is not open to submissions or nominations. Winners are chosen by the Society as and when suitable candidates arise.

Cartier Diamond Dagger
PO Box 273, Boreham Wood, WD6 2XA
- info@thecwa.co.uk
- www.thecwa.co.uk
Established 1986
Insider Info This award is sponsored by the Crime Writers Association, it is a lifetime achievement award for a crime writer who has made an outstanding contribution to crime writing in the English language. The award is presented annually. The dagger may be awarded to writers regardless of nationality, age or gender.
Genres Crime Fiction
Tips There are no submissions, this award is voted for by a committee of the CWA, and based on nominations from members.

CBI Bisto Book of the Year Award
First Floor, 17 North Great Georges Street, Dubin 1, Republic of Ireland
- 00353 1 872 7475
- 00353 1 872 7476
- info@childrensbooksireland.com
- www.childrensbooksireland.com
Competition/Award Director Mary Shine Thompson
Established 1990
Insider Info The awards consist of: CBI Bisto Book of the Year Award; three CBI Bisto Honour Awards (authors or illustrators); and The Eilís Dillon Award (for a first children's book). The awards are presented annually and the winner of the Book of the Year Award receives €10,000 as well as a perpetual trophy and framed certificate. Honour Awards winners share a prize fund of €6,000 and each receive a framed certificate. The Eilís Dillon winner wins €3,000, a trophy and a framed certificate. Writers and illustrators must be from Ireland, or resident in Ireland at the time of publication.
Genres Children's Books
Submission Guidelines Submissions must be received by December 15 each year. Titles must have been published between January 1and December 31 each year. Entries must be submitted

by publishers. Send 12 hard copies with an entry form.

C.B. Oldman Prize
Aberdeen University Library, Meston Walk, Aberdeen, AB24 3UE
- 01224 272590
- 01224 487048
- r.turbet@abdn.ac.uk
- www.iaml-uk-irl.org

Established 1987

Insider Info Sponsored by the International Association of Music Libraries, Archives and Documentation Centres (IAML), United Kingdom and Ireland. The C.B. Oldman Prize is awarded for the best book on music bibliography, librarianship or reference published in the UK. The prize is given annually and the winner receives £200. Writers must be resident in the UK.

Genres Non-Fiction

Submission Guidelines Submissions must be previously published.

Chapter One Promotions Children's Short Story Competition
PO Box 43667, London, SE22 9XU
- 0845 456 5364
- 0845 456 5347
- kidskorner@chapteronepromotions.com
- www.chapteronepromotions.com

Insider Info A short story competition for children writing stories of up to 1,000 words. Themes to choose from are published on the website. Individuals may enter, as may groups from particular schools or colleges. Age categories are: 7–9; 10–12; 13–15 and 16–18. In each category, 1st, 2nd and 3rd place winners will receive £150, £75 and £50 respectively. Open to any writer that either lives within the Commonwealth and is English speaking or an English national.

Submission Guidelines Submissions must be received by May 31 each year. There is a fee of £5 per story. Schools, colleges and youth clubs can submit group entries of up to 30 stories for £50. Submissions may be made online or by post, and may be typed or handwritten.

Tips Stories must relate to one of the set themes on the website.

Chapter One Promotions International Novel Competition
PO Box 43667, London, SE22 9XU
- 0845 456 5364
- 0845 456 5347
- info@chapteronepromotions.com
- www.chapteronepromotions.com

Insider Info This is an open competition for unpublished novels. Only the first two chapters and the closing chapter are required, and the novel need not have been finished. The competition is held every four years. The winner will receive support in completing their work, which will be published and available through the Book Cellar and Amazon.

Genres Novels

Submission Guidelines Submissions must be received by February 28 each year. There is a fee of £20 per novel. Titles should be previously unpublished.

Tips There is no word count and entries may be submitted by post or online. Entrants must declare if their work has been submitted to any other competitions, agents or publishers.

Chapter One Promotions International Open Poetry Competition
PO Box 43667, London, SE22 9XU
- 0845 456 5364
- 0845 456 5347
- poetry@chapteronepromotions.com
- www.chapteronepromotions.com

Insider Info An open competition for poems of up to 30 lines long in English. The competition is held annually and prizes consist of £1,000, £500 and £250 for 1st, 2nd and 3rd. The top 20 poems are selected by the poet Jacob Sam-La Rose and are published on the website. Users then vote for their favourite. Entrants must be over 18.

Genres Poetry

Submission Guidelines Submissions must be received by June 30 each year. Entry guidelines are available on the website. There is a £5 fee per poem. Poems must be previously unpublished.

Tips Accepts handwritten or typed poems, and both submissions and payments can be made either online or by post.

Chapter One Promotions International Short Story Competition
PO Box 43667, London, SE22 9XU
- 0845 456 5364
- 0845 456 5347
- shortstory@chapteronepromotions.com
- www.chapteronepromotions.com

Established 2005

Insider Info An international competition for short stories of up to 2,500 words. The competition takes place annually and prizes are: £2,500 for the winner; £1,000 for 2nd place; and £500 for 3rd place. The 13 top ranking entries are published in an anthology.

Genres Short Stories

Tips Details of entry procedures will be available on the website. This competition is open to any writer.

The Children's Laureate
Book House, 45 East Hill, London, SW18 2QZ
- 020 8875 4580
- 020 8516 2978
- childrenslaureate@booktrust.org.uk
- www.childrenslaureate.org.uk

Established 1999

Insider Info Administered by Booktrust and sponsored by the MLA Council, Waterstone's and various children's publishers. A title awarded to a writer or illustrator for children's books that has made an outstanding contribution to children's publishing. 2007–2009 laureate was Michael Rosen. Awarded every two years (odd years), the prize consists of the title, a medal and a bursary of £10,000.

Tips Nominations are usually accepted from organisations representing librarians, critics, writers and booksellers. Contact Nikki Marsh at the above email address for further details.

Cholmondeley Awards for Poets
The Society of Authors, 84 Drayton Gardens, London, SW10 9SB
- 020 7373 6642
- 020 7373 5768
- info@societyofauthors.org
- www.societyofauthors.org

Established 1966

Insider Info Founded by the late Dowager Marchioness of Cholmondeley to recognise the achievements of poets. These awards are honorary and submissions are not accepted. The winners are chosen by the board for their contribution to poetry. The awards are presented annually.

CILIP Carnegie Medal
7 Ridgmount Street, London, WC1E 7AE
- 020 7255 0650
- 020 7255 0651
- ckg@cilip.org.uk
- www.carnegiegreenaway.org.uk

Established 1936

Insider Info Awarded to an outstanding children's book in any category. The award is presented annually and the winner receives a golden medal and £500 worth of books to donate to a library of their choice. Books must be in English and have had their first publication in the UK, or have had a co-publication within a three month time lapse.

Genres Children's Fiction or Non-Fiction

Submission Guidelines Submissions must be previously published.

Tips Both e-books and short stories are eligible for this award. Nominations for the award are made by members of CILIP.

CILIP Kate Greenaway Medal
7 Ridgmount Street, London, WC1E 7AE
- 020 7255 0650
- 020 7255 0651
- ckg@cilip.org.uk
- www.carnegiegreenaway.org.uk

Established 1955

Insider Info Awarded for excellence in children's book illustrating during the previous year. The award is presented annually and the winner receives a golden medal and £500 worth of books to donate to a library of their choice. Winners are also granted the Colin Mears Award, which is worth £5,000.

Genres Illustrated Children's Books

Submission Guidelines Submissions must be previously published.

Tips Nominations are taken from members of CILIP. Books for both older and younger children are included.

Cinnamon Press Novella Award
Meirion House, Glan yr afon, Tanygrisiau, Blaenau Ffestiniog, Gwynedd, LL41 3SU
- jan@cinnamonpress.com
- www.cinnamonpress.com

Insider Info This competition is aimed at bringing attention to novellas and promoting their publication. A novella is defined as being between 20,000 and 45,000 words. The award is offered twice yearly. The winner will receive £200 and a contract for their first novella to be published by Cinnamon Press. The competition is open to published and unpublished writers.

Genres Novellas

Submission Guidelines Submissions must be received by June 30 and November 30 each year. There is a fee of £16 per collection – £14 for subscribers to *Envoi* magazine.

Tips Submit the first 10,000 words only to start with. Entries should be typed, single sided and double spaced.

Cinnamon Press Novel Writing Award
Meirion House, Glan yr afon, Tanygrisiau, Blaenau Ffestiniog, Gwynedd, LL41 3SU
- jan@cinnamonpress.com
- www.cinnamonpress.com

Insider Info An award aimed at allowing new writers their first full-length novel publication. Writers are invited to submit the first 10,000 words of their work. The award is offered twice yearly. The top five based on the samples will be invited to submit their full novel. The winner receives £500 and a contract for their novel of between 60,000 and 80,000 words to published by Cinnamon Press. Open to any writer who has never had a full length novel published.

Genres Novels

Submission Guidelines Submissions must be received June 30 and November 30 each year. Guidelines are available on the website. The entry fee is £20 per novel. Novels must be previously unpublished.

Tips Novels do not necessarily need to be finished at the closing date but writers need to be able to provide the full work within two months of the closing date if they are shortlisted. Work should be double spaced on single sided sheets. Handwritten entries will not be accepted.

Cinnamon Press Poetry Collection Award

Meirion House, Glan yr afon, Tanygrisiau, Blaenau Ffestiniog, Gwynedd, LL41 3SU
- jan@cinnamonpress.com
- www.cinnamonpress.com

Insider Info The award aims to give new writers the chance to publish a collection of poetry. Entrants are invited to submit ten poems of up to 40 lines each. Competition is offered twice yearly, and three shortlisted poets will be invited to submit ten further poems. The final winner will receive £100 and a contract with a view to publishing a collection of around 60 poems.

Genres Poetry

Submission Guidelines Deadlines are always June 30 and November 30. Guidelines are available on website. Entry fee of £16 per collection – £14 for subscribers to *Envoi* magazine. May include poems that have been previously published in small press anthologies or magazines.

Tips When submitting, do not put your name on any of the poems. Include a separate sheet with contact details and titles of poems. Each poem should be on a separate sheet.

Cinnamon Press Short Story Award

Meirion House, Glan yr afon, Tanygrisiau, Blaenau Ffestiniog, Gwynedd, LL41 3SU
- jan@cinnamonpress.com
- www.cinnamonpress.com

Insider Info A competition aiming to encourage the writing of short fiction of between 2,000 and 4,000 words. The award is offered twice yearly. The winner receives £100 and the story is published by Cinnamon Press. Up to ten others will be published in an anthology. This competition is open to new and published writers.

Genres Short Stories

Submission Guidelines Submissions must be received June 30 and November 30 each year. Guidelines are available on the website. There is a fee of £16 per collection – £14 for subscribers to *Envoi* magazine.

Tips Accepts postal entries only, typed on single sided sheets.

City of Derby Short Story & Poetry Competition

PO Box 7065, Derby, Derbyshire, DE1 OAD
- 01332 725362
- info@cityofderbywritingcompetition.org.uk
- www.cityofderbywritingcompetition.org.uk

Established 2006

Insider Info This competition is sponsored by *The Independent*. Short stories are invited of up to 5,000 words and poems of up to 40 lines. The primary purpose of the competition is to provide a vehicle for enabling new writers to receive recognition which they might not otherwise have known. Or, if their writing has been already recognised in some way, to give the writers in question further encouragement on the route to reaching a wider audience. The competition takes place annually. In each category of short stories/poetry there is a £500 1st prize, a £250 2nd prize and a £150 3rd prize. The judges are always established authors and poets. Entrants retain all rights to their work. Winning entries are published permanently on the competition website. The competition is open to all ages and nationalities.

Genres Poetry and Short Stories

Submission Guidelines Submissions must be received by 31 May each year. No entry form is required. Full entry details are contained within the website. There is a fee of £3 per entry. Poems and stories must be previously unpublished.

Tips Entries must be typed.

Commonwealth Writers' Prize

Marlborough House, Pall Mall, London, SW1Y 5HY
- 020 7930 3783
- 020 7839 8157
- j.sobol@commonwealth.int
- www.commonwealthfoundation.com/ culturediversity/writersprize

Competition/Award Director Jennifer Sobol
Established 1987

Insider Info The Commonwealth Writer's Prize is an annual award to reward and encourage new Commonwealth fiction. Any work of prose or fiction is eligible, i.e. a novel or collection of short stories. No drama or poetry. The work must be first written in

English by a citizen of the Commonwealth and be first published in the year before its entry for the prize. Entries must be submitted by the publisher to the region of the writer's Commonwealth citizenship. The four regions are: Africa, Europe and South East Asia and South Pacific, Caribbean and Canada. The Commonwealth Writers' Prize is international in its character and administration. In practice it consists of ten prizes. In four Commonwealth regions two prizes of £1,000 are given out: one for the Best Book and one for the Best First Book. The regional winners then go through to the final phase of the competition, where a pan-Commonwealth panel meets to decide the overall Commonwealth winners for Best Book and Best First Book. There will be one award of £10,000 for the Overall Best Book and one award of £5,000 for the Overall Best First Book.

Genres Fiction, Novels, Story collections
Submission Guidelines Deadlines change each year – see the website for details. Accepts simultaneous submissions. Submissions must be previously published between December 1 of the previous year, and December 31 of the year of application.
Tips Please visit the CWP website for more information.

Costa Book Awards
Booksellers Association, Minster House, 272 Vauxhall Bridge Road, London, SW1V 1BA
- 020 7802 0802
- naomi.gane@booksellers.org.uk
- www.costabookawards.com
Established 1971
Insider Info These awards have been designed to celebrate British contemporary writing and were formerly known as the Whitbread Book Awards. There are five categories: Novel; First Novel; Biography; Poetry; and Children's Books. The awards are held annually and each of the category winners receives £5,000, and the overall winner receives a further £25,000. Writers must have been resident in the UK or Ireland for at least six months of each of the previous three years, but do not necessarily have to be of UK or Irish nationality.
Genres Fiction and Non-Fiction.
Submission Guidelines Submissions must be received by the end of June each year. They must be previously published between 1 November of the previous year and 30 October in the current year.
Tips Short story collections are not accepted at present. Accepts submissions from publishers only. Contact the Booksellers Association for an application form.

Country Ghost Story Competition
14 The Park, Stow On The Wold, Cheltenham, Gloucestershire, GL54 1DX
- 01451 831053
- sales@parkpublications.co.uk
- www.parkpublications.co.uk
Competition/Award Director David Howarth
Established 1999
Insider Info This competition is sponsored by Park Publications and is for ghost stories of up to 2000 words with a rural setting. The competition takes place annually and there are three prizes of £75, £25 and £15 plus publication in *Countryside Tales* magazine. The Editor of the magazine judges the competition. Guidelines and entry forms are available for self-addressed SAEs. Park Publications reserves the right for first publication but the copyright remains with the author. The competition is open to any writer.
Genres Fiction
Submission Guidelines Submissions must be received by 31 January each year. There is an entry fee of £3 per entry. Stories must be previously unpublished.
Tips Read the writers' guidelines on the website and/or the magazine.

The CWA Gold Dagger
PO Box 273, Borehamwood, WD6 2XA
- info@thecwa.co.uk
- www.thecwa.co.uk
Established 2006
Insider Info Sponsored by the Crime Writers Association and Duncan Lawrie Private Bank. Formerly the Duncan Lawrie Dagger. Awarded annually for the best crime fiction novel written in English.
Submission Guidelines Work should be previously published.
Tips Check the website for prize details. Submissions from publishers only.

The CWA Gold Dagger for Non-fiction
PO Box 273, Borehamwood, WD6 2XA
- info@thecwa.co.uk
- www.thecwa.co.uk
Established 1978
Insider Info Sponsored by the Crime Writers Association. Awarded bi-annually to the best non-fiction crime book published in the previous year. The winner receives an ornamental dagger and £2,000. All judges have a publishing or legal background.
Genres Non-Fiction, Real-Life Crime/Criminology
Submission Guidelines Work should be published previously.

Tips The Gold Dagger is now awarded bi-annually, with the next to be made in 2010. Submissions by publishers only.

The CWA Short Story Dagger
PO Box 273, Borehamwood, WD6 2XA
- info@thecwa.co.uk
- www.thecwa.co.uk

Established 1995

Insider Info Sponsored by the Crime Writers Association. Awarded annually for short crime stories that may have been published in magazines or anthologies. Winners receive a gold pin of the CWA's crossed daggers emblem and £1,500. Judges are made up of authors, editors and agents.

Genres Short Stories

Submission Guidelines Work should be published previously.

Tips Submissions by publishers only.

The Dagger in the Library
PO Box 273, Borehamwood, WD6 2XA
- info@thecwa.co.uk
- www.thecwa.co.uk

Established 1994

Insider Info Sponsored by the Crime Writers Association and Random House Group. Awarded annually to a living crime fiction author who is deemed to have given readers the most pleasure. Writers are nominated by UK libraries. The prize consists of £1,500 and an ornamental dagger. Judged by librarians.

Submission Guidelines Work should be published previously.

Tips No submissions.

Daily Mail First Novel Competition
Transworld Publishers, 61–63 Uxbridge Road, London, W5 5SA
- www.mailonsunday.co.uk

Established 2008

Insider Info A competition for debut novelists (any genre) run by *The Daily Mail* in association with Transworld Publishers. The winning author receives a publishing deal with Transworld and a £30,000 advance.

Genres Fiction, Novels

Submission Guidelines Unpublished authors are asked to submit a manuscript of between 80,000 to 150,000 words, along with a 600 word synopsis, by post. Deadline for submissions is July.

Tips A valid entry must include the entrant's full name and contact details (including an address and telephone number) and be submitted as a hard copy with double spacing in font size 12 point 'Times New Roman'.

Dark Tales Short Story Competition
PO Box 681, Worcester, WR3 8WB
- www.darktales.co.uk

Insider Info This is a regular competition for stories of up to 3,000 words. The magazine is based around genre, fantasy and speculative fiction. The prizes are: £250 for 1st place; £50 for 2nd place; £25 for 3rd place and £5 for shortlisted entries. All winning entries are published in the magazine. The competition is open to any writer, UK or international.

Genres Short Stories

Submission Guidelines Submission guidelines are available on the website. There is a fee of £3 for non-subscribers and £1.50 for subscribers. Stories must be previously unpublished.

Tips Entrants are strongly advised to buy a copy of the magazine and look at previous winning articles. The competition is held regularly and details of upcoming deadlines are published on the website. Entries may be made by post or online.

David Berry Prize
University College London, Gower Street, London, WC1E 6BT
- 020 7387 7532
- 020 7387 7532
- royalhistsoc@ucl.ac.uk
- www.royalhistoricalsociety.org/grants.htm

Insider Info This award is sponsored by the Royal Historical Society and is presented to the writer of an outstanding essay or academic article on Scottish history. The award is offered annually and consists of £250 prize money.

Genres Essays and Articles

Submission Guidelines Submissions must be received by 30 October each year.

Tips Essays must be up to a maximum word limit of 10,000.

David Cohen Prize for Literature
14 Great Peter Street, London, SW1P 3NQ
- 0845 300 6200
- 020 7973 6590
- enquiries@artscouncil.org.uk
- www.artscouncil.org.uk

Insider Info This prize is sponsored by the Arts Council England and is awarded for a lifetime's achievement in British Literature. The award is presented every 2 years (odd years). An award of £40,000 is provided by the David Cohen Family Charitable Trust for the winner and an additional £12,500 (the Clarissa Luard Award) is provided by the Arts Council for the winner to give to an organisation of their choice that helps develop young writers and readers.

Tips Submissions are not accepted.

The David St John Thomas Charitable Trust & Awards
PO Box 6055, Nairn, IV12 4YB
- 01667 453351
- 01667 452365
- dsjtcharitynairn@fsmail.net

Competition/Award Director Lorna Edwardson

Insider Info A range of prizes are awarded annually by the trust including the annual ghost story and love story awards, self-publishing awards, writers group anthology and poetry awards, and many others. The prize money totals around £30,000. There are various other prizes including publication in *Writer's News* magazine for certain winners.

Submission Guidelines Guidelines, categories and entry forms available via large SAE.

Tips The David St John Thomas Charitable Trust is also closely associated with *Writers' News* magazine.

The David Watt Prize
2 Eastbourne Terrace, London, W2 6LG
- 020 781 1150
- davidwattprize@riotinto.com
- www.riotinto.com

Established 1988

Insider Info Sponsored by Rio Tinto PLC. Awarded annually in memory of David Watt for an article making an outstanding contribution to national, international or global current affairs. The winner receives £10,000.

Genres Articles of not more than 5,000 words published in English in the preceding calendar year.

Submission Guidelines One entry per author. Deadline for entries is the 31st of March. Work should be published previously.

Debut Dagger
PO Box 62121, London, NW1W 9TF
- debut.dagger@thecwa.co.uk
- www.thecwa.co.uk/daggers/debut

Insider Info The Debut Dagger award is sponsored by the Crime Writer's Association. It is an award designed to help launch the careers of unpublished crime writers and is presented annually. The prize consists of £500 and two tickets to the CWA Duncan Lawrie Dagger Awards, including a night's stay for two in a hotel. All shortlisted entrants receive a selection of crime novels and professional critiques of their entries, and will also be invited to the awards dinner. The award is open to any writer who has not previously had a novel published. Previously published writers in non-crime fiction areas

(including self-published writers) should email for advice on their individual eligibility.

Genres Crime Fiction

Submission Guidelines Submissions must be received between November 1 and February 7 each year. Guidelines for submissions are available on the website. Submit the first 3,000 words and a 500–1,000 word synopsis of the rest of the novel. Include a signed entry form, information for which is on the website. There is also the facility for online entry. There is a fee of £25 per story. The novel must be previously unpublished.

Tips Crime novels only, although 'crime' can be interpreted broadly. For a style guide and advice on writing crime novels, visit the website. Winning the Debut Dagger doesn't guarantee you'll get published, but it does mean your work will be seen by leading agents and top editors.

Delphi Award for Automotive Technology Journalism
Guild of Motoring Writers, 40 Baring Road, Bournemouth, BH6 4DT
- 01202 422424
- generalsec@gomw.co.uk
- www.guildofmotoringwriters.co.uk

Insider Info This is awarded for excellence in writing technical articles in the field of motoring. The award is presented annually and the winner receives £1,000.

Genres Non-Fiction, Essays, and Articles

Submission Guidelines Articles must be previously published.

Tips Winning articles or series must be of particular interest to specialists in the field, but also be accessible and appealing to a wider readership with a more limited technical knowledge.

The Dennis Potter Screenwriting Award
BBC Broadcasting House, Whiteladies Road, Bristol, BS8 2LR
- 0117 974 7586

Established 1995

Insider Info An annual award in memory of Dennis Potter in recognition of emerging screenwriters.

Genres Scripts

Tips Submissions are usually sought from the BBC TV drama department and winners are often already fairly high profile.

The Desmond Elliott Prize
Charitable Trust, 84 Godolphin Road, London, , W12 8JW
- 020 8222 6580
- ema.manderson@googlemail.com

① www.desmondelliottprize.com

Competition/Award Director Administrator, Emma Manderson

Established 2008

Insider Info The competition is administered by Academi with the financial assistance of Cardiff Council. The competition takes place annually, with a first prize of £10,000. The competition is judged by three established poets, with one acting as a filter judge. Copyright will remain with the competitor, but Academi reserves the right to arrange the first publication or broadcast of selected poems as it sees fit. The competition is open to poets of all nationalities, they do not have to be resident in Wales.

Genres Fiction (first novels)

Submission Guidelines United Kingdom publishers may enter up to two full-length novels per imprint, with scheduled publication dates between April 2008 and April 2009. Guidelines and entry forms are available online.

Dingle Prize

5 Woodcote Green, Fleet, Hampshire, GU51 4EY

① bshs@bshs.org.uk

① www.bshs.org.uk

Established 1997

Insider Info A biennial prize sponsored by the British Society for the History of Science. It is awarded for the best book in the following categories: History of Science and Technology; and Medicine. The book must be printed in the English language. The aim is to encourage accessible writing whilst maintaining rigorous historical methods. The prize is awarded every two years (odd years), and winners receive £300.

Genres Non-Fiction

Submission Guidelines Submissions must be received by the end of February each year. Books must have been published in the preceding three years to the award. Send three hard copies to Philip Crane, Executive Secretary at the above address.

Tips Nominations are accepted by publishers only.

Dolman Best Travel Book Prize

The Authors' Club, 40 Dover Street, London, W1S 4NP

① 020 7408 5092

① 020 7408 0913

① stella@authorsclub.co.uk

Insider Info This prize was initiated by William Dolman, a former Authors' Club chairman. It is awarded for an excellent first travel book published in Great Britain. The prize is offered annually and consists of £1,000. Only British writers are eligible.

Genres Travel Literature

Submission Guidelines Submissions must be received by the end of January each year. Titles must be previously published.

Tips Contact Stella Kane at the Authors' Club for more details on how to submit.

Drama Association of Wales One-Act Playwriting Competition

The Old Library, Singleton Road, Splott, Cardiff, CF24 2ET

① 029 2045 2200

① 029 2045 2277

① teresa@dramawales.org.uk

Insider Info An open competition for one-act plays in either English or Welsh. Aims to encourage the writing of material for amateur theatre. There are usually three categories: an open category; plays for performance by a cast of 16–25 year olds; and plays the Welsh language. The competition takes place annually. Winning plays are considered for publication and the winning writers in each category receive £200.

Genres Scripts

Submission Guidelines Plays must be 20–50 minutes long and have a minimum cast of two. Contact Teresa Hennessy at the Drama Association of Wales (see above for contact details) for an application form and for details of the next competition.

The Duff Cooper Prize

54 Saint Maur Road, London, SW6 4DP

① 020 7736 3729

① 020 7731 7638

Competition/Award Director Artemis Cooper

Insider Info Awarded annually for a literary work of history, biography, politics or poetry published in English or French. The prize consists of £5,000, a magnum of champagne and a presentation copy of Duff Cooper's autobiography *Old Men Forget*.

Genres Non-Fiction, Poetry

Submission Guidelines Work must have been published by a recognised British publisher within the preceding year.

Tips Only open to entries from publishers that fulfil the criteria.

The Duke of Westminster's Medal for Military Literature

Royal United Services Institute for Defence & Security Studies, Whitehall, London, SW1A 2ET

① 020 7930 2602

① 020 7321 0943

① www.rusi.org/westminstermedal

Established 1997

Insider Info Awarded to what is deemed to be the best book published on international or national security, or the military professions. The winner will be presented with a £1,000 cash prize and a medal.
Submission Guidelines Submissions should be published or due to publish six months either side of the closing date, usually January. Send two copies of the book to Professor Michael Clarke by post.
Tips Work must be in English, but there are no restrictions as to nationality, gender or age.

The Dundee International Book Prize
City of Discovery Campaign, Econ Dev Dept, Dundee City Council, 3 City Square, Dundee, DD1 3BA

- 01382 434214
- 01382 434650
- book.prize@dundeecity.gov.uk
- www.dundeebookprize.com

Established 1996
Insider Info Sponsored by Birlinn Ltd and the University of Dundee. Normally awarded every two years. The winning writer receives £10,000 and the publication of their novel.
Genres Fiction, Novels
Submission Guidelines Deadline for entry is the beginning of March every two years. Entrants must not have had a novel previously published. Children's novels are not eligible.
Tips There are no restrictions on theme or style. Entries may be made by post or by email, although online entries have an earlier closing date; see website for details.

Dylan Thomas Prize
The Dylan Thomas Centre, Ty Llên, Somerset Place, Swansea, SA1 1RR

- 01792 474051
- 01792 463993
- tim@dylanthomasprize.com
- www.dylanthomasprize.com

Competition/Award Director Tim Prosser
Established 2004
Insider Info This prize is sponsored by the University of Wales. An award of £60,000 will be given to the winner of this prize, which was established to encourage, promote and reward exciting new writing in the English speaking world, and to celebrate the poetry and prose of Dylan Thomas. Entrants should be the author of a published book (in English) and under the age of 30 (when the work was published). Writing must be within one of the following categories: poetry, novel, collection of short stories by one author, play that has been professionally performed, a broadcast radio play or a professionally produced screenplay that has resulted

in a feature-length film. Authors need to be nominated by their publishers, or producers in the case of performance art. The award is presented every two years (odd years) and winners participate in the Dylan Thomas Festival in Swansea. There is also a short residency programme for the winner at the University of Texas, Austin. An international panel is appointed for each prize.
Genres Fiction, Poetry, Scripts, Novels, Short Stories, Story Collections
Submission Guidelines Submissions must be received by 28 April each odd year. Guidelines and entry forms are available with self addressed SAE. There is an entry fee of £100. Submissions must be previously published.
Tips The judges are looking to reward an outstanding use of language.

Earlyworks Press Competitions
Creative Media Centre, 45 Robertson Street, Hastings, Sussex, TN34 1HL

- www.earlyworkspress.co.uk

Insider Info Earlyworks Press competitions offer at least three competitions a year and publish three resulting anthologies. First prize in each competition is usually £100 and publication in the anthology. Runners up are published and receive a complimentary copy of the book. Copyright remains with the author although Earlyworks Press retains the right to publish entries in their anthologies. Writers must be over 16.
Submission Guidelines Submission guidelines are available on the website. Fee is dependant on word count, see website for details. Work must be previously unpublished and must not be simultaneously entered for other competitions.
Tips Details of each new competition are published on the website, along with comprehensive terms and conditions.

Eleanor Farjeon Award
Children's Book Circle, 338 Euston Road, London, NW1 3BH

- www.childrensbookcircle.org.uk

Established 1965
Insider Info This award is sponsored by the Children's Book Circle and is awarded to a teacher, publisher, bookseller, librarian, writer, artist or other who has made an outstanding contribution to the world of children's books. The award is presented annually and the winner receives a cash sum of around £750.
Tips Nominations are from members of the Children's Book Circle only.

The Elizabeth Goudge Trophy

✉ jan@jan-jones.co.uk

🌐 www.rna-uk.org

Insider Info An annual competition sponsored by the Romantic Novelists' Association. Writers are invited to submit entries based on a romance theme set by the Chairman. The winner is presented with a silver bowl at the conference.

Genres Fiction

Submission Guidelines Work should be previously unpublished.

Tips Open to RNA members only.

The Elizabeth Longford Prize for Historical Biography

The Society of Authors, 84 Drayton Gardens, London, SW10 9SB

☎ 020 7373 6642

☎ 020 7373 5768

✉ info@societyofauthors.org

🌐 www.societyofauthors.org

Established 2003

Insider Info Sponsored by Flora Fraser and Peter Soros. Founded in memory of Elizabeth Long, a biographer, the prize is awarded annually to the best historical biography in the preceding year. The winner receives £5,000.

Genres Biography

Submission Guidelines Work should be published previously.

Tips No unsolicited submissions.

The Ellis Peters Award

PO Box 273, Borehamwood, WD6 2XA

✉ info@thecwa.co.uk

🌐 www.thecwa.co.uk

Established 1999

Insider Info Sponsored by the Crime Writers Association, the Estate of Ellis Peters, and publishers Hodder Headline and Little, Brown. Awarded annually for a crime novel with a historical background. The setting may be any period up to the 1960s. Winners receive £3,000 and an ornamental dagger, the judging panel is made up of the previous year's winner, historians and reviewers.

Genres Historical crime novels

Submission Guidelines Work should be previously published.

Tips Submissions by publishers only.

The Encore Award

84 Drayton Gardens, London, SW10 9SB

☎ 020 7373 6642

☎ 020 7373 5768

✉ info@societyofauthors.org

🌐 www.societyofauthors.org

Established 1990

Insider Info Sponsored by the Society of Authors. Awarded every two years (odd years) for the best 2nd published novel for a writer from the previous two years. The winner receives £10,000. Writers must be a British or Commonwealth citizen.

Genres Novels

Submission Guidelines Deadline for entry is the end of November int he year prior to the competition. Guidelines and entry forms available on the website. Entries must have been published in the UK in the previous two years.

Tips Entries from publishers only.

Enid McLeod Prize

2 Dovetail Studios, 465 Battersea Park Road, London, SW11 4LR

☎ 020 7924 3511

✉ execsec@francobritishsociety.org.uk

🌐 www.francobritishsociety.org.uk

Competition/Award Director Kate Brayn

Established 1982

Insider Info This award is sponsored by the Franco-British Society and is awarded to the writer of a book that is deemed to have contributed the most to Franco-British understanding. The award is presented annually and the winner receives £250. Any book published in English, and in the UK by a British or Commonwealth writer is eligible. Translations are also considered.

Genres Non-Fiction

Submission Guidelines Titles must be previously published between 1 January and 31 December that year.

Tips Submissions are accepted from publishers only. Contact the Franco-British Society for more information.

Envoi International Open Poetry Competition

Meirion House, Glan yr afon, Tanygrisiau, Burton-on-Trent, Gwynedd, LL41 3SU

🌐 www.cinnamonpress.com/envoi/competitions.htm

Insider Info This competition is sponsored by *Envoi Magazine* and is a competition for poems of up to 40 lines written in any style. The competition takes place three times a year. The prizes are: £150 for 1st place; £100 for 2nd place; and £50 for 3rd place. Poems are published in the magazine and complimentary copies are offered to all winners. Three runners up receive a subscription to the magazine.

Genres Poetry

Submission Guidelines Submissions must be received by 20 February, 20 June and 20 October each year. Submission guidelines are available on the website. There is a fee of £3 per poem and £12 for five poems. Poems must be previously unpublished and must not have been submitted to any other competitions.

Tips Accepts postal entries only.

The Eric Gregory Trust Fund Awards
The Society of Authors, 84 Drayton Gardens, London, SW10 9SB
- 020 7373 6642
- 020 7373 5768
- info@societyofauthors.org
- www.societyofauthors.org

Insider Info Prizes for young poets in memory of Eric Gregory. Prize money totals £24,000. Winners will be invited to give a reading at the prestigious Ledbury Poetry Festival at the discretion of the Trustees, and may also be invited to take part in an event hosted and promoted by the renowned Poetry Society. Entrants must be British by birth (excluding Eire and British colonies) and be under the age of 30.

Genres Poetry

Submission Guidelines Entry forms are available on the website. Works may be unpublished or published previously.

Tips The work submitted may be drama-poems or belles-lettres as well as a volume of poetry. No more than 30 poems should be submitted. Poems should be submitted on numbered sheets of A4 paper with a contents page that states the author's name. Submissions of unpublished poems should not be stapled or bound together. If you would like an acknowledgement and/or the return of your poems you need to provide SAEs.

Financial Times & Goldman Sachs Business Book of the Year Award
1 Southwark Bridge, London, SE1 9HL
- 020 7873 3000
- 020 7873 3072
- bookaward@ft.com
- www.ft.com/bookaward

Established 2005

Insider Info Awarded to the best business book published during the previous year. Winning books will have presented an exciting insight into modern business issues – including management, finance and economics. The award is presented annually and winners receive £30,000 and shortlisted writers receive £5,000 each. The judging panel is made up of business experts from around the world.

Genres Business Non-Fiction

Submission Guidelines Submissions must be received by 30 June each year. Titles must be previously published between 31 October in the previous year and 1 November in the current year.

Tips Submissions are accepted from publishers only.

Fish Awards
Fish Publishing, Durrus, Bantry, Co. Cork, Republic of Ireland
- info@fishpublishing.com
- www.fishpublishing.com

Insider Info There are two main Fish fiction prizes: The annual Fish Short Story Prize, closing 30th Nov, with a prize fund of €5,000, as well as publication in the annual Fish Anthology of Short Fiction for the best ten as chosen by the independent Judges. Entry on-line is €20 (£18), or by post for €25 (£22). Results announced 17th March and the anthology is launched in July. Word limit 5,000.

The Fish One Page Prize, closing 20th March, with a prize fund of €2,000 and an entry fee of €12 Euro or £10. Word limit is 250 and the best ten will be published in the Fish Anthology.

For other competitions, including poetry, and for information on the Fish Critique and Editorial Services, and for full details on all prizes, see the web site. Fish Publishing is supported by the Arts Council of Ireland.

Genres Fiction

Submission Guidelines Submission guidelines are available on the website.

The Forward Prizes for Poetry
Colman Getty PR, 28 Windmill Street, London, W1T 2JJ
- 020 7631 2666
- 020 7631 2699

Established 1991

Insider Info Awards for poetry published in three categories: poetry collection of the year; first collection; and single poem. Awarded annually, winners receive: £10,000 for best collection; £5,000 for best first collection; and £1,000 for best single poem.

Genres Poetry

Submission Guidelines Work should be published previously.

Tips No submissions. Nominations may be made by publishers and editors.

Frank O'Connor International Short Story Award
The Munster Literature Centre, Frank O'Connor House, 84 Douglas Street, Co. Cork, Republic of Ireland
- 00353 21 431 2955

munsterlit@eircom.net

www.munsterlit.ie

Insider Info Awarded for the best collection of short stories in English published anywhere in the world during the previous year. The award is presented at The Frank O'Connor International Short Story Festival. It is presented annually and the winner will receive 35,000 Euros (split between author and translator for translations). Any living author is eligible.

Genres Translations and Story Collections

Submission Guidelines Submissions must be received by the end of March each year. The short stories must be previously published between September the previous year and August of the current year. Submit seven copies of the book or proofs and details of publication for books published after the closing date.

Tips Submissions accepted by publishers only.

The Frogmore Poetry Prize
18 Nevill Road, Lewes, East Sussex, BN7 1PF

07751 251689

www.frogmorepress.co.uk

Established 1987

Insider Info Sponsored by *The Frogmore Papers* magazine – an annual open competition for poems no longer than 40 lines. The overall winner will receive 200 guineas and a two year subscription to *The Frogmore Papers*. 2nd and 3rd place winners receive 75 and 50 guineas respectively and a year's subscription to the papers. All winning and shortlisted poems will be published in the magazine. Copyright remains with the authors, but the Frogmore Press reserves the right to publish all poems shortlisted for the prize.

Genres Poetry

Submission Guidelines Deadline for entry is the end of May. Guidelines available on the website. Entry fee is £2 per poem. Work should be previously unpublished.

Tips All poetry submissions must be in English.

Geoffrey Faber Memorial Prize
3 Queen Square, London, WC1N 3AU

020 7465 0045

020 7465 0043

belinda.matthews@faber.co.uk

Established 1963

Insider Info This award is sponsored by Faber & Faber Ltd, and is awarded in alternate (even) years for a work of prose or poetry by a writer under 40. Special attention is paid to its literary merit. The winner receives £1,000. Writers must be a resident of the UK, Republic of Ireland or South Africa.

Genres Fiction and Poetry

Submission Guidelines Entries must have been published in the UK in the preceding two years.

Tips Entry is by nomination only, no submissions.

George Devine Award
9 Lower Mall, Hammersmith, London, W6 9DJ

Competition/Award Director Christine Smith

Insider Info A prize in memory of the former artistic director of the Royal Court Theatre, awarded to a new playwright. Prize money is usually £10,000.

Genres Scripts

Submission Guidelines Submissions must be received by the end of March each year. Contact Christine Smith in writing for details.

Tips Submissions are welcomed from individuals.

The George Orwell Memorial Prize
Blackwell Publishing, 9600 Garsington Road, Oxford, OX4 2DQ

01865 476255

01865 471255

Established 1993

Insider Info Sponsored by the George Orwell Memorial Fund and *The Political Quarterly* journal. Founded in memory of George Orwell to recognise excellence in political writing. The prize is split into two categories: Books; and Journalism. Awarded annually, the winners in each category receive £1,000 each.

Genres Fiction, Non-Fiction, Articles

Submission Guidelines Work should be published previously.

Tips Political writing can include politics, economics, social studies, cultural studies and fictional writing. Particular attention is paid to work that treats the writing as art and makes it accessible to the general public.

The Gladstone History Book Prize
University College London, Gower Street, London, WC1E 6BT

020 7387 7532

020 7387 7532

royalhistsoc@ucl.ac.uk

www.royalhistoricalsociety.org

Established 1998

Insider Info Sponsored by the Royal Historical Society. Awarded annually for an original work of historical research and writing on any subject other than an aspect of British history. The work must be the writer's first sole publication. The winner receives £1,000. Writers should be normally resident in the UK.

Genres Non-Fiction

Submission Guidelines Entry deadline is end of December. Work should have been published during the previous calendar year.

Tips Nominations from publishers only.

Golden PEN Award for Lifetime Distinguished Service to Literature
6–8 Amwell Street, London, EC1R 1UQ
- 020 7713 0023
- 020 7837 7838
- enquiries@englishpen.org
- www.englishpen.org

Insider Info This award is administered by English PEN, and is awarded to an established writer who is deemed by their peers to have made an outstanding contribution to the literary world. The award is offered annually. The award is voted for by members of the PEN committee.

Tips Nominations come from English PEN only. The award is normally awarded to senior writers with a long publishing history.

Goss First Novel Award
c/o Tourist Information Centre, Tunsgate, Guildford, GU1 3QT
- 01483 444334
- assistant@guildfordbookfestival.co.uk
- www.guildfordbookfestival.co.uk

Insider Info The award is adminstered by Guildford Book Festival and supported by The Country Club. It is awarded for the best first novel published in the year between Guildford Book Festivals, usually held in October. The winner receives £2,500. Entry is open to any writer whose first novel was published within the given time frame.

Genres Novels

Submission Guidelines Submissions must be previously published.

Tips Accepts submissions from publishers and agents only.

Grace Dieu Writers' Circle
c/o Rockside, 139 London Road, Coalville, Leicestershire, LE67 3JE
- 01530 450203
- 01530 811495
- kshatri@ntlworld.com

Contact Competition Organiser, Tony Gutteridge

Established 2004

Insider Info Annual short story and poetry competition to promote and challenge writing, and to provide reward both financially and by way of publication. £1 from each book sold will be donated to Rainbows Children's Hospice in Leicestershire. Short story prizes are £200/£100/£50/£25/£15, poetry prizes are £100/£75/£50/£25/£15. Winners agree to publication in Grace Dieu's anthology and on the website. All entries must be written in English observing usual competition rules, and competition is open to all.

Genres Fiction, Poetry

Submission Guidelines Submissions should be made by February 28 each year. Accepts simultaneous submissions and submissions from previously published authors. Entry fee for short story competition is £5, poetry fee is £3. Reduction for multiple entries (see website for further information). Submitted material must be unpublished.

The Guardian Children's Fiction Award
119 Farringdon Road, London, EC1R 3ER
- 020 7239 9694
- 020 7239 9933
- books@guardian.co.uk
- http://books.guardian.co.uk

Established 1967

Insider Info Awarded annually to the best children's fiction book for children aged 7+. Picture books are not eligible. The winner receives £1,500. The award is decided by the *Guardian* Children's Book Editor and a selection of authors. Writers must be a resident of Britain or the Commonwealth.

Genres Children's Fiction

Submission Guidelines Work should be published in the UK, in the year preceding the award.

Tips Submissions are usually made by publishers.

Guardian First Book Award
119 Farringdon Road, London, EC1R 3ER
- 020 7239 9694
- books@guardian.co.uk
- http://books.guardian.co.uk

Contact The Literary Editor

Established 1999

Insider Info Awarded for the best first book in the year preceding the award. Any type of book – fiction or non-fiction, is eligible except academic texts, children's books, television or radio tie-ins, educational books, directories and reprints. The award is offered annually and the winner receives £10,000 and is offered an advertising package across *The Guardian* and *The Observer*. This award is open to books in English that have been published in the UK.

Genres Fiction and Non-fiction

Submission Guidelines Submissions must be previously published.

Tips Accepts submissions from publishers only.

The Guild of Food Writers' Awards
255 Kent House Road, Beckenham, Kent, BR3 1JQ
- 020 8659 0422
- awards@gfw.co.uk
- www.gfw.co.uk

Established 1997

Insider Info *The Jeremy Round Award for Best First Book.*This award, which commemorates Jeremy Round, is given to a writer of any age or level of experience, provided that this is his or her first cookery book, or book about food.

*Food Book of the Year.*This may be biographical, historical, topographical; a guidebook, encyclopedia or compendium, even a technical handbook. Recipes, if they form part of the work, should serve to illuminate the text, rather than lead it.

*Cookery Book of the Year.*Recipes and, if appropriate, the practicalities of cooking should be the main focus. The subject may be any cuisine, historical period, specific ingredient or diet.

*Food Journalist of the Year.*This award is given to the writer of the best food-related articles published in a magazine, newspaper or newspaper supplement. Five pieces should be submitted; they may contain recipes, but recipes should not form the bulk of the text.

*The Evelyn Rose Award for Cookery Journalist of the Year.*This award was renamed in honour of Evelyn Rose, a former chair of the Guild. The award goes to the writer of the best recipe-led articles, columns or pages published in a magazine, newspaper, newspaper supplement or on the internet. Five such features should be submitted.

Genres Non-Fiction, Articles, Television or Radio Programmes/Websites

Submission Guidelines Deadline for entry is in March each year. Forms are available on the Guild's website. Work should be published previously, between January 1 and December 31.

Hans Christian Andersen Awards
British Section of IBBY, PO Box 20875, London, SE22 9WQ
- 020 8299 1641
- ann@lazim.demon.co.uk
- www.ibby.org

Established 1956

Insider Info This award is sponsored by IBBY and is awarded to a living writer and illustrator who is seen to have made a lasting contribution to children's literature. It is the highest international recognition in the field of children's books and her Majesty Queen Margrethe II of Denmark is the Patron. The award is offered every two years (even years). The prize consists of a gold medal and a diploma, presented during the biennial IBBY Congress.

Genres Illustrated Children's Books

Submission Guidelines Submissions must be previously published.

Tips Writer and illustrator prizes may be awarded separately, but both must have an entire body of work that has influenced children's literature over a period of time.

Harry Bowling Prize
Storytracks, 16 St Briac Way, Bystock, Exmouth, Devon, EX8 5RN
- www.harrybowlingprize.net

Established 2000

Insider Info An award for the best opening chapter and synopsis of a novel set in London. In memory of Harry Bowling, a successful writer who set much of his work in London. Held every two (even) years, the overall winner receives £1,000 and runners up receive £100 each. Judges include Jane Morpeth (Harry Bowling's Editor at Hodder Headline) and Laura Longrigg (his Agent at MBA). Entrants must not have published any adult works of fiction before, however they may have published short stories, scripts for television and radio, non-fiction and children's fiction and non-fiction.

Genres Fiction

Submission Guidelines Submissions should be received by March 31 each year. Guidelines are available online. Entry fee of £10.

Tips Submit up to 5,000 words and a 500 word synopsis by post, along with an entry form (available from the website), entry fee and SAE if receipt is required. A list of criteria that the judges are looking for is published on the website – read this thoroughly before entering.

The Hawthornden Prize
42a Hays Mews, Berkeley Square, London, W1X 7RU

Insider Info Sponsored by the Hawthornden Trust. Awarded annually for what is deemed to be the best and most imaginative work of literature published in the UK in the preceding year.

Submission Guidelines Work should be published previously.

Tips No entries, winners are chosen from nominations.

Henrietta Branford Writing Competition
c/o Kate Jones, Glebe House, Weobly, Hereford, HR4 8SD
- 01544 318901
- youngwriter@enterprise.net

🌐 www.branfordboaseaward.org.uk

Insider Info An annual competition for young writers up to the age of 19. Entrants must download two opening paragraphs from the website and finish the story in up to 1,500 words. Winners of the 2007 award were invited to meet Jacqueline Wilson at the Branford Boase Award party in London, and received copies of the shortlisted books for the main awards. The competition is judged by Kate Jones, director of *Young Writer Magazine*, to which you should also send entries at the above postal or email addresses. Writers may enter from all over the world.

Genres Short Stories

Submission Guidelines Submissions should be made by May each year. Further guidelines available on the website. Submission should be unpublished.

Tips Although there is a 1,500 word limit, stories that are much shorter are welcomed.

The Hessell-Tiltman Prize for Lyrical Poetry

6–8 Amwell Street, London, EC1R 1UQ

📞 020 7713 0023
📠 020 7837 7838
✉ enquiries@englishpen.org
🌐 www.englishpen.org

Established 2002

Insider Info Sponsored by English PEN. Awarded annually for a history text that is deemed to have a wide audience appeal. The author of the winning book receives £3,000.

Genres Non-Fiction.

Submission Guidelines Work should be published previously.

Tips Submissions by publishers only.

The Ian Fleming Steel Dagger

PO Box 273, Boreham Wood, WD6 2XA

✉ info@thecwa.co.uk
🌐 www.thecwa.co.uk

Established 2002

Insider Info Sponsored by the Crime Writers' Association and Ian Fleming (Glidrose) Publications Ltd. An annual award given for the best thriller novel published in the preceding year. The prize consists of an ornamental steel dagger and £2,000.

Genres Crime/Thriller Novels

Submission Guidelines Work should be published previously.

Tips Submissions by publishers only.

The Independent Foreign Fiction Prize

The Literature Department, Arts Council England, 14 Great Peter Street, London, SW1P 3NQ

📞 020 7973 5204
📠 020 7973 6983
✉ maddy.pickard@artscouncil.org.uk
🌐 www.artscouncil.org.uk

Insider Info Awarded annually for a contemporary work of fiction in translation. It is one of the only awards to honour the writer and translator in equal measure. The winning writer and translator receive £5,000 each. The judging panel changes each year. The author must be living at the time of publication and the work must have been published in the UK.

Genres Translations

Submission Guidelines Deadline for entry is end of December each year. Guidelines and entry forms are available on the website. Work should be published previously, between January 1 and December 31.

Tips Although the deadline is the end of each year, entries are accepted and encouraged much earlier than this. Send seven copies to Bethany King, Administrator.

The International Dagger

PO Box 273, Borehamwood, WD6 2XA

✉ info@thecwa.co.uk
🌐 www.thecwa.co.uk

Established 2006

Insider Info Sponsored by the Crime Writers Association and Duncan Lawrie Private Bank. Awarded annually to the year's best crime novel translated into English from another language. Formerly the Gold and Silver Daggers.

Submission Guidelines Work should be published previously.

Tips formerly known as the Duncan Lawrie International Dagger. Submissions by publishers only.

The International IMPAC Dublin Literary Award

Dublin City Library & Archive, 138–144 Pearse Street, Dublin 2, Republic of Ireland

📞 00353 1 674 4802
📠 00353 1 674 4879
✉ literaryaward@dublincity.ie
🌐 www.impacdublinaward.ie

Competition/Award Director Eileen Hendrick

Established 1994

Insider Info Sponsored by Dublin City Council and IMPAC. Awarded every two years (odd years) to a work of fiction in English, including translations into English. The winning writer receives €100,000 and a crystal trophy. If the book is a translation, a €25,000 share goes to the translator.

Genres Fiction, Novels, Translations

Submission Guidelines Deadline for entries is August. Work should be previously published – see the website for further details and submission guidelines.

Tips Nominations are to be made by libraries in capital cities all over the world.

International Playwrighting Festival
Warehouse Theatre, Dingwall Road, Croydon, CR0 2NF
- info@warehousetheatre.co.uk
- www.warehousetheatre.co.uk

Established 1986

Insider Info An annual competition for playwrights from all over the world aimed at encouraging new writing for the theatre. Scripts are invited for submission and later in the year four winning plays are performed at the festival. The festival is twinned with Premio Candoni – Arta Terme in Italy.

Genres Scripts

Submission Guidelines Submissions should be made by June 30 each year. Guidelines and entry forms are available on the website. Plays must not have been previously produced, although amateur performances do not count.

Tips There are no limitations to cast size or restrictions on theme, although scripts should be roughly 50–100 pages long, or a full length, completed play. Translations are eligible but adaptations are not. Contact Rose Marie Vernon for more information.

ISG (Cilip)/Nielsen BookDate Reference Awards
c/o Katharine Spackman, County Reference and Information Librarian, Cultural & Adult Learning Services, Oxfordshire County Council
- 01865 810210
- isgrefawards@cilip.org.uk
- www.cilip.org.uk

Established 1970

Insider Info Annual competition, sponsored by Nielsen Bookscan, consisting of three awards to mark achievements in reference works: The Besterman McColvin award for first editions of print titles; The Besterman McColvin award for new electronic publications; and The Walford award for contribution to bibliography. For the Besterman/McColvin awards, the prizes consist of £500 cash, a medal and a certificate. For the Walford award, the winner receives £500 and a certificate. Entries are judged by members of ISG, along with the multimedia Information and Technology Group for the electronic award. The Besterman/McColvin nominations must have been already published in the UK. The Walford nominees do not need to be resident in the UK.

Genres Non-Fiction

Submission Guidelines Submissions should be made by January 31 each year. Guidelines available on website. Submissions should have been published between January 1 and December 31 of the previous year.

Tips Works are judged on the scope of the content, the layout and quality of information and knowledge, the index and references, look and feel, innovation and whether it represents value for money.

James Cameron Award
City University Department of Journalism, Northampton Square, London, EC1V 0HB
- 020 7040 8221
- 020 7040 8594

Established 1985

Insider Info An annual award celebrating the UK journalist who is judged to have made an outstanding contribution to the media in the tradition of foreign correspondent, columnist and author James Cameron.

Tips This is not an open competition.

James Tait Black Memorial Prizes
Department of English Literature, The University of Edinburgh, David Hume Tower, George Square, Edinburgh, EH8 9JX
- 0131 650 3620
- 0131 650 6898
- www.englit.ed.ac.uk/jtbinf.htm

Established 1919

Insider Info Annual award with two prizes awarded for outstanding works of fiction or biography written in English. The winners in each category receive £10,000. The same writer may win both awards, but never the same award twice. Open to writers of any nationality.

Genres Fiction, Biography

Submission Guidelines Submissions should be made by December 1 of each year. Simultaneous submissions accepted. An information pamphlet may be downloaded from the website. Submissions should have been published between January 1 and December 31 of the previous year.

Tips Submissions are invited from publishers. Send one copy of the book as soon after its publication as possible, stating the exact date of publication. The award may also be presented to books that have not been submitted but have caught the judge's eye, although this is rare.

Jerwood Aldeburgh First Collection Prize
The Cut, 9 New Cut, Halesworth, Suffolk, IP19 8BY

☎ 01986 835950

📠 01986 874524

✉ info@thepoetrytrust.org

🌐 www.thepoetrytrust.org

Insider Info An annual competition, sponsored by The Poetry Trust, awarded for the best first poetry collection published in Britain or the Republic of Ireland in the previous year. The winner receives £3,000, one week's paid writing time in Aldeburgh, and an opportunity to read their poetry at the Aldeburgh Poetry Festival of the following year.

Genres Poetry

Submission Guidelines Submissions should be made by July 31 of each year. Submissions must have been published between August 31 and July 1 of the previous year.

Tips Submissions are invited from poets and publishers. Submit three bound copies along with publication details.

The Joan Hessayon New Writers' Scheme Award

✉ gillroger@tiscali.co.uk

🌐 www.rna-uk.org

Competition/Award Director Roger Sanderson

Insider Info Sponsored by the Romantic Novelists' Association. Awarded annually for a debut published romance novel from a member of their New Writers' Scheme. The writer must still be a member of the New Writers' Scheme at the time of the award and the winning novel in particular must have been developed through the scheme.

Genres Fiction, Novels

Submission Guidelines The book must either be published or under contract with a publisher.

Tips Any unpublished romantic novelist may apply to join the New Writers' Scheme. Entry forms are available from the website and fees are £90. Members will have access to all the events and services of the RNA and will be entitled to a manuscript appraisal service.

John D. Criticos Prize

The Hellenic Centre, 16–18 Paddington Street, London, W1U 5AS

Competition/Award Director Mr George Rodopoulos

Established 1996

Insider Info An annual award, sponsored by The London Hellenic Society, awarded to an artist, writer, or researcher for a book on an aspect of Hellenic culture. Prize money totals £10,000.

Genres Non-Fiction

Tips Particular areas of interest are archaeology, art, history and literature. Submissions are welcome from both individuals and publishers.

The John Dryden Translation Competition

School of Literature and Creative Writing, University of East Anglia, Norwich, NR4 7TJ

✉ transcomp@uea.ac.uk

🌐 www.bcla.org

Established 1983

Insider Info Sponsored by the British Comparative Literature Association and the British Centre for Literary Translation. Awarded annually for unpublished literary translations from any language into English. This can include prose, poetry or drama from any era. Winners will have their work published on the website, and extracts from winning entries may be published in the *Comparative Critical Studies* Journal. Judges include: Peter France, Editor of *The Oxford Guide to Literature in English Translation*; Stuart Gillespie, Editor of *Translation and Literature*; Amanda Hopkinson, Director of the British Centre for Literary Translation; and Elinor Shaffer, former Editor of *Comparative Criticism*. First prize: £350; second prize: £200; third prize: £100; other entries may receive commendations.

Genres Translations

Submission Guidelines Deadline for entries is February. Entry fee is £7 per entry. Work should be previously unpublished.

Tips Writers may submit a maximum of three entries each, none of which may have been previously entered for competitions or been published.

John Llewellyn Rhys Prize

Book House, 45 East Hill, London, SW18 2QZ

☎ 020 8516 2972

📠 020 8516 2978

✉ tarryn@booktrust.org.uk

🌐 www.booktrust.org.uk

Contact Tarryn McKay

Established 1942

Insider Info An annual competition, administered by Booktrust, awarded for a work of either fiction, non-fiction, poetry or drama by a British or Commonwealth writer aged 35 or under at the time of publication. The award is in memory of John Llewellyn Rhys, a young author killed in WWII. The winning author receives £5,000. Shortlisted authors receive £500 each. Although the authors may be from any Commonwealth country, the book must be in English (translations are not eligible), and published in the UK by a UK publisher.

Genres Fiction, Non-Fiction, Poetry, Drama

Submission Guidelines Submissions must be published during the year of the prize.

Tips Publisher submissions only.

The John Whiting Award

14 Great Peter Street, London, SW1P 3NQ

☎ 020 7973 6480

🌐 www.artscouncil.org.uk

Established 1965

Insider Info Sponsored by the Arts Council England. Awarded for a new play that bears reference to contemporary society, whilst being innovative in writing style. The winner receives £6,000.

Genres Scripts

Tips The award may be given to a writer who has had some previous involvement with the Arts Council, such as winning a previous grant or award, or having their play produced in an Arts Council-subsidised theatre.

Katharine Briggs Folklore Award

c/o The Warburg Institute, Woburn Square, London, WC1H 0AB

☎ 020 7862 8564

🌐 www.folklore-society.com

Insider Info An annual competition, sponsored by the Folklore Society, created to encourage the study and publication of folklore in Britain and Ireland, and to commemorate the life and work of Katharine Mary Briggs (1898–1980; Society president 1969–1972). The prize consists of an engraved goblet and £200. There are three judges, one of whom is the Society's President, Vice-President or Publications Officer. Open to all books in English having their first publication in the United Kingdom and/or Republic of Ireland.

Genres Non-Fiction

Submission Guidelines Submissions should be made by May 31 each year. Guidelines available on the website. Submissions must have been published between June 1 and May 31 of the previous year.

Tips Folklore can include all aspects of traditional and popular culture, narrative, beliefs, customs and folk arts, including studies with a literary, anthropological, linguistic, sociological or geographical slant. Entries are welcomed from both writers and publishers, as long as they meet all the criteria. Submit four hard copies, along with an application form, to the Convenor at the above address.

Keats-Shelley Prize

Bedford House, 76a Bedford Street, Leamington Spa, Warwickshire, CV32 5DT

📧 hello@keats-shelley.co.uk

🌐 www.keats-shelley.co.uk

Competition/Award Director Chairman, Harriet Cullen

Established 1998

Insider Info An annual competition sponsored by Barclays Bank PLC, The School of English, University of St Andrew's and The Cowley Foundation. The award is in two categories: poems that take their inspiration from the style of the romantic poets; and essays on the life and work of Keats or Shelley. The specific theme for the poetry category is chosen by the judges each year. The winners and runners up in each category receive a share of £3,000. The competition is open to anyone, although it tends to be heavily promoted through universities.

Genres Poetry, Essays

Submission Guidelines Submissions should be made by June 30 each year. Simultaneous submissions accepted.

Tips Essays of 2,000–3,000 words (including quotations) may be on any aspect of the life or work of John Keats, P.B. Shelley, Mary Shelley or Lord Byron. Poems may be up to 50 lines long. For an information leaflet, contact Sandra McDevitt at the above address.

Kelpies Prize

15 Harrison Gardens, Edinburgh, EH11 1SH

☎ 0131 337 2372

☎ 0131 347 9919

🌐 www.florisbooks.co.uk/kelpiesprize

Insider Info An annual competition, sponsored by Floris Books, for the best unpublished novel for children aged 9–12 set entirely, or mainly, in Scotland. Winners receive a cash prize and their novel will be published in the Kelpies series by Floris Books. Open to any writer, but the book must be set in Scotland. Writers may have been published before but the winning entry must not have been.

Genres Fiction, Novels, Older Children/Young Teenage Novels

Submission Guidelines Submissions should be made by February of each year. Guidelines are available on the website.

Tips The stories must appeal to both boys and girls within the relevant age group. Novels with animals as main characters and romantic novels are not generally recommended.

Kent & Sussex Poetry Society Open Competition

📧 info@kentandsussexpoetrysociety.org

🌐 www.kentandsussexpoetrysociety.org

Insider Info Annual international competition, with £1,350 total prize money. Submissions limited to 40 lines. Different, well known and respected judge each year. All entries should be submitted anonymously, and will be read by the judge. First prize is £700, with second and third prizes of £250 and £100. Four runners-up will each receive £75 and all winners will be published in the competition anthology.

Genres Poetry

Submission Guidelines Submissions should be made by January 31 each year. Simultaneous submissions accepted, but submitted pieces must be previously unpublished. Enter via the website or write to the competition organiser.

Kerry Group Irish Fiction Award
Writer's Week, 24 The Square, Listowel, Co. Kerry, Republic of Ireland
- 00353 682 1074
- 00353 682 2893
- info@writersweek.ie
- www.writersweek.ie

Insider Info Annual competition, sponsored by the Kerry Group PLC, awarded to a published fiction book by an Irish writer. The results are linked in with the Writers Week festival in Listowel. The winner receives €15,000.

Genres Fiction

Submission Guidelines Submissions must be previously published. See the website for further details.

Tips Details of other competitions that run with each festival appear on the website.

The Kim Scott Walwyn Prize
Booktrust, Book House, 45 East Hill, London, SW18 2QZ
- 020 8516 2960
- 020 8516 2978
- helen@booktrust.org.uk
- www.booktrust.org.uk

Insider Info An annual award to celebrate the achievements of women in publishing, in memory of Kim Scott Walwyn, former Director of Publishing at Oxford University Press. The prize is presented to an individual who is deemed to have made an outstanding professional contribution to the publishing industry over a period of time. The winner receives £3,000. The judges are a panel of female professionals in the publishing industry including agents, editors and broadcasters.

Submission Guidelines Deadline for entry is March. Guidelines are available on the website.

Tips Nominations may be made by the entrants themselves, or by sponsors. Email entries are encouraged – see the website for details of how to apply and what to include. Winners may be from any area of the publishing industry, including editorial, marketing, design, sales and production, and should show potential for future achievements as well as substantial existing career successes.

Kraszna-Krausz Book Awards
The National Media Museum, Bradford, West Yorkshire, BD1 1NQ
- awards@kraszna-krausz.org.uk
- www.kraszna-krausz.org.uk/book-awards

Established 1985

Insider Info Annual awards that alternate between being for books on photography and books on the moving image. Books may be about any technical or creative aspect of these areas. Books may have been published in any country and be written in any language.

Genres Non-Fiction

Submission Guidelines Submissions should be made by December of each year, and must be previously published.

Tips Nominations from publishers only. Entry forms and more details are available on the website.

Lakeland Book of the Year Awards
Windermere Road, Staveley, Cumbria, LA8 9PL
- 01539 825052
- 01539 825076
- slindsay@cumbriatourism.org
- www.golakes.co.uk

Contact Coordinator, Sheila Lindsay
Established 1984

Insider Info Annual competition run by Cumbria Tourism. This year celebrates 25 years of the Lakeland Book of the Year Awards which are now established as a prestigious event on the literary calendar. Authors (be they first-time or previously published) and publishers are encouraged to enter. Last year's awards saw a large number of entries all competing for the prestigious Hunter Davies Prize of The Lakeland Book of the Year. In addition to The Hunter Davies Prize for the Book of the Year there are five further categories. Prize is £100, plus certificate and publicity for each category.

Submission Guidelines Submissions should be made by March 9 each year. Simultaneous submissions are accepted. Submissions must have been published between January and December of the previous year.

Leaf Books Writing Competitions
GTi Suite, Valleys Innovations Centre, Navigation Park, Abercynon, Wales, CF45 4SN
- 029 2081 0726
- contact@leafbooks.co.uk
- www.leafbooks.co.uk

Competition/Award Director Sam Burns
Established 2005

Insider Info Ongoing competitions for Fiction, Short Stories, Micro-fiction and Poetry. Each competition is run in order to get the winning entries into print.

Prize consists of publication in a Leaf book and £100–200. Judged by named judges, or a panel of readers. Rights to submitted material remains with the author upon entry. Competition open to any writer.

Genres Fiction, Poetry, Short Stories, Micro-fiction
Submission Guidelines Guidelines and entry form available via SAE. Entry fee varies. Work should be previously unpublished.
Tips Read the guidelines on the website.

Legend Writing Award

39 Emmanuel Road, Hastings, East Sussex, TN34 3LB

- ⓦ www.legendwritingaward.com

Established 2001

Insider Info An annual open competition for short stories of less than 2,000 words. Stories may be on any theme but children's stories and poetry are not accepted. Prizes consist of: 1st £500; 2nd £250; 3rd £100; and three runners-up of £50 each. Copyright remains with the author but the work may be published in the Hastings Writers Group Anthology. The entry must not have been previously entered for any other award or competition.

Genres Short Stories

Submission Guidelines Deadline for entry is end of August. Guidelines and entry forms are available on the website. entry fee is £7 for first entry, and then £5 for each subsequent entry. Work should be previously unpublished.

Tips Postal entries only, including an entry form. They should be typed, single sided and double spaced. Legend also runs a flash fiction competition, details of which are on the website.

Lichfield & District Writers Short Story Competition

133 Park Road, Barton under Needwood, Burton on Trent, DE13 8DD

- ⓔ lichfield_writers@yahoo.co.uk
- ⓦ http://members.lycos.co.uk/lichfield_writers

Insider Info An annual open short story competition for pieces up to a maximum of 2,000 words. Prizes consist of: £125 for 1st place; £75 for 2nd place; and £25 for 3rd place. All short listed writers receive a certificate.

Genres Short Stories.

Submission Guidelines Deadline for entries is November. Guidelines available on the website. Entry fee is £3 for the first entry, £2 for subsequent entries. Work should be previously unpublished.

Tips Entrants are invited to include a further £4 per story if they would like a written appraisal. Entries should be typed and double spaced on single sided

sheets. Details of future closing dates will be published on the website.

London Press Club Awards

St Bride Institute, 14 Bride Lane, Fleet Street, London, EC4Y 8EQ

- ⓞ 020 7353 7086
- ⓞ 020 7353 7087
- ⓔ info@londonpressclub.co.uk
- ⓦ www.londonpressclub.co.uk

Insider Info Awards are presented annually across a variety of categories to celebrate British journalism and journalists. Judges are made up of industry professionals from the journalism, media and communications industry.

Tips Awards are voted for by the judging panel and do not need submissions.

London Writers Competition

Room 224a, The Town Hall, Wandsworth High Street, London, SW18 2PU

- ⓞ 020 8871 8711
- ⓞ 020 8871 7630
- ⓔ arts@wandsworth.gov.uk
- ⓦ www.wandsworth.gov.uk

Established 1977

Insider Info Sponsored by Wandsworth Council and Roehampton University. An annual competition designed to encourage people who work, live or study in London to write. The categories include poetry, story, play and fiction for children. There is a total prize fund of £5,000.

Genres Fiction, Poetry, Scripts, Children's Fiction
Submission Guidelines Work should be previously unpublished.
Tips Details of closing dates for future competitions will be published in the arts events section of the Wandsworth Council website.

Longman/History Today Book of the Year

History Today, 20 Old Compton Street, London, W1D 4TW

- ⓞ 020 7534 8000
- ⓔ p.furtado@historytoday.com
- ⓦ www.historytoday.com

Competition/Award Director Peter Furtado
Established 1993
Insider Info Awarded annually for a writer's first or second historical non-fiction book. The winner receives £1,000.
Genres Non-Fiction
Submission Guidelines Work should be published previously.
Tips Publisher submissions only.

L. Ron Hubbard's Writers of the Future Contest

PO Box 218, East Grinstead, RH19 4GH
Established 1984
Insider Info Aimed at encouraging new writing in the science fiction, and fantasy genres. The annual competition consists of four quarterly mini-contests with an annual overall winner. The 1st, 2nd and 3rd placed winners in each quarter receive £500, £375 and £250 respectively.
Genres Short Stories, Novelettes
Submission Guidelines Entrants must be previously unpublished. Short stories of up to 10,000 words and novelettes of up to 17,000 words may be submitted.
Tips Write to administrator Andrea Grant-Webb at the above address for more details. The competition no longer covers horror, and focuses solely on science fiction and fantasy.

Macmillan Prize for Children's Picture Book Illustration

Macmillan Children's Books, 20 New Wharf Road, London, N1 9RR
❶ 020 7014 6124
❷ 020 7014 6124
🌐 www.panmacmillan.com
Insider Info An annual competition to find the best original illustration for children's books. Entrants are invited to submit a 'mock book' based on their own story or an out of copyright text. Art and illustration students are usually invited to apply. The winner receives £1,000 and the possibility of being published with Macmillan.
Submission Guidelines Work should be previously unpublished.
Tips Details of the scheme are usually advertised through art colleges and the art departments of universities.

The Man Booker International Prize

c/o Colman Getty PR, 28 Windmill Street, London, W1T 2JJ
❶ 020 7631 2666
❷ 020 7631 2699
📧 lois@colmangetty.co.uk
🌐 www.themanbookerprize.com
Competition/Award Director Ion Trewin
Established 2004
Insider Info Awarded every two years (odd years) to a fiction writer who is deemed to have made an outstanding contribution to international literature with work written in, or translated to the English language. The winner receives £60,000. Open to writers of any nationality.
Genres Fiction, Translations

Submission Guidelines Work should be published previously.
Tips Contenders for the prize are decided by a panel of judges which changes every year. No unsolicited submissions.

The Man Booker Prize

c/o Colman Getty PR, 28 Windmill Street, London, W1T 2JJ
❶ 020 7631 2666
❷ 020 7631 2699
📧 lois@colmangetty.co.uk
🌐 www.themanbookerprize.com
Established 1968
Insider Info Sponsored by Colman Getty PR. Awards the best novel of the year written by a citizen of the Commonwealth or the Republic of Ireland. Prize is awarded annually. Prize money is £50,000. Judges change every year but normally include a literary critic, an academic, a literary editor and a novelist. Only open to writers of books published in the Commonwealth or Republic of Ireland.
Genres Fiction and Novels
Submission Guidelines Work should be published previously appearing between October 1 of the previous year and September 30 of the year of entry.
Tips Entrants must be nominated by UK publishers. Works must be in English. Translations, short story collections, novellas or self-published books may not be nominated.

Marsh Award for Children's Literature in Translation

National Centre for Research in Children's Literature, Roehampton University, Froebel College, Roehampton Lane, London, SW15 5PJ
❶ 020 8392 3008
❷ 020 8392 3819
📧 g.lathey@roehampton.ac.uk
Competition/Award Director Dr. Gillian Lathey
Established 1995
Insider Info Awarded to the best book translated into English and published by a British publisher. Competition takes place every two years (odd years), the winner receives £1,000.
Genres Fiction, Non-Fiction, Children's Books for ages four and over.
Submission Guidelines Work should be previously published.
Tips Encyclopedias, reference books, audio books and e-books are not eligible.

Marsh Biography Award

The English-Speaking Union, Dartmouth House, 37 Charles Street, London, W1J 5ED
❶ 020 7529 1550

○ 020 7495 6108
○ esu@esu.org
○ gillian_parker@esu.org
◍ www.esu.org
Contact Gillian Parker
Established 1985
Insider Info Awarded for the most influential biography published in Britain over the previous two years; competition takes place every two years (odd years). The winning biographer receives £4,000, a trophy and membership to the ESU. Writers must be British.
Genres Biography
Submission Guidelines Work should be published previously in the preceding two years.
Tips The award is usually given to a thoroughly researched biography, often of a historical figure.

Martha Gellhorn Trust Prize
Rutherfords, Herbert Road, Torquay, TQ8 8HN
Insider Info An award for journalism in honour of journalist Martha Gellhorn. Focuses on human interest stories and how people cope in the midst of larger scale news events.The competition takes place annually, and the winner receives £5,000.
Genres Articles
Submission Guidelines Work should be published previously.
Tips Postal submissions may be made. The deadline is usually in March.

Mary Vaughan Jones Award
Welsh Books Council, Castell Brychan, Aberystwyth, Ceredigion, SY23 2JB
○ 01970 624151
○ 01970 625385
○ wbc.children@wbc.org.uk
◍ www.wbc.org.uk
Established 1985
Insider Info Awarded to a person who has made a significant contribution to children's literature in Wales over a long period of time. Awarded every three years, with the next award in 2009. The winner receives a silver trophy.
Tips Not open to submissions.

McKitterick Prize
84 Drayton Gardens, London, SW10 9SB
○ 020 7373 6642
○ 020 7373 5768
○ info@societyofauthors.org
◍ www.societyofauthors.org
Insider Info Sponsored by the Society of Authors. Awarded for a first full length novel by a writer over the age of 40. Awarded annually, the winner receives

£4,000. The writer must be over the age of 40 on the December 31 in the year of submission.
Genres Novels
Submission Guidelines Guidelines available on the website. Previously published entries must have appeared in print between January 1 and December 31 the previous year. Accepts unpublished entries.
Tips Send four copies of the book (if published), or the first 30 pages of the manuscript (if unpublished), to Dorothy Sym at the Society of Authors. Entries are normally invited from late summer.

Me and My Movie
CBBC, BBC Television Centre, Wood Lane, London, W12 7RJ
○ 020 8743 8000
◍ www.bbc.co.uk/cbbc/meandmymovie
Established 2007
Insider Info An award in partnership with CBBC and BAFTA to recognise child film-makers. Winners will be awarded a special prize at the Children's BAFTAs.
Submission Guidelines Children are invited to submit their entire home-made films to CBBC, check the website for submission dates.
Tips Visit the website for tips on how to become involved with film making at a young age. Further details will appear on the website, or can be obtained from CBBC.

Medical Book Awards
Society of Authors, 84 Drayton Gardens, London, SW10 9SB
○ 020 7373 6642
○ 020 7373 5768
○ sbaxter@societyofauthors.org
◍ www.societyofauthors.org
Insider Info Sponsored by the Royal Society of Medicine. Awards are given for books written either for the medical profession, or for the general public on a medical theme. There are a number of categories for new books, new editions, specialist and general books. Awarded annually. The prizes are different for each category but winner usually receives a cash prize. Each category has a different set of entry criteria. See the website for details.
Genres Non-Fiction
Submission Guidelines Deadline for entry is April. Work should be published previously between May 1 and April 30.
Tips Entries from publishers only. Each publisher may submit ten books per imprint, per category.

Melissa Nathan Award for Comedy Romance
○ Online form
◍ www.melissanathan.com

Insider Info The Melissa Nathan Award is presented to a writer of a comedy romance title published during the previous year. The prize was set up by Nathan, a writer, before she died in 2006 and was first awarded in 2007. The winner receives a prize of £5,000 and a trophy.

Genres Romance/Comedy Novels

Submission Guidelines Use the online form on the website where there is an option to click on 'enter competition', for more information.

Tips Entries should link the two main elements – comedy and romance – together in a way that is 'compelling and natural'. The inaugural winner was bestseller Marian Keyes.

The Mercedes Benz Award for the Montagu of Beaulieu Trophy
Guild of Motoring Writers, 40 Baring Road, Bournemouth, BH6 4DT
- 01202 422424
- 01202 422424
- chris@whizzco.freeserve.co.uk
- www.guildofmotoringwriters.co.uk

Established 1972

Insider Info Sponsored by Mercedes Benz UK. The award is made to an individual who has contributed to highlighting and recording the history of motoring or motorcycling. It originated when Lord Montagu introduced it to celebrate the opening of the National Motor Museum at Beaulieu. The award is given annually. The winner receives £1,000 and a trophy.

Genres Non-Fiction, Essays, Scripts and Articles

Tips Multiple winners may be awarded in the same year. Books, television broadcasts, films, radio broadcasts, essays, research documents and articles are all eligible as long as they are publicly accessible.

Mere Literary Festival Open Competition
Lawrence's, Old Hollow, Mere, Warminster, Wiltshire, BA12 6EG
- 01747 860475
- howellatmere@aol.com

Competition/Award Director Mrs Adrienne Howell

Insider Info An open competition for both young people and adults. The subject may vary each year. The winners are announced at the festival which takes place annually.

Genres Short Stories

Submission Guidelines Guidelines and entry forms are also available on the website. Work should be previously unpublished.

Tips Although the competition is open to writers living all over the country, entrants living within a ten mile radius of Mere are often simultaneously entered for a separate prize.

Meyer-Whitworth Award
Arts Council England, 14 Great Peter Street, London, SW1P 3NQ
- 020 7973 6480
- charles.hart@artscouncil.org.uk
- www.artscouncil.org.uk

Insider Info Awarded to a playwright who has had a play produced in the preceding year, but no more than two produced in their career so far. The award is designed to help fully establish emerging writers for the theatre. Awarded annually, the winner receives £8,000. Plays must be in English and have been produced in the UK.

Genres Theatre productions

Submission Guidelines Work should be published previously.

Tips Nominations from theatre directors. Contact Charles Hart for more details.

MIND Book of the Year Award
Granta House, 15–19 Broadway, London, E15 4BQ
- 020 8519 2122
- 020 8522 1725
- contact@mind.org.uk
- www.mind.org.uk

Established 1981

Insider Info Awarded for a book published in the preceding year that has made significant advances in helping the public understanding of mental health issues. Awarded annually.

Genres Fiction, Non-Fiction

Submission Guidelines See the website for full submission guidelines.

Tips Memoir, fiction and non-fiction are eligible as long as the book has is publicly accessible and deals with issues in a way that appeals to general readers, rather than specialists.

Mitsubishi Motors Regional Motoring Journalist of the Year Award
Guild of Motoring Writers, 40 Baring Road, Bournemouth, BH6 4DT
- 01202 422424
- 01202 422424
- chris@whizzco.freeserve.co.uk
- www.guildofmotoringwriters.co.uk

Insider Info Presented to a regional journalist, freelancers included, who have made contributions to the field of motoring journalism. Awarded annually, the winner receives £1,000.

Genres Non-Fiction, Articles

Submission Guidelines Work should be published previously.

Tips The winners must be people who write for the local press and do not earn their main income from writing for national newspapers.

Momaya Press Short Story Competition

Momaya Press, 189a Balham High Road, London, SW12 9BE

📞 020 8673 9616

✉ infouk@momayapress.com

🌐 www.momayapress.com

Insider Info An open competition for any writer writing short stories in English up to 3,000 words long. Each year entrants are given a set theme on which to write. Awarded anually, prizes consist of: £110 for 1st place; £55 for 2nd place; and £30 for 3rd place. All winning stories are published in the *Momaya Annual Review* anthology.

Genres Short Stories

Submission Guidelines Deadline for entry is April. Guidelines available on the website. Entry fee is £8 per story. Submissions should be unpublished.

Tips Email entry only. Although there is a set theme, the style and subject matter are completely open.

Mslexia Women's Poetry Competition

Mslexia Publications Ltd, PO Box 656, Newcastle upon Tyne, NE99 1PZ

📞 0191 2616656

📞 0191 2616636

✉ postbag@mslexia.co.uk

🌐 www.mslexia.co.uk

Competition/Award Director Carol Seajay

Established 2004

Insider Info *Mslexia* invites poems in any style, of any length, on any subject by women writers. Awarded annually, with prizes of £1,000, £500 and £250. All winning poems will be published in *Mslexia* magazine. £5 entry fee allows you to enter five poems. Poems should be unpublished. Email submissions are accepted from outside the UK only. Purpose of the competition is to find the best contemporary poetry written by women. Copyright remains with author. *Mslexia* should be credited if the poem appears elsewhere after we have published it. Submissions invited from women of all ages and nationalities.

Genres Poetry

Submission Guidelines Deadline for entry is always the end of April each year; the exact day varies. Entry fee is £5 for a group of five poems. Work should be unpublished.

Nasen & TES Special Educational Needs Book Awards

Nasen House, 4–5 Amber Business Village, Amber Close, Amington, Tamworth, Staffordshire, B77 4RP

📞 01827 311500

📞 01827 313005

✉ janec@nasen.org.uk

🌐 www.nasen.org.uk

Insider Info Awards to celebrate writers and publishers of books that help and encourage children with special educational needs, as well as teachers. Categories include: Academic Book Award; Books for Teaching and Learning; and Children's Award. Awarded annually, the winners in each category receive £500. Books must have been published in the UK.

Genres Fiction, Non-Fiction, Children's Special Educational

Submission Guidelines Deadline for entry is June. Work must be published previously.

Tips The awards usually take place in October with a shortlist announced in August. Books that portray special educational needs in a positive light are often successful, especially in the children's category.

National Association of Writers Groups Creative Writing Competitions

The Arts Centre, Biddick Lane, Washington, Tyne and Wear, NE38 2AB

✉ nawg@tesco.net

🌐 www.nawg.co.uk

Insider Info The NAWG run a variety of annual competitions including the NAWG/Writers' News Short Story Competition. Other categories have included: Mini-Tale; Denise Robertson Trophy for the Best Group Anthology; Best Limerick; Free Verse Poem; Children's Poem; A Collection of Five Poems; Open Short Story; Short Story (with given last line); Children's Short Story; Novel (previously unpublished); Non-fictional Article in 'how-to' mode; and Fantasy/Science Fiction. Awarded annually, each category has different prizes but there are often small cash prizes, books and trophies on offer.

Genres Fiction, Non-Fiction, Poetry, Novels, Articles, Short Stories, Story Collections

Submission Guidelines There are various entry fees. Works should be unpublished.

Tips Details of further competitions, categories and closing dates will be published on the website along with shortlisted and winning entries from previous years.

National Poetry Anthology

United Press, Admail 3735, London, EC1B 1JB
- 0870 240 6190
- 0870 240 6191
- info@unitedpress.co.uk
- www.unitedpress.co.uk

Competition/Award Director Peter Quinn
Established 1998

Insider Info An open poetry competition. Writers are invited to submit up to three poems of up to 20 lines, or 160 words on any theme or subject. Awarded annually, winning entries are published in an anthology, a copy of which contributors receive for free. Every contributor then casts a vote for their favourite poem and the overall winner receives £1,000 and a trophy.

Genres Poetry

Submission Guidelines Deadline for entry is June each year. Guidelines and entry forms available via SAE. Work should be unpublished.

Tips Authors can submit up to three poems. Winners will be informed by November.

National Poetry Competition

22 Betterton Street, London, WC2H 9BX
- 020 7420 9880
- 020 7240 4818
- competition@poetrysociety.org.uk
- www.poetrysociety.org.uk

Established 1978

Insider Info Sponsored by The Poetry Society in association with *Aesthetica* magazine. An open competition for poets around the world, both published and unpublished. Entry forms are available from April. Awarded annually, prizes consist of: £5,000 for 1st place; £1,000 for 2nd place; £500 for 3rd place; and £50 for 10 runners up. All winners will also have the chance to read their poetry at the Ledbury Poetry Festival.

Genres Poetry

Submission Guidelines Deadline for entry is October. Guidelines and entry form available via SAE. Entry fee is £5 for the first poem and £3 per subsequent poem. Work should be unpublished.

Tips Entry forms will be available on the website, or by post in April. No submissions without completed forms.

The New Blood Dagger

PO Box 273, Borehamwood, WD6 2XA
- info@thecwa.co.uk
- www.thecwa.co.uk

Established 1973

Insider Info Sponsored by the Crime Writers Association and BBC Audio Books. It is awarded in memory of John Creasey, founder of the CWA, for first crime novels by previously unpublished writers. It was previously known as The John Creasey Memorial Award. The award is given annually. Winners receive an ornamental dagger and £1,000. Entries must be the first work of a writer who has no publishing history.

Genres Crime Novels

Tips Submissions must be made by publishers only.

New Writer Prose & Poetry Prizes

PO Box 60, Cranbrook, Kent, TN17 2ZR
- 01580 212626
- editor@thenewwriter.com
- www.thenewwriter.com

Competition/Award Director Merric Davidson
Established 1997

Insider Info Sponsored by *The New Writer* magazine. The prize is an open award for poets and writers. Categories include: Factual (essays, articles and interviews); Short stories (up to 4,000 words; Serials/Novellas (up to 20,000 words); Single poems (up to 40 lines); and Poetry collections (6–10 poems). Prize is awarded annually. For the factual category the prizes are £150, £100 and £50 for 1st, 2nd and 3rd respectively. For short stories the prizes are £300, £200, and £100. The winner of the serial/novella category receives £300. The single poem category prizes are £100, £75 and £50 and the poetry collection winners receive £300, £200 and £100. Winning entries may also be published in *The New Writer* 'Special Collection' anthology.

Genres Non-fiction, Poetry, Essays, Articles, Short Stories, Novellas

Submission Guidelines Submissions should be received by November 30. The entry fees are: £5 for articles, short stories or two single poems, £12 for poetry collections and £15 for serials/novellas. *New Writer* subscribers will receive a discount on entry fees. Work should be previously unpublished.

Tips Short entries may be submitted online, but longer entries should be submitted by post. An online entry form and payment system are published on the website.

Nielsen Gold & Platinum Book Awards

3rd Floor, Midas House, 62 Goldsworth Road, Woking, Surrey, GU21 6LQ
- 01483 712222
- 01483 712220
- gold&platinumawards@nielsenbookscan.co.uk
- www.nielsenbookscan.co.uk

Established 2000

Insider Info Sponsored by Nielsen BookScan. Awarded for consumer sales of books in UK shops. Gold standard is 500,000 copies; platinum is

1,000,000. The award consists of a plaque presented to the writer by their publisher.
Submission Guidelines An award for book sales.

Noma Award for Publishing in Africa
PO Box 128, Witney, Oxfordshire, OX8 5XU
- 01993 775235
- 01993 709265
- maryljay@aol.com
- www.nomaaward.org

Competition/Award Director Mary Jay
Established 1979
Insider Info Sponsored by Kodansha Ltd, Japan. An annual $10,000 award for a book by an African writer and published by an independent/autonomous African publishing house domiciled on the continent. Scholarly works, literature and children's books are eligible. Submission and entry must be made by publisher; maximum of three entries. The purpose is to encourage African scholars and writers to publish with African publishers, rather than abroad, with a view to strengthening African publishing. Judged by a panel of African and international scholars and book experts, chaired by Walter Bgoya, Tanzanian publisher. No entry fee. The writer must be an African national, wherever resident.
Genres Fiction, Non-Fiction, Poetry, Essays, Children's, Novels, Short Stories, Drama
Submission Guidelines Deadline for entry is the end of April each year. Guidelines and entry forms do not need SAE; they can be posted, emailed, or downloaded from the website. Previously published entries must appear in print between January 1 and December 31 the previous year.
Tips If interpretation of guidelines gives rise to questions of eligibility, the Secretariat can advise.

Olive Cook & Tom-Gallon Awards
84 Drayton Gardens, London, SW10 9SB
- 020 7373 6642
- 020 7373 5768
- info@societyofauthors.org
- www.societyofauthors.org

Insider Info Sponsored by the Society of Authors. Awarded by Miss Nellie Tom-Gallon in memory of her brother, and by Olive Cook, in alternate years for short story writers who have had at least one piece of work accepted for publication. Writers must have serious ambitions to become professional and their financial circumstances will be taken into consideration. The winners receive £1,000. Entrants must be residents of the UK, Commonwealth or the Republic of Ireland.
Genres Short Stories

Submission Guidelines Guidelines and entry form available on the website. The Tom-Gallon Award is presented bianually in odd years, the Olive Cook award in even years.
Tips The stories submitted must be traditional, rather than experimental and should be no longer than 5,000 words. Postal entries only, for the attention of Dorothy Sym.

Opening Pages Competition
- andrea@ukauthors.com
- www.ukauthors.com

Insider Info Sponsored by volunteer readers, professional editors and the UKA Press to support UK Authors writing site activities, this annual competition offers detailed feedback on the opening 3,000 words of a book. Run annually, 'feedback entrants' receive a five page detailed assessment on their writing, 65 pages of writing advice, and six to ten independent reader reports.
Submission Guidelines Entry fee is £5 per entry, and £18 per feedback entry. Work should be unpublished.
Tips The winning entry is offered publication by UKA Press, and shortlisted entries are invited to submit their work to be considered for publication. Check the UK Authors website for more details.

Orange Award for New Writers
Booktrust, Book House, 45 East Hill, London, SW18 2QZ
- 020 8516 2972
- 020 8516 2978
- tarryn@booktrust.org.uk
- www.orangeprize.co.uk

Established 2005
Insider Info An award for an emerging woman writer who has had her first work of fiction (novel, novella or collection of short stories) published and shows great potential. Awarded annually, the winner receives £10,000. Writers must be a woman of any nationality, who has had their first work of fiction published in the UK by a UK publisher. Previous publication outside the UK will not disqualify an author, but the work entered must be the first published.
Genres Fiction, Novels, Short Stories, Story Collections, Novellas
Submission Guidelines Work should be published previously between 1st April and the following 31st March.
Tips Submissions from publishers only. Awarded on the basis of future potential shown in first published work.

Orange Prize for Fiction

Booktrust, Book House, 45 East Hill, London, SW18 2QZ

- 020 8516 2972
- 020 8516 2978
- tarryn@booktrust.org.uk
- www.orangeprize.co.uk

Established 1996

Insider Info Awarded for a full length novel published in the UK by a female writer. Designed to celebrate and highlight the achievement of women in literature and publishing. Awarded annually, the winner receives £30,000 and a limited edition bronze figurine called the 'Bessie'. The judging panel changes each year and details are published on the website. Usually made up of media personalities, writers and publishing professionals. The award is not open to novels by men.

Genres Fiction, Novels

Submission Guidelines Work should be published in the UK by a UK publisher, between April 1 and the following March 31.

Tips Submissions by publishers only.

The Oscar Moore Screenwriting Prize

c/o Screen International, 33–39 Bowling Green Lane, London, EC1R 0DA

- 020 7505 8080
- 020 7505 8087
- www.screendaily.com

Established 1997

Insider Info Sponsored by The Oscar Moore Foundation. The prize is awarded for a best first draft of a screenplay in memory of Oscar Moore, a *Guardian* columnist and editor of *Screen International*. The prize is awarded annually. The winner receives £10,000 and often other prizes such as scriptwriting courses and a live performance of the play.

Genres Scripts

Submission Guidelines Work should be unpublished.

Tips Each year the competition has a different theme. In 2004 it was thrillers and in 2006 it was comedy. Details are available from the Foundation. There was deemed to be no entry good enough to win in 2006 so no award was made.

OWG Awards for Excellence

PO Box 520, Bamber Bridge, Preston, Lancashire, PR5 8LF

- 01772 321243
- 0870 137 8888
- secretary@owg.org.uk
- www.owg.org.uk

Established 1980

Insider Info Sponsored by the Outdoor Writers' Guild. Awards made in several categories including writing, journalism and broadcast about outdoor living and pursuits. Awarded annually.

Genres Non-Fiction, Articles

Submission Guidelines Deadline for entry is July. Work should be published previously.

Tips OWG members only. To join, send a CV and samples of published/produced work to memsec@owg.org.uk.

Oxford Weidenfeld Translation Prize

St Anne's College, Woodstock, Oxford, OX2 6HS

- 01865 274800
- 01865 274899
- sandra.madley@st-annes.ox.ac.uk
- www.st-annes.ox.ac.uk/about/translationprize.html

Competition/Award Director Dr. Matthew Reynolds

Established 1996

Insider Info Sponsored by St Anne's College, The Queen's College and New College, Oxford, and Lord Weidenfeld. The prize is for book-length English translations of fiction, poetry or drama written in any living European language by any author living or dead. Three copies of each translation must be submitted; it will not be possible to return them. The award aims to honour the craft of translation, and to recognise its cultural importance. Entries must be books, must have been published in the preceding calendar year, must be distributed in the UK, and may be the work of up to three translators. They must be submitted by the publisher rather than by the translator. Awarded annually, the prize of £2,000 is awarded at an event at St Anne's College Oxford, where all the shortlisted translators are invited to read from their work. The competition is judged by three Oxford academics and translators, plus a guest judge. No entry fee. Books must have been published in the preceding calendar year and must be distributed in the UK. Entries must be submitted by the publisher.

Genres Translations

Submission Guidelines Deadline for entry is the end of January each year. Publisher submission only. Work should be published previously between the beginning of January and the end of December.

The Paul Foot Award

6 Carlisle Street, London, W1D 3BN

- www.private-eye.co.uk

Established 2005

Insider Info Sponsored by *Private Eye* and *The Guardian*. Awarded in memory of Paul Foot for achievement in campaigning journalism. The award may be given to an individual, a team, or a newspaper for either a single article or an entire campaign. The award is given annually. 1st prize is £5,000 and five runners up will also receive £1,000.

Submission Guidelines Submissions should received by September 1. Work should be published previously having appeared between September 1 of the previous year and August 31 of the year of entry, and either be in print or online.

Tips Application forms and details on how to submit material will be available on the *Private Eye* website during the period the competition is open. Please do not send any broadcast material.

PEN/Ackerley Prize
English PEN, 6–8 Amwell Street, London, EC1R 1UQ
- 020 7713 0023
- 020 7837 7838
- enquiries@englishpen.org
- www.englishpen.org

Established 1982

Insider Info An annual competition awarded for an outstanding work of literary autobiography written in the previous year by a British writer. Prize money is £1,000.

Genres Autobiography

Submission Guidelines Submissions must be previously published.

Tips Nominations are from members of the judging panel and Ackerley trustees only. No public submissions.

The Petra Kenney Poetry Competition
PO Box 32, Filey, North Yorkshire, YO14 9YG
- morgan@kenney.uk.net
- www.petrapoetrycompetition.co.uk

Established 1995

Insider Info A set of poetry awards in the memory of Petra Kenney. The categories include a general category, comic verse and young poets (14–18). The competition is held annually, The prizes for the general category consist of: £1,000 and publication in *Writers Magazine* for the winner; £500 for 2nd place; and £250 for 3rd place. All three also win a Royal Brierley Crystal Vase. The winner of the comic verse receives £250 and the Young Poet winner receives £250 whilst the runner up receives £125. Open to UK and international writers (see website for fees in $US).

Genres Poetry

Submission Guidelines Submissions should be received by December 31 each year. Guidelines are available on the website. The entry fee is £3 per poem. Work should be unpublished.

Tips Poems should be no more than 80 lines and should be typed on A4 paper.

P.J. O'Connor Radio Drama Awards
RTÉ Radio Centre, Donnybrook, Dublin 4, Republic of Ireland
- 00353 1 208 3111
- 00353 1 208 3304
- radiodrama@rte.ie
- www.rte.ie

Insider Info Sponsored by RTÉ, this competition aims to find the best radio drama script from an new writer. Plays must last 15 minutes and be in either Irish or English. Awarded annually, prizes consist of: €3,000 for the 1st place; €2,000 for 2nd; and €1,000 for 3rd. All three plays are also professionally produced. RTÉ Radio have the right to broadcast all winning plays twice before having to pay fees. Writers must be either unproduced or have had a maximum of one hour's radio professionally produced.

Genres Scripts

Submission Guidelines Deadline for entry is April. Guidelines are available on the website. Work should be previously unpublished.

Tips Detailed advice on script layout and the construction of a successful radio drama are published along with the entry guidelines.

The Poetry Business Book & Pamphlet Competition
The Studio, Byram Arcade, Westgate, Huddersfield, HD1 1ND
- 01484 434840
- 01484 426566
- www.poetrybusiness.co.uk

Insider Info Competition for poetry collections. The purpose of this contest is to find and publish new or less-well-known poets. The competition is held annually. The first set of winners will have their collection published in pamphlet form. These winners can submit an extended manuscript and one will be chosen to be published in a full length collection under the Smith/Doorstop imprint. Winners will receive a cash prize of £250. The competition is open to any adult writer.

Genres Poetry

Submission Guidelines Submissions should be received by October. Guidelines and entry forms are available with SAE. The entry fee is £24.

Tips Please do not submit any poetry for children.

Poetry London Competition
81 Lambeth Walk, London, SE11 6DX
- 020 7735 8880
- 020 7735 8880

◉ editors@poetrylondon.co.uk
🌐 www.poetrylondon.co.uk
Established 2000
Insider Info Sponsored by *Poetry London* magazine, this annual poetry competition is judged by a guest judge each year. The judging process begins in July. Details of entry will be published in the magazine and on the website. First prize is £1,000, second prize is £500, third prize is £200. There are also four commendation prizes of £75 each.
Genres Poetry
Submission Guidelines Work should be previously unpublished.
Tips Each year the judges write a report on what they found successful and unsuccessful about the competition and its entries. These are published on the website for entrants to read.

The Portico Prize
The Portico Library, 57 Mosley Street, Manchester, M2 3HY
☎ 0161 236 6785
☎ 0161 236 6803
◉ librarian@theportico.org.uk
🌐 www.theportico.org.uk/portprize.htm
Established 1985
Insider Info Sponsored prize awarded for a work of fiction and a work of non-fiction set wholly or mainly in the North of England. The books should be of general interest whilst maintaining literary quality. Fiction and non-fiction shortlists are drawn up and prizes are awarded to one winner from each list. The prize is awarded every two years (even years). The prize (£8,000 in 2008) id divided between the two winners and a specially bound copy of their winning book presented at a later date.
Genres Fiction and Non-Fiction.
Submission Guidelines Work should be published between the last and the current closing dates – usually August 31st.
Tips Contact Emma Marigliano at the above email address for more details. The shortlisted books are selected from a long list (115 in 2008).

Practical Art Instruction Book of the Year
PO Box 32, Huntingdon, PE28 0QX
☎ 01832 710201
☎ 01832 710488
◉ award@acaward.com
🌐 www.acaward.com
Insider Info Sponsored by Artist's Choice book club, *The Leisure Painter* magazine and *The Artist* magazine, this is an annual award for best instructional art book. A shortlist is drawn up by the sponsors which

is then voted for by readers of the magazines through the award's website.
Genres Non-Fiction
Submission Guidelines Work should be published previously.
Tips No submissions – the magazine and book club editors shortlist their choice of books.

The Raymond Williams Community Publishing Prize
The Literature Department, 14 Great Peter Street, London, SW1P 3NQ
☎ 020 7973 6442
◉ info.literature@artscouncil.org.uk
🌐 www.artscouncil.org.uk
Insider Info The prize is sponsored by the Arts Council England and is awarded for works published to highlight and reflect the experiences of a particular community. Open to not-for-profit publishing companies only. The prize is awarded annually. The prizes are usually £3,000 for the winners and £2,000 for the runner-up.
Submission Guidelines Work should be published previously.
Tips At the time of going to press the award administration is under review and not open to submissions. New details and calls for submissions will be published on the website.

The Reader Classic Rescue Prize
English Department, University of Liverpool, Liverpool, L69 7ZR
Insider Info The prize is sponsored by *The Reader*. Writers and readers are asked to review a classic book that they would save if all the world's libraries were burning down. The only criteria is that the book must be more than 75 years old. The prize is awarded monthly. The winning review will be published in each month's *Reader* magazine and authors will receive 15 titles from Oxford World's Classic series.
Genres Book Reviews
Tips Reviews should be kept to under 850 words and sent by post to the address above. Be sure to include plenty of quotations in the entry.

Red House Children's Book Award
Freepost, 2 Laurel Drive, Oxted, RH8 9DT
☎ 01582 831506
◉ enquiries@rhcba.co.uk
🌐 www.redhousechildrensbookaward.co.uk
Contact Andrea Goodall
Established 1980
Insider Info Sponsored by The Federation of Children's Book Groups. This annual award voted for entirely by children is given in three categories:

Books for Younger Children; Books for Young Readers; and Books for Older Children. The top 50 titles are published in Red House's Pick of the Year list. The top ten writers and illustrators receive sets of children's letters and pictures relating to their book. Winners in each category receive an engraved silver bowl, and the overall winner receives an oak and silver trophy for a year and an engraved silver acorn to keep. Nominations are invited from children, writers, illustrators and publishers, and shortlisted books are published on the website. Children may then vote either individually or in groups through the website for the category winners and the overall winner. Books entered must have been published in the UK for the first time in the corresponding year.

Genres Children's Fiction

Submission Guidelines Deadline for entry is December each year. Nomination forms and submissions guidelines are available on the website. Work should be published previously, between January 1 and December 31 the same year.

Tips See the website for full submission details. The book must be original, although major re-workings of religious or folk stories are accepted.

Red Planet Prize

Unit 13, Doolittle Mill, Froghall Road, Ampthill, Bedfordshire, MK45 2ND

⊙ redplanetprize@redplanetpictures.co.uk
⊛ www.redplanetpictures.co.uk

Competition/Award Director Chief Executive, Tony Jordan

Established 2007

Insider Info An annual competition run by the Red Planet Pictures production house. The prize aims to find and develop new screenwriting talent. The winning entrant will receive £5,000, representation, and a script commission for Red Planet Pictures. The prize is judged by a panel of experts including Tony Jordan.

Genres Screenwriting

Submission Guidelines Submissions should be received before September 1st each year and must be previously unpublished. Send up to ten pages of a screenplay, including a half-page synopsis and author biography. Guidelines are available online.

Tips All submissions must be in English and in screenwriting format. Sending a complete screenplay will be grounds for disqualification.

Reginald Taylor & Lord Fletcher Essay Prize

Council for British Archaeology, St Mary's House, 66 Bootham, York, YO30 7BZ

⊙ 01904 671417
⊙ 01904 671384

⊙ info@britarch.ac.uk
⊛ www.britarch.ac.uk

Competition/Award Director Dr Martin Henig, Honorary Editor

Insider Info A prize for the best essay submitted in the areas of art history, archaeology or antiquarian subject. Awarded every two years (even years). The winning essay will be published in the *Journal of the British Archaeological Association* and read at a meeting.

Genres Essays

Submission Guidelines Deadline for entry is June. Work should be previously unpublished.

Tips Essay should be a maximum of 7,500 words. Contact The Hon. Editor for more details.

Regional Press Awards

Press Gazette, Wilmington Business Information, Paulton House, 8 Sheperdess Walk, N1 7LB

⊙ 020 7324 2337
⊙ 020 7566 5769
⊙ pged@pressgazette.co.uk
⊛ www.pressgazette.co.uk

Insider Info An annual awards ceremony to recognise regional newspapers and journalists. Freelancers and employees may be presented with prizes in a number of categories.

Genres Non-Fiction, Articles

Submission Guidelines Work should be published previously.

Tips The ceremony is usually held in June or July. Details are published in the events section of the Press Gazette website.

Renault UK Journalist of the Year Award

Guild of Motoring Writers, 40 Baring Road, Bournemouth, Dorset, BH6 4DT

⊙ 01202 422424
⊙ 01202 422424
⊙ chris@whizzco.freeserve.co.uk
⊛ www.guildofmotoringwriters.co.uk

Insider Info Awarded annually to an individual deemed to have made an outstanding contribution during the previous year to the field of motoring journalism. The winner receives £2,000.

Genres Non-Fiction, Articles

Submission Guidelines Work should be previously published.

Tips The awarding judges are looking for initiative and endeavour over an entire year. Tends to be awarded to bodies of work and series.

The Richard Imison Memorial Award

84 Drayton Gardens, London, SW10 9SB

⊙ 020 7373 6642

☎ 020 7373 5768

✉ jhodder@societyofauthors.org

🌐 www.societyofauthors.org

Established 1995

Insider Info Sponsored by The Society of Authors. The award was founded in memory of Richard Imison to encourage the writing of original radio drama by a writer, or writers who have never previously been published or produced. The award is given annually. Winners receive £1,500. Judges are made up from the Broadcasting Committee of the Society of Authors. Entries may include a one-off drama, or the first episode of a series or serial, but adaptions are not eligible.

Genres Scripts

Submission Guidelines Submissions should be received by January. Guidelines are available on the website. Work must have been previously broadcast having appeared between January 1 and December 31 of the previous year.

Tips Submissions may come from any source, including the writers themselves. Send three copies of the script along with its broadcast recording, a 250 word synopsis, an author biography and a completed entry form, to Jo Hodder at the address above.

RNA Romance Prize
13 Makepeace Avenue, London, N6 6EL

✉ normacurtisuk@yahoo.co.uk

🌐 www.rna-uk.org

Competition/Award Director Norma Curtis

Established 2003

Insider Info Sponsored by the Romantic Novelists' Association, this is an award for category romances by members of the RNA. Category romances are defined as short romances with a strong emphasis on the central relationship. They are usually published in a standard format and several similar books published each month. Serials in magazines are also eligible for the prize. Awarded annually, the winner receives £1,000 and an inscribed cup. Books must have been first published in the UK between the dates specified.

Genres Fiction, Novels

Submission Guidelines Deadline for entry is October. Entry forms and guidelines available on the website. Work should be published previously, between January 1 and December 31.

Tips Does not accept self-published or vanity novels. Send two copies along with an entry form to Norma Curtis.

Romantic Novel of the Year
Flat 2, 42 Lexham Gardens, London, W8 5JE

✉ rnaawardorganiser@hotmail.com

🌐 www.rna-uk.org

Contact Hon. Award Administrator, Pia Tapper Fenton

Established 1960

Insider Info Sponsored by the Romantic Novelists' Association, a prize for the most romantic novel of the year. The purpose of the competition is to celebrate good writing and to encourage excellence within the genre. Awarded annually, the prize is a cheque for £5,000 and a small trophy to the winner. The competition is open to any writer, but the book must be written in the English language and only books first published in the UK are eligible. Novels may be submitted in hardback or paperback form, but the original version must have been published within the period stated.

Genres Novels

Submission Guidelines Deadline for entry is October every year. See the RNA website for guidelines and entry form. Entries must be published in the UK between January 1 and December 31 of the year before the prize is awarded. Must be written in the English language.

Rose Mary Crawshay Prize
10 Carlton House Terrace, London, SW1Y 5AH

☎ 020 7969 5200

☎ 020 7969 5300

✉ chiefexec@britac.ac.uk

🌐 www.britac.ac.uk

Established 1888

Insider Info Sponsored by the British Academy. Presented to a woman who has produced historical or critical writing on any aspect of English Literature, particularly one of the poets Byron, Shelley or Keats. Usually awarded twice yearly. Writers may be of any nationality.

Genres Non-Fiction, Essays

Submission Guidelines Works should be published within three years prior to the award.

Tips Although preference is said to be given to work on the poets mentioned above, this has only been the case for one winner since 2003. A list of previous winners and their subject matters is published on the website.

Royal Mail Awards for Scottish Children's Books
Scottish Book Trust, Sandeman House, Trunks Close, 55 High Street, Edinburgh, EH1 1SR

☎ 0131 524 0160

☎ 0131 524 0161

🌐 www.scottishbooktrust.com/children-and-young-people/royal-mail-awards

Insider Info Awards presented for children's books across three categories, 0–7 years, 8–11 years and

12–16 years. Primarily for Scottish writers and illustrators resident in Scotland. Awarded annually, a shortlist is drawn up from nominated books. The category winners and runners up are then voted on entirely by children who register through their schools.

Genres Fiction, Non-Fiction, Poetry, Children's Books
Submission Guidelines Deadline for entry is January each year. Work should be published previously between January 1 and December 31.
Tips Submissions by publishers only. Books may be in English or Scots but must be available to buy in Scotland and by authors and illustrators living in Scotland.

The Royal Society of Literature Ondaatje Prize
Somerset House, Strand, London, WC2R 1LA
- 020 7845 4676
- 020 7845 4679
- paulaj@rslit.org
- www.rslit.org
Contact Paula Johnson
Insider Info Awarded to a distinguished work of fiction, non-fiction or poetry, published during the preceding year, that successfully evokes the spirit of a place. The prize is awarded annually. The winner receives £10,000. Writers must be resident in the UK, Ireland or the Commonwealth.
Genres Fiction, Non-Fiction, Poetry
Submission Guidelines Submissions must be received by December each year. Guidelines are available on the website. Work should be published previously having appeared between January 1 and December 1 of the year of entry.
Tips Do not submit short stories, novellas or children's literature. Submissions should be made by publishers only; submit four copies to Paula Johnson.

The Royal Society Prizes for Science Books
The Royal Society, 6–9 Carlton House Terrace, London, SW1Y 5AG
- 020 7451 2500
- 020 7930 2170
- sciencebooks@royalsoc.ac.uk
- www.royalsoc.ac.uk/sciencebooks
Established 1988
Insider Info Annual awards aimed at encouraging the writing, publishing and reading of popular science books. There are two separate categories: The Junior Prize, for books written for the under-14s; and the General Prize, for books written for a general audience. Prizes consist of £10,000 for each of the two category winners and £1,000 each for

shortlisted books. Books must be in the English language and be distributed in the UK.
Genres Popular, accessible science books
Submission Guidelines Submissions should be received by January 31. Guidelines are available on the website. Work should be published for the first time in the previous year.
Tips No purely educational textbooks, encyclopedias or books for a specialist audience. The aim of the prize is to award writers whose books make science accessible to an unknowledgeable audience. Entries must be submitted by publishers only.

RTÉ Radio 1 Short Story Competition
RTÉ Radio Centre, Donnybrook, Dublin 4, Republic of Ireland
- 00353 1 208 3111
- 00353 1 208 3080
- www.rte.ie/radio1/francismacmanus
Established 1985
Insider Info An open competition for radio short stories to commemorate the life of Francis MacManus, former writer and Head of Talks and Features in Radio Eireann. Awarded annually, the prize consists of: €3,000 and a commemorative trophy for the overall winner; €2,000 for 2nd place; and €1,000 for 3rd. The three winners, plus a selection of shortlisted stories will be broadcast on RTÉ Radio 1.
Genres Short Stories
Submission Guidelines Deadline for entries is October each year. Work should be unpublished.
Tips Entries may be in English or Irish, and should be by Irish writers, or writers living in Ireland.

Runciman Award
c/o Lady Fairweather, 39c Pembridge Villas, London, W11 3EP
- 020 7221 5227
- www.hellenicbookservice.com/ahl.runciman.htm
Established 1985
Insider Info Sponsored by The National Bank of Greece and The Anglo-Hellenic League. Awarded for a book of any type, published in English anywhere in the world, that focuses wholly or mainly on Greece or Hellenism. The purpose of the award is to promote an understanding of Greek culture and its impact on civilisation. Awarded annually, the winner receives £9,000. Work must be available for purchase in the UK at the time of the award presentation.
Genres Fiction, Non-Fiction, Poetry, Essays, Scripts, Novels, Articles, Short Stories, Story Collections, Biography

Submission Guidelines Deadline for entry is January each year. Work should be previously published.

Tips No works of translation. Other than this exception, no types of work are excluded. Work may reflect any time period from ancient Greece right up to present day life.

Saga Award for Wit
c/o Belinda Harley Associates, 22 South Audley Street, London, W1K 2NY
- 020 7499 4979
- 020 7499 4068
- info@belindaharley.com

Insider Info Sponsored by *Saga* magazine. Awarded annually to a work of comedy written by an author over the age of 50. The winner receives £20,000.

Genres Fiction, Non-Fiction

Submission Guidelines Work should be previously published.

Tips Nominations by publishers only.

Saltire History Book of the Year Award
9 Fountain Close, 22 High Street, Edinburgh, EH1 1TF
- 0131 556 1836
- 0131 557 1675
- saltire@saltiresociety.org.uk
- www.saltiresociety.org.uk

Established 1965

Insider Info Sponsored by The Saltire Society. An annual £1,500 award in memory of Dr Angus Mure MacKenzie for a work of Scottish historical research published during the preceding year.

Genres Non-Fiction

Submission Guidelines An entry form is available online. Work should be published previously.

Tips Nominations should be sent via the online form to the administrator.

The Saltire Scottish Literary Awards
9 Fountain Close, 22 High Street, Edinburgh, EH1 1TF
- 0131 556 1836
- 0131 557 1675
- saltire@saltiresociety.org.uk
- www.saltiresociety.org.uk

Insider Info The award is sponsored by The Saltire Society, Royal Mail Group, Faculty of Advocates and the National Library of Scotland. Prizes are awarded in two categories: Scottish Book of the Year; and Scottish First Book of the Year. To qualify, the book must be by a writer born or living in Scotland, or of Scottish descent, or alternatively must deal with a Scottish theme, event or situation. The award is given annually. The winner of the book of the year title receives £5,000. The first book winner receives £1,500.

Genres Fiction, Non-Fiction, Poetry, Essays, Scripts, Articles

Submission Guidelines Submissions should be received by September 8. Work should be published previously having appeared between September 1 of the previous year and August 31 of the year of entry.

Tips Nominations are invited from editors and reviewers working in Scotland, as well as producers of radio and television and publishers. Address nominations to Kathleen Munro, Administrator, at the above address.

Samuel Pepys Award
Colman Getty, 28 Windmill Street, London, W1T 2JJ
- 020 7631 2666
- 020 7631 2699
- hannah@colmangetty.co.uk
- www.pepys-club.org.uk

Established 2003

Insider Info Awarded for a book that has increased the understanding of Samuel Pepys, his era or his peers, and encouraged further study. Awarded every two years (odd years), the winner receives £2,000 and a silver medal.

Submission Guidelines Work should be published between July 1 and June 31. Submissions by publishers only. Send five copies to Hannah Blake at Colman Getty PR.

Science Writer Awards
PO Box 5824, Westcliff on Sea, Southend, SS1 9EW
- 0845 094 6367
- enquiries@science-writer.co.uk
- www.science-writer.co.uk

Competition/Award Director Dr Roger Highfield

Established 1987

Insider Info Sponsored by *The Daily Telegraph* and Bayer. A competition for science articles of around 700 words that successfully communicate a scientific subject in a clear and jargon-free way. There are two age groups: 15–19 and 20–28. Awarded annually, the winner in each group receives £1,000, a work placement at *The Daily Telegraph*, Bayer or The Royal Society, a year's subscription to *Nature* and *New Scientist* magazines, and the opportunity for their article to be published in the *Telegraph's* science section. The prize for 2nd place is £500, publication in the *Telegraph* and the magazine subscriptions. Nine runners up each receive £100.

Genres Non-Fiction, Essays, Articles

Submission Guidelines Deadline for submission is June. Guidelines are available on the website. Work should be previously unpublished.

Tips There are extensive tips and guidelines on the website along with previous winning entries and advice from top science writers. Entries must not exceed 800 words.

SciTalk Competitions
Plumbland House, Plumbland, Aspatria, Cumbria, CA7 2HD

✉ enquiries@scitalk.org.uk

🌐 www.scitalk.org.uk

Insider Info SciTalk is an organisation that promotes the inclusion of science and scientists in literature without limiting them to science fiction. Occasional competitions are offered with this aim in mind. A recent example is The Short Story Challenge where writers were invited to talks and lab tours from scientists and then challenged to write a short story including the information they had gathered. Prizes will vary with competitions but have included publication in *The Guardian*.

Tips New events and their linked competitions will be published in the events section on the website. The website may also be used as a research tool for writers and can put people in touch with scientists willing to help with information and ideas to be put into fiction writing.

The Scotsman & Orange Short Story Award
108 Holyrood Road, Edinburgh, EH8 8AS

☎ 0131 620 8620

🌐 www.scotsman.com

Insider Info An open short story competition centred around a different theme each year. The award is given annually. The winner receives £7,500 and a trip, including travel and accommodation, to the Orange Prize for Fiction. Five runners up receive £500 each. Writers must have been born in Scotland or be a current resident of Scotland.

Genres Short Stories

Submission Guidelines Work should be unpublished.

Tips Stories should be up to 3,000 words, double-spaced and single-sided. Details of future competitions, closing dates and entry forms will be published in *The Scotsman* newspaper and website.

Scribble Magazine Competitions
14 The Park, Stow on the Wold, Cheltenham, Gloucestershire, GL54 1DX

☎ 01451 831053

✉ sales@parkpublications.co.uk

🌐 www.parkpublications.co.uk

Insider Info Sponsored by Park Publications. Several competitions are offered by the magazine including an ongoing quarterly short story competition for stories of up to 3,000 words. Details of various other one-off writing competitions are published on the website. The prizes consist of £75, £25, and £15 for the top three published in each issue.

Genres Poetry, Articles, Short Stories

Submission Guidelines Guidelines and entry forms available via SAE. Entry fee of £3 per short story for the quarterly competition. Work should be previously unpublished.

Tips Guidelines are published on the submissions section of the website that advise writers how to best write for *Scribble*'s audience. Subscribers to the magazine get free entry to competitions.

The Shiva Naipaul Memorial Prize
22 Old Queen Street, London, SW1H 9HP

☎ 020 7961 0200

🌐 www.spectator.co.uk

Insider Info The prize is sponsored by *The Spectator* and is awarded to a writer who is able to powerfully convey a visit to a foreign place or culture. The prize is awarded annually. The winner receives £3,000. Entry is open to any writer under 35 who writes in English.

Genres Non-Fiction

Submission Guidelines Submissions should be received by May. Work should be unpublished.

Tips Although the award is essentially for travel writing, the judges look past this at how well a foreign culture is conveyed to the reader.

Sid Chaplin Short Story Competition
Shildon Town Council, Civic Hall Square, Shildon, Co. Durham, DL4 1AH

☎ 01388 772563

☎ 01388 775227

✉ council@shildon.gov.uk

🌐 www.shildon.gov.uk

Established 1988

Insider Info A short story competition. Entries are invited of up to 3,000 words. Annually, 1st prize is £300, 2nd is £150 and 3rd is £75. There are also be Junior prizes, split into various age groups from 8–17, and a further prize for the best entry from a resident of Shildon. Open to anyone aged 8+ years.

Genres Short Stories

Submission Guidelines Deadline for entry is the end of March. Entry fee is £2.50 for adults, children free. Work should be previously unpublished.

Tips The competition is open to stories on any theme. For more details contact Shildon town council.

Sir Banister Fletcher Award

40 Dover Street, London, W1S 4NP

- 020 7408 5092
- 020 7409 0913
- stella@theauthorsclub.co.uk

Established 1954

Insider Info Sponsored by the Authors' Club, awarded for the best book on architecture or the arts published in Britain. The prize consists of £1,000. Open to any books written by British authors and published under a British imprint.

Genres Non-Fiction

Submission Guidelines Work should be published previously. No submissions.

Sir William Lyons Award

40 Baring Road, Bournemouth, Dorset, BH6 4DT

- 01202 422424
- 01202 422424
- chris@whizzco.freeserve.co.uk
- www.guildofmotoringwriters.co.uk

Established 1966

Insider Info Sponsored by The Guild of Motoring Writers, an award open to people under the age of 23 who are interested in motor journalism. To be eligible for the award the entrant has to complete a number of tasks, including conducting and writing up an interview with a person in the motoring industry. Awarded annually, winners receive a cash prize and membership to The Guild of Motoring Journalists. Open to people who are British by nationality or live in Britain.

Submission Guidelines Deadline for entries is September each year. Entry forms are usually available in late spring.

Tips There is a useful tips document from a previous award winner available on the website.

Society of Theatre Research Book Prize

The Society for Theatre Research, PO Box 53971, London, SW15 6UL

- theatrebookprize@btinternet.com
- www.str.org.uk

Established 1998

Insider Info An award for the best piece of writing in English on British theatre published during the preceding year. Awarded annually, the winner receives £400. Writers may be of any nationality and the book does not have to have been published by a British publisher.

Genres Non-Fiction

Submission Guidelines Work should be previously published. Submissions invited from publishers. Write to the administrator at the above address for more information.

Somerset Maugham Awards

The Society of Authors, 84 Drayton Gardens, London, SW10 9SB

- 020 7373 6642
- 020 7373 5768
- info@societyofauthors.org
- www.societyofauthors.org

Insider Info Awards for a British work of fiction or non-fiction by a young writer. The award should be spent on foreign travel. Awarded annually with up to £12,000 in prize money. Writers must be under the age of 35 and be British by birth (excluding Eire and British colonies). The work submitted must be a full length book published within the previous year in Britain.

Genres Fiction, Poetry, Novels, Criticism, Biography, History, Philosophy, Belles-lettres, Travel

Submission Guidelines Entry form on website. Work should be published within the previous year.

Tips Entry are accepted from publishers only.

Sony Radio Academy Awards

47–48 Chagford Street, London, NW1 6EB

- 020 7723 0106
- 020 7724 6163
- secretariat@radioawards.org
- www.radioawards.org

Established 1983

Insider Info An annual awards ceremony to recognise excellence in radio broadcast during the preceding year. The awards are split into various categories that are subject to review each year.

Submission Guidelines Deadline for entries is January. Entries must have been broadcast on FM, AM, digital terrestrial, satellite or cable, streamed or been downloadable between January 1 and December 31 the previous year.

Tips Entries may only be submitted by OFCOM (or similar) licensed radio stations, BBC production departments, independent production companies and BFBS. Clear guidelines are published on the website, along with tips on how to submit winning entries and details of all individual prize categories.

Southport Writers' Circle International Poetry Competition

32 Dover Road, Birkdale, Southport, Merseyside, PR8 4TB

Insider Info An open poetry competition for poetry of up to 40 lines. Awarded annually, the winning poet receives £200. 2nd prize is £100 and 3rd prize is £50. There are additional £25 prizes for a humorous poem and local poet.

Genres Poetry

Submission Guidelines Deadline for entry is April each year. Entry fee is £2 per poem. Work should be previously unpublished.

Tips Writers with Liverpool or Preston postcodes should mark their entries with an 'L' in the top right corner for entry into the local prize.

Speakeasy Open Creative Writing Competition

46 Wealdstone Place, Springfield, Milton Keynes, Buckinghamshire, MK6 3JG

- 01908 663860
- speakeasy@writerbrock.co.uk
- www.mkweb.co.uk/speakeasy

Competition/Award Director Martin Brocklebank

Established 1996

Insider Info Sponsored by Speakeasy – Milton Keynes Writers' Group. Prizes in both the short story and poetry categories are awarded annually. 1st is £100, 2nd is £50 and 3rd is £25 for both short story and poetry. Judges vary each year. Open to all writers and poets.

Genres Poetry, Short Stories

Submission Guidelines Deadline for entry is the end of October each year. Guidelines and entry forms available via SAE or on , the website. Entry fee is £3 per poem or four for £10; £4 per short story or three for £10. Work should be previously unpublished.

Tips Please read the rules carefully and send in your entries with an entry form printed from the website, cheques made payable to Speakeasy with 'Comp 09' written on the reverse.

Strokestown International Poetry Competition

Strokestown Poetry Festival Office, Strokestown, County Roscommon, Republic of Ireland

- 00353 71 963 3759
- petersirr@eircom.net
- www.strokestownpoetry.org

Competition/Award Director Peter Sirr

Insider Info A poetry competition, administered by Strokestown International Poetry Festival, established to promote excellence in poetry and participation in the reading and writing of it. There are three awards: for an unpublished poem in English; for an unpublished poem in Irish or Scottish Gaelic language; and smaller on-the-spot prizes for witty verses during the festival. Awarded annually, prizes are €4,000, €2,000 and €1,000 for the two main poetry categories, and €500, €100, €80 for on-the-spot prizes. Poets may also be invited to read their poems at the festival for a fee and travel expenses. Judges are different for each category and are published on the website each year. Copyright

remains with the poet, but Strokestown Community Development Association reserves the right to arrange first publication or broadcast of selected poems. Poems must be unpublished and the original work of a living poet.

Genres Poetry

Submission Guidelines Deadline for entry is the end of January. Guidelines are on the website. Entry fee is £4 for each poem. Work should be previously unpublished.

Tips Entries must be typed or written on single sided paper. Entries will not be returned.

Sunday Times Young Writer of the Year Award

84 Drayton Gardens, London, SW10 9SB

- 020 7373 6642
- 020 7373 5768
- info@societyofauthors.org
- www.societyofauthors.org

Established 1991

Insider Info Sponsored by the Society of Authors. Awarded annually to a young writer under the age of 35 for a full length British publication in the preceding year. The winner receives £5,000. Writers must be usually resident in Britain and their work must be in English.

Genres Fiction, Non-Fiction, Poetry

Submission Guidelines Deadline for entry is October. Guidelines are available on the website. Work should be published previously, between January 1 and December 31.

Tips Submissions are only accepted from publishers; four copies of the work are required.

Sygenta ABSW Science Writers' Awards

58 Greenhill Road, Moseley, Birmingham, B13 9SS

- 07866 769381
- sciencewritersawards@clairejowett.com
- www.sciencewritersawards.co.uk

Established 1966

Insider Info Sponsored by the Association of British Science Writers. Awards given annually across eight categories for excellence in science journalism, including writing and broadcasting. The winners in each category receive £2,000.

Genres Non-Fiction, Essays, Scripts, Articles

Submission Guidelines Guidelines and entry forms available on the website.

Tips Of particular interest to new science journalists is the New Voice Award (formerly the Young Broadcaster), open to journalists aged 30 or under. Detailed guidelines for all categories are published on the website.

Templar Poetry Pamphlet & Collection Competition 2007
Templar Poetry, PO Box 7082, Bakewell, Derbyshire, DE45 9AF

☎ 01629 582500

✉ info@templarpoetry.co.uk

🌐 www.templarpoetry.co.uk

Competition/Award Director Alex McMillen

Established 2005

Insider Info The annual Templar Poetry Pamphlet & Collection competition is open to all poets writing in English. The competition aims to find and publish poetry from new and previously published writers. Four winners have their pamphlets published in a high quality perfect bound pamphlet. They also receive a prize of £500 each and the option to submit a full collection for publication. There is also a competition anthology containing the best individual poems from the remaining submissions. All writers will have the option of recording an audio CD containing a selection of their poems to be included free with their pamphlet or collection. All entrants receive a complimentary copy of the anthology. Submissions are invited of between 18–25 A4 pages of poetry of up to 40 lines per page. Authors retain their rights according to copyright law, but grant the permission to publish their work in the pamphlets, anthology and collections in the usual way, again in accordance with copyright law. Translated poetry is not eligible. There are no residency requirements or limitations.

Genres Poetry

Submission Guidelines Closing date for submissions is the first week of May every year. Further information and rules are available on the Templar Poetry website. Individual poems may have been previously published, but not the submission as a whole. The entry fee is £16.

Theakston's Old Peculier Prize for Crime Novel of the Year
Festival Office, Raglan House, Raglan Street, Harrogate, North Yorkshire, HG1 1LE

☎ 01423 562303

☎ 01423 521264

✉ crime@harrogate-festival.org.uk

🌐 www.harrogate-festival.org.uk

Established 2005

Insider Info Sponsored by Harrogate Crime Writing Festival and Theakston's Old Peculier. An award for a full length crime novel published in Britain and written by a British writer. Presented during the annual crime writing festival which takes place in July. The winner receives £3,000 and a handmade Theakston's beer cask. A shortlist is advertised and members of the public are invited to vote for the winner.

Genres Fiction, Novels

Submission Guidelines Work should be published previously.

Tips The shortlist is usually published around April on the festival's website and tends to include several commercial successes by high profile writers such as Ian Rankin and Val McDermid.

The Tir Na N-Og Award
Castell Brychan, Aberystwyth, Ceredigion, SY23 2JB

☎ 01970 624151

☎ 01970 625385

✉ wbc.children@wbc.org.uk

🌐 www.wbc.org.uk

Established 1976

Insider Info The award is sponsored by Cyngor Llyfrau Cymru (Welsh Books Council) and is an award for children's books. The award is split over three categories: English language books; Welsh language books, primary sector; and Welsh language books, secondary sector. The award is judged annually. The winner in each category receives £3,000.

Genres Children's Books

Submission Guidelines Work should be published previously.

The Translators Association Prizes
84 Drayton Gardens, London, SW10 9SB

☎ 020 7373 6642

☎ 020 7373 5768

✉ info@societyofauthors.org

🌐 www.societyofauthors.org

Insider Info The prizes are administered by the Society of Authors. Awards are given for translations in several categories: Dutch/Flemish Translation, The Vondel Translation Prize; French Translation, The Scott Moncrieff Prize; German Translation, The Schlegel-Tieck Prize; Greek Translation, The Hellenic Foundation for Culture Translation Prize; Italian Translation, The John Florio Prize; Portuguese Translation, The Calouste Gulbenkian Prize; Russian Translation, The Rossica International Prize; Spanish Translation, The Premio Valle Inclán; Swedish Translation, The Bernard Shaw Prize; and Arabic Translations, The Saif Ghobash Banipal Prize. Each prize may be given at different intervals. The prizes vary between £1,000 to £3,000.

Genres Translations

Submission Guidelines Submissions should be received by January 31 every year. Work should be published previously. Submissions should be made by publishers and five copies sent.

Tips For the criteria of each individual prize, visit the Society of Authors website.

Trevor Reese Memorial Prize

Institute of Commonwealth Studies, University of London, 28 Russell Square, London, WC1B 5DS

- ☎ 020 7862 8844
- 📠 020 7862 8820
- ✉ ics@sas.ac.uk
- 🌐 www.commonwealth.sas.ac.uk/reese.htm

Established 1979

Insider Info Awarded in memory of Trevor Reese, an academic in the field of Australian and Commonwealth history. Presented for a work which has made a significant contribution to the study of Imperial and Commonwealth History. The prize is awarded every two years (even years). The winner receives £1,000.

Genres Non-Fiction and Essays

Submission Guidelines Submissions should be received by February of the year before entry. Works must have been published in the two years preceding the year in which the award is presented. Please send two copies of the entry to Dee Burn, Development and Marketing Officer, at the above address.

Tips Submissions are welcome from publishers or writers.

TS Eliot Prize

Poetry Book Society, Fourth Floor, 2 Tavistock Place, London, WC1H 9RA

- ☎ 020 7833 9247
- 📠 020 7833 5990
- ✉ info@poetrybooks.co.uk
- 🌐 www.poetrybooks.co.uk

Insider Info The competition is administered by The Poetry Book Society. The competition takes place annually, with a first prize of £15,000 plus £1,000 for each shortlisted entry. The competition is judged by three judges, with one acting as the Chair. Copyright will remain with the competitor, but PBS reserves the right to publish up to five poems from each shortlisted entry in press releases and related material. The competition is open to poets in the UK or Republic of Ireland only.

Genres Poetry

Submission Guidelines Submissions should be received by the end of July every year and must be entered by the publisher, not the author. Guidelines are available on the website.

Tips The TS Eliot Prize is the largest poetry prize in the UK.

Undiscovered Authors

1st Floor, Blissett House, Roslin Road, London, W3 8DH

- ☎ 0844 800 5215
- ✉ generalenquiries@discoveredauthors.co.uk
- 🌐 www.discoveredauthors.co.uk

Competition/Award Director Graham Miller

Established 2005

Insider Info An annual competition, sponsored by Discovered Authors. The organisation looks for works in the categories of General Fiction, Non-Fiction and Academic. These three categories are open to unpublished writers, plus a new and separate category has been introduced for Previously Published Authors. There is a top National prize of £10,000 available, plus a publishing contract with Discovered Authors. The General Fiction category is split regionally across the UK and Ireland with a prize of £1,000 per region. All regional winners will be put forward to a national final to win a top prize of £10,000, along with three wild card entries, which will be selected from the favourite losing entries. Regional 2nd and 3rd placed entrants will also win a prize of publication. The Non-Fiction and Academic categories will be judged on a national level only – with the winners receiving a prize of £1,000. The Previously Published category is a new addition to the competition and is open to published writers – but the text they submit must be previously unpublished – the national winner in this category will win £2,500. A publication contract with Discovered Authors will be offered to all winners. No rights will be acquired at entry. The competition is open to all writers.

Genres Fiction, Non-Fiction, Poetry, Children's, Novels, Short Stories, Story Collections and Academic

Submission Guidelines Submissions should be received by the end of January every year. Guidelines and entry forms are available via email. A synopsis and completed work is required at entry. Registration details are available at www.undiscoveredauthors.co.uk. The entry fee is £10. Work should be unpublished.

Verity Bargate Award

Soho Theatre Company, 21 Dean Street, London, W1D 3NE

- ☎ 020 7287 5060
- 📠 020 7287 5061
- ✉ writers@sohotheatre.com
- 🌐 www.sohotheatre.com

Insider Info The award is sponsored by Soho Theatre Company and is a national competition to find the best play by a new or fledgling writer. The award is given every two years (odd years). The prize is £5,000 and a residency at the Soho Theatre. Open to writers resident in the UK or Republic of Ireland. The following are not eligible: writers with three or more professional productions to their credit; plays commissioned by Soho Theatre Company (STC); previous Verity Bargate Award winners; and plays that have already been rejected by the STC literary department.

Genres Scripts

Submission Guidelines Submissions should be received by the July of the year of entry. Guidelines are available on the website. Work should be unpublished and unproduced.

Tips Submit one full-length play of at least 70 minutes on any subject. Include a title page with contact details and two SAEs for acknowledgement letter and manuscripts. Also please include a career history of all publications/productions.

Ver Poets Open Competition
Room G1, St Albans School, Abbey Gateway, St Albans, AL1 4AH
- 01727 864898
- daphne.schiller@virgin.net
- www.verpoets.org.uk

Insider Info An open competition for poetry of up to 30 lines on any theme or subject. The competition is held annually. The overall winner receives £500, 2nd place wins £300 and 3rd place wins £100. There is also a Young Writers prize of £100. The copyright remains with the author.

Genres Poetry

Submission Guidelines Submissions should be received by the end of April of each year. Entry fees are: £3 per poem, £10 for 4 poems and £2 each for the 11th poem onwards. Work should be unpublished.

Tips Submit two copies of each poem with an application form, downloadable from the website. Do not submit any translations or poems that have been entered in any other competition.

Vogue Talent Contest
Vogue House, Hanover Square, London, W1S 1JU
- www.vogue.co.uk

Insider Info A competition for young journalists, or potential journalists, under the age of 25. Entrants are invited to submit three pieces of writing on set subjects. Previous awards have required a 600 word autobiography, a 600 word arts review or comment on a fashion trend, and an 800 word magazine-style profile of an important person in their life. The contest is held annually. The winner receives £1,000 and a month's paid work experience at *Vogue*. The runner up receives £500. Judges will include the

editor of *Vogue*, senior magazine staff and guest writers and editors. Copyright of entries belongs to Condé Nast Publications Ltd. Writers must be under 25 on the January 1 in the year of the award presentation.

Submission Guidelines Submissions should be received by April. Entries should be unpublished.

Tips The judges state they are looking for 'creativity, wit and stylish writing'. Studying several copies of *Vogue* magazine may give an idea of the magazine's style of writing.

VS Pritchett Memorial Prize
The Royal Society of Literature, Strand, London, WC2R 1LA
- 020 7845 4676
- 020 7845 4679
- info@rslit.org
- www.rslit.org

Established 1999

Insider Info Prize is sponsored by the Royal Society of Literature and Chatto & Windus and is awarded for a short story of between 2,000 and 5,000 words in memory of VS Pritchett. The prize is awarded annually. The winner receives £1,000 and publication of their story in *The London Magazine*. Writers must be resident in the UK or Ireland.

Genres Short Stories

Submission Guidelines Submissions should be received by January of each year. Writers wishing to enter the competition should email the above address for an entry form in November and it will be sent in the mail, alternatively the form is also available on the website. The cost for entry is £5 per story. Work should be unpublished.

Tips Entries should be double spaced on single sided A4 paper. Please do not send any handwritten entries. Entrants may read VS Pritchett's stories for inspiration.

Wadsworth Prize for Business History
Lloyds TSB Group Archives, 5th Floor, Princess House, 1 Suffolk Lane, London, EC4R 0AX
- 020 7489 3945
- www.businessarchivescouncil.org.uk

Established 1978

Insider Info Prize is sponsored by The Business Archives Council and is awarded to an individual who is deemed to have made an outstanding contribution to the study of business history in the preceding year. The prize is awarded annually.

Genres Non-Fiction

Submission Guidelines Work should be previously published.

Tips Nominations should be by publishers only. All correspondence should be addressed to Karen Sampson at the above address.

Wales Book of the Year Award
Academi, Third Floor, Mount Stuart House, Mount Stuart Square, Cardiff, CF10 5FQ
- 029 2047 2266
- 029 2049 2930
- post@academi.org
- www.academi.org/book-of-the-year

Competition/Award Director Chief Executive, Peter Finch

Established 1986

Insider Info The competition is administered by Academi with funding from the Arts Council of Wales. The prize is awarded annually to the best Welsh language and English language works in the fields of creative writing and literary criticism. Two winners, one English and one Welsh author, receive prizes of £10,000. Four runners-up each receive £1,000. Academi will only accept submissions of books published during the previous calendar year, from publishers only.

Genres Novels, Short Fiction Collections

Submission Guidelines The Academi will attempt to contact the publishers of all relevant books. Publishers who wish to nominate their authors are asked to send five copies of the book to Academi by post.

Ware Poets Open Poetry Competition
48 Highbury Road, Hitchen, SG4 9SA
- www.rockingham-press.co.uk

Insider Info An open competition for poetry of up to 50 lines on any theme or subject. The competition is held annually. The prizes are: £500 for 1st place, £200 for 2nd and £100 for 3rd. Winning entries will be published in the competition anthology.

Genres Poetry

Submission Guidelines Submissions should be received by April. Guidelines for the submission of entries are available on the website. Entry fees are: £3 per poem, £10 for four poems and £2.50 for the 11th poem onwards. Work should be unpublished.

Tips There is also a separate £100 prize for sonnets, sponsored by Redwing. Sonnets may therefore be considered for both prizes and should be marked with an 'S' in the top right-hand corner of the entry.

Wellington Town Council Short Story Competition
Civic Offices, Larkin Way, Tan Bank, Wellington, Telford, TF1 1LX
- 01952 567697
- 01952 567690
- welltowncl@aol.com
- www.wellington-shropshire.gov.uk

Contact Town Clerk, Derrick Drew

Established 1997

Insider Info Competition is sponsored by Wellington Town Council. The competition is open to persons regardless of age or location and it has no theme. Entries should not exceed 4,500 words. Prizes are awarded in the following three categories: Best story nationally; Best Story submitted by a Shropshire resident; Best Story written by a young person (aged 16 or younger). Competition is held annually. Cash prizes are awarded and there is a trophy for the winner of the Shropshire resident category and for that of the under 16 category. The competition is judged by Write Associates (www.writeassociates.co.uk).

Genres Fiction, Children's and Short Stories.

Submission Guidelines Submissions should be received by the end of August each year. Guidelines and entry form are available with SAE. Work should be unpublished.

The Wheatley Medal
Woodbourn Business Centre, 10 Jessell Street, Sheffield, S9 3HY
- 0114 244 9561
- 0114 244 9563
- info@indexers.org.uk
- www.indexers.org.uk

Insider Info Sponsored by the Society of Indexers. The Wheatley Medal is an award that recognises an outstanding index in any type of publication. The award is given annually. The winner receives £200, plus a medal and certificate.

Submission Guidelines Work should be published previously.

Tips A set of criteria that the judges will use to make the award is published on the Society of Indexers website.

Whitfield Prize
Royal Historical Society, University College London, Gower Street, London, WC1E 6BT
- 020 7387 7532
- 020 7387 7532
- royalhistsoc@ucl.ac.uk
- www.royalhistoricalsociety.org

Established 1977

Insider Info Prize is sponsored by the Royal Historical Society. The annual Whitfield Prize is awarded for a first published book on British history, published in the UK during the previous year. The winner receives £1,000. The submission must be the writer's first published history book.

Genres Non-Fiction

Submission Guidelines Submissions should be received by the end of December of the previous year. The work should be published previously.
Tips Submissions by authors or publishers are welcome. Please send three copies before the closing date.

The Wilfred Owen Award for Poetry

- woa@1914-18.co.uk
- www.1914-18.co.uk/owen

Established 1988
Insider Info The award is sponsored by Faber & Faber and The Royal College of Art and is awarded for poetry that is deemed to reflect the intentions and feel of Wilfred Owen's own poetry. The award is judged annually. The winner is presented with a piece of art.
Genres Poetry
Submission Guidelines Work should be published previously.
Tips Please do not send any submissions, the winner is selected by the Wilfred Owen Association. Winners and details of the award ceremony are published on the website.

William Hill Sports Book of the Year

William Hill, Greenside House, 50 Station Road, Wood Green, London, N22 7TP

- 020 8918 3731
- 020 8918 3728
- pressoffice@williamhill.co.uk
- www.williamhillmedia.com

Established 1989
Insider Info Awarded for the best book on a sporting theme, known as 'The Bookie Prize'. The award is usually announced in November and is held annually. The winner receives £20,000, a free £2,000 bet, and a specially commissioned hand-bound copy of their book.
Genres Sports Books
Submission Guidelines Submissions should be received by September 11. Work should be published previously, having appeared between September 30 of the previous year and September 29 of the year of entry.
Tips Books must be nominated and entered by publishers.

Wingate Literary Prize

Jewish Quarterly, PO Box 37645, London, NW7 1WB

- 020 8343 4675
- admin@jewishquarterly.org
- www.jewishquarterly.org

Established 1977

Insider Info The prize is sponsored by the Harold Hyam Wingate Foundation. The Wingate Literary Prize is an award designed to celebrate work that encourages an interest in Jewish themes and issues in a wider readership. The prize is awarded annually. The winner receives £4,000. Writers may be resident in the UK, the Commonwealth, Israel or the Republic of Ireland, but books must be published in the UK.
Genres Fiction and Non-Fiction
Submission Guidelines Work should be published previously.
Tips Translations and originals are eligible as long as they reflect Jewish concerns.

W.J.M. Mackenzie Book Prize

Political Studies Association, Department of Politics, University of Newcastle, Newcastle upon Tyne, NE1 7RU

- 0191 222 8021
- 0191 222 3499
- psa@ncl.ac.uk
- www.psa.ac.uk

Established 1987
Insider Info Awarded for a political science book published in the preceding year. Prize is awarded annually.
Genres Non-Fiction
Submission Guidelines Submissions should be received by October. Work should be published previously having appeared between January 1 and December 31 of the previous year.
Tips Nominations from members of the Political Studies Association only.

Wolfson History Prizes

The Wolfson Foundation, 8 Queen Anne Street, London, W1G 9LD

- 020 7323 5730
- 020 7323 3241
- www.wolfson.org.uk

Established 1972
Insider Info Prizes are sponsored by the Wolfson Foundation. They are awarded to promote and encourage the writing of history for the general public. Prizes are given for two works published during the year, with an occasional general award for an individual's outstanding contribution to the writing of history. The prizes are awarded annually. Writers must be British and normally resident in Britain, and the work must have also been published in Britain.
Genres Non-Fiction
Submission Guidelines Work should be published previously.
Tips Books are selected by judges, but suggestions for consideration may be made in writing. Books

should be academic, yet remain accessible to a more general readership.

Write a Story for Children Competition

The Academy of Children's Writers, PO Box 95, Huntingdon, Cambridgeshire, PE28 5RL

- 01487 832752
- 01487 832752
- enquiries@childrens-writers.co.uk
- www.childrens-writers.co.uk

Competition/Award Director Roger Dewar
Established 1985
Insider Info The competition is sponsored by the Academy of Children's Writers and is for a short story of up to 2,000 words aimed at children of any age up to teenage. The author must be over 18 and previously unpublished. The competition is held annually. The 1st Prize is £2,000, 2nd Prize is £300 and 3rd Prize is £200. The competition is judged by an independent panel. The competition is open to all.
Genres Fiction, Children's and Short Stories
Submission Guidelines Submissions should be received by the end of March each year. Guidelines and entry forms are available with SAE. The entry fee is £2.70.
Tips Full rules and conditions are available on the website.

The Writers Bureau Poetry & Short Story Competition

Sevendale House, 7 Dale Street, Manchester, M1 1JB

- 0161 228 2362
- 0161 236 9440
- advisory@writersbureau.com
- www.writersbureau.com

Established 1994
Insider Info An open poetry competition for poems of up to 40 lines and short stories of up to 2,000 words. The competition is held annually. Prizes are £1,000, £400, £200 and £100, plus six runner-up prizes of £50 in each category. Copyright remains with the author but first publication rights lay with The Writers Bureau once assigned from the writer, as does permission to include the work on The Writers Bureau website for up to 12 months.
Genres Poetry and Short Stories
Submission Guidelines Submissions should be received by 30th June. Entry fee is £5 per entry. Work should be unpublished.
Tips Online and postal entries accepted but entries by email will not be accepted. All posted sheets should be single sided and double spaced.

Writers Forum Poetry & Short Story Competitions

PO Box 3229, Bournemouth, BH1 1ZS

- 01202 589828
- 01202 587758
- editorial@writers-forum.com
- www.writers-forum.com

Insider Info Sponsored by *Writers Forum Magazine*. For the monthly poetry competition, readers may submit a poem of up to 40 lines. 1st prize is £100 and three runners-up win Chambers dictionaries. Similarly, readers may submit short stories of between 1,500 and 3,000 words. There is a minimum monthly 1st prize of £300, 2nd prize of £150 and 3rd prize of £100 – with an annual trophy and a cheque for £1,000 for the yearly winner. All entries receive critical feedback at no extra cost.
Genres Poetry and Short Stories
Submission Guidelines Poetry entries should be received by the 15th of each month. Short stories should be received by the 5th of each month. Guidelines and entry form are available on the website. Entry fees are: £5 for one poem, £7 for two, and £10 for each short story (a reading fee). Work should be previously unpublished.
Tips The guidelines state that by reading the magazine, writers are more likely to be successful.

Writers Inc Writers-of-the-Year Competition

14 Somerset Gardens, London, SE13 7SY

- 020 8305 8844
- 020 8469 2147

Established 1993
Insider Info An open competition for poetry and prose across various categories. The 2007 categories were: Poems; Extended sequences of poems; Short stories (50–2,500 words); and Writing for children (8–12 years, up to 20,000 words). The competition is held annually. The prize money totals £3,000 and winners will be invited to read their work at a Writers Inc event. A portion of the prize fund may be allocated as bursaries, awarded to writers from London to attend a writing weekend at the Abbey in Sutton Courtenay, Oxfordshire. One winner will be submitted to the Forward Poetry Prize and in the category for writing for children, the winning entry will be read by a London literary agency. Copyright remains with the author, but Writers Inc reserves the right to first publication after the closing date. The competition is open to any writer writing in English.
Genres Fiction, Poetry and Short Stories
Submission Guidelines Submissions should be received by April. Guidelines and entry form are available on the website. Entry fees are: £3 for poems up to 60 lines, £5 for poems over 60 lines, £8 for a

poetry sequence of up to 400 lines, £5 for a short story, £12 for three short stories and £4 for a children's story. Work should be previously unpublished.

Tips Competition categories may change from year to year, so please check the website for new competition details.

YoungMinds Book Award
48–50 St John Street, London, EC1M 4DG
- 020 7336 8445
- 020 7336 8446
- bookaward@youngminds.org.uk
- www.youngminds.org.uk

Established 2003

Insider Info Awarded to a publication that highlights and explores the ways a child takes in and makes sense of the world, or gives an insight into the minds of children. The competition is held annually. The winner receives £2,000.

Genres Fiction, Non-Fiction, Poetry, Novels and Memoirs

Submission Guidelines Work should be published previously.

Tips Only accepts submissions from publishers.

The Aldeburgh International Poetry Festival

The Poetry Trust, The Cut, 9 New Cut, Halesworth, Suffolk, IP19 8BY

- 01986 835950
- 01986 874524
- info@thepoetrytrust.org
- www.thepoetrytrust.org

Contact Festival Director, Naomi Jaffa

Dates November

About A mixture of free and ticketed poetry readings and events with an attendance of around 3,800.

Animated Exeter

Animated Exeter, Exeter City Council, Civic Centre, Paris Street, Exeter, EX1 1JN

- 01392 265208
- 01392 256366
- animatedexeter@exeter.gov.uk
- www.exeter.gov.uk/festival

Dates February

About A film and animation festival, including special screenings and workshops.

Aspects Festival

North Down Heritage Centre, Bangor, Co. Down, BT20 4BT

- 028 9127 8032
- www.northdown.gov.uk

Dates Late September

About A series of events to celebrate Irish writing. Many guest speakers across various genres of writing.

Athlone Literary Festival

Custume Place, Athlone, Co. Westmeath, Republic of Ireland

- 00353 90 643 4420
- literaryathlone@gmail.com
- www.athlone.ie/literaryfestival

Dates September

About Formerly known as the John Broderick Weekend, which celebrated the work of Broderick. It is now a broader literary festival. Guest speakers include writers, poets, agents and academics.

Aurthur Miller Centre International Literary Festival

Literary Festival Administrator, HUM Faculty Office, University of East Anglia, Norwich, NR4 7TJ

- 01603 592810
- 01603 507728
- s.alexander@uea.ac.uk
- www1.uea.ac.uk/cm/home/schools/hum/booksandwriters/litfest

Dates Spring

About An annual festival of events and talks by well known writers.

Ballymena Arts Festival

Leisure and Events Unit, Ballymena Showgrounds, Warden Street, Ballymena, Co. Antrine, BT43 7DR

- 028 2563 9853
- 028 2563 8549
- rosalind.lowry@ballymena.gov.uk
- www.ballymena.gov.uk

Contact Rosalind Lowry

Dates March/April

About A general arts festival that offers a varied programme of activities including music, dance, theatre, comedy and storytelling. The festival now takes place in The Braid, Northern Ireland's newest museum, arts and civic centre.

Bath Literature Festival

Bath Festivals Ltd, Abbey Chambers, Kingston Buildings, Bath, BA1 1NT

- 01225 462231
- 01225 445551
- info@bathfestivals.org.uk
- www.bathlitfest.org.uk

Contact Artistic Director, Sarah LeFanu

Dates February/March

About Ten days of literary events, encompassing writing in all its forms. The festival is fast gaining a reputation for presenting the very best in local, national and international writers to an ever-increasing audience.

Beverley Literature Festival

Wordquake, Council Offices, Skirlaugh, East Riding of Yorkshire, HU11 5HN

- 01482 392745
- john@bevlit.org
- www.beverley-literature-festival.org

Contact Festival Director, John Clarke

Dates October

About A series of literature events and readings, including some to live music. A children's programme runs alongside the main festival.

Birmingham Book Festival

Midland Creative Projects Ltd, Unit 116, Custard Factory, Gibb Street, Birmingham, B9 4AA

- 0121 246 2770
- 0121 246 2771
- www.birminghambookfestival.org

Contact Artistic Director, Jonathan Davidson; Programme Manager, Sara Beadle; Project Manager, Lucy Wood

Dates October

About An annual festival of books and writing. The festival is a not-for-profit charity and also runs an extensive 'writers in schools' programme (Write On! – Adventures in Writing) and undertakes year round events and activities.

Book Now! Literature Festival

London Borough of Richmond upon Thames, The Arts Service, Orleans House Gallery, Riverside, Twickenham, TW1 3DJ

- 020 8831 6494
- 020 8940 7568
- artsinfo@richmond.gov.uk
- www.richmond.gov.uk/ book_now_literature_festival

Contact Festival Programmer, Penny Bowles

Dates November

About A series of high-profile writers, from biographers, novelists and poets to leading figures from film, politics and media, give lectures on aspects of writing and literature.

Bournemouth Literary Festival

BLF, 20a Parkwood Road, Bournemouth, Dorset, BH5 2BH

- 01202 417535
- info@bournemouthliteraryfestival.co.uk
- www.bournemouthliteraryfestival.co.uk

Contact Director & Founder, Lillian Avon

Dates September/October

About Bournemouth's international and multicultural literary festival offers events for both adults and children, including authors' news, views and reviews, competitions, parties, performances and workshops. Each year has a theme, or set of themes, with events spread across September and October.

Brighton Children's Book Festival

Brighton Writers' Centre, 49 Grand Parade, Brighton, BN2 9QA

- 01273 571700
- cara@thesouth.org.uk
- www.bcbf.org.uk

Contact Festival Director, Cara Courage

Dates 10th and 11th July (2009)

About Brighton Children's Book Festival is an annual event celebrating children's book writing, illustrating and publishing. It is open to adults and young people, and aims to appeal to parents and children, teachers and librarians, aspiring and practising children's book authors and illustrators, and people working in electronic media, TV, film and publishing. The festival offers a combination of talks, hands-on workshops, and networking events, and runs on a different theme each year. The theme for 2007 was 'Children of the South', 2008's theme was 'Leaping from the Page' and the theme for 2009 is 'Get Real', which will look at writing for children based on real experience. The festival also runs a parallel series of community events in partnership with THE SOUTH.

Brighton Festival

12a Pavilion Buildings, Castle Square, Brighton, BN1 1EE

- 01273 700747
- info@brightonfestival.org
- www.brightonfestival.org

Contact Press Manager, Shelley Hughes

Dates May

About Brighton Festival features an exciting programme of theatre, dance, music, books and debate, children's and family shows, and outdoor spectacle.

Bristol Poetry Festival

Poetry Can, 12 Great George Street, Bristol, Bristol, BS1 5RH

- 0117 933 0900
- admin@poetrycan.co.uk
- www.poetrycan.co.uk

Dates September

About An annual festival featuring poetry readings, open mic nights, seminars, talks and workshops around Bristol. Organised by Poetry Can.

The British & Irish Contemporary Poetry Conference

St Anne's College, Woodstock Road, Oxford, OX2 6HS

- coordinator@poetryconference.org.uk
- www.poetryconference.org.uk

Contact Conference Coordinator, Clare Brown

Dates September
About A weekend conference for academics, designed to produce original, contemporary poetry.

Buxton Festival
3 The Square, Buxton, Derbyshire, SK17 6AZ
- 01298 70395
- 01298 72289
- info@buxtonfestival.co.uk
- www.buxtonfestival.co.uk

Contact Artistic Director, Andrew Greenwood
Dates July
About A music and literature festival, with an emphasis on opera.

Cambridge Wordfest
Bick Barn, Royston Lane, Comberton, CB23 7EE
- 01223 264404
- admin@cambridgewordfest.co.uk
- www.cambridgewordfest.co.uk

Contact Festival Director & Founder, Cathy Moore
Dates April
About A three-day literature festival with events for adults and children, taking place in the ADC Theatre. Also runs a Winter Wordfest one-day festival in Novmber, as well as the Wordfest Summer School.

Canterbury Festival
Festival Office, Christ Church Gate, The Precincts, Canterbury, Kent, CT1 2EE
- 01227 452853
- info@canterburyfestival.co.uk
- www.canterburyfestival.co.uk

Contact Festival Director, Rosie Turner; Festival Administrator, Sylviane Martell
Dates October
About The Canterbury Festival is Kent's International Arts Festival, the largest festival of arts and culture in the region. It attracts an audience of nearly 80,000 people, to over 200 events across two weeks.

The Charleston Festival
The Charleston Trust, Charleston Firle, Lewes, East Sussex, BN8 6LL
- 01323 811626
- info@charleston.org.uk
- www.charleston.org.uk/charlestonfestival

Dates May
About The Charleston Festival is held in May and hosts a programme of literary events, workshops and readings by guest speakers. Small Wonder, the short story festival, is held in September. See separate entry for details.

Chaucer Festival
Chaucer Heritage Trust, 22 St Peter's Street, Canterbury, CT1 2BQ
- 01227 470379

Dates Spring/Summer/Autumn
About An annual festival taking place at various locations throughout London, Canterbury and Kent during the spring, summer and autumn. Includes medieval fairs, readings, performances and schools programmes based around the works of Chaucer.

Chester Literature Festival
55-57 Watergate Row South, Chester, , CH1 2LE
- 01244 409113
- info@chesterlitfest.org.uk
- www.chesterfestivals.co.uk/literature

Contact Katherine Seddon
Dates October
About A literature festival with workshops, readings and other events.

Chichester Festivities
Canon Gate House, South Street, Chichester, West Sussex, PO19 1PU
- 01243 785718
- info@chifest.org.uk
- www.chifest.org.uk

Dates June/July
About An arts festival across various venues in Chichester, including workshops, talks and readings from literary speakers.

City of London Festival
Fitz Eylwin House, 25 Holborn Viaduct, London, EC1A 2BP
- 020 7583 3585
- 020 7353 0455
- admin@colf.org
- www.colf.org

Contact Festival Director, Ian Ritchie; General Manager, Lindsey Dear
Dates June/July
About An arts festival offering a varied programme including opera, literature, installations and exhibitions of visual arts, film screenings and architecture walks and talks. Many of the bigger events are broadcast by the BBC.

County Bookshop Peak Festival (Spring & Autumn)
Countrybookshop, Hassop Station, Nr Bakewell, Derbyshire, DE45 1NW
- www.countrybookshop.co.uk/peakfestival

Dates May/June and October/November

About Two large literary festivals, in Spring and Autumn, held in the Peak District with many well known authors. The Peak District Book of the Year Award is also presented as part of the festival.

The Cuirt International Festival of Literature
Galway Arts Centre, 47 Dominick Street, Co. Galway, Republic of Ireland
- 00353 91 565886
- 00353 91 568642
- maura@galwayartscentre.ie
- www.galwayartscentre.ie/cuirt

Contact Programme Director, Maura Kennedy
Dates April
About A festival of around 6,000 visitors, offering an eclectic mix of Irish and international writers. Includes readings, signings and workshops.

Derbyshire Literature Festival
Venues across Derbyshire
- 01773 831359
- alison.betteridge@derbyshire.gov.uk
- www.derbyshire.gov.uk

Contact Literature Development Officer, Alison Betteridge
Dates 1–14 June (2010)
About A biennial festival which takes place during the first two weeks in June. The next festival is in 2010. The festival takes place in venues all over Derbyshire and aims to encourage people to become involved in all kinds of literature and storytelling events.

Dorchester Festival
Dorchester Arts Centre, School Lane, The Grove, Dorchester, Dorset, DT1 1XR
- 01305 266926
- enquiries@dorchesterarts.org.uk
- www.dorchesterarts.org.uk

Dates May
About A local arts festival with a few literary events.

Dromineer Literary Festival
Arts Office, North Tipperary County Council, Civic Offices, Limerick Road, Nenagh, Co. Tipperary, Republic of Ireland
- 00353 87 753 5207
- festival@dromineer.net
- http://festival.dromineer.net

Contact Chair, Pat Kelly; Secretary, Eleanor Hooker
Dates September
About A weekend festival. The programme includes readings, storytelling and competitions.

Dublin Writers Festival
Dublin City Arts Office, The Lab, Foley Street, Dublin 1, Republic of Ireland
- 00353 1 222 5455
- office@dublinwritersfestival.com
- www.dublinwritersfestival.com

Contact Festival Director, Jack Gilligan; Programme Director, Liam Browne
Dates June
About A five-day writer's festival typically featuring over 40 Irish and international writers and poets, journalists, political commentators, and even lawyers for a series of readings, discussions, debates and public interviews. Some events are specifically for children.

Durham Book Festival
DCA (Durham City Arts), 2 The Cottages, Fowler's Yard, Back Silver Street, Durham City, DH1 3RA
- 0191 375 0763
- enquiries@durhamcityarts.org.uk
- www.bookfestival.org.uk

Dates October (2009)
About The longest running and largest literature festival in the North East comprising a range of literary events, readings, workshops and talks across Durham City and County.

The Dylan Thomas Festival
Dylan Thomas Centre, Somerset Place, Swansea, SA1 1RR
- 01792 463980
- 01792 463993
- dylanthomas.lit@swansea.gov.uk
- www.dylanthomas.com

Dates October/November
About An annual festival to celebrate the life and work of Dylan Thomas. The programme includes poetry readings, performances, films, talks and discussions. The Dylan Thomas Centre also organises year round literary events.

Edgeworth Literary Festival
Ballymahon Road, Edgeworthstown, Co. Longford, Republic of Ireland
- 00353 43 71801
- edgelocdev@eircom.net
- www.edgeworthliteraryfestival.com

Dates March
About A festival based around an annual literary competition, culminating in a gala weekend with events, readings, talks and discussions. Set in the town of Edgeworthstown.

Edinburgh International Book Festival

5a Charlotte Square, Edinburgh, EH2 4DR
- 0131 718 5666
- 0131 226 5335
- admin@edbookfest.co.uk
- www.edbookfest.co.uk

Contact Festival Director, Catherine Lockerbie
Dates August
About A world-class festival of literature and books, with around 220,000 visitors. Generally features over 600 authors, both new and famous, from over 30 different countries. A large selection of events for toddlers, young readers, teenagers and young adults also runs alongside the main festival.

Ennis BookClub Festival

25 Willsgrove, Cahercalla, Ennis, Co. Clare, Republic of Ireland
- 00353 87 972 3647
- info@ennisbookclubfestival.com
- www.ennisbookclubfestival.com

Dates March
About A three-day festival celebrating books of all types and genres. The festival is designed with the reader in mind. and aims to attract Book Clubs and Book Lovers from Ireland and abroad. Events include readings, lectures, music, workshops, exhibitions, cookery demonstrations and more.

Essex Poetry Festival

Cramphorn Theatre, Fairfield Road, Chelmsford, Essex, CM1 1JG
- 01245 606505
- derek@essex-poetry-festival.co.uk
- www.essex-poetry-festival.co.uk

Contact Derek Adams
Dates September/October
About A festival of poetry readings and talks. The festival incorporates the Young Essex Poet of the Year competition and the Essex Poetry Festival Competition.

Federation of Worker Writers & Community Publishers Festival of Writing

Burslem School of Art, Queen Street, Stoke on Trent, Staffordshire, ST6 3EJ
- 01782 822327
- thefwwcp@tiscali.co.uk
- http://myweb.tiscali.co.uk/thefwwcp/info.htm

Dates Spring
About An annual festival for members of the FWWCP, which includes workshops, readings and opportunities to write. The federation is a not-for-profit members organisation for writers' groups and community publishers.

Festival at the Edge

Festival at the Edge, The Morgan Library, Aston Street, Wem, Shropshire, SY4 5AU
- 01939 236626
- info@festivalattheedge.org
- www.festivalattheedge.org

Contact Sue Chand
Dates 3rd weekend in July (Friday to Sunday)
About Major UK Storytelling festival in Much Wenlock, Shropshire. Offers an exciting programme of storytelling and music performances including new storytelling commissions, open spot storyrounds, tales around the fire, workshops (both story and music), a full children's programme, craft stalls, on site catering and camping. A family friendly event.

Folkestone Literary Festival

Festival Office, 65-69 Tontine Street, Folkestone, CT20 1JR
- 01303 842192
- info@folkestonelitfest.co.uk
- www.folkestonelitfest.co.uk

Contact Festivals Manager, Roberta Spicer
Dates November
About Offers a range of different activities, literary workshops, screenings and discussions taking place over the course of nine days. The festival also runs a short story competition and a series of children's events.

Frome Festival

25 Market Place, Frome, BA11 1AH
- 01373 455420
- office@fromefestival.co.uk
- www.fromefestival.co.uk

Contact Founder, Martin Bax; Creative Director, Martin Dimery
Dates July
About A community arts festival with a literature element. The ten-day festival typically features over 150 events, from pop culture to horticulture.

The Guardian Hay Festival

The Drill Hall, 25 Lion Street, Hay-on-Wye, HR3 5AD
- 0870 787 2848
- 01497 821066
- admin@hayfestival.com
- www.hayfestival.com

Contact Festival Director, Peter Florence
Dates May

About Hay-on-Wye is a paradise for lovers of secondhand books. The Guardian Hay Festival is a major UK festival, which includes talks from a number of famous literary personalities. Webcasts and podcasts of events are made available, and the festival is generally covered on Sky Arts, Radio 4 and the Guardian website. The Hay Festival is now an international event, with festivals in Cartagena, Bogota, Alhambra and Segovia.

Guildford Book Festival
Venues around Guildford
- 01483 444334
- director@guildfordbookfestival.co.uk
- www.guildfordbookfestival.co.uk

Contact Festival Director, Glenis Pycraft
Dates 15-24 October (2009)
About Talks, workshops and events, in and around Guildford. 2009 is the 20th anniversary of the festival.

Harrogate Crime Writing Festival
Raglan House, Raglan Street, Harrogate, North Yorkshire, HG1 1LE
- 01423 562303
- 01423 521264
- info@harrogate-festival.org.uk
- www.harrogate-festival.org.uk/crime

Contact Festival Co-ordinator, Erica Morris
Dates July
About Launched in 2003 the Theakstons Old Peculier Crime Writing Festival has grown into the largest literary crime fiction event of its kind, and has achieved international acclaim for its programming, organisation and Festival atmosphere. Over 7,000 people including writers, editors, publicists, reviewers, press and aficionados attend the Festival each July.

The Humber Mouth Literature Festival
City Arts Unit, Central Library, Albion Street, Kingston upon Hull, HU1 3TF
- 01482 300300
- humbermouth@gmail.com
- www.humbermouth.org.uk

Contact Festival Director, Maggie Hannan; Festival Assistant, Colin Hurst
Dates June
About The Humber Mouth Literature Festival takes place in Hull during the last two weeks of June, presenting a wide range of events featuring authors, speakers and artists from the UK and around the world.

Ilkley Literature Festival
Manor House, 2 Castle Hill, Ilkley, West Yorkshire, LS29 9DT
- 01943 601210
- 01943 817079
- admin@ilkleyliteraturefestival.org.uk
- www.ilkleyliteraturefestival.org.uk

Contact Festival Director, Rachel Feldberg; Administrator, Gail Price
Dates October
About A two-week literature festival sponsored by Skipton Building Society. The festival includes a free fringe programme and a children's programme.

International Playwriting Festival
Warehouse Theatre, Dingwall Road, Croydon, CR20 2NF
- 020 8681 1257
- 020 8688 6699
- rose@warehousetheatre.co.uk
- www.warehousetheatre.co.uk/ipf.html

Contact Festival Administrator, Rose Marie Vernon
Dates November
About The IPF is held in two parts: The first is a competition with entries accepted from all over the world, which are judged by a panel of distinguished theatre practitioners. The second is a showcase of the selected plays which is held in November. Twinned with the Italian festival Premio Candoni Arta Terme.

Jewish Book Week
Jewish Book Council, ORT House, 126 Albert Street, London, NW1 7NE
- 020 7446 8771
- 020 7446 8777
- info@jewishbookweek.com
- www.jewishbookweek.com

Dates February/March
About A week celebrating Jewish books and writing, with international speakers and events for children.

King's Lynn Festival
5 Thoresby College, Queen Street, King's Lynn, Norfolk, PE30 1HX
- 01553 767557
- 01533 767688
- www.kingslynnfestival.org.uk

Contact Artistic Director, Ambrose Miller; Administrator, Joanne Mawson
Dates July
About An arts festival with an emphasis on musical performance, although literature talks and events are also held.

King's Lynn Literature Festivals

c/o Anthony Ellis, Hawkins Solicitors, 19 Tuesday Market Place, King's Lynn, Norfolk, PE30 1JW

- 01553 691661
- enquiries@lynnlitfests.com
- www.lynnlitfests.com

Contact Chairman, Anthony Ellis

Dates March & September

About A fiction festival in March and a poetry festival in September, both held over weekends. Programmes include presentations from international writers in different genres.

King's Sutton Literary Festival

Festival Tickets, 4 Church Avenue, King's Sutton, Banbury, Oxfon, OX17 3RJ

- 01295 810108
- info@kslitfest.co.uk
- www.kslitfest.co.uk

Contact Jackie Bradley

Dates March

About A weekend festival of literary events, sponsored by the Banbury Guardian, including readings and guest speakers.

Knutsford Literature Festival

76 Glebelands Road, Knutsford, Cheshire, WA16 9DZ

- 01565 722738
- knutsfordlitfest@yahoo.co.uk
- www.knutsfordlitfest.blogspot.com

Dates October

About A small, independent festival, offering a range of literary events.

Latitude

Festival Republic, 35 Bow Street, Covent Garden, London, WC2E 7AU

- 020 7009 3001
- info@latitudefestival.co.uk
- www.latitudefestival.co.uk

Dates July

About A weekend music festival at Henham Park, Suffolk, with elements of drama, poetry and other literary events. A campsite is available.

Ledbury Poetry Festival

Venues around Ledbury

- 0845 458 1743
- director@poetry-festival.com
- www.poetry-festival.com

Contact Director, Chloe Garner

Dates July

About Britain's largest poetry festival with a resident poet, over ten days every summer. Offers many events for both adults and children, including workshops and readings, and also runs an international poetry competition.

Lewes Live Literature Festival

PO Box 2766, Lewes, East Sussex, BN7 2WF

- 07972 037612
- info@leweslivelit.co.uk
- www.leweslivelit.co.uk

Contact Artistic Director, Mark Hewitt

Dates October

About The festival programme includes creative writing workshops, spoken word performances, readings, music, film, and visual arts events. LLL runs creative writing workshops throughout the year and plans are currently underway to stage a young people's festival of words that will take place in Lewes during June 2009. More information can be found at www.festivalofwords.org.uk.

Lincoln Book Festival

Venues around Lincoln

- 01522 873844
- arts@lincoln.gov.uk
- www.lincolnbookfestival.co.uk

Contact Karen Parsons

Dates May

About The Lincoln Book Festival programme includes talks, workshops, discussions, exhibitions and performances. There are also a wide range of activities and events for children and young readers, including the Lincolnshire Young People's Book Award.

Lit.Com

Venues around Lincolnshire

- 01472 323382
- charlotte.bowen@nelincs.gov.uk
- www.nelincs.gov.uk

Dates September/October

About A festival of literature and comedy, including live author events, the very best in UK stand up, film showings, theatre for families, poetry performances and writing workshops, a major exhibition, discussion groups, free-giveaways and design and craft sessions for kids. Held at various venues across North East Lincolnshire.

Lit Fest

PO Box 751, Lancaster, Lancashire, LA1 9AJ

- 01524 62166
- 0871 433 6449
- www.litfest.org

Contact Artistic Director, Andy Darby

Dates November

About An annual festival focusing on literature, poetry and writing. Includes newly commissioned performances each year. Literature development continues throughout the year in Lancaster.

London Literature Festival
Southbank Centre, Belvedere Road, London, SE1 8XX
- 0871 663 2501
- customer@southbankcentre.co.uk
- www.southbankcentre.co.uk

Dates July

About London Literature Festival is a new festival of literature, ideas, creative writing and performance taking place at the South Bank Centre. The festival lasts two weeks and also has many events for children.

London Lit Plus
- hello@londonlitplus.com
- www.londonlitplus.com

Dates July

About London Lit Plus is an 'open' festival, which means anyone can participate and anyone can hold an event. The festival is organised by a coalition of literary magazines and publishers and aims to provide an independent counterpoint to the London Literary Festival.

Lowdham Book Festival
The Bookcase, 50 Main Street, Lowdham, NG14 7BE
- 0115 966 4143
- janestreeter@thebookcase.co.uk
- www.lowdhambookfestival.co.uk

Contact Jane Streeter/Ross Bradshaw

Dates June

About Lowdham Festivals runs a major summer book festival, a winter weekend (in January) and a weekend of film in the spring. The summer festival has many different arts events, including talks, readings and live music.

Manchester Literature Festival
Beehive Mill, Jersey Street, Ancoats, Manchester, M4 6JG
- 0161 236 5555
- admin@manchesterliteraturefestival.co.uk
- www.manchesterliteraturefestival.co.uk

Contact Festival Director, Cathy Bolton; Festival Administrator/Events Manager, Jon Atkin

Dates October

About Manchester Literature Festival produces a programme of readings and events showcasing the best in regional and national independent

publishing, writing and production. It aims to challenge the boundaries of what is traditionally understood to be a literature event and also aims to promote internationalism, diversity and independence.

Mere Literary Festival
Mere, Wiltshire, BA12 6EG
- info@merelitfest.co.uk
- www.merelitfest.co.uk

Contact Festival Administrator, Adrienne Howell

Dates 11–17 October (2010)

About An annual festival beginning on the second monday of October. Events include talks, readings, workshops, shows and activities for children. Also runs the Mere Literary Festival Short Story Competition, with the awards ceremony taking place on the last day of the festival.

National Eisteddfod of Wales
40 Parc Ty Glas, Llanishen, Cardiff, CF14 5DU
- 029 2076 3777
- 029 2076 3737
- sionedmair@eisteddfod.org.uk
- www.eisteddfod.org.uk

Contact Festival Organiser, Hywel Wyn Edwards

Dates August

About The National Eisteddfod of Wales is a major arts and culture festival, attracting around 160,000 visitors annually. It aims to promote Welsh language and culture and also provides a launch pad for Wales' most talented new performers.

NAWG Open Festival of Writing
The Arts Centre, Biddick Lane, Washington, Tyne & Wear, NE38 2AB
- 01262 609228
- nawg@tesco.net
- www.nawg.co.uk

Contact Festival Administrator, Mike Wilson

Dates September

About A weekend of 36 workshops, seminars, readings, tutorials and fringe activities led by NAWG tutors.

New Writing Worlds
The New Writing Partnership, 14 Princes Street, Norwich, NR3 1AE
- 01603 877177
- 01603 625452
- info@newwritingpartnership.org.uk
- www.newwritingpartnership.org.uk

Contact Marketing Director, Katy Carr

Dates June

UK & IRELAND

FESTIVALS & CONFERENCES

LISTINGS

About A new festival, founded in 2008, with various events including author readings, creative workshops, debates and lectures on writing and environmental issues.

Norfolk & Norwich Festival
Festival Office, 1st Floor, Augustine Steward House, 14 Tombland, Norwich, NR3 1HF
- ☎ 01603 877750
- ☎ 01603 877766
- ✉ info@nnfestival.org.uk
- 🌐 www.nnfestival.org.uk

Contact Festival Director, Jonathan Holloway; General Assistant, Katherine Stapley
Dates First two weeks of May every year
About An International Arts Festival of classical music, contemporary music and contemporary performance, with a children's festival.

Northern Children's Book Festival
Gateshead CLC, Unit 6, Keel Row, The Watermark, Gateshead, NE11 9SZ
- ☎ 0191 460 2900
- ✉ peter.bolger@gateshead.org
- 🌐 www.ncbf.co.uk

Contact Peter Bolger
Dates November
About The largest annual reading celebration for young people in Europe. Authors and poets visit schools throughout the north of England, culminating in a gala day of workshops, talks, seminars and activities for children and their families. The Gala day is open to the general public but the other events are for schools only.

Oundle Festival of Literature
Ticket Sales, Oundle Tourist Information Centre, 14 West Street, Oundle
- ☎ 01832 274333
- ✉ enquiries@oundlelitfest.org.uk
- 🌐 www.oundlelitfest.org.uk

Contact Chair, Nick Turnball
Dates January/March
About A festival of fiction, theatre, poetry, history, politics, travel, gardening, cuisine, environmental issues and a community events programme. Some events are free, others are paid for.

Poetry International
Royal Festival Hall, South Bank Centre, Belvedere Road, London, SE1 8XX
- ☎ 0870 380 4300
- ☎ 0870 163 3896
- 🌐 www.rfh.org.uk/poetryinternational

About A six day biennial festival of poetry, with readings, workshops and projects.

Quite Literary
The Plough Arts Centre, 9–11 Fore Street, Great Torrington, Devon, EX38 8HQ
- ☎ 01805 622552
- ☎ 01805 622113
- 🌐 www.plough-arts.org

Contact Director, Richard Wolfenden Brown
About A year-round programme of literature events in and around Torrington. There are readings, workshops and community events.

Redbridge Book & Media Festival
3rd Floor, Central Library, Clements Road, Ilford, Essex, IG1 1EA
- ☎ 020 8708 2855
- ✉ arts&events@redbridge.gov.uk
- 🌐 www.redbridge.gov.uk

Dates April/May
About A festival of the written word in all its forms, including film screenings and performances, workshops, industry talks and visits from well known writers and performers. The media element to this festival, alongside the more traditional literature events, makes it unique.

Royal Court Young Writers' Festival
Royal Court Theatre, Sloane Square, London, SW1W 8AS
- ☎ 020 7565 5000
- ☎ 020 7565 5001
- ✉ info@royalcourttheatre.com
- 🌐 www.royalcourttheatre.com

Contact Artistic Director, Dominic Cooke
Dates January/March
About A biennial festival, the next of which will take place in 2010. Young people under the age of 26 may submit scripts to win the chance to see them developed and performed.

Rye Arts Festival
PO Box 33, Rye, East Sussex, TN31 7YB
- ☎ 01797 22442
- ✉ info@ryeartsfestival.co.uk
- 🌐 www.ryefestival.co.uk

Contact Chairman, Richard Thomas
Dates September
About One of the top ten small festivals in the UK, providing a diverse mixture of musical, literary and theatrical events with the emphasis on quality, intellectual weight, style and fun. The visual arts are also very well catered for with the galleries running shows especially for the festival.

Salisbury International Arts Festival

87 Crane Street, Salisbury, Wiltshire, SP1 2PU

- 01722 332977
- info@salisburyfestival.co.uk
- www.salisburyfestival.co.uk

Contact Festival Director, Maria Bota

Dates May/June

About An annual multi-arts festival focusing on dance, theatre and visual arts, with some literary events.

Small Wonder

Charleston, Firle, Lewes, East Sussex, BN8 6LL

- 01323 811626
- info@charleston.org.uk
- www.charleston.org.uk/smallwonder

Dates September

About Small Wonder is the UK's only festival dedicated entirely to the short story from. The festival features a two-day creative writing workshop, as well as talks and debates featuring contemporary writers, live events, and social gatherings. See the website to read the Small Wonder commissioned short story and for full programme details.

StAnza: Scotland's Poetry Festival

THe Byre Theatre, Abbey Street, St Andrews, Fife, KY16 9LA

- 01334 475000
- 01334 475370
- arts@stanzapoety.org
- www.stanzapoetry.org

Contact Festival Director, Brian Johnstone; Artistic Director, Eleanor Livingstone

Dates March

About The only regular festival dedicated to poetry in Scotland. StAnza is international in outlook and the programme typically includes workshops, master classes, readings, performances, discussions, exhibitions and much more. Visiting poets come from all over the world and there is also a children's programme.

Sting in the Tale

Venues around Dorset and Hampshire.

- 01202 886201
- rlimb@eastdorset.gov.uk
- www.stinginthetale.org.uk

Contact Festival Committee Chairman, Rachel Limb

Dates August

About Sting in the Tale is a festival of traditional oral storytelling, based in Dorset and Hampshire. Events include live stories and workshops at castles, crypts, woodlands and other historical locations, for both children and adults. All events must be booked in advance, including the free ones. See website for booking information.

Stratford Upon Avon Poetry Festival

The Shakespeare Centre, Henley Street, Stratford Upon Avon, CV37 6QW

- 01789 204016
- 01789 296083
- general@shakespeare.org
- www.shakespeare.org

Dates June/July

About An annual poetry festival with readings of poetry taking place, mainly on Sunday evenings, in various venues around Stratford. Famous actors read poems of the past, while contemporary poets present their work. There is also a children's event.

The Sunday Times Oxford Literary Festival

301 Woodstock Road, Oxford, OX2 7NY

- 01865 514149
- info@sundaytimes-oxfordliteraryfestival.co.uk
- www.sundaytimes-oxfordliteraryfestival.co.uk

Contact Festival Directors: Sally Dunsmore and Angela Prysor-Jones

Dates March/April

About Workshops and talks on many literary topics, including writing in different genres, and publishing. Generally has around 350 visiting authors. Children's literature is a special focus and there are plenty of events and workshops for children, as well as workshops on how to write for them.

Swindon Festival of Literature

Lower Shaw Farm, Shaw, Swindon, Wiltshire, SN5 5PJ

- 01793 771080
- swindonlitfest@lowershawfarm.co.uk
- www.swindonfestivaloflriterature.co.uk

Contact Festival Director, Matt Holland

Dates May

About A two-week festival with workshops, talks and speakers on literature and writing, in and around Swindon. Includes a family and children's weekend.

The Times Cheltenham Literature Festival

109–111 Bath Road, Cheltenham, Gloucestershire, GL53 7LS

- 01242 775861
- 01242 256457
- clair.greenaway@cheltenhamfestivals.com
- www.cheltenhamfestivals.com

Contact Executive Director, Clair Greenaway; Artistic Director, Sarah Smyth
Dates October (9-18 October, 2009)
About Ten days of literary workshops, events and performances, including some big name speakers. More information is available on the festival website and via podcasts on the *Times* website.

Tŷ Newydd Festival
Tŷ Newydd, Llanystumdwy, Criccieth, Gwynedd, LL52 0LW
☎ 01766 522811
☎ 01766 523095
✉ post@tynewydd.org
🌐 www.tynewydd.org
Dates April
About A biennial festival, the next of which will be held in 2011. It is a weekend festival with a poetry programme in both Welsh and English.

Ulster Bank Belfast Festival at Queen's
Culture & Arts Unit, Queen's University, 8 Fitzwilliam Street, Belfast, BT9 6AW
☎ 028 9097 1197
✉ g.farrow@qub.ac.uk
🌐 www.belfastfestival.com
Contact Festival Director, Graeme Farrow
Dates October
About A festival of arts – including music, theatre, film and writing. Previous festivals have featured over 450 visiting artists.

Warwick International Festival
Pageant House, Jury Street, Warwick, CV34 4EW
☎ 01926 410018
✉ director@warwickmusiclive.org.uk
🌐 www.warwickintfestival.org
Dates June/July
About A music and arts festival in and around Warwick, with some literary events.

Warwick Words
The Court House, Jury Street, Warwick, CV34 4EW
☎ 01926 427056
✉ info@warwickwords.co.uk
🌐 www.warwickwords.co.uk
Contact Patron, Andrew Davies
Dates October
About A festival of literature and the spoken word. Workshops, talks, performances and children's events are part of the programme.

Ways With Words Literature Festivals
Droridge Farm, Dartington, Totnes, Devon, TQ9 6JG
☎ 01803 867373
☎ 01803 863688
✉ office@wayswithwords.co.uk
🌐 www.wayswithwords.co.uk
Contact Festival Directors: Kay Dunbar and Stephen Bristow
Dates March, July & November
About Runs highly-regarded literature festivals at several locations across the UK: Keswick (March); Dartington (July); Southwold (November). Also runs retreats and events overseas.

Wellington Literary Festival
Venues around Wellington
☎ 01952 567697
✉ welltowncl@aol.com
🌐 www.wellington-shropshire.gov.uk
Dates October
About A series of free events and talks in Wellington, with several guest speakers.

Wells Festival of Literature
Venues around Somerset
☎ 01749 670929
🌐 www.wlitf.co.uk
Dates October
About A series of lectures and workshops on various topics within literature and writing. Also runs annual short story and poetry competitions.

Welsh Writing in English Annual Conference
Gregynog Hall, Newton, Powys, Wales
✉ daniel.g.williams@swansea.ac.uk
🌐 www.swan.ac.uk/english/awwe/annualconference
Contact Conference Organiser, Dr Daniel Williams
Dates March
About An annual weekend conference centred around Welsh writing in English, with a different theme every year.

West Cork Literary Festival
15 Glengarriff Road, Bantry, Co. Cork, Republic of Ireland
☎ 00353 27 55987
✉ info@westcorkliteraryfestival.ie
🌐 www.westcorkliteraryfestival.ie
Contact Festival Directors: Clem Cairns and Lorraine Bacchus
Dates July

About A week of literary events for writers, including the annual launch of the Fish Publishing anthology and short story prize.

Wigtown Book Festivals
County Buildings, Wigtown, Newton Stuart, Dumfries & Galloway, DG8 9JH
☎ 01988 402036
✉ mail@wigtownbookfestival.com
🌐 www.wigtownbookfestival.com
Contact Festival Director, Adrian Turpin
Dates September/October
About An annual festival in Wigtown, Scotland's national book town. Programme includes readings and events at various locations in Wigtown.

Winchester Writer's Conference
Faculty of Arts, University of Winchester, West Hill, Winchester, Hampshire, SO22 4NR
☎ 01962 827238
✉ barbara.large@winchester.ac.uk
🌐 www.writersconference.co.uk
Contact Founder/Director, Barbara Large
Dates June/July
About A weekend of workshops, events and talks. Also run a book fair.

Wonderful Words Book Festival
Penzance Library, Morrab Road, Penzance, Cornwall, TR18 4EY
☎ 0800 032 2345
☎ 01736 330644
✉ wonderfulwords06@yahoo.co.uk
🌐 http://db.cornwall.gov.uk/ww/ww
Dates August/October
About A festival of workshops, talks, readings and events throughout Cornwall. Many of the visiting speakers are big name authors, or media personalities.

Word
Office of External Affairs, University of Aberdeen, King's College, Aberdeen, AB24 3FX
☎ 01224 273874
☎ 01224 272086
✉ word@abdn.ac.uk
🌐 www.abdn.ac.uk/word
Contact Artistic Director, Alan Spence
Dates May
About A large festival with over 10,000 visitors. Programme includes readings, workshops, music sessions, art exhibitions, children's activities and film screenings.

World Book Day
🌐 www.worldbookday.com
Dates March (5th)
About World Book Day was designated by UNESCO as a worldwide celebration of books and reading, and is marked in over 100 countries around the globe. The UK World Book Day is celebrated on a different date to the International World Book Day to ensure that it falls within school term time. Special £1 books are created, and there are lots of events in schools throughout the country. The Bookseller and National Book Tokens Ltd host and sponsor the day.

Writers' Holiday at Caerleon
School Bungalow, Church Road, Pontnewydd, Cwmbran, NP44 1AT
✉ enquiries@writersholiday.net
🌐 www.writersholiday.net
Contact Anne Hobbs
Dates July
About A six day residential conference for everyone, from beginners to the more experienced. Around 150 delegates attend.

Writers' Week
24 The Square, Listowel, Co. Kerry, Republic of Ireland
☎ 00353 68 21074
☎ 00353 68 22893
✉ info@writersweek.ie
🌐 www.writersweek.ie
Contact Máire Logue; Chairman, Michael Lynch
Dates May
About Writers' Week is a literary festival devoted to the cause of writers. It aims to guide, direct and enthuse the emerging writer, to befriend the established writer and provide a practical platform for their artistic output. This ideal is achieved through annual literary competitions, three day workshops, readings, seminars, lectures, book launches and other events. Writers' Week aims to be inclusive and to make the arts accessible to everybody. To succeed with this ambition they have put in place a broad and comprehensive literary programme to cater for all tastes.

Writing on the Wall
60 Duke Street, Liverpool, L1 5AA
☎ 0151 707 4313
✉ info@writingonthewall.org.uk
🌐 www.writingonthewall.org.uk
Contact Festival Administrator, Janette Stowell
Dates May
About A not for profit organisation that runs a series of literature related events. These are designed to

encourage young people and the wider community to take part.

Young Readers Birmingham

Children's Office, Central Library, Chamberlain Square, Birmingham, B3 3HQ

☎ 0121 303 3368

☎ 0121 464 1004

✉ gena.gaynor@birmingham.gov.uk

🌐 www.birmingham.gov.uk/youngreaders

Contact Gena Gaynor

Dates May/June

About An annual two week festival for children and young people, to encourage them to enjoy books and reading. There are around 150 events across Birmingham during the two week period.

INDEX of Directory Listings

966